104TH YEAR

WISDEN

CRICKETERS' ALMANACK

1967

EDITED BY NORMAN PRESTON

PUBLISHED BY SPORTING HANDBOOKS LTD AT THIRTEEN BEDFORD SQUARE LONDON WCI FOR THE PROPRIETORS JOHN WISDEN AND CO LTD IN TWO EDITIONS, LIMP COVERS AT TWENTY-THREE SHILLINGS AND SIXPENCE NET, CLOTH BOARDS BINDING AT TWENTY-SEVEN SHILLINGS AND SIXPENCE NET

PREFACE

This, the 104th consecutive issue of *Wisden*, has been prepared amid all the controversy concerning the County Championship which has been thrown into the background of popular appeal with the ever increasing growth of Test Match cricket. On the eve of the printing of this latest *Wisden* came the news that the Counties had emphatically rejected the plan for two separate Championships, one at the week-ends on its usual three-day basis and the other in mid-week of only one day duration for each match. I am grateful to Charles Bray, one of the members of the D. G. Clark sub-committee who made their recommendations after a most exhaustive inquiry, for dealing with this important subject.

While congratulating Sir Neville Cardus, C.B.E., on his knighthood in the New Year Honours I also thank him for another of his delightful pen pictures, this time on *Garfield Sobers—The Lion of Cricket*. Also recently honoured was A. A. Thomson, M.B.E., another gifted writer on cricket, whose entertaining article *My Favourite Summer* will, I am sure, afford much pleasure. R. T. Simpson, the former Nottinghamshire captain, has completed our series of County Club histories by writing of the part his own county has played in the growth of cricket.

I have persuaded Dicky Rutnagur (India) and Ghulam Mustafa Khan (Pakistan) to look into the background of the two countries who are sharing a dual tour of England this summer. Rowland Bowen has supplied dates showing the evolution of cricket in the sub-continent of Asia and Stanley Conder has provided the Test averages of all the players who have represented India and Pakistan. I would mention that all statistics are up to the end of last September, except in the case of the Sobers article where, on page 133, we have been able to squeeze in his recent tour of India.

Again, E. M. Wellings has dealt comprehensively with the Public Schools and I would also thank him for his review and reports of the M.C.C. tour in Australia, 1965–66. John Arlott looks at the books published over the past year and to Leslie Smith goes the credit for revising Cricket Records, no easy task in these days of so much first-class cricket in many parts of the world. I would take this opportunity of thanking many vigilant readers who are good enough to write when they spot a discrepancy.

For the Five Cricketers of the Year I looked at those whose performances in these times of so much mediocrity do most to draw the crowds: R. W. Barber (Warwickshire), C. Milburn (Northamptonshire), B. L. d'Oliveira (Worcestershire), J. T. Murray (Middlesex) and S. M. Nurse (West Indies).

Finally, my thanks to F. H. C. Tatham (Sporting Handbooks) for his industry in reading and revising proofs and for his extensive Index; and to S. C. Griffith and D. B. Carr (M.C.C.), Frank Crompton (Minor Counties) and all the secretaries of the First-class and Second-class counties as well as those of the Leagues and Public Schools for their ready help and co-operation.

Besides those already mentioned there follows a list of contributors whose work has been most valuable in producing this edition of the Almanack.

NORMAN PRESTON

PRESS ASSOCIATION,
85 FLEET STREET,
LONDON, E.C.4.
February, 1967.

LIST OF CONTRIBUTORS

The Editor acknowledges with gratitude the generous assistance afforded in the preparation of the Almanack by all those whose names are enumerated in the Preface and by the following:—

H. E. A. Abel (London)
R. L. Arrowsmith
Alex Bannister (Herts.)
Mark Buxton (W. Australia)
Michael Carey (Derbyshire)
G. A. Copinger (London)
G. A. Chettle (South Africa)
E. Eden (Essex)
H. Gee (London)
J. E. Godfrey (Worcestershire)
T. L. Goodman (Australia)
Eric Hill (Somerset)
Horace Hutt (Gloucestershire)
John Kay (Lancashire)
J. M. Kilburn (Yorkshire)
Donald King (Canada)
W. King (Leicestershire)
Gordon Kitchen (Oxford)
W. M. McMurtrie (Scotland)
John I. Marder (U.S.A.)
John Morgan (Glamorgan)
Douglas Moore (Kent)
A. E. Rawlings (Hampshire)
Netta Rheinberg (Women's Cricket)
H. Richards (Nottinghamshire)
H. S. Scales (London)
Derek Scott (Ireland)
Christie Seneviratne (Ceylon)
John Solan (Warwickshire)
F. S. Speakman (Northamptonshire)
P. N. Sundaresan (India)
H. D. Vaidyasekera (Ceylon)
William Wanklyn (Warwickshire)
A. S. R. Winlaw (Cambridge)
A. G. Wiren (New Zealand)

limp 85020/0148. *cloth* 85020/0156

TABLE OF MAIN CONTENTS

(A complete Index appears on the following pages)

	PAGE
WEST INDIES RETAIN THE WISDEN TROPHY (PHOTOGRAPH)	61
WEST INDIES TEAM IN ENGLAND, 1966 (PHOTOGRAPH)	62
ENGLAND TEAM AT THE OVAL, 1966 (PHOTOGRAPH)	63
TOM GRAVENEY'S HAPPY RETURN (PHOTOGRAPH)	64
KEN HIGGS THE PERSISTENT ATTACKER (PHOTOGRAPH)	65
YORKSHIRE—COUNTY CHAMPIONS, 1966 (PHOTOGRAPH)	66
WARWICKSHIRE—GILLETTE CUP WINNERS, 1966 (PHOTOGRAPH)	67
C. MILBURN (NORTHAMPTONSHIRE) (PHOTOGRAPH)	68
S. M. NURSE (WEST INDIES) (PHOTOGRAPH)	69
B. L. D'OLIVEIRA (WORCESTERSHIRE) (PHOTOGRAPH)	70
J. T. MURRAY (MIDDLESEX) (PHOTOGRAPH)	71
R. W. BARBER (WARWICKSHIRE) (PHOTOGRAPH)	72
FIVE CRICKETERS OF THE YEAR	73
NOTES BY THE EDITOR	87
COUNTIES REJECT THE CLARK PLAN, BY CHARLES BRAY	96
THE TWO DAVID CLARK REPORTS	101
THE THROWING REPORT	114
MY FAVOURITE SUMMER, BY A. A. THOMSON	118
SOBERS—THE LION OF CRICKET, BY SIR NEVILLE CARDUS	126
NOTTINGHAMSHIRE'S NOTABLE PART IN THE GROWTH OF CRICKET, BY R. T. SIMPSON	134
INDIAN CRICKET—ITS PROBLEMS AND PLAYERS, BY DICKY RUTNAGUR	143
THE RISE OF CRICKET IN PAKISTAN, BY GHULAM MUSTAFA KHAN	153
TEST CRICKETERS, 1877–1966	161
CRICKET RECORDS	190
WEST INDIES IN ENGLAND, 1966	279
THE MARYLEBONE CLUB, 1966	321
OTHER MATCHES AT LORD'S, 1966	335
THE COUNTY CHAMPIONSHIP IN 1966	348
THE GILLETTE CUP	652
THE UNIVERSITIES IN 1966	668
OTHER MATCHES IN 1966	699
MINOR COUNTIES IN 1966	705
SECOND XI CHAMPIONSHIP IN 1966	726
LEAGUE CRICKET IN 1966	739
THE PUBLIC SCHOOLS IN 1966, BY E. M. WELLINGS	748
PUBLIC SCHOOL AVERAGES IN 1966	758
M.C.C. TEAM IN AUSTRALIA, 1965–66, BY E. M. WELLINGS	812
WORCESTERSHIRE IN JAMAICA	848
OVERSEAS CRICKET, 1965–66	850
WOMEN'S CRICKET, NEW ZEALANDERS IN ENGLAND, BY NETTA RHEINBERG	909
BIRTHS AND DEATHS OF CRICKETERS	913
OBITUARY	962
CRICKETERS OF THE YEAR	976
LAWS OF CRICKET	980
CRICKET BOOKS, 1966, BY JOHN ARLOTT	1011
FIXTURES FOR 1967	1030

INDEX

NOTE:—r. = runs; w. = wickets * Signifies "Not Out".

Abberley, R. N. (Warwickshire):—
Birthday....................913
Photograph....................599
Group....................67
1,315 r. in 1966....................270
117* v. Essex....................603
Abdul Dyer (Karachi Whites) (and Mushtaq Mohammad), 140 for 9th wkt....................205
Abdul Kadir (Pakistan), Test Cricket....................188
Abel, R. (Surrey):—
32,669 r....................198
Aggregate of 3,309....................206
Highest for Surrey....................193
74 Hundreds....................195
357* v. Somerset....................192, 193
247 v. Gentlemen....................259
195 v. Gentlemen....................259
132* v. Australia....................232
120 v. South Africa....................238
(and W. Brockwell), 379 for 1st wkt....................202
(and T. W. Hayward), 448 for 4th wkt....................204
(and D. L. A. Jephson), 364 for 1st wkt....................202
Abid Ali (Hyderabad):—
147 v. Vazir Sultan Colts....................888
140* v. K. M. Rangnekar's XI....................888
Abingdon School....................758
v. M.C.C....................331
Ackerman, H. (Border), 118* v. M.C.C. Schools....................902
Adastrian v. M.C.C....................331
Adcock, N. A. T. (South Africa):—
Test Cricket....................176
104 w. in Test Matches....................224
26 w. in Rubber v. England....................240
Addresses of Representative Bodies 492
Adhikari, H. R. (India), 114* v. West Indies....................256
Adhikari, S. G. (Bombay):—
126 v. Prof. Deodhar's XI....................888
110 v. Maharashtra....................883
ADVISORY COUNTY CRICKET COMMITTEE (A.C.C.C.)....................1002–3
Meetings....................1006–7
Afaq Hussain (Pakistan):—
Test Cricket....................188
(and Haseeb Ahsan), last wkt. record v. England....................248
(and Wallis Mathias), 135 for last wkt....................205
Aftab Gul (Punjab Univ.), 100 v. Sargodha....................890
Ahad Khan (Pakistan Railways) 9 w. for 7 r....................211
Aird, R. (Hampshire), M.C.C. Committee....................321
Akash Lal (Delhi), 104 v. North Punjab....................885
Akers-Douglas, I. S. (Eton and Kent), 158 v. Harrow....................337
Akhtar Javed (Pakistan), Test Cricket....................188
Alabaster, J. C. (New Zealand), Test Cricket....................183
Aldenham School....................758
v. M.C.C....................329
Alderman, A. E. (Derbyshire), First-Class Umpire....................1008
Aldershot Services v. M.C.C....................332
Alexander, F. C. M. (West Indies) (wkt.-kpr.):—
Birthday....................913
Captain v. India....................255
Captain v. Pakistan....................256
Test Cricket....................180
108 v. Australia....................251
23 w. in Test Rubber....................228
5 catches in Test Innings....................229
(and L. R. Gibbs), 8th wkt. record v. Australia....................252
(and W. W. Hall), 134 for 9th wkt....................205
(and W. W. Hall), 9th wkt. record v. Australia....................252
Alim-ud-Din (Pakistan):—
Test Cricket....................188
109 v. England....................247
103* v. India....................257
(and Fazal Mahmood), 8th wkt. record v. England....................248
(and Hanif Mohammad), 277 for 1st wkt....................203
(and Hanif Mohammad), 1st wkt. record v. England....................248
Allan, D. W. (West Indies) (wkt.-kpr.):—
Group....................62
Test Cricket....................180
Test Match Averages, 1966....................283
35 w. in 1966....................285
Allan, P. J. (Queensland):—
Test Cricket....................171
Test Match Averages, 1965–66 819, 820
10 w. in Innings v. Victoria....................210, 863

Allcock, G. (Yorkshire masseur), Group....................66
Allcott, C. F. W. (New Zealand):—
(and C. S. Dempster), 301 for 2nd wkt....................203
(and J. E. Mills), 190* for 8th wkt....................205
Allen, A. W. (Eton, Camb. Univ. and Northamptonshire):—
115 *v.* Oxford....................339
112 *v.* Harrow....................337
Allen, D. A. (Gloucestershire):—
Birthday....................913
Photograph....................406
All-Round....................216
Test Cricket....................161
Test Match Averages, 1965–66 819, 821
Test Match Averages, 1966. 282, 283
122 w. in Test Matches....................224
9 Lancashire w....................414
9 Warwickshire w....................607
(and P. H. Parfitt), 6th wkt. record *v.* Pakistan....................247
(and P. H. Parfitt), 8th wkt. record *v.* Pakistan....................247
(and J. B. Statham), last wkt. record *v.* Pakistan....................247
Allen, G. O. (Middlesex):—
Birthday....................913
Captain *v.* Australia....................231
Captain *v.* West Indies....................241
Treasurer of M.C.C....................321
122 *v.* New Zealand....................244
81 w. in Test Matches....................224
10 w. in Innings....................209
(and L. E. G. Ames), 8th wkt. record *v.* New Zealand....................244
Alletson, E. (Nottinghamshire):—
Fast Scoring....................199
34 r. in Over....................200
Alley, W. E. (Somerset):—
All-Round....................216
3,019 r. in Season....................206
1,104 r. in 1966....................271
2 Hundreds in 1966....................277
115 *v.* Nottinghamshire....................532
110* *v.* Glamorgan....................556
8 Sussex w....................560
25 catches in 1966....................369
Alleyn's School....................758
v. M.C.C....................327
Allhallows School....................759
v. M.C.C....................328
All-India State Bank Tour of Ceylon, 1966....................894
Allom, M. J. C. (Surrey):—
Hat-trick *v.* New Zealand. . 228, 245
M.C.C. Committee....................321
ALL-ROUND CRICKET....................215–17
Amarnath, L. (India):—
Captain *v.* Australia....................252
Amarnath, L. (India):—*contd.*
118 *v.* England on Test début 225, 246
(and R. S. Modi), 410 for 3rd wkt....................203
Amersham *v.* M.C.C....................334
Ames, L. E. G. (Kent) (wkt.-kpr.):—
Birthday....................914
Hon. Cricket Member, M.C.C. . 347
Secretary-Manager, Kent....................441
37,245 r....................197
2,434 r. in Test Matches....................222
1,000 r. (17 times)....................198
Aggregate of 3,058....................206
102 Hundreds....................195
3 Hundreds *v.* West Indies....................242
2 Hundreds *v.* New Zealand....................244
2 Hundreds *v.* South Africa....................238
2 Separate Hundreds....................196
201 *v.* Gentlemen....................259
120 *v.* Australia....................232
(wkt.-kpr.), 127 w. in Season....................218
(wkt.-kpr.), 1,919 r. and 121 w. . 216
415 Stumpings....................217
8 w. in Test Match....................229
(and G. O. Allen), 8th wkt. record *v.* New Zealand....................244
(and W. R. Hammond), 4th wkt. record *v.* South Africa....................238
(and W. R. Hammond), 5th wkt. record *v.* New Zealand....................244
Amir Elahi (India and Pakistan), Test Cricket....................185, 188
Amiss, D. L. (Warwickshire):—
Birthday....................914
Group....................63, 67
Test Cricket....................161
Test Match Averages, 1966....................282
1,765 r. in 1966....................270
2 Hundreds in 1966....................277
160* *v.* West Indies....................313
150* *v.* Scotland....................604
113 *v.* Glamorgan (Gillette Cup). 658
Ampleforth College....................759
v. I.Z....................269
v. M.C.C....................329
Andrew, K. V. (Northamptonshire) (wkt.-kpr.):—
Birthday....................914
Captain of Northamptonshire . . 510
Retirement....................510
Test Cricket....................161
55 w. in 1966....................369
7 catches in Innings....................217
Andrews, C. W. (Queensland) (and E. C. Bensted), 335 for 7th wkt....................204
Andrews, W. (Gentlemen of Ireland and Ulster), Obituary....................962
Andrews, W. H. R. (Somerset), All-Round....................216

Anson, Hon. R. (Middlesex), Obituary....................962
Appeals (Laws of Cricket)........993
against Light..................997
Appleyard, R. (Yorkshire), 200 w. in Season.................214
Apte, A. L. (India), Test Cricket...185
Apte, M. L. (India), 163* *v.* West Indies.....................256
Archer, R. G. (Queensland):—
128 *v.* West Indies.............251
(and K. R. Miller), 5th wkt. record *v.* West Indies......252
(and K. R. Miller), 6th wkt. record *v.* West Indies......252
Ardingly College................759
Arif Butt (Pakistan), Test Cricket..188
ARLOTT, JOHN ("Cricket Books, 1966")...............1011–29
Armstrong, N. F. (Leicestershire), 36 Hundreds.............196
Armstrong, W. W. (Victoria):—
All-Round..................216
Captain *v.* England............231
2,863 r. in Test Cricket.........222
2,172 r. *v.* England............237
45 Hundreds..................196
4 Hundreds *v.* England........234
2 Hundreds *v.* South Africa....248
303* *v.* Somerset..............193
87 w. in Test Matches.........224
(and M. A. Noble), 428 for 6th wkt.....................204
(and V. T. Trumper), 5th wkt. record *v.* South Africa......250
Army:—
v. Royal Air Force............345
v. Royal Navy.................345
Arnold, C. (Throwing Record)....219
Arnold, E. G. (Worcestershire):—
All-Round..................216
(and W. B. Burns), 393 for 5th wkt.....................204
Arnold, G. (Surrey), 8 Glamorgan w.......................395
Arnold, J. (Hampshire):—
37 Hundreds.................196
First-class Umpire...........1008
Asgarali, N. (West Indies), Test Cricket..................180
Asghar Quareshi (Lahore Greens), 100 *v.* Bahawalpur.........891
Ashby, D. (Canterbury, N.Z.), 5 w. for 2 r....................212
Ashdown, W. H. (Kent):—
Highest for Kent..............193
39 Hundreds.................196
332 *v.* Essex..............192, 193
307 r. in Day.................201
305* *v.* Derbyshire...........193
Ashes, The...............231, 509
Ashok Anand, P. R. (Mysore), 109 *v.* Kerala.................882
Ashton, Sir Hubert (Cambridge Univ. and Essex):—
President of Essex.............370
118 *v.* Oxford.................339
Ashville College................760
Ashworth, D. A. (Free Foresters), 120 *v.* Oxford Univ.........674
Asif Iqbal (Pakistan), Test Cricket.188
Aspinall, R. (Yorkshire), First-Class Umpire................1008
Astill, W. E. (Leicestershire):—
All-Round...................215
2,431 w......................214
100 w. (9 times)..............215
Atkins, G., 101 for Buckinghamshire....................709
Atkinson, C. R. M. (Somerset):—
Birthday.....................914
Photograph...................545
Captain of Somerset...........545
1,120 r. in 1966...............271
Atkinson, D. (West Indies):—
Captain *v.* New Zealand........204
Test Cricket..................180
219 *v.* Australia...............251
(and C. Depeiza), 347 for 7th wkt. *v.* Australia..204, 252, 258
Atkinson, B. G. W. (Northamptonshire, Middlesex and Scotland), Obituary..........962
Atkinson, F. (West Indies), Test Cricket..................180
Atkinson, G. (Somerset):—
1,307 r. in 1966...............271
2 Hundreds in 1966............277
148 *v.* Hampshire............433
127 *v.* Sussex................597
(and R. Virgin), 1st wkt. Hundreds..................203
Atkinson, N. S. M. (Middlesex), Obituary..................962
Atkinson-Clark, J. C. (Eton and Middlesex), 135 *v.* Harrow..337
ATTENDANCES AND GATE RECEIPTS 262–3, 1008
Attewell, W. (Nottinghamshire), 100 w. (10 times).............215
AUSTRALIA:—
Representative Body...........492
Summary of All Tests..........229
Test Cricketers (1877–1966)...170–6
AUSTRALIA *v.* ENGLAND........231–7
Highest Totals................232
Individual Hundreds.........232–6
Match Results................231
Record Partnerships...........232
Smallest Totals...............232
Visiting Captains..............231
AUSTRALIA *v.* ENGLAND, 1965–66:—
First Test (Brisbane).........831–2

AUSTRALIA v. ENGLAND, 1965–66:—*contd.*
Second Test (Melbourne) 834–5
Third Test (Sydney) 835–6
Fourth Test (Adelaide)......839–40
Fifth Test (Melbourne) 841–2
AUSTRALIA *v.* INDIA............252–3
AUSTRALIA *v.* NEW ZEALAND......250
AUSTRALIA *v.* PAKISTAN 253
AUSTRALIA *v.* SOUTH AFRICA...248–50
AUSTRALIA *v.* WEST INDIES......250–2
AUSTRALIAN CRICKET, 1965–66.849–72
Averages..................871–2
Inter-State Matches (T. L. Goodman)................849–71
Sheffield Shield Table..........849
Combined XI v. M.C.C. 825–6, 838–9
New South Wales:—
v. M.C.C..........829–30, 840–1
v. Queensland......851–2, 860–1
v. South Australia...858–9, 868–9
v. Victoria.........859–60, 865–6
v. Western Australia.854–5, 870–1
N.S.W. County Districts v. M.C.C. 832
Northern N.S.W. Country Districts. v M.C.C.........836–7
Prime Minister's XI v. M.C.C....832
Queensland:—
v. M.C.C................830–1
v. New South Wales.851–2, 860–1
v. South Australia...863–4, 867–8
v. Victoria.........862–3, 866–7
v. Western Australia.855–6, 864–5
Queensland Country Districts v. M.C.C................831
South Australia:—
v. M.C.C..........826–7, 832–3
v. New South Wales.858–9, 868–9
v. Queensland......863–4, 867–8
v. Victoria........852–3, 869–70
v. Western Australia.857–8, 861–2
South Australian Country Districts v. M.C.C................832
Tasmania v. M.C.C...........837–8
Victoria:—
v. M.C.C...............828–9.
v. New South Wales 859–60, 865–6
v. Queensland......862–3, 866–7
v. South Australia..852–3, 869–70
v. Western Australia 853–4, 856–7
Victorian Country Districts v. M.C.C..............827, 829
Western Australia:—
v. M.C.C...............824–5
v. New South Wales.854–5, 870–1
v. Queensland......855–6, 864–5
v. South Australia...857–8, 861–2
v. Victoria.........853–4, 856–7
Western Australia Country XI v. M.C.C..................824

Awasthy, B. (Services), 142 *v.* Jammu and Kashmir........885
Awdry, C. E. (Wiltshire), Obituary.975
Ayub Zonal Tournament.......890–2

Bacher, A. (South Africa), Test Cricket 176
Bacon, F. H. (Hampshire), 114 on début.....................194
Bad Light...................997
Badcock, C. L. (South Australia):—
325 *v.* Victoria...............192
118 *v.* England...............234
Baig, A. A. (India):—
Test Cricket..................185
159 *v.* North Zone.............887
147 *v.* Maharashtra Small Savings Minister's XI.........889
121 *v.* Andhra...............882
112 *v.* England on Test début 225, 246
Bailey, D., 114 for Durham 713
Bailey, J. (Hampshire):—
All-Round 216
7 w. for 7 r..................211
Bailey, J. A. (Essex), 13 w. *v.* Ireland 701
Bailey, T. E. (Essex):—
Birthday.....................915
All-Round 215
Captain of Essex..............370
Slow Scoring.................226
Test Cricket..................191
2,290 r. in Test Matches 222
1,000 r. (17 times)............198
134* *v.* New Zealand..........244
2,070 w.....................213
132 w. in Test Matches 224
100 w. (9 times)..............215
10 w. in Innings..............210
(and D. C. S. Compton), 5th wkt. record *v.* Pakistan.........247
(and T. G. Evans), 6th wkt. record *v.* West Indies........241
Bails, The (Laws of Cricket)......981
Baker, C. (Northern N.S.W. Country Districts), 101 *v.* M.C.C...................836
Baker, W. A. (Wellington, N.Z.), Obituary...................962
Bakewell, A. H. (Northamptonshire):—
107 *v.* West Indies............242
8 catches in Match............218
Balaskas, X. (South Africa), 122* v. New Zealand............254
Balderstone, J. C. (Yorkshire), 100* for Yorkshire II...........723
BALL, THE (Laws of Cricket)......981
Dead.......................986
Lifting the Seam.............992
Lost........................985

Ball, The (Laws of Cricket):—
contd.
New................981, 996, 1007
Polishing...............996, 1007
Size and Weight..............981
Bancroft's School..............760
v. M.C.C.......................332
Banerjee, S. N. (India) (and C. T. Sarwate), 249 for last wkt...205
Bannerman, C. (N.S.W.), 165* *v.* England on Test début.225, 234
Bannister, J. D. (Warwickshire):—
Benefit.......................263
Group.........................67
10 w. in Innings...............210
8 Worcestershire w............623
Barber, R. W. (Lancashire and Warwickshire):—
Birthday......................915
Photograph....................72
Group....................63, 67
Five Cricketers of the Year......73
Test Cricket..................161
Test Match Averages, 1965–66..819
Test Match Averages, 1966.....282
1,001 r. in Australia..........820
3 Hundreds in Australia.......822
185 *v.* Australia..........232, 836
126 *v.* Western Australia.......825
113 *v.* Combined XI...........826
113 *v.* Gloucestershire (Gillette Cup)...................663
(and G. A. R. Lock), 9th wkt. record *v.* India............246
(and G. Pullar), 1st wkt. record *v.* Pakistan...............247
Barclays Bank *v.* M.C.C..........331
Bardsley, W. (N.S.W.):—
2,469 r. in Test Matches.......222
53 Hundreds...................196
3 Hundreds *v.* England........234
3 Hundreds *v.* South Africa....248
2 Separate Test Hundreds..225, 234
(and C. E. Kelleway), 3rd wkt. record *v.* South Africa.....250
Barker, G. E. (Essex):—
1,301 r. in 1966...............271
107* on début..................194
Barlow, E. J. (South Africa):—
Birthday......................915
Test Cricket..................176
1,970 r. in Test Matches.......223
3 Hundreds *v.* Australia........249
142 *v.* Eastern Province.......874
138 *v.* England................239
111 *v.* Rhodesia...............874
106 *v.* Natal..................875
(and R. G. Pollock), 341 for 3rd wkt. *v.* Australia......203, 250
Barlow, R. G. (Lancashire):—
6 w. for 3 r...................212
3 Hat-tricks...................209
Barnard, H. M. (Hampshire):—
120 for Hampshire II..........729
20 catches in 1966.............369
Barnard Castle School..........760
v. M.C.C.......................331
Barnes, S. F. (Lancashire and Staffordshire):—
Birthday......................915
Hon. Cricket Member, M.C.C. .347
189 w. in Test Matches........223
106 w. *v.* Australia............237
49 w. in Rubber *v.* S. Africa....240
34 w. in Rubber *v.* S. Africa....240
17 w. in Match *v.* S. Africa 210, 227
14 w. in Test Match...........227
9 w. in Test Innings...........227
8 w. in Test Innings (twice) 227, 228
Barnes, S. G. (N.S.W.):—
2 Hundreds *v.* England......234
112 *v.* India..................253
(and D. G. Bradman), 405 for 5th wkt. *v.* England.......204, 232
Barnes, W. (Nottinghamshire), 134 *v.* Australia...............232
Barnet *v.* M.C.C.................332
Barnett, C. J. (Gloucestershire):—
Birthday......................915
Hon. Cricket Member, M.C.C...347
48 Hundreds...................196
11 Sixes in Innings............200
2 Hundreds *v.* Australia........232
Barratt, E. (Surrey), All 10 w. 209
Barratt, F. (Notts.), All-Round ...216
Barrington, K. F. (Surrey):—
Birthday......................915
Benefit.......................263
Fastest Test Hundred in 1966...268
Test Cricket..................162
Test Match Averages, 1965–66..819
Test Match Averages, 1966.....282
5,598 r. in Test Matches.......222
68 Hundreds...................195
5 Hundreds *v.* Australia........232
3 Hundreds in Australia.......823
3 Hundreds in 1966............277
3 Hundreds *v.* India...........245
3 Hundreds *v.* New Zealand....244
2 Hundreds *v.* South Africa....238
2 Hundreds *v.* West Indies.....242
158 *v.* Victoria................828
139 *v.* Pakistan...............247
117* *v.* Lancashire............474
115 *v.* Australia..........232, 842
106 *v.* Nottinghamshire........533
103* *v.* Northamptonshire......569
102 *v.* Australia..........232, 839
103* for Surrey II.............735
64 catches in Season..........218
(and M. C. Cowdrey), 4th wkt. record *v.* New Zealand.....244
(and J. H. Edrich), 2nd wkt. record *v.* New Zealand.....244

Barrington, K. F. (Surrey):—*contd.*
(and J. M. Parks), 6th wkt. record *v.* South Africa......238
(and G. Pullar), 2nd wkt. record *v.* India..........246
(and F. E. Rumsey), last wkt. record *v.* New Zealand.....244
(and M. J. K. Smith) 3rd wkt. record *v.* Pakistan..........247
Barrow, I. (West Indies), 105 *v.* England 242
Bartlett, G. A. (New Zealand):—
Test Cricket..................183
Test Match Averages, 1966.....821
Barton, P. T. (New Zealand):—
Test Cricket 183
109 *v.* South Africa 254
BAT, THE (Laws of Cricket).......981
Bates, D. L. (Sussex), 8 Essex w.....590
Bates, W. (Yorkshire), Hat-trick *v.* Australia.............228, 236
Bath, Plan of County Ground......546
BATSMAN (Laws of Cricket)....988–91
BATTING AVERAGES (1966) 270–3, 283–4
BATTING RECORDS..........191–207
Index.........................190
B.B.C. *v.* M.C.C..................327
Bear, M. J. (Essex):—
Birthday......................916
Photograph 370
1,833 r. in 1966...............270
105 *v.* Warwickshire..........603
Beasley, Rev. R. N. (Northamptonshire), Obituary...........962
Beaufort, Duke of, President, Gloucestershire...................406
Beaumont College................761
v. M.C.C......................328
v. Oratory.....................335
Beck, J. E. F. (New Zealand) (and L. C. Butler), 187 for 6th wkt)......................204
Bedford, P. I. (Middlesex), Obituary 962
Bedford School.................761
v. M.C.C......................327
BEDFORDSHIRE 708
Championship Table 707
Bedser, A. V. (Surrey):—
Birthday......................916
Benefit.......................263
Hon. Cricket Member, M.C.C...347
Test Selector 1006
236 w. in Test Matches 223
104 w. in Australia............237
100 w. (11 times)..............215
39 w. in Rubber *v.* Australia....236
14 w. in Test Match 227
Bell, A. J. (South Africa) (and H. G. Owen-Smith), last wkt. record *v.* England 238
Bell, T. A. (Hertfordshire), 105 *v.* Berkshire (Gillette Cup)....653
Benaud, R. (N.S.W.):—
Birthday......................916
All-Round 225
Captain *v.* England............231
Captain *v.* India 252
Captain *v.* Pakistan............253
Fast Scoring...................226
Test Cricket 171
2,201 r. in Test Matches 222
2 Hundreds *v.* South Africa.....248
121 *v.* West Indies.............251
11 Sixes in Innings.............200
248 w. in Test Matches.........224
(and A. K. Davidson), 7th wkt. record *v.* West Indies.......252
(and A. T. W. Grout), 8th wkt. record *v.* South Africa.....250
(and I. W. Johnson), 8th wkt. record *v.* West Indies.......252
(and G. D. McKenzie), 7th wkt. record *v.* South Africa.......250
Benefits and Testimonials in 1967..458
Benefits, Best 263
Bennett, G. (Kent), 7 w. for 9 r.....212
Bennett, Maj. G. G. M. (Berkshire), Obituary......................963
Bensted, E. C. (Queensland) (and C. W. Andrews), 335 for 7th wkt..........................204
Bentley, W., President of Leicestershire.......................475
Berkhamsted School.............761
v. M.C.C......................328
BERKSHIRE....................708–9
Championship Table 707
Championship Winners........266
Gillette Cup Matches...653–4, 656
Bernau, E. H. L. (Wellington, N.Z.), Obituary...................963
Berry, L. G. (Leicestershire):—
30,188 r.......................198
1,000 r. (18 times)..............198
45 Hundreds 196
Berry, R. (Lancashire, Worcestershire and Derbyshire), 10 w. in Innings...............210
Bestwick, W. (Derbyshire), 10 w. in Innings.....................209
Best Young Cricketer of the Year..266
Beuth, A. J. (Northern Districts, N.Z.), 9 Canterbury w.......879
Bevington, T. A. (Middlesex), Obituary.........................963
Bhandarkar, K. V. (Maharashtra) (and B. B. Nimbalkar), 455 for 2nd wkt............201, 203
Bibby, G. P. (New Zealand):—
Test Cricket...................183
Test Match Averages, 1966......821
161 *v.* Otago...................878

Bickley, J. (Nottinghamshire), 8 w. for 7 r. 211
Biddulph, K. D. (Somerset and Durham), 40 w. for Durham 714
Billimaria, B. M. (Parsees), 8 w. for 11 r. 211
Binks, J. G. (Yorkshire (wkt.-kpr.):—
Birthday 917
Photograph 634
Group 66
Benefit, 1967 458
Test Cricket 162
108 w. in Season 218
64 w. in 1966 369
5 catches in Test Innings 229
Binns, A. P. (West Indies) (and N. L. Bonitto), 283 for 5th wkt. 204
Bird, M. C. (Harrow and Surrey):—
100* and 131 *v.* Eton 337
(and J. W. H. T. Douglas), 7th wkt. record *v.* South Africa . 238
Birmingham and District League, 1966 746–7
Address of Secretary 492
Birmingham, Plan of Edgbaston Ground 600
Births and Deaths of Cricketers 913–61
Bisgood, B. L. (Somerset), 116* on début 194
Bishop's Stortford *v.* M.C.C. 334
Bishop's Stortford College 762
v. M.C.C. 330
Bissex, M. (Gloucestershire):—
Birthday 917
Photograph 406
Blackham, J. McC. (Victoria):—
Captain *v.* England 231
(and S. E. Gregory), 9th wkt. record *v.* England 232
Blackie, D. J. (Victoria), Oldest Australian Test début 259
Blair, R. W. (New Zealand), Test Cricket 183
Blanckenberg, J. M. (South Africa) (and E. P. Nupen), 9th wkt. record *v.* Australia 250
Bland, C. H. G. (Sussex), 10 w. in Innings 209
Bland, K. C. (South Africa):—
Birthday 917
Test Cricket 176
1,637 r. in Test Matches 223
2 Hundreds *v.* England 239
126 *v.* Australia 249
(and J. D. Lindsay), 6th wkt. record *v.* Australia 250
Blenkiron, W., 56 w. for Warwickshire II 737
Bligh, Hon. Ivo (Lord Darnley) (Kent), Captain *v.* Australia . 231
Bloomfield, H. O. (Surrey), 107* on début 194
Bloxham School 762
v. M.C.C. 330
Blues, List of (1880–1966):—
Cambridge 693–8
Oxford 688–93
Blundell's School 762
v. M.C.C. 329
Blunt, R. C. (New Zealand):—
338* *v.* Canterbury, N.Z. 192
(and W. Hawkesworth), 184 for last wkt. 205
(and M. L. Page), 4th wkt. record *v.* England 244
Obituary 963
Blythe, C. (Kent):—
2,506 w. 214
215 w. in Season 213
100 w. (14 times) 214
100 w. in Test Matches 224
17 w. in Day 210
17 w. in Match 210, 212
15 w. in Test Match 227
10 w. in Innings 209
8 w. in Test Innings 228
7 w. for 9 r. 212
Board of Control 1001–2
Meeting 1006
Boles, D. C. (Eton), 183 *v.* Harrow . 337
Bolton, B. A. (New Zealand), Test Cricket 183
Bolton School 762–3
v. M.C.C. 332
Bolus, J. B. (Yorkshire and Nottinghamshire):—
Slow Scoring 226
Test Cricket 162
1,393 r. in 1966 270
122* *v.* Sussex 539
105* for Nottinghamshire II 734
Bond, J. D. (Lancashire), 123 for Lancashire II 715
Bonitto, N. L. (Jamaica) (and A. P. Binns), 283 for 5th wkt. 204
Bonnor, G. J. (Australia), 128 *v.* England 234
Booth, A. (Lancashire II), 253 *v.* Lincolnshire 194
Booth, B. C. (N.S.W.):—
Birthday 917
Test Cricket 171
Test Match Averages, 1965–66 . . 819
1,775 r. in Test Matches 222
2 Hundreds *v.* England 234
2 Hundreds *v.* South Africa . . 248–9
117 *v.* West Indies 251
Booth, B. J. (Lancashire and Leicestershire):—
1,201 r. in 1966 270

Booth, B. J. (Lancashire and Leicestershire):—*contd.*
- 2 Hundreds in 1966 277
- 109 and 104 *v.* Middlesex 197
- 102* *v.* Surrey 575
- 101 *v.* Lancashire 483

Booth, M. W. (Yorkshire), All-Round....................216

Booth R. (Worcestershire) (wkt.-kpr.):—
- 100 w. in Season (twice)........218
- 72 w. in 1966.....................369

Borde, C. G. (India):—
- Test Cricket......................185
- 2,330 r. in Test Matches 223
- 177* *v.* Pakistan 257
- 109 *v.* New Zealand.............257
- 109 *v.* West Indies..............256
- (and A. S. Durani), 7th wkt. record *v.* England)........246
- (and Nawab of Pataudi), 5th wkt. record *v.* England.....246

Borland, A. F. (Natal), 4 w. with consecutive balls 208

Bosanquet, B. J. T. (Middlesex):—
- All-Round 216
- 2 Separate Hundreds...........196
- 8 w. in Test Innings............228

Botten, J. T. (South Africa), Test Cricket 176

BOUNDARY (Laws of Cricket) 985, 997, 1007
- Catch on...........................989

Bowditch, M. (Western Province):—
- 12 Natal w.........................875
- 9 Natal w. in innings............875

BOWEN, ROWLAND:—
- Some Dates in Indian Cricket History 147–50
- Some Dates in Pakistan Cricket History 157

Bowes, W. E. (Yorkshire):—
- Birthday............................918
- Benefit..............................263
- Hon. Cricket Member, M.C.C...347
- 100 w. (9 times)..................215

"Bowled" defined (Laws)..........988

BOWLER (Laws of Cricket).......986–7

Bowley, E. H. (Sussex):—
- 1,000 r. (15 times)...............198
- 52 Hundreds 196
- 109 *v.* New Zealand 244
- (and John Langridge), 490 for 1st wkt.. 201
- (and J. H. Parks), 368 for 1st wkt. 202

Bowley, F. L. (Worcestershire):—
- Highest for Worcestershire.....193
- 38 Hundreds 196

BOWLING:—
- Averages (1966)..........274–6, 284
- Crease (Laws of Cricket).......981

BOWLING RECORDS...........208–15
- Index................................190

Boyce, K. D. (Essex):—
- 13 Cambridge Univ. w. 378
- 9 Cambridge Univ. w. in Innings 267, 268, 378
- 42 w. for Essex II...............728

Boycott, G. (Yorkshire):—
- Birthday............................918
- Group 63, 66
- Test Cricket.......................162
- Test Match Averages, 1965–66 819, 821
- Test Match Averages, 1966.....282
- 1,854 r. in 1966..................270
- 6 Hundreds in 1966 276
- 164 *v.* Sussex.....................592
- 156 *v.* Combined XI.............838
- 136* *v.* Warwickshire...........606
- 131 *v.* West Indies...............319
- 123 *v.* M.C.C......................326
- 117 *v.* South Africa..............238
- 113 *v.* Australia..................232
- 103 and 105 *v.* Nottinghamshire 197, 267, 645

Boyd, A. N. A. (Eton), 100 *v.* Harrow 337

Boyle, H. F. (Australia), 6 w. for 3 r. 212

Bradburn, W. P. (New Zealand):—
- Test Cricket.......................183
- 107 *v.* Auckland..................879

Bradfield College...................763
- *v.* M.C.C............................332

Bradford Grammar School........763
- *v.* M.C.C............................331

Bradford League, 1966..........741–3
- Address of Secretary.............492

Bradley, W. M. (Kent), 3 Hat-tricks 209

Bradman, Sir Donald G. (N.S.W. and South Australia):—
- Birthday............................918
- Captain *v.* England..............231
- Fast Scoring.......................226
- Testimonial 263
- 6,996 r. in Tests..................222
- 5,028 r *v.* England...............237
- 1,690 r. in Australian Season ...206
- 1,000 r. (April 30–May 31) 207
- 1,000 r. (16 times)...............198
- 974 r. in Rubber *v.* England....236
- 452* *v.* Queensland..............191
- 369 *v.* Tasmania 192
- 357 *v.* Victoria...................192
- 334 *v.* England..........192, 193, 234
- 309 r. in Day.......................201
- 304 *v.* England..............193, 234
- 278 at Lord's......................263
- 270 *v.* England....................234
- 117 Hundreds 195
- 30 r. in Over 200
- 19 Hundreds *v.* England.......234

Bradman, Sir Donald G. (N.S.W. and South Australia):—*contd.*
13 Hundreds in Season........199
6 Hundreds in Succession......198
4 Hundreds in Succession......199
4 Hundreds *v.* India...........253
4 Hundreds *v.* South Africa.....249
2 Separate Hundreds...........196
2 Separate Test Hundreds..225, 253
2 Hundreds *v.* West Indies.....251
(and S. G. Barnes), 405 for 5th wkt. *v.* England.......204, 232
(and J. H. Fingleton), 6th wkt. record *v.* England.........232
(and A. L. Hassett), 3rd wkt. record *v.* England.........232
(and W. J. O'Reilly), 9th wkt. record *v.* South Africa....250
(and W. H. Ponsford), 451 for 2nd wkt. *v.* England 201, 203, 232
(and W. H. Ponsford), 2nd wkt. record *v.* West Indies.....252
(and W. H. Ponsford), 4th wkt. record *v.* England.........232
Brain, B. M. (Worcestershire), 9 Northamptonshire w.......516
Brain, W. H. (Gloucestershire) (wkt.-kpr.), Hat-trick......218
Brancker, R. C. (Barbados):—
Group.........................62
132 *v.* British Guiana.........897
Braund, L. C. (Somerset):—
All-Round.....................216
2 Hundreds *v.* Australia........232
104 *v.* S. Africa...............238
8 w. in Test Innings...........228
BRAY, CHARLES ("Counties Reject the Clark Plan").......96–100
Brearley, J. M. (Cambridge Univ., Middlesex and Cambridgeshire):—
2 Hundreds *v.* Oxford......260, 339
101 *v.* Yorkshire..............685
118 *v.* Isaacs' XI..............810
Brearley, W. (Lancashire):—
17 w. in Match.................210
4 w. with consecutive balls......208
Brentwood School..............763
v. M.C.C.....................328
Bridge, W. B. (Warwickshire), 5 w. for 2 r.....................212
Bridges, J. J. (Somerset), Obituary.963
Briggs, J. (Lancashire):
Hat-trick *v.* Australia......228, 236
2,221 w.......................214
118 w. in Test Matches.........224
100 w. (12 times)..............215
15 w. in Test Match............227
10 w. in Innings...............209
8 w. in Test Innings...........227
Briggs, J. (Lancashire):—*contd.*
8 w. for 11 r..............211, 227
121 *v.* Australia..............232
Brighton College...............764
v. M.C.C.....................331
Briscoe, A. W. (Transvaal) (and H. B. Cameron), 327 for 5th wkt..........................204
Bristol Grammar School.........764
v. M.C.C.....................329
Brockwell, W. (Surrey):—
All-Round.....................216
(and R. Abel), 379 for 1st wkt...202
Broderick, V. (Northamptonshire):—
All-Round.....................216
(and N. Oldfield), 361 for 1st wkt. 202
Bromfield, H. D. (South Africa), Test Cricket..................176
Bromley-Davenport, H. R. (Middlesex) (and C. W. Wright), 8th wkt. record *v.* South Africa..238
Bromsgrove School.............764
v. M.C.C.....................331
Brondesbury *v.* M.C.C..........332
Brookes, D. (Northamptonshire):—
30,874 r......................198
1,000 r. (17 times)............198
71 Hundreds...................195
Brook, G. W. (Worcestershire), Obituary.................963–4
Brooks, V. (London Schools), 128 *v.* All India Schools........904
Brotherton, E. J. (N. E. Transvaal), 111 *v.* Transvaal "B"........875
Brown, A. (Kent), Test Cricket....162
Brown, A. S. (Gloucestershire):—
8 Derbyshire w.................411
27 catches in 1966.............369
7 catches in Innings *v.* Nottinghamshire.........218, 268, 540
Brown, Maj., C. A., Sec., Essex....370
Brown, D. J. (Warwickshire):—
Birthday......................919
Photograph....................599
Group.........................67
Test Tricket..................162
Test Match Averages, 1965–66 819, 821
Test Match Averages, 1966 282, 283
8 Nottinghamshire w. (twice) 544, 613
Brown, F. R. (Surrey and Northamptonshire):—
Birthday......................919
All-Round.....................216
Captain *v.* Australia..........231
Captain *v.* New Zealand.......243
Fast Scoring...................200
M.C.C. Committee..............321
(and W. Voce), 7th wkt. record *v.* New Zealand..............244

Brown, G. (Hampshire), 37 Hundreds.....196
Brown, J. T. (Yorkshire):—
311 *v.* Sussex.....192
300 v. Derbyshire.....193
140 *v.* Australia.....232
(and J. Tunnicliffe), 554 for 1st wkt.....201
(and J. Tunnicliffe), 378 for 1st wkt.....202
Brown, J. W. (Scotland) (wkt.-kpr.), 7 w. in Innings.....217
Brown, W. A. (N.S.W. and Queensland):—
1,592 r. in Test Matches.....223
39 Hundreds.....196
3 Hundreds *v.* England.....234
121 *v.* South Africa.....249
(and J. H. Fingleton), 1st wkt. record *v.* South Africa.....250
Bruyns, A. (Isaacs' XI):—
101 *v.* Old Johnians.....810
100 *v.* Sidmouth.....809
Bryan, G. J. (Kent), 124 on début..194
Bryanston School.....765
Buckhurst Hill *v.* M.C.C.....333
BUCKINGHAMSHIRE.....709
Championship Table.....707
Championship Winners.....266
Buckle, W. (Queensland) 112 *v.* Western Australia.....856
Budge, N. (Western Province Colts), 113* *v.* M.C.C. Schools.....902
Bull, D. F. (Queensland), 167* *v.* Victoria.....863
Buller, J. S. (Worcestershire):—
First-Class Umpire.....1008
Test Panel.....1008
Burge, P. J. (Queensland):—
Birthday.....919
Test Cricket.....171
Test Match Averages, 1965–66..819
2,290 r. in Test Matches.....222
4 Hundreds *v.* England.....234
120 *v.* England.....234, 834
114* *v.* M.C.C.....830
111 *v.* New South Wales.....852
Burger, C. G. de V. (South Africa), Test Cricket.....176
Burke, J. W. (N.S.W.):—
Slow Scoring.....226
Test Cricket.....171
189 *v.* South Africa.....249
161 *v.* India.....253
101* *v.* England on Test début.....225, 234
Burke, S. F. (South Africa), Test Cricket.....176
Burki, J. (Pakistan):—
Captain *v.* England.....247
Test Cricket.....188
3 Hundreds *v.* England.....247
Burki, J. (Pakistan):—*contd.*
210 *v.* Ceylon.....895
137 *v.* Lahore Greens.....890
(and Hanif Mohammad), 3rd wkt. record *v.* England.....248
(and Mushtaq Mohammad), 4th wkt. record *v.* England.....248
(and Nasim-ul-Ghani), 7th wkt. record *v.* England.....248
Burley, J. (New Zealand Women), 9 w. *v.* England.....912
Burns, W. B. (Worcestershire):—
102* and Hat-trick *v.* Gloucestershire.....216
8 catches in Match.....218
(and E. G. Arnold), 393 for 5th wkt.....204
Burrow, B. W. (Griqualand West), 11 Transvaal "B" w.....876
Burrows, T. E., M.C.C. Committee 321
Burton, G. (Middlesex), All 10 w....209
Burton on Trent, Plan of County Ground.....353
Burtt, T. B. (New Zealand) (and J. Cowie), 9th wkt. record *v.* England.....245
Buss, A. (Sussex):—
Birthday.....919
Photograph.....581
120 w. in 1966.....275
9 Essex w.....377
9 Gloucestershire w.....420
9 Northamptonshire w.....588
9 Worcestershire w. (twice) 586, 633
Buss, M. A. (Sussex):—
Birthday.....919
Photograph.....581
136 *v.* Cambridge Univ.....591
24 catches in 1966.....369
Butcher, B. F. (West Indies):—
Birthday.....919
Group.....62
Test Cricket.....180
Test Match Averages, 1966.....283
1,858 r. in Test Matches.....223
1,105 r. in 1966.....283
3 Hundreds in 1966.....284
2 Hundreds *v.* England.....242
2 Hundreds *v.* India.....255
209* *v.* England.....242, 267, 303
137 *v.* M.C.C.....289
128 *v.* Warwickshire.....314
117 *v.* Australia.....251
Butler, H. J. (Nottinghamshire), 3 Hat-tricks.....209
Butler, L. C. (Wellington, N.Z.):—
8 w. *v.* N.Z. Under 23 XI.....880
(and J. E. F. Beck), 187 for 6th wkt.....204
Butler, S. E. (Oxford Univ.):—
All 10 Cambridge w.....209, 260
15 Cambridge w.....260

Butt, J. A. S. (Sussex), Obituary....964
Byes and Leg-byes (Laws).......987–8
Bynoe, M. R. (West Indies):—
Test Cricket....................180
104 *v.* Trinidad................897
Byrne, J. F. (Warwickshire), 100 on début....................194

Café Royal Trophy...............268
Caffyn, W. (Surrey), 7 w. for 7 r...211
Cahill, K. W. J. (Tasmania), Obituary....................964
Calthorpe, Hon. F. S. G. (Warwickshire:—
All-Round...................216
Captain *v.* West Indies.........241
CAMBRIDGE UNIVERSITY.......679–87
Averages.......................680
Results........................680
Blues (1880–1966)...........693–8
v. Lancashire..................683
v. Middlesex...............681–2
v. Northamptonshire........685–6
v. Scotland.................682–3
v. Warwickshire............683–4
v. West Indies..............290–1
v. Worcestershire..........683–4
v. Yorkshire................684–5
CAMBRIDGE *v.* OXFORD, 1966....337–9
CAMBRIDGESHIRE...................710
Championship Table..........707
Championship Winners........266
Cameron, F. J. (New Zealand), Test Cricket...............183
Cameron, H. B. (South Africa):—
Captain *v.* Australia..........248
Captain *v.* New Zealand.......254
30 r. in Over...................200
(and A. W. Briscoe), 327 for 5th wkt.....................204
CANADA:—
Cricket in 1966 (Donald King) 897–8
Representative Body..........492
v. United States............900–1
Canford School..................765
v. M.C.C........................331
CARDUS, SIR NEVILLE ("Sobers—The Lion of Cricket")...126–33
Carew. G. (West Indies):—
107 *v.* England.................242
(and A. G. Ganteaume), 1st wkt. record *v.* England.........242
Carew, M. C. (West Indies):—
Group..........................62
Test Cricket....................181
Test Match Averages, 1966.....283
132 *v.* Gloucestershire........296
Carlstein, P. R. (South Africa):—
Test Cricket....................176
102 *v.* Border..................876
Carr, A. W. (Nottinghamshire), 45 Hundreds.....................196
Carr, D. B. (Derbyshire):—
Asst. Sec., M.C.C..............321
103 *v.* Oxford Univ............674
Carr, Maj. D. J., Sec., Derbyshire.352
Carson, W. N. (Auckland) (and P. E. Whitelaw):—
Fast Scoring....................199
445 for 3rd wkt...........199, 203
Carter, R. G. M. (Worcestershire), 44 w. for Worcestershire II.738
Cartwright. T. W. (Warwickshire):—
Group..........................67
All-Round.....................216
Test Cricket....................162
100 w. in 1966.................274
13 Northamptonshire w.........616
23 catches in 1966..............369
Cassels, Gen. Sir James, M.C.C. Committee..................321
CATCHES IN 1966............285, 369
CATCHING RECORDS...............218
Caterham School.................765
Catterall, R. H. (South Africa):—
1,555 r. in Test Matches........223
3 Hundreds *v.* England.........239
Caught, Definition of (Laws)......989
Cave, H. B. (New Zealand):—
Captain *v.* India...............256
Captain *v.* Pakistan............258
Test Cricket....................183
(and I. B. Leggat), 239 for 9th wkt.....................205
Cazalet, P. V. F. (Eton), 100* *v.* Harrow.....................337
Central Lancashire League, 1966..740
Ceylon Cricket, 1965–66.......892–5
All-India State Bank Tour......894
Ceylon *v.* M.C.C...............824
Ceylon C.A. President's XI *v.* M.C.C.....................824
Ceylon Tour of Pakistan........895
M. J. Gopalan Trophy.........893
Madras Team in Ceylon.........893
Pentangular Tournament (Robert Senanayaka Trophy)......893–4
Chadwick, D. (Western Australia), 110 *v.* South Australia......858
Chalk, F. G. H. (Oxford Univ. and Kent), 108 *v.* Cambridge...339
Chaman Lal (Mehandra Coll., Patiala), 502* *v.* Govt. Coll., Rupar.....................194
Chandrasekhar, B. S. (India):—
Test Cricket....................185
10 Hyderabad w.................882
9 w. *v.* L. I. C. Chairman's XI...889
8 Kerala w......................882
8 Madras w.....................883
(and R. G. Nadkarni), last wkt. record *v.* England.........246

Chanmugam, N. (Mercantile Services, Ceylon), 9 Combined Services w. 893
Chapman, A. P. F. (Cambridge Univ. and Kent):—
Captain v. Australia 231
Captain v. South Africa 237
2 Hundreds v. Players 260
121 v. Australia 232, 260
118 on début 194
102* v. Oxford 260, 339
Chapman, J. (Derbyshire) (and A. R. Warren), 283 for 9th wkt. 205
Chappell, I. M. (South Australia):—
Test Cricket 171
Test Match Averages 819, 820
1,019 r. in 1965–66 871
134 v. Western Australia 862
129 v. Western Australia 858
113* v. M.C.C. 833
113 v. Victoria 869
Chapple, M. E. (New Zealand):—
Test Cricket 183
Test Match Averages, 1966 821
Charrington Trophy (Single-Wicket Championship) 703–4
Charterhouse 765–6
v. I. Z. 269
v. M.C.C. 329
Chatterjee, P. (Bengal), 10 w. in Innings 210, 211
Chaturvedi, A. K. (Madhya Pradesh), 130* v. Uttar Pradesh 884
Cheam v. M.C.C. 330
Cheesman, B. E. F., 102 for Berkshire 709
Cheetham, J. E. (South Africa):—
Captain v. Australia 248
Captain v. England 237
Captain v. New Zealand 254
(and P. N. F. Mansell), 7th wkt. record v. Australia 250
Cheltenham College 766
Plan of Ground 407
v. Haileybury 340–1
v. M.C.C. 328
Cherry-Downes, H. M. A. (Nottinghamshire II and Lincolnshire), Obituary 964
CHESHIRE 710–11
Championship Table 707
Gillette Cup 652
Chidgey, G. J. (Free Foresters), 113 on début 194
Chigwell School 766
v. M.C.C. 329
Chipperfield, A. G. (N.S.W.), 109 v. South Africa 249
Choudhry, Y. M. (Railways):—
102 v. North Punjab 885
100 v. Jammu and Kashmir 885
Christ Church, Oxford v. I.Z. 269
Christ College, Brecon 766
v. M.C.C. 330
Christiani, R. J. (West Indies), 107 v. India 255
Christ's Hospital 767
v. M.C.C. 329
Christy, J. A. J. (South Africa), 103 v. New Zealand 254
Chubb, G. W. A. (South Africa), Oldest South African Test début 259
City of London School 767
v. M.C.C. 330
Clark, D. G. (Kent):—
Committee on Future of County Cricket 87, 101–13
M.C.C. Committee 321
Clark, E. A. (Middlesex):—
1,365 r. in 1966 270
149 v. Kent 444
100* on début 194
Clarke, J., cricket writer, Obituary . 964
Clarke, W. (Nottinghamshire), 10 w. in Innings 209
Clarkson, A. (Somerset), 104 for Somerset II 719
Clay, J. C. (Glamorgan):—
President of Glamorgan 388
17 w. in Match 210
Clayesmore School 767
Clayton, G. (Lancashire and Somerset), (wkt.-kpr.), 85 w. in 1966 369
Cliff, A. T. (Worcestershire), Obituary 964
Clifton College 767–8
v. M.C.C. 333
v. Tonbridge 341–2
Clifton, E. G. (Middlesex) (wkt.-kpr.), 26 w. in 1966 369
Close, D. B. (Yorkshire):—
Birthday 921
Group 62, 66
All-Round 216
Benefit 263
Captain of Yorkshire 634
Test Cricket 163
Test Match Averages, 1966 . 282, 283
Youngest English Test Player . . . 259
1,335 r. in 1966 270
36 Hundreds 196
3 Hundreds in 1966 277
115* v. Nottinghamshire 541
105 v. Gloucestershire 409
103 v. Cambridge Univ. 685
8 Surrey w. 647
46 catches in 1966 369
Close of Play (Laws) 984
Club Cricket Association, National, Address of Secretary 492

Club Cricket Conference:—
Address of Secretary...........492
v. M.C.C......................327
Cobbold, R. H. (Eton), 100 *v.* Harrow 337
Cobden, F. C. (Cambridge Univ.), Hat-trick *v.* Oxford........260
Cockfosters *v.* M.C.C...........334
Code of Signalling (Umpires).....994
Coe, S. (Leicestershire), Highest for Leicestershire.............193
Coen, S. K. (South Africa) (and J. M. M. Commaille), 305 for 2nd wkt........................203
Cohen, R. A. (West Indies), Group.62
Colchester and E. Essex *v.* M.C.C..334
Coldwell, L. J. (Worcestershire):—
Test Cricket...................163
8 Northamptonshire w..........316
Coles, W. N. (Eton), 107 v. Harrow 337
Collinge, R. O. (New Zealand), Test Cricket...............183
Collins, A. E. J. (Clifton College), 628* *v.* North Town.......194
Collins, G. C. (Kent), 10 w. in Innings..................209
Collins, H. L. (N.S.W.):—
All-Round.....................216
Captain *v.* England............231
Captain *v.* South Africa........248
Slow Scoring...................226
3 Hundreds *v.* England.........234
203 *v.* South Africa............249
104 in Test début..............225
Comacho, S. (British Guiana), 106 *v.* Trinidad................896
Combined Services:—
Address of Secretary...........492
v. M.C.C. Schools XI..........344
Commaille, J. M. M. (S. Africa):—
(and S. K. Coen), 305 for 2nd wkt.....................203
(and A. W. Palm), 244* for 6th wkt.....................204
Commencement of Play (Laws)...983
Compton, D. C. S. (Middlesex):—
Birthday.......................922
Benefit........................263
Fast Scoring...................199
Hon. Cricket Member, M.C.C...347
38,942 r.......................197
5,807 r. in Test Matches........222
3,816 r. in Season..............205
1,000 r. (17 times).............198
753 r. in Rubber *v.* S. Africa....240
123 Hundreds..................195
18 Hundreds in Season.........199
7 Hundreds *v.* South Africa....238
5 Hundreds *v.* Australia........232
4 Successive Hundreds.........199
2 Hundreds *v.* New Zealand....244
Compton, D. C. S. (Middlesex):—*contd.*
2 Hundreds *v.* West Indies.....242
2 Separate Hundreds...........196
2 Separate Test Hundreds..225, 232
300 *v.* N. E. Transvaal.....193, 199
278 *v.* Pakistan...............247
273 r. in Day *v.* Pakistan.......236
(and T. E. Bailey), 5th wkt. record *v.* Pakistan..............247
(and W. J. Edrich) 424 for 3rd wkt.....................203
(and W. J. Edrich), 3rd wkt. record *v.* South Africa.238, 258
(and E. Paynter), 5th wkt. record *v.* Australia..............232
(and N. W. D. Yardley), 5th wkt. record *v.* South Africa.....238
Conder, Stanley:—
Indian Test Statistics........150–3
Pakistan Test Statistics.......158–9
Congdon, B. E. (New Zealand):—
Test Cricket...................183
Test Match Averages, 1966.....821
104 *v.* England..............244, 844
Connolly, A. N. (Victoria):—
Test Cricket...................171
Test Match Averages, 1965–66 819, 820
Constantine, Sir L. N. (West Indies):—
All-Round.....................216
107 and Hat-trick..............216
Contractor, N. J. (India):—
Captain *v.* West Indies.........255
Test Cricket...................185
1,611 r. in Test Matches........223
4 Successive Hundreds.........199
152 and 102* on début.........195
108 *v.* Australia...............253
Cook, C. (Gloucestershire), 100 w. (9 times)..................215
Cook, G. W. (Cambridge Univ.), 111* *v.* Oxford..............339
Cook, L. (Lancashire), 7 w. for 8 r..211
Cook, P. W. (Kent II), Obituary...964
Copson, W. H. (Derbyshire):—
4 w. with consecutive balls......208
3 Hat-tricks...................209
8 w. for 11 r...................211
First-Class Umpire............1008
Corbett, P. L. (N. E. Transvaal), 146 *v.* Griqualand West....876
Corling, G. E. (N.S.W.), Test Cricket...................171
CORNWALL.......................711
Championship Table..........707
Corrall, P. (Leicestershire) (wkt.-kpr.), 10 w. in Match.......217
Cosstick, S. (Victoria), 6 w. for 1 r..212
Cotter, A. (N.S.W.), 89 w. in Test Matches...................224

Cottrell, G. A. (Cambridge Univ.), Hon. Sec. of Cambridge, 1967....................679
COUNTIES REJECT THE CLARK PLAN (Charles Bray)............96–100
COUNTY CHAMPIONSHIP:—
Champion Counties..........265
Final Positions, 1966..........350
Fixtures, 1967............1030–4
Rules.....................1002–6
Experimental..........999, 1007
Scoring Rules..............350–1
Statistics for 1966............351
County Cricket, Clark Committee's Reports 87, 101–13
County Histories in *Wisden*.......142
County Secretaries' Meeting.....1009
Covering the Pitch (Laws) 982–3, 998, 1007
Cowdrey, M. C. (Oxford Univ. and Kent):—
Birthday....................922
Captain of Kent...............441
Test Cricket..................163
Test Match Averages, 1965–66 819, 821
Test Match Averages, 1966.....282
32,065 r.......................198
6,305 r. in Test Matches........222
1,081 r. in 1966................270
1,076 r. in Australasia..........822
1,000 r. (20 times).............198
78 Hundreds...................195
4 Hundreds *v.* Australia........233
4 Hundreds *v.* West Indies......242
3 Hundreds *v.* India............245
3 Hundreds *v.* South Africa...238–9
2 Hundreds in Australia.........823
2 Hundreds *v.* New Zealand....244
2 Hundreds *v.* Pakistan.........247
2 Separate Hundreds............196
307 *v.* South Australia......192, 193
116 *v.* Cambridge...............339
116 *v.* Suffolk (Gillette Cup).....655
108 *v.* Tasmania................837
104 *v.* Australia............233, 835
100* *v.* Oxford Univ............449
31 catches in 1966.............369
(and K. F. Barrington), 4th wkt. record *v.* New Zealand.....244
(and E. R. Dexter), 2nd wkt. record *v.* Pakistan.........247
(and P. B. H. May), 4th wkt. record *v.* West Indies..241, 258
(and A. C. Smith), 9th wkt. record *v.* New Zealand..244, 258
Cowie, J. (New Zealand):—
10 w. in Test Match..........227
6 w. for 3 r...................212
(and T. B. Burtt), 9th wkt. record *v.* England...............245
Cowie, J. (New Zealand)—*contd.*
(and F. L. H. Mooney), last wkt. record *v.* England.........245
Cowper, R. M. (Victoria):—
Birthday....................922
Test Cricket..................171
Test Match Averages, 1965–66 819, 820
1,418 r. in 1965–66............871
2 Hundreds *v.* West Indies....251
307 *v.* England...192, 193, 234, 842
143* *v.* M.C.C.................838
122* *v.* M.C.C.................826
113 *v.* Western Australia.......854
Cox, G. (Sussex), 50 Hundreds....196
Cox, G. R. (Sussex):—
17 w. in Match................210
7 w. for 8 r...................211
5 w. for 0 r...................212
Cragg, J. S., President of Lancashire 459
Craig, E. J. (Cambridge Univ. and Lancashire), 105 *v.* Oxford..339
Craig, I. D. (N.S.W.):—
Captain *v.* South Africa........248
Test Cricket..................172
Youngest Australian Test Player.259
Cranbrook School..............768
v. M.C.C....................332
Cranleigh *v.* M.C.C.............333
Cranleigh School...............768
v. M.C.C....................327
Cranston, K. (Lancashire), 4 w. for 0 r. *v.* South Africa.......241
Crapp, J. F. (Gloucestershire):—
38 Hundreds..................196
First-Class Umpire...........1008
Crawford, J. N. (Surrey and South Australia):—
All-Round 216
Fast Scoring..................200
Crawley, A. M. (Kent), M.C.C. Committee..................321
Crawley, L. G. (Harrow, Cambridge Univ., Worcestershire and Essex), 103 *v.* Eton.........337
Creases, The (Laws of Cricket) 981–2, 1000
Creber, A. B. (Scotland), Obituary.964
Cresswell, G. F. (New Zealand), Obituary...................964
CRICKET BOOKS, 1966 (John Arlott) 1011–29
CRICKET RECORDS (Leslie Smith) 190–266
Index.......................190
Cricket Societies, Addresses.......492
CRICKETERS OF THE YEAR, 1889–1966, Alphabetical List...976–9
Crisp, R. J. (South Africa and Worcestershire):—
4 w. with consecutive balls (twice).208

Crisp, R. J. (South Africa and Worcestershire):—*contd.*
3 Hat-tricks....209
Crump, B. (Northamptonshire):—
11 Gloucestershire w....513
9 Leicestershire w....526
Crutchley, E. (Harrow), 115 *v.* Eton 337
Cuckfield *v.* M.C.C....334
Cuffe, J. A. (Worcestershire), All-Round....216
Culford School....768
CUMBERLAND....711–12
Championship Table....707
Cunis, R. S. (New Zealand):—
Test Cricket....183
Test Match Averages, 1966....821
Cunningham, E. (North of Argentine and Brazil), Obituary....964
Currie Cup....873–7
Cuttell, W. R. (Lancashire), All-Round....216

Dacre, C. C. (New Zealand and Gloucestershire), 2 Separate Hundreds....196
Dallas Brooks, General Sir R. A. (Hampshire), Obituary....965
Dalton, E. L. (South Africa):—
2 Hundreds *v.* England....239
(and A. B. C. Langton), 9th wkt. record *v.* England....238
Damage to Pitch....999
Dansie, H. N. (South Australia):—
106 v. Queensland....868
101 *v.* Victoria....869
D'Arcy, J. W. (New Zealand), Test Cricket....183
Darling, J. (South Australia):—
Captain *v.* England....231
Captain *v.* South Africa....248
1,657 r. in Test Matches....222
3 Hundreds *v.* England....234
DATES OF FORMATION OF COUNTY CLUBS NOW FIRST-CLASS....264
DATES OF FORMATION OF MINOR COUNTIES....264
Davey, J., 54 w. for Gloucestershire II....729
Dauntsey's School *v.* M.C.C....329
Davidson, A. K. (N.S.W.):—
Test Cricket....172
186 w. in Test Matches....224
(and R. Benaud), 7th wkt record *v.* West Indies....252
Davidson, G. (Derbyshire):—
All-Round....216
Highest for Derbyshire....193
Davies, E. (Glamorgan):—
All-Round....215, 216
Highest for Glamorgan....193
1,000 r. (16 times)....198
Davies, E. (Glamorgan):—*contd.*
139 and Hat-trick *v.* Leicestershire....216
(and A. H. Dyson), 1st wkt. Hundreds....202
Davis, A. T. (Berkshire):—
129 *v.* Western Province Willows 808
119 for Berkshire....708
Davis, B. (West Indies):—
Test Cricket....181
(and C. C. Hunte), 1st wkt. record v. Australia....252
Davison, I. (Nottinghamshire), 8 Lancashire w....537
Dawkes, G. O. (Derbyshire) (wkt.-kpr.), Hat-trick....218
Dawson, E. W. (Eton, Camb. Univ. and Leicestershire), 159 *v.* Harrow....337
Day, S. H. (Kent), 101 on début....194
Dead Ball (Laws of Cricket)....986
Deakins, L. T., Sec., Warwickshire....599
Dean, H. (Lancashire):—
100 w. (8 times)....215
17 w. in Match....210
Dean Close School....769
Deane, H. G. (South Africa):—
Captain *v.* England....237
(and E. P. Nupen), 7th wkt. record *v.* England....238
(and H. W. Taylor), 4th wkt. record *v.* England....238
DECLARATIONS (Laws)....983, 997
de Courcy, J. H. (N.S.W.), 28 r. in Over....200
Deed, J. A. (Kent), 252 *v.* Surrey II....194
De Flamingo's Tour, 1966....810–11
v. M.C.C....334, 811
Dempster, C. S. (New Zealand and Leicestershire):—
2 Hundreds *v.* England....244
(and C. F. W. Allcott), 301 for 2nd wkt....203
(and J. E. Mills), 1st wkt. record *v.* England....244
(and M. L. Page), 3rd wkt. record *v.* England....244
Denmark *v.* Scotland....699
Denness, M. H. (Kent):—
1,606 r. in 1966....270
22 catches in 1966....369
Dennett, G. E. (Gloucestershire):—
2,147 w....214
201 w. in Season....213
100 w. (12 times)....215
10 w. in Innings....209
8 w. for 9 r....211
Denstone College....769
v. M.C.C....330
Denton, D. (Yorkshire):—
36,520 r....197
1,000 r. (21 times)....198

Denton, D. (Yorkshire):—*contd.*
69 Hundreds....................195
2 Separate Hundreds............196
104 *v.* South Africa...........239
Depeiza, C. (West Indies):—
122 *v.* Australia..................251
(and D. Atkinson), 347 for 7th wkt. *v.* Australia.204, 252, 258
DERBYSHIRE..................352–69
Averages........................354
Results...........................354
Championship Table...........350
Championship Winners........265
County Badge...................352
v. Essex.......................356–7
v. Glamorgan.................367–8
v. Gloucestershire...........365–6
v. Hampshire.................355–6
v. Kent.......................359–60
v. Lancashire.................364–5
v. Leicestershire.............362–3
v. Northamptonshire.........354–5
v. Nottinghamshire...........368–9
v. Oxford Univ................361–2
v. Somerset....................363–4
v. Sussex.......................357–8
v. Warwickshire...............360–1
v. West Indies..................292–3
v. Worcestershire.............366–7
v. Yorkshire....................358–9
Gillette Cup......................657
DERBYSHIRE II.....................727
Championship Table...........727
Desai, R. B. (India), Test Cricket..185
De Saram, F. C. (Oxford Univ.), 176 on début..............194
DEVON.........................712–13
Championship Table...........707
Devonshire, Duke of, President, Derbyshire...............352
Dewdney, T. (West Indies), Test Cricket.....................181
Dewes, J. G. (Cambridge Univ. and Middlesex) (and G. H. G. Doggart), 429* for 2nd wkt. 203
Dews, G. (Worcestershire), Fast Scoring......................200
Dexter, E. R. (Sussex):—
Birthday...........................924
Captain *v.* Australia............231
Captain *v.* India..................245
Captain *v.* New Zealand.........243
Captain *v.* Pakistan.............247
Test Cricket.......................163
4,405 r. in Test Matches........222
50 Hundreds.......................196
2 Hundreds *v.* Australia........233
2 Hundreds *v.* Pakistan........247
2 Hundreds *v.* West Indies......242
172 *v.* South Africa..............239
141 *v.* New Zealand.............244
126* *v.* India......................245
Dexter, E. R. (Sussex)—*contd.*
(and M. C. Cowdrey), 2nd wkt. record *v.* Pakistan.........247
(and P. H. Parfitt), 4th wkt. record *v.* Pakistan.........247
Dick, A. E. (New Zealand) (wkt.-kpr.):—
Test Cricket.......................183
23 w. in Test Rubber............228
Dickens, H. C., Obituary.........965
Dickinson, P. J. (Cambridge Univ. and Surrey), 100 *v.* Oxford..339
Dillon, E. W. (Kent), 108 on début.194
Dipper, A. E. (Gloucestershire):—
1,000 r. (15 times)...............198
53 Hundreds.......................196
Ditchling *v.* M.C.C.................334
Diwadkhar, S. J. (Bombay), 103 *v.* Gujarat Governor's XI.........888
Dixon, A. L. (Kent):—
115 w. in 1966....................274
11 Sussex w........................593
10 Leicestershire w...............454
8 Hampshire w.....................439
8 Leicestershire w.................491
8 Somerset w.......................552
Doggart, G. H. G. (Cambridge Univ. and Sussex):—
215* on début......................194
(and J. G. Dewes), 429 for 2nd wkt.............................203
d'Oliveira, B. L. (Worcestershire):—
Birthday...........................925
Photograph 70
Group..................................63
Five Cricketers of the Year....75–8
Test Cricket........................163
Test Match Averages, 1966.282, 283
1,536 r. in 1966...................270
2 Hundreds in 1966...............277
126 *v.* Essex........................632
123 *v.* Nottinghamshire.........620
101 *v.* Jamaica Invitation XI....849
23 catches in 1966................369
(and T. W. Graveney), 271 for 4th wkt. *v.* Essex.....267, 632
Doll, M. H. C. (Hertfordshire and Middlesex). Obituary......965
Dollery, H. E. (Warwickshire):—
1,000 r. (15 times)...............198
50 Hundreds........................196
Donnelly, M. P. (New Zealand, Oxford Univ. and Warwickshire):—
206 *v.* England............244, 260
162* *v.* Players.....................260
142 *v.* Cambridge.........260, 339
(and F. B. Smith), 5th wkt. record *v.* England.........244
Dooland, B. (South Australia and Notts.), All-Round.......216

Doreen, N. (Canterbury, N.Z.) (and J. L. Powell), 265 for 7th wkt. 204
Dorset ... 713
Championship Table ... 707
Douai School ... 769
v. M.C.C. ... 329
Douglas, J. (Middlesex) (and A. E. Stoddart), 1st wkt. Hundreds ... 202
Douglas, J. W. H. T. (Essex):—
All-Round ... 215
Captain *v.* Australia ... 231
Captain *v.* South Africa ... 237
119 *v.* South Africa ... 239
3 Hat-tricks ... 209
(and M. C. Bird), 7th wkt. record *v.* South Africa ... 238
Douglas-Home, Sir Alec (Middlesex), President of M.C.C., 1966–67 ... 93, 321
Dover, Plan of County Ground ... 442
Dover College ... 770
v. M.C.C. ... 331
Dowling, G. T. (New Zealand):—
Test Cricket ... 183
129 *v.* India ... 257
Downes, A. (Otago), 4 w. with consecutive balls ... 208
Downside School ... 770
v. M.C.C. ... 331
Dowty, Sir George, President of Worcestershire ... 617
Drag, Experimental Law ... 999, 1007
Drake, A. (Yorkshire):—
All-Round ... 216
10 w. in Innings ... 209
4 w. with consecutive balls ... 208
Driffield, L. T. (Cambridge Univ.), 7 w. for 7 r. ... 211
Drying of the Pitch ... 998, 1000
D'Souza, A. (Pakistan), Test Cricket ... 188
Ducat, A. (Surrey):—
52 Hundreds ... 196
306* *v.* Oxford Univ. ... 192
Duckworth, G. (Lancashire) (wkt.-kpr.)—
107 w. in Season ... 218
Obituary ... 965–6
Duff, R. A. (Australia):—
2 Hundreds *v.* England ... 234
104 on Test début ... 225
Duke of York's R.M.S. *v.* M.C.C. . 332
Duleepsinhji, K. S. (Sussex):—
Highest for Sussex ... 193
50 Hundreds ... 196
4 Successive Hundreds ... 199
2 Hundreds *v.* New Zealand ... 244
2 Separate Hundreds ... 196
333 *v.* Northamptonshire ... 192, 193
173 *v.* Australia ... 233
Duleep Trophy ... 887
Dulwich *v.* M.C.C. ... 330
Dulwich College ... 770
v. M.C.C. ... 330
Dumbrill, R. (South Africa), Test Cricket ... 177
Dunbar, J. G. (Charterhouse), Assistant Sec., M.C.C. ... 321
Duncan, A. (Western Province Willows), 100 *v.* Marlow ... 808
Durani, A. S. (India):—
Test Cricket ... 185
104 *v.* Madhya Pradesh ... 884
104 *v.* West Indies ... 256
(and C. G. Borde), 7th wkt. record *v.* England ... 246
Durham ... 713–14
Championship Table ... 707
Championship Winners ... 266
Dyer, A. W. (Oxford Univ.) (wkt.-kpr.), 29 w. in 1966 ... 369
Dyson, A. H. (Glamorgan) (and E. Davies), 1st wkt. Hundreds ... 202

Eady, C. J. (Tasmania), 566 *v.* Wellington ... 194
Eagar, E. D. R. (Hampshire), Sec., Hampshire ... 424
Ealham, A. (Kent), 30 catches in 1966 ... 369
Ealing *v.* M.C.C. ... 333
Earle, G. F. (Somerset), Obituary . . 966
East, R. (Essex), 9 Gloucestershire w. ... 374
Eastbourne, Plan of The Saffrons Ground ... 582
Eastbourne College ... 771
v. M.C.C. ... 329
Ebden, C. H. M. (Cambridge Univ., Sussex and Middlesex), 137 on début ... 194
Edinburgh Academy (The) ... 771
Edmeades, B. (Essex):—
Birthday ... 926
Photograph ... 370
106 w. in 1966 ... 274
9 Kent w. ... 448
Edmonds, R. B. (Warwickshire):—
Group ... 67
102* *v.* Scotland ... 604
Edrich, B. R. (Kent, Glamorgan and Oxfordshire), 101* for Oxfordshire ... 718
Edrich, J. H. (Surrey):—
Birthday ... 926
Group ... 63
Test Cricket ... 163
Test Match Averages, 1965–66 ... 819, 821
Test Match Averages, 1966 ... 282
1,978 r. in 1966 ... 270
1,060 r. in Australasia ... 822

Edrich, J. H. (Surrey):—*contd.*
45 Hundreds 196
3 Hundreds in Australia 823
3 Hundreds in 1966............277
3 Hundreds *v.* Australia.......233
310* *v.* New Zealand.......192, 244
137 *v.* Nottinghamshire........533
136* *v.* Lancashire.............570
133 *v.* Queensland.............830
132 *v.* Kent...................450
109 *v.* Australia............233, 836
21 catches in 1966.............369
(and K. F. Barrington), 2nd wkt. record *v.* New Zealand.....244
Edrich, W. J. (Middlesex and Norfolk):—
Birthday........................926
36,965 r.........................197
3,539 r. in Season..............205
2,440 r. in Test Matches.......222
1,010 r. (April 30–May 31).....207
1,000 r. (15 times)..............198
86 Hundreds....................195
3 Hundreds *v.* South Africa.....239
2 Hundreds *v.* Australia........233
100 *v.* New Zealand............244
(and D. C. S. Compton), 424 for 3rd wkt.......................203
(and D. C. S. Compton), 3rd wkt. record *v.* South Africa......238
(and P. A. Gibb), 2nd wkt. record *v.* South Africa..........238
Edwards, M. J. (Surrey):—
Birthday........................926
Photograph 563
1,064 r. in 1966...............270
116 *v.* Gloucestershire..........579
108* *v.* West Indies............307
40 catches in 1966.............369
Elgie, M. K. (South Africa), Test Cricket.....................177
Elizabeth College, Guernsey *v.* M.C.C......................328
Ellesmere College 771
v. M.C.C.........................331
Elliott, C. S. (Derbyshire):—
First-Class Umpire............1008
Test Panel.....................1008
Elliott, G. (Victoria), 9 w. for 2 r...211
Elliott, H. (Derbyshire) (wkt.-kpr.), 10 w. in Match............217
Eltham College...............771–2
Elviss, R. W. (Oxford Univ.):—
9 Royal Navy w................699
8 Lancashire w.................677
Emanuel School 772
v. M.C.C.........................331
Emmett, G. M. (Gloucestershire):—
37 Hundreds 196
2 Separate Hundreds 196
Emmett, T. (Yorkshire):—
16 w. in day....................212
Emmett, T. (Yorkshire):—*contd.*
7 w. for 9 r......................212
Endean, W. R. (South Africa):—
Test Cricket.....................177
1,630 r. in Test Matches 223
162* *v.* Australia...............249
116* *v.* England................239
116 *v.* New Zealand............254
(and J. H. B. Waite), 5th wkt. record *v.* Australia.........250
Engineer, F. M. (India):—
Test Cricket....................186
(and R. G. Nadkarni), 8th wkt. record *v.* England..........246
ENGLAND:—
Representative Body.........492
Summary of All Tests..........229
Test Cricketers (1877–1966)..161–70
England Team at The Oval, 1966, Photograph 63
ENGLAND *v.* AUSTRALIA........231–7
Highest Totals.................232
Individual Hundreds..........232–6
Match Results..................231
Record Partnerships...........232
Smallest Totals 232
Visiting Captains...............231
ENGLAND *v.* AUSTRALIA, 1965–66:—
First Test (Brisbane)........831–2
Second Test (Melbourne).....834–5
Third Test (Sydney).........835–6
Fourth Test (Adelaide)......839–40
Fifth Test (Melbourne).......841–2
England *v.* Australia, 1968, Dates and Venues...............1008
ENGLAND *v.* INDIA............245–6
Highest Totals.................245
Individual Hundreds..........245–6
Match Results..................245
Record Partnerships...........246
Smallest Totals................245
Visiting Captains...............245
ENGLAND *v.* INDIA, 1967, Test Fixtures....................1034
ENGLAND *v.* NEW ZEALAND 243–5
Highest Totals.................243
Individual Hundreds...........243
Match Results..................243
Record Partnerships..........244–5
Smallest Totals................243
Visiting Captains...............243
ENGLAND *v.* NEW ZEALAND, 1966:—
First Test (Christchurch).....843–4
Second Test (Dunedin).......845–6
Third Test (Auckland)........846–7
ENGLAND *v.* PAKISTAN..........247–8
Highest Totals.................247
Individual Hundreds...........247
Match Results..................247
Record Partnerships..........247–8
Smallest Totals................247
Visiting Captains...............247

ENGLAND *v.* PAKISTAN, 1967, Test Fixtures 1034
ENGLAND *v.* SOUTH AFRICA 237–41
Highest Totals 238
Individual Hundreds 238–40
Match Results 237
Record Partnerships 238
Smallest Totals 238
Visiting Captains 237
ENGLAND *v.* WEST INDIES 241–3
Highest Totals 241
Individual Hundreds 242–3
Record Partnerships 241–2
Smallest Totals 241
Visiting Captains 241
Wisden Trophy 241, 269
ENGLAND *v.* WEST INDIES, 1966:—
First Test (Manchester) 293–5
Second Test (Lord's) 297–9
Third Test (Trent Bridge) 301–3
Fourth Test (Leeds) 310–12
Fifth Test (Oval) 314–16
ENGLAND XI:—
v. Rest of the World XI . 346, 701–2
v. West Indies 347
English, C. R. (Griqualand West), 9 Border w. 875
English, E. A. (Hampshire), Obituary 966
English Schools C.A. *v.* Public Schools 343–4
Enthoven, H. J. (Cambridge Univ. and Middlesex), 2 Hundreds *v.* Oxford 260, 339
Entwistle, R. (Lancashire), 118 for Lancashire II 715
Epsom College 772
v. M.C.C. 332
Errata in *Wisden* 1966 59
ESSEX 370–87
Averages 372
Results 372
Championship Table 350
County Badge 370
v. Cambridge Univ. 378
v. Derbyshire 382
v. Glamorgan 383–4
v. Gloucestershire 374
v. Kent 381
v. Lancashire 382–3
v. Leicestershire 386–7
v. Northamptonshire 385–6
v. Nottinghamshire 376
v. Somerset 373
v. Surrey 379–80
v. Sussex 377
v. Warwickshire 380–1
v. West Indies 300–1
v. Worcestershire 375
v. Yorkshire 384–5
Gillette Cup Matches 657, 664
ESSEX II 728
Championship Table 727
Eton College 772–3
v. Harrow 335–6
v. M.C.C. 327
v. Winchester 806–7
Evans, D. L. (Glamorgan) (wkt.-kpr.), 34 w. in 1966 369
Evans, J. B. (Glamorgan and Leicestershire), 71 w. for Lincolnshire 716
Evans, T. G. (Kent) (wkt.-kpr.):—
Birthday 926
Fastest English Test Fifty 226
Hon. Cricket Member, M.C.C. .. 347
Test Cricket 163
104 *v.* India 245
104 *v.* West Indies 242
219 w. in Test Matches 228
20 w. in Test Rubber 229
(and T. E. Bailey), 6th wkt. record *v.* West Indies 241
(and T. W. Graveney), 6th wkt. record *v.* India 246
Evans Baillie, T. H., sports journalist, Obituary 966–7
Exeter School 773
Experimental County Championship Laws 1007

Fagg, A. E. (Kent):—
58 Hundreds 195
2 Double Hundreds 197
2 Separate Hundreds 196
First-Class Umpire 1008
Test Panel 1008
Fair and Unfair Play (Laws) 992
Fairbairn, A. (Middlesex), 108 on début 194
Fane, F. L. (Essex), 143 *v.* South Africa 239
Farooq Hamid (Pakistan), Test Cricket 188
Farrer, W. S. (South Africa):—
Test Cricket 177
207 *v.* Orange Free State 875
Farrimond, W. F. (Lancashire) (wkt.-kpr.), 7 w. in Innings . 217
Faulkner, G. A. (South Africa):—
All-Round 216
1,754 r. in Test Matches 223
3 Hundreds *v.* Australia 249
123 *v.* England 239
82 w. in Test Matches 224
Favell, L. E. (South Australia):—
Test Cricket 172
2 Separate Hundreds 196
101 *v.* India 253
Fazal Mahmood (Pakistan):—
Captain *v.* India 257
Test Cricket 188
139 w. in Test Matches 225

Fazal Mahmood (Pakistan):—
contd.
13 w. in Test Match 227
(and Alim-ud-Din), 8th wkt. record *v.* England 248
Fearnley, C. D. (Worcestershire), 112 *v.* Derbyshire...........630
Fellows-Smith, J. P. (South Africa), Test Cricket...............177
Felsted School...................773
v. M.C.C.......................329
Fender, P. G. H. (Surrey):—
All-Round 215
Fast Scoring.....................199
Fenner, F. P. (Cambridge Town), 17 w. in Match...............210
Ferguson, W. (West Indies), 11 w. in Test Match 227
Fernando, Dr. H. I. K. (Ceylon), 102* *v.* Madras...............893
Fernando, L. (Government Services), 129 *v.* Ceylon Schools......893
Ferris, J. J. (Australia and Gloucestershire):—
Australia *v.* England............172
England *v.* South Africa........164
Fettes College 773
Field, F. E. (Warwickshire), 6 w. for 2 r......................212
Fielder, A. (Kent):—
10 w. in Innings.................209
(and F. E. Woolley), 235 for last wkt.........................205
Fielders, Limitation of Onside 999, 1007
Fielding Statistics for 1966....285, 369
Fieldsman (Laws of Cricket).......991
Fiji, Representative Body, Address.492
Finchley *v.* M.C.C.................334
Fingleton, J. H. (N.S.W.):—
Birthday 927
4 Successive Test Hundreds.....199
3 Hundreds *v.* South Africa.....249
2 Hundreds *v.* England..........234
(and D. G. Bradman), 6th wkt. record *v.* England............232
(and W. A. Brown), 1st wkt. record *v.* South Africa.......250
Finlay, I., 103* for Surrey II......735
First-Class Match Defined........1001
FIRST-WICKET HUNDREDS.......201–3
Fishlock, L. B. (Surrey):—
56 Hundreds......................195
2 Separate Hundreds..............196
FIVE CRICKETERS OF THE YEAR...73–86
R. W. Barber (Warwickshire) 73–75
B. L. d'Oliveira (Worcestershire) 75–78
C. Milburn (Northamptonshire) 78–81
J. T. Murray (Middlesex).....84–86
S. M. Nurse (West Indies).....81–84
Fixture Making 88
FIXTURES FOR 1967:—
First Class...................1030–4
Gillette Cup....................1039
Indian Tour.....................1034
Minor Counties..............1035–7
Pakistan Tour...................1034
Second XI Competition.....1037–9
Flavell, J. A. (Worcestershire):—
Test Cricket.....................164
3 Hat-tricks.....................209
135 w. in 1966...................274
100 w. (8 times).................215
11 Surrey w......................628
10 Sussex w......................586
9 Kent w.........................621
9 Nottinghamshire w..............620
8 Middlesex w....................508
8 Sussex w.......................633
Fletcher, K. W. R. (Essex):—
1,550 r. in 1966.................270
2 Hundreds in 1966...............277
106 *v.* West Indies...............301
101* *v.* Leicestershire...........387
42 catches in 1966...............369
Flower, A. W., Sec., Middlesex....493
Flowers, W. (Nottinghamshire), All-Round.......................216
Folkestone *v.* M.C.C...............333
Following On (Laws).........983, 996
Forbes, C. (Nottinghamshire):—
109 w. in 1966...................275
9 Essex w........................376
9 Gloucestershire w..............540
Forbes, W. F., Throwing record...219
Foreman, D. J. (Sussex):—
110 for Sussex II................736
27 catches in 1966...............369
Forest School....................774
v. M.C.C.......................327
Forfeiture of Second Innings.997, 1007
FORMATION OF COUNTY CLUBS NOW FIRST-CLASS..................264
FORMATION OF MINOR COUNTIES...264
Foster, D. G. (Warwickshire), Throwing record...............219
Foster, F. R. (Warwickshire):—
All-Round 216
Highest for Warwickshire.......193
305* *v.* Worcestershire..........193
Foster, R. E. (Oxford Univ. and Worcestershire):—
2 Separate Hundreds......196, 197
287 *v.* Australia on Test début 193, 225, 233
171 *v.* Cambridge.................260
(and W. Rhodes), 10th wkt. record *v.* Australia 232
Foster, W. L. (Worcestershire) (and R. E. Foster), each 2 Separate Hundreds 197
Four w. with consecutive balls.....208

Fourth Innings, Heavy Scoring....221
Framlingham College............774
v. M.C.C......................327
Frank, C. N. (South Africa):—
152 *v.* Australia..............249
(and A. D. Nourse, sr.), 4th wkt. record *v.* Australia........250
Frederick, N. (Ceylon), 10 Ceylon Schools w...................893
Free Foresters *v.* Oxford University 673–4
Freeman, A. P. (Kent):—
3,776 w........................214
2,090 w. in Eight Seasons.......214
1,122 w. in Four Seasons.......214
304 w. in Season...............213
200 w. (8 times)............213–14
100 w. (17 times)..............214
100 w. by June 13.............214
17 w. in Match (twice).........210
10 w. in Innings (3 times)...209, 210
9 w. for 11 r...................211
3 Hat-tricks...................209
Freeman, D. L. (New Zealand), Youngest New Zealand Test Player.......................259
Front Foot Experiment.....999, 1007
Fry, C. B. (Sussex and Hampshire):—
Dates of Birth and Death.......928
30,886 r.......................198
Aggregate of 3,147.............206
94 Hundreds....................195
13 Hundreds in Season..........199
6 Successive Hundreds.........198
4 Successive Hundreds.........199
2 Separate Hundreds...........196
232* *v.* Players...............259
144 *v.* Australia..............233
129 *v.* South Africa...........239
(and J. Vine), 1st wkt. Hundreds.202
Fuller, E. R. H. (South Africa), Test Cricket..................177
Funston, K. J. (South Africa), Test Cricket.......................177
Fusilier Brigade *v.* I.Z...........269
Future Tours...................1001

Gaekwad, D. K. (India):—
Captain *v.* England............245
Test Cricket....................186
Gallop, D. L. (Canterbury, N.Z.), 124 *v.* Auckland................879
Galloway, J. O., Obituary.......967
Game, W. H., Throwing record....219
Ganteaume, A. G. (West Indies):—
112 *v.* England on Test début 225, 242
(and G. Carew), 1st wkt. record *v.* England...................242
Garnet, F. (Berkshire), 282 *v.* Wiltshire......................194
Gaskell, A., First-Class Umpire..1008
Gaunt, R. A. (Western Australia), Test Cricket..................172
Gavaskar, S. (All India Schools), 115 *v.* London Schools.....904
Geary, G. (Leicestershire):—
Birthday.......................928
Hon. Cricket Member, M.C.C...347
2,063 w........................214
100 w. (11 times)..............215
10 w. in Innings..........209, 210
7 w. for 7 r....................211
Gedye, S. G. (New Zealand), Test Cricket.......................184
GENTLEMEN *v.* PLAYERS..........259
Gentlemen of Leicester *v.* M.C.C...334
Ghorpade, J. M. (India), Test Cricket.......................186
Ghosh, H. (Railways), 166* *v.* North Punjab........................885
Ghulam Abbas (Pakistan Board of Control XI), 101 *v.* Ceylon..895
Ghulam Ahmed (India), Test Cricket.......................186
Ghulam Mohamed (India), Obituary.........................967
GHULAM MUSTAFA KHAN:—
"Pakistan Cricket, 1965–66" 889–92
"The Rise of Cricket in Pakistan" 153–6
Gibb, P. A. (Camb. Univ., Yorkshire and Essex):—
2 Hundreds *v.* South Africa.....239
122 *v.* Oxford...................339
106 on Test début..............225
(and W. J. Edrich), 2nd wkt. record *v.* South Africa.....238
(and J. Hardstaff, jr.), 5th wkt. record *v.* India...........246
Gibb, P. J. M. (Transvaal) (and E. A. B. Rowan), 342 for 4th wkt...........................204
Gibbons, H. H. I. (Worcestershire), 44 Hundreds..................196
Gibbs, G. (West Indies) (and L. Wight), 390 for 1st wkt. 201, 203
Gibbs, L. R. (West Indies):—
Birthday.......................928
Group...........................62
Hat-trick *v.* Australia......228, 252
Test Cricket....................181
Test Match Averages, 1966.....283
133 w. in Test Matches.........224
11 w. in Test Match............227
10 England w...................295
8 w. in Test Innings............227
(and F. C. M. Alexander), 8th wkt. record *v.* Australia....252
Gibbs, P. J. K. (Oxford Univ. and Derbyshire), 107 *v.* Warwickshire.........................608

Giffen, G. (South Australia):—
All-Round 216
161 v. England 234
113 and Hat-trick v. Lancashire.216
103 w. in Test Matches.....224, 237
17 w. in Match....................210
10 w. in Innings....................209
3 Hat-tricks....................209
Gifford, N. (Worcestershire):—
Birthday....................929
Photograph 617
Test Cricket....................164
12 Derbyshire w....................630
10 Glamorgan w....................391
8 Derbyshire w....................367
8 Somerset w....................561
Giggleswick School v. M.C.C......330
Gilchrist, R. (West Indies):—
Test Cricket....................181
117 w. in Central Lancashire League 740
GILLETTE CUP....................652–67
Final, 1966....................666
Fixtures, 1967 1039
Matches, 1966....................652–66
Past Winners....................666
Rules....................667
Gilliat, R. M. C. (Oxford Univ. and Hampshire), Captain of Oxford 668
Gilligan, A. E. R. (Sussex):—
Birthday....................929
All-Round 216
Captain v. Australia....................231
XI v. West Indies....................318
(and A. C. Russell), last wkt. record v. South Africa......238
Gilligan, A. H. H. (Sussex), Captain v. New Zealand....................243
Gimblett, H. (Somerset):—
Highest for Somerset....................193
50 Hundreds....................196
2 Separate Hundreds....................196
310 v. Essex....................192, 193
123 on début....................194
Gladwin, C. (Derbyshire), 100 w. (12 times) 215
GLAMORGAN....................388–405
Averages....................390
Results 390
Championship Table....................350
Championship Winners....................265
County Badge....................388
Minor Counties Championship..266
v. Cambridge Univ....................396
v. Derbyshire....................404–5
v. Essex....................401–2
v. Gloucestershire....................400–1
v. Hampshire....................393–4
v. Lancashire....................399–400
v. Leicestershire....................394
v. Middlesex....................397–8
GLAMORGAN:—*contd.*
v. Northamptonshire....................403–4
v. Nottinghamshire....................397
v. Somerset....................402–3
v. Surrey....................395
v. Sussex (P. M. Walker's Benefit) 398–9
v. Warwickshire....................392–3
v. West Indies....................309–10
v. Worcestershire....................391
Gillette Cup Matches....654, 657–8
GLAMORGAN II....................728–9
Championship Table 727
Championship Winners....................266
GLOUCESTERSHIRE....................406–23
Averages....................408
Results....................408
Championship Table 350
Championship Winners....................265
County Badge....................406
v. Cambridge Univ....................413
v. Derbyshire....................410–11
v. Glamorgan....................415–16
v. Hampshire....................409–10
v. Kent....................417–18
v. Lancashire....................413–14
v. Leicestershire....................414–15
v. Middlesex....................421–2
v. Northamptonshire....................422–3
v. Somerset....................418–19
v. Surrey....................420–1
v. Sussex....................419–20
v. Warwickshire....................412
v. West Indies....................295–6
v. Worcestershire (R. B. Nicholls' Benefit)....................416–17
v. Yorkshire....................409
Gillette Cup Matches....656–7, 663
GLOUCESTERSHIRE II....................729
Championship Table....................727
Championship Winners....................266
Goddard, J. D. (West Indies):—
Captain v. Australia....................250
Captain v. England....................241
Captain v. India....................255
Captain v. New Zealand....................254
Test Cricket....................181
(and O. G. Smith), 7th wkt. record v. England....................242
(and F. M. Worrell), 502 for 4th wkt....................201
Goddard, T. L. (South Africa):—
Birthday....................929
Captain v. Australia....................248
Captain v. New Zealand....................254
Test Cricket....................177
2,164 r. in Test Matches....................223
102 v. North....................877
88 w. in Test Matches....................224
6 w. for 3 r....................212
(and D. J. McGlew), 1st wkt. record v. Australia....................250

Goddard, T. W. (Gloucestershire):—
Hat-trick *v.* South Africa...228, 241
2,979 w....................214
200 w. (4 times)..........213, 214
100 w. (16 times)..............214
17 w. in Day..................212
17 w. in Match................210
10 w. in Innings...............210
6 Hat-tricks..................208
Obituary...................967–8
Goel, R. (Delhi), 9 Jammu and Kashmir w.................885
Goldstein, F. S. (Oxford Univ.):—
Secretary of Oxford, 1967......668
131 *v.* Royal Navy............699
Gomez, G. E. (West Indies):—
101 *v.* India..................255
(and J. B. Stollmeyer), 434 for 3rd wkt.......................203
Goodwin, K. (Lancashire) (wkt.-kpr.), 61 w. in 1966........369
Goonesena, G. (Cambridge Univ. and Nottinghamshire):—
All-Round 216
211 *v.* Oxford............260, 339
(M. J.) Gopalan Trophy..........893
Gopinath, C. D. (India), Test Cricket 186
Gordon, A.:—
120 for Warwickshire II........721
100* for Warwickshire II.......736
Gordonstoun School.............775
Gover, A. R. (Surrey):—
200 w. (twice)............213, 214
100 w. (8 times)...............215
4 w. with consecutive balls......208
Grace, Dr. E. M. (Gloucestershire), 10 w. in Innings..........209
Grace, Dr. W. G. (Gloucestershire):—
Dates of Birth and Death.......929
All-Round 215
Captain *v.* Australia...........231
Highest for Gloucestershire.....193
Testimonials...................263
Throwing the Cricket Ball......219
54,896 r......................197
Aggregate of 2,739.............206
1,000 r. (28 times).............198
1,000 r. in May................206
217 Hundreds in all Cricket....196
126 First-Class Hundreds.......195
15 Hundreds *v.* Players.........259
2 Hundreds *v.* Australia........233
2 Separate Hundreds............196
344 *v.* Kent...................192
318* *v.* Yorkshire..........192, 193
301 *v.* Sussex..................193
217 *v.* Players.................259
215 *v.* Players.................259
152 on Test début..............225
130 and 102* at Canterbury....196
Grace, Dr. W. G. (Gloucestershire):—*contd.*
123 and Hat-trick *v.* Kent......216
104 and 10 w..................217
2,876 w......................214
100 w. (10 times)..............215
17 w. in Match................210
10 w. in Innings..........209, 217
871 catches...................218
(and A. E. Stoddart), 1st wkt. Hundreds 202
Graham, H. (Australia):—
2 Hundreds *v.* England.........234
107 on Test début..............225
Graham, J. N. (Kent):—
63 w. for Kent II..............731
9 Lancashire w.................457
Grant, G. C. (West Indies):—
Captain *v.* Australia...........250
Captain *v.* England............241
Grant, R. S. (West Indies), Captain *v.* England 241
Graveney, J. K. (Gloucestershire), 10 w. in Innings............210
Graveney, T. W. (Gloucestershire and Worcestershire):—
Birthday......................930
Photograph 64
Group.........................63
Test Cricket..................164
Test Match Averages, 1966......282
41,831 r.....................197
3,566 r. in Test Matches........222
1,777 r. in 1966...............270
1,000 r. (19 times)............198
111 Centuries.................195
4 Hundreds in 1966............277
4 Hundreds *v.* West Indies......242
2 Hundreds *v.* Pakistan........247
2 Separate Hundreds 196
175 *v.* India 246
166 *v.* Essex..................632
165 *v.* West Indies.........242, 316
111 *v.* Australia...............233
109 *v.* Surrey 576
109 *v.* West Indies.........242, 303
20 catches in 1966.............369
(and B. d'Oliveira), 271 for 4th wkt. *v.* Essex..........267, 632
(and T. G. Evans), 6th wkt. record *v.* India..............246
(and C. Milburn), 5th wkt. record *v.* West Indies..241, 299
(and J. T. Murray), 8th wkt. record *v.* West Indies..241, 316
(and P. E. Richardson), 2nd wkt. record *v.* West Indies......241
(and F. S. Trueman), 9th wkt. record *v.* Pakistan.........247
Gray, J. R. (Hampshire) (and R. E. Marshall), 1st wkt. Hundreds 202

Gray, L. H. (Middlesex), First-Class Umpire............1008
GREAT TOTALS..................219
Green, D. J., 104 for Wiltshire....722
Green, D. M. (Lancashire):—
1,180 r. in 1966...............271
115 v. Nottinghamshire.........537
Greenhough, T. (Lancashire), Test Cricket 164
Green Jackets Club v. I.Z.........269
Greensword, S. (Leicestershire), 83 w. for Leicestershire II.....732
Gregory, C. W. (N.S.W.):—
383 v. Queensland..............192
318 r. in Day..................201
Gregory, J. M. (N.S.W.):—
Birthday.......................930
All-Round......................216
Fastest Test Century and Fifty..226
119 v. South Africa............249
100 v. England.................234
85 w. in Test Matches..........224
Gregory, R. J. (Surrey), 39 Hundreds..........................196
Gregory, S. E. (N.S.W.):—
Captain v. England.............231
Captain v. South Africa........248
2,282 r. in Test Matches.......222
2,193 r. v. England............237
4 Hundreds v. England.......234–5
(and J. McC. Blackham), 9th wkt. record v. England........232
Gresham's School...............775
v. M.C.C.......................330
Greswell, W. T. (Somerset), President of Somerset..........545
Grieves, K. J. (Lancashire):—
63 catches in Season...........218
8 catches in Match.............218
Griffin, G. (South Africa):—
Hat-trick v. England.......228, 241
Test Cricket...................177
Griffith, C. C. (West Indies):—
Birthday.......................930
Group...........................62
Test Cricket...................181
Test Match Averages, 1966.....283
(and W. W. Hall), 9th wkt. record v. England.....242, 315
Griffith, E. H. C. (Jamaica), 150 v. Windward and Leeward Islands.....................896
Griffith, K. (English Schools' C.A.), 100* v. Public Schools 343
Griffith, S. C. (Sussex):—
Birthday.......................930
Secretary, M.C.C...............321
Speech to County Secs.........1009
140 v. West Indies on Test début 225, 242
Griffiths, J. A., West Indies Scorer, Group...........................62
Grimmett, C. V. (South Australia):—
Birthday.......................930
216 w. in Test Matches.........224
44 w. in Rubber v. South Africa.250
14 w. v. South Africa...........227
10 w. in Innings...............209
Grinter, T. G. (Essex), Obituary..968
Grout, A. T. W. (Queensland):—
Birthday.......................930
Test Cricket...................172
Test Match Averages, 1965–66..819
187 w. in Test Matches.........228
23 w. in Test Rubber...........228
8 w. in Test Match (twice).....229
8 catches in Innings...........217
6 catches in Test Innings.......229
(and R. Benaud), 8th wkt. record v. South Africa............250
Grover, J. N. (Oxford Univ.), 121 v. Cambridge..................339
Guard, G. M. (India), Test Cricket.186
Guernsey Island v. M.C.C.......328
Guest, C. (Victoria), Test Cricket..172
Guillen, S. C. (West Indies and New Zealand), Test Cricket.181, 184
Guise, J. L. (Winchester, Oxford Univ. and Middlesex), 278 v. Eton 194
Gulrej Ali (Central Zone Schools), 135 v. London Schools.....904
Gunn, G. (Nottinghamshire):—
1,000 r. (20 times).............198
62 Hundreds....................195
2 Hundreds v. Australia.........233
2 Separate Hundreds............196
119 on Test début..............225
(and G. V. Gunn), Hundreds in Same Match...................197
(and W. W. Whysall), 1st wkt. Hundreds.....................202
Gunn, G. V. (Nottinghamshire) (and G. Gunn), Hundreds in Same Match...................197
Gunn, J. (Nottinghamshire):—
All-Round 216
41 Hundreds....................196
Gunn, T. (Sussex) (wkt.-kpr.), 21 w. in 1964 369
Gunn, W. (Nottinghamshire):—
48 Hundreds....................196
102* v. Australia 233
(and A. Shrewsbury), 398 for 2nd wkt...........................205
Gupte, B. P. (India), Test Cricket..186
Gupte, S. P. (India):—
Test Cricket...................186
149 w. in Test Matches.........224
10 w. in Innings...............210
9 w. in Test Innings...........227
Gurunathan, S. K., Indian cricket writer, Obituary..........968

Guy, J. W. (New Zealand):—
Test Cricket...184
102 *v.* India...257

Haberdashers' Aske's School, Elstree...775
v. M.C.C....329
Hadlee, W. A. (New Zealand):—
Captain *v.* England...243
116 *v.* England...244
(and M. L. Page), 6th wkt. record *v.* England...244
Hafeez, A. (India and Pakistan):—
Test Cricket...186, 188
See also Kardar, A. H.
Haig, N. E. (Middlesex):—
All-Round...216
Obituary...968–9
Haig, W. S. (Otago) (and B. Sutcliffe), 266 for 5th wkt...204
Haigh, S. (Yorkshire):—
All-Round...216
2,012 w...214
100 w. (11 times)...215
5 Hat-tricks...208
4 w. with consecutive balls...208
Haileybury and I.S.C....776
v. Cheltenham...340–1
v. M.C.C....328
Hale, K. F. H., (Eton) 109 *v.* Harrow...337
Hale, T. S., 104* for Cambridgeshire...710
Hall, G. G. (N. E. Transvaal):—
11 Orange Free State w...877
8 Griqualand West w...876
Hall, G. I. (South Africa), Test Cricket...177
Hall, I. W. (Derbyshire):—
102 *v.* Oxford Univ...362
101 and 101 *v.* Kent...197
Hall, P. M. (Oxford Univ. and Hampshire), 101 on début...194
Hall, W. W. (West Indies):—
Birthday...931
Group...62
Hat-trick *v.* Pakistan...228
Test Cricket...181
Test Match Averages, 1966...283
166 w. in Test Cricket...224
11 w. in Test Match...227
8 Minor Counties w...300
(and F. C. M. Alexander), 134 for 9th wkt...205
(and F. C. M. Alexander), 9th wkt. record *v.* Australia...252
(and C. C. Griffith), 9th wkt. record *v.* England...242, 315
(and A. L. Valentine), last wkt. record *v.* Australia...252
Hallam, M. R. (Leicestershire):—
1,502 r. in 1966...270

Hallam, M. R. (Leicestershire):—*contd.*
2 Separate Hundreds...196, 197
135 v. Hampshire...489
107* and 149* *v.* Worcestershire...197
30 catches in 1966...369
Halliwell, E. A. (South Africa) (and A. D. Nourse, sr.), 8th wkt. record *v.* Australia...250
Hallows, C. (Lancashire):—
1,000 r. in May...206
55 Hundreds...195
2 Separate Hundreds...196
(and F. Watson), 1st wkt. Hundreds...202
Hallows, J. (Lancashire), All-Round...216
Halse, C. G. (South Africa), Test Cricket...177
Hamence, R. A. (South Australia), 2 Separate Hundreds...196
Hamilton, C. P. (Army and Kent), 121 on début...194
Hammond, W. R. (Gloucestershire):—
Dates of Birth and Death...931
Captain *v.* Australia...231
Captain *v.* New Zealand...243
Captain *v.* South Africa...237
Fastest English Test Double Century...226
50,493 r...197
7,249 r. in Test Matches...222
3,323 r. in Season...206
2,852 r. *v.* Australia...237
1,281 r. in Month...207
1,042 r. in May...206
1,000 r. (22 times)...198
905 r. in Rubber *v.* Australia...236
167 Hundreds...195
15 Hundreds in Season...199
13 Hundreds in Season...199
9 Hundreds *v.* Australia...233
6 Hundreds *v.* South Africa...239
4 Hundreds *v.* New Zealand...244
4 Successive Hundreds...199
2 Hundreds *v.* India...246
2 Separate Hundreds...196
2 Separate Test Hundreds...225, 233
336* *v.* New Zealand...192, 244
317 *v.* Nottinghamshire...192
302* *v.* Glamorgan...193
302 *v.* Glamorgan...193
295 r. in Day in Test...226
138 *v.* West Indies...242
83 w. in Test Matches...224
78 catches in Season...218
10 catches in Match...218
(and L. E. G. Ames), 4th wkt. record *v.* South Africa...238
(and L. E. G. Ames), 5th wkt. record *v.* New Zealand...244

Hammond, W. R. (Gloucestershire):—*contd.*
(and J. Hardstaff, jr.), 3rd wkt. record *v.* New Zealand.....244
(and L. Hutton), 3rd wkt. record *v.* West Indies............241
(and D. R. Jardine), 3rd wkt. record *v.* Australia........232
(and E. Paynter), 4th wkt. record *v.* Australia..............232
(and T. S. Worthington), 4th wkt. record *v.* India...........246
HAMPSHIRE....................424–40
Averages.....................426
Results......................426
Championship Table...........350
Championship Winners.........265
County Badge.................424
v. Derbyshire..............435
v. Essex...................439–40
v. Glamorgan...............432–3
v. Gloucestershire.........428–9
v. Kent....................438–9
v. Lancashire..............437
v. Leicestershire..........430–1
v. Middlesex...............437–8
v. Nottinghamshire.........429–30
v. Somerset................433
v. Surrey..................427
v. Sussex..................434
v. Sussex (Friendly).......426
v. West Indies.............317–18
v. Worcestershire..........431–2
v. Yorkshire...............436
Gillette Cup Matches 652–3, 658–9, 662, 665
HAMPSHIRE II.................729–30
Championship Table...........727
Hampshire, J. H. (Yorkshire):—
Group........................66
1,179 r. in 1966.............271
25 catches in 1966...........369
Hampstead *v.* M.C.C..........334
Handled the Ball (Laws).......989
Instances in First-Class Cricket..207
Hanif Mohammad (Pakistan):—
Birthday.....................931
Captain *v.* Australia........253
Captain *v.* New Zealand......258
Longest First-Class Innings...192
Slow Scoring.................226
Test Cricket.................188
3,584 r. in Test Matches......223
891 r. in Pakistan Season.....206
43 Hundreds..................196
3 Hundreds *v.* New Zealand....258
2 Hundreds *v.* Australia......253
2 Hundreds *v.* England........247
2 Hundreds *v.* India..........257
2 Hundreds *v.* West Indies....256
2 Separate Hundreds..........196
2 Separate Test Hundreds..225, 247
Hanif Mohammad (Pakistan):—*contd.*
499 *v.* Bahawalpur............191
337 *v.* West Indies...........192, 256
114 *v.* Ceylon................895
(and Alim-ud-Din), 1st wkt. record *v.* England.........248
(and Alim-ud-Din), 277 for 1st wkt.......................203
(and J. Burki), 3rd wkt. record *v.* England...............248
(and Majid Jahangir), 217 for 6th wkt.......................204
Hanumant Singh (India):—
Test Cricket.................186
168* *v.* East Zone............887
106 *v.* Hyderabad.............888
105 *v.* England on Test début 225, 246
Harbottle, M. N. (Army and Dorset), 156 on début..............194
Hardikar, M. S. (India):—
Test Cricket.................186
112 *v.* State Bank of India...887
9 Rajasthan w................886
Hardinge, H. T. W. (Kent):—
33,519 r.....................198
1,000 r. (18 times)..........198
75 Hundreds..................195
4 Successive Hundreds........199
2 Separate Hundreds..........196
Hardstaff, J., jr. (Nottinghamshire):—
Birthday.....................931
31,841 r.....................198
1,636 r. in Test Matches......222
83 Hundreds..................195
2 Hundreds *v.* New Zealand....244
205* *v.* India................246
169* *v.* Australia............233
(and P. A. Gibb), 5th wkt. record *v.* India..................246
(and W. R. Hammond), 3rd wkt. record *v.* New Zealand.......244
(and L. Hutton), 6th wkt. record *v.* Australia..............232
Hare, T. (Eton), 103 *v.* Harrow....337
Harford, N. S. (New Zealand):—
Test Cricket.................184
103* *v.* Central Districts....879
Harman, R. (Surrey), 9 Glamorgan w..........................568
Harris, 4th Lord (Kent):—
Dates of Birth and Death......931
Captain *v.* Australia........231
Harris, C. B. (Nottinghamshire) (and W. W. Keeton), 1st wkt. Hundreds.....................202
Harris, L. R. (Transvaal "B"), 116 *v.* N.E. Transvaal..........875
Harris, M. J. (Middlesex):—
Birthday.....................931
Photograph...................493

Harris, M. J. (Middlesex):—*contd.*
114 *v.* Derbyshire..............504
100* for Middlesex II..........732
Harris, P. G. Z. (New Zealand):—
Slow Scoring..................226
Test Cricket..................184
101 *v.* South Africa..........254
Harris, R. (New Zealand), Test Cricket..................184
Harrison, W. P. (Cambridge Univ., Kent and Middlesex), Obituary..................975
Harrow School..................776
v. Eton..................335–6
v. I.Z..................269
v. M.C.C..................328
Hartigan, R. J. (N.S.W. and Queensland):—
116 *v.* England on Test début 225, 235
(and C. Hill), 8th wkt. record *v.* England..................232
Harvey, G. (Norfolk), Obituary....969
Harvey, J. F. (Derbyshire):—
1,112 r. in 1966..............271
103* *v.* Nottinghamshire.......538
Harvey, R. N. (Victoria and N.S.W.):—
Birthday..................932
Test Cricket..................172
6,149 r. in Test Matches........222
2,416 r. *v.* England............237
67 Hundreds..................195
8 Hundreds *v.* South Africa.....249
6 Hundreds *v.* England..........235
4 Hundreds *v.* India............253
3 Hundreds *v.* West Indies......251
(and C. C. McDonald), 3rd wkt. record *v.* West Indies.........252
(and K. R. Miller), 4th wkt. record *v.* South Africa.........250
Haseeb Ahsan (Pakistan):—
Test Cricket..................188
(and Afaq Hussain), last wkt. record *v.* England.........248
Hassett, A. L. (Victoria):—
Birthday..................932
Captain *v.* England............231
Captain *v.* South Africa.......248
3,073 r. in Test Matches........222
59 Hundreds..................195
4 Hundreds *v.* England.........235
3 Hundreds *v.* South Africa.....249
2 Hundreds *v.* West Indies......251
2 Separate Hundreds..........196
198* *v.* India..................253
(and D. G. Bradman), 3rd wkt. record *v.* England.........232
(and C. C. McDonald), 2nd wkt. record *v.* South Africa......250
(and K. R. Miller), 4th wkt. record *v.* West Indies.......252
Hastilow, C. A. F., M.C.C. Committee..................321
Hastings Festival..............700
Address of Secretary...........492
Hathorn, M. (South Africa), 102 *v.* England..................239
Hat-Tricks:—
Double..................208
In Test Matches..............228
Three and More..............208–9
Havant *v.* M.C.C..............334
Hawke, 7th Lord (Yorkshire):—
Dates of Birth and Death......932
Captain *v.* South Africa........237
(and R. Peel), 292 for 8th wkt....205
Hawke, N. J. N. (South Australia):—
Birthday..................932
Test Cricket..................173
Test Match Averages, 1965–66 819, 820
86 w. in Test Matches..........224
10 Queensland w..............864
9 Western Australian w.........862
Hawkesworth, W. (Otago) (and R. C. Blunt), 184 for last wkt..................205
Hayes, E. G. (Surrey and Leicestershire):—
1,000 r. (16 times).............198
48 Hundreds..................196
Hayes, J. A. (New Zealand), Test Cricket..................184
Hays, D. L. (Cambridge Univ.) (wkt.-kpr.), 23 w. in 1966...369
Hayward, T. W. (Surrey):—
Dates of Birth and Death.......932
All-Round..................216
43,518 r..................197
Aggregate of 3,518.............205
1,999 r. in Test Matches........222
1,000 r. (20 times)..............198
1,000 r. (April 16–May 31)......207
104 Hundreds..................195
13 Hundreds in Season.........199
4 Successive Hundreds.........199
2 Separate Hundreds.........196
2 Hundreds *v.* Australia........233
315* *v.* Lancashire............192
203 *v.* Gentlemen............259
122 *v.* South Africa............239
(and R. Abel), 448 for 4th wkt...204
(and J. B. Hobbs), 352 for 1st wkt..................202
(and J. B. Hobbs), 1st wkt. Hundreds..................202
Hazare, V. S. (India):—
Birthday..................932
Captain *v.* England............245
Captain *v.* West Indies.........255
2,192 r. in Test Matches........223
57 Hundreds..................195

Hazare, V. S. (India):—*contd.*
2 Hundreds *v.* Australia........253
2 Hundreds *v.* England........246
2 Hundreds *v.* West Indies.....256
2 Separate Hundreds..........196
2 Separate Test Hundreds..225, 253
316* *v.* Baroda...............192
309 *v.* Hindus.................192
146* *v.* Pakistan..............257
(and Gul Mahomed), 577 for 4th wkt..................201, 203
(and V. L. Manjrekar), 4th wkt. record *v.* England.........246
(and V. Mankad), 3rd wkt. record *v.* England...............246
(and V. M. Merchant), 3rd wkt. record *v.* England..........246
(and N. D. Nagarwalla), 245 for 9th wkt.....................205
(and D. G. Phadkar), 6th wkt. record *v.* England..........246
Hazell, H. L. (Somerset), 28 r. in Over.....................200
Headley, G. A. (West Indies):—
Birthday........................932
2,190 r. in Test Matches........223
8 Hundreds *v.* England.........242
2 Hundreds *v.* Australia........251
2 Separate Hundreds..........196
2 Separate Test Hundreds..225, 242
344* *v.* Lord Tennyson's Team..192
176 on Test début..............225
(and R. K. Nunes), 2nd wkt. record *v.* England.........242
(and C. C. Passalique), 487 for 6th wkt...............201, 204
Headley. R. G. A. (Worcestershire):—
1,028 r. in 1966...............271
137 *v.* Yorkshire..............625
39 catches in 1966.............369
Hearn, P. (Kent), 124 on début....194
Hearne, F. (Kent and S. Africa):—
England *v.* South Africa........164
South Africa *v.* England........177
Hearne. J. T. (Middlesex):—
3,061 w.........................214
257 w. in Season...............213
200 w. (3 times)................213
100 w. (15 times)...............214
100 w. by June 12..............214
4 Hat-tricks....................208
Hat-trick *v.* Australia.....228. 236
(and H. Wood), 9th wkt. record *v.* South Africa............238
Hearne, J. W. (Middlesex):—
All-Round.......................215
37,250 r.........................197
1,000 r. (19 times)..............198
96 Hundreds.....................195
114 *v.* Australia...............233
3 Hat-tricks.....................209
Heaslip, J. G. (Gentlemen of Ireland, Club Cricket Conference and Civil Service), Obituary...................969
Heath, G. C. (Natal "B"), 122 *v.* Orange Free State.........876
Heine, P. S. (South Africa), Test Cricket.....................177
Hemmings, E. E., 41 w. for Warwickshire II.................737
Hemsley, E. J. O. (Worcestershire), 105 for Worcestershire II...737
Henderson, W. A. (N.E. Transvaal):—
7 w. for 4 r....................211
4 w. with consecutive balls......208
Hendren, E. (Middlesex):—
Dates of Birth and Death.......933
57,610 r........................197
3,525 r. in Test Matches........222
1,000 r. (25 times)..............198
Aggregate of 3,311.............206
Aggregate of 1,765 in West Indies........................206
170 Hundreds...................195
13 Hundreds in Season.........199
3 Hundreds *v.* Australia.........233
2 Hundreds *v.* West Indies......242
2 Separate Hundreds...........196
301* *v.* Worcestershire.........193
277* at Lord's..................263
194* *v.* Gentlemen..............259
(and H. Larwood), 8th wkt. record *v.* Australia........232
Hendriks, J. L. (West Indies) (wkt.-kpr.):—
Photograph.......................64
Group............................62
Test Cricket....................181
Test Match Averages, 1966.....283
34 w. in 1966..................285
Hendry, H. L. (Victoria):—
325* *v.* New Zealand...........192
112 *v.* England................235
Henfield *v.* M.C.C..............333
(George) Heriot's School.........774
Herman, O. W. (Hampshire), First-Class Umpire...............1008
HERTFORDSHIRE...................714
Championship Table...........707
Championship Winners........266
Gillette Cup.................653–4
Heyhoe, R. (England Women), 113 *v.* New Zealand..............910
Hickton, W. (Lancashire), All 10 w. 209
Hide, J. B. (Sussex), 4 w. with consecutive balls..............208
Higgs, K. (Lancashire):—
Birthday........................933
Photograph..................65, 459
Group............................63
Test Cricket....................155

Higgs, K. (Lancashire):—*contd.*
Test Match Averages, 1965–66 819, 821
Test Match Averages, 1966.....282
8 Kent w....................457
8 West Indies w..............299
(and J. A. Snow), last wkt. record *v.* West Indies....241, 268, 316
Higgs, K. A. (Sussex), 101 on début 194
HIGHEST AGGREGATES:—
Individual....................205–6
Team.........................220–1
HIGHEST INDIVIDUAL SCORES....191–4
HIGHEST PARTNERSHIPS...........201
HIGHEST TOTAL FOR EACH COUNTY.219
Highgate School...............776
v. M.C.C.....................327
Hilder, A. L. (Kent), 103* on début 195
Hill, A. (Yorkshire), 3 Hat-tricks..209
Hill, A. J. L. (Hampshire), 124 *v.* South Africa..............239
Hill, C. (South Australia):—
Dates of Birth and Death.......933
3,412 r. in Test Matches........222
2,660 r. *v.* England............237
45 Hundreds....................196
4 Hundreds *v.* England.........235
3 Hundreds *v.* South Africa.....249
365* *v.* N.S.W..................192
(and R. J. Hartigan), 8th wkt. record *v.* England..........232
(and H. Trumble), 7th wkt. record *v.* England...........232
(and E. Walkley), 232 for 9th wkt. 205
Hill, N. (Nottinghamshire):—
Birthday.......................933
Captain of Nottinghamshire....528
1,003 r. in 1966...............271
20 catches in 1966.............369
Hill-Wood, W. W. (Derbyshire), M.C.C. Committee.......321
Hinde, Brigadier H. M. (Berkshire), Obituary...............975
Hinkly, E. (Kent), 10 w. in Innings.209
Hirst, G. H. (Yorkshire):—
Dates of Birth and Death.......933
All-Round......................215
Benefit........................263
Highest for Yorkshire.........193
36,203 r.......................197
1,000 r. (19 times)............198
60 Hundreds....................195
341 *v.* Leicestershire.......192, 193
2,739 w........................214
208 w. in Season...............213
100 w. (15 times)..............214
Hit the Ball Twice (Laws).........989
Instances in First-Class Cricket..207
Hit Wicket (Laws).............989–90
Hoad, E. L. G. (West Indies) (and H. C. Griffith), 138 for last wkt........................205
Hoare, D. G. (Western Australia), Test Cricket.............173
Hobbs, Sir J. B. (Surrey):—
Dates of Birth and Death.......933
Fast Scoring...................200
61,237 r.......................197
5,410 r. in Test Matches.......222
3,636 r. *v.* Australia..........237
Aggregate of 3,024.............206
1,000 r. (26 times)............198
244 Hundreds in all Cricket....196
197 First-Class Hundreds......195
16 Hundreds in Season.........199
16 Hundreds *v.* Gentlemen.....260
12 Hundreds *v.* Australia......233
4 Successive Hundreds.........199
2 Hundreds *v.* South Africa.....239
316* *v.* Middlesex at Lord's 192, 263
266* *v.* Gentlemen.............259
159 *v.* West Indies.............242
(and T. W. Hayward), 352 for 1st wkt........................202
(and T. W. Hayward), 1st wkt. Hundreds...................202
(and W. Rhodes), 1st wkt. record *v.* Australia...............232
(and A. Sandham), 428 for 1st wkt........................201
(and A. Sandham), 1st wkt. Hundreds.....................202
(and H. Sutcliffe), 1st wkt. Hundreds.....................202
Hobbs, R. N. S. (Essex):—
13 Glamorgan w................402
10 Yorkshire w.................651
35 catches in 1966.............369
Holder, J. W., 44 w. for Hampshire II.........................730
Holford, D. A. J. (West Indies):—
Group...........................62
Test Cricket...................181
Test Match Averages, 1966.....283
2 Hundreds in 1966............284
107* *v.* Lancashire............290
105 *v.* England..........242, 299
12 Cambridge Univ. w..........291
8 w. *v.* Jamaica................897
(and G. S. Sobers), 6th wkt. record *v.* England 242, 267, 299
Hollies, W. E. (Warwickshire):—
2,323 w........................214
100 w. (14 times)..............214
10 w. in Innings...............210
Holloway, G. J. W. (Gloucestershire), Obituary...........969
Holmes, E. R. T. (Oxford Univ. and Surrey), 113 *v.* Cambridge..339
Holmes, P. (Yorkshire):—
Birthday.......................934

Holmes, P. (Yorkshire):—*contd.*
30,574 r. 198
1,000 r. (15 times) 198
67 Hundreds. 195
315* *v.* Middlesex at Lord's 192, 263
302* *v.* Hampshire. 193
(and H. Sutcliffe), 555 for 1st wkt. 201, 203
(and H. Sutcliffe), 1st wkt. Hundreds 202
Holt, J. K. (West Indies):—
Test Cricket 181
166 *v.* England. 242
123 *v.* India. 255
(and C. A. McWatt), 8th wkt. record *v.* England. 242
Holt, R. A. A. (Harrow), 111 *v.* Eton. 337
Hone, B. W. (South Australia and Oxford Univ.), 167 *v.* Cambridge .339
Hong Kong, M.C.C. in. 847
Honourable Artillery Company:—
v. I.Z. 269
v. M.C.C. .327
Hooker, J. E. H. (N.S.W.):—
4 w. with consecutive balls 208
(and A. F. Kippax), 307 for last wkt. 205
Hooker, R. W. (Middlesex):—
102 *v.* Somerset. 558
8 West Indies w. 304
Hopwood, J. L. (Lancashire), All-Round. 216
Horak, D. J. (Transvaal "B"), 111 *v.* Border. 877
Horan, T. (Australia), 124 *v.* England 235
Horlicks Awards. 269
Horner, N. F. (Warwickshire) (and K. Ibadulla), 377* for 1st wkt. 202
Horton, H. (Hampshire):—
Birthday 934
Photograph 424
1,312 r. in 1966. 270
2 Hundreds in 1966 277
148* *v.* Middlesex 438
146* *v.* Leicestershire 489
(and D. A. Livingstone), 272 for 3rd wkt. *v.* Middlesex . .267, 438
Horton, M. J. (Worcestershire):—
All-Round .216
Test Cricket. 165
1,272 r. in 1966. 270
114 *v.* Hampshire (Gillette Cup). 665
Hotchkin, N. S. (Eton, Cambridge Univ. and Middlesex), 2 Hundreds *v.* Harrow. 337
Hough, K. W. (New Zealand), Test Cricket 184
Hours of Play (First-Class Matches) 994–5
Sunday 995
Household Brigade:—
v. I.Z. 269
v. Lords and Commons 278
v. M.C.C. 334
Howard, C. G., Sec., Surrey 563
Howard, K. (Lancashire), 8 Oxford Univ. w. 676
Howard, N. D. (Lancashire), Captain *v.* India 245
Howarth, J., 42 w. for Nottinghamshire II 734
Howell, H. (Warwickshire), 10 w. in Innings 209
Howell, M. (Oxford Univ. and Surrey), 170 *v.* Cambridge 260, 339
Howell, W. P. (N.S.W.):—
17 w. in Match. 210
10 w. in Innings. 209
Howorth, R. (Worcestershire):—
All-Round .216
100 w. (9 times) 215
Hoyos, W. F. B., Asst. Manager, West Indies Team, Group . . .62
Hubble, J. C. (Kent) (wkt.-kpr.), 10 w. in Match. 217
Hugo, D. (Western Province Colts), 102 *v.* M.C.C. Schools. 902
Huish, F. H. (Kent) (wkt.-kpr.):—
102 w. in Season 218
10 w. in Match. 217
Human, J. H. (Cambridge Univ. and Middlesex), 158* on début. .195
HUNDREDS:—
In 1966. . . . . .276–8, 284–5
Individual. 195–6
Most in Season. 199
On début 194–5
4 or more in succession. 198–9
2 Separate. 196–7
Hunte, C. C. (West Indies):—
Birthday 935
Group 62
Test Cricket 181
Test Match Averages, 1966. 283
2,986 r. in Test Matches 223
3 Hundreds *v.* England. 242
3 Hundreds *v.* Pakistan. 256
2 Hundreds in 1966. 285
206 *v.* Somerset 267, 306
142 on Test début 225
135 *v.* England. 242, 294
110 *v.* Australia 251
(and B. Davis), 1st wkt. record *v.* Australia. 252
(and R. B. Kanhai), 2nd wkt. record *v.* Australia. 252

Hunte, C. C. (West Indies):—*contd.*
(and G. S. Sobers), 446 for 2nd wkt....................203
Hunting, G. L. (Northumberland), Obituary.................969
Hurstpierpoint College...........777
v. M.C.C......................330
Hussain, A. (Assam), 120 *v.* Orissa.885
Hutchings, K. L. (Kent), 126 *v.* Australia..................233
Hutton, Sir Leonard (Yorkshire):—
Birthday.......................935
Benefit........................263
Captain *v.* Australia...........231
Captain *v.* New Zealand........243
Captain *v.* West Indies..........241
Hon. Cricket Member, M.C.C...347
40,140 r........................197
6,971 r. in Test Matches........222
3,429 r. in Season..............205
2,428 r. *v.* Australia............237
1,294 r. in Month...............207
1,050 r. in Month............. 207
1,000 r. (17 times)..............198
129 Hundreds...................195
5 Hundreds *v.* Australia.........233
5 Hundreds *v.* West Indies......242
4 Hundreds *v.* South Africa.....239
3 Hundreds *v.* New Zealand.....244
2 Hundreds *v.* India............246
2 Separate Hundreds...........196
364 *v.* Australia.......192, 193, 233
241 *v.* Gentlemen..............259
(and W. R. Hammond), 3rd wkt. record *v.* West Indies......241
(and J. Hardstaff, jr.), 6th wkt. record *v.* Australia.........232
(and M. Leyland), 2nd wkt. record *v.* Australia.........232
(and R. J. Simpson), 1st wkt. record *v.* New Zealand.....244
(and C. Washbrook), 359 for 1st wkt. *v.* South Africa...202, 238
(and C. Washbrook), 1st wkt. Hundreds................202

Ibadulla, K. (Warwickshire, Pakistan and Otago):—
Group...........................67
Test Cricket....................188
166 *v.* Australia on Test début 225, 253
1,044 r. in 1966.................271
111 *v.* Auckland................879
31 catches in 1966.............369
(and N. F. Horner), 377 for 1st wkt........................202
Ibrahim, K. C. (India) (and K. M. Rangnekar), 274 for 7th wkt. 204
Iddon, J. (Lancashire), 46 Hundreds 196
Ijaz Butt (Pakistan):—
Slow Scoring....................226
Test Cricket....................188
Ijaz Husain (Railway Reds):—
173 *v.* Lahore Reds.............891
158 *r.* Lahore Greens...........891
Ikin, J. T. (Lancashire and Staffordshire):—
Birthday.......................935
Hon. Cricket Member, M.C.C...347
Illingworth, R. (Yorkshire):—
Birthday.......................935
Group 63, 66
All-Round 215
Test Cricket....................165
Test Match Averages, 1966.282, 283
100 w. (8 times)................215
100 w. in 1966..................274
11 Leicestershire w.............482
22 catches in 1966.............369
(and R. Swetman), 7th wkt. record *v.* India............247
Imperial Cricket Conference, *see* International Cricket Conference
Imtiaz Ahmed (Pakistan) (wkt.-kpr.):—
Birthday.......................935
Test Cricket....................188
2,079 r. in Test Matches........223
209 *v.* New Zealand............258
135 *v.* India....................257
122 *v.* West Indies.............256
5 w. in Test Innings............229
(and Mushtaq Mohammad), 2nd wkt. record *v.* England.....248
(and Mushtaq Mohammad), 6th wkt. record *v.* England.....248
(and Waqar Hassan), 308 for 7th wkt........................204
Inder Dev, G. (Services):—
103* *v.* State Bank of India......888
10 South Punjab w..............884
9 Jammu and Kashmir w.........885
INDIA:—
"Cricket in 1965–66" (P. N. Sundaresan)...........880–9
"Indian Cricket—Its Problems and Players" (Dicky Rutnagur)................143–7
"Some Dates in Indian Cricket History" (Rowland Bowen) 147–50
Test Statistics (Stanley Conder) 150–3
Duleep Trophy..............887
Moin-ud-Dowla Tournament.887–8
Ranji Trophy 882–7
Representative Body...........492
Summary of All Tests..........230
Test Cricketers, 1932–65......185–7

INDIA:—*contd.*
Yeshwant Rao Memorial Tournament 888
INDIA *v.* AUSTRALIA............252–3
INDIA *v.* ENGLAND.............245–6
Highest Totals..................245
Individual Hundreds.........245–6
Lowest Totals...................245
Match Results...................245
Record Partnerships............246
Visiting Captains................245
INDIA *v.* ENGLAND, 1967, Test Fixtures....................1034
INDIA *v.* NEW ZEALAND.........256–7
INDIA *v.* PAKISTAN................257
INDIA *v.* WEST INDIES...........255–6
INDIA *v.* WEST INDIES, 1966–67 100
India Gymkhana *v.* M.C.C.......333
Individual Hundreds (35 or more) 195–6
Individual Hundreds in 1966 276–8, 284–5
Indrajitsingh, K. S. (India):—
Test Cricket 186
119 *v.* Prof. Deodhar's XI.......888
Inglis, R., 156* for Durham.......713
Inman, C. C. (Leics. and Ceylon):—
Birthday 935
Photograph 475
Fast Scoring.......................199
1,314 r. in 1966..................270
3 Hundreds in 1966..............277
113* *v.* Nottinghamshire.......543
110 *v.* Lancashire................474
109* *v.* Northamptonshire.......481
102 *v.* Governor's XI............895
32 r. in Over.......................200
Innings (Laws of Cricket).........983
Insole, D. J. (Essex):—
Birthday 935
Chairman of Selectors.........1006
M.C.C. Committee................321
Test Cricket 165
54 Hundreds.......................195
110* *v.* South Africa............239
INTERNATIONAL CRICKET CONFERENCE.........................1001
Meeting..................1007–8
Interval (Laws of Cricket) 983–4, 994–5
Intikhab Alam (Pakistan):—
Test Cricket 188
9 Ceylon w.........................895
Inverarity, R. J. (Western Australia):—
177 *v.* South Australia..........862
109 *v.* Queensland...............856
Ipswich School.....................777
v. M.C.C.............................330
Iqbal Awan (Bahawalpur):—
118 *v.* Multan.....................890
111 *v.* Lahore Greens............891
Iredale, F. A. (N.S.W.), 2 Hundreds *v.* England.................235
IRELAND:—
v. M.C.C.......................700–1
v. Middlesex......................699
v. Scotland..................699–700
Ireland, J. F. (Cambridge Univ), Hat-trick *v.* Oxford.........260
Iremonger, J. (Nottinghamshire) (and A. O. Jones), 1st wkt. Hundreds.....................202
IRISH CRICKET IN 1966..........906–8
(Wilfred) Isaacs' South Africans' Tour, 1966.............809–10
Isle of Wight *v.* M.C.C............334
Israr Ali (Pakistan):—
Test Cricket 188
6 w. for 1 r.........................212
I Zingari in 1966..................269
Jackman, R. D. (Surrey):—
42 w. for Surrey II...............735
8 Warwickshire w.................610
Jackson, A. A. (N.S.W.), 164 *v.* England on Test début.225, 235
Jackson, A. B. (Derbyshire), 10 Warwickshire w..............614
Jackson, Rt. Hon. Sir F. S. (Yorkshire):—
Dates of Birth and Death.......935
All-Round 216
5 Hundreds *v.* Australia........233
Jackson, Capt. G. R. (Derbyshire), Obituary.....................969
Jackson, H. L. (Derbyshire):—
Test Cricket 165
100 w. (10 times).................215
9 w. for 17 r.......................211
Jackson, V. E. (N.S.W. and Leicestershire), All-Round.....216
Jaisimha, M. L. (India):—
Slow Scoring.......................226
Test Cricket 186
1,625 r. in Test Matches........223
2 Hundreds *v.* England.........246
160 *v.* North Zone...............887
111 *v.* State Bank of India......888
Jakeman, F. (Northamptonshire), First-Class Umpire........1008
Jameson, J. A. (Warwickshire):—
Group 67
1,270 r. in 1966...................270
118* *v.* Somerset.................555
Jamshedji, R. J. (India), Oldest Indian Test début..........259
Jardine, D. R. (Surrey):—
Dates of Birth and Death.......936
Captain *v.* Australia.............231
Captain *v.* India..................245
Captain *v.* New Zealand........243
35 Hundreds.......................196
127 *v.* West Indies...............242

Jardine, D. R. (Surrey):—*contd.*
(and W. R. Hammond), 3rd wkt. record *v.* Australia........232
Jarman, B. N. (South Australia) (wkt.-kpr.):—
Test Cricket..................173
196 *v.* New South Wales........859
10 w. in Match...............217
5 w. in Test Innings...........229
Jarvis, T. W. (New Zealand):—
Test Cricket..................184
Test Match Averages, 1966......821
Javed Bhatti (Bahawalpur), 142 *v.* Multan....................890
Jayasinghe, S. (Leicestershire and Ceylon), 118 *v.* Pakistan....895
Jefferson, R. I. (Surrey):—
11 Yorkshire w................648
8 Derbyshire w................566
Jena, B. (Orissa), 110 *v.* Assam....885
Jenkins, R. O. (Worcestershire):—
All-Round....................216
Double Hat-trick..............208
Fast Scoring...................200
3 Hat-tricks..................209
Jephson, D. L. A. (Surrey) (and R. Abel), 364 for 1st wkt.......202
Jepson, A. (Nottinghamshire):—
First-Class Umpire...........1008
Test Panel....................1008
Jersey Island *v.* M.C.C...........328
Jessop, G. L. (Gloucestershire):—
Dates of Birth and Death.......936
All-Round..............215, 216
Fast Scoring...................199
Fastest English Test Century....226
53 Hundreds...................196
2 Separate Hundreds...........196
104 *v.* Australia..............233
28 r. in Over (twice)...........200
Jewell, J. E. (Surrey II and Orange Free State), Obituary.....969
Johnson, G., 111 for Kent II......730
Johnson, I. W. (Victoria):—
Captain *v.* England...........231
Captain *v.* India..............252
Captain *v.* Pakistan...........253
Captain *v.* West Indies.........250
109 w. in Test Matches.........224
(and R. Benaud), 8th wkt. record *v.* West Indies............252
Johnson, L. A. (Northamptonshire) (wkt.-kpr.):—
Birthday.....................936
Photograph...................510
10 catches in Match............217
10 w. in Match................217
Johnston, W. A. (Victoria), 160 w. in Test Matches...........224
Johnstone, C. P. (Kent), President of Kent..................441
Jones, A. (Glamorgan):—
1,865 r. in 1966...............270
2 Hundreds in 1966............277
161* *v.* West Indies...........310
104* *v.* Essex.................402
Jones, A. O. (Nottinghamshire):—
Captain *v.* Australia...........231
(and J. Iremonger), 1st wkt. Hundreds...................202
(and A. Shrewsbury), 391 for 1st wkt.......................201
Jones, C. J. E., Obituary.......969–70
Jones, E. (Glamorgan) (wkt.-kpr.), 27 w. in 1966..............369
Jones, I. J. (Glamorgan):—
Birthday.....................936
Photograph...................388
Test Cricket..................165
Test Match Averages, 1965–66 819, 821
Test Match Averages, 1966.282, 283
8 w. for 11 r...................211
Joshi, A. (Maharashtra):—
13 Gujerat w..................884
8 Saurashtra w................883
Joshi, C. G. (Rajasthan), 8 Mysore w...........................886
Joshi, P. G. (India), Test Cricket..186
Jowett, C. J. C. (Dorset), Obituary.970
Joy, F. D. H. (Somerset), Obituary.970
Judd, A. K. (Cambridge Univ. and Hampshire), 124 *v.* Oxford..339
Julian, R. (Leicestershire), Testimonial, 1967..............458

Kanhai, R. B. (West Indies):—
Birthday.....................936
Group.........................62
Test Cricket..................181
Test Match Averages, 1966.....283
3,923 r. in Test Matches........223
1,028 r. in 1966...............283
4 Hundreds *v.* Australia........251
3 Hundreds in 1966............284
3 Hundreds *v.* India...........255
2 Hundreds *v.* England......242–3
2 Separate Test Hundreds..225, 251
217 *v.* Pakistan...............256
192* *v.* Oxford University......287
104 *v.* England............243, 315
103 *v.* T. N. Pearce's XI.......319
(and C.C. Hunte), 2nd wkt. record *v.* Australia...............252
Kanitkar, H. S. (Maharashtra), 116 *v.* Baroda.................883
Kardar, A. H. (India and Pakistan):—
See also Hafeez, A.
Captain *v.* England...........247
Captain *v.* India..............257
Captain *v.* West Indies........256
Test Cricket........186, 188, 189

Keeton, W. W. (Nottinghamshire):—
Highest for Nottinghamshire ... 192
54 Hundreds ... 196
312* *v.* Middlesex ... 192, 193
(and C. B. Harris), 1st wkt. Hundreds ... 202
Kelleway, C. E. (N.S.W.):—
2 Hundreds *v.* South Africa ... 249
147 *v.* England ... 235
(and W. Bardsley), 3rd wkt. record *v.* South Africa ... 250
(and V. S. Ransford), 6th wkt. record *v.* South Africa ... 250
Kelly, J. J. (N.S.W.) (wkt.-kpr.), 8 w. in Test Match ... 229
Kelly, P. C. (Western Australia):—
132 *v.* New South Wales ... 855
119 and 108* *v.* M.C.C. ... 197, 825
103 *v.* New South Wales ... 870
Kelly College ... 777
Kenley *v.* M.C.C. ... 332
Kennedy, A. S. (Hampshire):—
All-Round ... 215
2,874 w. ... 214
204 w. in Season ... 213
100 w. (15 times) ... 214
10 w. in Innings ... 209
8 w. for 11 r. ... 211
7 w. for 8 r. ... 212
3 Hat-tricks ... 209
Kennington Oval ... 93–4, 564
Kenny, R. B. (India), Test Cricket ... 186
KENT ... 441–58
Averages ... 443
Results ... 443
Championship Table ... 350
Championship Winners ... 265
County Badge ... 441
v. Derbyshire ... 447
v. Essex ... 448
v. Glamorgan ... 445
v. Gloucestershire ... 450–1
v. Hampshire ... 455–6
v. Lancashire ... 456–7
v. Leicestershire ... 453–4
v. Middlesex ... 444
v. Northamptonshire ... 451–2
v. Nottinghamshire ... 457–8
v. Oxford Univ. ... 449
v. Surrey ... 450
v. Sussex ... 446
v. Warwickshire ... 454–5
v. West Indies ... 305
v. Worcestershire ... 452–3
Gillette Cup Matches ... 655–6, 658–9
KENT II ... 730–1
Championship Table ... 727
Championship Winners ... 266
Kent College ... 778
Kent Schools *v.* M.C.C. ... 334
Kenyon, D. (Worcestershire):—
Birthday ... 937
Kenyon, D. (Worcestershire):—*contd.*
Captain of Worcestershire ... 617
Fast Scoring ... 200
Test Selector ... 1006
35,843 r. ... 197
1,091 r. in 1966 ... 271
1,000 r. (18 times) ... 198
73 Hundreds ... 195
2 Hundreds in 1966 ... 277
114 *v.* Kent ... 621
103 *v.* Northamptonshire ... 626
Khan Mohammad (Pakistan), Test Cricket ... 188
Khawar Nabi (Hyderabad), 131 *v.* Khairpur ... 890
Kher, B. G. (Madhya Pradesh), 120 *v.* Uttar Pradesh ... 884
Killick, E. H. (Sussex):—
All-Round ... 216
5 w. for 2 r. ... 212
Killick, Rev. E. T. (Cambridge Univ. and Middlesex), 136 *v.* Oxford ... 339
Kilner, R. (Yorkshire):—
All-Round ... 216
Benefit ... 263
Kimbolton School ... 778
King, J. H. (Leicestershire):—
All-Round ... 216
2 Separate Hundreds ... 196
King, L. A. (West Indies), Test Cricket ... 181
Kippax, A. F. (N.S.W.):—
Birthday ... 937
43 Hundreds ... 196
2 Separate Hundreds ... 196
315* *v.* Queensland ... 192
146 *v.* West Indies ... 251
100 *v.* England ... 235
(and J. E. H. Hooker), 307 for last wkt. ... 205
King Edward's School, Birmingham ... 778
v. M.C.C. ... 332
King Henry VIII School, Coventry ... 779
King William's College ... 779
King's College School, Wimbledon ... 779–80
v. M.C.C. ... 332
King's College, Taunton ... 779
v. M.C.C. ... 329
King's School, Bruton ... 780
v. M.C.C. ... 329
King's School, Canterbury ... 780
v. M.C.C. ... 329
King's School, Ely ... 780
King's School, Macclesfield ... 781
King's School, Rochester ... 781
Kingston Grammar School *v.* M.C.C. ... 332

Kingswood School..............781
v. M.C.C.......................329
Kirsten, N. (Border) (wkt.-kpr.), 7 w. in Innings............217
Kitchen, M. (Somerset):—
Birthday.......................938
Photograph 545
1,422 r. in 1966...............270
2 Hundreds in 1966 277
111* *v.* Sussex...............597
100 *v.* Worcestershire..........631
Kline, L. F. (Victoria):—
Hat-trick *v.* South Africa ..228, 250
Test Cricket....................173
(and K. D. Mackay), last wkt. record *v.* West Indies......252
Knight, B. (Witney Town), Obituary 970
Knight, B. R. (Essex):—
Birthday.......................938
All-Round 216
Test Cricket....................165
Test Match Averages, 1965–66 819, 821
Test Match Averages, 1966.282, 283
127 *v.* India 246
125 *v.* New Zealand...........244
8 Sussex w......................590
20 catches in 1966..............369
(and P. H. Parfitt), 6th wkt. record *v.* West Indies.......244
Knock-Out Competition (Gillette Cup).....................652–67
Knott, A. (Kent) (wkt.-kpr.), 81 w. in 1966 369
Knox, G. K. (Lancashire):—
100 *v.* Derbyshire 468
27 catches in 1966..............369
Kripal Singh, A. G. (India):—
Test Cricket....................186
100* *v.* New Zealand on Test début...................225, 257
Kumar, V. V. (India), Test Cricket.186
Kunderam, B. K. (India) (wkt.-kpr.):—
Test Cricket....................186
2 Hundreds *v.* England 246
111* *v.* Andhra 882
101* *v.* Associated Cement Company 888
100 *v.* Central Zone 887
5 w. in Test Innings 229
(and D. N. Sardesai), 2nd wkt. record *v.* England.........246

Lacey, Sir F. E. (Hampshire), 323* *v.* Norfolk....................194
Laker, J. C. (Surrey and Essex):—
Birthday.......................938
Benefit.........................263
Test Cricket....................166
Laker, J. C. (Surrey and Essex):— *contd.*
193 w. in Test Matches 223
100 w. (11 times)...............215
46 w. in Rubber *v.* Australia....236
19 w. in Match *v.* Australia 210, 227, 236
10 w. in Innings (twice).........210
10 w. in Test Innings......210, 227
9 w. in Test Innings............227
8 w. for 2 r......................211
4 Hat-tricks.....................208
Lamb, M. (Western Province Willows), 131 *v.* Berkshire.....808
Lambert, W. (Sussex), 107 and 157 *v.* Epsom (1817)............196
LANCASHIRE....................459–74
Averages........................461
Results 461
Championship Table 350
Championship Winners..........265
County Badge...................959
v. Derbyshire..................467–8
v. Glamorgan...................464
v. Gloucestershire..............462
v. Hampshire..................468–9
v. Kent.......................472–3
v. Leicestershire..............473–4
v. Middlesex..................471–2
v. Nottinghamshire...........462–3
v. Somerset.................469–70
v. Surrey.......................474
v. Sussex.....................466–7
v. Warwickshire................465
v. West Indies..............289–90
v. Worcestershire.............465–6
v. Yorkshire..................470–1
Gillette Cup Matches 652, 660, 662–3
LANCASHIRE II...............715, 731
Championship Tables......707, 727
Championship Winners.........266
Lancashire League, 1966..........740
Address of Secretary............492
Lancaster Royal Grammar School 781–2
Lance, H. R. (South Africa):—
Test Cricket....................178
169 *v.* Natal.....................874
147 *v.* Western Province.........874
(and D. Mackay-Coghill), 174 for last wkt................205, 873
Lancing College..................782
v. M.C.C.......................328
Langford, B. A. (Somerset):—
112 w. in 1966...................274
11 Middlesex w 558
11 Northamptonshire w..........557
10 Gloucestershire w............551
8 Lancashire w 470
8 Nottinghamshire w............559
8 Surrey w.......................553

Langley, G. R. A. (South Australia) (wkt.-kpr.):—
21 w. in Test Rubber..........229
9 w. in Test Match..........229
5 w. in Test Innings (3 times)...229
Langridge, James (Sussex):—
All-Round..........215
31,716 r..........198
1,000 r. (20 times)..........198
42 Hundreds..........196
7 w. for 8 r..........212
Obituary..........970–1
Langridge, John (Sussex):—
34,380 r..........198
1,000 r. (17 times)..........198
76 Hundreds..........195
4 Successive Hundreds..........199
2 Separate Hundreds..........196
69 catches in Season..........218
First-Class Umpire..........1008
(and E. H. Bowley), 490 for 1st wkt..........201
Langton, A. B. C. (South Africa) (and E. L. Dalton), 9th wkt. record v. England..........238
Larrier, O. (United States), 11 w. v. Canada..........901
Larter, J. D. F. (Northamptonshire), Test Cricket..........166
Larwood, H. (Nottinghamshire):—
Birthday..........938
Hon. Cricket Member, M.C.C...347
100 w. (8 times)..........215
78 w. in Test Matches..........224
(and E. Hendren), 8th wkt. record v. Australia..........232
Lashley, P. D. (West Indies):—
Group..........62
Test Cricket..........181
Test Match Averages, 1966..........283
121* v. Jamaica..........897
121* v. Minor Counties..........300
120 v. Trinidad..........897
Last Over (Laws of Cricket)..........984
Latchman, H. C. (Middlesex), 8 Oxford Univ. w..........674
Latymer Upper School v. M.C.C...328
Laver, F. (Australia), 8 w. in Test Innings..........227
Lawrence, G. B. (South Africa):—
Test Cricket..........178
11 Western Province w..........874
9 Eastern Province w..........874
8 w. in Test Innings..........228
Lawrence, J. W. (Somerset and Lincolnshire), 50 w. for Lincolnshire..........716
Lawrence Trophy..........268
Lawry, W. M. (Victoria):—
Birthday..........938
Test Cricket..........173
Test Match Averages, 1965–66..819
Lawry, W. M. (Victoria):—*contd.*
2,876 r. in Test Matches..........222
1,445 r. in 1965–66..........871
38 Hundreds..........196
6 Hundreds v. England..........235
210 v. West Indies..........251
166 v. England..........235, 831
160 v. South Australia..........853
157 v. South Africa..........249
153 v M.C.C..........828
126* v. M.C.C..........838
119 v. England..........235, 840
108 v. England..........235, 842
(and R. B. Simpson), 1st wkt. record v. England..........232, 840
(and R. B. Simpson), 382 for 1st wkt. v. West Indies...201, 252
Law Society v. Lords and Commons..........278
LAWS OF CRICKET (1947 CODE) (2nd Edition)..........980–1006
Lay, R. S., First-Class Umpire 1008
LEAGUE CRICKET IN 1966..........739–47
Leamington v. M.C.C..........328
Leary, S. E. (Kent):—
Benefit, 1957..........458
29 catches in 1966..........399
Le Couteur, P. R. (Oxford Univ. and Victoria), 160 and 11 w. v. Cambridge..........260
Lee, F. S. (Somerset) (and J. W. Lee), 1st wkt. Hundreds..........202
Lee, H. W. (Middlesex):—
37 Hundreds..........196
2 Separate Hundreds..........196
Lee, I. S. (Victoria) (and S. O. Quin), 424 for 4th wkt..........204
Lee, J. W. (Somerset) (and F. S. Lee). 1st wkt. Hundreds....202
Leeds Grammar School..........782
Lees, W. (Surrey), Benefit..........262
Leese, Lt.-Gen. Sir Oliver:—
President of M.C.C..........321
President of Warwickshire..........599
Leg before Wicket (Laws)..89–90, 990
Leg-bye (Laws)..........987–8
Leggat, I. B. (New Zealand) (and H. B. Cave), 239 for 9th wkt..........205
Legge, G. B. (Kent), 196 v. New Zealand..........244
Leicester, Plan of County Ground.476
Leicester v. M.C.C..........330
LEICESTERSHIRE..........475–92
Averages..........477
Results..........477
Championship Table..........350
Championship Winners..........265
v. Derbyshire..........478–9
v. Essex..........478
v. Glamorgan..........489–90
v. Hampshire..........489

LEICESTERSHIRE:—*contd.*
v. Kent....................491
v. Lancashire.................482–3
v. Middlesex.................483–4
v. Northamptonshire..........480–1
v. Nottinghamshire...........485–6
v. Surrey....................484–5
v. Sussex...................479–80
v. Warwickshire..............486–7
v. West Indies..............316–17
v. Worcestershire............487–8
v. Yorkshire.................481–2
Gillette Cup....................659
LEICESTERSHIRE II...............731–2
Championship Table..............727
Championship Winners............726
Lenham, L. J. (Sussex), 1,198 r. in 1966....................271
Leslie, C. F. H. (Oxford Univ. and Middlesex), 111* on début..195
Lester, E. I. (Yorkshire):—
Group.............................66
2 Separate Hundreds..............196
Leveson Gower, Sir H. D. G. (Surrey), Captain *v.* South Africa 237
Lewis, A. R. (Cambridge Univ. and Glamorgan):—
Birthday.........................939
Photograph.......................388
2,198 r. in 1966.................270
5 Hundreds in 1966...............276
223 *v.* Kent................267, 445
146 *v.* Gloucestershire.........401
103* *v.* Oxford.................339
103 *v.* Northamptonshire........404
102 *v.* Middlesex...............497
100 *v.* Gloucestershire.........415
(and R. M. Prideaux), 1st wkt. Hundreds......................203
Lewis, C. (London Schools), 107 *v.* Madras Schools................904
Lewis, Sir Edward, M.C.C. Committee........................321
Leyland, M. (Yorkshire):—
Dates of Birth and Death.........939
Fast Scoring.....................200
33,660 r.........................198
2,764 r. in Test Matches.........222
1,000 r. (17 times)..............198
80 Hundreds......................195
7 Hundreds *v.* Australia........233
2 Hundreds *v.* South Africa....239
(and L. Hutton), 2nd wkt. record *v.* Australia...................232
Leys School, The.................782
v. M.C.C.......................328
Light (Laws of Cricket)....992–3, 997
Appeals against..................997
Lightfoot, A. (Northamptonshire) 8 Yorkshire w...................644
Lilley, A. A. (Warwickshire) (wkt.-kpr.), 84 w. *v.* Australia....236
Lillywhite, James, jr. (Sussex):—
Captain *v.* Australia...........231
10 w. in Innings.................209
LINCOLNSHIRE.................715–16
Championship Table...............707
Championship Winners.......266, 707
Gillette Cup...................652–3
Lindsay, J. D. (South Africa):—
Test Cricket.....................178
30 r. in Over....................200
(and K. C. Bland), 6th wkt. record *v.* Australia...........250
Lindsay, N. V. (Transvaal) (and G. R. McCubbin), 221 for 9th wkt.......................205
Lindwall, R. R. (N.S.W. and Queensland):—
Birthday.........................939
Test Cricket.....................173
1,502 r. in Test Matches.........223
118 *v.* West Indies..............251
100 *v.* England..................235
228 w. in Test Matches...........224
114 w. *v.* England...............237
Lister, J. (Worcestershire), Sec., Worcestershire...................617
Liverpool College................783
v. M.C.C.......................333
Livingstone, D. A. (Hampshire):—
116 *v.* Middlesex...............438
(and H. Horton), 272 for 3rd wkt. *v.* Middlesex...........267, 438
Llandovery College...............783
Llewellyn, C. B. (Hampshire and South Africa):—
All-Round........................216
2 Separate Hundreds..............196
(and L. J. Tancred), 2nd wkt. record *v.* Australia...........250
Lloyd, C. (British Guiana):—
194 *v.* Jamaica.................897
107 *v.* Barbados................897
Lloyd, D. (Lancashire), 10 Gloucestershire w..................414
Lloyds Bank *v.* M.C.C...........327
Loader, P. J. (Surrey):—
Hat-trick *v.* West Indies....228, 243
Test Cricket.....................166
9 w. for 17 r....................211
Lock, G. A. R. (Surrey, W. Australia and Leicestershire):—
Birthday.........................939
Captain of Leicestershire........475
Test Cricket.....................166
2,499 w..........................214
200 w. in Season (twice).........213
170 w. in Test Matches...........223
109 w. in 1966...................274
100 w. (13 times)................215
34 w. in Rubber *v.* New Zealand.245

Lock, G. A. R. (Surrey, W. Australia and Leicestershire):—*contd.*
12 Derbyshire w. 479
10 Derbyshire w. 363
10 w. in Innings. 210
8 South Australian w. 858
8 Warwickshire w. 487
5 w. for 2 r. 212
3 Hat-tricks 209
63 catches in Season. 218
38 catches in 1966. 369
8 catches in Match 218
(and R. W. Barber), 9th wkt. record *v.* India. 246
(and P. J. Sharpe), 9th wkt. record *v.* West Indies. 241
Lockwood, W. H. (Nottinghamshire and Surrey):—
All-Round 216
3 Hat-tricks 209
Lohmann, G. A. (Surrey):—
Hat-trick *v.* South Africa. . .228, 241
200 w. (3 times). 213
112 w. in Test Matches. 224
100 w. (8 times). 215
15 w. in Test Match 227
9 w. in Test Innings. 227
8 w. in Test Innings (3 times) 227, 228
8 w. for 7 r. 211, 227
London Schools in India and Ceylon, 1965–66. 903–4
London Schools' C.A. *v.* M.C.C. . . .332
Long, A. (Surrey) (wkt.-kpr.):—
57 w. in 1966. 369
11 catches in Match. 217
7 catches in Innings. 218
Lords and Commons, 1966. 278
v. M.C.C. 278, 332
LORD'S CRICKET GROUND. 263–4
Biggest Hit 265
Highest Individual Scores. 263
Highest Totals. 263–4
Plan of Ground. 494
Rebuilding and Redevelopment . 324
Three Grounds 263
Lord's Taverners XI *v.* Old England XI 335
Lord Wandsworth College. 783
Loretto School. 783–4
Lost Ball (Laws of Cricket). 985
Loughborough College *v.* M.C.C. . 328
Loughton *v.* M.C.C. 334
Lowe, R. G. H. (Cambridge Univ. and Kent), Hat-trick *v.* Oxford 260
Lowry, T. C. (New Zealand), Captain *v.* England 243
Loxton, S. J. (Victoria), 101 *v.* South Africa. 249
Luckhurst, B. W. (Kent):—
Birthday .940
Photograph 441
1,763 r. in 1966. 270
5 Hundreds in 1966 276
183 *v.* Surrey 450
133 *v.* Gloucestershire 451
110 *v.* Glamorgan. 445
104 *v.* West Indies. 305
101 *v.* Oxford Univ. 449
43 catches in 1966. 369
Lumb, J. L., 147 for Yorkshire II . 723
Luncheon Interval (Laws) 984, 994
Luthra, S. (North Punjab), 101 *v.* Services. 884
Luton Town *v.* M.C.C. 327
Lyons, J. J. (South Australia), 134 *v.* England 235

McAdam, K. P. W. J. (Cambridge Univ.), Hon. Sec. of Cambridge. 679
Macartney, C. G. (N.S.W.):—
Dates of Birth and Death. 940
Fast Scoring. 226
2,131 r. in Test Matches. 222
48 Hundreds. 196
5 Hundreds *v.* England. 235
4 Successive Hundreds. 199
2 Separate Hundreds. 196
2 Hundreds *v.* South Africa. 249
345 *v.* Nottinghamshire 192, 193, 201
Macaulay, G. G. (Yorkshire):—
211 w. in Season. 213
100 w. (10 times). 215
7 w. for 9 r. 212
6 w. for 3 r. 212
4 Hat-tricks. 208
Macaulay, M. J. (South Africa), Test Cricket 178
McCabe, S. J. (N.S.W.):—
Birthday .940
Fast Scoring 226
2,748 r. in Test Matches 222
4 Hundreds *v.* England 235
2 Hundreds *v.* South Africa 249
(and W. H. Ponsford), 389 for 3rd wkt. 203
McConnon, J. E. (Glamorgan), 28 r. in Over 200
McCool, C. L. (Queensland and Somerset), 104* *v.* England. 235
McCormack, V. C. (Jamaica), Obituary. 971
McCrudden, R. J. G., Sec., Gloucestershire. 406
McCubbin, G. R. (Transvaal) (and N. V. Lindsay), 221 for 9th wkt. .205
McDonald, C. C. (Victoria):—
Test Cricket 174

McDonald, C. C. (Victoria):—
contd.
3,106 r. in Test Matches 222
2 Hundreds *v.* England 235
2 Hundreds *v.* West Indies 251
154 *v.* South Africa 249
(and R. N. Harvey), 3rd wkt. record *v.* West Indies......252
(and A. L. Hassett), 2nd wkt. record *v.* South Africa.....250
McDonald, E. A. (Victoria and Lancashire):—
205 w. in season 213
3 Hat-tricks....................209
McDonald, N. (Natal "B"), 100* *v.* Griqualand West 877
McDonell, H. C. (Cambridge Univ., Surrey and Hampshire), Obituary.................971
McDonnell, P. S. (Australia):—
Captain *v.* England...........231
3 Hundreds *v.* England 235
MacGibbon, A. R. (New Zealand), Test Cricket..............184
McGlew, D. J. (South Africa):—
Captain *v.* England............237
Slow Scoring...................226
Test Cricket....................178
2,440 r. in Test Matches 223
3 Hundreds *v.* New Zealand....254
2 Hundreds *v.* Australia........249
2 Hundreds *v.* England 240
(and T. L. Goddard), 1st wkt. record *v.* Australia 250
McGregor, S. N. (New Zealand):—
Test Cricket...................184
111 *v.* Pakistan 258
McIntyre, A. J. (Surrey), Benefit..263
Mackay, K. D. (Queensland):—
Slow Scoring..................226
Test Cricket...................174
1,507 r. in Test Matches 223
(and L. F. Kline), last wkt. record *v.* West Indies 252
(and J. W. Martin), 9th wkt. record *v.* West Indies) 252
(and I. W. Meckiff), 9th wkt. record *v.* South Africa.....250
Mackay-Coghill, D. (Transvaal), (and H. R. Lance), 174 for last wkt...........205, 873
McKenzie, G. D. (Western Australia):—
Birthday.......................941
Test Cricket...................174
Test Match Averages, 1965–66 819, 820
137 w. in Test Matches 224
(and R. Benaud), 7th wkt. record *v.* South Africa...........250
Mackenzie, R., Throwing Record .219
McKinnon, A. H. (South Africa):—
Test Cricket...................178
11 Western Province w.........874
MacLaren, A. C. (Lancashire):—
Dates of Birth and Death......941
Captain *v.* Australia...........231
Highest for Lancashire.........193
1,931 r. in Test Matches 222
47 Hundreds 196
5 Hundreds *v.* Australia........233
424 *v.* Somerset 192, 193
108 on début...................195
(and R. H. Spooner), 368 for 1st wkt..........................202
MacLaren, G. (Lancashire), Obituary..........................971
McLean, R. A. (South Africa):—
Test Cricket...................178
2,120 r. in Test Matches 223
3 Hundreds *v.* England 240
2 Hundreds *v.* New Zealand....254
118 *v.* Col. Stevens' XI 810
McLeod, C. E. (Australia), 112 *v.* England 235
McMorris, E. D. (West Indies):—
Group..........................62
Test Cricket...................182
Test Match Averages, 1966.....283
2 Hundreds in 1966 285
190 *v.* British Guiana..........897
157* *v.* Derbyshire 212
134 *v.* Windward and Leeward Islands 896
127* *v.* Trinidad 896
125 *v.* India 255
116 *v.* Kent 305
McVicker, N. M., 71 w. for Lincolnshire 716
McWatt, C. A. (West Indies) (and J. K. Holt), 8th wkt. record *v.* England 242
Madras Team in Ceylon 893
Madray, I. S. (West Indies and Lincolnshire), Test Cricket.182
Magdalen College, Oxford *v.* I.Z..269
Magdalen College School 784
v. M.C.C......................330
Magdalene College, Cambridge *v.* I.Z...........................269
Mahendra Kumar, B. (Hyderabad):—
104* *v.* Kerala.................883
9 Kerala w.....................883
Mahmood Hussain (Pakistan), Test Cricket 188
Maidenhead and Bray *v.* M.C.C...333
Mailey, A. A. (N.S.W.):—
99 w. in Test Matches 224
36 w. in Rubber *v.* England 236
10 w. in Innings 209
9 w. in Test Innings...........227

Mailey, A. A. (N.S.W.):—*contd.*
(and J. M. Taylor), last wkt. record *v.* England 232
Majid Jahangir (Pakistan):—
Test Cricket 188
241 *v.* Bahawalpur 891
127* *v.* Punjab Univ..........891
(and Hanif Mohammad), 217 for 6th wkt. 204
(and Zafar Altaf), 346 for 4th wkt.........................204
(and Zulfiqar Ali), 171 for 8th wkt.........................205
Makepeace, H. (Lanchashire):—
43 Hundreds 196
117 *v.* Australia...............233
Malden Wanderers *v.* M.C.C. 333
Malvern College.................784
v. M.C.C.......................327
Manasseh, M. (Oxford Univ. and Middlesex), 100* *v.* Cambridge.......................339
Manchester Grammar School..784–5
v. M.C.C.......................331
Manjrekar, V. L. (India):—
Test Cricket....................186
3,209 r. in Test Matches 223
35 Hundreds 196
3 Hundreds *v.* England 246
3 Hundreds *v.* New Zealand....257
175 *v.* Mysore 886
119 *v.* Prof. Deodhar's XI......888
118 *v.* West Indies..............256
(and V. S. Hazare), 4th wkt. record *v.* England.........246
Mankad, V. (India):—
Birthday.........................941
All-Round 216
Captain *v.* Pakistan 257
Test Cricket.....................186
2,109 r. in Test Matches 223
2 Hundreds *v.* Australia........253
2 Hundreds *v.* New Zealand....257
184 *v.* England..................246
162 w. in Test Matches 224
8 w. in Test Innings (twice).....228
(and V. S. Hazare), 3rd wkt. record *v.* England...........246
(and P. Roy), 413 for 1st wkt. 201, 203, 258
Mann, E. J. (Norfolk and Middlesex II), Obituary..........975
Mann, F. G. (Middlesex):—
Captain *v.* South Africa........237
M.C.C. Committee..............321
136* *v.* South Africa 239
Mann, F. T. (Middlesex), Captain *v.* South Africa 237
Mansell, P. N. F. (South Africa) (and J. E. Cheetham), 7th wkt. record *v.* Australia....250
Maralanda, A. P. (Trinity Coll., Kandy), Obituary.........972
Marks, C. P., 101* for Derbyshire II 727
Marks, L. (South Australia), 127 *v.* Western Australia..........858
Marlborough College............785
v. M.C.C.......................332
v. Rugby........................340
Marlow, F. W. (Sussex), 144 on début.........................195
Marner, P. (Lancashire and Leicestershire):—
Birthday.........................942
Photograph 475
1,184 r. in 1966.................271
2 Hundreds in 1966 277
108 *v.* Oxford Univ.............677
104 *v.* Nottinghamshire.........543
11 Glamorgan w..................490
8 Kent w.........................491
35 catches in 1966..............369
Marriott, C. S. (Cambridge Univ., Lancashire and Kent), Obituary..........................972
Marriott, D. A. (Surrey), 54 w. for Surrey II.....................735
Marsh, J. F. (Cambridge Univ.), 172* *v.* Oxford...............260
Marshall, A. G., 40 w. for Wiltshire 722
Marshall, R. E. (West Indies and Hampshire):—
Birthday.........................942
Captain of Hampshire..........424
1,882 r. in 1966.................270
56 Hundreds 195
3 Hundreds in 1966 277
133 *v.* Warwickshire............611
110 *v.* Nottinghamshire.........429
106 *v.* Kent 439
(and J. R. Gray), 1st wkt. Hundreds.........................202
Martin, F. (Kent), 4 w. with consecutive balls.................208
Martin, F. R. (West Indies), 123* *v.* Australia 251
Martin, J. W. (New South Wales):—
Test Cricket.....................174
9 Queensland w..................861
(and K. D. Mackay), 9th wkt. record *v.* West Indies........252
Martin, S. H. (Worcestershire), All-Round 216
Martindale, E. A. (Barbados) (and E. A. V. Williams), 255 for 8th wkt. 205
Marx, W. F. E. (Transvaal), 240 on début..........................195
MARYLEBONE CLUB, THE (1966) 321–34
Annual Meeting (179th) 321–5
v. Abingdon School 331

MARYLEBONE CLUB, THE (1966):—*contd.*
v. Adastrians 331
v. Aldenham School 329
v. Aldershot Services 332
v. Alleyn's School 327
v. Allhallows School 328
v. Amersham 334
v. Ampleforth College 329
v. Bancroft's School 332
v. Barclays Bank 331
v. Barnard Castle School 331
v. Barnet 332
v. Beaumont College 328
v. Bedford School 327
v. Berkhamsted School 328
v. Bishop's Stortford C.C. 334
v. Bishop's Stortford College 330
v. Bloxham School 330
v. Blundell's School 329
v. Bolton School 332
v. Bradfield College 332
v. Bradford Grammar School 331
v. Brentwood School 328
v. Brighton College 331
v. Bristol Grammar School 329
v. B.B.C. 327
v. Bromsgrove School 331
v. Brondesbury 332
v. Buckhurst Hill 333
v. Cambridge University 328
v. Canford School 331
v. Charterhouse School 329
v. Cheam 330
v. Cheltenham College 328
v. Chigwell School 329
v. Christ College, Brecon 330
v. Christ's Hospital 329
v. City of London School 330
v. Clifton College 333
v. Club Cricket Conference 327
v. Cockfosters 334
v. Colchester and E. Essex 334
v. Cranbrook School 332
v. Cranleigh C.C. 333
v. Cranleigh School 327
v. Cuckfield 334
v. Dauntsey's School 329
v. de Flamingo's 334
v. Denstone College 330
v. Ditchling 334
v. Douai School 329
v. Dover College 331
v. Downside School 331
v. Duke of York's R.M.S. 332
v. Dulwich C.C. 330
v. Dulwich College 330
v. Ealing 333
v. Eastbourne College 329
v. Elizabeth College, Guernsey 328
v. Ellesmere College 331
v. Emanuel School 331

MARYLEBONE CLUB, THE (1966):—*contd.*
v. Epsom College 332
v. Eton College 327
v. Felsted School 329
v. Finchley 334
v. Folkestone 333
v. Forest School 327
v. Framlingham College 327
v. Gents. of Leicester 334
v. Giggleswick School 330
v. Gresham's School 330
v. Guernsey Island 328
v. Haberdashers' School 329
v. Haileybury and I.S.C. 328
v. Hampstead 334
v. Harrow School 328
v. Havant 334
v. Henfield 333
v. Highgate School 327
v. Honourable Artillery Company 327
v. Household Brigade 334
v. Hurstpierpoint College 330
v. Indian Gymkhana 333
v. Ipswich School 330
v. Ireland 334
v. Isle of Wight 334
v. Jersey Island 328
v. Kenley 332
v. Kent Schools 334
v. King Edward's School, Birmingham 332
v. King's College, Taunton 329
v. King's College School 332
v. King's School, Bruton 329
v. King's School, Canterbury 329
v. Kingston Grammar School 332
v. Kingswood School 329
v. Lancing College 328
v. Latymer Upper School 328
v. Leamington 328
v. Leicester 330
v. Leys School 328
v. Liverpool College 333
v. Lloyds Bank 327
v. London Schools' C.A. 332
v. Lords and Commons 278, 332
v. Loughborough College 328
v. Loughton 334
v. Luton Town 327
v. Magdalen College School 330
v. Maidenhead and Bray 333
v. Malden Wanderers 333
v. Malvern College 327
v. Manchester Grammar School 331
v. Marlborough College 332
v. Mayfield 334
v. Merchant Taylors' School 328
v. Merchant Taylors' School, Crosby 332
v. Middlesex G.S. 333

MARYLEBONE CLUB, THE (1966):—
contd.
v. Midland Bank 333
v. Midlands C.C.C. 332
v. Millfield School 329
v. Mill Hill School 328
v. Monkton Combe School 330
v. Monmouth School 330
v. National Provincial Bank 329
v. North Riding G.S. 332
v. Northwood 332
v. Nottingham High School 331
v. Nottingham University 330
v. Notts. Amateur 333
v. Oakham School 332
v. Oratory School 330
v. Oundle School 329
v. Perse School 327
v. Pocklington School 330
v. Radley College 328
v. R.A.F. College 332
v. Reading C.C. 329
v. Reading School 332
v. Reed's School 331
v. Reigate Priory 333
v. Repton School 327
v. R.M.A., Sandhurst 327
v. Roehampton 331
v. Rossall School 331
v. Rugby C.C. 332
v. Rugby School 327
v. Rydal School 333
v. St. Bartholomew's G.S. 333
v. St. Bees School 331
v. St. Dunstan's College 329
v. St. Edmund's College 330
v. St. Edward's School, Oxford .331
v. St. George's College, Weybridge 329
v. St. John's School, Leatherhead 331
v. St. Lawrence College, Ramsgate 330
v. St. Paul's School 332
v. St. Peter's School, York 330
v. Scotland 328
v. Sedbergh School 330
v. Sheffield University 329
v. Shepherd's Bush 333
v. Sherborne School 332
v. Shrewsbury School 329
v. Sidmouth 334
v. Sir George Monoux Grammar School 327
v. Slough 334
v. Solihull School 329
v. South Woodford 333
v. Spencer 333
v. Stamford School 331
v. Stonyhurst College 329
v. Stowe School 332
v. Stroud 333

MARYLEBONE CLUB, THE (1966):—
contd.
v. Sunbury 333
v. Surrey 326–7
v. Surrey Schools 333
v. Sussex Martlets 334
v. Sutton Valence School 329
v. Taunton School 331
v. Tiffin School 329
v. Tonbridge School 333
v. Trent College 329
v. Tring Park 333
v. Trinity School 333
v. United London Banks 330
v. University College School 331
v. Uppingham School 327
v. Victoria College, Jersey 328
v. Wanstead 330
v. Wellingborough School 331
v. Wellington College 333
v. Welsh Secondary Schools 330
v. Wembley 333
v. West Buckland School 333
v. Westcliff-on-Sea 334
v. West Herts 330
v. West Indies 288–9
v. West Kent 332
v. Westminster Bank 333
v. Westminster School 330
v. Weston-super-Mare 331
v. Whitgift School 327
v. Winchester College 327
v. Wisbech Town 325
v. Wolverhampton 334
v. Woodford Wells 331
v. Worksop College 331
v. Worthing 334
v. Wrekin College 328
v. Wycliffe College 330
v. Yorkshire 325–6
M.C.C. IN AUSTRALIA AND NEW ZEALAND, 1965–66 (E. M. Wellings) 812–18
Averages 819–22
Fielding Statistics 822
Individual Hundreds 822–3
Summary of Results 818–19
v. Combined XI (Hobart) 838–9
v. Combined XI (Perth) 825–6
v. New South Wales .829–30, 840–1
v. N.S.W. County Districts 832
v. Northern N.S.W. Country Districts 836–7
v. President's XI (Wellington) .842–3
v. Prime Minister's XI (Canberra) 832
v. Queensland 830–1
v. Queensland Country Districts .831
v. South Australia 826–7, 832–3
v. South Australian Country Districts 832
v. Tasmania 837–8

M.C.C. in Australia and New Zealand, 1965–66 (E. M. Wellings):—*contd.*
v. Victoria 828–9
v. Victorian Country Districts 827, 829
v. Western Australia.........824–5
v. Western Australia Country XI 824
M.C.C. in Ceylon 824
M.C.C. in Hong Kong..........847
M.C.C. President's XI *v.* West Indies 308–9
M.C.C. Schools in South Africa, 1965–66................901–2
M.C.C. Schools XI *v.* Combined Services..................344
M.C.C. Young Professionals:—
v. English Schools C.A.........345
v. London Federation of Boys' Clubs.....................345
v. Young Amateurs of Middlesex 345
Maslin, M., 103 for Lincolnshire..715
Mason, J. R. (Kent), All-Round ..216
Massie, R. J. A. (N.S.W.), Obituary.972
Mathias, Wallis (Pakistan):—
Test Cricket..................188
278* *v.* Railway Greens........891
(and Afaq Hussain), 135 for last wkt.......................205
(and Nasim-ul-Ghani), 216 for 5th wkt..................204
(and Salah-ud-Din), 388 for 3rd wkt.......................203
Matthews, F. C. L. (Nottinghamshire), 17 w. in match......210
Matthews, T. J. (Victoria):—
Double Hat-trick in Test 208, 228, 250
3 Hat-tricks...................209
Mattocks, D. E., 104 for Norfolk..716
May, P. B. H. (Surrey):—
Birthday......................942
Captain *v.* Australia 231
Captain *v.* New Zealand 243
Captain *v.* South Africa........237
Captain *v.* West Indies.........241
M.C.C. Committee.............321
Test Cricket..................166
Test Selector 1006
4,537 r. in Test Matches 222
85 Hundreds 195
4 Successive Hundreds.........199
3 Hundreds *v.* Australia........233
3 Hundreds *v.* New Zealand....244
3 Hundreds *v.* South Africa 239
3 Hundreds *v.* West Indies 242
2 Separate Hundreds 196
138 on Test début.............225
106 *v.* India 246
(and M. C. Cowdrey), 4th wkt. record *v.* West Indies .241, 258
Mayfield *v.* M.C.C...............334
Mayne, E. R. (South Australia and Victoria) (and W. H. Ponsford), 456 for 1st wkt...201, 203
Mayne, L. R. (Western Australia), Test Cricket..............174
Mead, C. P. (Hampshire):—
Dates of Birth and Death......942
55,060 r......................197
Aggregate of 3,179............206
1,000 r. (27 times)............198
153 Hundreds 195
13 Hundreds in Season 199
3 Hundreds *v.* South Africa 239
2 Separate Hundreds 196
223 *v.* Gentlemen 259
182* *v.* Australia.............233
Mead, W. (Essex):—
100 w. (10 times).............215
17 w. in Match (twice).........210
Meale, T. (New Zealand), Test Cricket 184
Meckiff, I. W. (Victoria):—
Test Cricket 174
(and K. D. Mackay), 9th wkt. record *v.* South Africa.....250
Meetings in 1966:—
Advisory County Cricket Committee 1006–7
Board of Control 1006, 1008
International Cricket Conference 1007–8
M.C.C. (179th) 321–5
Mehra, V. L. (India):—
Test Cricket..................186
Youngest Indian Test Player ...259
Melle, Dr. B. G. von B. (Western Province, Oxford Univ. and Hampshire), Obituary ...972–3
Melle, M. G. (South Africa), 8 w. for 8 r.....................211
Mellows, H., First-Class Umpire.1008
Melville, A. (South Africa):—
Captain *v.* England 237
4 Hundreds *v.* England 240
4 Successive Test Hundreds 199
2 Separate Test Hundreds ..225,240
(and B. Mitchell), 299 for 7th wkt.......................204
(and A. D. Nourse, jr.), 319 for 3rd wkt. *v.* England 238
Mendonca, I. (West Indies), Test Cricket 182
Mercer, J. (Sussex, Glamorgan and Northamptonshire):—
Testimonial, 1967.............458
100 w. (9 times)..............215
10 w. in Innings 210
Merchant, Uday (Bombay) (and M. N. Raiji), 360 for 5th wkt.......................204

Merchant, V. M. (India):—
Birthday....................943
43 Hundreds....................196
4 Successive Hundreds....................199
3 Hundreds *v.* England....................296
359* *v.* Maharashtra....................192
142 and Hat-trick....................216
(and V. S. Hazare), 3rd wkt. record *v.* England....................246
(and R. S. Modi), 371 for 6th wkt....................204
(and Mushtaq Ali), 1st wkt. record *v.* England....................246
Merchant Taylors' School....................785
v. M.C.C....................328
Merchant Taylors' School, Crosby.785
v. M.C.C....................332
Merryweather, J. H., 44 w. for Wiltshire....................722
Meyer, B. J. (Gloucestershire) (wkt.-kpr.), 71 w. in 1966..369
MIDDLESEX....................493–509
Results....................495
Averages....................495
Championship Table....................350
Championship Winners....................265
County Badge....................493
v. Derbyshire....................504–5
v. Essex....................505
v. Glamorgan....................497
v. Hampshire....................509
v. Kent....................496
v. Lancashire....................507
v. Leicestershire....................499
v. Northamptonshire....................503
v. Somerset....................502
v. Surrey....................506
v. Sussex (J. T. Murray's Benefit)....................500
v. Warwickshire....................498
v. West Indies....................287–8
v. Worcestershire....................508
v. Yorkshire....................501
Gillette Cup....................660
MIDDLESEX II....................732–3
Championship Table....................727
Championship Winners....................266
Middlesex Grammar Schools *v.* M.C.C....................333
Midland Bank *v.* M.C.C....................333
Midlands C.C.C. *v.* M.C.C....................332
Midwinter, W. E. (Australia and Gloucestershire):—
Australia *v.* England....................174
England *v.* Australia....................166
Milburn, C. (Northamptonshire):—
Birthday....................943
Photograph....................68
Fastest Hundred in 1966...268, 535
Five Cricketers of the Year...78–81
Test Cricket....................166
Test Match Averages, 1966....................282
Milburn, C. (Northamptonshire):— *contd.*
1,861 r. in 1966....................270
6 Hundreds in 1966....................276
203 *v.* Essex....................267, 386
171 *v.* Leicestershire....................481
137 *v.* Sussex....................585
130 *v.* Derbyshire....................355
126* *v.* West Indies....................242, 299
113 *v.* Nottinghamshire....................535
22 catches in 1966....................369
(and T. W. Graveney), 5th wkt. record *v.* West Indies..241, 299
(and R. M. Prideaux), 293 for 1st wkt. *v.* Essex....................267, 386
Milkha Singh, A. G. (India):—
Test Cricket....................186
115* *v.* Mysore....................883
108 *v.* West Zone....................887
Miller, H. D. (Glamorgan), 52 w. for Glamorgan II....................729
Miller, K. R. (Victoria and N.S.W.):—
Birthday....................943
2,958 r. in Test Matches....................222
41 Hundreds....................196
4 Hundreds *v.* West Indies....................251
3 Hundreds *v.* England....................235
170 w. in Test Matches....................224
(and R. G. Archer), 5th wkt. record *v.* West Indies....................252
(and R. G. Archer), 6th wkt. record *v.* West Indies....................252
(and R. N. Harvey), 4th wkt. record *v.* South Africa....................250
(and A. L. Hassett), 4th wkt. record *v.* West Indies....................252
Miller, L. S. M. (New Zealand), Test Cricket....................184
Miller, N. (Surrey), 124 on début..195
Miller, R. (Warwickshire), 9 Oxford Univ. w....................608
Millfield School....................786
v. M.C.C....................329
Mill Hill School....................786
v. M.C.C....................328
Millman, G. (Nottinghamshire):—
Test Cricket....................166
(and D. R. Smith), last wkt. record *v.* India....................246
Mills, J. E. (New Zealand):—
117 *v.* England on Test début 225, 244
(and C. F. W. Allcott), 190* for 8th wkt....................205
(and C. S. Dempster), 1st wkt. record *v.* England....................244
Mills, P. T. (Gloucestershire), 5 w. for 0 r....................212
Millyard, G., Throwing record....219
Milton, C. A. (Gloucestershire):—
Test Cricket....................166
1,646 r. in 1966....................270

Milton, C. A. (Gloucestershire):—
contd.
41 Hundreds 196
2 Hundreds in 1966 277
2 Separate Hundreds 196
138* *v.* Leicestershire 414
121 *v.* Nottinghamshire 540
104* *v.* New Zealand on Test début 225, 244
63 catches in Season 218
29 catches in 1966 369
8 catches in Match 218
Milton Abbey School *v.* I.Z. 269
MINOR COUNTIES 705–25
Averages, 1966 723–5
Championship Table 707
Championship Winners 266
Fixtures, 1967 1035–7
Formation of 264
Umpires, 1967 1008
v. West Indies 299–300
Miran Bux (Pakistan), Oldest Pakistan début 259
Misson, F. M. (N.S.W.), Test Cricket 174
Mitchell, A. (Yorkshire):—
44 Hundreds 196
4 Successive Hundreds 199
Mitchell, B. (South Africa):—
Birthday 943
3,471 r. in Test Matches 223
7 Hundreds *v.* England 240
2 Separate Test Hundreds . . 225, 240
113 *v.* New Zealand 254
(and A. Melville), 299 for 7th wkt. 204
(and I. J. Siedle), 1st wkt. record *v.* England 238
(and L. Tuckett), 8th wkt. record *v.* England 238
Mitchell, F. (Yorkshire and South Africa):—
Captain *v.* Australia 248
Captain *v.* England 237
England *v.* South Africa 167
South Africa *v.* England and *v.* Australia 178
Mitchell, T. B. (Derbyshire):—
100 w. (10 times) 215
10 w. in Innings 210
Mitra, S. S. (Bengal), 155 *v.* Assam . 886
Modi, R. S. (India):—
112 *v.* West Indies 256
(and L. Amarnath), 410 for 3rd wkt. 203
(and V. M. Merchant), 371 for 6th wkt. 204
Mohammad Farooq (Pakistan), Test Cricket 188
Mohammad Ilyas (Pakistan):—
Test Cricket 188
126 *v.* New Zealand 258
Mohammad Iqbal (Muslim Model H.S.), 475* *v.* Islamia H.S. 194
Mohammad Munaf (Pakistan), Test Cricket 188
Mohammad Sadiq (P.W.D.), 119 *v.* Karachi Blues 892
Mohammad Younis:—
1,048 r. for Surrey II 735
169* for Surrey II 735
Moin-ud-Dowla Gold Cup Tournament 887–8
Moir, A. M. (New Zealand), Test Cricket 184
Mold, A. (Lancashire):—
200 w. (twice) 213
100 w. (9 times) 215
4 w. with consecutive balls 208
Moloney, D. A. R. (New Zealand) (and A. W. Roberts), 8th wkt. record *v.* England 245
Monkton Combe School 786
v. M.C.C. 330
Monmouth School 787
v. M.C.C. 330
Montgomerie, R. D., 100 for Oxfordshire 718
Mooney, F. L. H. (New Zealand) (and J. Cowie), last wkt. record *v.* England 245
Moore, H. I. (Nottinghamshire):—
Birthday 943
Photograph 528
1,169 r. in 1966 271
100 *v.* Lancashire 537
Moore, R. H. (Hampshire):—
Highest for Hampshire 193
316 *v.* Warwickshire 192, 193
Morgan, D. C. (Derbyshire):—
Birthday 944
Photograph 352
Captain of Derbyshire 352
1,028 r. in 1966 271
11 Northamptonshire w. 515
9 Glamorgan w. 405
9 Gloucestershire w. 411
28 catches in 1966 369
Morgan, H. E. (Glamorgan), 254 *v.* Monmouthshire 194
Morgan, J. (Queensland), 8 South Australian w. 868
Morgan, J. T. (Cambridge Univ. and Glamorgan), 149 *v.* Oxford 339
Morgan, R. W. (New Zealand):—
Test Cricket 184
Test Match Averages, 1966 821
Morkel, D. P. B. (South Africa) (and S. S. L. Steyn), 222 for 8th wkt. 205
Morley, F. (Nottinghamshire):—
7 w. for 6 r. 211

Morley, F. (Nottinghamshire):—*contd.*
7 w. for 7 r....................211
7 w. for 9 r. (twice)...........212
Moroney, J. R. (N.S.W.):—
2 Hundreds *v.* South Africa.....249
2 Separate Test Hundreds ..225, 249
Morris, A. R. (N.S.W.):—
Birthday........................944
3,533 r. in Test Matches 222
2,080 r. *v.* England...........237
46 Hundreds 196
8 Hundreds *v.* England 235
2 Hundreds *v.* South Africa 249
2 Separate Hundreds 196
2 Separate Test Hundreds..225, 235
148 and 111 on début...........195
111 *v.* West Indies............251
100* *v.* India 253
Morris, I., 121 for Glamorgan II..728
Morrison, B. (New Zealand), Test Cricket.........................184
Mortimore, J. B. (Gloucestershire):—
Birthday........................944
All-Round 216
Captain of Gloucestershire.....406
Test Cricket....................167
8 Warwickshire w. 607
Morton, P. H. (Cambridge Univ.), Hat-trick *v.* Oxford........260
Moss, A. E. (Canterbury, N.Z.), 10 w. in Innings on first-class début...........209
Moss, A. E. (Middlesex), Test Cricket 167
Motz, R. C. (New Zealand):—
Test Cricket....................184
Test Match Averages, 1966.....821
Mowing the Pitch...............982
Muddiah, V. M. (India):—
Test Cricket....................186
5 w. for 2 r....................212
Mufasir-ul-Haq (Pakistan), Test Cricket........................188
Muncer, B. L. (Middlesex and Glamorgan), All-Round...216
Munir Malik (Pakistan):—
Test Cricket....................188
8 Punjab Univ. w...............891
Murawwat Hussain (Pakistan) (and Nazar Mohammad), 269 for 2nd wkt.........................203
Murdoch, W. L. (N.S.W. and Sussex):—
Dates of Birth and Death......944
Australia *v.* England..........174
Captain *v.* England............231
England *v.* South Africa 167
Slow Scoring 226
2 Hundreds *v.* England 235
321 *v.* Victoria...............192
Murray, A. R. A. (South Africa), 109 *v.* New Zealand.......254
Murray, D. L. (West Indies, Cambridge Univ., and Nottinghamshire) (wkt.-kpr.):—
Captain of Cambridge.........679
Test Cricket....................182
1,358 r. in 1966...............270
2 Hundreds in 1966 277
166* *v.* Surrey................578
133 *v.* Sussex.................591
40 w. in 1966...................369
24 w. in Test Rubber..........228
Murray, J. T. (Middlesex) (wkt.-kpr.):—
Birthday........................944
Photograph......................71
Group...........................63
Benefit Match 500
Five Cricketers of the Year....84–6
Test Cricket....................167
Test Match Averages, 1966.282, 821
1,025 r. and 104 w..............216
3 Hundreds in 1966 277
114 *v.* Sussex.................598
112 *v.* West Indies.........242, 316
110 *v.* South Australia.........833
100* *v.* West Indies...........289
100 w. in Season (twice) 218
38 w. in 1966...................369
20 w. in Australasia 822
(and T. W. Graveney), 8th wkt. record *v.* West Indies ..241, 316
(and P. H. Parfitt), 7th wkt. record *v.* Pakistan...........247
Murray-Wood, W. (Oxford Univ. and Kent), 106* on début..195
Mushtaq Ali (India):—
112 *v.* England................246
106 *v.* West Indies............256
(and V. M. Merchant), 1st wkt. record *v.* England) 246
Mushtaq Ali (Railways), 100 *v.* South Punjab..................885
Mushtaq Mohammad (Pakistan and Northamptonshire):—
Test Cricket....................188
Youngest Test Player..........259
1,179 r. in 1966...............271
3 Hundreds in 1966 277
129 *v.* Ceylon.................895
117 *v.* Gloucestershire 423
112 *v.* Leicestershire.........481
101 *v.* Ceylon.................895
101 *v.* India 257
100* *v.* England...............247
100* *v.* England XI............702
8 Glamorgan w. 404
24 catches in 1966.............369
(and Abdul Dyer), 140 for 9th wkt...........................205

Mushtaq Mohammad (Pakistan and Northamptonshire):—*contd.*
(and J. Burki), 4th wkt. record *v.* England 248
(and Imtiaz Ahmed), 2nd wkt. record *v.* England 248
(and Imtiaz Ahmed), 6th wkt. record *v.* England 248
Muzzell, R. K. (Western Province), 101* *v.* Transvaal 875
Mycroft, W. (Derbyshire), 17 w. in Match 210
My Favourite Summer (A. A. Thomson) 118–25

Nadkarni, R. G. (India):—
Test Cricket 187
122* *v.* England 246
(and B. S. Chandresekhar), last wkt. record *v.* England 246
(and F. M. Engineer), 8th wkt. record *v.* England 246
Nagarwalla, N. D. (Maharashtra) (and V. S. Hazare), 245 for 9th wkt. 205
Nagdev, R. (All India Schools), 100* *v.* London Schools 904
Najam Hussain (Mysore), 103 *v.* Hyderabad 882
Napier, G. G. (Cambridge Univ. and Middlesex), 9 w. for 17 r. 211
Nash, G. (Lancashire), 4 w. with consecutive balls 208
Nash, J. H., Sec., Yorkshire 634
Nasim-ul-Ghani (Pakistan):—
Test Cricket 188
101 *v.* England 247
(and J. Burki), 5th wkt. record *v.* England 248
(and Wallis Mathias), 216 for 5th wkt. 204
(and Saeed Ahmed), 7th wkt. record *v.* England 248
National Club Cricket Association, Address of Secretary 492
National Provincial Bank *v.* M.C.C. 329
Naushad Ali (Pakistan), Test Cricket 188
Nautical College, Pangbourne 787
Nayudu, C. K. (India):—
Captain *v.* England 245
11 Sixes in Innings 200
Nayudu, C. S. (India), Most Balls in Match 228
Nazar Mohammad (Pakistan):—
124* *v.* India 257
(and Murawwat Hussain), 269 for 2nd wkt. 203

Nel, J. (South Africa), Test Cricket 178
New Ball (Laws of Cricket) 981, 996, 1007
Newcastle Royal Grammar School . 787
Newham, W. (Sussex) (and K. S. Ranjitsinhji), 344 for 7th wkt. 204
Newman, F. C. W. (Bedfordshire and Surrey), Obituary 973
Newman, G. C. (Middlesex):—
M.C.C. Committee 321
President of Middlesex 493
Newman, J. (Hampshire)—
All-Round 215
2,033 w. 214
100 w. (9 times) 215
New South Wales—*See* Australia
Newton, H., 63 w. for Sussex II . . . 736
New Zealand:—
Representative Body 492
Summary of All Tests 230
Test Cricketers (1929–66) 183–5
New Zealand Cricket, 1965–66 (A. G. Wiren) 878–80
Plunket Shield Table 878
See also M.C.C. in Australia and New Zealand
New Zealand *v.* Australia 250
New Zealand *v.* England 243–5
Bowling Feats 245
Highest Totals 243
Individual Hundreds 244
Match Results 243
Record Partnerships 244–5
Smallest Totals 243
Visiting Captains 243
New Zealand *v.* England, 1966:—
First Test (Christchurch) 843–4
Second Test (Dunedin) 845–6
Third Test (Auckland) 846–7
New Zealand *v.* India 256–7
New Zealand *v.* Pakistan 258
New Zealand *v.* South Africa . . 254
New Zealand *v.* West Indies . . 254–5
Nichol, M. (Worcestershire), 104 on début 195
Nicholls, D. (Kent), 108 for Kent II 730
Nicholls, R. B. (Gloucestershire):—
Benefit Match 416–17
1,301 r. in 1966 271
127 *v.* Berkshire (Gillette Cup) . . 656
108 *v.* West Indies 295
(and D. M. Young), 395 for 1st wkt. 201
Nichols, M. S. (Essex):—
All-Round 215
100 w. (11 times) 215
Nicholson, A. G. (Yorkshire):—
Group 66
113 w. in 1966 274
9 Derbyshire w. 641

Nicolson, J. F. W. (Natal) (and I. J. Siedle), 424 for 1st wkt. 201, 203
Nimbalkar, B. B. (Maharashtra):—
443* *v.* Western Indian States...191
(and K. V. Bhandarkar), 445 for 2nd wkt....................203
No Ball (Laws of Cricket) 986–7, 993–4
See also Throwing
Noble, M. A. (N.S.W.):—
Dates of Birth and Death......945
Captain *v.* England............231
1,997 r. in Test Matches.......222
37 Hundreds..................196
133 *v.* England.................235
121 w. in Test Matches........224
(and W. W. Armstrong), 428 for 6th wkt....................204
NORFOLK.......................716
Championship Table..........707
Championship Winners........266
Norfolk, Duke of:—
President of Sussex...........581
XI *v.* I.Z.......................269
XI *v.* West Indies.............286
Norman, M. E. (Northamptonshire and Leicestershire):—
1,345 r. in 1966...............270
2 Hundreds in 1966...........277
132* *v.* Hampshire...........489
102 *v.* Northamptonshire......506
Northampton, Plan of County Ground.....................511
NORTHAMPTONSHIRE..........510–27
Averages.......................512
Results.........................512
Championship Table..........350
Championship Winners........265
County Badge..................510
Minor Counties Championship.266
v. Derbyshire..................515
v. Essex.......................518
v. Glamorgan..............524–5
v. Gloucestershire............513
v. Hampshire...............522–3
v. Kent....................519–20
v. Lancashire..................514
v. Leicestershire...........525–6
v. Middlesex................523–4
v. Nottinghamshire..........520–1
v. Somerset....................517
v. Warwickshire.............521–2
v. West Indies..............307–8
v. Worcestershire.............516
v. Yorkshire..................526–7
Gillette Cup....................654
NORTHAMPTONSHIRE II..............733
Championship Table..........727
Championship Winners........266
North Riding G.S. *v.* M.C.C......332
North Staffordshire and District League, 1966............745
North Staffordshire and South Cheshire League, 1966...743–4
NORTHUMBERLAND................717
Championship Table..........707
Northwood *v.* M.C.C.............332
NOTES BY THE EDITOR..........87–95
Nottingham, Plan of Trent Bridge Ground....................529
Nottingham High School.....787–8
v. M.C.C.......................331
Nottingham University *v.* M.C.C...330
NOTTINGHAMSHIRE...........528–44
"Nottinghamshire's Notable Part in the Growth of Cricket" (R. T. Simpson).......134–42
Averages.......................529
Results.........................529
Championship Table..........350
Championship Winners........265
County Badge..................528
v. Derbyshire..................538
v. Essex.......................542
v. Gloucestershire............540
v. Hampshire...............534–5
v. Kent....................530–1
v. Lancashire...............537–8
v. Leicestershire.............543
v. Middlesex................536–7
v. Northamptonshire........535–6
v. Somerset....................532
v. Surrey.......................533
v. Sussex.......................539
v. Warwickshire...............544
v. West Indies..............295–6
v. Yorkshire....................541
Gillette Cup....................661
NOTTINGHAMSHIRE II.....717–18, 734
Championship Tables.....707, 727
Notts. Amateur *v.* M.C.C.........333
Nourse, A. D., jr. (South Africa):—
Birthday........................945
Captain *v.* England............237
2,960 r. in Test Matches.......223
621 r. in Rubber *v.* England....240
41 Hundreds....................196
7 Hundreds *v.* England........240
2 Hundreds *v.* Australia.......249
(and A. Melville), 319 for 3rd wkt. *v.* England...........238
Nourse, A. D., sr. (South Africa):—
2,234 r. in Test Matches.......223
38 Hundreds....................196
304* *v.* Transvaal..............193
111 *v.* Australia................249
(and C. N. Frank), 4th wkt. record *v.* Australia........250
(and E. A. Halliwell), 8th wkt. record *v.* Australia........250
Nugent, Lt.-Col. Lord:—
President of Surrey............563

Nugent, Lt.-Col. Lord:—*contd.*
Trustee, M.C.C. 321
Nunes, R. K. (West Indies):—
Captain *v.* England.............241
(and G. A. Headley), 2nd wkt. record *v.* England.........242
Nupen, E. P. (South Africa):—
(and J. M. Blanckenberg), 9th wkt. record *v.* Australia....250
(and H. G. Deane), 7th wkt. record *v.* England..........238
Nurse, S. M. (West Indies):—
Birthday.....................945
Photograph 64, 69
Group..........................62
Five Cricketers of the Year....81–4
Test Cricket..................182
Test Match Averages, 1966......283
1,105 r. in 1966...............283
2 First-Class Hundreds in 1966 .284
201 *v.* Australia...............251
155 *v.* Essex...................301
153 *v.* Windward and Leeward Islands 896
137 *v.* England 243, 312
126 *v.* Jamaica.................897
102* *v.* Warwickshire..........320
(and G. S. Sobers), 5th wkt. record *v.* Australia 252
(and G. S. Sobers), 5th wkt. record *v.* England .242, 267, 312

Oakham School..................788
v. M.C.C.......................332
Oakman, A. S. M. (Sussex):—
9 Kent w.......................593
8 Leicestershire w. 479
21 catches in 1966.............369
Oates, T. W. (Nottinghamshire) (wkt.-kpr.), 10 w. in Match.217
OBITUARY.....................962–75
O'Brien, R. (Cambridge Univ.), 146 *v.* Oxford.................339
Obstructing the Field (Laws) 990
Instances in First-Class Cricket.207
O'Connor, J. (Essex):—
1,000 r. (16 times)..............198
72 Hundreds 195
Old England XI *v.* Lord's Taverners XI 335
OLDEST PLAYERS ON TEST DÉBUT..259
Oldfield, N. (Lancashire and Northamptonshire):—
38 Hundreds 196
(and V. Broderick), 361 for 1st wkt.........................202
Oldfield, W. A. (N.S.W.) (wkt.-kpr.):—
Birthday.......................945
130 w. in Test Matches 228
90 w. *v.* England...............236
5 w. in Test Innings...........229
Oldroyd, E. (Yorkshire), 37 Hundreds 196
O'Linn, S. (Kent and South Africa), Test Cricket...............178
Oliver, S., 101 w. in Lancashire League 740
O'Neill, N. C. (N.S.W.):—
Birthday.......................945
Test Cricket....................174
2,779 r. in Test Matches 222
37 Hundreds 196
2 Hundreds *v.* England 235
2 Hundreds *v.* India 253
181 *v.* West Indies.............251
140 *v.* Western Australia.......870
134 *v.* Pakistan 253
108 *v.* Victoria................860
O'Neill, W. P. (U.S.A.), Obituary.973
Oratory School..................788
v. Beaumont...................335
v. M.C.C......................330
O'Reilly, W. J. (N.S.W.):—
Birthday.......................945
144 w. in Test Matches 224
102 w. *v.* England.............237
(and D. G. Bradman), 9th wkt. record *v.* South Africa.....250
O'Riordan, A. J. (Ireland), 8 M.C.C. w...................701
Ormrod, J. A. (Worcestershire):—
Birthday.......................945
Photograph 617
1,284 r. in 1966...............271
20 catches in 1966.............369
Oundle School................788–9
v. M.C.C......................329
Out of his Ground (Laws).........988
OVER, THE (Laws of Cricket) 986
Number of balls 986
The last.......................984
OVERSEAS CRICKET, 1965–66 ..849–904
Overthrows (Laws of Cricket) 985
Owen-Smith, H. G. (South Africa):—
129 *v.* England................240
(and A. J. Bell), last wkt. record *v.* England 238
OXFORD UNIVERSITY..........668–78
Averages.......................669
Results........................669
Blues (1880–1966).........688–93
v. Essex...................675–6
v. Free Foresters............673–4
v. Gloucestershire.............670
v. Hampshire..................671
v. Lancashire...............676–7
v. Leicestershire...........677–8
v. Middlesex................674–5
v. Northamptonshire 678
v. Nottinghamshire..........672–3
v. West Indies..............286–7
v. Worcestershire..............672
v. Yorkshire................671–2

OXFORD v. CAMBRIDGE:—
Highest Individual Scores......260
Hundreds since 1919..........339
Largest Totals................260
Match Results since 1919......339
Smallest Totals...............260
Various Records...............260
OXFORD v. CAMBRIDGE, 1966....337–9
OXFORDSHIRE...................718
Championship Table...........707
Championship Winners.........266

Padgett, D. E. V. (Yorkshire):—
Group.........................66
Test Cricket..................167
1,194 in 1966.................271
Page, M.H. (Derbyshire), 22 catches in 1966...........369
Page, M. L. (New Zealand):—
Captain v. England............243
101 v. England................244
(and R. C. Blunt), 4th wkt. record v. England.........244
(and C. S. Dempster), 3rd wkt. record v. England.........244
(and W. A. Hadlee), 6th wkt. record v. England.........244
Pairaudeau, B. H. (West Indies):—
Test Cricket..................182
115 v. India on Test début..225, 255
PAKISTAN:—
"The Rise of Cricket in Pakistan" (Ghulam Mustafa Khan).153–6
"Some Dates in Pakistan Cricket History" (Rowland Bowen).157
Representative Body...........492
Summary of All Tests..........230
Test Cricketers (1952–65).....188–9
Test Records (Stanley Conder) 158–9
PAKISTAN CRICKET, 1965–66 (Ghulam Mustafa Khan).....889–92
Ayub Zonal Tournament.....890–2
Ceylon Tour of Pakistan........895
Quaid-e-Azam Trophy......889–90
PAKISTAN v. AUSTRALIA..........253
PAKISTAN v. ENGLAND..........247–8
Highest Totals................247
Individual Hundreds...........247
Match Results.................247
Record Partnerships........247–8
Smallest Totals...............247
Visiting Captains.............247
PAKISTAN v. INDIA..............257
PAKISTAN v. NEW ZEALAND.......258
PAKISTAN v. WEST INDIES.......256
Palm, A. W. (Western Province), (and J. M. M. Commaille), 244* for 6th wkt...........204
Palmer, C. H. (Worcestershire and Leicestershire), 8 w. for 7 r..211
Palmer, G. E. (Australia):—
All-Round.....................216
78 w. in Test Matches.........224
Palmer, J. F. (Natal "B"):—
8 Griqualand West w...........877
8 Orange Free State w.........876
Palmer, K. E. (Somerset):—
All-Round.....................216
Test Cricket..................167
118 v. Lancashire.............470
107 w. in 1966................274
9 Cambridge Univ. w...........554
9 Derbyshire w................363
9 Sussex w....................560
8 Yorkshire w.................642
23 catches in 1966............369
Parfitt, P. H. (Middlesex):—
Birthday......................946
Test Cricket..................167
Test Match Averages, 1966.....821
2,018 r. in 1966..............270
1,722 r. in Test Matches......222
41 Hundreds...................196
4 Hundreds v. Pakistan........247
2 Hundreds in 1966............277
2 Separate Hundreds...........196
131 v. New Zealand............244
122* v. South Africa..........239
121 v. India..................246
121 v. President's XI.........843
114* v. Yorkshire.............501
107 v. Sussex.................598
48 catches in 1966............369
(and D. A. Allen), 6th wkt. record v. Pakistan.........247
(and D. A. Allen), 8th wkt. record v. Pakistan.........247
(and E. R. Dexter), 4th wkt. record v. Pakistan.........247
(and B. R. Knight), 6th wkt. record v. New Zealand.....244
(and J. T. Murray), 7th wkt. record v. Pakistan.........247
Paris, C. G. A. (Hampshire), M.C.C. Committee...........321
Parker, C. W. L. (Gloucestershire):—
Double Hat-trick..............208
3,278 w.......................214
200 w. (5 times)..............213
100 w. (16 times).............214
100 w. by June 12.............214
17 w. in Match................210
10 w. in Innings..............209
6 Hat-tricks..................208
Parkhouse, W. G. A. (Glamorgan):—
Test Cricket..................167
1,000 r. (15 times)...........198
Parkin, C. H. (Lancashire), 200 w. (twice)...........213
Parks, H. W. (Sussex), 42 Hundreds 196

Parks, J. H. (Sussex):—
All-Round 215, 216
Aggregate of 3,003...........206
41 Hundreds...................196
(and E. H. Bowley), 368 for 1st wkt.......................202
Parks, J. M. (Sussex) (wkt.-kpr.):—
Birthday.......................946
Benefit.........................263
Captain of Sussex, 1967........581
Test Cricket...................167
Test Match Averages, 1965–66 819, 821
Test Match Averages, 1966......282
1,914 r. in Test Matches........222
1,225 r. in 1966.................270
45 Hundreds 196
2 Hundreds in 1966............278
119 *v.* Lancashire..............587
108* *v.* South Africa...........239
107* *v.* Western Australia.......825
101* *v.* Rest of the World XI....702
101* *v.* West Indies............242
61 w. in 1966....................369
38 w. in Australasia.............822
8 catches in Test *v.* New Zealand 229, 844
5 catches in Innings *v.* New Zealand.................229, 844
5 w. in Test Innings............229
(and K. F. Barrington), 6th wkt. record *v.* South Africa......238
(and M. J. K. Smith), 7th wkt. record *v.* West Indies......241
Parsons, Rev. J. H. (Warwickshire), 38 Hundreds 196
Partnerships, Highest..........201
Partridge, J. T. (South Africa):—
Test Cricket....................179
7 w. for 9 r.....................212
Passalique, C. C. (Jamaica) (and G. A. Headley), 487 for 6th wkt.................201, 204
Pataudi, Nawab of (Oxford Univ., Worcestershire, England and India):—
Captain *v.* England.............245
England *v.* Australia...........167
India *v.* England...............187
4 Successive Hundreds..........199
2 Hundreds *v.* Cambridge..260, 339
238* *v.* Cambridge........260, 339
106 *v.* Cambridge.........260, 339
102 *v.* Australia on Test début 225, 233
Pataudi, Nawab of (Oxford Univ., Sussex and India):—
Birthday........................946
Captain of Sussex..............581
Test Cricket....................187
2 Hundreds *v.* England 246
2 Hundreds *v.* New Zealand....257
Pataudi, Nawab of (Oxford Univ., Sussex and India):—*contd.*
2 Separate Hundreds......196, 197
175 *v.* Hyderabad XI.........888
132 *v.* West Zone 887
131 *v.* Cambridge 339
128* *v.* Australia..............253
24 catches in 1966.............369
(and C. G. Borde), 5th wkt. record *v.* England.........246
Patel, A. (Orissa), 8 Bihar w.......886
Patel, J. M. (Baroda), 106 *v.* Gujerat 883
Patel, J. S. (India):—
Test Cricket.....................187
14 w. in Test Match............227
9 w. in Test Innings............227
Paull, R., 130* for Somerset II....734
Pawson, H. A. (Oxford Univ. and Kent), 135 *v.* Cambridge...339
Payne, C. (London Schools), 100* *v.* South Zone Schools......904
Payne, C. A. L. (Oxford Univ. and Middlesex), 101 on début...195
Paynter, E. (Lancashire):—
Birthday........................946
Hon. Cricket Member, M.C.C...347
1,540 r. in Test Matches........222
653 r. in Rubber *v.* South Africa.240
45 Hundreds 196
3 Hundreds *v.* South Africa.....239
2 Separate Hundreds............196
2 Separate Test Hundreds..225, 239
322 *v.* Sussex...................192
216* *v.* Australia...............233
(and D. C. S. Compton), 5th wkt. record *v.* Australia 232
(and W. R. Hammond), 4th wkt. record *v.* Australia..........232
Payton, W. R. D. (Nottinghamshire), 39 Hundreds........196
Peach, H. A. (Surrey):—
Fast Scoring.....................199
4 w. with consecutive balls......208
Pearce, T. N. (Essex):—
M.C.C. Committee..............321
XI *v.* West Indies...........318–19
Pearson, A. J. G. (Cambridge Univ. and Somerset), 10 w. in Innings...................210
Pearson, F. (Worcestershire), All-Round.......................216
Peate, E. (Yorkshire):—
214 w. in Season................213
8 w. for 5 r.....................211
Peel, R. (Yorkshire):—
All-Round 216
102 w. in Test Matches.........224
100 w. (8 times) 215
(and Lord Hawke), 292 for 8th wkt..........................205

Pegler, S. J. (South Africa) (and L. A. Stricker), last wkt. record *v.* Australia........250
Pellew, C. E. (South Australia), 2 Hundreds *v.* England......235
Penn, A. (Kent), 6 w. for 3 r.........212
Pepper, C. G., First-Class Umpire 1008
Percival, R., Throwing Record....219
Perks, R. T. D. (Worcestershire):—
2,233 w........................214
100 w. (16 times)...............214
Perrin, P. A. (Essex):—
Highest for Essex..............193
1,000 r. (18 times)..............198
66 Hundreds....................195
2 Separate Hundreds............196
343* *v.* Derbyshire..........192, 193
Perse School, Cambridge..........789
v. M.C.C.........................327
Pervez Akhtar (Pakistan Railways), 337* *v.* Dera Ismail Khan...192
Pervez Sajjad (Pakistan), Test Cricket.......................188
Petrie, E. C. (New Zealand):—
Test Cricket....................184
Test Match Averages, 1966.....821
Phadkar, D. G. (India):—
Test Cricket....................187
123 *v.* Australia.................253
115 *v.* England..................246
(and V. S. Hazare), 6th wkt. record *v.* England.........246
Phillips, H. (Sussex) (wkt.-kpr.), 10 w. in Match.................217
Phillipson, W. E. (Lancashire), First-Class Umpire........1008
Philpott, P. I. (N.S.W.):—
Test Cricket....................175
Test Match Averages, 1965–66 819, 820
Piachaud, J. D. (Oxford Univ. and Hampshire), 9 Oxford Univ. w...........................673
Pickett, H. (Essex), 10 w. in Innings 209
Pieris, P. I. (Ceylon Prime Minister's XI), 10 w. *v.* All-India State Bank.........................894
Pilling, H. (Lancashire), 117 for Lancashire II..............715
Pimprikar, V. (Vidharba), 122* *v.* Madhya Pradesh..........884
Pinch, C. (South Australia), 2 Separate Hundreds.............196
Pinch, F. B. (Glamorgan), 138* on début.......................195
PITCH, THE (Laws of Cricket).......981
Care of........................982–3
Covering.......982–3, 998–9, 1007
Damage to......................999
Drying....................998, 1000
Mowing 982
PITCH, THE (Laws of Cricket):— *contd.*
Rolling.........................982
Sweeping.......................982
Watering.......................982
Pithey, A. J. (South Africa):—
Test Cricket....................179
154 *v.* England..................240
(and J. H. B. Waite), 5th wkt. record *v.* England..........238
Pithey, D. B. (South Africa):—
Test Cricket....................179
143 *v.* Eastern Province 874
Place, W. (Lancashire):—
36 Hundreds 196
107 *v.* West Indies...............242
(and C. Washbrook), 350* for 1st wkt...........................202
Players, The (Laws of Cricket)....980
Playle, W. R. (New Zealand and Western Australia):—
Slow Scoring....................226
Test Cricket....................184
132 *v.* Queensland...............865
116 *v.* Victoria..................857
Plunket Shield...............878–80
Plymouth College.................789
Pocklington School...........789–90
v. M.C.C.........................330
Pocock, P. I. (Surrey):—
10 Somerset w...................553
8 Middlesex w...................574
Podder, P. C. (Rajasthan), 176 *v.* Vidharba....................884
Polishing the Ball (Laws)....996, 1007
Pollard, R. (Lancashire), Benefit...263
Pollard, V. (New Zealand):—
Test Cricket....................184
(and B. Sutcliffe), 7th wkt. record *v.* England 244
Pollock, P. M. (South Africa):—
Birthday........................947
Test Cricket....................179
89 w. in Test Matches..........224
Pollock, R. G. (South Africa):—
Birthday........................947
Test Cricket....................179
2 Hundreds *v.* Australia.........249
2 Hundreds *v.* England..........240
(and E. J. Barlow), 341 for 3rd wkt. *v.* Australia......203, 250
Ponsford, W. H. (Victoria):—
Birthday........................947
2,122 r. in Test Matches.........222
47 Hundreds....................196
5 Hundreds *v.* England..........235
2 Hundreds *v.* West Indies......251
437 *v.* Queensland...............192
429 *v.* Tasmania.................192
352 *v.* New South Wales.........192
336 *v.* South Australia...........192
334 r. in Day....................201

Ponsford, W. H. (Victoria):—*contd.*
281* at Lord's 263
110 on Test début 225
(and D. G. Bradman), 451 for 2nd wkt. *v.* England . . . 201, 203, 232
(and D. G. Bradman), 2nd wkt. record *v.* West Indies 252
(and D. G. Bradman), 4th wkt. record *v.* England 232
(and S. J. McCabe), 389 for 3rd wkt. 203
(and E. R. Mayne), 456 for 1st wkt. 201, 203
(and W. M. Woodfull), 375 for 1st wkt. 202
Poole, K., 133 for Nottinghamshire II 717
Pooley, E. (Surrey) (wkt.-kpr.):—
12 w. in Match 217
10 w. in Match 217
Poore, R. M. (Hampshire):—
304 *v.* Somerset 193
(and E. G. Wynyard), 411 for 6th wkt. 204
Pope, G. H. (Derbyshire):—
All-Round 216
First-Class Umpire 1008
Popping Crease (Laws of Cricket) 981–2
Porchester, Lord:—
President of Hampshire 424
XI *v.* I.Z. 269
Portal of Hungerford, Marshal of R.A.F. Visct., M.C.C. Committee 321
Portsmouth Grammar School 790
Pothecary, J. E. (South Africa), Test Cricket 179
Potter, J. (Victoria), 221 *v.* New South Wales 860
Pougher, A. D. (Leicestershire), 5 w. for 0 r. 212
Poulton, R. M., Sec., Nottinghamshire 528
Powell, J. L. (Canterbury, N.Z.) (and N. Doreen), 265 for 7th wkt. 204
Prasanna, E. A. S. (India):—
Test Cricket 187
12 Rajasthan w. 886
11 Central Zone w. 887
8 w. *v.* Maharashtra Small Savings Minister's XI 889
Preece, C. A. (Worcestershire), Obituary 973
Pressdee, J. S. (Glamorgan and N.E. Transvaal):—
All-Round 216
101 *v.* Orange Free State 877
Pretlove, J. F. (Cambridge Univ. and Kent), 114 *v.* Oxford . . . 339
Pretty, Dr. H. C. (Surrey and Northamptonshire), 124 on début . 195
Price, J. S. E. (Middlesex):—
Birthday 948
Photograph 493
Test Cricket 167
9 Somerset w. 558
8 Derbyshire w. 505
8 Northamptonshire w. 503
8 Yorkshire w. 646
Price, W. F. (Middlesex) (wkt.-kpr.):—
7 w. in innings 217
First-Class Umpire 1008
Test Panel 1008
Prideaux, R. M. (Kent and Northamptonshire):—
Birthday 948
Photograph 510
1,947 r. in 1966 270
6 Hundreds in 1966 276
2 Separate Hundreds 196
153* *v.* Essex 386
135* *v.* Cambridge Univ. 686
109 *v.* Yorkshire 526
106 and 100 *v.* Nottinghamshire 197, 267, 535
101* *v.* Surrey 569
(and A. R. Lewis), 1st wkt. Hundreds 203
(and C. Milburn), 293 for 1st wkt. *v.* Essex 267, 386
Pritchard, G. C. (Essex), 41 w. for Essex II 72
Pritchard, T. L. (Warwickshire), 3 Hat-tricks 209
Proctor, M. H. (Natal), 129 *v.* Transvaal 875
Prodger, J. M. (Kent):—
114* *v.* Glamorgan 445
103 for Kent II 730
24 catches in 1966 369
8 catches in Match 218
Prout, J. A. (Wesley College), 459 *v.* Geelong College 194
PUBLIC SCHOOLS, THE, 1966 (E. M. Wellings) 748–57
PUBLIC SCHOOL CRICKET IN 1966 758–806
Public Schools *v.* English Schools' C.A. 343–4
Puckle, Sir F. H. (Uppingham and Lahore Europeans), Obituary 973
Pulbrook, R. (Harrow), 104 *v.* Eton 337
Pullar, G. (Lancashire):—
Benefit, 1967 458
Test Cricket 167
1,974 r. in Test Matches 222
1,184 r. in 1966 270
38 Hundreds 196

Pullar, G. (Lancashire):—*contd.*
2 Hundreds in 1966 278
2 Hundreds *v.* India 246
175 *v.* South Africa 239
167* *v.* West Indies 290
165 *v.* Pakistan 247
110 *v.* Leicestershire 483
(and R. W. Barber), 1st wkt. record *v.* Pakistan 247
(and K. F. Barrington) 2nd wkt. record *v.* India 246
(and P. E. Richardson), 1st wkt. record *v.* India 246
Puna, N. (New Zealand):—
Test Cricket 184
Test Match Averages, 1966 821
8 Auckland w. 879
8 Central Districts w. 879
Pye, D., physiotherapist, West Indies Team, Group 62

Quaid-e-Azam Trophy 889–90
Quaife, W. G. (Warwickshire):—
36,050 r. 197
1,000 r. (25 times) 198
72 Hundreds 195
Qualifications (Counties) 1002–6
Appeals 1006
Birth 1003, 1004
Overseas Players . . . 1004, 1005, 1008
Residential 1003, 1004
Special Registration 1005–6
University Players 1006
QUEEN, H.M. THE:—
Patron of Lancashire 459
Patron of M.C.C. 321
Patron of Surrey 563
Queen Elizabeth Grammar School, Wakefield 790
Queen's College, Taunton 790
QUEENSLAND—*See* Australia
Quin, S. O. (Victoria) (and I. S. Lee), 424 for 4th wkt. 204

Rabone, G. O. (New Zealand):—
Captain *v.* South Africa 254
Slow Scoring 226
107 *v.* South Africa 254
Radley College 791
v. M.C.C. 328
Radley, C. T. (Middlesex), 115 *v.* Cambridge Univ. 681
Rae, A. F. (West Indies):—
2 Hundreds *v.* England 243
2 Hundreds *v.* India 255
(and J. B. Stollmeyer), 355 for 1st wkt. 202
Raiji, M. N. (Bombay) (and Uday Merchant), 360 for 5th wkt. 204
Raikes, Rev. G. B. (Oxford Univ., Hampshire and Norfolk), Obituary 974
Rajinder Pal (India):—
Test Cricket 187
6 w. for 3 r. 212
Ramadhin, S. (West Indies and Lancashire):—
Birthday 949
Most balls in Single Innings 228
Most balls in Test Match 228
Test Cricket 182
158 w. in Test Matches 224
11 w. in Test Matches 227
(and F. M. Worrell), last wkt. record *v.* England 242
Ramchand, G. S. (India):—
Test Cricket 187
109 *v.* Australia 253
106* *v.* New Zealand 257
2 Hundreds *v.* New Zealand 257
(and S. G. Shinde), 9th wkt. record *v.* England 246
Rangnekar, K. M. (India) (and K. C. Ibrahim), 274 for 7th wkt. 204
Ranjane, V. B. (India), Test Cricket 187
Ranji Trophy 882–6
Winners, 1934–66 887
Ranjitsinhji, K. S. (H.H. The Jam Sahib of Nawanagar):—
Dates of Birth and Death 949
Aggregate of 3,159 206
72 Hundreds 195
2 Hundreds *v.* Australia 233
154* on Test début 225
(and W. Newham), 344 for 7th wkt. 204
Ransford, V. S. (Victoria):—
143* *v.* England 235
(and C. E. Kelleway), 6th wkt. record *v.* South Africa 250
(and W. J. Whitty), last wkt. record *v.* South Africa 250
Rao, J. S. (Services):—
Double Hat-trick 208
3 Hat-tricks 209
Ratcliffe, A. (Cambridge Univ. and Surrey):—
2 Hundreds *v.* Oxford 260, 339
201 *v.* Oxford 260, 339
Ratcliffe College, Leicester 791
Rayson, R. W. (Victoria), 10 South Australian w. 853
Read, W. W. (Surrey):—
Captain *v.* Australia 231
Captain *v.* South Africa 237
38 Hundreds 196
338 *v.* Oxford Univ. 192
Reading *v.* M.C.C. 329

Reading School....................791
v. M.C.C.....................332
Redmond, R. E. (N.Z. Under 23 XI), 10 Wellington w.......880
Redpath, I. R. (Victoria):—
Test Cricket....................175
Test Match Averages, 1965–66..819
180 *v.* Queensland...............863
161* *v.* New South Wales........866
107 *v.* South Australia...........853
Reed, B. L. (Hampshire), 1,096 r. in 1966....................271
Reed's School, Cobham...........792
v. M.C.C.....................331
Rees, A. (Glamorgan), 24 catches in 1966....................369
Rees, R. B. (South Australia), Obituary....................974
Rege, M. (All India Schools), 113 *v.* London Schools..........904
Rehman, R. (Leicestershire II):—
196* for Leicestershire II.......732
Obituary.......................974
Rehman, S. F. (Pakistan), Test Cricket....................189
Reid, C. (Mercantile C.A., Ceylon), 110* *v.* All-India State Bank 894
Reid, J. R. (New Zealand):—
Birthday.......................949
Captain *v.* England............243
Captain *v.* India...............256
Captain *v.* Pakistan............258
Captain *v.* South Africa........254
Test Cricket....................184
3,431 r. in Test Matches........223
1,915 r. in South Africa........206
39 Hundreds....................196
2 Hundreds *v.* India............257
2 Hundreds *v.* South Africa....254
128 *v.* Pakistan...............258
100 *v.* England................244
85 w. in Test Matches...........224
15 Sixes in Innings.............200
(and B. Sutcliffe), 2nd wkt. record *v.* England..............244
(and W. M. Wallace), 324 for 4th wkt..........................204
Reigate Priory *v.* M.C.C..........333
Relf, A. E. (Sussex):—
All-Round......................215
100 w. (11 times)...............215
Representative Bodies (Addresses).492
Repton School....................792
v. M.C.C.....................327
Rest *v.* Southern Schools.......342–3
Rest of the World XI:—
v. England XI..........346, 701–2
v. West Indies................346–7
Reynolds, B. L. (Northamptonshire):—
1,323 r. in 1966................271
22 catches in 1966..............369
Rhodes, A. E. G. (Derbyshire):—
5 Hat-tricks....................208
First-Class Umpire.............1008
Rhodes, H. J. (Derbyshire):—
Bowling Action.................1007
Test Cricket....................168
8 Surrey w......................566
Rhodes, W. (Yorkshire):—
Birthday.......................949
All-Round......................215
Hon. Cricket Member, M.C.C...347
39,797 r........................197
2,325 r. in Test Matches........222
1,000 r. (21 times).............198
58 Hundreds....................195
2 Separate Hundreds............196
179 *v.* Australia...............233
152 *v.* South Africa............239
4,187 w........................214
261 w. in Season...............213
200 w. (3 times)................213
127 w. in Test Matches.........224
100 w. (23 times)...............214
15 Australian w. in Match..227, 236
8 w. in Test Innings............228
(and R. E. Foster) last wkt. record *v.* Australia.........232
(and J. B. Hobbs), 1st wkt. record *v.* Australia..........232
Rhys, H. R. J. (Glamorgan), 149 on début..........................195
Richardson, A. J. (South Australia):—
280 *v.* M.C.C...................193
100 *v.* England.................235
Richardson, B. (Tasmania), 112 *v.* M.C.C.....................838
Richardson, B. A. (Warwickshire), 110* for Warwickshire II...736
Richardson, D. W. (Worcestershire):—
Benefit, 1967...................458
Test Cricket....................168
65 catches in Season...........218
31 catches in 1966.............369
Richardson, P. E. (Worcestershire and Kent):—
Slow Scoring...................226
Test Cricket....................168
2,061 r. in Test Matches........222
44 Hundreds....................196
2 Hundreds *v.* West Indies......242
117 *v.* South Africa............239
104 *v.* Australia...............233
100 *v.* New Zealand............244
(and T. W. Graveney), 2nd wkt. record *v.* West Indies......241
(and G. Pullar), 1st wkt. record *v.* India...................246
Richardson, T. (Surrey):—
Dates of Birth and Death.......949
2,105 w.........................21

Richardson, T. (Surrey):—*contd.*
1,005 w. in Four Seasons 214
290 w. in Season 213
200 w. (3 times)..............213
100 w. (10 times).............215
88 w. in Test Matches..........224
10 w. in Innings...............209
8 w. in Test Innings............228
4 Hat-tricks...................208
Richardson, V. Y. (South Australia):—
Captain *v.* South Africa........248
138 *v.* England...............235
Ricketts, J. (Lancashire), 195* on début....................195
Ridgway, F. (Kent), 4 w. with consecutive balls.............208
Ridley, G. N. S. (Oxford Univ. and Kent):—
Captain of Oxford, 1967........668
Secretary of Oxford, 1966.......668
Rigg, K. E. (Victoria), 127 *v.* South Africa..................249
Rippon, A. E. S. (Somerset), Obituary....................974
Roach, C. A. (West Indies), 2 Hundreds *v.* England...........243
Roberts, A. W. (New Zealand) (and D. A. R. Moloney), 8th wkt. record *v.* England.........245
Robertson, J. D. (Middlesex):—
Birthday.....................950
Highest for Middlesex.........193
31,914 r......................198
1,000 r. (15 times)............198
331 r. in Day.................201
67 Hundreds...................195
331* *v.* Worcestershire.....192, 193
133 *v.* West Indies...........242
121 *v.* New Zealand...........244
Robins, R. V. C. (Eton and Middlesex), 102 *v.* Harrow.......337
Robins, R. W. V. (Cambridge Univ. and Middlesex):—
Birthday.....................950
All-Round....................216
108 *v.* South Africa...........239
101* *v.* Oxford...............339
(and H. Verity), 8th wkt. record *v.* India.................246
Robinson, P. J. (Worcestershire and Somerset):—
11 Surrey w...................553
8 Glamorgan w.................403
8 Gloucestershire w............551
33 catches in 1966.............369
Robinson, R., Sec., Somerset......545
Rodriguez, W. V. (West Indies), Test Cricket..............182
Roe, B. (Somerset), 152* for Somerset II..................734
Roehampton *v.* M.C.C...........331
Roller, W. E. (Surrey), 204 and Hat-trick *v.* Sussex.............216
Rolling the Pitch (Laws)..........982
Rome, Cricket in 94–5
Root, C. F. (Worcestershire):—
All-Round...................216
219 w. in Season.............213
100 w. (9 times).............215
Rorke, G. (N.S.W.), Test Cricket..175
Rosendorff, N. (Orange Free State), 102 *v.* Griqualand West.....876
Rossall School.................792
v. M.C.C....................331
Rothman Cricket Films...........95
Rothman World Cup..........345–7
Rothwell, B. A. (New South Wales), 125 *v.* Queensland.........861
Rowan, E. A. B. (South Africa):—
1,965 r. in Test Matches........223
2 Hundreds *v.* England.........240
306* *v.* Natal................192
143 *v.* Australia..............249
(and P. J. M. Gibb), 342 for 4th wkt....................204
(and C. B. van Ryneveld), 2nd wkt. record *v.* England......238
Roy, A. (Bengal), 197 *v.* Orissa....886
Roy, P. (India):—
Test Cricket..................187
2,441 r. in Test Matches........223
4 Successive Hundreds.........199
2 Hundreds *v.* England.........246
2 Separate Hundreds...........196
150 *v.* West Indies............256
(and V. Mankad), 413 for 1st wkt...........201, 203, 258
Royal Air Force................345
R.A.F. College *v.* M.C.C..........332
Royal Artillery *v.* I.Z............269
Royal Masonic School.........792–3
Royal Military Academy:—
v. I.Z.......................269
v. M.C.C....................327
Royal Navy:—
v. Army.....................345
v. I.Z.......................269
v. Oxford Univ...............699
v. Royal Air Force............345
Rugby C.C. *v.* M.C.C............332
Rugby School..................793
v. Marlborough..............340
v. M.C.C....................327
Rumsey, F. E. (Somerset):—
Test Cricket..................168
100 w. in 1966...............274
8 Northamptonshire w.........517
(and K. F. Barrington), last wkt. record *v.* New Zealand.....244
Run (Laws of Cricket)...........984
Rungta, K. M. (Rajasthan), 128 *v.* Services................886
Run Out (Laws of Cricket)........990

Rushby, T. (Surrey), 10 w. in Innings....................209
Russell, A. C. (Essex):—
71 Hundreds....................195
3 Hundreds *v.* Australia........233
2 Separate Hundreds..........196
2 Separate Test Hundreds..225, 239
2 Hundreds *v.* South Africa.....239
(and A. E. R. Gilligan), last wkt. record *v.* South Africa......238
Russell, S. E. (Middlesex and Gloucestershire):—
107 *v.* Oxford Univ............670
109* for Gloucestershire II.....729
Russell, S.G. (Cambridge Univ.):—
Captain of Cambridge, 1967....697
8 w. *v.* Scotland..............682
Russell, W. E. (Middlesex):—
Birthday.......................951
Test Cricket...................168
Test Match Averages, 1965–66 819, 821
Test Match Averages, 1966.....282
1,513 r. in 1966...............270
3 Hundreds in 1966............277
2 Hundreds in Australia........823
146* *v.* Glamorgan............497
117* *v.* Worcestershire........623
110 *v.* Queensland............830
101* *v.* New South Wales.......841
101 *v.* Derbyshire............504
Rutnagur, Dicky ("Indian Cricket —Its Problems and Players") 143–7
Ryder, J. S. (Victoria):—
2 Hundreds *v.* England........235
142 *v.* South Africa...........249
Rydal School....................793
v. M.C.C......................333

Sadiq Mohammad, 9 Punjab Univ. w.........................892
Saeed Ahmed (Pakistan):—
Test Cricket...................189
2,562 r. in Test Matches........223
4 Successive Hundreds.........199
2 Hundreds *v.* India...........257
172 *v.* New Zealand............258
166 *v.* Australia..............253
150 *v.* West Indies.............256
100* *v.* Surrey................326
10 Ceylon w....................895
(and Nasim-ul-Ghani), 7th wkt. record *v.* England..........248
Saeed Butt (Railway Reds), 105 *v.* Lahore Reds...................891
Saggers, R. A. (N.S.W.) (wkt.-kpr.):—
21 w. in Test Rubber...........229
10 w. in Match.................217
7 w. in Innings.................217
Sainsbury, P. J. (Hampshire), 23 catches in 1966..............369
Sainsbury, S. D. D. (Eton), 100 *v.* Harrow....................337
St. Albans School...............793
St. Bartholomew's G.S. *v.* M.C.C..333
St. Bees School.................794
v. M.C.C......................331
St. Dunstan's College............794
v. M.C.C......................329
St. Edmund's College *v.* M.C.C...330
St. Edmund's School, Canterbury..794
St. Edward's School...........794–5
v. M.C.C......................331
St. George's College, Weybridge...795
v. M.C.C......................329
St. John's School, Leatherhead....795
v. M.C.C......................331
St. Lawrence College............795
v. M.C.C......................330
St. Paul's School................796
v. I.Z.........................269
v. Lords and Commons.........278
v. M.C.C......................332
St. Peter's School, York..........796
v. M.C.C......................330
Salah-ud-Din (Pakistan):—
Test Cricket...................189
(and Wallis Mathias), 388 for 3rd wkt........................203
Saldana, N. F. (Maharashtra), 142 *v.* Saurashtra..............883
Salim Altaf (Punjab Univ.), 11 w. *v.* Lahore Greens..............891
Sandham, A. (Surrey):—
Birthday.......................951
Hon. Cricket Member, M.C.C...347
41,284 r.......................197
1,977 r. in India...............206
1,000 r. (20 times).............198
107 Hundreds..................195
2 Hundreds *v.* West Indies......242
325 *v.* West Indies.........192, 242
219 *v.* Australians.............193
(and J. B. Hobbs), 428 for 1st wkt........................201
(and J. B. Hobbs), 1st wkt. Hundreds..................202
Santall, F. R. (Warwickshire), Fast Scoring....................200
Sanyal, R. (Bihar), 121 *v.* Assam...886
Sardesai, D. N. (India):—
Test Cricket...................187
2 Hundreds *v.* New Zealand.....257
101 *v.* Gujarat Governor's XI....888
(and B. K. Kunderam), 2nd wkt. record *v.* England..........246
Sarwate, C. T. (India):—
(and S. N. Banerjee), 249 for last wkt...................205
(and R. P. Singh), 236 for 8th wkt........................205
Saunders, J. G. (Oxford Univ.), 10 Lancashire w...............677

Saunders, J. V. (Victoria), 79 w. in Test Matches.............224
Savage, J. S. (Leicestershire), 9 Lancashire w.............483
Saville, S. H. (Cambridge Univ. and Middlesex), Obituary......974
Saxena, R. (Delhi), 122 *v.* Services.885
Sayer, D. M. (Kent), 8 Sussex w...446
SCARBOROUGH FESTIVAL..........701–2
Address of Secretary...........492
Scarlett, R. (West Indies), Test Cricket.................182
Schofield, R. (Central Districts, N.Z.), 7 catches in Innings..218
Schonegevel, D. J. (Griqualand West), 138* v. Natal "B"...877
Scorers (Laws of Cricket)..........980
Notes for.....................993–4
SCOTLAND:—
v. Cambridge Univ............682–3
v. Denmark......................699
v. Ireland..................699–700
v. M.C.C.......................328
v. Warwickshire.................604
v. West Indies...............312–13
Scott, H. J. H. (Australia):—
Captain *v.* England..............231
102 *v.* England..................235
Scott, J. C. G. (Sussex), 137 on début.....................195
SCOTTISH CRICKET IN 1966.......905–6
Scotton, W. H. (Nottinghamshire):—
Slow Scoring.....................226
(and W. W. Read), 9th wkt. record *v.* Australia..........232
Sealy, J. E. D. (West Indies):—
Youngest West Indian Test Player.....................259
8 w. for 8 r......................211
Sebright School...................796
SECOND XI CHAMPIONSHIP.....726–38
Championship Table..............727
Fixtures, 1967..............1037–9
Second Innings, Forfeiture of.997, 1007
Sedbergh School..................797
v. M.C.C........................330
Sellers, A. B. (Yorkshire), M.C.C. Committee....................321
Sellers, R. H. D. (S. Australia), Test Cricket................175
(Robert) Senanayaka Trophy.....893–4
Sengupta, A. K. (India), Test Cricket.....................187
Sevenoaks School.................797
Seymour, James (Kent):—
1,000 r. (16 times).............198
53 Hundreds.....................196
2 Separate Hundreds.............196
Seymour, M. A. (South Africa), Test Cricket.................179
Shabbir Hussain (Karachi Blues), 8 w. *v.* Lahore Greens.......890
Shackleton, D. (Hampshire):—
Birthday........................952
Benefit, 1967...................458
Test Cricket....................168
2,627 w.........................214
117 w. in 1966..................274
100 w. (18 times)...............214
9 Gloucestershire w.............410
8 Kent w........................456
8 Somerset w....................548
8 w. for 4 r....................211
Shacklock, F. (Nottinghamshire), 4 w. with consecutive balls..208
Shafqat Rana (Pakistan):—
Test Cricket....................189
110 *v.* Karachi Blues..........890
104 *v.* Dacca..................890
Shahid Mahmood (Pakistan), Test Cricket......................189
Shaikh, A. (Maharashtra), 8 Saurashtra w...................883
Shakoor Ahmad (Lahore Greens), 150* *v.* Karachi Blues.......890
Sharma, M. (Services), 170 *v.* North Punjab....................884
Sharp, J. (Lancashire):—
38 Hundreds.....................196
105 *v.* Australia..............233
Sharp, J. C. (Melbourne G.S.), 506* *v.* Geelong College........194
Sharpe, D. (Pakistan), Test Cricket.189
Sharpe, P. J. (Yorkshire):—
Birthday........................952
Photograph......................634
Group............................66
Test Cricket....................168
71 catches in Season............218
45 catches in 1966..............369
(and G. A. R. Lock), 9th wkt. record *v.* West Indies......241
Shaw, A. (Nottinghamshire and Sussex):—
Captain *v.* Australia..........231
2,072 w.........................214
201 w. in Season................213
100 w. (8 times)................215
10 w. in Innings................209
7 w. for 7 r....................211
Double Hat-trick................208
3 Hat-tricks....................209
Sheahan, A. P. (Victoria), 106* *v.* South Australia.............869
SHEFFIELD SHIELD (1892–1966).....872
Sheffield University *v.* M.C.C.....329
Shell Regional Tournament (West Indies)..................896–7
Shelmerdine, G. O. (Lancashire), M.C.C. Committee............321
Shepherd, B.K. (Western Australia) Test Cricket.................175

Shepherd, D. (Gloucestershire):—
118 *v.* Worcestershire..........416
108 on début..................195
Shepherd, D. J. (Glamorgan):—
Benefit, 1967..................458
111 w. in 1966.................274
100 w. (10 times)..............215
9 Middlesex w..................398
9 Yorkshire w..................648
8 Essex w. (twice).........384, 402
8 Somerset w...................403
7 w. for 7 r. *v.* Hampshire..211, 394
5 w. for 2 r...................212
Shepherd, J., 53 w. for Kent II.....731
Shepherd, T. F. (Surrey), 42 Hundreds..........................196
Shepherd's Bush *v.* M.C.C.........333
Sheppard, Rev. D. S. (Sussex):—
Birthday.......................952
Test Cricket...................168
45 Hundreds....................196
2 Hundreds *v.* Australia.........233
127 *v.* Oxford..................339
119 *v.* India...................246
Shepperd, J., 40 w. for Norfolk....716
Sherborne School...............797
v. M.C.C.......................332
Sher Mohammad (Delhi):—
109 *v.* Railways.................885
101 *v.* Services.................885
Sherwell, P. W. (South Africa):—
Captain *v.* Australia...........248
Captain *v.* England.............237
115 *v.* England.................240
Shiell, A. B. (South Australia), 202* *v.* M.C.C.......................833
Shillingford, I. (Windward and Leeward Islands), 113* *v.* Jamaica........................896
Shinde, S. G. (India) (and G. S Ramchand), 9th wkt. record *v.* England......................246
Shining of Ball, Artificial........996
Shippey, P. A., 137 for Cambridgeshire..........................710
Shodhan, D. S. (India), 110 *v.* Pakistan on Test début.225, 257
Short Run (Laws of Cricket).......984
Shrewsbury, A. (Nottinghamshire):—
Captain *v.* Australia...........231
59 Hundreds....................195
3 Hundreds *v.* Australia......233–4
(and W. Gunn), 398 for 2nd wkt..205
(and A. O. Jones), 391 for 1st wkt...........................201
Shrewsbury School..............798
v. M.C.C.......................329
Shrimpton, M. J. F. (New Zealand):—
Test Cricket...................185
Test Match Averages, 1966.....821
SHROPSHIRE.....................719
Championship Table............707
Shuja-ud-Din (Pakistan):—
Slow Scoring...................226
Test Cricket...................189
Sidmouth *v.* M.C.C...............334
Siedle, I. J. (South Africa):—
141 *v.* England.................240
(and B. Mitchell), 1st wkt. record *v.* England..........238
(and J. F. W. Nicolson), 424 for 1st wkt..............201, 203
Signalling, Code of (Umpires).....994
Sikdar, B. K. (Orissa), 105 *v.* Bihar.886
Silk, D. R. W. (Cambridge University and Somerset), 2 Hundreds *v.* Oxford.......260, 339
Simms, H. L. (Sussex and Warwickshire), All-Round..........216
Simpson, R. B. (New South Wales):—
Birthday.......................952
Captain *v.* England.............231
Captain *v.* India...............252
Captain *v.* Pakistan............253
Captain *v.* West Indies.........250
Test Cricket...................175
Test Match Averages, 1965–66 819, 820
3,354 r. in Test Matches.......222
49 Hundreds....................196
2 Hundreds *v.* England..........235
2 Hundreds *v.* Pakistan.........253
2 Separate Hundreds......196, 197
2 Separate Test Hundreds..225, 253
359 *v.* Queensland..............192
311 *v.* England............192, 235
225 *v.* England............235, 840
201 *v.* West Indies.............251
123 *v.* M.C.C...................840
113 *v.* Victoria................860
(and W. M. Lawry), 382 for 1st wkt. *v.* West Indies...201, 252
(and W. M. Lawry), 1st wkt. record *v.* England.....232, 840
Simpson, R. T. (Nottinghamshire):—
"Nottinghamshire's Notable Part in the Growth of Cricket" 134–42
Birthday.......................952
30,546 r.......................198
64 Hundreds....................195
156* *v.* Australia..............234
137 *v.* South Africa............239
103 *v.* New Zealand.............244
101 *v.* Pakistan................247
(and L. Hutton), 1st wkt. record *v.* New Zealand..........244
(and C. Washbrook), 1st wkt. record *v.* West Indies......241

Simpson, W. F., First-Class Umpire....................1008
Sims, Sir Arthur (and V. T. Trumper), 433 for 8th wkt.......205
Sims, J. M. (Middlesex):—
100 w. (8 times)...............215
10 w. in Innings...............210
Sinclair, B. W. (New Zealand):—
Test Cricket...................185
Test Match Averages, 1966......821
138 *v.* South Africa...........254
130 *v.* Pakistan...............258
114 *v.* England............244, 846
Sinclair, J. H. (South Africa):—
Fast Scoring...................226
2 Hundreds *v.* Australia........249
106 *v.* England................240
Sincock, D. J. (S. Australia):—
Test Cricket...................175
Test Match Averages, 1965–66 819, 820
9 Queensland w................868
Sinfield, R. A. (Gloucestershire), All-Round...............216
Singh, C. K. (West Indies), Test Cricket..................182
Singh, R. P. (Holkar) (and C. T. Sarwate), 236 for 8th wkt...205
Single-Wicket Championship (Charrington Trophy).........703–4
Past Winners..................704
Rules.........................704
Sir George Monoux Grammar School *v.* M.C.C...........327
Sixty-Five Overs Experiment 90, 348, 1006
List of Matches................349
Slack, J. K. E. (Cambridge Univ.), 135 on début..............195
Slade, W. (Glamorgan), 23 catches in 1966.....................369
Slater, K. (Western Australia), Test Cricket..............175
Slough *v.* M.C.C.................334
Smailes, T. F. (Yorkshire):—
All-Round.....................216
10 w. in Innings..............210
Smales, K. (Nottinghamshire), 10 w. in Innings..............210
SMALL TOTALS...............219–20
Smart, C. C. (Glamorgan), 32 r. in Over...................200
Smedley, M. J. (Nottinghamshire):—
1,266 r. in 1966...............270
134* *v.* Leicestershire..........543
Smith, A. C. (Warwickshire) (wkt.-kpr.):—
Group...........................67
Test Cricket...................168
59 w. in 1966..................369
(and M. C. Cowdrey), 9th wkt. record *v.* New Zealand.244, 258
Smith, C. (West Indies), Test Cricket...................182
Smith, C. A. (Sussex), Captain *v.* South Africa..............237
Smith, C. I. J. (Middlesex), Fast Scoring..................199
Smith, D. M. (Eton), 106 *v.* Harrow 336, 337
Smith, D. R. (Gloucestershire):—
Test Cricket...................168
10 Glamorgan w................415
(and G. Millman), last wkt. record *v.* India...........246
Smith, D. V. (Sussex), Test Cricket.168
Smith, E. (Derbyshire):—
13 Hampshire w................356
9 Surrey w....................566
8 Worcestershire w............366
Smith, E. J. (Warwickshire) (wkt.-kpr.):—
Birthday.......................953
Hon. Cricket Member, M.C.C...347
7 w. in Innings................217
Smith, F. B. (New Zealand) (and M. P. Donnelly), 5th wkt. record *v.* England..........244
Smith, G. J. (Essex), 8 Oxford Univ. w..........................676
SMITH, LESLIE ("Cricket Records") 190–266
Smith, M. J. K. (Oxford Univ., Leicestershire and Warwickshire):—
Birthday.......................953
Group...........................67
Captain of Warwickshire.......599
Captain *v.* Australia...........231
Captain *v.* India...............245
Captain *v.* New Zealand.......243
Captain *v.* South Africa........237
Test Cricket...................168
Test Match Averages, 1965–66 819, 821
Test Match Averages, 1966.....282
3,245 r. in Season.............206
2,138 r. in Test Matches.......222
1,824 r. in 1966...............270
1,079 r. in Australasia.........822
52 Hundreds...................196
4 Hundreds in 1966............277
3 Hundreds *v.* Cambridge..260, 339
2 First-Class Hundreds in Australia.........................823
201* *v.* Cambridge........260, 339
164 *v.* Country Districts........837
140 *v.* West Indies.............289
121 *v.* South Africa............239
117 *v.* Nottinghamshire........544
113* *v.* Hampshire............611
112* *v.* Combined XI..........826
108 *v.* South Australia.........833
108 *v.* West Indies.............242

Smith, M. J. K. (Oxford Univ., Leicestershire and Warwickshire):—*contd.*
103* *v.* Sussex....594
100 *v.* India....246
32 catches in 1966....369
27 catches in Australasia....822
(and K. F. Barrington), 3rd wkt. record *v.* Pakistan....247
(and J. M. Parks), 7th wkt. record *v.* West Indies....241
(and R. Subba Row), 3rd wkt. record *v.* India....246
Smith, M. S. (Natal) (wkt.-kpr.), 7 w. in Innings....217
Smith, O. G. ("Collie") (West Indies):—
Test Cricket....182
2 Hundreds *v.* England....243
104 *v.* Australia on Test début 225, 251
100 *v.* India....255
(and J. D. Goddard), 7th wkt. record *v.* England....242
(and C. L. Walcott), 6th wkt. record *v.* Australia....252
Smith, R. (Essex), All-Round....216
Smith, S. G. (West Indies, Northamptonshire and New Zealand):—
All-Round....216
4 w. with consecutive balls....208
Smith, T. P. B. (Essex), All-Round.216
Smith, V. I. (South Africa), 6 w. for 1 r....212
Smith, W. C. (Surrey), 247 w. in Season....213
Snellgrove, K. (Lancashire), 104 for Lancashire II....731
Snooke, S. J. (South Africa):—
103 *v.* Australia....249
8 w. in Test Innings....228
Snow, J. A. (Sussex):—
Birthday....953
Group....63
Test Cricket....168
Test Match Averages, 1966....282
126 w. in 1966....274
11 West Indies w....297
10 Yorkshire w....640
9 Worcestershire w....633
8 Derbyshire w....358
8 Gloucestershire w....420
(and K. Higgs), last wkt. record *v.* West Indies....241, 268, 316
Sobers, G. S. (West Indies and South Australia):—
"Sobers—The Lion of Cricket" (Sir Neville Cardus)....126–33
Birthday....953
Photographs...61, 64, 127, 129, 131
Group....62
Sobers, G. S. (West Indies and South Australia):—*contd.*
Captain *v.* England....241
Test Cricket....182
Test Figures....133
Test Match Averages, 1966....283
5,172 r. in Test Matches....223
1,349 r. in 1966....283
49 Hundreds....196
7 Hundreds *v.* England....243
5 Hundreds *v.* India....255
4 Hundreds in 1966....284
3 Hundreds *v.* Pakistan....256
2 Hundreds *v.* Australia....251
2 Separate Test Hundreds..225, 256
365* *v.* Pakistan....192, 256
204 *v.* British Guiana....897
174 *v.* England....243, 312
163* *v.* England....243, 299
161 *v.* England....243, 294
153 *v.* Nottinghamshire....288
120 *v.* Worcestershire....849
130 w. in Test Matches....224
9 Derbyshire w....293
9 Kent w. in Innings....267, 305
8 England w....312
23 catches in 1966....285
(and D. A. J. Holford), 6th wkt. record *v.* England.242, 267, 299
(and C. C. Hunte), 446 for 2nd wkt....203
(and S. M. Nurse), 5th wkt. record *v.* Australia....252
(and S. M. Nurse), 5th wkt. record *v.* England.242, 267, 312
(and C. L. Walcott), 4th wkt. record *v.* Australia....252
(and F. M. Worrell), 4th wkt. record *v.* England....242
Solihull School....798
v. M.C.C....329
Solomon, J. S. (West Indies):—
Group....62
Test Cricket....182
110 *v.* Trinidad....896
104 *v.* Somerset....306
100* *v.* India....255
SOMERSET....545–62
Averages....547
Results....547
Championship Table....350
County Badge....545
v. Cambridge Univ....554
v. Essex....562
v. Glamorgan....556
v. Gloucestershire....551
v. Hampshire....547–8
v. Kent....552
v. Leicestershire....549–50
v. Middlesex....558–9
v. Northamptonshire....557
v. Nottinghamshire....559

SOMERSET—*contd.*
v. Surrey 553
v. Sussex 560
v. Warwickshire 555
v. West Indies 305–6
v. Worcestershire 561
v. Yorkshire 548–9
Gillette Cup Matches
654–5, 660–1, 662–3, 664–5
SOMERSET II 719–20, 734–5
Championship Tables 707, 727
Championship Winners 266
Sood, M. M. (India), Test Cricket..187
SOUTH AFRICA:—
Representative Body 492
Summary of All Tests 230
Test Cricketers (1888–1965)..176–80
SOUTH AFRICA *v.* AUSTRALIA...248–50
Highest Totals 248
Individual Hundreds 248–9
Match Results 248
Record Partnerships 250
Smallest Totals 248
Visiting Captains 248
SOUTH AFRICA *v.* ENGLAND....237–41
Highest Totals 238
Individual Hundreds 238–40
Match Results 237
Record Partnerships 238
Smallest Totals 238
Visiting Captains 237
SOUTH AFRICA *v.* NEW ZEALAND...254
SOUTH AFRICAN CRICKET, 1965–66
(Geoffrey A. Chettle)....872–7
Southampton, Plan of County
Ground 425
SOUTH AUSTRALIA—*See* Australia
Southern Schools *v.* The Rest....342–3
Southerton, J. (Surrey):—
Oldest Test début 259
210 w. in Season 213
100 w. (9 times) 215
16 w. in Day 212
South Wales Cricket Association,
Address of Secretary 492
South Wales Hunts *v.* I.Z. 269
South Woodford *v.* M.C.C. 333
Sparling, J. T. (New Zealand), Test
Cricket 185
Special Regulations (Laws) 980
Spencer *v.* M.C.C. 333
Spencer, C. T. (Leicestershire):—
11 Worcestershire w. 629
21 catches in 1966 369
Spencer, T. W. (Kent), First-Class
Umpire 1008
Spofforth, F. R. (N.S.W., Victoria
and Derbyshire):—
Dates of Birth and Death 953
Hat-trick *v.* England 228, 236
218 w. in Season 213
94 w. in Test Matches 224

Spofforth, F. R. (N.S.W., Victoria
and Derbyshire):—*contd.*
14 English w. in Match.....227, 236
7 w. for 3 r. 211
3 Hat-tricks 209
Spooner, R. H. (Lancashire):—
119 *v.* S. Africa 239
(and A. C. MacLaren), 368 for 1st
wkt. 202
Squires, H.S. (Surrey), 37 Hundreds
196
Stackpole, K. R. (Victoria):—
Test Cricket 175
Test Match Averages, 1965–66
819, 820
9 Queensland w. 863
Staff College, Camberley *v.* I.Z....269
STAFFORDSHIRE 720
Championship Table 707
Championship Winners 266
Stamford School 798
v. M.C.C. 331
Standen, J. A. (Worcestershire), 50
w. for Worcestershire II....738
Stanger-Leathes, C. F. (Northumberland), Obituary 974
Stanyforth, Lt.-Col. R. T. (Yorks.),
Captain *v.* South Africa....237
Statham, J. B. (Lancashire):—
Birthday 954
Benefit 263
Captain of Lancashire 459
Test Cricket 169
2,098 w. 214
252 w. in Test Matches 223
102 w. in 1966 274
100 w. (13 times) 215
10 Kent w. 457
9 Hampshire w. 469
8 Derbyshire w. 364
8 Nottinghamshire w. 463
3 Hat-tricks 209
(and D. A. Allen), last wkt. record *v.* Pakistan 247
Stayers, C. (West Indies), Test
Cricket 182
Steel, A. G. (Cambridge Univ. and
Lancashire):—
Hat-trick *v.* Oxford 260
2 Hundreds *v.* Australia 234
Steele, D. S. (Northamptonshire):—
1,170 r. in 1966 270
2 Hundreds in 1966 278
118* *v.* Leicestershire 481
117 *v.* Gloucestershire 423
8 Lancashire w. 514
33 catches in 1966 369
Stevens, G. (South Australia), Test
Cricket 175
Stevens, G. T. S. (Middlesex), 466*
v. Lambda 194

Stewart, M. J. (Surrey):—
Birthday....954
Captain of Surrey....563
Test Cricket....169
41 Hundreds....196
2 Hundreds in 1966....278
102 *v.* Sussex....596
101 *v.* Leicestershire....575
77 catches in Season....218
31 catches in 1966....369
7 catches in Innings....218
Stewart, W. J. (Warwickshire):—
Benefit, 1967....458
166 *v.* Oxford Univ....608
17 Sixes in Match....200
Stewart-Brown, P. H. (Harrow), 102* *v.* Eton....337
Steyn, S. S. L. (Western Province) (and D. P. B. Morkel), 222 for 8th wkt....205
Stockport Grammar School....798–9
Stocks, F. W. (Nottinghamshire), 114 on début....195
Stoddart, A. E. (Middlesex):—
Captain *v.* Australia....231
2 Hundreds *v.* Australia....234
485 *v.* Stoics....194
(and J. Douglas) 1st wkt. Hundreds....202
(and W. G. Grace), 1st wkt. Hundreds....202
Stollmeyer, J. B. (West Indies):—
Group....62
West Indies Manager, 1966....281
2,159 r. in Test Matches....223
2 Hundreds *v.* India....255
324 *v.* British Guiana....192
152 *v.* New Zealand....255
104 *v.* Australia....251
(and G. E. Gomez), 434 for 3rd wkt....203
(and A. F. Rae), 355 for 1st wkt..202
Stonyhurst College....799
v. M.C.C....329
Storey, S. J. (Surrey):—
Birthday....954
Photograph....563
All-Round....216, 267
1,013 r. in 1966....271
109* *v.* Nottinghamshire....578
104 w. in 1966....274
10 Glamorgan w....395
8 Yorkshire w....648
Stowe School....799
v. M.C.C....332
Strathallan School....799
Stricker, L. A. (South Africa) (and S. J. Pegler), last wkt. record *v.* Australia....250
Stroud *v.* M.C.C....333
Strudwick, H. (Surrey) (wkt.-kpr.):—
Birthday....954
Hon. Cricket Member, M.C.C...347
1,493 Dismissals....217
1,235 catches....217
21 w. in Test Rubber....229
Strydom, S. (Orange Free State), 234 *v.* Transvaal "B"....876
Studd, C. T. (Middlesex), All-Round....216
Studd, P. M. (Harrow and Cambridge Univ.). 100* *v.* Eton.337
Stumped (Laws of Cricket)....991
Stumps, The (Laws of Cricket)....981
Subba Row, R. (Surrey and Northamptonshire):—
Highest for Northamptonshire..193
Test Cricket....169
2 Hundreds *v.* Australia....234
300 *v.* Surrey....193
100 *v.* West Indies....242
(and M. J. K. Smith), 3rd wkt. record *v.* India....246
Subramaniam, V. (India), Test Cricket....187
Substitutes (Laws of Cricket)....980
SUFFOLK....721
Championship Table....707
Championship Winners....266
Gillette Cup....655–6
Sully, H. (Northamptonshire):—
101 w. in 1966....274
9 Kent w....520
8 Essex w....386
8 Glamorgan w....404
8 Sussex w....585
Sunbury *v.* M.C.C....333
Sunday County Matches....1006
Hours of Play....995, 1006
Sunley, J., 100* for Lincolnshire...715
Surendranath, R. (India), Test Cricket....187
SURREY....563–80
Averages....565
Results....565
Championship Table....350
Championship Winners....265
County Badge....563
v. Cambridge Univ....572
v. Derbyshire....566
v. Essex....577
v. Glamorgan....568
v. Gloucestershire....578–9
v. Kent....571
v. Kent (Friendly)....700
v. Lancashire....570
v. Leicestershire....575
v. Middlesex....574
v. Northamptonshire....569
v. Nottinghamshire....577–8
v. Somerset....573

SURREY:—*contd.*
v. Sussex....................567
v. West Indies..............306–7
v. Worcestershire..............576
v. Yorkshire..............579–80
Gillette Cup Matches......659, 662
SURREY II....................735
Championship Table 727
Championship Winners....266, 727
Surrey Schools *v.* M.C.C..........333
Surti, R. S. (India), Test Cricket ..187
SUSSEX....................581–98
Averages....................583
Results 583
Championship Table 350
County Badge................581
v. Cambridge Univ. 591
v. Essex....................590
v. Glamorgan................584
v. Gloucestershire..........594–5
v. Hampshire................589
v. Kent....................593
v. Kent (Friendly)............700
v. Lancashire................587
v. Middlesex..............597–8
v. Northamptonshire 585
v. Nottinghamshire..........588
v. Somerset..............596–7
v. Surrey..................595–6
v. Warwickshire............593–4
v. West Indies..............296–7
v. Worcestershire..........586
v. Yorkshire................592
Gillette Cup................654–5
SUSSEX II....................736
Championship Table 727
Sussex Martlets *v.* M.C.C..........334
Sutcliffe, B. (New Zealand):—
Birthday....................955
Test Cricket................185
2,727 r. in Test Matches 223
45 Hundreds 196
3 Hundreds *v.* India............257
2 Hundreds *v.* England 244
2 Separate Hundreds 196
385 *v.* Canterbury............192
355 *v.* Auckland 192
(and W. S. Haig), 266 for 5th wkt. 204
(and V. Pollard), 7th wkt. record *v.* England 244
(and J. R. Reid), 2nd wkt. record *v.* England 244
(and D. D. Taylor), 1st wkt. Hundreds..................202
(and L. A. Watt), 373 for 1st wkt. 202, 203
Sutcliffe, H. (Yorkshire):—
Birthday....................955
Fast Scoring..................200
Hon. Cricket Member, M.C.C...347
50,135 r......................197
Sutcliffe, H. (Yorkshire):—*contd.*
4,555 r. in Test Matches........222
Aggregate of 3,336............206
2,741 r. *v.* Australia............237
1,000 r. (24 times)..............198
149 Hundreds..................195
14 Hundreds in Season..........199
13 Hundreds in Season 199
8 Hundreds *v.* Australia........234
6 Hundreds *v.* South Africa 239
4 Successive Hundreds..........199
2 Hundreds *v.* New Zealand....244
2 Separate Hundreds 196
2 Separate Test Hundreds 225, 234, 239
313 *v.* Essex....................192
(and J. B. Hobbs), 1st wkt. Hundreds..................202
(and P. Holmes), 555 for 1st wkt. 201, 203
(and P. Holmes), 1st wkt. Hundreds....................202
Suttle, K. G. (Sussex):—
1,500 r. in 1966..............270
37 Hundreds 196
3 Hundreds in 1966 277
172* *v.* Middlesex..............598
139* *v.* Leicestershire..........480
102 *v.* Surrey..................596
Sutton, J. A., 112 for Cheshire....710
Sutton Valence School............800
v. M.C.C.....................329
Swansea, Plan of St. Helen's Ground 389
Sweeping the Pitch (Laws)........982
Swetman, R. (Surrey and Nottinghamshire) (wkt.-kpr.):—
Birthday......................955
Photograph 528
Test Cricket..................169
115 *v.* Essex....................542
63 w. in 1966..................369
(and R. Illingworth), 7th wkt. record *v.* India..............246
Sydenham, D. A. D. (Surrey), Testimonial, 1967..................458

Tait, J., Surrey masseur, Obituary..974
Tallon, D. (Queensland) (wkt.-kpr.):—
20 w. in Test Rubber............229
12 w. in Match................217
7 w. in Innings................217
Tamhane, N. S. (India), Test Cricket 187
Tancred, L. J. (South Africa) (and C. B. Llewellyn), 2nd wkt. record *v.* Australia........250
Tanner, A. R. (Middlesex), Obituary..........................975
Tarilton, P. H. (Barbados), 304* *v.* Trinidad....................193

Tarrant, F. A. (Victoria and Middlesex):—
All-Round....................215
100 w. (8 times)...............215
5 Hat-tricks....................208
4 w. with consecutive balls......208
Tate, F. W. (Sussex), 5 w. for 1 r...212
Tate, M. W. (Sussex):—
All-Round....................215
100* v. South Africa...........239
2,783 w......................214
200 w. (3 times)...............213
155 w. in Test Matches........223
100 w. (14 times).............214
38 w. in Rubber v. Australia....236
3 Hat-tricks...................209
Tattersall, R. (Lancashire), 100 w. (8 times)...............215
Taunton School.................800
v. M.C.C.....................331
Tayfield, H. J. (South Africa):—
Test Cricket...................179
170 w. in Test Matches.........224
37 w. in Rubber v. England.....240
30 w. in Rubber v Australia.....250
26 w. in Rubber v. England.....240
13 w. in Test Innings...........227
9 w. in Test Innings...........227
8 w. in Test Innings...........228
Taylor, B. (Essex) (wkt.-kpr.):—
1,264 r. in 1966...............271
70 w. in 1966.................369
Taylor, B. R. (New Zealand):—
Test Cricket...................185
Test Match Averages, 1966......821
105 v. India in Test début..225, 257
Taylor, C. H. (Oxford Univ., Leicestershire and Buckinghamshire):—
109 v. Cambridge...............339
Obituary......................975
Taylor, H. W. (South Africa):—
Birthday......................955
Captain v. England............237
2,936 r. in Test Matches........223
582 r. in Rubber...............240
7 Hundreds v. England.........240
(and H. G. Deane), 4th wkt. record v. England.........238
Taylor, J. (West Indies), Test Cricket...................182
Taylor, J. M. (N.S.W.):—
108 v. England.................235
(and A. A. Mailey), last wkt. record v. England.........232
Taylor, K. (Yorkshire):—
Group.........................66
Test Cricket...................169
1,044 r. in 1966...............271
106 v. M.C.C..................326
Taylor, M. (Nottinghamshire), 21 catches in 1966............369
Taylor, R. W. (Derbyshire) (wkt.-kpr.):—
Birthday......................955
Photograph...................352
64 w. in 1966.................369
10 catches in Match...........217
7 catches in Innings v. Glamorgan 218, 268, 367
Tea Interval................984, 995
Tennyson, Hon. L. H. (3rd Lord Tennyson) (Hampshire), 110 on début...............195
Test Centuries after age of 39......92
TEST CRICKETERS (1877–1966)..161–89
Test Dates, 1968..............1008
Testimonials in 1967............458
TEST MATCH RULES...........1001–2
TEST MATCHES:—
Centuries on début............225
Fast Scoring..................226
Hat-tricks....................228
Largest Scorers...........222–3
Most wickets.........223–5, 227–8
Slow Scoring.................226
Summary of..............229–30
Wicket-Keeping Feats........228–9
Test Profits, 1966..............1008
Test Selectors for 1966..........1006
Thomas, G. (N.S.W.):—
Test Cricket..................175
Test Match Averages, 1965–66..819
1,171 r. in 1965–6.............871
229 v. Victoria................860
182 v. Queensland.............852
131 v. South Australia..........859
129 v. M.C.C..................840
Thompson, G. J. (Northamptonshire):—
All-Round....................216
100 w. (8 times)..............215
THOMSON, A. A. ("My Favourite Summer")............118–25
Thomson, N. I. (Sussex):—
Test Cricket..................169
100 w. (12 times).............215
10 w. in Innings...............210
THOUSAND RUNS IN MAY.......206–7
Throwing:—
Experimental Laws..999–1000, 1007
M.C.C. Sub-Cmte. Report ..114–17
New Definition..............1007
Rhodes' Action..............1007
Throwing Records..............219
TIE MATCHES...................261
Points for, in Championship....350
Tiffin School v. M.C.C...........329
Time-Wasting, Umpires' Action.998–9
Timms, B. S. V. (Hampshire) (wkt.-kpr.):—
120 v. Oxford Univ.............671
66 w. in 1966.................369

Tindall, R. A. E. (Surrey), Testimonial, 1967 458
Tissera, M. (Ceylon), 120* *v.* Pakistan 895
Titmus, F. J. (Middlesex):—
Birthday 956
All-Round 215
Captain of Middlesex 493
Charrington Trophy Winner 704
Hat-trick *v.* Somerset 268, 558
Test Cricket 169
Test Match Averages, 1965–66 819
Test Match Averages, 1966 .... 282, 283
114 *v.* Country Districts 837
136 w. in Test Matches 224
100 w. (12 times) 215
9 Somerset w. 559
8 N.S.W. w. 830
8 Yorkshire w. 646
Todd, L. J. (Kent):—
All-Round 216
38 Hundreds 196
Tolchard, R. W. (Leicestershire) (wkt.-kpr.), 60 w. in 1966 369
Tonbridge School 800
v. Clifton 341–2
v. M.C.C. 333
Toshack, E. R. H. (N.S.W.), 5 w. for 2 r. 212
Toss, The (Laws of Cricket) 983
Townsend, C. L. (Gloucestershire), All-Round 215, 216
Townsend, D. C. H. (Oxford Univ. and Durham):—
M.C.C. Committee 321
193 *v.* Cambridge 339
Townsend, L. F. (Derbyshire), All-Round 215, 216
Trent College 800–1
v. M.C.C. 329
Trevor, A. H. (Sussex), 103 on début 195
Trial Balls (Laws) 983
Tribe, G. E. (Victoria and Northamptonshire):—
All-Round 215
100 w. (8 times) 215
8 w. for 9 r. 211
Trimble, S. C. (Queensland):—
152 *v.* South Australia 867
140 *v.* Western Australia 856
101 *v.* Western Australia 865
Trimborn, P. H. J. (Natal), 8 Western Province w. 875
Tring Park *v.* M.C.C. 333
Trinity College, Cambridge *v.* I.Z. 269
Trinity College, Glenalmond 801
Trinity School, Croydon 801
v. M.C.C. 333
Trott, A. E. (Victoria and Middlesex):—
All-Round 215, 216
Trott, A. E. (Victoria and Middlesex):—*contd.*
Australia *v.* England 175
Double Hat-trick 208
England *v.* South Africa 169
Hit over Lord's Pavilion 265
200 w. (twice) 213
10 w. in Innings 209
8 w. in Test Innings 227
4 w. with consecutive balls 208
Trott, G. H. S. (Victoria):—
Captain *v.* England 231
143 *v.* England 235
Trueman, F. S. (Yorkshire):—
Birthday 956
Group 66
Benefit 263
Test Cricket 169
2,161 w. 214
307 w. in Test Matches 223
111 w. in 1966 274
100 w. (12 times) 215
10 Essex w. 643
8 w. in Test Innings 227
4 Hat-tricks 208
21 catches in 1966 369
(and T. W. Graveney), 9th wkt. record *v.* Pakistan 247
Trumble, H. (Victoria):—
All-Round 216
Hat-trick *v.* England (twice) 228, 236
141 w. in Test Matches 224
8 w. in Test Innings 228
3 Hat-tricks 209
(and C. Hill), 7th wkt. record *v.* England 232
(and A. Sims), 433 for 8th wkt. 205
Trumper, V. T. (N.S.W.):—
Dates of Birth and Death 956
Fast Scoring 226
3,163 r. in Test Matches 222
2,263 r. *v.* England 237
42 Hundreds 196
6 Hundreds *v.* England 235
2 Hundreds *v.* South Africa 249
300* *v.* Sussex 193
(and W. W. Armstrong), 5th wkt. record *v.* South Africa 250
Truscott, P. B. (New Zealand), Test Cricket 185
Tuck, G. S. (Royal Navy), 126 on début 195
Tuckett, L. (South Africa) (and B. Mitchell), 8th wkt. record *v.* England 238
Tunnicliffe, J. (Yorkshire):—
70 catches in Season 218
(and J. T. Brown), 554 for 1st wkt. 201
(and J. T. Brown), 378 for 1st wkt. 202

Turner, C. T. B. (N.S.W.):—
Dates of Birth and Death........956
283 w. in Season................213
101 w. in Test Matches.....224, 237
17 w. in Match..................210
9 w. for 15 r...................211
Turner, F. M., Sec., Leicestershire.475
Turner, K. C., Sec., Northamptonshire.....................510
Twining, R. H. (Middlesex), Trustee, M.C.C......................321
Tyldesley, E. (Lancashire):—
Dates of Birth and Death........956
38,874 r........................197
Aggregate of 3,024..............206
1,000 r. (19 times).............198
102 Hundreds....................195
4 Successive Hundreds..........199
2 Hundreds v. South Africa.....239
2 Separate Hundreds............196
122 v. West Indies..............242
Tyldesley, J. T. (Lancashire):—
Dates of Birth and Death........956
37,809 r........................197
Aggregate of 3,041..............206
1,661 r. in Test Matches........222
1,000 r. (19 times).............198
86 Hundreds.....................195
3 Hundreds v. Australia........234
2 Separate Hundreds............196
112 v. South Africa............239
Tyldesley, R. (Lancashire):—
100 w. (10 times)...............215
7 w. for 6 r....................211
5 w. for 0 r....................212
4 w. with consecutive balls......208
Tyler, E. J. (Somerset), 10 w. in Innings.................209
Tyson, C. (Yorkshire), 100* on début.....................195
Tyson, F. H. (Northamptonshire):—
Test Cricket....................169
76 w. in Test Matches...........224

Ulyett, G. (Yorkshire):—
149 v. Australia................234
4 w. with consecutive balls......208
Ullyett, R. B. (Rhodesia), 135 v. Eastern Province..........874
UMPIRES:—
Appeals to......................993
Appointment of..................980
Attendance of...................980
Changing........................980
Changing Ends...................991
Duties of.....................991–3
Notes for.....................993–4
Signalling Code.................994
Test Matches..................995–6
Umpires for 1967:—
First Class....................1008
Umpires for 1967:—contd.
Minor Counties.................1008
Test Panel.....................1008
Umrigar, P. R. (India):—
Birthday........................956
Test Cricket....................187
3,621 r. in Test Matches........223
50 Hundreds.....................196
5 Hundreds v. Pakistan..........257
3 Hundreds v. England...........246
3 Hundreds v. West Indies.......256
223 v. New Zealand..............257
Underwood, D. L. (Kent):—
Birthday........................957
Photograph......................441
Best Young Cricketer of the Year 266
Test Cricket....................169
Test Match Averages, 1966.282, 283
157 w. in 1966..................274
13 Essex w......................381
11 Somerset w...................552
11 Yorkshire w..................650
10 Lancashire w.................473
10 Middlesex w..................496
9 Essex w.......................448
9 Essex w. in Innings......267, 381
9 Leicestershire w..............454
9 Gloucestershire w.............451
8 Sussex w......................593
Unfair Play.....................992
United London Banks v. M.C.C...330
UNITED STATES:—
Cricket in 1966 (John I. Marder) 899–901
Address of Representative Body.492
v. Canada.....................900–1
UNIVERSITIES, THE, IN 1966.....668–87
University College School........801
v. M.C.C........................331
Uppingham School................802
v. M.C.C........................327

Valentine, A. L. (West Indies):—
Birthday........................957
Test Cricket....................182
139 w. in Test Matches..........224
11 w. in Test Match.............227
8 w. in Test Innings............228
(and W. W. Hall), last wkt. record v. Australia..........252
Valentine, B. H. (Kent):—
35 Hundreds.....................196
136 v. India on Test début..225, 246
112 v. South Africa.............239
Van der Byl, P. G. (South Africa), 125 v. England.............239
Van der Merwe, P. L. (South Africa):—
Captain v. England..............237
Test Cricket....................180

van Geloven, J. (Leicestershire and Northumberland):—
All-Round....................216
47 w. for Northumberland......717
van Ryneveld, C. B. (South Africa):—
Test Cricket..................180
(and E. A. B. Rowan), 2nd wkt. record v. England..........238
Varnals, G. D. (South Africa), Test Cricket..................180
Veivers, T. R. (Queensland):—
Test Cricket..................176
Test Match Averages, 1965–66 819, 820
Venkataraghavan, S. (India):—
Test Cricket..................187
11 Andhra w...................882
8 w. in Test Innings..........228
Verity, H. (Yorkshire):—
Dates of Birth and Death.......957
Memorial Fund.................263
200 w. (3 times)...............213
144 w. in Test Matches.........224
100 w. (9 times)...............215
17 w. in Day...................212
17 w. in Match.................210
15 Australian w. in Match..227, 236
10 w. in Innings (twice).....209, 210
9 w. for 12 r..................211
8 w. in Test Innings...........227
7 w. for 9 r...................212
(and R. W. V. Robins), 8th wkt. record v. India...........246
Vernon, M. (Western Australia):—
173 v. New South Wales.........870
118 v. M.C.C...................825
Versfeld, B. (Natal):—
201* v. Transvaal..............875
128 v. Transvaal...............874
141 v. Western Province........877
Vials, G. A. T. (Northamptonshire), President of Northamptonshire..............510
VICTORIA—*See* Australia
Victoria College, Jersey..........802
v. M.C.C.....................328
Viljoen, K. G. (South Africa):—
124 v. England.................240
111 v. Australia...............249
Vincent, C. L. (South Africa), 84 w. in Test Matches..........224
Vine, J. (Sussex):—
All-Round.....................216
(and C. B. Fry), 1st wkt. Hundreds.....................202
(and F. E. Woolley), 7th wkt. record v. Australia........232
Virgin, R. (Somerset):—
1,333 r. in 1966...............271
124 and 125* v. Warwickshire...197
42 catches in 1966.............369
Virgin, R. (Somerset):—*contd.*
(and G. Atkinson), 1st wkt. Hundreds...............203
Vivian, G. E. (New Zealand), Test Cricket..................185
Vivian, H. G. (New Zealand), 100 v. South Africa............254
Vizianagram, Maharaj of (India), Captain v. England........245
Voce, W. (Nottinghamshire):—
Birthday.......................957
Hon. Cricket Member, M.C.C...347
98 w. in Test Matches..........224
(and F. R. Brown), 7th wkt. record v. New Zealand.....244
Vogler, A. E. E. (South Africa):—
16 w. in Day...................212
10 w. in Innings...........209, 211

Waddington, A. (Yorkshire), 7 w. for 6 r...................211
Wade, H. F. (South Africa), Captain v. England...............237
Wade, W. W. (South Africa), 125 v. England..................240
Wadekar, A. L. (Bombay):—
185 v. Rajasthan..............886
157* v. Gujerat...............883
127 v. Maharashtra Small Savings Minister's XI............889
118* v. Ceylon Nationalised Services.....................894
108 v. Hyderabad..............888
105 v. Associated Cement Company......................888
101* v. Maharashtra...........883
100 v. Saurashtra.............883
Wainwright, E. (Yorkshire), All-Round..................216
Waite, J. H. B. (South Africa) (wkt.-kpr.):—
Birthday......................957
Test Cricket..................180
2,405 r. in Test Matches.......223
2 Hundreds v. Australia........249
113 v. England................240
101 v. New Zealand............254
141 w. in Test Matches.........228
26 w. in Test Rubber...........228
(and W. R. Endean), 5th wkt. record v. Australia........250
(and A. J. Pithey), 5th wkt. record v. England........238
(and P. L. Winslow), 6th wkt. record v. England........238
Walcott, C. L. (West Indies):—
Birthday......................957
Test Cricket..................182
3,798 r. in Test Matches........223
42 Hundreds...................196
5 Hundreds v. Australia........251

Walcott, C. L. (West Indies):—*contd.*
4 Hundreds *v.* England.........243
4 Hundreds *v.* India..........255
2 Separate Hundreds...........196
2 Separate Test Hundreds..225, 251
314* *v.* Trinidad..............192
145 *v.* Pakistan...............256
115 *v.* New Zealand............255
(and O. G. Smith), 6th wkt. record *v.* Australia.........252
(and G. S. Sobers), 4th wkt. record *v.* Australia........252
(and E. D. Weekes), 3rd wkt. record *v.* Australia........252
(and F. M. Worrell), 574 for 4th wkt..................201, 203
Walker, A. K. (Nottinghamshire), 4 w. with consecutive balls..208
Walker, I. D. (Middlesex), 102 on début......................195
Walker, P. M. (Glamorgan):—
All-Round......................216
Benefit Match...............398–9
Test Cricket...................170
1,213 r. in 1966................270
73 catches in Season............218
42 catches in 1966..............369
Walker, V. E. (Middlesex):—
108 and 10 w...................217
10 w. in Innings (twice).........209
Walkley, E. (South Australia) (and C. Hill), 232 for 9th wkt.....205
Wall, T. W. (South Australia), 10 w. in Innings.................210
Wallace, W. M. (New Zealand) (and J. R. Reid), 324 for 4th wkt..........................204
Wallasey Grammar School........802
Walsh, J. E. (Leicestershire), All-Round......................216
Walter, K. A. (South Africa):—
Test Cricket....................180
8 Griqualand West w...........876
Walters, C. F. (Glamorgan and Worcestershire), 102* *v.* India..........................246
Walters, K. D. (N.S.W.):—
Test Cricket....................176
Test Match Averages, 1965–66 819, 820
1,332 r. in 1965–66..............871
2 Hundreds *v.* England.......235–6
168 *v.* South Australia..........868
155 *v.* England on Test début 225, 235, 831
129 *v.* M.C.C...................829
115 *v.* England............236, 834
114 *v.* Western Australia........870
113* *v.* South Australia.........859
Wanstead *v.* M.C.C..............330
Waqar Hassan (Pakistan):—
Test Cricket....................189
189 *v.* New Zealand............258
(and Imtiaz Ahmed), 308 for 7th wkt..........................204
Ward, A. (Lancashire), 117 *v.* Australia.......................234
Ward, J. T. (New Zealand), Test Cricket.......................185
Ward, W. (M.C.C.), 278 at Lord's.263
Wardle, J. H. (Yorkshire and Cambridgeshire):—
Benefit.........................263
Test Cricket....................170
102 w. in Test Matches..........224
100 w. (10 times)...............215
110 w. in Lancashire League....740
69 w. for Cambridgeshire........710
Waring, J. (Yorkshire):—
Group............................66
10 Lancashire w.................638
Warner, G. S.:—
1,202 r. for Warwickshire II.....736
105* for Warwickshire II.........736
Warner, Sir Pelham F. (Middlesex):—
Dates of Birth and Death.......958
Captain *v.* Australia............231
Captain *v.* South Africa.........237
60 Hundreds....................195
132* *v.* South Africa on Test début.....................225, 239
Warren, A. R. (Derbyshire) (and J. Chapman), 283 for 9th wkt..........................205
Warwick School.................803
WARWICKSHIRE..............599–616
Averages.......................601
Results.........................601
Championship Table............350
Championship Winners..........265
County Badge...................599
v. Derbyshire...............613–14
v. Essex......................603
v. Glamorgan..................605
v. Gloucestershire...........606–7
v. Hampshire...............610–11
v. Lancashire.................609
v. Leicestershire..............602
v. Middlesex................601–2
v. Northamptonshire........615–16
v. Nottinghamshire.........612–13
v. Oxford Univ.................608
v. Scotland...................604
v. Somerset................614–15
v. Surrey...................609–10
v. West Indies..........313–14, 320
v. Worcestershire...........611–12
v. Yorkshire..................606
Gillette Cup Matches 657–8, 663, 664–5, 666
Winners.......................666
Photograph....................67

WARWICKSHIRE II 721–2, 736–7
Championship Tables. 707, 727
Championship Winners 266
Washbrook, C. (Lancashire):—
Birthday. .958
Benefit. 263
Hon. Cricket Member, M.C.C. . .347
34,101 r. .198
2,569 r. in Test Matches 222
1,000 r. (20 times) 198
76 Hundreds 195
2 Hundreds v. Australia 234
2 Hundreds v. West Indies. 242
195 v. South Africa. 239
103* v. New Zealand. 244
(and L. Hutton), 359 for 1st wkt. v. S. Africa. 202, 238
(and L. Hutton), 1st wkt. Hundreds .202
(and W. Place), 350* for 1st wkt. 202
(and R. T. Simpson), 1st wkt. record v. West Indies 241
Wass, T. (Nottinghamshire):—
100 w. (10 times). 215
16 w. in Day (twice). 212
6 w. for 3 r. 212
Wassell, A. R. (Hampshire), 52 w. for Hampshire II. 730
Watering the Pitch. 982
Watkins, A. J. (Glamorgan):—
All-Round 216
138* v. India. 246
111 v. South Africa. 239
Watson, C. (West Indies), Test Cricket 182
Watson, F. (Lancashire):—
50 Hundreds. 196
300* v. Surrey. 193
(and C. Hallows), 1st wkt. Hundreds 202
Watson, G. D. (Victoria):—
109 v. Queensland. 863
8 South Australian w.. 870
(George) Watson's College. 774–5
Watson, W. (Yorkshire and Leicestershire):—
Test Cricket 170
55 Hundreds 195
116 v. West Indies. 242
109 v. Australia 234
Watt, L. A. (New Zealand) (and B. Sutcliffe), 373 for 1st wkt. 202, 203
Watts, E. A. (Surrey), 10 w. in Innings 210
Watts, P. D. (Northamptonshire), 40 w. for Northamptonshire II 733
Watts, P. J. (Northamptonshire), 38 catches in 1966 369
Wazir Mohammad (Pakistan):—
Test Cricket 189
Wazir Mohammad (Pakistan):—*contd.*
2 Hundreds v. West Indies 256
(and Zulfiqar Ahmed), 9th wkt. record v. England 248
Weather and Light (Laws). 992–3
Webb, H. E. (Oxford Univ.), 145* v. Cambridge 339
Webster, R. V. (Warwickshire):—
Group 67
9 Cambridge Univ. w.. 684
8 Glamorgan w.. 605
8 Middlesex w.. 498
7 w. for 6 r. 211
Weekes, E. D. (West Indies):—
Birthday 958
Test Cricket 182
4,455 r. in Test Matches 223
940 r. in New Zealand. 206
36 Hundreds. 196
7 Hundreds v. India. 255
5 Successive Test Hundreds. 199
3 Hundreds v. England 243
2 Separate Test Hundreds. .225, 255
304* v. Cambridge Univ. 193
197 v. Pakistan. 256
139 v. Australia 251
(and C. L. Walcott), 3rd wkt. record v. Australia 252
(and F. M. Worrell), 4th wkt. record v. England 242
Weekes, K. H. (West Indies), 137 v. England 243
Weerasinghe, D. (Government Services), 130 v. Ceylon Schools . 893
Wellard, A. W. (Somerset):—
All-Round 216
100 w. (8 times) 215
31 r. in Over. 200
30 r. in Over. 200
Wellingborough School 803
v. M.C.C. 331
WELLINGS, E. M.:—
"M.C.C. Team in Australia and New Zealand, 1965–66". 812–18
"The Public Schools in 1966" 748–57
Wellington College 803
v. I.Z. 269
v. M.C.C. 333
Wellington School 803–4
Wells, J. (Kent), 4 w. with consecutive balls 208
Welsh Secondary Schools v. M.C.C. 330
Wembley v. M.C.C. 333
Wensley, A. F. (Sussex), All-Round 216
Wesley, C. (South Africa):—
Test Cricket 180
120 v. N. E. Transvaal. 876
West Buckland School v. M.C.C. . .333

Westcliff-on-Sea *v.* M.C.C. 334
Westcliff, Plan of County Ground .371
Westcott, R. J. (South Africa), Test Cricket 180
Western Australia, *see* Australia
Western Province Willows in England, 1966 807–8
West Herts. *v.* M.C.C. 330
West Indies:—
Representative Body. 492
Summary of All Tests. 230
Test Cricketers (1928–66). 180–3
West Indies Cricket, 1965–66. .896–7
See also Worcestershire in Jamaica
West Indies in England, 1966 279–320
Batting Averages. 283–4
Bowling Averages. 284
Fielding Statistics. 285
Group. 62
Individual Hundreds. 284–5
Match Results. 282
Test Match Averages. 283
v. Cambridge Univ. 290–1
v. Derbyshire. 292–3
v. England XI. 347
v. Essex. 300–1
v. A. E. R. Gilligan's XI. 318
v. Glamorgan. 309–10
v. Gloucestershire. 295–6
v. Hampshire. 317–18
v. Kent. 305
v. Lancashire. 289–90
v. Leicestershire. 316–17
v. M.C.C. 288–9
v. M.C.C. President's XI. 308–9
v. Middlesex. 303–4
v. Minor Counties 299–300
v. Duke of Norfolk's XI. 286
v. Northamptonshire. 307–8
v. Nottinghamshire. 287–8
v. Oxford Univ. 286–7
v. T. N. Pearce's XI. 318–19
v. Rest of the World XI. 346–7
v. Scotland. 312–13
v. Somerset. 305–6
v. Surrey. 306–7
v. Sussex. 296–7
v. Warwickshire. 313–14, 320
v. Worcestershire. 286
v. Yorkshire. 291–2
West Indies in India, 1966–67. . . .100
West Indies *v.* Australia. 250–2
West Indies *v.* England. 241–3
Highest Totals. 241
Individual Hundreds. 242–3
Match Results. 241
Record Partnerships. 241–2
Smallest Totals. 241
Visiting Captains. 241
West Indies *v.* England, 1966:—
First Test (Manchester). 293–5
Second Test (Lord's). 297–9
Third Test (Trent Bridge). 301–3
Fourth Test (Leeds). 310–12
Fifth Test (The Oval). 314–16
West Indies *v.* India. 255–6
West Indies *v.* New Zealand. . .254–5
West Indies *v.* Pakistan. 256
West Kent *v.* M.C.C. 332
Westminster Bank *v.* M.C.C. 333
Westminster School:—
v. Lords and Commons. 278
v. M.C.C. .330
Weston-super-Mare *v.* M.C.C. 331
Wheatley, O. S. (Glamorgan):—
Birthday. 958
Captain of Glamorgan. 388
103 w. in 1966. 274
9 Essex w. .384
8 Derbyshire w. 405
White, D. W. (Hampshire):—
Birthday. 959
Photograph 424
Test Cricket. 170
28 r. in Over. 201
109 w. in 1966. 274
10 Leicestershire w. 431
9 Leicestershire w. in Innings 267, 431
White, G. C. (South Africa), 2 Hundreds *v.* England. 240
White, J. C. (Somerset):—
Dates of Birth and Death. 959
All-Round .216
2,356 w. 214
100 w. (14 times). 214
16 w. in Day. 212
10 w. in Innings. 209
8 w. in Test Innings 228
White, R. C. (Gloucestershire and Transvaal):—
205 *v.* Griqualand West. 876
117 *v.* Western Province. 875
White, W. A. (West Indies), Test Cricket 183
Whitefield, D. (Western Province Willows) 8 Buckinghamshire w. 808
Whitehead, H. (Leicestershire) (and C. J. B. Wood), 380 for 1st wkt. 202
Whitehead, R. (Lancashire), 131* on début. 195
Whitelaw, P. E. (Auckland) (and W. N. Carson):—
Fast Scoring. 199
445 for 3rd wkt. 199, 203
Whitgift School. 804
v. M.C.C. 327
Whittaker, G. J. (Surrey), 253* *v.* Gloucestershire II. 194

Whittingham, B. (Nottinghamshire), 133 *v.* Hampshire..........534
Whitty, W. J. (South Australia) (and V. S. Ransford), last wkt. record *v.* South Africa......250
Whysall, W. W. (Nottinghamshire):—
51 Hundreds..................196
4 Successive Hundreds..........199
2 Separate Hundreds..........196
(and G. Gunn), 1st wkt. Hundreds..................202
Wicket-keeper (Laws)............991
WICKET-KEEPING FEATS.......217–18
WICKET RECORDS (1st to 10th)...203–5
Wicket, The (Laws of Cricket)....981
When "down"................988
See also "Pitch"
Wide Ball (Laws of Cricket)......987
Wight, L. (British Guiana) (and G. Gibbs), 390 for 1st wkt. 201, 203
Wight, P. B. (Somerset), First-Class Umpire..................1008
Wilcox, D. R. (Cambridge Univ. and Essex), 157 *v.* Oxford ..339
Wiles, C. A. (West Indies), Oldest West Indies Test début.....259
Willett, M. D. (Surrey), 112 for Surrey II..................735
Willetts, F. T. (Somerset):—
160 for Somerset II............734
104 for Somerset II............719
Willey, P., 126* for Northamptonshire II..................733
Williams, C. R. (Baroda), 8 Bombay w.........................883
Williams, E. A. V. (West Indies) (and E. A. Martindale), 255 for 8th wkt.................205
Williams, Col. P. C., Sec., Sussex..581
Wills, R. (Northamptonshire), 151* *v.* Cambridge Univ.............686
Wilmot, A. L. (Eastern Province), 222* *v.* Rhodesia..........874
Wilson, A. E. (Gloucestershire) (wkt.-kpr.), 10 catches in Match....................217
Wilson, D. (Yorkshire):—
Group..........................66
Hat-trick *v.* Kent..........268, 650
Hat-trick *v.* Nottinghamshire 268, 541
Test Cricket..................170
30 r. in Over..........200, 268, 651
100 w. in 1966.................274
9 Gloucestershire w............637
9 Nottinghamshire w...........541
3 Hat-tricks..................209
Wilson, E. R. (Cambridge Univ. and Yorkshire), 117* on début.......................195
Wilson, G. A. (Worcestershire), 3 Hat-tricks..................209
Wilson, R. C. (Kent), 1,025 r. in 1966.....................270
WILTSHIRE......................722
Championship Table..........707
Championship Winners........266
Winchester College.............804
v. Eton 806–7
v. I.Z. 269
v. M.C.C.....................327
Windows, A. R. (Gloucestershire), 8 West Indies w...........296
Winslow, L. (Sussex), 124 on début 195
Winslow, P. L. (South Africa):—
108 *v.* England................240
30 r. in Over.................200
(and J. H. B. Waite), 6th wkt. record *v.* England..........238
Wisbech Town *v.* M.C.C.........325
Wisden, J. (Sussex), 10 w. in Innings.....................209
Wisden Trophy.............241, 269
Photograph....................61
Wolverhampton *v.* M.C.C........334
WOMEN'S CRICKET IN 1966 (Netta Rheinberg)...........909–12
England *v.* New Zealand....909–12
Women's Cricket Association, Address of Secretary...........492
Wood, C. J. B. (Leicestershire):—
37 Hundreds 196
2 Separate Hundreds..........197
(and H. Whitehead), 380 for 1st wkt.......................202
Wood, H. (Surrey):—
134* *v.* South Africa...........239
(and J. J. Hearne), 9th wkt. record *v.* South Africa............238
Wood, J. B., Sec., Lancashire......459
Woodford Wells *v.* M.C.C........331
Woodfull, W. M. (Victoria):—
Dates of Birth and Death.......960
Captain *v.* England.............231
2,300 r. in Test Matches........222
49 Hundreds..................196
6 Hundreds *v.* England.........236
161 *v.* South Africa............249
(and W. H. Ponsford), 375 for 1st wkt.....................202
Woodhouse Grove School......804–5
Woods, S. M. J. (Australia and Somerset):—
Australia *v.* England...........176
England *v.* South Africa........170
10 w. in Innings...............209
Wooller, W. (Glamorgan):—
All-Round 216
Secretary of Glamorgan........388
Woolley, F. E. (Kent):—
Birthday.....................960
All-Round 215

Woolley, F. E. (Kent):—*contd.*
Hon. Cricket Member, M.C.C...347
58,969 r.........................197
Aggregate of 3,352.............205
3,283 r. in Test Matches.......222
1,000 r. (28 times)...............198
145 Hundreds 195
4 Successive Hundreds..........199
3 Hundreds *v.* South Africa.....239
2 Hundreds *v.* Australia........234
305* *v.* Tasmania...................192
2,068 w.............................214
100 w. (8 times)...................215
83 w. in Test Matches..........224
7 w. for 9 r.........................212
913 catches.........................218
(and A. Fielder), 235 for last wkt. 205
(and J. Vine), 7th wkt. record *v.* Australia.................232
Wootton, G. (Nottinghamshire):—
100 w. in Innings................209
8 w. for 9 r..........................211
Worcester Royal Grammar School.805
WORCESTERSHIRE................617–33
Averages............................619
Results...............................619
Championship Table 350
Championship Winners.........265
County Badge......................617
Minor Counties Championship..266
v. Derbyshire.......................630
v. Essex..............................632
v. Gloucestershire.................627
v. Hampshire........................624
v. Kent................................621
v. Leicestershire...................629
v. Middlesex....................623–4
v. Northamptonshire..............626
v. Nottinghamshire................620
v. Somerset..........................631
v. Surrey..............................628
v. Sussex...........................632–3
v. Warwickshire..................622–3
v. West Indies 286
v. Yorkshire..........................625
Gillette Cup Matches 661, 664, 665, 666
Worcestershire in Jamaica, 1966.847–8
WORCESTERSHIRE II............737–8
Championship Table 727
Championship Winners.........266
Worksop College...................805
v. M.C.C..............................331
World Cricket Cup..............345–7
Worrell, Sir F. M. (West Indies):—
Birthday.............................960
Captain *v.* Australia..............250
Captain *v.* England...............241
Test Cricket.........................183
Trophy................................250
3,860 r. in Test Matches.........223
Worrell, Sir F. M. (West Indies):—*contd.*
40 Hundreds........................196
6 Hundreds *v.* England...........243
308* *v.* Trinidad.....................192
237 *v.* India...........................255
108 *v.* Australia.....................251
100 *v.* New Zealand.................255
(and J. D. Goddard), 502 for 4th wkt.............................201
(and S. Ramadhin), last wkt. record *v.* England...........242
(and G. S. Sobers), 4th wkt. record *v.* England................242
(and C. L. Walcott), 574 for 4th wkt.........................201, 203
(and E. D. Weekes), 3rd wkt. record *v.* England...........242
Worsley, D. R. (Lancashire), 20 catches in 1966..................369
Worsley, Sir William, Bt. (Yorkshire), President of Yorkshire 634
Worthing *v.* M.C.C..................334
Worthington, T. S. (Derbyshire):—
128 *v.* India..........................246
(and W. R. Hammond), 4th wkt. record *v.* India...............246
Wrekin College..................805–6
v. M.C.C..............................328
Wright, C. W. (Nottinghamshire) (and H. R. Bromley-Davenport), 8th wkt. record *v.* South Africa 238
Wright, D. V. P. (Kent):—
Birthday.............................960
Hon. Cricket Member, M.C.C...347
2,056 w..............................212
108 w. in Test Matches.........222
100 w. (10 times).................213
7 Hat-tricks........................207
Wyatt, R. E. S. (Warwickshire and Worcestershire):—
Birthday.............................960
39,404 r..............................197
18,839 r. in Test Matches.......222
1,000 r. (18 times)...............198
85 Hundreds........................195
2 Hundreds *v.* South Africa.....239
124 and Hat-trick *v.* Ceylon.....216
Wycliffe College..................806
v. M.C.C..............................330
Wyggeston School.................806
Wynyard, E. G. (Hampshire) (and R. M. Poore), 411 for 6th wkt...............................204

Yardley, N. W. D. (Cambridge Univ. and Yorkshire):—
101 *v.* Oxford.......................339
(and D. C. S. Compton), 5th wkt. record *v.* South Africa.....238

Yardley, W. (Cambridge Univ. and Kent):—
2 Hundreds *v.* Oxford....260
Throwing record....219
Yarnold, H. (Worcestershire) (wkt.-kpr.):—
110 w. in Season....218
7 w. in Innings....217
First-Class Umpire....1008
Test Panel....1008
Yeshwant Rao Tournament....888
YORKSHIRE....634–51
Averages....636
Results....636
Championship Table....350
Championship Winners....265
County Badge....634
Group....66
v. Derbyshire....641
v. Essex....642–3
v. Glamorgan....648
v. Gloucestershire....636–7
v. Hampshire....639
v. Kent....650
v. Lancashire....638–9
v. M.C.C....651
v. Middlesex....646
v. Northamptonshire....644
v. Nottinghamshire....645
v. Somerset....642
v. Surrey....647–8
YORKSHIRE—*contd.*
v. Sussex....640
v. Warwickshire....649
v. West Indies....291–2
Gillette Cup....660–1
YORKSHIRE II....723
Championship Table....707
Championship Winners....266
Yorkshire Gentlemen *v.* I.Z....269
Young, D. M. (Gloucestershire):—
40 Hundreds....196
(and R. B. Nicholls), 395 for 1st wkt....201
Young, J. A. (Middlesex), 100 w. (8 times)....215
YOUNGEST TEST PLAYERS....259
Yuile, B. W. (New Zealand):—
Test Cricket....185
9 Canterbury w. in Innings....879

Zafar Altaf (Lahore Greens):—
268 *v.* Bahawalpur....891
(and Majid Jahangir), 346 for 4th wkt....204
Zulch, J. W. (South Africa), 2 Hundreds *v.* Australia....249
Zulfiqar Ahmed (Pakistan) (and Wazir Mohammad), 9th wkt. record *v.* England....248
Zulfiqar Ali (and Majid Jahangir), 171 for 8th wkt....205

ERRATA IN WISDEN 1966

Page 98. F. C. M. Alexander's highest Test innings is 108 not 70.

Page 127. In W. R. Hammond's centuries for Gloucestershire (113), one line to be added: v. Worcestershire (6): 265*, 178, 160, 122, 111*, 100. Also: Two Fifties in One Match, fourth line should read 55 and 51 v. Kent at Bristol in 1933 and not against Worcestershire.

Page 131. In Test Cricket: D. G. Bradman in 1930 in England scored 720 runs in his first four Test innings that season and therefore Hammond was not the only nor the first cricketer to accomplish the feat.

Pages 263 and 608. M. J. Horton's highest score in 1965 was 60.

Page 301. M. C. Cowdrey's average should be 68.50 not 48.50.

Pages 302 and 303. The match between Hampshire and the South Africans was played at Southampton.

Page 553. D. Gibson scored 996 runs in first-class cricket in 1965.

Page 569. The picture on the left is L. J. Lenham and not G. C. Cooper.

Page 816. In England's second innings read E. R. Dexter not out 5 and delete F. J. Titmus not out 5.

Page 819. The number of overs bowled by L. R. Mayne should read 82.

Page 820. Add 100's against Australia: S. M. Nurse (1): 201 for West Indies at Bridgetown (Fourth Test); R. B. Kanhai (2): 129 at Bridgetown (Fourth Test) and 121 at Port of Spain (Fifth Test).

Page 820. Add 100 for Australians: S. Trimble 164* *v.* Barbados Colts at Bridgetown (not first-class).

Page 836. Add 100's for Pakistan: Javed Burki, 139* *v.* Nelson at Nelson (not first-class); Saeed Ahmed (3) 142 *v.* Canterbury at Christchurch, 118 *v.* President's XI at Palmerston North, 105 *v.* New South Wales at Sydney.

Page 902. G. T. Dowling scored only 88 in the three innings against Pakistan and averaged 29.33.

Page 966. J. W. Hearne's highest innings in first-class cricket was 285 *v.* Essex at Leyton in 1929.

WEST INDIES RETAIN THE WISDEN TROPHY

[*Central Press*

Garfield Sobers proudly holds aloft the Wisden Trophy after it has been presented to him by the President of M.C.C., Lt. General Sir Oliver Leese, at the conclusion of the final Test at The Oval. West Indies won it first in 1963 when the Trophy was inaugurated to commemorate the one hundredth consecutive appearance of the Almanack.

WEST INDIES TEAM IN ENGLAND, 1966

[*Sport and General*

J. S. Solomon, B. F. Butcher, S. M. Nurse, J. L. Hendriks, P. D. Lashley, D. A. Allan, D. Pye (physiotherapist); *Middle row:* W. F. B. Hoyos (assistant manager), R. C. Brancker, D. A. J. Holford, R. A. Cohen, C. C. Griffith, M. C. Carew, E. D. McMorris, J. A. Griffiths (scorer);
Front row: L. R. Gibbs, R. B. Kanhai, J. B. Stollmeyer (manager), G. S. Sobers (captain), C. C. Hunte (vice-captain), W. W. Hall

ENGLAND TEAM AT THE OVAL, 1966

[*Central Press*

G. Boycott, J. H. Edrich, B. d'Oliveira, J. A. Snow, D. L. Amiss, R. W. Barber; *Front row:* R. Illingworth, T. W. Graveney, D. B. Close (captain), J. T. Murray, K. Higgs.

TOM GRAVENEY'S HAPPY RETURN

[*Sport and General*

By his skill and artistry Tom Graveney, scorer of over one hundred hundreds, gave pleasure to thousands of people, on his return to the England team after being left out for three years. He was the mainstay of the England batting and hit centuries at Trent Bridge and The Oval. In four Tests he made 459 runs, average 76.50. Here he has turned L. R. Gibbs to fine leg, watched by J. L. Hendriks, S. M. Nurse and G. S. Sobers.

KEN HIGGS THE PERSISTENT ATTACKER

[*Sport and General*

Ken Higgs alone among the 24 players called on by England kept his place in all five Tests. He maintained a persistent attack in the region of the off stump and finished with 24 wickets, average 25.45, including six victims in the first innings at Lord's.

YORKSHIRE—COUNTY CHAMPIONS, 1966

[*Sport and General*

G. Allcock (masseur), P. J. Sharpe, A. G. Nicholson, J. Waring, D. Wilson, J. H. Hampshire, D. E. V. Padgett, G. Boycott, E. Lester (scorer); *Front row:* J. G. Binks, F. S. Trueman, D. B. Close (captain), R. Illingworth, K. Taylor.

WARWICKSHIRE—GILLETTE CUP WINNERS, 1966

[*Sport and General*

M. J. K. Smith, the Warwickshire captain, displays the Gillette Cup, after receiving it at Lord's from Lt. General Sir Oliver Leese, the M.C.C. President and his own county President. Team: R. N. Abberley, R. B. Edmonds, K. Ibadulla, T. W. Cartwright, D. L. Amiss, J. A. Jameson, A. C. Smith, R. V. Webster, D. J. Brown, M. J. K. Smith, J. D. Bannister, R. W. Barber.

[*Sport and General*

C. MILBURN (Northamptonshire)

FIVE CRICKETERS OF THE YEAR

[*Central Press*

S. M. NURSE (West Indies)

[*Sport and General*

B. L. d'OLIVEIRA (Worcestershire)

FIVE CRICKETERS OF THE YEAR

[*Sport and General*

J. T. MURRAY (Middlesex)

FIVE CRICKETERS OF THE YEAR

[*Central Press*

R. W. BARBER (Warwickshire)

FIVE CRICKETERS OF THE YEAR

R. W. BARBER

LANCASHIRE coaches are not given to overstatement. It was high praise indeed when Stan Worthington, the Lancashire coach, first saw a tall, powerfully built young left-hander at the Old Trafford nets and told his Yorkshire-born father, "That one needs no help from me."

His assessment of the player concerned, ROBERT WILLIAM BARBER, who was born in Manchester on September 26, 1935, was to prove remarkably accurate. As a batsman he remains to this day virtually uncoached. Even as a bowler he had only an hour or two in the hands of that Australian back-of-the-hand specialist, George Tribe, whose maxim was "Spin first, length afterwards. Don't worry about the odd bad ball. They get wickets, too."

Barber, now the supreme individualist, scorns the orthodox routine that is so much a part of the contemporary game, and is one of the few English batsmen who can still draw the Australian crowds. Worthington could have had only one real regret. All Barber's best cricket came after he had switched allegiance to Warwickshire.

Even when at school at Ruthin, where he did the double, there were already signs that Barber could achieve heights far beyond the reach of the usual promising youngster and, in fact, he played for Lancashire while still a schoolboy. The coaching in leg-break bowling was arranged by his father, himself a very useful cricketer with Huddersfield League experience. Next came Cambridge, with a Blue for the javelin in addition to cricket.

The stormy passage of the Lancashire captaincy followed the University years. Lancashire were already showing signs of becoming a county of divided loyalties, according to some sound judges through their tendency to rule through committee rather than captain. But when they asked Barber to lead a side which was beginning to look a little thin in terms of seasoned professionals, the not inconsiderable honour was naturally accepted. It is easy to be wise after the event. There were no doubt errors of judgement on both sides. Like his predecessors, Barber found it impossible to please everyone.

He was criticised frequently for not bowling enough himself, but a young captain was understandably reluctant to play too prominent a role in this direction when he already had a specialist leg-spinner in the side. There was, in fact, a considerable measure of success in his first year as captain. Yorkshire eventually won the Championship after Lancashire's first successful "double" against their old rivals for more than sixty years. The eventual margin at the top of the table was exaggerated by the weather. The season proceeded amid controversial rulings on discipline on and off the field, many of which undoubtedly received publicity completely out of their true perspective.

In the following season, with more younger players in the side, Lancashire found it hard to finish matches on good pitches at Old Trafford. Again they decided on a change at the helm, ruling against the possibility of giving Barber any further opportunity to learn from whatever mistakes he may have made. In the light of subsequent administrative upheavals at Old Trafford there is no point in discussing the rights and wrongs of the matter here, but the outcome was that Lancashire lost Barber, not only as captain but also as a player. So far there had been little real chance for him to mature. That came with his arrival at Edgbaston in 1963, where he quickly settled down once initial tension had eased. The real transition followed Warwickshire's decision to ask him to resume his role as an opening batsman, a bold step which succeeded handsomely. Here again there was a preliminary period of uncertainty, but the real Barber soon emerged and he began to give full rein to his dynamic power as a challenger of opening bowling.

For his new county, he hit a brilliant hundred off the West Indies bowling that had humbled England in 1963. The following year he scored an even more spectacular century before lunch against the Australians. Often his cavalier tactics brought swift downfall, but whenever he survived there was cricket of breathtaking brilliance. The advent of the Gillette Cup provided an ideal outlet for a player who always ignores playing-in preliminaries. Bowlers with reputations for keeping the game "tight" suddenly found themselves without an answer against a batsman ever ready to leave the crease. For a left-hander an unusually high proportion of his runs came from a glorious array of strokes through cover and he was utterly fearless against fast bowling.

It is worthy of mention that Barber has made something of a personal corner in knock-out cricket. He has scored more Gillette Cup runs than any other player in the country and has won no fewer than four Man-of-the-Match awards.

Those who watched Barber's progress with Warwickshire were able to note increasing mental relaxation after the hangover from Old Trafford had vanished. At last he was enjoying his cricket. So did those who saw it.

England first tried him (as a bowler in one match) against South Africa at Edgbaston in 1960 and he toured India and Pakistan in 1961–62, and then they dropped him.

Further Test recognition was inevitable and he showed first in South Africa three winters ago, where he had a Test average of 72.50, and in Australia that he was an even more devastating force on good pitches. He maintained the happiest of relationships under the leadership of M. J. K. Smith, his own county captain, the pair between them constituting a leg-trap, the equal of any close-catching combination in the world.

In South Africa his activities were unfortunately curtailed by injury, but he was an automatic choice for Australia, reaching new heights with that memorable innings of 185 at Sydney. He was top scorer on this tour in Australia with 1,001 first-class runs for an average of 50.05, all scored with the same commanding approach which did so much to help restore the tarnished image of English Test cricket. The crowds loved him as a player. The Australians respected him as an opponent. It was a thousand pities that the England selectors were not prepared to accept this form as evidence enough for a place at the start of the West Indies series.

By that time other factors had emerged. As an executive in the group of companies of which his father is a director, and by now a family man, Barber felt he could no longer devote six days a week to county cricket. Warwickshire tried hard to persuade him to change his mind and he compromised by making himself available for a limited number of county games and all the Gillette Cup matches, but the selectors were not satisfied.

Barber has never been a man to speak out of turn. Whatever his thoughts on the selectors' ruling, he kept them strictly to himself; merely commenting that he had considered he was in better form on his return from Australia than he was a month later after half a dozen games on indifferent English wickets.

This is a topic on which Barber does have forthright views, frankly admitting that on under-prepared pitches he cannot maintain the standard he sets for personal performance. Belatedly chosen for the Fourth Test against the West Indies at Headingley, he hit a second-innings fifty after bowling Sobers and he again dismissed that remarkable player at The Oval.

When cricket's administrators finish their deliberations on possible changes in the structure of the game, one can only hope they evolve a pattern which will enable Barber and others like him to devote adequate time to business and domestic interests and still play regularly in a reduced programme of three- or four-day games. He is personally in favour of an extension of one-day matches. The game has so few personalities that it can ill afford to lose a Barber. It will be a major tragedy if he is not available for the West Indies' tour next winter.—W.G.W.

B. L. d'OLIVEIRA

The story of Basil d'Oliveira is a fairy tale come true; the story of a nonentity in the country of his birth who because of the colour of his skin was confined to cricket on crude mudheaps until he was 25, yet after only one season in the County Championship played for England. No Test player has had to overcome such tremendous disadvantages along the road to success as the Cape coloured d'Oliveira. Admirable though his achievements were against the West Indies in 1966, undoubtedly his triumph in ever attaining Test status was more commendable.

That he did not fall by the wayside of the stony path he was compelled to tread is a tribute to the courage and skill of this player from the land of apartheid. To say that he never contemplated giving up the game before reaching the hour of glory was hardly the case. The hazards he encountered were very nearly too great even for the stout-hearted d'Oliveira. Suffice to say that of the 25,000 South African coloured cricketers who would dearly love to make county grade over here d'Oliveira is the first to have done so. Hundreds of others are doomed to spend their lives in a class of cricket far beneath their skill. They will stay because no one ever sees them in this unfashionable outpost of the game.

Born in Cape Town on October 4, 1934, Basil Lewis d'Oliveira inherited his father's love for the game but until he was 15 practically the only cricket he played was in the street. There were no facilities at either of his schools, St Joseph's Catholic or Zonnebloem Training College, as money for the promotion of school sport was non-existent. His schooldays over, he joined St Augustine's, the club for which his father, Lewis d'Oliveira, played as an all-rounder for something like 40 years. There, in one of the South African leagues for non-Europeans, young "Dolly" began to blossom under the guidance of his father, as a right-handed batsman and medium-paced bowler. His team-mates would walk miles to a suitable strip of grassless earth, sand or gravel over which to lay a mat after first preparing their pitch with a spade and wheelbarrow. D'Oliveira thought nothing of walking ten miles to his home ground. The alternative was a four-mile stroll to the nearest bus stop. His club shared the ground with other teams and it was not uncommon for square-leg in one match to find himself standing near third-slip in the next.

Yet these primitive conditions served only to imbue d'Oliveira with a zest and enthusiasm for the game. He was deeply impressed on his visits to first-class matches in Cape Town, in particular to see Compton, Harvey and May. He never missed an opportunity to study closely the manner in which these and other great batsmen moved about the crease and into their strokes. He reasoned for himself why any particular stroke was made, and soon reports of his own phenomenal scoring feats began to trickle through. d'Oliveira scored 80 centuries in the Cape and once hit 225 in seventy minutes. In a federation tournament he thrashed 168 in ninety-eight minutes and in another innings made 46 in an eight-ball over. English professionals who went to South Africa coaching during the winter, spoke of him as a natural player who moved well and struck the ball hard. Yet, it seemed, it was not easy to convince anyone that he could be a top-class player against top-class opposition. He played, however, in one or two testimonial matches in South Africa against White teams, then against the Kenya Asians and went on an all-coloured team's tour of East Africa.

For a couple of years, John Arlott, the broadcaster and cricket writer, tried to get people in England to take an interest in d'Oliveira, and eventually, with the aid of the urgings of two other journalists, Middleton, of the Central Lancashire League, after failing to get several better known players, offered him a contract at £450 for the 1960 season. He was then 25. Raffles, fêtes and matches were organised in the locality of his tenement home in the coloured quarter of Cape Town to raise his fare to England. As an £8 10*s*. a week machine-minder for a printing firm there was little scope for savings of his own with a wife and baby to support. For an unproved player with the Manchester suburban club he was little or no better off to begin with. He had just enough to live frugally during the summer and pay his return fare home to bring back his wife.

At Middleton, d'Oliveira's competitors included Gary Sobers, Cecil Pepper, John McMahon and Salim Durani. So that with only 25 or so runs and three or four wickets to show for his endeavours after five matches in the League he was all set to pack his bags. He felt he was clearly out of his depth. Then, almost suddenly as the weather warmed up and pitches became faster, runs began to flow from d'Oliveira's bat as in his native South Africa. By the end of his first summer he had made 930 runs, average 48.95, which was slightly better than Sobers and the best of the League. For good measure he gained 71 wickets at 11.72 each. Middleton's gamble had paid off. The coloured cricketer from the Cape stayed for four years.

When he first arrived in England in April 1960 the extremely modest and well behaved d'Oliveira was quite stunned at being treated as an ordinary human being unaffected by any colour bar. He would have been perfectly content to have spent the rest of his life in Middleton where he established himself with more than 3,600 runs for an average of over 48, and 238 wickets at under 17 each. D'Oliveira considers he owed a great deal in his successful switch from matting to grass to the kindly advice and help he received at Middleton from Eric Price, the old Lancashire and Essex left-arm slow bowler who played in the league as an amateur. Hours and hours of net practice, sometimes with only schoolboys for company, illustrated his tremendous will to succeed.

It was Tom Graveney who persuaded "Dolly" that he was good enough to be a success at county level. They were on a private Commonwealth tour together, and in the face of competition from Gloucestershire (after Lancashire had turned him down) d'Oliveira joined Worcestershire. While qualifying by residence he spent the

1964 season with Kidderminster in the Birmingham League, averaging 78.44, and played the occasional non-Championship match. In the latter he showed his potential with 370 runs (average 61.66) in eight first-class innings, including 119 at Hastings for A. E. R. Gilligan's XI against R. B. Simpson's touring Australians.

And so to 1965, his first year of Championship cricket. If there were any lingering doubts that at the age of 30 his weaknesses would be exposed these were soon dispelled. He made five centuries, totalling 1,523 runs (average 43.51), and he and Graveney were the only batsmen in the Championship to exceed 1,500 that season. D'Oliveira also took 35 wickets, proved himself in the top flight as a slip fielder and gained the distinction in his first county season of helping Worcestershire in no small measure to retain the Championship pennant. As his captain, Don Kenyon, remarked at the end of a memorable summer, "D'Oliveira did everything we hoped he might do and a lot more . . . all the predictions that a turning ball might find him out proved utterly false." D'Oliveira himself considered that it was in 1965 he played his finest innings—51 not out on a turning pitch at Cheltenham against Allen and Mortimore.

Undoubtedly the most memorable year of his life was 1966, by which time he had become a British citizen. Although he had shown every promise in M.C.C. matches at Lord's, to be selected for England against the West Indies was beyond his wildest dreams. It was d'Oliveira himself who said after his Test debut at Lord's, "This is a fairy tale come true. Six years ago I was playing on mudheaps. Now I have played for England and met the Queen; what more could I possibly ask?"

It set the seal on the happiness he and his charming wife, Naomi, and sons Damian, aged six, and Shaun, aged two, have found since coming to this country. He went on to play successfully in the three subsequent Tests, making the jump to international grade in the same facile manner of his previous steps up in status. England had gained not only a skilful cricketer but a man of rare fighting qualities. People who have delighted in the manner in which he has savaged county bowling in Worcestershire's cause, consider that his best days for England are still to come. As he grows in confidence and experience in the Test sphere England could find themselves with one of the finest all-rounders in post-war cricket.—J.G.

C. MILBURN

On a mid-September day in 1959 at Sunderland that very fine judge, the late George Duckworth, watched with growing interest an unusually large seventeen-year-old schoolboy score 101 unusually good runs for Durham against the visiting Indians. Duckworth saw to it that the exceptional feat did not pass unrecognised, and one sequel was a paragraph, soberly headed COLIN MILBURN, in *Notes by the Editor* in the following edition of *Wisden*. Milburn, who had been marking each passing birthday by adding a stone in weight, was described as "a well-built lad". He was already 17 stones, and created no small surprise when he presented himself for a trial at Northampton.

Equally true was the Editor's use of the words to describe the prodigy's methods—"a fine attacking batsman". Milburn is still large and his outline is some way from the popular conception of an athletic Test cricketer, but what is far more important in these days of stereotyped mediocrity, he remains an attacking batsman. When things go right it can be truthfully said to be violent attack. Twice in 1966 Milburn hit centuries before lunch.

While he was in Australia last winter he reached 100 in seventy-seven minutes for Western Australia against South Australia. It was the fastest first-class hundred seen at Adelaide since 1928–29 when P. K. Lee attained three figures in seventy minutes.

Milburn is both a scientific hitter and a character. There is little doubt that he inherited his bulk and style from his father Jack, a well-known professional in the Tyneside Senior League. The young Milburn grew up in an atmosphere of cricket. While his father batted and bowled, his mother, Bertha, helped to serve the teas (and still does) at Burnopfield, where Colin was born on October 23, 1941. Burnopfield is a mining village in Co. Durham seven miles from Newcastle upon Tyne.

Though he had no coaching as such his precocious aptitude and parental encouragement won him a place in Burnopfield's 2nd XI when he was 11. By the time he was 13 he was opening the batting and bowling for the senior side. At the same age he was also chosen for Durham Schoolboys, and for two successive seasons played for the North against the South in the annual Schools' representative match, at Northampton (appropriately) and Oldham.

Yet the youthful Milburn had little cricket at the Secondary Modern School at Annfield Plain. On Saturday mornings he was engaged in a milk round! Later a little more sophisticated Milburn, now at Stanley Grammar School, represented Durham Public Schools, scoring 285 runs, average 57.

Half-way through the 1959 season Milburn became properly restless and ambitious. He decided his many successes at Burnopfield were not getting him anywhere, and he moved to Chester-le-Street, members of the Durham Senior League. At once he was a sensation. In three weeks he hit two centuries (one a score in the region of 150 being supported by a bowling performance of seven for three), and a near-century, and he was selected for Durham to play the Indians in the final match of their tour. It proved to be Milburn's first and only appearance for Durham.

Several first-class clubs were now very much interested in him.

On the recommendation of Bill Coverdale, a former player, Milburn had gone to Northampton for a trial in the Easter of 1959. He had also played once for Warwickshire's 2nd XI, and twice for their Club and Ground. Indeed a Warwickshire coach named Milburn as one of their two most promising players during a broadcast interview, which was heard by Mr. Ken C. Turner, secretary of Northamptonshire, while he was lying on the beach on holiday.

That was enough for the well-developed recruiting instinct of Mr. Turner, and Milburn finally went to Northamptonshire in April, 1960, having been offered ten shillings a week more than Warwickshire's terms, an investment which Northamptonshire do not regret! Milburn's first year was spent in qualifying, but still with the profitable return of 1,153 runs in 2nd XI cricket. His first-class debut against Cambridge University was scarcely memorable. His only score was an edged four.

In the following season Milburn opened the innings for the 2nd XI and began with 201 not out, out of a total of 256, against Middlesex II in the second match. Consistent scoring was crowned with two successive centuries off Kent II (including a century before lunch) and Somerset II. Fittingly his first championship match was at Edgbaston, less fittingly with scores of 28 and 0, and the next, at home, facing Surrey, brought a score of 63 out of 125. Yet he went back to the 2nd XI as a final polishing of his raw apprenticeship. He was then vulnerable to off-break bowling.

Mid-way through the following summer he gained a regular place in the championship side. In July there was his maiden first-class century for Northamptonshire off Cambridge University, and later that month he made 102 out of 182 against Derbyshire at Buxton. Milburn still considers this to be his best innings for his county, bearing in mind the quality of Derbyshire's attack and the state of the pitch. Of Northamptonshire's total Mick Norman made 58, and the other individual scores were: 5, 0, 1, 4, 0, 0, 3, 0 not out, and 0 with 9 Extras.

In the winter of 1962–63 Milburn rigorously fought his increasing weight. It had exceeded 18 stones. For five months, three times a week, he endured a strict routine of remedial exercises and circuit training. By the start of the season he was down to 16 stones 5 lb, and the slimmer Milburn took 48 and 123 (seven 6's and fourteen 4's) in the second game with Yorkshire. Later the West Indies conceded 100 and 88 to him, and if he could not stay at 16 stones the value of experience, and particularly of selection in the ball to hit, was beginning to tell.

When he made runs his innings were variously and inevitably described as exhilarating, brilliant or exciting. Gloucestershire were slogged for seven 6's and fifteen 4's in 152 not out, and during a short tour of East Africa with M. J. K. Smith's M.C.C. team, Milburn hit Noel Shuttleworth, a leg-break bowler, for six from each of the first five balls of an over. He was caught on the boundary off the sixth.

In 1966 he began with a fast century at Derby, and followed with an even faster one at Leicester. Winning a place in the first Test, he overcame the cruel blow of being run out without scoring in the first innings to slog 94 in the second. A century followed in his second Test at Lord's, and Milburn was one of the few personalities the public craved to see. He scored the quickest century of the season—in eighty-two minutes against Nottinghamshire—and spent the winter in Australia playing for Western Australia, an invitation that was a tribute in itself.

Milburn's average in an England team not famous for its batting strength was 52.66, second only to Tom Graveney, but he did not share in the final triumph at The Oval. His disappointment could be well tempered by the knowledge that the best of Milburn is still to come. He is also sensible enough to understand that his weight problems will be a handicap unless controlled. His level of performance must be that much better because of his size.

Unhappily his useful medium-pace bowling can no longer be used. Though the hard exercise of Squash and as a Rugby Union forward causes him no discomfort he has only to bowl and his back protests immediately. Nor can the complaint be diagnosed.

Forward short leg is his best fielding position, and any doubt of his mobility is answered by the fact that in 1964 he held 43 catches, a record for Northamptonshire.

Milburn is an even-tempered and modest personality. He is not confused or bothered by theory, which is perhaps the basic reason for his continued success. He has not consciously changed his style or technique since his Burnopfield days. "I just try and hit the ball" is his over-simplified explanation of his technique. "It is my way of playing the game, and I want it to stay that way." Words to shock and offend many a coach, but it is the essential Milburn, a pearl of great price in modern cricket. Few have been blessed with his genius for attack; fewer still with the nerve to go through with it come triumph or failure.—A.B.

S. M. NURSE

When Seymour Nurse set out from Barbados to begin the 1966 tour of England he said good-bye to identical twin daughters three months old. As a father of recent heritage, he had them constantly in his mind until nearly six months later he returned a man of additional stature in the cricket world. During the tour he had established himself in the eyes of the English followers as a strokemaker fit to line up with credit beside the likes of George Headley, Frank Worrell and Everton Weekes. For the first time he had played throughout a Test series, and in the process hit 501 runs, second only to his illustrious captain, Garfield Sobers. What more could any cricketer ask?

Certainly it was enough for Nurse, particularly as, then 32, he could so easily have become the player who always threatened to come from the shadows into the sun but never quite made the journey. Untimely injuries in Australia in 1960 and England in 1963 did not help but there was also a nagging thought that, while a delight to the purists, Nurse had a temperament not really suitable to the rigours of international cricket. True he hit 201 off the Australian bowlers at Bridgetown but up to 1966 and since his first Test appearance in 1959, eleven of his eighteen innings had produced under 20 runs apiece.

There was another more fundamental reason why the Test career of Nurse was of such in and out character. He belonged to an age of abundant talent. Kanhai filled the number three position he liked best and apart from Sobers, and Worrell for much of the time, there were Butcher and Solomon to compete for places in the middle order. Solomon, three years the senior of Nurse, and Butcher and Kanhai, respectively one and two years his junior, all got into the West Indies side first and they were not to be ousted easily. More credit, then, to Nurse for showing the perseverance which finally carried him to the top last summer. In his eight Test innings his aggregate was only 99 short of the total for his first 18.

SEYMOUR MACDONALD NURSE was born on November 10, 1933 in the parish of St. Michael, Barbados. Son of a carpenter, he was one of a family of two boys and two girls. His elder brother, Sinclair, was considered to have cornered the talent with leg-spin bowling. Most of the local clubs had an eye on him. But Sinclair possessed a shyness seldom associated with the people of his country and he never developed into a player of any great moment.

So it became the youngest of the four children, Seymour, who was to make his name on the field of play. At St. Stephen's Boys' School he showed an aptitude for most outdoor sports, with cricket and football his favourite pastimes. He was an opening batsman, and reflecting on the difficulties which his country experienced later in finding a suitable partner for Hunte, it could be said that he might have sidetracked disappointments had he continued to go in first.

Academically Nurse did well, too, moving into the sixth form, but even at this early age an impetuosity was evident. Anxious to earn a living rather than learn more, he left when 16, living, he says, to regret it. Next he played cricket for Bay Street Boys' Club in the Barbados League which boasted such as Sobers, Griffith and Hunte and from there progressed to the Empire Club, where he became associated with Everton Weekes, the man who really shaped his life. In the words of Nurse himself, Weekes made him into a first-class cricketer, a batsman able to get a line on the ball to know precisely where to hit it.

At the same time, Nurse played soccer for Empire, leading their attack and gaining representative honours for Barbados. Cricket remained his first love, but he doubted whether he would have given up football readily had he not received a nasty leg injury and also parental advice from his father to "stay in cricket and quit football, otherwise you are on your own. Football in Barbados is too rough." So Nurse did the next best thing and helped to form a club, named Black Spurs and now the recipients of first-hand information on why and how England won the World Cup. Nurse saw the Final at Wembley and every other game possible.

The first venture into big cricket came in 1959 when Nurse was already 25. In the December of that year, after only four first-class games, he faced M.C.C. and with a score of 213 in six and a quarter hours played a big part in the defeat of the touring team in their first major encounter. Said *Wisden* of this Barbados victory: "Nurse, a promising young batsman, and the established Sobers, shared a third-wicket stand of 306 and paved the way for the highest score ever made by a Colony side against M.C.C."

Even that could not earn him a place in the first Test and indeed it took an ankle injury to Worrell to bring about his Test debut in the third game of the series. Scores of 70 and 11 were reasonable enough but it was the last time that Nurse faced the England bowlers that tour. Walcott was recalled for the next Test.

Nevertheless, Nurse went to Australia for the 1960 tour with its tie and pulsating finale. His personal performances were mediocre, with the final blow coming when he fell and injured an ankle during play. This put him on crutches for a while and it took all the skills of the masseur, Manny Alves, to get him fit to take up his first engagement in English League cricket with Ramsbottom, an association which came about through the recommendation of Sobers and was to produce three happy summers, 1961, 1962 and 1964. Not only did Nurse find the locals a "good bunch" but he improved his batting tremendously. He never knew the ball moved about so much!

Misfortune again attended Nurse in 1963 on his first tour of England. The trip had hardly begun when, following an admirable century against Oxford University, he pulled a muscle. This left him lame for about a month and some fine batting in August, during which he hit a hundred against Glamorgan and 77 against Yorkshire, came too late to get him into the Test side.

When next he did appear it was as opening partner to Hunte in the first Test against Australia in 1965. That venture ended with scores of 15 and 17. So he disappeared again, returning for the third Test lower in the order, and in spite of mediocre results, 42 and 6, he was retained for the fourth, when the selectors received their reward. After Australia scored 650 with the help of 201 from Simpson and 210 for Lawry, Nurse came along with the third double hundred, 201, which he considers his best as well as his highest Test innings.

But Nurse left for a "duck" in the second innings and then for 9 and 1 when chosen for the fifth Test, so it seemed that inconsistency remained in his make-up. The West Indies' selectors never lost faith though, to the benefit of the English public in 1966. He may have got himself out at times by going for runs too soon but what a delight it was to witness the power and fluency of his strokes when things did go right. Anyone who saw his 93 in the first innings of the Nottingham Test will testify to that.—H.E.A.

J. T. MURRAY

Long before the fates made the magnificent atonement on late-summer days at The Oval, 1966, there must have been times when JOHN THOMAS MURRAY was left with nothing more than a cricketer's natural philosophy as balm to his wounds. His career as England's wicket-keeper began on the highest note of promise with five Tests and five impeccable performances against Australia in 1961.

None could have suspected his position would soon be assailed. Yet the first of his disappointments was round the corner. In the following winter of 1961–62 he had to return prematurely from M.C.C.'s tour of India and Pakistan to undergo an operation for varicose veins. Though he regained his place in the last three Tests against Pakistan in England in 1962, he faced successive competition from Alan Smith and Jim Parks.

Perhaps he did not find the form abroad for which he was famed at home, but in 1962–63 he made only one appearance, of the briefest nature, in the third Test. Early in the game he injured his shoulder making a brilliant catch to dismiss Bill Lawry. Smith returned for the last two Tests. Again in Australia, 1965–66, Parks was made the No. 1 wicket-keeper and played in all five Tests. As in 1963 Murray had one compensatory Test in New Zealand. Sandwiched between the two visits to Australasia was a tour of South Africa, and again Murray was on the side lines, the stand by for Parks. The final irony came in the last Test at Port Elizabeth when Murray was used as an opening batsman!

When Parks played in the first four Tests in the series with the West Indies last year Murray might have been forgiven for thinking his way for ever blocked by the selectors' preference for a batsman able to keep wicket. Without disrespect to Parks, who often justified his case with good scores, this represented a new line in cricket thought. To say the least it was hard luck for a specialist wicket-keeper.

The remodelled England team for the last Test at The Oval,

however, found Murray as the wicket-keeper, a choice which won considerable approval. But that he should score a century and take part in a stand with Tom Graveney, which laid the foundation of his side's victory, was a real quirk of mischievous fortune.

The sheer professionalism of Murray's wicket-keeping made an essential and vital difference to England's out-cricket, and understandably he regards his century as the greatest moment of his career. For one glorious hour the unobtrusive player became the glittering star. Yet his innings came within a fraction of failure.

Playing back to the first ball from Charlie Griffith he edged it on to his pads. There was a very loud, and what is generally termed, confident appeal. "Considering the noise that was going on from the crowd at the time it was a wonderful piece of umpiring by Syd Buller," acknowledges Murray. "I couldn't have complained if I'd gone first ball."

Earlier in the season for M.C.C., Murray had given the West Indies something to think about with his batting with an outstanding century, and there was a time when he opened for Middlesex. The strain had its effect when, after a long time in the field, he had to restart immediately. He now finds No. 5 ideal.

Born in North Kensington, London, on April 1, 1935, Murray became a wicket-keeper in what has always been the classical accident. He was playing in the final of the Boys' Clubs competition when his side's wicket-keeper broke a finger. Murray took over, and from that moment a Test wicket-keeper was born.

A member of the Rugby Boys' club (so called for its sponsorship by Rugby School), Murray had already had a successful trial as batsman-cum-bowler at Lord's. He had returned unwillingly to school as the leaving age was extended. Now Paul Pawson, the club warden, a distant relative of Tony Pawson, of Oxford University and Kent, was able to offer the extra recommendation of Murray's wicket-keeping. Archie Fowler, then head coach, took due note, and, on joining the staff in 1950, Murray kept wicket. So well, indeed, that only two years later he deputised for the injured Leslie Compton at Leicester. In 1953 Murray joined the R.A.F. for his two years' national Service.

Luckily for Murray his cricket progress was scarcely interrupted. He played for Combined Services against counties, and there was also plenty of Soccer. As an inside forward or wing half Murray was signed by the Arsenal as an amateur, and Tommy Lawton, then manager of Brentford, offered him professional terms. Murray's decision to concentrate on cricket was probably influenced by the fact that Leslie Compton was ready for retirement.

In 1956 Murray went straight into the Middlesex championship team. By 1960 he was groomed for Test status when he went to New Zealand with an M.C.C. "A" party under Dennis Silk.

He learned much by studying the methods and style of Wally

Grout, the Australian, during the 1961 series. "I felt as I watched him," says Murray, "that here was the perfect pair of hands. I felt I wanted to keep wicket like him. I came to understand how necessary it was to achieve balance, and to read the game in order to be in the right position at the right moment. Some would call that anticipation. I discovered Grout was hardly ever to be seen on the ground. His balance and anticipation were such that he didn't often need to be. Grout always made an impression on me, particularly when I watched him in 1961. All that he did emphasised the necessity of mastering the basic principles of keeping wicket."

Clearly Murray enjoys the intellectual exercise of his job, and none more so than when Fred Titmus, his Middlesex colleague and captain, is bowling. Murray explains: "Titmus never falls into a bowling routine, even when he is taking wickets. He is always experimenting, always trying something new, so much so that the keeper cannot relax." Equally impressive has been the experience of keeping wicket to Brian Statham and Freddie Trueman, and batsmen of the class of Graveney and Peter May.

Murray's reputation is built on polished orthodoxy and eschewing the spectacular for its own sake. He denies the need for flashiness, and is no subscriber to the theory that a wicket-keeper has to prove himself by standing up to pace bowling. To do so, he insists, is not a true test of ability. "If I am asked to do so I stand up," he says, "but I am certain that the best position for a keeper to stand is where he is best likely to take chances. And he must have a better chance standing back. You have to try and do what is in the best interests of your side."

As a batsman Murray looks for the opportunity to drive, the shot in which he excels. He bears the stamp of Lord's coaching, which many will regard as a good recommendation, and in 1957 he achieved the wicket-keeper's double of 1,025 runs and 104 dismissals (82 ct, 22 st), a feat which only Leslie Ames, of England and Kent, had previously accomplished. Such is the measure of Murray's value to Middlesex.

He has long passed 10,000 runs in first-class cricket, and been responsible for 1,000 dismissals. Statistics have no special appeal to Murray for he is sensible enough to know their worth. The years of frustration did not leave a trace of bitterness. Nor was a word of complaint uttered. As No. 1 or No. 2 wicket-keeper in any touring side he pulled his weight cheerfully. He is immaculate in his turn-out, and the key to his character is to be found in his own words: you have to try and do what is in the best interests of your side. That, in a nutshell, is John Thomas Murray.—A.B.

NOTES BY THE EDITOR

ENGLISH CRICKET AT THE CROSS ROADS

CRICKET at the present time seems to be flourishing everywhere except in England. The only ray of sunshine for a very long while came last August in the Final Test at The Oval where England, having already surrendered the rubber, outplayed the West Indies by an innings margin. On top of all the disappointments there remains the problems that have driven the crowds from the County Championship.

The standard of English first-class cricket has never been so low; not even after the first world war when England lost eight consecutive Tests to Australia was the outlook so depressing. That the authorities are alive to the situation cannot be denied. The latest findings among a long list of inquiries into the maladies affecting the game in England follow these Notes in the shape of two reports by the David Clark committee and comments by Charles Bray who was a member of that committee.

One-Day Championship Plan Rejected

For the time being the three-day County Championship remains unaltered, but although I would not like to see it cut down as was proposed it cannot last much longer in its present form without public support which has dwindled to next to nothing. Its salvation lies with the weather, pitches and the players, four of whom from each county were due to attend at Lord's before this season began to be briefed by the M.C.C. secretary. Mr. S. C. Griffith was also expected to talk to county committees. Another wise move by the Advisory Committee is the authority they have now given M.C.C. to set up machinery to ban cricket grounds reported as being unfit for first-class cricket.

Some people, and particularly the top players, think that all our troubles will be solved with a return to better pitches. Give us fast, true pitches and we will do better, say some England batsmen, and they refer to the attractive cricket played by M.C.C. on their last visit to Australia, but I remember many negative performances by Test teams of recent years in Australia, South Africa and West Indies. It is a matter of intention and will power. If both sides settle for a war of attrition rather than a game of cricket there can be little to amuse the spectator even if the players themselves are satisfied.

Nevertheless, I firmly believe that we in England will not produce anything like the number of top class cricketers there were before the war until pitches everywhere are brought back to the highest standard. That will be the first step in the right direction and at the same time every visiting county team must understand that they have an obligation to provide keen and attractive cricket for the home team's supporters. The County Championship would never have embraced as many as seventeen clubs had not this been understood in the beginning.

Fixture Making

When qualification rules were first agreed in 1873 only nine counties were considered first-class: The Big Six—Yorkshire, Lancashire, Nottinghamshire, Surrey, Kent and Middlesex—plus Derbyshire, Gloucestershire and Sussex. Gradually others gained admission to this august body, but first of all it was essential to obtain fixtures with the Big Six. To do this an ambitious county had to provide satisfactory evidence of playing strength and ability to provide attractive opposition. There were no guaranteed fixtures as there are to-day. Each county went to Lord's in the winter to the annual fixture meeting, some cap in hand in the hope of getting enough matches. They still hold the annual meeting, but it is merely a formality as far as fixtures are concerned; now-a-days these are made a year in advance.

As Sir Neville Cardus has so often pointed out, the finest players have always had flexibility of technique that has enabled them to deal adequately with changes of pitch, scene and climate. Cricket is inclined to reflect the prevailing social background and in this computer age it is utilitarian, freeze and squeeze, nothing generous about it. The odd player who rises above the commonplace is often derided. Hence, the batsman, like Milburn, who has contempt for all bowlers—and rightly so if a disciple of George Gunn—is termed "slogger", a word reserved for the daring tail enders of bygone years.

Lack of Personalities and Variety

Considering there is more leisure than ever with the five-day working week and universal annual holidays there must be other reasons besides the motor car and television that have caused attendances at county cricket to fall so alarmingly. Even members, though still paying their subscriptions, do not appear with any regularity. Surely it is because the pattern is always the same. One can scarcely tell one county from another; just a succession of seam bowlers against numerous batsmen static on their feet, ready to use their pads as their main line of defence against the ball not directed at the stumps, with a few deflections behind the wicket for the odd single. Last season I saw Underwood and Dixon bowl nearly all day on a beautiful pitch at Canterbury while Nottinghamshire laboriously compiled 210 in six hours and ten minutes—a typical example of the many dreary displays given by so many counties.

Commonplace Bowling

The prevalence of medium-fast bowling has brought about the almost complete disappearance of the genuine leg-spin bowler and the left-arm slow bowler. Hence, the authorities rightly complain that the over-rate—20 an hour is considered acceptable—has fallen. Bring back the slow bowlers with the shorter run-up and the over-rate must rise. Much as I dislike any restraint on captains as to their field placings and general conduct of the game, variety would be lent if there were a limitation on the number of overs permitted to seam bowlers during an innings. We know spinners occasionally use the seam, but umpires would know where to draw the line.

The way County Cricket has been allowed to drift towards disaster is surely a reflection upon the Advisory County Cricket Committee which was formed by the M.C.C. in 1904 to consider matters arising out of county cricket and other cricket. All first-class counties may send a representative to attend meetings and the minor counties are also represented. All decisions are subject to the approval of the M.C.C. Committee and I cannot recall any case in recent years of this being withheld. Sir Pelham Warner, long before he died in 1963, advocated a ten-year standstill to any change but his advice went unheeded as did Surrey's for a three-year period.

Constant Changes

For the past twenty years we have had one change after another, including the abolition of the distinction between amateur and professional, experiments on taking the new ball varying from 55 to 85 overs, declarations, limitation of the leg-side field, two years without the follow-on, boundaries limited to 75 yards, various pitch-covering rules, insistence of sight screens on all grounds, numerous ways of reckoning the County Championship, including number of matches played and the final abomination, the limit of 65 overs for the first innings in some matches in 1966. Also the controversies over throwing and the bowler's drag, polishing the ball, bowler's run-up limited to 20 yards and permission to captains to forfeit their second innings.

Small wonder that the ordinary follower of the game has become so utterly confused. I always keep a copy of the latest Playing Conditions by me when I go to report a match and I would imagine that every umpire must have one in his pocket to keep abreast of the situation. And what about the players? Surely this constant tampering with the rules has been of little benefit to them.

The L.B.W. Law

I always regretted the alteration of the lbw law in 1935. Most of our troubles seem to stem from that time when one must not forget there was a preponderance of pad play, heavy scoring and too many drawn games. I remember the warnings of many experts that the move would be the ruination of attractive batting. Herbert Sutcliffe and R. E. S. Wyatt were particularly insistent on the way cricket would be heading and now their words have been proved true. Is it too late to put the clock back thirty years and begin all over again? The change in the law has mattered most in England where the ball swings more in the air and off the pitch. To compensate the bowler, Wyatt would widen the wicket by two or three inches, encouraging him to attack the stumps and thus compel the batsman to use his bat. If this would lead to hard, positive cricket the leg-spinner could come into his own again.

The 65 Over Experiment

Opposition to the 65 over first-innings experiment—the list of matches involved is given in the County Championship section—stemmed mainly from the problem it set the middle-order batsmen. I felt that it succeeded in jolting the early-order batsmen, specially the openers, out of their lethargic habits. No longer could they be content in gathering 20 to 30 runs individually in the two-hour session before lunch and there was a notable improvement in this respect. On the other hand many young promising batsmen coming in later could not settle down to build an innings and often had to try and push the score along before they were ready. The experiment favoured the weaker bowling sides who knew their task was done when 65 overs were completed and a premium was put on the negative attack with corresponding fielding placings to keep down the runs rather than all-out endeavour to dismiss the opposition. Nearly two-thirds of the 102 matches, 61 to be exact, produced a definite result. Only once did a side make 300, Northamptonshire reaching 355 for seven against Nottinghamshire at Trent Bridge. The highest personal score was 171 by Colin Milburn for Northamptonshire against Leicestershire at Leicester.

What with a wet summer and the 65 overs experiment, only eight batsmen in 1966 achieved an average of 40 runs and only two reached 2,000, compared with 32 and 23 in the dry summer of 1959.

England's Lean Period

There has seldom been such a disappointing season for England as that of 1966. The M.C.C. team came back from Australia having drawn the rubber following many days of excellent cricket, yet at home little went right and the losing sequence against the major Test countries continued. Look at the depressing details of the last four years. In 18 home Tests against West Indies, Australia and South Africa, England have won only twice. West Indies were beaten at Edgbaston in 1963 when Trueman took twelve wickets for 119 and last August in that memorable match with West Indies, when they had already won the series, England triumphed by an innings. For the first time on record, England in 1966 had three captains in the same season, M. J. K. Smith, M. C. Cowdrey and D. B. Close. Australia once had four—back in 1884–85, as did West Indies in 1929–30.

Authoritative Batting was Needed

In the cases of Smith and Cowdrey, the selectors probably felt their diffident batting did not set the example required to inspire their men compared with the authority and brilliance that their rival Sobers exercised immediately he reached the crease. Before the summer ended the selectors themselves came in for adverse criticism. Examining the facts, one must remember that compared with other countries England have many more first-class players on the fringe of Test standard, yet few who can be termed automatic choices. The early retirement of P. B. H. May—now a selector—the car accident that put E. R. Dexter out of action and the breakdown of K. F. Barrington in the middle of the season robbed the team of three great batsmen. Then the order from M.C.C. that no bowler with a suspect action should be considered for England ruled out two or three men, notably H. J. Rhodes, who were taking plenty of wickets for their counties.

One of the biggest disappointments was the failure of the fast bowlers, I. J. Jones and D. J. Brown, to reproduce the form they showed earlier in the year in Australia. Here again the difference of the pitches, as in the case of batsmen, had a direct bearing. Fortunately, K. Higgs, having learned his art under the sound guidance of Brian Statham, showed the value of accurate length and direction. Higgs used the new ball to such purpose that he took 24 wickets and alone played in all five Tests. Altogether England called on 24 players, including J. S. E. Price who withdrew through injury.

Graveney's Majestic Return

The big surprise of the season was the return of Tom Graveney to the England team after being on the shelf for three years. One would imagine that a batsman with more than one hundred centuries to his name in first-class cricket would be certain of a place. Anyhow, in their dilemma after the disastrous first Test the selectors brought him back and in seven innings he made 459 runs, topping the batting with an average of 76.50. At the age of 39, Graveney batted better than ever. He certainly had nothing to worry about and his elegant style was a model for all young cricketers. He played straight down the line, a lesson for so many who play across when unwisely trying to force the ball away to leg. I am obliged to Mark Buxton for sending the following list of batsmen who have scored centuries in Test cricket in their fortieth year or over, with age at the completion of their last century. The last column shows the number of Test centuries hit after reaching the age of 39:—

Year	Month	Batsmen	Last Century		Venue	Year	Total
46	2	J. B. Hobbs	142	England *v.* Australia	Melbourne	1928–29	8
45	5	E. Hendren	132	England *v.* Australia	Manchester	1934	4
43	9	A. D. Nourse, sr.	111	S. Africa *v.* Australia	Jo'burg	1921–22	1
42	6	W. Bardsley	193*	Australia *v.* England	Lord's	1926	1
42	2	F. E. Woolley	154	England *v.* S. Africa	Manchester	1929	1
42	—	E. A. B. Rowan	236	S. Africa *v.* England	Leeds	1951	3
41	8	W. W. Armstrong	123*	Australia *v.* England	Melbourne	1920–21	3
41	8	H. W. Taylor	117	S. Africa *v.* England	Cape Town	1930–31	2
41	3	B. Sutcliffe	151*	N. Zealand *v.* India	Calcutta	1965	1
40	6	A. D. Nourse, jr.	208	S. Africa *v.* England	Nott'gham	1951	2
40	1	C. G. Macartney	109	Australia *v.* England	Manchester	1926	3
40	—	V. M. Merchant	154	India *v.* England	New Delhi	1951–52	1
39	11	B. Mitchell	120	S. Africa *v.* England	Cape Town	1948–49	1
39	11	D. G. Bradman	173*	Australia *v.* England	Leeds	1948	6
39	10	A. L. Hassett	104	Australia *v.* England	Lord's	1953	3
39	9	A. Sandham	325	England *v.* W. Indies	Kingston	1929–30	2
39	8	E. H. Bowley	109	England *v.* N.Z.	Auckland	1929–30	1
39	5	H. Makepeace	117	England *v.* Australia	Melbourne	1920–21	1
39	4	J. S. Ryder	112	Australia *v.* England	Melbourne	1928–29	1
39	4	E. Tyldesley	122	England *v.* W. Indies	Lord's	1928	1
39	2	T. W. Graveney	165	England *v.* W. Indies	The Oval	1966	2

John Murray Celebrates

Another come back was that of John Murray. He received the chance which had been denied him far too long, in the wholesale changes made after the Headingley Test that settled the rubber and the destiny of the *Wisden* Trophy. His neat wicket-keeping was a joy to watch and made England look so more efficient in the Final Test. Moreover, Murray proved his all-round ability by celebrating his return with a century in a crisis which swayed the issue England's way when he and Graveney put on 217 in a record seventh-wicket stand against West Indies. Finally, Snow and Higgs raised the total to 527 in their gallant last-wicket partnership of 128. Between them the last three England batsmen totalled 234.

Close's Captaincy

Brian Close, the latest England captain, was the third player to cover himself with glory on a belated return to the Test team. Back in 1949 he was the youngest cricketer at the age of 18 to appear for England, the youngest Yorkshireman to gain his county cap and the youngest player to accomplish the double. Since then his Test career has been intermittent. M.C.C. took him to Australia in 1950 —his only overseas tour—and on his single appearance at home against Australia at Manchester in 1961 his Test career seemed to have been completed when he was assailed on all sides for alleged reckless stroke play. Yet he was back in 1963 and batting courageously against the fiery bumpers of Hall and Griffith in all five Tests with West Indies. But strangely England did not pick him again until a captain was needed last August for the final Test at The Oval. He had proved his ability as a leader for Yorkshire and he led England in the same positive way; his bowling changes were successful, notably the early introduction of Barber, and his personal example close to the batsman at short leg made an aggressive set of fielders who took all the catches offered. Perhaps, luck did go his way for once. This forthright Yorkshireman was certainly the hero of the hour and it would appear he is destined to lead England in the West Indies next winter.

Six Test Nineties

The nervous nineties claimed a record number of six victims in the five Tests: C. Milburn 94, T. W. Graveney 96, J. M. Parks 91, S. M. Nurse 93, G. S. Sobers 94 and M. C. Cowdrey 96. Previously five such dismissals occurred in 1901–2 and 1962–3 when England visited Australia and in 1958–9 when West Indies were in India. There were also five nineties in 1953–4 between West Indies and England in the West Indies but in one instance Everton Weekes was 90 not out.

Sir Alec Douglas-Home

Cricket is certainly fortunate in this vital year with the structure of the first-class game in England in the balance to have such a compelling personality as Sir Alec Douglas-Home in the most important office of all, that of President of the M.C.C. He alone of all the Prime Ministers of England has played first-class cricket. At Eton, as Lord Dunglass, he played in the Eleven for two years, making top score, 66, against Harrow in 1922 when he also played for the Lord's Schools against The Rest. A medium-paced bowler and capable batsman, he played for Oxford University and is a Harlequin but he did not gain a Blue. He also played for Middlesex and in 1926–7 went on the M.C.C.'s tour to South America under the captaincy of Sir Pelham Warner. The only other Prime Minister who became President of M.C.C. was Lord Baldwin, in 1938. In those days the Committee met at four and took tea at half-past, a very different state of affairs compared with the many arduous all-day meetings of the present time.

The Proposed New Oval

While the one million pound new building scheme, including a luxury block of flats and the demolition of the old tavern at Lord's has got well under way, Surrey, like a bolt out of the blue, produced their plan at the beginning of the year for transforming

The Oval. It provides up-to-date amenities for Surrey C.C.C., players and spectators, including terraced seating for 22,000 and the erection of four to five hundred flats and nine shops at the Vauxhall side of the ground. There has been some imaginative thinking by the Surrey club, its Landlords, the Duchy of Cornwall and the developers and architects. It will mean a reduction of the vast playing area which will become a circle inside The Oval with a maximum seventy-five yard boundary. Spectators will enjoy a much closer view of the players and there is provision for plenty of car parking space on two levels under the flats and with the rake of the stands. The developer, M. Howard, is a brother of Geoffrey Howard, the Surrey Secretary.

The Dr. W. G. Grace

The first Public House to bear the name of the Grand Old Man of Cricket was opened last July at Elmers End. It stands within 200 yards of his grave and between the two sites is Birkbeck railway station. In the saloon bar is an attractive mirror tinged with copper with the head of Dr. Grace superimposed. The architect, a lover of cricket, attended the previous year's ceremony commemorating the fiftieth anniversary of the death of W.G. and so the new hostelry got its name. Cricket could not wish for a better advertisement, thousands of commuters to the City pass its doors, and some enter, day by day. The Rev. A. N. B. Sugden, a chaplain at the cemetery, who has since returned to his native Yorkshire as the Vicar of St. Peter's, Harrogate, blessed the house and pulled the first pint. The next day he was present when Mr. C. Stuart Chiesman, Chairman of Kent C.C.C. unveiled a commemorative plaque to W.G. on his final home, Fairmont, Mottingham, where he died in 1915. Downend House, Gloucestershire, the birthplace of W.G. was also in the news at the same time for it was sold by auction for £12,600 to a Bristol engineering design firm. In 1942, it fetched only £1,200.

Cricket in Rome

The English College in Rome can, like cricket itself, trace its history in some fashion to Anglo-Saxon times, when a hospice for English pilgrims was founded by the Tiber. Almost inevitably English Catholic men studying in Rome played, in the rolling fields round the city, the game which their co-religionist John Nyren, helped to immortalise. The serious history of English College cricket there began, however, just after the first world war, when the rector, afterwards Cardinal Hinsley, bought the old Portuguese monastery of Palazola by Lake Albano as a summer residence for the college.

The formation of the Rome Cricket Association came about in 1962 following a Cricket Gala competed for by teams from the British Embassy, the Australian Sports and Social Club, the Commonwealth War Graves Commission, the English College, the Beda College and the Food and Agricultural Organisation of the United Nations. This event, for which a trophy known as "The Rome Ashes" was presented, is now annual.

None of this would have been possible without the generous support of Donna Orietta and Don Frank Pogson Doria Pamphili in whose private park, the beautiful villa Doria Pamphili (a masterpiece created by Algardi when the head of the family was Pope Innocent X), the matches are played. Teams from England are regularly entertained and an Australian side has also played there. A fast matting wicket, quick outfield, generally superb weather and a happy atmosphere make cricket in Rome an exhilarating experience. No less, for the visitor, is the hospitality of the home teams. At least two members of the present Sacred College have played Roman cricket—Cardinal McCann of Capetown (a very capable player) and Cardinal Heenan of Westminster (a more light-hearted one).

A Splendid Film

Rothmans of Pall Mall have rendered spendid service to cricket in recent years, including the production of coloured films on various Test series. The latest, "West Indian Summer" lasts forty-seven minutes and deals with last season's Test series in England. It has a commentary by John Arlott and is available free to cricket clubs, societies and sports organisations all over the country. Many a long winter evening can be enlivened by recalling the exciting cricket witnessed the previous summer. Anyone interested should contact Desmond Smith, Rothmans of Pall Mall, Berk House, 8 Baker Street, London, W.1.

COUNTIES REJECT THE CLARK PLAN

By Charles Bray

The Clark committee's bold plan to give the County Championship a new look was killed before it was born. Its main recommendation (*see page 106*), which was to alter the existing championship and create an additional one of one-day games, was defeated by 16 votes to 4, a majority so emphatic that the counties may have signed their own death warrant.

Only time will tell. A mountain of labour produced a mouse of achievement. The only change the counties would sanction was a slight alteration in this 1967 season in the points scoring system (eight for a win and four for a first-innings lead) and a reduction in the qualifying period for an overseas player from two years to twelve months.

It would be as well at the outset, to give the reasons for the setting up of the Sub-Committee. Then to examine its composition, the manner in which it went about its work and finally the two reports which caused such widespread interest and controversy.

In 1950 close on 2,000,000 people paid to see championship cricket in this country. In 1966 the figure had dropped to 513,578. In the early fifties the decline was steady but not unduly alarming. Then the tempo increased at an alarming rate until in recent years it became positively frightening. Worse still was the abrupt halt in the overall increase in membership. In 1964 members totalled 141,707. In 1965 139,964 and in 1966 135,045. To combat the double drop in revenue, counties were compelled to increase subscriptions, which in itself caused a drop in membership.

It was then obvious to all, except those with their heads firmly buried in the sand, that first-class cricket in this country was only solvent because of the efforts of supporters' clubs with football pools and Test match profits.

An exhaustive and detailed investigation with perhaps drastic action was imperative, and a committee under the chairmanship of Mr. David Clark was set up. Its terms of reference couldn't have been wider. They were "to examine the future of County cricket in the widest possible terms and if thought fit to recommend alterations in the structure and playing conditions of the County Championship".

The sky was the limit and the men chosen to carry out the job combined playing, business and administrative experience. In view of certain criticism made of the Committee and its report, let us examine the respective members' qualifications.

D. G. CLARK, Chairman of the Kent Cricket Committee, former captain of the county. Took M.C.C. team to India in the winter of 1963–4. A successful farmer.

G. O. ALLEN, Treasurer of the M.C.C., who has had more experience of cricket administration than anyone in the world. Former England captain and Test cricketer. A stockbroker.

E. R. DEXTER, former captain of England and Sussex. One of the most dynamic batsmen in English cricket for many years. Several business interests, including close-circuit television.

D. J. INSOLE, Chairman of the England Test Selection Committee, former captain of Essex. Vice-chairman of Essex. Holds important position with well-known firm of contractors and property developers.

A. B. SELLERS, Captain of Yorkshire from 1933 to 1947. A former Test selector. Chairman of Yorkshire Cricket Committee. Runs a printing business in Bradford.

W. S. SURRIDGE, Chairman of Surrey Cricket Committee. A former and highly successful Surrey captain. Head of sports goods manufacturing firm.

E. H. KING, Chairman of Warwickshire. Partner in well-known firm of accountants in Birmingham. Financial adviser to Aston Villa F.C.

O. S. WHEATLEY, The Glamorgan captain.

F. J. TITMUS, Middlesex captain and Test cricketer.

C. G. HOWARD, Manager of several M.C.C. Overseas tours, former secretary of Lancashire. Now Surrey secretary.

K. C. TURNER, Northamptonshire secretary.

F. M. TURNER, Leicestershire secretary.

C. BRAY, Cricket correspondent of a national daily newspaper for 30 years. Played for Essex 1928–38. Reported cricket all over the world. Five tours of Australia, four of West Indies, and three of South Africa.

Ill health prevented Mr. F. M. Turner from attending many meetings and he resigned before the final report was drafted.

The sub-committee held its first meeting in September 1965 and its last in January 1967. Seven meetings were held during the 1965/6 winter. It restarted work in October 1966, met five times and submitted its final report.

To obtain the maximum amount of evidence and data, the sub-committee's first step was to circularise all the counties with a vast questionnaire. This had six main headings: (1) *Pitches*, (2) *Playing conditions*, (3) *Conduct of and approach to the game by players*, (4) *Structure of County cricket*, (5) *Sunday cricket*, (6) *Test matches.* Over thirty pertinent questions were asked and the counties also given the opportunity of offering their own solutions to the various problems.

An analysis of the replies showed that only three counties were satisfied that they had been able to produce fast, true wickets. Only four were entirely satisfied with the approach to the game of their own players and those satisfied with their opponents' approach were two. Seven were in favour of the existing structure. Eight were not satisfied and two were not sure. For Sunday cricket there was an overwhelming majority.

The sub-committee was unanimous in its belief that sub-standard pitches produced sub-standard cricket, a view well supported later by the capped players. Its next step was to call all the county groundsmen to Lord's for a conference. Much opinion and evidence was gathered at this meeting.

Each member of the sub-committee not only answered the questionnaire which had been sent to the counties but also submitted a paper giving in detail his own ideas as to the best way to re-orientate county cricket and put it back on its financial feet, as well as making the game more attractive to the spectator.

It was apparent from these individual papers that there existed in the sub-committee just as wide a divergence of opinion as there was outside. Yet on two major issues—pitches, and the approach to the game by the players—there was complete agreement. It was felt that pitches must be improved and counties should see to it that they were.

To improve the players' approach was a more intricate and delicate matter. The sub-committee, however, was convinced that it was the key factor and in both reports laid great emphasis on the need for an immediate improvement.

Derbyshire in a lengthy statement giving reasons for rejecting the sub-committee's new structure proposals, supported this view in the most forthright terms. "It is, however, quite clear", the county declared, "that ultimately an improvement will only follow through very tough action when necessary by County Committees through their captain".

One does not recall any such action being taken by Derbyshire, or for that matter by any other county with the possible exception of Yorkshire, who on more than one occasion have disciplined a player. Even their action was not directed against the wrong approach to the actual playing of the game but to club discipline off the field rather than on it.

During the summer of 1966 the *Daily Mail*, at the request of the sub-committee, commissioned the National Opinion Polls to carry out a national survey, the object of which was "to investigate the reasons for the fall in crowds at county grounds and in particular to find out how far the causes of it may be (*a*) counter attractions and present national social habits and (*b*) a feeling that there are defects in the game as a spectator sport on account of the way in which it is played or organised".

This vast document was of immense value to the sub-committee. In addition, counties were asked to carry out a postal survey of their members, in order to elicit more fully the possible contrast between the opinion of members and that of the cricket-watching public covered in the N.O.P. report.

Still with the object of getting the widest possible evidence and opinion, the sub-committee had a questionnaire sent to all "capped" players. Well over a hundred replied.

They were almost unanimous that modern pitches were largely to blame for the dull cricket and that modern first-class cricket was not good entertainment. It was significant that of the various suggested alterations in the structure of the county championship the players were emphatically against all but the one finally recommended by the Clark committee.

The counties for their part produced some remarkable suggestions. Hampshire were so satisfied with the *status quo* that they didn't want any change for at least three years, despite the state of their finances.

Glamorgan, whose secretary greeted the Clark report with "it's a lot of tommy rot" were in favour of leaving well alone, although the county lost £10,539 in 1966 and their gate receipts were £6,573 less than in the previous season.They were £5,344, the lowest since the war. A similar reduction this season would see the county paying spectators to watch its cricket.

Sussex went even further than Glamorgan. They suggested even more first-class cricket. In other words they want to give the public more of something of which, by its decreasing support, it has shown that it has too much already.

Gloucestershire put forward an interesting programme, which staggered championship matches to one a week in May, June and mid-July and then increased the number to two a week until the end of August. They also suggested that the qualification period for one overseas star player should be the period of one playing season, rather than twelve calendar months.

Derbyshire wanted no change and their main reason was that in their opinion they would lose ten per cent of their members. The Northamptonshire chairman put the loss at fifty per cent.

The Clark committee considered at great length the effect fewer matches might have on membership. It agreed in the end that the loss would not be anything like as big as estimated.

Unless something drastic was done to increase revenue counties would be compelled to go on increasing members' subscriptions. That would have a much greater effect on membership than a reduction in the amount of cricket.

The Clark committee found overwhelming evidence in favour

of Sunday championship cricket. It could and would be a decisive factor in increasing revenue, but it could not be assumed that it would be legalised by 1968, the earliest that any major alteration in the Championship could be made.

At the same time Sunday play was not the complete solution. A serious attempt had to be made: (*a*) to get a more positive and enthusiastic approach by the players, (*b*) to produce a structure that would cause a revival of public interest, and (*c*) to find ways and means of attracting more players into county cricket. In other words to establish a pyramid by which the budding first-class player could graduate from club to county without having to make first-class cricket his sole occupation, as he must do under existing conditions.

The Clark committee felt that its proposals would be the first definite step towards achieving that end.

The counties have decided otherwise. That was their prerogative, their right. But in doing so they have taken upon their own shoulders the full responsibility of saving our national summer sport.

One may well ask, "What next?" Few can be so sanguine as to believe that first-class cricket is going to recover on its own. A failure of football pools and most counties would be bankrupt.

Despite the rejection of its report the Clark committee did not work in vain. It gathered and analysed vital statistics and opinions. It stimulated interest by the controversial nature of its recommendations and it must have awakened the counties to the seriousness of the present situation and their responsibility to do something about it.

WEST INDIES IN INDIA, 1966–67

First Test: Bombay, December 13, 14, 16, 17, 18. West Indies won by six wickets. India 296 (C. G. Borde 121, A. S. Durani 55; C. C. Griffith three for 63, G. S. Sobers three for 46) and 316 (B. K. Kunderam 79, Nawab of Pataudi 51; L. R. Gibbs four for 67, D. A. J. Holford three for 94); West Indies 421 (C. C. Hunte 101, C. Lloyd 82, D. A. J. Holford 80, G. S. Sobers 50; B. S. Chandrasekhar seven for 157) and 192 for four (C. Lloyd 78 not out, G. S. Sobers 53 not out; B. S. Chandrasekhar four for 78).

Second Test: Calcutta, December 31, January 2, 3, 4, 5. West Indies won by an innings and 45 runs. West Indies 390 (R. B. Kanhai 90, G. S. Sobers 70, S. M. Nurse 56; B. S. Chandrasekhar three for 107); India 167 (L. R. Gibbs five for 51) and 178 (G. S. Sobers four for 56).

Third Test: Madras, January 13, 14, 16, 17, 18. Drawn. India 404 (C. G. Borde 125, F. M. Engineer 109, R. F. Surti 50 not out; L. R. Gibbs three for 87) and 323 (A. L. Wadekar 67, V. Subramanian 61, Hanumant Singh 50; L. R. Gibbs four for 96, C. C. Griffith four for 61); West Indies 406 (G. S. Sobers 95, R. B. Kanhai 77; B. S. Chandrasekhar four for 130; R. F. Surti three for 68) and 270 for seven (G. S. Sobers 74 not out, C. C. Griffith 40 not out; B. S. Bedi four for 81, E. A. S. Prasanna three for 106).

A full report with full scores of the tour will be given in the 1968 *Wisden.*

THE FIRST COUNTY CRICKET REPORT

FIRST INNINGS EXPERIMENT OF 65 OVERS

The Advisory County Cricket Committee on March 1, 1966 received and confirmed the report of the special sub-committee appointed to examine the future of County Cricket. The inquiry was under the chairmanship of D. G. Clark and included the following members: Lt.-Gen. Sir Oliver Leese (President of M.C.C.), G. O. Allen (Treasurer of M.C.C.), Charles Bray, E. R. Dexter, C. G. Howard, D. J. Insole E. H. King, A. B. Sellers, W. S. Surridge, F. M. Turner, O. S. Wheatley.

I Terms of Reference

To examine the future of County Cricket in the widest possible terms and, if thought fit, to recommend alterations in the Structure and Playing Conditions of the County Championship.

II Meetings of Sub-Committee

The Sub-Committee met on seven occasions. In addition, it convened a meeting of County Groundsmen at Lord's for the purpose of discussing the preparation of pitches on County grounds.

III Questionnaire

A Questionnaire was compiled and sent to all Counties and the replies to this have been very carefully considered by the Sub-Committee.

IV Criticism of present day County Cricket

The Sub-Committee believe that there is little wrong with the game of cricket if it is played in the right spirit, but they consider that present day County Cricket can be criticised on the following counts:—

(a) The negative approach towards the game of many players.
(b) Too much cricket is played, especially by the leading players.
(c) Pitches which bring about:—
  (i) lack of stroke play by batsmen;
  (ii) negative bowling, mainly of the seam variety.
(d) A steady decline in the run-rate, the over-rate and a reduction in slow bowling.
(e) The first innings have become a prolonged manoeuvre with resultant dull cricket on the first two days of County matches.
(f) Potential cricketers may be lost to the game, and some established players have retired prematurely on account of:—
  (i) The necessity to find permanent employment in business at an early age.
  (ii) The amount of cricket at present played, which almost excludes the part-time cricketer.
(g) Lack of spectator appeal. Paid attendances have continually declined and although membership has substantially increased over the years, there was, in fact, an overall reduction in County membership in 1965 for the first time.

V Analysis of the Problem

In considering the problem it is quite evident that there are two sides to the question:—

(a) How any action which may be taken will affect players and the standard of First-Class Cricket.
(b) How such action may affect the finances of County Clubs.

In coming to our conclusions and recommendations, when these two factors have conflicted, it has been the Sub-Committee's view that the standard of the game must have first priority, as unless this standard is maintained or improved, the finances of the game are certain, in the long run, to be affected adversely.

There were certain specific suggestions which the Sub-Committee were instructed to consider originally and these were extended by further instructions at the meeting of the Advisory County Cricket Committee on November 24, 1965. It was considered that most of these suggestions could be implemented in First-Class Cricket without delay, if thought desirable. Therefore, this Report is in the form of:—

(a) Short Term recommendations, which if agreed, could apply in First-Class Cricket in 1966.
(b) Long Term recommendations, which could not apply until 1967 at the earliest.

VI Specific Points that the Sub-Committee were instructed to consider

(*a*) *The extension of the season to mid-September to allow all Counties to play 32 three-day matches*

NOT RECOMMENDED BECAUSE:—

(i) It would increase Counties' costs and it is doubtful whether increased gates would cover these costs.
(ii) It is considered there should be a reduction in the amount of Cricket played rather than an increase.

(*b*) *One-innings matches each of two-days' duration*

NOT RECOMMENDED BECAUSE:—

It would have little spectator appeal.

(*c*) *Seven Test Matches of three days each, instead of five of five days*

NOT RECOMMENDED BECAUSE:—

(i) Results would be very infrequent.
(ii) Five-day Matches sustain interest over a longer period.

(*d*) *The Warwickshire proposal for complete covering of pitches during hours of play*

NOT RECOMMENDED BECAUSE:—

(i) Rain affected pitches have always been part of English Cricket.
(ii) When heavy rain occurs it is generally the surrounds which delay the resumption of play rather than the pitch itself.
(iii) Counties playing on small grounds with a very small groundstaff would have great difficulty in covering completely and quickly.
NOTE: Refer to Short Term Recommendation (d).

(*e*) *Glamorgan proposal that only one new ball per innings be allowed*

NOT RECOMMENDED BECAUSE:—

(i) The taking of a new ball after 85 overs frequently reduces the time taken to bowl out the "tail", and it is a factor believed to have a degree of spectator appeal.
(ii) The Committee believe that their recommendation under Short Term (e) for no polishing of the ball is more likely to achieve the object intended in the Glamorgan proposal.

(*f*) *The County Captains' Recommendations of Points in County Championship Matches*

NOT RECOMMENDED BECAUSE:—

Of experimental matches recommended under Short Term (f) and (g).

(*g*) *Limitation of the First Innings*

See Short Term Recommendation (f).

(*h*) 20 *three-day matches and* 16 *one-day matches to be played as a separate competition*

See Long Term Recommendation (b).

VII Short Term Recommendations

(*a*) *Pitches*

The majority of Counties agree that hard, fast pitches are desirable both for attractive cricket to be played, and for the development of good cricketers.

IT IS RECOMMENDED:—

That all Counties should take a much closer interest in the production of such pitches and that it should be generally agreed that the preparation of pitches to favour a home side should be discouraged.

NOTE:—The Soil Science Unit, University College of Wales, Aberystwyth, is carrying out a research programme, aimed at elucidating the factors involved and their relative importance for the production of pitches of a desirable, pre-determined standard. This information was received late in the proceedings of the Sub-Committee, and the Soil Science Unit has been asked to supply further details.

(*b*) *Over-Rate*

The majority of Counties agree that an increase in over-rate is essential.

However, 12 Counties state that they are satisfied that everything possible has been done to increase the over-rate by their teams. The Sub-Committee cannot agree that the over-rate could not be further improved and considers the attitude of many Counties in this matter to be over-complacent.

IT IS RECOMMENDED:—

(i) That County Committees should all agree to instruct their teams to bowl an average of 20 overs per hour and should make enquiries as to the reason on each occasion when this target is not achieved.
(ii) That at this stage legislation to improve the over-rate is undesirable as being difficult to implement under varying conditions, and would be difficult to enforce.

(*c*) *Attitude of Players to the game*

The Short Term Recommendations of the Sub-Committee are not likely to assist the problem.

However, the Sub-Committee feel that more could be done by County Committees to ensure their players adopt a more positive and enterprising approach to the game. The players should be made to realise that unless this is done their livelihood is in real jeopardy.

(*d*) *Covering of the Pitch*

IT IS RECOMMENDED:—

That the covering of pitches in County Championship games is brought into line with present Test Match practice in the United Kingdom, *i.e.*:—

(i) The whole pitch shall be covered:—

(a) The night before the match and, if necessary, until the first ball is bowled; and, whenever necessary and possible, at any time prior to that during the preparation of the pitch.
(b) On each night of the match and, if necessary, throughout Sunday. In addition, in the event of rain falling during the specified hours of play, the pitch shall be completely covered as soon as play has been abandoned for the day.

NOTE: During hours of daylight, and provided that it is not raining at the time, the covers should be removed whenever possible; this is particularly desirable when the sheet type cover laid flat on the ground is in use.

(ii) The bowling ends will be covered to a distance of 4 feet in front of the popping creases, if, during the hours of play, the match is suspended temporarily, owing to weather or light conditions.

The reasons for this recommendation are:—

(i) Overnight covering may reduce the occasions when overnight rain delays the start of play. Few things irritate spectators more than no play being possible on a fine day.
(ii) It may help groundsmen to produce hard, fast pitches.
(iii) In order to have one system of covering for all First-Class Cricket.

IT IS ALSO RECOMMENDED:—

That Ground Authorities should pay more attention to the covering of the bowlers' run-up.

(*e*) *New Ball and Interference with the Ball*

IT IS RECOMMENDED:—

That a New Ball may be taken after 85 overs; but that no interference with the natural condition of the ball shall be allowed. Wiping and cleaning the ball shall be allowed under the Umpires' supervision.

The reasons for this recommendation concerning interference with the ball are:—

(i) The present day factors of lush outfields and constant polishing combine to retain shine almost indefinitely and, thus, to discourage the use of spin bowlers.
(ii) It may help to increase the over-rate.
(iii) It has some support from Overseas Cricket Authorities.

(*f*) *Limitation of overs in First Innings*

IT IS RECOMMENDED:—

That as an experiment in 1966 each County should play.:—

16 three-day matches under normal Playing Conditions
and
12 three-day matches with the first innings of each team limited to a maximum of 65 overs, with no limitation on the number of overs per bowler

These 12 matches will be the first against those opponents played twice during the season.

The reasons for this recommendation are that limitation of the first innings could:—

(i) Produce more entertaining cricket on the first day, and ensure, subject to weather, that first day spectators see both sides bat.
(ii) Encourage the use of spin bowling in the second innings.
(iii) Encourage the production of good pitches.

(*g*) *Points Scoring System*

IT IS RECOMMENDED:—

That the existing points scoring system should be continued, with the exception that the team leading on the first innings and winning the match should retain the 2 points for first innings lead, making a total of 12 points.

(*h*) *Appointment and Duties of Umpires*

IT IS RECOMMENDED:—

(i) That a Committee of seven, including three senior County Captains, appointed by M.C.C. or the Advisory County Cricket Committee, should, in future, appoint Umpires.

The reason for this recommendation is that the Umpires would feel that there was less likelihood of bias in their re-election to the First-Class List if this re-election was in the hands of a Body, the majority of whom were not County Captains.

(ii) That the Captains should continue to submit reports on Umpires at the conclusion of each match.

(iii) That Umpires should be reminded that it is their duty to enforce the Laws, without fear or favour, and that, in doing so, they will be given the fullest support.

(*i*) *Discipline*

At the meeting of the Advisory County Cricket Committee on November 24, 1965, it was agreed by all Counties that any time-wasting of whatever nature should be considered "unfair play".

The existing Regulations are considered adequate but they may not have appeared to be so because of a past unwillingness to act firmly and strongly in implementing them.

It is, therefore, recommended that the Rules of the Advisory County Cricket Committee be altered so as to empower the Executive Committee, mentioned in Rule 2 (ii) (c), to act in any reported case of misconduct on the field, including time-wasting as laid down in the Advisory County Cricket Committee Rules.

(*j*) *Publicity and Public Relations*

IT IS RECOMMENDED:—

That a Committee should be appointed to consider the matter.

The Sub-Committee considered the question of Public Relations and Publicity and agreed there was room for considerable improvement. At the same time it was felt that this important question ought to be probed by a Small Special Sub-Committee, more competent to deal with a matter of such complexity.

VIII Long Term Recommendations

(*a*) *Survey of County Members and Supporters*

The Committee feel that, before any final decision is taken regarding the future structure of County Cricket, efforts should be made to ascertain the views of both County Members and their Supporters.

IT IS RECOMMENDED:—

That a survey be carried out on the following lines:—

(i) Counties should circularise all their Members with a questionnaire.

(ii) A survey of the Associated Clubs and Supporters' Associations should be carried out based on identical questions to those submitted to Members.

(*b*) *The Future Structure of County Cricket*

In considering this subject the basic conclusions of the Sub-Committee, subject to views expressed by Members and Supporters are:—

(i) That a minimum of 16 three-day games per County, unmolested by any change of basic rules, should form the basis of the County Championship.

(ii) That any programme of matches additional to those stated in (i) above should be so designed as to assure, as far as possible, the retention of membership at present levels and subscription rates, yet also make reductions in cost possible, if thought necessary or desirable by any County.

(iii) That the changes should not be so drastic as to prevent a reversion to a similar programme as at present played.

(iv) That the question of playing County Cricket on Sundays must, for the time being, be a matter for individual Counties to decide. The result of the survey may give a useful lead for future decisions on this matter.

(v) That the Gillette Cricket Cup should continue in its present form.

The Sub-Committee believes that the need to curtail the present programme of three-day matches may soon be forced upon the Counties, both as a means of effecting economies of staffing and of bringing back lost spectators by introducing the elements of scarcity and contrasting types of cricket, and, therefore, considers that it may be necessary for the future structure of County Cricket to be:—

(i) 16 matches of three days' duration
16 matches of one day's duration } In one Championship

or

(ii) 20 matches of three days' duration
16 matches of one day's duration } In separate Championships

(iii) In addition to (i) or (ii) above—The Gillette Cricket Cup.

IX Conclusion

Throughout its deliberations, the Sub-Committee has constantly been reminded of the fact that cricket in its traditional form is a great game, and factual evidence confirms the view that public interest in it has never been greater. As with most spectator sports, the attendance at matches often fails to reflect this interest, and the Sub-Committee regards the exclusive use of gate figures as a yardstick by which to measure the popularity of cricket, to be misleading.

The future of First-Class cricket depends upon two major factors—first, the spirit in which the game is played and the manner in which it is approached by the players and, second, the ability of administrators to encourage the proper approach and to present the game in a way which produces full and varied entertainment for the public.

With this in mind, the report offers spectators the wide choice of five-day Test Matches, three-day First-Class matches, and one-day matches of two sorts.

Some Counties may consider that the recommendations as presented are not sufficiently revolutionary. The Sub-Committee believes, however, that cricket must stand or fall on its merits as a game, and that no amount of "tinkering" with the Laws or regulations will do as much to make it worthwhile as an entertainment or as a sport to be enjoyed by players and spectators alike, as will an enlightened, lively and sporting approach.

THE SECOND COUNTY CRICKET REPORT

The Second Report of the Advisory County Cricket Committee Special Sub-Committee 1966 was issued on December 16, 1966.

Committee

Owing to the resignation of one member and invitations sent to two new members, the Committee was reconstituted as follows: *Chairman:* D. G. Clark; *Members:* G. O. Allen, C. Bray, E. R. Dexter, C. G. Howard, D. J. Insole, E. H. King, A. B. Sellers, W. S. Surridge, F. J. Titmus, K. C. Turner and O. S. Wheatley.

The Sub-Committee wish to record their sincere appreciation to the *Daily Mail* for having sponsored the National Opinion Poll, to the Counties who carried out surveys of their members and to the 'capped' players who responded so well to the questionnaire sent to them. The Sub-Committee also greatly appreciate the advice and comment of the President of M.C.C., The Rt. Hon. Sir Alec Douglas-Home, who attended the main meeting when decisions were made.

I Terms of Reference

The original terms of reference remain unaltered:

> "To examine the future of County Cricket in the widest possible terms and, if thought fit, to recommend alterations in the Structure and Playing Conditions of the County Championship."

II Meetings of the Sub-Committee

The Sub-Committee met on four occasions during the autumn of 1966.

III The Effect of the Short Term Recommendations in 1966

At their first meeting, the Sub-Committee agreed that the Short Term Recommendations, which had been accepted for the 1966 season, had had little or no effect on either the standard of play or on the entertainment value of County cricket. It was appreciated that cricket in 1966 suffered from bad weather and that most of the sporting public's interest was directed towards the World Cup in July. Although interest was maintained in Test Matches, County Championship attendances continued to decline alarmingly.

The Sub-Committee have the following comments to make on the Short Term Recommendations:

(a) *Pitches:*

In spite of the unanimous agreement by the Counties to try to produce hard, fast and true pitches, the general standard appears to have deteriorated still further.

The Soil Science Unit of the University College of Wales, Aberystwyth, carried out certain tests on some County grounds and it is hoped that the results of their research will be known at the end of the 1967 season.

(b) *Over-Rates:*

The average over-rate in 1966 showed a slight improvement on the previous season, but this was marginal and did not appear to have any significant effect on public interest.

(c) *Attitude of Players to the Game:*

There did not appear to be any difference in the attitude of the players in 1966 and their general approach continued, on many occasions, to be both negative and unenterprising.

(d) *Covering of the Pitch:*

The Sub-Committee's recommendation was not accepted by the Counties and a variety of covering regulations were adopted. It is difficult to assess the effect of this decision on the standard of pitches or on the game itself.

(e) *New Ball and Interference with the Ball:*

The decision to disallow any polishing of the ball did not reduce the amount of seam bowling, though this may have been due partly to the introduction of "65 over" matches. It is thought that the experiment will only have a significant effect in the long term.

(f) *Limitation of Overs in First Innings:*

The decision to discontinue this experiment was taken by the Advisory County Cricket Committee in November 1966 for the following reasons:

(i) it encouraged negative fielding and bowling tactics;
(ii) it adversely affected middle-order batsmen;
(iii) it discouraged spin bowling.

Many spectators, however, appear to have enjoyed these matches, though attendances were not affected.

(g) *Points Scoring System:*

The ratio of 10 points for a win to 2 points for first-innings lead did not encourage positive cricket in the first innings. It may even have tended to penalise those Counties who produced good pitches.

(h) *Appointment and Duties of Umpires:*

This recommendation was not designed to improve the standards of play, but received the wholehearted support of the Umpires.

(i) *Discipline:*

Although no cases of deliberate time wasting or unfair play were reported, there was no significant improvement.

(j) *Publicity and Public Relations:*

The recommendation of the Publicity and Public Relations Sub-Committee was not accepted by the Advisory County Cricket Committee. This Sub-Committee regrets that decision, as it is convinced that improved publicity and public relations are of paramount importance. M.C.C. have been asked to consider the matter further.

IV The Future of County Cricket

The Sub-Committee very strongly believe that County cricket in 1966 could still be criticised on all the counts listed in paragraph IV of their last Report, as follows:

"(*a*) The negative approach towards the game of many players.
(*b*) Too much cricket is played, especially by the leading players.
(*c*) Pitches which bring about:
  (i) lack of stroke play by batsmen;
  (ii) negative bowling, mainly of the seam variety.
(*d*) A steady decline in the run-rate, the over-rate and a reduction in slow bowling. (There was, however, a slight improvement in 1966.)
(*e*) The first innings have become a prolonged manoeuvre with resultant dull cricket on the first two days of County matches.
(*f*) Potential cricketers may be lost to the game, and some established players have retired prematurely on account of:
  (i) The necessity to find permanent employment in business at an early age.
  (ii) The amount of cricket at present played, which almost excludes the part-time cricketer.
(*g*) Lack of spectator appeal. Paid attendances have continually declined and although membership has substantially increased over the years, there was, in fact, an overall reduction in County membership in 1965 for the first time. (This again occurred in 1966.)"

The existing structure of County cricket has produced a situation, whereby substantial financial losses are incurred annually. In 1965, the last year for which accurate figures are available, Cricket income, including Test Match, television and tourist match receipts, failed to cover the total cost of running County Cricket by approximately £150,000. Extraneous sources of income did, of course, reduce this figure. It is almost certain that 1966 will show a further deterioration in the financial position.

If no action is taken, the Sub-Committee believe this trend will continue, and ultimately result in some County Clubs being forced to leave the County Championship. It is felt that such a situation would be most undesirable and could, in fact, be avoided.

The Sub-Committee is optimistic for the future, in view of the unimpaired interest in County cricket; but it considers that it is essential to institute changes in the playing programme and the way the game is played, with a view to this wide interest in the County game being translated into active support.

The Sub-Committee believe that the principal objectives, when considering the future of County cricket and its structure, must be:

(*a*) To produce the highest possible standard of play in all classes of cricket.
(*b*) To provide a form of entertainment which will appeal to spectators and will be available when the majority are able to attend.
(*c*) To improve the financial position of all Counties, particularly those who are, at present, in difficulties.

V Views of Players, Members and the General Public

The Sub-Committee examined the views of players, Members and the public on a wider basis than ever before. They considered in detail the National Opinion

Poll taken in June 1966, and the Surveys of County Members and Capped Players, which have been carried out since the conclusion of the season. The following points have emerged clearly from these surveys:

(*a*) Interest in cricket is as great as ever, and the game is played and watched by a vast number of people. For various reasons County cricket attendances have declined alarmingly.

(*b*) The Members and public condemn present-day County cricket as being dull and unattractive, owing mainly to the negative approach of the players.

(*c*) There is overwhelming support for County cricket to be played on Sundays.

(*d*) Of those County members who replied to questionnaires, approximately 62 per cent are not satisfied with the present structure; yet there is no majority support for any particular alternative.

(*e*) There is some support amongst Members, and substantial support from the general public, for a greater number of one-day matches.

(*f*) The players condemn the standard of pitches, which, in their opinion, is the principal cause of the lack of entertainment value.

(*g*) A large majority of the players considered that the necessity to produce good averages has an adverse effect.

(*h*) Of the alternative structures put before the players, the one which received most support was 16 three-day matches and 16 one-day matches in separate Championships.

VI Recommendations

A. STRUCTURE:

The Sub-Committee recommend that the following structure of County Cricket should apply in 1968:

(i) A County Championship of 16 three-day matches.
(ii) A separate Championship of 16 one-day matches.
(iii) The continuation of the Gillette Cricket Cup as at present.

In addition, the Sub-Committee recommend that consideration should be given to playing a full Second XI Championship of 16 two-day matches.

Editor's Note: The Counties rejected (i) and (ii) at the meeting at Lord's, January 25, 1967.

B. PLAYING CONDITIONS:

The Sub-Committee recommend that the Playing Conditions should be:

(i) *Three-day Championship:*

(*a*) Matches to be played, in the main, over the weekend—Saturday, Sunday and Monday, unless a County is unwilling to play on Sundays. Counties wishing to play a limited number of mid-week three-day matches may do so provided they can obtain opponents willing to play them.

(*b*) Standard hours of play should be: Saturday, 11.30 a.m. to 7 p.m.; Sunday, 2.00 p.m. to 7 p.m.; Monday, 11.0 a.m. to 6.30 p.m.

Other matches to be of 20 hours duration, including intervals and extra time.

(*c*) The points scoring system should be:

(i) Should a match be finished the winning side to score 8 points, plus any points scored in the first innings.

(ii) Should a match be finished and the scores be equal (a "Tie") each side to score 6 points plus any points scored in the first innings.

(iii) Should the scores be equal in a drawn match, the side batting in the fourth innings to score 6 points, plus any points scored in the first innings.

(iv) The side which leads on the first innings shall score 4 points. If the scores in the completed first innings are equal each side shall score 2 points. If the scores are equal in the first innings in a drawn match, in which the first innings is not completed, only the side batting second shall score 2 points. First innings' points shall be retained and added to any other points scored.

(v) If a match is drawn, each side shall score 2 points, plus any points scored in the first innings. Points for a drawn match shall only be awarded if a result has been achieved in the first innings.

(vi) Even should there be no play for any reason, or no result obtained in the first innings, every match shall be included in the table of results as a "match played", in these cases neither side to score points.

(vii) The side which has the highest aggregate of points gained at the end of the season shall be the Champion County. Should two or more sides be equal on points, the side with most wins will have priority.

Editor's Note: The above points system has been adopted for 1967.

(ii) *One-day Championship:*

(*a*) The Laws of Cricket and First-Class Playing Conditions will apply.

(*b*) Matches to be played, in the main, mid-week on the most suitable day for the home County.

(*c*) Hours of play should be: 11.00 a.m. to 7.00 p.m.

(*d*) Points scoring should be:—

(i) 4 points for a win;
(ii) 2 points for a tie;
(iii) 1 point for a draw;
(iv) 2 points for a side batting second in a drawn game when the scores are equal.

(*e*) A strong recommendation should be made to the International Cricket Conference that matches in this Competition should be designated First-Class.

(*f*) The Sub-Committee consider it is most important that a suitable name is found for this Competition.

(iii) *Gillette Cricket Cup:*

The Sub-Committee recommend that the Rules should remain as at present.

C. RULES GOVERNING THE REGISTRATION AND QUALIFICATION OF CRICKETERS IN COUNTY CRICKET:

The Sub-Committee recommend that the Registration Rules should be amended to allow one of the two overseas-born players per County, permitted under Rule 5 (*d*), to be qualified to play for that County after a residential period of 12 months instead of 24 months. Such a player should not be eligible for registration by another County within a period of five years, after which time he would be considered an English-born cricketer (see Rule 7 (*d*)) and the County could then register another overseas-born cricketer in the same way.

Before an overseas-born cricketer could commence his 12-month residential qualifying period, the County concerned would have to notify the Registration Committee.

D. SPONSORSHIP:

The Sub-Committee recommend that the question of sponsorship of the three-day Championship, the one-day Championship and the Second XI Championship should be carefully examined.

E. PITCHES

The Sub-Committee recommend that consideration should be given to the banning of any County ground on which a number of bad reports have been submitted.

VII Reasons for Recommendations

The Sub-Committee believe that the objectives referred to in paragraph 4 would be achieved by the acceptance of the recommendations, for the following reasons:

A. STANDARD OF PLAY:

(i) Under the proposed structure, involving a reduction in the amount of County cricket played, some Counties might still feel inclined to retain a sizeable full-time professional staff. They might fear that a reduction in staff would automatically cause a drop in standards.

The Sub-Committee do not believe that this need be the case, if the following action is taken:

(*a*) Lessen the wide gulf in the standard of play between County cricket and Club cricket, by a closer liaison.

(*b*) The introduction of progressive training schemes whereby regular mid-week evening practice sessions are organised at County grounds for all potential County cricketers.

(*c*) The setting up of a fully-organised coaching scheme for both Clubs and schools throughout the County, utilising the permanent staff on some of their free days.

The Sub-Committee believe that top standards can be maintained or increased if a "pyramid" is formed in each County, whereby the best players can progress through school to Club, to County Second XI, to County First XI and, perhaps, to international level.

(ii) It is appreciated that many of the best players, at present in County cricket, have originated from Minor Counties, and it is not intended that the proposed structure should prevent these players from entering First-Class cricket. The best of them could certainly be offered full-time contracts, whereas others may well be prepared to take outside employment within a First-Class County.

(iii) The Survey of County players has shown that a number of them are worried about their future livelihood, and this affects their method of play. It is considered that, if the younger players were not completely dependent upon cricket for their living, and had the opportunity of regular coaching and good competitive cricket, they would develop just as quickly and would not suffer from the present fear for their future.

The Sub-Committee firmly believe that it is wrong not to give young men the opportunity of following an alternative career, whilst being trained as a County cricketer; and furthermore, by allowing players this greater opportunity, some of the more senior and higher-class cricketers will continue in the game for a longer period.

(iv) The proposal to shorten the qualification period for overseas players will, it is thought, encourage them to enter County cricket. It is emphasised that the majority of the public, and, indeed, many of the players, support this proposal, provided it does not give the overseas player preferential treatment. It is thought that overseas star players will not only raise the standard of County teams by their individual prowess, but they should also have a beneficial effect on the young men who play with them.

(v) The proposed points scoring system would:

(*a*) Result in teams making greater efforts to bowl out their opponents, rather than, by means of containment, waiting for the inevitable declaration.

(*b*) Suitably reward the team behind on the first innings who have managed to save the game—circumstances which often produce an exciting finish.

(*c*) Encourage the preparation of better pitches, since there will be less emphasis placed on the final result.

(vi) The Survey of County players has emphasised the Sub-Committee's conviction that the production of a better standard of pitches is essential.

The future standard of English County and Test Match cricket is being imperilled by the production of indifferent pitches, since moderate bowlers appear to be far better than they are, and the development of batsmen is seriously handicapped.

It is thought that the production of poor pitches is due either to unsuitable direction from County authorities anxious for results, or to the incompetence of groundsmen; and that consideration should be given to the wisdom of direction in this connection and to the payment of salaries which will attract the best groundsmen in the country.

(vii) The introduction of a one-day Championship, played according to the Laws of Cricket, should encourage a freer approach by the players, similar to that seen on a number of the third days of County matches at present. The hours of play suggested would allow for a good game of cricket and the players would not be affected by any over limitation. It is also thought that First-Class status for these games and possible sponsorship rewards would add to the players' incentive to make the proposed Competition a success.

B. ENTERTAINMENT VALUE:

The vast majority of spectators and, indeed, most of the players feel that present-day County cricket is dull to watch and lacks entertainment value. The Sub-Committee accepts that this is partly due to the poor standard of pitches. However, it is thought to be mainly due to the ultra professional approach, where efficiency and a misguided belief that negative tactics pay, has produced a stereotyped pattern which is deadly to watch and which gives the appearance of being boring to play. The Sub-Committee also believe that additional reasons for the lack of entertainment value are:

(i) The continuous "grind" of six days per week cricket, in which it is difficult to retain enthusiasm, unless a team is still running for the Championship.
(ii) The belief of some players that their future career depends on the production of satisfactory figures and averages. This applies particularly to the young player.

Whilst increased entertainment value must basically stem from better cricket, as envisaged under "Standard of Play" in section A, it is considered that the majority of spectators would enjoy the opportunity of having a greater variety of cricket to watch.

Under the proposed structure, matches would be played at times when the majority would be able to attend. The one-day matches should certainly provide better entertainment than a single day of a mid-week three-day match, although it is realised that they would not have the tension of the Gillette Cup matches with its knock-out element.

The easier introduction of overseas players should also add to the attraction and entertainment value of County cricket.

C. FINANCIAL IMPLICATIONS:

The Sub-Committee considered the financial implications of the proposed new structure under the following four headings:

(i) Effect on Membership.
(ii) Effect on outer gate receipts.
(iii) Possible reductions in expenditure.
(iv) Additional sources of income.

(i) *Effect on Membership:*

The Sub-Committee realise that County administrators fear a loss of Membership, if less cricket is played. It is appreciated that Membership is, and will continue to be, the most important source of a County Club's revenue; and it would be wrong to take any action which would affect Membership income adversely. However, the Sub-Committee do not believe that the proposed structure would reduce Membership, when it is realised that nearly all County cricket would be played at times when Members could watch. Furthermore, the pattern of the programme suggested would have a much-needed variety and more matches would be played. In the event of the introduction of a new Second XI Championship, played at home at the weekend when the First XI is away, it should provide Members with further good cricket and the chance to take an active interest in the younger County players.

It will be recalled that the majority of Members, who answered the questionnaire, expressed dissatisfaction with the present structure and called for more one-day matches.

(ii) *Effect on Outer Gate Receipts:*

The outer gate receipts for County matches have shown an alarmingly large decline in recent years, which, to some extent, has been offset by increased Membership. It is evident, however, that the casual spectator has become even less inclined to attend County cricket, because it lacks appeal, and he is, therefore, less inclined to become a Member. The Sub-Committee have no doubt that the introduction of one-day matches would prove popular with the general public, when they knew that they could see the whole match, or could come for a few hours at the end of the day to see the climax.

It is also considered that the scarcity of three-day matches would make each of them a more important event, and this would inevitably attract larger crowds. The Sub-Committee believe that not only could the decline in outer gates be halted but attendances would, in due course, improve. The greater number of "free" days would also give the Press, both local and national, a greater opportunity to "build up" forthcoming matches rather than continually reporting what has gone before.

(iii) *Possible Reduction in Expenditure:*

The proposed structure should certainly mean a reduction in expenditure for County Clubs.

The greatest financial saving offered by the proposed structure, is clearly the opportunity to reduce the size of the full-time playing staffs, if Counties so wish. It is realised that many Counties are not particularly embarrassed financially, owing to outside sources of income, and these might wish to retain their playing staffs, at any rate, for the time being.

Also the playing of 10 days less cricket, both at home and away, would automatically reduce match expenses by £1,000 to £1,500 at a conservative estimate.

Travelling costs on one-day matches away from home would be reduced, where it was possible to arrange two consecutive matches on a Wednesday and Thursday in the same region. Similarly, for those who might wish to hold cricket weeks at home, two one-day matches prior to or following a three-day match could be arranged.

The Sub-Committee considered zoning the one-day Championship matches, in order to reduce costs. It was decided, however, that the saving in cost did not outweigh the disadvantage of not entertaining each other County at least once at home during the season.

(iv) *Additional Sources of Income:*

The Sub-Committee are recommending that the possibility of sponsorship of all Championship cricket should be examined. It is appreciated that previous suggestions of sponsorship of the County Championship have been turned down as being unsuitable for a traditional Competition of this sort. It is felt, however, that, provided sponsors could be found who could act with as great a dignity and lack of interference as the Gillette Company, no harm would be done to the image of cricket; and the financial benefits might be considerable.

VIII Conclusion

The Sub-Committee is convinced that the time is ripe for a change in the structure of County cricket. It is abundantly clear that the vast public which is interested in cricket is expecting change and will welcome it. The weight of public opinion is clearly on the side of change and it is felt that, if this does not take place, the long-term effect on County cricket might well prove disastrous.

The Sub-Committee believe that the introduction of the proposed structure would cause the revival of enthusiasm for County cricket both as far as the players and the public are concerned.

All the proposals contained in this Report will be worthless, unless County Committees ensure that the approach of Captains and players to the actual playing of the game is wholly positive and enthusiastic.

It is vital, too, that the implications of the present situation are fully understood and appreciated by Committees and players alike.

THE THROWING REPORT

SPECIAL COMMITTEE TO DEAL WITH SUSPECTS

The throwing sub-committee set up by M.C.C. in August 1965 published their findings and recommendations, which were accepted by the Advisory County Cricket Committee on March 1, 1966. The committee comprised: F. G. Mann (chairman), G. O. Allen, T. E. Bailey, E. R. Dexter, C. S. Elliott, D. J. Insole, W. F. Price, R. Subba Row and R. H. Twining.

Terms of Reference

The Sub-Committee was instructed to look into further ways and means of eliminating suspect bowling actions from all grades of cricket in the United Kingdom.

The Committee's Approach to the Problem

The Committee recognised that their main objectives were:—

(A) The elimination of throwing from First-Class cricket as fairly and as quickly as possible.

(B) Its elimination from other grades of cricket in the United Kingdom.

(C) As a means of achieving these two main objectives, it was considered essential to produce an improved definition, which would assist umpires in all grades of cricket in the uniform interpretation of the Law. It was appreciated that any recommended definition must be one which would be acceptable to all members of the International Cricket Conference.

(A) First-Class Cricket

(I) Present Situation

The Sub-Committee considered that the existing system, whereby an umpire "called" a bowler when satisfied that the ball had been "thrown", and had to submit a report on the actions of all bowlers after each match, had helped considerably in producing a clearer picture of the Umpires' opinions on the fairness or otherwise of bowlers in County Cricket. It was thought that, in the long run, this system might have the desired effect of eliminating suspect bowlers from the First-Class game. The Captains' reports had also helped to clarify the position.

Nevertheless, it was felt that this system had not proved entirely satisfactory for the following main reasons:—

(a) Judging from reports received from Umpires and Captains and from the viewing of a number of films, it was evident that there were still bowlers with suspect actions.

(b) The difficulty the Umpire has in making an accurate judgement due to:—

(i) The speed of the bowler's arm in the delivery swing.
(ii) The variation in the action of bowlers considered to be suspect.
(iii) The position in which he normally stands at square-leg, which is not always ideal.

(c) The additional difficulty facing an umpire because of his understandable reluctance to become involved in unpleasant incidents or publicity.

(d) As a result of the above difficulties, there has been a wide variation in the opinion expressed and the action taken by umpires.

(e) In some cases, only a limited number of umpires have been sufficiently doubtful about a bowler's action to "report" him, or confident enough of their opinion to "call" him. In these circumstances, Counties have continued to play bowlers who may have been throwing consistently.

(II) Other Factors Considered by the Committee

(a) The Committee viewed a large number of films which convinced them of their value and necessity, as they showed far more clearly than the naked eye the details of a bowler's action. They would always be of assistance and in some cases could be an essential aid in forming a firm opinion.

(b) The desirability of giving some assistance to the umpires in the present situation was considered. The view was expressed by both Mr. Elliott and Mr. Price that all the First-Class Umpires would welcome support and assistance from an outside body. This would be particularly appreciated if, as a result of their "calling" or "reporting" a player, some form of sanction could be imposed. These views were supported unanimously by the Committee.

(III) Recommendations

It was recommended that:—

(1) The existing system of "calling" and "reporting" shall continue.

(2) In addition, a Special Sub-Committee shall be set up to adjudicate on bowlers who have been "called" or "reported", which shall have the power to suspend a player from bowling until the end of a season.

The composition and procedure of the Committee be as follows:—

(a) The following members be invited to form the Committee:—

F. G. Mann (chairman); G. O. Allen (vice-chairman); F. S. Lee and J. H. Parks (retired umpires); D. J. Insole and A. V. Bedser (Board of Control selectors); T. E. Bailey, D. B. Close, M. J. K. Smith and O. S. Wheatley (current players); L. E. G. Ames and R. T. Simpson (county representatives).

It was appreciated that this Committee was rather large, but it was felt that attendance during the summer, when a meeting might be called at short notice, could prove difficult.

(b) The minimum number of members required to form a quorum when adjudicating on any bowler shall be seven. Included in this number shall be:—

Chairman or Vice-Chairman
One retired umpire
Three from the list of B.O.C. Selectors, Current Players and County Representatives.

(c) Before the Committee decide to suspend a bowler, at least two-thirds of those present shall have shown to be in favour of suspension. Should a member of the Committee be connected with the County of the bowler concerned, he should have no vote, nor be counted as present for the purpose of calculating the voting percentage.

(d) The following procedure should be adopted:—

(i) After one report by an umpire or captain, or on the recommendation of a member of the Committee, the player shall be filmed in black and white in at least two matches from varying angles and at varying speeds, including slow motion. Members of the Committee will also watch him, if possible.

(ii) After two reports by umpires, the Committee shall adjudicate on a bowler's action, though they should have power to do this after only one report, if they so wished.

(iii) Having decided that a bowler's basic action is unfair, the Committee shall have power to suspend him from bowling until the end of the season.

(iv) The Committee might, at their discretion, following four reports by umpires on one bowler, suspend him immediately until such time as they have the opportunity of adjudicating.

(v) In cases where the Committee "clear" a bowler's basic action, but regard him as an "occasional" thrower, it is intended that they shall, at their discretion, make whatever additional comments they may think proper for the assistance of umpires in the light of the evidence they have seen and heard.

(vi) In the cases where the Committee completely clear a bowler, the County Committee and umpires concerned, will be notified accordingly. At the same time it will be pointed out that this clearance does not preclude umpires from "calling" or "reporting" the bowler in the future.

(vii) In 1966 and in subsequent seasons bowlers shall start with a "clean sheet" unless a County make a particular request for adjudication before the commencement of the season.

(viii) The County concerned in a particular case, shall be entitled to express its views to the Committee, if it wishes to do so.

(3) Prior to the 1966 season, a special meeting of the First-Class Umpires shall be held at Lord's, at which the machinery of the new Committee will be explained. The umpires will also be invited to view films of both fair and suspect bowlers, but in the latter category they shall be players who have retired from First-Class Cricket.

(B) Other Grades of Cricket

Undoubtedly there are throwers in other grades of cricket and steps shall be taken to move towards their elimination.

The Committee make the following recommendations:—

(*i*) *Minor County Umpires*

That the Minor County Umpires, as with the First-Class Umpires, be invited to Lord's at the beginning of the coming season, for a discussion and to view films.

(*ii*) *Umpires in Other Grades of Cricket*

That steps be taken to contact the Association of Cricket Umpires and the Yorkshire Federation of Cricket Umpires, to seek their advice and co-operation. Firm proposals will be made later.

(*iii*) *Coaches and Players*

That a new coaching film on bowling shall be produced, which will be concerned principally with instruction of the correct bowling action. It shall, however, include some examples of "suspect" actions and shall point out the "danger signs" of which a coach shall take particular notice and correct before it is too late.

(C) Definition of a Throw

(*I*) *Present situation in the United Kingdom*

The existing definition, which applies in all countries at the present time, and should, in the opinion of the Sub-Committee, continue to be used in this country until the International Cricket Conference decides otherwise, reads as follows:—

"A ball shall be deemed to have been thrown if, in the opinion of either Umpire, the bowling arm, having been bent at the elbow, whether the wrist is backward of the elbow or not, is suddenly straightened immediately prior to the instant of delivery. The bowler shall nevertheless be at liberty to use the wrist freely in the delivery action."

(*II*) *Views of the International Cricket Conference*

Following a discussion at the last meeting of the International Cricket Conference, the delegates recommended the following definition for consideration by their respective Boards:—

"A ball shall be deemed to have been thrown if, in the opinion of either Umpire, the bowling arm is straightened, whether partially or completely, immediately prior to the ball leaving the hand. This definition shall not debar the bowler from the use of the wrist in delivering the ball."

Most countries have accepted the above proposal, but Australia have not supported it, since they consider that the words "immediately prior to . . ." are open to doubt in interpretation and that there appears to be a body of opinion in some countries who have maintained that, under the existing definition, which also includes these words, a bowler is "fair", provided his arm is straight at the instant of delivery. The Committee believe that there is some substance in Australia's objection.

(*III*) *Other Factors Considered by the Committee*

When considering alternative definitions, the Committee have borne in mind that bowlers who contravene the Law vary in their methods, in that they straighten their arms in different ways and start to do so at different points in their delivery swings. They are, nevertheless, convinced that, for a bowler to "throw", the arm must be in the process of straightening during the final stages of the delivery swing, *i.e.* in the 50° to 60° before the ball leaves the hand, though, of course, some bowlers begin to straighten well before this point.

During their deliberations the Committee considered the possibility of defining a fair delivery based on the bowler maintaining a fully extended arm from the horizontal until the ball leaves the hand. In spite of its apparent simplicity of interpretation, this suggestion is not supported for the reasons stated in the previous paragraph and for the fact that, although such a definition might be slightly easier to interpret, umpires would still have the difficulty of judging whether or not a bowler's arm was bent in the latter part of the delivery swing. The Committee decided that any recommended definition should be clear to interpret, should, if possible, overcome the objections raised by Australia and should be fair to the bowlers. They feel that any definition designed to catch the "guilty", but capable of penalising the "innocent" should be avoided.

(*IV*) *Recommendation*

It was recommended that the following definition be submitted to the International Cricket Conference in July, 1966:—

> "A ball shall be deemed to have been thrown if, in the opinion of either umpire, the process of straightening the bowling arm, whether it be partial or complete, takes place during that part of the delivery swing which directly precedes the ball leaving the hand. This definition shall not debar the bowler from the use of the wrist in delivering the ball."

The reasons for this recommendation are:—

(*a*) The sole objection to the definition recommended by the International Cricket Conference in 1965 has been that the words "immediately prior to . . ." could be taken to mean that if a bowler's arm is straight at the instant of delivery, the ball is fair.

(b) In the recommended definition above the Committee believe that this possible misinterpretation has been precluded by the introduction of the following words: **"the process of straightening the bowling arm"** and **"takes place during that part of the delivery swing which directly precedes . . ."**

COUNTY CAPS AWARDED IN 1966

Kent: J. C. Dye.
Lancashire: D. R. Worsley.
Leicestershire: M. E. Norman, R. W. Tolchard.
Northamptonshire: H. Sully.
Nottinghamshire: M. J. Smedley, R. Swetman, R. A. White.
Somerset: M. Kitchen, P. J. Robinson.
Surrey: M. J. Edwards.
Warwickshire: R. N. Abberley.
Worcestershire: J. A. Ormrod.

MY FAVOURITE SUMMER

By A. A. Thomson

My favourite summer is 1902. I had not then played any cricket, except in the back garden, and I had never seen a first-class match. I was eight years old at the time, but my knowledge of the season was, and remains, considerable. My information came from two main sources: my step-Uncle Walter and *Wisden Cricketers' Almanack* for 1903. I learned, as history students must, partly from patriotic narrative and partly from sober factual report.

Uncle Walter, now in heaven, departed this life in 1935, not long after Yorkshire's innings defeat by Essex at Huddersfield. (At 87 he should have been sheltered from such shocks.) *Wisden* for 1903 happily sits in front of me. If the B.B.C. were to maroon me on a desert island and, according to their pleasant custom, demand to know what book I should like to take with me, there would be no difficulty. *Pickwick* I know by heart and, though I revere Tolstoi, to read *War and Peace* under the breadfruit trees would be too much like starting to watch an innings by J. W. H. T. Douglas and waking up to find that Trevor Bailey was still batting. But *Wisden* for 1903 is the perfect companion. It has almost everything the heart of man could desire.

I doubt, of course, if any historian between Macaulay and Churchill could have produced so glowing, so romantic a tale as Uncle Walter's account of the game at Headingley on June 2 and 3, 1902, in which Hirst and Rhodes dismissed the mighty Australians for 23 and Yorkshire struggled desperately towards the 48 runs needed for victory until Irving Washington, with a cannon-shot clear of mid-on, made it 50. "Finest innings of Irving's life", Uncle Walter would conclude, "and would you believe me if I told you he didn't even get double figures?"

Naturally I believed him, just as I believed what he told me about the Spanish Armada, the Death of Nelson, and Jessop's 101 in forty minutes, scored on our own town ground, to Uncle Walter's mingled horror and delight. One at least of these stories was an eye-witness account. Nevertheless it is arguable that *Wisden's* unemotional version may have given an even vivider picture:

	Overs	Mdns	Runs	Wkts.
Hirst ..	7	4	9	5
Jackson ..	7	1	12	5

As for Washington's titanic battle with fate, *Wisden* rightly leaves its heights and depths to our imaginations:

I. Washington not out........................ 9

One of the human things about cricket is that it changes continually, but does not change very much. The features that I instinctively look for in *Wisden* to-day—the Five Cricketers of the Year, the Notes by the Editor, the complete first-class results and averages, the Births and Deaths and the Obituaries—are all to be found in the older Almanack. The 40th volume, containing 672 pages, is a little smaller than the 103rd, which takes up 1,084. I think myself that 672 pages make a tidy book and I sadly sympathise with the Editor whose "only difficulty is to deal with the immense number of matches crowded into a season within the limits of a volume published at a shilling".

In the matter of illustrations *Wisden* to-day, with its wealth of photographs, scores heavily over "my" *Wisden* which, apart from some sketches of austere-looking stumping gloves in the advertisements, has no pictures except those of the Five Cricketers, which look as though they had come out of a family album with brass clasps. Since this was an Australian summer, three of the Cricketers are Australians. The two Englishmen are C. J. Burnup of Kent and J. Iremonger of Nottinghamshire. Burnup was one of those players who, like the Fosters, the Days and D. J. Knight, were brought up in the graceful batting tradition of Malvern. His best year was 1902, and it was only the immense strength of England's batting in that deplorably wet summer that robbed him of an England cap. The brightest of his hundreds was scored at Tunbridge Wells, a ground which I now associate with its blaze of rhododendrons in June and the spiral stairway which eternally obtrudes the horrors of vertigo between the correspondent and the press-box.

Iremonger, who played full-back for Nottingham Forest, was a sturdy, if rather stiff, batsman who, though no aristocrat, held his own among such masters as Shrewsbury, William Gunn and A. O. Jones. Playing up to the outbreak of the first war, he toured Australia without appearing in a Test, and scored 32 centuries, the oddest of which included one of 1902's oddest incidents. In the Notts game against M.C.C. at Lord's, enamelled stumps were used with the enamel still wet, and when a ball moved one of his stumps, the bail remained faithful. From that moment nothing stopped Iremonger from going ahead to his hundred.

The three Australians were perhaps of heavier metal. Australia has never lacked wicket-keepers and J. J. Kelly, with 36 caps, was the most eminent, I think, between Blackham (35 caps) and Oldfield (54). His reserve wicket-keeper on this tour was Hanson Carter, by profession an undertaker, but Kelly himself presided at the obsequies of 35 victims (23 caught and 12 stumped). His is the most striking of my five faded photographs, because his face was adorned by the most luxurious moustache in cricket history. Like tropical foliage, it cascaded down from his upper lip and I cannot imagine how, as he crouched on duty, he managed to avoid contravening Law 43, which decrees that no part of the wicket-keeper's person shall advance in front of the wicket before the ball arrives, or words to that effect.

Those who saw the gargantuan Warwick Armstrong, when his hard-bitten warriors crushingly defeated England in 1921, might not have recognised the slim boyish figure of the 1902 tour's most gifted all-rounder, who scored 1,087 runs and captured 81 wickets, mainly with deliveries so far outside the leg-stump that the batsmen would get themselves out chasing them in sheer exasperation. This was the first of his four visits and, when *Wisden* said "It is not unreasonable to expect a great future for him", an understatement was being released that was virtually to become a curse upon our country.

Some cricketers may be judged by statistics; some by eccentricity and some by massive achievement. A rare and enchanted few are remembered for the sheer beauty they brought to the game. Victor Trumper was a superb batsman with, as was said, three strokes for every ball; a vivid fielder and a personality of compelling charm. He did not, in the foolish phrase, "hate" the bowler; he merely thought the poor fellow couldn't bowl. In that desolate summer Trumper made more runs than anybody else, English or Australian, and every one of his 2,570 runs bore the hallmark of supreme artistry. Is is one of *Wisden*'s steadfast virtues to be soberly discriminating; this enables it to reserve its highest praise for the noblest and best.

With Trumper it could go to town: "No-one has been at once so brilliant and so consistent since W. G. Grace was at his best.... He seemed independent of varying conditions, being able to play just as dazzling a game after a night's rain as when the wickets were hard and true. All bowling came alike to him ... in the Tests at Sheffield and Manchester he reduced our best bowlers to the level of the village green.... The way in which he took good-length balls off the middle stump and sent them to the boundary, had to be seen to be believed.... For the moment he is unapproachable."

Who were the batsmen of 1902 who could not approach him? The first-class averages mention them: Shrewsbury, Ranjitsinhji, Abel, Grace, R. E. Foster, Fry, Jessop, Jackson, MacLaren, Warner, Palairet and Hayward, to name but a dozen. And who were the village green trundlers whom he cut to ribbons? They were Hirst, Rhodes, Braund, Barnes, Jackson, Lockwood, Cranfield, Trott and Tate who, perhaps as a consolation for his nightmare Test at Old Trafford, finished the season with 180 wickets at 15 runs apiece. In 1902 those nine bowlers took over 1,200 wickets between them and Trumper just felt sorry for them.

The Australian tour of 1902 produced a rubber more exciting than any in history except, and until, the electrifying series between Australia and the West Indies of 1960–61 which began with the fantastic tied match at Brisbane and ended with Australia's heart-hammering victory by two wickets at Melbourne. The 1902 rubber began at Edgbaston with a rain-wrecked game, which England must have won if a full third day's play had been possible. This match had everything except a positive ending. It had what was reckoned the best integrated side that England ever put into the field: MacLaren, Fry, Tyldesley, Ranjitsinhji, Jackson, Braund, Jessop, Hirst, Lilley, Lockwood and Rhodes. It saw a swordsman's century by Tyldesley which dragged England's batting back from the abyss; it staged Australia's dismissal for 36 (Hirst, three for 15 and Rhodes seven for 17) of which total Trumper magnificently scored half; it then alas, suffered an almost empty last day. (C. B. Fry told me long afterwards that, though Rhodes took seven wickets, it was Hirst who broke the batting's back.) For full measure the score card carried a classic misprint which sets down the extras as three wides. There were, of course, really three byes, probably due to Hirst's terrific swerve. I doubt if Hirst ever bowled three wides in a season or Rhodes three wides in his whole career.

The second match, at Lord's, began sensationally and ended, after less than two hours, in torrential rain. By the end of the fourth over, Fry and Ranjitsinhji were out for ducks, and after 19 runs had been scored, 15 of them by Jackson, rain drove the players off. When they returned MacLaren and Jackson hit 83 more at a run a minute. After that the deluge. The Australians were unlucky in that our abominable climate had hit half of them with influenza; in a minor sense, on the other hand, they were lucky, not to have to play out the game in that state.

It was the third Test, at Bramall Lane, that gave Australia victory by 143, and a grip on the rubber they never relaxed. "They played the finer all-round cricket," said *Wisden* judicially, "and fully deserved their victory, but it is no more than the truth to say that all the luck of the game went their way." They owed their win to superlative batting by Trumper and Hill and equally splendid bowling by Noble. England endured the worst of the wicket, the worst of the light, the worst of the decision to leave out Lockwood, and the worst of Barnes's ineffectiveness in the second innings after he had bowled like an angel in the first. On England's side MacLaren and Jessop batted heroically and Rhodes finished Australia's second innings by taking four wickets in 19 balls. As he said of the Oval Test twenty-four years later. "They should have put me on sooner. . . ."

The fourth and fifth games of the rubber were, always excepting the 1960–61 tie at "the Gabba", the most dramatic in Test history. Both have been celebrated in nobler prose than mine and it is not for me to paint the lily in recalling the wonder of Trumper, whose pulling on a fast drying wicket was "a marvel of ease and certainty"; or the bowling of Lockwood, recalled after the Sheffield *débâcle*, who took six for 48 and five for 28; or Jackson's defiant hundred, practically unsupported, or the torments inflicted on the hapless Tate, who missed a vital catch and, after nerve-racking suspense, was bowled, attempting to batter the four which would have won the match. I will only quote, not *Wisden*, but Uncle Walter who, to his dying day, believed England's defeat to be a dreadful retribution from on high for leaving out George Hirst. "I knew it would happen", he said. "*Things can only go so far....*"

The fifth Test at the Oval was Jessop's and only one game in history has been more memorable. Australia's first innings total of 324 looked high enough to win and, when England has six down for 83, it looked higher still. Hirst and Braund rallied the broken ranks and when Hirst, driving furiously, was caught and bowled, England still needed 38 to save the follow-on. It was Lockwood who saved it, with a mixture of fortitude and fortune, by a mere ten runs, and when Australia batted again, it was Lockwood, whose deadly bowling, backed by grand fielding, pulled the game round. Everybody knows how England lost MacLaren, Palairet, Tyldesley, Hayward and Braund for 48; how Jessop, joining Jackson, played his early overs quietly and then, first with Jackson and afterwards with Hirst he burst forth in any apocalyptic blend of high art and controlled violence. In an hour and a quarter his score, enriched by a 5 and seventeen 4's, leaped to 104 out of 139.

"... A more astonishing display", says the temperate chronicler, "has never been seen. What he did would have been scarcely possible under the same circumstances to any other living batsman. The rest of the match was simply one crescendo of excitement...."

Everybody knows, too, how when Rhodes joined Hirst 15 runs were still wanted and how Hirst said, or did not say: "We'll get 'em in singles." Fifty years later Rhodes told me it was only a tale and Hirst said: "At a time like that you don't remember *what* you say." They did not in fact get them in singles but get them they did in their own good time. This was without question Jessop's match, but close to Jessop came Hirst, bold, imperturbable, the symbol of the bonnie fighter. Scoring 101 for once out, he twice saved the day and the myth that he was no more than a good county player should have lain down and died at the Oval that day.

With so fierce a Test series, you might have imagined the county season to be comparatively dull. Not so. For the third successive time Yorkshire headed the table with three times as many points as Sussex, the runners-up. The method of reckoning was one point for a win, minus one for a loss and nothing for a draw, but no system could have been devised by human brain that would have dislodged Yorkshire from the top. Systems of rewarding excellence, or indeed of assessing any form of merit, are frequently changed on the grounds that they are unjust to somebody. True, but, in an unjust world, the well-meant changes merely transfer the injustice to someone else. The best teams will still come out on top, the least talented at the bottom, and minor variations will occur only in the middle.

That Yorkshire side which beat the Australians were probably as well equipped as any county team have ever been. With an attack which consisted of Hirst, Rhodes, Haigh and Jackson, nothing could compare with it until the Yorkshire bowling of the 1920's and Surrey's in the 1950's. Their early batting—Brown, Tunnicliffe, Jackson and Taylor—was not quite as strong as that of Sussex—Fry, Vine, Killick and Ranjitsinhji—but it was powerful enough for all practical purposes. Denton was developing that cavalier approach which later made him Tyldesley's most dashing rival for the post of England's No. 3; Washington, a maternal uncle of the Kilners, played for Yorkshire and, had illness not shortened his career, would have played for England the left-handed part which Leyland played later with rugged resolution. Hunter, whose luxuriant moustache challenged even J. J. Kelly's, might well have worn England's gloves, but for Arthur Augustus Lilley, of Warwickshire, who appeared to occupy the place behind the stumps on a long lease. T. L. Taylor (1,517 runs) and Haigh (158 wickets) both had their turn as England's twelfth man and Lord Hawke, then a young 41, was the shrewdest of contemporary captains. I would not argue with anyone who denied that Rhodes was England's best bowler.

Could such a side be beaten? Yes, they could. In their three seasons' triumph Yorkshire lost only two matches, both to Somerset who, under the volatile and exuberant leadership of S. M. J. (Sammy) Woods showed time and again a remarkable talent for the unexpected. Sammy, an Australian by birth and an England rugby forward by inclination, radiated such elemental force in hard hitting, fast bowling and electrical fielding that he might have been the forerunner of Sir Learie Constantine. His team had, in L. C. H. Palairet, the most purely graceful batsman in the country, who even to-day is looked back on as the epitome of elegance; in Leonard Braund they had a batsman-bowler who, even with Hirst, Lockwood and F. S. Jackson in the reckoning, was often deemed the finest all-rounder of the day.

Yorkshire's progress in 1902 was hard to hinder. On Whit Monday, mainly through the bowling of Sydney Barnes, they were put out by Lancashire for 148 and yet this scanty total gave them an innings win, Jackson taking eight for 13. They beat Warwickshire, Kent, Gloucestershire and Middlesex twice; Nottinghamshire by 227 and Surrey by an innings and 102. The second Middlesex game was almost a recording of the first Roses match. Yorkshire made well under 200, but easily won by an innings. (Rhodes, ten for 56, Haigh, nine for 53). Immediately after this they met Somerset, on a fiendish wicket at Bramall Lane. Somerset, for whom

Palairet and Braund scored 44 for the first wicket, scarcely realised that this would be the best stand of the match. Yorkshire were all at sea with the bowling of Braund and Robson and then, after another bold stand by Palairet and Braund and some furious hitting by Gill, Somerset meekly gave in to Haigh who, taking six for 19, hit the stumps five times, three of them for a hat-trick. Asked to make a mere 119, Yorkshire were doomed from the start and Braund (nine for 41) demolished them with his whippy leg-breaks. Altogether, he took fifteen for 71 and hit 65. Very few among the other twenty-one players scored 20 for twice out. It was the one occasion of the season when Yorkshire lost their grip on a game and it was Braund who prised it loose.

You could not say there was a dull county. Sussex, the runners-up, could never be tedious with Fry and Ranjitsinhji on their strength, while Nottinghamshire, who came third, leaned a little on the over-forties, as represented by Shrewsbury and William Gunn, but had a fast bowler, Wass, who took 140 wickets and was faster than he looked, which was a feat in itself; this for a county in which Larwood was not to be born for a further two years and Voce for another seven.

Surrey before Hobbs was not necessarily drama before Shakespeare. There have always been outstanding batsmen under the shadow of the gasometers. The firm of Brockwell and Abel was to change to Abel and Hayward before it changed to Hayward and Hobbs. In Hayward's benefit match at the Oval a total of 1,427 runs were scored for 24 wickets and, though the game ended in a draw, it never grew wearisome. The wicket was good and the batsmen were good; could it be that the bowling was feeble? As the bowlers included Hirst, Rhodes, Haigh, Jackson, Richardson and Lockwood (who took seven for 159) I should say not. Perhaps—this is a daring suggestion—they were all enjoying themselves.

In the rest of the 15 counties—Northamptonshire and Glamorgan were not yet with them—were many who to-day are freshl remembered. Lancashire's MacLaren was England's captain and Tyldesley England's most dashing professional batsman; Warwickshire gave England in Lilley an almost irreplaceable wicket-keeper; Kent had Blythe, next in prestige to Rhodes; Worcestershire boasted a "pride" of Fosters, of whom R. E. was the most brilliant; Warren and Bestwick were neither the first nor the last of Derbyshire's dreaded pairs of fast bowlers; Leicestershire had C. J. B. Wood, King and Knight, all more than locally famous; Middlesex glittered almost too brightly for their collective success with such names as P. F. Warner, C. M. Wells, Trott, Hearne (J. T.) and the only begetter of the googly, B. J. T. Bosanquet. Essex had their twins, Perrin and McGahey; Gloucestershire, though modestly placed, owned the magnificent Jessop, and Hampshire, at the bottom of the table, could be proud of the tireless all-rounder, C. B. Llewellyn, who scored nearly 1,000 runs, took 170 wickets and was in the 14 from whom England's most illustrious eleven were chosen at Edgbaston.

Besides the first-class counties there was London County, captain and secretary, W. G. Grace. This club, founded by W. G. after leaving Gloucestershire under a cloud—the cloud was the county's, not W.G.'s—was presided over by the Old Man himself and his friend, W. L. (Billy) Murdoch. The two, nicknaming each other Father and Muvver, rollicked through the season like schoolboys. At W. G.'s command the club could conscript virtually any cricketer in the land, so that often they could field something like a Test team. In one of their matches at the Crystal Palace against M.C.C. there was a global total of well over 1,000 runs for 30 wickets, garnished with hundreds by C. J. B. Wood, L. O. S. Poidevin and, need you ask, W. G. In this game played Mr. J. Gilman who, still youthful at 88, has recently told delightful stories of those days, including one of W. G. and Murdoch, who in attempting to alight from a hansom, so vied with each other in elephantine politeness—"After you, Father." "No, after you, Muvver."—that their combined thirty-five stone or so went slap through the bottom of the cab.

In the same match appeared the man who, apart from the Graces, was the most celebrated of cricketing doctors, a brisk batsman stumped on his way to a lively 50. There is a legend that, while entering the pavilion at the start of this match, he was accosted by a small autograph-hunting boy.

"Please, sir, is your name Conan Doyle?"

"Yes, sonny. How did you guess?"

"Elementary, my dear Sir Arthur," said the lad. "I saw it on your cricket bag."

So we bid farewell to my favourite summer, with a nostalgic glance at the advertisements in my favourite *Wisden*. You could buy men's white buck leg-guards for 5*s*. 11*d*. and guaranteed Australian catgut-sewn cricket balls for 5*s*. Best of all there were bats with specially selected blades and handles (I quote) *of a particularly resilient nature*, price, with double splice, 18*s*. 6*d*. That I have survived those golden days so long does not argue any virtue in me, but it does prove one thing.

I am of a particularly resilient nature.

SOBERS—THE LION OF CRICKET

By Sir Neville Cardus

Garfield St. Aubrun Sobers, thirty years old in July 1966—the most renowned name of any cricketer since Bradman's high noon. He is, in fact, even more famous than Bradman ever was; for he is accomplished in every department of the game, and has exhibited his genius in all climes and conditions. Test matches everywhere, West Indies, India, Pakistan, Australia, New Zealand, England; in Lancashire League and Sheffield Shield cricket. We can safely agree that no player has proven versatility of skill as convincingly as Sobers has done, effortlessly, and after the manner born.

He is a stylish, prolific batsman; two bowlers in one, fastish left-arm, seaming the new ball, and slow to medium back-of-the-hand spinner with the old ball; a swift, accurate, slip fieldsman in the class of Hammond and Simpson, and generally an astute captain. Statistics concerning him speak volumes.

Sobers holds a unique Test double, over 5,500 runs, and close on 150 wickets. Four years ago he set up an Australian record when playing for South Australia by scoring 1,000 runs and taking 50 wickets in the same season. To emphasize this remarkable feat he repeated it the following summer out there.

Only last January he established in India a record for consecutive Test appearances, surpassing J. R. Reid's 58 for New Zealand. He is also amongst the select nine who have hit a century and taken five or more wickets in one Test, joining J. H. Sinclair, G. A. Faulkner, C. E. Kelleway, J. M. Gregory, V. Mankad, K. R. Miller, P. R. Umrigar and B. R. Taylor.

Is Sobers the greatest all-round cricketer in history? Once upon a time there was W. G. Grace, who in his career scored 54,896 runs and took 2,876 wickets, many of which *must* really have been out; also W.G. was a household name, an eminent Victorian, permanent in the National gallery of representative Englishmen. Aubrey Faulkner, South African, a "googly" bowler too, scored 1,754 runs in Test matches, average 40.79, and took 82 wickets, average 26.58. In 1906, George Hirst achieved the marvellous double performance of 2,385 runs and 208 wickets. When asked if he thought anybody would ever equal this feat he replied, "Well, whoever does it will be tired." But Hirst's record in Test matches was insignificant compared with Sobers', over a period. (All the same, shouldn't we estimate a man by his finest hour?)

There was Wilfred Rhodes, let us not forget. In his career he amassed no fewer than 39,802 runs, average 30.83, and his wickets amounted to 4,187, average 16.71. In first for England with Jack Hobbs at Melbourne in 1912, and colleague in the record first-wicket stand against Australia of 323; and in last for England in

G. S. SOBERS—THE SQUARE CUT.

1903, partner of R. E. Foster in a last-wicket stand of 130. Again, what of Frank Woolley, 39,802 runs in Tests, 83 wickets?

It is, of course, vain to measure ability in one age with ability in another. Material circumstances, the environment which moulds technique, are different. Only providence, timeless and all-seeing, is qualified to weigh in the balance the arts and personality of a Hammond and a Sobers. It is enough that the deeds of Sobers are appreciated in our own time, as we have witnessed them. He has, as I have pointed out, boxed the compass of the world of present-day cricket, revealing his gifts easefully, abundantly. And here we touch on his secret: power of relaxation and the gift of holding himself in reserve. Nobody has seen Sobers obviously in labour. He makes a stroke with moments to spare. His fastest ball—and it can be very fast—is bowled as though he could, with physical pressure, have bowled it a shade faster. He can, in the slips catch the lightning snick with the grace and nonchalance of Hammond himself. The sure sign of mastery, of genius of any order, is absence of strain, natural freedom of rhythm.

In the Test matches in England last summer, 1966, his prowess exceeded all precedents: 722 runs, average 103.14, twenty wickets, average 27.25, and ten catches. In the first game, at Manchester, 161 and three wickets for 103; in the second, at Lord's, 46 and 163 not out and one wicket for 97; in the third, at Nottingham, 3 and 94, five wickets for 161; in the fourth, at Leeds, 174 and eight wickets for 80; in the fifth, at The Oval, 81 and 0, with three wickets for 104. A writer of highly-coloured boys' school stories wouldn't dare to presume that the hero could go on like this, staggering credulity match after match. I am not sure that his most impressive assertion of his quality was not seen in the Lord's Test. Assertion is too strenuous a word to apply to the 163 not out scored then; for it was done entirely free of apparent exertion, even though at one stage of the proceedings the West Indies seemed beaten beyond salvage. When the fifth second-innings wicket fell, the West Indies were leading by nine runs only. Nothing reliable to come in the way of batsmanship, nobody likely to stay with Sobers, excepting Holford. As everybody concerned with cricket knows, Sobers and his cousin added, undefeated, 274. It is easy to argue that Cowdrey, England's captain, did not surround Sobers with a close field. Sobers hinted of no technical flaw, no mental or temperamental anxiety. If he slashed a ball when 93, to Cowdrey's hands, Cowdrey merely let us know that he was mortal when he missed a blistering chance. Bradman has expressed his opinion that few batsmen of his acquaintance hits with the velocity and strength of Sobers. And a sliced shot can travel at murderous pace.

At his best, Sobers scores as easily as any left-handed batsman I have seen since Frank Woolley. He is not classical in his grammar of batsmanship as, say, Martin Donnelly was. To describe

G. S. SOBERS—THE FAST BOWLER.

F

Sobers' method I would use the term lyrical. His immense power is concealed, or lightened, to the spectator's eye, by a rhythm which has in it as little obvious propulsion as a movement of music by Mozart (who could be as dramatically strong as Wagner!). A drive through the covers by Sobers sometimes appears to be quite lazy, until we see an offside fieldsman nursing bruised palms, or hear the impact of ball striking the fence. His hook is almost as majestic as MacLaren's, though he hasn't MacLaren's serenity of poise as he makes it. I have actually seen Sobers carried round, off foot balance, while making a hook; it is his only visibly violent stroke—an assault. MacLaren, as I have written many times before, dismissed the ball from his presence. The only flaw in Sobers' technique of batsmanship, as far as I and better judges have been able so far to discern, is a tendency to play at a dangerously swinging away off-side ball "with his arms"—that is to say, with his bat a shade (and more) too far from his body. I fancy Sydney F. Barnes would have concentrated on this chink in the generally shining armour.

He is a natural product of the West Indies' physical and climatic environment, and of the condition of the game in the West Indies, historical and material, in which he was nurtured. He grew up at a time when the first impulses of West Indies' cricket were becoming rationalised; experience was being added to the original instinctive creative urge, which established the general style and pattern—a creative urge inspired largely by Constantine, after George Challenor had laid a second organised basis of batting technique. Sobers, indeed, flowered as West Indies' cricket was "coming of age". As a youth he could look at Worrell, at Weekes, at Walcott, at Ramadhin, at Valentine. The amazing thing is that he learned from all these superb and definitely formative, constructive West Indies cricketers; for each of them made vintage of the sowings of Challenor, George Headley, Constantine, Austin, Nunes, Roach, and Browne—to name but a few pioneers. Sobers began at the age of ten to bowl orthodox slow left-arm; he had no systematic coaching. (Much the same could safely be said of most truly gifted and individual cricketers.) Practising in the spare time given to him from his first job as a clerk in a shipping house, he developed his spin far enough to win a place, 16 years old now, in a Barbados team against an Indian touring side; moreover, he contrived to get seven wickets in the match for 142.

In the West Indies season of 1953–1954, Sobers, now 17, received his Test match baptism at Sabina Park, Kingston. Valentine dropped out of the West Indies XI because of physical disability and Sobers was given his chance—as a bowler, in the Fifth game of the rubber. His order in the batting was ninth but he bowled 28 overs, 5 balls for 75 runs, 4 wickets, when England piled-up 414, Hutton 215. In two innings he made 14 not out, and 26.

G. S. SOBERS—THE SPINNER.

Henceforward he advanced as a predestined master, opening up fresh aspects of his rich endowment of gifts. He began to concentrate on batsmanship, so much so that in 1955, against Australia in the West Indies, he actually shared the opening of an innings, with J. K. Holt, in the fourth Test. Facing Lindwall and Miller, after Australia had scored 668, he assaulted the greatest fast bowlers of the period to the tune of 43 in a quarter of an hour. Then he suffered the temporary set-back which the fates, in their wisdom, inflict on every budding talent, to prove strength of character. On a tour to New Zealand, the young man, now rising twenty, was one of a West Indies contingent. His Test match record there was modest enough—81 runs in five innings and two wickets for 49.

He first played for the West Indies in England in 1957, and his form could scarcely have given compensation to his disappointed compatriots when the rubber was lost by three victories to none. His all-round record then was 10 innings, 320 runs, with five wickets costing 70.10 each. Next he became a professional for Radcliffe in the Central Lancashire League, where, as a bowler, he relied on speed and swing. In 1958/9 he was one of the West Indies team in India and Pakistan; and now talent burgeoned prodigiously. On the hard wickets he cultivated his left-arm "googlies", and this new study did not in the least hinder the maturing of his batsmanship. Against India he scored 557, average 92.83 and took ten for 292. Against Pakistan he scored 160, average 32.0 and failed to get anybody out for 78.

The course of his primrose procession since then has been constantly spectacular, rising to a climax of personal glory in Australia in 1960–1961. He had staggered cricketers everywhere by his 365 not out v. Pakistan in 1958; as a batsman he has gone on and on, threatening to debase the Bradman currency, all the time swinging round a crucial match the West Indies' way by removing an important opposing batsman, or by taking a catch of wondrous rapidity. He has betrodden hemispheres of cricket, become a national symbol of his own islands, the representative image on a postage stamp. Best of all, he has generally maintained the *art* of cricket at a time which day by day—especially in England—threatens to change the game into (a) real industry or (b) a sort of out-of-door "Bingo" cup jousting. He has demonstrated, probably unaware of what he has been doing, the worth of trust in natural-born ability, a lesson wasted on most players here. If he has once or twice lost concentration at the pinch—as he did at Kennington Oval in the Fifth Test last year—well, it is human to err, occasionally, even if the gods have lavished on you a share of grace and skill not given to ordinary mortals. The greatest ever ?—certainly the greatest all-rounder today, and for decades. And all the more precious is he now, considering the general nakedness of the land.

SOBERS IN TEST CRICKET

Season	Country	Tests	Batting						Bowling			Fielding
			Innings	Not Outs	Runs	Highest Innings	100's	Average	Runs	Wickets	Average	
1953–54	v. England	1	2	1	40	26	—	40.00	81	4	20.25	—
1955	v. Australia	4	8	2	231	64	—	38.50	213	6	35.50	1
1956	in N.Z.	4	5	0	81	27	—	16.20	49	2	24.50	4
1957	in England	5	10	0	320	66	—	32.00	355	5	70.10	1
1957–58	v. Pakistan	5	8	2	824	365*	3	137.33	377	4	94.25	2
1958–59	in India	5	8	2	557	198	3	92.82	292	10	29.20	5
1958–59	in Pakistan	3	5	0	160	72	—	32.00	77	0	—	2
1959–60	v. England	5	8	1	709	226	3	101.28	356	9	39.55	7
1960–61	in Australia	5	10	0	430	168	2	43.00	588	15	39.20	12
1962	v. India	5	7	1	424	153	2	70.66	473	23	20.56	11
1963	in England	5	8	0	322	102	1	40.25	571	20	28.55	8
1965	v. Australia	5	10	1	352	69	—	39.11	492	12	41.00	8
1966	in England	5	8	1	722	174	3	103.14	545	20	27.25	10
1966–67	in India	3	5	2	342	95	—	114.00	397	18	22.05	7
	TOTALS	60	102	13	5514	365*	17	61.95	4866	148	32.87	78

NOTTINGHAMSHIRE'S NOTABLE PART IN THE GROWTH OF CRICKET

By R. T. Simpson

Reginald Thomas Simpson, born at Sherwood, Nottingham on February 27, 1920, had to wait until the war was over before making his county debut in 1946. He gained his county cap the same season and was appointed captain in 1951, a post he held for ten years. He played in 27 Tests for England, made four overseas tours and when he retired in 1963 he had scored 30,546 runs, average 38.32, 64 centuries. An opening batsman, his pleasing upright stance and general style bore a marked resemblance to Joe Hardstaff with whom he played in his early years for the county.

[Editor]

Although it is not known when cricket was first played in Nottinghamshire there are records of a match in 1771 between Nottingham and Sheffield, which suggests that the game had already flourished in the county for many years. Between 1771 and 1867 twenty-eight matches are known to have taken place between the two towns, Nottingham winning 17, Sheffield eight and the remaining three drawn. Unfortunately, it cannot be said that the spirit of the game was high in the list of priorities in these matches, many of which were played for money and the rivalry being keen, bad blood and ill feeling often resulted.

M.C.C. come to Nottingham

Not even the dates of the inauguration or disbandment of the Nottingham Old Club have survived, but in 1791 an event occurred which must be regarded as a red letter mark in the county's history for in August of that year they were visited by the M.C.C. Although this now famous club had been in existence for only four years its fame had spread from one end of the country to the other, and even then its position as the recognised head of the game was firmly established. On this occasion, although the play of the Nottinghamshire cricketers excited the admiration and applause of their opponents they were nevertheless defeated by ten wickets, being unacquainted with the system of playing adopted by the Marylebone Club.

The first captain of the Nottingham club was J. Gilbert and perhaps one of the first of a long line of outstanding players was Thomas Warsop, an under-hand bowler, who continued for many years.

The Father of Nottinghamshire Cricket

It was not until 1817, in June, that Nottinghamshire had another great day in cricket. This was when the M.C.C. sent Eleven players to play Twenty-two of Nottingham. This match aroused tremendous interest and was witnessed by 12,000 to 14,000 spectators, who paid admission charges of 2*s.* 6*d* per day. The game was again won by the M.C.C., by 30 runs. Making his second appearance for Nottinghamshire was a young player named William Clarke, then 18 years of age, and destined to become one of the outstanding personalities of Nottinghamshire and English cricket. In this particular game he scored 1 and 0 and as far as can be judged did not bowl. However, no-one in the history of Nottinghamshire cricket has stood out more prominently than William Clarke, the celebrated slow bowler, who captained the Nottingham team and, practically unaided, for many years conducted all affairs respecting the county's cricket.

He established the Trent Bridge ground, and lastly, founded and led the All England Eleven which did so much missionary work for the game. There is no doubt that he will always be recalled as one of the game's chief characters and exponents, and his career was an unusually long and busy one. He was actually 37 when he first played at Lord's and it was not until he was 47 that he was chosen for the Players. That was in the year 1846, but all in all for 30 years he was a terror to batsmen.

Near the main gates erected in 1933 to the memory of J. A. Dixon, captain of Nottinghamshire for many years, is this inscription:

> "THIS THE COUNTY GROUND OF THE NOTTINGHAMSHIRE CRICKET CLUB, FAMOUS THROUGHOUT THE WORLD AS 'TRENT BRIDGE', WAS ORIGINALLY A MEADOW ADJOINING THE OLD TRENT BRIDGE INN AT THE TIME WHEN ITS LANDLORD WAS WILLIAM CLARKE, THE INCOMPARABLE SLOW BOWLER, LATER TO EARN THE HONOURED TITLE OF 'FATHER OF NOTTINGHAMSHIRE CRICKET.' THE GROUND, PREPARED BY HIM, WAS OPENED ON MAY 28, 1838. THE FIRST INTER-COUNTY CONTEST TO BE FOUGHT HERE BEING BETWEEN NOTTINGHAMSHIRE AND SUSSEX ON JULY 27 AND 28, 1840. SINCE WHEN AS THE SCENE OF NOTTINGHAMSHIRE MATCHES AND TEST MATCHES ITS HISTORY HAS BEEN STEADILY ILLUSTRIOUS."

During Clarke's reign another great Notts player emerged, Tom Barker, one of the first of a line of fast bowlers produced by Nottinghamshire. In 1834 he had the distinction of being the first Nottinghamshire man to play in the Gentlemen v. Players match, and continued to represent the latter until 1845.

According to available records the first match to be played at Trent Bridge was on May 28, 1838, between The Forest Club and the South of the Trent; the spectators were charged an admission fee of sixpence, which was much resented by the Forest Club whose spectators were allowed to watch them on the Forest free.

The Lion of the North

After William Clarke's death the All England Eleven was managed by George Parr, who next to Clarke was one of the greatest influences in Nottinghamshire cricket and was sometimes referred to as "The Lion of the North". He is immortal by reason of his leg-side hitting, which often landed the ball out of the ground, but more often than not in an elm which still stands at Trent Bridge and is affectionately known as Parr's Tree.

Next to Parr as an outstanding personality in those early days was Richard Daft, who was considered a model for the young cricketers. He was an outstanding fielder, and athlete, and a leading batsman of the time, but the actual successor to William Clarke in the bowling line was considered to be Alfred Shaw, who first played for Nottinghamshire in 1864 and whose chief asset was his great control of length and pace. Apparently he had no superior in the way of stamina and accuracy. Like many opening bowlers a large number of his great feats were accomplished with another great bowler of his day, Fred Morley, one of the mainstays of Nottinghamshire until 1884, when he died at the early age of 33, not long after touring Australia.

Morley had no successor as a fast bowler until the arrival of Tom Wass in 1896, except for the brief appearance of Frank Shacklock who made a name for himself by bowling out Surrey at The Oval in 1892 when Nottinghamshire won. To mark this shining event everyone on the winning side was given a medal and each of the professionals twenty guineas. Over 60,000 people watched this match on the first two days.

Hallam and Wass

Tom Wass, on his day, was considered to be the most deadly bowler in England and during his career took more wickets than any one else in the county's history, 1,679. During most of his illustrious reign the bowler at the other end was Hallam, who, with his gentle pace, provided the contrast, and the combination of Hallam and Wass became a byword with the cricketers of Nottinghamshire.

William Gunn and Shrewsbury

Returning to batsmen, one of the most famous of an impressive list of great Nottinghamshire cricketers was Arthur Shrewsbury, who came into the side in 1875 at the age of 19 and continued to play until 1902. It was said that "W.G." was his only superior, which gives some idea of his fame in those distant years. Soon the famous partnership of Gunn and Shrewsbury was formed, and they still hold the record for the highest opening partnership for Nottinghamshire; 398 against Sussex at Trent Bridge in 1890. Shrewsbury's partner, the giant William Gunn, played for his county from 1880 to 1905, when he was succeeded by his nephews, John Gunn, the slow bowler and left-handed all-rounder, and George Gunn, his brother. Between 1895 and 1925, John Gunn made 24,601 runs, took 1,243 wickets and held 233 catches, and like many great bowlers it was said of him that on grounds which helped him he was unplayable.

George Gunn's Wonderful Record

George Gunn, perhaps the most famous of all the Nottinghamshire batsmen, made 35,190 runs, the highest number ever reached by a Nottinghamshire cricketer and one that may well stand for all time. He was everything a batsman could be and simply played as the mood took him. Sometimes a stone-waller, sometimes pure virtuoso and sometimes, as one umpire said, he would go to sleep. Typical of the man was the occasion when the lunch hour at Trent Bridge was changed from 1.30 p.m. to 2 p.m. Almost the first time the new hours were used George happened to be still batting at 1.30 p.m. and when he saw the clock immediately started to walk towards the pavilion at the end of the appropriate over. When it was pointed out to him that lunch was at 2 p.m., he returned to the crease, gave a dolly of a catch, and walked out with the remark, "I always take my lunch at 1.30 p.m.", and this when his score was in the 90's.

Returning for a moment to the combination of William Gunn and Shrewsbury, their partnerships were particularly fruitful at Hove, where it used to be said that if Nottinghamshire won the toss all except the first four players felt free to go down to the sea to bathe. Shrewsbury's defensive powers, coupled with his inexhaustible patience, were undoubtedly the chief factors of his greatness, although his late cutting and back play were considered as near perfection as possible, and he had a favourite lofting stroke over mid-off's head which frequently brought him a couple of runs.

It was considered that because of the tactics used against him by the bowlers of his day, who apparently acknowledged him as their master, he was regarded as a slow player. Here it is interesting to note, bearing in mind the present-day theories for the causes of slow play, that it was stated in an article in 1892 regarding Shrewsbury's slow play "That runs are much more difficult to obtain now than formerly on account of the bowlers' off theory (note 'off' theory). . . . more attractive and all round cricket would be seen if bowlers would try and hit the wicket, instead of deliberately trying to miss it."

Alfred Shaw

It was also said at that time that the critics quite overlooked the fact that bowlers, just as readily as batsmen, can make play dull and uninteresting (modern captains and bowlers please note). It is interesting also to dwell on the remarks of Alfred Shaw that same year. This wise old player believed that the loss of appreciation of good play was due in part to the excitement provided for spectators at football matches and he commented, "It will not be a good day for English cricket when batsmen are required to assimilate their style to the aspirations of the ignoramus who thinks the higher the hit the better the cricket, and who yells his approval or boos his discontent accordingly." Interesting to know that cricket had such difficulties in 1892 and that comments such as this had to be made.

Alfred Shaw, who first played for Nottinghamshire in 1864 and continued for 23 years, was one of the greatest of all Nottinghamshire bowlers. He bowled medium pace and could turn the ball either way. Throughout his career he never sent down a wide, over half the number of overs he bowled were maidens and he accomplished the unique feat of bowling more overs to batsmen than they took runs off him. He set up a record by clean bowling "W.G." twenty times and was the first captain to lead a county in four successive years to the top of the Championship, 1883–86.

As Nottinghamshire's cricket is at the moment in the doldrums it is interesting to read an article written by the Editor of this illustrious Almanack in 1901, "The outlook for Notts in the future is not hopeful and the committee must use every possible effort to discover fresh talent. For the decreased skill amongst the young players all over the county it is thought that the immense popularity of football is in some measure responsible. Cricket is now being played in the various villages and small towns with less eagerness and enthusiasm than was once the case." The present Nottinghamshire committee should take heart from this because after that was written Nottinghamshire had some of their greatest years.

A player who should be mentioned along with William Gunn and Shrewsbury and who performed many great batting feats with this celebrated pair was William Barnes, also a fine bowler, who toured Australia three times, and who in his day was considered probably the best player of fast bowling on a hard wicket.

The First Noted Left-Hander

The first left-handed batsman of note to play for Nottinghamshire was William Henry Scotton. After starting his career as a fast scorer and hard hitter, he became the most pronounced stone-waller of his day. On one occasion in 1885 when playing for Nottinghamshire against Gloucestershire he batted for sixty minutes without scoring and in his side's innings of 291 there were 165 maidens. Nevertheless he visited Australia three times.

In 1887 and 1888 Nottinghamshire were captained by that famous wicket-keeper, Mordecai Sherwin, the last professional to do so for over 70 years. The first amateur to take control, in 1889, was J. A. Dixon, who led the team for the following ten years and in whose commemoration, as I have already mentioned, the main gates at Trent Bridge were built. In 1892 one of the most famous amateurs in the history of the game came into the side. That was A. O. Jones, who eventually formed another of those renowned opening partnerships with James Iremonger, and they proceeded to reach the hundred on no fewer than 24 occasions. Jones was a fine fielder, particularly in the gully, and his tally of catches for Nottinghamshire was over 500. His top score was 296. Iremonger played for the county from 1897 until 1921, when he became the coach until the late 30's, a position he held with great distinction, being recognised as the finest coach the county have ever had.

Spirit of the Game

It is interesting to note the philosophy regarding Nottinghamshire cricket in the period between 1890 and 1900. The side ran into rather lean times and many people boldly asserted that unenterprising tactics were responsible for the lack of public support. Nevertheless, it was agreed that if a team had to choose between losing prettily and endeavouring to avoid defeat by painstaking play, the captain was thoroughly justified in adopting the latter course. So much for the spirit of the game in those days!

A most disheartening year for Nottinghamshire was 1895 when the team sank to a lower level than at any previous period in the club's history; the cricket shown was considered utterly unworthy of a side with such great traditions. Between 1873 and 1889 Nottinghamshire won the County Championship six times and shared the Championship on four other occasions. In March 1895, the club made an important appointment when they secured the services of Mr. H. Turner as secretary. He displayed much energy and under his skilful guidance the club's position improved in every respect, and apart from an increased membership and a healthier financial state, he was mainly responsible for an innovation in April 1897 that had a considerable bearing on cricket itself. An attempt was made to train young players. A staff of bowlers was attached to the ground and coached by Mr. Walter Marshall—a policy which proved most gratifying in its success almost from the moment of its inception.

One of the leading bowlers during this depressing period of Nottinghamshire's cricket was William Attewell. He alone was really reliable and did a tremendous amount of work, often taking twice as many wickets as any other bowler and at a smaller cost. Shortly after the turn of the century there appeared two more players destined to join the ranks of the more famous Nottinghamshire cricketers, Thomas William Oates, the wicket-keeper, and Joseph Hardstaff, father of perhaps an even more famous Hardstaff, young Joe. For sometime it was assumed that Hardstaff senior's short stature would prevent him from developing into a first-rate player, but fortunately he was persevered with and consequently served his county and country for many years, later becoming a famous umpire.

Alletson's Famous Innings

Other names to hit the headlines before World War One were Wilfred Payton, an extremely sound player for the county for very many years, and, in particular, Edward Alletson. He achieved renown as one of the most vigorous hitters in the game and became nationally famous in 1911 for his innings of 189 out of 227 runs against Sussex at Hove in only ninety minutes. During this innings he took 34 runs off E. H. Killick in one over. Unfortunately, his successes with the bat were very rare and he lasted for only about seven seasons. Still he had been connected with the side that won the Championship again in 1907, but success on this occasion was entirely the result of the tremendous bowling of Hallam and Wass. Hallam took 156 wickets at 12.18 apiece, and Wass at 14.28 apiece.

Immense Batting Power

For sixteen years after World War One, Nottinghamshire were always well placed in the County Championship, which they won in 1929. In the early twenties they had a very strong batting side, including Arthur Carr, the captain, Whysall, Walker, George and John Gunn, Payton and Hardstaff senior. The chief bowlers at that time were burly Fred Barratt, Matthews, Sam Staples, the great off-spin bowler, and "Tich" Richmond, the leg-break bowler who season after season took his hundred wickets and held the record for the greatest numbers of wickets in a season for the county until the advent of Bruce Dooland.

Larwood and Voce

During this period the groundsman was Walter Marshall, a character, who created pitches that were very fast and very true, the back-cloth for great fast bowlers, which were of tremendous assistance to one of the finest and perhaps easily the most famous of Nottinghamshire fast bowlers, Harold Larwood, who made his first appearance in 1925. Not long afterwards he was joined by Bill

Voce, a devastating fast left-arm bowler, and with such a combination Nottinghamshire simply had to win the Championship sooner or later. It was, indeed, surprising that it happened only once whilst Nottinghamshire had this very great side. Eventually the acrimonious body-line controversy led to the retirement of Arthur Carr and had much to do with Larwood leaving first-class cricket when he did.

In 1935 Nottinghamshire were jointly led by S. D. Rhodes and G. F. H. Heane, but thereafter the latter captained them until 1947, when he was superseded by W. A. Sime. After winning the Championship in 1929 Nottinghamshire suffered a gradual decline in their fortunes, due to a very noticeable falling off in the standard of bowling, and although the batting was still well above average with the great success of a new generation of batsmen in Keeton and Harris, who made a fine opening pair, and the beautifully upright, straight-hitting Joe Hardstaff, no new bowlers could be found apart from Harold Butler. Hardstaff could not help but enthrall anyone who watched him play. His record but for the War would have been tremendous, and as it was he scored 31,841 runs, made 83 centuries, averaged 44.34 and played in 23 Test matches—a wonderful record.

Harold Butler did sterling work for Nottinghamshire but apart from Test matches against South Africa in this country and the ill-fated Tour of the West Indies in 1947, he never received the recognition that his bowling really warranted. Probably doubts regarding his fitness were the major factors. The combination of Butler and Jepson served Nottinghamshire well for many years but their bowling, particularly that of the latter, had not really the penetration to raise the side from the lower rungs of the table, and it was not until the advent of Bruce Dooland, from Australia that this occurred.

Dooland's Influence

This was the first time Nottinghamshire had broken with tradition and engaged a player from overseas However, with his extremely accurate leg-spin bowling, coupled with his wrong 'un and "flipper" he completely mesmerised the majority of batsmen in this country—in fact all of them in his first two years—with the result that Notts jumped from next to the bottom in the Championship to eighth place in his first year and in his second year there was a further improvement. Dooland achieved the double in 1955 and 1957, and created a Nottinghamshire record of 181 wickets in a season. His decision to return to Australia at the end of the 1957 season was a very big blow to the club, and the following years were mostly a time of lamentation and woe, the biggest disappointment to many being the fact that no young players from the county itself were showing promise.

The only bright spot in recent years was the success of Brian Bolus, obtained under special registration from Yorkshire, who scored 2,190 runs and was selected for the last two Test matches against the West Indies in 1963. His fine attacking batsmanship had a wonderful tonic on the side and they finished ninth in the Championship. Unfortunately this improvement has not been maintained and Nottinghamshire are once again in the throes of team building for there is still great faith in the future of Nottinghamshire cricket.

Finally, some words on Trent Bridge. It is the considered opinion of many lovers of cricket that no great cricket ground in these islands has a more charming situation than that of Trent Bridge. The accommodation and amenities for public and players alike are more than ample. The playing area exceeds six and a half acres and the wicket is one of the best, if not the best, in the country. During its existence the ground has been the scene of many very stern and heroic contests, helping to make cricket history. A match which provided a perfect example of the fact that the wicket is not so entirely one-sided as some would have us believe was the match played against the Australians in 1921. Nottinghamshire were bowled out for scores of 58 and 100, whilst Australia, thanks to a famous innings of 345 scored in four hours by Macartney, amassed the huge total of 675.

Ever since the ground was established Nottinghamshire players have been extremely fortunate in having had the opportunity to play their cricket on such a wonderful piece of turf. There was actually a period shortly after the last war when the label "featherbed" was attached to the wicket, but that was often proved erroneous by the outstanding performance of many bowlers, especially from overseas. However, since the re-turfing took place in the late '50s to dispense with the marl, it has proved to be an excellent cricket wicket, culminating in the fact that in 1966 it was considered by all to be the best in the country.

COUNTY HISTORIES IN WISDEN

Derbyshire, 1953, by W. T. Taylor
Essex, 1960, by Charles Bray
Glamorgan, 1949, by J. H. Morgan
Gloucestershire, 1957, by H. F. Hutt
Hampshire, 1952, by E. D. R. Eagar
Kent, 1966, by R. L. Arrowsmith
Lancashire, 1951, by Neville Cardus
Leicestershire, 1964, by Brian Chapman
Middlesex, 1965, by I. A. R. Peebles
Northamptonshire, 1958, by James D. Coldham
Nottinghamshire, 1967, by R. T. Simpson
Somerset, 1959, by Eric Hill
Surrey, 1946, by H. D. G. Leveson Gower.
Sussex, 1954, by A. E. R. Gilligan
Warwickshire, 1950, by M.F.K. Fraser
Worcestershire, 1963, by Noel Stone
Yorkshire, 1955, by J. M. Kilburn

INDIAN CRICKET—ITS PROBLEMS AND PLAYERS

By DICKY RUTNAGUR, the noted Indian Cricket Writer

Of all the forms of their culture the British brought to India, none thrust its roots as deep as cricket. Though India has dominated international hockey for almost four decades, cricket is far more a part of the national scene than the only team game at which we have been world champions.

Growing audiences at Test matches do not alone indicate the extent of cricket's popularity in the country. More significant is the appreciable rise each year in the number of clubs and tournaments at all levels—a sure sign that the game is constantly recruiting more players.

The only pity is that cricket in India, for social and economic reasons, will always be an urban game and its growth, therefore, is in peril of being retarded by the shortage of grounds in the over-crowded towns and cities. This handicap must be overcome if the enthusiasm for the game is to be reflected truly in playing standards at the highest level.

Finance, fortunately, has been no problem in recent years. A succession of tours has made for the accumulation of large reserves and the enthusiasm whipped up by Test cricket has spread to Ranji Trophy matches which, in many places, are more largely attended than at any time since the war. Of course, the money taken at these games is not sufficient to support the whole structure of the game, but at least there is plenty left over from Test match receipts to develop cricket at school and university level.

The continuance of this happy state of affairs depends largely on the 1967 Indian team. They tour both England and Australia within the year and if they take back sizeable returns, the Government of India will in future be more free in sanctioning foreign exchange for inward tours and minor tours abroad, like the proposed Colts' visit to England two years ago, which never came off because sterling was not made available.

Their approach, even more than results, will bring the Indians the goodwill they need. Their undoing on the last two visits was their outlook, and I have always felt that better cricket could have been extracted from both the 1952 and 1959 sides by captains more imaginative than Hazare and Gaekwad.

Some of the more successful members of the 1959 party have now bowed out, and few really exciting players have since emerged. Durani, a genius if ever there was one, faded away too quickly after two triumphant series, in 1961–62. An unfortunate accident deprived India of the full value of Pataudi's flair. Chandrasekhar has had greater days, but being a sort of "mystery" bowler, his effectiveness tends to wane with the progress of a series. His worth would have been greater if he were part of a strong bowling combination and could have been bowled in shorter spells. Venkataraghavan, whose experience is yet limited, is a gifted off-spinner, and the fortunes of the team in England will largely hinge on his success.

This stock-taking, however, does not leave me utterly pessimistic. Far from it. It is strange, but often a side without great names excels on tour, and I know there is material available which a shrewd and understanding captain could mould into a fine team.

India's Test fortunes have been mixed during the eight years since they were last in England. In this span, they have played six series at home and one abroad, and of the 32 Tests involved, five were won and eight lost, while 19 were drawn. India won two of the seven series, and lost two.

This is by no means a glittering record, but certainly more striking than what was achieved in earlier years. The ratio between defeats and wins is small, but considering that no part was played by the weather, the large proportion of unfinished matches is depressing. I saw every one of these 19 draws, and by my estimate, at least half of them did no credit to the approach of the players.

In the one series played abroad, West Indies beat India 5–0, a fate similar to that we suffered in England, in 1959. But to be fair to the vanquished, the similarity between the two calamities ended with this statistic. In the West Indies, there were times when the Indians played very enjoyable cricket, and, far from implying that they ever had a chance of beating one of the three greatest Test teams of all time, I thought they were a singularly unlucky side.

Among the five Tests won, two victories in successive matches gave India their first rubber against England, in the winter of 1961–62; Australia were beaten once in each of two series, while the fifth win was over New Zealand.

Considering that the English and Australian sides beaten on these occasions were a lot more formidable than England in India (1951–52), the Pakistanis of 1962 and the New Zealanders of 1955, who gave India their five earlier wins, one would be inclined to believe that the cream of Indian cricketing talent between 1959 and 1964 was richer than ever before. Frankly, I would not give expression to such a thought for fear of being laughed at, but there is no denying that latterly we have marshalled our resources more capably than at other times.

Not many months ago, some of us sat round to pick an Indian team of all-time greats. Anybody who has indulged in this popular pastime knows how much argument it can produce, but on this occasion, the matter was settled quickly, tempers were not roused and few claims were greatly disputed. The team decided was:

V. M. MERCHANT, S. WAZIR ALI, L. AMARNATH, V. S. HAZARE, V. L. MANJREKAR, C. K. NAYUDU, VINOO MANKAD, L. AMARSINGH, N. S. TAMHANE, M. NISSAR, S. P. GUPTE.

To touch briefly on the discussions that prefaced this nomination, all except Wazir Ali, Manjrekar and Tamhane were selected unanimously. Mushtaq Ali for Wazir Ali and B. E. Kapadia or D. D. Hindlekar for Tamhane were the alternatives proposed, while there was a claim for Umrigar to be preferred to Manjrekar on his merit as a close fielder. Indeed Umrigar's omission was embarrassing to all concerned and a postscript to the "selection" was that on certain wickets, Ghulum Ahmed would be more valuable than Gupte.

Thus, be it noted, of the 16 players who came into reckoning, nine first played for India before the war, and from amongst the others, Mankad and Hazare would have been capped in the 30's, had there been occasion; in fact, they both first appeared in unofficial "Tests" in 1937, against Lord Tennyson's team. Ghulam Ahmed made his mark only just afterwards, and to be very precise, recent or contemporary talent is represented only by Manjrekar, Gupte and Tamhane.

It is logical to ask why, if the pre-war maestros were such giants, India's star did not shine more brightly in their time. The answers, without going too deeply into the background, are that firstly, there was not enough first-class cricket in India in their day to prepare them fully for Test cricket. It must be remembered that the Ranji Trophy tournament was not instituted till 1934–35. Secondly, the cast supporting the stars was hardly ever the best available, for patronage in those days dictated selection.

India's first Test tour to England was in 1932, when they were allotted just one Test. The tour as a whole was more successful than any other India have made here, except perhaps the one in 1946. The Test match was lost by 158 runs, but it began with England losing three wickets for 29, and that was not the last crisis they had to survive before victory was sighted. It needs to be noted that India were without Merchant, then only 21, but already a heavy scorer at home, and L. P. Jai, who came in 1936 as almost a veteran. Both were selected, but could not make themselves available.

However, Lord's, the public and the press did not judge the 1932 side in terms of wins and losses. They rather looked on Indian cricket as a rough diamond, and welcomed the team's dashing approach. This image of the Indians being happy, natural cricketers was created mainly by C. K. Nayudu, a man of tremendous bearing, whose batting was stylish and immensely virile. There was gushing admiration for the bowling of Amarsingh and Nissar, one of the fastest bowlers of his time. Amarsingh, at medium-fast, was not only compared to Tate, but was described by many leading batsmen of the time as the finest bowler to visit England since World War I. These great cricketers gave India a magnificent start in the international sphere and before passing to later events, one should mention that the 1932 side were superb in the field, an attribute applied to few Indian sides afterwards.

Two winters later, India played England at home and lost the series, but not without honour. However, when they came back to England in 1936, they not only failed to advance their reputation, but completely destroyed the image the 1932 team had left behind.

Never has any side done itself less justice than that unfortunate 1936 team. This is hardly the occasion to go into the sordid details of the incidents that wrecked the tour, but lest the poor cricketers of the time be saddled with all the blame, it should be recorded that the whole venture was doomed at the moment the captain was selected. The dismissal from the team of L. Amarnath led to a commission inquiring into the failure of the tour, and Sir John Beaumont, then Chief Justice of Bombay, who was the one-man tribunal, came to the conclusion that the good prince of Vizianagram was no born leader of men.

An unofficial series against Lord Tennyson's team, in the winter of 1937–38, and then Indian cricket was pushed into isolation by the war. The next contact with cricketers from abroad was eight years later, when we were visited by the Australian Services. In the meanwhile the game in India was given a new concept by the batting rivalry between the two Vijays, Merchant and Hazare, and we entered an era of high scoring. This period also saw an *en masse* invasion of the scene by spinners, and the ranks of the fast bowlers grew thinner and thinner.

Bradman, Hammond and Hutton never played in India, but their batting records in the years immediately preceding the war had an undeniable influence on Vijay Merchant. He was a batsman with strokes, who in full flight was a delight to watch. But he seemed to believe that the only way to fame was through making enormous scores. The rising batsman of the day, Vijay Hazare, also cast himself in the same mould and every time either Merchant or Hazare went to the wicket, he looked upon his innings as an opportunity to outdo the other. Of course, this trend was encouraged by the perfect wickets at India's new cricket headquarters, the Brabourne Stadium, where both played so many matches.

It was inevitable that other batsmen, too, aimed for high scores and, as a result, cricket as a team game suffered, for the interest of the side was transcended by personal ambition. And when batsmen of lesser talent than Merchant and Hazare set out to make colossal scores, cricket became slower and less spectacular.

If Indian batsmen score slowly on occasions to-day, it is not that they are still under the spell of the exploits of Merchant and Hazare. More often than not, they are inhibited by the knowledge that our bowling resources are frighteningly thin and that any score less than 300 would lead to disaster.

Many theories have been advanced to explain the rarity of top class bowlers in India to-day. There is substance in each of them, but none is wholly true. It is claimed that with a large chunk of north India going to Pakistan, we have lost the biggest breeding ground of fast bowlers. If so, where are the Nissars in the Pakistan team to-day? Then they say that slow, unresponsible wickets have taken away the incentive from the bowler. But then, our wickets were not all that dead till about six years ago and moreover, there are wickets elsewhere which are not much quicker. In fact, I remember Garfield Sobers telling me during a radio interview in Bombay, immediately after the West Indies' historic tour of Australia, that except Perth, he did not think most Australian wickets were faster than the ones he knew in India.

These theories are not without foundation, but the real cause, I feel, lies deeper. Generally speaking, there is not the strength of will to work assiduously at a task that is exacting and usually less rewarding than that of the batsman in the conditions that obtain.

To take one more glimpse into the past, three Indian teams came to England before 1932. The first two were really private tours by the Parsees, the first Indians to be lured to the game. They found themselves utterly out of their depth, and in analysing their failures, a great cricketer of the time said that the Parsee batsmen were overwhelmed because they tried to hit every ball they received out of sight.

Poor, unsophisticated souls. They lacked guile and science, but there could not have been a keener band of cricketers, and all they sought from the game was the enjoyment of playing it.

This spirit did not desert India's cricketers immediately they learnt its grammar and discovered its intricacies. Till even a few years ago, we were blessed with players like Nayudu, Amarsingh, Mushtaq Ali and Nissar.

Nayudu's brilliance has been immortalised in some delightfully romantic passages by Mr. Cardus, tributes of one genius to another. I wish the 1967 tourists would read them, not just as literature, but as a reminder of their heritage.

SOME DATES IN INDIAN CRICKET HISTORY

Compiled by Rowland Bowen

1721 Cricket played by mariners of the East India Company's ships at Cambay.

1792 The Calcutta Cricket Club already in existence (perhaps the second oldest cricket club in the world) as a match was played against Barrackpore and Dum Dum.

1797 Cricket being played in Bombay.
1804 First recorded century in India: 102 by Robert Vansittart for Old Etonians v. Rest of Calcutta.
1840 Indians known to be taking part in cricket matches.
1846 Madras Cricket Club formed.
1847 Cricket being played in Karachi.
1848 Parsis in Bombay form Orient C.C.
c. 1850 Cricket being regularly played in Lahore.
1854 First known publication on cricket in India—"Calcutta Cricket Club matches 1844–54"—this is also the first known book of scores outside the British Isles.
1864 First known match between Madras and Calcutta.
1866 Hindus in Bombay form the Union C.C.
1867 First known instructional book on cricket in Hindi: the same book translated into Urdu in 1868: both were published in Agra, United Provinces.
1872 First recorded double century in India: 228 by Private Sheiring at Shahjehanpur.
1878–9 Proposed Parsi tours to England, and to Australia, fell through.
1880 First total of over 600 made in India: 678 by Bolan Pass XI v. Subordinates, at Peshawar.
1883 Muslims in Bombay form Mohammedan C.C. (became Muslim Gymkhana in 1893).
1884 First match between Bombay Gymkhana (Europeans) and Parsi Gymkhana: latter won by innings and 38 runs. From this encounter developed the Bombay Presidency matches and later Tournaments.
1886 First Indian team to tour overseas—Parsi Gentlemen to U.K.
1888 Second tour by Parsi Gentlemen to U.K.
1888–9 First tour by English team—G. F. Vernon's XI.
1889 First known instructional book on cricket in Marathi—published in Baroda.
1890 Parsi Cricket Club formed in Shanghai: probably the first Indian cricket club to be established outside India.
1891 H.H. Maharao Umedsinghji of Kotah became first Indian to take all ten wickets in an innings (at Mayo College).
1892 First Presidency match in Bombay—Europeans v. Parsis.
1892–3 Second tour by English team, Lord Hawke's: won the only representative match.
1894 Hindu Gymkhana formed in Bombay.
1896 Badeshi Ram became first Indian to score double century (219) in India.
1898 K. S. Ranjitsinhji and Colonel K. M. Mistri became first Indians to make a partnership of over 300 (376)—for Patiala v. Ambala.
1902–3 Third tour by English team to India: Oxford University Authentics, who established a new Indian record by scoring 696 v. Peshawar.
1904 Proposed All India tour to England fell through after fixtures agreed, for financial reasons.
1905 First score of over 300 in India: 309 by G. H. S. Fowke at Peshawar.
1906 First representative match between Hindus and Parsis at Bombay: Hindus won.
1907 Bombay Tournament became triangular with admission of Hindus.
1908 First Presidency match in Madras—Europeans v. Indians. The match lapsed until 1915 when it was revived, and played regularly until 1946.
1911 First All India team toured England.
1912 Bombay Tournament became Quadrangular with admission of Muslims.
1914 P. N. Polishwalla published first of his many publications on cricket, all of which partook of the nature of cricket annuals and some of which were so entitled: last of eight was published in 1934.
1916 Sind Tournament first played: Parsis beat Hindus. Revived in 1919, the tournament was played in most years up to 1946–7, and was revived after partition (see "Some Dates in Pakistan Cricket History", 1950–1).
1922 First visit to India of team of South African Indians.
First All India cricket tournament at New Delhi, won by Maharajah of Patiala's XI. The tournament was played in most years until the early 1930s.

1922–3 Lahore Quadrangular Tournament instituted: first winners Europeans. This tournament was subsequently played only in 1924, 1925, 1926, 1928 and 1939.
1926 India admitted to Imperial Cricket Conference.
1926–7 First visit by M.C.C. team (fourth visit by English team) to India: in two representative matches, M.C.C. beat All India, but could only draw with All India (Indians).
1927 The Indian Cricket Board of Control formed in April.
1929 First score of over 700 made in India, 726 by 4/7th Dragoon Guards.
1930–1 Moin-ud-Dowlah Tournament instituted: first-class at the start, it deteriorated and eventually ceased to be played but was revived in 1962.
1931 In April the first Indian cricket magazine commenced—*Illustrated Cricket & Sporting News*: name changed in 1932 to *Indian Cricketer* but did not last beyond 1933.
1932 Second tour by All India to England: lost the only Test played.
1932–3 First tour by All Ceylon to India: drew both unofficial Tests.
1933–4 D. R. Havewalla scored 515, the record for all grades of Indian cricket. His team was thereby enabled to make 721 (the highest score hitherto by an Indian team) in reply to its opponents 446, and to win by an innings. Second tour by M.C.C.: won two Tests and drew the other.
1934 First issue of a fresh Indian cricket magazine, in October: *Indian Cricket*, a well produced publication, which however ceased shortly after the outbreak of war in 1939.
1934–5 Ranji Trophy instituted: first winners Bombay (who have won it seven times to 1965–6).
1935–6 Rohinton Baria Tournament instituted for inter-University cricket: not first-class. The Marajah of Patiala sponsored the first (unofficial) tour by Australians to India: won two and drew two of the unofficial Tests.
1936 Third tour by All India to England. Lost two Tests and drew the other.
1936–7 Proposed tour to New Zealand by Nawanagar led by Jam Sahib fell through at last moment.
1937–8 Bombay Tournament became Pentangular with the admission of "The Rest". This tournament lasted until 1945–6 in communal form, and for two more seasons thereafter as a non-communal tournament. Sixth tour by an English team, Lord Tennyson's: won two and lost three unofficial tests.
1939–40 *Crickinia* Indian Cricketers Annual made its debut: lasted six issues, last 1944–5.
1940 Maharashtra made 798 v. Northern India at Poona, establishing a fresh Indian record.
1940–1 Second tour by All Ceylon: lost one and drew the other of two unofficial tests.
1944–5 First tour by All India to Ceylon: drew the unofficial test.
1945–6 Australian Services toured India, the second Australian team to do so: won one and drew two of the unofficial tests. Holkar made 212 for eight v. Mysore and thus established the record innings total for India in any grade of cricket.
1946 Fourth tour by All India to England: lost one and drew the other two Tests. In scoring 249 for the last wicket v. Surrey, C. T. Sarwate and S. N. Bannerjee, numbers ten and eleven who each scored centuries, established a record for that wicket in England and in other respects performed a feat unlikely to be easily surpassed.
1946–7 The world record partnership for the fourth wicket established by V. S. Hazare and Gul Mohammed—557 unbroken for Baroda v. Holkar. The annual *Indian Cricket* instituted—now in its 20th edition.
1947–8 First tour to Australia by a team representing undivided India, although it took place after partition: four Tests lost and one drawn.
1948–9 First tour to India by West Indies: won one and drew four Tests. B. B. Nimbalkar in making the record first-class score of 443* for Maharastra v. Kathiawar, assisted in establishing the world record partnership of 455 for the second wicket.

1949–50 First Commonwealth tour to India: won two, lost one and drew two of the unofficial tests.
1950–1 Second Commonwealth tour to India: lost two and drew three of the unofficial tests.
1951–2 Third M.C.C. tour to India: won one, lost one and drew three Tests. India's first victory in an official Test was at Madras.
1952 First tour to England by post-partition India (fifth in all): lost three and drew one Test.
1952–3 First tour to India by Pakistan: won one, lost two and drew two Tests.
1953 First tour to West Indies by India: lost one and drew four Tests.
1953–4 Third Commonwealth tour to India: won two, lost one and drew two of the unofficial tests.
1954–5 First tour to Pakistan by India: drew all five Tests.
1955–6 First tour by New Zealand to India: lost two and drew three Tests.
1956 First tour to India by official Australian team (third in all): won two and drew one Test.
1956–7 Second tour by All India to Ceylon: drew the only unofficial test.
1957 Sunder C.C. of Bombay—a strong combination with many first-class players—toured East Africa and lost v. Combined East Africa.
1957–8 *Indian Cricket-Field Annual* first appeared: eight issues in all, last for 1964–5.
1958–9 Second tour by West Indies to India: won three and drew two Tests.
1959 Sixth tour to England by India: lost all five Tests.
1959–60 Second official tour by Australians to India: won two, lost one and drew two Tests.
First tour by Indian Starlets, to Pakistan: a team of young Indian cricketers sent for experience.
1960 Second tour by an Indian team to East Africa: Gujarat C.A. (a contender in the Ranji Trophy)—lost one and drew two matches v. Combined East Africa.
1960–1 Second tour by Pakistan to India: drew all five Tests.
1961–2 A cricket annual appeared in Gujarati.
Duleep Trophy instituted for inter-zonal competition: first winners, West Zone.
Fourth M.C.C. tour to India: lost two and drew three Tests.
1962 Second tour by India to West Indies: lost all five Tests.
Moin-ud-Dowlah Gold Cup Tournament successfully revived.
1963–4 Fifth M.C.C. tour to India: all five Tests drawn.
1964 Third unofficial tour by Australia to India: won one, lost one and drew one Test.
1964–5 Third tour by All Ceylon to India: won one and lost two unofficial tests.
1965 Second tour by New Zealand to India: lost one and drew three Tests.
1965–6 First tour by English schoolboys to India, members of the London Schools Cricket Association: drew four and lost the fifth match against All-India schools.
1966–7 Third tour by West Indies to India.
1967 First official tour to East Africa by an Indian team.
Seventh tour to U.K. by India: three five-day Tests to be played.

TEST CAREERS OF INDIAN PLAYERS

STATISTICS by STANLEY CONDER

BATTING and BOWLING

	M.	I.	N.O.	Runs	H.S.	Aver.	Ct.	Runs	Wkts.	Aver.
Adhikari, H. R.	21	36	8	872	114	31.14	8	82	3	27.33
Ali, S. Nazir	2	4	0	30	13	7.25	–	83	4	20.75
Ali, S. Wazir	7	14	0	237	42	16.92	1	25	0	—
Amarnath, L.	24	40	4	878	118	24.38	13	1481	45	32.91
Amar Singh	7	14	1	292	51	22.46	3	858	28	30.64
Amir Elahi	1	2	0	17	13	8.50	–	–	–	—
Apte, A. L.	1	2	0	15	8	7.50	–	–	–	—
Apte, M. L.	7	13	2	542	163*	49.27	2	3	0	—

	M.	I.	N.O.	Runs	H.S.	Aver.	Ct.	Runs	Wkts.	Aver.
Baig, A. A.	8	14	0	376	112	26.85	5	15	0	—
Banerjee, S. N.	1	2	0	13	8	6.50	–	127	5	25.40
Banerjee, S. S.	1	1	0	0	0	0.00	3	181	5	36.20
Bhandari, P.	3	4	0	77	39	19.25	1	39	0	—
Borde, C. G.	40	68	9	2230	177*	37.79	26	2416	52	46.46
Chandrasekhar, R. S.	8	7	2	25	16	5.00	3	820	27	30.37
Chowdhury, N.	2	2	1	3	3*	3.00	–	205	1	205.00
Colah, S. H. M.	2	4	0	69	31	17.25	2	–	–	—
Contractor, N. J.	31	52	1	1611	108	31.58	18	82	1	82.00
Dani, H. T.	1	–	–	–	–	—	1	19	1	19.00
Desai, R. B.	26	41	11	359	85	11.96	9	2624	72	36.44
Divecha, R. V.	5	5	0	60	26	12.00	5	361	11	32.81
Durani, A. S.	22	38	2	863	104	23.97	11	2312	70	33.02
Engineer, F. M.	11	19	1	428	90	23.77	15 & 1 st.	–	–	—
Gadkari, C. V.	6	10	4	132	50*	22.00	6	45	0	—
Gaekwad, D. K.	11	20	1	350	52	19.44	5	12	0	—
Gaekwad, H. G.	1	2	0	22	14	11.00	–	47	0	—
Ghorpade, J. M.	8	15	0	229	41	15.26	4	131	0	—
Ghulam Ahmed	22	31	9	192	50	8.72	11	2052	68	30.17
Gopalan, M. J.	1	2	1	18	11*	18.00	3	39	1	39.00
Gopinath, C. D.	8	12	1	242	50*	22.00	2	11	1	11.00
Guard, G.	2	2	0	11	7	5.50	2	182	3	60.66
Gul Mahomed	8	15	0	166	34	11.06	3	24	2	12.00
Gupte, B. P.	3	3	2	28	17*	28.00	–	349	3	116.33
Gupte, S. P.	36	42	13	183	21	6.31	14	4402	149	29.54
Hafeez, A.	3	5	0	80	43	16.00	1	–	–	—
Hanumant Singh	9	14	2	471	105	39.25	11	24	0	—
Hardikar, M. S.	2	4	1	56	32*	18.66	3	55	1	55.00
Hazare, V. S.	30	52	6	2192	164*	47.65	11	1220	20	24.40
Handlekar, D. D.	4	7	2	71	26	14.20	3	–	–	—
Hussain, Dilawar	3	6	0	254	59	42.33	6 & 1 st.	–	–	—
Ibrahim, K. C.	4	8	0	169	85	21.12	–	–	–	—
Indrajitsingh, K. S.	3	5	1	32	23	8.00	5 & 3 st.	–	–	—
Irani, J. K.	2	3	2	3	2*	3.00	2 & 1 st.	–	–	—
Jahangir Khan	4	7	0	39	13	5.57	4	255	4	63.75
Jai, L. P.	1	2	0	19	19	9.50	–	–	–	—
Jaisimha, M. L.	27	49	2	1625	129	34.57	11	636	7	90.85
Jamshedji, R. J.	1	2	2	5	4*	—	2	137	3	45.66
Jilani, M. Baqa	1	2	1	16	12	16.00	–	55	0	—
Joshi, P. G.	12	20	1	207	52*	10.89	18 & 9 st.	–	–	—
Kenny, R. B.	5	10	1	245	62	27.22	1	–	–	—
Kischenchand, G.	5	10	0	89	44	8.90	1	–	–	—
Kripal Singh, A. G.	14	20	5	422	100*	28.13	4	584	10	58.40
Kumar, V.	2	2	0	6	6	3.00	2	202	7	28.85
Kunderam, B. K.	14	26	4	751	192	34.13	19 & 8 st.	–	–	—
Lall Singh	1	2	0	44	29	22.00	1	–	–	—
Maka, E. S.	2	1	1	2	2*	—	2 & 1 st.	–	–	—
Manjrekar, V. L.	55	92	10	3209	189	39.13	18 & 2 st.	43	1	43.00
Mankad, V.	44	72	5	2109	231	31.47	33	5235	162	32.31
Mantri, M. K.	4	8	1	67	39	9.57	8 & 1 st.	–	–	—
Meherhomji, K. R.	1	1	1	0	0*	—	1	–	–	—
Mehra, V.	8	14	1	329	62	25.30	1	6	0	—
Merchant, V. M.	10	18	0	859	154	47.72	7	40	0	—
Milkha Singa, A. G.	4	6	0	92	35	15.33	2	2	0	—
Modi, R. S.	10	17	1	736	112	46.00	3	14	0	—
Muddiah, V. M.	2	3	1	11	11	5.50	–	134	3	44.66
Mushtaq Ali	11	20	1	612	112	32.21	7	202	3	67.33
Nadkarni, R. G.	33	54	12	1265	122*	30.11	22	2050	71	28.87
Naoomal Jeoomal	3	5	1	108	43	27.00	–	68	2	34.00
Navle, J. G.	2	4	0	42	13	10.50	1	–	–	—
Nayudu, C. K.	7	14	0	350	81	25.00	4	386	9	42.88

	M.	I.	N.O.	Runs	H.S.	Aver.	Ct.	Runs	Wkts.	Aver.
Nayudu, C. S.	11	19	3	147	36	9.18	3	359	2	179.50
Nissar Mohommad	6	11	3	55	14	6.87	2	707	25	28.28
Nyalchand, K.	1	2	1	7	6*	7.00	–	97	3	32.33
Palia, P. E.	2	4	1	29	16	9.66	–	13	0	—
Patankar, C. T.	1	2	1	14	13	14.00	3 & 1 st.	–	–	—
Pataudi, Nawab of	3	5	0	55	22	11.00	–	–	–	—
Pataudi, Nawab of (son of the above)	18	31	2	1231	203*	42.44	9	59	1	59.00
Patel, J. S.	7	10	1	25	12	2.77	2	636	29	21.93
Patiala, Yuvraj of	1	2	0	84	60	42.00	2	–	–	—
Patil, S. R.	1	1	1	14	14*	—	1	51	2	25.50
Phadkar, D. G.	31	45	7	1229	123	32.60	21	2285	62	36.85
Prasanna, E. A. S.	2	4	2	33	17	16.50	1	161	4	40.25
Punjabi, P. L.	5	10	0	164	33	16.40	5	–	–	—
Rai Singh	1	2	0	26	24	13.00	–	–	–	—
Rajindernath, V.	1	–	–	–	–	—	– & 4 st.	–	–	—
Rajinder Pal	1	2	1	6	3*	6.00	–	22	0	—
Ramaswami, C.	2	4	1	170	60	56.66	–	–	–	—
Ramchand, G. S.	33	53	5	1180	109	24.58	20	1900	41	46.34
Ramji, L.	1	2	0	1	1	0.50	1	64	0	—
Rangachari, C.	4	6	3	8	8*	2.66	–	493	9	54.77
Rangnekar, K. M.	3	6	0	33	18	5.50	1	–	–	—
Ranjane, V. B.	7	9	3	40	16	6.66	1	649	19	34.15
Rege, M. R.	1	2	0	15	15	7.50	1	–	–	—
Roy, P.	43	79	4	2441	173	32.54	16	66	1	66.00
Sardesai, D. N.	15	28	3	1060	200*	42.40	4	33	0	—
Sarwate, C. T.	9	17	1	208	37	13.00	–	374	3	124.66
Sen, P.	14	18	4	165	25	11.78	19 & 12 st.	–	–	—
Sengupta, A. K.	1	2	0	9	8	4.50	–	–	–	—
Shinde, S. G.	7	11	5	85	14	14.16	–	717	12	59.75
Shodhan, D. H.	3	4	1	181	110	60.33	1	26	0	—
Sohoni, S. W.	4	7	2	83	29*	16.60	2	202	2	101.00
Sood, M. M.	1	2	0	3	3	1.50	–	–	–	—
Subramaniam, V.	1	1	0	9	9	9.00	–	35	2	17.50
Sunderram, G.	2	1	1	3	3*	—	–	164	3	54.66
Surendranath, R.	11	20	7	136	27	10.46	4	1053	26	40.50
Surti, R.	11	18	2	387	64	24.18	4	808	11	73.45
Swamy, V.	1	–	–	–	–	—	–	45	0	—
Tamhane, N. S.	21	27	5	222	54*	10.09	35 & 16 st.	–	–	—
Tarapor, K. K.	1	1	0	2	2	2.00	–	72	0	—
Umrigar, P. R.	59	94	8	3621	223	42.10	33	1475	35	42.14
Venkataranghavan, S.	4	4	1	18	7	6.00	4	399	21	19.00
Vizianagram, Maharaj Sir Vijaya	3	6	2	33	19*	8.25	1	–	–	—
Substitutes							22			

RUNS SCORED FOR AND AGAINST OTHER COUNTRIES IN TEST MATCHES BY INDIA

	FOR					AGAINST				
Against	Runs	Extras	Wkts.	Absent	Aver.	Runs	Extras	Wkts.	Run Out	Aver.
England	15,624	665	569	4	27.45	15,929	740	416	11	38.24
Australia	6,384	337	294	–	21.74	7,121	247	198	10	35.91
New Zealand	4,714	261	90	–	52.37	4,273	194	137	5	31.18
Pakistan	5,416	316	164	–	33.02	6,343	250	224	15	28.31
West Indies	10,391	561	367	6	28.31	11,447	342	250	16	45.78
Totals	42,529	2,140	1,484	10		45,113	1,773	1,225	57	
	2,140	20				1,773		57		
	40,389		1,474			43,340		1,168		

MODE OF DISMISSAL OF OTHER COUNTRIES IN TEST MATCHES AGAINST INDIA

Opponents	Bowled	Caught	L.B.W.	Run Out	Stumped	Hit Wkt.	Absent	Total
England.........	100	228	54	10	21	2	1	416
Australia.........	63	81	30	7	11	3	3	198
New Zealand....	37	63	28	3	4	0	2	137
Pakistan.........	46	114	34	15	15	0	0	224
West Indies......	56	122	46	16	9	1	0	250
Totals....	302	608	192	51	60	6	6	1,225
				Less Run out and Absent				57
								1,168

MODE OF DISMISSAL OF INDIAN BATSMEN IN TEST MATCHES

Opponents	Bowled	Caught	L.B.W.	Run Out	Stumped	Hit Wkt.	Absent	Total
England.........	175	282	66	21	20	1	4	569
Australia.........	91	163	28	4	7	1	0	294
New Zealand....	36	46	2	4	1	1	0	90
Pakistan.........	64	79	14	5	2	0	0	164
West Indies......	91	191	43	20	11	5	6	367
Totals	457	761	153	54	41	8	10	1,484
						Less Absent		10
								1,474

* * * * *

THE RISE OF CRICKET IN PAKISTAN

By Ghulam Mustafa Khan

Pakistan Cricket has had a chequered career spreading over a period of fifteen years. In the year 1952 Pakistan earned merited admission into the Imperial Cricket Conference (now International Cricket Conference) after showing her worth against Nigel Howard's M.C.C. team of 1951. The period was full of incidents, sometimes cricket soaring to great heights and at other times descending to the depths. Since then, apart from South Africa, we have played against every cricketing country, great or small. And happily, Pakistan have had the proud privilege of winning at least one Test Match against every such country.

English crowds must still remember the young and immature Pakistan team of 1954, then earning the title of "babes of International Cricket" being thrown against the full might of England.

Their initial showings prompted some critics to write them off, but as the tour progressed and the players got used to one of the wettest summers, the team improved beyond recognition. On Tuesday, August 17, at Kennington Oval, Pakistan covered themselves with glory by being the only side to win a Test match on a first visit to England. That victory enabled Pakistan to draw the rubber.

Over the years Pakistan have suffered from retirements and replacements, inevitable in the course of life. Yet, one is struck by the sustaining power of their present captain, the diminutive Hanif Mohammad, who has survived all these years, maintaining his consistent form. All his 1954 colleagues, including the captain, Hafeez Kardar, Fazal Mahmood, Imtiaz Ahmad and Khan Mohammad, have thrown in the towel by force of circumstances. Hanif, therefore, forms a happy link between the past and present, and who knows for how many more years he will continue to guide the destiny of Pakistan Cricket?

This will be Pakistan's third tour to the motherland. Since 1954 England have held the upper hand, in England in 1962 and a year earlier in Pakistan. Unfortunately our cricket in those gloomy times had fallen on lean days, for everything went wrong, though good performances were achieved by Pakistan against other countries. If we flick back the pages of history we find Pakistan on her first Test series in 1952 containing India on her first tour of that country. Considering the odds against Pakistan when playing her maiden Test series, the loss of two Tests against one was, indeed, creditable. Two years later, our maiden tour of England raised Pakistan's status in International Cricket.

Then followed India's barren tour of Pakistan in 1954–55, when not a single match was won or lost, owing to the defensive tactics employed by the Indians and the reluctance on both sides to come seriously to grips with each other.

After that came the hectic activities which saw Pakistan emerge from her shell and beat some of the major cricketing countries of the world. She won a three-Test series against New Zealand and administered the same medicine to the young M.C.C. "A" team. As if to justify these victories, Pakistan lowered the colours of Ian Johnson's 1956 Australian team in the only Test at Karachi.

Next came a strenuous tour of West Indies in 1958 when tall scoring was the order of the day. Pakistan drew the first Test after having fallen in arrear by 473 runs. Their recovery was due mainly to the monumental innings of 337 by Hanif Mohammad which also, incidentally, won for him a record for the longest stay at the wicket of sixteen hours and thirty-nine minutes. Then at the height of their power, with the legendary Garfield Sobers emerging as a new star on the cricket horizon, West Indies almost completely overwhelmed Pakistan in the next three Tests. Yet who would believe that Kardar's men fully avenged their defeats and beat West Indies by an innings in the fifth and final Test? Soon afterwards, the West Indies paid a return visit only to be beaten in two Tests while winning one. These victories sent a wave of optimism among Pakistan supporters and showed the world that cricket in Pakistan was of the highest class.

The Australians came in 1959–60, and being then in their peak form under Richie Benaud, unquestionably had the better of the series, winning two of the three Tests. Norman O'Neill and Neil Harvey excelled with the bat and Benaud, 47 victims, and Alan Davidson, 41, were the chief wicket-takers. Only Hanif and Saeed Ahmed shone as run-getters for Pakistan. Fazal alone of the bowlers achieved respect.

The 1960–61 tour of Pakistan in India may well be forgotten. All the five Tests and the nine other matches resulted in draws. It established a world record, for the two countries, India and Pakistan, in thirteen Tests had now failed to come to a decision. This was a dubious distinction that no cricket-playing country could ever be proud of.

For a year or so Pakistan were confronted by England, who not only beat Pakistan in Pakistan (in one out of the three Tests played), but also in England where they dictated terms almost completely in all the five Tests. Pakistan's only consolation was to draw one Test, thus preventing England making a clean sweep. This tour threw Pakistan cricket in the doldrums again. Gradually the feeling of despondency began to disappear, bringing in a fresh wave of optimism and hope, when Pakistan did well to draw the only Test against Australia at Karachi in 1964.

Pakistan's first tour of Australia and New Zealand served only to add to the genuine confidence in the Pakistan team, as no match in Australia, including the lone Test, was lost. In spite of being sent into bat at Melbourne, Hanif showed his greatness and carried his men with innings of 104 and 93.

In New Zealand the sodden wickets did not permit the Pakistanis to give of their best. The only redeeming feature of the series was that although they were in a tight corner in three Tests they managed to hit their way out of trouble. More than six years had elapsed and Pakistan had not won a Test match. The stalemate was broken in Rawalpindi in March, 1965, when Pakistan beat New Zealand by an innings in the first Test played there. Perhaps it constituted a modern record that a Test was finished in two days and forty minutes. The series went in Pakistan's favour.

Where does Pakistan stand today, after having played 50 Tests of which she has won 10 and lost 14, with the remaining 26 drawn? In terms of wins there may not be anything to boast about. Most of the victories were achieved when she had a string of fighters who could truly be called the pioneers of cricket in our country. Gradually they vanished from the scene and cricket began to deteriorate.

Happily there are encouraging signs of revival. Proof of this was found in the recent showing against foreign teams, including the 1963 Commonwealth team which had such stalwarts as Griffith—a dreaded bowler—Kanhai, Butcher and Graveney.

Unfortunately so far Pakistan has not been able to find pacemen like Fazal Mahmood, Mahmood Hussain or Khan Mohammad. In spin, Intikhab Alam has acquired some viciousness and Pervez Sajjad is a medium-slow tight bowler who shuns flight. Salah-ud-din is an off-spinner of some promise who has already made a good impression. With Hanif, there is a string of dependable batsmen who have already gone through the ordeal of experience in every country and climate. One, therefore, hopes that these players in whom the Pakistanis have pinned high hopes will show in England that it is not only the winning or losing that matters, but that there is some such thing as attractive cricket which tickles the appetite of the crowd.

We hope that English spectators will see in action at their best the cricket prodigy, little Hanif Mohammad and his younger brother Mushtaq Mohammad. Both have carved out names for themselves—the rise to eminence of Mushtaq being more sudden than Hanif's. They belong to a family of five cricketers (in the order of their ages: Wazir, Raees, Hanif, Mushtaq and Sadiq).

In the 1954–55 Quaid-e-Azam Trophy final, Wazir, Raees and Hanif scored a century each against Services. Their presence created a world record in 1961 when all of them played in the Ayub Cricket Trophy during a match—two of the brothers were pitted against the other three who played for the opposite side. A lot of world records have fallen to this cricketing family. Hanif holds the world record for the highest individual score in first-class cricket: 499 against Bahawalpur in the year 1958–59 (which broke Sir Don Bradman's feat of 452). He scored 891 runs that season. He also has the record of staying at the wicket for sixteen hours and thirty-nine minutes in the first Test against the West Indies at Bridgetown in 1958, when he finished with a triple century, 337. Hanif has also scored the largest number of Test centuries (11) by a Pakistani player. Mushtaq Mohammad is the youngest Test cricketer in the world, for he appeared for Pakistan in the Lahore Test against the West Indies in 1959 when his age was 15 years and 124 days. He has shown maturity and an aggressive approach to batting that has delighted crowds everywhere.

And talking of Hanif, two years back, we in Pakistan had lost all hopes of his staging a come-back to cricket, when he was so very lame—but he recovered from the operation on his leg, and like a true fighter, he resumed and successfully picked up his bat again after a long period of inactivity. It was most heart-warming. We hope that in 1966, Hanif will again be the Master Batsman.

SOME DATES IN PAKISTAN CRICKET HISTORY

Compiled by Rowland Bowen

1947 Pakistan came into existence.

1948–9 First tour to Pakistan, by West Indies. The one unofficial Test was drawn. Pakistan undertook first away tour, to Ceylon: won both unofficial tests.

1949 May 1: Board of Control for Cricket in Pakistan formed. *Cricket in Pakistan* Annual first issued—two more issues, 1951 and 1954. Ceylon undertook tour to Pakistan: lost both unofficial tests.

1949–50 First tour to Pakistan by Commonwealth team. The one unofficial test was drawn.

1950–1 Karachi: the Pentangular Tournament revived for first time since partition.

1951–2 First tour by M.C.C. to Pakistan: drew one and lost the other unofficial test.

1952 Pakistan admitted to Imperial Cricket Conference. The first of eight tours to the U.K. undertaken by the Pakistan Eaglets, teams of young Pakistani cricketers sent on tour for experience.

1952–3 First tour to India by Pakistan: won one and drew two Tests. Also visited Burma.

1953–4 Pakistan Services team visited Ceylon, Quaid-e-Azam Trophy instituted: first winners, Bahawalpur.

1954 First tour by Pakistan to U.K.: won one, lost one and drew two Tests. First match between Pakistan and Canada: Pakistan won.

1954–5 First tour by India to Pakistan: all five Tests drawn. First appearance of a team from East Pakistan in the Quaid-e-Azam Trophy.

1955–6 Second tour by M.C.C.—an "A" team: won one, lost two and drew one of the unofficial tests. First tour by New Zealand to Pakistan: lost two and drew one Test.

1956 Pakistan team toured East Africa under the name of "Pakistan Cricket Writers": it included Test and other first-class players. Lost only unofficial test v. E. Africa. First Australian team to Pakistan: lost the only Test.

1958 First tour by Pakistan to West Indies: won one, lost three and drew the other Test. Also visited Bermuda, Canada and U.S.A.

1958–9 Second tour by West Indies to Pakistan: won one and lost two Tests World record first-class innings of 499 compiled by Hanif Mohammad for Karachi v. Bahawalpur.

1959–60 Second tour by Australians to Pakistan: won two Tests and drew the other. Matting wickets henceforth prohibited in Quaid-e-Azam Trophy matches.

1960–1 Second tour by Pakistan to India: all five Tests drawn.
Pakistan Eaglets undertook tour to Ceylon and Malaya.
Ayub Zonal Trophy instituted: first winners, Railways—Quetta.

1961–2 Third tour by M.C.C. to Pakistan: won one and drew two Tests.

1962 Second tour by Pakistan to U.K.: lost four Tests and drew the other.

1963–4 Second tour by Commonwealth team to Pakistan: drew all three unofficial tests.

1964 Third tour by Australians to Pakistan: drew the only Test.
Pakistan International Airways team, consisting solely of Test and other first-class players, toured East Africa: beat Invitation XI at Mombasa (virtually Combined E. Africa)

1964–5 Pakistan record first-class score of 910 for six wickets declared made by Railways v. Dera Ismail Khan.
First tour by Pakistan to Australia (drew only Test) and to New Zealand (drew all three Tests).
Pakistan "A" team visited Ceylon and drew only unofficial test.

1965 Second tour by New Zealand to Pakistan: lost 2 and drew the other Test.

1966 First Official Cricket Annual, issued by Pakistan Cricket Board of Control, covering 1964–5 (also first cricket annual issued by a governing body).

1966–7 Second tour by Ceylon to Pakistan: lost all three unofficial Tests.

1967 Third tour by Pakistan to U.K.: three five-day Tests to be played.

TEST CAREER RECORDS OF PAKISTAN PLAYERS

STATISTICS by STANLEY CONDER

BATTING and BOWLING

	M.	I.	N.O.	Runs	H.S.	Aver.	Ct.	Runs	Wkts.	Aver.
Abdul Kadir.........	4	8	0	272	95	34.00	– 1st.	–	–	—
Afaq Hussain........	2	4	4	64	33*	64.00	2	106	1	106.00
Agha Saadet Ali......	1	1	1	8	8*	8.00	3	–	–	—
Alim-ud-Din..........	25	45	2	1091	109	25.37	8	76	1	76.00
Amir Elahi..........	5	7	1	65	47	10.83	–	248	7	35.42
Anwar Hussain........	4	6	0	42	17	7.00	–	29	1	29.00
Arif Butt............	3	5	0	59	20	11.80	–	288	14	20.28
Asif Iqbal..........	8	14	1	303	56	23.30	6	619	28	22.10
D'Souza, A..........	6	10	8	76	23*	38.00	3	745	17	43.82
Farooq Hamid.......	1	2	0	3	3	1.50	–	107	1	107.00
Fazal Mahmood.....	34	50	6	620	60	14.09	11	3437	139	24.72
Ghazali, M. E. Z......	2	4	0	32	18	8.00	–	18	0	—
Gul Mahomed.......	1	2	1	39	27*	39.00	–	–	–	—
Hanif Mohammad....	48	86	6	3584	337	44.80	31	87	1	87.00
Haseeb Ahsan........	12	16	7	61	14	6.77	2	1330	27	49.25
Ibadulla, Khalid......	2	4	0	206	166	51.50	2	52	0	—
Ijaz Butt.............	8	16	2	279	58	19.21	5	–	–	—
Imtiaz Ahmed.......	41	72	1	2079	209	29.28	77 & 16st.	0	0	—
Intikhab Alam	17	30	6	507	61	21.12	9	1296	27	48.00
Israr Ali............	4	8	1	33	10	4.71	1	165	6	27.50
Javed Akhtar........	1	2	1	4	2*	4.00	–	52	0	—
Javed Burki..........	21	40	3	1220	140	32.94	6	23	0	—
Kardar, A. H.........	23	37	3	847	93	24.91	15	953	21	45.38
Khalid Hassan.......	1	2	1	17	10	17.00	–	116	2	58 00
Khalid Wazir........	2	3	1	14	9*	7.00	–	–	–	—
Khan Mohammad....	13	17	7	100	26*	10.00	4	1294	54	23.96
Mahmood Hussain...	27	39	6	336	35	10.18	5	2628	68	38.64
Majid Jahangir.......	4	5	0	147	80	29.40	6	267	6	44.50
Maqsood Ahmed.....	16	27	1	507	99	19.50	13	191	3	63.66
Mathias, Wallis......	21	36	3	783	77	23.72	21	20	0	—
Miran Bux...........	2	3	2	1	1*	1.00	–	115	2	57.50
Mohammad Aslam...	1	2	0	34	18	17.00	–	–	–	—
Mohammad Ilyas.....	7	13	0	396	126	30.46	3	62	0	—
Mohammad Farooq..	7	9	4	85	47	17.00	1	682	21	32.47
Mohammad Munaf...	4	7	2	63	19	12.60	–	339	11	30.81
Mufasir-ul-Haq	1	1	1	8	8*	—	1	84	3	28.00
Munir Malik.........	3	4	1	7	4	2.33	1	358	9	39.77
Mushtaq Mohammad.	14	25	2	868	101	37.73	1	67	0	—
Nasim-ul-Ghani......	26	45	5	659	101	16.47	8	1871	48	38.97
Naushad Ali.........	6	11	0	156	39	14.18	9	–	–	—
Nazar Mohammad...	5	8	1	277	124*	39.57	7	4	0	—
Pervez Sajjad........	7	9	6	57	18	19.00	2	505	22	22.95
Rahman, S. F........	1	2	0	10	8	5.00	1	99	1	99.00
Saeed Ahmed........	32	62	3	2562	172	43.42	8	402	12	33.50
Salahuddin..........	3	4	2	93	34	46.50	2	187	7	26.71
Shafqat Rana........	1	2	0	24	24	12.00	–	1	0	—
Shahid Mahmood....	1	2	0	25	16	12.50	–	23	0	—
Sharpe, D...........	3	6	0	134	56	22.33	2	–	–	—
Shuja-ud-Din........	19	32	6	395	47	15.19	8	801	20	40.05
Waqar Hassan.......	21	35	1	1071	189	31.50	10	10	0	—
Wazir Mohammad....	20	33	4	801	189	27.62	5	15	0	—
Zulfiqar Ahmed......	9	10	4	200	63*	33.33	5	365	20	18.25
Substitutes							7			

RUNS SCORED FOR AND AGAINST OTHER COUNTRIES IN TEST MATCHES BY PAKISTAN

	FOR					AGAINST				
Against	Runs	Extras	Wkts.	Absent	Aver.	Runs	Extras	Wkts.	Run Out	Aver.
England ..	5,219	172	217	–	23.62	5,243	196	114	4	45.99
Australia...	2,901	134	107	–	27.11	2,572	146	80	1	32.15
New Zealand	3,843	211	122	–	31.50	3,597	216	151	5	23.82
India......	6,343	250	224	–	28.31	5,416	316	164	5	33.02
West Indies	4,112	237	138	2	29.79	4,364	181	114	8	38.28
Totals	22,328	1,004	808	2	27.63	21,192	1,055	623	23	34.01
	1,004		2			1,055		23		
	21,324		806			20,137		600		

MODE OF DISMISSAL OF OTHER COUNTRIES IN TEST MATCHES AGAINST PAKISTAN

Opponents	Bowled	Caught	L.B.W.	Run Out	Stumped	Hit Wkt.	Total
England..............	30	64	12	4	3	1	114
Australia.............	24	41	11	1	2	1	80
India.................	64	79	14	5	2	0	164
West Indies...........	28	53	17	8	8	0	114
New Zealand..........	53	74	17	5	2	0	151
Totals......	199	311	71	23	17	2	623

MODE OF DISMISSAL BY PAKISTAN PLAYERS IN TEST MATCHES

Opponents	Bowled	Caught	L.B.W.	Run Out	Stumped	Hit Wkt.	Total
England..............	71	125	14	5	1	1	217
Australia.............	25	61	9	5	5	2	107
India.................	46	114	34	15	15	0	224
West Indies...........	54	55	15	8	4	0	136
New Zealand..........	41	62	11	5	3	0	122
Totals......	237	417	83	38	28	3	806

TEST CRICKETERS

FULL LIST FROM 1877 TO AUGUST 31, 1966

These lists have been compiled on a home and abroad basis, appearances abroad being printed in *italics*.

Abbreviations.—E: England. A: Australia. SA: South Africa. WI: West Indies. NZ: New Zealand. In: India. P: Pakistan.

All appearances are placed in this order of seniority. Hence, any England cricketer playing against Australia in England has that achievement recorded first and the remainder of his appearances at home (if any) are set down before passing to matches abroad. Although the distinction between amateur and professional was abolished in 1963, initials of English professionals before that date are still given in brackets. The figures immediately following each name represent the total number of appearances in *all* Tests.

Where the season embraces two different years, the first year is given, i.e. 1876 indicates 1876–77.

When South Africa left the British Commonwealth in 1961 they ceased membership of the International Cricket Conference and ford official Test status. To maintain continuity of the records the arances of all players engaged in Tests played by South Africa continue to be included.

ENGLAND

Abel (R.) 13: v A 1888 (3) 1896 (3) 1902 (2); *v A 1891 (3)*; *v SA 1888 (2)*
Absolom, C. A. 1: *v A 1878*
Allen (D. A.) 39: v A 1961 (4) 1964 (1); v SA 1960 (2); v WI 1963 (2) 1966 (1); v P 1962 (4); *v A 1962 (1) 1965 (4)*; *v SA 1964 (4)*; *v WI 1959 (5)*; *v NZ 1965 (3)*; *v In 1961 (5)*; *v P 1961 (3)*
Allen, G. O. 25: v A 1930 (1) 1934 (2); v WI 1933 (1); v NZ 1931 (3); v In 1936 (3); *v A 1932 (5) 1936 (5)*; *v WI 1947 (3)*; *v NZ 1932 (2)*
Allom, M. J. C. 5: *v SA 1930 (1)*; *v NZ 1929 (4)*
Ames (L. E. G.) 47: v A 1934 (5) 1938 (2); v SA 1929 (1) 1935 (4); v WI 1933 (3); v NZ 1931 (3) 1937 (3); v In 1932 (1); *v A 1932 (5) 1936 (5)*; *v SA 1938 (5)*; *v WI 1929 (4)*; *1934 (4)*; *v NZ 1932 (2)*
Amiss, D. L. 1: v WI 1966
Andrew (K. V.) 2: v WI 1963(1); *v A 1954(1)*
Appleyard (R.) 9: v A 1956 (1); v SA 1955 (1); v P 1954 (1); *v A 1954 (4)*; *v NZ 1954 (2)*
Archer, A. G. 1: *v SA 1898*
Armitage (T.) 2: *v A 1876 (2)*
Arnold (E. G.) 10: v A 1905 (4); v SA 1907 (2); *v A 1903 (4)*
Arnold (J.) 1: v NZ 1931
Astill (W. E.) 9: *v SA 1927 (5)*; *v WI 1929 (4)*
Attewell (W.) 10: v A 1890 (1); *v A 1884 (5) 1887 (1) 1891 (3)*

Bailey, T. E. 61: v A 1953 (5) 1956 (4); v SA 1951 (2) 1955 (5); v WI 1950 (2) 1957 (4); v NZ 1949 (4) 1958 (4); v P 1954 (3); *v A 1950 (4) 1954 (5) 1958 (5)*; *v SA 1956 (5)*; *v WI 1953 (5)*; *v NZ 1950 (2) 1954 (2)*
Bakewell (A. H.) 6: v SA 1935 (2); v WI 1933 (1); v NZ 1931 (2); *v In 1933 (1)*
Barber, R. W. 27: v A 1964 (1): v SA 1960 (1) 1965 (3); v WI 1966 (2); v NZ 1965 (3); *v A 1965 (5)*; *v SA 1964 (4)*; *v In 1961 (5)*; *v P 1961 (3)*
Barber (W.) 2: v SA 1935 (2)
Barlow (R. G.) 17: v A 1882 (1) 1884 (3) 1886 (3); *v A 1881 (4) 1882 (4) 1886 (2)*

Barnes (S. F.) 27: v A 1902 (1) 1909 (3) 1912 (3); v SA 1912 (3); *v A 1901 (3) 1907 (5) 1911 (5); v SA 1913 (4)*
Barnes (W.) 21: v A 1880 (1) 1882 (1) 1884 (2) 1886 (2) 1888 (3) 1890 (2); *v A 1882 (4) 1884 (5) 1886 (1)*
Barnett (C. J.) 20: v A 1938 (3); 1948 (1); v SA 1947 (3); v WI 1933 (1); v NZ 1937 (3); v In 1936 (1); *v A 1936 (5); v In 1933 (3)*
Barratt (F.) 5: v SA 1929 (1); *v NZ 1929 (4)*
Barrington (K. F.) 68: v A. 1961 (5) 1964 (5); v SA 1955 (2) 1960 (4) 1965 (3); v WI 1963 (5) 1966 (2); v NZ 1965 (2); v In 1959 (5); v P 1962 (4); *v A 1962 (5) 1965 (5); v SA 1964 (5); v WI 1959 (5); v NZ 1962 (3); v In 1961 (5) 1963 (1); v P 1961 (2)*
Barton (V. A.) 1: *v SA 1891*
Bates (W.) 15: *v A 1881 (4) 1882 (4) 1884 (5) 1886 (2)*
Bean (G.) 3: *v A 1891 (3)*
Bedser (A. V.) 51: v A 1948 (5) 1953 (5); v SA 1947 (2) 1951 (5) 1955 (1); v WI 1950 (3); v NZ 1949 (2); v In 1946 (3) 1952 (4); v P 1954 (2); *v A 1946 (5) 1950 (5) 1954 (1); v SA 1948 (5); v NZ 1947 (1) 1950 (2)*
Berry (R.) 2: v WI 1950 (2)
Binks, J. G. 2: *v In 1963 (2)*
Bird, M. C. 10: *v SA 1909 (5) 1913 (5)*
Bligh, Hon. Ivo 4: *v A 1882 (4)*
Blythe (C.) 19: v A 1905 (1) 1909 (2); v SA 1907 (3); *v A 1901 (5) 1907 (1); v SA 1905 (5) 1909 (2)*
Board (J. H.) 6: *v SA 1898 (2) 1905 (4)*
Bolus, J. B. 7: v WI 1963 (2); *v In 1963 (5)*
Booth (M. W.) 2: *v SA 1913 (2)*
Bosanquet, B. J. T. 7: v A 1905 (3); *v A 1903 (4)*
Bowden, M. P. 2: *v SA 1888 (2)*
Bowes (W. E.) 15: v A 1934 (3) 1938 (2); v SA 1935 (4); v WI 1939 (2); v In 1932 (1); 1946 (1); *v A 1932 (1); v NZ 1932 (1)*
Bowley (E. H.) 5: v SA 1929 (2); *v NZ 1929 (3)*
Boycott, G. 24: v A 1964 (4); v SA 1965 (2) v WI 1966 (4); v NZ 1965 (2); *v A 1965 (5); v SA 1964 (5); v NZ 1965 (2).*
Bradley, W. M. 2: v A 1899 (2)
Braund (L. C.) 23: v A 1902 (5); v SA 1907 (3); *v A 1901 (5) 1903 (5) 1907 (5)*
Brearley, W. 4: v A 1905 (2) 1909 (1); v SA 1912 (1)
Brennan, D. V. 2: v SA 1951 (2)
Briggs (John) 33: v A 1886 (3) 1888 (3) 1893 (2) 1896 (1) 1899 (1); *v A 1884 (5) 1886 (2) 1887 (1) 1891 (3) 1894 (5) 1897 (5); v SA 1888 (2)*
Brockwell (W.) 7: v A 1893 (1) 1899 (1); *v A 1894 (5)*
Bromley-Davenport, H. R. 4: *v SA 1895 (3) 1898 (1)*
Brookes (D.) 1: *v WI 1947*
Brown (A.) 2: *v In 1961 (1); v P 1961 (1)*
Brown, D. J. 9: v SA 1965 (2); v WI 1966 (1); *v A 1965 (4); NZ 1965 (2).*
Brown, F. R. 22: v A 1953 (1); v SA 1951 (5); v WI 1950 (1); v NZ 1931 (2) 1937 (1) 1949 (2); v In 1932 (1); *v A 1950 (5); v NZ 1932 (2) 1950 (2)*
Brown (G.) 7: v A 1921 (3); *v SA 1922 (4)*
Brown (J. T.) 8: v A 1896 (2) 1899 (1); *v A 1894 (5)*
Buckenham (C. P.) 4: *v SA 1909 (4)*
Butler (H. J.) 2: v SA 1947 (1); *v WI 1947 (1)*
Butt (H. R.) 3: *v SA 1895 (3)*

Calthorpe, Hon. F. S. G. 4: *v WI 1929 (4)*
Carr, A. W. 11: v A 1926 (4); v SA 1929 (2); *v SA 1922 (5)*
Carr, D. B. 2: *v In 1951 (2)*
Carr, D. W. 1: v A 1909
Cartwright, T. W. 5: v A 1964 (2); v SA 1965 (1); v NZ 1965 (1); *v SA 1964 (1)*
Chapman, A. P. F. 26: v A 1926 (4) 1930 (4); v SA 1924 (2); v WI 1928 (3); *v A 1924 (4) 1928 (4); v SA 1930 (5)*
Charlwood (H.) 2: *v A 1876 (2)*
Chatterton (W.) 1: *v SA 1891*
Christopherson, S. 1: v A 1884
Clark (E. W.) 8: v A 1934 (2); v SA 1929 (1); v WI 1933 (2); *v In 1933 (3)*

Clay, J. C. 1: v SA 1935
Close (D. B.) 13: v A 1961 (1); v SA 1955 (1); v WI 1957 (2) 1963 (5) 1966 (1); v NZ 1949 (1); v In 1959 (1); *v A 1950 (1)*
Coldwell (L. J.) 7: v A 1964 (2); v P 1962 (2); *v A 1962 (2); v NZ 1962 (1)*
Compton (D. C. S.) 78: v A 1938 (4) 1948 (5) 1953 (5) 1956 (1); v SA 1947 (5) 1951 (4) 1955 (5); v WI 1939 (3) 1950 (1); v NZ 1937 (1) 1949 (4); v In 1946 (3) 1952 (2); v P 1954 (4); *v A 1946 (5) 1950 (4) 1954 (4); v SA 1948 (5) 1956 (5); v WI 1953 (5); v NZ 1947 (1) 1950 (2)*
Cook (C.) 1: v SA 1947
Copson (W. H.) 3: v SA 1947 (1); v WI 1939 (2)
Cornford (W.) 4: *v NZ 1929 (4)*
Coventry, Hon. C. J. 2: *v SA 1888 (2)*
Cowdrey, M. C. 90: v A 1956 (5) 1961 (4) 1964 (3); v SA 1955 (1) 1960 (5) 1965 (3); v WI 1957 (5) 1963 (2) 1966 (4); v NZ 1958 (4) 1963 (3); v In 1959 (5); v P 1962 (4); *v A 1954 (5) 1958 (5) 1962 (5) 1965 (4); v SA 1956 (5); WI 1959 (5); v NZ 1954 (2) 1958 (2) 1962 (3) 1965 (3); v In 1963 (3)*
Coxon (A.) 1: v A 1948
Cranston, J. 1: v A 1890
Cranston, K. 8: v A 1948 (1); v SA 1947 (3); *v WI 1947 (4)*
Crapp (J. F.) 7: v A 1948 (3); *v SA 1948 (4)*
Crawford, J. N. 12: v SA 1907 (2); *v A 1907 (5); v SA 1905 (5)*
Cuttell (W. R.) 2: *v SA 1898 (2)*

Dawson, E. W. 5: *v SA 1927 (1); v NZ 1929 (4)*
Dean (H.) 3: v A 1912 (2); v SA 1912 (1)
Denton (D.) 11: v A 1905 (1); *v SA 1905 (5) 1909 (5)*
Dewes, J. G. 5: v A 1948 (1); v WI 1950 (2); *v A 1950 (2)*
Dexter, E. R. 60: v A 1961 (5) 1964 (5); v SA 1960 (5); v WI 1963 (5); v NZ 1958 (1) 1965 (2); v In 1959 (2); v P 1962 (5); *v A 1958 (2) 1962 (5); v SA 1964 (5); v WI 1959 (5); v NZ 1958 (2) 1962 (3); v In 1961 (5); v P 1961 (3)*
Dipper (A. E.) 1: v A 1921
Doggart, G. H. G. 2: v WI 1950 (2)
d'Oliveira, B. 4: v WI 1966 (4)
Dollery (H. E.) 4: v A 1948 (2); v SA 1947 (1); v WI 1950 (1)
Dolphin (A.) 1: *v A 1920*
Douglas, J. W. H. T. 23: v A 1912 (1) 1921 (5); v SA 1924 (1); *v A 1911 (5); 1920 (5) 1924 (1); v SA 1913 (5)*
Druce, N. F. 5: *v A 1897 (5)*
Ducat (A.) 1: v A 1921
Duckworth (G.) 24: v A 1930 (5); v SA 1924 (1) 1929 (4) 1935 (1); v WI 1928 (1); v In 1936 (3); *v A 1928 (5); v SA 1930 (3); v NZ 1932 (1)*
Duleepsinhji, K. S. 12: v A 1930 (4); v SA 1929 (1); v NZ 1931 (3); *v NZ 1929 (4)*
Durston (F. J.) 1: v A 1921

Edrich, J. H. 19: v A 1964 (3); v SA 1965 (1); v WI 1963 (3) 1966 (1); v NZ 1965 (1); *v A 1965 (5); v NZ 1965 (3); v In 1963 (2)*
Edrich, W. J. 39: v A. 1938 (4) 1948 (5) 1953 (3); v SA 1947 (4); v WI 1950 (2); v NZ 1949 (4); v In 1946 (1); v P 1954 (1); *v A 1946 (5) 1954 (4); v SA 1938 (5); v NZ 1947 (1)*
Elliott (H.) 4: v WI 1928 (1); *v SA 1927 (1); v In 1933 (2)*
Emmett (G. M.) 1: v A 1948
Emmett (T.) 7: *v A 1876 (2) 1878 (1) 1881 (4)*
Evans, A. J. 1: v A 1921
Evans (T. G.) 91: v A 1948 (5) 1953 (5) 1956 (5); v SA 1947 (5) 1951 (3) 1955 (3); v WI 1950 (3) 1957 (5); v NZ 1949 (4) 1958 (5); v In 1946 (1) 1952 (4) 1959 (2); v P 1954 (4); *v A 1946 (4) 1950 (5) 1954 (4) 1958 (3); v SA 1948 (3) 1956 (5); v WI 1947 (4) 1953 (4); v NZ 1947 (1) 1950 (2) 1954 (2)*

Fagg (A. E.) 5: v WI 1939 (1); v In 1936 (2); *v A 1936 (2)*
Fane, F. L. 14: *v A 1907 (4); v SA 1905 (5) 1909 (5)*
Farnes, K. 15: v A 1934 (2) 1938 (4); *v A 1936 (2); v SA 1938 (5); v WI 1934 (2)*
Farrimond (W.) 4: v SA 1935 (1); *v SA 1930 (2); v WI 1934 (1)*
Fender, P. G. H. 13: v A 1921 (2); v SA 1924 (2) 1929 (1); *v A 1920 (3); v SA 1922 (5)*

Ferris, J. J. 1: *v SA 1891*
Fielder (A.) 6: *v A 1903 (2) 1907 (4)*
Fishlock (L. B.) 4: v In 1936 (2) 1946 (1); *v A 1946 (1)*
Flavell (J. A.) 4: v A 1961 (2) 1964 (2)
Flowers (W.) 8: v A 1893 (1); *v A 1884 (5) 1886 (2)*
Ford, F. G. J. 5: *v A 1894 (5)*
Foster, F. R. 11: v A 1912 (3); v SA 1912 (3); *v A 1911 (5)*
Foster, R. E. 8: v SA 1907 (3); *v A 1903 (5)*
Fothergill (A. J.) 2: *v SA 1888 (2)*
Freeman (A. P.) 12: v SA 1929 (3); v WI 1928 (3); *v A 1924 (2)*; *v SA 1927 (4)*
Fry, C. B. 26: v A 1899 (5) 1902 (3) 1905 (4) 1909 (3) 1912 (3); v SA 1907 (3) 1912 (3); *v SA 1895 (2)*

Gay, L. H. 1: *v A 1894*
Geary (G.) 14: v A 1926 (2) 1930 (1) 1934 (2); v SA 1924 (1) 1929 (2); *v A 1928 (4)*; *v SA 1927 (2)*
Gibb, P. A. 8: v In 1946 (2); *v A 1946 (1)*; *v SA 1938 (5)*
Gifford, N. 2: v A 1964 (2)
Gilligan, A. E. R. 11: v SA 1924 (4); *v A 1924 (5)*; *v SA 1922 (2)*
Gilligan, A. H. H. 4: *v NZ 1929 (4)*
Gimblett (H.) 3: v WI 1939 (1); v In 1936 (2)
Gladwin (C.) 8: v SA 1947 (2); v NZ 1949 (1); *v SA 1948 (5)*
Goddard (T. W.) 8: v A 1930 (1); v WI 1939 (2); v NZ 1937 (2); *v SA 1938 (3)*
Gover (A. R.) 4: v NZ 1937 (2); v In 1936 (1) 1946 (1)
Grace, E. M. 1: v A 1880
Grace, G. F. 1: v A 1880
Grace, W. G. 22: v A 1880 (1) 1882 (1) 1884 (3) 1886 (3) 1888 (3) 1890 (2) 1893 (2) 1896 (3) 1899 (1); *v A 1891 (3)*
Graveney (T. W.) 59: v A 1953 (5) 1956 (2); v SA 1951 (1) 1955 (5); v WI 1957 (4) 1966 (4); v NZ 1958 (4); v In 1952 (4); v P 1954 (3) 1962 (4); *v A 1954 (2) 1958 (5) 1962 (3)*; *v WI 1953 (5)*; *v NZ 1954 (2) 1958 (2)*; *v In 1951 (4)*
Greenhough (T.) 4: v SA 1960 (1); v In 1959 (3)
Greenwood (A.) 2: *v A 1876 (2)*
Grieve, B. A. F. 2: *v SA 1888 (2)*
Griffith, S. C. 3: *v SA 1948 (2)*; *v WI 1947 (1)*
Gunn (G.) 15: v A 1909 (1); *v A 1907 (5) 1911 (5)*; *v WI 1929 (4)*
Gunn (J.) 6: v A 1905 (1); *v A 1901 (5)*
Gunn (W.) 11: v A 1888 (2) 1890 (2) 1893 (3) 1896 (1) 1899 (1); *v A 1886 (2)*

Haig, N. E. 5: v A 1921 (1); *v WI 1929 (4)*
Haigh (S.) 11: v A 1905 (2) 1909 (1); 1912 (1); *v SA 1898 (2) 1905 (5)*
Hallows (C.) 2: v A 1921 (1); v WI 1928 (1)
Hammond, W. R. 85: v A 1930 (5) 1934 (5) 1938 (4); v SA 1929 (4) 1935 (5); v WI 1928 (3) 1933 (3) 1939 (3); v NZ 1931 (3) 1937 (3); v In 1932 (1) 1936 (2) 1946 (3); *v A 1928 (5) 1932 (5) 1936 (5) 1946 (4)*; *v SA 1927 (5) 1930 (5) 1938 (5)*; *v NZ 1932 (2) 1947 (1)*; *v WI 1934 (4)*
Hardinge (H. T. W.) 1: v A 1921
Hardstaff (J.) 5: *v A 1907 (5)*
Hardstaff (J., Jnr.) 23: v A 1938 (2) 1948 (1); v SA 1935 (1); v WI 1939 (3); v NZ 1937 (3); v In 1936 (2) 1946 (2); *v A 1936 (5) 1946 (1)*; *v WI 1947 (3)*
Harris, Lord 4: v A 1880 (1) 1884 (2); *v A 1878 (1)*
Hartley, J. C. 2: *v SA 1905 (2)*
Hawke, Lord 5: *v SA 1895 (3) 1898 (2)*
Hayes (E. G.) 5: v A 1909 (1); v SA 1912 (1); *v SA 1905 (3)*
Hayward (T. W.) 35: v A 1896 (2) 1899 (5) 1902 (1) 1905 (5) 1909 (1); v SA 1907 (3); *v A 1897 (5) 1901 (5) 1903 (5)*; *v SA 1895 (3)*
Hearne (A.) 1: *v SA 1891*
Hearne (F.) 2: *v SA 1888 (2)*
Hearne (G. G.) 1: *v SA 1891*
Hearne (J. T.) 12: v A 1896 (3) 1899 (3); *v A 1897 (5)*; *v SA 1891 (1)*
Hearne (J. W.) 24: v A 1912 (3) 1921 (1) 1926 (1); v SA 1912 (2) 1924 (3); *v A 1911 (5) 1920 (2) 1924 (4)*; *v SA 1913 (3)*

Hendren (E.) 51: v A 1921 (2) 1926 (5) 1930 (2) 1934 (4); v SA 1924 (5) 1929 (4) v WI 1928 (1); *v A 1920 (5) 1924 (5) 1928 (5); v SA 1930 (5); v WI 1929 (4) 1934 (4)*
Heseltine, C. 2: *v SA 1895 (2)*
Higgs, K. 10: v WI 1966 (5); v SA 1965 (1); *v A 1965 (1); v NZ 1965 (3)*
Hill (A.) 2: *v A 1876 (2)*
Hill, A. J. L. 3: *v SA 1895 (3)*
Hilton (M. J.) 4: v SA 1951 (1); v WI 1950 (1); *v In 1951 (2)*
Hirst (G. H.) 24: v A 1899 (1) 1902 (4) 1905 (3) 1909 (4); v SA 1907 (3); *v A 1897 (4) 1903 (5)*
Hitch (J. W.) 7: v A 1912 (1) 1921 (1); v SA 1912 (1); *v A 1911 (3) 1920 (1)*
Hobbs (J. B.) 61: v A 1909 (3) 1912 (3) 1921 (1) 1926 (5) 1930 (5); v SA 1912 (3) 1924 (4) 1929 (1); v WI 1928 (2); *v A 1907 (4) 1911 (5) 1920 (5) 1924 (5) 1928 (5); v SA 1909 (5) 1913 (5)*
Hollies (E.) 13: v A 1948 (1); v SA 1947 (3); v WI 1950 (2); v NZ 1949 (4); *v WI 1934 (3)*
Holmes, E. R. T. 5: v SA 1935 (1); *v WI 1934 (4)*
Holmes (P.) 7: v A 1921 (1); v In 1932 (1); *v SA 1927 (5)*
Hone, L. 1: *v A 1878*
Hopwood (J. L.) 2: v A 1934 (2)
Hornby, A. N. 3: v A 1882 (1) 1884 (1); *v A 1878 (1)*
Horton (M. J.) 2: v In 1959 (2)
Howard, N. D. 4: *v In 1951 (4)*
Howorth (R.) 5: v SA 1947 (1); *v WI 1947 (4)*
Howell (H.) 5: v A 1921 (1); v SA 1924 (1); *v A 1920 (3)*
Humphries (J.) 3: *v A 1907 (3)*
Hunter (J.) 5: *v A 1884 (5)*
Hutchings, K. L. 7: v A 1909 (2); *v A 1907 (5)*
Hutton (L.) 79: v A 1938 (3) 1948 (4) 1953 (5); v SA 1947 (5) 1951 (5); v WI 1939 (3) 1950 (3); v NZ 1937 (3) 1949 (4); v In 1946 (3) 1952 (4); v P 1954 (2); *v A 1946 (5) 1950 (5) 1954 (5); v SA 1938 (4) 1948 (5); v WI 1947 (2) 1953 (5); v NZ 1950 (2) 1954 (2)*

Iddon (J.) 5: v SA 1935 (1); *v WI 1934 (4)*
Ikin (J. T.) 18: v SA 1951 (3) 1955 (1); v In 1946 (2); 1952 (2); *v A 1946 (5); v NZ 1946 (1); v WI 1947 (4)*
Illingworth (R.) 23: v A 1961 (2); v SA 1960 (4); WI 1966 (2); v NZ 1958 (1) 1965 (1); v In 1959 (2); v P 1962 (1); *v A 1962 (2); v WI 1959 (5); NZ 1962 (3)*
Insole, D. J. 9: v A 1956 (1); v SA 1955 (1); v WI 1950 (1) 1957 (1); *v SA 1956 (5)*

Jackson (H. L.) 2: v A 1961 (1); v NZ 1949 (1)
Jackson, Rt. Hon. Sir F. S. 20: v A 1893 (2) 1896 (3) 1899 (5) 1902 (5) 1905 (5)
Jardine, D. R. 22: v WI 1928 (2) 1933 (2); v NZ 1931 (3); v In 1932 (1); *v A 1928 (5) 1932 (5); v NZ 1932 (1); v In 1933 (3)*
Jenkins (R. O.) 9: v WI 1950 (2); v In 1952 (2); *v SA 1948 (5)*
Jessop, G. L. 18: v A 1899 (1) 1902 (4) 1905 (1) 1909 (2); v SA 1907 (3) 1912 (2); *v A 1901 (5)*
Jones, A. O. 12: v A 1899 (1) 1905 (2) 1909 (2); *v A 1901 (5) 1907 (2)*
Jones, I. J. 10: v WI 1966 (2); *v A 1965 (4); v NZ 1965 (3); v In 1963 (1)*
Jupp (H.) 2: *v A 1876 (2)*
Jupp, V. W. C. 8: v A 1921 (2); v WI 1928 (2); *v SA 1922 (4)*

Keeton (W. W.) 2: v A 1934 (1); v WI 1939 (1)
Kennedy (A. S.) 5: *v SA 1922 (5)*
Kenyon (D.) 8: v A 1953 (2); v SA 1955 (3); *v In 1951 (3)*
Killick, E. T. 2: v SA 1929 (2)
Kilner (R.) 9: v A 1926 (4); v SA 1924 (2); *v A 1924 (3)*
King (J. H.) 1: v A 1909
Kinneir (S. P.) 1: *v A 1911*
Knight (A. E.) 3: *v A 1903 (3)*
Knight (B. R.) 22: v WI 1966 (1); v P 1962 (2); *v A 1962 (1) 1965 (2); v NZ 1962 (3) 1966 (2); v In 1961 (4) 1963 (5); v P 1961 (2)*
Knight, D. J. 2: v A 1921 (2)
Knox, N. A. 2: v SA 1907 (2)

Laker (J. C.) 46: v A 1948 (3) 1953 (3) 1956 (5); v SA 1951 (2) 1955 (1); v WI 1950 (1) 1957 (4); v NZ 1949 (1) 1958 (4); v In 1952 (4); v P 1954 (1); *v A 1958 (4)*; *v SA 1956 (5)*; *v WI 1947 (4) 1953 (4)*
Langridge (James) 8: v SA 1935 (1); v WI 1933 (2); v In 1936 (1) 1946 (1); *v In 1933 (3)*
Larter (J. D. F.) 10: v SA 1965 (2); v NZ 1965 (1); v P 1962 (1); *v NZ 1962 (3)*; *v In 1963 (3)*
Larwood (H.) 21: v A 1926 (2) 1930 (3); v SA 1929 (3); v WI 1928 (2); v NZ 1931 (1); *v A 1928 (5) 1932 (5)*
Leadbeater (E.) 2: *v In 1951 (2)*
Lee (H. W.) 1: *v SA 1930*
Lees (W.) 5: *v SA 1905 (5)*
Legge, G. B. 5: *v SA 1927 (1)*; *v NZ 1929 (4)*
Leslie, C. F. H. 4: *v A 1882 (4)*
Leveson Gower, H. D. G. 3: *v SA 1909 (3)*
Levett, W. H. V. 1: *v In 1933*
Leyland (M.) 41: v A 1930 (3) 1934 (5) 1938 (1); v SA 1929 (5) 1935 (4); v WI 1928 (1) 1933 (1); v In 1936 (2); *v A 1928 (1) 1932 (5) 1936 (5) v SA 1930 (5)*; *v WI 1934 (3)*
Lilley (A. A.) 35: v A 1896 (3) 1899 (4) 1902 (5) 1905 (5) 1909 (5); v SA 1907 (3); *v A 1901 (5) 1903 (5)*
Lillywhite (Jas. Jnr.) 2: *v A 1876 (2)*
Loader (P. J.) 13: v SA 1955 (1); v WI 1957 (2); v NZ 1958 (3); v P 1954 (1); *v A 1958 (2)*; *v SA 1956 (4)*
Lock (G. A. R.) 47: v A 1953 (2) 1956 (4) 1961 (3); v SA 1955 (3); v WI 1957 (3) 1963 (3); v NZ 1958 (5); v In 1952 (2); v P 1962 (3); *v A 1958 (4)*; *v SA 1956 (1)*; *v WI; 1953 (5)*; *v NZ 1958 (2)*; *v In 1961 (5)*; *v P 1961 (2)*
Lockwood (W. H.) 12: v A 1893 (2) 1899 (1) 1902 (4); *v A 1894 (5)*
Lohmann (G. A.) 18: v A 1886 (3) 1888 (3) 1890 (2) 1896 (1); *v A 1886 (2) 1887 (1) 1891 (3)*; *v SA 1895 (3)*
Lowson (F. A.) 7: v SA 1951 (2) 1955 (1); *v In 1951 (4)*
Lucas, A. P. 5: v A 1880 (1) 1882 (1) 1884 (2); *v A 1878 (1)*
Lyttelton, Rt. Hon. A. 4: v A 1880 (1) 1882 (1) 1884 (2)

Macaulay (G. G.) 8: v A 1926 (1); v SA 1924 (1); v WI 1933 (2); *v SA 1922 (4)*
MacBryan, J. C. W. 1: v SA 1924
McConnon (J. E.) 2: v P 1954 (2)
McGahey, C. P. 2: *v A 1901 (2)*
MacGregor, G. 8: v A 1890 (2) 1893 (3); *v A 1891 (3)*
McIntyre (A. J.) 3: v SA 1955 (1); v WI 1950 (1); *v A 1950 (1)*
MacKinnon, F. A. 1: *v A 1878*
MacLaren, A. C. 35: v A 1896 (2) 1899 (4) 1902 (5) 1905 (4) 1909 (5); *v A 1894 (5) 1897 (5) 1901 (5)*
McMaster, J. E. P. 1: *v SA 1888*
Makepeace (H.) 4: *v A 1920 (4)*
Mann, F. G. 7: v NZ 1949 (2); *v SA 1948 (5)*
Mann, F. T. 5: *v SA 1922 (5)*
Marriott, C. S. 1: v WI 1933
Martin (F.) 2: v A 1890 (1); *v SA 1891 (1)*
Martin, J. W. 1: v SA 1947
Mason, J. R. 5: *v A 1897 (5)*
Matthews (A. D. G.) 1: v NZ 1937
May, P. B. H. 66: v A 1953 (2) 1956 (5) 1961 (4); v SA 1951 (2) 1955 (5); v WI 1957 (5); v NZ 1958 (5); v In 1952 (4) 1959 (3); v P 1954 (4); *v A 1954 (5) 1958 (5)*; *v SA 1956 (5)*; *v WI 1953 (5) 1959 (3)*; *v NZ 1954 (2) 1958 (2)*
Mead (C. P.) 17: v A 1921 (2); *v A 1911 (4) 1928 (1)*; *v SA 1913 (5) 1922 (5)*
Mead (W.) 1: v A 1899
Midwinter (W. E.) 4: *v A 1881 (4)*
Milburn, C. (4): v WI 1966 (4)
Miller, A. M. 1: *v SA 1895*
Milligan, F. W. 2: *v SA 1898 (2)*
Millman (G.) 6: v P 1962 (2); *v In 1961 (2)*; *v P 1961 (2)*
Milton (C. A.) 6: v NZ 1958 (2); v In 1959 (2); *v A 1958 (2)*

Mitchell (A.) 6: v SA 1935 (2); v In 1936 (1); *v In 1933 (3)*
Mitchell, F. 2: *v SA 1898 (2)*
Mitchell (T. B.) 5: v A 1934 (2); v SA 1935 (1) *v A 1932 (1)*; *v NZ 1932 (1)*
Mitchell-Innes, N. S. 1: v SA 1935
Mold (A.) 3: v A 1893 (3)
Moon, L. J. 4: *v SA 1905 (4)*
Morley (F.) 4: v A 1880 (1); *v A 1882 (3)*
Mortimore (J. B.) 9: v A 1964 (1); v In 1959 (2); *v A 1958 (1)*; *v NZ 1958 (2)*; *v In 1963 (3)*
Moss (A. E.) 9: v A 1956 (1); v SA 1960 (2); v In 1959 (3); *v WI 1953 (1) 1959 (2)*
Murdoch, W. L. 1: *v SA 1891*
Murray (J. T.) 17: v A 1961 (5); v WI 1966 (1); v P 1962 (3); *v A 1962 (1)*; *v SA 1964 (1)*; *v NZ 1962 (1) 1965 (1)*; *v In 1961 (3)*; *v P 1961 (1)*

Newham (W.) 1: *v A 1887*
Nichols (M. S.) 14: v A 1930 (1); v SA 1935 (4); v WI 1933 (1) 1939 (1); *v NZ 1929 (4)*; *v In 1933 (3)*

Oakman (A. S. M.) 2: v A 1956 (2)
O'Brien, Sir T. C. 5: v A 1884 (1) 1888 (1); *v SA 1895 (3)*
O'Connor (J.) 4: v SA 1929 (1); *v WI 1929 (3)*
Oldfield (N.) 1: v WI 1939

Padgett (D. E. V.) 2: v SA 1960 (2)
Paine (G. A. E.) 4: *v WI 1934 (4)*
Palairet, L. C. H. 2: v A 1902 (2)
Palmer, C. H. 1: *v WI 1953*
Palmer, K. E. 1: *v SA 1964*
Parfitt (P. H.) 33: v A 1964 (4); v SA 1965 (2); v NZ 1965 (2); v P 1962 (5); *v A 1962 (2)*; *v SA 1964 (5) v NZ 1962 (3) 1965 (3)*; *v In 1961 (2) 1963 (3)*; *v P 1961 (2)*
Parker (C. W. L.) 1: v A 1921
Parkhouse (W. G. A.) 7: v WI 1950 (2); v In 1959 (2); *v A 1950 (2)*; *v NZ 1950 (1)*
Parkin (C. H.) 10: v A 1921 (4); v SA 1924 (1); *v A 1920 (5)*
Parks (J. H.) 1: v NZ 1937
Parks (J. M.) 43: v A 1964 (5); v SA 1960 (5) 1965 (3); v WI 1963 (4) 1966 (4); v NZ 1965 (3); v P 1954 (1); *v A 1965 (5)*; *v SA 1964 (5)*; *v WI 1959 (1)*; *v NZ 1965 (2)*; *v In 1963 (5)*
Pataudi, Nawab of 3: v A 1934 (1); *v A 1932 (2)*
Paynter (E.) 20: v A 1938 (4); v WI 1939 (2); v NZ 1931 (1) 1937 (2); v In 1932 (1); *v A 1932 (3)*; *v SA 1938 (5)*; *v NZ 1932 (2)*
Peate (E.) 9: v A 1882 (1) 1884 (3) 1886 (1); *v A 1881 (4)*
Peebles, I. A. R. 13: v A 1930 (2); v NZ 1931 (3); *v SA 1927 (4) 1930 (4)*
Peel (R.) 20: v A 1888 (3) 1890 (1) 1893 (1) 1896 (1); *v A 1884 (5) 1887 (1) 1891 (3) 1894 (5)*
Penn, F. 1: v A 1880
Perks (R. T. D.) 2: v WI 1939 (1); *v SA 1938 (1)*
Philipson, H. 5: *v A 1891 (1) 1894 (4)*
Pilling (R.) 8: v A 1884 (1) 1886 (1) 1888 (1); *v A 1881 (4) 1887 (1)*
Place (W.) 3: *v WI 1947 (3)*
Pollard (R.) 4: v A 1948 (2); v In 1946 (1); *v NZ 1947 (1)*
Poole (C. J.) 3: *v In 1951 (3)*
Pope (G. H.) 1: v SA 1947
Pougher (A. D.) 1: *v SA 1891*
Price, J. S. E. 10: v A 1964 (2); *v SA 1964 (4)*; *v In 1963 (4)*
Price (W. F.) 1: v A 1938
Pullar (G.) 28: v A 1961 (5); v SA 1960 (3); v In 1959 (3); v P 1962 (2); *v A 1962 (4)*; *v WI 1959 (5)*; *v In 1961 (3)*; *v P 1961 (3)*

Quaife (W. G.) 7: v A 1899 (2); *v A 1901 (5)*

Ranjitsinhji, K. S. 15: v A 1896 (2) 1899 (5) 1902 (3); *v A 1897 (5)*
Read, H. D. 1: v SA 1935
Read (J. M.) 17: v A 1882 (1) 1890 (2) 1893 (1); *v A 1884 (5) 1886 (2) 1887 (1) 1891 (3)*; *v SA 1888 (2)*
Read, W. W. 18: v A 1884 (2) 1886 (3) 1888 (3) 1890 (2) 1893 (2); *v A 1882 (4) 1887 (1)*; *v SA 1891 (1)*

Relf (A. E.) 13: v A 1909 (1); *v A 1903* (2); *v SA 1905* (5) *1913* (5)
Rhodes (H. J.) 2: v In 1959 (2)
Rhodes (W.) 58: v A 1899 (3) 1902 (5) 1905 (4) 1909 (4) 1912 (3) 1921 (1) 1926 (1); v SA 1912 (3); *v A 1903* (5) *1907* (5) *1911* (5) *1920* (5); *v SA 1909* (5) *1913* (5) *v WI 1929* (4)
Richardson (D. W.) 1: v WI 1957
Richardson (P. E.) 34: v A 1956 (5); v WI 1957 (5) 1963 (1); v NZ 1958 (4); *v A 1958* (4); *v SA 1956* (5); *v NZ 1958* (2); *v In 1961* (5); *v P 1961* (3)
Richardson (T.) 14: v A 1893 (1) 1896 (3); *v A 1894* (5) *1897* (5)
Richmond (T. L.) 1: v A 1921
Ridgway (F.) 5: *v In 1951* (5)
Robertson (J. D.) 11: v SA 1947 (1); v NZ 1949 (1); *v WI 1947* (4); *v In 1951* (5)
Robins, R. W. V. 19: v A 1930 (2); v SA 1929 (1) 1935 (3); v WI 1933 (2); v NZ 1931 (1) 1937 (3); v In 1932 (1) 1936 (2); *v A 1936* (4)
Root (C. F.) 3: v A 1926 (3)
Royle, V. P. F. A. 1: *v A 1878*
Rumsey, F. E. 5: v A 1964 (1); v SA 1965 (1); v NZ 1965 (3)
Russell (A. C.) 10: v A 1921 (2); *v A 1920* (4); *v SA 1922* (4)
Russell (W. E.) 9: v SA 1965 (1) v WI 1966 (2); *v A 1965* (*1*); *v NZ 1965* (*3*); *v In 1961* (*1*); *v P 1961* (*1*)

Sandham (A.) 14: v A 1921 (1); v SA 1924 (2); *v A 1924* (2); *v SA 1922* (5); *WI 1929* (4)
Schultz, S. S. 1: *v A 1878*
Scotton (W. H.) 15: v A 1884 (1) 1886 (3); *v A 1881* (4) *1884* (5) *1886* (2)
Selby (J.) 6: *v A 1876* (2) *1881* (4)
Shackleton (D.) 7: v SA 1951 (1); v WI 1950 (1) 1963 (4); *v In 1951* (*1*)
Sharp (J.) 3: v A 1909 (3)
Sharpe (J. W.) 3: v A 1890 (1); *v A 1891* (2)
Sharpe, P. J.: 6: v A 1964 (2); v WI 1963 (3); *v In 1963* (*1*)
Shaw (A.) 7: v A 1880 (1); *v A 1876* (2) *1881* (4)
Sheppard, Rev. D. S. 22: v A 1956 (2); v WI 1950 (1) 1957 (2); v In 1952 (2); v P 1954 (2) 1962 (2); *v A 1950* (2) *1962* (5); *v NZ 1950* (*1*) *1962* (3)
Sherwin (M.) 3: v A 1888 (1); *v A 1886* (2)
Shrewsbury (A.) 23: v A 1884 (3) 1886 (3) 1890 (2) 1893 (3); *v A 1881* (4) *1884* (5) *1886* (2) *1887* (*1*)
Shuter, J. 1: v A 1888
Sims (J. M.) 4: v SA 1935 (1); v In 1936 (1); *v A 1936* (2)
Simpson, R. T. 27: v A 1953 (3); v SA 1951 (3); v WI 1950 (3); v NZ 1949 (2); v In 1952 (2); v P 1954 (3); *v A 1950* (5) *1954* (*1*); *v SA 1948* (*1*); *v NZ 1950* (2) *1954* (2)
Simpson-Hayward, G. H. 5: *v SA 1909* (5)
Sinfield (R. A.) 1: v A 1938
Smailes (T. F.) 1: v In 1946
Smith, A. C. 6: *v A 1962* (4); *v NZ 1962* (2)
Smith, C. A. 1: *v SA 1888*
Smith (C. I. J.) 5: v NZ 1937 (1); *v WI 1934* (4)
Smith (D.) 2: v SA 1935 (2)
Smith (D. R.) 5: *v In 1961* (5)
Smith (D. V.) 3: v WI 1957 (3)
Smith (E. J.) 11: v A 1912 (3); v SA 1912 (3); *v A 1911* (4); *v SA 1913* (*1*)
Smith (H.) 1: v WI 1928
Smith, M. J. K. 47: v A 1961 (1); v SA 1960 (4) 1965 (3); v WI 1966 (1); v NZ 1958 (3) 1965 (3); v In 1959 (2); *v A 1965* (5); *v SA 1964* (5); *v WI 1959* (5); *v. NZ 1965* (3); *v In 1961* (4) *1963* (5); *v P 1961* (3)
Smith (T. P. B.) 4: v In 1946 (1); *v A 1946* (2); *v NZ 1947* (*1*)
Smithson (G. A.) 2: *v WI 1947* (2)
Snow, J. A. 5: v SA 1965 (1); v WI 1966 (3); v NZ 1965 (1)
Southerton (J.) 2: *v A 1876* (2)
Spooner, R. H. 10: v A 1905 (2) 1909 (2) 1912 (3); v SA 1912 (3)
Spooner (R. T.) 7: v SA 1955 (1); *v In 1951* (5); *v WI 1953* (*1*)
Stanyforth, R. T. 4: *v SA 1927* (4)

Staples (S. J.) 3: *v SA 1927 (3)*
Statham (J. B.) 70: v A 1953 (1) 1956 (3) 1961 (4); v SA 1951 (2) 1955 (4) 1960 (5) 1965 (1); v WI 1957 (3); 1963 (2); v NZ 1958 (2); v In 1959 (3); v P 1954 (4) 1962 (3); *v A 1954 (5) 1958 (4) 1962 (5); SA 1956 (4); v NZ 1950 (1) 1954 (2); v WI 1953 (4) 1959 (3); v In 1951 (5)*
Steel, A. G. 13: v A 1880 (1) 1882 (1) 1884 (3) 1886 (3) 1888 (1); *v A 1882 (4)*
Stevens, G. T. S. 10: v A 1926 (2): *v SA 1922 (1) 1927 (5); v WI 1929 (2)*
Stewart (M. J.) 8: v. WI 1963 (4); v P 1962 (2); *v In 1963 (2)*
Stoddart, A. E. 16: v A 1893 (3) 1896 (2); *v A 1887 (1) 1891 (3) 1894 (5) 1897 (2)*
Storer (W.) 6: v A 1899 (1); *v A 1897 (5)*
Street (G. B.) 1: *v SA 1922*
Strudwick (H.) 28: v A 1921 (2) 1926 (5); v SA 1924 (1); *v A 1911 (1) 1920 (4) 1924 (5); v SA 1909 (5) 1913 (5)*
Studd, C. T. 5: v A 1882 (1); *v A 1882 (4)*
Studd, G. B. 4: *v A 1882 (4)*
Sugg (F. H.) 2: v A 1888 (2)
Subba Row, R. 13: v A 1961 (5); v SA 1960 (4); v NZ 1958 (1); v In 1959 (1); *v WI 1959 (2)*
Sutcliffe (H.) 54: v A 1926 (5) 1930 (4) 1934 (4); v SA 1924 (5) 1929 (5) 1935 (2); v WI 1928 (3) 1933 (2); v NZ 1931 (2); v In 1932 (1); *v A 1924 (5) 1928 (4) 1932 (5); v SA 1927 (5); v NZ 1932 (2)*
Swetman (R.) 11: v In 1959 (3); *v A 1958 (2); v WI 1959 (4); v NZ 1958 (2)*

Tate (F. W.) 1: v A 1902
Tate (M. W.) 39: v A 1926 (5) 1930 (5); v SA 1924 (5) 1929 (3) 1935 (1); v WI 1928 (3); v NZ 1931 (1); *v A 1924 (5) 1928 (5); v SA 1930 (5); v NZ 1932 (1)*
Tattersall (R.) 16: v A 1953 (1); v SA 1951 (5); v P 1954 (1); *v A 1950 (2); v NZ 1950 (2); v In 1951 (5)*
Taylor (K.) 3: v A 1964 (1); v In 1959 (2)
Tennyson, Lord, 9: v A 1921 (4); *v SA 1913 (5)*
Thompson (G. J.) 6: v A 1909 (1); *v SA 1909 (5)*
Thomson, N. I. 5: *v SA 1964 (5)*
Titmus (F. J.) 45: v A 1964 (5); v SA 1955 (2) 1965 (3); v WI 1963 (4) 1966 (3); v NZ 1965 (3); v P 1962 (2); *v A 1962 (5) 1965 (5); v SA 1964 (5); v NZ 1962 (3); v In 1963 (5)*
Townsend, C. L. 2: v A 1899 (2)
Townsend, D. C. H. 3: *v WI 1934 (3)*
Townsend (L. F.) 4: *v WI 1929 (1); v In 1933 (3)*
Tremlett (M. F.) 3: *v WI 1947 (3)*
Trott (A. E.) 2: *v SA 1898 (2)*
Trueman (F. S.) 67: v A 1953 (1) 1956 (2) 1961 (4) 1964 (4); v SA 1955 (1) 1960 (5); v WI 1957 (5) 1963 (5); v NZ 1958 (5) 1965 (2); v In 1952 (4) 1959 (5); v P 1962 (4); *v A 1958 (3) 1962 (5); v WI 1953 (3) 1959 (5); v NZ 1958 (2) 1962 (2)*
Tufnell, N. C. 1: *v SA 1909*
Turnbull, M. J. 9: v WI 1933 (2); v In 1936 (1); *v SA 1930 (5); v NZ 1929 (1)*
Tyldesley (E.) 14: v A 1921 (3) 1926 (1); v SA 1924 (1); v WI 1928 (3); *v A 1928 (1); v SA 1927 (5)*
Tyldesley (J. T.) 31: v A 1899 (2) 1902 (5) 1905 (5) 1909 (4); v SA 1907 (3); *v A 1901 (5) 1903 (5); v SA 1898 (2)*
Tyldesley (R.) 7: v A 1930 (2); v SA 1924 (4); *v A 1924 (1)*
Tylecote, E. F. S. 6: v A 1886 (2); *v A 1882 (4)*
Tyler (E. J.) 1: *v SA 1895*
Tyson (F. H.) 17: v A 1956 (1); v SA 1955 (2); v P 1954 (1); *v A 1954 (5) 1958 (2); v SA 1956 (2); v NZ 1954 (2) 1958 (2)*

Ulyett (G.) 25: v A 1882 (1) 1884 (3) 1886 (3) 1888 (2) 1890 (1); *v A 1876 (2) 1878 (1) 1881 (4) 1884 (5) 1887 (1); v SA 1888 (2)*
Underwood, D. L. 2: v WI 1966 (2)

Valentine, B. H. 7: *v SA 1938 (5); v In 1933 (2)*
Verity (H.) 40: v A 1934 (5) 1938 (4); v SA 1935 (4); v WI 1933 (2) 1939 (1); v NZ 1931 (2) 1937 (1); v In 1936 (3); *v A 1932 (4) 1936 (5); v SA 1938 (5); v NZ 1932 (1); v In 1933 (3)*
Vernon, G. F. 1: *v A 1882*

Vine (J.) 2: *v A 1911 (2)*
Voce (W.) 27: v NZ 1931 (1) 1937 (1); v In 1932 (1) 1936 (1) 1946 (1); *v A 1932 (4) 1936 (5) 1946 (2); v SA 1930 (5); v NZ 1932 (2); v WI 1929 (4)*

Waddington (A.) 2: *v A 1920 (2)*
Wainwright (E.) 5: v A 1893 (1); *v A 1897 (4)*
Walker (P. M.) 3: v SA 1960 (3)
Walters, C. F. 11: v A 1934 (5); v WI 1933 (3); *v In 1933 (3)*
Ward (A.) 7: v A 1893 (2); *v A 1894 (5)*
Wardle (J. H.) 28: v A 1953 (3) 1956 (1); v SA 1951 (2) 1955 (3); v WI 1950 (1) 1957 (1); v P 1954 (4); *v A 1954 (4); v SA 1956 (4); v WI 1947 (1) 1953 (2); v NZ 1954 (2)*
Warner, Sir Pelham, 15: v A 1909 (1) 1912 (1); v SA 1912 (1); *v A 1903 (5); v SA 1898 (2) 1905 (5)*
Warr, J. J. 2: *v A 1950 (2)*
Warren (A. R.) 1: v A 1905
Washbrook (C.) 37: v A 1948 (4) 1956 (3); v SA 1947 (5); v WI 1950 (2); v NZ 1937 (1) 1949 (2); v In 1946 (3); *v A 1946 (5) 1951 (5); v SA 1948 (5); v NZ 1947 (1) 1951 (1)*
Watkins (A. J.) 15: v A 1948 (1); v NZ 1949 (1); v In 1952 (3); *v SA 1948 (5); v In 1951 (5)*
Watson (W.) 23: v A 1953 (3) 1956 (2); v SA 1951 (5) 1955 (1); v NZ 1958 (2); v In 1952 (1); *v A 1958 (2); v WI 1953 (5); v NZ 1958 (2)*
Webbe, A. J. 1: *v A 1878*
Wellard (A. W.) 2: v A 1938 (1); v NZ 1937 (1)
Wharton (A.) 1: v NZ 1949
White, J. C. 15: v A 1921 (1) 1930 (1); v SA 1929 (3); v WI 1928 (1); *v A 1928 (5); v SA 1930 (4)*
White (D. W.) 2: *v P 1961 (2)*
Whysall (W. W.) 4: v A 1930 (1); *v A 1924 (3)*
Wilkinson (L. L.) 3: *v SA 1938 (3)*
Wilson, C. E. M. 2: *v SA 1898 (2)*
Wilson, D. 5: *v In 1963 (5)*
Wilson, E. R. 1: *v A 1920*
Wood (A.) 4: v A 1938 (1); v WI 1939 (3)
Wood, G. E. C. 3: v SA 1924 (3)
Wood (H.) 4: v A 1888 (1); *v SA 1888 (2) 1891 (1)*
Wood (R.) 1: *v A 1886*
Woods, S. M. J. 3: *v SA 1895 (3)*
Woolley (F. E.) 64: v A 1909 (1) 1912 (3) 1921 (5) 1926 (5) 1930 (2) 1934 (1) v SA 1912 (3) 1924 (5) 1929 (3); v NZ 1931 (1); v In 1932 (1); *v A 1911 (5) 1920 (5) 1924 (5); v SA 1909 (5) 1913 (5) 1922 (5); v NZ 1929 (4)*
Worthington (T. S.) 9: v In 1936 (2); *v A 1936 (3); v NZ 1929 (4)*
Wright, C. W. 3: *v SA 1895 (3)*
Wright (D. V. P.) 34: v A 1938 (3) 1948 (1); v SA 1947 (4); v WI 1939 (3) 1950 (1); v NZ 1949 (1); v In 1946 (2); *v A 1946 (5) 1950 (5); v SA 1938 (3) 1948 (3); v NZ 1947 (1) 1950 (2)*
Wynyard, E. G. 3: v A 1896 (1); *v SA 1905 (2)*
Wyatt, R. E. S. 40: v A 1930 (1) 1934 (4); v SA 1929 (2) 1935 (5); v WI 1933 (2); v In 1936 (1); *v A 1932 (5) 1936 (2); v SA 1927 (5) 1930 (5); v WI 1929 (2) 1934 (4); v NZ 1932 (2)*

Yardley, N. W. D. 20: v A 1948 (5); v SA 1947 (5); v WI 1950 (3); *v A 1946 (5); v SA 1938 (1); v NZ 1947 (1)*
Young (H.) 2: v A 1899 (2)
Young (J. A.) 8: v A 1948 (3); v SA 1947 (1); v NZ 1949 (2); *v SA 1948 (2)*
Young, R. A. 2: *v A 1907 (2)*

AUSTRALIA

a'Beckett, E. L. 4: v E 1928 (2) v SA 1931 (1); *v E 1930 (1)*
Alexander, G. 2: v E 1884 (1); *v E 1880 (1)*
Alexander, H. H. 1: v E 1932
Allan, F. E. 1: v E 1878

Allan, P. J. 1: v E 1965
Allen, R. 1: v E 1886
Andrews, T. J. E. 16: v E 1924 (3); *v E 1921 (5) 1926 (5)*; *v SA 1921 (3)*
Archer, K. A. 5: v E 1950 (3); v WI 1951 (2)
Archer, R. G. 19: v E 1954 (4); v SA 1952 (1); *v E 1953 (3) 1956 (5)*; *v WI 1955 (5)*; *v P 1956 (1)*
Armstrong, W. W. 50: v E 1901 (4) 1903 (3) 1907 (5) 1911 (5) 1920 (5); v SA 1910 (5); *v E 1902 (5) 1905 (5) 1909 (5) 1921 (5)*; *v SA 1902 (3)*

Badcock, C. L. 7: v E 1936 (3); *v E 1938 (4)*
Bannerman, A. C. 28: v E 1878 (1) 1881 (3) 1882 (4) 1884 (4) 1886 (1) 1887 (1) 1891 (3); *v E 1880 (1) 1882 (1) 1884 (3) 1888 (3) 1893 (3)*
Bannerman, C. 3: v E 1876 (2) 1878 (1)
Bardsley, W. 41: v E 1911 (4) 1920 (5) 1924 (3); v SA 1910 (5); *v E 1909 (5) 1912 (3) 1921 (5) 1926 (5)*; *v SA 1912 (3) 1921 (3)*
Barnes, S. G. 13: v E 1946 (4); v In 1947 (3); *v E 1938 (1) 1948 (4)*; *v NZ 1946 (1)*
Barnett, B. A. 4: *v E 1938 (4)*
Barrett, J. E. 2: *v E 1890 (2)*
Benaud, R. 63: v E 1954 (5) 1958 (5) 1962 (5); v SA 1952 (4) 1963 (4); v WI 1951 (1) 1960 (5); *v E 1953 (3) 1956 (5) 1961 (4)*; *v SA 1957 (5)*; *v WI 1955 (5)*; *v In 1956 (3) 1959 (5)*; *v P 1956 (1) 1959 (3)*
Blackham, J. McC. 35: v E 1876 (2) 1878 (1) 1881 (4) 1882 (4) 1884 (2) 1886 (1) 1887 (1) 1891 (3) 1894 (1); *v E 1880 (1) 1882 (1) 1884 (3) 1886 (3) 1888 (3) 1890 (2) 1893 (3)*
Blackie, D. J. 3: v E 1928 (3)
Bonnor, G. J. 17: v E 1882 (4) 1884 (3); *v E 1880 (1) 1882 (1) 1884 (3) 1886 (2) 1888 (3)*
Booth, B. C. 29: v E 1962 (5) 1965 (3); v SA 1963 (4); v P 1964 (1); *v E 1961 (2) 1964 (5)*; *v WI 1965 (5)*; *v 1964 (3)*; *v P 1964 (1)*
Boyle, H. F. 12: v E 1878 (1) 1881 (4) 1882 (1) 1884 (1); *v E 1880 (1) 1882 (1) 1884 (3)*
Bradman, D. G. 52: v E 1928 (4) 1932 (4) 1936 (5) 1946 (5); v SA 1931 (5); v WI 1930 (5); v In 1947 (5); *v E 1930 (5) 1934 (5) 1938 (4) 1948 (5)*
Bromley, E. H. 2: v E 1932 (1); *v E 1934 (1)*
Brown, W. A. 22: v E 1936 (2); v In 1947 (3); *v E 1934 (5) 1938 (4) 1948 (2)*; *v SA 1935 (5)*; *v NZ 1946 (1)*
Bruce, W. 14: v E 1884 (2) 1891 (3) 1894 (4); *v E 1886 (2) 1893 (3)*
Burn, K. E. 2: *v E 1890 (2)*
Burge, P. J. 42: v E 1954 (1) 1958 (1) 1962 (3) 1965 (4); v SA 1963 (5); v WI 1960 (2); *v E 1956 (3) 1961 (5) 1964 (5)*; *v SA 1957 (1)*; *v WI 1955 (1)*; *v In 1956 (3)*; *1959 (2) 1964 (3)*; *v P 1959 (2) 1964 (1)*
Burke, J. W. 24: v E 1950 (2) 1954 (2) 1958 (5); v WI 1951 (1); *v E 1956 (5)*; *v SA 1957 (5)*; *v In 1956 (3)*; *v P 1956 (1)*
Burton, F. J. 2: v E 1886 (1) 1887 (1)

Callaway, S. T. 3: v E 1891 (2) 1894 (1)
Carkeek, W. 6: v E 1912 (3); v SA 1912 (3)
Carter, H. 28: v E 1907 (5) 1911 (5) 1920 (2); v SA 1910 (5); *v E 1909 (5) 1921 (4)*; *v SA 1921 (2)*
Chappell, I. M. 3: v E 1965 (2); v P 1964 (1)
Charlton, P. C. 2: *v E 1890 (2)*
Chipperfield, A. G. 14: v E 1936 (3); *v E 1934 (5) 1938 (1)*; *v SA 1935 (5)*
Collins, H. L. 19: v E 1920 (5) 1924 (5); *v E 1921 (3) 1926 (3)*; *v SA 1921 (3)*
Coningham, A. 1: v E 1894
Connolly, A. N. 6: v E 1965 (1) v SA 1963 (3); *v In 1964 (2)*
Cooper, B. B. 1: v E 1876
Cooper, W. H. 2: v E 1881 (1) 1884 (1)
Corling, G. E. 5: *v E 1964 (5)*
Cottam, J. 1: v E 1886
Cotter, A. 21: v E 1903 (2) 1907 (2) 1911 (4); v SA 1910 (5); *v E 1905 (3) 1909 (5)*
Coulthard, G. 1: v E 1881
Cowper, R. M. 14: v E 1965 (4); v P 1964 (1); *v E 1964 (1)*; *v WI 1965 (5)*; *v In 1964 (2)*; *v P. 1964 (1)*

Craig, I. D. 11: v SA 1952 (1); *v E 1956 (2)*; *v SA 1957 (5)*; *v In 1956 (2)*; *v P 1956 (1)*
Crawford, P. 4: *v E 1956 (1)*; *v In 1956 (3)*

Darling, J. 34: v E 1894 (5) 1897 (5) 1901 (3); *v E 1896 (3) 1899 (5) 1902 (5) 1905 (5)*; *v SA 1902 (3)*
Darling, L. S. 12: v E 1932 (2) 1936 (1); *v E 1934 (4)*; *v SA 1935 (5)*
Davidson, A. K. 44: v E 1954 (3) 1958 (5) 1962 (5); v WI 1960 (4); *v E 1953 (5) 1956 (2) 1961 (5)*; *v SA 1957 (5)*; *v In 1956 (1) 1959 (5)*; *v P 1956 (1) 1959 (3)*
de Courcy, J. H. 3: *v E 1953 (3)*
Donnan, H. 5: v E 1891 (2); *v E 1896 (3)*
Dooland, B. 3: v E 1946 (2); v In 1947 (1)
Duff, R. A. 22: v E 1901 (4) 1903 (5); *v E 1902 (5) 1905 (5)*; *v SA 1902 (3)*

Eady, C. J. 2: v E 1901 (1); *v E 1896 (1)*
Ebeling, H. I. 1: *v E 1934*
Edwards, J. D. 3: *v E 1888 (3)*
Emery, S. H. 4: *v E 1912 (2)*; *v SA 1912 (2)*
Evans, E. 6: v E 1881 (2) 1882 (1) 1884 (1): *v E 1886 (2)*

Fairfax, A. 10: v E 1928 (1); v WI 1930 (5); *v E 1930 (4)*
Favell, L. E. 19: v E 1954 (4) 1958 (2); v WI 1960 (4); *v WI 1955 (2)*; *v In 1959 (4)*; *v P 1959 (3)*
Ferris, J. J. 8: v E 1886 (2) 1887 (1); *v E 1888 (3) 1890 (2)*
Fingleton, J. H. 18: v E 1932 (3) 1936 (5); v SA 1931 (1); *v E 1938 (4)*; *v SA 1935 (5)*
Fleetwood-Smith, L. O'B. 10: v E 1936 (3); *v E 1938 (4)*; *v SA 1935 (3)*
Freer, F. 1: v E 1946

Garrett, T. W. 19: v E 1876 (2) 1878 (1) 1881 (3) 1882 (3) 1884 (3) 1886 (2) 1887 (1); *v E 1882 (1) 1886 (3)*
Gaunt, R. A. 3: v SA 1963 (1); *v E 1961 (1)*; *v SA 1957 (1)*
Gehrs, D. R. A. 6: v E 1903 (1); v SA 1910 (4); *v E 1905 (1)*
Giffen, G. 31: v E 1881 (3) 1882 (4) 1884 (3) 1891 (3) 1894 (5); *v E 1882 (1) 1884 (3) 1886 (3) 1893 (3) 1896 (3)*
Giffen, W. F. 3: v E 1886 (1) 1891 (2)
Graham, H. 6: v E 1894 (2); *v E 1893 (3) 1896 (1)*
Gregory, D. W. 3: v E 1876 (2) 1878 (1)
Gregory, E. J. 1: v E 1876
Gregory, J. M. 24: v E 1920 (5) 1924 (5) 1928 (1); *v E 1921 (5) 1926 (5)*; *v SA 1921 (3)*
Gregory, R. 2: v E 1936 (2)
Gregory, S. E. 58: v E 1891 (1) 1894 (5) 1897 (5) 1901 (5) 1903 (4) 1907 (2) 1911 (1); *v E 1890 (2) 1893 (3) 1896 (3) 1899 (5) 1902 (5) 1905 (3) 1909 (5) 1912 (3)*; *v SA 1902 (3) 1912 (3)*
Grimmett, C. V. 37: v E 1924 (1) 1928 (5) 1932 (3); v SA 1931 (5); v WI 1930 (5); *v E 1926 (3) 1930 (5) 1934 (5)*; *v SA 1935 (5)*
Groube, T. U. 1: *v E 1880*
Grout, A. T. W. 51: v E 1958 (5) 1962 (2) 1965 (5); v SA 1963 (5); v WI 1960 (5); *v E 1961 (5) 1964 (5)*; *v SA 1957 (5)*; *v WI 1965 (5)*; *v In 1959 (4) 1964 (1)*; *v P 1959 (3) 1964 (1)*
Guest, C. 1: v E 1962

Hamence, R. A. 3: v E 1946 (1); v In 1947 (2)
Harry, J. 1: v E 1894
Hartigan, R. J. 2: v E 1907 (2)
Hartkopf, A. E. V. 1: v E 1924
Harvey, M. 1: v E 1946
Harvey, R. N. 79: v E 1950 (5) 1954 (5) 1958 (5); 1962 (5); v SA 1952 (5); v WI 1951 (5) 1960 (4); v In 1947 (2); *v E 1948 (2) 1953 (5) 1956 (5) 1961 (5)*; *v SA 1949 (5) 1957 (4)*; *v WI 1955 (5)*; *v In 1956 (3) 1959 (5)*; *v P 1956 (1) 1959 (3)*
Hassett, A. L. 43: v E 1946 (5) 1950 (5); v SA 1952 (5); v WI 1951 (4); v In 1947 (4); *v E 1938 (4) 1948 (5) 1953 (5)*; *v SA 1949 (5)*; *v NZ 1946 (1)*

Hawke, N. J. N. 22: v E 1962 (1) 1965 (4); v SA 1963 (4); v P 1964 (1); *v E 1964 (5); v WI 1965 (5); v In 1964 (1); v P 1964 (1)*
Hazlitt, G. R. 9: v E 1907 (2) 1911 (1); *v E 1912 (3); v SA 1912 (3)*
Hendry, H. L. 11: v E 1924 (1) 1928 (4); *v E 1921 (4); v SA 1921 (2)*
Hill, Clem, 49: v E 1897 (5) 1901 (5) 1903 (5) 1907 (5) 1911 (5); v SA 1910 (5); *v E 1896 (3) 1899 (3) 1902 (5) 1905 (5); v SA 1902 (3)*
Hill, J. C. 3: *v E 1953 (2); v WI 1955 (1)*
Hoare, D. 1: v WI 1960
Hodges, J. 2: v E 1876 (2)
Hole, G. B. 18: v E 1950 (1) 1954 (3); v SA 1952 (4); v WI 1951 (5); *v E 1953 (5)*
Hopkins, A. J. 20: v E 1901 (2) 1903 (5); *v E 1902 (5) 1905 (3) 1909 (2); v SA 1902 (3)*
Horan, T. 15: v E 1876 (1) 1878 (1) 1881 (4) 1882 (4) 1884 (4); *v E 1882 (1)*
Hordern, H. V. 7: v E 1911 (5); v SA 1910 (2)
Hornibrook, P. M. 6: v E 1928 (1); *v E 1930 (5)*
Howell, W. P. 18: v E 1897 (3) 1901 (4) 1903 (3); *v E 1899 (5); 1902 (1); v SA 1902 (2)*
Hunt, W. A. 1: v SA 1931
Hurwood, A. 2: v WI 1930 (2)

Iredale, F. A. 14: v E 1894 (5) 1897 (4); *v E 1896 (2) 1899 (3)*
Ironmonger, H. 14: v E 1928 (2) 1932 (4); v SA 1931 (4); v WI 1930 (4)
Iverson, J. 5: v E 1950 (5)

Jackson, A. A. 8: v E 1928 (2); v WI 1930 (4); *v E 1930 (2)*
Jarman, B. N. 7: v E 1962 (3); v P 1964 (1); *v In 1959 (1) 1964 (2)*
Jarvis, A. H. 11: v E 1884 (3) 1894 (4); *v E 1886 (2) 1888 (2)*
Jennings, C. B. 6: *v E 1912 (3); v SA 1912 (3)*
Johnson, I. W. 45: v E 1946 (4) 1950 (5) 1954 (4); v SA 1952 (1); v WI 1951 (4); v In 1947 (4); *v E 1948 (4) 1956 (5); v SA 1949 (5); v WI 1955 (5); v NZ 1946 (1); v In 1956 (2); v P 1956 (1)*
Johnson, L. 1: v In 1947
Johnston, W. A. 40: v E 1950 (5) 1954 (4); v SA 1952 (5); v WI 1951 (5); v In 1947 (4); *v E 1948 (5) 1953 (3); v SA 1949 (5); v WI 1955 (4)*
Jones, E. 19: v E 1894 (1) 1897 (5) 1901 (2); *v E 1896 (3) 1899 (5) 1902 (2); v SA 1902 (1)*
Jones, S. P. 12: v E 1881 (2) 1884 (4) 1886 (1) 1887 (1); *v E 1882 (1) 1886 (3)*

Kelleway, C. E. 26: v E 1911 (4) 1920 (5) 1924 (5) 1928 (1); v SA 1910 (5); *v E 1912 (3); v SA 1912 (3)*
Kelly, J. J. 36: v E 1897 (5) 1901 (5) 1903 (5); *v E 1896 (3) 1899 (5) 1902 (5) 1905 (5); v SA 1902 (3)*
Kelly, T. J. D. 2: v E 1876 (1) 1878 (1)
Kendall, T. 2: v E 1876 (2)
Kippax, A. F. 22: v E 1924 (1) 1928 (5) 1932 (1); v SA 1931 (4); v WI 1930 (5); *v E 1930 (5) 1934 (1)*
Kline, L. F. 13: v E 1958 (2); v WI 1960 (2); *v SA 1957 (5); v In 1959 (3); v P 1959 (1)*

Laver, F. 15: v E 1901 (1) 1903 (1); *v E 1899 (4) 1905 (5) 1909 (4)*
Langley, G. R. 26: v E 1954 (2); v SA 1952 (5); v WI 1951 (5); *v E 1953 (4) 1956 (3); v WI 1955 (4); v In 1956 (2); v P 1956 (1)*
Lawry, W. M. 35: v E 1962 (5) 1965 (5); v SA 1963 (5); v P 1964 (1); *v E 1961 (5) 1964 (5); v WI 1965 (5); v In 1964 (3); v P 1964 (1)*
Lee, P. K. 2: v E 1932 (1); v SA 1931 (1)
Lindwall, R. R. 61: v E 1946 (4) 1950 (5) 1954 (4) 1958 (2); v SA 1952 (4); v WI 1951 (5); v In 1947 (5); *v E 1948 (5) 1953 (5) 1956 (4); v SA 1949 (4); v WI 1955 (5); v NZ 1946 (1); v In 1956 (3) 1959 (2); v P 1956 (1) 1959 (2)*
Love, H. S. 1: v E 1932
Loxton, S. J. 12: v E 1950 (3); v In 1947 (1); *v E 1948 (3); v SA 1949 (5)*
Lyons, J. J. 14: v E 1886 (1) 1891 (3) 1894 (3) 1897 (1); *v E 1888 (1) 1890 (2) 1893 (3)*

Macartney, C. G. 35: v E 1907 (5) 1911 (1) 1920 (2); v SA 1910 (4); *v E 1909 (5) 1912 (3) 1921 (5) 1926 (5); v SA 1912 (3) 1921 (2)*

Mackay, K. D. 37: v E 1958 (5) 1962 (3); v WI 1960 (5); *v E 1956 (3) 1961 (5); v SA 1957 (5); v In 1956 (3) 1959 (5); v P 1959 (3)*
Maddocks, L. 7: v E 1954 (3); *v E 1956 (2); v WI 1955 (1); v In 1956 (1)*
Mailey, A. A. 21: v E 1920 (5) 1924 (5); *v E 1921 (3) 1926 (5); v SA 1921 (3)*
Marr, P. 1: v E 1884
Martin, J. W. 7: v SA 1963 (1); v WI 1960 (3); *v In 1964 (2); v P 1964 (1)*
Massie, H. H. 9: v E 1881 (4) 1882 (3) 1884 (1); *v E 1882 (1)*
Matthews, T. J. 8: v E 1911 (2); *v E 1912 (3); v SA 1912 (3)*
Mayne, E. R. 4: *v E 1912 (1); v SA 1912 (1) 1921 (2)*
Mayne, L. R. 3: *v WI 1965 (3)*
McAlister, P. A. 8: v E 1903 (2) 1907 (4); *v E 1909 (2)*
McCabe, S. J. 39: v E 1932 (5) 1936 (5); v SA 1931 (5); v WI 1930 (5); *v E 1930 (5) 1934 (5) 1938 (4); v SA 1935 (5)*
McCool, C. L. 14: v E 1946 (5); v In 1947 (3); *v SA 1949 (5); v NZ 1946 (1)*
McCormick, E. L. 12: v E 1936 (4); *v E 1938 (3); v SA 1935 (5)*
McDonald, C. C. 47: v E 1954 (2) 1958 (5); v SA 1952 (5); v WI 1951 (1) 1960 (5); *v E 1956 (5) 1961 (3); v SA 1957 (5); v WI 1955 (5); v In 1956 (2) 1959 (5); v P 1956 (1) 1959 (3)*
McDonald, E. A. 11: v E 1920 (3); *v E 1921 (5); v SA 1921 (3)*
McDonnell, P. S. 19: v E 1881 (4) 1882 (3) 1884 (2) 1886 (2) 1887 (1); *v E 1880 (1) 1884 (3) 1888 (3)*
McKenzie, G. D. 32: v E 1962 (5) 1965 (4); v SA 1963 (5); v P 1964 (1); *v E 1961 (3) 1964 (5); v WI 1965 (5); v In 1964 (3); v P 1964 (1)*
McLaren, J. W. 1: v E 1911
McLeod, C. E. 17: v E 1894 (1) 1897 (5) 1901 (2) 1903 (3); *v E 1899 (1) 1905 (5)*
McLeod, R. W. 6: v E 1891 (3); *v E 1893 (3)*
Meckiff, I. W. 18: v E 1958 (4); v SA 1963 (1); v WI 1960 (2); *v SA 1957 (4); v In 1959 (5); v P 1959 (2)*
Meuleman, K. 1: *v NZ 1946*
Midwinter, W. E. 8: v E 1876 (2) 1882 (1) 1886 (2); *v E 1884 (3)*
Miller, K. R. 55: v E 1946 (5) 1950 (5) 1954 (4); v SA 1952 (4); v WI 1951 (5); v In 1947 (5); *v E 1948 (5) 1953 (5) 1956 (5); v SA 1949 (5); v WI 1955 (5); v NZ 1946 (1); v P 1956 (1)*
M'Ilwraith, J. 1: *v E 1886*
Minnett, R. B. 9: v E 1911 (5); *v E 1912 (1); v SA 1912 (3)*
Misson, F. M. 5: v WI 1960 (3); *v E 1961 (2)*
M'Kibbin, T. R. 5: v E 1894 (1) 1897 (2); *v E 1896 (2)*
Moroney, J. R. 7: v E 1950 (1); v WI 1951 (1); *v SA 1949 (5)*
Morris, A. R. 46: v E 1946 (5) 1950 (5) 1954 (4); v SA 1952 (5); v WI 1951 (4); v In 1947 (4); *v E 1948 (5) 1953 (5); v SA 1949 (5); v WI 1955 (4).*
Morris, S. 1: v E 1884
Moses, H. 6: v E 1886 (2) 1887 (1) 1891 (2) 1894 (1)
Moule, W. H. 1: *v E 1880*
M'Shane, P. G. 3: v E 1884 (1) 1886 (1) 1887 (1)
Murdoch, W. L. 18: v E 1876 (1) 1878 (1) 1881 (4) 1882 (4) 1884 (1); *v E 1880 (1) 1882 (1) 1884 (3) 1890 (2)*
Musgrove, H. 1: v E 1884

Nagel, L. E. 1: v E 1932
Nash, L. J. 2: v E 1936 (1); v SA 1931 (1)
Nitschke, H. C. 2: v SA 1931 (2)
Noble, M. A. 42: v E 1897 (4) 1901 (5) 1903 (5) 1907 (5); *v E 1899 (5) 1902 (5) 1905 (5) 1909 (5); v SA 1902 (3)*
Noblet, G. 3: v SA 1952 (1); v WI 1951 (1); *v SA 1949 (1)*
Nothling, O. E. 1: v E 1928

O'Brien, L. P. 5: v E 1932 (2) 1936 (1); *v SA 1935 (2)*
O'Connor, J. A. 4: v E 1907 (3); *v E 1909 (1)*
Oldfield, W. A. 54: v E 1920 (3) 1924 (5) 1928 (5) 1932 (4) 1936 (5); v SA 1931 (5); v WI 1930 (5); *v E 1921 (1) 1926 (5) 1930 (5) 1934 (5); v SA 1921 (1) 1935 (5)*
O'Neill, N. C. 42: v E 1958 (5) 1962 (5); v SA 1963 (4); v WI 1960 (5); *v E 1961 (5) 1964 (4); v WI 1965 (4); v In 1959 (5) 1964 (2); v P 1959 (3)*

O'Reilly, W. J. 27: v E 1932 (5) 1936 (5); v SA 1931 (2); *v E 1934 (5) 1938 (4); v SA 1935 (5); v NZ 1946 (1)*
Oxenham, R. K. 7: v E 1928 (3); v SA 1931 (1); v WI 1930 (3)

Palmer, G. E. 17: v E 1881 (4) 1882 (4) 1884 (2); *v E 1880 (1) 1884 (3) 1886 (3)*
Park, R. L. 1: v E 1920
Pellew, C. E. 10: v E 1920 (4): *v E 1921 (5)* ; *v SA 1921 (1)*
Philpott, P. I. 8: v E 1965 (3); *v WI 1965 (5)*
Ponsford, W. H. 29: v E 1924 (5) 1928 (2) 1932 (3); v SA 1931 (4); v WI 1930 (5); *v E 1926 (2) 1930 (4) 1934 (4)*
Pope, R. J. 1: v E 1884

Ransford, V. S. 20: v E 1907 (5) 1911 (5); v SA 1910 (5); *v E 1909 (5)*
Redpath, I. R. 10: v E 1965 (1); v SA 1963 (1); *v E 1964 (5)*; *v In 1964 (2)*; *v P 1964 (1)*
Reedman, J. C. 1: v E 1894
Richardson, A. J. 9: v E 1924 (4); *v E 1926 (5)*
Richardson, V. Y. 19: v E 1924 (3) 1928 (2) 1932 (5); *v E 1930 (4)*; *v SA 1935 (5)*
Rigg, K. E. 8: v E 1936 (3); v SA 1931 (4); v WI 1930 (1)
Ring, D. 13: v SA 1952 (5); v WI 1951 (5); v In 1947 (1); *v E 1948 (1) 1953 (1)*
Robertson, W. R. 1: v E 1884
Robinson, R. 1: v E 1936
Rorke, G. 4: v E 1958 (2); *v In 1959 (2)*
Rutherford, J. 1: *v In 1956*
Ryder, J. S. 20: v E 1920 (5) 1924 (3) 1928 (5); *v E 1926 (4)*; *v SA 1921 (3)*

Saggers, R. A. 6: *v E 1948 (1)*; *v SA 1949 (5)*
Saunders, J. V. 14: v E 1901 (1) 1903 (2) 1907 (5); *v E 1902 (4)*; *v SA 1902 (2)*
Scott, H. J. H. 8: v E 1884 (2); *v E 1884 (3) 1886 (3)*
Sellars, R. H. D. 1: *v In 1964*
Sievers, M. 3: v E 1936 (3)
Shepherd B. 9: v E 1962 (2); v SA 1963 (4); v P 1964 (1); *v WI 1965 (2)*
Simpson, R. B. 44: v E 1958 (1) 1962 (5) 1965 (3); v SA 1963 (5); v WI 1960 (5); v P 1964 (1); *v E 1961 (5) 1964 (5)*; *v SA 1957 (5)*; *v WI 1965 (5)*; *v In 1964 (3)*; *v P 1964 (1)*
Sincock, D. J. 3: v E 1965 (1); v P 1964 (1); *v WI 1965 (1)*
Slater, K. 1: v E 1958
Slight, J. 1: *v E 1880*
Smith, D. 2: *v E 1912 (2)*
Spofforth, F. R. 18: v E 1876 (1) 1878 (1) 1881 (1) 1882 (4) 1884 (3) 1886 (1); *v E 1882 (1) 1884 (3) 1886 (3)*
Stackpole, K. R. 2: v E 1965 (2)
Stevens, G. 4: *v In 1959 (2)*; *v P 1959 (2)*

Tallon, D. 21: v E 1946 (5) 1950 (5); v In 1947 (5); *v E 1948 (4) 1953 (1)*; *v NZ 1946 (1)*
Taylor, J. M. 20: v E 1920 (5) 1924 (5); *v E 1921 (5) 1926 (3)*; *v SA 1921 (2)*
Thomas, G. 8: v E 1965 (3); *v WI 1965 (5)*
Thompson, N. 2: v E 1876 (2)
Thoms, G. 1: v WI 1951
Thurlow, H. M. 1: v SA 1931
Toshack, E. R. H. 12: v E 1946 (5); v In 1947 (2); *v E 1948 (4)*; *v NZ 1946 (1)*
Travers, J. F. 1: v E 1901
Tribe, G. E. 3: v E 1946 (3)
Trott, A. E. 3: v E 1894 (3)
Trott, G. H. S. 24: v E 1891 (3) 1894 (5) 1897 (5); *v E 1888 (3) 1890 (2) 1893 (3) 1896 (3)*
Trumble, H. 32: v E 1894 (1) 1897 (5) 1901 (5) 1903 (4); *v E 1890 (2) 1893 (3) 1896 (3) 1899 (5) 1902 (3)*; *v SA 1902 (1)*
Trumble, J. W. 7: v E 1884 (4); *v E 1886 (3)*
Trumper, V. T. 48: v E 1901 (5) 1903 (5) 1907 (5) 1911 (5); v SA 1910 (5); *v E 1899 (5) 1902 (5) 1905 (5) 1909 (5)*; *v SA 1902 (3)*
Turner, C. T. B. 17: v E 1886 (2) 1887 (1) 1891 (3) 1894 (3); *v E 1888 (3) 1890 (2) 1893 (3)*

Veivers, T. R. 17: v E 1965 (4); v SA 1963 (3); v P 1964 (1); *v E 1964 (5)*; *v In 1964 (3)*; *v P 1964 (1)*
Waite, M. G. 2: *v E 1938 (2)*
Wall, T. W. 18: v E 1928 (1) 1932 (4); v SA 1931 (3); v WI 1930 (1); *v E 1930 (5) 1934 (4)*
Walters, F. H. 1: v E 1884
Walters, K. D. 5: v E 1965 (5)
Ward, F. A. 4: v E 1936 (3); *v E 1938 (1)*
Watson, W. 4: v E 1954 (1); *v WI 1955 (3)*
Whitty, W. J. 14: v E 1911 (2); v SA 1910 (5); *v E 1909 (1) 1912 (3)*; *v SA 1912 (3)*
Wilson, J. 1: *v In 1956*
Woodfull, W. M. 35: v E 1928 (5) 1932 (5); v SA 1931 (5); v WI 1930 (5): *v E 1926 (5) 1930 (5) 1934 (5)*
Woods, S. M. J. 3: *v E 1888 (3)*
Worrall, J. 11: v E 1884 (1) 1887 (1) 1894 (1) 1897 (1); *v E 1888 (3) 1899 (4)*

SOUTH AFRICA

Adcock, N. A. T. 26: v E 1956 (5); v A 1957 (5); v NZ 1953 (5) 1961 (2); *v E 1955 (4) 1960 (5)*
Anderson, J. H. 1: v A 1902
Ashley, W. H. 1: v E 1888

Bacher, A. 3; *v E 1965 (3)*
Balaskas, X. C. 9: v E 1930 (2) 1938 (1); v A 1935 (3); *v E 1935 (1)*; *v NZ 1931 (2)*
Barlow, E. J. 21: v E 1964 (5); v NZ 1961 (5); *v E 1965 (3)*; *v A 1963 (5)*; *v NZ 1963 (3)*
Baumgartner, H. V. 1: v E 1913
Beaumont, R. 5: v E 1913 (2); *v E 1912 (1)*; *v A 1912 (2)*
Begbie, D. W. 5: v E 1948 (3); v A 1949 (2)
Bell, A. J. 16: v E 1930 (3); *v E 1929 (3) 1935 (3)*; *v A 1931 (5)*; *v NZ 1931 (2)*
Bisset, M. 3: v E 1898 (2) 1909 (1)
Bissett, G. F. 4: v E 1927 (4)
Blanckenberg, J. M. 18: v E 1913 (5) 1922 (5); v A 1921 (3); *v E 1924 (5)*
Bland, K. C. 20: v E 1964 (5); v NZ 1961 (5); *v E 1965 (3)*; *v A 1963 (4)*; *v NZ 1963 (3)*
Bock, E. G. 1: v A 1935
Bond, G. E. 1: v E 1938
Botten, J. T. 3: *v E 1965 (3)*
Brann, W. H. 3: v E 1922 (3)
Briscoe, A. W. 2: v E 1938 (1); v A 1935 (1)
Bromfield, H. D. 9: v E 1964 (3); v NZ 1961 (5); *v E 1965 (1)*
Brown, L. S. 2: *v A 1931 (1)*; *v NZ 1931 (1)*
Burger, C. 2: v A 1957 (2)
Burke, S. F. 2: v E 1964 (1); v NZ 1961 (1)
Buys, I. D. 1: v E 1922

Cameron, H. B. 26: v E 1927 (5) 1930 (5); *v E 1929 (4) 1935 (5)*; *v A 1931 (5)*; *v NZ 1931 (2)*
Campbell, T. 5: v E 1909 (4); *v E 1912 (1)*
Carlstein, P. 8: v A 1957 (1); *v E 1960 (5)*; *v A 1963 (2)*
Carter, C. P. 10: v E 1913 (2); v A 1921 (3); *v E 1912 (2) 1924 (3)*
Catterall, R. H. 24: v E 1922 (5) 1927 (5) 1930 (4); *v E 1924 (5) 1929 (5)*
Chapman, H. W. 2: v E 1913 (1); v A 1921 (1)
Cheetham, J. E. 24: v E 1948 (1); v A 1949 (3); v NZ 1953 (5); *v E 1951 (5) 1955 (3)*; *v A 1952 (5)*; *v NZ 1952 (2)*
Christy, J. A. J. 10: v E 1930 (1); *v E 1929 (2)*; *v A 1931 (5)*; *v NZ 1931 (2)*
Chubb, G. W. A. 5: *v E 1951 (5)*
Cochran, J. A. K. 1: v E 1930
Coen, S. K. 2: v E 1927 (2)
Commaille, J. M. M. 12: v. E 1909 (5) 1927 (2); *v E 1924 (5)*
Conyngham, D. P. 1: v E 1922
Cook, F. J. 1: v E 1895

Cooper, A. H. C. 1: v E 1913
Cox, J. L. 3: v E 1913 (3)
Cripps, G. 1: v E 1891
Crisp, R. J. 9: v A 1935 (4); *v E 1935 (5)*
Curnow, S. H. 7: v E 1930 (3); *v A 1931 (4)*

Dalton, E. L. 15: v E 1930 (1) 1938 (4); v A 1935 (1); *v E 1929 (1) 1935 (4); v A 1931 (2); v NZ 1931 (2)*
Davies, E. Q. 5: v E 1938 (3); v A 1935 (2)
Dawson, O. C. 9: v E 1948 (4); *v E 1947 (5)*
Deane, H. G. 17: v E 1927 (5) 1930 (2); *v E 1924 (5) 1929 (5)*
Dixon, C. D. 1: v E 1913
Dower, R. R. 1: v E 1898
Draper, R. G. 2: v A 1949 (2)
Duckworth, C. A. R. 2: v E 1956 (2)
Dumbrill, R. 3: *v E 1965 (3)*
Duminy, J. P. 3: v E 1927 (2); *v E 1929 (1)*
Dunell, O. R. 2: v E 1888 (2)
Du Toit, J. F. 1: v E 1891
Dyer, D. V. 3: *v E 1947 (3)*

Elgie, M. K. 3: v NZ 1961 (3)
Endean, W. R. 28: v E 1956 (5); v A 1957 (5); v NZ 1953 (5); *v E 1951 (1) 1955 (5); v A 1952 (5);* v *NZ 1952 (2)*

Farrer, W. R. 6: v NZ 1961 (3); *v NZ 1963 (3)*
Faulkner, G. A. 25: v E 1905 (5) 1909 (5); *v E 1907 (3) 1912 (3) 1924 (1); v A 1910 (5) 1912 (3)*
Fellows-Smith, J. P. 4: *v E 1960 (4)*
Fichardt, C. G. 2: v E 1891 (1) 1895 (1)
Finlason, C. E. 1: v E 1888
Floquet, C. E. 1: v E 1909
Francis, H. H. 2: v E 1898 (2)
Francois, C. M. 5: v E 1922 (5)
Frank, C. N. 3: v A 1921 (3)
Frank, W. H. B. 1: v E 1895
Fuller, E. R. H. 7: v A 1957 (1); *v E 1955 (2); v A 1952 (2); v NZ 1952 (2)*
Fullerton, G. M. 7: v A 1949 (2); *v E 1947 (2) 1951 (3)*
Funston, K. J. 18: v E 1956 (3); v A 1957 (5); v NZ 1953 (3); *v A 1952 (5) v NZ 1952 (2)*

Gleeson, R. A. 1: v E 1895
Glover, G. K. 1: v E 1895
Goddard, T. L. 33: v E 1956 (5) 1964 (5); v A (1957 (5); *v E 1955 (5) 1960 (5); v A 1963 (5); v NZ 1963 (3)*
Gordon, N. 5: v E 1938 (5)
Graham, R. 2: v E 1898 (2)
Grieveson, R. E. 2: v E 1938 (2)
Griffin, G. 2: *v E 1960 (2)*

Hall, A. E. 7: v E 1922 (4) 1927 (2) 1930 (1)
Hall, G. I. 1: v E 1964
Halliwell, E. A. 8: v E 1891 (1) 1895 (3) 1898 (1); v A 1902 (3)
Halse, C. G. 3; *v A 1963 (3)*
Hands, P. A. M. 7: v E 1913 (5); v A 1921 (1); *v E 1924 (1)*
Hands, R. H. M. 1: v E 1913
Hanley, M. A. 1: v E 1948
Harris, T. A. 3: v E 1948 (1); *v E 1947 (2)*
Hartigan, G. P. D. 5: v E 1912 (3); *v E 1912 (1); v A 1912 (1)*
Harvey, R. L. 2: v A 1935 (2)
Hathorn, M. 12: v E 1905 (5); v A 1902 (3); *v E 1907 (3); v A 1910 (1)*
Hearne, F. 4: v E 1891 (1) 1895 (3)
Hearne, G. A. L. 3: v E 1922 (2); *v E 1924 (1)*
Heine, P. 14: v E 1956 (5); v A 1957 (4); v NZ 1961 (1); *v E 1955 (4)*

Hime, C. F. W. 1: v E 1895
Hutchinson, P. 2: v E 1888 (2)

Innes, A. R. 2: v E 1888 (2)
Ironside, D. E. J. 3: v NZ 1953 (3)

Johnson, C. L. 1: v E 1895
Jones, P. S. T. 1: v A 1902

Keith, H. J. 8: v E 1956 (3); *v E 1955 (4)*; *v A 1952 (1)*
Kempis, G. A. 1: v E 1888
Kotze, J. J. 3: v A 1902 (2); *v E 1907 (1)*
Kuys, F. 1: v E 1898

Lance, H. R. 5: v NZ 1961 (2); *v E 1965 (3)*
Langton, A. B. C. 15: v E 1938 (5); v A 1935 (5); *v E 1935 (5)*
Lawrence, G. B. 5: v NZ 1961 (5)
Le Roux, F. le S. 1: v E 1913
Lewis, P. T. 1: v E 1913
Lindsay, D. 12: v E 1964 (3); *v E 1965 (3)*; *v A 1963 (3)*; *v NZ 1963 (3)*
Lindsay, J. D. 3: *v E 1947 (3)*
Lindsay, N. V. 1: v A 1921
Ling, W. V. S. 6: v E 1922 (3); v A 1921 (3)
Llewellyn, C. B. 15: v E 1895 (1) 1898 (1); v A 1902 (3); *v E 1912 (3)*; *v A 1910 (5) 1912 (2)*
Lundie, E. B. 1: v E 1913

Macaulay, M. J. 1: v E 1964
Mann, N. B. F. 19: v E 1948 (5); v A 1949 (5); *v E 1947 (5) 1951 (4)*
Mansell, P. N. F. 13: *v E 1951 (2) 1955 (4)*; *v A 1952 (5)*; *v NZ 1952 (2)*
Markham, L. A. 1: v E 1948
Marx, W. F. E. 3: v A 1921 (3)
McCarthy, C. N. 15: v E 1948 (5); v A 1949 (5); *v E 1951 (5)*
McGlew, D. J. 34: v E 1956 (1); v A 1957 (5); v NZ 1953 (5) 1961 (5); *v E 1951 (2) 1955 (5) 1960 (5)*; *v A 1952 (4)*; *v NZ 1952 (2)*
McKinnon, A. H. 6: v E 1964 (2); v NZ 1961 (1); *v E 1960 (1) 1965 (2)*
McLean, R. A. 40: v E 1956 (5) 1965 (2); v A 1957 (4); v NZ 1953 (4) 1961 (5); *v E 1951 (3) 1955 (5) 1960 (5)*; *v A 1952 (5)*; *v NZ 1952 (2)*
McMillan, Q. 13: v E 1930 (5); *v E 1929 (2)*; *v A 1931 (4)*; *v NZ 1931 (2)*
Meintjes, D. J. 2: v E 1922 (2)
Melle, M. G. 7: v A 1949 (2); *v E 1951 (1)*; *v A 1952 (4)*
Melville, A. 11: v E 1938 (5) 1948 (1); *v E 1947 (5)*
Middleton, J. 6: v E 1895 (2) 1898 (2); v A 1902 (2)
Mills, C. 1: v E 1891
Milton, W. H. 3: v E 1888 (2) 1891 (1)
Mitchell, B. 42: v E 1930 (5) 1938 (5) 1948 (5); v A 1935 (5); *v E 1929 (5) 1935 (5) 1947 (5)*; *v A 1931 (5)*; *v NZ 1931 (2)*
Mitchell, F. 3: *v E 1912 (1)*; *v A 1912 (2)*
Morkel, D. P. B. 16: v E 1927 (5); *v E 1929 (5)*; *v A 1931 (5)*; *v NZ 1931 (1)*
Murray, A. R. A. 10: v NZ 1953 (4); *v A 1952 (4)*; *v NZ 1952 (2)*

Nel, J. 6: v A 1949 (5) 1957 (1)
Newberry, C. 4: v E 1913 (4)
Newson, E. S. 3: v E 1930 (1) 1938 (2)
Nicholson, F. 4: v A 1935 (4)
Nicolson, J. F. W. 3: v E 1927 (3)
Norton, N. O. 1: v E 1909
Nourse, A. D. 45: v E 1905 (5) 1909 (5) 1913 (5) 1922 (5); v A 1902 (3) 1921 (3); *v E 1907 (3) 1912 (3) 1924 (5)*; *v A 1910 (5) 1912 (3)*
Nourse, Jnr., A. D. 34: v E 1938 (5) 1948 (5); v A 1935 (5) 1949 (5); *v E 1935 (4) 1947 (5) 1951 (5)*
Nupen, E. P. 17: v E 1922 (4) 1927 (5) 1930 (3); v A 1921 (2) 1935 (1); *v E 1924 (2)*

Ochse, A. E. 2: v E 1888 (2)
Ochse, A. L. 3: v E 1927 (1); *v E 1929 (2)*
O'Linn, S. 7: v NZ 1961 (2); *v E 1960 (5)*

Owen-Smith, H. G. 5: *v E 1929* (*5*)

Palm, A. W. 1: v E 1927
Parker, G. M. 2: *v E 1924* (*2*)
Parkin, D. C. 1: v E 1891
Partridge, J. T. 11: v E 1964 (3); *v A 1963* (*5*); *v NZ 1963* (*3*)
Pearse, O. C. 3: *v A 1910* (*3*)
Pegler, S. J. 16: v E 1909 (1); *v E 1912* (*3*) *1924* (*5*); *v A 1910* (*4*) *1912* (*3*)
Pithey, A. J. 17: v E 1956 (3) 1964 (5); *v E 1960* (*2*); *v A 1963* (*4*); *v NZ 1963* (*3*)
Pithey, D. B. 6: *v A 1963* (*3*); *v NZ 1963* (*3*)
Plimsoll, J. B. 1: *v E 1947*
Pollock, P. M. 19: v E 1964 (5); v NZ 1961 (3); *v E 1965* (*3*); *v A 1963* (*5*); *v NZ 1963* (*3*)
Pollock, R. G. 14: v E 1964 (5); *v E 1965* (*3*); *v A 1963* (*5*); *v NZ 1963* (*1*)
Poore, R. M. 3: v E 1895 (3)
Pothecary, J. E. 3: *v E 1960* (*3*)
Powell, A. W. 1: v E 1898
Prince, C. F. 1: v E 1898
Promnitz, H. L. E. 2: v E 1927 (2)

Quinn, N. A. 12: v E 1930 (1); *v E 1929* (*4*); *v A 1931* (*5*); *v NZ 1931* (*2*)

Reid, N. 1: v A 1921
Richards, A. 1: v E 1895
Richards, W. H. 1: v E 1888
Robertson, J. B. 3: v A 1935 (3)
Routledge, T. 4: v E 1891 (1) 1895 (3)
Rowan, A. M. B. 15: v E 1948 (5); *v E 1947* (*5*) *1951* (*5*)
Rowan, E. A. B. 26: v E 1938 (4) 1948 (4); v A 1935 (3) 1949 (5); *v E 1935* (*5*) *1951* (*5*)
Rowe, G. A. 5: v E 1895 (2) 1898 (2); v A 1902 (1)

Samuelson, S. V. 1: v E 1909
Schwarz, R. O. 20: v E 1905 (5) 1909 (4); *v E 1907* (*3*) *1912* (*1*); *v A 1910* (*5*) *1912* (*2*)
Seccull, A. W. 1; v E 1895
Seymour, M. A. 6: v E 1964 (2); *v A 1963* (*4*)
Shalders, W. A. 12: v E 1898 (1) 1905 (5); v A 1902 (3); *v E 1907* (*3*)
Shepstone, G. H. 2: v E 1895 (1) 1898 (1)
Sherwell, P. W. 13: v E 1905 (5); *v E 1907* (*3*); *v A 1910* (*5*)
Siedle, I. J. 18: v E 1927 (1) 1930 (5); v A 1935 (5); *v E 1929* (*3*) *1935* (*4*)
Sinclair, J. H. 25: v E 1895 (3) 1898 (2) 1905 (5) 1909 (4); v A 1902 (3); *v E 1907* (*3*); *v A 1910* (*5*)
Smith, C. J. E. 3; v A 1902 (3)
Smith, F. W. 3: v E 1888 (2) 1895 (1)
Smith, V. I. 9: v A 1949 (3) 1947 (1); *v E 1947* (*4*) *1955* (*1*)
Snooke, S. D. 1: v E 1907
Snooke, S. J. 26: v E 1905 (5) 1909 (5) 1922 (3); *v E 1907* (*3*) *1912* (*3*); *v A 1910* (*5*) *1912* (*2*)
Solomon, W. R. 1: v E 1898
Stewart, R. B. 1: v E 1888
Stricker, L. A. 13: v E 1909 (4); *v E 1912* (*2*); *v A 1910* (*5*) *1912* (*2*)
Susskind, M. J. 5: *v E 1924* (*5*)

Taberer, H. M. 1: v A 1902
Tancred, A. B. 2: v E 1888 (2)
Tancred, L. J. 14: v E 1905 (5) 1913 (1); v A 1902 (3); *v E 1907* (*1*) *1912* (*2*); *v A 1912* (*2*)
Tancred, V. M. 1: v E 1898
Tapscott, L. E. 2: v E 1922 (2)
Tapscott, L. G. 1: v E 1913
Tayfield, H. J. 37; v E 1956 (5); v A 1949 (5) 1957 (5); v NZ 1953 (5); *v E 1955* (*5*) *1960* (*5*); *v A 1952* (*5*); *v NZ 1952* (*2*)
Taylor, A. I. 1: v E 1956
Taylor, D. 2: v E 1913 (2)

Taylor, H. W. 42: v E 1913 (5) 1922 (5) 1927 (5) 1930 (4); v A 1921 (3); *v E 1912 (3) 1924 (5) 1929 (3)*; *v A 1912 (3) 1931 (5)*; *v NZ 1931 (1)*
Theunissen, N. H. 1: v E 1888
Thornton, G. 1: v A 1902
Tomlinson, D. S. 1: *v E 1935*
Tuckett, L. 9: v E 1948 (4); *v E 1947 (5)*
Tuckett, L. R. 1: v E 1913

van der Byl, P. G. 5: v E 1938 (5)
van der Merwe, E. A. 2: v A 1935 (1); *v E 1929 (1)*
van der Merwe, P. L. 10: v E 1964 (2); *v E 1965 (3)*; *v A 1963 (3)*; *v NZ 1963 (2)*
van Ryneveld, C. B. 19: v E 1956 (5); v A 1957 (4); v NZ 1953 (5); *v E 1951 (5)*
Varnals, G. D. 3: v E 1964 (3)
Viljoen, K. G. 27: v E 1930 (3) 1938 (4) 1948 (2); v A 1935 (4); *v E 1935 (4) 1947 (5)*; *v A 1931 (4)*; *v NZ 1931 (1)*
Vincent, C. L. 25: v E 1927 (5) 1930 (5); *v E 1929 (4) 1935 (4)*; *v A 1931 (5)*; *v NZ 1931 (2)*
Vintcent, C. H. 3: v E 1888 (2) 1891 (1)
Vogler, A. E. E. 15: v E 1905 (5) 1909 (5); *v E 1907 (3)*; *v A 1910 (2)*

Wade, H. F. 10: v A 1935 (5); *v E 1935 (5)*
Wade, W. W. 11: v E 1938 (3) 1948 (5); v A 1949 (3)
Waite, J. H. B. 50: v E 1956 (5) 1964 (2); v A 1957 (5); v NZ 1953 (5) 1961 (5); *v E 1951 (4) 1955 (5) 1960 (5)*; *v A 1952 (5) 1963 (4)*; *v NZ 1952 (2) 1963 (3)*
Walter, K. A. 2: v NZ 1961 (2)
Ward, T. A. 23: v E 1913 (5) 1922 (5); v A 1921 (3); *v E 1912 (2) 1924 (5)*; *v A 1912 (3)*
Watkins, J. C. 15: v E 1956 (2); v A 1949 (3); v NZ 1953 (3); *v A 1952 (5)*; *v NZ 1952 (2)*
Wesley, C. 3: *v E 1960 (3)*
Westcott, R. J. 5: v A 1957 (2); v NZ 1953 (3)
White, G. C. 17: v E 1905 (5) 1909 (4); *v E 1907 (3) 1912 (2)*; *v A 1912 (3)*
Willoughby, J. T. I. 2: v E 1895 (2)
Wimble, C. S. 1: v E 1891
Winslow, P. L. 5: v A 1949 (2); *v E 1955 (3)*
Wynne, O. E. 6: v E 1948 (3); v A 1949 (3)

Zulch, J. W. 16: v E 1909 (5) 1913 (3); v A 1921 (3); *v A 1910 (5)*

WEST INDIES

Achong, E. 6: v E 1929 (1) 1934 (2); *v E 1933 (3)*
Alexander, F. C. M. 25: v E 1959 (5); v P 1958 (5); *v E 1957 (2)*; *v A 1960 (5)* *v In 1958 (5)*; *v P 1958 (3)*
Allan, D. W. 5: v A 1965 (1); v In 1962 (2); *v E 1966 (2)*
Asgarali, N. 2: *v E 1957 (2)*
Atkinson, D. 22: v E 1953 (4); v A 1955 (4); v P 1958 (1); *v E 1957 (2)*; *v A 1951 (2)*; *v NZ 1951 (1) 1955 (4)*; *v In 1948 (4)*
Atkinson, F. 8: v P 1958 (3); *v In 1958 (3)*; *v P 1958 (2)*

Barrow, I. 11: v E 1929 (1) 1934 (1); *v E 1933 (3) 1939 (1)*; *v A 1930 (5)*
Bartlett, E. L. 5: *v E 1928 (1)*; *v A 1930 (4)*
Betancourt, N. 1: v E 1929
Binns, A. P. 5: v A 1955 (1); v In 1952 (1); *v NZ 1955 (3)*
Birkett, L. S. 4: *v A 1930 (4)*
Browne, C. R. 4: v E 1929 (2); *v E 1928 (2)*
Butcher, B. F. 25: v E 1959 (2); v A 1965 (5); *v E 1963 (5) 1966 (5)*; *v In 1958 (5)*; *v P 1958 (3)*
Butler, L. 1: v A 1955
Bynoe, R. 1: *v P 1958*

Caires, F. I. de 3: v E 1929 (3)
Cameron, F. J. 5: *v In 1948 (5)*
Cameron, J. H. 2: *v E 1939 (2)*
Carew, G. 4: v E 1934 (1) 1947 (2); *v In 1948 (1)*

Carew, M. C. 3: *v E 1963 (2) 1966 (1)*
Challenor, G. 3: *v E 1928 (3)*
Christiani, C. M. 4: v E 1934 (4)
Christiani, R. J. 22: v E 1947 (4) 1953 (1); v In 1952 (2); *v E 1950 (4); v A 1951 (5); v NZ 1951 (1); v In 1948 (5)*
Clarke, C. B. 3: *v E 1939 (3)*
Constantine, L. N. 18: v E 1929 (3) 1934 (3); *v E 1928 (3) 1933 (1) 1939 (3); v A 1930 (5)*
Costa, O. C. da, 5: v E 1929 (1) 1934 (1); *v E 1933 (3)*

Davis, B. 4: v A 1965 (4)
Depeiza, C. 5: v A 1955 (3); *v NZ 1955 (2)*
Dewdney, T. 9: v A 1955 (2); v P 1958 (3); *v E 1957 (1); v NZ 1955 (3)*

Ferguson, W. 8: v E 1947 (4) 1953 (1); *v In 1948 (3)*
Fernandes, M. P. 2: v E 1929 (1); *v E 1928 (1)*
Francis, G. N. 10: v E 1929 (1); *v E 1928 (3) 1933 (1); v A 1930 (5)*
Frederick, M. 1: v E 1953
Fuller, R. L. 1: v E 1934
Furlonge, H. 3: v A 1955 (1); *v NZ 1955 (2)*

Ganteaume, A. G. 1: v E 1947
Gaskin, B. 2: v E 1947 (2)
Gibbs, G. 1: v A 1955
Gibbs L. R. 31: v A 1965 (5); v In 1962 (5); v P 1958 (4); *v E 1963 (5) 1966 (5); v A 1960 (3); v In 1958 (1); v P 1958 (3)*
Gilchrist, R. 13: v P 1958 (5); *v E 1957 (4); v In 1958 (4)*
Gladstone, G. 1: v E 1929
Goddard, J. D. 27: v E 1947 (4); *v E 1950 (4) 1957 (5); v A 1951 (4); v NZ 1951 (2) 1955 (3); v In 1948 (5)*
Gomez, G. E. 29: v E 1947 (4) 1953 (4); v In 1952 (4); *v E 1939 (2) 1950 (4); v A 1951 (5); v NZ 1951 (1); v In 1948 (5)*
Grant, G. C. 12: v E 1934 (4); *v E 1933 (3); v A 1930 (5)*
Grant, R. S. 7: v E 1934 (4); *v E 1939 (3)*
Grell, M. 1: v E 1929
Griffith, C. C. 16: v E 1959 (1); v A 1965 (5); *v E 1963 (5) 1966 (5)*
Griffith, H. C. 13: v E 1929 (3); *v E 1928 (3) 1933 (2); v A 1930 (5)*
Guillen, S. C. 5: *v A 1951 (3); v NZ 1951 (2)*

Hall W. W. 38: v E 1959 (5); v A 1965 (5); v In 1962 (5); *v E 1963 (5) 1966 (5); v A 1960 (5); v In 1958 (5); v P 1958 (3)*
Headley, G. A. 22: v E 1929 (4) 1934 (4) 1947 (1) 1953 (1); *v E 1933 (3) 1939 (3); v A 1930 (5); v In 1948 (1)*
Hendriks, J. L. 8: v A 1965 (4); v In 1962 (1); *v E 1966 (3)*
Hoad, E. L. G. 4: v E 1929 (1); *v E 1928 (1) 1933 (2)*
Holford, D. A. J. 5: *v E 1966 (5)*
Holt, J. K. 17: v E 1953 (5); v A 1955 (5); *v In 1958 (5); v P 1958 (2)*
Hunte, C. C. 41: v E 1959 (5); v A 1965 (5); v In 1962 (5); v P 1958 (5); *v E 1963 (5) 1966 (5); v A 1960 (5); v In 1958 (5); v P 1958 (1)*
Hunte, E. 3: v E 1929 (3)
Hylton, L. G. 6: v E 1934 (4); *v E 1939 (2)*

Johnson, H. H. 3: v E 1947 (1); *v E 1950 (2)*
Johnson, T. 1: *v E 1939*
Jones, C. M. 4: v E 1929 (1) 1934 (3)
Jones, P. E. 9: v E 1947 (1); *v E 1950 (2); v A 1951 (1); v In 1948 (5)*

Kanhai, R. B. 48: v E 1959 (5); v A 1965 (5); v In 1962 (5); v P 1958 (5); *v E 1957 (5) 1963 (5) 1966 (5); v A 1960 (5); v In 1958 (5); v P 1958 (3)*
Kentish, E. 2: v E 1947 (1) 1953 (1)
King, F. 14: v E 1953 (3); v A 1955 (4); v In 1952 (5); *v NZ 1955 (2)*
King, L. 1: v In 1962

Lashley, P. D. 4: *v E 1966 (2) v A 1960 (2)*
Legall, R. 4: v In 1952 (4)

Madray, I. S. 2: v P 1958 (2)
Marshall, N. 1: v A 1955
Marshall, R. E. 4: *v A 1951 (2)*; *v NZ 1951 (2)*
Martin, F. R. 9: v E 1929 (1); *v E 1928 (3)*; *v A 1930 (5)*
Martindale, E. A. 10: v E 1934 (4); *v E 1933 (3) 1939 (3)*
McMorris, E. D. 13: v E 1959 (4); v In 1962 (4); v P 1958 (1); *v E 1963 (2) 1966 (2)*
McWatt, C. A. 6: v E 1953 (5); v A 1955 (1)
Mendonca, I. 2: v In 1962 (2)
Merry, C. A. 2: *v E 1933 (2)*
Miller, R. 1: v In 1952
Moodie, G. H. 1: v E 1934
Murray, D. L. 5: *v E 1963 (5)*

Neblett, J. M. 1: v E 1934
Nunes, R. K. 4: v E 1929 (1); *v E 1928 (3)*
Nurse, S. M. 14: v E 1959 (1); v A 1965 (4); v In 1962 (1); *v E 1966 (5)*; *v A 1960 (3)*

Pairaudeau, B. H. 13: v E 1953 (2); v In 1952 (5); *v E 1957 (2)*; *v NZ 1955 (4)*
Passalique, C. C. 1: v E 1929
Pierre, L. R. 1: v E 1947

Rae, A. F. 15: v In 1952 (2); *v E 1950 (4)*; *v A 1951 (3)*; *v NZ 1951 (1)*; *v In 1948 (5)*
Ramadhin, S. 43: v E 1953 (5) 1959 (4); v A 1955 (4); v In 1952 (4); *v E 1950 (4) 1957 (5)*; *v A 1951 (5) 1960 (2)*; *v NZ 1951 (2) 1955 (4)*; *v In 1958 (2)*; *v P 1958 (2)*
Rickards, K. 2: v E 1947 (1); *v A 1951 (1)*
Roach, C. A. 16: v E 1929 (4) 1934 (1); *v E 1928 (3) 1933 (3)*; *v A 1930 (5)*
Roberts, A. 1: *v NZ 1955*
Rodriguez, W. V. 4: v A 1965 (1); v In 1962 (2); *v E 1963 (1)*

St. Hill, E. 2: v E 1929 (2)
St. Hill, W. H. 3: v E 1929 (1) *v E 1928 (2)*
Scarlett, R. 3: v E 1959 (3)
Scott, A. P. H. 1: v In 1952
Scott, O. C. 8: v E 1929 (1); *v E 1928 (2)*; *v A 1930 (5)*
Sealey, B. J. 1: *v E 1933*
Sealy, J. E. D. 11: v E 1929 (2) 1934 (4); *v E 1939 (3)*; *v A 1930 (2)*
Singh, C. K. 2: v E 1959 (2)
Small, J. A. 3: v E 1929 (1); *v E 1928 (2)*
Smith, C. 5: v In 1962 (1); *v A 1960 (4)*
Smith, O. G. 26: v A 1955 (4); v P 1958 (5); *v E 1957 (5)*; *v NZ 1955 (4)*; *v In 1958 (5)*; *v P 1958 (3)*
Sobers, G. S. 57: v E 1953 (1) 1959 (5); v A 1955 (4) 1965 (5); v In 1962 (5); v P 1958 (5); *v E 1957 (5) 1963 (5) 1966 (5)*; *v A 1960 (5)*; *v NZ 1955 (4)*, *v In 1958 (5)*; *v P 1958 (3)*
Solomon, J. S. 27: v E 1959 (2); v A 1965 (4); v In 1962 (4); *v E 1963 (5)*; *v A 1960 (5)*; *v In 1958 (4)*; *v P 1958 (3)*
Stayers, C. 4: v In 1962 (4)
Stollmeyer, J. B. 32: v E 1947 (2) 1953 (5); v A 1955 (2); v In 1952 (5); *v E 1939 (3) 1950 (4)*; *v A 1951 (5)*; *v NZ 1951 (2)*; *v In 1948 (4)*
Stollmeyer, V. H. 1: *v E 1939*

Taylor, J. 3: v P 1958 (1); *v In 1958 (1)*; *v P 1958 (1)*
Trim, J. 4: v E 1947 (1); *v A 1951 (1)*; *v In 1948 (2)*

Valentine, A. L. 36: v E 1953 (3); v A 1955 (3); v In 1952 (5) 1962 (2); v P 1958 (1); *v E 1950 (4) 1957 (2)*; *v A 1951 (5) 1960 (5)*; *v NZ 1951 (2) 1955 (4)*
Valentine, V. A. 2: *v E 1933 (2)*

Walcott, C. L. 44: v E 1947 (4) 1953 (5) 1959 (2); v A 1955 (5); v In 1952 (5); v P 1958 (4); *v E 1950 (4) 1957 (5)*; *v A 1951 (3)*; *v NZ 1951 (2)*; *v In 1948 (5)*
Walcott, L. A. 1: v E 1929
Watson, C. 7: v E 1959 (5); v In 1962 (1); *v A 1960 (1)*
Weekes, E. D. 48: v E 1947 (4) 1953 (4); v A 1955 (5); v In 1952 (5); v P 1958 (5); *v E 1950 (4) 1957 (5)*; *v A 1951 (5)*; *v NZ 1951 (2) 1955 (4)*; *v In 1948 (5)*

Weekes, K. H. 2: *v E 1939 (2)*
White, W. A. 2: v A 1965 (2)
Wight, C. V. 2: v E 1929 (1); *v E 1928 (1)*
Wight, L. 1: v In 1952
Wiles, C. A. 1: *v E 1933*
Williams, E. A. V. 4: v E 1947 (3); *v E 1939 (1)*
Wishart, K. L. 1: v E 1934
Worrell, F. M. 51: v E 1947 (3) 1953 (4) 1959 (4); v A 1955 (4); v In 1952 (5) 1962 (5); *v E 1950 (4) 1957 (5) 1963 (5); v A 1951 (5) 1960 (5); v NZ 1951 (2)*

NEW ZEALAND

Alabaster, J. C. 15: v E 1962 (2); v WI 1955 (1); *v E 1958 (2); v SA 1961 (5); v In 1955 (4); v P 1955 (1)*
Allcott, C. F. W. 6: v E 1929 (2); v SA 1931 (1); *v E 1931 (3)*
Anderson, W. M. 1: v A 1946

Badcock, F. T. 7: v E 1929 (3) 1932 (2); v SA 1931 (2)
Barber, R. T. 1: v WI 1955
Bartlett, G. A. 8: v E 1965 (2); v P 1965 (1); *v SA 1961 (5)*
Barton, P. T. 7: v E 1962 (3); *v SA 1961 (4)*
Beard, D. D. 4: v WI 1951 (2) 1955 (2)
Beck, J. E. F. 8: v WI 1955 (4); *v SA 1953 (4)*
Bell, W. 2: *v SA 1953 (2)*
Bilby, G. B. 2: v E 1965 (2)
Blair, R. W. 19: v E 1954 (1) 1958 (2) 1962 (2); v SA 1952 (2) 1963 (3); v WI 1955 (2); *v E 1958 (3); v SA 1953 (4)*
Blunt, R. C. 9: v E 1929 (4); v SA 1931 (2); *v E 1931 (3)*
Bolton, B. A. 2: v E 1958 (2)
Bradburn, W. P. 2: v SA 1963 (2)
Burke, C. C. 1: v A 1946
Burtt, T. B. 10: v E 1946 (1) 1950 (2); v SA 1952 (1); v WI 1951 (2); *v E 1949 (4)*
Butterfield, L. A. 1: v A 1946

Cameron, F. J. 19: v E 1962 (3); v SA 1963 (3); v P 1965 (3); *v E 1965 (2); v SA 1961 (5); v In 1965 (1); v P 1965 (2)*
Cave, H. B. 19: v E 1954 (2); v WI 1955 (3); *v E 1949 (4) 1958 (2); v In 1955 (5); v P 1955 (3)*
Chapple, M. E. 14: v E 1954 (1) 1965 (1); v SA 1952 (1) 1963 (3); v WI 1955 (1); *v SA 1953 (5) 1961 (2)*
Cleverley, D. C. 2: v SA 1931 (1); v A 1946 (1)
Collinge, R. O. 10: v P 1965 (3); *v E 1965 (3); v In 1965 (2); v P 1965 (2)*
Colquhoun, I. A. 2: v E 1954 (2)
Congdon, B. E. 13: v E 1965 (3); v P 1965 (3); *v E 1965 (3); v In 1965 (3); v P 1965 (1)*
Cowie, J. 9: v E 1946 (1); v A 1946 (1); *v E 1937 (3) 1949 (4)*
Cresswell, G. F. 3: v E 1950 (2); *v E 1949 (1)*
Cromb, I. B. 5: v SA 1931 (2); *v E 1931 (3)*
Cunis, R. S. 4: v E 1965 (3); v SA 1963 (1)

D'Arcy, J. W. 5: *v E 1958 (5)*
Dempster, C. S. 10: v E 1929 (4) 1932 (2); v SA 1931 (2); *v E 1931 (2)*
Dempster, E. W. 5: v SA 1952 (1); *v SA 1953 (4)*
Dick, A. E. 17: v E 1962 (3); v SA 1963 (2); v P 1965 (2); *v E 1965 (2); v SA 1961 (5); v P 1965 (3)*
Dickinson, G. R. 3: v E 1929 (2); v SA 1931 (1)
Donnelly, M. P. 7: *v E 1937 (3) 1949 (4)*
Dowling, G. T. 19: v E 1962 (3); v SA 1963 (1); v P 1965 (2); *v E 1965 (3); v SA 1961 (4); v In 1965 (4); v P 1965 (2)*
Dunning, J. A. 4: v E 1932 (1); *v E 1937 (3)*

Emery, R. W. G. 2: v WI 1951 (2)

Fisher, F. E. 1: v SA 1952
Foley, H. 1: v E 1929
Freeman, D. L. 2: v E 1932 (2)

Gallichan, N. M. 1: *v E 1937*
Gedye, S. G. 4: v SA 1963 (3); v P 1965 (1)
Guillen, S. C. 3: v WI 1955 (3)
Guy, J. W. 12: v E 1958 (2); v WI 1955 (2); *v SA 1961 (2)*; *v In 1955 (5)*; *v P 1955 (1)*

Hadlee, W. A. 11: v E 1946 (1) 1950 (2); v A 1946 (1); *v E 1937 (3) 1949 (4)*
Harford, N. S. 8: *v E 1958 (4)*; *v In 1955 (2)*; *v P 1955 (2)*
Harris, P. G. Z. 9: v P 1965 (1); *v SA 1961 (5)*; *v In 1955 (1)*; *v P 1955 (2)*
Harris, R. 2: v E 1958 (2)
Hayes, J. A. 15: v E 1950 (2) 1954 (1); v WI 1951 (2); *v E 1958 (4)*; *v In 1955 (5)*; *v P 1955 (1)*
Henderson, M. 1: v E 1929
Hough, K. W. 2: v E 1958 (2)

James, K. C. 11: v E 1929 (4) 1932 (2); v SA 1931 (2); *v E 1931 (3)*
Jarvis, T. W. 6: v E 1965 (1); *v In 1965 (2)*; *v P 1965 (3)*

Kerr, J. L. 7: v E 1932 (2); v SA 1931 (1); *v E 1931 (2) 1937 (2)*

Leggat, I. B. 1: *v SA 1953*
Leggat, J. G. 9: v E 1954 (1); v SA 1952 (1); v WI 1951 (1) 1955 (1); *v In 1955 (3)*; *v P 1955 (2)*
Lissette, A. F. 2: v WI 1955 (2)
Lowry, T. C. 7: v E 1929 (4); *v E 1931 (3)*

MacGibbon, A. R. 26: v E 1950 (2) 1954 (2); v SA 1952 (1); v WI 1955 (3); *1958 (5)*; *v SA 1953 (5)*; *v In 1955 (5)*; *v P 1955 (3)*
McGirr, H. M. 2: v E 1929 (2)
McGregor, S. N. 25: v E 1954 (2) 1958 (2); v SA 1963 (3); v WI 1955 (4); v P 1965 (2); *v SA 1961 (5)*; *v In 1955 (4)*; *v P 1955 (3)*
McLeod, E. A. 1: v E 1929
McMahon, T. G. 5: v WI 1955 (1); *v In 1955 (3)*; *v P 1955 (1)*
McRae, D. A. N. 1: v A 1946
Maloney, D. A. R. 3: *v E 1937 (3)*
Matheson, A. M. 2: v E 1929 (1); *v E 1931 (1)*
Meale, T. 2: *v E 1958 (2)*
Merritt, W. E. 6: v E 1929 (4); *v E 1931 (2)*
Meuli, E. M. 1: v SA 1952
Miller, L. S. M. 13: v SA 1952 (2); v WI 1955 (3); *v E 1958 (4)*; *v SA 1953 (4)*
Mills, J. W. E. 7: v E 1929 (3) 1932 (1); *v E 1931 (3)*
Moir, A. M. 17: v E 1950 (2) 1954 (2) 1958 (2); v SA 1952 (1); v WI 1951 (2) 1955 (1); *v E 1958 (2)*; *v In 1955 (2)*; *v P 1955 (3)*
Mooney, F. L. H. 14: v E 1950 (2); v SA 1952 (2); v WI 1951 (2); *v E 1949 (3)*; *v SA 1953 (5)*
Morgan, R. W. 14: v E 1965 (2); v P 1965 (2); *v E 1965 (3)*; *v In 1965 (4)*; *v P 1965 (3)*
Morrison, B. (1): E 1962
Motz, R. C. 22: v E 1962 (2) 1965 (3); v SA 1963 (2); v P 1965 (3); *v E 1965 (3)*; *v SA 1961 (5)*; *v In 1965 (3)*; *v P 1965 (1)*

Newman, J. 3: v E 1932 (2); v SA 1931 (1)

Overton, G. W. F. 3: *v SA 1953 (3)*

Page, M. L. 14: v E 1929 (4) 1932 (2); v SA 1931 (2); *v E 1931 (3) 1937 (3)*
Petrie, E. C. 14: v E 1958 (2) 1965 (3); *v E 1958 (5)*; *v In 1955 (2)*; *v P 1955 (2)*
Playle, W. R. 8: v E 1962 (3); *v E 1958 (5)*
Pollard, V. 13: v E 1965 (3); *v E 1965 (3)*; *v In 1965 (4)*; *v P 1965 (3)*
Poore, M. B. 14: v E 1954 (1); v SA 1952 (1); *v SA 1953 (5)*; *v In 1955 (4)*; *v P 1955 (3)*
Puna, N. 3: v E 1965 (3)

Rabone, G. O. 12: v E 1954 (2); v SA 1952 (1); v WI 1951 (2); *v E 1949 (4)*; *v SA 1953 (3)*
Reid, J. R. 58: v E 1950 (2) 1954 (2) 1958 (2) 1962 (3); v SA 1952 (2) 1963 (3); v WI 1951 (2) 1955 (4); v P 1965 (3); *v E 1949 (2) 1958 (5) 1965 (3)*; *v SA 1953 (5) 1961 (5)*; *v In 1955 (5) 1965 (4)*; *v P 1955 (3) 1965 (3)*

Roberts, A. W. 5: v E 1929 (1); v SA 1931 (2); *v E 1937 (2)*
Rowe, C. G. 1: v A 1946

Scott, R. H. 1: v E 1946
Scott, V. J. 10: v E 1946 (1) 1950 (2); v A 1946 (1); v WI 1951 (2); *v E 1949 (4)*
Shrimpton, M. J. F. 6: v E 1962 (2) 1965 (3); v SA 1963 (1)
Sinclair, B. W. 19: v E 1962 (3) 1965 (3); v SA 1963 (3); v P 1965 (2); *v E 1965 (3)*; *v In 1965 (2)*; *v P 1965 (3)*
Sinclair, I. M. 2: v WI 1955 (2)
Smith, D. 1: v E 1932
Smith, F. B. 4: v E 1946 (1); v WI 1951 (1); *v E 1949 (2)*
Snedden, C. A. 1: v E 1946
Sparling, J. T. 11: v E 1958 (2) 1962 (1); v SA 1963 (2); *v E 1958 (3)*; *v SA 1961 (3)*
Sutcliffe, B. 42: v E 1946 (1) 1950 (2) 1954 (2) 1958 (2); v SA 1952 (2); v WI 1951 (2) 1955 (2); *v E 1949 (4) 1958 (4) 1965 (1)*; *v SA 1953 (5)*; *v In 1955 (5) 1965 (4)*; *v P 1955 (3) 1965 (3)*

Taylor, B. R. 9: v E 1965 (1); *v E 1965 (2)*; *v In 1965 (3)*; *v P 1965 (3)*
Taylor, D. D. 3: v E 1946 (1); v WI 1955 (2)
Tindill, E. W. 5: v E 1946 (1); v A 1946 (1); *v E 1937 (3)*
Truscott, P. B. 1: v P 1965

Vivian, G. E. 1: *v In 1965*
Vivian, H. G. 7: v E 1932 (1); v SA 1931 (1); *v E 1931 (2) 1937 (3)*

Wallace, W. M. 13: v E 1946 (1) 1950 (2); v A 1946 (1); v SA 1952 (2); *v E 1937 (3) 1949 (4)*
Ward, J. T. 7: v SA 1963 (1); v P 1965 (1); *v E 1965 (1)*; *v In 1965 (4)*
Watt, L. A. 1: v E 1954
Weir, G. L. 11: v E 1929 (3) 1932 (2); v SA 1931 (2); *v E 1931 (3) 1937 (1)*
Whitelaw, P. E. 2: v E 1932 (2)

Yuile, B. W. 10: v E 1962 (2); v P 1965 (3); *v E 1965 (1)*; *v In 1965*; *v P 1965 (1)*

INDIA

Adhikari, H. R. 21: v E 1951 (3); v A 1956 (2); v WI 1948 (5) 1958 (1); v P 1952 (2); *E 1952 (3)*; *v A 1947 (5)*
Ali, S. Nazir, 2: v E 1933 (1); *v E 1932 (1)*
Ali, S. Wazir, 7: v E 1933 (3); *v E 1932 (1) 1936 (3)*
Amarnath, L. 24: v E 1933 (3) 1951 (3); v WI 1948 (5); v P 1952 (5); *v E 1946 (3)*; *v A 1947 (5)*
Amar Singh 7: v E 1933 (3); *v E 1932 (1) 1936 (3)*
Amir Elahi 1: *v A 1947*
Apte, A. L. 1: *v E 1959*
Apte, M. L. 7: v P 1952 (2); *v WI 1952 (5)*

Baig, A. A. 8: v A 1959 (3); v P 1960 (3); *v E 1959 (2)*
Banerjee, S. N. 1: v WI 1948
Banerjee, S. S. 1: v WI 1948
Bhandari, P. 3: v A 1956 (1); v NZ 1955 (1); *v P 1954 (1)*
Borde, C. G. 40: v E 1961 (5) 1963 (5); v A 1959 (5) 1964 (3); v WI 1958 (4); v NZ 1965 (4); v P 1960 (5); *v E 1959 (4)*; *v WI 1962 (5)*

Chandrasekhar, B. S. 8: v E 1963 (4); v A 1964 (2); v NZ 1965 (2)
Chowdhury, N. 2: v E 1951 (1); v WI 1948 (1)
Colah, S. H. M. 2: v E 1933 (1); *v E 1932 (1)*
Contractor, N. J. 31: v E 1961 (5); v A 1956 (1) 1959 (5); v WI 1958 (5); v NZ 1955 (4); v P 1960 (5); *v E 1959 (4)*; *v WI 1962 (2)*

Dani, H. T. 1: v P 1952
Desai, R. B. 26: v E 1961 (4) 1963 (2); v A 1959 (3); v WI 1958 (1); v NZ 1965 (3); v P 1960 (5); *v E 1959 (5)*; *v WI 1962 (3)*
Divecha, R. V. 5: v E 1951 (2); v P 1952 (1); *v E 1952 (2)*
Durani, A. S. 22: v E 1961 (5) 1963 (5); v A 1959 (1) 1964 (3); v NZ 1965 (3); *v WI 1962 (5)*

Engineer, F. M. 11: v E 1961 (4); v NZ 1965 (4); *v WI 1962 (3)*

Gadkari, C. V. 6: *v WI 1952 (3); v P 1954 (3)*
Gaekwad, D. K. 11: v WI 1958 (1); v P 1952 (2) 1960 (1); *v E 1952 (1) 1959 (4); v WI 1952 (2)*
Gaekwad, H. G. 1: v P 1952
Ghorpade, J. M. 8: v A 1956 (1); v WI 1958 (1); v NZ 1955 (1); *v E 1959 (3); v WI 1952 (2)*
Ghulam Ahmed 22: v E 1951 (2); v A 1956 (2); v WI 1948 (3) 1958 (2); v NZ 1955 (1); v P 1952 (4); *v E 1952 (4); v P 1954 (4)*
Gopalan, M. J. 1: v E 1933
Gopinath, C. D. 8: v E 1951 (3); v A 1959 (1); v P 1952 (1); *v E 1952 (1); v P 1954 (2)*
Guard, G. M. 2: v A 1959 (1); v WI 1958 (1)
Gul Mahomed 8: v P 1952 (2); *v E 1946 (1); v A 1947 (5)*
Gupte, B. P. 3: v E 1963 (1); v NZ 1965 (1); v P 1960 (1)
Gupte, S. P. 36: v E 1951 (1) 1961 (2); v A 1956 (3); v WI 1958 (5); v NZ 1955 (5); v P 1952 (2) 1960 (3); *v E 1959 (5); v WI 1952 (5); v P 1954 (5)*

Hafeez, A. 3: *v E 1946 (3)*
Hanumant Singh 9: v E 1963 (2); v A 1964 (3); v NZ 1965 (4)
Hardikar, M. S. 2: v WI 1958 (2)
Hazare, V. S. 30: v E 1951 (5); v WI 1948 (5); v P 1952 (3); *v E 1946 (3) 1952 (4); v A 1947 (5); v WI 1952 (5)*
Hindlekar, D. D. 4: *v E 1936 (1) 1946 (3)*
Hussain, Dilawar, 3: v E 1933 (2); *v E 1936 (1)*

Ibrahim, K. C. 4: v WI 1948 (4)
Indrajitsingh, K. S. 3: v A 1964 (3)
Irani, J. K. 2: *v A 1947 (2)*

Jai, L. P. 1: v E 1933
Jaisimha, M. L. 27: v E 1961 (5) 1963 (5); v A 1959 (1) 1964 (3); v NZ 1965 (4); v P 1960 (4); *v E 1959 (1); v WI 1962 (4)*
Jamshedji, R. J. 1: v E 1933
Jahangir Khan, M. 4: *v E 1932 (1) 1936 (3)*
Jliani, M. Baqa, 1: *v E 1936*
Joshi, P. G. 12: v E 1951 (2); v A 1959 (1); v WI 1958 (1); v P 1952 (1) 1960 (1); *v E 1959 (3); v WI 1952 (3)*

Kardar, A. H., *see* Hafeez
Kenny, R. B. 5: v A 1959 (4); v WI 1958 (1)
Kischenchand, G. 5: v P 1952 (1); *v A 1947 (4)*
Kripal Singh, A. G. 14: v E 1961 (3) 1963 (2); v A 1956 (2) 1964 (1); v WI 1958 (1); v NZ 1955 (4); *v E 1959 (1)*
Kumar, V. V. 2: v E 1961 (1); v P 1960 (1)
Kunderam, B. K. 14: v E 1961 (1) 1963 (5); v A 1959 (3); v NZ 1965 (1); v P 1960 (2); *v WI 1962 (2)*

Lall Singh 1: *v E 1932*

Maka, E. S. 2: v P 1952 (1); *v WI 1952 (1)*
Manjrekar, V. L. 55: v E 1951 (2) 1961 (5) 1963 (4); v A 1956 (3) 1964 (3); v WI 1959 (4); v NZ 1955 (5) 1965 (1); v P 1952 (3) 1960 (5); *v E 1952 (4) 1959 (2); v WI 1952 (4) 1962 (5); v P 1954 (5)*
Mankad, V. 44: v E 1951 (5); v A 1956 (3); v WI 1948 (5) 1958 (2); v NZ 1955 (4); v P 1952 (4); *v E 1946 (3) 1952 (3); v A 1947 (5); v WI 1952 (5); v P 1954 (5)*
Mantri, M. K. 4: v E 1951 (1); *v E 1952 (2); v P 1954 (1)*
Meherhomji, K. R. 1: *v E 1936*
Mehra, V. L. 8: v E 1961 (1) 1963 (2); v NZ 1955 (2); *v WI 1962 (3)*
Merchant, V. M. 10: v E 1933 (3) 1951 (1); *v E 1936 (3) 1946 (3)*
Milkha Singh, A. G. 4: v E 1961 (1); v A 1959 (1); v P 1960 (2)
Modi, R. S. 10: v E 1951 (1); v WI 1948 (5); v P 1952 (1); *v E 1946 (3)*
Muddiah, V. M. 2: v A 1959 (1); v P 1960 (1)
Mushtaq Ali 11: v E 1933 (2) 1951 (1); v WI 1948 (3); *v E 1936 (3) 1946 (2)*

Naoomal Jeoomal 3: v E 1933 (2); *v E 1932 (1)*
Nadkarni, R. G. 33: v E 1961 (1) 1963 (5); v A 1959 (5) 1964 (3); v WI 1958 (1); v NZ 1955 (1) 1965 (4); v P 1960 (4); *v E 1959 (4)*; *v WI 1962 (5)*
Navle, J. G. 2: v E 1933 (1); *v E 1932 (1)*
Nayudu, C. K. 7: v E 1933 (3); *v E 1932 (1) 1936 (3)*
Nayudu, C. S. 11: v E 1933 (2) 1951 (1); *v E 1936 (2) 1946 (2)*; *v A 1947 (4)*
Nissar, Mahomed 6: v E 1933 (2); *v E 1932 (1) 1936 (3)*
Nyalchand, K. 1: v P 1952

Palia, P. E. 2: *v E 1932 (1) 1936 (1)*
Patankar, C. T. 1: v NZ 1955
Pataudi, Nawab of, 3: *v E 1946 (3)*
Pataudi, Nawab of (son of the above) 18: v E 1961 (3) 1963 (5); v A 1964 (3); v NZ 1965 (4); *v WI 1962 (3)*
Patel, J. S. 7: v A 1956 (2) 1959 (3); v NZ 1955 (1); *v P 1954 (1)*
Patil, S. R. 1: v NZ 1955
Patiala, Yuvraj of, 1: v E 1933
Phadkar, D. G. 31: v E 1951 (4); v A 1956 (1); v WI 1948 (4) 1958 (1); v NZ 1955 (4); v P. 1952 (2); *v E 1952 (4)*; *v A 1947 (4)*; *v WI 1952 (4)*; *v P 1954 (3)*
Prasanna, E. A. S. 2: v E 1961 (1); *v WI 1962 (1)*
Punjabi, P. L. 5: *v P 1954 (5)*

Rai Singh 1: *v A 1947*
Rajindernath, V. 1: v P 1952
Rajinder Pal 1: v E 1963
Ramaswami, C. 2: *v E 1936 (2)*
Ramchand, G. S. 33: v A 1956 (3) 1959 (5); v WI 1958 (3); v NZ 1955 (5); v P 1952 (3); *v E 1952 (4)*; *v WI 1952 (5)*; *v P 1954 (5)*
Ramji, L. 1: v E 1933
Rangachari, C. 4: v WI 1948 (2); *v A 1947 (2)*
Rangnekar, K. M. 3: *v A 1947 (3)*
Ranjane, V. B. 7: v E 1961 (3) 1963 (1); v A 1964 (1); v WI 1958 (1); *v WI 1962 (1)*
Rege, M. R. 1: v WI 1948
Roy, P. 43: v E 1951 (5); v A 1956 (3) 1959 (5); v WI 1958 (5); v NZ 1955 (3); v P 1952 (3) 1960 (1); *v E 1952 (4) 1959 (5)*; *v WI 1952 (4)*; *v P 1954 (5)*

Sardesai, D. N. 15: v E 1961 (1) 1963 (5); v A 1964 (3); v NZ 1965 (3); *v WI 1962 (3)*
Sarwate, C. T. 9: v E 1951 (1); v WI 1948 (2); *v E 1946 (1)*; *v A 1947 (5)*
Sen, P. 14: v E 1951 (2); v WI 1948 (5); v P 1952 (2); *v E 1952 (2)*; *v A 1947 (3)*
Sengupta, A. K. 1: v WI 1958
Shinde, S. G. 7: v E 1951 (3); v WI 1948 (1); *v E 1946 (1) 1952 (2)*
Shodhan, D. H. 3: v P 1952 (1); *v WI 1952 (2)*
Sohoni, S. W. 4: v E 1951 (1); *v E 1946 (2)*; *v A 1947 (1)*
Sood, M. M. 1: v A 1959
Subramaniam, V. 1: v NZ 1965
Sunderram, G. 2: v NZ 1955 (2)
Surendranath, R. 11: v A 1959 (2); v WI 1958 (2); v P 1960 (2); *v E 1959 (5)*
Surti, R. S. 11: v E 1963 (1); v A 1964 (2); v NZ 1965 (1); v P 1960 (2); *v WI 1962 (5)*
Swamy, V. 1: v NZ 1955

Tamhane, N. S. 21: v A 1956 (3) 1959 (1); v WI 1958 (4); v NZ 1955 (4); v P 1960 (2); *v E 1959 (2)*; *v P 1954 (5)*
Tarapore, K. K. 1: v WI 1948

Umrigar, P. R. 59: v E 1951 (5) 1961 (4); v A 1956 (3) 1959 (3); v WI 1948 (1) 1958 (5); v NZ 1955 (5); v P 1952 (5) 1960 (5); *v E 1952 (4) 1959 (4)*; *v WI 1952 (5) 1962 (5)*; *v P 1954 (5)*

Venkataraghavan, S.4: v NZ 1965 (4)
Vizianagram, Maharaj Sir Vijaya 3: *v E 1936 (3)*

Note.—Hafeez, on going later to Oxford University, took his correct name, Kardar.

PAKISTAN

Abdul Kadir 4: v A 1964 (1); *v A 1964 (1)*; *v NZ 1964 (2)*
Afaq Hussain 2: v E 1961 (1); *v A 1964 (1)*
Agha Saadat Ali 1: v NZ 1955
Akhtar Javed 1: *v E 1962*
Alim-ud-Din 25: v E 1961 (2); v A 1956 (1) 1959 (1); v WI 1958 (1); v NZ 1955 (3); v In 1954 (5); *v E 1954 (3) 1962 (3)*; *v WI 1958 (5)*; *v In 1960 (1)*
Amir Elahi 5: *v In 1952 (5)*
Anwar Hussain 4: *v In 1952 (4)*
Arif Butt 3: *v A 1964 (1)*; *v NZ 1964 (2)*
Asif Iqbal 8: v A 1964 (1); v NZ 1965 (3); *v A 1964 (1)*; *v NZ 1964 (3)*

Burki, J. 21: v E 1961 (3); v A 1964 (1); v NZ 1965 (3); *v E 1962 (5)*; *v A 1964 (1)*; *v NZ 1964 (3)*; *v In 1960 (5)*

D'Souza, A. 6: v E 1961 (2); v WI 1958 (1); *v E 1962 (3)*

Farooq Hamid 1: *v A 1964*
Fazal Mahmood 34: v E 1961 (1); v A 1956 (1) 1959 (2); v WI 1958 (3); v NZ 1955 (2); v In 1954 (4); *v E 1954 (4) 1962 (2)*; *v WI 1958 (5)*; *v In 1952 (5) 1960 (5)*

Ghazali, M. E. Z. 2: *v E 1954 (2)*
Gul Mahomed 1: v A 1956

Hanif Mohammad 48: v E 1961 (3); v A 1956 (1) 1959 (3) 1964 (1); v WI 1958 (1); v NZ 1955 (3) 1965 (3); v In 1954 (5); *v E 1954 (4) 1962 (5)*; *v A 1964 (1)*; *v WI 1958 (5)*; *v NZ 1965 (3)*; *v In 1952 (5) 1960 (5)*
Haseeb Ahsan 12: v E 1961 (2); v A 1959 (1); v WI 1958 (1); *v WI (3)*; *v In 1960 (5)*

Ibadulla, K. 2: v A 1964 (1); *v NZ 1964 (1)*
Ijaz Butt 8: v A 1959 (2); v WI 1958 (3); *v E 1962 (3)*
Imtiaz Ahmed 41: v E 1961 (3); v A 1956 (1) 1959 (3); v WI 1958 (3); v NZ 1955 (3); v In 1954 (5); *v E 1954 (4)*; *v E 1962 (4)*; *v WI 1958 (5)*; *v In 1952 (5) 1960 (5)*
Intikhab Alam 17: v E 1961 (2); v A 1959 (1) 1964 (1); v NZ 1965 (3); *v E 1962 (3)*; *v A 1964 (1)*; *v NZ 1964 (3)*; *v In 1960 (3)*
Israr Ali 4: v A 1959 (2); *v In 1952 (2)*

Kardar, A. H. 23: v A 1956 (1); v NZ 1955 (3); v In 1954 (5); *v E 1954 (4)*; *v WI 1958 (5)*; *v In 1952 (5)*
Khalid Hassan 1: *v E 1954*
Khalid Wazir 2: *v E 1954 (2)*
Khan Mohammad 13: v A 1956 (1); v NZ 1955 (3); v In 1954 (4); *v E 1954 (2)*; *v WI 1958 (2)*; *v In 1952 (1)*

Mahmood Hussain 27: v E 1961 (1); v WI 1958 (3); v NZ 1955 (1); v In 1954 (5); *v E 1954 (2)*; *v E 1962 (3)*; *v WI 1958 (3)*; *v In 1952 (4) 1960 (5)*
Majid Jahangir 4: v A 1964 (1); v NZ 1965 (3)
Maqsood Ahmed 16: v NZ 1955 (2); v In 1954 (5); *v E 1954 (4)*; *v In 1952 (5)*
Mathias, Wallis 21: v E 1961 (1); v A 1956 (1) 1959 (2); v WI 1958 (3); v NZ 1955 (1); *v E 1962 (3)*; *v WI 1958 (5)*; *v In 1960 (5)*
Miran Bux 2: v In 1954 (2)
Mohammad Aslam 1: *v E 1954*
Mohammad Farooq 7: v NZ 1965 (3); *v E 1962 (2)*; *v In 1960 (2)*
Mohammad Ilyas 7: v NZ 1965 (3); *v A 1964 (1)*; *v NZ 1964 (3)*
Mohammad Munaf 4: v E 1961 (2); v A 1959 (2)
Mufasir-ul-Haq 1: *v NZ 1964*
Munir Malik 3: v A 1959 (1); *v E 1962 (2)*
Mushtaq Mohammad 14: v E 1961 (3); v WI 1958 (1); *v E 1962 (5)*; *v In 1960 (5)*

Nasim-ul-Ghani 26: v E 1961 (2); v A 1959 (2) 1964 (1); v WI 1958 (3); *v E 1962 (5)*; *v A 1964 (1)*; *v WI 1958 (5)*; *v NZ 1964 (3)*; *v In 1960 (4)*
Naushad Ali 6: v NZ 1965 (3); *v NZ 1964 (3)*
Nazar Mohammad 5: *v In 1952 (5)*

Pervez Sajjad 7: v A 1964 (1); v NZ 1965 (3); *v NZ 1964 (3)*

Rahman, S. F. 1: *v WI 1958 (1)*

Saeed Ahmed 32: v E 1961 (3); v A 1959 (3) 1964 (1); v WI 1958 (3); v NZ 1965 (3); *v E 1962 (5); v A 1964 (1); v WI 1958 (5); v NZ 1964 (3); v In 1960 (5)*
Salah-ud-Din 3: v NZ 1965 (3)
Shafqat Rana 1: v A 1964
Shahid Mahmood 1: *v E 1962*
Sharpe, D. 3: v A 1959 (3)
Shuja-ud-Din 19: v E 1961 (2); v A 1959 (3); v WI 1958 (3); v NZ 1955 (3); v In 1954 (5); *v E 1954 (3)*

Waqar Hassan 21: v A 1956 (1) 1959 (1); v WI 1958 (1); v NZ 1955 (3); v In 1954 (5); *v E 1954 (4); v WI 1958 (1); v In 1952 (5)*
Wazir Mohammad 20: v A 1956 (1) 1959 (1); v WI 1958 (3); v NZ 1955 (2); v In 1954 (5); *v E 1954 (2); v WI 1958 (5); v In 1952 (1)*

Zulfiqar Ahmed 9: v A 1956 (1); v NZ 1955 (3); *v E 1954 (2); v In 1952 (3)*

Twelve cricketers have appeared for two countries in Test Matches, namely:

Amir Elahi, *India and Pakistan.*
J. J. Ferris, *Australia and England.*
S. C. Guillen, *West Indies and NZ.*
Gul Mahomed, *India and Pakistan.*
F. Hearne, *England and South Africa.*
A. H. Kardar *India and Pakistan.*
W. E. Midwinter, *England and Australia.*
F. Mitchell, *England and South Africa.*
W. L. Murdoch, *Australia and England.*
Nawab of Pataudi, *England and India.*
A. E. Trott, *Australia and England.*
S. M. J. Woods, *Australia and England.*

CRICKET RECORDS

AMENDED BY LESLIE SMITH TO SEPTEMBER 30, 1966

Unless otherwise stated, all records, apart from Throwing the Cricket Ball, apply only to first-class cricket.

* Denotes "not out" or an unfinished partnership.

(A), (S.A.), (W.I.), (N.Z.), (I) or (P) indicates either the nationality of the player, or the country in which the record was made.

When South Africa left the British Commonwealth in 1961 they ceased membership of the International Cricket Conference and forfeited official Test status. To maintain continuity of the records the appearances and achievements of all players engaged in Tests played by South Africa will continue to be included.

INDEX

BATTING

	PAGE
Individual Scores of 300 or More	191
Highest Individual Scores in England and Australia	193
Highest Innings for each First-Class County	193
Highest in Minor Counties	194
Hundred on Debut in England	194
Most Individual Hundreds	195
Two Separate Hundreds in a Match	196
Batsmen who have Scored 30,000 Runs	197
1,000 Runs in a Season Fifteen Times or more	198
Four Hundreds or More in Succession	198
Most Hundreds in a Season	199
Fast Scoring	199
Record Hit	200
Most Personal Sixes in an Innings	200
Most Runs Scored off One Over	200
300 Runs in One Day	201
Highest Partnerships	201
Partnerships for First Wicket	201
First-Wicket Hundreds in Both Innings	202
Wicket Records for All Countries	203
Highest Aggregates in a Season	205
Largest Aggregates Outside England	206
1,000 Runs in May	206
1,000 Runs in Two Separate Months	207
Handled Ball	207
Obstructing the Field	207
Hit the Ball Twice	207

BOWLING AND FIELDING

Four Wickets with Consecutive Balls	208
Double Hat-Trick, Most Hat-Tricks	208
Ten Wickets in One Innings	209
Nineteen Wickets in a Match	210
Remarkable Analyses	210
Sixteen or More Wickets in a Day	212
200 or More Wickets in a Season	213
Bowlers who have taken 2,000 Wickets	214
Bowlers who have taken 100 Wickets in a Season Eight Times	214
All-round Cricket	215
Century and Hat-Trick	216
Century and All Ten Wickets	217
Wicket-keeping Feats	217

PAGE
Most Catches—Excluding Wicket-keepers 218
Throwing the Cricket Ball 219

THE SIDES

Great Totals. Small Totals 219
Smallest Total in a Match 220
Lowest for Each County 220
Highest Aggregates 220
Heavy Scoring in Fourth Innings 221
Biggest Victories 221

TEST MATCH RECORDS

Scorers of 1,500 Runs in Tests 222
Bowlers with 75 Wickets in Tests 223
Century on Test Debut 225
Two Separate Hundreds in a Test Match 225
Fastest Test Fifties 226
Fastest Test Centuries 226
Fastest Test Double Centuries 226
Most Runs in a Day by a Batsmen 226
Most Runs in a Day (Both Sides and One Side) 226
Slow Individual Test Batting 226
Lowest Test Scores in One Full Day's Play 227
Most Wickets in a Test and in a Test Innings 227
Test Hat-Tricks 228
Most Balls Bowled in a Test Match 228
Wicket-keeping Feats 228
Summary of All Test Matches to October 31, 1966 229
Same Captain Winning Toss All Five Tests 230
England v. Australia 231
England v. South Africa 237
England v. West Indies 241
England v. New Zealand 243
England v. India 245
England v. Pakistan 247
Australia v. South Africa 248
Australia v. New Zealand 250
Australia v. West Indies 250
Australia v. India 252
Australia v. Pakistan 253
South Africa v. New Zealand 254
West Indies v. New Zealand 254
West Indies v. India 255
West Indies v. Pakistan 256
India v. New Zealand 256
India v. Pakistan 257
Pakistan v. New Zealand 258
Highest Test Wicket Partnerships 258
Youngest Test Players: Oldest Players 259

VARIA

Gentlemen v. Players 259
Oxford v. Cambridge 260
Tie Matches 261
Matches Begun and Finished in One Day 261
Large Attendances and Gate Receipts 262
Best Benefits 263
County Championship 265

INDIVIDUAL SCORES OF 300 OR MORE

499 Hanif Mohammad, Karachi v. Bahawalpur, at Karachi 1958–59
452* D. G. Bradman, New South Wales v. Queensland, at Sydney .. 1929–30
443* B. B. Nimbalkar, Maharashtra v. Western India States, at Poona 1948–49

Score	Batsman, match and ground	Season
437	W. H. Ponsford, Victoria v. Queensland, at Melbourne	1927–28
429	W. H. Ponsford, Victoria v. Tasmania, at Melbourne	1922–23
424	A. C. MacLaren, Lancashire v. Somerset, at Taunton	1895
385	B. Sutcliffe, Otago v. Canterbury, at Christchurch	1952–53
383	C. W. Gregory, New South Wales v. Queensland, at Brisbane	1906–07
369	D. G. Bradman, South Australia v. Tasmania, at Adelaide	1935–36
365*	C. Hill, South Australia v. New South Wales, at Adelaide	1900–01
365*	G. S. Sobers, West Indies v. Pakistan, at Kingston	1957–58
364	L. Hutton, England v. Australia, at The Oval	1938
359*	V. M. Merchant, Bombay v. Maharashtra, at Bombay	1943–44
359	R. B. Simpson, New South Wales v. Queensland, at Brisbane	1963–64
357*	R. Abel, Surrey v. Somerset, at The Oval	1899
357	D. G. Bradman, South Australia v. Victoria, at Melbourne	1935–36
355	B. Sutcliffe, Otago v. Auckland, at Dunedin	1949–50
352	W. H. Ponsford, Victoria v. New South Wales, at Melbourne	1926–27
345	C. G. Macartney, Australia v. Nottinghamshire, at Nottingham	1921
344*	G. A. Headley, All Jamaica v. Lord Tennyson's Team, at Kingston	1931–32
344	W. G. Grace, M.C.C. v. Kent, at Canterbury	1876
343*	P. A. Perrin, Essex v. Derbyshire, at Chesterfield	1904
341	G. H. Hirst, Yorkshire v. Leicestershire, at Leicester	1905
340*	D. G. Bradman, New South Wales v. Victoria, at Sydney	1928–29
338*	R. C. Blunt, Otago v. Canterbury, at Christchurch	1931–32
338	W. W. Read, Surrey v. Oxford University, at The Oval	1888
337†	Hanif Mohammad, Pakistan v. West Indies, at Barbados	1957–58
337*	Pervez Akhtar, Railways v. Dera Ismail Khan, at Lahore	1964
336	W. H. Ponsford, Victoria v. South Australia, at Melbourne	1927–28
336*	W. R. Hammond, England v. New Zealand, at Auckland	1932–33
334	D. G. Bradman, Australia v. England, at Leeds	1930
333	K. S. Duleepsinhji, Sussex v. Northamptonshire, at Hove	1930
332	W. H. Ashdown, Kent v. Essex, at Brentwood	1934
331*	J. D. Robertson, Middlesex v. Worcestershire, at Worcester	1949
325*	H. L. Hendry, Victoria v. New Zealand, at Melbourne	1925–26
325	C. L. Badcock, South Australia v. Victoria, at Adelaide	1935–36
325	A. Sandham, England v. West Indies, at Kingston	1929–30
324	J. B. Stollmeyer, Trinidad v. British Guiana, at Port of Spain	1946–47
322	E. Paynter, Lancashire v. Sussex, at Hove	1937
321	W. L. Murdoch, New South Wales v. Victoria, at Sydney	1881–82
319	Gul Mahomed, Baroda v. Holkar, at Baroda	1946–47
318*	W. G. Grace, Gloucestershire v. Yorkshire, at Cheltenham	1876
317	W. R. Hammond, Gloucestershire v. Notts, at Gloucester	1936
316*	V. S. Hazare, Maharashtra v. Baroda, at Poona	1939–40
316*	J. B. Hobbs, Surrey v. Middlesex, at Lord's	1926
316	R. H. Moore, Hampshire v. Warwickshire, at Bournemouth	1937
315*	T. Hayward, Surrey v. Lancashire, at The Oval	1898
315*	P. Holmes, Yorkshire v. Middlesex, at Lord's	1925
315*	A. F. Kippax, New South Wales v. Queensland, at Sydney	1927–28
314*	C. L. Walcott, Barbados v. Trinidad, at Port of Spain	1945–46
313	H. Sutcliffe, Yorkshire v. Essex at Leyton	1932
312*	W. W. Keeton, Nottinghamshire v. Middlesex, at The Oval	1939
311	J. T. Brown, Yorkshire v. Sussex, at Sheffield	1897
311	R. B. Simpson, Australia v. England, at Manchester	1964
310*	J. H. Edrich, England v. New Zealand, at Leeds	1965
310	H. Gimblett, Somerset v. Sussex, at Eastbourne	1948
309	V. S. Hazare, The Rest v. Hindus, at Brabourne Stadium	1943–44
308*	F. M. Worrell, Barbados v. Trinidad, at Bridgetown	1943–44
307	M. C. Cowdrey, M.C.C. v. South Australia, at Adelaide	1962–63
307	R. M. Cowper, Australia v. England, at Melbourne	1965–66
306*	A. Ducat, Surrey v. Oxford University, at The Oval	1919
306*	E. A. B. Rowan, Transvaal v. Natal, at Johannesburg	1939–40
305*	F. E. Woolley, M.C.C. v. Tasmania, at Hobart	1911–12

† Hanif Mohammad batted for 16 hours 39 minutes—the longest innings in first-class cricket.

305* F. R. Foster, Warwickshire v. Worcestershire, at Dudley .. 1914
305* W. H. Ashdown, Kent v. Derbyshire, at Dover 1935
304* P. H. Tarilton, Barbados v. Trinidad, at Bridgetown 1919–20
304* A. D. Nourse. sen., Natal v. Transvaal, at Johannesburg .. 1919–20
304* E. D. Weekes, West Indies v. Cambridge University, at Cambridge 1950
304 R. M. Poore, Hampshire v. Somerset, at Taunton 1899
304 D. G. Bradman, Australia v. England, at Leeds 1934
303* W. W. Armstrong, Australia v. Somerset, at Bath 1905
302* P. Holmes, Yorkshire v. Hampshire, at Portsmouth 1920
302* W. R. Hammond, Gloucestershire v. Glamorgan, at Bristol .. 1934
302 W. R. Hammond, Gloucestershire v. Glamorgan, at Newport .. 1939
301 W. G. Grace, Gloucestershire v. Sussex, at Bristol 1896
301* E. Hendren, Middlesex v. Worcestershire, at Dudley 1933
300* Imtiaz Ahmed, Prime Minister's XI v. Commonwealth XI, at Bombay 1950–51
300* V. T. Trumper, Australia v. Sussex, at Hove 1899
300* F. Watson, Lancashire v. Surrey, at Manchester 1928
300 J. T. Brown, Yorkshire v. Derbyshire, at Chesterfield 1898
300 D. C. S. Compton, M.C.C. v. N. E. Transvaal, at Benoni .. 1948–49
300 R. Subba Row, Northamptonshire v. Surrey, at The Oval .. 1958

HIGHEST FOR TEAMS

INDIVIDUAL SCORES

FOR ENGLISH TEAMS IN AUSTRALIA

307 M. C. Cowdrey, M.C.C. v. South Australia, at Adelaide .. 1962–63
287 R. E. Foster, England v. Australia, at Sydney (Highest in a Test) 1903–04

AGAINST AUSTRALIANS IN ENGLAND

364 L. Hutton, for England v. Australia, at The Oval 1938
219 A. Sandham, for Surrey, at The Oval (record for any county) .. 1934

FOR AUSTRALIAN TEAMS IN ENGLAND

345 C. G. Macartney, v. Nottinghamshire, at Nottingham 1921
334 D. G. Bradman, Australia v. England, at Leeds 1930

AGAINST ENGLISH TEAMS IN AUSTRALIA

307 R. M. Cowper, Australia v. England, at Melbourne 1965–66
280 A. J. Richardson, South Australia v. M.C.C., at Adelaide .. 1922–23

FOR EACH FIRST-CLASS COUNTY

Derbyshire ..	274	G. Davidson, v. Lancashire, at Manchester ..	1896
Essex	343*	P. A. Perrin, v. Derbyshire, at Chesterfield ..	1904
Glamorgan ..	287*	E. Davies, v. Gloucestershire, at Newport ..	1939
Gloucestershire ..	318*	W. G. Grace, v. Yorkshire, at Cheltenham ..	1876
Hampshire ..	316	R. H. Moore, v. Warwickshire, at Bournemouth	1937
Kent	332	W. H. Ashdown, v. Essex, at Brentwood ..	1934
Lancashire ..	424	A. C. MacLaren, v. Somerset, at Taunton ..	1895
Leicestershire ..	252*	S. Coe, v. Northamptonshire, at Leicester ..	1914
Middlesex ..	331*	J. D. Robertson, v. Worcestershire, at Worcester	1949
Northamptonshire	300	R. Subba Row, v. Surrey, at The Oval	1958
Nottinghamshire	312*	W. W. Keeton, v. Middlesex, at The Oval‡ ..	1939
Somerset	310	H. Gimblett, v. Sussex, at Eastbourne	1948
Surrey	357*	R. Abel, v. Somerset, at The Oval	1899
Sussex	333	K. S. Duleepsinhji, v. Northants, at Hove ..	1930
Warwickshire ..	305*	F. R. Foster, v. Worcestershire, at Dudley ..	1914
Worcestershire ..	276	F. L. Bowley, v. Hampshire, at Dudley ..	1914
Yorkshire ..	341	G. H. Hirst, v. Leicestershire, at Leicester ..	1905

‡ On this date Eton played Harrow at Lord's.

HIGHEST IN A MINOR COUNTY MATCH

23* F. E. Lacey, Hampshire v. Norfolk, at Southampton 1887

HIGHEST IN MINOR COUNTIES CHAMPIONSHIP

282 F. Garnet, Berkshire v. Wiltshire, at Reading 1908
254 H. E. Morgan, Glamorgan v. Monmouthshire, at Cardiff .. 1901
253* G. J. Whittaker, Surrey II v. Gloucestershire II, at The Oval .. 1950
253 A. Booth, Lancashire II v. Lincolnshire, at Grimsby 1950
252 J. A. Deed, Kent II v. Surrey II, at The Oval (On debut) .. 1924

HIGHEST FOR ENGLISH PUBLIC SCHOOL

278 J. L. Guise, Winchester v. Eton, at Eton 1921

HIGHEST IN OTHER MATCHES

628* A. E. J. Collins, Clark's House v. North Town, at Clifton College. (A Junior House match. His innings of 6 hours 50 minutes was spread over five afternoons) 1899
566 C. J. Eady, Break-o'-Day v. Wellington, at Hobart 1901–02
515 D. R. Havewalla, B.B. and C.I. Rly. v. St. Xavier's, at Bombay 1933–34
506* J. C. Sharp, Melbourne G.S. v. Geelong Coll., at Melbourne .. 1914–15
502* Chaman Lal, Mehandra College, Patiala v. Government College, Rupar, at Patiala 1956–57
485 A. E. Stoddart, Hampstead v. Stoics, at Hampstead 1886
475* Mhd. Iqbal, Muslim Model H.S. v. Islamia H.S. Sialkot, at Lahore 1958–59
466* G. T. S. Stevens, Beta v. Lambda (University College School House Match), at Neasden 1919
459 J. A. Prout, Wesley Coll. v. Geelong Coll., at Geelong 1908–09

HUNDRED ON DEBUT IN ENGLAND

(The following list does not include instances of players who have previously appeared in first-class cricket outside England.)

114 F. H. Bacon, Hampshire v. Warwickshire, at Birmingham .. 1894
107* G. E. Barker, Essex v. Canadians, at Clacton .. .. .. †1954
116* B. L. Bisgood, Somerset v. Worcestershire, at Worcester 1907
107* H. O. Bloomfield, Surrey v. Northamptonshire, at Northampton.. 1921
124 G. J. Bryan, Kent v. Nottinghamshire, at Nottingham .. .. †1920
100 J. F. Byrne, Warwickshire v. Leicestershire, at Birmingham .. 1897
118 A. P. F. Chapman, Cambridge University v. Essex, at Cambridge 1920
113 G. J. Chidgey, Free Foresters v. Cambridge University, at Cambridge 1962
100* E. A. Clark, Middlesex v. Cambridge University, at Cambridge .. 1959
101* S. H. Day, Kent v. Gloucestershire, at Cheltenham .. .. †1897
176 F. C. de Saram, Oxford University v. Gloucestershire, at Oxford .. 1934
108 E. W. Dillon, London County v. Worcestershire, at Crystal Palace 1900
215* G. H. G. Doggart, Cambridge University v. Lancashire, at Cambridge 1948
137 C. H. M. Ebden, Camb. U. v. Leveson Gower's XI, at Cambridge 1902
108 A. Fairbairn, Middlesex v. Somerset, at Taunton .. .. .. †‡1947
123 H. Gimblett, Somerset v. Essex, at Frome 1935
101 P. M. Hall, Oxford University v. Free Foresters, at Oxford .. 1919
121 C. P. Hamilton, Army v. West Indies, at Aldershot 1933
156 M. N. Harbottle, Army v. Oxford University, at Camberley .. 1938
124 P. Hearn, Kent v. Warwickshire, at Gillingham 1947
101 K. A. Higgs, Sussex v. Worcestershire, at Hove 1920

103*	A. L. Hilder, Kent v. Essex, at Gravesend	†1924
158*	J. H. Human, Camb. U. v. Leveson Gower's XI, at Eastbourne ..	1932
111*	C. F. H. Leslie, Oxford U., v. M.C.C. and Ground, at Oxford ..	1881
108	A. C. MacLaren, Lancashire v. Sussex, at Hove	1890
144	F. W. Marlow, Sussex v. M.C.C. and Ground, at Lord's	1891
124	N. Miller, Surrey v. Sussex, at Hove	1899
106*	W. Murray Wood, Oxford University v. Gloucestershire, at Oxford	1936
104	M. Nichol, Worcestershire v. West Indies, at Worcester	1928
101	C. A. L. Payne, M.C.C. and Ground v. Derbyshire, at Lord's ..	1905
138*	F. B. Pinch, Glamorgan v. Worcestershire, at Swansea	1921
124	H. C. Pretty, Surrey v. Nottinghamshire, at The Oval	1899
149	H. R. J. Rhys, Free Foresters v. Cambridge U., at Cambridge ..	1929
195*	J. Ricketts, Lancashire v. Surrey, at The Oval	1867
137	J. G. C. Scott, Sussex v. Oxford University, at Eastbourne ..	1907
108	D. Shepherd, Gloucestershire v. Oxford U., at Oxford	1965
135	J. K. E. Slack, Cambridge University v. Middlesex, at Cambridge ..	1954
114	F. W. Stocks, Nottinghamshire v. Kent, at Nottingham	1946
110	Hon. L. H. Tennyson, M.C.C. and Ground v. Oxford U., at Lord's	†1913
103	A. H. Trevor, Sussex v. Kent, at Hove	†1880
125	G. S. Tuck, Royal Navy v. New Zealanders, at Portsmouth ..	1927
100*	C. Tyson, Yorkshire v. Hampshire, at Southampton	1921
102	I. D. Walker, Middlesex v. Surrey at The Oval	1862
131*	R. Whitehead, Lancashire v. Nottinghamshire, at Manchester ..	1908
117*	E. R. Wilson, A. J. Webbe's XI v. Cambridge U., at Cambridge ..	1899
124	L. Winslow, Sussex v. Gloucestershire, at Hove	1875

† In second innings. S. H. Day, schoolboy at Malvern, aged 18.

‡ A. Fairbairn (Middlesex) in 1947 scored centuries in the second innings of his first two matches in first-class cricket: 108 Middlesex v. Somerset, at Taunton 110* Middlesex v. Nottinghamshire, at Nottingham.

A number of players abroad have also made a century on a first appearance. The highest Innings on debut was hit by W. F. E. Marx when he made 240 for Transvaal against Griqualand West at Johannesburg in 1920–21.

The following feats stand alone for a cricketer making two separate hundreds on debut: A. R. Morris, New South Wales, 148 and 111 against Queensland in 1940–41, and N. J. Contractor, Gujerat, 152 and 102 not out against Baroda in 1952–53.

MOST INDIVIDUAL HUNDREDS

(35 OR MORE)

	Hundreds Total	Abr'd	100th 100		Hundreds Total	Abr'd	100th 100
J. B. Hobbs ...	197	22	1923	D. C. S. Compton	123	31	1952
E. Hendren....	170	19	1928	D. G. Bradman	117	41	1947–8
W. R. Hammond	167	33	1935	T. W. Graveney	111	28	1964
C. P. Mead....	153	8	1927	A. Sandham ..	107	20	1935
H. Sutcliffe	149	14	1932	T. Hayward ...	104	4	1913
F. E. Woolley..	145	10	1929	L. E. G. Ames.	102	13	1950
L. Hutton	129	24	1951	E. Tyldesley ...	102	8	1934
W. G. Grace ..	126	1	1895				

J. W. Hearne	96	D. Kenyon	73	G. Gunn	62
C. B. Fry.........	94	J. O'Connor	72	G. H. Hirst........	60
W. J. Edrich	86	W. G. Quaife	72	P. F. Warner	60
J. T. Tyldesley	86	K. S. Ranjitsinhji ..	72	A. L. Hassett	59
P. B. H. May	85	D. Brookes	71	A. Shrewsbury	59
R. E. S. Wyatt	85	A. C. Russell	71	A. E. Fagg	58
J. Hardstaff, junr ..	83	D. Denton........	69	W. Rhodes	58
M. Leyland........	80	K. F. Barrington ..	68	V. S. Hazare......	57
M. C. Cowdrey ...	78	R. N. Harvey	67	L. B. Fishlock	56
John Langridge ...	76	P. Holmes	67	R. E. Marshall	56
C. Washbrook	76	J. D. Robertson ...	67	C. Hallows	55
H. T. W. Hardinge	75	P. A. Perrin	66	W. Watson	55
R. Abel	74	R. T. Simpson	64	D. J. Insole	54

W. W. Keeton	54	J. H. Edrich	45	W. R. D. Payton	39
W. Bardsley	53	Clem Hill	45	J. R. Reid	39
A. E. Dipper	53	J. M. Parks	45	F. Bowley	38
G. L. Jessop	53	E. Paynter	45	J. F. Crapp	38
James Seymour	53	Rev. D. S. Sheppard	45	W. M. Lawry	38
E. H. Bowley	52	B. Sutcliffe	45	A. D. Nourse, senr.	38
A. Ducat	52	H. H. I. Gibbons	44	N. Oldfield	38
M. J. K. Smith	52	A. Mitchell	44	Rev. J. H. Parsons	38
W. W. Whysall	51	P. E. Richardson	44	G. Pullar	38
G. Cox, junr.	50	Hanif Mohammad	43	W. W. Read	38
E. R. Dexter	50	A. F. Kippax	43	J. Sharp	38
H. E. Dollery	50	H. Makepeace	43	L. J. Todd	38
K. S. Duleepsinhji	50	V. M. Merchant	43	J. Arnold	37
H. Gimblett	50	James Langridge	42	G. Brown	37
P. R. Umrigar	50	H. W. Parks	42	G. M. Emmett	37
F. Watson	50	T. F. Shepherd	42	H. W. Lee	37
R. B. Simpson	49	V. T. Trumper	42	M. A. Noble	37
G. S. Sobers	49	C. L. Walcott	42	E. Oldroyd	37
W. M. Woodfull	49	J. Gunn	41	N. C. O'Neill	37
C. J. Barnett	48	K. R. Miller	41	H. S. Squires	37
W. Gunn	48	C. A. Milton	41	K. G. Suttle	37
E. G. Hayes	48	A. D. Nourse, junr.	41	C. J. B. Wood	37
C. G. Macartney	48	P. H. Parfitt	41	N. F. Armstrong	36
A. C. MacLaren	47	J. H. Parks	41	D. B. Close	36
W. H. Ponsford	47	M. J. Stewart	41	W. Place	36
J. Iddon	46	F. M. Worrell	40	E. D. Weekes	36
A. R. Morris	46	D. M. Young	40	C. S. Dempster	35
W. W. Armstrong	45	W. H. Ashdown	39	D. R. Jardine	35
L. G. Berry	45	W. A. Brown	39	V. L. Manjrekar	35
A. W. Carr	45	R. J. Gregory	39	B. H. Valentine	35

In all cricket J. B. Hobbs hit 244 hundreds and W. G. Grace hit 217.

TWO SEPARATE HUNDREDS IN A MATCH

Seven Times: W. R. HAMMOND.

Six Times: J. B. HOBBS.

Five Times: C. B. FRY.

Four Times: D. G. BRADMAN, L. B. FISHLOCK, T. W. GRAVENEY, H. T. W. HARDINGE, E. HENDREN, G. L. JESSOP, P. A. PERRIN, B. SUTCLIFFE, H. SUTCLIFFE.

Three Times: L. E. G. AMES, D. C. S. COMPTON, M. C. COWDREY D. DENTON, K. S. DULEEPSINHJI, R. E. FOSTER, W. G. GRACE, G. GUNN, M. R. HALLAM, HANIF MOHAMMAD, T. HAYWARD, V. S. HAZARE, L. HUTTON, P. B. H. MAY, C. P. MEAD, A. C. RUSSELL, J. T. TYLDESLEY.

Twice: B. J. T. BOSANQUET, C. C. DACRE, G. M. EMMETT, A. E. FAGG, L. E. FAVELL, H. GIMBLETT, C. HALLOWS, R. A. HAMENCE, A. L. HASSETT, G. A. HEADLEY, J. H. KING, A. F. KIPPAX, JOHN LANGRIDGE, H. W. LEE, E. LESTER, G. C. B. LLEWELLYN, C. G. MACARTNEY, C. A. MILTON, A. R. MORRIS, NAWAB OF PATAUDI, JNR., P. H. PARFITT, E. PAYNTER, C. PINCH, R. M. PRIDEAUX, W. RHODES, P. ROY, JAS. SEYMOUR, R. B. SIMPSON, E. TYLDESLEY, C. L. WALCOTT, W. W. WHYSALL.

W. Lambert scored 107 and 157 for Sussex v. Epsom at Lord's in 1817 and it was not until W. G. Grace made 130 and 102* for South of the Thames v. North of the Thames at Canterbury in 1868 that the feat was repeated.

T. Hayward (Surrey) set up a unique record in 1906, when in one week—six days—he hit four successive hundreds, 144 and 100 v. Nottinghamshire at Nottingham, and 143 and 125 v. Leicestershire at Leicester.

A. E. Fagg alone has scored two double hundreds in the same match; 244 and 202* for Kent v. Essex at Colchester. 1938.

M. R. Hallam (Leicestershire), opening the batting each time, achieved the following treble: 210* and 157 v. Glamorgan at Leicester, 1959; 203* and 143* v. Sussex at Worthing, 1961; 107* and 149* v. Worcestershire at Leicester, 1965. In the last two matches he was on the field the whole time as was C. J. B. Wood when he scored 107* and 117* for Leicestershire against Yorkshire at Bradford, 1911.

W. L. Foster, 140 and 172*, and R. E. Foster, 134 and 101*, at Worcester against Hampshire in July 1899, set up a record by brothers both scoring two separate hundreds in the same first-class match. This remains unequalled.

G. Gunn, 183 and G. V. Gunn, 100* for Notts. v. Warwickshire at Birmingham in 1931, provide the only instance of father and son each hitting a century in the same innings of a first-class match.

Most Recent Instances

In 1964–65:—

130 and 107* Nawab of Pataudi Delhi and Districts v. Services, at Delhi.
121 and 142* R. B. Simpson New South Wales v. South Australia at Sydney.

In 1965:—

109 and 104 B. J. Booth Leicestershire v. Middlesex, at Lord's.
107* and 149* M. R. Hallam Leicestershire v. Worcestershire, at Leicester.
101 and 101 I. W. Hall Derbyshire v. Kent, at Folkestone.
124 and 125* R. Virgin Somerset v. Warwickshire, at Birmingham.

In 1965–66:—

119 and 108* P. C. Kelly Western Australia v. M.C.C., at Perth.

In 1966:—

103 and 105 G. Boycott Yorkshire v. Nottinghamshire, at Bradford.
106 and 100 R. M. Prideaux Northamptonshire v. Nottinghamshire, at Nottingham.

BATSMEN WHO HAVE SCORED 30,000 RUNS

	Career	Runs	Inns.	Times Not Out	Highest Inns.	100's	Average
J. B. Hobbs	1905–34	61237	1315	106	316*	197	50.65
F. E. Woolley	1906–38	58969	1532	85	305*	145	40.75
E. Hendren........	1907–38	57610	1300	166	301*	170	50.80
C. P. Mead........	1905–36	55060	1340	185	280*	153	47.67
W. G. Grace	1865–1908	54896	1493	105	344	126	39.55
W. R. Hammond ..	1920–51	50493	1004	104	336*	167	56.10
H. Sutcliffe........	1919–45	50135	1087	123	313	149	52.00
T. Hayward	1893–1914	43518	1137	96	315	104	41.80
T. W. Graveney....	1948–66	41831	1044	126	258	111	45.56
A. Sandham.......	1911–37	41284	1002	81	325	107	44.82
L. Hutton	1934–60	40140	814	91	364	129	55.51
W. Rhodes	1898–1930	39797	1532	236	267*	58	30.70
R. E. S. Wyatt.....	1923–57	39404	1141	157	232	85	40.04
D. C. S. Compton..	1936–64	38942	842	89	300	123	51.71
E. Tyldesley	1909–36	38874	961	106	256*	102	45.46
J. T. Tyldesley	1895–1923	37809	991	62	295*	86	40.69
J. W. Hearne	1909–35	37250	1024	116	285*	96	41.02
L. E. G. Ames.....	1926–51	37245	950	95	295	102	43.56
W. J. Edrich.......	1934–58	36965	964	92	267*	86	42.39
D. Denton	1894–1920	36520	1164	70	221	69	33.38
G. H. Hirst	1889–1929	36203	1215	152	341	60	34.05
W. G. Quaife......	1894–1928	36050	1204	186	255*	72	35.41
D. Kenyon........	1946–66	35843	1110	54	259	73	33.94
G. Gunn..........	1902–32	35190	1062	82	222	62	35.90

	Career	Runs	Inns.	Times Not Out	Highest Inns.	100's	Average
John Langridge	1928–55	34380	984	66	250*	76	37.45
C. Washbrook.....	1933–64	34101	906	107	251*	76	42.67
M. Leyland	1920–48	33660	932	101	263	80	40.50
H. T. W. Hardinge.	1902–33	33519	1021	103	263*	75	36.51
R. Abel...........	1881–1904	32669	994	73	357*	74	35.47
M. C. Cowdrey	1950–66	32065	818	88	307	78	43.92
J. D. Robertson....	1937–59	31914	897	46	331*	67	37.50
J. Hardstaff, junr...	1930–55	31841	812	94	266	83	44.34
James Langridge ...	1924–53	31716	1058	157	167	42	35.20
C. B. Fry	1892–1921	30886	658	43	258*	94	50.22
D. Brookes........	1934–59	30874	925	70	257	71	36.10
P. Holmes.........	1913–35	30574	810	84	315	67	42.11
R. T. Simpson	1944–5–63	30546	852	55	259	64	38.32
L. G. Berry	1924–51	30188	1048	57	232	45	30.46

1,000 RUNS IN A SEASON

(OVERSEAS TOURS INCLUDED)

28 Times: W. G. GRACE 2,000 (6); F. E. WOOLLEY 3,000 (1), 2,000 (12).

27 Times: C. P. MEAD 3,000 (2), 2,000 (9).

26 Times: J. B. HOBBS 3,000 (1), 2,000 (16).

25 Times: E. HENDREN 3,000 (3), 2,000 (12); W. G. QUAIFE 2,000 (1).

24 Times: H. SUTCLIFFE 3,000 (3), 2,000 (12).

22 Times: W. R. HAMMOND 3,000 (3), 2,000 (9).

21 Times: D. DENTON 2,000 (5); W. RHODES 2,000 (2).

20 Times: M. C. COWDREY 2,000 (2); G. GUNN; T. HAYWARD 3,000 (2), 2,000 (8); JAMES LANGRIDGE 2,000 (1); A. SANDHAM 2,000 (8); C. WASHBROOK 2,000 (2).

19 Times: T. W. GRAVENEY 2,000 (7); J. W. HEARNE 2,000 (4); G. H. HIRST 2,000 (3); E. TYLDESLEY 3,000 (1), 2,000 (5); J. T. TYLDESLEY 3,000 (1), 2,000 (4).

18 Times: L. G. BERRY 2,000 (1); H. T. W. HARDINGE 2,000 (5); D. KENYON 2,000 (7); P. A. PERRIN; R. E. S. WYATT 2,000 (5).

17 Times: L. E. G. AMES 3,000 (1), 2,000 (5); T. E. BAILEY 2,000 (1); D. BROOKES 2,000 (6); D. C. S. COMPTON 3,000 (1), 2,000 (5); L. HUTTON 3,000 (1), 2,000 (8); JOHN LANGRIDGE 2,000 (11); M. LEYLAND 2,000 (3).

16 Times: D. G. BRADMAN 2,000 (4); EMRYS DAVIES 2,000 (1); E. G. HAYES 2,000 (2); J. O'CONNOR 2,000 (4); JAMES SEYMOUR 2,000 (1).

15 Times: E. H. BOWLEY 2,000 (4); A. E. DIPPER 2,000 (5); H. E. DOLLERY 2,000 (2); W. J. EDRICH 3,000 (1), 2,000 (8); P. HOLMES 2,000 (7); W. G. A. PARKHOUSE 2,000 (1); J. D. ROBERTSON 2,000 (9).

FOUR HUNDREDS OR MORE IN SUCCESSION

Six in Succession

C. B. FRY: in 1901. D. G. BRADMAN: in 1938–39.

Five in Succession

E. D. WEEKES: in 1955–56.

Four in Succession

D. G. BRADMAN: 1931–32, 1948–49.
W. R. HAMMOND: 1936–37, 1945–46.
J. B. HOBBS: 1920, 1925.
H. SUTCLIFFE: 1931, 1939.
D. C. S. COMPTON: 1946–47.
N. J. CONTRACTOR: 1957–58.
K. S. DULEEPSINHJI: 1931.
C. B. FRY: 1911.
T. HAYWARD: 1906.
H. T. W. HARDINGE: 1913.
JOHN LANGRIDGE: 1949.
C. G. MACARTNEY: 1921.
P. B. H. MAY: 1956–57.
V. M. MERCHANT: 1941–42.
A. MITCHELL: 1933.
NAWAB OF PATAUDI: 1931.
P. ROY: 1962–63.
SAEED AHMED: 1961–62.
E. TYLDESLEY: 1926.
W. W. WHYSALL: 1930.
F. E. WOOLLEY: 1929.

Five Hundreds in Successive Test Innings

E. D. Weekes (West Indies), 141 v. England, 1947–48; 128, 194, 162 and 101 v. India, 1948–49.

Four Hundreds in Successive Test Innings

J. H. Fingleton (Australia), 112, 108, 118 in South Africa, 1935–36, and 100 v. England in Australia, 1936–37.

A. Melville (South Africa), 103 v. England in South Africa, 1938–39, 189, 104* and 117 in England, 1947.

MOST HUNDREDS IN A SEASON

Eighteen: D. C. S. Compton, in 1947. These included six centuries against the South Africans in which matches his average was 84.78. His aggregate for the season was 3,816, also a record.

Sixteen: J. B. Hobbs, in 1925, when aged 42, played 16 three-figure innings in first-class matches. It was during this season that he exceeded the number of hundreds obtained in first-class cricket by W. G. Grace.

Fifteen: W. R. Hammond, in 1938.

Fourteen: H. Sutcliffe, in 1932.

Thirteen: D. G. Bradman in 1938, C. B. Fry in 1901, W. R. Hammond in 1933 and 1937, T. Hayward in 1906, E. Hendren in 1923, 1927 and 1928, C. P. Mead in 1928, and H. Sutcliffe in 1928 and 1931.

FAST SCORING

E. Alletson, for Notts v. Sussex, at Hove, in 1911, scored 189 out of 227 runs obtained whilst at the wicket in ninety minutes.

D. C. S. Compton, for M.C.C. v. N.E. Transvaal, at Benoni, in 1948–49, scored 300 out of 399 in 181 minutes.

P. G. H. Fender, for Surrey v. Northamptonshire, at Northampton, in 1920, scored 113* out of 171 in forty-two minutes. He reached 50 in nineteen minutes and 100 in thirty-five minutes. Fender and H. A. Peach added 171 in forty-two minutes.

G. L. Jessop, for Gloucestershire v. Yorkshire, at Harrogate, in 1897, scored 101 out of 118 in forty minutes.

G. L. Jessop, for Gentlemen of South v. Players of South, at Hastings, in 1907, scored 191 runs out of 234 in ninety minutes. He reached 50 in twenty-four minutes, 100 in forty-two, and 150 in sixty-three.

C. I. J. Smith, in June 1938, made 69 in twenty minutes for Middlesex against Sussex at Lord's, and ten days later against Gloucestershire at Bristol he scored 66 in eighteen minutes—the first 50 coming in eleven minutes.

C. C. Inman, in 1965, made 51 in eight minutes for Leicestershire v. Nottinghamshire, at Nottingham, including 32 in an over when full tosses were presented to him to hit.

For Auckland v. Otago, at Dunedin in 1936–37, P. E. Whitelaw and W. N. Carson added 445 runs for the third wicket in 268 minutes—a world's record.

Worcestershire, set to make 131 in forty minutes against Nottinghamshire at Worcester in 1951, hit off the runs in thirty-five minutes for the loss of D. Kenyon's wicket. The other batsmen were G. Dews and R. O. Jenkins.

Kent scored 219 in seventy-one minutes when beating Gloucestershire at Dover, 1937. They averaged nine runs an over.

F. R. Santall (201) scored 173 out of 230 in 116 minutes before lunch on the third day for Warwickshire v. Northants at Northampton, 1933.

F. R. Brown made 168 out of 206 in 125 minutes for Surrey v. Kent, Blackheath, 1932. He advanced from 100 to 150 in fifteen minutes.

H. Sutcliffe (194) and M. Leyland (45) hit 102 off six consecutive overs for Yorkshire v. Essex, Scarborough, 1932.

J. B. Hobbs (47) and J. N. Crawford (48) made 96 without loss in thirty-two minutes at The Oval, 1919, after Kent left Surrey to get 95 in forty-two minutes.

RECORD HIT

The Rev. W. Fellows, while at practice on the Christchurch Ground at Oxford in 1856, drove a ball bowled by Charles Rogers 175 yards from hit to pitch.

MOST PERSONAL SIXES IN AN INNINGS

15	J. R. Reid (296)	Wellington v. Northern Districts, at Wellington	1962–63
11	C. K. Nayudu (153)	Hindus v. M.C.C., at Bombay	1926–27
11	C. J. Barnett (194)	Gloucestershire v. Somerset, at Bath	1934
11	R. Benaud (135)	Australians v. T. N. Pearce's XI, at Scarborough	1953

W. J. Stewart (Warwickshire) hit 17 sixes in the match v. Lancashire at Blackpool, July 29, 30, 31, 1959, 10 in his first innings of 155 and seven in the second innings of 125.

MOST RUNS SCORED OFF ONE OVER

34	E. Alletson	off E. H. Killick, Notts v. Sussex, at Hove (including two no-balls)	1911
32	C. C. Inman	off N. Hill, Leicestershire v. Nottinghamshire, at Nottingham (full tosses were provided for him to hit)	1965
32	C. Smart	off G. Hill, Glamorgan v. Hampshire, at Cardiff	1935
31	A. W. Wellard	off F. E. Woolley, Somerset v. Kent, at Wells (including five 6's)	1938
30	D. G. Bradman	off A. P. Freeman, Australians v. England XI, at Folkestone	1934
30	H. B. Cameron	off H. Verity, South Africans v. Yorkshire, at Sheffield	1935
30	J. D. Lindsay	off W. T. Greensmith, South African Fezela XI v. Essex, at Chelmsford (five successive 6's to win the match)	1961
30	A. W. Wellard	off T. R. Armstrong, Somerset v. Derbyshire, at Wells (five 6's)	1936
30	D. Wilson	off R. N. S. Hobbs, Yorkshire v. M.C.C., at Scarborough	1966
30	P. L. Winslow	off J. T. Ikin, South Africans v. Lancashire, at Manchester	1955
28	H. T. Bartlett	off T. P. B. Smith, Gentlemen v. Players, at Lord's	1938
28	J. H. de Courcy	off W. T. Greensmith, Australians v. Essex, at Southend	1953
28	H. L. Hazell	off H. Verity, Somerset v. Yorkshire, at Bath	1936
28	G. L. Jessop	off L. C. Braund, Gloucestershire v. Somerset, at Bristol	1904
28	G. L. Jessop	off R. D. Burrows, Gloucestershire v. Worcestershire, at Stourbridge	1910
28	J. E. McConnon	off N. I. Thomson, Glamorgan v. Sussex, at Cardiff	1955

28 D. W. White off J. D. Piachaud, Hampshire v. Oxford University, at Oxford 1960

(All the above instances refer to six-ball overs.)

300 RUNS IN ONE DAY

345	C. G. Macartney	Australians v. Nottinghamshire	Nottingham	1921
334	W. H. Ponsford	Victoria v. New South Wales	Melbourne	1926–27
333	K. S. Duleepsinhji	Sussex v. Northamptonshire	Hove	1930
331*	J. D. Robertson	Middlesex v. Worcestershire	Worcester	1949
322	E. Paynter	Lancashire v. Sussex	Hove	1937
318	C. W. Gregory	New South Wales v. Queensland	Brisbane	1906–7
316	R. H. Moore	Hampshire v. Warwickshire	Bournemouth	1937
315*	R. C. Blunt	Otago v. Canterbury	Christchurch	1931–32
309	D. G. Bradman	Australia v. England	Leeds	1930
307	W. H. Ashdown	Kent v. Essex	Brentwood	1934
306	A. Ducat	Surrey v. Oxford University	The Oval	1919
305	F. R. Foster	Warwickshire v. Worcestershire	Dudley	1914

HIGHEST PARTNERSHIPS

577 V. S. Hazare (288) and Gul Mahomed (319), fourth wicket for Baroda v. Holkar, at Baroda 1946–47

574 F. M. Worrell (255*) and C. L. Walcott (314*), fourth wicket for Barbados v. Trinidad, at Port of Spain 1945–46

555 P. Holmes (224*) and H. Sutcliffe (313), first wicket, Yorkshire v. Essex, at Leyton 1932

554 J. T. Brown (300) and J. Tunnicliffe (243), first wicket, Yorkshire v. Derbyshire, at Chesterfield 1898

502 F. M. Worrell (308*) and J. D. Goddard (218*), fourth wicket, Barbados v. Trinidad, at Bridgetown 1943–44

490 E. H. Bowley (283) and John Langridge (195), first wicket, Sussex v. Middlesex, at Hove 1933

487 G. A. Headley (344*) and C. C. Passalique (261*), sixth wicket Jamaica v. Lord Tennyson's XI, at Kingston 1931–32

456 E. R. Mayne (209) and W. H. Ponsford (248), first wicket, Victoria v. Queensland, at Melbourne 1923–24

455 B. B. Nimbalkar (443*) and K. V. Bhandarkar (205), second wicket for Maharashtra v. Western India States, at Poona 1948–49

451 D. G. Bradman (244) and W. H. Ponsford (266), second wicket, 5th Test, Australia v. England, at Kennington Oval 1934

PARTNERSHIP FOR FIRST WICKET

555 P. Holmes and H. Sutcliffe, Yorkshire v. Essex, at Leyton .. 1932

554 J. T. Brown and J. Tunnicliffe, Yorkshire v. Derbyshire, at Chesterfield 1898

490 E. H. Bowley and John Langridge, Sussex v. Middlesex, at Hove 1933

456 E. R. Mayne and W. H. Ponsford, Victoria v. Queensland, at Melbourne 1923–24

428 J. B. Hobbs and A. Sandham, Surrey v. Oxford U., at The Oval 1926

424 J. F. W. Nicolson and I. J. Siedle, Natal v. Orange Free State, at Bloemfontein 1926–27

413 V. Mankad and P. Roy, India v. New Zealand, at Madras .. 1955–56 (World Test Record)

395 D. M. Young and R. B. Nicholls, Gloucestershire v. Oxford University, at Oxford 1962

391 A. O. Jones and A. Shrewsbury, Notts v. Glos., at Bristol .. 1899

390 L. Wight and G. Gibbs, British Guiana v. Barbados, at Georgetown 1951–52

382 R. B. Simpson and W. M. Lawry, Australia v. West Indies, at Bridgetown 1965

380 H. Whitehead and C. J. B. Wood, Leicestershire v. Worcestershire, at Worcester 1906
379 R. Abel and W. Brockwell, Surrey v Hampshire, at The Oval.. 1897
378 J. T. Brown and J. Tunnicliffe, Yorkshire v. Sussex, at Sheffield 1897
377 N. F. Horner and K. Ibadulla, Warwickshire v. Surrey, at The Oval (unbroken) 1960
375 W. H. Ponsford and W. M. Woodfull, Victoria v. New South Wales, at Melbourne 1926–27
373 B. Sutcliffe and L. A. Watt, Otago v. Auckland, at Auckland .. 1950–51
368 A. C. MacLaren and R. H. Spooner, Lancashire v. Gloucestershire, at Liverpool 1903
368 E. H. Bowley and J. H. Parks, Sussex v. Glos., at Hove 1929
364 R. Abel and D. L. A. Jephson, Surrey v. Derbyshire, at The Oval 1900
361 N. Oldfield and V. Broderick, Northamptonshire v. Scotland, at Peterborough 1953
359 L. Hutton and C. Washbrook, England v. South Africa, at Johannesburg 1948–49
355 A. F. Rae and J. B. Stollmeyer, West Indies v. Sussex, at Hove .. 1950
352 T. Hayward and J. B. Hobbs, Surrey v. Warwickshire, at The Oval 1909
350 C. Washbrook and W. Place, Lancashire v. Sussex, at Manchester (unbroken) 1947

FIRST-WICKET HUNDREDS IN BOTH INNINGS

B. Sutcliffe and D. D. Taylor, for Auckland v. Canterbury in 1948–49, scored for the first wicket 220 in the first innings and 286 in the second innings. This is the only instance of two double century opening stands in the same match.

T. Hayward and J. B. Hobbs in 1907 accomplished a performance without parallel by scoring over 100 together for the first wicket of Surrey four times in one week: 106 and 125 v. Cambridge University, at The Oval, and 147 and 105 v. Middlesex, at Lord's.

L. Hutton and C. Washbrook, in three consecutive innings which they opened together for England in Test Matches with Australia in 1946–47, made 138 in the second innings at Melbourne, and 137 and 100 at Adelaide. They also opened with 168 and 129 at Leeds in 1948.

J. B. Hobbs and H. Sutcliffe, in three consecutive innings which they opened together for England in Test matches with Australia in 1924–25, made 157 and 110 at Sydney and 283 at Melbourne. On 26 occasions—15 times in Test matches—Hobbs and Sutcliffe took part in a three-figure first-wicket partnership. Seven of these stands exceeded 200.

P. Holmes and H. Sutcliffe made 100 or more runs for the first wicket of Yorkshire on sixty-nine occasions; J. B. Hobbs and A. Sandham of Surrey on sixty-three; W. W. Keeton and C. B. Harris of Notts on forty-six; T. Hayward and J. B. Hobbs of Surrey on forty; G. Gunn and W. W. Whysall of Notts on forty; C. B. Fry and J. Vine of Sussex on thirty-three; R. E. Marshall and J. R. Gray of Hampshire on thirty-three; E. Davies and A. H. Dyson of Glamorgan on thirty-two; and A. O. Jones and J. Iremonger of Notts on twenty-four.

J. Douglas and A. E. Stoddart in 1896 scored over 150 runs for the first wicket of Middlesex three times within a fortnight. In 1901, J. Iremonger and A. O. Jones obtained over 100 for the first wicket of Nottinghamshire four times within eight days, scoring 134 and 144* v. Surrey at The Oval, 238 v. Essex at Leyton and 119 v. Derbyshire at Welbeck.

J. W. Lee and F. S. Lee, brothers, in 1934, for Somerset, scored over 100 runs thrice in succession in the County Championship.

W. G. Grace and A. E. Stoddart in three consecutive innings against the Australians in 1893 made over 100 runs for each opening partnership.

In consecutive innings for Lancashire in 1928 C. Hallows and F. Watson opened with 200, 202, 107, 118; reached three figures twelve times, 200 four times.

J. B. Hobbs during his career, which extended from 1905 to 1934, helped to make 100 or more for the first wicket in first-class cricket 166 times—15 of them in 1926, when in consecutive innings he helped to make 428, 182, 106 and 123 before a wicket fell. As many as 117 of the 166 stands were made for Surrey.

In the period 1919–1939 inclusive, H. Sutcliffe shared in 145 first-wicket partnerships of 100 runs or more.

There were four first-wicket hundred partnerships in the match between Somerset and Cambridge University at Taunton in 1960. G. Atkinson and R. Virgin scored 172 and 112 for Somerset and R. M. Prideaux and A. R. Lewis 198 and 137 for Cambridge University.

WICKET RECORDS FOR ALL COUNTRIES

Best First-Wicket Stands

English ..	555	P. Holmes (224*) and H. Sutcliffe (313), Yorkshire v. Essex, at Leyton	1932
Australian ..	456	W. H. Ponsford (248) and E. R. Mayne (209), Victoria v. Queensland, at Melbourne ..	1923–24
South African..	424	J. F. W. Nicolson (252*) and I. J. Siedle (174), Natal v. Orange Free State, at Bloemfontein	1926–27
Indian	413	V. Mankad (231) and P. Roy (173), India v. New Zealand, at Madras	1955–56
West Indian ..	390	L. Wight (262*) and G. Gibbs (216). British Guiana v. Barbados, at Georgetown ..	1951–52
New Zealand ..	373	B. Sutcliffe (275) and L. A. Watt (96), Otago v. Auckland, at Auckland	1950–51
Pakistan ..	277	Hanif Mohammad (146*) and Alim-ud-Din (131*), Karachi "A" v. Sind "A", at Karachi	1957–58

Best Second-Wicket Stands

Indian	455	B. B. Nimbalkar (443*) and K. V. Bhandarkar (205), Maharashtra v. W.I. States, at Poona	1948–49
Australian ..	451	D. G. Bradman (244) and W. H. Ponsford (266), Australia v. England, at The Oval ..	1934
West Indian ..	446	C. C. Hunte (260) and G. S. Sobers (365*), West Indies v. Pakistan, at Kingston	1957–58
English ..	429	J. G. Dewes (204*) and G. H. G. Doggart (219*), Cambridge U. v. Essex, at Cambridge	1949
South African..	305	S. K. Coen (165) and J. M. M. Commaille (186), Orange Free State v. Natal, at Bloemfontein	1926–27
New Zealand ..	301	C. S. Dempster (180) and C. F. W. Allcott (131), N.Z'drs. v. Warwicks., at Birmingham	1927
Pakistan ..	269	Nazar Mohammad (170) and Murawwat Hussain (100), Pakistan v. Ceylon, at Ceylon Oval	1948–49

Best Third-Wicket Stands

New Zealand ..	445	P. E. Whitelaw (195) and W. N. Carson (290), Auckland v. Otago, at Dunedin	1936–37
West Indian ..	434	J. B. Stollmeyer (324) and G. E. Gomez (190), Trinidad v. British Guiana, at Port of Spain	1946–47
English ..	424	D. C. S. Compton (252*) and W. J. Edrich (168*), Middlesex v. Somerset, at Lord's ..	1948
Indian	410	L. Amarnath (262) and R. S. Modi (156), Indians v. The Rest, at Calcutta	1946–47
Australian ..	389	S. J. McCabe (192) and W. H. Ponsford (281*), Australians v. M.C.C., at Lord's	1934
Pakistan ..	388	Salah-ud-Din (169) and Wallis Mathias (228), Karachi Blues v. Hyderabad, at Karachi .	1964–65
South African..	341	E. J. Barlow (201) and R. G. Pollock (175), South Africa v. Australia, at Adelaide ..	1963–64

Best Fourth-Wicket Stands

Indian	577	V. S. Hazare (288) and Gul Mahomed (319), Baroda v. Holkar, at Baroda	1946–47
West Indian ..	574	F. M. Worrell (255*) and C. L. Walcott (314*), Barbados v. Trinidad, at Port of Spain ..	1945–46

English ..	448	R. Abel (193) and T. Hayward (273), Surrey v. Yorkshire, at The Oval	1899
Australian ..	424	I. S. Lee (258) and S. O. Quin (210), Victoria v. Tasmania, at Melbourne	1933–34
Pakistan ..	346	Zafar Altaf (268) and Majid Jahangir (241), Lahore Greens v. Bahawalpur, at Lahore ..	1966
South African..	342	E. A. B. Rowan (196) and P. J. M. Gibb (203), Transvaal v. N.E. Transvaal, at Johannesburg	1952–53
New Zealand ..	324	W. M. Wallace (197) and J. R. Reid (188*), N. Z'drs. v. Camb. U., at Cambridge ..	1949

Best Fifth-Wicket Stands

Australian ..	405	D. G. Bradman (234) and S. G. Barnes (234), Australia v. England, at Sydney	1946–47
English ..	393	E. G. Arnold (200*) and W. B. Burns (196), Worcs. v. Warwicks., at Birmingham ..	1909
Indian	360	Uday Merchant (217) and M. N. Raiji (170), Bombay v. Hyderabad, at Bombay	1947–48
South African..	327	A. W. Briscoe (191) and H. B. Cameron (182), Transvaal v. Griqualand West, at Jo'burg..	1934–35
West Indian ..	283	N. L. Bonitto (207) and A. P. Binns (157), Jamaica v. British Guiana, at Georgetown..	1951–52
New Zealand ..	266	B. Sutcliffe (355) and W. S. Haig (67), Otago v. Auckland, at Dunedin	1949–50
Pakistan ..	216	Wallis Mathias (129) and Nasim-ul-Ghani (117), Karachi "A" v. East Pakistan, at Karachi	1962–63

Best Sixth-Wicket Stands

West Indian ..	487	G. A. Headley (344*) and C. C. Passalique (261*), Jamaica v. Lord Tennyson's XI, at Kingston	1931–32
Australian ..	428	W. W. Armstrong (172*) and M. A. Noble (284), Australians v. Sussex, at Hove ..	1902
English ..	411	R. M. Poore (304) and E. G. Wynyard (225), Hampshire v. Somerset, at Taunton ..	1899
Indian	371	V. M. Merchant (359*) and R. S. Modi (168), Bombay v. Maharashtra, at Bombay ..	1943–44
South African..	244	J. M. M. Commaille (132*) and A. W. Palm (106*), Western Province v. Griqualand West, at Johannesburg	1923–24
Pakistan ..	217	Hanif Mohammad (203*) and Majid Jahangir (80), Pakistan v. New Zealand, at Lahore ..	1965
New Zealand ..	187	J. E. F. Beck (103*) and L. C. Butler (101*) Wellington v. Central Districts, at New Plymouth	1961–62

Best Seventh-Wicket Stands

West Indian ..	347	D. Atkinson (219) and C. Depeiza (122), West Indies v. Australia, at Bridgetown	1954–55
English ..	344	K. S. Ranjitsinhji (230) and W. Newham (153), Sussex v. Essex, at Leyton..	1902
Australian ..	335	C. W. Andrews (253) and E. C. Bensted (155), Queensland v. New South Wales, at Sydney	1934–35
Pakistan ..	308	Waqar Hassan (189) and Imtiaz Ahmed (209), Pakistan v. New Zealand, at Lahore.. ..	1955–56
South African..	299	B. Mitchell (159) and A. Melville (153), Transvaal v. Griqualand West, at Kimberley	1946–47
Indian	274	K. C. Ibrahim (250) and K. M. Rangnekar (138), Bijapur XI v. Bengal XI, at Bombay..	1942–43
New Zealand ..	265	J. L. Powell (164) and N. Doreen (105*), Canterbury v. Otago, at Christchurch ..	1929–30

Best Eighth-Wicket Stands

Australian ..	433	A. Sims (184*) and V. T. Trumper (293), An Australian XI v. Canterbury, at Christchurch	1913–14
English ..	292	Lord Hawke (166) and R. Peel (210*), Yorkshire v. Warwickshire, at Birmingham ..	1896
West Indian ..	255	E. A. V. Williams (131*) and E. A. Martindale (134), Barbados v. Trinidad, at Bridgetown	1935–36
Indian	236	C. T. Sarwate (235) and R. P. Singh (88), Holkar v. Delhi and Dis., at New Delhi ..	1949–50
South African..	222	D. P. B. Morkel (114) and S. S. L. Steyn (261*), Western Province v. Border, at Cape Town	1929–30
New Zealand ..	190	J. E. Mills (104*) and C. F. W. Allcott (102*), New Zealanders v. Civil Service, at Chiswick,	1927
Pakistan ..	171	Majid Jahangir (108) and Zulfiqar Ali (90) Lahore Board v. P.I.A. at Lahore	1964–65

Best Ninth-Wicket Stands

English ..	283	J. Chapman (165) and A. R. Warren (123), Derbyshire v. Warwickshire, at Blackwell ..	1910
Indian	245	V. S. Hazare (316)* and N. D. Nagarwalla (98), Maharashtra v. Baroda, at Poona ..	1939–40
New Zealand ..	239	H. B. Cave (118) and I. B. Leggat (142*), Central Districts v. Otago, at Dunedin ..	1952–53
Australian ..	232	C. Hill (365*) and E. Walkley (53), South Australia v. N.S.W., at Adelaide	1900–01
South African..	221	N. V. Lindsay (160*) and G. R. McCubbin (97). Transvaal v. Rhodesia, at Bulawayo ..	1922–23
Pakistan ..	140	Mushtaq Mohammad (87) and Abdul Dyer (45), Karachi Whites v. Hyderabad, at Hyderabad	1956–57
West Indian ..	134	W. W. Hall (77) and F. C. M. Alexander (36), E. D. Weekes's XI v. C. L. Walcott's XI, at Port of Spain	1956–57

Best Tenth-Wicket Stands

Australian ..	307	A. F. Kippax (260*), and J. E. H. Hooker (62) New South Wales v. Victoria, at Melbourne	1928–29
Indian	249	C. T. Sarwate (124*) and S. N. Banerjee (121), Indians v. Surrey, at The Oval	1946
English ..	235	A. Fielder (112*) and F. E. Woolley (185), Kent v. Worcestershire, at Stourbridge ..	1909
New Zealand ..	184	R. C. Blunt (338*) and W. Hawkesworth (21), Otago v. Canterbury, at Christchurch ..	1931–32
South African..	174	H. R. Lance (169) and D. Mackay-Coghill (57*), Transvaal v. Natal, at Johannesburg ..	1965–66
West Indian ..	138	E. L. G. Hoad (149*) and H. C. Griffith (84), West Indies v. Sussex, at Hove	1933
Pakistan ..	135	Wallis Mathias (144*) and Afaq Hussain (87), Karachi "A" v. Karachi "B" at Karachi ..	1962–63

(All the English record wicket partnerships were made in the County Championship with the exception of the second, for which the best county stand is: 398, W. Gunn (196) and A. Shrewsbury (267), Notts v. Sussex, at Nottingham, 1890.)

HIGHEST AGGREGATES IN A SEASON: OVER 3,000

		Inns.	Times Not Out	Runs	Highest Score	No. of 100's	Average
1947	D. C. S. Compton	50	8	3816	246	18	90.85
1947	W. J. Edrich....	52	8	3539	267*	12	80.43
1906	T. Hayward	61	8	3518	219	13	66.37
1949	L. Hutton	56	6	3429	269*	12	68.58
1928	F. E. Woolley ..	59	4	3352	198	12	60.94

		Inns.		Times Not Out		Runs		Highest Score		No. of 100's		Average
1932	H. Sutcliffe	52	..	7	..	3336	..	313	..	14	..	74.13
1933	W. R. Hammond	54	..	5	..	3323	..	264	..	13	..	67.81
1928	E. Hendren.....	54	..	7	..	3311	..	209*	..	13	..	70.44
1901	R. Abel........	68	..	8	..	3309	..	247	..	7	..	55.15
1937	W. R. Hammond	55	..	5	..	3252	..	217	..	13	..	65.04
1959	M. J. K. Smith .	67	..	11	..	3245	..	200*	..	8	..	57.94
1933	E. Hendren.....	65	..	9	..	3186	..	301*	..	11	..	56.89
1921	C. P. Mead.....	52	..	6	..	3179	..	280*	..	10	..	69.10
1904	T. Hayward	63	..	5	..	3170	..	205	..	11	..	54.65
1899	K. S. Ranjitsinhji	58	..	8	..	3159	..	197	..	8	..	63.18
1901	C. B. Fry	43	..	3	..	3147	..	244	..	13	..	78.67
1900	K. S. Ranjitsinhji	40	..	5	..	3065	..	275	..	11	..	87.57
1933	L. E. G. Ames ..	57	..	5	..	3058	..	295	..	9	..	58.80
1901	J. T. Tyldesley ..	60	..	5	..	3041	..	221	..	9	..	55.29
1928	C. P. Mead.....	50	..	10	..	3027	..	180	..	13	..	75.67
1925	J. B. Hobbs	48	..	5	..	3024	..	266*	..	16	..	70.32
1928	E. Tyldesley	48	..	10	..	3024	..	242	..	10	..	79.57
1961	W. E. Alley	64	..	11	..	3019	..	221*	..	11	..	56.96
1938	W. R. Hammond	42	..	2	..	3011	..	271	..	15	..	75.27
1923	E. Hendren.....	51	..	12	..	3010	..	200*	..	13	..	77.17
1931	H. Sutcliffe.....	42	..	11	..	3006	..	230	..	13	..	96.96
1937	J. H. Parks....	63	..	4	..	3003	..	168	..	11	..	50.89
1928	H. Sutcliffe.....	44	..	5	..	3002	..	228	..	13	..	76.97

W. G. Grace scored 2,739 runs in 1871 when every stroke was run out. He made ten centuries and twice exceeded 200, with an average of 78.25 all first-class matches and the over was four balls.

LARGEST AGGREGATES OUTSIDE ENGLAND

		Inns.	Not out	Runs	Highest Score	No. of 100's	Average
In Australia							
1928–29	D. G. Bradman	24	6	1690	340*	7	93.88
In South Africa							
1961–62	J. R. Reid	30	2	1915	203	7	68.39
In West Indies							
1929–30	E. Hendren........	18	5	1765	254*	6	135.76
In New Zealand							
1955–56	E. D. Weekes......	10	1	940	146	6	104.44
In India							
1926–27	A. Sandham.......	33	4	1977	150	8	68.17
In Pakistan							
1958–59	Hanif Mohammad .	8	2	891	499	4	148.50

1,000 RUNS IN MAY

Three batsmen have scored 1,000 runs in May, and three others—D. G. Bradman twice—have made 1,000 runs before June. Their innings-by-innings records are as follows:—

	Runs	Average
W. G. GRACE, May 9 to May 30, 1895 (22 days):		
13, 103, 18, 25, 288, 52, 257, 73*, 18, 169	1016	112.88
"W.G." was within two months of completing his 47th year.		
W. R. HAMMOND, May 7 to May 31, 1927 (25 days):		
27, 135, 108, 128, 17, 11, 99, 187, 4, 30, 83, 7, 192, 14 ..	1042	74.42
Hammond scored his 1,000th run on May 28, thus equalling "W.G.'s" record of 22 days.		
C. HALLOWS, May 5 to May 31, 1928 (27 days):		
100, 101, 51*, 123, 101*, 22, 74, 104, 58, 34*, 232	1000	125.00

T. HAYWARD, April 16 to May 31, 1900:
120*, 55, 108, 131*, 55, 193, 120, 5, 6, 3, 40, 146, 92 .. 1074 97.63
Hayward scored 120 not out on April 16.
D. G. BRADMAN, April 30 to May 31, 1930:
236, 185*, 78, 9, 48*, 66, 4, 44, 252*, 32, 47* 1001 143.00
On April 30 Bradman scored 75 not out.
D. G. BRADMAN, April 30 to May 31, 1938:
258, 58, 137, 278, 2, 143, 145*, 5, 30* 1056 150.85
Bradman scored 258 on April 30, and his 1,000th run on May 27.
W. J. EDRICH, April 30 to May 31, 1938:
104, 37, 115, 63, 20*, 182, 71, 31, 53*, 45, 15, 245, 0, 9, 20* 1010 84.16
Edrich scored 21 not out on April 30. All his runs were scored at Lord's.

1,000 RUNS IN TWO SEPARATE MONTHS

L. Hutton, by scoring 1,294 in June 1949, made more runs in a single month than anyone else. The previous best was by W. R. Hammond, 1,281, in August 1936. Hutton also made 1,050 in August 1949, and thus joined C. B. Fry, K. S. Ranjitsinhji and H. Sutcliffe, who scored over 1,000 in each of two months in the same season.

HANDLED BALL

1857 J. Grundy, M.C.C. v. Kent, at Lord's.
1872 G. Bennett, Kent v. Sussex, at Hove.
1886–87 W. H. Scotton, Smokers v. Non-Smokers, at East Melbourne.
1893 C. W. Wright, Nottinghamshire v. Gloucestershire, at Bristol.
1894–95 E. Jones, South Australia v. Victoria, at Melbourne.
1907 A. D. Nourse, Snr., South Africans v. Sussex, at Brighton.
1929–30 E. T. Benson, Auckland v. M.C.C., at Auckland.
1952–53 A. Gilbertson, Otago v. Auckland, at Auckland.
1956–57 W. R. Endean, South Africa v. England, at Cape Town.
1958–59 P. J. Burge, Queensland v. New South Wales, at Sydney.
1959–60 Dildar Awan, Services v. Lahore, at Lahore.
1960–61 Mahmood Hasan, Karachi Univ. v. Railways-Quetta, at Karachi.
1965 A. Rees, Glamorgan v. Middlesex, at Lord's.

OBSTRUCTING THE FIELD

1868 C. A. Absolom, Cambridge University v. Surrey, at The Oval.
1899 T. Straw, Worcestershire v. Warwickshire, at Worcester.
1901 T. Straw, Worcestershire v. Warwickshire, at Birmingham.
1901 J. P. Whiteside, Leicestershire v. Lancashire, at Leicester.
1951 L. Hutton, England v. South Africa, at The Oval.
1954–55 J. A. Hayes, Canterbury v. Central Districts, at Christchurch.
1956–57 D. D. Deshpande, Madhya Pradesh v. Uttar Pradesh, at Benares.
1963 K. Ibadulla, Warwickshire v. Hampshire, at Coventry.

HIT THE BALL TWICE

1864 H. E. Bull, M.C.C. v. Oxford Univ., at Lord's.
1872 H. Charlwood, Sussex v. Surrey, at Hove.
1873–74 I. J. Salmon, Wellington v. Hawke's Bay, at Wellington.
1878 R. G. Barlow, North v. South, at Lord's.
1892–93 P. S. Wimble, Transvaal v. Griqualand West, at Kimberley.
1896 G. B. Nicholls, Somerset v. Gloucestershire, at Bristol.
1897 A. A. Lilley, Warwickshire v. Yorkshire, at Birmingham.
1906 J. H. King, Leicestershire v. Surrey, at The Oval.
1956–57 A. P. Binns, Jamaica v. British Guiana, at Georgetown.

BOWLING AND FIELDING RECORDS

Four Wickets With Consecutive Balls

J. Wells, Kent v. Sussex, at Brighton	1862
G. Ulyett, England v. New South Wales, at Sydney	1878–79
G. Nash, Lancashire v. Somerset, at Manchester	1882
J. B. Hide, Sussex v. M.C.C. and Ground, at Lord's	1890
F. Shacklock, Notts v. Somerset, at Nottingham	1893
A. Downes, Otago v. Auckland, at Dunedin	1893–94
F. Martin, M.C.C. and Ground v. Derbyshire, at Lord's	1895
A. Mold, Lancashire v. Notts, at Nottingham	1895
W. Brearley, Lancashire v. Somerset, at Manchester (Not all in same innings)	1905
S. Haigh, M.C.C. v. Army XI, at Pretoria	1905–06
A. E. Trott, Middlesex v. Somerset, at Lord's (It was Trott's benefit match and he did the hat-trick also in the same innings)	1907
F. A. Tarrant, Middlesex v. Gloucestershire, at Bristol	1907
A. Drake, Yorkshire v. Derbyshire, at Chesterfield	1914
S. G. Smith, Northamptonshire v. Warwickshire, at Edgbaston	1914
H. A. Peach, Surrey v. Sussex, at The Oval	1924
A. F. Borland, Natal v. Griqualand West, at Kimberley	1926–27
J. E. H. Hooker, New South Wales v. Victoria, at Sydney (Not all in same innings)	1928–29
R. Tyldesley, Lancashire v. Derbyshire, at Derby (Not all in same innings)	1929
R. J. Crisp, Western Province v. Griqualand West, at Johannesburg	1931–32
R. J. Crisp, Western Province v. Natal, at Durban	1933–34
A. R. Gover, Surrey v. Worcestershire, at Worcester	1935
W. H. Copson, Derbyshire v. Warwickshire, at Derby	1937
W. A. Henderson, North-Eastern Transvaal v. Orange Free State at Bloemfontein	1937–38
F. Ridgway, Kent v. Derbyshire, at Folkestone	1951
A. K. Walker, Notts v. Leicestershire, at Leicester	1956

(Walker dismissed Firth with the last ball of the first innings and Lester, Tompkin and Smithson with the first three balls of the second innings, a feat without parallel.)

In their match with England at The Oval in 1863, Surrey lost four wickets in the course of a four-ball over from G. Bennett. From his first H. H. Stephenson was stumped, from his second W. Caffyn was run out, E. Dowson was bowled by his third, and G. Griffiths was caught off his fourth.

Double Hat-Trick

Besides Trott's performance, which is given in the preceding section, the following instances are recorded of players having performed the hat-trick twice in the same match:—

A. Shaw, Notts v. Gloucestershire, at Trent Bridge, 1884.
T. J. Matthews, Australia v. South Africa, at Manchester, 1912.
C. W. L. Parker, Gloucestershire v. Middlesex, at Bristol, 1924.
R. O. Jenkins, Worcestershire v. Surrey, at Worcester, 1949.
J. S. Rao, Services v. Northern Punjab, at Amritsar, 1963–64 (*Rao performed his feat twice in the same innings*).

Most Hat-Tricks

Seven Times	Five Times	Four Times
D. V. P. Wright.	S. Haigh.	J. T. Hearne.
	V. W. C. Jupp.	J. C. Laker.
Six Times	A. E. G. Rhodes.	G. G. Macaulay.
T. W. Goddard.	F. A. Tarrant.	T. Richardson.
C. W. L. Parker.		F. S. Trueman.

THREE TIMES		
R. G. Barlow.	G. Giffen.	T. L. Pritchard.
W. M. Bradley.	J. W. Hearne.	J. S. Rao.
H. J. Butler.	A. Hill.	A. Shaw.
W. H. Copson.	R. O. Jenkins.	F. R. Spofforth.
R. J. Crisp.	A. S. Kennedy.	J. B. Statham.
J. W. H. T. Douglas.	G. A. R. Lock.	M. W. Tate.
J. A. Flavell.	W. H. Lockwood.	H. Trumble.
A. P. Freeman.	E. A. McDonald.	D. Wilson.
	T. J. Matthews.	G. A. Wilson.

TEN WICKETS IN ONE INNINGS

	O.	M.	R.		
W. Clarke (Notts)				v. Leicester., at Nottingham	1845
E. Hinkly (Kent)				v. England, at Lord's	1848
J. Wisden (North)				v. South, at Lord's	1850
V. E. Walker (England)	43		74	v Surrey, at The Oval	1859
E. M. Grace (M.C.C.)	32.2	7	69	v. Gents. of Kent, at Canterbury	1862
V. E. Walker (Middlesex) ..	44.2		104	v. Lancashire, at Manchester	1865
G. Wootton (All England)..				v. Yorkshire, at Sheffield ...	1865
W. Hickton (Lancashire) ...	36.2	19	46	v. Hampshire, at Manchester	1870
S. E. Butler (Oxford)	24.1	11	38	v. Cambridge, at Lord's....	1871
Jas. Lillywhite (South)	60.2	22	129	v. North, at Canterbury....	1872
A. Shaw (M.C.C.)	36.2	8	73	v. North, at Lord's	1874
E. Barratt (Players)	29	11	43	v. Australians, at The Oval	1878
G. Giffen (Fourth Aust. XI)	26	10	66	v. The Rest, at Sydney.....	1883–84
W. G. Grace (M.C.C.)	36.2	17	49	v. Oxford U., at Oxford ...	1886
G. Burton (Middlesex)	52.3	25	59	v. Surrey, at The Oval	1888
†A. E. Moss (Canterbury) ..	21.3	10	28	v. Wellington, at Christchurch	1889–90
S. M. J. Woods (Cambridge U.)	31	6	69	v. Thornton's XI, at Cambridge	1890
T. Richardson (Surrey)	15.3	3	45	v. Essex, at The Oval	1894
H. Pickett (Essex)	27	11	32	v. Leicester., at Leyton	1895
E. J. Tyler (Somerset)	34.3	15	49	v. Surrey, at Taunton	1895
W. P. Howell (Australians)	23.2	14	28	v. Surrey, at The Oval	1899
C. H. G. Bland (Sussex) ...	25.2	0	48	v. Kent, at Tonbridge	1899
J. Briggs (Lancashire)	28.5	7	55	v. Worcester., at Manchester	1900
A. E. Trott (Middlesex) ...	14.2	5	42	v. Somerset, at Taunton ...	1900
A. Fielder (Players)	24.5	1	90	v. Gentlemen, at Lord's....	1906
G. E. Dennett (Gloucester.)	19.4	7	40	v. Essex, at Bristol	1906
A. E. E. Vogler (Eastern Prov.)	12	2	26	v. Griq. West, at Johannesburg	1906–07
C. Blythe (Kent)	16	7	30	v. Northants, at Northampton	1907
A. Drake (Yorkshire)	8.5	0	35	v. Somerset, at Weston	1914
W. Bestwick (Derbyshire) ..	19	2	40	v. Glamorgan, at Cardiff...	1921
A. A. Mailey (Australians)..	28.4	5	66	v. Glos., at Cheltenham....	1921
C. W. L. Parker (Gloucester.)	40.3	13	79	v. Somerset, at Bristol	1921
T. Rushby (Surrey)	17.5	4	43	v. Somerset, at Taunton ...	1921
J. C. White (Somerset)	42.2	11	76	v. Worcester., at Worcester.	1921
G. C. Collins (Kent)	19.3	4	65	v. Notts, at Dover	1922
H. Howell (Warwicks.)	25.1	5	51	v. Yorkshire, at Birmingham	1923
A. S. Kennedy (Players)....	22.4	10	37	v. Gentlemen, at The Oval..	1927
G. O. Allen (Middlesex) ...	25.3	10	40	v. Lancashire, at Lords	1929
A. P. Freeman (Kent)	42	9	131	v. Lancashire, at Maidstone	1929
G. Geary (Leicester)	16.2	8	18	v. Glamorgan, at Pontypridd	1929
C. V. Grimmett (Australians)	22.3	8	37	v. Yorkshire, at Sheffield ...	1930
A. P. Freeman (Kent)	30.4	8	53	v. Essex, at Southend	1930
H. Verity (Yorkshire)	18.4	6	36	v. Warwicks., at Leeds.....	1931

† *On debut in first-class cricket.*

	O.	M.	R.		
A. P. Freeman (Kent)	36.1	9	79	v. Lancashire, at Manchester	1931
V. W. C. Jupp (Northants).	39	6	127	v. Kent, at Tunbridge Wells	1932
H. Verity (Yorkshire)......	19.4	16	10	v. Notts, at Leeds	1932
T. W. Wall (Sth. Australia).	12.4	2	36	v. N.S.W., at Sydney	1932–33
T. B. Mitchell (Derbyshire).	19.1	4	64	v. Leicester., at Leicester...	1935
J. Mercer (Glamorgan)	26	10	51	v. Worcester., at Worcester.	1936
T. W. Goddard (Gloucester.)	28.4	4	113	v. Worcester., at Cheltenham	1937
T. F. Smailes (Yorkshire) ..	17.1	5	47	v. Derbyshire, at Sheffield..	1939
E. A. Watts (Surrey).......	24.1	8	67	v. Warwicks., at Birmingham	1939
W. E. Hollies (Warwicks.)..	20.4	4	49	v. Notts, at Birmingham ...	1946
J. M. Sims (East)	18.4	2	90	v. West, at Kingston	1948
T. E. Bailey (Essex)	39.4	9	90	v. Lancs., at Clacton	1949
J. K. Graveney (Gloucester.)	18.4	2	66	v. Derby., at Chesterfield...	1949
R. Berry (Lancashire)......	36.2	9	102	v. Worcester., at Blackpool.	1953
S. P. Gupte (Bombay)	24.2	7	78	v. Comb. XI, at Bombay..	1954–55
J. C. Laker (Surrey)	46	18	88	v. Australians, at The Oval.	1956
J. C. Laker (England)......	51.2	23	53	v. Australia, at Manchester.	1956
G. A. R. Lock (Surrey)	29.1	18	54	v. Kent, at Blackheath	1956
K. Smales (Notts)	41.3	20	66	v. Gloucestershire, at Stroud	1956
P. Chatterjee (Bengal)	19	11	20	v. Assam, at Jhorat	1956–57
J. D. Bannister (Warwicks.)	23.3	11	41	v. Comb. Ser. at Birmingham	1959
A. J. G. Pearson (Cambridge U.)	30.3	8	78	v. Leicestershire, at Loughborough	1961
N. I. Thomson (Sussex)....	34.2	19	49	v. Warwickshire, at Worthing	1964
P. J. Allan (Queensland)...	15.6	3	61	v. Victoria, at Melbourne .	1965–66

NINETEEN WICKETS IN A MATCH

J. C. Laker, England v. Australia at Manchester, for 90 runs 1956

SEVENTEEN WICKETS IN A MATCH

F. P. Fenner, Cambridge Town Club v. The University, at Cambridge 1844
W. Mycroft, for 103 runs, Derbyshire v. Hampshire, at Southampton 1876
W. G. Grace, for 89 runs, Gloucestershire v. Notts, at Cheltenham .. 1877
G. Giffen, for 201 runs, South Australia v. Victoria, at Adelaide .. 1885–86
C. T. B. Turner, for 50 runs, Australians v. An England Eleven, at Hastings 1888
W. Mead for 205 runs, Essex v. Australians, at Leyton 1893
W. Mead, for 119 runs, Essex v. Hampshire, at Southampton 1895
W. P. Howell, for 54 runs, Australians v. Western Province, at Cape Town 1902–03
W. Brearley, for 137 runs, Lancashire v. Somerset, at Manchester .. 1905
C. Blythe, for 48 runs, Kent v. Northants, at Northampton 1907
H. Dean, for 91 runs, Lancashire v. Yorkshire, at Liverpool 1913
S. F. Barnes, for 159 runs, England v. South Africa, at Johannesburg 1913–14
A. P. Freeman, for 67 runs, Kent v. Sussex, at Brighton 1922
F. C. L. Matthews, for 89 runs, Notts v. Northants. at Nottingham .. 1923
C. W. L. Parker, for 56 runs, Gloucestershire v. Essex, at Gloucester 1925
G. R. Cox, for 106 runs, Sussex v. Warwickshire, at Horsham .. 1926
A. P. Freeman, for 92 runs, Kent v. Warwickshire, at Folkestone .. 1932
H. Verity, for 91 runs, Yorkshire v. Essex, at Leyton 1933
J. C. Clay, for 212 runs, Glamorgan v. Worcestershire, at Swansea .. 1937
T. W. Goddard, for 106 runs, Gloucestershire v. Kent, at Bristol .. 1939

REMARKABLE ANALYSES

(Also see Ten Wickets in One Innings on preceding pages)

	O.	M.	R.	W.		
H. Verity (Yorkshire)......	19.4	16	10	10	v. Notts, at Leeds	1932
G. Geary (Leicestershire)...	16.2	8	18	10	v. Glamorgan, at Pontypridd.............	1929

	O.	M.	R.	W.	
P. Chatterjee (Bengal)	19	11	20	10	v. Assam, at Jhorat ...1956–57
A. E. E. Vogler (Eastern Province)	12	2	26	10	v. Griqualand West, at Johannesburg 1906
G. Elliott (Victoria)	19	—	2	9	v. Tasmania, at Launceston 1857–58
Ahad Khan (Railways)	6.3	4	7	9	v. Dera Ismail Khan ..1964–65
A. P. Freeman (Kent)......	10	4	11	9	v. Sussex, at Brighton .. 1922
H. Verity (Yorkshire)......	6.3	3	12	9	v. Kent, at Sheffield 1936
C. T. B. Turner (Australia) .	17.1	10	15	9	v. An England XI, at Stoke 1888
H. L. Jackson (Derbyshire).	17.3	9	17	9	v. Univ., at Cambridge . 1959
P. J. Loader (Surrey)	15.5	6	17	9	v. Warwickshire, at The Oval 1958
G. G. Napier (Europeans) .	14.5	9	17	9	v. Parsees, at Poona...1909–10
J. C. Laker (England)......	14	12	2	8	v. The Rest, at Bradford 1950
D. Shackleton (Hampshire).	11.1	7	4	8	v. Somerset, at Weston . 1955
E. Peate (Yorkshire).......	16	11	5	8	v. Surrey, at Holbeck... 1883
G. A. Lohmann (England) .	9.4	5	7	8	v. South Africa, at Port Elizabeth 1896
J. Bickley (England)	14	—	7	8	v. Kent and Sussex at Lord's............ 1856
C. H. Palmer (Leic.).......	14	12	7	8	v. Surrey, at Leicester .. 1955
J. E. D. Sealy (Barbados) ..	6.7	2	8	8	v. Trinidad, at Bridgetown 1942
M. G. Melle (Transvaal) ...	12	7	8	8	v. Griqualand West, at Johannesburg 1950–51
G. E. Dennett (Gloucestershire)	6	1	9	8	v. Northants, at Gloucester 1907
G. E. Tribe (Northants)....	14.2	10	9	8	v. Yorkshire, at Northampton 1958
G. Wootton (M.C.C.)	13.2	9	9	8	v. Sussex, at Lord's 1863
B. M. Billimaria (Parsees) .	11.4	6	11	8	v. Europeans, at Poona 1896–97
G. Freeman (Yorkshire) ...	13	8	11	8	v. Lancashire, at Holbeck 1868
J. Briggs (English XI)......	14.2	5	11	8	v. South Africa XI, at Cape Town 1889
A. S. Kennedy (Hampshire)	13	7	11	8	v. Glamorgan, at Cardiff 1921
W. H. Copson (Derbyshire)	8.2	2	11	8	v. Warwickshire, at Derby 1937
I. J. Jones (Glamorgan) ...	13	9	11	8	v. Leicestershire at Leicester 1965
F. R. Spofforth (Australia) .	8.3	6	3	7	v. Eng. XI, at B'ham ... 1884
W. A. Henderson (N.E. Transvaal)	9.3	7	4	7	v. Orange Free State, at Bloemfontein.....1937–38
F. Morley (M.C.C.)	22	18	6	7	v. Univ.,at Oxford 1877
A. Waddington (Yorkshire).	7	4	6	7	v. Sussex, at Hull 1922
R. Tyldesley (Lancashire) ..	14	12	6	7	v. Northants, at Liverpool 1924
R. V. Webster (Warwick.)..	12.4	7	6	7	v. Yorkshire, at Birmingham............. 1964
W. Caffyn (Surrey)	24	20	7	7	v. Kent, at Canterbury . 1862
F. Morley (Notts)	10.2	7	7	7	v. Derbyshire, at Nottingham 1879
A. Shaw (Notts)	41.2	36	7	7	v. M.C.C., at Lord's.... 1875
L. T. Driffield (Cambridge)	6.4	3	7	7	v. M.C.C., at Cambridge 1900
J. Bailey (Hampshire)......	7	3	7	7	v. Notts, at Southampton...... 1932
G. Geary (Leicestershire)...	13.3	8	7	7	v. Warwickshire, at Hinckley......... 1936
D. J. Shepherd (Glamorgan)	9.1	6	7	7	v. Hampshire, at Cardiff 1966
L. Cook (Lancashire)	14	9	8	7	v. Derbyshire, at Chesterfield 1920
G. R. Cox (Sussex)........	16	9	8	7	v. Derbyshire, at Hove.. 1920

	O.	M.	R.	W.		
A. S. Kennedy (Hampshire)	10	7	8	7	v. Warwickshire, at Portsmouth	1927
James Langridge (Sussex) ..	11.5	7	8	7	v. Glos., at Cheltenham	1932
G. Bennett (Kent)	10	—	9	7	v. Sussex, at Brighton ..	1857
C. Blythe (Kent)	7.5	3	9	7	v. Leics., at Leicester ...	1912
T. Emmett (Yorkshire).....	9.3	6	9	7	v. Sussex, at Hove	1878
G. G. Macaulay (Yorkshire)	14	7	9	7	v. Northants, at Kettering	1933
F. Morley (Notts)	22	15	9	7	v. Kent, at Town Malling	1878
F. Morley (Notts)	19.2	12	9	7	v. Surrey, at The Oval ..	1880
J. T. Partridge (Rhodesia) .	12.1	8	9	7	v. Border, at Bulawayo	1959–60
H. Verity (Yorkshire)......	6	1	9	7	v. Sussex, at Hove	1939
F. E. Woolley (Kent)	6.3	3	9	7	v. Surrey, at The Oval ..	1911
V. I. Smith (South Africans)	4.5	3	1	6	v. Derbyshire, at Derby.	1947
S. Cosstick (Victoria)	21.1	20	1	6	v. Tasmania, at Melbourne	1868–69
Israr Ali (Bahawalpur).....	11	10	1	6	v. Dacca U., at Bahawalpur	1957–58
F. E. Field (Warwickshire) .	8.4	7	2	6	v. Worcs., at Dudley ...	1914
T. Wass (Notts)	4.4	3	3	6	v. M.C.C., at Lord's....	1907
H. F. Boyle (Australia)	8.1	6	3	6	v. M.C.C., at Lord's....	1878
A. Penn (Kent)	13.3	11	3	6	v. Sussex, at Tunbridge Wells.............	1878
R. G. Barlow (Lancashire) .	10.1	9	3	6	v. Derbyshire, at Derby	1881
G. G. Macaulay (Yorkshire)	7	4	3	6	v. Derbyshire, at Hull ..	1921
J. Cowie (New Zealand) ...	8	5	3	6	v. Ireland, at Dublin ...	1937
T. L. Goddard (Natal).....	11	9	3	6	v. Border, at East London	1959–60
Rajinder Pal (Delhi)	9	8	3	6	v. Jammu and Kashmir, at Srinagar	1960–61
A. D. Pougher (M.C.C.) ...	3	3	0	5	v. Australians, at Lord's	1896
G. R. Cox (Sussex)	6	6	0	5	v. Somerset, at Weston .	1921
R. Tyldesley (Lancashire) ..	4	4	0	5	v. Leics., at Manchester.	1924
P. T. Mills (Gloucestershire)	6.4	6	0	5	v. Somerset, at Bristol ..	1928
F. W. Tate (Sussex)	4	3	1	5	v. Kent, at Tonbridge ..	1888
D. Ashby (Canterbury)	15.2	13	2	5	v. Auckland, at Auckland.............	1877–78
E. H. Killick (Sussex)......	6.1	4	2	5	v. Hants, at Chichester..	1907
J. C. Clay (Glamorgan)	5.2	4	2	5	v. Somerset, at Cardiff..	1922
E. R. H. Toshack (Australia)	2.3	1	2	5	v. India, at Brisbane...	1947–48
G. A. R. Lock (Surrey)	5.3	4	2	5	v. Worcs., at Oval......	1954
W. B. Bridge (Warwickshire)	5.1	4	2	5	v. Kent, at Blackheath..	1961
V. M. Muddiah (Services) ..	4	2	2	5	v. Jammu and Kashmir, at Delhi	1961–62
D. J. Shepherd (Glamorgan)	10	8	2	5	v. Leicestershire at Ebbw Vale	1965

SIXTEEN OR MORE WICKETS IN A DAY

17	C. Blythe, Kent v. Northants, at Northampton (for 48 runs) ..	1907
17	H. Verity, Yorkshire v. Essex, at Leyton (for 91 runs)	1933
17	T. W. Goddard, Gloucestershire v. Kent, at Bristol (for 106 runs)	1939
16	T. Emmett, Yorkshire v. Cambridgeshire, at Hunslet (for 38 runs)	1869
16	J. Southerton, South v. North, at Lord's (for 52 runs)	1875
16	T. Wass, Nottinghamshire v. Lancashire, at Liverpool (for 69 runs)	1906
16	A. E. E. Vogler, Eastern Province v. Griqualand West, at Johannesburg (for 38 runs)	1906
16	T. Wass, Nottinghamshire v. Essex, at Nottingham (for 103 runs)	1908
16	J. C. White, Somerset v. Worcestershire, at Bath (for 83 runs) ..	1919

200 OR MORE WICKETS IN A SEASON

			Overs	Maidens	Runs	Wickets	Average
	1928	A. P. Freeman	1976.1	423	5489	304	18.05
	1933	A. P. Freeman	2039	651	4549	298	15.26
(2)	1895	T. Richardson	1690.1	463	4170	290	14.37
(1)	1888	C. T. B. Turner** .	2427.2	1127	3307	283	11.68
	1931	A. P. Freeman	1618	360	4307	276	15.60
	1930	A. P. Freeman	1914.3	472	4632	275	16.84
(2)	1897	T. Richardson	1603.4	495	3945	273	14.45
	1929	A. P. Freeman	1670.5	381	4879	267	18.27
	1900	W. Rhodes........	1553	455	3606	261	13.81
(2)	1896	J. T. Hearne.......	2003.1	818	3670	257	14.28
	1932	A. P. Freeman	1565.5	404	4149	253	16.39
	1901	W. Rhodes........	1565	505	3797	251	15.12
	1937	T. W. Goddard ...	1478.1	359	4158	248	16.76
	1910	W. C. Smith.......	1423.2	420	3225	247	13.05
(2)	1896	T. Richardson	1656.2	526	4015	246	16.32
(2)	1899	A. E. Trott	1772.4	587	4086	239	17.09
	1947	T. W. Goddard ...	1451.2	344	4119	238	17.30
	1925	M. W. Tate	1694.3	472	3415	228	14.97
(2)	1898	J. T. Hearne.......	1802.2	781	3120	222	14.05
	1925	C. W. L. Parker ...	1512.3	478	3311	222	14.91
(2)	1890	G. A. Lohmann ...	1759.1	737	2998	220	13.62
	1923	M. W. Tate	1608.5	331	3061	219	13.97
	1925	C. F. Root	1493.2	416	3770	219	17.21
	1931	C. W. L. Parker ...	1320.4	386	3125	219	14.26
(1)	1884	F. R. Spofforth*** .	1625	672	2732	218	12.53
	1936	H. Verity	1289.3	463	2847	216	13.18
	1955	G. A. R. Lock	1408.4	497	3109	216	14.39
	1909	C. Blythe	1273.5	343	3128	215	14.54
(1)	1882	E. Peate	1853.1	868	2466	214	11.52
(2)	1895	A. Mold	1629	598	3400	213	15.96
	1902	W. Rhodes........	1306.3	405	2801	213	13.15
	1926	C. W. L. Parker ...	1739.5	556	3920	213	18.40
(2)	1893	J. T. Hearne.......	1741.4	667	3492	212	16.47
	1935	A. P. Freeman	1503.2	320	4562	212	21.51
	1957	G. A. R. Lock	1194.1	449	2550	212	12.02
	1900	A. E. Trott	1547.1	363	4923	211	23.33
	1925	G. G. Macaulay ...	1338.2	307	3268	211	15.48
	1935	H. Verity	1279.2	453	3032	211	14.36
(1)	1870	J. Southerton......	1863.2	696	3069	210	14.61
(1)	1888	G. A. Lohmann ...	1649.1	783	2280	209	10.90
	1923	C. H. Parkin	1356.2	356	3543	209	16.94
	1906	G. H. Hirst	1306.1	271	3434	208	16.50
(2)	1894	A. Mold	1288.3	456	2548	207	12.30
	1922	C. W. L. Parker ...	1294.5	445	2712	206	13.16
	1922	A. Kennedy	1346.4	366	3444	205	16.80
	1924	M. W. Tate	1469.5	465	2818	205	13.74
	1925	E. A. McDonald...	1249.4	282	3828	205	18.67
	1934	A. P. Freeman	1744.4	440	4753	205	23.18
	1924	C. W. L. Parker ...	1303.5	411	2913	204	14.27
(2)	1889	G. A. Lohmann ...	1614.1	646	2714	202	13.43
	1937	H. Verity	1386.2	487	3168	202	15.68
(1)	1878	A. Shaw	2630	—	2203	201	10.96
	1907	G. E. Dennett	1216.2	305	3227	201	16.05
	1937	A. R. Gover.......	1219.4	191	3816	201	18.98
	1924	C. H. Parkin	1162.5	357	2735	200	13.67
	1935	T. W. Goddard ...	1553	384	4073	200	20.36

** *Exclusive of matches not reckoned as first-class.*

*** *Including Smokers v. Non-Smokers, at Lord's, and all matches of the Australians' tour.*

		Overs	Maidens	Runs	Wickets	Average
1936	A. R. Gover.......	1159.2	185	3547	200	17.73
(3) 1939	T. W. Goddard ...	819	139	2973	200	14.86
1951	R. Appleyard	1313.2	391	2829	200	14.14

(1) *Indicates* 4-*ball;* (2) 5-*ball; and* (3) 8-*ball overs. All others were* 6-*ball overs.*

In four consecutive seasons (1928–31), A. P. Freeman took 1,122 wickets, and in eight consecutive seasons (1928–35), 2,090 wickets. In each of these eight seasons he took over 200 wickets.

T. Richardson took 1,005 wickets in four consecutive seasons (1894–97).

In 1896, J. T. Hearne took his 100th wicket as early as June 12th. In 1931, C. W. L. Parker did the same and A. P. Freeman obtained his 100th wicket a day later.

BOWLERS WHO HAVE TAKEN 2,000 WICKETS

	Career	Wickets	Runs	Average
W. Rhodes	1898–1930	4187	69993	16.71
A. P. Freeman.............	1914–36	3776	69577	18.42
C. W. L. Parker	1903–35	3278	63821	19.46
J. T. Hearne	1888–1923	3061	54342	17.75
T. W. Goddard............	1922–52	2979	59116	19.84
W. G. Grace	1865–1908	2876	51545	17.92
A. S. Kennedy.............	1907–36	2874	61044	21.24
M. W. Tate	1912–37	2783	50544	18.16
G. H. Hirst	1889–1919	2739	51300	18.72
D. Shackleton	1948–66	2627	49400	18.80
C. Blythe	1899–1914	2506	42136	16.81
G. A. R. Lock	1946–66	2499	47326	19.09
W. E. Astill	1906–39	2431	57784	23.76
J. C. White	1909–37	2356	43759	18.57
W. E. Hollies..............	1932–57	2323	48656	20.94
R. T. D. Perks	1930–55	2233	53770	24.07
J. Briggs..................	1879–1900	2221	35390	15.93
F. S. Trueman	1949–66	2161	39018	18.28
G. E. Dennett	1903–26	2147	42568	19.82
T. Richardson	1892–1905	2105	38794	18.42
J. B. Statham..............	1950–66	2098	34236	16.31
A. Shaw	1864–97	2072	24827	11.97
T. E. Bailey	1945–66	2070	47788	23.08
F. E. Woolley	1906–38	2068	41066	19.85
G. Geary	1912–39	2063	41339	20.03
D. V. P. Wright............	1932–57	2056	49309	23.98
J. Newman................	1906–30	2032	51211	25.20
S. Haigh	1895–1913	2012	32091	15.94

BOWLERS WHO HAVE TAKEN 100 WICKETS IN A SEASON EIGHT TIMES OR MORE

23 Times: W. RHODES 200 wickets (3).

18 Times: D. SHACKLETON.

17 Times: A. P. FREEMAN 300 wickets (1), 200 wickets (7).

16 Times: T. W. GODDARD 200 wickets (4); C. W. L. PARKER 200 wickets (5); R. T. D. PERKS.

15 Times: J. T. HEARNE 200 wickets (3); G. H. HIRST 200 wickets (1); A. S. KENNEDY 200 wickets (1).

14 Times: C. BLYTHE 200 wickets (1); W. E. HOLLIES; M. W. TATE 200 wickets (3); J. C. WHITE.

13 Times: G. A. R. LOCK 200 wickets (2); J. B. STATHAM.

12 Times: J. BRIGGS; G. E. DENNETT 200 wickets (1); C. GLADWIN; N. I. THOMSON; F. J TITMUS; F. S. TRUEMAN.

11 Times: A. V. BEDSER; G. GEARY; S. HAIGH; J. C. LAKER; M. S. NICHOLS; A. E. RELF.

10 Times: W. ATTEWELL; W. G. GRACE; H. L. JACKSON; V. W. C. JUPP; G. G. MACAULAY 200 wickets (1); W. MEAD; T. B. MITCHELL; T. RICHARDSON 200 wickets (3); D. J. SHEPHERD; R. TYLDESLEY; J. H. WARDLE; T. WASS; D. V. P. WRIGHT.

9 Times: W. E. ASTILL; T. E. BAILEY; W. E. BOWES; C. COOK; R. HOWORTH; J. MERCER; A. MOLD 200 wickets (2); J. NEWMAN; C. F. ROOT 200 wickets (1); J. SOUTHERTON 200 wickets (1); H. VERITY 200 wickets (3).

8 Times: H. DEAN; J. A. FLAVELL; A. R. GOVER 200 wickets (2); R. ILLINGWORTH; H. LARWOOD; G. A. LOHMANN 200 wickets (3); R. PEEL; A. SHAW; J. M. SIMS; F. A. TARRANT; R. TATTERSALL; G. J. THOMPSON; G. E. TRIBE; A. W. WELLARD; F. E. WOOLLEY; J. A. YOUNG.

ALL-ROUND CRICKET

2,000 RUNS AND 200 WICKETS IN A SEASON

1906 G. H. Hirst 2,385 runs and 208 wickets

3,000 RUNS AND 100 WICKETS IN A SEASON

1937 J. H. Parks 3,003 runs and 101 wickets

2,000 RUNS AND 100 WICKETS IN A SEASON

		Runs	Wickets			Runs	Wickets
1873	W. G. Grace	2139	106	1914	F. E. Woolley	2272	125
1876	W. G. Grace	2622	129	1920	J. W. Hearne	2148	142
1899	C. L. Townsend	2440	101	1921	V. W. C. Jupp	2169	121
1900	G. L. Jessop	2210	104	1921	F. E. Woolley	2101	167
1904	G. H. Hirst	2501	132	1922	F. E. Woolley	2022	163
1905	G. H. Hirst	2266	110	1923	F. E. Woolley	2091	101
1909	W. Rhodes	2094	141	1933	L. F. Townsend	2268	100
1911	W. Rhodes	2261	117	1937	E. Davies	2012	103
1911	F. A. Tarrant	2030	111	1937	Jas. Langridge	2081	101
1913	J. W. Hearne	2036	124	1959	T. E. Bailey	2011	100
1914	J. W. Hearne	2116	123				

1,000 RUNS AND 200 WICKETS IN A SEASON

1899	A. E. Trott	1175	239	1923	M. W. Tate	1168	219
1900	A. E. Trott	1337	211	1924	M. W. Tate	1419	205
1922	A. S. Kennedy	1129	205	1925	M. W. Tate	1290	228

The double feat of scoring 1,000 runs and taking 100 wickets in one season of first-class cricket has been accomplished as follows:—

SIXTEEN
W. Rhodes

FOURTEEN
G. H. Hirst

TEN
V. W. C. Jupp

NINE
W. E. Astill

EIGHT
T. E. Bailey
W. G. Grace
M. S. Nichols
A. E. Relf
F. A. Tarrant
M. W. Tate
F. E. Woolley

SEVEN
F. J. Titmus
G. E. Tribe

SIX
P. G. H. Fender
R. Illingworth
Jas. Langridge

FIVE
J. W. H. T. Douglas
J. W. Hearne
A. S. Kennedy
J. Newman

FOUR

E. G. Arnold
J. Gunn
R. Kilner
B. R. Knight

THREE

W. W. Armstrong (Australia)
L. C. Braund
G. Giffen (Australia)
N. E. Haig
R. Howorth
C. B. Llewellyn
J. B. Mortimore
Ray Smith
S. G. Smith
L. F. Townsend
A. W. Wellard

TWO

W. H. R. Andrews
F. R. Brown
D. B. Close
J. N. Crawford
E. Davies
B. Dooland
F. R. Foster
G. Goonesena
J. L. Hopwood
M. J. Horton
R. O. Jenkins
G. L. Jessop
W. H. Lockwood
S. H. Martin
J. H. Parks
G. H. Pope
J. S. Pressdee
R. A. Sinfield
C. T. Studd
G. J. Thompson
C. L. Townsend
A. E. Trott
A. J. Watkins
J. C. White

ONE

D. A. Allen
W. E. Alley
J. Bailey
F. Barratt
M. W. Booth
B. J. T. Bosanquet
W. Brockwell
V. Broderick
Hon. F. S. G. Calthorpe
T. W. Cartwright
H. L. Collins (Australia)
L. N. Constantine (West Indies)
J. A. Cuffe
W. R. Cuttell
G. Davidson
A. Drake
G. A. Faulkner (South Africa)
W. Flowers
A. E. R. Gilligan
J. M. Gregory (Australia)
S. Haigh
J. Hallows
T. Hayward
F. S. Jackson
V. E. Jackson
E. H. Killick
J. H. King
V. Mankad (India)
J. R. Mason
B. L. Muncer
G. E. Palmer (Australia)
K. E. Palmer
F. Pearson
R. Peel
R. W. V. Robins
C. F. Root
H. L. Simms
T. F. Smailes
T. B. P. Smith
S. J. Storey
L. J. Todd
H. Trumble (Australia
J. van Geloven
J. Vine
E. Wainwright
P. M. Walker
J. E. Walsh
A. F. Wensley
W. Wooller

L. E. G. Ames, in 1928 scored 1,919 runs and obtained 121 wickets while keeping wicket. In 1929 his aggregates were, 1,795 runs and 127 wickets, and in 1932, 2,482 runs and 100 wickets.

J. T. Murray, in 1957, scored 1,025 runs and obtained 104 wickets while keeping wicket.

CENTURY AND HAT-TRICK

1874 W. G. Grace, M.C.C. v. Kent, at Canterbury, 123 and 5 for 82 and 6 for 47 including hat-trick (12-a-side).

1884 G. Giffen, Australians v. Lancashire, at Manchester, 13 and 113 and 6 for 55 including hat-tricks.

1885 W. E. Roller, Surrey v. Sussex, at The Oval, 204 and 4 for 28 including hat-trick and 2 for 16.

1913 W. B. Burns, Worcestershire v. Gloucestershire, at Worcester, 102* and 3 for 56 including hat-trick and 2 for 21.

1921 V. W. C. Jupp, Sussex v. Essex, at Colchester, 102 and 6 for 61 including hat-trick and 6 for 78.

1927 R. E. S. Wyatt, M.C.C. v. Ceylon, at Colombo, 124 and 5 for 39 including hat-trick.

1928 L. N. Constantine, West Indies v. Northamptonshire, at Northampton, 7 for 45 including hat-trick, 107 (five 6's) and 6 for 67.

1937 Emrys Davies, Glamorgan v. Leicestershire, at Leicester, 139 and 4 for 27 and 3 for 31 including hat-trick.

1946–47 V. M. Merchant, Dr. C. R. Pereira's XI v. Sir Homi Mehta's XI, at Bombay, 1 and 142 and 3 for 31 including hat-trick and 0 for 17.

CENTURY AND ALL TEN WICKETS

1859 V. E. Walker, England v. Surrey at The Oval, 10 wickets for 74 and four for 17, 20* and 108.

1886 W. G. Grace, M.C.C. v. Oxford University at Oxford two wickets for 60 and 10 for 49, 104.

WICKET-KEEPING FEATS

Most dismissals: H. Strudwick (1902–27) 1,493
Most Catches: H. Strudwick (1902–27) 1,235
Most Stumpings: L. E. G. Ames (1926–50) 415

12 wickets in match, ct. 8, st. 4, E. Pooley, Surrey v. Sussex, at The Oval 1868
12 wickets in match, ct. 9, st. 3, D. Tallon, Queensland v. New South Wales, at Sydney 1938–39
11 wickets in match, all ct. A. Long, Surrey v. Sussex, at Hove .. 1964
10 wickets in match, all ct., A. E. Wilson, Gloucestershire v. Hampshire, at Portsmouth 1953
10 wickets in match, all ct., L. A. Johnson, Northamptonshire v. Sussex, at Worthing 1963
10 wickets in match, all ct., R. W. Taylor, Derbyshire v. Hampshire, at Chesterfield 1963
10 wickets in match, ct. 5, st. 5, H. Phillips, Sussex v. Surrey, at The Oval 1878
10 wickets in match, ct. 2, st. 8, E. Pooley, Surrey v. Kent, at The Oval 1872
10 wickets in match, ct. 9, st. 1, T. W. Oates, Nottinghamshire v. Middlesex, at Nottingham 1908
10 wickets in match, ct. 1, st. 9, F. H. Huish, Kent v. Surrey, at The Oval.. 1910
10 wickets in match, ct. 9, st. 1, J. C. Hubble, Kent v. Gloucestershire, at Cheltenham 1923
10 wickets in match, ct. 8, st. 2, H. Elliott, Derbyshire v. Lancashire, at Manchester 1935
10 wickets in match, ct. 7, st. 3, P. Corrall, Leicestershire v. Sussex, at Hove 1936
10 wickets in match, ct. 9, st. 1, R. A. Saggers, New South Wales v. Combined XI at Brisbane 1940–41
10 wickets in match, ct. 7, st. 3, B. N. Jarman, South Australia v. New South Wales, at Adelaide 1961–62
10 wickets in match, ct. 8, st. 2, L. A. Johnson, Northamptonshire v. Warwickshire, at Birmingham 1965
8 wickets in an innings, all ct., A. T. W. Grout, Queensland v. Western Australia, at Brisbane 1959–60
7 wickets in innings, ct. 4, st. 3, E. J. Smith, Warwickshire v. Derbyshire, at Edgbaston 1926
7 wickets in innings, ct. 6, st. 1, W. F. Farrimond, Lancashire v. Kent at Manchester 1930
7 wickets in innings, all ct., W. F. Price, Middlesex v. Yorkshire, at Lord's 1937
7 wickets in innings, ct. 3, st. 4, D. Tallon, Queensland v. Victoria, at Brisbane 1938–39
7 wickets in innings, ct. 7, R. A. Saggers, New South Wales v. Combined XI, at Brisbane 1940–41
7 wickets in innings, ct. 1, st. 6, H. Yarnold, Worcestershire v. Scotland, at Broughty Ferry 1951
7 wickets in innings, ct. 4, st. 3, J. W. Brown, Scotland v. Ireland, at Dublin 1957
7 wickets in innings, ct. 6, st. 1, N. Kirsten, Border v. Rhodesia, at East London 1959–60
7 wickets in an innings, all ct. M. S. Smith, Natal v. Border, at East London 1959–60
7 wickets in innings, all ct. K. V. Andrew, Northamptonshire v. Lancashire, at Manchester 1962

7 wickets in innings, all ct. A. Long, Surrey v. Sussex, at Hove .. 1964
7 wickets in innings, all ct. R. Schofield, Central Districts v. Wellington, at Wellington 1964
7 wickets in innings, all ct. R. W. Taylor, Derbyshire v. Glamorgan, at Derby 1966

Three men stumped off successive balls, W. H. Brain, Gloucestershire v. Somerset, at Cheltenham, 1893. (The bowler thus credited with the hat-trick was C. L. Townsend.)

Three men caught off successive balls by the wicket-keeper, G. O. Dawkes, Derbyshire v. Worcestershire, at Kidderminster, 1958. (The bowler thus credited with the hat-trick was H. L. Jackson.)

127 wickets in a season, ct. 79, st. 48, L. E. G. Ames, of Kent 1929
121 wickets in a season, ct. 69, st. 52, L. E. G. Ames, of Kent 1928
110 wickets in a season, ct. 62, st. 48, H. Yarnold, of Worcestershire .. 1949
108 wickets in a season, ct. 97, st. 11, J. G. Binks, of Yorkshire 1960
107 wickets in a season, ct. 77, st. 30, G. Duckworth, of Lancashire .. 1928
104 wickets in a season, ct. 82, st. 22, J. T. Murray, of Middlesex .. 1957
102 wickets in a season, ct. 70, st. 32, F. H. Huish, of Kent 1913
102 wickets in a season, ct. 95, st. 7, J. T. Murray, of Middlesex 1960
101 wickets in a season, ct. 85, st. 16, R. Booth, of Worcestershire .. 1960
100 wickets in a season, ct. 36, st. 64, L. E. G. Ames, of Kent 1932
100 wickets in a season, ct. 91, st. 9, R. Booth, of Worcestershire 1964
100 wickets in a season, ct. 62, st. 38, F. H. Huish, of Kent 1911

J. G. Binks has made 334 consecutive appearances since 1955 for Yorkshire in County Championship matches. G. O. Dawkes (Derbyshire) made 289, 1950–61; H. G. Davies (Glamorgan) 282, 1947–57; H. Elliott (Derbyshire) 226, 1929–37; A. Wood (Yorkshire) 222, 1928–35.

MOST CATCHES—EXCLUDING WICKET-KEEPERS

In a Career

913 F. E. Woolley
871 W. G. Grace

In a Season

78	W. R. Hammond	1928	65	D. W. Richardson	1961
77	M. J. Stewart	1957	65	J. Tunnicliffe	1895
73	P. M. Walker	1961	65	P. M. Walker	1959
71	P. J. Sharpe	1962	64	K. F. Barrington	1957
70	J. Tunnicliffe	1901	64	J. Tunnicliffe	1904
69	John Langridge	1955	63	K. Grieves	1950
69	P. M. Walker	1960	63	G. A. R. Lock	1957
65	W R. Hammond	1925	63	C. A. Milton	1956

In a Match

10 W. R. Hammond, Gloucestershire v. Surrey, Cheltenham 1928
8 W. B. Burns, Worcestershire v. Yorkshire, Bradford 1907
8 A. H. Bakewell, Northamptonshire v. Essex, Leyton 1928
8 W. R. Hammond, Gloucestershire, v. Worcestershire, Cheltenham .. 1932
8 K. Grieves, Lancashire v. Sussex, Manchester 1951
8 C. A. Milton, Gloucestershire v. Sussex, Hove 1952
8 G. A. R. Lock, Surrey v. Warwickshire, The Oval 1957
8 J. M. Prodger, Kent v. Gloucestershire, Cheltenham 1961

In an Innings

7 M. J. Stewart, Surrey v. Northamptonshire, Northampton 1957
7 A. S. Brown, Gloucestershire v. Nottinghamshire, at Nottingham .. 1966

THROWING THE CRICKET BALL

140 yards 2 feet, R. Percival, on the Durham Sand Racecourse 1884
140 yards 9 inches, Ross Mackenzie, at Toronto 1872

W. F. Forbes, on March 16th, 1876, threw 132 yards at the Eton College Sports. He was then 18 years of age.

William Yardley, while a boy at Rugby, threw 100 yards with his right hand and 78 yards with his left.

Charles Arnold, of Cambridge, once threw 112 yards with the wind and 108 against. W. H. Game, at The Oval, in 1875. threw the ball 111 yards and then back the same distance. W. G. Grace threw 109 yards one way and back 105, and George Millyard 108 with the wind and 103 against. At The Oval in 1868, W. G. Grace made three successive throws of 116, 117 and 118 yards, and then threw back over 100 yards. D. G. Foster (Warwickshire) has thrown 133 yards, and in 1930 he made a Danish record with 120.1 metres—about 130 yards.

THE SIDES—GREAT TOTALS

1107	Victoria v. New South Wales, at Melbourne	1926–27
1059	Victoria v. Tasmania, at Melbourne	1922–23
918	New South Wales v. South Australia, at Sydney	1900–01
912	(eight wkts., dec.), Holkar v. Mysore, at Indore	1945–46
910	(six wkts., dec.), Railways v. Dera Ismail Khan, at Lahore	1964–65
903	(seven wkts.), England v. Australia, at The Oval	1938
887	Yorkshire v. Warwickshire, at Edgbaston	1896
849	England v. West Indies, at Kingston	1929–30
843	Australians v. Oxford and Cambridge Universities Past and Present, at Portsmouth	1893

HIGHEST FOR EACH FIRST-CLASS COUNTY

Derbyshire	645 v. Hampshire, at Derby	1898
Essex	692 v. Somerset, at Taunton	1895
Glamorgan	587 (eight wickets) v. Derbyshire, at Cardiff	1951
Gloucesterhire	653 (six wickets) v. Glamorgan, at Bristol	1928
Hampshire	672 (seven wickets) v. Somerset, at Taunton	1899
Kent	803 (four wickets) v. Essex, at Brentwood	1934
Lancashire	801 v. Somerset, at Taunton	1895
Leicestershire	701 (four wickets) v. Worcestershire, at Worcester	1906
Middlesex	642 (three wickets) v. Hampshire, at Southampton	1923
Northamptonshire	557 (six wickets) v. Sussex, at Hove	1914
Nottinghamshire	739 (seven wickets) v. Leicestershire, at Nottingham	1903
Somerset	675 (nine wickets) v. Hampshire, at Bath	1924
Surrey	811 v. Somerset, at The Oval	1899
Sussex	705 (eight wickets) v. Surrey at Hastings	1902
Warwickshire	657 (six wickets), v. Hampshire, at Edgbaston	1899
Worcestershire	633 v. Warwickshire, at Worcester	1906
Yorshire	887 v. Warwickshire, at Edgbaston	1896

SMALL TOTALS

12	Oxford University v. M.C.C. and Ground, at Oxford	†1877
12	Northamptonshire v. Gloucestershire, at Gloucester	1907
13	Nottinghamshire v. Yorkshire, at Nottingham	1901
15	M.C.C. v. Surrey, at Lord's	1839
15	Victoria v. M.C.C., at Melbourne	†1903–04
15	Northamptonshire v. Yorkshire, at Northampton	†1908
15	Hampshire v. Warwickshire, at Edgbaston	1922

(Following on, Hampshire scored 521 and won by 155 runs)

† *Signifies that one man was absent.*

16	M.C.C. and Ground v. Surrey, at Lord's	1872
16	Derbyshire v. Nottinghamshire, at Nottingham	1879
16	Surrey v. Nottinghamshire, at The Oval	1880
16	Warwickshire v. Kent, at Tonbridge	1913
16	Trinidad v. Barbados, at Bridgetown	1941–42
16	Border v. Natal, at East London (first innings)	1959–60
17	Gloucestershire v. Australians, at Cheltenham	1896
18	Kent v. Sussex, at Gravesend	†1867
18	Australians v. M.C.C. and Ground, at Lord's	†1896
18	Border v. Natal, at East London (second innings)	1959–60
19	Sussex v. Surrey, at Godalming	1830
19	Sussex v. Nottinghamshire, at Hove	†1873
19	M.C.C. and Ground v. Australians, at Lord's	1878

† *Signifies that one man was absent.*

SMALLEST TOTAL IN A MATCH

34 (16 and 18) Border v. Natal, at East London 1959–60

LOWEST FOR EACH COUNTY

Derbyshire	16 v. Nottinghamshire, at Nottingham	1879
Essex	30 v. Yorkshire, at Leyton	1901
Glamorgan	22 v. Lancashire, at Liverpool	1924
Gloucestershire	17 v. Australians, at Cheltenham	1896
Hampshire	15 v. Warwickshire, at Birmingham	1922
Kent	18 v. Sussex, at Gravesend	1867
Lancashire	25 v. Derbyshire, at Manchester	1871
Leicestershire	25 v. Kent, at Leicester	1912
Middlesex	20 v. M.C.C., at Lord's	1864
Northamptonshire	12 v. Gloucestershire, at Gloucester	1907
Nottinghamshire	13 v. Yorkshire, at Nottingham	1901
Somerset	25 v. Gloucestershire, at Bristol	1947
Surrey	16 v. Nottinghamshire, at The Oval	1880
Sussex	19 v. Nottinghamshire, at Hove	1873
Warwickshire	16 v. Kent, at Tonbridge	1913
Worcestershire	24 v. Yorkshire, at Huddersfield	1903
Yorkshire	23 v. Hampshire, at Middlesbrough	1965

HIGHEST AGGREGATES

2376 for 38 wickets,	Maharashtra v. Bombay, at Poona	1948–49
2078 for 40 wickets,	Bombay v. Holkar, at Bombay	1944–45
1981 for 35 wickets,	England v. South Africa, at Durban	1938–39
1929 for 39 wickets,	New South Wales v. South Australia, at Sydney	1925–26

In England

1723 for 31 wickets,	England v. Australia, at Leeds	1948
1601 for 29 wickets,	England v. Australia, at Lord's	1930
1502 for 28 wickets,	M.C.C. v. New Zealand, at Lord's	1927
1499 for 31 wickets,	T. N. Pearce's XI v. Australians, at Scarborough	1961
1496 for 24 wickets,	England v. Australia, at Nottingham	1938
1494 for 37 wickets,	England v. Australia, at The Oval	1934
1492 for 33 wickets,	Worcestershire v. Oxford University, at Worcester	1904

1477 for 32 wickets, Hampshire v. Oxford University, at Southampton 1913
1477 for 33 wickets, England v. South Africa, at The Oval 1947
1475 for 27 wickets, Northamptonshire v. Surrey, at Northampton .. 1920

HEAVY SCORING IN FOURTH INNINGS

654 (five wickets), England v. South Africa, at Durban 1938–39
(After being set 696 to win. The match was left drawn on the tenth day.)
604 Maharashtra v. Bombay, at Poona 1948–49
(After being set 959 to win.)
576 (eight wickets), Trinidad v. Barbados, at Port of Spain 1946
(After being set 672 to win. Match drawn on fifth day.)
572 New South Wales v. South Australia, at Sydney 1907–08
(After being set 593 to win.)
529 (nine wickets), Combined XI v. South Africans, at Perth .. 1963–64
(After being set 579 to win.)
518 Victoria v. Queensland, at Brisbane.. 1926–27
(When set 753 to win)
507 (seven wickets), Cambridge University v. M.C.C. and Ground, at Lord's 1896
502 (six wickets), Middlesex v. Nottinghamshire, at Trent Bridge .. 1925
(Game won by an unfinished stand of 271: county record)
502 (eight wickets), Players v. Gentlemen, at Lord's 1900

(Unless otherwise stated, the side making the runs won the match.)

BIGGEST VICTORIES

Yorkshire (555 for one wkt., dec.) beat Essex at Leyton on June 15, 16, 17, 1932, by an innings and 313 runs. Holmes and Sutcliffe made 555, the world's highest first-wicket partnership.

Middlesex (464 for one wkt., dec.) beat Essex at Leyton on May 23, 25, 26, 1914, by an innings and 56 runs.

Lancashire beat Leicestershire without having a batsman dismissed in either innings at Manchester in 1956 by ten wickets. A. Wharton and J. Dyson were the two men concerned.

Railways beat Jammu and Kashmir without having a batsman dismissed in either innings at Srinager in 1960 by ten wickets, V. L. Mehra and B. K. Kunderam were the two men concerned.

Railways (910 for six wkts., dec.) beat Dera Ismail Khan by an innings and 851 runs at Lahore, 1964–65.

Victoria (1,059) beat Tasmania by an innings and 666 runs at Melbourne, 1922–23.

Victoria (1,107) beat New South Wales by an innings and 656 runs at Melbourne, 1926–27.

New South Wales (918) beat South Australia by an innings and 605 runs at Sydney, 1900–01.

England (903 for seven wkts., dec.) beat Australia by an innings and 579 runs at The Oval in 1938.

England (521 and 342 for eight wkts., dec.) beat Australia by 675 runs at Brisbane in 1928–29.

Australians (675) beat Nottinghamshire by an innings and 517 runs at Nottingham in 1921. In their previous game they defeated Northamptonshire by an innings and 484 runs.

New South Wales (235 and 761 for eight wkts., dec.) beat Queensland by 685 runs at Sydney in 1929–30.

Karachi "A" defeated Sind "A" by an innings without losing a wicket. Karachi "A" 277 for 0 dec. (Hanif Mohammed 146*, Alim-ud-din 131*); Sind "A" 99 and 108, 1957–58.

TEST MATCH RECORDS

SCORERS OF 1,500 RUNS IN TESTS

ENGLAND

	Tests	Inns.	Not Outs	Runs	Highest Score	100's	Average
W. R. Hammond ..	85	140	16	7249	336*	22	58.45
L. Hutton	79	138	15	6971	364	19	56.67
M. C. Cowdrey	90	149	14	6305	182	18	46.70
D. C. S. Compton..	78	131	15	5807	278	17	50.06
K. F. Barrington...	68	110	12	5598	256	16	57.12
J. B. Hobbs	61	102	7	5410	211	15	56.94
H. Sutcliffe........	54	84	9	4555	194	16	60.73
P. B. H. May......	66	106	9	4537	285*	13	46.77
E. R. Dexter	60	98	8	4405	205	9	48.95
T. W. Graveney....	59	92	12	3566	258	8	44.57
E. Hendren........	51	83	9	3525	205*	7	47.63
F. E. Woolley	64	98	7	3283	154	5	36.07
M. Leyland	41	65	5	2764	187	9	46.06
C. Washbrook	37	66	6	2569	195	6	42.81
W. J. Edrich.......	39	63	2	2440	219	6	40.00
T. G. Evans	91	133	14	2439	104	2	20.69
L. E. G. Ames.....	47	72	12	2434	149	8	40.56
W. Rhodes	58	98	21	2325	179	2	30.19
T. E. Bailey	61	91	14	2290	134*	1	29.74
M. J. K. Smith	47	72	6	2138	121	3	32.39
P. E. Richardson ..	34	56	1	2061	126	5	37.47
T. Hayward	35	60	2	1999	137	3	34.46
G. Pullar..........	28	49	4	1974	175	4	43.86
A. C. MacLaren ...	35	61	4	1931	140	5	33.87
J. M. Parks	43	64	7	1914	108*	2	33.57
R. E. S. Wyatt	40	64	6	1839	149	2	31.70
P. H. Parfitt	33	44	5	1722	131*	7	44.15
J. T. Tyldesley	31	55	1	1661	138	4	30.75
J. Hardstaff, junr...	23	38	3	1636	205*	4	46.74
E. Paynter	20	31	5	1540	243	4	59.23

AUSTRALIA

	Tests	Inns.	Not Outs	Runs	Highest Score	100's	Average
D. G. Bradman ...	52	80	10	6996	334	29	99.94
R. N. Harvey	79	137	10	6149	205	21	48.41
A. R. Morris	46	79	3	3533	206	12	46.48
C. Hill	49	89	2	3412	191	7	39.21
R. B. Simpson	44	77	7	3354	311	5	47.91
V. T. Trumper	48	89	8	3163	214*	8	39.04
C. C. McDonald ..	47	83	4	3106	170	5	39.31
A. L. Hassett	43	69	3	3073	198*	10	46.56
K. R. Miller	55	87	7	2958	147	7	36.97
W. M. Lawry......	35	63	6	2876	210	8	50.45
W. W. Armstrong..	50	84	10	2863	159*	6	38.68
N. C. O'Neill......	42	69	8	2779	181	6	45.55
S. J. McCabe	39	62	5	2748	232	6	48.21
W. Bardsley	41	66	5	2469	193*	6	40.47
W. M. Woodfull ...	35	54	4	2300	161	7	46.00
P. J. Burge	42	68	8	2290	181	4	38.16
S. E. Gregory......	58	100	7	2282	201	4	24.53
R. Benaud	63	97	7	2201	122	3	24.42
C. G. Macartney...	35	55	4	2131	170	7	41.78
W. H. Ponsford ...	29	48	4	2122	266	7	48.22
M. A. Noble	42	73	7	1997	133	1	30.25
B. C. Booth	29	48	5	1773	169	5	41.23
J. Darling	34	60	2	1657	178	3	28.56

	Tests	Inns.	Not Outs	Runs	Highest Score	100's	Average
W. A. Brown	22	35	1	1592	206*	4	46.82
K. Mackay........	37	52	7	1507	89	0	33.48
R. R. Lindwall	61	84	13	1502	118	2	21.15
			SOUTH AFRICA				
B. Mitchell	42	80	9	3471	189*	8	48.88
A. D. Nourse, junr.	34	62	7	2960	231	9	53.81
H. W. Taylor......	42	76	4	2936	176	7	40.77
D. J. McGlew	34	64	6	2440	255*	7	42.06
J. H. B. Waite	50	86	6	2405	134	4	30.06
A. D. Nourse, senr.	45	83	8	2234	111	1	29.78
T. L. Goddard.....	33	64	4	2164	112	1	36.06
R. A. McLean	40	73	3	2120	142	5	30.28
E. J. Barlow	21	41	2	1970	201	4	50.51
E. A. B. Rowan....	26	50	5	1965	236	3	43.66
G. A. Faulkner	25	47	4	1754	204	4	40.79
K. C. Bland	20	37	5	1637	144*	3	51.15
W. R. Endean	28	52	4	1630	162*	3	33.96
R. H. Catterall	24	43	2	1555	120	3	37.29
			WEST INDIES				
G. S. Sobers	57	97	11	5172	365*	17	60.13
E. D. Weekes	48	81	5	4455	207	15	58.61
R. B. Kanhai......	48	84	2	3923	256	10	47.48
F. M. Worrell	51	87	9	3860	261	9	49.48
C. L. Walcott......	44	74	7	3798	220	15	56.68
C. C. Hunte	41	73	6	2986	260	7	44.56
G. A. Headley	22	40	4	2190	270*	10	60.83
J. B. Stollmeyer	32	56	5	2159	160	4	42.33
B. F. Butcher	25	43	4	1858	209*	5	47.64
			NEW ZEALAND				
J. R. Reid	58	108	5	3431	142	6	33.31
B. Sutcliffe	42	76	8	2727	230*	5	40.10
			INDIA				
P. R. Umrigar	59	94	8	3621	223	12	42.10
V. L. Manjrekar ...	55	92	10	3209	189*	7	39.13
P. Roy...........	43	79	4	2441	173	5	32.54
C. G. Borde	40	68	9	2230	177*	3	37.79
V. S. Hazare	30	52	6	2192	164*	7	47.65
V. Mankad	44	72	5	2109	231	5	31.47
M. L. Jaisimha	27	49	2	1625	129	2	34.57
N. J. Contractor ...	31	52	1	1611	108	1	31.58
			PAKISTAN				
Hanif Mohammad .	48	86	6	3584	337	11	44.80
Saeed Ahmed	32	62	3	2562	172	5	43.42
Imtiaz Ahmed	41	72	1	2079	209	3	29.28

BOWLERS WITH 75 WICKETS IN TESTS

ENGLAND

	Tests	Runs	Wickets	Average
F. S. Trueman	67	6625	307	21.57
J. B. Statham..............	70	6261	252	24.84
A. V. Bedser	51	5876	236	24.89
J. C. Laker................	46	4099	193	21.23
S. F. Barnes	27	3106	189	16.43
G. A. R. Lock..............	47	4240	170	24.94
M. W. Tate	39	4051	155	26.13

	Tests	Runs	Wickets	Average
H. Verity	40	3510	144	24.37
F. J. Titmus	45	4273	136	31.41
T. E. Bailey	61	3856	132	29.21
W. Rhodes	58	3425	127	26.96
D. A. Allen	39	3778	122	30.76
J. Briggs	33	2094	118	17.74
G. A. Lohmann	18	1205	112	10.75
D. V. P. Wright	34	4224	108	39.11
R. Peel	20	1715	102	16.81
J. H. Wardle	28	2080	102	20.39
C. Blythe	19	1863	100	18.63
W. Voce	27	2733	98	27.88
T. Richardson	14	2220	88	25.22
W. R. Hammond	85	3127	83	37.67
F. E. Woolley	64	2815	83	33.91
G. O. Allen	25	2379	81	29.37
H. Larwood	21	2216	78	28.41
F. H. Tyson	17	1411	76	18.56
AUSTRALIA				
R. Benaud	63	6706	248	27.04
R. R. Lindwall	61	5257	228	23.05
C. V. Grimmett	37	5231	216	24.21
A. K. Davidson	44	3828	186	20.58
K. R. Miller	55	3905	170	22.97
W. A. Johnston	40	3825	160	23.90
W. J. O'Reilly	27	3254	144	22.59
H. Trumble	32	3072	141	21.78
G. D. McKenzie	32	3914	137	28.56
M. A. Noble	42	3027	121	25.01
I. W. Johnson	45	3182	109	29.19
G. Giffen	31	2791	103	27.09
C. T. B. Turner	17	1670	101	16.53
A. A. Mailey	21	3358	99	33.91
F. R. Spofforth	18	1731	94	18.41
A. Cotter	21	2549	89	28.64
W. W. Armstrong	50	2923	87	33.59
N. J. N. Hawke	22	2327	86	27.05
J. M. Gregory	24	2648	85	31.15
J. V. Saunders	14	1797	79	22.74
G. E. Palmer	17	1678	78	21.51
SOUTH AFRICA				
H. J. Tayfield	37	4405	170	25.91
N. A. T. Adcock	26	2195	104	21.10
P. M. Pollock	19	2078	89	23.34
T. L. Goddard	33	2601	88	29.35
C. L. Vincent	25	2631	84	31.32
G. A. Faulkner	25	2180	82	26.58
WEST INDIES				
W. W. Hall	38	4080	166	24.07
S. Ramadhin	43	4577	158	28.96
A. L. Valentine	36	4215	139	30.32
L. R. Gibbs	31	3147	133	23.66
G. S. Sobers	57	4469	130	34.37
NEW ZEALAND				
J. R. Reid	58	2840	85	33.41
INDIA				
V. Mankad	44	5235	162	32.31
S. P. Gupte	36	4402	149	29.54

PAKISTAN

	Tests	Runs	Wickets	Average
Fazal Mahmood	34	3437	139	24.72

Note: R. Benaud (Australia) is the only player to score 2,000 *runs and take* 200 *wickets.*

CENTURY ON TEST DEBUT

C. Bannerman (165*) Australia v. England, at Melbourne	1876–77
W. G. Grace (152) England v. Australia, at The Oval	1880
H. Graham (107) Australia v. England, at Lord's	1893
K. S. Ranjitsinhji (154*) England v. Australia, at Manchester	1896
P. F. Warner (132*) England v. South Africa, at Johannesburg ..	1898–99
R. A. Duff (104) Australia v. England, at Melbourne	1901–02
R. E. Foster (287) England v. Australia, at Sydney	1903–04
G. Gunn (119) England v. Australia, at Sydney	1907–08
R. J. Hartigan (116) Australia v. England, at Adelaide	1907–08
H. L. Collins (104) Australia v. England, at Sydney	1920–21
W. H. Ponsford (110) Australia v. England, at Sydney	1924–25
A. A. Jackson (164) Australia v. England, at Adelaide	1928–29
G. A. Headley (176) West Indies v. England, at Barbados	1929–30
J. E. Mills (117) New Zealand v. England, at Wellington	1929–30
Nawab of Pataudi (102) England v. Australia, at Sydney	1932–33
L. Amarnath (118) India v. England, at Bombay	1933–34
B. H. Valentine (136) England v. India, at Bombay	1933–34
P. A. Gibb (106) England v. South Africa, at Johannesburg	1938–39
A. G. Ganteaume (112) West Indies v. England, at Trinidad	1947–48
S. C. Griffith (140) England v. West Indies, at Trinidad	1947–48
J. W. Burke (101*) Australia v. England, at Adelaide	1950–51
P. B. H. May (138) England v. South Africa, at Leeds	1951
B. H. Pairaudeau (115) West Indies v. India, at Trinidad	1952–53
D. H. Shodhan (110) India v. Pakistan, at Calcutta	1952–53
O. G. Smith (104) West Indies v. Australia, at Kingston	1954–55
A. G. Kripal Singh (100*) India v. New Zealand, at Hyderabad ..	1955–56
C. C. Hunte (142) West Indies v. Pakistan, at Barbados	1957–58
C. A. Milton (104*) England v. New Zealand, at Leeds	1958
A. A. Baig (112) India v. England, at Manchester	1959
Hanumant Singh (105) India v. England, at Delhi	1963–64
Khalid Ibadulla (166) Pakistan v. Australia, at Karachi	1964
B. R. Taylor (105) New Zealand v. India, at Calcutta	1965
K. D. Walters (155) Australia v. England, at Brisbane	1965–66

TWO SEPARATE HUNDREDS IN A TEST MATCH

Twice in one Series: C. L. Walcott v. Australia (1954–55).

Twice: H. Sutcliffe v. Australia (1924–25), South Africa (1929).
G. A. Headley v. England (1929–30 and 1939).

Once: W. Bardsley v. England (1909).
A. C. Russell v. South Africa (1922–23).
W. R. Hammond v. Australia (1928–29).
E. Paynter v. South Africa (1938–39).
D. C. S. Compton v. Australia (1946–47).
A. R. Morris v. England (1946–47).
A. Melville v. England (1947).
B. Mitchell v. England (1947).
D. G. Bradman v. India (1947–48).
V. S. Hazare v. Australia (1947–48).
E. D. Weekes v. India (1948–49).
J. R. Moroney v. South Africa (1949–50).
G. S. Sobers v. Pakistan (1957–58).
R. B. Kanhai v. Australia (1960–61).
Hanif Mohammad v. England (1961–62).
R. B. Simpson v. Pakistan (1964).

FASTEST TEST FIFTIES

J. M. Gregory, Australia v. South Africa, at Johannesburg, 1921–22—35 minutes.
C. G. Macartney, Australia v. South Africa, at Sydney 1910–11—35 minutes.
J. H. Sinclair, South Africa v. Australians, at Cape Town, 1902–03—35 minutes.
R. Benaud, Australia v. West Indies, at Kingston, 1954–55—38 minutes.
T. G. Evans, England v. India, at Nottingham, 1959—42 minutes.
S. J. McCabe, Australia v. South Africa, at Johannesburg, 1935–36—42 minutes.

FASTEST TEST CENTURIES

J. M. Gregory, Australia v. South Africa, at Johannesburg, 1921–22—70 minutes.
G. L. Jessop, England v. Australia, at The Oval, 1902—75 minutes.
R. Benaud, Australia v. West Indies, at Kingston, 1954–55—78 minutes.
J. H. Sinclair, South Africa v. Australia, at Cape Town, 1902–03—80 minutes.
D. G. Bradman, Australia v. England, at Leeds, 1930—90 minutes.

FASTEST TEST DOUBLE CENTURIES

D. G. Bradman, Australia v. England, at Leeds, 1930—214 minutes
S. J. McCabe, Australia v. England, at Nottingham, 1938—225 minutes.
V. T. Trumper, Australia v. South Africa, at Adelaide, 1910–11—226 minutes.
W. R. Hammond, England v. New Zealand, at Auckland, 1932–33—240 minutes.
D. C. S. Compton, England v. Pakistan, at Nottingham, 1954—245 minutes.

MOST RUNS IN A DAY BY A BATSMAN

D. G. Bradman, Australia v. England, at Leeds, 1930 309
W. R. Hammond, England v. New Zealand, at Auckland, 1932–33 .. 295
D. C. S. Compton, England v. Pakistan, at Nottingham, 1954 273
D. G. Bradman, Australia v. England, at Leeds, 1934 271

MOST RUNS IN A DAY (BOTH SIDES)

England (398/6); India (190/0) at Manchester, 1936 .. .. .. 588/6
England (503/2); South Africa (19/0) at Lord's, 1924 .. .. .. 522/2
England (221/2); South Africa (287/6) at The Oval, 1935 .. .. .. 508/8

MOST RUNS IN A DAY (ONE SIDE)

England v. South Africa, at Lord's, 1924 .. .. 503/2
Australia v. South Africa, at Sydney, 1910–11 .. .. 494/6
Australia v. England, at The Oval, 1934 .. .. 475/2
England v. India, at The Oval, 1936 .. .. 471/8
Australia v. England, at Leeds, 1930 .. .. 458/3
Australia v. England, at Leeds, 1934 .. .. 455/1

SLOW INDIVIDUAL TEST BATTING

18 in 194 minutes—W. R. Playle, New Zealand v. England, Leeds .. 1958
18 in 180 minutes—G. O. Rabone, New Zealand v. England, Dunedin 1954–55
19 not out in 150 minutes—W. L. Murdoch, Aust. v. Engl., Melbourne 1882–83
20 in 195 minutes—Hanif Mohammad, Pakistan v. England, Lord's .. 1954
21 in 210 minutes—P. G. Z. Harris, New Zealand v. Pakistan, Karachi 1955–56
28 not out in 250 minutes—J. W. Burke, Australia v. England, Brisbane 1958–59
31 in 266 minutes—K. Mackay, Australia v. England, Lord's 1956
38 in 260 minutes—T. E. Bailey, England v. Australia, Leeds 1953
40 in 295 minutes—H. L. Collins, Australia v. England, Manchester .. 1921
45 in 318 minutes—Shuja-ud-Din, Pakistan v. Australia, Lahore .. 1959–60
58 in 367 minutes—Ijaz Butt, Pakistan v. Australia, Karachi 1959–60
68 in 458 minutes—T. E. Bailey, England v. Australia, Brisbane .. 1958–59
74 in 393 minutes—M. L. Jaisimha, India v. Australia, Calcutta .. 1959–60
82 in 360 minutes—W. H. Scotton, England v. Australia, Adelaide .. 1884–85
88 in 415 minutes—J. B. Bolus, England v. India, Madras 1963–64
99 in 500 minutes—M. L. Jaisimha, India v. Pakistan, Kanpur .. 1960–61
105 in 575 minutes—D. J. McGlew, South Africa v. Australia, Durban (He took 545 minutes to reach 100) 1957–58
117 in 530 minutes—P. E. Richardson, England v. South Africa, Johannesburg (He took 490 minutes to reach 100) 1956–57

LOWEST TEST SCORES IN ONE FULL DAY'S PLAY

95 At Karachi, October 1956, Australia 80 all out; Pakistan 15 for two wickets.

104 At Karachi, December 1959, Pakistan 0 for no wicket to 104 for five wickets (fourth day).

106 At Brisbane, December 1958, England 92 for 2 wickets to 198 all out v. Australia.

112 At Karachi, October 1956, Australia 138 for six wickets to 187 all out; Pakistan 63 for one wicket (fourth day).

117 At Madras, October 1956, India 117 for five wickets v. Australia.

119 At Johannesburg, February 1958, South Africa 7 for no wicket to 126 for two wickets v. Australia.

120 At Calcutta, November 1956, India 15 for no wicket to 135 for eight wickets v. Australia.

122 At Port Elizabeth, March 1957. England's last wicket fell after first twenty minutes without addition. South Africa then made 122 for seven wickets in five and a half hours.

122 At Brisbane, December 1958, Australia 156 for six wickets to 186 all out; England 92 for two wickets.

125 At Dunedin, March 1955, New Zealand 125 all out v. England.

128 At Barbados, February 9, 1954. England added only 128 on the third day v. West Indies

MOST WICKETS IN A TEST

19/90	J. C. Laker, England v. Australia, Manchester	1956
17/159	S. F. Barnes, England v. South Africa, Johannesburg	1913–14
15/28	J. Briggs, England v. South Africa, Cape Town	1888–89
15/45	G. A. Lohmann, England v. South Africa, Port Elizabeth	1895–96
15/99	C. Blythe, England v. South Africa, Leeds	1907
15/104	H. Verity, England v. Australia, Lord's	1934
15/124	W. Rhodes, England v. Australia, Melbourne	1903–04
14/90	F. R. Spofforth, Australia v. England, Oval	1882
14/99	A. V. Bedser, England v. Australia, Nottingham	1953
14/124	J. S. Patel, India v. Australia, Kanpur	1959–60
14/144	S. F. Barnes, England v. South Africa, Durban	1913–14
14/199	C. V. Grimmett, Australia v. South Africa, Adelaide	1931–32

The best for South Africa is 13/165 by H. J. Tayfield against Australia at Melbourne, 1952–53.

The best for West Indies is 11 wickets by W. Ferguson, L. R. Gibbs, W. W. Hall, S. Ramadhin and A. L. Valentine.

The best for New Zealand is 10/137 by J. Cowie against England at Manchester, 1937.

The best for Pakistan is 13/114 by Fazal Mahmood against Australia at Karachi, 1956–57.

MOST WICKETS IN A TEST INNINGS

10/53	J. C. Laker, England v. Australia, at Manchester	1956
9/28	G. A. Lohmann, England v. South Africa, at Johannesburg	1895–96
9/37	J. C. Laker, England v. Australia, at Manchester	1956
9/69	J. S. Patel, India v. Australia, at Kanpur	1959–60
9/102	S. P. Gupte, India v. West Indies, at Kanpur	1958–59
9/103	S. F. Barnes, England v. South Africa, at Johannesburg	1913–14
9/113	H. J. Tayfield, South Africa v. England, at Johannesburg	1956–57
9/121	A. A. Mailey, Australia v. England, at Melbourne	1920–21
8/7	G. A. Lohmann, England v. South Africa, at Port Elizabeth	1895–96
8/11	J. Briggs, England v. South Africa, at Cape town	1888–89
8/29	S. F. Barnes, England v. South Africa, at The Oval	1912
8/31	F. Laver, Australia v. England, at Manchester	1909
8/31	F. S. Trueman, England v. India, at Manchester	1952
8/35	G. A. Lohmann, England v. Australia, at Sydney	1886–87
8/38	L. R. Gibbs, West Indies v. India, at Barbados	1962
8/43	A. E. Trott, Australia v. England, at Adelaide	1894–95
8/43	H. Verity, England v. Australia, at Lord's	1934

8/52	V. Mankad, India v. Pakistan, at Delhi	1952–53
8/53	G. B. Lawrence, South Africa v. New Zealand, at Johannesburg	1961–62
8/55	V. Mankad, India v. England, at Madras..	1951–52
8/56	S. F. Barnes, England v. South Africa, at Johannesburg ..	1913–14
8/58	G. A. Lohmann, England v. Australia, at Sydney	1891–92
8/59	C. Blythe, England v. South Africa, at Leeds	1907
8/65	H. Trumble, Australia v. England, at The Oval	1902
8/68	W. Rhodes, England v. Australia, at Melbourne	1903–04
8/69	H. J. Tayfield, South Africa v. England, at Durban	1956–57
8/70	S. J. Snooke, South Africa v. England, at Johannesburg ..	1905–06
8/72	S. Venkataraghavan, India v. New Zealand, at New Delhi ..	1965
8/81	L. C. Braund, England v. Australia, at Melbourne	1903–04
8/94	T. Richardson, England v. Australia, at Sydney	1897–98
8/104	A. L. Valentine, West Indies v. England, at Manchester ..	1950
8/107	B. J. T. Bosanquet, England v. Australia, at Nottingham ..	1905
8/126	J. C. White, England v. Australia, at Adelaide	1928–29

TEST HAT-TRICKS

L. R. Gibbs, West Indies v. Australia, Adelaide	1960–61
G. Griffin, South Africa v. England, Lord's	1960
W. W. Hall, West Indies v. Pakistan, Lahore	1958–59
L. F. Kline, Australia v. South Africa, Capetown	1957–58
P. J. Loader, England v. West Indies, Leeds	1957
T. W. Goddard, England v. South Africa, Johannesburg	1938–39
M. J. C. Allom, England v. New Zealand, Christchurch	1929–30
T. J. Matthews / T. J. Matthews } Australia v. South Africa, Manchester	1912
H. Trumble, Australia v. England, Melbourne	1903–4
H. Trumble, Australia v. England, Melbourne	1901–2
J. T. Hearne, England v. Australia, Leeds	1899
G. A. Lohmann, England v. South Africa, Port Elizabeth	1895–96
J. Briggs, England v. Australia, Sydney	1891–92
W. Bates, England v. Australia, Melbourne	1882–83
F. R. Spofforth, Australia v. England, Melbourne	1878–79

T. J. Matthews did the hat-trick in each innings of the same match.

MOST BALLS BOWLED IN A TEST MATCH

S. Ramadhin (West Indies) sent down 774 balls in 129 overs against England at Birmingham, 1957. It was the most delivered by any bowler in a Test, beating H. Verity's 766 for England against South Africa at Durban, 1939. In this match Ramadhin also bowled most balls (588) in any single first-class innings, including Tests. The highest number of balls bowled by one man in a first-class match is 917 by C. S. Nayudu for Holkar v. Bombay, 1944–45. It should be noted that six balls were bowled to the over in the Australia v. England Test series of 1928–29 and 1932–33 when the eight-ball over was otherwise in force in Australia.

WICKET-KEEPING FEATS

MOST VICTIMS IN A TEST CAREER

T. G. Evans (England).	219 in 91 matches
A. T. W. Grout (Australia)	187 in 51 matches
J. H. B. Waite (South Africa)	141 in 50 matches
W. A. Oldfield (Australia).	130 in 54 matches

MOST VICTIMS IN A TEST SERIES

26 (23 c 3 s)	J. H. B. Waite, South Africa v. New Zealand	1961–62
24 (22 c 2 s)	D. L. Murray, West Indies v. England	1963
23 (22 c 1 s)	F. C. M. Alexander, West Indies v. England	1959–60
23 (21 c 2 s)	A. E. Dick, New Zealand v. South Africa	1961–62
23 (20 c 3 s)	A. T. W. Grout, Australia v. West Indies	1960–61

23 (16 c 7 s)	J. H. B. Waite, South Africa v. New Zealand	1953-54
21 (20 c 1 s)	A. T. W. Grout, Australia v. England	1961
21 (16 c 5 s)	G. R. Langley, Australia v. West Indies	1951-52
21 (13 c 8 s)	R. A. Saggers, Australia v. South Africa..	1949-50
21 (15 c 6 s)	H. Strudwick, England v. South Africa	1913-14
20 (18 c 2 s)	T. G. Evans, England v. South Africa	1956-57
20 (17 c 3 s)	A. T. W. Grout, Australia v. England	1958-59
20 (16 c 4 s)	G. R. Langley, Australia v. West Indies	1954-55
20 (16 c 4 s)	D. Tallon, Australia v. England	1946-47

MOST VICTIMS IN A TEST INNINGS

6 (all c)	A. T. W. Grout, Australia v. South Africa, at Jo'burg ..	1957-58
5 (1 c 4 s)	W. A. Oldfield, Australia v. England, at Melbourne ..	1924-25
5 (2 c 3 s)	G. R. Langley, Australia v. West Indies, at Georgetown	1954-55
5 (all c)	G. R. Langley, Australia v. West Indies, at Kingston ..	1954-55
5 (all c)	G. R. Langley, Australia v. England, at Lord's	1956
5 (4 c 1 s)	A. T. W. Grout, Australia v. South Africa, at Durban ..	1957-58
5 (all c)	A. T. W. Grout, Australia v. Pakistan, at Lahore ..	1959-60
5 (4 c 1 s)	Imtiaz Ahmed, Pakistan v. Australia, at Lahore	1959-60
5 (all c)	F. C. M. Alexander, West Indies v. England, at Bridgetown	1959-60
5 (4 c 1 s)	A. T. W. Grout, Australia v. West Indies, at Brisbane ..	1960-61
5 (all c)	A. T. W. Grout, Australia v. England, at Lord's	1961
5 (3 c 2 s)	B. K. Kunderam, India v. England, at Bombay	1961-62
5 (all c)	J. G. Binks, England v. India, at Calcutta	1963-64
5 (4 c 1 s)	B. N. Jarman, Australia v. Pakistan, at Melbourne ..	1964-65
5 (all c)	A. T. W. Grout, Australia v. England, at Sydney ..	1965-66
5 (3 c 2 s)	J. M. Parks, England v. Australia, at Sydney	1965-66
5 (all c)	J. M. Parks, England v. New Zealand, at Christchurch ..	1966

MOST VICTIMS IN ONE TEST

9 (8 c 1 s)	G. R. Langley, Australia v. England, at Lord's	1956
8 (6 c 2 s)	L. E. G. Ames, England v. West Indies, at The Oval ..	1933
8 (6 c 2 s)	A. T. W. Grout, Australia v. Pakistan, at Lahore ..	1959-60
8 (all c)	A. T. W. Grout, Australia v. England, at Lord's	1961
8 (all c)	J. J. Kelly, Australia v. England, at Sydney	1901-02
8 (all c)	G. R. Langley, Australia v. West Indies, at Kingston ..	1954-55
8 (all c)	J. M. Parks, England v. New Zealand, at Christchurch ..	1966

SUMMARY OF ALL TEST MATCHES TO OCT. 31, 1966

ENGLAND

Against	Won	Lost	Drawn	Tied	Total
Australia	65	79	54	0	198
South Africa	46	18	38	0	102
West Indies	17	16	17	0	50
New Zealand	17	0	20	0	37
India	15	3	16	0	34
Pakistan	6	1	5	0	12
Totals	166	117	150	0	433

AUSTRALIA

Against	Won	Lost	Drawn	Tied	Total
England	79	65	54	0	198
South Africa	28	4	12	0	44
West Indies	14	5	5	1	25
New Zealand	1	0	0	0	1
India	9	2	5	0	16
Pakistan	2	1	3	0	6
Totals	133	77	79	1	290

SOUTH AFRICA

Against	Won	Lost	Drawn	Tied	Total
England	18	46	38	0	102
Australia	4	28	12	0	44
New Zealand	9	2	6	0	17
Totals	31	76	56	0	163

WEST INDIES

Against	Won	Lost	Drawn	Tied	Total
England	16	17	17	0	50
Australia	5	14	5	1	25
New Zealand	4	1	1	0	6
India	10	0	10	0	20
Pakistan	4	3	1	0	8
Totals	39	35	34	1	109

NEW ZEALAND

Against	Won	Lost	Drawn	Tied	Total
England	0	17	20	0	37
Australia	0	1	0	0	1
South Africa	2	9	6	0	17
West Indies	1	4	1	0	6
India	0	3	6	0	9
Pakistan	0	4	5	0	9
Totals	3	38	38	0	79

INDIA

Against	Won	Lost	Drawn	Tied	Total
England	3	15	16	0	34
Australia	2	9	5	0	16
West Indies	0	10	10	0	20
New Zealand	3	0	6	0	9
Pakistan	2	1	12	0	15
Totals	10	35	49	0	94

PAKISTAN

Against	Won	Lost	Drawn	Tied	Total
England	1	6	5	0	12
Australia	1	2	3	0	6
West Indies	3	4	1	0	8
India	1	2	12	0	15
New Zealand	4	0	5	0	9
Totals	10	14	26	0	50

SAME CAPTAIN WINNING TOSS ALL FIVE TESTS

1905 Hon. F. S. Jackson, for England v. Australia.
1909 M. A. Noble, for Australia v. England.
1927–28 H. G. Deane, for South Africa v. England.
1948–49 J. D. C. Goddard, for West Indies, v. India.
1953 A. L. Hassett, for Australia v. England.
1960 M. C. Cowdrey, for England v. South Africa.
1963–64 Nawab of Pataudi, for India v. England.
1966 G. S. Sobers, for West Indies v. England.

P. B. H. May (3) and M. C. Cowdrey (2) won in all five Tests for England in West Indies, 1959–60.

ENGLAND v. AUSTRALIA

THE ASHES

Season	Visiting Captain	Won by England	Won by Australia	Drawn	Total
1876–77	J. Lillywhite ....(E.)	1	1	0	2
1878–79	Lord Harris ....(E.)	0	1	0	1
1880	W. L. Murdoch.......(A.)	1	0	0	1
1881–82	A. Shaw ....(E.)	0	2	2	4
1882	W. L. Murdoch.......(A.)	0	1	0	1
1882–83	Hon. Ivo Bligh ....(E.)	2	2	0	4
1884	W. L. Murdoch.......(A.)	1	0	2	3
1884–85	A. Shrewsbury........(E.)	3	2	0	5
1886	H. J. H. Scott ....(A.)	3	0	0	3
1886–87	A. Shrewsbury........(E.)	2	0	0	2
1887–88	W. W. Read ....(E.)	1	0	0	1
1888	P. S. McDonnell ......(A)	2	1	0	3
1890*	W. L. Murdoch.......(A.)	2	0	0	2
1891–92	W. G. Grace ....(E.)	1	2	0	3
1893	J. McC. Blackham ....(A.)	1	0	2	3
1894–95	A. E. Stoddart........(E.)	3	2	0	5
1896	G. H. S. Trott ....(A.)	2	1	0	3
1897–98	A. E. Stoddart........(E.)	1	4	0	5
1899	J. Darling ....(A.)	0	1	4	5
1901–2	A. C. MacLaren ......(E.)	1	4	0	5
1902	J. Darling ....(A.)	1	2	2	5
1903–4	P. F. Warner ....(E.)	3	2	0	5
1905	J. Darling ....(A.)	2	0	3	5
1907–8	A. O. Jones ....(E.)	1	4	0	5
1909	M. A. Noble ....(A.)	1	2	2	5
1911–12	J. W. H. T. Douglas ..(E.)	4	1	0	5
1912	S. E. Gregory.........(A.)	1	0	2	3
1920–21	J. W. H. T. Douglas ..(E.)	0	5	0	5
1921	W. W. Armstrong .....(A.)	0	3	2	5
1924–25	A. E. R. Gilligan......(E.)	1	4	0	5
1926	H. L. Collins ....(A.)	1	0	4	5
1928–29	A. P. F. Chapman ....(E.)	4	1	0	5
1930	W. M. Woodfull ......(A.)	1	2	2	5
1932–33	D. R. Jardine ....(E.)	4	1	0	5
1934	W. M. Woodfull ......(A.)	1	2	2	5
1936–37	G. O. Allen ....(E.)	2	3	0	5
1938*	D. G. Bradman ......(A.)	1	1	2	4
1946–47	W. R. Hammond .....(E.)	0	3	2	5
1948	D. G. Bradman ......(A.)	0	4	1	5
1950–51	F. R. Brown..........(E.)	1	4	0	5
1953	A. L. Hassett ....(A.)	1	0	4	5
1954–55	L. Hutton............(E.)	3	1	1	5
1956	I. W. Johnson ....(A.)	2	1	2	5
1958–59	P. B. H. May.........(E.)	0	4	1	5
1961	R. Benaud ....(A.)	1	2	2	5
1962–63	E. R. Dexter ....(E.)	1	1	3	5
1964	R. B. Simpson ....(A.)	0	1	4	5
1965–66	M. J. K. Smith ....(E.)	1	1	3	5
	In Australia	40	55	12	107
	In England	25	24	42	91
	Totals	65	79	54	198

* *The matches at Manchester in 1890 and 1938 were abandoned without a ball bowled.*

HIGHEST TOTALS FOR AN INNINGS

By England

903	(7 wkts.), The Oval ..	1938
658	(8 wkts.), Nottingham	1938
636	.. Sydney	1928–29
627	(9 wkts.), Manchester	1934
611	.. Manchester	1964

By Australia

729	(6 wkts.), Lord's	1930
701	.. The Oval	1934
695	.. The Oval	1930
659	(8 wkts.), Sydney	1946–47
656	(8 wkts.), Manchester.	1964
645	.. Brisbane	1946–47
604	.. Melbourne	1936–37
601	(8 wkts.), Brisbane ...	1954–55

SMALLEST TOTALS FOR AN INNINGS

36	.. Australia	.. Edgbaston	1902
42	.. Australia	.. Sydney	1887–88
44	.. Australia	.. The Oval	1896
45	.. England	.. Sydney	1886–87

RECORD PARTNERSHIP FOR EACH WICKET

By England

323 for 1st	J. B. Hobbs and W. Rhodes, at Melbourne	1911–12
382 for 2nd	L. Hutton and M. Leyland, at The Oval	1938
262 for 3rd	W. R. Hammond and D. R. Jardine, at Adelaide ..	1928–29
222 for 4th	W. R. Hammond and E. Paynter, at Lord's	1938
206 for 5th	E. Paynter and D. C. S. Compton, at Nottingham ..	1938
215 for 6th	L. Hutton and J. Hardstaff, at The Oval	1938
143 for 7th	J. Vine and F. E. Woolley, at Sydney	1911–12
124 for 8th	E. Hendren and H. Larwood, at Brisbane	1928–29
151 for 9th	W. W. Read and W. H. Scotton, at The Oval	1884
130 for 10th	R. E. Foster and W. Rhodes, at Sydney	1903–04

By Australia

244 for 1st	R. B. Simpson and W. M. Lawry, at Adelaide	1965–66
451 for 2nd	W. H. Ponsford and D. G. Bradman, at The Oval ..	1934
276 for 3rd	D. G. Bradman and A. L. Hassett, at Brisbane	1946–47
388 for 4th	W. H. Ponsford and D. G. Bradman, at Leeds	1934
405 for 5th	S. G. Barnes and D. G. Bradman, at Sydney	1946–47
346 for 6th	D. G. Bradman and J. H. Fingleton, at Melbourne	1936–37
165 for 7th	C. Hill and H. Trumble, at Melbourne	1897–98
243 for 8th	C. Hill and R. J. Hartigan, at Adelaide	1907–08
154 for 9th	J. McC. Blackham and S. E. Gregory, at Sydney ..	1894–95
127 for 10th	J. M. Taylor and A. A. Mailey, at Sydney	1924–25

INDIVIDUAL HUNDREDS IN THE MATCHES 1876–1966

For England (140)

132*	R. Abel, Sydney	1891–2
120	L. E. G. Ames, Lord's	1934
185	R. W. Barber, Sydney	1965–6
134	W. Barnes, Adelaide .	1884–5
129	C. J. Barnett, Adelaide	1936–7
126	C. J. Barnett, Nottingham.............	1938
132*	K. F. Barrington, Adelaide	1962–3
101	K. F. Barrington, Sydney	1962–3
256	K. F. Barrington, Manchester	1964
102	K. F. Barrington, Adelaide	1965–6
115	K. F. Barrington, Melbourne	1965–6
113	G. Boycott, The Oval.	1964
103*	L. C. Braund, Adelaide	1901–2
102	L. C. Braund, Sydney	1903–4
121	J. Briggs, Melbourne .	1884–5
140	J. T. Brown, Melbourne	1894–5
121	A. P. F. Chapman, Lord's	1930
102†	D. C. S. Compton, Nottingham......	1938
147 } 103* }	D. C. S. Compton, Adelaide	1946–7
184	D. C. S. Compton, Nottingham......	1948
145*	D. C. S. Compton, Manchester	1948

102 M. C. Cowdrey, Melbourne 1954–5
100* M. C. Cowdrey, Sydney 1958–9
113 M. C. Cowdrey, Melbourne 1962–3
104 M. C. Cowdrey, Melbourne 1965–6
180 E. R. Dexter, B'ham .. 1961
174 E. R. Dexter, Manchester 1964
173† K. S. Duleepsinhji, Lord's 1930
120† J. H. Edrich, Lord's... 1964
109 J. H. Edrich, Melbourne 1965–6
103 J. H. Edrich, Sydney .. 1965–6
119 W. J. Edrich, Sydney .. 1946–7
111 W. J. Edrich, Leeds ... 1948
287† R. E. Foster, Sydney .. 1903–4
144 C. B. Fry, The Oval .. 1905
152† W. G. Grace, The Oval 1880
170 W. G. Grace, The Oval 1886
111 T. W. Graveney, Sydney 1954–5
119† G. Gunn, Sydney 1907–8
122* G. Gunn, Sydney 1907–8
102* W. Gunn, Manchester 1893
251 W. R. Hammond, Sydney 1928–9
200 W. R. Hammond, Melbourne 1928–9
119* } W. R. Hammond,
177 } Adelaide 1928–9
113 W. R. Hammond, Leeds 1930
112 W. R. Hammond, Sydney 1932–3
101 W. R. Hammond, Sydney 1932–3
231* W. R. Hammond, Sydney 1936–7
240 W. R. Hammond, Lord's 1938
169* J. Hardstaff, junr., The Oval 1938
130 T. Hayward, Manchester 1899
137 T. Hayward, The Oval 1899
114 J. W. Hearne, Melbourne 1911–12
127* E. Hendren, Lord's ... 1926
169 E. Hendren, Brisbane . 1928–9
132 E. Hendren, Manchester 1934
126* J. B. Hobbs, Melbourne 1911–12
187 J. B. Hobbs, Adelaide . 1911–12
178 J. B. Hobbs, Melbourne 1911–12
107 J. B. Hobbs, Lord's ... 1912
122 J. B. Hobbs, Melbourne 1920–1
123 J. B. Hobbs, Adelaide . 1920–1
115 J. B. Hobbs, Sydney .. 1924–5
154 J. B. Hobbs, Melbourne 1924–5
119 J. B. Hobbs, Adelaide . 1924–5
119 J. B. Hobbs, Lord's ... 1926
100 J. B. Hobbs, The Oval. 1926
142 J. B. Hobbs, Melbourne 1928–9
126 K. L. Hutchings, Melbourne 1907–8

100† L. Hutton, Nottingham 1938
364 L. Hutton, The Oval .. 1938
122* L. Hutton, Sydney 1946–7
156* L. Hutton, Adelaide... 1950–1
145 L. Hutton, Lord's..... 1953
103 Hon. F. S. Jackson, The Oval 1893
118 Hon. F. S. Jackson, The Oval 1899
128 Hon. F. S. Jackson Manchester 1902
144* Hon. F. S. Jackson, Leeds 1905
113 Hon. F. S. Jackson, Manchester 1905
104 G. L. Jessop, The Oval 1902
137† M. Leyland, Melbourne 1928–9
109 M. Leyland, Lord's ... 1934
153 M. Leyland, Manchester 1934
110 M. Leyland, The Oval 1934
126 M. Leyland, Brisbane . 1936–7
111* M. Leyland, Melbourne 1936–7
187 M. Leyland, The Oval . 1938
130 A. C. MacLaren, Melbourne 1894–5
109 A. C. MacLaren, Sydney 1897–8
124 A. C. MacLaren, Adelaide 1897–8
116 A. C. MacLaren, Sydney 1901–2
140 A. C. MacLaren, Nottingham 1905
117 H. Makepeace, Melbourne 1920–1
104 P. B. H. May, Sydney . 1954–5
101 P. B. H. May, Leeds .. 1956
113 P. B. H. May, Melbourne 1958–9
182* C. P. Mead, The Oval 1921
102† Nawab of Pataudi, Sydney 1932–3
216* E. Paynter, Nottingham 1938
154*† K. S. Ranjitsinhji, Manchester 1896
175 K. S. Ranjitsinhji, Sydney 1897–8
117 W. W. Read, The Oval 1884
179 W. Rhodes, Melbourne 1911–12
104 P. E. Richardson, Manchester 1956
135 A. C. Russell, Adelaide 1920–1
101 A. C. Russell, Manchester 1921
102* A. C. Russell, The Oval 1921
105 J. Sharp, The Oval 1909
113 Rev. D. S. Sheppard, Manchester 1956
113 Rev. D. S. Sheppard, Melbourne 1962–3
105* A. Shrewsbury, Melbourne 1884–5

164 A. Shrewsbury, Lord's . 1886
106 A. Shrewsbury, Lord's . 1893
156* R. T. Simpson, Melbourne 1950–1
135* A. G. Steel, Sydney ... 1882–3
148 A. G. Steel, Lord's ... 1884
134 A. E. Stoddart, Adelaide 1891–2
173 A. E. Stoddart, Melbourne 1894–5
112† R. Subba Row, B'ham. 1961
137 R. Subba Row, The Oval 1961
115† H. Sutcliffe, Sydney ... 1924–5
176, 127 H. Sutcliffe, Melbourne 1924–5
143 H. Sutcliffe, Melbourne 1924–5
161 H. Sutcliffe, The Oval . 1926
135 H. Sutcliffe, Melbourne 1928–9
161 H. Sutcliffe, The Oval . 1930
194 H. Sutcliffe, Sydney ... 1932–3
138 J. T. Tyldesley, Edgbaston 1902
100 J. T. Tyldesley, Leeds . 1905
112* J. T. Tyldesley, The Oval 1905
149 G. Ulyett, Melbourne . 1881–2
117 A. Ward, Sydney 1894–5
109† W. Watson, Lord's.... 1953
112 C. Washbrook, Melbourne 1946–7
143 C. Washbrook, Leeds . 1948
133* F. E. Woolley, Sydney . 1911–12
123 F. E. Woolley, Sydney. 1924–5

Note.—In consecutive innings in 1928–29 W. R. Hammond scored 251 at Sydney, 200 and 32 at Melbourne, and 119* and 177 at Adelaide.

For Australia (153)

133* W. W. Armstrong, Melbourne 1907–8
158 W. W. Armstrong, Sydney 1920–1
121 W. W. Armstrong, Adelaide 1920–1
123* W. W. Armstrong, Melbourne 1920–1
118 C. L. Badcock, Melbourne 1936–7
165*† C. Bannerman, Melbourne 1876–7
136, 130 W. Bardsley, The Oval 1909
193* W. Bardsley, Lord's ... 1926
234 S. G. Barnes, Sydney .. 1946–7
141 S. G. Barnes, Lord's .. 1948
128 G. J. Bonnor, Sydney . 1884–5
112 B. C. Booth, Brisbane . 1962–3
103 B. C. Booth, Melbourne 1962–3
112 D. G. Bradman, Melbourne 1928–9
123 D. G. Bradman, Melbourne 1928–9
131 D. G. Bradman, Nottingham 1930
254 D. G. Bradman, Lord's 1930
334 D. G. Bradman, Leeds 1930
232 D. G. Bradman, The Oval 1930
103* D. G. Bradman, Melbourne 1932–3
304 D. G. Bradman, Leeds 1934
244 D. G. Bradman, The Oval 1934
270 D. G. Bradman, Melbourne 1936–7
212 D. G. Bradman, Adelaide 1936–7
169 D. G. Bradman, Melbourne 1936–7
144* D. G. Bradman, Nottingham 1938
102* D. G. Bradman, Lord's 1938
103 D. G. Bradman, Leeds 1938
187 D. G. Bradman, Brisbane 1946–7
234 D. G. Bradman, Sydney 1946–7
138 D. G. Bradman, Nottingham 1948
173* D. G. Bradman, Leeds 1948
105 W. A. Brown, Lord's.. 1934
133 W. A. Brown, Nottingham 1938
206* W. A. Brown, Lord's.. 1938
181 P. J. Burge, Oval 1961
103 P. J. Burge, Sydney ... 1962–3
160 P. J. Burge, Leeds..... 1964
120 P. J. Burge, Melbourne 1965–6
101*† J. W. Burke, Adelaide 1950–1
104† H. L. Collins, Sydney . 1920–1
162 H. L. Collins, Adelaide 1920–1
114 H. L. Collins, Sydney 1924–5
307 R. M. Cowper, Melbourne 1965–6
101 J. Darling, Sydney 1897–8
178 J. Darling, Adelaide .. 1897–8
160 J. Darling, Sydney 1897–8
104† R. A. Duff, Melbourne 1901–2
146 R. A. Duff, The Oval.. 1905
100 J. H. Fingleton, Brisbane 1936–7
136 J. H. Fingleton, Melbourne 1936–7
161 G. Giffen, Sydney..... 1894–5
107† H. Graham, Lord's ... 1893
105 H. Graham, Sydney... 1894–5
100 J. M. Gregory, Melbourne 1920–1
201 S. E. Gregory, Sydney. 1894–5

103	S. E. Gregory, Lord's .	1896
117	S. E. Gregory, The Oval	1899
112	S. E. Gregory, Adelaide	1903–4
116†	R. J. Hartigan, Adelaide	1907–8
112†	R. N. Harvey, Leeds ..	1948
122	R. N. Harvey, Manchester	1953
162	R. N. Harvey, Brisbane	1954–5
167	R. N. Harvey, Melbourne	1958–9
114	R. N. Harvey, B'ham..	1961
154	R. N. Harvey, Adelaide	1962–3
128	A. L. Hassett, Brisbane	1946–7
137	A. L. Hassett, Nottingham...............	1948
115	A. L. Hassett, Nottingham...............	1953
104	A. L. Hassett, Lord's .	1953
112	H. L. Hendry, Sydney	1928–9
188	C. Hill, Melbourne....	1897–8
135	C. Hill, Lord's	1899
119	C. Hill, Sheffield......	1902
160	C. Hill, Adelaide	1907–8
124	T. Horan, Melbourne .	1881–2
140	F. A. Iredale, Adelaide .	1894–5
108	F. A. Iredale, Manchester	1896
164†	A. A. Jackson, Adelaide	1928–9
147	C. E. Kelleway, Adelaide	1920–1
100	A. F. Kippax, Melbourne	1928–9
130	W. M. Lawry, Lord's .	1961
102	W. M. Lawry, Manchester	1961
106	W. M. Lawry, Manchester	1964
166	W. M. Lawry, Brisbane	1965–6
119	W. M. Lawry, Adelaide	1965–6
108	W. M. Lawry, Melbourne	1965–6
100	R. R. Lindwall, Melbourne	1946–7
134	J. J. Lyons, Sydney ...	1891–2
170	C. G. Macartney, Sydney	1920–1
115	C. G. Macartney, Leeds	1921
133*	C. G. Macartney, Lord's	1926
151	C. G. Macartney, Leeds	1926
109	C. G. Macartney, Manchester	1926
187*	S. J. McCabe, Sydney ..	1932–3
137	S. J. McCabe, Manchester	1934
112	S. J. McCabe, Melbourne	1936–7
232	S. J. McCabe, Nottingham..............	1938
104*	C. L. McCool, Melbourne	1946–7
170	C. C. McDonald, Adelaide	1958–9
133	C. C. McDonald, Melbourne	1958–9
147	P. S. McDonnell, Sydney	1881–2
103	P. S. McDonnell, The Oval	1884
124	P. S. McDonnell, Adelaide	1884–5
112	C. E. McLeod, Melbourne	1897–8
141*	K. R. Miller, Adelaide .	1946–7
145*	K. R. Miller, Sydney .	1950–1
109	K. R. Miller, Lord's ..	1953
155	A. R. Morris, Melbourne	1946–7
122 } 124* }	A. R. Morris, Adelaide	1946–7
105	A. R. Morris, Lord's .	1948
182	A. R. Morris, Leeds ...	1948
196	A. R. Morris, The Oval	1948
206	A. R. Morris, Adelaide.	1950–1
153	A. R. Morris, Brisbane	1954–5
153*	W. L. Murdoch, The Oval	1880
211	W. L. Murdoch, The Oval	1884
133	M. A. Noble, Sydney..	1903–4
117	N. C. O'Neill, Oval ...	1961
100	N. C. O'Neill, Adelaide	1962–3
116	C. E. Pellew, Melbourne	1920–1
104	C. E. Pellew, Adelaide .	1920–1
110†	W. H. Ponsford, Sydney	1924–5
128	W. H. Ponsford, Melbourne	1924–5
110	W. H. Ponsford, The Oval	1930
181	W. H. Ponsford, Leeds .	1934
266	W. H. Ponsford, The Oval	1934
143*	V. S. Ransford, Lord's .	1909
100	A. J. Richardson, Leeds	1926
138	V. Y. Richardson, Melbourne	1924–5
201*	J. S. Ryder, Adelaide .	1924–5
112	J. S. Ryder, Melbourne	1928–9
102	H. J. H. Scott, The Oval	1884
311	R. B. Simpson, Manchester	1964
225	R. B. Simpson, Adelaide	1965–6
108	J. M. Taylor, Sydney ..	1924–5
143	G. H. S. Trott, Lord's .	1896
135*	V. T. Trumper, Lord's .	1899
104	V. T. Trumper, Manchester	1902
185*	V. T. Trumper, Sydney	1903–4
113	V. T. Trumper, Adelaide	1903–4
166	V. T. Trumper, Sydney	1907–8
113	V. T. Trumper, Sydney	1911–12
155†	K. D. Walters, Brisbane	1965–6

115	K. D. Walters, Melbourne	1965–6	107	W. M. Woodfull, Melbourne	1928–9
141	W. M. Woodfull, Leeds	1926	102	W. M. Woodfull, Melbourne	1928–9
117	W. M. Woodfull, Manchester	1926	155	W. M. Woodfull, Lord's	1930
111	W. M. Woodfull, Sydney	1928–9			

† *Signifies hundred on first appearance in England–Australia Tests.*

D. G. Bradman's scores in 1930 were 8 and 131 at Nottingham, 254 and 1 at Lord's, 334 at Leeds, 14 at Manchester, and 232 at The Oval.

D. G. Bradman scored a hundred in six consecutive Test Matches v. England —three in 1936–37 and three in 1938.

K. D. Walters hit centuries in each of his first two Tests.

No right-handed batsman has obtained two 100's for Australia in a Test Match against England. H. Sutcliffe, in his first two games for England, scored 59 and 115 at Sydney and 176 and 127 at Melbourne in 1924–25. In the latter match, which lasted into the seventh day, he was on the field throughout except for 86 minutes, namely 27 hours 52 minutes.

C. Hill made 98 and 97 at Adelaide in 1901–02, and F. E. Woolley 95 and 93 at Lord's in 1921.

C. G. Macartney in 1926, H. Sutcliffe in 1924–25 and A. R. Morris in 1946–47 made three hundreds in consecutive innings.

J. B. Hobbs and H. Sutcliffe shared in eleven first-wicket three-figure partnerships.

L. Hutton and C. Washbrook have twice made three-figure stands in each innings, at Adelaide in 1946–47 and at Leeds in 1948.

H. Sutcliffe, during his highest score of 194, v. Australia in 1932–33, took part in three stands each exceeding 100, viz. 112 with R. E. S. Wyatt for the first wicket, 188 with W. R. Hammond for the second wicket, and 123 with the Nawab of Pataudi for the third wicket. In 1903–04 R. E. Foster, in his historic innings of 287, added 192 for the fifth wicket with L. C. Braund, 115 for the ninth with A. E. Relf, and 130 for the tenth with W. Rhodes.

When L. Hutton scored 364 at The Oval in 1938 he added 382 for the second wicket with M. Leyland, 135 for the third wicket with W. R. Hammond and 215 for the sixth wicket with J. Hardstaff, junr.

D. C. S. Compton and A. R. Morris at Adelaide in 1946–47 provide the only instance of a player on each side hitting two separate hundreds in a Test match.

MOST RUNS IN A RUBBER

For England—905, average 113.12 by W. R. Hammond, 1928–29.
For Australia—974, average 139.14, by D. G. Bradman, 1930.

MOST WICKETS IN A RUBBER

For England—46, for 9.60 runs each, in 1956, by J. C. Laker.
For England—39, for 17.48 runs each, in 1953, by A. V. Bedser.
For England—38, for 23.18 runs each, in 1924–25, by M. W. Tate.
For Australia—36, for 26.27 runs each, in 1920–21, by A. A. Mailey.

MOST WICKETS IN A MATCH

For England—19, for 90 runs, J. C. Laker, at Manchester, 1956.
For England—15, for 124 runs, W. Rhodes, at Melbourne, 1903–04.
For England—15, for 104 runs, H. Verity, at Lord's, 1934.
For Australia—14, for 90 runs, F. R. Spofforth, at The Oval, 1882.

THE HAT-TRICK

For England			For Australia		
W. Bates	Melbourne	1882–83	F. R. Spofforth	Melbourne	1878–79
J. Briggs	Sydney	1891–92	H. Trumble	Melbourne	1901–02
J. T. Hearne	Leeds	1899	H. Trumble	Melbourne	1903–04

WICKET-KEEPING

W. A. Oldfield in Tests v. England dismissed 90 men: 59 caught, 31 stumped.
A. A. Lilley dismissed 84 Australians.

SCORERS OF OVER 2,000 RUNS

	Innings	Not Outs	Runs	Highest Innings	Average
D. G. Bradman	63	7	5028	334	89.78
J. B. Hobbs	71	4	3636	187	54.26
W. R. Hammond	58	3	2852	251	51.85
H. Sutcliffe	46	5	2741	194	66.85
C. Hill	76	1	2660	188	35.46
L. Hutton	49	6	2428	364	56.46
R. N. Harvey	68	5	2416	167	38.34
V. Trumper	74	5	2263	185*	32.79
S. E. Gregory	92	7	2193	201	25.80
W. W. Armstrong	71	9	2172	158	35.03
A. R. Morris	43	2	2080	206	50.73

BOWLERS WITH 100 WICKETS

	Runs	Wickets	Average
H. Trumble	2945	141	20.88
M. A. Noble	2862	115	24.88
R. R. Lindwall	2559	114	22.44
W. Rhodes	2616	109	24.00
S. F. Barnes	2288	106	21.58
C. V. Grimmett	3439	106	32.44
A. V. Bedser	2859	104	27.49
G. Giffen	2791	103	27.09
W. J. O'Reilly	2587	102	25.36
R. Peel	1715	102	16.81
C. T. B. Turner	1670	101	16.53

ENGLAND v. SOUTH AFRICA

Season	Visiting Captain	Won by England	Won by South Africa	Drawn	Total
1888–89	C. A. Smith (E.)	2	0	0	2
1891–92	W. W. Read (E.)	1	0	0	1
1895–96	Lord Hawke (E.)	3	0	0	3
1898–99	Lord Hawke (E.)	2	0	0	2
1905–06	P. F. Warner (E.)	1	4	0	5
1907	P. W. Sherwell (S.A.)	1	0	2	3
1909–10	H. D. G. Leveson Gower (E.)	2	3	0	5
1912	F. Mitchell (S.A.)	3	0	0	3
1913–14	J. W. H. T. Douglas (E.)	4	0	1	5
1922–23	F. T. Mann (E.)	2	1	2	5
1924	H. W. Taylor (S.A.)	3	0	2	5
1927–28	Capt. R. T. Stanyforth (E.)	2	2	1	5
1929	H. G. Deane (S.A.)	2	0	3	5
1930–31	A. P. F. Chapman (E.)	0	1	4	5
1935	H. F. Wade (S.A.)	0	1	4	5
1938–39	W. R. Hammond (E.)	1	0	4	5
1947	A. Melville (S.A.)	3	0	2	5
1948–49	F. G. Mann (E.)	2	0	3	5
1951	A. D. Nourse (S.A.)	3	1	1	5
1955	J. E. Cheetham (S.A.)	3	2	0	5
1956–57	P. B. H. May (E.)	2	2	1	5
1960	D. J. McGlew (S.A.)	3	0	2	5
1964–65	M. J. K. Smith (E)	1	0	4	5
1965	P. L. van der Merwe (S.A.)	0	1	2	3
	In South Africa	25	13	20	58
	In England	21	5	18	44
	Totals	46	18	38	102

HIGHEST TOTALS

By England

654 (5 wkts.)	Durban	1938–39
608 ..	Johannesburg	1948–49
559 (9 wkts., dec.)	Cape Town	1938–39
554 (8 wkts.)	Lord's	1947
551 ..	Nottingham	1947
534 (6 wkts.)	The Oval	1935
531 (2 wkts.)	Lord's	1924

By South Africa

538 ..	Leeds	1951
533 ..	Nottingham	1947
530 ..	Durban	1938–39
521 (8 wkts.)	Manchester	1955
513 (8 wkts.)	Cape Town	1930–31
500 ..	Leeds	1955
492 (8 wkts.)	The Oval	1929

SMALLEST TOTALS

By England

76 ..	Leeds	1907

By South Africa

30 ..	Port Elizabeth	1895–96
30 ..	Edgbaston	1924
35 ..	Cape Town	1898–99

RECORD PARTNERSHIPS FOR EACH WICKET

By England

359 for 1st	L. Hutton and C. Washbrook, at Johannesburg	1948–49
280 for 2nd	P. A. Gibb and W. J. Edrich, at Durban	1938–39
370 for 3rd	W. J. Edrich and D. C. S. Compton, at Lord's	1947
197 for 4th	W. R. Hammond and L. E. G. Ames, at Cape Town	1938–39
237 for 5th	D. C. S. Compton and N. W. D. Yardley, at Nottingham	1947
206 for 6th	K. F. Barrington and J. M. Parks, at Durban	1964–65
115 for 7th	M. C. Bird and J. W. H. T. Douglas, at Durban	1913–14
154 for 8th	H. R. Bromley-Davenport and C. W. Wright, at Johannesburg	1895–96
71 for 9th	H. Wood and J. T. Hearne, at Cape Town	1891–92
92 for 10th	A. C. Russell and A. E. R. Gilligan, at Durban	1922–23

By South Africa

260 for 1st	I. J. Siedle and B. Mitchell, at Cape Town	1930–31
198 for 2nd	E. A. B. Rowan and C. B. van Ryneveld, at Leeds	1951
319 for 3rd	A. Melville and A. D. Nourse, junr., at Nottingham	1947
214 for 4th	H. W. Taylor and H. G. Deane, at The Oval	1929
157 for 5th	A. J. Pithey and J. H. B. Waite, at Johannesburg	1964–65
171 for 6th	P. L. Winslow and J. H. B. Waite, at Manchester	1955
123 for 7th	H. G. Deane and E. P. Nupen, at Durban	1927–28
109 for 8th	B. Mitchell and L. Tuckett, at The Oval	1947
137 for 9th	E. L. Dalton and A. B. C. Langton, at The Oval	1935
103 for 10th	H. G. Owen-Smith and A. J. Bell, at Leeds	1929

INDIVIDUAL HUNDREDS IN THE MATCHES

For England (87)

120	R. Abel, Cape Town	1888–9
148*	L. E. G. Ames, The Oval	1935
115	L. E. G. Ames, Cape Town	1938–9
148*	K. F. Barrington, Durban	1964–5
121	K. F. Barrington, Johannesburg	1964–5
117	G. Boycott, Port Elizabeth	1964–5
104†	L. C. Braund, Lord's	1907
208	D. C. S. Compton, Lord's	1947
163†	D. C. S. Compton, Nottingham	1947
115	D. C. S. Compton, Manchester	1947
113	D. C. S. Compton, The Oval	1947
114	D. C. S. Compton, Johannesburg	1948–9
114	D. C. S. Compton, Nottingham	1951
158	D. C. S. Compton, Manchester	1955
101	M. C. Cowdrey, Cape Town	1956–7
155	M. C. Cowdrey, The Oval	1960

105	M. C. Cowdrey, Nottingham	1965
104	D. Denton, Johannesburg	1909–10
172	E. R. Dexter, Johannesburg	1964–5
119†	J. W. H. T. Douglas Durban	1913–14
219	W. J. Edrich, Durban	1938–9
191	W. J. Edrich, Manchester	1947
189	W. J. Edrich, Lord's	1947
143	F. L. Fane, Johannesburg	1905–6
129	C. B. Fry, The Oval	1907
106†	P. A. Gibb, Johannesburg	1938–9
120	P. A. Gibb, Durban	1938–9
138*	W. R. Hammond, Birmingham	1929
136*	W. R. Hammond, Durban	1930–1
101*	W. R. Hammond, The Oval	1929
181	W. R. Hammond, Cape Town	1938–9
120	W. R. Hammond, Durban	1938–9
140	W. R. Hammond, Durban	1938–9
122	T. Hayward, Johannesburg	1895–6
132	E. Hendren, Leeds	1924
142	E. Hendren, The Oval	1924
124	A. J. L. Hill, Cape Town	1895–6
187	J. B. Hobbs, Cape Town	1909–10
211	J. B. Hobbs, Lord's	1924
100	L. Hutton, Leeds	1947
158	L. Hutton, Johannesburg	1948–9
123	L. Hutton, Johannesburg	1948–9
100	L. Hutton, Leeds	1951
110*	D. J. Insole, Durban	1956–7
102	M. Leyland, Lord's	1929
161	M. Leyland, The Oval	1935
136*	F. G. Mann, Port Elizabeth	1948–9
138†	P. B. H. May, Leeds	1951
112	P. B. H. May, Lord's	1955
117	P. B. H. May, Manchester	1955
102	C. P. Mead, Jo'burg	1913–14
117	C. P. Mead, Port Elizabeth	1913–14
181	C. P. Mead, Durban	1922–3
122*	P. H. Parfitt, Johannesburg	1964–5
108*	J. M. Parks, Durban	1964–5
117† / 100	E. Paynter, Johannesburg	1938–9
243	E. Paynter, Durban	1938–9
175	G. Pullar, The Oval	1960
152	W. Rhodes, Jo'burg	1913–14
117†	P. E. Richardson, Jo'burg	1956–7
108	R. W. V. Robins, Manchester	1935
140 / 111	A. C. Russell, Durban	1922–3
137	R. T. Simpson, Nottingham	1951
121	M. J. K. Smith, Cape Town	1964–5
119†	R. H. Spooner, Lord's	1912
122	H. Sutcliffe, Lord's	1924
102	H. Sutcliffe, Jo'burg	1927–8
114	H. Sutcliffe, Birmingham	1929
100	H. Sutcliffe, Lord's	1929
104 / 109*	H. Sutcliffe, The Oval	1929
100*	M. W. Tate, Lord's	1929
122	E. Tyldesley, Jo'burg	1927–8
100	E. Tyldesley, Durban	1927–8
112	J. T. Tyldesley, Cape Town	1898–9
112	B. H. Valentine, Cape Town	1938–9
132*†	P. F. Warner, Jo'burg	1898–9
195	C. Washbrook, Jo'burg	1948–9
111	A. J. Watkins, Jo'burg	1948–9
134*	H. Wood, Cape Town	1891–2
115*	F. E. Woolley, Jo'burg	1922–3
134*	F. E. Woolley, Lord's	1924
154	F. E. Woolley, Manchester	1929
113	R. E. S. Wyatt, Manchester	1929
149	R. E. S. Wyatt, Nottingham	1935

For South Africa (58)

138	E. J. Barlow, Cape Town	1964–5
144*	K. C. Bland, Johannesburg	1964–5
127	K. C. Bland, The Oval	1965
125	P. G. Van der Byl, Durban	1938–9
120	R. H. Catterall, B'ham	1924
120	R. H. Catterall, Lord's	1924
119	R. H. Catterall, Durban	1927–8
117	E. L. Dalton, The Oval	1935
102	E. L. Dalton, Jo'burg	1938–9
116*	W. R. Endean, Leeds	1955
123	G. A. Faulkner, Jo'burg	1909–10
112	T. L. Goddard, Johannesburg	1964–5
102	M. Hathorn, Jo'burg	1905–6

104*	D. J. McGlew, Manchester	1955
133	D. J. McGlew, Leeds	1955
142	R. A. McLean, Lord's	1955
100	R. A. McLean, Durban	1956–7
109	R. A. McLean, Manchester	1960
103	A. Melville, Durban	1938–9
189 } 104* }	A. Melville, Nottingham	1947
117	A. Melville, Lord's	1947
123	B. Mitchell, Cape Town	1930–1
164*	B. Mitchell, Lord's	1935
128	B. Mitchell, The Oval	1935
109	B. Mitchell, Durban	1938–9
120 } 189* }	B. Mitchell, The Oval	1947
120	B. Mitchell, Cape Town	1948–9
120	A. D. Nourse, junr., Cape Town	1938–9
103	A. D. Nourse, junr., Durban	1938–9
149	A. D. Nourse, junr., Nottingham	1947
115	A. D. Nourse, junr., Manchester	1947
129*	A. D. Nourse, junr., Johannesburg	1948–9
112	A. D. Nourse, junr., Cape Town	1948–9
208	A. D. Nourse, junr., Nottingham	1951
129	H. G. Owen-Smith, Leeds	1929
154	A. J. Pithey, Cape Town	1964–5
137	R. G. Pollock, Port Elizabeth	1964–5
125	R. G. Pollock, Nottingham	1965
156*	E. A. B. Rowan, Johannesburg	1948–9
236	E. A. B. Rowan, Leeds	1951
115	P. W. Sherwell, Lord's	1907
141	I. J. Siedle, Cape Town	1930–1
106	J. H. Sinclair, Cape Town	1898–9
109	H. W. Taylor, Durban	1913–14
176	H. W. Taylor, Jo'burg	1922–3
101	H. W. Taylor, Jo'burg	1922–3
102	H. W. Taylor, Durban	1922–3
101	H. W. Taylor, Jo'burg	1927–8
121	H. W. Taylor, The Oval	1929
117	H. W. Taylor, Cape Town	1930–1
124	K. G. Viljoen, Manchester	1935
125	W. W. Wade, Port Elizabeth	1948–9
113	J. H. B. Waite, Manchester	1955
147	G. C. White, Jo'burg	1905–6
118	G. C. White, Durban	1909–10
108	P. L. Winslow, Manchester	1955

† *Signifies hundred on debut in England–South Africa Tests.*

P. F. Warner carried his bat through the second innings.

The highest score by a South African batsman on debut is 93* by A. D. Nourse sen., at Johannesburg in 1905–6.

P. N. F. Mansell made 90 at Leeds in 1951, the best on debut in England.

A. Melville, B. Mitchell, E. Paynter, A. C. Russell and H. Sutcliffe are the only players who have made two separate hundreds in a match in these Tests.

HIGHEST RUN AGGREGATES BY A BATSMAN IN A RUBBER

England in England	753 (av. 94.12)	D. C. S. Compton	1947
England in South Africa	653 (av. 81.62)	E. Paynter	1938–39
South Africa in England	621 (av. 69.00)	A. D. Nourse, junr.	1947
South Africa in South Africa	582 (av. 64.66)	H. W. Taylor	1922–23

HIGHEST WICKET AGGREGATES BY A BOWLER IN A RUBBER

England in England	34 (av. 8.29)	S. F. Barnes	1912
England in South Africa	49 (av. 10.93)	S. F. Barnes	1913–14
South Africa in England	26 (av. 21.84)	H. J. Tayfield	1955
South Africa in England	26 (av. 22.57)	N. A. T. Adcock	1960
South Africa in South Africa	37 (av. 17.18)	H. J. Tayfield	1956–57

HIGHEST MATCH AGGREGATES

1,981 for 35 wkts., at Durban	1938–39
1,477 for 33 wkts., at The Oval	1947
1,458 for 31 wkts., at Nottingham	1947

LOWEST MATCH AGGREGATES

378 for 30 wkts., at The Oval	1912
382 for 30 wkts., at Cape Town	1888–89

THE HAT-TRICK

For England		For South Africa	
G. A. Lohmann, Port Elizabeth	1895–96	G. Griffin, Lord's	1960
T. W. Goddard, Jo'burg	1938–39		

At Leeds in 1947 K. Cranston finished South Africa's second innings by taking 4 wickets in one over of six balls for no runs but this did not include the hat-trick.

ENGLAND v. WEST INDIES

THE WISDEN TROPHY

Season	Visiting Captain	Won by England	Won by West Indies	Drawn	Total
1928	R. K. Nunes (W.I.)	3	0	0	3
1929–30	F. S. G. Calthorpe (E.)	1	1	2	4
1933	G. C. Grant (W.I.)	2	0	1	3
1934–35	R. E. S. Wyatt (E.)	1	2	1	4
1939	R. S. Grant (W.I.)	1	0	2	3
1947–48	G. O. Allen (E.)	0	2	2	4
1950	J. D. Goddard (W.I.)	1	3	0	4
1953–54	L. Hutton (E.)	2	2	1	5
1957	J. D. Goddard (W.I.)	3	0	2	5
1959–60	P. B. H. May (E.)	1	0	4	5
1963	F. M. Worrell (W.I.)	1	3	1	5
1966	G. S. Sobers (W.I.)	1	3	1	5
	In West Indies	5	7	10	22
	In England	12	9	7	28
	Totals	17	16	17	50

HIGHEST TOTALS FOR AN INNINGS

By England

849	Kingston	1930
619	(6 wkts.), Nottingham	1957
583	(4 wkts.), Birmingham	1957
537	Port of Spain	1954

By West Indies

681	(8 wkts.), Port of Spain	1954
563	(8 wkts.), Bridgetown	1960
558	Nottingham	1950
535	(7 wkts.), Kingston	1935
503	The Oval	1950

LOWEST TOTALS FOR AN INNINGS

By England

103	Kingston	1935
103	The Oval	1950

By West Indies

86	The Oval (2nd inns.)	1957
89	The Oval (1st inns.)	1957
91	Birmingham	1963
97	Lord's	1933

RECORD PARTNERSHIPS FOR EACH WICKET

By England

212 for 1st	C. Washbrook and R. T. Simpson, at Nottingham	1950
266 for 2nd	P. E. Richardson and T. W. Graveney, at Nottingham	1957
264 for 3rd	L. Hutton and W. R. Hammond, at The Oval	1939
411 for 4th	P. B. H. May and M. C. Cowdrey, at Birmingham	1957
130 for 5th	C. Milburn and T. W. Graveney, at Lord's	1966
161 for 6th	T. E. Bailey and T. G. Evans, at Manchester	1950
197 for 7th	M. J. K. Smith and J. M. Parks, at Port of Spain	1960
217 for 8th	T. W. Graveney and J. T. Murray, at The Oval	1966
89 for 9th	P. J. Sharpe and G. A. R. Lock at Birmingham	1963
128 for 10th	K. Higgs and J. A. Snow, at The Oval	1966

By West Indies

173 for 1st	G. Carew and A. G. Ganteaume, at Port of Spain	..	1947–48
228 for 2nd	R. K. Nunes and G. A. Headley, at Kingston ..	..	1929–30
338 for 3rd	E. D. Weekes and F. M. Worrell, at Port of Spain	..	1953–54
399 for 4th	G. S. Sobers and F. M. Worrell, at Bridgetown ..	..	1959–60
265 for 5th	S. M. Nurse and G. S. Sobers, at Leeds	..	1966
274 for 6th	G. S. Sobers and D. A. J. Holford, at Lord's ..	..	1966
154 for 7th	O. G. Smith and J. D. Goddard, at Nottingham	..	1957
99 for 8th	C. A. McWatt and J. K. Holt, at Georgetown ..	..	1953–54
36 for 9th	C. C. Griffith and W. W. Hall, at The Oval ..	..	1966
55 for 10th	F. M. Worrell and S. Ramadhin, at Nottingham	..	1957

INDIVIDUAL HUNDREDS IN THE MATCHES

For England (48)

105	L. E. G. Ames, Port of Spain	1930
149	L. E. G. Ames, Kingston	1930
126	L. E. G. Ames, Kingston	1935
107†	A. H. Bakewell, The Oval	1933
128†	K. F. Barrington, Bridgetown	1960
121	K. F. Barrington, Port of Spain	1960
120†	D. C. S. Compton, Lord's	1939
133	D. C. S. Compton, Port of Spain	1954
154†	M. C. Cowdrey, Birmingham...............	1957
152	M. C. Cowdrey, Lord's..	1957
114	M. C. Cowdrey, Kingston	1960
119	M. C. Cowdrey, Port of Spain	1960
136*†	E. R. Dexter, Bridgetown	1960
110	E. R. Dexter, Georgetown	1960
104	T. G. Evans, Manchester	1950
258	T. W. Graveney, Nottingham...............	1957
164	T. W. Graveney, The Oval	1957
109	T. W. Graveney, Nottingham	1966
165	T. W. Graveney, The Oval	1966
140†	S. C. Griffith, Port of Spain	1948
138	W. R. Hammond, The Oval	1939
205*	E. Hendren, Port of Spain	1930
123	E. Hendren, Georgetown	1930
159	J. B. Hobbs, The Oval...	1928
196†	L. Hutton, Lord's.......	1939
165*	L. Hutton, The Oval	1939
202*	L. Hutton, The Oval	1950
169	L. Hutton, Georgetown..	1954
205	L. Hutton, Kingston	1954
127	D. R. Jardine, Manchester	1933
135	P. B. H. May, Port of Spain	1954
285*	P. B. H. May, Birmingham	1957
104	P. B. H. May, Nottingham	1957
126*	C. Milburn, Lord's......	1966
112†	J. T. Murray, The Oval ..	1966
101*†	J. M. Parks, Port of Spain	1960
107	W. Place, Kingston	1948
126	P. E. Richardson, Nottingham...............	1957
107	P. E. Richardson, The Oval	1957
133	J. D. Robertson, Port of Spain	1948
152†	A. Sandham, Bridgetown	1930
325	A. Sandham, Kingston ..	1930
108	M. J. K. Smith, Port of Spain	1960
100†	R. Subba Row, Georgetown	1960
122†	E. Tyldesley, Lord's.....	1928
114†	C. Washbrook, Lord's ..	1950
102	C. Washbrook, Nottingham...............	1950
116†	W. Watson, Kingston ...	1954

For West Indies (48)

105	I. Barrow, Manchester...	1933
133	B. F. Butcher, Lord's ...	1963
209*	B. F. Butcher, Nottingham...............	1966
107	G. Carew, Port of Spain	1948
112†	A. G. Ganteaume, Port of Spain	1948
176†	G. A. Headley, Bridgetown	1930
114 } 112 }	G. A. Headley, Georgetown	1930
223	G. A. Headley, Kingston	1930
169*	G. A. Headley, Manchester	1933
270*	G. A. Headley, Kingston	1935
106 } 107 }	G. A. Headley, Lord's ..	1939
105*	D. A. J. Holford, Lord's .	1966
166	J. K. Holt, Bridgetown ..	1954
182	C. C. Hunte, Manchester	1963
108*	C. C. Hunte, The Oval ..	1963
135	C. C. Hunte, Manchester	1966
110	R. B. Kanhai, Port of Spain	1960

104 R. B. Kanhai, The Oval . 1966
137 S. M. Nurse, Leeds 1966
106 A. F. Rae, Lord's 1950
109 A. F. Rae, The Oval 1950
122 C. A. Roach, Bridgetown 1930
209 C. A. Roach, Georgetown 1930
161† O. G. Smith, Birmingham 1957
168 O. G. Smith, Nottingham 1957
226 G. S. Sobers, Bridgetown 1960
147 G. S. Sobers, Kingston .. 1960
145 G. S. Sobers, Georgetown 1960
102 G. S. Sobers, Leeds 1963
161 G. S. Sobers, Manchester 1966
163* G. S. Sobers, Lord's 1966
174 G. S. Sobers, Leeds 1966
168* C. L. Walcott, Lord's ... 1950
220 C. L. Walcott, Bridgetown 1954
124 C. L. Walcott, Port of Spain 1954
116 C. L. Walcott, Kingston . 1954
141 E. D. Weekes, Kingston . 1948
129 E. D. Weekes, Nottingham 1950
206 E.D.Weekes, Port of Spain 1954
137 K. H. Weekes, The Oval 1939
131* F. M. Worrell, Georgetown 1948
261 F. M. Worrell, Nottingham................ 1950
138 F. M. Worrell, The Oval. 1950
167 F. M. Worrell, Port of Spain 1954
191* F. M. Worrell, Nottingham 1957
197* F. M. Worrell, Bridgetown 1960

† Signifies hundred on debut in England–West Indies Test. S. C. Griffith provided the only instance for England of a player hitting his maiden century in first-class cricket in his FIRST Test.

HAT-TRICK

P. J. Loader for England, at Leeds............ 1957

ENGLAND v. NEW ZEALAND

THE W. J. JORDAN TROPHY

Season	Visiting Captain	Won by England	Won by New Zealand	Drawn	Total
1929–30	A. H. H. Gilligan .....(E.)	1	0	3	4
1931	T. C. Lowry ....(N.Z.)	1	0	2	3
1932–33	D. R. Jardine ....(E.)	0	0	2	2
1937	M. L. Page ....(N.Z.)	1	0	2	3
1946–47	W. R. Hammond .....(E.)	0	0	1	1
1949	W. A. Hadlee.......(N.Z.)	0	0	4	4
1950–51	F. R. Brown..........(E.)	1	0	1	2
1954–55	L. Hutton ....(E.)	2	0	0	2
1958	J. R. Reid ....(N.Z.)	4	0	1	5
1958–59	P. B. H. May.........(E.)	1	0	1	2
1962–63	E. R. Dexter ....(E.)	3	0	0	3
1965	J. R. Reid..........(N.Z.)	3	0	0	3
1965–66	M. J. K. Smith ....(E.)	0	0	3	3
	In New Zealand	8	0	11	19
	In England	9	0	9	18
	Totals	17	0	20	37

HIGHEST TOTALS FOR AN INNINGS

BY ENGLAND

562 (7 wkts., dec.) Auckland 1962–3
560 (8 wkts., dec.), Christchurch 1932–33
550 Christchurch 1950–51
548 (7 wkts., dec.), Auckland............... 1932–33

BY NEW ZEALAND

484 Lord's 1949
469 (9 wkts., dec.), Lord's . 1931
440 Wellington........... 1929–30

LOWEST TOTALS FOR AN INNINGS

BY ENGLAND

181 Christchurch 1929–30

BY NEW ZEALAND

26 Auckland 1954–55
47 Lord's 1958
67 Leeds 1958

INDIVIDUAL HUNDREDS IN THE MATCHES

For England (39)

122† G. O. Allen, Lord's 1931
137† L. E. G. Ames, Lord's... 1931
103 L. E. G. Ames, Christchurch 1933
134* T. E. Bailey, Christchurch 1951
126† K. F. Barrington, Auckland.................1962–3
163 K. F. Barrington, Leeds 1965
137 K. F. Barrington, Birmingham................. 1965
109 E. H. Bowley, Auckland.. 1930
114 D. C. S. Compton, Leeds 1949
116 D. C. S. Compton, Lord's 1949
128* M. C. Cowdrey, Wellington 1962–3
119 M. C. Cowdrey, Lord's .. 1965
141 E. R. Dexter, Christchurch 1959
117 K. S. Duleepsinhji, Auckland................. 1930
109 K. S. Duleepsinhji, The Oval 1931
310*†J. H. Edrich, Leeds...... 1965
100 W. J. Edrich, The Oval . 1949
100* W. R. Hammond, The Oval 1931
227 W. R. Hammond, Christchurch 1933
336* W. R. Hammond, Auckland.................. 1933
140 W. R. Hammond, Lord's 1937
114† J. Hardstaff, Lord's 1937
103 J. Hardstaff, The Oval .. 1937
100 L. Hutton, Manchester .. 1937
101 L. Hutton, Leeds 1949
206 L. Hutton, The Oval 1949
125† B. R. Knight, Auckland .1962–3
196 G. B. Legge, Auckland .. 1930
113* P. B. H. May, Leeds 1958
101 P. B. H. May, Manchester 1958
124* P. B. H. May, Auckland. 1959
104*†C. A. Milton, Leeds 1958
131*†P. H. Parfitt, Auckland..1962–3
100† P. E. Richardson, Birmingham................. 1958
121† J. D. Robertson, Lord's . 1949
103† R. T. Simpson, Manchester 1949
117† H. Sutcliffe, The Oval ... 1931
109* H. Sutcliffe, Manchester . 1931
103* C. Washbrook, Leeds ... 1949

For New Zealand (11)

104 B. E. Congdon, Christchurch 1966
136 C. S. Dempster, Wellington 1930
120 C. S. Dempster, Lord's .. 1931
206 M. P. Donnelly, Lord's .. 1949
116 W. A. Hadlee, Christchurch 1947
117† J. E. Mills, Wellington .. 1930
104 M. L. Page, Lord's...... 1931
100 J. R. Reid, Christchurch 1962–3
114 B. W. Sinclair, Auckland 1966
101 B. Sutcliffe, Manchester . 1949
116 B. Sutcliffe, Christchurch 1951

† *Signifies hundred on first appearance in England–N.Z. Tests.*

RECORD PARTNERSHIPS FOR EACH WICKET

For England

147 for 1st	L. Hutton and R. T. Simpson, at The Oval	1949
369 for 2nd	J. H. Edrich and K. F. Barrington, at Leeds	1965
245 for 3rd	W. R. Hammond and J. Hardstaff, at Lord's	1937
166 for 4th	K. F. Barrington and M. C. Cowdrey, at Auckland ..	1962–63
242 for 5th	W. R. Hammond and L. E. G. Ames, at Christchurch ..	1932–33
240 for 6th	P. H. Parfitt and B. R. Knight, at Auckland	1962–63
108 for 7th	F. R. Brown and W. Voce, at Christchurch	1932–33
246 for 8th	L. E. G. Ames and G. O. Allen, at Lord's	1931
163 for 9th	M. C. Cowdrey and A. C. Smith, at Wellington ..	1962–3
41 for 10th	K. F. Barrington and F. E. Rumsey, at Birmingham ..	1965

For New Zealand

276 for 1st	C. S. Dempster and J. E. Mills, at Wellington	1929–30
131 for 2nd	B. Sutcliffe and J. R. Reid, at Christchurch	1950–51
118 for 3rd	C. S. Dempster and M. L. Page, at Lord's	1931
142 for 4th	M. L. Page and R. C. Blunt, at Lord's	1931
120 for 5th	F. B. Smith and M. P. Donnelly, at Lord's	1949
99 for 6th	W. A. Hadlee and M. L. Page, at Manchester	1937
104 for 7th	B. Sutcliffe and V. Pollard, at Birmingham	1965

104 for 8th	A. W. Roberts and D. A. R. Moloney, at Lord's ..	1937
64 for 9th	J. Cowie and T. B. Burtt, at Christchurch	1946–47
57 for 10th	F. L. H. Mooney and J. Cowie, at Leeds	1949

MOST WICKETS IN A RUBBER

G. A. R. Lock, 34 wickets for 7.47 in five Tests, 1958.

HAT-TRICK

M. J. C. Allom, in his first Test match, England v. New Zealand at Christchurch in 1929–30, dismissed T. C. Lowry, K. C. James and F. T. Badcock with consecutive balls and took four wickets in five balls.

ENGLAND v. INDIA

Season	Visiting Captain	Won by England	Won by India	Drawn	Total
1932	C. K. Nayudu............(I.)	1	0	0	1
1933–34	D. R. Jardine ....(E.)	2	0	1	3
1936	Maharaj of Vizianagram..(I.)	2	0	1	3
1946	Nawab of Pataudi ....(I.)	1	0	2	3
1951–52	N. D. Howard ....(E.)	1	1	3	5
1952	V. S. Hazare ....(I.)	3	0	1	4
1959	D. K. Gaekwad ....(I.)	5	0	0	5
1961–62	E. R. Dexter ....(E.)	0	2	3	5
1963–64	M. J. K. Smith ....(E.)	0	0	5	5
	In England	12	0	4	16
	In India.....................	3	3	12	18
	Totals	15	3	16	34

HIGHEST TOTALS FOR AN INNINGS

BY ENGLAND

571	.. (8 wkts.), Manchester	1936
559	.. (8 wkts.), Kanpur...	1963–64
537	.. Lord's	1952
500	.. (8 wkts.), Bombay ..	1961–62
497	.. (5 wkts.), Kanpur...	1961–62
490	.. Manchester	1959
483	.. (8 wkts.), Leeds.....	1959
471	.. (8 wkts.), The Oval .	1936
456	.. Bombay	1951–52

BY INDIA

485	.. (9 wkts.), Bombay ..	1951–52
467	.. (8 wkts.), Kanpur...	1961–62
466	.. New Delhi	1961–62
463	.. (4 wkts.), Delhi.....	1963–64
457	.. (9 wkts.), Madras ..	1951–52
457	.. (7 wkts.), Madras...	1963–64

LOWEST TOTAL FOR AN INNINGS

BY ENGLAND

134	.. Lord's	1936

BY INDIA

58	.. Manchester	1952
82	.. Manchester	1952
93	.. Lord's	1936
98	.. The Oval	1952

INDIVIDUAL HUNDREDS IN THE MATCHES

FOR ENGLAND (25)

151	K. F. Barrington Bombay	1961–2
172	K. F. Barrington, Kanpur	1961–2
113*	K. F. Barrington, New Delhi..............	1961–2
160	M. C. Cowdrey, Leeds .	1959
107	M. C. Cowdrey, Calcutta	1963–64
151	M. C. Cowdrey, Delhi.	1963–64
126*	E. R. Dexter, Kanpur ..	1961–2
104	T. G. Evans, Lord's....	1952

175† T. W. Graveney, Bombay 1951–2
167 W. R. Hammond, Manchester 1936
217 W. R. Hammond, The Oval 1936
205* J. Hardstaff, junr., Lord's 1946
150 L. Hutton, Lord's...... 1952
104 L. Hutton, Manchester . 1952
127 B. R. Knight, Kanpur.. 1963–64
106 P. B. H. May, Nottingham.......... 1959
121 P. H. Parfitt, Kanpur.. 1963–64
131 G. Pullar, Manchester . 1959
119 G. Pullar, Kanpur 1961–2
119 D. S. Sheppard, The Oval 1952
100† M. J. K. Smith, Manchester 1959
136† B. H. Valentine, Bombay 1933–4
102 C. F. Walters, Madras .. 1933–4
138*† A. J. Watkins, New Delhi 1951–2
128 T. S. Worthington, The Oval 1936

For India (26)

118† L. Amarnath, Bombay . 1933–4
112† A. A. Baig, Manchester. 1959
105† Hanumant Singh, Delhi 1963–64
164* V. S. Hazare, New Delhi 1951–2
155 V. S. Hazare, Bombay .. 1951–2
127 M. L. Jaisimha, New Delhi.......... 1961–2
129 M. L. Jaisimha, Calcutta 1963–64
192 B. K. Kunderam, Madras.......... 1963–64
100 B. K. Kunderam, Delhi 1963–64
133 V. L. Manjrekar, Leeds 1952
189* V. L. Manjrekar, New Delhi.......... 1961–2
108 V. L. Manjrekar, Madras.......... 1963–64
184 V. Mankad, Lord's 1952
114 V. M. Merchant, Manchester 1936
128 V. M. Merchant, The Oval 1946
154 V. M. Merchant, New Delhi.......... 1951–2
112 Mushtaq Ali, Manchester 1936
122* R. G. Nadkarni, Kanpur 1963–64
103 Nawab of Pataudi, Madras.......... 1961–2
203* Nawab of Pataudi, Delhi.......... 1963–64
115 D. G. Phadkar, Calcutta 1951–2
140 P. Roy, Bombay....... 1951–2
111 P. Roy, Madras 1951–2
130* P. R. Umrigar, Madras. 1951–2
118 P. R. Umrigar, Manchester 1959
147* P. R. Umrigar, Kanpur. 1961–2

† *Signifies hundred on debut in England–India Tests.*

RECORD PARTNERSHIPS FOR EACH WICKET

For England

159 for 1st	P. E. Richardson and G. Pullar, at Bombay	1961–62
164 for 2nd	G. Pullar and K. F. Barrington, at Delhi	1961–62
169 for 3rd	R. Subba Row and M. J. K. Smith, at The Oval ..	1959
266 for 4th	W. R. Hammond and T. S. Worthington, at The Oval	1936
182 for 5th	J. Hardstaff and P. A. Gibb, at Lord's..	1946
159 for 6th	T. W. Graveney and T. G. Evans, at Lord's	1952
102 for 7th	R. Illingworth and R. Swetman, at The Oval	1959
138 for 8th	R. W. V. Robins and H. Verity, at Manchester ..	1936
81 for 9th	R. W. Barber and G. A. R. Lock, at Kanpur ..	1961–62
55 for 10th	G. Millman and D. R. Smith, at Madras	1961–62

For India

203 for 1st	V. M. Merchant and Mushtaq Ali, at Manchester ..	1936
143 for 2nd	B. K. Kunderam and D. N. Sardesai, at Madras ..	1963–64
211 for 3rd	V. M. Merchant and V. S. Hazare, at New Delhi ..	1951–52
	V. Mankad and V. S. Hazare, at Lord's	1952
222 for 4th	V. S. Hazare and V. L. Manjrekar, at Leeds	1952
190 for 5th	Nawab of Pataudi and C. G. Borde, at Delhi	1963–64
105 for 6th	V. S. Hazare and D. G. Phadkar, at Leeds	1952
153 for 7th	C. G. Borde and A. S. Durani, at Bombay	1963–64
101 for 8th	R. G. Nadkarni and F. M. Engineer, at Madras ..	1961–62
54 for 9th	G. S. Ramchand and S. G. Shinde, at Lord's	1952
51 for 10th	R. G. Nadkarni and B. S. Chandrasekhar, at Calcutta	1963–64

ENGLAND v. PAKISTAN

Season	Visiting Captain		Won by England	Won by Pakistan	Drawn	Total
1954	A. H. Kardar	(P.)	1	1	2	4
1961–62	E. R. Dexter	(E.)	1	0	2	3
1962	Javed Burki	(P.)	4	0	1	5
	In England		5	1	3	9
	In Pakistan		1	0	2	3
	Totals		6	1	5	12

HIGHEST TOTALS FOR AN INNINGS

By England		By Pakistan	
558 for 6 Nottingham	1954	404 for 8 Karachi	1961–62
544 for 5 Birmingham	1962	393 for 7 Dacca	1961–62
507 .. Karachi	1961–62	387 for 9 Lahore	1961–62
480 for 5 The Oval	1962	355 .. Lord's	1962

LOWEST TOTALS FOR AN INNINGS

By England		By Pakistan	
130 .. The Oval	1954	87 .. Lord's	1954

INDIVIDUAL HUNDREDS IN THE MATCHES

By England (14)

139†	K. F. Barrington, Lahore	1961–62
278	D. C. S. Compton, Nottingham	1954
159†	M. C. Cowdrey, Birmingham	1962
182	M. C. Cowdrey, The Oval	1962
205	E. R. Dexter, Karachi	1961–62
172	E. R. Dexter, The Oval	1962
153	T. W. Graveney, Lord's	1962
114	T. W. Graveney, Nottingham	1962
111	P. H. Parfitt, Karachi	1961–62
101*	P. H. Parfitt, Birmingham	1962
119	P. H. Parfitt, Leeds	1962
101*	P. H. Parfitt, Nottingham	1962
165	G. Pullar, Dacca	1961–62
101	R. T. Simpson, Nottingham	1954

By Pakistan (8)

109	Alim-ud-Din, Karachi	1961–62
138†	Javed Burki, Lahore	1961–62
140	Javed Burki, Dacca	1961–62
101	Javed Burki, Lord's	1962
111 } 104 }	Hanif Mohammad, Dacca	1961–62
100*	Mushtaq Mohammad, Nottingham	1962
101	Nasim-ul-Ghani, Lord's	1962

† *Signifies hundred on debut in England–Pakistan Tests.*

RECORD PARTNERSHIPS FOR EACH WICKET

For England

198 for 1st	G. Pullar and R. W. Barber, at Dacca	1961–62
248 for 2nd	M. C. Cowdrey and E. R. Dexter, at The Oval	1962
192 for 3rd	K. F. Barrington and M. J. K. Smith, at Lahore	1961–62
188 for 4th	E. R. Dexter and P. H. Parfitt, at Karachi	1961–62
192 for 5th	D. C. S. Compton and T. E. Bailey, at Nottingham	1954
153 for 6th	P. H. Parfitt and D. A. Allen, at Birmingham	1962
67 for 7th	P. H. Parfitt and J. T. Murray, at Leeds	1962
99 for 8th	P. H. Parfitt and D. A. Allen, at Leeds	1962
76 for 9th	T. W. Graveney and F. S. Trueman, at Lord's	1962
51 for 10th	D. A. Allen and J. B. Statham, at Leeds	1962

FOR PAKISTAN

122 for 1st	Hanif Mohammad and Alim-ud-Din, at Dacca.. ..	1961–62
137 for 2nd	Imtiaz Ahmed and Mushtaq Mohammad, at The Oval	1962
156 for 3rd	Hanif Mohammad and Javed Burki, at Dacca	1961–62
153 for 4th	Javed Burki and Mushtaq Mohammad, at Lahore ..	1961–62
197 for 5th	Javed Burki and Nasim-ul-Ghani, at Lord's	1962
81 for 6th	Imtiaz Ahmed and Mushtaq Mohammad, at Karachi	1961–62
51 for 7th	Saeed Ahmed and Nasim-ul-Ghani, at Nottingham ..	1962
49 for 8th	Alim-ud-Din and Fazal Mahmood, at Karachi.. ..	1961–62
58 for 9th	Wazir Mohammad and Zulfiqar Ahmed, at The Oval..	1954
52 for 10th	Afaq Hussain and Haseeb Ahsan, at Lahore	1961–62

AUSTRALIA v. SOUTH AFRICA

Season	Visiting Captain	Won by Australia	Won by S. Africa	Drawn	Total
1902–03	J. Darling .... (A.)	2	0	1	3
1910–11	P. W. Sherwell (S.A.)	4	1	0	5
1912	S. E. Gregory (A.) F. Mitchell ....(S.A.)	2	0	1	3
1921–22	H. L. Collins ....(A.)	1	0	2	3
1931–32	H. B. Cameron.........(S.A.)	5	0	0	5
1935–36	V. Y. Richardson ......(A.)	4	0	1	5
1949–50	A. L. Hassett ....(A.)	4	0	1	5
1952–53	J. E. Cheetham ....(S.A.)	2	2	1	5
1957–58	I. D. Craig.............(A.)	3	0	2	5
1963–64	T. L. Goddard........(S.A.)	1	1	3	5
	In South Africa	14	0	7	21
	In Australia	12	4	4	20
	In England	2	0	1	3
	Totals	28	4	12	44

HIGHEST TOTALS FOR AN INNINGS

BY AUSTRALIA

578 ..	Melbourne.......	1910–11
554 ..	Melbourne.......	1931–32
549 for 7	Port Elizabeth ...	1949–50
530 ..	Adelaide	1952–53
528 ..	Sydney	1910–11
526 for 7	Cape Town	1949–50
520 ..	Melbourne.......	1952–53
513 ..	Adelaide.........	1931–32

BY SOUTH AFRICA

595 ..	Adelaide	1963–64
506 ..	Melbourne.......	1910–11
491 ..	Johannesburg	1935–36
482 ..	Adelaide	1910–11
472 for 8	Johannesburg	1921–22

SMALLEST TOTALS FOR AN INNINGS

BY AUSTRALIA

75 ..	Durban..........	1949–50
153 ..	Melbourne.......	1931–32
163 ..	Durban..........	1957–58

BY SOUTH AFRICA

36 & 45†	Melbourne.......	1931–32
80 ..	Melbourne.......	1910–11
85 ..	Johannesburg	1902–03

† The aggregate of 81 (12 extras) for two innings is the smallest in Test cricket.

INDIVIDUAL HUNDREDS IN THE MATCHES

FOR AUSTRALIA (53)

159*	W. W. Armstrong, Johannesburg..............	1902–3
132	W. W. Armstrong, Melbourne	1910–11
132†	W. Bardsley, Sydney ..	1910–11
121	W. Bardsley, Manchester	1912
164	W. Bardsley, Lord's...	1912
122	R. Benaud, Johannesburg	1957–58
100	R. Benaud, Johannesburg	1957–58
169†	B. C. Booth, Brisbane..	1963–64

102* B. C. Booth, Sydney .. 1963–64
226† D. G. Bradman, Brisbane 1931–2
112 D. G. Bradman, Sydney 1931–2
167 D. G. Bradman, Melbourne 1931–2
299* D. G. Bradman, Adelaide 1931–2
121 W. A. Brown, Cape Town 1935–6
189 J. W. Burke, Cape Town 1957–58
109† A. G. Chipperfield, Durban........... 1935–6
203 H. L. Collins, Johannesburg 1921–2
112 J. H. Fingleton Cape Town 1935–6
108 J. H. Fingleton, Johannesburg........... 1935–6
118 J. H. Fingleton, Durban 1935–6
119 J. M. Gregory, Johannesburg........... 1921–2
178 R. N. Harvey, Cape Town 1949–50
151 R. N. Harvey, Durban. 1949–50
116 R. N. Harvey, Port Elizabeth 1949–50
100 R. N. Harvey, Johannesburg 1949–50
109 R. N. Harvey, Brisbane 1952–53
190 R. N. Harvey, Sydney.. 1952–53
116 R. N. Harvey, Adelaide 1952–53
205 R. N. Harvey, Melbourne 1952–53
112† A. L. Hassett, Johannesburg........... 1949–50
167 A. L. Hassett, Port Elizabeth 1949–50
163 A. L. Hassett, Adelaide 1952–53
142† C. Hill, Johannesburg.. 1902–3
191 C. Hill, Sydney 1910–11
100 C. Hill, Melbourne.... 1910–11
114 C. E. Kelleway, Manchester 1912
102 C. E. Kelleway, Lord's 1912
157 W. M. Lawry, Melbourne 1963–64
101† S. J. Loxton, Johannesburg 1949–50
137 C. G. Macartney, Sydney 1910–11
116 C. G. Macartney, Durban 1921–2
149 S. J. McCabe, Durban. 1935–6
189* S. J. McCabe, Johannesburg........... 1935–6
154 C. C. McDonald, Adelaide 1952–53
111 A. R. Morris, Johannesburg........... 1949–50
157 A. R. Morris, Port Elizabeth 1949–50
118 } 101* } J. R. Moroney, Johannesburg 1949–50
127† K. E. Rigg, Sydney .. 1931–2
142 J. S. Ryder, Cape Town 1921–2
159 V. T. Trumper, Melbourne 1910–11
214* V. T. Trumper, Adelaide 1910–11
161 W. M. Woodfull, Melbourne 1931–2

For South Africa (25)

114† E. J. Barlow, Brisbane. 1963–64
109 E. J. Barlow, Melbourne 1963–64
201 E. J. Barlow, Adelaide. 1963–64
126 K. C. Bland, Sydney .. 1963–64
162* W. R. Endean, Melbourne 1952–53
204 G. A. Faulkner, Melbourne 1910–11
115 G. A. Faulkner, Adelaide 1910–11
122* G. A. Faulkner, Manchester 1912
152 C. N. Frank, Johannesburg 1921–2
108 D. J. McGlew, Johannesburg........... 1957–58
105 D. J. McGlew, Durban 1957–58
111 A. D. Nourse, senr., Johannesburg 1921–2
231 A. D. Nourse, junr., Johannesburg 1935–6
114 A. D. Nourse, junr., Cape Town 1949–50
122 R. G. Pollock, Sydney. 1963–64
175 R. G. Pollock, Adelaide 1963–64
143 E. A. B. Rowan, Durban 1949–50
101 J. H. Sinclair, Johannesburg 1902–3
104 J. H. Sinclair, Cape Town 1902–3
103 S. J. Snooke, Adelaide. 1910–11
111 K. G. Viljoen, Melbourne 1931–2
115 J. H. B. Waite, Johannesburg........... 1957–58
134 J. H. B. Waite, Durban 1957–58
105 J. W. Zulch, Adelaide.. 1910–11
150 J. W. Zulch, Sydney... 1910–11

† *Signifies hundred on debut in Australia–South Africa Tests.*

RECORD PARTNERSHIPS FOR EACH WICKET

For Australia

233 for 1st	J. H. Fingleton and W. A. Brown, at Cape Town ..	1935–36
275 for 2nd	C. C. McDonald and A. L. Hassett, at Adelaide ..	1952–53
242 for 3rd	W. Bardsley and C. E. Kelleway, at Lord's	1912
168 for 4th	R. N. Harvey and K. R. Miller, at Sydney	1952–53
143 for 5th	W. W. Armstrong and V. T. Trumper, at Melbourne ..	1910–11
107 for 6th	C. E. Kelleway and V. S. Ransford, at Melbourne ..	1910–11
160 for 7th	R. Benaud and G. D. McKenzie, at Sydney	1963–64
89 for 8th	R. Benaud and A. T. W. Grout, at Johannesburg ..	1957–58
78 for 9th	D. G. Bradman and W. J. O'Reilly, at Adelaide ..	1931–32
	K. D. Mackay and I. W. Meckiff, at Johannesburg ..	1957–58
82 for 10th	V. S. Ransford and W. J. Whitty, at Johannesburg ..	1910–11

For South Africa

176 for 1st	D. J. McGlew and T. L. Goddard, at Johannesburg ..	1957–58
173 for 2nd	L. J. Tancred and C. B. Llewellyn, at Johannesburg ..	1902–03
341 for 3rd	E. J. Barlow and R. G. Pollock, at Adelaide	1963–64
206 for 4th	C. N. Frank and A. D. Nourse, senr., at Johannesburg	1921–22
129 for 5th	J. H. B. Waite and W. R. Endean, at Johannesburg ..	1957–58
118 for 6th	K. C. Bland and J. D. Lindsay, at Sydney	1963–64
111 for 7th	J. E. Cheetham and P. N. F. Mansell, at Melbourne ..	1952–53
124 for 8th	A. D. Nourse, senr. and E. A. Halliwell, at Johannesburg	1902–03
54 for 9th	J. M. Blanckenberg and E. P. Nupen, at Johannesburg	1921–22
53 for 10th	S. J. Pegler and L. A. Stricker, at Adelaide	1910–11

MOST WICKETS IN A RUBBER

44, for 14.59 runs in five Tests, C. V. Grimmett, for Australia in 1935–36.
30, for 28.10 runs in five Tests, H. J. Tayfield, for South Africa in 1952–53.

HAT-TRICKS

T. J. Matthews (Australia), twice on the same afternoon in separate innings against South Africa at Manchester, 1912. A feat without parallel in Test cricket.

L. F. Kline (Australia), Cape Town, 1957–58.

AUSTRALIA v. NEW ZEALAND

One match has been played, at Wellington, where Australia beat New Zealand by an innings and 103 runs in March 1946. No centuries were scored.

AUSTRALIA v. WEST INDIES

THE F. M. WORRELL TROPHY

Season	Visiting Captain	Won by W. Indies	Won by Australia	Drawn	Tie	Total
1930–31	G. C. Grant.......(W.I.)	1	4	0	0	5
1951–52	J. D. Goddard.....(W.I.)	1	4	0	0	5
1954–55	I. W. Johnson ......(A.)	0	3	2	0	5
1960–61	F. M. Worrell .....(W.I.)	1	2	1	1	5
1964–65	R. B. Simpson ......(A.)	2	1	2	0	5
	In Australia	3	10	1	1	15
	In West Indies	2	4	4	0	10
	Totals	5	14	5	1	25

HIGHEST TOTALS FOR AN INNINGS

By Australia			By West Indies		
758–8*	Kingston	1954–5	573	Bridgetown	1965
668	Bridgetown	1954–5	510	Bridgetown	1954–5
650–6*	Bridgetown	1965			
600–9*	Port of Spain	1954–5			
558	Brisbane	1930–1			
516	Port of Spain	1965			
515–9*	Kingston	1954–5			

LOWEST TOTALS FOR AN INNINGS

By Australia			By West Indies		
82	Adelaide	1951–2	78	Sydney	1951–2
			90	Sydney	1930–1
			99	Melbourne	1930–1

INDIVIDUAL HUNDREDS IN THE MATCHES

For Australia (26)

128	R. G. Archer, Kingston	1954–5
121	R. Benaud, Kingston	1954–5
117	B. C. Booth, Port of Spain	1965
223	D. G. Bradman, Brisbane	1930–1
152	D. G. Bradman, Melbourne	1930–1
143	R. M. Cowper, Port of Spain	1965
102	R. M. Cowper, Bridgetown	1965
133	R. N. Harvey, Kingston	1954–5
133	R. N. Harvey, Port of Spain	1954–5
204	R. N. Harvey, Kingston	1954–5
132	A. L. Hassett, Sydney	1951–2
102	A. L. Hassett, Melbourne	1951–2
146†	A. F. Kippax, Adelaide	1930–1
210	W. M. Lawry, Bridgetown	1965
118	R. R. Lindwall, Bridgetown	1954–5
110	C. C. McDonald, Port of Spain	1954–5
127	C. C. McDonald, Kingston	1954–5
129	K. R. Miller, Sydney	1951–2
147	K. R. Miller, Kingston	1954–5
137	K. R. Miller, Bridgetown	1954–5
109	K. R. Miller, Kingston	1954–5
111	A. R. Morris, Port of Spain	1954–5
181†	N. C. O'Neill, Brisbane	1960–1
183	W. H. Ponsford, Sydney	1930–1
109	W. H. Ponsford, Brisbane	1930–1
201	R. B. Simpson, Bridgetown	1965

For West Indies (24)

108	F C. M. Alexander, Sydney	1960–1
219	D. Atkinson, Bridgetown	1954–5
117	B. F. Butcher, Port of Spain	1965
122	C. Depeiza, Bridgetown	1954–5
102*	G. A. Headley, Brisbane	1930–1
105	G. A. Headley, Sydney	1930–1
110	C. C. Hunte, Melbourne	1960–1
117 } 115 }	R. B. Kanhai, Adelaide	1960–1
129	R. B. Kanhai, Bridgetown	1965
121	R. B. Kanhai, Port of Spain	1965
123*	F. R. Martin, Sydney	1930–1
201	S. M. Nurse, Bridgetown	1965
104†	O. G. Smith, Kingston	1954–5
132	G. S. Sobers, Brisbane	1960–1
168	G. S. Sobers, Sydney	1960–1
104	J. B. Stollmeyer, Sydney	1951–2
108	C. L. Walcott, Kingston	1954–5
126 } 110 }	C. L. Walcott, Port of Spain	1954–5
155 } 110 }	C. L. Walcott, Kingston	1954–5
139	E. D. Weekes, Port of Spain	1954–5
108	F. M. Worrell, Melbourne	1951–2

† Signifies hundred on debut in Australia–W. Indies Tests. F. C. M. Alexander hit the only century of his career in a Test Match.

RECORD PARTNERSHIPS FOR EACH WICKET

For Australia

382 for 1st	W. M. Lawry and R. B. Simpson, at Bridgetown ..	1965
229 for 2nd	W. H. Ponsford and D. G. Bradman, at Brisbane ..	1930–31
295 for 3rd	C. C. McDonald and R. N. Harvey, at Kingston ..	1954–55
235 for 4th	A. L. Hassett and K. R. Miller, at Sydney	1951–52
220 for 5th	K. R. Miller and R. G. Archer, at Kingston	1954–55
206 for 6th	K. R. Miller and R. G. Archer, at Bridgetown.. ..	1954–55
134 for 7th	A. K. Davidson and R. Benaud, at Brisbane	1960–61
137 for 8th	R. Benaud and I. W. Johnson, at Kingston	1954–55
97 for 9th	K. D. Mackay and J. W. Martin, at Melbourne ..	1960–61
66 for 10th	K. D. Mackay and L. F. Kline, at Adelaide	1960–61

For West Indies

145 for 1st	C. C. Hunte and B. Davis, at Bridgetown	1965
163 for 2nd	C. C. Hunte and R. B. Kanhai, at Adelaide	1960–61
242 for 3rd	C. L. Walcott and E. D. Weekes, at Port of Spain ..	1954–55
179 for 4th	C. L. Walcott and G. S. Sobers, at Kingston	1954–55
128 for 5th	G. S. Sobers and S. M. Nurse, at Sydney	1960–61
138 for 6th	C. L. Walcott and O. G. Smith, at Kingston	1954–55
347 for 7th	C. Depeiza and D. Atkinson, at Bridgetown	1954–55
74 for 8th	F. C. M. Alexander and L. R. Gibbs, at Sydney ..	1960–61
86 for 9th	F. C. M. Alexander and W. W. Hall, at Brisbane ..	1960–61
31 for 10th	W. W. Hall and A. L. Valentine, at Brisbane	1960–61

The 347 *partnership for the 7th wicket is the highest for this wicket in* 1*st class cricket.*

HAT-TRICK

L. R. Gibbs (West Indies), Adelaide 1960–61

AUSTRALIA v. INDIA

Season	Visiting Captain		Won by Australia	Won by India	Drawn	Total
1947–48	L. Amarnath................	(I.)	4	0	1	5
1956–57	I. W. Johnson	(A.)	2	0	1	3
1959–60	R. Benaud	(A.)	2	1	2	5
1964	R. B. Simpson	(A.)	1	1	1	3
	In Australia		4	0	1	5
	In India........................		5	2	4	11
	Totals		9	2	5	16

HIGHEST TOTALS FOR AN INNINGS

By Australia

674 Adelaide............ 1947–48
575 (8 wkts., dec.), Melbourne 1947–48

By India

381 Adelaide............ 1947–48

LOWEST TOTALS FOR AN INNINGS

By Australia

105 Kanpur............. 1959–60
107 Sydney 1947–48

By India

58 Brisbane............ 1947–48
67 Melbourne.......... 1947–48

INDIVIDUAL HUNDREDS IN THE MATCHES

For Australia (15)

112 S. G. Barnes, Adelaide. 1947–8
201 D. G. Bradman, Adelaide 1947–8
185† D. G. Bradman, Brisbane 1947–8
132 } D. G. Bradman, Mel-
127* } bourne 1947–8
161 J. W. Burke, Bombay.. 1956–7
101 L. Favell, Madras..... 1959–60
153 R. N. Harvey, Melbourne 1947–8
140 R. N. Harvey, Bombay. 1956–7
114 R. N. Harvey, New Delhi............ 1959–60
102 R. N. Harvey, Bombay. 1959–60
198* A. L. Hassett, Adelaide 1947–8
100* A. R. Morris, Melbourne 1947–8
163 N. C. O'Neill, Bombay 1959–60
113 N. C. O'Neill, Calcutta 1959–60

For India (8)

108 N. J. Contractor, Bombay 1959–60
145 } V. S. Hazare, Adelaide. 1947–8
116 }
116 V. Mankad, Melbourne 1947–8
111 V. Mankad, Melbourne 1947–8
128*†Nawab of Pataudi, Madras........... 1964
123 D. G. Phadkar, Adelaide 1947–8
109 G. S. Ramchand, Bombay 1956–7

† *Signifies hundred on debut in Australia–India Tests.*

AUSTRALIA v. PAKISTAN

Season	Visiting Captain	Won by Australia	Won by Pakistan	Drawn	Total
1956–57	I. W. Johnson (A.)	0	1	0	1
1959–60	R. Benaud (A.)	2	0	1	3
1964	R. B. Simpson (A.)	0	0	1	1
1964	Hanif Mohammad (P.)	0	0	1	1
	Totals	2	1	3	6

HIGHEST TOTALS FOR AN INNINGS

By Australia

448 Melbourne 1964

By Pakistan

414 Karachi............ 1964

LOWEST TOTALS FOR AN INNINGS

By Australia

80 Karachi 1956–57

By Pakistan

134 Dacca 1959–60

INDIVIDUAL HUNDREDS IN THE MATCHES

For Australia (3)

134 N. C. O'Neill, Lahore. 1959–60
153† } R. B. Simpson,
115 } Karachi......... 1964

For Pakistan (4)

101* Hanif Mohammad, Karachi.......... 1959–60
104 Hanif Mohammad, Melbourne....... 1964
166† K. Ibadulla, Karachi . 1964
166 Saeed Ahmad, Lahore 1959–60

† *Signifies hundred on debut in Australia–Pakistan Tests.*

SOUTH AFRICA v. NEW ZEALAND

Season	Visiting Captain	Won by S. Africa	Won by N. Zealand	Drawn	Total
1931–32	H. B. Cameron........(S.A.)	2	0	0	2
1952–53	J. E. Cheetham ....(S.A.)	1	0	1	2
1953–54	G. O. Rabone ....(N.Z.)	4	0	1	5
1961–62	J. R. Reid ....(N.Z.)	2	2	1	5
1963–64	T. L. Goddard.........(S.A.)	0	0	3	3
	In South Africa	6	2	2	10
	In New Zealand	3	0	4	7
	Totals	9	2	6	17

HIGHEST TOTALS:—South Africa, 524 for 8, Wellington, 1952–53.
New Zealand, 505, Cape Town, 1953–54.

LOWEST TOTALS:—South Africa, 148, Johannesburg, 1953–54.
New Zealand, 79, Johannesburg, 1953–54.

INDIVIDUAL HUNDREDS IN THE MATCHES

FOR SOUTH AFRICA (11)

122* X. Balaskas, Wellington 1931–2
103† J. A. J. Christy, Christchurch 1931–2
116 W. R. Endean, Auckland. 1952–3
255*† D. J. McGlew, Wellington 1952–3
127 D. J. McGlew, Durban 1961–2
120 D. J. McGlew, Johannesburg 1961–2
113 R. A. McLean, Cape Town 1961–2
101 R. A. McLean, Durban. 1953–4
113† B. Mitchell, Christchurch 1931–2
109† A. R. A. Murray, Wellington 1952–3
101 J. H. B. Waite, Johannesburg 1961–2

FOR NEW ZEALAND (7)

109 P. T. Barton, Port Elizabeth................ 1961–2
101 P. G. Harris, Cape Town 1961–2
107 G. O. Rabone, Durban.. 1953–4
135 J. R. Reid, Cape Town.. 1953–4
142 J. R. Reid, Johannesburg 1961–2
138 B. W. Sinclair, Auckland................ 1963–4
100† H. G. Vivian, Wellington 1931–2

† *Signifies hundred on debut in South Africa–New Zealand Tests.*

WEST INDIES v. NEW ZEALAND

Season	Visiting Captain	Won by West Indies	Won by New Zealand	Drawn	Total
1951–52	J. D. Goddard (W.I.)	1	0	1	2
1955–56	D. Atkinson (W.I.)	3	1	0	4
	Totals	4	1	1	6

HIGHEST TOTALS FOR AN INNINGS

BY WEST INDIES

546 for 6 Auckland 1951–52

BY NEW ZEALAND

255 Auckland 1955–56

LOWEST TOTALS FOR AN INNINGS

By West Indies			By New Zealand		
77	Auckland	1955–56	74	Dunedin	1955–56

E. Weekes scored 123, 103 and 156 in three successive Tests in 1956.
J. B. Stollmeyer (152), C. L. Walcott (115) and F. M. Worrell (100) have also scored hundreds for West Indies. No instances for N.Z.

WEST INDIES v. INDIA

Season	Visiting Captain	Won by West Indies	Won by India	Drawn	Total
1948–49	J. D. Goddard..........(W.I.)	1	0	4	5
1952–53	V. S. Hazare..............(I.)	1	0	4	5
1958–59	F. C. M. Alexander......(W.I.)	3	0	2	5
1961–62	N. J. Contractor ....(I.)	5	0	0	5
	In West Indies	6	0	4	10
	In India........................	4	0	6	10
	Totals	10	0	10	20

HIGHEST TOTALS FOR AN INNINGS

By West Indies			By India		
644 for 8	New Delhi	1958–59	454	New Delhi	1948–49
631 for 8	Kingston	1961–62	444	Kingston	1952–53
631	New Delhi	1948–49	422	Port of Spain	1961–62
629 for 6	Bombay	1948–49	417	Port of Spain	1952–53

LOWEST TOTALS FOR AN INNINGS

By West Indies			By India		
222	Kanpur..............	1958–59	98	Port of Spain	1961–62
228	Bridgetown	1952–53	124	Calcutta	1958–59

INDIVIDUAL HUNDREDS IN THE MATCHES

For West Indies (33)

103	B. F. Butcher, Calcutta.	1958–9
142	B. F. Butcher, Madras..	1958–9
107†	R. J. Christiani, New Delhi..............	1948–9
101†	G. E. Gomez, New Delhi	1948–9
123	J. K. Holt, New Delhi..	1958–9
256	R. B. Kanhai, Calcutta .	1958–9
138	R. B. Kanhai, Kingston.	1961–2
139	R. B. Kanhai, Port of Spain	1961–2
125	E. D. McMorris, Kingston	1961–2
115†	B. H. Pairaudeau, Port of Spain	1952–3
104	A. F. Rae, Bombay	1948–9
109	A. F. Rae, Madras	1948–9
100	O. G. Smith, New Delhi	1958–9
142*	G. S. Sobers, Bombay ..	1958–9
198	G. S. Sobers, Kanpur ..	1958–9
106*	G. S. Sobers, Calcutta ..	1958–9
153	G. S. Sobers, Kingston .	1961–2
104	G. S. Sobers, Kingston .	1961–2
100*	J. S. Solomon, New Delhi	1958–9
160	J. B. Stollmeyer, Madras	1948–9
104*	J. B. Stollmeyer, Port of Spain	1952–3
152†	C. L. Walcott, New Delhi	1948–9
108	C. L. Walcott, Calcutta.	1948–9
125	C. L. Walcott, Georgetown	1952–3
118	C. L. Walcott, Kingston	1952–3
128†	E. D. Weekes, New Delhi	1948–9
194	E. D. Weekes, Bombay .	1948–9
162 / 101	E. D. Weekes, Calcutta .	1948–9
207	E. D. Weekes, Port of Spain	1952–3
161	E. D. Weekes, Port of Spain	1952–3
109	E. D. Weekes, Kingston	1952–3
237	F. M. Worrell, Kingston	1952–3

For India (13)

114*†H. R. Adhikari, New Delhi 1948–9
163* M. L. Apte, Port of Spain 1952–3
109 C. G. Borde, New Delhi 1958–9
104 A. S. Durani, Port of Spain 1961–2
134* V. S. Hazare, Bombay .. 1948–9
122 V. S. Hazare, Bombay .. 1948–9
118 V. L. Manjrekar, Kingston 1952–3
112 R. S. Modi, Bombay 1948–9
106† Mushtaq Ali, Calcutta .. 1948–9
150 P. Roy, Kingston 1952–3
130 P. R. Umrigar, Port of Spain 1952–3
117 P. R. Umrigar, Kingston 1952–3
172* P. R. Umrigar, Port of Spain 1961–2

† *Signifies hundred on debut in West Indies–India Tests.*

WEST INDIES v. PAKISTAN

Season	Visiting Captain	Won by West Indies	Won by Pakistan	Drawn	Total
1957–58	A. H. Kardar ....(P.)	3	1	1	5
1958–59	F. C. M. Alexander (W.I.)	1	2	0	3
	Totals	4	3	1	8

HIGHEST TOTALS FOR AN INNINGS

By West Indies

790 for 3 Kingston 1957–58
579 for 9 Bridgetown 1957–58

By Pakistan

657 for 8 Bridgetown 1957–58

LOWEST TOTALS FOR AN INNINGS

By West Indies

76 Dacca 1958–59
146 Karachi 1958–59

By Pakistan

104 Lahore 1958–59
106 Bridgetown 1957–58

INDIVIDUAL HUNDREDS IN THE MATCHES

For West Indies (9)

142† C. C. Hunte, Bridgetown 1957–58
260 C. C. Hunte, Kingston 1957–58
114 C. C. Hunte, Georgetown 1957–58
217 R. B. Kanhai, Lahore . 1958–59
365* G. S. Sobers, Kingston 1957–58
125 } 109* } G. S. Sobers, Georgetown 1957–58
145 C. L. Walcott, Georgetown 1957–58
197† E. D. Weekes, Bridgetown 1957–58

For Pakistan (6)

337† Hanif Mohammad, Bridgetown 1957–58
103 Hanif Mohammad, Karachi 1958–59
122 Imtiaz Ahmed, Kingston 1957–58
150 Saeed Ahmed, Georgetown 1957–58
106 Wazir Mohammad, Kingston 1957–58
189 Wazir Mohammad, Port of Spain 1957–58

† *Signifies hundred on debut in West Indies–Pakistan Tests.*

INDIA v. NEW ZEALAND

Season	Visiting Captain	India	New Zealand	Drawn	Total
1955–56	H. B. Cave.......(N.Z.)	2	0	3	5
1965	J. R. Reid ....(N.Z.)	1	0	3	4
		3	0	6	9

Highest Totals:—India 537 (for three wickets, dec.), Madras, 531 (for seven wickets, dec.), and New Delhi, 1955–56. New Zealand 462 (for nine wickets dec.), Calcutta, 1965.

Lowest Totals:—India 132, Calcutta. New Zealand 136, Bombay.

INDIVIDUAL HUNDREDS IN THE MATCHES

For India (15)

109	C. G. Borde, Bombay ..	1965
177	V. L. Manjrekar, New Delhi..............	1955–6
118	V. L. Manjrekar, Hyderabad	1955–6
102	V. L. Manjrekar, Madras	1965
231	V. Mankad, Madras....	1955–6
223	V. Mankad, Bombay ...	1955–6
153	Nawab of Pataudi, Calcutta	1965
113	Nawab of Pataudi, New Delhi..............	1965
106*	G. S. Ramchand, Calcutta	1955–6
173	P. Roy, Madras	1955–6
100	P. Roy, Calcutta.......	1955–6
100*†	Kripal Singh, Hyderabad	1955–6
200*	D. N. Sardesai, Bombay	1965
106	D. N. Sardesai, New Delhi..............	1965
223	P. R. Umrigar, Hyderabad	1955–6

For New Zealand (8)

129	G. T. Dowling, Bombay	1965
102	J. W. Guy, Hyderabad .	1955–6
120	J. R. Reid, Calcutta....	1955–6
119*	J. R. Reid, New Delhi..	1955–6
230*	B. Sutcliffe, New Delhi .	1955–6
137*	B. Sutcliffe, Hyderabad .	1955–6
151*	B. Sutcliffe, Calcutta ...	1965
105†	B. R. Taylor, Calcutta..	1965

† *Signifies hundred on debut in India–New Zealand Tests.*

INDIA v. PAKISTAN

Season	Visiting Captain		Won by India	Won by Pakistan	Drawn	Total
1952–53	A. H. Kardar.........	(P.)	2	1	2	5
1954–55	V. Mankad	(I.)	0	0	5	5
1960–61	Fazal Mahmood	(P.)	0	0	5	5
	In India...................		2	1	7	10
	In Pakistan...............		0	0	5	5
	Totals		2	1	12	15

Highest Totals:—India, 539 (9 wkts., dec.), Madras, 1960–61. Pakistan 448 (8 wkts., dec.), Madras, 1960–61.

Lowest Totals:—India, 106, Lucknow, 1952–53. Pakistan, 150, Delhi, 1952–53.

INDIVIDUAL HUNDREDS IN THE MATCHES

For India (8)

177*	C. G. Borde, Madras...	1960–1
146*	V. S. Hazare, Bombay..	1952–3
110†	D. S. Shodhan, Calcutta	1952–3
102	P. R. Umrigar, Bombay	1952–3
108	P. R. Umrigar, Peshawar	1954–5
115	P. R. Umrigar, Kanpur.	1960–1
117	P. R. Umrigar, Madras.	1960–1
112	P. R. Umrigar, New Delhi..............	1960–1

For Pakistan (8)

103*	Alim-ud-Din, Karachi..	1954–5
135	Imtiaz Ahmed, Madras.	1960–1
142	Hanif Mohammad, Bahawalpur	1954–5
160	Hanif Mohammad, Bombay	1960–1
101	Mushtaq Mohammad, New Delhi	1960–1
124*	Nazar Mohammad, Lucknow	1952–3
121	Saeed Ahmed, Bombay.	1960–1
103	Saeed Ahmed, Madras..	1960–1

† *Signifies hundred on debut in India–Pakistan Tests.*

PAKISTAN v. NEW ZEALAND

Season	Visiting Captain	Won by Pakistan	Won by New Zealand	Drawn	Total
1955–56	H. B. Cave ....(N.Z.)	2	0	1	3
1965	Hanif Mohammad (P.)	0	0	3	3
1965	J. R. Reid .....(N.Z.)	2	0	1	3
	In Pakistan..............	4	0	2	6
	In New Zealand..........	0	0	3	3
	Totals................	4	0	5	9

HIGHEST TOTALS FOR AN INNINGS

By Pakistan

561 .. Lahore 1955–56

By New Zealand

482 for 6 dec. Lahore 1965

LOWEST TOTALS FOR AN INNINGS

By Pakistan

187 .. Wellington 1965

By New Zealand

70 .. Dacca 1955–56
79 .. Rawalpindi 1965

INDIVIDUAL HUNDREDS IN THE MATCHES

For Pakistan (7)

103 Hanif Mohammad, Dacca.................. 1955–6
100* Hanif Mohammad, Christchurch 1965
203* Hanif Mohammad, Lahore................ 1965
209 Imtiaz Ahmed, Lahore . 1955–6
126 Mohammad Ilyas, Karachi 1965
172 Saeed Ahmed, Lahore .. 1965
189 Waqar Hassan, Lahore . 1955–6

For New Zealand (3)

111 S. N. McGregor, Lahore 1955–6
128 J. R. Reid, Lahore 1965
130 B. W. Sinclair, Lahore.. 1965

HIGHEST TEST WICKET PARTNERSHIPS

413 for 1st	V. Mankad (231) and P. Roy (173) for India v. New Zealand, at Madras	1955–56
451 for 2nd	W. H. Ponsford (266) and D. G. Bradman (244) for Australia v. England, at The Oval	1934
370 for 3rd	W. J. Edrich (189) and D. C. S. Compton (208) for England v. South Africa, at Lord's	1947
411 for 4th	P. B. H. May (285*) and M. C. Cowdrey (154) for England v. West Indies, at Birmingham	1957
405 for 5th	S. G. Barnes (234) and D. G. Bradman (234) for Australia v. England, at Sydney	1946–47
346 for 6th	J. H. Fingleton (136) and D. G. Bradman (270) for Australia v. England, at Melbourne	1936–37
347 for 7th	D. Atkinson (219) and C. Depeiza (122) for West Indies v. Australia, at Bridgetown	1954–55
246 for 8th	L. E. G. Ames (137) and G. O. Allen (122) for England v. New Zealand, at Lord's	1931
163 for 9th	M. C. Cowdrey (128*) and A. C. Smith (69*) for England v. New Zealand, at Wellington	1962–63
130 for 10th	R. E. Foster (287) and W. Rhodes (40*) for England v. Australia, at Sydney	1903–04

YOUNGEST TEST PLAYERS

15 years 124 days	Mushtaq Mohammad	**Pakistan v. West Indies, at Lahore, 1958–59.**
16 years 248 days	Nasim-ul-Ghani	**Pakistan v. West Indies, at Barbados, 1957–58.**
16 years 352 days	Khalid Hassan	**Pakistan v. England, at Nottingham, 1954.**
17 years 122 days	J. E. D. Sealy	**West Indies v. England, at Kensington Oval, Barbados, 1929–30.**
17 years 239 days	I. D. Craig	**Australia v. South Africa, at Melbourne, 1952–53.**
17 years 245 days	G. S. Sobers	**West Indies v. England, at Kingston, 1953–54.**
17 years 265 days	V. L. Mehra	**India v. New Zealand, at Bombay, 1955–56.**
17 years 300 days	Hanif Mohammad	**Pakistan v. India, at New Delhi, 1952–53.**
18 years 44 days	Khalid Wazir	**Pakistan v. England, at Lord's, 1954.**
18 years 105 days	J. B. Stollmeyer	**West Indies v. England, at Lord's, 1939.**
18 years 149 days	D. B. Close	**England v. New Zealand, at Manchester, 1949.**
18 years 197 days	D. L. Freeman	**New Zealand v. England, at Christchurch, 1932–33**
18 years 232 days	T. W. Garrett	**Australia v. England, at Melbourne, 1876–77.**
18 years 267 days	H. G. Vivian	**New Zealand v. England, at Manchester, 1931.**

OLDEST PLAYERS ON TEST DEBUT

49 years 119 days	J. Southerton	**England v. Australia, Melbourne, 1876–77.**
47 years 275 days	Miran Bux	**Pakistan v. India, at Lahore, 1954–55.**
46 years 273 days	D. J. Blackie	**Australia v. England, Sydney, 1928–29.**
41 years 337 days	E. R. Wilson	**England v. Australia, Sydney, 1920–21.**
41 years 275 days	H. Ironmonger	**Australia v. England, Brisbane, 1928–29.**
41 years 28 days	R. J. Jamshedji	**India v. England, Bombay, 1933.**
40 years 346 days	C. A. Wiles	**West Indies v. England, Manchester, 1933.**
40 years 110 days	H. W. Lee	**England v. South Africa, Johannesburg, 1930–31.**
40 years 56 days	G. W. A. Chubb	**South Africa v. England, Nottingham, 1951.**
40 years 37 days	C. Ramaswami	**India v. England, Manchester, 1936.**
39 years 361 days	G. Challoner	**West Indies v. England, Lord's, 1928.**
39 years 360 days	A. Wood	**England v. Australia, The Oval, 1938.**
39 years 306 days	B. M. Gaskin	**West Indies v. England, at Bridgetown, 1948**

GENTLEMEN v. PLAYERS

The highest individual scores were:—

266*	J. B. Hobbs	Scarboro'	1925	**215**	W. G. Grace	The Oval	**1870**
247	R. Abel	The Oval	1901	203	T. Hayward	The Oval	**1904**
241	L. Hutton	Scarboro'	1953	201	L. E. G. Ames	Folkestone	**1933**
232*	C. B. Fry	Lord's	1903	195	R. Abel	The Oval	**1899**
223	C. P. Mead	Scarboro'	1911	**194***	E. Hendren	The Oval	**1932**
217	W. G. Grace	Brighton	1871				

W. G. Grace played no fewer than fifteen three-figure innings for Gentlemen v. Players. On his fifty-eighth birthday—at The Oval in July 1906—he scored 74.

J. B. Hobbs in all matches under this title scored 16 three-figure innings, and had an aggregate of 4,052 runs with an average of 54.75.

The match, first played in 1806, has not been contested since 1962, owing to the abolition of the amateur status in first-class cricket.

There were 137 matches played at Lord's from 1806; Players won 68, Gentlemen won 41 and 28 were drawn—Individual hundreds and results since 1919 appeared in *Wisden* 1963 page 358.

OXFORD v. CAMBRIDGE

Largest totals

503	Oxford	1900		432‡	Cambridge	1936
457	Oxford	1947		431	Cambridge	1932
453†	Oxford	1931		425	Cambridge	1938

Smallest totals

32	Oxford	1878		42	Oxford	1890
39	Cambridge	1858		47	Cambridge	1838

Highest individual scores

238*	Nawab of Pataudi (O.)	1931		193	D. C. H. Townsend (O.)	1934
211	G. Goonesena (C.)	1957		172*	J. F. Marsh (C.)	1904
201*	M. J. K. Smith (O.)	1954		171	R. E. Foster (O.)	1900
201	A. Ratcliffe (C.)	1931		170	M. Howell (O.)	1919

† For eight wickets. ‡ For nine wickets.

A. P. F. Chapman and M. P. Donnelly enjoy the following distinction: Chapman scored a century at Lord's in the University match (102*, 1922); for Gentlemen v. Players (160, 1922), (108, 1926); and for England v. Australia (121, 1930). M. P. Donnelly scored a century at Lord's in the University match (142, 1946); for Gentlemen v. Players (162*, 1947); and for New Zealand v. England (206, 1949).

A. Ratcliffe's 201 for Cambridge remained a record for the match for only one day, being beaten by the Nawab of Pataudi's 238* for Oxford next day.

M. J. K. Smith (Oxford) is the only player who has scored three hundreds; *201 in 1954, 104 in 1955 and 117 in 1956. His aggregate, 477, surpassed the previous best, 457, by the Nawab of Pataudi, 1929–31.

The following players have scored two hundreds: W. Yardley (Cambridge) 100 in 1870 and 130 in 1872; H. J. Enthoven (Cambridge) 104 in 1924 and 129 in 1925; The Nawab of Pataudi (Oxford) 106 in 1929 and 238 not out in 1931; A. Ratcliffe (Cambridge) 201 in 1931 and 124 in 1932; D. R. W. Silk (Cambridge) 116* in 1953 and 118 in 1954; J. M. Brearley (Cambridge) 113* in 1962 and 119 in 1964.

F. C. Cobden, in the Oxford and Cambridge match in 1870, performed the hat-trick by taking the last three wickets and won an extraordinary game for Cambridge by two runs. The feat is without parallel in first-class cricket. Cobden obtained the last three wickets of Oxford in each innings—a curious coincidence. Other hat-tricks, all for Cambridge, have been credited to A. G. Steel (1879), P. H. Morton (1880), J. F. Ireland (1911), and R. G. H. Lowe (1926).

S. E. Butler, in the 1871 match, took all the wickets in the Cambridge first innings. The feat is unique in University matches. He bowled 24 overs and a ball. In the follow-on he took 5 wickets for 57, making 15 for 95 runs in the match.

P. R Le Couteur scored 160 and took eleven Cambridge wickets for 66 runs in 1910—the best all-round performance in the history of the match.

Of the 122 matches played, Cambridge have won 50 and Oxford 44. The remaining twenty-eight games have been drawn. The match dates back to 1827.

TIE MATCHES IN FIRST-CLASS CRICKET

There have been twenty since the First World War:—

Somerset v. Sussex, at Taunton 1919
(The last Sussex batsman not allowed to bat under Law 45.)
Orange Free State v. Eastern Province, at Bloemfontein 1925–26
(Eastern Province had two wickets to fall.)
Essex v. Somerset, at Chelmsford 1926
(Essex had one man to go in, and the M.C.C. ruled that the game should rank as a tie. The ninth wicket fell half a minute before time.)
Gloucestershire v. Australians, at Bristol 1930
Victoria v. M.C.C., at Melbourne 1932–33
(Victoria's third wicket fell to the last ball of the match when one run was needed to win.)
Somerset, v. Worcestershire, at Kidderminster 1939
Southern Punjab v. Baroda, at Patiala 1945–46
Essex v. Northamptonshire, at Ilford 1947
Hampshire v. Lancashire, at Bournemouth 1947
D. G. Bradman's XI v. A. L. Hassett's XI, at Melbourne (Bradman's Testimonial) 1948–49
Hampshire v. Kent, at Southampton 1950
Sussex v. Warwickshire, at Hove 1952
Essex v. Lancashire, at Brentwood 1952
Northamptonshire v. Middlesex, at Peterborough.. 1953
Yorkshire v. Leicestershire, at Huddersfield 1954
Sussex v. Hampshire, at Eastbourne 1955
Victoria v. New South Wales, at Melbourne 1956–57
T. N. Pearce's XI v. New Zealanders, at Scarborough 1958
Essex v. Gloucestershire, at Leyton 1959
Australia v. West Indies (1st Test), at Brisbane 1960–61
Bahawalpur v. Lahore "B", at Bahawalpur 1961–62

Note.—Since 1948 a tie has been recognised only when the scores are level with all the wickets down in the fourth innings. This ruling applies to all grades of Cricket, and in the case of a one-day match to the second innings, provided that the match has not been brought to a further conclusion.

MATCHES BEGUN AND FINISHED IN ONE DAY

The most notable instances during the nineteenth and present centuries are:—

The B's v. England, at Lord's, June 13 1831
Cambridge University v. M.C.C. and Ground, at Cambridge, May 18 1837
M.C.C. and Ground v. Cambridge University, at Lord's, June 19 .. 1848
Gentlemen of Kent v. Gentlemen of England, at Lord's, July 1 .. 1850
North v. South, at Lord's, July 15.. 1850
M.C.C. and Ground v Sussex, at Lord's, June 2 1856
Surrey v. Sussex, at The Oval, July 16 1857
Kent v. England. at Lord's, July 5.. 1858
M.C.C. and Ground v. Oxford University, at Lord's, June 18 1863
North of Thames v. South of Thames, at Lord's July 8.. 1863
M.C.C. and Ground v. Surrey, at Lord's, May 14 1872
Middlesex v. Oxford University, at Prince's, June 18 1874
North v. South, at Lord's, May 17 1875
M.C.C. and Ground v. Oxford University. at Oxford. May 24 .. 1877
M.C.C. and Ground v. Australians, at Lord's, May 27 1878
M.C.C. and Ground v. Oxford University. at Oxford. May 28 .. 1880
An England XI v. Australians, at Aston Lower Grounds, Birmingham, May 26 1884
M.C.C. and Ground v. Lancashire, at Lord's, May 18 1886
North v. South, at Lord's, May 30 1887
Lancashire v. Surrey, at Manchester, August 2 1888

M.C.C. and Ground v. Notts, at Lord's, June 1	1891
Lancashire v. Somerset, at Old Trafford, August 9	1892
M.C.C. and Ground v. Sussex, at Lord's, May 2	1894
Lancashire v. Somerset, at Old Trafford, July 17	1894
Yorkshire v. Somerset, at Huddersfield, July 19	1894
Leicestershire v. Surrey, at Leicester, June 10	1897
Hampshire v. Yorkshire, at Southampton, May 27 (H. Baldwin's benefit)	1898
Middlesex v. Somerset, at Lord's, May 23 (W. Flowers' benefit) ..	1899
Yorkshire v. Worcestershire, at Bradford, May 7	1900
M.C.C. and Ground v. London County at Lord's, May 20	1903
Transvaal v. Orange Free State, at Johannesburg	1906
Middlesex v. Gentlemen of Philadelphia, at Lord's, July 20	1908
Gloucestershire v. Middlesex, at Bristol, August 26	1909
Kent v. Sussex, at Tonbridge, June 21	1919
Lancashire v. Somerset, at Manchester, May 21	1925
Madras v. Mysore, at Madras, November 4	1934
Ireland v. New Zealanders, at Dublin, September 11	1937
Derbyshire v. Somerset, at Chesterfield, June 11..	1947
Lancashire v. Sussex, at Manchester, July 12	1950
Surrey v. Warwickshire, at The Oval, May 16	1953
Somerset v. Lancashire, at Bath, June 6 (H. T. F. Buse's benefit) ..	1953
Kent v. Worcestershire, at Tunbridge Wells, June 15	**1960**

LARGE ATTENDANCES AND GATE RECEIPTS

933,513 persons (exclusive of about 10,000 who watched the last day's play of the Fifth Test free of charge) were present at the five Test matches between England and Australia in 1936–37, receipts amounting to £A90,909. The third Test at Melbourne broke the records for attendance: 350,534 persons were present.

£201,432, record receipts for any series, was paid by the 322,361 people who attended the five Tests between England and West Indies in England in 1966.

£200,194, was paid by the 549,650 people who attended the five Tests between England and Australia in England, 1953.

£58,602 is the largest sum of money taken at any cricket match in the world when England met West Indies at Lord's, 1966.

£57,716 was taken when England met Australia at Lord's, 1953. The attendance, 137,915, at that match remains the highest for Lord's.

90,800 attended the second day of the Fifth Test match between Australia and West Indies at Melbourne. The aggregate attendance was 274,404, the total receipts £A65,054 13s. 10d., a world record in Australian currency, but in sterling £52,040, 1960–61.

£A47,933 was taken in Australia when England played at Melbourne in the Third Test, 1954–55. The attendance at that match was 300,270. The full figures for the five Tests in 1954–55 were 707,510; receipts £A119,059.

Over 158,000 persons were present during the five days of the England v. Australia match at Leeds, and the total receipts were £34,000	1948
116,000 people were present during the four days of the England v. South Africa Test at Leeds, a record for any Test between the two countries	1951
Just under 115,000 persons were present during the four days of the England v. Australia match, at Lord's	1930
112,000 people attended first Test between South Africa and Australia, at Johannesburg, which was a record aggregate for South Africa	1957–58
99,614 people were present at the Fourth Test Match, England v. Australia, at Leeds (over in three days). (75,614 paid: receipts £14,189) ..	1938
Over 80,000 persons watched the play, Surrey v. Yorkshire, at The Oval, (Lees' benefit—£2,300—66,923 paid for admission)	July 1906
78,792 persons watched the play, Yorkshire v. Lancashire, at Leeds, (Hirst's benefit—£3,703)	August 1904

78,617 persons were present at the match between Lancashire and Yorkshire, at Manchester 1926
About 76,000 watched the play in the Surrey v. Kent match at The Oval 1920

BEST BENEFITS

£14,000	C. Washbrook, Lancashire v. Australians	1948
£13,047	J. B. Statham, Lancashire v. Australians	1961
£12,866	A. V. Bedser, Surrey v. Yorkshire	1953
£12,200	D. C. S. Compton, Middlesex v. Sussex	1949
£11,000	J. C. Laker, Surrey v. Yorkshire	1956
£10,702	K. F. Barrington, Surrey v. Yorkshire	1964
£9,750	J. M. Parks, Sussex (no match allotted)	1964
£9,713	L. Hutton, Yorkshire v. Middlesex	1950
£9,331	F. S. Trueman, Yorkshire v. Surrey	1962
£8,846	J. D. Bannister, Warwickshire v. Worcestershire	1964
£8,600	A. J. McIntyre, Surrey v. Yorkshire	1955
£8,154	D. B. Close, Yorkshire v. Surrey	1961
£8,129	J. H. Wardle, Yorkshire v. Surrey	1957
£8,083	W. E. Bowes, Yorkshire v. Middlesex	1947
£8,000	R. Pollard, Lancashire v. Derbyshire	1949

The following figures were records at the respective date of each match:

£4,106	R. Kilner, Yorkshire v. Middlesex	1925
£3,703	G. H. Hirst, Yorkshire v. Lancashire	1904

Sir Donald Bradman received £A10,000 from his Testimonial match, D. G. Bradman's XI v. A. L. Hassett's XI, 1948–49.

W. G. Grace was given three Testimonials which raised £1,458, £2,377 and £5,000, a total of £8,835.

Hedley Verity's Memorial Fund in 1945 yielded £8,233.

LORD'S CRICKET GROUND

Lord's and the M.C.C. were founded in 1787. The Club has enjoyed an uninterrupted career since that date, but there have been three grounds known as Lord's. The first (1787–1810) was situated where Dorset Square now is; the second (1809–13), at North Bank, had to be abandoned owing to the cutting of the Regent's Canal; and the third, opened in 1814, is that where the game is played to-day. It was not until 1866 that the freehold of Lord's was secured by the M.C.C. The present pavilion was erected in 1890 at a cost of £21,000.

THE LARGEST INDIVIDUAL SCORES MADE AT LORD'S ARE:—

316*	J. B. Hobbs, Surrey v. Middlesex	1926
315*	P. Holmes, Yorkshire v. Middlesex	1925
281*	W. H. Ponsford, Australians v. M.C.C.	1934
278	W. Ward, M.C.C. v. Norfolk (with E. H. Budd, T. Vigne and F. Ladbroke)	1820
278	D. G. Bradman, Australians v. M.C.C.	1938
277*	E. Hendren, Middlesex v. Kent	1922

THE GREATEST TOTALS OBTAINED THERE ARE:—

FIRST-CLASS MATCHES

729	(six wickets), Australia v. England	1930
665	West Indies v. Middlesex	1939
612	(eight wickets), Middlesex v. Nottinghamshire	1921
610	(five wickets), Australians v. Gentlemen of England	1948
609	(eight wickets), Cambridge University v. M.C.C. and Ground	1913
608	(seven wickets), Middlesex v. Hampshire	1919
607	M.C.C. and Ground v. Cambridge University	1902

MINOR MATCH

735 (nine wickets), M.C.C. and Ground v. Wiltshire 1888

DATES OF FORMATION OF COUNTY CLUBS NOW FIRST CLASS

County	First known county organisation	Present Club	
		Original date	Reorganisation, if substantial
DERBYSHIRE	Nov. 4 1870	Nov. 4 1870	—
ESSEX	By May 1790	Jan. 14 1876	—
GLAMORGAN	1864	July 6 1888	—
GLOUCESTERSHIRE	Nov. 3 1863	1871	—
HAMPSHIRE	April 3 1849	Aug. 12 1863	July 1879
KENT	Aug. 6 1842	Mar. 1 1859	Dec. 6 1870
LANCASHIRE	Jan. 12 1864	Jan. 12 1864	—
LEICESTERSHIRE	By Aug. 1820	Mar. 25 1879	—
MIDDLESEX	Dec. 15 1863	Dec. 15 1863	—
NORTHAMPTONSHIRE	1820	1820	July 31 1878
NOTTINGHAMSHIRE	Mar./Apr. 1841	Mar./Apr. 1841	Dec. 11 1866
SOMERSET	Oct. 15 1864	Aug. 18 1875	—
SURREY	Aug. 22 1845	Aug. 22 1845	—
SUSSEX	June 16 1836	Mar. 1 1839	Aug. 1857
WARWICKSHIRE	May 1826	Jan. 19 1884	—
WORCESTERSHIRE	1844	Mar. 5 1865	—
YORKSHIRE	March 7 1861	Jan. 8 1863	Dec. 10 1891

DATES OF FORMATION OF ENGLISH MINOR COUNTIES

County	First known county organisation	Present Club
BEDFORDSHIRE	May 1847	Nov. 3 1899
BERKSHIRE	By May 1841	March 17 1895
BUCKINGHAMSHIRE	Nov. 1864	Jan. 15 1891
CAMBRIDGESHIRE	March 13 1844	June 6 1891
CHESHIRE	1819	Sept. 29 1908
CORNWALL	1813	Nov. 12 1894
CUMBERLAND	Jan. 2 1884	April 10 1948
DEVON	1824	Nov. 26 1899
DORSET	1862 *or* 1871	Feb. 5 1896
DURHAM	Jan. 24 1874	May 10 1882
HERTFORDSHIRE	1838	March 8 1876
HUNTINGDONSHIRE	1831	Sept. 15 1948
LINCOLNSHIRE	1853	Feb. 18 1921
NORFOLK	Jan. 11 1827	Oct. 14 1876
NORTHUMBERLAND	1838	Dec. 1895
OXFORDSHIRE	1787	Dec. 14 1921
SHROPSHIRE	1819 *or* 1829	June 28 1956
STAFFORDSHIRE	Nov. 24 1872	Nov. 24 1872
SUFFOLK	July 27 1864	August 1932
WILTSHIRE	Feb. 24 1881	Jan. 1893

The remaining three counties have also had county cricket clubs, but these no longer exist. Details:—

HEREFORDSHIRE. First known club 1836, lasted till about 1905–6. Revived 1950 but disbanded 1955.

RUTLAND. First known club about 1881–2; lasted 5 or 6 years. Occasional county matches still played.

WESTMORLAND. First known club 1835 (only reference). There have been several county matches.

BIGGEST HIT AT LORD'S

The only known instance of a batsman hitting a ball over the present pavilion at Lord's occurred when A. E. Trott, appearing for M.C.C. against Australians at Lord's, July 31, August 1, 2, 1899, drove M. A. Noble so far and high that the ball struck a chimney pot and fell behind the building.

CHAMPION COUNTY SINCE 1864

1864	Surrey
1865	Nottinghamshire
1866	Middlesex
1867	Yorkshire
1868	Nottinghamshire
1869	Nottinghamshire, Yorkshire
1870	Yorkshire
1871	Nottinghamshire
1872	Nottinghamshire
1873	Gloucestershire, Nottinghamshire
1874	Gloucestershire
1875	Nottinghamshire
1876	Gloucestershire
1877	Gloucestershire
1878	Undecided
1879	Nottinghamshire, Lancashire
1880	Nottinghamshire
1881	Lancashire
1882	Nottinghamshire, Lancashire
1883	Nottinghamshire
1884	Nottinghamshire
1885	Nottinghamshire
1886	Nottinghamshire
1887	Surrey
1888	Surrey
1889	Surrey, Lancashire, Nottinghamshire
1890	Surrey
1891	Surrey
1892	Surrey
1893	Yorkshire
1894	Surrey
1895	Surrey
1896	Yorkshire
1897	Lancashire
1898	Yorkshire
1899	Surrey
1900	Yorkshire
1901	Yorkshire
1902	Yorkshire
1903	Middlesex
1904	Lancashire
1905	Yorkshire
1906	Kent
1907	Nottinghamshire
1908	Yorkshire
1909	Kent
1910	Kent
1911	Warwickshire
1912	Yorkshire
1913	Kent
1914	Surrey
1919	Yorkshire
1920	Middlesex
1921	Middlesex
1922	Yorkshire
1923	Yorkshire
1924	Yorkshire
1925	Yorkshire
1926	Lancashire
1927	Lancashire
1928	Lancashire
1929	Nottinghamshire
1930	Lancashire
1931	Yorkshire
1932	Yorkshire
1933	Yorkshire
1934	Lancashire
1935	Yorkshire
1936	Derbyshire
1937	Yorkshire
1938	Yorkshire
1939	Yorkshire
1946	Yorkshire
1947	Middlesex
1948	Glamorgan
1949	Middlesex, Yorkshire
1950	Lancashire, Surrey
1951	Warwickshire
1952	Surrey
1953	Surrey
1954	Surrey
1955	Surrey
1956	Surrey
1957	Surrey
1958	Surrey
1959	Yorkshire
1960	Yorkshire
1961	Hampshire
1962	Yorkshire
1963	Yorkshire
1964	Worcestershire
1965	Worcestershire
1966	Yorkshire

The title has been won outright as follows:—Yorkshire 29 times, Surrey 17, Nottinghamshire 12, Lancashire 8, Middlesex 5, Kent 4, Gloucestershire 3, Warwickshire 2, Worcestershire 2, Derbyshire 1, Glamorgan 1, Hampshire 1.

Seven times the title has been shared as follows: Nottinghamshire 5, Lancashire 4, Surrey 2, Yorkshire 2, Gloucestershire 1, and Middlesex 1.

The earliest date the Championship has been won in any season since it was expanded in 1895 was August 12, 1910, by Kent.

CONSTITUTION OF COUNTY CHAMPIONSHIP

When qualification rules were first agreed in July 1873 (that no cricketer should play for more than one county during the same season), the following counties were considered first-class: Derbyshire, Gloucestershire, Kent, Lancashire, Middlesex, Notts, Surrey, Sussex and Yorkshire. In 1887 Derbyshire fell out. Hampshire were considered first-class from 1874–78, and perhaps from 1880–85, but not again till they were added in 1895. Some contemporary authorities considered Somerset first-class from 1881–85, but they were not regularly accepted till 1891. There was a further extension in 1894, as Essex, Derbyshire, Leicestershire and Warwickshire were admitted to the group. Worcestershire who came in for 1899, have since played regularly except for 1919, the first season after the First World War. Northamptonshire were raised for 1905, and Glamorgan were adopted in 1921.

THE MINOR COUNTIES CHAMPIONSHIP

Year	Winner	Year	Winner
1895	Norfolk Durham Worcestershire	1929	Oxfordshire
		1930	Durham
		1931	Leicestershire Second XI
1896	Worcestershire	1932	Buckinghamshire
1897	Worcestershire	1933	Undecided
1898	Worcestershire	1934	Lancashire Second XI
1899	Northamptonshire Buckinghamshire	1935	Middlesex Second XI
		1936	Hertfordshire
1900	Glamorgan Durham Northamptonshire	1937	Lancashire Second XI
		1938	Buckinghamshire
		1939	Surrey Second XI
1901	Durham	1946	Suffolk
1902	Wiltshire	1947	Yorkshire Second XI
1903	Northamptonshire	1948	Lancashire Second XI
1904	Northamptonshire	1949	Lancashire Second XI
1905	Norfolk	1950	Surrey Second XI
1906	Staffordshire	1951	Kent Second XI
1907	Lancashire Second XI	1952	Buckinghamshire
1908	Staffordshire	1953	Berkshire
1909	Wiltshire	1954	Surrey Second XI
1910	Norfolk	1955	Surrey Second XI
1911	Staffordshire	1956	Kent Second XI
1912	In abeyance	1957	Yorkshire Second XI
1913	Norfolk	1958	Yorkshire Second XI
1920	Staffordshire	1959	Warwickshire Second XI
1921	Staffordshire	1960	Lancashire Second XI
1922	Buckinghamshire	1961	Somerset Second XI
1923	Buckinghamshire	1962	Warwickshire Second XI
1924	Berkshire	1963	Cambridgeshire
1925	Buckinghamshire	1964	Lancashire Second XI
1926	Durham	1965	Somerset Second XI
1927	Staffordshire	1966	Lincolnshire
1928	Berkshire		

SECOND ELEVEN CHAMPIONSHIP

Year	Winner	Year	Winner
1959	Gloucestershire Second XI	1963	Worcestershire Second XI
1960	Northamptonshire Second XI	1964	Lancashire Second XI
1961	Kent Second XI	1965	Glamorgan Second XI
1962	Worcestershire Second XI	1966	Surrey Second XI

BEST YOUNG CRICKETER OF THE YEAR

The following are the winners of the annual trophy awarded by the Cricket Writers Club:

1950 R. Tattersall
1951 P. B. H. May
1952 F. S. Trueman
1953 M. C. Cowdrey
1954 P. J. Loader
1955 K. F. Barrington
1956 B. Taylor
1957 M. J. Stewart
1958 A. C. D. Ingleby-Mackenzie
1959 G. Pullar
1960 D. A. Allen
1961 P. H. Parfitt
1962 P. J. Sharpe
1963 G. Boycott
1964 J. M. Brearley
1965 A. Knott
1966 D. L. Underwood

FEATURES OF 1966

Double Hundreds

223 A. R. Lewis, Glamorgan v. Kent, at Gravesend.
209* B. F. Butcher, West Indies v. England, at Nottingham.
206 C. C. Hunte, West Indies v. Somerset, at Taunton.
203 C. Milburn, Northamptonshire v. Essex, at Clacton.

Hundreds in Each Innings

G. Boycott, 103 and 105 (Yorkshire v. Nottinghamshire, at Sheffield).
R. M. Prideaux, 106 and 100 (Northamptonshire v. Nottinghamshire, at Nottingham).

First to 1,000 Runs

C. Milburn (Northamptonshire), June 21.

First to 2,000 Runs

A. R. Lewis (Glamorgan), August 25.

Stands of 250 or Over

293 for first wicket, by C. Milburn and R. M. Prideaux (Northamptonshire v. Essex, at Clacton).
274 (unbroken) for sixth wicket, by G. S. Sobers and D. A. J. Holford (West Indies v. England, at Lord's).
272 for third wicket, by H. Horton and D. A. Livingstone (Hampshire v. Middlesex, at Bournemouth).
271 for fourth wicket, by T. W. Graveney and B. d'Oliveira (Worcestershire v. Essex, at Worcester).
265 for fifth wicket, by S. M. Nurse and G. S. Sobers (West Indies v. England, at Leeds).

The Double

S. J. Storey (Surrey), 1,013 runs; 104 wickets (August 31).

Totals of 500

527 England v. West Indies, at The Oval.
500 for 9 dec., West Indies v. England, at Leeds.

First to 100 Wickets

D. L. Underwood (Kent), July 28.

Nine Wickets in an Innings

D. L. Underwood (Kent v Essex, at Westcliff) 9 for 37.
D. W. White (Hampshire v. Leicestershire, at Portsmouth) 9 for 44.
G. S. Sobers (West Indies v. Kent, at Canterbury) 9 for 49.
K. D. Boyce (Essex v. Cambridge University, at Brentwood) 9 for 61.

Hat-trick

F. J. Titmus (Middlesex v. Somerset, at Weston-super-Mare).
D. Wilson (Yorkshire v. Nottinghamshire, at Worksop).
D. Wilson (Yorkshire v. Kent, at Harrogate).

Totals Under 60

36 Cambridge University v. Warwickshire, at Cambridge.
38 Warwickshire v. Derbyshire, at Coventry.
43 Somerset v. Middlesex, at Weston-super-Mare.
52 Glamorgan v. Warwickshire, at Birmingham.
57 Lancashire v. Yorkshire, at Leeds.
58 Derbyshire v. Gloucestershire, at Derby.

Fastest 100

C. Milburn, Northamptonshire v. Nottinghamshire, at Nottingham, reached 100 in 82 minutes and won the Café Royal trophy and 100 guineas for the fastest hundred in the County Championship.

K. F. Barrington, England v. Australia, at Melbourne, 100 off 122 balls won the Lawrence Trophy for the fastest century in Test cricket in 1966.

Unique Century Stand

For the first time in any Test Match numbers ten and eleven shared a three figure stand when K. Higgs (63) and J. A. Snow (59*) added 128 for England's last wicket against West Indies at The Oval.

Miscellaneous

Northamptonshire hit 355 for seven wickets against Nottinghamshire, at Nottingham, the highest in the first innings under the 65-over regulations and the only total over 300.

R. M. Prideaux (Northamptonshire) hit three hundreds in successive innings, 135 not out against Cambridge University at Cambridge and 106 and 100 against Nottinghamshire at Nottingham.

D. Wilson (Yorkshire) hit 30 runs off nine overs by R. N. S. Hobbs against M.C.C. at Nottingham.

P. J. Robinson (Somerset) had an analysis of 17.2—14—10—7 in the second innings against Nottinghamshire, at Nottingham.

D. J. Shepherd (Glamorgan) had an analysis of 9.1—6—7—7 in the second innings against Hampshire, at Cardiff.

K. D. Boyce took nine for 61 against Cambridge University, at Brentwood, his first match for Essex.

T. W. Cartwright (Warwickshire) bowled throughout the second day against Northamptonshire, at Birmingham. His figures for the two innings were 31.5—18—40—6 and 20.2—4—57—7.

D. L. Underwood (Kent) had an analysis of 10.1—7—9—6 in the first innings against Lancashire, at Blackpool.

A. B. Jackson (Derbyshire) gained an analysis of 13.3—5—8—8 in the first innings against Warwickshire, at Coventry.

N. Gifford (Worcestershire) had figures of 25—13—28—6 in the first innings against Somerset, at Yeovil.

J. A. Bailey (M.C.C.) had this bowling analysis against Ireland in Dublin: 32.1—22—24—8.

A. S. Brown (Gloucestershire) held seven catches in an innings against Nottinghamshire, at Nottingham, equalling the world record.

R. W. Taylor (Derbyshire) held seven catches behind the wicket against Glamorgan, at Derby.

A. Knott (Kent) twice dismissed six batsmen in an innings, four caught and two stumped against Middlesex, at Gravesend, and five caught and one stumped against Northamptonshire, at Maidstone.

R. B. Kanhai held five catches in an innings for West Indies against Gloucestershire, at Bristol.

A. Ealham held five catches in an innings, all off the bowling of D. L. Underwood, for Kent against Gloucestershire at Folkestone.

C. Milburn and R. M. Prideaux shared century stands for the first wicket (141 and 127 unbroken) in each innings of the match between Northamptonshire and Sussex, at Hove.

The Horlicks Awards

For each of the five Tests between England and West Indies, Horlicks Ltd. offered £200 for the best batting and £200 for the best bowling and £500 to the side that won the series. G. S. Sobers won the batting in the first, second and fourth Tests and he also won the bowling in the fourth Test. S. M. Nurse won the batting in the third Test and T. W. Graveney and J. T. Murray shared the prize in the fifth Test. L. R. Gibbs won the bowling in the first Test, K. Higgs in the second and third and J. A. Snow in the fifth. West Indies won the £500 team prize.

The Wisden Trophy

Lieut. General Sir Oliver Leese, President of M.C.C., presented The Wisden Trophy and the replicas to the West Indies players and manager at the finish of the Oval Test for winning the series, 3–1.

I ZINGARI RESULTS 1966

Played 23; *Won* 8, *Lost* 9, *Drawn* 6

April 30	v.	St. Paul's School	Won by 8 wickets
May 7	v.	Charterhouse School	Won by 7 wickets
May 7	v.	Honourable Artillery Company	Won by 5 wickets
May 14	v.	Magdalene College, Cambridge	Lost by 5 wickets
May 14	v.	Magdalen College, Oxford	Won by 5 wickets
May 21	v.	Harrow School	Drawn
May 21	v.	Christ Church, Oxford	Drawn
May 21	v.	Trinity College, Cambridge	Lost by 60 runs
June 4	v.	Royal Artillery	Won by 4 wickets
June 11	v.	Green Jackets Club	Drawn
June 11	v.	Lord Porchester's XI	Lost by 51 runs
June 21	v.	Winchester College	Lost by 91 runs
June 25	v.	Household Brigade	Drawn
June 25	v.	Royal Navy	Drawn
July 2	v.	Milton Abbey School	Won by 139 runs
July 9	v.	Wellington College	Drawn
July 9	v.	Fusilier Brigade	Lost by 4 wickets
July 10	v.	Duke of Norfolk's XI	Lost by 3 wickets
July 16	v.	Royal Military Academy, Sandhurst	Lost by 57 runs
July 17	v.	Ampleforth College	Lost by 6 wickets
July 30	v.	Staff College, Camberley	Won by 113 runs
Aug. 20	v.	South Wales Hunts	Won by 9 wickets
Aug. 27	v.	Yorkshire Gentlemen	Lost by 38 runs

FIRST-CLASS AVERAGES, 1966

BATTING

(Qualification: 8 innings; average 10.00)

† *Denotes a left-handed batsman.* * *Signifies not out.*

	Innings	Not Outs	Runs	Highest Innings	Average
T. W. Graveney (*Worcestershire*)	40	6	1777	166	52.26
C. Milburn (*Northamptonshire*) .	44	6	1861	203	48.97
W. J. Stewart (*Warwickshire*)...	14	3	505	166	45.90
M. J. K. Smith (*Warwickshire*)..	50	9	1824	140	44.48
†J. H. Edrich (*Surrey*)..........	49	3	1978	137	43.00
A. R. Lewis (*Glamorgan*)........	61	8	2198	223	41.47
†P. H. Parfitt (*Middlesex*).......	57	8	2018	114*	41.18
R. M. Prideaux (*Northants.*)....	55	7	1947	153*	40.56
G. Boycott (*Yorkshire*)........	50	3	1854	164	39.44
B. d'Oliveira (*Worcestershire*)...	45	5	1536	126	38.40
D. L. Amiss (*Warwickshire*)....	52	5	1765	160*	37.55
J. T. Murray (*Middlesex*).......	28	7	784	114	37.33
†G. Pullar (*Lancashire*).........	38	6	1184	167*	37.00
K. F. Barrington (*Surrey*).......	33	6	987	117*	36.55
R. E. Marshall (*Hampshire*)....	54	2	1882	133	36.19
B. W. Luckhurst (*Kent*)........	53	3	1763	183	35.26
E. A. Clark (*Middlesex*)........	47	8	1365	149	35.00
†A. Jones (*Glamorgan*)..........	57	3	1865	161*	34.53
F. S. Goldstein (*Oxford Univ.*)..	17	0	583	87	34.29
W. E. Russell (*Middlesex*)......	52	5	1513	146*	32.19
†M. J. Bear (*Essex*)............	58	1	1833	105	32.15
H. Horton (*Hampshire*)........	53	12	1312	148*	32.00
M. C. Cowdrey (*Kent*).........	40	6	1081	100*	31.79
M. H. Denness (*Kent*).........	55	4	1606	97	31.49
M. R. Hallam (*Leicestershire*)...	51	3	1502	135	31.29
D. Bennett (*Middlesex*)	10	3	218	50	31.14
M. J. Edwards (*Surrey*)........	35	0	1064	116	30.40
M. J. Horton (*Worcestershire*)..	49	7	1272	91	30.28
D. L. Murray (*Nottinghamshire*)	51	6	1358	166*	30.17
M. J. Smedley (*Nottinghamshire*)	54	12	1266	134*	30.14
†R. W. Barber (*Warwickshire*)...	23	0	693	84	30.13
N. J. Cosh (*Cambridge Univ.*)...	26	3	693	98	30.13
B. J. Booth (*Leicestershire*).....	45	5	1201	102*	30.02
R. W. Hooker (*Middlesex*).....	31	7	719	102	29.95
C. A. Milton (*Gloucestershire*)..	58	3	1646	138*	29.92
D. P. Toft (*Oxford Univ.*)......	13	0	386	84	29.69
†D. B. Close (*Yorkshire*).......	56	11	1335	115*	29.66
J. A. Jameson (*Warwickshire*)...	53	10	1270	118*	29.53
†K. G. Suttle (*Sussex*).........	56	5	1500	172*	29.41
M. J. Harris (*Middlesex*).......	36	3	962	114	29.15
†D. R. Worsley (*Lancashire*).....	34	5	843	76	29.06
M. E. Norman (*Leicestershire*)..	52	5	1345	132*	28.61
R. N. Abberley (*Warwickshire*).	51	5	1315	117*	28.58
†C. C. Inman (*Leicestershire*)....	49	3	1314	113*	28.56
J. M. Parks (*Sussex*)...........	52	9	1225	119	28.48
K. W. R. Fletcher (*Essex*)......	63	8	1550	106	28.18
M. Kitchen (*Somerset*)........	54	3	1422	111*	27.88
D. S. Steele (*Northamptonshire*).	48	6	1170	118*	27.85
†R. C. Wilson (*Kent*)..........	39	2	1025	88	27.70
P. M. Walker (*Glamorgan*).....	50	6	1213	95*	27.56
J. B. Bolus (*Nottinghamshire*)...	54	3	1393	122*	27.31

	Innings	Not Outs	Runs	Highest Innings	Average
J. A. Ormrod (*Worcestershire*) . .	53	6	1284	72	27.31
P. J. Sainsbury (*Hampshire*)	40	10	819	75	27.30
D. Kenyon (*Worcestershire*)	41	1	1091	114	27.27
H. I. Moore (*Nottinghamshire*) . .	49	5	1169	100	26.56
A. W. Dyer (*Oxford Univ.*)	23	4	504	67	26.52
†D. A. Livingstone (*Hampshire*) . .	38	6	845	116	26.40
†R. M. C. Gilliat (*Oxford & Hants.*)	37	4	869	86	26.33
P. Marner (*Leicestershire*)	48	3	1184	108	26.31
†M. A. Buss (*Sussex*)	33	3	787	136	26.23
C. R. M. Atkinson (*Somerset*) . .	52	9	1120	89	26.04
G. E. Barker (*Essex*)	57	7	1301	95*	26.02
R. A. E. Tindall (*Surrey*)	24	4	519	81	25.95
B. L. Reynolds (*Northants.*)	55	4	1323	89	25.94
†C. D. Fearnley (*Worcestershire*) .	17	2	384	112	25.60
P. J. K. Gibbs (*Oxford & Derby.*)	24	0	614	107	25.58
R. B. Nicholls (*Gloucestershire*) .	56	5	1301	108	25.50
D. E. V. Padgett (*Yorkshire*)	52	5	1194	79	25.40
Mushtaq Mohammad (*Northamptonshire*)	53	6	1179	117	25.08
K. Ibadulla (*Warwickshire*)	46	4	1044	62	24.85
K. Taylor (*Yorkshire*)	45	3	1044	106	24.85
S. J. Storey (*Surrey*)	45	4	1013	109*	24.70
†R. Wills (*Northamptonshire*)	14	1	321	151*	24.69
†B. Whittingham (*Notts.*)	25	3	543	133	24.68
G. Atkinson (*Somerset*)	55	2	1307	148	24.66
D. N. F. Slade (*Worcestershire*) .	15	6	219	46*	24.33
I. W. Hall (*Derbyshire*)	41	1	973	102	24.32
†A. Lightfoot (*Northamptonshire*)	24	5	462	58	24.31
R. Virgin (*Somerset*)	56	1	1333	98	24.23
A. S. M. Oakman (*Sussex*)	47	7	966	86*	24.15
†R. G. A. Headley (*Worcs.*)	47	4	1028	137	23.90
M. J. Stewart (*Surrey*)	49	7	997	102	23.73
R. B. Edmonds (*Warwickshire*) .	18	3	355	102*	23.66
L. J. Lenham (*Sussex*)	55	4	1198	86	23.49
D. C. Morgan (*Derbyshire*)	52	8	1028	96	23.36
G. Cross (*Leicestershire*)	15	4	257	45*	23.36
M. Bissex (*Gloucestershire*)	41	0	953	80	23.24
J. H. Hampshire (*Yorkshire*)	55	4	1179	76	23.11
†W. E. Alley (*Somerset*)	51	3	1104	115	23.00
C. T. Radley (*Middlesex*)	32	4	644	115	23.00
†B. Taylor (*Essex*)	57	2	1264	77	22.98
R. Entwistle (*Lancashire*)	11	1	227	60	22.70
R. Swetman (*Nottinghamshire*) . .	50	11	880	115	22.56
P. J. Sharpe (*Yorkshire*)	49	5	992	72	22.54
J. D. Bond (*Lancashire*)	38	5	743	90	22.51
Nawab of Pataudi (*Sussex*)	43	4	876	67	22.46
K. E. Palmer (*Somerset*)	50	10	898	118	22.45
T. E. Bailey (*Essex*)	37	9	627	77	22.39
†B. L. Reed (*Hampshire*)	51	2	1096	93	22.36
A. Rees (*Glamorgan*)	46	7	869	65	22.28
D. M. Green (*Lancashire*)	53	0	1180	115	22.26
J. F. Harvey (*Derbyshire*)	52	2	1112	103*	22.24
†D. Lloyd (*Lancashire*)	37	10	588	77	21.77
A. Knott (*Kent*)	46	11	761	48*	21.74
M. J. Smith (*Middlesex*)	30	2	605	68	21.60
R. Illingworth (*Yorkshire*)	39	8	669	98*	21.58
D. Shepherd (*Gloucestershire*) . . .	54	8	981	118	21.32
L. W. Hill (*Glamorgan*)	13	3	210	50	21.00
†N. Hill (*Nottinghamshire*)	50	2	1003	96	20.89
†D. Constant (*Leicestershire*)	38	6	667	80	20.84

	Innings	Not Outs	Runs	Highest Innings	Average
S. E. Leary (*Kent*)	49	4	936	67*	20.80
A. C. Smith (*Warwickshire*).....	39	7	665	85	20.78
†D. W. Richardson (*Worcs.*).....	40	7	685	87*	20.75
D. Brown (*Gloucestershire*).....	50	4	952	92*	20.69
M. Taylor (*Nottinghamshire*)....	48	9	807	69	20.69
†P. D. Watts (*Northamptonshire*).	15	3	247	69	20.58
†M. D. Mence (*Gloucestershire*)..	23	7	329	76*	20.56
†T. J. P. Eyre (*Derbyshire*)......	31	4	553	88	20.48
M. Hill (*Derbyshire*)...........	44	3	838	61	20.43
M. G. Griffith (*Sussex*)........	43	7	735	67	20.41
D. J. Foreman (*Sussex*)........	36	5	632	68	20.38
†G. R. Cass (*Essex*)............	44	6	772	65	20.31
G. Burgess (*Somerset*).........	21	1	406	69	20.30
†W. A. Smith (*Surrey*)..........	29	2	548	62	20.29
M. D. Willett (*Surrey*).........	35	7	561	78*	20.03
S. E. Russell (*Gloucestershire*)...	39	1	758	107	19.94
B. R. Knight (*Essex*)..........	42	3	776	73	19.89
H. L. Johnson (*Derbyshire*).....	40	3	733	90	19.81
D. L. Hays (*Cambridge Univ.*)...	26	0	510	72	19.61
J. M. Allan (*Warwickshire*).....	25	10	291	55*	19.40
G. K. Knox (*Lancashire*).......	45	2	828	100	19.25
M. H. Page (*Derbyshire*........	43	6	706	79*	19.08
J. S. Waring (*Yorkshire*).......	13	8	95	26	19.00
†R. A. White (*Nottinghamshire*)..	53	5	911	68	18.97
A. Ealham (*Kent*).............	36	7	549	59	18.93
F. J. Titmus (*Middlesex*).......	41	5	678	81*	18.83
A. G. M. Watson (*Oxford Univ.*)	15	6	169	65*	18.77
B. Crump (*Northamptonshire*)...	39	9	563	76*	18.76
†J. Birkenshaw (*Leicestershire*)...	26	4	408	68	18.54
K. Shuttleworth (*Lancashire*)...	17	4	241	34*	18.53
K. J. Wheatley (*Hampshire*)....	28	4	441	46	18.37
B. Hedges (*Glamorgan*)........	39	3	659	65	18.30
B. S. V. Timms (*Hampshire*)....	34	8	475	120	18.26
T. W. Cartwright (*Warwicks.*)..	35	7	504	65*	18.00
G. A. R. Lock (*Leicestershire*)..	43	6	658	56	17.78
†P. J. Watts (*Northamptonshire*)..	46	6	711	60	17.77
†P. J. Robinson (*Somerset*)......	41	12	515	66	17.75
†K. P. W. J. McAdam (*Cambs. U.*)	24	0	424	50	17.66
R. Booth (*Worcestershire*)......	41	10	546	43	17.61
R. E. J. Chambers (*Cambs. Univ.*)	22	0	386	58	17.54
P. E. Russell (*Derbyshire*).....	14	1	227	56	17.46
G. C. Cooper (*Sussex*).........	12	1	192	33	17.45
†P. J. Graves (*Sussex*).........	34	5	502	64	17.31
†K. Higgs (*Lancashire*)........	27	7	346	63	17.30
P. Lever (*Lancashire*).........	40	4	617	83	17.13
R. W. Taylor (*Derbyshire*)......	47	5	719	42	17.11
R. I. Jefferson (*Surrey*)........	36	9	459	45*	17.00
G. J. Saville (*Essex*)..........	42	8	577	48*	16.97
I. R. Buxton (*Derbyshire*)......	37	5	542	68	16.93
G. Arnold (*Surrey*)...........	13	6	118	32	16.85
J. M. Prodger (*Kent*).........	26	3	384	114*	16.69
J. G. Binks (*Yorkshire*).......	42	11	517	60*	16.67
G. A. Cottrell (*Cambridge Univ.*)	26	2	398	44*	16.58
B. Edmeades (*Essex*)..........	47	8	647	47	16.58
G. R. J. Roope (*Surrey*).......	15	4	181	35	16.45
A. Brown (*Kent*).............	18	5	213	52*	16.38
J. Sullivan (*Lancashire*).......	30	1	474	56	16.34
J. B. Mortimore (*Gloucs.*)......	50	8	685	75	16.30
H. Pilling (*Lancashire*)........	26	2	390	70	16.25
D. A. Allen (*Gloucestershire*)....	42	11	502	82*	16.19

	Innings	Not Outs	Runs	Highest Innings	Average
†D. Wilson (*Yorkshire*)	42	6	578	52	16.05
J. Cotton (*Leicestershire*)	20	11	142	25	15.77
A. Clarkson (*Somerset*)	16	1	234	74*	15.60
J. R. Eyre (*Derbyshire*)	37	2	542	61	15.48
B. Wood (*Lancashire*)	15	1	216	39	15.42
J. C. Balderstone (*Yorkshire*)	13	1	183	64	15.25
†R. G. Caple (*Hampshire*)	17	4	196	35	15.07
A. T. Castell (*Hampshire*)	11	2	134	39	14.88
D. A. Bick (*Middlesex*)	34	7	400	63*	14.81
H. M. Barnard (*Hampshire*)	18	2	233	54	14.56
T. E. Barwell (*Somerset*)	10	0	144	56	14.40
R. D. Jackman (*Surrey*)	10	5	71	19	14.20
P. R. V. Ledden (*Sussex*)	9	3	85	28	14.16
R. W. Tolchard (*Leicestershire*)	42	11	433	44*	13.96
J. A. Snow (*Sussex*)	34	14	279	71	13.95
†N. Gifford (*Worcestershire*)	31	13	249	32	13.83
†E. Lewis (*Glamorgan*)	33	2	428	56	13.80
G. Clayton (*Somerset*)	50	5	620	63	13.77
A. E. Cordle (*Glamorgan*)	25	4	285	38	13.57
W. D. Slade (*Glamorgan*)	26	1	338	69	13.52
D. R. Walsh (*Oxford Univ.*)	12	2	135	56	13.50
V. P. Malalasekera (*Camb. U.*)	24	0	323	80	13.45
A. B. Palfreman (*Camb. Univ.*)	18	1	227	67	13.35
†R. J. Langridge (*Sussex*)	16	0	212	68	13.25
A. L. Dixon (*Kent*)	41	6	462	44*	13.20
B. Stead (*Nottinghamshire*)	20	10	132	19*	13.20
P. Willey (*Northamptonshire*)	9	1	105	78	13.12
D. Shackleton (*Hampshire*)	25	8	223	42*	13.11
R. Davis (*Glamorgan*)	23	2	273	52	13.00
F. J. Davis (*Glamorgan*)	15	5	129	28*	12.90
D. J. Brown (*Warwickshire*)	23	8	192	34	12.80
B. Roe (*Somerset*)	8	0	102	32	12.75
†B. A. Richardson (*Warwicks.*)	9	2	89	25*	12.71
B. J. Meyer (*Gloucestershire*)	38	18	244	31*	12.20
R. V. Webster (*Warwickshire*)	25	2	280	47	12.17
G. N. S. Ridley (*Oxford Univ.*)	19	3	193	32	12.06
R. N. S. Hobbs (*Essex*)	50	15	442	40	12.05
†D. W. White (*Hampshire*)	33	6	324	50*	12.00
†D. Nicholls (*Kent*)	15	0	179	53	11.93
H. J. Rhodes (*Derbyshire*)	33	18	179	28	11.93
A. R. Garofall (*Oxford Univ.*)	9	0	107	26	11.88
D. R. Smith (*Gloucestershire*)	15	7	95	21*	11.87
A. S. Brown (*Gloucestershire*)	49	4	529	33*	11.75
I. Morris (*Glamorgan*)	8	1	82	38	11.71
D. A. Ashworth (*Oxford Univ.*)	8	0	93	25	11.62
R. Harman (*Surrey*)	19	12	81	23	11.57
J. R. Gray (*Hampshire*)	9	3	69	21	11.50
E. J. O. Hemsley (*Worcs.*)	8	2	69	24*	11.50
F. S. Trueman (*Yorkshire*)	43	4	448	43	11.48
A. Buss (*Sussex*)	42	6	412	35	11.44
P. I. Pocock (*Surrey*)	32	8	271	45*	11.29
T. Greenhough (*Lancashire*)	21	6	167	22*	11.13
A. R. Windows (*Gloucestershire*)	34	4	329	40*	10.96
A. G. Nicholson (*Yorkshire*)	28	16	130	41	10.83
K. V. Andrew (*Northants*)	29	10	203	21	10.68
A. M. Jorden (*Essex*)	34	13	223	29*	10.61
†C. Forbes (*Nottinghamshire*)	36	9	281	38	10.40
M. E. Scott (*Northamptonshire*)	21	6	154	24*	10.26
A. V. E. Gould (*Cambridge Univ.*)	22	0	225	38	10.22
M. H. J. Allen (*Derbyshire*)	8	3	50	17*	10.00

BOWLING

(Qualification: 10 wickets in 10 innings)

† *Denotes a left-arm bowler.*

	Overs	Maidens	Runs	Wickets	Average
†D. L. Underwood (*Kent*).......	1104.5	475	2167	157	13.80
J. A. Flavell (*Worcestershire*)...	822.3	199	1891	135	14.00
J. B. Statham (*Lancashire*)......	624.4	135	1479	102	14.50
A. G. Nicholson (*Yorkshire*)....	879.3	297	1752	113	15.50
O. S. Wheatley (*Glamorgan*)....	865.3	269	1642	103	15.94
†N. Gifford (*Worcestershire*)....	806.5	366	1458	91	16.02
D. J. Shepherd (*Glamorgan*)....	1025	427	1844	111	16.61
D. R. Smith (*Gloucestershire*)...	358.1	73	947	57	16.61
R. Illingworth (*Yorkshire*)......	830.1	341	1680	100	16.80
Mushtaq Mohammad (*Northamptonshire*)..........	403	113	976	57	17.12
†D. S. Steele (*Northamptonshire*).	235	82	505	29	17.41
†D. Wilson (*Yorkshire*).........	861	341	1753	100	17.53
B. A. Langford (*Somerset*).....	1026.4	438	1971	112	17.59
D. Shackleton (*Hampshire*).....	1306.2	574	2088	117	17.84
T. W. Cartwright (*Warwicks.*)..	842.5	304	1795	100	17.95
K. E. Palmer (*Somerset*).......	717.1	148	1935	107	18.08
F. S. Trueman (*Yorkshire*).....	859.5	203	2040	111	18.37
S. J. Storey (*Surrey*)..........	935.5	300	1913	104	18.39
E. Smith (*Derbyshire*).........	803.3	320	1605	87	18.44
H. J. Rhodes (*Derbyshire*)......	664	192	1441	78	18.47
B. Edmeades (*Essex*)..........	725	145	1971	106	18.59
J. S. E. Price (*Middlesex*).......	728	158	1762	94	18.74
J. N. Graham (*Kent*)..........	257.3	89	493	26	18.96
G. Arnold (*Surrey*)...........	424.4	85	1124	59	19.05
A. B. Jackson (*Derbyshire*).....	625.1	176	1222	64	19.09
J. A. Snow (*Sussex*)...........	903.2	196	2406	126	19.09
†F. E. Rumsey (*Somerset*).......	812	199	1911	100	19.11
R. V. Webster (*Warwickshire*)..	510.4	112	1368	70	19.54
†G. A. R. Lock (*Leicestershire*)..	956.1	324	2132	109	19.55
D. W. White (*Hampshire*)......	856.1	185	2153	109	19.75
A. Lightfoot (*Northamptonshire*)	79	16	198	10	19.80
D. C. Morgan (*Derbyshire*).....	861.2	312	1735	87	19.94
W. E. Alley (*Somerset*).........	519	170	1015	50	20.30
P. J. Watts (*Northamptonshire*)..	527.1	152	1158	57	20.31
†R. Harman (*Surrey*)...........	455.1	156	1020	50	20.40
A. E. Cordle (*Glamorgan*)......	342.5	86	824	40	20.60
R. M. H. Cottam (*Hampshire*)..	583.1	130	1287	62	20.75
B. d'Oliveira (*Worcestershire*)...	763.5	264	1516	73	20.76
K. Higgs (*Lancashire*)..........	863.2	205	1994	96	20.77
L. J. Coldwell (*Worcestershire*) .	627.4	164	1480	71	20.84
B. R. Knight (*Essex*)..........	674.4	123	1757	83	21.16
J. D. Bannister (*Warwickshire*)..	411.4	128	912	43	21.20
B. Crump (*Northamptonshire*)...	874.5	257	1845	87	21.20
H. Sully (*Northamptonshire*)....	860.1	241	2145	101	21.23
A. L. Dixon (*Kent*)............	1022.5	329	2460	115	21.39
†P. J. Robinson (*Somerset*)......	693.3	287	1499	70	21.41
R. D. Jackman (*Surrey*)	239	61	557	26	21.42
A. J. Durose (*Northamptonshire*)	375.4	73	948	44	21.54
J. S. Waring (*Yorkshire*).......	206.2	49	542	25	21.68
R. W. Hooker (*Middlesex*).....	572.5	157	1389	64	21.70
P. I. Pocock (*Surrey*)..........	747	222	1780	81	21.97
D. A. Allen (*Gloucestershire*)...	850.5	269	1761	80	22.01
D. M. Sayer (*Kent*)...........	634	159	1540	69	22.31
R. W. Stewart (*Middlesex*).....	673.3	183	1571	70	22.44

	Overs	Maidens	Runs	Wickets	Average
A. Buss (*Sussex*)	977.3	212	2707	120	22.55
A. T. Castell (*Hampshire*)	312.5	58	812	36	22.55
D. B. Close (*Yorkshire*)	563.3	201	1362	60	22.70
P. Lever (*Lancashire*)	672.1	140	1681	74	22.71
T. E. Bailey (*Essex*)	440	106	1028	45	22.84
†R. Miller (*Warwickshire*)	340.4	106	916	40	22.90
†C. Forbes (*Nottinghamshire*)	1012.2	280	2515	109	23.07
†G. N. S. Ridley (*Oxford Univ.*)	456.1	181	969	42	23.07
C. T. Spencer (*Leics.*)	626	136	1671	72	23.20
D. J. Brown (*Warwickshire*)	690.2	143	1828	78	23.43
R. G. M. Carter (*Worcs.*)	183.3	40	520	22	23.63
R. Bailey (*Northamptonshire*)	244.1	40	598	25	23.92
†J. C. Dye (*Kent*)	466.1	155	890	37	24.05
J. Cotton (*Leicestershire*)	457.2	100	1188	49	24.24
J. B. Mortimore (*Gloucestershire*)	849.2	278	1805	74	24.39
†D. Lloyd (*Lancashire*)	297.4	77	796	32	24.87
T. Greenhough (*Lancashire*)	484.2	157	1026	41	25.02
D. L. Bates (*Sussex*)	683.5	161	1783	71	25.11
D. A. Bick (*Middlesex*)	518	170	1207	48	25.14
F. J. Titmus (*Middlesex*)	996	317	2115	84	25.17
†M. E. Scott (*Northamptonshire*)	393.1	130	883	35	25.22
M. J. Horton (*Worcestershire*)	342.3	111	732	29	25.24
†S. G. Russell (*Cambridge Univ.*)	338.4	72	1035	41	25.24
K. Shuttleworth (*Lancashire*)	241.3	58	610	24	25.41
T. J. P. Eyre (*Derbyshire*)	289	64	865	34	25.44
P. Marner (*Leicestershire*)	688.3	133	1964	77	25.50
C. R. M. Atkinson (*Somerset*)	137.1	34	359	14	25.64
R. N. S. Hobbs (*Essex*)	752.4	177	2268	88	25.77
A. Brown (*Kent*)	399	97	1089	42	25.92
R. I. Jefferson (*Surrey*)	673.5	148	1714	66	25.96
B. M. Brain (*Worcestershire*)	337.3	61	1050	40	26.25
R. B. Edmonds (*Warwickshire*)	301	99	670	25	26.80
R. W. Elviss (*Oxford Univ.*)	499.4	184	1133	42	26.97
H. C. Latchman (*Middlesex*)	380.3	122	1012	37	27.35
E. Lewis (*Glamorgan*)	378.1	100	1155	42	27.50
J. Birkenshaw (*Leicestershire*)	164.5	36	469	17	27.58
J. S. Savage (*Leicestershire*)	700.2	226	1545	55	28.09
I. Davison (*Nottinghamshire*)	650.3	129	1916	68	28.17
K. F. Barrington (*Surrey*)	92	18	282	10	28.20
†D. A. Marriott (*Surrey*)	220.4	46	536	19	28.21
K. J. Wheatley (*Hampshire*)	449.1	174	893	31	28.80
R. B. Hiller (*Oxford Univ.*)	166.2	36	494	17	29.05
G. R. J. Roope (*Surrey*)	160	42	407	14	29.07
R. A. White (*Nottinghamshire*)	499.5	159	1254	43	29.16
†P. M. Walker (*Glamorgan*)	272.5	90	672	23	29.21
†J. M. Allan (*Warwickshire*)	418.5	120	1143	39	29.30
A. S. M. Oakman (*Sussex*)	653	185	1526	52	29.34
I. R. Buxton (*Derbyshire*)	374.2	128	800	27	29.62
A. R. Windows (*Gloucestershire*)	577.3	132	1576	53	29.73
†I. J. Jones (*Glamorgan*)	613	140	1616	54	29.92
†D. N. F. Slade (*Worcestershire*)	203.3	87	389	13	29.92
A. B. Palfreman (*Cambridge U.*)	245.1	62	786	26	30.23
A. S. Brown (*Gloucestershire*)	941.2	202	2452	81	30.27
R. W. Barber (*Warwickshire*)	204.3	41	606	20	30.30
M. Bissex (*Gloucestershire*)	217.4	77	546	18	30.33
†F. J. Davis (*Glamorgan*)	177.3	68	486	16	30.37
D. L. Acfield (*Cambridge Univ. & Essex*)	652.5	199	1648	53	31.09
M. Taylor (*Nottinghamshire*)	708.2	169	1842	59	31.22
†N. Sinker (*Cambridge Univ.*)	279.1	74	656	21	31.23
D. R. Worsley (*Lancashire*)	230	59	610	19	32.10

	Overs	Maidens	Runs	Wickets	Average
R. Roopnaraine (*Camb. Univ.*)..	461.5	165	1061	32	33.15
R. East (*Essex*)..............	238	59	673	20	33.65
R. S. Herman (*Middlesex*)......	146	31	380	11	34.54
†B. Stead (*Nottinghamshire*).....	435.1	85	1284	37	34.70
J. N. C. Easter (*Oxford Univ.*)...	221.4	60	676	19	35.57
A. Johnson (*Nottinghamshire*)..	263.3	44	785	22	35.68
A. G. M. Watson (*Oxford Univ.*)	235.3	58	774	21	36.85
A. M. Jorden (*Essex*)..........	576.5	73	1779	47	37.85
K. Ibadulla (*Warwickshire*).....	286.4	65	840	22	38.18
G. A. Cottrell (*Cambridge U.*)...	265	72	776	20	38.80
D. M. Green (*Lancashire*)......	164.2	35	457	11	41.54
P. J. Sainsbury (*Hampshire*)....	425.2	167	885	21	42.14
M. D. Mence (*Gloucestershire*)..	254	40	825	18	45.83
K. G. Suttle (*Sussex*)	220.2	70	523	11	47.54
M. A. Buss (*Sussex*)...........	186.3	62	494	10	49.40
K. Gillhouley (*Nottinghamshire*)	223.3	64	579	10	57.90

The following bowled in less than ten innings:

	Overs	Maidens	Runs	Wickets	Average
J. A. Bailey (*M.C.C.*)..........	51.3	29	57	13	4.38
K. D. Boyce (*Essex*)...........	55.5	7	172	14	12.28
A. J. O'Riordan (*Ireland*)......	84	24	196	14	14.00
J. G. Saunders (*Oxford Univ.*)...	98.3	47	163	10	16.30
B. Lewis (*Glamorgan*)..........	118.5	31	330	17	19.41
K. Howard (*Lancashire*)........	151.3	63	299	15	19.93
J. F. Fitzgerald (*Camb. Univ.*)...	107.2	33	324	15	21.60
D. Barr (*Scotland*)............	141.5	29	380	13	29.23

INDIVIDUAL SCORES OF 100 AND OVER

There were 158 three-figure innings in first-class cricket in 1966, nine more than in 1965. The list included 103 hit in County Championship matches and 35 in other first-class games, but not the 20 by members of the West Indies Touring team which can be found in their own section.

G. Boycott (6)
164 Yorks. v. Sussex: Hove.
136* Yorks. v. War.: Birmingham.
131 T. N. Pearce's XI v. West Indies: Scarborough.
123 Yorks v. M.C.C.: Lord's.
103 }
105 } Yorks. v. Notts.: Sheffield.

C. Milburn (6)
203 Northants v. Essex: Clacton.
171 Northants v. Leics.: Leicester.
137 Northants v Sussex: Hove.
130 Northants v. Derby.: Derby.
126* England v. West Indies: Lord's.
113 Northants v. Notts: Nottingham.

R. M. Prideaux (6)
153* Northants v. Essex: Clacton.
135* Northants v Camb. U.: Cambridge.
109 Northants v. Yorks.: Northampton.
106 }
100 } Northants v. Notts.: Nottingham.
101* Northants v. Surrey: The Oval.

A. R. Lewis (5)
223 Glam. v. Kent: Gravesend.
146 Glam. v. Glos.: Cardiff.
103 Glam. v Northants: Neath.
102 Glam. v. Middx.: Lord's.
100 Glam. v. Glos: Gloucester.

B. W. Luckhurst (5)
183 Kent v. Surrey: Blackheath.
133 Kent v. Glos: Folkestone.
110 Kent v. Glam.: Gravesend.
104 Kent v. West Indies: Canterbury.
101 Kent v. Oxford U.: Canterbury.

T. W. Graveney (4)
166 Worcs. v. Essex: Worcester.
165 England v. West Indies: The Oval.
109 England v. West Indies: Nottingham.
109 Worcs. v. Surrey: The Oval.

M. J. K. Smith (4)
140 M.C.C. v. West Indies: Lord's.
117 War. v. Notts.: Nottingham.
113* War. v. Hants: Birmingham.
103* War. v. Sussex: Hastings.

K. F. Barrington (3)
117* Surrey v. Lancs.: Manchester.
106 Surrey v. Notts.: Nottingham.
103* Surrey v. Northants: The Oval.

D. B. Close (3)
115* Yorks. v. Notts.: Worksop.
105 Yorks. v. Glos.: Bristol.
103 Yorks. v. Camb. U.: Cambridge.

J. H. Edrich (3)
137 Surrey v. Notts.: Nottingham.
136* Surrey v. Lancs.: The Oval.
132 Surrey v. Kent: Blackheath.

C. C. Inman (3)
113* Leics. v. Notts.: Nottingham.
110 Leics. v. Lancs.: Manchester.
109* Leics. v. Northants: Leicester.

R. E. Marshall (3)
133 Hants v. War.: Birmingham.
110 Hants v. Notts.: Bournemouth.
106 Hants v. Kent: Bournemouth.

J. T. Murray (3)
114 Middx. v. Sussex: Hove.
112 England v. West Indies: The Oval.
100* M.C.C. v. West Indies: Lord's.

Mushtaq Mohammad (3)
117 Northants v. Glos.: Bristol.
112 Northants v. Leics.: Leicester.
100* Rest of the World v. England XI: Scarborough.

W. E. Russell (3)
146* Middx. v. Glam.: Lord's.
117* Middx. v. Worcs.: Worcester.
101 Middx. v. Derby.: Lord's.

K. G. Suttle (3)
172* Sussex v. Middx.: Hove.
139* Sussex v. Leics.: Leicester.
102 Sussex v. Surrey: Eastbourne.

W. E. Alley (2)
115 Somerset v. Notts.: Nottingham.
110* Somerset v. Glam.: Taunton.

D. L. Amiss (2)
160* War. v. West Indies: Birmingham.
150* War. v. Scotland: Birmingham.

G. Atkinson (2)
148 Somerset v. Hants: Bournemouth.
127 Somerset v. Sussex: Eastbourne

B. J. Booth (2)
102* Leics. v. Surrey: The Oval.
101 Leics. v. Lancs: Leicester.

B. d'Oliveira (2)
126 Worcs. v. Essex: Worcester.
123 Worcs. v. Notts.: Worcester

K. W. R. Fletcher (2)
106 Essex v. West Indies: Southend.
101* Essex v. Leics.: Clacton.

H. Horton (2)
148* Hants v. Middx.: Bournemouth.
146* Hants v. Leics.: Coalville.

A. Jones (2)
161* Glam. v. West Indies: Swansea.
104* Glam. v. Essex: Swansea.

D. Kenyon (2)
114 Worcs. v. Kent: Worcester.
103 Worcs. v. Northants: Worcester.

M. Kitchen (2)
111* Somerset v. Sussex: Eastbourne.
100 Somerset v. Worcs.: Worcester.

P. Marner (2)
108 Leics. v. Oxford U.: Oxford.
104 Leics. v. Notts.: Nottingham.

C. A. Milton (2)
138* Glos. v. Leics.: Bristol.
121 Glos. v. Notts.: Nottingham.

D. L. Murray (2)
166* Notts. v. Surrey: The Oval.
133 Camb. U. v. Sussex: Hove.

M. E. Norman (2)
132* Leics. v. Hants: Coalville.
102 Leics. v. Northants: Northampton.

P. H. Parfitt (2)
114* Middx. v. Yorks.: Lord's.
107 Middx. v. Sussex: Hove.

J. M. Parks (2)
119 Sussex v. Lancs.: Hove.
101* England XI v. Rest of the World: Scarborough.

G. Pullar (2)
167* Lancs. v. West Indies: Manchester.
110 Lancs. v. Leics.: Leicester.

D. S. Steele (2)
118* Northants v. Leics.: Leicester.
117 Northants v. Glos.: Bristol.

M. J. Stewart (2)
102 Surrey v. Sussex: Eastbourne.
101 Surrey v. Leics.: The Oval.

The following thirty-seven each played one three-figure innings:—

R. N. Abberley, 117*, War. v. Essex, Birmingham.

M. Bear, 105, Essex v. War., Birmingham; J. B. Bolus, 122*, Notts. v. Sussex, Nottingham; J. M. Brearley, 101, Camb. U. v. Yorks., Cambridge; M. A. Buss, 136, Sussex v. Camb. U., Hove.

E. A. Clark, 149, Middx. v. Kent, Gravesend; M. C. Cowdrey, 100*, Kent v. Oxford U., Canterbury.

R. B. Edmonds, 102*, War. v. Scotland, Birmingham; M. J. Edwards 116, Surrey v. Glos., The Oval.

C. D. Fearnley, 112, Worcs. v. Derby., Kidderminster.

P. J. K. Gibbs, 107, Oxford U. v. War., Birmingham; D. M. Green, 115, Lancs. v. Notts., Newark.

I. W. Hall, 102, Derby. v. Oxford U., Derby; M. R. Hallam, 135, Leics. v. Hants, Coalville; M. J. Harris, 114, Middx. v. Derby., Lord's; J. F. Harvey, 103*, Derby. v. Notts., Nottingham; R. G. A. Headley, 137, Worcs. v. Yorks., Worcester; R. W. Hooker, 102, Middx. v. Somerset, Weston.

J. A. Jameson, 118*, War. v. Somerset, Taunton.

G. K. Knox, 100, Lancs. v. Derby, Manchester.

D. A. Livingstone, 116, Hants v. Middx., Bournemouth.

H. I. Moore, 100, Notts. v. Lancs., Newark.

R. B. Nicholls, 108, Glos. v. West Indies, Bristol.

K. E. Palmer, 118, Somerset v. Lancs., Southport; J. M. Prodger, 114*, Kent v. Glam., Gravesend.

C. T. Radley, 115, Middx. v. Camb. U., Cambridge; S. E. Russell, 107, Glos. v. Oxford U., Oxford.

Saeed Ahmed 100*, M.C.C. v. Surrey, Lord's; D. Shepherd, 118, Glos. v. Worcs. Worcester; M. J. Smedley, 134*, Notts. v. Leics., Nottingham; W. J. Stewart, 166, War. v. Oxford U., Birmingham; S. J. Storey, 109*, Surrey v. Notts., The Oval; R. Swetman, 115, Notts. v. Essex, Nottingham.

K. Taylor, 106, Yorks. v. M.C.C., Lord's; B. S. V. Timms, 120, Hants v. Oxford U., Oxford.

B. Whittingham, 133, Notts. v. Hants, Nottingham; R. Wills, 151*, Northants v. Camb. U., Cambridge

---

LORDS AND COMMONS 1966

Played 5: *Lost* 4, *Drawn* 1

Lords and Commons (XII)	174 for 5 dec.	Westminster School	131 for 10
Lords and Commons	96	St. Paul's School	98 for 3
Lords and Commons	96	The Law Society	98 for 5
Lords and Commons	108	Household Brigade	112 for 2
M.C.C.	239 for 6 dec.	Lords and Commons	122

WEST INDIES IN ENGLAND, 1966

The West Indies team of 1966 was the seventh to visit England and play a series of Test Matches over a period of thirty-nine years and inasmuch as they outplayed the old country in three of the five Tests they proved highly successful. Yet, overall, the combination led by Garfield Sobers failed by a long way to reveal the power of the team that came three years earlier under Sir Frank Worrell, the first to win The Wisden Trophy. In 1963, Worrell's men won fifteen of their thirty first-class engagements whereas Sobers' men could point to only eight wins in twenty-seven matches. The wet summer partly contributed to the number of draws but it seemed that this latest side was not so well balanced and relied too much on the all-round excellence of the captain. Moreover, England, until the last Test, in which the West Indies themselves were outplayed, proved most disappointing, and were at their lowest ebb for many years.

For the left-handed Sobers, the Tests were one triumph after another with bat and ball as well as in the field as a master tactician and fantastic catcher close to the bat. Sobers scored 722 in the five Tests: 161 at Old Trafford; 46 and 163 not out at Lord's, 3 and 94 at Trent Bridge, 174 at Headingley and 81 and 0 at The Oval. He averaged 103.14 an innings and his aggregate beat the record of 709 he set up for his country against England in the West Indies in 1959–60. A brilliant stroke player. Sobers always made his runs at a tempo to suit the situation. If the West Indies were in difficulties, he would proceed steadily until things improved and then he dealt out heavy punishment, showing himself the complete master.

Originally a left-arm slow bowler, Sobers, apart from his batting, would be worth his place in the attack of any current Test side. Excelling in three different roles, Sobers was a genuine opening bowler with an occasional extremely fast ball, an orthodox slow left-arm bowler and, thirdly, a skilful exponent of wrist spin in the tradition of George Tribe who taught him the art. Only Gibbs took more wickets than Sobers for West Indies in the Tests, 21 to 20, but in all first-class matches Sobers finished with most wickets, 60 at 20.58 runs each. He also gained the distinction of being the first bowler from the West Indies to take nine wickets in an innings in England. That feat was achieved against Kent on a perfect pitch at Canterbury where his figures were nine for 49.

Sobers had the good fortune to win the toss in all five Tests—May and Cowdrey did so for England in the West Indies in 1959–60—yet in three of their first innings, at Lord's, Trent Bridge and The Oval, they were put out for 269, 235 and 268, which rather suggested that sometimes batting first when the pitches were fresh and lively was a more difficult hazard than taking second knock.

What mattered most was that Sobers won the toss in the first

Test at Old Trafford. There the surface soon deteriorated and England, who faced a total of 484, gave a pathetic display at their first attempt. Another important factor was the ability of this West Indies team to extricate themselves from critical situations as they did in the Tests at Lord's and Trent Bridge. They came as World Champions and by their skill and determination they retained the title.

Twelve of the seventeen players had previously toured England. The selectors preferred to rely on experience, but there were occasions, particularly in the matches against the Counties, when the resources of the side were severely tested. Some of the older batsmen like Solomon, McMorris and Carew could not be termed successes and of the five newcomers, Holford, Hendriks, Lashley, Brancker and Cohen, only the first two really proved their worth.

For this tour the West Indies agreed on the system of umpires calling and/or reporting cases of suspicious bowling actions as applied in 1965 when New Zealand and South Africa were in England. On the previous West Indies tour in 1963 there was no reporting.

The side was chosen in two batches. In the first list, announced several months ahead, Lester King, the Jamaica fast bowler who came in 1963, was included, but a cartilage operation caused his place to be given to Cohen, who at 23 was the youngest member of the party. The average age was thirty.

Undoubtedly the side would have been stronger had King been fit enough to come. Cohen lacked experience; too much work could not be thrown on Hall, the key man of the attack, and Griffith, of the controversial action, came under fire in the press, especially from Test player-writers. This was an unpleasant feature of the tour. Day after day we had the unsatisfactory spectacle of umpires scrutinising his action from square leg and point. In mid-May Griffith was called for throwing by Umpire Fagg in the match against Lancashire at Old Trafford and during the Headingley Test he was warned by Umpire Elliott for an illegal delivery. When Griffith attempted his fullest pace, or his bouncer or his yorker, he seemed to have to take care and was seldom the same deadly bowler as on his previous visit. At times, Sobers preferred to take the new ball himself. Hall did not strike his best form until the second Test at Lord's and reserved his biggest triumph for the fourth Test at Headingley where his speed in the first innings sent England headlong towards defeat.

Another valuable member of the attack was Gibbs who maintained his reputation as the world's leading exponent of off-spin. He made the most of his opportunity on the crumbling Old Trafford pitch in the first Test and headed the Test bowling averages, despite much punishment at The Oval.

As in 1963 the West Indies failed to solve the problem of

providing a reliable opening batting partner to Hunte; McMorris, Carew and Lashley all being tried. Even Hunte faded after giving them a noble start with 135 at Old Trafford—a repetition of his success in 1963—for he scored only 108 runs in the four remaining Tests. Kanhai performed in reverse and did not really blossom forth until the fifth when he hit his tenth Test century but only his first in England.

The reliable consistency of Nurse was a great asset, his only failure in eight Test innings being on the opening day at The Oval. He hit 137 at Headingley and altogether helped himself to 501 runs from the England bowlers. Moreover he always made his runs attractively. Butcher, like Nurse, finished with a Test average of 60, but nearly half his runs came from his not-out double century at Trent Bridge where he stood in the breach with Kanhai when England threatened to break through.

Holford, one of only three members of the party without previous Test experience, soon established for himself a permanent place. A cousin of Sobers, he came to the rescue at Lord's after five second-innings wickets had gone for 95, by hitting 105 in an unbroken stand of 274 with Sobers that staved off the possibility of defeat. Standing over six feet, he drove splendidly and did some useful work as a leg-break bowler besides being a fine close-up fielder. Brancker, a left-handed slow bowler, could never seriously challenge Sobers for a place in that art. Lashley was a diminutive left-handed batsman, very restricted in his forcing strokes, but in his solitary spell as a Test bowler, he removed Boycott and began England's second-innings slide at Headingley.

The side was adequately served by the wicket-keepers. Indeed, Hendriks, after being kept out of the first two Tests by a hand injury, proved extremely efficient; Allan, on his second visit, performed admirably at Old Trafford but was less confident on the faster pitch at Lord's.

The West Indies players brought a heap of criticism on themselves midway through the tour by their apparent lack of interest in many county engagements. Possibly a contributory factor was the short interval of only three years between their previous tour and the poor standard of some pitches which drew adverse comment from their popular manager, Jeffrey Stollmeyer. Anyhow, they put up some drab batting displays and did not gain their first victory over any county until they overcame Derbyshire on the eve of the first Test. Immediately after that Test, they drew with Gloucestershire with the scores level and then lost to Sussex on a frightful pitch at Hove. They later lost to Northamptonshire, both these matches being over in two days.

During a season when football intervened, with England staging the World Cup, the West Indies played a vital part in keeping cricket alive. Unfortunately it was a wet summer with many days ruined by rain but happily the Tests met with little interference nor did the dates clash with the Soccer matches during July. Nevertheless, although record crowds attended the Tests at Lord's and Trent Bridge, and 90,000 went during the four days at The Oval, the profits fell by nearly half compared with 1963.—N.P.

WEST INDIES RESULTS

Test Matches—Played 5; *Won* 3, *Lost* 1, *Drawn* 1.

First-Class Matches—Played 27; *Won* 8, *Lost* 4, *Drawn* 15.

All Matches—Played 34; *Won* 13, *Lost* 5, *Drawn* 16.

Wins—England (3), Duke of Norfolk's XI (one-day match), Cambridge University, Derbyshire, Minor Counties (two days), Kent, Surrey (one day), Warwickshire, Leicestershire, Warwickshire (one day), Rest of the World (one day).

Losses—England, Sussex, Northamptonshire, T. N. Pearce's XI, An England XI (one day).

Draws—England, Worcestershire, Oxford University, Nottinghamshire, M.C.C., Lancashire, Yorkshire, Gloucestershire, Essex, Middlesex, Somerset, President of M.C.C.'s XI, Glamorgan, Scotland (one day), Hampshire, A. E. R. Gilligan's XI.

TEST MATCH AVERAGES

ENGLAND

BATTING

	Matches	Inns.	Not Outs	Runs	Highest Inns.	Average
T. W. Graveney	4	7	1	459	165	76.50
C. Milburn	4	8	2	316	126*	52.66
B. d'Oliveira	4	6	0	256	88	42.66
R. W. Barber	2	3	0	97	55	32.33
M. C. Cowdrey	4	8	0	252	96	31.50
G. Boycott	4	7	0	186	71	26.57
J. M. Parks	4	8	0	181	91	22.62
J. A. Snow	3	5	2	62	59*	20.66
K. Higgs	5	8	0	147	63	18.37
W. E. Russell	2	4	0	61	26	15.25
K. F. Barrington	2	4	0	59	30	14.75
F. J. Titmus	3	5	0	61	22	12.20
D. L. Underwood	2	4	2	22	12*	11.00
R. Illingworth	2	3	0	7	4	2.33
I. J. Jones	2	3	3	0	0*	—

Played in one match: J. T. Murray 112; D. A. Allen 37 and 1; J. H. Edrich 35; D. J. Brown 14 and 10; D. L. Amiss 17; M. J. K. Smith 5 and 6; B. R. Knight 6; D. B. Close 4.

* *Signifies not out.*

BOWLING

	Overs	Maidens	Runs	Wickets	Average
K. Higgs	236.4	49	611	24	25.45
R. W. Barber	51.1	7	182	6	30.33
J. A. Snow	138.5	29	451	12	37.58

	Overs	Maidens	Runs	Wickets	Average
F. J. Titmus	81	20	190	5	38.00
B. d'Oliveira	160	48	329	8	41.12
R. Illingworth	63	24	165	4	41.25
B. R. Knight	51	3	169	4	42.25
D. L. Underwood	69	25	172	1	172.00
I. J. Jones	74	11	259	1	259.00

Also bowled: D. A. Allen 31.1—8—104—2; D. B. Close 12—3—28—1 D. J. Brown 28—4—84—0.

WEST INDIES

BATTING

	Matches	Inns.	Not Outs	Runs	Highest Inns.	Average
G. S. Sobers	5	8	1	722	174	103.14
S. M. Nurse	5	8	0	501	137	62.62
B. F. Butcher	5	8	1	420	209*	60.00
R. B. Kanhai	5	8	0	324	104	40.50
D. A. J. Holford	5	8	2	227	105*	37.83
C. C. Hunte	5	8	0	243	135	30.37
P. D. Lashley	2	3	0	81	49	27.00
W. W. Hall	5	6	2	69	30*	17.25
C. C. Griffith	5	6	1	82	30	16.40
E. D. McMorris	2	3	0	26	14	8.66
L. R. Gibbs	5	6	3	22	12	7.33
D. W. Allan	2	2	0	14	13	7.00
J. L. Hendriks	3	4	1	11	9*	3.66

Played in one match: M. C. Carew 2 and 0.

* *Signifies not out.*

BOWLING

	Overs	Maidens	Runs	Wickets	Average
L. R. Gibbs	273.4	103	520	21	24.76
G. S. Sobers	269.4	78	545	20	27.25
W. W. Hall	175.3	35	555	18	30.83
C. C. Griffith	144.3	27	438	14	31.28
D. A. J. Holford	90.5	13	302	5	60.40

Also bowled: P. D. Lashley 3—2—1—1; M. C. Carew 3—0—11—1; C. C. Hunte 13—2—41—0.

WEST INDIES FIRST-CLASS AVERAGES

BATTING

† *Denotes left-handed batsman.*

	Birthplace	Matches	Inns.	Not Outs	Runs	Highest Inns.	Average
†G. S. Sobers	*Barbados*	18	25	3	1349	174	61.31
B. F. Butcher	*Guyana*	19	25	2	1105	209*	48.04
S. M. Nurse	*Barbados*	19	26	1	1105	155	44.20
R. B. Kanhai	*Guyana*	19	28	1	1028	192*	38.07
D. A. J. Holford	*Barbados*	19	26	6	759	107*	37.95
C. C. Hunte	*Barbados*	19	27	0	970	206	35.92

* *Signifies not out.*

	Birthplace	Matches	Inns.	Not Outs	Runs	Highest Inns.	Average
J. S. Solomon . . .	*Guyana*	17	21	4	585	104*	34.41
†P. D. Lashley . .	*Barbados*	18	24	2	647	78	29.40
E. D. McMorris .	*Jamaica*	17	25	3	634	157*	28.81
†M. C. Carew . . .	*Trinidad*	18	29	1	720	132	25.71
C. C. Griffith	*Barbados*	16	20	6	297	63*	21.21
†R. C. Brancker .	*Barbados*	16	19	1	329	37	18.27
D. W. Allan	*Barbados*	14	15	2	209	56	16.07
W. W. Hall	*Barbados*	19	21	5	246	34*	15.37
J. L. Hendriks . . .	*Jamaica*	14	16	5	144	20	13.09
R. A. Cohen	*Jamaica*	18	15	8	72	32	10.28
L. R. Gibbs	*Guyana*	17	18	8	98	19	9.80

* *Signifies not out.*

BOWLING

† *Denotes left-arm bowler.*

	Overs	Maidens	Runs	Wickets	Average
C. C. Griffith	357	86	998	49	20.36
†G. S. Sobers	557.2	158	1235	60	20.58
R. A. Cohen	283.3	59	969	40	24.22
L. R. Gibbs	608.4	207	1190	47	25.31
†R. C. Brancker	330.4	81	861	33	26.09
D. A. J. Holford	507	117	1459	51	28.60
P. D. Lashley	162.2	40	407	14	29.07
M. C. Carew	233	78	531	17	31.23
W. W. Hall	439	104	1280	39	32.82
R. B. Kanhai	5.1	0	47	1	47.00
C. C. Hunte	32	8	93	1	93.00
J. S. Solomon	54	10	204	1	204.00

Also bowled: B. F. Butcher 2—0—7—0; S. M. Nurse 2—0—3—0.

WEST INDIES HUNDREDS

The following twenty-two three-figure innings were hit for West Indies, two not ranking as first-class:

G. S. Sobers (4):
174 v. England (Fourth Test) at Leeds
163* v. England (Second Test), at Lord's
161 v. England (First Test) at Manchester
153 v. Nottinghamshire at Nottingham

B. F. Butcher (3):
209* v. England (Third Test) at Nottingham
137 v. M.C.C. at Lord's
128 v. Warwickshire at Birmingham

R. B. Kanhai (3):
192* v Oxford University at Oxford.
104 v. England (Fifth Test) at The Oval
103 v. T. N. Pearce's XI at Scarborough

S. M. Nurse (3):
155 v. Essex at Southend
137 v. England (Fourth Test) at Leeds
†102* v. Warwickshire at Birmingham

D. A. J. Holford (2):
107* v. Lancashire at Manchester
105* v. England (Second Test) at Lord's

C. C. Hunte (2):
206 v. Somerset at Taunton
135 v. England (First Test) at Manchester

E. D. McMorris (2):
157* v. Derbyshire at Derby
116 v. Kent at Canterbury

M. C. Carew (1):
132 v. Gloucestershire at Bristol

P. D. Lashley (1):
†121* v. Minor Counties at Lakenham

J. S. Solomon (1):
104* v. Somerset at Taunton

* *Signifies not out.* † *Signifies not first-class.*

HUNDREDS AGAINST WEST INDIES

The following fourteen three-figure innings were played against West Indies, one not first-class:

T. W. Graveney (2):
165 for England (Fifth Test) at The Oval
109 for England (Third Test) at Nottingham

J. T. Murray (2):
112 for England (Fifth Test) at The Oval
100* for M.C.C. at Lord's

D. L. Amiss (1):
160* for Warwickshire at Birmingham

G. Boycott (1):
131 for T. N. Pearce's XI at Scarborough

M. J. Edwards (1):
†108* for Surrey at The Oval

K. W. R. Fletcher (1):
106 for Essex at Southend

A. Jones (1):
161* for Glamorgan at Swansea

B. W. Luckhurst (1):
104 for Kent at Canterbury

C. Milburn (1):
126* for England (Second Test) at Lord's

R. B. Nicholls (1):
108 for Gloucestershire at Bristol

G. Pullar (1):
167* for Lancashire at Manchester

M. J. K. Smith (1):
140 for M.C.C. at Lord's.

† *Not first-class.* * *Signifies not out.*

WEST INDIES—FIELDING

D. W. Allan (27 caught, 8 stumped) 35; J. L. Hendriks (24 caught, 10 stumped) 34; G. S. Sobers 23; S. M. Nurse 17; P. D. Lashley 15; R. B. Kanhai 13; D. A. J. Holford 12; R. C. Brancker 10; M. C. Carew 9; R. A. Cohen 9; L. R. Gibbs 9; C. C. Hunte 9; B. F. Butcher 8; W. W. Hall 6; J. S. Solomon 6, C. C. Griffith 4; E. D. McMorris 2. (First-class matches.)

DUKE OF NORFOLK'S XI v. WEST INDIES

At Arundel, April 30. Duke of Norfolk's XI 221 for seven declared (K. F. Barrington 73, T. W. Graveney 58; R. C. Brancker three for 50); West Indies 223 for six (S. M. Nurse 61, P. D. Lashley 61, M. C. Carew 54). West Indies won by four wickets.

WORCESTERSHIRE v. WEST INDIES

At Worcester. May 4, 5, 6. Drawn without a first-innings decision. The glorious sunshine which had greeted the West Indies at Arundel four days earlier, turned to rain for their opening first-class match. Only four hours' play out of the eighteen was possible and the tourists never went into bat. The whole of the third day was washed out. Ormrod made a promising 72 to equal his previous highest and, with Headley, put on a useful 69 for the second wicket. Confronted by the spin of Gibbs and Brancker, who bowled 28 overs in an hour at one stage, Graveney quickly produced handsome drives into the covers and wide of mid-on, and the county got to 152 for 2. With Brancker then dismissing Graveney, the innings deteriorated.

Worcestershire

*D. Kenyon c Hendriks b Sobers	4	†R. Booth run out	1
R. G. A. Headley st Hendriks b Gibbs	35	D. N. F. Slade not out	25
J. A. Ormrod st Hendriks b Brancker	72	N. Gifford not out	6
T. W. Graveney c Sobers b Brancker	41	B 1, l-b 4, w 1, n-b 1	7
B. d'Oliveira c Gibbs b Brancker	7	1/9 2/78 3/152 4/163 (7 wkts.)	206
D. W. Richardson b Gibbs	8	5/164 6/165 7/178	

L. J. Coldwell and J. A. Flavell did not bat.

Bowling: Hall 14—3—45—0; Sobers 13—3—37—1; Gibbs 32—12—58—2; Solomon 9—3—28—0; Brancker 34—9—31—3.

West Indies

C. C. Hunte, M. C. Carew, R. B. Kanhai, *G. S. Sobers, S. M. Nurse, B. F. Butcher, J. S. Solomon, R. C. Brancker, †J. L. Hendriks, W. W. Hall, and L. R. Gibbs.

Umpires: J. S. Buller and C. S. Elliott.

OXFORD UNIVERSITY v. WEST INDIES

At Oxford, May 7, 9, 10. Drawn. A display of exhilarating batting by Kanhai, who made 192 not out, and the bowling of Griffith were the notable features of this game which was spoilt through the loss of the second day through rain. In the Oxford first innings all eyes were on Griffith, playing his first game of the tour. His action, first at medium-pace then at quicker speed, was watched by Umpire Jepson from deep point as well as from square-leg. Griffith made good use of his yorker and thoroughly deserved his four wickets. Kanhai, in his opening first-class innings of the season, recorded his highest score in England. After the blank Monday he went from 50 not out to 192 in great style, driving, cutting, glancing, pulling and hooking in delightful vein. He reached his century with an almost straight six off Ridley, a steady left-arm spin bowler, and earned an ovation when he took out his bat after staying four hours and hitting twenty-three 4's and three 6's. Oxford, needing 221 to avoid an innings defeat, gallantly held out after Gibbs, the off-spinner, had taken the first five wickets to fall for 31, out of 129. For Oxford, Ridley made 50, including two 6's.

Oxford University

P. J. K. Gibbs b Griffith	23 — c Hunte b Gibbs	40
F. S. Goldstein lbw b Cohen	3 — b Gibbs	22
D. P. Toft b Griffith	3 — c Griffith b Gibbs	11
*R. M. C. Gilliat run out	25 — b Gibbs	5
M. G. M. Groves c Cohen b Holford	21 — b Gibbs	28
†A. W. Dyer c Allan b Griffith	28 — st Allan b Holford	20
G. N. S. Ridley lbw b Holford	6 — not out	50
A. H. Barker c Lashley b Holford	28 — c Allan b Lashley	15
A. G. M. Watson not out	2 — c Lashley b Cohen	0
R. W. Elviss c Cohen b Gibbs	5 — not out	2
J. N. C. Easter b Griffith	0	
B 9, l-b 6, w 1	16	B 17, l-b 1 18
1/26 2/30 3/37 4/67 5/81 6/97 7/139 8/149 9/158	160	1/46 2/74 3/85 4/92 5/129 6/137 7/198 8/203 (8 wkts.) 211

Bowling: *First Innings*—Griffith 12.5—2—35—4; Cohen 12—2—30—1; Solomon 5—3—12—0; Gibbs 12—6—27—1; Holford 15—5—40—3. *Second Innings*—Griffith 4—1—9—0; Cohen 8—1—17—1; Solomon 10—0—56—0; Gibbs 32—15—45—5; Holford 24—9—48—1; Lashley 5—1—18—1.

West Indies

*C. C. Hunte b Ridley	20
E. D. McMorris b Barker	45
R. B. Kanhai not out	192
B. F. Butcher c Barker b Ridley	0
P. D. Lashley b Ridley	28
J. S. Solomon c Dyer b Watson	20
D. A. J. Holford c Groves b Barker	19
†D. W. Allan c Ridley b Watson	19
C. C. Griffith not out	31
B 1, l-b 6	7
1/69 2/71 3/71 4/137 5/180 6/248 7/320 (7 wkts., dec.)	381

L. R. Gibbs and R. A. Cohen did not bat.

Bowling: Watson 18—4—68—2; Easter 10—2—49—0; Ridley 37—9—105—3; Barker 41—11—107—2; Elviss 9—2—25—0; Groves 3—0—20—0.

Umpires: W. F. Price and A. Jepson.

NOTTINGHAMSHIRE v. WEST INDIES

At Nottingham, May 11, 12, 13. Drawn. After rain had ruled out the first day's play Nottinghamshire won the toss and, as usual with touring sides, put them in. Lacking batting practice, the West Indies played cautiously, McMorris and Carew not hurrying during an opening stand of 72, but there was a drastic change when Sobers arrived at the wicket. He began quietly, spending twenty minutes over his first three runs. Then his innings blossomed into a glorious affair and at the end of two hours and forty minutes of attractive stroke play he reached 153 out of 221 helped by five 6's and twenty 4's. Nottinghamshire batted soundly and Hill, Swetman and Moore each exceeded fifty. The West Indies attack, although showing plenty of variety, did not look too impressive. Nottinghamshire declared 76 runs behind with only six wickets down, to give the spectators a brief glance of the West Indies batting a second time.

West Indies

First Innings		Second Innings	
M. C. Carew c Bolus b Forbes	40	— c Swetman b Forbes	36
E. D. McMorris run out	40	— c Hill b Bolus	35
S. M. Nurse lbw b Davison	17	— b Bolus	7
*G. S. Sobers c White b Gillhouley	153		
P. D. Lashley b Johnson	28		
R. C. Brancker c Whittingham b White	25		
D. A. J. Holford c Swetman b Davison	10	— not out	1
D. W. Allan not out	10		
L-b 9, w 1, n-b 2	12	L-b 1, n-b 1	2
1/72 2/94 3/104 4/179 5/280 6/315 7/335 (7 wkts., dec.)	335	1/66 2/73 3/81 (3 wkts.)	81

†J. L. Hendriks, W. W. Hall and R. A. Cohen did not bat.

Bowling: *First Innings*—Davison 16.3—0—44—2; Johnson 15—3—51—1; Forbes 23—4—86—1; Gillhouley 24—4—65—1; White 12—1—77—1. *Second Innings*—Davison 4—2—6—0; Johnson 7—2—17—0; Gillhouley 6—0—24—0; Bolus 7—2—24—2; Forbes 3—0—6—1; Moore 1—0—2—0.

Nottinghamshire

*N. Hill retired hurt	61
J. B. Bolus lbw b Cohen	8
†R. Swetman c Cohen b Brancker	57
I. Moore c Nurse b Lashley	63
R. A. White c Sobers b Brancker	6
M. J. Smedley not out	33
B. Whittingham c Nurse b Lashley	2
C. Forbes lbw b Hall	1
K. Gillhouley not out	11
B 14, l-b 2, n-b 1	17
1/24 2/113 3/187 4/220 5/222 6/223 (6 wkts., dec.)	259

A. Johnson and I. Davison did not bat.

Bowling: Hall 16—5—29—1; Cohen 13—5—31—1; Brancker 24—5—45—2; Holford 26—4—69—0; Sobers 12—2—35—0; Carew 8—1—16—0; Lashley 11—4—17—2.

Umpires: A. E. Rhodes and T. W. Spencer.

M.C.C. v. WEST INDIES

At Lord's, May 14, 16, 17. Drawn. For the most part West Indies were in a light hearted mood, but twice recovered well. A grand innings of 137 by Butcher on the ground where he hit a splendid Test century in 1963 delighted the Saturday crowd of 13,000. Clean driving and cutting brought him the majority of his thirteen 4's. Nurse also drove firmly and he and Butcher added 143 in under two hours. Brown and Higgs were M.C.C.'s best bowlers throughout the match. On Monday, M. J. K. Smith made himself favourite for the Test captaincy (which was announced next day) by scoring 140 in three hours, ten minutes. He was very severe on the left-arm slows of Brancker whom he swept for several of his sixteen 4's. Murray carried on the assault and completed his century in two hours, fifty minutes. Earlier, Milburn with a punishing innings of 64 showed that the West Indies attack carried little danger. A bruised foot prevented him fielding again or batting. West Indies faced a crisis when four second-innings wickets fell for 37 and left them only three runs ahead. Russell missed Nurse off Slade at 57 whereupon Butcher, Nurse. Sobers and Brancker saw them safe. When Sobers made a token declaration M.C.C. wanted 213 in less than two hours, a task they did not attempt to achieve.

West Indies

C. C. Hunte b Higgs	10	—	lbw b Higgs	23
M. C. Carew run out	17	—	c Murray b Brown	3
R. B. Kanhai c Brown b Slade	47	—	b Higgs	8
B. F. Butcher c Milburn b Brown	137	—	c Cowdrey b Walker	56
S. M. Nurse b Slade	65	—	c Smith b Walker	47
*G. S. Sobers c Murray b Higgs	40	—	c and b Lewis	34
R. C. Brancker lbw b Higgs	8	—	lbw b Lewis	37
†J. L. Hendriks lbw b Walker	0	—	b Brown	12
C. C. Griffith not out	21	—	not out	11
W. W. Hall b Brown	1	—	not out	4
L. R. Gibbs not out	0	—	b Brown	2
B. 1, l-b 2	3		B 2, l-b 4, w 1, n-b 2	9
1/25 2/32 3/88 4/231 (9 wkts., dec.)	349		1/11 2/25 3/34 (9 wkts., dec.)	246
5/298 6/312 7/313 8/334 9/342			4/37 5/133 6/158	
			7/178 8/215 9/236	

Bowling: *First Innings*—Brown 23—6—70—2; Higgs 24—4—58—3; Walker 20—6—55—1; Slade 30—9—89—2; Lewis 20—2—74—0. *Second Innings*—Brown 19—4—37—3; Higgs 16—2—38—2; Walker 20—5—75—2; Slade 8—2—30—0; Lewis 16—3—57—2.

M.C.C.

W. E. Russell b Hall	13	—	not out	25
C. Milburn c Nurse b Sobers	64			
J. H. Edrich c Carew b Gibbs	8	—	b Sobers	17
M. C. Cowdrey c Hendriks b Brancker	15	—	lbw b Hunte	13
*M. J. K. Smith b Hall	140	—	not out	10
P. M. Walker c Sobers b Brancker	11			
†J. T. Murray not out	100			
E. Lewis c Hendriks b Griffith	0			
D. N. F. Slade b Hall	0			
B. 8, l-b 8, n-b 16	32		N-b 2	2
1/22 2/92 3/100 4/119 (8 wkts., dec.)	383		1/26 2/46 (2 wkts.)	67
5/157 6/357 7/371 8/383				

D. J. Brown and K. Higgs did not bat.

Bowling: *First Innings*—Hall 15—2—60—3; Griffith 17—1—71—1; Sobers 19—5—47—1; Gibbs 29—6—61—1; Brancker 17—0—85—2; Carew 4—0—27—0. *Second Innings*—Hall 5—0—19—0; Sobers 6—2—14—1; Griffith 1—0—2—0; Hunte 7—2—10—1; Carew 7—2—10—0; Nurse 2—0—3—0; Butcher 2—0—7—0.

Umpires: W. H. Copson and H. Yarnold.

LANCASHIRE v. WEST INDIES

At Manchester, May 18, 19, 20. Drawn. Indifferent weather kept the crowd down to meagre proportions, but on a pitch that was green and easy-paced Lancashire did exceedingly well to dismiss the first five West Indies batsmen for 132. Nurse batted just over two hours and hit five 4's in his 69, but the turning point in the innings came when Holford arrived at that stage and stayed three and a quarter hours. He hit ten 4's in his maiden century in this country and his first of any consequence in big cricket. With sound defensive support from Allan, Griffith and Gibbs the tourists reached 295 for eight by close of play and declared on the morning of the second day, when rain limited play to twenty-five minutes in which time Lancashire replied with 27 for the loss of Green. On the last day

Pullar batted fluently for five and a half hours for his not-out 167 and Lancashire took the lead in the final over with only four wickets down. Entwistle gave Pullar splendid support by batting two and a half hours and hitting five boundaries. The feature of the West Indies attack was the first glimpse of Griffith at anything near top pace. The giant fast bowler was no-balled eight times for over-stepping, and once for throwing by Umpire A. E. Fagg, standing at square leg, an incident that escaped general notice until the Lancashire players drew attention to it the following day.

West Indies

*C. C. Hunte c Goodwin b Statham 2
E. D. McMorris b Greenhough ... 31
S. M. Nurse c Goodwin b Higgs.. 69
B. F. Butcher lbw b Greenhough.. 12
P. D. Lashley b Statham......... 0
J. S. Solomon c Knox b Greenhough 12
D. A. J. Holford not out.........107
†D. W. Allan c Snellgrove b Lloyd 20
C. C. Griffith lbw b Greenhough.. 10
L. R. Gibbs not out............. 17
B 7, l-b 4, n-b 4........... 15

1/6 2/79 3/117 (8 wkts., dec.) 295
4/118 5/132 6/137 7/188 8/213

Bowling: Statham 20—2—55—2; Higgs 22—5—55—1; Lever 24—6—57—0; Greenhough 33—9—83—4; Lloyd 11—3—30—1.

Lancashire

D. M. Green b Griffith........... 12
G. Pullar not out................167
G. K. Knox c McMorris b Griffith 16
R. Entwistle c Allan b Griffith ... 60
K. Snelgrove c Lashley b Griffith . 0
D. Lloyd not out................ 22
B 8, l-b 4, n-b 7.......... 19

1/20 2/71 3/221 4/221 (4 wkts.) 296

P. Lever, K. Higgs, †K. Goodwin, T. Greenhough and *J. B. Statham did not bat.

Bowling: Griffith 18—5—55—4; Cohen 15—2—51—0; Holford 29—5—80—0; Gibbs 29—10—48—0; Lashley 14—7—26—0; Solomon 6—1—17—0.

Umpires: F. Jakeman and A. E. Fagg.

CAMBRIDGE UNIVERSITY v. WEST INDIES

At Cambridge, May 21, 22, 24. West Indies won by 174 runs. This was the West Indies' first win of their tour. The West Indies visits to Fenner's since the war have provided some memorable batting feats—notably in 1950 when E. D. Weekes scored 304 not out in a total of 730 for three declared, and in 1963 when W. W. Hall hit a remarkably unorthodox hundred in only sixty-five minutes. There was nothing quite to compare with those deeds this time, but Sobers played an attractive innings of 83 in just over an hour and a half, Kanhai hit 45 in thirty-eight minutes, and later Lashley, with 78, and Solomon, with 73 not out, helped to take West Indies to a first-innings total of 345. Cambridge lost their first five wickets for 63, but then Cosh, a 19-year-old Freshman from Dulwich, and Barnwell put on 92 for the sixth wicket. Cosh went on to score 98, and was last man out, caught at mid-off, two runs away from his maiden hundred. Cambridge, thanks to Cosh's fine innings, saved the follow-on, but the West Indies, with a lead of 125, scored 169 for six declared in their second innings, leaving the University 295 to win in six hours on the third day. Things did not start too well for the West Indies on the final morning, as an hour and a half was lost through rain, and the Cambridge opening pair made 54 for the first wicket. After lunch, the leg-spinner, Holford, in spite of the handicap of bowling with a wet ball, took the first six wickets to fall for 19 runs in 10 overs. Cambridge then soon succumbed, and Holford finished with eight wickets for 52 runs.

West Indies

M. C. Carew c Sinker b Palfreman	2	— c Murray b Acfield	67
E. D. McMorris b Roopnaraine	30	— b Barnwell	1
R. B. Kanhai c and b Palfreman	45	— c Barnwell b Acfield	38
R. C. Brancker b Acfield	12	— c Murray b Roopnaraine	28
*G. S. Sobers lbw b Roopnaraine	83		
P. D. Lashley c Sinker b Palfreman	78	— not out	1
J. S. Solomon not out	73		
D. A. J. Holford c Murray b Palfreman	0	— b Roopnaraine	6
†J. L. Hendriks lbw b Acfield	13		
W. W. Hall lbw b Sinker	1	— c Murray b Sinker	20
R. A. Cohen lbw b Sinker	0	— not out	0
B 7, l-b 1	8	B 7, l-b 1	8
1/2 2/64 3/89 4/89 5/211 6/282 7/292 8/334 9/335	345	1/2 2/84 3/138 4/142 5/168 6/168 (6 wkts., dec.)	169

Bowling: *First Innings*—Palfreman 24—9—62—4; Barnwell 15—2—55—0; Roopnaraine 35—9—88—2; Acfield 22—6—73—2; Sinker 32.2—7—59—2. *Second Innings*—Palfreman 8—0—33—0; Barnwell 4—2—11—1; Acfield 23—6—52—2; Sinker 10—3—32—1; Roopnaraine 16—4—33—2.

Cambridge University

K. P. W. J. McAdam b Cohen	10	— lbw b Holford	4
R. E. J. Chambers c and b Sobers	16	— c Hendriks b Holford	32
J. M. Brearley b Holford	9	— b Holford	4
*†D. L. Murray c Hall b Sobers	0	— c Hendriks b Sobers	11
D. L. Hays b Holford	24	— c Brancker b Holford	4
N. J. Cosh c Carew b Holford	98	— c Brancker b Holford	0
L. M. L. Barnwell c Holford b Sobers	46	— st Hendriks b Holford	27
A. B. Palfreman c Hendriks b Holford	6	— b Sobers	20
R. Roopnaraine run out	1	— c and b Holford	0
N. Sinker run out	0	— c Solomon b Holford	5
D. C. Acfield not out	4	— not out	0
B 3, l-b 3	6	B 12, l-b 1	13
1/17 2/30 3/30 4/44 5/63 6/155 7/177 8/191 9/197	220	1/54 2/62 3/69 4/79 5/82 6/87 7/89 8/92 9/116	120

Bowling: *First Innings*—Hall 13—5—23—0; Cohen 3—0—12—1; Brancker 16—4—38—0; Solomon 6—2—15—0; Sobers 20—4—56—3; Holford 28.5—14—63—4; Carew 5—3—7—0. *Second Innings*—Hall 3—1—7—0; Cohen 5—2—10—0; Sobers 20.1—6—38—2; Holford 18—4—52—8.

Umpires: J. S. Buller and W. F. Price.

YORKSHIRE v. WEST INDIES

At Bradford, May 25, 26, 27. Drawn. The loss of all Wednesday and an hour of Thursday morning because of rain and saturated turf left little possibility of outright victory as a result. Yorkshire gained the satisfaction of a first-innings advantage after having been sent in to bat and declaring with six wickets down. The pitch, which was protected against rain for this match, was firmer than the surrounds, but never permitted confident batting and only Hunte, not out 17 overnight, recorded an individual 50 for either side. He concentrated on defence in a stay of more than three hours and after his departure Trueman undermined the innings by dismissing Nurse and Brancker in one over. Sobers drove Wilson for 6 and 4 before edging a slip catch and Griffith and Hall added 23 runs in fifteen minutes, but Yorkshire won a first-innings lead of 9 runs as consolation for spectators enduring cold, dull weather.

Yorkshire

G. Boycott c Allan b Griffith	40	— c Sobers b Hall	14
K. Taylor c Sobers b Gibbs	19	— not out	32
D. E. V. Padgett st Allan b Brancker	13	— b Sobers	5
J. H. Hampshire b Griffith	3	— lbw b Hall	3
*D. B. Close b Sobers	34	— not out	7
P. J. Sharpe c Butcher b Gibbs	18		
R. Illingworth not out	28		
†J. G. Binks not out	20		
L-b 1, w 1	2	B 1, n-b 2	3
1/49 2/62 3/68 4/83 5/112 6/144 (6 wkts., dec.)	177	1/25 2/30 3/39 (3 wkts.)	64

D. Wilson, F. S. Trueman and J. Waring did not bat.

Bowling: *First Innings*—Griffith 12—6—17—2; Sobers 17—4—38—1; Hall 13—6—29—0; Gibbs 29—9—51—2; Brancker 9—0—24—1; Carew 7—0—16—0. *Second Innings*—Hall 9—0—35—2; Griffith 5—1—6—0; Sobers 6—3—6—1; Carew 5—3—3—0; Hunte 4—1—10—0; Kanhai 1—0—1—0.

West Indies

C. C. Hunte c Close b Wilson	66
M. C. Carew c Sharpe b Close	19
R. B. Kanhai c Binks b Taylor	0
B. F. Butcher lbw b Trueman	11
S. M. Nurse lbw b Trueman	20
*G. S. Sobers c Sharpe b Wilson	20
R. C. Brancker lbw b Trueman	0
†D. W. Allan c Sharpe b Waring	3
C. C. Griffith c Illingworth b Waring	14
W. W. Hall c Binks b Close	9
L. R. Gibbs not out	0
B 11, l-b 3, w 2, n-b 3	19
1/55, 2/56 3/97 4/114 5/116 6/116 7/145 8/145 9/168	168

Bowling: Trueman 19—4—46—3; Waring 15.3—6—25—2; Illingworth 4—1—17—0; Wilson 8—3—23—2; Close 11—6—14—2; Taylor 14—4—24—1.

Umpires: C. S. Elliott and J. Langridge.

DERBYSHIRE v. WEST INDIES

At Derby, May 28, 30, 31. West Indies won by an innings and 32 runs. Derbyshire were without their injured off-spinner, Smith, and with Morgan unable to bowl and Jackson later suffering a recurrence of a finger injury, the tourists took a heavy toll of a weakened attack on a beautiful batting surface. Hunte and McMorris made the biggest opening stand of the tour before Hunte was out two short of his century. McMorris struck one 6 and eighteen 4's in his not-out 157 and with Sobers making 49 at more than a run a minute the West Indies declared after batting for six hours. Sobers, swinging the ball prodigiously, upset Derbyshire after a good start. His first five wickets cost only 9 runs and Derbyshire followed on 266 behind. Johnson played well, equalling the highest score by a Derbyshire player against the West Indies, but the spin of Sobers took the tourists to victory before lunch on the third day.

West Indies

C. C. Hunte c Page b Buxton	98
E. D. McMorris not out	157
S. M. Nurse c Taylor b Page	54
*G. S. Sobers not out	49
B 3, l-b 4, n-b 6	13
1/182 2/292 (2 wkts. dec.)	371

B. F. Butcher, J. S. Solomon, P. D. Lashley, D. A. J. Holford, †J. L. Hendriks, C. C. Griffith and R. A. Cohen did not bat.

Bowling: Jackson 19—8—33—0; Rhodes 21—10—24—0; Buxton 26—6—59—1; Eyre 28—6—134—0; Page 28—4—108—1.

Derbyshire

I. W. Hall b Sobers	19	— b Holford	47
J. F. Harvey c Hendriks b Sobers	16	— c Hendriks b Griffith	0
J. R. Eyre b Cohen	1	— b Holford	14
H. L. Johnson lbw b Cohen	1	— b Sobers	90
I. R. Buxton lbw b Sobers	0	— b Griffith	25
M. Hill b Griffith	0	— st Hendriks b Holford	18
†R. W. Taylor b Sobers	11	— c and b Sobers	2
*D. C. Morgan b Sobers	0	— c Sobers b Cohen	29
M. H. Page c sub. b Sobers	22	— c and b Sobers	5
H. J. Rhodes not out	23	— not out	0
A. B. Jackson absent hurt	0	— absent hurt	0
B 4, l-b 4, n-b 4	12	B 1, l-b 3	4
1/37 2/40 3/42 4/42 5/46 6/57 7/57 8/58 9/105	105	1/0 2/22 3/91 4/143 5/186 6/210 7/224 8/230 9/234	234

Bowling: *First Innings*—Griffith 11—4—22—1; Cohen 15—4—60—2; Sobers 9.2—4—11—6. *Second Innings*—Sobers 10.2—4—36—3; Griffith 17—9—20—2; Cohen 10—1—33—1; Lashley 8—3—14—0; Holford 35—8—94—3; Solomon 9—0—33—0.

Umpires: A. Jepson and R. Aspinall.

ENGLAND v. WEST INDIES

First Test

At Manchester, June 2, 3, 4. West Indies won by an innings and 40 runs with two days to spare. It was the first time England had lost in three days since they went down to Australia at Leeds in 1938 and it was the first time they had been beaten so soon in a five-day Test. No doubt, West Indies were fortunate to win the toss and bat on a newly prepared pitch before it turned in favour of spin. Only thirty wickets went down in the match and of these 24 fell to the slow bowlers. Titmus and Allen took seven for England, but easily the most deadly artist in this important phase of the game was Gibbs, who with five wickets in each innings, finished with a full analysis of ten for 106. Holford, in his first Test, and Sobers gave sound support and between them claimed seven victims with varied leg spin.

The match was favoured with three days of really hot weather. The England selectors made B. d'Oliveira twelfth man and committed the side to carrying an excessively long tail, which proved a great mistake. The play followed very much the pattern of the 1963 match on the same ground. Then West Indies batting first scored 501 for six declared, with Hunte 182, and they won by ten wickets, Gibbs's figures being eleven for 157.

Now Hunte dominated the cricket for five hours and made 135 (nineteen 4's) of the first day's total of 343 for five wickets, he being fifth out to the new ball at 283 when he fell to a grand catch at short fine leg. The cavalier treatment of the England bowlers began with the very first ball which Jones pitched short and Hunte square cut for four with a handsome stroke. Yet in Jones's second over Hunte, when seven and the total 10, was dropped by Higgs on the leg boundary; Higgs appeared to sight the ball very late against the distant background of dark coated spectators.

At times, Jones, Brown and Higgs made the ball fly awkwardly but the West Indies batsmen were adept in punishing anything a shade loose. England began well when Higgs disposed of McMorris and Kanhai (yorked middle stump) in six deliveries but Butcher, Nurse and Sobers helped Hunte in stands of 74, 99 and 68.

In the last two hours Sobers set the seal on the day's play with a devastating exhibition during which he helped himself to 83 while the score rose by 128. Holford arrived for the last hour while Sobers, his elder cousin, collared the bowling, Holford's share of an unbroken stand of 60 amounting to six.

Fielding blunders cost England dearly. Sobers, for all his brilliance, was let off four times; the first when 63, Brown misjudging a high catch from Higgs at long-on. Next morning the West Indies captain offered three more chances when in the "nineties" and altogether he stayed four hours and eight minutes for his 161, which contained one 6 and twenty-six 4's, being ninth out at 482 just before the innings, which lasted eight hours and ten minutes, closed for 484.

The respect Titmus commanded and the spin he acquired in taking five for 83 in thirty-five overs helped to undermine the confidence of the England batsmen who realised the pitch had already turned in favour of the spin bowling.

England began their reply at half past two on Friday and at once disaster overtook them, Milburn, on his first Test appearance, being run out for a duck. He pushed Hall straight to Gibbs at cover, went for a single, only to be sent back by Russell, but Gibbs had time to sprint across and break the wicket. Although Russell stayed for ninety minutes, England never recovered from that early reverse and when Smith was fifth to leave Gibbs had already cast his net, his figures reading 9—6—3—3. Parks and Allen batted sensibly for an hour while adding 58, but the end of the second day found England 163 for eight, needing 122 to save the follow on.

Consequently, just before noon on Saturday, England faced the task of getting 317 to avoid an innings defeat, a feat they did not achieve though they put up a better show at the second attempt.

The two big boys, Milburn and Cowdrey, were the mainstays. Milburn redeemed his duck with a powerful display of big hitting. Dropped three times, he enjoyed plenty of good luck on this sporting pitch and moreover he provided plenty of entertainment for the big crowd. This time Sobers, against the wind, opened the bowling while Griffith and Hall attacked in turn from the Stretford end. Milburn hooked Hall for 6 and he reached 94 when he hooked Gibbs for 6. Then he slashed across the line of the ball and was bowled, having made his runs out of 166 in two and a half hours. He also hit twelve 4's.

Thereafter, Cowdrey alone proved equal to dealing with Sobers, Gibbs and Holford who were able to make the ball lift and turn in disconcerting fashion. By watchful defence and clean hitting, Cowdrey (nine 4's), stayed for two hours and ten minutes. When heavy clouds threatened rain, Brown remained an hour, making 6 in a stand of 50 with Cowdrey.

With the light indifferent, Sobers stuck to his spinners, who finished the match by a quarter to six. Sobers was the central figure in his side's success. He followed his 161 with skilful leadership, and long spells of bowling in three different forms which earned his three wickets, and he held five catches, four of them in the leg trap.

During the match Griffith was no-balled nine times for overstepping the crease. In turn, each umpire scrutinised his action from square leg, sometimes crossing to point. Hall, with a run of 35 yards, which he covered in 17 paces, was erratic in length and direction, most of his deliveries going down the leg side.

The total attendance for the three days was 61,127; receipts £26,500. N.P.

West Indies

C. C. Hunte c Smith b Higgs......	135	C. C. Griffith lbw b Titmus.......	30
E. D. McMorris c Russell b Higgs.	11	W. W. Hall b Allen..............	1
R. B. Kanhai b Higgs...........	0	L. R. Gibbs not out.............	1
B. F. Butcher c Parks b Titmus....	44		
S. M. Nurse b Titmus...........	49	B 8, l-b 10, n-b 1..........	19
*G. S. Sobers c Cowdrey b Titmus.	161		——
D. A. J. Holford c Smith b Allen ..	32	1/38 2/42 3/116 4/215 5/283	484
†D. W. Allan lbw b Titmus.......	1	6/410 7/411 8/471 9/482	

Bowling: Jones 28—6—100—0; Brown 28—4—84—0; Higgs 31—5—94—3; Allen 31.1—8—104—2; Titmus 35—10—83—5.

England

C. Milburn run out	0	— b Gibbs	94
W. E. Russell c Sobers b Gibbs	26	— b Griffith	20
K. F. Barrington c and b Griffith	5	— c Nurse b Holford	30
M. C. Cowdrey c and b Gibbs	12	— c Butcher b Sobers	69
*M. J. K. Smith c Butcher b Gibbs	5	— b Gibbs	6
†J. M. Parks c Nurse b Holford	43	— c and b Sobers	11
F. J. Titmus b Holford	15	— c Butcher b Sobers	12
D. A. Allen c Sobers b Gibbs	37	— c Allan b Gibbs	1
D. J. Brown b Gibbs	14	— c Sobers b Gibbs	10
K. Higgs c Sobers b Holford	1	— st Allan b Gibbs	5
I. J. Jones not out	0	— not out	0
B 1, l-b 4, n-b 4	9	B 11, l-b 1, n-b 7	19
1/11 2/24 3/42 4/48 5/65 6/85 7/143 8/153 9/163	167	1/53 2/142 3/166 4/184 5/203 6/217 7/218 8/268 9/276	277

Bowling: *First Innings*—Hall 14—6—43—0; Griffith 10—3—28—1; Sobers 7—1—16—0; Gibbs 28.1—13—37—5; Holford 15—4—34—3. *Second Innings*—Sobers 42—11—87—3; Hall 5—0—28—0; Griffith 6—1—25—1; Gibbs 41—16—69—5; Holford 14—2—49—1.

Umpires: J. S. Buller and C. S. Elliott.

GLOUCESTERSHIRE v. WEST INDIES

At Bristol, June 8, 9, 10. Drawn with the scores level. Gloucestershire punished an indifferent attack and their 332 for nine declared was the highest at that stage by any county against the West Indies. Nicholls gave one of his best displays and hit his 108, which included fourteen 4's, in three and a half hours. His innings came to a close through one of Kanhai's five catches which assisted Brancker to take six wickets for 101. The tourists failed badly against the seamers of Windows, whose inspired bowling earned him his best analysis, eight for 78. Hunte, 68, alone held the innings together. Gloucestershire led by 181 but did not enforce the follow-on. They set West Indies 285 to win in four hours and five minutes. The county attack was mastered by Carew. He hit his first century of the tour, an attractive innings which included twelve 4's and came in two and three-quarter hours. In the last over West Indies with five wickets in hand needed 12 to win. They obtained 11 and then required a single off the last ball. Holford made a mighty swing but was bowled, leaving the scores level.

Gloucestershire

R. B. Nicholls c Kanhai b Brancker	108	— c Carew b Cohen	13
C. A. Milton lbw b Cohen	19	— c Hunte b Hall	0
H. Jarman c Kanhai b Brancker	28	— c Hunte b Hall	1
S. E. Russell c Kanhai b Brancker	3	— c Holford b Cohen	29
D. Shepherd c Kanhai b Brancker	29	— b Cohen	2
D. A. Allen c Allan b Cohen	34	— c Allan b Lashley	17
*J. B. Mortimore c Kanhai b Brancker	64	— b Lashley	12
A. S. Brown b Cohen	8	— c Brancker b Carew	10
A. R. Windows c Cohen b Brancker	25	— c Brancker b Lashley	11
M. D. Mence not out	2	— not out	2
L-b 6, n-b 3, w 3	12	B 1, l-b 5	6
1/45 2/128 3/154 4/188 5/204 6/260 7/274 8/320 9/332 (9 wkts., dec.)	332	1/9 2/17 3/30 4/41 5/58 6/79 7/80 8/96 9/103 (9 wkts., dec.)	103

†B. J. Meyer did not bat.

Bowling: *First Innings*—Hall 16—4—45—0; Cohen 21—3—59—3; Holford 26—6—68—0; Lashley 13—2—36—0; Brancker 37.3—11—101—6; Carew 9—3—11—0. *Second Innings*—Hall 19—5—39—2; Cohen 18—6—35—3; Lashley 5—1—15—3; Carew 4.5—2—8—1.

West Indies

M. C. Carew lbw b Brown	7	— b Brown	132
E. D. McMorris c Milton b Windows	2	— c Mortimore b Brown	1
R. B. Kanhai b Windows	4	— c Mortimore b Mence	13
*C. C. Hunte lbw b Windows	68	— run out	43
P. D. Lashley c Mortimore b Windows	3		
J. S. Solomon c Milton b Windows	11	— c Windows b Brown	39
R. C. Brancker lbw b Windows	28		
D. A. J. Holford c Meyer b Windows	22	— b Brown	27
†D. W. Allan b Windows	0		
W. W. Hall b Brown	3	— not out	13
R. A. Cohen not out	1		
B 1, l-b 1	2	B 5, l-b 9, n-b 2	16
1/6 2/14 3/14 4/17 5/47 6/119 7/132 8/138 9/141	151	1/11 2/112 3/150 4/222 5/267 6/284 (6 wkts.)	284

Bowling: *First Innings*—Brown 23—5—52—2; Windows 24.1—8—78—8; Mence 5—0—15—0; Mortimore 1—0—4—0. *Second Innings*—Brown 11—0—61—4; Windows 16—1—63—0; Allen 19—4—46—0; Mence 23—5—77—1; Mortimore 11—3—21—0.

Umpires: W. E. Phillipson and J. F. Crapp.

SUSSEX v. WEST INDIES

At Hove, June 11, 13. Sussex won by nine wickets. The West Indies, asked to bat first, were visibly shaken out of their stride by a "green" Hove pitch and an atmosphere helping swing, so that they played unimpressive cricket in losing for the first time on the tour. They were beaten with an hour and half of the second day, not to mention all the third, to spare. Their first innings lasted three and a quarter hours and they were out for 67 in two and a quarter hours at the second attempt.

This was the second lowest total ever recorded by a West Indies team in England, being nine more than the 58 of R. K. Nunes's side against Yorkshire in 1928, a year when Sussex also beat them, by an innings and 87 runs. The only stand of any consequence in the West Indies second innings was of 34 by Solomon and Lashley. No other batsman got into double figures. Three West Indians managed it in the first innings, Carew with 56, Nurse 24 and Butcher 12. Even then, Carew had a charmed life and the kindest comment on his knock was to say that he did not let the good fortune affect him. He played each ball on merit.

Snow, bowling up the hill, took seven for 29 in the initial collapse of the touring team, tearing out the heart of their innings in his second spell with six for 14. He also returned the same figures as his fellow seamer Buss on the Monday, four for 18, and finished with match figures of eleven for 47. Parks took seven catches behind the wicket, which perhaps reflected the lack of resolution in the batting.

Sussex had their worries, too, when facing Cohen and Griffith, but they were steered into a first-innings lead of 62 by Graves in only his second game of the summer. This 20-year old left-hander showed a more sensible approach than older colleagues and opponents. Finally, Sussex needed only six to win but even this produced something out of the ordinary. Sobers gave the opening over to Griffith, whose first ball rose and struck Suttle on the jaw. He went to hospital for an X-ray, which showed nothing more serious than bruising.

West Indies

M. C. Carew lbw b Snow	56	— c Pataudi b Buss	3
E. D. McMorris c Pataudi b Snow	1	— c Pataudi b Buss	0
S. M. Nurse b Bates	24	— c Foreman b Buss	8
B. F. Butcher lbw b Suttle	12	— lbw b Snow	0
*G. S. Sobers c Parks b Bates	0	— b Buss	8
J. S. Solomon c Parks b Snow	6	— c Parks b Snow	17
P. D. Lashley b Snow	6	— c Parks b Snow	14
C. C. Griffith c Parks b Snow	1	— c Parks b Bates	1
†J. L. Hendriks c Lenham b Snow	8	— b Snow	3
L. R. Gibbs b Snow	5	— c Parks b Bates	7
R. A. Cohen not out	1	— not out	2
L-b 3	3	L-b 1, n-b 1	4
1/14 2/45 3/60 4/61 5/77 6/97 7/108 8/109 9/118	123	1/2 2/7 3/12 4/16 5/20 6/54 7/55 8/55 9/63	67

Bowling: *First Innings*—Snow 16.5—5—29—7; Buss 15—5—27—0; Suttle 6—1—18—1; Bates 17—1—46—2. *Second Innings*—Snow 11.3—4—18—4; Buss 11—6—18—4; Bates 10—3—19—2; Suttle 4—1—8—0.

Sussex

K. G. Suttle b Griffith	0	— retired hurt	0
L. J. Lenham b Cohen	0	— not out	4
*Nawab of Pataudi c Hendriks b Cohen	32		
†J. M. Parks c Hendriks b Cohen	3	— not out	1
M. G. Griffith c Hendriks b Cohen	0		
D. J. Foreman c Lashley b Griffith	2		
P. J. Graves c Solomon b Griffith	64	— lbw b Griffith	0
A. S. M. Oakman c Lashley b Cohen	31		
A. Buss c Sobers b Griffith	21		
J. A. Snow b Cohen	5		
D. L. Bates not out	10		
L-b 8, n-b 8, w 1	17	N-b 1	1
1/0 2/2 3/16 4/18 5/38 6/40 7/99 8/131 9/158	185	1/1 (1 wkt.)	6

Bowling: *First Innings*—Griffith 17.4—6—43—4; Cohen 17—3—71—6; Sobers 14—5—36—0; Gibbs 5—1—18—0. *Second Innings*—Griffith 1—1—0—1; Solomon 2—1—4—0; Lashley 1.2—1—1—0.

Umpires: J. Langridge and L. H. Gray.

ENGLAND v. WEST INDIES

Second Test

At Lord's, June 16, 17, 18, 20, 21. Drawn. Despite losing the toss again, England, who had a different captain in Cowdrey, gave a much better account of themselves than in the first Test. In fact, this match was splendidly contested throughout, interest being sustained right to the end.

Again Sobers was a key figure for West Indies and he thwarted England on the fourth day when victory seemed just round the corner for the old country. Having gained a lead of 86, England took the first five West Indies second-innings wickets for 95 and looked to be romping home. Then Sobers was joined by his young cousin, Holford, and they remained together for five hours and twenty minutes until Sobers declared at ten minutes to one on Tuesday. This unbroken stand of 274 was a record for the fifth wicket for West Indies against England.

Sobers, who batted ten minutes longer, hit thirteen 4's in his excellent 163 and Holford showed six boundaries in his 105.

Holford gained the distinction of hitting his maiden Test century on only his second appearance and later in the day Milburn, three 6's and seventeen 4's, wound up this grand struggle by emulating Holford's feat and taking out his bat for 126, made in three hours.

Over the five days, four hours and fifty minutes' play was lost through rain, there being only two and three-quarter hours' cricket on the first day when West Indies reached 155 for four wickets. Personal honours went to Higgs who prised through the early West Indies batsmen, taking three wickets for 14 runs in his first nine overs. He kept a splendid length and moved the ball slightly each way.

The next morning Nurse and Sobers lasted an hour together while they carried their stand to 86 and the total to 205 before d'Oliveira, playing in his first Test, deceived Nurse with a fine ball from the Nursery end which turned up the slope and took his leg stump.

Nurse did not offer a stroke, nor did Sobers when he covered up and was lbw to Knight so that at lunch time on Friday West Indies were 247 for six. Higgs and Jones took the new ball directly after the interval and the remaining four wickets were captured for 22 more runs. Higgs, with three for 11 in five overs, finished with six for 91, a grand effort, and Parks claimed Gibbs as his 100th Test victim.

The return of Graveney to Test cricket after an interval of three years during which England played 38 Tests proved a wise move by the selectors. Milburn went cheaply on Friday but Boycott and Graveney progressed steadily in a stand of 115 and at nightfall England were 145 for two; Graveney 65, Barrington 8.

Next day, only d'Oliveira and Parks rose to the occasion against some much improved bowling. There was no excuse for the poor displays of Barrington, Cowdrey, Knight and Titmus. Sobers attacked persistently and Hall and Griffith kept more in line with the stumps, yet Graveney batted almost without blemish for four hours and twenty minutes. He wanted only four for his hundred when he cut at a rising ball from Hall and was taken by the wicket-keeper. He hit eleven 4's.

Even the new ball did not disturb Parks and d'Oliveira and their partnership of 48 was in full sail when Parks drove back so fast that the ball went off d'Oliveira's heel and bounced back from the broken wicket. Hall, with commendable presence of mind, swept up the ball and pulled up the stump with both hands without the South African making any attempt to recover his ground.

It was left to the left-handed Higgs to keep up his end while Parks hit freely so that the ninth stand yielded 59, but altogether England occupied eight and a quarter hours for their total of 355.

A fine leg slip catch by Knight disposed of Carew on Saturday evening when West Indies finished the third day 18 for one. The pitch sweated under the covers during the week-end when more rain soaked the outfield and by ten minutes to one on Monday, following a prompt start, four more wickets had gone and West Indies faced a hopeless position. At least, so it seemed, but there followed that wonderful partnership between Sobers and Holford which meant that England were set to get 284 to win in four hours.

Rain reduced the time by an hour, but at first West Indies made a brave attempt to achieve success. Griffith disposed of Boycott and Barrington for 43 and at 67 Sobers switched Hall to the nursery end where he removed Cowdrey and Parks with his first two deliveries.

It had not been intended that Graveney should bat owing to a badly bruised right thumb, but he came to the rescue, averted a hat-trick, and stayed with Milburn for the last hour and fifty minutes while they added 130 in England's highest fifth-wicket stand against West Indies. Graveney batted almost one handed, continually drawing away the other, but while he defended, Milburn followed up his 94 at Manchester with another amazing display of powerful hitting. This was a much better effort. He hoisted Holford, Gibbs and Hall in turn for 6 and made very few false strokes.

England, who did not claim the extra half hour, fell 87 short of their target. The receipts of £58,000 were a record for a cricket match in any part of the world. The full attendance was estimated to be 125,500, of whom 104,000 paid the six shillings outer gate admission fee. N.P.

West Indies

C. C. Hunte c Parks b Higgs	18	c Milburn b Knight	13
M. C. Carew c Parks b Higgs	2	c Knight b Higgs	0
R. B. Kanhai c Titmus b Higgs	25	c Parks b Knight	40
B. F. Butcher c Milburn b Knight	49	lbw b Higgs	3
S. M. Nurse b d'Oliveira	64	c Parks b d'Oliveira	35
*G. S. Sobers lbw b Knight	46	not out	163
D. A. J. Holford b Jones	26	not out	105
†D. W. Allan c Titmus b Higgs	13		
C. C. Griffith lbw b Higgs	5		
W. W. Hall not out	8		
L. R. Gibbs c Parks b Higgs	4		
B 2, l-b 7	9	L-b 8, n-b 2	10
1/8 2/42 3/53 4/119 5/205 6/213 7/252 8/252 9/261	269	1/2 2/22 3/25 4/91 5/95 (5 wkts. dec.)	369

Bowling: *First Innings*—Jones 21—3—64—1; Higgs 33—9—91—6; Knight 21—0—63—2; Titmus 5—0—18—0; d'Oliveira 14—5—24—1. *Second Innings*—Jones 25—2—95—0; Higgs 34—5—82—2; Knight 30—3—106—2; d'Oliveira 25—7—46—1; Titmus 19—3—30—0.

England

G. Boycott c Griffith b Gibbs	60	c Allan b Griffith	25
C. Milburn lbw b Hall	6	not out	126
T. W. Graveney c Allan b Hall	96	not out	30
K. F. Barrington b Sobers	19	b Griffith	5
*M. C. Cowdrey c Gibbs b Hall	9	c Allan b Hall	5
†J. M. Parks lbw b Carew	91	b Hall	0
B. d'Oliveira run out	27		
B. R. Knight b Griffith	6		
F. J. Titmus c Allan b Hall	6		
K. Higgs c Holford b Gibbs	13		
I. J. Jones not out	0		
B 7, l-b 10, n-b 5	22	B 4, l-b 2	6
1/8 2/123 3/164 4/198 5/203 6/251 7/266 8/296 9/355	355	1/37 2/43 3/67 4/67 (4 wkts.)	197

Bowling: *First Innings*—Sobers 39—12—89—1; Hall 36—2—106—4; Griffith 28—4—79—1; Gibbs 37.3—18—48—2; Carew 3—0—11—1. *Second Innings*—Hall 14—1—65—2; Griffith 11—2—43—2; Gibbs 13—4—40—0; Sobers 8—4—8—0; Holford 9—1—35—0.

Umpires: J. S. Buller and W. F. Price.

MINOR COUNTIES v. WEST INDIES

At Lakenham, June 23, 24. West Indies won by an innings and 33 runs. Throwing off the cares of Test cricket, they displayed some magnificent bowling and free-hitting batting. After Kanhai, captain for the first time, had put the Minor Counties in, Hall produced a superb spell of fast bowling which accounted for seven batsmen, and an eighth, Millett, was sent to hospital with a broken finger. Hall's figures of seven for 31 were deserved reward for an unchanged spell of one and three-quarter hours during which he extracted maximum life from a firm pitch. West Indies, starting their reply before lunch, took the lead after only seventy-two minutes. Butcher and Kanhai, with fierce hitting, both exceeded 50, but Lashley proved more subdued, taking two hours and fifty minutes to reach his first century of the tour. West Indies added 36 on the second morning. Kanhai then employed his slow bowlers almost exclusively, and the ball was tossed up invitingly, giving the batsmen a chance to redeem themselves Most accepted the opportunity before falling to skiers, none more than Edrich, whose 61 occupied only forty minutes and contained four 6's and six 4's. Maslin, with three, and Rose, one, brought the total of 6's for the innings to eight, but wickets fell regularly and West Indies won with two and a half hours to spare.

Minor Counties

R. Inglis (*Durham*) c Gibbs b Hall	8	— b Hall	5
†I. D. Prior (*Suffolk*) c Brancker b Hall	9	— b Gibbs	11
F. W. Millett (*Cheshire*) retired hurt	2	— absent	0
N. Cooley (*Bedfordshire*) c McMorris b Hall	14	— b Holford	44
M. Maslin (*Lincolnshire*) c Kanhai b Hall	10	— c Cohen b Holford	66
D. J. Mordaunt (*Berkshire*) c Butcher b Hall	9	— c Holford b Brancker	4
H. J. Bailey (*Durham*) c Cohen b Hall	3	— c Kanhai b Brancker	0
*W. J. Edrich (*Norfolk*) c Cohen b Hall	0	— c Cohen b Kanhai	61
N. M. McVicker (*Lincolnshire*) c Holford b Brancker	1	— c and b Solomon	1
W. Rose (*Norfolk*) not out	7	— c Allan b Kanhai	12
J. Waring (*Yorkshire*) c sub. b Brancker	1	— not out	4
N-b 1	1	L-b 3	3
1/8 2/19 3/31 4/49 5/54 6/54 7/57 8/57 9/65	65	1/6 2/32 3/92 4/107 5/115 6/151 7/166 8/206 9/211	211

Bowling: *First Innings*—Hall 12—3—31—7; Cohen 5—0—28—0; Lashley 4—3—1—0; Brancker 2.2—0—4—2. *Second Innings*—Hall 4—0—15—1; Cohen 3—2—8—0; Gibbs 12—4—31—1; Brancker 21—4—72—2; Solomon 3—1—11—1; Holford 9—0—35—2; Kanhai 2.1—0—31—2; McMorris 1—0—5—0.

West Indies

E. D. McMorris b McVicker	14	D. A. J. Holford not out	28
R. C. Brancker b Waring	13		
B. F. Butcher c Edrich b Bailey	54	B 2, l-b 3, w 1, n-b 1	7
P. D. Lashley not out	121		
J. S. Solomon c Prior b Rose	5	1/28 2/31 3/106 (5 wkts., dec.)	309
*R. B. Kanhai c Prior b Waring	67	4/133 5/261	

†D. W. Allan, W. W. Hall, L. R. Gibbs and R. A. Cohen did not bat.

Bowling: Waring 24—5—96—2; McVicker 24—3—64—1; Bailey 11—4—30—1; Mordaunt 7—1—31—0; Rose 10—1—68—1; Edrich 3—0—13—0.

Umpires: C. E. Dunn and G. E. Hart.

ESSEX v. WEST INDIES

At Southend, June 25, 27, 28. Drawn. Essex began so badly against the pace of Hall that four wickets fell for 52. Then Fletcher, whose splendidly-executed strokes all round brought him two 6's and fifteen 4's in a stay of three and a quarter hours, shared in a stand of 120 with Bailey—in fifty minutes longer for 63 fewer runs. The West Indies also made a moderate start, but the strong-driving Nurse played his highest innings in England, hitting two 6's and thirteen 4's in four hours ten minutes. Lashley, less free, helped him put on 172 in three hours for the fourth wicket and good batting by Solomon preceded a declaration 124 ahead. Interruptions by rain ruled out the possibility of a definite result.

Essex

G. E. Barber c Hendriks b Hall	0	— c Carew b Lashley	22
M. J. Bear lbw b Lashley	14	— c Hunte b Hall	0
†B. Taylor c Cohen b Hall	22	— c Lashley b Cohen	15
K. W. R. Fletcher c Hendriks b Brancker	106	— lbw b Cohen	28
B. R. Knight lbw b Hall	1	— not out	8
*T. E. Bailey not out	43	— not out	2
G. J. Saville c Cohen b Brancker	5		
K. D. Boyce c Hendriks b Hall	0		
B. Edmeades c Nurse b Cohen	10		
R. N. S. Hobbs b Cohen	18		
R. East b Cohen	5		
B 5, l-b 1	6		
1/0 2/22 3/51 4/52 5/172 6/178 7/179 8/198 9/220	230	1/1 2/33 3/53 4/73 (4 wkts.)	75

Bowling: *First Innings*—Hall 25—8—63—4; Cohen 20.3—4—67—3; Lashley 2—1—2—1; Brancker 29—16—31—2; Carew 14—6—29—0; Hunte 8—3—32—0. *Second Innings*—Hall 6—0—27—1; Cohen 6—0—30—2; Lashley 7—1—18—1.

West Indies

M. C. Carew c Taylor b Boyce	3	R. C. Brancker b Knight	12
*C. C. Hunte c Taylor b Knight	6	†J. L. Hendriks not out	16
R. B. Kanhai c Knight b Edmeades	25	B 11, l-b 7, n-b 10	28
S. M. Nurse st Taylor b East	155		
P. D. Lashley c Taylor b East	54	1/4 2/22 3/57 (6 wkts., dec.)	354
J. S. Solomon not out	55	4/229 5/278 6/311	

E. D. McMorris, W. W. Hall and R. A. Cohen did not bat.

Bowling: Knight 26—1—69—2; Boyce 19—2—64—1; Edmeades 18—2—64—1; Bailey 14—4—34—0; Hobbs 7—0—40—0; East 18—2—55—2.

Umpires: J. F. Crapp and C. G. Pepper.

ENGLAND v. WEST INDIES

Third Test

At Trent Bridge, June 30, July 1, 2, 4, 5. West Indies won by 139 runs. Again they proved the superior side and extricated themselves from an inferior position. They fell 90 behind on the first innings and then lost two wickets for 65, yet were able to declare with only five men out and set England the reasonable task of scoring 393 in six and a half hours, a rate of exactly 60 an hour.

England caused much surprise just before the match began by omitting Barrington on the grounds that he was suffering from physical and nervous strain through playing too much cricket in the past six years. They also left out Knight (twelfth man) and introduced Underwood to Test cricket, there being altogether four changes compared with the Lord's Test. Lashley and Hendriks made their first Test appearances in England for the West Indies.

For the third time in the series Sobers won the toss and again the West Indies captain played a notable part. Besides hitting 94 in just over two hours when it was necessary to press for runs, Sobers took five wickets, including that of Boycott with the second ball in England's first innings, and he held five catches, besides handling his bowlers and setting his field with marked skill. Nurse and Butcher both played profitable innings.

England were indebted to Graveney for a fine century, his third in successive Test appearances at Trent Bridge and to Cowdrey who helped the Worcestershire player to a valuable stand of 169 after the first three wickets had gone for 13. d'Oliveira hit splendidly in both innings and like Higgs, bowled well, but England were guilty once again of poor fielding. They dropped Butcher five times and Boycott, at cover, alone stood out in a favourable light.

The Nottinghamshire groundsman must be congratulated on preparing a fast true pitch which encouraged the pace bowlers, especially in the early stages of the match. They enjoyed a notable first day when thirteen wickets went down for 268 runs. Snow and Higgs were lively and aggressive for England, but Lashley, with a short back lift and receiving at least one life, proved stubborn while staying over three hours for 49. Time and again the batsmen were saved by their pads; even Nurse had his anxious moments. Still, his was a fine display for he made 93, including eleven 4's, in two and three-quarter hours, but fell as soon as Snow took the second new ball.

When England batted for the last fifty minutes it was the same tale of the previous year on this ground against South Africa who twice captured cheap wickets by night fall. This time, Boycott, Milburn and Russell all failed so that Graveney and Cowdrey had to play through the final half hour. They took the score to 33 for three.

Next day, in heavy cloudy weather, the England fourth pair had to use all their skill and resource to combat the menacing attack of Hall, Sobers, Griffith, Gibbs and Holford. Only 36 runs came in the first hour, but by lunch, when the total was 128, each had reached his fifty and Graveney had pulled Gibbs for 6. Subsequently, a barrage of bumpers increased the batsmen's problems, Cowdrey suffering painful blows under the heart from Hall. There were two stoppages for bad light and it was after tea, at 4.40, that Graveney went to a brilliant left-handed catch in the gully, having scored 109, out of 172 in three hours fifty minutes. In addition to his 6, he hit eleven 4's.

Cowdrey saw England go ahead and then at 238, having batted over five hours for 96 and hit only six 4's he was taken at the wicket. As Illingworth failed England were 254 for seven at the close.

The ground was full on Saturday when in warm sunshine England consolidated their position, thanks to Underwood keeping up his end for eighty-five minutes with d'Oliveira while 65 runs were added, a record for England's last wicket against West Indies, d'Oliveira hit ten 4's in his excellent 76. Next, he disposed of Hunte and Lashley, the latter taking one and three-quarter hours for 23.

Butcher joined Kanhai at 3.45 p.m. and with their side in a precarious position they added only 73 runs in the remaining two and a half hours before the close. Underwood, left arm medium over the wicket, who bowled unchanged from 3.30 p.m. till 6 o'clock had these figures 22—13—17—0 but he failed to take his first wicket in Test cricket, d'Oliveira missing a slip catch from Kanhai, who was then 36.

On Monday, the West Indies wasted no time in piling on 334 runs in five and a quarter hours. The hero was Butcher. Severely criticised for his stonewalling on Saturday, he went on to punish England for 209 not out in seven and three-quarter hours and he hit twenty-two 4's. His double century had only been bettered for West Indies in England by F. M. Worrell—261 at Trent Bridge, 1950. Moreover, Butcher had the rare distinction of taking part in three successive three-figure stands, with Kanhai, Nurse and Sobers. His partnership with Sobers of 173 in two hours was a whirlwind affair.

England had a poor day in the field. Higgs alone of the five bowlers maintained his best form. Snow found the pitch lifeless and his attempts to produce bouncers presented no difficulties.

England began their second innings with half an hour left on Monday and this time Boycott and Milburn survived. Milburn hooked Hall for 6, but was fortunate in the final over to be missed off the same bowler by Lashley at third slip. So on the last morning England resumed at 30 without loss, but the fifth ball of the first over accounted for Milburn who mishooked Hall to mid-on. Boycott faced the situation with rare skill, his defence being superb, but Russell never appeared confident and West Indies, in the two and a half hours session before lunch, gained absolute control, taking five wickets for the addition of 112 runs. Boycott pulled Sobers for 6 and also hit six 4's in his 71, made in two and a half hours.

Griffith delivered some vicious bouncers, one only just missing Cowdrey's head. Again d'Oliveira hit freely and he was particularly aggressive on being joined by Higgs. There were ten 4's in his 54. Snow withstood the bowling for half an hour and, when Underwood again resisted, Griffith brought forth wholesale condemnation by producing another of his bouncers which struck the Kent bowler in the mouth.

In the end, West Indies won with eighty-five minutes to spare. The weather remained fine and a crowd of 105,000 produced receipts of £36,396, a record for a Trent Bridge Test. N.P.

West Indies

C. C. Hunte lbw b Higgs	9	— c Graveney b d'Oliveira	12
P. D. Lashley c Parks b Snow	49	— lbw b d'Oliveira	23
R. B. Kanhai c Underwood b Higgs	32	— c Cowdrey b Higgs	63
B. F. Butcher b Snow	5	— not out	209
S. M. Nurse c Illingworth b Snow	93	— lbw b Higgs	53
*G. S. Sobers c Parks b Snow	3	— c Underwood b Higgs	94
D. A. J. Holford lbw b d'Oliveira	11	— not out	17
†J. L. Hendriks b d'Oliveira	2		
C. C. Griffith c Cowdrey b Higgs	14		
W. W. Hall b Higgs	12		
L. R. Gibbs not out	0		
B 3, l-b 2	5	L-b 6, w 5	11
1/19 2/68 3/80 4/140 5/144 6/180 7/190 8/215 9/228	235	1/29 2/65 3/175 4/282 5/455 (5 wkts., dec.)	482

Bowling: *First Innings*—Snow 25—7—82—4; Higgs 25.4—3—71—4; d'Oliveira 30—14—51—2; Underwood 2—1—5—0; Illingworth 8—1—21—0. *Second Innings*—Snow 38—10—117—0; Higgs 38—6—109—3; d'Oliveira 34—8—77—2; Underwood 43—15—86—0; Illingworth 25—7—82—0.

England

G. Boycott lbw b Sobers	0	— c Sobers b Griffith	71
C. Milburn c Sobers b Hall	7	— c Griffith b Hall	12
W. E. Russell b Hall	4	— c Sobers b Gibbs	11
T. W. Graveney c Holford b Sobers	109	— c Hendriks b Griffith	32
*M. C. Cowdrey c Hendriks b Griffith	96	— c Sobers b Gibbs	32
†J. M. Parks c Butcher b Sobers	11	— c Lashley b Hall	7
B. d'Oliveira b Hall	76	— lbw b Griffith	54
R. Illingworth c Lashley b Griffith	0	— c Lashley b Sobers	4
K. Higgs c Lashley b Sobers	5	— c Sobers b Gibbs	4
J. A. Snow b Hall	0	— b Griffith	3
D. L. Underwood not out	12	— not out	10
L-b 2, n-b 3	5	B 8, l-b 2, n-b 3	13
1/0 2/10 3/13 4/182 5/221 6/238 7/247 8/255 9/260	325	1/32 2/71 3/125 4/132 5/142 6/176 7/181 8/222 9/240	253

Bowling: *First Innings*—Sobers 49—12—90—4; Hall 34.3—8—105—4; Griffith 20—5—62—2; Gibbs 23—9—40—0; Holford 8—2—23—0. *Second Innings*—Sobers 31—6—71—1; Hall 16—3—52—2; Griffith 13.3—3—34—4; Gibbs 48—16—83—3.

Umpires: C. S. Elliott and A. Jepson.

MIDDLESEX v. WEST INDIES

At Lord's, July 6, 7, 8. Drawn, though for a period on the last afternoon Middlesex stood near their first victory over a touring side for thirty years. Sent in, the West Indies progressed with dismal slowness, disregarding their reputation and the crowd's expectancy. They achieved only 187 runs in five hours, off 95.2 overs against bowling that never proved hostile. Mindful of the need to keep the match moving, Hunte declared overnight. His move brought initial success, for the first five Middlesex wickets fell for 42, Griffith producing extreme pace from the occasional delivery to account for four of them. Then the alliance of Clark and Hooker brought about a transformation. Playing strokes with confidence, they added 48 in fifty minutes before lunch, and their partnership eventually realised 131 before Clark, seeking his hundred, lashed out at Carew and was stumped. He batted three hours and hit one 6 and seven 4's. Hooker continued to flourish, but became another victim of Griffith shortly before the declaration, having hit one 6 and nine 4's.

Middlesex made their runs, 56 more than the West Indies, in 32.2 overs less, and actually went into the lead in 45 less overs than the West Indies had taken. The tourists lost three wickets on the second evening, and a fourth early on the last morning. They relied on caution to save them. Immediately after lunch they stood only 110 on with five wickets left, Hunte having spent four hours over 82. Butcher and Brancker, by adding 72 in under an hour, put a better face on matters, and Middlesex eventually required 187 in two hours, twenty minutes. This difficult task was rendered impossible when the West Indies took sixteen minutes to bowl their first three overs and bad light caused a ten-minute stoppage just before tea. So a match which won the West Indies no admirers finished in a tame draw.

West Indies

*C. C. Hunte lbw b Price	21	— c Clark b Hooker	82
E. D. McMorris c Titmus b Hooker	15	— b Stewart	12
P. D. Lashley lbw b Hooker	14	— c Parfitt b Titmus	19
J. S. Solomon c Titmus b Hooker	38	— c Hooker b Parfitt	4
M. C. Carew b Hooker	34	— lbw b Hooker	26
R. B. Kanhai lbw b. Bick	18	— c Clark b Hooker	4
B. F. Butcher c Russell b Bick	29	— lbw b Price	36
R. C. Brancker not out	10	— c and b Stewart	32
†D. W. Allan lbw b Hooker	3	— c Clifton b Price	12
C. C. Griffith not out	1	— b Price	2
R. A. Cohen (did not bat)		— not out	2
L-b 3, n-b 1	4	B 2, l-b 8, n-b 1	11
1/26 2/42 3/61 4/110 5/129 6/160 7/177 8/186 (8 wkts., dec.)	187	1/22 2/58 3/62 4/83 5/155 6/163 7/166 8/228 9/234	242

Bowling: *First Innings*—Price 19—6—29—1; Stewart 21—4—50—0; Hooker 25.2—9—53—5; Titmus 19—3—34—0; Bick 11—2—17—2. *Second Innings*—Price 21—3—54—3; Stewart 14.3—3—33—2; Hooker 20—4—46—3; Bick 18—8—39—0; Titmus 14—4—36—1; Parfitt 12—5—23—1.

Middlesex

W. E. Russell c Lashley b Griffith	18	— not out	41
M. J. Harris lbw b Griffith	2	— c Kanhai b Griffith	6
P. H. Parfitt c Allan b Cohen	3	— b Lashley	9
E. A. Clark st Allan b Carew	99	— not out	28
M. J. Smith c Allan b Griffith	0		
*F. J. Titmus b Griffith	4		
R. W. Hooker c Hunte b Griffith	81		
D. A. Bick b Griffith	18		
†E. G. Clifton not out	1		
R. W. Stewart not out	4		
B 1, l-b 11, n-b 1	13	L-b 1	1
1/9 2/12 3/30 4/32 5/42 6/173 7/231 8/238 (8 wkts., dec.)	243	1/15 2/34 (2 wkts.)	85

J. S. E. Price did not bat.

Bowling: *First Innings*—Griffith 22—5—69—6; Cohen 10—1—36—1; Lashley 9—2—28—0; Brancker 13—1—74—0; Solomon 2—0—7—0; Carew 7—1—16—1. *Second Innings*—Griffith 5—1—12—1; Cohen 6—0—18—0; Lashley 12—0—33—1; Carew 10—4—21—0.

Umpires: O. W. Herman and W. E. Phillipson.

KENT v. WEST INDIES

At Canterbury, July 9, 11, 12. West Indies won by an innings and 56 runs. They outplayed Kent who on a fast dry pitch gave two woeful displays of batting, apart from Luckhurst. McMorris defended stoutly for a long time but finished with four 6's and nine 4's in his 116 which was notable for his powerful driving. Kent were baffled by spin bowling. Luckhurst alone showed ability to deal with Brancker's flighted left-arm slows and he hit his fourth hundred (eleven 4's) in nine innings during a stay of three hours ten minutes. When Kent followed on 180 behind, Sobers soon dismissed Denness at his fast pace, two wickets being down for 19 at the close. Next day he finished the innings three-quarters of an hour before lunch by taking the eight remaining wickets for 39 runs. Sobers full analysis read 19.4—6—49—9 and he became the first West Indies cricketer to take nine wickets in an innings in England. On that last morning Sobers adopted his unorthodox left-arm spin and the Kent players fell victims one after the other to the "chinaman".

West Indies

E. D. McMorris c Sayer b Dixon	116
P. D. Lashley lbw b Dixon	27
R. C. Brancker lbw b Sayer	26
D. A. J. Holford c Ealham b Luckhurst	55
*G. S. Sobers c Leary b Dixon	5
J. S. Solomon c Denness b Dixon	42
M. C. Carew b Sayer	20
S. M. Nurse lbw b Dixon	1
†J. L. Hendriks c Knott b Underwood	28
W. W. Hall b Dye	5
R. A. Cohen not out	32
B 10, l-b 12, w 2, n-b 1	25
1/45 2/94 3/235 4/244 5/247 6/297 7/298 8/308 9/320	382

Bowling: Sayer 23—6—51—2; Dye 25—5—76—1; Dixon 43—15—138—5; Underwood 19.2—3—54—1; Luckhurst 12—3—30—1; Leary 1—0—8—0.

Kent

M. H. Denness c Hendriks b Carew	20	c Brancker b Sobers	22
B. W. Luckhurst c and b Brancker	104	c Hendriks b Sobers	5
D. Nicholls b Carew	0	lbw b Holford	0
*M. C. Cowdrey c Holford b Brancker	19	c Hendriks b Sobers	1
S. E. Leary st Hendriks b Brancker	7	c Nurse b Sobers	38
A. Ealham c Carew b Brancker	24	c Carew b Sobers	13
†A. Knott lbw b Brancker	0	st Hendriks b Sobers	15
A. L. Dixon c Brancker b Holford	7	c Hall b Sobers	5
D. L. Underwood c and b Brancker	10	c Hall b Sobers	10
D. M. Sayer b Brancker	7	b Sobers	1
J. C. Dye not out	2	not out	1
W 1, n-b 1	2	B 9, l-b 4	13
1/40 2/42 3/79 4/91 5/147 6/147 7/164 8/184 9/193	202	1/15 2/18 3/27 4/37 5/38 6/60 7/78 8/100 9/118	124

Bowling: *First Innings*—Hall 3—1—3—0; Cohen 6—0—26—0; Sobers 2—0—7—0; Carew 20—9—32—2; Brancker 31.3—8—78—7; Holford 18—0—54—1. *Second Innings*—Cohen 4—2—8—0; Sobers 19.4—6—49—9; Carew 1—1—0—0; Brancker 10—5—17—0; Holford 10—2—37—1.

Umpires: G. H. Pope and P. A. Gibb.

SOMERSET v. WEST INDIES

At Taunton, July 16, 18, 19. Drawn. Rain restricted play to twenty-five minutes on the third day, preventing heavy defeat for Somerset, who were still 100 behind with four wickets left. The West Indies innings was dominated by Hunte, who made 206 out of 319 in five hours, a superb effort containing thirty 4's and two 6's. On the second day Solomon completed his first tour century in three and a quarter hours and then Cohen, taking three for five in six overs upset Somerset's start. Thereafter, Somerset heartily attacked the spinners, but lost wickets regularly to Holford, whose leg breaks earned him six for 59. Following on 287 behind, the Somerset second innings followed much the same pattern as the first with Burgess, in his first County outing, showing aggressive promise. On the final day, C. R. M. Atkinson had time to complete 51 in seventy-five minutes before the rain came.

West Indies

*C. C. Hunte c Rumsey b C. R. M. Atkinson....................206
R. C. Brancker lbw b C. R. M. Atkinson.................... 28
M. C. Carew c Burgess b Langford 16
R. B. Kanhai c Kitchen b Rumsey 12
B. F. Butcher run out............ 13
J. S. Solomon not out............104
D. A. J. Holford not out......... 59
B 1, l-b 4, n-b 2........... 7

1/95 2/120 3/147 (5 wkts., dec.) 445
4/194 5/319

†D. W. Allan, W. W. Hall, L. R. Gibbs and R. A. Cohen did not bat.

Bowling: Rumsey 25—3—105—1; Burgess 28—4—101—0; C. R. M. Atkinson 20—4—66—2; Alley 6—3—18—0; Langford 30—12—83—1; Robinson 15—2—65—0.

Somerset

G. Atkinson c Allan b Cohen..........	0	— b Carew	17
R. Virgin b Cohen....................	0	— b Cohen	4
M. Kitchen b Cohen...................	17	— c Allan b Brancker.........	6
A. Clarkson b Holford................	26	— c Allan b Brancker.........	19
W. E. Alley b Holford	33	— st Allan b Gibbs...........	34
*C. R. M. Atkinson c Solomon b Holford	32	— not out	51
G. Burgess c Gibbs b Brancker.........	1	— b Holford.................	35
†G. Clayton c Solomon b Holford......	10	— not out	11
P. J. Robinson not out...............	35		
B. A. Langford c Solomon b Holford...	2		
F. E. Rumsey b Holford	0		
B 1, l-b 1......................	2	B 4, l-b 2, w 1, n-b 3....	10
1/1 2/5 3/19 4/72 5/82 6/97 7/111 8/130 9/158	158	1/5 2/33 3/33 4/86 5/90 6/169 (6 wkts.)	187

Bowling: *First Innings*—Cohen 7—3—21—3; Hall 6—1—25—0; Gibbs 8—1—24—0; Holford 17.5—5—59—6; Brancker 10—4—27—1. *Second Innings*—Hall 8—4—13—0; Cohen 3—1—8—1; Carew 9—4—23—1; Brancker 18—1—65—2; Gibbs 11—5—26—1; Holford 13—3—42—1.

Umpires: A. E. Fagg and H. Mellows.

SURREY v. WEST INDIES

At The Oval, July 22. West Indies won by seven wickets. This match, restricted to 60 overs and each bowler to ten overs, did not rank as first-class. It was arranged because the original three-day game was ruined by rain, no play being possible on Wednesday and Thursday. The decision to play on the final day under knock-out rules proved a great success and the attractive but nevertheless serious cricket was enjoyed by a crowd of over 3,000. Edwards had the satisfaction of hitting his first century for Surrey, which he completed in the sixtieth over.

Two powerful drives by him went for 6 and he also hit twelve 4's in a most impressive display. At one stage Griffith took three wickets in seven deliveries. Hunte and Kanhai began with some fine strokes for West Indies and Nurse showed his class while scoring 73 in a stand of 116 with Lashley in seventy-five minutes. Lashley, slow in the early stages, later cut and drove freely and made the winning hit with his eighth boundary, West Indies winning with twelve overs to spare.

Surrey

J. H. Edrich c Butcher b Lashley..	14	†A. Long c Griffith b Hunte......	2
M. J. Edwards not out...........	108	P. I. Pocock st Hendriks b Holford	3
M. D. Willett c Hunte b Brancker.	13	G. Arnold not out...............	3
*M. J. Stewart c Solomon b Hunte	21	L-b 2, n-b 1..............	3
Mohammed Younis c and b Sobers	18		——
R. A. E. Tindall lbw b Griffith....	3	1/27 2/55 3/90 (9 wkts., 60 overs)	188
S. J. Storey b Griffith............	0	4/140 5/158 6/158 7/160	
R. I. Jefferson b Griffith..........	0	8/165 9/175	

Bowling: Griffith 10—0—26—3; Sobers 10—3—13—1; Lashley 10—3—39—1; Brancker 10—1—33—1; Hunte 10—2—23—2; Holford 10—2—51—1.

West Indies

C. C. Hunte c Long b Arnold.....	11	D. A. J. Holford not out.........	11
P. D. Lashley not out............	75		
R. B. Kanhai b Jefferson.........	21		——
S. M. Nurse hit wkt. b Tindall....	73	1/12 2/43 3/159 (3 wkts.)	191

B. F. Butcher, *G. S. Sobers, J. S. Solomon, R. C. Brancker, †J. L. Hendriks and C. C. Griffith did not bat.

Bowling: Arnold 10—1—30—1; Jefferson 10—0—33—1; Storey 10—0—37—0; Pocock 10—0—48—0; Tindall 5—1—25—1; Willett 3—1—14—0; Stewart 0.1—0—4—0.

Umpires: F. Jakeman and R. Aspinall.

NORTHAMPTONSHIRE v. WEST INDIES

At Northampton, July 23, 25. Northamptonshire won by four wickets, gaining their second victory over the West Indies—the other was in 1933—an hour after tea on the second day. On a remarkable first day twenty-five wickets fell and 353 runs were scored. The conditions aided seam bowling, the heavy atmosphere making the ball swing considerably on the first morning, when the pitch was fairly green. As the West Indies batsmen went for their shots the young pace bowlers, Durose and Kettle, performed most effectively. Sobers hit a characteristically enterprising 45 but Nurse alone gave him much support. Milburn attacked immediately in the Northamptonshire innings, hitting 55 out of 77 in an hour, including two 6's and eight 4's. Even so Gibbs promised to give the tourists the lead until Durose hit 30 out of a last-wicket stand of 40, with two 6's and four 4's. Before the close the West Indies lost five more wickets for 68 and began the second day only 35 ahead. Solomon batted efficiently for 38 and Griffith scored 45. Kettle produced fine bowling for his five wickets. Northamptonshire needed 131. Despite useful batting by Reynolds, Lightfoot, and Mushtaq, they lost five wickets for 85 by tea. Then Milburn, batting with a runner owing to injury, joined Watts, and they were within five of victory when Watts was dismissed. Milburn drove his second 6 of the innings, this time off Kanhai, for the winning stroke.

West Indies

First innings		Second innings	
C. C. Hunte lbw b Durose	17	lbw b Kettle	8
P. D. Lashley c Reynolds b Kettle	4	c Kettle b Durose	10
M. C. Carew c Watts b Durose	5	run out	15
R.B . Kanhai c Kettle b Durose	3	b Kettle	12
S. M. Nurse c Reynolds b Watts	29	c Andrew b Durose	7
*G. S. Sobers b Kettle	45	c Steele b Kettle	4
J. S. Solomon c Watts b Sully	2	c Lightfoot b Sully	38
†D. W. Allan c Kettle b Sully	0	c Mushtaq b Durose	9
C. C. Griffith b Sully	1	c Andrew b Kettle	45
L. R. Gibbs not out	10	c Andrew b Kettle	6
R. A. Cohen b Watts	6	not out	0
N-b 4	4	B 4, n-b 5	9
1/10 2/23 3/27 4/32 5/85 6/92 7/92 8/94 9/110	126	1/18 2/18 3/45 4/46 5/61 6/83 7/93 8/125 9/155	163

Bowling: *First Innings*—Durose 13—2—40—3; Kettle 12—3—30—2; Watts 9.5—1—23—2; Lightfoot 4—0—17—0; Sully 5—3—10—3; Steele 1—0—2—0. *Second Innings*—Kettle 19.4—2—58—5; Durose 16—2—47—3; Watts 10—1—22—0; Sully 6—2—17—1; Mushtaq 4—0—10—0.

Northamptonshire

First innings		Second innings	
C. Milburn c Hunte b Gibbs	57	not out	26
B. L. Reynolds b Griffith	0	c Griffith b Gibbs	21
A. Lightfoot c Solomon b Cohen	5	lbw b Sobers	22
Mushtaq Mohammad c Lashley b Cohen	9	c Kanhai b Gibbs	24
D. S. Steele c and b Gibbs	16	c Nurse b Sobers	0
R. Wills c Hunte b Sobers	0	c Allan b Griffith	1
P. J. Watts c Kanhai b Sobers	14	b Gibbs	26
M. J. Kettle run out	0	not out	2
H. Sully c Sobers b Gibbs	0		
*†K. V. Andrew not out	14		
A. J. Durose c Kanhai b Gibbs	30		
B 12, l-b 1, n-b 1	14	B 2, l-b 12	14
1/1 2/21 3/47 4/77 5/88 6/96 7/101 8/103 9/119	159	1/6 2/49 3/57 4/59 5/85 6/126 (6 wkts.)	136

Bowling: *First Innings*—Griffith 7—1—27—1; Cohen 5—1—36—2; Sobers 13—6—40—2; Gibbs 13.4—5—42—4. *Second Innings*—Sobers 23—9—44—2; Griffith 8—4—14—1; Gibbs 31—11—44—3; Cohen 6—3—11—0; Carew 4—2—3—0; Kanhai 0.1—0—6—0.

Umpires: A. E. Rhodes and H. Yarnold.

M.C.C. PRESIDENT'S XI v. WEST INDIES

At Lord's, July 27, 28, 29. Drawn. The fixture seemed ill-fated and proved a sad disappointment. Late changes weakened the President's team, all under 25, and injuries caused Arnold and Sobers to drop out of the game. Apart from Amiss (one 6, seven 4's) who, following a careful start, drove well in a stay of just over three hours, and a little brisk hitting by Shuttleworth, the President's men batted timidly in the first innings, even though Hall and Sobers did not bowl after getting down three wickets for 25. Nor was the West Indies batting more attractive. Butcher spent three hours ten minutes over 74, and he and Holford, badly missed when 10, added 75, but not till Kanhai (one 6, four 4's) attacked the bowling was really bright cricket seen. Kanhai was unluckily run out when a return by Hall off Shuttleworth was deflected by the bowler's boot on to the stumps. The President's team lost two wickets in clearing arrears of 63, and though Amiss again played well for one and three-quarter hours, an abandonment through rain soon after four o'clock on Friday came as something of a relief. In dismissing Gibbs, Underwood became first to take 100 wickets during this season.

M.C.C. President's XI

M. J. Harris b Hall	0	— c Kanhai b Hall	14
R. N. Abberley c Butcher b Sobers	10	— c Gibbs b Holford	24
D. L. Amiss b Holford	69	— st Hendriks b Gibbs	47
K. W. R. Fletcher b Hall	4	— c sub b Holford	39
J. A. Ormrod lbw b Lashley	12	— c Hendriks b Holford	14
*R. M. C. Gilliat run out	15	— not out	12
†A. Knott st Hendriks b Brancker	0	— not out	24
D. L. Underwood lbw b Holford	2		
K. Shuttleworth c Hall b Holford	27		
P. I. Pocock b Gibbs	16		
G. Arnold not out	1		
B 6, l-b 2	8	B 6, l-b 2	8
1/2 2/20 3/25 4/64 5/90 6/95 7/115 8/130 9/153	164	1/33 2/45 3/111 4/136 5/145 (5 wkts.)	182

Bowling: *First Innings*—Hall 10—4—21—2; Sobers 8—3—6—1; Lashley 18—4—36—1; Brancker 22—9—31—1; Gibbs 14.2—3—32—1; Holford 9—3—30—3. *Second Innings*—Hall 15.3—8—20—1; Lashley 7—2—15—0; Holford 37—16—67—3; Gibbs 26—10—54—1; Brancker 10—3—18—0.

West Indies

P. D. Lashley run out	10
E. D. McMorris c Knott b Shuttleworth	13
R. C. Brancker c and b Fletcher	13
B. F. Butcher c Harris b Underwood	74
†J. L. Hendriks not out	16
D. A. J. Holford c Fletcher b Pocock	30
S. M. Nurse b Pocock	10
*G. S. Sobers retired hurt	2
R. B. Kanhai run out	36
W. W. Hall b Underwood	11
L. R. Gibbs b Underwood	3
L-b 9	9
1/15 2/26 3/69 4/144 5/152 6/167 7/200 8/221 9/227	227

Bowling: Arnold 10—2—22—0; Shuttleworth 26—6—57—1; Underwood 36.2—15—56—3; Pocock 29—4—64—2; Fletcher 1—1—0—1; Amiss 4—0—19—0.

Umpires: J. F. Crapp and J. Langridge.

GLAMORGAN v. WEST INDIES

At Swansea, July 30, August 1, 2. Drawn. A. Jones played probably his best innings of the season, but rain prevented an interesting finish when the West Indies were struggling to avoid defeat. In the Glamorgan first innings Jones carried his bat for 161 and dominated the batting to such an extent that he scored his first 50 runs out of 60 in an hour, though he took three and a half hours to reach his century. E. Lewis took part with Jones in a punishing eighth-wicket partnership of 84, Lewis hitting three 6's and eight 4's. West Indies just saved the follow on, finishing 144 behind Glamorgan, who soon declared after rain had intervened and challenged West Indies to get 198 to win in three hours. They lost two wickets for 33 when more rain caused the match to be abandoned. Hunte, who captained the tourists, was dismissed for "a pair" for the first time in his career.

Glamorgan

A. Jones not out	161		
B. Hedges c Allan b Griffith	0	— not out	27
R. Davis c Holford b Hall	3	— b Hall	4
A. R. Lewis c Carew b Holford	28	— not out	6
A. Rees lbw b Carew	6		
P. M. Walker lbw b Holford	5	— b Hall	14
W. Slade run out	23		
A. E. Cordle st Allan b Holford	4		
E. Lewis c Allan b Brancker	56		
†D. L. Evans not out	38		
B 9, l-b 1, w 1, n-b 2	13	L-b 2	2
1/4 2/15 3/115 4/130 5/135 6/175 7/179 8/263 (8 wkts., dec.)	337	1/11 2/39 (2 wkts., dec.)	53

*O. S. Wheatley did not bat.

Bowling: *First Innings*—Hall 8—1—35—1; Griffith 13—3—50—1; Cohen 6—2—21—0; Brancker 13—2—44—1; Holford 31—7—100—3; Carew 26—9—74—1. *Second Innings*—Hall 9—3—24—2; Griffith 8—0—27—0.

West Indies

*C. C. Hunte c Evans b Cordle	0	— c Davis b Cordle	0
E. D. McMorris lbw b Wheatley	0	— not out	9
R. C. Brancker c Davis b Slade	31		
B. F. Butcher c Walker b E. Lewis	40		
J. S. Solomon b E. Lewis	2	— lbw b Cordle	6
M. C. Carew c Jones b Davis	26		
D. A. J. Holford c and b Walker	46	— not out	13
C. C. Griffith c Evans b Cordle	8		
W. W. Hall b Wheatley	27		
†D. W. Allan not out	11		
R. A. Cohen lbw b Wheatley	0		
B 1, n-b 1	2	B 1, l-b 4	5
1/0 2/0 3/66 4/74 5/78 6/124 7/148 8/177 9/183	193	1/0 2/8 (2 wkts.)	33

Bowling: *First Innings*—Cordle 16—8—34—2; Wheatley 14.2—5—29—3; Slade 14—6—27—1; E. Lewis 19—3—58—2; Davis 8—0—34—1; Walker 2—0—9—1. *Second Innings*—Cordle 5—0—12—2; Wheatley 4—1—6—0; Davis 3—0—8—0; E. Lewis 2—1—2—0.

Umpires: G. H. Pope and J. Arnold.

ENGLAND v. WEST INDIES

Fourth Test

At Leeds, August 4, 5, 6, 8. West Indies won by an innings and 55 runs just after three o'clock on the fourth day with a day to spare. So they completed three wonderful years in which they twice won the rubber convincingly in England—and twice carried off the Wisden trophy—and for the first time beat Australia in a series. They achieved their ambition like World Champions and, while they excelled as a team, standing high above the rest of them was their captain, Sobers, who in this match made the top score, 174, and took eight wickets for 80 runs, besides directing his men with masterly skill. In the four Tests Sobers had then scored 641 runs, average 128.20 and taken 17 wickets, as well as holding ten catches close to the bat.

As for England, this was a sorry performance and one felt at the end of the match that the selectors would have to take drastic action. This they did. They dropped Cowdrey, Milburn, Parks, Titmus, Underwood and Snow, although Snow played at The Oval owing to the withdrawal of Price, the Middlesex fast bowler.

For this Leeds match, England played Barber for the first time since his triumphs in Australia and recalled Titmus, leaving out Russell and Illingworth. West Indies relied on the eleven which played at Trent Bridge and at once Sobers gained a big advantage for his side by winning the toss for the fourth time and batting on an excellent pitch that lasted well and never offered bowlers undue help.

On a restricted first day when rain and bad light limited the cricket to three and a quarter hours England fared pretty well in dismissing Lashley, Kanhai and Hunte for 137. Another success came early the next morning when Butcher was out off the second ball of the day that he received from Higgs, the fourth wicket falling at 154.

Thereupon, Sobers and Nurse took charge and for four hours the England bowlers toiled in vain while Sobers hit his seventeenth Test century, his seventh against England and his third of the series. Moreover, he never offered a chance while making 174 out of 265, the highest West Indies stand for the fifth wicket against England. Sobers struck twenty-four 4's and he had the rare experience of hitting a hundred between lunch and tea. During the course of his great display, in which he square cut, hooked, pulled and drove as he pleased, he became the first cricketer to attain a Test aggregate of 5,000 runs and also 100 wickets. In addition, in this, his eighteenth innings of the tour, he completed his 1,000 for the summer.

The fact that Nurse hit his first hundred against England passed almost unnoticed, yet he played a most valuable innings of 137 out of 367 which covered five and three-quarter hours and contained two 6's and fourteen 4's.

The England bowlers simply could not penetrate the defences of these two fine players. Cowdrey tried to unsettle them by ringing his bowling changes. Perhaps he should have used Barber earlier, for West Indies had made 324 before the wrist-spinner was introduced. Barber certainly puzzled Nurse and he bowled Sobers, but by then the West Indies captain was a tired man. Sobers declared at 500, West Indies highest total of the tour, and Barber and Boycott scored four from the four overs delivered by Hall and Griffith before the end of the day.

An opening spell of eighty minutes by Hall at his fastest and best destroyed England on Saturday when he sent back Boycott, Cowdrey and Graveney. Sheer speed led each batsman into error and Milburn also suffered through not offering a stroke to a ball that struck him such a painful blow on the left elbow that he had to retire. When Milburn returned three and a half hours later he could only defend as he lacked power in that arm to hit with his usual freedom.

When the England total stood at 18 for two, just before mid-day, Griffith was cautioned against throwing by umpire Elliott after he had delivered a vicious bouncer to Graveney. Both umpires conferred and later Elliott said: "I told Syd Buller that in my opinion that delivery was illegal. We agreed that I should speak to Griffith about it. I then said to him: 'You can bowl, Charlie. Any more like that and I will have to call you. That delivery to Graveney was illegal.' " Following the incident, much of Griffith's pace disappeared and he took only one more wicket in the match when d'Oliveira skied a loose ball to cover.

Sobers eventually relieved Hall and adopting his quick pace soon removed Parks (with his first ball) and Titmus so that six wickets were down for 83 and England's fate was a foregone conclusion.

At last, d'Oliveira and Higgs made a stand, putting on 96 together. The South African played his third consecutive Test innings of over fifty. He hit four 6's one a magnificent straight drive from Hall, of all people, and eight 4's. Higgs also hit two 6's and played his longest and highest innings in first-class cricket, two and a quarter hours for 49 while the total rose by 155.

Sobers finally put in two spells of mixed spin and picked up the last three wickets in four balls so that England followed on 260 behind. They batted for fifty minutes before bad light caused over an hour to be lost at the end of Saturday and during that time, Lashley, with his first spell in Test cricket, trapped Boycott with his third delivery, Hendriks holding a smart catch wide and low of the off stump.

Only Barber and Milburn really troubled the West Indies bowlers on Monday when the remaining nine second-innings wickets went down for 165 runs. Barber, top scorer, defended soundly and drove and hit to leg confidently. Milburn, batting number seven—d'Oliveira went in at three—hit Holford for five 4's and hooked Gibbs over the square-leg pavilion for 6, he and Titmus adding 51 in twenty-five minutes. That was England's final fling against slow bowlers prepared to buy their wickets.

Gibbs bowled splendidly, sometimes with plenty of pace and skilful variation of flight rather than prodigious spin. He took six for 39, England's last five wickets falling in under an hour for 77.—N.P.

West Indies

C. C. Hunte lbw b Snow	48	C. C. Griffith b Higgs	0
P. D. Lashley b Higgs	9	†J. L. Hendriks not out	9
R. B. Kanhai c Graveney b Underwood	45	W. W. Hall b Snow	1
B. F. Butcher c Parks b Higgs	38	L. R. Gibbs not out	2
S. M. Nurse c Titmus b Snow	137	B 1, l-b 12	13
*G. S. Sobers b Barber	174	1/37 2/102 3/128 (9 wkts., dec.)	500
D. A. J. Holford b Higgs	24	4/154 5/419 6/467 7/467 8/489 9/491	

Bowling: Snow 42—6—146—3; Higgs 43—11—94—4; d'Oliveira 19—3—52—0; Titmus 22—7—59—0; Underwood 24—9—81—1; Barber 14—2—55—1.

England

R. W. Barber c Hendriks b Griffith	6	— b Sobers	55
G. Boycott c Holford b Hall	12	— c Hendriks b Lashley	14
C. Milburn not out	29	— b Gibbs	42
T. W. Graveney b Hall	8	— b Gibbs	19
*M. C. Cowdrey b Hall	17	— lbw b Gibbs	12
B. d'Oliveira c Hall b Griffith	88	— c Butcher b Sobers	7
†J. M. Parks lbw b Sobers	2	— c Nurse b Gibbs	16
F. J. Titmus c Hendriks b Sobers	6	— b Gibbs	22
K. Higgs c Nurse b Sobers	49	— c Hunte b Sobers	7
D. L. Underwood c Gibbs b Sobers	0	— c Kanhai b Gibbs	0
J. A. Snow c Holford b Sobers	0	— not out	0
B 12, l-b 11	23	B 8, l-b 1, n-b 2	11
1/10 2/18 3/42 4/49 5/63 6/83 7/179 8/238 9/240	240	1/28 2/70 3/84 4/109 5/128 6/133 7/184 8/205 9/205	205

Bowling: *First Innings*—Hall 17—5—47—3; Griffith 12—2—37—2; Sobers 19.3—4—41—5; Gibbs 20—5—49—0; Holford 10—3—43—0. *Second Innings*—Sobers 20.1—5—39—3; Griffith 12—0—52—0; Lashley 3—2—1—1; Hall 8—2—24—0; Gibbs 19—6—39—6; Holford 9—0—39—0.

Umpires: J. S. Buller and C. S. Elliott.

SCOTLAND v. WEST INDIES

At Hamilton Crescent, Glasgow, August 10, 11. *60 overs.* Drawn. As rain prevented play on the first day, a 60-overs match was arranged for Thursday, but this too was interrupted by the weather soon after Scotland had begun to reply to the West Indies, who had been dismissed for 193, mainly due to some excellent medium-fast bowling by Thompson, who took six for 55. Ford fielded brilliantly in catching Carew and Lashley and running out Brancker. Kanhai hit splendidly for 68, but the tail did little.

West Indies

M. C. Carew c Ford b Dow...... 34
E. D. MacMorris c Brown b Thompson.................. 29
R. B. Kanhai c Dudman b Thompson......................... 68
J. S. Solomon run out............ 8
*C. C. Hunte c Brown b Thompson 0
P. D. Lashley c Ford b Thompson. 18
R. C. Brancker run out........... 17
J. B. Stollmeyer b Allan.......... 6
†D. W. Allan c Brown b Thompson 8
C. C. Griffith c Allan b Thompson 0
R. A. Cohen not out............ 0
B 4, n-b 1................ 5

1/56 2/72 3/90 4/93 5/149 193
6/164 7/185 8/185 9/186

Bowling: Dow 17—2—61—1; Barr 11—2—57—0; Thompson 16.1—1—55—6; Allan 4—1—15—1.

Scotland

R. H. E. Chisholm c Allan b Cohen 10
L. C. Dudman not out........... 2
J. C. Laing not out............... 2
L-b 2.................. 2

1/11 (1 wkt.) 16

H. K. Moore, T. B. Racionzer, G. M. C. Ford, J. M. Allan, D. Barr, *†J. Brown, W. D. F. Dow and E. R. Thompson did not bat.

Bowling: Griffith 3—0—10—0; Cohen 2—1—4—1.

Umpires: D. R. McCulloch and R. J. Ritchie.

WARWICKSHIRE v. WEST INDIES

At Birmingham, August 13, 15, 16. West Indies won by ten wickets, with ten minutes to spare. Faint murmurings from some counties about the West Indies' casual approach will not be supported in Birmingham. Sobers put Warwickshire in to bat and they were bowled out in three hours. Hall found the pitch too slow but Cohen had the county batsmen struggling, although he was inclined to be erratic. A century by Butcher on the second day and a stand of 122 between Solomon and Allan provided splendid entertainment and gave the tourists a lead of 268, which proved far too much for Warwickshire, despite an innings of 160 not out by Amiss, the highest of his career. Normally a number three, he opened the innings and carried his bat through his stay of three hours and ten minutes, hitting two 6's, one 5 and fifteen 4's. Amiss and M. J. K. Smith put on 109 in eighty-four minutes.

Warwickshire

K. Ibadulla b Cohen................ 6 — c Nurse b Sobers........... 24
D. L. Amiss b Cohen................ 19 — not out..................160
*M. J. K. Smith c Allan b Cohen....... 12 — c Gibbs b Carew.......... 44
J. A. Jameson c Sobers b Hall......... 10 — c McMorris b Sobers....... 9
W. J. Stewart c Cohen b Gibbs......... 20 — absent hurt............... 0
T. W. Cartwright c Allan b Gibbs...... 18 — b Carew.................. 16
R. B. Edmonds b Gibbs............... 44 — c and b Holford........... 13
R. V. Webster b Holford.............. 17 — c Butcher b Gibbs 10
J. M. Allan c Allan b Holford......... 7 — c sub b Cohen.............. 14
†E. Legard not out.................. 10 — c Holford b Cohen.......... 0
D. J. Brown b Sobers................ 9 — c Gibbs b Sobers........... 11
N-b 1......................... 1 B 10, l-b 1, n-b 3....... 14

1/11 2/29 3/45 4/52 5/83 173 1/46 2/155 3/180 4/200 5/233 315
6/88 7/113 8/131 9/162 6/254 7/296 8/296 9/315

Bowling: *First Innings*—Hall 10—1—27—1; Cohen 8—0—48—3; Sobers 9.3—3—18—1; Gibbs 17—2—41—3; Holford 11—1—38—2. *Second Innings*—Hall 8—3—16—0; Cohen 10—5—22—2; Sobers 30.4—6—89—3; Gibbs 26—4—51—1; Holford 25—4—87—1; Carew 18—7—36—2.

West Indies

E. D. McMorris c Allan b Brown	61	— not out	20
M. C. Carew c Legard b Brown	10	— not out	28
S. M. Nurse b Webster	4		
B. F. Butcher c Ibadulla b Jameson	128		
D. A. J. Holford lbw b Jameson	46		
*G. S. Sobers b Webster	36		
J. S. Solomons c Ibadulla b Allan	77		
†D. W. Allan c Jameson b Ibadulla	56		
W. W. Hall c Ibadulla b Allan	4		
L. R. Gibbs not out	3		
R. A. Cohen c Amiss b Allan	1		
L-b 14, n-b 1	15	B 2	2
1/23 2/38 3/103 4/251 5/262 6/309 7/431 8/436 9/439	441	(No wkt.)	50

Bowling: *First Innings*—Brown 25—6—55—2; Webster 21—2—74—2; Cartwright 26—8—66—0; Allan 32—3—141—3; Ibadulla 19—3—66—1; Jameson 7—1—24—2. *Second Innings*—Brown 5—0—10—0; Cartwright 4—0—32—0; Smith 0.1—0—6—0.

Umpires: A. E. Alderman and R. S. Lay.

ENGLAND v. WEST INDIES
Fifth Test

At The Oval, August 18, 19, 20, 22. England won by an innings and 34 runs fifteen minutes after lunch on Monday with nearly ten hours to spare. It was a great triumph after so many humiliations during the summer and proved that England was not so poverty stricken in talent as previous performances suggested. Personal honours went to Brian Close, captain of his country for the first time and one of the six changes the selectors made after the rubber was lost in the fourth Test at Headingley. Close set his men a splendid example at short leg and silly mid off and he used his bowlers shrewdly, not being afraid to introduce Barber with his wrist spin early in the proceedings. Moreover, Barber took five wickets.

Sharing the honours with Close were Graveney, Murray, Higgs and Snow, all of whom batted magnificently after England, facing a total of 268, lost their first seven wickets for 166. At that stage everything pointed to another run-away win for West Indies, but once again the glorious uncertainty of cricket was demonstrated by these heroes who caused 361 runs to be added for the last three wickets so that West Indies, batting a second time, faced a deficit of 259.

Never before in Test cricket had the last three wickets produced 361 runs, nor had the last three men scored one hundred and two fifties. Murray, moreover, became only the third number nine to make a Test hundred. In 1931 at Lord's, G. O. Allen scored 122 and with L. E. G. Ames (137) added 246 for the eighth wicket against New Zealand and in 1946–47 at Melbourne R. R. Lindwall hit 100 out of 185 against England in under two hours.

The match was favoured with fine weather, the first three days cricket being played in a heat wave with the ground crowded to capacity. In spite of Sobers winning the toss for the fifth time, England took the initiative by dismissing Hunte, McMorris, Butcher and Nurse before lunch for 83. There followed a find stand for West Indies with Kanhai hitting his first Test century in England. He batted for three and three-quarter hours and many of his fourteen 4's came from drives past cover and mid-off. Sobers, never in difficulty, drove, cut and pulled freely until he mis-hit a short ball, giving mid-off an easy catch. The partnership yielded 122 and then only the last pair offered real opposition, the innings being completed in five hours and ten minutes, but before the end of the day England lost Boycott for 20.

Sobers, bowling his unorthodox left-handed spin, caused England trouble first thing on Friday. His third ball, a googly, accounted for Barber, and though Edrich and Amiss batted stubbornly, by the lunch interval five wickets had fallen and worse followed before Graveney at last found a reliable partner in Murray, whose neat and efficient wicket-keeping earlier had done so much towards bringing the fielding up to Test standard.

Graveney shouldered the early burden of keeping his end intact amid numerous failures. He showed the determination to build a long innings and when Murray settled down both men drove gracefully and hit to leg with power. When stumps were drawn on Friday, this pair had seen England take the lead; the total reached 330 with Graveney 132 and Murray 81. The form of Murray, who incidentally hit a century in May against the West Indies for M.C.C., was a revelation. He looked every bit as good as Graveney.

On Saturday the same batsmen continued serenely until Gibbs smartly ran out Graveney, who had spent six hours hitting his 165, which included nineteen 4's. Murray went on to 112, more than double his previous best Test score, before he was leg before to Sobers at 399. He batted four and a half hours and hit thirteen 4's.

The West Indies bowlers must have looked forward to an early rest, but the England opening bowlers, Higgs and Snow, displayed their talent for batting in a highly diverting partnership of 128 in two hours, defying all the pace and spin the West Indies could offer and the new ball. Before Higgs left to a return catch this plucky pair came within two runs of the world test record last wicket stand, 130 by R. E. Foster and W. Rhodes for England against Australia at Sydney in 1903–4. Neither Higgs nor Snow had previously completed fifty in first-class cricket.

Snow, who kept his place in the England team only at the last minute owing to an injury to Price, further distinguished himself in conjunction with Murray by disposing of McMorris and Hunte for 12 to be followed by d'Oliveira who upset Kanhai's wicket. Butcher hit spiritedly with nine 4's in his 60 in under an hour and a half before slamming a full toss into the hands of Barber at mid-wicket so that on Saturday evening, with West Indies 135 for four and still 124 behind, England were in sight of victory provided they could contain Sobers on the two remaining days.

This they did. In fact, England captured the remaining six wickets on Monday in two and a quarter hours. After a maiden over by Higgs to Nurse, the third and fourth deliveries of the day from Snow ruined any prospect West Indies entertained of saving the match. Holford unwisely went for a third run when Illingworth at third man was returning the ball on top of the stumps to Murray. Sobers, next in, went first ball, Close, waiting square in the leg trap, having directed Snow to try a bouncer. Sobers tried to hook this gift, only to give his rival captain a simple catch.

Nurse alone of the class batsmen remained. He pierced the closely set field with splendid drives and strong strokes to leg until Close recalled Barber at 164. Nurse pulled the first ball to the boundary (his fourteenth 4) and swept the next but it went high to Edrich deep behind the square leg umpire and the fielder held it at the second attempt. Nurse had stayed two hours, ten minutes for his 70 before being eighth to leave at 168. Griffith and Hall defended dourly for fifty minutes and finally Gibbs gave a return catch to Barber, West Indies being all out for 225, their lowest total of the series.

During the four days the attendance reached 90,000 and the receipts £45,494. N.P.

West Indies

C. C. Hunte b Higgs	1	— c Murray b Snow	7
E. D. McMorris b Snow	14	— c Murray b Snow	1
R. B. Kanhai c Graveney b Illingsworth	104	— b d'Oliveira	15
B. F. Butcher c Illingworth b Close	12	— c Barber b Illingworth	60
S. M. Nurse c Graveney b d'Oliveira	0	— c Edrich b Barber	70
*G. S. Sobers c Graveney b Barber	81	— c Close b Snow	0
D. A. J. Holford c d'Oliveira b Illingworth	5	— run out	7
†J. L. Hendriks b Barber	0	— b Higgs	0
C. C. Griffith c Higgs b Barber	4	— not out	29
W. W. Hall not out	30	— c d'Oliveira b Illingworth	17
L. R. Gibbs c Murray b Snow	12	— c and b Barber	3
B 1, l-b 3, n-b 1	5	B 1, l-b 14, n-b 1	16
1/1 2/56 3/73 4/74 5/196 6/218 7/218 8/223 9/223	268	1/5 2/12 3/50 4/107 5/137 6/137 7/142 8/168 9/204	225

Bowling: *First Innings*—Snow 20.5—1—66—2; Higgs 17—4—52—1; d'Oliveira 21—7—35—1; Close 9—2—21—1; Barber 15—3—49—3; Illingworth 15—7—40—2. *Second Innings*—Snow 13—5—40—3; Higgs 15—6—18—1; d'Oliveira 17—4—44—1; Illingworth 15—9—22—2; Barber 22.1—2—78—2; Close 3—1—7—0.

England

R. W. Barber c Nurse b Sobers	36
G. Boycott b Hall	4
J. H. Edrich c Hendriks b Sobers	35
T. W. Graveney run out	165
D. L. Amiss lbw b Hall	17
B. d'Oliveira b Hall	4
*D. B. Close run out	4
R. Illingworth c Hendriks b Griffith	3
†J. T. Murray lbw b Sobers	112
K. Higgs c and b Holford	63
J. A. Snow not out	59
B 8, l-b 14, n-b 3	25
1/6 2/72 3/85 4/126 5/130 6/150 7/166 8/383 9/399	527

Bowling: Hall 31—8—85—3; Griffith 32—7—78—1; Sobers 54—23—104—3; Holford 25.5—1—79—1; Gibbs 44—16—115—0; Hunte 13—2—41—0.

Umpires: J. S. Buller and C. S. Elliott.

LEICESTERSHIRE v. WEST INDIES

At Leicester, August 24, 25, 26. West Indies won by seven wickets. The touring team made six changes from the side beaten in the final Test but were still too good for Leicestershire. Griffith, even at half pace, caused trouble to all the batsmen and only a defiant stand between Birkenshaw and Duddleston, making his senior debut, enabled the county to reach a reasonable score. The West Indies themselves were unsure in their batting but the last pair, Lashley and Cohen, who added 47, helped them to a lead of 55. Lock, who completed 100 wickets in a season for the thirteenth time, claimed five for 51. Leicestershire made a better start to their second innings but collapsed against the leg spin of Holford who, in two maidens, sent back Duddleston, Tolchard, Lock and Savage at the same score, 201. Left to get 153 to win the West Indies hurried to their target after a second-wicket assault by Kanhai and Carew who put on 92 in an hour.

Leicestershire

M. R. Hallam b Cohen	2	run out	47
M. E. Norman c Allan b Griffith	27	st Allan b Brancker	43
B. J. Booth c Allan b Griffith	20	c Nurse b Holford	38
C. C. Inman c Nurse b Lashley	11	lbw b Brancker	38
J. Birkenshaw c Lashley b Carew	68	c Allan b Holford	4
S. Greensword c Kanhai b Griffith	4	st Allan b Brancker	20
B. Duddleston c Allan b Carew	24	c Nurse b Holford	4
†R. W. Tolchard c Nurse b Griffith	5	c Lashley b Holford	0
*G. A. R. Lock c Allan b Griffith	10	c Nurse b Holford	0
J. S. Savage b Griffith	1	b Holford	0
C. T. Spencer not out	2	not out	0
L-b 2, w 1, n-b 2	5	B 10, l-b 3	13
1/3 2/44 3/56 4/70 5/83 6/136 7/149 8/167 9/173	179	1/60 2/136 3/140 4/168 5/190 6/201 7/201 8/201 9/201	207

Bowling: *First Innings*—Griffith 24—6—59—6; Cohen 11—2—38—1; Lashley 11—3—19—1; Carew 13.5—5—34—2; Holford 6—0—24—0. *Second Innings*—Griffith 5—2—11—0; Cohen 4—0—16—0; Lashley 2—0—13—0; Carew 18—8—32—0; Holford 27—8—68—6; Brancker 25.2—6—54—3.

West Indies

*C. C. Hunte c Hallam b Greensword	3	— c Lock b Spencer	0
M. C. Carew c Spencer b Savage	28	— b Birkenshaw	42
R. B. Kanhai b Lock	35	— b Birkenshaw	62
S. M. Nurse c and b Lock	66	— not out	27
J. S. Solomon b Savage	3	— not out	24
P. D. Lashley not out	59		
D. A. J. Holford lbw b Savage	5		
R. C. Brancker c Greensword b Savage	0		
†D. W. Allan st Tolchard b Lock	1		
C. C. Griffith b Lock	6		
R. A. Cohen c Hallam b Lock	18		
B 7, l-b 2, n-b 1	10		
1/3 2/83 3/103 4/121 5/128 6/167 7/168 8/173 9/187	234	1/0 2/92 3/111 (3 wkts.)	155

Bowling: *First Innings*—Spencer 16—2—47—0; Greensword 15—5—41—1; Savage 29—9—66—4; Lock 25.1—6—51—5; Birkenshaw 6—0—19—0. *Second Innings*—Spencer 6—1—21—1; Greensword 2—0—12—0; Savage 8—1—35—0; Lock 12—1—54—0; Birkenshaw 11—2—25—2; Booth 0.3—0—8—0.

Umpires: R. Aspinall and H. Mellows.

HAMPSHIRE v. WEST INDIES

At Southampton, August 27, 29, 30. Drawn. No play was possible owing to rain on the second day and prospect of a good finish was ruined by more rain which caused the match to be given up when Hampshire, with eight wickets in hand, needed 81 more runs in sixty-five minutes to win. Good bowling by Castell, who took four wickets for 33 runs, helped to dismiss the West Indies for 191. Lashley and Sobers put on 64 for the fourth wicket, and Lashley's 73 contained two 6's, but the last five wickets fell for only 37 runs. Hampshire made 103 for two wickets by the end of the day. West Indies, thanks to enterprising play by Butcher, Sobers and Hall left Hampshire to get 223 to win in as many minutes. Marshall again batted well and with Horton put on 88 for the second wicket. Soon after Horton completed his fifty, rain put an end to the match.

West Indies

M. C. Carew c Horton b Marshall	26	— c Wassell b Shackleton	18
E. D. McMorris lbw b Shackleton	1	— c Timms b Castell	7
P. D. Lashley c and b Wassell	73	— c Horton b Marshall	11
B. F. Butcher run out	10	— c Livingstone b Castell	35
*G. S. Sobers c Horton b Wassell	35	— c and b Castell	23
J. S. Solomon c Timms b Castell	6		
R. C. Brancker lbw b Castell	0		
†J. L. Hendriks lbw b Castell	20	— not out	4
W. W. Hall c Caple b Castell	4	— not out	34
L. R. Gibbs b Shackleton	4		
R. A. Cohen not out	2		
B 5, l-b 5	10	B 2	2
1/3 2/59 3/75 4/139 5/154 6/155 7/160 8/166 9/186	191	1/20 2/28 3/55 4/91 5/108 (5 wkts., dec.)	134

Bowling: *First Innings*—Shackleton 23—10—49—2; Castell 23—7—33—4; Marshall 8—3—22—1; Wheatley 10—2—24—0; Wassell 24—8—53—2. *Second Innings*—Shackleton 11—4—28—1; Castell 11—4—25—3; Marshall 6—1—29—1; Wheatley 7—0—50—0.

Hampshire

*R. E. Marshall b Lashley	44	— c Cohen b Lashley	54
B. L. Reed b Sobers	36	— c Lashley b Cohen	5
H. Horton not out	14	— not out	54
D. A. Livingstone not out	5	— not out	27
B 2, n-b 2	4	L-b 2	2
1/69 2/94 (2 wkts., dec.)	103	1/6 2/94 (2 wkts.)	142

K. J. Wheatley, R. M. C. Gilliat, R. G. Caple, †B. S. V. Timms, A. T. Castell, A. R. Wassell and D. Shackleton did not bat.

Bowling: *First Innings*—Hall 4—0—29—0; Cohen 3—0—15—0; Sobers 10—3—18—1; Lashley 9—3—29—1; Gibbs 7—3—8—0. *Second Innings*—Hall 7—2—15—0; Cohen 5—1—24—1; Lashley 11—0—49—1; Gibbs 9—0—31—0; Brancker 2—0—14—0; Sobers 6—1—7—0.

Umpires: J. Arnold and W. H. Copson.

A. E. R. GILLIGAN'S XI v. WEST INDIES

At Hastings, August 31, September 1, 2. Drawn. This match suffered from rain, there being no cricket after the first day. Arthur Gilligan, with twelve of the seventeen counties engaged in the Championship, found difficulty in getting together a strong side. He included Greig, a South African qualifying for Sussex. David Brown, the Gloucestershire batsman, bowled for the first time in first-class cricket, taking a wicket in his first over. The West Indies gave a carefree batting display, hitting six 6's, five from Brown's off-breaks and one off Forbes. Griffith's 63 was his highest score of the tour.

West Indies

*C. C. Hunte run out	54	C. C. Griffith not out	63
E. D. McMorris c Bolus b Davison	11	L. R. Gibbs b Greig	19
R. B. Kanhai c Brown b Greig	33	R. A. Cohen b Jones	2
S. M. Nurse c Brown b Greig	7		
P. D. Lashley st Murray b Brown	60	B 13, l-b 5	18
D. A. J. Holford c Jones b Brown	4		
R. C. Brancker c Bolus b Brown	29	1/28 2/94 3/105 4/106 5/123	351
†D. W. Allan st Murray b Forbes	51	6/198 7/227 8/282 9/346	

Bowling: Jones 18.5—0—80—1; Davison 7—1—26—1; Greig 16—4—51—3; Marner 7—0—13—0; Forbes 25—4—79—1; Brown 15—1—84—3.

A. E. R. Gilligan's XI

J. B. Bolus c and b Brancker	38	M. J. Smedley not out	7
M. E. Norman lbw b Cohen	8	B 5, l-b 4, w 1, n-b 1	11
D. Brown c Kanhai b Cohen	1		
C. C. Inman c Hunte b Gibbs	5	1/30 2/36 3/51 4/70 (4 wkts.)	70

P. Marner, A. Greig, *†D. L. Murray, C. Forbes, I. Davison and I. J. Jones did not bat.

Bowling: Griffith 4—1—11—0; Cohen 7—2—24—2; Lashley 4—2—5—0; Gibbs 4—1—9—1; Brancker 3.2—0—10—1.

Umpires: John Langridge and A. E. Fagg.

T. N. PEARCE'S XI v. WEST INDIES

At Scarborough, September 3, 5, 6. T. N. Pearce's XI won by two wickets. The tourists were beaten on merit by a determined side under the leadership of Brian Close, captain of Yorkshire, the Champion County, and of England, but provided attractive cricket the whole time. Close had the pleasure, after being delayed in a traffic jam on the opening day, to find that his rivals had lost their opening pair for 36 by the time he reached the ground; then he himself took three for 68. Holford and Sobers entertained the crowd with their forceful and stylish strokes. Holford pulled Close for two 6's and Sobers on-drove him for another. On the second day the spectators found their chief interest in seeing Boycott reach his sixth hundred of the summer. Driving well, he hit twelve 4's and a 6, taking 4, 6, 4, 4, 2 off five successive balls from Kanhai before being stumped off the sixth. A deficit of 66 did not dismay Sobers, who opened his side's second innings with Carew and punished Trueman severely in a partnership of 70 in thirty-five minutes. Kanhai found his best driving and cutting form and two huge drives for 6 off successive balls from Close brought him his third century. He also hit thirteen 4's. Quick scoring next morning by Lashley and Butcher enabled Sobers to set Pearce's side 277 to make in three hours and fifty minutes. Boycott and Prideaux gave them a fine start with a partnership of 139 and although Carew, with flighted spinners, bowled skilfully, the result was rarely in doubt. Trueman hit three 4's off Carew when a bout of hitting was needed, and Pearce's XI won with half an hour to spare.

West Indies

M. C. Carew b Higgs	6	— c Parks b Knight	33
P. D. Lashley lbw b Knight	17	— st Parks b Hampshire	50
R. B. Kanhai b Knight	14	— b Underwood	103
B. F. Butcher c Prideaux b Underwood	48	— not out	44
D. A. J. Holford c Underwood b Close	62	— b Underwood	20
*G. S. Sobers c Underwood b Close	46	— c Parfitt b Trueman	44
J. S. Solomon c Prideaux b Close	6		
R. C. Brancker lbw b Trueman	2	— b Underwood	8
†J. L. Hendriks not out	11	— run out	2
W. W. Hall c Parfitt b Trueman	8	— c Lewis b Close	33
R. A. Cohen run out	5		
B 1, l-b 7, n-b 1	9	L-b 4, n-b 1	5
1/27 2/27 3/43 4/126 5/191 6/201 7/207 8/210 9/229	234	1/70 2/97 3/178 4/232 5/241 6/256 7/323 8/342 (8 wkts., dec.)	342

Bowling: *First Innings*—Trueman 18.5—3—51—2; Higgs 15—2—42—1; Knight 9—1—17—2; Underwood 16—3—47—1; Close 11—0—68—3. *Second Innings*—Trueman 6—1—40—1; Higgs 20—0—77—0; Knight 11—1—55—1; Close 15—1—60—1; Underwood 18—3—71—3; Hampshire 4—0—34—1.

T. N. Pearce's XI

G. Boycott st Hendriks b Kanhai	131	— b Hall	65
R. M. Prideaux run out	45	— st Hendriks b Carew	72
P. H. Parfitt c and b Carew	7	— b Carew	31
A. R. Lewis c and b Brancker	15	— c and b Sobers	40
J. H. Hampshire c Hall b Solomon	44	— c and b Carew	18
*D. B. Close not out	32	— c Cohen b Carew	9
†J. M. Parks not out	21	— not out	15
B. R. Knight (did not bat)		— b Sobers	1
F. S. Trueman (did not bat)		— b Carew	15
K. Higgs (did not bat)		— not out	1
L-b 3, n-b 2	5	B 3, l-b 7	10
1/29 2/112 3/149 4/245 5/245 (5 wkts., dec.)	300	1/139 2/141 3/218 4/226 5/243 6/248 7/251 8/268 (8 wkts.)	277

D. L. Underwood did not bat.

Bowling: *First Innings*—Hall 12—1—35—0; Cohen 9—2—33—0; Lashley 5—0—8—0; Sobers 7—0—22—0; Holford 9.3—0—37—0; Carew 17—5—42—1; Brancker 9—1—46—1; Solomon 5—0—32—1; Kanhai 4—0—40—1. *Second Innings*—Hall 9—1—41—1; Cohen 10—1—58—0; Lashley 5—1—24—0; Carew 22.2—3—80—5; Brancker 7—0—28—0; Sobers 12—1—36—2.

Umpires: T. W. Spencer and W. E. Phillipson.

WARWICKSHIRE v. WEST INDIES

At Birmingham, September 10, *50 overs*. West Indies won by 19 runs. They played their full Test side in this challenge match against the Gillette Cup winners. While the left-handed Carew batted steadily, Nurse (thirteen 4's) completed his brilliant not-out century in the last over of the innings in four minutes under two hours and was named the man of the match. Barber excelled for Warwickshire, punishing Griffith for 23 in two overs and the county passed 200 in the fortieth over, but in the quest for runs they broke down. Hunte, who seldom bowled during the tour, proved too accurate, finishing with four for 38. Dr. Webster, born in Barbados, experienced a lean time in his last match for Warwickshire before emigrating to New Zealand.

West Indies

C. C. Hunte c A. C. Smith b Brown 0
M. C. Carew c A. C. Smith b Cartwright 78
R. B. Kanhai c sub b Webster 18
B. F. Butcher c M. J. K. Smith b Cartwright 25
S. M. Nurse not out 102
*G. S. Sobers not out 28
L-b 6 6

1/0 2/27 3/74 4/203 (4 wkts., 50 overs) 257

D. A. J. Holford, †J. L. Hendriks, C. C. Griffith, W. W. Hall and L. R. Gibbs did not bat.

Bowling: Brown 10—2—46—1; Webster 10—1—61—1; Bannister 10—0—39—0; Cartwright 10—0—54—2; Ibadulla 10—0—51—0.

Warwickshire

R. W. Barber b Hunte 63
K. Ibadulla c Hunte b Hall 4
D. L. Amiss c Holford b Carew 76
*M. J. K. Smith st Hendriks b Gibbs 4
J. A. Jameson c Sobers b Gibbs 17
R. N. Abberley b Hunte 16
†A. C. Smith b Nurse 26
T. W. Cartwright b Hunte 14
R. V. Webster c Hunte b Carew 0
D. J. Brown b Hunte 2
J. D. Bannister not out 2
B 1, l-b 13 14

1/15 2/92 3/111 4/161 5/175 6/212 7/221 8/224 9/231 238

Bowling: Hall 6—1—18—1; Griffith 2—0—26—0; Sobers 8—0—33—0; Hunte 9.1—0—38—4; Gibbs 10—1—27—2; Carew 10—0—60—2; Nurse 2—0—22—1.

Umpires: A. E. Rhodes and R. Aspinall.

At Lord's, September 12, 13, West Indies played two matches in the "Rothman World Cup" tournament. (See OTHER MATCHES AT LORD'S.)

THE MARYLEBONE CRICKET CLUB

PATRON—HER MAJESTY THE QUEEN

President—LT.-GENERAL SIR OLIVER LEESE

President-Designate—SIR ALEC DOUGLAS-HOME

Treasurer—G. O. ALLEN

Secretary—S. C. GRIFFITH

(Lord's Cricket Ground, St. John's Wood Road, N.W.8)

Assistant Secretaries—J. G. DUNBAR and D. B. CARR

Trustees—R. H. TWINING, LT.-COLONEL THE LORD NUGENT, CAPTAIN LORD CORNWALLIS

Committee—F. G. MANN, G. C. NEWMAN, G. O. SHELMERDINE, M. J. C. ALLOM, F. R. BROWN, T. E. BURROWS, T. N. PEARCE, MARSHAL OF THE R.A.F. VISCOUNT PORTAL OF HUNGERFORD, D. C. H. TOWNSEND, GENERAL SIR JAMES CASSELS, D. G. CLARK, C. A. F. HASTILOW, W. W. HILL-WOOD, D. J. INSOLE, A. B. SELLERS, R. AIRD, A. M. CRAWLEY, SIR EDWARD LEWIS, P. B. H. MAY, C. G. A. PARIS.

At the 179th Annual Meeting of M.C.C. at Lord's on May 4, Sir Alec Douglas-Home was nominated President-Designate in succession to Lt.-General Sir Oliver Leese, the appointment to take effect from October 1, 1966.

With deep regret the Committee recorded the passing of Sir Winston Churchill who honoured the club by accepting Life Membership at the close of the Second World War.

The club also mourned the loss of two of its most distinguished administrators: Viscount Monckton of Brenchley who was President in 1956–57. He kept wicket for Harrow in Fowler's match in 1910 and was a member of Harlequins and I.Z. His skill and distinction as lawyer and statesman were of enormous benefit to cricket and especially to M.C.C. and Surrey whose President he was in 1950–52 and again in 1959–64.

H. S. Altham was President in 1959–60, Treasurer 1950–63 and was appointed Trustee, 1964. Cricketer; coach; historian; administrator. At Repton he was given his colours in 1905 by J. N. Crawford and he led the great eleven of 1908. After two years in the Oxford XI he went as a master to Winchester College, where, for the rest of his life he delighted to instil into generations of boys his own unquenchable enthusiasm for the game. He was always happy in the company of the young and in his later years it was, perhaps, his work as the first chairman of the M.C.C. Youth Cricket Association which gave him the deepest pleasure. From 1908 to 1913 he played for Surrey, but after the First World War he transferred to the county of his adoption, Hampshire, to whom he gave devoted service as player, advisor and president until the day of his death. In 1926 he published "A History of Cricket", the most authoritative history of the game, and he had an expert knowledge of cricket pictures and *objets d'art*. He was a brilliant speaker on the game and at Lilleshall when he addressed participants in the coaching courses run by the Youth Cricket Association, he held his audiences spellbound. He never spared himself, and it was characteristic that his death came, as he would surely have wished, after addressing an evening function of a distant cricket society. With the passing of Mr. Altham, M.C.C. and the cricket world in general have lost a great champion and a wise counsellor.

The Committee also made special mention of the following members who died during the year: A. P. Freeman, Captain T. O. Jameson, R. C. Robertson-Glasgow, W. R. Hammond, Max Woosnam, W. M. Woodfull, R. A. Roberts, E. S. Snell, J. W. Hearne, J. Barton King, and Maharaj Kumar Sir Vijaya Ananda of Vizianagram.

Membership

On December 31, 1965, the Club consisted of 9,343 Full Members and 2,961 Associate Members, 132 Honorary Life Members and 23 Honorary Cricket Members.

At the Special General Meeting on January 11, 1966 the number of Associate Members was increased from 3,000 to 4,000. Subscriptions were raised: Full Members £6 to £9; Associate Members £4 to £6. Entrance Fee £5. Reduced rates were introduced for Country Members having a residential or business address beyond a radius of 100 miles of Hyde Park Corner. Members attaining the age of 65, or under 25, could also apply for reduced subscriptions.

Finance

The accounts for the year 1965, after transferring £5,000 to the Building Fund, showed an excess of expenditure over income amounting to £9,677. The amount received from all firms having catering rights and concessions was £4,000.

New Zealand and South African Tours

The experiment of a "Double Tour" was tried for the first time in 1965. The New Zealanders, under the captaincy of Mr. J. R. Reid and managed by Mr. W. A. Hadlee, visited the United Kingdom during the first half of the summer, and the South Africans, under the captaincy of Mr. P. L. van der Merwe and managed by Mr. J. B. Plimsoll, came for the latter part of the season.

The New Zealanders were unfortunate in meeting the worst of the English weather and their playing results suffered accordingly. They lost all three Test Matches, but, in spite of this disappointment, they proved themselves a most popular touring team.

The South Africans played some exciting and entertaining cricket and are to be congratulated on winning the series by the only victory at Nottingham. Their attacking batsmanship and brilliant fielding caused great delight to many thousands of English cricket followers.

For the first time, two Test Matches were played at Lord's, both of which produced fine games of cricket and, in spite of causing a certain congestion of fixtures, this experiment is considered to have proved successful.

M.C.C. Tour to Australia and New Zealand 1965–66

A M.C.C. team, under the captaincy of Mr. M. J. K. Smith and managed by Mr. S. C. Griffith, the Secretary of M.C.C., toured Australia and New Zealand during the winter. The team is to be congratulated on playing much splendid attacking cricket, which was typified by the fine victory in the Third Test Match at Sydney, and the splendid Test Match centuries scored by R. W. Barber and K. F. Barrington. Special note must be made of the brilliant catching of the captain and one of the most encouraging features of the tour was the success attained by the young fast bowlers, D. J. Brown and I. J. Jones. The team was extremely popular both on and off the field wherever it went in Australia and great credit is due to the manager and captain.

M.C.C. Schools Tour to South Africa 1965–66

For the first time, M.C.C. sent a representative schoolboys' team to tour overseas and they visited South Africa for four and half weeks. Unfortunately, the uncertainty of the situation in Rhodesia caused the Committee to cancel the team's visit to that country at short notice, but the South African Nuffield Schools Cricket Authorities kindly extended the tour in South Africa by a week.

The team was selected following trials held at Lord's between a Public Schools XI and the English Schools Cricket Association XI. Mr. D. R. Walsh (Marlborough) was elected captain, and Mr. M. R. Ricketts managed the team.

Thirteen one-day matches were played, of which six were won, three drawn and four lost. Four of these matches were played against strong adult teams, and, of the fixtures against representative Provincial Schools XIs, five matches were drawn and only one was lost.

Match and Practice Grounds

The Head Groundsman and his staff are again to be congratulated on the very high standard of pitch preparation. It was generally agreed by both our overseas visiting teams and many of the countries that the pitches at Lord's were about the best in the country.

The new outfield drainage system, installed during the previous winter, proved very successful, and it is considered that many hours of cricket, including a considerable proportion of the New Zealand Test Match, were saved as a direct result. Additional sheet covers for use on the surrounding areas of the square have been purchased and it is hoped that they will further reduce playing time lost owing to wet weather conditions.

Building and Works

Rebuilding and Redevelopment—At the Special General Meeting held on October 20, 1965, at Lord's, the details of the rebuilding project were presented to members. It was resolved, however, to refer the project back to the Committee for further examination and so that full particulars could be circulated to all members, prior to the matter being reconsidered at another Special General Meeting.

At a further Special General Meeting, held on January 11, 1966, at Seymour Hall, authority was granted to the Trustees and the Custodian Trustee to exercise their powers of borrowing and charging the property and assets of the Club as provided for in Rule XX to an extent necessary to implement the Committee's proposals for the rebuilding and modernisation of the Old Tavern and Clock Tower Blocks, and the construction of a New Tavern and Restaurant to the west of the Grace Gates, subject to consideration being given to a modified stand costing less than the £280,000 at present envisaged.

After consultation with the Club's Architect, it has been decided that one tier of boxes shall be excluded, thereby reducing the overall cost by over £30,000. It is estimated that the stand, including a new score board and catering equipment in the bars, will cost £187,300. The cost of demolition will be approximately £18,000. Provision of new lavatories, roads and boundary walls will add a further £13,000 to the total. Finally, professional fees in connection with the rebuilding will amount to some £30,000. It is estimated that the seating capacity of the New Stand, including ten 24-seater boxes, will be 3,469, some 600 more than the existing seating capacity.

It is hoped that the existing Tavern and Clock Tower Block will be demolished after the cricket season, in September, 1966. It is expected that the new tavern unit to the west of the Grace

Gates will be ready for use by the spring of 1967. The New Stand, however, will be only partially completed for the 1967 season.

Refreshment Department

Negotiations have been concluded with Ring & Brymer (Birch's) Ltd., to terminate their agreement on September 30, 1966, some six months earlier than the contracted date, to enable building operations to begin in the autumn. For the winter months, there will be no catering facilities at Lord's for dinners and other functions. However, it is hoped that, when the new tavern unit is in operation, the new banqueting facilities will be used to the full. The tavern unit has been let to Watney Combe Reid and Co. Ltd. on a 21-year lease at a rental of £12,500 per annum. Watneys have sub-contracted the catering concessions to Pattison-Hughes Catering Co. Ltd., of Birmingham. The firm already has considerable cricket catering experience, as they undertake the catering both at Edgbaston and Old Trafford.

Arts and Library

The Club is once more indebted to members and others for gifts and bequests to the M.C.C. Collection. The fine china bowl specially executed by the Worcester Royal Porcelain Company to mark the 150th anniversary of the present Lord's Ground was presented to the Club by Lord Cobham at a special ceremony in October.

M.C.C. RESULTS

First-Class Matches—Played 5; *Won* 2, *Drawn* 3

Other Matches—Played 195, *Won* 94, *Lost* 32, *Drawn* 69, *Abandoned* 14

At Wisbech, April 27, 28. Wisbech Town C.C., 75 for 7 dec. and 119; M.C.C. 82 for 5 dec. and 57. M.C.C. lost by 55 runs.

M.C.C. v. YORKSHIRE

At Lord's, April 30, May 2, 3. Drawn. Yorkshire thought they had won when the ninth wicket went down with M.C.C. still 48 runs short of the winning target of 254 but Mr. S. C. Griffith, the M.C.C. secretary, ruled otherwise. He said that it was a draw as Gibson, who had taken no part in the game after the first day because of an injured leg, did not have time to reach the wicket. Generally honours were even on a pitch made for runs. A laborious century by Boycott meant little as M.C.C. with the help of Green and Russell at first and then Green and d'Oliveira replied with some attractive stroke play but Boycott later showed a greater willingness to attack as he and Taylor swung the balance back to Yorkshire. They put on 177 in two and a half hours, with Taylor batting five more minutes to complete 106 (two 6's and fourteen 4's). d'Oliveira again batted well but a rate of 73 an hour for the best part of four hours always looked too much for M.C.C.

Yorkshire

First Innings		Second Innings	
G. Boycott c Smedley b d'Oliveira	123	c Mortimore b Hobbs	68
K. Taylor c Smedley b Gibson	6	c Hobbs b Cottam	106
D. E. V. Padgett run out	40	not out	41
J. H. Hampshire c Hobbs b d'Oliveira	40	c Hobbs b Mortimore	11
*D. B. Close c sub b d'Oliveira	27	c Edrich b Green	20
P. J. Sharpe not out	23		
R. Illingworth lbw b Green	2		
†J. G. Binks not out	16		
L-b 4	4	B 7, l-b 1	8
1/14 2/98 3/175 4/239 5/242 6/249 (6 wkts., dec.)	281	1/177 2/183 3/200 4/254 (4 wkts., dec.)	254

D. Wilson, A. G. Nicholson and J. Waring did not bat.

Bowling: *First Innings*—Cottam 20—4—61—0; Gibson 14—5—36—1; d'Oliveira 30—16—49—3; Hobbs 20—5—58—0; Mortimore 25—5—57—0; Green 7—2—16—1. *Second Innings*—Cottam 25—7—47—1; d'Oliveira 9—3—15—0; Green 14.2—2—45—1; Mortimore 20—4—47—1; Hobbs 21—7—92—1.

M.C.C.

First Innings		Second Innings	
W. E. Russell c Binks b Waring	44	c Nicholson b Close	34
D. M. Green c Hampshire b Illingworth	81	c Illingworth b Waring	1
J. H. Edrich c Boycott b Wilson	1	c Binks b Waring	4
B. d'Oliveira c Hampshire b Waring	80	b Illingworth	83
K. W. R. Fletcher not out	37	c Binks b Wilson	23
M. J. Smedley not out	30	c Hampshire b Close	12
*J. B. Mortimore (did not bat)	—	c Waring b Close	0
†R. W. Taylor (did not bat)	—	c Boycott b Nicholson	24
R. N. S. Hobbs (did not bat)	—	c Binks b Nicholson	22
R. M. Cottam (did not bat)	—	not out	0
B 3, l-b 5, n-b 1	9	L-b 2, n-b 1	3
1/75 2/76 3/180 4/219 (4 wkts., dec.)	282	1/4 2/12 3/55 4/118 5/142 6/142 7/161 8/206 9/206 (9 wkts.)	206

D. Gibson did not bat.

Bowling: *First Innings*—Nicholson 9—1—36—0; Waring 12—0—58—2; Wilson 25—12—49—1; Illingworth 18—5—44—1; Close 11—1—39—0; Boycott 7—3—21—0; Hampshire 3—1—17—0; Taylor 4—1—9—0. *Second Innings*—Nicholson 11—3—32—2; Waring 10—2—26—2; Close 11—0—52—3; Illingworth 22—6—49—1; Wilson 16—5—44—1.

Umpires: H. P. Sharp and L. J. Todd.

M.C.C. v. SURREY

At Lord's, May 4, 5, 6. Drawn. Rain limited play to half an hour on the first day and about three hours on the second. Conditions were miserable but despite this Cowper, the Australian, and Saeed Ahmed, from Pakistan, shared a bright stand of 81. Saeed went on to reach a century in two and a half hours, hitting seven 4's while scoring his second fifty in forty minutes.

M.C.C.

J. H. Hampshire c Willett b Marriott	16
R. Virgin c Long b Arnold	5
R. M. Cowper c Edrich b Storey	53
Saeed Ahmed not out	100
*D. B. Close not out	13
B 3, l-b 2	5
1/12 2/34 3/115 (3 wkts., dec.)	192

C. G. Borde, †M. G. Griffith, M. D. Mence, B. A. Langford, K. E. Palmer and F. E. Rumsey did not bat.

Bowling: Arnold 14—0—61—1; Marriott 11—1—40—1; Storey 10—2—18—1; Harman 13—2—48—0; Pocock 13—5—20—0.

Surrey

*M. J. Stewart, J. H. Edrich, R. A. E. Tindall, K. F. Barrington, M. D. Willett, S. J. Storey, †A. Long, P. I. Pocock, G. Arnold, R. Harman, D. A. Marriott.

Umpires: H. P. Sharp and L. J. Todd.

May 7 New Malden	M.C.C. B.B.C. Club	181 163–9	Drawn
May 14 Framlingham	M.C.C. Framlingham College	175 for 9* 178 for 4	Lost by six six wickets

At Lord's, May 14, 16, 17. M.C.C. drew with West Indies. (See West Indies section.)

May 14 Rugby	Rugby School M.C.C.	51 52 for 1	Won by nine wickets
May 17 Winchester	M.C.C. Winchester College	97 85	Won by 12 runs
May 18, 19 Ealing	Club Cricket Conference M.C.C.	246 for 2* and 204 for 5* 214 and 164	Lost by 72 runs
May 18 Snaresbrook	M.C.C. Forest School	165 for 6* 48	Won by 117 runs
May 19 New Beckenham	M.C.C. Lloyds Bank C.C.	172 for 9* 87 for 2	Drawn (rain)
May 19 Luton	M.C.C. Luton Town C.C.	179 for 5* 54 for 1	Drawn (rain)
May 19 Repton	M.C.C. Repton School	187 for 4* 71 for 1	Drawn (rain)
May 21 Bedford	M.C.C. Bedford School	200 for 6* 142 for 7	Drawn
May 21 Eton	M.C.C. Eton College	186 for 4* 119	Won by 67 runs
May 21 City Road	Honourable Artillery Co. M.C.C.	173 134	Lost by 39 runs
May 21 Cambridge	M.C.C. Perse School	126 113	Won by 13 runs
May 21 Uppingham	Uppingham School M.C.C.	195 for 8* 121 for 8	Drawn
May 24 Cranleigh	Cranleigh School M.C.C.	160 161 for 8	Won by two wickets
May 24 Great Malvern	Malvern College M.C.C.	223 for 6* 225 for 5	Won by five wickets
May 24 Walthamstow	M.C.C. Sir George Monoux G.S.	191 for 9* 147	Won by 44 runs
May 25 Highgate	Highgate School M.C.C.	—	Abandoned (rain)
May 25 Camberley	M.C.C. R.M.A. Sandhurst	—	Abandoned (rain)
May 25 South Croydon	Whitgift School M.C.C.	119 for 6* 116 for 5	Drawn
May 26 Dulwich	M.C.C. Alleyn's School	156 for 7* 81	Won by 75 runs

May 26 Harrow	M.C.C. Harrow School	150 124	Won by 26 runs
May 26 Loughborough	Loughborough College M.C.C.	188 for 7* 140 for 6	Drawn
May 27 Brentwood	M.C.C. Brentwood School	208 for 5* 82	Won by 126 runs
May 27 Wellington	M.C.C. Wrekin College	192 for 9* 92	Won by 100 runs
May 28 Berkhamsted	Berkhamsted School M.C.C.	81 82 for 1	Won by nine wickets
May 28 Cheltenham	Cheltenham College M.C.C.	279 for 7* 214	Lost by 65 runs
May 28 Haileybury	M.C.C. Haileybury and I.S.C.	124 125 for 9	Lost by one wicket
May 28 Cambridge	Leys School M.C.C.	158 161 for 1	Won by nine wickets
May 28 Radley	Radley College M.C.C.	173 177 for 5	Won by five wickets
May 30 Old Windsor	Beaumont College M.C.C.	51 52 for 2	Won by eight wickets
May 30 Leamington Spa	Leamington C.C. M.C.C.	244 for 6* 215	Lost by 29 runs
May 31 Shoreham-by-Sea	Lancing College M.C.C.	120 121 for 1	Won by nine wickets
May 31 Du Cane Road, W.12	M.C.C. Latymer Upper School	225 for 6* 97	Won by 128 runs
May 31 Wills Grove, N.W.7	M.C.C. Mill Hill School	176 135	Won by 41 runs

M.C.C. v. SCOTLAND

At Lord's, June 2, 3. Drawn. M.C.C. 233 for two wickets, declared (A. R. Day 77, B. Ward 70). and 121 for two wickets, declared (B. Ward 49 not out); Scotland 134 for nine wickets, declared (A. R. Day five for 35) and 134 for six (R. H. E. Chisholm 62 not out).

M.C.C. v. CAMBRIDGE UNIVERSITY

At Lord's, June 4, 5. Drawn. Cambridge University 110 (R. A. Hutton four for 41) and 197 for six wickets (D. L. Hays 82, N. J. Cosh 53 not out); M.C.C. 203 (M. H. Stevenson 60; D. L. Acfield four for 59).

CHANNEL ISLANDS TOUR

June 1 Guernsey	Elizabeth College M.C.C.	86 87 for 4	Won by six wickets
June 2 Guernsey	M.C.C. Guernsey Island C.C.	224 for 7* 116 for 9	Drawn.
June 3 Jersey	M.C.C. Jersey Island C.C.	239 for 6* 90 for 6	Drawn
June 4 Jersey	M.C.C. Victoria College	268 for 9* 95	Won by 173 runs
June 6 Jersey	Jersey Island C.C. M.C.C.	106 108 for 1	Won by nine wickets

June 1 Rousdon	M.C.C. Allhallows School	242 for 5* 105	Won by 137 runs
June 1 Northwood	M.C.C. Merchant Taylors' School	216 for 4* 145	Won by 71 runs

June 1 Catford	M.C.C. St. Dunstan's College	164 for 6* 83	Won by 81 runs
June 1 Stonyhurst	M.C.C. Stonyhurst College	229 for 4* 131 for 6	Drawn
June 2 Bristol	Bristol Grammar School M.C.C.	102 104 for 6	Won by four wickets
June 2 Godalming	M.C.C. Charterhouse School	201 139 for 6	Drawn
June 2 Felsted	M.C.C. Felsted School	259 for 6* 166	Won by 93 runs
June 2 New Beckenham	M.C.C. National Provincial Bank	213 for 7* 131	Won by 82 runs
June 3 Weybridge	M.C.C. St. George's College	221 for 5* 79	Won by 142 runs
June 4 Letchmore Heath	Aldenham School M.C.C.	52 54 for 0	Won by ten wickets
June 4 Woolhampton	M.C.C. Douai School	109 85	Won by 24 runs
June 4 Oundle	M.C.C. Oundle School	179 89	Won by 90 runs
June 4 Earley	Reading C.C. M.C.C.	222 for 8* 168 for 9	Drawn
June 4 Shrewsbury	Shrewsbury School M.C.C.	145 146 for 2	Won by eight wickets
June 4 Long Eaton	M.C.C. Trent College	143 85	Won by 58 runs

WESTERN SCHOOLS WEEK

June 6 Bruton	M.C.C. King's School	202 for 4* 154	Won by 48 runs
June 7 Street	M.C.C. Millfield School	232 202 for 8	Drawn
June 8 Tiverton	Blundell's School M.C.C.	133 135 for 2	Won by eight wickets
June 9 Taunton	M.C.C. King's College	8 for 0 —	Drawn (rain)
June 10 Bath	Kingswood School M.C.C.	83 86 for 4	Won by six wickets
June 11 West Lavington	M.C.C. Dauntsey's School	206 for 9* 149	Won by 57 runs

June 7 Solihull	M.C.C. Solihull School	235 for 6* 154	Won by 81 runs
June 7 Sutton Valence	M.C.C. Sutton Valence School	204 for 4* 105	Won by 99 runs
June 7 East Molesey	M.C.C. Tiffin School	224 for 5* 139	Won by 85 runs
June 7 Sheffield	M.C.C. Sheffield University	178 122	Won by 56 runs
June 8 Ampleforth	M.C.C. Ampleforth College	244 for 3* 167 for 5	Drawn
June 8 Chigwell	M.C.C. Chigwell School	222 148 for 9	Drawn
June 8 Christ's Hospital	M.C.C. Christ's Hospital	192 for 4* 103	Won by 89 runs
June 8 Elstree	M.C.C. Haberdashers' School	183 for 7* 61	Won by 122 runs
June 9 Eastbourne	M.C.C. Eastbourne College	205 for 7* 198 for 8	Drawn
June 9 Canterbury	M.C.C. King's School	129 132 for 7	Lost by three wickets

Date / Venue	Teams	Score	Result
June 9	M.C.C.	203 for 5*	Drawn
Sedbergh	Sedbergh School	151 for 9	
June 9	M.C.C.	188 for 8*	Won by 110 runs
Vincent Square	Westminster School	78	
June 10	M.C.C.	163	Drawn
Dulwich	Dulwich C.C.	163 for 9	
June 11	M.C.C.	216 for 6*	Won by 87 runs
Dulwich	Dulwich College	129	
June 11	M.C.C.	176 for 9*	Won by 23 runs
Holt	Gresham's School	153	
June 11	M.C.C.	177 for 7*	Drawn
Leicester	Leicester C.C.	137 for 7	
June 11	M.C.C.	153 for 8*	Won by 74 runs
Oxford	Magdalen College School	79	
June 11	M.C.C.	150	Won by 27 runs
Ware	St. Edmund's College	123	
June 11	M.C.C.	196 for 9*	Won by 63 runs
Ramsgate	S. Lawrence College	133	
June 11	Wanstead C.C.	182	Lost by 56 runs
Wanstead	M.C.C.	126	
June 14	M.C.C.	193 for 9*	Drawn
Bishop's Stortford	Bishop's Stortford Coll.	128 for 8	
June 14	M.C.C.	228 for 8*	Won by 126 runs
Banbury	Bloxham School	102	
June 14	M.C.C.	203 for 9*	Won by 113 runs
Brecon	Christ College	90	
June 14	M.C.C.	176 for 8*	Won by 100 runs
York	Pocklington School	76	
June 14	M.C.C.	218 for 8*	Won by 108 runs
Watford	West Herts. C.C.	110	
June 15	M.C.C.	256 for 3*	Won by 89 runs
Lee	City of London School	167	
June 15	Hurstpierpoint College	147	Won by five wickets
Hassocks	M.C.C.	151 for 5	
June 15	M.C.C.	174	Won by 1 run
York	St. Peter's School	173	
June 15	M.C.C.	109	Lost by seven wickets
New Beckenham	United London Banks C.A.	112 for 3	
June 16	M.C.C.	193 for 4*	Drawn (rain)
Giggleswick	Giggleswick School	19 for 1	
June 21	M.C.C.	157	Won by 40 runs
Stonehouse	Wycliffe College	117	
June 22	Denstone College	122	Drawn (rain)
Uttoxeter	M.C.C.	64 for 2	
June 22	M.C.C.	129	Lost by two wickets
Woodcote	Oratory School	132 for 8	
June 22	M.C.C.	141	Drawn
Nottingham	Nottingham University	98 for 7	
June 22	Welsh Secondary Schools	125	Drawn
Cardiff	M.C.C.	72 for 8	
June 23	M.C.C.	191 for 5*	Drawn
Cheam	Cheam C.C.	143 for 9	
June 23	M.C.C.	222 for 6*	Drawn
Ipswich	Ipswich School	188 for 6	
June 23	M.C.C.	139 for 8*	Drawn (rain)
Monkton Combe	Monkton Combe School	0 for 0	
June 23	M.C.C.	81	Won by 39 runs
Monmouth	Monmouth School	42	

June 23	M.C.C.	114 for 1	Drawn (rain)
Putney Heath	Roehampton C.C.	—	
June 24	M.C.C.	187 for 8*	Drawn
Woodford Green	Woodford Wells C.C.	147 for 7	
June 25	M.C.C.	97	Drawn (rain)
Abingdon	Abingdon School	—	
June 25	M.C.C.	231 for 5	Drawn (rain)
Hillingdon	Adastrian C.C.	—	
June 25	M.C.C.	134	Drawn (rain)
Canford Magna	Canford School	78 for 3	
June 25	M.C.C.	233 for 8*	Lost by five wickets
Dover	Dover College	238 for 5	
June 25	M.C.C.	133 for 3*	Drawn
Ellesmere	Ellesmere College	92 for 7	
June 25	M.C.C.	217 for 5*	Drawn (rain)
Wandsworth Common	Emanuel School	47 for 6	
June 25	Taunton School	162	Drawn (rain)
Taunton	M.C.C.	50 for 1	
June 27	M.C.C.	—	Abandoned (rain)
St. Bees	St. Bees School	—	
June 28	M.C.C.	115	Won by 21 runs
Bradford	Bradford Grammar School	94	
June 28	Nottingham High School	183 for 9*	Drawn
Nottingham	M.C.C.	161 for 7	
June 29	M.C.C.	175 for 9*	Won by 63 runs
Stratton-on-the-Fosse	Downside School	112	
June 29	M.C.C.	183 for 4*	Drawn
Fleetwood	Rossall School	167 for 6	
June 29	M.C.C.	118	Won by 14 runs
Stamford	Stamford School	104	
June 30	M.C.C.	210 for 9*	Won by 112 runs
Brighton	Brighton College	98	
June 30	M.C.C.	90	Lost by six wickets
Bromsgrove	Bromsgrove School	94 for 4	
June 30	M.C.C.	200 for 9*	Drawn
Weston-super-Mare	Weston-super-Mare C.C.	149 for 7	
July 2	M.C.C.	204 for 5*	Won by 142 runs
Oxford	St. Edward's School	62	
July 2	St. John's School	157	Won by eight wickets
Leatherhead	M.C.C.	160 for 2	
July 2	M.C.C.	254 for 3*	Won by 104 runs
Wellingborough	Wellingborough School	150	
July 2	Worksop College	179	Lost by 93 runs
Worksop	M.C.C.	86	
July 5	M.C.C.	103 for 4	Drawn (rain)
Rusholme	Manchester Grammar School	—	
July 5	M.C.C.	129 for 4	Drawn (rain)
Cricklewood	University College School	—	
July 6	M.C.C.	240 for 5*	Won by 124 runs
Barnard Castle	Barnard Castle School	116	
July 6	M.C.C.	197 for 9*	Won by 50 runs
Cobham	Reed's School	147	
July 7	M.C.C.	144	Won by 46 runs
Norbury	Barclays Bank C.C.	98	

July 8, 9 Aldershot	Aldershot Services C.C.	184 and 212 for 9*	Drawn
	M.C.C.	227 for 7* and 160 for 7	
July 8 Kenley	M.C.C.	156	Lost by eight wickets
	Kenley C.C.	159 for 2	
July 9 Dover	M.C.C.	167 for 7*	Won by 19 runs
	Duke of York's R.M.S.	148	
July 9 Epsom	Epsom College	215	Won by three wickets
	M.C.C.	216 for 7	
July 9 Marlborough	Marlborough College	213 for 4*	Lost by 125 runs
	M.C.C.	88	
July 9 Cranwell	M.C.C.	155	Lost by four wickets
	R.A.F. College	157 for 6	
July 9 Sherborne	Sherborne School	194 for 5*	Drawn
	M.C.C.	191 for 9	
July 9 Stowe	M.C.C.	165 for 3*	Drawn
	Stowe School	143 for 7	
July 11 Birmingham	M.C.C.	143	Lost by two wickets
	King Edward's School	145 for 8	
July 12 Cranbrook	M.C.C.	200 for 8*	Won by 112 runs
	Cranbrook School	88	
July 12 Thames Ditton	M.C.C.	154	Won by 62 runs
	Kingston Grammar School	92	
July 12 Reading	M.C.C.	197 for 6*	Won by 63 runs
	Reading School	134	
July 12 Rugby	Rugby C.C.	143	Won by two wickets
	M.C.C.	146 for 8	
July 13 Woodford Green	M.C.C.	239 for 6*	Drawn
	Bancroft's School	117 for 6	
Huly 13 Bolton	M.C.C.	130	Drawn (rain)
	Bolton School	17 for 1	
July 13 Hurlingham	M.C.C.	239 for 6*	Won by 117 runs
	Lords and Commons C.C.	122	
July 14 Barnet Hill	M.C.C.	234 for 6*	Drawn
	Barnet C.C.	197 for 8	
July 14 Cricklewood	M.C.C.	204 for 9*	Drawn
	Brondesbury C.C.	104 for 9	
July 14 Lee	M.C.C.	168	Won by 11 runs
	London Schools' C.A.	157	
July 14 Halesowen	Midlands C.C.C.	200 for 6*	Lost by 20 runs
	M.C.C.	180	
July 14 Scarborough	M.C.C.	184 for 7*	Won by 97 runs
	North Riding G.S.C.A.	87	
July 15 Crosby	M.C.C.	210 for 6*	Drawn (rain)
	Merchant Taylors' School	11 for 0	
July 15 Chislehurst Common	M.C.C.	218 for 6*	Drawn (rain)
	West Kent C.C.	3 for 0	
July 16 Bradfield	M.C.C.	201 for 6*	Lost by three wickets
	Bradfield College	202 for 7	
July 16 Wimbledon	M.C.C.	218 for 6*	Drawn
	King's College School	152 for 6	
July 16 Northwood	M.C.C.	102 for 9*	Lost by six wickets
	Northwood C.C.	103 for 4	
July 16 Oakham	M.C.C.	186 for 3*	Lost by six wickets
	Oakham School	189 for 4	
July 16 West Kensington	M.C.C.	176 for 8*	Won by 94 runs
	St. Paul's School	82	

July 16 Crowthorne	Wellington College M.C.C.	200 135 for 9	Drawn
July 16 Near Barnstaple	M.C.C. West Buckland School	185 for 8* 143 for 9	Drawn
July 18 Ealing	M.C.C. Ealing C.C.	180 181 for 6	Lost by four wickets
July 19 Bristol	M.C.C. Clifton College	176 for 6* 96	Won by 80 runs
July 19 Mossley Hill	M.C.C. Liverpool College	245 for 3* 77	Won by 168 runs
July 19 Tonbridge	M.C.C. Tonbridge School	— —	Abandoned (rain)
July 20 Reigate	M.C.C. Reigate Priory C.C.	— —	Abandoned (rain)
July 20 Colwyn Bay	Rydal School M.C.C.	211 212 for 3	Won by seven wickets
July 20 Tring	M.C.C. Tring Park C.C.	167 87 for 1	Drawn (rain)
July 20 Croydon	M.C.C. Trinity School	— —	Abandoned (rain)
July 21 Woodford Bridge	M.C.C. South Woodford C.C.	155 156 for 4	Lost by six wickets
July 21 Norbury	M.C.C. Westminster Bank C.C.	— —	Abandoned (rain)
July 22 Newbury	M.C.C. St. Bartholomew's G.S.	232 for 8* 147	Won by 85 runs
July 22 Sudbury	Wembley C.C. M.C.C.	99 100 for 3	Won by seven wickets
July 23 Goosedale Farm	M.C.C. Notts. Amateur C.C.	95 96 for 1	Lost by nine wickets
July 25 New Malden	M.C.C. Malden Wanderers C.C.	193 for 7* 178 for 6	Drawn
July 26 Cranleigh Common	M.C.C. Cranleigh C.C.	255 for 8* 185 for 8	Drawn
July 26 East Acton Lane	M.C.C. Shepherd's Bush C.C.	173 for 3* 170	Won by 3 runs
July 27 New Beckenham	M.C.C. Midland Bank C.C.	152 for 9* 105 for 8	Drawn
July 27 Burntwood Lane	M.C.C. Spencer	159 160 for 5	Lost by five wickets
July 28 Stroud	M.C.C. Stroud C.C.	172 176 for 6	Lost by four wickets
July 28 Sunbury-on-Thames	M.C.C. Sunbury C.C.	224 for 8* 154	Won by 70 runs
July 28 East Croydon	M.C.C. Surrey Schools' C.A.	162 63	Won by 99 runs
July 29 Buckhurst Hill	M.C.C. Buckhurst Hill C.C.	194 for 3* 11 for 3	Drawn (rain)
July 29 Ealing	M.C.C. Middlesex G.S.C.A.	189 for 7* 31 for 2	Drawn (rain)
July 30 Folkestone	Folkestone C.C. M.C.C.	52 for 1 —	Drawn (rain)
July 30 Osterley	M.C.C. Indian Gymkhana C.C.	165 for 7 —	Drawn (rain)
August 1 Bray	Maidenhead and Bray C.C. M.C.C.	176 for 6* 178 for 7	Won by three wickets
August 2 Henfield Common	M.C.C. Henfield C.C.	114 62	Won by 52 runs

August 2	M.C.C.	204 for 8*	Drawn (rain)
Chalkwell Park	Westcliff-on-Sea C.C.	122 for 2	
August 3	M.C.C.	—	Abandoned
Bishop's Stortford	Bishop's Stortford C.C.		(rain)
August 3	M.C.C.	—	Abandoned
Worthing	Worthing C.C.	—	(rain)
August 4	M.C.C.	—	Abandoned
Finchley	Finchley C.C.	—	(rain)
August 4	M.C.C.	118	Won by 4 runs
Shanklin	Isle of Wight C.C.A.	114	
August 4	M.C.C.	—	Abandoned
Loughton	Loughton C.C.	—	(rain)
August 5	M.C.C.	201 for 6*	Won by 86 runs
Cuckfield Park	Cuckfield C.C.	115	
August 5	M.C.C.	213 for 8*	Won by 94 runs
Slough	Slough C.C.	119	
August 6	M.C.C.	150 for 5	Drawn (rain)
Hampstead	Hampstead C.C.	—	
August 6	M.C.C.	—	Abandoned
Havant	Havant C.C.	—	(rain)
August 8	M.C.C.	178	Lost by four
Sidmouth	Sidmouth C.C.	179 for 6	wickets
August 9	M.C.C.	147 for 4	Drawn (rain)
Oakham School	Gents. of Leicester C.C.	—	
August 10	M.C.C.	222 for 8*	Won by 156 runs
Cockfosters	Cockfosters C.C.	66	
August 10	Household Brigade C.C.	209	Lost by 39 runs
Burton Court	M.C.C.	170	
August 10	M.C.C.	—	Abandoned
Mayfield	Mayfield C.C.	—	(rain)
August 11	M.C.C.	139	Lost by three
Beckenham	Kent Schools' C.A.	142 for 7	wickets
August 12	Colchester and E.	255 for 8*	Drawn
Colchester	Essex C.C.		
	M.C.C.	220 for 6	
August 13	M.C.C.	164	Drawn
Ditchling	Ditchling C.C.	141 for 5	
August 17	de Flamingo's	194	Won by five
Lord's	M.C.C.	198 for 5	wickets
August 20	M.C.C.	230 for 9*	Lost by four
Amersham	Amersham C.C.	231 for 6	wickets
August 23	M.C.C.	185 for 9*	Lost by two
Hove	Sussex Martlets	186 for 8	wickets
August 30	M.C.C.	—	Abandoned
Tettenhall	Wolverhampton C.C.	—	(rain)

At Dublin, September 3, 5 and 6. M.C.C. beat IRELAND by 36 runs. (See OTHER MATCHES.)

At Scarborough, September 10, 12, 13. M.C.C. beat YORKSHIRE by 83 runs. (See YORKSHIRE section.)

* *Signifies declared.*

OTHER MATCHES AT LORD'S, 1966

June 1. Oratory 157 (R. Murphy 50; C. Haywood five for 39); Beaumont 159 for two wickets (P. J. Kinsella 69). Beaumont won by eight wickets.

OLD ENGLAND XI v. LORD'S TAVERNERS XI

June 11. Old England XI won by three wickets. Two England stalwarts of not long ago, Compton and May, batting in their varying styles, helped to bring about the victory with thirty-seven minutes to spare. Compton, partnered at first by his former Middlesex ally, Edrich, in a stand of 33, showed many of his inimitable strokes while scoring 50 quickly and May seemed to have lost little of his lustre in contributing 43. Compton's noted " all-sorts " brought him the game's best bowling figures too, four for 62, during a Taverners' innings which would indeed have been a sorry sight but for a ninth-wicket stand of 56 between Laker and Clarke.

Lord's Taverners

J. D. Robertson c Edrich b Compton	30	E. A. Bedser c May b Ikin	20
A. H. Phebey b A. V. Bedser	5	Dr. C. B. Clarke b Compton	42
B. A. Barnett b Perks	4	J. C. Laker c McIntyre b Ikin	39
L. Livingston c McIntyre b Edrich	23	J. W. Martin not out	2
R. Benaud b Watkins	4		
J. F. Pretlove b Compton	19	1/5 2/18 3/52 4/57 5/73	190
D. Frost b Compton	2	6/81 7/92 8/118 9/174	

Bowling: A. V. Bedser 6—1—14—1; Perks 6—1—11—1; Watkins 5—0—16—1; Edrich 9—0—35—1; Wright 6—1—15—0; Compton 10.4—0—62—4; Ikin 9—1—37—2.

Old England XI

R. T. Simpson b Laker	33	A. J. Watkins run out	3
J. G. Dewes b Laker	37	A. J. McIntyre not out	3
W. J. Edrich c Pretlove b E. A. Bedser	14	A. V. Bedser not out	4
D. C. S. Compton c Pretlove b Benaud	50	L-b 3	3
P. B. H. May b Pretlove	43	1/71 2/72 3/105 4/141 (7 wkts.)	191
J. T. Ikin b E. A. Bedser	1	5/146 6/157 7/186	

R. T. D. Perks and D. V. P. Wright did not bat.

Bowling: Martin 8—0—35—0; Livingston 2.3—1—1—0; E. A. Bedser 18—6—43—2; Laker 10—1—28—2; Benaud 18—2—47—1; Clarke 6—1—14—0; Pretlove 5.4—0—20—1.

Umpires: T. C. Burrell and H. P. Sharp.

June 16, 17, 18, 20, 21. ENGLAND drew with WEST INDIES in the Second Test Match. (See WEST INDIES section.)

ETON v. HARROW

July 1, 2. Drawn. A century by Smith, the first for thirteen years in these matches, enabled Eton to make a fine start. Hodges helped him put on 131 in one hour, forty minutes, for the opening partnership and by lunch the score had mounted to 164. Then came a collapse, with Smith, who batted two hours, fifty minutes and hit one 6 and fourteen 4's, a victim as the remaining eight wickets went down for 63 runs. Harrow also prospered at the start of their innings and then faltered, their later batsmen making little of Lawrie. He took five for 13 in eleven overs as the score slumped from 107 for three to 149 all out. Smith, helped mainly by Wilson this time, again batted attractively, but Eton were unable to force a win on leaving Harrow to get 252 in just under three hours. Lindsay, who carried his bat in the first innings, was again not out when the end came with neither side in sight of victory.

Eton

*D. M. Smith b Herbert	106	— c sub b Dunkels	42
P. M. Hodges run out	43	— b Dunkels	9
B. L. H. Powell c Wathen b Dunkels	0	— c sub b Coomaraswamy	36
G. E. N. S. Wilson c Webster b Dunkels	28	— not out	59
P. G. Lowndes b Herbert	0	— not out	20
H. R. B. Fawcett lbw b Herbert	0		
C. A. Lawrie b Chichester	12		
R. H. G. Fulton b Chichester	4		
Viscount Crowhurst not out	14		
†R. C. Kinkead-Weekes b Dunkels	0		
A. R. T. Peebles b Chichester	0		
B 13, l-b 1, n-b 6	20	B 4, l-b 2, n-b 1	7
1/131 2/131 3/176 4/176 5/178 6/195 7/201 8/208 9/221	227	1/19 2/70 3/106 (3 wkts., dec.)	173

Bowling: *First Innings*—Dunkels 22—4—63—3; Herbert 19—4—53—3; Chichester 13.2—5—26—3; Webster 8—1—29—0; Coomaraswamy 12—1—36—0. *Second Innings*—Dunkels 15—0—46—2; Herbert 9—0—39—0; Chichester 3—0—27—0; Coomaraswamy 14—1—54—1.

Harrow

*R. W. Evans b Crowhurst	1	— lbw b Crowhurst	9
R. E. Lindsay not out	72	— not out	27
M. B. A. Nobbs lbw b Lawrie	22	— b Peebles	5
R. S. Crawley b Wilson	13	— lbw b Smith	16
N. G. Stogdon c Wilson b Lawrie	15	— b Fulton	59
I. Coomaraswamy b Lawrie	5	— c K.-Weekes b Fulton	0
D. S. S. Chichester b Lawrie	4		
P. R. Dunkels b Lawrie	1		
†S. W. J. Wathen b Lawrie	0		
D. R. ap G. Herbert run out	1		
A. P. Webster run out	4	— not out	8
B 8, l-b 2, w 1	11	B 17	17
1/2 2/62 3/79 4/107 5/125 6/135 7/137 8/137 9/139	149	1/18 2/25 3/45 4/120 5/120 (5 wkts.)	141

Bowling: *First Innings*—Crowhurst 20—8—25—1; Peebles 8—2—12—0; Smith 5—0—13—0; Wilson 12—4—29—1; Lawrie 19—5—31—6; Fulton 16—7—28—0. *Second Innings*—Crowhurst 10—4—14—1; Peebles 14—4—34—1; Smith 7—1—29—1; Lawrie 12—4—28—0; Fulton 16—12—19—2.

Umpires: N. Cooper and H. E. Robinson.

ETON v. HARROW RESULTS AND HUNDREDS

Of the 131 matches played Eton have won 47, Harrow 41 and 43 have been drawn. This is the generally published record, but Harrow men object very strongly to the first game in 1805 being treated as a regular contest between the two schools, contending that it is no more correct to count that one than the fixture in 1857 which has been rejected.

The matches played during the war years 1915–1918 and 1940–1945 are not reckoned as belonging to the regular series.

Results since the First World War:—

1919	Eton won by 202 runs	1946	Drawn
1920	Eton won by nine wickets	1947	Drawn
1921	Eton won by seven wickets	1948	Drawn
1922	Drawn	1949	Eton won by seven wickets
1923	Drawn	1950	Drawn
1924	Drawn	1951	Drawn
1925	Drawn	1952	Harrow won by seven wickets
1926	Drawn	1953	Eton won by ten wickets
1927	Drawn	1954	Harrow won by nine wickets
1928	Eton won by 28 runs	1955	Eton won by 38 runs
1929	Drawn	1956	Drawn
1930	Eton won by eight wickets	1957	Drawn
1931	Eton won by inns. and 16 runs	1958	Drawn
1932	Drawn	1959	Drawn
1933	Drawn	1960	Harrow won by 124 runs
1934	Drawn	1961	Harrow won by inns. and 12 runs
1935	Drawn	1962	Drawn
1936	Drawn	1963	Drawn
1937	Eton won by seven wickets	1964	Eton won by eight wickets
1938	Drawn	1965	Harrow won by 48 runs
1939	Harrow won by eight wickets	1966	Drawn

Forty-one three-figure innings have been played in matches between these two schools. Those since 1918:—

159	E. W. Dawson	(in 1923), Eton	104	R. Pulbrook	(in 1932), Harrow
158	I. Akers-Douglas	(in 1928), Eton	103	L. G. Crawley	(in 1921), Harrow
153	N. S. Hotchkin	(in 1931), Eton	103	T. Hare	(in 1947), Eton
135	J. Atkinson-Clark	(in 1930), Eton	102*	P. H. Stewart-Brown	(in 1923), Harrow
115	E. Crutchley	(in 1939), Harrow	102	R. V. C. Robins	(in 1953), Eton
112	A. W. Allen	(in 1931), Eton	100	R. H. Cobbold	(in 1923), Eton
111	R. A. Holt	(in 1937), Harrow	100*	P. V. F. Cazalet	(in 1926), Eton
109	K. F. H. Hale	(in 1929), Eton	100	A. N. A. Boyd	(in 1934), Eton
109	N. S. Hotchkin	(in 1932), Eton	100*	P. M. Studd	(in 1935), Harrow
107	W. N. Coles	(in 1946), Eton	100	S. D. D. Sainsbury	(in 1947), Eton
106	D. M. Smith	(in 1966), Eton			

**** Signifies not out.***

In 1904, D. C. Boles, of Eton making 183, set up a new record for the match, beating the 152 obtained for Eton in 1841 by Emilius Bayley, afterwards the Rev. Sir John Robert Laurie Emilius Bayley Laurie, Eton. M. C. Bird, Harrow, in 1907, scored 100 not out and 131, the only batsman who has made two 100's in the match. N. S. Hotchkin, Eton, played the following innings: 1931, 153; 1932, 109 and 96; 1933, 88 and 12.

For other particulars see Records.

OXFORD v. CAMBRIDGE

July 9, 11, 12. Oxford won by an innings and nine runs, so bringing to an end the longest run of drawn matches between the Universities, six. In so doing, they won by an innings for the first time since 1948, when A. H. Kardar, later to captain Pakistan, and C. B. van Ryneveld, South Africa, were in the side and the opposition contained D. J. Insole, T. E. Bailey, G. H. G. Doggart and J. G. Dewes, all of whom became England players.

The standard this time did not suggest any possible return to those halcyon days but Oxford, with a willingness to attack, certainly brightened up this annual affair. Despite losing the opening pair for 52, they went solidly for runs, led by their captain, Gilliat. He and Toft put on 135 in just over two hours for the third wicket, Gilliat hitting eleven 4's in an attractive innings. Groves, a South African, followed his example, striking one 6 and fourteen 4's in scoring 80 in ninety-eight minutes, so that Gilliat was able to give Cambridge an awkward half an hour's batting at the end of the first day. They lost two wickets for 25 runs in that time and never recovered.

The spin bowlers, Ridley and Elviss, who made the initial breakthrough, troubled them most and when the match closed with little over an hour of the third day taken up, they had between them captured twelve wickets and bowled nearly 100 overs. Elviss operated for one period of two and a half hours unchanged on the second day, and in this time 19 of his 32 overs were maidens. Ridley bowled 12 maidens in 19 overs. Thus were Cambridge tied down, and eventually well beaten. Murray, their captain, and a West Indies Test cricketer, played the only defiant innings; 72 not out in three and a quarter hours.

Oxford

P. J. K. Gibbs (*Hanley G.S. and University*) c. Murray b Russell 25
F. S. Goldstein (*Falcon College, Bulawayo and St. Edmund Hall*) c Hays b Cottrell 25
*R. M. C. Gilliat (*Charterhouse and Christ Church*) c Hays b Murray 86
D. P. Toft (*Tonbridge and University*) b Russell 61
M. G. M. Groves (*Diocesan College S.A. and St. Edmund Hall*) not out 80
M. R. J. Guest (*Rugby and Magdalen*) c Cosh b Russell 6
†A. W. Dyer (*Mill Hill and St. Catherine's*) c and b Russell 1
G. N. S. Ridley (*Milton, Rhodesia and Pembroke*) lbw b Russell 0
A. G. M. Watson (*St. Lawrence, Ramsgate and Corpus Christi*) not out 8
B 5, l-b 3 8

1/38 2/52 3/187 4/207 5/264 6/266 7/266 (7 wkts., dec.) 300

R. W. Elviss (*Leeds G.S. and Trinity*) and R. B. Hiller (*Bec and St. Edmund Hall*) did not bat.

Bowling—Russell 25—8—60—5; Palfreman 21—8—68—0; Cottrell 10—2—19—1; Sinker 18—3—48—0; Roopnaraine 19—7—51—0; Murray 6—1—46—1.

Cambridge

Batsman	First innings		Second innings	
K. P. J. W. McAdam (*Prince of Wales, Nairobi, Millfield and Clare*)	b Ridley	13	c Dyer b Watson	0
R. E. J. Chambers (*Forest and Queens'*)	b Elviss	4	c and b Hiller	20
G. A. Cottrell (*Kingston G.S. and St. Catharine's*)	b Hiller	4	c Goldstein b Hiller	21
N. D. Sinker (*Winchester and Jesus*)	c Dyer b Watson	9	b Elviss	0
†D. L. Hays (*Highgate and Selwyn*)	c Guest b Ridley	35	b Watson	20
*D. L. Murray (*Queen's Royal College, Trinidad and Jesus*)	lbw b Ridley	20	not out	72
N. J. Cosh (*Dulwich and Queens'*)	not out	38	c Hiller b Ridley	6
V. P. Malalasekera (*Royal Colombo and Fitzwilliam*)	c Watson b Ridley	0	lbw Elviss	2
A. B. Palfreman (*Nottingham H.S. and Emmanuel*)	c Hiller b Elviss	5	c Dyer b Hiller	0
R. Roopnaraine (*Queen's College, Guyana and St. John's*)	c Dyer b Watson	0	c Watson b Elviss	0
S. G. Russell (*Tiffin and Trinity Hall*)	lbw b Elviss	1	b Ridley	0
	B 11	11	B 4, l-b 5, n-b 1	10
	1/21 2/23 3/25 4/47 5/81 6/92 7/92 8/97 9/116	140	1/0 2/27 3/49 4/61 5/70 6/141 7/141 8/146 9/150	151

Bowling: *First Innings*—Watson 11—5—31—2; Hiller 8—2—37—1; Ridley 22—8—35—4; Elviss 19.2—10—26—3. *Second Innings*—Watson 10—2—26—2; Hiller 15—5—48—3; Ridley 21.5—12—29—2; Elviss 34—20—26—3; Guest 5—2—12—0.

Umpires: C. S. Elliott and C. G. Pepper.

OXFORD v. CAMBRIDGE RESULTS AND HUNDREDS

The University match dates back to 1827. Altogether there have been 122 official matches, Cambridge winning 50, Oxford 44 with 28 drawn. Results since the First World War:—

1919	Oxford won by 45	1946	Oxford won by six wickets
1920	Drawn	1947	Drawn
1921	Cambridge won by inns. and 24	1948	Oxford won by inns. and 8
1922	Cambridge won by inns. and 100	1949	Cambridge won by seven wickets
1923	Oxford won by inns. and 227	1950	Drawn
1924	Cambridge won by nine wickets	1951	Oxford won by 21
1925	Drawn	1952	Drawn
1926	Cambridge won by 24	1953	Cambridge won by two wickets
1927	Cambridge won by 116	1954	Drawn
1928	Drawn	1955	Drawn
1929	Drawn	1956	Drawn
1930	Cambridge won by 205	1957	Cambridge won by inns. and 186
1931	Oxford won by eight wickets	1958	Cambridge won by 99
1932	Drawn	1959	Oxford won by 85
1933	Drawn	1960	Drawn
1934	Drawn	1961	Drawn
1935	Cambridge won by 195	1962	Drawn
1936	Cambridge won by eight wickets	1963	Drawn
1937	Oxford won by seven wickets	1964	Drawn
1938	Drawn	1965	Drawn
1939	Oxford won by 45	1966	Oxford won by an innings and 9
1940 to 1945	No official matches		

Seventy-five three-figure innings have been played in the University matches. For those scored before 1919 see 1940 *Wisden*. Those subsequent to 1919 include the four highest as shown here:—

238*	Nawab of Pataudi	1931	Oxford	118	H. Ashton	1921	Cam.
211	G. Goonesena	1957	Cam.	118	D. R. W. Silk	1954	Cam.
201*	M. J. K. Smith	1954	Oxford	117	M. J. K. Smith	1956	Oxford
201	A. Ratcliffe	1931	Cam.	116*	D. R. W. Silk	1953	Cam.
193	D. C. H. Townsend	1934	Oxford	116	M. C. Cowdrey	1953	Oxford
170	M. Howell	1919	Oxford	115	A. W. Allen	1934	Cam.
167	B. W. Hone	1932	Oxford	114	J. F. Pretlove	1955	Cam.
157	D. R. Wilcox	1932	Cam.	113	E. R. T. Holmes	1927	Oxford
149	J. T. Morgan	1929	Cam.	113*	J. M. Brearley	1962	Cam.
146	R. O'Brien	1956	Cam.	111*	G. W. Cook	1957	Cam.
145*	H. E. Webb	1948	Oxford	109	C. H. Taylor	1923	Oxford
142	M. P. Donnelly	1946	Oxford	108	F. G. H. Chalk	1934	Oxford
136	E. T. Killick	1930	Cam.	105	E. J. Craig	1961	Cam.
135	H. A. Pawson	1947	Oxford	106	Nawab of Pataudi	1929	Oxford
131	Nawab of Pataudi	1960	Oxford	104	H. J. Enthoven	1924	Cam.
129	H. J. Enthoven	1925	Cam.	104	M. J. K. Smith	1955	Oxford
127	D. S. Sheppard	1952	Cam.	103*	A. R. Lewis	1962	Cam.
124	A. K. Judd	1927	Cam.	102*	A. P. F. Chapman	1922	Cam.
124	A. T. Ratcliffe	1932	Cam.	101*	R. W. V. Robins	1928	Cam.
122	P. A. Gibb	1938	Cam.	101	N. W. D. Yardley	1937	Cam.
121	J. N. Grover	1937	Oxford	100	P. J. Dickinson	1939	Cam.
119	J. M. Brearley	1964	Cam.	100*	M. Manasseh	1964	Oxford

* *Signifies not out.*

For other particulars see Records.

RUGBY v. MARLBOROUGH

July 20, 21. Match abandoned without a ball bowled—rain.

Rugby

R. A. Goodhart, R. N. R. Jenkins, P. W. G. Evans, *A. D. B. Poole, J. N. B. Wright, P. N. Turner, E. G. Leburn, C. M. Forsyth, J. L. Burrows, G. M. Bloom, W. T. Hartley.

Marlborough

C. M. Page, P. R. Phillimore, I. C. R. Brown, *N. P. G. Rosse, A. C. Forbes, R. N. H. Style, T. S. A. Block, R. E. Percival, R. J. Freedman, R. St. G. Thwaites, J. W. Grimke-Drayton.

Umpires: H. P. Sharp and B. Ward.

Of 107 matches, Rugby have won 43 and Marlborough 32; 30 drawn, two abandoned. The match was first played in 1855. All matches, excepting the following, were played at Lord's: Oval—1857, 1863, 1867; Middlesex Ground, Islington 1864; Rugby—1868, 1915, 1917; Marlborough—1870, 1916, 1918, 1944. No match took place in 1858, 1859 and 1861 owing to the weakness of **Marlborough cricket in those early years, and in 1940 and 1947 when Rugby were unable to play.**

CHELTENHAM v. HAILEYBURY

July 22, 23. Cheltenham won by six wickets. Generally they held the upper hand after sending in their opponents on drying turf, though a ninth-wicket stand of 53 between Tice and Braybon in the first innings and the highest knock of the match, 62, by Hollington in the second, kept Haileybury well in the game. Cheltenham had twenty-five minutes to spare when Hibbert completed victory with 6 into the grandstand.

Haileybury

H. B. Hollington c Boone b Jessop	4	— c Boone b Boal	62
B. R. Kirkpatrick c Powdrill b Angier	21	— c and b Jessop	3
*S. Warner Jones c Whitaker b Jessop	12	— c Sheepshanks b Angier	0
R. J. Walton c Chida b Boal	19	— c Powdrill b Angier	25
†R. M. Young b Angier	1	— b Mermagen	0
N. P. Moore b Boal	23	— c Chida b Angier	4
A. F. Stewart b Angier	10	— b Jessop	18
A. W. L. Tice b Mermagen	43	— lbw b Jessop	25
C. W. Gray b Jessop	13	— c Whitaker b Boal	13
D. R. Braybon lbw b Boal	24	— c Chida b Boal	2
J. K. S. Denniston not out	0	— not out	0
B 9, n-b 4	13	B 2, l-b 1, n-b 6	9
1/6 2/24 3/62 4/62 5/64 6/79 7/104 8/128 9/181	183	1/26 2/27 3/69 4/70 5/81 6/101 7/128 8/157 9/160	161

Bowling: *First Innings*—Angier 17—4—43—3; Jessop 18—4—55—3; Boal 17.2—5—53—3; Sheepshanks 2—0—10—0; Mermagen 3—1—9—1. *Second Innings*—Angier 18—3—59—3; Jessop 14—5—46—3; Boal 12.2—6—22—3; Mermagen 7—1—25—1.

Cheltenham

	First Innings		Second Innings	
*I. A. Boal b Gray		0	run out	28
S. M. Powdrill c Braybon b Denniston		22	c W. Jones b Denniston	17
A. F. C. Whitaker c Braybon b Stewart		37	c sub b Denniston	39
G. G. Angier b Denniston		0	not out	19
†R. N. Boone c Stewart b Tice		44	c sub b Stewart	4
D. G. Burton c Hollington b Braybon		15		
J. C. Hibbert b Gray		46	not out	15
M. Z. U. Chida c Young b Braybon		0		
R. J. Sheepshanks b Stewart		26		
J. D. Mermagen not out		21		
J. W. H. Jessop c sub b Denniston		1		
B 7, l-b 3		10	B 5	5
1/0 2/44 3/50 4/90 5/128 6/159 7/163 8/184 9/219		222	1/40 2/74 3/94 4/108 (4 wkts.)	127

Bowling: *First Innings*—Gray 13—2—41—2; Tice 16—4—60—1; Braybon 13—3—19—2; Denniston 13.3—4—37—3; Warner Jones 3—0—19—0; Stewart 13—3—36—2. *Second Innings*—Gray 6—2—21—0; Tice 2—0—3—0; Braybon 3—0—12—0; Denniston 16—2—48—2; Stewart 11—1—38—1.

Umpires: S. H. Moore and L. D'Arcy.

CHELTENHAM v. HAILEYBURY RESULTS

Of the 68 matches played from 1893, Haileybury have won 21, Cheltenham 21, 25 drawn, one abandoned.

CLIFTON v. TONBRIDGE

July 25, 26. Drawn. The most notable feature was the batting of Harris, who with Hinton put on 72 runs for the third Clifton wicket. His 60 included one 6 and eight 4's and took only eighty minutes. Even so, Tonbridge led on the first innings. On a rain spoiled second day, Tonbridge made a sporting declaration, leaving Clifton to make 111 in ninety minutes. The weather reduced it to seventy minutes during which the two quick bowlers managed only 17 overs, but five wickets fell and for some of the time there was a right-handed and left-handed batsman together and the wet ball had to be wiped.

Tonbridge

First Innings		Second Innings	
P. G. A. Montgomery b Hobson	6	lbw b Hamersley	33
*†A. St. J. Thomson lbw b Tovey	32	b Hobson	0
R. G. Scoones b Peel	5	b Hamersley	14
J. S. Rodd c and b Hamersley	53	c Caisley b Hinton	6
G. B. Morgan b Hamersley	0		
R. J. Brown b Hobson	13	not out	29
T. J. Mills c and b Hamersley	34	not out	22
A. J. Thomas not out	9		
W. A. J. P. Breen b Hamersley	0		
S. C. M. Baguley c Hobson b Peel	3		
P. G. Roffey b Peel	0		
B 9, l-b 4, w 4	17	B 2, l-b 1	3
1/13 2/30 3/89 4/102 5/111 6/142 7/160 8/164 9/170	172	1/17 2/47 3/54 4/54 (4 wkts., dec.)	107

Bowling: *First Innings*—Peel 10—3—18—3; Hobson 24—8—51—2; Hamersley 33—16—48—4; Tovey 17—2—38—1. *Second Innings*—Peel 8—2—33—0; Hobson 16—3—25—1; Hamersley 12—1—26—2; Tovey 2—1—1—0; Hinton 3—1—4—1; Caisley 3—0—15—0.

Clifton

A. S. Dixon b Roffey	3	— c Thomson b Roffey	9
E. F. Peel c Thomas b Morgan	7	— c Brown b Roffey	11
P. C. Hinton not out	52	— c Thomson b Breen	6
L. R. Harris b Breen	60	— c Brown b Roffey	28
*H. R. St. G. Hamersley b Breen	0	— not out	29
A. C. Caisley b Roffey	4	— not out	4
R. F. M. Gwynn b Roffey	4		
D. Hobson lbw b Baguley	13	— b Breen	4
R. G. Tovey b Thomas	2		
M. F. R. Martin b Thomas	9		
†J. W. R. Capper lbw b Roffey	0		
B 10, l-b 4, w 1	15	L-b 3	3
1/6 2/20 3/92 4/92 5/114 6/122 7/150 8/153 9/169	169	1/20 2/21 3/40 4/62 5/76 (5 wkts.)	94

Bowling: *First Innings*—Breen 20—4—52—2; Roffey 23.1—11—38—4; Morgan 10—7—13—1; Thomas 10—3—35—2; Baguley 10—2—16—1; Montgomery 1—1—0—0. *Second Innings*—Breen 9—0—46—2; Roffey 8—0—45—3.

Umpires: T. W. Higginson and P. B. Jones.

Clifton v. Tonbridge Results

First played at Lord's in 1914, Clifton winning by nine wickets. Of 42 matches at Lord's from 1919, Tonbridge have won 18, Clifton 10, 13 drawn, one abandoned.

July 27, 28, 29. President of M.C.C.'s XI drew with West Indies. (See West Indies section.)

SOUTHERN SCHOOLS v. THE REST

July 30, August 1. Drawn. Rain reduced the first day to twenty minutes and cut the second by nearly three hours, so ruining the match. There was some spirited batting by Owen-Thomas and his 57 included one 6 and five 4's. Johnson did even better for The Rest with five 6's and seven 4's.

Southern Schools

*R. D. V. Knight (*Dulwich*) c Evans b Angier	8
D. M. Smith (*Eton*) c Evans b Angier	4
R. L. Burchnall (*Winchester*) c Hollington b Flitton	21
D. R. Owen-Thomas (*K.C.S. Wimbledon*) c Lander b Grimsdick	57
T. E. N. Jameson (*Taunton*) c Lander b Flitton	17
J. H. Aten (*Cranleigh*) c Grimsdick b Johnson	37
A. O. L. Green (*Bedford*) c Datt b Grimsdick	2
C. R. J. Black (*Stowe*) not out	19
C. M. Page (*Marlborough*) not out	4
B 2, l-b 5, w 2, n-b 1	10
1/10 2/20 3/47 4/82 5/144 6/148 7/163 (7 wkts., dec.)	179

N. P. Bond (*Blundell's*) and R. M. W. Longmore (*Winchester*) did not bat.

Bowling: Flitton 11—1—34—2; Angier 7—2—37—2; Lander 6—0—36—0; Johnson 6—1—42—1; Grimsdick 5—1—20—2.

The Rest

C. Johnson (*Pocklington*) not out.. 88
H. B. Hollington (*Haileybury*) b Bond........................ 35
P. J. Allerton (*Malvern*) c Aten b Green........................ 12
S. D. Datt (*Oakham*) c Jameson b Green........................ 0
G. G. Angier (*Cheltenham*) c Owen-Thomas b Jameson............ 11
R. L. Short (*Denstone*) b Bond.... 3
P. N. Gill (*Repton*) not out....... 2
B 4, l-b 4, w 1............ 9

1/64 2/110 3/110 4/141 5/157 (5 wkts.) 160

*J. M. H. Grimsdick (*Merchant Taylors'*), †V. G. Evans (*Warwick*). S. J. Lander (*Bishop's Stortford*) and C. R. Flitton (*Pocklington*) did not bat.

Bowling: Black 8—0—33—0; Page 7—1—25—0; Green 13—4—27—2; Bond 8—1—23—2; Knight 4—1—20—0; Jameson 2—0—23—1.

Umpires: W. Wignall and P. B. Jones.

PUBLIC SCHOOLS v. ENGLISH SCHOOLS' C.A.

August 2, 3. Drawn. The first day's play was marked by a fine century from Griffith, a Worcestershire boy who earlier had taken two wickets with impressive spin bowling. In helping his captain, Cragg, to stem a collapse by adding 170 runs in two hours, Griffith reached three figures in two and a quarter hours, hitting one 6 and fifteen 4's. Soon afterwards rain stopped play, and the next day limited cricket to an hour and a half.

Public Schools

C. Johnson (*Pocklington*) b Walker..... 5 — c Walker b Griffith........ 6
H. B. Hollington (*Haileybury*) b Walker. 24 — not out.................. 45
R. L. Burchnall (*Winchester*) b Walker.. 0 — st Beale b Johnson......... 14
D. R. Owen-Thomas (*K.C.S. Wimbledon*) c Beale b Johnson................. 32 — not out.................. 1
*R. D. V. Knight (*Dulwich*) run out.... 18
P. J. Allerton (*Malvern*) c Ikin b Johnson 3
J. M. H. Grimsdick (*Merchant Taylors'*) b Griffith........................ 1
A. L. O. Green (*Bedford*) c Harrison b Griffith........................ 1
C. J. R. Black (*Stowe*) c Ikin b Johnson.. 14
†V. G. Evans (*Warwick*) b Johnson..... 0
N. P. Bond (*Blundell's*) not out......... 1
B 2, n-b 5.................... 7 B 1, w 1, n-b 2......... 4

1/17 2/17 3/32 4/76 5/88 6/89 7/91 8/92 9/95 106 1/16 2/62 (2 wkts.) 70

Bowling: *First Innings*—Denman 7—0—18—0; Walker 6—1—21—3; Boyers 4—0—16—0; Ikin 6—1—18—0; Griffith 7—1—11—2; Johnson 5—2—15—4. *Second Innings*—Denman 6—2—16—0; Walker 5—1—8—0; Ikin 4—2—10—0; Griffith 10—1—19—1; Johnson 6—2—13—1.

English Schools' C.A.

T. Harrison (*Hampshire*) run out.. 6
R. Brookes (*Lancashire*) c Knight b Black...................... 5
M. J. Ikin (*Staffordshire*) lbw b Grimsdick.................. 15
*J. R. A. Cragg (*Cheshire*) b Black. 67
K. Griffith (*Worcestershire*) not out.........................100
W. Barlow (*Cheshire*) not out..... 0
B 12, l-b 3.............. 15

1/5 2/22 3/27 4/197 (4 wkts., dec.) 208

P. D. Johnson (*Nottinghamshire*), †M. E. Beale (*Dorset*), J. H. Walker (*Cheshire*), J. Denman (*Sussex*) and M. Boyers (*London*) did not bat.

Bowling: Black 19—5—44—2; Bond 15—4—42—0; Grimsdick 10—4—15—1; Knight 11—2—54—0; Green 8—1—24—0; Johnson 5—2—14—0.

Umpires: W. Wignall and P. B. Jones.

M.C.C. SCHOOLS XI v. COMBINED SERVICES

August 4, 5. Combined Services won by 50 runs. The Services, who did not enforce the follow-on, were in command throughout. Willson contributed a sound 80 and Dove-Dixon (three 6's) and Robinson (twelve 4's) much entertainment in laying the foundations. The fast bowling of Gooding in the first innings and the spin of Dover in the second proved too much for a disappointing Schools side.

Combined Services

Lt.-Comdr. G. G. Tordoff c Beale b Walker	11	— c Griffith b Black	22
F/Lt. B. J. Willson b Denman	80	— c Johnson b Ikin	26
F/Lt. B. Dove-Dixon c Denman b Johnson	40	— c Hollington b Black	1
L/S M. Robinson c Black b Denman	67	— c Cragg b Ikin	13
Capt. D. S. Williams not out	30	— not out	20
*Sqn. Ldr. M. D. Fenner not out	15	— run out	8
S.A.C. S. Hull (did not bat)		— not out	1
B 2, l-b 6, n-b 8	16	B 1, l-b 4, n-b 2	7
1/11 2/95 3/175 4/226 (4 wkts., dec.)	259	1/50 2/52 3/54 4/70 5/92 (5 wkts., dec.)	98

2nd Lt. W. G. Dover, †2nd Lt. C. E. P. Carter, F/O G. M. Gibson and L/Cpl. O. Gooding did not bat.

Bowling: *First Innings*—Denman 18—1—57—2; Walker 12—2—48—1; Black 7—0—25—0; Griffith 4—0—19—0; Ikin 10—3—40—0; Johnson 12—2—54—1. *Second Innings*—Denman 6—0—32—0; Walker 4—0—12—0; Black 7—0—27—2; Ikin 8—1—20—2.

M.C.C. Schools XI

H. B. Hollington (*Haileybury*) c Carter b Gibson	1	— b Dover	23
M. J. Ikin (*Newcastle G.S.*) c Carter b Gibson	9	— lbw b Dover	25
D. R. Owen-Thomas (*K.C.S. Wimbledon*) lbw b Gooding	8	— b Willson	29
*J. R. A. Cragg (*King's, Macclesfield*) c Gooding b Gibson	1	— b Dover	15
K. Griffith (*R.G.S., Worcester*) c Hull b Gooding	24	— lbw b Dover	25
R. D. V. Knight (*Dulwich*) c Williams b Dover	9	— c Carter b Dover	0
P. D. Johnson (*Nottingham H.S.*) b Gooding	1	— not out	13
†M. E. Beale (*Hardye's, Dorchester*) b Gooding	9	— c Williams b Gooding	2
C. J. R. Black (*Stowe*) b Gooding	23	— c Robinson b Dover	22
J. Denman (*Ifield G.S.*) not out	5	— c Willson b Hull	7
J. H. Walker (*King's, Macclesfield*) c Fenner b Gooding	11	— b Gibson	0
B 7, l-b 7, n-b 7	21	B 8, l-b 7, n-b 9	24
1/6 2/26 3/26 4/31 5/55 6/59 7/77 8/97 9/106	122	1/42 2/75 3/106 4/106 5/106 6/109 7/144 8/165 9/168	185

Bowling: *First Innings*—Gooding 18—3—47—6; Gibson 16—4—28—3; Willson 7—1—13—0; Dover 8—4—13—1. *Second Innings*—Gooding 18—6—50—1; Gibson 16—4—31—1; Willson 9—3—31—1; Dover 21—6—46—6; Hull 1.4—0—3—1.

Umpires—W. Wignall and P. B. Jones.

August 11, 12. Single-Wicket Tournament. (See special section.)

INTER-SERVICES TOURNAMENT

August 18. Army won by four wickets. R.A.F. 198 (F. R. C. Rudolph 44 not out); Army 199 for six (W. G. Dover 59 not out).

August 19. Army won by eight runs. Army 187 for nine, innings closed (J. Fawkes 57; G. S. Ibberson three for 23); Royal Navy 179 (W. J. Foster 56; N. J. Knott three for 37).

August 20. R.A.F. won by four runs. R.A.F. 189 (F. R. C. Rudolph 54, B. J. Willson 41; G. G. Tordoff five for 40); Royal Navy 185 for nine, innings closed (M. Robinson 52 not out; G. M. Gibson three for 27).

August 22. M.C.C. Young Professionals 174 for five, declared (J. D. Hopkins 55); London Federation of Boys' Clubs 89 for nine (M. P. Molony four for 24). Drawn.

August 23. English Schools C.A. 201 for seven wickets declared (M. J. Ikin 75; A. Blount three for 51); M.C.C. Young Professionals 141 (G. J. Timmins 46; M. J. Ikin five for 25). English Schools C.A. won by 60 runs.

August 27. M.C.C. Young Professionals 205 for seven wickets declared (R. W. A. Dermont 83, M. A. Lambert 40 not out; G. A. Carter four for 58); Young Amateurs of Middlesex 138 (B. R. Heighes five for 34, T. P. Charrington three for 39). M.C.C. Young Professionals won by 67 runs.

September 3. WARWICKSHIRE beat WORCESTERSHIRE in the Gillette Cup Final by five wickets. (See GILLETTE CUP section.)

WORLD CRICKET CUP

The Rothman World Cup, introduced for the first time and well won by England, provided three one-day matches of considerable interest. A Rest of the World side gathered from far and near were beaten by both England and West Indies in the first two matches. The South African Graeme Pollock played a fine knock of 65 (two 6's and nine 4's) and Nadkarni, the Indian left-arm spin bowler, tied the batsmen down with his nagging length, but generally it was clear that much of the great talent lay dormant because of lack of match practice.

So the destination of the trophy lay on the last game between England and West Indies. Sobers put England in to bat and maybe felt satisfied in tying down the opening pair, Edrich and Parfitt. With half the permitted 50 overs, a maximum of eleven per bowler, gone, 78 runs were on the board. Only one wicket had been lost, too, and with the sensible use of a longer handle subsequently, the very respectable average of 4.34 runs an over resulted.

West Indies could never challenge such a rate, largely because Dexter, captain while Cowdrey sat in the pavilion with a strained leg muscle, brought to bear the considerable knowledge gained in leading Sussex successfully in the Gillette Cup. After the first few overs he dispensed with his slips, bringing back an attacking field only for a short time as each batsman arrived at the wicket. Against such tactics, the West Indies were always struggling. Over the three days, 13,036 people paid at the turnstiles.

ENGLAND XI v. REST OF THE WORLD XI

September 10. England XI won by 82 runs.

England XI

J. H. Edrich b P. M. Pollock	0
P. H. Parfitt c Hanif b McKenzie	11
E. R. Dexter st Murray b Nadkarni	32
*M. C. Cowdrey lbw b Mushtaq	10
J. M. Parks c P. M. Pollock b Nadkarni	42
B. d'Oliveira c Mushtaq b P. M. Pollock	49
†J. T. Murray b Nadkarni	25
B. R. Knight not out	16
F. J. Titmus not out	6
B 4, l-b 6	10
1/9 2/15 3/39 4/88 5/105 6/165 7/184 (7 wkts., 50 overs)	201

K. Higgs and J. A. Snow did not bat.

Bowling: P. M. Pollock 11—1—51—2; McKenzie 11—3—45—1; Mushtaq Mohammad 8—0—32—1; Bland 9—0—32—0; Nadkarni 11—2—31—3.

Rest of the World XI

*R. B. Simpson lbw b Knight	38
Hanif Mohammad c Knight b Higgs	20
G. Thomas c Parks b Higgs	4
R. G. Pollock c Cowdrey b d'Oliveira	10
K. C. Bland c Murray b d'Oliveira	5
Nawab of Pataudi b Higgs	13
Mushtaq Mohammad b Knight	3
†D. L. Murray b Higgs	12
R. G. Nadkarni b Higgs	2
P. M. Pollock c Higgs b Knight	1
G. D. McKenzie not out	0
B 2, l-b 9	11
1/35 2/52 3/81 4/83 5/87 6/90 7/114 8/118 9/119	119

Bowling: Snow 3—0—19—0; Higgs 11—0—34—5; Titmus 10—1—21—0; Knight 8.3—1—19—3; d'Oliveira 4—1—15—2.

Umpires: C. S. Elliott and A. E. Fagg.

WEST INDIES v. REST OF THE WORLD XI

September 12. West Indies won by 18 runs.

West Indies

C. C. Hunte c McKenzie b Bland	57
M. C. Carew c Murray b McKenzie	2
R. B. Kanhai b P. M. Pollock	5
B. F. Butcher c McKenzie b Bland	15
S. M. Nurse c Murray b McKenzie	88
*G. S. Sobers c Hanif b P. M. Pollock	23
D. A. J. Holford run out	19
P. D. Lashley not out	23
W. W. Hall not out	4
B 7, l-b 11	18
1/4 2/11 3/50 4/117 5/169 6/204 7/246 (7 wkts., 50 overs)	254

†J. L. Hendriks and L. R. Gibbs did not bat.

Bowling: P. M. Pollock 11—0—54—2; McKenzie 11—0—39—2; Bland 9—0—50—2; Nadkarni 10—0—51—0; Mushtaq Mohammad 7—0—24—0; Simpson 2—0—18—0.

Rest of the World XI

*R. B. Simpson b Sobers	6
Hanif Mohammad b Hall	63
G. Thomas c Lashley b Hall	0
R. G. Pollock st Hendriks b Gibbs	65
K. C. Bland b Sobers	4
Nawab of Pataudi c and b Carew	24
Mushtaq Mohammad c Butcher b Hall	17
†D. L. Murray not out	19
G. D. McKenzie c Butcher b Hall	3
P. M. Pollock not out	19
B 2, l-b 13, n-b 1	16
1/9 2/18 3/114 4/123 5/161 6/190 7/190 8/200 (8 wkts., 50 overs)	236

R. G. Nadkarni did not bat.

Bowling: Hall 10—0—40—4; Sobers 11—4—25—2; Lashley 7—0—44—0; Hunte 5—0—38—0; Gibbs 11—1—27—1; Carew 6—0—46—1.

Umpires: C. S. Elliott and A. E. Fagg.

ENGLAND XI v. WEST INDIES

September 13. England XI won by 67 runs.

England XI

J. H. Edrich run out	33	B. R. Knight not out	10
P. H. Parfitt c sub b Lashley	25	F. J. Titmus not out	19
E. R. Dexter b Hall	26		
J. M. Parks st Kanhai b Carew	33	B 4, l-b 8	12
B. d'Oliveira c Hunte b Lashley	14		
*M. C. Cowdrey b Lashley	19	1/36 2/83 3/104 (7 wkts., 50 overs)	217
†J. T. Murray b Hunte	26	4/140 5/144 6/181 7/189	

K. Higgs and J. A. Snow did not bat.

Bowling: Sobers 11—2—28—0; Hall 11—2—29—1; Lashley 10—0—46—3; Gibbs 11—1—54—0; Carew 5—0—30—1; Hunte 2—0—18—1.

West Indies

C. C. Hunte c Parks b Snow	27	R. C. Brancker c and b d'Oliveira	20
M. C. Carew c Murray b Higgs	1	†J. L. Hendriks b Higgs	0
R. B. Kanhai b Knight	14	L. R. Gibbs not out	6
B. F. Butcher c Murray b Knight	0		
S. M. Nurse lbw b Higgs	58	L-b 12	12
*G. S. Sobers c Knight b Snow	3		
P. D. Lashley c Higgs b Titmus	9	1/9 2/28 3/28 4/65 5/92	150
W. W. Hall b Higgs	0	6/118 7/118 8/118 9/124	

Bowling: Higgs 11—1—50—4; Knight 6—2—17—2; Snow 11—0—34—2; Titmus 11—2—32—1; d'Oliveira 1.4—0—5—1.

Umpires: C. S. Elliott and A. E. Fagg.

M.C.C. HONORARY CRICKET MEMBERS

ENGLAND PLAYERS

L. E. G. Ames
S. F. Barnes
C. J. Barnett
A. V. Bedser
W. E. Bowes
D. C. S. Compton
T. G. Evans
G. Geary
Sir Leonard Hutton
J. T. Ikin
H. Larwood
E. Paynter
W. Rhodes
A. Sandham
E. J. Smith
H. Strudwick
H. Sutcliffe
W. Voce
C. Washbrook
F. E. Woolley
D. V. P. Wright

THE COUNTY CHAMPIONSHIP IN 1966

For the first time in the history of the County Championship the first innings of 102 matches in a total of 238 were restricted to 65 overs. These were the first 12 matches played by each of the 17 counties on a home and an away basis. Where counties met only once in the season normal conditions prevailed, as they did in the return matches. On the whole the experiment did not succeed, although in some matches it produced excellent cricket.

For most of the summer Yorkshire led the way and they won the title for the twenty-ninth time. They went to the top at the end of May and on August 5th appeared to be romping away as they were 40 points in front of their nearest challengers, Kent. Then Worcestershire, the reigning Champions, made a wonderful recovery as they had done in 1965 when they snatched the title in their final engagement. This time Yorkshire and Worcestershire each had seven matches in hand, but whereas Yorkshire in their next six gained only 12 points, being beaten by Surrey, Northamptonshire (for the second time) and Warwickshire, Worcestershire beat Derbyshire twice, Somerset and Middlesex.

Consequently, at the end of August when Yorkshire and Worcestershire each had one match to play, Worcestershire stood only six points behind. As it was, Sussex virtually settled the issue at Worcester where Snow and A. Buss with 18 wickets between them, defeated Worcestershire, while Yorkshire—held up by rain at Harrogate—were engaged in a hard struggle with Kent for whom Underwood took 11 wickets. At three o'clock came the news of Worcestershire's reverse which made Yorkshire Champions at a time when Kent threatened to win. A drying wind came to assist the Yorkshire slow bowlers and a hat-trick by Wilson helped Yorkshire home four minutes from time with a margin of 18 points.

Kent fell away in August and defeat in two days by Lancashire at Dover, where Statham and Higgs captured 18 wickets, was the crowning blow, but they were a much improved side in their most successful season since the war. Somerset by finishing third equalled their previous best and their 13 wins were the most they had achieved since gaining a place in the Championship of 1891. They owed much to their captain, C. R. M. Atkinson, as did Leicestershire, who under Lock rose six places in finishing eighth. Sussex too fared better under the Nawab of Pataudi, ascending from the sixteenth position to number 10.

On the other hand, Middlesex, with Titmus out of form after so much round the year cricket, dropped from sixth to thirteenth and Glamorgan, for all the fine batting of A. R. Lewis, the first man to complete 2,000 runs, fell 11 places to number 14. Essex, hit by injury, could not climb out of the doldrums and Nottinghamshire finished last for the third time in six years.

For those who would like an easy reference to the 65 over matches here is the list:

May 4, Derbyshire v. Northamptonshire; Lancashire v. Gloucestershire; Leicestershire v. Essex; Nottinghamshire v. Kent; Sussex v. Glamorgan; Warwickshire v. Middlesex. *May 7*, Lancashire v. Nottinghamshire; Middlesex v. Kent; Somerset v. Hampshire; Warwickshire v. Leicestershire; Yorkshire v. Gloucestershire. *May 11*, Leicestershire v. Derbyshire; Middlesex v. Glamorgan; Northamptonshire v. Gloucestershire; Somerset v. Yorkshire; Surrey v. Sussex; Warwickshire v. Essex. *May 14*, Derbyshire v. Hampshire; Essex v. Somerset; Surrey v. Glamorgan. *May 18*, Sussex v. Worcestershire. *May 25*, Derbyshire v. Essex; Glamorgan v. Warwickshire; Gloucestershire v. Hampshire; Middlesex v. Leicestershire; Nottinghamshire v. Somerset; Sussex v. Lancashire; Worcestershire v. Kent. *May 28*, Essex v. Worcestershire; Glamorgan v. Hampshire; Leicestershire v. Northamptonshire; Middlesex v. Sussex; Nottinghamshire v. Surrey; Somerset v. Gloucestershire; Yorkshire v. Lancashire.

June 1, Essex v. Nottinghamshire; Northamptonshire v. Worcestershire; Surrey v. Lancashire. *June 4*, Gloucestershire v. Derbyshire; Kent v. Sussex; Leicestershire v. Lancashire; Middlesex v. Yorkshire; Nottinghamshire v. Hampshire; Somerset v. Surrey; Worcestershire v. Warwickshire. *June 8*, Essex v. Sussex; Glamorgan v. Leicestershire; Kent v. Derbyshire; Middlesex v. Somerset; Nottinghamshire v. Northamptonshire; Warwickshire v. Yorkshire. *June 11*, Derbyshire v. Yorkshire; Gloucestershire v. Warwickshire; Lancashire v. Glamorgan; Northamptonshire v. Somerset; Surrey v. Kent; Worcestershire v. Middlesex; *June 15*, Kent v. Essex; Lancashire v. Warwickshire; Sussex v. Nottinghamshire; Yorkshire v. Hampshire. *June 18*, Hampshire v. Leicestershire; Northamptonshire v. Essex; Yorkshire v. Sussex. *June 25*, Leicestershire v. Surrey; Middlesex v. Northamptonshire; Somerset v. Warwickshire; Worcestershire v. Hampshire. *June 29*, Derbyshire v. Warwickshire; Essex v. Surrey; Leicestershire v. Nottinghamshire; Northamptonshire v. Kent; Somerset v. Glamorgan; Sussex v. Hampshire.

July 2, Lancashire v. Derbyshire. *July 6*, Kent v. Gloucestershire; Yorkshire v. Essex. *July 9*, Gloucestershire v. Glamorgan; Lancashire v. Hampshire; Leicestershire v. Worcestershire; Nottinghamshire v. Derbyshire; Surrey v. Middlesex. *July 13*, Gloucestershire v. Worcestershire; Yorkshire v. Northamptonshire. *July 16*, Yorkshire v. Nottinghamshire. *July 20*, Northamptonshire v. Warwickshire. *July 23*, Surrey v. Worcestershire. *July 27*, Glamorgan v. Essex. *July 30*, Kent v. Leicestershire; Sussex v. Gloucestershire.

August 3, Lancashire v. Middlesex; Somerset v. Sussex. *August 6*, Derbyshire v. Worcestershire; Northamptonshire v. Glamorgan; Warwickshire v. Nottinghamshire. *August 13*, Kent v. Hampshire; Yorkshire v. Surrey. *August 17*, Gloucestershire v. Surrey; Hampshire v. Middlesex; Lancashire v. Kent; Worcestershire v. Somerset. *August 20*, Derbyshire v. Glamorgan.

FINAL COUNTY CHAMPIONSHIP TABLE

	Played	Won	Lost	Drn.	No decn.	First inns. lead	Pts.
Points awarded...........	—	10	—	—	—	2	—
Yorkshire (4).............	28	15	5	8	0	17	184
Worcestershire (1).........	28	13	5	9	1	18	166
Somerset (7)..............	28	13	7	7	1	13	156
Kent (5)..................	28	11	8	8	1	17	144
Northamptonshire (2)......	28	10	9	9	0	15	130
Warwickshire (11).........	28	8	8	10	2	16	113
Surrey (8)................	28	8	3	16	1	15	110
Leicestershire (14)........	28	8	7	12	1	14	108
Derbyshire (9)............	28	8	12	7	1	8	96
Sussex (16)...............	28	6	11	11	0	16	92
Hampshire (12)............	28	5	4	18	1	16	87
Lancashire (13)...........	28	6	11	8	3	13	86
Middlesex (6).............	28	6	5	14	3	13	86
Glamorgan (3).............	28	6	8	13	1	10	85
Gloucestershire (10).......	28	6	12	9	1	7	75
Essex (15)................	28	4	10	11	3	10	60
Nottinghamshire (17)......	28	3	11	12	2	8	46

Warwickshire and Gloucestershire records include one point each for tie on first innings. Hampshire and Glamorgan records include five points in drawn match when scores finished level and they were batting.

(Figures in brackets indicate* 1965 *positions.)

SCORING IN THE COUNTY CHAMPIONSHIP

The scheme for scoring in the County Championship was as follows:—

(*a*) Should a match be finished the winning side to score 10 points, plus any points scored in the first innings (see (*d*) below).

(*b*) Should a match be finished and the scores be equal (a "Tie") each side to score 5 points, plus any points scored in the first innings (see (*d*) below).

(*c*) Should the scores be equal in a drawn match the side batting in the fourth innings to score 5 points, plus any points scored in the first innings (see (*d*) below).

(*d*) The side which leads on the first innings shall score 2 points. If the scores on the first innings are equal, each side shall score 1 point.

(*e*) If there is no play in the first two-thirds (measured by playing hours) of a match, and it is not carried to a further conclusion than that of the first innings, the side which leads on the first innings shall score 6 points.

(*f*) Should the scores be equal in a drawn match in which there has been no play in the first two-thirds (measured by playing hours) of a match the side batting second to score 3 points.

(*g*) Even should there be no play for any reason, or no result obtained on the first innings, every match shall be included in the table of results as a "match played", in these cases neither side to score points.

(*h*) The side which has the highest aggregate of points gained at the end of the season shall be the Champion County. Should two or more sides be equal on points, the side with most wins have priority.

COUNTY CHAMPIONSHIP STATISTICS FOR 1966

	For			Against		
County	Runs	Wickets	Average	Runs	Wickets	Average
Derbyshire	8,486	452	18.77	8,350	387	21.57
Essex	8,684	415	20.92	8,998	366	24.58
Glamorgan	8,914	452	19.72	8,581	402	21.34
Gloucestershire	8,827	446	19.79	9,438	365	25.85
Hampshire	8,111	354	22.91	8,324	378	22.02
Kent	8,615	379	22.73	8,704	440	19.78
Lancashire	7.495	388	19.31	7.552	348	21.70
Leicestershire	9,170	390	23.51	9,076	379	23.94
Middlesex	8,869	349	25.41	9,130	371	24.60
Northamptonshire	9,623	393	24.48	9,417	430	21.90
Nottinghamshire	9,192	429	21.42	10,040	343	29.27
Somerset	9,433	429	21.98	8,862	456	19.43
Surrey	9,116	362	25.18	9,468	428	22.12
Sussex	9,221	434	21.24	9,381	370	25.35
Warwickshire	9,156	352	26.01	8,726	384	22.72
Worcestershire	9,373	363	25.82	8,617	452	19.06
Yorkshire	8,650	383	22.58	8,271	471	17.56
	150,935	6,770	22.29	150,935	6,770	22.29

DERBYSHIRE

President—THE DUKE OF DEVONSHIRE

Secretary—MAJOR D. J. CARR, County Cricket Ground, Nottingham Road, Derby

Captain—D. C. MORGAN

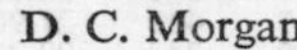

D. C. Morgan

County Badge

R. W. Taylor

After a mixed season during which they lost more matches than any other side in the Championship, Derbyshire remained ninth, the position they occupied in 1965. No bowler took 100 wickets and only Harvey, of the batsmen, made 1,000 runs in Championship matches. Yet, although the side bore an ill-balanced appearance at times, victories were gained over such formidable opponents as Kent, Northamptonshire, Surrey and Warwickshire (twice), and Worcestershire were among teams who could have been beaten.

Injury robbed the side of their off-spinner, Smith—he bowled extremely well in his testimonial year—Rhodes and Jackson at various times, while Rhodes was obviously still conscious of the throwing controversy despite taking wickets cheaply in several games. Morgan performed prodigiously as a stock bowler, mixing cut with swing as conditions demanded, and delivered more overs than any other player. Late in the season he rediscovered his batting form, making just over 1,000 runs in all matches and as he took the 500th catch of his career, the county's debt to his all-round ability was considerable.

No batsman averaged more than 23; the only two individual centuries were made against Oxford University and Nottinghamshire and this failure to make runs clearly cost many points. Derbyshire rarely succeeded in the fourth innings and too often there was a lack of fight and application, particularly against the turning ball. Hall, like Buxton, had his season curtailed by football and the side seldom received a sound start. M. Hill, from Nottinghamshire, played many fluent innings, but often got out through lack of concentration and like other middle-order batsmen was prevented by the 65-over rule from laying a firm foundation to an innings.

Towards the end of the season T. J. P. Eyre emerged as an aggressive left-hander, and a young all-rounder, Russell, showed promise, but Page again failed to harness dedication to his undoubted ability and finished an unhappy summer by losing his place. Taylor, the wicket-keeper, played many valuable innings in difficult circumstances, but, at times, his work behind the stumps seemed to lack its customary edge. Johnson, who took to wearing spectacles during the season, and Allen, the left-arm spinner, decided to retire.

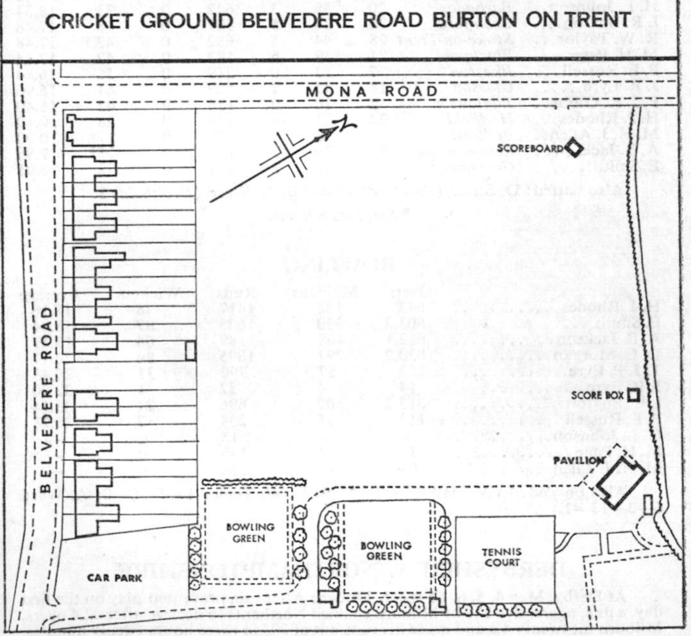

DERBYSHIRE RESULTS

All First-Class Matches—Played 30, *Won* 9, *Lost* 13, *Drawn* 8.

County Championship Matches—Played 28, *Won* 8, *Lost* 12, *Drawn* 7, *No Decision* 1

COUNTY CHAMPIONSHIP AVERAGES

BATTING

	Birthplace	Mtchs.	Inns.	Not Outs	Runs	100's	Highest Inns.	Aver.
D. C. Morgan..	*Muswell Hill*	28	48	7	962	0	96	23.46
J. F. Harvey....	*Cambridge*	26	48	2	1060	1	103*	23.04
I. W. Hall	*Sutton Scarsdale*	19	37	1	794	0	74	22.05
M. Hill........	*Scunthorpe*	23	41	3	810	0	61	21.31
T. J. P. Eyre....	*Brough Bradwell*	18	31	4	553	0	88	20.48
H. L. Johnson..	*Barbados*	20	38	3	642	0	73	18.34
I. R. Buxton....	*Cromford*	20	34	5	507	0	68	17.48
R. W. Taylor...	*Stoke-on-Trent*	28	44	5	682	0	42	17.48
M. H. Page....	*Blackpool*	21	39	5	583	0	42	17.14
P. E. Russell...	*Ilkeston*	7	13	0	219	0	56	16.84
J. R. Eyre......	*Glossop*	18	35	2	527	0	61	15.96
P. J. K. Gibbs..	*Buglawton*	5	10	0	154	0	43	15.40
H. J. Rhodes...	*Hadfield*	22	31	16	156	0	28	10.40
M. H. J. Allen..	*Bedford*	5	8	3	50	0	17*	10.00
A. B. Jackson..	*Kettleshulme*	21	26	13	118	0	25*	7.86
E. Smith......	*Grassmoor*	25	37	2	211	0	22	6.05

Also batted: D. Smith (*Bradford*) 15 and 0; A. Ward (*Dronfield*) 3.

* *Signifies not out.*

BOWLING

	Overs	Maidens	Runs	Wickets	Average
H. J. Rhodes............	643	182	1417	78	18.16
E. Smith................	803.3	320	1605	87	18.44
A. B. Jackson...........	612.1	168	1189	64	18.57
D. C. Morgan...........	830.2	297	1695	84	20.17
T. J. P. Eyre............	257	57	790	31	25.48
J. R. Eyre...............	14	4	32	1	32.00
I. R. Buxton............	313.2	100	696	21	33.14
P. E. Russell............	113	35	254	7	36.28
H. L. Johnson...........	4	0	15	0	—
M. H. Page.............	39	7	140	0	—
M. H. J. Allen..........	69.5	19	156	0	—

Also bowled: I. W. Hall 0.2—0—4—0; R. W. Taylor 1—1—0—0; A. Ward 6—3—13—1.

DERBYSHIRE v. NORTHAMPTONSHIRE

At Derby, May 4, 5, 6. *65 overs.* Drawn. After rain prevented play on the first day, a fine, aggressive 130 by Milburn enabled Northants to declare after 62.4 overs. Milburn hit twenty 4's and made his runs out of 205 in three hours twenty minutes.

Harvey and Buxton batted well for Derbyshire, who at one stage became so tied down by accurate bowling that they were in danger of following on (under two-day rules) with only four wickets down. Northamptonshire had a lead of 74, but after Milburn had failed in his second innings, rain washed out the rest of the match on the last afternoon.

Northamptonshire

C. Milburn c Eyre b Rhodes	130	— b Rhodes	1
R. M. Prideaux b Buxton	36	— not out	35
B. L. Reynolds c Johnson b Morgan	7	— not out	10
Mushtaq Mohammad not out	26		
D. S. Steele c Taylor b Rhodes	0		
P. J. Watts not out	0		
B 1, l-b 3, n-b 5	9	N-b 4	4
1/88 2/110 3/205 4/208 (4 wkts., dec.)	208	1/1 (1 wkt.)	50

P. D. Watts, B. Crump, M. Scott, *‡K. V. Andrew and J. D. F. Larter did not bat.

Bowling: *First Innings*—Jackson 15—3—34—0; Rhodes 15.4—2—65—2; Morgan 17—1—46—1; Buxton 14—1—52—1; Smith 1—0—2—0. *Second Innings*—Jackson 12—5—15—0; Rhodes 8—5—4—1; Morgan 3—1—6—0; Smith 9—8—1—0; Allen 8.5—4—20—0.

Derbyshire

J. F. Harvey b P. J. Watts	40	M. H. Page not out	6
J. R. Eyre c Milburn b Larter	0	L-b 5, w 1, n-b 1	7
H. L. Johnson c P. J. Watts b Larter	17		
I. R. Buxton not out	51	1/8 2/46 (4 wkts., 65 overs)	134
*D. C. Morgan c Andrew b Steele	13	3/75 4/109	

†R. W. Taylor, E. Smith, M. H. J. Allen, H. J. Rhodes and A. B. Jackson did not bat.

Bowling: Larter 16—7—24—2; Crump 22—7—24—0; P. J. Watts 15—4—31—1; Scott 7—0—33—0; Steele 4—0—14—1; Mohammad 1—1—0—0.

Umpires: C. G. Pepper and H. Yarnold.

At The Oval, May 7, 9, 10. DERBYSHIRE beat SURREY by seven runs.

At Leicester, May 11, 12, 13. DERBYSHIRE drew with LEICESTERSHIRE.

DERBYSHIRE v. HAMPSHIRE

At Chesterfield, May 14, 16, 17. *65 overs.* Drawn. With Shackleton bowling unchanged at one end, Derbyshire were contained to 145. The Hampshire last-wicket pair put on 21 to give them a lead of two runs, Sainsbury playing well against an attack that lacked Jackson, injured. Smith, the off-spinner, bowled 27 of Derbyshire's 65 overs, taking seven for 59 on an unresponsive pitch. Agains an attack which included spin for the first time, Derbyshire batted consistently in their second innings. Wheatley, a young off-spinner, bowled well for Hampshire. Needing 280 to win, Hampshire again lost wickets to Smith, whose six for 60 gave him match figures of thirteen for 119, his best in championship cricket. Reed batted impressively for 93 and held up Derbyshire. After play had continued in steady rain for some time the end came with Sainsbury and Cottam again defying the Derbyshire bowlers.

Derbyshire

First Innings		Second Innings	
J. F. Harvey b Cottam	20	st Timms b Wheatley	22
J. R. Eyre c Barnard b Shackleton	1	c Timms b Wheatley	39
H. L. Johnson c Timms b Shackleton	2	c Livingstone b Sainsbury	36
I. R. Buxton lbw b Shackleton	28	b Wheatley	68
*D. C. Morgan lbw b Shackleton	13	c and b Sainsbury	11
M. Hill c White b Cottam	31	lbw b Wheatley	13
†R. W. Taylor b Cottam	20	b Cottam	42
T. J. P. Eyre c Barnard b Cottam	9	c Marshall b White	33
E. Smith not out	11	not out	4
M. H. J. Allen lbw b Cottam	2	b White	4
H. J. Rhodes not out	2	not out	0
B 1, l-b 4, n-b 1	6	B 4, l-b 4, n-b 1	9
1/4 2/12 3/42 4/56 5/68 6/115 7/126 8/131 9/137 (9 wkts., 65 overs)	145	1/51 2/63 3/156 4/174 5/192 6/201 7/273 8/273 9/280 (9 wkts., dec.)	281

Bowling: *First Innings*—Shackleton 33—10—70—4; White 15—2—41—0; Cottam 17—5—28—5. *Second Innings*—Shackleton 30—15—53—0; White 18—5—38—2; Cottam 18—0—59—1; Wheatley 30—17—51—4; Sainsbury 29—11—71—2.

Hampshire

First Innings		Second Innings	
*R. E. Marshall c T. J. P. Eyre b Smith	30	lbw b Rhodes	6
B. L. Reed b Smith	11	lbw b Smith	93
H. Horton c Morgan b Smith	0	c Johnson b Smith	27
D. A. Livingstone b Smith	21	run out	5
H. M. Barnard c Allen b Smith	11	c Taylor b Smith	14
P. J. Sainsbury not out	46	not out	19
†B. S. V. Timms c Johnson b Rhodes	6		
K. J. Wheatley b Rhodes	11	c Morgan b Smith	4
D. Shackleton c Morgan b Smith	0	c Johnson b Smith	8
D. W. White b Smith	1	c Harvey b Smith	6
R. M. Cottam not out	3	not out	4
L-b 2, n-b 5	7	L-b 2, n-b 2	4
1/46 2/46 3/47 4/48 5/81 6/106 7/122 8/123 9/126 (9 wkts., 65 overs)	147	1/9 2/83 3/103 4/148 5/153 6/157 7/165 8/171 (8 wkts.)	190

Bowling: *First Innings*—Morgan 16—4—39—0; Rhodes 22—6—42—2; Smith 27—8—59—7. *Second Innings*—Morgan 14—6—22—0; Rhodes 12—2—23—1; Smith 35—20—60—6; Buxton 3—1—10—0; Allen 32—9—71—0.

Umpires: A. E. Fagg and T. W. Spencer.

At Northampton, May 18, 19, 20. DERBYSHIRE beat NORTHAMPTONSHIRE by 22 runs.

At Chesterfield, May 21. DERBYSHIRE lost to ESSEX by two wickets. (See GILLETTE CUP.)

DERBYSHIRE v. ESSEX

At Ilkeston, May 25, 26, 27. *65 overs.* Drawn. Lively bowling by Knight on a helpful pitch and in poor light undermined Derbyshire and they were all out for 110 in the 64th over. Essex also had to struggle for runs against bowling spearheaded by Rhodes and with Knight absent to attend a court hearing they were 15 behind on first innings. Confident batting by Harvey and Johnson as the wicket grew easier enabled Derbyshire to declare leaving Essex to make 225 in under three hours. There was an early breakthrough, but Fletcher, Taylor and Edmeades found little difficulty on a slow-paced pitch and neither side was in sight of victory when the game ended after fifteen minutes of the extra half hour.

Derbyshire

I. W. Hall b Knight	12	— c Taylor b Jorden	14
J. F. Harvey c Fletcher b Knight	7	— c Hobbs b Edmeades	76
J. R. Eyre c Taylor b Knight	8	— c Fletcher b Hobbs	15
H. L. Johnson b Knight	3	— c sub b Edmeades	49
I. R. Buxton c Taylor b Knight	4		
*D. C. Morgan c Taylor b Edmeades	23	— c Taylor b Edmeades	11
M. Hill c and b Hobbs	6	— not out	3
†R. W. Taylor b Presland	27		
M. H. Page not out	6	— not out	28
H. J. Rhodes b Edmeades	0		
A. Ward run out	3		
B 5, l-b 5, n-b 1	11	B 3, l-b 7, n-b 3	13
1/23 2/24 3/34 4/39 5/44 6/57 7/86 8/102 9/103	110	1/33 2/56 3/153 4/176 5/200 (5 wkts., dec.)	209

Bowling: *First Innings*—Jorden 12.3—1—29—0; Knight 22—8—25—5; Edmeades 8—2—14—2; Hobbs 16—8—21—1; Presland 5—1—10—1. *Second Innings*—Jorden 25—5—73—1; Edmeades 4—7—57—3; Hobbs 16—3—46—1; Presland 9—2—19—0; East 1—0—1—0.

Essex

*G. E. Barker c Page b Ward	7	— c Taylor b Rhodes	3
M. J. Bear b Rhodes	0	— c Eyre b Morgan	31
G. J. Saville b Rhodes	0	— c Taylor b Buxton	5
K. W. R. Fletcher c Taylor b Morgan	25	— c Hill b Morgan	58
†B. Taylor lbw b Rhodes	22	— not out	32
B. Edmeades b Rhodes	1	— not out	30
E. R. Presland b Morgan	15		
R. N. S. Hobbs b Buxton	5		
A. M. Jorden not out	8		
R. East c Page b Buxton	6		
B. R. Knight, absent			
B 4, l-b 2	6	L-b 1	1
1/2 2/6 3/7 4/51 5/56 6/63 7/76 8/88 9/95	95	1/3 2/12 3/96 4/106 (4 wkts.)	160

Bowling: *First Innings*—Buxton 22.5—8—27—2; Rhodes 20—11—21—4; Ward 6—3—13—1; Morgan 14—3—28—2. *Second Innings*—Buxton 12—6—21—1; Rhodes 8—4—15—1; J. R. Eyre 3—2—1—0; Morgan 22—7—46—2; Page 21—4—72—0; Johnson 1—0—4—0.

Umpires: R. Aspinall and R. S. Lay.

At Derby, May 28, 30, 31. WEST INDIES beat DERBYSHIRE by an innings and 32 runs. (See WEST INDIES section.)

DERBYSHIRE v. SUSSEX

At Chesterfield, June 1, 2, 3. Drawn. Lenham gave Sussex a good start on a pitch inclined to lift awkwardly at one end. Suttle retired after being struck by a ball from Rhodes, but returned and made a valuable fifty. Derbyshire fell 35 behind on the first innings and were handicapped when Rhodes could not bowl at the start of the Sussex second innings because of illness. Pataudi set Derbyshire to make 213 in three and three-quarter hours and they lost two wickets in Snow's first over. Eyre played courageously and a sixth-wicket stand between Morgan and Hill gave Derbyshire hopes of victory. When they were both out trying to force the pace, Snow broke through and the game ended with the last pair playing out time.

Sussex

K. G. Suttle b Buxton	52	— c Smith b Jackson	14
L. J. Lenham b Jackson	86	— c Morgan b Jackson	11
*Nawab of Pataudi c Hall b Smith	10	— c Hall b Rhodes	34
M. G. Griffith c and b Jackson	30	— c Smith b Buxton	35
G. C. Cooper c Taylor b Smith	13	— b Buxton	32
D. J. Foreman c Hill b Smith	15	— c Page b Morgan	0
A. S. M. Oakman c Hill b Buxton	9	— not out	33
A. Buss lbw b Eyre	5	— b Rhodes	0
†T. Gunn run out	3	— st Taylor b Morgan	2
J. A. Snow not out	12	— not out	12
D. L. Bates c Morgan b Jackson	2		
B 2, w 1, n-b 2	5	L-b 4	4
1/35 2/130 3/141 4/152 5/180 6/217 7/218 8/224 9/230	242	1/21 2/34 3/73 4/115 5/120 6/144 7/147 8/163 (8 wkts., dec.)	177

Bowling: *First Innings*—Jackson 23.5—4—66—3; Rhodes 12—5—19—0; Morgan 25—9—55—0; Smith 30—13—54—3; Buxton 22—9—37—2; Eyre 4—2—6—1. *Second Innings*—Jackson 16—2—55—2; Morgan 22—4—40—2; Smith 4—1—9—0; Rhodes 11—1—33—2; Buxton 12.5—5—36—2.

Derbyshire

I. W. Hall b Suttle	48	— c Pataudi b Snow	1
J. R. Eyre c Gunn b Buss	12	— c Cooper b Bates	47
H. L. Johnson c Gunn b Snow	5	— b Oakman	24
*D. C. Morgan c Foreman b Bates	39	— c Bates b Buss	54
M. Hill c Suttle b Bates	22	— c Suttle b Buss	30
M. H. Page c Gunn b Oakman	12	— c Griffith b Snow	0
†R. W. Taylor not out	38	— b Snow	5
L. R. Buxton c Pataudi b Buss	4	— not out	6
E. Smith c Oakman b Snow	1	— c Foreman b Snow	0
A. B. Jackson c Gunn b Snow	1	— not out	0
H. J. Rhodes b Suttle	7	— c Gunn b Snow	0
B 7, l-b 6, w 4, n-b 1	18	B 8, l-b 4, w 5	17
1/40 2/51 3/91 4/125 5/140 6/149 7/161 8/172 9/188	207	1/2 2/6 3/67 4/95 5/158 6/174 7/178 8/178 9/178 (9 wkts.)	184

Bowling: *First Innings*—Snow 32—7—59—3; Buss 27—6—55—2; Bates 23—4—35—2; Oakman 10—3—24—1; Suttle 15.4—8—16—2. *Second Innings*—Snow 16—4—33—5; Buss 15—1—54—2; Oakman 11—3—21—1; Bates 11—0—46—1; Suttle 3—0—13—0.

Umpires: A. Jepson and O. W. Herman.

At Bristol, June 4, 6, 7. DERBYSHIRE lost to GLOUCESTERSHIRE by nine runs.

At Tunbridge Wells, June 8, 9, 10. DERBYSHIRE beat KENT by 80 runs.

DERBYSHIRE v. YORKSHIRE

At Chesterfield, June 11, 13. *65 overs.* Yorkshire won by an innings and 15 runs. Yorkshire batted aggressively after bad light delayed the start. Boycott and Close put on 144 in 40 overs and later Illingworth and Binks punished the bowling. Derbyshire collapsed in startling fashion on Monday morning, losing their last seven wickets while only eight runs were scored. They became the first county to follow on in a game governed by the 65 over experimental rule. Batting again 169 behind, they showed more resistance, but Yorkshire took advantage of a rain-affected wicket to force victory after using eight minutes of the extra half hour.

Yorkshire

G. Boycott b T. J. P. Eyre........ 63
*D. B. Close c Morgan b Rhodes.. 77
D. E. V. Padgett c Hall b T. J. P. Eyre........................ 1
J. H. Hampshire c Page b T. J. P. Eyre........................ 15
P. J. Sharpe b Morgan........... 13
R. Illingworth not out........... 45
J. C. Balderstone b Morgan....... 7
†J. G. Binks not out............. 29
B 1, l-b 2, n-b 5........... 8

1/144 2/145 (6 wkts., 65 overs) 258
3/146 4/162 5/180 6/190

F. S. Trueman, J. Waring and A. G. Nicholson did not bat.

Bowling: Rhodes 19—3—56—1; T. J. P. Eyre 20—4—88—3; Smith 5—1—28—0; Morgan 15—2—50—2; Russell 6—1—28—0.

Derbyshire

I. W. Hall c Sharpe b Illingworth....... 38 — run out.................. 19
J. R. Eyre c Binks b Trueman........... 14 — c Balderstone b Nicholson... 5
H. L. Johnson c Binks b Nicholson..... 8 — c Hampshire b Illingworth... 26
*D. C. Morgan b Nicholson........... 0 — c Sharpe b Close........... 8
M. Hill c Hampshire b Trueman....... 16 — c Balderstone b Close....... 16
M. H. Page lbw b Illingworth.......... 2 — c Binks b Trueman......... 4
†R. W. Taylor b Trueman............ 0 — b Waring................. 10
T. J. P. Eyre c Trueman b Illingworth... 0 — c Binks b Close........... 27
P. E. Russell b Nicholson............. 4 — c Sharpe b Nicholson....... 12
E. Smith c Trueman b Nicholson....... 0 — c Binks b Nicholson........ 13
H. J. Rhodes not out................. 2 — not out.................. 1
L-b 4, n-b 1................... 5 B 6, l-b 4, n-b 3....... 13

1/17 2/34 3/34 4/81 5/81 89 1/11 2/53 3/58 4/69 5/79 154
6/81 7/82 8/87 9/87 6/95 7/119 8/128 9/153

Bowling: *First Innings*—Trueman 18—4—44—3; Nicholson 14—3—22—4; Waring 6—3—11—0; Illingworth 8.4—4—7—3. *Second Innings*—Trueman 19—5—28—1; Nicholson 25.5—10—33—3; Waring 14—3—21—1; Illingworth 26—13—39—1; Close 9—1—20—3.

Umpires: C. G. Pepper and R. S. Lay.

DERBYSHIRE v. KENT

At Derby, June 18, 19, 20. Kent won by seven wickets. Harvey's 97, which was Derbyshire's highest individual score at that stage of the season, enabled them to declare at 262. Play continued on Sunday, Derbyshire's first experiment, and was watched by more spectators than Saturday's play. In the two hours and forty minutes permitted by rain Kent took their score to 142 for four and on Monday declared 74 behind on the first innings. Derbyshire, in turn, declared their second innings after some brisk scoring, inviting Kent to make 174 to win in two hours, forty minutes on a slow pitch and outfield. This they accomplished with eight minutes to spare, largely because Luckhurst took out his bat for 86 (twelve 4's). Much of the Derbyshire bowling lacked its usual accuracy.

Derbyshire

J. F. Harvey b Luckhurst............ 97 — c Prodger b Dixon......... 10
J. R. Eyre c Prodger b Dye............ 27 — c Knott b Dye............. 7
M. H. Page b Underwood............. 33 — c Leary b Underwood...... 24
H. L. Johnson c Prodger b Dye........ 32 — not out.................. 47
*D. C. Morgan c Luckhurst b Sayer.... 0
M. Hill not out..................... 39 — not out.................. 11
†R. W. Taylor c Denness b Luckhurst.. 26
B 2, l-b 6..................... 8 0

1/69 2/135 3/185 (6 wkts., dec.) 262 1/15 2/21 (3 wkts., dec.) 99
4/187 5/200 6/262 3/79

T. J. P. Eyre, E. Smith, H. J. Rhodes and A. B. Jackson did not bat.

Bowling: *First Innings*—Sayer 30—11—53—1; Dye 28—8—67—2; Dixon 22—4—71—0; Underwood 31—14—49—1; Luckhurst 8.5—1—14—2. *Second Innings*—Sayer 6—2—12—0; Dye 6—1—7—1; Underwood 9—1—35—1; Dixon 9—3—45—1.

Kent

M. H. Denness b Jackson	27	— c Johnson b Rhodes	12
B. W. Luckhurst c Taylor b Morgan	39	— not out	86
D. Nicholls lbw b Morgan	0	— b Morgan	4
S. E. Leary c Taylor b Jackson	48	— c Johnson b Morgan	36
R. C. Wilson run out	32	— not out	27
J. M. Prodger b Rhodes	3		
†A Knott not out	18		
*A. L. Dixon not out	15		
B 2, l-b 2, n-b 2	6	L-b 9	9
1/50 2/51 3/95 4/122 5/153 6/155 (6 wkts., dec.)	188	1/17 2/31 3/131 (3 wkts.)	174

D. M. Sayer, D. L. Underwood and J. C. Dye did not bat.

Bowling: *First Innings*—T. J. P. Eyre 3—1—9—0; Rhodes 19—5—46—1; Smith 25—11—41—0; Jackson 16—6—25—2; Morgan 20—5—61—2. *Second Innings*—Jackson 12—3—28—0; Rhodes 17—3—56—1; Morgan 12.1—2—52—2; Smith 5—0—29—0.

Umpires: R. Aspinall and W. F. Simpson.

At Sheffield, June 25, 27, 28. DERBYSHIRE lost to YORKSHIRE by ten wickets.

DERBYSHIRE v. WARWICKSHIRE

At Buxton, June 29, 30. *65 overs.* Derbyshire won by eight wickets. Warwickshire were put in on a soft wicket from which the ball lifted slowly, but recovered well after losing two wickets for 12. Abberley batted bravely after being struck several times by lifting deliveries, laying the foundation for more aggressive batting by Jameson, Stewart and A. C. Smith. Derbyshire were in trouble as the ball began to lift more quickly and were 47 behind on first innings. Next morning, although the wicket had eased, Warwickshire batted badly against Rhodes and Smith and were all out for 73, leaving Derbyshire with a comfortable target which they reached for the loss of two wickets, the match ending in two days.

Warwickshire

R. N. Abberley b Smith	36	— c Morgan b Smith	10
K. Ibadulla c Taylor b Rhodes	0	— b Jackson	6
D. L. Amiss c Johnson b Rhodes	9	— c Taylor b Rhodes	5
*M. J. K. Smith b Jackson	16	— c and b Smith	22
J. A. Jameson c Buxton b Morgan	39	— c Taylor b Rhodes	17
W. J. Stewart not out	43	— b Smith	3
T. W. Cartwright b Smith	0	— b Smith	0
†A. C. Smith not out	35	— b Rhodes	2
R. Miller (did not bat)		— b Rhodes	0
R. V. Webster (did not bat)		— c Johnson b Smith	0
D. Brown (did not bat)		— not out	0
B 6, l-b 1, n-b 1	8	L-b 2, n-b 6	8
1/1 2/12 3/48 4/100 5/108 6/114 (6 wkts., 65 overs)	186	1/10 2/35 3/45 4/49 5/49 6/56 7/73 8/73 9/73	73

Bowling: *First Innings*—Jackson 20—8—36—1; Rhodes 13—3—24—2; Morgan 12—4—31—1; Buxton 14—2—65—0; Smith 6—3—22—2. *Second Innings*—Jackson 9—7—5—1; Rhodes 11—2—30—4; Buxton 4—1—7—0; Smith 10.4—3—23—5.

Derbyshire

I. W. Hall c A. C. Smith b Webster..... 7 — c and b Miller.......... 46
J. F. Harvey c Cartwright b Brown..... 6 — c A. C. Smith b Cartwright.. 30
M. H. Page c Amiss b Webster......... 7 — not out.................. 24
H. L. Johnson c M. J. K. Smith b Cartwright........................ 26 — not out.................. 18
M. Hill c Cartwright b Webster........ 7
I. R. Buxton c Jameson b Cartwright... 17
*D. C. Morgan b Brown............. 4
†R. W. Taylor c M. J. K. Smith b Cartwright......................... 6
E. Smith c M. J. K. Smith b Brown.... 18
H. J. Rhodes b Brown................ 15
A. B. Jackson not out................ 25
L-b 1.......................... 1 B 1, n-b 2.............. 3

1/13 2/13 3/24 4/36 5/64 6/69 7/75 8/82 9/100 139 1/49 2/88 (2 wkts.) 121

Bowling: *First Innings*—Brown 19.5—6—59—4; Webster 10—4—25—3; Cartwright 14—2—44—3; Miller 2—0—10—0. *Second Innings*—Brown 11—4—32—0; Webster 12—4—29—0; Cartwright 12—7—8—1; Ibadulla 6—2—24—0; Miller 8—4—19—1; A. C. Smith 2—0—3—0; M. J. K. Smith 1.3—1—3—0.

Umpires: H. Mellows and A. E. Fagg.

At Manchester, July 2, 4, 5. DERBYSHIRE beat LANCASHIRE by 30 runs.

DERBYSHIRE v. OXFORD UNIVERSITY

At Derby, July 6, 7, 8. Derbyshire won by five wickets. Derbyshire left out four established players and the new ball was shared in the first innings by Eyre and Ward. Goldstein batted aggressively for the University and a brisk, not-out 70 by Groves enabled them to declare. Derbyshire closed their innings 11 behind after Hall had made the county's first century of the season, putting on 168 for the second wicket with Page. The pitch gave considerable assistance to the seam bowlers when Oxford batted again and they could not recover from a poor start, despite a long, patient innings by Groves. Buxton, who took five wickets, conceded only 16 runs in 27 overs. Derbyshire had an easy task, but the Oxford spinners bowled well and made them struggle for their runs.

Oxford University

P. J. K. Gibbs c Russell b Eyre........ 2 — c Taylor b Russell.......... 6
F. S. Goldstein b Eyre................ 87 — c Russell b Buxton......... 11
D. P. Toft b Eyre.................... 28 — b Buxton................... 3
*R. M. C. Gilliat c Hill b Allen........ 16 — c Taylor b Russell.......... 2
M. G. M. Groves not out.............. 70 — c Russell b Morgan........ 47
M. R. J. Guest b Allen................ 4 — b Buxton................... 7
†A. W. Dyer not out.................. 3 — st Taylor b Buxton......... 20
G. N. S. Ridley (did not bat).......... — run out................... 0
A. G. M. Watson (did not bat)......... — b Buxton.................. 0
R. W. Elviss (did not bat)............ — not out................... 1
R. B. Hiller (did not bat)............. — run out................... 0
L-b 1.......................... 1 L-b 3.................... 3

1/16 2/110 3/121 4/142 5/148 (5 wkts., dec.) 211 1/19 2/19 3/25 4/25 5/80 6/98 7/98 8/98 9/99 100

Bowling: *First Innings*—Eyre 22—6—49—3; Ward 14—3—46—0; Russell 9—2—19—0; Allen 13—4—45—2; Page 7—1—21—0; Morgan 1—0—1—0; Buxton 8—2—29—0. *Second Innings*—Eyre 10—1—26—0; Morgan 15—8—14—1; Russell 9—5—5—2; Buxton 27—20—16—5; Allen 18—7—36—0.

Derbyshire

First innings		Second innings	
I. W. Hall c Holdstein b Ridley	102	— b Watson	14
J. F. Harvey b Hiller	13	— c Dyer b Guest	23
M. H. Page not out	79	— lbw b Ridley	17
M. Hill (did not bat)		— c and b Ridley	10
I. R. Buxton (did not bat)		— c Guest b Ridley	10
*D. C. Morgan (did not bat)		— not out	21
P. E. Russell (did not bat)		— not out	8
L-b 5, n-b 1	6	B 7, l-b 4	11
1/32 2/200 (2 wkts., dec.)	200	1/30 2/47 3/47 4/72 5/105 (5 wkts.)	114

†R. W. Taylor, T. J. P. Eyre, M. H. J. Allen and A. Ward did not bat.

Bowling: *First Innings*—Watson 10—2—37—0; Hiller 10—0—49—1; Guest 10—1—30—0; Groves 5—1—19—0; Ridley 15.5—8—26—1; Elviss 7—1—33—0. *Second Innings*—Watson 8—1—20—1; Hiller 5—0—22—0; Ridley 19—11—21—3; Guest 6—1—19—1; Elviss 12—5—17—0; Gibbs 1.2—1—4—0; Goldstein 1—1—0—0.

Umpires: J. Arnold and W. F. Simpson.

At Nottingham, July 9, 11, 12. DERBYSHIRE beat NOTTINGHAMSHIRE by eight wickets.

At Lord's, July 13, 14, 15. DERBYSHIRE drew with MIDDLESEX.

DERBYSHIRE v. LEICESTERSHIRE

At Chesterfield, July 16, 18, 19. Leicestershire won by 120 runs. After winning the toss, Leicestershire occupied almost all the first day in totalling 264 on a pitch from which the ball often bounced variably. In poor light the scoring rate did not reach two runs an over until late in the innings and Derbyshire's accurate bowling was offset by a number of dropped catches. Derbyshire also batted solidly, rather than spectacularly, and fell 49 runs behind on the first innings. Leicestershire consolidated their position, Hallam, Constant and Marner all playing well and left Derbyshire to make 254 in three hours and ten minutes. The loss of three early wickets ended their bid. Lock, turning the occasional ball sharply and backed by excellent close catching, bowled Leicestershire to their first win over their neighbours since 1958, taking seven for 50.

Leicestershire

First innings		Second innings	
M. R. Hallam lbw b Morgan	32	— c Taylor b Eyre	49
M. E. Norman c Morgan b Jackson	45	— c Taylor b Jackson	9
D. Constant c Taylor b Eyre	36	— c Taylor b Eyre	69
C. C. Inman run out	10	— c Morgan b Smith	9
P. Marner lbw b Eyre	57	— b Jackson	30
J. Birkenshaw b Eyre	37	— c Taylor b Morgan	17
†R. W. Tolchard run out	4	— not out	13
*G. A. R. Lock c Hall b Jackson	25	— b Morgan	0
C. T. Spencer b Eyre	10	— b Morgan	1
J. S. Savage c Taylor b Jackson	1	— not out	5
J. Cotton not out	0		
B 1, l-b 6	7	L-b 2	2
1/71 2/83 3/104 4/162 5/191 6/203 7/236 8/263 9/264	264	1/39 2/77 3/88 4/144 5/179 6/179 7/191 8/192 (8 wkts., dec.)	204

Bowling: *First Innings*—Jackson 29—8—55—3; Buxton 27—5—62—0; Eyre 23.3—5—58—4; Morgan 23—12—27—1; Smith 27—15—55—0. *Second Innings*—Jackson 23—4—49—2; Eyre 18—2—66—2; Morgan 19—3—55—3; Smith 7—1—32—1.

Derbyshire

J. F. Harvey b Spencer	11	c and b Spencer	2
†R. W. Taylor run out	31	not out	6
I. W. Hall lbw b Marner	24	c Hallam b Savage	34
M. H. Page c Savage b Cotton	14	lbw b Lock	5
H. L. Johnson b Cotton	19	b Cotton	11
M. Hill b Cotton	23	lbw b Lock	39
I. R. Buxton c Hallam b Lock	41	c Marner b Lock	0
*D. C. Morgan c Tolchard b Lock	10	c Cotton b Lock	4
T. J. P. Eyre c Hallam b Savage	34	c Constant b Lock	5
E. Smith c Marner b Lock	3	lbw b Lock	0
A. B. Jackson not out	0	c Savage b Lock	14
N-b 5	5	B 4, l-b 9	13
1/30 2/49 3/72 4/89 5/122 6/125 7/148 8/210 9/215	215	1/5 2/14 3/27 4/89 5/92 6/96 7/96 8/103 9/103	133

Bowling: *First Innings*—Spencer 21—5—56—1; Cotton 18—4—55—3; Marner 23—4—66—1; Lock 15.5—9—20—3; Savage 8—3—13—1. *Second Innings*—Spencer 6—1—11—1; Cotton 4—1—6—1; Lock 26.1—15—50—7; Savage 18—7—36—1; Birkenshaw 5—1—17—0.

Umpires: C. G. Pepper and P. A. Gibb.

At Colchester, July 20, 21, 22. DERBYSHIRE drew with ESSEX.

DERBYSHIRE v. SOMERSET

At Burton-on-Trent, July 23, 25, 26. Somerset won by ten wickets. Derbyshire made 56 for one after winning the toss, but Palmer after changing to the down-wind end, moved the ball each way off the seam in a hostile spell of bowling six wickets fell in 25 minutes while only eight runs were scored. The innings ended at 96, Palmer finishing with seven for 59. At the start of the Somerset innings, Rhodes bowled with umpire Buller at square leg for the first time since the 1965 "throwing" incident. Mr. Buller watched three overs, one from point and then indicated to the Derbyshire captain that his action was not satisfactory. Rhodes was taken off and bowled for the rest of the innings at the other end where he was "passed" by umpire Jepson. Sound contributions by Kitchen, Burgess, C. R. M. Atkinson and Palmer enabled Somerset to lead by 153. Derbyshire lost six wickets for 79 as the pitch wore, but with only two wickets left managed to prolong the match until the third morning, despite the extra half hour.

Derbyshire

I. W. Hall b Palmer	23	c Virgin b Langford	31
J. F. Harvey c Burgess b Rumsey	1	c Langford b Rumsey	4
M. H. Page c Kitchen b Alley	29	c Virgin b Rumsey	0
H. L. Johnson b Palmer	2	lbw b Rumsey	4
P. J. K. Gibbs c Clayton b Palmer	4	b Palmer	11
I. R. Buxton b Alley	0	c Kitchen b Langford	51
*D. C. Morgan not out	16	c Palmer b Langford	8
†R. W. Taylor c Burgess b Palmer	0	b Langford	10
H. J. Rhodes c Burgess b Palmer	8	not out	10
E. Smith c Robinson b Palmer	2	run out	11
A. B. Jackson b Palmer	5	c Kitchen b Palmer	0
L-b 2, w 1, n-b 3	6	B 2, l-b 5, w 1, n-b 5	13
1/3 2/56 3/58 4/58 5/59 6/63 7/64 8/86 9/88	96	1/11 2/12 3/24 4/51 5/65 6/79 7/130 8/130 9/152	153

Bowling: *First Innings*—Rumsey 8—3—16—1; Palmer 21—2—59—7; Alley 18—10—15—2. *Second Innings*—Rumsey 21—6—36—3; Palmer 15.2—4—30—2; Alley 7—4—6—0; Langford 30—15—54—4; Burgess 6—1—14—0.

Somerset

G. Atkinson c Morgan b Jackson	13		
R. Virgin c Taylor b Rhodes	5		
M. Kitchen c Taylor b Jackson	85		
W. E. Alley c Hall b Rhodes	7		
G. Burgess c Page b Morgan	42		
C. R. M. Atkinson c Smith b Buxton	31		
K. E. Palmer lbw b Jackson	34		
G. Clayton b Buxton	7	— not out	4
P. J. Robinson c Hall b Rhodes	16		
B. A. Langford not out	0	— not out	0
B 1, l-b 1, n-b 7	9		
1/6 2/49 3/56 4/148 5/162 6/215 7/224 8/246 9/249 (9 wkts., dec.)	249	(no wkt.)	4

F. E. Rumsey did not bat.

Bowling: *First Innings*—Jackson 30—6—54—3; Rhodes 27.1—9—47—3; Morgan 27—11—48—1; Buxton 24—6—53—2; Smith 16—3—38—0. *Second Innings*—Taylor 1—1—0—0; Hall 0.2—0—4—0.

Umpires: J. S. Buller and A. Jepson.

DERBYSHIRE v. LANCASHIRE

At Chesterfield, July 27, 28, 29. Lancashire won by seven wickets. The Derbyshire batsmen struggled against accurate seam bowling on a pitch of variable bounce until Rhodes and Smith briskly put on 48 for the ninth wicket. Solid displays by Green and Pullar enabled Lancashire to lead by 77 and Statham and Higgs soon had Derbyshire in more trouble. Four wickets were down for 39 and although Morgan, Eyre and Taylor played bravely on a rain-affected surface on the last morning, the innings ended at 132. Lancashire needed only 56 for victory but Rhodes gave them some anxious moments before it was achieved. He took three wickets in a lively spell during which he conceded only four runs.

Derbyshire

I. W. Hall c Worsley b Higgs	3	— lbw b Statham	22
J. F. Harvey b Statham	4	— b Statham	7
M. H. Page lbw b Greenhough	16	— c Wood b Higgs	5
I. R. Buxton b Statham	2	— b Statham	4
P. E. Russell c Knox b Higgs	4	— c Goodwin b Statham	0
*D. C. Morgan c Goodwin b Lever	4	— not out	38
T. J. P. Eyre b Lever	14	— c Knox b Lever	24
†R. W. Taylor c Goodwin b Lever	12	— b Higgs	21
H. J. Rhodes c Worsley b Statham	28	— c Goodwin b Lever	0
E. Smith lbw b Lever	19	— b Statham	4
A. B. Jackson not out	0	— c Statham b Higgs	0
L-b 6, n-b 4	10	L-b 5, n-b 2	7
1/7 2/11 3/20 4/27 5/33 6/41 7/60 8/68 9/116	116	1/28 2/29 3/39 4/39 5/43 6/84 7/112 8/117 9/131	132

Bowling: *First Innings*—Statham 11.1—1—33—3; Higgs 8—4—9—2; Lever 15—3—42—4; Greenhough 10—3—22—1. *Second Innings*—Statham 17—2—44—5; Higgs 26—5—58—3; Lever 9—1—23—2.

Lancashire

D. M. Green lbw b Morgan	60	— b Rhodes	21
G. K. Knox c Buxton b Rhodes	9	— c Page b Rhodes	13
J. D. Bond c Taylor b Rhodes	0	— c Page b Rhodes	1
G. Pullar c Taylor b Smith	64	— not out	10
D. R. Worsley c Buxton b Rhodes	4	— not out	10
B. Wood c Hall b Morgan	2		
P. Lever lbw b Jackson	18		
K. Higgs b Smith	8		
K. Goodwin b Eyre	8		
T. Greenhough not out	6		
J. B. Statham c Taylor b Smith	8		
B 1, l-b 2, n-b 3	6	L-b 1	1
1/33 2/33 3/110 4/115 5/134 6/146 7/166 8/179 9/179	193	1/27 2/33 3/40 (3 wkts.)	56

Bowling: *First innings*—Jackson 26—11—44—1; Rhodes 23—7—50—3; Eyre 12-2-38-1; Morgan 16-8-20-2; Smith 22.3—10—34—3. *Second Innings*—Jackson 11—0—37—0; Rhodes 10.5—2—18—3.

Umpires: J. S. Buller and A. Jepson.

At Southampton, July 30, August 1, 2. DERBYSHIRE drew with HAMPSHIRE.

DERBYSHIRE v. GLOUCESTERSHIRE

At Derby, August 3, 4, 5. Gloucestershire won by 60 runs. Because of rain only three hours' play was possible on the first two days. Gloucestershire, who struggled for runs after winning the toss, declared their first innings on the last morning and, after Derbyshire had declared 47 runs behind, eventually set the home county a target of 119 to win in ninety-five minutes. Although the pitch was slow and moist at one end, the odds seemed in favour of the batting side, but they collapsed in startling fashion against the spin of Allen and the left-arm Bissex. These two did not enter the attack until Derbyshire had passed 20 for the loss of one wicket, yet the innings lasted only one hour. Five wickets fell while the score moved from 51 to 52, Allen taking three in one over without cost. The ball turned, but many batsmen fell to poor strokes.

Gloucestershire

C. A. Milton c Taylor b Jackson	11	— not out	30
M. Bissex c J. R. Eyre b Buxton	13	— lbw b Jackson	0
D. Brown c Harvey b Buxton	38	— b Buxton	0
D. Shepherd b Jackson	0	— c sub b Morgan	34
R. B. Nicholls c Hall b Buxton	21	— not out	7
M. D. Mence b Jackson	5		
*J. B. Mortimore not out	2		
L-b 9	9		
1/26 2/31 3/37 4/85 5/ 97 6/99 (6 wkts., dec.)	99	1/0 2/1 3/56 (3 wkts., dec.)	71

D. A. Allen, A. S. Brown, †B. J. Meyer and D. R. Smith did not bat.

Bowling: *First Innings*—Jackson 21—10—18—3; Rhodes 9—3—7—0; Buxton 24—11—36—3; Morgan 11—6—14—0; Page 5—1—15—0. *Second Innings*—Jackson 5—4—3—1; Buxton 8—2—16—1; Morgan 9—2—33—1; Page 3—0—19—0.

Derbyshire

I. W. Hall c Meyer b Smith	1	— b A. S. Brown	1
J. R. Eyre not out	37	— c Nicholls b Bissex	18
M. H. Page not out	12	— b Allen	15
J. F. Harvey (did not bat)		— c A. S. Brown b Allen	4
M. Hill (did not bat)		— c D. Brown b A. S. Brown	4
I. R. Buxton (did not bat)		— c Mortimore b Bissex	8
*D. C. Morgan (did not bat)		— c A. S. Brown b Allen	0
T. J. P. Eyre (did not bat)		— c Nicholls b Allen	0
†R. W. Taylor (did not bat)		— lbw b Allen	0
A. B. Jackson (did not bat)		— not out	5
H. J. Rhodes (did not bat)		— c Nicholls b Bissex	1
L-b 2	2	L-b 2	2
1/4 (1 wkt., dec.)	52	1/5 2/26 3/32 4/37 5/51 6/52 7/52 8/52 9/52	58

Bowling: *First Innings*—Brown 5—2—15—0; Smith 8—2—17—1; Mortimore 3—1—18—0. *Second Innings*—Smith 3—0—14—0; A. S. Brown 6—0—17—2; Allen 7—0—25—5; Bissex 3.3—3—0—3.

Umpires: T. W. Spencer and W. F. Simpson.

DERBYSHIRE v. WORCESTERSHIRE

At Ilkeston, August 6, 8, 9. *65 overs.* Worcestershire won by three runs. On a slow-paced, sparsely grassed pitch, Worcestershire struggled for runs after winning the toss, but later, helped by fielding lapses, stepped up their scoring rate. Richardson and Booth both played aggressively before falling to Smith. Harvey batted well, becoming the first Derbyshire player to pass 1,000 runs, but despite sound contributions from Page and Hill they finished 30 behind. Worcestershire were restricted to 107 in nearly four hours by the accuracy of Smith and Morgan on a drying surface and Derbyshire, needing 138 to win, made 40 for one. On the last morning, however, Gifford took full advantage of the worn wicket and achieved his best bowling figures for Worcestershire, eight for 54, but Derbyshire, helped by J. R. Eyre hitting his best score, reached lunch needing four for victory with two wickets left. Afterwards, they lost them both without adding to their score.

Worcestershire

M. J. Horton c Taylor b Smith	35	— c Page b Smith	16
C. D. Fearnley b T. J. P. Eyre	11	— b Morgan	9
*D. Kenyon c and b Smith	34	— c Hill b Smith	10
J. A. Ormrod b T. J. P. Eyre	24	— c Buxton b Morgan	3
R. G. A. Headley c Jackson b Smith	15	— b Smith	8
D. W. Richardson b Smith	36	— lbw b Morgan	8
†R. Booth b Smith	36	— lbw b Jackson	20
N. Gifford not out	13	— not out	17
L. J. Coldwell c Harvey b T. J. P. Eyre	0	— b Jackson	4
R. G. M. Carter not out	0	— run out	0
J. A. Flavell (did not bat)		— b Morgan	5
L-b 6	6	B 4, l-b 3	7
1/39 2/65 3/84 4/117 5/122 6/186 7/199 8/208 (8 wkts., 65 overs)	210	1/6 2/20 3/37 4/42 5/53 6/64 7/80 8/94 9/107	107

Bowling: *First Innings*—Jackson 12—2—34—0; Buxton 9—5—17—0; T. J. P. Eyre 19—5—62—3; Smith 23—5—74—5; Morgan 2—0—17—0. *Second Innings*—Jackson 12—6—16—2; T.J.P. Eyre 10—4—15—0; Smith 30—12—33—3; Morgan 29.5—15—36—4.

Derbyshire

I. W. Hall c Booth b Flavell	14	c Richardson b Gifford	1
J. R. Eyre b Coldwell	1	st Booth b Gifford	61
M. H. Page run out	34	c Ormrod b Gifford	17
J. F. Harvey b Flavell	49	c Headley b Gifford	3
M. Hill lbw b Carter	32	c Headley b Gifford	2
I. R. Buxton lbw b Coldwell	12	c Ormrod b Gifford	15
*D. C. Morgan c Richardson b Coldwell	11	c Ormrod b Gifford	0
T. J. P. Eyre not out	20	c sub b Horton	5
†R. W. Taylor b Coldwell	0	b Gifford	18
E. Smith run out	0	lbw b Flavell	0
A. B. Jackson not out	2	not out	0
B 1, l-b 4	5	B 3, l-b 7, w 2	12
1/2 2/20 3/77 4/124 5/142 6/150 7/165 8/165 9/168 (9 wkts., 65 overs)	180	1/12 2/50 3/56 4/60 5/75 6/92 7/92 8/133 9/134	134

Bowling: *First Innings*—Flavell 16—3—51—2; Coldwell 19—7—40—4; Gifford 14—8—19—0; Carter 7—0—30—1; Horton 9—1—35—0. *Second Innings*—Flavell 10.4—5—11—1; Coldwell 10—6—13—0; Gifford 35—16—54—8; Horton 26—9—44—1.

Umpires: T. W. Spencer and W. F. Simpson.

At Kidderminster, August 13, 15, 16. DERBYSHIRE lost to WORCESTERSHIRE by seven wickets.

At Coventry, August 17, 18, 19. DERBYSHIRE beat WARWICKSHIRE by ten wickets.

DERBYSHIRE v. GLAMORGAN

At Derby, August 20, 22, 23. *65 overs*. Glamorgan won by 78 runs. A sound innings by Rees formed the backbone of Glamorgan's total, but Derbyshire led by 12 on first innings after some brisk scoring by Morgan and Taylor. Glamorgan took advantage of a good wicket to build up a solid second innings, during which Taylor, the Derbyshire wicket-keeper, held seven catches, breaking the county's record and equalling the best for championship cricket. Once again, batting last proved an ordeal for Derbyshire's suspect batting and the Glamorgan bowlers, helped by some good close catching, took their side to victory.

Glamorgan

A. Jones c J. R. Eyre b Russell	27	c Taylor b Russell	48
W. Slade b Jackson	1	c Taylor b T. J. P. Eyre	14
P. M. Walker b T. J. P. Eyre	7	c Russell b Jackson	31
A. R. Lewis c T. J. P. Eyre b Smith	29	c T. J. P. Eyre b Russell	39
A. Rees not out	53	c Taylor b Jackson	0
R. Davis not out	2	c Harvey b T. J. P. Eyre	52
†D. L. Evans b Jackson	7	c Taylor b Jackson	16
A. E. Cordle run out	18	c Taylor b T. J. P. Eyre	10
D. J. Shepherd c Morgan b T. J. P. Eyre	0	c Taylor b Jackson	0
*O. S. Wheatley (did not bat)		c Taylor b Jackson	9
I. J. Jones (did not bat)		not out	13
B 1, l-b 8	9	B 6, l-b 5	11
1/1 2/12 3/42 4/98 5/130 6/147 7/148 (7 wkts., 65 overs)	153	1/32 2/101 3/103 4/105 5/177 6/208 7/221 8/221 9/224	243

Bowling: *First Innings*—Jackson 15—2—33—2; T. J. P. Eyre 15—2—29—2; Russell 18—6—40—1; Morgan 4—1—7—0; Smith 13—4—35—1. *Second Innings*—Jackson 32—8—68—5; T. J. P. Eyre 35—13—66—3; Russell 24—6—41—2; Morgan 14—6—25—0; Smith 24—12—32—0.

Derbyshire

J. R. Eyre b Shepherd	11	— c Walker b I. J. Jones	4
P. J. K. Gibbs b Cordle	43	— c Walker b Shepherd	29
J. F. Harvey c Walker b Cordle	0	— b Wheatley	26
M. Hill c Evans b Cordle	1	— c A. Jones b Shepherd	5
H. L. Johnson run out	1	— b Wheatley	4
P. E. Russell b I. J. Jones	14	— c Rees b Shepherd	28
*D. C. Morgan not out	46	— run out	15
T. J. P. Eyre c I. J. Jones b Wheatley	15	— c I. J. Jones b Shepherd	11
†R. W. Taylor not out	31	— b Cordle	16
E. Smith (did not bat)		— c Walker b Cordle	4
A. B. Jackson (did not bat)		— not out	0
N-b 3	3	B 4, w 4, n-b 3	11
1/3 2/40 3/46 4/49 (7 wkts., 65 overs)	165	1/25 2/66 3/66 4/71 5/81	153
5/63 6/87 7/119		6/111 7/129 8/146 9/152	

Bowling: *First Innings*—I. J. Jones 13—4—35—1; Wheatley 18—4—50—1; Cordle 16—3—34—3; Shepherd 18—7—43—1. *Second Innings*—I. J. Jones 8—2—16—1; Wheatley 10—3—16—2; Cordle 18.2—3—44—2; Shepherd 27—13—48—4; Walker 6—0—18—0.

Umpires: W. F. Price and L. H. Gray.

DERBYSHIRE v. NOTTINGHAMSHIRE

At Chesterfield, August 24, 25, 26. Derbyshire won by 159 runs. Nottinghamshire's decision to field first was thwarted by Derbyshire who took advantage of some moderate bowling to recover from a poor start and were able to declare. A brilliant not-out 90 by Murray, the West Indian, showed up the rest of the Nottinghamshire batsmen. Hooking and cutting superbly, he refused to be dominated by the attack and ran out of partners when he seemed certain to reach his century. Morgan also played fluently against more wayward bowling before falling to the last ball of the day seven short of his century. On the last day Nottinghamshire found their target of 309 far beyond their capabilities.

Derbyshire

J. R. Eyre b Johnson	11	— c Swetman b Stead	18
P. J. K. Gibbs lbw b Stead	4	— lbw b Stead	33
J. F. Harvey run out	14	— lbw b Stead	9
M. Hill c Swetman b Forbes	42	— lbw b Stead	1
*D. C. Morgan c White b Forbes	31	— c Smedley b Johnson	93
P. E. Russell c Smedley b Taylor	56	— c Smedley b Johnson	19
T. J. P. Eyre c and b Forbes	80	— c Swetman b Taylor	0
†R. W. Taylor c Smedley b Taylor	19	— not out	15
H. J. Rhodes not out	0		
E. Smith b Johnson	1		
B 6, l-b 11, w 4, n-b 11	32	L-b 4, w 1, n-b 3	8
1/19 2/19 3/59 4/105 (9 wkts., dec.)	290	1/41 2/57 3/59 (7 wkts., dec.)	196
5/118 6/260 7/280 8/281 9/290		4/105 5/149 6/152 7/196	

A. B. Jackson did not bat.

Bowling: *First Innings*—Stead 20—4—55—1; Johnson 23—3—52—2; Forbes 29—9—59—3; Taylor 22—7—53—2; White 19—6—39—0. *Second Innings*—Stead 18—4—57—4; Johnson 14.4—1—55—2; Forbes 10—2—35—0; Taylor 15—3—41—1; White 1—1—0—0.

Nottinghamshire

*N. Hill c Hill b Rhodes	12	—	c Taylor b Russell	39
J. B. Bolus b Rhodes	11	—	c Russell b Jackson	1
D. L. Murray not out	90	—	lbw b Jackson	6
H. I. Moore b Rhodes	0	—	c Smith b Jackson	5
M. J. Smedley b Morgan	4	—	c Morgan b T. J. P. Eyre	6
R. A. White lbw b Russell	9	—	c Taylor b Russell	2
†R. Swetman lbw b Rhodes	3	—	b T. J. P. Eyre	7
M. Taylor lbw b Morgan	35	—	lbw b Smith	36
A. Johnson c and b Morgan	0	—	b Jackson	4
C. Forbes lbw b Smith	0	—	not out	19
B. Stead lbw b Smith	5	—	c J. R. Eyre b Rhodes	19
B 1, l-b 7, n-b 1	9		B 2, l-b 2, n-b 1	5
1/25 2/32 3/32 4/56 5/79 6/84 7/161 8/162 9/169	178		1/7 2/16 3/22 4/36 5/43 6/52 7/107 8/107 9/122	149

Bowling: *First Innings*—Jackson 18—5—26—0; Rhodes 19—4—46—4; Smith 15.4—5—28—2; T. J. P. Eyre 2—0—9—0; Morgan 21—7—48—3; Russell 9—5—12—1. *Second Innings*—Jackson 18—8—33—4; Rhodes 17.5—5—30—1; Smith 8—5—8—1; T. J. P. Eyre 13—3—46—2; Morgan 6—4—4—0; Russell 13—6—23—2.

Umpires: L. H. Gray and P. A. Gibb.

At Colwyn Bay, August 27, 29, 30. DERBYSHIRE lost to GLAMORGAN by 63 runs.

FIELDING STATISTICS FOR 1966

85 G. Clayton (75 c, 10 st)
81 A. Knott (73 c, 8 st)
72 R. Booth (64 c, 8 st)
71 B. J. Meyer (64 c, 7 st)
70 B. Taylor (61 c, 9 st)
66 B. S. V. Timms (57 c, 9 st)
64 R. W. Taylor (61 c, 3 st)
64 J. G. Binks (54 c, 10st)
63 R. Swetman (61 c, 2st)
61 J. M. Parks (56 c, 5 st)
61 K. Goodwin (59 c, 2 st)
60 R. W. Tolchard (54 c, 6 st)
59 A. C. Smith (56 c, 3 st)
57 A. Long (45 c, 12 st)
55 K. V. Andrew (51 c, 4 st)
48 P. H. Parfitt
46 D. B. Close
45 P. J. Sharpe
43 B. W. Luckhurst
42 K. W. R. Fletcher
42 R. Virgin
42 P. M. Walker
40 D. L. Murray (33 c, 7 st)
40 M.J. Edwards
39 R. G. A. Headley
38 G. A. R. Lock
38 J. T. Murray (31 c, 7 st)
38 P. J. Watts
35 P. Marner
35 R. N. S. Hobbs
34 D. L. Evans (32 c, 2 st)
33 P. J. Robinson
33 D. S. Steele
32 M. J. K. Smith
31 M. C. Cowdrey
31 K. Ibadulla
31 D. W. Richardson
31 M. J. Stewart
30 A. Ealham
30 M. R. Hallam
29 A. W. Dyer (25 c, 4 st)
29 S. E. Leary
29 C. A. Milton
28 D. C. Morgan
27 A. S. Brown
27 D. J. Foreman
27 E. Jones (26 c, 1 st)
27 G. K. Knox
26 E. G. Clifton (24 c, 2 st)
25 W. E. Alley
25 J. H. Hampshire
24 M. A. Buss
24 Mushtaq Mohammad
24 Nawab of Pataudi
24 J. M. Prodger
24 A. Rees
23 T. W. Cartwright
23 D. L. Hays (21 c, 2 st)
23 K. E. Palmer
23 P. J. Sainsbury
23 W. Slade
23 B. d'Oliveira
22 M. H. Denness
22 R. Illingworth
22 C. Milburn
22 M. H. Page
22 B. L. Reynolds
21 J. H. Edrich
21 T. Gunn (21 c)
21 A. S. M. Oakman
21 C. T. Spencer
21 M. Taylor
21 F. S. Trueman
20 H. M. Barnard
20 T. W. Graveney
20 N. Hill
20 B. R. Knight
20 J. A. Ormrod
20 D. R. Worsley

ESSEX

President—Sir Hubert Ashton

Secretary—Major C. A. Brown, 60 London Road, Chelmsford

Captain—T. E. Bailey

M. J. Bear

County Badge

B. Edmeades

From all points of view Essex again fared badly and remained dangerously near the bottom of the Championship. The need for economy left them with disturbingly attenuated playing resources and increased financial troubles led to cuts in the administrative staff at the end of the season. Often they found it difficult to field a team of county strength and Trevor Bailey, the captain, played for most of the summer under the handicap of a leg strain which greatly reduced his all-round effectiveness.

So far as bowling was concerned, this meant that added responsibility fell upon Edmeades, of fast-medium pace, and he responded admirably. Indeed, he took four or more wickets in an innings on eleven occasions, achieved the best analysis of his career when dismissing seven Glamorgan batsmen for 37 runs at Leyton and, in all matches, obtained more than 100 wickets for the first time. Furthermore he played some useful innings and was not the least noticeable in the field, where the team, whatever its shortcomings, generally performed smartly. Hobbs, the leg-spinner, also put in much work with distinct credit, attaining special success against Glamorgan at Swansea, where he took 13 wickets for 164 runs. In his first season, Jorden revealed both pace and promise and might well have gained a better record. The slow left-hander, East, did not fulfil hopes, but Acfield, the Cambridge off-spinner, did some useful things after the University match.

The batting once more proved far from reliable, too much depending upon too few. Only once did Essex reach a total of 300 and fifteen times they were disposed of for fewer than 150. Of the four men who exceeded 1,000 runs, Barker, acting captain when

Bailey stood down, played steadily, putting together a first-rate not out 95 against Worcestershire at Romford, and Bear, the left-hander, taking part in 13 more innings than in the previous year, increased his aggregate by 867 and his average by over 12.

Taylor, who again kept wicket skilfully, effectively blended aggression with spells of unaccustomed defence, but he could have made more runs but for a tendency to lose concentration when well set. Possibly because he so often forbore to employ the variety of brilliant strokes which brought him early prominence, Fletcher did not do so well as in 1965. Yet, when free of the seemingly haunting spectre of Championship points, he played a grand innings of 106 against the West Indies at Southend. Following a good opening, Knight finished the season in excellent form, but in between experienced so lean a spell that 19 innings yielded him no more than 151 runs. Cass occasionally appeared to advantage.

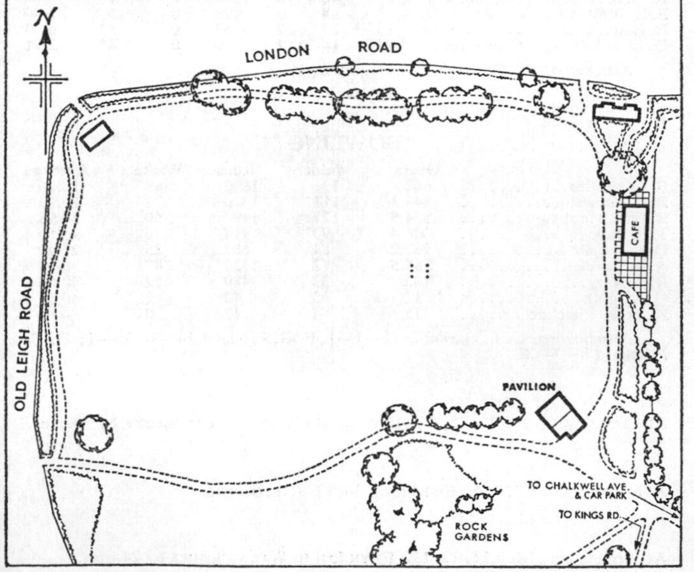

ESSEX RESULTS

All First-Class Matches—Played 32, *Won* 7, *Lost* 10, *Drawn* 15
County Championship Matches—Played 28, *Won* 4, *Lost* 10, *Drawn* 11, *No Decision* 3

COUNTY CHAMPIONSHIP AVERAGES

BATTING

	Birthplace	Mtchs.	Inns.	Not Outs	Runs	100's	Highest Inns.	Aver.
M. J. Bear.....	*Brentwood*	27	50	1	1571	1	105	32.06
G. E. Barker...	*Leeds*	27	51	7	1170	0	95*	26.59
K.W. R. Fletcher	*Worcester*	27	49	5	1042	1	101*	23.68
B. Taylor......	*West Ham*	28	51	1	1107	0	77	22.14
B. R. Knight...	*Chesterfield*	22	34	2	676	0	73	21.12
G. R. Cass.....	*Halifax*	23	40	5	641	0	53	18.31
T. E. Bailey....	*Westcliff*	20	33	7	466	0	31*	17.92
G. J. Saville....	*Leytonstone*	20	35	8	458	0	48*	16.96
B. Edmeades...	*Matlock*	25	40	8	542	0	47	16.93
G. J. Smith....	*Braintree*	2	4	0	47	0	26	11.75
A. M. Jorden...	*Radlett*	28	33	12	216	0	29*	10.28
R. N. S. Hobbs.	*Chippenham*	28	40	10	237	0	34	7.90
E. R. Presland..	*Loughton*	3	4	0	28	0	15	7.00
R. East........	*Manningtree*	13	16	7	57	0	9*	6.33
D. L. Acfield...	*Chelmsford*	14	14	7	19	0	4*	2.71

Also batted: G. C. Pritchard (*Farnborough*) 0.

* *Signifies not out.*

BOWLING

	Overs	Maidens	Runs	Wickets	Average
B. Edmeades............	662	131	1800	98	18.36
B. R. Knight...........	544.1	111	1370	71	19.29
R. N. S. Hobbs..........	534.3	127	1497	60	24.95
T. E. Bailey............	388.4	90	918	36	25.50
D. L. Acfield...........	267.2	84	685	25	27.40
A. M. Jorden............	565.5	72	1722	47	36.63
R. East................	162	33	480	12	40.00
G. J. Smith	12	3	40	1	40.00
K. W. R. Fletcher........	15	4	42	0	—

Also bowled: G. E. Barker 2—1—1—1; E. R. Presland 14—3—29—1; G. C. Pritchard 8—3—21—0.

At Cambridge, April 27, 28, 29. Essex beat Cambridge University by 50 runs.

At Leicester, May 4, 5, 6. Essex drew with Leicestershire.

At Birmingham, May 11, 12, 13. Essex lost to Warwickshire by 24 runs.

ESSEX v. SOMERSET

At Ilford, May 14, 15, 16. *65 overs.* Drawn. The first county match to involve Sunday play proved a financial success. Although no admission fee could be charged on Sunday, the sale of score-cards, stand seats and collections yielded nearly £500 from 6,000 spectators. Somerset failed in the first innings against the pace of Knight and Bailey and though Essex also struggled, bold batting by Knight took them to a lead of 54. Steady batting by Virgin and a partnership of 143 between G. Atkinson and Kitchen featured a Somerset recovery and Essex needed 290 for victory. Fletcher displayed patience while Taylor obtained twelve 4's in 77 scored in eighty-five minutes and Essex would have won had Hobbs been able to hit the last ball for 6.

Somerset

First Innings		Second Innings	
B. Roe c Taylor b Knight	12	c Taylor b Jorden	0
R. Virgin c Taylor b Bailey	29	lbw b Hobbs	51
M. Kitchen c Fletcher b Knight	0	lbw b Jorden	76
G. Atkinson st Taylor b Bailey	15	b Knight	76
W. E. Alley lbw b Bailey	6	c Knight b Jorden	19
*C. R. M. Atkinson c Barker b Knight	0	not out	35
K. E. Palmer lbw b Knight	6	not out	30
†G. Clayton lbw b Knight	0	c Hobbs b Bailey	42
P. J. Robinson b Knight	12		
B. Langford not out	14		
F. E. Rumsey b Bailey	3		
B 4, n-b 1	5	L-b 7, n-b 7	14
1/34 2/40 3/46 4/54 5/57 6/63 7/63 8/79 9/91	102	1/0 2/79 3/103 4/246 5/255 6/277 (6 wkts. dec.)	343

Bowling: *First Innings*—Knight 24—2—36—6; Jorden 9—1—24—0; Bailey 21.2—4—37—4. *Second Innings*—Jorden 24—3—61—3; Knight 25—3—86—1; Bailey 24—5—63—1; Hobbs 29—8—70—1; East 18—4—49—0.

Essex

First Innings		Second Innings	
G. E. Barker b Alley	20	c Rumsey b Robinson	26
M. J. Bear run out	2	run out	37
G. J. Saville lbw b Alley	12	c Alley b Langford	10
K. W. R. Fletcher c Clayton b Palmer	0	b Rumsey	73
†B. Taylor b Alley	26	c Virgin b Alley	77
B. R. Knight c Alley b Rumsey	56	c Clayton b Alley	30
*T. E. Bailey b Langford	17	not out	19
G. R. Cass lbw b Langford	7	b Palmer	1
R. N. S. Hobbs c G. Atkinson b Langford	0	not out	2
A. M. Jorden not out	3		
R. East c Clayton b Langford	0		
B 6, l-b 6, n-b 1	13	B 5, l-b 3, w 1, n-b 2	11
1/14 2/41 3/44 4/44 5/89 6/135 7/147 8/147 9/156	156	1/35 2/68 3/77 4/178 5/239 6/273 7/282 (7 wkts.)	286

Bowling: *First Innings*—Rumsey 15—3—53—1; Palmer 15—2—44—1; Alley 11—2—36—3; Langford 7.4—4—10—4. *Second Innings*—Rumsey 19—2—61—1; Alley 20—1—59—2; Palmer 10—2—29—1; Langford 24—8—63—1; Robinson 18—6—63—1.

Umpires: W. F. Price and W. F. Simpson.

ESSEX v. GLOUCESTERSHIRE

At Ilford, May 18, 19, 20. Drawn. Given a good start by Barker and Bear, Essex batted solidly on the opening day, Knight (one 6, eight 4's) providing the brightest innings. Thanks to Nicholls and Milton, Gloucestershire also began well, but rain caused time to be lost and Mortimore declared on the last morning when 81 behind. Though troubled by the spin of Mortimore, Essex were able to close their innings for a second time, leaving Gloucester to get 205 to win in two and a half hours. The total reached 38 by the time the first wicket fell, but five more went for 55 against the left-arm slows of East, and the task proved too heavy. In the match, East took nine wickets for 100 runs.

Essex

G. E. Barker c A. S. Brown b Mortimore	48	— b Mortimore	22
M. J. Bear c Windows b Mortimore	50	— c Russell b Mortimore	35
†B. Taylor lbw b Allen	1	— c Meyer b Mortimore	1
K. W. R. Fletcher b Allen	21	— not out	42
B. R. Knight c Meyer b Windows	51	— retired hurt	16
*T. E. Bailey c Meyer b Windows	20		
G. J. Saville lbw b Windows	15	— not out	6
G. R. Cass c Milton b Windows	21	— c Meyer b Mortimore	1
R. N. S. Hobbs not out	13		
L-b 1	1		
1/83 2/84 3/112 4/128 5/191 6/192 7/226 8/241 (8 wkts., dec.)	241	1/45 2/55 3/58 4/113 (4 wkts. dec.)	123

A. M. Jorden and R. East did not bat.

Bowling: *First Innings*—A. S. Brown 17—3—40—0; Windows 27.2—5—55—4; Mortimore 43—16—76—2; Allen 34—14—69—2; *Second Innings*—A. S. Brown 6—0—26—0; Windows 5—0—17—0; Mortimore 13—4—26—4; Bissex 13—1—54—0.

Gloucestershire

R. B. Nicholls c and b East	41	— c and b East	35
C. A. Milton b East	38	— c Saville b Bailey	17
S. E. Russell c sub. b East	10	— c and b East	2
M. Bissex c and b East	17	— c Barker b Bailey	10
D. Brown not out	24	— c and b East	19
D. Shepherd not out	21	— c Barker b East	1
*J. B. Mortimore (did not bat)		— not out	40
A. S. Brown (did not bat)		— c Fletcher b East	20
D. A. Allen (did not bat)		— not out	1
B 4, l-b 4, n-b 1	9	L-b 2	2
1/74 2/93 3/94 4/120 (4 wkts., dec.)	160	1/38 2/49 3/60 4/78 5/85 6/93 7/143 (7 wkts.)	147

A. R. Windows and †B. J. Meyer did not bat.

Bowling: *First Innings*—Knight 19—7—29—0; Jorden 22—4—53—0; Bailey 16—2—26—0; East 15—4—43—4. *Second Innings*—Jorden 10—1—27—0; Bailey 11—2—18—2; Knight 6—0—14—0; East 17—4—57—5; Fletcher 7—1—29—0.

Umpires: W. F. Price and W. F. Simpson.

At Chesterfield, May 21. ESSEX beat DERBYSHIRE by two wickets. (See GILLETTE CUP.)

At Ilkeston, May 25, 26, 27. ESSEX drew with DERBYSHIRE.

ESSEX v. WORCESTERSHIRE

At Romford, May 28, 30, 31. *65 overs.* Worcestershire won by four wickets. Barker, the Essex acting captain, carried his bat on the first day after hitting eleven 4's in three and a half hours and Taylor drove hard while helping to add 51. Ormrod turned an early life to good account with a steady innings lasting two hours forty minutes. He and Graveney put on 88, but not till the final over did Worcester take over the lead. Then Essex fought for runs against the medium-paced off-breaks of d'Oliveira, who achieved his best analysis for Worcestershire, six for 57. Even so, the Midland county required 183 to win and despite another sturdy display by Ormrod, who shared a partnership of 82 with Graveney, took more than four hours to get them.

Essex

First innings		Second innings	
*G. E. Barker not out	95	— c d'Oliveira b Coldwell	31
M. J. Bear b Gifford	5	— c Headley b d'Oliveira	27
†B. Taylor b Horton	42	— hit wkt. b d'Oliveira	18
K. W. R. Fletcher c Headley b Brain	22	— c Headley b d'Oliveira	5
B. R. Knight c Booth b Coldwell	4	— c Coldwell b d'Oliveira	9
G. R. Cass not out	26	— run out	4
B. Edmeades (did not bat)		— b Gifford	27
E. R. Presland (did not bat)		— c Graveney b d'Oliveira	9
R. N. S. Hobbs (did not bat)		— c Graveney b d'Oliveira	34
A. M. Jorden (did not bat)		— lbw b Slade	15
R. East (did not bat)		— not out	8
L-b 16	16	B 2, l-b 1	3
1/69 2/120 3/133 4/153 (4 wkts., 65 overs)	210	1/46 2/70 3/77 4/84 5/88 6/105 7/119 8/141 9/180	190

Bowling: *First Innings*—Coldwell 16—2—53—1; Brain 17—1—68—1; d'Oliveira 11—6—19—0; Horton 6—1—11—1; Gifford 11—3—22—1; Slade 4—0—21—0. *Second Innings*—Coldwell 11—3—40—1; Brain 3—0—21—0; d'Oliveira 30—11—57—6; Horton 8—2—17—0; Gifford 25—9—45—1; Slade 4.1—2—7—1.

Worcestershire

First innings		Second innings	
*D. Kenyon c Fletcher b Knight	13	— lbw b Hobbs	48
R. G. A. Headley c Taylor b Jorden	1	— b Edmeades	9
J. A. Ormrod b Knight	67	— c Taylor b Edmeades	51
T. W. Graveney b Jorden	33	— c Knight b Edmeades	36
B. d'Oliveira b Knight	16	— b Hobbs	6
M. J. Horton c Knight b Jorden	5	— not out	13
†R. Booth c Jorden b Edmeades	34	— lbw b Edmeades	2
D. N. F. Slade not out	33	— not out	4
N. Gifford not out	6		
B 1, l-b 7, n-b 2	10	B 11, l-b 2, n-b 1	14
1/2 2/26 3/114 4/130 5/139 6/153 7/201 (7 wkts., 65 overs)	218	1/40 2/75 3/157 4/158 5/166 6/171 (6 wkts.)	183

B. M. Brain and L. J. Coldwell did not bat.

Bowling: *First Innings*—Knight 22—2—74—3; Jorden 19—2—67—3; Edmeades 14—2—40—1; Hobbs 7—1—24—0; East 3—1—3—0. *Second Innings*—Knight 7—3—7—0; Jorden 9—1—32—0; Hobbs 24—4—54—2; Edmeades 18—6—31—4; East 26—10—45—0.

Umpires: P. A. Gibb and P. B. Wight.

ESSEX v. NOTTINGHAMSHIRE

At Romford, June 1, 2, 3. *65 overs.* Essex won by 56 runs. Batsmen fared indifferently on a pitch always helpful to bowlers and 40 wickets fell for an aggregate of 510 runs. Bear (ten 4's) saved Essex on the opening day. Hill, struck in the face when trying to hook Jorden, dropped out of the match early in the Nottinghamshire innings and despite stubborn play by Moore, Essex gained a lead of 36. Barker proved so successful at the second attempt that by lunch-time on Thursday the total stood at 95 for two wickets. Then the innings closed for another 50 runs, Forbes completing a match analysis of nine wickets for 72. Again Nottinghamshire collapsed, the game ending after five minutes on the third morning.

Essex

*G. E. Barker c. Swetman b Davison	10	— c and b Forbes	53
M. J. Bear c Johnson b Forbes	78	— lbw b Forbes	26
†B. Taylor c Moore b Johnson	2	— b Taylor	24
K. W. R. Fletcher lbw b Forbes	10	— c Moore b White	6
B. R. Knight c Hill b Forbes	15	— c Swetman b Taylor	7
G. R. Cass c Hill b Taylor	7	— c Taylor b Forbes	10
B. Edmeades c Parkin b Taylor	8	— c and b White	0
E. R. Presland c Swetman b Forbes	1	— c Whittingham b Forbes	3
R. N. S. Hobbs not out	0	— b Forbes	1
A. M. Jorden b Taylor	1	— b Davison	6
R. East run out	1	— not out	0
L-b 2, n-b 3	5	L-b 8, n-b 1	9
1/22 2/35 3/70 4/108 5/121 6/130 7/135 8/135 9/137	138	1/44 2/90 3/101 4/123 5/123 6/124 7/129 8/131 9/144	145

Bowling: *First Innings*—Davison 11—1—42—1: Johnson 10—4—16—1; Forbes 19—6—39—4; Taylor 19—4—36—3. *Second Innings*—Davison 6.5—0—24—1; Johnson 7—0—35—0; Forbes 22—6—33—5; Taylor 6—4—5—2; White 13—4—39—2.

Nottinghamshire

*N. Hill retired hurt	4	— absent hurt	0
J. B. Bolus c Taylor b Jorden	5	— c Presland b Edmeades	23
B. Whittingham b Edmeades	19	— b Hobbs	22
I. Moore not out	41	— c Fletcher b Edmeades	5
R. A. White lbw b Edmeades	2	— b Edmeades	14
†R. Swetman b Jorden	4	— c Presland b Edmeades	3
J. M. Parkin c Fletcher b Jorden	0	— c Taylor b Hobbs	3
M. Taylor b Knight	7	— c Barker b Knight	13
C. Forbes c Barker b Knight	10	— c Hobbs b Knight	17
A. Johnson c Hobbs b Knight	4	— st Taylor b Hobbs	6
I. Davison lbw b Knight	3	— not out	12
L-b 2, n-b 1	3	L-b 4, n-b 3	7
1/19 2/31 3/35 4/45 5/45 6/59 7/76 8/86	102	1/43 2/49 3/55 4/58 5/76 6/77 7/84 8/106	125

Bowling: *First Innings*—Jorden 16—2—28—3; Edmeades 12—1—32—2; Hobbs 6—1—12—0; Knight 9.4—0—27—4. *Second Innings*—Jorden 12—3—35—0; Edmeades 11—4—20—4; Hobbs 14—7—22—3; Knight 10.4—3—30—2; East 4—0—11—0.

Umpires: P. A. Gibb and P. B. Wight.

At Oxford, June 4, 6, 7. ESSEX beat OXFORD UNIVERSITY by 162 runs.

ESSEX v. SUSSEX

At Brentwood, June 8, 9, 10. *65 overs.* Sussex won by 64 runs on a pitch which always helped bowlers. They began by losing half the side for 71, but Oakman (eleven 4's), batting skilfully for two and a half hours, effected a recovery, he and Griffith adding 50. The first five Essex wickets fell for 49, all to Buss, and though Barker batted pluckily and Bailey and Edmeades put on 50, Sussex gained a lead of 84. This time Suttle and Lenham began with a stand of 62, but thanks mainly to Edmeades and Hobbs, the innings ended for another 104. Barker and Bear hit off 53 of the 251 Essex needed for victory, but apart from Taylor and a partnership of 42 by Smith and Edmeades, later resistance was negligible.

Sussex

K. G. Suttle b Edmeades	23	— b Knight	40
L. J. Lenham c Jorden b Knight	1	— c Taylor b East	29
*Nawab of Pataudi b Jorden	0	— c Bailey b Edmeades	28
†J. M. Parks c Taylor b Jorden	11	— b Hobbs	12
M. G. Griffith b Jorden	36	— c Bailey b Hobbs	11
D. J. Foreman c Knight b Edmeades	10	— lbw b Edmeades	1
A. S. M. Oakman not out	86	— c Taylor b Edmeades	0
P. J. Graves c Barker b Knight	11	— b Edmeades	12
A. Buss lbw b Bailey	9	— st Taylor b Hobbs	20
J. A. Snow c Bailey b Knight	0	— not out	1
D. L. Bates b Jorden	4	— c Fletcher b Hobbs	0
B 1, l-b 1	2	B 5, l-b 6, w 1	12
1/1 2/2 3/20 4/47 5/71 6/121 7/160 8/179 9/180	193	1/62 2/95 3/116 4/116 5/121 6/121 7/129 8/165 9/165	166

Bowling: *First Innings*—Knight 18—3—48—3; Jorden 14—2—50—4; Edmeades 15—2—36—2; Bailey 11—1—39—1; Hobbs 3—0—4—0; Smith 3—1—14—0. *Second Innings*—Knight 10—1—22—1; Jorden 7—0—25—0; Edmeades 11—3—28—4; Bailey 4—1—12—0; Hobbs 16.4—4—41—4; Smith 5—2—13—0; East 4—1—13—1.

Essex

G. E. Barker c Parks b Buss	30	— run out	56
M. J. Bear c Foreman b Buss	7	— lbw b Buss	16
†B. Taylor c Foreman b Buss	0	— b Buss	30
K. W. R. Fletcher c and b Buss	7	— c Lenham b Oakman	0
B. R. Knight c Foreman b Buss	2	— lbw b Snow	20
*T. E. Bailey c Oakman b Snow	24	— c Suttle b Oakman	0
G. J. Smith c Griffith b Bates	1	— c Snow b Buss	26
B. Edmeades c Graves b Oakman	28	— c and b Buss	21
R. N. S. Hobbs lbw b Snow	1	— lbw b Snow	8
A. M. Jorden lbw b Snow	0	— b Snow	4
R. East not out	7	— not out	1
B 1, l-b 1	2	B 2, w 1, n-b 1	4
1/18 2/18 3/44 4/46 5/49 6/50 7/100 8/101 9/102	109	1/53 2/58 3/59 4/92 5/107 6/125 7/167 8/180 9/180	186

Bowling: *First Innings*—Snow 13.5—4—35—3; Buss 20—2—50—5; Bates 7—1—21—1; Oakman 1—1—0—1; Foreman 1—0—1—0. *Second Innings*—Snow 15.2—4—48—3; Buss 22—5—71—4; Oakman 15—4—46—2; Suttle 1—0—3—0; Bates 3—0—6—0; Graves 2—0—8—0.

Umpires: J. Arnold and L. H. Gray.

ESSEX v. CAMBRIDGE UNIVERSITY

At Brentwood, June 11, 13, 14. Essex won by 188 runs a match rendered notable by the performance of Boyce who, on his debut for the county, took nine wickets for 61 runs in the University first innings. His pace proved too much for all but the experienced Murray. Taylor hit eight boundaries in 33; Cass (one 6, eleven 4's) and Bailey put on 101 and Hobbs enlivened the later stages of the county first innings with free scoring. Though leading by 157, Essex did not enforce the follow-on and hard driving by Bear (one 6, ten 4's) and Taylor (ten 4's) led to a declaration which left Cambridge to get 396 to win. Six men were out for 62, but Palfreman followed good bowling with an excellent innings and he and Cottrell delayed the end with a stand of 110.

Essex

First innings		Second innings	
M. J. Bear c Acfield b Palfreman	13	c Murray b Palfreman	79
G. J. Saville c Murray b Palfreman	23	c Cosh b Palfreman	15
*B. Taylor b Cottrell	33	c Palfreman b Acfield	59
K. W. R. Fletcher c Malalasekera b Acfield	37	c Murray b Roopnaraine	8
G. R. Cass c Malalasekera b. Acfield	65	not out	39
K. D. Boyce c Murray b Cottrell	0	c Chambers b Palfreman	6
*T. E. Bailey c Chambers b Acfield	39		
B. Edmeades c Chambers b Acfield	18	c Russell b Palfreman	10
R. N. S. Hobbs c Chambers b Acfield	40	c Hays b Palfreman	21
A. M. Jorden not out	7		
R. East lbw b Acfield	0		
B 5, l-b 1, w 1, n-b 2	9	N-b 1	1
1/19 2/50 3/86 4/117 5/117 6/218 7/223 8/246 9/284	284	1/40 2/60 3/88 4/168 5/172 6/183 7/238 (7 wkts., dec.)	238

Bowling: *First Innings*—Russell 21—4—77—0; Palfreman 15—3—53—2; Cottrell 11—6—29—2; Acfield 29.3—14—69—6; Roopnaraine 19—8—47—0. *Second Innings*—Russell 5—0—28—0; Palfreman 26.1—7—63—5; Roopnaraine 12—2—50—1; Acfield 24—4—68—1; Cottrell 4—1—28—0.

Cambridge University

First innings		Second innings	
K. P. W. J. McAdam c Bailey b Boyce	15	c East b Boyce	22
R. E. J. Chambers b Boyce	18	c Cass b Boyce	10
D. L. Hays b Boyce	6	c Taylor b Hobbs	7
V. P. Malalasekera c Fletcher b Boyce	4	b Hobbs	2
*†D. L. Murray not out	58	b Boyce	12
N. J. Cosh b Boyce	4	c Taylor b Boyce	0
G. A. Cottrell c Fletcher b Boyce	6	c Edmeades b East	44
A. B. Palfreman b Edmeades	1	lbw b East	67
R. Roopnaraine c Taylor b Boyce	9	c Cass b Hobbs	20
D. L. Acfield b Boyce	0	not out	3
S. G. Russell b Boyce	5	st Taylor b Hobbs	11
L-b 1	1	L-b 1, n-b 8	9
1/33 2/34 3/40 4/45 5/55 6/81 7/90 8/121 9/121	127	1/29 2/38 3/44 4/45 5/53 6/62 7/172 8/179 9/195	207

Bowling: *First Innings*—Jorden 7—0—34—0; Boyce 18.5—4—61—9; Hobbs 6—1—13—0; Edmeades 6—1—18—1. *Second Innings*—Jorden 4—1—23—0; Boyce 18—1—47—4; Hobbs 18.2—2—71—4; East 20—7—57—2.

Umpires: J. Arnold and T. W. Spencer.

At Dartford, June **15, 16, 17. ESSEX beat KENT by four runs.**

At Peterborough, June 18, 20, 21. ESSEX lost to NORTHAMPTONSHIRE by six wickets.

At Worcester, June 22. ESSEX lost to WORCESTERSHIRE by 82 runs. (See GILLETTE CUP.)

At Southend, June 25, 27, 28. ESSEX drew with WEST INDIES. (See WEST INDIES section.)

ESSEX v. SURREY

At Southend, June 29, 30, July 1. *65 overs.* Drawn after a remarkably even contest. Cass took the batting honours in the Essex first innings and Stewart in that of Surrey who, despite good bowling by Edmeades, gained a lead of three runs. At the second attempt Essex lost four men for 87, but Fletcher, restrained for four hours ten minutes, hit ten 4's and effected a recovery. Cass and Saville helped him in stands of 56 and 88. Surrey needed 298 in four and three-quarter hours and, as the wearing pitch did not afford bowlers the help expected, Edrich and Edwards scored 119 before the first wicket fell. Storey hit 60 in just over an hour, leaving 86 required in seventy minutes, but two men were foolishly run out and in the end Surrey were satisfied to play out time.

Essex

G. E. Barker c Long b Jefferson	0	— c Long b Harman	34
M. J. Bear c Roope b Storey	20	— c Stewart b Jefferson	0
†B. Taylor b Storey	33	— b Storey	19
K. W. R. Fletcher c Harman b Roope	10	— b Pocock	91
*T. E. Bailey c Storey b Pocock	16	— c Roope b Harman	11
G. R. Cass run out	53	— c Edwards b Jefferson	38
R. N. S. Hobbs b Storey	0	— not out	19
G. J. Saville not out	15	— b Pocock	44
B. Edmeades not out	9	— c Edrich b Pocock	22
A. M. Jorden (did not bat)		— not out	5
B 2, l-b 9	11	B 13, l-b 4	17
1/0 2/53 3/62 4/68 5/117 6/124 7/148 (7 wkts., 65 overs)	167	1/6 2/35 3/67 4/87 5/143 6/231 7/267 8/287 (8 wkts., dec.)	300

R. East did not bat.

Bowling: *First Innings*—Jefferson 8—0—28—1; Roope 19—4—45—1; Storey 27—8—55—3; Pocock 11—4—28—1. *Second Innings*—Storey 32—8—73—1; Jefferson 22—6—57—2; Roope 11—4—25—0; Harman 22—3—71—2; Pocock 36—16—55—3; Edwards 2—1—2—0.

Surrey

J. H. Edrich c Taylor b Jorden	35	— c Barker b Jorden	61
M. J. Edwards b Edmeades	37	— c and b Hobbs	65
W. A. Smith lbw b Edmeades	0	— c Taylor b Edmeades	13
I. Finlay b Edmeades	1	— not out	5
S. J. Storey c Cass b Bailey	15	— c Taylor b Bailey	60
*M. J. Stewart not out	65	— not out	40
P. I. Pocock lbw b Edmeades	1	— run out	3
R. I. Jefferson c East b Jorden	0	— c Barker b Edmeades	10
G. R. J. Roope lbw b Bailey	13	— run out	0
†A. Long not out	1		
L-b 1, n-b 1	2	L-b 3	3
1/69 2/70 3/72 4/79 5/105 6/107 7/118 8/169 (8 wkts., 65 overs)	170	1/119 2/131 3/150 4/212 5/223 6/234 7/238 (7 wkts.)	260

R. Harman did not bat.

Bowling: *First Innings*—Jorden 20—4—46—2; Bailey 15—3—33—2; Edmeades 24—3—72—4; Hobbs 6—2—17—0. *Second Innings*—Jorden 9—1—34—1; Bailey 25—5—44—1; Edmeades 22—7—69—2; Hobbs 25.4—6—73—1; East 14—1—34—0; Fletcher 2—0—3—0.

Umpires: J. F. Crapp and C. G. Pepper.

At Hove, July 2, 4. ESSEX beat SUSSEX by ten wickets.

At Bradford, July 6, 7, 8. ESSEX lost to YORKSHIRE by 139 runs.

ESSEX v. WARWICKSHIRE

At Westcliffe, July 9, 11, 12. Essex won by four wickets with fifteen minutes to spare after being set to get 249 in four hours. Good batting by Abberley, M. J. K. Smith (ten 4's) and Cartwright assured a good Warwickshire total on Saturday. Thanks to the left-handers, Bear and Taylor, Essex began well, but finished 88 behind despite plucky play by Saville. Warwickshire appeared safe in declaring on the last day, but Barker and Bear hit 80 in fifty minutes for the opening stand and runs continued to come freely. Fletcher (nine 4's) brought victory within sight and a capital innings from Cass completed the task.

Warwickshire

R. W. Barber c Fletcher b Hobbs	25	— c Hobbs b Edmeades	41
R. N. Abberley lbw b Edmeades	54	— not out	9
D. L. Amiss c Fletcher b Hobbs	25	— c Fletcher b Hobbs	8
*M. J. K. Smith run out	73	— c and b Edmeades	28
J. A. Jameson c Taylor b Hobbs	1	— not out	10
K. Ibadulla lbw b Bailey	48	— c Saville b Hobbs	47
T. W. Cartwright b Edmeades	51		
†A. C. Smith lbw b Edmeades	21		
R. Miller not out	4		
R. V. Webster c Taylor b Edmeades	9		
J. D. Bannister b Jorden	1		
B 5, l-b 2, w 1, n-b 1	9	B 5, l-b 1, n-b 1	7
1/43 2/83 3/145 4/152 5/217 6/244 7/293 8/308 9/321	321	1/62 2/81 3/124 4/131 (4 wkts., dec.)	150

Bowling: *First Innings*—Jorden 12.2—1—47—1; Bailey 17—0—42—1; Edmeades 25—6—62—4; Hobbs 34—6—103—3; East 16—3—58—0. *Second Innings*—Jorden 4—0—18—0; Edmeades 20—5—47—2; Hobbs 21—4—43—2; East 6—0—35—0.

Essex

G. E. Barker b Webster	5	— lbw b Miller	46
M. J. Bear c M. J. K. Smith b Barber	44	— b Miller	39
†B. Taylor c Miller b Barber	41	— c A. C. Smith b Cartwright	22
K. W. R. Fletcher b Miller	0	— c Cartwright b Bannister	52
*T. E. Bailey c A. C. Smith b Cartwright	26	— c Jameson b Miller	23
G. R. Cass c Ibadulla b Miller	24	— not out	41
G. J. Saville not out	48	— c Barber b Bannister	6
B. Edmeades c Cartwright b Bannister	12	— not out	9
R. N. S. Hobbs b Webster	3		
A. M. Jorden c Amiss b Webster	3		
R. East c Ibadulla b Barber	8		
L-b 8, n-b 1	9	B 5, l-b 6	11
1/9 2/72 3/79 4/99 5/138 6/152 7/187 8/192 9/198	223	1/80 2/85 3/111 4/169 5/199 6/223 (6 wkts.)	249

Bowling: *First Innings*—Bannister 14—6—16—1; Webster 20—4—62—3; Cartwright 17—8—28—1; Barber 26.2—4—66—3; Miller 27—10—42—2. *Second Innings*—Bannister 25—6—51—2; Webster 3—0—14—0; Miller 17—2—69—3; Barber 13—1—56—0; Cartwright 16.1—5—48—1.

Umpires: J. S. Buller and W. F. Price.

ESSEX v. KENT

At Westcliff, July 13, 14. Kent won by eight wickets. So pronounced was the mastery of the bowlers on a pitch dusty from the start that 32 wickets fell for an aggregate of 292 runs and the match ended before lunch on the second day. Underwood in the second Essex innings proved so effective with left-arm deliveries of medium pace that in 20 overs he dismissed nine batsmen at a cost of 37 runs—the best analysis of the season—bringing his match-record to 13 wickets for 57 runs. Leary, whose bold methods brought Kent a lead of 42, and Barker, defending stoutly during the whole of the two hours ten minutes the Essex second innings lasted were the only batsmen to achieve anything of note.

Essex

*G. E. Barker b Dixon	15	— not out	36
M. J. Bear c Knott b Dye	2	— b Underwood	2
G. J. Saville c Cowdrey b Sayer	0	— c Leary b Underwood	0
K. W. R. Fletcher c Cowdrey b Sayer	4	— st Knott b Underwood	12
†B. Taylor b Underwood	7	— b Underwood	0
G. R. Cass c Prodger b Underwood	10	— c Ealham b Underwood	0
B. Edmeades c Cowdrey b Underwood	19	— c Luckhurst b Underwood	7
R. N. S. Hobbs c Luckhurst b Underwood	0	— c Knott b Underwood	6
A. M. Jorden c Leary b Dixon	1	— c Cowdrey b Underwood	7
R. East b Dixon	2	— b Dixon	6
D. L. Acfield not out	0	— c Luckhurst b Underwood	0
B 4	4	L-b 4	4
1/4 2/11 3/17 4/32 5/32 6/61 7/61 8/62 9/64	64	1/10 2/10 3/24 4/24 5/26 6/38 7/52 8/70 9/79	80

Bowling: *First Innings*—Sayer 9—2—14—2; Dye 9—4—9—1; Underwood 11.3—5—20—4; Dixon 6—1—17—3. *Second Innings*—Sayer 3—0—6—0; Dye 2—1—4—0; Underwood 20—5—37—9; Dixon 19—3—29—1.

Kent

M. H. Denness lbw b Edmeades	4	— not out	18
B. W. Luckhurst c Hobbs b Edmeades	3	— c Fletcher b Jorden	10
J. M. Prodger c Taylor b Jorden	0		
*M. C. Cowdrey c Hobbs b Edmeades	7		
S. E. Leary c Taylor b Edmeades	35	— not out	6
A. Ealham c Fletcher b Edmeades	8		
†A. Knott b Jorden	11		
A. L. Dixon st Taylor b East	14	— b Jorden	6
D. L. Underwood b Jorden	5		
D. M. Sayer b Jorden	12		
J. C. Dye not out	4		
B 2, l-b 1	3	B 1, l-b 1	2
1/7 2/8 3/8 4/29 5/48 6/63 7/83 8/88 9/89	106	1/16 2/30 (2 wkts.)	42

Bowling: *First Innings*—Jorden 13.2—3—34—4; Edmeades 15—4—58—5; Hobbs 2—0—10—0; East 1—0—1—1. *Second Innings*—Jorden 7.1—0—20—2; Edmeades 3—0—8—0; East 5—0—12—0.

Umpires: J. S. Buller and W. F. Price.

At Lord's, July 16, 18, 19. ESSEX drew with MIDDLESEX.

ESSEX v. DERBYSHIRE

At Colchester, July 20, 21, 22. Drawn. Rain prevented cricket on the first two days and rendered the Castle Park ground unplayable. So the venue for the last day was switched to the Garrison ground and though seventeen wickets fell for 246 runs, not even a first-innings decision could be reached. Apart from Harvey, who hit only one 4 in a stay of two and a half hours, the Derbyshire batsmen failed against an attack in which Edmeades and Hobbs did best. Left two hours' batting, Essex lost four men for 51. Bear and Cass added 33 inside twenty minutes, but when the seventh wicket fell at 92, Bailey and Edmeades turned to defence.

Derbyshire

I. W. Hall b Edmeades	18	T. J. P. Eyre c and b Edmeades	1
J. F. Harvey c Barker b Edmeades	58	E. Smith c Bailey b Edmeades	0
M. H. Page c Hobbs b Acfield	22	A. B. Jackson not out	0
H. L. Johnson run out	13		
M. Hill b Knight	0	B 1, l-b 5, n-b 1	7
I. R. Buxton c Edmeades b Hobbs	6		
*D. C. Morgan st Taylor b Hobbs	12	1/34 2/82 3/101 4/104 5/123	147
†R. W. Taylor c Taylor b Hobbs	10	6/124 7/138 8/141 9/141	

Bowling: Jorden 9—2—20—0; Knight 16—3—32—1; Edmeades 15—3—34—4; Acfield 10—0—35—1; Hobbs 8.4—0—19—3.

Essex

G. E. Barker b Jackson	7	*T. E. Bailey not out	0
M. J. Bear c and b Morgan	40	B. Edmeades not out	6
†B. Taylor c Page b Jackson	2		
K. W. R. Fletcher lbw b Smith	3	B 1	1
B. R. Knight c Hall b Morgan	19		
G. R. Cass b Smith	17	1/12 2/24 3/32 4/51	(7 wkts.) 99
R. N. S. Hobbs lbw b Morgan	4	5/84 6/92 7/92	

A. M. Jorden and D. L. Acfield did not bat.

Bowling: Jackson 9—3—17—2; Eyre 3—0—7—0; Smith 18—9—35—2; Morgan 14—6—39—3; Buxton 1—1—0—0.

Umpires: W. E. Phillipson and W. H. Copson.

ESSEX v. LANCASHIRE

At Colchester, July 23, 25, 26. Drawn. Following the fall of three Lancashire wickets for 36, Wood, making his first appearance for the county, joined Worsley in a partnership of 92 and Lever (eleven 4's), hitting the highest score of his career, completed the recovery in a seventh-wicket stand of 80 with Higgs. Essex displayed little batting enterprise. Even Taylor was subdued and Fletcher, occupying an hour over his first four runs, altogether spent four hours twenty minutes at the crease. All this was profitless, for though Cass did a little hitting, Higgs finished off the innings with Essex 12 behind. Pullar, slow and forceful in turn, did most to lead to a declaration which left Essex to get 184 in two hours ten minutes. Taylor hit strongly, but any chance of a definite result was ruined by torrential rain.

Lancashire

D. M. Green lbw b Knight	10	— b Knight	0
G. Pullar b Hobbs	19	— c Taylor b Acfield	71
J. D. Bond b Knight	0	— c Acfield b Jorden	37
D. R. Worsley c Hobbs b Jorden	60	— not out	39
B. Wood b Acfield	39	— b Acfield	7
J. Sullivan c Knight b Hobbs	12	— not out	8
P. Lever c Hobbs b Edmeades	83		
K. Higgs b Edmeades	9		
†K. Goodwin b Bailey	6		
T. Greenhough b Bailey	8		
*J. B. Statham not out	11		
B 3, l-b 8, w 4	15	B 6, l-b 1, n-b 2	9
1/21 2/21 3/36 4/128 5/140 6/166 7/246 8/247 9/253	272	1/0 2/85 3/122 4/147 (4 wkts., dec.)	171

Bowling: *First Innings*—Jorden 15—4—48—1; Knight 22—7—42—2; Acfield 19—9—27—1; Edmeades 18—4—60—2; Hobbs 19—7—52—2; Bailey 10.3—3—28—2. *Second Innings*—Knight 9—1—38—1; Jorden 22—3—46—1; Hobbs 12—4—23—0; Bailey 11—4—13—0; Acfield 16—7—42—2.

Essex

G. E. Barker lbw b Higgs	27	— not out	36
M. J. Bear lbw b Higgs	18	— b Lever	2
†B. Taylor c Sullivan b Statham	48	— c Statham b Lever	41
K. W. R. Fletcher b Statham	68	— not out	26
*T. E. Bailey b Statham	1		
B. R. Knight c Goodwin b Greenhough	10		
G. R. Cass b Higgs	48		
B. Edmeades b Higgs	2		
R. N. S. Hobbs b Higgs	2		
A. M. Jorden b Higgs	15		
D. L. Acfield not out	4		
B 4, l-b 7, n-b 6	17	L-b 10, n-b 1	11
1/41 2/64 3/117 4/121 5/138 6/230 7/236 8/240 9/241	260	1/6 2/71 (2 wkts.)	116

Bowling: *First Innings*—Statham 30—4—96—3; Higgs 27.3—6—58—6; Greenhough 32—13—42—1; Lever 19—5—47—0; Worsley 1—1—0—0. *Second Innings*—Higgs 11—2—26—0; Lever 9—0—43—2; Worsley 4—0—21—0; Green 4—0—15—0.

Umpires: W. E. Phillipson and W. H. Copson.

At Swansea, July 27, 28, 29. ESSEX drew with GLAMORGAN.

At The Oval, July 30, August 1, 2. ESSEX lost to SURREY by seven wickets.

ESSEX v. GLAMORGAN

At Leyton, August 3, 4, 5. Drawn. A pitch affected by rain told against batsmen during the first two days, each of which was shortened by rain. In the first Glamorgan innings only A. R. Lewis and Walker, adding 75 in two and a quarter hours, offered much resistance to Edmeades, whose analysis of seven wickets for 37 runs was the best of his career. Essex fared even worse against the off-spin of Shepherd and the pace of Wheatley and they finished 63 behind on the first innings. Walker and A. R. Lewis sharing a stand of 51, Glamorgan were able to declare and leave Essex to get 183 to win in three hours. While Bear and Fletcher stayed, a chance existed that Essex might achieve the feat, but the effort to score quickly cost wickets and in the end they were glad to play out time.

Glamorgan

A. Jones c Bear b Edmeades	10	— b Bailey	7
B. Hedges c Jorden b Edmeades	5	— c Taylor b Acfield	18
P. M. Walker c Saville b Edmeades	48	— not out	53
A. R. Lewis c Fletcher b Acfield	37	— c Cass b Bailey	25
A. Rees b Acfield	8	— c Cass b Bailey	0
R. Davis b Edmeades	0	— not out	9
†D. L. Evans b Acfield	7		
E. Lewis c Barker b Edmeades	3		
*O. S. Wheatley not out	5		
I. J. Jones c Taylor b Edmeades	0		
D. J. Shepherd b Edmeades	3		
B 1, l-b 10	11	B 5, n-b 2	7
1/14 2/23 3/98 4/109 5/109 6/118 7/127 8/131 9/133	137	1/10 2/33 3/84 4/84 (4 wkts., dec.)	119

Bowling: *First Innings*—Jorden 10—2—26—0; Bailey 12—3—19—0; Edmeades 29.2—11—37—7; Acfield 28—14—26—3; Hobbs 9—3—18—0. *Second Innings*—Edmeades 8—6—27—0; Bailey 20—9—46—3; Acfield 7—1—25—1; Hobbs 4—2—3—0; Jorden 2—0—11—0.

Essex

G. E. Barker c Walker b Shepherd	7	— c Rees b Shepherd	12
M. J. Bear c Walker b Shepherd	16	— b I. J. Jones	45
†B. Taylor c Rees b Shepherd	5	— lbw b Wheatley	5
K. W. R. Fletcher c sub b Wheatley	9	— c A. Jones b Shepherd	29
*T. E. Bailey c Evans b Wheatley	3	— b Wheatley	31
G. R. Cass c Walker b Wheatley	3	— not out	25
G. J. Saville lbw b Wheatley	0	— not out	0
B. Edmeades c Evans b Wheatley	1	— c and b Shepherd	0
R. N. S. Hobbs c Walker b Shepherd	7	— b Wheatley	2
A. M. Jorden b Wheatley	12	— c Rees b Shepherd	0
D. L. Acfield not out	0		
B 9, l-b 2	11	B 3, l-b 3, n-b 3	9
1/21 2/31 3/32 4/47 5/48 6/51 7/55 8/62 9/72	74	1/26 2/52 3/79 4/103 5/150 6/151 7/154 8/157 (8 wkts.)	158

Bowling: *First Innings*—I. J. Jones 4—0—12—0; Wheatley 19.3—7—27—6; Shepherd 19—8—24—4. *Second Innings*—I. J. Jones 16—3—42—1; Wheatley 19—6—32—3; Shepherd 22—10—37—4; E. Lewis 6—1—28—0; Davis 2—0—10—0.

Umpires: F. Jakeman and A. E. Fagg.

ESSEX v. YORKSHIRE

At Leyton, August 6, 8, 9. Drawn. Essex began well, a stand by Barker and Bear, which yielded 98 before rain ended the opening day's play, altogether realising 118. Then the pitch developed difficulties as it dried and Wilson bowled so effectively, with great support in the field from Close, that the innings ended for another 69. Though Sharpe and Taylor hit 33 together, Yorkshire struggled for the remainder of the day. Next morning, bold batting by Wilson and Binks saw 43 runs added in half an hour, but the innings closed six runs behind. Again Essex found runs difficult to get, but declared, leaving Yorkshire 156 to win. Four wickets fell for 45, but Close and Illingsworth put on 85, taking their side to within 26 of success when rain intervened fifteen minutes from time.

Essex

G. E. Barker c Sharpe b Trueman	62	— b Trueman	0
M. J. Bear c Illingworth b Nicholson	54	— lbw b Illingworth	38
†B. Taylor c Old b Wilson	30	— c and b Illingworth	24
K. W. R. Fletcher b Trueman	1	— c Sharpe b Wilson	1
*T. E. Bailey not out	18	— b Close	23
B. R. Knight c Close b Wilson	0	— c Wilson b Illingworth	11
G. R. Cass c Close b Wilson	0	— b Close	21
B. Edmeades c Close b Illingworth	9	— not out	8
R. N. S. Hobbs run out	4	— c Old b Close	7
A. M. Jorden c Taylor b Wilson	0	— lbw b Wilson	0
D. L. Acfield c Close b Wilson	0	— not out	0
B 2, l-b 3, n-b 4	9	B 10, l-b 6	16
1/118 2/118 3/121 4/161 5/161 6/161 7/178 8/186 9/187	187	1/0 2/48 3/49 4/73 5/86 6/118 7/135 8/143 9/145 (9 wkts., dec.)	149

Bowling: *First Innings*—Trueman 16—6—26—2; Nicholson 22—5—41—1; Close 10—3—25—0; Wilson 19.5—6—59—5; Illingworth 18—7—27—1. *Second Innings*—Trueman 3—1—12—1; Nicholson 4—1—12—0; Wilson 17—6—41—2; Illingworth 24.1—8—46—3; Close 15—8—22—3.

Yorkshire

K. Taylor c Barker b Acfield	29	— c Hobbs b Knight	2
P. J. Sharpe c Bailey b Knight	15	— c Hobbs b Edmeades	1
D. E. V. Padgett c Fletcher b Acfield	7		
J. H. Hampshire lbw b Edmeades	11	— b Knight	17
*D. B. Close b Hobbs	18	— not out	55
R. Illingworth c Knight b Edmeades	3	— not out	32
†J. G. Binks b Knight	42		
F. S. Trueman c Knight b Hobbs	12		
D. Wilson b Knight	28	— b Knight	15
C. Old run out	0		
A. G. Nicholson not out	6		
B 6, l-b 3, n-b 1	10	L-b 8	8
1/33 2/49 3/56 4/64 5/72 6/93 7/109 8/165 9/167	181	1/2 2/15 3/23 4/45 (4 wkts.)	130

Bowling: *First Innings*—Knight 15.4—1—50—3; Edmeades 15—2—39—2; Acfield 20—6—46—2; Hobbs 6—0—36—2. *Second Innings*—Knight 9—0—45—3; Edmeades 10.4—0—56—1; Acfield 1—0—6—0; Jorden 3—0—15—0.

Umpires: A. E. Fagg and F. Jakeman.

At Nottingham, August 13, 15, 16. ESSEX drew with NOTTINGHAMSHIRE.

ESSEX v. NORTHAMPTONSHIRE

At Clacton, August 17, 18, 19. Northamptonshire won by seven wickets. The feature of the match was undoubtedly the batting of Milburn. Omitted from the England team for the final Test, he drove, hooked and hit to leg with such power that he registered four 6's and twenty-two 4's while scoring 203—the highest innings of his career—in a partnership of 293 in four hours ten minutes with Prideaux (eighteen 4's). This stand beat a forty-years-old record for the Northamptonshire first wicket. Against the off-spin of Sully, Essex rarely looked like saving the follow-on and though Bear drove strongly for eighty minutes and Fletcher brought off some hard strokes, Northamptonshire required no more than 55 to win. Despite the loss of Milburn and Prideaux without a run on the board, the result was never in doubt.

Northamptonshire

First innings		Second innings	
C. Milburn c Bear b Acfield	203	c and b Knight	0
R. M. Prideaux not out	153	c Knight b Jorden	0
B. L. Reynolds c Fletcher b Hobbs	4	c Knight b Barker	18
Mushtaq Mohammad not out	42	not out	31
D. S. Steele (did not bat)		not out	4
L-b 10, n-b 1	11	L-b 2, n-b 1	3
1/293 2/308 (2 wkts., dec.)	413	1/0 2/0 3/48 (3 wkts.)	56

P. J. Watts, B. Crump, *†K. V. Andrew, M. E. Scott, H. Sully and A. J. Durose did not bat.

Bowling: *First Innings*—Knight 25—4—69—0; Jorden 11—1—62—0; Edmeades 19—1—77—0; Hobbs 30—3—94—1; Acfield 23—3—99—1; Barker 1—0—1—0. *Second Innings*—Knight 5—2—12—1; Jorden 8—0—35—1; Hobbs 2—0—6—0; Barker 1—1—0—1.

Essex

First innings		Second innings	
G. J. Saville c Andrew b Durose	29	c Watts b Mushtaq	22
M. J. Bear c Watts b Durose	3	c Steele b Sully	65
*G. E. Barker c Milburn b Sully	34	lbw b Scott	23
K. W. R. Fletcher c Watts b Sully	24	c Watts b Scott	41
†B. Taylor lbw b Sully	43	c Steele b Scott	20
B. R. Knight c Andrew b Sully	2	c Sully b Scott	22
G. R. Cass c Watts b Sully	29	c Reynolds b Scott	4
B. Edmeades lbw b Sully	47	c Watts b Durose	8
R. N. S. Hobbs b Crump	4	b Crump	16
A. M. Jorden c Andrew b Sully	4	not out	7
D. L. Acfield not out	0	lbw b Crump	0
B 6, l-b 4, n-b 5	15	B 2, l-b 1, w 1, n-b 1	5
1/5 2/68 3/68 4/112 5/136 6/149 7/203 8/215 9/220	234	1/42 2/86 3/122 4/122 5/157 6/190 7/207 8/222 9/233	233

Bowling: *First Innings*—Crump 29—8—47—1; Durose 11—1—36—2; Watts 11—4—26—0; Sully 36—12—69—7; Mushtaq 8—2—15—0; Scott 17—6—26—0. *Second Innings*—Durose 8—2—14—1; Crump 9.4—1—28—2; Mushtaq 10—4—21—1; Scott 33—9—69—5; Sully 16—2—69—1; Steele 8—1—27—0.

Umpires: H. Yarnold and A. Jepson.

ESSEX v. LEICESTERSHIRE

At Clacton, August 20, 22, 23. Leicestershire won by four wickets. Essex began badly, losing five men for 92, but Knight drove and cut hard and he and Edmeades put on 103. Few of the Leicestershire batsmen showed to advantage against the seam bowlers and Essex led by 37. Bear and Saville started with a stand of 52 and Barker, despite a damaged hand, shared in an unfinished partnership of 172 with Fletcher. Very enterprising after a quiet start, Fletcher scored freely all round, with twelve 4's his chief hits. A declaration left Leicestershire to get 262 in three hours five minutes. Progress was slow for a long time, but Inman (one 6, ten 4's) transformed the situation by scoring 74 in forty-eight minutes and Marner drove well for an hour, so that victory was achieved with ten minutes to spare.

Essex

First Innings		Second Innings	
M. J. Bear c Hallam b Spencer	32	c Marner b Cotton	33
G. J. Saville c Tolchard b Spencer	13	c Hallam b Spencer	15
*G. E. Barker lbw b Cotton	9	not out	68
K. W. R. Fletcher b Marner	20	not out	101
†B. Taylor c Marner b Cotton	13		
B. R. Knight c Hallam b Marner	73		
B. Edmeades c Tolchard b Marner	40		
A. M. Jorden not out	29		
R. N. S. Hobbs lbw b Spencer	8		
R. East c Tolchard b Spencer	7		
D. L. Acfield c Tolchard b Cotton	1		
B 5, l-b 2, n-b 6	13	L-b 2, n-b 5	7
1/28 2/56 3/57 4/83 5/92 6/195 7/218 8/234 9/247	258	1/52 2/52 (2 wkts., dec.)	224

Bowling: *First Innings*—Spencer 18—4—39—4; Cotton 22.5—7—58—3; Marner 29—6—66—3; Lock 16—5—38—0; Savage 6—0—34—0; Birkenshaw 1—0—10—0. *Second Innings*—Spencer 24—3—66—1; Cotton 19—4—72—1; Marner 8—0—31—0; Lock 15—1—48—0.

Leicestershire

First Innings		Second Innings	
M. R. Hallam b Edmeades	32	b Knight	6
M. E. Norman c Taylor b Jorden	6	c Taylor b Jorden	26
†R. W. Tolchard c Fletcher b Knight	30		
B. J. Booth c Acfield b Jorden	24	c Fletcher b Acfield	45
C. C. Inman b Knight	1	c Knight b Acfield	74
P. Marner c Jorden b Edmeades	43	not out	63
J. Birkenshaw b Jorden	35	not out	9
*G. A. R. Lock c Taylor b Edmeades	5	c Saville b Acfield	18
J. S. Savage b Knight	16		
J. Cotton not out	23		
C. T. Spencer c Hobbs b Edmeades	1	c East b Jorden	10
L-b 2, n-b 3	5	B 4, l-b 5, n-b 2	11
1/18 2/51 3/75 4/85 5/129 6/141 7/146 8/181 9/220	221	1/18 2/58 3/148 4/175 5/205 6/246 (6 wkts.)	262

Bowling: *First Innings*—Knight 21—4—44—3; Jorden 25—2—74—3; Edmeades 26.2—1—95—4; Hobbs 3—1—3—0. *Second Innings*—Knight 7—0—25—1; Edmeades 8—0—34—0; Jorden 9.4—0—43—2; Hobbs 13—0—69—0; East 3—0—26—0; Acfield 10—1—54—3.

Umpires: H. Yarnold and A. Jepson.

At Portsmouth, August 24, 25, 26. ESSEX drew with HAMPSHIRE.

At Worcester, August 27, 29, 30. ESSEX drew with WORCESTERSHIRE.

At Taunton, August 31, September 1, 2. ESSEX lost to SOMERSET by 101 runs.

GLAMORGAN

President—J. C. Clay

Secretary—W. Wooller, 6 High Street, Cardiff

Captain—O. S. Wheatley

A. R. Lewis

County Badge

I. J. Jones

After being strong challengers for the championship the previous season Glamorgan declined in 1966, which was a big disappointment to all connected with the club and all Welsh cricket enthusiasts. With the exception of J. Pressdee, the same playing staff was available, and although there was no doubt that the absence of this outstanding all-rounder upset the balance of the side one had to search more deeply for the lack of success which resulted in Glamorgan being at the foot of the table for most of the season. True, they rallied by winning their last three games, but even this was achieved by individual brilliance rather than sound team work, and only confirmed that Glamorgan's fall from grace was due to a lack of balance.

Too many middle order batsmen failed. In match after match they were unable to build on the solid foundation laid by A. Jones and A. R. Lewis, each of whom scored his record number of runs for the season. Lewis with 2,052 just failed to beat the record aggregate of W. G. A. Parkhouse.

In addition, Wheatley and Shepherd each took more than 100 wickets, and it was indeed remarkable that with these four players figuring so high in the personal honours list Glamorgan did not do better. Walker and Rees played some good innings, but were inconsistent, though perhaps Glamorgan erred when they dropped Rees midway through the season. Not only was he one of the finest fielders in the country, but when in an attacking mood he could turn an innings, as he proved on his return to the side.

Generally Glamorgan suffered because the young batsmen they introduced did not seem to have the right temperament, even if they possessed the skill demanded of first-class status. This will be Glamorgan's big problem of the future.

Another adverse factor was the number of matches affected by bad weather. None of the six games played at Swansea produced a decisive result. Glamorgan always used to reckon on winning four or five matches a season at Swansea where Shepherd and Pressdee were so often " monarchs of all they surveyed ".

But the 1966 season marked two new milestones. For the first time Glamorgan played a home match at Colwyn Bay in North Wales and they have now played in Glamorgan, Carmarthenshire, Monmouthshire and Denbighshire. " Started to serve a county they grew to represent a nation." The last game, however, was played at Cardiff Arms Park which has been in existence as a cricket ground for over one hundred years. Now Glamorgan have moved to the adjoining Sophia Gardens.

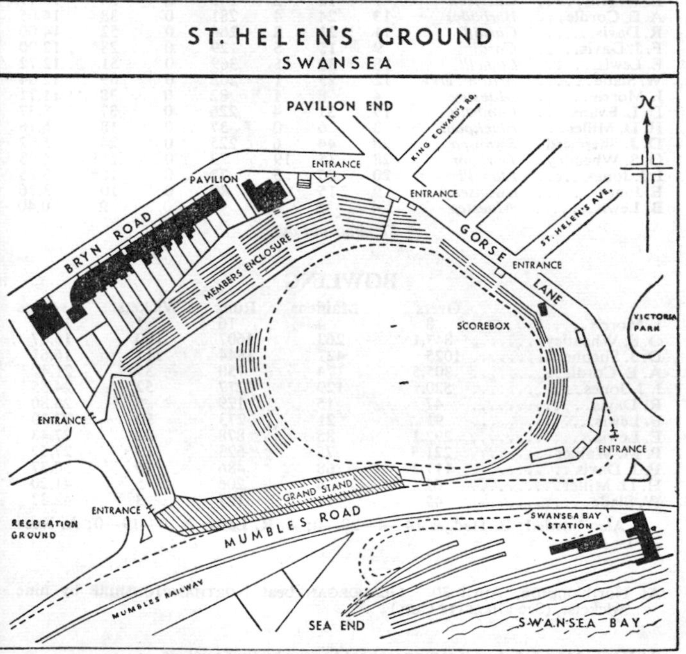

GLAMORGAN RESULTS

All First-Class Matches—Played 29, *Won* 6, *Lost* 8, *Drawn* 15.
County Championship Matches—Played 28, *Won* 6, *Lost* 8, *Drawn* 13, *No Decision* 1

COUNTY CHAMPIONSHIP AVERAGES

BATTING

	Birthplace	Mtchs.	Inns.	Not Outs	Runs	100's	Highest Inns.	Aver.
A. R. Lewis....	*Neath*	27	51	4	1960	5	223	41.70
A. Jones.......	*Swansea*	28	54	2	1626	1	104*	31.26
P. M. Walker..	*Bristol*	24	45	6	1135	0	95*	29.10
A. Rees.......	*Port Talbot*	24	45	7	863	0	65	22.71
B. Hedges.....	*Pontypridd*	20	37	2	632	0	65	18.05
L. W. Hill.....	*Caerleon*	7	11	2	142	0	34*	15.77
A. E. Cordle...	*Barbados*	13	24	4	281	0	38	14.05
R. Davis.......	*Cardiff*	11	21	2	266	0	52	14.00
F. J. Davis.....	*Cardiff*	9	15	5	129	0	28*	12.90
E. Lewis.......	*Llanelli*	18	30	1	369	0	51	12.72
W. Slade......	*Briton Ferry*	12	23	1	265	0	69	12.04
I. Morris......	*Maesteg*	4	8	1	82	0	38	11.71
D. L. Evans....	*Lambeth*	19	31	4	226	0	37	8.37
H. D. Miller...	*Blackpool*	3	6	0	37	0	18	6.16
D. J. Shepherd.	*Swansea*	28	44	6	225	0	24	5.92
O. S. Wheatley.	*Durham*	28	35	19	79	0	15*	4.93
I. J. Jones......	*Llanelli*	20	25	5	77	0	18*	3.85
E. Jones.......	*Swansea*	9	15	2	49	0	10	3.76
B. Lewis.......	*Maesteg*	4	5	0	2	0	2	0.40

* *Signifies not out.*

BOWLING

	Overs	Maidens	Runs	Wickets	Average
I. Morris............	8	4	16	1	16.00
O. S. Wheatley........	847.1	263	1607	100	16.07
D. J. Shepherd........	1025	427	1844	111	16.61
A. E. Cordle..........	305.5	74	750	35	21.42
I. J. Jones............	520.1	129	1277	52	24.55
R. Davis.............	47	15	129	5	25.80
B. Lewis.............	91	21	273	10	27.30
E. Lewis.............	292.1	85	878	32	27.43
P. M. Walker.........	221.5	75	523	19	27.52
F. J. Davis	117.3	68	486	16	30.37
H. D. Miller..........	62	8	206	5	41.20
W. Slade.............	45	11	127	3	42.33

Also bowled: B. Hedges 14—4—28—0; A. R. Lewis 2—0—19—0; A. Rees 2—1—4—0.

At Northampton, April 30. GLAMORGAN beat NORTHAMPTONSHIRE by nine wickets. (See GILLETTE CUP.)

At Hove, May 4, 5, 6. GLAMORGAN beat SUSSEX by four wickets.

GLAMORGAN v. WORCESTERSHIRE

At Pontypridd, May 7, 9, 10. Worcestershire won by six wickets. A rain-affected wicket posed a problem for both sides, but no one exploited it more than Gifford, who was Worcestershire's match winner. In the Glamorgan first innings he caused a collapse after lunch when six wickets fell for 22 runs, Gifford's share being four for 8. Worcestershire were also worried by the spin of Shepherd and E. Lewis, and despite stubborn batting by Headley, who took two hours over 29 runs, they finished four behind on the first innings. The spinners continued to hold the mastery and in their second innings Glamorgan were dismissed for 111, the only redeeming feature being the improved batting of E. Lewis, who scored 50 out of 75 in just under two hours. Needing only 116 to win, Worcestershire did not allow any crisis to develop because of the steady batting of Kenyon and Graveney, who brought their experience to bear in the closing stages.

Glamorgan

A. Jones c d'Oliveira b Flavell	13	— c Booth b Flavell	0
B. Hedges c Headley b Slade	31	— b Flavell	15
P. M. Walker b Coldwell	4	— c Graveney b Flavell	0
A. R. Lewis b Gifford	49	— b Flavell	14
E. Lewis c Booth b Gifford	10	— b Coldwell	51
A. Rees c Booth b Gifford	2	— b Gifford	0
F. J. Davis not out	5	— b d'Oliveira	8
†D. L. Evans b Gifford	3	— b Gifford	8
D. J. Shepherd c Flavell b Slade	5	— c Graveney b Gifford	1
I. J. Jones b Gifford	0	— st Booth b Gifford	3
*O. S. Wheatley c Headley b Gifford	1	— not out	5
B 4, l-b 1, n-b 1	6	L-b 6	6
1/32 2/38 3/86 4/107 5/113 6/114 7/120 8/125 9/125	129	1/0 2/0 3/19 4/46 5/47 6/94 7/94 8/97 9/102	111

Bowling: *First Innings*—Flavell 5—2—23—1; Coldwell 6—1—22—1; Gifford 21.3—9—31—6; Slade 26—12—32—2; d'Oliveira 7—2—15—0. *Second Innings*—Flavell 15—2—32—4; Coldwell 12—3—22—1; Gifford 19.2—9—36—4; Slade 3—0—8—0; d'Oliveira 3—1—7—1.

Worcestershire

*D. Kenyon b Wheatley	1	— lbw b Wheatley	46
R. G. A. Headley c Walker b E. Lewis	29	— c Walker b Wheatley	5
A. Ormrod c Evans b I. J. Jones	30	— lbw b Davis	28
T. W. Graveney c Walker b E. Lewis	2	— not out	30
B. d'Oliveira c Walker b E. Lewis	22	— not out	5
D. W. Richardson c A. Jones b Wheatley	15		
†R. Booth c Hedges b Shepherd	22		
D. N. F. Slade c Davis b Shepherd	1	— c Davis b I. J. Jones	3
N. Gifford c Davis b Wheatley	2		
L. J. Coldwell b Shepherd	1		
J. A. Flavell not out	0		
		L-b	1
1/9 2/42 3/44 4/76 5/98 6/100 7/111 8/124 9/125	125	1/8 2/8 3/73 4/104 (4 wkts.)	118

Bowling: *First Innings*—I. J. Jones 16—5—20—1; Wheatley 20.3—7—21—3; Shepherd 22—10—31—3; E. Lewis 24—9—48—3; Davis 7—5—5—0. *Second Innings*—I. J. Jones 13—2—31—1. Wheatley 11—3—28—2; Shepherd 9—2—16—0; E. Lewis 10.5—3—28—0; Davis 8—4—14—1.

Umpires: C. S. Elliott and H. Mellows.

At Lord's, May 11, 12, 13. GLAMORGAN drew with MIDDLESEX.

At The Oval, May 14, 16, 17. GLAMORGAN drew with SURREY.

At Gravesend, May 18, 19, 20. GLAMORGAN drew with KENT.

GLAMORGAN v. WARWICKSHIRE

At Swansea, May 25, 26, 27. *65 overs.* Drawn. After a lot of good cricket the finish of this match was in the nature of an anti-climax, as Warwickshire refused to take up the challenge of scoring 201 to win in two and a half hours. M. J. K. Smith said afterwards that he did not think a win was possible because of the bad start they made to their second innings. Smith himself and Jameson gave Warwickshire a chance by their bold batting in a fourth-wicket partnership which added 59 in twenty-five minutes, but when they were separated all the adventure went out of the game. Earlier Glamorgan had seized the initiative. In their 65 overs they scored 230 for four, with Alan Jones being the pace maker. His opening partnership with Hedges realised 134 runs in just under two hours and gave Glamorgan a flying start. M. J. K. Smith was Warickshire's most successful batsman. He made 50 out of 66 in fifty-three minutes, but Warwickshire could score only 187 for nine in their 65 overs, which gave Glamorgan a first-innings lead of 43 runs.

Glamorgan

B. Hedges c M. J. K. Smith b Miller	65	— b Webster	1
A. Jones c A. C. Smith b Brown	79	— c A. C. Smith b Bannister	29
W. Slade c Ibadulla b Allan	0	— c Abberley b Webster	8
A. R. Lewis not out	40	— not out	56
A. Rees c Webster b Miller	35	— c Bannister b Miller	21
D. J. Shepherd not out	4		
B. Lewis (did not bat)		— c M. J. K. Smith b Allan	0
†D. L. Evans (did not bat)		— lbw b Allan	0
D. J. Shepherd (did not bat)		— c and b Miller	14
F. J. Davis (did not bat)		— not out	23
B 5, l-b 2	7	B 5	5
1/134 2/135 3/150 4/219 (4 wkts., 65 overs)	230	1/7 2/21 3/41 4/85 5/86 6/86 7/103 (7 wkts. dec.)	157

*O. S. Wheatley did not bat.

Bowling: *First Innings*—Brown 8—0—27—1; Webster 7—1—27—0; Bannister 11—3—35—0; Allan 17—4—55—1; Miller 22—7—79—2. *Second Innings*—Brown 8—0—21—0; Webster 8—2—12—2; Miller 15—2—53—2; Bannister 8—3—12—1; Allan 9—0—46—2; Ibadulla 2—0—8—0.

Warwickshire

K. Ibadulla c Rees b Davis	36	— run out	28
R. N. Abberley b Wheatley	5	— b B. Lewis	20
D. L. Amiss c A. Jones b Davis	34	— c A. R. Lewis b Shepherd	18
*M. J. K. Smith hit wkt. b Shepherd	53	— c I. J. Jones b Davis	38
J. A. Jameson c Rees b Shepherd	16	— not out	45
†A. C. Smith c Wheatley b Shepherd	15	— not out	5
R. Miller c Slade b I. J. Jones	14		
J. M. Allan b Shepherd	0		
R. V. Webster b Davis	5		
D. J. Brown not out	7		
J. D. Bannister not out	2		
1/18 2/74 3/79 4/126 5/148 6/165 7/173 8/178 9/178 (9 wkts., 65 overs)	187	1/36 2/53 3/77 4/136 (4 wkts.)	154

Bowling: *First Innings*—I. J. Jones 12—4—20—1; Wheatley 7—4—7—1; Davis 16—5—63—3; Shepherd 25—4—73—4; B. Lewis 5—0—24—0. *Second Innings*—I. J. Jones 3—1—12—0; Wheatley 5—3—3—0; Shepherd 14—4—33—1; Davis 14—6—32—1; B. Lewis 22—5—74—1.

Umpires: L. H. Gray and C. G. Pepper.

GLAMORGAN v. HAMPSHIRE

At Cardiff, May 28, 30, 31. *65 overs.* Glamorgan won by 46 runs. A remarkable spell of bowling by Shepherd was responsible for the rout of Hampshire in their second innings, when they wanted only 122 to win. In his first four overs Shepherd snapped up three wickets without conceding a run and when Hampshire were skittled out for 75 his analysis read seven for seven. Yet during the previous two days Hampshire appeared to be in command. They gained a first-innings lead of 24 runs and in the Glamorgan second innings only the sound batting of Alan Jones prevented Hampshire from consolidating their position. Seventh to leave at 135, Jones had held out against Hampshire's array of seam bowlers almost single handed for three and three-quarter hours for his 78, which included nine 4's.

Glamorgan

First innings		Second innings	
B. Hedges b Shackleton	0	b Shackleton	0
A. Jones c Reed b White	4	lbw b Cottam	78
E. Lewis lbw b White	10	lbw b Shackleton	7
A. R. Lewis c Barnard b White	43	b Wheatley	21
A. Rees st Titmus b Shackleton	26	c Sainsbury b Wheatley	1
I. Morris c Livingstone b White	38	lbw b Wheatley	6
F. J. Davis c Cottam b Shackleton	9	lbw b Shackleton	1
D. J. Shepherd c Reed b Cottam	10	not out	6
†D. L. Evans b Cottam	1	b Cottam	12
I. J. Jones run out	8	b Cottam	0
*O. S. Wheatley not out	0	b White	0
B 4, l-b 7, w 1, n-b 6	18	B 6, l-b 5, n-b 2	13
1/11 2/16 3/27 4/74 5/115 6/143 7/146 8/151 9/167	167	1/2 2/33 3/68 4/70 5/90 6/103 7/135 8/144 9/144	145

Bowling: *First Innings*—Shackleton 23—9—56—3; White 20—6—46—4; Cottam 14—2—32—2; Sainsbury 8—3—15—0. *Second Innings*—Shackleton 20—9—32—3; White 11.5—0—30—1; Cottam 17—3—26—3; Wheatley 18—8—30—3; Sainsbury 8—3—14—0.

Hampshire

First innings		Second innings	
*R. E. Marshall c and b Wheatley	5	c Evans b I. J. Jones	3
B. L. Reed c Evans b I. J. Jones	41	lbw b I. J. Jones	28
H. Horton c Rees b I. J. Jones	47	c Rees b I. J. Jones	17
D. A. Livingstone c A. R. Lewis b I. J. Jones	55	c Davis b. Shepherd	2
H. M. Barnard c Evans b Wheatley	18	c A. R. Lewis b Shepherd	1
D. W. White not out	7	b Shepherd	0
P. J. Sainsbury not out	5	c Morris b Shepherd	8
†B. S. V. Timms (did not bat)		lbw b Shepherd	0
K. J. Wheatley (did not bat)		not out	13
D. Shackleton (did not bat)		c Morris b Shepherd	0
R. M. Cottam (did not bat)		c and b Shepherd	0
L-b 13	13	B 2, n-b 1	3
1/13 2/81 3/120 4/179 5/185 (5 wkts., 65 overs)	191	1/4 2/32 3/47 4/49 5/49 6/61 7/67 8/67 9/67	75

Bowling: *First Innings*—I. J. Jones 24—7—64—3; Wheatley 22—6—62—2; Shepherd 12—2—26—0; E. Lewis 4—1—13—0; Davis 3—1—13—0. *Second Innings*—I. J. Jones 12—3—41—3; Wheatley 8—0—24—0; Shepherd 9.1—6—7—7.

Umpires: C. G. Pepper and L. H. Gray.

At Birmingham, June 1, 2, 3. GLAMORGAN lost to WARWICKSHIRE by 155 runs.

GLAMORGAN v. LEICESTERSHIRE

At Swansea, June 8, 9, 10. *65 overs.* Drawn. Rain seriously affected this game. There was no play on the second day and cricket was only possible before lunch on the third day. As a result, interest was confined to first-innings points, which Leicestershire won through a fine innings by Booth. Glamorgan batted first, scoring 177 off the 65 overs. As so often happened during the season Alan Jones and A. R. Lewis provided the backbone of the batting and they added 51 in a brisk third-wicket partnership. Jones took two and a quarter hours over his 58, hitting two 6's and six 4's. For Leicestershire, Booth batted three and a quarter hours for 74, which included seven 4's.

Glamorgan

A. Jones c Tolchard b Lock	58	— c Booth b Marner	0
R. Davis b Cross	11	— c Hallam b Savage	9
B. Hedges c Birkenshaw b Savage	24		
A. R. Lewis c and b Cross	48	— c Hallam b Savage	55
P. M. Walker c Lock b Marner	0	— not out	67
A. Rees c Tolchard b Marner	13		
D. J. Shepherd b Cross	4		
A. E. Cordle not out	4	— b Marner	9
†D. L. Evans c Lock b Cross	0		
F. J. Davis not out	0		
B 4, l-b 10, w 1	15		
1/27 2/68 3/119 4/124 5/156 6/164 7/173 8/173 (8 wkts., 65 overs)	177	1/0 2/23 3/116 4/140 (4 wkts.)	140

*O. S. Wheatley did not bat.

Bowling: *First Innings*—Marner 23—5—55—2; Cross 21—2—55—4; Savage 14—3—31—1; Lock 7—2—21—1. *Second Innings*—Marner 16.5—7—39—2; Cross 12—4—27—0; Lock 11—2—27—0; Savage 15—1—47—2.

Leicestershire

M. R. Hallam run out	36
B. J. Booth not out	74
C. C. Inman c Jones b Wheatley	7
P. Marner c Evans b Cordle	22
G. Cross b Cordle	8
*G. A. R. Lock b Cordle	11
M. E. Norman b Wheatley	2
D. Constant not out	10
B 4, l-b 6	10
1/67 2/82 3/129 4/141 5/155 6/162 (6 wkts., 65 overs)	180

J. Birkenshaw, †R. W. Tolchard and J. S. Savage did not bat.

Bowling: Wheatley 19—4—51—2; Cordle 16—3—45—3; Shepherd 18—6—33—0; F. J. Davis 12—2—41—0.

Umpires: A. E. Rhodes and O. W. Herman.

At Liverpool, June 11, 13, 14. GLAMORGAN drew with LANCASHIRE.

GLAMORGAN v. SURREY

At Cardiff, June 18, 20, 21. Surrey won by 198 runs. A fighting innings by Edrich proved decisive and this was followed up by some hostile seam bowling by Storey and Arnold, with the result that Glamorgan were overwhelmed. Surrey were given a flying start by Edrich, who reached his 50 out of 82 with a 6. Rain threatened to interfere with play but the hold up lasted only ninety minutes and did not unsettle Edrich who batted two hours and forty minutes for 78, which also included eight 4's. Glamorgan made a disastrous reply, losing their first four wickets for 17 runs and only a stout-hearted effort by Walker prevented a complete collapse. Edrich again batted magnificently for Surrey, hitting one 6 and five 4's in his 62. Surrey left Glamorgan 282 to win in three and a half hours and more splendid bowling by Storey and Arnold brought this innings to a close for only 83.

Surrey

First innings		Second innings	
*M. J. Stewart c Cordle b Walker	17	c E. Jones b Cordle	7
J. H. Edrich c E. Jones b Cordle	78	c E. Jones b Walker	62
I. Finlay c E. Jones b E. Lewis	8	b Wheatley	44
M. D. Willett lbw b Wheatley	11	not out	8
M. J. Edwards c Hedges b Wheatley	4		
S. J. Storey lbw b Wheatley	14	b Wheatley	23
G. R. J. Roope lbw b Cordle	35		
†D. J. Taylor c Davis b Walker	4		
P. I. Pocock lbw b Wheatley	26	c Wheatley b Walker	0
G. Arnold not out	3		
R. Harman c Rees b Cordle	0		
B 1, l-b 4, n-b 4	9	B 6, l-b 6, n-b 6	18
1/33 2/69 3/118 4/120 5/124 6/145 7/167 8/205 9/207	209	1/30 2/112 3/141 4/142 5/162 (5 wkts., dec.)	162

Bowling: *First Innings*—Wheatley 28—11—52—4; Cordle 23.5—4—66—3; Walker 13—10—5—2; Shepherd 22—6—46—0; E. Lewis 11—5—31—1. *Second Innings*—Wheatley 19—5—31—2; Cordle 9—1—29—1; Shepherd 11—7—12—0; E. Lewis 10—5—23—0; Davis 8—2—27—0; Walker 9—4—22—2.

Glamorgan

First innings		Second innings	
R. Davis lbw b Storey	0	c Storey b Arnold	3
A. E. Cordle c Finlay b Arnold	0	c Edwards b Roope	6
E. Lewis b Storey	15	c Willett b Storey	6
A. Jones b Arnold	2	c Stewart b Arnold	4
P. M. Walker lbw b Arnold	46	b Storey	19
A. R. Lewis c Taylor b Arnold	8	c Edwards b Arnold	11
B. Hedges c Edwards b Storey	5	b Storey	4
A. Rees c Edwards b Storey	1	st Taylor b Storey	13
†E. Jones c Taylor b Arnold	2	c Edrich b Roope	0
D. J. Shepherd b Storey	3	b Storey	6
*O. S. Wheatley not out	0	not out	0
N-b 8	8	B 8, n-b 3	11
1/0 2/2 3/17 4/17 5/56 6/67 7/69 8/86 9/88	90	1/6 2/25 3/29 4/37 5/47 6/60 7/61 8/71 9/78	83

Bowling: *First Innings*—Storey 21.2—13—17—5; Arnold 20—5—51—5; Roope 9—3—14—0. *Second Innings*—Arnold 10—4—35—3; Storey 13.1—7—22—5; Roope 4—1—15—2.

Umpires: P. A. Gibb and H. Yarnold.

GLAMORGAN v. CAMBRIDGE UNIVERSITY

At Cardiff, June 22, 23, 24. Drawn. This was Glamorgan's ninth game out of twelve to be seriously curtailed by rain. Play did not start on the first day until after the tea interval and Glamorgan did not even take any money at the turnstiles. The handful of spectators who were admitted free saw Glamorgan score briskly. Again the foundation was laid by Alan Jones and A. R. Lewis. The latter hit a very good 50 in ninety minutes. With so much time lost through rain Glamorgan declared their first innings closed with only four wickets down. There was more delay on the second day, when Cambridge were dismissed for 182, D. L. Hays providing all the sparkle in a hard hitting innings. In only half an hour he scored 62 of 82, which included three 6's and ten 4's—58 in boundaries. When Glamorgan declared a second time Cambridge needed 196 to win in two and three-quarter hours and just held out.

Glamorgan

A. Jones b Roopnaraine	41	c Acfield b Sinker	37
W. Slade run out	29	c Cosh b Palfreman	21
P. M. Walker b Russell	18	c Gould b Acfield	30
*A. R. Lewis b Sinker	54	not out	4
L. Hill not out	18	b Roopnaraine	50
†E. Jones not out	0	lbw b Roopnaraine	38
F. Nash (did not bat)		b Acfield	16
E. Lewis (did not bat)		not out	3
B 6, l-b 2	8	B 9, n-b 1	10
1/65 2/77 3/111 4/168 (4 wkts., dec.)	168	1/41 2/77 3/118 4/140 5/199 6/199 (6 wkts., dec.)	209

B. Lewis, H. D. Miller and A. E. Cordle did not bat.

Bowling: *First Innings*—Russell 13—0—58—1; Palfreman 14—2—34—0; Sinker 22—10—21—1; Roopnaraine 28—12—41—1; Acfield 7—3—6—0. *Second Innings*—Roopnaraine 32—13—85—2; Palfreman 6—4—6—1; Acfield 25—5—63—2; Sinker 14—5—34—1; Russell 3—0—11—0.

Cambridge University

K. P. W. J. McAdam st E. Jones b Nash	34	run out	16
R. E. Chambers c Hill b B. Lewis	56	b E. Lewis	23
A. V. E. Gould lbw b Nash	0	c Slade b E. Lewis	6
D. L. Hays c A. R. Lewis b. E. Lewis	62	c Slade b E. Lewis	10
*†D. L. Murray c Slade b B. Lewis	7	lbw b B. Lewis	9
N. J. Cosh c Walker b B. Lewis	1	not out	17
A. B. Palfreman c Slade b E. Lewis	3	c B. Lewis b Slade	17
R. Roopnaraine c and b B. Lewis	1	b E. Lewis	0
N. Sinker c Miller b B. Lewis	2	b Cordle	4
D. L. Acfield c Walker b B. Lewis	5	not out	0
S. G. Russell not out	1		
B 2, l-b 5, w 1, n-b 2	10	B 8, l-b 4, n-b 1	13
1/68 2/68 3/150 4/169 5/170 6/170 7/172 8/176 9/178	182	1/36 2/47 3/57 4/72 5/72 6/98 7/99 8/107 (8 wkts.)	115

Bowling: *First Innings*—Cordle 6—0—13—0; Miller 9—1—37—0; Nash 6—1—30—2; B. Lewis 14.5—4—41—6; E. Lewis 13—2—51—2. *Second Innings*—Nash 6—2—12—0; E. Lewis 16—4—35—4; B. Lewis 13—6—16—1; Walker 9—4—10—0; Cordle 10—4—15—1; Slade 5—2—6—1; Miller 3—0—8—0; A. R. Lewis 1—1—0—0.

Umpires: H. Yarnold and D. Evans.

GLAMORGAN v. NOTTINGHAMSHIRE

At Swansea, June 25, 27, 28. Drawn. Rain prevented a ball being bowled on the first two days with the result that it was reduced to a one-day match, with the sides battling for first-innings lead and six points. Both lacked adventure and a rain-ruined match ended in a pointless draw.

Glamorgan

W. Slade retired ill	4	B. Lewis b Stead	0
A. Jones b Taylor	22	I. J. Jones not out	2
P. M. Walker c Smedley b Forbes	20	†E. Jones not out	1
A. R. Lewis c Bolus b Taylor	4	B 12, l-b 3, n-b 3	18
B. Hedges run out	28		
L. Hill c Taylor b Forbes	28	1/44 2/54 3/56 4/110 (7 wkts., dec.)	140
D. J. Shepherd b Forbes	13	5/136 6/137 7/137	

*O. S. Wheatley did not bat.

Bowling: Davison 8—0—29—0; Stead 10—3—31—1; Forbes 18.4—4—25—3; Taylor 14—4—24—2; White 8—1—13—0.

Nottinghamshire

*N. Hill c A. R. Lewis b Wheatley	2	†R. Swetman lbw b Wheatley	16
J. B. Bolus lbw b Wheatley	2		
R. A. White c sub b Shepherd	9	W 1	1
H. I. Moore b Shepherd	35		
M. J. Smedley not out	52	1/4 2/5 3/16 4/86 5/117 (5 wkts.)	117

B. Whittingham, M. Taylor, C. Forbes, B. Stead and I. Davison did not bat.

Bowling: I. J. Jones 8—2—13—0; Wheatley 7—3—5—3; Shepherd 14—2—50—2; Walker 15—8—29—0; A. R. Lewis 2—0—19—0.

Umpires: J. Langridge and H. Yarnold.

At Taunton, June 29, 30, July 1. GLAMORGAN lost to SOMERSET by four wickets.

GLAMORGAN v. MIDDLESEX

At Cardiff, July 2, 4, 5. Drawn. Middlesex had to be content with first-innings points, after holding the initiative for most of the game, which again was seriously interrupted by rain. On the last day Glamorgan had to get 297 in five hours, twenty minutes, but scored only 21 in the first hour and were well behind the clock when rain caused the match to be abandoned as a draw. In their first innings Middlesex, after losing half their wickets for 96, rallied through a hard-hit fifty by Bick in seventy-five minutes. It included nine 4's. Only A. R. Lewis batted with any consistency for Glamorgan, who finished 81 behind. Lewis scored 78 of Glamorgan's total of 140, hitting one 6 and nine 4's in a stay of three hours.

Middlesex

M. J. Harris c and b Walker	20	— c E. Jones b Wheatley	10
M. J. Smith lbw b Wheatley	26	— c E. Jones b Wheatley	1
P. H. Parfitt c Walker b Shepherd	16	— c Wheatley b Shepherd	88
E. A. Clark c Walker b Shepherd	18	— b E. Lewis	8
D. Bennett b E. Lewis	50	— c and b Shepherd	36
*F. J. Titmus c Hedges b Shepherd	11	— b I. J. Jones	21
R. W. Hooker b Shepherd	6	— b Shepherd	12
D. A. Bick c and b E. Lewis	52	— c E. Lewis b Shepherd	0
H. C. Latchman c A. Jones b Walker	1	— c Wheatley b I. J. Jones	7
†E. G. Clifton not out	15	— c A. Jones b Shepherd	16
J. S. E. Price c Slade b E. Lewis	0	— not out	1
L-b 4, n-b 2	6	L-b 12, n-b 3	15
1/27 2/48 3/77 4/82 5/96 6/104 7/194 8/197 9/207	221	1/1 2/23 3/48 4/146 5/177 6/183 7/183 8/194 9/204	215

Bowling: *First Innings*—I. J. Jones 12—3—36—0; Wheatley 20—10—38—1; E. Lewis 16.3—4—47—3; Walker 16—4—35—2; Shepherd 27—10—59—4. *Second Innings*—I. J. Jones 20—5—59—2; Wheatley 15—5—18—2; Walker 5—1—11—0; E. Lewis 9—3—35—1; Shepherd 29.4—11—55—5; Slade 7—1—22—0.

Glamorgan

First Innings		Second Innings	
A. Jones c Harris b Titmus	9	lbw b Hooker	13
W. Slade c Clifton b Titmus	10	c Clifton b Hooker	2
P. M. Walker b Price	3	c Price b Hooker	12
A. R. Lewis c Harris b Titmus	78	not out	43
B. Hedges c Parfitt b Titmus	6	not out	10
L. Hill c Parfitt b Latchman	17		
†E. Jones b Titmus	1		
E. Lewis c Parfitt b Latchman	0		
D. J. Shepherd b Titmus	2		
I. J. Jones c Parfitt b Titmus	5		
*O. S. Wheatley not out	0		
L-b 2, n-b 7	9	L-b 1	1
1/20 2/22 3/31 4/61 5/98 6/99 7/106 8/123 9/137	140	1/15 2/16 3/42 (3 wkts.)	81

Bowling: *First Innings*—Price 21—8—32—1; Hooker 8—2—18—0; Titmus 33.3—17—58—7; Bick 3—0—9—0; Latchman 10—2—14—2. *Second Innings*—Price 10—3—24—0; Hooker 14—6—29—3; Titmus 11—7—11—0; Latchman 3—1—12—0; Bick 1—0—4—0.

Empires: J. S. Buller and W. H. Copson.

At Southampton, July 6, 7, 8. GLAMORGAN drew with HAMPSHIRE.

GLAMORGAN v. SUSSEX

(P. M. Walker's Benefit)

At Swansea, July 13, 14, 15. Drawn. This match would have been a financial disaster had it not been for continuous rain on the third day which enabled Walker to draw £700 insurance money. The rain also meant another home draw, although Sussex obtained first-innings points by 32 runs. Glamorgan were given a flying start by their most reliable batsmen, A. Jones and A. R. Lewis, who put on 87 for the third wicket. Jones batted three hours and forty minutes for 83 which included eleven 4's. After lunch Glamorgan collapsed, losing their seven remaining wickets for 43. Sussex were in dire trouble when they lost half their wickets for 65, but Oakman led a rearguard action, scoring 50 out of 86 in seventy-five minutes, and assured Sussex of first-innings lead.

Glamorgan

First Innings		Second Innings	
A. Jones c Griffith b A. Buss	83	b A. Buss	13
W. Slade lbw b A. Buss	4	c M. A. Buss b Oakman	69
P. M. Walker c Foreman b Snow	6	c Foreman b Snow	32
A. R. Lewis b A. Buss	40	c M. A. Buss b Oakman	46
A. Rees b Snow	2	lbw b Oakman	9
L. Hill c and b A. Buss	1	c Parks b Snow	0
†E. Jones b Snow	9	b Snow	0
E. Lewis b Bates	12	c Griffith b Bates	13
D. J. Shepherd c Snow b Bates	0	c Parks b Snow	14
I. J. Jones b A. Buss	0	b Bates	0
*O. S. Wheatley not out	0	not out	0
B 2, l-b 2, w 1	5	L-b 4	4
1/13 2/32 3/119 4/126 5/127 6/139 7/155 8/155 9/162	162	1/16 2/88 3/158 4/172 5/173 6/173 7/173 8/196 9/196	200

Bowling: *First Innings*—Snow 21—6—45—3; A. Buss 24—8—59—5; Bates 9—2—19—2; Oakman 10—4—17—0; M. A. Buss 4—0—17—0. *Second Innings*—Snow 20—7—52—4; A. Buss 16—2—41—1; Bates 12.5—6—23—2; Oakman 20—5—45—3; M. A. Buss 17—11—25—0; Suttle 6—3—10—0.

Sussex

L. J. Lenham lbw b Wheatley	4	— not out	6
M. A. Buss c Slade b Walker	9	— not out	4
K. G. Suttle c E. Jones b Wheatley	16		
*†J. M. Parks b Wheatley	7		
M. G. Griffith b Wheatley	16		
P. J. Graves lbw b Shepherd	42		
D. J. Foreman lbw b Shepherd	30		
A. S. M. Oakman not out	54		
A. Buss c E. Jones b Wheatley	6		
D. L. Bates c Walker b I. J. Jones	1		
J. A. Snow c E. Jones b Wheatley	0		
B 2, l-b 5, n-b 2	9		
1/14 2/24 3/36 4/39 5/65 6/109 7/154 8/184 9/189	194	(no wkt.)	10

Bowling: *First Innings*—I. J. Jones 27—11—56—1; Wheatley 32—11—60—6; Walker 14—6—29—1; Shepherd 15—10—16—2; E. Lewis 6—4—18—0; Slade 2—1—6—0. *Second Innings*—I. J. Jones 1—0—5—0; Wheatley 0.3—0—5—0.

Umpires: O. W. Herman and H. Mellows.

GLAMORGAN v. LANCASHIRE

At Ebbw Vale, July 16, 18, 19. Glamorgan won by 95 runs. This was Glamorgan's first win since the end of May, and marked a revival in the form of I. J. Jones who had disappointed as a pace bowler since his successful tour of Australia. In reply to Glamorgan's first-innings total of 168 of which A. Jones, with 50 in two hours and twenty minutes, was the anchor man, Lancashire scored only 109; I. J. Jones starting the collapse when he captured three wickets in his opening spell for 18 runs and finished with five for 52. With a first-innings lead of 59 Glamorgan went out for quick runs and steady partnerships for the second and fourth wickets enabled them to declare. Left all the third day in which to get 311 to win, Lancashire batted soundly, if slowly, until an hour before the close, when they lost their last three wickets quickly, and were all out for 215.

Glamorgan

A. Jones c Higgs b Worsley	51	— run out	89
W. Slade c Goodwin b Higgs	2	— c Knox b Lever	2
P. M. Walker c Goodwin b Higgs	1	— c Knox b Worsley	24
A. R. Lewis c Worsley b Higgs	12	— not out	75
A. Rees c Greenhough b Worsley	39	— not out	58
L. Hill lbw b Greenhough	6		
†E. Jones lbw b Greenhough	0		
E. Lewis b Higgs	23		
I. J. Jones not out	18		
D. J. Shepherd b Greenhough	5		
*O. S. Wheatley run out	1		
B 4, l-b 4, w 1, n-b 1	10	L-b 1, n-b 2	3
1/7 2/17 3/49 4/110 5/119 6/119 7/119 8/144 9/161	168	1/6 2/108 3/121 (3 wkts., dec.)	251

Bowling: *First Innings*—Higgs 21.5—11—37—4; Lever 12—4—32—0; Worsley 27—8—55—2; Greenhough 16—5—34—3. *Second Innings*—Higgs 23—4—66—0; Lever 20—4—36—1; Worsley 20—1—67—1; Greenhough 20—3—52—0; Green 7—1—27—0.

Lancashire

*D. M. Green c E. Jones b Walker	29	— c A. Jones b E. Lewis	38
G. K. Knox c Slade b I. J. Jones	5	— c Walker b I. J. Jones	14
J. D. Bond c E. Jones b I. J. Jones	8	— c E. Lewis b Shepherd	15
G. Pullar b I. J. Jones	19	— c E. Jones b I. J. Jones	0
†K. Goodwin c Slade b I. J. Jones	4	— c Slade b E. Lewis	4
D. R. Worsley c E. Jones b Wheatley	8	— lbw b E. Lewis	40
J. Sullivan lbw b I. J. Jones	2	— lbw b Wheatley	25
H. Pilling lbw b Walker	14	— b E. Lewis	11
P. Lever b Wheatley	11	— c Rees b E. Lewis	50
K. Higgs not out	2	— c E. Jones b Shepherd	10
T. Greenhough c E. Jones b Walker	0	— not out	2
B 6, l-b 1	7	B 3, l-b 3	6
1/11 2/22 3/52 4/63 5/68 6/72 7/80 8/92 9/109	109	1/51 2/57 3/57 4/70 5/117 6/147 7/155 8/201 9/209	215

Bowling: *First Innings*—I. J. Jones 28—7—52—5; Wheatley 23—8—34—2; E. Lewis 1—0—4—0; Walker 5.5—2—12—3; Shepherd 2—2—0—0. *Second Innings*—I. J. Jones 13—2—47—2; Wheatley 11—4—29—1; Shepherd 30—21—28—2; Walker 10—5—25—0; E. Lewis 24.5—8—80—5.

Umpires: J. Langridge and O. W. Herman.

GLAMORGAN v. GLOUCESTERSHIRE

At Cardiff, July 20, 21, 22. Drawn. Dropped catches helped Gloucestershire to build up a first-innings total of 344. Milton who batted four hours for 95 which included thirteen 4's was missed in the gully when 37 and Bissex and D. Brown also had "lives". Glamorgan made a spirited reply, thanks to A. R. Lewis who reached his fourth century of the season in two hours and fifty minutes. Altogether he hit one 6 and eighteen 4's. Rees gave him best support in a fourth-wicket partnership of 141. Finally, Gloucestershire challenged Glamorgan to get 189 to win in two hours. Glamorgan scored 84 in the first hour, but with Mortimore tempting the batsmen five wickets fell quickly. They had to get 56 in half an hour and when the hard-hitting Shepherd was bowled the last few batsmen concentrated on saving the game.

Gloucestershire

C. A. Milton c Slade b Shepherd	95	— c Rees b E. Lewis	55
M. Bissex c Walker b Miller	26	— c Miller b I. J. Jones	3
D. Brown b E. Lewis	37	— lbw b Wheatley	14
D. Shepherd c A. R. Lewis b E. Lewis	25	— lbw b Wheatley	0
R. B. Nicholls c E. Jones b I. J. Jones	32	— c Miller b Shepherd	37
S. E. Russell c E. Lewis b Shepherd	19	— c Slade b Wheatley	10
D. A. Allen lbw b I. J. Jones	8	— lbw b Shepherd	5
*J. B. Mortimore lbw b Wheatley	4	— lbw b Wheatley	10
A. S. Brown lbw b Shepherd	28	— run out	4
†B. J. Meyer not out	31	— not out	20
D. R. Smith c Walker b Shepherd	5		
B 8, l-b 17, n-b 9	34	L-b 1, w 1, n-b 2	4
1/58 2/143 3/177 4/213 5/253 6/267 7/274 8/276 9/328	344	1/6 2/32 3/32 (9 wkts., dec.) 4/91 5/113 6/128 7/135 8/137 9/162	162

Bowling: *First Innings*—I. J. Jones 21—4—68—2; Wheatley 20—3—34—1; Miller 27—5—87—1; Walker 4—0—19—0; Shepherd 32.1—13—41—4; E. Lewis 24—5—61—2. *Second Innings*—I. J. Jones 4—0—10—1; Wheatley 23—10—28—4; Miller 12—2—35—0; E. Lewis 8—2—29—1; Shepherd 28.2—8—44—2; Walker 6—0—12—0.

Glamorgan

A. Jones c Shepherd b Mortimore	24	— c Bissex b Allen	29
W. Slade c Meyer b Smith	7	— st Meyer b Allen	33
P. M. Walker b Bissex	53	— c Bissex b Mortimore	23
A. R. Lewis c Bissex b A. S. Brown	146	— c Russell b Mortimore	16
A. Rees c Meyer b Smith	50	— c Milton b Mortimore	6
H. D. Miller lbw b Smith	6	— lbw b Mortimore	0
†E. Jones lbw b A. S. Brown	10	— c Milton b Mortimore	0
E. Lewis c Meyer b Smith	0	— b Allen	7
I. J. Jones b A. S. Brown	0	— not out	0
D. J. Shepherd c D. Brown b A. S. Brown	3	— b Bissex	20
*O. S. Wheatley not out	4	— not out	0
B 4, l-b 9, w 1, n-b 1	15	B 8, l-b 10, w 2	20
1/14 2/59 3/108 4/249 5/255 6/304 7/309 8/309 9/309	318	1/56 2/93 3/112 4/112 5/120 6/127 7/133 8/140 9/154	(9 wkts.) 154

Bowling: *First Innings*—Smith 22—4—69—4; A. S. Brown 28.5—6—82—4; Mortimore 31—8—61—1; Allen 20—6—37—0; Bissex 20—7—54—1. *Second Innings*—Smith 6—1—20—0; A. S. Brown 9—3—13—0; Mortimore 12—1—58—5; Allen 10—0—39—3; Bissex 2—1—4—1; Nicholls 1—1—0—0.

Umpires: J. Langridge and R. S. Lay.

At Coalville, July 23, 25. GLAMORGAN lost to LEICESTERSHIRE by ten wickets.

GLAMORGAN v. ESSEX

At Swansea, July 27, 28, 29. *65 overs.* Drawn. In a "photo" finish Glamorgan failed by just one run with one wicket left to win a splendidly contested game. But with the scores level they obtained five points as the side batting last in an unfinished match. Glamorgan wanted nine runs to win in the last over. Shepherd obtained eight off the first four balls; played and missed the fifth and was caught on the edge of the boundary off the last. Glamorgan needed 234 to win in four hours on a sporting wicket which in their first innings had suited Hobbs' leg spinners so completely that in one spell he took four wickets for four runs. His final analysis of eight for 63 was the best of his career.

Essex

G. E. Barker c Miller b Shepherd	28	— c Rees b Davis	14
M. J. Bear c Walker b Shepherd	46	— c Wheatley b Davis	34
†B. Taylor b Shepherd	28	— b Shepherd	45
B. R. Knight b Davis	9	— c Evans b E. Lewis	48
G. R. Cass c A. R. Lewis b Shepherd	7	— c Walker b Wheatley	18
*T. E. Bailey not out	30	— c Rees b E. Lewis	7
G. J. Saville b Shepherd	11	— lbw b Shepherd	16
B. Edmeades c Rees b Shepherd	1	— not out	14
R. N. S. Hobbs not out	0	— not out	4
B 2, l-b 7	9	B 4, l-b 2	6
1/54 2/108 3/111 4/119 5/128 6/153 7/167	(7 wkts., 65 overs) 169	1/48 2/48 3/126 4/152 5/152 6/175 7/189	(7 wkts., dec.) 206

A. M. Jorden and D. L. Acfield did not bat.

Bowling: *First Innings*—Wheatley 13—5—27—0; Miller 3—0—15—0; Shepherd 30—10—64—6; E. Lewis 6—0—26—0; Davis 13—5—28—1. *Second innings*—Wheatley 13.5—6—42—1; Miller 5—0—13—0; Shepherd 35—12—71—2; E. Lewis 17—6—49—2; Davis 11—4—25—2.

Glamorgan

B. Hedges c Saville b Acfield	28	— c Hobbs b Acfield	28
A. Jones b Hobbs	37	— not out	104
A. R. Lewis c Knight b Hobbs	8	— c Taylor b Hobbs	8
A. Rees not out	42	— c Cass b Hobbs	4
R. Davis c Bailey b Hobbs	0	— lbw b Edmeades	16
P. M. Walker c and b Hobbs	0	— c Bailey b Hobbs	0
H. D. Miller c Saville b Hobbs	0	— c Hobbs b Edmeades	7
E. Lewis c Knight b Hobbs	14	— c Jorden b Hobbs	32
†D. L. Evans c Bailey b Hobbs	2	— c Taylor b Edmeades	0
D. J. Shepherd c sub b Hobbs	3	— c Knight b Hobbs	24
*O. S. Wheatley b Acfield	0		
L-b 8	8	B 6, l-b 2, n-b 2	10
1/50 2/75 3/80 4/81 5/81 6/85 7/109 8/132 9/140	142	1/54 2/94 3/119 4/131 5/134 6/179 7/194 8/194 9/233 (9 wkts.)	233

Bowling: *First Innings*—Jorden 5—0—9—0; Edmeades 12—3—20—0; Hobbs 27—10—63—8; Acfield 19.2—4—42—2. *Second Innings*—Jorden 3—1—10—0; Edmeades 20—2—51—3; Bailey 14—4—49—0; Acfield 10—6—12—1; Hobbs 30—7—101—5.

Umpires: G. H. Pope and J. Arnold.

At Swansea, July 30, August 1, 2. GLAMORGAN drew with WEST INDIES. (See WEST INDIES section.)

At Leyton, August 3, 4, 5. GLAMORGAN drew with ESSEX.

A Wellingborough, August 6, 8, 9. GLAMORGAN drew with NORTHAMPTONSHIRE.

GLAMORGAN v. SOMERSET

At Cardiff, August 13, 15, 16. Somerset won by 71 runs. This was the last County championship match to be played at Cardiff Arms Park, which had been used as a cricket ground for one hundred years, but Glamorgan could not mark the occasion with a win. Throughout Somerset were better in all phases. In their first innings, after they had lost half their wickets for 96, they had to thank Alley, who scored 50 out of 79 in two hours, before becoming one of Shepherd's six victims. Glamorgan failed by 29 runs to obtain a first-innings lead, and although Somerset could not build up a commanding position, they set Glamorgan the task of getting 223 to win in three hours. The opening batsmen went for the runs, with A. Jones scoring 50 out of 90 in eighty minutes, but suddenly they lost six wickets for only 37. Glamorgan were handicapped through E. Lewis, suffering from an eye infection, being unable to bat in either innings.

Somerset

G. Atkinson c Walker b Wheatley	16	— c Shepherd b Slade	15
R. Virgin c Walker b Shepherd	8	— c Evans b Cordle	10
M. Kitchen c Evans b Shepherd	1	— c A. Jones b Shepherd	48
G. Burgess b Shepherd	6	— c A. R. Lewis b Slade	13
W. E. Alley c Wheatley b Shepherd	55	— c Slade b Cordle	28
*C. R. M. Atkinson c Evans b Cordle	20	— c Slade b Shepherd	0
K. E. Palmer lbw b Wheatley	6	— not out	21
†G. Clayton c Rees b Shepherd	16	— c Walker b Wheatley	9
P. J. Robinson c Evans b E. Lewis	25	— c Walker b Cordle	28
B. A. Langford c Walker b Shepherd	25	— run out	2
F. E. Rumsey not out	0	— not out	1
L-b 2, n-b 4	6	B 8, l-b 4, w 5, n-b 2	19
1/18 2/20 3/28 4/46 5/96 6/116 7/122 8/146 9/178	184	1/17 2/56 3/82 (9 wkts., dec.) 4/126 5/126 6/130 7/140 8/187 9/189	194

Bowling: *First Innings*—Cordle 23—5—56—1; Wheatley 25—8—42—2; Shepherd 38.3—17—64—6; E. Lewis 9—4—16—1. *Second Innings*—Cordle 24—7—48—3; Wheatley 15—5—28—1; Shepherd 34—17—51—2; Slade 18—4—46—2; Walker 4—3—2—0.

Glamorgan

A. Jones b Robinson	48	— c Alley b Langford	51
B. Hedges c Robinson b Palmer	2	— run out	11
P. M. Walker c Clayton b Rumsey	9	— c G. Atkinson b Robinson	20
A. R. Lewis c Robinson b Langford	0	— c and b Robinson	5
A. Rees not out	35	— c Kitchen b Robinson	6
W. Slade c Alley b Langford	0	— b Langford	4
†D. L. Evans c Burgess b Robinson	15	— b Langford	1
A. E. Cordle b Langford	25	— c Alley b Robinson	28
D. J. Shepherd c Alley b Robinson	7	— not out	13
*O. S. Wheatley b Robinson	5	— b Langford	0
E. Lewis absent ill	0	— absent ill	0
B 2, l-b 4, w 1, n-b 3	10	L-b 6, w 5, n-b 1	12
1/4 2/21 3/72 4/72 5/100 6/109 7/137 8/147 9/156	156	1/48 2/91 3/91 4/97 5/106 6/106 7/115 8/127 9/151	151

Bowling: *First Innings*—Rumsey 12—5—18—1; Palmer 13—6—27—1; Langford 35—24—45—3; Alley 16—8—20—0; Robinson 18.5—6—36—4. *Second Innings*—Rumsey 6—1—23—0; Palmer 12—5—24—0; Langford 16—5—41—4; Robinson 9.3—2—51—4.

Umpires: J. F. Crapp and F. Jakeman.

At Scarborough, August 17, 18, 19. GLAMORGAN lost to YORKSHIRE by two wickets.

At Derby, August 20, 22, 23. GLAMORGAN beat DERBYSHIRE by 78 runs.

GLAMORGAN v. NORTHAMPTONSHIRE

At Neath, August 24, 25, 26. Glamorgan won by 72 runs. The batting of A. R. Lewis was a decisive factor in Glamorgan's success. Northamptonshire gained a narrow first-innings lead of seven runs through a fine spell of bowling by Sully, who at one stage took four wickets for three runs and finished with six for 36. But Glamorgan recaptured the initiative when A. R. Lewis hit his fifth century of the season in just over three hours and also became the first batsman in the country to complete 2,000 runs for the season. He was fortunate to be dropped by Prideaux when only seven. Losing their last four wickets for two runs, Glamorgan left Northamptonshire needing 252 to win on the whole of the third day. They failed on a spinner's wicket before the joint attack of Shepherd and B. Lewis. Lightfoot alone played the turning ball with any assurance. Mushtaq, eight wickets in the match for 82, bowled his leg-breaks cleverly for Northamptonshire.

Glamorgan

R. Davis c Prideaux b Mushtaq	34	— c Mushtaq b Sully	13
A. Jones c Andrew b Durose	14	— b Sully	23
P. M. Walker c Steele b Sully	17	— b Durose	59
A. R. Lewis lbw b Mushtaq	25	— c Durose b Crump	103
A. Rees c Lightfoot b Sully	0	— lbw b Mushtaq	6
I. Morris c Mushtaq b Sully	16	— c Steele b Mushtaq	5
A. E. Cordle b Sully	2	— b Mushtaq	8
†D. L. Evans c Prideaux b Sully	3	— c Scott b Crump	37
B. Lewis lbw b Mushtaq	2	— b Mushtaq	0
*O. S. Wheatley b Sully	0	— not out	0
D. J. Shepherd not out	0	— c Scott b Mushtaq	0
B 4, l-b 1	5	B 1, l-b 3	4
1/26 2/59 3/73 4/78 5/107 6/111 7/113 8/118 9/118	118	1/16 2/78 3/124 4/156 5/168 6/180 7/256 8/258 9/258	258

Bowling: *First Innings*—Durose 6—1—12—1; Crump 6—3—5—0; Watts 9—3—16—0; Mushtaq 23—9—34—3; Sully 27.4—9—36—6; Scott 6—1—10—0. *Second Innings*—Durose 6—1—18—1; Crump 10—3—15—2; Watts 4—0—9—0; Mushtaq 26—11—48—5; Sully 41—9—99—2; Scott 13—2—57—0; Steele 3—0—8—0.

Northamptonshire

R. M. Prideaux lbw b Walker	7	— b B. Lewis	7
B. L. Reynolds b Wheatley	2	— b Cordle	0
Mushtaq Mohammad b Cordle	43	— c Morris b Shepherd	29
D. S. Steele c Rees b B. Lewis	7	— b Shepherd	23
A. Lightfoot b Shepherd	24	— b Shepherd	58
P. J. Watts c Evans b B. Lewis	16	— c Morris b B. Lewis	2
B. Crump lbw b Shepherd	19	— c and b B. Lewis	26
M. E. Scott lbw b Wheatley	1	— c A. Jones b B. Lewis	16
*†K. V. Andrew not out	4	— b B Lewis	1
H. Sully c Morris b Cordle	0	— not out	1
A. J. Durose b Cordle	0	— lbw b Shepherd	2
L-b 1, n-b 1	2	B 6, l-b 5, n-b 3	14
1/6 2/11 3/39 4/47 5/70 6/101 7/114 8/125 9/125	125	1/3 2/30 3/79 4/118 5/123 6/129 7/155 8/173 9/174	179

Bowling: *First Innings*—Cordle 6.3—4—5—3; Wheatley 19—5—40—2; Walker 5—1—12—1; Shepherd 20—9—28—2; B. Lewis 11—2—37—2; Morris 1—0—1—0. *Second Innings*—Cordle 14—4—37—1; Wheatley 13—4—19—0; Shepherd 30.1—13—48—4; B. Lewis 34—12—56—5; Morris 4—3—5—0.

Umpires: W. E. Phillipson and A. E. Alderman.

GLAMORGAN v DERBYSHIRE

At Colwyn Bay, August 27, 29, 30. Glamorgan won by 63 runs. This was the first county championship match to be played in North Wales. The Colwyn Bay Cricket Club guaranteed Glamorgan £400 and the gate receipts just covered the guarantee, and it was certain that Glamorgan, having now played in four different counties, would repeat the experiment. Glamorgan obtained a first-innings lead of 65 and again the batting of A. Jones proved decisive. For Derbyshire, the man of the match was Morgan, whose seven for 47 in the Glamorgan first innings was his best of the season. He also scored 44 not out in a low total. Wheatley, taking six wickets for 42, completed his 100 wickets for the season, but A. R. Lewis failed by 20 runs to create a new record for the most runs scored in a season held by W. G. A. Parkhouse with 2,071. Needing 285 to win in five and three-quarter hours, Derbyshire put up a good fight through brisk batting by Harvey and Eyre who each hit 50 in seventy minutes, but Shepherd halted the visitors when they were in full cry by taking three wickets in eight balls for four runs.

Glamorgan

R. Davis lbw b Rhodes	5	— b E. Smith	21
A. Jones c D. Smith b Morgan	62	— c and b E. Smith	64
P. M. Walker c Russell b Morgan	39	— b Morgan	35
A. R. Lewis lbw b Morgan	1	— lbw b Morgan	15
A. Rees not out	42	— not out	51
I. Morris b Morgan	2	— not out	7
A. E. Cordle b Morgan	12	— lbw b Rhodes	19
†D. L. Evans lbw b Morgan	7		
B. Lewis lbw b Rhodes	0		
*O. S. Wheatley c Taylor b Rhodes	10		
D. J. Shepherd lbw b Morgan	0		
B 1, l-b 1, n-b 1	3	L-b 3, n-b 4	7
1/5 2/76 3/78 4/123 5/125 6/137 7/153 8/162 9/180	183	1/55 2/116 3/124 4/153 5/194 (5 wkts., dec.)	219

Bowling: *First Innings*—Jackson 5—0—20—0; Rhodes 16—5—40—3; Eyre 6—0—29—0; Morgan 32—16—47—7; Russell 19—6—44—0. *Second Innings*—Jackson 4—1—6—0; Rhodes 24—7—49—1; Eyre 12—3—40—0; Morgan 22—11—35—2; Russell 3—0—13—0; E. Smith 32—15—69—2.

Derbyshire

D. Smith c and b Morris	15	— lbw b Wheatley	0
P. J. K. Gibbs b Wheatley	11	— c Cordle b Shepherd	9
J. F. Harvey lbw b Walker	2	— c Rees b Walker	20
M. Hill c Walker b Cordle	19	— c A. Jones b B. Lewis	54
*D. C. Morgan not out	44	— c Walker b B. Lewis	19
P. E. Russell b Wheatley	2	— run out	31
T. J. P. Eyre c Evans b Wheatley	0	— b Shepherd	53
†R. W. Taylor b Wheatley	1	— lbw b Wheatley	22
H. J. Rhodes b Cordle	3	— b Shepherd	0
E. Smith lbw b Wheatley	7	— c Morris b Shepherd	4
A. B. Jackson b Wheatley	2	— not out	0
B 9, n-b 3	12	B 4, l-b 2, n-b 3	9
1/25 2/28 3/52 4/68 5/75 6/75 7/92 8/103 9/112	118	1/3 2/30 3/32 4/66 5/113 6/184 7/207 8/211 9/215	221

Bowling: *First Innings*—Cordle 22—6—43—2; Wheatley 28.3—10—42—6; Walker 12—6—9—1; Shepherd 3—2—8—0; B. Lewis 1—0—4—0; Morris 1—1—0—1. *Second Innings*—Cordle 8—2—20—0; Wheatley 15.1—4—43—2; Walker 8—3—20—1; Shepherd 32—15—41—4; B. Lewis 18—2—78—2; Morris 2—0—10—0.

Umpires: W. E. Phillipson and A. Jepson.

GLOUCESTERSHIRE

President—The Duke of Beaufort

Secretary—R. J. G. McCrudden, County Ground, Bristol

Captain—J. B. Mortimore

M. Bissex

County Badge

D. A. Allen

Despite the fact that Gloucestershire gained six victories, only one fewer than in 1965, they fell from tenth to fifteenth in the Championship and only on three occasions had they been in that position or lower since 1919. The reasons for their decline were mainly instability in the middle-order batting, the inability to find quickly enough a suitable partner to open the innings with Milton and the absence for two months of their pace bowler, Smith, who underwent a cartilage operation on his right knee in May.

Two of the younger batsmen did not make the progress expected, namely David Brown and Shepherd. Russell failed to produce the encouraging form of 1965, and was dropped for several matches. Nicholls, deposed from opening the innings, did better lower down and finished with over 1,000 for the tenth consecutive season—his benefit year.

At 38, the experienced Milton, again an opening batsman, was the most successful run-getter and his 1,646, his highest aggregate for eight years, carried him to the top of the county averages. His best partner was the last one to be tried—the 21-year-old Bissex. He showed a pleasing style which emanated mainly from good foot work and a readiness to discern the hittable ball and punish it.

Promise was also shown by Mence, released by Warwickshire, and taken on as a pace bowler. He, too, liked to attack the bowling, and is a left-hander Gloucestershire have needed for some seasons. He has a chance to make good with Gloucestershire for he can expect more opportunities as a pace bowler next season with Windows, the Cambridge Blue, retiring to study law.

When Smith returned, he captured 57 wickets in thirteen games

—just less than half the full season—and headed the averages. In 1965 he was the only bowler to secure 100 wickets and 1966 was only the fourth time in the last twenty years that no Gloucestershire bowler had reached that target. Tony Brown sent down nearly 1,000 overs, and in all matches he gained more wickets, 84, than anyone else but they cost him more. Windows was also employed more and the batting of both appeared to be affected.

Bissex, left-arm slow gained more control over length and spin, and became a useful member of the attack. He added variety and gave relief to the off-spinners Mortimore and Allen, who, bowling with customary steadiness, took 151 victims between them, very much the same as in the previous season.

There were occasions when the fielding was not quite up to the high Gloucestershire standard but Milton and Tony Brown brought off many fine catches close to the wickets. Again, Meyer kept in all county games—for the eighth year in succession—and his 64 catches equalled his best.

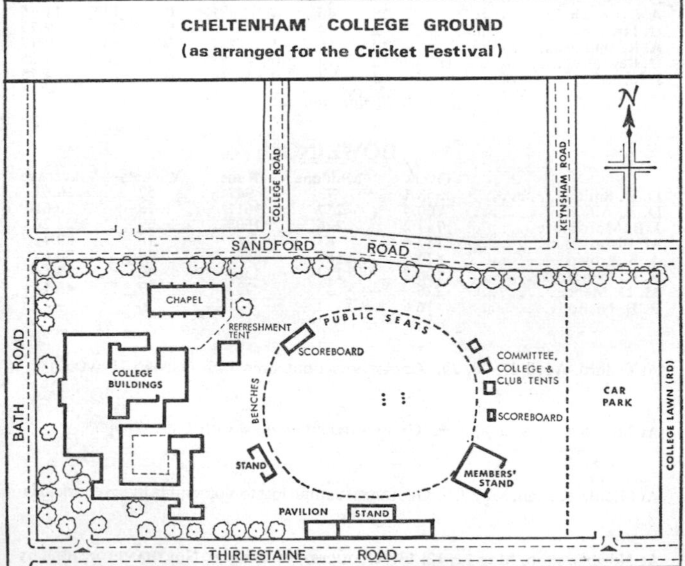

GLOUCESTERSHIRE RESULTS

All First-Class Matches—Played 31, *Won* 6, *Lost* 12, *Drawn* 13
County Championship Matches—Played 28, *Won* 6, *Lost* 12, *Drawn* 9, *No Decision* 1

COUNTY CHAMPIONSHIP AVERAGES

BATTING

	Birthplace	Mtchs.	Inns.	Not Outs	Runs	100's	Highest Inns.	Aver.
C. A. Milton...	*Bristol*	28	53	3	1526	2	138*	30.52
R. B. Nicholls..	*Sharpness*	28	52	5	1162	0	69	24.72
M. Bissex......	*Bath*	21	39	0	856	0	80	21.94
D. Brown......	*Cheltenham*	25	46	3	923	0	92*	21.46
D. Shepherd...	*Northam*	25	49	6	893	1	118	20.76
M. D. Mence...	*Newbury*	14	21	5	325	0	76*	20.31
S. E. Russell....	*Feltham*	19	35	1	592	0	62	17.41
D. A. Allen....	*Bristol*	26	38	11	413	0	82*	15.29
J. B. Mortimore	*Bristol*	27	46	8	581	0	75	15.28
B. J. Meyer....	*Bournemouth*	28	37	18	244	0	31*	12.84
D. R. Smith....	*Bristol*	13	15	7	95	0	21*	11.87
A. S. Brown....	*Bristol*	28	46	4	481	0	33*	11.45
H. Jarman.....	*Bristol*	2	4	0	39	0	28	9.75
A. R. Windows.	*Bristol*	20	31	3	257	0	40*	9.17
D. Bevan......	*Gloucester*	2	4	0	21	0	14	5.25
J. King.......	*Bristol*	2	4	0	19	0	10	4.75

* *Signifies not out.*

BOWLING

	Overs	Maidens	Runs	Wickets	Average
D. R. Smith..........	358.1	73	947	57	16.61
D. A. Allen...........	800.4	257	1611	78	20.65
J. B. Mortimore.......	744.2	236	1605	69	23.26
M. Bissex............	187.4	63	483	16	30.18
A. S. Brown..........	874.2	187	2266	74	30.62
A. R. Windows........	508.2	112	1367	42	32.54
M. D. Mence.........	226	35	733	17	43.11
R. B. Nicholls.........	6	1	21	0	—

At Oxford, April 27, 28, 29. GLOUCESTERSHIRE drew with OXFORD UNIVERSITY.

At Manchester, May 4, 5, 6. GLOUCESTERSHIRE drew with LANCASHIRE.

At Middlesbrough, May 7, 9. GLOUCESTERSHIRE lost to YORKSHIRE by seven wickets

At Northampton, May 11, 12, 13. GLOUCESTERSHIRE beat NORTHAMPTONSHIRE by one wicket.

GLOUCESTERSHIRE v. YORKSHIRE

At Bristol, May 14, 16, 17. Drawn. Rain at 2.45 p.m. on the final day ruined any chance of a finish and Yorkshire were then 192 ahead with one wicket standing. Close was the mainstay of the Yorkshire first innings and his 105 in three and a quarter hours included twelve boundaries. By the consistent batting of their top six Gloucestershire gained a useful lead of 82, and two points. When they went on to capture six of Yorkshire's second-innings wickets for 132 they seemed on the pathway to victory. They were baulked by a partnership of 104 for the seventh wicket between Illingworth and Balderstone. The former, who batted four hours for his 98 would surely have reached his century except for the rain; he was master of the attack. Balderstone's 64 was his highest in first-class cricket.

Yorkshire

K. Taylor b Windows	12	— b Mortimore	48
*D. B. Close c D. Brown b A. S. Brown	105	— c Meyer b A. S. Brown	4
D. E. V. Padgett c Milton b Windows	23	— lbw b A. S. Brown	4
J. H. Hampshire lbw b Mortimore	11	— b A. S. Brown	0
P. J. Sharpe c Meyer b Mortimore	1	— b Allen	5
R. Illingworth st Meyer b Mortimore	1	— not out	98
†J. G. Binks c Meyer b Windows	3	— c Meyer b Mortimore	32
J. C. Balderstone c Meyer b Allen	18	— c Bissex b A S. Brown	64
F. S. Trueman lbw b A. S. Brown	3	— c Nicholls b Allen	1
D. Wilson lbw b Allen	5	— c Milton b Allen	1
J. Waring not out	4	— not out	3
L-b 4	4	B 4, l-b 8, n-b 2	14
1/17 2/84 3/101 4/105 5/113 6/122 7/173 8/177 9/181	190	1/9 2/15 3/15 4/67 5/67 6/132 7/236 8/240 9/243 (9 wkts.)	274

Bowling: *First Innings*—A. S Brown 24—6—50—2; Windows 19—5—48—3; Allen 17.4—4—43—2; Mortimore 16—3—45—3; Bissex 1—1—0—0. *Second Innings*—A. S. Brown 34—8—64—4, Windows 14—3—31—0; Allen 40—17—58—3; Mortimore 31—8—74—2; Bissex 6—1—26—0: Nicholls 1—0—7—0.

Gloucestershire

R. B. Nicholls b Illingworth	31	D. A. Allen c Padgett b Illingworth	8
C. A. Milton hit wkt b Wilson	62	A. R. Windows b Trueman	6
S. E. Russell lbw b Illingworth	25	†B. J. Meyer not out	0
M. Bissex lbw b Waring	52		
D. Brown c Waring b Illingworth	20	B 2, l-b 5, n-b 2	9
D. Shepherd b Wilson	31		
*J. B. Mortimore lbw b Illingworth	9	1/84 2/110 3/134 4/192 5/196	272
A. S. Brown c Close b Trueman	19	6/231 7/243 8/252 9/263	

Bowling: Trueman 18.2—2—58—2; Waring 14—6—25—1; Close 11—1—31—0; Illingworth 50—19—75—5; Taylor 5—2—9—0; Wilson 36—16—65—2.

Umpires: W. E. Phillipson and C. G. Pepper.

At Ilford, May 18, 19, 20. GLOUCESTERSHIRE drew with ESSEX.

At Reading, May 21. GLOUCESTERSHIRE beat BERKSHIRE by 135 runs. (See GILLETTE CUP.)

GLOUCESTERSHIRE v. HAMPSHIRE

At Bristol, May 25, 26, 27. *65 overs.* Hampshire won by eight wickets. Gloucestershire never recovered from being dismissed in their first innings for 87. White was mainly responsible, for he took three of the first four wickets and finished with six for 46. Nicholls, who carried his bat for the first time in his career, alone faced him confidently, but he obtained only 26. Hampshire, apart from a quick 21 by Marshall, showed little inclination to attack the bowling but they reached 154 off the full quota of overs for the loss of only two batsmen. Horton batted patiently but surely for his 57. Shackleton ruined Gloucestershire's second innings by taking five for 17, which gave him a match analysis of nine for 43. Gloucestershire fought stubbornly in the hope of improving their position but could only give their opponents the formality of having to obtain 29 to win. Hampshire lost two wickets in that simple task and so won the match for the loss of only four batsmen.

Gloucestershire

First innings		Second innings	
R. B. Nicholls not out	26	c Barnard b Shackleton	0
C. A. Milton c Timms b White	6	c Timms b Wheatley	24
S. E. Russell b White	2	b Shackleton	28
M. Bissex c Wheatley b Shackleton	0	b Wheatley	0
D. Brown b White	0	c Barnard b Cottam	19
D. Shepherd c Barnard b Shackleton	10	c Livingstone b Sainsbury	11
*J. B. Mortimore b White	1	b Sainsbury	0
A. S. Brown b Shackleton	15	c Livingstone b Shackleton	3
D. A. Allen c Sainsbury b White	19	not out	2
A. R. Windows b Shackleton	3	b Shackleton	0
†B. J. Meyer b White	0	lbw b Shackleton	1
L-b 2, n-b 3	5	B 3, l-b 3, n-b 1	7
1/8 2/11 3/12 4/13 5/31 6/34 7/55 8/82 9/85	87	1/0 2/45 3/49 4/67 5/84 6/84 7/90 8/93 9/93	95

Bowling: *First Innings*—Shackleton 22—14—26—4; White 14.5—2—46—6; Cottam 7—2—10—0. *Second Innings*—Shackleton 27.1—17—17—5; White 9—3—22—0; Cottam 11—3—16—1; Wheatley 20—8—28—2; Sainsbury 15—13—5—2.

Hampshire

First innings		Second innings	
*R. E. Marshall b A. S. Brown	21	c Shepherd b A. S. Brown	7
B. L. Reed lbw b Windows	41	run out	13
H. Horton not out	57	not out	9
D. A. Livingstone not out	31	not out	0
L-b 2, n-b 2	4		
1/23 2/105 (2 wkts., 65 overs)	154	1/8 2/28 (2 wkts.)	29

P. J. Sainsbury, H. M. Barnard, †B. S. V. Timms, K. J. Wheatley, D. Shackleton, D. W. White and R. M. Cottam did not bat.

Bowling: *First Innings*—A. S. Brown 24—7—50—1; Windows 18—4—42—1; Allen 14—3—30—0; Mortimore 9—1—28—0. *Second Innings*—A. S. Brown 7.4—0—22—1; Windows 5—3—3—0; Bissex 2—1—4—0.

Umpires: A. Gaskell and H. Yarnold.

At Bath, May 28, 30, 31. GLOUCESTERSHIRE lost to SOMERSET by 139 runs.

GLOUCESTERSHIRE v. DERBYSHIRE

At Bristol, June 4, 6, 7. *65 overs*. Gloucestershire won by nine runs. Close fights for first-innings lead and the match were the features of this game. Gloucestershire recovered from a poor position in their first innings through a sound 58 by Shepherd, but Derbyshire appeared capable of exceeding their opponents' 158 without difficulty, mainly through a splendid innings by Harvey. Then fine bowling by Brown brought them to the position of needing a single off the last ball of the 65th over to go ahead. Rhodes tapped it forward and the batsmen scrambled the last run. Another attractive innings by Shepherd was chiefly responsible for Derbyshire needing 263 to win. Ample time of five hours fifty minutes remained, but this appeared a disadvantage to Derbyshire. The early batsmen made slow progress. Hall's workmanlike 59 gave them sight of victory before the bowling of Mortimore and Brown swung the game Gloucestershire's way. The last pair required 14 in twenty minutes but could only add four. Derbyshire were all out at 253 and Gloucestershire won with ten minutes left.

Gloucestershire

R. B. Nicholls c Page b Smith.......... 12 — c Taylor b Smith.......... 32
C. A. Milton run out.................. 19 — lbw b Morgan.............. 22
M. Bissex b Morgan.................... 20 — lbw b Rhodes.............. 1
S. E. Russell c Taylor b Smith......... 0 — b Morgan.................. 5
D. Shepherd lbw b Smith............... 58 — c sub b Morgan............ 88
H. Jarman b Smith...................... 0 — c Eyre b Morgan........... 8
*J. B. Mortimore lbw b Morgan.......... 5 — b Morgan.................. 56
A. S. Brown run out................... 10 — c Taylor b Rhodes......... 4
A. R. Windows c and b Morgan.......... 13 — b Rhodes.................. 6
M. D. Mence not out................... 16 — lbw b Morgan.............. 19
†B. J. Meyer not out................... 3 — not out................... 0
N-b 2.................................. 2 B 4, l-b 8, n-b 10....... 22

1/33 2/33 3/33 (9 wkts., 65 overs) 158 1/43 2/44 3/65 4/65 5/111 263
4/111 5/111 6/111 7/125 8/128 9/141 6/201 7/207 8/213 9/262

Bowling: *First Innings*—Buxton 11—3—33—0; Rhodes 10—1—26—0; Morgan 22—4—51—3; Smith 17—8—33—4; Eyre 5—0—13—0. *Second Innings*—Buxton 11—3—34—0; Rhodes 28—8—72—3; Smith 22—7—35—1; Morgan 33.1—15—55—6; Page 9—2—29—0; Johnson 1—0—4—0; Eyre 2—0—12—0.

Derbyshire

I. W. Hall run out.................... 11 — c Meyer b Windows......... 59
J. R. Eyre lbw b Windows............... 0 — c Meyer b Windows......... 19
J. F. Harvey not out.................. 73 — b Mence................... 29
H. L. Johnson b Brown................. 10 — c and b Mortimore......... 35
I. R. Buxton lbw b Windows............. 0 — lbw b Windows............. 1
*D. C. Morgan c and b Mence........... 35 — c and b Mortimore......... 12
M. Hill b Brown....................... 17 — lbw b Brown............... 4
M. H. Page lbw b Brown................. 0 — b Brown................... 35
†R. W. Taylor b Brown.................. 5 — b Brown................... 25
E. Smith b Brown....................... 0 — lbw b Mortimore........... 13
H. J. Rhodes not out................... 2 — not out................... 2
L-b 5, n-b 1........................... 6 L-b 17, n-b 2............ 19

1/2 2/18 3/31 4/32 (9 wkts., 65 overs) 159 1/40 2/98 3/120 4/124 5/155 253
5/83 6/142 7/142 8/156 9/156 6/164 7/175 8/234 9/249

Bowling: *First Innings*—Brown 23—8—42—5; Windows 22—4—47—2; Mortimore 10—2—29—0; Mence 10—2—35—1. *Second Innings*—Brown 34—10—69—3; Windows 31—7—63—3; Mortimore 42.4—23—51—3; Mence 25—9—51—1.

Umpires: F. Jakeman and W. E. Phillipson.

At Bristol, June 8, 9, 10. GLOUCESTERSHIRE drew with WEST INDIES, scores level. (See WEST INDIES section.)

GLOUCESTERSHIRE v. WARWICKSHIRE

At Bristol, June 11, 13, 14. *65 overs.* Drawn. Gloucestershire were set 227 to win in three hours but the task proved beyond them despite a sound innings of 92 not out by David Brown and they were never on level terms with the clock. Warwickshire claimed the extra time in an endeavour to force a win but could capture only one wicket and at the close Gloucestershire were 182 for seven, thus 45 from their target. On the first day Abberley and Amiss, who both just missed centuries, gave a delightful display of forceful batting and in a second-wicket stand hit 179 in two and a half hours. They were responsible for Warwickshire making 252 for four wickets off the 65 overs. Rain restricted play to the last hour on the second day and Gloucestershire declared next morning at 214 for seven, thus conceding a lead to their opponents of 38 and with 11 deliveries untaken. Warwickshire, chiefly through some hard hitting by M. J. K. Smith and Jameson, were able to declare at 188 for five, to try to get a decision.

Warwickshire

R. N. Abberley lbw b A. S. Brown	91	— c A. S. Brown b Windows	0
R. W. Barber c Mortimore b Windows	5	— lbw b A. S. Brown	9
D. L. Amiss b A. S. Brown	97	— c Shepherd b Allen	44
*M. J. K. Smith c Windows b Mence	9	— c Mence b Allen	62
J. A. Jameson not out	37	— not out	44
K. Ibadulla not out	8	— b Allen	11
T. W. Cartwright (did not bat)		— not out	10
B 1, l-b 3, n-b 1	5	B 2, l-b 4, n-b 2	8
1/7 2/186 3/205 4/207 (4 wkts., 65 overs)	252	1/0 2/12 3/98 4/125 5/165 (5 wkts., dec.)	188

†A. C. Smith, J. M. Allan, R. V. Webster and D. J. Brown did not bat.

Bowling: *First Innings*—Mence 17—1—79—1; A. S. Brown 27—4—89—2; Windows 21—7—79—1. *Second Innings*—A. S. Brown 9—1—35—1; Windows 7—2—18—1; Mence 11—1—41—0; Allen 18—4—41—3; Mortimore 11—1—36—0; Nicholls 2—0—9—0.

Gloucestershire

R. B. Nicholls b Ibadulla	46	— c Cartwright b Barber	18
C. A. Milton b Brown	19	— c Amiss b Brown	9
D. Brown c Webster b Ibadulla	6	— not out	92
S. E. Russell c Allan b Cartwright	45	— c Amiss b Allan	22
D. Shepherd c Webster b Cartwright	40	— c Amiss b Allan	1
*J. B. Mortimore not out	18	— c A. C. Smith b Barber	0
A. S. Brown b Cartwright	21	— c A. C. Smith b Brown	17
A. R. Windows b Brown	15	— b Barber	4
D. A. Allen (did not bat)		— not out	12
L-b 4	4	B 7	7
1/31 2/64 3/74 4/145 5/167 6/199 7/214 (7 wkts., dec.)	214	1/11 2/53 3/92 4/101 5/104 6/109 7/157 (7 wkts.)	182

M. D. Mence and †B. J. Meyer did not bat.

Bowling: *First Innings*—D. J. Brown 17.1—3—56—2; Webster 12—1—40—0; Ibadulla 15—2—37—2; Cartwright 19—5—77—3. *Second Innings*—D. J. Brown 9—3—16—2; Webster 6—1—15—0; Cartwright 5—1—14—0; Barber 23—5—49—3; Allan 11—1—31—2; Ibadulla 12—1—50—0.

Umpires: A. E. Rhodes and H. Yarnold.

At Birmingham, June 18, 20, 21. GLOUCESTERSHIRE beat WARWICKSHIRE by five runs.

At Birmingham, June 22. GLOUCESTERSHIRE lost to WARWICKSHIRE by six wickets. (See GILLETTE CUP.)

GLOUCESTERSHIRE v. CAMBRIDGE UNIVERSITY

At Lydney, June 25, 26, 27. Drawn with only two and a half hours of play owing to rain. Gloucestershire's first experiment with Sunday play was ruined by the weather and only an hour was possible on that day. Not a ball was bowled on the third day.

Gloucestershire

C. A. Milton b Cottrell	69	D. Shepherd not out	13
J. King c Russell b Cottrell	28	B 4, l-b 2	6
D. Brown c Acfield b Cottrell	0		
H. Jarman not out	44	1/41 2/45 3/147 (3 wkts.)	160

M. Bissex, *J. B. Mortimore, A. R. Windows, †R. Etheridge, D. Smith and J. Davey did not bat.

Bowling: Russell 10—1—43—0; Cottrell 22—5—56—3; Roopnaraine 7—2—11—0; Acfield 13—1—44—0.

Cambridge University

K. P. W. J. McAdam, R. E. J. Chambers, A. V. E. Gould, *†D. L. Murray, N. J. Cosh, V. P. Malalasekara, G. A. Cottrell, R. Roopnaraine, N. Sinker, D. L. Acfield and S. G. Russell.

Umpires: J. S. Buller and P. A. Gibb.

GLOUCESTERSHIRE v. LANCASHIRE

At Lydney, June 29, 30, July 1. Lancashire beat Gloucestershire by 60 runs. There was instability in the Gloucestershire batting when they needed 193 in three hours and twenty-five minutes to win and indiscretion in selecting the right ball to hit. They were unable to master the young left-arm bowler Lloyd, who spun Lancashire to victory, finishing with seven wickets for 38. Gloucestershire's chances were bright at 106 for four, with eighty minutes left for the remaining 87, but Lloyd put paid to their prospects when he captured three wickets in nine deliveries without cost. Gloucestershire gained first-innings points, chiefly through skilful bowling by Allen, who played a major part in the dismissal of Lancashire for 176, and a steady 53 by Nicholls around which the total of 202 was built. Lancashire gained a grip on the game in the second innings through a sixth-wicket stand of 81 between Pullar and Lever.

Lancashire

D. M. Green b A. S. Brown	17	— run out	38
G. K. Knox hit wkt. b Allen	9	— b Windows	9
J. D. Bond c Mortimore b Allen	47	— b Allen	18
G. Pullar b Mortimore	23	— c D. Brown b Mortimore	77
A. M. Beddow lbw b Allen	13	— b Allen	8
D. Lloyd b Allen	3	— lbw b Mortimore	1
P. Lever b Allen	31	— c A. S. Brown b Mortimore	32
K. Shuttleworth c Meyer b Bissex	14	— c D. Brown b Mortimore	16
†K. Goodwin c Allen b Bissex	3	— c Milton b Allen	1
T. Greenhough lbw b Allen	10	— b Mortimore	10
*J. B. Statham not out	1	— not out	2
L-b 5	5	L-b 6	6
1/24 2/28 3/89 4/109 5/116 6/119 7/150 8/162 9/174	176	1/20 2/63 3/67 4/87 5/100 6/181 7/194 8/204 9/205	218

Bowling: *First Innings*—A. S. Brown 13—2—27—1; Windows 4—1—5—0; Allen 47—18—74—6; Mortimore 38—13—48—1; Bissex 9.5—3—17—2. *Second Innings*—A. S. Brown 10—1—28—0; Windows 9—1—22—1; Allen 53—29—68—3; Mortimore 45.3—17—74—5; Bissex 10—2—20—0.

Gloucestershire

R. B. Nicholls c Knox b Greenhough... 53 — c Goodwin b Statham 0
C. A. Milton c Goodwin b Shuttleworth. 29 — c Goodwin b Lever......... 4
D. Brown b Greenhough............. 1 — lbw b Lloyd............... 31
A. R. Windows c Pullar b Greenhough.. 10 — c Goodwin b Lloyd......... 3
S. E. Russell c Shuttleworth b Lloyd.... 31 — st Goodwin b Lloyd........ 34
D. Shepherd not out................ 36 — c Goodwin b Lloyd......... 22
M. Bissex b Greenhough............. 0 — c Knox b Lloyd........... 8
D. A. Allen lbw b Greenhough .... 10 — c Pullar b Lloyd 1
*J. B. Mortimore c Shuttleworth b Lloyd 4 — c Green b Greenhough...... 15
A. S. Brown run out................ 9 — c Statham b Lloyd.......... 6
†B. J. Meyer c Goodwin b Lloyd....... 9 — not out 0
B 4, l-b 3, n-b 3............... 10 L-b 6, n-b 2.......... 8

1/49 2/57 3/77 4/126 5/134 202 1/0 2/15 3/59 4/82 5/106 132
6/134 7/166 8/177 9/190 6/106 7/108 8/124 9/131

Bowling: *First Innings*—Statham 7—3—10—0; Lever 7—1—21—0; Greenhough 41—20—57—5; Shuttleworth 13—4—28—1; Lloyd 26.5—7—76—3. *Second Innings*—Statham 5—1—5—1; Lever 6—1—18—1; Shuttleworth 5—0—19—0; Greenhough 19—5—44—1; Lloyd 15.1—2—38—7.

Umpires: J. S. Buller and P. A. Gibb.

GLOUCESTERSHIRE v. LEICESTERSHIRE

At Bristol, July 2, 4, 5. Drawn. On the last day rain limited play to sixty-five minutes and prevented any opportunity of a finish. The game was given up with Gloucestershire 33 ahead and six second innings wickets standing. Milton carried his bat for the third time in his career and obtained the last three runs to complete his century in partnership with the last man, Meyer. Once this was accomplished the last-wicket pair were responsible for the best stand of the innings—68 in an hour. A partnership of 152 for the fifth wicket by Constant and Marner, not only enabled Leicestershire to recover from a disastrous start, but to gain a first-innings lead of 22, although a brisk fifty by Lock played an important part. On the third morning Marner started to play havoc with Gloucestershire's second innings and took all four wickets for 19.

Gloucestershire

R. B. Nicholls c Tolchard b Greensword. 23 — b Marner 18
C. A. Milton not out ....138 — b Marner 2
D. Brown c Constant b Lock .... 2 — b Marner 6
S. E. Russell lbw b Savage............ 1 — c Spencer b Marner........ 19
D. Shepherd run out................ 0 — not out 5
M. D. Mence run out................ 5 — not out 0
D. A. Allen c Tolchard b Lock......... 8
*J. B. Mortimore b Savage 20
A. S. Brown c Tolchard b Spencer...... 10
A. R. Windows b Spencer............. 5
†B. J. Meyer b Spencer............... 27
B 7, l-b 6, n-b 1............... 14 L-b 5................. 5

1/48 2/53 3/80 4/84 5/101 253 1/12 2/26 3/47 (4 wkts.) 55
6/112 7/150 8/171 9/185 4/54

Bowling: *First Innings*—Spencer 24.3—4—73—3; Marner 15—3—38—0; Lock 36—18—61—2; Greensword 11—1—25—1; Savage 22—6—42—2. *Second Innings*—Spencer 10—0—25—0; Marner 13—5—19—4; Greensword 4—1—6—0.

Leicestershire

B. J. Booth c Mayer b A. S. Brown	16	*G. A. R. Lock b Mortimore	51
M. E. Norman b A. S. Brown	13	C. T. Spencer c Allen b Mence	3
M. R. Hallam c Meyer b Allen	1	J. S. Savage not out	1
C. C. Inman c Allen b A. S. Brown	3		
P. Marner c Windows b Mortimore	73	B 10, l-b 2, n-b 3	15
D. Constant lbw b A. S. Brown	80		
S. Greensword lbw b Windows	7	1/27 2/30 3/32 4/34 5/186	275
†R. W. Tolchard b Mortimore	12	6/202 7/202 8/264 9/267	

Bowling: A. S. Brown 32—8—73—4; Windows 24—7—57—1; Allen 21—6—49—1; Mence 16—3—26—1; Mortimore 27.3—9—55—3.

Umpires: W. F. Price and O. W. Herman.

At Folkestone, July 6, 7, 8. GLOUCESTERSHIRE lost to KENT by 173 runs.

GLOUCESTERSHIRE v. GLAMORGAN

At Gloucester, July 9, 11, 12. *65 overs.* Gloucestershire won by two wickets. Windows off-drove the fourth ball of the last over, bowled by Wheatley, to the boundary to record a remarkable victory. The ninth-wicket pair came together with 56 needed in thirty-five minutes when Glamorgan had a firm grip on the game, but Windows and Meyer hit the runs off. Gloucestershire's achievement of securing 241 in three and a half hours was remarkable. Despite a steady 52 by Milton, they were well behind the clock until Shepherd's breezy 69, which included two 6's and seven 4's in eighty minutes. Even so, Wheatley's hostile bowling seemed to have brought a Glamorgan victory in sight, for eight men were out for 185. The exciting finish followed a close fight for first-innings lead, which went to Gloucestershire by five runs, despite an excellent innings by Rees. In the Glamorgan second innings A. R. Lewis was the dominating figure and his immaculate batting earned him 100 (eleven 4's). Smith, after a long absence through knee trouble, played a large part in Gloucestershire's success with a match analysis of ten for 92.

Glamorgan

A. Jones b Smith	17	— c Meyer b Smith	45
W. Slade c Meyer b Windows	18	— b Smith	1
P. M. Walker lbw b Smith	0	— c Milton b Allen	22
A. R. Lewis c Nicholls b A. S. Brown	23	— c Meyer b Smith	100
A. Rees c Windows b Smith	65	— c King b Smith	18
L. Hill c Allen b A. S. Brown	3	— c Meyer b Windows	16
†E. Jones b A. S. Brown	0	— b A. S. Brown	10
E. Lewis run out	22	— c King b A. S. Brown	18
D. J. Shepherd c Allen b Smith	0	— c Nicholls b Smith	0
I. J. Jones c Meyer b A. S. Brown	1	— b Smith	4
*O. S. Wheatley not out	0	— not out	0
B 1, l-b 3	4	B 6, l-b 1, w 4	11
1/23 2/23 3/53 4/77 5/85 6/89 7/152 8/152 9/153	153	1/8 2/47 3/139 4/190 5/204 6/218 7/241 8/241 9/245	245

Bowling: *First Innings*—Smith 23—2—58—4; A. S. Brown 20.1—3—56—4; Windows 8—2—21—1; Mortimore 11—6—14—0. *Second Innings*—Smith 22.3—9—34—6; A. S. Brown 16—3—39—2; Allen 36—12—65—1; Mortimore 17—2—54—0; Windows 15—5—42—1.

Gloucestershire

First Innings		Second Innings	
C. A. Milton c Rees b I. J. Jones	38	c Walker b Shepherd	52
J. King c Hill b I. J. Jones	10	c E. Jones b I. J. Jones	0
D. Brown lbw b Shepherd	53	b E. Lewis	19
D. Shepherd lbw b Walker	4	c Walker b Wheatley	69
R. B. Nicholls not out	21	c Slade b Shepherd	5
*J. B. Mortimore b Walker	1	c Rees b Wheatley	15
A. S. Brown c Slade b Wheatley	20	b Wheatley	0
A. R. Windows b Wheatley	6	not out	40
D. A. Allen not out	2	lbw b Wheatley	15
†B. J. Meyer (did not bat)		not out	19
L-b 2, w 1	3	B 5, l-b 3, n-b 2	10
1/12 2/78 3/102 4/108 (7 wkts., 65 overs) 5/109 6/146 7/154	158	1/0 2/54 3/113 4/119 (8 wkts.) 5/165 6/168 7/168 8/185	244

D. R. Smith did not bat.

Bowling: *First Innings*—I. J. Jones 20—5—59—2; Wheatley 17—4—29—2; Shepherd 15—3—32—1; Walker 13—2—35—2. *Second Innings*—I. J. Jones 11—2—28—1; Wheatley 13.4—3—38—4; Shepherd 22—6—66—2; E. Lewis 20—4—68—1; Slade 4—0—16—0; Walker 5—0—18—0.

Umpires: A. Jepson and P. B. Wight.

GLOUCESTERSHIRE v. WORCESTERSHIRE
(R. B. Nicholls' Benefit)

At Gloucester, July 13, 14, 15. *65 overs.* Drawn. Rain washed out what might have been an interesting finish, for Worcestershire, set 301 in four hours and ten minutes, had scored only four without loss before repeated heavy showers caused the match to be abandoned. This game was an outstanding example of the success of the 65 overs experimental rule, for on the first day 436 runs were scored for the loss of twelve wickets. An attractive second-wicket stand between Milton and David Brown which yielded 126 off forty overs was the feature of Gloucestershire's innings. Worcestershire gained a first-innings lead through a workmanlike innings by Horton who fourth out at 183, hit one 6 and seven 4's. Gloucestershire quickly liquidated the arrears in their second innings, in which Shepherd's first century in championship cricket included three 6's and twelve 4's. Allen pushed home the advantage and his 82 not out enabled Gloucestershire to declare.

Gloucestershire

First Innings		Second Innings	
C. A. Milton c Ormrod b Flavell	76	c d'Oliveira b Gifford	16
J. King b Flavell	3	b Brain	6
D. Brown lbw b Flavell	63	b Brain	23
D. Shepherd lbw b Flavell	18	c Gifford b d'Oliveira	118
R. B. Nicholls lbw b Flavell	0	c d'Oliveira b Brain	48
*J. B. Mortimore not out	18	lbw b Brain	22
A. S. Brown b Flavell	0	not out	33
A. R. Windows not out	0		
D. A. Allen (did not bat)		not out	82
B 4, l-b 7, w 1, n-b 1	13	B 1, l-b 4, n-b 1	6
1/25 2/151 3/152 4/158 5/191 6/191 (6 wkts., 65 overs)	191	1/11 2/37 3/51 4/197 5/232 6/293 (6 wkts., dec.)	354

†B. J. Meyer and D. R. Smith did not bat.

Bowling: *First Innings*—Flavell 27—10—49—6; Brain 16—3—65—0; Gifford 10—6—18—0; d'Oliveira 12—1—46—0. *Second Innings*—Flavell 33—11—79—0; Brain 40.1—10—107—4; Gifford 42—15—87—1; d'Oliveira 27—11—50—1; Horton 9—2—25—0.

Worcestershire

C. D. Fearnley c Meyer b Smith .... 0 — not out 3
M. J. Horton b A. S. Brown........... 86 — not out 1
J. A. Ormrod c Milton b Allen......... 17
*T. W. Graveney retired hurt 7
B. d'Oliveira c Meyer b Smith.......... 36
R. G. A. Headley c Milton b Smith..... 37
D. W. Richardson not out.............. 27
†R. Booth b A. S. Brown............... 3
N. Gifford not out.................... 11
B 7, l-b 14........................ 21

1/3 2/41 3/121 (6 wkts., 65 overs) 245 (no wkt.) 4
4/183 5/215 6/228

B. M. Brain and J. A. Flavell did not bat.

Bowling—*First Innings*—Smith 19—1—76—3; Windows 8—1—30—0; Mortimore 13—3—32—0; Allen 14—3—37—1; A. S. Brown 11—1—49—2. *Second Innings*—Smith 1—1—0—0; A. S. Brown 0.4—0—4—0.

Umpires: A. Jepson and J. Langridge.

At Worcester, July 16, 18. GLOUCESTERSHIRE lost to WORCESTERSHIRE by ten wickets.

At Cardiff, July 20, 21, 22. GLOUCESTERSHIRE drew with GLAMORGAN.

At Nottingham, July 23, 25, 26. GLOUCESTERSHIRE lost to NOTTINGHAMSHIRE by 88 runs.

GLOUCESTERSHIRE v. KENT

At Bristol, July 27, 28, 29. Gloucestershire gained an unexpected victory in the last over by four wickets. An opening stand of 115 by Denness and Luckhurst was the foundation of Kent's 316, and Cowdrey and Leary were together in a fourth-wicket partnership of 103. Gloucestershire, who batted grimly in reply, were in danger of following-on, but Mence saved them with a fine hard-hitting innings. Kent's lead was only 86 and Cowdrey in a bid to win the game declared just before lunch on the third day after Luckhurst had shaped splendidly for 81 not out. Set 200 to win in three hours they lost three wickets for 39 in forty-five minutes and judged by their first-innings performance of 230 in over six hours the task looked beyond them. A sparkling innings by Nicholls, whose 64 contained eight 4's, effected a recovery and placed them on the pathway to victory. When Sayer began the last over Gloucestershire needed three to win. Mortimore did not score off the first two deliveries but the third glanced off his pads and went for four leg-byes.

Kent

M. H. Denness c D. Brown b Windows . 80 — c D. Brown b A. S. Brown .. 0
B. W. Luckhurst c Bissex b Allen....... 57 — not out 81
†D. Nicholls lbw b Allen.............. 12
*M. C. Cowdrey c Windows b Mence... 87 — not out 3
S. E. Leary b A. S. Brown............. 48 — c Mortimore b Mence 5
A. L. Dixon c Mence b Windows....... 2 — b Mence.................. 8
A. Ealham c Milton b Mence.......... 21 — b Windows................ 0
D. M. Sayer not out.................. 2
R. C. Wilson (did not bat)........... — b Mortimore 12
L-b 5, n-b 2 .... 7 L-b 3, n-b 1 4

1/115 2/137 3/161 4/264 (7 wkts., dec.) 316 1/0 2/42 (5 wkts., dec.) 113
5/269 6/308 7/316 3/77 4/105 5/106

J. N. Graham and J. C. Dye did not bat.

Bowling: *First Innings*—A. S. Brown 31—6—71—1; Windows 24—1—80—2; Mence 7.2—0—31—2; Mortimore 22—6—54—0; Allen 23—8—40—2; Bissex 14—5—33—0. *Second Innings*—A. S. Brown 11—2—32—1; Windows 9—2—19—1; Mortimore 9—3—27—1; Mence 8—0—31—2.

Gloucestershire

First Innings		Second Innings	
C. A. Milton c Cowdrey b Dye	5	c Leary b Dye	16
M. Bissex lbw b Sayer	32	c Denness b Sayer	16
D. Brown c Nicholls b Sayer	15	c Cowdrey b Dye	6
D. Shepherd c Nicholls b Sayer	32	c Sayer b Leary	25
R. B. Nicholls c Nicholls b Dye	11	c Luckhurst b Graham	64
M. D. Mence not out	76	c Ealham b Dixon	33
D. A. Allen c Nicholls b Graham	14		
*J. B. Mortimore b Graham	3	not out	9
A. S. Brown c Ealham b Graham	7	not out	24
A. R. Windows b Graham	9		
†B. J. Meyer c Luckhurst b Sayer	22		
L-b 2, n-b 2	4	L-b 7, n-b 1	8
1/9 2/50 3/59 4/91 5/110 6/140 7/144 8/163 9/187	230	1/28 2/38 3/39 4/83 5/147 6/177 (6 wkts.)	201

Bowling: *First Innings*—Graham 45—18—68—4; Dye 24—3—46—2; Sayer 26—7—68—4; Dixon 23—9—44—0. *Second Innings*—Sayer 8.3—0—25—1; Dye 14—5—31—2; Graham 12—3—50—1; Dixon 12—0—41—1; Leary 9—0—46—1.

Umpires: O. W. Herman and F. Jakeman.

At Hove, July 30, August 1, 2. GLOUCESTERSHIRE drew with SUSSEX.

At Derby, August 3, 4, 5. GLOUCESTERSHIRE beat DERBYSHIRE by 68 runs.

GLOUCESTERSHIRE v. SOMERSET

At Bristol, August 6, 7, 8. Drawn. Not a ball was bowled on Saturday because of rain and the match commenced on Sunday. Somerset never recovered from a disastrous start against Smith and A. S. Brown, who obtained some help from the pitch, which was damp on top, and they were all out for 90 in two hours. Gloucestershire, mainly through a capital 60 by Bissex out of an opening stand of 118, were 125 for two at the end of the day and declared next morning. Somerset at first accepted the challenge to go for a decision but, at 65 for four, realised they could not score fast enough to declare and set their opponents a target. They defended stubbornly, failed to seize scoring chances, even ignoring slow full tosses and their 170 occupied five hours. A section of the crowd by slow handclapping displayed their disapproval of the lack of enterprise. Gloucestershire showed willingness to embark on the almost impossible task of scoring 136 in seventy-five minutes, but when 40 for three in half an hour they gave up. The experiment of Sunday cricket in Bristol was a success, the attendance being about 4,000 and the proceeds amounting to £311.

Somerset

First innings		Second innings	
F. T. Willetts c Meyer b Smith	7	c Meyer b A. S. Brown	6
R. Virgin b Smith	0	c A. S. Brown b Mence	30
M. Kitchen c Meyer b A. S. Brown	0	c Meyer b Mence	20
G. Burgess b A. S. Brown	17	c Shepherd b Allen	5
G. Atkinson c Meyer b A. S. Brown	6	c Meyer b A. S. Brown	25
*C. R. M. Atkinson b Smith	1	lbw b Allen	35
W. E. Alley run out	15	c Smith b Mortimore	7
K. E. Palmer lbw b Mortimore	14	b Smith	8
†G. Clayton b Allen	24	lbw b Mortimore	4
P. J. Robinson c Meyer b Mortimore	0	not out	16
B. A. Langford not out	0	b Smith	2
B 3, l-b 2, w 1	6	B 4, l-b 7, w 1	12
1/0 2/12 3/14 4/32 5/33 6/49 7/51 8/85 9/89	90	1/11 2/59 3/64 4/65 5/130 6/138 7/142 8/148 9/164	170

Bowling: *First Innings*—Smith 14—5—29—3; A. S. Brown 15—3—40—3; Mence 4—0—11—0; Allen 3—1—4—1; Mortimore 1—1—0—2. *Second Innings*—Smith 22.3—9—30—2; A. S. Brown 25—10—48—2; Mence 18—4—39—2; Allen 27—16—28—2; Mortimore 17—12—8—2; Bissex 2—1—3—0; Nicholls 1—0—2—0.

Gloucestershire

First innings		Second innings	
C. A. Milton not out	48		
M. Bissex c Robinson b Alley	60	c C. R. M. Atkinson b Alley	22
D. Brown lbw b Alley	0		
D. Shepherd not out	3	lbw b Alley	3
A. S. Brown (did not bat)	—	b Palmer	0
R. B. Nicholls (did not bat)	—	not out	17
*J. B. Mortimore (did not bat)	—	b Palmer	0
M. D. Mence (did not bat)	—	not out	0
B 7, l-b 6, w 1	14	B 4, l-b 1, n-b 2	7
1/118 2/122 (2 wkts., dec.)	125	1/7 2/12 3/40 4/48 (4 wkts.)	49

D. A. Allen, †B. J. Meyer and D. R. Smith did not bat.

Bowling: *First Innings*—Palmer 12—2—28—0; Alley 11—1—23—2; Langford 9—3—17—0; C. R. M. Atkinson 5—1—11—0; Burgess 7—1—18—0; Robinson 4—1—14—0. *Second Innings*—Palmer 6—0—28—2; Alley 6—1—14—2; Langford 1—1—0—0.

Umpires: J. Arnold and G. H. Pope.

GLOUCESTERSHIRE v. SUSSEX

At Cheltenham, August 13, 15. Sussex won by ten wickets in two days. Gloucestershire were only 53 in arrears on the first innings but, their batsmen floundered in their second innings against the devastating bowling of Snow and Tony Buss on a helpful pitch and were dismissed for 96. When Gloucestershire slumped to 39 for seven against the opening attack, they looked like being dismissed for a very small total, but the tail-enders saved them from a complete rout. Still, Sussex only wanted 44 to win and soon hit them without any trouble, and without any loss. Michael Buss, who batted so confidently against the spinners Mortimore and Allen in the first innings, contributed 24. Sussex stayed to play a £100 challenge match under Gillette Cup rules on the Tuesday for Nicholls's benefit and the gate realised £125. Gloucestershire won by 22.

Gloucestershire

C. A. Milton c Oakman b A. Buss	13 — lbw b A. Buss	5
M. Bissex b Snow	32 — b A. Buss	7
D. Brown c Parks b Snow	11 — c Parks b Snow	0
D. Shepherd c and b A. Buss	1 — lbw b Snow	3
R. B. Nicholls lbw b Snow	35 — c Foreman b A. Buss	8
M. D. Mence c M. A. Buss b A. Buss	6 — b Snow	10
A. S. Brown c Oakman b Bates	20 — c Parks b A. Buss	1
D. A. Allen c Pataudi b Bates	2 — lbw b A. Buss	17
*J. B. Mortimore lbw b A. Buss	8 — b Snow	20
†B. J. Meyer not out	9 — c Parks b Snow	11
D. R. Smith c Oakman b Bates	6 — not out	7
L-b 2, w 1, n-b 3	6 B 4, l-b 2, n-b 1	7
1/23 2/57 3/58 4/60 5/78 6/116 7/123 8/126 9/139	149 1/11 2/12 3/12 4/25 5/33 6/39 7/39 8/67 9/89	96

Bowling: *First Innings*—A. Buss 20—6—49—4; Snow 18—3—37—3; Oakman 18—5—27—0; M. A. Buss 5—2—7—0; Bates 13.5—2—23—3. *Second Innings*—Snow 18.2—3—37—5; A. Buss 21—10—35—5; Oakman 3—0—17—0.

Sussex

L. J. Lenham c A. S. Brown b Allen	25 — not out	13
M. A. Buss b Allen	51 — not out	24
J. A. Snow lbw b Mortimore	1	
K. G. Suttle b Allen	46	
†J. M. Parks c Milton b Bissex	23	
*Nawab of Pataudi c Meyer b Bissex	0	
A. S. M. Oakman c Meyer b Mortimore	2	
P. J. Graves c Meyer b Mortimore	3	
D. J. Foreman c A. S. Brown b Mortimore	34	
A. Buss c Nicholls b Allen	3	
D. L. Bates not out	6	
B 3, l-b 5	8 B 5, l-b 2	7
1/54 2/59 3/108 4/140 5/140 6/143 7/153 8/193 9/193	202 (no wkt.)	44

Bowling: *First Innings*—Smith 9—1—30—0; A. S. Brown 14—1—32—0; Allen 31—10—58—4; Mortimore 36—16—49—4; Bissex 7—0—25—2. *Second Innings*—A. S. Brown 3—0—11—0; Mortimore 4—0—7—0; Allen 4—3—1—0; Bissex 3—1—15—0; Nicholls 1—0—3—0.

Umpires: W. H. Copson and C. G. Pepper.

GLOUCESTERSHIRE v. SURREY

At Cheltenham, August 17, 18. *65 overs.* Surrey won by seven wickets five minutes before the normal close on the second day. Their success was largely due to an entertaining third-wicket stand of 115 between Barrington and Stewart. This partnership was the foundation of their first-innings lead of 81 over Gloucestershire, who had given an indifferent batting display in being dismissed for 119 off 44.2 overs. Barrington gave a brilliant exhibition, hitting one 6 and ten 4's in his 76 in two hours. All six Surrey wickets fell to Smith for 44, a splendid performance. The Gloucestershire batting improved in their second innings, due mostly to Mortimore, who had put himself in at number four as night-watchman. Next morning he hit 75, which included six 6's and five 4's. His innings was a mixture of watchful defence and big hitting, and lasted three and three-quarter hours. All his sixes were off Pocock, though the off-spinner took four for 69. Mortimore's heroic effort was of no avail, as Surrey wanted only 109 and obtained them mainly through some lively hitting by Smith.

Gloucestershire

C. A. Milton lbw b Jackman	15	— b Harman	9
M. Bissex c Edwards b Storey	10	— c Long b Jackman	0
S. E. Russell run out	16	— b Harman	22
D. Bevan b Storey	4	— c Edwards b Pocock	1
R. B. Nicholls lbw b Harman	18	— c Edwards b Harman	27
M. D. Mence c Long b Jefferson	18	— c Storey b Pocock	3
A. S. Brown c Long b Pocock	1	— c Willett b Pocock	21
D. A. Allen run out	5	— c Edwards b Jackman	7
*J. B. Mortimore c Willett b Pocock	5	— b Jackman	75
†B. J. Meyer not out	12	— b Pocock	6
D. R. Smith c Edwards b Harman	7	— not out	4
L-b 8	8	B 6, l-b 6, n-b 1, w 1	14
1/25 2/31 3/45 4/50 5/81 6/82 7/87 8/95 9/105	119	1/0 2/22 3/51 4/116 5/119 6/133 7/149 8/157 9/184	189

Bowling: *First Innings*—Jackman 12—4—27—1; Jefferson 7—1—36—1; Storey 11—7—14—2; Pocock 8—1—20—2; Harman 6.2—0—14—2. *Second Innings*—Jackman 21—7—27—3; Storey 15—6—22—0; Pocock 26—7—69—4; Harman 35—17—42—3; Jefferson 11—6—11—0; Barrington 2—1—4—0.

Surrey

M. J. Edwards lbw b Smith	5	— c Brown b Allen	29
W. A. Smith c Allen b Smith	18	— c Meyer b Smith	50
*M. J. Stewart c Russell b Smith	55	— lbw b Mortimore	19
K. F. Barrington c Meyer b Smith	76	— not out	9
S. J. Storey not out	28		
R. I. Jefferson c Milton b Smith	6		
P. I. Pocock b Smith	0		
M. D. Willett not out	1	— not out	1
B 4, l-b 5, n-b 1, w 1	11	L-b 1	1
1/12 2/38 3/153 4/169 5/176 6/176 (6 wkts., 65 overs)	200	1/51 2/89 3/105 (3 wkts.)	109

†A. Long, R. Harman and R. D. Jackman did not bat.

Bowling: *First Innings*—Smith 25—5—44—6; Brown 13—3—33—0; Allen 12—1—20—0; Bissex 4—1—21—0; Mortimore 5—1—21—0; Mence 6—0—50—0. *Second Innings*—Smith 9—1—32—1; Brown 5—3—5—0; Mortimore 9.4—2—24—1; Allen 11—4—26—1; Bissex 6—1—21—0.

Umpires: C. G. Pepper and W. H. Copson.

GLOUCESTERSHIRE v. MIDDLESEX

At Cheltenham, August 20, 22, 23. Middlesex won by nine wickets. They followed Sussex and Surrey in winning at the Cheltenham Festival, but they had to wait until half an hour before lunch on the third day to record their victory. Gloucestershire never really recovered from being dismissed for 102 in their first innings, when they could not master Hooker, who took five for 35. Middlesex gained a first innings lead of 158, which kept them on top. For that advantage they were indebted to a grand innings of 96 by Parfitt, the left-hander hitting thirteen 4's, most of them by perfectly timed cover driving. Smith caused something of a minor collapse when he took the new ball, for he captured five for 30, which gave him six for 91 in the innings. Gloucestershire's batting was more stable in the second innings following an opening stand of 85, but Stewart, who had received a trial for Gloucestershire at the start of the season, secured five for 63. Gloucestershire's total, the only time they reached 200 in the festival, left Middlesex needing 75 to win, which they reached in under an hour.

Gloucestershire

C. A. Milton b Price	7	c and b Stewart	56
M. Bissex c Clifton b Stewart	0	run out	32
S. E. Russell lbw b Price	1	lbw b Stewart	27
R. B. Nicholls c Clifton b Hooker	12	c Clifton b Bick	29
D. Bevan c Parfitt b Hooker	14	c Clifton b Stewart	2
*J. B. Mortimore c Clifton b Price	2	c Stewart b Bick	21
M. D. Mence c sub b Hooker	6	c Smith b Price	0
A. S. Brown c sub b Hooker	24	c Russell b Stewart	10
D. A. Allen lbw b Stewart	6	lbw b Price	28
†B. J. Meyer not out	21	c Russell b Stewart	1
D. R. Smith c Clifton b Hooker	5	not out	21
N-b 4	4	B 2, l-b 1, n-b 2	5
1/6 2/7 3/10 4/31 5/38 6/40 7/44 8/66 9/91	102	1/85 2/92 3/130 4/136 5/170 6/170 7/170 8/202 9/204	232

Bowling: *First Innings*—Price 18—6—48—3; Stewart 11—3—15—2; Hooker 19.4—6—35—5; Titmus 1—1—0—0. *Second Innings*—Price 32.2—4—85—2; Stewart 29—9—63—5; Hooker 5—0—19—0; Titmus 26—6—52—0; Bick 10—5—8—2.

Middlesex

W. E. Russell c Meyer b Allen	36	lbw b Smith	16
M. J. Smith c Meyer b Smith	7	not out	31
P. H. Parfitt c Allen b Bissex	96	not out	25
E. A. Clark c Meyer b Mortimore	35		
C. T. Radley lbw b Smith	25		
R. W. Hooker lbw b Brown	13		
*F. J. Titmus c Brown b Smith	9		
D. A. Bick c Brown b Smith	9		
†E. G. Clifton not out	21		
R. W. Stewart lbw b Smith	0		
J. S. E. Price c Meyer b Smith	1		
L-b 6, w 2	8	B 2, l-b 1	3
1/28 2/64 3/136 4/200 5/220 6/220 7/233 8/238 9/254	260	1/28 (1 wkt.)	75

Bowling: *First Innings*—Smith 24.2—1—91—6; Brown 34—11—70—1; Mortimore 24—9—44—1; Allen 24—10—40—1; Bissex 4—1—7—1. *Second Innings*—Smith 9—1—41—1; Brown 6—0—22—0; Mence 2.4—0—9—0.

Umpires: W. H. Copson and P. B. Wight.

At The Oval, August 24, 25, 26. GLOUCESTERSHIRE drew with SURREY.

GLOUCESTERSHIRE v. NORTHAMPTONSHIRE

At Bristol, August 27, 29 and 30. Northamptonshire won by an innings and 23 after ten minutes of the extra half hour. They gained this decisive victory in the Bank Holiday fixture because they won the toss and batted first on a hard true pitch. The feature was the fourth-wicket stand between Steele and Mushtaq Mohammad, who put on 220 in as many minutes and each hit 117. Steele hit two 6's and thirteen 4's, while Mushtaq hit one 6 and sixteen 4's. They mastered the attack as their partnership progressed, particularly when Gloucestershire were handicapped by the loss of Smith who had a recurrence of his knee trouble. Rain damaged the pitch on Monday and Tuesday and curtailed play, and even when the game was resumed conditions were hardly fit. Gloucestershire on Monday, when play did not commence until 2.45, were dismissed for 131 and had to follow on 195 in arrear. Bissex, who hit six 4's in a breezy 48 and Nicholls, who was last out for a hard-earned 58, tried to save Gloucestershire, but defeat was inevitable. Scott bowled with rare skill and accuracy to finish with seven for 46.

Northamptonshire

R. M. Prideaux c Milton b Allen	14	P. Willey c Nicholls b Mortimore	2
B. L. Reynolds lbw b Bissex	32	P. J. Watts not out	14
A. Lightfoot c A. S. Brown b Allen	1	H. Sully not out	1
D. S. Steele c sub b A. S. Brown	117		
Mushtaq Mohammad c and b A. S. Brown	117	B 7, l-b 10, w 1	18
B. Crump lbw b A. S. Brown	6	1/30 2/34 3/59 (8 wkts., dec.)	326
M. E. Scott b A. S. Brown	4	4/279 5/291 6/304 7/309 8/309	

*†K. V. Andrew did not bat.

Bowling: Smith 14—6—18—0; A. S. Brown 25—6—66—4; Allen 37—13—76—2; Mortimore 27—13—77—1; Bissex 32—12—71—1.

Gloucestershire

C. A. Milton c Mushtaq b Crump	1	— c Andrew b Scott	33
M. Bissex lbw b Watts	15	— c Prideaux b Scott	48
S. E. Russell b Mushtaq	40	— c Watts b Scott	2
D. Shepherd b Watts	0	— c Reynolds b Scott	4
R. B. Nicholls c Mushtaq b Watts	18	— c Mushtaq b Crump	58
D. Brown c Watts b Sully	7	— lbw b Scott	0
*J. B. Mortimore not out	33	— c Watts b Sully	8
A. S. Brown c Andrew b Sully	0	— c Prideaux b Scott	2
D. A. Allen c and b Sully	10	— c Mushtaq b Crump	9
†B. J. Meyer c Mushtaq b Watts	2	— c Andrew b Scott	0
D. R. Smith b Mushtaq	1	— not out	2
B 4	4	B 3, l-b 3	6
1/3 2/21 3/21 4/76 5/78 6/86 7/86 8/98 9/130	131	1/63 2/69 3/87 4/88 5/88 6/118 7/128 8/149 9/164	172

Bowling: *First Innings*—Crump 8—2—15—1; Watts 21—9—32—4; Willey 4—2—2—0; Sully 13—6—42—3; Mushtaq 23.2—10—36—2. *Second Innings*—Crump 8—2—21—2; Watts 9—3—16—0; Sully 27—10—49—1; Mushtaq 10—2—21—0; Scott 35—18—46—7; Lightfoot 4—0—13—0.

Umpires: A. E. Alderman and G. H. Pope.

HAMMOND'S ASHES

The ashes of Walter Hammond, former cricket captain of England and Gloucestershire, who died in July 1965, were scattered on the square of the county ground at Bristol in August 1966.

The ceremony took place in the presence of his widow, three children and four officials of Gloucestershire County Cricket Club. The ashes were brought home from South Africa, where Hammond died.

HAMPSHIRE

President—LORD PORCHESTER

Secretary—E. D. R. EAGAR, County Ground, Southampton

Captain—R. E. MARSHALL

H. Horton

County Badge

D. W. White

Hampshire finished eleventh in the Championship, one place higher than in 1965, but it was a disappointing season, with the failure of the middle batting the main reason for poor performances. While they were beaten only four times they had more drawn games than any other county.

In his first year as captain, Marshall led his side with sound judgment and showed that the cares of captaincy did not affect his run-getting. His total of 1,882 runs was 238 more than in 1965. He hit three centuries and thirteen other scores of over 50. How much Hampshire depended on him for runs was shown by the fact that only three other batsmen hit centuries, Horton two, and Livingstone and Timms one each. Reed, who in his first full season reached 1,000 runs, helped to form with Marshall a reliable opening pair.

Lower in the batting order Hampshire looked in vain for runs. Horton, who finished second to Marshall in aggregate, served the county well again, and against Middlesex at Bournemouth he took part in a third-wicket partnership of 272 with Livingstone, whose share of the runs brought him his first century for two seasons. Timms hit his maiden century in first-class cricket against Oxford University.

Once again the 42-year-old Shackleton formed with White the spearhead of the Hampshire attack. Since he made his first appearance for Hampshire in 1948 he has taken 100 wickets in a season 18 times, a figure exceeded only by Wilfred Rhodes. Shackleton headed the bowling averages and his 117 wickets took this remarkable bowler's total in first-class cricket to 2,627. Only nine bowlers in cricket history have taken more. Shackleton's great service to

Hampshire has been recognised by his being granted a second benefit in 1967, an honour accorded by the county to only one other player, Philip Mead.

The highlight of the season for White was his nine wickets for 44 against Leicestershire at Portsmouth, the best performance of his career. Cottam proved a valuable support for Shackleton and White, and Castell, who changed from leg-spinner to seamer, took 36 wickets.

While the season was somewhat disappointing to Hampshire, the introduction of some young players held out hopes for the future. Wheatley, who began batting at number eight and finished at five, showed enough ability with bat and ball to suggest that he will develop into a useful all-rounder.

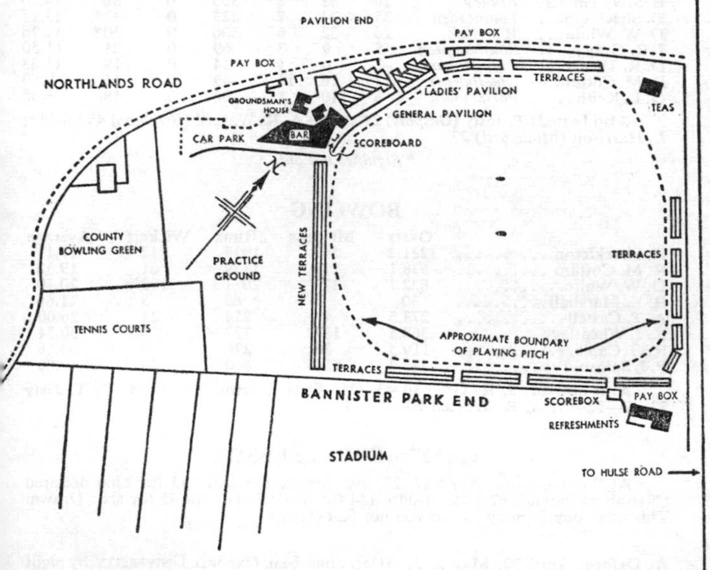

HAMPSHIRE RESULTS

All First-Class Matches—Played 30, *Won* 6, *Lost* 4, *Drawn* 20

County Championship Matches—Played 28, *Won* 5, *Lost* 4, *Drawn* 18, *No Decision* 1

COUNTY CHAMPIONSHIP AVERAGES

BATTING

	Birthplace	Mtchs.	Inns.	Not Outs	Runs	100's	Highest Inns.	Aver.
R. E. Marshall.	*Barbados*	27	50	2	1685	3	133	33.10
H. Horton.....	*Hereford*	27	49	9	1223	2	148*	30.57
P. J. Sainsbury.	*Southampton*	26	39	10	794	0	75	27.37
D. A. Livingstone	*Antigua*	20	34	3	776	1	116	25.03
B. L. Reed.....	*Southsea*	25	45	2	957	0	93	22.25
K. J. Wheatley.	*Farnham*	21	27	4	401	0	46	17.43
R. M. C. Gilliat.	*Ware*	7	11	3	139	0	32*	17.37
R. G. Caple....	*Chiswick*	12	17	4	196	0	35	15.07
A. T. Castell...	*Oxford*	10	11	2	134	0	39	14.88
H. M. Barnard.	*Portsmouth*	11	18	2	233	0	54	14.56
B. S. V. Timms.	*Ropley*	26	33	8	355	0	36	14.20
D. Shackleton..	*Todmorden*	25	24	7	223	0	42*	13.11
D. W. White...	*Warwick*	26	32	6	306	0	50*	11.76
J. R. Gray.....	*Southampton*	5	9	3	69	0	21	11.50
D. R. Turner...	*Chippenham*	2	4	1	34	0	19	11.33
R. M. Cottam..	*Cleethorpes*	18	16	11	49	0	16	9.80
G. L. Keith....	*Portsmouth*	6	10	1	86	0	19	9.55

Also batted: T. Jesty (*Gosport*) 2* and 0; A. R. Wassell (*Brighton*) 4 and 14*; L. Harrison (*Mudeford*) 23.

* *Signifies not out.*

BOWLING

	Overs	Maidens	Runs	Wickets	Average
D. Shackleton...........	1231.2	549	1917	112	17.11
R. M. Cottam	538.1	119	1179	61	19.32
D. W. White............	822.1	179	2071	103	20.10
R. E. Marshall..........	30	6	65	3	21.66
A. T. Castell............	278.5	47	754	29	26.00
K. J. Wheatley..........	368.5	137	733	24	30.54
R. G. Caple.............	119.5	36	276	9	30.66
P. J. Sainsbury..........	386.2	154	800	20	40.00

Also bowled: J. R. Gray 10—3—24—0; H. Horton 0.3—0—4—0; T. Jesty 23—9—52—0; A. R. Wassell 20—4—73—1.

HAMPSHIRE v. SUSSEX

At Southampton, April 27, 28, 29. Sussex 103 and 173 for nine declared (Nawab of Pataudi 67); Hampshire 134 for six declared and 45 for six. Drawn. This three-day friendly match was not first-class.

At Oxford, April 30, May 2, 3. HAMPSHIRE beat OXFORD UNIVERSITY by eight wickets.

At Southampton, May 5. HAMPSHIRE beat LINCOLNSHIRE by 31 runs. (See GILLETTE CUP.)

At Bristol, May 7, 9, 10. HAMPSHIRE drew with SOMERSET.

At Chesterfield, May 14, 16, 17. HAMPSHIRE drew with DERBYSHIRE.

HAMPSHIRE v. SURREY

At Basingstoke, May 18, 19, 20. Drawn. This first Championship match at Basingstoke for twenty-eight years was hindered by rain, sixty-five minutes being lost. Hampshire declared twice and Surrey once in an effort to get a result. Surrey, set to make 179 in two hours, twenty minutes to win, lost six wickets for 78, but held on for a draw. White hit a whirlwind 50 to be top scorer in the Hampshire first innings which was marked by consistent scoring by most of the batsmen. The county coach, Harrison, replaced the injured wicket-keeper, Timms, in the Hampshire side, this being his first game for four years.

Hampshire

*R. E. Marshall c Edrich b Storey	34	— c Long b Jefferson	25
B. L. Reed c Storey b Pocock	34	— not out	26
H. Horton c Long b Jefferson	36	— not out	8
D. A. Livingstone c Barrington b Storey	33		
H. M. Barnard not out	30		
P. J. Sainsbury c and b Willett	8		
†L. Harrison lbw b Harman	23		
D. W. White not out	50		
B 7, l-b 2, n-b 2	11	L-b 1, n-b 2	3
1/54 2/95 3/131 4/155 5/168 6/206 (6 wkts., dec.)	259	1/41 (1 wkt., dec.)	62

K. J. Wheatley, D. Shackleton and R. M. Cottam did not bat.

Bowling: *First Innings*—Arnold 22—8—37—0; Jefferson 27—5—60—1; Storey 28—8—45—2; Pocock 22—6—59—1; Harman 15—6—40—1; Willett 6—3—7—1. *Second Innings*—Arnold 3—0—16—0; Jefferson 7—1—17—1; Barrington 5—1—18—0; Pocock 1—0—8—0.

Surrey

*M. J. Stewart c Cottam b White	0	— c Harrison b White	13
J. H. Edrich c Harrison b White	6	— c Barnard b Shackleton	8
R. A. E. Tindall c Marshall b Wheatley	25	— not out	7
K. F Barrington lbw b Shackleton	8	— c Shackleton b Sainsbury	22
M. D. Willett c Livingstone b Shackleton	9	— c Sainsbury b Wheatley	5
S. J. Storey b Cottam	56	— c Reed b White	0
R. I. Jefferson b Sainsbury	22	— b Shackleton	21
P. I. Pocock c Reed b Sainsbury	6	— not out	4
†A. Long not out	0		
G. Arnold not out	7		
B 1, l-b 2, w 1	4	B 2, n-b 1	3
1/5 2/6 3/20 4/46 5/69 6/118 7/136 8/136 (8 wkts., dec.)	143	1/17 2/21 3/21 4/56 5/70 6/78 (6 wkts.)	83

R. Harman did not bat.

Bowling: *First Innings*—Shackleton 18—8—27—2; White 15—5—32—2; Cottam 10—2—23—1; Wheatley 11—3—33—1; Sainsbury 8—2—24—2. *Second Innings*—Shackleton 17—11—24—2; White 8—3—21—2; Cottam 5—1—19—0; Wheatley 8—7—4—1; Sainsbury 6—3—12—1.

Umpires: P. B. Wight and C. S. Elliott.

At Southampton, May 21. HAMPSHIRE beat KENT by 54 runs. (See GILLETT CUP.)

At Bristol, May 25, 26, 27. HAMPSHIRE beat GLOUCESTERSHIRE by eight wickets.

At Cardiff, May 28, 30, 31. HAMPSHIRE lost to GLAMORGAN by 46 runs.

HAMPSHIRE v. GLOUCESTERSHIRE

At Southampton, June 1, 2, 3. Hampshire won by 224 runs. Superior both in batting and bowling, Hampshire coasted to an easy victory before lunch on the third day. Two fine innings by Marshall dominated the Hampshire score. In the first innings he made 89 out of a total of 133 in two and a half hours, hitting eleven 4's, and in the second he hit 52 in forty-five minutes (one 6 and eight 4's). Sainsbury enjoyed a useful match with 75 for once out, and Barnard made 54 in the second innings. Gloucestershire failed miserably in their first innings against the seam bowling of Shackleton, White and Cottam, and Milton alone faced them with any confidence. Although Gloucestershire fell 160 behind, Hampshire did not enforce the follow-on, but, declaring at tea-time on the second day, set Gloucestershire the task of getting 363 to win. Except for a fifth-wicket stand by Nicholls and Jarman, Gloucestershire again failed, though this time Wheatley did most damage with his off-spin.

Hampshire

First innings		Second innings	
*R. E. Marshall c Mence b Windows	89	b A. S. Brown	52
B. L. Reed c Meyer b A. S. Brown	2	b A. S. Brown	29
H. Horton c Meyer b Mence	15	c Meyer b Mence	12
D. A. Livingstone c Milton b Windows	1	lbw b A. S. Brown	0
H. M. Barnard b Windows	11	c Milton b Windows	54
P. J. Sainsbury c Shepherd b Mence	36	not out	39
†B. S. V. Timms c A. S. Brown b Mortimore	29	not out	8
K. J. Wheatley lbw b Mortimore	10		
D. Shackleton not out	23		
D. W. White c Meyer b A. S. Brown	7		
R. M. Cottam b Windows	16		
B 2, l-b 9, w 1, n-b 2	14	L-b 8	8
1/4 2/63 3/66 4/118 5/133 6/195 7/197 8/210 9/217	253	1/80 2/87 3/87 4/105 5/176 (5 wkts., dec.)	202

Bowling: *First Innings*—A. S. Brown 25—9—47—2; Windows 24.3—6—64—4; Mence 19—4—62—2; Mortimore 25—6—66—2. *Second Innings*—A. S. Brown 16—1—65—3; Windows 17—3—58—1; Mence 11—0—36—1; Mortimore 13—1—35—0.

Gloucestershire

First innings		Second innings	
R. B. Nicholls lbw b White	10	c Sainsbury b Wheatley	63
C. A. Milton c Barnard b Cottam	37	c Timms b White	5
S. E. Russell b Cottam	4	c Timms b Shackleton	9
D. Shepherd c Sainsbury b White	13	c Barnard b Wheatley	9
D. Brown c Horton b White	2	c Timms b Shackleton	6
*J. B. Mortimore b White	3	c Barnard b Cottam	0
H. Jarman run out	3	c Livingstone b Wheatley	28
A. R. Windows c Barnard b Shackleton	8	lbw b Cottam	0
A. S. Brown lbw b Shackleton	5	c Reed b Sainsbury	15
M. D. Mence not out	1	c White b Wheatley	1
†B. J. Meyer c Timms b Shackleton	0	not out	0
B 1, n-b 6	7	L-b 1, n-b 1	2
1/20 2/37 3/56 4/70 5/74 6/79 7/87 8/87 9/93	93	1/6 2/17 3/27 4/28 5/100 6/113 7/114 8/126 9/138	138

Bowling: *First Innings*—Shackleton 24.3—16—14—3; White 15—3—44—4; Cottam 13—5—22—2; Wheatley 4—2—6—0. *Second Innings*—Shackleton 23—14—19—2; White 17—4—33—1; Cottam 21—4—56—2; Wheatley 17.3—10—24—4; Sainsbury 2—1—4—1.

Umpires: W. F. Price and L. H. Gray.

At Nottingham, June 4, 5, 6. HAMPSHIRE drew with NOTTINGHAMSHIRE, scores level.

HAMPSHIRE v. NOTTINGHAMSHIRE

At Bournemouth, June 11, 13, 14. Nottinghamshire won by seven wickets. They gained their first win of the season by scoring 141 with ten minutes to spare. Hampshire found no answer to the fast bowling of Forbes in their first innings, the batting being redeemed only by a sixth-wicket partnership of 42 between Sainsbury and Timms and one of 41 between Timms and Wheatley. Hampshire, 69 behind on the first innings, made a bad start to the second, losing four wickets for 20 runs. Marshall, however, played an outstanding innings, curbing his natural scoring pace to meet the situation, and while he remained Hampshire had hope. He and Sainsbury put on 162 for the fifth wicket, and Marshall completed his first century of the season early on the third day. White finished the Hampshire innings and Nottinghamshire were left to get 141 to win in three and three-quarter hours. Bolus steered them to victory with 41 in two hours forty minutes, and when he left 52 runs were needed in sixty-five minutes.

Hampshire

*R. E. Marshall c Davison b Forbes	14	— lbw b Taylor	110
B. L. Reed lbw b Forbes	15	— c White b Davison	0
H. Horton c Swetman b Forbes	7	— c Swetman b Forbes	2
D. A. Livingstone b Forbes	14	— lbw b Davison	6
H. M. Barnard c Swetman b Stead	0	— b Davison	1
P. J. Sainsbury run out	12	— c Forbes b White	49
*B. S. V. Timms b White	36	— not out	9
K. J. Wheatley run out	25	— c Forbes b White	2
D. Shackleton c Stead b Forbes	3	— b White	9
D. W. White b Forbes	8	— c Stead b White	3
R. M. Cottam not out	1	— lbw b White	0
L-b 9, w 1, n-b 5	15	B 2, l-b 4, w 1, n-b 11	18
1/20 2/38 3/41 4/48 5/53 6/95 7/136 8/140 9/142	150	1/1 2/8 3/15 4/20 5/182 6/182 7/184 8/202 9/209	209

Bowling: *First Innings*—Davison 13—2—35—0; Forbes 26.1—15—34—6; Stead 12—4—17—1; White 15—4—42—1; Taylor 3—1—7—0. *Second Innings*—Davison 19—5—50—3; Forbes 32—11—69—1; Stead 9—4—24—0; White 14.5—5—35—5; Taylor 9—4—13—1.

Nottinghamshire

*J. B. Bolus lbw b Cottam	7	— c Barnard b Sainsbury	41
B. Whittingham c Timms b Shackleton	16	— b White	11
R. A. White lbw b White	47	— c Reed b Cottam	20
I. Moore c Horton b Shackleton	41	— not out	30
M. J. Smedley b White	9	— not out	26
†R. Swetman c Timms b White	0		
J. Parkin b Sainsbury	11		
M. Taylor c Cottam b Sainsbury	25		
C. Forbes c Timms b White	14		
I. Davison lbw b Cottam	27		
B. Stead not out	17		
L-b 3, n-b 2	5	B 8, l-b 1, n-b 4	13
1/20 2/36 3/101 4/123 5/123 6/125 7/160 8/160 9/191	219	1/15 2/58 3/89 (3 wkts.)	141

Bowling: *First Innings*—Shackleton 35—18—48—2; White 26—6—69—4; Cottam 25.2—5—58—2; Wheatley 6—2—13—0; Sainsbury 11—4—26—2. *Second Innings*—Shackleton 14—6—24—0; White 7—2—15—1; Cottam 23—8—35—1; Wheatley 16—10—25—0; Sainsbury 13.2—5—29—1.

Umpires: A. E. Fagg and P. A. Gibb.

At Bradford, June 15, 16, 17. HAMPSHIRE drew with YORKSHIRE.

HAMPSHIRE v. LEICESTERSHIRE

At Portsmouth, June 18, 20, 21. *65 overs.* Drawn. Marshall and Reed gave Hampshire a good start and at lunch the score was 115 for two wickets. Later against Lock (four for 32) they failed badly and were all out in 63 overs for 189, of which Horton made 51. Leicestershire, thanks to Inman, were 98 for four at the close, but on Monday were all out for 135, adding only 37 more runs. The damage was done by White, whose figures on that day were 8—3—15—6, giving him an analysis for the innings of 23—7—44—9. This represented not only his own best career figures, but the best bowling of the season till then. When Hampshire went in they lost six wickets for 63, but Sainsbury and Wheatley held out and on the third day took their seventh-wicket partnership to 60. Leicestershire had to make 224 to win in four hours but there was no serious attempt to get the runs, and the score after two hours was 72 for two.

Hampshire

First innings		Second innings	
*R. E. Marshall lbw b Spencer	32	c Tolchard b Cotton	2
B. L. Reed c Marner b Cotton	16	b Spencer	21
H. Horton c Marner b Lock	51	lbw b Spencer	16
G. L. Keith c Hallam b Lock	16	lbw b Spencer	0
R. G. Caple run out	25	c Cross b Cotton	4
P. J. Sainsbury lbw b Savage	5	c Lock b Savage	43
†B. S. V. Timms c and b Lock	10	c Tolchard b Cotton	1
D. W. White c Lock b Savage	3	b Savage	12
K. J. Wheatley st Tolchard b Lock	11	c Tolchard b Spencer	32
D. Shackleton run out	2	not out	19
R. M. Cottam not out	0	c Marner b Savage	0
B 13, l-b 5	18	B 12, l-b 2, w 4, n-b 1	19
1/37 2/68 3/115 4/126 5/133 6/161 7/171 8/181 9/188	189	1/10 2/44 3/44 4/47 5/57 6/63 7/123 8/145 9/169	169

Bowling: *First Innings*—Cotton 7—1—33—1; Spencer 11—1—35—1; Marner 12—1—29—0; Lock 20—7—32—4; Savage 13—2—42—2. *Second Innings*—Cotton 22—5—38—3; Spencer 27—9—49—4; Marner 9—3—22—0; Lock 7—4—14—0; Savage 10.3—3—27—3.

Leicestershire

First innings		Second innings	
M. R. Hallam c Horton b White	5	c Reed b White	15
B. J. Booth c Timms b White	12		
M. E. Norman b White	2	c Timms b Sainsbury	35
C. C. Inman c Timms b White	73	c Timms b Sainsbury	0
P. Marner lbw b Shackleton	21	st Timms b Sainsbury	36
G. Cross b White	7	not out	45
†R. W. Tolchard c Timms b White	0		
*G. A. R. Lock c Cottam b White	2	not out	20
J. Cotton c Horton b White	1		
C. T. Spencer not out	6		
J. S. Savage c Wheatley b White	0		
L-b 1, n-b 5	6	L-b 3, n-b 2	5
1/13 2/20 3/25 4/75 5/106 6/106 7/108 8/113 9/135	135	1/27 2/72 3/72 4/124 (4 wkts.)	156

Bowling: *First Innings*—White 23—7—44—9; Shackleton 25—9—52—1; Cottam 5—1—29—0; Sainsbury 1—0—4—0. *Second Innings*—Shackleton 16—5—32—0; White 15—4—34—1; Cottam 16—3—35—0; Sainsbury 16—2—50—3.

Umpires: A. E. Alderman and L. H. Gray.

At Bournemouth, June 23. HAMPSHIRE beat SURREY by seven wickets. (See GILLETTE CUP.)

At Dudley, June 25, 27, 28. HAMPSHIRE drew with WORCESTERSHIRE.

At Hove, June 29, 30. HAMPSHIRE beat SUSSEX by nine wickets.

HAMPSHIRE v. WORCESTERSHIRE

At Portsmouth, July 2, 3, 4. Drawn. Worcestershire batted through on the first day for 283 for eight declared, with Headley and Ormrod associated in a third-wicket partnership of 78. Hampshire missed the bowling of Shackleton, who had a knee injury, but Castell came in to bowl seamers for a career-best performance of six wickets for 69. Hampshire batted on a somewhat difficult wicket, and, dismissed for 119, had to follow on. Coldwell bowled well to take five wickets for 38. Marshall and Reed gave the second innings a good start with a stand of 90, but once they had gone there was little substance in the rest of the batting. Nearly three hours were lost in four breaks through rain on the third day, when, thanks to a long patient innings of 30 by Sainsbury, helped by 36 not out by White, Hampshire avoided defeat.

Worcestershire

M. J. Horton c Castell b White	56
C. D. Fearnley c Wheatley b Castell	40
R. G. A. Headley c Timms b Castell	64
J. A. Ormrod lbw b Castell	70
D. W. Richardson c Castell b Wheatley	8
E. J. O. Hemsley c Timms b Castell	1
D. N. F. Slade b Castell	7
*†R. Booth c Timms b Castell	22
N. Gifford not out	1
L. J. Coldwell not out	1
B 4, l-b 3, n-b 6	13
1/86 2/124 3/202 4/218 5/219 6/229 7/281 8/282 (8 wkts., dec.)	283

J. A. Flavell did not bat.

Bowling: White 23—1—72—1; Cottam 21—0—58—0; Gray 8—3—13—0; Castell 27—4—69—6; Wheatley 16—5—28—1; Sainsbury 10—5—30—0.

Hampshire

*R. E. Marshall b Coldwell	20	c Richardson b Gifford	57
B. L. Reed lbw b Flavell	16	b Horton	63
H. Horton c Slade b Coldwell	8	c Ormrod b Horton	3
J. R. Gray c Booth b Coldwell	3	c Headley b Gifford	2
G. L. Keith c Booth b Coldwell	4	lbw b Horton	4
P. J. Sainsbury b Gifford	31	not out	30
†B. S. V. Timms lbw b Slade	25	c Richardson b Gifford	13
K. J. Wheatley c Booth b Coldwell	3	lbw b Flavell	7
A. T. Castell c Headley b Gifford	0	c Slade b Flavell	1
D. W. White b Gifford	3	not out	36
R. M. Cottam not out	0	c Slade b Flavell	2
L-b 6	6	B 4, l-b 3	7
1/39 2/45 3/51 4/54 5/57 6/102 7/105 8/108 9/116	119	1/90 2/112 3/118 4/130 5/137 6/140 7/164 8/184 9/188 (9 wkts.)	225

Bowling: *First Innings*—Flavell 19—3—47—1; Coldwell 20—6—38—5; Gifford 9.3—3—18—3; Slade 5—3—2—1; Horton 1—0—8—0. *Second Innings*—Flavell 25—10—42—3; Coldwell 14—7—35—0; Gifford 33—20—53—3; Hemsley 5—1—22—0; Slade 16—9—24—0; Horton 21—6—42—3.

Umpires: P. A. Gibb and R. Aspinall.

HAMPSHIRE v. GLAMORGAN

At Southampton, July 6, 7, 8. Drawn. On a rain-affected wicket Glamorgan took nearly five hours on the opening day to make 158 for four after three hold-ups because of the weather. The next day Hampshire, with the new ball, took five wickets for 30 in three-quarters of an hour, and Glamorgan declared. Thereupon I. J. Jones quickly broke through and six Hampshire wickets fell for 57, including that of Marshall, who spent almost two hours for 27. More enterprising batting by the later batsmen enabled Hampshire to restrict Glamorgan's lead to 44. Eventually Hampshire were set 186 runs for victory in two and a half hours. Thanks to Marshall and Horton they were up with the clock at one time but afterwards lost wickets cheaply and only just held out to avoid defeat after Glamorgan had claimed the extra half-hour.

Glamorgan

First innings		Second innings	
A. Jones c Barnard b Castell	46	lbw b White	0
W. Slade c Sainsbury b Cottam	20	c Sainsbury b Cottam	1
P. M. Walker b White	30	c Castell b White	49
A. R. Lewis c Reed b Cottam	43	c Barnard b White	54
B. Hedges b Cottam	7	c Castell b White	6
L. Hill b White	24	not out	5
†E. Jones c Timms b White	0	not out	7
E. Lewis b Cottam	17	c Barnard b Cottam	12
D. J. Shepherd not out	2		
I. J. Jones c Sainsbury b Cottam	3		
L-b 5, n-b 9	14	L-b 3, n-b 4	7
1/55 2/88 3/110 4/120 5/177 6/178 7/199 8/200 9/206 (9 wkts., dec.)	206	1/0 2/2 3/22 4/120 5/129 6/132 (6 wkts., dec.)	141

*O. S. Wheatley did not bat.

Bowling: *First Innings*—White 29—7—70—3; Cottam 27.2—8—52—5; Castell 18—7—33—1; Wheatley 19—11—25—0; Sainsbury 6—3—12—0; *Second Innings*—White 14—3—29—4; Cottam 16—3—27—2; Castell 8—0—33—0; Wheatley 8—1—30—0; Sainsbury 6—2—15—0.

Hampshire

First innings		Second innings	
*R. E. Marshall c E. Jones b Shepherd	27	c Slade b Shepherd	40
B. L. Reed c I. J. Jones b Wheatley	4	c E. Jones b I. J. Jones	5
H. Horton b I. J. Jones	4	lbw b Shepherd	37
J. R. Gray c Walker b I. J. Jones	1	not out	8
H. M. Barnard c E. Jones b I. J. Jones	7	c E. Jones b Walker	12
P. J. Sainsbury c E. Jones b Shepherd	5	lbw b E. Lewis	5
†B. S. V. Timms c E. Jones b Walker	33	lbw b E. Lewis	4
K. J. Wheatley run out	24	c Walker b I. J. Jones	4
A. T. Castell c A. Jones b I. J. Jones	25	not out	0
D. W. White b I. J. Jones	17	b Shepherd	0
R. M. Cottam not out	3		
L-b 10, n-b 2	12	L-b 2, n-b 1	3
1/13 2/19 3/21 4/31 5/52 6/57 7/103 8/127 9/159	162	1/24 2/60 3/94 4/99 5/100 6/103 7/113 8/117 (8 wkts.)	118

Bowling: *First Innings*—I. J. Jones 28.5—6—56—5; Wheatley 24—8—40—1; Shepherd 30—19—25—2; E. Lewis 10—3—18—0; Walker 6—3—11—1. *Second Innings*—I. J. Jones 12—4—36—2; Wheatley 5—3—7—0; Shepherd 17—9—20—3; Walker 10—4—24—1; E. Lewis 12—7—28—2.

Umpires: P. A. Gibb and R. Aspinall.

At Manchester, July 9, 11, 12. HAMPSHIRE lost to LANCASHIRE by three wickets.

HAMPSHIRE v. SOMERSET

At Bournemouth, July 13, 14, 15. Drawn. Rain restricted play on the third day to four overs between lunch and six o'clock and robbed Somerset of victory. Hampshire gave a dismal display when they won the toss. Rumsey took their first four wickets for 13 runs and finished with six for 28. Horton kept the innings together by scoring 50 in two hours fifty minutes. For Somerset, G. Atkinson and Virgin made 60 without being separated before the close, and next day took their partnership to 208 before Virgin was caught at the wicket for 98. Atkinson hit his twenty-first century and his first of the season. Somerset declared and dismissed Timms in the last over of the day. Next day Marshall reached his 50 out of 65 in fifty-five minutes, but in spite of a useful 47 by Livingstone, Hampshire were on the way to defeat with five men out for 129 at lunch. After an almost blank afternoon Somerset went out again for the last thirty-five minutes in the outside hope of winning, but they could get only one more wicket in the extra time. Hampshire still needed 62 more runs to avoid the innings defeat when play ended.

Hampshire

*R. E. Marshall c Kitchen b Rumsey	5	— b Langford	67
B. L. Reed c Virgin b Rumsey	5	— b Langford	11
H. Horton c Clayton b Robinson	50	— c Clayton b Langford	0
D. A. Livingstone c Clayton b Rumsey	0	— c Clayton b Palmer	47
H. M. Barnard c Clayton b Rumsey	8	— c Robinson b Langford	2
P. J. Sainsbury c Alley b C. R. M. Atkinson	9	— not out	13
†B. S. V. Timms c Palmer b Robinson	21	— c Clayton b Rumsey	6
K. J. Wheatley not out	20	— not out	4
A. T. Castell lbw b Langford	0		
D. Shackleton c Robinson b Rumsey	14		
D. W. White b Rumsey	0		
B 1, l-b 2, w 1	4	L-b 3	3
1/8 2/13 3/13 4/29 5/45 6/91 7/98 8/101 9/134	136	1/10 2/46 3/46 4/109 5/115 6/143 (6 wkts.)	153

Bowling: *First Innings*—Rumsey 18.1—5—28—6; Palmer 10—0—24—0; Alley 7—2—9—0; Langford 27—13—37—1; C. R. M. Atkinson 4—1—6—1; Robinson 28—15—28—2. *Second Innings*—Rumsey 11—2—37—1; Palmer 6—2—21—1; Langford 22.3—7—43—4; Robinson 21—5—49—0.

Somerset

G. Atkinson c Barnard b White	148
R. Virgin c Timms b White	98
M. Kitchen b Shackleton	43
W. E. Alley lbw b White	1
*C. R. M. Atkinson run out	1
A. Clarkson c Marshall b White	4
†G. Clayton c Sainsbury b Castell	20
K. E. Palmer b Castell	14
P. J. Robinson not out	8
B 3, l-b 11	14
1/208 2/299 3/300 4/300 5/301 6/314 7/330 8/351 (8 wkts., dec.)	351

B. A. Langford and F. E. Rumsey did not bat.

Bowling: Shackleton 40—14—75—1; White 32—11—71—4; Castell 25—6—72—2; Wheatley 22—1—68—0; Sainsbury 20—5—51—0.

Umpires: J. F. Crapp and A. E. Rhodes.

HAMPSHIRE v. SUSSEX

At Bournemouth, July 16, 18, 19. Drawn. Rain prevented any play on the third day and the match had to be abandoned in an interesting state. Sussex took nearly six hours to make 213 when they won the toss. Both their openers were caught at slip with the score at seven, but Parks and Suttle added 53 before Hampshire met with further success. An attractive 60 scored by Oakman in two hours gave character to the innings but no other batsman looked comfortable against Shackleton and White who shared seven of the wickets. Hampshire made a disastrous start as both Marshall and Reed were out for 11 runs. On the second day they effected a brave recovery after losing seven wickets for 63. Sainsbury and Castell revived their hopes with an eighth-wicket stand of 92, and at the close Hampshire were only 31 behind. Sainsbury took nearly four hours for 75, his best score so far of the season.

Sussex

L. J. Lenham c Castell b White	5	— c Reed b Shackleton	11
M. A. Buss c Barnard b Shackleton	2	— b White	9
K. G. Suttle c Sainsbury b White	36	— c Livingstone b White	3
*†J. M. Parks c sub b Castell	25	— not out	18
M. G. Griffith run out	23		
P. J. Graves c Timms b White	0		
D. J. Foreman b Sainsbury	22		
A. S. M. Oakman c Horton b Shackleton	60	— not out	14
A. Buss b White	23		
D. L. Bates b Shackleton	11		
J. A. Snow not out	1		
L-b 5	5	N-b 1	1
1/7 2/7 3/60 4/80 5/81 6/101 7/145 8/187 9/210	213	1/19 2/23 3/23 (3 wkts.)	56

Bowling: *First Innings*—Shackleton 31.1—15—42—3; White 29—1—93—4; Castell 24—1—54—1; Sainsbury 20—11—19—1. *Second Innings*—Shackleton 12—6—9—1; White 9—0—25—2; Castell 6—0—15—0; Sainsbury 3—1—6—0.

Hampshire

*R. E. Marshall b A. Buss	7
B. L. Reed lbw b Snow	1
H. Horton c M. A. Buss b Bates	32
†B. S. V. Timms c Foreman b A. Buss	4
D. A. Livingstone c Foreman b Snow	1
P. J. Sainsbury lbw b Snow	75
K. J. Wheatley c Foreman b Bates	0
H. M. Barnard c Foreman b A. Buss	0
A. T. Castell c Lenham b Snow	39
D. Shackleton not out	16
D. W. White c Griffith b A. Buss	4
L-b 1, n-b 2	3
1/6 2/11 3/20 4/21 5/62 6/62 7/63 8/155 9/169	182

Bowling: Snow 30—12—38—4; A. Buss 29.3—10—45—4; Bates 17—6—34—2; Oakman 23—9—46—0; M. A. Buss 1—0—3—0; Suttle 7—2—13—0.

Umpires: A. E. Rhodes and P. B. Wight.

At Coalville, July 20, 21, 22. HAMPSHIRE drew with LEICESTERSHIRE.

At Birmingham, July 23, 25, 26. HAMPSHIRE beat WARWICKSHIRE by six wickets

At Kettering, July 27, 28, 29. HAMPSHIRE drew with NORTHAMPTONSHIRE.

HAMPSHIRE v. DERBYSHIRE

At Southampton, July 30, August 1, 2. Drawn. Three outstanding bowling performances were features of this low-scoring match which was spoilt by rain on the third day. When Derbyshire batted first Castell bowled with great effect and took six wickets for 49 runs, the best figures of his career. Derbyshire took a little under five hours to reach 157, and owed most to Hall, who scored 62 in three hours. A seventh-wicket partnership between Timms and Castell put Hampshire within sight of the lead, but 16 runs were still needed when White, the last man, came in. White hit the 16 runs off nine balls, and Hampshire finished one run in front. Rhodes took five wickets for 28. Derbyshire were again dismissed cheaply with White taking six wickets for 37. Left to get 142 for victory in three hours, Hampshire had made 10 without loss when rain caused the game to be abandoned.

Derbyshire

I. W. Hall c Caple b Castell	62	— c Livingstone b White	6
J. R. Eyre b Caple	12	— c Timms b Shackleton	0
M. H. Page c Sainsbury b Castell	5	— c Sainsbury b White	5
J. F. Harvey c Sainsbury b Castell	25	— c Gilliat b White	2
I. R. Buxton b Caple	5	— lbw b White	31
*D. C. Morgan lbw b Castell	30	— c Castell b Shackleton	19
T. J. P. Eyre b Castell	10	— c Gilliat b White	45
†R. W. Taylor b Castell	0	— c Timms b Shackleton	22
H. J. Rhodes not out	1	— not out	4
E. Smith c Marshall b Caple	2	— b White	0
A. B. Jackson run out	2	— c and b Shackleton	0
B 2, l-b 1	3	B 5, l-b 1, n-b 2	8
1/33 2/50 3/99 4/112 5/112 6/145 7/147 8/152 9/155	157	1/8 2/13 3/27 4/30 5/66 6/72 7/137 8/137 9/140	142

Bowling: *First Innings*—Shackleton 18—10—19—0; White 17—4—36—0; Castell 27—5—49—6; Caple 22.5—7—37—3; Sainsbury 4—0—13—0. *Second Innings*—Shackleton 31.5—17—39—4; White 26—9—37—6; Castell 15—3—28—0; Caple 15—8—29—0; Sainsbury 4—3—1—0.

Hampshire

*R. E. Marshall b Rhodes	4	— not out	8
B. L. Reed c Taylor b Rhodes	16	— not out	2
H. Horton c Page b Rhodes	15		
D. A. Livingstone c Morgan b Jackson	37		
P. J. Sainsbury c T. J. P. Eyre b Rhodes	0		
R. M. C. Gilliat c Taylor b T. J. P. Eyre	8		
R. G. Caple c Taylor b T. J. B. Eyre	6		
†B. S. V. Timms c Smith b T. J. P. Eyre	28		
A. T. Castell c J. R. Eyre b T. J. P. Eyre	24		
D. Shackleton c Taylor b Rhodes	0		
D. W. White not out	16		
L-b 1, n-b 3	4		
1/11 2/25 3/49 4/49 5/65 6/81 7/92 8/135 9/142	158	(no wkt.)	10

Bowling: *First Innings*—Jackson 24—6—42—1; Rhodes 21.4—7—28—5; Smith 11—6—11—0; Buxton 2—0—6—0; T. J. P. Eyre 14—3—43—4; Morgan 13—4—24—0. *Second Innings*—Jackson 3—1—6—0; Rhodes 2—1—4—0.

Umpires: H. Mellows and A. E. Alderman.

HAMPSHIRE v. YORKSHIRE

At Portsmouth, August 3, 4, 5. Drawn. Hampshire were in a bad position when rain, on the third day, prevented play until late in the day. Against a tight Hampshire attack on the first day Yorkshire scored 205 for six wickets. Illingworth was 52 not out and with Binks put on 53 for the sixth wicket. Next day Illingworth took his score to 86 not out before Close declared. On a drying wicket Hampshire fared disastrously and were put out for their lowest total of the season. Nicholson, who took four wickets for 16 in the first innings, struck quickly when Hampshire followed on and dismissed Marshall cheaply for the second time in the match. At the close Hampshire had lost three wickets for 38, but next day Yorkshire were unable to press home their advantage until after mopping-up operations (in which Yorkshire players joined) on a rain soaked pitch.

Eventually one hour and fifty minutes was available, but with Hampshire losing only one more wicket, and Livingstone and Gilliat putting on 59 in an unbroken fifth-wicket partnership, Yorkshire left twenty minutes of the extra half hour unclaimed.

Yorkshire

K. Taylor c Timms b Shackleton	32
P. J. Sharpe c Sainsbury b Shackleton	18
D. E. V. Padgett run out	31
J. H. Hampshire c Livingstone b Castell	33
*D. B. Close c Timms b Castell	11
R. Illingworth not out	86
†J. G. Binks b Shackleton	24
C. Old c Horton b Shackleton	3
F. S. Trueman c Marshall b White	12
D. Wilson c Caple b White	23
L-b 6, n-b 1	7
1/24 2/76 3/91 4/127 5/128 6/181 7/225 8/248 9/280 (9 wkts., dec.)	280

A. G. Nicholson did not bat.

Bowling: Shackleton 47—21—84—4; White 37.2—12—83—2; Castell 26—5—65—2; Caple 7—2—17—0; Sainsbury 10—3—24—0.

Hampshire

*R. E. Marshall c Illingworth b Nicholson	9	c Padgett b Nicholson	3
B. L. Reed b Nicholson	7	lbw b Trueman	5
H. Horton lbw b Illingworth	9	c Illingworth b Close	10
D. A. Livingstone b Nicholson	0	not out	54
P. J. Sainsbury c Close b Wilson	10	c Wilson b Illingworth	8
R. M. C. Gilliat lbw b Wilson	2	not out	32
R. G. Caple c Binks b Trueman	1		
†B. S. V. Timms lbw b Nicholson	12		
A. T. Castell not out	4		
D. Shackleton c Illingworth b Trueman	1		
D. W. White c Old b Trueman	7		
L-b 1, n-b 1	2	B 4, l-b 2, n-b 1	7
1/11 2/17 3/17 4/32 5/38 6/39 7/39 8/53 9/56	64	1/3 2/18 3/28 4/60 (4 wkts.)	119

Bowling: *First Innings*—Trueman 10—2—22—3; Nicholson 15—10—16—4; Wilson 11—3—20—2; Illingworth 10—8—4—1. *Second Innings*—Trueman 18—9—27—1; Nicholson 21—10—25—1; Illingworth 8—3—18—1; Wilson 11—4—21—0; Close 10—5—13—1; Old 3—1—8—0.

Umpires: H. Mellows and A. E. Alderman.

HAMPSHIRE v. LANCASHIRE

At Portsmouth, August 6, 8, 9. Drawn. No play was possible on the first day and only eighty minutes on the third because of rain. Hampshire made good progress after being sent in to bat. Reed was missed in Statham's second over and went on to make 48. Marshall, meanwhile, had been caught off a skier, after making 20 out of 26. Livingstone and Sainsbury were severe on Worsley, Sainsbury hitting him for four boundaries on the leg side. Livingstone punished Worsley and Lloyd each for 6. Marshall declared and Hampshire took three Lancashire wickets for 54 by the close. Next day Lancashire declared after eighty minutes but no further play was possible. Castell bowled well, taking four for 29.

Hampshire

*R. E. Marshall c Wood b Statham	20	R. G. Caple not out	1
B. L. Reed c Lloyd b Worsley	48	†B. S. V. Timms not out	2
H. Horton c Green b Worsley	21		
D. A. Livingstone c Worsley b Green	54	B 4, l-b 5, n-b 1	10
P. J. Sainsbury c Wood b Lloyd	18	1/26 2/82 3/95 (6 wkts., dec.)	180
R. M. C. Gilliat c Wood b Worsley	6	4/124 5/157 6/177	

A. T. Castell, D. Shackleton and D. W. White did not bat.

Bowling: Statham 8—1—17—1; Lever 10—2—23—0; Shuttleworth 6—0—15—0; Worsley 19—5—52—3; Lloyd 10—1—41—1; Green 6—1—22—1.

Lancashire

D. M. Green c Sainsbury b White	4	K. Shuttleworth st Timms b Castell	0
H. Pilling b White	3	†K. Goodwin c Timms b Castell	12
J. D. Bond c White b Caple	45		
D. R. Worsley c Timms b Castell	7	B 2, l-b 3	5
B. Wood run out	14		
D. Lloyd b Castell	7	1/5 2/12 3/28 4/55 (8 wkts., dec.)	106
P. Lever not out	9	5/75 6/87 7/90 8/106	

G. Pullar and *J. B. Statham did not bat.

Bowling: Shackleton 19—10—22—0; White 11—5—17—2; Castell 15.2—3—29—4; Caple 12—5—29—1; Sainsbury 4—2—4—0.

Umpires: R. S. Lay and J. Langridge.

At Worcester, August 10. HAMPSHIRE lost to WORCESTERSHIRE by 99 runs. (*See* GILLETTE CUP.)

At Gillingham, August 13, 15, 16. HAMPSHIRE drew with KENT.

HAMPSHIRE v. MIDDLESEX

At Bournemouth, August 17, 18, 19. *65 overs.* Hampshire won by 80 runs. By beating Middlesex, Hampshire ended a run of twenty-four Championship matches on the Dean Park ground without a win. Their previous victory there in the Championship was against Leicestershire in 1962. The foundation for their win was a third-wicket partnership of 272 in the second innings between Horton and Livingstone. Both made centuries and set a record for any Hampshire wicket at Bournemouth. It was Livingstone's only century of the season. During the match Reed, in his first full season, completed his 1,000 runs, and Shackleton took his hundredth wicket for the eighteenth time. Marshall set Middlesex to get 312 to win in five and a half hours, but good bowling by Cottam and Sainsbury kept Hampshire on top and they had an hour to spare.

Hampshire

*R. E. Marshall b Stewart	62	— c Smith b Stewart	3
B. L. Reed b Stewart	24	— c Clifton b Hooker	5
H. Horton b Hooker	13	— not out	148
D. A. Livingstone b Hooker	19	— c Latchman b Hooker	116
P. J. Sainsbury b Stewart	22		
R. M. C. Gilliat b Stewart	23		
D. W. White b Stewart	16		
R. G. Caple not out	3		
†B. S. V. Timms not out	7		
B 4, l-b 11	15	B 7, l-b 3, w 1	11
1/85 2/92 3/117 4/134 5/168 6/188 7/197 (7 wkts., 65 overs)	204	1/9 2/11 3/283 (3 wkts., dec.)	283

D. Shackleton and R. M. Cottam did not bat.

Bowling: *First Innings*—Stewart 21—4—73—5; Hooker 27—7—59—2; Titmus 17—1—57—0. *Second Innings*—Stewart 25—3—76—1; Hooker 21—7—49—2; Titmus 13—4—22—0; Latchman 10—4—20—0; Bick 18—2—87—0; Parfitt 7—0—18—0.

Middlesex

W. E. Russell b Cottam	19	— b Sainsbury	54
M. J. Smith lbw b Shackleton	11	— c Timms b Shackleton	4
P. H. Parfitt b Shackleton	83	— b Sainsbury	35
E. A. Clark run out	4	— run out	46
R. W. Hooker b Shackleton	21	— b Cottam	42
*F. J. Titmus c Reed b Shackleton	17	— lbw b Cottam	13
C. T. Radley c Gilliat b Shackleton	4	— c Sainsbury b Caple	1
D. A. Bick b Cottam	0	— b Cottam	22
H. C. Latchman st Timms b Shackleton	3	— lbw b Sainsbury	0
†E. G. Clifton not out	1	— not out	4
R. W. Stewart (did not bat)		— c Caple b Cottam	0
B 5, l-b 6, n-b 2	13	L-b 7, n-b 3	10
1/19 2/57 3/88 4/142 5/149 6/157 7/158 8/172 (9 wkts., 65 overs)	176	1/6 2/92 3/99 4/114 5/171 6/193 7/202 8/212 9/231	231

Bowling: *First Innings*—Shackleton 33—12—69—6; White 16—3—53—0; Cottam 16—1—41—2. *Second Innings*—Shackleton 8—2—17—1; White 10—5—18—0; Cottam 20.2—4—51—4; Sainsbury 36—12—97—3; Caple 12—3—34—1; Marshall 1—0—4—0.

Umpires: G. H. Pope and W. F. Simpson.

HAMPSHIRE v. KENT

At Bournemouth, August 20, 22, 23. Kent won by nine wickets. Marshall scored his third century of the season to help Hampshire to a total of 257 on the first day. He made 106 in just over two and a half hours, hitting twelve 4's. Kent made 34 for one by the end of the day and then, on the second day, took nearly six and a half hours to take their total to 238. Cowdrey was the mainstay of his side's long innings and was at the wicket over four hours for his 73. Hampshire gave a poor display in their second innings and Dixon and Underwood put them out for only 97. The seventeen-year-old Turner made his first appearance for Hampshire and batted coolly for 15 not out after getting a duck in the first innings. Hampshire were handicapped by muscle injuries to White and Sainsbury, and neither was able to bowl in the Kent second innings when Denness and Luckhurst began with a stand of 64.

Hampshire

*R. E. Marshall c Wilson b Underwood	106	— c Denness b Underwood	14
H. Horton lbw b Dixon	7	— c Ealham b Dixon	20
R. G. Caple c Luckhurst b Underwood	35	— c Knott b Dixon	0
D. A. Livingstone c Luckhurst b Dixon	6	— b Dixon	19
P. J. Sainsbury c Cowdrey b Graham	39	— lbw b Dixon	2
R. M. C. Gilliat c Luckhurst b Underwood	4	— c Knott b Underwood	1
D. R. Turner b Dixon	0	— not out	15
K. J. Wheatley c Knott b Sayer	46	— c Leary b Underwood	9
†B. S. V. Timms lbw b Graham	1	— b Dixon	1
D. Shackleton c Denness b Sayer	0	— c Ealham b Sayer	10
D. W. White not out	0	— c Leary b Sayer	0
B 10, l-b 3	13	L-b 6	6
1/27 2/138 3/153 4/163 5/180 6/181 7/246 8/257 9/257	257	1/24 2/33 3/48 4/59 5/60 6/73 7/78 8/82 9/96	97

Bowling: *First Innings*—Sayer 14.4—2—49—2; Graham 17—6—38—2; Dixon 35—8—108—3; Underwood 39—19—49—3. *Second Innings*—Sayer 5.4—2—8—2; Graham 8—4—12—0; Dixon 15—5—44—5; Underwood 19—12—27—3.

Kent

M. H. Denness c Turner b Wheatley	9	— not out	44
B. W. Luckhurst c Horton b White	26	— b Shackleton	38
D. M. Sayer lbw b White	21		
R. C. Wilson b Shackleton	41	— not out	28
*M. C. Cowdrey not out	73		
S. E. Leary c Timms b White	22		
A. Ealham b White	4		
†A. L. Knott st Timms b Shackleton	26		
A. L. Dixon lbw b Shackleton	0		
D. L. Underwood st Timms b Shackleton	5		
J. N. Graham b Shackleton	0		
B 5, l-b 4, n-b 2	11	B 2, l-b 5, n-b 1	8
1/30 2/43 3/88 4/119 5/167 6/175 7/228 8/228 9/236	238	1/64 (1 wkt.)	118

Bowling: *First Innings*—Shackleton 44.1—23—59—5; White 32—8—75—4; Wheatley 32—11—52—1; Caple 7—1—16—0; Sainsbury 14—7—25—0. *Second Innings*—Shackleton 18—7—19—1; Wheatley 17—5—47—0; Caple 7—2—20—0; Marshall 6—1—20—0; Horton 0.3—0—4—0.

Umpires: A. E. Rhodes and G. H. Pope.

HAMPSHIRE v. ESSEX

At Portsmouth, August 24, 25, 26. Drawn. Hampshire were without four regular bowlers White, Cottam, Sainsbury and Castell through injuries and included for the first time a nineteen-year-old all-rounder, Jesty. Marshall put Essex in and after giving Jesty six overs went on to bowl himself. He soon took three wickets and Essex plunged to 69 for five when there was a break for rain. The day ended with the score 186 for nine and they were soon out next day. Shackleton's figures were five for 83—the seventh time in the season he had taken five or more wickets in an innings. Hampshire were bowled out cheaply and then Essex batted steadily before Bailey declared on the third day. Essex seemed to be heading for victory, thanks to some good leg-spin bowling by Hobbs (five for 65) but Timms and Wassell checked them with an unbroken last-wicket partnership of 29, which held up Essex for seventy minutes and prevented them from winning.

Essex

First Innings		Second Innings	
M. J. Bear lbw b Shackleton	38	not out	82
G. J. Saville c Livingstone b Marshall	11		
G. E. Barker c Jesty b Marshall	3	not out	30
K. W. R. Fletcher c Horton b Shackleton	2		
*T. E. Bailey c Timms b Marshall	1	lbw b Shackleton	17
B. R. Knight c Livingstone b Shackleton	30		
†B. Taylor c Livingstone b Wassell	49	b Shackleton	75
B. Edmeades c and b Shackleton	29		
A. M. Jorden not out	16		
R. N. S. Hobbs c Jesty b Shackleton	0		
D. L. Acfield c Timms b Wheatley	2		
B 8, l-b 2	10	B 1, l-b 5	6
1/43 2/49 3/52 4/55 5/69 6/121 7/163 8/170 9/170	191	1/49 2/157 (2 wkts., dec.)	210

Bowling: *First Innings*—Shackleton 43—16—83—5; Jesty 6—1—20—0; Marshall 16—3—29—3; Wassell 6—3—10—1; Wheatley 16.3—3—39—1. *Second Innings*—Shackleton 37—11—80—2; Jesty 17—8—32—0; Marshall 7—3—12—0; Wassell 14—1—63—0; Wheatley 6—1—17—0.

Hampshire

First Innings		Second Innings	
*R. E. Marshall c Barker b Edmeades	16	c Fletcher b Knight	2
H. Horton lbw b Hobbs	34	c Barker b Edmeades	18
R. G. Caple c Fletcher b Bailey	0	c and b Hobbs	18
D. A. Livingstone c Taylor b Edmeades	0	c and b Hobbs	69
K. J. Wheatley c Jorden b Knight	32	c Barker b Edmeades	27
R. M. C. Gilliat c Fletcher b Knight	1	lbw b Bailey	23
D. R. Turner c Bailey b Jorden	19	c and b Hobbs	0
†B. S. V. Timms c Taylor b Acfield	9	not out	11
T. Jesty not out	2	c Knight b Hobbs	0
D. Shackleton lbw b Jorden	0	c Fletcher b Hobbs	4
A. R. Wassell c Taylor b Jorden	4	not out	14
B 1, l-b 1	2	B 4, l-b 2	6
1/24 2/25 3/26 4/74 5/75 6/96 7/113 8/113 9/113	119	1/2 2/32 3/43 4/114 5/163 6/163 7/163 8/163 9/168 (9 wkts.)	192

Bowling: *First Innings*—Knight 10—2—21—2; Jorden 13—4—31—3; Edmeades 12—3—30—2; Bailey 10—6—13—1; Acfield 4—1—6—1; Hobbs 8—4—16—1. *Second Innings*—Knight 11—4—21—1; Jorden 8—3—21—0; Edmeades 10—1—28—2; Bailey 11—6—18—1; Acfield 18—9—31—0; Hobbs 29—10—65—5; Fletcher 5—3—2—0.

Umpires: A. E. Rhodes and R. S. Lay.

At Southampton, August 27, 29, 31. HAMPSHIRE drew with WEST INDIES. (See WEST INDIES section.)

At Lord's, August 31, September 1, 2. HAMPSHIRE v. MIDDLESEX abandoned without a ball bowled.

KENT

President—C. P. JOHNSTONE

Secretary-Manager—L. E. G. AMES, St. Lawrence Ground, Canterbury

Captain—M. C. COWDREY

B. W. Luckhurst

County Badge

D. L. Underwood

Kent climbed yet another place in the county table to finish fourth, their highest position for nineteen years. Underwood, who although only twenty-one, took over 100 wickets for the third time in four seasons, causing his county officials to rake through past records as he moved from distinction to distinction throughout the summer. Selected for two Tests, he was first in the country to reach 100 wickets and headed the national bowling averages, the first time this had been achieved by a Kent bowler since Colin Blythe did so in 1914. His total of 144 wickets for Kent was the highest since 1935 when "Tich" Freeman topped the 200 mark. Underwood and the county's popular all-rounder, Dixon, who led the side splendidly whenever Cowdrey was absent, carried all before them with the ball.

Dixon, switching from seamers to off-spin when the need demanded, took 115 wickets, the third successive season he has topped 100. The prominent part he and Underwood played was underlined by the fact that twelve and thirteen times respectively they took five or more wickets in an innings.

The pace bowling did not earn such rewards. Sayer was the most consistent wicket-taker but Brown and the left-arm bowler, Dye, who was awarded his county cap in June, both had spells out of the side.

Probably the most disappointing feature of the campaign was the lack of success of the middle-order batsmen. The new 65 overs-rule and some bad pitches may not have helped matters, but Wilson only managed to reach his 1,000 runs for the county in the last match of the season, Leary failed by 64 and Cowdrey by 199.

Indeed, the Kent captain, hit only one century for his county during the summer—100 not out against Oxford University—which marked his completion of ten years as county captain. No one is more determined to lead Kent to a Championship success and he himself has great confidence in the material at his command.

Fortunately Kent were wonderfully served by the opening batsmen, Luckhurst and Denness, who formed one of the most successful partnerships in the country. Both played some memorable innings and finished with their best aggregates in first-class cricket.

In the field Kent performed as well as, if not better than, any side in the championship and behind the stumps Knott again confirmed his high promise. Twice he equalled a county record by dismissing six victims in an innings. Competition for a place in the side was keen—a good thing—with Ealham establishing himself in his first season on the staff.

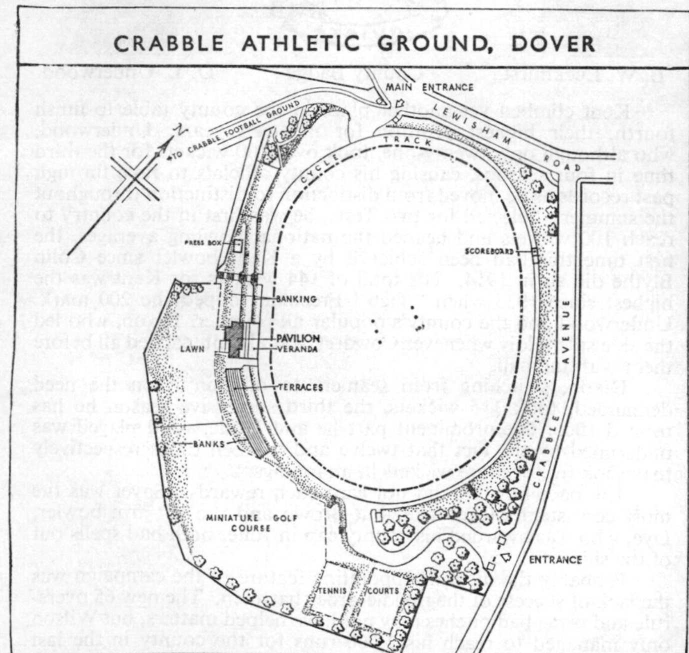

KENT RESULTS

All First-Class Matches—Played 30, *Won* 12, *Lost* 9, *Drawn* 9
County Championship Matches—Played 28, *Won* 11, *Lost* 8, *Drawn* 8, *No Decision* 1

COUNTY CHAMPIONSHIP AVERAGES

BATTING

	Birthplace	Mtchs.	Inns.	Not Outs	Runs	100's	Highest Inns.	Aver.
B. W. Luckhurst	*Sittingbourne*	28	50	3	1553	3	183	33.04
M. H. Denness.	*Ayrshire*	26	47	3	1409	0	97	32.02
M. C. Cowdrey.	*Bangalore, India*	18	27	5	681	0	87	30.95
R. C. Wilson...	*Bapchild*	23	39	2	1025	0	88	27.70
A. Knott......	*Erith*	27	40	9	658	0	48*	21.22
S. E. Leary.....	*Cape Town*	28	46	4	873	0	67*	20.78
A. Ealham.....	*Ashford*	21	33	6	493	0	59	18.25
A. Brown......	*Rainworth*	13	18	5	213	0	52*	16.38
J. M. Prodger..	*Forest Hill*	16	25	3	332	1	114*	15.09
D. Nicholls....	*Dereham*	8	13	0	179	0	53	13.76
A. L. Dixon....	*Dartford*	26	39	6	450	0	44*	13.63
A. J. Hooper...	*Blackheath*	2	3	1	26	0	15	13.00
D. M. Sayer....	*Romford*	24	27	9	168	0	39	9.33
J. C. Dye.....	*Rochester*	16	14	9	38	0	11	7.60
J. N. Graham..	*Hexham*	8	6	2	24	0	12	6.00
D. L. Underwood	*Bromley*	23	25	8	94	0	21*	5.52

Also batted: E. W. J. Fillary (*Heathfield*) 1 and 7.

* *Signifies not out.*

BOWLING

	Overs	Maidens	Runs	Wickets	Average
D. L. Underwood.......	921.1	410	1745	143	12.20
J. N. Graham...........	257.3	89	493	26	18.96
A. L. Dixon............	917.4	287	2225	105	21.19
D. M. Sayer............	611	153	1489	67	22.22
J. C. Dye..............	406.1	133	787	33	23.84
A. Brown..............	399	97	1089	42	25.92
A. J. Hooper...........	32	8	89	3	29.66
B. W. Luckhurst........	60.2	15	175	5	35.00
S. E. Leary............	54	8	193	5	38.60

Also bowled: M. C. Cowdrey 2—0—13—0; A. Ealham 5—0—15—0; E. W. J. Fillary 4—0—8—0.

At Ipswich, April 30. KENT beat SUFFOLK by 113 runs. (See GILLETTE CUP.)

At Nottingham, May 4, 5, 6. KENT drew with NOTTINGHAMSHIRE.

At Lord's, May 7, 9, 10. KENT beat MIDDLESEX by 117 runs.

KENT v. MIDDLESEX

At Gravesend, May 14, 16, 17. Drawn. A match which produced many highlights on the first two days, ended on the third in a not unfamiliar manner with Middlesex running out of time in which to bowl out their opponents who, in turn, were short of the target. A best performance by the Middlesex forcing right-hand batsman, Clark, who featured in a third-wicket stand of 162 in two and a half hours with Parfitt, enabled Middlesex to build up an impressive total. Clark proved that aggression paid handsomely on this perfect batting wicket which Kent, in their first innings, apart from Wilson, failed to appreciate until their last pair came together. Then the fast bowlers, Brown and Sayer, hit a whirlwind 94 in exactly an hour, with the former recording his highest score. It was a thrilling last-wicket stand which, in his forty years' experience of Kent cricket, secretary-manager Leslie Ames did not think had been bettered for Kent by batsmen numbers ten and eleven. During the Middlesex first innings, the young Kent wicket-keeper Knott equalled the Kent wicket-keeping record by dismissing six batsmen—four of them caught and two stumped.

Middlesex

M. J. Harris c Knott b Brown	28	— c Luckhurst b Underwood	56
C. T. Radley c Knott b Sayer	1	— c Knott b Underwood	57
P. H. Parfitt c Knott b Sayer	85	— c Knott b Brown	1
E. A. Clark lbw b Dixon	149	— c Brown b Dixon	24
*F. J. Titmus c Underwood b Sayer	32	— lbw b Dixon	25
R. W. Hooker c Knott b Underwood	27	— run out	21
M. J. Smith st Knott b Underwood	10	— not out	17
D. A. Bick c Luckhurst b Dixon	0	— not out	11
H. C. Latchman not out	1		
†E. G. Clifton st Knott b Dixon	0		
R. W. Stewart b Dixon	1		
L-b 2, w 1	3	B 5, l-b 4, n-b 1	10
1/1 2/39 3/201 4/283 5/316 6/324 7/333 8/334 9/335	337	1/113 2/114 3/114 4/159 5/186 6/206 (6 wkts., dec.)	222

Bowling: *First Innings*—Brown 20—1—94—1; Sayer 22—4—62—3; Dixon 32—9—90—4; Underwood 23—5—80—2; Fillary 4—0—8—0. *Second Innings*—Brown 20—7—38—1; Sayer 11—0—39—0; Dixon 21—5—64—2; Underwood 30—11—71—2.

Kent

E. W. J. Fillary c Parfitt b Latchman	1	— c Parfitt b Latchman	7
B. W. Luckhurst c Clifton b Stewart	20	— c Titmus b Stewart	10
D. Nicholls c Parfitt b Titmus	1	— lbw b Hooker	23
R. C. Wilson c Hooker b Titmus	74	— c Stewart b Titmus	53
S. E. Leary b Latchman	18	— lbw b Bick	46
J. M. Prodger c Radley b Bick	5	— b Bick	21
†A. Knott run out	4	— lbw b Titmus	36
*A. L. Dixon c Titmus b Bick	30	— not out	44
D. L. Underwood lbw b Stewart	0	— c Clifton b Bick	5
A. Brown not out	52	— not out	0
D. M. Sayer b Clark	39		
B 1, l-b 11, n b 1	13	B 9, l-b 12, w 1	22
1/11 2/18 3/33 4/78 5/110 6/125 7/132 8/133 9/163	257	1/31 2/35 3/118 4/156 5/164 6/194 7/216 8/235 (8 wkts.)	267

Bowling: *First Innings*—Stewart 25—10—36—2; Hooker 17—5—53—0; Latchman 17—4—57—2; Titmus 29—8—50—2; Bick 16—5—45—2; Clark 2.2—1—3—1. *Second Innings*—Stewart 9—2—27—1; Hooker 13—0—41—1; Latchman 8—3—21—1; Titmus 27—7—76—2; Bick 21—6—69—3; Smith 2—0—11—0.

Umpires: A. E. Alderman and R. S. Lay.

KENT v. GLAMORGAN

At Gravesend, May 18, 19, 20. Drawn. Glamorgan, unfortunate enough to be caught by a shower of rain which freshened the wicket and dismissed for 83 in their first innings, recovered well when they followed on and a glorious double century by A. R. Lewis enabled them easily to save the game. Lewis hit two 6's and thirty-two 4's in a stay of over five hours and he figured in a second-wicket stand of 190 with A. Jones. Not afraid to take chances, the Cambridge Blue punished the Kent attack unmercifully. So the Welsh county, without all-rounder Walker who sustained an injured foot from the first ball he received in that unfortunate first innings, made up for their dismal showing when the seam bowlers, Brown, Sayer and Dixon were getting some response from the wicket. Kent owed their large total mainly to centuries by the opening batsman, Luckhurst, and Prodger who hit his first hundred for two seasons and displayed many attractive shots in front of the wicket.

Kent

B. W. Luckhurst b I. J. Jones.....110	†A Knott not out................ 48
D. Nicholls lbw b Shepherd 26	
R. C. Wilson c Shepherd b E. Lewis 11	B 6, l-b 3................ 9
*M. C. Cowdrey b Davis......... 4	
S. E. Leary c. A. Jones b I. J. Jones 0	1/47 2/71 3/80 (5 wkts., dec.) 322
J. M. Prodger not out............114	4/93 5/222

A. L. Dixon, A. Brown, D. M. Sayer and D. L. Underwood did not bat.

Bowling: I. J. Jones 21—4—53—2; Wheatley 23—7—47—0; Walker 13—4—33—0; Davis 29—13—68—1; Shepherd 20—3—77—1; E. Lewis 9—2—35—1.

Glamorgan

A. Jones c Luckhurst b Sayer	20	— c Leary b Dixon	81
B. Hedges b Dixon	22	— c Knott b Brown..........	0
P. M. Walker retired hurt	0		
A. R. Lewis c Luckhurst b Brown	14	— c Nicholls b Luckhurst	223
E. Lewis c Knott b Brown..............	0	— b Leary..................	6
A. Rees c Cowdrey b Dixon	9	— lbw b Dixon..............	29
F. J. Davis c Nicholls b Brown.........	6	— not out	28
†D. L. Evans c Underwood b Dixon....	7	— not out	2
D. J. Shepherd c Brown b Sayer........	1		
I. J. Jones c Cowdrey b Sayer..........	0		
*O. S. Wheatley not out...............	1		
L-b 3	3	B 12, l-b 1, w 1, n-b 2..	16
1/32 2/52 3/53 4/58 5/66 6/79 7/82 8/82 9/83	83	1/1 2/191 3/206 4/353 5/354 (5 wkts.)	385

Bowling: *First Innings*—Brown 21—7—36—3; Sayer 14.5—3—29—3; Dixon 14—6—15—3. *Second Innings*—Brown 20—3—57—1; Sayer 15—2—39—0; Dixon 33—11—76—2; Underwood 25—10—82—0; Leary 19—4—73—1; Luckhurst 10—4—29—1; Cowdrey 2—0—13—0.

Umpires: A. E. Alderman and R. S. Lay.

At Southampton, May 21. KENT lost to HAMPSHIRE by 54 runs. (See GILLETTE CUP.)

At Worcester, May 25, 26, 27. KENT lost to WORCESTERSHIRE by 80 runs.

At Bath, June 1, 2, 3. KENT beat SOMERSET by 164 runs.

KENT v. SUSSEX

At Tunbridge Wells. June 4, 6, 7. *65 overs.* Kent won by five wickets. Kent were always in command of this game and although they only took first innings points by 26 runs the pace attack of Sayer and Brown went to work on Sussex in the second innings and shot them out for 159. They shared eight wickets between them and Sayer had also taken four wickets in the Sussex first innings when only Suttle offered real resistance. In the Sussex second innings, Lenham and Foreman fought to retrieve a bad start with a fighting fourth wicket stand of 84, but Kent were left an easy task to win. Denness who batted beautifully in the first innings and shared an opening stand of 124 with Luckhurst, was dismissed in the second innings without a run being scored, but Luckhurst and Wilson steered Kent out of trouble and then it was only a question of how long they would take to win.

Sussex

K. G. Suttle lbw b Dixon	79	— c Wilson b Brown	1
L. J. Lenham lbw b Dixon	14	— c Denness b Underwood	62
*Nawab of Pataudi c Brown b Sayer	35	— c Denness b Brown	4
M. G. Griffith c Knott b Sayer	10	— c Luckhurst b Brown	19
G. C. Cooper b Sayer	29	— c Knott b Sayer	3
D. J. Foreman lbw b Sayer	1	— c Knott b Brown	32
A. S. M. Oakman c sub b Underwood	10	— c Knott b Sayer	18
J. A. Snow c Wilson b Underwood	9	— c Wilson b Underwood	5
A. Buss not out	2	— b Sayer	5
†T. Gunn not out	4	— c Luckhurst b Sayer	0
D. L. Bates (did not bat)		— not out	1
B 4, l-b 3	7	B 5, n-b 4	9
1/73 2/98 3/120 4/151 5/165 6/170 7/190 8/194 (8 wkts., 65 overs)	200	1/3 2/7 3/37 4/121 5/128 6/147 7/149 8/150 9/150	159

Bowling: *First Innings*—Brown 11—0—45—0; Sayer 21—6—53—4; Dixon 14—2—50—2; Underwood 19—8—45—2. *Second Innings*—Brown 15—3—45—4; Sayer 20—6—49—4; Underwood 31—20—41—2; Luckhurst 4—1—15—0.

Kent

M. H. Denness c Oakman b Snow	95	— c Bates b Snow	0
B. W. Luckhurst c Pataudi b Bates	55	— b Buss	34
R. C. Wilson run out	29	— c Griffith b Snow	38
A. Ealham b Snow	1	— b Snow	10
S. E. Leary c Snow b Buss	1	— c Suttle b Bates	15
A. Brown c Gunn b Snow	25		
D. M. Sayer not out	5		
D. L. Underwood not out	1		
J. M. Prodger (did not bat)		— not out	25
†A. Knott (did not bat)		— not out	12
B 4, l-b 10	14	B 1, l-b 2	3
1/124 2/178 3/186 4/193 5/215 6/225 (6 wkts., 65 overs)	226	1/0 2/68 3/84 4/88 5/105 (5 wkts.)	137

*A. L. Dixon did not bat.

Bowling: *First Innings*—Snow 21—2—74—3; Buss 18—1—82—1; Bates 17—8—38—1; Suttle 9—4—18—0. *Second Innings*—Snow 17—2—47—3; Buss 11—3—40—1; Bates 9—3—19—1; Suttle 1—0—4—0; Oakman 9.4—2—24—0.

Umpires: W. F. Price and H. Mellows.

KENT v. DERBYSHIRE

At Tunbridge Wells, June 8, 9, 10. *65 overs.* Derbyshire won by 80 runs. After seeming to have this game, with maximum points, well under control, Kent faded badly in their second innings when the Derbyshire bowlers, Rhodes and Morgan, were afforded some help from the pitch and bowled their side to victory. In the restricted first innings, Kent took the two points by a narrow margin and then their fast bowler Brown had Derbyshire in real trouble. The visitors lost their first four wickets for 36 runs but Harvey and subsequently their captain, Morgan, pulled them round to great effect. When Kent went in again they were never comfortable against the Derbyshire attack and after a second-wicket partnership of 50 by Luckhurst and Leary had been broken, Derbyshire carried all before them and romped home to an easy victory.

Derbyshire

I. W. Hall c Ealham b Dye	26	— c Knott b Brown	0
J. R. Eyre c Knott b Sayer	1	— c Luckhurst b Brown	0
J. F. Harvey c Prodger b Dye	26	— c Leary b Underwood	63
H. L. Johnson c Knott b Brown	34	— c Prodger b Brown	2
I. R. Buxton b Brown	9	— c Knott b Dye	12
*D. C. Morgan c Knott b Underwood	9	— c Knott b Dye	88
M. Hill b Sayer	39	— c Ealham b Brown	8
M. H. Page c Dye b Underwood	7	— c Prodger b Underwood	10
†R. W. Taylor run out	6	— c Underwood b Leary	11
T. J. P. Eyre not out	2	— c Knott b Sayer	8
H. J. Rhodes not out	0	— not out	6
B 5, l-b 3, n-b 1	9	b 1, l-b 2, n-b 1	4
1/12 2/44 3/65 4/98 (9 wkts., 65 overs) 5/107 6/107 7/159 8/159 9/168	168	1/0 2/11 3/17 4/36 5/96 6/126 7/160 8/198 9/199	212

Bowling: *First Innings*—Brown 16—3—44—2; Sayer 12—2—32—2; Dye 14—5—32—2; Underwood 23—10—51—2. *Second Innings*—Brown 23—6—59—4; Sayer 17.2—3—58—1; Dye 20—9—38—2; Underwood 29—5—48—2; Leary 2—0—5—1.

Kent

M. H. Denness b T. J. P. Eyre	15	— c Johnson b Rhodes	1
B. W. Luckhurst c Harvey b Buxton	50	— c Taylor b Rhodes	37
S. E. Leary c Taylor b T. J. P. Eyre	2	— b Morgan	25
*R. C. Wilson c Morgan b T. J. P. Eyre	0	— c Taylor b Rhodes	9
J. M. Prodger c T. J. P. Eyre b Buxton	22	— c Taylor b Rhodes	0
A. Brown c Taylor b T. J. P. Eyre	12	— b Morgan	4
A. Ealham c Taylor b Morgan	19	— c T. J. P. Eyre b Morgan	14
†A. Knott c Hill b Rhodes	35	— c Morgan b Rhodes	14
D. M. Sayer lbw b Morgan	8	— not out	5
D. L. Underwood b Morgan	0	— b Morgan	4
J. C. Dye not out	5	— c sub b T. J. P. Eyre	0
L-b 4, n-b 6	10	l-b 4, n-b 5	9
1/45 2/47 3/49 4/96 5/96 6/118 7/144 8/164 9/164	178	1/3 2/53 3/65 4/69 5/93 6/99 7/110 8/113 9/121	122

Bowling: *First Innings*—Buxton 10—7—17—2; Rhodes 21—5—58—1; Morgan 21—7—54—3; T. J. P. Eyre 11—1—39—4. *Second Innings*—Buxton 7—0—19—0; Rhodes 20—9—31—5; Morgan 23—8—37—4; T. J. P. Eyre 7.3—9—21—1; Page 1—0—5—0.

Umpires: W. F. Price and H. Mellows.

At The Oval, June 11, 12, 13. KENT drew with SURREY.

KENT v. ESSEX

At Dartford, June 15, 16, 17. *65 overs.* Essex won by four runs. Essex had the last laugh on a pitch which always had the batsmen troubled because the ball came through at varying heights. Bear and Barker successfully pursued a bold course but Essex faltered and at the end of the first day Kent looked in a sound position, being only 35 runs behind with eight wickets in hand. A fine spell of bowling, however, by Edmeades cut the Kent lead to 26, but when Essex batted again they ran into trouble against Underwood who in nine overs took five wickets for 13 and in spite of an enterprising innings of 50 by Taylor, Kent were left to score 87 to win which, despite the pitch, did not seem an unreasonable task. Denness did his best to prove that the pitch might not be as bad as it looked, but good spells by Edmeades and Bailey sent Kent crashing to a surprising but exciting defeat.

Essex

First Innings		Second Innings	
G. E. Barker lbw b Brown	2	lbw b Brown	8
M. J. Bear c Leary b Underwood	30	c Luckhurst b Underwood	23
†B. Taylor c Luckhurst b Dixon	27	c Wilson b Underwood	50
K. W. R. Fletcher c Denness b Underwood	32	c Luckhurst b Underwood	0
G. R. Cass c Luckhurst b Brown	11	c Prodger b Underwood	3
G. J. Smith b Dye	16	c Leary b Underwood	4
B. Edmeades c and b Dye	1	c Knott b Underwood	7
*T. E. Bailey b Underwood	22	lbw b Dixon	9
R. N. S. Hobbs not out	10	not out	2
A. M. Jorden not out	1	c and b Dixon	3
G. C. Pritchard (did not bat)		c Leary b Dixon	0
B 4, l-b 1	5	L-b 3	3
1/6 2/63 3/65 4/88 5/112 6/114 7/134 8/156 (8 wkts., 65 overs)	157	1/14 2/73 3/83 4/84 5/88 6/92 7/99 8/108 9/112	112

Bowling—*First Innings*—Brown 15—1—44—2; Dye 16—6—20—2; Dixon 9—2—27—1; Underwood 25—10—61—3. *Second Innings*—Brown 18—5—47—1; Dye 10—4—20—0; Dixon 9.3—3—22—3; Underwood 16—11—20—6.

Kent

First Innings		Second Innings	
M. H. Denness c Cass b Bailey	32	c Bailey b Edmeades	38
B. W. Luckhurst lbw b Jorden	1	b Jorden	0
D. Nicholls c Taylor b Edmeades	32	c Taylor b Edmeades	4
S. E. Leary c Taylor b Edmeades	48	c Fletcher b Smith	0
R. C. Wilson c Bailey b Edmeades	8	c Bailey b Edmeades	0
J. M. Prodger lbw b Edmeades	13	c Taylor b Edmeades	1
A. Brown b Edmeades	2	c Hobbs b Bailey	3
†A. Knott not out	18	c Smith b Bailey	19
*A. L. Dixon not out	7	b Bailey	3
D. L. Underwood (did not bat)		run out	10
J. C. Dye (did not bat)		not out	0
B 9, l-b 12, n-b 1	22	l-b 2, n-b 2	4
1/11 2/50 3/123 4/137 5/142 6/146 7/161 (7 wkts., 65 overs)	183	1/1 2/29 3/30 4/39 5/45 6/60 7/68 8/70 9/82	82

Bowling: *First Innings*—Jorden 9—1—16—1; Pritchard 8—3—21—0; Edmeades 21—2—55—5; Bailey 23—3—53—1; Hobbs 4—2—16—0. *Second Innings*—Jorden 4—0—11—1; Bailey 11.2—4—25—3; Smith 4—0—13—1; Edmeades 11—3—29—4.

Umpires: L. H. Gray and P. B. Wight.

At Derby, June 18, 19, 20. KENT beat DERBYSHIRE by seven wickets.

KENT v. OXFORD UNIVERSITY

At Canterbury, June 25, 27, 28. Kent won by 139 runs. The Kent batsmen, needing to recover form, took full advantage of this match against Oxford and both Luckhurst and Cowdrey scored centuries, with Prodger making a half century, as an impressive first innings total was manufactured. The University made a good start with an opening stand of 80 and later Guest and Dyer played useful innings, while easily dispelling any possibility of a follow on. The Kent West Indian all-rounder Shepherd, making his County debut, and Dixon, shared eight University wickets. In the Kent second innings Denness also took the opportunity to give a good display and the University were finally set 247 to win in three hours, fifty minutes. They never looked like achieving their target. Half the side were dismissed for 50 and Leary, bowling his leg spinners, brought the proceedings to an abrupt close with four wickets for three runs

Kent

First Innings		Second Innings	
M. H. Denness b Watson	8	not out	75
B. W. Luckhurst b Ridley	101		
S. E. Leary c Dyer b Guest	18		
J. M. Prodger c and b Ridley	52		
*M. C. Cowdrey not out	100		
J. Shepherd lbw b Easter	17		
A. Ealham not out	19		
E. W. J. Fillary (did not bat)	—	b Elviss	44
†A. Knott (did not bat)	—	not out	35
B 4, l-b 6, w 2, n-b 1	13	B 3, w 1, n-b 3	7
1/8 2/35 3/118 4/237 5/275 (5 wkts., dec.)	328	1/96 (1 wkt., dec.)	161

A. L. Dixon and J. C. Dye did not bat.

Bowling: *First Innings*—Watson 18—2—72—1; Easter 16.4—4—57—1; Barker 20—9—48—0; Guest 11—1—37—1; Ridley 18—6—53—2; Elviss 19—7—48—0. *Second Innings*—Watson 14—6—26—0; Easter 7—2—21—0; Barker 10—1—36—0; Guest 6—2—17—0; Ridley 6—0—31—0; Elviss 17—8—23—1.

Oxford University

First Innings		Second Innings	
P. J. K. Gibbs c Luckhurst b Shepherd	35	c Knott b Dye	13
F. S. Goldstein b Fillary	68	b Dye	19
D. P. Toft c Prodger b Dixon	29	b Dixon	5
*R. M. C. Gilliat c Luckhurst b Fillary	1	b Dye	0
M. R. J. Guest c Knott b Shepherd	58	b Shepherd	3
†A. W. Dyer c Knott b Dixon	33	c Luckhurst b Fillary	18
G. N. S. Ridley c Fillary b Shepherd	0	c Luckhurst b Leary	32
A. G. M. Watson lbw b Dixon	0	lbw b Leary	12
A. H. Barker c Dye b Shepherd	8	lbw b Leary	0
R. W. Elviss not out	0	not out	1
J. N. C. Easter b Dixon	0	c Prodger b Leary	0
B 5, l-b 6	11	L-b 4	4
1/80 2/114 3/120 4/155 5/231 6/233 7/233 8/235 9/243	243	1/29 2/38 3/40 4/40 5/50 6/75 7/102 8/106 9/107	107

Bowling: *First Innings*—Dye 19—7—18—0; Shepherd 25—6—71—4; Dixon 36.1—18—40—4; Luckhurst 27—13—47—0; Fillary 21—4—56—2. *Second Innings*—Dye 16—10—9—3; Shepherd 12—5—14—1; Dixon 26—9—57—1; Luckhurst 4—2—5—0; Fillary 10—5—15—1; Leary 4.2—2—3—4.

Umpires: J. Arnold and O. W. Herman.

At Northampton, June 29, 30, July 1. KENT lost to NORTHAMPTONSHIRE by 77 runs.

KENT v. SURREY

At Blackheath, July 2, 4, 5. Drawn. Both sides defied the reputation of the Blackheath pitch to cause batsmen discomfort by running up big scores on the first two days. Then when the wicket really was awkward on the third day, an interesting finish was denied by the intervention of the weather after Graham and Dixon had caused Surrey to collapse in their second innings. On the opening day Edrich and Edwards figured in a century partnership. Edrich went on to score 132, hitting two 6's and sixteen 4's in a stay of five hours and Stewart helped himself to fourteen boundaries in an innings of just over two hours. When Kent lost half their side for 156 runs on the second day it appeared that the pitch had already helped the bowlers to gain the upper hand but Luckhurst with 183, his highest innings on the ground when he scored his first century in County cricket, enabled Kent to recover. Luckhurst hit twenty-nine 4's in a stay of just over five hours and thanks to good support from Knott and Dixon plus a thrilling last-wicket stand, Kent won an exciting struggle for first-innings lead. For Surrey, Storey bowled splendidly in taking six wickets for 100.

Surrey

J. H. Edrich c Luckhurst b Dixon	132	— c Nicholls b Dixon	28
M. J. Edwards run out	65	— lbw b Dixon	15
M. D. Willett c Knott b Dixon	10	— c Ealham b Graham	1
R. A. E. Tindall lbw b Graham	12	— c Sayer b Graham	8
*M. J. Stewart run out	77	— c Denness b Dixon	9
S. J. Storey c Dixon b Sayer	0	— lbw b Dixon	6
G. R. J. Roope not out	31	— b Graham	0
R. I. Jefferson c Ealham b Graham	12	— c Luckhurst b Graham	0
†A. Long not out	0	— c Knott b Dixon	0
P. I. Pocock (did not bat)		— not out	0
R. Harman (did not bat)		— not out	1
B 9, l-b 10, w 1, n-b 1	21	B 6, l-b 2	8
1/125 2/156 3/199 4/283 5/283 6/334 7/356 (7 wkts., dec.)	360	1/30 2/33 3/51 4/61 5/67 6/69 7/69 8/73 9/75 (9 wkts.)	76

Bowling: *First Innings*—Sayer 18—3—63—1; Dye 18—6—42—0; Graham 28—6—54—2; Dixon 47—11—147—2; Luckhurst 13—2—33—0. *Second Innings*—Sayer 6—3—14—0; Dye 2—1—1—0; Graham 14—4—20—4; Dixon 17—10—33—5.

Kent

M. H. Denness c Edwards b Harman	28
B. W. Luckhurst c Tindall b Storey	183
D. Nicholls c Edwards b Storey	21
S. E. Leary b Storey	4
J. M. Prodger c Edwards b Storey	2
A. Ealham c Edwards b Jefferson	4
†A. Knott c Stewart b Pocock	46
*A. L. Dixon lbw b Pocock	41
D. M. Sayer lbw b Storey	3
J. N. Graham b Storey	12
J. C. Dye not out	6
B 8, l-b 4	12
1/50 2/139 3/143 4/147 5/156 6/236 7/308 8/343 9/348	362

Bowling: Jefferson 30—8—75—1; Storey 37.4—8—100—6; Harman 19—3—77—1; Pocock 17—3—64—2; Tindall 5—1—20—0; Roope 5—0—14—0.

Umpires: P. B. Wight and C. G. Pepper.

KENT v. GLOUCESTERSHIRE

At Folkestone, July 6, 7, 8. *65 overs.* Kent won by 173 runs. A spell of three wickets for one run in six balls by Mortimore, the Gloucestershire captain, had Kent struggling in their first innings, but Ealham and Knott launched a recovery and Ealham was later responsible for Gloucestershire being in even worse trouble when they batted. He took five catches in the same place in the deep, all off Underwood, whose figures of six for 52 completed Gloucestershire's first-innings downfall. A fine century by Luckhurst was a feature of the Kent second innings which ensured that Gloucestershire were left a formidable target. Milton defied the Kent attack for two and a half hours but the only other real resistance came from Mence and Kent eventually pulled off a convincing victory.

Kent

M. H. Denness lbw b Allen............ 28 — lbw b Allen................ 39
B. W. Luckhurst c and b Mortimore.... 33 — c Meyer b Mence 133
D. Nicholls c Milton b Mortimore...... 0 — c Milton b Mence.......... 53
S. E. Leary lbw b Mortimore 22
*M. C. Cowdrey c D. Brown b Mortimore 0
A. Ealham c Meyer b A. S. Brown....... 44 — not out 28
†A. Knott c D. Brown b A. S. Brown... 47 — c Russell b A. S. Brown..... 11
A. L. Dixon st Meyer b Windows ...... 20 — not out 26
D. L. Underwood run out............ 1
D. M. Sayer not out................. 0
B 2, l-b 7, n-b 1................ 10 B 1, l-b 5............. 6

1/64 2/67 3/68 4/68 (9 wkts., 65 overs) 205 1/71 2/199 (4 wkts., dec.) 296
5/107 6/167 7/202 8/205 9/205 3/224 4/246

J. C. Dye did not bat.

Bowling: *First Innings*—A. S. Brown 12—1—46—2; Windows 15—1—59—1; Allen 21—6—53—1; Mortimore 17—5—37—4. *Second Innings*—A. S. Brown 17—0—84—1; Windows 20—2—70—0; Allen 14—3—56—1; Mortimore 7—4—8—0; Mence 21—4—72—2.

Gloucestershire

R. B. Nicholls b Sayer................ 29 — c Denness b Sayer.......... 2
C. A. Milton c Sayer b Underwood..... 27 — hit wkt. b Underwood 43
D. Brown c Ealham b Underwood...... 8 — b Dye 12
S. E. Russell c Ealham b Underwood ... 6 — c Leary b Underwood 7
D. Shepherd b Dye.................. 4 — c Cowdrey b Sayer 12
M. D. Mence c Ealham b Underwood... 0 — c Luckhurst b Dye 55
*J. B. Mortimore c Ealham b Underwood 10 — c Cowdrey b Leary......... 20
A. S. Brown b Sayer................. 13 — lbw b Sayer 24
A. R. Windows c Ealham b Underwood. 16 — lbw b Sayer 0
D. A. Allen not out .... 10 — hit wkt. b Leary 16
†B. J. Meyer not out................. 6 — not out 0
L-b 2...................... 2 B 4, l-b 2 6

1/56 2/56 3/63 4/71 (9 wkts., 65 overs) 131 1/10 2/37 3/51 4/66 5/84 197
5/74 6/74 7/90 8/101 9/115 6/117 7/143 8/197 9/197

Bowling: *First Innings*—Sayer 22—8—45—2; Dixon 6—0—19—0; Underwood 26—10—52—6; Dye 11—6—13—1. *Second Innings*—Sayer 16—2—32—4; Dixon 18—8—44—0; Underwood 21—16—21—2; Dye 16.2—6—31—2; Leary 18—1—63—2.

Umpires: P. B. Wight and C. G. Pepper.

At Canterbury, July 9, 11, 12. KENT lost to WEST INDIES by an innings and 56 runs. (See WEST INDIES section.)

At Westcliff, July 13, 14. KENT beat ESSEX by eight wickets.

KENT v. NORTHAMPTONSHIRE

At Maidstone, July 16, 18, 19. Drawn. Rain ruined this match after Kent had played themselves into a sound position. Northamptonshire made a shocking start, losing three wickets for 20 runs and half the side was dismissed for 72. The left-handed Wills, who the previous season had twice defied the Kent attack to get him out, defended soundly and was last out, having batted nearly five and a half hours for his highest first-class score, 82. Knott, for the second time in the summer, equalled the Kent wicket-keeping record by dismissing six batsmen in an innings. Kent were given a wonderful start by Denness and the left-handed Wilson, whose second-wicket partnership realised 154. On the third day rain prevented any play and Kent had to be content with two points.

Northamptonshire

C. Milburn c Ealham b Sayer	0	B. Crump c Knott b Sayer	10
R. Wills c Knott b Dye	82	H. Sully c Knott b Dye	1
D. S. Steele c Knott b Dixon	0	*†K. V. Andrew lbw b Sayer	21
B. L. Reynolds c Knott b Dye	5	A. Durose not out	6
Mushtaq Mohammad st Knott b Underwood	13	L-b 5, n-b 6	11
P. J. Watts c and b Dixon	12	1/6 2/7 3/20 4/48 5/72	180
A. Lightfoot b Dye	19	6/122 7/138 8/139 9/168	

Bowling: Sayer 29—10—40—3; Dixon 27—10—46—2; Dye 24.5—4—41—4; Underwood 27—14—42—1.

Kent

M. H. Denness c Steele b Lightfoot	96	†A. Knott not out	17
B. W. Luckhurst b Crump	15		
R. C. Wilson st Andrew b Sully	88	L-b 5	5
*M. C. Cowdrey not out	41		
A. L. Dixon c Steele b Sully	19	1/35 2/189 3/203 4/237 (4 wkts.)	281

S. E. Leary, A. Ealham, D. L. Underwood, D. M. Sayer and J. C. Dye did not bat.

Bowling: Crump 22—3—80—1; Durose 19—4—48—0; Lightfoot 22—4—52—1; Sully 17—5—52—2; Mushtaq 3—0—12—0; Watts 12—2—32—0.

Umpires: A. E. Alderman and J. F. Crapp.

KENT v. WORCESTERSHIRE

At Maidstone, July 20, 21, 22. Kent won by 32 runs. The second game of the Maidstone week was also spoilt by the weather but this time the teams triumphed over the rain. Only seventy-seven minutes' play was possible on the first day, the second day was completely washed out, but the final day, with three declarations, produced an exciting finish. Kent declared first after a three-figure stand by their openers, Denness and Luckhurst; Worcestershire batted for two overs before lunch, scored one run and declared at the interval. Kent went in again and lost seven wickets for 57 runs in an hour, leaving Worcestershire to get 192. Thanks to Underwood who took seven for 50, Kent were rewarded twelve minutes from the end of the extra half hour, after first Graveney and then Booth had threatened to dash their hopes.

Kent

M. H. Denness not out	79	— b Flavell	4
B. W. Luckhurst c Booth b d'Oliveira	51	— b Brain	13
A. L. Dixon not out	1	— b Horton	19
A. Ealham (did not bat)		— b Gifford	7
D. M. Sayer (did not bat)		— lbw b Horton	2
R. C. Wilson (did not bat)		— c Headley b Horton	1
*M. C. Cowdrey (did not bat)		— not out	11
S. E. Leary (did not bat)		— c Booth b Gifford	0
†A. Knott (did not bat)		— not out	0
B 1, l-b 3	4		
1/129 (1 wkt., dec.)	135	1/4 2/28 3/39 (7 wkts., dec) 4/43 5/45 6/48 7/55	57

D. L. Underwood and J. C. Dye did not bat.

Bowling: *First Innings*—Flavell 5—1—12—0; Brain 10—2—29—0; Gifford 25—12—43—0; d'Oliveira 14—3—28—1; Horton 7—0—19—0. *Second Innings*—Flavell 3—0—15—1; Brain 4—0—16—1; Gifford 5—0—16—2; Horton 3.4—1—10—3.

Worcestershire

M. J. Horton not out	1	— c Cowdrey b Underwood	11
†R. Booth not out	0	— c and b Underwood	41
*D. Kenyon (did not bat)		— c Knott b Underwood	6
J. A. Ormrod (did not bat)		— run out	15
R. G. A. Headley (did not bat)		— b Underwood	0
D. W. Richardson (did not bat)		— c Luckhurst b Dixon	4
T. W. Graveney (did not bat)		— c Denness b Underwood	34
B. d'Oliveira (did not bat)		— c Denness b Underwood	13
N. Gifford (did not bat)		— not out	16
B. M. Brain (did not bat)		— b Dixon	10
J. A. Flavell (did not bat)		— c Dixon b Underwood	1
		B 8	8
(no wkt., dec.)	1	1/9 2/20 3/26 4/36 5/36 6/86 7/89 8/142 9/157	159

Bowling: *First Innings*—Sayer 1—0—1—0; Dye 1—1—0—0. *Second Innings*—Sayer 4—1—10—0; Dye 1—0—6—0; Underwood 23.3—10—50—7; Dixon 21—6—73—2; Luckhurst 2—0—12—0.

Umpires: A. E. Alderman and J. F. Crapp.

At Hastings, July 23, 25. KENT beat SUSSEX by four wickets.

At Bristol, July 27, 28, 29. KENT lost to GLOUCESTERSHIRE by four wickets.

KENT v. LEICESTERSHIRE

At Canterbury, July 30, August 1, 2. *65 overs.* Kent won by 66 runs. Only three minutes of extra time were left when Kent took the last Leicestershire wicket to gain an exciting victory. Rain reduced the first two days to four and a half hours and Leicestershire still had eight of their first-innings wickets standing when the third day began. The Kent spin pair, Dixon and Underwood, found the drying wicket to their liking and soon tumbled Leicestershire out. Kent scored briskly in their second-innings before leaving Leicestershire a target of 130 in one hour fifty minutes. Again the visitors struggled against Dixon and Underwood. Norman alone of the early batsmen offered real resistance and Kent's task looked comparatively easy when, with forty-five minutes remaining, they needed to take only three wickets. Lock, always a fighter, relished the situation, and even when he was prised out the last-wicket pair looked capable of holding on until Cotton chose the wrong one from Dixon to turn his back on. Dixon and Underwood shared all the eighteen Leicestershire wickets which fell in just under three and a half hours on the third day.

Kent

First Innings		Second Innings	
M. H. Denness c Marner b Lock	30	c Hallam b Spencer	6
B. W. Luckhurst c Marner b Cotton	1	c Marner b Spencer	2
R. C. Wilson c Hallam b Marner	24	c Savage b Cotton	33
*M. C. Cowdrey c Tolchard b Marner	0	b Savage	11
S. E. Leary c Tolchard b Marner	20	not out	26
A. Ealham st Tolchard b Lock	17	not out	1
†A. Knott not out	25		
A. L. Dixon c Spencer b Lock	0	b Spencer	1
D. L. Underwood not out	6		
L-b 5	5	B 8, l-b 1	9
1/6 2/53 3/54 4/69 5/96 6/106 7/110 (7 wkts., dec.)	128	1/10 2/12 3/15 4/35 5/77 (5 wkts., dec.)	89

J. C. Dye and J. N. Graham did not bat.

Bowling: *First Innings*—Spencer 5—0—17—0; Cotton 8—5—18—1; Lock 24—9—39—3; Savage 1—0—4—0; Marner 22—2—45—3. *Second Innings*—Spencer 8—2—12—3; Cotton 7—3—10—1; Lock 6—2—28—0; Savage 5.2—0—30—1.

Leicestershire

First Innings		Second Innings	
M. R. Hallam lbw b Dye	2	c Leary b Underwood	4
M. E. Norman c Leary b Underwood	6	c Cowdrey b Underwood	22
B. J. Booth c Ealham b Underwood	31	c Leary b Underwood	2
D. Constant c Cowdrey b Dixon	17	b Dixon	0
C. C. Inman c Underwood b Dixon	8	b Dixon	2
P. Marner c Ealham b Dixon	2	c Luckhurst b Dixon	0
†R. W. Tolchard c Luckhurst b Underwood	0	b Underwood	0
*G. A. R. Lock b Dixon	9	b Dixon	16
C. T. Spencer c Wilson b Dixon	0	b Underwood	0
J. S. Savage not out	4	not out	5
J. Cotton c Dye b Underwood	3	lbw b Dixon	10
B 3, l-b 3	6	L-b 2	2
1/4 2/10 3/57 4/59 5/71 6/71 7/71 8/75 9/81	88	1/5 2/19 3/30 4/30 5/32 6/32 7/36 8/40 9/52	63

Bowling: *First Innings*—Dye 7—4—7—1; Graham 9—5—4—0; Underwood 20.3—4—46—4; Dixon 13—4—25—5. *Second Innings*—Dye 3—1—5—0; Graham 2—2—0—0; Underwood 15—8—23—5; Dixon 15—5—33—5; Leary 1—1—0—0.

Umpires: O. W. Herman and L. H. Gray.

KENT v. WARWICKSHIRE

At Canterbury, August 3, 4, 5. Drawn. One of the worst ever Canterbury Weeks from the weather point of view ended with Kent not only failing to get any points but at one stage on the last day having been threatened with defeat. Warwickshire batted solidly throughout most of the first day and although Dixon toiled away with his mixture of medium pace and off-spin, Amiss, M. J. K. Smith and Stewart made sure that their side reached a respectable total. Kent, 18 for one overnight, had only seven balls bowled at them on the second day before torrential rain washed out play. On the final day they found themselves trapped on a wicket made for the seam bowling of Cartwright and Edmonds who shot them out for 99. Kent were forced to follow on, but although Cartwright removed Denness and Wilson cheaply, defeat was easily avoided.

Warwickshire

R. N. Abberley c Knott b Dixon..	0	R. B. Edmonds not out..........	26
K. Ibadulla lbw b Sayer..........	18	J. M. Allan b Luckhurst.........	11
D. L. Amiss c Denness b Hooper..	55	D. J. Brown c Hooper b Luckhurst	3
*M. J. K. Smith c Knott b Dixon..	42		
J. A. Jameson c Dixon b Hooper..	15	B 6, l-b 3, n-b 5...........	14
W. J. Stewart c Ealham b Dixon..	41		
T. W. Cartwright lbw b Dixon....	17	1/2 2/31 3/117 4/123 5/148	250
†A. C. Smith lbw b Dixon........	8	6/186 7/191 8/204 9/244	

Bowling: *First Innings*—Dye 22—7—33—0; Dixon 44—17—72—5; Sayer 13—3—43—1; Hooper 26—7—78—2; Luckhurst 3.3—0—10—2.

Kent

M. H. Denness c Brown b Cartwright...	21	— c Ibadulla b Cartwright.....	2
B. W. Luckhurst b Cartwright	8	— not out	21
†A. Knott c A. C. Smith b Edmonds....	4		
R. C. Wilson c Allan b Cartwright......	4	— lbw b Cartwright...........	8
S. E. Leary lbw b Cartwright	5	— not out	0
J. M. Prodger c Jameson b Edmonds ...	2		
A. Ealham c Jameson b Edmonds......	0		
*A. L. Dixon b Allan.................	21		
D. M. Sayer c Edmonds b Allan	4		
A. J. Hooper c A. C. Smith b Brown....	15		
J. C. Dye not out......................	7		
B 1, l-b 7..........................	8		
1/18 2/33 3/35 4/40 5/45 6/46 7/48 8/71 9/82	99	1/7 2/29 (2 wkts.)	31

Bowling: *First Innings*—Brown 12.3—2—42—1; Cartwright 25—17—18—4; Allan 9—3—14—2; Edmonds 17—9—17—3. *Second Innings*—Brown 4—3—2—0; Cartwright 13—8—14—2; Allan 6—4—5—0; Edmonds 3—1—10—0.

Umpires: A. E. Rhodes and L. H. Gray.

At Leicester, August 6, 8, 9. KENT lost to LEICESTERSHIRE by seven wickets.

KENT v. HAMPSHIRE

At Gillingham, August 13, 15, 16. *65 overs.* Drawn. Slow progress by Kent on the second day and the morning of the final day against accurate bowling, resulted in them running out of time to bowl at Hampshire. Shackleton and Cottam gave Kent a nasty jolt on the opening day when they were saved by Wilson. Thanks to Marshall, Hampshire made a flying start. Dropped when he had scored four, the Hampshire captain scored 74 out of 103, hitting two 6's and eleven 4's in a stay of one hour, fifty minutes. With Livingstone also in good form, Hampshire gained a lead of 64. A second-wicket stand of 139 by Denness and Wilson put Kent on the road to a useful second-innings total, but when Denness was out they could never raise their batting tempo. Hampshire wanted 199 to win but after losing three wickets for 45 runs, Livingstone and Gilliat made sure of saving the game and leaving Kent pointless.

Kent

	First Innings		Second Innings	
M. H. Denness b Cottam	14	—	c Sainsbury b White	97
B. W. Luckhurst c Reed b Shackleton	23	—	b Shackleton	5
R. C. Wilson c Gilliat b Cottam	53	—	c Horton b Cottam	59
*M. C. Cowdrey b Shackleton	12	—	b White	5
S. E. Leary c Gilliat b Cottam	15	—	b White	4
A. Ealham lbw b Shackleton	1	—	c Sainsbury b Shackleton	16
†A. Knott b Shackleton	18	—	c Marshall b White	21
A. L. Dixon b Shackleton	0	—	b White	19
D. L. Underwood b Cottam	2	—	lbw b Cottam	6
D. M. Sayer not out	3	—	not out	2
J. C. Dye c Timms b Shackleton	1	—	c Reed b Cottam	11
L-b 2, n-b 1	3		B 5, l-b 5, n-b 7	17
1/19 2/55 3/84 4/105 5/110 6/120 7/120 8/129 9/141	145		1/7 2/146 3/170 4/177 5/184 6/215 7/228 8/247 9/247	262

Bowling: *First Innings*—Shackleton 28.3—9—59—6; White 15—0—37—0; Cottam 17—2—46—4. *Second Innings*—Shackleton 44—25—45—2; White 34—6—68—5; Cottam 31.3—7—58—3; Caple 6—2—20—0; Sainsbury 20—6—54—0.

Hampshire

	First Innings		Second Innings	
*R. E. Marshall b Dixon	74	—	c Knott b Dixon	17
B. L. Reed b Sayer	0	—	c Knott b Sayer	13
H. Horton lbw b Sayer	24	—	c Leary b Sayer	9
D. A. Livingstone c Ealham b Sayer	57	—	b Sayer	49
P. J. Sainsbury not out	37	—	c Cowdrey b Underwood	8
R. M. C. Gilliat not out	13	—	not out	26
R. G. Caple (did not bat)		—	not out	3
B 2, l-b 2	4		B 12, l-b 8	20
1/5 2/97 3/103 (4 wkts., 65 overs)	209		1/33 2/43 3/45 4/84 5/136 (5 wkts.)	145

†B. S. V. Timms, D. Shackleton, D. W. White and R. M. Cottam did not bat.

Bowling: *First Innings*—Sayer 27—4—85—3; Dye 18—6—54—0; Underwood 9—3—25—0; Dixon 11—3—41—1. *Second Innings*—Sayer 12—4—24—3; Dye 4—0—20—0; Underwood 12—6—26—1; Dixon 20—8—49—1; Leary 5—2—6—0.

Umpires: W. F. Simpson and H. Yarnold.

At Blackpool, August 17, 18. KENT beat LANCASHIRE by an innings and 30 runs.

At Bournemouth, August 20, 22, 23. KENT beat HAMPSHIRE by nine wickets.

KENT v. LANCASHIRE

At Dover, August 24, 25, 26. Lancashire won by four wickets. A fine spell of bowling by Statham soon had Kent in trouble and they fared little better in their second effort against the combination of Statham and Higgs. Lancashire also found the going tough, but Pilling resisted and with some useful contributions following, the visiting county obtained a very helpful first-innings lead of 31. This was achieved despite a good performance by Graham, Kent's tall seam bowler, who returned the best figures of his career. Graham did not repeat his performance in the second innings and although Underwood snatched four cheap wickets, Lancashire, with a useful contribution from Knox, gained maximum points.

Kent

M. H. Denness b Lever	34	— c Knox b Higgs	8
B. W. Luckhurst c Goodwin b Statham	3	— lbw b Higgs	0
R. C. Wilson b Statham	26	— b Statham	44
*M. C. Cowdrey c Goodwin b Lever	10	— c Worsley b Statham	2
S. E. Leary b Higgs	12	— c Goodwin b Statham	22
A. Ealham b Statham	0	— c Bond b Higgs	18
†A. Knott b Higgs	8	— b Statham	2
A. L. Dixon b Statham	7	— c Statham b Higgs	22
D. L. Underwood not out	0	— lbw b Higgs	7
D. M. Sayer lbw b Statham	0	— b Higgs	2
J. N. Graham b Statham	1	— not out	3
B 9, l-b 6, n-b 6	21	L-b 1, n-b 4	5
1/17 2/43 3/79 4/96 5/96 6/108 7/120 8/120 9/120	122	1/0 2/11 3/20 4/75 5/88 6/97 7/107 8/124 9/126	135

Bowling: *First Innings*—Statham 15.4—2—32—6; Higgs 20—3—41—2; Lever 9—2—21—2; Green 4—2—7—0. *Second Innings*—Statham 17—5—42—4; Higgs 17—6—42—6; Lever 13—0—32—0; Green 3—0—14—0.

Lancashire

D. M. Green c Leary b Graham	2	— c Knot b Underwood	13
H. Pilling c Ealham b Graham	35	— lbw b Graham	6
G. K. Knox lbw b Sayer	1	— c Denness b Graham	29
D. R. Worsley b Underwood	28	— c Ealham b Underwood	19
J. D. Bond lbw b Graham	10	— b Underwood	13
B. Wood run out	5	— not out	5
J. Sullivan c Knott b Graham	23	— c Wilson b Underwood	7
P. Lever b Graham	18	— not out	7
K. Higgs c Knott b Graham	6		
†K. Goodwin c Knott b Graham	14		
*J. B. Statham not out	2		
B 2, l-b 5, w 1, n-b 1	9	L-b 6	6
1/4 2/5 3/70 4/70 5/85 6/85 7/120 8/135 9/142	153	1/21 2/23 3/50 4/76 5/84 6/94 (6 wkts.)	105

Bowling: *First Innings*—Sayer 4—0—13—1; Graham 30.5—10—70—7; Dixon 24—9—51—0; Underwood 5—2—10—1. *Second Innings*—Graham 24.4—5—55—2; Dixon 10—2—27—0; Underwood 20—12—17—4.

Umpires: J. Langridge and H. Yarnold.

KENT v. NOTTINGHAMSHIRE

At Canterbury, August 27, 29, 30. Drawn. The rain which had plagued Canterbury Cricket Week earlier in the summer returned again and prevented any chance of a decision in this match. Nottinghamshire, batting first, soon lost two wickets to the former Trent Bridge ground-staff bowler, Brown, returning to the Kent side after a lengthy absence. Following a sparkling innings from the West Indian, Murray, they struggled painfully for runs. Smedley and White extricated them from a bad start (45 for four) with a stand of 78, but Smedley took two and a half hours for his 49 and Swetman nearly the same time for 40. At one stage Underwood claimed three wickets in ten overs without conceding a run. Kent were left little time at the end of the day and resuming on the Monday at seven without loss and in a day punctuated by rain they took their score to 135 for five, with Wilson showing grand form. Kent scored their runs much faster, but on the third day only 27 balls could be bowled before rain washed out the proceedings.

Nottinghamshire

*N. Hill b Brown	2	M. Taylor c Leary b Underwood	8
J. B. Bolus c Knott b Brown	11	C. Forbes b Underwood	26
D. L. Murray lbw b Dixon	31	A. Johnson not out	3
H. I. Moore lbw b Dixon	0	B. Stead c Knott b Graham	0
M. J. Smedley c Knott b Underwood	49	L-b 5, n-b 1	6
R. A. White c Wilson b Underwood	34		
†R. Swetman c Wilson b Underwood	40	1/2 2/45 3/45 4/45 5/123 6/133 7/149 8/205 9/205	210

Bowling: Brown 24—7—60—2; Graham 31.3—11—51—1; Dixon 28—4—65—2; Underwood 27—19—28—5.

Kent

M. H. Denness c Moore b Forbes	15	A. Ealham not out	17
B. W. Luckhurst c Swetman b Johnson	26	†A. Knott not out	0
R. C. Wilson c Moore b Taylor	47	L-b 6, n-b 5	11
*M. C. Cowdrey c Murray b Johnson	20		
S. E. Leary c Moore b Johnson	2	1/36 2/61 3/107 4/111 5/133 (5 wkts.)	138

A. L. Dixon, D. L. Underwood, J. N. Graham and A. Brown did not bat.

Bowling: Forbes 20—7—37—1; Stead 4—2—8—0; Taylor 7—2—19—1; Johnson 13.5—1—50—3; White 5—1—13—0.

Umpires: J. Langridge and H. Yarnold.

At Harrogate, August 31, September 1, 2. KENT lost to YORKSHIRE by 24 runs.

BENEFITS AND TESTIMONIALS IN 1967

Benefits

D. W. Richardson—Worcestershire v. Warwickshire at Worcester, June 3.

D. Shackleton—Hampshire v. Yorkshire at Bournemouth, July 29.

S. E. Leary—Kent v. Leicestershire at Canterbury, August 5.

W. J. Stewart—Warwickshire v. Worcestershire at Edgbaston, August 5.

J. G. Binks—Yorkshire v. Surrey at Headingly, June 24.

G. Pullar—Lancashire v. Yorkshire at Old Trafford, May 27.

D. J. Shepherd—Glamorgan. Match to be announced.

Testimonials

R. Julian (Leicestershire), J. Mercer (Northamptonshire), R. A. E. Tindall and D. A. D. Sydenham (Surrey).

LANCASHIRE

PATRON—HER MAJESTY THE QUEEN

President—J. S. Cragg

Secretary—J. B. Wood, County Cricket Ground, Old Trafford, Manchester 16

Captain—J. B. Statham

J. B. Statham

County Badge

K. Higgs

Although Lancashire climbed one position in the championship table and gained six victories, the 1966 season was a very disappointing one inasmuch as few of the younger players showed improvement and the lack of a progressive policy behind the scenes became more and more apparent as the season progressed. The fact that twenty-four players were called for the first team indicated the seriousness of the situation and apart from the seam bowling in which Statham, the captain, Higgs, Lever and Shuttleworth, all produced excellent work at times, there was a decided lack of purpose about the side's cricket.

Only two batsmen, Green and Pullar, topped 1,000 runs and both these experienced run-scorers failed to improve or maintain their form of the previous season with Green a great disappointment. For a batsman who hit over 2,000 runs and seldom failed to reach the thirties in 1965, Green, essentially an attacking batsman, became an anxious and apprehensive stroke player who mustered only 1,073 runs in 49 innings for an average of 21. Pullar, plagued by injury late in the season and frequently shuffled in the batting order, headed the averages with 1,184 runs, average 37, without suggesting he was back to his best form.

Worsley, awarded his county cap in the final match of the season, showed signs of becoming an increasingly valuable batsman who, once assured of his place in the side and established in the middle order instead of at the beginning of an innings, played some useful innings and also bowled off-spinners with promise on occasions. Pilling and Bond, along with Knox, were sound at times but in the main inconsistent and Lancashire's inability to score steadily constantly nullified the splendid efforts of their seam attack in which Statham again completed 100 wickets and Lever showed considerable improvement with 74 wickets. Higgs, alone called upon by England for all five Test matches against the West Indies, was again a model of persevering endeavour and his return of 63 victims left Lancashire with no qualms about their pace bowling. The side was certainly deficient in spin where Greenhough, capturing 41 victims and representing the most experienced spinner on the staff, had his engagement terminated at the end of the season.

Howard's off-spinners never came up to requirements and he also left Old Trafford—at his own request—leaving only the raw promise of Lloyd and the little used potential of Worsley to offer any kind of balance to a seam battery as good as any in the country. A lop-sided attack and lack of consistent batting are faults Lancashire must iron out before progress can be achieved. Fortunately for the club Statham has again accepted the captaincy for 1967. His experience and consideration for his men will again do much to bridge the gap, but Lancashire's need is threefold. They require better batsmen, experienced spin bowlers and top-class slip fieldsmen before Statham can be expected to surmount difficulties increased by his committee's decision to uncover the Old Trafford pitches and failure to pursue any sort of a settled team policy. It was ironical, although not unexpected, to see Lancashire's decision to leave their pitches at the mercy of the weather play into the opposition hands, for Smith (Derbyshire), Illingworth (Yorkshire) and Lock (Leicestershire) all produced match-winning figures under conditions ideal for the sort of bowlers Lancashire, themselves, lacked.—John Kay.

LANCASHIRE RESULTS

All First-Class Matches—Played 31, *Won* 7, *Lost* 12, *Drawn* 12
County Championship Matches—Played 28, *Won* 6, *Lost* 11, *Drawn* 8, *No Decision* 3

COUNTY CHAMPIONSHIP AVERAGES

BATTING

	Birthplace	Mtchs.	Inns.	Not Outs	Runs	100's	Highest Inns.	Aver.
G. Pullar......	*Swinton*	20	34	5	894	1	110	30.82
D. R. Worsley..	*Bolton*	19	32	5	792	0	76	29.33
J. D. Bond.....	*Kearsley*	21	36	5	737	0	90	23.77
D. M. Green...	*Llanengan*	25	45	0	1021	1	115	22.68
G. K. Knox....	*North Shields*	23	41	2	708	1	100	19.70
D. Lloyd......	*Accrington*	22	33	8	472	0	77	18.88
K. Higgs......	*Stoke-on-Trent*	16	17	6	195	0	29	17.72
P. Lever.......	*Todmorden*	26	37	4	559	0	83	16.93
H. Pilling......	*Ashton-under-Lyne*	15	25	2	374	0	70	16.26
J. Sullivan.....	*Stalybridge*	15	27	1	401	0	56	15.42
B. Wood......	*Ossett*	10	15	1	216	0	39	15.42
K. Shuttleworth	*St. Helens*	10	15	3	182	0	34*	15.16
R. Entwistle....	*Burnley*	5	9	1	116	0	37*	14.50
K. Howard....	*Manchester*	4	3	2	13	0	9*	13.00
T. Greenhough.	*Rochdale*	16	21	6	167	0	22*	11.13
J. B. Statham...	*Manchester*	24	21	8	114	0	31	8.76
K. Goodwin...	*Oldham*	28	34	9	180	0	21	7.20
K. Snellgrove..	*Somerset*	2	3	0	20	0	16	6.66
R. Bennett.....	*Bacup*	2	3	0	16	0	5	5.33
A. M. Beddow.	*St. Helens*	4	6	1	25	0	13	5.00

Also batted: J. Cumbes (*East Didsbury*) 0* and 0*.

** Signifies not out.*

BOWLING

	Overs	Maidens	Runs	Wickets	Average
J. B. Statham.........	604.4	133	1424	100	14.24
K. Higgs.............	501.4	139	1047	61	17.16
P. Lever..............	586.4	117	1471	64	22.98
D. Lloyd.............	213.3	46	644	27	23.85
K. Howard...........	88	29	185	7	26.42
T. Greenhough........	418.2	136	899	32	28.09
D. R. Worsley.........	204	54	519	18	28.83
K. Shuttleworth.......	181.3	39	486	16	30.37
D. M. Green..........	120	27	334	7	47.71

Also bowled: A. M. Beddow 8—1—25—0; J. Cumbes 17—4—42—4; G. K. Knox 10—3—33—1; G. Pullar 1—0—4—0; J. Sullivan 4—0—10—0; B. Wood 6—0—36—0.

At Macclesfield, April 28. Lancashire beat Cheshire by 42 runs. **(See Gillette Cup.)**

LANCASHIRE v. GLOUCESTERSHIRE

At Manchester, May 4, 5, 6. *65 overs.* Drawn. Rain prevented play on the first day and intervened early on the second day. Although Lancashire batted soundly against an attack consisting of all seam bowling except for one over by Mortimore, the Gloucestershire captain, they were never able to score freely enough to suggest any other outcome than a first-innings points decision. Chosen to play, Green developed foot trouble during the first day and withdrew to allow the inclusion of Beddow. Knox, who batted ten minutes short of two hours and Entwistle showed the best form for Lancashire in an innings of just over three hours. On the third day Gloucestershire had batted only for quarter of an hour, losing Milton in the process, before a storm flooded the ground and summarily ended play in mid-afternoon.

Lancashire

G. K. Knox c Meyer b Smith	47
G. Pullar b A. S. Brown	10
H. Pilling c Nicholls b A. S. Brown	25
J. Sullivan c Mortimore b Smith	34
R. Entwistle not out	37
A. M. Beddow c Mortimore b Smith	0
D. Lloyd not out	4
L-b 2	2
1/39 2/83 3/85 4/142 5/152 (5 wkts., 65 overs)	159

P. Lever, †K. Goodwin, K. Higgs and *J. B. Statham did not bat.

Bowling: Smith 19—4—43—3; A. S. Brown 25—3—63—2; Windows 20—4—49—0; Mortimore 1—0—2—0.

Gloucestershire

R. B. Nicholls not out	5
C. A. Milton c Beddow b Higgs	1
S. E. Russell not out	1
1/6 (1 wkt.)	7

M. Bissex, D. Brown, *J. B. Mortimore, A. S. Brown, D. A. Allen, A. R. Windows, †B. J. Meyer and D. R. Smith did not bat.

Bowling: Statham 2.4—0—5—0; Higgs 2—0—2—1.

Umpires: J. F. Crapp and W. H. Copson.

LANCASHIRE v. NOTTINGHAMSHIRE

At Manchester, May 7, 9. *65 overs.* Lancashire won by six wickets. Splendid seam bowling by Statham, Higgs and Lever had Nottinghamshire in trouble on an easy-paced but green pitch, and with the elimination of the 75-yard-boundary ropes, batsmen had to run for the majority of their scoring strokes. Bolus showed sound defence for ninety-five minutes in compiling top score after Nottinghamshire had won the toss, but the innings ended within the over limit for a modest 113; Lancashire had reached 105 for 3 with Pullar unbeaten for a stylish 50 at close of play after 51 overs had been bowled. On the second day, Lancashire found it difficult to score freely after topping their opponent's score, but Pullar was unbeaten for 75 when the innings ended for a lead of 47. The accuracy of Statham and Higgs again proved too much for Nottinghamshire in their second innings although Moore batted with determination for 53 out of 125. Left to hit 79 for victory, Lancashire did so by claiming the extra half-hour on the second day with Pullar, again unbeaten, making the winning hit in the final over.

Nottinghamshire

*N. Hill c Green b Higgs	21	— run out	15
J. B. Bolus c Sullivan b Lloyd	23	— c Lloyd b Statham	20
†R. Swetman lbw b Higgs	6	— lbw b Statham	1
I. Moore lbw b Lever	5	— c Lloyd b Higgs	53
R. A. White lbw b Statham	16	— c and b Lever	1
M. J. Smedley c Entwistle b Higgs	14	— lbw b Lloyd	11
B. Whittingham c Entwistle b Statham	10	— not out	20
M. Taylor c Goodwin b Lever	1	— b Statham	1
C. Forbes not out	11	— b Statham	0
A. Johnson b Lever	0	— b Statham	0
I. Davison b Statham	2	— lbw b Higgs	0
L-b 2, n-b 2	4	L-b 2, w 1	3
1/29 2/49 3/56 4/65 5/78 6/94 7/95 8/103 9/109	113	1/25 2/32 3/41 4/46 5/65 6/117 7/124 8/124 9/124	125

Bowling: *First Innings*—Statham 16.3—5—28—3; Higgs 22—7—38—3; Lloyd 7—3—13—1; Lever 16—4—30—3. *Second Innings*—Statham 20—8—31—5; Higgs 20.1—9—33—2; Lever 8—5—12—1; Lloyd 16—9—23—1; Knox 7—2—23—0.

Lancashire

D. M. Green c Moore b Forbes	22	— b Davison	17
G. Pullar not out	75	— not out	23
H. Pilling c Swetman b Davison	10	— b Davison	0
J. Sullivan c Taylor b Davison	0	— c Swetman b Davison	0
R. Entwistle c Moore b Johnson	21	— b Forbes	9
G. K. Knox c Hill b Johnson	0	— not out	26
D. Lloyd not out	29		
L-b 3	3	L-b 5, w 1	6
1/31 2/44 3/48 4/107 5/107 (5 wkts., 65 overs)	160	1/20 2/21 3/29 4/41 (4 wkts.)	81

P. Lever, †K. Goodwin, K. Higgs and *J. B. Statham did not bat.

Bowling: *First Innings*—Davison 20—4—55—2; Forbes 17—3—48—1; Taylor 18—7—36—0; Johnson 10—2—18—2. *Second Innings*—Davison 11—3—22—3; Johnson 2—0—8—0; Taylor 15.2—7—32—0; Forbes 7—3—13—1.

Umpires: W. H. Copson and J. F. Crapp.

At Cambridge, May 11, 12, 13. LANCASHIRE beat CAMBRIDGE UNIVERSITY by an innings and 48 runs.

At Northampton, May 14, 16, 17. LANCASHIRE lost to NORTHAMPTONSHIRE by seven wickets.

At Manchester, May 18, 19, 20. LANCASHIRE drew with WEST INDIES. (See WEST INDIES section.)

At Lord's, May 21. LANCASHIRE beat MIDDLESEX by 63 runs. (See GILLETTE CUP.)

At Hove, May 25, 26, 27. LANCASHIRE drew with SUSSEX.

At Leeds, May 28, 30. LANCASHIRE lost to YORKSHIRE by ten wickets.

At The Oval, June 1, 2, 3. LANCASHIRE lost to SURREY by ten wickets.

At Manchester, June 2, 3, 4. WEST INDIES beat ENGLAND in the First Test Match by an innings and 40 runs. (See WEST INDIES section.)

At Leicester, June 4, 6, 7. LANCASHIRE lost to LEICESTERSHIRE by two wickets.

At Oxford, June 8, 9, 10. LANCASHIRE lost to OXFORD UNIVERSITY by 75 runs.

LANCASHIRE v. GLAMORGAN

At Liverpool, June 11, 13, 14. *65 overs.* Drawn. Seam bowlers dominated the game on a green and lively pitch with rain interrupting play for four hours and twenty minutes on the second day and preventing play on the third. Lancashire, who took two points for a first innings lead of 40, won the toss but apart from Green, and later Lloyd and Goodwin, none of their batsmen could master the pace bowling of Wheatley, I. J. Jones and Shepherd. A plucky innings by Lloyd, a nineteen-year-old left-hander, finally allowed Lancashire a degree of respectability. Glamorgan found just as much trouble and only Hedges and Cordle, producing his best innings to date, faced Statham, Higgs and Lever with any confidence. Lancashire were faring little better when rain interrupted their second innings shortly before tea on the second day.

Lancashire

D. M. Green c Lewis b Shepherd	29	— c A. Jones b Wheatley	4
G. Pullar c Evans b Wheatley	10	— lbw b I. J. Jones	16
G. K. Knox b I. J. Jones	0	— not out	8
D. R. Worsley c Evans b Wheatley	14	— b I. J. Jones	4
J. D. Bond b I. J. Jones	7	— not out	1
D. Lloyd not out	44		
P. Lever c Evans b Wheatley	1		
†K. Goodwin c and b Wheatley	21		
K. Higgs not out	8		
L-b 5	5	L-b 4	4
1/24 2/25 3/47 4/62 5/65 6/71 7/118 (7 wkts., 65 overs)	139	1/7 2/32 3/36 (3 wkts.)	37

K. Howard and *J. B. Statham did not bat.

Bowling: *First Innings*—I. J. Jones 16—3—31—2; Wheatley 18—3—36—4; Cordle 12—2—36—0; Shepherd 19—10—31—1. *Second Innings*—I. J. Jones 8.2—2—15—2; Wheatley 9—3—13—1; Shepherd 8—4—5—0.

Glamorgan

A. Jones b Statham	0	D. J. Shepherd b Statham	1
R. Davis lbw b Higgs	0	I. J. Jones b Statham	0
P. M. Walker lbw b Statham	8	*O. S. Wheatley not out	0
A. R. Lewis lbw b Statham	9		
B. Hedges c Goodwin b Lever	25	B 1, l-b 2, n-b 2	5
A. Rees c Goodwin b Higgs	10		
A. E. Cordle c Knox b Higgs	38	1/0 2/5 3/9 4/25 5/48	99
†D. L. Evans lbw b Statham	3	6/72 7/87 8/99 9/99	

Bowling—Statham 22.1—9—41—6; Higgs 22—10—26—3; Lever 9—0—27—1.

Umpires: W. H. Copson and W. F. Simpson.

LANCASHIRE v. WARWICKSHIRE

At Old Trafford, June 15, 16, 17. *65 overs.* Drawn. After allowing Warwickshire to reach a total of 151 before Statham bowled Brown in the final over, Lancashire lost Green and Pullar, their opening batsmen, with only six runs scored, rain having just previously held up play for ten minutes. Bond and Worsley then batted soundly and Lloyd found a useful partner in Goodwin but Lancashire seldom looked capable of passing the Warwickshire total in the limited number of overs. Statham bowled with sustained accuracy and hostility in the Warwickshire first innings and was again in good form when they batted a second time. The Lancashire captain claimed four of the five wickets to fall before the close of play on the second day but was prevented from continuing his good work when rain ruled out play on the final day, so Statham had to be satisfied with a match return of nine wickets for 99 runs.

Warwickshire

R. N. Abberley lbw b Statham	44	— b Statham	11
K. Ibadulla c Goodwin b Statham	51	— not out	10
D. L. Amiss c Howard b Lever	0	— c Howard b Lever	1
*M. J. K. Smith c Goodwin b Lever	9	— b Statham	5
J. A. Jameson c Goodwin b Lever	13	— lbw b Statham	8
T. W. Cartwright c Howard b Lever	3		
†A. C. Smith b Statham	11	— c Goodwin b Statham	23
R. B. Edmonds b Statham	0		
R. V. Webster c Worsley b Lever	0		
J. M. Allan not out	10	— not out	15
D. J. Brown b Statham	4		
L-b 3, n-b 3	6	L-b 2, n-b 1	3
1/95 2/98 3/98 4/111 5/121 6/134 7/136 8/136 9/136	151	1/2 2/9 3/22 4/27 5/56 (5 wkts.)	76

Bowling: *First Innings*—Statham 27.3—7—60—5; Lever 25—4—51—5; Green 7—1—18—0; Howard 5—1—16—0. *Second Innings*—Statham 18—4—39—4; Lever 19—7—27—1; Howard 7—6—1—0; Worsley 2—0—6—0.

Lancashire

D. M. Green c Allan b Brown	2
G. Pullar c A. C. Smith b Webster	0
G. K. Knox c M. J. K. Smith b Webster	15
J. D. Bond c M. J. K. Smith b Cartwright	37
D. R. Worsley c Brown b Cartwright	34
K. Snellgrove b Brown	0
D. Lloyd c Cartwright b Webster	15
P. Lever c A. C. Smith b Cartwright	2
†K. Goodwin not out	20
K. Howard not out	9
L-b 1, n-b 2	3
1/0 2/6 3/26 4/67 5/68 6/95 7/102 8/113 (8 wkts., 65 overs)	137

*J. B. Statham did not bat.

Bowling: Brown 18—3—41—2; Webster 19—5—39—3; Cartwright 26—11—50—3; Edmonds 2—1—4—0.

Umpires: W. H. Copson and W. F. Simpson.

LANCASHIRE v. WORCESTERSHIRE

At Old Trafford, June 18, 20, 21. Worcestershire won by six wickets. Consistent batting on an easy-paced pitch saw Lancashire reach 178 before Statham declared and succeeded in capturing the wicket of Kenyon by close of play on the first day. Flavell's seamers and Gifford's variations in flight and length coupled with a little spin had made runs hard to acquire. On the second day Worcestershire ran into Lever in top form and the Lancashire bowler achieved his best figures to date by capturing six wickets for 25 runs. Shuttleworth gave him splendid support in dismissing the opposition for 91. Although Lancashire found Flavell and Coldwell two accurate seam bowlers in their second innings, they left Worcestershire to make 203 for victory. It appeared an arduous task but a splendid innings by Horton, who had carried his bat through the first innings for 53 and now hit 61, and fifty from Ormrod saw the Champions home.

Lancashire

First innings		Second innings	
G. Pullar c Booth b Horton	45	— c Booth b Flavell	6
D. R. Worsley c Richardson b Flavell	5	— c Ormrod b Flavell	0
G. K. Knox c Booth b Flavell	17	— c Booth b Gifford	32
J. D. Bond c Booth b Gifford	26	— c Headley b Flavell	11
K. Snellgrove b Coldwell	16	— c Richardson b Coldwell	4
D. Lloyd c Ormrod b Gifford	16	— c Ormrod b Flavell	18
P. Lever c and b Flavell	22	— b Coldwell	27
K. Shuttleworth not out	20	— c Richardson b Gifford	4
†K. Goodwin b Gifford	5	— c Booth b Coldwell	0
K. Howard (did not bat)		— not out	4
*J. B. Statham (did not bat)		— c Slade b Horton	0
B 1, l-b 5	6	L-b 9	9
1/9 2/67 3/85 4/109 5/119 6/145 7/153 8/178 (8 wkts., dec.)	178	1/3 2/10 3/36 4/42 5/71 6/84 7/96 8/101 9/112	115

Bowling: *First Innings*—Flavell 23—4—50—3; Coldwell 21—4—39—1; Hemsley 5—0—12—0; Gifford 22.1—13—33—3; Horton 19—9—26—1; Slade 9—4—12—0. *Second Innings*—Flavell 18—5—35—4; Coldwell 22—5—42—3; Hemsley 3—0—12—0; Gifford 6—2—14—2; Horton 1.5—1—3—1.

Worcestershire

First innings		Second innings	
*D. Kenyon c Knox b Lever	1	— b Lever	2
M. J. Horton not out	53	— c Worsley b Statham	61
R. G. A. Headley b Lever	12	— b Lloyd	23
J. A. Ormrod b Shuttleworth	16	— not out	59
D. W. Richardson c Worsley b Lever	0	— c Goodwin b Shuttleworth	23
E. J. O. Hemsley c Goodwin b Shuttleworth	0	— not out	24
D. N. F. Slade b Shuttleworth	0		
†R. Booth c Goodwin b Lever	0		
N. Gifford c Lloyd b Lever	2		
L. J. Coldwell c Bond b Lever	0		
J. A. Flavell b Statham	0		
B 3, l-b 4	7	B 7, l-b 3, n-b 1	11
1/1 2/26 3/66 4/67 5/70 6/70 7/73 8/88 9/90	91	1/11 2/77 3/100 4/152 (4 wkts.)	203

Bowling: *First Innings*—Statham 12.3—0—32—1; Lever 19—7—25—6; Shuttleworth 21—8—27—3. *Second Innings*—Statham 16—3—28—1; Lever 22—3—63—1; Shuttleworth 9.3—3—21—1; Howard 26—10—40—0; Lloyd 13—3—40—1.

Umpires: F. Jakeman and A. E. Rhodes.

At Taunton, June 22. LANCASHIRE lost to SOMERSET by four wickets. (See GILLETTE CUP.)

LANCASHIRE v. SUSSEX

At Old Trafford, June 25, 27, 28. Lancashire won by seven wickets. Rain limited play to less than two and a half hours on the first day when Sussex, always struggling against some accurate bowling, scored only 69 for one wicket with

Lenham plodding to a sedate 28 in that time and Pataudi doing little better. A blank second day because of rain was followed by three declarations and an exciting finish. After Parks and Graves had hit well to take Sussex to 140 for four in their second innings Lancashire were left to make 147 in even time. They had lost Green and Knox for 44 and were falling behind the clock when Bond and Pullar joined forces to add 101 for the third wicket before Bond was stumped in the final over of the match after batting splendidly for 59. Lever came in to hit the fourth delivery for four and snatch victory for Lancashire, Pullar having contributed a watchful 35.

Sussex

K. G. Suttle c Goodwin b Lever	19	— c Beddow b Statham	1
L. J. Lenham not out	28	— c Knox b Statham	4
*Nawab of Pataudi not out	21	— lbw b Greenhough	9
†J. M. Parks (did not bat)		— not out	72
M. G. Griffith (did not bat)		— run out	3
P. J. Graves (did not bat)		— not out	43
N-b 1	1	L-b 7, n-b 1	8
1/32 (1 wkt., dec.)	69	1/4 2/9 3/38 4/49 (4 wkts., dec.)	140

D. J. Foreman, A. S. M. Oakman, P. R. V. Ledden, A. Buss and J. A. Snow did not bat.

Bowling: *First Innings*—Statham 13—4—24—0; Higgs 11—4—17—0; Lever 10—4—12—1; Greenhough 9—4—15—0. *Second Innings*—Statham 6—1—18—2; Higgs 8.2—1—24—0; Lever 7—3—11—0; Greenhough 12—2—52—1; Lloyd 2—0—27—0.

Lancashire

D. M. Green b Snow	6	— c Pataudi b Snow	25
G. K. Knox c Foreman b Buss	4	— lbw b Snow	16
J. D. Bond not out	24	— st Parks b Suttle	59
G. Pullar b Oakman	26	— not out	35
A. M. Beddow not out	2		
P. Lever (did not bat)		— not out	4
B 1	1	B 1, l-b 9	10
1/10 2/10 3/47 (3 wkts., dec.)	63	1/39 2/44 3/145 (3 wkts.)	149

D. Lloyd, †K. Goodwin, K. Higgs, T. Greenhough and *J. B. Statham did not bat.

Bowling: *First Innings*—Snow 6—1—14—1; Buss 4—1—16—1; Oakman 7—2—21—1; Suttle 6—3—11—0. *Second Innings*—Snow 14—1—32—2; Buss 14—1—63—0; Suttle 5.4—0—25—1; Ledden 5—1—19—0.

Umpires: R. Aspinall and G. H. Pope.

At Lydney, June 29, 30, July 1. LANCASHIRE beat GLOUCESTERSHIRE by 60 runs.

LANCASHIRE v. DERBYSHIRE

At Old Trafford, July 2, 4, 5. *65 overs.* Derbyshire won by 30 runs. On a pitch that had little to offer either pace or spin Derbyshire, winning the toss, batted solidly with Hill making a patient 60 in a total of 189 before their 65 over allocation was up. With Knox and Sullivan batting splendidly Lancashire passed that figure with only two wickets down and went on to gain a lead of 38. Then Hill again batted well and Morgan compiled an attractive 45 not out so that Derbyshire left Lancashire what appeared to be a comfortable task—120 for victory. The off-spin of Smith, however, proved a vital factor on the last day when several Lancashire batsmen hitting out wildly, Derbyshire ran through the opposition for 89. Smith finished with six wickets for 21 runs.

Derbyshire

Batsman	First Innings		Second Innings	
I. W. Hall	b Lever	0	c Goodwin b Statham	0
J. F. Harvey	b Statham	13	b Lever	10
M. H. Page	lbw b Greenhough	34	c Green b Statham	0
H. L. Johnson	b Statham	0	lbw b Shuttleworth	33
M. Hill	c Lloyd b Greenhough	60	b Greenhough	46
I. R. Buxton	not out	34	lbw b Greenhough	9
*D. C. Morgan	not out	31	not out	45
†R. W. Taylor	(did not bat)		b Lever	5
E. Smith	(did not bat)		c Goodwin b Lever	4
H. J. Rhodes	(did not bat)		b Statham	0
A. B. Jackson	(did not bat)		c Goodwin b Lever	0
	L-b 6, n-b 11	17	L-b 4, n-b 1	5
	(5 wkts., 65 overs)	189		157

1/7 2/17 3/17 4/94 5/124 — 1/0 2/0 3/20 4/79 5/90 6/113 7/137 8/143 9/154

Bowling: *First Innings*—Statham 16—2—40—2; Lever 17—3—48—1; Shuttleworth 11—2—33—0; Beddow 8—1—25—0; Greenhough 13—6—26—2. *Second Innings*—Statham 16—1—43—3; Lever 15—1—45—4; Shuttleworth 9—2—29—1; Greenhough 13—5—25—2; Lloyd 3—0—10—0.

Lancashire

Batsman	First Innings		Second Innings	
D. M. Green	c and b Morgan	39	c and b Rhodes	17
G. K. Knox	c Hill b Rhodes	100	c Hill b Smith	21
J. Sullivan	c Harvey b Rhodes	56	run out	4
D. Lloyd,	not out	22	c Jackson b Smith	1
A. M. Beddow	run out	2	c Morgan b Smith	0
H. Pilling	not out	0	c Hall b Morgan	4
P. Lever	(did not bat)		c Page b Smith	15
K. Shuttleworth	(did not bat)		c Morgan b Smith	13
†K. Goodwin	(did not bat)		c Taylor b Morgan	3
T. Greenhough	(did not bat)		c Johnson b Smith	9
*J. B. Statham	(did not bat)		not out	1
	L-b 5, n-b 3	8	N-b 1	1
	(4 wkts., 65 overs)	227		89

1/116 2/119 3/212 4/220 — 1/19 2/24 3/28 4/30 5/41 6/63 7/63 8/78, 9/84

Bowling: *First Innings*—Rhodes 23—1—89—2; Jackson 15—2—30—0; Morgan 13—2—41—1; Smith 14—0—59—0. *Second Innings*—Jackson 3—0—14—0; Rhodes 10—0—29—1; Smith 19.1—12—21—6; Morgan 12—3—24—2.

Umpires: J. Arnold and H. Yarnold.

At Newark, July 6, 7, 8. LANCASHIRE drew with NOTTINGHAMSHIRE.

LANCASHIRE v. HAMPSHIRE

At Old Trafford, July 9, 11, 12. *65 overs.* Lancashire won by three wickets. The seam bowling of Shackleton and Statham dominated the match which Lancashire won after being set to hit 181 for victory on a wearing pitch. Worsley led the way with a patient and chanceless 62. The stubborn batting of Reed was the main feature of the Hampshire first innings and Shackleton's immaculate control of length and direction proved far too much for Lancashire when they replied. Bowling 23 overs for 25 runs and six wickets, Shackleton seldom bowled a loose ball, nor did Statham when Hampshire batted again. The Lancashire captain gained the excellent figures of seven for 24 and transformed the game. For once, he failed to hit the stumps, but he was given splendid support in the field and only Horton, Gray and Sainsbury stayed any length of time in an innings all over in less than two and a half hours.

Hampshire

*R. E. Marshall c Worsley b Statham	24	— c Goodwin b Higgs	9
B. L. Reed c Knox b Lever	66	— lbw b Statham	0
H. Horton c Lloyd b Greenhough	7	— c Knox b Statham	29
J. R. Gray lbw b Statham	18	— c Higgs b Statham	0
H. M. Barnard not out	32	— b Lever	14
P. J. Sainsbury lbw b Greenhough	9	— c Worsley b Higgs	16
D. W. White b Lever	0	— c Higgs b Statham	0
†B. S. V. Timms not out	20	— lbw b Statham	0
K. J. Wheatley (did not bat)		— lbw b Statham	0
D. Shackleton (did not bat)		— c Worsley b Statham	6
R. M. Cottam (did not bat)		— not out	2
B 4, l-b 10, n-b 4	18	B 4, l-b 2, n-b 1	7
1/32 2/61 3/108 4/132 (6 wkts., 65 overs) 5/157 6/160	194	1/9 2/11 3/11 4/40 5/71 6/71 7/71 8/79 9/79	83

Bowling: *First Innings*—Statham 13—2—36—2; Higgs 11—2—36—0; Lever 18—0—48—2; Greenhough 21—5—51—2; Lloyd 2—0—5—0. *Second Innings*—Statham 14—5—24—7; Higgs 20—5—29—2; Lever 2—0—9—1; Greenhough 4—0—14—0.

Lancashire

D. M. Green lbw b Shackleton	13	— b Shackleton	0
G. K. Knox c Timms b Shackleton	13	— c Barnard b White	39
J. D. Bond c Gray b Shackleton	21	— c Barnard b White	24
D. R. Worsley b Shackleton	0	— not out	62
J. Sullivan b Shackleton	4	— lbw b Cottam	21
D. Lloyd c Wheatley b White	2	— c Sainsbury b Cottam	3
P. Lever b White	9	— b Cottam	0
K. Higgs c Gray b Shackleton	5	— st Timms b Wheatley	22
†K. Goodwin c Sainsbury b White	1	— not out	2
T. Greenhough not out	22		
*J. B. Statham b White	4		
N-b 3	3	B 2, l-b 5, n-b 1	8
1/15 2/36 3/36 4/46 5/51 6/62 7/65 8/70 9/70	97	1/0 2/65 3/72 (7 wkts.) 4/104 5/108 6/117 7/174	181

Bowling: *First Innings*—Shackleton 23—13—25—6; White 19.2—8—49—4; Cottam 9—2—20—0. *Second Innings*—Shackleton 45—26—32—1; White 21—5—49—2; Cottam 33.3—15—44—3; Wheatley 28—13—32—1; Sainsbury 8—5—16—0.

Umpires: L. H. Gray and W. F. Simpson.

At Birmingham, July 13, 14, 15. LANCASHIRE drew with WARWICKSHIRE.

At Ebbw Vale, July 16, 18, 19. LANCASHIRE lost to GLAMORGAN by 95 runs.

LANCASHIRE v. SOMERSET

At Southport, July 20, 21, 22. Somerset won by an innings and 15 runs. A remarkable all-round performance by Palmer who captured seven wickets for 56 runs and then hit up 118 paved the way for an easy Somerset victory before lunch on the third day. Winning the toss and taking first use of an easy-paced pitch, Lancashire were in trouble from the start against the lively seam bowling of Rumsey, Palmer and Alley. Pullar alone played with any assurance and

Lancashire were dismissed for 97. Statham and Higgs then proceeded to capture the first five Somerset wickets for 29 before Burgess, playing in his first Championship match, and Palmer came together. They added 145 for the sixth wicket and enabled their side to gain a lead of 226. Lancashire batted much better in their second innings with Bond and Worsley each reaching fifty. Clayton, the former Lancashire wicket-keeper, enjoyed a good match against his old colleagues, taking five catches in the first innings and another, as well as a stumping, in the second.

Lancashire

D. M. Green c Virgin b Palmer	7	— b Rumsey	0
G. K. Knox c Clayton b Palmer	4	— st Clayton b Langford	22
J. D. Bond c Clayton b Rumsey	1	— c Virgin b Langford	52
G. Pullar b Palmer	37	— c and b Langford	23
D. R. Worsley c Clayton b Palmer	8	— c Clayton b Langford	55
J. Sullivan c Clayton b Palmer	10	— c Virgin b Langford	30
P. Lever lbw b Alley	0	— c Virgin b Langford	0
K. Higgs c Virgin b Langford	10	— b Rumsey	18
†K. Goodwin not out	4	— c and b Langford	0
T. Greenhough c Robinson b Palmer	0	— b Rumsey	4
*J. B. Statham c Clayton b Palmer	9	— not out	1
B 1, l-b 5, n-b 1	7	B 1, l-b 4, n-b 1	6
1/9 2/10 3/14 4/34 5/52 6/53 7/76 8/83 9/83	97	1/0 2/59 3/100 4/102 5/152 6/152 7/205 8/205 9/210	211

Bowling: *First Innings*—Rumsey 12—3—18—1; Palmer 17.1—1—56—7; Alley 12—4—15—1; Langford 3—2—1—1. *Second Innings*—Rumsey 8.1—1—25—3; Alley 5—1—4—0; Palmer 7—2—11—0; Langford 40—18—99—7; Robinson 29—11—65—0; Virgin 1—1—0—0; C. R. M. Atkinson 1—0—1—0.

Somerset

G. Atkinson c Knox b Statham	0
R. Virgin run out	20
M. Kitchen c Goodwin b Statham	1
W. E. Alley c Goodwin b Higgs	2
*C. R. M. Atkinson b Statham	2
G. Burgess b Statham	66
K. E. Palmer c Pullar b Worsley	118
†G. Clayton c and b Greenhough	10
P. J. Robinson c Bond b Greenhough	66
B. A. Langford not out	3
F. E. Rumsey c Goodwin b Worsley	0
B 8, l-b 15, n-b 12	35
1/0 2/2 3/7 4/12 5/29 6/174 7/200 8/318 9/323	323

Bowling: Statham 27—6—58—4; Higgs 24—4—40—1; Greenhough 29—7—73—2; Lever 31—6—79—0; Worsley 17.3—6—38—2.

Umpires: C. G. Pepper and T. W. Spencer.

At Colchester, July 23, 25, 26. LANCASHIRE drew with ESSEX.

At Chesterfield, July 27, 28, 29. LANCASHIRE beat DERBYSHIRE by seven wickets.

LANCASHIRE v. YORKSHIRE

At Old Trafford, July 30, August 1, 2. Yorkshire won by 12 runs. Cricket history was made in this match when, after play had been limited to ninety-five minutes on the first day and washed out completely on the second, Yorkshire became the first side to forfeit an innings. They did so after declaring at lunch time on the third day and in answer to a Lancashire declaration immediately afterwards. To make the match even more memorable Yorkshire gained victory with the last ball of the match when Greenhough was lbw to Illingworth with

Lancashire 13 runs short of victory. A fine 54 from Close led up to the Yorkshire declaration and after Goodwin had taken a single from the second delivery bowled by Trueman the battle was joined with Yorkshire fighting for twelve points and Lancashire chasing ten. Nicholson at once dismissed Knox and Bond and later came Illingworth with his off-spinners to capture five for 33 and earn Yorkshire a thrilling victory. Close's captaincy and aggressive field placings also played an important part.

Yorkshire

G. Boycott c Worsley b Lever	0	D. Wilson c Shuttleworth b Lloyd	6
K. Taylor b Shuttleworth	30	P. J. Sharpe c Goodwin b Lloyd	2
D. E. V. Padgett c Lloyd b Shuttleworth	5	R. Illingworth not out	9
J. H. Hampshire c Worsley b Lloyd	38	L-b 1, n-b 1	2
*D. B. Close not out	54		
F. S. Trueman c Shuttleworth b Lloyd	0	1/0 2/15 3/50 4/95 5/101 6/118 7/121 (7 wkts., dec.)	146

†J. G. Binks and A. G. Nicholson did not bat. Yorkshire forfeited their second innings.

Bowling: Lever 14—3—34—1; Shuttleworth 13—3—33—2; Green 2—0—3—0; Worsley 11—1—35—0; Lloyd 11—1—39—4.

Lancashire

†K. Goodwin not out	1	— not out	4
T. Greenhough not out	0	— lbw b Illingworth	14
*D. M. Green (did not bat)		— c Close b Wilson	21
G. K. Knox (did not bat)		— c Hampshire b Nicholson	0
J. D. Bond (did not bat)		— c Binks b Nicholson	4
G. Pullar (did not bat)		— c Trueman b Illingworth	18
D. R. Worsley (did not bat)		— c Close b Illingworth	19
B. Wood (did not bat)		— b Illingworth	10
D. Lloyd (did not bat)		— b Close	26
K. Shuttleworth (did not bat)		— run out	2
P. Lever (did not bat)		— b Illingworth	1
		B 8, l-b 1, w 4, n-b 1	14
(no wkt.)	1	1/12 2/22 3/44 4/56 5/80 6/83 7/90 8/102 9/110	133

Bowling: *First Innings*—Trueman 1—0—1—0. *Second Innings*—Trueman 3—0—4—0; Nicholson 6—2—13—2; Illingworth 27—14—33—5; Wilson 23—5—62—1; Close 7—4—7—1.

Umpires: J. S. Buller and T. W. Spencer.

LANCASHIRE v. MIDDLESEX

At Old Trafford, August 3, 4, 5. *65 overs*. Drawn. Rain prevented play on the first two days and on the third Middlesex batted soundly to reach 187 for the loss of only two wickets before declaring. Parfitt and Clark put on 151 for an unfinished third-wicket partnership, Middlesex batting 45.4 overs and challenging Lancashire to hit 188. After losing Green with only three runs scored and Bond and Pullar by the time they had reached 40, Lancashire's chance had gone. Knox batted soundly for 27, but Worsley produced the best and was unbeaten for 49 when the match was left drawn without reward for either side. Lancashire undoubtedly missed Higgs who was on Test duty at Leeds, but the weather was the overruling factor.

Middlesex

W. E. Russell b Statham	13
M. J. Smith b Green	18
P. H. Parfitt not out	87
E. A. Clark not out	62
B 4, l-b 3	7
1/28 2/36 (2 wkts., dec.)	187

*†J. T. Murray, C. T. Radley, R. W. Hooker, M. Manasseh, D. A. Bick, J. S. E. Price and R. W. Stewart did not bat.

Bowling: Statham 12—2—23—1; Lever 7.4—2—19—0; Green 9—0—40—1; Worsley 5—1—18—0; Lloyd 6—0—44—0; Wood 6—0—36—0.

Lancashire

D. M. Green b Stewart	2
G. K. Knox lbw b Bick	27
J. D. Bond b Price	14
G. Pullar run out	6
D. R. Worsley not out	49
H. Pilling c Manasseh b Hooker	16
P. Lever b Parfitt	7
B. Wood b Price	3
D. Lloyd not out	1
B 2, l-b 3	5
1/3 2/34 3/40 4/51 5/85 6/95 7/112 (7 wkts.)	130

†K. Goodwin and *J. B. Statham did not bat.

Bowling: Price 9—1—34—2; Stewart 7—2—19—1; Bick 20—9—36—1; Manasseh 4—2—7—0; Hooker 8—2—10—1; Parfitt 9—3—19—1.

Umpires: R. Aspinall and A. Jepson.

At Portsmouth, August 6, 8, 9. LANCASHIRE drew with HAMPSHIRE.

At Lord's, August 13, 15, 16. LANCASHIRE drew with MIDDLESEX.

LANCASHIRE v. KENT

At Blackpool, August 17, 18, 19. *65 overs.* Kent won by an innings and 30 runs. Winning the toss presented problems for Green, the acting Lancashire captain, for the pitch was of doubtful lasting qualities, though its state alone could not excuse two feeble batting displays. The left-arm spin of Underwood completely undermined Lancashire in the first innings but when the early moisture disappeared the pitch played easily. Capturing six wickets for only nine runs, Underwood was the entire master yet Kent scored 251 for eight before their 65 overs were completed. The first five batsmen all showed good form with Cowdrey leading the way. Lancashire fought back admirably in their second innings with Worsley hitting splendidly for 76 without being able to save the game for his side or extend it into the third day. Again Underwood was Kent's most successful bowler and his full haul of ten wickets for 68 runs was a masterly piece of bowling.

Lancashire

H. Pilling c Knott b Underwood	13	— c Cowdrey b Graham	0
*D. M. Green c Denness b Sayer	0	— c Wilson b Sayer	2
J. D. Bond c Knott b Sayer	1	— c Luckhurst b Underwood	17
D. R. Worsley c Luckhurst b Underwood	14	— run out	76
B. Wood c Leary b Underwood	1	— c Knott b Graham	31
J. Sullivan c Underwood b Dixon	2	— b Underwood	15
P. Lever c Dixon b Underwood	0	— c Luckhurst b Underwood	0
D. Lloyd c Ealham b Underwood	6	— c Wilson b Dixon	0
K. Shuttleworth c and b Underwood	11	— b Dixon	6
†K. Goodwin b Sayer	13	— c Cowdrey b Underwood	4
J. Cumbes not out	0	— not out	0
L-b 1	1	B 2, l-b 4, w 1, n-b 1	8
1/4 2/6 3/21 4/29 5/30 6/32 7/35 8/38 9/62	62	1/3 2/3 3/48 4/112 5/136 6/137 7/137 8/148 9/155	159

Bowling: *First Innings*—Sayer 12—6—13—3; Graham 11—6—17—0; Underwood 10.1—7—9—6; Dixon 7—2—22—1. *Second Innings*—Sayer 5—1—17—1; Graham 6—2—15—2; Underwood 33—15—59—4; Dixon 36.4—17—56—2; Luckhurst 3—2—4—0.

Kent

B. W. Luckhurst b Cumbes...... 40
M. H. Denness c Worsley b Cumbes 45
R. C. Wilson c Worsley b Green... 47
*M. C. Cowdrey c Goodwin b Green 56
S. E. Leary lbw b Lever.......... 22
A. Ealham c Shuttleworth b Cumbes 21
†A. Knott c Goodwin b Cumbes.. 1
A. L. Dixon c Goodwin b Lever.. 3
D. L. Underwood not out........ 7
D. M. Sayer not out............ 1
L-b 5, n-b 3 8

1/84 2/87 3/175 (8 wkts., 65 overs) 251
4/212 5/239 6/239 7/242 8/244

J. N. Graham did not bat.

Bowling: Lever 15—1—61—2; Shuttleworth 11—1—40—0; Worsley 12—1—42—0; Cumbes 17—4—42—4; Lloyd 5—0—26—0; Green 5—0—32—2.

Umpires: R. Aspinall and T. W. Spencer.

At Dover, August 24, 25. LANCASHIRE beat KENT by four wickets.

LANCASHIRE v. LEICESTERSHIRE

At Old Trafford, August 27, 28, 29. Leicestershire won by eight wickets. Lancashire's first experiment with Sunday cricket proved highly encouraging, with receipts of £251 against £40 on the Saturday, but from the playing point of view the home county were well mastered by an aggressive side splendidly captained by Lock. The bowling of Marner, who took five wickets for 68 runs in the first innings confined Lancashire to a modest total on an easy-paced pitch and Leicestershire, thanks to an attractive century by Inman and an aggressive 64 from Marner, built up a lead of 132. They went on to dismiss Lancashire for 165 in their second innings, despite a fine innings of 73 from Worsley, who was awarded his county cap after consistent batting in the closing matches of the season. Set to hit 34 for victory, Leicestershire had to battle against an advancing storm.

Lancashire

First innings		Second innings	
*D. M. Green c Lock b Cotton	5	b Cotton	7
H. Pilling lbw b Spencer	24	b Cotton	12
G. K. Knox c Cotton b Spencer	3	lbw b Spencer	1
D. R. Worsley c Tolchard b Marner	8	c Spencer b Birkenshaw	73
J. D. Bond c Tolchard b Marner	21	c Hallam b Lock	20
J. Sullivan b Marner	27	c Inman b Lock	0
B. Wood c Birkenshaw b Marner	28	lbw b Lock	24
D. Lloyd c Tolchard b Lock	27	b Birkenshaw	21
P. Lever b Cotton	2	b Lock	0
K. Shuttleworth c Tolchard b Marner	26	b Lock	3
†K. Goodwin not out	0	not out	0
B 4, l-b 1, w 1	6	L-b 4	4
1/5 2/12 3/29 4/45 5/71 6/111 7/117 8/128 9/173	177	1/9 2/12 3/30 4/100 5/132 6/132 7/155 8/155 9/163	165

Bowling: *First Innings*—Spencer 14—2—50—2; Cotton 12—1—48—2; Marner 23.4—5—68—5; Lock 9—7—5—1. *Second Innings*—Spencer 13—3—43—1; Cotton 17—5—22—2; Marner 5—0—14—0; Lock 25.4—8—40—5; Savage 15—5—41—0; Birkenshaw 6—5—1—2.

Leicestershire

M. R. Hallam c Goodwin b Lloyd	43	— c and b Lloyd	8
M. E. Norman b Lever	3	— not out	21
B. J. Booth b Lloyd	31	— lbw b Lloyd	2
C. C. Inman b Worsley	110		
P. Marner lbw b Lever	64		
J. Birkenshaw c Sullivan b Lloyd	21	— not out	2
†R. W. Tolchard lbw b Worsley	0		
*G. A. R. Lock lbw b Lever	5		
J. S. Savage c Worsley b Lever	0		
J. Cotton not out	10		
C. T. Spencer c Goodwin b Worsley	11		
B 1, l-b 9, n-b 1	11	L-b 1	1
1/17 2/77 3/94 4/155 5/261 6/261 7/285 8/285 9/288	309	1/24 2/30 (2 wkts.)	34

Bowling: *First Innings*—Lever 26—5—71—4; Shuttleworth 13—2—49—0; Green 22—5—44—0; Lloyd 21—3—77—3; Worsley 19.3—2—57—3. *Second Innings*—Lever 3—0—6—0; Green 2—0—10—0; Lloyd 4.2—1—5—2; Worsley 5—1—12—0.

Umpires: J. F. Crapp and P. A. Gibb.

LANCASHIRE v. SURREY

At Old Trafford, August 31, September 2, 3. Drawn. No decision. An admirable chanceless century from Barrington who was unbeaten for 117 in five and three-quarter hours after his side had lost their first four wickets for 20 runs enabled Surrey, who won the toss, to declare, despite Statham, four for 47, completing his 100 wickets of the season for the thirteenth time in a career that began in 1950. During the Surrey innings Storey became the only cricketer of the season to record the double of 100 wickets and 1,000 runs. Although Bennett failed, Lancashire reached 100 for the loss of three wickets, but three more falling at 104 they struggled desperately in face of aggressive bowling and fielding. Rain ended play for the day at tea time on the second day and with no improvement in the weather the match was abandoned at lunch time on the third day.

Surrey

M. J. Edwards b Statham	4
W. A. Smith b Statham	4
*M. J. Stewart c Pilling b Higgs	0
K. F. Barrington not out	117
M. D. Willett b Higgs	5
S. J. Storey b Statham	37
R. D. Jackman b Lever	5
†A. Long b Lever	1
P. I. Pocock b Worsley	17
G. Arnold b Statham	30
R. Harman not out	3
L-b 3, n-b 8	11
1/7 2/8 3/8 4/20 5/83 6/112 7/125 8/165 9/215 (9 wkts., dec.)	234

Bowling: Statham 23—4—47—4; Higgs 32—7—87—2; Lever 24—8—48—2; Worsley 10—5—13—1; Lloyd 10—1—28—0.

Lancashire

R. Bennett c Edwards b Arnold	11
H. Pilling c Arnold b Harman	32
B. Wood b Storey	39
D. R. Worsley c Storey b Jackman	11
J. D. Bond c Long b Storey	3
J. Sullivan c Long b Jackman	0
D. Lloyd not out	1
P. Lever not out	6
B 4, l-b 1, n-b 4	9
1/24 2/68 3/96 4/104 5/104 6/104 (6 wkts.)	112

K. Higgs, †K. Goodwin and *J. B. Statham did not bat.

Bowling: Arnold 15—2—39—1; Jackman 19.1—7—28—2; Storey 19—10—20—2; Harman 6—2—16—1; Pocock 1—1—0—0.

Umpires: P. A. Gibb and T. W. Spencer.

LEICESTERSHIRE

President—WILLIAM BENTLEY

Secretary—MICHAEL TURNER, Spencer Chambers, 4 Market Place, Leicester

Captain—G. A. R. LOCK

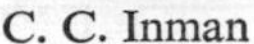

C. C. Inman

County Badge

P. Marner

Leicestershire, in 1966, lifted themselves six places to a final position of eighth in the County Championship. In so doing, they fulfilled the confident hopes of several people, among them the new captain, Tony Lock. His own contribution to the much improved performance was made with all-round excellence—he took more than one hundred wickets, scored over 600 runs and held thirty-odd catches, but equally important was his highly stimulating lead. The former Surrey and England player was clearly resolved to make a success of his captaincy, and infected his team with his own exuberance which was an important factor in recording eight wins, the most since 1961. That year was the last in which Leicestershire had topped one hundred points, and in 1966 they reached a total of 108, compared with 58 in 1965.

Lock's urgent approach to his duties delighted supporters and brought a lively response from the players, evidence of which was often to be seen in the field. Indeed, Leicestershire were rated among the best fielding sides in the country. In two respects the county made striking progress: their middle and late batting frequently came to the rescue, and their wicket-taking ability much increased compared with the previous season. Especially pleasing was the return of Spencer as the spearhead, while Marner produced match-winning spells with his accuracy at just above medium pace. Lock could always come along with a destructive burst of highly skilled spin bowling, which sometimes encouraged the belief that he should be recalled to Test cricket.

Young contenders made their mark, among them the former

Devon wicket-keeper, Tolchard, who supplemented his impressive work behind the stumps with some valuable batting in critical situations. The one-time Kent left-hander, Constant, was given more scope than previously and seized his chance avidly. Birkenshaw displayed a flair for arresting a slump with his dogged batting, and could still snatch important wickets when most needed.

The season should prove to have been most useful in rebuilding Leicestershire's morale and the effects of this ought soon to be seen in 1967.

Lock returned to the Antipodes for the Australian summer where he again captained Western Australia. Bowling as well as ever he established a Sheffield Shield record by surpassing the 47 wickets by G. S. Sobers for South Australia in 1963–64.

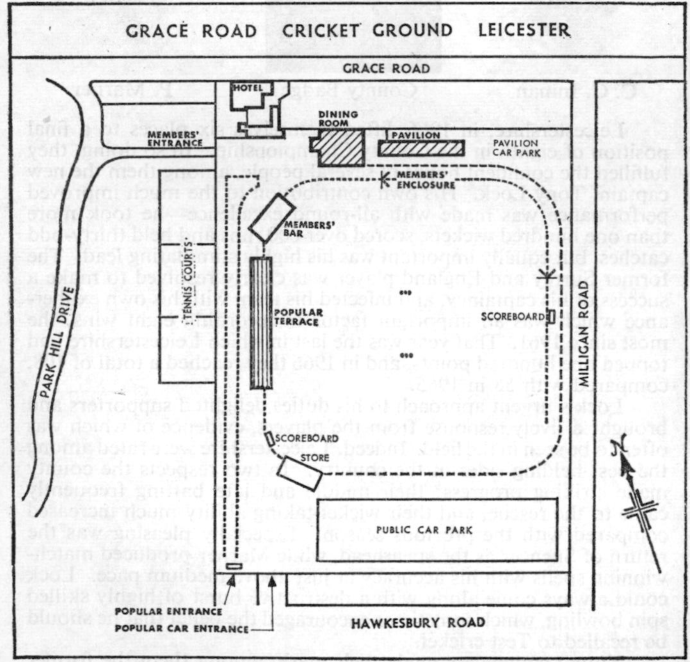

LEICESTERSHIRE RESULTS

All First Class Matches—Played 30, *Won* 9, *Lost* 8, *Drawn* 13
County Championship Matches—Played 28, *Won* 8, *Lost* 7, *Drawn* 12, *No Decision* 1

COUNTY CHAMPIONSHIP AVERAGES

BATTING

	Birthplace	Mtchs.	Inns.	Not Outs	Runs	100's	Highest Inns.	Aver.
M. R. Hallam..	*Leicester*	27	49	3	1453	1	135	31.58
M. E. Norman.	*Northampton*	27	47	5	1233	2	132*	29.35
C. C. Inman....	*Colombo, Ceylon*	28	46	3	1260	3	113*	29.30
B. J. Booth.....	*Blackburn*	24	41	4	1078	2	102*	29.13
P. Marner.....	*Oldham*	28	46	3	1063	1	104	24.72
G. Cross.......	*Leicester*	9	15	4	257	0	45*	23.36
D. Constant....	*Bradford-on-Avon*	23	36	5	621	0	80	20.03
G. A. R. Lock..	*Limpsfield*	27	40	6	627	0	56	18.44
J. Birkenshaw..	*Rothwell*	17	24	4	336	0	58	16.80
R. W. Tolchard	*Torquay*	28	39	11	426	0	44*	15.21
S. Greensword.	*Philadelphia, Co. Durham*	3	5	0	39	0	18	7.80
J. S. Savage....	*Ramsbottom*	25	29	13	122	0	16	7.62
J. Cotton......	*Newstead*	18	19	11	117	0	23*	6.50
C. T. Spencer..	*Leicester*	24	31	5	167	0	22	6.42

* *Signifies not out.*

BOWLING

	Overs	Maidens	Runs	Wickets	Average
G. A. R. Lock..........	875	300	1941	97	20.01
C. T. Spencer..........	604	133	1603	71	22.57
J. Cotton..............	432.2	96	1134	45	25.20
P. Marner..............	660.4	126	1905	74	25.74
J. S. Savage...........	607.2	195	1358	48	28.29
J. Birkenshaw..........	147.5	34	425	15	28.33
S. Greensword..........	17	3	33	1	33.00
G. Cross...............	92	17	305	6	50.83

LEICESTERSHIRE v. ESSEX

At Leicester, May 4, 5, 6. *65 overs*. Drawn. Rain prevented play on the first and second days, and enforced two brief stoppages on the third day. Knight, with seven 4's in his not-out 61, came in with the Essex score at 68 for three, and lost his captain, Bailey, who retired with a leg muscle strain when the fifth-wicket partnership was going smoothly. A declaration left Leicestershire one hour and fifty minutes to score 173, which never appeared likely, especially after Hallam had been caught off Knight at 67.

Essex

G. E. Barker b Marner	33	*T. E. Bailey retired hurt	14
M. J. Bear c Spencer b Cotton	0	G. R. Cass not out	24
†B. Taylor b Cotton	6		
K. W. R. Fletcher c Norman b Marner	32	L-b 2	2
B. R. Knight not out	61	1/3 2/13 3/68 4/73 (4 wkts., dec.)	172

G. J. Saville, B. Edmeades, R. N. S. Hobbs and A. M. Jorden did not bat.

Bowling: Cotton 15—2—65—2; Spencer 14—0—34—0; Marner 19—3—71—2.

Leicestershire

M. R Hallam c Barker b Knight	44
B. J. Booth not out	32
P. Marner not out	4
L-b 1, n-b 4	5
1/67 (1 wkt.)	85

M. E. Norman, C. C. Inman, J. Birkenshaw, D. Constant, †R. W. Tolchard, *G. A. R. Lock, C. T. Spencer and J. Cotton did not bat.

Bowling: Knight 6—0—22—1; Edmeades 7—0—31—0; Jorden 8—0—26—0; Hobbs 1—0—1—0.

Umpires: R. S. Lay and A. E. Alderman.

At Nuneaton, May 7, 9, 10. LEICESTERSHIRE lost to WARWICKSHIRE by 39 runs.

LEICESTERSHIRE v. DERBYSHIRE

At Leicester, May 11, 12, 13. *65 overs.* Drawn. For the second successive match at Grace Road, rain was the spoiler, there being no cricket on the first day. A turning, lifting wicket was welcomed by Lock, the Leicestershire captain, when Derbyshire took first innings. The former Surrey and England spin bowler's seven wickets for 31 runs was his best to date for his adopted county, Eyre and Hill being despatched by successive balls, and a leg-side catch from Smith was typical Lock. Taylor offered stubborn late resistance after preventing a hat trick. Rhodes bowled Hallam when Leicestershire had made 12 and again hit the stumps to dismiss Marner, Leicestershire being hard put to secure the lead, which came from a straight 4 by Lock off his rival captain, Morgan. Lock made this his match with a vengeance when he took five more wickets for a full analysis of twelve for 71, but his feat was in vain. Derbyshire batted on well into the last afternoon, and the Leicestershire openers, Hallam and Booth, made no serious attempt to go for the required 142, for which seventy-three minutes were allowed.

Derbyshire

J. F. Harvey c Tolchard b Lock	18	— b Birkenshaw	34
J. R. Eyre c Hallam b Lock	33	— c sub. b Lock	27
H. L. Johnson b Lock	1	— c Hallam b Lock	13
I. R. Buxton b Marner	6	— b Birkenshaw	0
T. J. P. Eyre c Inman b Lock	1	— not out	16
*D. C. Morgan b Lock	12	— b Birkenshaw	8
M. Hill c Marner b Lock	0	— c Spencer b Lock	15
†R. W. Taylor not out	31	— c and b Lock	14
E. Smith c Lock b Marner	5	— st Tolchard b Lock	18
M. H. J. Allen b Lock	6	— not out	2
H. J. Rhodes run out	5		
L-b 3, w 1	4	B 3, l-b 3	6
1/47 2/49 3/58 4/59 5/65 6/65 7/80 8/105 9/114	122	1/56 2/63 3/65 (8 wkts., dec.) 4/81 5/87 6/113 7/114 8/138	153

Bowling: *First Innings*—Cotton 6—3—14—0; Spencer 8—4—8—0; Marner 26.4—4—65—2; Lock 23—11—31—7. *Second Innings*—Spencer 9—2—36—0; Marner 11—2—34—0; Lock 25—7—40—5; Birkenshaw 21—5—37—3.

Leicestershire

M. R. Hallam b Rhodes.............. 6 — not out 14
B. J. Booth run out.................. 28 — not out 17
M. E. Norman st Taylor b Smith 23
P. Marner b Rhodes 4
C. C. Inman c Harvey b Morgan....... 19
J. Birkenshaw b Smith 27
D. Constant not out.................. 7
*G. A. R. Lock c Rhodes b Morgan.... 13
B 2, l-b 1, w 2, n-b 2 7

1/12 2/57 3/64 4/64 (7 wkts. dec.) 134 (no wkt.) 31
5/99 6/117 7/134

†R. W. Tolchard, C. T. Spencer and J. Cotton did not bat.

Bowling: *First Innings*—Buxton 13—5—22—0; Rhodes 17—4—40—2; Smith 16—5—30—2; Allen 7—2—12—0; Morgan 11.1—3—23—2. *Second Innings*—Buxton 2—1—1—0; Rhodes 1—0—3—0; Smith 4—1—6—0; Allen 8—3—11—0; Morgan 2—0—3—0; Johnson 2—0—7—0.

Umpires: A. E. Fagg and F. Jakeman.

LEICESTERSHIRE v. SUSSEX

At Leicester, May 14, 16, 17. Sussex won by eight wickets. Suttle, in his benefit year, gained the distinction of being on the field for the entire match, scoring 228 runs not out, taking three wickets for 67 runs and making one catch. He began by parting the Leicestershire openers when they had put on 124, holding a return catch from Booth. The patient Norman kept his wicket intact, and Lock, at number nine, offered a rousing 56 in fifty minutes, with seven 4's, the runs being out of 62 for the eighth wicket. When Sussex replied, all but Suttle fell to the Leicestershire spinners; he stayed three hours, forty-five minutes for his 89, with five boundaries. With a lead of 105, Leicestershire succumbed to Oakman's off spin, leaving Sussex to get 265 to win in four hours, thirty-five minutes. They did so with ten minutes to spare, Suttle striking a splendid 139 that demanded much running, there being one 6 and nine 4's in his innings. Langridge was brilliantly run out by Norman after participating in a second-wicket stand of 146.

Leicestershire

M. R. Hallam c M. A. Buss b Oakman .. 64 — b Oakman 18
B. J. Booth c and b Suttle............. 55 — c Pataudi b Oakman 30
M. E. Norman not out .... 47 — b Oakman 2
P. Marner c Bates b Suttle .... 2 — b Suttle.................... 35
C. C. Inman c Lenham b Oakman...... 12 — c Parks b A. Buss 34
J. Birkenshaw c Langridge b Snow ..... 17 — run out 11
D. Constant b A. Buss................ 5 — c Parks b Snow............ 16
†R. W. Tolchard b Snow.............. 0 — not out 3
*G. A. R. Lock c Oakman b Snow ..... 56 — b Oakman 1
C. T. Spencer c Lanham b Snow........ 0 — c Langridge b Oakman 5
J. S. Savage b A. Buss .... 2 — b Oakman 0
B 6......................... 6 B 2, l-b 2.............. 4

1/124 2/124 3/127 4/156 5/189 266 1/24 2/32 3/79 4/119 5/123 159
6/200 7/201 8/263 9/263 6/126 7/132 8/155 9/156

Bowling: *First Innings*—Snow 23—7—63—4; A. Buss 21.5—5—65—2; Oakman 30—9—60—2; M. A. Buss 16—7—23—0; Bates 4—0—13—0; Suttle 33—16—36—2. *Second Innings*—Snow 10—5—7—1; A. Buss 8—2—18—1; Oakman 29.5—2—94—6; M. A. Buss 5—3—5—0; Suttle 10—1—31—1.

Sussex

L. J. Lenham c Inman b Lock	10	— b Lock	43
K. G. Suttle not out	89	— not out	139
R. J. Langridge lbw b Lock	3	— run out	68
†J. M. Parks c Marner b Birkenshaw	31	— not out	12
*Nawab of Pataudi c Spencer b Birkenshaw	7		
A. S. M. Oakman c Lock b Birkenshaw	7		
M. G. Griffith c Tolchard b Lock	6		
M. A. Buss c Marner b Savage	2		
A. Buss c Lock b Savage	0		
D. L. Bates run out	1		
J. A. Snow b Savage	2		
L-b 3	3	B 1, l-b 2	3
1/31 2/38 3/72 4/87 5/110 6/133 7/152 8/152 9/155	161	1/94 2/240 (2 wkts.)	265

Bowling: *First Innings*—Spencer 4—1—16—0; Marner 5—2—10—0; Lock 24—4—40—3; Savage 17.2—4—37—3; Birkenshaw 26—5—55—3. *Second Innings*—Spencer 11—1—50—0; Marner 10.4—1—28—0; Birkenshaw 19—3—56—0; Savage 29—6—74—0; Lock 28—9—54—1.

Umpires: C. S. Elliott and A. E. Rhodes.

At Taunton, May 18, 19, 20. LEICESTERSHIRE lost to SOMERSET by three wickets.

At Leicester, May 21. LEICESTERSHIRE lost to SURREY by 46 runs. (See GILLETTE CUP.)

At Lord's, May 25, 26, 27. LEICESTERSHIRE drew with MIDDLESEX.

LEICESTERSHIRE v. NORTHAMPTONSHIRE

At Leicester, May 28, 29, 30. *65 overs.* Drawn. This match introduced Sunday play in the county championship to the Midlands, and the experiment was described by the Leicestershire secretary, F. M. Turner, as "an unqualified success". Of the estimated 10,000 who attended, 5,000 were present on the Sunday, when the sale of a special programme realised £420, total receipts being £880, considerably more than at any match in the previous season. Played beneath cloudless skies throughout, the match yielded 1,158 runs while twenty-three wickets fell and there were three Northamptonshire centuries and one from Leicestershire. On the first day Milburn, blending belligerence with his great gift of timing, hit a magnificent 171, the highest of his career, including four 6's and twenty-two 4's. He was nine short of his century before learning that Test selector Alec Bedser was watching. His side established a new record of 291 runs in 65 overs. The following day Milburn's triumph was completed by the news of his inclusion in England's twelve. With Inman the next century-maker (thirteen 4's) being supported by Cross in a sixth-wicket stand of 74, Leicestershire failed by only 19 in their bid for innings lead. Next came Mushtaq Mohammad's first hundred for Northamptonshire and another personal record, 118 not out from Steele, before Andrew declared, leaving Leicestershire six hours and twenty minutes in which to score 334. Although no wicket was lost for just over two hours, runs came far too slowly, and the match moved to a tense finish with Northamptonshire's efforts to take two wickets in the last over successfully resisted.

Northamptonshire

C. Milburn c Marner b Cotton	171	— c Cotton b Marner	18
R. M. Prideaux lbw b Marner	1	— c Tolchard b Cross	19
B. L. Reynolds st Tolchard b Lock	48	— b Marner	0
Mushtaq Mohammad b Marner	25	— c and b Lock	112
P. D. Watts not out	33	— c Lock b Savage	10
P. J. Watts not out	8	— b Lock	29
D. S. Steele (did not bat)		— not out	118
B. Crump (did not bat)		— not out	3
B 1, l-b 3, n-b 1	5	B 4, l-b 2	6
1/2 2/112 3/239 4/273 (4 wkts., 65 overs)	291	1/27 2/27 3/47 4/69 5/249 6/308 (6 wkts., dec.)	315

H. Sully, *†K. V. Andrew and R. Bailey did not bat.

Bowling: *First Innings*—Cotton 19—3—56—1; Marner 14—1—68—2; Lock 14—1—52—1; Savage 3—0—18—0; Birkenshaw 2—0—20—0: Cross 13—1—72—0. *Second Innings*—Cotton 19—2—38—0; Marner 17—3—69—2; Cross 15—2—52—1; Savage 15—3—51—1; Lock 21—1—86—2; Birkenshaw 2—0—13—0.

Leicestershire

M. R. Hallam c Crump b Sully	22	— run out	58
M. E. Norman lbw b Bailey	9	— c Bailey b P. J. Watts	45
P. Marner b Bailey	4	— c P. J. Watts b Crump	27
C. C. Inman not out	109	— b Crump	13
J. Birkenshaw b Sully	58	— c Andrew b Sully	12
D. Constant c P. D. Watts b Sully	15	— c P. D. Watts b Mushtaq	38
G. Cross not out	42	— c Bailey b Mushtaq	35
†R. W. Tolchard (did not bat)		— not out	24
*G. A. R. Lock (did not bat)		— c P. J. Watts b Sully	10
J. Cotton (did not bat)		— not out	0
B 9, l-b 5	14	B 14, l-b 3	17
1/24 2/28 3/46 4/167 5/199 (5 wkts., 65 overs)	273	1/88 2/134 3/144 4/167 5/183 6/239 7/248 8/273 (8 wkts.)	279

J. S. Savage did not bat.

Bowling: *First Innings*—Crump 24—4—53—0; Bailey 15—2—51—2; Sully 13—0—76—3; Steele 2—0—18—0; P. J. Watts 11—0—61—0. *Second Innings*—Crump—18—5—41—2; Bailey 21—7—28—0; P. J. Watts 9—0—32—1; Sully 39—10—105—2; Steele 9—4—16—0; P. D. Watts 6—0—29—0; Mushtaq 6—2—11—2.

Umpires: W. H. Copson and R. S. Lay.

LEICESTERSHIRE v. YORKSHIRE

At Leicester, June 1, 2, 3. Yorkshire won by seven wickets. Illingworth, with match figures of eleven wickets for 126 runs, an important 43 in Yorkshire's first innings, and two catches was the chief agent of this conclusive victory. The other vital factor was fifty-five minutes' exhilarating batting by the Yorkshire opening pair at the end of the first day when Taylor used daring methods on a pitch that helped spin bowlers from the start. He hit boldly all round the wicket to score 60 out of 78 with Boycott, and their eventual stand of 123 was the foundation on which Yorkshire built a lead of 47. Leicestershire had manfully assembled 253, of which Hallam's share was a fine 96, scored in just under four hours, with five 4's. In their second innings, Leicestershire were no match for Illingworth and Wilson on the crumbling wicket, and although the loss of three men for 17 runs caused a ripple of excitement, Yorkshire, thanks to Sharpe, easily made the 54 needed to win, by a quarter past twelve on the last day.

Leicestershire

M. R. Hallam c Close b Illingworth	96 — c Illingworth b Wilson	8
M. E. Norman c Banks b Trueman	44 — b Trueman	11
P. Marner c Nicholson b Illingworth	8 — c Sharpe b Wilson	10
C. C. Inman c Close b Illingworth	2 — c and b Illingworth	19
J. Birkenshaw b Close	14 — b Illingworth	2
D. Constant c Sharpe b Illingworth	14 — c Waring b Wilson	9
G. Cross b Wilson	22 — b Illingworth	14
†R. W. Tolchard c Sharpe b Close	1 — lbw b Illingworth	18
*G. A. R. Lock b Illingworth	14 — not out	5
C. T. Spencer b Trueman	22 — c Close b Illingworth	2
J. S. Savage not out	3 — b Illingworth	0
B 2, l-b 9, n-b 2	13 L-b 1, w 1	2
1/81 2/114 3/116 4/167 5/177 6/205 7/206 8/227 9/235	253 1/15 2/30 3/51 4/51 5/53 6/78 7/93 8/93 9/100	100

Bowling: *First Innings*—Trueman 12.4—3—27—2; Nicholson 12—1—31—0; Illingworth 34—5—96—5; Wilson 28—12—46—1; Waring 1—0—10—0; Close 19—10—30—2. *Second Innings*—Trueman 4—1—22—1; Nicholson 3—1—5—0; Illingworth 17.3—5—30—6; Wilson 16—6—40—3; Close 1—0—1—0.

Yorkshire

G. Boycott c Inman b Birkenshaw	34 — b Savage	10
K. Taylor c Constant b Savage	87 — b Spencer	0
D. E. V. Padgett lbw b Birkenshaw	43 — c Tolchard b Spencer	7
*D. B. Close c Norman b Birkenshaw	39 — not out	0
P. J. Sharpe c Constant b Savage	9 — not out	36
R. Illingworth b Savage	43	
†J. G. Binks b Birkenshaw	17	
F. S. Trueman lbw b Lock	11	
D. Wilson c and b Spencer	1	
A. G. Nicholson c Lock b Spencer	0	
J. Waring not out	1	
B 12, l-b 2, n-b 1	15 N-b 1	1
1/123 2/127 3/212 4/219 5/236 6/284 7/295 8/296 9/296	300 1/1 2/17 3/17	(3 wkts.) 54

Bowling: *First Innings*—Spencer 11—2—34—2; Marner 9—1—25—0; Cross 4—1—12—0; Savage 23.5—10—44—3; Lock 33—7—93—1; Birkenshaw 25—6—77—4. *Second Innings*—Spencer 6.1—2—19—2; Savage 6—2—34—1.

Umpires: R. S. Lav and G. H. Pope.

LEICESTERSHIRE v. LANCASHIRE

At Leicester, June 4, 6, 7. *65 overs*. Leicestershire won by two wickets. This was their first victory in a succession of seventeen championship matches, and a tense affair it became. As in the foregoing match, spin bowlers were always being encouraged by a pitch that started to wear early, but at 189 for four Leicestershire, needing 15 to win, were cruising home when Worsley, whose ten wickets in first-class matches had cost him 65 runs apiece, sent back Marner, Birkenshaw and Cross with his off-spinners and Howard accounted for Booth, all four batsmen leaving while three runs were added. Cotton, using the extremity of the bat to take four runs behind the slips, thus made the score 200 and his captain, Lock, hit the winning boundary to long on, off his opposite number, Statham. The match was exceptional for the part played by Lancastrians in a Midlands success. Marner was top scorer of the first innings; Savage, from Ramsbottom, then took seven for 64 and finally Booth hit the century (fourteen 4's) which exposed Lancashire's bowling limitations. The first innings of the match was notable for Pullar's quite resplendent 110, including twelve boundaries, while Green blazed the trail in typically aggressive fashion, though his second knock was an essay in patience.

Lancashire

G. Pullar c and b Cotton	110	— c Lock b Savage	22
D. M. Green b Savage	54	— c Lock b Savage	62
G. K. Knox c Booth b Savage	37	— c Marner b Savage	10
D. R. Worsley not out	15	— c Cross b Lock	10
J. D. Bond not out	7	— not out	38
D. Lloyd (did not bat)		— lbw b Savage	4
P. Lever (did not bat)		— lbw b Savage	0
T. Greenhough (did not bat)		— c Lock b Birkenshaw	13
†K. Goodwin (did not bat)		— lbw b Lock	2
K. Howard (did not bat)		— c Marner b Savage	0
*J. B. Statham (did not bat)		— c Marner b Savage	6
L-b 4, n-b 1	5	B 5, l-b 3	8
1/98 2/204 3/208 (3 wkts., 65 overs)	228	1/55 2/69 3/107 4/111 5/119 6/119 7/146 8/152 9/153	175

Bowling: *First Innings*—Cotton 16—2—51—1; Cross 7—1—34—0; Marner 9—1—35—0; Lock 15—2—49—0; Savage 18—4—54—2. *Second Innings*—Cotton 7—1—20—0; Cross 3—2—4—0; Savage 39.2—17—64—7; Lock 37—14—53—2; Birkenshaw 5—0—26—1.

Leicestershire

B. J. Booth c Knox b Howard	13	— c Lloyd b Howard	101
M. E. Norman c Statham b Howard	48	— b Howard	8
D. Constant c Lloyd b Howard	6	— b Greenhough	23
C. C. Inman st Goodwin b Howard	16	— c Goodwin b Worsley	36
P. Marner b Lever	59	— c Statham b Worsley	11
G. Cross c Green b Howard	14	— c and b Worsley	3
J. Birkenshaw b Greenhough	3	— c Goodwin b Worsley	0
†R. W. Tolchard c Howard b Lever	12	— lbw b Lloyd	1
*G. A. R. Lock lbw b Statham	18	— not out	4
J. Cotton b Lever	4	— not out	8
J. S. Savage not out	1		
L-b 6	6	B 8, l-b 1	9
1/34 2/46 3/82 4/91 5/102 6/130 7/159 8/182 9/187	200	1/17 2/22 3/74 4/151 5/189 6/189 7/191 8/192 (8 wkts.)	204

Bowling: *First Innings*—Statham 12—2—36—1; Lever 12—0—41—3; Howard 20—3—60—5; Greenhough 20—7—57—1. *Second Innings*—Statham 10.1—2—19—0; Lever 3—1—4—0; Howard 30—9—68—2; Lloyd 21—3—57—1; Greenhough 10—3—26—1; Worsley 10—4—21—4.

Umpires: G. H. Pope and A. Jepson.

At Swansea, June 8, 9, 10. LEICESTERSHIRE drew with GLAMORGAN.

At Oxford, June 11, 13, 14. LEICESTERSHIRE beat OXFORD UNIVERSITY by seven wickets.

LEICESTERSHIRE v. MIDDLESEX

At Leicester, June 15, 16, 17. Drawn. A man-of-the-match adjudicator would have had no difficulty in making his award, for Lock, having taken five Middlesex wickets for 33 in 16.3 overs, clubbed the bowling to such purpose that he and Tolchard, the 21-year-old wicket-keeper, lifted Leicestershire from 91 for seven to 161 for eight. After the captain had gone, Tolchard effected the hit that gave Leicestershire the two points emerging from this rain-mauled match. On the first and second days, three hours and forty minutes were lost to the weather, and the third day was restricted to forty minutes. It was a melancholy affair for Russell, the Middlesex opening batsman who had lost his England place, and returned to register a "pair". He was bowled middle stump by Spencer's first delivery of the match, and, at the second attempt, fell to a close-range catch in the same bowler's second over. Once more, the Grace Road wicket began to crumble on the first day, and there was high merit in Parfitt's stay of two and a quarter hours.

Middlesex

W. E. Russell b Spencer	0	— c Cross b Spencer	0
M. J. Harris c Tolchard b Spencer	20	— not out	4
P. H. Parfitt b Savage	57	— not out	8
E. A. Clark c Tolchard b Lock	33		
*†J. T. Murray c Inman b Lock	0		
M. J. Smith c Lock b Savage	23		
R. W. Hooker c Marner b Lock	20		
D. A. Bick c Savage b Lock	8		
H. C. Latchman not out	0		
J. S. E. Price c Spencer b Savage	0		
R. W. Stewart lbw b Lock	0		
L-b 2	2		
1/0 2/41 3/93 4/93 5/120 6/147 7/161 8/161 9/163	163	1/0 (1 wkt.)	12

Bowling: *First Innings*—Spencer 12—2—36—2; Marner 9—0—28—0; Savage 21—7—58—3; Cross 2—0—6—0; Lock 16.3—8—33—5. *Second Innings*—Spencer 4—2—3—1; Marner 2—1—2—0; Lock 4—2—7—0; Savage 2.5—3—0—0.

Leicestershire

M. R. Hallam b Price	16
B. J. Booth b. Price	22
M. E. Norman lbw b Stewart	16
C. C. Inman c Murray b Bick	16
P. Marner b Stewart	1
J. Birkenshaw b Bick	8
G. Cross c Clark b Bick	1
†R. W. Tolchard not out	23
*G. A. R. Lock c Stewart b Parfitt	56
C. T. Spencer not out	3
B 4, l-b 4	8
1/18 2/55 3/61 4/68 5/80 6/84 7/91 8/161 (8 wkts. dec.)	170

J. S. Savage did not bat.

Bowling: Price 19—7—42—2; Stewart 25—7—59—2; Hooker 11—2—32—0; Bick 13—6—22—3; Parfitt 3—1—7—1.

Umpires: C. S. Elliott and J. F. Crapp.

At Portsmouth, June 18, 20, 21. LEICESTERSHIRE drew with HAMPSHIRE.

LEICESTERSHIRE v. SURREY

At Leicester, June 25, 26, 27. *65 overs.* Drawn. This was the second experiment with Sunday play at Leicester and it did not enjoy the brilliant weather of the first occasion, but the presence of about 2,500 spectators, and £230 receipts from the sale of the match programme were felt to be encouraging. On the Saturday, the Bishop of Leicester, Dr. R. R. Williams, opened the new pavilion, and 150 guests were entertained by the President, Mr W. Bentley. The match, abandoned at ten minutes past three on a cricket-less third day, will be remembered as a frustrating affair for Leicestershire. Badly needing a win, they moved within sight of one by bowling out Surrey for 81 and gaining a first-innings lead of 114. The Sunday crowd had full value in the success of the home bowlers on a damp wicket,

Marner at one stage having taken three for 2. Surrey tumbled to 19 for six before Long led a rearguard action. The Leicestershire batting on the first day was notable for Hallam's 91 on a difficult pitch, and his fourth-wicket stand with Marner which realised 97. By the end of the second day Leicestershire had gained a lead of 137, with two wickets down.

Leicestershire

	First innings		Second innings	
M. R. Hallam lbw b Arnold	91	—	not out	14
B. J. Booth run out	1	—	c Long b Roope	3
M. E. Norman c Edrich b Storey	6	—	c Long b Roope	6
C. C. Inman c Arnold b Roope	24			
P. Marner b Arnold	52			
G. Cross c Finlay b Storey	7			
*G. A. R. Lock c Pocock b Arnold	13			
C. T. Spencer b Arnold	0			
D. Constant not out	0			
†R. W. Tolchard not out	0	—	not out	0
N-b 1	1			
1/8 2/19 3/74 4/171 5/174 6/186 7/195 8/195 (8 wkts., 65 overs)	195		1/8 2/18 (2 wkts.)	23

J. S. Savage did not bat.

Bowling: *First Innings*—Arnold 24—2—77—4; Storey 21—1—60—2; Roope 9—2—26—1; Pocock 11—1—31—0. *Second Innings*—Arnold 1—0—8—0; Roope 5—3—7—2; Storey 5—0—8—0.

Surrey

*M. J. Stewart b Marner	1
J. H. Edrich b Spencer	10
I. Finlay c Hallam b Marner	0
K. F. Barrington c Lock b Marner	2
S. J. Storey c Lock b Marner	4
M. J. Edwards b Spencer	2
G. R. J. Roope c Hallam b Lock	7
†A. Long c Lock b Savage	28
P. I. Pocock c Marner b Lock	6
G. Arnold not out	4
R. Harman b Lock	13
B 4	4
1/7 2/11 3/13 4/13 5/19 6/19 7/46 8/64 9/64	81

Bowling: Spencer 15—8—19—2; Marner 16—6—25—4; Lock 12—6—18—3; Savage 7—3—15—1.

Umpires: A. E Rhodes and C. S. Elliott.

LEICESTERSHIRE v. NOTTINGHAMSHIRE

At Leicester, June 29, 30, July 1. *65 overs.* Leicestershire won by one wicket. This second victory in the championship was gained excitingly, before lunch on the third day. The Leicestershire bowlers had left their batsmen a modest task of 128 but the first four were out on the second evening, having contributed 27 in the face of lively new-ball activity by Forbes. Marner struck a priceless 43, and Constant assisted in a fifth-wicket stand of 54 on the last morning, which turned the match. Four cheap wickets for the off-spinner White heightened tension, but Lock kept his county's chance alive, and when he left, six were needed. With two required, Spencer was caught on the boundary, and the last man Savage joined the patient Constant, whose single to backward point levelled the scores. When Constant cut Davison square to the boundary, this former Kent left-hander not only ended a two-hour stay by winning the match but clinched his place for the next game, at Bristol (in which, incidentally, he went on to make his top score of 80). Both sides were hampered by brittle batting, and among the few exceptions was White, with a solid 61 in the first innings.

Nottinghamshire

	First Innings		Second Innings	
*N. Hill	b Spencer	6	c Tolchard b Lock	33
M. Taylor	run out	18	c Spencer b Lock	17
R. A. White	run out	61	c Spencer b Marner	0
H. I. Moore	c Hallam b Lock	0	b Spencer	40
M. J. Smedley	b Spencer	44	c Booth b Spencer	14
†R. Swetman	b Spencer	19	c Tolchard b Lock	36
H. M. Winfield	lbw b Lock	6	lbw b Spencer	7
J. Parkin	not out	5	c Spencer b Lock	1
K. J. Gillhouley	not out	8	c Tolchard b Savage	7
C. Forbes	(did not bat)		b Lock	0
I. Davison	(did not bat)		not out	0
	L-b 8, n-b 2	10	B 1, l-b 2	3
	1/12 2/45 3/45 4/118 5/147 6/162 7/162 (7 wkts, 65 overs)	177	1/23 2/24 3/62 4/94 5/101 6/106 7/143 8/158 9/158	158

Bowling: *First Innings*—Spencer 20—7—41—3; Marner 8—3—24—0; Cross 3—0—6—0; Savage 12—3—30—0; Lock 22—5—66—2. *Second Innings*—Spencer 14—4—26—3; Marner 8—1—21—1; Savage 32—11—45—1; Lock 32.4—9—63—5.

Leicestershire

	First Innings		Second Innings	
M. R. Hallam	lbw b Taylor	47	c Swetman b Forbes	5
B. J. Booth	b Davison	59	c Swetman b Forbes	0
C. C. Inman	c Winfield b Forbes	12	lbw b Forbes	8
M. E. Norman	c Hill b Taylor	14	lbw b Taylor	14
P. Marner	lbw b Davison	6	c Winfield b Taylor	43
D. Constant	b Forbes	0	not out	25
G. Cross	b Forbes	13	c Smedley b White	8
†R. W. Tolchard	not out	22	b. White	0
*G. A. R. Lock	not out	21	b White	17
C. T. Spencer	(did not bat)		c Taylor b White	4
J. S. Savage	(did not bat)		not out	0
	B 3, l-b 3, n-b 8	14	B 5, l-b 2	7
	1/101 2/129 3/129 4/138 5/142 6/155 7/172 (7 wkts., 65 overs)	208	1/4 2/7 3/23 4/35 5/89 6/98 7/98 8/122 9/126 (9 wkts.)	131

Bowling: *First Innings*—Davison 20—4—52—2; Forbes 19—0—74—3; Taylor 17—2—38—2; Gillhouley 9—1—30—0. *Second Innings*—Davison 16.4—4—47—0; Forbes 15—5—21—3; Taylor 7—3—11—2; Gillhouley 4—0—21—0; White 9—3—24—4.

Umpires: J. Langridge and W. F. Simpson.

At Bristol, July 2, 4, 5. LEICESTERSHIRE **drew with** GLOUCESTERSHIRE.

LEICESTERSHIRE v. WARWICKSHIRE

At Leicester, July 6, 7, 8. Drawn. Leicestershire had the limited satisfaction of taking two points from their neighbours, and Lock's bowling was his best for the county, but the possibility of an exciting scamper by Warwickshire soon faded and the closing stages were tinged with farce. M. J. K. Smith won the toss and put the home county in, but his hopes of success for the seam bowlers on a damp pitch steadily diminished while Hallam and Inman joined forces for a third wicket partnership of 102. With Tolchard and Marner batting in similar vein, Leicestershire passed 300 for the first time in the season, and declared. The Warwickshire first innings was largely controlled by Lock, with some able catching in support, and he set himself a new record for Leicestershire of eight for 85. Flashes of brilliant defiance came from Amiss, with nine 4's in a significantly polished innings, and Jameson, hitting one 6 and twelve 4's, kept the chance of a lead alive, Brown unearthing latent batting skill in a last-wicket stand of 82. The Warwickshire bowlers tried commendably to hold the door to victory open but Leicestershire batted on to a point at which only one and threequarter hours were left for their opponents to get 179.

Leicestershire

M. R. Hallam c A. C. Smith b Webster	91	— lbw b Cartwright	31
B. J. Booth lbw b Cartwright	8	— b Brown	14
M. E. Norman lbw b Cartwright	10	— lbw b Ibadulla	14
C. C. Inman b Webster	69	— c Miller b Cartwright	9
P. Marner lbw b Cartwright	40	— c Cartwright b Ibadulla	10
D. Constant c M. J. K. Smith b Webster	0	— b Webster	4
S. Greensword run out	18	— c Abberley b Cartwright	1
†R. W. Tolchard not out	44	— c Webster b Miller	24
*G. A. R. Lock c Abberley b Cartwright	2	— c Brown b Webster	21
C. T. Spencer c Ibadulla b Webster	13	— c A. C. Smith b Barber	0
J. S. Savage not out	12	— not out	0
B 5, l-b 4, n-b 9	18	B 1, l-b 1, n-b 2	4
1/40 2/83 3/185 4/191 (9 wkts. dec.) 5/195 6/237 7/250 8/252 9/280	325	1/23 2/54 3/71 4/72 5/82 6/83 7/87 8/121 9/122	132

Bowling: *First Innings*—Brown 23—3—73—0; Webster 26—5—63—4; Cartwright 33—11—81—4; Ibadulla 6—0—37—0; Miller 20—8—45—0; Barber 2—0—8—0. *Second Innings*—Webster 14—2—44—2; Brown 9—1—17—1; Miller 10.1—5—16—1; Cartwright 20—12—40—3; Ibadulla 13—8—9—2; Barber 6—4—2—1.

Warwickshire

R. W. Barber c Tolchard b Lock	41	— c Tolchard b Spencer	30
R. N. Abberley lbw b Spencer	3	— c Tolchard b Marner	7
D. L. Amiss c Constant b Lock	72	— c and b Marner	35
*M. J. K. Smith c Lock b Spencer	9	— not out	12
J. A. Jameson not out	94	— not out	9
K. Ibadulla c Constant b Lock	5		
T. W. Cartwright c Marner b Lock	0		
†A. C. Smith c Hallam b Lock	2		
R. Miller lbw b Lock	6		
R. V. Webster c Hallam b Lock	0		
D. J. Brown b Lock	34		
B 5, l-b 7, w 1	13	L-b 1, w 1	2
1/5 2/58 3/100 4/153 5/166 6/171 7/181 8/197 9/197	279	1/11 2/65 3/85 (3 wkts.)	95

Bowling: *First Innings*—Spencer 20—5—60—2; Marner 12—0—49—0; Savage 24—4—72—0; Lock 33.2—12—85—8. *Second Innings*—Spencer 9—0—35—1; Marner 9—0—48—2; Greensword 2—1—2—0; Lock 4—3—8—0; Savage 2—2—0—0.

Umpires: T. W. Spencer and H. Mellows.

LEICESTERSHIRE v. WORCESTERSHIRE

At Leicester, July 9, 11, 12. *65 overs.* Worcestershire won by four wickets. Leicestershire could never quite match the batting power and bowling penetration of the Champions, and R. Booth made the winning hit just before noon on the third day. The home batsmen edged their way out cheaply in the first innings, when

R. Booth took three catches at the wicket and Richardson a similar number at slip. Flavell and Brain were always difficult to deal with, though Lock and Constant found means in a seventh-wicket stand of 41. Kenyon gave Worcestershire a fine start, he and Horton raising 71, and later came Headley to strike out boldly, and win a lead of 53. After B. J. Booth had been caught by his namesake, Leicestershire again found a partnership for the seventh wicket valuable, Lock and Tolchard adding 41. The honours went to d'Oliveira, with five for 49, and at the end of the second day Worcestershire, 39 for one, needed only 69 more. They got them after Savage and Lock had caused some concern by spinning out six batsmen.

Leicestershire

M. R. Hallam c d'Oliveira b Flavell	13	— c Booth b Gifford	21
B. J. Booth c Booth b Flavell	17	— c Booth b Brain	37
S. Greensword c Booth b Brain	2	— lbw b Brain	11
C. C. Inman c Richardson b Brain	24	— b d'Oliveira	2
P. Marner c Booth b Brain	1	— b d'Oliveira	3
†R. W. Tolchard c Richardson b d'Oliveira	8	— b Gifford	20
D. Constant c Richardson b d'Oliveira	38	— b d'Oliveira	5
*G. A. R. Lock b Brain	32	— b Horton	20
C. T. Spencer b Flavell	8	— b d'Oliveira	20
J. S. Savage c Horton b Flavell	2	— not out	2
J. Cotton not out	11	— c Richardson b d'Oliveira	0
L-b 2, w 1, n-b 1	4	B 13, l-b 6	19
1/20 2/33 3/33 4/34 5/56 6/70 7/111 8/130 9/140	160	1/37 2/66 3/75 4/77 5/81 6/91 7/132 8/148 9/160	160

Bowling: *First Innings*—Flavell 23—4—51—4; Brain 21—6—62—4; d'Oliveira 15.1—5—43—2. *Second Innings*—Flavell 8—3—12—0; Brain 15—6—31—2; d'Oliveira 31.3—12—49—5; Gifford 23—10—31—2; Horton 9—2—18—1.

Worcestershire

*D. Kenyon b Marner	57	— c Spencer b Lock	18
M. J. Horton c Savage b Lock	32	— c Constant b Savage	5
J. A. Ormrod c Hallam b Cotton	21	— lbw b Lock	14
T. W. Graveney c Marner b Cotton	29	— b Savage	20
B. d'Oliveira b Cotton	18	— not out	11
R. G. A. Headley not out	41	— c Marner b Savage	10
D. W. Richardson run out	3	— c Greensword b Savage	6
†R. Booth not out	7	— not out	7
L-b 3, n-b 2	5	B 16, w 1	17
1/71 2/94 3/124 4/144 5/187 6/190 (6 wkts, 65 overs)	213	1/20 2/44 3/45 4/69 5/85 6/97 (6 wkts.)	108

N. Gifford, B. M. Brain and J. A. Flavell did not bat.

Bowling: *First Innings*—Spencer 23—3—75—0; Cotton 22—3—86—3; Lock 14—6—25—1; Marner 6—1—22—1. *Second Innings*—Spencer 3—0—7—0; Cotton 2—0—5—0; Lock 17.4—3—50—2; Savage 17—6—29—4.

Umpires: T. W. Spencer and J. Arnold.

At The Oval, July 13, 14, 15. LEICESTERSHIRE drew with SURREY.

At Chesterfield, July 16, 18, 19. LEICESTERSHIRE beat DERBYSHIRE by 120 runs.

LEICESTERSHIRE v. HAMPSHIRE

At Coalville, July 20, 21, 22. Drawn. Leicester returned to the Snibston Colliery ground at Coalville after five years' absence, and found it a handsomely appointed recreation centre, but despite the facilities and the good weather, the public response was poor. The match afforded two examples of monumental patience, and centuries by three players on the best batting wicket they had then encountered. Yet, as a contest it failed lamentably, because neither captain could foresee removing his opponents twice on such a pitch, and the game was allowed to expire dismally after a brief suggestion of challenge for the lead by Hampshire. Hallam, reaching his first century of the season in three hours with thirteen 4's, batted with characteristic grace and urgency. His partner, Norman, needed five hours for his first hundred as a Leicestershire player, but Hampshire's Horton was only five minutes inside this time, and went on to bat for all but thirty minutes of the seven and threequarter hours of the innings. With one 6 and eleven 4's in his 146, Horton made his final exit from the wicket—not out—just over twenty-four hours after he had first taken guard. White, in a last-wicket stand of 39, made a gallant attempt to take Hampshire ahead, but they finished 22 behind, and Leicestershire played out time.

Leicestershire

M. R. Hallam b Shackleton .... 135 — not out 37
M. E. Norman not out................. 132 — not out 14
D. Constant b White 3
C. C. Inman c Timms b White......... 43
P. Marner not out..................... 4
B 6, l-b 4, w 5 .... 15 W 2.................. 2

1/242 2/225 3/327 (3 wkts. dec.) 332 (no wkt.) 53

J. Birkenshaw, †R. W. Tolchard, *G. A. R. Lock, C. T. Spencer, J. S. Savage and J. Cotton did not bat.

Bowling: *First Innings*—Shackleton 40—12—79—1; White 25—4—64—2; Castell 30—7—89—0; Sainsbury 24—6—56—0; Wheatley 7—1—29—0. *Second Innings*—Shackleton 3—0—7—0; White 5—2—10—0; Wheatley 6—2—14—0; Castell 2—0—14—0; Caple 2—1—6—0.

Hampshire

*R. E. Marshall c Tolchard b Cotton 11
B. L. Reed c Marner b Lock...... 25
H. Horton not out..............146
D. A. Livingstone c Marner b Lock 0
P. J. Sainsbury c Birkenshaw b Lock 2
K. J. Wheatley c Spencer b Savage 19
R. G. Caple c Norman b Savage.. 35
†B. S. V. Timms c Tolchard b Cotton 0
A. T. Castell c Lock b Savage..... 33
D. Shackleton run out........... 1
D. W. White b Cotton........... 30
L-b 6, n-b 2............. 8

1/13 2/74 3/74 4/78 5/110 6/192 7/193 8/262 9/271 310

Bowling: Spencer 16—3—34—0; Cotton 28.4—10—55—3; Marner 2—1—3—0; Lock 55—28—94—3; Savage 57—19—108—3; Birkenshaw 2—1—8—0.

Umpires: W. F. Price and P. B. Wight.

LEICESTERSHIRE v. GLAMORGAN

At Coalville, July 23, 25. Leicestershire won by ten wickets. This fourth Leicestershire victory was quite the most conclusive, the twelve points being collected at 4.40 p.m. on the second day. The animated pitch called for aggressive batting and good length bowling, both of which the home county supplied in much greater measure than the Welshmen. Two key performances were the match return of eleven for 86 by the seam bowler Marner, including a personal record in the Glamorgan second innings of seven for 29, and Inman's 97, which contained sixteen boundaries. Having won the toss, Glamorgan found the pitch quite unmanageable, though E. Lewis gave a brief sample of what was needed in a stay of seventy minutes. Marner, making the ball hurry off the pitch and sometimes lift, and Lock, taking four of the last five wickets, were assisted by efficient catching. Hallam and Constant, the latter in a stand of 79 for the second wicket with Inman, took Leicestershire to a fine position at the end of the first day, then they led by 56. On Monday morning, Miller emulated the Leicestershire bowlers by dismissing four men for two runs, and six Leicestershire wickets fell for 30, but a Welsh collapse followed, leaving Leicestershire to get eight to win. This was achieved with due solemnity by Savage and Tolchard in eight overs.

Glamorgan

A. Jones b Cotton	6	— c Tolchard b Marner	18
R. Davis c Tolchard b Marner	22	— c Constant b Marner	1
P. Walker b Marner	2	— b Marner	0
A. R. Lewis c Tolchard b Marner	26	— c Hallam b Lock	8
A. Rees c Hallam b Marner	6	— lbw b Lock	29
H. D. Miller c and b Lock	18	— lbw b Marner	6
F. J. Davis c Tolchard b Lock	0	— lbw b Marner	7
E. Lewis c Birkenshaw b Lock	36	— c Cotton b Marner	0
†D. L. Evans not out	17	— not out	10
D. J. Shepherd c Marner b Lock	1	— b Lock	1
*O. S. Wheatley run out	0	— c and b Marner	2
L-b 6, n-b 1	7	B 1, l-b 8, w 2	11
1/15 2/20 3/31 4/56 5/69 6/72 7/117 8/126 9/141	141	1/11 2/13 3/24 4/39 5/51 6/77 7/77 8/81 9/82	93

Bowling: *First Innings*—Cotton 15—8—17—1; Marner 27—10—57—4; Lock 21—7—48—4; Savage 8.1—3—12—0. *Second Innings*—Cotton 12—3—19—0; Marner 23.3—7—29—7; Lock 15—8—20—3; Savage 10—6—14—0.

Leicestershire

M. R. Hallam b E. Lewis	41		
M. E. Norman c Walker b Miller	5		
D. Constant c Evans b E. Lewis	48		
C. C. Inman c Evans b Wheatley	97		
B. J. Booth lbw b Shepherd	7		
†R. W. Tolchard c R. Davis b Miller	15	— not out	1
P. Marner c Walker b Miller	1		
J. Birkenshaw not out	3		
*G. A. R. Lock c A. Jones b Miller	0		
J. S. Savage c Rees b Wheatley	2	— not out	7
B 8	8		
1/70 2/149 3/180 4/213 5/217 6/218 7/223 8/223 9/227 (9 wkts. dec.)	227	(no wkt.)	8

J. Cotton did not bat.

Bowling: *First Innings*—Wheatley 22—3—56—2; Miller 15—1—56—4; Shepherd 13—8—24—1; Walker 4—1—20—0; E. Lewis 15—4—40—2; F. J. Davis 7—1—23—0. *Second Innings*—Shepherd 4—4—0—0; F. J. Davis 2—1—4—0; E. Lewis 2—0—4—0.

Umpires: W. F. Price and P. B. Wight.

At Canterbury, July 30, August 1, 2. LEICESTERSHIRE lost to KENT by 66 runs.

At Worcester, August 3, 4, 5. LEICESTERSHIRE beat WORCESTERSHIRE by 60 runs.

LEICESTERSHIRE v. KENT

At Leicester, August 6, 8, 9. Leicestershire won by seven wickets. The big danger to Leicestershire was the weather, their sixth championship win being gained in heavy rain. Lock ran to the crease when Inman had been bowled after taking his county to the brink of success with a fierce assault on the bowling. This included four boundary hits in one over from Dixon. Two runs were needed when Inman left, and the winning four was struck by Norman when he square cut Dixon. In doing so, Norman completed a memorable day during which he was awarded his county cap and completed his thousand runs for the season. Major credit for the result went to the bowlers, notably Marner, with his match figures of eight for 105. Early in the day Kent had lost their last three wickets for the addition of eight runs and Leicestershire were required to make 108. Leaving at 42, Hallam was Dixon's ninety-ninth victim of the season, and Booth was run out before lunch. Then Inman led the fourth-wicket stand of 55 with Norman.

Kent

M. H. Denness c Tolchard b Marner	7	— lbw b Marner	12
B. W. Luckhurst c Tolchard b Cotton	57	— lbw b Cotton	4
R. C. Wilson c Spencer b Marner	0	— c Hallam b Spencer	24
S. E. Leary b Marner	0	— b Spencer	23
J. M. Prodger b Marner	8	— b Cotton	5
A. Ealham c Tolchard b Cotton	54	— b Spencer	5
†A. Knott c Hallam b Cotton	10	— c Marner b Spencer	0
*A. L. Dixon b Spencer	33	— c Tolchard b Cotton	12
D. M. Sayer c Inman b Marner	13	— c Spencer b Marner	5
A. J. Hooper not out	9	— c Lock b Marner	2
J. C. Dye run out	3	— not out	0
B 1, l-b 1, n-b 1	3	B 3, l-b 5	8
1/23 2/23 3/23 4/33 5/120 6/135 7/140 8/173 9/188	197	1/6 2/25 3/62 4/62 5/71 6/75 7/87 8/92 9/100	100

Bowling: *First Innings*—Spencer 20.1—3—45—1; Cotton 13—4—25—3; Marner 26—4—74—5; Lock 10—2—33—0; Savage 8—2—17—0. *Second Innings*—Spencer 15—7—27—4; Cotton 9—4—14—3; Marner 16.2—2—31—3; Savage 7—4—4—0; Lock 8—4—16—0.

Leicestershire

M. R. Hallam b Sayer	28	— lbw b Dixon	29
M. E. Norman c Knott b Dye	29	— not out	38
B. J. Booth lbw b Dixon	11	— run out	6
C. C. Inman c Knott b Dixon	1	— b Dye	33
P. Marner st Knott b Dixon	20		
D. Constant b Dixon	24		
†R. W. Tolchard b Hooper	27		
*G. A. R. Lock b Dixon	10	— not out	0
J. S. Savage c Luckhurst b Dixon	8		
J. Cotton not out	10		
C. T. Spencer lbw b Dixon	6		
B 2, l-b 7, n-b 7	16	B 1, l-b 1, n-b 2	4
1/41 2/62 3/66 4/90 5/97 6/153 7/153 8/171 9/176	190	1/42 2/51 3/106 (3 wkts.)	110

Bowling: *First Innings*—Sayer 30—8—63—1; Dixon 35.2—14—58—7; Dye 23—6—40—1; Luckhurst 3—1—5—0; Hooper 3—0—8—1. *Second Innings*—Dye 15—5—32—1; Dixon 19.1—6—57—1; Sayer 3—0—14—0; Hooper 3—1—3—0.

Umpires: W. E. Phillipson and R. Aspinall.

At Northampton, August 13, 14, 15. LEICESTERSHIRE lost to NORTHAMPTONSHIRE by 80 runs.

At Nottingham, August 17, 18, 19. LEICESTERSHIRE drew with NOTTINGHAMSHIRE.

At Clacton, August 20, 22, 23. LEICESTERSHIRE beat ESSEX by four wickets.

At Leicester, August 24, 25, 26. LEICESTERSHIRE lost to WEST INDIES by seven wickets. (See WEST INDIES section.)

At Manchester, August 27, 28, 29. LEICESTERSHIRE beat LANCASHIRE by eight wickets.

ADDRESSES OF REPRESENTATIVE BODIES

ENGLAND: M.C.C., Lord's Cricket Ground, St. John's Wood, London, N.W.8.
AUSTRALIA: Australian Cricket Board of Control, Alan Barnes, Cricket House, 254, George Street, Sydney, N.S.W.
SOUTH AFRICA: Cricket Association, P.O. Box 9, P.O. Northlands, Johannesburg.
WEST INDIES: West Indies Board of Control, (Acting Secretary) P.B.D. Short, P.O. Box 103, Bridgetown, Barbados.
INDIA: India Cricket Board of Control, S. Sriraman, 26III Main Road, Raja Annamalaipuram, Madras, 28.
NEW ZEALAND: New Zealand Cricket Council, P.O. Box 958. Christchurch, N.Z.
PAKISTAN: Board of Control for Cricket in Pakistan Bashir Ahmad, Hon. Sec., B.C.C.P., Chief Admin. Officer, G.H.Q., Rawalpindi.
CANADA: Canadian Cricket Association, Donald King, 534a, Eglington Avenue West, Toronto, 12, Ontario.
FIJI: Fiji Cricket Association, P.O. Box 177, Suva, Fiji Islands.
BIRMINGHAM LEAGUE: J. Williams, 51, Beeches Road, West Bromwich Staffs.
BRADFORD LEAGUE: E. W. Sharpe, 14, Newforth Grove, Bradford, 5.
CLUB CRICKET CONFERENCE: Major S. W. Woods, 64A, Hill Road, London, S.W.19.
COMBINED SERVICES CRICKET ASSOCIATION, c/o Army Sports Control Board Lansdowne House, War Office, Berkeley Square, London, W1.
CRICKET SOCIETY: E. C. Rice, 2, Steep Hill, Streatham, London, S.W.16.
CRICKET SOCIETY OF SCOTLAND: B. L. Mellis, 10, Montrose Gardens, Milngavie, Dumbartonshire.
HASTINGS FESTIVAL: Major E. H. Flear, Central Cricket Ground, Hastings, Sussex.
LANCASHIRE CRICKET LEAGUE: J. Isherwood, 118, Manor Street, Accrington.
LANCASHIRE AND CHESHIRE CRICKET SOCIETY: W. G. Smith, 40, Crescent Road, Hale, Cheshire.
MIDLAND CLUB CRICKET CONFERENCE: W. L. Jones, 43, Chesterwood Road, King's Heath, Birmingham, 14.
NATIONAL CLUB CRICKET ASSOCIATION: W. E. Lindsey, 30, Sandhurst Road, Mile End, Stockport, Cheshire.
NORTHERN CRICKET SOCIETY: C. R. Yeomans, 88, Church Lane, Cross Gates, Leeds 15.
NORTH STAFFORDSHIRE AND SOUTH CHESHIRE LEAGUE: W. L. Johnson, 72 Wolstanton Road, Chesterton, Staffs.
NORTH STAFFORDSHIRE AND DISTRICT LEAGUE: J. Bradburn, 30 Woodland Avenue, Norton-le-Moors, Stoke-on-Trent.
SCARBOROUGH FESTIVAL: J. Midgley, North Marine Road, Scarborough, Yorks.
SOUTH WALES CRICKET ASSOCIATION: M. K. Jenkins, 13, Pembrey Road, Llanelli.
SUSSEX CRICKET SOCIETY: P. Edwards, 41, Hill Drive, Hove 4.
UNITED STATES CRICKET ASSOCIATION: Dr. M. A. Verity, Dept. of Pathology, U. C. L. A. Medical Centre, Los Angeles, California.
WOMBWELL CRICKET SOCIETY: J. Sokell, 42, Woodstock Road, Barnsley, Yorkshire.
WOMEN'S CRICKET ASSOCIATION: Miss E. M. Riley, Corner Farm, Frittenden, Cranbrook, Kent.
YORKSHIRE COUNCIL: N. Stead, 337, Leeds Road, Scholes, Leeds.

The addresses of the First-Class Counties, Universities and Minor Counties are given at the head of each separate section.

MIDDLESEX

President—G. C. NEWMAN

Secretary—A. W. FLOWER, Lord's Cricket Ground, St. John's Wood Road, London, N.W.8

Captain—F. J. TITMUS

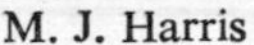

M. J. Harris

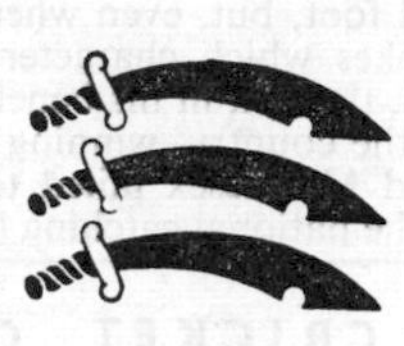

County Badge

J. S. E. Price

Middlesex, who seemed to have found their contemporary niche, finishing sixth for the last three seasons, disappointed by tumbling to equal twelfth. Their failure to win more than six matches cannot be entirely explained by the loss of ten full Championship days. They failed to get away to their usual good start at Lord's, not winning until Whitsun. Victories were then heavily punctuated by draws, and they did not win at Lord's after June, though they lost only five matches all told, as few as the Champions, Yorkshire. Their old deficiency dogged them—difficulty in getting sides out.

The bowling lacked penetration all round, though Price, after a year beset by injury, rediscovered his pace and hostility. He returned only at Whitsun, but still took 90 wickets, regaining his Test place at The Oval. However, injury struck again, and he stood down. Titmus, seeming to be suffering from a surfeit of cricket, lost his form, 1966 being the first season since 1960 that he failed to take 100 wickets for the county. His deterioration twice cost him his Test place during the series. Stewart, a West Indian fast-medium bowler, signed from Gloucestershire after the start of the season, proved a useful acquisition. His best performance came in his first game against Glamorgan, where he displayed the virtues of straightness and length. A lower arm-action reduced Herman's effectiveness, and Latchman's speciality as a leg-break bowler in modern cricket diminished his chances. Hooker, another dogged by injuries, took 31 wickets fewer.

The batting was held together by Parfitt, who, playing as well as ever, achieved his highest aggregate for the county. Russell, depressed by Test Match failures and his rhythm broken by opening with a succession of different partners, saw his average and aggregate fall sharply. His technique also proved fallible on occasions, a preference for playing straight balls away to mid-wicket often accounting for his dismissal. Of his partners only Harris, given an extended trial, afforded sufficient support. Harris promised much with his fighting approach and high-quality strokes, but he was dropped during the side's late failures. Murray was absent for a month with a poisoned foot, but, even when fit, he seldom reproduced the flowing strokes which characterised his two centuries against the West Indies, though, in his benefit year, he kept wicket as well as anybody in the country, winning back his place for the last Test. In the field Middlesex failed to scintillate as before, though Parfitt topped the national catching list.

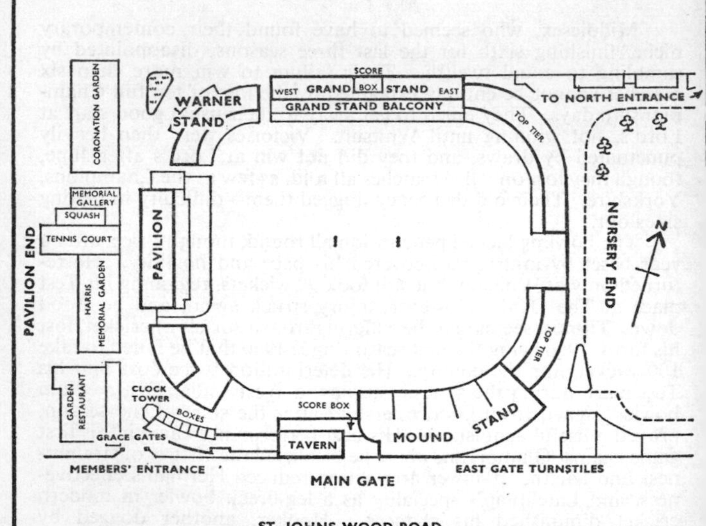

MIDDLESEX RESULTS

All First-Class Matches—Played 31, *Won* 8, *Lost* 5, *Drawn* 18
County Championship Matches—Played 28, *Won* 6, *Lost* 5, *Drawn* 14, *No Decision* 3

COUNTY CHAMPIONSHIP AVERAGES

BATTING

	Birthplace	Mtchs.	Inns.	Not Outs	Runs	100's	Highest Inns.	Aver.
P. H. Parfitt ...	*Billingford*	26	50	8	1860	2	114*	44.28
E. A. Clark....	*Balham*	25	42	7	1197	1	149	34.20
W. E. Russell..	*Glasgow*	22	42	3	1277	3	146*	32.74
M. J. Harris....	*St. Just-in-Roseland*	15	29	3	767	1	114	29.50
J. T. Murray...	*Kensington*	15	23	6	474	1	114	27.88
R. W. Hooker..	*Shoreditch*	21	28	6	573	1	102	26.04
D. Bennett.....	*Wakefield*	4	8	2	140	0	50	23.33
M. J. Smith....	*Enfield*	16	26	2	520	0	68	21.66
C. T. Radley...	*Hertford*	17	29	4	515	0	75	20.60
F. J. Titmus....	*Kentish Town*	21	32	5	530	0	81*	19.62
D. A. Bick	*Hampstead*	24	31	6	337	0	63*	13.48
E. G. Clifton...	*Lambeth*	11	16	7	80	0	21*	8.88
H. C. Latchman	*Kingston, Jamaica*	19	23	6	139	0	28	8.17
R. S. Herman..	*Southampton*	5	4	2	7	0	4	3.50
J. S. E. Price...	*Harrow*	20	20	4	43	0	13*	2.68
R. W. Stewart..	*Portland, Jamaica*	21	17	3	18	0	5*	1.28

Also batted: T. Selwood (*Prestatyn*), 0 and 17; M. Manasseh (*Calcutta*) 19; D. J. Ling (*Enfield*) played in one match but did not bat.

* *Signifies not out.*

BOWLING

	Overs	Maidens	Runs	Wickets	Average
M. Manasseh...........	12	4	31	3	10.33
J. S. E. Price...........	688	149	1679	90	18.65
R. W. Stewart..........	605.2	164	1435	64	22.42
R. W. Hooker..........	509.3	140	1248	55	22.69
F. J. Titmus.............	818	272	1733	72	24.06
D. A. Bick..............	412.4	127	1031	37	27.86
P. H. Parfitt.............	50	10	117	4	29.25
H. C. Latchman.........	296.5	81	882	24	36.75
R. S. Herman...........	112	20	310	8	38.75

Also bowled: D. Bennett 17—2—51—2; E. A. Clark 5.2—2—6—1; D. J. Ling 23—5—60—1; C. T. Radley 5—3—7—1; M. J. Smith 3—0—19—0.

At Cambridge, April 30, May 2, 3. MIDDLESEX beat CAMBRIDGE UNIVERSITY by 232 runs.

At Birmingham, May 4, 5, 6. MIDDLESEX v. WARWICKSHIRE abandoned.

MIDDLESEX v. KENT

At Lord's, May 7, 9, 10. *65 overs.* Kent won by 117 runs. In their first encounter with the 65-over limitation Middlesex displayed little idea of how to build an innings in this type of cricket. They could never shake off the burden of having spent 20 overs over their first 27 runs on the first evening. Wickets had to be sacrificed against accurate bowling on the second day in the vain attempt to match Kent's carefully compiled 170 for five. Middlesex finished 58 behind, and were denied the breakthrough they urgently needed in Kent's second innings when the opening batsmen, Luckhurst and Denness, put on 93. Nearly an hour's batting on the last day set Middlesex 320 in five hours, a target they never approached. Underwood took another five wickets, bringing his match analysis to ten for 87, deserved reward for mature bowling.

Kent

First innings		Second innings	
B. W. Luckhurst c Latchman b Bennett	17	— c Hooker b Bick	44
M. H. Denness c Murray b Hooker	26	— b Titmus	42
R. C. Wilson c Radley b Titmus	24	— c Parfitt b Hooker	14
*M. C. Cowdrey not out	53	— b Herman	41
A. L. Dixon c Latchman b Titmus	0	— b Titmus	2
S. E. Leary c Herman b Bennett	31	— not out	67
J. M. Prodger not out	6	— b Hooker	2
†A. Knott (did not bat)		— c Titmus b Herman	14
D. L. Underwood (did not bat)		— not out	21
B 3, l-b 5, w 1, n-b 4	13	B 1, l-b 9, w 1, n-b 3	14
1/45 2/49 3/107 4/107 5/163 (5 wkts., 65 overs)	170	1/93 2/93 3/140 4/174 5/177 6/200 7/222 (7 wkts. dec.)	261

A. Brown and D. M. Sayer did not bat.

Bowling: *First Innings*—Herman 13—4—25—0; Hooker 20—6—48—1; Titmus 22—6—60—2; Bennett 10—2—24—2. *Second Innings*—Herman 16—2—49—2; Hooker 21—4—58—2; Titmus 27—9—65—2; Bennett 7—0—27—0; Bick 12—2—21—1; Latchman 9—4—27—0.

Middlesex

First innings		Second innings	
W. E. Russell b Sayer	27	— b Underwood	24
C. T. Radley c Knott b Brown	5	— c Luckhurst b Underwood	33
P. H. Parfitt c Sayer b Brown	5	— b Dixon	20
D. A Bick c Luckhurst b Brown	6	— c Denness b Underwood	0
E. A. Clark c Prodger b Sayer	8	— c Knott b Dixon	42
†J. T. Murray c Luckhurst b Underwood	23	— c Denness b Dixon	14
*F. J. Titmus b Underwood	4	— c Denness b Dixon	12
R. W. Hooker c Brown b Underwood	15	— not out	31
D. Bennett not out	9	— c Leary b Underwood	17
H. C. Latchman c Prodger b Underwood	2	— c Prodger b Dixon	0
R. S. Herman c Prodger b Underwood	3	— b Underwood	4
B 1, l-b 1, w 2, n-b 1	5	L-b 4, w 1	5
1/5 2/23 3/35 4/51 5/58 6/74 7/98 8/98 9/100	112	1/43 2/78 3/78 4/121 5/150 6/151 7/191 8/196 9/197	202

Bowling: *First Innings*—Brown 17—7—31—3; Sayer 21—9—38—2; Underwood 14.1—5—29—5; Dixon 6—2—9—0. *Second Innings*—Brown 10—4—24—0; Sayer 8—3—18—0; Underwood 30.3—11—58—5; Dixon 32—8—97—5.

Umpires: J. Langridge and G. H. Pope.

MIDDLESEX v. GLAMORGAN

At Lord's, May 11, 12, 13. *65 overs*. Drawn. In a tense finish the Glamorgan wicket-keeper, Evans, failed to hit the six off the last ball of the match, bowled by Stewart, which would have given Glamorgan victory. Set 251 in three hours and ten minutes, Glamorgan came very close, through a magnificent century by A. R. Lewis. Lewis added 92 in an hour with Walker for the third wicket, and while he remained Glamorgan seemed to have the task in hand, but on his departure, twenty minutes from the end, they lost their grip. Middlesex batted entertainingly in the morning, adding 215 in two hours, forty minutes, Russell's elegant 146 not out being the cornerstone. Only six hours' cricket proved possible on the first day. Middlesex declared well within their permitted overs, and Glamorgan easily overtook their swiftly made 137 for two.

Middlesex

W. E. Russell st Evans b Davis	61	— not out	146
C. T. Radley not out	51	— c E. Lewis b Wheatley	3
P. H. Parfitt c A. R. Lewis b Davis	10	— lbw b Wheatley	3
E. A. Clark not out	11	— c A. Jones b Davis	66
†J. T. Murray (did not bat)		— b Walker	14
*F. J. Titmus (did not bat)		— b Shepherd	12
R. W. Hooker (did not bat)		— not out	1
L-b 4	4	L-b 5, n-b 1	6
1/96 2/116 (2 wkts. dec.)	137	1/13 2/19 3/149 4/214 5/243 (5 wkts. dec.)	251

D. A. Bick, H. C. Latchman, R. S. Herman and R. W. Stewart did not bat.

Bowling: *First Innings*—I. J. Jones 14—1—39—0; Wheatley 9—2—21—0; Walker 10—2—31—0; Shepherd 6—0—20—0; Davis 5.3—1—22—2. *Second Innings*—I. J. Jones 9—2—31—0; Wheatley 9—0—19—2; E. Lewis 5—0—28—0; Davis 18—6—69—1; Shepherd 23—3—62—1; Walker 10—2—36—1.

Glamorgan

A. Jones not out	80	— c and b Latchman	37
B. Hedges c Parfitt b Titmus	21	— b Stewart	10
P. M. Walker not out	32	— b Stewart	45
A. R. Lewis (did not bat)		— b Herman	102
A. Rees (did not bat)		— c Hooker b Stewart	23
D. J. Shepherd (did not bat)		— c Radley b Stewart	1
E. Lewis (did not bat)		— c Titmus b Stewart	7
†D. L. Evans (did not bat)		— c Hooker b Stewart	7
F. J. Davis (did not bat)		— not out	1
B 1, l-b 2, n-b 2	5	B 2, l-b 9, n-b 1	12
1/41 (1 wkt. dec.)	138	1/37 2/61 3/170 4/216 5/223 6/235 7/243 8/245 (8 wkts.)	245

I. J. Jones and *O. S. Wheatley did not bat.

Bowling: *First Innings*—Herman 8—1—18—0; Stewart 7—3—11—0; Latchman 7.5—4—36—0; Hooker 4—0—16—0; Titmus 14—5—27—1; Bick 9—2—25—0. *Second Innings*—Herman 12—2—40—1; Stewart 21—1—65—6; Hooker 6—0—22—0; Latchman 9—1—52—1; Bick 3—0—14—0; Titmus 12—2—40—0.

Umpires: G. H. Pope and H. Yarnold.

At Gravesend, May 14, 16, 17. MIDDLESEX drew with KENT.

MIDDLESEX v. WARWICKSHIRE

At Lord's, May 18, 19, 20. Drawn. In a rain-interrupted match, only a superb spell of hostile fast bowling by Webster prevented Middlesex recording their first Championship win. Set to make 194 runs in two and a half hours, Middlesex seemed to have victory within their grasp, but Webster undermined their attempt by taking the first five wickets for 46 runs in a 13-over spell which lasted one hour forty minutes, and the Middlesex last man, Herman, experienced great difficulty in preventing a Warwickshire win. The highlights of the early play were Barber's first Championship innings of the season, in which he displayed a tantalizing glimpse of his attacking abilities, on an abbreviated first day, and Parfitt's resolute effort on the second, which proved the basis of a successful bid for the lead by Middlesex, to which Titmus finally steered them with a bold innings that contained ten 4's.

Warwickshire

First innings		Second innings	
R. W. Barber c Hooker b Stewart	19	c Russell b Herman	26
R. M. Abberley c and b Hooker	29	c Latchman b Bick	43
D. L. Amiss b Hooker	66	lbw b Titmus	3
*M. J. K. Smith c Russell b Titmus	44	c Radley b Bick	21
J. A. Jameson c Murray b Stewart	26	c Parfitt b Hooker	41
†A. C. Smith b Herman	2	c Bick b Hooker	16
R. Miller st Murray b Hooker	1	b Hooker	8
J. M. Allan not out	15	b Latchman	2
R. V. Webster b Latchman	16	not out	15
J. D. Bannister c Parfitt b Latchman	4	not out	4
D. J. Brown not out	16		
B 8, l-b 3, w 1	12	B 7, l-b 8	15
1/22 2/69 3/152 4/190 5/191 6/191 7/199 8/226 9/232 (9 wkts. dec.)	250	1/44 2/54 3/93 4/117 5/163 6/168 7/171 8/189 (8 wkts. dec.)	194

Bowling: *First Innings*—Herman 16—2—47—1; Stewart 20—9—45—2; Hooker 21.5—9—48—3; Titmus 18—3—48—1; Bick 7—1—17—0; Latchman 7—1—33—2. *Second Innings*—Herman 9—2—30—1; Stewart 12—2—27—0; Hooker 14—4—33—3; Titmus 18—5—43—1; Bick 14—2—42—2; Latchman 1—0—4—1.

Middlesex

First innings		Second innings	
W. E. Russell lbw b Webster	5	b Webster	9
C. T. Radley c Jameson b Webster	14	c A. C. Smith b Webster	40
P. H. Parfitt c Barber b Bannister	85	c A. C. Smith b Webster	32
E. A. Clark c A. C. Smith b Webster	0	b Webster	20
†J. T. Murray c Barber b Miller	33	b Webster	0
*F. J. Titmus not out	81	c Bannister b Allan	16
R. W. Hooker c M. J. K. Smith b Brown	29	run out	29
D. A. Bick not out	0	not out	18
H. C. Latchman (did not bat)	—	lbw b Miller	0
R. W. Stewart (did not bat)	—	c Jameson b Brown	2
R. S. Herman (did not bat)	—	not out	0
B 1, l-b 2, n-b 1	4	B 2, l-b 4, n-b 1	7
1/11 2/24 3/24 4/104 5/163 6/247 (6 wkts. dec.)	251	1/11 2/61 3/98 4/98 5/112 6/136 7/162 8/169 9/173 (9 wkts.)	173

Bowling: *First Innings*—Brown 14—3—29—1; Webster 15.4—4—36—3; Bannister 15—6—22—1; Miller 16—3—58—1; Allan 14—3—43—0; Jameson 12—2—46—0; Amiss 3—1—13—0. *Second Innings*—Brown 7—2—33—1; Webster 13—2—46—5; Bannister 5—1—8—0; Barber 14—3—51—0; Allan 4—0—26—1; Miller 1—0—2—1.

Umpires: J. Arnold and W. H. Copson.

MIDDLESEX v. LEICESTERSHIRE

At Lord's, May 25, 26, 27. *65 overs.* Drawn. The loss of the first day proved an insurmountable obstacle to a definite result. The Leicestershire first innings came to life only during the final few overs. Most of their batsmen seemed out of form. Booth, whose 51 occupied two and three-quarter hours and included only two 4's, in particular was unable to keep the score moving. Despite defensive bowling and field-placing, Middlesex achieved the lead with eight overs left. Parfitt turned the scales for them, hitting 61 out of 96 in an hour. Leicestershire again batted without aggressive intent, taking four hours and 91 overs to make 189 for five on the last day, although Middlesex rested their two main bowlers, Titmus and Hooker. Set to score 188 in an hour and fifty-five minutes to win, Middlesex never attempted the task.

Leicestershire

First innings		Second innings	
M. R. Hallam st Murray b Hooker	35	c Titmus b Radley	61
B. J. Booth c Stewart b Hooker	51	c Parfitt b Stewart	0
P. Marner c Radley b Ling	3	st Murray b Bick	13
M. E. Norman b Hooker	10	c Latchman b Bick	82
C. C. Inman b Hooker	0	c Stewart b Bick	1
G. Cross not out	34	not out	4
*G. A. R. Lock st Murray b Hooker	17		
J. Birkenshaw c Russell b Hooker	4	not out	18
†R. W. Tolchard not out	1		
B 4, l-b 5, w 1	10	B 6, l-b 4	10
1/49 2/52 3/81 4/85 5/128 6/152 7/162 (7 wkts., 65 overs)	165	1/1 2/120 3/140 4/141 5/180 (5 wkts. dec.)	189

C. T. Spencer and J. S. Savage did not bat.

Bowling: *First Innings*—Stewart 12—6—23—0; Ling 11—2—40—1; Hooker 27—5—55—6; Titmus 14—4—37—0; Latchman 1—1—0—0. *Second Innings*—Stewart 12—2—20—1; Ling 12—3—20—0; Hooker 3—0—7—0; Latchman 24—6—58—0; Bick 23—6—44—3; Parfitt 9—1—20—0; Radley 5—3—7—1; Clark 3—1—3—0.

Middlesex

First innings		Second innings	
W. E. Russell c and b Lock	22	not out	41
C. T. Radley run out	16	c Birkenshaw b Spencer	7
P. H. Parfitt c Lock b Cross	61	not out	20
E. A. Clark c Lock b Marner	29		
†J. T. Murray not out	26		
*F. J. Titmus not out	8		
L-b 4 w 1	5		
1/36 2/44 3/132 4/132 (4 wkts. dec.)	167	1/27 (1 wkt.)	68

R. W. Hooker, D. A. Bick, D. J. Ling, H. C. Latchman and R. W. Stewart did not bat.

Bowling: *First Innings*—Spencer 9—2—32—0; Marner 28—5—72—1; Lock 14—4—36—1; Cross 6—2—22—1. *Second Innings*—Spencer 7—2—21—1; Cross 6—2—15—0; Savage 8—3—15—0; Birkenshaw 7—4—17—0.

Umpires: H. Mellows and J. S. Buller.

MIDDLESEX v. SUSSEX

(J. T. Murray's Benefit)

At Lord's, May 28, 30, 31. *65 overs.* Middlesex won by seven wickets, their first Championship victory always seeming probable after two incisive spells of bowling had dislocated the Sussex first innings. First Hooker dismissed the illustrious trio of Dexter, Parks and the Nawab of Pataudi, all without scoring within the space of five balls. Then Price, in his first Championship match since July 1965, swept aside Cooper, Oakman, and Buss in four balls, the intervening delivery being a no-ball. Middlesex paced their reply superbly. Parfitt and Clark built on the solid foundations laid by Russell and Radley, adding 110 in well under an hour. Altogether Middlesex, on the second morning, scored 130 runs in seventy minutes off 21 overs, establishing a lead of 123. The Sussex fight-back was centred round Lenham and Dexter, whose second-wicket partnership produced 112 runs, but nobody else could stay long enough to make Middlesex hurry over the 168 they needed to win.

Sussex

K. G. Suttle b Stewart	23	— lbw b Stewart	14
L. J. Lenham b Price	18	— b Price	52
E. R. Dexter b Hooker	0	— b Price	63
†J. M. Parks c Titmus b Hooker	0	— c Latchman b Titmus	16
*Nawab of Pataudi c Clark b Hooker	0	— b Titmus	32
G. C. Cooper c Clark b Price	18	— c Clark b Latchman	12
M. G. Griffith not out	52	— c Radley b Price	10
A. S. M. Oakman lbw b Price	2	— not out	42
A. Buss b Price	0	— c Murray b Stewart	7
J. A. Snow b Latchman	9	— c Parfitt b Bick	6
D. L. Bates not out	9	— c Radley b Titmus	3
B 4, l-b 4, n-b 4	12	B 6, l-b 21, n-b 6	33
1/39 2/42 3/42 4/46 5/48 6/71 7/73 8/74 9/112 (9 wkts., 65 overs)	143	1/30 2/142 3/147 4/166 5/207 6/213 7/225 8/238 9/276	290

Bowling: *First Innings*—Price 15—2—41—4; Stewart 12—6—18—1; Hooker 20—8—38—3; Titmus 14—6—26—0; Latchman 4—2—8—1. *Second Innings*—Price 21—3—49—3; Stewart 28—11—29—2; Titmus 40.2—13—67—3; Hooker 13—7—25—0; Latchman 26—10—61—1; Bick 9—5—26—1.

Middlesex

W. E. Russell b Oakman	62	— c A. Buss b Bates	61
C. T. Radley lbw b Snow	75	— lbw b Snow	1
P. H. Parfitt run out	78	— b Oakman	33
E. A. Clark not out	38	— not out	63
†J. T. Murray not out	6	— not out	10
L-b 6, n-b 1	7	B 2, n-b 1	3
1/114 2/150 3/260 (3 wkts., 65 overs)	266	1/5 2/52 3/141 (3 wkts.)	171

*F. J. Titmus, R. W. Hooker, D. A. Bick, J. S. E. Price, H. C. Latchman and R. W. Stewart did not bat.

Bowling: *First Innings*—Snow 26—3—113—1; Buss 20—2—83—0; Suttle 2—0—5—0; Bates 8—1—34—0; Oakman 9—0—24—1. *Second Innings*—Snow 9—3—9—1; A. Buss 8—1—21—0; Oakman 15—2—59—1; Suttle 17—7—39—0; Bates 7—2—17—1; Cooper 5—2—15—0; Dexter 0.3—0—8—0.

Umpires: H. Mellows and W. E. Phillipson.

At Oxford, June 1, 2. MIDDLESEX beat OXFORD UNIVERSITY by an innings and 11 runs.

MIDDLESEX *v.* YORKSHIRE

At Lord's, June 4, 6, 7. *65 overs.* Drawn, an almost inevitable result in view of the slow scoring by both sides. Pace bowlers held sway on the first day, Trueman and Nicholson limiting Middlesex to 190 off their full quota of overs. That Middlesex achieved so much was due to a spirited sixth-wicket partnership between Smith and Hooker which produced 56 runs. Yorkshire compiled only 70 from 32 overs on the first evening, and their later attempts to hurry met with no success, though they used up all but three balls of their 65 overs. With a lead of 15, Middlesex allowed themselves to be confined, Illingworth at one point on the second evening bowling ten consecutive maidens. The efforts of Clark, Murray and Hooker to break the deadlock foundered, and Parfitt decided upon mere survival. As the danger of a Middlesex defeat receded on the last morning, he scored with more freedom, reaching 114 after five hours, twenty-five minutes. Yorkshire set 250 in three and a half hours, again shuffled their batting order, and though Padgett displayed some superb strokes, they never kept pace with the clock.

Middlesex

C. T. Radley c Binks b Trueman	4	— lbw b Trueman	1
M. J. Harris c Binks b Waring	15	— c Binks b Illingworth	27
P. H. Parfitt c Wilson b Trueman	43	— not out	114
E. A. Clark c Binks b Waring	9	— c Waring b Wilson	5
*†J. T. Murray c Taylor b Nicholson	26	— c Nicholson b Illingworth	16
M. J. Smith b Nicholson	30	— run out	41
R. W. Hooker b Trueman	33	— c Waring b Close	4
D. A. Bick c Waring b Trueman	17	— lbw b Nicholson	1
H. C. Latchman b Nicholson	3	— not out	14
J. S. E. Price run out	0		
R. W. Stewart not out	0		
B 1, w 2, n-b 7	10	L-b 7, n-b 4	11
1/11 2/39 3/61 4/89 5/106 6/162 7/181 8/186 9/190	190	1/2 2/55 3/66 4/90 5/100 6/192 7/193 (7 wkts. dec.)	234

Bowling: *First Innings*—Trueman 20—3—70—4; Nicholson 29—9—60—3; Waring 13—0—37—2; Close 3—0—13—0. *Second Innings*—Trueman 20—3—49—1; Nicholson 19—8—41—1; Waring 10—3—25—0; Wilson 18—6—40—1; Illingworth 23—15—22—2; Close 17—1—46—1.

Yorkshire

G. Boycott c Parfitt b Stewart	56	— c Hooker b Price	35
K. Taylor c Murray b Price	1	— c Parfitt b Latchman	20
D. E. V. Padgett lbw b Hooker	23	— not out	70
*D. B. Close b Hooker	24	— c Radley b Bick	6
F. S. Trueman c Harris b Stewart	1	— c Clark b Bick	2
D. Wilson c Murray b Hooker	14	— b Latchman	1
P. J. Sharpe c sub b Stewart	8	— c Clark b Parfitt	26
R. Illingworth c Stewart b Price	1	— not out	21
†J. G. Binks not out	11		
J. Waring c Bick b Stewart	26		
A. G. Nicholson b Price	0		
B 4, l-b 4, n-b 2	10	B 8, l-b 2, n-b 4	14
1/8 2/57 3/103 4/114 5/114 6/129 7/138 8/138 9/175	175	1/42 2/81 3/92 4/95 5/98 6/149 (6 wkts.)	195

Bowling: *First Innings*—Price 20.3—4—47—3; Stewart 22—3—64—4; Hooker 21—3—52—3; Latchman 1—0—2—0. *Second Innings*—Price 10—5—22—1; Latchman 27—4—106—2; Bick 17—5—37—2; Parfitt 6—1—12—1; Stewart 3—2—4—0.

Umpires: H. Yarnold and T. W. Spencer.

MIDDLESEX v. SOMERSET

At Lord's, June 8, 9, 10. *65 overs.* Middlesex won by six wickets. The Somerset first innings proved typical of limited-over cricket. 35 runs came in the first hour, 72 in the second, and every run was squeezed out of the remaining time. Middlesex partially recovered from losing two wickets in their first over to Rumsey, but when Hooker retired early on the second morning after he was struck in the face when hooking at a ball from Rumsey, the innings wilted. Somerset could not consolidate their lead of 37. Wickets fell regularly and cheaply to Price, Bick and Latchman, and Middlesex began their quest for 222 runs with well over a day of the match remaining. They barely attempted to score in the hour and a half of the second evening, but on the last morning Clark, although giving three chances, initiated and maintained an aggressive attitude. With Parfitt he added 115 in two hours, five minutes, and he remained not out just short of a century, having hit five 6's, all off Langford, and seven 4's.

Somerset

G. Atkinson c Murray b Hooker	52	— b Latchman	13
R. Virgin c Russell b Titmus	9	— c Parfitt b Latchman	20
M. Kitchen c Parfitt b Price	38	— c Murray b Price	27
W. E. Alley c Bick b Hooker	2	— lbw b Price	4
T. E. Barwell c Murray b Titmus	0	— c Parfitt b Price	42
*C. R. M. Atkinson not out	36	— not out	35
K. E. Palmer c Parfitt b Titmus	16	— lbw b Bick	6
†G. Clayton b Titmus	1	— b Bick	1
P. J. Robinson not out	11	— lbw b Bick	11
B. A. Langford (did not bat)		— b Price	2
F. E. Rumsey (did not bat)		— b Titmus	0
B 10 l-b 8, n-b 2	20	B 20, l-b 3	23
1/35 2/107 3/110 (7 wkts., 65 overs) 4/114 5/118 6/160 7/162	185	1/32 2/39 3/96 4/104 5/123 6/132 7/142 8/175 9/177	184

Bowling: *First Innings*—Price 15—1—44—1; Hooker 20—6—50—2; Titmus 23—6—48—4; Bick 7—2—23—0. *Second Innings*—Price 15—3—30—4; Titmus 21.3—6—41—1; Latchman 19—6—54—2; Bick 16—8—36—3.

Middlesex

W. E. Russell lbw b Rumsey	21	— b Robinson	22
C. T. Radley b Rumsey	0	— c Virgin b Rumsey	11
P. H. Parfitt c Virgin b Rumsey	0	— c Clayton b Langford	54
E. A. Clark b Alley	37	— not out	95
†J. T. Murray c and b Alley	37	— c Alley b Robinson	8
*F. J. Titmus c Robinson b Palmer	15	— not out	13
M. J. Smith b Rumsey	12		
R. W. Hooker retired hurt	10		
D. A. Bick c Clayton b Rumsey	2		
H. C. Latchman c Langford b Alley	2		
J. S. E. Price not out	1		
B 8, l-b 3	11	B 10, l-b 4, n-b 5	19
1/1 2/2 3/52 4/73 5/112 6/120 7/143 8/146 9/148	148	1/36 2/43 3/158 4/173 (4 wkts.)	222

Bowling: *First Innings*—Rumsey 17—4—29—5; Palmer 9—1—27—1; Alley 14.5—4—34—3; Langford 12—1—47—0. *Second Innings*—Rumsey 19—7—38—1; Palmer 8—1—14—0; Robinson 32—13—73—2; Langford 32.2—13—70—1; Alley 3—0—8—0.

Umpires: T. W. Spencer and A. E. Alderman.

At Worcester, June 11, 13, 14. MIDDLESEX drew with WORCESTERSHIRE.

At Leicester, June 15, 16, 17. MIDDLESEX drew with LEICESTERSHIRE.

At Nottingham, June 18, 20, 21. MIDDLESEX drew with NOTTINGHAMSHIRE.

MIDDLESEX v. NORTHAMPTONSHIRE

At Lord's, June 25, 27, 28. *65 overs.* Middlesex won by nine wickets. Only a defiant innings by their opening batsman, Prideaux, saved Northamptonshire in their first innings. He was seventh out, having made his 80, which contained seven 4's, out of 156 in three and a quarter hours. Brisk hitting by Parfitt, Clark and Titmus took Middlesex into the lead after their innings had begun uncertainly, and an immediate declaration brought reward. Unfortunately for Northamptonshire Prideaux could not repeat his effort, and, with the rest of the batting capitulating again, Middlesex were faced with a simple task, though they batted laboriously to their target in 43 overs.

Northamptonshire

C. Milburn b Price	13	— c Clifton b Stewart	39
R. M. Prideaux b Stewart	80	— b Price	3
Mushtaq Mohammad lbw b Hooker	1	— lbw b Hooker	0
B. L. Reynolds lbw b Price	6	— c Harris b Hooker	13
D. S. Steele lbw b Hooker	5	— b Hooker	0
P. J. Watts c Clifton b Price	34	— c Clifton b Price	5
B. Crump b Price	1	— lbw b Titmus	11
M. E. Scott not out	20	— lbw b Price	0
H. Sully b Hooker	2	— lbw b Latchman	6
*†K. V. Andrew not out	12	— not out	4
R. Bailey (did not bat)		— c Russell b Price	0
B 3, l-b 4, n-b 2	9	B 1, l-b 4, n-b 2	7
1/18 2/19 3/34 (8 wkts., 65 overs) 4/45 5/109 6/117 7/156 8/169	183	1/11 2/45 3/45 4/47 5/64 6/64 7/65 8/78 9/88	88

Bowling: *First Innings*—Price 20—2—53—4; Stewart 16—4—38—1; Hooker 25—5—69—3; Titmus 4—1—14—0. *Second Innings*—Price 16.5—3—44—4; Hooker 21—13—18—3; Stewart 9—1—13—1; Latchman 5—3—4—1; Titmus 1—0—2—1.

Middlesex

W. E. Russell b Crump	11	— b Sully	29
M. J. Harris b Crump	24	— not out	43
P. H. Parfitt c Andrew b Crump	36	— not out	11
E. A. Clark c Scott b Crump	57		
*F. J. Titmus c Watts b Bailey	29		
M. J. Smith c Prideaux b Bailey	1		
R. W. Hooker not out	16		
H. C. Latchman lbw b Bailey	0		
L-b 9, n-b 1	10	B 1, l-b 2, n-b 2	5
1/20 2/68 3/75 4/144 5/148 6/181 7/184 (7 wkts. dec.)	184	1/64 (1 wkt.)	88

†E. G. Clifton, J. S. E. Price and R. W. Stewart did not bat.

Bowling: *First Innings*—Crump 32—9—78—4; Bailey 20.3—0—68—3; Watts 11—3—28—0. *Second Innings*—Crump 6—3—11—0; Bailey 3—0—3—0; Mushtaq 12—2—23—0; Scott 15.1—5—30—0; Sully 7—2—16—1.

Umpires: P. B. Wight and W. E. Phillipson.

At Cardiff, July 2, 4, 5. MIDDLESEX drew with GLAMORGAN.

At Lord's, July 6, 7, 8. MIDDLESEX drew with WEST INDIES. (See WEST INDIES section.)

At The Oval, July 9, 11, 12. MIDDLESEX lost to SURREY by 105 runs.

MIDDLESEX v. DERBYSHIRE

At Lord's, July 13, 14, 15. Drawn. The Middlesex opening batsmen, Russell and Harris, dominated the first day. Both hit centuries, the first time such a feat had been achieved for Middlesex since Russell and R. A. Gale scored 120 and 106 respectively against Kent at Gravesend in 1960. It was Harris's maiden hundred, as, coincidentally, was it Russell's on the former occasion. Both centuries were restrained innings, Russell's occupying three and a half hours, and Harris taking four hours. Magnificent fast bowling by Price provided the feature of the second day. His straight, full-length deliveries brought him 8 for 48, by far the best of his career, of which five were bowled. Derbyshire's last pair saved the follow-on and Middlesex did their best to increase their advantage, eventually setting Derbyshire 286 in just under five hours. Then the batsmen were frustrated by two interruptions for rain, and Middlesex by Price's failure to emulate his first-innings hostility.

Middlesex

W. E. Russell c Taylor b Jackson	101	— b Jackson	3
M. J. Harris b Buxton	114	— c Page b Smith	23
P. H. Parfitt lbw b Smith	0	— c and b Morgan	19
E. A. Clark c Johnson b Jackson	35	— b Morgan	24
C. T. Radley not out	14	— not out	33
*F. J. Titmus c Taylor b Buxton	21	— b Morgan	21
D. A. Bick not out	1	— c Gibbs b Smith	1
H. C. Latchman (did not bat)		— b Morgan	4
†E. G. Clifton (did not bat)		— c Page b Smith	2
B 1, l-b 5, n-b 3	9	— B 11, l-b 1, n-b 2	14
1/195 2/195 3/242 4/268 5/293 (5 wkts. dec.)	295	1/6 2/36 3/64 4/82 5/122 6/129 7/135 8/144 (8 wkts. dec.)	144

J. S. E. Price and R. S. Herman did not bat.

Bowling: *First Innings*—Jackson 25—5—51—2; Rhodes 17—2—62—0; Buxton 15.4—3—55—2; Morgan 27—10—48—0; Smith 20—2—70—1. *Second Innings*—Jackson 10—1—27—1; Buxton 2—0—3—0; Morgan 24—9—30—4; Smith 26—4—70—3.

Derbyshire

I. W. Hall b Price	14	— c Clifton b Titmus	42
P. J. K. Gibbs b Price	2	— c Parfitt b Price	8
†R. W. Taylor b Price	21		
M. H. Page b Titmus	38	— c Parfitt b Titmus	42
H. L. Johnson c Latchman b Price	1	— c Radley b Titmus	39
J. F. Harvey c Parfitt b Price	44	— run out	17
I. R. Buxton b Price	3	— not out	9
*D. C. Morgan b Price	1	— not out	5
E. Smith c Clifton b Price	2		
H. J. Rhodes not out	13		
A. B. Jackson b Titmus	8		
B 2, l-b 2, w 1, n-b 2	7	B 14, l-b 5, n-b 5	24
1/5 2/37 3/42 4/44 5/126 6/126 7/128 8/131 9/132	154	1/23 2/100 3/101 4/149 5/168 (5 wkts.)	186

Bowling: *First Innings*—Price 26—9—48—8; Herman 12—5—27—0; Titmus 26.5—10—40—2; Latchman 6—1—11—0; Bick 8—2—21—0. *Second Innings*—Price 21—5—42—1; Herman 5—0—11—0; Titmus 33—13—70—3; Latchman 5—1—8—0; Bick 13—5—26—0; Parfitt 3—2—5—0.

Umpires: R. Aspinall and W. F. Simpson.

MIDDLESEX v. ESSEX

At Lord's, July 16, 18, 19. Drawn, rain allowing less than half an hour's play on the last day. The pitch gave assistance to the spin bowlers all through, and Titmus confined Essex to such an extent that their total of 138 came only after four hours and ten minutes' toil. Middlesex fared little better on the second day when the crowd were treated to a sight too seldom seen in modern cricket, a superb exhibition of leg-break bowling. Hobbs, spinning the ball down the hill in a long spell, caused difficulty to all the batsmen who faced him and fully deserved the last six wickets. Middlesex finally struggled to a lead of 15. Essex, losing their first six for 55, seemed in trouble, but Saville shared fruitful partnerships with Edmeades and Hobbs which might have worried Middlesex had not the rain interfered.

Essex

First Innings		Second Innings	
*G. E. Barker b Titmus	9	b Stewart	5
M. J. Bear lbw b Price	27	st Clifton b Titmus	30
†B. Taylor b Titmus	0	c Smith b Price	1
K. W. R. Fletcher c Russell b Stewart	8	b Price	5
B. R. Knight b Price	13	c Clifton b Stewart	3
G. R. Cass c Parfitt b Stewart	18	b Bick	7
G. J. Saville lbw b Titmus	2	not out	19
B. Edmeades b Titmus	33	c Smith b Titmus	28
R. N. S. Hobbs b Stewart	6	not out	22
A. M. Jorden not out	12		
D. L. Acfield lbw b Bick	3		
B 4, l-b 3	7	L-b 6, n-b 4	10
1/21 2/21 3/44 4/52 5/75 6/81 7/85 8/98 9/123	138	1/7 2/8 3/18 4/27 5/55 6/55 7/93 (7 wkts.)	130

Bowling: *First Innings*—Price 24—5—52—2; Stewart 22—10—25—3; Titmus 30—13—49—4; Bick 5.4—1—5—1. *Second Innings*—Price 16—5—29—2; Stewart 20.4—8—32—2; Titmus 22—13—44—2; Bick 9—4—15—1.

Middlesex

M. J. Smith lbw b Knight	20
M. J. Harris b Jorden	1
P. H. Parfitt c Taylor b Jorden	33
D. A. Bick c Taylor b Knight	20
W. E. Russell c Fletcher b Hobbs	8
E. A. Clark c Barker b Hobbs	16
C. T. Radley st Taylor b Hobbs	27
*F. J. Titmus b Hobbs	19
†E. G. Clifton not out	2
R. W. Stewart c Fletcher b Hobbs	0
J. S. E. Price b Hobbs	5
B 1, l-b 1	2
1/1 2/46 3/65 4/83 5/83 6/110 7/138 8/147 9/147	153

Bowling: Jorden 16—5—39—2; Knight 18—6—29—2; Edmeades 19—6—40—0; Hobbs 22.3—8—31—6; Acfield 7—2—12—0.

Umpires: W. F. Simpson and F. Jakeman.

At Belfast, July 20, 21. MIDDLESEX beat IRELAND by an innings and 21 runs.

At Sheffield, July 23, 25, 26. MIDDLESEX lost to YORKSHIRE by 120 runs.

At Weston-super-Mare, July 27, 28. MIDDLESEX beat SOMERSET by 164 runs.

At Northampton, July 30, August 1, 2. MIDDLESEX beat NORTHAMPTONSHIRE by six wickets.

At Manchester, August 3, 4, 5. MIDDLESEX drew with LANCASHIRE.

MIDDLESEX v. SURREY

At Lord's, August 6, 8, 9. Drawn, rain claiming the best part of the first and last afternoons. For Surrey, Edrich and Edwards achieved their sixth opening partnership of over 100 in the eleven matches since their association began. Stewart's confident declaration was fully justified when Pocock, maintaining an immaculate length and spinning the ball sharply, broke the back of the Middlesex batting, the innings occupying only two hours, ten minutes. Surrey also found themselves in trouble on the last morning against hostile seam bowling, but a patient 62 by Smith in two and three-quarter hours enabled Stewart to declare again, setting Middlesex 229 to win in three and a half hours. With the game poised, three long interruptions for rain prevented a serious attempt being made to get the runs.

Surrey

J. H. Edrich c Murray b Bick	60	— st Murray b Bick	9
M. J. Edwards c Murray b Stewart	72	— lbw b Price	0
W. A. Smith c Latchman b Stewart	8	— b Hooker	62
K. F. Barrington c Hooker b Stewart	0	— c Stewart b Hooker	20
*M. J. Stewart not out	15	— lbw b Price	0
S. J. Storey b Price	0	— b Hooker	8
R. I. Jefferson not out	36	— c Clark b Stewart	1
†A. Long (did not bat)		— b Hooker	0
P. I. Pocock (did not bat)		— b Stewart	2
R. Harman (did not bat)		— not out	2
R. D. Jackman (did not bat)		— not out	9
B 3, l-b 4, n-b 2	9	B 8, l-b 1, n-b 1	10
1/116 2/140 3/140 4/151 5/152 (5 wkts.)	200	1/0 2/27 3/83 (9 wkts., dec.) 4/90 5/103 6/104 7/110 8/111 9/112	123

Bowling: *First Innings*—Price 20—5—34—1; Stewart 19—4—48—3; Hooker 25—4—75—0; Bick 17—6—34—1. *Second Innings*—Price 20—3—56—2; Stewart 14—7—24—2; Hooker 12—5—15—4; Bick 5—4—4—1; Latchman 10—4—14—0.

Middlesex

W. E. Russell b Pocock	10	— b Pocock	18
M. J. Harris b Jackman	3	— not out	16
P. H. Parfitt b Pocock	12	— not out	23
E. A. Clark c Stewart b Pocock	28		
*†J. T. Murray c Stewart b Storey	12		
M. J. Smith b Harman	11		
R. W. Hooker b Pocock	0		
D. A. Bick b Pocock	4		
H. C. Latchman lbw b Harman	10		
J. S. E. Price not out	0		
R. W. Stewart b Pocock	4		
L-b 1	1		
1/5 2/24 3/25 4/58 5/66 6/66 7/70 8/88 9/95	95	1/27 (1 wkt.)	57

Bowling: *First Innings*—Jefferson 4—2—11—0; Jackman 8—2—16—1; Pocock 17.2—5—43—6; Storey 11—5—20—1; Harman 3—2—4—2. *Second Innings*—Jefferson 9—2—16—0; Jackman 9—3—17—0; Pocock 3—1—14—1; Storey 3—0—9—0; Smith 1—0—1—0.

Umpires: A. E. Rhodes and O. W. Herman.

MIDDLESEX v. LANCASHIRE

At Lord's, August 13, 15, 16. Drawn. The game concluded in dramatic fashion. On the fall of their ninth wicket. Lancashire needed three runs to win, but, with ninety seconds remaining, the umpire, Fagg, took off the bails. Fagg said: "There was a minute and a half left by the Nursery clock, and under the two-minute rule—the time allowed for a batsman to come in—I decided the match was at an end when Statham was out. Had he played the ball (the last of an over from Price) I would have allowed another over." Thus both sides were denied the chance of a success they had done little to deserve. None of the recognised batsmen, except Pilling and Parfitt on the second day, showed any ability to dominate the bowlers on a good, firm pitch. Two tail-enders, Higgs and Statham, had no such inhibitions. They came together 24 behind the Middlesex first innings, and, driving magnificently, took Lancashire into a lead of 27. Tentative Middlesex batting on the last morning left Lancashire with four hours to obtain 167, but their course to the target was such a meandering one that they never got there. Not a moment was lost to the weather over the three days, but only 692 runs were compiled, at an overall rate of 38 an hour.

Middlesex

W. E. Russell c and b Higgs	28	— lbw b Worsley	47
M. J. Smith b Higgs	58	— b Lever	23
P. H. Parfitt b Lever	1	— c Goodwin b Lever	61
E. A. Clark c Goodwin b Lever	1	— not out	12
R. W. Hooker b Statham	2	— lbw b Lloyd	38
†J. T. Murray c Goodwin b Green	7	— b Worsley	2
*F. J. Titmus b Lever	0	— c Higgs b Lever	1
D. A. Bick b Green	3	— b Higgs	1
R. W. Stewart lbw b Higgs	4	— b Lloyd	0
H. C. Latchman run out	28	— lbw b Lever	2
J. S. E. Price not out	13	— b Higgs	0
B 1, l-b 5, n-b 3	9	B 4, l-b 1, n-b 1	6
1/46 2/47 3/53 4/69 5/76 6/84 7/93 8/112 9/118	154	1/39 2/104 3/108 4/148 5/150 6/151 7/154 8/193 9/193	193

Bowling: *First Innings*—Statham 12—2—24—1; Higgs 19.1—5—34—3; Lever 22—4—62—3; Green 16—5—21—2; Worsley 2—1—4—0. *Second Innings*—Statham 2—0—7—0; Higgs 19.2—6—32—2; Lever 13—3—33—4; Green 9—3—25—0; Worsley 26—10—63—2; Lloyd 12—4—27—2.

Lancashire

D. M. Green b Hooker	11	— b Titmus	13
H. Pilling b Bick	70	— c Murray b Price	14
J. D. Bond c Murray b Hooker	1	— c Murray b Latchman	21
D. R. Worsley b Titmus	1	— c Parfitt b Titmus	8
B. Wood c Russell b Price	8	— c Murray b Latchman	0
J. Sullivan lbw b Price	0	— c Russell b Price	48
D. Lloyd lbw b Titmus	5	— c sub b Latchman	23
P. Lever b Bick	17	— run out	11
K. Higgs not out	24	— not out	11
†K. Goodwin st Murray b Bick	4		
*J. B. Statham c Titmus b Stewart	31	— b Price	0
B 1, l-b 5, n-b 3	9	B 11, l-b 4	15
1/23 2/31 3/38 4/58 5/58 6/75 7/121 8/122 9/130	181	1/26 2/28 3/59 4/63 5/67 6/116 7/137 8/164 9/164 (9 wkts.)	164

Bowling: *First Innings*—Price 24—7—56—2; Stewart 14.4—4—20—1; Hooker 8—4—8—2; Titmus 26—12—48—2; Latchman 3—0—18—0; Bick 12—5—22—3. *Second Innings*—Price 24—8—37—3; Stewart 6—1—16—0; Titmus 31—10—48—2; Latchman 13—5—26—3; Bick 8—3—22—0.

Umpires: A. Jepson and A. E. Fagg.

At Bournemouth, August 17, 18, 19. MIDDLESEX lost to HAMPSHIRE by 80 runs.

At Cheltenham, August 20, 22, 23. MIDDLESEX beat GLOUCESTERSHIRE by nine wickets.

MIDDLESEX v. WORCESTERSHIRE

At Lord's, August 24, 25. Worcestershire won by an innings and 41 runs. On a pitch which required circumspection, but which seldom allowed the ball to do anything extravagant, Middlesex twice batted badly, seeming to have no heart for the long, applied innings which Graveney proved was necessary. Coldwell wrecked their first innings with a spell of four for 7 in 26 balls. Harris withstood this hostile period, hitting a solid 50 in two hours, ten minutes, but still the innings lasted under three hours. Most of the Worcestershire batsmen found difficulty in coping with Price and Stewart, but when Headley joined Graveney, Worcestershire moved to a lead on the first evening. They carried this to 104 in the morning, Graveney completing a patient but masterly 72. Middlesex then collapsed. Russell and Harris batted for an hour, putting on 38 without alarm, but in just over an hour from Russell's dismissal the innings was ended by high-class seam bowling from Flavell and d'Oliveira, Worcerstershire winning just after tea on the second day.

Middlesex

W. E. Russell lbw b Coldwell	16	— c Ormrod b d'Oliveira	14
M. J. Harris c Headley b Gifford	50	— b Flavell	27
P. H. Parfitt c Graveney b Coldwell	1	— b Flavell	3
E. A. Clark lbw b Coldwell	0	— c Headley b d'Oliveira	1
M. J. Smith b Coldwell	2	— b d'Oliveira	0
C. T. Radley c Booth b Flavell	19	— lbw b Flavell	2
*F. J. Titmus lbw b Gifford	7	— c Richardson b d'Oliveira	1
†E. G. Clifton not out	0	— c Kenyon b Flavell	0
D. A. Bick b Gifford	14	— not out	11
J. S. E. Price b Flavell	3	— c Richardson b Flavell	1
R. W. Stewart lbw b Flavell	0	— c Coldwell b d'Oliveira	0
L-b 3	3	L-b 3	3
1/33 2/37 3/37 4/45 5/87 6/93 7/99 8/112 9/115	115	1/38 2/46 3/47 4/47 5/47 6/50 7/50 8/50 9/60	63

Bowling: *First Innings*—Flavell 11.5—1—32—3; Coldwell 13—5—26—4; d'Oliveira 5—2—5—0; Gifford 18—2—40—3; Horton 4—0—9—0. *Second Innings*—Flavell 16—7—28—5; Coldwell 7—1—18—0; d'Oliveira 11.4—5—14—5.

Worcestershire

M. J. Horton c Parfitt b Stewart	3
*D. Kenyon b Stewart	33
J. A. Ormrod b Stewart	1
T. W. Graveney c Smith b Titmus	72
B. d'Oliveira lbw b Price	13
D. W. Richardson b Price	3
R. G. A. Headley c Titmus b Stewart	24
†R. Booth c Parfitt b Price	24
N. Gifford not out	20
L. J. Coldwell run out	0
J. A. Flavell c Clark b Titmus	8
B 3, l-b 3, n-b 12	18
1/26 2/29 3/47 4/71 5/81 6/160 7/182 8/193 9/196	219

Bowling: Price 28—4—83—3; Stewart 20—5—55—4; Titmus 32—13—44—2; Bick 10—5—19—0.

Umpires: J. Arnold and P. B. Wight.

At Hove, August 27, 29, 30. MIDDLESEX drew with SUSSEX.

MIDDLESEX v. HAMPSHIRE

At Lord's, August 31, September 1, 2. Match abandoned without a ball being bowled.

Middlesex

W. E. Russell, M. J. Harris, P. H. Parfitt, E. A. Clark, *†J. T. Murray, R. W. Hooker, M. Manasseh, D. Bennett, D. A. Bick, J. S. E. Price, R. W. Stewart.

Hampshire

***R. E. Marshall, B. L. Reed, H. Horton, D. A. Livingstone, K. J. Wheatley, R. M. C. Gilliat, †B. S. V. Timms, A. T. Castell, D. W. White, R. M. Cottam, D. Shackleton.**

Umpires: J. S. Buller and W. H. Copson.

THE ASHES

The Ashes were originated in 1882 when, on August 29th, Australia defeated the full strength of England on English soil for the first time. The Australians won by the narrow margin of seven runs, and the following day the *Sporting Times* printed a mock obituary notice, written by Shirley Brooks, son of an editor of *Punch*, which read:

"In affectionate remembrance of English Cricket which died at The Oval, 29th August, 1882. Deeply lamented by a large circle of sorrowing friends and acquaintances. R.I.P. N.B. The body will be cremated and the Ashes taken to Australia."

The following winter the Hon. Ivo Bligh, afterwards Lord Darnley, set out to Australia to recover these mythical Ashes. Australia won the first match by nine wickets, but England won the next two, and the real ashes came into being when some Melbourne women burnt a stump used in the third game and presented the ashes in an urn to Ivo Bligh.

When Lord Darnley died in 1927, the urn, by a bequest in his will, was given to M.C.C., and it held a place of honour in the Long Room at Lord's until 1953 when, with other cricket treasures, it was moved to the newly built Imperial Cricket Memorial near the pavilion. There it stands permanently, together with the velvet bag in which the urn was originally given to Lord Darnley and the score card of the 1882 match.

NORTHAMPTONSHIRE

President—G. A. T. VIALS

Secretary—K. C. TURNER, County Ground, Wantage Road, Northampton

Captain—K. V. ANDREW

R. M. Prideaux

County Badge

L. A. Johnson

Northamptonshire finished fifth, with 130 points and ten wins, a creditable performance. Yet after attaining third and second places in the two preceding seasons it was a considerable disappointment, especially to the captain Keith Andrew in his last season, not to secure the club's first-ever title. The reasons? The absence for much of the season through injuries of two bowlers, Larter, fast, and Scott, left-arm slow. This left the team under-equipped to exploit some pitches where their own batsmen struggled. Close catching, although still generally capable, and occasionally brilliant, fell below the previous season's high standard. The absence of Milburn through representative calls and injuries left the early batting more defensive and uncertain than when he was opening in aggressive style.

At their best the team looked worthy of Championship honours, notably when completing a double over the eventual Champions, Yorkshire, and beating the West Indies. Against that, defeats occurred from four counties finishing in the bottom five, stressing the greatest problem, inconsistency.

The individual successes were the opening batsmen, Milburn and Prideaux, and the off-spinner, Sully. Milburn enjoyed a memorable season. Twice he compiled his highest scores, 171 and 203. The first batsman to make 1,000 runs in the country, he also hit the season's fastest century, in 82 minutes at Trent Bridge, and most sixes, 31. He made five centuries for Northamptonshire and missed the chance of his first 2,000 through a broken finger.

Although overshadowed by his brilliant partner, Prideaux was equally valuable. Second to Milburn for the 1,000, Prideaux's determined play, wide range of strokes, and admirable concentration made him the bulwark of the batting. He hit six centuries, establishing a Northamptonshire record with three in successive innings. Steele and Reynolds played valuable innings, if not so consistent as in some years. Mushtaq fell below his Pakistan reputation, probably due to the trials of the two years' qualification and variable pitches, but in August he demonstrated his ability with better innings.

Sully claimed one hundred wickets in his first full season, being rewarded with his county cap. He promised to establish himself as a successful off-spinner. Mushtaq also displayed skill with his leg-breaks. Crump again proved a competent stock bowler and P. J. Watts and Steele gave capable support, while the twenty-one-year-old Durose raised considerable hopes with his pace bowling after being promoted in July.

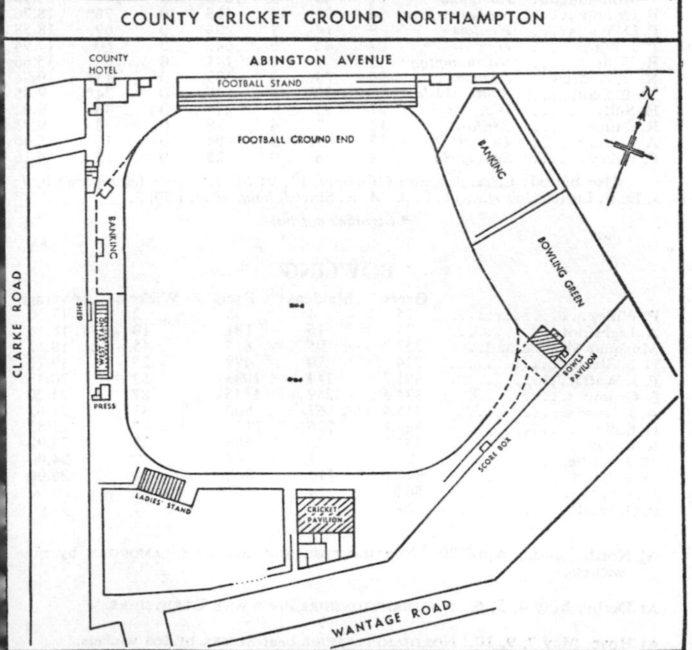

NORTHAMPTONSHIRE RESULTS

All First-Class Matches—Played 31, *Won* 12, *Lost* 9, *Drawn* 10

County Championship Matches—Played 28, *Won* 10, *Lost* 9, *Drawn* 9

COUNTY CHAMPIONSHIP AVERAGES

BATTING

	Birthplace	Mtchs.	Inns.	Not Outs	Runs	100's	Highest Inns.	Aver.
C. Milburn....	*Burnopfield*	17	33	3	1398	5	203	46.60
R. M. Prideaux.	*Chelsea*	26	51	5	1670	5	153*	36.30
D. S. Steele....	*Stoke-on-Trent*	27	43	5	1080	2	118*	28.42
B. L. Reynolds.	*Kettering*	28	52	4	1291	0	89	26.89
A. Lightfoot...	*Woore, Crewe*	12	22	5	435	0	58	25.58
Mushtaq Mohammad.	*Junagadh*	27	48	5	1028	2	117	23.90
B. Crump......	*Stoke-on-Trent*	28	39	9	563	0	76*	18.76
P. D. Watts....	*Henlow*	8	14	3	204	0	69	18.58
P. J. Watts.....	*Henlow*	27	42	6	646	0	60	17.94
R. Wills.......	*Northampton*	5	9	0	141	0	82	15.66
K. V. Andrew..	*Oldham*	26	28	9	189	0	18*	9.94
M. E. Scott....	*South Shields*	15	20	6	138	0	24*	9.85
H. Sully.......	*Watchet*	27	33	9	231	0	48	9.62
R. Bailey......	*Bedford*	10	7	4	28	0	8	9.33
A. J. Durose...	*Dukinfield*	13	15	5	64	0	16	6.40
P. Willey......	*Sedgefield*	4	6	0	25	0	12	4.16

Also batted: L. A. Johnson (*Horsley*), 1*, 0; M. J. Kettle (*Stamford*) 0, 7; J. D. F. Larter (*Inverness*) 6, 0; A. M. R. Sim (*Johannesburg*) 20, 2.

* *Signifies not out.*

BOWLING

	Overs	Maidens	Runs	Wickets	Average
P. Willey..............	15	4	35	2	17.50
A. Lightfoot...........	75	16	181	10	18.10
Mushtaq Mohammad....	337.2	95	815	45	18.11
D. S. Steele............	214	70	479	25	19.16
P. J. Watts.............	491.2	144	1083	53	20.43
B. Crump...............	874.5	257	1845	87	21.20
A. J. Durose...........	315.4	67	800	37	21.62
H. Sully...............	849.1	236	2118	97	21.83
R. Bailey..............	244.1	40	598	25	23.92
M. J. Kettle...........	21	4	48	2	24.00
M. E. Scott............	344.1	110	808	31	26.06
J. D. F. Larter.........	56.3	14	148	5	29.60
P. D. Watts............	24	5	78	2	39.00

At Northampton, April 30. NORTHAMPTONSHIRE lost to GLAMORGAN by nine wickets.

At Derby, May 4, 5, 6. NORTHAMPTONSHIRE drew with DERBYSHIRE.

At Hove, May 7, 9, 10. NORTHAMPTONSHIRE beat SUSSEX by ten wickets.

NORTHAMPTONSHIRE v. GLOUCESTERSHIRE

At Northampton, May 11, 12, 13. *65 overs.* Gloucestershire won by one wicket with one ball remaining. In a thrilling finish Gloucestershire lost two wickets in six balls before Meyer, needing three, played the fifth ball of the last over for a quick single. Mushtaq's throw missed the stumps by a fraction and the ball went past a fielder, enabling the batsmen to take the two further runs needed. On an under-prepared pitch, with rain restricting play on the first day to five overs and causing two more hold-ups on the second, wickets fell cheaply. Neither side reached their overs limit. Windows and Mortimore did the damage for Gloucestershire, while Crump took six for 14 in reply. Prideaux, Steele and Crump enabled Northamptonshire to declare their second innings, setting the visitors to score 133 in two hours forty minutes. Crump and Jim Watts bowled effectively but D. Brown and Shepherd, aided by two missed catches, sustained the innings for the exciting finish.

Northamptonshire

C. Milburn c Meyer b A. S. Brown	1	— c Allen b A. S. Brown	9
R. M. Prideaux b Windows	0	— c Milton b Allen	40
B. L. Reynolds c Allen b Windows	13	— c Nicholls b Allen	13
Mushtaq Mohammad c Meyer b A. S. Brown	3	— c Milton b Bissex	3
D. S. Steele b Windows	5	— c Meyer b Mortimore	24
P. J. Watts c A. S. Brown b Windows	5	— st Meyer b Bissex	0
P. D. Watts st Meyer b Mortimore	23	— lbw b Allen	9
B. Crump c A. S. Brown b Allen	12	— not out	22
H. Sully b Mortimore	0	— not out	4
J. D. F. Larter lbw b Mortimore	0		
*†K. V. Andrew not out	5		
B 4, l-b 1	5	L-b 2	2
1/0 2/14 3/14 4/19 5/25 6/27 7/58 8/61 9/61	72	1/16 2/62 3/65 4/65 5/71 6/82 7/118 (7 wkts., dec.)	126

Bowling: *First Innings*—A. S. Brown 12—4—23—2; Windows 14—8—23—4; Allen 8—3—16—1; Mortimore 5.1—2—5—3. *Second Innings*—A. S. Brown 11—4—25—1; Windows 7—0—10—0; Mortimore 16—5—33—1; Allen 21—6—44—3; Bissex 8—5—12—2.

Gloucestershire

R. B. Nicholls c Steele b Larter	0	— c Reynolds b Crump	13
C. A. Milton c Milburn b Crump	20	— lbw b P. J. Watts	7
S. E. Russell c P. J. Watts b Crump	14	— lbw b Crump	16
M. Bissex c Milburn b P. J. Watts	2	— c Reynolds b Crump	10
D. Brown c P. J. Watts b Crump	12	— b P. J. Watts	33
D. Shepherd c P. D. Watts b Crump	0	— b P. J. Watts	30
*J. B. Mortimore c Steele b Sully	0	— b Crump	4
A. S. Brown c Andrew b Crump	3	— c and b P. J. Watts	5
D. A. Allen c Larter b Sully	8	— not out	6
A. R. Windows lbw b Crump	3	— c Reynolds b Crump	0
†B. J. Meyer not out	0	— not out	3
L-b 1, n-b 3	4	L-b 2, w 1, n-b 3	6
1/0 2/26 3/28 4/50 5/51 6/51 7/51 8/56 9/66	66	1/17 2/21 3/40 4/49 5/92 6/99 7/108 8/129 9/130 (9 wkts.)	133

Bowling: *First Innings*—Larter 8—2—16—1; Crump 17—10—14—6; P. J. Watts 10—3—25—1; Sully 6.2—1—7—2. *Second Innings*—Larter 7—2—16—0; Crump 21.5—9—44—5; P. J. Watts 19—6—44—4; Sully 4—0—18—0; Steele 1—0—5—0.

Umpires: J. Langridge and A. E. Alderman.

NORTHAMPTONSHIRE v. LANCASHIRE

At Northampton, May 14, 16, 17. Northamptonshire won by seven wickets. The Northampton wicket was again difficult owing to under-preparation during April's bad weather and batsmen found run-getting much harder than normal on this ground. Green, missed three times, and Pullar began with a stand of 64. Pullar batted three hours five minutes, scoring 64, with eight 4's, and giving no chance. Afterwards Northamptonshire's varied attack took control. Northamptonshire fell 10 short despite an innings of nearly four hours for 69 by Peter Watts, sent in as night-watchman on Saturday. After Green had hit brilliantly for 76, with thirteen 4's, Lancashire collapsed against the left-arm slow bowler, Steele, who gained a career-best of eight for 29. Statham soon dismissed Northamptonshire's opening pair but Mushtaq and Reynolds ensured a home victory in a brisk third-wicket stand of 109. Mushtaq produced some splendid strokes.

Lancashire

D. M. Green c Andrew b Sully	38	c Andrew b Steele	76
G. Pullar c Reynolds b Scott	64	c Reynolds b Steele	16
H. Pilling c Sully b Mushtaq	10	c Steele b Sully	5
J. Sullivan st Andrew b Mushtaq	2	c Scott b Steele	1
R. Entwistle c Steele b Sully	3	c Andrew b Steele	0
G. K. Knox c Andrew b Sully	12	c P. D. Watts b Steele	10
D. Lloyd c P. D. Watts b P. J. Watts	15	c P. D. Watts b Steele	0
P. Lever b P. J. Watts	28	c Andrew b Steele	9
†K. Goodwin b Crump	3	not out	4
T. Greenhough not out	15	c Andrew b Sully	3
*J. B. Statham b Crump	6	b Steele	1
B 4, w 1	5		
1/64 2/84 3/86 4/99 5/125 6/129 7/173 8/176 9/180	201	1/67 2/78 3/79 4/87 5/103 6/103 7/116 8/117 9/124	125

Bowling: *First Innings*—Crump 12.5—5—35—2; P. J. Watts 12—5—22—2; Sully 37—15—67—3; Scott 31—12—50—1; Steele 3—1—5—0; Mushtaq 9—1—17—2. *Second Innings*—Crump 4—0—13—0; P. J. Watts 3—1—8—0; Sully 28—10—47—2; Scott 11—4—24—0; Steele 23.1—10—29—8; Mushtaq 3—1—4—0.

Northamptonshire

R. M. Prideaux lbw b Statham	10	b Statham	2
R. Wills c Goodwin b Statham	22	c Goodwin b Statham	0
B. L. Reynolds run out	14	not out	56
P. D. Watts run out	69	not out	9
Mushtaq Mohammad c Knox b Green	19	c Pilling b Knox	64
D. S. Steele lbw b Greenhough	0		
P. J. Watts c Sullivan b Statham	32		
B. Crump c Lloyd b Statham	0		
M. E. Scott b Lever	2		
H. Sully lbw b Greenhough	9		
*†K. V. Andrew not out	7		
B 5, l-b 2	7	B 4, l-b 1	5
1/18 2/50 3/68 4/99 5/102 6/162 7/162 8/167 9/181	191	1/1 2/4 3/113 (3 wkts.)	136

Bowling: *First Innings*—Statham 28—8—45—4; Lever 33—9—68—1; Greenhough 29.2—14—40—2; Lloyd 8—3—13—0; Green 16—8—18—1. *Second Innings*—Statham 5—1—8—2; Lever 5—2—6—0; Lloyd 8—2—23—0; Greenhough 16—4—44—0; Green 7—1—36—0; Knox 3—1—10—1; Pullar 0.1—0—4—0.

Umpires: J. S. Buller and O. W. Herman.

NORTHAMPTONSHIRE v. DERBYSHIRE

At Northampton, May 18, 19, 20. Derbyshire won by 22 runs. This low-scoring game, badly interfered with by rain on the second day, was a triumph for Morgan, the Derbyshire captain, whose match figures were eleven for 60. He always caused problems for Northamptonshire. Rhodes, persistently hostile, and Smith gave excellent support. Although Taylor hit a bold 40 for Derbyshire, Northamptonshire gained a one run first-innings lead when Sully drove Morgan for 6. A second-wicket stand of 56 by Harvey and Johnson proved the turning point, for although Sully and Jim Watts routed the later batsmen, Derbyshire set Northamptonshire a final target of 123. This proved too severe on a badly worn pitch. Although struck some nasty blows on the hand Prideaux hit bravely for 47, with three 6's off Smith. Afterwards only Steele, in one hour, fifty minutes' defiance, reached double figures.

Derbyshire

First Innings		Second Innings	
J. F. Harvey c Steele b P. J. Watts	0	c Andrew b P. J. Watts	35
J. R. Eyre c and b P. J. Watts	11	b P. J. Watts	5
H. L. Johnson c Andrew b Crump	2	c Scott b Crump	31
I. R. Buxton c Crump b Sully	14	b P. J. Watts	23
*D. C. Morgan b P. J. Watts	7	c Steele b P. J. Watts	0
M. Hill c Milburn b Sully	10	c Milburn b Sully	6
†R. W. Taylor b Scott	40	c Steele b Sully	0
T. J. P. Eyre c Scott b Steele	4	c Crump b Sully	6
E. Smith lbw b Steele	1	c P. J. Watts b. Sully	1
M. H. J. Allen not out	17	lbw b Sully	12
H. J. Rhodes c Andrew b Mushtaq	8	not out	1
L-b 1	1	L-b 3	3
1/4 2/11 3/27 4/28 5/42 6/62 7/77 8/79 9/98	115	1/14 2/70 3/78 4/78 5/97 6/97 7/107 8/108 9/115	123

Bowling: *First Innings*—Crump 16—4—24—1; P. J. Watts 22—8—30—3; Sully 26—10—40—2; Steele 11—5—10—2; Scott 8—4—8—1; Mushtaq 2—0—2—1. *Second Innings*—Crump 11—3—24—1; P. J. Watts 27—6—64—4; Sully 13.3—6—22—5; Steele 13—8—10—0.

Northamptonshire

First Innings		Second Innings	
C. Milburn b Rhodes	19	c Taylor b Rhodes	6
R. M. Prideaux c Hill b Morgan	19	b Morgan	47
B. L. Reynolds c Taylor b Smith	6	c Allen b Morgan	0
Mushtaq Mohammad b Morgan	9	c Allen b Smith	2
P. D. Watts c J. R. Eyre b Morgan	26	c Hill b. Smith	0
D. S. Steele b Morgan	5	c Allen b Rhodes	25
P. J. Watts b Rhodes	0	c Buxton b Morgan	0
B. Crump b Morgan	5	b Smith	1
*†K. V. Andrew b Rhodes	0	lbw b Morgan	8
M. E. Scott not out	1	c Rhodes b Morgan	5
H. Sully c Johnson b Morgan	12	not out	1
B 8, n-b 6	14	L-b 1, n-b 4	5
1/26 2/37 3/54 4/67 5/74 6/80 7/91 8/95 9/99	116	1/7 2/12 3/17 4/28 5/70 6/72 7/75 8/91 9/97	100

Bowling: *First Innings*—Buxton 4—1—8—0; Rhodes 21—10—34—3; Morgan 22.4—8—36—6; Smith 11—4—22—1; Allen 3-1—2-0. *Second Innings*—Morgan 21.5—12—24—5; Rhodes 17—9—20—2; Smith 21—11—39—3; Allen 3—0—12—0.

Umpires: T. W. Spencer and H. Mellows.

At The Oval, May 25, 26, 27. NORTHAMPTONSHIRE drew with SURREY.

At Leicester, May 28, 29, 30. NORTHAMPTONSHIRE drew with LEICESTERSHIRE.

NORTHAMPTONSHIRE v. WORCESTERSHIRE

At Northampton, June 1, 2, 3. *65 overs.* Worcestershire won by 180 runs. Despite a gallant innings by Crump, Northamptonshire never promised to score the 309 runs they needed in five hours and twenty minutes when Worcestershire declared at their Thursday night total. Crump batted just over two hours for his not-out 71, including ten 4's. The Worcestershire pace bowlers, Brain and Coldwell, held control and took half the wickets for 27. This pair had bowled unchanged in the first innings, and their match figures were Brain, nine for 110, and Coldwell, eight for 103. The Worcestershire batsmen also had some trouble, but each innings produced one fine individual effort. Graveney hit 82 not out in an unblemished display, with ten 4's and on the second day Richardson was equally dominating with 87 not out. Worcestershire were noticeably superior in close-in catching, particularly by Ormrod and Headley.

Worcestershire

C. D. Fearnley c Mushtaq b Bailey	24	— lbw b Sully	27
R. G. A. Headley c Andrew b Bailey	3	— c Reynolds b Scott	34
J. A. Ormrod c Andrew b Crump	9	— b Scott	44
*T. W. Graveney not out	82	— c Steele b Mushtaq	24
D. W. Richardson lbw b Crump	3	— not out	87
M. J. Horton c Reynolds b P. J. Watts	1	— lbw b Mushtaq	0
†R. Booth b Bailey	15	— b Mushtaq	5
D. N. F. Slade not out	46	— c Andrew b Mushtaq	20
N. Gifford (did not bat)		— not out	0
B 1, l-b 8	9	B 2, l-b 13, w 4, n-b 3	22
1/4 2/35 3/47 (6 wkts., 65 overs) 4/53 5/54 6/108	192	1/42 2/107 (7 wkts., dec.) 3/114 4/154 5/162 6/183 7/247	263

L. J. Coldwell and B. M. Brain did not bat.

Bowling: *First Innings*—Crump 33—9—92—2; Bailey 20—4—62—3; P. J. Watts 12—2—29—1. *Second Innings*—Crump 10—2—28—0; Bailey 23—6—40—0; Sully 31—13—47—1; Mushtaq 21—5—59—4; P. J. Watts 8—0—25—0; Scott 19—5—42—2.

Northamptonshire

B. L. Reynolds c Fearnley b Brain	9	— c Ormrod b Brain	10
R. M. Prideaux lbw b Coldwell	13	— c Headley b Coldwell	6
Mushtaq Mohammad c Ormrod b Brain	27	— c Ormrod b Brain	29
P. D. Watts c Graveney b Coldwell	8	— c Ormrod b Coldwell	2
D. S. Steele b Coldwell	9	— c Headley b Coldwell	0
P. J. Watts b Brain	6	— b Brain	0
B. Crump lbw b Coldwell	0	— not out	71
M. E. Scott b Brain	4	— c Booth b Coldwell	5
H. Sully b Brain	48	— c Graveney b Horton	1
*†K. V. Andrew c Headley b Brain	18	— absent hurt	—
R. Bailey not out	1	— st Booth b Slade	4
L-b 3, w 1	4		
1/22 2/30 3/43 4/68 5/70 6/74 7/76 8/89 9/144	147	1/16 2/18 3/26 4/26 5/27 6/58 7/105 8/109 9/128	128

Bowling: *First Innings*—Coldwell 31—6—65—4; Brain 30.2—5—78—6. *Second Innings*—Coldwell 17—6—38—4; Brain 12—2—32—3; Gifford 8—2—7—0; Slade 15.2—5—30—1; Horton 6—2—21—1.

Umpires: J. Langridge and A. E. Rhodes.

At Cambridge, June 4, 6, 7. NORTHAMPTONSHIRE beat CAMBRIDGE UNIVERSITY by 183 runs.

At Nottingham, June 8, 9, 10. NORTHAMPTONSHIRE beat NOTTINGHAMSHIRE by 244 runs.

NORTHAMPTONSHIRE v. SOMERSET

At Northampton, June 11, 12, 13. *65 overs.* Drawn. Somerset narrowly failed to secure a victory, Northamptonshire's last batsman coming in with five balls of the final over remaining. Northamptonshire, set 290 in four and a quarter hours, lost Reynolds and Mushtaq to the first two balls of Rumsey's second over. Steele hit an amazing 76, with 12 fours, before being fifth out at 92. Somerset then appeared certain of success until late resistance came from P. J. Watts, Crump and Sully. Somerset gained a first-innings lead of 17 after Virgin and Kitchen established their batting with a second-wicket stand of 104. Clayton hit fifty in thirty-eight minutes, followed by 63 in the second innings when Graham Atkinson produced some fine batting. Northamptonshire found Rumsey's hostile bowling a difficult proposition in both innings.

Somerset

First Innings		Second Innings	
G. Atkinson c Steele b Crump	0	c Mushtaq b Steele	78
R. Virgin c Sully b Crump	42	c P. D. Watts b Sully	13
M. Kitchen c Sully b Crump	68	st Johnson b P. D. Watts	2
W. E. Alley c Crump b Bailey	4	b Scott	20
T. E. Barwell b Crump	17	c Johnson b Sully	5
*C. R. M. Atkinson c P. D. Watts b Bailey	2	c Steele b Crump	21
K. E. Palmer b Bailey	0	c and b Scott	23
†G. Clayton not out	52	b Mushtaq	63
P. J. Robinson c Prideaux b P. J. Watts	6	c Reynolds b Sully	20
B. A. Langford not out	0	not out	7
F. E. Rumsey (did not bat)		not out	10
L-b 3, n-b 1	4	B 8, l-b 2	10
1/0 2/104 3/116 4/118 5/127 6/127 7/187 8/194 (8 wkts., 65 overs)	195	1/27 2/48 3/63 4/96 5/177 6/190 7/215 8/248 9/254 (9 wkts., dec.)	272

Bowling: *First Innings*—Crump 24—2—62—4; Bailey 14—2—43—3; P. J. Watts 9—0—39—1; Scott 10—2—21—0; Sully 8—1—26—0. *Second Innings*—Crump 15—5—24—1; P. J. Watts 4—2—3—0; Bailey 12—4—15—0; Scott 22—4—62—2; Sully 33—11—66—3; P. D. Watts 7—1—33—1; Steele 8—4—9—1; Mushtaq 15—1—50—1.

Northamptonshire

First Innings		Second Innings	
*R. M. Prideaux b Rumsey	10	c and b Robinson	4
B. L. Reynolds lbw b Rumsey	40	lbw b Rumsey	1
Mushtaq Mohammad c Clayton b Palmer	19	c Clayton b Rumsey	0
D. S. Steele c Robinson b Rumsey	44	c Kitchen b Robinson	76
P. D. Watts c Clayton b C. R. M. Atkinson	2	lbw b Langford	10
P. J. Watts c Barwell b C. R. M. Atkinson	4	c Clayton b Rumsey	60
B. Crump c C. R. M. Atkinson b Alley	29	c Rumsey b Robinson	11
M. E. Scott not out	18	c Palmer b Langford	6
H. Sully b Rumsey	0	not out	16
†L. A. Johnson not out	1	b Rumsey	0
R. Bailey (did not bat)		not out	5
L-b 5, w 2, n-b 4	11	B 11, l-b 1, w 1	13
1/22 2/54 3/108 4/115 5/129 6/129 (8 wkts., 65 overs)	178	1/1 2/1 3/53 4/82 5/92 6/129 7/140 8/187 9/197 (9 wkts.)	202

Bowling: *First Innings*—Rumsey 23—7—45—4; Palmer 14—1—55—1; Alley 12—3—32—1; Langford 5—2—11—0; C. R. M. Atkinson 11—5—24—2. *Second Innings*—Rumsey 13—4—45—4; Alley 5—1—18—0; Langford 40—23—43—2; Robinson 34—16—69—3; Palmer 2—0—6—0; C. R. M. Atkinson 2—1—8—0.

Umpires: C. S. Elliott and R. Aspinall.

At Oxford, June 15, 16, 17. NORTHAMPTONSHIRE drew with OXFORD UNIVERSITY.

NORTHAMPTONSHIRE v. ESSEX

At Peterborough, June 18, 20, 21. *65 overs.* Northamptonshire won by six wickets in the first over after lunch on the third day. The pitch was always difficult. First it was two-paced, rain having got under the covers. Underprepared, it progressively deteriorated and the match would have finished in two days but for considerable rain after tea on Monday. The Essex opening pair, Barker and Bear, found the best batting conditions. The later batsmen slumped against the consistent Crump, Sully and Watts. Bailey and Edmeades exploited the conditions, but Northamptonshire gained a first-innings lead of 15 through enterprising hitting by Steele, Reynolds and Mushtaq. Bear played a second good innings but Essex again fell quickly to Crump and Watts so that Northamptonshire needed only 71. Once more Bailey's hostile bowling on a broken pitch required bold hitting tactics. On the final day it was announced that no more games would be played on this ground, because it no longer reached championship standards. When Bear hit Scott out of the ground for 6 on the first morning it went through a house window. The housewife refused to return the ball until the window was repaired at a cost of 25/–.

Essex

First Innings		Second Innings	
G. E. Barker c sub b Sully	33	— c Wills b Crump	0
M. J. Bear c Wills b Scott	45	— b Sully	25
†B. Taylor c Andrew b P. J. Watts	11	— b Crump	12
K. W. R. Fletcher lbw b Sully	4	— lbw b P. J. Watts	5
*T. E. Bailey b Crump	17	— c Wills b Sully	4
G. R. Cass c Andrew b P. J. Watts	0	— c Andrew b Crump	13
G. J. Saville b Sully	6	— c Bailey b P. J. Watts	6
B. Edmeades lbw b Crump	3	— c and b P. J. Watts	13
R. N. S. Hobbs c Sully b Crump	3	— c Steele b Crump	1
A. M. Jorden not out	5	— c Mushtaq b P. J. Watts	1
R. East not out	0	— not out	1
B 1, l-b 6, w 1, n-b 1	9	L-b 4	4
1/69 2/90 3/94 (9 wkts., 65 overs) 4/97 5/100 6/109 7/118 8/124 9/135	136	1/2 2/28 3/38 4/46 5/61 6/63 7/78 8/32 9/84	85

Bowling: *First Innings*—Crump 13—3—22—3; Bailey 4—1—11—0; P. J. Watts 20—9—24—2; Sully 24—7—49—3; Scott 4—0—21—1. *Second Innings*—Crump 22—9—24—4; Bailey 4—0—13—0; Sully 21—11—33—2; P. J. Watts 20.3—11—11—4.

Northamptonshire

First Innings		Second Innings	
R. M. Prideaux c Edmeades b East	25	— c Jorden b Edmeades	14
R. Wills c Taylor b Bailey	2	— lbw b Bailey	0
Mushtaq Mohammad lbw b Bailey	24	— c Cass b Bailey	24
B. L. Reynolds b Jorden	20	— not out	16
D. S. Steele run out	38	— c Jorden b Bailey	5
P. J. Watts run out	11	— not out	13
B. Crump b Edmeades	1		
M. E. Scott c Hobbs b Bailey	3		
H. Sully b Edmeades	14		
*†K. V. Andrew b Edmeades	0		
R. Bailey not out	3		
B 2, l-b 6, n-b 2	10	B 1, l-b 1	2
1/10 2/55 3/63 4/97 5/123 6/129 7/129 8/146 9/146	151	1/4 2/29 3/40 4/54 (4 wkts.)	74

Bowling: *First Innings*—Jorden 13—1—26—1; Bailey 21.4—5—47—3; Edmeades 14—3—35—3; East 16—4—33—1. *Second Innings*—Jorden 4—0—9—0; Bailey 12.4—2—40—3; Edmeades 10—1—23—1.

Umpires: A. Jepson and G. H. Pope.

At Lord's, June 25, 27, 28. NORTHAMPTONSHIRE lost to MIDDLESEX by nine wickets.

NORTHAMPTONSHIRE v. KENT

At Northampton. June 29, 30, July 1. *65 overs.* Northamptonshire won by 77 runs. On an entertaining first day, Northamptonshire secured a first-innings lead of 106, and lost a wicket without scoring at the end of the day. Northamptonshire scored 100 in 46 overs, then hit 102 off the remaining 19. Prideaux started slowly became the second player in the country to reach 1,000 runs when 24, then fiercely punished the bowling. He hit eleven boundaries. Reynolds provided lively support with nine 4's. Dixon, Kent's only effective bowler, earned five wickets. Then Kent collapsed for 96 in 49.2 overs against Bailey and Sully, who took five wickets each. Reynolds, 89 in four hours, and Crump, 76 not out in just over two hours, enabled Northamptonshire to set Kent a final target of 359 in just under six and a half hours. They lost their opening batsmen on the second night for 58. Yet on the third morning Kent hit 153 in two hours before lunch. Leary and Wilson, each with seven boundaries, added 85. Then Ealham, four 6's and five 4's, and Knott put on 81 for the sixth wicket. Brown hit bravely but Kent's task was too big against the spin of Sully and Steele, and pace of Bailey.

Northamptonshire

R. M. Prideaux b Dixon	84	— b Sayer	16
D. S. Steele c and b Dixon	32	— b Sayer	6
Mushtaq Mohammad c Luckhurst b Dixon	0	— c Luckhurst b Dye	34
B. L. Reynolds c Knott b Dixon	65	— c Prodger b Sayer	89
P. J. Watts c Wilson b Sayer	3	— c Prodger b Dye	18
H. Sully run out	8		
M. E. Scott not out	1	— not out	8
*†K. V. Andrew c Denness b Dixon	1	— c Prodger b Sayer	0
P. Willey (did not bat)		— c Knott b Dye	0
B. Crump (did not bat)		— not out	76
L-b 8	8	B 2, l-b 2, n-b 1	5
1/51 2/51 3/187 4/191 5/197 6/200 7/202 (7 wkts., 65 overs)	202	1/0 2/21 3/26 4/73 5/113 6/113 7/227 (7 wkts., dec.)	252

R. Bailey did not bat.

Bowling: *First Innings*—Brown 15—2—67—0; Sayer 16—4—42—1; Dye 16—5—32—0; Dixon 18—4—53—5. *Second Innings* Sayer 26—8—47—4; Brown 15—2—56—0; Dye 24—7—65—3; Dixon 36—15—58—0; Luckhurst 3—0—21—0.

Kent

M. H. Denness c Bailey b Sully	12	— b Mushtaq	11
B. W. Luckhurst c Prideaux b Sully	24	— b Sully	7
S. E. Leary c Andrew b Bailey	14	— c Bailey b Sully	54
R. C. Wilson lbw b Sully	6	— c Watts b Sully	51
J. M. Prodger c Prideaux b Sully	9	— c Reynolds b Sully	6
A Ealham c Andrew b Bailey	0	— c Watts b Steele	59
†A. Knott not out	18	— lbw b Steele	37
*A. L. Dixon c Bailey b Sully	5	— b Bailey	10
A. Brown b Bailey	3	— b Bailey	36
D. M. Sayer b Bailey	2	— c Sully b Steele	2
J. C. Dye b Bailey	0	— not out	0
B 1, l-b 2	3	— l-b 5, n-b 3	8
1/35 2/37 3/47 4/67 5/67 6/72 7/77 8/80 9/96	96	1/11 2/35 3/120 4/128 5/147 6/228 7/229 8/252 9/261	281

Bowling: *First Innings*—Crump 17—6—22—0; Bailey 14.2—4—27—5; Willey 3—0—10—0; Sully 15—4—34—5. *Second Innings*—Crump 14—10—10—0; Bailey 11.2—2—24—2; Sully 30—6—91—4; Mushtaq 15—3—49—1; Scott 10—1—43—0; Steele 17—6—56—3.

Umpires: F. Jakeman and T. W. Spencer.

NORTHAMPTONSHIRE v. NOTTINGHAMSHIRE

At Northampton, July 2, 3, 4. Nottinghamshire won by three wickets with five minutes of extra time to spare. They had been set to score 189 in three and a half hours and achieved the target on a dusty, difficult wicket, mainly through the determined batting of Moore. He made 58 not out in two and a half hours. Nottinghamshire never really lost the initiative, after Davison dismissed Prideaux with the first ball of the game. Their captain, Hill, earned most credit with a stalwart innings of 96 in four hours. After his dismissal the Nottinghamshire batsmen collapsed to Mushtaq's leg-breaks. Despite a poor start to their second innings Northamptonshire reached the stage of deciding Nottinghamshire's final task through a fourth-wicket stand of 156 by Prideaux and Steele. This pair began a long, slow battle against the hostile Davison and Forbes with defensive batting, but gradually took control, and finished their effort scoring freely.

Northamptonshire

R. M. Prideaux c Swetman b Davison	0	— c Swetman b White	68
A. M. R. Sim c Moore b Taylor	20	— lbw b Davison	2
Mushtaq Mohammad c Swetman b Johnson	9	— c. Swetman b Davison	4
B. L. Reynolds c Swetman b Taylor	12	— c Johnson b Forbes	5
D. S. Steele b White	39	— b Gillhouley	91
P. J. Watts c Swetman b White	27	— run out	11
P. Willey c Forbes b White	10	— b Davison	12
B. Crump c Johnson b Forbes	15	— c Taylor b Forbes	11
H. Sully c White b Forbes	18	— not out	1
*†K. V. Andrew not out	5		
R. Bailey c Johnson b Forbes	8		
L-b 3, n-b 5	8	L-b 3, n-b 3	6
1/0 2/15 3/40 4/55 5/109 6/123 7/124 8/156 9/158	171	1/5 2/9 3/18 4/174 5/174 6/199 7/201 8/211 (8 wkts. dec.)	211

Bowling: *First Innings*—Davison 13—5—23—1; Johnson 10—1—36—1; Forbes 14.3—6—20—3; Taylor 20—6—43—2; White 15—6—29—3; Gillhouley 9—3—12—0. *Second Innings*—Davison 19—5—31—3; Forbes 20.1—7—38—2; Taylor 12—3—28—0; White 25—9—56—1; Johnson 5—2—13—0; Gillhouley 14—3—39—1.

Nottinghamshire

*N. Hill b Mushtaq	96	— b Mushtaq	20
M. Taylor c Sim b Willey	17	— b Steele	18
R. A. White c Andrew b Willey	0	— b Sully	19
I. Moore run out	3	— not out	58
M. J. Smedley c Sully b Watts	35	— c Reynolds b Watts	35
†R. Swetman run out	0	— c Reynolds b Watts	0
J. Parkin c Andrew b Mushtaq	15	— b Watts	9
K. Gillhouley lbw b Mushtaq	2	— not out	16
C. Forbes c Andrew b Mushtaq	8		
A. Johnson lbw b Crump	0	— c Andrew b Crump	0
I. Davison not out	1		
B 8, l-b 5, n-b 4	17	B 4, l-b 9, n-b 2	15
1/32 2/40 3/58 4/149 5/150 6/166 7/184 8/185 9/188	194	1/34 2/40 3/66 4/127 5/131 6/155 7/156 (7 wkts.)	190

Bowling: *First Innings*—Crump 18—5—29—1; Bailey 20—4—50—0; Willey 5—1—13—2; Sully 10—2—33—0; Steele 17—5—18—0; Mushtaq 17—9—19—4; Watts 8—1—15—1. *Second Innings*—Crump 6—0—14—1; Bailey 3—0—11—0; Watts 13—2—34—3; Mushtaq 14—3—35—1; Steele 25.5—8—51—1; Sully 9—1—30—1.

Umpires: L. H. Gray and H. Mellows.

At Worcester, July 6, 7, 8. NORTHAMPTONSHIRE drew with WORCESTERSHIRE.

At Glastonbury, July 9, 11, 12. NORTHAMPTONSHIRE lost to SOMERSET by nine wickets.

At Leeds, July 13, 14, 15. NORTHAMPTONSHIRE beat YORKSHIRE by 66 runs.

At Maidstone, July 16, 18, 19. NORTHAMPTONSHIRE drew with KENT.

NORTHAMPTONSHIRE v. WARWICKSHIRE

At Northampton, July 20, 21, 22. *65 overs*. Drawn. On the first day, reduced by eighty minutes through four interruptions due to bad light and rain, the Northamptonshire batting produced two bright features. Milburn hit aggressively for 69, with twelve 4's. Other men went cheaply to Bannister, who bowled well. Finally, Lightfoot and Crump took 59 off the last ten overs. Until the attractive Abberley was run out Warwickshire promised to go ahead, but in an hour after lunch on the second day the last five wickets fell for 31 to Durose and Sully. The twenty-one year-old Durose also took three wickets in the second innings, showing much promise. Northamptonshire batted steadily in their second innings to consolidate their lead, with Prideaux, Reynolds and Steele contributing sound efforts. Set to score 263 in three hours, forty minutes, Warwickshire did not continue their attempt after their fifth wicket fell at 129, made in two and a quarter hours. Their captain, M. J. K. Smith, scored 84, with nine 4's. First, he gave Warwickshire a chance of victory, but when wickets fell, he helped to save them by defending for the last hour for 13 runs. Smith could not find a sufficiently successful partner.

Northamptonshire

C. Milburn c Barber b Bannister	69	— c Bannister b Brown	18
R. M. Prideaux c A. C. Smith b Bannister	7	— run out	55
R. Wills c Amiss b Cartwright	11	— c Cartwright b Barber	9
B. L. Reynolds b Bannister	4	— lbw b Brown	43
D. S. Steele c Stewart b Bannister	8	— c A. C. Smith b Brown	47
P. J. Watts c Cartwright b Brown	18	— b Bannister	11
A. Lightfoot not out	29	— c M. J. K. Smith b Barber	9
B. Crump not out	44	— not out	21
B 4, l-b 5, n-b 1	10	B 4, l-b 8	12
1/20 2/80 3/96 4/101 5/116 6/131 (6 wkts., 65 overs)	200	1/36 2/51 3/123 4/131 5/158 6/174 7/225 (7 wkts., dec.)	225

H. Sully, *†K. V. Andrew and A. J. Durose did not bat.

Bowling: *First Innings*—Brown 19—3—56—1; Bannister 25—9—61—4; Cartwright 14—4—34—1; Edmonds 7—1—39—0. *Second Innings*—Brown 18.1—6—35—3; Bannister 16—3—59—1; Edmonds 32—12—59—0; Cartwright 9—3—24—0; Barber 15—4—36—2.

Warwickshire

R. W. Barber c and b Watts	16	— c Andrew b Durose	7
R. N. Abberley run out	44	— c Reynolds b Durose	5
D. L. Amiss c Andrew b Crump	19	— c Wills b Sully	15
*M. J. K. Smith c Sully b Durose	25	— not out	84
J. A. Jameson c Wills b Durose	14	— c Wills b Durose	20
W. J. Stewart c Durose b Sully	9	— c Crump b Sully	4
T. W. Cartwright b Sully	16	— not out	30
†A. C. Smith c Andrew b Sully	0		
R. B. Edmonds b Durose	11		
D. J. Brown not out	1		
J. D. Bannister run out	0		
L-b 5, n-b 3	8	B 10, l-b 1	11
1/35 2/71 3/95 4/121 5/126 6/132 7/137 8/150 9/163	163	1/12 2/15 3/69 4/120 5/129 (5 wkts.)	176

Bowling: *First Innings*—Durose 22—6—40—3; Crump 10—1—36—1; Watts 11—5—15—1; Lightfoot 7—1—23—0; Sully 12—1—41—3. *Second Innings*—Durose 16—2—28—3; Watts 6—2—7—0; Sully 24—1—96—2; Steele 11—4—25—0; Crump 7—4—9—0.

Umpires: A. E. Rhodes and H. Yarnold.

At Northampton, July 23, 25. NORTHAMPTONSHIRE beat WEST INDIES by four wickets.

NORTHAMPTONSHIRE v. HAMPSHIRE

At Kettering, July 27, 28, 29. Drawn. Rain badly affected this game. Only seventy-five minutes' play was possible on the last day after 90 minutes had been lost on the second day. On a pitch whence the ball came off rather slowly and tended to keep low, Northamptonshire batted for six hours on the first day, scoring 280. They were consistently sound, with Prideaux taking three hours, twenty-five minutes for 68. The more aggressive Watts hit 53 in an hour and forty minutes, with two 6's and five 4's. Then in the final twenty minutes Hampshire lost five wickets for six runs in five overs. Durose claimed four wickets without cost in his first two overs. Next day Marshall retrieved the position with a masterly 94 (three 6's and eleven 4's), being adequately supported by Sainsbury and Shackleton. This followed a lengthy and accurate bowling performance on the first day by Shackleton, who fully deserved his six wickets. Reynolds and Prideaux followed their first innings opening stand of 73 with another of 74 in the second, but rain prevented the final struggle developing.

Northamptonshire

B. L. Reynolds c Reed b Caple	38	— b White	48
R. M. Prideaux c Timms b Shackleton	68	— c Castell b White	38
A. Lightfoot b Shackleton	28	— not out	3
Mushtaq Mohammad b Castell	13	— not out	4
P. J. Watts c Sainsbury b Shackleton	53		
D. S. Steele b Castell	34		
B. Crump not out	15		
M. J. Kettle b Shackleton	0		
H. Sully c Marshall b Castell	12		
*†K. V. Andrew b Shackleton	5		
A. J. Durose lbw b Shackleton	0		
B 3, l-b 11	14	L-b 2, n-b 1	3
1/73 2/141 3/146 4/171 5/241 6/253 7/254 8/269 9/280	280	1/74 2/91 (2 wkts.)	96

Bowling: *First Innings*—Shackleton 41—14—85—6; White 20—4—63—0; Castell 20—4—53—3; Sainsbury 14—6—21—0; Caple 9—2—16—1; Wheatley 11—3—28—0. *Second Innings*—Shackleton 18—7—42—0; White 17.1—4—41—2; Castell 4—0—10—0.

Hampshire

B. L. Reed c Watts b Kettle...... 4	*R. E. Marshall c Reynolds b Sully 94
†B. S. V. Timms b Durose....... 0	A. T. Castell c Mushtaq b Crump. 3
K. J. Wheatley c Watts b Durose . 0	D. Shackleton not out........... 42
R. C. Caple lbw b Sully.......... 19	D. W. White c Mushtaq b Crump. 1
H. Horton c Steele b Durose... .. 0	B 6, l-b 2, n-b 2.......... 10
D. A. Livingstone c Mushtaq b Durose 0	1/0 2/4 3/4 4/4 5/4 218
P. J. Sainsbury c and b Watts..... 45	6/40 7/105 8/116 9/209

Bowling: *First Innings*—Durose 13—7—18—4; Kettle 7—1—18—1; Crump 26—5—52—2; Sully 23—7—68—2; Mushtaq 9—4—25—0; Watts 8—2—27—1.

Umpires: R. S. Lay and C. S. Elliott.

NORTHAMPTONSHIRE v. MIDDLESEX

At Northampton, July 30, Aug. 1, 2. Middlesex won by six wickets, with twenty minutes to spare. Rain reduced play by thirty-five minutes before lunch and affected the wicket later on the first day when Northamptonshire were dismissed for 218 and Middlesex lost Smith and Harris for 32. No play at all was possible on the second day. At the start of the game the wicket looked one of the best of the season at Northampton. Capable batting was seen, notably from Lightfoot, Reynolds and Mushtaq. After the rain Hooker and Titmus caused some trouble, but the pitch was in fine condition again on the third day when each team declared after an hour's batting in order to secure a finish. Middlesex needed 221 in three hours, and got home with twenty minutes to spare. Smith and Harris set the pace in a brisk opening stand of 88. Then Parfitt hit 64 in just over an hour, with two 6's and seven 4's. When Parfitt was fourth out 39 were needed in thirty-five minutes. Murray and Hooker scored them in only a quarter of an hour.

Northamptonshire

C. Milburn lbw b Price	29	— not out	39
R. M. Prideaux c Parfitt b Stewart	10	— c Radley b Hooker	17
A. Lightfoot c and b Titmus	55	— not out	15
B. L. Reynolds c Hooker b Stewart	38		
Mushtaq Mohammad c Parfitt b Titmus	37		
P. J. Watts c Hooker b Bick	5		
D. S. Steele c Murray b Hooker	8		
B. Crump c and b Hooker	10		
*†K. V. Andrew lbw b Price	8		
H. Sully b Hooker	2		
A. J. Durose not out	8		
B 1, l-b 7	8		
1/18 2/51 3/109 4/171 5/176 6/176 7/194 8/201 9/204	218	1/30 (1 wkt., dec.)	71

Bowling: *First Innings*—Price 15.2—1—47—2; Stewart 15—4—38—2; Hooker 24—7—64—3; Titmus 28—13—41—2; Bick 11—4—20—1. *Second Innings*—Price 4—1—12—0; Stewart 8—0—37—0; Hooker 5—1—22—1.

Middlesex

M. J. Smith b Crump	10	— c Steele b Crump	63
M. J. Harris c Milburn b Crump	8	— c Crump b Steele	34
P. H. Parfitt st Andrew b Steele	29	— c Reynolds b Steele	64
D. A. Bick b Steele	11		
E. A. Clark c Lightfoot b Mushtaq	4	— c Watts b Sully	15
C. T. Radley not out	4		
†J. T. Murray not out	2	— not out	28
R. W. Hooker (did not bat)		— not out	14
L-b 1	1	L-b 2, n-b 2	4
1/13 2/32 3/54 4/59 5/67 (5 wkts., dec.)	69	1/88 2/105 3/177 4/182 (4 wkts.)	222

*F. J. Titmus, R. W. Stewart and J. S. E. Price did not bat.

Bowling: *First Innings*—Durose 10—4—14—0; Crump 11—3—19—2; Watts 2—1—2—0; Sully 1—1—0—0; Steele 8—3—16—2; Mushtaq 7.3—2—17—1. *Second Innings*—Crump 18—1—59—1; Durose 8—0—40—0; Lightfoot 4—0—15—0; Sully 8.2—1—40—1; Steele 9—1—42—2; Mushtaq 1—0—12—0; Watts 2—0—10—0.

Umpires: R. S. Lay and C. G. Pepper.

NORTHAMPTONSHIRE v. GLAMORGAN

At Wellingborough, August 6, 8, 9. *65 overs.* Drawn. Rain ended play on the third day when Northamptonshire required 91 runs from their last nine wickets in two hours, forty minutes. An opening stand of 76 by Reynolds and Prideaux, who batted soundly against Shepherd and Wheatley, gave Northamptonshire a fair chance, although left to score the biggest total of the game, 175, on a pitch where runs were always hard to get. Glamorgan possessed the most successful batsman, Walker, with fifty in each innings, and a total of 119 for once out. Each team began their first innings steadily, and then lost wickets when the overs limitation demanded acceleration. Crump, with three wickets in four balls, caused Glamorgan to slump to 42 for five in their second innings, but Walker and Evans staged a recovery. Rain had also prevented any play after tea on the first day.

Glamorgan

A. Jones run out	5	— b Kettle	3
B. Hedges b Crump	30	— c Kettle b Crump	11
P. M. Walker b Durose	50	— not out	69
A. R. Lewis c Andrew b Watts	25	— c Watts b Crump	10
A. Rees b Watts	0	— lbw b Crump	0
A. E. Cordle c Prideaux b Durose	8	— b Crump	0
†D. L. Evans b Watts	8	— lbw b Watts	15
E. Lewis c Andrew b Durose	6	— b Crump	11
*O. S. Wheatley not out	5	— b Watts	1
D. J. Shepherd b Watts	0	— run out	0
I. J. Jones not out	1	— lbw b Watts	0
L-b 7, n-b 9	16	B 7, l-b 1, n-b 1	9
1/13 2/82 3/114 4/117 5/128 6/131 7/139 8/153 9/153 (9 wkts., 65 overs)	154	1/5 2/30 3/42 4/42 5/42 6/96 7/122 8/129 9/129	129

Bowling: *First Innings*—Crump 18—6—36—1; Kettle 9—2—21—0; Durose 15—3—36—3; Sully 12—4—22—0; Steele 1—0—6—0; Watts 10—4—17—4. *Second Innings*—Crump 32.4—19—42—5; Durose 10—5—15—0; Kettle 5—1—9—1; Watts 25—12—32—3; Sully 7—2—22—0.

Northamptonshire

B. L. Reynolds c E. Lewis b Wheatley	23 — b Shepherd	35
R. M. Prideaux b Cordle	24 — not out	37
A. Lightfoot b Shepherd	1 — not out	1
Mushtaq Mohammad c E. Lewis b Cordle	0	
P. J. Watts c E. Lewis b Shepherd	2	
D. S. Steele c Evans b I. J. Jones	23	
B. Crump c E. Lewis b Shepherd	0	
M. J. Kettle b Wheatley	7	
*†K. V. Andrew not out	1	
A. J. Durose c A. Jones b Wheatley	9	
H. Sully c Evans b Wheatley	1	
B 5, l-b 8, n-b 5	18	B 5, l-b 5, n-b 1 11
1/47 2/53 3/56 4/59 5/63 6/66 7/98 8/98 9/108	109	1/76 (one wkt.) 84

Bowling: *First Innings*—I. J. Jones 13—4—22—1; Wheatley 17.4—6—26—4; Shepherd 17—8—27—3; Cordle 12—6—16—2. *Second Innings*—I. J. Jones 2—0—9—0; Wheatley 10—4—10—0; Shepherd 17—9—19—1; E. Lewis 3—0—21—0; Cordle 6.3—2—14—0.

Umpires: W. F. Price and C. G. Pepper.

NORTHAMPTONSHIRE v. LEICESTERSHIRE

At Northampton, August 13, 14, 15. Northamptonshire won by 80 runs After a keen low-scoring contest Northamptonshire only undermined Leicestershire's advantage when their eighth and ninth second-innings wickets produced 54 runs. This extended Leicestershire's final task to the reasonable figure of 152 in two hours, forty minutes. But the visitors fell for 71 against accurate, hostile bowling by Crump, Watts and Mushtaq. Effective bowling by Lock made Northamptonshire struggle in their first innings despite hard-hitting by Reynolds and Watts. Then Norman, a former Northamptonshire batsman, helped Leicestershire to a lead of 71 runs, though he occupied over five hours for 102. This was the first century of the season on the Northampton ground. Leicestershire held the initiative until lunch on the third day and then the late Northamptonshire batsmen, followed by the bowlers and fine catching, turned the tables.

Northamptonshire

C. Milburn c Lock b Spencer	21 — c Booth b Cotton	38
R. M. Prideaux c Spencer b Marner	5 — lbw b Marner	39
A. Lightfoot lbw b Lock	6 — c Inman b Savage	1
B. L. Reynolds c Lock b Marner	57 — b Savage	38
Mushtaq Mohammad b Lock	0 — run out	7
D. S. Steele lbw b Lock	10 — b Savage	26
P. J. Watts c Tolchard b Lock	35 — c Hallam b Savage	9
B. Crump st Tolchard b Savage	18 — lbw b Marner	22
*†K. V. Andrew c Tolchard b Savage	12 — not out	18
M. Sully c Spencer b Lock	0 — b Cotton	18
A. J. Durose not out	0 — b Cotton	0
B 4, l-b 4, w 1, n-b 1	10	L-b 6 6
1/27 2/27 3/61 4/61 5/105 6/107 7/150 8/168 9/174	174	1/47 2/49 3/99 4/107 5/154 6/159 7/168 8/186 9/222 222

Bowling: *First Innings*—Spencer 11—1—42—1; Cotton 7—1—25—0 Marner 8—3—34—2; Savage 16—8—30—2; Lock 23.1—13—33—5. *Second Innings*—Spencer 9—1—49—0; Cotton 11.4—2—30—3; Lock 30—13—57—0; Savage 39—23—33—4; Marner 13—1—47—2.

Leicestershire

First Innings		Second Innings	
M. R. Hallam c Andrew b Crump	0	lbw b Crump	4
M. E. Norman b Crump	102	b Durose	8
B. J. Booth c and b Steele	42	b Crump	4
C. C. Inman c Andrew b Watts	24	c Andrew b Watts	16
P. Marner b Crump	2	c Steele b Watts	1
D. Constant b Lightfoot	8	b Watts	12
†R. W. Tolchard lbw b Crump	2	not out	17
*G. A. R. Lock c Crump b Sully	34	c Reynolds b Crump	0
J. S. Savage b Crump	12	c Steele b Mushtaq	7
J. Cotton not out	12	c Steele b Mushtaq	0
C. T. Spencer b Crump	0	c and b Mushtaq	0
L-b 2, n-b 5	7	L-b 1, n-b 1	2
1/0 2/90 3/129 4/132 5/162 6/180 7/213 8/229 9/245	245	1/6 2/17 3/19 4/29 5/40 6/43 7/49 8/67 9/71	71

Bowling: *First Innings*—Crump 37.4—14—57—6; Durose 20—4—52—0; Watts 21—7—42—1; Sully 12—2—33—1; Steele 14—4—37—1; Lightfoot 6—2—13—1; Mushtaq 2—1—4—0. *Second Innings*—Crump 16—6—24—3; Durose 7—2—15—1; Watts 8—4—14—3; Mushtaq 3—2—4—3; Sully 2—0—12—0.

Umpires: W. F. Price and H. Mellows.

At Clacton, August 17, 18, 19. NORTHAMPTONSHIRE beat ESSEX by seven wickets.

NORTHAMPTONSHIRE v. YORKSHIRE

At Northampton, August 20, 22, 23. Northamptonshire won by 34 runs. In an exciting final afternoon Yorkshire attacked the bowling in a bid to score 268 in three hours, but failed narrowly. The accuracy of Crump, who bowled unchanged, aided by Durose, Mushtaq and Scott, prevented any batsman sustaining his effort long enough to take Yorkshire to the points they needed in their challenge for the championship. Northamptonshire gained a grip on the game when batting throughout Saturday. Prideaux scored 109 in four and three-quarter hours. Trueman bowled spiritedly but three catches missed off him probably affected the final result. The Yorkshire first innings, like their second, was revived by strong late hitting. Only the capable Sharpe held together the early part of the innings, scoring 72 out of 117 for six. Although Milburn broke a finger in Northamptonshire's second effort, Steele put them in a declaring position with 83 not out, including one 6 and thirteen 4's, following his 45 not out on the first day.

Northamptonshire

First Innings		Second Innings	
C. Milburn c Taylor b Nicholson	28	retired hurt	22
R. M. Prideaux b Hutton	109	c Taylor b Nicholson	19
B. L. Reynolds lbw b Trueman	39	b Trueman	4
Mushtaq Mohammad c Binks b Hutton	35	c Trueman b Hutton	29
A. Lightfoot b Nicholson	24	c Binks b Trueman	1
D. S. Steele not out	45	not out	83
B. Crump c Taylor b Nicholson	4	c Trueman b Hutton	0
*†K. V. Andrew b Nicholson	5		
M. E. Scott c Trueman b Nicholson	4	not out	24
L-b 2, n-b 5	7	L-b 1, n-b 3	4
1/44 2/123 3/175 4/222 5/270 6/274 7/284 8/300 (8 wkts., dec.)	300	1/48 2/48 3/62 4/95 5/95 (5 wkts., dec.)	186

H. Sully and A. J. Durose did not bat.

Bowling: *First Innings*—Trueman 22—7—49—1; Nicholson 24—4—83—5; Hutton 20—6—66—2; Wilson 22—13—27—0; Cope 26—12—68—0. *Second Innings*—Trueman 17.5—5—66—2; Nicholson 16—4—51—1; Hutton 8—1—31—2; Wilson 8—2—23—0; Cope 5—2—11—0.

Yorkshire

K. Taylor c Milburn b Durose	0	— b Crump	25
P. J. Sharpe c Mushtaq b Scott	72	— b Durose	28
D. E. V. Padgett c Andrew b Durose	9	— c Sully b Scott	34
J. H. Hampshire lbw b Crump	12	— c Lightfoot b Crump	28
B. Leadbetter lbw b Mushtaq	4	— run out	7
R. A. Hutton lbw b Mushtaq	16	— b Crump	4
†J. G. Binks b Crump	23	— b Crump	0
*F. S. Trueman c Andrew b Durose	32	— c Sully b Scott	5
D. Wilson c Durose b Mushtaq	41	— c Crump b Durose	52
G. Cope b Mushtaq	1	— not out	3
A. G. Nicholson not out	1	— b Mushtaq	41
L-b 6, n-b 2	8	B 4, l-b 2	6
1/8 2/30 3/50 4/74 5/101 6/117 7/165 8/217 9/217	219	1/27 2/34 3/50 4/102 5/103 6/108 7/171 8/175 9/189	233

Bowling: *First Innings*—Durose 19—6—57—3; Crump 25—2—69—2; Lightfoot 6—2—12—0; Mushtaq 13.3—3—55—4; Scott 5—1—18—1. *Second Innings*—Durose 11—2—44—2; Crump 26—5—86—4; Mushtaq 10.4—1—52—1; Scott 5—0—45—2.

Umpires: W. E. Phillipson and H. Mellows.

At Neath, August 24, 25, 26. NORTHAMPTONSHIRE lost to GLAMORGAN by 72 runs.

At Bristol, August 27, 29, 30. NORTHAMPTONSHIRE beat GLOUCESTERSHIRE by an innings and 23 runs.

At Birmingham, August 31, September 1, 2. NORTHAMPTONSHIRE lost to WARWICKSHIRE by an innings and 89 runs.

NOTTINGHAMSHIRE

President—R. J. de C. Barber

Secretary—R. M. Poulton, County Cricket Ground, Nottingham

Captain—Norman Hill

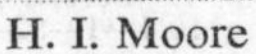

H. I. Moore

County Badge

R. Swetman

Nottinghamshire's hope that under their new captain, Norman Hill, they would rise in the County Championship table was not realised and for the second year in succession they finished last. The side was strengthened by two special registrations in Swetman, the former Surrey wicket-keeper who came out of retirement, and White, of Middlesex. The latter did not make as many runs as had been expected but his emergence as an off-spin bowler proved most valuable. Swetman kept wicket splendidly and made many useful contributions with the bat.

Four players topped 1,000 runs, Bolus, Smedley, Moore and Hill, but generally there was a lack of consistency and although Bolus made more runs than any of his colleagues his painstaking methods were not always appreciated by the spectators.

Nottinghamshire's main failing was the absence of variety in attack. For the second season in succession, the left-arm medium-paced bowling of Forbes was outstanding and again he was rewarded with over 100 wickets. Davison began well as opening partner to Forbes, but beset in mid-season by injury he faded and eventually lost his place. He has now accepted a business appointment.

Two medium-fast bowlers, Johnson and Stead (left-arm), were drafted into the side on occasion and their performances were steady rather than spectacular. White's off-spin was the only alternative to seam bowling, for Gillhouley, whose left-arm slow attack was badly needed, ran into "throwing" trouble, and his form suffered accordingly so that his appearances were severely restricted. The outlook was not entirely black. Nottinghamshire's keenness in the field was refreshing and Hill, generally, made the best of his most limited resources.

A new young batting personality in Smedley made further progress and his style and manner of making runs was most pleasing. The West Indies Test cricketer, Murray, who captained Cambridge University, later played for Nottinghamshire and his exciting batting helped to brighten the gloomy season. Murray is expected to be available in 1967 when the much-needed variation in attack could be supplied by P. D. Watts, the Northamptonshire leg-spinner, who, on being released by that county, agreed to join Nottinghamshire on special registration.

In addition to Davison there were other notable departures from the staff, two Yorkshiremen, Gillhouley and the left-handed batsman, Whittingham, both being released.

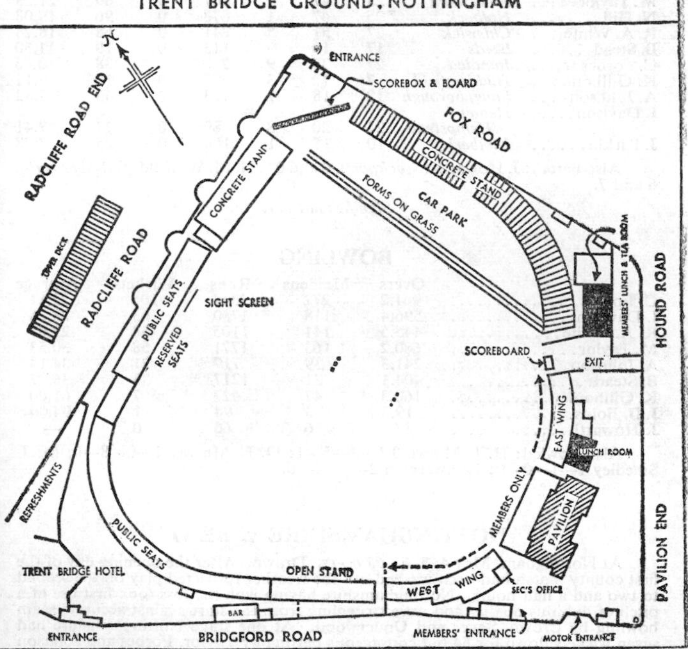

NOTTINGHAMSHIRE RESULTS

All First-Class Matches—Played 30, *Won* 3, *Lost* 11, *Drawn* 16
County Championship Matches—Played 28, *Won* 3, *Lost* 11, *Drawn* 12, *No Decision*

COUNTY CHAMPIONSHIP AVERAGES

BATTING

	Birthplace	Mtchs.	Inns.	Not Outs	Runs	100's	Highest Inns.	Aver.
D. L. Murray..	*Trinidad*	12	23	3	672	1	166*	33.60
M. J. Smedley..	*Maltby*	26	49	9	1121	1	134*	28.02
H. I. Moore....	*Sleaford*	26	47	5	1104	1	100	26.28
J. B. Bolus.....	*Leeds*	26	50	2	1253	1	122*	26.10
B. Whittingham	*Silsden*	13	22	2	461	1	133	23.05
R. Swetman....	*Croydon*	28	49	11	823	1	115	21.65
M. Taylor.....	*Amersham*	28	47	9	807	0	69	21.23
N. Hill.........	*Holbeck*	25	47	1	878	0	96	19.08
R. A. White....	*Chiswick*	27	51	5	841	0	68	18.28
B. Stead.......	*Leeds*	17	19	9	113	0	19	11.30
C. Forbes......	*Jamaica*	27	35	9	280	0	38	10.76
K. Gillhouley..	*Huddersfield*	7	12	3	82	0	16*	9.11
A. Johnson....	*Loughborough*	12	18	1	133	0	45	7.82
I. Davison.....	*Hemel Hempstead*	21	20	8	89	0	27	7.41
J. Parkin......	*Kimberley*	10	15	1	100	0	25	7.28

Also batted: J. Howarth (*Stockport*), 0 and 0*; H. M. Winfield (*Gainsborough*), 6 and 7.

* *Signifies not out.*

BOWLING

	Overs	Maidens	Runs	Wickets	Average
C. Forbes...............	961.2	272	2344	106	22.11
I. Davison..............	596.4	118	1780	63	28.25
R. A. White............	445.5	141	1105	38	29.07
M. Taylor..............	680.2	163	1771	58	30.53
A. Johnson.............	241.3	39	717	21	34.14
B. Stead................	404.1	81	1217	33	36.87
K. Gillhouley...........	160.3	47	427	7	61.00
J. B. Bolus..............	19.3	3	94	1	94.00
J. Howarth.............	27	6	60	0	—

Also bowled: H. I. Moore 3.1—2—5—1; D. L. Murray 1—0—8—0; M. J. Smedley 1—1—0—0; R. Swetman 2—0—4—0.

NOTTINGHAMSHIRE v. KENT

At Nottingham, May 4, 5, 6. *65 overs.* Drawn. After the opening day of the first county match had been washed out the weather restricted play on the second to two and a half hours. Nottinghamshire having won the toss took first use of a pitch of dubious quality and were struggling from the start against accurate seam bowling by Brown, Sayer and Underwood. At one stage Nottinghamshire had seven wickets down for 54 but courageous batting by Taylor, Forbes and Johnson helped them to total 133 in 53 overs. Kent, faced with steady medium-paced left-arm bowling by the West Indian, Forbes, fared even worse and in just over 50 overs were dismissed for 100. Only Cowdrey and Knott played Forbes competently. Forbes finished with seven wickets for 19 runs, the best performance of his career. In the remaining short time available Nottinghamshire took the opportunity to get in some batting practice.

Nottinghamshire

*N. Hill c Cowdrey b Sayer	16	— b Dixon	14
J. B. Bolus c Luckhurst b Sayer	5	— not out	27
†R. Swetman c Cowdrey b Sayer	15	— not out	8
I. Moore c Cowdrey b Brown	11		
M. J. Smedley b Brown	6		
B. Whittingham c Knott b Brown	0		
J. Parkin c Luckhurst b Sayer	0		
M. Taylor not out	23		
C. Forbes c and b Underwood	38		
A. Johnson b Underwood	16		
I. Davison c Prodger b Underwood	0		
B 1, l-b 1, n-b 1	3	W 1	1
1/17 2/24 3/44 4/54 5/54 6/54 7/54 8/109 9/133	133	1/33 (1 wkt.)	50

Bowling: *First Innings*—Brown 23—7—53—3; Sayer 26—4—63—4; Underwood 4—2—14—3. *Second Innings*—Brown 2—0—7—0; Sayer 4—2—7—0; Dixon 14—6—20—1; Underwood 8—5—8—0; Luckhurst 3—1—7—0.

Kent

B. W. Luckhurst c Forbes b Johnson	1	D. L. Underwood c and b Forbes	0
M. H. Denness c Hill b Forbes	11	A Brown b Davison	4
R. C. Wilson b Forbes	0	D. M. Sayer not out	0
*M. C. Cowdrey lbw b Forbes	39		
S. E. Leary b Forbes	7	N-b 2	2
J. M. Prodger lbw b Forbes	3		
†A. Knott c Swetman b Davison	33	1/8 2/10 3/13 4/30 5/48	100
A. L. Dixon c Johnson b Forbes	0	6/67 7/73 8/79 9/91	

Bowling: Johnson 11—4—24—1; Forbes 19—11—19—7; Davison 10.2—2—33—2; Taylor 10—2—22—0.

Umpires: G. H. Pope and F. Jakeman.

At Manchester, May 7, 9. NOTTINGHAMSHIRE lost to LANCASHIRE by six wickets.

At Nottingham, May 11, 12, 13. NOTTINGHAMSHIRE drew with WEST INDIES. (See WEST INDIES section.)

At Oxford, May 18, 19, 20. NOTTINGHAMSHIRE drew with OXFORD UNIVERSITY.

At Worcester, May 21. NOTTINGHAMSHIRE lost to WORCESTERSHIRE by 19 runs. (See GILLETTE CUP.)

NOTTINGHAMSHIRE v. SOMERSET

At Nottingham, May 25, 26, 27. *65 overs.* Somerset won by 178 runs. Somerset won the toss but began disastrously losing their first two wickets for 3 runs and a third at 24. G. Atkinson, however, played a sound innings of 59 and Alley, the veteran Australian, provided the sparkle with a dashing innings of 36. His captain, C. R. M. Atkinson, also batted well. Nottinghamshire's early batsmen were not too convincing, half the side being out for 75; then Swetman and Taylor came together in a useful seventh-wicket partnership of 88. Despite this Nottinghamshire finished 21 runs behind when their allotted overs ran out. Alley was in even more devastating form in the Somerset second innings for having been missed when one, he ran up 115. This, and a useful 54 not out from Palmer, enabled the visitors to declare at 219 for seven. Hill and Bolus put on 37 for Nottinghamshire's opening stand in the second innings but the slow left-arm bowler, Robinson, created havoc by fine bowling on a pitch which was still good and his final figures of seven for 10, the best of his career, resulted in Nottinghamshire collapsing for 62.

Somerset

First innings		Second innings	
R. Virgin c Swetman b Johnson	3	c Swetman b Forbes	26
A. Clarkson c Hill b Davison	0	c Swetman b Davison	0
M. Kitchen c Swetman b Johnson	7	lbw b Davison	0
G. Atkinson b Davison	59	c White b Johnson	1
W. E. Alley c Bolus b Taylor	36	c Bolus b White	115
*C. R. M. Atkinson c Swetman b Forbes	36	c Hill b Forbes	0
K. E. Palmer b Davison	6	not out	54
†G. Clayton c Swetman b Forbes	17	c White b Gillhouley	0
P. J. Robinson not out	11		
B. A. Langford c Johnson b Forbes	1		
F. E. Rumsey not out	1		
L-b 6, w 1, n-b 5	12	B 9, l-b 7, w 1, n-b 6	23
1/3 2/3 3/24 4/68 5/145 6/153 7/175 8/181 9/184 (9 wkts., 65 overs)	189	1/0 2/0 3/4 4/75 5/75 6/218 7/219 (7 wkts., dec.)	219

Bowling: *First Innings*—Davison 19—4—48—3; Johnson 15—3—50—2; Forbes 19—3—47—3; Taylor 12—6—32—1. *Second Innings*—Davison 12—1—37—2; Johnson 11—2—31—1; Forbes 11—3—36—2; Gillhouley 14.3—1—58—1; Taylor 5—0—15—0; White 5—0—19—1.

Nottinghamshire

First innings		Second innings	
*N. Hill c Robinson b Rumsey	12	c C. R. M. Atkinson b Robinson	22
J. B. Bolus c G. Atkinson b Alley	22	c Palmer b Langford	18
B. Whittingham c Clayton b Palmer	16	b Robinson	0
R. A. White lbw b Rumsey	12	c and b Robinson	4
M. J. Smedley c Alley b Rumsey	5	c Langford b Robinson	0
†R. Swetman not out	41	c and b Robinson	0
M. Taylor c Clayton b Rumsey	48	b Robinson	1
A. Johnson run out	1	run out	0
K. Gillhouley not out	0	c Kitchen b Rumsey	10
C. Forbes (did not bat)		lbw b Robinson	3
I. Davison (did not bat)		not out	0
L-b 6, n-b 5	11	B 1, w 1, n-b 2	4
1/30 2/42 3/64 4/69 5/75 6/163 7/167 (7 wkts., 65 overs)	168	1/37 2/41 3/47 4/47 5/47 6/47 7/59 8/59 9/62	62

Bowling: *First Innings*—Rumsey 21—3—44—4; Palmer 18—5—61—1; Alley 26—7—52—1. *Second Innings*—Rumsey 11—3—18—1; Palmer 5—0—19—0; Langford 12—5—11—1; Robinson 17.2—14—10—7.

Umpires: F. Jakeman and W. F. Simpson.

NOTTINGHAMSHIRE v. SURREY

At Nottingham, May 28, 30, 31. *65 overs*. Drawn. Nottinghamshire won the toss and put Surrey in. Despite losing Stewart at 11, the visitors batted powerfully. Edrich never gave a chance in a stay of three and a half hours, which brought him 137, including twenty 4's. Though facing a formidable total, Nottinghamshire made a brave effort to gain first-innings lead and failed by only seven runs. Bolus hit 54 and Moore bolstered the score with a capable innings of 65. When Surrey batted again Barrington took the limelight. He spent exactly three hours making 106. Tindall, 81, helped him to put on 153. Finally, Stewart left Nottinghamshire to score 338 at the rate of 65 an hour. They never looked equal to the challenge and only some brave batting by Swetman and Taylor averted defeat. As it was, Stewart claimed the extra half hour—in vain.

Surrey

First Innings		Second Innings	
*M. J. Stewart c Taylor b Davison	4	b Johnson	8
J. H. Edrich c Moore b Forbes	137	b Davison	23
R. A. E. Tindall c and b Forbes	19	b Davison	81
K. F. Barrington not out	49	c Johnson b White	106
S. J. Storey c White b Forbes	0	not out	51
R. I. Jefferson not out	17	not out	7
M. D. Willett (did not bat)	—	c Johnson b Forbes	35
B 1, l-b 4, n-b 8	13	L-b 7, n-b 13	20
1/11 2/74 3/213 4/213 (4 wkts., 65 overs)	239	1/23 2/54 3/207 4/231 5/313 (5 wkts., dec.)	331

P. I. Pocock, G. Arnold, †A Long and R. Harman did not bat.

Bowling: *First Innings*—Davison 16—2—58—1; Johnson 15—1—47—0; Forbes 18—0—74—3; Taylor 16—4—47—0. *Second Innings*—Davison 23—3—71—2; Johnson 16—0—55—1; Forbes 23—5—87—1; Taylor 15—4—37—0; White 19—6—61—1.

Nottinghamshire

First Innings		Second Innings	
J. B. Bolus c Tindall b Pocock	54	lbw b Jefferson	5
*N. Hill c Edrich b Storey	23	c Tindall b Harman	28
B. Whittingham c Tindall b Pocock	7	c Tindall b Jefferson	10
I. Moore not out	65	c and b Barrington	35
A. Johnson c Arnold b Storey	37		
R. A. White c Arnold b Storey	5	c Barrington b Storey	36
†R. Swetman st Long b Storey	8	c and b Barrington	58
J. Parkin st Long b Storey	2	c Long b Barrington	13
M. Taylor b Arnold	10	not out	59
C. Forbes not out	1	not out	10
B 8, l-b 11, n-b 2	21	B 5, l-b 2	7
1/56 2/74 3/113 4/155 5/174 6/192 7/198 8/229 (8 wkts., 65 overs)	233	1/7 2/25 3/58 4/90 5/116 6/147 7/232 (7 wkts.)	261

I. Davison did not bat.

Bowling: *First Innings*—Arnold 15—2—58—1; Jefferson 9—0—30—0; Storey 26—6—76—5; Pocock 15—6—48—2. *Second Innings*—Arnold 4—1—6—0; Jefferson 20—3—57—2; Storey 16—7—29—1; Pocock 25—8—37—0; Harman 28—6—76—1; Barrington 22—7—45—3; Willett 3—2—4—0.

Umpires: T. W. Spencer and W. F. Simpson.

At Romford, June 1, 2, 3. NOTTINGHAMSHIRE lost to ESSEX by 56 runs.

NOTTINGHAMSHIRE v. HAMPSHIRE

At Nottingham, June 4, 5, 6. *65 overs.* Drawn. Nottinghamshire's first county game ever to include Sunday play proved a memorable one, with Hampshire gaining seven points, two for first innings lead and five because the scores finished level with the visitors having five wickets in hand. It was fully half an hour after the game had ended before the result was known because of some doubt about the legitimacy of the run off the last ball which levelled the scores. Horton played the ball a short way along the pitch and then as the bowler went to collect it the batsman in the excitement kicked the ball away and he and Wheatley completed the vital run. It appeared a clear case of obstruction but Bolus the acting Nottinghamshire captain later said no appeal had been made against Horton although it appeared as though Swetman, the wicket-keeper, had given a shout. At the time of the incident Nottinghamshire committee members were meeting and their deliberations were suspended until the result had been sorted out.

The fight for first innings lead was also close. The Hampshire last pair were together with the scores level when Shackleton was missed by Parkin at first slip. The unlucky bowler was Davison who in this innings finished with five wickets for 71. In the Nottinghamshire second innings the left-handed Whittingham reached his best score, 133. He batted five hours fifty minutes and hit sixteen 4's. On the Sunday, with admission free, 1/– each was charged for scorecards and with other fund raising activities £178 was taken.

Nottinghamshire

*J. B. Bolus c Reed b White	42	— c Marshall b Cottam	16
B. Whittingham c Livingstone b Shackleton	25	— c Livingstone b Shackleton	133
R. A. White b Shackleton	42	— c White b Wheatley	14
H. I. Moore run out	22	— b Cottam	6
M. J. Smedley c Livingstone b Shackleton	5	— c Livingstone b Sainsbury	27
†R. Swetman not out	22	— b Shackleton	2
J. Parkin run out	8	— c Marshall b Shackleton	25
M. Taylor c Timms b Cottam	11	— b Sainsbury	3
C. Forbes b Cottam	0	— c Timms b Shackleton	5
I. Davison (did not bat)		— c Barnard b White	9
B. Stead (did not bat)		— not out	3
L-b 7, n-b 1	8	B 4, l-b 5	9
1/46 2/83 3/128 4/140 5/147 6/159 7/185 8/185 (8 wkts., 65 overs)	185	1/27 2/64 3/77 4/100 5/103 6/162 7/234 8/240 9/240	252

Bowling: *First Innings*—Shackleton 32—7—77—3; White 20—4—54—1; Cottam 13—1—46—2. *Second Innings*—Shackleton 40—21—52—4; White 19—1—62—1; Cottam 24—7—50—2; Wheatley 24—7—47—1; Sainsbury 25—12—32—2.

Hampshire

*R. E. Marshall c Swetman b Davison	51	— c Bolus b Forbes	28
B. L. Reed c Parkin b Davison	6	— c Taylor b Stead	72
H. Horton c Swetman b Forbes	46	— not out	66
D. A. Livingstone c Taylor b Davison	0	— b Davison	23
H. M. Barnard b Taylor	5	— c Davison b Stead	13
P. J. Sainsbury c Swetman b Forbes	18		
†B. S. V. Timms c Forbes b Davison	19		
K. J. Wheatley c Stead b Forbes	12	— not out	9
D. Shackleton not out	14		
D. W. White c Taylor b Davison	10	— c Bolus b Taylor	18
R. M. Cottam not out	8		
L-b 3, n-b 8	11	L-b 3, w 1, n-b 4	8
1/19 2/89 3/90 4/112 5/120 6/142 7/166 8/167 9/179 (9 wkts., 65 overs)	200	1/64 2/114 3/163 4/188 5/225 (5 wkts.)	237

Bowling: *First Innings*—Davison 23—3—71—5; Stead 11—0—39—0; Taylor 6—1—26—1; Forbes 25—9—53—3. *Second Innings*—Davison 14—1—74—1; Forbes 15—1—65—1; Stead 11—1—60—2; Taylor 7—0—30—1.

Umpires: W. H. Copson and C. G. Pepper.

NOTTINGHAMSHIRE v. NORTHAMPTONSHIRE

At Nottingham, June 8, 9, 10. *65 overs.* Northamptonshire won by 245 runs, Northamptonshire dominated the game throughout after winning the toss. From the start Milburn attacked the bowling and it took him eighty two minutes and just seventy-seven deliveries to hit the season's fastest century to date. He scored 113 of an opening partnership of 157 in thirty-eight scoring strokes, his major hits being three 6's and eighteen 4's. Prideaux, too, made a century in just under three hours (one 6, thirteen 4's). At the end of sixty-five overs free hitting Northamptonshire had amassed 355 for seven, the highest then achieved in a limited overs game. Moore hit a compact 81 and Smedley 89 not out but at the end of Nottinghamshire's over allotment they had made 220 for four and were well behind. Prideaux completed a century for the second time in the match in three hours twenty minutes (eleven 4's) to become the first Northamptonshire player to do so since D. Brookes in 1946, and only the third in their history. After Northamptonshire declared, the accurate left-arm bowling of Scott (five for 30) and the spin of Mushtaq (four for 16) proved too much for Nottinghamshire, who collapsed badly on a pitch still in good order.

Northamptonshire

C. Milburn c Swetman b Davison	113	— b Davison	6
*R. M. Prideaux c Smedley b Taylor	106	— c Bolus b White	100
B. L. Reynolds c Whittingham b Davison	60	— c Swetman b Forbes	67
Mushtaq Mohammad c Smedley b Forbes	29	— c Davison b White	22
P. J. Watts c Swetman b Davison	22	— not out	1
D. S. Steele b Forbes	2	— not out	23
B. Crump not out	9		
H. Sully b Davison	1		
L-b 9, n-b 4	13	B 1, l-b 7, n-b 3	11
1/157 2/262 3/301 4/341 5/342 6/350 7/355 (7 wkts., 65 overs)	355	1/8 2/166 3/192 4/223 (4 wkts., dec.)	230

M. E. Scott, †L. A. Johnson and R. Bailey did not bat.

Bowling: *First Innings*—Davison 19—2—96—4; Forbes 21—4—89—2: Stead 11—1—61—0; Taylor 11—0—72—1; White 3—0—24—0. *Second Innings*—Davison 15—2—31—1; Forbes 17—5—42—1; Taylor 24—0—88—0; Stead 11—0—40—0; White 5—0—18—2.

Nottinghamshire

*J. B. Bolus c Johnson b Crump	1	— c Mushtaq b Watts	13
B. Whittingham c Scott b Crump	0	— lbw b Scott	45
R. A. White b Scott	41	— b Scott	16
H. I. Moore c Crump b Bailey	81	— st. Johnson b Mushtaq	10
M. J. Smedley not out	89	— c Reynolds b Scott	5
†R. Swetman not out	7	— c Mushtaq b Scott	4
J. Parkin (did not bat)		— c and b Mushtaq	0
M. Taylor (did not bat)		— not out	19
C. Forbes (did not bat)		— b Mushtaq	2
I. Davison (did not bat)		— c Prideaux b Scott	0
B. Stead (did not bat)		— c Milburn b Mushtaq	2
W 1	1	B 2, l-b 2	4
1/1 2/9 3/85 4/169 (4 wkts., 65 overs)	220	1/29 2/70 3/77 4/91 5/95 6/95 7/95 8/98 9/99	120

Bowling: *First Innings*—Crump 18—3—51—2; Bailey 13—0—48—1; Watts 12—0—50—0; Sully 8—0—23—0; Scott 12—3—31—1; Mushtaq 2—0—16—0. *Second Innings*—Crump 13—5—22—0; Bailey 2—0—3—0; Sully 14—4—15—0; Watts 9—1—30—1; Scott 24—13—30—5; Mushtaq 13.4—7—16—4.

Umpires: W. F. Simpson and C. G. Pepper.

At Bournemouth, June 11, 13, 14. NOTTINGHAMSHIRE beat HAMPSHIRE by seven wickets.

At Hove, June 15, 16, 17. NOTTINGHAMSHIRE lost to SUSSEX by eight wickets.

NOTTINGHAMSHIRE v. MIDDLESEX

At Nottingham, June 18, 20, 21. Drawn. Nottinghamshire won the toss and put Middlesex in to bat on a pitch left damp after overnight rain. The gamble failed: the visitors batted carefully, Russell, Murray and Bick each making fifty. The Nottinghamshire batsmen were worried by the bowling of Stewart (five for 42) and Hill declared 100 runs behind in the hope of forcing a definite result. Middlesex, however, disappointed the small crowd by delaying the closure of their second innings until after Parfitt had hit a competent half century. This left Nottinghamshire the difficult target of scoring 226 runs for victory at 85 an hour and the match petered out into a tame draw.

Middlesex

W. E. Russell st Swetman b Taylor	59	— c Swetman b Davison	24
M. J. Harris lbw b White	39	— c White b Stead	4
P. H. Parfitt c Smedley b Davison	5	— not out	54
E. A. Clark lbw b Johnson	3		
M. J. Smith c Swetman b Stead	18	— run out	12
*†J. T. Murray b Taylor	53	— not out	30
R. W. Hooker c Taylor b Davison	3		
D. A. Bick not out	63		
H. C. Latchman not out	18		
B 9, l-b 3, n-b 3	15	N b 1	1
1/88 2/100 3/111 4/128 5/180 6/190 7/207 (7 wkts., dec.)	276	1/22 2/35 3/63 (3 wkts., dec.)	125

J. S. E. Price and R. W. Stewart did not bat.

Bowling:—*First Innings*—Davison 24—5—67—2; Stead 23—6—43—1; Johnson 19—4—51—1; Taylor 25—5—63—2; White 18—8—37—1. *Second Innings*—Davison 11.3—1—34—1; Stead 11—2—37—1; Taylor 3—0—36—0; White 2—0—17—0.

Nottinghamshire

*N. Hill c Parfitt b Hooker	13	— c Parfitt b Stewart	19
J. B. Bolus c Clark b Stewart	14	— c Parfitt b Bick	25
B. Whittingham c Price b Bick	45	— c Russell b Stewart	8
H. I. Moore c Parfitt b Stewart	37	— c Price b Latchman	15
R. A. White c Murray b Stewart	0	— not out	25
M. J. Smedley lbw b Stewart	0	— run out	0
†R. Swetman c Parfitt b Stewart	4	— not out	35
M. Taylor not out	36		
B. Stead b Latchman	16		
I Davison not out	0		
A. Johnson (did not bat)		— b Parfitt	45
B 5, l b 5, n-b 1	11	L-b 1, n-b 1	2
1/28 2/30 3/116 4/118 5/118 6/124 7/124 8/153 (8 wkts. dec.)	176	1/21 2/37 3/68 4/68 5/125 6/125 (6 wkts.)	174

Bowling: *First Innings*—Price 21—6—39—0; Stewart 28—12—42—5; Hooker 10—2—33—1; Latchman 8—2—39—1; Bick 11—6—12—1. *Second Innings*—Price 8—0—26—0; Stewart 3—0—24—2; Latchman 13—2—55—1; Bick 15—2—49—1; Hooker 2—1—2—0; Parfitt 3—1—8—1; Smith 1—0—8—0.

Umpires: W. E. Phillipson and R. S. Lay.

At Swansea, June 25, 27, 28. NOTTINGHAMSHIRE drew with GLAMORGAN.

At Leicester, June 28, 29, July 1. NOTTINGHAMSHIRE lost to LEICESTERSHIRE by one wicket.

NOTTINGHAMSHIRE v. LANCASHIRE

At Newark, July 6, 7, 8. Drawn. It was a pity that the first county game to be staged at Newark should peter out into a tame draw. Lancashire appeared over-cautious in scoring less than 40 runs an hour over four hours in their second innings before declaring and setting Nottinghamshire to make an unrealistic 87 an hour for victory on a pitch which never permitted runs to be obtained quickly. Green batted splendidly for Lancashire and in the first innings scored his first century since July 1964, staying three and a half hours for 115. He was also top scorer in the second innings with 65. Nottinghamshire also had a century maker, Moore hitting his first of the season—100 in three hours. Nottinghamshire, despite their best total of the summer, 289, finished 11 runs in arrears on the first innings. The later stages of the game were remarkable only for the slow scoring.

Lancashire

First innings		Second innings	
D. M. Green c Parkin b Taylor	115	c Taylor b Gillhouley	65
G. K. Knox b Davison	25	b Davison	21
J. D. Bond b Davison	4	not out	39
G. Pullar run out	32	not out	2
J. Sullivan c Swetman b Gillhouley	28	c Bolus b Gillhouley	7
D. Lloyd b Taylor	20	b Davison	0
P. Lever c Taylor b Davison	40	c Swetman b Davison	23
K. Higgs b Davison	9		
†K. Goodwin b Taylor	7		
T. Greenhough not out	2		
*J. B. Statham c White b Davison	2		
B 6, l-b 8, n-b 2	16	B 1, l-b 3, n-b 1	5
1/49 2/53 3/117 4/155 5/226 6/257 7/276 8/295 9/295	300	1/33 2/44 3/108 4/122 5/159 (5 wkts., dec.)	162

Bowling: *First Innings*—Davison 27.1—6—77—5; Forbes 27—6—78—0; Taylor 18—6—37—3; Gillhouley 26—10—61—1; White 25—11—31—0. *Second Innings*—Davison 28—6—72—3; Forbes 21—12—17—0; Taylor 5—2—24—0; Gillhouley 21—11—30—2; White 10—5—14—0.

Nottinghamshire

First innings		Second innings	
*N. Hill c Goodwin b Higgs	13	c Statham b Lever	21
M. Taylor b Higgs	0	b Higgs	28
J. B. Bolus b Statham	64	c Goodwin b Lloyd	2
H. I. Moore b Lever	100	c Goodwin b Higgs	0
M. J. Smedley c Goodwin b Greenhough	4	not out	1
R. A. White c Higgs b Statham	68	not out	7
†R. Swetman lbw b Greenhough	4		
J. Parkin c Bond b Greenhough	4		
K. Gillhouley lbw b Statham	7		
C. Forbes not out	10		
I. Davison lbw b Statham	0		
B 2, l-b 10, n-b 3	15	L-b 3	3
1/6 2/17 3/154 4/188 5/190 6/205 7/221 8/251 9/289	289	1/48 2/49 3/49 4/54 (4 wkts.)	62

Bowling: *First Innings*—Statham 26.2—2—92—4; Higgs 28—9—59—2; Lever 21—3—67—1; Greenhough 24—6—52—3; Lloyd 1—0—4—0. *Second Innings*—Statham 5—0—29—0; Higgs 10—2—17—2; Lever 6—3—5—1; Lloyd 3—1—2—1; Greenhough 3—0—6—0.

Umpires: L. H. Gray and A. E. Rhodes.

NOTTINGHAMSHIRE v. DERBYSHIRE

At Nottingham, July 9, 11, 12. *65 overs.* Derbyshire won by eight wickets. Nottinghamshire won the toss, but their early batsmen were in trouble against the Derbyshire seam attack and despite ultra-caution three wickets fell for 30 runs. Moore and Smedley put on 107 in one hour fifty minutes but when the innings closed only 173 runs had been scored. Derbyshire made easy work of passing this total, Johnson, batting for the first time in spectacles, scored a powerful 73. Although Nottinghamshire faced a deficit of 57, sound batting by Taylor and Moore enabled them to reach 247 in their second innings. Derbyshire, however, proceeded serenely to victory, the foundation being laid by an opening stand of 164 by Hall and Harvey. They were together three and a quarter hours and it was their first century partnership of the season. Harvey's 103 not out took him just under three and three-quarter hours and he hit thirteen 4's.

Nottinghamshire

First Innings		Second Innings	
*N. Hill b Rhodes	7	c Smith b Rhodes	24
M. Taylor b Rhodes	0	b Morgan	69
J. B. Bolus c Taylor b Jackson	10	c Hall b Jackson	33
H. I. Moore c Hill b Jackson	64	c Taylor b Smith	57
M. J. Smedley not out	64	b Smith	2
R. A. White not out	21	c Buxton b Jackson	10
†R. Swetman (did not bat)		c Buxton b Smith	20
K. Gillhouley (did not bat)		b Smith	13
C. Forbes (did not bat)		b Jackson	5
A. Johnson (did not bat)		c Page b Jackson	2
I. Davison (did not bat)		not out	0
L-b 2, n-b 5	7	B 4, l-b 2, w 1, n-b 5	12
1/7 2/9 3/30 4/137 (4 wkts., 65 overs)	173	1/62 2/132 3/134 4/142 5/162 6/212 7/230 8/240 9/246	247

Bowling: *First Innings*—Buxton 13—6—23—0; Rhodes 14—4—37—2; Jackson 16—4—32—2; Smith 13—2—35—0; Morgan 9—1—39—0. *Second Innings*—Jackson 23.2—4—36—4; Rhodes 23—7—71—1; Smith 41—17—64—4; Morgan 42—19—55—1; Buxton 4—1—9—0.

Derbyshire

First Innings		Second Innings	
I. W. Hall b Forbes	52	b White	74
J. F. Harvey c Johnson b Forbes	13	not out	103
M. H. Page c Moore b Johnson	33	lbw b Moore	4
H. L. Johnson c Smedley b Johnson	73	not out	1
M. Hill b Forbes	47		
I. R. Buxton not out	5		
L-b 5, n-b 2	7	B 5, l-b 2, w 1, n-b 1	9
1/49 2/78 3/154 4/211 5/230 (5 wkts., 65 overs)	230	1/164 2/190 (2 wkts.)	191

*D. C. Morgan, †R. W. Taylor, E. Smith, H. J. Rhodes and A. B. Jackson did not bat.

Bowling: *First Innings*—Davison 13—1—45—0; Forbes 26—6—87—3; Johnson 26—6—91—2. *Second Innings*—Davison 5—1—15—0; Johnson 8—1—27—0; Forbes 11—3—21—0; White 32—11—59—1; Gillhouley 14—6—29—0; Taylor 10—2—21—0; Moore 3.1—2—5—1; Bolus 2—1—5—0; Smedley 1—1—0—0.

Umpires: F. Jakeman and H. Yarnold.

At Sheffield, July 16, 18, 19. NOTTINGHAM lost to YORKSHIRE by 229 runs.

NOTTINGHAMSHIRE *v.* SUSSEX

At Nottingham, July 20, 21, 22. Drawn. Although Nottinghamshire must have been disappointed at failing to win a match which they commanded almost throughout, they had cause for satisfaction in the return to form of Bolus. In the first innings he scored his first century since August 1964, although he was nearly four and a half hours reaching three figures. He and Smedley put on 143 for the fourth wicket. When Sussex replied they were unconvincing and the left-arm medium-paced Forbes bowled well in capturing five wickets for 50 runs. After brisk hitting in their second innings Nottinghamshire declared. Sussex needed to get 276 runs for victory at 69 an hour and when time ran out they were 26 runs short of the target with only two wickets left. Oakman was the main stumbling block to Nottinghamshire after Lenham and M. A. Buss had figured in an opening partnership of 99.

Nottinghamshire

*N. Hill c Oakman b A. Buss	7	— c Parks b Bates	45
M. Taylor c Parks b A. Buss	24	— c M. A. Buss b Snow	10
J. B. Bolus not out	122	— c A. Buss b Snow	35
B. Whittingham b Bates	24		
M. J. Smedley c M. A. Buss b Oakman	59	— not out	17
D. L. Murray b Oakman	14	— not out	20
R. A. White b A. Buss	14	— b A. Buss	6
†R. Swetman not out	26		
B 4, l-b 11, n-b 3	18	L-b 3, w 1	4
1/11 2/37 3/76 4/219 5/240 6/262 (6 wkts., dec.)	308	1/26 2/90 3/99 4/100 (4 wkts., dec.)	137

C. Forbes, B. Stead and I. Davison did not bat.

Bowling: *First Innings*—Snow 19—2—74—0; A. Buss 36—7—100—3; Bates 28—5—59—1; Suttle 6—2—22—0; Oakman 16—3—35—2. *Second Innings*—A. Buss 17—4—43—1; Bates 18—1—48—1; Snow 11—0—42—2.

Sussex

L. J. Lenham lbw b Stead	10	— c Taylor b Davison	51
M. A. Buss b Stead	30	— c Swetman b Taylor	51
K. G. Suttle b Forbes	4	— b Stead	22
A. S. M. Oakman c Swetman b Forbes	38	— c and b Taylor	68
*†J. M. Parks b Stead	2	— c Hill b Forbes	11
M. G. Griffith c Taylor b Forbes	1	— c Hill b Taylor	17
P. J. Graves c Swetman b Taylor	32	— run out	2
D. J. Foreman c Swetman b Forbes	21	— b Taylor	0
A. Buss c Murray b Forbes	4	— not out	0
D. L. Bates b White	8		
J. A. Snow not out	12	— not out	10
B 2, l-b 4, n-b 2	8	B 5, l-b 5, n-b 8	18
1/32 2/43 3/57 4/60 5/69 6/100 7/141 8/145 9/148	170	1/99 2/122 3/146 4/165 5/218 6/231 7/231 8/244 (8 wkts.)	250

Bowling: *First Innings*—Davison 18—4—64—0; Stead 23—10—34—3; Forbes 23—7—50—5; Taylor 9—3—10—1; White 1—0—4—1. *Second Innings*—Davison 15—4—56—1; Stead 18—1—57—1; Forbes 16—3—59—1; White 11—3—21—0; Taylor 14—1—39—4.

Umpires: P. A. Gibb and J. S. Buller.

NOTTINGHAMSHIRE v. GLOUCESTERSHIRE

At Nottingham, July 23, 25, 26. Nottinghamshire won by 88 runs. After winning the toss Nottinghamshire batted so soundly that they were able to declare at 363 for nine wickets, their highest total of the season. Hill and Bolus paved the way with an opening partnership of 115 scored at a fast rate. Both batsmen topped the half century as did Smedley and White later. The fastest scoring of an exhilarating opening day came in the last half hour when White and Forbes added 62 runs. Gloucestershire made a brave reply reaching 294, helped by Milton's 121 in just over four hours. In this innings Nottinghamshire's left-arm slow bowler Gillhouley was taken off after a long consultation between the square-leg umpire Herman and Hill, the Nottinghamshire captain. Bowlers came more into their own in the second innings. Allen claimed five for 51 with his off-spin and Nottinghamshire were tumbled out for 123, but Gloucestershire fared even worse on the rain-affected pitch and with Forbes taking seven for 31 were routed for 104. A. S. Brown equalled a fielding record by taking seven catches in the Nottinghamshire second innings.

Nottinghamshire

*N. Hill b Smith	50	— c Meyer b Smith	2
J. B. Bolus c Milton b Mortimore	79	— c and b A. S. Brown	15
M. Taylor c Allen b Smith	12	— c A. S. Brown b Allen	10
H. I. Moore c Allen b Smith	0	— c A. S. Brown b Smith	13
M. J. Smedley c D. Brown b Smith	71	— c A. S. Brown b Bissex	38
D. L. Murray c Meyer b Mortimore	30	— c A. S. Brown b Allen	1
R. A. White not out	55	— c A. S. Brown b Allen	9
†R. Swetman c Nicholls b Smith	20	— lbw b Mortimore	0
K. Gillhouley b A. S. Brown	3	— c A. S. Brown b Allen	10
C. Forbes b Windows	33	— not out	10
B. Stead (did not bat)		— lbw b Allen	0
L-b 8, n-b 2	10	B 9, l-b 5, w 1	15
1/115 2/138 3/144 4/145 (9 wkts., dec.)	363	1/11 2/23 3/39 4/43 5/54	123
5/201 6/252 7/296 8/301 9/363		6/86 7/87 8/98 9/116	

Bowling: *First Innings*—A. S. Brown 23—2—102—1; Smith 27—7—74—5; Windows 22.5—5—91—1; Mortimore 22—8—45—2; Allen 28—13—41—0. *Second Innings*—A. S. Brown 12—2—18—1; Windows 1—0—2—0; Smith 14—3—22—2; Allen 23—6—51—5; Mortimore 9—2—15—1; Bissex 1—1—0—1.

Gloucestershire

C. A. Milton c Smedley b Taylor	121	— c Taylor b Forbes	0
M. Bissex b Gillhouley	53	— c and b Stead	10
D. Brown c and b Gillhouley	55	— c Taylor b Forbes	4
D. Shepherd c White b Stead	1	— b White	39
R. B. Nicholls lbw b Stead	8	— c Hill b Forbes	2
A. R. Windows b Forbes	19	— c Bolus b Forbes	2
D. A. Allen lbw b Stead	1	— b Forbes	0
*J. B. Mortimore run out	9	— c Gillhouley b White	24
A. S. Brown b Stead	5	— not out	5
†B. J. Meyer lbw b Forbes	8	— c Moore b Forbes	2
D. R. Smith not out	10	— c Murray b Forbes	12
L-b 3, n-b 1	4	B 4	4
1/118 2/225 3/233 4/233 5/244	294	1/5 2/9 3/17 4/22 5/36	104
6/252 7/268 8/272 9/278		6/36 7/79 8/85 9/88	

Bowling: *First Innings*—Forbes 34.1—11—63—2; Stead 29—5—79—4; Taylor 21—6—58—1; Gillhouley 16—3—52—2; White 11—3—30—0; Murray 1—0—8—0. *Second Innings*—Forbes 20.2—10—31—7; Stead 4—1—6—1; Taylor 4—1—16—0; White 12—2—47—2.

Umpires: O. W. Herman and H. Mellows.

NOTTINGHAMSHIRE v. YORKSHIRE

At Worksop, July 27, 28, 29. Yorkshire won by ten wickets. Yorkshire won the toss and put Nottinghamshire in to bat. Close's gamble looked like succeeding when half the Nottinghamshire wickets fell for 57, but late resistance came from White and Swetman. The Nottinghamshire attack held little terror for Yorkshire as Close was in particularly good form. He reached his third century of the season in three hours ten minutes. When he declared Yorkshire held a first-innings lead of 128 and he was 115 not out. Nottinghamshire began their second innings more confidently, Hill and Bolus putting on 56, but when they were separated the visitors made swift strides towards victory. The left-arm slow bowler Wilson claimed the second hat-trick of his career in dismissing Swetman, Forbes and White. The first time he achieved the feat was also against Nottinghamshire, at Middlesbrough in 1959. On the turning pitch Wilson finished with five wickets for 46 and Illingworth took five for 54.

Nottinghamshire

*N. Hill c Binks b Nicholson	0	— c Sharpe b Illingworth	22
J. B. Bolus b Nicholson	10	— c Nicholson b Wilson	53
M. Taylor lbw b Nicholson	15	— c Close b Illingworth	0
H. I. Moore b Wilson	23	— b Illingworth	1
M. J. Smedley c Close b Wilson	2	— lbw b Illingworth	1
D. L. Murray c Close b Wilson	26	— c Hampshire b Wilson	0
R. A. White c Close b Wilson	48	— c Taylor b Wilson	13
†R. Swetman c Wilson b Trueman	52	— c Nicholson b Wilson	23
C. Forbes b Illingworth	7	— c Close b Wilson	0
B. Stead b Nicholson	4	— not out	1
I. Davison not out	0	— c Taylor b Illingworth	13
B 4, l-b 9, n-b 4	17	B 4, l-b 1, n-b 2	7
1/6 2/19 3/35 4/52 5/57 6/100 7/162 8/194 9/202	204	1/56 2/56 3/61 4/77 5/79 6/79 7/118 8/118 9/119	134

Bowling: *First Innings*—Trueman 16.3—3—33—1; Nicholson 18—7—36—4; Close 3—0—11—0; Wilson 26—8—66—4; Illingworth 25—10—41—1. *Second Innings*—Trueman 4—1—5—0; Nicholson 3—2—5—0; Illingworth 20.4—5—54—5; Wilson 14—4—46—5; Close 7—2—17—0.

Yorkshire

G. Boycott c Swetman b Forbes	25		
K. Taylor c Swetman b Forbes	29	— not out	7
D. E. V. Padgett b Forbes	25		
J. H. Hampshire c Bolus b Davison	6		
*D. B. Close not out	115		
P. J. Sharpe c Smedley b Davison	48		
R. Illingworth lbw b Forbes	9		
F. S. Trueman c Stead b Davison	24		
D. Wilson c Bolus b Davison	29		
†J. G. Binks not out	0	— not out	1
B 5, l-b 9, n-b 8	22	W 1	1
1/58 2/61 3/70 4/111 5/230 6/254 7/285 8/329 (8 wkts., dec.)	332	(for no wkt.)	9

A. G. Nicholson did not bat.

Bowling: *First Innings*—Davison 31—6—109—4; Stead 11—1—69—0; Forbes 28—11—68—4; Taylor 13—2—37—0; White 13—3—27—0; *Second Innings*—Swetman 2—0—4—0; Bolus 1.3—1—4—0.

Umpires: P. B. Wight and W. F. Price.

At Weston-super-Mare, July 30, August 1, 2. NOTTINGHAMSHIRE drew with SOMERSET.

At The Oval, August 3, 4, 5. NOTTINGHAMSHIRE drew with SURREY.

At Birmingham, August 6, 8, 9. NOTTINGHAMSHIRE drew with WARWICKSHIRE.

NOTTINGHAMSHIRE v. ESSEX

At Nottingham, August 13, 15, 16. Drawn. Essex, put in to bat on a damp, greenish pitch, scored slowly but steadily and Barker, Bear and Taylor helped the total reach three figures before the second wicket fell. Subsequently Forbes and Taylor, both medium-pace, caused a slump. When Nottinghamshire batted Swetman sent in as " night watchman ", achieved his best score, 115, which occupied just over four hours and contained fifteen 4's. To a second-wicket stand of 127 Boius contributed only 28. Essex did better when batting a second time thanks mainly to Bear and Barker and left Nottinghamshire 201 to make at 100 an hour. Despite the severity of the task they went for the runs but when the extra half hour ran out they were tottering on the brink of defeat with one wicket left and 44 runs short of their target.

Essex

*G. E. Barker b Forbes	25	— c Hill b Forbes	15
M. J. Bear run out	39	— c Swetman b Stead	98
†B. Taylor c Murray b Forbes	41	— b Forbes	1
K. W. R. Fletcher c White b Taylor	0	— b White	39
B. R. Knight c Taylor b Forbes	19	— c and b White	1
G. R. Cass b Taylor	24	— c Hill b White	26
G. J. Saville b Taylor	26	— not out	22
B. Edmeades lbw b White	0	— c White b Forbes	15
R. N. S. Hobbs c Forbes b White	0	— not out	0
A. M. Jorden c Forbes b Stead	8		
D. L. Acfield not out	2		
B 8, l-b 7, w 1, n-b 1	17	L-b 6, w 1, n-b 4	11
1/49 2/101 3/102 4/114 5/155 6/156 7/158 8/176 9/176	201	1/29 2/92 3/96 4/171 5/173 6/188 7/224 (7 wkts., dec.)	228

Bowling: *First Innings*—Stead 20—8—34—1; Howarth 14—2—42—0; Forbes 34—9—73—3; Taylor 18.1—10—17—3; White 17—8—18—2. *Second Innings*—Forbes 24—9—54—3; Stead 15.1—3—50—1; White 33—14—58—3; Howarth 7—1—15—0; Taylor 19—4—40—0.

Nottinghamshire

†R. Swetman c and b Hobbs	115	— c Fletcher b Hobbs	9
*N. Hill lbw b Knight	2	— c Hobbs b Jorden	36
J. B. Bolus c Knight b Acfield	28	— c Saville b Knight	72
D. L. Murray run out	10	— c Bear b Hobbs	0
H. I. Moore not out	39	— run out	16
M. J. Smedley not out	20	— c and b Hobbs	10
R. A. White (did not bat)		— c Knight b Acfield	7
M. Taylor (did not bat)		— c Knight b Hobbs	0
C. Forbes (did not bat)		— b Hobbs	0
B. Stead (did not bat)		— not out	2
J. Howarth (did not bat)		— not out	0
B 14, l-b 1	15	L-b 3, n-b 2	5
1/6 2/133 3/149 4/170 (4 wkts., dec.)	229	1/95 2/95 3/128 4/128 5/142 6/146 7/146 8/154 9/157 (9 wkts.)	157

Bowling: *First Innings*—Acfield 14—4—36—1; Knight 25—7—41—1; Jorden 16—5—35—0; Edmeades 18—5—33—0; Hobbs 22—5—69—1. *Second Innings*—Knight 5—1—22—1; Jorden 11—0—56—1; Hobbs 15—3—63—5; Acfield 3—1—3—1; Fletcher 1—0—8—0.

Umpires: J. S. Buller and C. S. Elliott.

NOTTINGHAMSHIRE v. LEICESTERSHIRE

At Nottingham, August 17, 18, 19. Drawn. Before the start Hill, the Nottinghamshire captain, awarded county caps to Smedley, Swetman and White. Smedley celebrated by making his second century—134 not out and his highest score. He took three and a quarter hours and hit seventeen 4's. After declaring, Nottinghamshire bowled their opponents out for 213, of which Marner helped himself to 104, one 6 and sixteen 4's. Taylor took four wickets for 21 runs. Nottinghamshire again batted soundly before declaring a second time and set Leicestershire to score 316 in four hours—79 an hour. They accepted the challenge and Inman hit magnificently for 113 (twenty 4's) in under two and a half hours. When the last over of extra time began Leicestershire, with only three wickets down, wanted six to win. Three runs were still needed off the last ball but the hard-hitting Marner, trying to make sure with a boundary, failed to connect and was bowled.

Nottinghamshire

*N. Hill c Marner b Lock	27	— c Lock b Spencer	36
J. B. Bolus c Hallam b Lock	61	— lbw b Spencer	13
D. L. Murray lbw b Cotton	36	— c and b Spencer	35
H. I. Moore lbw b Spencer	39	— run out	11
M. J. Smedley not out	134	— c Marner b Lock	29
R. A. White c Tolchard b Marner	16	— run out	25
†R. Swetman c Tolchard b Marner	0	— not out	17
M. Taylor not out	9	— not out	21
B 4, l-b 11	15	L-b 3, n-b 1	4
1/63 2/129 3/137 4/234 5/295 6/295 (6 wkts., dec.)	337	1/28 2/85 3/90 4/101 5/142 6/159 (6 wkts., dec.)	191

C. Forbes, B. Stead and I. Davison did not bat.

Bowling: *First Innings*—Spencer 17—6—49—1; Cotton 16—3—42—1; Marner 13—1—68—2; Lock 41—9—99—2; Savage 22—4—64—0. *Second Innings*—Spencer 14—3—51—3; Cotton 7—0—31—0; Marner 2—0—9—0; Lock 12—1—59—1; Savage 14—0—37—0.

Leicestershire

M. R. Hallam c Hill b Taylor	30	— c Murray b Davison	0
M. E. Norman c Swetman b Taylor	27	— lbw b Taylor	55
B. J. Booth c Davison b Forbes	2	— b Taylor	83
C. C. Inman c Davison b Taylor	4	— not out	113
P. Marner st Swetman b White	104	— b Forbes	49
D. J. Constant run out	7		
†R. W. Tolchard c Swetman b White	5		
*G. A. R. Lock c Swetman b Stead	0		
J. S. Savage b White	11		
J. Cotton not out	16		
C. T. Spencer b Taylor	1		
L-b 3, n-b 3	6	B 1, l-b 9, n-b 3	13
1/51 2/54 3/59 4/80 5/108 6/123 7/124 8/175 9/211	213	1/0 2/84 3/228 4/313 (4 wkts.)	313

Bowling: *First Innings*—Davison 14—2—43—0; Stead 14—2—38—1; Forbes 23—7—48—1; Taylor 15.5—6—21—4; White 15—4—57—3. *Second Innings*—Davison 5—2—13—1; Stead 19—3—81—0; Forbes 16—4—59—1; Taylor 19—3—90—2; White 12—0—57—0.

Umpires: P. B. Wight and O. W. Herman.

NOTTINGHAMSHIRE v. WARWICKSHIRE

At Nottingham, August 20, 21, 22. Warwickshire won by an innings and 41 runs. Nottinghamshire gave a dismal batting display on a good pitch and were dismissed for 91 runs with the pace men, Brown (four for 34) and Bannister (three for 23) doing most damage. By contrast Warwickshire were in no trouble at the crease and M. J. K. Smith was in good form. Rain curtailed the Sunday play and considerably restricted the attendance, but Smith took his contribution to 117 in three hours and ten minutes, the next best performance being Abberley's 76. The Nottinghamshire batting was again undistinguished and Warwickshire swept to a resounding victory. In their innings Brown again bowled well with four wickets for 45. The medium-paced Cartwright also played a big part (four for 54) and the only serious resistance was offered by Murray who hit defiantly.

Nottinghamshire

*N. Hill b Brown	13	— c Edmonds b Brown	17
J. B. Bolus c Cartwright b Brown	6	— c Bannister b Cartwright	22
D. L. Murray b Cartwright	7	— c Gordon b Bannister	41
H. I. Moore c Cartwright b Allan	4	— c Bannister b Brown	27
M. J. Smedley c Gordon b Bannister	16	— c Allan b Bannister	0
R. A. White c Gordon b Brown	13	— c Gordon b Cartwright	0
†R. Swetman lbw b Brown	6	— c Ibadulla b Cartwright	7
M. Taylor c Cartwright b Bannister	14	— c M. J. K. Smith b Brown	9
A. Johnson c A. C. Smith b Bannister	0	— c Brown b Cartwright	0
C. Forbes b Cartwright	4	— lbw b Brown	9
B Stead not out	7	— not out	2
L-b 1	1		
1/15 2/22 3/26 4/44 5/51 6/65 7/68 8/69 9/80	91	1/39 2/39 3/97 4/97 5/107 6/107 7/118 8/118 9/129	134

Bowling: *First Innings*—Brown 18—8—34—4; Bannister 17—4—23—3; Cartwright 11.1—2—28—2; Allan 4—2—5—1. *Second Innings*—Brown 20.3—9—45—4; Bannister 10—3—20—2; Cartwright 24—6—54—4; Allan 4—2—5—0; Edmonds 3—0—10—0.

Warwickshire

K. Ibadulla c Swetman b Stead	2	J. M. Allan not out	3
R. N. Abberley b White	76	D. J. Brown c Swetman b Stead	10
A. Gordon c Hill b Taylor	11	J. D. Bannister not out	4
*M. J. K. Smith c Stead b Johnson	117		
R. B. Edmonds c Swetman b Stead	18	B 7, l-b 1	8
J. A. Jameson c Swetman b Johnson	12		
†A. C. Smith c Bolus b Taylor	4	1/2 2/48 3/148 4/211 (9 wkts., dec.)	266
T. W. Cartwright b Taylor	1	5/233 6/244 7/244 8/247 9/261	

Bowling: Stead 26—7—59—3; Johnson 15—1—43—2; Taylor 25—4—77—3; Forbes 19.2—4—58—0; White 11—6—21—1.

Umpires: O. W. Herman and R. Aspinall.

At Chesterfield, August 24, 25, 26. NOTTINGHAMSHIRE lost to DERBYSHIRE by 159 runs.

At Canterbury, August 27, 29, 30. NOTTINGHAMSHIRE drew with KENT.

SOMERSET

President—W. T. GRESWELL

Secretary—RICHARD ROBINSON, County Cricket Ground, St. James's Street, Taunton

Captain—C. R. M. ATKINSON

C. R. M. Atkinson

County Badge

M. Kitchen

Somerset enjoyed their most successful season since joining the Championship in 1891. They equalled the previous highest position attained, third, and by winning thirteen Championship matches established a new record. Indeed, partisans could produce a case that Somerset should have won the competition, considering that two of their leading bowlers were injured early in the game against Yorkshire, the eventual Champions, which was lost by 49 runs, and last-wicket stands denied them victory over Surrey and Northamptonshire. Somerset also enjoyed a fine run in the Gillette Cup before they went down in the semi-final to the new holders, Warwickshire. The Cup successes helped to adjust some disturbing losses in membership and gate receipts.

Colin Atkinson, in his second year of captaincy, displayed much more authority and confidence than in 1965. Besides setting an inspiring example in the field, he revealed invaluable batting attributes which saved many an apparently lost cause and passed 1,000 runs for the first time. Kitchen, given a long trial at number three, succeeded excellently and Robinson, in spite of a mid-season eclipse, showed further development with his left-arm slows. He also revealed considerable batting ability and, like Kitchen, gained his county cap.

Perhaps the most interesting newcomer was Burgess, of Glastonbury, a well-built twenty-three-year-old with a flair for any ball game. His brisk right-arm bowling, occasional brilliant fielding and most attractive stroke play could develop into something of great benefit to the county and the game.

For the first time, three Somerset bowlers each took 100 wickets. Langford, the first there, passed 1,000 wickets in his Testimonial year; Rumsey completed his 100 with the final delivery of Somerset's Championship season and K. E. Palmer, after his long battle against injury in 1965, made a splendid return with 109 wickets and 898 runs.

Although both opening batsmen, Graham Atkinson and Virgin, were quietly successful on the many unreliable surfaces they did not often come off together, a fact that made Kitchen's efforts so praiseworthy. Virgin underlined his virtues with some brilliant close-wicket fielding that brought him 42 catches, a county record.

The remarkable contribution Alley has made to Somerset continued to the tune of over 1,000 runs and 50 wickets and Clayton's wicket-keeping varied little from the high standard he set in his first year.

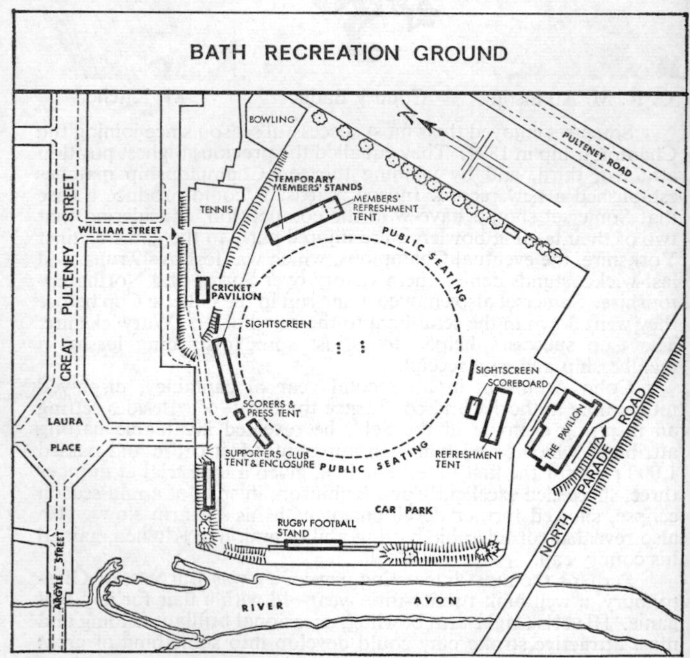

SOMERSET RESULTS

All First-Class Matches—Played 30, *Won* 14, *Lost* 7, *Drawn* 9
County Championship Matches—Played 28, *Won* 13, *Lost* 7, *Drawn* 7, *No Decision* 1

COUNTY CHAMPIONSHIP AVERAGES

BATTING

	Birthplace	Mtchs.	Inns.	Not Outs	Runs	100's	Highest Inns.	Aver.
M. Kitchen....	*Nailsea*	28	50	3	1360	2	111*	28.93
G. Atkinson....	*Lofthouse*	28	51	2	1280	2	148	26.12
C. R. M. Atkinson	*Thornaby-on-Tees*	28	48	8	1026	0	89	25.65
R. Virgin......	*Taunton*	28	51	1	1255	0	98	25.10
W. E. Alley....	*Sydney*	28	47	3	968	2	110*	22.00
K. E. Palmer...	*Winchester*	28	47	8	851	1	118	21.82
G. Burgess.....	*Glastonbury*	12	19	1	370	0	69	20.55
P. J. Robinson.	*Worcester*	26	40	11	480	0	66	16.55
T. E. Barwell...	*Transvaal*	4	8	0	130	0	56	16.27
A. Clarkson....	*Killinghall*	8	14	1	189	0	74*	14.53
G. Clayton.....	*Mossley*	28	46	4	594	0	63	14.14
B. Roe........	*Cleethorpes*	4	8	0	102	0	32	12.75
B. A. Langford.	*Birmingham*	27	36	14	220	0	55*	10.00
F. E. Rumsey..	*Stepney*	26	29	17	90	0	18*	7.50
C. Greetham...	*Wargrave*	2	4	0	26	0	19	6.50

Also batted: R. Palmer (*Devizes*), 5 and 1; F. T. Willetts (*Warwickshire*), 7 and 6.

* *Signifies not out.*

BOWLING

	Overs	Maidens	Runs	Wickets	Average
B. A. Langford..........	996.4	426	1888	111	17.00
F. E. Rumsey...........	753	193	1723	95	18.13
K. E. Palmer...........	685.2	143	1838	98	18.75
W. E. Alley............	503	162	986	50	19.72
P. J. Robinson..........	678.3	285	1434	70	20.48
C. R. M. Atkinson.......	106.1	28	272	11	24.72
R. Palmer.............	57.4	15	174	7	24.85
G. Burgess.............	15.4	2	45	0	—

Also bowled: R. Virgin 1—1—0—0.

At Taunton, April 30. SOMERSET beat SUSSEX by four wickets. (See GILLETTE CUP.)

SOMERSET v. HAMPSHIRE

At the Imperial Ground, Bristol, May 7, 9, 10. *65 overs.* Drawn. A stout rearguard action by their captain, C. R. M. Atkinson and Palmer saved Somerset after they had been outplayed for much of the game. Marshall's gay attack brought him 65 of 99 in eighty-five minutes, and useful innings by Horton and Reed gave the pace bowlers Shackleton and Cottam an opportunity to build up an important first-innings advantage, which they did in excellent style. Only

G. Atkinson prospered at all, and Hampshire led by 88. Rumsey with the greenish pitch still reacting to the new ball, struck back firmly, with a spell of six for 35, until Wheatley, Shackleton and White, the latter hitting three 6's, rescued the innings from 47 for seven. Somerset, needing 235 to win in four and a quarter hours, collapsed against Shackleton, whose first twenty-five overs brought him four for 18 as the score ran to 61 for five, with two and a quarter hours left. G. Atkinson again defended stoutly and his captain and Palmer stayed together for seventy minutes, the game being given up ten minutes before the scheduled end.

Hampshire

First innings		Second innings	
*R. E. Marshall b Alley	65	lbw b Rumsey	9
B. L. Reed b Palmer	49	lbw b Palmer	0
H. Horton c Roe b Alley	42	c Clayton b Rumsey	14
D. A. Livingstone lbw b Alley	4	b Rumsey	1
G. L. Keith not out	14	c Alley b Rumsey	10
P. J. Sainsbury not out	2	lbw b Rumsey	8
†B. S. V. Timms (did not bat)		c Clayton b Rumsey	3
K. J. Wheatley (did not bat)		c Clayton b Alley	23
D. Shackleton (did not bat)		b Alley	37
D. W. White (did not bat)		b Rumsey	28
R. M. Cottam (did not bat)		not out	6
B 4, l-b 12, n-b 5	21	B 1, l-b 3, n-b 3	7
1/98 2/160 3/175 4/186 (4 wkts., 65 overs)	197	1/2 2/12 3/19 4/28 5/43 6/46 7/47 8/98 9/134	146

Bowling: *First Innings*—Rumsey 15—3—35—0; Palmer 17—3—65—1; Alley 28—9—54—3; C. R. M. Atkinson 5—0—22—0. *Second Innings*—Rumsey 29—7—48—7; Palmer 18—4—49—1; Alley 16.2—5—41—2; Langford 2—1—1—0.

Somerset

First innings		Second innings	
R. Virgin c Timms b Shackleton	5	lbw b Shackleton	5
B. Roe c Timms b Cottam	19	c Horton b Shackleton	32
M. Kitchen c Timms b White	7	lbw b Shackleton	15
G. Atkinson c Timms b Shackleton	40	c Keith b Sainsbury	14
C. Greetham c Marshall b Cottam	0	c Reed b Cottam	3
W. E. Alley b Cottam	16	b Shackleton	0
*C. R. M. Atkinson c Reed b Shackleton	9	not out	46
K. E. Palmer c Keith b Cottam	9	not out	37
†G. Clayton c Horton b Shackleton	2		
B. Langford not out	1		
F. E. Rumsey c Keith b Cottam	0		
B 1	1	B 5	5
1/11 2/22 3/43 4/45 5/71 6/84 7/102 8/108 9/109	109	1/17 2/49 3/54 4/61 5/61 6/95 (6 wkts.)	157

Bowling: *First Innings*—Shackleton 30—9—43—4; White 16—3—37—1; Cottam 13.1—4—28—5. *Second Innings*—Shackleton 32—18—25—4; White 12—1—41—0; Cottam 12—2—19—1; Sainsbury 18—9—27—1; Wheatley 16—3—40—0.

Umpires: W. E. Phillipson and R. Aspinall.

SOMERSET v. YORKSHIRE

At Taunton, May 11, 12, 13. *65 overs.* Yorkshire won by eight wickets. After many delays on the first two days of the game, the Yorkshire spinners came into their own on a drying pitch on the final day, the match ending twenty minutes after lunch. A moderate Somerset first innings total owed a good deal to the seventh-wicket pair, C. R. M. Atkinson and Palmer, who added 52 valuable runs in the last ten overs. Yorkshire's lead of 36 depended largely on a second-wicket stand of 96 in even time from Taylor and Padgett, while in the later stages, Sharpe played attractively, and Trueman swung willingly, hitting Rumsey for 6. Yorkshire declared after 63.2 overs, but Wilson and Illingworth changed the picture completely when after a stand of 30 for the second wicket Virgin and Kitchen were both out to stumpings. In twenty-seven minutes, seven wickets fell for 11 runs as the ball spun quickly, but less devastatingly than the score suggested. Langford and Rumsey made 20 for the last wicket, but the innings took only one hour, forty minutes to complete. Langford made Yorkshire struggle but the necessary 35 came in an hour

Somerset

First Innings		Second Innings	
R. Virgin st Binks b Close	32	st Binks b Wilson	17
B. Roe b Nicholson	9	c Hampshire b Trueman	0
M. Kitchen c Binks b Trueman	21	st Binks b Illingworth	13
G. Atkinson lbw b Nicholson	36	c Trueman b Illingworth	0
C. Greetham c Trueman b Wilson	19	c Close b Wilson	4
W. E. Alley lbw b Nicholson	6	run out	0
*C. R. M. Atkinson not out	28	c Waring b Wilson	0
K. E. Palmer not out	21	c Hampshire b Wilson	5
†G. Clayton (did not bat)		c and b Wilson	4
B. Langford (did not bat)		lbw b Illingworth	14
F. E. Rumsey (did not bat)		not out	13
B 2, l-b 2, n-b 2	6		
1/9 2/55 3/71 4/116 5/121 6/126 (6 wkts., 65 overs)	178	1/0 2/30 3/30 4/32, 5/32 6/34 7/35 8/41 9/50	70

Bowling: *First Innings*—Trueman 18—2—47—1; Nicholson 23—6—45—3; Waring 5—0—20—0; Close 12—5—31—1; Wilson 7—1—29—1. *Second Innings*—Trueman 4—1—8—1; Nicholson 1—1—0—0; Waring 2—0—5—0; Wilson 12—3—40—5; Illingworth 12—4—17—3.

Yorkshire

First Innings		Second Innings	
K. Taylor b C. R. M. Atkinson	54	b Langford	12
*D. B. Close c Clayton b Rumsey	12	b Langford	9
D. E. V. Padgett b Palmer	63	not out	7
J. H. Hampshire b Palmer	2	not out	8
P. J. Sharpe not out	40		
R. Illingworth c Clayton b Palmer	5		
F. S. Trueman not out	27		
B 1, l-b 7, w 1, n-b 2	11		
1/17 2/113 3/120 4/162 5/170 (5 wkts., dec.)	214	1/11 2/26 (2 wkts.)	36

†J. G. Binks, D. Wilson, A. G. Nicholson and J. Waring did not bat.

Bowling: *First Innings*—Rumsey 15.2—4—38—1; Palmer 22—5—60—3; Alley 11—2—49—0; Langford 4—1—23—0; C. R. M. Atkinson 11—3—33—1. *Second Innings*—Rumsey 3—0—4—0; Palmer 3—0—5—0; Langford 8.2—3—20—2; Alley 8—4—7—0.

Umpires: R. Aspinall and W. E. Phillipson.

At Ilford, May 14, 15, 16. SOMERSET drew with ESSEX.

SOMERSET v. LEICESTERSHIRE

At Taunton, May 18, 19, 20. Somerset won by three wickets. Alley swung at the final possible ball, and edged it high over the wicket-keeper for the deciding boundary that gave Somerset their first points of the season. Fortunes fluctuated rapidly throughout, Leicestershire being bowled out for 178 after Hallam with 72 in three hours and Norman, two and a half hours for 33, had put on 95 for the second wicket. Palmer's most successful spell of the season brought him six for 28. Rumsey previously achieved the important break. A finely sustained spell by Spencer kept Somerset in check and despite 41 from Alley and 51 not out by Palmer, Somerset fell 11 runs short on the final morning, rain having made deep inroads. Again, Leicestershire started soundly, the second wicket falling at 63, but this time the slow left-arm, Robinson, and Langford changed the scene. Norman defended stoutly for two and three-quarter hours, but Robinson with five for 28 and two notable close catches opened the game. Somerset needed 139 to win in one hour fifty minutes, but seemed to have little chance when Clayton joined Alley with four wickets and half an hour left to get another 52. By most bold methods they put on 46, Alley and Robinson taking nine runs off the last five balls. Alley's 42 came off thirty-two balls.

Leicestershire

First Innings		Second Innings	
M. R. Hallam b Rumsey	72	c Clayton b Alley	18
B. J. Booth c Clayton b Rumsey	2	st Clayton b Robinson	25
M. E. Norman b Rumsey	33	c Robinson b Langford	35
P. Marner c Roe b Langford	17	c Palmer b Robinson	0
C. C. Inman c Clayton b Palmer	6	b Robinson	0
J. Birkenshaw lbw b Palmer	0	b Rumsey	0
D. Constant c Clayton b Palmer	14	c Roe b Robinson	12
†R. W. Tolchard c Kitchen b Palmer	21	c Kitchen b. Robinson	0
*G. A. R. Lock c Alley b Palmer	3	c Clayton b Rumsey	14
C. T. Spencer not out	0	c Robinson b Langford	10
J. S. Savage b Palmer	0	not out	2
L-b 9, n-b 1	10	B 7, l-b 3, n-b 1	11
1/7 2/102 3/115 4/133 5/137 6/138 7/173 8/177 9/178	178	1/26 2/63 3/67 4/67 5/68 6/90 7/92 8/94 9/116	127

Bowling: *First Innings*—Rumsey 22—10—35—3; Palmer 14.2—3—28—6; Alley 16—7—24—0; C. R. M. Atkinson 11—3—22—0; Langford 31—11—42—1; Robinson 8—2—17—0. *Second Innings*—Rumsey 13.4—3—29—2; Palmer 3—1—14—0; Alley 4—1—8—1; Langford 28—12—37—2; Robinson 23—15—28—5.

Somerset

First Innings		Second Innings	
R. Virgin c and b Marner	18	c Hallam b Marner	23
B. Roe lbw b Spencer	15	c Tolchard b Spencer	15
M. Kitchen run out	11	c Inman b Marner	21
G. Atkinson run out	0	c Tolchard b Marner	2
W. E. Alley c Booth b Lock	41	not out	42
*C. R. M. Atkinson b Spencer	10	run out	8
K. E. Palmer not out	51	c Marner b Lock	6
†G. Clayton b Spencer	1	c Norman b Spencer	18
P. J. Robinson c Lock b Marner	12	not out	3
B. Langford lbw b Spencer	0		
F. E. Rumsey b Spencer	4		
B 1, l-b 3	4	L-b 3	3
1/33 2/33 3/36 4/51 5/61 6/109 7/110 8/156 9/157	167	1/22 2/47 3/49 4/70 5/76 6/87 7/133 (7 wkts.)	141

Bowling: *First Innings*—Spencer 34—10—50—5; Marner 31—13—84—2; Lock 14—4—29—1. *Second Innings*—Spencer 10—1—40—2; Marner 16—1—68—3; Lock 7—1—30—1.

Umpires: C. G. Pepper and A. Jepson.

At Taunton, May 21, SOMERSET beat YORKSHIRE by 40 runs. (See GILLETTE CUP.)

At Nottingham, May 25, 26, 27. Somerset beat Nottinghamshire by 178 runs.

SOMERSET v. GLOUCESTERSHIRE

At Bath, May 28, 30, 31. *65 overs.* Somerset won by 139 runs, an achievement largely due to their spinners; Langford took ten wickets for 82 and Robinson eight for 99. Bright batting by Clayton and Palmer rescued Somerset's innings on a turning pitch, but after a good start from Milton, Robinson made Gloucestershire fight for first innings lead, which came off the last possible ball, Meyer skying Robinson for two. C. R. M. Atkinson in his innings for Somerset hit two sixes and eight 4's and saved them in their second attempt. Consequently with good support from the tail, 81 for six became 238 all out. Gloucestershire, needing 238 to win, again started briskly, but three cheap wickets to Langford overnight destroyed the innings. Apart from some fine strokes Shepherd, the batting folded without spirit. The last seven wickets added only 53, Langford taking eight for 26.

Somerset

First innings		Second innings	
G. Atkinson c Nicholls b Allen	15	— c Mortimore b A. S. Brown	2
R. Virgin c A. S. Brown b Allen	9	— b Allen	21
M. Kitchen c Shepherd b Windows	29	— lbw b Allen	3
A. Clarkson c and b Windows	8	— c Bissex b Allen	9
W. E. Alley lbw b Windows	17	— b Mortimore	32
*C. R. M. Atkinson c Meyer b Allen	4	— lbw b A. S. Brown	89
K. E. Palmer not out	36	— c D. Brown b Mortimore	8
†G. Clayton c Milton b Windows	35	— c Milton b Mortimore	23
P. J. Robinson b Windows	0	— b Bissex	30
B. A. Langford run out	10	— c A. S. Brown b Allen	15
F. E. Rumsey (did not bat)		— not out	0
B 1, l-b 10	11	B 2, l-b 4	6
1/22 2/37 3/67 4/74 5/91 6/91 7/154 8/164 9/174 (9 wkts., 65 overs)	174	1/4 2/25 3/28 4/40 5/76 6/81 7/111 8/166 9/238	238

Bowling: *First Innings*—A. S. Brown 15—4—40—0; Windows 23—7—61—5; Allen 23—10—46—3; Mortimore 4—0—16—0. *Second Innings*—A. S. Brown 17.1—5—28—2; Windows 8—2—16—0; Allen 35—11—79—4; Mortimore 27—3—86—3; Bissex 9—4—23—1.

Gloucestershire

First innings		Second innings	
R. B. Nicholls run out	14	— c Alley b Langford	13
C. A. Milton c Clayton b Robinson	69	— c Alley b Langford	23
S. E. Russell b Langford	31	— c Virgin b Langford	0
M. Bissex st Clayton b Robinson	0	— c Virgin b Langford	15
D. Brown c Clayton b Robinson	14	— b Langford	6
D. Shepherd c C. R. M. Atkinson b Robinson	1	— b Langford	20
*J. B. Mortimore b Langford	2	— b Robinson	3
A. S. Brown b Robinson	9	— c Clarkson b Robinson	5
D. A. Allen st Clayton b Robinson	12	— not out	5
A. R. Windows not out	7	— c Robinson b Langford	1
†B. J. Meyer not out	2	— b Langford	0
B 5, l-b 8, n-b 1	14	B 4, l-b 2, n-b 1	7
1/53 2/113 3/123 4/139 5/141 6/141 7/143 8/158 9/173 (9 wkts., 65 overs)	175	1/36 2/36 3/37 4/46 5/48 6/65 7/86 8/93 9/93	98

Bowling: *First Innings*—Rumsey 7—2—24—0; Alley 7—2—19—0; C. R. M. Atkinson 2—0—7—0; Robinson 26—7—55—6; Langford 23—4—56—2. *Second Innings*—Rumsey 3—0—12—0; Palmer 2—0—9—0; Robinson 21—10—44—2; Langford 20.1—9—26—8.

Umpires—J. Arnold and A. Gaskell.

SOMERSET v. KENT

At Bath, June 1, 2, 3. Kent won by 164 runs, a remarkable effort considering they lost three wickets in the first fifteen minutes for 14 runs. The composed stroke-making of Denness on a slow, wearing pitch which admitted extravagant turn, saved the first innings. He made 97 out of 215 in four and a half hours and followed this with a superb effort—87 out of 137 in two hours, twenty minutes, his splendid batting being quite out of context with the struggles of the others. In both their innings, Somerset collapsed before Dixon (eight for 104) and Underwood (eleven for 133). The last morning was enlivened by some big hitting by Alley, who made 29 in fifteen minutes, and Barwell, whose 56 occupied only an hour. The game lasted one hour and forty minutes on the final morning, Somerset's last eight wickets adding 149, a bold response to the well-nigh impossible task of getting 352 to win.

Kent

First Innings		Second Innings	
B. W. Luckhurst c Clayton b Palmer	3	c Clayton b Robinson	14
M. H. Denness c Virgin b Palmer	97	st Clayton b Robinson	87
D. Nicholls b Palmer	0	c Virgin b Langford	3
S. E. Leary b Rumsey	3	c Clayton b Palmer	13
J. M. Prodger c and b Robinson	36	c Virgin b Robinson	9
A. Ealham c Alley b Robinson	37	not out	57
†A. Knott c Kitchen b Langford	1	c and b Langford	14
*A. Dixon c C. R. M. Atkinson b Langford	12	b Palmer	11
A. Brown b Rumsey	20	not out	9
D. M. Sayer not out	16		
D. L. Underwood b Rumsey	1		
B 1, n-b 1	2	B 4, l-b 10	14
1/11 2/11 3/14 4/67 5/117 6/118 7/151 8/191 9/215	228	1/62 2/83 3/118 4/132 5/137 6/160 7/201 (7 wkts., dec.)	231

Bowling: *First Innings*—Rumsey 15.2—4—36—3; Palmer 13—2—44—3; Alley 2—0—9—0; Robinson 36—14—61—2; Langford 32—12—76—2. *Second Innings*—Rumsey 4—1—20—0; Palmer 8—1—40—2; Langford 34—13—64—2; Robinson 30—10—93—3.

Somerset

First Innings		Second Innings	
G. Atkinson b Dixon	29	c Prodger b Underwood	10
R. Virgin c Brown b Dixon	16	run out	24
M. Kitchen b Dixon	1	c Leary b Dixon	5
T. E. Barwell lbw b Dixon	0	c Knott b Underwood	56
W. E. Alley b Dixon	0	c Leary b Dixon	29
*C. R. M. Atkinson c Prodger b Underwood	1	c Leary b Underwood	15
K. E. Palmer c Prodger b Underwood	22	b Underwood	6
†G. Clayton c Nicholls b Underwood	14	b Underwood	14
P. J. Robinson c Knott b Underwood	8	c Ealham b Dixon	8
B. Langford not out	11	not out	6
F. E. Rumsey c Brown b Underwood	0	c Brown b Underwood	6
B 4, l-b 2	6	B 4, l-b 4	8
1/25 2/26 3/26 4/26 5/27 6/75 7/75 8/93 9/102	108	1/27 2/34 3/45 4/45 5/78 6/148 7/150 8/171 9/177	187

Bowling: *First Innings*—Brown 6—2—10—0; Sayer 3—0—8—0; Underwood 23.2—11—55—5; Dixon 21—10—29—5. *Second Innings*—Brown 3—1—11—0; Sayer 2—0—15—0; Underwood 22.3—6—78—6; Dixon 22—5—75—3.

Umpires: J. Arnold and A. E. Fagg.

SOMERSET v. SURREY

At Bath, June 4, 6. *65 overs.* Somerset won by two wickets, the wearing, breaking pitch accounting for 38 wickets falling for 444 runs during the ten hours the match lasted. Four bowlers took 36 wickets, the leading performers being Pocock (ten for 84) and Robinson (eleven for 87). Surrey began reasonably, then collapsed against Robinson, while Somerset, after a disastrous beginning against Storey, recovered through their middle batting to gain a first-innings lead of 17. Within eighty-five minutes of the second day, Surrey reached 39 for nine, but some lusty play from Pocock, who hit five 6's in 45 not out, his highest championship score, found response from Harman. Together they added 68 for the final wicket. G. Atkinson and Alley attacked to some purpose as Somerset needed 91 to win, but wickets fell steadily around Kitchen. At tea, Pocock and Storey had reduced Somerset to 82 for eight, but two fine boundaries from Kitchen, who had played excellently for seventy-eight minutes, eventually carried the day.

Surrey

J. H. Edrich lbw b Langford	32	— c Virgin b Robinson	11
W. A. Smith c Clayton b Langford	16	— c Palmer b Langford	11
R. A. E. Tindall c and b Robinson	22	— c Robinson b Langford	7
*M. J. Stewart c Virgin b Langford	0	— st Clayton b Langford	0
M. D. Willett c Virgin b Robinson	14	— c Clayton b Langford	5
S. J. Storey c Barwell b Robinson	0	— c Barwell b Robinson	1
M. J. Edwards c Rumsey b Robinson	2	— c Robinson b Langford	0
R. I. Jefferson c Palmer b Robinson	12	— c Rumsey b Robinson	4
P. I. Pocock c Barwell b Robinson	0	— not out	45
†A. Long b Robinson	6	— c Rumsey b Robinson	0
R. Harman not out	2	— st Clayton b Alley	23
L-b 7, n-b 1	8		
1/37 2/56 3/58 4/75 5/84 6/85 7/103 8/105 9/109	114	1/16 2/29 3/29 4/32 5/35 6/35 7/36 8/39 9/39	107

Bowling: *First Innings*—Rumsey 4—1—13—0; Palmer 3—0—16—0; Robinson 22.5—11—48—7; Langford 22—8—29—3. *Second Innings*—Rumsey 7—2—10—0; Alley 2.5—2—4—1; Robinson 20—12—39—4; Langford 24—10—54—5.

Somerset

G. Atkinson lbw b Storey	1	— c Stewart b Pocock	22
R. Virgin c Stewart b Pocock	12	— c Edwards b Pocock	8
M. Kitchen c Harman b Storey	0	— not out	33
T. E. Barwell c Tindall b Storey	7	— b Pocock	3
W. E. Alley c Edwards b Pocock	24	— c Stewart b Pocock	15
*C. R. M. Atkinson lbw b Pocock	21	— c Edwards b Pocock	0
K. E. Palmer c Edrich b Pocock	18	— c Long b Pocock	1
†G. Clayton c Willett b Storey	24	— b Storey	2
P. J. Robinson c Edwards b Jefferson	7	— lbw b Storey	2
B. A. Langford c Long b Storey	4	— not out	2
F. E. Rumsey not out	3		
B 4, l-b 6	10	L-b 4	4
1/1 2/1 3/8 4/45 5/50 6/77 7/108 8/118 9/127	131	1/24 2/33 3/41 4/67 5/67 6/71 7/78 8/82	(8 wkts.) 92

Bowling: *First Innings*—Jefferson 9.5—4—15—1; Storey 22—10—29—5; Pocock 20—7—46—4; Harman 7—1—31—0. *Second Innings*—Storey 15—1—46—2; Jefferson 7—4—4—0; Pocock 17.5—6—38—6.

Umpires: A. E. Fagg and A. E. Alderman.

At Lord's, June 8, 9, 10. SOMERSET lost to MIDDLESEX by six wickets.

At Northampton, June 11, 12, 13. SOMERSET drew with NORTHAMPTONSHIRE.

SOMERSET v. CAMBRIDGE UNIVERSITY

At Taunton, June 18, 20, 21. Somerset won by two wickets. This closely fought match found batsmen for the most part in difficulties against bowlers who exploited the help they received from the pitch, which was affected by rain on all three days. Cambridge won the toss when the pitch was dry, but soon lost three wickets before the first heavy storm occurred. Somerset missed several catches, whereas Cambridge excelled in the slips. Russell and Palfreman took the first five county wickets which fell on Saturday for 69. On Monday, the brothers Palmer added 40 for the ninth wicket on a dry pitch and Somerset led by seven runs. A sound fifty by Chambers enabled Cambridge to reach 116 for four by the close of the second day, but he was run out next morning when K. E. Palmer on a damp pitch claimed the five remaining wickets, catching Sinker off his brother's bowling. Due largely to the steadiness of Virgin and the brisk hitting of Alley, Somerset, who needed 159 to win in three hours and twenty minutes, just managed to complete their task.

Cambridge University

K. P. W. J. McAdam b Rumsey	23	— b Rumsey	13
R. E. Chambers b R. Palmer	0	— run out	58
A. V. E. Gould c Virgin b Rumsey	1	— lbw b K. E. Palmer	7
*D. L. Murray run out	0	— b K. E. Palmer	0
†D. L. Hays c Greetham b K. E. Palmer	40	— b Greetham	22
V. P. Malalasekera c Virgin b Rumsey	10	— b K. E. Palmer	15
G. A. Cottrell lbw b C. R. M. Atkinson	13	— b K. E. Palmer	14
A. B. Palfreman not out	20	— b K. E. Palmer	15
N. Sinker b K. E. Palmer	7	— c K. E. Palmer b R. Palmer	5
D. L. Acfield c Clayton b K. E. Palmer	0	— not out	5
S. G. Russell b Greetham	2	— c and b K. E. Palmer	1
L-b 3, w 4	7	L-b 5, w. 4, n-b 1	10
1/2 2/5 3/9 4/41 5/55 6/85 7/93 8/110 9/110	123	1/26 2/46 3/46 4/103 5/118 6/129 7/144 8/149 9/161	165

Bowling: *First Innings*—Rumsey 10—0—27—3; R. Palmer 9—0—31—1; K. E. Palmer 12—2—38—3; Alley 4—2—2—0; C. R. M. Atkinson 6—1—13—1; Greetham 2—1—5—1. *Second Innings*—Rumsey 11—0—34—1; R. Palmer 12—1—36—1; K. E. Palmer 19.5—3—59—6; C. R. M. Atkinson 5—1—8—0; Alley 6—3—9—0; Greetham 5—2—9—1.

Somerset

G. Atkinson b Russell	5	— c McAdam b Russell	5
R. Virgin c Cottrell b Palfreman	14	— b Acfield	55
M. Kitchen c Murray b Palfreman	27	— c Hays b Cottrell	12
T. E. Barwell b Russell	5	— c Russell b Acfield	9
W. E. Alley c Acfield b Russell	13	— c Malalasekera b Acfield	56
*C. R. M. Atkinson c Hays b Russell	2	— st Hays b Sinker	9
C. Greetham c Chambers b Palfreman	7	— c Hays b Acfield	5
K. E. Palmer not out	43	— not out	4
†G. Clayton c Hays b Russell	5	— b Sinker	0
R. Palmer b Sinker	5	— not out	0
F. E. Rumsey b Sinker	0		
L-b 4	4	B 2, l-b 4	6
1/6 2/46 3/53 4/53 5/59 6/76 7/78 8/90 9/130	130	1/14 2/37 3/58 4/115 5/144 6/153 7/157 8/157 (8 wkts.)	161

Bowling: *First Innings*—Russell 23—5—60—5; Palfreman 23—4—66—3; Sinker 3—3—0—2. *Second Innings*—Russell 6—2—19—1; Palfreman 11—3—24—0; Cottrell 8—2—29—1; Acfield 13.4—2—44—4; Sinker 11—2—39—2.

Umpires: J. Langridge and O. W. Herman.

At Taunton, June 22. SOMERSET beat LANCASHIRE by four wickets. (See GILLETTE CUP.)

SOMERSET v. WARWICKSHIRE

At Taunton, June 25, 27 28. *65 overs.* Warwickshire won by 53 runs. With the pitch damp on top, Warwickshire, having won the toss, quickly met trouble, losing two wickets and Ibadulla, hit in the mouth by a lifter, in brief time. However, Jameson hit one 6 and eighteen 4's in a very fine not out 118; he was helped by his captain in a stand of 168 which established the innings. Despite a useful 52 from Virgin, and a fighting 39 by Clarkson, the seam attack gave Warwickshire a lead of 55 which proved decisive. Hostile bowling by Rumsey, who took seven for 35, and a serious eye injury to Richardson put Warwickshire in trouble, but Amiss played with much fortitude for three hours. Needing 187 for victory, Somerset lost three wickets for seven runs, and after Alley and C. R. M. Atkinson had proved valuable partners to Virgin who hit another notable fifty, Allan and Ibadulla broke through the middle batting and Brown removed the tail.

Warwickshire

R. N. Abberley c Virgin b R. Palmer	17	— b Rumsey	0
K. Ibadulla retired hurt	1	— c Clayton b K. E. Palmer	28
D. L. Amiss b R. Palmer	0	— c Robinson b Rumsey	58
*M. J. K. Smith c Clarkson b Rumsey	66	— lbw b Rumsey	0
J. A. Jameson not out	118	— c K. E. Palmer b Rumsey	3
B. A. Richardson c C. R. M. Atkinson b R. Palmer	15	— retired hurt	3
T. W. Cartwright not out	8	— c Alley b Rumsey	20
J. M. Allan (did not bat)		— lbw b Rumsey	6
†A. C. Smith (did not bat)		— b R. Palmer	1
R. V. Webster (did not bat)		— b Rumsey	3
D. J. Brown (did not bat)		— not out	6
L-b 8, n-b 2	10	L-b 2, n-b 1	3
1/5 2/24 3/192 4/221 (4 wkts., 65 overs)	235	1/0 2/15 3/19 4/31 5/69 6/111 7/122 8/122 9/131	131

Bowling: *First Innings*—Rumsey 22—5—73—1; R. Palmer 20—5—72—3; Alley 11—4—31—0; K. E. Palmer 9—0—36—0; Robinson 3—0—13—0. *Second Innings*—Rumsey 18.1—4—35—7; R. Palmer 13—7—31—1; K. E. Palmer 12—3—33—1; Alley 11—4—20—0; Robinson 2—0—9—0.

Somerset

G. Atkinson c A. C. Smith b Brown	10	— b Webster	0
R. Virgin c Cartwright b Webster	52	— b Ibadulla	50
M. Kitchen c A. C. Smith b Webster	27	— lbw b Brown	0
A. Clarkson b Brown	39	— c A. C. Smith b Webster	3
W. E. Alley c Allan b Cartwright	13	— c Ibadulla b Brown	31
K. E. Palmer lbw b Cartwright	20	— c M. J. K. Smith b Ibadulla	5
*C. R. M. Atkinson not out	12	— b Allan	20
†G. Clayton b Brown	0	— b Allan	2
P. J. Robinson not out	1	— b Brown	6
R. Palmer (did not bat)		— b Brown	5
F. E. Rumsey (did not bat)		— not out	0
B 2, l-b 4	6	B 4, l-b 7	11
1/30 2/90 3/99 4/114 5/151 6/179 7/179 (7 wkts., 65 overs)	180	1/1 2/4 3/7 4/58 5/100 6/107 7/110 8/128 9/128	133

Bowling: *First Innings*—Brown 18—2—48—3; Webster 20—3—46—2; Cartwright 27—8—80—2. *Second Innings*—Brown 12.2—3—20—4; Webster 10—2—23—2; Cartwright 12—1—30—0; Allan 8—0—19—2; Ibadulla 10—2—30—2.

Umpires: W. F. Price and R. S. Lay.

SOMERSET v. GLAMORGAN

At Taunton, June 29, 30, July 1. *65 overs.* Somerset won by four wickets. After a fine start, especially by Hedges, on a good pitch, Glamorgan were completely subdued by Langford, who began with a spell of 12—11—11—2. Alley, in brilliant form, hit 110 not out in two and a half hours and gave Somerset a lead of 40, the brisk fourth wicket stand of 102 with Clarkson setting the scene. Glamorgan lost their openers before going ahead, but Walker and A. R. Lewis steadily made ground against the spinners. Walker's long and valuable innings held things together at one end, and as he cleverly organised the strike, the eighth wicket brought 46 runs. Somerset, with all the third day to get 123 to win began briskly, an opening partnership of 76 suggesting an easy victory. Then Cordle led a sharp counter-attack, and the final 47 runs occupied no fewer than two hours and ten minutes, six wickets falling around C. R. M. Atkinson, who stayed two hours for 24 not out.

Glamorgan

A. Jones c Kitchen b Langford	31	— b Rumsey	5
B. Hedges c Virgin b Alley	40	— c Clayton b Palmer	21
P. M. Walker b Langford	34	— not out	95
A. R. Lewis c Clayton b Rumsey	4	— c Palmer b Robinson	23
L. Hill not out	34	— st. Clayton b Langford	8
†E. Jones c Alley b Rumsey	9	— lbw b Langford	0
E. Lewis not out	9	— b Palmer	0
A. E. Cordle (did not bat)		— lbw b Palmer	0
D. J. Shepherd (did not bat)		— b Palmer	2
I. J. Jones (did not bat)		— c Virgin b Rumsey	4
*O. S. Wheatley (did not bat)		— lbw b Palmer	0
B 1, l-b 6, w 1	8	L-b 1, w 1, n-b 2	4
1/60 2/94 3/115 4/115 5/139 (5 wkts., 65 overs)	169	1/26 2/28 3/74 4/97 5/97 6/99 7/99 8/115 9/161	162

Bowling: *First Innings*: Rumsey 15—4—38—2; Palmer 7—0—31—0; Alley 22—7—51—1; C. R. M. Atkinson 6—0—20—0; Langford 15—12—21—2. *Second Innings*—Rumsey 16—4—40—2; Palmer 19.3—6—52—5; Robinson 24—9—34—1; Langford 32—17—32—2.

Somerset

G. Atkinson c E. Jones b Walker	18	— lbw b Cordle	29
R. Virgin c Walker b Wheatley	26	— c E. Jones b Shepherd	42
M. Kitchen lbw b Wheatley	2	— c Walker b I. J. Jones	9
A. Clarkson c Hedges b Wheatley	27	— lbw b Cordle	0
W. E. Alley not out	110		
*C. R. M. Atkinson c Walker b I. J. Jones	1	— not out	24
K. E. Palmer b Wheatley	20	— b Cordle	6
†G. Clayton not out	2	— b Cordle	1
P. J. Robinson (did not bat)		— not out	5
L-b 3	3	L-b 9, w 1, n-b 1	11
1/45 2/45 3/48 4/150 5/152 6/195 (6 wkts., 65 overs)	209	1/76 2/76 3/77 4/99 5/113 6/117 (6 wkts.)	127

B. A. Langford and F. E. Rumsey did not bat.

Bowling: *First Innings*—I. J. Jones 19—7—45—1; Wheatley 24—3—77—4; Cordle 6—0—29—0; Walker 11—3—35—1; Shepherd 5—2—20—0. *Second Innings*—I. J. Jones 19—10—32—1; Wheatley 12—3—19—0; E. Lewis 8—1—36—0; Shepherd 16—10—12—1; Cordle 13—5—17—4.

Umpires: W. F. Price and R. S. Lay.

At Sheffield, July 2, 4, 5. SOMERSET lost to YORKSHIRE by 49 runs.

At The Oval, July 6, 7, 8. SOMERSET drew with SURREY.

SOMERSET v. NORTHAMPTONSHIRE

At Glastonbury, July 9, 11, 12. Somerset won by nine wickets. Their total of 274 was founded on a fortunate opening stand of 76, and an attractive fifth wicket partnership of 113 between Kitchen, who batted for three hours, and C. R. M. Atkinson. With the pitch showing signs of wear, Northamptonshire were in the toils for most of the rest of the game. Palmer began their troubles by taking three wickets for seven in five overs and one ball. Then Langford dominated the remainder of the play. Taking eleven for 91 in 69 overs he was held up by a last-wicket stand of 32 between Lightfoot, who played excellently, and Durose. Following on 158 behind, Northamptonshire again broke down until the last morning when Lightfoot, attacking boldly, with 50 in seventy minutes, made positive efforts to take the initiative. He and P. J. Watts put on 69, then, with rain threatening, the tail fought a determined rearguard action. Sully batted one and three-quarter hours for 11 not out, and in the end, Northamptonshire, having begun the day 84 behind with only five second-innings wickets left, delayed Somerset's victory until 3.50 p.m. When Langford dismissed Mushtaq Mohammad in the second innings, he completed 1,000 wickets in a career which began in 1953.

Somerset

G. Atkinson b Durose	44	— not out	23
R. Virgin b Sully	40	— c Watts b Steele	12
M. Kitchen c Milburn b Durose	87	— not out	6
A. Clarkson b Crump	0		
W. E. Alley c Crump b Sully	7		
*C. R. M. Atkinson b Durose	52		
†G. Clayton c Watts b Durose	14		
P. Robinson c Lightfoot b Durose	7		
K. E. Palmer not out	6		
B. A. Langford b Crump	7		
F. E. Rumsey b Crump	0		
B 7, n-b 3	10	L-b 3, w 1, n-b 2	6
1/76 2/106 3/107 4/119 5/232 6/260 7/260 8/272 9/272	274	1/40	(1 wkt.) 47

Bowling: *First Innings*—Crump 38.3—12—83—3; Durose 26—7—64—5; Watts 15—1—48—0; Steele 3—2—6—0; Sully 18—5—41—2; Mushtaq 4—0—22—0. *Second Innings*—Crump 3—0—7—0; Durose 3—0—8—0; Sully 2—0—11—0; Lightfoot 4—1—13—0; Steele 2—1—2—1.

Northamptonshire

C. Milburn c C. R. M. Atkinson b Palmer	8	— b Langford	16
R. M. Prideaux b Palmer	11	— b Langford	19
D. S. Steele c Clayton b Rumsey	2	— c Kitchen b Langford	11
B. L. Reynolds c Palmer b Langford	17	— b Langford	15
Mushtaq Mohammad lbw b Palmer	0	— c Alley b Langford	0
P. J. Watts b Langford	14	— b Robinson	36
A. Lightfoot not out	38	— lbw b Robinson	50
B. Crump c Clarkson b Langford	0	— b Langford	4
H. Sully c Virgin b Rumsey	1	— not out	11
*†K. V. Andrew b Langford	4	— c Alley b Palmer	5
A. Durose b Robinson	11	— lbw b Langford	16
B 1, l-b 7, n-b 2	10	B 5, l-b 10, w 1, n-b 5	21
1/16 2/21 3/29 4/29 5/54 6/71 7/71 8/73 9/84	116	1/36 2/41 3/55 4/55 5/74 6/143 7/154 8/174 9/180	204

Bowling: *First Innings*—Rumsey 27—9—36—2; Palmer 14—5—25—3; Langford 20—12—28—4; Alley 4—2—10—0; Robinson 3.4—1—7—1. *Second Innings*—Rumsey 19—11—24—0; Palmer 15—3—28—1; Robinson 37—18—68—2; Langford 49—25—63—7.

Umpires: J. Langridge and A. E. Alderman.

At Bournemouth, July 13, 14, 15. SOMERSET drew with HAMPSHIRE.

At Taunton, July 16, 18, 19. SOMERSET drew with WEST INDIES. (See WEST INDIES section.)

At Southport, July 20, 21, 22. SOMERSET beat LANCASHIRE by an innings and 15 runs.

SOMERSET v. MIDDLESEX

At Weston-super-Mare, July 27, 28. Middlesex won by 164 runs. A brilliant innings by Hooker, who reached 100 in eighty-nine minutes, with one 6 and thirteen 4's dominated a match which otherwise was in complete charge of the bowlers. The dry pitch wore badly at a very early stage, and the process was quickened by the heavy rolling ordered by Middlesex. Hooker, who came in at 110 for five, scored his 102 out of 120 with a superb attacking display. Later, Somerset faced the possibility of following on at 80 for eight before a most effective counter-attack by Langford, who hit 55 in eighty-three minutes, reduced the deficit to 81. Clark led a hectic Middlesex attack on Rumsey but Langford, as batting conditions neared the impossible stage, took six for 60 and Somerset wanted 208 to win. They were all out in an hour for 43, Price taking six for 12. Titmus performed the first hat-trick of a career which began against Somerset at Bath in 1949.

Middlesex

First innings		Second innings	
W. E. Russell c Palmer b Langford	21	b Langford	11
T. Selwood c Clayton b Rumsey	0	c Robinson b Rumsey	17
P. H. Parfitt c Robinson b Langford	1	c Clayton b Rumsey	0
E. A. Clark c Virgin b Langford	43	c Palmer b Langford	35
C. T. Radley c Virgin b Robinson	33	c Robinson b Langford	4
*F. J. Titmus lbw b Langford	12	c Palmer b Langford	13
R. W. Hooker c C. R. M. Atkinson b Palmer	102	c Virgin b Langford	14
D. A. Bick c Clayton b Langford	0	b Langford	12
†E. G. Clifton run out	11	not out	4
R. W. Stewart not out	5	lbw b Rumsey	0
J. S. E. Price b Palmer	4	b Rumsey	0
L-b 3, n-b 4	7	B 12, l-b 1, n-b 3	16
1/2 2/13 3/28 4/90 5/110 6/128 7/131 8/223 9/230	239	1/15 2/16 3/45 4/59 5/95 6/95 7/115 8/122 9/126	126

Bowling: *First Innings*—Rumsey 15—4—39—1; Palmer 9.4—1—21—2; Langford 30—11—103—5; Alley 8—3—19—0; Robinson 17—5—50—1. *Second Innings*—Rumsey 22—5—46—4; Palmer 1—0—4—0; Langford 20—3—60—6.

Somerset

First innings		Second innings	
G. Atkinson c Russell b Price	2	b Titmus	11
R. Virgin c and b Price	27	c and b Price	0
M. Kitchen c Clifton b Price	10	lbw b Price	0
W. E. Alley b Titmus	14	c Selwood b Price	4
G. Burgess lbw b Titmus	0	c Parfitt b Titmus	4
*C. R. M. Atkinson c Russell b Titmus	7	c Clark b Price	2
K. E. Palmer c Bick b Titmus	22	c Russell b Price	10
†G. Clayton c Stewart b Bick	7	b Titmus	0
P. J. Robinson c Parfitt b Bick	0	not out	7
B. A. Langford not out	55	lbw b Titmus	0
F. E. Rumsey c Hooker b Titmus	5	c Clifton b Price	0
B 4, l-b 3, n-b 2	9	B 4, l-b 1	5
1/7 2/31 3/54 4/54 5/54 6/71 7/80 8/80 9/111	158	1/1 2/21 3/21 4/24 5/29 6/29 7/29 8/29 9/35	43

Bowling: *First Innings*—Price 23—7—52—3; Stewart 2—1—4—0; Titmus 28.4—8—58—5; Bick 9—1—35—2. *Second Innings*—Price 8.1—3—12—6; Stewart 1—0—2—0; Titmus 7—0—24—4.

Umpires: P. A. Gibb and W. H. Copson.

SOMERSET v. NOTTINGHAMSHIRE

At Weston-super-Mare, July 30, August 1, 2. Drawn. Rain ended the game at lunch-time on the third day when it had reached its most interesting state. Nottinghamshire were 115 ahead with six wickets down and three hours, twenty minutes remained. A heavily watered wicket produced some dull, slow cricket on the first two days. Moore and Smedley added 74 in two hours to redress a poor start by Nottinghamshire and the innings continued on Monday; it occupied altogether six and a quarter hours. That the Somerset deficit was only 32 was largely due to C. R. M. Atkinson, who, making 55 in ten minutes under three hours, stretched the score from 132 for six to 230 all out. On the final morning, with the pitch now dry and wearing considerably, Langford took six for 18. No other bowler could match his effectiveness, and as Swetman and Taylor counter-attacked briskly with a partnership of 48 Nottinghamshire were very much back in the game when the rain concluded proceedings.

Nottinghamshire

*N. Hill c C. R. M. Atkinson b Robinson	14	— c and b Langford	5
J. B. Bolus b Langford	7	— b Langford	16
D. L. Murray c Palmer b Langford	39	— c Palmer b Langford	0
H. I. Moore c Virgin b Rumsey	50	— c and b Langford	0
M. J. Smedley lbw b Palmer	51	— c Virgin b Langford	3
R. A. White b Alley	24	— c Clayton b Langford	6
†R. Swetman c Clayton b Palmer	4	— not out	33
M. Taylor b Rumsey	35	— not out	16
J. Parkin b Alley	4		
C. Forbes not out	11		
I. Davison b Palmer	9		
L-b 7, n-b 7	14	L-b 4	4
1/20 2/24 3/79 4/153 5/175 6/185 7/235 8/239 9/243	262	1/12 2/12 3/16 4/20 5/34 6/35 (6 wkts.)	83

Bowling: *First Innings*—Rumsey 25—4—65—2; Palmer 20.3—3—61—3; Langford 44—24—68—2; Robinson 29—13—45—1; Alley 11—6—9—2. *Second Innings*—Rumsey 7—4—13—0; Palmer 1—0—2—0; Langford 31—17—36—6; Robinson 24—15—28—0.

Somerset

G. Atkinson lbw b Taylor	9
R. Virgin c Hill b Forbes	21
M. Kitchen c Taylor b White	28
W. E. Alley c Forbes b White	0
G. Burgess c and b White	28
*C. R. M. Atkinson c Hill b Forbes	55
K. E. Palmer c Swetman b Davison	14
†G. Clayton b Taylor	29
P. J. Robinson not out	12
B. A. Langford c Hill b Forbes	9
F. E. Rumsey b Davison	2
B 9, l-b 9, w 1, n-b 4	23
1/13 2/43 3/50 4/80 5/99 6/132 7/199 8/211 9/223	230

Bowling: Davison 18.2—4—40—2; Taylor 25—10—45—2; Forbes 35—14—60—3; White 27—6—62—3.

Umpires: P. A. Gibb and W. H. Copson.

SOMERSET v. SUSSEX

At Weston-super-Mare, August 3, 4, 5. *65 overs.* Somerset won by ten wickets. A remarkable and unbroken opening partnership of 178 in even time between Graham Atkinson and Virgin, ended this contest in completely unexpected fashion. On a pitch showing generous signs of wear, their steady beginning and subsequent range of stroke quite confounded Sussex in a match previously very much in the grip of the bowlers. Suttle, who had retired hurt at 2, having swept a ball from Alley into his face, returned and bravely extended the Sussex innings from 87 for seven to 158 all out, despite Alley taking seven for 58. The substance of the Somerset first innings was provided by Burgess and Kitchen. Bates, however, struck back firmly and taking five for 63 sent Somerset from 97 for two to 152 all out, Langford having been sent to bed with a stomach upset for the first two days of the game. Sussex, six ahead, soon met trouble at 26 for three, but after a dogged innings of three hours from Oakman, Palmer continued his destructive efforts on the wearing pitch, finishing with eight for 59, his best figures of the season. Somerset needed 176 in four and a half hours for their ninth victory of the year, and against all expectation, Virgin and Atkinson completed the job with ninety-seven minutes to spare.

Sussex

L. J. Lenham c Palmer b Alley	16	— b Palmer	31
M. A. Buss lbw b Palmer	19	— c and b Palmer	1
K. G. Suttle not out	44	— b Rumsey	2
*Nawab of Pataudi c and b Alley	10	— lbw b Palmer	14
A. S. M. Oakman c Clayton b Rumsey	12	— c Clayton b Palmer	55
M. G. Griffith b Alley	0	— b Alley	7
P. J. Graves b Rumsey	3	— lbw b Palmer	11
D. J. Foreman c Clayton b Alley	16	— b Palmer	1
A. Buss b Alley	28	— lbw b Palmer	17
†T. Gunn c Clayton b Alley	0	— c Alley b Palmer	11
D. L. Bates st Clayton b Alley	2	— not out	4
L-b 5, w 1, n-b 2	8	B 6, l-b 8, n-b 1	15
1/26 2/48 3/55 4/55 5/60 6/71 7/87 8/134 9/134	158	1/2 2/5 3/26 4/77 5/110 6/128 7/141 8/147 9/148	169

Bowling: *First Innings*—Rumsey 24—7—72—2; Palmer 11—4—20—1; Alley 29.4—7—58—7. *Second Innings*—Rumsey 19—3—47—1; Palmer 29.1—9—59—8; Alley 23—12—16—1; Robinson 14—7—26—0; Langford 5—2—6—0.

Somerset

G. Atkinson c Oakman b Bates	4	— not out	82
R. Virgin lbw b A. Buss	13	— not out	86
M. Kitchen c and b Bates	52		
G. Burgess c Foreman b Bates	41		
W. E. Alley c Pataudi b Oakman	9		
*C. R. M. Atkinson b Bates	9		
K. E. Palmer c Pataudi b Bates	8		
†G. Clayton b Oakman	5		
P. J. Robinson c Gunn b Oakman	4		
F. E. Rumsey not out	0		
B. A. Langford absent ill	0		
B 2, l-b 1, n-b 4	7	B 6, l-b 4	10
1/16 2/24 3/97 4/109 5/127 6/139 7/144 8/148 9/152	152	(for no wkt.)	178

Bowling: *First Innings*—A. Buss 16—2—57—1; Bates 26—4—63—5; Oakman 20—8—25—3. *Second Innings*—A. Buss 12—3—36—0; Bates 19—5—38—0; Oakman 17—4—42—0; Suttle 5—1—15—0; M. A. Buss 9—2—21—0; Foreman 1.2—0—11—0; Lenham 1—0—5—0.

Umpires: P. A. Gibb and W. H. Copson.

At Bristol, August 6, 7, 8. SOMERSET drew with GLOUCESTERSHIRE.

At Cardiff, August 13, 15, 16. SOMERSET beat GLAMORGAN by 71 runs.

SOMERSET v. WORCESTERSHIRE

At Yeovil, August 20, 22, 23. Worcestershire won by eight wickets. A notable all-round performance by Horton, who made 84 and 55 not out, as well as taking five wickets for 74 in 42 overs followed a decisive first-innings spell of six for 28 by Gifford which gave the Champions an easy victory with ninety-five minutes to spare. The pitch was never entirely reliable. Horton, third out at 160, hit eleven 4's, while putting his side on the way to a large score. Langford, however, with a remarkable spell of six for 8 in 57 deliveries restricted the first-innings lead to 83. Next an opening partnership of 53 between Virgin and G. Atkinson, suggested that Somerset would make a fight but Horton took four wickets and altered things again. Clayton, Palmer and Robinson fought sternly to pose a task of 121 in nearly four hours. Fearnley was out immediately, but Kenyon and Ormrod provided excellent assistance for Horton, who hit seven boundaries in his 55 not out which occupied two and a quarter hours.

Somerset

First Innings		Second Innings	
G. Atkinson c Booth b Gifford	19	c Headley b Horton	16
R. Virgin c Ormrod b Coldwell	13	lbw b Gifford	40
M. Kitchen run out	23	c Ormrod b Horton	16
G. Burgess c Ormrod b Gifford	12	c and b Horton	10
W. E. Alley b Gifford	0	st Booth b Horton	24
*C. R. M. Atkinson b Horton	11	c and b Gifford	8
K. E. Palmer c Ormrod b Gifford	5	c Booth b Brain	33
†G. Clayton c Horton b Gifford	0	c Headley b Coldwell	28
P. J. Robinson not out	13	b Coldwell	18
B. A. Langford lbw b Gifford	6	b Brain	0
F. E. Rumsey b Brain	5	not out	1
B 1, l-b 2	3	B 4, l-b 4, n-b 1	9
1/25 2/40 3/66 4/66 5/70 6/83 7/85 8/85 9/103	110	1/53 2/77 3/77 4/100 5/111 6/125 7/167 8/195 9/197	203

Bowling: *First Innings*—Coldwell 11—7—10—1; Brain 11—3—21—1; Carter 7—1—25—0; Gifford 25—13—28—6; Horton 18—7—23—1. *Second Innings*—Coldwell 24.5—11—41—2; Brain 13—4—27—2; Carter 5—0—6—0; Gifford 33—15—69—2; Horton 24—10—51—4.

Worcestershire

First Innings		Second Innings	
M. J. Horton b Alley	84	not out	55
C. D. Fearnley b Rumsey	32	c Kitchen b Palmer	2
*D. Kenyon b Rumsey	24	c Virgin b Alley	29
J. A. Ormrod c Kitchen b Langford	23	not out	24
R. G. A. Headley c Virgin b Langford	9		
D. W. Richardson c Virgin b Langford	0		
†R. Booth c Burgess b Langford	12		
N. Gifford lbw b Langford	1		
L. J. Coldwell not out	1		
B. M. Brain b Alley	0		
R. G. M. Carter b Langford	0		
L-b 6, n-b 1	7	B 4, l-b 4, n-b 4	12
1/75 2/114 3/160 4/174 5/174 6/177 7/187 8/192 9/192	193	1/2 2/61 (2 wkts.)	122

Bowling: *First Innings*—Rumsey 21—3—49—2; Palmer 11—3—33—0; Alley 21—7—27—2; Langford 27.4—13—43—6; Robinson 12—2—34—0. *Second Innings*—Rumsey 10—2—20—0; Palmer 8—0—36—1; Alley 6—2—8—1; Langford 11—2—32—0; Robinson 4—3—1—0; Burgess 2.4—0—13—0.

Umpires: J. Arnold and A. E. Fagg.

At Eastbourne, August 24, 25, 26. SOMERSET beat SUSSEX by six wickets.

At Birmingham, August 27, 29, 30. SOMERSET drew with WARWICKSHIRE.

SOMERSET v. ESSEX

At Taunton, August 31, September 1, 2. Somerset won by 101 runs. Put in by Essex on a slightly damp pitch, Somerset prospered at first, but Knight, with five for 15 in seven overs upset the middle batting. C. R. M. Atkinson, however, drove strongly for 88 in two hours, Rumsey supporting him in a last-wicket stand of 73. Palmer, Rumsey, and Alley had Essex struggling, but Cass defended stoutly for nearly two and a half hours. Knight's enterprise brought him 52, but Somerset led by 43. Knight and Bailey soon reduced Somerset to 13 for three before Virgin, C. R. M. Atkinson and Robinson launched a recovery and Alley, with a spirited 56, left Essex to score 227 in three and a quarter hours. Bear gave them a splendid start, hitting one 6 and four 4's to reach 50 in seventy-four minutes, but two good close catches by Virgin allowed the spinners to break through. Palmer returned a spell of four for 7 in four overs, assisted by a fine diving catch by Rumsey, and as Essex, sorely hit by injury, which early in the game also robbed them of Jorden's bowling, continued to play shots and the last seven wickets fell in under half an hour. Somerset won with seventy minutes to spare, completing their thirteenth championship victory, the most since joining the Competition in 1891.

Somerset

G. Atkinson lbw b Knight	46	— b Bailey	3
R. Virgin lbw b Bailey	49	— b Knight	42
M. Kitchen run out	12	— c Taylor b Knight	6
G. Burgess c Edmeades b Hobbs	0	— c Cass b Bailey	1
W. E. Alley c Cass b Knight	5	— b Edmeades	56
*C. R. M. Atkinson b Edmeades	88	— lbw b Edmeades	24
K. E. Palmer lbw b Knight	1	— lbw b Acfield	1
†G. Clayton b Knight	2	— st Cass b Acfield	16
P. J. Robinson b Knight	4	— c Bailey b Acfield	25
B. A. Langford c Cass b Edmeades	2	— c Acfield b Edmeades	0
F. E. Rumsey not out	13	— not out	0
L-b 1, w 1	2	B 9	9
1/76 2/102 3/102 4/111 5/130 6/132 7/134 8/144 9/151	224	1/5 2/12 3/13 4/58 5/105 6/105 7/115 8/181 9/181	183

Bowling: *First Innings*—Knight 24—3—73—5; Jorden 6—0—16—0; Edmeades 15.4—3—43—2; Bailey 12—1—23—1; Acfield 10—4—19—0; Hobbs 16—3—48—1. *Second Innings*—Knight 19—7—24—2; Edmeades 24—6—41—3; Bailey 9—4—14—2; Acfield 24.3—9—67—3; Hobbs 7—0—28—0.

Essex

M. J. Bear lbw b Palmer	18	— c Virgin b Robinson	50
G. J. Saville b Palmer	9	— b Langford	11
*T. E. Bailey c Clayton b Rumsey	1	— b Langford	1
K. W. R. Fletcher c Clayton b Alley	10	— lbw b Palmer	29
B. Taylor b Rumsey	0	— b Palmer	10
B. R. Knight b Alley	52	— c Rumsey b Palmer	4
†G. R. Cass not out	39	— c Virgin b Langford	0
B. Edmeades c Clayton b Rumsey	20	— b Palmer	0
A. M. Jorden c and b Robinson	17	— not out	5
R. N. S. Hobbs c Robinson b Alley	5	— st Clayton b Langford	6
D. L. Acfield not out	3	— b Rumsey	4
L-b 7	7	B 3, w 1, n-b 1	5
1/23 2/30 3/30 4/55 5/55 6/70 7/135 8/141 9/167 (9 wkts., dec.)	181	1/53 2/53 3/67 4/97 5/109 6/110 7/110 8/116 9/116	125

Bowling: *First Innings*—Rumsey 17—9—30—3; Palmer 29—7—77—2; Alley 24—9—35—3; Langford 14—6—20—0; Robinson 4—2—12—1. *Second Innings*—Rumsey 9.3—1—25—1; Palmer 9—2—20—4; Alley 3—0—11—0; Langford 14—2—46—4; Robinson 7—3—18—1.

Umpires: J. Arnold and O. W. Herman.

SURREY

PATRON—HER MAJESTY THE QUEEN

President—Lieutenant Colonel The Lord Nugent

Secretary—C. G. Howard, Kennington Oval, London, S.E.11

Captain—M. J. Stewart

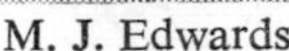

M. J. Edwards

County Badge

S. Storey

Injury, illness and loss of form by leading players bedevilled Surrey's season. That they finished as high as seventh was not so much a testimony to their resilience, for at their best they were a side of modest quality, as a commentary on the low standard of county cricket. Cartilage trouble put Gibson out of the game at the outset. Arnold was again prone to muscular injury. Barrington suffered a breakdown in health in mid-season, and, playing generally restrained cricket, he did not score 1,000 during the season. All the leading batsmen were out of form in the early weeks, and Stewart in the first two months was not even as effective with the bat as Pocock. The latter scored usefully as a tail-ender until he was, for no obvious reason, dropped to number ten in the order.

Edrich alone of the leading batsmen was true to himself, with nearly 2,000 runs, and near the end of June he found an admirable partner in Edwards. After a series of failures in the middle of the order Edwards began opening, with such success that in each of the next four matches he and Edrich scored more than 100 together in one innings or the other. Twice more they passed 100 together and also shared several other stands between 60 and 100. Edwards was the most improved batsman on the side and shared the main honours of the season with Edrich and Storey. The latter was the first Surrey cricketer since F. R. Brown in 1932 to do the all-rounder's double. Storey took nearly twice as many wickets as in 1965, a splendidly consistent medium pacer. He also played some excellent innings without yet realising his true potential.

Pocock also made progress as an off spinner, perhaps as much as could be expected in the current restricting conditions for slow bowlers, which have grievously set back Harman in the past two years. Neither Jefferson nor Willett, who were incapacitated for most of the previous summer, quite recaptured their form, though Willett, a magnificent trier in the field, made some superb catches. Jefferson and Tindall retired at the end of the season. A newcomer, Jackman, had some success as a medium-paced bowler, but Surrey needed more penetrative bowling to become a championship prospect. They needed also more positive leadership. Even in 1966 a higher position could have been attained by more aggressive cricket. Servile batting, for instance, cost them 10 points in their opening match against Derbyshire.

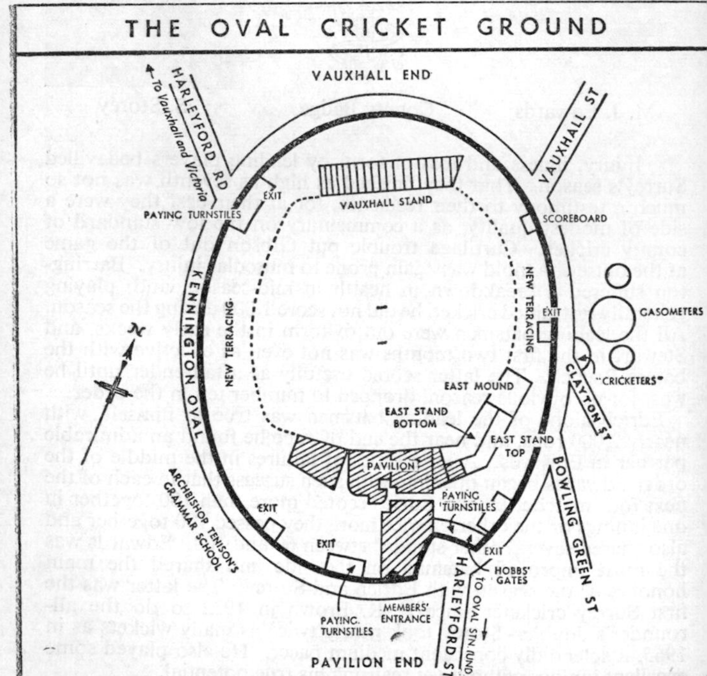

SURREY RESULTS

All First-Class Matches—Played 30, *Won* 9, *Lost* 3, *Drawn* 18
County Championship Matches—Played 28, *Won* 8, *Lost* 3, *Drawn* 16, *No Decision* 1

COUNTY CHAMPIONSHIP AVERAGES

BATTING

	Birthplace	Mtchs.	Inns.	Not Outs	Runs	100's	Highest Inns.	Aver
J. H. Edrich....	*Blofield*	24	44	3	1913	3	137	46.65
K. F. Barrington	*Reading*	17	29	6	928	3	117*	40.34
M. J. Edwards..	*Balham*	20	34	0	1033	1	116	30.38
R. A. E. Tindall.	*Streatham*	13	24	4	519	0	81	25.95
S. J. Storey.....	*Worthing*	28	45	4	1013	1	109*	24.70
M. J. Stewart...	*Herne Hill*	28	48	7	982	2	102	23.95
W. A. Smith...	*Salisbury*	17	28	2	525	0	62	20.19
M. D. Willett..	*W. Norwood*	20	34	7	494	0	78*	18.29
R. I. Jefferson..	*Frimley*	23	36	9	459	0	45*	17.00
G. R. J. Roope.	*Fareham*	10	14	4	170	0	35	17.00
I. Finlay.......	*Woking*	3	5	1	58	0	44	14.50
G. Arnold.....	*Earlsfield*	12	11	5	85	0	30	14.16
R. D. Jackman.	*Simla, India*	9	9	5	52	0	19	13.00
P. I. Pocock....	*Bangor*	26	31	8	255	0	45*	11.08
R. Harman....	*Hersham*	23	18	11	67	0	23	9.57
A. Long.......	*Cheam*	27	30	7	149	0	28	6.47
D. A. Marriott.	*Jamaica*	7	5	1	5	0	3	1.25

Also batted: D. J. Taylor (*Amersham*), 4.

* *Signifies not out.*

BOWLING

	Overs	Maidens	Runs	Wickets	Average
G. Arnold.............	373	77	985	54	18.24
S. J. Storey............	925.5	298	1895	103	18.39
R. Harman.............	390	126	913	43	21.23
P. I. Pocock............	705	213	1696	79	21.46
R. D. Jackman..........	221	56	513	22	23.31
R. I. Jefferson..........	673.5	148	1714	66	25.96
G. R. J. Roope.........	147	38	381	14	27.21
D. A. Marriott..........	209.4	45	496	18	27.55
K. F. Barrington........	92	18	282	10	28.20
R. A. E. Tindall.........	59.2	19	124	3	41.33

Also bowled: M. J. Edwards 2—1—2—0; W. A. Smith 1—0—1—0; M. J. Stewart 3—1—7—0; M. D. Willett 9—5—11—1.

At Lord's, May 4, 5, 6. SURREY drew with M.C.C.

SURREY v. DERBYSHIRE

At The Oval, May 7, 9, 10. Derbyshire won by seven runs. The pitch favoured bowlers throughout, though less in the fourth innings, when Surrey's lack of enterprise played into the hands of the Derbyshire bowlers. These lacked Jackson, who was injured on the first day. Smith, however, bowled his off-breaks so well opposite the pace of Rhodes that only Barrington, who batted two hours and fifty minutes in a painstaking innings of 48, stood out against them long. Smith had a match record of nine for 70, and, with Pocock being similarly successful in the only innings in which Surrey used his bowling, off spin accounted for thirteen wickets for 109. Jefferson was another successful bowler. On returning to the game after illness had cost him most of the 1965 season, he took the first three Derbyshire wickets that fell for 10. Altogether he had eight for 69. In five and a quarter hours on the second day twenty wickets tumbled for only 168. Surrey were left to make 54 with six wickets standing on the third day in improving conditions. They tried to get home by the hard, slow way, but though they lingered 36 overs, those six fell for 46. Derbyshire deserved to win because they played the more positive cricket.

Derbyshire

J. F. Harvey c Long b Jefferson	1	— c Harman b Jefferson	1
J. R. Eyre c Barrington b Jefferson	8	— c Harman b Jefferson	5
H. L. Johnson c Barrington b Harman	8	— c Edrich b Jefferson	0
I. R. Buxton c Long b Jefferson	0	— c Jefferson b Storey	29
*D. C. Morgan b Jefferson	0	— b Jefferson	18
M. Hill c Stewart b Harman	32	— b Storey	10
†R. W. Taylor c Storey b Pocock	38	— c Barrington b Marriott	9
E. Smith c Marriott b Pocock	22	— b Storey	4
M. H. J. Allen c Stewart b Pocock	5	— not out	2
H. J. Rhodes not out	9	— b Storey	4
A. B. Jackson c Smith b Pocock	9	— absent injured	—
L-b 2, n-b 2	4	N-b 3	3
1/9 2/10 3/10 4/10 5/35 6/65 7/100 8/107 9/120	136	1/5 2/6 3/6 4/36 5/47 6/71 7/77 8/78 9/85	85

Bowling: *First Innings*—Jefferson 22—9—29—4; Marriott 14—7—18—0; Storey 4—3—2—0; Pocock 19.2—9—39—4; Harman 14—6—23—2; Barrington 8—0—21—0. *Second Innings*—Jefferson 15—5—40—4; Marriott 6—1—10—1; Harman 3—1—12—0; Storey 11.5—4—20—4.

Surrey

*M. J. Stewart c and b Smith	32	— c Taylor b Rhodes	10
J. H. Edrich b Smith	6	— c Smith b Buxton	1
W. A. Smith lbw b Smith	11	— b Smith	12
K. F. Barrington b Smith	0	— c Harvey b Smith	48
M. D. Willett c Allen b Rhodes	7	— b Buxton	22
S. J. Storey c Johnson b Rhodes	30	— c and b Buxton	2
R. I. Jefferson c Allen b Rhodes	1	— b Rhodes	14
†A. Long c Morgan b Smith	0	— not out	3
P. I. Pocock c Hill b Smith	1	— lbw b Rhodes	0
R. Harman not out	8	— b Rhodes	0
D. A. Marriott c Hill b Rhodes	0	— c Allen b Smith	1
N-b 1	1	— B 2, l-b 1, n-b 1	4
1/25 2/49 3/49 4/50 5/86 6/87 7/88 8/88 9/94	97	1/5 2/21 3/25 4/69 5/73 6/106 7/114 8/115 9/115	117

Bowling: *First Innings*—Smith 26—12—26—6; Rhodes 18.5—7—21—4; Jackson 7—1—14—0; Morgan 2—0—7—0; Allen 8—0—28—0. *Second Innings*—Buxton 21—7—27—3; Rhodes 27—6—40—4; Smith 18.1—6—44—3; Morgan 8—7—2—0.

Umpires: R. S. Lay and O. W. Herman.

SURREY v. SUSSEX

At The Oval, May 11, 12, 13. *65 overs.* Surrey won by nine wickets. Pocock's off spin on a sticky wicket clinched Surrey's victory on the third day, when Storey, persistently accurate at medium pace, helped him to destroy Sussex resistance. On the second day of this 65-over limit match, Sussex also bowled on a rain-affected pitch, but they played into Surrey's hands by excessive use of seam bowling designed to keep the scoring down. Their own first innings was timidly conducted until Oakman and Griffith hit 40 off the last six overs. Storey was mainly responsible for Surrey's lead of 61, for in fifty minutes he hit 46 in a stand of 59 with Barrington, after which Jefferson and Pocock hit freely. Surrey's last 79 came off 13 overs after the tea interval. Only Parks, who was aggressive, and Griffith showed any ability to counter the sticky pitch conditions in the final day. Although at one period severely mauled by Parks, who hit him for two 6's in one over, Pocock finished with seven for 57, the best figures of his career. He bowled well in conditions unfamiliar to a young bowler brought up in an age of pitch covering.

Sussex

First Innings		Second Innings	
K. G. Suttle b Marriott	13	lbw b Storey	17
L. J. Lenham c Smith b Marriott	56	c Long b Pocock	14
R. J. Langridge c Stewart b Storey	2	b Pocock	1
†J. M. Parks c Long b Storey	19	c and b Storey	22
*Nawab of Pataudi b Jefferson	4	b Pocock	0
A. S. M. Oakman not out	37	c Stewart b Pocock	0
A. Buss c Smith b Storey	1	c Harman b Pocock	10
M. G. Griffith not out	11	c Stewart b Pocock	24
M. A. Buss (did not bat)		c Willett b Pocock	0
J. A. Snow (did not bat)		st Long b Storey	0
D. L. Bates (did not bat)		not out	5
B 4, l-b 6, n-b 2	12	B 3, l-b 6	9
1/32 2/39 3/62 4/79 5/110 6/115 (6 wkts., 65 overs)	155	1/27 2/28 3/34 4/57 5/59 6/61 7/64 8/80 9/80	102

Bowling: *First Innings*—Jefferson 21—5—41—1; Marriott 18—3—43—2; Storey 26—7—59—3. *Second Innings*—Jefferson 4—0—10—0; Marriott 3—2—3—0; Storey 19—8—22—3; Pocock 19.1—4—58—7; Harman 1—1—0—0.

Surrey

First Innings		Second Innings	
*M. J. Stewart c M. A. Buss b Snow	11	not out	26
J. H. Edrich c Parks b Bates	30	c Lenham b M. A. Buss	12
W. A. Smith c Parks b A. Buss	27	not out	2
K. F. Barrington c Pataudi b Bates	41		
M. D. Willett c M. A. Buss b A. Buss	8		
S. J. Storey c Griffith b Bates	46		
R. I. Jefferson not out	22		
†A. Long run out	0		
P. I. Pocock not out	26		
L-b 5	5	L-b 1, n-b 1	2
1/12 2/55 3/89 4/104 5/163 6/167 7/167 (7 wkts., 65 overs)	216	1/40 (1 wkt.)	42

D. A. Marriott and R. Harman did not bat.

Bowling: *First Innings*—Snow 27—10—81—1; A. Buss 23—6—66—2; Oakman 2—0—5—0; Bates 13—3—59—3. *Second Innings*—A. Buss 3—0—18—0; Snow 1—1—0—0; Oakman 9—6—10—0; Suttle 1—0—2—0; M. A. Buss 6.3—3—10—1.

Umpires:—H. Mellows and O. W. Herman.

SURREY v. GLAMORGAN

At The Oval, May 14, 16, 17. *65 overs*. Drawn. Slow batting on the second day after they established a lead of 51 cost Glamorgan their chance of winning. On a soft, placid pitch Glamorgan could manage only 131. Surrey spin played a notable part in this 65-over innings, which is normally the preserve of seam bowlers, and Pocock's spell of two for 14 in 11 overs was particularly good. Surrey fared even worse and never recovered from the loss of their first three wickets for 13 in as many overs. The fast bowling of I. J. Jones and two fine pieces of fielding by Rees, which put out Barrington and Storey, earned the substantial Welsh lead. After a brisk second innings start of 62 before Hedges fell to Harman's spin, Glamorgan scored only 78 in two hours and five minutes between lunch and tea. After an uncertain start Surrey, needing 304, never looked like accomplishing their run-a-minute task, though they had little difficulty in drawing the game. Storey, who reached 50 inside fifty minutes, attacked spendidly to make 63 of a stand of 74 with Willett, but by then Surrey were far behind the clock.

Glamorgan

A. Jones st Long b Pocock	23	— st Long b Harman	37
B. Hedges b Arnold	0	— c Tindall b Harman	39
W. Slade c Storey b Pocock	20	— lbw b Barrington	24
A. R. Lewis c Arnold b Storey	32	— c Stewart b Arnold	59
A. Rees b Arnold	0	— c Stewart b Harman	48
F. J. Davis c Barrington b Harman	9	— c Storey b Harman	8
A. E. Cordle c Storey b Harman	0	— c Long b Jefferson	2
†D. L. Evans c and b Harman	6	— c Storey b Arnold	5
D. J. Shepherd b Arnold	18	— b Harman	9
I. J. Jones c Tindall b Arnold	15	— c and b Harman	0
*O. S. Wheatley not out	2	— not out	5
B 1, l-b 2, n-b 3	6	B 5, l-b 6, n-b 5	16
1/2 2/39 3/48 4/51 5/87 6/88 7/88 8/97 9/125	131	1/62 2/91 3/119 4/197 5/200 6/219 7/234 8/244 9/244	252

Bowling: *First Innings*—Arnold 15.1—3—24—4; Jefferson 12—2—29—0; Pocock 11—5—14—2; Storey 15—5—30—1; Harman 11—1—28—3. *Second Innings*—Arnold 33—7—66—2; Jefferson 14—4—28—1; Pocock 28—10—44—0; Storey 5—2—7—0; Harman 36.3—14—85—6; Barrington 9—3—6—1.

Surrey

*M. J. Stewart c Hedges b I. J. Jones	2	— c Slade b Davis	34
W. A. Smith c Wheatley b Shepherd	28	— c Slade b I. J. Jones	10
R. A. E. Tindall c Davis b I. J. Jones	2	— run out	9
K. F. Barrington run out	2	— c Rees b Davis	10
M. D. Willett c Shepherd b Cordle	1	— not out	78
S. J. Storey c Rees b Wheatley	12	— c Evans b Shepherd	63
R. I. Jefferson c Davis b I. J. Jones	6	— b Slade	0
†A. Long b I. J. Jones	2	— run out	3
P. I. Pocock c and b Cordle	6	— not out	30
G. Arnold c Evans b Cordle	5		
R. Harman not out	1		
B 6, l-b 4, n-b 3	13	B 4, l-b 4, w 1	9
1/3 2/7 3/13 4/19 5/38 6/56 7/62 8/69 9/78	80	1/23 2/57 3/58 4/76 (7 wkts.) 5/150 6/161 7/173	246

Bowling: *First Innings*—I. J. Jones 19—7—25—4; Wheatley 14—5—26—1; Cordle 14.5—8—15—3; Shepherd 6—5—1—1. *Second Innings*—I. J. Jones 12—1—30—1; Wheatley 10—5—17—0; Cordle 8—1—15—0; Davis 31—12—60—2; Shepherd 38—20—74—1; Slade 14—5—37—1; Rees 2—1—4—0.

Umpires: G. H. Pope and H. Mellows.

At Basingstoke, May 18, 19, 20. SURREY drew with HAMPSHIRE.

At Leicester, May 21. SURREY beat LEICESTERSHIRE by 46 runs. (See GILLETTE CUP.)

SURREY v. NORTHAMPTONSHIRE

At The Oval, May 25, 27, 28. Drawn. Three declarations could not contrive a definite result after bad weather had prevented any play on the opening day. Thanks to Milburn, who hit 50 of an opening stand of 70 in an hour, and Prideaux, Northamptonshire hit their first 100 off 25 overs, but the remaining batsmen were less enterprising. With the exception of Barrington, who ran into form with an innings of much good stroke play curiously punctuated with pauses, Surrey batted weakly against the medium quick bowling of Bailey and the flighted off breaks of Sully. In the Northamptonshire second innings the same two opening batsmen excelled themselves with a stand of 78 in only forty-five minutes, and Prideaux went on playing splendidly free cricket to reach 101 off 44 overs. Yet by delaying the declaration until he reached his hundred Northamptonshire sacrificed their chance of winning. In the remaining 170 minutes not even a run-a-minute 65 by Storey could put Surrey into a position from which to challenge for victory.

Northamptonshire

	First Innings		Second Innings	
C. Milburn b Jefferson	50	—	b Pocock	38
R. M. Prideaux c Willett b Pocock	59	—	not out	101
B. L. Reynolds c Willett b Pocock	28	—	c Long b Arnold	13
Mushtaq Mohammad b Arnold	12	—	b Storey	21
P. D. Watts c Willett b Arnold	3	—	not out	0
D. S. Steele b Storey	14			
P. J. Watts not out	34			
B. Crump not out	0			
B 2, n-b 5	7		L-b 4, n-b 4	8
1/70 2/124 3/147 4/156 5/159 6/191 (6 wkts., dec.)	207		1/78 2/107 3/174 (3 wkts., dec.)	181

H. Sully, *†K. V. Andrew and R. Bailey did not bat.

Bowling: *First Innings*—Arnold 18—3—36—2; Jefferson 15—1—72—1; Storey 11—2—29—1; Pocock 22—6—38—2; Harman 5.1—0—25—0. *Second Innings*—Arnold 12—3—56—1; Jefferson 3—0—24—0; Storey 12—2—28—1; Pocock 15—3—53—1; Harman 2—0—12—0.

Surrey

	First Innings		Second Innings	
*M. J. Stewart c Steele b Bailey	4	—	b Crump	26
J. H. Edrich c and b Sully	29	—	c Milburn b Sully	26
R. A. E. Tindall lbw b Bailey	1	—	lbw b P. D. Watts	12
K. F. Barrington not out	103	—	c Milburn b Crump	1
M. D. Willett c P. D. Watts b Sully	6	—	b Sully	11
S. J. Storey c Milburn b Sully	1	—	lbw b P. J. Watts	65
R. I. Jefferson c P. D. Watts b Sully	0	—	c Prideaux b Bailey	19
P. I. Pocock c Prideaux b Sully	0	—	not out	13
G. Arnold b Bailey	2	—	not out	4
†A. Long c Milburn b Bailey	7			
R. Harman not out	1			
N-b 3	3		B 1, l-b 3	4
1/10 2/14 3/74 4/102 5/105 6/109 7/115 8/120 9/130 (9 wkts., dec.)	157		1/52 2/56 3/64 4/126 5/143 6/156 7/174 (7 wkts.)	181

Bowling: *First Innings*—Bailey 17—1—39—4; Crump 6—1—12—0; Sully 23—5—70—5; Mohammad 6—0—20—0; P. D. Watts 6—2—13—0. *Second Innings*—Bailey 13—0—36—1; Crump 19—7—48—2; Sully 20.5—2—84—2; Steele 1—0—1—0; P. J. Watts 1—0—5—1; P. D. Watts 5—2—3—1.

Umpires: T. W. Spencer and P. A. Gibb.

SURREY v. LANCASHIRE

At The Oval, June 1, 2, 3. *65 overs.* Surrey won by ten wickets. Edrich scored his second century in successive matches and a total of 187 without being dismissed in the match to play the leading part in the overthrow of Lancashire. What he began the Surrey spinners, Pocock and Harman, virtually completed on the second afternoon. After an innings of modest calibre by the weak Lancashire batting side, Surrey attacked so well that they averaged 4.3 an over. Edrich, who hit one 6 and ten 4's, and Storey put on 150. Lancashire again batted indifferently, and Harman began his most impressive bowling of the season by taking two wickets in his first seven overs without conceding a run. Where his seniors had failed Lloyd, a promising all-rounder, made his highest score, 77, in first-class cricket. He saved his side from an innings defeat by putting on 68 for the last two wickets with Greenhough and Statham, and so carried the match into the third morning.

Lancashire

G. Pullar c Edrich b Marriott	5	— c Stewart b Marriott	17
D. M. Green c Harman b Marriott	23	— b Pocock	15
G. K. Knox c Long b Storey	36	— st Long b Harman	5
D. R. Worsley c Willett b Storey	23	— c Harman b Jefferson	29
R. Bennett c Stewart b Pocock	5	— c and b Harman	0
D. Lloyd run out	0	— b Jefferson	77
P. Lever lbw b Pocock	15	— c Long b Jefferson	2
K. Shuttleworth not out	34	— st Long b Harman	4
†K. Goodwin b Pocock	0	— b Pocock	4
T. Greenhough c Long b Jefferson	22	— b Harman	14
*J. B. Statham b Marriott	9	— not out	6
B 1, l-b 1, n-b 2	4	— B 1, l-b 1, n-b 1	3
1/12 2/40 3/77 4/88 5/92 6/106 7/110 8/110 9/160	176	1/28 2/37 3/37 4/43 5/91 6/97 7/101 8/108 9/144	176

Bowling: *First Innings*—Jefferson 13—2—38—1; Marriott 9.3—2—35—3; Storey 22—4—61—2; Pocock 19—6—38—3. *Second Innings*—Jefferson 17.3—1—54—3; Marriott 17—2—54—1; Pocock 28—17—30—2; Harman 25—15—31—4; Tindall 4—4—0—0; Storey 3—2—4—0.

Surrey

J. H. Edrich not out	136	— not out	51
W. A. Smith c Bennett b Shuttleworth	14	— not out	22
R. A. E. Tindall lbw b Greenhough	33		
M. D. Willett b Lever	1		
S. J. Storey c Knox b Lever	73		
R. I. Jefferson run out	7		
*M. J. Stewart not out	6		
L-b 8, n-b 2	10	B 1	1
1/31 2/96 3/107 4/257 5/266 (5 wkts., 65 overs)	280	(no wkt.)	74

P. I. Pocock, †A. Long, R. Harman and D. A. Marriott did not bat.

Bowling: *First Innings*—Statham 22—2—95—0; Shuttleworth 17—1—68—1; Lever 16—2—74—2; Greenhough 10—1—33—1. *Second Innings*—Shuttleworth 3—0—11—0; Lever 5—0—15—0; Statham 2—0—8—0; Lloyd 7.5—2—22—0; Greenhough 7—2—17—0.

Umpires: H. Mellows and H. Yarnold.

At Bath, June 4, 6. SURREY lost to SOMERSET by two wickets.

SURREY v. KENT

At The Oval, June 11, 12, 13. *65 overs*. Drawn. For the first time Surrey staged Sunday cricket and drew a crowd of 8,000 on that day. Unfortunately the cricket on Sunday was dull, Barrington playing the first part of an innings of 68 that lasted three and a half hours. The Surrey declaration accordingly did not leave enough time for their bowlers to complete the dismissal of Kent on a pitch taking spin freely. By contrast to Barrington's troubles, Denness on the last day played beautiful aggressive cricket, making the first 49 of his 52 in an hour. Cowdrey also batted successfully. He and Leary were responsible for Kent's first-innings lead when they put on 120 for the third wicket. In the second innings Knott outdid Cowdrey by scoring 36 of their stand of 59 in fifty minutes, after which the spin of Pocock and Harman took Surrey to the brink of victory. Earlier Arnold, four for 14 on the second day, and Underwood bowled excellently.

Surrey

*M. J. Stewart b Sayer	19	— c Prodger b Sayer	14
J. H. Edrich c Knott b Dye	39	— c and b Dye	57
R. A. E. Tindall run out	27	— b Underwood	6
K. F. Barrington c Ealham b Underwood	7	— c Dye b Brown	68
S. J. Storey c Prodger b Brown	15	— b Underwood	19
M. D. Willett c Leary b Brown	5	— b Brown	20
R. I. Jefferson b Dye	4	— b Underwood	3
P. I. Pocock not out	25	— c Ealham b Underwood	0
†A. Long b Dye	0	— b Dye	23
G. Arnold c Knott b Sayer	5	— c Cowdrey b Underwood	10
R. Harman not out	6	— not out	0
L-b 4	4	B 5, l-b 3, w 1	9
1/44 2/73 3/92 4/93 (9 wkts., 65 overs)	156	1/45 2/72 3/78 4/143 5/176	229
5/113 6/117 7/136 8/140 9/145		6/180 7/190 8/198 9/229	

Bowling: *First Innings*—Brown 18—3—47—2; Sayer 14—2—42—2; Dye 16—5—28—3; Underwood 17—7—35—1; *Second Innings*—Brown 20—6—44—2; Sayer 17—7—38—1; Dye 28—13—41—2; Underwood 44.4—24—57—5; Ealham 5—0—15—0; Luckhurst 7—3—25—0.

Kent

M. H. Denness b Arnold	14	— c Edrich b Harman	52
B. W. Luckhurst b Arnold	4	— run out	2
S. E. Leary c Long b Jefferson	57	— c Storey b Harman	9
*M. C. Cowdrey c and b Arnold	68	— c Long b Harman	48
J. M. Prodger b Arnold	10	— b Pocock	0
A. Brown b Arnold	0	— not out	8
D. M. Sayer b Jefferson	13	— c Harman b Pocock	0
A. Ealham not out	4	— c Harman b Pocock	3
†A. Knott b Arnold	0	— st Long b Harman	36
D. L. Underwood not out	4	— c Willett b Pocock	5
J. C. Dye (did not bat)		— not out	0
L-b 5	5	B 2, l-b 2, n-b 1	5
1/11 2/26 3/146 (8 wkts., 65 overs)	179	1/14 2/50 3/86 (9 wkts.)	168
4/148 5/148 6/171		4/87 5/95 6/154	
7/175 8/175		7/155 8/160 9/167	

Bowling: *First Innings*—Arnold 22—4—49—6; Jefferson 20—2—57—2; Storey 16—5—39—0; Pocock 7—2—29—0. *Second Innings*—Arnold 9—1—20—0; Jefferson 2—0—12—0; Storey 14—3—32—0; Harman 27—10—62—4; Pocock 20—8—36—4; Barrington 1—0—1—0.

Umpires: J. S. Buller and A. E. Alderman.

SURREY v. CAMBRIDGE UNIVERSITY

At The Oval, June 15, 16, 17. Surrey won by an innings and 64 runs. In his first match for the County the medium-paced Jakeman took three wickets in his first over in the second innings. Only Cottrell played aggressively in a weak Cambridge batting side that tumbled to heavy defeat, when they lost their last seven wickets for 70 in two hours and ten minutes on the last day.

Surrey

*M. J. Stewart b Palfreman	15	R. D. Jackman b Palfreman	19
I. Finlay c Hays b Roopnaraine	23	G. Arnold b Acfield	32
M. D. Willett lbw b Sinker	67	R. Harman not out	14
W. A. Smith c and b Roopnaraine	23		
K. B. McEntyre b Sinker	15	B 6, l-b 5, w 1	12
M. J. Edwards c and b Acfield	31		
G. R. J. Roope run out	11	1/34 2/44 3/92 4/133 5/160	302
†D. J. Taylor b Roopnaraine	40	6/176 7/197 8/221 9/226	

Bowling: Palfreman 15—4—55—2; Cottrell 13—5—26—0; Roopnaraine 24.5—12—65—3; Acfield 31—9—81—2; Sinker 27—8—63—2.

Cambridge University

K. P. W. J. McAdam c and b Arnold	29	— c Jackman b Harman	35
R. E. Chambers c Smith b Jackman	1	— c Willett b Jackman	0
A. V. E. Gould b Arnold	7	— c Stewart b Jackman	2
†D. L. Hays lbw b Willett	0	— c Stewart b Jackman	0
N. J. Cosh run out	32	— c and b Harman	21
V. P. Malalasekera c Roope b Harman	19	— c Edwards b Willett	0
G. A. Cottrell c Roope b Harman	0	— b Arnold	36
A. B. Palfreman c Smith b Harman	26	— c Arnold b Willett	13
*R. Roopnaraine c Roope b Harman	7	— c Taylor b Willett	0
N. Sinker b Harman	1	— not out	2
D. L. Acfield not out	0	— b Arnold	0
B 1, l-b 1	2	B 4, w 1	5
1/4 2/23 3/27 4/48 5/83 6/87 7/94 8/116 9/123	124	1/0 2/2 3/2 4/56 5/59 6/59 7/83 8/86 9/114	114

Bowling—*First Innings*—Arnold 23—5—47—2; Jackman 10—3—18—1; Harman 25.1—11—37—5; Willett 9—5—7—1; Roope 7—2—13—0. *Second Innings*—Arnold 4.4—1—9—2; Jackman 8—2—26—3; Roope 6—2—13—0; Harman 27—17—22—2; Willett 21—10—36—3; Edwards 3—2—3—0.

Umpires: A. Jepson and G. H. Pope.

At Cardiff, June 18, 20, 21 SURREY beat GLAMORGAN by 198 runs.

At Bournemouth, June 22. SURREY lost to HAMPSHIRE by seven wickets. (See GILLETTE CUP.)

At Leicester, June 25, 26, 27. SURREY drew with LEICESTERSHIRE.

At Southend, June 29, 30, July 1. SURREY drew with ESSEX.

At Blackheath, July 2, 4, 5. SURREY drew with KENT.

SURREY v. SOMERSET

At The Oval, July 6, 7, 8. Drawn. Marriott, the last Surrey batsman, safely played the last five balls of the match from Langford with every Somerset fielder clustered round the bat. Spin bowlers failed to take advantage of a pitch giving them generous encouragement. A stubborn innings of 74 unfinished in four and a quarter hours by Clarkson was the backbone of a dull first innings by Somerset. Surrey were more enterprising, particularly Edrich, whose hearty attack on Langford was responsible for putting the off-spinner out of his stride. He hit one 6 and eleven 4's, and his partnership of 116 with Edwards, who also played purposeful cricket, was one of four century opening stands between these two in successive matches. Except for some intelligent stroke play by C. R. M. Atkinson the Somerset second innings was little improvement on the first. They finally set Surrey to make 201 in two and a quarter hours. After a stand of 71 by Edrich and Edwards the batting was so ill-judged that five wickets fell for 22 in five overs. Tindall, batting for fifty minutes, and finally Marriott were hard pressed to rescue Surrey from the consequences of their own reckless excesses.

Somerset

G. Atkinson c Stewart b Pocock	40	— run out	36
R. Virgin c Roope b Jefferson	0	— c Roope b Jefferson	14
M. Kitchen c Edwards b Storey	31	— b Marriott	40
A. Clarkson not out	74	— b Storey	22
W. E. Alley c Edrich b Marriott	6	— c Marriott b Jefferson	21
*C. R. M. Atkinson c Jefferson b Pocock	4	— c Pocock b Storey	56
K. E. Palmer b Marriott	31	— c Tindall b Pocock	11
†G. Clayton c Tindall b Pocock	26	— not out	12
P. J. Robinson run out	28	— c Edwards b Pocock	6
B. A. Langford b Storey	1	— not out	1
R. Palmer lbw b Pocock	1		
B 1, l-b 2, w 2	5	B 1, l-b 2, n-b 5	8
1/1 2/59 3/78 4/87 5/102 6/163 7/207 8/245 9/246	247	1/42 2/59 3/102 4/129 5/150 6/204 7/211 8/225 (8 wkts., dec.)	227

Bowling: *First Innings*—Jefferson 27—6—47—1; Marriott 22—4—49—2; Storey 26—7—43—2; Roope 10—1—22—0; Pocock 30.2—7—62—4; Tindall 10—3—19—0. *Second Innings*—Jefferson 20—8—42—2; Marriott 22—5—48—1; Pocock 25—5—72—2; Storey 14.2—3—47—2; Tindall 3—0—10—0.

Surrey

M. J. Edwards b K. E. Palmer	49	— lbw b K. E. Palmer	28
J. H. Edrich c Robinson b R. Palmer	86	— c Virgin b Alley	46
M. D. Willett c Clayton b K. E. Palmer	24	— b Langford	19
R. A. E. Tindall c Clayton b K. E. Palmer	25	— not out	12
*M. J. Stewart c Clayton b K. E. Palmer	2	— c Robinson b Alley	5
S. J. Storey c Clarkson b Robinson	6	— c Robinson b Alley	9
G. R. J. Roope lbw b K. E. Palmer	1	— c and b Langford	12
R. I. Jefferson not out	45	— c Clayton b K. E. Palmer	0
†A. Long c Clayton b R. Palmer	13	— b Langford	4
P. I. Pocock c K. D. Palmer b R. Palmer	12	— run out	0
D. A. Marriott (did not bat)		— not out	0
B 3, l-b 8	11	L-b 2, w 1	3
1/116 2/153 3/176 4/184 5/199 6/199 7/200 8/248 9/274 (9 wkts., dec.)	274	1/71 2/81 3/90 4/91 5/93 6/93 7/110 8/128 9/138 (9 wkts.)	138

Bowling: *First Innings*—R. Palmer 19.4—3—47—3; C. R. M. Atkinson 4—1—11—0; K. E. Palmer 27—6—56—5; Alley 8—2—29—0; Langford 34—12—66—0; Robinson 14—3—54—1. *Second Innings*—R. Palmer 5—0—24—0; Alley 12—0—37—3; K. E. Palmer 9—2—29—2; Robinson 8—4—14—0; Langford 10—5—31—3; C. R. M. Atkinson 1—1—0—0.

Umpires: A. E. Alderman and J. Langridge.

SURREY v. MIDDLESEX

At The Oval, July 9, 10, 11. *65 overs.* Surrey won by 105 runs. On a pitch that was again encouraging to spinners, the faster bowlers, particularly Price, who was fast and lively, had rather more cause for satisfaction. Thanks to Edrich, who played another fine innings after a slow, uncomfortable start, and Stewart, his partner in a quick-fire stand of 89, Surrey made good use of their 65 overs, despite making only 14 off the first ten. For Middlesex, Parfitt played well, but the best-timed innings was Hooker's aggressive 50, made under the handicap of a strained back, which deprived Middlesex of his bowling. Again Edrich and Edwards, both of whom were missed early off Price, set Surrey on the way to victory by scoring 120 together, and in the final innings spin at length prevailed. After an opening stand of 91 between Russell and Harris, full of fluent stroke play, the last nine Middlesex wickets tumbled for 94.

Surrey

First Innings		Second Innings	
M. J. Edwards c Clark b Price	2	b Stewart	56
J. H. Edrich b Price	76	c Clifton b Titmus	67
M. D. Willett st Clifton b Hooker	28	c Clifton b Price	27
*M. J. Stewart c Parfitt b Titmus	44	b Price	19
S. J. Storey b Titmus	2	c and b Titmus	8
R. A. E. Tindall b Price	26	b Price	43
R. I. Jefferson b Price	31	not out	9
P. I. Pocock b Titmus	2		
G. R. J. Roope not out	6	not out	34
†A. Long b Titmus	1		
R. D. Jackman not out	1		
N-b 1	1	B 6, l-b 10	16
1/4 2/46 3/135 4/144 5/155 6/208 7/211 8/213 9/214 (9 wkts., 65 overs)	220	1/120 2/138 3/177 4/180 5/201 6/267 (6 wkts., dec.)	279

Bowling: *First Innings*—Price 22—4—69—4; Stewart 17—4—47—0; Hooker 8—0—46—1; Titmus 18—4—57—4. *Second Innings*—Price 25—4—64—3; Stewart 20—3—64—1; Titmus 32—6—70—2; Latchman 12—1—46—0; Parfitt 6—0—19—0.

Middlesex

First Innings		Second Innings	
W. E. Russell c Edwards b Pocock	29	c Pocock b Tindall	48
M. J. Harris c Long b Jefferson	11	c Storey b Tindall	73
P. H. Parfitt b Jefferson	67	c Stewart b Storey	11
E. A. Clark c Jackman b Pocock	11	c Roope b Pocock	5
D. Bennett c Roope b Pocock	13	c Edrich b Pocock	0
*F. J. Titmus st Long b Pocock	17	c Roope b Storey	13
R. W. Hooker st Long b Jackman	50	c Willett b Pocock	10
H. C. Latchman c Roope b Storey	1	not out	16
†E. G. Clifton c Stewart b Storey	0	b Jefferson	0
R. W. Stewart not out	2	c Edwards b Pocock	0
J. S. E. Price run out	3	c Willett b Jefferson	1
B 4, l-b 1	5	B 6, l-b 2	8
1/25 2/63 3/89 4/114 5/150 6/156 7/171 8/199 9/205	209	1/91 2/105 3/112 4/113 5/138 6/159 7/182 8/183 9/184	185

Bowling: *First Innings*—Jefferson 22—5—62—2; Jackman 10—1—34—1; Pocock 19—4—70—4; Storey 12.3—2—38—2. *Second Innings*—Jefferson 16.1—6—23—2; Jackman 10—3—28—0; Pocock 25—2—74—4; Tindall 12—5—16—2; Storey 19—7—36—2.

Umpires: A. E. Fagg and R. Aspinall.

SURREY v. LEICESTERSHIRE

At The Oval, July 13, 14, 15. Drawn. Leicestershire spent most of the first day scoring 275, and a game generally behind schedule was finally beaten by rain. Booth, whose sound century came in three and a half hours, had his nose broken when Storey's return from the boundary struck him while he was acknowledging the applause of the crowd. Norman batted sluggishly for his 66 and shared a stand of 110 with Booth, after which wickets fell steadily and mainly to the medium pace of Roope. Stewart's first century of the season and his stand of 154 with Tindall were the features of Surrey's innings. Stewart attacked well after passing 50 and was finally unluckily dismissed when his foot flicked the stump as he was hitting to leg. On the last rain-damaged day a stand of 110 between Marner and Inman prevented Surrey from exploiting their first innings advantage. On Sunday, £830 was taken with 7,000 spectators in the ground.

Leicestershire

*M. R. Hallam c Roope b Jackman	10	— b Tindall	16
B. J. Booth retired hurt	102		
M. E. Norman lbw b Jackman	66	— run out	25
C. C. Inman b Roope	1	— not out	72
P. Marner b Roope	0	— b Roope	53
D. Constant c Long b Pocock	13	— not out	1
J. Birkenshaw c Long b Storey	28		
†R. W. Tolchard c Edrich b Roope	15	— c Roope b Storey	41
C. T. Spencer c Tindall b Roope	20		
J. S. Savage not out	8		
J. Cotton b Storey	4		
B 6, l-b 2	8	B 4, l-b 2	6
1/21 2/176 3/176 4/197 5/197 6/234 7/260 8/260	275	1/16 2/78 3/93 4/203 (4 wkts.)	214

Bowling: *First Innings*—Jefferson 22—5—41—0; Jackman 22—7—47—2; Roope 21—2—69—4; Storey 21.4—4—45—2; Pocock 18—5—39—1; Tindall 11—1—26—0. *Second Innings*—Jefferson 9—2—28—0; Jackman 10—1—26—0; Pocock 28—8—71—0; Tindall 14.2—5—33—1; Roope 11—5—23—1; Storey 17—8—27—1.

Surrey

J. H. Edrich c Tolchard b Marner	54
M. J. Edwards c Constant b Marner	50
M. D. Willett lbw b Marner	0
*M. J. Stewart hit wkt b Cotton	101
R. A. E. Tindall not out	67
S. J. Storey c Cotton b Birkenshaw	19
B 10, l-b 12, n-b 1	23
1/87 2/87/3/121 4/275 5/314 (5 wkts., dec.)	314

R. I. Jefferson, G. R. J. Roope, †A. Long, P. I. Pocock and R. D. Jackman did not bat.

Bowling: Cotton 22—4—54—1; Spencer 19—1—58—0; Marner 25—3—84—3; Savage 21—9—52—0; Birkenshaw 16.5—3—43—1.

Umpires: C. S. Elliott and G. H. Pope.

At Coventry, July 16, 18, 19. Surrey beat Warwickshire by five wickets.

At The Oval, July 20, 21, 22. Surrey lost to West Indies by seven wickets in a one-day match. (See West Indies section.)

SURREY v. WORCESTERSHIRE

At The Oval, July 23, 25, 26. *65 overs.* Drawn. Worcestershire, and particularly Graveney, dominated a game which was rained off on the third afternoon. Graveney played delightful cricket for his first county century of the season, hitting fifteen 4's, mainly from perfectly timed drives. Ormrod and d'Oliveira also batted finely to share with him respectively stands of 83 and 164. Surrey lost their chance of first-innings lead by taking 51 overs to make 125 for three on the first day. Slogging then brought them 62 for five more wickets from the final 14. Edrich and Edwards continued their successful partnership by scoring 95 and 62 together. The match, however, was lifted above the mediocre only in the second Worcestershire innings by Graveney and his partners.

Worcestershire

First innings		Second innings	
*D. Kenyon b Arnold	0	c Edwards b Arnold	22
M. J. Horton c Long b Arnold	2	c Long b Arnold	2
J. A. Ormrod c Roope b Storey	43	c Edwards b Storey	38
T. W. Graveney c Roope b Jefferson	9	c Smith b Arnold	109
B. d'Oliveira lbw b Pocock	24	c Long b Roope	96
R. G. A. Headley c Edwards b Jefferson	31	b Arnold	6
D. W. Richardson b Storey	19	b Roope	25
†R. Booth not out	32	not out	4
N. Gifford not out	19		
B 4, l-b 6, w 1, n-b 3	14	B 4, l-b 10, n-b 9	23
1/1 2/12 3/31 4/77 5/106 6/133 7/147 (7 wkts., 65 overs)	193	1/11 2/28 3/111 4/275 5/284 6/310 7/325 (7 wkts., dec.)	325

B. M. Brain and J. A. Flavell did not bat.

Bowling: *First Innings*—Arnold 14—4—52—2; Jefferson 18—5—49—2; Storey 25—9—53—2; Pocock 8—0—25—1. *Second Innings*—Arnold 25—4—69—4; Jefferson 17—2—65—0; Storey 28—12—47—1; Pocock 18—4—63—0; Roope 13.2—0—58—2.

Surrey

First innings		Second innings	
J. H. Edrich c Gifford b d'Oliveira	53	c Booth b d'Oliveira	32
M. J. Edwards lbw b Flavell	45	c Booth b d'Oliveira	32
M. D. Willett lbw b Flavell	0	not out	17
*M. J. Stewart c Richardson b Brain	35	not out	12
W. A. Smith lbw b d'Oliveira	16		
S. J. Storey c Booth b d'Oliveira	6		
R. I. Jefferson c Booth b Flavell	13		
G. R. J. Roope not out	8		
P. I. Pocock c Gifford b Brain	1		
†A. Long not out	2		
B 5, l-b 3	8	B 4, n-b 1	5
1/95 2/99 3/117 4/141 5/149 6/167 7/177 8/184 (8 wkts., 65 overs)	187	1/62 2/79 (2 wkts.)	98

G. Arnold did not bat.

Bowling: *First Innings*—Flavell 22—2—50—3; Brain 10—0—45—2; d'Oliveira 24—8—64—3; Horton 6—1—20—0; Gifford 3—3—0—0. *Second Innings*—Flavell 9—1—17—0; Brain 10—2—26—0; d'Oliveira 17—6—29—2; Gifford 8.5—2—21—0.

Umpires: L. H. Gray and A. E. Alderman.

At Worcester, July 27, 28, 29. SURREY lost to WORCESTERSHIRE by an innings and 14 runs.

SURREY v. ESSEX

At The Oval, July 30, 31, August 1. Surrey won by seven wickets. Another century stand by Edrich and Edwards decided a match of give and take in favour of Surrey. A rain-marred first day was followed by a series of declarations and more weather interruptions. In the first Essex innings Knight with seven 4's hit 60 of 80 added with Bailey, after Marriott had taken three for eight in seven overs. Barrington, returning to the first-class game after suffering ill-health, batted forty-five minutes for his 19. On the last day Surrey were set to make 165 in two hours, twenty-five minutes, and Edrich and Edwards made the first 108 in one hundred minutes.

Essex

G. E. Barker run out	11	— c Long b Jefferson	5
M. J. Bear b Marriott	30	— b Marriott	10
†B. Taylor b Marriott	8	— c Edrich b Jefferson	0
K. W. R. Fletcher c Long b Marriott	2	— not out	54
*T. E. Bailey not out	21	— c Edwards b Jefferson	4
B. R. Knight b Storey	60	— b Storey	11
G. R. Cass (did not bat)		— b Jefferson	0
B. Edmeades (did not bat)		— not out	27
B 4, l-b 4, n-b 1	9	L-b 4	4
1/20 2/44 3/50 4/61 5/141 (5 wkts., dec.)	141	1/11 2/13 3/17 4/41 5/48 (6 wkts., dec.)	115

R. N. S. Hobbs, A. M. Jorden and D. L. Acfield did not bat.

Bowling: *First Innings*—Jefferson 13—1—46—0; Marriott 21—2—44—3; Storey 15.3—5—26—1; Pocock 5—2—16—0. *Second Innings*—Jefferson 14—2—40—4; Marriott 9—1—25—1; Storey 6—3—10—1; Pocock 8—1—31—0; Harman 4—1—5—0.

Surrey

J. H. Edrich not out	47	— c Taylor b Hobbs	69
M. J. Edwards lbw b Knight	1	— c Cass b Acfield	53
W. A. Smith lbw b Edmeades	10		
K. F. Barrington b Knight	19	— not out	13
*M. J. Stewart not out	14		
S. J. Storey (did not bat)		— c Taylor b Acfield	0
R. I. Jefferson (did not bat)		— not out	21
W 1	1	B 3, l-b 6	9
1/5 2/27 3/68 (3 wkts., dec.)	92	1/108 2/109 3/135 (3 wkts.)	165

R. Harman, †A. Long, P. I. Pocock and D. A. Marriott did not bat.

Bowling: *First Innings*—Knight 11—3—28—2; Jorden 9—0—47—0; Edmeades 7—1—16—1. *Second Innings*—Knight 14—1—58—0; Jorden 5—0—14—0; Acfield 8.3—2—24—2; Edmeades 3—0—12—0; Bailey 4—1—19—0; Hobbs 5—0—29—1.

Umpires: J. F. Crapp and A. E. Rhodes.

SURREY v. NOTTINGHAMSHIRE

At The Oval, August 3, 4, 5. Drawn. Murray's 166 with twenty-two 4's in five and a quarter hours, his highest score in first-class cricket, earned a draw for Nottinghamshire. On a green pitch they were skittled by Jefferson and Harman on the first day. On the second Storey's first century of the season, a dashing innings, put Surrey in command. Storey batted only two hours, ten minutes for 109 and hit one 6 and seventeen 4's. He and Pocock put on 63 in half an hour. Surrey were still in control when they took the first six second-innings wickets for 164. In the next two and a half hours Murray and Taylor scored 158 together and saved the match.

U

Nottinghamshire

*N. Hill c Barrington b Jefferson	6	— lbw b Harman	37
J. B. Bolus lbw b Storey	22	— lbw b Jefferson	15
D. L. Murray c Long b Jefferson	16	— not out	166
H. I. Moore c Storey b Harman	33	— c and b Pocock	13
M. J. Smedley lbw b Storey	1	— run out	20
R. A. White c Edwards b Marriott	3	— c Long b Storey	4
†R. Swetman lbw b Jefferson	17	— c Barrington b Storey	1
M. Taylor c Jefferson b Harman	0	— lbw b Harman	62
B. Stead c Stewart b Harman	10	— not out	8
C. Forbes b Jefferson	2	— c Stewart b Barrington	3
I. Davison not out	1		
B 4, l-b 1	5	B 12, l-b 8, n-b 3	23
1/16 2/38 3/58 4/60 5/73 6/100 7/102 8/102 9/114	116	1/58 2/60 3/92 4/149 5/160 6/164 7/322 8/336 (8 wkts.)	352

Bowling: *First Innings*—Jefferson 21—6—52—4; Marriott 18—6—32—1; Storey 15—7—25—2; Harman 6—4—2—3. *Second Innings*—Jefferson 22—5—62—1; Marriott 23—3—60—0; Storey 30—11—60—2; Harman 29—10—51—2; Pocock 30—7—62—1; Barrington 7—2—27—1; Stewart 3—1—7—0.

Surrey

J. H. Edrich c Davison b White	68
M. J. Edwards lbw b Stead	0
W. A. Smith c White b Forbes	16
K. F. Barrington c Swetman b Taylor	36
*M. J. Stewart c Moore b Taylor	4
S. J. Storey not out	109
R. I. Jefferson c Swetman b Stead	18
†A. Long b Stead	0
P. I. Pocock not out	25
B 4, l-b 3	7
1/0 2/43 3/119 4/121 5/136 6/220 7/220 (7 wkts., dec.)	283

R. Harman and D. A. Marriott did not bat.

Bowling—Davison 25—5—80—0; Stead 22—4—63—3; Taylor 16—6—30—2; Forbes 21—4—60—1; White 14—5—43—1.

Umpires: W. F Price and J. F. Crapp.

At Lord's, August 6, 8, 9. SURREY drew with MIDDLESEX.

At Bradford, August 13, 15, 16. SURREY beat YORKSHIRE by 31 runs.

At Cheltenham, August 17, 18. SURREY beat GLOUCESTERSHIRE by seven wickets.

At The Oval, August 18, 19, 20, 22. ENGLAND beat WEST INDIES in the fifth Test by an innings and 34 runs. (See WEST INDIES section.)

At Eastbourne, August 20, 22, 23. SURREY drew with SUSSEX.

SURREY v. GLOUCESTERSHIRE

At The Oval, August 24, 25, 26. Drawn. At the close Gloucestershire needed two runs for victory with their last pair together, after being set to make 222 in three hours, twenty minutes. Edwards made his first first-class century for the county, batting three and three-quarter hours, and on the other side Bissex played delightfully in both innings. His perfectly timed stroke play was the feature of the match. Bissex hit his first 51 in forty-seven minutes, but subsequently Gloucestershire scored slowly, and against Arnold and Jefferson their last four wickets added only 25. A brisk stand of 134 between Edrich and Barrington accelerated Surrey's final declaration. Bissex, who was partnered by Russell while 66 were added, had put Gloucestershire in a favourable position, when Barrington swung the game by taking three wickets for 16 in twenty balls. In the final over, bowled by Jefferson, four runs were scored and the ninth wicket fell to a brilliant diving catch by Stewart in the covers.

Surrey

J. H. Edrich c Milton b Smith	5	— c Meyer b Smith	83
M. J. Edwards c Shepherd b Bissex	116	— c Meyer b Smith	3
W. A. Smith c Milton b Smith	49		
K. F. Barrington lbw b Smith	0	— not out	57
*M. J. Stewart c Meyer b Smith	71		
S. J. Storey c Meyer b Mence	41	— b A. S. Brown	5
R. I. Jefferson not out	16		
†A. Long not out	7		
B 5, l-b 10, w 1	16	B 4, l-b 6	10
1/22 2/122 3/122 4/230 5/264 6/304 (6 wkts., dec.)	321	1/17 2/24 3/158 (3 wkts., dec.)	158

R. Harman, P. I. Pocock and G. Arnold did not bat.

Bowling: *First Innings*—Smith 25—7—71—4; A. S. Brown 26—2—81—0; Mence 15—1—48—1; Allen 22—6—57—0; Bissex 23—9—48—1. *Second Innings*—Smith 13.5—0—39—2; A. S. Brown 19—5—38—1; Mence 13—1—50—0; Allen 4—1—12—0; Bissex 3—1—9—0.

Gloucestershire

C. A. Milton c Long b Storey	18	— c Barrington b Storey	12
M. Bissex lbw b Storey	79	— lbw b Barrington	64
S. E. Russell c Storey b Pocock	21	— c Edwards b Barrington	39
D Shepherd c Arnold b Jefferson	17	— c Jefferson b Barrington	8
R. B. Nicholls c Barrington b Storey	46	— b Arnold	30
D Brown b Jefferson	39	— run out	11
M. D. Mence c Smith b Arnold	22	— c Harman b Arnold	5
A. S. Brown c Arnold b Jefferson	12	— not out	23
*D. A. Allen c Edwards b Arnold	0	— not out	1
†B. J. Meyer c Barrington b Arnold	1	— b Jefferson	4
D. R. Smith not out	0	— c Stewart b Jefferson	11
L-b 2, n-b 1	3	B 7, l-b 3, n-b 2	12
1/76 2/118 3/118 4/141 5/199 6/233 7/249 8/252 9/258	258	1/47 2/113 3/132 4/135 5/145 6/176 7/185 8/199 9/219 (9 wkts.)	220

Bowling: *First Innings*—Arnold 25.2—3—88—3; Jefferson 20—3—73—3; Storey 27—6—68—3; Harman 12—5—17—0; Pocock 12—7—9—1. *Second Innings*— Arnold 20—5—41—2; Jefferson 6—1—16—2; Storey 15—4—38—1; Harman 9—1—26—0; Barrington 13—0—87—3.

Umpires: A. E. Fagg and F. Jakeman.

SURREY v. YORKSHIRE

At The Oval, August 27, 29, 30. Drawn. No play was possible on the final day of a match dominated by the bowlers. Arnold bowled splendidly for Surrey, taking the first four wickets for nine in fourteen overs of fast, accurate swing bowling, and Yorkshire's batting broke down. Close, however, emulated Arnold by taking the first four Surrey wickets in six overs for 16, including three in five balls. That Surrey gained a slender lead of seven was due to Willett and Jackman, who scored 57 for the ninth wicket. At the end of a personally disappointing season Willett showed his true quality in an innings of magnificent determination. Jackman prospered by swinging his bat straight down the line of the ball, a virtue not sufficiently observed by county batsmen in 1966.

Yorkshire

G. Boycott c Edwards b Arnold	0	— not out	44
P. J. Sharpe c Barrington b Arnold	40	— c Barrington b Jackman	5
D. E. V. Padgett c Long b Arnold	18	— c Long b Jackman	9
J. H. Hampshire b Arnold	7	— b Storey	28
*D. B. Close c Long b Jackman	11	— c Edrich b Storey	10
R. Illingworth lbw b Storey	7	— c Long b Arnold	1
R. A. Hutton c Harman b Storey	6	— not out	3
†J. G. Binks b Harman	7		
F. S. Trueman c and b Arnold	15		
D. Wilson c Barrington b Arnold	20		
A. G. Nicholson not out	7		
N-b 5	5	B 6, l-b 2	8
1/0 2/59 3/63 4/76 5/82 6/91 7/100 8/112 9/116	143	1/8 2/22 3/76 4/98 5/99 (5 wkts.)	108

Bowling: *First Innings*—Arnold 18.1—10—33—6; Jackman 18—4—38—1; Storey 20—2—45—2; Harman 11—3—22—1. *Second Innings*—Arnold 15—3—26—1; Jackman 11—2—28—2; Storey 11.4—1—31—2; Harman 5—1—15—0.

Surrey

J. H. Edrich c Sharpe b Close	5
M. J. Edwards c Close b Illingworth	40
W. A. Smith c Binks b Close	8
K. F. Barrington c Sharpe b Close	0
*M. J. Stewart c Padgett b Close	0
M. D. Willett not out	52
†A. Long c Close b Illingworth	0
S. J. Storey lbw b Illingworth	15
G. Arnold c and b Illingworth	0
R. D. Jackman c Hampshire b Close	19
R. Harman c Sharpe b Close	0
B 7, n-b 4	11
1/19 2/37 3/37 4/37 5/73 6/73 7/93 8/93 9/150	150

Bowling: Trueman 13—3—26—0; Nicholson 1.5—0—3—0; Close 15.5—7—27—6; Hutton 13—2—31—0; Illingworth 20—7—36—4; Wilson 6—1—16—0.

Umpires: J. S. Buller and P. B. Wight.

At Manchester, August 31, September 1, 2. SURREY drew with LANCASHIRE.

SUSSEX

President—THE DUKE OF NORFOLK

Secretary—COL. P. C. WILLIAMS, County Ground, Eaton Place, Hove 3

Captain in 1966—THE NAWAB OF PATAUDI; 1967—J. M. PARKS

M. A. Buss

County Badge

A. Buss

There are some things in cricket difficult to explain. For example, the performances of Sussex in 1966. They won only eight of their 30 first-class matches, yet three of the victories were at the expense of the strongest sides, West Indies, Yorkshire, the champions, and Worcestershire, the runners-up. They also beat Gloucestershire, Essex and Nottinghamshire, all low in the table, and Leicestershire, eighth, as well as Cambridge University. A mixed bag if ever there was one.

The relaying of part of the square at Hove, where four games ended inside two days, had much to do with the summary defeat of the West Indies, beaten for the first time on the tour. Yet no vagaries of turf supplied the reason for the two-day victory over Yorkshire at Leeds or the success over Worcestershire when the Midland county still held a chance of retaining the championship.

Credit for the majority of the victories belonged to the three seamers, Snow, Tony Buss and Bates. Snow took eleven for 47 against West Indies at Hove and he followed this with ten for 120 at Leeds, where Buss returned five for 91. These two each took nine wickets in the defeat of Worcestershire, Snow for 88 and Buss for 86. Bates meanwhile returned his best figures, eight for 51, against Essex and Buss took eight for 23 against Nottinghamshire. Between them, the three accounted for 317 of the 413 wickets taken by Sussex bowlers.

Snow blossomed forth as a batsman, too, in the latter part of the season. Included in the last Test because Price of Middlesex was unfit, he hit his first 50 in helping Higgs put on 128, only two runs short of the record last-wicket stand in Test cricket. He followed with 21 and 71 against Somerset.

As a whole, the batting did not match the bowling. Suttle in his benefit year did best but even he with an average of 29.41 from 56 innings and a total of 1,500 runs, could not get higher than 37th in the overall averages. Parks, who gained his 100th Test victim at Lord's, and Lenham were the only other batsmen to exceed 1,000 runs, with Michael Buss, who hit his maiden century against Cambridge, scoring 787 runs in 32 innings.

The absence of Dexter for all but two matches was a big blow. The Nawab of Pataudi took over from him as captain successfully in one capacity, the tossing of the coin. He won the choice in the first eleven matches. His batting lacked consistency and there were times when a more dynamic approach might have proved beneficial. Still, the side finished tenth in the table as against sixteenth twelve months earlier, a step in the right direction.

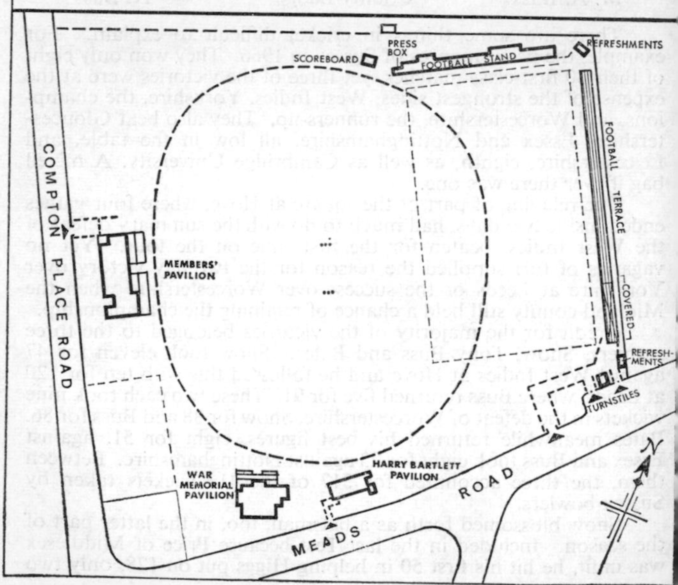

SUSSEX RESULTS

All First-Class Matches—Played 30, *Won* 8, *Lost* 11, *Drawn* 11
County Championship Matches—Played 28, *Won* 6, *Lost* 11, *Drawn* 11

COUNTY CHAMPIONSHIP AVERAGES

BATTING

	Birthplace	Mtchs.	Inns.	Not Outs	Runs	100's	Highest Inns.	Aver.
K. G. Suttle....	*Kensington*	28	53	4	1439	3	172*	29.36
J. M. Parks....	*Haywards Heath*	21	38	5	897	1	119	27.18
A. S. M. Oakman	*Hastings*	28	46	7	935	0	86*	23.97
L. J. Lenham...	*Lancing*	27	53	3	1194	0	86	23.88
M. A. Buss....	*Brightling*	17	32	3	651	0	65	22.44
Nawab of Pataudi.....	*Bhopal*	21	40	3	774	0	67	20.91
D. J. Foreman..	*Cape Town*	21	33	5	584	0	68	20.85
E. R. Dexter...	*Milan*	2	4	0	83	0	63	20.75
M. G. Griffith..	*Beaconsfield*	23	39	7	614	0	57*	19.18
P. J. Graves....	*Hove*	18	30	5	435	0	43*	17.40
G. C. Cooper..	*East Grinstead*	5	10	1	149	0	32	16.55
J. A. Snow.....	*Peopletown*	22	28	12	212	0	71	13.25
R. J. Langridge.	*Brighton*	7	14	0	165	0	68	11.78
A. Buss........	*Brightling*	28	41	6	391	0	35	11.17
P. R. V. Ledden	*Scarborough*	5	7	2	44	0	28	8.80
D. L. Bates....	*Hove*	25	31	13	146	0	18	8.11
H. Newton....	*Little Lever*	2	4	2	16	0	16*	8.00
T. Gunn.......	*Bradford*	7	11	2	40	0	17*	4.44

A. Jones (*Horley*) played in one match but did not bat.

** Signifies not out.*

BOWLING

	Overs	Maidens	Runs	Wickets	Average
J. A. Snow.............	736.1	158	1908	103	18.52
A. Buss..............	951.3	201	2662	116	22.94
H. Newton.............	66	20	141	6	23.50
D. L. Bates............	616.5	149	1596	64	24.93
A. S. M. Oakman........	653	185	1526	52	29.34
K. G. Suttle............	209.2	68	486	10	48.60
M. A. Buss............	157.3	49	431	5	86.20
P. R. V. Ledden	24	4	92	1	92.00
D. J. Foreman..........	2.3	0	12	0	—

Also bowled: G. C. Cooper 5—2—15—0; E. R. Dexter 0.3—0—8—0; P. J. Graves 3—0—22—0; A. Jones 14—3—50—2; L. J. Lenham 1.4—0—9—0; Nawab of Pataudi 0.3—0—1—0.

At Southampton, April 27, 28, 29. SUSSEX drew with HAMPSHIRE.

At Taunton, April 30. SUSSEX lost to SOMERSET by four wickets. (See GILLETTE CUP.)

SUSSEX v. GLAMORGAN

At Hove, May 4, 5, 6. *65 overs.* Glamorgan won by four wickets in a thrilling finish, with the winning run hit three minutes from time, but it took two declarations after a blank day to produce the climax. Wheatley made the first when he called in his players 21 behind. Sussex, for whom Parks and the Nawab of Pataudi saved a collapse in the first innings with a stand of 85, then found trouble facing the off-breaks of Euros Lewis, who conceded 64 runs in taking all seven wickets to fall, but they batted fast enough for Pataudi to tempt Glamorgan with a target of 184 in two hours, thirty-five minutes. At 72 for three the game was evenly balanced but when Tony Lewis and Euros Lewis put on 50 in half an hour for the fourth wicket the advantage was all with Glamorgan.

Sussex

K. G. Suttle lbw b Wheatley	10	— c and b E. Lewis	51
L. J. Lenham lbw b I. J. Jones	11	— c Wheatley b E. Lewis	47
R. J. Langridge b Wheatley	0	— st Evans b E. Lewis	11
†J. M. Parks c Evans b I. J. Jones	57	— c A. R. Lewis b E. Lewis	16
*Nawab of Pataudi c E. Lewis b Shepherd	40	— c Hedges b E. Lewis	13
A. S. M. Oakman b Shepherd	2	— b E. Lewis	0
G. C. Cooper b Shepherd	3	— not out	11
M. A. Buss c Evans b Shepherd	25	— b E. Lewis	0
A. Buss c Evans b Wheatley	2	— not out	10
J. A. Snow run out	2		
D. L. Bates not out	2		
B 2, l-b 3, n-b 2	7	L-b 2, n-b 1	3
1/21 2/21 3/22 4/107 5/117 6/124 7/128 8/143 9/150	161	1/99 2/99 3/117 4/126 5/136 6/141 7/141 (7 wkts. dec.)	162

Bowling: *First Innings*—I. J. Jones 18—3—60—2; Wheatley 13—4—25—3; Cordle 7—0—22—0; Walker 7—1—20—0; Shepherd 18.5—8—27—4. *Second Innings*—I. J. Jones 6—1—20—0; Wheatley 4—0—11—0; E. Lewis 21—4—64—7; Cordle 5—0—21—0; Shepherd 15—2—43—0.

Glamorgan

A. Jones c Oakman b Snow	15	— c Lenham b Oakman	20
B. Hedges c Parks b Oakman	31	— b Snow	0
P. M. Walker c Pataudi b Bates	27	— run out	29
A. R. Lewis c M. A. Buss b Snow	27	— c Pataudi b Snow	50
E. Lewis b Snow	2	— b A. Buss	20
A. Rees c Langridge b Snow	5	— c A. Buss b Snow	24
†D. L. Evans not out	10		
A. E. Cordle not out	11	— not out	35
D. J. Shepherd (did not bat)		— not out	0
B 3, l-b 2, n-b 7	12	L-b 3, n-b 3	6
1/27 2/79 3/88 4/106 5/118 6/119 (6 wkts., 65 overs)	140	1/0 2/32 3/72 4/122 5/126 6/183 (6 wkts.)	184

I. J. Jones and *O. S. Wheatley did not bat.

Bowling: *First Innings*—Snow 17—4—43—4; A. Buss 16—4—25—0; Suttle 7—2—18—0; Bates 12—2—23—1; Oakman 5—1—19—1. *Second Innings*—Snow 12.5—1—42—3; A. Buss 10—0—65—1; Oakman 12—5—27—1; Suttle 2—0—12—0; Bates 8—1—32—0.

Umpires: P. A. Gibb and J. Arnold.

SUSSEX v. NORTHAMPTONSHIRE

At Hove, May 7, 9, 10. Northampton won by ten wickets, taking ten points to two by Sussex. This comfortable victory after Sussex had started with a partnership of 103 in one hour, fifty minutes between Suttle and Lenham and gone on to total over 300 was the outcome of good performances with both bat and ball. Milburn scored his second century in three Championship innings, hitting with all his known power in scoring 92 of his 137 runs in boundaries. He and Prideaux put on 141 for the first wicket, Prideaux's share being 38. Even so, Northamptonshire were 17 behind on the first innings and it took some fine off-spin bowling by Sully to put them on the path to success. He took seven wickets for 29 runs, figures which surpassed his previous best. Then Milburn and Prideaux were together in their second-century stand, scoring the 127 runs needed in one hour, forty minutes.

Sussex

K. G. Suttle c Mushtaq b Larter	45	— c Mushtaq b Sully	29
L. J. Lenham c Steele b Larter	84	— c Andrew b P. J. Watts	16
R. J. Langridge c Prideaux b Sully	25	— lbw b Sully	6
*J. M. Parks b P. J. Watts	24	— c Crump b Sully	4
*Nawab of Pataudi c P. J. Walls b Scott	30	— c Larter b Sully	3
A. S. M. Oakman c P. J. Watts b Mushtaq	9	— b Scott	4
M. G. Griffith not out	38	— c Steele b Sully	3
M. A. Buss c Steele b Crump	31	— lbw b Sully	0
A. Buss b Crump	4	— c Steele b Sully	35
D. L. Bates not out	3	— not out	5
A. Jones (did not bat)		— absent ill	
B 6, n-b 6, l-b 1	13	L-b 3, n-b 1	4
1/103 2/142 3/184 4/192 (8 wkts. dec.) 5/217 6/227 7/271 8/294	306	1/22 2/31 3/35 4/47 5/57 6/62 7/62 8/83 9/109	109

Bowling: *First Innings*—Larter 21.3—3—73—2; Crump 22—8—34—2; P. J. Watts 16—6—41—1; Sully 14—2—56—1; Scott 19—7—52—1; Mushtaq 18—5—37—1. *Second Innings*—Larter 4—0—19—0; Crump 5—2—10—0; P. J. Watts 3—0—6—1; Sully 23.3—9—29—7; Scott 18—7—41—1.

Northamptonshire

C. Milburn c and b A. Buss	137	— not out	68
R. M. Prideaux c Parks b Jones	38	— not out	48
B. L. Reynolds c Jones b Oakman	0		
Mushtaq Mohammad c Langridge b Oakman	38		
D. S. Steele c Pataudi b Jones	21		
P. J. Watts b Oakman	8		
B. Crump c Pataudi b Oakman	1		
H. Sully not out	20		
M. E. Scott c Parks b A. Buss	2		
*†K. V. Andrew lbw b A. Buss	7		
J. D. F. Larter b A. Buss	6		
B 3, l-b 8	11	B 10, n-b 1	11
1/141 2/146 3/194 4/230 5/251 6/252 7/253 8/265 9/275	289	(no wkt.)	127

Bowling: *First Innings*—A Buss 27.1—5—70—4; Bates 19—4—64—0; Jones 14—3—50—2; Oakman 40—13—80—4; Suttle 4—1—14—0. *Second Innings*—A. Buss 5—1—17—0; Bates 3—0—7—0; Oakman 15—5—46—0; M. A. Buss 13—3—42—0; Lenham 4—0—4—0.

Umpires: P. A. Gibb and J. Arnold.

At The Oval, May 11, 12, 13. SUSSEX lost to SURREY by nine wickets.

At Leicester, May 14, 16, 17. SUSSEX beat LEICESTERSHIRE by eight wickets.

SUSSEX v. WORCESTERSHIRE

At Hove, May 18, 19, 20. *65 overs.* **Drawn. At 157 for two in trying to score 215 to win, Worcestershire seemed to be in an excellent position. Kenyon (one 6 and seven 4's) had set them on the path with 64 of an opening partnership of 84 with Headley. Then the fast bowlers Snow and Buss caused such a collapse that when Flavell went to the wicket he had to play the last ball surrounded by fieldsmen to prevent Sussex from winning. This inconsistency on the part of batsmen was marked throughout the match. Parks, having been involved in a car accident overnight, found himself batting with Pataudi 10 minutes after the start to save the situation for Sussex and only Graveney showed any assurance for Worcestershire in the first innings. Then Sussex were glad of another good knock from Pataudi after the opening batsmen had been dismissed without scoring.**

Sussex

K. G. Suttle b Coldwell	16	— lbw b Flavell	0
L. J. Lenham c Booth b Flavell	1	— c Headley b Coldwell	0
R. J. Langridge c Booth b Coldwell	0	— c Booth b. Gifford	7
†J. M. Parks lbw b Flavell	63	— c Headley b Flavell	16
*Nawab of Pataudi lbw b Flavell	58	— b Flavell	67
G. C. Cooper c Booth b d'Oliveira	0	— c Headley b Gifford	28
M. G. Griffith not out	23	— c Gifford b Flavell	0
A. S. M. Oakman b Coldwell	44	— c Gifford b Flavell	1
A. Buss not out	1	— c Graveney b Flavell	16
D. L. Bates (did not bat)		— c Headley b Flavell	10
J. A. Snow (did not bat)		— not out	3
B 1, l-b 4	5	B 2, l-b 4	6
1/2 2/3 3/28 4/137 5/138 6/138 7/210 (7 wkts., 65 overs)	211	1/0 2/0 3/37 4/57 5/122 6/122 7/123 8/124 9/145	154

Bowling: *First Innings*—Flavell 19—0—63—3; Coldwell 22—2—69—3; d'Oliveira 10—1—22—1; Gifford 14—4—52—0. *Second Innings*—Flavell 24.3—7—40—7; Coldwell 10—3—28—1; d'Oliveira 14—4—35—0; Gifford 26—15—37—2; Horton 4—1—8—0.

Worcestershire

*D. Kenyon c Cooper b A. Buss	7	— c Snow b A. Buss	64
R. G. A. Headley run out	12	— run out	84
J. A. Ormrod b Snow	4	— c Cooper b Oakman	14
T. W. Graveney b A. Buss	77	— b Snow	4
B. d'Oliveira c Suttle b Bates	11	— c and b A. Buss	2
D. W. Richardson c Lenham b A. Buss	9	— c Parks b A. Buss	0
M. J. Horton c Suttle b A. Buss	5	— b A. Buss	8
†R. Booth c Suttle b Bates	6	— b Snow	11
N. Gifford b A. Buss	14	— not out	8
L. J. Coldwell not out	1	— c Parks b Snow	0
J. A. Flavell c Griffith b Bates	3	— not out	0
L-b 2	2	L-b 7, n-b 1	8
1/13 2/23 3/26 4/64 5/84 6/103 7/123 8/147 9/148	151	1/84 2/157 3/170 4/174 5/174 6/175 7/192 8/200 9/203 (9 wkts.)	203

Bowling: *First Innings*—Snow 18—4—38—1; A. Buss 28—5—63—5; Bates 14.5—5—42—3; Suttle 4—1—6—0. *Second Innings*—Snow 24—5—84—3; A. Buss 21—4—50—4; Oakman 10—5—39—1; Bates 8—2—22—0.

Umpires: R. Aspinall and L. H. Gray.

SUSSEX v. LANCASHIRE

At Hove, May 25, 26, 27. *65 overs.* Drawn. In cold, cheerless conditions this match which did not begin until after tea on the first day, developed into a battle between batsmen and seam bowlers. The latter came out best, though it took a leg-spinner, Greenhough, to dismiss the most successful batsman, Parks. He hit one 6 and sixteen 4's in scoring 119 in three hours when Sussex, having lost four wickets with 12 runs of the first innings arrears still to clear, were in a parlous position. By his efforts it was possible to leave Lancashire to get 143 in two hours, ten minutes to win, a target which, with the attack monopolised by seamers, proved too much. The game received added interest through a decision by Dexter to make himself available for Test cricket again. He played his first match for nearly a year, but without distinction, scoring two off 19 balls in the first innings and 18 off 30 in the second.

Sussex

K. G. Suttle b Statham	13	— c Lloyd b Higgs	15
L. J. Lenham b Higgs	0	— lbw b Higgs	1
E. R. Dexter c Shuttleworth b Higgs	2	— c Knox b Higgs	18
†J. M. Parks c Goodwin b Higgs	4	— c Knox b Greenhough	119
*Nawab of Pataudi b Statham	28	— c Knox b Statham	21
R. J. Langridge b Statham	11	— c Goodwin b Shuttleworth	12
M. G. Griffith b Shuttleworth	0	— c Knox b Shuttleworth	0
A. S. M. Oakman b Shuttleworth	5	— c and b Statham	18
A. Buss b Shuttleworth	1	— c Lloyd b Higgs	10
D. L. Bates not out	0	— b Statham	1
J. A. Snow b Statham	1	— not out	5
L-b 3, n-b 1	4	B 4, l-b 10, n-b 2	16
1/4 2/16 3/16 4/27 5/59 6/61 7/61 8/67 9/68	69	1/2 2/33 3/44 4/82 5/133 6/147 7/192 8/220 9/226	236

Bowling: *First Innings*—Statham 17.1—8—19—4; Higgs 16—5—32—3; Shuttleworth 10—3—14—3. *Second Innings*—Statham 26—4—72—3; Higgs 25.2—5—70—4; Shuttleworth 11—2—40—2; Greenhough 11—1—38—1.

Lancashire

G. Pullar b Buss	1	— b Buss	6
D. M. Green c Pataudi b Buss	56	— c Bates b Buss	32
G. K. Knox c Parks b Snow	6	— c Suttle b Bates	17
H. Pilling c Parks b Snow	8	— not out	22
R. Entwistle c Parks b Snow	17	— c Parks b Buss	8
D. Lloyd not out	49	— not out	24
K. Shuttleworth b Bates	4		
K. Higgs c Parks b Snow	3		
†K. Goodwin c Pataudi b Bates	12		
T. Greenhough c Parks b Snow	1		
*J. B. Statham not out	0		
L-b 4, n-b 2	6	L-b 4	4
1/2 2/34 3/55 4/76 5/108 6/119 7/130 8/153 9/163 (9 wkts., 65 overs)	163	1/8 2/59 3/60 4/68 (4 wkts.)	113

Bowling: *First Innings*—Snow 25—4—59—5; Buss 19—5—43—2; Bates, 21—4—55—2. *Second Innings*—Snow 12—1—31—0; Buss 15—0—52—3; Bates 9—2—26—1.

Umpires: W. F. Price and A. E. Alderman.

At Lord's, May 28, 30, 31. SUSSEX lost to MIDDLESEX by seven wickets.

At Chesterfield, June 1, 2, 3. SUSSEX drew with DERBYSHIRE.

At Tunbridge Wells, June 4, 6, 7. SUSSEX lost to KENT by five wickets.

At Brentwood, June 8, 9, 10. SUSSEX beat ESSEX by 64 runs.

At Hove, June 11, 13. SUSSEX beat WEST INDIES by nine wickets. (See WEST INDIES section.)

SUSSEX v. NOTTINGHAMSHIRE

At Hove, June 15, 16. *65 overs.* Sussex won by eight wickets, following their win over the West Indies with an equally decisive victory on a pitch of similar character. It became particularly hostile when hot sunshine followed rain on the second day. Then Buss took eight wickets for 23 runs and in so doing not only surpassed his previous best but also put his side on the brink of success. He dismissed White, Smedley and Bolus in four balls. Sussex had already gained a first innings lead of 42 and only once could Pataudi have regretted losing the toss for the first time in the season. That was when Smedley and Swetman with cool, determined batting added 63 in one hour, twenty-five minutes after the first five Nottinghamshire wickets had gone down for 62 runs.

Nottinghamshire

First Innings		Second Innings	
J. B. Bolus c Gunn b Bates	11	— c Gunn b Buss	10
B. Whittingham c Foreman b Buss	1	— c Suttle b Buss	7
R. A. White c Gunn b Snow	18	— c Suttle b Buss	4
H. I. Moore c Oakman b Bates	3	— c Foreman b Buss	3
M. J. Smedley c Graves b Snow	52	— c Gunn b Buss	0
*N. Hill c Pataudi b Snow	3	— c Oakman b Buss	5
†R. Swetman not out	49	— not out	23
M. Taylor c Gunn b Snow	1	— c Lenham b Snow	3
C. Forbes not out	3	— c Gunn b Snow	0
B. Stead (did not bat)		— c Bates b Buss	6
I. Davison (did not bat)		— lbw b Buss	2
B 9, l-b 8, n-b 1	18	B 1, n-b 2	3
1/8 2/22 3/28 4/58 5/62 6/125 7/135 (7 wkts., 65 overs)	159	1/5 2/14 3/18 4/29 5/29 6/32 7/46 8/46 9/59	66

Bowling: *First Innings*—Snow 21—5—38—4; Buss 21—6—43—1; Bates 19—6—50—2; Suttle 4—0—10—0. *Second Innings*—Snow 13—1—29—2; Buss 20.5—8—23—8; Oakman 8—3—11—0.

Sussex

First Innings		Second Innings	
K. G. Suttle lbw b Davison	16	— c sub b Stead	7
L. J. Lenham lbw b Taylor	25	— c sub b Davison	1
*Nawab of Pataudi c Swetman b Forbes	23	— not out	15
M. G. Griffith retired hurt	21		
P. J. Graves c Swetman b Forbes	29	— not out	0
D. J. Foreman not out	41		
A. S. M. Oakman lbw b Taylor	9		
A. Buss not out	30		
L-b 3, n-b 4	7	N-b 2	2
1/26 2/63 3/71 4/125 5/154 (5 wkts., 65 overs)	201	1/5 2/16 (2 wkts.)	25

†T. Gunn, J. A. Snow and D. L. Bates did not bat.

Bowling: *First Innings*—Davison 12—2—37—1; Forbes 29—6—93—2; Taylor 24—8—64—2. *Second Innings*—Stead 4—1—8—1; Davison 4.4—3—15—1.

Umpires: T. W. Spencer and A. E. Fagg.

At Leeds, June 18, 20. SUSSEX beat YORKSHIRE by 22 runs.

At Old Trafford, June 25, 27, 28. SUSSEX lost to LANCASHIRE by seven wickets.

SUSSEX v. HAMPSHIRE

At Hove, June 29, 30. *65 overs*. Hampshire won by nine wickets. Having won the last three matches at Hove inside two days, Sussex received similar treatment handed out by Hampshire. The final tormentor was Marshall, who in his inimitable style made the task of scoring 125 runs look ridiculously simple. These came in an hour and three-quarters, with Marshall hitting one 6 over cover as well as thirteen 4's in scoring 92 in that time. Bowlers had been on top up to that point, with a newcomer to the Sussex team, 31 year-old Newton, returning the best figures of five for 54 with his pace deliveries. His first victim was Marshall, bowled.

Sussex

First Innings		Second Innings	
K. G. Suttle lbw b Shackleton	11	c Timms b Shackleton	10
L. J. Lenham lbw b Cottam	27	b White	2
*Nawab of Pataudi b White	13	c Timms b Shackleton	16
M. G. Griffith b White	53	b Shackleton	0
P. J. Graves c Timms b White	13	c Cottam b Wheatley	23
D. J. Foreman c Timms b Shackleton	1	b White	21
A. S. M. Oakman c Wheatley b White	0	c Timms b Wheatley	13
P. R. V. Ledden run out	5	c Keith b Wheatley	4
A. Buss c Gray b Cottam	5	c Gray b Wheatley	4
†T. Gunn run out	0	lbw b White	0
H. Newton not out	16	not out	0
L-b 5, n-b 4	9	B 4, n-b 2	6
1/22 2/44 3/65 4/83 5/91 6/96 7/109 8/120 9/120	153	1/12 2/12 3/15 4/40 5/70 6/91 7/95 8/95 9/95	99

Bowling: *First Innings*—Shackleton 29—10—45—2; White 20.4—2—68—4; Cottam 15—4—31—2. *Second Innings*—Shackleton 14—7—21—3; White 12—5—30—3; Cottam 10—4—16—0; Gray 2—0—11—0; Wheatley 6.5—2—15—4.

Hampshire

First Innings		Second Innings	
*R. E. Marshall b Newton	14	not out	92
B. L. Reed lbw b Buss	0	b Buss	7
H. Horton c Gunn b Buss	11	not out	21
J. R. Gray c Graves b Buss	21		
G. L. Keith c Oakman b Newton	5		
P. J. Sainsbury c Oakman b Newton	8		
†B. S. V. Timms c Oakman b Newton	7		
K. J. Wheatley c Griffith b Newton	33		
D. Shackleton not out	14		
D. W. White b Buss	4		
R. M. Cottam not out	4		
L-b 4, n-b 3	7	L-b 5	5
1/8 2/17 3/31 4/48 5/60 6/64 7/81 8/115 9/122 (9 wkts., 65 overs)	128	1/25 (1 wkt.)	125

Bowling: *First Innings*—Buss 32—5—63—4; Newton 32—11—54—5; Suttle 1—0—4—0. *Second Innings*—Buss 6—0—21—1; Newton 10—1—46—0; Suttle 8—2—35—0; Oakman 13—4—17—0; Pataudi 0.3—0—1—0.

Umpires: A. E. Alderman and W. E. Phillipson.

SUSSEX v. ESSEX

At Hove, July 2, 4. Essex won by ten wickets. The events of the fourth successive two-day finish at Hove promoted the Sussex committee to exonerate publicly the new groundsman, W. L. Creese. Presumably the dry spell had interfered with his efforts to improve a poor surface. Be that as it may, the pitch was all in favour of bowlers, and particularly those of seam. The bounce from it was most unrealiable. Bailey read the conditions right in asking Sussex to bat and Essex put them out for 86, Knight and Edmeades taking nine of the wickets. Then Bates did better than either with eight wickets for 51 runs, so surpassing his previous best, but even that could not alter the balance. Essex led by 67 and after their seam bowlers had done their work again, only 66 runs were needed. Victory came with about an hour of the second day to spare.

Sussex

K. G. Suttle c Taylor b Jorden	1	— c Fletcher b Knight	4
L. J. Lenham c Bailey b Knight	17	— c Taylor b Jorden	3
*Nawab of Pataudi c Hobbs b Edmeades	10	— c Taylor b Knight	5
M. G. Griffith lbw b Edmeades	16	— c Fletcher b Knight	19
P. J. Graves c Jorden b Knight	1	— c Fletcher b Edmeades	25
D. J. Foreman b Edmeades	3	— lbw b Edmeades	30
A. S. M. Oakman c Taylor b Knight	3	— not out	11
A. Buss b Knight	0	— c Fletcher b Jorden	17
†T. Gunn not out	17	— c Taylor b Edmeades	3
H. Newton c Fletcher b Edmeades	0	— lbw b Jorden	0
D. L. Bates c Taylor b Knight	18	— run out	10
		L-b 3, n-b 2	5
1/4 2/23 3/41 4/42 5/46 6/49 7/51 8/51 9/51	86	1/5 2/13 3/13 4/41 5/88 6/89 7/110 8/113 9/114	132

Bowling: *First Innings*—Knight 20.3—11—24—5; Jorden 8—0—18—1; Edmeades 13—0—44—4. *Second Innings*—Knight 14—4—27—3; Jorden 15—2—47—3; Bailey 9.1—1—24—0; Edmeades 15—3—29—3.

Essex

G. E. Barker b Bates	10	— not out	34
M. J. Bear c Pataudi b Bates	53		
†B. Taylor run out	2		
K. W. R. Fletcher c Pataudi b Bates	2		
B. R. Knight c Gunn b Newton	9		
*T. E. Bailey c Foreman b Bates	8		
G. R. Cass c Graves b Bates	24		
G. J. Saville c Griffith b Bates	18	— not out	27
B. Edmeades c Lenham b Bates	2		
R. N. S. Hobbs lbw b Bates	11		
A. M. Jorden not out	7		
B 4, l-b 1, n-b 2	7	B 4, n-b 1	5
1/37 2/55 3/58 4/73 5/77 6/111 7/116 8/118 9/138	153	(no wkt.)	66

Bowling: *First Innings*—Buss 24—6—52—0; Bates 29.3—10—51—8; Newton 20—8—28—1; Oakman 8—4—15—0. *Second Innings*—Buss 6—0—25—0; Bates 7—3—23—0; Newton 4—0—13—0; Oakman 2—2—0—0.

Umpires: A. E. Alderman and W. E. Phillipson.

SUSSEX v. CAMBRIDGE UNIVERSITY

At Hove, July 6, 7, 8. Sussex won by five wickets. Cambridge began their last match before Lord's by losing their opening pair to Ledden in his first over but they recovered well enough to take Sussex to within six minutes of the end before the county made the winning hit. Sussex led by 141 on the first innings, thanks largely to a maiden century by the twenty-two-year-old M. A. Buss, the younger of the two brothers. To this Murray, the Cambridge captain replied with his side's solitary three-figure innings of the summer, despite the fact that he was handicapped by a foot injury. Finally Sussex needed 133 in two hours fifty minutes and Greig, a young South African on debut, who took three wickets in one over in the Cambridge first innings, emphasised his usefulness with an enterprising knock.

Cambridge University

R. E. J. Chambers c Griffith b Ledden	0	— b Buss	30
A. V. E. Gould c Foreman b Ledden	1	— b Cooper	18
D. L. Hays run out	47	— b Buss	6
*†D. L. Murray c Gunn b Ledden	0	— c Buss b Bates	133
N. J. Cosh c Suttle b Cooper	54	— b Bates	90
V. P. Malalasekera b Greig	6	— lbw b Buss	14
G. A. Cottrell c Foreman b Greig	2	— b Buss	26
A. B. Palfreman c Buss b Greig	0	— c Gunn b Buss	17
N. Sinker c Gunn b Ledden	9	— not out	19
D. C. Acfield not out	3	— lbw b Bates	9
S. G. Russell c Gunn b Ledden	1	— b Foreman	0
B 6, w 1, n-b 1	8	B 11	11
1/2 2/5 3/17 4/75 5/85 6/87 7/87 8/123 9/127	131	1/45 2/59 3/61 4/277 5/302 6/304 7/336 8/349 9/372	373

Bowling: *First Innings*—Bates 16—6—43—0; Ledden 14.2—3—43—5; Greig 11—3—27—3; Cooper 9—6—9—1; Suttle 1—0—1—0. *Second Innings*—Bates 24—2—79—3; Ledden 20—3—72—0; Greig 19—6—67—0; Cooper 31—12—55—1; Suttle 3—0—10—0; Buss 29—13—63—5; Graves 6—3—14—0; Langridge 1—1—0—0; Foreman 4.3—3—2—1.

Sussex

D. J. Foreman c Palfreman b Russell	27	— lbw b Palfreman	19
M. A. Buss st Murray b Sinker	136		
R. J. Langridge b Palfreman	13	— c Cosh b Russell	34
*K. G. Suttle c Murray b Palfreman	61		
M. G. Griffith b Sinker	67	— c Hays b Russell	2
P. J. Graves c Murray b Palfreman	0	— c Hays b Palfreman	3
G. C. Cooper c Malalasekera b Acfield	10	— c Hays b Acfield	33
A. Greig c Murray b Russell	26	— not out	25
P. R. V. Ledden c Russell b Acfield	23	— not out	18
†T. Gunn not out	0		
B 1, l-b 4, w 1, n-b 3	9	L-b 1	1
1/40 2/105 3/240 4/242 5/244 6/260 7/293 8/372 9/372 (9 wkts., dec.)	372	1/43 2/47 3/86 4/90 5/98 (5 wkts.)	135

D. L. Bates did not bat.

Bowling: *First Innings*—Russell 32—8—87—2; Palfreman 33—6—111—3; Cottrell 12—3—53—0; Sinker 22—3—80—2; Acfield 23.2—10—32—2. *Second Innings*—Russell 15—3—36—2; Palfreman 11—2—33—2; Cottrell 10—3—17—0; Acfield 15—5—37—1.

Umpires: R. S. Lay and J. F. Crapp.

SUSSEX v. YORKSHIRE

At Hove, July 9, 11, 12. Drawn. The bat mastered the ball for a change on the Hove square where four of the previous five matches had ended in two days. So Yorkshire, already 40 points clear at the top of the table at the halfway mark, were pegged back to two points. They gained these comfortably enough, with Boycott and Taylor replying to the Sussex total of 276 for nine with an opening stand of 135 in the first two and a half hours of the second day. Boycott went on to complete his century and then added another 64 with enterprise, his complete innings occupying five and a half hours. During the afternoon of the second day the Sussex bowlers employed negative tactics to stem the flow of runs, so the chances of a definite result quickly receded.

Sussex

First Innings		Second Innings	
L. J. Lenham b Trueman	49	c Wilson b Balderstone	40
M. A. Buss c Boycott b Wilson	65	run out	28
K. G. Suttle b Wilson	6	lbw b Wilson	52
*†J. M. Parks c Sharpe b Wilson	25	c Binks b Wilson	53
M. G. Griffith b Trueman	0	not out	28
P. J. Graves b Wilson	42	not out	0
D. J. Foreman c Hampshire b Close	23		
A. S. M. Oakman b Close	34		
A. Buss not out	7		
J. A. Snow b Close	0		
D. L. Bates not out	12		
L-b 8, n-b 5	13	B 15, l-b 5, n-b 2	22
1/115 2/121 3/126 4/127 5/187 6/194 7/240 8/261 9/261 (9 wkts., dec.)	276	1/61 2/113 3/145 4/223 (4 wkts.)	223

Bowling: *First Innings*—Trueman 19—5—46—2; Nicholson 28—7—60—0; Close 35—9—99—3; Wilson 28—10—49—4; Balderstone 3—1—9—0. *Second Innings*—Trueman 9.1—3—10—0; Nicholson 4—2—7—0; Wilson 34—15—53—2; Close 18—8—37—0; Balderstone 13—2—39—1; Hampshire 16—2—55—0.

Yorkshire

G. Boycott c Parks b A. Buss	164
K. Taylor c Parks b Bates	60
D. E. V. Padgett c Suttle b M. A. Buss	20
J. H. Hampshire lbw b Snow	19
*D. B. Close c Parks b A. Buss	36
P. J. Sharpe c A. Buss b Bates	1
J. C. Balderstone c Parks b Snow	17
†J. G. Binks c and b A. Buss	19
F. S. Trueman not out	18
D. Wilson not out	12
B 4, l-b 12, n-b 1	17
1/135 2/179 3/256 4/283 5/284 6/323 7/353 8/353 (8 wkts., dec.)	383

A. G. Nicholson did not bat.

Bowling: Snow 31—6—93—2; A. Buss 30—5—95—3; Bates 33—6—77—2; Oakman 17—3—48—0; Suttle 8—2—20—0; M. A. Buss 8—3—33—1.

Umpires: R. S. Lay and J. F. Crapp.

At Swansea, July 13, 14, 15. SUSSEX drew with GLAMORGAN.

At Bournemouth, July 16, 18, 19. SUSSEX drew with HAMPSHIRE.

At Nottingham, July 20, 21, 22. SUSSEX drew with NOTTINGHAMSHIRE.

SUSSEX v. KENT

At Hastings, July 23, 25. Kent won by four wickets. Sussex, having been involved in four two-day finishes at Hove in the previous six weeks, got the worst of another two-day match, this time at Hastings. On a drying pitch 24 wickets fell on the first day for 198 runs, Kent gaining a first-innings lead of 15. Graves and A. Buss hit back with a lively stand of 45, the highest of the match, but even so Kent always seemed to have the game in hand. Under the difficult conditions, Cowdrey showed his class, playing some handsome strokes as he steered his side towards the required 109. The combined efforts of Dixon, eleven for 77 in the match, and Underwood, eight for 63, saw Kent to their win, though the best figures for an innings went to Oakman of Sussex whose off-spin earned him six for 16.

Sussex

L. J. Lenham c Ealham b Underwood	19	— c Leary b Dixon	9
M. A. Buss c Cowdrey b Dixon	21	— b Dye	3
K. G. Suttle c Knott b Dixon	8	— lbw b Dixon	6
A. S. M. Oakman c Cowdrey b Dixon	0	— c Knott b Dixon	1
*†J. M. Parks c and b Underwood	1	— lbw b Dixon	6
M. G. Griffith c Leary b Underwood	0	— c Cowdrey b Underwood	2
P. J. Graves lbw b Dixon	0	— b Dixon	22
D. J. Foreman st Knott b Underwood	18	— c Knott b Underwood	1
A. Buss c Sayer b Dixon	1	— c Luckhurst b Underwood	23
D. L. Bates c Leary b Dixon	2	— c Denness b Underwood	10
J. A. Snow not out	3	— not out	14
L-b 1, n-b 1	2	B 10, l-b 14, n-b 2	26
1/35 2/47 3/47 4/48 5/48 6/49 7/51 8/57 9/70	75	1/6 2/17 3/25 4/33 5/36 6/36 7/44 8/89 9/89	123

Bowling: *First Innings*—Sayer 4—0—5—0; Dye 5—2—5—0; Underwood 15—7—26—4; Dixon 14—4—37—6. *Second Innings*—Sayer 3—1—3—0; Dye 8—2—17—1; Underwood 29.2—15—37—4; Dixon 27—14—40—5.

Kent

M. H. Denness b A. Buss	7	— lbw b Suttle	10
B. W. Luckhurst c Graves b A. Buss	8	— c sub b Snow	44
S. E. Leary c Graves b Oakman	9	— c and b Oakman	2
*M. C. Cowdrey c Snow b A. Buss	18	— c Foreman b Oakman	26
R. C. Wilson st Parks b Oakman	15	— c Griffith b Oakman	16
A. Ealham c Snow b Oakman	0	— not out	8
†A. Knott c Graves b Oakman	9	— b Snow	0
A. L. Dixon b Snow	14	— not out	5
D. L. Underwood c Foreman b Oakman	0		
D. M. Sayer b Oakman	4		
J. C. Dye not out	1		
B 2, l-b 3	5		
1/8 2/22 3/42 4/47 5/52 6/65 7/72 8/72 9/86	90	1/22 2/27 3/70 4/96 5/101 6/103 (6 wkts.)	111

Bowling: *First Innings*—Snow 9—4—24—1; A. Buss 13—2—45—3; Oakman 15.1—5—16—6. *Second Innings*—Snow 8—2—25—2; A. Buss 6—1—14—0; Oakman 27—9—42—3; Suttle 21—9—30—1.

Umpires: R. Aspinall and W. F. Simpson.

SUSSEX v. WARWICKSHIRE

At Hastings, July 27, 28, 29. Drawn. Parks conceded first innings to Warwickshire, no doubt mindful of the two-day defeat on the same square in the previous match. With the score 123 for nine, at which point A. Buss had taken seven for 47, he looked to have made the right decision, but there was a remarkable last-wicket stand of 79 between Edmonds, who surpassed his previous best, and Allan. Webster consolidated the position for Warwickshire by taking five for 19 before the end of the first day and subsequently M. J. K. Smith hit his second hundred in successive matches. It included fourteen 4's. So Sussex, after making such a good start, were asked to score 265 to win and in the end were thankful for the rain which washed out the last two hours. At 147 for seven they seemed to be facing defeat.

Warwickshire

First Innings		Second Innings	
K. Ibadulla c Suttle b A. Buss	16	c Griffith b Bates	30
A. Gordon b A. Buss	14	c Parks b M. A. Buss	22
*M. J. K. Smith run out	24	not out	103
G. S. Warner c and b A. Buss	2	c Langridge b M. A. Buss	47
J. A. Jameson c Parks b A. Buss	29	not out	20
B. A. Richardson b Oakman	1		
T. W. Cartwright c Oakman b A. Buss	19		
†A. C. Smith c Foreman b A. Buss	4		
R. V. Webster lbw b A. Buss	0		
R. B. Edmonds not out	61		
J. M. Allan b Oakman	25		
L-b 7	7	B 2, l-b 2, n-b 1	5
1/17 2/32 3/34 4/85 5/87 6/95 7/100 8/100 9/123	202	1/42 2/65 3/180 (3 wkts., dec.)	227

Bowling: *First Innings*—A. Buss 21—9—67—7; Bates 8—3—16—0; Oakman 28.1—8—71—2; Suttle 7—1—22—0; M. A. Buss 7—0—19—0. *Second Innings*—A. Buss 19—2—56—0; Bates 23—6—59—1; Oakman 19—6—46—0; M. A. Buss 25—9—61—2.

Sussex

First Innings		Second Innings	
R. J. Langridge c A. C. Smith b Webster	10	c Warner b Webster	9
M. A. Buss c Allan b Webster	16	c Jameson b Cartwright	6
K. G. Suttle c M. J. K. Smith b Webster	3	c A. C. Smith b Edmonds	24
A. S. M. Oakman c A. C. Smith b Cartwright	69	c and b Allan	44
*†J. M. Parks c Edmonds b Webster	0	b Edmonds	2
A. Buss c Richardson b Webster	0		
M. G. Griffith c Gordon b Ibadulla	23	c M. J. K. Smith b Allan	14
P. J. Graves c M. J. K. Smith b Cartwright	5	c M. J. K. Smith b Allan	15
D. J. Foreman c Jameson b Cartwright	23	not out	29
P. R. V. Ledden c and b Cartwright	5	not out	0
D. L. Bates not out	0		
B 4, l-b 2, n-b 5	11	B 4	4
1/15 2/29 3/32 4/34 5/34 6/92 7/103 8/156 9/164	165	1/9 2/23 3/57 4/59 5/97 6/106 7/147 (7 wkts.)	147

Bowling: *First Innings*—Webster 28—11—57—5; Cartwright 33.2—17—46—4; Edmonds 8—3—18—0; Ibadulla 16—5—27—1; Allan 11—8—6—0. *Second Innings*—Webster 11—1—38—1; Cartwright 24—6—60—1; Edmonds 8—2—18—2; Allan 13—7—27—3.

Umpires: R. Aspinall and W. F. Simpson.

SUSSEX v. GLOUCESTERSHIRE

At Hove, July 30, August 1, 2. *65 overs.* Drawn. After an opening day on which the cricket failed to match the weather, Sussex won an interesting struggle for first-innings lead. M. A. Buss, who took four catches at slip in Gloucestershire's first innings, led the reply with a sound if unspectacular 53. Rain reduced the second day to three-quarters of an hour, so to get the lead Sussex needed 21 runs off four overs when the last day began. This they did with the help of some hard hitting by Parks. Bissex and D. Brown emulated him in a bid to keep the game alive but on the declaration, which left Sussex to score 194 in two hours, the rain returned. On the last day, Snow became the second bowler to take his 100th wicket during the summer.

Gloucestershire

C. A. Milton b Bates	20	— c Graves b Bates	19
M. Bissex c Graves b A. Buss	11	— c M. A. Buss b Snow	80
D. Brown c M. A. Buss b A. Buss	10	— not out	74
D. Shepherd lbw b A. Buss	21	— not out	8
R. B. Nicholls c M. A. Buss b A. Buss	0		
M. D. Mence c Griffith b Bates	44		
A. S. Brown c Graves b A. Buss	9		
*J. B. Mortimore c Griffith b Snow	3		
A. R. Windows c M. A. Buss b Snow	11		
D. A. Allen c M. A. Buss b Snow	14		
†B. J. Meyer not out	4		
B 5, l-b 9, n-b 1	15	B 2, l-b 6, n-b 5	13
1/13 2/33 3/61 4/63 5/67 6/85 7/88 8/124 9/156	162	1/51 2/179 (2 wkts., dec.)	194

Bowling: *First Innings*—Snow 24—6—63—3; A. Buss 24—8—51—5; Bates 11—1—33—2. *Second Innings*—Snow 17—2—49—1; A. Buss 13—1—50—0; Bates 10—1—34—1; Oakman 10—0—33—0; M. A. Buss 5—1—15—0.

Sussex

L. J. Lenham c Meyer b Mence	27
M. A. Buss c Bissex b A. S. Brown	53
K. G. Suttle b A. S. Brown	19
A. S. M. Oakman run out	28
*†J. M. Parks not out	28
P. J. Graves not out	0
L-b 8	8
1/79 2/89 3/115 4/155 (4 wkts., 65 overs)	163

M. G. Griffith, D. J. Foreman, A. Buss, J. A. Snow and D. L. Bates did not bat.

Bowling: A. S. Brown 28—7—61—2; Windows 15—6—32—0; Mence 22—5—62—1.

Umpires: F. Jakeman and H. Yarnold.

At Weston-super-Mare, August 3, 4, 5. SUSSEX lost to SOMERSET by ten wickets.

At Cheltenham, August 13, 15. SUSSEX beat GLOUCESTERSHIRE by ten wickets.

SUSSEX v. SURREY

At Eastbourne, August 20, 22, 23. Drawn. At the end of an interesting game, Surrey stood 13 runs short of a target of 234 with two wickets left. So honours were even. Spectators wondered whether this would have been so had Stewart, who hit a sound century (one 6, eleven 4's), tried to build up a big first-innings lead instead of declaring 42 ahead with six wickets in hand. Once back in the game, Sussex made the most of things, with Suttle and Foreman, by adding 114 runs in an hour and three-quarters, enabling their captain to make a timely declaration. Suttle hit fifteen 4's in scoring 102 in three and a half hours on the eve of his 350th consecutive county match. Surrey's bid to get the 234 wanted stuttered with the loss of Smith for nought but Barrington and Storey restored the balance with a stand of 66 in forty minutes, Storey striking three 6's and eight 4's.

Sussex

M. A. Buss b Harman	45	— c Stewart b Arnold	26
L. J. Lenham b Arnold	53	— c and b Pocock	24
K. G. Suttle c Long b Barrington	30	— lbw b Pocock	102
†J. M. Parks b Barrington	5	— not out	28
*Nawab of Pataudi c Smith b Harman	26	— b Arnold	0
A. S. M. Oakman c Pocock b Harman	20	— c Edwards b Arnold	0
P. J. Graves not out	34	— lbw b Arnold	1
D. J. Foreman c Long b Jefferson	8	— c Barrington b Pocock	68
P. R. V. Ledden c Edwards b Arnold	1	— not out	1
A. Buss c Stewart b Jefferson	3		
D. L. Bates b Arnold	5		
B 1, l-b 6	7	B 8, l-b 10, n-b 7	25
1/71 2/117 3/133 4/143 5/179 6/202 7/224 8/225 9/228	237	1/58 2/88 3/90 (7 wkts., dec.) 4/99 5/101 6/215 7/256	275

Bowling: *First Innings*—Arnold 16.2—1—48—3; Jefferson 16—3—38—2; Storey 9—2—27—0; Harman 21—5—47—3; Pocock 15—6—36—0; Barrington 15—4—34—2. *Second Innings*—Arnold 16—2—50—4; Jefferson 9—1—28—0; Pocock 24—7—68—3; Harman 13—3—41—0; Storey 14—6—24—0; Barrington 10—0—39—0.

Surrey

M. J. Edwards c M. A. Buss b Oakman	58	— c sub b Ledden	32
W. A. Smith lbw b A. Buss	43	— c Graves b Bates	0
*M. J. Stewart c Suttle b Oakman	102	— c Ledden b A. Buss	7
K. F. Barrington c Suttle b Bates	27	— b A. Buss	50
M. D. Willett not out	31	— b Bates	2
S. J. Storey (did not bat)		— c sub b Bates	64
R. I. Jefferson (did not bat)		— c and b Oakman	10
P. I. Pocock (did not bat)		— c Pataudi b A. Buss	0
†A. Long (did not bat)		— not out	27
G. Arnold (did not bat)		— not out	15
B 6, l-b 5, n-b 7	18	B 3, l-b 6, w 4, n-b 1	14
1/78 2/130 3/201 4/279 (4 wkts., dec.)	279	1/0 2/22 3/78 4/144 (8 wkts.) 5/160 6/162 7/163 8/172	221

R. Harman did not bat.

Bowling: *First Innings*—A. Buss 21—5—66—1; Bates 27—8—80—1; Oakman 28.2—8—47—2; Suttle 3—1—5—0; M. A. Buss 13—4—30—0; Ledden 11—2—33—0. *Second Innings*—A. Buss 15—2—39—3; Bates 15—4—52—3; Oakman 16—5—48—1; M. A. Buss 5—0—34—0; Ledden 4—1—20—1; Graves 1—0—14—0.

Umpires: W. F. Simpson and F. Jakeman.

SUSSEX v. SOMERSET

At Eastbourne, August 24, 25, 26. Somerset won by six wickets. The match sprung to life on the second day following some dismal batting. Graham Atkinson and Kitchen caused the transformation while 193 runs were hit in the afternoon session of two hours, twenty minutes, both recording centuries. Atkinson hit nineteen 4's, one more than Kitchen. So Somerset led by 56 runs with only two wickets down on the declaration, and their position quickly improved further when Rumsey with some fine fast bowling took three wickets for 16 runs in 29 balls. Sussex began the last day 96 for five, only 40 on and seemingly in a hopeless position. That Somerset finally had to get 185 to win in under two hours was a tribute to the subsequent efforts of Snow, who followed his fine Test batting at The Oval a week earlier by scoring 71 in one hour, twenty minutes. He contributed 53 of a last-wicket stand of 55 with Bates, who hit a single. The other run was an extra.

Sussex

M. A. Buss b Palmer	22	— b Rumsey	10
L. J. Lenham b Palmer	16	— c Robinson b Rumsey	10
K. G. Suttle c Clayton b Palmer	15	— b Rumsey	4
†J. M. Parks c Robinson b Langford	46	— c Virgin b Robinson	14
*Nawab of Pataudi b Langford	51	— c and b Robinson	41
D. J. Foreman b Robinson	0	— c Langford b Robinson	18
A. S. M. Oakman c Burgess b Rumsey	32	— run out	33
P. J. Graves b Langford	14	— c Clayton b Palmer	16
A. Buss run out	0	— c Virgin b Robinson	12
J. A. Snow b Palmer	21	— c Rumsey b Robinson	71
D. L. Bates not out	0	— not out	1
B 4, l-b 9, n-b 1	14	L-b 8	8
1/33 2/48 3/87 4/141 5/146 6/156 7/192 8/192 9/217	231	1/19 2/24 3/25 4/69 5/90 6/111 7/145 8/155 9/183	238

Bowling: *First Innings*—Rumsey 15—2—58—1; Palmer 28.4—11—65—4; Alley 10—5—8—0; Langford 24—9—40—3; Robinson 20—7—46—1. *Second Innings*—Rumsey 23—5—56—3; Palmer 21—3—51—1; Alley 4—1—8—0; Robinson 33.2—15—67—5; Langford 18—5—48—0.

Somerset

G. Atkinson c Parks b Bates	127	— c Snow b Bates	30
R. Virgin c Oakman b Bates	31	— lbw b A. Buss	19
M. Kitchen not out	111	— run out	59
G. Burgess not out	6	— b A. Buss	9
W. E. Alley (did not bat)		— not out	30
*C. R. M. Atkinson (did not bat)		— not out	30
B 1, l-b 6, w 4, n-b 1	12	B 4, l-b 4	8
1/79 2/259 (2 wkts., dec.)	287	1/30 2/90 3/99 4/123 (4 wkts.)	185

K. E. Palmer, †G. Clayton, P. J. Robinson, B. A. Langford and F. E. Rumsey did not bat.

Bowling: *First Innings*—Snow 14—5—30—0; A. Buss 20—4—65—0; Bates 21—5—68—2; Oakman 22—4—58—0; M. A. Buss 5—1—30—0; Suttle 3—0—24—0. *Second Innings*—Snow 12—2—41—0; A. Buss 12—0—85—2; Bates 8—0—51—1; Foreman 0.1—0—0—0.

Umpires: W. F. Price and C. S. Elliott.

SUSSEX v. MIDDLESEX

At Hove, August 27, 29, 30. Drawn. Middlesex seemed to have established a considerable advantage through a third-wicket stand of 185 in two hours, forty minutes between Murray and Parfitt. Both batsmen reached centuries, with Murray, having batted so well in the Test, looking the more certain of his strokeplay. He hit eighteen 4's. The wicket of Michael Buss before the end of the first day followed by that of Lenham at 16 advanced the position of Middlesex even further, but at that point Suttle went to the wicket and changed the situation. Though receiving several painful blows, this aggressive little batsman playing in his 351st consecutive county game was still there five hours later when Sussex declared one run ahead. His 172 not out included one 6 and seventeen 4's. Thereafter Middlesex struggled and Sussex also failed to rise to the occasion when left to score 163 in five minutes under two hours.

Middlesex

First Innings		Second Innings	
W. E. Russell c and b Bates	16	c Foreman b Oakman	10
M. J. Harris c M. A. Buss b Snow	37	c Suttle b Oakman	24
P. H. Parfitt c A. Buss b Oakman	107	c Graves b Bates	43
†J. T. Murray c Foreman b M. A. Buss	114	c Graves b Bates	2
*F. J. Titmus not out	27	c Parks b Bates	7
D. Bennett not out	1	c Pataudi b Bates	14
M. Manasseh (did not bat)		c Parks b Bates	19
D. A. Bick (did not bat)		c Snow b Oakman	32
J. S. E. Price (did not bat)		c A. Buss b Oakman	4
R. S. Herman (did not bat)		not out	0
B 1, l-b 5	6	B 3, l-b 5	8
1/43 2/59 3/244 4/303 (4 wkts., dec.)	308	1/17 2/58 3/73 4/91 5/101 6/151 7/154 8/159 9/163 (9 wkts., dec.)	163

R. W. Stewart did not bat.

Bowling: *First Innings*—Snow 19—4—46—1; A. Buss 20—4—52—0; Suttle 1—0—5—0; Bates 23—5—66—1; Oakman 25—4—77—1; M. A. Buss 13—0—56—1. *Second Innings*—Snow 12—4—25—0; A. Buss 8—1—21—0; Oakman 30.1—9—78—4; Bates 19—11—31—5.

Sussex

First Innings		Second Innings	
L. J. Lenham c Murray b Stewart	6	c Parfitt b Price	0
M. A. Buss c Parfitt b Herman	2	c Price b Manasseh	11
A. Buss c Herman b Titmus	24		
K. G. Suttle not out	172	c Murray b Herman	8
†J. M. Parks c Price b Titmus	30	c Price b Stewart	55
*Nawab of Pataudi c Murray b Price	2	not out	16
D. J. Foreman b Manasseh	58	not out	25
A. S. M. Oakman b Manasseh	2		
P. J. Graves c sub b Herman	9		
J. A. Snow not out	0		
L-b 3, n-b 1	4	B 2	2
1/3 2/16 3/58 4/100 5/131 6/255 7/261 8/284 (8 wkts., dec.)	309	1/0 2/11 3/68 4/80 (4 wkts.)	117

D. L. Bates did not bat.

Bowling: *First Innings*—Price 27.2—2—94—1; Herman 18—2—45—2; Stewart 26—4—77—1; Titmus 14—3—41—2; Bick 10—0—37—0; Manasseh 3—0—11—2. *Second Innings*—Price 5—3—5—1; Herman 3—0—18—1; Bick 7—2—24—0; Stewart 10—3—55—1; Manasseh 5—2—13—1.

Umpires: C. S. Elliott and A. E. Fagg.

At Worcester, August 31, September 1, 2. SUSSEX beat WORCESTERSHIRE by 31 runs.

WARWICKSHIRE

President—Lieut.-Gen. Sir Oliver Leese, Bart.

Secretary—L. T. Deakins, County Ground, Birmingham 5

Captain—M. J. K. Smith

R. N. Abberley

County Badge

D. J. Brown

If to say that Warwickshire had a worthy season smacks of damning with faint praise, it is perhaps still a valid judgment. Winning three out of their four last matches and landing the Gillette Cup was some compensation for their supporters who had hoped for better things, especially as they had begun by winning four of their first seven matches, the first, moreover, being abandoned without a ball being bowled. It is no simple matter to decide what happened to them in the interval between these two successful phases. Certainly they had their share of interference by the weather when matters looked bright for them, and they suffered the rubs of the green in other ways not unknown to cricketers everywhere.

One factor militating against them was that Barber's presence in the side was only occasional. This is not to say that they always did well when he was playing, but, welcome as his batting was, his absence could not but have an unsettling effect on the side. Warwickshire, and the public, would have liked Barber all the time.

As a generalisation, failure to bowl a side out after declaring in a strong position, was a reason for the mid-season slump. The defeat at Westcliff was a notable example. Slow pitches handicapped Brown, while Webster, who has now left the county for New Zealand, did not have one of his better seasons and was absent several times through injury. The bulk of the work fell on Cartwright, but frequently the pitches did not suit his medium-paced bowling. He finished with a great burst, however, and was rewarded by his 100th wicket in the last match, in which he took thirteen. The side was again lamentably short of spin, J. M. Allan (specially registered) not being able to repair the deficiency. The other left-arm slow bowler, Miller, had an indifferent season, and, after being more out of the side than in it, resigned before it was completed.

The batting, though uneven, provided a better account, and the prospects, here, looked promising. Abberley, an opener who looks more mature than one would expect after only one full season, and Amiss, who played in the final Test against the West Indies, are two of the younger school for whom the future holds great possibilities. Jameson was one of the scores of batsmen throughout the country who suffered from the 65-over rule, either not getting in at all or doing so at a time when the pressure to score provided no opportunity to settle down.

M. J. K. Smith's own performances were uneven. He showed himself still capable of turning a situation but not with the devastating effect of former years. Enterprising moves in captaincy were too often negatived by failure of either the batting or the bowling to substantiate them.

EDGBASTON (BIRMINGHAM) CRICKET GROUND

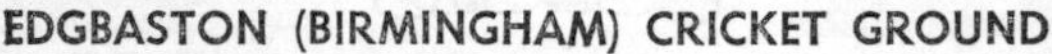

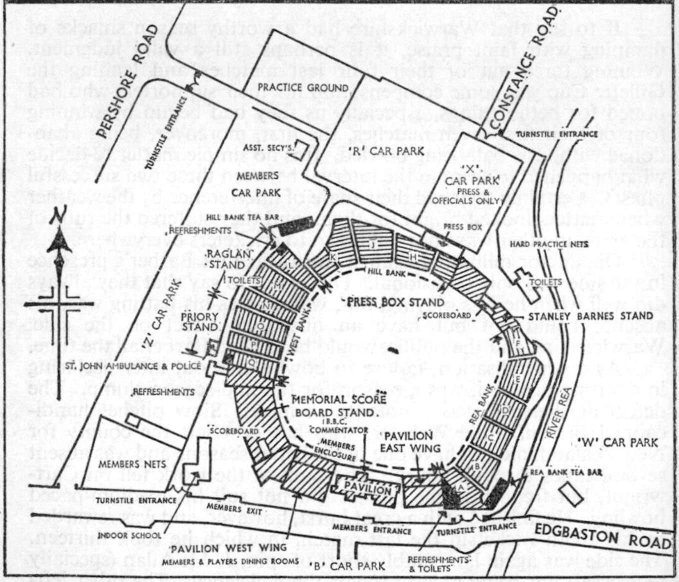

WARWICKSHIRE RESULTS

All First-Class Matches—Played 32, *Won* 9, *Lost* 9, *Drawn* 14
County Championship Matches—Played 28, *Won* 8, *Lost* 8, *Drawn* 10, *No Decision* 2

COUNTY CHAMPIONSHIP AVERAGES

BATTING

	Birthplace	Mtchs.	Inns.	Not Outs	Runs	100's	Highest Inns.	Aver.
M. J. K. Smith.	*Leicester*	25	44	8	1607	3	117	44.63
J. A. Jameson..	*Bombay*	27	46	10	1183	1	118*	32.86
W. J. Stewart...	*Carmarthen-shire*	6	10	2	259	0	64*	32.37
D. L. Amiss....	*Birmingham*	24	44	3	1258	0	97	30.68
R. W. Barber...	*Manchester*	10	19	0	553	0	84	29.10
R. M. Abberley	*Birmingham*	25	46	5	1110	1	117*	27.07
K. Ibadulla....	*Pakistan*	23	39	4	883	0	62	25.22
A. C. Smith....	*Birmingham*	27	36	7	557	0	85	19.20
T. W. Cartwright	*Coventry*	24	33	7	470	0	65*	18.07
R. B. Edmonds.	*Birmingham*	15	14	2	190	0	61*	15.83
J. M. Allan....	*Leeds*	19	19	8	148	0	25	13.45
D. J. Brown....	*Walsall*	22	19	8	148	0	34	13.45
A. Gordon.....	*Coventry*	3	5	0	55	0	22	11.00
R. V. Webster..	*Barbados*	18	22	2	215	0	47	10.75
B. A. Richardson	*Kenilworth*	4	7	1	62	0	17	10.33
R. Miller......	*Co. Durham*	9	9	1	63	0	17	7.87
J. D. Bannister.	*Wolverhampton*	15	15	9	21	0	4*	3.50

Also batted: G. S. Warner (*Darlaston*), 2 and 47.

* *Signifies not out.*

BOWLING

	Overs	Maidens	Runs	Wickets	Average
T. W. Cartwright........	812.5	296	1697	100	16.97
J. D. Bannister..........	363.5	109	802	42	19.09
R. V. Webster...........	439.4	93	1167	57	20.47
D. J. Brown.............	590.2	123	1572	71	22.14
J. M. Allan..............	280.4	82	782	31	25.22
R. Miller................	206.3	52	647	25	25.88
R. B. Edmonds..........	299	98	669	25	26.76
R. W. Barber...........	131.2	28	367	11	33.36
K. Ibadulla.............	200.4	45	596	14	42.57

Also bowled: D. L. Amiss 7—2—22—0; J. A. Jameson 17—3—60—1; B. A. Richardson 12—1—32—1; A. C. Smith 3.3—0—9—0; M. J. K. Smith 1—1—7—0.

WARWICKSHIRE v. MIDDLESEX

At Birmingham, May 4, 5, 6. *65 overs.* Abandoned. Warwickshire won the toss and elected to bat, but the game was given up without a ball having been bowled.

Warwickshire

K. Ibadulla, R. N. Abberley, D. L. Amiss, *M. J. K. Smith, J. A. Jameson, T. W. Cartwright, †A. C. Smith, J. M. Allan, R. Miller, J. D. Bannister, D. J. Brown.

Middlesex

W. E. Russell, M. J. Smith, P. H. Parfitt, E. A. Clark, †J. T. Murray, *F. J. Titmus, D. Bennett, R. W. Hooker, D. A. Bick, M. J. Harris, R. S. Herman.

Umpires: W. E. Phillipson and P. B. Wight.

WARWICKSHIRE v. LEICESTERSHIRE

At Nuneaton, May 7, 9, 10. *65 overs.* Warwickshire won by 39 runs. A blank second day had the effect of dividing the match into two Gillette-style games, and Warwickshire won both. M. J. K. Smith scored 67 in a little more than an hour and Abberley 56 towards their first-innings total of 212, and despite an innings of 75 by Inman, Leicestershire could manage no more than 177. On the last day they were bowled out by the two left-arm spinners, Allan and Miller, who took four wickets apiece. Inman was again Leicestershire's mainstay, being last man out with 40. With an hour left and needing 90 runs with six wickets standing, they were not unfavourably placed, but apart from Lock, Inman could find no support.

Warwickshire

K. Ibadulla c Spencer b Lock	24	— c Tolchard b Marner	14
R. N. Abberley b Cotton	56	— c and b Birkenshaw	26
D. L. Amiss lbw b Spencer	0	— b Spencer	79
*M. J. K. Smith c Birkenshaw b Marner	67	— c Tolchard b Lock	15
J. A. Jameson not out	36	— c Constant b Spencer	15
T. W. Cartwright not out	23		
†A. C. Smith (did not bat)		— not out	4
L-b 6	6	L-b 2	2
1/42 2/52 3/149 4/152 (4 wkts., 65 overs)	212	1/27 2/56 3/119 4/142 5/155 (5 wkts., dec.)	155

J. M. Allan, R. Miller, J. D. Bannister and D. J. Brown did not bat.

Bowling: *First Innings*—Spencer 16—6—31—1; Cotton 18—1—54—1; Lock 18—7—65—1; Marner 13—1—56—1. *Second Innings*—Cotton 5—1—16—0; Spencer 11.4—2—34—2; Marner 8—1—25—1; Birkenshaw 10—1—45—1; Lock 8—0—33—1.

Leicestershire

M. R. Hallam b Brown	9	— c Jameson b Bannister	19
B. J. Booth c Cartwright b Miller	26	— c Bannister b Allan	29
M. E. Norman c Miller b Allan	16	— lbw b Brown	0
C. C. Inman c Abberley b Bannister	75	— c Abberley b Allan	40
P. Marner c A. C. Smith b Brown	6	— c and b Miller	24
J. Birkenshaw c Ibadulla b Allan	3	— c Bannister b Allan	7
D. Constant c A. C. Smith b Brown	8	— c and b Miller	4
†R. W. Tolchard b Brown	7	— b Miller	0
*G. A. R. Lock not out	25	— b Allan	18
C. T. Spencer not out	2	— b Miller	7
J. Cotton (did not bat)		— not out	0
		B 1, l-b 2	3
1/14 2/45 3/61 4/78 5/91 6/143 6/143 8/170 (8 wkts., 65 overs)	177	1/27 2/28 3/68 4/94 5/115 6/124 7/145 8/149 9/149	151

Bowling: *First Innings*—Brown 20—3—49—4; Bannister 19—6—64—1; Cartwright 3—1—8—0; Allan 17—8—37—2; Miller 6—1—19—1. *Second Innings* Brown 5—0—13—1; Bannister 4—1—16—1; Miller 11—0—69—4; Allan 8.4—0—50—4.

Umpires: J. S. Buller and P. B. Wight.

WARWICKSHIRE v. ESSEX

At Birmingham, May 11, 12, 13. *65 overs.* Warwickshire won by 24 runs. There was no play until after tea on the second day because of rain, and M. J. K. Smith declared Warwickshire's innings closed at 92 for one off 18 overs. Essex then batted until five minutes from the close at 95 for two off 28 overs. A maiden century by the young Warwickshire opener, Abberley, paved the way for another declaration by Smith at 217 for 2, which left Essex requiring 215 in ten minutes under three hours. They approached their task enthusiastically but with consequent losses to Miller and Allan who took three wickets each. A century by Bear kept them within range. With three wickets left and 30 needed in fifteen minutes, they were nearer success than failure, but Allan was recalled and removed Saville, Warwickshire's last serious obstacle.

Warwickshire

K. Ibadulla c Jorden b Knight	5	— c Jorden b Knight	18
R. N. Abberley not out	31	— not out	117
D. L. Amiss not out	51	— c Fletcher b Hobbs	30
*M. J. K. Smith (did not bat)		— not out	43
L-b 5	5	B 4, l-b 3, w 2	9
1/8 (1 wkt., dec.)	92	1/48 2/133 (2 wkts., dec.)	217

J. A. Jameson, †A. C. Smith, J. M. Allan, R. Miller, R. V. Webster, J. D. Bannister and D. J. Brown did not bat.

Bowling: *First Innings*—Knight 8—0—45—1; Jorden 5—0—14—0; Bailey 4—0—19—0; East 1—0—9—0. *Second Innings*—Knight 20—5—43—1; Jorden 12—1—47—0; East 9—1—37—0; Hobbs 16—1—81—1.

Essex

G. E. Barker not out	45	— c. A. C. Smith b Brown	0
M. J. Bear c Jameson b Miller	21	— lbw b Brown	105
†B. Taylor c Allan b Miller	22	— c Bannister b Webster	30
K. W. R. Fletcher not out	2	— lbw b Allan	0
*T. E. Bailey (did not bat)		— c and b Miller	14
B. R. Knight (did not bat)		— b Miller	7
R. N. S. Hobbs (did not bat)		— b Allan	2
G. R. Cass (did not bat)		— c Jameson b Miller	2
G. J. Saville (did not bat)		— b Allan	25
A. M. Jorden (did not bat)		— not out	0
R. East (did not bat)		— b Brown	0
B 4, l-b 1	5	L-b 5	5
1/42 2/80 (2 wkts., dec.)	95	1/0 2/58 3/58 4/87 5/106 6/119 7/126 8/188 9/188	190

Bowling: *First Innings*—Brown 4—1—8—0; Bannister 5—0—10—0; Webster 5—0—10—0; Miller 9—0—39—2; Allan 5—0—23—0. *Second Innings*—Brown 10.4—2—44—3; Bannister 6—3—15—0; Webster 5—1—15—1; Allan 15—2—50—3; Miller 11—3—28—3; Ibadulla 5—0—33—0.

Umpires: J. F. Crapp and C. G. Pepper.

At Cambridge, May 14, 16. WARWICKSHIRE beat CAMBRIDGE UNIVERSITY by an innings and 74 runs.

At Lord's, May 18, 19, 20. WARWICKSHIRE drew with MIDDLESEX.

At Swansea, May 21. WARWICKSHIRE beat GLAMORGAN by 165 runs. (See GILLETTE CUP.)

At Swansea, May 25, 26, 27. WARWICKSHIRE drew with GLAMORGAN.

WARWICKSHIRE v. SCOTLAND

At Birmingham, May 28, 30, 31. Drawn. An unnecessarily prolonged first innings on the part of Warwickshire, who scored 401 for four before declaring, virtually doomed the match to stalemate from the beginning. As their principal entertainment on Saturday, spectators had to be content with a maiden century from Edmonds whose elevation to number six in the batting order was not so much a tribute to his talent in this direction as evidence that the county fielded a scratch side. Their acting captain, Ibadulla, having accommodated Edmonds by extending their first innings, delayed his second declaration until lunch. Scotland, who had taken all the second day to score 257 to avoid following on, were now asked to make roughly the same number of runs in about half the time. They finished 120 runs short but with four wickets standing.

Warwickshire

*K. Ibadulla b Barr	47	— c Laing b Barr	29
R. N. Abberley lbw b Barr	79	— c Thompson b Dow	11
D. L. Amiss not out	150	— run out	45
J. A. Jameson b Allan	9	— c Brown b Barr	9
B. A. Richardson b Allan	2	— not out	25
R. B. Edmonds not out	102	— c and b Thompson	6
E. E. Hemmings (did not bat)		— not out	0
L-b 10, n-b 2	12	L-b 2	2
1/98 2/149 3/170 4/182 (4 wkts., dec.)	401	1/22 2/66 3/84 (5 wkts., dec.) 4/105 5/119	127

R. Miller, R. V. Webster, †E. Legard and W. Blenkiron did not bat.

Bowling: *First Innings*—Dow 20—4—91—0; Thompson 17—4—56—0; Barr 34—3—138—2; Allan 41.1—11—89—2; Chisholm 5—0—15—0. *Second Innings*—Barr 23—5—61—2; Dow 10—1—29—1; Thompson 12—2—35—1.

Scotland

R. H. E. Chisholm run out	47	— b Hemmings	35
L. C. Dudman c Legard b Webster	11	— b Blenkiron	40
M. H. Denness c Jameson b Webster	28	— c Ibadulla b Miller	9
J. G. Laing b Miller	27	— not out	38
M. K. More lbw b Blenkiron	12	— lbw b Blenkiron	9
T. B. Racilner c Abberley b Miller	15	— b Blenkiron	2
J. M. Allan not out	55	— c Jameson b Hemmings	0
D. Barr b Blenkiron	5	— not out	17
*†J. Brown b Blenkiron	46		
W. D. F. Gow lbw b Miller	0		
E. R. Thompson b Blenkiron	0		
B 4, l-b 3, w 2, n-b 2	11	N-b 1	1
1/23 2/67 3/118 4/123 5/140 6/148 7/158 8/252 9/253	257	1/71 2/84 3/84 4/109 5/114 6/123 (6 wkts.)	151

Bowling: *First Innings*—Webster 24—7—51—2; Blenkiron 33—12—53—4; Amiss 3—0—12—0; Hemmings 18—4—50—0; Miller 35—15—51—3; Ibadulla 15—6—29—0. *Second Innings*—Webster 3—1—8—0; Blenkiron 18—7—24—3; Amiss 6—2—9—0; Miller 28—9—58—1; Ibadulla 4—0—15—0; Hemmings 12—4—26—2; Edmonds 2—1—1—0; Jameson 4—1—9—0.

Umpires: J. Langridge and F. Jakeman.

WARWICKSHIRE *v.* GLAMORGAN

At Birmingham, June 1, 2, 3. Warwickshire won by 155 runs. This was Webster's match. Having scored 47, going in number ten, Warwickshire's Barbadian fast bowler then took the first six Glamorgan wickets for 30 runs and they were all out for 52. Warwickshire declared at 278 for eight, of which Amiss and Abberley contributed 152 between them. Glamorgan put up a better fight in their second innings, Hedges particularly being hard to remove, but they had left themselves too much to do and Warwickshire's four seam bowlers were able to take advantage of the fact.

Warwickshire

K. Ibadulla c Evans b Shepherd	20	— c Cordle b F. J. Davis	24
R. N. Abberley lbw b Wheatley	9	— c Lewis b R. Davis	70
D. L. Amiss lbw b Shepherd	15	— c Morris b F. J. Davis	82
J. A. Jameson c Evans b Cordle	11	— c Evans b R. Davis	7
T. W. Cartwright lbw b Wheatley	8	— c Cordle b F. J. Davis	20
*†A. C. Smith b Wheatley	0	— not out	35
R. B. Edmonds c Morris b Cordle	28	— c Rees b F. J. Davis	6
J. M. Allan c R. Davis b Wheatley	1	— not out	7
R. Miller c and b Shepherd	17	— lbw b Shepherd	13
R. V. Webster c Morris b Cordle	47	— c Rees b F. J. Davis	2
J. D. Bannister not out	0		
B 1, l-b 1, w 1	3	B 6, l-b 6	12
1/30 2/34 3/53 4/65 5/65 6/65 7/71 8/98 9/155	159	1/40 2/114 3/126 4/185 5/205 6/218 7/237 8/245 (8 wkts. dec.)	278

Bowling: *First Innings*—Cordle 15.1—3—47—3; Wheatley 28—12—40—4; Shepherd 32—11—69—3. *Second Innings*—Wheatley 16—6—35—0; Cordle 18.4—4—55—0; F. J. Davis 25—11—72—5; Shepherd 23—10—37—1; Hedges 14—4—28—0; R. Davis 13—4—39—2.

Glamorgan

A. Jones lbw b Webster	0	— lbw b Bannister	22
R. Davis c Amiss b Webster	12	— lbw b Bannister	30
A. Rees not out	22	— b Webster	12
A. R. Lewis c Smith b Webster	6	— c Ibadulla b Cartwright	22
B. Hedges c Ibadulla b Webster	2	— b Ibadulla	59
I. Morris c Amiss b Webster	4	— c Ibadulla b Cartwright	4
F. J. Davis c Smith b Webster	1	— lbw b Webster	23
†D. L. Evans lbw b Cartwright	1	— b Bannister	0
A. E. Cordle lbw b Cartwright	0	— c Cartwright b Ibadulla	18
D. J. Shepherd c Ibadulla b Cartwright	2	— b Miller	19
*O. S. Wheatley b Bannister	0	— not out	15
L-b 1, n-b 1	2	L-b 4, n-b 2	6
1/0 2/18 3/24 4/28 5/34 6/38 7/39 8/41 9/43	52	1/38 2/63 3/63 4/74 5/91 6/99 7/167 8/195 9/197	230

Bowling: *First Innings*—Webster 18—6—30—6; Bannister 9.1—2—17—1; Cartwright 9—7—3—3. *Second Innings*—Webster 14—2—44—2; Bannister 16—7—39—3; Cartwright 21—9—40—2; Allan 14—10—18—0; Ibadulla 14—1—54—2; Edmonds 8—4—14—0; Miller 10.2—4—15—1.

Umpires: W. E. Phillipson and W. F. Simpson.

At Worcester, June 4, 6, 7. WARWICKSHIRE beat WORCESTERSHIRE by 167 runs.

WARWICKSHIRE v. YORKSHIRE

At Birmingham, June 8, 9, 10. *65 overs.* Yorkshire won by eight wickets. Warwickshire began so slowly that only nine runs came off the first eight overs, but M. J. K. Smith and Amiss adjusted matters in a stand of 101 for the third wicket. Smith reached 89 by the end of Warwickshire's 65 overs, and a score of 223 appeared a useful one. Thanks to a forthright 136 by Boycott, Yorkshire had no difficulty in capping it. Nor did they find Warwickshire much trouble a second time, dismissing them for 148, and leaving themselves only 80 runs for victory on the third day. Boycott sank from the heights, being bowled by Brown for nothing, but Close and Padgett scored freely and it was all over in an hour.

Warwickshire

R. N. Abberley b Wilson	42	— c Sharpe b Wilson	11
K. Ibadulla c Boycott b Close	19	— run out	6
D. L. Amiss c Sharpe b Nicholson	50	— c Sharpe b Illingworth	5
*M. J. K. Smith not out	89	— b Illingworth	26
J. A. Jameson c Wilson b Nicholson	6	— lbw b Illingworth	46
T. W. Cartwright c Padgett b Trueman	9	— c Balderstone b Wilson	5
†A. C. Smith c Close b Trueman	3	— b Illingworth	14
R. V. Webster not out	1	— b Illingworth	4
R. B. Edmonds (did not bat)		— b Illingworth	0
J. M. Allan (did not bat)		— run out	6
D. J. Brown (did not bat)		— not out	12
B 1, l-b 1, n-b 2	4	B 11, l-b 1, n-b 1	13
1/37 2/78 3/179 4/199 5/210 6/222 (6 wkts., 65 overs)	223	1/10 2/21 3/31 4/73 5/80 6/110 7/110 8/125 9/125	148

Bowling: *First Innings*—Trueman 18—3—58—2; Nicholson 19—5—75—2; Close 11—4—25—1; Illingworth 11—1—45—0; Wilson 6—1—16—1. *Second Innings*—Trueman 4—0—16—0; Nicholson 4—2—4—0; Wilson 33—15—49—2; Close 5—5—0—0; Illingworth 27.5—9—66—6.

Yorkshire

G. Boycott not out	136	— b Brown	0
*D. B. Close c A. C. Smith b Webster	8	— not out	60
D. E. V. Padgett b Webster	79	— c Amiss b Ibadulla	59
J. H. Hampshire not out	10	— not out	11
L-b 9	9		
1/28 2/218 (2 wkts., 65 overs)	242	1/0 2/111 (2 wkts.)	130

P. J. Sharpe, R. Illingworth, J. C. Balderstone, †J. G. Binks, F. S. Trueman, D. Wilson and A. G. Nicholson did not bat.

Bowling: *First Innings*—Brown 9—1—35—0; Webster 14—0—67—2; Cartwright 21—4—61—0; Edmonds 18—4—64—0; Ibadulla 3—0—6—0. *Second Innings*—Brown 5—2—9—1; Webster 4—1—11—0; Cartwright 9—4—17—0; Edmonds 12—5—24—0; Allan 10—1—34—0; Ibadulla 9.4—1—35—1.

Umpires: J. S. Buller and A. Jepson.

At Bristol, June 11, 13, 14. WARWICKSHIRE drew with GLOUCESTERSHIRE.

At Manchester, June 15, 16, 17. WARWICKSHIRE drew with LANCASHIRE.

WARWICKSHIRE v. GLOUCESTERSHIRE

At Birmingham, June 18,20, 21. Gloucestershire won by five runs. Gloucestershire found scoring difficult on a slow wicket and with the weather interfering, scored 192 on the first day off 90 overs. They went to 251 before declaring and

Warwickshire, after falling away from an opening partnership of 107 between Abberley and Barber, reached exactly the same total but for the loss of all their wickets. Much the same happened to them when they were set 193 in just under two hours. They raced to 112 in fifty-five minutes for the loss of two wickets, but collapsed spectacularly against the off-breaks of Mortimore and Allen, being dismissed for 187. As the first-innings scores were level, Gloucestershire gained 11 points and Warwickshire one.

Gloucestershire

R. B. Nicholls c Cartwright b Webster	0	— st A. C. Smith b Allan	69
C. A. Milton lbw b Cartwright	17	— c Richardson b Jameson	52
D. Brown lbw b Allan	63	— c Brown b Allan	21
S. E. Russell c Webster b Barber	62		
D. Shepherd c Amiss b Barber	10	— not out	13
D. A. Allen not out	45		
*J. B. Mortimore b Cartwright	37	— not out	1
A. S. Brown b Cartwright	2		
A. R. Windows b Cartwright	11	— c M. J. K. Smith b Richardson	23
B 1, l-b 3	4	B 8, l-b 5	13
1/3 2/25 3/126 4/154 5/155 6/237 7/239 8/251 (8 wkts., dec.)	251	1/96 2/135 3/164 4/182 (4 wkts., dec.)	192

M. D. Mence and †B. J. Meyer did not bat.

Bowling: *First Innings*—Brown 20—6—47—0; Webster 26—8—51—1; Cartwright 16.2—2—35—4; Amiss 4—1—9—0; Allan 31—12—58—1; Barber 17—5—47—2. *Second Innings*—Brown 6—0—15—0; Webster 6—3—5—0; Cartwright 6—1—10—0; Allan 23—4—75—2; Barber 11—2—28—0; Jameson 5—1—14—1; Richardson 12—1—32—1.

Warwickshire

R. N. Abberley c Milton b Mortimore	56	— run out	11
R. W. Barber c Shepherd b Mortimore	56	— c. Allen b Mortimore	14
D. L. Amiss c Allen b Mortimore	45	— c Mence b A. S. Brown	40
*M. J. K. Smith c Mence b Allen	4	— c Meyer b Mortimore	56
J. A. Jameson c D. Brown b Allen	16	— b Allen	44
B. A. Richardson lbw b Allen	10	— c Windows b Mortimore	5
T. W. Cartwright c D. Brown b Allen	1	— c Milton b Mortimore	6
†A. C. Smith c D. Brown b Allen	23	— b Allen	2
R. V. Webster c D. Brown b Mortimore	3	— b Allen	0
J. M. Allan not out	10	— not out	6
D. J. Brown b Windows	19	— b Allen	0
B 4, l-b 4	8	L-b 3	3
1/107 2/114 3/123 4/150 5/171 6/173 7/199 8/207 9/222	251	1/43 2/54 3/132 4/157 5/160 6/169 7/172 8/172 9/176	187

Bowling: *First Innings*—A. S. Brown 18—3—45—0; Windows 12.5—2—39—1; Mortimore 37—12—94—4; Allen 32—6—65—5. *Second Innings*—A. S. Brown 7—0—46—1; Windows 5—0—40—0; Mortimore 14.3—0—48—4; Allen 13—0—50—4.

Umpires: J. Arnold and C. S. Elliott.

At Birmingham, June 22. WARWICKSHIRE beat GLOUCESTERSHIRE by six wickets. (See GILLETTE CUP.)

At Taunton, June 25, 27, 28. WARWICKSHIRE beat SOMERSET by 53 runs.

At Buxton, June 29, 30. WARWICKSHIRE lost to DERBYSHIRE by eight wickets.

WARWICKSHIRE v. OXFORD UNIVERSITY

At Birmingham, July 2, 4, 5. Drawn. Big scores on both sides demonstrated the easiness of the pitch. The University made rather a mess of their first innings, collapsing dismally against Ibadulla and the left-arm spinner, Miller, who took five for 39 and five for 57 respectively. They had been given a splendid start by Gibbs, who scored 107, Goldstein and Toft, but were all out for 204. The Warwickshire batting was also uneven, but a commanding innings of 166 by Stewart raised them to a total of 327. Big scores by Gibbs, Toft, Gilliat and Groves in a total of 347 for seven declared was more than the Warwickshire batting could sustain.

Oxford University

First Innings		Second Innings	
P. J. K. Gibbs st Legard b Ibadulla	107	c Jameson b Miller	74
F. S. Goldstein c and b Ibadulla	37	c and b Blenkiron	2
D. P. Toft c Smith b Miller	38	c Gordon b Ibadulla	84
*R. M. C. Gilliat b Miller	2	c Legard b Blenkiron	74
M. C. M. Groves b Ibadulla	0	c Bannister b Miller	80
M. R. J. Guest c Miller b Ibadulla	7	c Jameson b Miller	21
†A. W. Dyer c Smith b Miller	8	st Legard b Miller	1
G. N. S. Ridley c and b Ibadulla	0	not out	3
A. G. M. Watson not out	4		
R. W. Elviss lbw b Miller	0		
R. B. Hiller c Legard b Miller	0		
B 1	1	B 3, l-b 5	8
1/58 2/139 3/164 4/167 5/179 6/200 7/200 8/204 9/204	204	1/4 2/127 3/212 4/257 5/314 6/320 7/347 (7 wkts., dec.)	347

Bowling *First Innings*—Bannister 8—2—42—0; Blenkiron 5—2—10—0; Ibadulla 21—8—39—5; Miller 33.3—16—57—5; Allan 30—13—44—0; Smith 3—0—11—0. *Second Innings*—Bannister 22—9—32—0; Blenkiron 20—1—56—2; Miller 29.1—7—93—4; Allan 22—7—63—0; Ibadulla 22—1—87—1; Smith 3—0—8—0.

Warwickshire

First Innings		Second Innings	
*A. C. Smith c Dyer b Hiller	50	c Gilliat b Ridley	53
K. Ibadulla c Dyer b Hiller	5	c Guest b Hiller	11
A. Gordon c Goldstein b Watson	0	lbw b Elviss	25
J. A. Jameson c Watson b Ridley	24	c Watson b Ridley	26
W. J. Stewart c Goldstein b Ridley	166	not out	46
G. S. Warner c Gilliat b Ridley	7	not out	8
J. M. Allan c Goldstein b Guest	32		
R. Miller b Watson	7	c Ridley b Elviss	0
W. Blenkiron b Elviss	14	b Elviss	0
†E. Legard c Gilliat b Watson	10		
J. D. Bannister not out	0		
B 4, l-b 7, n-b 1	12	L-b 4	4
1/18 2/21 3/70 4/102 5/151 6/217 7/238 8/313 9/317	327	1/50 2/80 3/114 4/127 5/137 6/137 (6 wkts.)	173

Bowling: *First Innings*—Watson 19.2—4—68—3; Hiller 18—3—51—2; Elviss 34—10—82—1; Ridley 39—21—101—3; Guest 10—5—13—1. *Second Innings*—Watson 6—1—40—0; Hiller 13—4—34—1; Ridley 22—9—54—2; Elviss 11—3—41—3.

Umpires: A. E. Fagg and T. W. Spencer.

At Leicester, July 6, 7, 8. WARWICKSHIRE drew with LEICESTERSHIRE.

At Westcliff, July 9, 11, 12. WARWICKSHIRE lost to ESSEX by four wickets.

WARWICKSHIRE v. LANCASHIRE

At Birmingham, July 13, 14, 15. Drawn. Statham accepted the hospitality of a pitch which might have been prepared with him specially in mind, bowling Warwickshire out for 84. The total would have been even more meagre, but for middle-order resistance by Jameson, Ibadulla and Cartwright. Statham's figures were six for 31. Lancashire scored 297 for seven before declaring, a poor start being adjusted by Bond, with 90, and strong support from all the batsmen in turn. The weather took a hand, however, and lengthy interruptions, allied to staunch batting by Barber, Amiss and Ibadulla denied Lancashire the victory they deserved.

Warwickshire

R. N. Abberley b Higgs	3	— lbw b Higgs	1
R. W. Barber c Higgs b Statham	10	— c Goodwin b Higgs	75
D. L. Amiss lbw b Higgs	1	— not out	76
*M. J. K. Smith b Statham	1	— c Worsley b Greenhough	2
J. A. Jameson c Bond b Shuttleworth	18	— lbw b Shuttleworth	10
K. Ibadulla b Higgs	20	— not out	10
T. W. Cartwright b Statham	26		
†A. C. Smith c Goodwin b Statham	1		
R. Miller b Statham	0		
D. J. Brown not out	2		
J. D. Bannister b Statham	0		
L-b 2	2	B 4, l-b 3, n-b 2	9
1/10 2/11 3/16 4/16 5/42 6/81 7/81 8/81 9/84	84	1/2 2/130 3/149 4/152 (4 wkts.)	183

Bowling: *First Innings*—Statham 18.5—7—31—6; Higgs 21—6—35—3; Shuttleworth 7—1—16—1. *Second Innings*—Statham 19—10—31—0; Higgs 18—6—37—2; Shuttleworth 22—7—43—1; Greenhough 29—15—38—1; Worsley 13—7—15—0; Sullivan 4—0—10—0.

Lancashire

D. M. Green b Bannister	7
G. K. Knox b Bannister	0
J. D. Bond c A. C. Smith b Cartwright	90
D. R. Worsley c and b Miller	59
J. Sullivan c M. J. K. Smith b Cartwright	35
H. Pilling c A. C. Smith b Cartwright	39
K. Higgs lbw b Cartwright	29
K. Shuttleworth not out	25
†K. Goodwin not out	8
L-b 4, n-b 1	5
1/2 2/13 3/127 4/182 5/203 6/258 7/265 (7 wkts., dec.)	297

T. Greenhough and *J. B. Statham did not bat.

Bowling—Brown 27—2—68—0; Bannister 19—7—32—2; Cartwright 29—13—63—4; Ibadulla 15—6—45—0; Miller 21—3—84—1.

Umpires: J. Arnold and W. E. Phillipson.

WARWICKSHIRE v. SURREY

At Coventry, July 16, 18, 19. Surrey won by five wickets. A disciplined innings by Barber, and A. C. Smith's marshalling of the lower order batsmen enabled Warwickshire to reach 168 in the first innings against lively bowling by Jackman, who took five for 71. Surrey, in their turn, found Brown, Webster and Cartwright difficult to manage, with the result that they conceded Warwickshire a lead of 12. Warwickshire then crashed badly, losing their first five wickets for 49 and Surrey were left to make 160 in three and a half hours, which they achieved principally because of a dominant innings by Storey.

Warwickshire

First innings		Second innings	
R. W. Barber b Jackman	56	run out	4
R. N. Abberley c Roope b Jackman	0	lbw b Jefferson	2
D. L. Amiss c Edrich b Jackman	0	b Jackman	11
*M. J. K. Smith c Edrich b Storey	12	b Pocock	31
J. A. Jameson c Edrich b Storey	1	c Roope b Jackman	2
W. J. Stewart b Storey	14	c Edwards b Storey	8
T. W. Cartwright b Jackman	0	c Long b Jackman	21
†A. C. Smith not out	42	c Storey b Jefferson	45
R. V. Webster b Storey	23	b Storey	9
D. J. Brown c Edrich b Roope	15	b Jefferson	12
J. D. Bannister b Jackman	1	not out	0
B 1, l-b 2, n-b 1	4	B 1, n-b 1	2
1/2 2/16 3/41 4/55 5/77 6/78 7/85 8/124 9/161	168	1/3 2/16 3/22 4/34 5/49 6/63 7/102 8/113 9/146	147

Bowling: *First Innings*—Jefferson 12—2—28—0; Jackman 23.5—4—71—5; Storey 27—13—49—4; Roope 11—5—16—1. *Second Innings*—Jefferson 10.1—1—23—3; Jackman 19—2—64—3; Storey 23—13—24—2; Pocock 13—5—28—1; Roope 5—2—6—0.

Surrey

First innings		Second innings	
M. J. Edwards c Jameson b Webster	0	run out	23
J. H. Edrich lbw b Cartwright	37	c A. C. Smith b Bannister	28
M. D. Willett c Amiss b Cartwright	20	b Brown	10
*M. J. Stewart c Barber b Bannister	0	c Stewart b Brown	7
R. A. E. Tindall b Webster	21	not out	28
S. J. Storey c A. C. Smith b Webster	1	c Barber b Webster	50
G. R. J. Roope c A. C. Smith b Brown	18		
R. I. Jefferson b Brown	40	not out	14
†A. Long c M. J. K. Smith b Brown	11		
P. I. Pocock lbw b Cartwright	1		
R. D. Jackman not out	5		
L-b 1, n-b 1	2	L-b 3	3
1/1 2/35 3/36 4/72 5/79 6/80 7/138 8/139 9/142	156	1/30 2/61 3/63 4/70 5/143	(5 wkts.) 163

Bowling: *First Innings*—Brown 21.2—6—44—3; Webster 19—9—36—3; Bannister 14—4—25—1; Cartwright 29—11—49—3. *Second Innings*—Brown 14—4—22—2; Webster 16—2—67—1; Cartwright 15—0—39—0; Bannister 11—4—28—1; M. J. K. Smith 0.4—0—4—0.

Umpires: A. Jepson and G. H. Pope.

At Nottingham, July 20, 21, 22. WARWICKSHIRE drew with NORTHAMPTONSHIRE.

WARWICKSHIRE v. HAMPSHIRE

At Birmingham, July 23, 25, 26. Hampshire won by six wickets. Marshall proved the stumbling block to Warwickshire, as he has been to other counties, over the years. He topped M. J. K. Smith's 113, the chief contribution to Warwickshire's first-innings total with 133, but whereas the Warwickshire captain could not repeat his performance, Marshall scored 79 in his second innings. Hampshire fell 31 short of Warwickshire's first innings and M. J. K. Smith's second declaration required them to score 203 in two and three-quarter hours. They approached their task with relish, and the opening stand of 136 by Marshall and Reed assured success.

Warwickshire

First Innings		Second Innings	
K. Ibadulla run out	62	c Livingstone b Castell	41
R. N. Abberley c Timms b White	4	b Caple	26
D. L. Amiss c Sainsbury b White	36	c Timms b White	40
*M. J. K. Smith not out	113	b Caple	3
J. A. Jameson c Timms b White	24	c Horton b Castell	5
W. J. Stewart c Timms b White	52	c Horton b Caple	21
T. W. Cartwright lbw b Castell	3	not out	21
†A. C. Smith not out	24	c Livingstone b Castell	2
L-b 1, n-b 3	4	L-b 6, n-b 6	12
1/4 2/75 3/129 4/166 5/280 6/290 (6 wkts., dec.)	322	1/59 2/97 3/116 4/118 5/135 6/166 7/171 (7 wkts., dec.)	171

R. B. Edmonds, D. J. Brown and J. D. Bannister did not bat.

Bowling: *First Innings*—Shackleton 36—12—74—0; White 29—4—95—4; Cottam 17—1—58—0; Castell 11—1—62—1; Sainsbury 15—9—29—0. *Second Innings*—Shackleton 11—6—11—0; White 10—5—17—1; Castell 20.3—1—79—3; Caple 20—3—52—3.

Hampshire

First Innings		Second Innings	
*R. E. Marshall c Amiss b Edmonds	133	c and b Cartwright	79
B. L. Reed lbw b Brown	1	b Cartwright	48
H. Horton c M. J. K. Smith b Cartwright	10	not out	4
D. A. Livingstone lbw b Cartwright	11	c and b Edmonds	41
P. J. Sainsbury c Abberley b Cartwright	62		
R. G. Caple b Edmonds	35	not out	7
†B. S. V. Timms not out	21		
D. W. White b Brown	4	c M. J. K. Smith b Edmonds	15
A. T. Castell b Edmonds	5		
D. Shackleton c Abberley b Brown	0		
R. M. Cottam not out	0		
L-b 8, n-b 1	9	B 4, l-b 7	11
1/9 2/41 3/57 4/190 5/246 6/274 7/283 8/288 9/291 (9 wkts., dec.)	291	1/136 2/148 3/167 4/201 (4 wkts.)	205

Bowling: *First Innings*—Brown 26—2—79—3; Bannister 7—0—17—0; Cartwright 33—5—66—3; Ibadulla 29—6—65—0; Edmonds 25—8—55—3. *Second Innings*—Brown 10—0—62—0; Cartwright 21—4—68—2; Edmonds 21.1—4—64—2.

Umpires: G. H. Pope and J. Arnold.

At Hastings, July 27, 28, 29. WARWICKSHIRE drew with SUSSEX.

WARWICKSHIRE v. WORCESTERSHIRE

At Birmingham, July 30, August 1, 2. Worcestershire won by three wickets in a tense finish. Warwickshire held the initiative firmly until the last afternoon when Graveney and d'Oliveira in an aggressive stand of 109 in an hour, wrested it from them. The loss of the last hour on the first day disposed M. J. K. Smith to encroach to that extent on the second, before declaring. Despite Kenyon's example and 59 from d'Oliveira, Worcestershire fell 129 short and Warwickshire, though scoring slowly on the last morning, increased their neighbour's final obligation to 247 in three hours. At tea, Worcestershire's chance of succeeding looked remote, but Graveney and d'Oliveira transformed the situation. The last stage developed dramatically, so that there was only one ball left when Worcestershire got home.

Warwickshire

R. W. Barber b d'Oliveira	84	— c Headley b d'Oliveira	24
R. N. Abberley lbw b Carter	19	— c Gifford b Flavell	1
D. L. Amiss c Booth b Carter	12	— not out	49
*M. J. K. Smith b Horton	42	— b d'Oliveira	2
J. A. Jameson c Kenyon b Gifford	13	— not out	40
K. Ibadulla b Carter	59		
T. W. Cartwright not out	65		
†A. C. Smith not out	14		
L-b 5	5	L-b 1	1
1/46 2/60 3/128 4/146 5/180 6/287 (6 wkts., dec.)	313	1/5 2/45 3/49 (3 wkts., dec.)	117

R. B. Edmonds, J. M. Allan and D. J. Brown did not bat.

Bowling: *First Innings*—Flavell 24—3—76—0; Carter 37—6—109—3; d'Oliveira 21—7—68—1; Gifford 22—11—30—1; Horton 14—5—25—1. *Second Innings*—Flavell 10—3—22—1; Carter 10—3—31—0; d'Oliveira 15—2—41—2; Gifford 8—4—22—0.

Worcestershire

*D. Kenyon c Abberley b Allan	56	— b Cartwright	18
M. J. Horton c Barber b Brown	1	— b Allan	33
J. A. Ormrod b Brown	0	— c Allan b Cartwright	7
T. W. Graveney c M. J. K. Smith b Cartwright	24	— c M. J. K. Smith b Brown	94
B. d'Oliveira c M. J. K. Smith b Edmonds	59	— c M. J. K. Smith b Brown	70
R. G. A. Headley b Cartwright	30	— run out	4
D. W. Richardson b Allan	0	— not out	16
†R. Booth c Brown b Allan	1	— c Cartwright b Edmonds	0
N. Gifford c Cartwright b Brown	1	— not out	1
J. A. Flavell b Brown	0		
R. G. M. Carter not out	0		
B 7, l-b 4, n-b 1	12	B 1, l-b 5, n-b 1	7
1/3 2/3 3/50 4/125 5/155 6/161 7/169 8/184 9/184	184	1/20 2/28 3/106 4/215 5/220 6/244 7/245 (7 wkts.)	250

Bowling: *First Innings*—Brown 23—7—45—4; Cartwright 21.2—13—23—2; Ibadulla 4—1—14—0; Edmonds 24—8—47—1; Allan 21—8—43—3. *Second Innings*—Brown 15—2—65—2; Cartwright 10—4—30—2; Barber 4—0—24—0; Edmonds 19.5—2—70—1; Allan 11—1—54—1.

Umpires: A. E. Fagg and W. F. Price.

At Canterbury, August 3, 4, 5. WARWICKSHIRE drew with KENT.

WARWICKSHIRE v. NOTTINGHAMSHIRE

At Birmingham, August 6, 8, 9. *65 overs.* Drawn. One of Edgbaston's " experimental " wickets, on the portion of the square dug up two years ago in an attempt to achieve more bounce, proved satisfactory so far as Brown and Cartwright were concerned. They bowled Nottinghamshire out in their first innings for 103, the last eight wickets falling for 21 runs in a little more than an hour A stand of 136 in ninety minutes between M. J. K. Smith and Stewart enabled Warwickshire to build a lead of 115 off their 65 overs, but Nottinghamshire displayed a stubborn streak on the last morning, and the match was abandoned in the afternoon.

Nottinghamshire

*N.Hill c A. C. Smith b Cartwright	38	— c A. C. Smith b Webster	16
J. B. Bolus lbw b Brown	13	— c Stewart b Webster	15
D. L. Murray c Ibadulla b Cartwright	25	— c M. J. K. Smith b Brown	65
H. I. Moore b Brown	6	— c Ibadulla b Brown	1
M. J. Smedley c Cartwright b Brown	3	— not out	34
R. A. White c A. C. Smith b Cartwright	1	— not out	1
†R. Swetman not out	12		
M. Taylor b Brown	0		
C. Forbes c Cartwright b Brown	3		
B. Stead c Edmonds b Cartwright	2		
J. Howarth lbw b Brown	0		
		L-b 1, n-b 4	5
1/21 2/71 3/82 4/82 5/86 6/86 7/87 8/95 9/100	103	1/30 2/39 3/50 4/132 (4 wkts.)	137

Bowling: *First Innings*—Brown 20.5—5—46—6; Webster 10—0—25—0; Cartwright 19—7—32—4. *Second Innings*—Brown 16—3—56—2; Webster 17—1—42—2; Cartwright 16—6—34—0; Allan 1—1—0—0.

Warwickshire

K. Ibadulla c Murray b Forbes	21
†A. C. Smith c White b Forbes	20
D. L. Amiss c Stead b Taylor	10
*M. J. K. Smith not out	85
J. A. Jameson lbw b Taylor	11
W. J. Stewart not out	64
B 4, l-b 3	7
1/38 2/53 3/57 4/82 (4 wkts., 65 overs)	218

T. W. Cartwright, R. B. Edmonds, R. V. Webster, J. M. Allan and D. J. Brown did not bat.

Bowling: Stead 15—1—61—0; Howarth 6—3—3—0; Forbes 26—3—99—2; Taylor 18—3—48—2.

Umpires: A. Jepson and P. B. Wight.

At Birmingham, August 10. WARWICKSHIRE beat SOMERSET by ten wickets.

At Birmingham, August 13, 15, 16. WARWICKSHIRE lost to WEST INDIES by ten wickets. (See WEST INDIES section.)

WARWICKSHIRE v. DERBYSHIRE

At Coventry, August 17, 18, 19. Derbyshire won by eight wickets. Warwickshire began well and finished dismally. Not only did they allow four substantial Derbyshire partnerships to develop after getting four wickets for 24, but were then themselves bowled out for 38, their lowest score of the season. Following on 243 runs behind, they collapsed again, but A. C. Smith and Webster saved them from the second two-day defeat by the same opposition. On the last morning, however, Jackson, who had upset them in the first innings, took their last three wickets, leaving a formal task for the Derbyshire openers.

Derbyshire

I. W. Hall b Bannister	12	— not out	1
J. R. Eyre b Brown	5	— not out	5
M. H. Page c and b Brown	2		
J. F. Harvey c Bannister b Cartwright	3		
M. Hill c Bannister b Ibadulla	61		
P. E. Russell c Ibadulla b Bannister	34		
*D. C. Morgan c Ibadulla b Brown	96		
T. J. P. Eyre lbw b Ibadulla	25		
†R. W. Taylor c Jameson b Cartwright	39		
E. Smith lbw b Cartwright	0		
A. B. Jackson not out	0		
N-b 4	4	L-b 6	6
1/11 2/18 3/22 4/24 5/81 6/142 7/194 8/281 9/281	281	(no wkt.)	12

Bowling: *First Innings*—Brown 24—10—47—3; Webster 13—2—39—0; Bannister 23—6—71—2; Cartwright 8.2—4—28—3; Edmonds 17—2—44—0; Ibadulla 10—0—48—2. *Second Innings*—Edmonds 1—1—0—0; A. C. Smith 1.2—0—6—0.

Warwickshire

K. Ibadulla c Taylor b Jackson	0	— b Smith	55
R. N. Abberley c Hall b Jackson	8	— c Hall b Smith	12
R. B. Edmonds c Smith b Jackson	0	— lbw b Morgan	0
A. Gordon c Russell b Jackson	4	— c Morgan b Jackson	4
*M. J. K. Smith c T. Eyre b Jackson	15	— c Taylor b T. Eyre	11
J. A. Jameson b Smith	1	— b Morgan	19
T. W. Cartwright c Hall b Jackson	3	— c Jackson b Smith	5
†A. C. Smith c Hall b Jackson	3	— c Hall b Jackson	85
R. V. Webster run out	2	— c Hall b Jackson	42
D. J. Brown c Page b Jackson	0	— c Page b Jackson	4
J. D. Bannister not out	1	— not out	2
N-b 1	1	B 8, l-b 6	14
1/0 2/0 3/13 4/18 5/19 6/28 7/32 8/34 9/37	38	1/32 2/37 3/67 4/93 5/102 6/169 7/170 8/232 9/242	253

Bowling: *First Innings*—Jackson 13.3—5—18—8; Smith 13—6—19—1. *Second Innings*—Jackson 21.2—8—31—4; Smith 53—25—65—3; T. J. P. Eyre 13—2—63—1; Morgan 29—15—66—2; Russell 2—0—14—0.

Umpires: R. S. Lay and A. E. Alderman.

At Nottingham, August 20, 21, 22. WARWICKSHIRE beat NOTTINGHAMSHIRE by an innings and 41 runs.

At Hull, August 24, 25, 26. WARWICKSHIRE beat YORKSHIRE by three wickets.

WARWICKSHIRE v. SOMERSET

At Birmingham, August 27, 29, 30. Drawn. A courageous innings by Alley gave what character there was to the first day's play. Admittedly, the weather was uncongenial and Cartwright's accuracy, sustained over the best part of the day, made batting no easy business. Only an hour's play was possible on the second day and none at all on the third.

Somerset

G. Atkinson b Cartwright........ 25
R. Virgin b Brown.............. 13
M. Kitchen lbw b Cartwright..... 40
G. Burgess c Brown b Cartwright.. 36
W. E. Alley lbw b Edmonds...... 62
*C. R. M. Atkinson c A. C. Smith b Edmonds.................. 6
K. E. Palmer lbw b Cartwright.... 47
†G. Clayton b Brown............ 27
P. J. Robinson run out........... 6
B. A. Langford not out.......... 6
F. E. Rumsey not out............ 4
L-b 1, n-b 1.............. 2

1/27 2/64 3/111 (9 wkts., dec.) 274
4/118 5/145 6/196 7/244 8/264 9/265

Bowling: Brown 25—1—78—2; Bannister 17—4—36—0; Cartwright 36—12—30—4; Edmonds 19—6—37—2; Allan 11—1—41—0.

Warwickshire

K. Ibadulla b Palmer............ 3
R. N. Abberley not out.......... 11
D. L. Amiss lbw b Alley.......... 5
*M. J. K. Smith not out.......... 5
L-b 4, n-b 1.............. 5

1/10 2/15 (2 wkts.) 29

J. A. Jameson, †A. C. Smith, T. W. Cartwright, R. B. Edmonds, J. M. Allan, D. J. Brown and J. D. Bannister did not bat.

Bowling: Palmer 8—4—4—1; Alley 5—2—10—1; Rumsey 3.1—0—10—0.

Umpires: O. W. Herman and T. W. Spencer.

WARWICKSHIRE v. NORTHAMPTONSHIRE

At Birmingham, August 31, September 1. Warwickshire won by an innings and 89 runs. In the course of the Warwickshire innings, to which M. J. K. Smith subscribed 99, Sully, the visitors' off-spinner from Somerset, took his 100th wicket. A more remarkable achievement was reached on the second day, however, by Cartwright who needed 13 for his 100 wickets when play began and got them when he split the last Northamptonshire pair to give Warwickshire victory in two days. Andrew, the Northamptonshire captain and wicket-keeper, made his last appearance for his county.

Warwickshire

K. Ibadulla c Scott b Sully........ 33
R. W. Barber c Andrew b Durose.. 11
D. L. Amiss lbw b Scott.......... 9
*M. J. K. Smith c Scott b Durose.. 99
J. A. Jameson c Reynolds b Sully.. 75
R. N. Abberley c Prideaux b Mushtaq.......................... 23
†A. C. Smith c Reynolds b Durose 7
T. W. Cartwright b Mushtaq..... 11
R. B. Edmonds b Mushtaq....... 19
J. M. Allan not out.............. 0
R. V. Webster b Mushtaq........ 0
L-b 1, n-b 3.............. 4

1/15 2/35 3/110 4/214 5/232 291
6/242 7/247 8/286 9/291

Bowling—Crump 12—6—25—0; Durose 26—5—59—3; Sully 50—16—106—2; Scott 20—6—49—1; Mushtaq 12.4—1—38—4; Willey 3—1—10—0.

Northamptonshire

R. M. Prideaux c Ibadulla b Edmonds..	15	— c M. J. K. Smith b Cartwright	1
B. L. Reynolds c A. C. Smith b Cartwright	5	— b Cartwright..............	43
A. Lightfoot c Cartwright b Edmonds...	31	— lbw b Cartwright..........	20
P. J. Watts lbw b Cartwright..........	5	— c Ibadulla b Edmonds......	16
Mushtaq Mohammed c A. C. Smith b Cartwright....................	0	— b Cartwright..............	4
P. Willey c Ibadulla b Cartwright......	0	— b Edmonds.................	1
B. Crump b Edmonds.................	10	— st A. C. Smith b Cartwright..	3
*†K. V. Andrew lbw b Cartwright......	8	— c Abberley b Cartwright	2
M. E. Scott c Abberley b Cartwright....	4	— st A. C. Smith b Edmonds ..	10
H. Sully lbw b Edmonds	0	— not out	4
A. J. Durose not out.................	0	— c A. C. Smith b Cartwright..	0
B 6, l-b 4, n-b 1	11	B 2, l-b 4, w 1, n-b 2 ...	9
1/8 2/36 3/45 4/45 5/45 6/56 7/75 8/81 9/85	89	1/8 2/64 3/73 4/82 5/82 6/85 7/102 8/107 9/113	113

Bowling: *First Innings*—Webster 8—2—17—0; Cartwright 31.5—18—40—6; Edmonds 24—16—17—4; Allan 1—0—4—0. *Second Innings*—Webster 3—0—17—0; Cartwright 20.2—4—57—7; Edmonds 9—3—12—3; Ibadulla 9—3—18—0.

Umpires: L. H. Gray and P. B. Wight.

At Lord's, September 3. WARWICKSHIRE beat WORCESTERSHIRE by five wickets in the Cup Final. (See GILLETTE CUP.)

At Birmingham, September 10. WARWICKSHIRE (Gillette Cup Winners) lost to WEST INDIES by 19 runs. (See WEST INDIES section.)

WORCESTERSHIRE

President—SIR GEORGE DOWTY

Secretary—J. LISTER, County Ground, Worcester

Captain—DONALD KENYON

J. A. Ormrod

County Badge

N. Gifford

While unpleasant weather for most of the summer did not result in quite the same heart-pounding cricket for Worcestershire followers as in the memorable championship seasons of 1964 and 1965, there was nevertheless a lot to commend the 1966 season. How otherwise when the side was not deprived of their county title until the final afternoon of their first-class programme and then wound up the year in the Gillette Cup final against neighbouring Warwickshire the following day?

The Cup for the Championship pennant would have been a nice exchange with Yorkshire. But it was not to be. In the final analysis Worcestershire emerged with nothing to show for their endeavours. Nothing that is, other than the acclaim of their host of admirers for a bold effort. It was no mean achievement to finish runners-up in both competitions. Indeed, it was a unique distinction.

With interruptions in twenty-one of the twenty-eight Championship matches, the weather was far from kind to Worcestershire's cause. Yet one could point to batting breakdowns rather than to the elements for most failures. With Graveney and d'Oliveira required by England for four Test matches and Kenyon away with them on Test selector duties, the batting resources were stretched to the limit. The experienced batsmen, perhaps more than the younger members of the side, failed to rise to the occasion.

In the final weeks when Yorkshire were faltering after establishing a lead of 43 points by August 1, Worcestershire lost three home matches. Twice they were dismissed for under 100 runs by Leicestershire, then for 182 and 125 by Somerset and finally by Sussex for 77 and 150. Earlier, Warwickshire put them out for 138 and 87, also at Worcester. While these scores were clearly not Championship class, Worcestershire's form on opponents' grounds could not be faulted. Ten of fourteen victories were achieved in their travels, with defeat by Kent at Maidstone when Kenyon declared at 0—0, the only reverse away from home.

The biggest and most spectacular contributions again came from Graveney and Flavell. The old maestro, Graveney, finished with most runs for the county, 1,277, at an average of nearly 12 better than the next highest, d'Oliveira. The latter was the side's—as well as England's—outstanding all-rounder. As a middle-order batsman d'Oliveira often found himself running out of time in restricted-over innings, yet managed approximately 1,500 runs in all first-class matches and gained more than 70 wickets.

The evergreen Flavell once more carried the burden in attack, with 135 wickets, taking five or more in an innings nine times. It was significant that Flavell finished second in the first-class averages, while the other giant of the side, Graveney, finished top of the country's batting.

Kenyon and Horton, after a particularly lean year in 1965, showed better form and for much of the season were back as opening batting partners. Of the younger players, Gifford did splendidly to take ninety wickets in a season in which experimental rules did not encourage spin.

The only player to be newly capped, Ormrod, promised well for the first half of the summer, at one time averaging 48, but his batting fell away unaccountably. In his last 23 innings he averaged only 21, and with Headley and Richardson, the left-handers, both having particularly lean seasons with the bat, instead of the 1965 all-powerful finish being repeated, the county had to be content with six wins from their last ten matches.

This proved two wins too few for the championship hat-trick. But the image of Worcestershire cricket generally was tarnished very little.

WORCESTERSHIRE RESULTS

All First-Class Matches—Played 31, *Won* 14, *Lost* 5, *Drawn* 11, *Abandoned* 1

County Championship Matches—Played 28, *Won* 13, *Lost* 5, *Drawn* 9, *No Decision* 1

COUNTY CHAMPIONSHIP AVERAGES

BATTING

	Birthplace	Mtchs.	Inns.	Not Outs	Runs	100's	Highest Inns.	Aver.
T. W. Graveney	*Riding Mill*	19	32	5	1277	2	166	47.29
L. J. Coldwell..	*Newton Abbot*	20	20	4	73	0	12	45.62
B. d'Oliveira...	*Cape Town*	20	33	5	1004	2	126	35.85
M. J. Horton...	*Worcester*	26	47	6	1173	0	86	28.60
D. Kenyon.....	*Wordsley*	22	39	1	1038	1	114	27.31
J. A. Ormrod...	*Ramsbottom*	27	48	5	1138	0	70	26.46
C. D. Fearnley.	*Pudsey*	9	17	2	384	1	112	25.60
R. G. A. Headley	*Jamaica*	27	44	4	992	1	137	24.80
D. N. F. Slade..	*Feckenham*	9	13	5	194	0	46*	24.25
D.W. Richardson	*Hereford*	25	38	7	640	0	87*	20.64
R. Booth......	*Marsden*	28	39	10	509	0	43	17.55
N. Gifford.....	*Ulverston*	27	29	12	242	0	32	14.23
E. J. O. Hemsley	*Stoke-on-Trent*	5	8	2	69	0	24*	11.50
R. G. M. Carter	*Horden*	6	9	6	27	0	13	9.00
B. M. Brain....	*Worcester*	12	8	1	44	0	15	6.28
J. A. Flavell....	*Wall Heath*	25	21	8	59	0	13	4.53

Also batted: J. A. Standen (*Edmonton*), 6.

* *Signifies not out.*

BOWLING

	Overs	Maidens	Runs	Wickets	Average
J. A. Flavell............	822.3	199	1891	135	14.00
N. Gifford.............	780.5	349	1429	90	15.87
B. d'Oliveira...........	507.4	178	1011	57	17.73
L. J. Coldwell..........	627.4	164	1480	71	20.84
D. N. F. Slade..........	165.3	76	270	11	24.54
B. M. Brain............	318.3	60	974	37	26.32
M. J. Horton...........	328.3	102	718	27	26.59
R. G. M. Carter........	161.5	36	449	16	28.06

Also bowled: J. A. Standen 24—8—45—1; E. J. O. Hemsley 13—1—46—0.

At Worcester, May 4, 5, 6. WORCESTERSHIRE drew with WEST INDIES. (See WEST INDIES section.)

At Pontypridd, May 7, 9, 10. WORCESTERSHIRE beat GLAMORGAN by six wickets.

At Oxford, May 11, 12, 13. WORCESTERSHIRE v. OXFORD UNIVERSITY abandoned.

WORCESTERSHIRE v. NOTTINGHAMSHIRE

At Worcester, May 14, 16, 17. Drawn. Worcestershire were rescued by d'Oliveira, whose share in an eighth-wicket stand of 107 with Brain was 101. D'Oliveira, thirty minutes over his first run, reached his century in two hours twenty minutes, and his 123 contained seventeen 4's. Nottinghamshire lost half their side for 47 to the lively pace of Flavell and Coldwell and though improving in their second innings the visitors never looked equal to the task of scoring 344 for victory with more than a day left. The pitch looked perfect for batting as Worcestershire moved to 260 for three declared after an opening stand of 119 by Horton and Headley, but Nottinghamshire were still 220 short with four wickets remaining when rain ended the match three hours five minutes early. The Champions were robbed of almost certain success. Flavell, who celebrated his 37th birthday during the game, came out with a match analysis of nine for 74.

Worcestershire

M. J. Horton b Davison	0	— c Swetman b Bolus	62
R. G. A. Headley c Hill b Davison	29	— c Swetman b Forbes	52
J. A. Ormrod lbw b Taylor	21	— not out	59
*T. W. Graveney b Taylor	11	— b Taylor	26
B. d'Oliveira c Smedley b Forbes	123	— not out	49
D. W. Richardson c Taylor b Davison	18		
†R. Booth b Davison	0		
N. Gifford c Booth b Taylor	0		
B. M. Brain b Forbes	4		
L. J. Coldwell not out	0		
J. A. Flavell c Smedley b Davison	1		
L-b 6, n-b 1	7	B 2, l-b 8, n-b 2	12
1/2 2/48 3/64 4/64 5/101 6/101 7/106 8/213 9/213	214	1/119 2/131 3/177 (3 wkts., dec.)	260

Bowling: *First Innings*—Davison 19.1—6—55—5; Forbes 25—9—38—2; Johnson 10—3—15—0; Taylor 28—2—70—3; Bolus 5—0—29—0. *Second Innings*—Davison 17—7—29—0; Forbes 20—4—45—1; Taylor 22—3—88—1; Bolus 11—1—56—1; White 7—1—30—0.

Nottinghamshire

*N. Hill c Graveney b Flavell	8	— c Richardson b Flavell	0
J. B. Bolus b Coldwell	12	— c Headley b Flavell	21
†R. Swetman b Coldwell	18	— c Headley b Brain	13
H. I. Moore b Flavell	1	— lbw b Flavell	2
R. A. White lbw b Coldwell	5	— c Gifford b Brain	13
M. J. Smedley b Flavell	14	— c d'Oliveira b Brain	23
B. Whittingham b Flavell	8	— not out	34
M. Taylor not out	25	— not out	18
C. Forbes b Flavell	15		
A. Johnson c Brain b Gifford	15		
I. Davison b Flavell	10		
1/20 2/20 3/21 4/32 5/47 6/59 7/68 8/96 9/115	131	1/0 2/33 3/35 4/37 5/69 6/80 (6 wkts.)	124

Bowling: *First Innings*—Flavell 26.3—9—50—6; Coldwell 20—4—61—3; Gifford 6—2—20—1. *Second Innings*—Flavell 16—5—24—3; Coldwell 9—2—27—0; Brain 13—3—55—3; Gifford 8—2—18—0; Horton 1—1—0—0.

Umpires: A. Jepson and J. F. Crapp.

At Hove, May 18, 19, 20. WORCESTERSHIRE drew with SUSSEX.

At Worcester, May 21. WORCESTERSHIRE beat NOTTINGHAMSHIRE by 19 runs. (See GILLETTE CUP.)

WORCESTERSHIRE v. KENT

At Worcester, May 25, 26, 27. *65 overs.* Worcestershire won by 80 runs. Kenyon regained form and his century, the seventy-second of his career, which came in two and a half hours out of 156, contained some glorious back foot cover drives and straight hits. Headley helped his captain in an opening stand of 98, and Ormrod and Kenyon followed with a bright association worth 97. Flavell and Coldwell, in hostile mood, wrought havoc with the Kent batsmen and eight were dismissed for 43 after fourteen overs. Cowdrey was out first ball, taking a painful blow on the neck, whence the ball dropped on his stumps. Worcestershire found Underwood's accuracy and spin troublesome in their second innings and were all out for 162, leaving Kent seven and a half hours to obtain 307 to win. Their hopes were raised when 150 was reached for the loss of only Luckhurst, but upon Denness being bowled by Horton for a well hit 83, a collapse ensued. The last eight wickets fell to pace and spin for 76 runs, and Flavell's new ball spell of four for 9 gave him match figures of nine for 71.

Worcestershire

*D. Kenyon c Brown b Underwood	114	— c Knott b Brown	37
R. G. A. Headley c Cowdrey b Underwood	27	— c Knott b Sayer	0
J. A. Ormrod c Prodger b Brown	43	— c Cowdrey b Brown	5
T. W. Graveney not out	16	— c and b Underwood	33
B. d'Oliveira not out	5	— c Denness b Underwood	4
M. J. Horton (did not bat)		— st Knott b Dixon	19
†R. Booth (did not bat)		— b Underwood	43
N. Gifford (did not bat)		— b Underwood	2
B. M. Brain (did not bat)		— b Dixon	0
L. J. Coldwell (did not bat)		— b Brown	12
J. A. Flavell (did not bat)		— not out	0
B 3, l-b 13	16	B 6, l-b 1	7
1/98 2/195 3/195 (3 wkts., 65 overs)	221	1/0 2/31 3/67 4/77 5/80 6/127 7/130 8/145 9/162	162

Bowling: *First Innings*—Brown 16—5—41—1; Sayer 14—2—56—0; Dixon 15—1—58—0; Underwood 20—5—50—2. *Second Innings*—Brown 22—7—62—3; Sayer 15—6—34—1; Underwood 28.1—14—39—4; Dixon 11—3—20—2.

Kent

M. H. Denness c Gifford b Coldwell	16	— b Horton	83
B. W. Luckhurst lbw b Flavell	9	— b d'Oliveira	34
R. C. Wilson b Coldwell	2	— b Horton	38
*M. C. Cowdrey b Coldwell	0	— b Gifford	8
S. E. Leary c Kenyon b Flavell	6	— c d'Oliveira b Flavell	15
J. M. Prodger c and b Gifford	30	— c Headley b Gifford	0
†A. Knott b Flavell	0	— b Flavell	29
A. L. Dixon c Booth b Flavell	4	— c d'Oliveira b Flavell	2
A. Brown b Coldwell	0	— run out	6
D. M. Sayer b Flavell	4	— c Booth b Flavell	0
D. L. Underwood not out	2	— not out	1
L-b 4	4	B 2, l-b 8	10
1/15 2/22 3/22 4/31 5/33 6/36 7/42 8/43 9/73	77	1/72 2/150 3/171 4/171 5/171 6/204 7/215 8/215 9/225	226

Bowling: *First Innings*—Flavell 11—2—32—5; Coldwell 11—1—29—4; Gifford 1—0—12—1. *Second Innings*—Flavell 16.3—2—39—4; Coldwell 18—3—42—0; Brain 14—3—38—0; Gifford 29—17—33—2; d'Oliveira 9—3—21—1; Horton 21—10—43—2.

Umpires: W. H. Copson and J. Arnold.

At Romford, May 28, 30, 31. WORCESTERSHIRE beat ESSEX by four wickets.

At Northampton, June 1, 2, 3. WORCESTERSHIRE beat NORTHAMPTONSHIRE by 180 runs.

WORCESTERSHIRE v. WARWICKSHIRE

At Worcester, June 4, 6, 7. *65 overs.* Warwickshire beat Worcestershire by 167 runs. This was the Champions' first defeat in eleven months and followed a feeble batting performance. Ibadulla and A. C. Smith led an enterprising attack on the home bowling after half the Warwickshire side were out for 73, and the last five wickets boosted the score by 112 runs in 25 overs. Although Headley and Graveney put on 67 for the Worcestershire third wicket, forcing shots of note against accurate seam bowling were few. When the visitors went in again leading by 55, Jameson, with 80, held the innings together as the spinners threatened destruction, and Worcestershire were left a target of 255. With the score 44 for one at the start of the final day they were fully expected to put up a bold fight to preserve their proud record, but in a frail effort the remaining nine wickets fell to seam bowling for 43 runs. Webster began the slide with a wicket in each of his first two overs, and Bannister completed the rout with five of the last six for 10 runs in 7.2 overs.

Warwickshire

First Innings		Second Innings	
K. Ibadulla c Kenyon b Brain	60	lbw b Flavell	3
R. N. Abberley b Flavell	0	c Booth b Brain	13
D. L. Amiss c d'Oliveira b Flavell	0	c Ormrod b Slade	23
J. A. Jameson lbw b d'Oliveira	23	c Booth b Slade	80
B. A. Richardson b d'Oliveira	17	c d'Oliveira b Coldwell	11
T. W. Cartwright b Brain	9	c Richardson b d'Oliveira	31
*†A. C. Smith b d'Oliveira	35	c Richardson b d'Oliveira	6
R. V. Webster c d'Oliveira b Brain	25	c Graveney b d'Oliveira	9
R. B. Edmonds b Flavell	8	lbw b Slade	2
J. M. Allan lbw b Flavell	9	c Graveney b Slade	12
J. D. Bannister not out	2	not out	0
B 1, l-b 4	5	B 7, l-b 2	9
1/1 2/1 3/46 4/64 5/73 6/120 7/169 8/175 9/186	193	1/14 2/40 3/46 4/71 5/136 6/148 7/161 8/182 9/191	199

Bowling: *First Innings*—Flavell 19—4—68—4; Coldwell 11—2—30—0; Brain 20—4—56—3; d'Oliveira 15—6—34—3. *Second Innings*—Flavell 17—4—38—1; Coldwell 13—4—25—1; Brain 5—0—21—1; Slade 31—14—53—4; d'Oliveira 24—7—53—3.

Worcestershire

First Innings		Second Innings	
*D. Kenyon b Bannister	1	c Smith b Webster	31
R. G. A. Headley lbw b Ibadulla	28	c Smith b Webster	10
J. A. Ormrod lbw b Webster	0	lbw b Bannister	8
T. W. Graveney lbw b Cartwright	49	c Ibadulla b Cartwright	13
B. d'Oliveira c Smith b Ibadulla	5	c Webster b Bannister	6
D. W. Richardson c Abberley b Cartwright	11	b Cartwright	2
†R. Booth c Smith b Cartwright	2	c Ibadulla b Bannister	3
D. N. F. Slade c Richardson b Bannister	18	not out	6
B. M. Brain not out	9	b Webster	4
L. J. Coldwell b Bannister	6	lbw b Bannister	4
A. Flavell not out	5	b Bannister	0
L-b 4	4		
1/1 2/4 3/71 4/83 5/83 6/86 7/117 8/117 9/124 (9 wkts., 65 overs)	138	1/40 2/44 3/45 4/58 5/71 6/74 7/76 8/79 9/87	87

Bowling: *First Innings*—Webster 11—1—36—1; Bannister 16—4—32—3; Cartwright 23—4—45—3; Ibadulla 15—6—21—2. *Second Innings*—Webster 16—3—39—3; Bannister 12.2—2—32—5; Cartwright 18—12—16—2.

Umpires: O. W. Herman and A. E. Rhodes.

At Cambridge, June 8, 9, 10. WORCESTERSHIRE beat CAMBRIDGE UNIVERSITY by nine wickets.

WORCESTERSHIRE v. MIDDLESEX

At Worcestershire, June 11, 13, 14. *65 overs.* Drawn. The Worcestershire batsmen, eager to play strokes, made their highest total in six matches of 65-over cricket. Graveney, with glorious straight drives, reached 88 in one hour fifty minutes, ten of his thirteen 4's coming from the off-spin of Titmus and Bick. D'Oliveira helped Graveney in a gay association of three quarters of an hour to add 79. In a disappointing Middlesex innings, Parfitt alone showed authority against either pace or spin and Worcestershire led by 105. Their batsmen remained untroubled and a most pleasing 70 by d'Oliveira, who struck one 6 and nine 4's, helped the side to set the visitors a huge victory target of 364 in six hours. Though they never looked equal to this, Middlesex were much improved after their first day effort. Russell, his upper lip cut and swollen as a result of being hit the previous day, became the first century maker of the season at the expense of the Champions. He was helped by Smith in a second-wicket stand of 109 and on a slow turning pitch Russell remained unbeaten after four and three quarter hours with 117, having hit thirteen 4's.

Worcestershire

First Innings		Second Innings	
*D. Kenyon c Harris b Price	19	b Price	10
M. J. Horton c Parfitt b Titmus	22	c Stewart b Bick	67
J. A. Ormrod c Parfitt b Bick	45	run out	34
T. W. Graveney c Stewart b Price	88		
B. d'Oliveira not out	42	c Murray b Price	70
D. W. Richardson not out	4	not out	47
D. N. F. Slade (did not bat)		not out	18
B 4, l-b 12, n-b 1	17	B 4, l-b 8	12
1/27 2/64 3/141 4/220 (4 wkts., 65 overs)	237	1/14 2/77 3/146 4/210 (4 wkts., dec.)	258

†R. Booth, N. Gifford, L. J. Coldwell and J. A. Flavell did not bat.

Bowling: *First Innings*—Price 16—1—63—2; Stewart 12—0—39—0; Titmus 23—7—67—1; Bick 14—2—51—1. *Second Innings*—Price 20—3—56—2; Stewart 21—4—61—0; Titmus 26—11—49—0; Bick 18—6—42—1; Parfitt 1—0—4—0; Latchman 14—4—34—0.

Middlesex

First Innings		Second Innings	
W. E. Russell b Flavell	1	not out	117
M. J. Harris run out	13	lbw b Coldwell	19
P. H. Parfitt c Gifford b d'Oliveira	51	st Booth b d'Oliveira	32
E. A. Clark lbw b Gifford	8	not out	5
†J. T. Murray c Booth b Coldwell	11		
*F. J. Titmus c Gifford b d'Oliveira	13		
M. J. Smith b Coldwell	3	lbw b Gifford	68
D. A. Bick b Flavell	14		
H. C. Latchman not out	5		
J. S. E. Price b Flavell	0		
R. W. Stewart b Coldwell	0		
B 2, l-b 11	13	L-b 8	8
1/6 2/29 3/42 4/73 5/104 6/108 7/121 8/131 9/131	132	1/31 2/140 3/223 (3 wkts.)	249

Bowling: *First Innings*—Flavell 19—5—35—3; Coldwell 26.1—11—38—3; Gifford 8—3—24—1; d'Oliveira 11—4—22—2. *Second Innings*—Flavell 13—2—47—0; Coldwell 21—5—48—1; Gifford 23—12—40—1; Slade 20—9—41—0; d'Oliveira 23—10—38—1; Horton 13—1—27—0.

Umpires: J. F. Crapp and G. H. Pope.

At Manchester, June 18, 20, 21. WORCESTERSHIRE beat LANCASHIRE by seven wickets.

At Worcester, June 22. WORCESTERSHIRE beat ESSEX by 82 runs. (See GILLETTE CUP.)

WORCESTERSHIRE v. HAMPSHIRE

At Dudley, June 25, 27, 28. *65 overs.* Drawn. This match was so badly hit by rain on the first two days that in spite of three declarations victory to either side rarely looked likely. Kenyon made the visitors a present of first innings points in a bid to keep the game alive, yet there was so little resolve by batsmen to push on that when Worcestershire again declared only two hours remained. This left Hampshire a tempting target of 145 runs but Marshall appeared to be the only batsman who considered a win possible. He gained 43 of the first 68 that came in a little over a run a minute, but with the Hampshire captain's dismissal there was no further aggression, the match ending after five minutes of extra time.

Worcestershire

*D. Kenyon not out	21	— b Shackleton	2
M. J. Horton c Wheatley b White	3	— b Cottam	76
J. A. Ormrod not out	8	— b Cottam	4
D. N. F. Slade (did not bat)		— c Keith b Shackleton	4
B. d'Oliveira (did not bat)		— c Keith b Cottam	16
D. W. Richardson (did not bat)		— not out	41
R. G. A. Headley (did not bat)		— run out	0
†R. Booth (did not bat)		— not out	9
B 4, l-b 1, n-b 3	8	L-b 4, w 1, n-b 2	7
1/11 (1 wkt.)	40	1/2 2/16 3/31 4/84 5/120 6/127 (6 wkts., dec.)	159

N. Gifford, L. J. Coldwell and J. A. Flavell did not bat.

Bowling: *First Innings*—Shackleton 11—5—11—0; White 6—0—14—1; Cottam 5—1—7—0. *Second Innings*—Shackleton 26—12—42—2; White 11—0—48—0; Cottam 20—6—40—3; Sainsbury 8—2—14—0; Wheatley 3—1—8—0.

Hampshire

*R. E. Marshall lbw b Flavell	14	— c Slade b Gifford	43
B. L. Reed c Booth b Flavell	6	— lbw b Coldwell	19
H. Horton b Coldwell	10	— not out	14
J. R. Gray not out	10	— not out	6
G. L. Keith lbw b Flavell	1		
P. J. Sainsbury not out	14		
		L-b 3	3
1/15 2/26 3/32 4/33 (4 wkts., dec.)	55	1/62 2/68 (2 wkts.)	85

†B. S. V. Timms, K. J. Wheatley, D. Shackleton, D. W. White and R. M. Cottam did not bat.

Bowling: *First Innings*—Flavell 10—3—28—3; Coldwell 10—1—27—1. *Second Innings*—Flavell 6—0—12—0; Coldwell 15—2—32—1; d'Oliveira 3—0—16—0; Gifford 6—1—22—1.

Umpires: F. Jakeman and W. H. Copson.

WORCESTERSHIRE v. YORKSHIRE
(R. Bouth's Benefit)

At Worcester, June 29, 30, July 1. Drawn. Headley's first century oft summer followed a lean period and prevented a threatened Worcestershire collapse. In a painstaking stay of six hours and five minutes the left hander struck twenty 4's and played a number of excellent strokes though these were isolated. Without the presence of Graveney and d'Oliveira, both on Test duty, Worcestershire, with the aid of three dropped catches, reached 302 after seven and a quarter hours. The pitch held too much pace for the Yorkshire batsmen, and Coldwell, with inswing, took five for 57 in helping his side to a lead of 122. Sharpe missed slip chances from Kenyon and Horton early in the Worcestershire second innings and these opening partners strengthened the position with a stand of 85. Kenyon, however, with an exaggerated respect for Yorkshire batting, delayed his declaration and the visitors showed no serious interest in the task set them of obtaining 295 runs in just over three hours. Taylor and Padgett, without attaining anything like the required rate of 98 runs an hour, played the bowling attractively for more than two hours in a second-wicket partnership of 140.

Worcestershire

*D. Kenyon c Sharpe b Nicholson	26	— b Trueman	41
M. J. Horton c and b Nicholson	11	— run out	52
R. G. A. Headley c Binks b Trueman	137	— b Waring	6
J. A. Ormrod c Binks b Trueman	4	— c sub b Trueman	15
D. W. Richardson c and b Nicholson	29	— not out	36
E. J. O. Hemsley c Binks b Wilson	15	— not out	3
D. N. F. Slade b Nicholson	34		
†R. Booth c Binks b Trueman	18		
N. Gifford run out	3		
L. J. Coldwell b Nicholson	5		
J. A. Flavell not out	0		
B 6, l-b 7, w 1, n-b 6	20	B 5, l-b 7, n-b 7	19
1/39 2/44 3/58 4/117 5/171 6/261 7/291 8/294 9/302	302	1/85 2/106 3/114 4/154 (4 wkts., dec.)	172

Bowling: *First Innings*—Trueman 32—6—66—3; Nicholson 31.5—9—60—5; Waring 19—5—45—0; Close 27—13—58—0; Wilson 23—15—53—1. *Second Innings*—Trueman 23—5—65—2; Nicholson 14—4—25—0; Waring 14—1—53—1; Close 1—0—10—0.

Yorkshire

K. Taylor b Coldwell	26	— c Kenyon b Gifford	86
*D. B. Close c Booth b Coldwell	10	— b Flavell	0
D. E. V. Padgett c Headley b Flavell	11	— st Booth b Slade	51
J. H. Hampshire c Hemsley b Coldwell	12	— not out	1
P. J. Sharpe c Booth b Horton	37	— not out	5
J. C. Balderstone c Richardson b Slade	19		
†J. G. Binks c Slade b Flavell	27		
F. S. Trueman b Gifford	3		
D. Wilson b Coldwell	24		
J. Waring b Coldwell	6		
A. G. Nicholson not out	0		
L-b 5	5	B 1, l-b 3, n-b 1	5
1/20 2/43 3/47 4/85 5/112 6/132 7/135 8/166 9/180	180	1/1 2/141 3/143 (3 wkts.)	148

Bowling: *First Innings*—Flavell 15.1—3—42—2; Coldwell 18—2—57—5; Slade 17—12—10—1; Gifford 14—1—51—1; Horton 14—6—15—1. *Second Innings*—Flavell 5—0—30—1; Coldwell 11—3—30—0; Slade 15—6—30—1; Horton 10—1—36—0; Gifford 9—3—17—1.

Umpires: W. H. Copson and G. H. Pope.

At Portsmouth, July 2, 4, 5. **Worcestershire drew with Hampshire.**

WORCESTERSHIRE v. NORTHAMPTONSHIRE

At Worcester, July 6, 7, 8. Drawn. In a match in which there were three current England batsmen, 42-year-old Test selector Kenyon took chief honours with his second century of the summer. After early anxiety on a pitch which helped seam bowling throughout the innings, the home captain produced many crisp drives and cuts and his fighting 103 in four hours contained eleven 4's. Headley also played the pacemen soundly for his not out 72 which contained two 6's and seven 4's. Northamptonshire were in immediate difficulties against the pace of Flavell and Brain and lost their top seven batsmen for 54. Flavell whisked out five of the first six for 22 in thirteen lively overs and Worcestershire had a lead of 133. Led by Horton with a brisk 54, they reached 211 for five declared, but with the pitch becoming increasingly placid they never appeared likely to dismiss the visitors a second time. On the other hand a victory target of 345 in six hours was never within Northamptonshire's sights. Almost an hour was lost through bad light and at the close a leisurely unbroken partnership for the fourth wicket by Reynolds and Mushtaq realised 101.

Worcestershire

*D. Kenyon c Crump b Steele	103	— c Mushtaq b Crump	9
M. J. Horton c Steele b Durose	22	— c Watts b Sully	54
J. A. Ormrod run out	15	— c Mushtaq b Sully	35
T. W. Graveney b Watts	18	— c Andrew b Sully	48
B. d'Oliveira c Steele b Bailey	2	— b Crump	26
R. G. A. Headley not out	72	— not out	17
†R. Booth c Sully b Steele	2	— not out	12
J. A. Standen c Durose b Steele	6		
N. Gifford c sub b Sully	5		
B. M. Brain c Milburn b Durose	2		
J. A. Flavell c Andrew b Durose	0		
L-b 3, n-b 2	5	B 4, l-b 4, n-b 2	10
1/45 2/74 3/115 4/126 5/176 6/182 7/196 8/231 9/252	252	1/17 2/96 3/125 4/168 5/192 (5 wkts., dec.)	211

Bowling: *First Innings*—Crump 15—4—46—0; Bailey 14—3—26—1; Durose 20.4—0—55—3; Mushtaq 12—3—28—0; Watts 15—6—22—1; Sully 13—5—28—1; Steele 13—3—42—3. *Second Innings*—Durose 12—2—47—0; Crump 17—4—46—2; Watts 6—2—17—0; Sully 17—2—72—3; Steele 4—0—17—0; Mushtaq 2—0—2—0.

Northamptonshire

C. Milburn c Ormrod b Flavell	6	— c Ormrod b Flavell	14
R. M. Prideaux c Graveney b Brain	4	— c Headley b d'Oliveira	27
D. S. Steele c Booth b Flavell	16	— b Flavell	15
B. L. Reynolds b Standen	16	— not out	74
H. Sully b Flavell	10		
Mushtaq Mohammad lbw b Flavell	0	— not out	57
P. J. Watts c d'Oliveira b Flavell	0		
B. Crump c Booth b Brain	32		
*†K. V. Andrew b Brain	14		
A. J. Durose st Booth b Gifford	12		
R. Bailey not out	7		
B 1, l-b 1	2	B 5, l-b 1	6
1/10 2/10 3/30 4/50 5/50 6/50 7/54 8/96 9/105	119	1/24 2/44 3/92 (3 wkts.)	193

Bowling: *First Innings*—Flavell 22—7—39—5; Brain 17—2—44—3; Gifford 8.5—4—7—1; Standen 7—2—16—1; d'Oliveira 3—0—11—0. *Second Innings*—Flavell 22—6—51—2; Brain 14—3—48—0; Gifford 17—7—25—0; Standen 17—6—29—0; Horton 9—3—23—0; d'Oliveira 21—15—11—1.

Umpires: A. Jepson and A. E. Fagg.

At Leicester, July 9, 11, 12. WORCESTERSHIRE beat LEICESTERSHIRE by four wickets.

At Gloucester, July 13, 14, 15. WORCESTERSHIRE drew with GLOUCESTERSHIRE.

WORCESTERSHIRE v. GLOUCESTERSHIRE

At Worcester, July 16, 18. Worcestershire won by ten wickets. In helping Worcestershire establish a lead of 115 d'Oliveira followed up his best bowling figures of six for 34 by making 80, top score of the match. He and Flavell worried Gloucestershire with lift and movement off the pitch on the first day, d'Oliveira having an afternoon spell of five for ten in fourteen overs. With the visitors' attack not nearly as menacing, d'Oliveira and Headley in an enterprising hour put on 77 before bad light ended play nearly an hour early. By then Worcestershire were within eleven runs of the lead with six wickets left. The spin of Gifford was largely responsible for Gloucestershire's undoing on the second day. The left-hander made the occasional ball turn and lift sharply, and though Nicholls held out defiantly for one and three-quarter hours and Windows struck two 6's in a last-wicket show of aggression victory was forced in the extra half hour, with a day to spare.

Gloucestershire

First Innings		Second Innings	
M. Bissex b d'Oliveira	64	— c Booth b Brain	16
C. A. Milton lbw b Flavell	42	— lbw b Flavell	10
D. Brown c Booth b d'Oliveira	5	— c Horton b Gifford	27
D. Shepherd b d'Oliveira	6	— lbw b Flavell	3
R. B. Nicholls c Booth b Flavell	5	— b Gifford	26
D. A. Allen c d'Oliveira b Flavell	1	— c Richardson b Gifford	10
*J. B. Mortimore c Booth b d'Oliveira	1	— c Richardson b Gifford	4
A. S. Brown c Headley b Flavell	1	— run out	[illegible]
A. R. Windows c Headley b d'Oliveira	3	— c Headley b d'Oliveira	28
†B. J. Meyer not out	0	— c Kenyon b Gifford	5
D. R. Smith c Brain b d'Oliveira	0	— not out	[illegible]
L-b 3	3	L-b 2	2
1/106 2/108 3/120 4/120 5/125 6/126 7/128 8/129 9/131	131	1/19 2/27 3/44 4/74 5/84 6/94 7/103 8/104 9/116	141

Bowling: *First Innings*—Flavell 22—9—34—4; Brain 9—0—44—0; d'Oliveira 26.3—11—34—6; Gifford 7—2—16—0. *Second Innings*—Flavell 13—1—26—2; Brain 16—1—40—1; d'Oliveira 19.5—4—40—1; Gifford 24—14—33—5.

Worcestershire

First Innings		Second Innings	
*D. Kenyon b A. S. Brown	28		
M. J. Horton b A. S. Brown	12	— not out	15
J. A. Ormrod c Nicholls b Allen	1		
B. d'Oliveira b Smith	80		
R. G. A. Headley c Allen b Smith	42		
D. W. Richardson c Meyer b Smith	1		
C. D. Fearnley c D. Brown b Mortimore	31	— not out	7
†R. Booth c Meyer b Allen	10		
N. Gifford lbw b Smith	16		
B. M. Brain c Mortimore b A. S. Brown	15		
J. A. Flavell not out	0		
B 2, l-b 8	10	B 8	8
1/28 2/41 3/41 4/118 5/123 6/193 7/208 8/217 9/242	246	(for no wicket)	30

Bowling: *First Innings*—Smith 28—3—95—4; A. S. Brown 29.5—8—75—3; Allen 21—11—31—2; Windows 12—3—30—0; Mortimore 7—5—5—1. *Second Innings*—Bissex 4.2—1—16—0; Mortimore 4—1—6—0.

Umpires: C. S. Elliott and R. S. Lay.

At Maidstone, July 20, 21, 22. WORCESTERSHIRE lost to KENT by 32 runs.

At The Oval, July 23, 25, 26. WORCESTERSHIRE drew with SURREY.

WORCESTERSHIRE v. SURREY

At Worcester, July 27, 28, 29. Worcestershire won by an innings and 14 runs. In conditions well suited to quick bowling Surrey were most unhappy after electing to bat. Flavell swung the ball appreciably in a heavy atmosphere and made good length balls lift spitefully off the moist turf. In helping to reduce the visitors to 91 for five by lunch, Flavell had three for 39 and an afternoon spell of four for 19 gave him seven for 58. Edwards alone played Flavell with authority, and Worcestershire passed their opponents' total with seven wickets remaining after an excellent opening partnership of 93 by Kenyon and Horton. With Surrey's weakened attack posing few problems, Worcestershire led by 143. A two-day victory looked likely when by the middle of the afternoon Surrey were 46 for the loss of their openers. Then on a pitch of unpredictable bounce, Smith and Stewart now played Flavell firmly to double the score before rain brought play to a close shortly before tea. With the pitch rejuvenated by showers, Flavell and Gifford brought about an astonishing collapse on the third morning. In one and a quarter hours Surrey lost their remaining eight wickets for 37 runs, Gifford having a final spell of three for six and Flavell four for nine to gain a match analysis of eleven for 96.

Surrey

First Innings		Second Innings	
J. H. Edrich b Carter	7	c Hemsley b d'Oliveira	27
M. J. Edwards b Gifford	54	b Carter	9
W. A. Smith lbw b Flavell	1	c Booth b Flavell	39
*M. J. Stewart lbw b Flavell	3	c Graveney b Gifford	33
R. A. E. Tindall b Flavell	26	lbw b d'Oliveira	0
S. J. Storey lbw b Flavell	16	lbw b Flavell	6
G. R. J. Roope c Richardson b Flavell	3	b Gifford	2
†A. Long c Richardson b Flavell	7	c Graveney b Flavell	2
R. Harman not out	2	c Kenyon b Flavell	0
R. D. Jackman b Flavell	4	not out	4
D. A. Marriott lbw b Carter	3	c d'Oliveira b Gifford	1
		B 4, l-b 2	6
1/11 2/14 3/26 4/91 5/91 6/109 7/114 8/119 9/123	126	1/21 2/46 3/100 4/105 5/112 6/121 7/124 8/124 9/128	129

Bowling: *First Innings*—Flavell 26—4—58—7; Carter 17.5—6—40—2; d'Oliveira 8—3—17—0; Gifford 5—4—11—1. *Second Innings*—Flavell 25—9—38—4; Carter 13—4—26—1; d'Oliveira 18—6—38—2; Gifford 10.3—3—21—3; Horton 1—1—0—0.

Worcestershire

*D. Kenyon b Storey	40
M. J. Horton lbw b Harman	46
R. G. A. Headley b Harman	25
T. W. Graveney b Marriott	31
B. d'Oliveira st Long b Storey	5
D. W. Richardson b Storey	18
E. J. O. Hemsley b Storey	3
†R. Booth lbw b Marriott	32
N. Gifford b Marriott	32
J. A. Flavell b Jackman	13
R. G. M. Carter not out	2
B 12, l-b 5, n-b 5	22
1/93 2/111 3/125 4/138 5/181 6/190 7/190 8/232 9/245	269

Bowling: Marriott 27.1—7—75—3; Jackman 12—4—28—1; Storey 33—11—65—4; Roope 13—6—41—0; Harman 14—5—38—2.

Umpires: W. E. Phillipson and A. E. Fagg.

At Birmingham, July 30, August 1, 2. WORCESTERSHIRE beat WARWICKSHIRE by three wickets.

WORCESTERSHIRE v. LEICESTERSHIRE

At Worcester, August 3, 4, 5. Leicestershire won by 60 runs. On a pitch uneven in bounce, eighteen wickets fell to seam bowling on the first day, though the wet outfield held up the start until after lunch. Leicestershire, dismissed for under 100 runs for the third successive innings, stormed back with four Worcestershire wickets for 14. Cotton claimed three for 7, but Worcestershire gained a lead of four runs, with the last man in, Flavell, lifting the ball over cover to the boundary before retiring with a damaged finger nail. Going in again Leicestershire slumped to 79 for six before Carter and Coldwell, but Constant and Lock stemmed the slide in a fighting stand of 52. Although they were weakened by Test demands, a Worcestershire victory seemed probable when Fearnley and Ormrod put on 57 to take their side to within 97 of the 160 target. On the third morning, however, the batsmen were shattered by an opening blast of six for 18 by Spencer, whose match figures were eleven for 65.

Leicestershire

M. R. Hallam b Flavell	1	— c Headley b Carter	16
M. E. Norman c Booth b Carter	17	— c and b Carter	32
B. J. Booth b Flavell	12	— lbw b Coldwell	2
C. C. Inman b Carter	8	— b Coldwell	5
P. Marner c Richardson b Flavell	20	— lbw b Carter	15
D. Constant b Carter	6	— b Gifford	44
†R. W. Tolchard lbw b Flavell	11	— b Flavell	4
*G. A. R. Lock b Coldwell	5	— lbw b Carter	36
C. T. Spencer c Booth b Coldwell	2	— not out	0
J. S. Savage c Gifford b Coldwell	8	— b Flavell	3
J. Cotton not out	0	— b Gifford	5
		N-b 1	1
1/2 2/28 3/38 4/42 5/61 6/65 7/72 8/74 9/90	90	1/23 2/30 3/42 4/63 5/72 6/79 7/131 8/143 9/154	163

Bowling: *First Innings*—Flavell 13.3—3—29—4; Coldwell 13—5—20—3; Carter 13—3—41—3. *Second Innings*—Coldwell 18—5—49—2; Carter 26—7—54—4; Flavell 26—8—46—2; Gifford 8.4—5—13—2; Horton 1—1—0—0.

Worcestershire

M. J. Horton c Norman b Cotton	7	— c Marner b Cotton	2
C. D. Fearnley lbw b Cotton	2	— lbw b Spencer	34
J. A. Ormrod lbw b Spencer	2	— lbw b Spencer	30
R. G. A. Headley c Tolchard b Cotton	2	— b Spencer	7
D. W. Richardson c Tolchard b Marner	20	— b Spencer	11
E. J. O. Hemsley b Marner	23	— lbw b Spencer	0
*†R. Booth lbw b Spencer	18	— b Spencer	2
N. Gifford c Marner b Spencer	0	— run out	1
L. J. Coldwell c Norman b Spencer	9	— c Tolchard b Spencer	8
R. G. M. Carter not out	0	— not out	0
J. A. Flavell retired hurt	5	— absent hurt	0
N-b 6	6	L-b 2, w 1, n-b 1	4
1/9 2/9 3/14 4/14 5/45 6/71 7/72 8/82 9/89	94	1/6 2/63 3/64 4/72 5/78 6/78 7/84 8/94	99

Bowling: *First Innings*—Spencer 17—4—32—4; Cotton 14.1—3—26—3; Marner 9—1—26—2; Lock 1—0—4—0. *Second Innings*—Spencer 13.3—4—33—7; Cotton 11—0—31—1; Marner 7—1—22—0; Lock 3—0—9—0.

Umpires: W. E. Phillipson and P. B. Wight.

At Ilkeston, August 6, 8, 9. WORCESTERSHIRE beat DERBYSHIRE by three runs.

At Worcester, August 10. WORCESTERSHIRE beat HAMPSHIRE by 99 runs. (See GILLETTE CUP.)

WORCESTERSHIRE *v.* DERBYSHIRE

At Kidderminster, August 13, 15, 16. Worcestershire won by seven wickets. After Derbyshire lost their first six batsmen for 103 on drying turf, T. J. P. Eyre thrashed the bowling for 88 runs in just over two hours. He struck four 6's and eleven 4's, Smith and Jackson helping him put on 97 for the last two wickets. Fearnley, an hour over his first run in opening Worcestershire's reply, was rewarded for his patience with a maiden century. His 112 occupied more than five and a half hours, but his side would have been in a bad way without the left-hander who lost five partners before Richardson, another left-hander, helped him put on 114. In hastening Derbyshire's dismissal for 188 in the second innings Gifford took six for 55 and his match figures were twelve for 146. Thus in three Derbyshire innings in eight days the left-hand spinner harvested twenty wickets. Worcestershire hit off the 135 runs for victory in two hours, Graveney's winning 6 over mid-wicket being the ninth of the match.

Derbyshire

I. W. Hall c Richardson b Gifford	21	— lbw b Gifford	47
J. R. Eyre b Gifford	15	— c Richardson b Gifford	45
M. H. Page c Booth b Gifford	30	— c Richardson b Gifford	2
J. F. Harvey b Flavell	24	— b Horton	4
M. Hill lbw b Flavell	4	— c Coldwell b Horton	19
P. E. Russell c d'Oliveira b Gifford	3	— c Richardson b Horton	12
*D. C. Morgan c Headley b Gifford	16	— b Gifford	0
T. J. P. Eyre b Flavell	88	— c Horton b Gifford	0
†R. W. Taylor b Coldwell	3	— c Richardson b Horton	11
E. Smith c Booth b Gifford	6	— b Gifford	17
A. B. Jackson not out	8	— not out	25
B 4, l-b 8	12	L-b 5, n-b 1	6
1/31 2/40 3/91 4/97 5/101 6/103 7/122 8/133 9/173	230	1/78 2/80 3/85 4/119 5/119 6/119 7/119 8/137 9/146	188

Bowling: *First Innings*—Flavell 22.4—10—60—3; Coldwell 27—9—58—1; Gifford 42—16—91—6; d'Oliveira 7—1—9—0. *Second Innings*—Flavell 6—2—16—0; Coldwell 7—2—22—0; Gifford 34.3—17—55—6; d'Oliveira 3—2—4—0; Horton 30—9—85—4.

Worcestershire

M. J. Horton b Russell	40	— b Jackson	14
C. D. Fearnley b Smith	112	— c Page b Smith	10
J. A. Ormrod c Morgan b Smith	31	— not out	43
B. d'Oliveira b Smith	0	— c Page b Morgan	28
T. W. Graveney c Morgan b Jackson	5	— not out	35
R. G. A. Headley c Taylor b Smith	12		
D. W. Richardson b Smith	56		
*†R. Booth not out	14		
N. Gifford not out	4		
B 1, l-b 10	11	B 4, w 1	5
1/48 2/109 3/109 4/116 5/149 6/263 7/270 (7 wkts., dec.)	285	1/18 2/26 3/82 (3 wkts.)	135

L. J. Coldwell and J. A. Flavell did not bat.

Bowling: *First Innings*—Jackson 25—10—38—1; Smith 45—19—102—5; T. J. P. Eyre 11—4—24—0; Russell 16—4—35—1; Morgan 27—7—75—0. *Second Innings*—Jackson 8—2—36—1; Russell 3—1—4—0; Smith 19.2—9—52—1; Morgan 14—3—38—1.

Umpires: J. Langridge and O. W. Herman.

WORCESTERSHIRE v. SOMERSET

At Worcestershire, August 17, 18, 19. *65 overs.* Somerset won by 127 runs. Kitchen, having missed a century by two runs on this ground two years previously, made his maiden hundred in just under three and a half hours. The left-hander hit thirteen 4's and with his captain, C. R. M. Atkinson, put on a splendid 126 after four men were out for 77. Somerset's 225 was the biggest total off Worcestershire's attack in their twelve matches under the experimental 65 over rule. Ormrod strove to prop a tottering Worcestershire innings with 51 not out in a score of 125 for four on the first day. Rumsey and Palmer then demolished the remaining wickets for the addition of 57. Aided by several dropped catches and a dour three-figure partnership for the third wicket by Kitchen and Burgess, Somerset struggled to 209 in 96 overs. Left a target of 253, Worcestershire were always labouring on an unpredictable pitch and, after reaching 78 for three in two and a quarter hours, collapsed. Seven wickets fell for the addition of 49 runs to the lunch score, Alley claiming three of them to finish with five for 39.

Somerset

G. Atkinson lbw b Coldwell	3	— c Booth b Carter	6
R. Virgin c Richardson b Gifford	23	— b Coldwell	12
M. Kitchen lbw b Flavell	100	— lbw b Horton	59
G. Burgess b Gifford	5	— c Booth b Flavell	69
W. E. Alley c Booth b Carter	9	— lbw b Coldwell	9
*C. R. M. Atkinson c Gifford b Coldwell	57	— c Coldwell b Horton	27
†G. Clayton c Booth b Coldwell	3	— b Gifford	2
K. E. Palmer lbw b Flavell	0	— c Richardson b Gifford	6
P. J. Robinson not out	7	— lbw b Flavell	7
B. A. Langford b Flavell	0	— b Coldwell	5
F. E. Rumsey not out	0	— not out	1
B 4, l-b 13, w 1	18	L-b 2, w 2, n-b 2	6
1/20 2/46 3/64 4/77 (9 wkts., 65 overs) 5/203 6/207 7/210 8/223 9/223	225	1/14 2/18 3/118 4/127 5/183 6/186 7/192 8/197 9/207	209

Bowling: *First Innings*—Flavell 18—2—48—3; Coldwell 16—1—58—3; Carter 16—4—63—1; Gifford 12—3—25—2; Horton 3—0—13—0. *Second Innings*—Flavell 16—3—46—2; Coldwell 19.4—2—50—3; Carter 10—2—24—1; Gifford 24—12—35—2; Horton 26—9—48—2.

Worcestershire

M. J. Horton c Clayton b C. R. M. Atkinson	2	— c Clayton b Rumsey	25
C. D. Fearnley c Alley b Rumsey	3	— lbw b Alley	37
*D. Kenyon c and b Langford	33	— c C. R. M. Atkinson b Palmer	1
J. A. Ormrod c Alley b Rumsey	52	— c and b Alley	2
R. G. A. Headley c Alley b Palmer	15	— b Alley	12
D. W. Richardson b Palmer	27	— b Rumsey	2
†R. Booth b Palmer	8	— not out	11
N. Gifford c Virgin b Palmer	7	— b Alley	2
L. J. Coldwell b Rumsey	3	— b Rumsey	11
J. A. Flavell run out	10	— run out	2
R. G. M. Carter not out	12	— c C. R. M. Atkinson b Alley	13
B 1, l-b 6, n-b 3	10	B 4, l-b 3	7
1/5 2/9 3/63 4/106 5/136 6/140 7/154 8/159 9/163	182	1/32 2/38 3/54 4/78 5/82 6/82 7/86 8/101 9/103	125

Bowling: *First Innings*—Rumsey 19.3—3—53—3; Palmer 23—2—70—4; C. R. M. Atkinson 8—2—23—1; Langford 11—3—26—1. *Second Innings*—Rumsey 18—6—34—3; Palmer 12—2—33—1; Langford 6—1—12—0; Alley 21.2—8—39—5.

Umpires: J. Langridge and H. Mellows.

At Yeovil, August 20, 22, 23. WORCESTERSHIRE beat SOMERSET by eight wickets.

At Lord's. August 24, 25. WORCESTERSHIRE beat MIDDLESEX by an innings and 41 runs.

WORCESTERSHIRE v. ESSEX

At Worcester, August 27, 29, 30. Drawn. In a grand partnership of just over three hours, Graveney and d'Oliveira lashed an Essex attack hit by injuries for 271 runs, six short of the Worcestershire fourth-wicket record. When Edmeades dismissed both in the same over and completed 100 wickets for the season, Graveney in a handsome 166, had struck one 6 and twenty-two 4's in just over four and a half hours. D'Oliveira's 126 contained two 6's and fifteen 4's. After a first day revel of 405 for six declared, Worcestershire were dealt an unkind blow by the weather. Rain shortened play to less than an hour on each of the next two days and the sharp inroads which Flavell and Coldwell made into the visitors' batting were of no avail.

Worcestershire

*D. Kenyon b Jorden	17	D. W. Richardson c Taylor b Knight	2
M. J. Horton c Taylor b Knight	53		
J. A. Ormrod c Saville b Edmeades	26	B 2, l-b 12	14
T. W. Graveney c and b Edmeades	166		——
B. d'Oliveira c Acfield b Edmeades	126	1/23 2/61 3/131 (6 wkts., dec.)	405
R. G. A. Headley not out	1	4/402 5/402 6/405	

†R Booth, N. Gifford, L. J. Coldwell and J. A. Flavell did not bat.

Bowling: Knight 21.3—2—97—2; Jorden 18—1—69—1; Edmeades 27—6—92—3; Bailey 15—1—60—0; Acfield 15—1—73—0.

Essex

G. E. Barker c Richardson b Flavell	34	G. J. Saville not out	4
M. J. Bear c Booth b Coldwell	0	B. Edmeades not out	10
*T. E. Bailey b Flavell	10	A. M. Jorden c Graveney b Flavell	6
K. W. R. Fletcher c Flavell b Coldwell	12		——
†B. Taylor b Flavell	44	1/6 2/40 3/49 4/61 5/87 (7 wkts.)	122
B. R. Knight b Flavell	2	6/97 7/108	

R. N. S. Hobbs and D. L. Acfield did not bat.

Bowling: Flavell 19—5—51—5; Coldwell 19—3—59—2; Gifford 2—0—6—0; d'Oliveira 2—2—0—0; Horton 1—0—6—0.

Umpires: R. S. Lay and H. Mellows.

WORCESTERSHIRE v. SUSSEX

At Worcester, August 31, September 1, 2. Sussex won by 31 runs. Twenty wickets fell on rain-affected turf on the first day, fifteen in under two and three-quarter hours after lunch for 88 runs. In his first five overs of the afternoon, d'Oliveira, with lift and movement off the pitch, gained four Sussex wickets for nought. The visitors hit back by whisking out seven batsmen for 30 runs in under an hour. The hostile A. Buss had four of the first five for eight runs in 32 balls and Worcestershire, for the fifth time of the summer, were all out for under 100 runs. After trailing by 68 runs, they were brought back into the game by Flavell. Following further rain, the brothers Buss were the only batsmen to play this seam bowler with any measure of certainty and accounted for 89 of the Sussex total of 113. Requiring 182 to win, Worcestershire appeared to be heading for success with Gifford and Graveney putting on 65 for the fifth wicket and getting within 68 runs of their objective. A. Buss then delivered a mortal blow when he dismissed Graveney, Richardson and Headley in the course of seven balls. In a match in which thirty-seven wickets fell to seam bowling, A. Buss and Snow each claimed nine.

Sussex

L. J. Lenham b d'Oliveira	16	— lbw b Flavell	0
M. A. Buss b d'Oliveira	27	— not out	57
K. G. Suttle lbw b d'Oliveira	32	— c Headley b Gifford	1
†J. M. Parks c Richardson b Coldwell	15	— b Flavell	5
*Nawab of Pataudi lbw b Coldwell	18	— lbw b d'Oliveira	1
D. J. Foreman b d'Oliveira	0	— lbw b Flavell	0
A. S. M. Oakman c Booth b d'Oliveira	3	— lbw b Flavell	2
M. G. Griffith c Headley b d'Oliveira	3	— c Booth b Flavell	3
A. Buss c d'Oliveira b Gifford	15	— lbw b Gifford	32
J. A. Snow not out	4	— b Flavell	8
D. L. Bates c Booth b Flavell	10	— b Flavell	0
L-b 1, n-b 1	2	L-b 4	4
1/37 2/62 3/87 4/93 5/93 6/99 7/109 8/117 9/132	145	1/17 2/25 3/37 4/53 5/79 6/80 7/83 8/95 9/109	113

Bowling: *First Innings*—Flavell 13—3—31—1; Coldwell 22—7—52—2; Gifford 9—5—15—1; d'Oliveira 26—9—40—6; Horton 1—0—5—0. *Second Innings*—Flavell 17.1—1—36—7; Coldwell 16—5—27—0; Gifford 13—10—13—2; d'Oliveira 20—7—31—1; Horton 1—0—2—0.

Worcestershire

*D. Kenyon c Griffith b Snow	1	— b A. Buss	15
M. J. Horton c Parks b A. Buss	0	— c Parks b Snow	0
J. A. Ormrod c Parks b Snow	16	— c M. A. Buss b Snow	17
T. W. Graveney c Parks b A. Buss	2	— c M. A. Buss b A. Buss	50
B. d'Oliveira c Lenham b A. Buss	0	— b A. Buss	15
R. G. A. Headley b A. Buss	7	— c Parks b A. Buss	0
D. W. Richardson c Foreman b Snow	23	— b A. Buss	0
†R. Booth b Snow	1	— not out	20
N. Gifford c Snow b Bates	17	— c Parks b Bates	21
L. J. Coldwell c A. Buss b Snow	2	— b Snow	5
J. A. Flavell not out	3	— c Oakman b Snow	3
L-b 3, w 1, n-b 1	5	L-b 3, w 1	4
1/2 2/2 3/8 4/8 5/26 6/28 7/30 8/72 9/74	77	1/1 2/17 3/46 4/49 5/114 6/120 7/120 8/121 9/146	150

Bowling: *First Innings*—Snow 13—3—28—5; A. Buss 12—5—19—4; Bates 10.5—4—20—1; Oakman 3—1—5—0. *Second Innings*—Snow 24.1—1—60—4; A. Buss 28—8—67—5; Bates 12—3—19—1; Oakman 1—1—0—0.

Umpires: R. S. Lay and G. H. Pope.

At Lord's, September 3. WORCESTERSHIRE lost to WARWICKSHIRE in the CUP FINAL by five wickets. (See GILLETTE CUP.)

YORKSHIRE

President—Sir William Worsley, Bart.

Secretary—J. H. Nash, Headingley Cricket Ground, Leeds 6

Captain—D. B. Close

P. J. Sharpe

County Badge

J. G. Binks

Although Yorkshire headed the championship table throughout the season their eventual success was in no way a runaway triumph. They seemed beyond challenge in early August with a lead of 40 points but in seven successive matches they could complete only one outright victory and when they reached Harrogate for their final engagement in the competition they found Worcestershire, also with one match to play, only six points behind.

As events turned out Worcestershire were beaten by Sussex and Yorkshire took full points from Kent, so the final margin of leadership became more convincing. Nevertheless, Yorkshire could not be described as great champions. They were beaten five times, twice by Northamptonshire, once by Sussex, Surrey and Warwickshire, and as four of the defeats were on home grounds disappointment among their supporters was inevitable.

The most outspoken complaint was against the batting, which was never impressive, and by the measure of figures could only be regarded as weak. Five players reached 1,000 runs in all matches but only Boycott and Close averaged over 30 and in few matches was an innings given the secure foundation that indicates alliance of talent and good form.

To some extent the lack of solidity was obscured by the 65-over rule which discourages constructive batsmanship, but an even more potent influence was the untrustworthy pitch on which so much of the season's cricket had to be undertaken. Yorkshire could make no complaint in this regard. The pitches on their home grounds were as unprepared as any in the country and though exceptional talent will reveal itself in any circumstances, poor pitches produce lack of assurance and consequent limitation of batting range.

As the batting was hambered so the bowling was helped by the underprepared pitches and the compulsory declarations. In all matches four bowlers, Nicholson, Trueman, Illingworth and Wilson took 100 wickets, yet there were times when the Yorkshire attack looked altogether undistinguished.

Trueman was clearly not the masterful authority of his great years and needed helpful conditions to rouse his enthusiasm for long spells. Nicholson, embarrassed for months by a protracted examination of his action (which was eventually passed as acceptable), presented late swing and unexpected pace from the pitch to be troublesome to the early batsmen of most opponents. Illingworth was usually unable to fulfil the particular obligations of the moment and though Wilson remained notably uncertain in length and direction for a bowler of his type he returned one or two remarkable analyses and, against Nottinghamshire at Worksop and Kent at Harrogate, he claimed the only Yorkshire hat-tricks of the season.

The bowling was invariably supported, indeed augmented, by enterprising fielding in which Close played the leading part expected of a captain. At either short leg or silly point he stationed himself alarmingly near to the bat and was fortunate to avoid injury, but his courage enabled him to create many spectacular catches and his example in concentration and effort was a vital factor in the winning of the championship.

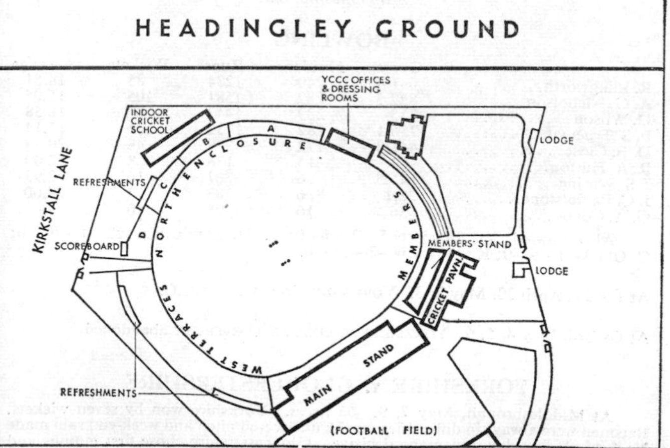

YORKSHIRE RESULTS

All First-Class Matches—Played 33, *Won* 16, *Lost* 6, *Drawn* 11, *Abandoned* 1

County Championship Matches—Played 28, *Won* 15, *Lost* 5 *Drawn* 8

COUNTY CHAMPIONSHIP AVERAGES

BATTING

	Birthplace	Mtchs.	Inns.	Not Outs	Runs	100's	Highest Inns.	Aver.
G. Boycott.....	*Fitzwilliam*	18	31	3	1097	4	164	39.17
D. B. Close....	*Rawdon*	26	43	8	1060	2	115*	30.28
D.E.V. Padgett.	*Bradford*	27	45	4	1054	0	79	25.70
J. H. Hampshire	*Thurnscoe*	26	44	4	988	0	76	24.70
R. Illingworth..	*Pudsey*	21	31	7	568	0	98*	23.66
K. Taylor......	*Huddersfield*	23	41	2	881	0	87	22.58
P. J. Sharpe....	*Shipley*	28	43	3	875	0	72	21.87
J. S. Waring....	*Ripon*	9	10	6	78	0	26	19.50
D. Wilson......	*Settle*	27	39	6	527	0	52	15.96
J.C.Balderstone	*Huddersfield*	11	13	1	183	0	64	15.25
J. G. Binks.....	*Hull*	28	37	8	383	0	42	13.20
F. S. Trueman..	*Stainton*	28	37	3	409	0	43	12.02
A. G. Nicholson	*Dewsbury*	26	25	15	120	0	41	12.00
R. A. Hutton...	*Pudsey*	3	6	1	40	0	16	8.00
B. Leadbeater..	*Leeds*	2	4	0	14	0	7	3.50
G. A. Cope....	*Leeds*	3	5	2	7	0	3*	2.33

Also batted: C. Old (*Middlesbrough*), 3 and 0.

* *Signifies not out.*

BOWLING

	Overs	Maidens	Runs	Wickets	Average
R. Illingworth..........	631.4	240	1234	85	14.51
A. G. Nicholson.........	822.3	282	1581	105	15.05
D. Wilson...............	733	289	1443	87	16.58
F. S. Trueman...........	756.1	182	1732	101	17.14
D. B. Close.............	441.3	172	979	48	20.39
R. A. Hutton............	63	15	176	8	22.00
J. S. Waring............	145.5	36	367	16	22.93
J. C. Balderstone........	28.1	6	83	3	28.00
G. A. Cope.............	36	16	98	0	—

Also bowled: G. Boycott 5—2—4—0; J. H. Hampshire 22—4—76—0; C. Old 3—1—8—0; K. Taylor 6—2—13—0.

At Lord's, April 30, May 2, 3. YORKSHIRE drew with M.C.C.

At Oxford, May 4, 5, 6. YORKSHIRE v. OXFORD UNIVERSITY abandoned.

YORKSHIRE v. GLOUCESTERSHIRE

At Middlesbrough, May 7, 9. *65 overs.* Yorkshire won by seven wickets. Batsmen were always in difficulties on the uncovered pitch and week-end rain made Yorkshire's first-day advantage decisive. Gloucestershire chose first innings and were dismissed by mid-afternoon on Saturday after an unenterprising batting display on a pitch permitting the ball to lift and turn. Yorkshire made a more forthright approach, Boycott and Taylor putting on 63 for the first wicket and Trueman and Wilson hitting boldly to secure a lead of 36 after the sixth wicket had fallen at 91. On Monday the drying pitch offered ample scope for spin bowling and Illingworth and Wilson shared the Gloucestershire wickets in an innings that never seemed likely to last long. Close, Padgett and Sharpe held brilliant catches to emphasize the bowling domination. Firm driving was the feature of two invaluable innings by Taylor for Yorkshire.

Gloucestershire

R. B. Nicholls c and b Close	15	— c Padgett b Illingworth	9
C. A. Milton c Illingworth b Trueman	0	— c Close b Wilson	13
S. E. Russell b Trueman	10	— b Illingworth	11
M. Bissex st Binks b Wilson	28	— c Sharpe b Wilson	0
D. Brown run out	13	— c Padgett b Wilson	2
D. Shepherd b Wilson	15	— c Boycott b Illingworth	0
*J. B. Mortimore c Hampshire b Illingworth	15	— not out	21
A. S. Brown c Padgett b Wilson	2	— c Close b Wilson	8
D. A. Allen not out	13	— c Trueman b Wilson	0
A. R. Windows c Close b Illingworth	5	— b Wilson	0
†B. J. Meyer c Padgett b Nicholson	12	— b Illingworth	3
B 6, l-b 1	7	B 1, w 1	2
1/7 2/15 3/42 4/64 5/85 6/86 7/102 8/103 9/110	135	1/16 2/30 3/34 4/37 5/37 6/37 7/48 8/48 9/48	69

Bowling: *First Innings*—Trueman 12—2—30—2; Nicholson 10.5—3—22—1; Close 9—4—21—1; Illingworth 15—4—36—2; Boycott 5—2—4—0; Wilson 12—6—15—3. *Second Innings*—Trueman 6—1—9—0; Nicholson 4—3—1—0; Illingworth 21—6—42—4; Wilson 19—12—15—6.

Yorkshire

G. Boycott c Meyer b Windows	23	— c Nicholls b Mortimore	3
K. Taylor b Allen	47	— not out	23
D. E. V. Padgett c Allen b Windows	6	— c A. S. Brown b Mortimore	2
J. H. Hampshire lbw b Allen	0	— c and b Mortimore	1
*D. B. Close c Milton b Allen	0	— not out	3
P. J. Sharpe c and b Allen	5		
R. Illingworth c Russell b Allen	16		
F. S. Trueman run out	18		
†J. G. Binks st Meyer b Allen	17		
D. Wilson st Meyer b Windows	33		
A. G. Nicholson not out	2		
L-b 4	4	B 2	2
1/63 2/71 3/71 4/73 5/80 6/91 7/113 8/127 9/156	171	1/13 2/27 3/29 (3 wkts.)	34

Bowling: *First Innings*—A. S. Brown 20—5—57—0; Windows 19.5—2—40—3; Allen 25—1—70—6. *Second Innings*—A. S. Brown 2—1—2—0; Windows 1—0—4—0; Mortimore 7.2—1—14—3; Allen 7—2—12—0.

Umpires: T. W. Spencer and A. E. Rhodes.

At Taunton, May 11, 12, 13. YORKSHIRE beat SOMERSET by eight wickets.

At Bristol, May 14, 16, 17. YORKSHIRE drew with GLOUCESTERSHIRE.

At Cambridge, May 18, 19, 20. YORKSHIRE beat CAMBRIDGE UNIVERSITY by eight wickets.

At Taunton, May 21. YORKSHIRE lost to SOMERSET by 40 runs. (See GILLETTE CUP.)

At Bradford, May 25, 26, 27. YORKSHIRE drew with WEST INDIES. (See WEST INDIES section.)

YORKSHIRE v. LANCASHIRE

At Headingley, May 28, 30. *65 overs.* Yorkshire won by ten wickets. A dismal batting display on the first morning placed Lancashire in a position from which they were not allowed to recover and Yorkshire completed an overwhelming victory by early evening on the second day. Trueman and Waring proved so dominant on the Saturday morning that Lancashire lost their first five wickets for 15 runs, Trueman's opening spell of 11 overs bringing him four wickets for 7 runs. Bowling at fast-medium pace with admirable control of length and swing, he was scarcely challenged by a recognizable stroke from the hesitant batsmen. Sterner opposition was raised from the Lancashire bowlers and Yorkshire were able to score only 165 runs from 61 overs by close of play but on Whit Monday morning they added 31 before compulsory declaration and by lunch time Lancashire, again batting feebly, had lost five second-innings wickets. Knox and Lever stayed together for nearly an hour and a half but after Knox had been brilliantly caught, left-handed in the gully, Waring hurried the match to its end by taking the last five wickets in succession with accurate fast-medium bowling. Attendances in warm, sunny weather were 8,000 on Saturday and 16,000 on Monday.

Lancashire

G. Pullar c Sharpe b Trueman	2	— c Sharpe b Waring	4
D. M. Green c Binks b Trueman	3	— b Trueman	1
G. K. Knox c Binks b Waring	1	— c Illingworth b Waring	44
R. Entwistle run out	13	— c Binks b Waring	8
H. Pilling b Trueman	0	— b Trueman	1
D. Lloyd b Trueman	0	— c Boycott b Wilson	8
P. Lever b Waring	21	— b Waring	38
†K. Goodwin c Padgett b Wilson	2	— b Waring	4
K. Higgs not out	8	— not out	13
T. Greenhough b Trueman	3	— b Waring	9
*J. B. Statham b Waring	4	— c Illingworth b Waring	10
		L-b 4	4
1/5 2/6 3/6 4/11 5/15 6/30 7/32 8/43 9/52	57	1/2 2/10 3/28 4/29 5/44 6/88 7/107 8/112 9/124	144

Bowling: *First Innings*—Trueman 14—6—18—5; Waring 13.5—7—23—3; Close 6—3—8—0; Wilson 5—4—2—1; Illingworth 5—3—6—0. *Second Innings*—Trueman 13—1—26—2; Waring 21.3—8—40—7; Close 7—4—25—0; Wilson, 15—8—28—1; Illingworth 22—15—21—0.

Yorkshire

G. Boycott b Higgs	6		
K. Taylor b Greenhough	24		
D. E. V. Padgett c Knox b Greenhough	26		
J. H. Hampshire b Lever	21		
*D. B. Close not out	48		
P. J. Sharpe lbw b Higgs	26		
R. Illingworth c Greenhough b Statham	10		
†J. G. Binks run out	9	— not out	4
F. S. Trueman c Knox b Statham	4		
D. Wilson c Green b Higgs	8	— not out	2
J. Waring not out	5		
L-b 9	9		
1/13 2/47 3/76 (9 wkts., 65 overs) 4/78 5/126 6/153 7/177 8/181 9/189	196	(no wkt.)	6

Bowling: *First Innings*—Statham 13—2—52—2; Higgs 18—5—62—3; Greenhough 20—5—41—2; Lever 14—1—32—1. *Second Innings*—Green 1—0—2—0; Lloyd 0.2—0—4—0.

Umpires: A. E. Rhodes and O. W. Herman.

At Leicester, June 1, 2, 3. YORKSHIRE beat LEICESTERSHIRE by seven wickets.

At Lord's, June 4, 6, 7. YORKSHIRE drew with MIDDLESEX.

At Birmingham, June 8, 9, 10. YORKSHIRE beat WARWICKSHIRE by eight wickets.

At Chesterfield, June 11, 13. YORKSHIRE beat DERBYSHIRE by an innings and 15 runs.

YORKSHIRE v. HAMPSHIRE

At Bradford, June 15, 16, 17. *65 overs.* Drawn. With Hampshire leading by 112 runs and having six wickets in hand, not a ball could be bowled on the third day. Hampshire gained first-innings points through masterful bowling by Shackleton, White and Cottam, who had reduced Yorkshire to 87 for seven in 37 overs when bad light stopped play on the first evening. Batsmen were never at home on a damp, untrustworthy pitch and the outstanding innings of the match was played by Reed, who hit one 6 and nine 4's as a lead to the Hampshire first innings. When Hampshire batted a second time Reed was ill and could not open the innings and deliberately defensive batting produced only 75 runs in two and a half hours before heavy rain ended the second day's cricket in mid-afternoon.

Hampshire

*R. E. Marshall b Close	12	— c Cope b Wilson	16
B. L. Reed c Binks b Nicholson	59		
H. Horton c Cope b Close	34	— lbw b Nicholson	3
G. L. Keith c Hampshire b Trueman	19	— c Binks b Wilson	13
R. G. Caple c Sharpe b Close	0	— b Wilson	4
P. J. Sainsbury c Wilson b Nicholson	3	— not out	25
†B. S. V. Timms lbw b Nicholson	1	— not out	8
K. J. Wheatley c Cope b Nicholson	21		
D. W. White not out	0		
D. Shackleton not out	0		
L-b 1, n-b 1	2	B 3, n-b 3	6
1/24 2/99 3/121 4/121 5/126 6/127 7/151 8/151 (8 wkts., 65 overs)	151	1/27 2/34 3/34 4/49 (4 wkts.)	75

R. M. Cottam did not bat.

Bowling: *First Innings*—Trueman 19—5—54—1; Nicholson 24—4—52—4; Close 21—10—39—3; Taylor 1—0—4—0. *Second Innings*—Trueman 9—4—21—0; Nicholson 14—7—13—1; Wilson 23—12—16—3; Cope 5—2—19—0.

Yorkshire

K. Taylor lbw b Shackleton	6
D. E. V. Padgett c Horton b Cottam	20
P. J. Sharpe c Keith b Shackleton	0
J. H. Hampshire b Cottam	25
*D. B. Close c Timms b Cottam	4
J. C. Balderstone b Shackleton	0
†J. G. Binks c Keith b Shackleton	1
F. S. Trueman c Reed b White	29
D. Wilson c Sainsbury b White	8
A. G. Nicholson not out	5
G. A. Cope c Keith b White	2
N-b 4	4
1/5 2/13 3/43 4/51 5/56 6/57 7/66 8/90 9/100	104

Bowling—Shackleton 18—10—31—4; White 10—0—30—3; Cottam 15—3—39—3.

Umpires: C. G. Pepper and W. E. Phillipson.

YORKSHIRE v. SUSSEX

At Headingley, June 18, 20. *65 overs.* Sussex won by 22 runs. Yorkshire met their first championship defeat of the season in extra time on the second day. They were 29 runs in arrears on first innings and though they gave themselves a chance of victory by dismissing Sussex for 121 on the second day their batting proved unequal to the final task. Sussex scored readily on the Saturday and had lost only four wickets at the compulsory declaration, Pataudi and Lenham each hitting nine boundaries and Griffith maintaining the policy of enterprise on a pitch that played easily. Yorkshire had lost four wickets for 97 in 38 overs by the close, but on Monday morning Wilson and Nicholson added 44 in a last-wicket partnership and Illingworth and Close, finding response to their off-breaks, kept the match balanced. Yorkshire batted uneasily in the fourth innings, losing the first three wickets for 10 runs to Snow and Buss. Sharpe and Illingworth checked the fast bowlers, but again the innings collapsed to 94 for eight and after a determined stand by Binks and Wilson, Snow returned to take the last two wickets at 128.

Sussex

K. G. Suttle b Trueman	1	— c and b Close	31
L. J. Lenham c Padgett b Trueman	80	— lbw b Close	10
*Nawab of Pataudi c Sharpe b Nicholson	55	— lbw b Illingworth	14
M. G. Griffith not out	57	— st Binks b Close	0
P. J. Graves c Sharpe b Wilson	19	— b Close	8
D. J. Foreman not out	10	— not out	24
A. S. M. Oakman (did not bat)		— c Trueman b Illingworth	1
P. R. V. Ledden (did not bat)		— b Illingworth	28
A. Buss (did not bat)		— b Illingworth	0
†T. Gunn (did not bat)		— c Trueman b Illingworth	0
J. A. Snow (did not bat)		— c Wilson b Nicholson	0
B 2, l-b 5, n-b 2	9	L-b 5	5
1/2 2/92 3/161 4/192 (4 wkts., 65 overs)	231	1/42 2/47 3/51 4/57 5/67 6/68 7/116 8/116 9/120	121

Bowling: *First Innings*—Trueman 12—1—38—2; Nicholson 19—6—52—1; Illingworth 20—3—71—0; Wilson 14—2—61—1. *Second Innings*—Trueman 3—0—12—0; Nicholson 3.2—2—4—1; Illingworth 24—9—42—5; Wilson 10—4—20—0; Close 14—5—38—4.

Yorkshire

*D. B. Close c Gunn b Buss	28	— c Griffith b Buss	0
K. Taylor lbw b Snow	3	— c Pataudi b Suttle	9
D. E. V. Padgett b Snow	10	— b Snow	2
J. H. Hampshire c Graves b Snow	34	— b Snow	3
P. J. Sharpe c Ledden b Oakman	19	— lbw b Snow	26
R. Illingworth b Buss	21	— c Suttle b Oakman	32
J. C. Balderstone c Oakman b Buss	9	— b Suttle	1
F. S. Trueman lbw b Snow	23	— c Graves b Suttle	7
†J. G. Binks c Gunn b Snow	5	— not out	26
D. Wilson c Foreman b Buss	31	— b Snow	10
A. G. Nicholson not out	11	— b Snow	0
B 2, l-b 6	8	— B 10, l-b 2	12
1/14 2/32 3/48 4/80 5/114 6/126 7/127 8/155 9/158	202	1/2 2/2 3/10 4/65 5/81 6/82 7/82 8/94 9/128	128

Bowling: *First Innings*—Snow 23—4—79—5; Buss 26.1—6—71—4; Ledden 4—0—20—0; Oakman 9—3—24—1. *Second Innings*—Snow 18.4—4—41—5; Buss 6—1—20—1; Oakman 14—5—37—1; Suttle 8—2—18—3.

Umpires—T. W. Spencer and W. H. Copson.

YORKSHIRE v. DERBYSHIRE

At Sheffield, June 25, 27, 28. Yorkshire won by 10 wickets. Although rain prevented any play on the second day feeble Derbyshire batting permitted Yorkshire to complete victory by lunch time on Tuesday. In the whole match no Derbyshire batsman reached an individual score of 20. On the Saturday, when Derbyshire batted first after winning the toss, completion of an innings by each side left Yorkshirr 64 runs ahead, but seven wickets had been lost before they secured the lead, and only Illingworth's resolution and Trueman's later hitting checked the bowling domination of the day in conditions always favouring swing. After the rain Derbyshire had little chance to recover lost ground and they avoided an innings defeat only when their last batsmen were together. In the match Nicholson conceded no more than 24 runs from 39 overs, though in the second innings he had to bowl at reduced pace because of a strained leg.

Derbyshire

First Innings		Second Innings	
I. W. Hall c Sharpe b Nicholson	1	— c Illingworth b Nicholson	6
J. F. Harvey b Trueman	0	— b Trueman	0
M. H. Page lbw b Trueman	8	— c Close b Illingworth	13
H. L. Johnson b Nicholson	10	— lbw b Illingworth	2
M. Hill c Hampshire b Trueman	4	— b Nicholson	12
*D. C. Morgan c Close b Nicholson	2	— b Nicholson	1
†R. W. Taylor b Nicholson	0	— st Binks b Wilson	16
T. J. P. Eyre not out	15	— c Binks b Trueman	2
E. Smith c Wilson b Close	12	— c Padgett b Trueman	2
H. J. Rhodes b Nicholson	19	— not out	5
A. B. Jackson b Close	12	— c Close b Nicholson	0
N-b 2	2	B 1, l-b 4, n-b 1	6
1/1 2/1 3/15 4/19 5/26 6/26 7/28 8/44 9/66	85	1/1 2/19 3/21 4/34 5/36 6/36 7/49 8/53 9/62	65

Bowling: *First Innings*—Trueman 20—5—61—3; Nicholson 21—12—12—5; Close 7.4—3—10—2. *Second Innings*—Trueman 9—3—15—3; Nicholson 17.4—11—12—4; Illingworth 17—6—32—2; Wilson 2—2—0—1.

Yorkshire

First Innings		Second Innings	
G. Boycott c Page b Rhodes	5	— not out	0
*D. B. Close c Hill b Jackson	10		
D. E. V. Padgett c Harvey b Rhodes	8		
J. H. Hampshire b Jackson	10		
P. J. Sharpe c Page b Rhodes	9		
R. Illingworth b Jackson	28		
J. C. Balderstone b Morgan	5		
†J. G. Binks c Hall b Eyre	11		
F. S. Trueman c Hill b Morgan	43		
D. Wilson c Page b Morgan	6	— not out	2
A. G. Nicholson not out	1		
B 6, l-b 5, n-b 2	13		
1/12 2/21 3/30 4/43 5/55 6/70 7/78 8/99 9/141	149	(no wkt.)	2

Bowling: *First Innings*—Jackson 18—3—35—3; Rhodes 17—7—31—3; Eyre 9—2—38—1; Morgan 11.3—4—32—3. *Second Innings*—Jackson 0.1—0—2—0.

Umpires: H. Mellows and A. E. Fagg.

At Worcester, June 29, 30, July 1. YORKSHIRE drew with WORCESTERSHIRE.

YORKSHIRE v. SOMERSET

At Sheffield, July 2, 4, 5. Yorkshire won by 49 runs. Yorkshire made hard work of winning after batting through most of the first day when Rumsey had to retire with injury and could not bowl again in the match. Somerset, batting mainly in poor light, were 99 behind on the first innings but countered by taking seven Yorkshire wickets for 85 in the evening of the second day, Palmer and C. R. M. Atkinson bowling steadily to meet attempts to force the pace. Somerset were left with more than four hours to bat and Virgin and Kitchen gave them hope of victory with a second-wicket partnership of 58 but Yorkshire were subsequently held up only by Palmer and C. R. M. Atkinson.

Yorkshire

K. Taylor b Rumsey	24	— run out	1
P. J. Sharpe lbw b Rumsey	13	— c Clayton b Palmer	13
D. E. V. Padgett lbw b Palmer	48	— c Kitchen b C. R. M. Atkinson	5
J. H. Hampshire c Virgin b Robinson	22	— c Virgin b C. R. M. Atkinson	25
*D. B. Close c Clayton b Palmer	53	— c sub b C. R. M. Atkinson	24
J. C. Balderstone c Clarkson b Robinson	25	— b C. R. M. Atkinson	4
†J. G. Binks c Clayton b Palmer	0	— c Clayton b C. R. M. Atkinson	1
F. S. Trueman c Langford b Robinson	14	— b Palmer	9
D. Wilson c Clayton b Palmer	39	— c Clayton b Palmer	8
J. Waring not out	13	— not out	4
A. G. Nicholson b C. R. M. Atkinson	3	— c Virgin b Palmer	9
B 1, l-b 9, n-b 3	13	L-b 1	1
1/31 2/40 3/95 4/150 5/188 6/190 7/210 8/210 9/262	267	1/9 2/14 3/30 4/68 5/69 6/71 7/74 8/89 9/92	104

Bowling: *First Innings*—Rumsey 15—3—22—2; Palmer 26—10—47—4; C. R. M. Atkinson 15.1—7—33—1; Langford 36—17—87—0; Robinson 24—8—65—3. *Second Innings*—Palmer 21—2—52—4; C. R. M. Atkinson 20—3—51—5.

Somerset

G. Atkinson c Trueman b Wilson	5	— c Padgett b Trueman	4
R. Virgin b Nicholson	45	— c Sharpe b Trueman	31
†G. Clayton c Sharpe b Trueman	11	— b Balderstone	0
M. Kitchen c Nicholson b Wilson	37	— lbw b Close	30
A. Clarkson c Padgett b Wilson	0	— c Wilson b Nicholson	3
W. E. Alley b Nicholson	13	— b Wilson	2
*C. R. M. Atkinson c Binks b Trueman	0	— c Taylor b Wilson	47
K. E. Palmer b Trueman	3	— lbw b Nicholson	26
P. J. Robinson b Waring	22	— c Trueman b Balderstone	2
B. A. Langford c Trueman b Nicholson	3	— b Wilson	6
F. E. Rumsey not out	18	— not out	0
B 4, l-b 4, n-b 3	11	L-b 2, n-b 1	3
1/12 2/32 3/94 4/95 5/111 6/112 7/118 8/120 9/139	168	1/7 2/65 3/68 4/68 5/78 6/131 7/132 8/148 9/154	154

Bowling *First Innings*—Trueman 25—6—57—3; Nicholson 24—9—29—3; Close 12—4—23—0; Wilson 15—5—27—3; Waring 5.3—0—21—1. *Second Innings*—Trueman 12—5—19—2; Nicholson 17—4—29—2; Waring 3—0—12—0; Close 14—7—25—1; Wilson 25—7—48—3; Balderstone 7.1—1—18—2.

Umpires: G. H. Pope and A. E. Rhodes.

YORKSHIRE v. ESSEX

At Bradford, July 6, 7, 8. *65 overs.* Yorkshire won by 139 runs. Averaging more than four runs an over to the compulsory declaration, Yorkshire established a first-day advantage that was never lost, though rain had prevented a start to the match until after lunch. Essex made no challenge for first-innings lead and were faced with the possibility of following-on when their eighth wicket had fallen at 92. Bailey's patient defence and determination by Jorden enabled the indignity to be avoided, but Trueman, bowling at fast-medium pace, finished with eight wickets for 37 runs—a return among the best of his career. Yorkshire declared on the second evening with a lead of 261 and had taken three Essex wickets by the close, but on the last morning Fletcher, Bailey and Cass prevented a rout. Knight, injured in the field, could not bowl after the first afternoon.

Yorkshire

G. Boycott lbw b Knight	28	— c Hobbs b Bailey	23
H. Taylor b Bailey	55	— b Edmeades	5
D. E. V. Padgett c Fletcher b Knight	8	— not out	44
J. H. Hampshire c Taylor b Edmeades	35	— lbw b Jorden	42
*D. B. Close run out	58		
P. J. Sharpe c Taylor b Bailey	47		
F. S. Trueman c Jorden b Bailey	1		
D. Wilson b Edmeades	1		
J. C. Balderstone not out	10		
†J. G. Binks not out	6		
B 11, l-b 2, n-b 1	14	B 4, l-b 5	9
1/34 2/44 3/114 (8 wkts., 65 overs)	263	1/26 2/32 (3 wkts., dec.)	123
4/161 5/221 6/240 7/242 8/252		3/123	

A. G. Nicholson did not bat.

Bowling: *First Innings*—Knight 14—1—40—2; Jorden 11—0—52—0; Edmeades 18—1—77—2; Bailey 19—2—67—3; East 3—0—13—0. *Second Innings*—Jorden 6.5—0—26—1; Knight 0.1—0—0—0; Bailey 15—5—27—1; Edmeades 14—2—38—1; Hobbs 5—0—23—0.

Essex

G. E. Barker lbw b Trueman	4	— lbw b Trueman	0
G. J. Saville c Binks b Trueman	4	— c Binks b Nicholson	1
†B. Taylor b Trueman	13	— c Binks b Trueman	4
K. W. R. Fletcher c Binks b Trueman	8	— st Binks b Close	35
B. R. Knight run out	0	— c Sharpe b Nicholson	0
*T. E. Bailey not out	31	— b Nicholson	23
G. R. Cass lbw b Close	11	— c Taylor b Close	24
B. Edmeades c Wilson b Trueman	20	— c Close b Nicholson	5
R. N. S. Hobbs b Trueman	2	— lbw b Nicholson	17
A. M. Jorden b Trueman	15	— c Hampshire b Nicholson	0
R. East b Trueman	1	— not out	9
B 5, l-b 6, n-b 5	16	L-b 1, n-b 3	4
1/5 2/21 3/29 4/31 5/38	125	1/0 2/3 3/5 4/18 5/48	122
6/62 7/87 8/92 9/123		6/89 7/89 8/95 9/102	

Bowling: *First Innings*—Trueman 23.2—7—37—8; Nicholson 24—11—35—0; Close 10—6—20—1; Wilson 7—1—17—0. *Second Innings*—Trueman 15—1—30—2; Nicholson 19.3—11—32—6; Close 13—5—27—2; Wilson 9—4—11—0; Balderstone 5—2—18—0.

Umpires: F. Jakeman and H. Yarnold.

At Hove, July 9, 11, 12. YORKSHIRE drew with SUSSEX.

YORKSHIRE v. NORTHAMPTONSHIRE

At Headingley, July 13, 14, 15. *65 overs.* Northamptonshire won by 66 runs. Yorkshire were 113 for three with 24 overs to come at the end of the first day but the remainder of their first innings was controlled by Lightfoot and they took the lead only when their last batsmen were together. Lightfoot, bowling at medium pace, with admirable accuracy, conceded only 25 runs from 14 overs and took seven wickets, six of them on the second morning. Milburn began the Northamptonshire second innings by scoring 40 of the first 41 runs from the bat and when he was caught at short leg he had hit two 6's and seven 4's. Northamptonshire were only 109 ahead when their sixth wicket fell, but Watts and Crump put on 52 and Yorkshire, needing 190 in the last innings, lost Boycott and Taylor before close of play on Thursday. Hampshire and Close stayed together for an hour on the last morning but on a deteriorating pitch the bowling could not be mastered. Reynolds and Hampshire played notable innings in the earlier stages of the match.

Northamptonshire

First Innings		Second Innings	
C. Milburn c Trueman b Nicholson	10	c Hampshire b Nicholson	58
R. Wills c Close b Wilson	14	lbw b Nicholson	1
D. S. Steele c Sharpe b Trueman	9	b Wilson	10
B. L. Reynolds c Sharpe b Nicholson	72	b Nicholson	0
Mushtaq Mohammad c Binks b Trueman	4	b Illingworth	7
P. J. Watts c Binks b Wilson	28	c Sharpe b Wilson	39
A. Lightfoot b Close	17	run out	4
B. Crump c Trueman b Nicholson	4	lbw b Trueman	36
H. Sully c Trueman b Nicholson	4	b Illingworth	4
*†K. V. Andrew not out	3	c Sharpe b Trueman	11
A. J. Durose c Sharpe b Trueman	0	not out	0
B 2, l-b 3, n-b 4	9	B 10, l-b 8, n-b 2	20
1/16 2/29 3/46 4/62 5/116 6/155 7/161 8/169 9/169	174	1/47 2/78 3/78 4/82 5/102 6/110 7/162 8/175 9/181	190

Bowling: *First Innings*—Trueman 19.4—5—43—3; Wilson 12—4—35—2; Nicholson 25—5—66—4; Close 8—2—21—1. *Second Innings*—Trueman 15.4—5—40—2; Nicholson 24—8—33—3; Wilson 19—6—41—2; Illingworth 21—8—56—2.

Yorkshire

First Innings		Second Innings	
G. Boycott b Crump	2	c Watts b Crump	6
K. Taylor c Milburn b Durose	9	b Crump	9
D. E. V. Padgett c Andrew b Lightfoot	30	c Milburn b Lightfoot	19
J. H. Hampshire st Andrew b Lightfoot	76	lbw b Sully	26
P. J. Sharpe c Milburn b Lightfoot	4	c Wills b Watts	11
*D. B. Close c Crump b Lightfoot	9	c Andrew b Watts	32
R. Illingworth c Durose b Crump	29	lbw b Sully	1
F. S. Trueman c Durose b Lightfoot	2	c Mushtaq b Sully	0
D. Wilson c Durose b Lightfoot	2	not out	0
†J. G. Binks c Crump b Lightfoot	2	c Milburn b Sully	11
A. G. Nicholson not out	0	b Watts	0
L-b 7, w 1, n-b 2	10	B 1, l-b 7	8
1/9 2/15 3/109 4/115 5/125 6/158 7/162 8/167 9/171	175	1/18 2/27 3/50 4/52 5/101 6/112 7/113 8/119 9/123	123

Bowling: *First Innings*—Crump 23.4—3—63—2; Durose 11—1—47—1; Watts 10—4—16—0; Lightfoot 14—5—25—7; Mushtaq 2—0—11—0; Sully 1—0—3—0. *Second Innings*—Crump 16—5—29—2; Durose 6—1—14—0; Steele 3—0—9—0; Watts 11.5—3—25—3; Sully 11—4—23—4; Lightfoot 8—1—15—1.

Umpires: W. H. Copson and L. H. Gray.

YORKSHIRE v. NOTTINGHAMSHIRE

At Sheffield, July 16, 18, 19. *65 overs.* Yorkshire won by 229 runs. Yorkshire never lost the advantage created in an opening partnership of 135 by Boycott and Sharpe on the first day and they had completed victory before lunch on the third morning. Although Nottinghamshire played out their 65 overs in the first innings they could not score at a rate to bring them within reach of the Yorkshire total and Bolus alone showed confidence against the containing bowling. His dismissal early on the last day was prelude to the final surrender of batting weakened through the absence of Moore, who split his hand in a fielding accident. Boycott completed two separate centuries in a match for the first time in his career. His second innings was notably more laborious than his first and in both he was indebted to Nottinghamshire failures in catching.

Yorkshire

G. Boycott run out	103	— c Murray b Taylor	105
P. J. Sharpe c Hill b Forbes	50	— c White b Forbes	32
D. E. V. Padgett c sub b Stead	52	— run out	39
J. H. Hampshire c Smedley b Stead	13	— c Smedley b Stead	55
D. Wilson c White b Forbes	0		
*D. B. Close c Swetman b Forbes	7	— not out	8
R. Illingworth run out	2	— not out	2
J. C. Balderstone c Murray b Forbes	4		
†J. G. Binks c Murray b Forbes	0		
F. S. Trueman not out	0		
L-b 2, n-b 1	3	L-b 1, n-b 1	2
1/135 2/182 3/202 (9 wkts., 65 overs) 4/208 5/228 6/228 7/234 8/234 9/234	234	1/77 2/167 (4 wkts., dec.) 3/200 4/240	243

A. G. Nicholson did not bat.

Bowling: *First Innings*—Forbes 25—2—85—5; Stead 21—2—76—2; Taylor 14—1—47—0; White 5—0—23—0. *Second Innings*—Forbes 20—3—41—1; Stead 12—1—30—1; Gillhouley 33—9—95—0; White 13—5—37—0; Taylor 13—1—38—1.

Nottinghamshire

*N. Hill c Binks b Trueman	13	— lbw b Trueman	14
M. Taylor c Illingworth b Trueman	11	— lbw b Trueman	9
J. B. Bolus run out	90	— c Close b Nicholson	10
D. L. Murray c Trueman b Close	10	— c Binks b Trueman	4
M. J. Smedley c Illingworth b Nicholson	4	— c Binks b Illingworth	12
R. A. White c Illingworth b Trueman	11	— b Wilson	10
†R. Swetman b Nicholson	11	— c Binks b Wilson	4
K. Gillhouley b Nicholson	2	— b Illingworth	4
C. Forbes not out	1	— c Balderstone b Nicholson	0
B. Stead not out	0	— not out	9
H. I. Moore (did not bat)		— absent hurt	0
L-b 2, w 1, n-b 7	10	L-b 7, w 1, n-b 1	9
1/24 2/30 3/65 4/87 (8 wkts., 65 overs) 5/126 6/149 7/155 8/162	163	1/25 2/32 3/42 4/44 5/67 6/67 7/76 8/76 9/85	85

Bowling: *First Innings*—Trueman 19—2—52—3; Nicholson 31—6—76—3; Close 15—6—25—1. *Second Innings*—Trueman 11—3—24—3; Nicholson 11.1—4—19—2; Illingworth 11—6—12—2; Wilson 11—4—21—2.

Umpires: T. W. Spencer and J. Arnold.

YORKSHIRE v. MIDDLESEX

At Sheffield, July 23, 25, 26. Yorkshire won by 120 runs. After losing first-innings points, Yorkshire achieved an astonishing victory by taking the last eight Middlesex wickets in less than an hour on the third afternoon. Middlesex were making no attempt to score the 235 runs they needed and had refused many scoring opportunities, to the irritation of the few vociferous spectators, before Wilson stirred Yorkshire's dying hopes by dismissing Clark. With only a possible hour remaining Parfitt, well-set, skied a catch into the long field and in the same over Radley, playing no stroke, was lbw. Yorkshire immediately crowded the batsmen with an attacking field and Wilson and Illingworth, who had failed to confuse the earlier batsmen on a wearing pitch, became irrepressible. Having instigated their own collapse, Middlesex were unable to control it. During the first two days the match was evenly fought, Hampshire and Clark playing admirable first innings.

Yorkshire

G. Boycott c Clifton b Price	4	— run out	53
K. Taylor lbw b Price	10	— c sub b Latchman	33
D. E. V. Padgett b Price	9	— c Hooker b Titmus	17
J. H. Hampshire c Radley b Titmus	78	— c Titmus b Price	16
*D. B. Close lbw b Latchman	29	— b Price	22
P. J. Sharpe b Titmus	42	— c Hooker b Price	12
R. Illingworth c Hooker b Latchman	2	— c Radley b Titmus	32
†J. G. Binks c Hooker b Titmus	8	— b Price	1
F. S. Trueman c Russell b Titmus	16	— c Clark b Titmus	29
D. Wilson not out	7	— c Parfitt b Price	9
A. G. Nicholson c Clifton b Titmus	3	— not out	9
B 4, l-b 2	6	B 1, l-b 6	7
1/8 2/17 3/40 4/131 5/139 6/149 7/181 8/203 9/204	214	1/81 2/105 3/107 4/122 5/147 6/169 7/177 8/222 9/222	240

Bowling: *First Innings*—Price 17—4—32—3; Hooker 16—6—45—0; Titmus 26.1—10—63—5; Bick 11—3—28—0; Latchman 16—3—35—2; Parfitt 3—1—5—0. *Second Innings*—Price 30.3—7—76—5; Hooker 19—3—54—0; Titmus 28—9—76—3; Latchman 8—2—27—1.

Middlesex

W. E. Russell c Hampshire b Trueman	17	— c Sharpe b Trueman	0
M. J. Harris lbw b Nicholson	1	— b Wilson	23
P. H. Parfitt c Sharpe b Wilson	15	— c Illingworth b Wilson	42
E. A. Clark c Close b Nicholson	71	— lbw b Wilson	21
C. T. Radley c Hampshire b Close	30	— lbw b Wilson	0
*F. J. Titmus not out	37	— c Hampshire b Illingworth	3
R. W. Hooker lbw b Trueman	0	— not out	10
D. A. Bick c Close b Trueman	3	— c Sharpe b Wilson	1
H. C. Latchman c Boycott b Nicholson	17	— lbw b Illingworth	5
†E. G. Clifton c Sharpe b Close	4	— c Close b Wilson	0
J. S. E. Price b Trueman	6	— b Trueman	0
B 11, l-b 4, n-b 4	19	L-b 5, n-b 4	9
1/18 2/20 3/70 4/151 5/151 6/151 7/159 8/198 9/214	220	1/0 2/44 3/85 4/94 5/94 6/102 7/103 8/108 9/109	114

Bowling: *First Innings*—Trueman 23—5—51—4; Nicholson 32—15—43—3; Wilson 22—8—52—1; Illingworth 18—9—31—0; Close 8—2—24—2. *Second Innings*—Trueman 8.1—4—11—2; Nicholson 7—3—14—0; Close 6—6—0—0; Wilson 14—6—22—6; Illingworth 22—10—37—2; Hampshire 6—2—21—0.

Umpires: C. G. Pepper and C. S. Elliott.

At Worksop, July 27, 28, 29. YORKSHIRE beat NORTHAMPTONSHIRE by ten wickets.

At Manchester, July 30, August 1, 2. YORKSHIRE beat LANCASHIRE by 12 runs.

At Portsmouth, August 3, 4, 5. YORKSHIRE drew with HAMPSHIRE.

At Leeds, August 4, 5, 6, 8. WEST INDIES beat ENGLAND in the Fourth Test by an innings and 55 runs. (See WEST INDIES section.)

At Leyton, August 6, 8, 9. YORKSHIRE drew with ESSEX.

YORKSHIRE v. SURREY

At Bradford, August 13, 15, 16. *65 overs.* Surrey won by 21 runs. No play was possible on the Saturday because of heavy rain but in the sunny weather of Monday and Tuesday four innings were completed to leave Surrey with the victory they had anticipated after being favoured by winning the toss. The bowling figures were flattering because the pitch, damp underneath and quickly broken on the surface, made orthodox batting virtually impracticable. The good length ball, even at medium pace, frequently lifted shoulder high. Jefferson and Storey made best use of the conditions, sharing all the Yorkshire wickets. The outstanding innings were played by Edwards and Hampshire but their success was inevitably dependent on errors in the field and the excitement in the progress of the match had to compensate for the limited technical merit in the cricket.

Surrey

J. H. Edrich c Sharpe b Close	33	— lbw b Close	11
M. J. Edwards c Hampshire b Nicholson	53	— b Illingworth	29
W. A. Smith c Boycott b Illingworth	24	— c Boycott b Close	11
K. F. Barrington b Close	33	— b Illingworth	4
S. J. Storey c and b Close	14	— not out	13
R. I. Jefferson b Nicholson	5	— c Close b Nicholson	13
*M. J. Stewart c Binks b Close	3	— c Trueman b Illingworth	6
P. I. Pocock c Taylor b Close	3	— b Nicholson	0
†A. Long b Close	0	— c Sharpe b Illingworth	1
R. Harman not out	5	— c Close b Nicholson	0
R. D. Jackman not out	5	— c Binks b Nicholson	0
L-b 5, n-b 6	11	B 6, l-b 2, n-b 2	10
1/72 2/113 3/120 (9 wkts., 65 overs)	189	1/40 2/42 3/46 4/64 5/78	98
4/145 5/164 6/172 7/177 8/177 9/182		6/96 7/96 8/97 9/98	

Bowling: *First Innings*—Trueman 10—1—33—0; Nicholson 22—7—37—2; Waring 4—0—19—0; Close 14—3—47—6; Wilson 8—3—20—0; Illingworth 7—1—22—1. *Second Innings*—Trueman 5—2—7—0; Nicholson 12—5—19—4; Close 10—4—22—2; Illingworth 10—2—37—4; Wilson 2—1—3—0.

Yorkshire

G. Boycott c Stewart b Jefferson	11	— c Edwards b Jefferson	5
K. Taylor run out	13	— c Edwards b Jefferson	4
P. J. Sharpe b Jefferson	0	— b Storey	21
J. H. Hampshire c Edwards b Jefferson	51	— b Jefferson	55
*D. B. Close c Edwards b Storey	2	— c Jefferson b Storey	33
R. Illingworth c Barrington b Jefferson	0	— c Long b Storey	5
†J. G. Binks lbw b Storey	3	— lbw b Jefferson	1
F. S. Trueman b Storey	7	— b Storey	3
D. Wilson c Stewart b Jefferson	17	— c Edwards b Jefferson	4
J. Waring c Jackman b Storey	3	— c Stewart b Jefferson	13
A. G. Nicholson not out	1	— not out	2
L-b 7	7	L-b 1, n-b 4	5
1/17 2/17 3/73 4/84 5/84	115	1/7 2/16 3/42 4/112 5/122	151
6/84 7/94 8/103 9/113		6/128 7/131 8/131 9/148	

Bowling: *First Innings*—Jackman 7—4—10—0; Jefferson 18—7—51—5; Pocock 5—1—14—0; Storey 14.1—6—33—4. *Second Innings*—Jefferson 32.1—4—49—6; Jackman 9—1—24—0; Storey 20—4—56—4; Pocock 2—0—17—0.

Umpires: P. A. Gibb and L. H. Gray.

YORKSHIRE v. GLAMORGAN

At Scarborough, August 17, 18. Yorkshire won by two wickets. Although in arrears on first innings, Yorkshire struggled to an unimpressive victory in the extra half-hour of the second day. Poor batting against earnest bowling rather than any deficiencies in the pitch was responsible for the low scoring, no total exceeding 137 and no individual making 50. Glamorgan were so unenterprising in their first innings that they allowed Wilson to bowl 25 overs for 22 runs and the whole of their second innings contained only two boundaries. Padgett provided the batting stability for Yorkshire and Sharpe and Hampshire played purposefully against the steady Glamorgan bowling.

Glamorgan

First innings		Second innings	
A. Jones c Binks b Nicholson	10	lbw b Nicholson	10
B. Hedges b Hutton	26	not out	1
P. M. Walker b Nicholson	2	lbw b Hutton	13
A. Rees b Nicholson	27	c Binks b Trueman	13
W. Slade run out	10	c Hampshire b Nicholson	11
R. Davis c Sharpe b Hutton	16	lbw b Wilson	10
†D. L. Evans b Hutton	4	b Trueman	12
A. E. Cordle not out	21	lbw b Trueman	7
*O. S. Wheatley b Wilson	1	b Nicholson	7
D. J. Shepherd b Trueman	7	b Nicholson	1
I. J. Jones b Trueman	0	b Wilson	0
B 4, l-b 3, n-b 6	13	L-b 2, n-b 4	6
1/15 2/22 3/56 4/84 5/84 6/104 7/113 8/114 9/137	137	1/22 2/37 3/37 4/57 5/72 6/77 7/81 8/81 9/82	91

Bowling: *First Innings*—Trueman 13—4—27—2; Nicholson 14—3—36—3; Hutton 18—5—39—3; Wilson 25—17—22—1. *Second Innings*—Trueman 19—4—45—3; Nicholson 15.4—6—28—4; Hutton 4—1—9—1; Wilson 7—5—3—2.

Yorkshire

First innings		Second innings	
K. Taylor b Wheatley	17	lbw b I. J. Jones	0
P. J. Sharpe b Shepherd	45	lbw b Wheatley	4
D. E. V. Padgett not out	35	c Walker b Cordle	28
J. H. Hampshire c Slade b Shepherd	5	c Slade b Shepherd	40
B. Leadbeater lbw b Wheatley	1	c Slade b Wheatley	2
R. A. Hutton c Evans b Shepherd	2	b Shepherd	9
†J. G. Binks b Wheatley	0	b Shepherd	1
*F. S. Trueman b Shepherd	5	c Slade b Shepherd	6
D. Wilson run out	0	not out	5
A. G. Nicholson b Wheatley	10		
G. Cope b Shepherd	0	not out	1
B 1, l-b 2, n-b 1	4	B 1, l-b 6, n-b 2	9
1/55 2/69 3/81 4/84 5/87 6/95 7/97 8/97 9/104	124	1/1 2/20 3/28 4/69 (8 wkts.) 5/83 6/84 7/90 8/99	105

Bowling: *First Innings*—I. J. Jones 9—1—24—0; Wheatley 27.5—9—40—4; Cordle 4—0—21—0; Shepherd 15—6—35—5. *Second Innings*—I. J. Jones 8—1—23—1; Wheatley 21—6—37—2; Cordle 3—1—15—1; Shepherd 16.1—10—21—4.

Umpires: L. H. Gray and P. A. Gibb.

At Northampton, August 20, 22, 23. YORKSHIRE lost to NORTHAMPTONSHIRE by 34 runs.

YORKSHIRE v. WARWICKSHIRE

At Hull, August 24, 25, 26. Warwickshire won by three wickets. In a closely fought match, on a pitch drying out after flooding earlier in the week, the decisive innings was played by Abberley, who stayed for more than two and a half hours on the third day in an impressive display of concentration and technical ability. Batsmen were never at ease throughout the match, varying their methods from attack with some appearance of desperation to such uncompromising defence as Ibadulla's 41 in three and a half hours during the Warwickshire first innings. With the pitch at its most awkward on the second day, Yorkshire made a feeble showing against the medium-pace bowling of Bannister and Cartwright and were dismissed in three hours, only Boycott and Close offering any prolonged resistance.

Yorkshire

G. Boycott c Allan b Bannister	12	— b Cartwright	52
P. J. Sharpe c Jameson b Cartwright	67	— lbw b Brown	0
D. E. V. Padgett lbw b Cartwright	2	— c Ibadulla b Bannister	2
J. H. Hampshire c Bannister b Edmonds	43	— c Edmonds b Bannister	5
*D. B. Close c A. C. Smith b Cartwright	6	— c M. J. K. Smith b Bannister	16
K. Taylor c Allan b Edmonds	0	— b Bannister	8
R. Illingworth c A. C. Smith b Edmonds	2	— b Cartwright	9
†J. G. Binks c A. C. Smith b Bannister	22	— not out	1
F. S. Trueman c Abberley b Edmonds	3	— c A. C. Smith b Cartwright	2
D. Wilson b Allan	28	— b Cartwright	0
A. G. Nicholson not out	1	— c Amiss b Bannister	3
B 5, l-b 6	11	N-b 3	3
1/31 2/48 3/133 4/134 5/135 6/141 7/141 8/145 9/195	197	1/3 2/6 3/23 4/65 5/84 6/86 7/95 8/98 9/98	101

Bowling—*First Innings*—Bannister 15—6—23—2; Brown 15—1—38—0; Ibadulla 7—1—35—0; Cartwright 26—12—31—3; Edmonds 21—6—46—4; Allan 2—0—13—1. *Second Innings*—Brown 7—1—16—1; Bannister 22.2—9—38—5; Cartwright 16—5—44—4.

Warwickshire

K. Ibadulla c Close b Trueman	41	— c Binks b Nicholson	0
R. N. Abberley lbw b Nicholson	0	— not out	54
D. L. Amiss c Close b Nicholson	5	— c Binks b Illingworth	20
*M. J. K. Smith lbw b Nicholson	16	— lbw b Wilson	8
J. A. Jameson lbw b Nicholson	48	— c Padgett b Illingworth	1
†A. C. Smith b Wilson	39	— c Sharpe b Illingworth	4
T. W. Cartwright lbw b Trueman	15	— not out	13
R. B. Edmonds b Trueman	11		
J. M. Allan c Hampshire b Trueman	2	— c Trueman b Nicholson	8
D. J. Brown not out	3	— b Trueman	0
J. D. Bannister run out	0		
B 5, l-b 6, n-b 2	13	L-b 1	1
1/16 2/24 3/44 4/110 5/127 6/173 7/177 8/188 9/191	193	1/5 2/8 3/17 4/49 5/68 6/69 7/75 (7 wkts.)	109

Bowling: *First Innings*—Trueman 22—7—33—4; Nicholson 30.5—6—62—4; Close 15—5—48—0; Wilson 13—7—10—1; Illingworth 13—7—27—0. *Second Innings*—Trueman 10—3—10—1; Nicholson 12—2—35—2; Close 6—1—14—0; Illingworth 18—10—25—3; Wilson 10.1—2—24—1.

Umpires: J. F. Crapp and C. G. Pepper.

At The Oval, August 27, 29, 30. YORKSHIRE drew with SURREY.

YORKSHIRE v. KENT

At Harrogate, August 31, September 1, 2. Yorkshire won by 24 runs. Yorkshire entered their last championship engagement knowing that outright victory would assure them of the title but that any other result might leave them in second place. The pitch was soft after heavy rain and first innings was a speculation but Boycott's determined batting laid the foundation for a total that proved beyond Kent's reach and left Yorkshire with an advantage of 91 when they went in again on the second day. This time they were dominated by Underwood who took seven wickets in succession on the difficult pitch, but Yorkshire's ultimate anxiety was rain that threatened abandonment of the match. Remarkable drying in a timely strong wind permitted play after lunch on the third day and though Kent had reached 143 when the fourth wicket fell the pitch gave its final favours to the spin bowlers and Yorkshire were able to complete victory in the extra half-hour.

Yorkshire

G. Boycott c Ealham b Brown	80	— c Knott b Underwood	9
P. J. Sharpe c Knott b Brown	0	— c Cowdrey b Underwood	18
D. E. V. Padgett c Knott b Underwood	31	— c and b Underwood	12
J. H. Hampshire b Underwood	29	— c Ealham b Underwood	9
*D. B. Close c Underwood b Dixon	1	— b Underwood	3
K. Taylor c Cowdrey b Brown	17	— lbw b Underwood	4
R. Illingworth c and b Brown	8	— c Knott b Brown	8
†J. G. Binks b Underwood	15	— b Underwood	3
F. S. Trueman st Knott b Underwood	4	— c Leary b Brown	18
D. Wilson c Luckhurst b Brown	14	— c Ealham b Graham	21
A. G. Nicholson not out	3	— not out	2
B 4, l-b 2, n-b 2	8	W 1, n-b 1	2
1/1 2/77 3/119 4/129 5/156 6/167 7/175 8/181 9/196	210	1/22 2/37 3/44 4/51 5/53 6/56 7/62 8/81 9/89	109

Bowling: *First Innings*—Brown 20—8—30—5; Graham 8—2—21—0; Underwood 35.5—9—105—4; Dixon 21—12—46—1. *Second Innings*—Brown 9—0—37—2; Graham 10.3—5—18—1; Underwood 20—7—30—7; Dixon 8—0—22—0.

Kent

M. H. Denness lbw b Trueman	1	— b Trueman	0
B. W. Luckhurst b Nicholson	5	— c Binks b Wilson	62
R. C. Wilson b Illingworth	22	— b Nicholson	17
*M. C. Cowdrey lbw b Trueman	1	— c Close b Illingworth	37
S. E. Leary c Hampshire b Wilson	15	— b Illingworth	39
A. Ealham lbw b Wilson	14	— c Sharpe b Wilson	1
†A. Knott c Close b Nicholson	16	— st Binks b Wilson	0
A. L. Dixon b Trueman	9	— b Illingworth	3
D. L. Underwood c Illingworth b Nicholson	0	— c Trueman b Illingworth	1
A. Brown b Trueman	19	— not out	10
J. N. Graham not out	8	— c Padgett b Illingworth	0
B 8, l-b 1	9	B 2, l-b 2, n-b 2	6
1/6 2/6 3/9 4/44 5/64 6/72 7/88 8/88 9/92	119	1/0 2/19 3/86 4/143 5/145 6/145 7/156 8/158 9/176	176

Bowling: *First Innings*—Trueman 10.5—3—25—4; Nicholson 10—3—36—3; Illingworth 7—1—26—1; Wilson 8—2—23—2. *Second Innings*—Trueman 14—4—19—1; Nicholson 19—13—31—1; Illingworth 17.5—3—55—5; Close 6—3—19—0; Wilson 17—5—46—3.

Umpires: C. G. Pepper and W. F. Simpson.

YORKSHIRE v. M.C.C.

At Scarborough, September 10, 12, 13. M.C.C. won by 83 runs. Yorkshire looked a tired team after their Championship exertions and anxieties and gave an unimpressive display of batting and bowling. M.C.C. were able to declare in both innings, but Yorkshire's only batting of note was an eighth-wicket partnership on the third day in which Binks and Wilson put on 76 runs in half an hour. Wilson drove four 6's in an over from Hobbs that yielded 30 runs. Hobbs took five wickets in each innings with his alluring leg-breaks and Underwood and Morgan bowled economically in a match of generally modest standards of cricket.

M.C.C.

D. M. Green c Hampshire b Trueman	6	— c Trueman b Wilson	19
M. H. Denness b Waring	10	— b Illingworth	25
A. R. Lewis b Nicholson	7	— not out	34
K. W. R. Fletcher c Hampshire b Wilson	47	— not out	26
*D. C. Morgan c Binks b Wilson	16		
M. G. Griffith b Close	52		
K. E. Palmer lbw b Illingworth	0		
†A. Knott c Padgett b Illingworth	29		
D. L. Underwood st Binks b Wilson	16		
R. N. S. Hobbs not out	29		
F. E. Rumsey not out	36		
L-b 3, n-b 1	4	B 1, n-b 2	3
1/6 2/16 3/32 4/60 5/93 6/97 7/158 8/187 9/187 (9 wkts., dec.)	252	1/44 2/54 (2 wkts.)	107

Bowling: *First Innings*—Trueman 7.1—2—18—1; Nicholson 8—2—20—1; Waring 9—3—19—1; Close 11—5—9—1; Illingworth 34—13—80—2; Wilson 29—11—102—3. *Second Innings*—Trueman 9—2—16—0; Nicholson 10—0—41—0; Illingworth 10—3—19—1; Wilson 9—1—28—1.

Yorkshire

G. Boycott c Griffith b Underwood	17	— b Palmer	10
P. J. Sharpe b Underwood	21	— b Palmer	9
D. E. V. Padgett b Morgan	3	— run out	8
*D. B. Close c Palmer b Hobbs	8	— b Hobbs	4
J. H. Hampshire b Morgan	28	— b Underwood	0
R. Illingworth c Denness b Underwood	3	— c Morgan b Hobbs	14
†J. G. Binks c and b Hobbs	16	— not out	60
F. S. Trueman c Palmer b Hobbs	6	— c Palmer b Hobbs	4
D. Wilson b Hobbs	4	— b Underwood	41
J. Waring not out	0	— b Hobbs	8
A. G. Nicholson c Underwood b Hobbs	6	— c and b Hobbs	0
L-b 5	5	L-b 1	1
1/23 2/33 3/48 4/57 5/62 6/101 7/107 8/109 9/111	117	1/15 2/22 3/25 4/32 5/32 6/58 7/62 8/138 9/159	159

Bowling: *First Innings*—Rumsey 8—2—13—0; Palmer 7—1—19—0; Underwood 13—8—11—3; Morgan 9—5—13—2; Hobbs 11.2—0—56—5. *Second Innings*—Rumsey 5—1—9—0; Palmer 5—0—13—2; Underwood 12—8—11—2; Hobbs 17.3—2—113—5; Morgan 6—2—12—0.

Umpires: J. S. Buller and T. W. Spencer.

THE GILLETTE CUP

FIRST ROUND

CHESHIRE v. LANCASHIRE

At Macclesfield, April 28. Lancashire won by 42 runs. Although Cheshire contained the first-class county splendidly, restricting them to 104 runs and capturing nine wickets, their batsmen were not good enough. Hardstaff shook Lancashire with a hostile spell which brought him three wickets for one run in eight deliveries and only a fine innings by Entwistle, with one 6 and four 4's, saved them from more serious trouble. It also earned him the man of the match award. The Minor County soon found the pace and accuracy of Higgs and Statham, the Test match bowlers, too much for them and despite a stubborn 24 in two and three-quarter hours by Millett, they totalled only 62.

Lancashire

D. M. Green c. Collins b Hardstaff	16
G. Pullar b Hardstaff	1
H. Pilling c and b Shillinglaw	9
J. Sullivan c Shillinglaw b Hardstaff	0
K. Snellgrove b Hardstaff	10
R. Entwistle not out	43
P. Lever c Millett b Shillinglaw	5
K. Shuttleworth c and b Millett	7
†K. Goodwin c Shillinglaw b Digman	0
K. Higgs c Cox b Digman	0
*J. B. Statham not out	8
L-b 3, n-b 2	5
1/18 2/21 3/21 4/40 5/42 6/50 7/67 8/68 9/74 (9 wkts., 60 overs)	104

Bowling: Hardstaff 12—2—31—4; Digman 12—5—10—2; Shillinglaw 12—4—21—2; Millett 12—6—15—1; Sutton 10—4—16—0; Halsall 2—0—6—0.

Cheshire

*F. W. Millett b Higgs	24
J. A. Sutton c Goodwin b Statham	0
S. F. Wood run out	0
D. F. Cox b Higgs	2
R. Collins c Shuttleworth b Lever	1
P. A. C. Kelly c Pilling b Lever	3
G. Hardstaff b Lever	0
N. R. Halsall c Goodwin b Green	4
A. L. Shillinglaw c Entwistle b Higgs	22
R. J. Digman c Entwistle b Higgs	0
†K. F. Holding not out	4
B 1, l-b 1	2
1/1 2/3 3/5 4/17 5/22 6/22 7/27 8/57 9/58	62

Bowling: Statham 10—3—16—1; Higgs 10.3—5—10—4; Shuttleworth 9—4—13—0; Lever 12—5—16—3; Green 4—1—5—1.

Umpires: F. Jakeman and A. E. Rhodes.

HAMPSHIRE v. LINCOLNSHIRE

At Southampton, May 4, 5. Hampshire won by 31 runs. No play was possible on May 4 because of rain but the match was completed the next day and Lincolnshire gave Hampshire a closer game than might have been expected. A splendid innings of 92 by Livingstone was the foundation of Hampshire's total of 226 for nine in their 60 overs. He and Horton put on 124 for the third wicket. Lincolnshire made a good start and Robinson and Johnson scored 74 for the first wicket, but subsequently they were unable to cope with White's pace and his four wickets cost him only 36 runs. Madray alone among the later batsmen showed confidence and his 58 was top score on his side. Man of the match award went to Livingstone.

Hampshire

*R. E. Marshall c Johnson b Evans 10
B. L. Reed c Beeson b McVicker.. 9
H. Horton run out.............. 54
D. A. Livingstone c Sunley b McVicker.................. 92
G. L. Keith c Maslin b Sunley.... 0
P. J. Sainsbury not out........... 17
†B.S.V. Timms c Beeson b Camplin 1
A.R. Wassell c McVicker b Camplin 11
D. W. White b Camplin......... 9
D. Shackleton c Johnson b McVicker................... 9
R. M. Cottam not out.......... 1

B 9, l-b 4 13

1/23 2/29 3/153 (9 wkts., 60 overs) 226
4/154 5/173 6/176 7/198 8/204 9/222

Bowling: McVicker 12—1—61—3; Evans 12—5—26—1; Camplin 12—1—38—3; Lawrence 7—11—37—0; Maslin 12—3—23—0; Madray 3—0—19—0; Sunley 2—0—9—1.

Lincolnshire

G. Robinson run out............ 40
D. Johnson b Sainsbury......... 35
C. A. Richardson c Keith b Wassell 16
M. Maslin c and b Wassell....... 6
I. S. Madray c Sainsbury b White.. 58
J. Sunley b White............... 14
*†R .N. Beeson c Livingstone b White....................... 0
N. M. McVicker c Reed b White.. 16
J. W. Lawrence not out.......... 2
J. B. Evans c and b Cottam....... 1
G. B. Camplin b Cottam......... 0

B 1, l-b 4, n-b 2.......... 7

1/74 2/77 3/86 4/117 5/163 195
6/164 7/187 8/192 9/195

Bowling: Shackleton 12—1—47—0; White 10—1—36—4; Cottam 10.4—0—42—2; Sainsbury 12—5—18—1; Wassell 12—1—45—2.

Umpires: J. Langridge and A. E. Fagg.

HERTFORDSHIRE v. BERKSHIRE

At Hitchin, April 30. Berkshire won by two wickets, a smaller margin than seemed likely when, with only two wickets down, they were within 23 runs of victory. Hertfordshire owed everything to Bell whose fine 105—the first century by a Minor Counties player in the competition—brought him the man of the match award. Berkshire, benefiting from dropped catches were comfortably placed after a second-wicket stand of 86 but there came the sensational collapse in which five men were dismissed for 22 runs.

Hertfordshire

T. A. Bell c Mordaunt b Watts....105
A. R. Day c Fortin b Mordaunt... 2
R. H. Wacey b Denness.......... 1
J. P. Fellows-Smith c Cheesman b Simpkins...................... 7
L. R. Gardner run out........... 14
T. L. Clough lbw b Cheesman.... 10
H. W. Tilly b Denness........... 3
†R. G. Simons c Brooks b Mordaunt......................... 7
*C. V. L. Marques run out........ 13
J. D. Appleyard not out.......... 0
J. Iberson b Mordaunt 0

B 1, l-b 3, n-b 1........... 5

1/20 2/21 3/31 4/66 5/87 167
6/104 7/146 8/155 9/167

Bowling: Denness 12—3—28—2; Mordaunt 11.3—1—24—3; Simpkins 12—3—33—1; Baines 12—4—23—0; Cheesman 9—1—37—1; Watts 2—0—17—1.

Berkshire

*A. T. Davis st Simons b Iberson.. 17
B. E. F. Cheesman c Gardner b Iberson.......... 31
F. S. Neate c Simons b Fellows-Smith.......... 38
D. J. Mordaunt lbw b Fellows-Smith.......... 53
†R. C. G. Fortin lbw b Tilly...... 1
C. E. W. Brooks lbw b Tilly...... 0
P. A. Baker run out.............. 5
P. W. Watts st Simons b Iberson.. 5
F. C. Baines not out.............. 4
A. C. Denness not out............ 0
B 7, l-b 4, n-b 6........... 17

1/59 2/59 3/145 4/154 (8 wkts.) 171
5/154 6/156 7/167 8/167

P. A. Simpkins did not bat.

Bowling: Tilly 12—2—34—2; Fellows-Smith 10.2—1—30—2; Iberson 11—3—37—3; Wacey 1—0—2—0; Appleyard 8—2—35—0; Marques 4—0—16—0.

Umpires: L. H. Gray and O. W. Herman.

NORTHAMPTONSHIRE v. GLAMORGAN

At Northampton, April 30. Glamorgan won by nine wickets, their first away victory in the competition. I. J. Jones, with four for 12, proved almost unplayable and only Reynolds of the early batsmen offered much resistance. Northamptonshire were all out soon after lunch in the 37th over and although Glamorgan lost Hedges with only 19 on the board, A. Jones and Walker steered them home with an unbroken stand of 51. Man of the match: I. J. Jones.

Northamptonshire

C. Milburn b Wheatley.......... 1
R. M. Prideaux c Evans b I. J. Jones 2
B. L. Reynolds b Walker......... 23
Mushtaq Mohammad c Cordle b Walker.......... 1
P. D. Watts c A. Jones b Cordle... 1
D. S. Steele run out............. 8
A. Lightfoot b I. J. Jones........ 13
B. Crump c Evans b I. J. Jones.... 8
*†K. V. Andrew b Cordle........ 0
M. J. Kettle not out............. 3
J. D. F. Larter c Evans b I. J. Jones 0
B 6, l-b 1................ 7

1/1 2/15 3/27 4/30 5/31 67
6/54 7/58 8/59 9/67

Bowling: I. J. Jones 11—2—12—4; Wheatley 8—3—18—1; Cordle 9—1—16—2; Walker 5—1—11—2; Shepherd 4—3—3—0.

Glamorgan

B. Hedges b Crump............. 11
A. Jones not out................ 37
P. M. Walker not out........... 21
L-b 1..................... 1

1/19 (1 wkt.) 70

A. R. Lewis, E. Lewis, A. Rees, †D. L. Evans, A. E. Cordle, D. J. Shepherd, I. J. Jones and *O. S. Wheatley did not bat.

Bowling: Larter 5—1—12—0; Crump 7—2—5—1; Lightfoot 6—1—23—0; Kettle 5—0—25—0; Steele 1—0—4—0.

Umpires: H. Yarnold and R. Aspinall.

SOMERSET v. SUSSEX

At Taunton, April 30. Somerset won by four wickets. A remarkable performance by the 47-year-old Alley brought about the quick dismissal from the competition of Sussex, winners in 1963 and 1964. With a spell of four for 14 he had Sussex toppling to 63 for six and, later in the day when Somerset were in danger of defeat, he hit one 6 and five 4's in an adventurous 38 not out to take the man of the match award. Pataudi had earlier stopped the Sussex slide, enabling the total to reach 175, and Buss put Sussex back into the game with three wickets for four runs in 20 balls. Then Alley took over.

Sussex

K. G. Suttle lbw b C. R. M. Atkinson	20	M. G. Griffith not out	32
A. S. M. Oakman c Greetham b K. E. Palmer	7	A. Buss st Clayton b Greetham	28
E. R. Dexter c Clayton b Alley	10	J. A. Snow not out	13
†J. M. Parks c R. Palmer b Alley	7	B 3, l-b 6, n-b 5	14
*Nawab of Pataudi b R. Palmer	42		
G. C. Cooper b Alley	2	1/13 2/36 3/46 (8 wkts., 60 overs)	175
P. R. V. Ledden c Kitchen b Alley	0	4/54 5/63 6/63 7/106 8/153	

D. L. Bates did not bat.

Bowling: Rumsey 12—5—17—0; K. E. Palmer 12—2—31—1; Alley 12—6—14—4; C. R. M. Atkinson 8—1—28—1; R. Palmer 12—0—56—1; Greetham 4—1—15—1.

Somerset

*C. R. M. Atkinson st Parks b Suttle	15	C. Greetham lbw b Buss	7
B. Roe b Snow	30	K. E. Palmer not out	12
M. Kitchen c Parks b Buss	21	B 1, l-b 6, w 1, n-b 3	11
G. Atkinson c Pataudi b Bates	21		
R. Virgin c Parks b Buss	4	1/37 2/59 3/107 4/118 (6 wkts.)	179
W. E. Alley not out	38	5/127 6/135	

†G. Clayton, F. E. Rumsey and R. Palmer did not bat.

Bowling: Snow 11—1—27—1; Buss 11—1—28—3; Bates 12—2—36—1; Suttle 12—3—38—1; Ledden 8.3—0—39—0.

Umpires: W. E. Phillipson and J. F. Crapp.

SUFFOLK v. KENT

At Ipswich, April 30. Kent won by 113 runs, their first victory in the competition. Cowdrey rescued them from a bad start with a sparkling century in two and a quarter hours, receiving excellent support from Leary. Prior and Flack, facing a Kent total of 284, batted well in an opening stand of 85 but they were never up with the clock. Some big hitting from Cunnell forced Cowdrey to change his tactics but the Kent captain, named the man of the match, had the last word when he dismissed Hargreaves in the final over.

Kent

B. W. Luckhurst b Hargreaves	3	J. M. Prodger not out	30
M. H. Denness c Prior b Scrutton	49	A. L. Dixon not out	6
R. C. Wilson c English b Hargreaves	0		
*M. C. Cowdrey c R. E. Cunnell b English	116	L-b 4	4
S. E. Leary c C. J. Cunnell b R. E. Cunnell	76	1/5 2/5 3/105 (5 wkts., 60 overs)	284
		4/116 5/257	

†A. Knott, D. L. Underwood, D. M. Sayer and A. Brown did not bat.

Bowling.—Hargreaves 11—2—44—2; Rutterford 11—1—49—0; Scrutton 12—1—45—1; Perkins 12—1—31—0; English 7—0—59—1; Cadman 4—1—24—0; R. E. Cunnell 3—0—28—1.

Suffolk

*†I. D. Prior c Prodger b Sayer....	41	J.M.Hargreaves c Wilson b Cowdrey..........................	2
R.E.Flack c Cowdrey b Luckhurst	46	C. Rutterford not out............	1
C. J. Cunnell b Underwood.......	3		
N. E. Scrutton b Luckhurst......	14		
R. E. Cunnell b Sayer............	40	B 3, l-b 1	4
J.F.Cadman c Underwood b Leary	7		
J. E. Green not out..............	13	1/85 2/92 3/93 (8 wkts., 60 overs)	171
R. J. English b Sayer.............	0	4/127 5/144 6/158 7/158 8/164	

G. C. Perkins did not bat.

Bowling: Brown 10—2—16—0; Sayer 11—2—24—3; Dixon 12—2—33—0; Luckhurst 12—1—58—2; Underwood 9—6—11—1; Leary 5—1—18—1; Cowdrey 1—0—7—1.

Umpires: W. F. Price and R. S. Lay.

Derbyshire, Essex, Gloucestershire, Leicestershire, Middlesex, Nottinghamshire, Surrey, Warwickshire, Worcestershire and Yorkshire each received a bye into the second round.

SECOND ROUND

BERKSHIRE v. GLOUCESTERSHIRE

At Reading, May 21. Gloucestershire won by 135 runs. Their 327 for seven established a new record for the competition, beating the 317 for four scored by Yorkshire in the 1965 final against Surrey. Nicholls won the man of the match award for his superb 127—he reached his century before lunch—which included one 6 and sixteen 4's. The Minor County soon lost two wickets, but their rate of progress was always respectable and they were far from disgraced. Only one other non-championship side has scored more runs in the Gillette Cup—Lincolnshire against Hampshire in the previous round.

Gloucestershire

R. B. Nicholls c Neate b Watts....	127	D. Brown not out...............	50
C. A. Milton b Simpkins.........	20	A. S. Brown c Baines b Denness...	9
A. R. Windows b Simpkins.......	13	D. A. Allen not out..............	5
S. E. Russell c Neate b Denness...	62	B 4, l-b 8, n-b 1........	13
*J. B. Mortimore c Mordaunt b Denness......................	4	1/56 2/84 3/209 (7 wkts., 60 overs)	327
M. Bissex b Denness..............	24	4/233 5/233 6/296 7/314	

†B. J. Meyer and J. Andrew did not bat.

Bowling: Denness 11—0—56—4; Mordaunt 12—0—61—0; Simpkins 12—0—54—2; Baines 12—0—50—0; Watts 9—0—65—1; Cheesman 2—0—16—0; Brooks 2—0—12—0.

Berkshire

*A. T. Davis c Windows b Mortimore........................	47	P. A. Baker c Meyer b Bissex......	9
B. E. F. Cheesman b A. S. Brown..	5	P. W. Watts b Andrew...........	4
F. W. Neate b Andrew...........	16	A. C. Denness c Meyer b Nicholls.	18
D. J. Mordaunt c Russell b Windows.........................	31	F. C. Baines not out.............	4
†R. C. G. Fortin b Mortimore....	18	L-b 3..................	3
C. E. W. Brooks not out..........	37	1/7 2/40 3/88 (8 wkts., 60 overs)	192
		4/107 5/128 6/145 7/154 8/188	

P. A. Simpkins did not bat.

Bowling: A. S. Brown 5—1—9—1; Windows 9—2—34—1; Allen 12—2—41—0; Andrew 12—1—37—2; Mortimore 10—1—36—2; Russell 1—1—0—0; Bissex 10—2—28—1; Nicholls 1—0—4—1.

Umpires: P. B. Wight and H. Yarnold.

DERBYSHIRE v. ESSEX

At Chesterfield, May 21. Essex won by two wickets, their first victory against a Championship side in the competition, and gained revenge for their defeat at Brentwood the previous season. Derbyshire passed 100 for the loss of only two wickets but the middle batting faltered and Morgan was called upon to prevent a complete collapse. Essex started briskly with an opening stand of 61 and Bear, continuing to play well, was made man of the match for his breezy 71. A partnership of 50 between Bailey and Knight took Essex to 171 for five but there were still a few shocks in store before victory came with two overs left.

Derbyshire

J. F. Harvey c Bailey b Jorden	29	M. H. J. Allen c Barker b Edmeades	0
J. R. Eyre lbw b Jorden	38	H. J. Rhodes not out	9
H. L. Johnson b Knight	25	A. Ward c Presland b Knight	3
I. R. Buxton c Taylor b Jorden	12		
*D. C. Morgan c Bailey b Knight	42	L-b 3	3
M. Hill lbw b Edmeades	17		
†R. W. Taylor b Presland	17	1/39 2/87 3/105 4/106 5/131	199
T. J. P. Eyre c Jorden b Edmeades	4	6/164 7/175 8/181 9/193	

Bowling: Knight 11.5—3—33—3; Jorden 12—0—41—3; Bailey 10—1—30—0; East 5—0—20—0; Edmeades 12—1—32—3; Presland 9—0—40—1.

Essex

G. E. Barker c Taylor b Ward	23	E. R. Presland not out	7
M. J. Bear run out	71	A. M. Jorden not out	0
†B. Taylor c and b Ward	9		
K. W. R. Fletcher c Taylor b Rhodes	7		
*T. E. Bailey run out	38		
B. R. Knight lbw b Ward	17	B 6, l-b 8 n-b 6	20
B. Edmeades run out	7		
G. J. Saville c T. J. P. Eyre b Buxton	1	1/61 2/81 3/112 4/121 (8 wkts.)	200
		5/171 6/191 7/193 8/194	

R. East did not bat.

Bowling: Morgan 12—0—42—0; Rhodes 12—5—17—1; Ward 12—2—36—3; Allen 6.4—1—29—0; Buxton 12—1—35—1; T. J. P. Eyre 2—0—16—0; J. R. Eyre 1—0—5—0.

Umpires: F. Jakeman and W. E. Phillipson.

GLAMORGAN v. WARWICKSHIRE

At Swansea, May 21. Warwickshire won by 165 runs. Any chance Glamorgan had of offering a serious challenge to Warwickshire's big total was virtually destroyed in Brown's first over in which he dismissed A. Jones and A. R. Lewis without a run scored. The Glamorgan innings never really got off the ground and Warwickshire won with ease. Brown's five for 18 earned him the man of the match award but the choice between him and Amiss must have been a difficult one, for the young batsman hit fourteen 4's in a splendid century in two hours ten minutes, sharing a third-wicket stand with M. J. K. Smith of 126 in eighty-five minutes.

Warwickshire

R. W. Barber c E. Jones b Wheatley	25	R. V. Webster c Miller b I. J. Jones	11
R. N. Abberley c Hedges b Wheatley	15	R. B. Edmonds not out	12
D. L. Amiss c Rees b I. J. Jones	113	D. J. Brown not out	12
*M. J. K. Smith c Rees b I. J. Jones	48	L-b 9, n-b 1	10
J. A. Jameson run out	16		
K. Ibadulla c Slade b Shepherd	2	1/40 2/40 3/166 (8 wkts., 60 overs)	266
†A. C. Smith run out	2	4/193 5/212 6/218 7/241 8/244	

J. D. Bannister did not bat.

Bowling: I. J. Jones 12—1—51—3; Wheatley 12—0—46—2; Miller 12—0—58—0; Cordle 12—0—49—0; Shepherd 12—1—52—1.

Glamorgan

A. Jones c A. C. Smith b Brown	0	D. J. Shepherd not out	1
W. Slade lbw b Edmonds	28	I. J. Jones b Ibadulla	6
A. R. Lewis b Brown	0	*O. S. Wheatley b Brown	3
A Rees c Barber b Brown	9		
†E. Jones b Ibadulla	3	L-b 7	7
B. Hedges b Bannister	32		
H. D. Miller lbw b Bannister	3	1/0 2/0 3/16 4/23 5/70	101
A. E. Cordle b Brown	9	6/75 7/82 8/91 9/98	

Bowling: Brown 7.3—2—18—5; Webster 5—1—4—0; Ibadulla 8—1—22—2; Bannister 10—2—32—2; Edmonds 4—0—18—1.

Umpires: J. Arnold and W. H. Copson.

HAMPSHIRE v. KENT

At Southampton, May 21. Hampshire won by 54 runs. Their former captain, Ingleby-Mackenzie, came in for his first game of the season to keep wicket in place of the injured Timms and won the man of the match award for a forceful 59 not out, which rescued Hampshire after six wickets were down for 105. Marshall had given them a good start but the middle batsmen failed. Ingleby-Mackenzie hit the ball out of the ground for two 6's and he also hit six 4's, sharing a ninth-wicket stand of 57 with Shackleton. Kent soon lost Denness but Luckhurst and Wilson took the score to 114 before the second wicket fell. Kent seemed to be well placed to win, but their later batsmen collapsed. The last six wickets fell for only 14 runs.

Hampshire

*R. E. Marshall b Dixon	46	D. W. White c Sayer b Underwood	0
J. R. Gray b Sayer	10	D. Shackleton c Brown b Sayer	22
H. Horton c Knott b Luckhurst	13	R. M. Cottam c and b Sayer	2
D. A. Livingstone lbw b Luckhurst	9		
B. L. Reed b Dixon	2		
P. J. Sainsbury run out	11		
H. M. Barnard st Knott b Underwood	17	B 4, l-b 4	8
†A. C. D. Ingleby-Mackenzie not out	59	1/24 2/65 3/72 4/79 5/85 6/105 7/123 8/127 9/184	199

Bowling: Brown 12—1—57—0; Sayer 11.5—1—38—3; Dixon 12—1—28—2; Underwood 12—3—17—2; Luckhurst 12—2—51—2.

Kent

M. H. Denness lbw b Shackleton . . 4
B. W. Luckhurst c Barnard b Sainsbury 65
R. C. Wilson c Horton b Cottam . . 44
J. M. Prodger run out 0
*M. C. Cowdrey c and b Sainsbury. 12
S. E. Leary c Ingleby-Mackenzie b Cottam 0
†A. Knott not out 5
A. L. Dixon st Ingleby-Mackenzie b Shackleton 3
A. Brown b Shackleton 1
D. M. Sayer c Horton b Gray 0
D. L. Underwood c Shackleton b Gray 0
L-b 8, w 1, n-b 2 11

1/8 2/114 3/115 4/116 5/131 6/131 7/142 8/144 9/145 145

Bowling: Shackleton 10—3—12—3; White 8—1—20—0; Gray 8.4—1—34—2; Cottam 11—1—28—2; Sainsbury 12—1—40—2.

Umpires: J. F. Crapp and G. H. Pope.

LEICESTERSHIRE *v.* SURREY

At Leicester, May 21. Surrey won by 46 runs. Winning the toss, Surrey founded their victory on a third-wicket partnership of 98 between Edrich and Barrington, on a pitch that encouraged seam bowlers. Edrich, making only four boundaries, was inclined to stay in a minor key, but gave a steadfast display of immense value to his side. Barrington, who hit a straight 6 off his old colleague, Lock, was adjudged man of the match by W. J. Edrich, but Leicestershire's Cross must have been a close runner-up. He was the most penetrative home bowler and his fifty towered over the rest of the Leicestershire batting, with the exception of Inman. Arnold dealt searching blows with well controlled bowling. Leicestershire are still without a win in Gillette Cup cricket.

Surrey

*M. J. Stewart c Booth b Cross 23
J. H. Edrich c Cross b Cotton 77
R. A. E. Tindall b Spencer 21
K. F. Barrington c Marner b Cotton 61
S. J. Storey b Cross 7
R. I. Jefferson b Cross 2
M. D. Willett not out 21
P. I. Pocock st Tolchard b Birkenshaw 0
G. Arnold run out 2
B 8, l-b 9 17

1/42 2/93 3/191 4/193 5/196 6/217 7/222 8/231 (8 wkts., 60 overs) 231

W. A. Smith and †A. Long did not bat.

Bowling: Cotton 12—0—41—2; Spencer 12—0—49—1; Marner 12—2—32—0; Cross 11—0—36—3; Lock 12—1—52—0; Birkenshaw 1—0—4—1.

Leicestershire

M. R. Hallam c Barrington b Jefferson 7
B. J. Booth hit wkt b Arnold 0
M. E. Norman c and b Arnold 8
P. Marner c Willett b Pocock 16
C. C. Inman b Pocock 47
J. Birkenshaw b Jefferson 28
G. Cross not out 53
*G. A. R. Lock b Arnold 1
†R. W. Tolchard run out 12
C. T. Spencer b Arnold 0
J. Cotton not out 9
B 1, l-b 3 4

1/1 2/15 3/23 4/56 5/102 6/119 7/126 8/145 9/145 (9 wkts., 60 overs) 185

Bowling: Arnold 12—3—28—4; Jefferson 12—3—23—2; Storey 12—3—37—0; Pocock 12—1—39—2; Willett 10—0—41—0; Barrington 2—0—13—0.

Umpires: C. S. Elliott and A. Jepson.

MIDDLESEX v. LANCASHIRE

At Lord's, May 21. Lancashire won by 63 runs. They virtually settled the issue by lunch-time with a splendid opening stand of 125 off 34 overs between Green and Pullar. Green in particular demoralized the Middlesex pace attack with firm hitting which brought him the man of the match award. After his dismissal the bowlers gained some control, but Middlesex still needed to score at over four runs an over to win, a rate they never approached in the face of straight, well-pitched fast bowling from Statham, Higgs and Shuttleworth. Clark and Murray, in a partnership of 77 for the fifth wicket, rekindled Middlesex hopes, but the running-out of Clark sped Lancashire to victory.

Lancashire

D. M. Green c Radley b Stewart	81	†K. Goodwin run out	6
G. Pullar c Herman b Hooker	57	K. Higgs run out	3
G. K. Knox run out	22	*J. B. Statham not out	6
R. Entwistle b Titmus	19	L-b 12, w 1, n-b 2	15
K. Snellgrove c Murray b Herman	9		
H. Pilling st Murray b Titmus	13	1/125 2/161 (9 wkts., 60 overs)	243
P. Lever c Titmus b Herman	3	3/178 4/195 5/198 6/208	
K. Shuttleworth b Herman	9	7/222 8/228 9/229	

Bowling: Price 12—1—41—0; Stewart 12—0—41—1; Hooker 12—1—50—1; Herman 11—0—63—3; Titmus 12—1—25—2; Clark 1—0—8—0.

Middlesex

W. E. Russell b Shuttleworth	19	J. S. E. Price c Goodwin b Lever	10
R. A. Gale b Statham	1	R. W. Stewart c Goodwin b Lever	0
P. H. Parfitt b Higgs	1	R. S. Herman run out	0
E. A. Clark run out	51		
C. T. Radley b Shuttleworth	0	L-b 7, n-b 1	8
†J. T. Murray c Green b Statham	54		
*F. J. Titmus lbw b Statham	1	1/3 2/6 3/44 4/50 5/127	180
R. W. Hooker not out	35	6/129 7/133 8/159 9/159	

Bowling: Statham 12—2—28—3; Higgs 12—1—49—1; Lever 9—1—36—2; Shuttleworth 9—2—27—2; Green 9—0—32—0.

Umpires: T. W. Spencer and P. A. Gibb.

SOMERSET v. YORKSHIRE

At Taunton, May 21. Somerset won by 40 runs. They again owed much to Alley, who made 58 not out and took three more wickets. Kitchen stepped initially into the breach after two wickets had fallen for four runs, hitting seven 4's in his 55, and Alley completed the recovery with two 6's and seven 4's, adding 56 with C. R. M. Atkinson from nine overs. Yorkshire made a characteristically solid start in defence of their title, but R. Palmer, man of the match, with four for 33 in twelve overs, changed the course of the game. Despite a late challenge from Illingworth and Sharpe, Yorkshire collapsed again when Alley came on.

Somerset

B. Roe c Hampshire b Nicholson	1	C. Greetham c and b Wilson	8
R. Virgin run out	0	*C. R. M. Atkinson run out	15
M. Kitchen c Nicholson b Illingsworth	55	†G. Clayton not out	4
		L-b 7	7
G. Atkinson c Sharpe b Close	7		
K. E. Palmer b Wilson	35	1/1 2/4 3/28 (7 wkts., 60 overs)	190
W. E. Alley not out	58	4/88 5/105 6/129 7/185	

F. E. Rumsey and R. Palmer did not bat.

Bowling: Trueman 12—1—39—0; Nicholson 12—6—23—1; Close 12—6—22—1; Boycott 3—0—12—0; Taylor 5—0—26—0; Illingworth 7—1—23—1; Wilson 9—1—38—2.

Yorkshire

G. Boycott c Clayton b Alley...... 21
K. Taylor b R. Palmer............ 27
D. E. V. Padgett c Greetham b R. Palmer.................. 15
J. H. Hampshire c Virgin b R. Palmer.................. 14
*D. B. Close c Clayton b R. Palmer 29
P. J. Sharpe c Alley b C. R. M. Atkinson..................... 10
R. Illingworth not out 29
F. S. Trueman c C. R. M. Atkinson b. Alley 0
†J. G. Binks c Clayton b Alley.... 0
D. Wilson c C. R. M. Atkinson b Rumsey.................... 3
A. G. Nicholson run out.......... 0
L-b 2..................... 2

1/43 2/55 3/70 4/101 5/107 6/133 7/133 8/133 9/148 — 150

Bowling: Rumsey 10—1—27—1; K. E. Palmer 8—1—18—0; Alley 11.1—3—35—3; R. Palmer 12—1—33—4; C. R. M. Atkinson 9—2—35—1.

Umpires: O. W. Herman and A. E. Rhodes.

WORCESTERSHIRE v. NOTTINGHAMSHIRE

At Worcester, May 21. Worcestershire won by 19 runs, despite an astonishing collapse after lunch in which their last eight wickets fell for 68 runs. Headley's 64 earned him the man of the match award and only he and Ormrod, who were associated in a second-wicket stand of 95, batted with any freedom. Johnson's persistent accuracy brought him a return of four for 37 but Nottinghamshire were unable to build as they might upon an opening partnership of 58 by Bolus and Hill. They fell behind the clock and lost wickets trying to force the pace.

Worcestershire

*D. Kenyon c and b Forbes...... 10
R. G. A. Headley b Stead........ 64
J. A. Ormrod c Swetman b Davison 31
T. W. Graveney lbw b Johnson.... 26
B. d'Oliveira c Hill b Taylor...... 1
D. W. Richardson b Johnson..... 9
†R. Booth lbw b Taylor......... 6
N. Gifford b Johnson............ 4
B. M. Brain b Stead 16
L. J. Coldwell b Johnson......... 0
J. A. Flavell not out............ 1
L-b 10, n-b 1............. 11

1/13 2/108 3/113 4/118 5/148 6/153 7/157 8/167 9/167 — 179

Bowling: Davison 12—4—20—1; Forbes 12—4—35—1; Johnson 11—1—37—4; Stead 10.4—2—33—2; Taylor 12—1—43—2.

Nottinghamshire

*N. Hill c Booth b Gifford........ 27
J. B. Bolus c Flavell b Brain....... 28
B. Whittingham c Booth b Brain.. 3
R. A. White lbw b Gifford........ 39
M. J. Smedley c Graveney b d'Oliveira.................. 9
†R. Swetman c Kenyon b Gifford.. 6
M. Taylor not out.............. 16
C. Forbes c Graveney b Flavell.... 1
A. Johnson b Flavell............ 21
B. Stead b d'Oliveira............ 1
I. Davison c Gifford b Brain...... 2
L-b 7.................. 7

1/58 2/58 3/66 4/104 5/118 6/119 7/122 8/150 9/151 — 160

Bowling: Flavell 12—3—35—2; Coldwell 10—2—25—0; Brain 11—2—31—3; Gifford 12—4—28—3; d'Oliveira 11—3—34—2.

Umpires: C. G. Pepper and R. Aspinall.

THIRD ROUND

HAMPSHIRE v. SURREY

At Bournemouth, June 22. Hampshire won by seven wickets. A brilliant innings of 85 by Marshall took them to the semi-final for the first time. Surrey were unable to make the best use of their luck in winning the toss and batting first. Although they lost their last five wickets in five overs for 13 runs their total was respectable, but not as large as the efforts of their early batsmen, Edrich, Smith and Barrington deserved. Marshall and Reed gave Hampshire a fine start, putting on 128 for the first wicket in 28 overs before Marshall was out for 85. It was the first time he had made 50 in a Cup match. Hitting one 6 and thirteen 4's, Marshall made his runs in eighty-five minutes. The match was virtually won by the time Marshall went and he won the man of the match award.

Surrey

*M. J. Stewart c Ingleby-Mackenzie b Shackleton	0
J. H. Edrich c Ingleby-Mackenzie b Gray	37
W. A. Smith c Barnard b Gray	33
K. F. Barrington b White	46
M. D. Willett b Gray	1
S. J. Storey c Barnard b Cottam	10
R. I. Jefferson b Cottam	21
P. I. Pocock not out	7
G. R. J. Roope b White	2
†D. J. Taylor b Cottam	2
G. Arnold b White	1
B 6, l-b 3, n-b 4	13
1/0 2/65 3/102 4/110 5/126 6/160 7/162 8/165 9/168	173

Bowling: Shackleton 12—4—22—1; White 10.1—1—41—3; Gray 12—4—28—3; Cottam 11—0—40—3; Sainsbury 12—3—29—0.

Hampshire

*R. E. Marshall c Pocock b Jefferson	85
B. L. Reed b Arnold	46
H. Horton c Stewart b Pocock	15
D. A. Livingstone not out	14
H. M. Barnard not out	2
L-b 7, n-b 5	12
1/128 2/138 3/166 (3 wkts.)	174

†A. C. D. Ingleby-Mackenzie, P. J. Sainsbury, J. R. Gray, D. Shackleton, D. W. White and R. M. Cottam did not bat.

Bowling: Arnold 12—2—38—1; Jefferson 9—0—43—1; Storey 7—1—36—0; Roope 5—0—27—0; Pocock 10—2—18—1.

Umpires: L. H. Gray and A. E. Alderman.

SOMERSET v. LANCASHIRE

At Taunton, June 22. Somerset won by four wickets. They could not have envisaged such a fight after capturing the first five Lancashire wickets for 16, Roy Palmer taking four of them for three runs in 23 balls. Bond and Lever added 27 and Higgs hit out boldly in a last-wicket stand of 21 with Statham so that Lancashire reached 103, Palmer finishing with five for 18 to take the man of the match award. Statham, Lever and Shuttleworth made Somerset struggle even though the pitch played more easily later in the day, but a fine innings from Kitchen ensured their passage into the semi-finals for the first time.

Lancashire

G. Pullar c Virgin b R. Palmer	5
D. M. Green c Virgin b R. Palmer	9
G. K. Knox c Clayton b Rumsey	1
J. D. Bond c Clayton b Rumsey	29
A. M. Beddow b R. Palmer	0
D. Lloyd b R. Palmer	0
P. Lever c Virgin b K. E. Palmer	11
K. Shuttleworth b Alley	6
†K. Goodwin b R. Palmer	6
K. Higgs c Clayton b Greetham	25
*J. B. Statham not out	2
L-b 4, w 1, n-b 4	9
1/11 2/16 3/16 4/16 5/16 6/43 7/53 8/66 9/82	103

Bowling: Rumsey 12—4—22—2; R. Palmer 12—5—18—5; Alley 10—5—12—1; K. E. Palmer 12—6—22—1; C. R. M. Atkinson 3—0—19—0; Greetham 5—0—1—1.

Somerset

G. Atkinson lbw b Shuttleworth	16	K. E. Palmer not out	9
R. Virgin b Statham	1	*C. R. M. Atkinson not out	4
M. Kitchen c and b Lever	32	B 1, l-b 13, n-b 2	16
W. E. Alley b Shuttleworth	4		
B. Roe run out	20	1/9 2/36 3/48 4/75 (6 wkts.)	104
C. Greetham b Statham	2	5/78 6/84	

†G. Clayton, F. E. Rumsey and R. Palmer did not bat.

Bowling: Statham 10.1—7—10—2; Higgs 12—2—30—0; Lever 12—4—16—1; Beddow 4—0—12—0; Shuttleworth 12—3—20—2.

Umpires: J. Langridge and P. A. Gibb.

WARWICKSHIRE v. GLOUCESTERSHIRE

At Edgbaston, June 22. Warwickshire won by six wickets. A magnificent 113 in two hours five minutes by Barber carried Warwickshire to victory. He hit seventeen 4's and the adjudicator Cyril Washbrook, in naming him the man of the match, described the innings as the best he had seen in the competition. The extent of his aggression was reflected in Warwickshire's startling rate of progress: fourteen overs for the first 50, nine for the second and six for the third. Gloucestershire reached 100 with only three wickets down but the early promise was not maintained and their total of 193 proved within easy reach of the electrifying Barber.

Gloucestershire

C. A. Milton b Ibadulla	38	D. A. Allen b Ibadulla	2
A. R. Windows b Brown	12	†B. J. Meyer b Brown	2
D. Brown c Jameson b Bannister	28	J. Andrew not out	6
S. E. Russell b Ibadulla	47		
D. Shepherd c Abberley b Cartwright	7		
R. B. Nicholls lbw b Cartwright	0	L-b 5	5
*J. B. Mortimore b Brown	27		
A. S. Brown c A. C. Smith b Bannister	19	1/27 2/58 3/89 4/100 5/100 6/152 7/164 8/166 9/175	193

Bowling: Brown 12—1—33—3; Webster 12—0—39—0; Cartwright 12—2—36—2; Bannister 9.1—2—35—2; Ibadulla 12—0—45—3.

Warwickshire

R. N. Abberley lbw b A. S. Brown	10	J. A. Jameson not out	0
R. W. Barber c Andrew b Russell	113	K. Ibadulla not out	4
D. L. Amiss c Meyer b Andrew	62	B 1, l-b 2, n-b 1	4
*M. J. K. Smith c Shepherd b Andrew	4	1/15 2/177 3/193 4/193 (4 wkts.)	197

T. W. Cartwright, †A. C. Smith, R. V. Webster, J. D. Bannister and D. J. Brown did not bat.

Bowling: A. S. Brown 10—4—41—1; Windows 7—0—41—0; Andrew 9—0—41—2; Mortimore 5—0—29—0; Allen 7—0—37—0; Russell 2—0—4—1.

Umpires: H. Mellows and J. Arnold.

WORCESTERSHIRE v. ESSEX

At Worcester, June 22. Worcestershire won by 82 runs. Their opening bowlers, Flavell and Coldwell, wrecked the start of the Essex innings by dismissing four men for 29 runs in 13 overs and thereafter only Knight, 52 in ninety-five minutes, and Taylor, who hit six 4's in 31, made any real headway. The backbone of the Worcestershire total of 211 was a second-wicket partnership of 87 between Horton and Ormrod after Kenyon had left with only three on the board. Horton hit 51 and took two Essex wickets for 20 to win the man of the match award.

Worcestershire

*D. Kenyon c Cass b Jorden	2	B. M. Brain c Taylor b Bailey	10
M. J. Horton c Bailey b Presland	51	L. J. Coldwell not out	7
J. A. Ormrod run out	50	J. A. Flavell b Jorden	0
B. d'Oliveira c Bear b Jorden	39		
D. W. Richardson run out	23	B 1, l-b 7	8
R. G. A. Headley c Presland b Bailey	10		
D. N. F. Slade c Taylor b Knight	0	1/3 2/90 3/115 4/157 5/181	211
†R. Booth run out	11	6/181 7/184 8/197 9/211	

Bowling: Knight 12—3—30—1; Jorden 12—1—46—3; Edmeades 12—2—29—0; Hobbs 5—0—18—0; Presland 7—0—28—1; Bailey 12—0—52—2.

Essex

G. E. Barker b Coldwell	9	E. R. Presland lbw b Coldwell	10
M. J. Bear lbw b Flavell	0	R. N. S. Hobbs c Headley b d'Oliveira	13
*T. E. Bailey c Headley b Coldwell	2		
K. W. R. Fletcher c Slade b Flavell	0	A. M. Jorden not out	0
†B. Taylor st Booth b Horton	31	B 5	5
B. R. Knight c Headley b Coldwell	52		
G. R. Cass c and b Horton	1	1/3 2/8 3/11 4/29 5/57	129
B. Edmeades c Booth b d'Oliveira	6	6/63 7/105 8/106 9/129	

Bowling: Flavell 10—3—24—2; Coldwell 12—3—42—4; Brain 9—2—19—0; Horton 10—3—20—2; d'Oliveira 6.1—1—19—2.

Umpires: W. F. Simpson and A. E. Rhodes.

SEMI-FINALS

WARWICKSHIRE v. SOMERSET

At Birmingham, August 10. Warwickshire won by five wickets with eight overs to spare. Somerset made a solid start but slumped after lunch from 97 for one to 189 all out in less than two hours. G. Atkinson's sheet-anchor role occupied three hours and included only three 4's. Bannister ended the Somerset innings by dismissing C. R. M. Atkinson, Palmer and Clayton in four balls. Barber gave Warwickshire a good start and then Amiss, man of the match, and Smith shared a third-wicket stand of 105 in 29 overs to ensure Warwickshire's place in the final.

Somerset

G. Atkinson c Stewart b Ibadulla	72	C. Greetham c Jameson b Brown	7
R. Virgin run out	15	†G. Clayton b Bannister	10
M. Kitchen b Cartwright	26	R. Palmer c Webster b Bannister	0
W. E. Alley b Webster	6	F. E. Rumsey not out	0
F. T. Willetts lbw b Webster	0	L-b 17	17
G. Burgess c M. J. K. Smith b Ibadulla	20	1/40 2/98 3/108 4/110 5/137	189
*C. R. M. Atkinson b Bannister	16	6/153 7/172 8/189 9/189	

Bowling: Brown 12—3—22—1; Webster 12—4—26—2; Cartwright 12—1—29—1; Bannister 11.4—1—47—3; Ibadulla 12—2—48—2.

Warwickshire

R. W. Barber b Alley 45	W. J. Stewart b Burgess 4
K. Ibadulla lbw b Alley 5	T. W. Cartwright not out 0
D. L. Amiss not out 80	B 4, l-b 2, n-b 3 9
*M. J. K. Smith c Willetts b Rumsey 47	1/41 2/60 3/165 (5 wkts.) 190
J. A. Jameson b Rumsey 0	4/165 5/183

†A. C. Smith, R. V. Webster, D. J. Brown and J. D. Bannister did not bat.

Bowling: Rumsey 12—2—39—2; Palmer 6—0—46—0; Alley 12—5—15—2; C. R. M. Atkinson 8—1—32—0; Greetham 9—0—39—0; Burgess 4.4—2—10—1.

Umpires: J. S. Buller and T. W. Spencer.

WORCESTERSHIRE v. HAMPSHIRE

At Worcester, August 10. Worcestershire won by 99 runs. Driving powerfully and cutting effectively, Horton struck sixteen 4's in a stay of three hours nine minutes and his attractive second-wicket stand of 95 in ninety minutes with Ormrod enabled the later batsmen to play their shots. Hampshire began encouragingly with Marshall and Reed scoring well, but when they left the last eight wickets fell for 73, Coldwell taking four of them for 6 runs in his final spell. Man of the match: Horton.

Worcestershire

M. J. Horton b Cottam 114	D. W. Richardson not out 19
R. G. A. Headley c Ingleby-Mackenzie b Cottam 16	B 2, l-b 10, n-b 2 14
J. A. Ormrod b Shackleton 44	
B. d'Oliveira b Castell 24	1/45 2/140 (4 wkts., 60 overs) 253
*T. W. Graveney not out 22	3/195 4/216

†R. Booth, N. Gifford, L. J. Coldwell, R. G. M. Carter and J. A. Flavell did not bat.

Bowling: Shackleton 12—3—21—1; White 12—1—89—0; Cottam 12—0—45—2; Sainsbury 12—2—32—0; Castell 12—0—52—1.

Hampshire

*R. E. Marshall lbw b Flavell 37	A. T. Castell b Coldwell 3
B. L. Reed c Booth b Carter 37	D. Shackleton b Coldwell 10
H. Horton b Gifford 7	D. W. White not out 15
D. A. Livingstone c Graveney b. d'Oliveira 18	R. M. Cottam b Flavell 0
P. J. Sainsbury c Booth b Carter 1	
H. M. Barnard c d'Oliveira b Coldwell 18	L-b 6, n-b 1 7
†A. C. D. Ingleby-Mackenzie b Coldwell 1	1/59 2/81 3/83 4/84 5/118 6/124 7/126 8/138 9/153 154

Bowling: Flavell 10.2—4—32—2; Coldwell 12—3—39—4; Carter 12—5—33—2; Gifford 8—1—24—1; d'Oliveira 6—2—19—1.

Umpires: R. S. Lay and W. H. Copson.

THE FINAL

WARWICKSHIRE v. WORCESTERSHIRE

At Lord's, September 3. Warwickshire won by five wickets after a tremendous struggle against Worcestershire, their Midland neighbours, with 3.2 overs to spare. So in the course of two days Worcestershire, aspirants for the double, were deprived of the County Championship and the Cup, but they put up a noble fight. Warwickshire were greatly indebted to three men, Barber, top scorer of the day with 66, Cartwright, the most successful bowler, three wickets for 16, and Alan Smith, who, in the crisis, after being dropped before scoring by Graveney, hit a 6 and three 4's, getting all the last 21 runs after his colleagues had dithered.

Worcestershire's trouble began early when their captain, Kenyon, hit his wicket. Then Cartwright, swinging the ball awkwardly, penetrated deep into the Worcestershire batting by removing Ormrod, d'Oliveira and Graveney. They slumped to 104 in 49 overs before Gifford hit fearlessly while 50 were added from the remaining 11 overs, 43 coming in the last six. Gifford hit two 6's and five 4's but Warwickshire needed only 156 to win. They pursued a cautious path most of the way. Barber, whom Peter May named the man of the match, an award he has now won four times, alone showed any enterprise in the first two hours, and he hit six 4's, making 66 out of 95 in 39 overs. On his departure Amiss drove firmly and also hit one 6 and five 4's in 44, but Warwickshire still needed 17 from seven overs when Graveney at square leg failed to hold a sweep from Alan Smith off d'Oliveira. Smith rode his luck and saw Warwickshire home in a tense finish which roused the capacity crowd of 24,000 to lusty cheering for both teams.

Worcestershire

*D. Kenyon hit wkt. b Webster	13	†R. Booth c A. C. Smith b Bannister	0
M. J. Horton b Cartwright	20	N. Gifford b Ibadulla	38
J. A. Ormrod c A. C. Smith b Cartwright	9	B. M. Brain not out	14
T. W. Graveney c Ibadulla b Cartwright	18	L. J. Coldwell not out	1
B. d'Oliveira c Ibadulla b Brown	12	B 1, l-b 6	7
D. W. Richardson b Ibadulla	23	1/33 2/33 3/48 4/65 5/86 6/88 7/104 8/154 (8 wkts., after 60 overs)	155

J. A. Flavell did not bat.

Bowling: Brown 12—2—27—1; Webster 12—2—28—1; Cartwright 12—4—16—3; Bannister 12—3—27—1; Ibadulla 9—3—33—2; Barber 3—1—17—0.

Warwickshire

R. W. Barber c Horton b d'Oliveira	66	†A. C. Smith not out	21
K. Ibadulla c Horton b Gifford	10		
D. L. Amiss c Booth b Coldwell	44	L-b 2, n-b 1	3
*M. J. K. Smith b Brain	12		
J. A. Jameson c Booth b Flavell	0	1/44 2/95 3/130 4/133 5/138 (5 wkts.)	159
R. N. Abberley not out	3		

T. W. Cartwright, R. V. Webster, D. J. Brown and J. D. Bannister did not bat.

Bowling: Flavell 12—2—31—1; Coldwell 12—1—34—1; d'Oliveira 10—3—26—1; Gifford 11—3—32—1; Brain 11.4—2—33—1.

Umpires: J. S. Buller and C. S. Elliott.

Past Winners

1963	Sussex	1965	Yorkshire
1964	Sussex	1966	Warwickshire

GILLETTE CUP RULES

The Playing Conditions for First-Class matches in the United Kingdom will apply except where specified below.

Duration of Matches

The matches will consist of one innings per side and each innings will be limited to 60 overs. The matches are intended to be completed in one day, but three days will be allocated in case of weather interference.

Hours of play will be 10.45 a.m. to 7.30 p.m. The Umpires may order extra time if, in their opinion, a finish can be obtained.

In the event of the match starting not less than 30 *minutes nor more than* 90 *minutes late, owing to weather or the state of the ground, each innings shall be limited to* 50 *overs. If, however, the start of play is delayed for more than* 90 *minutes, the* 60*-over limit shall apply.*

Intervals

The normal intervals will be as follows: Lunch, 12.45 p.m.–1.15 p.m. Between innings, 10 minutes. Tea (15 minutes) to be taken after 1½ hours batting by the side batting second, or at 4.15 p.m. whichever is the earlier.

Adjustments can be made to the times of intervals by agreement between the Ground Authority and the two Captains.

Covering of the Pitch

The pitch will be completely covered throughout the match in the event of rain.

Limitations of Overs by any one bowler

No bowler may bowl more than 12 overs in an innings.

In the event of a bowler breaking down and being unable to complete an over, the remaining balls will be bowled by another bowler. Such part of an over will count as a full over only in so far as each bowler's limit is concerned.

The Result

(a) A Tie

In the event of a Tie, the result will be decided in favour of the side losing the least number of wickets. If both sides have lost the same number of wickets, the result will be decided on the higher rate of scoring in the first 20 overs of each innings. In the event of both sides being all out, in or under 60 overs, the overall scoring rate of both sides will be the deciding factor.

(b) Unfinished Match

If a match remains unfinished after three days, the winner will be the side which has scored the faster in runs per over throughout the innings provided that at least 20 overs have been bowled at the side batting second. If the scoring rate is the same, the side losing the least number of wickets in the first 20 overs of each innings, will be the winner.

If, however, at 3.00 p.m. on the third day, in the opinion of the Umpires, no result can be achieved in the match, whatever the weather, the Umpires will order a match of 10 overs each side to be started, if to do so is humanly possible.

If no play is possible on the first and second days, the Captains, bearing in mind the time remaining, will be empowered to re-arrange the number of overs to be bowled by each side to achieve a result. In the event of the number of overs being re-arranged, a minimum of 10 overs for each innings will apply.

If, owing to conditions, it is not possible to obtain a result, the two Captains will arrange another match of a minimum of 10 overs each side, to be played within 10 days on a ground to be mutually agreed.

THE UNIVERSITIES IN 1966

OXFORD

Captain—R. M. C. Gilliat (Charterhouse and Christ Church)
Secretary—G. N. S. Ridley (Milton, Rhodesia and Pembroke)
Captain for 1967—G. N. S. Ridley
Secretary—F. S. Goldstein (Falcon, Rhodesia and St. Edmund Hall)

Oxford's season finished triumphantly with a resounding win by an innings over Cambridge at Lord's, ending an exasperatingly long sequence of six drawn games in this annual fixture.

Oxford, who began the season with eight Blues still available, thus justified their pre-match position as favourites, earned by some noteworthy, if not always consistent, performances. Victories were gained in The Parks against Lancashire—the first against the county since 1946—and against the Royal Navy and The Army on tour.

Two pronounced weaknesses showed themselves often; a lack of technique against spin bowling and the failure of the last five batsmen to score runs. In some of the early matches when, as is usual nowadays with the inexorable demands of examinations, Oxford were compelled to play much below strength, there was not enough fighting spirit.

In the event Gilliat welded his side into a well-balanced and effective unit, and his excellent leadership was recognised by his being chosen to lead the M.C.C. President's XI against the West Indies.

The University's own match against the tourists, like so many others, was hit by rain, although Kanhai was seen in superlative form in making 192 not out. When defeat for Oxford looked certain the visitors were thwarted by an excellent rearguard action.

So bad was the weather in The Parks that two games, against Yorkshire and Worcestershire, were abandoned without a ball being delivered.

The University were fortunate in having their best opening pair for many years. Goldstein, in his first year, hit form straight away with an impressive combination of solid defence and enterprising attacking strokes, and both he and the experienced Gibbs made centuries.

Toft was not always successful in The Parks, but once his selection was announced this correct stroke player showed his true form. Gilliat himself contributed some innings of typical polish and once again Groves proved his forcefulness. Despite an extended trial, Daniels was unable to make any impression.

In bowling, Oxford could call on a well-varied and talented array. The Rugby Blue, Hiller, had enough " bite " to win him a place as attack opener with Watson. Easter began with a promising challenge for this vacancy, but failed to sustain it.

An important feature in Oxford's progress was the emergence of Elviss as an off-spinner of considerable merit. In the previous year the Dark Blues used two left-arm spin blowlers; this time Ridley sufficed and Barker, who had had little opportunity to play in earlier games, was left out.

With the selection of Ridley as captain and Goldstein as secretary, Oxford's affairs in 1967 are in the hands of two Rhodesians. G.K.

OXFORD UNIVERSITY RESULTS

First-Class Matches—Played 13: *Won* 2, *Lost* 6, *Drawn* 5, *Abandoned* 2

FIRST-CLASS AVERAGES

BATTING

	Matches	Inns.	Not Outs	Runs	Highest Inns.	Average
M. G. M. Groves	4	7	2	326	80*	65.20
F. S. Goldstein	9	17	0	583	87	34.29
P. J. K. Gibbs	8	14	0	460	107	32.85
D. P. Toft	7	13	0	386	84	29.69
R. M. C. Gilliat	13	24	0	703	86	29.29
A. W. Dyer	13	23	4	504	67	26.52
A. G. M. Watson	10	15	6	169	65*	18.77
J. P. R. F. Stephens	2	4	0	72	27	18.00
H. D. F. Marshall	3	5	0	86	48	17.20
A. H. Morgan	2	4	1	50	26	16.66
J. G. Saunders	2	4	1	48	47*	16.00
M. R. J. Guest	4	7	0	106	58	15.14
D. R. Walsh	6	12	2	135	56	13.50
G. N. S. Ridley	12	19	3	193	50*	12.06
A. R. Garofall	5	9	0	107	26	11.88
D. A. Ashworth	4	8	0	93	25	11.62
A. H. Barker	3	5	0	58	28	11.60
R. C. Daniels	3	6	0	67	26	11.16
R. B. Hiller	8	11	1	87	64	8.70
R. W. Elviss	13	18	5	57	9	4.38
J. N. C. Easter	10	14	6	24	12	3.00

Played in one match: A. D. Curtis 15; P. W. Neate 3.

**Signifies not out.*

BOWLING

	Overs	Maidens	Runs	Wickets	Average
J. G. Saunders	98.3	47	163	10	16.30
G. N. S. Ridley	456.1	181	969	42	23.07
R. W. Elviss	499.4	184	1,133	42	26.97
R. B. Hiller	166.2	36	494	17	29.05
J. N. C. Easter	221.4	60	676	19	35.57
A. G. M. Watson	235.3	58	774	21	36.85

Also bowled: A. H. Barker 73—23—191—2; R. C. Daniels 27—6—96—1; A. R. Garofall 0.1—0—4—0; P. J. K. Gibbs 1.2—1—4—0; F. S. Goldstein 1—1—0—0; M. G. M. Groves 8—1—39—0; M. R. J. Guest 48—12—128—3; P. W. Neate 29—13—53—0; D. R. Walsh 13—4—31—2.

OXFORD UNIVERSITY v. GLOUCESTERSHIRE

At Oxford, April 27, 28, 29. Drawn. Gloucestershire left the University to get 296 to win in four hours twenty minutes, but although the pitch remained perfect throughout the match the inexperience of the middle-order batsmen made this target unattainable. The Rhodesian Freshman, Goldstein, made a notable debut, with fifty in each innings. Concentration in defence and an ability to drive the ball effectively were his chief assets and his 78 in the second innings included eleven boundaries. For Gloucestershire, Russell, the former Middlesex player, played an attractive second innings to make 107 (eighteen 4's), which was cricket's first century of the season. Bissex helped him put on 176 in quick time for the third wicket. Elviss, the off-spinner, took five for 100 in his first bowling spell for the University. After this match R. W. Stewart played for Middlesex.

Gloucestershire

R. B. Nicholls c Dyer b Easter	9	— b Easter	9
C. A. Milton c Daniels b Ridley	26	— lbw b Watson	6
S. E. Russell c Dyer b Elviss	27	— c Gilliat b Ridley	107
M. Bissex c Gilliat b Elviss	20	— st Dyer b Elviss	77
D. Brown b Elviss	0	— not out	28
D. Shepherd c Dyer b Watson	33	— not out	11
*J. B. Mortimore b Elviss	28		
A. S. Brown c Gilliat b Elviss	30		
A. R. Windows not out	36		
R. W. Stewart c Walsh b Ridley	9		
†B. J. Meyer lbw b Ridley	0		
B 2, l-b 1	3	B 5, l-b 1	6
1/23 2/53 3/67 4/67 5/106 6/132 7/154 8/185 9/221	221	1/7 2/25 3/201 4/201 (4 wkts., dec.)	244

Bowling: *First Innings*—Watson 21—7—40—1; Easter 13—4—37—1; Ridley 18.3—9—41—3; Elviss 26—5—100—5. *Second Innings*—Watson 15—3—64—1; Easter 18—2—67—1; Ridley 20—7—45—1; Elviss 11—1—46—1; Walsh 6—2—16—0.

Oxford University

D. P. Toft lbw b Windows	32	— b Stewart	21
F. S. Goldstein c Windows b Mortimore	65	— c A. S. Brown b Bissex	78
*R. M. C. Gilliat b Windows	4	— lbw b Bissex	24
D. R. Walsh b Mortimore	3	— not out	20
R. C. Daniels b Stewart	4	— lbw b Mortimore	19
A. H. Morgan c Shepherd b Mortimore	26	— not out	11
†A. W. Dyer lbw b A. S. Brown	18		
G. N. S. Ridley b Windows	0		
A. G. M. Watson b Stewart	2		
R. W. Elviss not out	2		
J. N. C. Easter b Stewart	0		
B 6, l-b 7, n-b 1	14	B 1, l-b 2	3
1/51 2/67 3/76 4/85 5/129 6/148 7/151 8/168 9/168	170	1/44 2/107 3/124 4/150 (4 wkts.)	176

Bowling: *First Innings*—A. S. Brown 20—9—37—1; Windows 17—7—30—3; Mortimore 29—17—31—3; Stewart 20.4—10—27—3; Bissex 11—3—31—0. *Second Innings*—A. S. Brown 13—1—36—0; Stewart 12—2—26—1; Mortimore 29—13—40—1; Windows 12—4—38—0; Bissex 19—11—32—2; Nicholls 2—1—1—0.

Umpires: J. S. Buller and A. E. Alderman.

OXFORD UNIVERSITY v. HAMPSHIRE

At Oxford, April 30, May 2, 3. Hampshire won by eight wickets. Oxford made a good start after winning the toss and their captain Gilliat, a left-hander, hit 62. The Freshman, Walsh, from Marlborough, contributed 56 and Gilliat was able to declare at 285 for seven. The young off-spinner, Wheatley, bowled skilfully in a long spell of 39 overs. Hampshire topped the Oxford score due mainly to an excellent maiden century by their wicket-keeper, Timms, in two hours forty minutes, including sixteen boundaries. Batting again 43 behind, the University did not fare nearly so well against the pace of White (five for 47) and the spin of Wheatley (four for 22) and were all out for 136, leaving the county to make only 94 to win. Marshall raced to a typically breezy 50, with the help of ten boundaries.

Oxford University

D. P. Toft c Keith b Shackleton	51	— lbw b Shackleton	20
F. S. Goldstein lbw b Wheatley	23	— c Timms b White	6
*R. M. C. Gilliat b Wheatley	62	— c Timms b Wheatley	38
D. R. Walsh c Reed b Wassell	56	— c Timms b White	0
R. C. Daniels b White	0	— c Keith b White	26
A. H. Morgan c Marshall b Wassell	9	— c Shackleton b Wheatley	4
†A. W. Dyer st Timms b Wheatley	32	— b White	17
G. N. S. Ridley not out	24	— b Wheatley	3
A. G. M. Watson not out	16	— c Wheatley b White	3
R. W. Elviss (did not bat)		— b Wheatley	8
J. N. C. Easter (did not bat)		— not out	0
B 8, l-b 4	12	L-b 11	11
1/49 2/113 3/141 4/146 5/160 6/236 7/242 (7 wkts., dec.)	285	1/10 2/12 3/54 4/75 5/89 6/112 7/117 8/127 9/130	136

Bowling: *First Innings*—Shackleton 26—7—60—1; White 15—1—35—1; Sainsbury 30—8—72—0; Wheatley 39—20—64—3; Wassell 25—12—42—2; Marshall 3—3—0—0. *Second Innings*—Shackleton 15—4—34—1; White 19—5—47—5; Wheatley 24.2—15—22—4; Wassell 11—7—9—0; Sainsbury 9—5—13—0.

Hampshire

*R. E. Marshall c Goldstein b Easter	47	— b Ridley	52
B. L. Reed c Toft b Easter	15	— c Dyer b Ridley	31
H. Horton c Ridley b Elviss	19	— not out	2
D. A. Livingstone c Dyer b Watson	26	— not out	11
G. L. Keith b Elviss	0		
P. J. Sainsbury c Dyer b Ridley	25		
†B. S. V. Timms c Gilliat b Elviss	120		
K. J. Wheatley b Easter	40		
A. R. Wassell b Elviss	10		
D. Shackleton not out	0		
D. W. White c Dyer b Watson	18		
B 5, l-b 2, n-b 1	8	L-b 1	1
1/48 2/69 3/92 4/102 5/110 6/160 7/247 8/291 9/310	328	1/69 2/84 (2 wkts.)	97

Bowling: *First Innings*—Watson 23.3—6—83—2; Easter 20—5—79—3; Ridley 34—15—57—1; Elviss 21—6—65—4; Daniels 15—5—36—0. *Second Innings*—Watson 7—2—24—0; Easter 8—1—21—0; Ridley 8—1—20—2; Daniels 7—1—31—0.

Umpires: J. S. Buller and A. E. Alderman.

OXFORD UNIVERSITY v. YORKSHIRE

At Oxford, May 4, 5, 6. Match abandoned without a ball being bowled.

Oxford University

P. J. K. Gibbs, F. S. Goldstein, D. P. Toft, *R. M. C. Gilliat, D. R. Walsh, †A. W. Dyer, A. H. Barker, G. N. S. Ridley, A. G. M. Watson, R. W. Elviss, J. N. C. Easter.

Yorkshire

From G. Boycott, K. Taylor, D. E. V. Padgett, P. J. Sharpe, R. Illingworth, G. A. Cope, †J. G. Binks, *F. S. Trueman, D. Wilson, J. Waring, A. G. Nicholson, B. Wood.

Umpires: W. F. Price and W. F. Simpson.

At Oxford, May 7, 9, 10. OXFORD UNIVERSITY drew with WEST INDIES. (See WEST INDIES section.)

OXFORD UNIVERSITY v. WORCESTERSHIRE

At Oxford, May 11, 12, 13. Abandoned without a ball being bowled.

Oxford University

D. P. Toft, F. S. Goldstein, J. F. Stephens, *R. M. C. Gilliat, D. R. Walsh, †A. W. Dyer, G. N. S. Ridley, A. G. M. Watson, P. W. Neate, R. W. Elviss, J. N. C. Easter.

Worcestershire

*D. Kenyon, R. G. A. Headley, J. A. Ormrod, T. W. Graveney, B. d'Oliveira, D. W. Richardson, †R. Booth, D. N. F. Slade, N. Gifford, L. J. Coldwell, J. A. Flavell.

Umpires: P. B. Wight and A. Jepson.

OXFORD UNIVERSITY v. NOTTINGHAMSHIRE

At Oxford, May 18, 19, 20. Drawn. Oxford were never likely to get the 193 runs needed in two hours twenty minutes for victory, but earned a comfortable draw, mainly due to a fifth-wicket partnership between Dyer and Walsh. White, Whittingham and Smedley figured in quick-scoring stands for Nottinghamshire against amiable bowling. Despite an innings of 69 by their captain, Gilliat, and other useful scores by Dyer and Goldstein in a rain-interrupted day, Oxford fell 43 runs behind. When Nottinghamshire batted again, Bolus showed some of his old aggression and was not out 81 at the declaration. A feature of the match was the emergence of White, the former Middlesex batsman, as an off-spin bowler with ability to turn the ball considerably.

Nottinghamshire

*N. Hill b Ridley	37	— c Ridley b Elviss	27
J. B. Bolus c Dyer b Ridley	13	— not out	81
B. Whittingham b Daniels	42	— not out	38
I. Moore c Neate b Ridley	2		
R. A. White c Dyer b Easter	64		
M. J. Smedley c Stephens b Easter	63		
M. Taylor c Ridley b Easter	0		
K. Gillhouley c Neate b Watson	2		
†F. B. Hassan b Watson	11		
B. Stead not out	19		
I. Davison c Gilliat b Elviss	16		
B 14	14	L-b 2, w 1	3
1/47 2/62 3/74 4/130 5/224 6/224 7/229 8/242 9/254	283	1/59 (1 wkt., dec.)	149

Bowling: *First Innings*—Watson 19—8—51—2; Easter 20—5—58—3; Neate 22—11—36—0; Ridley 22—8—38—3; Elviss 25.2—11—57—1; Daniels 5—0—29—1. *Second Innings*—Watson 4—1—9—0; Easter 5—0—13—0; Ridley 24—6—55—0; Elviss 16—3—52—1; Neate 7—2—17—0.

Oxford University

First Innings		Second Innings	
F. S. Goldstein b White	40	— run out	16
J. F. Stephens b Taylor	18	— c Hassan b Stead	24
*R. M. C. Gilliat c Moore b Gillhouley	69	— b White	12
D. R. Walsh c Taylor b White	9	— not out	9
R. C. Daniels b White	18	— c Hassan b Gillhouley	0
†A. W. Dyer c Hassan b Stead	47	— not out	37
G. N. S. Ridley lbw b Stead	15		
A. G. M. Watson c Hassan b Davison	9		
P. W. Neate b Davison	3		
R. W. Elviss c Moore b Stead	7		
J. N. C. Easter not out	0		
B 2, l-b 2, n-b 1	5	L-b 1	1
1/55 2/65 3/97 4/135 5/171 6/204 7/223 8/231 9/240	240	1/36 2/42 3/42 4/54 (4 wkts.)	99

Bowling: *First Innings*—Davison 17.2—6—34—2; Stead 23—4—42—3; Taylor 25—6—57—1; White 27—11—53—3; Gillhouley 21—9—49—1. *Second Innings*—Davison 9—2—26—0; Stead 8—0—25—1; White 15—6—19—1; Gillhouley 12—4—14—1; Taylor 3—0—14—0.

Umpires: J. S. Buller and H. P. Sharp.

OXFORD UNIVERSITY v. FREE FORESTERS

At Oxford, May 28, 30, 31. (Not first-class.) Free Foresters won by 125 runs. The Foresters made a splendid recovery after being led by 161 runs on the first innings. This will be remembered above all as Carr's match. The M.C.C. assistant secretary and former Derbyshire and Oxford captain, scored a whirlwind century in eighty-six minutes, including one 6 and seventeen 4's, the second 50 coming in twenty-two minutes of perfectly-timed stroke play. He took four for 39 with his left-arm slows in Oxford's second innings, held three catches—and was no-balled for having too many fielders behind the popping crease on the leg side! Another old Oxford Blue, Piachaud, did considerable damage with his off-breaks, but Oxford gave up the ghost too easily. Ashworth, loaned by the University to the Foresters, hit an excellent 120.

Oxford University

First Innings		Second Innings	
F. S. Goldstein lbw b Carr	27	— c Carr b Coghlan	1
J. F. Stephens run out	11	— b Piachaud	13
*R. M. C. Gilliat b Piachaud	39	— c Howland b Piachaud	28
A. R. Garofall c and b Piachaud	27	— c Howland b Piachaud	5
D. R. Walsh c Howland b Bailey	53	— b Carr	11
†A. W. Dyer c Ainsworth b Bailey	4	— c Metcalfe b Piachaud	5
G. N. S. Ridley c Carr b Coghlan	38	— c and b Carr	0
A. G. M. Watson st Howland b Piachaud	29	— run out	26
R. W. Elviss c Howland b Piachaud	27	— st Howland b Carr	6
R. B. Hiller b Piachaud	4	— lbw b Carr	8
J. N. C. Easter not out	4	— not out	2
B 8, l-b 1, n-b 2	11	B 4	4
1/19 2/72 3/82 4/131 5/140 6/206 7/206 8/235 9/245	274	1/4 2/35 3/45 4/48 5/62 6/67 7/68 8/76 9/94	109

Bowling: *First Innings*—Bailey 38—13—58—2; Coghlan 13—2—40—1; Scott 3—0—21—0; Piachaud 49—21—88—5; Carr 26—5—56—1. *Second Innings*—Coghlan 12—3—23—1; Scott 6—1—21—0; Piachaud 18.4—10—22—4; Carr 13—4—39—4.

Free Foresters

S. G. Metcalfe b Watson	8	— st Dyer b Ridley	24
R. C. G. Fortin b Watson	8	— b Elviss	19
C. A. Fry b Hiller	13	— b Ridley	24
D. B. Carr c Garofall b Elviss	28	— c Goldstein b Ridley	103
D. A. Ashworth c Gilliat b Ridley	0	— b Ridley	120
*M. L. Y. Ainsworth c and b Ridley	12	— b Easter	41
†C. B. Howland c and b Elviss	6	— c Hiller b Elviss	20
T. B. L. Coghlan c Walsh b Ridley	20	— c Dyer b Elviss	3
P. J. R. Scott lbw b Elviss	0	— b Elviss	0
J. D. Piachaud c Goldstein b Elviss	2	— st Dyer b Elviss	16
J. A. Bailey not out	8	— not out	4
B 8	8	B 11, l-b 10	21
1/8 2/27 3/39 4/55 5/69 6/77 7/89 8/95 9/97	113	1/46 2/46 3/108 4/199 5/281 6/343 7/370 8/372 9/374	395

Bowling: *First Innings*—Watson 8—2—20—2; Hiller 10—13—14—1; Easter 6—3—12—0; Ridley 15.2—5—34—3; Elviss 12—5—25—4. *Second Innings*—Watson 15—3—64—0; Hiller 14—1—47—0; Elviss 42.1—11—119—5; Ridley 50—11—127—4; Easter 8—3—17—1.

Umpires: J. F. Crapp and G. H. Pope.

OXFORD UNIVERSITY v. MIDDLESEX

At Oxford, June 1, 2. Middlesex won by an innings and 11 runs. A youthful, largely unseasoned Middlesex XI proved much too good for an Oxford side lacking spirit and won in two days. Oxford were put out for 140 on a good, hard wicket. Goldstein resisted firmly and Ridley showed what could be achieved with positive stroke play. By contrast, Middlesex went on to make 307 by a display of competent, all-round batting that never faltered even when wickets were falling. In their second innings the University were bemused by spin, and the West Indian leg-break bowler, Latchman, took half their wickets for 43, finishing with a match analysis of eight for 68. He received useful support from Bick and Parfitt; Oxford were beaten with eleven minutes of extra time left.

Oxford University

F. S. Goldstein c Parfitt b Latchman	42	— c Radley b Latchman	39
*R. M. C. Gilliat b Ling	19	— b Latchman	35
A. R. Garofall run out	9	— lbw b Latchman	0
D. R. Walsh c Parfitt b Herman	1	— c Murray b Bick	1
D. A. Ashworth b Latchman	4	— c Ling b Latchman	25
†A. W. Dyer c Radley b Latchman	0	— b Latchman	6
G. N. S. Ridley c Murray b Ling	27	— c Murray b Bick	2
A. G. M. Watson c Clark b Parfitt	13	— c Parfitt b Bick	25
R. W. Elviss lbw b Ling	7	— c Clark b Parfitt	4
R. B. Hiller run out	4	— b Parfitt	5
J. N. C. Easter not out	1	— not out	0
B 13	13	B 9, l-b 4, n-b 1	14
1/31 2/64 3/67 4/79 5/79 6/88 7/122 8/129 9/135	140	1/51 2/88 3/94 4/106 5/112 6/114 7/118 8/137 9/150	156

Bowling: *First Innings*—Herman 12—6—16—1; Ling 15—8—24—3; Bick 19—8—33—0; Latchman 15—9—25—3; Parfitt 9—2—17—1; White 6—3—12—0. *Second Innings*—Herman 5—0—12—0; Ling 5—2—24—0; Bick 29.2—15—49—3; Latchman 30—15—43—5; Parfitt 9—6—6—2; White 3—1—8—0.

Middlesex

C. T. Radley lbw b Watson	4	H. C. Latchman b Hiller	2
M. J. Smith c Gilliat b Ridley	47	R. F. White not out	7
M. J. Harris c Elviss b Easter	58	R. S. Herman c Elviss b Watson	9
P. H. Parfitt c Gilliat b Easter	23		
E. A. Clark c Ridley b Easter	25	B 2, l-b 4, n-b 2	8
D. J. Ling b Elviss	40		
D. A. Bick c Walsh b Elviss	38	1/5 2/93 3/125 4/153 5/184	307
*†J. T. Murray c Goldstein b Ridley	46	6/210 7/289 8/289 9/292	

Bowling—Watson 17.4—2—57—2; Hiller 8—0—31—1; Easter 20—6—64—3; Elviss 33—11—91—2; Ridley 18—5—56—2.

Umpires: J. F. Crapp and A. E. Alderman.

OXFORD UNIVERSITY v. ESSEX

At Oxford, June 4, 6, 7. Essex won by 162 runs. Batting failures by Oxford on a wicket taking spin gave Essex a comfortable victory. A splendid knock of 89 by Fletcher was the chief feature of the county's first innings. Oxford fared disastrously in reply against Hobbs and Smith but Watson and Hiller came to the rescue with a ninth-wicket partnership of 124, well-earned by some hearty and correct stroke play. Essex were given another good start by Bear and Saville, and Fletcher again proved a stumbling-block, passing 50 for the second time and remaining undefeated. The task of scoring 300 to win was well beyond Oxford's capabilities. The county slow bowlers were right on top again, and the last six University wickets collapsed for 30 runs.

Essex

*G. E. Barker c Stephens b Elviss	38	— c Dyer b Walsh	4
M. J. Bear c Dyer b Elviss	46	— c Ashworth b Ridley	42
G. J. Saville b Ridley	24	— c Walsh b Easter	42
K. W. R. Fletcher c Ashworth b Watson	89	— not out	51
B. R. Knight b Elviss	0	— b Easter	16
G. J. Smith lbw b Ridley	12	— c Elviss b Walsh	13
†G. R. Cass lbw b Elviss	0	— c Hiller b Elviss	27
B. Edmeades c Garofall b Elviss	17	— b Hiller	18
R. N. S. Hobbs b Hiller	19	— not out	16
G. C. Pritchard not out	0		
R. East c Easter b Watson	0		
B 8, l-b 1, n-b 4	13	B 8, l-b 1, n-b 2	11
1/72 2/119 3/119 4/130 5/149 6/156 7/212 8/258 9/258	258	1/82 2/107 3/131 4/143 5/174 6/186 7/215 (7 wkts., dec.)	240

Bowling: *First Innings*—Watson 9—1—36—2; Hiller 6—1—11—1; Easter 11—1—51—0; Elviss 37—11—90—5; Ridley 28—12—57—2. *Second Innings*—Watson 5—1—22—0; Hiller 19—6—51—1; Elviss 24—7—66—1; Ridley 11—3—29—1; Easter 19—7—46—2; Walsh 7—2—15—2.

Oxford University

G. F. Stephens lbw b Edmeades	3	— c and b Fletcher	27
D. A. Ashworth c Saville b Hobbs	6	— c Hobbs b Smith	18
*R. M. C. Gilliat st Cass b Hobbs	14	— lbw b Hobbs	5
A. R. Garofall c and b Smith	6	— c Fletcher b Smith	19
D. R. Walsh c Cass b Hobbs	0	— lbw b Smith	30
†A. W. Dyer lbw b Hobbs	19	— b East	6
G. N. S. Ridley lbw b Smith	0	— lbw b East	2
A. G. M. Watson not out	65	— not out	10
R. W. Elviss b Smith	0	— c Smith b East	0
R. B. Hiller c Cass b Smith	64	— b East	0
J. N. C. Easter b Knight	12	— c Hobbs b Smith	6
B 2, l-b 8	10	B 6, l-b 7, w 1	14
1/9 2/11 3/24 4/24 5/46 6/48 7/48 8/48 9/172	199	1/33 2/50 3/56 4/107 5/114 6/114 7/124 8/130 9/130	137

Bowling: *First Innings*—Pritchard 11—3—17—0; Edmeades 17—6—34—1; Hobbs 30—12—63—4; East 8—4—13—0; Smith 17—8—35—4; Knight 7.3—0—27—1. *Second Innings*—Knight 3—1—3—0; Edmeades 4—2—4—0; Hobbs 20—7—36—1; East 17—10—19—4; Smith 19.5—9—34—4; Fletcher 10—3—27—1.

Umpires: J. Langridge and R. S. Lay.

OXFORD UNIVERSITY v. LANCASHIRE

At Oxford, June 8, 9, 10. Oxford won by 71 runs and gained their first success over Lancashire since 1946. Oxford recovered after losing their openers, Gibbs and Ashworth, for nothing and reached 241 through some sound batting by Gilliat, Marshall, Dyer and Saunders on a pitch that favoured the spinners. The Dark Blues' off spinners, Saunders and Elviss, took full advantage of the conditions and bowled the county out for 203 of which Pullar contributed a handsome 60. Oxford left Lancashire to score 263 runs to win in four hours after half centuries by Gibbs and Gilliat and another useful innings by Dyer enabled them to declare at 224 for eight wickets. Green and Pullar accepted the challenge and put the county ahead of the clock with an opening stand of 64 in half an hour, but with their departure the innings collapsed before Saunders and Elviss and Oxford won with an hour to spare. Saunders, in his first game for the University finished with match figures of ten for 102 and Elviss took nine for 166.

Oxford University

P. J. K. Gibbs c Krikken b Lever	0	— b Howard	53
D. A. Ashworth b Lever	0	— c Krikken b Lever	22
*R. M. C. Gilliat c and b Howard	38	— c Pullar b Howard	58
A. R. Garofall b Lever	20	— b Howard	9
D. R. Walsh c Howard b Lever	2	— c Knox b Lloyd	4
H. D. F. Marshall c Sullivan b Worsley	48	— c Green b Howard	0
†A. W. Dyer c Worsley b Green	67	— not out	43
R. W. Elviss c Worsley b Howard	4	— b Howard	3
J. G. Saunders not out	47	— b Howard	0
R. B. Hiller b Green	1	— not out	8
J. N. C. Easter c Krikken b Lever	2		
B 5, w 1, n-b 6	12	B 16, l-b 4, n-b 4	24
1/0 2/5 3/48 4/55 5/67 6/140 7/155 8/226 9/230	241	1/24 2/115 3/145 4/151 5/155 6/157 7/164 8/164 (8 wkts., dec.)	224

Bowling: *First Innings*—Lever 21.3—7—43—5; Green 9—0—34—2; Howard 24—14—37—2; Lloyd 19—5—48—0; Sullivan 2—1—8—0; Thomas 8—5—7—0; Worsley 12—2—52—1; *Second Innings*—Lever 17—3—54—1; Green 4—2—7—0; Worsley 14—3—39—0; Howard 39.3—20—77—6; Lloyd 16—6—23—1.

Lancashire

*D. M. Green c Dyer b Hiller	2	— c Hiller b Saunders	24
G. Pullar c sub b Elviss	60	— b Elviss	3[illegible]
G. K. Knox lbw b Elviss	39	— b Saunders	1[illegible]
D. R. Worsley c Gilliatt b Saunders	32	— c Gibbs b Elviss	1[illegible]
J. D. Bond b Saunders	1	— c Ashworth b Saunders	[illegible]
J. Sullivan c Easter b Elviss	11	— c Gilliat b Saunders	2[illegible]
D. Lloyd c Garofall b Saunders	0	— st Dyer b Elviss	2[illegible]
A. Thomas c Garofall b Elviss	4	— c Garofall b Elviss	[illegible]
P. Lever c and b Saunders	32	— c Marshall b Saunders	2[illegible]
†B. Krikken c Gibbs b Saunders	4	— c Garofall b Elviss	[illegible]
K. Howard not out	0	— not out	[illegible]
B 15, l-b 3	18	B 19, l-b 4, w 1	2[illegible]
1/2 2/89 3/112 4/117 5/148 6/160 7/160 8/181 9/194	203	1/64 2/78 3/84 4/100 5/134 6/144 7/144 8/177 9/177	19[illegible]

Bowling: *First Innings*—Hiller 14—2—37—1; Easter 10—6—15—0; Elviss 47—22—83—4; Saunders 39.3—25—50—5. *Second Innings*—Hiller 4—1—17—0; Easter 3—0—15—0; Saunders 34—18—52—5; Elviss 35—15—83—5.

Umpires: H. Yarnold and F. Jakeman.

OXFORD UNIVERSITY v. LEICESTERSHIRE

At Oxford, June 11, 13, 14. Leicestershire won by seven wickets with ten minutes to spare. The University batsmen were never happy against the speed of Cotton and spin of Lock and were dismissed for 172. The exception was Gilliat who hit magnificently for 85. Leicestershire made a bad start in reply, losing three wickets for 48, but a partnership of 157 between Marner (108) and Constant enabled them to gain a lead of 108. Lock really came into his own in the second innings with four wickets and three excellent close-to-the-wicket catches. The opening bat Gibbs hit 67 and Dyer was 52 not out when Oxford were all out for 204, leaving Leicestershire to score 97 to win. They achieved their target only after two and a half hours of listless batting.

Oxford University

First Innings		Second Innings	
P. J. K. Gibbs b Marner	15	c Savage b Lock	67
D. A. Ashworth c Norman b Cotton	13	c Lock b Marner	5
*R. M. C. Gilliat b Marner	85	c Lock b Matthews	13
A. R. Garofall c Marner b Cotton	1	c Lock b Matthews	26
H. D. F. Marshall c Lock b Matthews	12	b Savage	17
†A. W. Dyer c Norman b Cotton	7	not out	52
G. N. S. Ridley c Matthews b Lock	22	b Savage	5
R. W. Elviss b Lock	4	b Savage	0
J. G. Saunders c Constant b Lock	0	c Greensword b Lock	1
R. B. Hiller c Tolchard b Cotton	2	c and b Lock	3
J. N. C. Easter not out	3	c Constant b Lock	0
L-b 6, n-b 2	8	B 7, l-b 5, n-b 3	15
1/25 2/29 3/31 4/56 5/72 6/97 7/111 8/111 9/138	172	1/12 2/38 3/64 4/124 5/150 6/160 7/171 8/193 9/193	204

Bowling: *First Innings*—Cotton 17—3—34—4; Marner 8.5—3—18—2; Greensword 6—1—16—0; Savage 22—11—22—0; Matthews 13—2—39—1; Lock 8—1—35—3. *Second Innings*—Cotton 8—1—20—0; Marner 12—4—28—1; Savage 34—10—64—3; Lock 36—16—51—4; Matthews 11—4—26—2.

Leicestershire

First Innings		Second Innings	
B. J. Booth b Elviss	15	not out	50
R. Rehman lbw b Hiller	18	c Garofall b Ridley	4
M. E. Norman b Ridley	9	c Hiller b Ridley	25
P. Marner c Ridley b Easter	108	lbw b Easter	13
D. Constant c Dyer b Hiller	45	not out	1
S. Greensword lbw b Easter	13		
†R. W. Tolchard lbw b Hiller	2		
A. Matthews c Dyer b Easter	0		
*G. A. R. Lock b Easter	21		
J. Cotton b Hiller	25		
J. S. Savage not out	6		
B 5, l-b 9, n-b 4	18	L-b 5, n-b 1	6
1/30 2/38 3/48 4/205 5/209 6/223 7/223 8/227 9/249	280	1/61 2/65 3/81 (3 wkts.)	99

Bowling: *First Innings*—Hiller 21.2—5—53—4; Easter 21—6—51—4; Elviss 48—19—67—1; Ridley 33—16—56—1; Saunders 13—2—35—0. *Second Innings*—Hiller 7—4—12—0; Easter 14—6—20—1; Ridley 20—8—31—2; Saunders 12—2—26—0; Garofall 0.1—0—4—0.

Umpires: O. W. Herman and F. Jakeman.

OXFORD UNIVERSITY v. NORTHAMPTONSHIRE

At Oxford, June 15, 16, 17. Drawn. Oxford's last match in the University Parks was abandoned as a draw after rain had curtailed play to a little over six hours in the first two days and prevented any on the last day. Oxford again showed their inability to deal with spin bowling and were shot out for 102. Ridley, the University slow left-arm bowler, took four wickets for 29 runs on a pitch that gave him some assistance. At the end of the second day the game was delicately poised with the county leading by one run with four wickets standing, but hopes of an exciting finish the next day were dashed by the weather.

Oxford University

P. J. K. Gibbs c Johnson b Watts	0
A. D. Curtis b Willey	15
*R. M. C. Gilliat b Willey	16
A. R. Garofall c Johnson b Steele	17
H. D. F. Marshall c Scott b Steele	9
†A. W. Dyer c and b Steele	21
G. N. S. Ridley c Watts b Steele	2
A. H. Barker c Scott b Mushtaq	7
R. W. Elviss st Johnson b Mushtaq	9
R. B. Hiller b Mushtaq	0
J. N. C. Easter not out	0
L-b 4, n-b 2	6
1/0 2/22 3/49 4/52 5/63 6/76 7/90 8/90 9/90	102

Bowling: Watts 8—3—11—1; Durose 13—1—17—0; Willey 11—2—21—2; Scott 8—5—11—0; Steele 20—12—24—4; Mushtaq 11.1—3—12—3.

Northamptonshire

R. Wills b Ridley	6
A. M. R. Sim lbw b Ridley	14
B. L. Reynolds b Elviss	11
P. J. Watts c and b Ridley	6
Mushtaq Mohammad c Dyer b Hiller	9
D. S. Steele b Ridley	21
*R. M. Prideaux not out	25
P. Willey not out	2
B 4, l-b 3, n-b 2	9
1/18 2/25 3/41 4/50 5/56 6/94 (6 wkts.)	103

M. E. Scott, †L. A. Johnson and A. J. Durose did not bat.

Bowling: Hiller 18—3—41—1; Easter 6—3—12—0; Elviss 14—7—12—1; Ridley 19—7—29—4.

Umpires: J. Arnold and H. Mellows.

At Chatham, June 22, 23. OXFORD UNIVERSITY beat ROYAL NAVY by ten wickets. (Not first-class.)

At Canterbury, June 25, 27, 28. OXFORD UNIVERSITY lost to KENT by 139 runs.

At Aldershot, June 29, 30, July 1. OXFORD UNIVERSITY beat THE ARMY by 155 runs. (Not first-class.)

At Birmingham, July 2, 4, 5. OXFORD UNIVERSITY drew with WARWICKSHIRE.

At Derby, July 6, 7, 8. OXFORD UNIVERSITY lost to DERBYSHIRE by five wickets.

At Lord's, July 9, 11, 12. OXFORD beat CAMBRIDGE by an innings and nine runs. (See OTHER MATCHES AT LORD'S.)

CAMBRIDGE

Captain—D. L. Murray (Queen's Royal College, Trinidad and Jesus)

Hon. Secretary—K. P. W. J. McAdam (Millfield and Clare)

Captain in 1967—S. G. Russell (Tiffin's and Trinity)

Hon. Secretary—G. A. Cottrell (Kingston G.S. and St. Catharine's)

There have been several instances in past years when University cricketers with a poor record have risen above themselves at Lord's and beaten, or at least had the better of the match, against the hot favourites, but the disappointing form of the 1966 Cambridge side continued to the end. Oxford beat them quite convincingly by an innings and nine runs. There is little doubt that this was the weakest Cambridge team in the last twenty years. Cambridge men have become so accustomed since the war to a flow of talent through their hands—there have been eleven Test cricketers, including four International captains—that the failure of last year's side was particularly hard to bear. The barrel, for the time being, has clearly run dry, and although they did rather better on tour than they did at Fenner's, they never really over-troubled the counties.

The season got off to a controversial start when the captain, D. L. Murray, announced that he would select the team to play Oxford only from those who had made themselves available during the term. This immediately excluded two of his main bowlers, A. A. McLachlan and M. Whitaker, who had their noses over books in May and June. McLachlan had been in the side the two previous years as a leg-break bowler, and Whitaker, at medium pace, had been the most successful bowler in 1965 before falling ill. In fact, as it turned out, it was the batting rather than the bowling which proved the weaker.

The captain showed his class on several occasions, including an innings of 133 against Sussex at Hove, where Cambridge scored 373 in their second innings, but on the whole Murray was too erratic for a player of such ability. The secretary, K. P. W. J. McAdam, had a disappointing season as an opener, with an average of 17.66 and a top score of 50, while D. L. Hays and V. P. Malalasakera from Ceylon, flattered only to deceive too often.

The one really encouraging aspect for Cambridge was the batting of N. J. Cosh, the Dulwich Freshman, who the previous winter had toured South Africa with the M.C.C. Schools team. From the first match against Essex, when he scored 42, Cosh revealed the technique and temperament to succeed against the counties, and at the end he finished at the head of the averages, with nearly 700 runs and a top score of 98 against the West Indies.

The best of the bowlers was the old Blue, S. G. Russell, with 41 wickets. In the University Match, Russell, who is the new captain, took five for 60. The off-spinner, R. Roopnaraine, had an impressive match against Worcestershire at Fenner's, when his analysis in the first innings was 49—23—78—5, but, alas, he was never as accurate again. Finally, although Cambridge were so soundly beaten at Lord's, at least they never resorted to negative tactics in the field, and their batting, although so unsuccessful, was not without a certain degree of spirit all the way through. A.S.R.W.

CAMBRIDGE UNIVERSITY RESULTS

First-Class Matches—Played 16: *Won* 1, *Lost* 13, *Drawn* 2

FIRST-CLASS AVERAGES

BATTING

	Matches	Inns.	Not Outs	Runs	Highest Inns.	Average
N. J. Cosh	14	26	3	693	98	30.13
J. M. Brearley	2	4	0	114	101	28.50
D. L. Murray	14	26	6	626	133	26.08
D. L. Hays	13	26	0	510	72	19.61
L. M. L. Barnwell	3	6	0	107	46	17.83
K. P. W. J. McAdam	13	24	0	424	50	17.66
R. E. J. Chambers	12	22	0	386	58	17.54
G. A. Cottrell	14	26	2	398	44*	16.58
V. P. Malalasakera	13	24	0	323	80	13.45
A. B. Palfreman	9	18	1	227	67	13.35
A. V. E. Gould	12	22	0	225	38	10.22
N. Sinker	11	20	4	150	31*	9.37
R. Roopnaraine	12	22	3	172	50*	9.05
D. L. Acfield	12	22	10	77	19*	6.41
R. W. Cutler	2	4	0	25	12	6.25
D. R. Aers	2	4	0	17	16	4.25
J. F. Fitzgerald	3	6	1	21	7	4.20
S. G. Russell	14	25	6	67	12	3.52

Played in one match: A. J. Cross 19 and 17.

* *Signifies not out.*

BOWLING

	Overs	Maidens	Runs	Wickets	Average
J. F. Fitzgerald	107.2	33	324	15	21.60
S. G. Russell	338.4	72	1,035	41	25.24
A. B. Palfreman	245.1	62	786	26	30.23
N. Sinker	279.1	74	650	21	31.23
R. Roopnaraine	461.5	165	1,061	32	33.15
D. L. Acfield	385.3	115	963	28	34.39
G. A. Cottrell	265	72	776	20	38.80

Also bowled: L. M. L. Barnwell 19—4—66—1; J. M. Brearley 2—1—7—0 R. E. J. Chambers 0.5—0—4—0; N. J. Cosh 5—1—22—1; A. J. Cross 6—1—19—0; R. W. Cutler 42—14—119—1; A. V. E. Gould 5.2—1—16—1; D. L. Hay 2—1—5—0; V. P. Malalasakera 3—1—5—0; K. P. W. J. McAdam 2—0—2—0 D. L. Murray 12—3—66—1.

In the 1966 *Wisden, Cambridge were credited with a victory over Combined Services in* 1965 *which was not a first-class match. The record should have read: Played* 10: *Lost* 8, *Drawn* 2.

CAMBRIDGE UNIVERSITY v. MIDDLESEX

At Cambridge, April 30, May 2, 3. Middlesex won by 232 runs. An attractive hundred in the first innings by the Middlesex opening batsman, Radley, was the feature of a very comfortable win for Middlesex. The Cambridge bowlers were attacked with confidence in both innings, and the situation was made worse for Cambridge in the first innings when their opening bowler, Russell, pulled a muscle in the eighth over of the morning and took no further part in the first day's play. Middlesex, after bowling Cambridge out for 142, had a lead of 223, but they did not enforce the follow-on, and in their second innings Harris, opening in place of Radley, scored 81. On the third day Cambridge were left with the mammoth task of scoring 416 to win, and although the captain Murray played well for 51, Middlesex won, as expected, with plenty of time to spare.

Middlesex

First innings		Second innings	
M. J. Smith c Hays b Cottrell	26	c Hays b Russell	12
C. T. Radley c Cosh b Fitzgerald	115	b Russell	10
M. J. Harris c Hays b Cutler	34	c Cottrell b Fitzgerald	81
E. A. Clark c Murray b Fitzgerald	13	b Russell	3
†J. T. Murray c Cutler b Fitzgerald	44	c Murray b Fitzgerald	8
*F. J. Titmus c Murray b Cottrell	30	c Cosh b Fitzgerald	18
D. Bennett st Hays b Roopnaraine	36	not out	42
R. W. Hooker b Fitzgerald	50	not out	15
D. A. Bick not out	7		
B 4, l-b 5, w 1	10	B 2, l-b 1	3
1/42 2/153 3/184 4/193 5/252 6/290 7/333 8/365 (8 wkts., dec.)	365	1/14 2/28 3/44 4/67 5/97 6/172 (6 wkts., dec.)	192

H. C. Latchman and R. S. Herman did not bat.

Bowling: *First Innings*—Russell 3.1—1—8—0; Cutler 20—5—73—1; Cottrell 18—4—52—2; Fitzgerald 41.2—10—139—4; Roopnaraine 29—8—83—1. *Second Innings*—Russell 15—4—33—3; Cottrell 8—1—28—0; Cutler 5—2—13—0; Roopnaraine 8—1—26—0; Fitzgerald 17—6—54—3; Murray 4—0—20—0; Malalasekera 2—1—1—0; Cosh 2—0—6—0; Gould 2—0—6—0; McAdam 2—0—2—0.

Cambridge University

First innings		Second innings	
K. P. W. J. McAdam c Murray b Latchman	8	c Clark b Bennett	5
A. V. E. Gould b Hooker	12	c Hooker b Herman	0
†D. L. Hays c Radley b Bennett	0	lbw b Titmus	39
*D. L. Murray b Latchman	30	b Titmus	51
V. P. Malalasekera c Murray b Bennett	11	b Bick	30
N. J. Cosh lbw b Bick	25	b Bick	24
G. A. Cottrell b Bick	15	c Smith b Titmus	4
J. F. Fitzgerald b Bick	5	b Bick	0
R. W. Cutler b Herman	1	st Murray b Latchman	7
R. Roopnaraine c Clark b Latchman	19	not out	9
S. G. Russell not out	5	c and b Latchman	3
B 4, l-b 6, n-b 1	11	B 7, l-b 3, w 1	11
1/18 2/20 3/42 4/56 5/73 6/107 7/108 8/110 9/119	142	1/1 2/13 3/92 4/109 5/158 6/159 7/163 8/163 9/171	183

Bowling: *First Innings*—Herman 10—2—27—1; Bennett 16—4—45—2; Latchman 19—10—21—3; Hooker 8—2—25—1; Titmus 5—1—6—0; Bick 8—4—7—3. *Second Innings*—Herman 7—3—15—1; Bennett 9—3—29—1; Hooker 10—2—17—0; Latchman 19.4—7—41—2; Titmus 20—6—39—3; Bick 20—6—31—3.

Umpires: C. S. Elliott and A. Jepson.

CAMBRIDGE UNIVERSITY v. SCOTLAND

At Cambridge, May 7, 9, 10. Cambridge University won by one wicket. On their first visit to Fenner's, Scotland appeared certain to beat Cambridge, but a last-wicket partnership of 42 by Roopnaraine and Russell gave the University an exciting win by one wicket. In a low-scoring match Scotland gained a first-innings lead of 4, but in their second innings lost the first four wickets—all to Russell—for 27. More and the captain, Brown, then batted well for Scotland, but they were all out after tea on the second day for 192, leaving Cambridge with 197 to win. At one stage Cambridge were 75 for six, but a stand of 57 between Cosh and Cottrell put them back in the hunt. However at 155 for nine, Scotland looked home and dry only to find victory snatched from their grasp by Roopnaraine, whose 50 not out was his highest score, and the last man, Russell.

Scotland

First innings		Second innings	
R. H. E. Chisholm c Cosh b Russell	15	b Russell	0
L. C. Dudman c Hays b Sinker	13	c Hays b Russell	7
J. G. Laing c Chambers b Cottrell	31	c McAdam b Russell	4
T. N. Gallacher b Russell	2	lbw b Russell	8
H. K. More c Hays b Russell	11	c Chambers b Roopnaraine	50
D. Barr c McAdam b Roopnaraine	2	lbw b Roopnaraine	22
G. F. Goddard c Cottrell b Roopnaraine	20	c Hays b Cottrell	6
*†J. Brown c Cosh b Sinker	8	b Russell	67
E. R. Thompson c Chambers b Sinker	21	c Hays b Cottrell	0
D. Livingstone not out	5	run out	12
G. Hutton b Sinker	0	not out	0
B 6, l-b 4, n-b 6	16	B3, l-b 6, n-b 7	16
1/30 2/30 3/39 4/64 5/69 6/103 7/105 8/132 9/138	144	1/0 2/9 3/12 4/27 5/88 6/103 7/116 8/120 9/174	192

Bowling: *First Innings*—Russell 19—4—49—3; Cottrell 19—7—42—1; Sinker 17.2—10—10—4; Roopnaraine 17—7—27—2. *Second Innings*—Russell 14.3—6—41—5; Cottrell 13—4—46—2; Sinker 23—8—50—0; Roopnaraine 32—14—39—2.

Cambridge University

First innings		Second innings	
R. E. J. Chambers b Barr	6	b Barr	18
L. M. Barnwell c Brown b Thompson	21	c Brown b Hutton	9
A. V. E. Gould b Livingstone	29	b Barr	13
K. P. W. J. McAdam st Brown b Livingstone	46	lbw b Barr	7
†D. L. Hays lbw b Livingstone	0	c Hutton b Livingstone	17
N. J. Cosh lbw b Livingstone	0	st Brown b Chisholm	28
D. R. Aers b Livingstone	0	b Livingstone	1
G. A. Cottrell run out	6	run out	34
*R. Roopnaraine b Thompson	5	not out	50
N. Sinker b Barr	11	b Hutton	3
S. G. Russell not out	4	not out	7
B 4, n-b 8	12	L-b 7, n-b 3	10
1/12 2/63 3/73 4/77 5/78 6/78 7/87 8/98 9/129	140	1/21 2/27 3/41 4/61 5/71 6/75 7/132 8/140 9/155	(9 wkts.) 197

Bowling: *First Innings*—Thompson 20—8—36—2; Barr 19.5—4—41—2; Hutton 6—2—12—0; Livingstone 17—8—16—5; Chisholm 7—1—23—0. *Second Innings*—Barr 26—5—65—3; Thompson 26—3—38—0; Hutton 9—5—16—2; Livingstone 23—8—34—2; Chisholm 10—1—21—1; Goddard 3—0—13—0.

Umpires: L. H. Gray and W. F. Simpson.

CAMBRIDGE UNIVERSITY v. LANCASHIRE

At Cambridge, May 11, 12, 13. Lancashire won by an innings and 48 runs. Some disappointing batting in both innings by Cambridge gave Lancashire an easy win. The only resistance came in a spirited innings at the end by Cottrell, who was left with 44 not out. In the Lancashire innings Lloyd, a 19-year-old left-hander, scored an attractive 72 in only eighty minutes. He and Shuttleworth put on 94 in seventy minutes for the eighth wicket before Lancashire declared. Cambridge were bowled out for 120, and following-on the principal batsmen again failed against the skilful spin bowling of Greenhough and the pace of Shuttleworth, who took four wickets for 49.

Lancashire

*D. M. Green c Malalasekera b Russell	14
G. Pullar c Murray b Roopnaraine	30
H. Pilling c McAdam b Roopnaraine	16
J. Sullivan b Russell	36
R. Entwistle c Cottrell b Russell	51
G. K. Knox lbw b Acfield	52
D. Lloyd not out	72
P. Lever c Murray b Russell	2
K. Shuttleworth not out	32
B 7, l-b 8, n-b 1	16
1/40 2/57 3/77 4/105 5/209 6/217 7/227 (7 wkts., dec.)	321

†K. Goodwin and T. Greenhough did not bat.

Bowling: Russell 23—4—74—4; Cottrell 16—4—43—0; Roopnaraine 40—7—104—2; Acfield 34—11—84—1.

Cambridge University

K. P. W. J. McAdam lbw b Greenhough	24	— b Shuttleworth	0
L. M. Barnwell c Knox b Lever	0	— b Shuttleworth	4
A. V. E. Gould lbw b Shuttleworth	38	— c and b Lever	16
D. L. Hays c Knox b Greenhough	6	— lbw b Greenhough	13
*†D. L. Murray run out	16	— c Goodwin b Lloyd	26
V. P. Malalasekera b Shuttleworth	0	— lbw b Greenhough	9
N. J. Cosh not out	23	— lbw b Shuttleworth	23
G. A. Cottrell lbw b Shuttleworth	0	— not out	44
R. Roopnaraine c Sullivan b Lloyd	4	— c Goodwin b Shuttleworth	3
D. L. Acfield lbw b Lever	1	— c Knox b Greenhough	9
S. G. Russell b Lever	0	— c Sullivan b Lloyd	1
B 1, l-b 4, n-b 3	8	B 4, n-b 1	5
1/0 2/51 3/61 4/85 5/87 6/93 7/93 8/103 9/115	120	1/0 2/5 3/33 4/33 5/53 6/83 7/112 8/126 9/152	153

Bowling: *First Innings*—Shuttleworth 17—10—18—3; Lever 10—3—25—3; Lloyd 26—13—29—1; Greenhough 19—7—19—2; Green 10—2—21—0. *Second Innings*—Shuttleworth 17—3—49—4; Lever 13—4—31—1; Greenhough 14—5—25—3; Lloyd 12.1—4—22—2; Sullivan 7—0—21—0.

Umpires: L. H. Gray and W. F. Simpson.

CAMBRIDGE UNIVERSITY v. WARWICKSHIRE

At Cambridge, May 14, 15. Warwickshire won by an innings and 74 runs. For the second match in succession the Cambridge batting failed and they were again beaten by an innings. Cambridge were bowled out for 36 in the first innings, after losing their first five wickets for 10 runs. Warwickshire's fast bowler, Webster, took eight wickets for 19—the best figures of his career. Barber and Abberley needed only twenty minutes to give Warwickshire the lead, and after Barber, playing his first game of the season, had scored 43 in even time, Abberley went on to make 81 in a most promising innings. In their second innings Cambridge, needing 254 to avoid an innings defeat, were given their best start in four matches when McAdam and Chambers put on 37, and although Chambers batted well for his fifty, scored in just over an hour, Cambridge were all out for 180, three-quarters of an hour after lunch on the second day.

Cambridge University

K. P. W. J. McAdam c Allan b Webster	0	— lbw b Webster	22
R. E. J. Chambers b Webster	8	— c Ibadulla b Allan	55
D. R. Aers b Webster	0	— lbw b Allan	16
A. V. E. Gould b Ibadulla	2	— c Ibadulla b Barber	4
*†D. L. Murray c Barber b Webster	0	— b Miller	36
V. P. Malalasekera b Webster	5	— b Allan	1
G. A. Cottrell c Smith b Webster	10	— c and b Barber	10
A. B. Palfreman c Smith b Webster	0	— c Miller b Barber	12
D. L. Acfield not out	1	— run out	0
J. F. Fitzgerald b Webster	6	— not out	3
S. G. Russell b Bannister	0	— b Miller	12
B 4	4	B 2, l-b 5, w 1, n-b 1	9
1/3 2/3 3/10 4/10 5/10 6/18 7/26 8/29 9/35	36	1/37 2/96 3/99 4/107 5/111 6/130 7/154 8/154 9/164	180

Bowling: *First Innings*—Bannister 9.5—6—5—1; Webster 14—8—19—8; Ibadulla 5—2—8—1; *Second Innings*—Webster 9—1—49—1; Bannister 8—2—31—0; Barber 22—6—57—3; Allan 13—4—24—3; Miller 8.3—5—10—2.

Warwickshire

R. W. Barber b Palfreman	43	J. M. Allan not out	35
R. N. Abberley st Murray b Fitzgerald	81	R. Miller b Acfield	18
J. A. Jameson lbw b Palfreman	0	R. V. Webster lbw b Acfield	38
D. L. Amiss c and b Palfreman	0	J. D. Bannister c and b Fitzgerald	10
K. Ibadulla c Acfield b Russell	39	B 5, l-b 1, n-b 1	7
W. J. Stewart c Chambers b Acfield	14	1/76 2/76 3/80 4/126 5/171	290
*†A. C. Smith b Russell	5	6/176 7/194 8/215 9/265	

Bowling: Russell 15—1—77—2; Palfreman 15—4—75—3; Cottrell 1—0—7—0; Fitzgerald 19.4—6—57—2; Acfield 29—9—67—3.

Umpires: P. A. Gibb and J. Langridge.

CAMBRIDGE UNIVERSITY v. YORKSHIRE

At Cambridge, May 18, 19, 20. Yorkshire won by eight wickets. The Cambridge captain took the unusual step in this match of bringing in a player who was not going to be eligible to represent the University against Oxford at Lord's. After the low scores by Cambridge in the previous matches, Brearley, who captained Cambridge in 1963 and 1964 and who was back in residence on a post-graduate course, came into the side to provide support for the less experienced batsmen. Brearley was out for 0 in the first innings, but proved his worth by scoring 101 out of the Cambridge total of 247 in the second innings. Cosh shared a stand of 114 for the fourth wicket with Brearley, but Cambridge had lost too much ground in the first innings when bowled out for 81, and Yorkshire were left with only 94 to win in two hours and ten minutes. The Yorkshire first innings had been dominated by their captain, Close, who scored 103 out of the first 147. Illingworth, whose off-breaks caused Cambridge considerable trouble, also batted well in an innings of 47.

Cambridge University

First Innings		Second Innings	
J. M. Brearley b Nicholson	0	c Sharpe b Wilson	101
R. E. J. Chambers b Nicholson	6	b Trueman	0
D. L. Hays b Nicholson	1	c Binks b Nicholson	9
*†D. L. Murray c Boycott b Waring	32	b Nicholson	34
N. J. Cosh c Close b Waring	5	c Close b Wilson	47
V. P. Malalasekera c Wilson b Illingworth	17	c and b Illingworth	3
G. A. Cottrell b Wilson	5	lbw b Wilson	2
R. Roopnaraine b Wilson	0	c Boycott b Illingworth	23
N. Sinker b Illingworth	8	b Illingworth	1
D. L. Acfield st Binks b Illingworth	2	not out	9
S. G. Russell not out	0	b Trueman	3
B 3, l-b 1, n-b 1	5	L-b 12, n-b 3	15
1/5 2/6 3/27 4/43 5/53 6/66 7/70 8/70 9/80	81	1/1 2/20 3/85 4/199 5/206 6/206 7/212 8/240 9/240	247

Bowling: *First Innings*—Trueman 7—4—11—0; Nicholson 8—3—21—3; Waring 7—1—19—2; Wilson 11—6—11—2; Illingworth 12.3—8—8—3; Close 7—4—6—0. *Second Innings*—Trueman 12.4—3—29—2; Nicholson 11—6—21—2; Wilson 30—14—53—3; Illingworth 35—16—64—3; Waring 7—1—28—0; Close 10—4—19—0; Hampshire 5—0—18—0.

Yorkshire

First Innings		Second Innings	
G. Boycott c Murray b Russell	11	b Russell	8
*D. B. Close b Roopnaraine	103		
D. E. V. Padgett run out	30		
J. H. Hampshire b Sinker	0	c Brearley b Cosh	28
P. J. Sharpe c Cosh b Sinker	0	not out	47
R. Illingworth c Cosh b Russell	47		
†J. G. Binks c Murray b Sinker	22		
F. S. Trueman lbw b Roopnaraine	0	not out	12
D. Wilson lbw b Roopnaraine	6		
A. G. Nicholson not out	4		
J. Waring not out	9		
B 1, l-b 2	3	B 1	1
1/30 2/123 3/132 4/134 5/150 6/183 7/188 8/218 9/220 (9 wkts., dec.)	235	1/16 2/77 (2 wkts.)	96

Bowling: *First Innings*—Russell 15—3—41—2; Cottrell 8—0—35—0; Acfield 13—2—34—0; Roopnaraine 34—13—90—3; Sinker 19—5—32—3. *Second Innings*—Russell 14—4—38—1; Cottrell 12—4—33—0; Roopnaraine 3—2—5—0; Cosh 2—1—8—1; Brearley 2—1—7—0; Chambers 0.5—0—4—0.

Umpires: P. A. Gibb and J. Langridge.

At Cambridge, May 21, 23, 24. CAMBRIDGE UNIVERSITY lost to WEST INDIES by 174 runs. (See WEST INDIES section.)

CAMBRIDGE UNIVERSITY v. NORTHAMPTONSHIRE

At Cambridge, June 4, 6, 7. Northamptonshire won by 183 runs. Cambridge made an encouraging start by taking the first five Northamptonshire wickets for 88. The Northamptonshire captain, Prideaux, led a successful recovery, scoring 135 not out before he declared. In reply Cambridge reached 261 which was then their highest total of the season. Malalasekera batted attractively for 72, and he and Murray put on 77 for the fourth wicket. Cambridge lost the initiative after tea on the second day when Wills and Willey put on 155 without loss for the first wicket. These two went on to score 171 together before Willey was out for 78. Willey was making his first-class debut at the age of sixteen. Northamptonshire declared their second innings, thanks mainly to Wills, who hit splendidly for 151 not out. Next, their spin bowlers soon had the Cambridge batsmen in trouble and they were all out for 124.

Northamptonshire

R. Wills c Murray b Palfreman	22	— not out 151
P. Willey b Russell	0	— c McAdam b Cottrell 78
D. S. Steele lbw b Cottrell	28	— not out 25
P. J. Watts c Cosh b Cottrell	19	
Mushtaq Mohammad b Cottrell	9	
*R. M. Prideaux not out	135	
P. D. Watts b Acfield	43	
M. E. Scott c Cosh b Russell	16	
†L. A. Johnson not out	17	
B 5, l-b 2, n-b 5	12	B 5, l-b 4, n-b 4 13
1/1 2/51 3/53 4/67 5/88 6/195, 7/236 (7 wkts., dec.)	301	1/171 (1 wkt., dec.) 267

J. D. F. Larter and A. J. Durose did not bat.

Bowling: *First Innings*—Russell 23—3—64—2; Palfreman 19—5—73—1; Cottrell 21—8—61—3; Acfield 22—9—40—1; Sinker 17—0—51—0. *Second Innings*—Russell 13—5—33—0; Palfreman 4—1—19—0; Acfield 28—8—75—0; Sinker 21—4—72—0; Cross 6—1—19—0; Cosh 1—0—8—0; Cottrell 7—3—28—1.

Cambridge University

K. P. W. J. McAdam lbw b Larter	15	— lbw b P. J. Watts 20
A. V. E. Gould b Durose	24	— lbw b Scott 17
N. J. Cosh c P. D. Watts b Larter	11	— lbw b Scott 21
*†D. L. Murray c Johnson b P. D. Watts	43	— c Steele b P. D. Watts 8
V. P. Malalasekera c Scott b Willey	72	— c P. J. Watts b P. D. Watts 1
A. J. Cross c Johnson b Scott	19	— b Mushtaq 17
G. A. Cottrell lbw b Scott	7	— c Wills b P. D. Watts 20
A. B. Palfreman c Wills b P. D. Watts	0	— c P. J. Watts b Mushtaq 5
N. Sinker not out	31	— not out 4
D. L. Acfield c Willey b Mushtaq	6	— b Mushtaq 0
S. G. Russell b Larter	8	— lbw b Mushtaq 0
B 12, l-b 11, n-b 2	25	B 6, l-b 2, w 3 11
1/50 2/58 3/63 4/140 5/193 6/199 7/206 8/206 9/229	261	1/30 2/52 3/75 4/75 5/80 6/100 7/120 8/120 9/120 124

Bowling: *First Innings*—Larter 17.1—2—71—3; Durose 15—1—36—1; Scott 21—7—39—2; P. D. Watts 30—5—64—2; Mushtaq 12—8—19—1: Willey 3—1—7—1. *Second Innings*—Larter 1—0—1—0; Durose 3—0—8—0; P. J. Watts 8—3—19—1; Scott 20—8—25—2; Mushtaq 6.2—2—16—4; P. D. Watts 21—9—44—3.

Umpires: R. Aspinall and P. B. Wight.

CAMBRIDGE UNIVERSITY v. WORCESTERSHIRE

At Cambridge, June 8, 9, 10. Worcestershire won by nine wickets. This was another heavy defeat for Cambridge, with Worcestershire winning comfortably after only three-quarters of an hour's play on the third morning. However, there were two encouraging innings played for the University by Hays, and a long impressive spell of off-spin bowling by Roopnaraine during the Worcestershire innings. Hays was helped each time by Cottrell but there was not enough support from the others. For Worcestershire, Horton, after a lean period, came back to form in an innings of 91, and they batted right through for a first-innings lead of 154. It would have been even bigger, but for some remarkably accurate bowling by Roopnaraine, who in 49 overs conceded only 78 runs, and took five wickets.

Cambridge University

R. E. J. Chambers b Brain	23 — b Carter	2
A. V. E. Gould c Headley b Carter	0 — lbw b Brain	0
*†D. L. Murray b Carter	13 — lbw b Brain	0
D. L. Hays c Gifford b Horton	54 — c Headley b d'Oliveira	72
N. J. Cosh b Horton	38 — c Booth b Carter	7
V. P. Malalasekera c Headley b d'Oliveira	15 — c d'Oliveira b Gifford	3
G. A. Cottrell not out	32 — st Booth b Baylis	20
R. Roopnaraine c Booth b Baylis	2 — b d'Oliveira	10
N. Sinker c Horton b Baylis	9 — b Carter	20
D. L. Acfield c Booth b d'Oliveira	1 — not out	19
S. G. Russell c Horton b Baylis	0 — lbw b Carter	0
L-b 11, n-b 1	12 B 8, l-b 7, n-b 1	16
1/3 2/25 3/47 4/124 5/139 6/172 7/175 8/196 9/198	199 1/2 2/2 3/13 4/46 5/69 6/89 7/126 8/126 9/169	169

Bowling: *First Innings*—Carter 9—2—33—2; Brain 10—0—40—1; d'Oliveira 19—5—39—2; Baylis 18.3—3—54—3; Gifford 11—8—8—0; Horton 12—8—13—2. *Second Innings*—Carter 12.4—2—38—4; Brain 9—1—36—2; Gifford 15—9—21—1; d'Oliveira 19—10—31—2; Baylis 9—2—26—1; Horton 2—1—1—0.

Worcestershire

*D. Kenyon lbw b Roopnaraine	49	
M. J. Horton c Cottrell b Russell	91 — not out	8
R. G. A. Headley c Hays b Roopnaraine	0 — c Acfield b Gould	1
J. A. Ormrod b Sinker	42 — not out	6
B. d'Oliveira lbw b Acfield	37	
D. W. Richardson b Russell	37	
†R. Booth b Roopnaraine	36	
N. Gifford lbw b Russell	1	
K. Baylis b Roopnaraine	26	
B. M. Brain c Cottrell b Roopnaraine	5	
R. G. M. Carter not out	0	
B 10, l-b 13, w 2, n-b 4	29 B 1	1
1/107 2/111 3/186 4/206 5/277 6/281 7/284 8/338 9/350	353 1/9 (1 wkt.)	16

Bowling: *First Innings*—Cottrell 10—2—37—0; Sinker 25—6—65—1; Roopnaraine 49—23—78—5; Acfield 33—11—94—1; Malalasekera 1—0—4—0; Russell 18—3—46—3. *Second Innings*—Hays 2—1—5—0; Gould 3.2—1—10—1; Murray 2—2—0—0.

Umpires: R. Aspinall and P. B. Wight.

At Brentwood, June 11, 13, 14. CAMBRIDGE UNIVERSITY lost to ESSEX by 188 runs.

At The Oval, June 15, 16, 17. CAMBRIDGE UNIVERSITY lost to SURREY by an innings and 64 runs.

At Taunton, June 18, 20, 21. CAMBRIDGE UNIVERSITY lost to SOMERSET by two wickets.

At Cardiff, June 22, 23, 24. CAMBRIDGE UNIVERSITY drew with GLAMORGAN.

At Lydney, June 25, 26, 27. CAMBRIDGE UNIVERSITY drew with GLOUCESTERSHIRE.

At Lord's, July 4, 5. CAMBRIDGE UNIVERSITY drew with M.C.C.

At Hove, July 6, 7, 8. CAMBRIDGE UNIVERSITY lost to SUSSEX by five wickets.

At Lord's, July 9, 11, 12. CAMBRIDGE lost to OXFORD by an innings and nine runs.

LIST OF BLUES

From 1880–1966

To save space, Blues prior to 1880 are omitted, except some of special interest for personal or family reasons.

OXFORD

Abell, G. E. B. (Marlborough), 1924, 1926–27
Allan, J. M. (Edinburgh Academy), 1953–56
Altham, H. S. (Repton), 1911–12
Arenhold, J. A. (Diocesan Coll., S.A.), 1954
Arkwright, H. A. (Eton), 1895
Arnall-Thompson, H. T. (Rugby), 1886
Asher, A. G. G. (Loretto), 1883
Awdry, R. W. (Winchester), 1904

Baig, A. A. (Osmania Univ.), 1959–62
Baig, M. A. (Osmania Univ.), 1962–64
Bailey, J. A. (Christ's Hospital) (Capt. in 1958), 1956–58
Ballance, T. G. L. (Uppingham), 1935, 1937
Bannon, B. D. (Tonbridge), 1898
Barber, A. T. (Shrewsbury) (Capt. in 1929), 1927–29
Bardsley, R. V. (Shrewsbury), 1911–13
Bardswell, G. R. (Uppingham) (Capt. in 1897), 1894, 1896–97
Barker, A. H. (Charterhouse), 1964–65
Barlow, E. A. (Shrewsbury), 1932–34
Barnard, F. H. (Charterhouse), 1922, 1924
Barnes, R. G. (Harrow), 1906–07
Bartlett, J. N. (Chichester), 1946, 1951
Barton, M. R. (Winchester), 1936–37
Bassett, H. (Bedford House, Oxford), 1889–91
Bastard, E. W. (Sherborne), 1883–85
Bathurst, F. (Winchester), 1848
Bathurst, L. C. V. (Radley), 1893–94
Bathurst, R. A. (Winchester), 1838–39
Bathurst, S. E. (Winchester), 1836
Bell, G. F. (Repton), 1919
Belle, B. H. (Forest School), 1936
Benn, A. (Harrow), 1935
Benson, E. T. (Blundell's), 1928–29
Berkeley, G. F. H. (Wellington), 1890–93
Bettington, R. H. B. (The King's School, Parramatta) (Capt. in 1923), 1920–23
Bickmore, A. F. (Clifton), 1920–21
Bird, W. S. (Malvern) (Capt. in 1906), 1904–06
Birrell, H. B. (St. Andrews, South Africa), 1953–54
Blagg, P. H. (Shrewsbury), 1939
Blaikie, K. G. (Maritzburg), 1924
Blake, P. D. S. (Eton) (Capt. in 1952), 1950–52
Bloy, N. C. F. (Dover), 1946–47
Boger, A. J. (Winchester), 1891
Bolitho, W. E. T. (Harrow), 1883, 1885
Bonham-Carter, M. (Winchester), 1902
Boobbyer, B. (Uppingham), 1949–52
Bosanquet, B. J. T. (Eton), 1898–1900
Boswell, W. G. K. (Eton), 1913–14
Bowman, R. (Fettes), 1957
Bowring, T. (Rugby), 1907–08
Bradby, H. C. (Rugby), 1890
Braddell, R. L. (Charterhouse), 1910–11
Bradshaw, W. H. (Malvern), 1930–31
Brain, J. H. (Clifton) (Capt. in 1887), 1884–87
Brain, W. H. (Clifton), 1891–93
Brandt, D. R. (Harrow), 1907
Branston, G. T. (Charterhouse), 1904–06
Brett, P. J. (Winchester), 1929
Bristowe, O. C. (Eton), 1914
Bromley-Martin, G. E. (Eton), 1897–98
Brooke, R. H. J. (St. Edward's, Oxford), 1932
Brougham, H. (Wellington), 1911
Brownlee, L. D. (Clifton), 1904
Bruce, C. N. (now Lord Aberdare) (Winchester), 1907–08
Buckland, E. H. (Marlborough), 1884–87
Burki, J. (Punjab Univ.), 1958–60
Burn, R. C. W. (Winchester), 1902–05
Bush, J. E. (Magdalen Coll. Sch.), 1952
Butterworth, R. E. C. (Harrow), 1927
Buxton, R. V. (Eton), 1906

Campbell, I. P. (Camford), 1949–50
Campbell, I. P. F. (Repton) (Capt. in 1913), 1911–13
Carlisle, K. M. (Harrow) (Capt. in 1905), 1903–05
Carr, D. B. (Repton) (Capt. in 1950), 1949–51
*Case, T. B. (Winchester), 1891–92
Cazalet, P. V. F. (Eton), 1927
Chalk, F. G. H. (Uppingham) (Capt. in 1934), 1931–34

* Case came into the game of 1891, by permission of the Cambridge captain, through the Hon. F. J. N. Thesiger being injured soon after play began.

Champain, F. H. B. (Cheltenham) (Capt. in 1899), 1897–1900
Chesterton, G. H. (Malvern), 1949
Clube, S. V. M. (St. John's, Leatherhead), 1956
Cobb, A. R. (Winchester), 1886
Cochrane, A. H. J. (Repton), 1885–86, 1888
Colebrooke, E. L. (Charterhouse), 1880
Collins, L. P. (Marlborough), 1899
Colman, G. R. R. (Eton), 1913–14
Corran, A. J. (Gresham's), 1958–60
Coutts, I. D. F. (Dulwich), 1952
Cowdrey, M. C. (Tonbridge) (Capt. in 1954), 1952–54
Coxon, A. J. (Harrow C.S.), 1952
Crawford, J. W. F. (Merchant Taylors), 1900–01
Crawley, A. M. (Harrow), 1927–30
Croome, A. C. M. (Wellington), 1888–89
Crutchley, G. E. V. (Harrow), 1912
Cunliffe, F. H. E. (Eton) (Capt. in 1898), 1895–98
Curwen, W. J. H. (Charterhouse), 1906
Cuthbertson, J. L. (Rugby), 1962–63

Darwall-Smith, R. F. H. (Charterhouse), 1935–38
Dauglish, M. J. (Harrow), 1889–90
Davidson, W. W. (Brighton), 1947–48
Davies, P. H. (Brighton), 1913–14
Davis, F. J. (Blundell's), 1963
Delisle, G. P. S. (Stoneyhurst), 1955–56
De Montmorency, R. H. (Cheltenham and St. Paul's), 1899
de Saram, F. C. (Royal College, Colombo), 1934–35
Dillon, E. W. (Rugby), 1901–02
Divecha, R. V. (Bombay University), 1950–51
Dixon, E. J. H. (St. Edward's, Oxford) (Capt. in 1939), 1937–39
Donnelly, M. P. (Canterbury University, New Zealand) (Capt. in 1947), 1946–47
Dowding, A. L. (St. Peter's, Adelaide) (Capt. in 1953), 1952–53
Drybrough, C. D. (Highgate) (Capt. in 1961–62), 1960–62
Duff, A. R. (Radley), 1960–61
Dyer, A. W. (Mill Hill), 1965–66
Dyson, E. M. (Queen Eliz. G.S., Wakefield), 1958
Dyson, J. H. (Charterhouse), 1936

Eagar, E. D. R. (Cheltenham), 1939
Eagar, M. A. (Rugby), 1956–59
Eccles, A. (Repton), 1897–99
Eggar, J. D. (Winchester), 1938
Elviss, R. W. (Leeds G.S.), 1966
Evans, A. H. (Rossall and Clifton) (Capt. in 1881), 1878–81
Evans, A. J. (Winchester) (Capt. in 1911), 1909–12
Evans, E. N. (Haileybury), 1932
Evans, G. (St. Asaph), 1939
Evans, W. H. B. (Malvern) (Capt. in 1904), 1902–05
Evelyn, F. L. (Rugby), 1880

Fane, F. L. (Charterhouse), 1897–98
Fasken, D. K. (Wellington), 1953–55
Fellows-Smith, J. P. (Durban High School, South Africa), 1953–55
Fillary, E. W. J. (St. Lawrence), 1963–65
Findlay, W. (Eton) (Capt. in 1903), 1901–03
Fisher, C. D. (Westminster), 1900
Forbes, D. H. (Eton), 1894
Ford, N. M. (Harrow), 1928–30
Forster, H. W. (Eton), 1887–89
Foster, G. N. (Malvern), 1905–08
Foster, H. K. (Malvern), 1894–96
Foster, R. E. (Malvern) (Capt. in 1900), 1897–1900
Fowler, G. (Clifton), 1888
Fowler, H. (Clifton) 1877, 1879–80
Fox, R. W. (Wellington), 1897–98
Franklin, H. W. F. (Christ's Hospital), 1924
Fraser, J. N. (Church of England Grammar School, Melbourne, and Melbourne University), 1912–13
Frazer, J. E. (Winchester), 1924
Fry, C. A. (Repton), 1959–61
Fry, C. B. (Repton) (Capt. in 1894), 1892–95

Garland-Wells, H. M. (St. Paul's), 1928–30
Garthwaite, P. F. (Wellington), 1929
Gibbs, P. J. K. (Hanley G.S.), 1964–66
Gibson, I. (Manchester G.S.), 1955–58
Gilbert, H. (Charterhouse), 1907–09
Gilliat, I. A. W. (Charterhouse), 1925
Gilliat, R. M. C. (Charterhouse) (Capt. in 1966), 1964–66
Gilligan, F. W. (Dulwich) (Capt. in 1920), 1919–20
Goldstein, F. S. (Falcon, Buluwayo, Rhodesia), 1966
Gordon, J. H. (Winchester), 1906–07
Green, D. M. (Manchester G.S.), 1959–61
Greene, A. D. (Clifton) (Capt. in 1880), 1877–80
Greenstock, J. W. (Malvern), 1925–27
Gresson, F. H. (Winchester), 1887–89
Grover, J. N. (Winchester) (Capt. in 1938), 1936–38
Groves, M. G. M. (Diocesan College, S.A.), 1964–66
Guest, M. R. J. (Rugby), 1964–66
Guise, J. L. (Winchester) (Capt. in 1925), 1924–25

Halliday, J. G. (City of Oxford High School), 1935
Hamilton, W. D. (Haileybury), 1882
Harris, C. R. (Buckingham R. L. S.), 1964
Harris (Lord), G. R. C. (Eton), 1871–72, 1874
Harrison, G. C. (Malvern and Clifton), 1880–81
Hart, T. M. (Strathallan), 1931–32
Hartley, J. C. (Marlborough and Tonbridge), 1896–97
Hatfeild, C. E. (Eton), 1908
Hedges, L. P. (Tonbridge), 1920–22
Henderson, D. (St. Edwards, Oxford), 1950
Henley, D. F. (Harrow), 1947
Henley, F. A. H. (Forest School), 1905
Hewetson, E. P. (Shrewsbury), 1923–25
Hewett, H. T. (Harrow), 1886
Hildyard, L. D'Arcy (Private), 1844–86
Hiller, R. B. (Bec), 1966
Hill, V. T. (Winchester), 1892
Hill-Wood, C. K. (Eton), 1928–30
Hill-Wood, D. J. (Eton), 1928
Hine-Haycock, T. R. (Wellington), 1883–84
Hirst, E. T. (Rugby), 1878–80
Hobbs, J. A. D. (Liverpool Coll.), 1957
Hofmeyr, M. B. (Pretoria, South Africa) (Capt. in 1951), 1949–51
Holdsworth, R. L. (Repton), 1919–22
Hollins, A. M. (Eton), 1899
Hollins, F. H. (Eton), 1901
Holmes, E. R. T. (Malvern) (Capt. in 1927), 1925–27
Hone, B. W. (Adelaide University) (Capt. in 1933), 1931–33
Hooman, C. V. L. (Charterhouse), 1909–10
Hopkins, H. O. (St. Peter's College, Adelaide), 1923
Howell, M. (Repton) (Capt. in 1919), 1914, 1919
Hurst, C. S. (Uppingham) (Capt. in 1909), 1907–09

Jackson, K. L. T. (Rugby), 1934
Jakobson, T. R. (Charterhouse), 1961
Jardine, D. R. (Winchester), 1920–21, 1923
Jardine, M. R. (Fettes) (Capt. in 1891), 1889–92
Jenkins, V. G. J. (Llandovery), 1933
Jones, R. T. (Eton), 1892
Jose, A. D. (Adelaide U.), 1950–51
Jowett, D. C. P. R. (Sherborne), 1952–55
Jowett, R. L. (Bradford G.S.), 1957–59

Kamm, A. (Charterhouse), 1954
Kardar, A. H. (Punjab University), 1947–49
Keighley, W. G. (Eton), 1947–48
Kelly, G. W. F. (Stonyhurst), 1901–02
Kemp, M. C. (Harrow) (Capt. in 1883–84), 1881–84
Kentish, E. S. M. (Cornwall College, Jamaica), 1956
Key, K. J. (Clifton), 1884–87
Kimpton, R. C. M. (Melbourne University), 1935, 1937–38
Kingsley, P. G. T. (Winchester) (Capt. in 1930), 1928–30
Knight, D. J. (Malvern), 1914, 1919
Knight, N. S. (Uppingham), 1934
Knott, C. H. (Tonbridge) (Capt. in 1924), 1922–24
Knott, F. H. (Tonbridge) (Capt. in 1914), 1912–14
Knox, F. P. (Dulwich) (Capt. in 1901), 1899–1901

Lagden, R. O. (Marlborough), 1909–12
Le Couteur, P. R. (Warrnambool Academy and Melbourne University), 1909–11
Lee, E. C. (Winchester), 1898
Legard, A. R. (Winchester), 1932, 1935
Legge, G. B. (Malvern) (Capt. in 1926), 1925–26
Leslie, C. F. H. (Rugby), 1881–83
Leveson Gower, H. D. G. (Winchester) (Capt. in 1896), 1893–96
Lewis, D. J. (Cape Town University) 1951
Lewis, R. P. (Winchester), 1894–96
Lindsay, W. O'B. (Harrow), 1931
Llewelyn, W. D. (Eton), 1890–91
Lomas, J. M. (Charterhouse), 1938–39
Lowe, J. C. M. (Uppingham), 1907–09
Lowndes, W. G. L. F. (Eton), 1921
Lyon, B. H. (Rugby), 1922–23
Lyon, G. W. F. (Brighton), 1925

McBride, W. N. (Westminster), 1926
McCanlis, M. A. (Cranleigh) (Capt. in 1928), 1926–28
Macindoe, D. H. (Eton) (Capt. in 1946), 1937–39, 1946
McIntosh, R. I. F. (Uppingham), 1927–28
M'Iver, C. D. (Forest School), 1903–04
McKinna, G. H. (Manchester Grammar School), 1953
M'Lachlan, N. (Loretto) (Capt. in 1882), 1879–82
Majendie, N. L. (Winchester), 1962–63
Mallett, A. W. H. (Dulwich), 1947–48
Manasseh, M. (Epsom), 1964
Marshall, J. C. (Rugby), 1953
Marsham, A. J. B. (Eton), 1939
Marsham, C. D. B. (Private) (Capt. in 1857–58), 1854–58

Marsham, C. H. B. (Eton) Capt. in 1902), 1900–02
Marsham, C. J. B. (Private), 1851
Marsham, R. H. B. (Private), 1856
Marsland, G. P. (Rossall), 1954
Martin, E. G. (Eton), 1903–06
Martin, J. D. (Magdalen Coll. Sch.), (Capt. in 1965), 1962–65
Martyn, H. (Exeter Grammar School), 1899–1900
Matthews, M. H. (Westminster), 1936–37
Maudsley, R. H. (Malvern), 1946–47
Mayhew, J. F. N. (Eton), 1930
Medlicott, W. S. (Harrow), 1902
Melle, B. G. von B. (South African College School and South African College, Cape Town), 1913–14
Melville, A. (Michaelhouse, South Africa) (Capt. in 1931–32), 1930–33
Melville, C. D. (Michaelhouse S.A.), 1957
Metcalfe, S. G. (Leeds Grammar School), 1956
Minns, R. E. F. (King's, Canterbury), 1962–63
Mitchell, R. A. H. (Eton) (Capt. in 1863–65), 1862–65
Mitchell, W. M. (Dulwich), 1951–52
Mitchell-Innes, N. S. (Sedbergh) (Capt. in 1936), 1934–37
Monro, R. W. (Harrow), 1860
Moore, D. N. (Shrewsbury) (Capt. in 1931, when he did not play v. Cambridge owing to illness), 1930
Mordaunt, G. J. (Wellington) (Capt. in 1895), 1893–96
More, R. E. (Westminster), 1900–01
Moss, R. H. (Radley), 1889
Mountford, P. N. G. (Bromsgrove), 1963
Munn, J. S. (Forest School), 1901
Murray-Wood, W. (Mill Hill), 1936

Naumann, F. C. G. (Malvern), 1914, 1919
Neate, F. W. (St. Paul's), 1961–62
Nepean, E. A. (Sherborne), 1887–88
Neser, V. H. (South African College, Cape Town), 1921
Newman, G. C. (Eton), 1926–27
Newton, A. E. (Eton), 1885
Newton-Thompson, J. O. (Diocesan College, Rondebosch, South Africa), 1946
Nicholls, B. E. (Winchester), 1884
Nunn, J. A. (Sherborne), 1926–27

O'Brien, T. C. (St. Charles' College, Notting Hill), 1884–85
Oldfield, P. C. (Repton), 1932–33
Ottaway, C. J. (Eton) (Capt. in 1873), 1870–73
Owen-Smith, H. G. (Diocesan College, South Africa), 1931–33

Page, H. V. (Cheltenham) (Capt. in 1885–86), 1883–86
Palairet, L. C. H. (Repton) (Capt. in 1892–93), 1890–93
Palairet, R. C. N. (Repton), 1893–94
Pataudi, Nawab of (Chief's College, Lahore), 1929–31
Pataudi, Nawab of (Winchester) (Capt. in 1961 when he did not play against Cambridge owing to a car accident and 1963), 1960, 1963
Patten, M. (Winchester), 1922–23
Patterson, J. I. (Chatham House, Ramsgate), 1882
Patterson, W. H. (Chatham House), Ramsgate and Harrow), 1880–81
Pawson, A. C. (Winchester), 1903
Pawson, A. G. (Winchester) (Capt. in 1910), 1908–11
Pawson, H. A. (Winchester) (Capt. in 1948), 1947–48
Payne, A. (Private) (Capt. in 1856), 1852, 1854–56
Payne, A. F. (Private), 1855
Payne, C. A. L. (Charterhouse), 1906–07
Peake, E. (Marlborough), 1881–83
Pearse, G. V. (Maritzburg College, Natal), 1919
Peat, C. U. (Sedbergh), 1913
Peebles, I. A. R. (Glasgow Academy) 1930
Pershke, W. J. (Uppingham), 1938
Pether, S. (Magdalen College School), 1939
Philipson, H. (Eton) (Capt. in 1889), 1887–89
Phillips, F. A. (Rossall), 1892, 1894–95
Phillips, J. B. (King's, Canterbury), 1955
Piachaud, J. D. (St. Thomas's College, Colombo), 1958–61
Pilkington, C. C. (Eton), 1896
Pilkington, H. C. (Eton), 1899–1900
Pilkington, W. (Midhurst), 1827
Pithey, D. B. (Univ. of Capetown), 1961–62
Potter, I. C. (King's, Canterbury), 1961–62
Potts, H. J. (Stand G.S.), 1950
Price, V. R. (Bishop's Stortford) (Capt. in 1921), 1919–22
Proud, R. B. (Winchester), 1939
Pycroft, J. (Bath), 1836

Raikes, D. C. G. (Shrewsbury), 1931
Raikes, G. B. (Shrewsbury), 1894–95

Raikes, T. B. (Winchester), 1922–24
Randolph, B. M. (Charterhouse), 1855–56
Randolph, C. (Eton), 1844–45
Randolph, L. C. (Westminster), 1843
Randolph, L. C. (Westminster), 1845
Raphael, J. E. (Merchant Taylors) 1903–05
Rashleigh, W. (Tonbridge) (Capt. in 1888), 1886–89
Raybould, J. G. (Leeds G.S.), 1959
Rice, R. W. (Cardiff), 1893
Richardson, J. V. (Uppingham), 1925
Ricketts, G. W. (Winchester), 1887
Ridding, A. (Winchester), 1846–50
Ridding, C. H. (Winchester), 1845–49
Ridding, W. (Winchester) (Capt. in 1849 and 1852, also in 1851 but did not play v. Cambridge, owing to illness), 1849–50, 1852–53
Ridley, G. N. S. (Milton, Buluwayo, Rhodesia), 1965–66
Robertson-Glasgow, R. C. (Charterhouse), 1920–23
Robinson, G. E. (Burton), 1881–83
Robinson, H. B. (North Shore College, Vancouver), 1947–48
Robinson, R. L. (St. Peter's College, Adelaide, and Adelaide University), 1908–09
Royle, Vernon (Rossall), 1875–76
Rucker, C. E. S. (Charterhouse), 1914
Rucker, P. W. (Charterhouse), 1919
Rudd, C. R. D. (Eton), 1949
Ruggles-Brise, H. G. (Winchester), 1883
Rumbold, J. S. (St. Andrew's College, New Zealand), 1946

Sabine, P. N. B. (Marlborough), 1963
Sale, R. (Repton), 1910
Sale, R. (Repton), 1939, 1946
Salter, M. G. (Cheltenham), 1909–10
Samson, O. M. (Cheltenham), 1903
Saunders, C. J. (Lancing), 1964
Sayer, D. M. (Maidstone G.S.), 1958–60
Schwann, H. S. (Clifton), 1890
Scott, Lord Geo. (Eton), 1887–89
Scott, M. D. (Winchester), 1957
Scott, K. B. (Winchester), 1937
Scott, R. S. G. (Winchester), 1931
Seamer, J. W. (Marlborough), 1934–36
Seitz, J. A. (Scotch College and Melbourne University), 1909
Shaw, E. A. (Marlborough), 1912, 1914
Shaw, E. D. (Forest School), 1882
Simpson, E. T. B. (Harrow), 1888
Sinclair, E. H. (Winchester), 1924
Singleton, A. P. (Shrewsbury) (Capt. in 1937), 1934–37
Skeet, C. H. L. (St. Paul's), 1920
Skene, R. W. (Sedbergh), 1928
Smith, A. C. (King Edward's, Birmingham) (Capt. in 1959–60), 1958–60
Smith, E. (Clifton), 1890–91
Smith, G. O. (Charterhouse), 1895–9
Smith, M. J. K. (Stamford) (Capt. in 1956), 1954–56
Stainton, R. G. (Malvern), 1933
Stanning, J. (Winchester), 1939
Stephenson, J. S. (Shrewsbury), 1925–26
Stevens, G. T. S. (University College School) (Capt. in 1922), 1920–23
Stewart-Brown, P. H. (Harrow), 1925–26
Stocks, F. W. (Lancing and Denstone), 1898–99
Sutton, M. A. (Ampleforth), 1946

Taylor, C. H. (Westminster), 1923–26
Teesdale, H. (Winchester), 1908
*Thesiger, F. J. N., 1st Visct. Chelmsford (Winchester) (Capt. in 1890), 1888, 1890
Thomas, R. J. A. (Radley), 1965
Thornton, W. A. (Winchester), 1879–82
Tindall, R. G. (Winchester), 1933–34
Toft, D. P. (Tonbridge), 1966
Townsend, D. C. H. (Winchester), 1933–34
Travers, B. H. (Sydney University), 1946, 1948
Trevor, A. H. (Winchester), 1880–81
Tuff, F. N. (Malvern), 1910
Twining, R. H. (Eton) (Capt. in 1912), 1910–13
Tylecote, E. F. S. (Clifton) (Capt. in 1871–72), 1869–72
Tylecote, H. G. (Clifton), 1874–77

Udal, N. R. (Winchester), 1905–06

Van der Bijl, P. G. (Diocesan College, South Africa), 1932
Van Ryneveld, C. B. (Diocesan College South Africa) (Capt. in 1949), 1948–50
Vidler, J. L. S. (Repton), 1910–12
Von Ernsthausen, A. C. (Uppingham), 1902–04

Waddy, P. S. (The King's School, Parramatta), 1896–97
Waldock, F. A. (Uppingham), 1919–20
Walford, M. M. (Rugby), 1936, 1938
Walker, D. F. (Uppingham) (Capt. in 1935), 1933–35
Walker, J. G. (Loretto), 1882–83
Walker, R. D. (Harrow), 1861–65

* Thesiger began to play in the game of 1891, but retired injured soon after the start. The Cambridge captain allowed his place to be taken by T. B. Case.

Walton, A. C. (Radley) (Capt. in 1957), 1955–57
Walshe, A. P. (Milton, Rhodesia), 1953, 55–56
Ward, H. P. (Shrewsbury), 1919, 1921
Warner, P. F. (Rugby), 1895–96
Watson, A. G. M. (St. Lawrence), 1965–66
Watson, A. K. (Harrow), 1889
Watson, H. D. (Harrow), 1891
Webb, H. E. (Winchester), 1948
Webbe, A. J. (Harrow) (Capt. in 1877–78), 1875–78
Webbe, H. R. (Winchester) (Capt. in 1879), 1877–79
Wellings, E. M. (Cheltenham), 1929, 1931
Wheatley, G. A. (Uppingham), 1946
Whitby, H. O. (Leamington), 1884–87
Whitcombe, P. A. (Winchester), 1947–49
Whitcombe, P. J. (Worcester G.S.), 1951–52
White, H. (Denstone), 1900
Whitehouse, P. M. (Marlborough), 1938
Whiting, A. O. (Sherborne), 1881–82
Wickham, A. P. (Marlborough), 1878
Wiley, W. G. E. (Diocesan Coll., Rondebosch, S.A.), 1952
Wilkinson, W. A. C. (Eton), 1913
Williams, C. C. P. (Westminster) (Capt. in 1955), 1953–55
Williams, R. A. (Winchester), 1901–02
Wilson, G. L. (Brighton), 1890–91
Wilson, R. W. (Warwick), 1957
Wilson, T. S. B. (Bath College), 1892–93
Winn, C. E. (King's College School, Wimbledon), 1948–51
Wood, J. B. (Marlborough), 1892–93
Woodcock, R. G. (Worcester R.G.S.), 1957–58
Wordsworth, Chas. (Harrow) (Capt. both years, First Oxford Capt.), 1827, 1829
Worsley, D. R. (Bolton), (Capt. in 1964), 1961–64
Wright, E. C. (Clergy Orphan School), 1897
Wright, E. L. (Winchester) (Capt. in 1907–08), 1905–08
Wrigley, M. H. (Harrow), 1949
Wyld, H. J. (Harrow), 1901–03

Young, D. E. (King's College School, Wimbledon), 1938

CAMBRIDGE

Aird, R. (Eton), 1923
Alexander, F. C. M. (Wolmer's Coll., Jamaica), 1952–53
Allen, A. W. (Eton), 1933–34
Allen, B. O. (Clifton), 1933
Allen, G. O. (Eton), 1922–23
Allom, M. J. C. (Wellington), 1927–28
Arnold, A. C. P. (Malvern), 1914
Ashton, C. T. (Winchester) (Capt. in 1923), 1921–23
Ashton, G. (Winchester) (Capt. in 1921), 1919–21
Ashton, H. (Winchester) (Capt. in 1922), 1920–22
Atkins, G. (Challenors), 1960
Austin, H. M. (Melbourne), 1924

Baggallay, M. E. C. (Eton), 1911
Bagnall, H. F. (Harrow), 1923
Bailey, T. E. (Dulwich), 1947–48
Baily, E. P. (Harrow), 1872, 1874
Baily, R. E. H. (Harrow), 1908
Bainbridge, H. W. (Eton) (Capt. in 1886), 1884–86
Barber, R. W. (Ruthin), 1956–57
Baker, E. C. (Brighton), 1912, 1914
Bartlett, H. T. (Dulwich) (Capt. in 1936), 1934–36
Benke, A. F. (Cheltenham), 1962
Bennett, C. T. (Harrow) (Capt. in 1925), 1923, 1925
Bernard, J. R. (Clifton), 1958–60
Blake, J. P. (Aldenham), 1939
Blaker, R. N. (Elizabeth College, Guernsey), 1842–43
Blaker, R. N. R. (Westminster), 1900–02
Bligh, Ivo F. W. (Lord Darnley) (Eton) (Capt. in 1881), 1878–81
Block, S. A. (Marlborough), 1929
Blofeld, H. C. (Eton), 1959
Blundell, E. D. (Waitaki, New Zealand), 1928–29
Bodkin, P. E. (Bradfield) (Capt. in 1946), 1946
Bray, E. (Westminster), 1871–72
Bray, E. H. (Charterhouse), 1896–97
Brearley, J. M. (City of London) (Capt. in 1963–64), 1961–64
Bridgeman, W. C. (Eton), 1887
Brocklebank, J. M. (Eton), 1936
Brodhurst, A. H. (Malvern), 1939
Brodie, J. B. (Union H.S., S. Africa), 1960
Brodrick, P. D. (Royal G.S., Newcastle), 1961
Bromley-Davenport, H. R. (Eton), 1892–93
Brooke-Taylor, G. P. (Cheltenham), 1919–20

Brown, F. R. (Leys), 1930–31
Browne, F. B. R. (Aldro School and Eastbourne College), 1922
Brunton, J. du V. (Lancaster Grammar School), 1894
Bryan, J. L. (Rugby), 1921
Buchanan, J. N. (Charterhouse) (Capt. in 1909), 1906–09
Buckston, G. M. (Eton), 1903
Burnett, A. C. (Lancing), 1949
Burnup, C. J. (Malvern), 1896–98
Burrough, J. (King's School, Bruton, and Shrewsbury), 1895
Bushby, M. H. (Dulwich) Capt. in 1954), 1952–54
Butler, E. M. (Harrow), 1888–89
Butterworth, H. R. W. (Rydal Mount), 1929
Buxton, C. D. (Harrow) (Capt. in 1888), 1885–88

Calthorpe, F. S. G. (Repton), 1912–14, 1919
Cameron, J. H. (Taunton), 1935–37
Cangley, B. G. (Felsted), 1947
Carris, B. D. (Harrow), 1938–39
Carris, H. E. (Mill Hill), 1930
Cawston, E. (Lancing), 1932
Chambers, R. E. J. (Forest), 1966
Chapman, A. P. F. (Oakham and Uppingham), 1920–22
Christopherson, J. C. (Uppingham), 1931
Close, P. A. (Haileybury), 1965
Cobbold, P. W. (Eton), 1896
Cobbold, R. H. (Eton), 1927
Cobden, F. C. (Harrow), 1870–72
Cockett, J. A. (Aldenham), 1951
Coghlan, T. B. L. (Rugby), 1960
Colbeck, L. G. (Marlborough), 1905–06
Collins, D. C. (Wellington College, Wellington, N.Z.), 1910–11
Comber, J. T. H. (Marlborough), 1931–33
Conradi, E. R. (Oundle), 1946
Coode, A. T. (Fauconberge School, Beccles), 1898
Cook, G. W. (Dulwich), 1957–58
Cosh, N. J. (Dulwich), 1966
Cottrell, G. A. (Kingston G.S.), 1966
Cowie, A. G. (Charterhouse), 1910
Craig, E. J. (Charterhouse), 1961–63
Crawley, E. (Harrow), 1887–89
Crawley, L. G. (Harrow), 1923–25
Croft, P. D. (Gresham's, Holt), 1955
Crookes, D. V. (Michaelhouse, South Africa), 1953
Cumberlege, B. S. (Durham), 1913

Daniell, J. (Clifton), 1899–1901
Daniels, D. M. (Rutlish), 1964–65
Datta, P. B. (Asutosh College, Calcutta), 1947
Davies, G. B. (Rossall), 1913–14
Davies, J. G. W. (Tonbridge), 1933–34
Dawson, E. W. (Eton) (Capt. in 1927), 1924–27
Day, S. H. (Malvern) (Capt. in 1901), 1899–1902
De Little, E. R. (Geelong Grammar School), 1889
De Paravicini, P. J. (Eton), 1882–85
De Zoete, H. W. (Eton), 1897–98
Dewes, J. G. (Aldenham), 1948–50
Dexter, E. R. (Radley) (Capt. in 1958), 1956–58
Dickinson, D. C. (Clifton), 1953
Dickinson, P. J. (K.C.S., Wimbledon), 1939
Doggart, A. G. (Bishop's Stortford), 1921–22
Doggart, G. H. G. (Winchester) (Capt. in 1950), 1948–50
Dorman, A. W. (Dulwich), 1886
Douglas, J. (Dulwich), 1892–94
Douglas, R. N. (Dulwich), 1890–92
Douglas-Pennant, S. (Eton), 1959
Downes, K. D. (Rydal), 1939
Dowson, E. M. (Harrow) (Capt. in 1903), 1900–03
Driffield, L. T. (Leatherhead), 1902
Druce, N. F. (Marlborough) (Capt. in 1897), 1894–97
Druce, W. G. (Marlborough) (Capt. in 1895), 1894–95
Duleepsinhji, K. S. (Cheltenham), 1925–26, 1928

Ebden, C. H. M. (Eton), 1902–03
Elgood, B. C. (Bradfield), 1948
Enthoven, H. J. (Harrow) (Capt. in 1926), 1923–26
Estcourt, N. S. D. (Plumtree, Southern Rhodesia), 1954
Evans, R. G. (King Edward, Bury St. Edmunds), 1921
Eyre, C. H. (Harrow) (Capt. in 1906), 1904–06

Fabian, A. H. (Highgate), 1929–31
Fairbairn, G. A. (Church of England Grammar School, Geelong), 1913–14, 1919
Falcon, M. (Harrow) (Capt. in 1910), 1908–11
Fargus, A. H. C. (Clifton and Haileybury), 1900–01
Farnes, K. (Royal Liberty School, Romford), 1931–33
Fernie, A. E. (Wellingborough), 1897, 1900
Fiddian-Green, C. A. (Leys), 1921–22
Field, E. (Clifton), 1894
Foley, C. P. (Eton), 1889–91

Foley, C. W. (Eton), 1880
Ford, A. F. J. (Repton), 1878–81
Ford, F. G. J. (Repton) (Capt. in 1889), 1887–90
Ford, W. J. (Repton), 1873
Francis, T. E. S. (Tonbridge), 1925
Franklin, W. B. (Repton), 1912
Fraser, T. W. (Jeppe, S. Africa), 1937
Freeman-Thomas, F. (Lord Willingdon) (Eton), 1886–89
Frere, J. (Eton), 1827
Fry, K. R. B. (Cheltenham), 1904

Gaddum, F. D. (Uppingham and Rugby), 1882
Gay, L. H. (Marlborough and Brighton), 1892–93
Gibb, P. A. (St. Edward's, Oxford), 1935–38
Gibson, C. H. (Eton), 1920–21
Gillespie, D. W. (Uppingham), 1939
Gilligan, A. E. R. (Dulwich), 1919–20
Gilman, J. (St. Paul's), 1902
Godsell, R. T. (Clifton), 1903
Goodfellow, A. (Marlborough), 1961–62
Goodwin, H. J. (Marlborough), 1907–08
Goonesena, G. (Royal Coll., Colombo) (Capt. in 1957), 1954–57
Gosling, R. C. (Eton), 1888–90
Grace, W. G., junr. (Clifton), 1895–96
Grant, G. C. (Trinidad), 1929–30
Grant, R. S. (Trinidad), 1933
Gray, H. (Perse), 1894–95
Green, C. E. (Uppingham) (Capt. in 1868), 1865–68
Green, D. J. (Burton G.S.) (Capt. in 1959), 1957–59
Grierson, H. (Bedford Grammar), 1911
Griffith, M. G. (Marlborough), 1963–65
Griffith, S. C. (Dulwich), 1935
Griffiths, W. H. (Charterhouse), 1946–48
Grimshaw, J. W. T. (King William's College, Isle of Man), 1934–35

Hadingham, A. W. G. (St. Paul's), 1932
Hale, H. (Hutchins School, Hobart), 1887, 1889–90
Hall, P. J. (Geelong), 1949
Harbinson, W. K. (Marlborough), 1929
Harper, L. V. (Rossall), 1901–03
Harrison, W. P. (Rugby), 1907
Harvey, J. R. W. (Marlborough), 1965
Hawke, M. B. (Lord) (Eton) (Capt. in 1885), 1882–83, 1885
Hawkins, H. H. B. (Whitgift), 1898–99
Hays, D. L. (Highgate), 1966
Hayward, W. I. D. (St. Peter's College, Adelaide), 1950–51, 1953
Hazelrigg, A. G. (Eton) (Capt. in 1932), 1930–32
Hemingway, W. McG. (Uppingham), 1895–96
Henery, P. J. T. (Harrow), 1882–83
Hewan, G. E. (Marlborough), 1938
Hill, A. J. L. (Marlborough), 1890–93
Hill-Wood, W. W. (Eton), 1922
Hind, A. E. (Uppingham), 1898–1901
Hobson, B. S. (Taunton), 1946
Holloway, N. J. (Leys), 1910–12
Hone, N. T. (Rugby), 1881
Hopley, F. J. V. (Harrow), 1904
Hopley, G. W. V. (Harrow), 1912
Hotchkin, N. S. (Eton), 1935
Howard-Smith, G. (Eton), 1903
Howland, C. B. (Dulwich) (Capt. in 1960), 1958–60
Hughes, G. (Cardiff H. S.), 1965
Hughes, O. (Malvern), 1910
Hunt, R. G. (Aldenham), 1937
Human, J. H. (Repton) (Capt. in 1934), 1932–34
Human, R. H. C. (Repton), 1930–31
Hurd, A. (Chigwell), 1958–60
Hutton, R. A. (Repton), 1962–64

Imlay, A. D. (Clifton), 1907
Insole, D. J. (Monoux, Walthamstow) (Capt. in 1949), 1947–49
Ireland, J. F. (Marlborough) (Capt. in 1911), 1908–11
Irvine, L. G. (Taunton), 1926–27

Jackson, F. S. (Harrow) (Capt. in 1892–93), 1890–93
Jagger, S. T. (Malvern), 1925–26
Jahangir Khan, M. (Lahore), 1933–36
James, R. M. (St. John's, Leatherhead), 1956–58
Jefferson, R. I. (Winchester), 1961
Jenner, C. H. (Eton), 1829
Jenner, Herbert (Eton) (Capt. in 1827, First Cambridge Capt.), 1827
Jenner, H. L. (Harrow), 1841
Jephson, D. L. A. (Manor House, Clapham), 1890–92
Jessop, G. L. (Cheltenham Grammar) (Capt. in 1899), 1896–99
Johnson, P. R. (Eton), 1901
Johnstone, C. P. (Rugby), 1919–20
Jones, A. O. (Bedford Modern), 1893
Jones, R. S. (Chatham House, Ramsgate), 1879–80
Judd, A. K. (St. Paul's), 1927

Kaye, M. A. C. P. (Harrow), 1938
Keigwin, R. P. (Clifton), 1903–06
Kelland, P. A. (Repton), 1950
Kemp, G. M. (Mill Hill and Shrewsbury), 1885–86, 1888
Kemp-Welch, G. D. (Charterhouse) (Capt. in 1931), 1929–31
Kenny, C. J. M. (Ampleforth), 1952
Kerslake, R. C. (Kingswood), 1963–64

Khanna, B. C. (Lahore), 1937
Kidd, E. L. (Wellington) (Capt. in 1912), 1910–13
Killick, E. T. (St. Paul's), 1928–30
King, F. (Dulwich), 1934
Kirby, D. (St. Peter's, York) (Capt. in 1961), 1959–61
Kirkman, M. C. (Dulwich), 1963
Knatchbull-Hugessen, C. M. (Eton), 1886
Knightley-Smith, W. (Highgate), 1953

Lacey, F. E. (Sherborne), 1882
Lacy-Scott, D. G. (Marlborough), 1946
Lagden, R. B. (Marlborough), 1912–14
Lancashire, O. P. (Lancing), 1880
Lang, A. H. (Harrow), 1913
Langley, J. D. A. (Stowe), 1938
Latham, P. H. (Malvern) (Capt. in 1894), 1892–94
Lawrence, A. S. (Harrow), 1933
Lewis, A. R. (Neath G.S.) (Capt. in 1962), 1960–62
Lewis, L. K. (Taunton), 1953
Lockhart, J. H. B. (Sedbergh), 1909–10
Longfield, T. C. (Aldenham), 1927–28
Longman, G. H. (Eton) (Capt. in 1874–75), 1872–75
Longman, H. K. (Eton), 1901
Longrigg, E. F. (Rugby), 1927–28
Lowe, R. G. H. (Westminster), 1925–27
Lowe, W. W. (Malvern), 1895
Lowry, T. C. (Christ's College, N.Z.) (Capt. in 1924), 1923–24
Lucas, A. P. (Uppingham), 1875–78
Lumsden, V. R. (Munro College, Jamaica), 1953–55
Lyon, M. D. (Rugby), 1921–22
Lyttelton, 4th Lord (Eton), 1838
Lyttelton, Alfred (Eton) (Capt. in 1879), 1876–79
Lyttelton, C. F. (Eton), 1908–09
Lyttelton, C. G. (Lord Cobham) (Eton), 1861-64
Lyttelton, Edward (Eton) (Capt. in 1878), 1875–78
Lyttelton, G. W. S. (Eton), 1866–67

McAdam, K. P. W. J. (Millfield), 1965–66
MacBryan, J. C. W. (Exeter), 1920
McCarthy, C. N. (Pietermaritzburg Coll., S.A.), 1952
McDonell, H. C. (Winchester), 1903–05
MacGregor, G. (Uppingham) (Capt. in 1891), 1888–91
Machin, R. S. (Lancing), 1927
Mackinnon, F. A. (Harrow), 1870
McLachlan, A. A. (St. Peter's, Adelaide), 1964–65
McLachlan, I. M. (St. Peter's, Adelaide), 1957–58
MacLeod, K. G. (Fettes), 1908–09
Mainprice, H. (Blundell's), 1906
Malalasekera, V. P. (R.C., Colombo), 1966
Mann, E. W. (Harrow) (Capt. in 1905), 1903–05
Mann, F. G. (Eton), 1938–39
Mann, F. T. (Malvern), 1909–11
Mann, J. E. F. (Geelong), 1924
Mansfield, J. W. (Winchester), 1883–84
Marchant, F. (Rugby and Eton) (Capt. in 1887), 1884–87
Marlar, R. G. (Harrow) (Capt. in 1953), 1951–53
Marriott, C. S. (St. Columba's), 1920–21
Marriott, H. H. (Malvern), 1895–98
Marsh, J. F. (Amersham Hall), 1904
Martineau, L. (Uppingham), 1887
Mathews, K. P. A. (Felsted), 1951
May, P. B. H. (Charterhouse), 1950–52
May, P. R. (Private), 1905–06
Melluish, M. E. L. (Rossall) (Capt. in 1956), 1954–56
Meyer, R. J. O. (Haileybury), 1924–26
Meyrick-Jones, F. (Marlborough), 1888
Miller, M. E. (Prince Henry G.S.), 1963
Mills, J. M. (Oundle) (Capt. in 1948), 1946–48
Mischler, N. M. (St. Paul's), 1946–47
Mitchell, F. (St. Peter's, York) (Capt. in 1896), 1894–97
Money, W. B. (Harrow) (Capt. in 1870), 1868–71
Moon, L. J. (Westminster), 1899–1900
Morcom, A. F. (Repton), 1905–07
Mordaunt, H. J. (Eton), 1888–89
Morgan, J. T. (Charterhouse) (Capt. in 1930), 1928–30
Morgan, M. N. (Marlborough), 1954
Morris, R. J. (Blundell's), 1949
Morrison, J. S. F. (Charterhouse) (Capt. in 1919), 1912, 1914, 1919
Morton, P. H. (Rossall), 1878–80
Mugliston, F. H. (Rossall), 1907–08
Mulholland, H. G. H. (Eton) (Capt. in 1913), 1911–13
Murray, D. L. (Queen's R. C. Trinidad) (Capt. in 1966), 1965–66

Napier, G. G. (Marlborough), 1904–07
Nason, J. W. W. (University School, Hastings), 1909–10
Naumann, J. H. (Malvern), 1913, 1919
Nelson, R. P. (St. George's, Harpenden), 1936
Norman, C. L. (Eton), 1852–53
Norman, F. H. (Eton) (Capt. in 1860), 1858–60

O'Brien, R. (Wellington), 1955–56
Olivier, E. (Repton), 1908–09
Orford, L. A. (Uppingham), 1886–87

Page, C. C. (Malvern), 1905–06
Palfreman, A. B. (Nottingham), 1966
Palmer, C. (Uppingham), 1907
Parker, G. W. (Crypt, Gloucester) (Capt. in 1935), 1934–35
Parry, D. M. (Merchant Taylors), 1931
Parsons, A. B. D. (Brighton), 1954–55
Partridge, N. E. (Malvern), 1920
Patterson, W. S. (Uppingham) (Capt. in 1877), 1875–77
Pawle, J. H. (Harrow), 1936–37
Payne, A. U. (St. Edmund's, Canterbury), 1925
Payne, M. W. (Wellington) (Capt. in 1907), 1904–07
Payton, W. E. G. (Nottingham High School), 1937
Pearson, A. J. G. (Downside), 1961–63
Pelham, A. G. (Eton), 1934
Pelham, F. G. (Eton) (Capt. in 1866–67) 1864–67
Penn, E. F. (Eton), 1899, 1902
Pepper, J. (The Leys), 1946–48
Perkins, H. (Bury St. Edmunds), 1854
Perkins, T. T. N. (Leatherhead), 1893–94
Phillips, E. S. (Marlborough), 1904
Pickering, E. H (Eton) (Capt. in 1829), 1827, 1829
Pickering, W. P. (Eton) 1840, 1842
Pieris, P. I. (St. Thomas, Colombo), 1957–58
Ponsonby, F. G. B. (Lord Bessborough) (Harrow), 1836
Pope, C. G. (Harrow), 1894
Popplewell, O. B. (Charterhouse), 1949–51
Powell, A. G. (Charterhouse), 1934
Prest, E. B. (Eton), 1850
Prest, H. E. W. (Malvern), 1909, 1911
Pretlove, J. F. (Alleyn's), 1954–56
Pritchard, G. C. (King's Canterbury), 1964
Pryer, B. J. K. (City of London), 1948
Prideaux, R. M. (Tonbridge), 1958–60

Ramsay, R. C. (Harrow), 1882
Ranjitsinhji, K. S. (Rajkumar College, India), 1893
Ratcliffe, A. (Rydal School), 1930–32
Reddy, N. S. K. (Doon School, Doura Dun, India), 1959–61
Rees-Davies, W. R. (Eton), 1938
Riddell, V. H. (Clifton), 1926
Riley, W. N. (Worcester Grammar School), 1912
Rimell, A. G. J. (Charterhouse), 1949–50
Roberts, F. B. (Rossall), 1903
Robertson, W. P. (Harrow), 1901
Robins, R. W. V. (Highgate), 1926–28
Robinson, J. J. (Appleby), 1894
Rock, C. W. (Launceston Grammar School, Tasmania), 1884–86
Roe, W. N. (Clergy Orphan School, Canterbury), 1883
Roopnaraine, R. (Queen's R. C., B.G.), 1965–66
Rose, M. H. (Pocklington), 1963–64
Rotherham, G. A. (Rugby), 1919
Rought-Rought, D. C. (Private), 1937
Rought-Rought, R. C. (Private), 1930, 1932
Rowe, F. C. C. (Harrow), 1881
Rowell, W. I. (Marlborough), 1891
Russell, S. G. (Tiffin), 1965–66

Savile, A. (Eton), 1840
Savile, G. (Eton and Rossall), 1868
Saville, S. H. (Marlborough) (Capt. in 1914), 1911–14
Seabrook, F. J. (Haileybury) (Capt. in 1928), 1926–28
Seddon, R. (Bridgnorth Grammar School), 1846–47
Shelmerdine, G. O. (Cheltenham), 1922
Sheppard, D. S. (Sherborne) (Capt. in 1952), 1950–52
Sherwell, N. B. (Tonbridge), 1923–25
Shine, E. B. (King Edward VI School, Saffron Walden), 1896–97
Shirley, W. R. (Eton), 1924
Shirreff, A. C. (Dulwich), 1939
Shuttleworth, G. M. (Queen Elizabeth Grammar School), 1946–48
Silk, D. R. W. (Christ's Hospital) (Capt. in 1955), 1953–55
Singh, S. (Khalsa and Punjab U.), 1955–56
Sinker, N. D. (Winchester), 1966
Slack, J. K. E. (U.C.S.), 1954
Smith, C. A. (Charterhouse), 1882–85
Smith, C. S. (William Hulme's G.S.), 1954–57
Smith, D. J. (Stockport G.S.), 1955–56
Spencer, R. (Harrow), 1881
Spiro, D. G. (Harrow), 1884
Stanning, J. (Rugby), 1900
Steel, A. G. (Marlborough) (Capt. in 1880), 1878–81
Steel, D. Q. (Uppingham), 1876–79
Stevenson, M. H. (Rydal), 1949–52
Stogdon, J. H. (Harrow), 1897–99
Streatfeild, E. C. (Charterhouse), 1890–93
Studd, C. T. (Eton) (Capt. in 1883), 1880–83
Studd, G. B. (Eton) (Capt. in 1882), 1879–82
Studd, J. E. K. (Eton) (Capt. in 1884), 1881–84
Studd, P. M. (Harrow) (Capt. in 1939) 1937–39
Studd, R. A. (Eton), 1895

Subba Row, R. (Whitgift), 1951–53
Sutthery, A. M. (Uppingham and Oundle), 1887
Swift, B. T. (St. Peter's, Adelaide), 1957

Taylor, T. L. (Uppingham) (Capt. in 1900), 1898–1900
Thompson, J. R. (Tonbridge), 1938–39
Thomson, R. H. (Bexhill), 1961–62
Thornton, C. I. (Eton) (Capt. in 1872), 1869–72
Thwaites, I. G. (Eastbourne College), 1964
Tindall, M. (Harrow) (Capt. in 1937), 1935–37
Tomlinson, W. J. V. (Felsted), 1923
Topham, H. G. (Repton), 1883–84
Toppin, C. (Sedbergh), 1885–87
Tordoff, G. G. (Normanton G.S.), 1952
Trapnell, B. M. W. (U.C.S.), 1946
Tufnell, N. C. (Eton), 1909–10
Turnbull, M. J. (Downside) (Capt. in 1929), 1926, 1928–29
Turner, J. A. (Uppingham), 1883–86

Urquhart, J. R. (King Edward VI School, Chelmsford), 1948

Valentine, B. H. (Repton), 1929
Vincent, H. G. (Haileybury), 1914

Wait, O. J. (Dulwich), 1949, 1951
Ward, E. E., Rev. (Bury St. Edmunds), 1870–71
Warr, J. J. (Ealing County Grammar School) (Capt. in 1951), 1949–52
Watts, H. E. (Downside), 1947
Webster, J. (Bradford G.S.), 1939
Webster, W. H. (Highgate), 1932
Weedon, M. J. H. (Harrow), 1962
Weigall, G. J. V. (Wellington), 1891–92
Wells, C. M. (Dulwich), 1891–93
Wells, T. U. (King's College, Auckland, N.Z.), 1950
Wheatley, O. S. (King Edward's, Birmingham), 1957–58
Wheelhouse, A. (Nottingham H.S.), 1959
White, A. F. T. (Uppingham), 1936
White, A. H. (Geelong), 1924
White, R. C. (Hilton, S.A.), 1962–65
Whitfield, H. (Eton), 1878–81
Wilcox, D. R. (Dulwich) (Capt. in 1933), 1931–33
Wild, J. V. (Taunton), 1938
Wilenkin, B. C. G. (Harrow), 1956
Willard, M. J. L. (Judd), 1959–61
Willatt, G. L. (Repton) (Capt. in 1947), 1946–47
Wilson, C. E. M. (Uppingham) (Capt. in 1898), 1895–98
Wilson, C. P. (Uppingham and Marlborough), 1880–81
Wilson, E. R. (Rugby) (Capt. in 1902), 1899–1902
Wilson, F. B. (Harrow) (Capt. in 1904), 1902–04
Wilson, G. (Harrow), 1919
Windows, A. R. (Clifton), 1962–64
Winlaw, R. de W. K. (Winchester), 1932–34
Winter, A. H. (Westminster), 1865–67
Winter, C. E. (Uppingham), 1902
Winter, G. E. (Winchester), 1898–99
Wood, G. E. C. (Cheltenham) (Capt. in 1920), 1914, 1919–20
Woodroffe, K. H. C. (Marlborough), 1913–14
Woods, S. M. J. (Brighton) (Capt. in 1890), 1888–91
Wooller, W. (Rydal), 1935–36
Wright, C. C. G. (Tonbridge), 1907–08
Wright, C. W. (Charterhouse), 1882–85
Wright, P. A. (Wellingborough), 1922–24
Wykes, N. G. (Oundle), 1928

Yardley, N. W. D. (St. Peter's, York) (Capt. in 1938), 1935–38
Yardley, W. (Rugby) (Capt. in 1871), 1869–72
Young, R. A. (Repton) (Capt. in 1908), 1905–08

OTHER MATCHES IN 1966

SCOTLAND v. DENMARK

At Edinburgh, June 21, 22. Scotland 114 for five wickets declared (J. M. C. Ford 65 not out) and 41 for one wicket; Denmark 126 (K. M. Hardie eight for 48). Drawn.

ROYAL NAVY v. OXFORD UNIVERSITY

At Chatham, June 22, 23. Royal Navy 162 for nine wickets declared (M. Robinson 61; R. W. Elviss five for 30) and 150 (R. W. Elviss four for 48); Oxford University 312 for four wickets declared (F. S. Goldstein 131, D. P. Toft 74, P. J. K. Gibbs 52) and 4 for no wicket. Oxford University won by ten wickets.

IRELAND v. MIDDLESEX

At Belfast, July 20, 21. Ireland 113 and 112 (D. A. Bick six for 19); Middlesex 246 (P. H. Parfitt 93, J. T. Murray 50; R. Torrens four for 77). Middlesex won by an innings and 21 runs.

SCOTLAND v. IRELAND

At Edinburgh, July 30, August 1, 2. Scotland won by six wickets, just reward for their enterprise after they had put in the opposition. With the opening day washed out by rain, they declared 21 runs behind and when left to score 136 in just under two hours, went for the runs with commendable enthusiasm. The winning hit came with six minutes to spare. Dudman and Laing, both from the Perthshire club, were the main architects with a second-wicket stand of 86. Dudman reached his second 50 of the match in one hour, six minutes. Another notable feature was the work of Colhoun, who in catching Moore helped in a dismissal for the fifty-fourth time, a wicket-keeping record for Ireland.

Ireland

M. C. McCall c Brown b Barr	19	— c Ellis b Dow	14
D. R. Pigot c Barr b Dow	32	— c Barr b Dow	13
B. A. O'Brien c Dudman b Hardy	32	— c Ford b Barr	6
I. Anderson c Laing b Barr	11	— b Barr	19
A. J. O'Riordan c Thompson b Hardy	0	— c Brown b Hardy	13
G. O. Duffy c Brown b Dow	19	— b Thompson	1
F. S. A. Hewitt b Dow	36	— c Dudman b Ellis	17
C. Corry not out	1	— st Brown b Hardy	6
D. Goodwin (did not bat)		— b Hardy	21
†O. D. Colhoun (did not bat)		— not out	0
*S. S. Huey (did not bat)		— b Hardy	0
W 1, n-b 1	2	L-b 3, n-b 1	4
1/33 2/53 3/80 4/83 5/98 6/145 7/152 (7 wkts., dec.)	152	1/23 2/31 3/49 4/58 5/69 6/69 7/89 8/95 9/114	114

Bowling: *First Innings*—Barr 23—7—46—2; Dow 19—7—33—3; Thompson 13—4—23—0; Hardy 18—5—48—2; *Second Innings*—Hardy 13.4—6—23—4; Ellis 5—4—5—1; Thompson 12—3—16—1; Dow 8—1—26—2; Barr 16—5—29—2; Chisholm 3—1—11—0.

Scotland

R. H. E. Chisholm c Huey b O'Riordan	20	— c Duffy b O'Riordan	5
L. C. Dudman b Huey	59	— not out	73
J. G. Laing b O'Riordan	0	— c Colhoun b O'Riordan	41
H. K. Moore not out	38	— c Colhoun b O'Riordan	7
J. M. C. Ford not out	9	— c Hewitt b O'Riordan	6
D. Barr (did not bat)		— not out	4
B 4, n-b 1	5	W 1	1
1/57 2/57 3/114 (3 wkts., dec.)	131	1/16 2/102 3/118 4/132 (4 wkts.)	137

*†J. Brown, R. Ellis, W. D. F. Dow, K. M. Hardy and K. G. H. R. Thompson did not bat.

Bowling: *First Innings*—O'Riordan 23—8—41—2; Hewitt 5—0—26—0; Goodwin 11—3—25—0; Huey 10—3—20—1; Duffy 2—1—3—0; Anderson 2—0—11—0. *Second Innings*—O'Riordan 15—3—57—4; Hewitt 3—0—18—0; Goodwin 8.3—1—34—0; Huey 4—0—27—0.

Umpires: S. G. Walker and W. J. Green.

HASTINGS FESTIVAL

At Hastings, August 31, September 1, 2. A. E. R. GILLIGAN'S XI drew with WEST INDIES. (See WEST INDIES section.)

At Hastings, September 3. KENT 100; SUSSEX 96 (A. L. Dixon four for 9). Kent won by four runs.

At Hastings, September 5. SURREY 122 (J. C. Dye four for 21); KENT 106. Surrey won by 16 runs.

IRELAND v. M.C.C.

At Dublin, September 3, 5, 6. M.C.C. won by 36 runs. Despite an excellent recovery in which O'Riordan, getting a fair amount of pace, took six wickets for 35 runs as M.C.C. slumped to 67 all out in their second innings, Ireland could not avert another defeat which followed those against Middlesex and Scotland. They were "destroyed" by Bailey, the former Essex and Oxford University medium-pace bowler, who took thirteen for 57 in the match. He controlled the last day, which began with Ireland seemingly well placed, needing 90 to win with seven wickets in hand. The only score over fifty came from Pretlove, formerly of Cambridge University and Kent. He hit 81 for M.C.C. in just over two and a half hours.

M.C.C.

*M. H. Bushby b O'Riordan	2	— hit wkt b Anderson	5
B. L. Reed c Huey b Torrens	41	— c Hope b O'Riordan	11
R. A. Gale b Torrens	0	— absent hurt	0
J. F. Pretlove b O'Riordan	81	— c and b O'Riordan	9
M. A. Eagar c Colhoun b Lang	8	— lbw b O'Riordan	0
A. R. Duff not out	30	— c McCall b O'Riordan	0
†C. B. Howland run out	1	— b O'Riordan	21
P. I. Bedford b Anderson	21	— c Lang b Anderson	0
J. D. Piachaud c and b Anderson	7	— not out	17
J. A. Bailey c Pigot b Huey	8	— c Pigot b O'Riordan	0
G. H. Chesterton b Anderson	0	— b Anderson	0
B 1, l-b 7, n-b 3	11	B 1, l-b 1, w 1, n-b 1	4
1/17 2/22 3/92 4/135 5/139 6/141 7/182 8/190 9/209	210	1/17 2/20 3/20 4/20 5/37 6/38 7/50 8/56 9/67	67

Bowling: *First Innings*—O'Riordan 29—7—63—2; Torrens 14—5—37—2; Lang 17—4—36—1; Huey 15—3—51—1; Anderson 4.3—1—12—3. *Second Innings*—O'Riordan 17—6—35—6; Anderson 10—2—18—3; Torrens 2—1—8—0; Huey 6—4—2—0.

Ireland

H. C. McCall c Duff b Piachaud	33	— b Bailey	6
D. R. Pigot b Bailey	4	— c Eagar b Bailey	0
B. A. O'Brien c sub b Duff	29	— c Howland b Bailey	22
I. Anderson b Bailey	44	— lbw b Bailey	12
A. J. O'Riordan c Reed b Duff	8	— lbw b Duff	19
D. M. Pratt b Duff	5	— b Bailey	8
K. W. Hope lbw b Bailey	0	— not out	0
†O. D. Colhoun st Howland b Duff	0	— b Duff	0
D. Lang not out	0	— b Bailey	1
R. Torrens b Bailey	4	— b Bailey	0
*S. S. Huey b Bailey	0	— c Eagar b Bailey	0
B 18, l-b 4	22	B 15, l-b 4, w 2, n-b 3	24
1/5 2/49 3/107 4/115 5/137 6/138 7/145 8/145 9/149	149	1/5 2/16 3/35 4/44 5/59 6/81 7/91 8/92 9/92	92

Bowling: *First Innings*—Bailey 19.2—7—33—5; Chesterton 9—7—9—0; Piachaud 22—8—46—1; Pretlove 12—7—12—0; Duff 21—9—27—4. *Second Innings*—Bailey 32.1—22—24—8; Chesterton 11—9—3—0; Piachaud 4—1—14—0; Duff 20—13—27—2.

Umpires: J. Connerton and K. Orme.

SCARBOROUGH FESTIVAL

At Scarborough, September 3, 5, 6. T. N. PEARCE'S XI beat WEST INDIES by two wickets. (See WEST INDIES section.)

AN ENGLAND XI v. REST OF THE WORLD XI

At Scarborough, September 7, 8, 9. England XI won by five wickets. This challenge match, sponsored by Rothmans, was seriously—though entertainingly—fought. Many of the Rest of the World team, flown to England, lacked recent match practice. On the opening day, Mushtaq, a model of concentration, made a sound not-out hundred, and excellent stroke-play by Pataudi and Deryck Murray brought recovery for the Rest from three wickets for 19 to 289 for six declared. Higgs bowled accurately and fast. Next day, d'Oliveira hit three 6's—one of them straight off Peter Pollock—in an aggressive display, but England fell 32 behind on the first innings. Hanif and Simpson, in their second innings, put their team in a sound position with a partnership of 66 and on the last morning lively batting by their colleagues enabled Simpson to declare at lunch when he set England to score 299 in three and a half hours. Parks proved the match winner. Dexter drove dashingly for 43, but England were 191 for five when Close, their captain, was out. Then Parks, in company with Lewis, his partner in an unbroken stand of 110 in an hour, mastered the varied Rest attack. Parks drove particularly well, and hit one 6 and eleven 4's in his century, which he reached just before Lewis glanced the winning boundary off Pataudi. Parks made his runs in ninety-five minutes. The game attracted an aggregate attendance of nearly 32,000 people.

Rest of the World XI

*R. B. Simpson b Trueman	4 — c d'Oliveira b Titmus	37
Hanif Mohammad b Higgs	2 — b Titmus	45
G. Thomas c d'Oliveira b Higgs	9 — st Parks b Hobbs	39
R. G. Pollock c and b d'Oliveira	22 — b Hobbs	29
K. C. Bland b Higgs	24 — c Close b Hobbs	15
Nawab of Pataudi b Titmus	66 — not out	4
Mushtaq Mohammad not out	100	
†D. L. Murray not out	50 — c and b Higgs	10
R. G. Nadkarni (did not bat)	— not out	29
P. M. Pollock (did not bat)	— st Parks b Hobbs	25
G. D. McKenzie (did not bat)	— c d'Oliveira b Close	19
B 2, l-b 4, n-b 6	12 B 8, l-b 6	14
1/4 2/8 3/19 4/48 5/76 6/196 (6 wkts., dec.)	289 1/66 2/97 3/135 4/154 5/177 6/277 7/250 8/261 (8 wkts., dec.)	266

Bowling: *First Innings*—Trueman 16—2—69—1; Higgs 20—3—46—3; d'Oliveira 16.1—2—39—1; Close 16—4—45—0; Titmus 18—4—41—1; Hobbs 10—2—37—0. *Second Innings*—Trueman 8—0—28—0; Higgs 8—1—20—1; d'Oliveira 3—2—3—0; Hobbs 24—1—111—4; Titmus 21—7—36—2; Dexter 5—2—11—0; Close 7—1—43—1.

An England XI

G. Boycott c Thomas b Mushtaq	33 — b Nadkarni	51
P. H. Parfitt c Simpson b McKenzie	62 — c Murray b Bland	23
E. R. Dexter c Murray b P. M. Pollock	37 — c Thomas b Nadkarni	43
A. R. Lewis c Murray b McKenzie	15 — not out	35
B. d'Oliveira c Thomas b Mushtaq	51 — b Nadkarni	18
*D. B. Close b P. M. Pollock	2 — c McKenzie b Nadkarni	12
†J. M. Parks st Murray b Simpson	6 — not out	101
F. J. Titmus st Murray b Nadkarni	35	
F. S. Trueman b Mushtaq	2	
K. Higgs b Mushtaq	3	
R. N. S. Hobbs not out	0	
L-b 11	11 B 11, l-b 7	18
1/59 2/117 3/148 4/149 5/155 6/190 7/239 8/245 9/257	257 1/36 2/121 3/131 4/173 5/191 (5 wkts.)	301

Bowling: *First Innings*—P. M. Pollock 14—0—72—2; McKenzie 18—5—31—2; Bland 1—0—1—0; Mushtaq 17.1—4—50—4; Nadkarni 14—5—45—1; Simpson 14—3—44—1; R. G. Pollock 1—0—3—0. *Second Innings*—P. M. Pollock 9—1—39—0; McKenzie 10—1—43—0; Bland 10—1—35—1; Nadkarni 21—1—107—4; Mushtaq 15—1—54—0; Nawab of Pataudi 0.4—0—5—0.

Umpires: J. S. Buller and W. E. Phillipson.

At Scarborough, September 10, 12, 13. YORKSHIRE lost to M.C.C. by 83 runs. (See YORKSHIRE section.)

SINGLE-WICKET CHAMPIONSHIP IN 1966

F. J. Titmus, the Middlesex captain and England cricketer, won the Charrington Breweries Single Wicket Championship and the top prize of £250 in the two-day competition held at Lord's on August 11, 12. He was the highest scorer with 149 runs in his four innings and in the semi-final and final he made 56 and 42 without being dismissed.

The final provided a match between England and Australia, with Cowper, of Victoria, opposing Titmus who, contrary to the general trend, batted on winning the toss. He scored steadily through the eight overs and later beat Cowper with the last ball of his third over. The Australian touched it to the feet of the wicket-keeper, Murray, moved out of his ground not knowing where the ball had gone, and Murray easily stumped him.

Titmus had a much closer struggle in his semi-final when Boycott sent him in to bat, and confined him to nine runs in four overs. Then Titmus pulled him for 6 and proceeded to make 47 from the next four overs. Boycott, wanting 57 to win had to run nearly all his runs. Taylor (Derbyshire) missed stumping him when he was 44 but he needed only eight from the last seven deliveries when he popped up a soft catch to forward short leg.

On the first day each match in the preliminary and first rounds was restricted to five overs instead of eight because rain prevented play before lunch. All three Yorkshire representatives, Trueman, Illingworth and Boycott won their first round ties. Boycott had a very tight match against Underwood who took him to the last ball, the Yorkshireman being credited with seven extras with Taylor behind the stumps. Underwood swung his bat freely.

Both West Indies representatives, Hall and Holford, fell at the first hurdle to Australians, Stackpole and Cowper. Five 6's were hit on the first day by Knight, Parfitt, Illingworth, Benaud and Stackpole.

A feature of the cricket on both days was the excellent fielding of the M.C.C. ground staff. Terry Charrington (most appropriately named) won the prize for the best fielder. He threw down the middle stump at the bowler's end from deep point in helping Titmus to knock out the Australian, Stackpole.

Preliminary Round

K. R. Stackpole (Australia) 20 not out (14 balls) beat W. W. Hall (West Indies) 16 (17 balls).

B. R. Knight (Essex) 27 not out (30 balls) beat D. A. Allen (Gloucestershire) 7 (13 balls).

First Round

W. E. Russell (Middlesex) 22 (26 balls) lost to F. S. Trueman (Yorkshire) 23 not out (17 balls).

P. H. Parfitt (Middlesex) 31 (24 balls) beat Saeed Ahmed (Pakistan) 6 (eight balls).

R. Illingworth (Yorkshire) 31 (28 balls) beat R. Benaud (Australia) 14 (18 balls).

D. A. J. Holford (West Indies) 10 (10 balls) lost to R. M. Cowper (Australia) 11 not out (19 balls).

D. L. Underwood (Kent) 23 (28 balls) lost to G. Boycott (Yorkshire) 24 not out (30 balls).

K. F. Barrington (Surrey) 19 (21 balls) lost to Mushtaq Mohammad (Northamptonshire) (holder), 20 (23 balls).

F. J. Titmus (Middlesex) 26 (30 balls) beat G. Milburn (Northamptonshire) 11 (14 balls).

K. R. Stackpole (Australia) 15 (9 balls) beat B. R. Knight (Essex) 8 (9 balls).

Quarter-Finals

P. H. Parfitt (Middlesex) 8 (12 balls) lost to F. S. Trueman (Yorkshire) 9 not out (4 balls).

R. Illingworth (Yorkshire) 18 (19 balls) lost to R. M. Cowper (Australia) 22 not out (25 balls).

Mushtaq Mohammad (Northamptonshire) 2 (7 balls) lost to G. Boycott (Yorkshire) 3 not out (13 balls).

F. J. Titmus (Middlesex) 25 (39 balls) beat K. R. Stackpole (Australia) 7 (12 balls).

Semi-Finals

R. M. Cowper (Australia) 26 (30 balls) beat F. S. Trueman (Yorkshire) 4 (5 balls).

F. J. Titmus (Middlesex) 56 not out (48 balls) beat G. Boycott (Yorkshire) 49 (42 balls).

FINAL

F. J. Titmus (Middlesex) 42 not out (48 balls) beat R. M. Cowper (Australia) 9 (18 balls).

Wicket-keeper's Prize

R. W. Taylor (Derbyshire) 15 (16 balls) lost to J. T. Murray (Middlesex) 17 not out (15 balls).

Past Winners

1963 at Scarborough:	K. E. Palmer (Somerset)
1964 at Lord's:	B. R. Knight (Essex)
1965 at Lord's:	Mushtaq Mohammad (Pakistan and Northamptonshire)
1966 at Lord's:	F. J. Titmus (Middlesex)

RULES

1. The Championship is played, on a knock-out basis, between individuals matched in accordance with a draw made before the event starts.

2. Each player bats for eight overs (or until out—whichever is sooner) against his opponent's bowling. Positions are then reversed; his opponent bats while he bowls. The player with the highest score wins and goes into the next round.

3. Each player is supported, while bowling, by a normal complement of nine fielders and a wicket-keeper. The field is not changed, unless injury makes it necessary during any match.
Except that there is only one batsman and one bowler in each innings, normal cricket rules apply. The bowler chooses the end at which the innings will commence, and changes ends after each six-ball over. At the beginning of each innings, the bowler chooses a ball from six offered him; none of them is brand new.

4. The batsman must continue any run, once he has crossed a marker half-way between the wickets. After making a run (or runs) which leaves him at the bowling end, the batsman must not return to his own wicket until told to by the bowling-end umpire; otherwise he shall be deemed to be taking a further run.

5. A tie is resolved by playing two extra overs on each side until the match is decided.

6. The winner of the Championship will receive a prize of £250; the runner-up £100; the two semi-finalists £50 each; and the quarter finalists £10 each.

THE MINOR COUNTIES IN 1966

Lincolnshire, one of the true Minor Counties, won the Championship for the first time since the club was founded in 1853. **Somerset II,** who finished top the previous year, came second, but did not seek a challenge match. Lincolnshire's success was based on three factors; the inspired leadership of R. W. Beeson, their captain and wicket-keeper—he claimed 38 victims in twelve matches—the enterprising stroke play of several batsmen who did not mind sacrificing their wickets for runs; and splendid bowling supported by very fine fielding. Some phenomenal catches were taken and very few chances were missed. Though injury deprived them of one key bowler in G. B. Camplin, they possessed a penetrative opening attack in N. M. McVicker and J. B. Evans and as usual J. W. Lawrence was a deadly spinner. Maslin led the batting in which two nineteen-year-olds, J. Sunley and C. A. Richardson, deserved special mention.

Cambridgeshire, who rose fourteen places and finished fourth, were fortunate in having the services of J. M. Brearley; he kept wicket ably and opened the innings consistently well. Perhaps the most encouraging aspect was the continued improvement of P. A. Shippey, who headed the batting. J. H. Wardle again did most of the bowling, taking 69 wickets, and he received steady support from D. C. Wing, who took 30 wickets for the first time. **Warwickshire** finished fifth, their identical position in 1965. They were rarely short of runs, the most successful batsmen being A. Gordon and J. W. Warrington, both from Coventry and new to the professional staff. Gordon hit two centuries and showed outstanding ability as a slip catcher. Warrington, a left-hander, played for the English Schools Cricket Association under Fifteen XI in 1964, together with E. E. Hemmings, who as in 1965, was again the main wicket-taker.

Bad weather early in the season soon dampened **Lancashire**'s Championship aspirations, but they met with only one defeat. R. Bennett led the side with marked keenness and the batting was always adequate with H. Pilling, R. Entwistle and J. D. Bond often scoring freely. J. Cumbes had his best season with the ball and formed a lively spearhead with K. Shuttleworth, but the spinners lacked the necessary penetration to finish matches in two days.

After an indifferent start, **Bedfordshire** showed much improvement and rose from sixteenth to seventh place. G. Millman (Nottinghamshire) and M. Ashenden (Gloucestershire) returned and added strength to the side, but N. Cooley, who headed the Minor Counties batting in 1965, could not appear regularly and was greatly missed as were other key players. Bad weather was another severe handicap.

D. Banton captained **Oxfordshire** with imagination and sagacity and the side rose seven places in the competition. This success was also due in no small way to B. R. Edrich, who in his first season with the club scored 329 runs, including two centuries, in the four games he played. D. Parrott, born and bred in Oxford, but with several years' experience with Leicestershire, J. E. Bush and J. Love also batted consistently well and R. D. Montgomerie hit his maiden century for the county. D. J. Laitt, the most penetrative bowler, has now taken 542 Minor County wickets in fifteen seasons. R. Matthews and A. C. Buck were two young bowlers of great promise and M. W. Smith again excelled as one of the best wicket-keepers in the competition.

Durham, once again most ably led by D. W. Hardy, enjoyed a successful season. They possessed notable batsmen in R. Inglis, H. J. Bailey and David Bailey and two newcomers, J. Kennedy and F. M. Westcott, made runs consistently. K. D. Biddulph, S. H. Young and M. J. Tate bowled well. **Yorkshire** under their new captain, J. D. H. Blackburn, had a moderate season, finishing tenth compared with sixth in 1965. The policy was again to give trials to young players and no fewer than 35 took part in the 12 matches. J. Lumb, B. Leadbeater and R. E. Crossley were the most successful batsmen and P. Stringer, G. A. Cope, J. White and D. L. Ash the outstanding bowlers. D. A. Pullan and N. Smith each kept wicket efficiently.

Berkshire had a mixed season and many matches were affected by the weather. They were weakened by the limited availability in August of some experienced players, particularly D. J. Mordaunt. The play of some younger members augured well for the future. Two of these, J. A. Scholfield and P. W. Neate, produced a remarkable stand of 100 in the last hour which enabled Berkshire to beat Wiltshire after losing their first five wickets for 46 runs.

Northumberland, after a disastrous start which yielded three points from four matches, took part in three thrilling finishes. They scored 101 runs in seventy-five minutes when beating Staffordshire; against Cheshire first-innings win points were gained with a few minutes to spare, and set to score 172 in two hours and five minutes against Cumberland, they failed by two runs with three wickets in hand to reach their target. J. van Geloven took 47 wickets in his first season, and A. S. Thompson and R. Jowsey gave some entertaining batting displays.

Rain prevented definite results in half of **Staffordshire**'s matches. John Ikin, the captain, again headed the batting and was well supported by S. A. Neal and D. A. Hancock. C. V. Lindo proved a splendid all-rounder with most wickets, 37, and 270 runs. **Dorset** also suffered, like most of the counties, from the weather and had to be content with one victory. There was plenty of depth in the batting, D. M. Daniels leading with 499 runs. The bowling proved disappointing, P. D. Stuckley being absent through injury. H. W. Stephenson had an excellent season behind the stumps.

Cornwall reserved their best performance for the last match when Wiltshire were defeated for the first time since fixtures were resumed in 1960. Another praiseworthy performance occurred at Taunton where Somerset were put out for 86, R. W. Hosen, the captain taking seven for 36, including the hat-trick. G. R. Parsons distinguished himself in his first game for the club by hitting 99 against Somerset. **Shropshire,** who suffered nine defeats, were not downcast and decided to improve by engaging a professional for the first time in their history in 1967, when all the counties anxiously hope that the sun will shine on their efforts.

MINOR COUNTIES IN 1966

	Played	Won	Lost	Won 1st Inns.	Lost 1st Inns.	No Result	Points	Average
Lincolnshire......	12	9	0	2	0	1	98	8.16
Somerset II.......	8	4	0	2	2	0	48	6.00
Nottinghamshire II	10	5	3*	0	1	1	56	5.60
Cambridgeshire...	10	4	3†	2	1	0	53	5.30
Warwickshire II...	10	4	1	1	4	0	47	4.70
Lancashire II.....	12	4	1	1	3	3	52	4.33
Bedfordshire......	10	3	3*	3	1	0	43	4.30
Oxfordshire.......	10	3	0	2	4	1	42	4.20
Durham..........	12	3	2*	5	2	0	50	4.16
Yorkshire II......	12	4	2	0	5	1	47	3.91
Norfolk..........	12	4	4	1	3	0	46	3.83
Cheshire.........	10	2	2*	3	1	2	37	3.70
Devon...........	10	2	2*	1	3	2	33	3.30
Berkshire.........	10	2	1	1	3	3	32	3.20
Suffolk..........	8	1	3*	3	0	1	24	3.00
Hertfordshire.....	10	2	2	1	4	1	29	2.90
Northumberland ..	12	1	2*	6	3	0	34	2.83
Staffordshire......	12	2	3	3	3	1	34	2.83
Dorset...........	10	1	3*	4	1	1	28	2.80
Wiltshire.........	10	1	3*	4	1	1	28	2.80
Cornwall.........	8	1	3*	1	2	1	20	2.50
Buckinghamshire..	10	0	3*	2	2	3	17	1.70
Cumberland......	10	0	7*	1	1	1	9	0.90
Shropshire........	10	0	9	1	0	0	3	0.30

* 1st Innings' points (3) in one match lost.
† 1st Innings' points in two matches lost.

METHOD OF SCORING:

Ten points for a win in a completed two-day match and for a lead on the first innings when there is no play on the first day of a two-day match, provided it cannot be played out.

Should a two-day match not be completed the side leading on the first innings scores three points and its opponents one point. In the event of a tie on the first innings in an unfinished match each side gets two points. In matches in which no result shall have been attained each side will be awarded two points. In the event of a tie the ten points shall be equally divided.

First innings qualifying points (3) gained shall be retained irrespective of the final result of a match, provided that a County shall receive not more than ten points.

In a one-day match, there having been no play on the first day, a tie is recorded if the scores of the completed first innings are equal, providing only if the match has not been played out to a further conclusion.

Somerset Second XI surrendered their right to challenge and Lincolnshire automatically became Champion County according to Rule 13.

* *Denotes Captain.* † *Wicket-keeper.*

BEDFORDSHIRE

Secretary—FRANK CROMPTON, High Knoll, Richmond Road, Bedford.

Matches 10: *Won—Cambridgeshire, Shropshire* (*twice*) *Lost—Lincolnshire* (*twice*), *Staffordshire. Won on first innings—Hertfordshire* (*twice*), *Staffordshire Lost on first innings—Cambridgeshire.*

Batting Averages

	Innings	Not Outs	Runs	Highest Inns.	Average
P. M. Taylor	16	4	485	82*	40.41
A. W. Durley	11	2	361	80	40.11
D. J. F. Hoare	9	1	298	72	37.25
†G. Millman	16	1	485	95	32.33
W. Chamberlain	7	2	141	61*	28.20
W. Bushby	9	3	167	49*	27.83
†N. Cooley	6	1	126	50	25.20
F. Moore	10	3	125	32*	17.85
G. Dawson	10	2	131	35	16.37
M. Ashenden	8	3	78	21*	15.60
*J. Smith	11	2	104	29	11.55
B. D. Robinson	12	1	122	33	11.09

Also batted: T. Brown 24, 3*; G. Jarrett 26, 0; T. G. A. Morley 4*, 7, 2 A. Ingledew 0, 11*, 2; J. Mordue 9, 0; G. Darlow 6*; T. Beck 5; R. White 3*, 0.

Bowling Averages

	Overs	Maidens	Runs	Wickets	Average
R. White	45.4	8	125	10	12.50
J. Smith	278.4	97	593	36	16.47
G. Jarrett	104.1	24	314	19	16.52
W. Bushby	168.4	42	463	28	16.53
A. Ingledew	51	12	186	9	20.66
T. Brown	58	13	190	8	23.75
T. Beck	47.1	10	167	6	27.83
M. Ashenden	194.2	37	567	20	28.35
T. G. A. Morley	117.1	27	283	8	35.37

Also bowled: J. Mordue 0 for 103.

BERKSHIRE

Secretary—H. L. LEWIS, White House, Pangbourne.

Matches 10: *Won—Devon, Wiltshire. Lost—Oxfordshire. Won on first innings—Dorset. Lost on first innings—Wiltshire, Buckinghamshire, Dorset. No Result—Buckinghamshire, Devon, Oxfordshire.*

Batting Averages

	Innings	Not Outs	Runs	Highest Inns.	Average
J. Scholfield	9	3	196	43*	36.67
*A. T. Davis	17	3	452	119	32.28
†R. C. G. Fortin	8	0	200	59	25.00

	Innings	Not outs	Runs	Highest Inns.	Average
B. E. F. Cheesman......	17	2	333	102	22.20
D. Johnston..........	11	2	179	49*	19.89
P. W. Neate..........	9	3	114	52*	19.00
F. W. Neate..........	10	0	179	56	17.90
C. E. W. Brooks........	10	2	133	45	16.63

Also batted: D. J. Mordaunt, W. Perkins, P. J. West, P. A. Baker, A. C. Denness, P. Watts, F. C. Baines, P. A. Simpkins, J. E. Flower, K. Salter, G. B. Jarrett, D. W. Stokes, J. Norman.

Bowling Averages

	Overs	Maidens	Runs	Wickets	Average
P. A. Simpkins.........	273.1	104	620	38	16.32
J. E. Flower...........	108.2	29	304	17	17.88
F. C. Baines...........	193	79	347	17	20.41
A. C. Denness..........	234.1	41	688	33	20.85
B. E. F. Cheesman......	159.5	35	436	18	24.22

Also bowled: P. W. Neate, G. B. Jarrett, D. J. Mordaunt, P. Watts, C. E. W. Brooks, K. Salter.

BUCKINGHAMSHIRE

Secretary—C. ANTHONY PRINCE, 16, Park View Road, London, W.5.

Matches 10: *Lost—Norfolk (twice), Oxfordshire. Won on first innings—Berkshire, Oxfordshire. Lost on first innings—Hertfordshire, Suffolk. No result—Berkshire, Suffolk, Hertfordshire.*

Batting Averages

	Innings	Not Outs	Runs	Highest Inns.	Average
C. W. Leach..........	5	1	133	80	33.25
C. Lever..............	15	0	402	95	26.80
G. Atkins.............	11	1	203	101	20.30
N. V. Butler..........	6	0	114	28	19.00
B. J. Tustian.........	10	1	162	52	18.00
D. F. V. Johns........	10	0	131	37	13.10
R. J. Hughes..........	5	2	37	15	12.33
†G. D. Hudson.........	13	4	100	29*	11.11
K. P. W. J. McAdam....	4	0	41	32	10.25
F. W. Harris..........	5	1	43	14*	10.15
*B. C. Janes..........	13	0	132	28	10.15
H. H. Huntley.........	7	0	69	28	9.86
J. K. E. Slack........	3	0	28	16	9.33
A. C. Waite...........	9	5	33	7*	8.25
J. E. Palmer..........	9	0	66	32	7.33
B. G. Sidaway.........	8	1	35	13*	5.00

Also batted: C. R. Harris 5*, 3, 0; R. W. A. Bray 37, 0; I. Feasey 7*; L. E. Hitchings 15*; W. Rawlings 0*. Played but did not bat: D. A. Pratt, D. A. Janes and †B. W. Poll.

Bowling Averages

	Overs	Maidens	Runs	Wickets	Average
N. V. Butler..........	55	25	92	7	13.15
F. W. Harris..........	155.3	64	321	22	14.59
D. A. Pratt...........	72	3	113	6	18.83
B. G. Sidaway	133	34	293	14	20.93
A. C. Waite...........	198.2	60	509	23	22.13
C. Lever..............	146.5	45	336	11	30.55

Also bowled: D. F. V. Johns 19—6—51—3; B. C. Janes 17—7—19—1; C. R. Harris 14—2—30—1; J. E. Palmer 22—4—68—2; R. H. Huntley 45.2—12—34—2; I. Feasey 3.2—0—12—0; W. Rawlings 5—0—19—0.

CAMBRIDGESHIRE

Secretary—R. A. TAYLOR, Field View, Linton.

Matches 10: *Won—Nottinghamshire II, Shropshire (twice), Hertfordshire. Lost—Nottinghamshire II, Lincolnshire, Bedfordshire. Won on first innings—Bedfordshire, Hertfordshire. Lost on first innings—Lincolnshire.*

Batting Averages

	Innings	Not Outs	Runs	Highest Inns.	Average
P. A. Shippey	19	2	645	137	37.94
T. S. Hale	17	3	466	104*	33.28
†J. M. Brearley	19	2	516	85	30.35
P. A. Goodman	11	2	205	46	22.78
D. H. R. Fairley	16	2	296	98	21.14
*R. A. Gautrey	13	1	228	48	19.00
J. H. Wardle	14	2	226	39	18.83
C. B. Gadsby	12	4	122	27	15.25
A. M. Ponder	8	0	119	47	14.87
D. C. Wing	11	6	50	12*	10.00

Also batted: R. F. Hawes 4, 2; A. Darbyshire 6, 1; D. Farnell 5, 14, 7, 15, 0; A. B. Fitton 11, 5, 1, 7, 7*; D. Lyon 10, 0*, 0, 0, 0; R. Pearl 6, 15; A. R. Wilson 0, 0, 6*, 0*.

Bowling Averages

	Overs	Maidens	Runs	Wickets	Average
J. H. Wardle	378.5	117	863	69	12.50
D. Lyon	77	22	203	10	20.30
D. C. Wing	254.1	61	674	30	22.46
A. R. Wilson	135	45	281	12	23.41
C. B. Gadsby	127.4	52	232	9	25.77
D. H. R. Fairey	38.1	5	114	2	57.00

Also bowled: R. Pearl 10—2—24—1; D. Farnell 23.4—4—85—3; R. A Gautrey 9—3—23—0.

CHESHIRE

Secretary—B. S. JONES, Tattenhall Road, Tattenhall, nr. Chester

Matches 10: *Won—Staffordshire, Northumberland. Lost—Yorkshire II (twice) Won on first innings—Lancashire II, Warwickshire II (twice). Lost on first innings—Northumberland. No result—Staffordshire, Lancashire II.*

Batting Averages

	Innings	Not Outs	Runs	Highest Inns.	Average
J. A. Sutton	12	0	490	112	40.83
*F. W. Millett	12	0	418	73	34.83
R. A. Richardson	8	1	224	65	32.00
D. F. Cox	9	0	268	88	29.77
S. E. Wood	9	2	157	52	22.42
R. Collins	11	1	215	60	21.50
N. R. Halsall	11	2	155	61*	17.22
P. A. C. Kelly	10	1	135	77*	15.00
†T. Hodson	11	7	37	16	9.25

Also batted: N. Gamble, T. A. H. Woodcock, W. Blackburn, P. D. Briggs J. R. A. Cragg, G. Hardstaff, D. Atkin, R. J. Digman, D. E. Costain, B. S. Jones C. D. B. Barker, E. Williams, D. Webb, R. C. Hulme, S. Davies, E. Barnes, A. L Shillinglaw.

Bowling Averages

	Overs	Maidens	Runs	Wickets	Average
G. Hardstaff	64.4	17	135	13	10.38
R. Collins	188.3	63	352	24	14.66
N. R. Halsall	163	42	406	21	19.33
J. A. Sutton	129.4	45	237	11	21.54
F. W. Millett	97.5	23	283	12	23.58

Also bowled: D. E. Costain, W. Blackburn, R. C. Hulme, R. J. Digman, S. Davies, D. F. Cox, N. Gamble, E. Williams, E. Barnes, C. D. R. Barker, A. L. Shillinglaw, R. A. Richardson.

CORNWALL

Secretary—ARTHUR LUGG, "Wendron", 18, Trevean Road, Truro.

Matches 8: *Won—Wiltshire. Lost—Somerset II, Devon, Dorset. Won on first innings—Somerset II. Lost on first innings—Dorset, Wiltshire. No result—Devon.*

Batting Averages

	Innings	Not Outs	Runs	Highest Inns.	Average
G. R. Harvey	14	0	436	71	31.14
G. R. Parsons	15	1	305	99	21.78
C. R. M. Chaplin	12	1	234	51	21.27
R. L. Mason	12	4	149	31*	18.62
P. N. Hodgson	9	0	156	55	17.33
C. J. B. Taylor	15	1	164	36	11.71
*R. W. Hosen	14	0	154	55	11.00
C. J. C. Kendall	7	2	54	18	10.80
*W. J. Lawry	9	7	18	7	9.00
A. M. May	6	0	44	27	7.33
B. Read	10	1	41	10	4.55
. Vercoe	6	2	10	4	2.50

Also batted: B. Laity 38, 1; D. C. R. Hall 26, 6; W. M. Buzza 15, 0; R. Harris ?, 0; M. O. Trenwith 2*, 0, 0; G. H. C. Sloggett 0.

Bowling Averages

	Overs	Maidens	Runs	Wickets	Average
R. W. Hosen	201	48	543	34	15.97
B. Read	206.3	48	632	30	21.06
C. J. C. Kendall	67.3	12	191	8	23.87

Also bowled: R. L. Mason 35—9—108—4; M. O. Trenwith 32—5—87—3; C. R. M. Chaplin 31—8—73—2; G. H. C. Sloggett 13.4—2—56—1; C. J. B. Taylor 14—0—57—0.

CUMBERLAND

Secretary—N. WISE, 18, Banklands, Workington.

Matches 10: *Lost—Warwickshire II (twice), Yorkshire II (twice), Durham (twice), Lancashire II. Won on first innings—Northumberland. Lost on first innings—Northumberland. No result—Lancashire II (abandoned).*

Batting Averages

	Innings	Not Outs	Runs	Highest Inns.	Average
A. J. C. Gray	10	1	334	71*	37.11
. B. Parker	8	0	202	63	25.25
. Wood	4	1	64	38	21.33
. Ellwood	10	5	95	45	19.00

	Innings	Not Outs	Runs	Highest Inns.	Average
†R. S. Jakeman.........	14	0	231	45	16.50
M. Saunders...........	4	0	66	56	16.50
*J. H. Millican.........	12	1	181	38*	16.45
†M. Beaty.............	6	0	97	47	16.16
J. K. Graham..........	14	0	183	51	13.07
W. S. Singleton.........	7	0	91	36	13.00
P. Sarjeant.............	8	1	72	30	10.28
W. A. Talbot...........	6	0	59	18	9.83
K. McCourt...........	11	0	103	67	9.36
W. B. Norgrove........	8	1	62	16	8.85
R. F. Dawson..........	6	0	46	22	7.66
A. Wishart.............	6	0	42	21	7.00
G. H. Hall.............	9	2	38	21	5.42
P. N. Broughton........	15	4	43	19	3.90

Also batted: I. Farish 7*, 5, 5, 2; M. Parker 1, 1, 0; G. Pickup 0, 1, 0, 1, 0; K. White 1, 21, 0, 4; J. I. Coulthard 5, 4; A. Catterall 0, 5; A. Newton 2, 1; A. Clapperton 0, 6; J. Denver 13, 0, 1, 8; A. Postlethwaite 10, 7.

Bowling Averages

	Overs	Maidens	Runs	Wickets	Average
G. Pickup.............	61	9	198	8	24.75
G. H. Hall.............	118	24	341	13	26.23
P. N. Broughton........	185.5	34	618	19	32.52
K. McCourt...........	66.1	21	245	7	35.00
E. Ellwood............	108.1	11	301	8	37.62
A. Wishart.............	11.5	2	46	1	46.00
J. H. Millican..........	72	14	208	4	52.00

Also bowled: K. Graham 3.2—0—19—1; R. B. Parker 3—1—7—1; K. Woo 5—0—27—0; W. S. Singleton 1—0—8—0; P. Sarjeant 4—0—20—1; R. S Jakeman 1—0—1—0.

DEVON

Secretary—T. H. Kirkham, "Ewelme", 17, Shiphay Lane, Torquay

Matches 10: *Won—Cornwall, Dorset. Lost—Berkshire, Somerset II. Wo on first innings—Oxfordshire. Lost on first innings—Oxfordshire, Dorset, Somerse II. No result—Berkshire, Cornwall.*

Batting Averages

	Innings	Not Outs	Runs	Highest Inns.	Averag
*D. H. Cole............	16	3	505	96*	38.84
†R. J. Newman.........	16	1	438	86	29.20
W. Shepherd...........	10	5	128	33*	25.60
J. G. Tolchard..........	14	1	299	60	23.00
S. J. B. Newsom........	12	5	149	34*	21.28
G. J. Lomax...........	5	0	95	35	19.00
C. Newman............	5	0	90	28	18.00
†P. J. Eele.............	9	0	144	36	16.00
G. Trump.............	9	3	67	32	11.16
R. G. Collard..........	8	0	73	17	9.12
J. Swinburne..........	10	3	45	15	6.42
D. I. Yeabsley..........	8	4	18	8*	4.50

Also batted: D. Martin 1, 4, 7; B. V. Crawford 2, 10, 1; D. J. Semmenc 4, 8, 45; J. C. Patrick 63, 6, 77; B. Stockhill 25, 19; B. Williams 0.

Bowling Averages

	Overs	Maidens	Runs	Wickets	Average
B. V. Crawford	87.4	29	192	14	13.71
W. Shepherd	117.3	44	264	16	16.50
J. Swinburne	192.4	61	531	27	19.66
D. I. Yeabsley	234.1	73	463	22	21.04
G. J. Lomax	60	16	115	5	23.00
G. Trump	229	73	517	20	25.85

Also bowled: D. H. Cole 46—20—97—5; S. J. B. Newsom 42—16—94—4; B. Williams 13—2—55—1; D. Martin 11.3—1—49—3; D. J. Semmence 3—2—1—0; J. G. Tolchard 1—0—4—0.

DORSET

Secretary—S. Hey, "Greenoaks", Bradford Road, Sherborne.

Matches 10: *Won—Cornwall. Lost—Wiltshire, Devon, Oxfordshire. Won on first innings—Cornwall, Oxfordshire, Devon, Berkshire. Lost on first innings—Berkshire. No result—Wiltshire.*

Batting Averages

	Innings	Not Outs	Runs	Highest Inns.	Average
D. M. Daniels	17	0	499	93	29.35
†H. W. Stephenson	12	3	228	42	25.33
C. M. G. Hunter	17	1	363	72	22.69
M. Hardwicke	14	2	235	66	19.58
C. Roper	9	0	173	52	19.22
J. Baker	15	0	283	73	18.87
R. K. Whiley	17	2	277	57	18.48
D. R. Hayward	10	1	145	48	16.11
*D. J. W. Bridge	10	2	126	39	15.75
M. E. Doggrell	8	1	94	38*	13.43

Also batted: A. A. Adams 8*, 2; M. E. Beale 25, 3*, 10, 7, 5, 1*; P. A. Close 1, 0, 6; J. W. Crabb 0; R. J. G. Deighton 0, 12; R. S. Miller 1, 13; D. R. Pheasant 0, 2; A. D. Robertson 3, 1, 5, 6; J. S. Stoker 0, 0*, 11, 0*, 0*, 0*; H. G. Wylie 0*, 0*, 0*.

Bowling Averages

	Overs	Maidens	Runs	Wickets	Average
J. Baker	143.5	54	348	26	13.38
D. R. Hayward	217.5	71	479	24	19.96
C. M. G. Hunter	171	61	404	18	22.44
M. E. Doggrell	224	68	462	14	33.00
D. J. W. Bridge	101.1	20	308	9	34.50
J. W. Crabb	66	15	202	4	50.50

Also bowled: D. M. Daniels 3—1—12—0; M. Hardwicke 2—1—4—0; R. S. Miller 28.5—8—75—9; D. R. Pheasant 3.4—0—16—2; J. S. Stoker 56—10—187—1; R. K. Whiley 1—0—7—0; H. G. Wylie 11.2—4—17—2.

DURHAM

Secretary—J. Iley, "Roselea", Springwell Avenue, Durham City.

Matches 12: *Won—Cumberland (twice), Lancashire II. Lost—Lancashire II, Warwickshire II. Won on first innings—Northumberland, Staffordshire (twice), Yorkshire II (twice). Lost on first innings—Warwickshire II, Northumberland.*

Batting Averages

	Innings	Not Outs	Runs	Highest Inns.	Average
R. Inglis	21	4	839	156*	49.35
D. Bailey	12	1	519	114	47.18
J. Kennedy	9	1	289	72	36.12

	Innings	Not Outs	Runs	Highest Inns.	Average
*D. W. Hardy	12	6	208	56	34.66
H. J. Bailey	18	1	495	87	29.11
F. M. Westcott	10	1	241	61	26.77
J. G. Barkass-Williamson	7	1	114	48	19.00
A. J. Burridge	14	0	218	33	15.57
J. G. March	9	1	102	25*	12.75
D. W. Soakell	6	0	72	42	12.00
S. H. Young	7	3	47	12	11.75
M. J. Tate	5	2	26	13	8.66
K. D. Biddulph	8	1	53	16	7.57
R. Cole	6	2	8	4*	2.00

Bowling Averages

	Overs	Maidens	Runs	Wickets	Average
S. H. Young	170.1	41	399	26	15.34
M. J. Tate	201.1	39	460	26	17.69
K. D. Biddulph	326.5	119	787	40	19.67
J. G. March	106.3	34	242	12	20.16
C. Storey	90.2	20	236	10	23.60
R. Inglis	104	24	286	11	26.00
H. J. Bailey	111.5	25	282	9	31.33

HERTFORDSHIRE

Secretary—C. O. Harrison, 39, Eleanor Cross Road, Waltham Cross.

Matches 10: *Won—Norfolk, Suffolk. Lost—Cambridgeshire, Norfolk. Won on first innings—Buckinghamshire. Lost on first innings—Bedfordshire (twice), Cambridgeshire, Suffolk. No result—Buckinghamshire (abandoned). Six matches were spoilt by rain.*

Batting Averages

	Innings	Not Outs	Runs	Highest Inns.	Average
R. Pankhurst	6	2	266	96*	66.50
A. R. Day	12	1	367	77	33.36
†P. L. Lord	4	3	32	15*	32.00
C. I. M. Jones	10	2	237	45	29.62
E. B. Natley	7	1	175	88	29.16
P. R. Martins	7	1	160	42	22.85
T. L. Clough	14	1	272	62*	20.92
B. H. Skingle	6	1	95	43*	19.00
*C. V. L. Marques	10	3	131	30	18.71
H. W. Tilly	13	0	234	53	18.00
R. H. Wacey	6	1	90	49	18.00
T. A. Bell	12	0	208	54	17.33
V. R. H. Garling	9	1	123	47*	15.37
J. D. Appleyard	8	3	72	23	14.40
†R. G. Simons	7	2	60	21*	12.00
J. Iberson	4	2	11	6*	5.50

Also batted: H. B. Hollington 29, 32, 9; J. P. Fellows Smith 15; D. Haines 0, 7; B. G. Collins 2[illegible], 0; T. Burges 1, 0.

Bowling Averages

	Overs	Maidens	Runs	Wickets	Average
J. Iberson	206	74	438	36	12.16
J. D. Appleyard	176.5	47	451	25	18.04
*C. V. L. Marques	113.4	19	393	16	24.56
H. W. Tilly	239.4	52	665	19	35.00
R. H. Wacey	125	35	311	6	51.83

Also bowled: C. I. M. Jones 1 for 10, E. B. Natley 4 for 60, A. R. Day, 2 for 69, B. G. Collins 1 for 68, J. P. Fellows Smith 0 for 40, B. H. Skingle 0 for 5.

LANCASHIRE SECOND ELEVEN

Secretary—J. B. Wood, Old Trafford, Manchester, 16.

Matches 12: Won—Cumberland, Durham, Northumberland, Staffordshire. Lost—Durham. Won on first innings—Yorkshire II. Lost on first innings—Cheshire. Northumberland, Staffordshire. No result—Cheshire, Cumberland, Yorkshire II.

Batting Averages

	Innings	Not Outs	Runs	Highest Inns.	Average
H. Pilling	6	1	352	117	70.40
R. Entwistle	12	3	458	118	50.88
J. D. Bond	5	0	230	123	46.00
*R. Bennett	11	1	421	75	42.10
F. Hayes	5	3	63	31	31.50
B. E. Krikken	7	5	56	18	28.00
J. Sullivan	6	0	157	68	26.16
A. Thomas	8	3	87	24*	17.40
A. M. Beddow	11	2	150	30*	16.66
K. Snellgrove	12	2	156	35	15.60

Also batted: D. R. Worsley 46, 27, 2*; P. W. Sutcliffe 4; D. Hughes 1, 3, 20*; K. Howard 2, 3*; K. Shuttleworth 13*; B. Wood 83, 22, 68*, 72; T. Greenhough 0, 12; J. Cumbes 1, 2*; E. M. N. Ransom 29*; B. Cole 4*, 1, 3; P. Lever 5; K. Eccleshare 0*; N. O'Brien 6; J. Cockcroft 1; L. Moore 2, 23; A. Bermingham 0, 3; G. Gibson 8, 10*; David Lloyd 21*, 46, 48*; G. K. Knox 17, 24, 30; S. Westley 8; R. Westley 4.

Bowling Averages

	Overs	Maidens	Runs	Wickets	Average
J. Cumbes	143.5	38	299	29	10.31
T. Greenhough	54.2	20	117	10	11.70
David Lloyd	73	28	147	12	12.25
K. Shuttleworth	67.2	22	119	9	13.22
K. Howard	103	35	252	16	15.75
P. W. Sutcliffe	45.3	7	121	7	17.28
D. Hughes	56	12	170	7	24.29
A. Thomas	162	41	438	17	25.76
A. M. Beddow	153.2	45	362	9	40.22

Also bowled: J. Sullivan 52—11—171—4; B. Wood 24—6—55—3; D. R. Worsley 47.2—11—112—3; M. Staziger 23—5—66—2; K. Snellgrove 9—2—43—2; P. Lever 18—5—36—2; K. Eccleshare 15—1—37—1; J. Cockcroft 22—2—74—1; A. Bermingham 2—0—18—0; N. O'Brien 15—5—46—1; F. Hayes 6—1—19—1; G. Gibson 5—1—10—0; R. Westley 16.4—3—70—3.

LINCOLNSHIRE

Secretary—R. J. Charlton, 36, Park Drive, Grimsby.

Matches 12: Won—Bedfordshire (twice), Yorkshire II (twice), Shropshire (twice), Nottinghamshire II, Norfolk, Cambridgeshire. Won on first innings—Norfolk, Cambridgeshire. No result—Nottinghamshire II.

Batting Averages

	Innings	Not Outs	Runs	Highest Inns.	Average
M. Maslin	18	3	581	103	38.73
H. Pougher	3	0	91	42	30.33
J. Sunley	10	1	268	100*	29.76
J. V. Wilson	3	0	76	37	25.33
G. Robinson	19	1	437	66	24.27
C. A. Richardson	17	4	283	59	21.76

	Innings	Not Outs	Runs	Highest Inns.	Average
N. M. McVicker........	14	4	213	62*	21.30
J. B. Evans............	14	3	223	83	20.27
I. S. Madray...........	17	1	310	88	19.37
T. Johnson............	7	1	114	54	19.00
D. Johnson............	13	1	196	50	16.33
*†R. N. Beeson.........	12	2	111	28	11.10
J. W. Lawrence.........	14	4	103	26*	10.30
G. Plaskitt............	5	2	23	14	7.69

Also batted: D. Buckthorpe 11, 0; G. B. Camplin 2, 1, 0; P. Barnes 0.

Bowling Averages

	Overs	Maidens	Runs	Wickets	Average
J. W. Lawrence.........	317.5	97	597	50	11.94
N. M. McVicker........	475.5	192	885	71	12.46
G. B. Camplin..........	44.2	14	116	8	14.50
J. B. Evans............	534.4	190	1132	71	15.94
J. Sunley..............	18	3	40	2	20.00
M. Maslin..............	11	2	45	2	22.50
I. S. Madray	26	7	56	1	56.00
G. Plaskitt	31	6	95	0	—

NORFOLK

Secretary—DAVID ARMSTRONG, Ranchi House, Holt.

Matches 12: *Won—Hertfordshire, Buckinghamshire* (*twice*), *Nottinghamshire II. Lost—Hertfordshire, Suffolk, Lincolnshire, Staffordshire. Won on first innings—Nottinghamshire II. Lost on first innings—Suffolk, Lincolnshire, Staffordshire.*

Batting Averages

	Innings	Not Outs	Runs	Highest Inns.	Average
I. P. Mercer	12	1	362	84*	32.91
*W. J. Edrich...........	21	2	496	93	26.16
D. G. Pilch............	21	0	489	89	23.29
J. A. Donaldson.........	6	0	113	34	18.83
†D. E. Mattocks.........	18	1	302	104	17.76
J. Shepperd............	19	2	253	59	14.88
J. P. Atkins............	7	0	103	37	14.71
R. D. Huggins...........	19	0	278	39	14.63
G. G. Fiddler	10	2	114	45	14.25
T. G. Bland............	16	4	166	31*	13.83
W. Rose................	18	6	149	27	12.43
I. M. Watts............	7	0	71	33	10.14
M. Woolstencroft.......	7	0	61	26	8.71
C. McManus............	8	1	49	19	7.00
T. I. Moore............	17	6	69	23*	6.28

Also batted: T. Allcock 4, 12, 0, 0, 0; T. D. Bowsett 29, 8, 2, 0; R. Goodwin 0*, 2*, 2*; H. Waters 6, 4.

Bowling Averages

	Overs	Maidens	Runs	Wickets	Average
W. J. Edrich...........	175.4	50	482	29	16.62
J. Shepperd............	252.2	69	675	40	16.87
W. Rose................	241.3	70	649	33	19.67
T. I. Moore............	189.1	42	553	28	19.75
T. G. Bland............	190.5	37	710	28	25.35

Also bowled: R. Goodwin 20—6—80—4; D. G. Pilch 25—5—122—4.

NORTHUMBERLAND

Secretary—GEORGE HUTCHINSON, 2, Slingsby Gardens, Newcastle upon Tyne, 7.

Matches 12: *Won—Staffordshire. Lost—Lancashire II, Cheshire. Won on first innings—Yorkshire II (twice), Lancashire II, Cheshire, Cumberland, Durham. Lost on first innings—Cumberland, Durham, Staffordshire.*

Batting Averages

	Innings	Not Outs	Runs	Highest Inns.	Average
A. S. Thompson........	8	1	242	70	34.57
R. Jowsey.............	15	1	404	76	28.85
F. J. B. Taylor..........	4	1	83	40	27.66
J. Thewlis...............	15	4	283	65*	25.72
R. W. Smithson.........	13	1	267	40	22.25
J. M. Crawhall.........	18	0	373	45	20.72
†H. B. Henderson.......	12	6	109	30*	18.16
*R. G. Clough.........	15	1	226	47*	16.14
J. van Geloven	17	4	182	33*	14.00
C. Pearson.............	9	1	103	62	12.87
P. D. Broderick.........	8	2	77	21	12.82
A. Brown...............	13	2	140	33	12.72
M. E. Robson..........	7	0	54	23	7.71
K. Norton..............	6	3	23	14*	7.66

Also batted: J. M. Douglas 14*, 0; R. E. Wood, 23, 0; H. D. Bell 8, 0; G. Heatley 7, 3, 0; F. Suffield 4, 0; M. E. Latham 4*, 0; J. Pettigrew 5; C. Cairns 3; E. Sisterson 2; S. Allen 0, 0; H. Dyson 0.

Bowling Averages

	Overs	Maidens	Runs	Wickets	Average
J. van Geloven.........	386.5	114	801	47	17.04
K. Norton..............	228.4	62	659	36	18.30
G. Heatley.............	29	8	92	5	18.40
A. Brown...............	263.4	68	689	32	21.53
C. Pearson.............	95.2	28	249	11	22.63
P. D. Brodrick.........	127.4	37	324	12	27.00

Also bowled: J. M. Douglas 7—1—25—1; E. Sisterson 10—1—46—1; H. Dyson 29—7—78—1; M. E. Latham 17—3—82—1; R. Jowsey 6—0—41—0; S. Allen 7—0—42—0; F. Suffield 4—1—11—0; J. Pettigrew 8—0—29—0; J. M. Crawhall 1—0—2—0.

NOTTINGHAMSHIRE SECOND ELEVEN

Secretary—R. M. POULTON, County Cricket Ground, Nottingham.

Matches 10: *Won—Cambridgeshire, Shropshire (twice), Suffolk (twice). Lost—Cambridgeshire, Lincolnshire, Norfolk. Lost on first innings—Norfolk. No result—Lincolnshire.*

Batting Averages

	Innings	Not Outs	Runs	Highest Inns.	Average
C. Grant...............	9	1	279	79*	34.87
K. Poole...............	6	0	208	133	34.66
B. Whittingham........	4	0	113	87	28.25
A. Johnson............	10	2	217	42*	27.12
H. I. Moore............	5	1	103	66*	25.75
J. Parkin..............	10	0	187	61	25.30
†G. Thornley..........	10	0	200	74	20.00
P. Bickley.............	8	0	145	33	18.12
H. M. Winfield.........	17	1	288	51	18.00
D. Hayward............	7	0	125	73	17.85
J. Howarth............	12	6	96	35*	16.00

	Innings	Not Outs	Runs	Highest Inns.	Average
B. Stead...............	6	0	84	62	14.00
K. Gillhouley..........	10	1	79	32	8.77
A. Bull................	16	0	117	20	7.31

Also batted: M. Smedley; A. B. Palfreman; J. D. Springall; J. D. Clay; J. Loates; J. B. Bolus; D. Guy.

Bowling Averages

	Overs	Maidens	Runs	Wickets	Average
J. D. Springall..........	21	10	42	6	7.00
K. Gillhouley...........	115	40	274	20	13.20
B. Stead................	139	42	323	22	14.68
A. B. Palfreman........	53	14	159	10	15.90
J. Howarth.............	167	52	406	25	16.24
A. Johnson.............	163.4	33	466	28	16.64
A. Bull................	176.5	58	496	29	17.10
M. Tebbutt.............	20	4	58	3	19.30
P. Johnson.............	25	5	96	3	32.00

OXFORDSHIRE

Secretary—L. B. Frewer, 58 Sunderland Avenue, Oxford.

Matches 10: *Won—Buckinghamshire, Berkshire, Dorset. Won on first innings—Wiltshire, Devon. Lost on first innings—Dorset, Buckinghamshire, Wiltshire, Devon. No result—Berkshire.*

Batting Averages

	Innings	Not Outs	Runs	Highest Inns.	Average
B. R. Edrich	8	2	329	101*	54.83
†M. W. Smith..........	6	5	40	14*	40.00
D. Parrott..............	6	1	164	65	32.80
J. E. Bush..............	10	0	265	81	26.50
J. Love.................	16	1	392	98	26.13
*D. Banton.............	13	6	175	43*	25.00
R. D. Montgomerie.....	14	2	291	100	24.25
J. S. Baxter............	4	1	70	25	23.33
K. T. Tallboys..........	9	0	199	74	22.11
D. J. Laitt.............	6	2	88	24*	22.00
M. D. Nurton...........	14	1	261	52	20.76
I. B. Moffatt...........	7	2	71	25	14.20
A. C. Buck..............	4	1	30	13	10.00
P. B. Smith.............	11	2	89	29	9.88
D. J. Castle............	5	1	33	13	8.25

Also batted: R. W. G. White 7, 1, 0; R. Matthews 3*; A. T. Tame 27*, 0, 0; S. H. Hahn 57.

Bowling Averages

	Overs	Maidens	Runs	Wickets	Average
D. J. Laitt......... ..	194	75	398	34	11.70
R. Matthews............	83.3	26	185	11	16.81
P. B. Smith.............	70.4	9	255	13	19.61
A. C. Buck..............	68	19	205	10	20.50
D. Banton..............	229.4	68	519	22	23.59
B. R. Edrich	38	5	138	5	27.60
I. B. Moffatt...........	40	12	115	2	57.50
R. W. G. White........	41	7	151	2	75.50

Also bowled: J. Livermore 14.1—3—33—4; J. Love 11—2—43—2; A. T. Tame 14—2—34—1; T. V. Strange 20—5—59—1; B. J. Peaper 2.5—2—3—0; D. Parrott 2—0—8—0.

SHROPSHIRE

Secretary—H. Botfield, 1, The Crescent, Much Wenlock, Shropshire.

Matches 10: *Lost—Cambridge (twice), Lincolnshire (twice), Warwickshire II, Nottinghamshire II (twice), Bedfordshire (twice). Won on first innings—Warwickshire II.*

Batting Averages

	Innings	Not Outs	Runs	Highest Inns.	Average
D. Jones	18	0	371	69	20.61
P. W. Gough	18	0	347	57	19.28
D. F. Lowe	5	0	89	33	17.80
A. Taylor	8	1	117	85	16.71
B. Hughes	7	6	16	6	16.00
R. Burton	8	0	118	42	14.75
R. M. Claffey	17	1	216	34	13.50
E. J. Everall	8	0	93	46	11.62
P. Scott	8	1	81	32	11.57
G. V. Othen	12	0	128	28	10.66
D. L. York	18	5	132	31	10.15
C. Hemsley	5	0	49	17	9.80
R. Everall	5	0	41	18	8.20
D. Barnes	5	0	37	14	7.40
K. Arch	14	1	92	17	7.07
S. Maddocks	12	0	60	20	5.00

Also batted: P. Bromley 4—1—83—55; E. Marsh 4—0—43—36; D. Breakwell 4—1—11—6; M. Picken 4—0—22—20; T. M. Pitt 1, 0; D. Toward 2, 0; B. Everall 1, 0; R. Jones 8, 3; J. Tranter 11, 0; J. Phillips 0*, 0; G. Roberts 26, 0.

Bowling Averages

	Overs	Maidens	Runs	Wickets	Average
D. L. York	203.2	39	727	34	21.38
K. Arch	124.5	22	480	22	21.82
G. V. Othen	133	35	392	16	24.50
B. Hughes	76.2	22	233	9	25.88
S. Maddocks	20.5	2	117	4	29.25

Also bowled: P. Scott 33—6—93—3; D. Barnes 49.5—9—158—3; E. J. Everall 1—0—1—1; R. Everall 15—1—56—1; T. M. Pitt 7—0—35—0; D. Breakwell 19—3—96—3; D. Toward 7—0—45—0; D. F. Lowe 1—0—4—0; R. Jones 3—0—19—0; A. Taylor 1—0—2—0; R. Burton 0.5—0—5—0; J. Phillips 19—2—92—0.

SOMERSET SECOND ELEVEN

Secretary—R. Robinson, County Cricket Ground, Taunton.

Matches 8: *Wins—Cornwall, Warwickshire II (twice), Devon, Wiltshire. Won on first innings—Devon. Lost on first innings—Cornwall, Wiltshire.*

Batting Averages

	Innings	Not Outs	Runs	Highest Inns.	Average
M. G. M. Groves	8	2	322	79	53.66
F. T. Willetts	14	1	426	104	52.76
B. Roe	15	1	423	81*	30.21
R. Paull	12	3	212	37*	23.55
C. H. M. Greetham	12	0	274	82	22.83
†T. E. Barwell	11	3	165	47	20.62

Also batted: A. Clarkson 8—4—254—106*; J. Shaw 5—3—112—56*; R. Palmer 6—2—99—31; G. Burgess 2—0—44—24*; N. Parker 3—0—15—15; B. Lobb 2—1—1—1; M. Trescothick 1—0—9—9; E. Langford 1—0—0—0; G. Lloyd 1—0—1—1; O. Sheard 1—0—0—0; A. Chapple 1—0—0—0; †R. Brooks 1—1—3—3*; J. Fitzgerald 3—1—13—8; J. D. Martin 3—2—24—12.

Bowling Averages

	Overs	Maidens	Runs	Wickets	Average
B. Palmer..............	191.5	40	572	33	17.33
*B. Lobb...............	240	83	547	30	18.23
J. Shaw................	72	21	189	10	18.90
C. H. M. Greetham......	189	68	443	22	20.13
J. Fitzgerald..........	85.1	38	197	9	21.88

Also bowled: J. D. Martin 43.5—6—147—3; G. Burgess 16—0—47—3; A. Clarkson 29—10—79—2; A. Chapple 14—4—38—0; E. Langford 6—1—12—0; N. Parker 4—0—18—1; B. Roe 1—0—1—0; R. Paull 25.5—3—140—2.

STAFFORDSHIRE

Secretary—L. W. Hancock, 4, Kingsland Avenue, Oakhill, Stoke-on-Trent.

Matches 12: *Won—Norfolk, Bedfordshire. Lost—Cheshire, Northumberland, Lancashire II. Won on first innings—Northumberland, Norfolk, Lancashire II. Lost on first innings—Durham* (*twice*), *Bedfordshire. No result—Cheshire.*

Batting Averages

	Innings	Not Outs	Runs	Highest Inns.	Average
*J. T. Ikin............	19	1	628	85	34.88
S. A. Neal.............	12	1	312	70	28.36
D. A. Hancock	17	2	390	64	26.00
P. Tunnicliffe.........	13	0	271	60	20.84
C. V. Lindo............	16	2	270	38	19.28
R. W. Flower...........	8	2	114	35*	19.00
M. Perkins.............	8	0	150	41	18.75
P. A. Brown............	5	0	90	53	18.00
C. L. Price............	4	0	68	59	17.00
†I. Frost..............	7	1	99	45	16.50
P. J. Kavanagh.........	6	0	97	64	16.16
N. G. W. Banks.........	11	2	145	35	16.11
†L. Rolinson...........	11	1	157	72	15.70
B. James...............	4	2	24	13	12.00
R. T. DeVille..........	6	0	70	34	11.66
P. Shardlow............	10	0	116	37	11.60
J. Steele..............	6	1	49	19	9.80
J. Young...............	7	5	18	10*	9.00
D. H. Henson...........	6	1	42	13*	8.40
P. Harvey..............	8	3	39	28	7.80

Also batted: V. R. Babb 4, 19, 40; R. H. Downend 32, 8; P. N. Gill 8, 11; L. Lowe 4, 12; P. Timmis 15, 0*; B. Cooke 11*, 2; H. Boon 9, 2; J. T. Finney 3, 6; M. Hill 6.

Bowling Averages

	Overs	Maidens	Runs	Wickets	Average
R. T. DeVille..........	60	18	135	10	13.50
D. H. Henson...........	146.4	51	278	18	15.44
C. V. Lindo............	259.3	79	637	37	17.21
J. Young...............	135.4	35	373	18	20.72
N. G. W. Banks.........	53	11	139	6	23.16
J. T. Ikin	71.1	11	167	7	23.85
P. Harvey..............	132	29	453	16	28.31
B. James...............	42	8	145	5	29.00
R. W. Flower...........	84	17	219	7	31.28

Also bowled: R. H. Downend 23—2—75—2; P. N. Gill 8.2—1—25—1; B. Cooke 19—5—48—1; P. Timmis 15—2—74—1; J. Steele 26—2—84—1; P. Tunnicliffe 2—0—5—0; P. Shardlow 6—2—7—0; L. Lowe 5—1—24—0.

SUFFOLK

Secretary—C. H. C. PIPER, Barrack Corner Garage, Ipswich.

Matches 8 *Won—Norfolk. Lost—Nottinghamshire II* (*twice*), *Hertfordshire. Won on first innings—Buckinghamshire, Hertfordshire, Norfolk. No result—Buckinghamshire.*

Batting Averages

	Innings	Not Outs	Runs	Highest Inns.	Average
A. J. Watkins..........	7	1	188	53	31.33
R. J. English...........	13	4	281	83	31.22
M. E. Scrutton.........	4	1	86	43	28.66
*†I. D. Prior...........	11	1	277	53	27.70
R. L. Flack............	15	2	330	50	25.38
A. G. Warrington.......	14	1	309	64	23.76
R. E. Cunnell..........	14	3	221	43*	20.09
J. R. Moyes............	11	0	148	47	13.45
C. J. Cunnell...........	14	1	165	40*	12.69
J. M. Hargreaves.......	10	2	69	20*	8.62
C. R. Layne............	8	3	40	15	8.00
†C. H. C. Piper.........	4	1	21	11	7.00
C. Rutterford...........	4	0	15	8	3.75
G. C. Perkins...........	5	1	7	4*	1.75

Also batted: M. G. T. Carter, 1, 14.

Bowling Averages

	Overs	Maidens	Runs	Wickets	Average
R. E. Cunnell..........	12.2	1	47	4	11.75
G. C. Perkins...........	220.2	80	412	30	13.73
M. E. Scrutton.........	33	9	71	5	14.20
A. J. Watkins..........	80	27	208	11	18.90
J. M. Hargreaves.......	222	61	607	32	18.96
R. J. English...........	172.1	47	423	19	22.26
C. R. Layne............	132.4	41	312	12	26.00

Also bowled: C. Rutterford 48—11—106—0.

WARWICKSHIRE SECOND ELEVEN

Secretary—L. T. DEAKINS, County Ground, Edgbaston, Birmingham 5

Matches 10: *Won—Cumberland* (*twice*), *Shropshire, Durham. Lost—Somerset* (*twice*). *Won on first innings—Durham. Lost on first innings—Cheshire* (*twice*) *Shropshire.*

Batting Averages

	Innings	Not Outs	Runs	Highest Inns.	Average
B. A. Richardson.......	6	1	247	79	49.40
R. Miller...............	7	4	122	49*	40.66
A. Gordon..............	16	2	560	120	40.00
R. B. Edmonds.........	5	2	91	54*	30.33
J. H. Gough...........	4	0	118	52	29.50
*R. E. Hitchcock.......	11	2	257	81	28.55
D. R. Oakes...........	13	1	323	63	26.91
†G. S. Warner..........	13	2	290	72*	26.36
†E. Legard............	8	4	107	51*	26.25
J. W. Warrington.......	14	0	346	85	24.71
W. Blenkiron..........	7	4	62	35*	20.66
T. E. N. Jameson.......	5	1	62	28	15.50
J. M. Allan	6	0	87	44	14.50
C. F. Antrobus.........	5	1	44	19	11.00

	Innings	Not Outs	Runs	Highest Inns.	Average
R. V. Vijayasarathy.....	4	1	30	17*	10.00
D. R. Kench...........	3	0	27	16	9.00
E. E. Hemmings........	11	0	59	13	5.36
P. Graham............	7	3	20	6	5.00

Also batted: K. Ibadulla 67, 18; W. J. Stewart 21*, 6; J. Barnfield 19; M. Cheslin 7, 0; R. N. Abberley 4, 0.

Bowling Averages

	Overs	Maidens	Runs	Wickets	Average
J. D. Bannister.........	21	11	21	3	7.00
R. B. Edmonds.........	93	49	130	12	10.83
P. Graham.............	110.1	35	273	20	13.65
R. Miller..............	119.2	43	342	19	18.00
E. E. Hemmings........	239.4	73	661	30	22.03
J. M. Allan............	78	21	216	9	24.00
W. Blenkiron..........	164.2	48	316	13	24.30
K. Ibadulla............	19	2	87	3	29.00
T. E. N. Jameson.......	68	15	205	7	29.28
B. A. Richardson.......	4.4	2	30	1	30.00
C. F. Antrobus........	163.5	26	488	13	37.54

Also bowled: R. N. Abberley 2—0—12—0; R. E. Hitchcock 1—0—2—0; D. R. Oakes 2—0—2—0; R. V. Vijayasarathy 4—1—9—0.

WILTSHIRE

Secretary—C. O. S. Eales, 66, Queen's Road, Devizes.

Matches 10: *Won—Dorset. Lost—Berkshire, Cornwall, Somerset II. Won on first innings—Berkshire. Cornwall, Oxfordshire, Somerset II. Lost on first innings—Oxfordshire. No result—Oxfordshire.*

Batting Averages

	Innings	Not Outs	Runs	Highest Inns.	Average
D. Essenhigh...........	16	2	472	69	33.71
D. Hughes.............	11	5	194	72	32.66
R. Gulliver............	8	1	170	62	24.29
D. J. Green............	15	1	334	104	23.14
J. Ridge...............	13	1	260	62	21.66
D. Gardner............	7	0	143	70	20.44
M. Scott...............	9	1	155	47	19.44
A. H. Barker...........	11	1	185	58	18.50
A. G. Marshall.........	13	2	197	41	17.86
J. Savin...............	9	6	40	9	13.33
M. R. Guest...........	7	0	90	32	12.86
J. H. Merryweather.....	7	2	33	8	6.60

Also batted: J. Scollen 0, 0, 2; P. Hough 0, 4, 1, 6, 4; I. R. Lomax 27, 16; B. White 0, 23, 0, 46, 19; D. Othen 35, 1, 0, 21; C. Eales 6, 7.

Bowling Averages

	Overs	Maidens	Runs	Wickets	Average
J. Ridge...............	35	15	70	7	10.00
J. H. Merryweather.....	288	110	612	44	13.98
A. G. Marshall.........	330	105	778	40	19.45
M. R. Guest...........	23	2	81	3	27.00
R. Gulliver............	45	19	92	3	30.66
A. H. Barker...........	125	38	381	11	34.64
J. Savin	143	30	401	9	44.56

Also bowled: P. Meehan 4—0—19—0; I. R. Lomax 12—4—41—0; D. Essenhigh 2—0—7—0; D. J. Green 7—2—31—1; D. Othen 3—1—9—0; P. Hough 3—1—7—2.

YORKSHIRE SECOND ELEVEN

Secretary—J. H. Nash, Headingley Cricket Ground, Leeds 6.

Matches 12:—*Won—Cumberland* (*twice*), *Cheshire* (*twice*). *Lost—Lincolnshire* (*twice*). *Lost on first innings—Lancashire II, Northumberland* (*twice*), *Durham* (*twice*). *No result—Lancashire II.*

Batting Averages

	Innings	Not Outs	Runs	Highest Inns.	Average
J. L. Lumb	18	1	719	147	39.94
W. Roberts	7	0	258	53	36.85
†D. A. Pullan	4	2	70	56*	35.00
B. Leadbeater	17	3	487	92	34.78
R. E. Crossley	11	4	223	42	31.85
G. I. Grace	3	1	61	28	30.50
G. A. Cope	4	0	101	55	25.25
J. Crowhurst	8	1	133	52*	19.00
A. Dalton	4	0	75	40	18.75
J. Waring	3	1	37	21*	18.50
*J. D. H. Blackburn	12	3	165	53	18.33
C. M. Old	19	2	289	58	17.00
C. Calvert	4	2	33	30	16.50
D. L. Ash	15	3	192	40	16.00
J. Senior	8	1	103	35	14.71
P. Stringer	11	2	121	40	13.44
†N. Smith	9	1	92	50*	11.50
J. White	3	0	17	13	5.66
D. W. Sharp	5	1	14	7	3.50

Also batted: J. C. Balderstone 100*, 13; S. Armitage 52*, 0; J. A. White 46; A. Batty 21, 8; K. Jackson 12*; D. H. Burnett 10; A. G. Nicholson 8; C. Johnson 14, 2; R. W. Elviss 6, 1; M. C. Fearnley 8, 1, 0; G. V. H. Bradby 2, 2; C. Clifford 4, 0, 0; C. Robson 0*; P. Hardcastle 0; M. Jackson 0, 0.

J. Eddings played once but did not bat.

Bowling Averages

	Overs	Maidens	Runs	Wickets	Average
D. Middlewood	53	14	129	9	14.33
J. White	65	23	159	11	14.45
G. A. Cope	153	57	329	19	17.31
D. L. Ash	76	20	257	14	18.35
P. Stringer	217	56	595	28	21.25
G. I. Grace	66	13	212	8	26.50
C. Clifford	77	14	266	10	26.60
C. M. Old	140	26	420	15	28.00

Also bowled: R. W. Elviss 33—9—50—3; J. C. Balderstone 25—8—60—3; S. Armitage 32—13—44—2; M. Jackson 27—0—95—4; J. D. H. Blackburn 23—1—81—3; D. M. Burnett 9—2—28—1; C. Robson 6—1—29—1; K. Jackson 30—10—83—2; A. G. Nicholson 17—3—49—1; M. C. Fearnley 62—10—205—3; J. Crowhurst 1—1—0—0; D. M. Batty 7—1—23—0; J. A. White 10—0—29—0.

MINOR COUNTIES AVERAGES, 1966

BATTING

(Qualification: 8 innings, average 25.00)

	County	Innings	Not Outs	Runs	Highest Inns.	Average
B. R. Edrich	*Oxfordshire*	8	2	329	101*	54.83
M. G. M. Groves	*Somerset II*	8	2	322	79	53.66
R. Entwistle	*Lancashire II*	12	3	458	118	50.88
R. Inglis	*Durham*	21	4	839	156*	49.35
D. Bailey	*Durham*	12	1	519	114	47.18

	County	Innings	Not Outs	Runs	Highest Inns.	Average
R. Bennett	*Lancashire II*	11	1	421	75	42.10
J. A. Sutton	*Cheshire*	12	0	490	112	40.83
P. M. Taylor	*Bedfordshire*	16	4	485	82*	40.41
A. W. Durley	*Bedfordshire*	11	2	361	80	40.11
A. Gordon	*Warwickshire II*	16	2	560	120	40.00
J. L. Lumb	*Yorkshire II*	18	1	719	147	39.94
D. H. Cole	*Devon*	16	3	505	96*	38.84
M. Maslin	*Lincolnshire*	18	3	581	103	38.73
P. A. Shippey	*Cambridgeshire*	19	2	645	137	37.94
D. J. F. Hoare	*Bedfordshire*	9	1	298	72	37.25
A. J. C. Gray	*Cumberland*	10	1	334	71*	37.11
J. Scholfield	*Berkshire*	9	3	196	43*	36.67
J. Kennedy	*Durham*	9	1	289	72	36.12
J. T. Ikin	*Staffordshire*	19	1	628	85	34.88
C. Grant	*Nottinghamshire II*	9	1	279	79*	34.87
F. W. Millett	*Cheshire*	12	0	418	73	34.83
B. Leadbeater	*Yorkshire II*	17	3	487	92	34.78
D. W. Hardy	*Durham*	12	6	208	56	34.66
A. S. Thompson ..	*Northumberland*	8	1	242	70	34.57
D. Essenhigh	*Wiltshire*	16	2	472	69	33.71
A. R. Day	*Hertfordshire*	12	1	367	77	33.36
T. S. Hale	*Cambridgeshire*	17	3	466	104*	33.28
I. P. Mercer	*Norfolk*	12	1	362	84*	32.91
F. T. Willetts	*Somerset II*	14	1	426	104	32.76
D. Hughes	*Wiltshire*	11	5	194	72	32.66
G. Millman	*Bedfordshire*	16	1	485	95	32.33
A. T. Davis	*Berkshire*	17	3	452	119	32.28
R. A. Richardson .	*Cheshire*	8	1	224	65	32.00
R. E. Crossley	*Yorkshire II*	11	4	223	42	31.85
R. J. English	*Suffolk*	13	4	281	83	31.22
G. R. Harvey	*Cornwall*	14	0	436	71	31.14
J. M. Brearley	*Cambridgeshire*	19	2	516	85	30.35
B. Roe	*Somerset II*	15	1	423	81*	30.21
D. F. Cox	*Cheshire*	9	0	268	88	29.77
J. Sunley	*Lincolnshire*	10	1	268	100*	29.76
C. I. M. Jones	*Hertfordshire*	10	2	237	45	29.62
D. M. Daniels	*Dorset*	17	0	499	93	29.35
R. J. Newman	*Devon*	16	1	438	86	29.30
H. J. Bailey	*Durham*	18	1	495	87	29.11
R. Jowsey	*Northumberland*	15	1	404	76	28.85
R. E. Hitchcock ..	*Warwickshire II*	11	2	257	81	28.55
S. A. Neal	*Staffordshire*	12	1	312	70	28.36
W. J. Bushby	*Bedfordshire*	9	3	167	49*	27.83
I. D. Prior	*Suffolk*	11	1	277	53	27.70
A. Johnson	*Nottinghamshire II*	10	2	217	42*	27.12
D. R. Oakes	*Warwickshire II*	13	1	323	63	26.91
C. Lever	*Buckinghamshire*	15	0	402	95	26.80
F. M. Westcott ...	*Durham*	10	1	241	61	26.77
J. E. Bush	*Oxfordshire*	10	0	265	81	26.50
G. S. Warner	*Warwickshire II*	13	2	290	72*	26.36
W. J. Edrich	*Norfolk*	21	2	496	93	26.16
J. Love	*Oxfordshire*	16	1	392	98	26.13
D. A. Hancock	*Staffordshire*	17	2	390	64	26.00
J. Thewlis	*Northumberland*	15	4	283	65*	25.72
W. Shepherd	*Devon*	10	5	128	33*	25.60
R. L. Flack	*Suffolk*	15	2	330	50	25.38
H. W. Stephenson	*Dorset*	12	3	228	42	25.33
J. Parkin	*Nottinghamshire II*	10	0	187	61	25.30
R. B. Parker	*Cumberland*	8	0	202	63	25.25

** Signifies not out.*

	County	Innings	Not Outs	Runs	Highest Inns.	Average
R. C. G. Fortin...	*Berkshire*	8	0	200	59	25.00
D. Banton.......	*Oxfordshire*	13	6	175	43*	25.00

** Signifies not out.*

BOWLING

(Qualification: 20 wickets, average 24)

	County	Overs	Maidens	Runs	Wickets	Average
J. Cumbes.......	*Lancashire II*	143.5	38	299	29	10.31
D. J. Laitt.......	*Oxfordshire*	194	75	398	34	11.70
J. W. Lawrence...	*Lincolnshire*	317.5	97	597	50	11.94
J. Iberson........	*Hertfordshire*	206	74	438	36	12.16
N. M. McVicker..	*Lincolnshire*	475.5	192	885	71	12.46
J. H. Wardle.....	*Cambridgeshire II*	378.5	117	863	69	12.50
K. Gillhouley....	*Nottinghamshire II*	115	40	274	20	13.20
J. Baker.........	*Dorset*	143.4	54	348	26	13.38
P. Graham........	*Warwickshire II*	110.1	35	273	30	13.65
G. C. Perkins....	*Suffolk*	220.2	80	412	30	13.73
J. H. Merryweather	*Wiltshire*	288	110	612	44	13.98
F. W. Harris.....	*Buckinghamshire*	155.3	64	321	22	14.59
R. Collins........	*Cheshire*	188.3	63	352	24	14.66
B. Stead.........	*Nottinghamshire II*	139	42	323	22	14.68
S. H. Young......	*Durham*	170.1	41	399	26	15.34
J. B. Evans.......	*Lincolnshire*	534.4	190	1132	71	15.94
R. W. Hosen.....	*Cornwall*	201	48	543	34	15.97
J. Howarth.......	*Nottinghamshire II*	167	52	406	25	16.24
P. A. Simpkins....	*Berkshire*	273.1	104	620	38	16.32
J. Smith.........	*Bedfordshire*	278.4	97	593	36	16.47
W. J. Bushby.....	*Bedfordshire*	168.4	42	463	28	16.53
W. J. Edrich......	*Norfolk*	175.4	50	482	29	16.62
A. Johnson.......	*Nottinghamshire II*	163.4	33	466	28	16.64
J. Sheppard......	*Norfolk*	252.2	69	675	40	16.87
J. van Geloven...	*Northumberland*	386.5	114	801	47	17.04
A. Bull..........	*Yorkshire II*	176.5	58	496	29	17.10
C. V. Lindo......	*Staffordshire*	259.3	79	637	37	17.21
R. Palmer.......	*Somerset II*	191.5	40	572	33	17.33
M. J. Tate........	*Durham*	201.1	39	460	26	17.69
J. D. Appleyard..	*Hertfordshire*	176.5	47	451	25	18.04
B. Lobb..........	*Somerset II*	240	83	547	30	18.23
K. Norton.......	*Northumberland*	228.4	62	659	36	18.30
J. M. Hargreaves.	*Suffolk*	222	61	607	32	18.96
N. R. Halsall.....	*Cheshire*	163	42	406	21	19.33
A. G. Marshall...	*Wiltshire*	330	105	778	40	19.45
J. Swinburne.....	*Devon*	192.4	61	531	27	19.66
K. D. Biddulph...	*Durham*	326.5	119	787	40	19.67
W. Rose.........	*Norfolk*	241.3	70	649	33	19.67
T. I. Moore......	*Norfolk*	189.1	42	553	28	19.75
D. R. Hayward...	*Dorset*	217.5	71	479	24	19.96
C. H. M. Greetham	*Somerset II*	189	68	443	22	20.13
A. C. Denness....	*Berkshire*	234.1	41	688	33	20.85
D. I. Yeabsley....	*Devon*	234.1	73	463	22	21.04
B. Read.........	*Cornwall*	206.3	48	632	30	21.06
P. Stringer.......	*Yorkshire II*	217	56	595	28	21.25
D. York.........	*Shropshire*	203.2	39	727	34	21.38
A. Brown........	*Northumberland*	263.4	68	689	32	21.53
K. Arch.........	*Shropshire*	124.5	22	480	22	21.82
E. E. Hemmings..	*Warwickshire II*	239.4	73	661	30	22.03
A. C. Waite......	*Buckinghamshire*	198.2	60	509	23	22.13
D. C. Wing......	*Cambridgeshire*	254.1	61	674	30	22.46
D. Banton.......	*Oxfordshire*	229.4	68	519	22	23.53

SECOND XI CHAMPIONSHIP

Surrey, twelfth the previous year, won the Second Eleven Championship for the first time since it was inaugurated in 1959. Their success was largely a team effort with special emphasis on the captaincy of A. J. McIntyre, the county coach. Mohammed Younis, a brother of Saeed Ahmed, the Pakistan Test player, scored 1,048 runs, including three centuries, and I. Finlay also shone with the bat. D. A. Marriott bowled consistently well and D. J. S. Taylor shone as wicket-keeper. **Nottinghamshire** found an attacking batsman in S. B. Hassan, from Kenya, and three local boys, G. Frost, P. Bickley and J. Loates made runs attractively. J. Howarth and A. Bull were promising bowlers.

Following the example of the senior sides, all first innings were restricted to 55 overs (65 overs in three-day games). This arrangement certainly suited **Hampshire**, who, finishing fourth (fifteenth in 1965) eight times took two points for first-innings lead. They, too, owed much to their captain, Leo Harrison, and produced a talented 17-year-old left-handed batsman in D. Turner. R. Lewis, aged 19, also made strides as a run-getter.

Middlesex, who finished last and without a win the previous season, showed much improved form by rising to fifth place while gaining six wins. M. Manasseh, the Oxford Blue, did well as an all-rounder and of the new players, D. R. Abbey, D. J. Ling and D. G. Ottley deserved mention. The main reason for **Glamorgan** dropping from first to sixth was bad catching close to the wicket. In every match catches went down which normally would be held by Glamorgan players.

Sussex won four of their first five matches; then gave D. J. Foreman, M. A. Buss and P. J. Graves to the first team and did not win again. **Warwickshire**, who improved on their previous season's record, introduced an interesting newcomer in T. Jameson, from Taunton School, who has now gone to Durham University. His elder brother is the number five county batsman. E. Legard kept wicket splendidly.

Kent rejoiced in the grand all-round form of J. Shepherd, from Barbados, while he was qualifying to play for the County in 1967. J. N. Graham, fast-medium, a model of accuracy, was easily the best bowler and R. Maybank looked a promising young wicket-keeper. **Essex** called on 37 cricketers, giving trials to several youngsters, some of whom will surely find their way into the county eleven. K. D. Boyce, from the West Indies on a two-year qualifying period, proved an exciting find in batting, bowling and fielding and R. East, who is 19, played several times in the first team, such was his improved form.

The most encouraging aspect of the **Derbyshire** season was the great advance of two young players, P. E. Russell, an all-rounder who entered the first team, and C. P. Marks, a young batsman from Staffordshire.

SECOND XI COMPETITION

	Played	Won	Lost	Drawn	No Decision	1st Inns. 2 Pts.	Points	Aver.
Surrey	16	10	1	4	1	10	116	7.25
Somerset	14	6	2	4	2	9	78	5.57
Nottinghamshire	14	5	2	7	–	11	71	5.07
Hampshire	14	5	3	5	1	8	66	4.71
Middlesex	16	6	4	4	2	5	65	4.06
Glamorgan	14	4	7	2	1	7	54	3.85
Lancashire	10	3	2	2	3	4	38	3.80
Sussex	15	4	5	5	1	8	56	3.73
Warwickshire	24	7	5	9	3	10	86	3.58
Kent	18	3	2	13	–	10	49	2.72
Gloucestershire	14	3	5	4	2	3	36	2.57
Worcestershire	21	4	3	12	2	7	50	2.38
Leicestershire	18	3	10	3	2	6	42	2.33
Essex	12	2	6	3	1	2	24	2.00
Derbyshire	12	1	4	6	1	5	20	1.66
Northamptonshire	22	2	7	11	2	8	35	1.59

Scoring: 10 Points for a win. 2 Points for side leading on 1st innings. 6 Points to side winning in match restricted to one innings, when no play possible on first day.

The Surrey, Middlesex, Warwickshire and Worcestershire records include six points for a side winning on the first innings in a match restricted to one day.

The Nottinghamshire, Middlesex, Kent and Northamptonshire records include one point for a tie on the first innings.

DERBYSHIRE SECOND ELEVEN

Matches 12: *Won—Leicestershire II. Lost—Lancashire II, Northamptonshire II, Warwickshire II, Worcestershire II. Won on first innings—Leicestershire II, Northamptonshire II, Nottinghamshire II, Warwickshire II. Lost on first innings—Nottinghamshire II, Worcestershire II. No Result—Lancashire II.*

Batting Averages

	Innings	Not Outs	Runs	Highest Inns.	Average
H. L. Johnson	5	2	218	77*	72.66
P. E. Russell	17	2	573	88	38.20
C. P. Marks	17	6	410	101*	37.27
T. J. P. Eyre	7	1	192	66*	32.00
J. R. Eyre	10	0	238	57	23.80
D. H. K. Smith	19	3	354	52	22.12
K. F. Mohan	8	2	120	43	20.00
B. Ward	8	0	145	43	18.12
*G. C. Turner	13	4	158	35	17.55

Bowling Averages

	Overs	Maidens	Runs	Wickets	Average
M. H. J. Allen	161.2	51	398	25	15.92
A. Blount	39	7	163	10	16.30
T. J. P. Eyre	84.1	12	257	12	21.41
A. Ward	103	23	303	13	23.30
P. E. Russell	154.3	30	414	15	27.60

No regular wicket-keeper.

ESSEX SECOND ELEVEN

Matches 12: *Won—Northamptonshire II, Sussex II. Lost—Sussex II, Surrey II (twice), Kent II, Middlesex II, Worcestershire II. Drawn—Kent II, Northamptonshire II, Worcestershire II. No result—Middlesex (abandoned).*

Batting Averages

	Innings	Not Outs	Runs	Highest Inns.	Average
E. R. Presland	8	0	205	68	25.62
H. Sherman	22	3	465	90*	24.47
K. D. Boyce	19	1	388	66*	21.55
†R. Kilby	8	0	170	80	21.25
R. East	7	3	82	31*	20.50
R. W. Wrightson	6	1	102	55	20.40
V. Brookes	8	2	103	30*	17.16
R. Nayes	6	0	100	40	16.66
N. Chapman	20	1	249	38	13.10
T. Dash	16	4	148	38*	12.33
G. C. Pritchard	14	4	71	21	7.10
*F. Rist	6	3	10	4*	3.33

Bowling Averages

	Overs	Maidens	Runs	Wickets	Average
R. East	95.4	23	260	21	12.38
K. D. Boyce	242.3	50	729	42	17.35
G. C. Pritchard	259.4	39	766	41	18.68
E. R. Presland	129.5	31	347	14	24.78

GLAMORGAN SECOND ELEVEN

Matches 14: *Won—Warwickshire II, Leicestershire II, Gloucestershire II, Somerset II. Lost—Nottinghamshire II (twice), Worcestershire II, Surrey II (twice) Gloucestershire II, Somerset II. Drawn—Leicestershire II, Warwickshire II. No result—Worcestershire II (abandoned).*

Batting Averages

	Innings	Not Outs	Runs	Highest Inns.	Average
A. Rees	4	1	198	74*	66.00
L. Hill	6	1	169	90*	33.80
†E. Jones	18	1	456	57	26.82
W. Slade	16	1	400	97*	26.66
R. Davis	18	1	449	81	26.41
K. Jarrett	4	0	103	56	25.75
I. Morris	20	1	426	121	22.42
E. Lewis	6	0	132	64	22.00
W. Jones	8	2	120	30	20.00
M. Nash	22	5	331	41	19.47
A. E. Cordle	12	0	222	63	18.50
B. Lewis	16	2	227	52	16.21
H. D. Miller	17	1	255	57	15.97
J. Davis	15	3	189	71	15.75
*P. B. Clift	15	9	90	21*	15.00
P. Stimpson	4	0	50	30	12.50
G. Hughes	4	0	19	11	4.75

Also batted: K. Lyons 3—2—92—72*; D. Lewis 3—6—1—3*; H. Jenkins 3—1—24—10*; A. Walker 40, 21; A. Wright 29; E. Thomas 26, 25; A. Durban 46, 1; D. Morris 14, 5; G. Kingston 20, 15; R. Bastian 10, 6; A. Geohegan 25, 7; R. Williams 23, 5; D. Parry-Jones 19, 4; J. Bevan 8; B. Hedges 9, 1; P. M. Walker 5, 4; J. Lewis 5, 3; R. Evans 7, 0; N. Owen 0*.

Bowling Averages

	Overs	Maidens	Runs	Wickets	Average
D. Lewis	36.3	10	92	11	8.38
N. Owen	33	5	75	6	12.50
H. D. Miller	317.3	78	890	52	17.11
E. Lewis	64.4	12	196	9	21.77
M. Nash	258.4	77	661	30	22.03
J. Davis	162	57	364	16	22.75
G. Hughes	34.4	3	124	5	24.80
A. Wright	35	7	112	4	28.00
P. B. Clift	13.4	2	59	2	29.50
R. Davis	68	17	193	6	32.16
A. E. Cordle	194.5	35	605	18	33.61
B. Lewis	156.2	37	410	10	41.00
I. Morris	55	12	190	4	47.50
W. Slade	71.3	20	218	4	54.50
R. Bastian	32	9	104	1	104.00

Also bowled: K. Jarrett 6—0—24—1; P. M. Walker 13—6—22—0; D. Morris 6—2—23—0; A. Durban 2—0—16—0; K. Lyons 1—0—8—0.

GLOUCESTERSHIRE SECOND ELEVEN

Matches 14: *Won—Glamorgan II, Sussex II, Worcestershire II. Lost—Glamorgan II, Hampshire II (twice), Somerset II, Sussex II. Drawn* 4*—Kent II (twice), Somerset II, Worcestershire II. No result—Warwickshire II (twice) abandoned both times.*

Batting Averages

	Innings	Not Outs	Runs	Highest Inns.	Average
H. Jarman	15	7	563	84*	70.37
S. E. Russell	9	1	332	109*	41.50
M. D. Mence	13	4	350	64	38.88
M. Bissex	9	0	242	64	26.88
J. King	20	2	463	95	25.72
D. Bevan	16	1	363	53	24.25
M. Ridley	15	6	199	51*	22.11
*G. Wiltshire	14	6	171	37	21.38
†R. J. Etheridge	20	2	377	60	20.94
A. R. Windows	6	0	121	58	20.16
J. Sullivan	26	6	356	68*	17.80
A. Parker	11	8	121	24	15.12

Bowling Averages

	Overs	Maidens	Runs	Wickets	Average
M. Bissex	90	15	321	15	21.40
H. Jarman	70	16	202	9	22.44
J. Davey	441	86	1256	54	23.25
M. D. Mence	206	36	650	19	34.22
G. Wiltshire	312	58	966	26	37.15
A. R. Windows	68	12	223	6	37.16

HAMPSHIRE SECOND ELEVEN

Matches 14: *Won—Middlesex II, Kent II, Gloucestershire II (twice), Warwickshire II. Lost—Surrey II, Sussex II, Somerset II. Drawn—Warwickshire II, Middlesex II, Sussex II, Kent II, Surrey II. No result—Somerset II.*

Batting Averages

	Innings	Not Outs	Runs	Highest Inns.	Average
H. M. Barnard	13	2	664	120	60.36
J. R. Gray	8	2	254	74*	42.33
D. R. Turner	15	5	415	88*	41.50

	Innings	Not outs	Runs	Highest Inns.	Average
R. G. Caple............	14	4	403	91	40.30
A. T. Castell..........	9	3	160	31	26.66
D. A. Livingstone.......	7	0	182	75	26.00
G. L. Keith............	21	3	420	80	23.33
K. J. Wheatley.........	9	2	154	44*	22.00
A. Dindar............	8	2	129	34	21.50
B. R. S. Harrison.......	8	1	138	52	19.71
A. R. Wassell..........	12	3	166	40	18.44
T. E. Jesty............	16	3	235	34*	18.07
R. V. Lewis............	19	1	304	57	16.88
*†L. Harrison..........	12	6	76	26*	12.66
J. Jolder...............	13	4	98	24	10.88

Also batted: D. O. Baldry 40, 11*; T. Binks 29, 3, 9; R. M. C. Gilliat 22; J. A. Shippey 9, 8; M. E. Beale 8*; M. E. Wigger 11, 4, 1*; C. Harrison 5; T. M. A. Harrison 1*, 0*, 2; J. M. Shaw 2; E. G. Weller 1*; B. H. White 33, 1; O. Gooding 0, 0; R. M. Cottam 0; B. S. V. Timms 0.

Bowling Averages

	Overs	Maidens	Runs	Wickets	Average
K. J. Wheatley.........	130	39	304	20	15.20
A. R. Wassell..........	368.4	115	918	52	17.65
J. W. Holder...........	305	53	958	44	21.77
A. T. Castell..........	134.4	24	368	11	33.45
T. E. Jesty............	151	35	527	15	35.13

Also bowled: R. G. Caple 52—18—102—5; D. O. Baldry 30—9—89—3; A. Dindar 36—11—97—2; G. L. Keith 42—14—112—2; J, M. Shaw 84—12—341—4; R. M. Cottam 8—5—5—1.

KENT SECOND ELEVEN

Matches 18: *Won—Somerset II, Sussex II, Essex II. Lost—Surrey II. Hants II. Drawn—Somerset II, Northamptonshire II (twice), Gloucestershire II (twice), Surrey II, Hampshire II, Sussex II, Essex II, Middlesex II (twice), Worcestershire II (twice).*

Batting Averages

	Innings	Not Outs	Runs	Highest Inns.	Average
A. Ealham.............	13	4	343	84*	38.11
D. Nicholls...........	26	1	809	108	32.36
J. Shepherd...........	33	5	873	96*	31.17
J. M. Prodger..........	10	2	243	103	30.37
E. W. J. Fillary.........	36	4	795	80	24.84
G. Johnson............	33	2	631	111	20.35
T. Brett...............	20	2	355	68	19.72
†R. Maybank..........	21	8	213	43*	16.38
D. Toft...............	10	0	148	41	14.80
A. Brown..............	10	3	94	55*	13.42
R. Woolmer	10	4	64	12	10.66
E. Page..............	13	6	48	11*	6.85
R. Burnett............	14	4	66	24*	6.60
*J. C. Page............	9	5	19	4*	4.75
J. N. Graham..........	10	1	32	9	3.55

Also batted: T. Perry 6, 50, 22, 51, 1, 23, 7*; R. C. Wilson 23, 0, 36*, 6, 58*; R. Standen 4*, 15*, 26*, 2, 1, 4, 0; N. Hodge 11, 16, 5, 5, 3, 6; D. Laycock 70*, 13, 17, 0; D. G. Ufton 54, 13; R. Daniels 36, 18; C. Fagg 5, 5; R. Walker 7*, 4; J. C. Dye 0*, 0*; A. Hooper 14; R. Scott 13*; M. Burridge 6; R. Vizard 2; J. Dixon, 0.

Bowling Averages

	Overs	Maidens	Run	Wickets	Average
J. C. Page	54	23	139	12	11.58
J. N. Graham	441	149	929	63	14.74
G. Johnson	231	66	629	35	17.97
J. C. Dye	81	19	228	12	19.00
J. Shepherd	380	83	1071	53	20.20
A. Brown	174	38	503	21	23.95
A. Hooper	58	21	145	5	29.00
E. Page	201	33	715	24	29.79
R. Burnett	48	13	170	4	42.25
E. W. J. Fillary	110	31	438	7	62.57

Also bowled: R. Woolmer 12—2—44—0; T. Brett 4—0—38—0; R. Scott 4—1—21—0; T. Dixon 4—1—9—0; A. Ealham 3—2—4—1; R. Vizard 3—0—19—0.

LANCASHIRE SECOND ELEVEN

Matches 10: *Won—Derbyshire II, Northamptonshire II, Nottinghamshire II. Lost—Warwickshire II, Leicestershire II. Drawn—Northamptonshire II, Nottinghamshire II. No result—Derbyshire II, Warwickshire II, Leicestershire II.*

Batting Averages

	Innings	Not Outs	Runs	Highest Inns.	Average
A. M. Beddow	11	5	319	73	53.33
K. Snellgrove	12	4	388	104	48.50
J. Sullivan	6	1	224	81	44.80
R. Entwistle	10	1	372	94*	41.33
H. Pilling	10	1	311	96	34.55
D. R. Worsley	6	3	99	49	33.00
B. Wood	11	1	254	67	25.40
*R. Bennett	12	2	199	51	19.90
A. Thomas	6	1	65	36*	13.00

Also batted: J. D. Bond 45; P. W. Sutcliffe 7; D. Hughes 4, 8*, 0; Douglas Lloyd 4*, 4; K. Shuttleworth 2*, 11*; C. D. Moore 69, 5, 3, 6; R. Kelsall 0, 0, 0*, 1; T. Greenhough 5*, 0; J. Cumbes 0*, 0; E. M. N. Ranson 2; B. E. Krikken 1*, 10; F. Hayes 41*, 16*, 8; N. Hakin 49, 4; E. Williams 0.

Bowling Averages

	Overs	Maidens	Runs	Wickets	Average
K. Shuttleworth	54	19	76	14	5.42
T. Greenhough	55.5	23	94	15	6.26
J. Cumbes	181.2	35	445	23	19.34
D. Hughes	55.1	21	125	5	25.00
R. Kelsall	68	20	218	8	27.25
B. Wood	68	14	182	6	30.32
A. M. Beddow	87.4	20	240	7	34.28
A. Thomas	114.1	25	369	9	41.00

Also bowled: K. Howard 20—6—62—0; J. Sullivan 22—4—73—3; D. R. Worsley 69—19—187—4; M. Staziger 29—7—60—1; K. Snellgrove 4—1—9—0; N. England 2—0—10—2; P. Timmins 15—0—65—2; E. Williams 13—2—47—1.

LEICESTERSHIRE SECOND ELEVEN

Matches 18: *Won—Lancashire II, Northamptonshire II, Worcestershire II. Lost—Derbyshire II, Glamorgan II, Nottinghamshire II (twice), Somerset II, Warwickshire II (twice), Worcestershire II, Middlesex II (twice). Drawn—Derbyshire II, Glamorgan II, Northamptonshire II. No result—Lancashire II, Somerset II.*

Batting Averages

	Innings	Not Outs	Runs	Highest Inns.	Average
R. Rehman	14	1	738	196*	56.76
I. d'Oliveira	6	0	216	88	36.00
D. Constant	5	0	145	60	29.00
R. Oakley	10	1	220	53	24.44
P. Haywood	21	5	375	82	23.43
B. Dudleston	30	4	604	68*	23.23
A. Mathews	26	3	465	84	20.21
J. Birkenshaw	13	0	253	77	19.46
S. Greensword	32	0	615	70	19.21
G. Cross	5	0	84	62	16.80
*G. Lester	20	14	89	21*	14.83
N. Briers	14	6	116	22*	14.57
†R. Julian	29	6	318	39*	13.82
F. M. Turner	6	2	45	13	11.25
C. Tompkin	13	0	141	40	10.84
J. Pearson	14	1	124	30	9.53
R. J. Barratt	17	0	114	28	6.70
R. Smith	5	0	29	15	5.80
G. Goode	5	0	23	10	4.60
D. Kirby	6	0	25	7	4.18
M. Hendrick	7	2	10	6	2.00

Also batted: H. Bailey 1, 2, 12*, 0*; I. Phillipe 4, 13, 1; J. Franklin 21, 34; B. Andrews 3, 14*; C. T. Spencer 20, 2; M. Willis 7, 2*; K. Preston 7, 2; L. Robinson 5, 0; J. Ramskill 3, 0; B. J. Booth 78; C. C. Inman 66.

Bowling Averages

	Overs	Maidens	Runs	Wickets	Average
S. Greensword	624.4	155	1587	83	19.12
J. Birkenshaw	140.1	37	377	19	19.84
I. d'Oliveira	47	8	144	7	20.57
G. Cross	45	8	149	7	21.28
J. Ramskill	27	2	93	4	23.25
N. Briers	197	48	597	22	27.13
C. T. Spencer	36	10	82	3	27.33
R. J. Barratt	286.4	83	781	27	28.92
A. Mathews	274.4	52	983	33	29.78
R. Rehman	35	4	112	3	37.33
M. Hendrick	89	21	298	7	42.57

Also bowled: B. Dudleston 24—4—88—1; F. M. Turner 10—2—58—2; D. Kirby 9—1—39—2; M. Willis 17—0—64—1; B. Andrews 9—6—3—0; K. Preston 16—4—52—0; J. Franklin 2—0—15—0; L. Robinson 7—2—20—0.

MIDDLESEX SECOND ELEVEN

Matches 16: *Won—Northamptonshire II (twice), Essex II, Leicestershire II (twice), Surrey II. Lost—Surrey II, Sussex II, Hampshire II, Warwickshire II. Drawn—Warwickshire II, Hampshire II, Kent II (twice). No result—Essex II (abandoned), Sussex II.*

Batting Averages

	Innings	Not Outs	Runs	Highest Inns.	Average
M. Manasseh	15	5	477	91*	47.70
†M. J. Harris	15	2	465	100*	35.76
M. J. Smith	11	2	313	77*	34.77
D. G. Ottley	17	2	502	87	33.46
T. Selwood	26	3	726	92	31.56
*D. Bennett	14	3	311	78	28.27
D. J. Ling	14	1	272	47	20.92

	Innings	Not Outs	Runs	Highest Inns.	Average
R. S. Herman..........	9	5	83	36*	20.75
D. R. Abbey............	11	0	182	69	16.54
†J. Butterfield..........	17	2	155	43	10.33
†E. G. Clifton..........	10	2	60	41	7.50
R. F. White............	12	4	42	11	5.25

Also batted: *R. V. C. Robins, C. T. Radley, S. P. Daverin, †C. J. Payne, T. M. Watson, *M. P. Murray, H. C. Latchman, A. H. Crawley, S. F. Way, R. A. Gale, K. O. Edwards, D. L. Ash, R. M. Edrupt, D. Y. Carmichael, E. A. Clark, M. Oriel, R. Pearman, R. W. Dermont, G. Carter, †M. O. C. Sturt, *P. I. Bedford, D. L. Hays, †M. J. Heaffey, D. Douiff. Did not bat: J. S. E. Price, R. W. Stewart.

Bowling Averages

	Overs	Maidens	Runs	Wickets	Average
D. J. Ling.............	153.4	40	421	27	15.05
M. Manasseh..........	147	59	350	20	17.50
T. M. Watson..........	80	18	229	13	17.61
D. R. Abbey...........	92.5	52	249	14	17.78
R. S. Herman..........	249.3	72	690	33	20.90
R. F. White...........	278	86	793	31	25.48

Among those who also bowled were: M. J. Harris 6.2—1—30—3; H. C. Latchman 43.3—12—98—9; R. W. Stewart 38—13—77—5; M. Oriel 22—9—49—3; D. Y. Carmichael 47—14—94—5; D. L. Ash 70.1—22—224—7; R. M. Edrupt 40—12—141—4; T. Selwood 91.5—22—294—7; R. W. Dermont 29—6—86—2; R. V. C. Robins 30.2—2—143—3; S. F. Way 27—4—97—2.

NORTHAMPTONSHIRE SECOND ELEVEN

Matches 22: *Won—Derbyshire II, Nottinghamshire II. Lost—Essex II, Middlesex II* (*twice*), *Lancashire II, Warwickshire II, Somerset II, Leicestershire II. Drawn—Kent II* (*twice*), *Worcestershire II, Warwickshire II, Somerset II, Surrey II* (*twice*), *Lancashire II, Essex II, Derbyshire II, Nottinghamshire II. No result—Worcestershire II, Glamorgan II.*

Batting Averages

	Innings	Not Outs	Runs	Highest Inns.	Average
P. D. Watts...........	21	4	558	88*	32.82
A. M. R. Sim..........	34	6	821	85*	29.32
P. Willey..............	29	3	712	126*	25.84
A. Lightfoot...........	19	4	337	87*	22.46
R. Wills...............	29	1	590	66	21.07
†L. A. Johnson.........	18	7	177	47*	16.09
I. Bell................	23	4	301	39	15.84
M. K. Kettle...........	18	3	215	57*	14.33
J. Turner..............	18	3	140	46*	9.33
D. Breakwell...........	22	3	175	22	9.21

Captain: Dennis Brookes.

Bowling Averages

	Overs	Maidens	Runs	Wickets	Average
R. Bailey..............	58.1	19	139	11	12.63
J. D. F. Larter.........	113.4	42	263	20	13.15
A. J. Durose...........	225	51	530	38	13.94
M. E. Scott............	95.3	29	231	13	17.76
P. Lee................	177.1	38	539	25	21.56
M. K. Kettle...........	187.2	51	448	19	23.57
P. D. Watts............	302	68	957	40	23.92
P. Willey..............	180	45	510	21	24.28
D. Breakwell...........	260.2	82	798	32	24.93

NOTTINGHAMSHIRE SECOND ELEVEN

Matches 14: *Won—Warwickshire II, Glamorgan II* (*twice*), *Leicestershire II* (*twice*). *Lost—Northamptonshire II, Lancashire II. Drawn—Derbyshire II* (*twice*), *Worcestershire II* (*twice*), *Warwickshire II, Lancashire II, Northamptonshire II.*

Batting Averages

	Innings	Not Outs	Runs	Highest Inns.	Average
G. Frost	6	2	246	97*	61.50
J. D. Springall	7	3	149	50	37.25
B. Whittingham	4	2	73	54*	36.50
S. B. Hassan	22	2	417	78	25.70
R. Beilby	20	1	419	66	23.41
J. Loates	7	0	158	61	22.57
K. Gillhouley	12	3	197	51	21.88
I. Garda	17	3	278	42	21.10
C. Grant	3	0	65	50	20.16
A. Bull	16	6	183	53*	18.30
*H. M. Winfield	21	1	322	32*	16.10
J. Parkin	12	0	176	31	14.60
A. Johnson	11	0	148	66	13.45

Also batted: P. Bickley 7—0—33—60; *J. D. Clay 9—4—17—44; B. Stead 5—2—12—20; J. Howarth 13—2—19*—61; J. B. Bolus 105*; N. Hill 50; R. Swetman 32; H. I. Moore 71, 17.

Bowling Averages

	Overs	Maidens	Runs	Wickets	Average
K. Gillhouley	172	56	447	32	13.96
A. Johnson	224.3	48	583	28	20.82
B. Stead	123	23	358	17	21.05
A. Bull	166	38	500	23	21.73
J. Howarth	299	64	914	42	21.76
K. Whittle	35	8	97	4	24.25
M. Tebbutt	30	8	105	4	26.25

Also bowled: J. D. Springall 34—12—56—2; J. Dooley 39—18—78—2; R. W. Dermont 21.4—2—80—2; P. Plummer 16—5—8—31—3; A. B. Palfreman 53—17—143—2.

SOMERSET SECOND ELEVEN

Matches 14: *Won—Worcestershire II, Leicestershire II, Hampshire II, Northamptonshire II, Glamorgan II, Gloucestershire II. Lost—Kent II, Glamorgan II. Drawn—Kent II, Northamptonshire II, Gloucestershire II, Worcestershire II. No result—Leicestershire II, Hampshire II.*

Batting Averages

	Innings	Not Outs	Runs	Highest Inns.	Average
B. Roe	19	3	732	152*	45.75
F. T. Willetts	19	1	575	160	31.94
R. Paull	11	1	315	130*	31.50
G. Burgess	11	1	312	83	31.20
A. Clarkson	12	2	308	68*	30.80
C. H. M. Greetham	17	1	483	49	30.18
†T. E. Barwell	14	3	193	47	17.54
R. Palmer	10	4	72	18	12.00

Also batted: P. J. Robinson 5—1—146—82; J. Bethell 3—1—98—79*; B. Howe 5—2—21—6; J. D. Martin 8—4—24—7; N. Parker 6—2—46—27*; J. Shaw 4—1—48—26; M. G. M. Groves 3—0—45—29; G. Atkinson 18, 1; M. Kitchen 48, 1; C. R. M. Atkinson 13, 10; G. Clayton 19, 2; M. Wiseman 2, 1, 1, 0; B. Thompson 1*; H. More 30, 10; C. Spratt 1*; D. Isles 68, 36; J. Scott 7, 1, 1; J. Tolliday 14; L. Weston 6; A. Pearson 13*, 0; B. Lobb 4; C. Carter 6; M. Beak 0*; J. Maltby 3.

Bowling Averages

	Overs	Maidens	Runs	Wickets	Average
G. Burgess	228.5	50	589	32	18.40
C. H. M. Greetham	238.5	84	580	30	19.33
R. Palmer	268	53	855	31	27.58
*B. Lobb	143.2	48	374	13	28.76
J. D. Martin	222.1	39	663	16	41.43

Also bowled: C. R. M. Atkinson 22—4—74—3; P. J. Robinson 63.4—24—134—9; R. Spiller 2—0—6—0; C. Spratt 8—1—42—0; J. Ingram 24—8—56—5; A. Clarkson 94—30—246—8; J. Scott 15—4—35—0; N. Parker 33—6—104—5; T. Pearson 27—3—118—0; J. Fitzgerald 18.2—9—25—1; R. Paull 10.2—3—19—2; J. Shaw 79—17—232—5; M. Beak 8—2—29—2.

SURREY SECOND ELEVEN

Matches 16: *Won—Essex II* (*twice*), *Hampshire II, Sussex II, Middlesex II, Kent II, Warwickshire II* (*twice*), *Glamorgan II* (*twice*). *Lost—Middlesex II. Drawn—Northamptonshire II, Sussex II, Kent II, Hampshire II. No result—Northamptonshire II* (*abandoned*).

Batting Averages

	Innings	Not Outs	Runs	Highest Inns.	Average
Mohammed Younis	29	7	1048	169*	47.63
M. D. Willett	6	0	197	112	32.83
I. Finlay	25	1	742	103*	30.91
J. M. M. Hooper	19	6	388	67	29.84
M. J. Edwards	8	0	233	69	29.12
G. A. Cottrell	8	3	131	45*	26.20
P. Carling	7	1	146	32	24.33
R. A. E. Tindall	6	2	95	34	23.75
W. A. Smith	11	0	257	63	23.36
K. B. McEntyre	25	1	472	69	19.66
†D. J. S. Taylor	21	5	310	68	19.37
G. R. J. Roope	17	2	260	46	17.46
*A. J. McIntyre	6	2	42	24*	10.50
R. D. Jackman	15	5	90	31*	9.00
D. A. Marriott	14	4	74	24	7.40
C. E. Waller	8	4	29	9*	7.25

Also batted: G. Arnold 12, 7, 1*; K. F. Barrington 31, 5, 103*; J. Cope 0; M. E. Gear 2; D. Gibson 12, 6, 2, 5; R. Harman 4*; K. Jones 23; R. D. F. Knight 4, 41, 28; A. Long 24, 1; E. G. Neller 17; G. Treadwell 8*, 28, 0.

Played in matches, but did not bat: J. N. C. Easter, R. I. Jefferson, K. Rhodes, A. Taylor.

Bowling Averages

	Overs	Maidens	Runs	Wickets	Average
R. A. E. Tindall	92.5	32	195	18	10.83
G. Arnold	62.3	19	160	13	12.30
R. D. Jackman	256.5	58	666	42	15.85
D. A. Marriott	379.4	107	892	54	16.51
G. A. Cottrell	87.1	23	237	14	16.92
C. E. Waller	226.5	65	645	33	19.54
G. R. J. Roope	221.3	59	583	26	22.42

Also bowled: K. F. Barrington 7—3—18—1; J. N. C. Easter 16—4—51—0; M. J. Edwards 17.5—1—81—4; I. Finlay 8—1—20—0; D. Gibson 8—1—34—0; R. Harman 33—7—101—5; J. M. M. Hooper 46—12—95—1; R. I. Jefferson 19—6—29—5; K. Jones 25—4—83—2; K. Rhodes 6—2—12—1; A. Taylor 26.4—5—76—3; M. D. Willett 12—2—29—2; Mohammed Younis 34—8—103—5.

SUSSEX SECOND ELEVEN

Matches 15: *Won—Hampshire II, Middlesex II, Essex II, Gloucestershire II. Lost—Surrey II, Kent II, Warwickshire II, Gloucestershire II, Essex II. Drawn—Worcestershire II, Surrey II, Hampshire II, Kent II, Warwickshire II. No result—Middlesex II.*

Batting Averages

	Innings	Not Outs	Runs	Highest Inns.	Average
D. J. Semmence	10	5	207	46*	41.40
*D. J. Foreman	6	1	192	110	38.40
P. J. Graves	9	0	329	77	36.55
M. A. Buss	7	0	209	85	29.85
*R. J. Langridge	20	3	461	82	27.12
*G. C. Cooper	13	1	212	60	23.00
A. Greig	20	4	362	64	22.62
M. Sylvester	14	4	221	43	22.10
†R. H. C. Waters	15	2	283	88*	21.77
P. R. V. Ledden	16	3	299	55*	19.90
G. K. Honeysett	16	6	196	47	19.60
D. R. Walsh	7	1	109	31	18.17
†T. Gunn	17	1	233	45	14.56
H. Newton	11	1	76	31	7.60

Bowling Averages

	Overs	Maidens	Runs	Wickets	Average
P. R. V. Ledden	184.4	37	551	34	16.21
H. Newton	494.2	149	1250	63	20.00
A. Greig	312	78	892	42	21.24
G. K. Honeysett	47	5	137	6	22.83
M. A. Buss	46.5	12	162	7	23.14
G. C. Cooper	135	49	318	10	31.80
A. Jones	186.5	35	589	17	34.65

Also bowled: D. J. Foreman 30—15—49—5; P. J. Graves 28—7—76—4.

WARWICKSHIRE SECOND ELEVEN

Matches 24: *Won—Leicestershire II* (*twice*), *Derbyshire II, Lancashire II, Sussex II, Northamptonshire II, Middlesex II. Lost—Glamorgan II, Nottinghamshire II, Surrey II* (*twice*), *Hampshire II. Drawn—Worcestershire II* (*twice*), *Sussex II, Northamptonshire II, Middlesex II, Hampshire II, Derbyshire II, Glamorgan II, Nottinghamshire II. No result—Lancashire II, Gloucestershire II* (*twice*).

Batting Averages

	Innings	Not Outs	Runs	Highest Inns.	Average
W. J. Stewart	11	3	387	64*	48.37
G. S. Warner	39	4	1202	105*	34.34
A. Gordon	32	2	919	100*	30.63
B. A. Richardson	31	3	830	110*	29.64
R. B. Edmonds	8	2	152	44	25.33
K. Stokes	2	0	48	46	24.00
D. R. Oakes	17	2	319	48*	21.26
O. Williams	2	1	21	12*	21.00
*R. E. Hitchcock	27	10	345	60	20.29
J. W. Warrington	21	2	377	78	19.84
†E. Legard	27	12	280	35*	18.66
R. N. Abberley	8	0	147	39	18.37
W. Blenkiron	13	7	96	22	16.00
J. M. Allan	4	0	54	46	13.50
D. E. R. Stewart	7	2	67	23	13.40
E. E. Hemmings	31	3	364	62	13.00

	Innings	Not Outs	Runs	Highest Inns.	Average
K. G. Bedford..........	4	0	47	23	11.75
R. V. Vijayasarathy.....	4	0	45	23	11.25
R. Miller..............	9	0	74	49	8.22
T. E. N. Jameson.......	10	0	78	21	7.80
P. Graham.............	8	6	13	6*	6.50
J. Barnfield............	2	0	11	6	5.50
C. F. Antrobus..........	18	4	73	14	5.21
B. Packwood...........	2	1	4	4*	4.00
M. D. Mence...........	4	0	8	5	2.00

Also batted: B. J. Sewell 12*; R. Bielby 1, 0 and 0; J. D. Gray 6; J. McDowall 7, 6.

Bowling Averages

	Overs	Maidens	Runs	Wickets	Average
M. J. Sanders..........	25.1	6	58	8	7.25
T. J. Hawkes...........	54.1	12	154	9	17.11
W. Blenkiron..........	416.5	115	974	56	17.39
J. M. Allan.............	50	13	158	9	17.55
P. Graham.............	210	47	640	36	17.77
R. Miller..............	144.1	51	375	21	17.85
R. B. Edmonds.........	131	51	249	12	20.75
M. D. Mence...........	51	12	168	8	21.00
O. Williams............	86.2	24	245	11	22.27
S. J. Rouse............	25	4	67	3	22.33
T. E. N. Jameson.......	169.5	38	435	16	27.18
C. F. Antrobus.........	251.1	53	754	25	30.16
J. D. Gray.............	30	4	96	3	32.00
E. E. Hemmings........	487.5	116	1498	41	36.53
B. Packwood..........	16	4	39	1	39.00
B. A. Richardson.......	44.5	13	140	3	46.66
G. S. Warner.........	12	1	64	1	64.00

Also bowled: D. R. Oakes 2—2—0—0; R. Bielby 2.1—1—7—1.

WORCESTERSHIRE SECOND ELEVEN

Matches 21: *Won—Leicestershire II, Glamorgan II, Essex II, Derbyshire II Lost—Somerset II, Gloucestershire II, Leicestershire II. Drawn—Derbyshire II Nottinghamshire II* (*twice*), *Kent II* (*twice*), *Somerset II, Essex II, Gloucestershire II Sussex II, Northamptonshire II, Warwickshire II* (*twice*). *No result—Northamptonshire II, Glamorgan II.*

Batting Averages

	Innings	Not Outs	Runs	Highest Inns.	Average
C. D. Fearnley.........	24	4	732	80	36.60
E. J. O. Hemsley........	23	2	729	105	34.20
A. R. Barker..........	22	4	434	55	24.10
H. Martin.............	28	8	469	83*	23.45
*J. Lister.............	11	5	135	39*	22.50
J. T. Yardley..........	28	4	528	94	22.00
D. N. F. Slade.........	11	2	194	50	21.50
J. A. Standen..........	23	2	357	65	17.00
L. J. Beel............	15	3	191	69	15.91
P. C. Birtwisle.........	19	2	258	63	15.17
B. M. Brain...........	10	0	119	25	11.90
K. Wilkinson..........	11	3	66	20	8.25
K. R. Baylis...........	18	2	115	29	7.18
†J. W. Elliott..........	9	3	25	8	4.16
R. G. M. Carter........	8	8	20	7*	—

Bowling Averages

	Overs	Maidens	Runs	Wickets	Average
J. A. Standen	380	93	583	50	11.66
D. N. F. Slade	105.2	42	266	16	16.62
H. Martin	101	26	313	18	17.38
B. M. Brain	207.1	53	504	23	21.91
R. G. M. Carter	365.1	70	1056	44	24.00
K. R. Baylis	219	59	787	29	27.13
L. J. Beel	197	49	632	21	30.19

LEAGUE CRICKET IN 1966

East Lancashire and Stockport had things very much their own way in the Lancashire and Central Lancashire Leagues. Both sides completed impressive "doubles" by capturing the Worsley Cup and the Wood Cup in addition to running away with the League Championship. East Lancashire had a margin of 14 points at the head of the Lancashire League in reaching 66 points against the challenge of Rishton who finished runners-up with 52 points and, in addition, the Blackburn club took the Worsley Cup by beating Todmorden in a keenly contested final.

Stockport's superiority in the Central Lancashire League was equally pronounced. They won 14 out of their 26 matches, finishing with 68 points against Crompton's 53 and in addition they beat Castleton Moor in the Wood Cup final. The Cheshire side also took honours in the Second Division and captured the Aggregate Trophy. In a season often marred by bad weather East Lancashire had a fine professional in Bob Cowper, the Australian Test batsman. He hit 769 runs and captured 70 wickets at a cheap rate. Backed up by capable amateurs, Cowper made East Lancashire an attractive side to watch and a happy one to play with and against. His influence at the nets was also profound and it was with great regret that the club failed to sign Cowper for a second season. He returned to Australia to pick up the threads of his business career and resume a cricketing career which he hopes will bring him to England as an Australian tourist next summer.

Cowper's Test colleague, Keith Stackpole, was the League's leading run scorer with 824 runs, average 45.77, but, taking over from Tony Lock at Ramsbottom, Stackpole lacked the sort of amateur support accorded to Cowper and his club finished at the bottom of the table, winning only three matches although Stackpole backed up his sound batting with 58 wickets at a reasonable cost. Once again Johnny Wardle, the former Yorkshire and England left-hander, impressed as an all-rounder capable of holding his own in any company and his return of 501 runs and 110 wickets enabled Rishton to outpace all but the champions in a summer that saw gate receipts slump from £6,223 in 1965 to £5,207 in 1966.

The West Indian all-rounder Syd Oliver had a great season with Todmorden, hitting 520 runs and capturing 101 wickets to vie with Wardle as the leading all-rounder. Other West Indians to the fore were C. Wright, who claimed 99 wickets for Colne, and the ever-dangerous Chester Watson whose haul of 88 wickets failed, however, to lift Church out of the doldrums in the lower half of the League table. Chandu Borde, the Indian Test player, enjoyed himself with the bat in hitting 36 runs for Rawtenstall, but his bowling form completely deserted him, as a return of 18 wickets clearly indicated.

The leading amateur run-scorer was E. M. Ransom, of Enfield, who batted soundly for an aggregate of 694 runs in 18 innings, average 46.46, and his work left all the other unpaid players in the League well behind. Among the amateur bowlers none did better than S. H. Minhas, the Lowerhouse captain, who had seen professional service in several minor leagues. He proved his worth by capturing 1 victims at a trifle over 11 runs each. League officials were not unduly concerned at an apparent lack of good amateurs and pointed out that several clubs embarked upon a policy of giving youngsters in their 'teens every chance. It is a policy that will pay in a year or so and there is optimism in league circles that if only the weather improved the crowds would return.

In the Central Lancashire League, Stockport, like East Lancashire, owed a great deal to an Australian professional, Ken Grieves. The former Lancashire captain returned to the club after four years absence, hit 679 runs and captured 0 wickets. His influence at the nets and on the field with a young side were equally valuable assets to a team that always strove to play attractive cricket and usually succeeded. Grieves had an able batting recruit in Nigel Hakin who hit 03 runs and an all-rounder of merit in Bobby Kelsall whose batting return of 53 runs and bowling figures of 35 wickets attracted the attention of Lancashire County officials.

Leading bowlers in the league were the West Indians, George Rock, who claimed 88 victims for 8.98 in his first season at Heywood, and the once fiery Roy Gilchrist, who was the only bowler to top 100 wickets in capturing 117 victims for Crompton. With the bat, the New Zealand Test star, Mike Shrimpton, hit 679 runs in his first season at Royton and he, like Kelsall, aroused Lancashire's curiosity with his splendid consistency in a team that gave him very ordinary amateur support. In the amateur ranks Charlie Moore, a West Indian who works on the railway, proved a big hitter with Radcliffe, for whom he scored two centuries in reaching an aggregate of 722 runs, in spite of an absence at one time through injury. Moore's hard hitting was matched by an old favourite in Dennis Heywood, of Werneth, whose final figures put even the professionals to shame. Hitting 884 runs in 23 innings, Heywood had an average of 44.20 and broke a club record previously held by Geoff Pullar before he joined Lancashire and went on to reach Test status.

League officials again found fault with the weather and although there was more Sunday cricket than ever before they did not regard this as the complete answer to dwindling gates and some lack-lustre play. During the winter they made great efforts to rephrase vague rules but the biggest need is for players in general and captains in particular to make aggressive cricket their policy. Far too many matches were left drawn and there were frequent complaints of an over-cautious approach—in the middle and from the dressing rooms.—JOHN KAY.

LANCASHIRE LEAGUE

	P.	W.	D.	L.	Pts.	Pros.	Runs	Av.	Wkts.	Av.
East Lancs..	26	14	10	2	66	R. M. Cowper	769	38.45	70	9.02
Rishton	26	10	12	4	52	J. H. Wardle	501	33.40	110	8.21
Todmorden.	26	9	12	5	48	S. Oliver	520	30.58	101	8.04
Enfield	26	8	15	3	47	K. Barker	321	26.75	55	13.02
Burnley	26	8	14	4	46	R. Carter	175	11.66	60	11.63
Accrington.	26	8	13	5	45	G. Griffiths	399	19.85	73	11.83
Nelson	26	7	11	8	39	Saeed Ahmed	561	29.53	82	9.96
Colne	26	6	10	10	34	C. Wright	66	4.15	99	10.22
Haslingden.	26	6	10	10	34	C. Depeiza	223	20.11	71	10.44
Lowerhouse	26	6	10	10	34	R. Collins	342	18.00	45	15.48
Church	26	5	12	9	32	C. Watson	215	10.24	88	10.66
Rawtenstall.	26	4	13	9	29	C. G. Borde	736	46.00	18	23.5
Bacup	26	3	16	7	28	I. Elahi	735	43.23	45	16.8
Ramsbottom	26	3	12	11	24	K. R. Stackpole	824	45.77	58	14.2

CENTRAL LANCASHIRE LEAGUE

	P.	W.	D.	L.	Pts.	Pros.	Runs	Av.	Wkts.	Av.
Stockport	26	14	11*	1	68	K. Grieves	679	42.44	60	11.8
Crompton	26	12	5	9	53	R. Gilchrist	125	6.58	117	9.4
Radcliffe	26	10	8*	8	49	O. Williams	143	7.94	59	14.6
Oldham	26	10	8	8	48	C. Hilton	166	10.38	83	12.9
Werneth	26	10	8	8	48	D. Doughty	297	14.85	20	22.9
Walsden	26	9	10	7	46	J. D. Springall	616	29.93	24	18.7
Middleton	26	9	9	8	45	J. Mitchinson	595	23.80	49	13.8
Heywood	26	8	10*	8	43	G. Rock	393	19.65	88	8.9
Ashton	26	7	14	5	42	R. Scarlett	472	22.48	53	16.8
Littleboro	26	7	11	8	39	S. Mohamed	506	22.00	57	16.2
Milnrow	26	8	5	13	37	R. Digman	133	7.39	57	15.7
Castleton M.	26	6	11	9	35	A. Barratt	454	22.70	72	12.4
Royton	26	4	11*	11	28	M. J. F. Shrimpton	679	33.95	47	16.8
Rochdale	26	4	7	15	23	(no professional)				

** Indicates one match tied.*

BRADFORD LEAGUE

DIVISION ONE

	Played	Won 5 pts.	Lost	Drawn 3 pts.	Drawn 1 pt.	Points
Idle	22	14	3	0	5	75
Pudsey St. Lawrence	22	12	4	4	2	74
Lightcliffe	22	10	5	1	6	59
Undercliffe	22	9	4	2	7	58
Eccleshill	22	9	7	3	2	58
Bradford	22	9	7	1	5	53
Lidget Green	22	7	7	2	6	47
Keighley	22	6	5	2	9	45
Bowling Old Lane	22	5	11	0	6	31
East Bierley	22	3	11	2	5	28
Laisterdyke	22	4	10	0	8	28
Farsley	22	1	15	0	6	11

Eccleshill and East Bierley each received two points when they tied.

DIVISION TWO

	Played	Won 5 pts.	Lost	Drawn 3 pts.	Drawn 1 pt.	Points
Bingley	22	12	2	2	6	72
Great Horton	22	12	5	0	5	65
Spen Victoria	22	11	3	1	7	65
Baildon	22	9	8	1	4	52
Hartshead Moor	22	8	7	1	6	49
Windhill	22	7	7	1	7	45
Bankfoot	22	7	7	1	7	45
Salts	22	6	6	2	8	44
Queensbury	22	8	10	0	4	44
Brighouse	22	7	10	0	5	40
Yeadon	22	4	12	0	6	26
Saltaire	22	2	16	1	3	16

BATTING

		Inns.	Not Outs	Runs	Highest Inns.	Aver.
D. H. K. Smith	*Undercliffe*	16	4	572	74	47.66
F. A. Lowson	*Bradford*	18	2	679	102*	42.43
B. Sutherland	*Pudsey St. Law.*	16	6	406	61*	40.60
. K. Harrison	*Bingley*	18	6	484	80*	40.33
. D. Woodford	*Spen Victoria*	19	3	580	87	36.25
†K. B. Standring	*Bingley*	21	3	644	105*	35.78
A. Aspinall	*Great Horton*	19	2	556	96	32.70
†S. Smith	*Idle*	21	3	587	91	32.61
. Moule	*Queensbury*	17	3	421	85*	32.39
†L. Pickles	*Pudsey St. Law*	21	1	645	82	32.25
R. A. Fisher	*Lidget Green*	20	2	571	106	31.72
F. B. Terry	*Great Horton*	20	4	477	54*	29.81
G. B. Sugden	*Bankfoot*	19	1	531	89	29.50
L. C. Brailsford	*Undercliffe*	20	2	530	77	29.44
R. S. Heywood	*Brighouse*	21	3	528	69*	29.33
E. Slingsby	*East Bierley*	20	0	580	69	29.00
. Warren	*Lightcliffe*	18	3	416	72*	27.73
W. E. Rhodes	*Eccleshill*	20	1	525	98	27.63
D. Barlow	*Lidget Green*	17	0	457	81	26.88
. Roe	*Bradford*	18	1	455	62	26.72
W. B. Moore	*Eccleshill*	18	3	398	66	26.53
D. Dobson	*Great Horton*	18	3	394	97	26.26

* *Signifies not out.* † *Signifies professional.*

		Inns.	Not Outs	Runs	Highest Inns.	Aver.
T. Evans	*Hartshead Moor*	21	2	498	60	26.21
R. J. Parker	*Pudsey St. Law.*	18	1	443	89	26.06
P. Atkinson	*Lidget Green*	19	4	390	51	26.00
G. Aspinall	*Brighouse*	21	1	514	112	25.70
E. Harris	*Keighley*	20	2	458	83*	25.44
†B. Jenkinson	*Bradford*	20	6	355	59*	25.37
L. P. Squire	*Hartshead Moor*	15	3	300	73*	25.00
†J. Hainsworth	*Laisterdyke*	21	3	418	52*	24.59
B. Ellison	*Bowling Old Lane*	19	1	437	72	24.28
J. K. Dickinson	*Brighouse*	19	0	451	116	23.74
B. Clough	*Bowling Old Lane*	16	3	302	93	23.23
H. Gill	*Laisterdyke*	18	1	395	63	23.23
A. G. Parker	*Pudsey St. Law*	19	1	418	76	23.22
H. R. Waterhouse	*Lightcliffe*	19	1	417	70	23.17
A. J. Jennings	*Bradford*	20	1	438	94	23.05
J. Walker	*Bowling Old Lane*	19	2	388	47	22.82

* *Signifies not out.* † *Signifies professional.*

BOWLING

		Overs	Maidens	Runs	Wickets	Aver.
†L. Jackson	*Undercliffe*	327	88	570	63	9.05
B. J. Whitham	*Lightcliffe*	223	57	565	57	9.91
E. G. Smith	*Bingley*	218	42	541	52	10.40
†M. C. Fearnley	*Bradford*	371	104	1008	93	10.84
G. Blackburn	*Keighley*	249	57	705	61	11.56
A. J. Burnett	*Bradford*	183	51	448	38	11.79
N. Fell	*Eccleshill*	200	28	509	43	11.83
†B. Redfearn	*Hartshead M.*	243	52	615	52	11.84
J. Smith	*Yeadon*	205	38	533	45	11.84
N. Allinson	*Pudsey St. Law.*	197	51	504	42	12.00
P. Davico	*Lidget Green*	143	37	372	31	12.00
D. Douglas	*Great Horton*	154	35	420	35	12.00
†D. A. Batty	*Bingley*	182	28	525	43	12.21
†R. Sherred	*Idle*	268	80	998	81	12.32
P. Warner	*Salts*	205	44	574	46	12.48
†G. D. Beaumont	*Lightcliffe*	281	71	713	57	12.51
†M. Swift	*Bingley*	156	35	426	34	12.53
R. Bradley	*Baildon*	152	20	530	41	12.9
†D. Bateson	*East Brierley*	253	49	615	47	13.0
†P. E. Watson	*Spen Victoria*	319	65	821	62	13.2
K. D. Robinson	*Great Horton*	277	73	628	47	13.36
†M. Sherred	*Idle*	324	94	803	59	13.61
W. Metcalfe	*Baildon*	190	38	472	33	14.30
B. Askham	*Eccleshill*	278	76	659	46	14.3
G. Maloney	*Queensbury*	183	41	507	35	14.49
†E. Rollinson	*Windhill*	311	67	769	52	14.80
G. Williams	*Yeadon*	192	39	490	33	14.8
D. Robinson	*Baildon*	212	49	551	37	14.8
R. Pawson	*Bankfoot*	167	31	465	31	15.00
†P. Stringer	*Pudsey St. Law.*	173	47	451	30	15.0
†R. T. Tindall	*Brighouse*	276	67	798	53	15.0
L. Hanson	*Lidget Green*	239	61	697	46	15.1
T. G. Webster	*Brighouse*	191	38	573	36	15.9
†J. White	*Pudsey St.Law*	290	58	881	55	16.0
M. Collins	*Bankfoot*	149	20	545	30	16.1
R. A. Rowe	*Salts*	254	60	680	42	16.1
A. Clarke	*Bankfoot*	267	53	763	47	16.2
A. Broadbent	*Salts*	300	57	897	55	16.3
A. Fielding	*Saltaire*	190	25	557	33	16.8

† *Signifies professional.*

		Overs	Maidens	Runs	Wickets	Aver.
†G. Tempest.........	*Windhill*	244	42	711	42	16.93
'H. Rider...........	*Bowling O.L.*	378	80	965	57	16.93
'M. Naylor..........	*Bowling O.L.*	326	46	774	45	17.20
‹. Pickersgill........	*Great Horton*	252	58	746	43	17.35

† *Signifies professional.*

NORTH STAFFORDSHIRE AND SOUTH CHESHIRE LEAGUE

Longton won the Championship after a fine tussle with Stone. Much of he honour should be attributed to Nasim-ul-Ghani (Pakistan), the Longton rofessional, who hit two grand centuries, 110 not out and 104. The runners-up, tone, found consolation in winning the Talbot Cup, beating Sneyd in the final at he Porthill Park ground.

Norton missed the prowess of Garfield Sobers, the West Indies captain, and nust eagerly await his return in their effort to regain the Championship in 1967. 'heir position, ninth of twelve teams, was the lowest in the history of the club. tone were the most improved side in the League and in Peter Harvey and Jeremy 'oung possessed the best opening pace attack in the League.

DIVISION ONE

	Played	Won	Lost	Drawn	Points
ongton....................	22	9	2	11	38
tone......................	22	8	3	11	35
ignall End................	22	7	2	13	34
Newcastle and Hartshill......	22	6	4	12	30
neyd......................	22	6	4	12	30
rewe L.M.R................	22	6	7	9	27
'orthill Park	22	3	4	15	24
Knypersley.................	22	2	3	17	23
Jorton....................	22	4	7	11	23
Great Chell................	22	4	8	10	22
eek......................	22	3	8	11	20
Jantwich..................	22	2	8	12	18

BATTING

		Inns.	Not Outs	Runs	Highest Inns.	Aver.
Jasim-ul-Ghani...	*Longton*	18	5	612	110*	47.07
. Young.........	*Stone*	11	10	47	12	47.00
). F. Cox.........	*Great Chell*	18	3	636	80	42.40
. T. Ikin.........	*Bignall End*	16	4	448	70	37.33
1. J. Ikin.........	*Bignall End*	9	2	246	92	35.14
. Henshall.......	*Knypersley*	17	8	310	38	34.44
Frost..........	*Knypersley*	19	0	519	60	27.31
. Whittaker......	*Longton*	16	3	348	61*	26.76
. James.........	*Knypersley*	8	5	80	33	26.66
. M. Shardlow...	*Stone*	12	2	266	67	26.60
. Harrison.......	*Sneyd*	18	3	373	56	24.86
. J. Furnival.....	*Bignall End*	14	4	243	70*	24.30
Bailey..........	*Knypersley*	13	3	242	89	24.20
. C. Hardstaff....	*Crewe L.M.R*	10	2	190	65*	23.75
W. Raine.......	*Stone*	17	4	303	53	23.30
. V. Lindo.......	*Sneyd*	17	1	370	70	23.12
. J. Clarke.......	*Crewe L.M.R.*	18	2	367	71	22.93
. F. Sobers......	*Norton*	16	0	366	82	22.87
7. Boon.........	*Knypersley*	12	6	136	50*	22.66
Sherratt.......	*Nantwich*	11	2	203	59*	22.58
Wood.........	*Crewe L.M.R*	19	2	378	71	22.23
. Robins........	*Nantwich*	18	2	355	105	22.18
. H. Downend...	*Norton*	10	1	195	66	21.66

* *Signifies not out.*

		Inns.	Not Outs	Runs	Highest Inns.	Aver.
A. W. Morley	*Newcastle*	19	1	383	64	21.27
B. Shreeve	*Nantwich*	18	1	357	73	21.00
R. J. DeVille	*Longton*	15	2	267	57	20.53
P. Tunnicliffe	*Newcastle*	17	2	308	73	20.53
N. G. W. Banks	*Stone*	17	2	307	49	20.51
B. Sherratt	*Knypersley*	18	2	325	67	20.31
T. Machin	*Knypersley*	13	2	221	41*	20.09
Les Lowe	*Knypersley*	18	1	331	42	19.47
D. A. Hancock	*Porthill*	15	2	246	40	18.92
B. Tatton	*Leek*	16	2	263	57*	18.78
M. Perkins	*Bignall End*	15	0	281	77	18.73
B. W. Griffiths	*Crewe L.M.R.*	11	1	184	35	18.40
V. C. Brewster	*Norton*	18	2	287	45	17.93
G. Griffiths	*Porthill*	15	0	266	57	17.7
C. Marks	*Longton*	13	2	195	52*	17.6
C. Robinson	*Nantwich*	10	1	157	37	17.44
J. Steele	*Sneyd*	15	1	243	54*	17.3
B. Street	*Great Chell*	19	2	287	48	16.8
V. R. Babb	*Stone*	13	1	201	52*	16.7
J. S. Williams	*Leek*	15	4	184	36	16.77
J. Dyson	*Newcastle*	15	1	232	57	16.57

** Signifies not out.*

BOWLING

		Overs	Maidens	Runs	Wickets	Aver
D. H. Henson	*Longton*	147	49	290	35	8.2
E. Barnes	*Crewe L.M.R.*	105	28	232	26	8.9
A. Burgess	*Bignall End*	262	71	532	56	9.5
J. Young	*Stone*	243	76	502	53	9.8
G. C. Hardstaff	*Crewe L.M.R.*	144	49	309	30	10.3
P. Harvey	*Stone*	257	65	616	59	10.4
Nasim-ul-Ghani	*Longton*	288	99	589	54	10.9
K. Brayford	*Sneyd*	185	60	412	37	11.1
P. Timmis	*Porthill*	235	49	590	51	11.5
C. V. Lindo	*Sneyd*	260	72	611	51	11.9
R. H. Downend	*Norton*	123	37	343	28	12.2
A. Mumford	*Crewe L.M.R.*	172	53	388	31	12.5
K. Young	*Knypersley*	139	38	328	26	12.6
S. M. Norcup	*Newcastle*	199	42	459	36	12.7
R. J. Furnival	*Bignall End*	139	32	363	28	12.9
A. Billings	*Great Chell*	198	44	497	38	13.0
W. Boon	*Knypersley*	194	69	381	29	13.1
Les Lowe	*Knypersley*	101	24	309	23	13.4
J. Tooth	*Newcastle*	241	49	610	44	13.8
R. J. DeVille	*Longton*	141	24	432	31	13.9
P. J. Howell	*Bignall End*	239	69	490	35	14.0
J. Dyson	*Newcastle*	233	57	633	45	14.0
D. F. Cox	*Great Chell*	186	40	516	35	14.7
J. Steele	*Sneyd*	189	43	443	30	14.7
Parvez Butt	*Leek*	174	33	507	34	14.9
K. Gallimore	*Longton*	181	44	422	28	15.0
N. G. W. Banks	*Stone*	150	30	386	25	15.4
A. Waterfall	*Leek*	132	20	433	28	15.4
V. C. Brewster	*Norton*	207	39	572	35	16.3
J. M. Ellsmore	*Porthill*	207	47	549	33	16.6
B. James	*Knypersley*	246	66	647	38	17.0
D. Wilson	*Norton*	208	55	532	30	17.7
E. Stubbs	*Nantwich*	184	40	613	30	20.4
B. Tatton	*Leek*	183	35	528	24	22.0

NORTH STAFFORDSHIRE AND DISTRICT LEAGUE

Ashcombe Park wrested the championship of the Senior "A" Section from the holders, Cheadle, in the last match of the season, the latter team having been in the lead for the whole of the season up to that time. Kidsgrove, third in the table, remained within striking distance of the leaders throughout the season but their batsmen failed to give sufficient support to their bowlers, who were outstanding, and so the final challenge was never made. At the other end Boltons, long established in the section, failed to respond to the task before them on the final day and, managing a draw only, occupied the bottom position by two points and, therefore, suffer relegation to the "B" section.

SENIOR "A"

	Played	Won	Lost	Drawn	Points
Ashcombe	18	10	5	3	43
Cheadle	18	8	2	8	40
Kidsgrove	18	9	8	1	37
Congleton	18	5	4	9	29
Crewe R. R.	18	4	3	11	27
Burslem	18	5	7	6	26
Audley	18	4	6	8	24
Sandyford	18	5	9	4	24
Silverdale	18	5	9	4	24
Boltons	18	3	5	10	22

BATTING

		Inns.	Not Outs	Runs	Highest Inns.	Aver.
F. R. Bailey	*Audley*	12	2	515	87*	51.50
T. Finney	*Boltons*	9	2	302	77*	43.14
C. Prophett	*Crewe R.R.*	10	2	297	102*	37.12
K. Danks	*Congleton*	15	3	413	87	34.41
B. Nixon	*Silverdale*	17	2	508	101*	33.86
A. Gilbert	*Boltons*	12	2	328	65*	32.80
J. Brindley	*Ashcombe Park*	11	1	326	68	32.60
T. Ratcliffe	*Audley*	14	4	313	91*	31.30
D. Boden	*Cheadle*	17	4	364	80*	28.00
B. Hewitt	*Crewe R.R.*	15	2	347	70*	26.69
H. Collis	*Cheadle*	16	3	340	72	26.15

* *Signifies not out.*

BOWLING

		Overs	Maidens	Runs	Wickets	Aver.
R. Vickers	*Kidsgrove*	264	111	408	61	6.68
R. Ryles	*Sandyford*	242	93	462	58	7.96
B. Williams	*Burslem*	117	38	262	30	8.73
E. Welch	*Kidsgrove*	142	38	346	39	8.87
W. Jennings	*Audley*	101	24	230	25	9.20
B. J. Cooke	*Congleton*	77	16	205	22	9.32
D. J. Stubbs	*Cheadle*	207	74	406	43	9.44
J. Clayton	*Crewe R.R.*	256	95	458	47	9.74
P. Edwards	*Silverdale*	83	21	225	22	10.22
J. Shaw	*Ashcombe Park*	213	76	438	42	10.42
G. Cartwright	*Kidsgrove*	102	25	208	19	10.90

BIRMINGHAM AND DISTRICT LEAGUE

FIRST DIVISION

	Played	Won	Drawn	Lost	Bonus Points	Points
Walsall	18	4	13	1	12	37
Kidderminster	18	4	12	2	13	37
Moseley	18	5	12	1	8	35
Dudley	18	4	12	2	7	31
Old Hill	18	4	12	2	7	31
Mitchell & Butlers	18	3	12	3	6	27
Smethwick	18	2	13	3	6	25
West Bromwich Dartmouth	18	1	14	3	6	23
Aston Unity	18	2	10	6	3	19
Stourbridge	18	0	12	6	3	15

BATTING

(Qualification: 8 innings)

		Inns.	Not Outs	Runs	Highest Inns.	Aver.
R. G. Carter	*M. & B.*	9	6	154	46	51.33
R. Barker	*Dudley*	10	2	392	111*	49.00
G. S. Warner	*Smethwick*	13	3	487	100*	48.70
P. M. Harris	*Kidderminster*	17	1	763	138	47.68
A. E. Fletcher	*Walsall*	17	1	687	83	42.94
B. Rowley	*Smethwick*	14	3	448	72*	40.72
G. Benson	*Smethwick*	13	4	361	74	40.10
R. Parsons	*Old Hill*	10	7	120	20*	40.00
A. Morton	*W.B.D.*	10	1	356	84	39.55
A. Townsend	*M. & B.*	14	2	469	100*	39.08
J. P. Fellows-Smith	*W.B.D.*	14	3	416	79*	37.81
D. R. Kench	*Moseley*	16	5	402	67*	36.55
R. J. Newman	*Kidderminster*	13	3	355	45	35.50
D. Jones	*Old Hill*	15	1	466	72	33.28
C. Price	*Aston Unity*	16	0	519	86	32.44
P. G. Heard	*Kidderminster*	15	1	443	74	31.64
R. Harper	*Old Hill*	8	1	214	75	30.57
J. Day	*W.B.D.*	10	6	121	28*	30.25
H. J. Latham	*Moseley*	12	4	239	63	29.87
D. M. Heath	*Moseley*	16	1	444	83*	29.60
R. Silvester	*Dudley*	10	5	148	37	29.60
M. Hill	*Stourbridge*	18	3	435	53*	29.00
H. R. A. Kelleher	*Old Hill*	9	4	144	37*	28.80
J. H. Gough	*Moseley*	13	1	322	68	26.83
J. B. Sedgley	*Old Hill*	14	3	280	60*	25.45
R. Devereux	*Walsall*	17	2	375	61	25.00
R. McHenry	*M. & B.*	12	1	269	49*	24.45
B. E. Fletcher	*Moseley*	13	4	220	65	24.44
K. Kelmere	*Dudley*	16	1	353	65	23.53
T. Jones	*Dudley*	16	3	302	37	23.23
D. A. Russell	*Stourbridge*	13	4	208	43	23.11
R. Bielby	*M. & B.*	8	1	154	52	22.00
T. Whitehouse	*Dudley*	17	2	326	92	21.73
R. Keeling	*Old Hill*	14	2	259	77	21.58
J. Burgess	*Walsall*	14	0	301	63	21.50
T. Pearsall	*Smethwick*	13	0	277	66	21.30
R. Williams	*W.B.D.*	10	0	203	66	20.30
F. King	*W.B.D.*	11	2	181	48	20.11

* *Signifies not out.*

BOWLING

(Qualification: 10 wickets)

		Overs	Maidens	Runs	Wickets	Aver.
B. Rowley.........	*Smethwick*	152.3	35	368	39	9.43
G. Kenrick.........	*Dudley*	57.0	6	182	14	13.00
D. Dewsbery........	*Walsall*	75.0	22	184	14	13.14
H. J. Latham.......	*Moseley*	262.2	63	621	45	13.80
B. V. Wintle	*Moseley*	117.5	29	299	21	14.24
R. G. Carter........	*M. & B.*	235.0	52	657	44	14.93
G. Gregory.........	*Walsall*	194.5	61	452	30	15.06
A. Millichamp.....	*M. & B.*	193.5	42	510	32	15.93
A. Field...........	*M. & B.*	115.1	21	295	18	16.38
F. King............	*W.B.D.*	102.3	18	306	18	17.00
D. Gale	*W.B.D.*	107.4	22	327	19	17.21
R. Abell	*Moseley*	162.5	45	481	27	17.81
B. Barrett	*Moseley*	153.0	23	509	28	18.18
R. Helme...........	*Dudley*	80.0	11	276	15	18.40
B. M. Brain	*Stourbridge*	153.0	38	390	21	18.57
R. Jenkins.........	*W.B.D.*	243.2	42	743	40	18.57
H. R. A. Kelleher...	*Old Hill*	320.4	83	797	42	18.98
R. Carter..........	*Dudley*	172.0	31	514	27	19.03
R. Bent...........	*Aston Unity*	131.2	20	448	23	19.48
L. Beel............	*Kidderminster*	204.1	40	561	28	20.03
D. L. York.........	*Old Hill*	198.1	26	616	30	20.53
K. J. Aldridge......	*Kidderminster*	330.1	76	928	45	20.62
G. Jackson........	*Aston Unity*	163.0	33	414	20	20.70
L. Cooke	*Aston Unity*	177.1	39	509	24	21.20
A. J. Harvey-Walker	*Stourbridge*	93.0	22	297	14	21.20
C. Hoppitt.........	*Stourbridge*	137.4	33	374	17	22.00
R. Snow..........	*Stourbridge*	160.1	29	475	20	23.75
D. Pearson.........	*Dudley*	123.0	26	316	13	24.30
T. Hope...........	*Walsall*	162.0	37	496	20	24.80

THE PUBLIC SCHOOLS IN 1966

By E. M. Wellings

The summer of 1966 brought partial eclipse to the major schools. Many of the best players came from the smaller and less publicised schools. The sign of the season was the drubbing given at Lord's to the Public Schools by the English Schools Cricket Association. This was only the second year in which the E.S.C.A. had taken part in the schools fortnight at Lord's. That the contribution they can make to it is large was thus quickly made evident. Two of their leading players were also qualified to play for the other side, J. R. A. Cragg of *King's, Macclesfield*, and K. Griffith of *Worcester Royal Grammar School*, but that does not detract from the merit of their performance on this occasion. Five others of the E.S.C.A. side won places in the representative Schools XI against Combined Services, and only four of the Public Schools side. Never before have the larger cricketing schools been left out in the cold to such an extent. Increasingly of late years they have been challenged by players from schools less well known. Now in 1966 H. B. Hollington (*Haileybury*) was the only player from those schools who annually play at Lord's to be chosen for the final representative team. *Winchester*, *Charterhouse* and *Bradfield* were others without representation.

It is impossible to say with any degree of certainty whether the change has been brought about by a decline in the playing standards of the old established cricketing schools, or a marked improvement in the newer cricketing nurseries. A combination of both is the probable answer. In theory the larger schools, with their greater coaching facilities, should produce the leading boy players. So much coaching to-day is, however, so stereotyped as to stifle natural talent that tends away from the orthodox that those offering fewer opportunities for coaching may actually be at an advantage. It may be, of course, that the approach to the playing of cricket is more virile and uninhibited in the latter schools. That thought is prompted by the report of one cricket master on his team's performance during the summer.

"A first XI cricketer should be naturally very fit," he wrote, "but there is a lethargic and slow footed air about our cricket and, indeed, the cricket of other first XIs. One wonders whether schoolboys go to bed too late nowadays or eat too much of the wrong type of food; or is it simply unfashionable to try as hard as is physically and mentally possible?"

Happily signs of bad sleeping and eating habits and of a wrong attitude to the game were not evident at Lord's, when the E.S.C.A. and the Public Schools met. The tempo of the play and the brand of cricket were highly satisfying, a relief from the boredom of so many of the season's county matches. A year earlier the E.S.C.A. pioneers in novel circumstances did not do themselves justice, with the exception of M. J. Ikin (Staffordshire), the son of a Test-playing father. This time they gave of their best, and the batting of Cragg and Griffith was a delight. Together they put on 170 in two hours, and to their credit the Public School bowlers sent down 45 overs in that time. Cragg, a grandson of Lancashire's President, was the more polished. He looked the best batsman in the match, neatly correct, with sure footwork to take him down the pitch to challenge slow bowlers, and his driving in the region of extra cover was admirable. As in 1965 he carried the batting in his school side with 495 runs and an average of 45. Griffith, who was only 16 at the time, was magnificently vigorous, a tough, resolute batsman with a pleasing upright stance. His defence was sound, and he not only walloped the loose ball with fine crisp strokes but unerringly found the gaps in the field. His century was an exhilarating affair containing a 6 and fifteen 4's. Griffith placed his scoring strokes so well between the fielders that he should have made the bowlers, particularly the spinners, wonder if the modern split field can be any sort of answer to a resolutely aggressive opponent.

The E.S.C.A. were also responsible for most of the good bowling. Here again Griffith was prominent. Indeed, he impressed me as the most complete bowler on the two sides. He bowled off breaks from a good lively action, which suggested pace off the pitch, and he imparted emphatic spin to the ball. The Public Schools had no slow bowling comparable to that of this side. Ikin, a thoroughly good all-round cricketer, was another off-spinner, who, however, tended to bowl with a trajectory too flat to worry anyone in the air, and P. Johnson from *Nottingham High School* was a decidedly good leg spinner despite an awkward action. Johnson, who has amassed the remarkable total of 244 wickets for the High School, and Griffith were responsible for the last six Public School wickets falling for 29. Earlier the in-swing of J. Walker (Cheshire) had started the innings on the wrong note by toppling the first three batsmen in quick succession.

Yet the pace bowling of the boys was less impressive than the spin. Of the five on show only C. J. R. Black of *Stowe* had a sideways-on action. The others were in varying degrees open-chested bowlers, effective enough on pitches such as green-tops where the turf does the work. In such conditions the pace bowler merely has to put the ball somewhere on a length and allow the ball's seam to do the rest. On true pitches the bowler has to do the work and one of his most important weapons is nip off the turf. But the open-chester, swinging the arm without the accompanying swing of the body, which accounts for pace off the pitch, is without that weapon.

Black accordingly was the most pleasing of the five. He had the groundwork of a good bowler. Already he was fast, and two corrections to his method might bring him into the express class. As yet his long run was virtually the same pace from start to finish, and at the wicket he reached a delivery position with his backside thrust out. He could with advantage study Trueman to note how that classic bowler brings his run to a climax and arches his back at the moment of delivery.

Walker was quite a lively in-swinger, and a resilient cricketer willing to take the rough with the smooth. His start at Lord's could hardly have been more depressing. In his first over he was smitten for a six and a four. In his second he bowled three no-balls and yet came back to take wickets with each of the last two balls of the over. His opening partner was J. Denman of Sussex, who was in his second year as a representative boy cricketer at Lord's. He was again an eminently steady medium pacer. Black's opening partner for the Public Schools was N. P. Bond (*Blundell's*). He achieved little on the day but nevertheless looked a good schoolboy bowler. The Public Schools attack, however, was generally weak, composed of all-round cricketers, several of whom put more emphasis on their batting than their bowling. J. H. M. Grimsdick was the only class spinner on the side, a neat left-hander, but he was clearly tiring after a season of solid work with both bat and ball for *Merchant Taylors'*. What success the school side gained they owed almost entirely to him. Only one other batsman and one other bowler gave him much support while he was taking 52 wickets at 11.2 each and scoring 546 runs with an average of nearly 50. The other Public School slow bowlers at Lord's were a rough lot with horrible actions and low deliveries.

The batting of the Public Schools was disappointing. Although number 11, Bond, had scored 554 and averaged 46 for *Blundell's*, which suggested powerful batting from top to bottom, they fell easy prey to Walker and the E.S.C.A. spinners. Only Hollington, D. R. Owen-Thomas (*K.C.S., Wimbledon*) and R. D. V. Knight (*Dulwich*) achieved anything of note. Hollington, a left-hander strong on the front foot, drove vigorously at the start, and again in the second innings, and Owen-Thomas and Knight shared a stand of 44. Owen-Thomas revealed his skill at cutting and off driving, and Knight, another left-hander, was an obviously well equipped batsman. Unfortunately, the paper strength of the batting was such that Black batted number nine, where he had barely time to refresh us by his emphatic treatment of half volleys. He also batted low against Combined Services, when he rattled up a couple of twenties.

Whatever the reputations of the other batsmen, I feel that the cause of cricket would have benefited, if Black had been given a higher position. The aggressive stroke-making batsman is scurvily treated in the modern game, where the grafter is usually more popular with skippers than the go-getter; where, in fact, the match-saver is, alas, more highly regarded than the potential match-winner. Black was undoubtedly a match-winner for *Stowe*, who defeated four other schools, his bowling too fast for most schoolboys and his striking too vigorous for most opposing bowlers. He hit 124 in eighty-five minutes against Oxford University Authentics, 99 in sixty-six minutes against *The Leys* and other speedy fifties. Such batsmen should be encouraged to continue batting in that vein. To give them tail-end positions is apt to give them the idea that they must become more defensive in order to attain higher rating. And what a misfortune that would be. The same applied to A. L. O. Green, of *Bedford*, who was number eight in the Public Schools side. Green, who made 622 with an average of 44 for his school, hit centuries against *The Leys* and *Haileybury* at above a run a minute. Unfortunately, he came and went speedily both against the E.S.C.A. and in the preceding match when playing for Southern Schools against The Rest.

In the latter game C. Johnson (*Pocklington*) lived up to his school reputation, based impressively on the scoring of 668 runs at an average of 111, by making 88 not out. He batted in such scintillating manner that he hit five sixes and seven fours. Two quick dismissals by Walker and Griffith in the next match cost him his place in the representative Schools XI, but he was clearly one of the best cricketers of the school year. Others helped Johnson to enliven that first game. The 57 of Owen-Thomas was a sparkling innings, and J. H. Aten (*Cranleigh*) shared with him a stand of 62 inside forty minutes. Aten's part was 37 with two vast sixes out of Lord's and into St. John's Wood Road, which has not often been invaded since Jim Smith ceased to scythe his bat for Middlesex. Others who created good impressions with the bat were Hollington, R. L. Burchnall (*Winchester*) and T. E. N. Jameson (*Taunton*). The bowling was less encouraging.

In the final match the Schools were rather easily defeated by the Services. Those batsmen who got going were dismissed just when they should have been set. There were seven scores above 20 but not one above 30. Griffith made two of the twenties, but strangely he was allowed only four overs in the match. The boys on this occasion did not do themselves justice, but it was nevertheless a pretty good year for schools cricket. Those boys who played in the three matches at Lord's approached their cricket in a positive manner, refreshing indeed to anyone accustomed to the spectacle of so much negative play in the county game. The influence of the first-class game on the young is naturally great, and the bad habits tend to spread faster than the good. It is greatly to the credit of the games masters and coaches that the spirit of schools cricket as shown in these representative games, has remained so good despite the bad influence of adult players.

That games masters and coaches have a task demanding constant watchfulness at this time is clear. They can no longer advise their boy players with confidence to watch their county sides and be guided by what they see. Much of what they are liable to see needs to be speedily forgotten, and that is easier said than done in the case of the impressionable young. This past year I heard murmurings about a "blatant chucker" among the bowlers of one West Country school. At Lord's in the *Clifton-Tonbridge* match we had an example of time wasting, for which the example set by the county players is directly responsible.

After a Tonbridge declaration, Clifton began the final innings with seventy minutes in which to make 111, but Tonbridge allowed them only 17 overs, a wretched average of 87 balls an hour. Correspondence I had with the games masters of the two schools refuted the suggestion made at the time that the time wasting was deliberate. Time wasting, however, there most certainly was to a degree which reflected badly on Public Schools cricket. Not long afterwards I saw the West Indies bowl 36 overs in seventy-five minutes on the same ground. All but one were bowled by spinners, whereas Tonbridge used pace throughout their seventy minutes. Yet, when all pertinent allowances have been made, including damp conditions for Tonbridge, the difference is vast.

Much muddled thinking accompanied this innings. I was told that, in condemning the slow over rate, I was overlooking the fact that by declaring Tonbridge had made a most sporting move to revive a game spoiled by the weather. The inference was that they could not then be expected to bowl their overs with despatch. In my view the declaration was ridiculous, but, having made it, Tonbridge should not have slowed the game down in order to avoid its consequences. I condemn the declaration because it falsified the play. Tonbridge had no hope of bowling an entire side out in the ninety minutes they anticipated, but which was in fact reduced to seventy minutes. The declaration was an embarrassing gift to the opposition, and victory in such circumstances would have been hollow. A match that cannot be won genuinely is not worth winning on the misguided altruism of opponents. Too many matches to-day which deserve to be drawn are doped to produce an artificial finish. No disgrace is attached to drawing a game, and it is against the spirit of games playing to throw it at the opponents in order to avoid such a result. A side goes into a match with the object of winning it. If they reach a position where they have no chance of winning, they should strive for the next best result, a draw. The only good declarations are those made to give the declarers a chance of winning. Any that are designed in the main to give the other side a chance are bad ones. Each side, in fact, should look after their own interests without concern for the welfare of opponents. That is not to say that declarations which dangle a carrot should not be made, but the carrot should not be too fat. Rain had wrecked the Clifton-Tonbridge match as a contest beyond repair. No time remained for genuine manoeuvre, and the Tonbridge batsmen should have been allowed to play the match out to its logical result. Cricketers need to be realistic, not romantic, in such circumstances.

The number of drawn games in 1966 indicated that cricket was not played so improvidently elsewhere. The wettest part of the summer came during the main match-playing period in the schools. The Scots were particularly hard hit by what a cricket master reported was "an unusually wet summer even by Scottish standards". Four of *Glenalmond*'s fixtures were never started, and only four of the other eleven were decided. Twice they played in absurdly wet conditions. Thus a potentially strong side were hamstrung, though D. R. A. Emslie had enough playing time to reveal himself as an outstandingly good wicket-keeper. *George Watson's* had eight draws in 13 games, but their season was made memorable by the bowling of A. P. Greening and R. B. Thompson, who put out *Loretto* for 23 and *Merchiston* for 74 in successive weeks. Yet *Loretto* overall had one of the best Scottish records with seven wins against two defeats. For the second year running A. H. Francis took over 50 wickets cheaply for them. *Fettes* too did well, being beaten only by the Masters, and *Edinburgh Academy*'s sound batting and superb fielding brought them victory in four inter-school matches. For *George Heriot's*, W. J. Dishington and D. O. Lee shared two opening century partnerships.

This seemed to be a notably good year for wicket-keepers. M. Beale from Dorset, who kept for the representative Schools XI was up to the very best school standard. He was big for the job, but he was a neat mover, and his hands were sure. The first choice of the Public Schools was V. G. Evans (*Warwick*), and he was not far below Beale's standard. *Ellesmere* were blessed with two unusually good stumpers, J. L. Beresford-Bourne, who made eight stumpings, and K. R. Bayliss. These two boys were taught by E. J. Rowe, the former Nottinghamshire wicket-keeper. They stood up to all the Ellesmere bowlers, and that is certainly something to boast about in these long-stop days. *Berkhamsted*'s wicket-keeper, G. S. May, brought his total of victims in three years to 54. B. R. Lawrence behind the wicket contributed materially with the all-rounders, Black and J. N. Dixey, to *Stowe*'s good season. Some excellent bags by wicket-keepers included 24 by M. J. Esplin for *Bradfield*, 27 including 10 stumpings for A. Clarke (*Lancing*) and 33 for I. A. R. Murray (*Malvern*).

Murray was a key member of a splendid fielding and strong

batting side that brought *Malvern* nine wins in 13 games. They won six of their school matches and drew the other, a record amply rewarding the excellent captaincy of G. B. Treverton-Jones, who was also the leading bowler. P. J. Allerton, young enough to have another year at school, scored 633 in 10 completed innings and was chosen for the trial games at Lord's. In addition to his wicket-keeping successes Murray contributed a batting average of 39.5. *Malvern* were clearly the leading side in the West, where the school game flourished more perhaps than in most parts during 1966. After a long lean period *Cheltenham*, I am happy to record, enjoyed one of their best seasons since the war with four wins in school matches. Their batting was steady, and their catching helped to make the opening bowlers, G. G. Angier and J. W. H. Jessop, a match winning pair. Angier's 45 wickets at only 13.26 runs each was a notable performance. Nearby, *Dean Close* also had a successful inter-school summer and a fast bowler, S. A. H. Chapple, whose 40 wickets cost fewer than 10 runs each. *King's College, Taunton*, for whom R. W. Poynton started the season with seven successive fifties and had a final average of 78, went through the season unbeaten. *Millfield*, though inexperienced, again had a good record. They were captained by Tom Graveney's nephew, a son of J. K., who took 40 wickets at 11 runs each and routed *Hardye's* by taking nine for 17.

Worcester Royal Grammar School had one of the best seasons in the school's history, to which Griffith contributed much. With the bat he made 454 and in the field was one of the three spin bowlers on whom the success was based. Griffith's 40 wickets cost 9.45, D. E. Perryman, another off spinner, had 42 at 10.35, and the slow left-hander J. C. H. Lee took 37 at only 7.5. *Taunton*, like their neighbours at *King's*, thrived with four wins in school matches. Jameson, who represented the school in the first game at Lord's, had a batting average of 57.75 and a bowling average of 15.7. Though they were less successful than *Malvern* and *Cheltenham*, *Marlborough* and *Clifton* maintained the standard of cricket in the West schools. Overall *Marlborough*'s results were average, but they were not beaten by another school, and when they walloped M.C.C. by 125 runs, I. C. R. Brown, the son of F.R., hit 98. N. P. G. Ross, the captain, and C. M. Page emerged with fine all-round records. *Clifton*, who tied with *Sherborne* at 141, also had average results, which would surely have been better if the fielding had been up to the standard of the batting and bowling, in both of which their captain, H. R. St. G. Hamersley, was prominent. A. S. Dixon's 111 against luckless *Downside*, who finished the season without a single win, was the first century scored for *Clifton* for five years.

It is always difficult, and usually impossible, to name the best side of the year. In 1966, *Dulwich* undoubtedly had the proudest record in the south, while *Pocklington* and *St. Peter's, York*, led the way in the north. *Dulwich*, who were beaten only by M.C.C., claimed 1966 as their best season for 25 years, which would take them back to the days of T. E. Bailey and A. W. H. Mallett. For Knight in particular the summer was a triumph. His four centuries represented a school record; in seven games against other schools he made 545 with an average of 109; his grand total in all matches was 742 with an average of 74.2.

On the whole the other leading cricketing schools of the south did not enjoy outstanding seasons, but it must be remembered that in their club games they meet generally tougher opposition than schools in most other parts of the country. *Charterhouse*, most of whose matches were left drawn, had a young side promising much for 1967. Despite the Charterhouse pitch, which offers little to slow bowlers, their spinners were more successful than the pace bowlers. N. G. Woodwark, an off-spinner aged 16, took 38 wickets and two similarly youthful opening batsmen, J. M. Bennett and R. E. W. Wild, each scored in the neighbourhood of 400 runs in support of J. R. Ginson's 564. One of their defeats was at the hands of *Eton*, who scored 185 for two in one hundred minutes to win. Yet Eton had a modest record, as did *Harrow* with a fragile batting side. *Bradfield*'s batting was also unreliable, and they achieved less than in recent years. *Winchester*, who did well against club sides and less well against schools, relied over much for runs on R. L. Burchnall, whose total was 610. *Tonbridge* were another side with shaky batting, but they had two excellent opening bowlers in P. G. Roffey and W. A. J. P. Breen.

Among the most successful southern sides were *Cranleigh* and *K.C.S., Wimbledon*. *Cranleigh*, adventurously led by Aten, who was also a brilliant fielder, won five of their seven school matches. Aten made runs, and his three pace bowlers did the rest. J. H. Chuter did a hat-trick, C. M. Lee hit the stumps seven times against *Christ's Hospital*, and K. R. Sunderland took six for 7 against *St. John's, Leatherhead*. Owen-Thomas played the major part in the most successful season *K.C.S.* have ever enjoyed with nine wins against a single defeat. He was top of both batting and bowling averages with 605 runs and 38 wickets. Although *King's, Canterbury* suffered from weak batting, several Kent schools prospered. *Sevenoaks*, nine wins to one defeat, had their best season for many years. *Dover*, who won twice as often as they lost, had a season of exciting finishes. T. C. D. Craven-Phillips hit two centuries for them and averaged 56. *St. Lawrence, Ramsgate*, had a really fast bowler in their captain, J. W. Nagenda, who took 45 wickets, and a highly successful all-rounder in R. P. R. Dixon. The latter made 534 runs and took 38 wickets with left-arm spin. *Kent College* began with only two old colours and yet won eight games.

Other schools in the south were deserving of mention. *Forest* became the first and only school to beat *Brentwood* in four years, but with an unusually young side *Brentwood* still won more matches than they lost. *Canford* had the distinction of beating *Bryanston* by an innings in a single day. Their captain, W. S. Rippon-Swayne, took his total of wickets during four years in the school team to 129. *Ardingly* lost only one of their eight inter-school matches, to *Lancing*, and won four. *Eastbourne*, thriving on the bowling of R. A. D. Perkins and P. F. Hepburn, were equally prominent against other schools. They won five times and lost only to *Cranleigh*. After losing their first two matches narrowly to *Cheltenham* and *Bradfield*, whose margin was only six runs, *St. Edward's, Oxford* lost subsequently only to M.C.C. Their leading batsman at the tender age of 15 was P. R. Thackeray with 366 runs. *Haileybury*'s season was distinguished by the batting of Hollington, who made 533 in 10 completed innings and his opening stand of 218, a *Haileybury* record, with B. R. Kirkpatrick against *Uppingham*. *Uppingham* lost only once, but bad weather combined with some indifferent catching caused them to leave nine of their 12 matches drawn. If the record of *St. Paul's* was modest, they could take pleasure from the excellence of their fielding.

In the north, *Pocklington*'s only defeat was inflicted by M.C.C. Against that solitary set-back they set ten victories and had only two drawn matches. In addition to Johnson, C. R. Flitton distinguished himself greatly by taking 55 wickets at the paltry cost of 6.8 runs each. *St. Peter's, York*, enjoying one of their best seasons, also won ten times, losing three matches, and were unbeaten in school matches. They have indeed lost only seven games to other schools in ten years. They fielded finely and generally played attacking cricket with a splendid all-round side. *St. Bees*, seven wins and two defeats, had such a strong and varied battery of bowlers that no opponent scored a fifty against them, and the highest total against them was only 122 by Lancaster University. K. Bursall, their left-arm spinner, took 37 wickets at 5.05. Another unbeaten side in School matches was *Denstone*, for whom R. L. Short made 775 and scored two centuries, but they had a narrow escape against *Wrekin*. At the close the scores were level at 141 with the last *Wrekin* pair at the wicket. *Wrekin* themselves had their best season for many years. They were another side with ten wins, though they lost five.

Lancaster R.G.S. for the third year and *King's, Macclesfield*, for the second came through unbeaten by another school. *Lancaster*'s most successful bowler was a leg spinner, M. J. Bather. He took nine for 13 against *Bradford G.S.* and finished the term with 44 wickets at 7.8. *Kimbolton* scored too slowly to achieve much success, but they had a highly successful fast bowler, M. W. Roddis, who has played for the Northamptonshire second team.

Roddis took seven for 18 against *Stamford*, six for 17 against *Perse* and nine for 14 against *Wellingborough*, who were put out for 28. *Rossall* also had a match-winning fast bowler, J. R. Roberts, a left-hander, and came out on the right side with a team of modest calibre.

Newcastle R.G.S., who won seven times, had a curious finish to their match with *Durham*. When the last ball was bowled, *Durham*'s last pair were together and they needed two to win. The ball passed through the wicket without removing a bail, struck the astonished wicket-keeper, and a bye was run. The result a draw, Newcastle 144, Durham 144 for 9.

Another odd finish was that in which *Warwick* suffered their only defeat of the season. *Worcester R.G.S.* also needed two off the last ball, and they ran them when Warwick missed a simple catch. Nevertheless, *Warwick*, with eight wins, had a fine season under the captaincy of D. I. Dollery, son of the former Warwickshire captain and Test cricketer. Young Dollery was the leading bowler. *Worcester* were involved in another tight finish with *Sebright*, who had their most successful season with nine wins against one defeat. On that occasion *Worcester* set *Sebright* to make 166, and they raced the clock by scoring them in two minutes under two hours. *Sebright*'s outstanding bowler was P. D. Markwick-Smith, a left-arm googly type spinner whose 60 wickets cost only 6.48.

Monmouth were another school to indulge in some fast scoring, for their captain, J. S. Jarrett, was not only their leading bowler but also a hard-hitting batsman. He played innings of 40 in twenty-three minutes and 60 in fifty-four minutes. However, the batting generally was not good enough, and their results were not striking.

Several schools up and down the country had frustrating seasons, not least *King William's, Isle of Man*. As though a wet summer was not sufficient handicap, they suffered also the effects of the seamen's strike. *Shrewsbury* looked like having a very successful season when they won four of their first six games. Then injury kept their captain, J. G. Matthews, out of the next two, and the side lost its impetus. *Rugby* had a good all-round side but kept on narrowly failing to win and so won only three of their 12 matches and left six drawn. *Wellington* did not gain a single win. They also just missed getting home. *Marlborough* beat them by one wicket; M.C.C. hung on grimly at 135 for 9 to draw when set to score 200. *Wellington* were not alone in failing to win a match.

In 1967 school cricket at Lord's is hit by the extra Test match which has to be staged there in a dual-tour season. The Public Schools v. E.S.C.A. match has had to be cut to one day, which is a grave, but seemingly unavoidable, misfortune, and the only two-day game remaining, apart from *Eton* v. *Harrow* earlier in the season, is the representative game against Combined Services.

THE SCHOOLS

** Indicates not out.* *† Indicates captain.*

ABINGDON SCHOOL

Played 15, *Won* 4, *Lost* 4, *Drawn* 7

Batting

	Innings	Not outs	Runs	Highest inns.	Average
R. B. Davis	15	0	369	69	24.60
N. D. Brice	15	2	289	48	22.23
M. J. Heading	13	6	125	28	17.85
P. H. Blackburn	8	1	125	50*	17.85
R. A. Jackson	15	1	216	32	15.42
A. J. Varley	12	1	165	43	15.00
†D. W. Penney	12	2	127	27	12.70

Bowling

	Overs	Maidens	Runs	Wickets	Average
D. W. Penney	193.3	53	502	35	14.34
M. J. Heading	180.7	52	537	31	17.32
N. D. Brice	106.2	24	293	16	18.31
A. J. Varley	94.2	19	241	12	20.08

ALDENHAM SCHOOL

Played 11, *Won* 3, *Lost* 5, *Drawn* 3, *Abandoned* 1

Batting

	Innings	Not outs	Runs	Highest inns.	Average
P. L. Warnock	12	1	167	43	15.18
D. A. Cooke	11	2	131	53	14.55
A. J. Bingham	12	0	166	38	13.83
J. R. Palmer	12	1	139	51	12.63
G. A. Wilson	9	0	113	18	12.55

Bowling

	Overs	Maidens	Runs	Wickets	Average
†J. A. Jeff	168	34	589	36	16.36
P. L. Warnock	128	17	436	18	24.22
J. A. Iddon	102	11	318	10	31.80

ALLEYN'S SCHOOL

Played 10, *Won* 3, *Lost* 2, *Drawn* 5, *Abandoned* 2

Batting

	Innings	Not outs	Runs	Highest inns.	Average
†A. P. L. Williams	11	3	403	110*	50.37
G. P. Dennis	11	2	305	111*	33.88
C. N. Williams	7	2	136	55	27.20
E. R. Ayling	9	0	201	53	22.33
L. E. Smith	10	1	132	46	14.66
B. Ware-Lane	11	1	102	31	10.20

Bowling

	Overs	Maidens	Runs	Wickets	Average
G. P. Dennis	62.1	12	206	16	12.87
A. P. L. Williams	88	36	179	13	13.76
C. N. Williams	113	26	315	14	22.50
P. Bateman	179.2	53	425	18	23.61

ALLHALLOWS SCHOOL

Played 14, *Won* 1, *Lost* 13, *Drawn* 0, *Abandoned* 1

Batting

	Innings	Not outs	Runs	Highest inns.	Average
J. D. Pagliero	15	1	422	87	30.14
G. H. Farthing	10	1	125	52	13.88
A. G. Shoobridge	15	0	200	40	13.33
C. R. Davidson	12	0	154	52	12.83
R. C. C. Hole	13	0	147	36	11.30

Bowling

	Overs	Maidens	Runs	Highest inns.	Average
B. R. W. Bayly	164	16	621	37	16.78
A. N. Monkhouse	100.1	13	371	13	28.54
J. D. Pagliero	101.1	11	367	10	36.70
R. C. Hopkins	131.3	19	446	12	37.16

AMPLEFORTH COLLEGE

Played 13, *Won* 3, *Lost* 4, *Drawn* 6

Batting

	Innings	Not outs	Runs	Highest inns.	Average
P. Spencer	15	1	471	64*	33.64
A. C. Walsh	15	0	403	99	26.86
P. Shepherd	15	2	320	77*	24.61
P. Henry	14	2	287	54*	23.91
†D. R. Tufnell	15	2	250	66*	19.23
A. O'Brien	11	1	163	31	16.30
H. Colville	9	0	129	54	14.33

Bowling

	Overs	Maidens	Runs	Wickets	Average
D. R. Tufnell	159	27	593	32	18.53
P. Henry	151	28	400	21	19.04
M. B. Grabowski	170.3	31	591	24	24.62
D. J. Craig	148.3	32	388	15	25.86

ARDINGLY COLLEGE

Played 13, *Won* 5, *Lost* 3, *Drawn* 5

Batting

	Innings	Not outs	Runs	Highest inns.	Average
J. E. Hall	13	5	506	144*	63.25
†H. R. S. Truscott	12	4	202	51	25.25
R. J. B. Tait	13	1	260	62	21.66
N. M. Hendrickson	9	1	159	66*	19.87
N. C. Bunch	10	3	117	33	16.71
P. R. Magness	12	0	173	68	14.41
J. F. Barker	10	2	103	25	12.87

Bowling

	Overs	Maidens	Runs	Wickets	Average
B. H. Wakeford	55	9	203	14	14.50
J. E. Hall	217	69	538	32	16.81
H. R. S. Truscott	171	38	590	30	19.66
P. R. Magness	115	20	439	18	24.38

ASHVILLE COLLEGE

Played 13, *Won* 1, *Lost* 11, *Drawn* 1, *Abandoned* 1

Batting

	Innings	Not outs	Runs	Highest inns.	Average
D. A. Hitchen	13	1	183	50*	15.25
H. C. Tomlinson	14	1	188	30*	14.46
B. Elsworth	14	2	159	32*	13.25
R. G. Middleton	13	1	141	37*	11.75
L. S. Couldwell	14	0	157	33	11.21

Bowling

	Overs	Maidens	Runs	Wickets	Average
H. C. Tomlinson	94.3	8	332	26	12.76
R. G. Middleton	100.1	24	319	20	15.95
A. J. McFarlane	112.5	27	326	17	19.17
†P. R. Barkes	129	24	432	17	25.41

BANCROFT'S SCHOOL

Played 12, *Won* 4, *Lost* 3, *Tied* 1, *Drawn* 4, *Abandoned* 2

Batting

	Innings	Not outs	Runs	Highest inns.	Average
M. G. Stedman	13	4	512	102	56.88
J. S. Smith	8	4	129	44	32.25
A. D. B. Wade	12	4	241	52*	30.12
D. G. Warne	13	2	219	45*	19.90
R. J. Turner	9	1	127	38	15.87
K. Stride	14	0	211	36	15.07
†D. Shoben	10	2	102	51	12.75

Bowling

	Overs	Maidens	Runs	Wickets	Average
D. Shoben	155.2	31	446	28	15.92
K. Stride	129.5	28	374	22	17.00
A. D. B. Wade	124.3	26	373	18	20.72
M. Turner	77	15	297	10	29.70

BARNARD CASTLE SCHOOL

Played 9, *Won* 3, *Lost* 5, *Drawn* 1, *Abandoned* 3

Batting

	Innings	Not outs	Runs	Highest inns.	Average
M. R. Douglas	9	0	153	58	17.00
†D. W. Riches	9	1	110	37*	13.75
K. Fawcett	10	2	110	25*	13.75
D. J. Wilford	11	1	115	34	11.50
R. A. Wilkinson	11	1	100	26	10.00

Bowling

	Overs	Maidens	Runs	Wickets	Average
D. W. Riches	97.5	29	211	24	8.79
G. M. Seaman	120.4	28	303	32	9.46
A. G. Yuill	129.2	45	287	18	15.94
J. A. Brown	67	10	182	10	18.20

BEAUMONT COLLEGE

Played 12, *Won* 3, *Lost* 7, *Drawn* 2

Batting

	Innings	Not outs	Runs	Highest inns.	Average
P. J. Kinsella	14	1	402	146*	30.92
J. Hoghton	14	3	216	49*	19.63
C. M. Haywood	8	2	109	51*	18.16
N. D. Kennedy	14	0	234	45	16.71
G. Ciuffardi	8	1	108	44	15.42
R. Collard	12	2	147	33	14.70
R. G. Kettlewell	14	1	168	49	12.92

Bowling

	Overs	Maidens	Runs	Wickets	Average
R. G. Kettlewell	169	38	407	25	16.28
C. M. Haywood	130	22	377	22	17.13
P. J. Kinsella	118	18	323	17	19.00
P. Sutton	124	19	445	19	23.42

BEDFORD SCHOOL

Played 13, *Won* 2, *Lost* 2, *Drawn* 9, *Abandoned* 1

Batting

	Innings	Not outs	Runs	Highest inns.	Average
A. L. O. Green	15	1	622	139	44.42
J. A. K. Lyon	14	6	312	105	39.00
J. C. Dalzell	16	1	502	59	33.46
†J. D. Poustie	16	1	412	62	27.46
F. W. N. Paterson	15	3	291	59*	24.25
J. H. Mytton	15	1	324	100*	23.14
C. A. Randall	10	4	102	26	17.00
W. R. L. Goodall	11	3	104	39	13.00

Bowling

	Overs	Maidens	Runs	Wickets	Average
J. K. Dicks	131.5	21	453	20	22.65
A. L. O. Green	271	93	740	31	23.87
F. W. N. Paterson	170.4	33	566	17	33.29
B. D. Harte	139	37	456	13	35.07

BERKHAMSTED SCHOOL

Played 10, *Won* 3, *Lost* 2, *Drawn* 5, *Abandoned* 2

Batting

	Innings	Not outs	Runs	Highest inns.	Average
A. N. Campbell	12	3	530	117*	58.88
R. E. Glenister	10	4	178	46*	29.66
I. O. Phillips	12	2	232	61*	23.20
S. D. Brice	6	1	101	42*	20.20
R. J. Drew	10	1	175	64	19.44
T. A. Pountney	9	0	172	62	19.11
J. J. L. Bone	7	1	113	59*	18.83
†G. S. May	8	2	100	26*	16.66

Bowling

	Overs	Maidens	Runs	Wickets	Average
R. E. Glenister	42	5	156	12	13.00
R. J. Drew	132.2	31	328	24	13.66
S. K. Gibbs	47	8	155	11	14.09
M. R. Keeling	95.3	13	287	10	28.70

BISHOP'S STORTFORD COLLEGE

Played 12, *Won* 2, *Lost* 3, *Drawn* 7, *Abandoned* 1

Batting

	Innings	Not outs	Runs	Highest inns.	Average
A. P. P. Smith	11	5	196	49	32.66
G. V. Gilmour	12	0	360	101	30.00
†S. J. Lander	13	2	268	75	24.36
J. E. B. White	14	1	224	60	17.23
W. J. Moore	13	1	187	48*	15.58

Bowling

	Overs	Maidens	Runs	Wickets	Average
S. J. Lander	254.3	58	696	46	15.13
J. B. M. Tidd	143	30	445	17	26.17
D. S. Linsell	135.2	19	341	11	31.00

BLOXHAM SCHOOL

Played 11, *Won* 1, *Lost* 7, *Drawn* 3, *Abandoned* 3

Batting

	Innings	Not outs	Runs	Highest inns.	Average
†J. R. Bulow	13	1	379	94	31.58
S. C. Earp	12	2	135	39	13.50
N. H. May	13	1	155	33	12.91
B. E. Hopkins	12	0	153	77	12.75
P. C. Hirst	10	1	104	45	11.55

Bowling

	Overs	Maidens	Runs	Wickets	Average
A. G. W. King	71	7	258	15	17.20
A. B. Todd	152.3	48	487	28	17.39
B. E. Hopkins	51	11	174	10	17.40
W. N. V. Weller	118.2	20	465	10	46.50

BLUNDELL'S SCHOOL

Played 13, *Won* 2, *Lost* 6, *Drawn* 5

Batting

	Innings	Not outs	Runs	Highest inns.	Average
N. P. Bond	14	2	554	100*	46.16
C. A. M. Walker	14	0	425	106	30.35
P. C. Kent	13	4	164	54	18.22
†J. R. K. Rose	14	0	210	99	15.00
A. G. A. Hillman	14	0	179	56	12.78
J. R. Wood	13	1	123	27	10.25

Bowling

	Overs	Maidens	Runs	Wickets	Average
N. P. Bond	211	66	524	35	14.97
C. E. Lloyds	118.2	25	422	28	15.07
H. Stoneman	186.2	59	391	19	20.57

BOLTON SCHOOL

Played 15, *Won* 6, *Lost* 2, *Drawn* 7, *Abandoned* 3

Batting

	Innings	Not outs	Runs	Highest inns.	Average
V. C. Williams	18	3	509	100*	33.93
M. G. Richardson	12	4	261	53	32.62
†A. J. Sadler	18	4	281	43*	20.07
W. K. Hindley	15	1	191	48	13.64
P. B. Syddall	16	1	184	29	12.26
R. Wakelin	18	0	164	24	9.11

Bowling

	Overs	Maidens	Runs	Wickets	Average
I. D. Nuttall	183.2	74	354	40	8.85
A. J. Sadler	26.5	4	89	10	8.90
V. C. Williams	158.4	44	329	35	9.40
R. J. Powell	85.5	31	189	19	9.94
I. W. Gibson	125.1	34	308	19	16.21

BRADFIELD COLLEGE

Played 14, *Won* 6, *Lost* 5, *Drawn* 3, *Abandoned* 1

Batting

	Innings	Not outs	Runs	Highest inns.	Average
N. R. C. Fyler	6	1	136	83	27.20
†K. Michel	15	2	271	55*	20.84
J. G. Melrose	10	1	181	76	20.11
G. E. Harrison	15	0	285	51	19.00
B. M. Huxley	15	2	201	47	15.46
S. E. Kirkness	14	5	129	27*	14.33
N. P. Blake	15	0	202	50	13.46
J. W. W. Wickham	14	1	179	33	12.76

Bowling

	Overs	Maidens	Runs	Wickets	Average
W. P. Seward	190	55	440	32	13.75
S. E. Kirkness	129	30	391	24	16.29
J. W. W. Wickham	163.2	40	382	19	20.10
N. F. Russell	207	46	571	28	20.39

BRADFORD GRAMMAR SCHOOL

Played 9, *Won* 4, *Lost* 3, *Drawn* 2, *Abandoned* 1

Batting

	Innings	Not outs	Runs	Highest inns.	Average
†S. A. Verity	10	1	242	64	26.88
I. R. Shackleton	10	1	157	79	17.44
P. S. Sykes	9	1	121	36	15.12

Bowling

	Overs	Maidens	Runs	Wickets	Average
J. M. Petrie	31	2	83	13	6.38
A. P. Smith	93	32	163	21	7.76
R. S. Brewerton	68.2	15	162	14	11.57
P. S. Sykes	80.3	24	189	16	11.81

BRENTWOOD SCHOOL

Played 15, *Won* 5, *Lost* 4, *Drawn* 6

Batting

	Innings	Not outs	Runs	Highest inns.	Average
S. W. French	16	2	488	111*	34.85
T. J. Edwards	8	3	150	53	30.00
B. L. Baker	15	1	408	56	29.14
D. G. Cameron	11	2	183	71*	20.33
P. M. Thomas	15	0	312	59	20.80
D. J. Anderson	15	1	129	36	9.21

Bowling

	Overs	Maidens	Runs	Wickets	Average
S. W. French	120	36	303	19	15.94
G. Ellis	219.4	56	659	37	17.81
P. M. Thomas	288.3	80	764	38	20.10
†M. C. W. Unwin	150	32	453	19	23.84

BRIGHTON COLLEGE

Played 14, *Won* 3, *Lost* 7, *Drawn* 4

Batting

	Innings	Not outs	Runs	Highest inns.	Average
C. J. Wilhelm	14	0	567	113	40.50
R. N. P. Smyth	15	1	371	68	26.50
H. A. Greaves	14	1	221	63	17.00
I. M. Jenkin	15	1	214	70*	15.28
F. A. Cornish	13	0	127	38	9.76

Bowling

	Overs	Maidens	Runs	Wickets	Average
M. E. Thomson	201.3	58	518	33	15.69
†J. D. Byford	198.5	63	513	27	18.96
F. A. Cornish	100.3	19	303	14	21.64
H. A. Elphick	133.5	39	334	12	27.83

BRISTOL GRAMMAR SCHOOL

Played 15, *Won* 4, *Lost* 5, *Drawn* 6, *Abandoned* 1

Batting

	Innings	Not outs	Runs	Highest inns.	Average
D. J. Rees	9	2	123	59*	17.57
R. A. Williams	15	1	218	32	15.57
D. A. L. Bunker	11	2	124	27	13.77
A. J. Peacock	14	0	184	58	13.14
D. A. Guest	15	2	169	36	13.00
P. R. Leary	14	0	141	30	10.07

Bowling

	Overs	Maidens	Runs	Wickets	Average
A. J. Peacock	93.3	32	232	33	7.03
†K. Richards	164.5	46	362	26	13.92
B. G. Charles	139.3	33	337	23	14.65
M. G. G. Saunders	52	5	209	12	17.41

BROMSGROVE SCHOOL

Played 12, *Won* 4, *Lost* 4, *Drawn* 4, *Abandoned* 2

Batting

	Innings	Not outs	Runs	Highest inns.	Average
D. V. Powell	14	1	318	67*	24.46
D. G. Priest	14	1	264	53*	20.30
W. J. E. Jay	13	2	209	55*	19.00
A. A. Cox	7	1	101	52*	16.83
A. Martyn-Smith	14	1	208	64	16.00
G. I. Sanders	15	0	182	35	12.13
†M. W. Nicholls	12	1	111	36	10.09

Bowling

	Overs	Maidens	Runs	Wickets	Average
N. B. Evans	148.5	49	339	32	10.59
M. W. Nicholls	166.1	48	424	32	13.25
D. G. Priest	67.1	20	181	11	16.45
G. I. Sanders	112.5	18	400	19	21.05

BRYANSTON SCHOOL

Played 10, *Won* 2, *Lost* 7, *Drawn* 1

Batting

	Innings	Not outs	Runs	Highest inns.	Average
R. P. Leet	7	0	127	57	18.14
†C. G. Murray	11	0	179	37	16.27

Bowling

	Overs	Maidens	Runs	Wickets	Average
D. Hamilton	60	13	143	12	11.91
J. M. Ensor	93	18	259	19	13.63
J. D. R. Cashin	96	21	244	15	16.26
S. Neubert	57	5	221	11	20.09

CANFORD SCHOOL

Played 13, *Won* 5, *Lost* 5, *Drawn* 3

Batting

	Innings	Not outs	Runs	Highest inns.	Average
R. P. Buckle	13	0	386	72	29.69
S. R. Moore	14	1	261	70	20.07
N. F. G. Taylor	13	2	179	42	16.27
P. N. Callender	14	0	217	39	15.50
P. W. N. Griffith	10	1	118	44	13.11
A. M. Broom	14	1	132	26*	10.15

Bowling

	Overs	Maidens	Runs	Wickets	Average
†W. S. Rippon-Swaine	200	49	471	44	10.70
S. R. Moore	177	58	421	32	13.15
N. F. G. Taylor	67	14	171	10	17.10
R. J. Wilson	101	1	385	19	20.26

CATERHAM SCHOOL

Played 9, *Won* 0, *Lost* 8, *Drawn* 1

Batting

	Innings	Not outs	Runs	Highest inns.	Average
R. Fogden	10	2	126	39	15.75
N. Whittaker	8	0	108	44	13.50
M. Button	10	1	129	52	14.33

Bowling

	Overs	Maidens	Runs	Wickets	Average
R. Fogden	129	32	214	20	10.70
J. C. Turner	132	21	326	12	27.16

CHARTERHOUSE

Played 13, *Won* 2, *Lost* 3, *Drawn* 8, *Abandoned* 1

Batting

	Innings	Not outs	Runs	Highest inns.	Average
J. R. Gimson	14	3	564	67	51.27
J. M. Bennett	15	1	395	90*	28.21
R. E. W. Wild	15	0	411	57	27.40
†W. M. Gray	15	0	384	80	25.60
P. F. Howard	15	2	235	54	18.07
N. C. Provis	14	1	232	62	17.84
N. V. M. Wilkinson	10	2	129	39*	16.12

Bowling

	Overs	Maidens	Runs	Wickets	Average
N. G. Woodwark	231	44	726	38	19.10
N. V. M. Wilkinson	80	19	287	11	26.09
J. E. S. Herrick	126.3	22	421	12	35.08

CHELTENHAM COLLEGE

Played 13, *Won* 7, *Lost* 4, *Drawn* 2

Batting

	Innings	Not outs	Runs	Highest inns.	Average
A. F. C. Whitaker	16	1	503	81	33.53
R. N. Boone	16	4	340	50*	28.33
G. G. Angier	16	2	348	55	24.85
S. M. Powdrill	16	0	377	85	23.56
J. C. Hibbert	13	3	218	46*	21.80
†I. A. Boal	14	2	182	55*	15.16
M. M. Kassim	8	0	103	53	12.87

Bowling

	Overs	Maidens	Runs	Wickets	Average
G. G. Angier	191.5	41	597	45	13.26
J. W. H. Jessop	208	40	670	39	17.17
I. A. Boal	95	37	531	27	19.66
J. D. Mermagen	101	23	256	13	19.69

CHIGWELL SCHOOL

Played 12, *Won* 1, *Lost* 4, *Drawn* 7

Batting

	Innings	Not outs	Runs	Highest inns.	Average
J. E. Smith	12	2	432	73*	43.20
†A. P. Latham	12	1	331	62	30.09
P. A. Rand	11	1	176	38	17.60
B. J. Sutton	12	0	189	33	15.75
J. P. Ottaway	9	1	103	31	12.87

Bowling

	Overs	Maidens	Runs	Wickets	Average
J. E. Smith	84	4	301	17	17.70
D. G. Chambers	98.5	21	274	15	18.26
S. J. Wright	107	20	303	16	18.93
R. J. Wiggs	72.5	6	277	13	21.30

CHRIST COLLEGE, BRECON

Played 9, *Won* 4, *Lost* 3, *Drawn* 2

Batting

	Innings	Not outs	Runs	Highest inns.	Average
†D. H. Stephens	9	3	119	52*	19.83
P. R. Moll	9	2	113	38*	16.14
D. T. Ford	9	1	105	30	13.12

Bowling

	Overs	Maidens	Runs	Wickets	Average
D. H. Stephens	102.2	36	148	18	8.22
R. M. Thomas	100	21	218	17	12.82
M. S. Nicholls	70	23	149	11	13.54
P. A. J. Henderson	57	12	152	10	15.20

CHRIST'S HOSPITAL

Played 8, *Won* 0, *Lost* 7, *Drawn* 1

Batting

	Innings	Not outs	Runs	Highest inns.	Average
R. E. D. Case	8	0	143	45	17.87

Bowling

	Overs	Maidens	Runs	Wickets	Average
P. F. H. Apsey	68.4	16	152	10	15.20
A. G. Talbot	165	49	356	23	15.47
†S. F. Pott	92.3	20	281	11	25.54

CITY OF LONDON SCHOOL

Played 16, *Won* 7, *Lost* 4, *Drawn* 5

Batting

	Innings	Not outs	Runs	Highest inns.	Average
S. H. Courtney	16	1	511	74	34.06
G. L. Anderson	14	2	278	84*	23.16
†C. A. Messenger	15	1	311	57*	22.21
D. C. Graddon	13	5	165	34*	20.62
H. M. Dowsett	15	3	247	57*	20.58
P. J. Sharnock	16	1	278	38*	18.53

Bowling

	Overs	Maidens	Runs	Wickets	Average
G. Hewitt	121.2	13	443	25	17.72
H. M. Dowsett	128.1	17	428	24	17.83
S. H. Courtney	118.2	21	336	17	19.76
C. A. Messenger	186.5	43	515	24	21.45
M. A. Simons	183.2	47	480	22	21.81

CLAYESMORE SCHOOL

Played 11, *Won* 2, *Lost* 8, *Drawn* 1

Batting

	Innings	Not outs	Runs	Highest inns.	Average
N. M. V. Wallrock	11	1	126	42	12.60
†D. R. Fangen	11	0	125	52	11.36
D. C. Mitchell	10	1	102	21	11.33

Bowling

	Overs	Maidens	Runs	Wickets	Average
N. M. V. Wallrock	122.5	39	249	26	9.57
N. J. Goumas	67.2	10	214	19	11.26
M. H. Gregory	106.3	21	307	23	13.34

CLIFTON COLLEGE

Played 16, *Won* 3, *Lost* 4, *Tied* 1, *Drawn* 8

Batting

	Innings	Not outs	Runs	Highest inns.	Average
†H. R. St. G. Hamersley	18	4	395	85*	28.21
L. R. Harris	16	2	376	66*	26.85
P. C. Hinton	18	1	444	94	26.11
A. S. Dixon	17	0	393	111	23.11
D. Hobson	14	1	170	35	13.07

Bowling

	Overs	Maidens	Runs	Wickets	Average
P. C. Hinton	74.1	15	255	18	14.16
D. Hobson	161.5	53	398	26	15.30
H. R. St. G. Hamersley	255.2	66	659	41	16.07
R. G. Tovey	142.2	28	427	20	21.35
E. F. Peel	199.3	47	484	20	24.20

CRANBROOK SCHOOL

Played 13, *Won* 3, *Lost* 5, *Drawn* 5

Batting

	Innings	Not outs	Runs	Highest inns.	Average
N. R. Lawrence	8	3	214	81	42.80
N. B. Bovingdon	13	1	339	58	28.25
S. A. West	12	2	178	82*	17.80
R. C. Holliday	10	1	157	35	17.44
J. W. W. Taylor	11	2	142	63	15.77
R. J. Marks	11	1	113	24	11.30
S. W. C. Winchester	13	0	135	34	10.38

Bowling

	Overs	Maidens	Runs	Wickets	Average
R. C. Holliday	102.1	25	272	19	14.31
R. J. Marks	257.4	72	632	35	18.05
A. R. Fernau	187	64	407	21	19.38

CRANLEIGH SCHOOL

Played 12, *Won* 6, *Lost* 5, *Drawn* 1, *Abandoned* 1

Batting

	Innings	Not outs	Runs	Highest inns.	Average
†J. H. Aten	13	1	386	96	32.16
P. S. Evans	8	3	119	38*	23.80
P. J. Croad	13	2	236	62	21.45
C. G. Walters	6	0	128	49	21.33
K. R. Sunderland	12	1	146	52*	13.27

Bowling

	Overs	Maidens	Runs	Wickets	Average
C. M. Lee	159	44	379	41	9.24
K. R. Sunderland	95	30	203	21	9.66
J. H. Chuter	122	30	333	23	14.47

CULFORD SCHOOL

Played 10, *Won* 6, *Lost* 1, *Drawn* 3, *Abandoned* 3

Batting

	Innings	Not outs	Runs	Highest inns.	Average
†P. J. Hudson	11	5	212	57*	35.33
A. D. Crawford	12	1	203	45	18.45
R. C. Theobald	12	1	187	37	17.00

Bowling

	Overs	Maidens	Runs	Wickets	Average
D. F. Leeder	133.2	33	356	38	9.36
P. J. Hudson	178.2	37	410	30	13.66
S. K. Rakshit	112.3	22	304	22	13.81
J. E. Dixon	75.4	20	174	12	14.50

DEAN CLOSE SCHOOL

Played 9, *Won* 3, *Lost* 2, *Drawn* 4, *Abandoned* 4

Batting

	Innings	Not outs	Runs	Highest inns.	Average
M. J. O'H. Wigley	10	1	305	86	33.88
C. J. Badger	10	1	216	79*	24.00
K. P. Tarsnane	9	0	141	44	15.66
M. Bateman	10	1	122	44*	13.55

Bowling

	Overs	Maidens	Runs	Wickets	Average
†S. A. H. Chapple	180	47	383	40	9.47
M. J. O'H. Wigley	132	25	320	21	15.23
C. J. Badger	101	17	209	11	19.00

DENSTONE COLLEGE

Played 15, *Won* 4, *Lost* 3, *Drawn* 8

Batting

	Innings	Not outs	Runs	Highest inns.	Average
R. L. Short	17	0	775	120	45.58
†K. B. Turnbull	13	2	396	91*	36.00
G. H. Marshall	17	2	352	51*	23.46
R. F. Peach	11	3	143	49*	17.87
I. R. Tyson	12	3	131	25*	14.55
J. K. S. Edwards	17	1	171	29*	10.68

Bowling

	Overs	Maidens	Runs	Wickets	Average
A. J. Walton	269.1	96	548	45	12.17
K. B. Turnbull	148.5	38	410	22	18.63
J. H. L. Richards	153.4	44	451	16	28.18

DOUAI SCHOOL

Played 13, *Won* 6, *Lost* 5, *Drawn* 2

Batting

	Innings	Not outs	Runs	Highest inns.	Average
†B. Coultas	13	1	211	56	17.58
B. Lowe	10	0	160	39	16.00
J. Dunlop	13	0	150	50	11.53
D. Reddin-Clancy	13	0	150	28	11.53
P. Usher-Somers	13	1	138	35	11.50
W. Osborn	12	2	105	31*	10.50
M. Kulesza	13	0	115	36	8.84

Bowling

	Overs	Maidens	Runs	Wickets	Average
B. Lowe	29.4	10	68	12	5.66
W. Osborn	167.5	54	325	57	5.70
P. Ashforth	67.4	16	197	16	12.31
B. Coultas	79.5	16	156	12	13.00

DOVER COLLEGE

Played 11, *Won* 6, *Lost* 3, *Drawn* 2, *Abandoned* 1

Batting

	Innings	Not outs	Runs	Highest inns.	Average
T. C. D. Craven-Phillips	12	4	448	107	56.00
R. A. H. Wright	12	1	269	61	24.45
A. H. Lloyd	12	0	200	58	16.66
†S. W. Ross	11	2	150	58	16.66
J. J. Lacey	11	0	160	59	14.54
R. S. F. Burnett	10	1	117	26*	13.00
G. J. Pitts	11	0	125	52	11.36

Bowling

	Overs	Maidens	Runs	Wickets	Average
A. R. Baker	86	21	181	17	10.64
S. W. Ross	160.4	36	410	31	13.22
M. P. G. Moody	59	14	162	12	13.50
R. S. F. Burnett	105	29	298	16	18.62
J. J. Lacey	97	27	282	11	25.63

DOWNSIDE SCHOOL

Played 11, *Won* 0, *Lost* 5, *Drawn* 6

Batting

	Innings	Not outs	Runs	Highest inns.	Average
G. R. Beach	12	0	267	47	22.25
N. G. Daly	10	3	155	53	22.14
C. J. Reid	12	0	229	47	19.08
J. Barrington	12	0	205	37	17.08
†G. E. Zacal	11	2	148	51	16.44
M. Gatehouse	10	1	119	59	13.22

Bowling

	Overs	Maidens	Runs	Wickets	Average
A. P. Nolan	84	5	352	21	16.76
T. M. Reeve-Tucker	74	21	195	10	19.50
G. E. Zacal	138	24	411	18	22.83

DULWICH COLLEGE

Played 14, *Won* 7, *Lost* 1, *Drawn* 6

Batting

	Innings	Not outs	Runs	Highest inns.	Average
†R. D. V. Knight	14	4	742	163*	74.20
A. P. Ross	9	5	166	34*	41.50
P. C. Howland	11	3	290	96*	36.25
J. S. Street	13	1	271	78	22.58
J. M. Fordham	10	2	131	55	16.37
B. B. Henfrey-Smith	14	1	212	72	16.30

Bowling

	Overs	Maidens	Runs	Wickets	Average
M. A. Terry	96	23	263	23	11.43
S. Dyson	197.4	66	494	34	14.53
R. D. V. Knight	165.3	47	339	20	16.95
R. J. D. Linnecar	117	29	324	14	23.14
J. M. Fordham	161.4	47	390	15	26.00

EASTBOURNE COLLEGE

Played 13, *Won* 6, *Lost* 2, *Drawn* 5

Batting

	Innings	Not outs	Runs	Highest inns.	Average
C. S. Soole	14	2	430	90*	35.83
N. P. Benedict	13	3	336	54	33.60
A. Trigg	9	2	182	58	26.00
M. T. Barford	13	0	327	101	25.15
P. K. L. Pearson	9	2	147	69*	21.00
D. N. West	11	1	190	75	19.00

Bowling

	Overs	Maidens	Runs	Wickets	Average
R. A. D. Perkins	279.4	92	665	45	14.77
†P. F. Hepburn	227	60	608	39	15.58

THE EDINBURGH ACADEMY

Played 12, *Won* 6, *Lost* 3, *Drawn* 3, *Abandoned* 3

Batting

	Innings	Not outs	Runs	Highest inns.	Average
K. M. Forrester-Paton	11	0	440	114	40.00
P. W. Black	12	2	366	86	36.60
N. D. Jackson	10	2	202	53*	25.25
R. W. Willis	11	2	214	90	23.77
J. L. Burtt	8	1	145	37*	20.71

Bowling

	Overs	Maidens	Runs	Wickets	Average
I. A. T. Donald	67	19	156	16	9.75
R. M. S. Allison	179	41	423	39	10.85
J. N. Dundas	171	60	365	31	11.77
J. L. Burtt	113	33	251	13	19.30

ELLESMERE COLLEGE

Played 13, *Won* 4, *Lost* 4, *Drawn* 5

Batting

	Innings	Not outs	Runs	Highest inns.	Average
N. M. Harvey	6	1	179	55*	35.80
K. R. Bayliss	13	2	304	55	27.63
S. J. Bunting	11	1	212	63	21.20
D. A. Yoxall	13	3	141	39*	14.10

Bowling

	Overs	Maidens	Runs	Wickets	Average
H. B. E. Hotz	72	9	275	18	15.27
R. F. Knight	153	33	427	26	16.42
D. A. Yoxall	92.3	19	249	14	17.78
M. Brereton	67.3	21	192	10	19.20

ELTHAM COLLEGE

Played 9, *Won* 2, *Lost* 3, *Drawn* 4, *Abandoned* 1

Batting

	Innings	Not outs	Runs	Highest inns.	Average
†C. E. Day	8	2	197	95*	32.83
N. J. Milne	10	1	123	37	13.66
D. L. Hodgson	9	1	106	52*	13.25
I. A. K. Drewer	9	0	118	50	13.11

Bowling

	Overs		Maidens		Runs		Wickets		Average
P. J. Brown	142.3	..	48	..	296	..	30	..	9.86
C. J. Evans	67	..	15	..	168	..	16	..	10.50
A. Hassan	105	..	31	..	252	..	22	..	11.45

EMANUEL SCHOOL

Played 20, *Won* 5, *Lost* 11, *Drawn* 4, *Abandoned* 2

Batting

	Innings		Not outs		Runs		Highest inns.		Average
P. W. Sawyer	20	..	1	..	491	..	60	..	25.84
†J. A. Blanchard	21	..	1	..	302	..	46*	..	15.10
P. R. Needham	21	..	3	..	249	..	52*	..	13.83
R. R. Lobb	22	..	2	..	243	..	54	..	12.15
I. A. Blair	22	..	1	..	253	..	54	..	12.04
C. A. Clark	15	..	0	..	175	..	42	..	11.66
S. W. Bone	20	..	3	..	140	..	25	..	8.23

Bowling

	Overs		Maidens		Runs		Wickets		Average
P. W. Sawyer	281.1	..	70	..	797	..	49	..	16.26
P. R. Needham	241	..	60	..	675	..	40	..	16.87
D. J. Webb	58.2	..	11	..	214	..	12	..	18.83

EPSOM COLLEGE

Played 12, *Won* 2, *Lost* 6, *Drawn* 4, *Abandoned* 1

Batting

	Innings		Not outs		Runs		Highest inns.		Average
J. S. Goldsmith	12	..	1	..	266	..	120	..	24.18
D. S. Goldsack	13	..	0	..	256	..	71	..	19.69
S. Sanai	13	..	1	..	235	..	75	..	19.58
†P. J. H. Glynn	12	..	1	..	200	..	73	..	18.18
R. H. Clark	13	..	0	..	203	..	61	..	15.61
A. Tibbits	13	..	1	..	186	..	39	..	15.50
R. P. D. Cape	13	..	0	..	147	..	43	..	11.30

Bowling

	Overs		Maidens		Runs		Wickets		Average
R. P. D. Cape	162	..	42	..	516	..	29	..	17.79
A. Tibbits	111	..	19	..	408	..	16	..	25.50
M. J. Caton	139	..	19	..	563	..	22	..	25.59
R. H. Clark	120	..	24	..	419	..	13	..	32.23

ETON COLLEGE

Played 11, *Won* 4, *Lost* 2, *Drawn* 5

Batting

	Innings		Not outs		Runs		Highest inns.		Average
A. P. G. Lowndes	10	..	3	..	272	..	78*	..	38.85
G. E. W. S. Wilson	13	..	3	..	333	..	109*	..	33.30
B. L. H. Powell	13	..	2	..	355	..	67*	..	32.27
†D. M. Smith	14	..	2	..	386	..	106	..	32.16
P. M. Hodges	14	..	1	..	286	..	45	..	22.00
C. A. Lawrie	8	..	0	..	143	..	77	..	17.87
H. R. B. Fawcett	9	..	2	..	104	..	39	..	14.85

Bowling

	Overs	Maidens	Runs	Wickets	Average
C. A. Lawrie	150	38	495	32	15.46
Viscount Crowhurst	220	72	529	33	16.03
G. E. W. S. Wilson	109	32	313	17	18.41
A. R. T. Peebles	118	20	333	10	33.30

EXETER SCHOOL

Played 10, *Won* 3, *Lost* 3, *Drawn* 4

Batting

	Innings	Not outs	Runs	Highest inns.	Average
†D. F. Whibley	10	1	243	87*	27.00
R. W. Rumbelow	10	1	163	61*	18.11
P. S. Bruce-Kidman	10	2	140	32	17.50
P. Brierley	10	0	114	29	11.40

Bowling

	Overs	Maidens	Runs	Wickets	Average
R. C. Price	62	14	191	18	10.61
M. J. D. Warren	75.5	20	193	14	13.78
G. Bawden	108.5	18	360	16	22.50

FELSTED SCHOOL

Played 15, *Won* 4, *Lost* 9, *Drawn* 2

Batting

	Innings	Not outs	Runs	Highest inns.	Average
†A. R. Bird	15	1	518	94	37.00
B. J. Youngs	14	3	271	66	24.63
G. H. Pearce	12	4	187	49	23.37
P. A. E. Neil	16	1	344	51	22.93
K. R. Bailey	15	5	223	79*	22.30
A. J. Linforth	13	1	261	54*	21.75
D. R. Lendrum	16	1	301	59	20.06
D. W. James	14	2	211	46*	17.58

Bowling

	Overs	Maidens	Runs	Wickets	Average
T. D. Lofts	232	59	617	33	18.69
P. A. E. Neil	122	21	399	18	22.16
D. W. James	144	28	490	22	22.27
G. H. Pearce	166	31	529	22	24.04
A. R. Bird	153	27	449	14	32.07

FETTES COLLEGE

Played 13, *Won* 5, *Lost* 1, *Drawn* 7

Batting

	Innings	Not outs	Runs	Highest inns.	Average
K. W. W. Brown	5	2	116	49*	38.66
D. A. Smith	14	5	318	60*	35.33
†D. J. L. Hardie	13	5	257	55*	32.12
J. W. D. McGlashan	11	1	210	48	21.00
E. M. Todd	9	2	145	57	20.71

Bowling

	Overs	Maidens	Runs	Wickets	Average
K. W. W. Brown	54.5	8	150	22	6.81
J. K. Foot	203.2	66	376	40	9.40
D. MacIntyre	150.4	42	294	28	10.50
M. B. Stewart	101	36	203	12	16.91

FOREST SCHOOL

Played 12, *Won* 2, *Lost* 5, *Tied* 1, *Drawn* 4, *Abandoned* 3

Batting

	Innings	Not outs	Runs	Highest inns.	Average
N. E. Herd	13	1	295	102*	24.58
L. P. Beschizza	12	2	219	60*	21.90
C. H. I. Brown	13	1	240	71	20.00
R. B. Hayes	10	3	117	36*	16.71
D. J. Lynch	10	0	123	38	12.30
M. Pearse	9	0	105	37	11.66
S. B. Duncombe	12	1	117	22*	10.63

Bowling

	Overs	Maidens	Runs	Wickets	Average
M. Pearse	130.4	28	414	22	18.81
S. B. Duncombe	104.0	25	312	16	19.50
G. S. Green	83.1	14	271	11	24.63
R. B. Hayes	122.0	22	362	12	30.17

FRAMLINGHAM COLLEGE

Played 9, *Won* 4, *Lost* 3, *Drawn* 2, *Abandoned* 3

Batting

	Innings	Not outs	Runs	Highest inns.	Average
G. A. Reason	12	0	368	68	30.66
S. D. Molyneux	10	2	221	61*	27.62
†A. J. G. Parsons	12	1	291	74	26.45
A. de R. Pearse	10	4	108	20	18.00
R. M. Daniels	11	0	178	62	16.18
D. J. Bonner	10	0	121	45	12.10

Bowling

	Overs	Maidens	Runs	Wickets	Average
J. M. Rutter	100.4	8	406	23	17.65
R. M. Daniels	85.1	11	257	13	19.76
R. W. R. Smith	173.2	49	463	23	20.13

GEORGE HERIOT'S SCHOOL

Played 9, *Won* 4, *Lost* 1, *Drawn* 4, *Abandoned* 1

Batting

	Innings	Not outs	Runs	Highest inns.	Average
†W. J. Dishington	10	3	384	86*	54.85
D. O. Lee	10	1	250	64	27.77
M. D. Guild	9	2	107	34*	15.28

Bowling

	Overs	Maidens	Runs	Wickets	Average
D. O. Lee	46	21	55	15	3.66
M. J. Dow	143.2	49	248	21	11.80
W. J. Dishington	127.3	47	212	14	15.14

GEORGE WATSON'S COLLEGE

Played 13, *Won* 3, *Lost* 2, *Drawn* 8, *Abandoned* 1

Batting

	Innings	Not outs	Runs	Highest inns.	Average
D. L. Bell	14	4	398	64	39.80
D. F. Paton	10	5	125	39	25.00
K. I. S. Currie	9	2	142	41	20.28
D. I. M. Lamb	13	2	199	50	18.09

Bowling

	Overs	Maidens	Runs	Wickets	Average
R. B. Thompkins	163	51	345	33	10.45
†A. P. Greening	167	51	433	30	14.43
S. A. Crawford	61	16	199	12	16.58

GORDONSTOUN SCHOOL

Played 8, *Won* 3, *Lost* 4, *Drawn* 1

Bowling

	Overs	Maidens	Runs	Wickets	Average
W. B. T. Kennedy	36	11	80	17	4.70
J. Braithwaite	29.2	6	75	13	5.76
A. A. Vlasto	38.2	15	88	13	6.76
G. F. Ritson	39	9	100	11	9.09

GRESHAM'S SCHOOL

Played 13, *Won* 4, *Lost* 6, *Drawn* 3

Batting

	Innings	Not outs	Runs	Highest inns.	Average
M. J. Owers	12	1	285	59*	25.90
†T. H. Cook	13	1	298	125*	24.83
R. D. Lees	13	3	248	51*	24.80
C. P. Hood	11	3	177	45*	22.12
G. H. Wells	11	1	196	65	19.60
A. R. Whipple	13	0	224	37	17.23

Bowling

	Overs	Maidens	Runs	Wickets	Average
M. J. Owers	58.3	13	155	14	11.07
I. S. R. Colquhoun	156	39	400	28	14.28
R. D. Lees	113.3	23	317	17	18.64
J. C. Henderson	82	17	237	12	19.75
C. P. Hood	70	13	240	11	21.81
J. A. Fordham	97.4	13	345	11	31.36

HABERDASHERS' ASKE'S SCHOOL, ELSTREE

Played 15, *Won* 3, *Lost* 5, *Drawn* 7, *Abandoned* 1

Batting

	Innings	Not outs	Runs	Highest inns.	Average
P. S. Mackie	16	4	294	56*	24.50
C. R. Done	16	0	356	80	22.25
A. J. Quick	16	2	296	55*	21.14
†G. S. Haslehurst	13	0	233	55	17.92
R. M. Wilkinson	15	2	224	38*	17.33
A. P. Scott	15	0	125	26	8.33
A. J. Phipps	13	0	105	19	8.07

Bowling

	Overs	Maidens	Runs	Wickets	Average
P. M. Wakely	164.2	39	453	28	16.17
R. M. Wilkinson	91	23	248	14	17.71
G. R. Bottoms	185.4	38	544	29	18.75
A. P. Scott	60	3	284	15	18.93
R. A. Foster	92.1	18	304	13	23.38
R. D. Woolerton	93	16	311	13	23.92

HAILEYBURY AND I.S.C.

Played 10, *Won* 3, *Lost* 4, *Drawn* 3

Batting

	Innings	Not outs	Runs	Highest inns.	Average
H. B. Hollington	12	2	533	144	53.30
R. J. Walton	9	3	274	133*	45.66
B. R. Kirkpatrick	12	3	231	69	25.66
A. W. L. Tice	8	1	178	43	25.42
†S. Warner Jones	10	0	251	74	25.10
N. P. Moore	7	1	131	45	21.83
R. M. Young	9	1	122	35	15.25

Bowling

	Overs	Maidens	Runs	Wickets	Average
D. R. Braybon	143.1	40	390	18	21.66
J. K. S. Denniston	154.3	39	426	18	23.66
C. W. Gray	193.2	56	555	22	25.22
A. W. L. Tice	137.1	23	445	17	26.17

HARROW SCHOOL

Played 13, *Won* 2, *Lost* 4, *Drawn* 7

Batting

	Innings	Not outs	Runs	Highest inns.	Average
R. E. Lindsay	15	4	418	120*	38.00
†R. W. Evans	15	0	500	122	33.33
N. G. Stogdon	15	2	325	69	25.00
R. S. Crawley	15	0	368	60	24.53
I. Coomaraswamy	12	2	177	84*	17.70
N. B. A. Nobbs	9	0	150	60	16.66
P. R. Dunkels	12	0	140	49	11.66
A. P. Webster	13	4	103	18*	11.44

Bowling

	Overs	Maidens	Runs	Wickets	Average
A. P. Webster	123.5	43	308	20	15.40
D. S. S. Chichester	86	20	231	14	16.50
P. R. Dunkels	216.4	38	658	32	20.56
D. R. ap G. Herbert	207.5	48	538	25	21.52
I. Coomaraswamy	239.1	80	539	21	25.66

HIGHGATE SCHOOL

Played 13, *Won* 3, *Lost* 4, *Drawn* 6, *Abandoned* 2

Batting

	Innings	Not outs	Runs	Highest inns.	Average
D. A. J. Chamberlain	13	2	361	102	32.81
A. E. Gibson	13	1	366	68	30.50
P. N. Hewitt	14	2	243	42*	20.25
†R. E. Norman	11	3	152	36	19.00
R. J. Smethers	12	1	167	45	15.18

Bowling

	Overs	Maidens	Runs	Wickets	Average
R. F. M. Edmonds	203.1	64	511	44	11.61
A. E. Gibson	117.2	28	327	17	19.23
E. M. B. King	112.3	15	401	20	20.05
O. S. Ritchie	114.1	19	384	18	21.33

HURSTPIERPOINT COLLEGE

Played 12, *Won* 1, *Lost* 5, *Drawn* 6

Batting

	Innings	Not outs	Runs	Highest inns.	Average
J. P. Ruddlesdin	11	0	388	110	35.27
S. C. Westoby	8	1	212	55*	30.28
P. G. Morgan	10	2	197	58	24.62
G. de W. Waller	11	5	147	34	24.50
E. H. R. Goodacre	12	0	264	68	22.00
†C. D. Henderson	12	1	217	79	19.72
R. O. Goode	12	2	166	41	16.60
C. H. Such	8	0	128	40	16.00

Bowling

	Overs	Maidens	Runs	Wickets	Average
J. P. Ruddlesdin	134.5	19	394	20	19.70
R. H. Roth	124	26	344	17	20.23
S. C. Westoby	115	31	285	13	21.92
R. T. Edgelow	141.1	11	474	19	24.94

IPSWICH SCHOOL

Played 12, *Won* 6, *Lost* 5, *Drawn* 1, *Abandoned* 2

Batting

	Innings	Not outs	Runs	Highest inns.	Average
J. R. D. Collett	11	4	212	61*	30.28
J. S. C. Smith	14	2	344	49	28.66
H. E. Staunton	14	1	371	98	28.53
B. Mayes	13	4	248	59*	27.55
S. Roberts	12	2	228	52*	22.80
S. K. H. Marks	11	0	203	64	18.45
†N. J. Newell	13	1	168	54	14.00

Bowling

	Overs	Maidens	Runs	Wickets	Average
J. Caston	47	9	158	12	13.16
B. Mayes	89	15	345	19	18.15
J. R. D. Collett	188	52	459	24	19.12
S. K. H. Marks	200	41	505	23	21.95
C. M. Lingard	135.2	24	381	15	25.40

KELLY COLLEGE

Played 12, *Won* 5, *Lost* 4, *Drawn* 3

Batting

	Innings	Not outs	Runs	Highest inns.	Average
R. J. Polglase	10	5	148	40*	29.60
†T. M. Walker	12	1	311	72	28.27
P. L. May	12	1	269	73*	24.45
D. F. B. Kemp	12	1	185	43	16.81
[illegible]. T. Bloxam	12	0	124	32	10.33

Bowling

	Overs	Maidens	Runs	Wickets	Average
R. J. Polglase	134.2	40	283	30	9.43
D. L. Blunden	89.3	31	171	17	10.05
T. M. Walker	95.4	19	289	22	13.13

KENT COLLEGE

Played 17, *Won* 8, *Lost* 4, *Drawn* 5, *Abandoned* 2

Batting

	Innings	Not outs	Runs	Highest inns.	Average
†A. Q. Kopp	16	0	439	68	27.43
F. P. Hallsworth	17	1	395	82*	24.68
J. S. Tamsett	10	2	107	21	13.37
M. J. Allworthy	15	0	180	30	12.00
D. P. Thompson	13	2	111	25	10.09
B. J. Packington	12	0	110	33	9.16

Bowling

	Overs	Maidens	Runs	Wickets	Average
F. P. Hallsworth	190	45	505	37	13.64
D. P. Thompson	80	18	249	18	13.83
R. A. Casement	133	30	378	24	15.75
B. W. Davy	121	18	398	18	22.11
D. H. Garrett	96	4	398	18	22.11

KIMBOLTON SCHOOL

Played 11, *Won* 3, *Lost* 3, *Drawn* 5, *Abandoned* 1

Batting

	Innings	Not outs	Runs	Highest inns.	Average
†M. W. Roddis	10	0	168	53	16.80
J. P. Tanner	11	1	148	36	14.80
D. J. Sandifer	12	1	148	57	13.45
D. P. Colyer	10	2	102	41	12.75
C. D. Pusey	11	2	100	20	11.11

Bowling

	Overs	Maidens	Runs	Wickets	Average
M. W. Roddis	111.1	29	229	33	6.93
H. O. Christmas	43	7	137	11	12.45
S. T. Crotty	136.3	44	296	20	14.80

KING EDWARD'S SCHOOL, BIRMINGHAM

Played 18, *Won* 6, *Lost* 11, *Drawn* 1, *Abandoned* 3

Batting

	Innings	Not outs	Runs	Highest inns.	Average
J. Pickering	11	0	303	70	27.54
A. M. Paul	19	3	413	77*	25.81
K. A. Ogden	18	4	265	46*	18.92
†M. W. Davis	19	0	350	91	18.42
J. S. Lee	19	0	264	55	13.89
S. A. Shaw	17	1	161	28	10.06

Bowling

	Overs	Maidens	Runs	Wickets	Average
A. M. Paul	211	56	523	35	14.94
J. P. Evans	216	45	505	27	18.70
J. S. Lee	104	28	287	14	20.50
K. A. Ogden	249	67	627	29	21.62
S. A. Shaw	147	34	392	17	23.05

KING HENRY VIII SCHOOL, COVENTRY

Played 13, *Won* 4, *Lost* 5, *Drawn* 4, *Abandoned* 2

Batting

	Innings	Not outs	Runs	Highest inns.	Average
B. Mills	10	1	108	51*	12.00
P. A. G. Green	12	2	105	48*	10.50

Bowling

	Overs	Maidens	Runs	Wickets	Average
†E. A. McCutcheon	42.5	19	217	30	7.23
P. Horner	86.5	19	231	16	14.43
J. Edwards	90	21	265	18	14.72
B. Mills	55	10	161	10	16.10

KING WILLIAM'S COLLEGE

Played 11, *Won* 3, *Lost* 6, *Drawn* 2

Batting

	Innings	Not outs	Runs	Highest inns.	Average
R. F. Carr	11	2	204	86	22.66
R. A. Hanson	8	1	148	48	21.14

Bowling

	Overs	Maidens	Runs	Wickets	Average
M. R. Roman	141	32	344	28	12.28
T. P. Ledsham	67	16	191	14	13.64

KING'S COLLEGE, TAUNTON

Played 12, *Won* 8, *Lost* 0, *Drawn* 4, *Abandoned* 3

Batting

	Innings	Not outs	Runs	Highest inns.	Average
R. W. Poynton	13	6	546	85*	78.00
†S. J. E. Goldie	14	2	467	78	38.91
R. M. Coverley	9	4	126	38*	25.20
F. G. Dawson	13	2	209	94	19.00
B. D. Evans	13	1	219	62	18.25
J. F. Morley	7	0	110	38	15.71
M. A. Evans	11	0	160	52	14.54

Bowling

	Overs	Maidens	Runs	Wickets	Average
R. W. Poynton	101	25	224	30	7.46
J. F. Morley	80	13	201	21	9.57
S. J. E. Goldie	153	40	390	30	13.00
M. A. Evans	154	48	322	24	13.41
R. M. Coverley	67	17	188	13	14.46

KING'S COLLEGE SCHOOL, WIMBLEDON

Played 15, *Won* 9, *Lost* 1, *Drawn* 5, *Abandoned* 2

Batting

	Innings	Not outs	Runs	Highest inns.	Average
D. R. Owen-Thomas	15	2	605	106*	46.53
S. C. Buchanan	9	5	118	25*	29.50
†D. R. Holland	15	1	357	87*	25.50
J. G. Poole	15	2	331	90	25.46
P. C. A. Bell	15	2	328	57*	25.23
A. J. W. Thompson	12	2	233	45	23.30
V. G. B. Cushing	13	1	216	63	18.00

KING'S SCHOOL, MACCLESFIELD

Played 16, *Won* 5, *Lost* 3, *Drawn* 8, *Abandoned* 1

Batting

	Innings	Not outs	Runs	Highest inns.	Average
†J. R. A. Cragg	17	6	495	70	45.00
J. H. Walker	16	5	277	84*	25.18

Bowling

	Overs	Maidens	Runs	Wickets	Average
J. S. Grose	134.4	58	214	26	8.23
J. H. Walker	184.5	72	383	42	9.11
A. Sherratt	47.3	15	94	10	9.40
P. J. Taylor	86.4	17	213	20	10.65
C. H. Jones	62.3	14	137	11	12.45

KING'S SCHOOL, ROCHESTER

Played 9, *Won* 1, *Lost* 7, *Drawn* 1, *Abandoned* 1

Batting

	Innings	Not outs	Runs	Highest inns.	Average
K. B. Bonsu	9	1	179	58*	22.37
†C. M. N. Sugden	9	1	125	29	15.62
K. U. Madden	10	1	118	41	13.11

Bowling

	Overs	Maidens	Runs	Wickets	Average
R. M. Fagg	119	36	277	16	17.31

KINGSWOOD SCHOOL

Played 11, *Won* 3, *Lost* 4, *Drawn* 4, *Abandoned* 2

Batting

	Innings	Not outs	Runs	Highest inns.	Average
B. P. Mole	11	4	299	67*	42.71
S. Bakhtiar	10	1	184	68*	20.44
M. A. Gaunt	11	1	171	37	17.10
†S. J. Frenkel	10	3	109	50*	15.57
J. S. Okell	11	1	121	27	12.10
W. M. Maddocks	10	0	112	35	11.20

Bowling

	Overs	Maidens	Runs	Wickets	Average
J. C. Burnell	54.2	22	111	11	10.09
D. W. N. Bibby	146	51	319	27	11.81
I. T. Tanner	52	10	151	11	13.72
S. Bakhtiar	137.1	33	450	25	18.00

LANCASTER ROYAL GRAMMAR SCHOOL

Played 12, *Won* 9, *Lost* 0, *Drawn* 3, *Abandoned* 2

Batting

	Innings	Not outs	Runs	Highest inns.	Average
†S. A. Westley	13	1	447	88	37.25
K. J. Roberts	8	2	133	34	22.16
S. K. Higgins	13	0	280	66	21.53
J. S. H. Fitton	12	0	227	83	18.91
D. S. Molyneaux	13	3	186	64	18.60
N. J. Bather	10	4	108	38	18.00

Bowling

	Overs	Maidens	Runs	Wickets	Average
N. J. Bather	196.2	85	344	44	7.81
S. K. Higgins	150.5	45	269	32	8.40
J. S. H. Fitton	87.4	28	155	12	12.91

LANCING COLLEGE

Played 17, *Won* 5, *Lost* 8, *Drawn* 4

Batting

	Innings	Not outs	Runs	Highest inns.	Average
H. O. Addo	9	2	198	80	28.28
R. H. Davey	17	0	390	68	22.94
†J. F. S. Milsom	17	1	364	49	22.75
S. D. Lincoln	15	6	194	34*	21.55
A. Ollennu	17	2	253	52*	16.86
A. Clarke	13	0	151	49	11.61
M. J. D. Stallibrass	16	0	184	44	11.50
G. F. Green	13	1	102	29	8.50

Bowling

	Overs	Maidens	Runs	Wickets	Average
M. Mildred	172.2	60	417	41	10.17
J. F. S. Milsom	60	13	191	11	17.36
R. J. Nonhebel	242.1	92	696	39	17.84
A. Ollennu	135	20	497	22	22.59
D. A. R. Barnes	97.1	20	417	16	26.06

LEEDS GRAMMAR SCHOOL

Played 11, *Won* 6, *Lost* 2, *Drawn* 3, *Abandoned* 1

Batting

	Innings	Not outs	Runs	Highest inns.	Average
†A. J. Dalton	12	5	611	123*	87.28
I. D. Nicholson	12	2	121	50*	12.10
B. W. Hunt	10	0	100	26	10.00

Bowling

	Overs	Maidens	Runs	Wickets	Average
B. W. Hunt	60.3	13	154	21	7.33
I. G. Skirrow	81	23	186	22	8.45
F. R. Futrell	89.2	17	232	21	11.04
A. J. Dalton	94.4	29	204	14	14.57

THE LEYS SCHOOL

Played 11, *Won* 4, *Lost* 4, *Drawn* 3, *Abandoned* 1

Batting

	Innings	Not outs	Runs	Highest inns.	Average
R. P. Hartley	10	2	198	46*	24.75
†R. S. Plant	11	1	208	39*	20.80
S. A. Murrills	12	2	203	57	20.30
P. J. Raper	8	1	135	56*	19.28
R. W. W. Jackson	11	2	145	32*	16.11
S. A. Kelshall	11	1	115	40	11.50

Bowling

	Overs	Maidens	Runs	Wickets	Average
G. J. H. Marcanik	141.2	32	397	28	14.17
M. Pink	106	26	331	23	14.39
S. A. Murrills	101.3	20	368	23	16.00
D. G. Mahon	62.5	15	162	10	16.20

LIVERPOOL COLLEGE

Played 9, *Won* 0, *Lost* 7, *Drawn* 2, *Abandoned* 3

Batting

	Innings	Not outs	Runs	Highest inns.	Average
†P. J. C. Winter	9	0	190	58	21.11
A. W. Bowes	9	1	130	38*	16.25

Bowling

	Overs	Maidens	Runs	Wickets	Average
D. R. Carter	115.2	22	350	22	15.90
P. Brewer	58.2	6	241	12	20.08
J. M. Wicks	135.3	37	417	12	34.75

LLANDOVERY COLLEGE

Played 13, *Won* 3, *Lost* 6, *Drawn* 4

Batting

	Innings	Not outs	Runs	Highest inns.	Average
D. E. A. Evans	13	2	208	55*	18.90
M. J. C. Andrea	13	1	219	54	18.25
M. P. Jones	13	0	185	51	14.23
D. M. T. Rogers	13	0	136	28	10.46
E. A. Jones	13	2	106	41	9.63
G. F. Davies	13	0	121	27	9.30

Bowling

	Overs	Maidens	Runs	Wickets	Average
J. R. L. Jones	73	6	215	21	10.23
E. A. Jones	140	11	473	36	13.13
D. E. A. Evans	138	25	364	19	19.15
D. M. T. Rogers	114	13	311	12	25.91

LORD WANDSWORTH COLLEGE

Played 13, *Won* 3, *Lost* 6, *Drawn* 4

Batting

	Innings	Not outs	Runs	Highest inns.	Average
†A. Dyson	13	2	262	47	23.81
R. P. Gribble	10	1	210	52*	23.33
E. G. Clode	13	1	279	71	23.25
D. N. Ainley	10	2	165	45	20.62
D. G. Wheatley	11	1	141	30	14.10
P. G. B. Evelegh	12	0	161	58	13.41
G. Ridler	10	1	113	37	12.55
R. P. M. Rendall	13	0	105	25	8.07

Bowling

	Overs	Maidens	Runs	Wickets	Average
E. G. Clode	146.5	31	384	40	9.60
G. Ridler	70.5	8	205	12	17.08
D. R. Glasson	79	11	252	13	19.38
P. G. B. Evelegh	68	6	241	10	24.10
A. J. Work	103.3	22	323	12	26.91

LORETTO SCHOOL

Played 15, *Won* 7, *Lost* 2, *Drawn* 6

Batting

	Innings	Not outs	Runs	Highest inns.	Average
A. J. Lawson	17	2	373	92	24.86
G. M. Waters	13	1	201	59	16.75
I. G. Rennie	10	2	133	47*	16.62

	Innings	Not outs	Runs	Highest inns.	Average
K. D. M. Wilson	14	6	126	37*	15.75
I. McDonald	18	1	262	67*	15.41
W. J. Watt	15	0	220	56	14.66
K. D. Brodie	12	1	122	47	11.09
R. W. K. McLean	12	1	121	27	11.00

Bowling

	Overs	Maidens	Runs	Wickets	Average
†A. H. Francis	266	72	563	53	10.62
J. C. A. Sconce	182	54	378	33	11.45
M. R. King	85.4	22	218	18	12.11

MAGDALEN COLLEGE SCHOOL

Played 10, *Won* 2, *Lost* 5, *Drawn* 3, *Abandoned* 1

Batting

	Innings	Not outs	Runs	Highest inns.	Average
R. H. Wallis	11	3	274	51*	34.25
S. J. Heath	11	0	229	62	20.81
J. D. Rosenthal	11	0	200	55	18.18

Bowling

	Overs	Maidens	Runs	Wickets	Average
J. D. Rosenthal	44	8	143	10	14.30
†P. J. Harlow	139.1	26	437	24	18.20
R. H. Wallis	102	19	371	18	20.61

MALVERN COLLEGE

Played 13, *Won* 9, *Lost* 2, *Drawn* 2, *Abandoned* 2

Batting

	Innings	Not outs	Runs	Highest inns.	Average
P. J. Allerton	13	3	633	100*	63.30
H. J. Tunnicliffe	13	3	437	92	43.70
I. A. R. Murray	13	5	316	62	39.50
A. C. R. James	16	1	430	101	28.66
P. M. Townend	13	3	243	54	24.30
W. J. Maidlow	14	3	263	48	23.90
S. J. Broughton	11	2	195	53	21.66
A. W. H. Charles	12	4	159	44*	19.87

Bowling

	Overs	Maidens	Runs	Wickets	Average
†G. B. Treverton-Jones	195.1	61	466	34	13.70
H. T. Tunnicliffe	194.1	58	508	27	18.81
C. M. Fernie	283	93	624	27	23.11
P. M. Townend	313.5	84	921	28	32.89

MANCHESTER GRAMMAR SCHOOL

Played 15, *Won* 9, *Lost* 2, *Drawn* 4, *Abandoned* 4

Batting

	Innings	Not outs	Runs	Highest inns.	Average
R. D. Stark	16	4	260	42*	21.60
H. Boyd	11	5	116	41*	19.33
A. G. Thornton	16	0	253	54	15.19
†D. B. Adams	17	1	229	35	14.31
R. J. Hope	16	0	196	54	12.25
J. E. Hewison	15	1	152	44	10.85

Bowling

	Overs	Maidens	Runs	Wickets	Average
I. R. Ashton	209	55	476	53	8.98
J. E. Hewison	244	85	487	52	9.36
H. Boyd	80	30	150	15	10.00

MARLBOROUGH COLLEGE

Played 12, *Won* 3, *Lost* 3, *Drawn* 6, *Abandoned* 1

Batting

	Innings	Not outs	Runs	Highest inns.	Average
C. M. Page	13	1	439	73	36.58
†N. P. G. Ross	13	1	387	77	32.25
I. C. R. Brown	13	1	309	98	25.75
A. C. Forbes	13	2	239	62	21.72
R. N. Style	12	2	170	47	17.00

Bowling

	Overs	Maidens	Runs	Wickets	Average
P. R. Phillimore	107	28	214	15	14.26
N. P. G. Ross	76.4	6	253	17	14.88
C. M. Page	116	35	255	17	15.00
R. St. G. Thwaites	94.2	25	283	16	17.68
J. W. Grimke-Drayton	79	12	245	13	18.84
R. J. Freedman	108.3	29	289	11	26.27

MERCHANT TAYLORS' SCHOOL, CROSBY

Played 8, *Won* 2, *Lost* 1, *Drawn* 5, *Abandoned* 1

Batting

	Innings	Not outs	Runs	Highest inns.	Average
M. J. O'Flaherty	9	2	159	41*	22.71
P. G. Brown	9	2	117	50	16.71
G. E. Webb	9	2	105	40*	15.00
J. D. P. Adams	9	0	128	34	14.22

Bowling

	Overs	Maidens	Runs	Wickets	Average
D. J. Harris	87	18	235	24	9.79
M. J. O'Flaherty	81.1	28	166	14	11.85
†J. N. Wallace	107	35	205	15	13.66

MERCHANT TAYLORS' SCHOOL, NORTHWOOD

Played 16, *Won* 4, *Lost* 6, *Drawn* 6

Batting

	Innings	Not outs	Runs	Highest inns.	Average
†J. M. H. Grimsdick	14	3	546	96	46.93
R. B. Newfield	14	2	313	47	26.08
C. J. L. Baker	12	0	136	42	11.33
M. J. Aaronson	12	0	134	44	11.16
M. N. Tollit	11	1	107	38*	10.70
A. S. F. Robertson	14	0	145	40	10.35

Bowling

	Overs	Maidens	Runs	Wickets	Average
J. M. H. Grimsdick	268.5	85	584	52	11.23
D. W. Heydon	196	48	484	25	19.36

MILLFIELD SCHOOL

Played 18, *Won* 8, *Lost* 2, *Drawn* 8

Batting

	Innings	Not outs	Runs	Highest inns.	Average
C. J. Perry	19	4	503	69	33.53
K. F. Weatherley	17	3	385	93	27.50
D. A. Browne	16	3	323	72	24.84
P. Denning	14	3	235	39	21.36
O. R. Sheard	8	3	101	44	20.20
†D. A. W. Hardick	12	2	188	53	18.80
A. T. D. Lerwill	13	2	204	43	18.54
J. I. Graveney	12	4	104	30	13.00

Bowling

	Overs	Maidens	Runs	Wickets	Average
J. I. Graveney	181.1	56	451	41	11.00
E. D. Cox	108	17	309	25	12.36
E. C. Ellett	207.2	59	524	36	14.55
O. R. Sheard	160.2	43	377	24	15.70
S. R. Heerey	113	30	318	16	19.87

MILL HILL SCHOOL

Played 12, *Won* 3, *Lost* 4, *Drawn* 5, *Abandoned* 2

Batting

	Innings	Not outs	Runs	Highest inns.	Average
†M. J. Hatchett	14	2	411	102*	34.25
R. W. Rudd	14	0	419	77	29.92
W. D. Mills	14	0	317	64	22.64
P. C. Windle-Taylor	14	0	250	55	17.85
N. W. Wray	14	4	132	26	13.20
D. J. Stevens	14	0	181	33	12.92

Bowling

	Overs	Maidens	Runs	Wickets	Average
M. J. Hatchett	210.4	62	458	36	12.72
P. C. Windle-Taylor	134.3	30	351	21	16.71
R. B. Morris	53	9	173	10	17.30
J. R. Hume	127.5	31	330	17	19.41

MONKTON COMBE SCHOOL

Played 10, *Won* 1, *Lost* 4, *Drawn* 5, *Abandoned* 2

Batting

	Innings	Not outs	Runs	Highest inns.	Average
P. J. Mulrenan	10	1	263	63	29.22
M. S. Watson	10	1	228	87*	25.33
A. G. Brooks	9	1	106	33*	13.25

Bowling

	Overs	Maidens	Runs	Wickets	Average
P. J. Mulrenan	187.2	55	382	43	8.88
R. C. Winter	111.4	32	285	19	15.00
J. J. H. Light	71.0	11	236	11	21.45

MONMOUTH SCHOOL

Played 11, *Won* 2, *Lost* 6, *Drawn* 3

Betting

	Innings	Not outs	Runs	Highest inns.	Average
A. J. Jones	11	3	215	71*	26.87
†K. S. Jarrett	11	1	206	60	20.60
J. R. Williams	10	0	100	27	10.00

Bowling

	Overs	Maidens	Runs	Wickets	Average
K. S. Jarrett	194	55	461	38	12.13
N. J. Keeves	83.3	27	222	11	20.18
A. B. Morgan	97	17	278	10	27.80

NAUTICAL COLLEGE, PANGBOURNE

Played 12, *Won* 2, *Lost* 2, *Drawn* 8, *Abandoned* 1

Batting

	Innings	Not outs	Runs	Highest inns.	Average
R. W. de la C. Shirley	11	0	322	145	29.27
B. M. Kirby	15	4	309	65*	28.09
P. J. Thomson	11	3	168	32*	21.00
†H. C. F. Howard	15	0	300	66	20.00
C. D. Horsfall	14	3	200	57	18.18
A. N. Sawrey-Cookson	12	0	114	47	9.50

Bowling

	Overs	Maidens	Runs	Wickets	Average
C. J. Masterman	94	9	281	25	11.24
H. C. F. Howard	177	50	539	39	13.82
R. W. de la C. Shirley	115	19	308	21	14.66
B. M. Kirby	139	34	429	18	23.83

NEWCASTLE ROYAL GRAMMAR SCHOOL

Played 16, *Won* 7, *Lost* 3, *Drawn* 6, *Abandoned* 1

Batting

	Innings	Not outs	Runs	Highest inns.	Average
J. S. Campbell	16	2	307	57*	21.92
†W. B. Hogg	16	3	283	57*	21.76
A. I. Douglass	14	4	175	32*	17.50
D. Morrison	16	0	224	55	14.00
D. L. Heslop	15	0	197	48	13.13
A. P. Cottier	11	1	104	30	10.40

Bowling

	Overs	Maidens	Runs	Wickets	Average
A. Dickinson	163.2	35	379	38	9.97
A. Adams	67.3	10	196	15	13.06
P. A. Thompson	155	37	383	28	13.67
W. B. Hogg	82	14	197	14	14.07
W. R. Dempster	109.5	29	293	13	22.53

NOTTINGHAM HIGH SCHOOL

Played 19, *Won* 8, *Lost* 6, *Drawn* 5, *Abandoned* 1

Batting

	Innings	Not outs	Runs	Highest inns.	Average
P. D. Johnson	19	5	529	87	37.78
P. A. Warsop	20	2	427	49	23.72
R. W. Nelson	10	4	139	32*	23.16

	Innings	Not outs	Runs	Highest inns.	Average
D. H. Quinney	20	2	340	40	18.88
B. E. D. Storer	14	5	134	41*	14.88
†M. J. Hodgkins	18	0	161	21	8.94
M. J. Brookes	17	2	131	18	8.73
P. H. Moody	17	0	125	28	7.35

Bowling

	Overs	Maidens	Runs	Wickets	Average
P. H. Moody	284.5	77	766	49	15.63
R. G. D. Ashworth	168.1	32	574	36	15.94
P. D. Johnson	248.5	47	741	43	17.23

OAKHAM SCHOOL

Played 14, *Won* 3, *Lost* 4, *Drawn* 7, *Abandoned* 1

Batting

	Innings	Not outs	Runs	Highest inns.	Average
S. D. Datt	14	1	442	146	34.00
D. N. Brooks	13	3	248	62	24.80
C. B. Glassey	13	0	292	67	22.46
†D. G. Jackson	11	0	204	46	18.54
M. T. Minta	12	4	144	41*	18.00
R. H. Robinson	14	2	202	72	16.83

Bowling

	Overs	Maidens	Runs	Wickets	Average
C. B. Glassey	153.5	44	411	25	16.44
P. E. Odell	65	8	255	12	21.25
M. K. Orchard	96.2	8	320	13	24.61
G. W. Hunter	109.1	15	352	14	25.14
D. G. Jackson	171.2	38	455	16	28.43

ORATORY SCHOOL

Played 13, *Won* 2, *Lost* 6, *Drawn* 5, *Abandoned* 3

Batting

	Innings	Not outs	Runs	Highest inns.	Average
R. St. J. Murphy	15	2	246	50	18.92
J. P. de Albuquerque	15	0	259	59	17.26
J. H. Bodenham	15	0	241	42	16.06
A. C. McEntegart	11	1	165	37	16.50
†W. A. Marshall	13	3	120	24	12.00
I. A. Duncan	13	2	131	30*	11.90

Bowling

	Overs	Maidens	Runs	Wickets	Average
W. A. Marshall	155.3	53	306	26	11.76
A. C. McEntegart	156.1	38	356	27	13.18
A. A. Cairns	104.5	20	319	21	15.19

OUNDLE SCHOOL

Played 14, *Won* 2, *Lost* 3, *Drawn* 9, *Abandoned* 1

Batting

	Innings	Not outs	Runs	Highest inns.	Average
†R. H. Wilson	15	5	278	61	27.80
J. C. Poore	14	1	357	68	27.46
J. Loder	15	0	333	63	22.20
J. M. C. Watson	9	2	151	47	21.57
J. V. Lishman	15	1	268	45	19.14
D. A. L. Joyce	12	2	176	37	17.60
M. D. S. Butler	16	3	222	32*	17.07

Bowling

	Overs	Maidens	Runs	Wickets	Average
J. Loder	158	38	453	25	18.12
R. H. Wilson	148	19	490	25	19.60
J. R. Hughes	162	28	495	25	19.80
J. M. C. Watson	96	31	272	13	20.92
D. A. L. Joyce	150	28	429	16	26.81

PERSE SCHOOL, CAMBRIDGE

Played 16, *Won* 4, *Lost* 2, *Drawn* 10, *Abandoned* 1

Batting

	Innings	Not outs	Runs	Highest inns.	Average
D. L. Cutting	6	1	107	42	21.40
P. A. Vallins	16	1	287	66	19.13
G. D. Sinclair	12	2	177	52	17.70
A. P. Peel	17	0	290	57	17.05
G. Coles	15	1	205	43	14.64
D. R. Simmons	13	1	142	46	11.83
I. A. Spooner	16	1	149	48*	9.93
M. J. Beloe	14	2	116	23	9.66
P. D. Robinson	16	1	132	35	8.80

Bowling

	Overs	Maidens	Runs	Wickets	Average
G. M. Thomas	159.5	54	322	38	8.47
D. R. Simmons	132.1	34	339	28	12.10
M. J. Beloe	161.3	26	410	30	13.66
†A. R. Pitman	78	21	235	12	19.33

PLYMOUTH COLLEGE

Played 17, *Won* 7, *Lost* 7, *Drawn* 3

Batting

	Innings	Not outs	Runs	Highest inns.	Average
†M. P. Griffiths	16	4	260	50	21.66
N. J. W. Hale	16	4	237	52	19.75
B. L. Spear	13	3	181	50	18.10
J. C. A. Pearn	15	1	235	51	16.78
A. J. Pople	16	0	237	39	14.81
R. D. Oliver	14	2	169	32	14.08

Bowling

	Overs	Maidens	Runs	Wickets	Average
J. C. A. Pearn	87	24	265	23	11.32
P. G. Babb	158	54	372	32	11.62
M. P. Griffiths	145	28	394	31	12.70

POCKLINGTON SCHOOL

Played 13, *Won* 10, *Lost* 1, *Drawn* 2, *Abandoned* 1

Batting

	Innings	Not outs	Runs	Highest inns.	Average
†C. Johnson	13	7	668	101*	111.33
P. M. Jackson	12	3	326	80	36.22
D. Briggs	9	4	160	51*	32.00
C. Aldred	9	3	128	58	21.33

Bowling

	Overs		Maidens		Runs		Wickets		Average
G. R. Flitton...........	203	..	70		374	..	55	..	6.80
M. C. Hillmann........	59.2	..	11	..	125	..	13	..	9.61
C. Johnson............	168.2	..	44	..	372	..	31	..	12.00
M. J. Lewis............	102.2	..	17	..	290	..	21	..	13.80

PORTSMOUTH GRAMMAR SCHOOL

Played 14, *Won* 10, *Lost* 2, *Drawn* 2

Batting

	Innings		Not outs		Runs		Highest inns.		Average
R. P. Broom...........	11	..	1	..	243	..	87	..	24.30
†R. Fawkner Corbett..	13	..	1	..	208	..	36	..	17.33
W. le Breton...........	10	..	1	..	135	..	41	..	15.00
B. S. Larkman..........	12	..	1	..	158	..	38	..	14.36
R. Wilkinson...........	12	..	1	..	156	..	34	..	14.18

Bowling

	Overs		Maidens		Runs		Wickets		Average
R. J. McIlwaine	187	..	60	..	408	..	53	..	7.69
P. Thomas.............	51	..	9	..	192	..	16	..	12.00
P. Rogers..............	177	..	46	..	406	..	25	..	15.24

QUEEN ELIZABETH GRAMMAR SCHOOL, WAKEFIELD

Played 13, *Won* 3, *Lost* 3, *Drawn* 7, *Abandoned* 2

Batting

	Innings		Not outs		Runs		Highest inns.		Average
R. P. Hodson..........	13	..	6	..	190	..	50*	..	27.14
M. Coope...............	14	..	3	..	221	..	64*	..	20.09
R. A. J. Corkett.......	14	..	0	..	253	..	61	..	18.07
J. A. Crapper..........	9	..	2	..	123	..	35*	..	17.57
N. D. Date.............	14	..	1	..	194	..	32	..	14.92
F. Spawforth..........	11	..	2	..	109	..	24*	..	12.11

Bowling

	Overs		Maidens		Runs		Wickets		Average
C. N. M. Pounder......	51.4	..	8	..	180	..	17	..	10.58
†C. Toone.............	159.3	..	42	..	354	..	33	..	10.72
D. Garforth...........	118	..	23	..	335	..	16	..	20.93

QUEEN'S COLLEGE, TAUNTON

Played 15, *Won* 7, *Lost* 4, *Drawn* 4

Batting

	Innings		Not outs		Runs		Highest inns.		Average
†M. C. H. Stringer.....	15	..	3	..	449	..	87*	..	37.41
I. G. Hopkins..........	15	..	1	..	419	..	78	..	29.92
A. T. Abery...........	14	..	2	..	171	..	24	..	14.25
R. J. Clapp............	14	..	0	..	159	..	42	..	11.35

Bowling

	Overs		Maidens		Runs		Wickets		Average
W. P. Costeloe........	130.2	..	47	..	287	..	31	..	9.25
G. I. Harwood.........	87.0	..	14	..	135	..	14	..	9.64
R. J. Clapp............	76.0	..	21	..	156	..	13	..	12.00
I. G. Hopkins..........	151.3	..	51	..	299	..	21	..	14.23
J. W. A. Andress.......	66.3	..	9	..	190	..	10	..	19.00

RADLEY COLLEGE

Played 14, *Won* 3, *Lost* 6, *Drawn* 5, *Abandoned* 1

Batting

	Innings	Not outs	Runs	Highest inns.	Average
A. W. Blackwell	15	2	473	110*	36.38
R. M. d'A. Samuda	5	1	129	53	32.25
R. J. S. Bucknall	15	1	301	118*	21.50
R. S. Gardner	15	0	267	60	17.80
R. J. Hill	9	2	111	42*	15.85
†R. J. U. Harington	14	0	199	61	14.21
J. D. Dallmeyer	14	0	139	40	9.92

Bowling

	Overs	Maidens	Runs	Wickets	Average
J. A. Barron	148	33	449	21	21.38
D. T. Pinsent	150	32	442	20	22.10
R. J. S. Bucknall	230.5	46	729	30	24.30
L. R. M. Smith	150.4	37	414	13	31.84

RATCLIFFE COLLEGE, LEICESTER

Played 15, *Won* 4, *Lost* 3, *Drawn* 8

Batting

	Innings	Not outs	Runs	Highest inns.	Average
M. P. Clarke	15	3	469	75*	39.08
M. C. O. Parker	14	1	308	66	23.69
W. T. Coates	14	0	316	76	22.57
M. A. Weston	13	1	234	105*	19.50
A. B. C. Gamble	12	3	131	31*	14.55
P. J. C. Shipster	11	3	116	28*	14.50

Bowling

	Overs	Maidens	Runs	Wickets	Average
W. T. Coates	199	76	417	45	9.26
A. B. C. Gamble	125	30	369	17	21.70
P. J. Hurrell	97	25	257	11	23.36
D. E. A. Pepper	157	48	484	20	24.20

READING SCHOOL

Played 14, *Won* 4, *Lost* 7, *Drawn* 3, *Abandoned* 3

Batting

	Innings	Not outs	Runs	Highest inns.	Average
†J. A. Scholfield	15	2	630	115	48.46
A. J. Llewellyn	15	3	290	81	24.16
D. W. Long	10	0	192	58	19.20
P. J. McHugh	12	0	191	43	15.91
D. J. Green	13	2	139	27	12.63
M. N. Calvert	14	0	166	28	11.85
R. J. Bull	14	3	103	24	9.36

Bowling

	Overs	Maidens	Runs	Wickets	Average
M. N. Calvert	234.4	43	675	45	15.00
A. J. Llewellyn	36.5	2	192	10	19.20
J. A. Scholfield	112	20	365	14	26.07
P. J. McHugh	106.2	20	331	11	30.09

REED'S SCHOOL, COBHAM

Played 11, *Won* 6, *Lost* 3, *Drawn* 2

Batting

	Innings	Not outs	Runs	Highest inns.	Average
A. McCulley	12	2	233	58	23.30
A. Mundy	12	0	279	73	23.25
R. P. Mortimore	8	0	118	46	14.75
M. A. Elson	11	2	131	41	14.55

Bowling

	Overs	Maidens	Runs	Wickets	Average
N. W. L. Simmons	48	12	113	10	11.30
S. L. Kerr	130	31	316	27	11.70
P. R. Williamson	293	27	316	26	12.15
D. L. Bowerman	112.1	32	356	28	12.71
A. Mundy	69.5	12	199	11	18.09

REPTON SCHOOL

Played 14, *Won* 2, *Lost* 6, *Drawn* 6, *Abandoned* 3

Batting

	Innings	Not outs	Runs	Highest inns.	Average
†P. N. Gill	17	3	456	62	32.57
J. G. West	16	2	367	102	26.21
A. C. Shuttleworth	18	2	329	81	20.56
M. R. Howarth	15	4	158	49*	14.36

Bowling

	Overs	Maidens	Runs	Wickets	Average
A. C. S. Clarke	74	13	175	12	14.58
P. N. Gill	202.4	61	466	31	15.03
M. H. Windridge	102	24	242	13	18.61
R. W. H. Hudson	242.2	50	625	31	20.16
T. J. Pywell	178	33	405	17	23.82

ROSSALL SCHOOL

Played 13, *Won* 4, *Lost* 1, *Drawn* 8

Batting

	Innings	Not outs	Runs	Highest inns.	Average
J. C. S. Herapath	8	2	148	55	24.66
J. R. Roberts	13	4	207	52*	23.00
J. D. Maude	10	4	128	26	21.33
†C. H. Lavery	14	1	259	60	19.92
D. A. Carr	14	1	257	65*	19.76
A. J. Garlick	14	0	269	77	19.21

Bowling

	Overs	Maidens	Runs	Wickets	Average
J. R. Roberts	228.3	60	523	44	11.88
R. M. Arnold	143.2	34	353	21	16.80
J. D. Maude	111.3	24	300	15	20.00
J. R. Smith	107	22	269	10	26.90

ROYAL MASONIC SCHOOL

Played 9, *Won* 2, *Lost* 7, *Drawn* 0

Batting

	Innings	Not outs	Runs	Highest inns.	Average
B. S. Nesbitt	7	0	83	45	11.85
A. S. Jamieson	5	0	54	24	10.80
M. A. Holborn	9	0	92	56	10.22
R. Gillbanks	5	0	48	35	9.60

Bowling

	Overs	Maidens	Runs	Wickets	Average
M. A. Holborn	75.4	33	136	18	7.55
†J. B. M. Poulter	106.4	41	205	24	8.54

RUGBY SCHOOL

Played 12, *Won* 3, *Lost* 3, *Drawn* 6, *Abandoned* 2

Batting

	Innings	Not outs	Runs	Highest inns.	Average
†A. D. B. Poole	13	4	416	102*	46.22
P. W. G. Evans	14	3	451	100*	41.00
R. A. G. Goodhart	13	0	343	65	26.38
J. N. B. Wright	12	1	242	51	22.00
P. N. N. Turner	11	1	200	45	20.00
R. N. R. Jenkins	10	0	192	53	19.20

Bowling

	Overs	Maidens	Runs	Wickets	Average
J. N. B. Wright	132.2	32	333	20	16.65
W. T. Hartley	168.4	42	391	23	17.00
P. N. N. Turner	145.4	31	473	26	18.19

RYDAL SCHOOL

Played 12, *Won* 6, *Lost* 5, *Drawn* 1, *Abandoned* 2

Batting

	Innings	Not outs	Runs	Highest inns.	Average
†M. S. R. Byrne	11	3	362	121*	45.25
J. R. Crossley-Holland	10	2	213	60	26.62
M. H. Trinder	12	2	246	58*	24.60
A. B. Gregory	8	1	163	36	23.28

Bowling

	Overs	Maidens	Runs	Wickets	Average
A. B. Gregory	67	20	153	16	9.56
M. S. R. Byrne	117.3	33	290	25	11.60
R. R. Plant	155.5	32	342	28	12.21

ST. ALBANS SCHOOL

Played 11, *Won* 4, *Lost* 4, *Drawn* 3, *Abandoned* 1

Batting

	Innings	Not outs	Runs	Highest inns.	Average
†M. J. Gatford	11	2	294	86*	32.66
P. J. Morgan	10	3	215	50*	30.71
P. A. Cockbain	8	1	104	44	14.85
R. J. Ashby	11	0	148	40	13.45
J. G. Keighley	11	1	110	26	11.00

Bowling

	Overs	Maidens	Runs	Wickets	Average
J. B. Hopwood	147	43	357	35	10.20
R. J. Ashby	75.3	11	224	20	11.20
P. A. Gittins	108	35	241	18	13.38

ST. BEES SCHOOL

Played 10, *Won* 7, *Lost* 2, *Drawn* 1, *Abandoned* 1

Batting

	Innings		Not outs		Runs		Highest inns.		Average
†C. P. Mackey	10	..	0	..	214	..	76	..	21.40
K. Bursell	11	..	2	..	163	..	68*	..	18.11
N. R. Harrison	11	..	4	..	110	..	42*	..	15.71
R. C. B. Astin	11	..	0	..	159	..	53	..	14.45

Bowling

	Overs		Maidens		Runs		Wickets		Average
K. Bursell	111.1	..	43	..	187	..	37	..	5.05
H. W. Redway	40.2	..	6	..	105	..	10	..	10.50
N. R. Harrison	35.4	..	12	..	106	..	10	..	10.60
O. L. Farrall	135.1	..	69	..	214	..	20	..	10.70
P. H. Swales	109.4	..	45	..	215	..	14	..	15.35

ST. DUNSTAN'S COLLEGE

Played 10, *Won* 2, *Lost* 3, *Drawn* 5, *Abandoned* 1

Batting

	Innings		Not outs		Runs		Highest inns.		Average
R. B. Hobson	10	..	5	..	151	..	47*	..	30.20
R. G. Fletcher	10	..	0	..	174	..	88	..	17.40
P. J. Barton	10	..	0	..	170	..	30	..	17.00
M. J. Lambert	9	..	0	..	137	..	45	..	15.22
D. E. Bettles	10	..	1	..	110	..	32	..	12.22

Bowling

	Overs		Maidens		Runs		Wickets		Average
R. M. Powell	140.1	..	38	..	316	..	30	..	10.53
D. E. Fletcher	42	..	7	..	121	..	11	..	11.00
P. J. Lockwood	120.1	..	31	..	361	..	21	..	17.19

ST. EDMUND'S SCHOOL, CANTERBURY

Played 12, *Won* 3, *Lost* 5, *Drawn* 4, *Abandoned* 3

Batting

	Innings		Not outs		Runs		Highest inns.		Average
B. M. J. Toogood	12	..	2	..	404	..	68	..	40.40
A. O. B. Green	12	..	1	..	246	..	85	..	22.36
M. G. Madgin	12	..	3	..	149	..	32	..	16.55
C. S. Davis	11	..	2	..	108	..	32	..	12.00
†P. F. Atkins	13	..	2	..	118	..	34	..	10.72

Bowling

	Overs		Maidens		Runs		Wickets		Average
A. O. B. Green	183.3	..	40	..	545	..	43	..	12.67
D. P. Cann	141.3	..	20	..	573	..	28	..	20.46
A. H. Parkinson	71.3	..	3	..	309	..	13	..	23.76

ST. EDWARD'S SCHOOL, OXFORD

Played 13, *Won* 6, *Lost* 3, *Drawn* 4

Batting

	Innings		Not outs		Runs		Highest inns.		Average
P. R. Thackeray	14	..	3	..	366	..	65*	..	33.27
R. A. Purdon	13	..	2	..	357	..	85*	..	32.45
R. C. Rivett	13	..	3	..	261	..	71*	..	26.10
G. E. Bennett	13	..	1	..	300	..	55	..	25.00
R. D. Barnett	8	..	3	..	100	..	30*	..	20.00
†D. E. Radcliffe	10	..	2	..	145	..	21*	..	18.12
S. A. Baldwin	9	..	1	..	109	..	71	..	13.62
J. E. D. Hodson	11	..	3	..	105	..	44	..	13.12

Bowling

	Overs	Maidens	Runs	Wickets	Average
R. A. Purdon	151	35	377	32	11.78
D. E. Radcliffe	217	53	483	28	17.25
S. A. Baldwin	109	37	236	13	18.15
T. A. Kirkpatrick	95	17	292	10	29.20
T. W. Kyle	94	19	326	10	32.60

ST. GEORGE'S COLLEGE, WEYBRIDGE

Played 14, *Won* 4, *Lost* 5, *Drawn* 5, *Abandoned* 2

Batting

	Innings	Not outs	Runs	Highest inns.	Average
C. J. Hughes	16	1	465	87	31.00
J. O'Keeffe	15	0	363	103	24.20
R. N. Low	15	3	266	77	22.16
J. Champion	15	1	184	43	13.14
P. A. Dwyer	11	0	128	55	11.63
P. G. Frawley	12	3	100	23*	11.11

Bowling

	Overs	Maidens	Runs	Wickets	Average
P. G. Edwards	57.1	11	181	17	10.64
A. J. Dew	154	39	398	22	18.09
G. P. Hewitt	150.3	33	426	18	23.66

ST. JOHN'S SCHOOL, LEATHERHEAD

Played 14, *Won* 2, *Lost* 9, *Drawn* 3

Batting

	Innings	Not outs	Runs	Highest inns.	Average
R. T. C. Gray	13	0	312	122	24.00
D. A. J. Peachey	14	2	266	54*	22.17
J. R. Henderson	14	0	238	69	17.00

Bowling

	Overs	Maidens	Runs	Wickets	Average
S. J. Neathercoat	165	28	501	26	19.27
J. R. Henderson	180	47	606	21	28.86

ST. LAWRENCE COLLEGE

Played 14, *Won* 5, *Lost* 5, *Drawn* 4, *Abandoned* 1

Batting

	Innings	Not outs	Runs	Highest inns.	Average
R. P. R. Dixon	14	1	534	129*	41.07
T. R. Alston	14	2	460	79*	38.33
†J. W. Nagenda	14	1	333	49	25.61
D. C. Hamill	14	2	258	50*	21.50
G. C. Nankivell	14	1	254	92*	19.53
H. R. D. Anderson	14	0	183	77	13.07

Bowling

	Overs	Maidens	Runs	Wickets	Average
J. W. Nagenda	249.4	69	677	45	15.04
R. P. R. Dixon	223.1	48	613	38	16.13
C. C. Townsend	81.1	20	256	13	19.69
M. A. Dawood	70.5	4	305	10	30.50

ST. PAUL'S SCHOOL

Played 13, *Won* 3, *Lost* 5, *Drawn* 5, *Abandoned* 2

Batting

	Innings	Not outs	Runs	Highest inns.	Average
†A. R. Gregory	12	2	269	74	26.90
C. R. Lambert	13	2	198	55	18.00
D. J. Barnett	12	1	186	36	16.90
G. W. Brook	15	2	204	34	15.69
J. D. Stephany	10	2	116	31	14.50
N. B. Butcher	13	1	153	49	12.75
J. Khateeli	15	1	149	27	10.64

Bowling

	Overs	Maidens	Runs	Wickets	Average
P. K. O. Crosthwaite	154.5	35	417	20	20.85
C. R. Lambert	126.4	17	432	17	25.41
R. J. Armstrong	128.1	26	399	15	26.60
A. R. Gregory	195.5	53	520	15	34.66

ST. PETER'S SCHOOL, YORK

Played 17, *Won* 10, *Lost* 3, *Drawn* 4, *Abandoned* 1

Batting

	Innings	Not outs	Runs	Highest inns.	Average
R. D. Harding	18	4	453	73	32.35
J. J. Vooght	15	3	354	72	29.50
D. M. Rawlings	19	1	493	93	27.38
W. J. Roebuck	16	2	383	96	27.35
D. R. Waller	16	1	287	55	19.13
J. C. Richardson	14	1	235	50	18.07
N. G. A. Morris	15	3	173	45	14.41

Bowling

	Overs	Maidens	Runs	Wickets	Average
W. J. Roebuck	32.1	0	104	12	8.66
†W. R. Pickersgill	227	54	544	39	13.94
J. E. Dickinson	216.5	52	607	38	15.97
D. R. Waller	173.2	49	408	18	22.66

SEBRIGHT SCHOOL

Played 15, *Won* 9, *Lost* 1, *Drawn* 5

Batting

	Innings	Not outs	Runs	Highest inns.	Average
M. I. Abdullah	15	1	388	60	27.71
P. R. Baker	15	2	280	61	21.53
R. Wassell	14	3	210	58	19.09
†P. D. Markwick-Smith	11	1	132	30	13.20

Bowling

	Overs	Maidens	Runs	Wickets	Average
P. D. Markwick-Smith	130	24	389	60	6.48
R. Howell	91.5	28	183	22	8.31
A. B. McDowell	133	40	299	17	17.58
T. J. Griffiths	79.3	8	222	11	20.18

SEDBERGH SCHOOL

Played 10, *Won* 3, *Lost* 5, *Tied* 1, *Drawn* 1, *Abandoned* 1

Batting

	Innings	Not outs	Runs	Highest inns.	Average
W. H. Shucksmith	11	1	247	85	24.73
†D. A. Turnbull	11	1	232	45	23.25
S. P. Berry	10	0	197	61	19.74
M. T. Bruce-Lockhart	9	0	129	47	14.33

Bowling

	Overs	Maidens	Runs	Wickets	Average
M. F. Cockcroft	61.2	16	112	11	10.01
C. C. Barraclough	160	37	409	30	13.63
J. de G. Walford	85	25	184	11	16.72
T. M. Chapman	118	32	245	14	17.50

SEVENOAKS SCHOOL

Played 12, *Won* 9, *Lost* 1, *Drawn* 2

Batting

	Innings	Not outs	Runs	Highest inns.	Average
T. A. McGavin	12	2	432	79	43.20
J. M. H. Hornsby	12	1	362	87	32.90
†J. R. Symes	12	2	327	64	32.70
F. R. Kemp	11	2	253	53*	28.11
S. L. Blow	7	2	121	30	24.20

Bowling

	Overs	Maidens	Runs	Wickets	Average
†J. R. Symes	181.3	58	368	46	8.00
D. A. R. Williams	67	14	147	16	9.18
M. C. Cowell	62.1	15	148	10	14.80
A. J. Cole	120.3	36	264	12	22.00

SHERBORNE SCHOOL

Played 11, *Won* 2, *Lost* 3, *Tied* 1, *Drawn* 5

Batting

	Innings	Not outs	Runs	Highest inns.	Average
N. H. E. Stamp	7	1	161	49	26.83
A. C. Charter	10	1	234	67	26.00
T. M. S. Geake	11	1	223	84*	22.30
N. H. Bates	11	2	164	56*	18.22
A. D. W. Robertson	10	1	154	39	17.11
A. M. Southall	11	1	171	46	17.10
†R. W. J. Hardie	10	0	141	39	14.10

Bowling

	Overs	Maidens	Runs	Wickets	Average
D. A. Haworth	123.2	29	330	24	13.77
A. M. Southall	132	32	406	22	18.45
R. R. M. Lytle	127.3	37	326	16	20.37
R. W. J. Hardie	95.5	22	251	11	22.81

SHREWSBURY SCHOOL

Played 12, *Won* 5, *Lost* 3, *Drawn* 4, *Abandoned* 1

Batting

	Innings	Not outs	Runs	Highest inns.	Average
P. Mucklow	11	3	238	53*	29.75
N. A. Wainwright	13	4	259	69	28.77
†J. G. Matthews	11	2	233	58*	25.88
R. H. Gilkes	14	1	292	57*	22.46
R. F. R. Lloyd	12	2	200	44*	20.00
C. S. Moser	12	0	212	76	17.66
R. P. C. Shaw	14	0	229	60	16.35

Bowling

	Overs	Maidens	Runs	Wickets	Average
R. T. Tudor	115.4	35	282	25	11.28
J. G. Matthews	75.4	25	202	15	13.46
N. J. Owen	111	35	238	13	18.30
P. S. Bryan	171.4	38	514	28	18.35

SOLIHULL SCHOOL

Played 14, *Won* 3, *Lost* 5, *Drawn* 6, *Abandoned* 2

Batting

	Innings	Not outs	Runs	Highest inns.	Average
†J. G. Woolman	15	5	456	60	45.60
H. J. C. Taylor	15	3	492	72*	41.00
A. K. C. Jones	13	1	383	78	31.91
T. T. Mokoena	16	1	159	29	10.60

Bowling

	Overs	Maidens	Runs	Wickets	Average
R. J. Wyatt	217.2	58	599	37	16.18
M. P. Probert	172.5	30	544	24	22.66
M. K. Mokoena	94	8	445	19	23.42
H. J. C. Taylor	90	14	348	12	29.00

STAMFORD SCHOOL

Played 10, *Won* 3, *Lost* 4, *Drawn* 3, *Abandoned* 3

Batting

	Innings	Not outs	Runs	Highest inns.	Average
P. W. Harris	8	2	155	71*	25.83
P. J. Furmer	10	0	195	43	19.50
B. T. Wilson	10	1	153	54	17.00
A. E. Searby	10	3	107	45*	15.28
D. T. Gill	7	0	100	33	14.28

Bowling

	Overs	Maidens	Runs	Wickets	Average
T. W. Patrick	97.5	28	226	20	11.30
P. W. Harris	147.5	40	327	26	12.57
R. H. A. Wright	93.2	24	209	15	13.93
S. L. Gooch	84.1	21	239	15	15.93

STOCKPORT GRAMMAR SCHOOL

Played 9, *Won* 4, *Lost* 2, *Tied* 1, *Drawn* 2, *Abandoned* 1

Batting

	Innings	Not outs	Runs	Highest inns.	Average
T. J. Lingard	9	3	126	61*	21.00
A. J. Shipsides	9	0	118	26	13.11
J. A. Battersby	9	1	103	28	12.87

Bowling

	Overs		Maidens		Runs		Wickets		Average
M. S. Parnell..........	42	..	8	..	90	..	13	..	6.92
T. J. Lingard..........	114	..	44	..	216	..	28	..	7.71
†P. W. Taylor..........	39	..	10	..	123	..	10	..	12.30
J. A. Battersby........	63	..	12	..	168	..	12	..	14.00

STONYHURST COLLEGE

Played 11, *Won* 1, *Lost* 7, *Drawn* 3

Batting

	Innings		Not outs		Runs		Highest inns.		Average
M. P. O'Meara	12	..	1	..	231	..	54*	..	21.00
J. Coltman...........	12	..	0	..	180	..	51	..	15.00
J. G.Colvill..........	12	..	0	..	157	..	43	..	13.08

Bowling

	Overs		Maidens		Runs		Wickets		Average
C. A. Marshall	191	..	53	..	435	..	36	..	12.08
M. P. O'Meara	172	..	48	..	404	..	24	..	16.83

STOWE SCHOOL

Played 11, *Won* 4, *Lost* 4, *Drawn* 3, *Abandoned* 1

Batting

	Innings		Not outs		Runs		Highest inns.		Average
C. J. R. Black.........	12	..	1	..	473	..	124	..	43.00
J. N. Dixey...........	12	..	2	..	293	..	65*	..	29.30
B. S. Davies..........	8	..	0	..	124	..	36	..	15.50
†W. P. Durlacher......	12	..	0	..	181	..	62	..	15.08
J. P. Raw.............	9	..	0	..	135	..	46	..	15.00
A. P. Greig...........	10	..	2	..	104	..	33	..	13.00
S. A. Stock...........	11	..	0	..	134	..	33	..	12.18

Bowling

	Overs		Maidens		Runs		Wickets		Average
C. J. R. Black.........	192	..	51	..	448	..	45	..	9.95
S. T. D. Ritchie.......	68	..	7	..	192	..	15	..	12.80
J. N. Dixey...........	171	..	39	..	463	..	22	..	21.04

STRATHALLAN SCHOOL

Played 14, *Won* 3, *Lost* 9, *Drawn* 2, *Abandoned* 1

Batting

	Innings		Not outs		Runs		Highest inns.		Average
T. N. W. Trusdale.....	12	..	2	..	295	..	67	..	29.50
†W. B. Melville........	14	..	2	..	266	..	76*	..	22.16
C. J. W. Mauchline....	12	..	0	..	241	..	57	..	20.08
A. F. Spence..........	13	..	0	..	159	..	39	..	12.23

Bowling

	Overs		Maidens		Runs		Wickets		Average
R. M. M. Lang........	77.1	..	17	..	198	..	14	..	14.14
R. J. Elder...........	115.2	..	25	..	304	..	20	..	15.20
A. D. Turner..........	167	..	40	..	426	..	27	..	15.77
W. B. Melville.........	100.2	..	21	..	262	..	14	..	18.71

SUTTON VALENCE SCHOOL

Played 15, *Won* 4, *Lost* 4, *Drawn* 7

Batting

	Innings	Not outs	Runs	Highest inns.	Average
†A. W. Dixon	15	4	597	126*	54.27
N. C. Whitlock	12	2	201	42	20.10
R. H. Miles	15	0	287	66	19.13
P. R. F. Hudson	15	0	257	78	17.13
G. B. L. Harrison	15	2	219	38	16.84
M. J. C. Phillips	13	3	140	25	14.00

Bowling

	Overs	Maidens	Runs	Wickets	Average
P. R. F. Hudson	209.5	39	561	37	15.16
N. T. Richards	178	32	479	26	18.42
G. J. Francis	81	4	373	17	21.94
G. B. L. Harrison	115.3	21	377	13	29.00

TAUNTON SCHOOL

Played 11, *Won* 6, *Lost* 2, *Drawn* 3, *Abandoned* 1

Batting

	Innings	Not outs	Runs	Highest inns.	Average
†T. E. N. Jameson	11	3	462	62	57.75
J. R. Maunders	4	1	134	54*	44.66
P. J. W. Wood	7	1	131	104*	21.83
A. B. Sayers	8	1	108	30	15.42

Bowling

	Overs	Maidens	Runs	Wickets	Average
C. C. W. Wheeler	196.2	54	504	32	15.75
T. E. N. Jameson	254.2	71	568	36	15.77

TONBRIDGE SCHOOL

Played 11, *Won* 3, *Lost* 3, *Drawn* 5, *Abandoned* 1

Batting

	Innings	Not outs	Runs	Highest inns.	Average
P. G. A. Montgomery	13	1	353	104	29.41
R. J. Brown	10	2	196	39	24.50
J. S. Rodd	11	1	234	53	23.40
T. J. Mills	9	2	151	35	21.57
†A. St. J. Thomson	13	1	202	43	16.83
R. G. Scoones	12	0	187	69	15.58
G. B. Morgan	10	0	128	38	12.80

Bowling

	Overs	Maidens	Runs	Wickets	Average
P. G. Roffey	122.2	33	347	31	11.19
S. N. Baguley	92.8	20	279	16	17.43
W. A. J. P. Breen	158.3	37	422	24	17.58
G. B. Morgan	104	29	287	15	19.13

TRENT COLLEGE

Played 18, *Won* 6, *Lost* 10, *Drawn* 2, *Abandoned* 2

Batting

	Innings	Not outs	Runs	Highest inns.	Average
†D. A. Wilding	17	5	367	110*	30.58
N. I. Image	19	2	398	63	23.41
R. N. Musson	14	2	186	63	15.50

	Innings	Not outs	Runs	Highest inns.	Average
N. J. Tompkin	19	5	178	33	12.71
N. D. Askew	14	0	163	46	11.64
K. J. Macdonald	16	2	159	35	11.35

Bowling

	Overs	Maidens	Runs	Wickets	Average
D. A. Wilding	194.1	36	549	50	10.98
R. O. Rowley	187.5	29	578	42	13.76
K. J. Macdonald	203.4	42	544	36	15.11
O. D. R. Dixon	182.3	32	529	22	24.04

TRINITY COLLEGE, GLENALMOND

Played 11, *Won* 2, *Lost* 2, *Drawn* 7, *Abandoned* 4

Batting

	Innings	Not outs	Runs	Highest inns.	Average
C. M. N. Wilson	11	3	231	57	28.87
†G. A. M. Begg	12	2	215	44*	21.50
C. B. Macmillan	7	1	101	26*	16.83
D. S. Gordon	11	3	121	26*	15.12
D. R. A. Emslie	11	0	147	26	13.36

Bowling

	Overs	Maidens	Runs	Wickets	Average
J. W. S. Bentley	68	32	78	18	4.33
C. B. Macmillan	168	54	341	15	22.73

TRINITY SCHOOL, CROYDON

Played 13, *Won* 2, *Lost* 4, *Drawn* 7, *Abandoned* 3

Batting

	Innings	Not outs	Runs	Highest inns.	Average
†C. F. Warren	13	2	295	72*	26.81
M. Seymour	12	2	232	51	23.20
P. N. Cosh	12	0	177	44	14.75

Bowling

	Overs	Maidens	Runs	Wickets	Average
P. Bennett	137	28	375	24	15.62
G. R. Godfrey	97.1	23	307	18	17.05
D. R. Wright	73.3	12	229	13	17.61
W. R. Jones	120.3	34	305	16	19.06

UNIVERSITY COLLEGE SCHOOL

Played 12, *Won* 2, *Lost* 5, *Drawn* 5, *Abandoned* 2

Batting

	Innings	Not outs	Runs	Highest inns.	Average
M. Cartwright	12	1	269	52	24.45
M. J. Cowtan	13	1	181	32	15.08
M. J. Fox	12	1	141	53	12.81
G. W. Lewis	13	0	144	27	11.07
J. H. Gillett	13	2	117	28	10.63

Bowling

	Overs	Maidens	Runs	Wickets	Average
G. C. Timbrell	187	48	386	27	14.29
J. C. M. Wise	127	20	426	26	16.38
C. S. Thomson	144	27	449	26	17.23
M. Cartwright	118	29	327	14	23.35

UPPINGHAM SCHOOL

Played 12, *Won* 2, *Lost* 1, *Drawn* 9

Batting

	Innings	Not outs	Runs	Highest inns.	Average
J. N. Musson	13	1	339	112	28.25
W. R. Ward	5	0	118	53	23.60
A. C. Howeson	14	5	202	42*	22.44
†I. D. Hendry	15	2	282	81	21.69
A. M. P. Falk	15	0	294	49	19.60
C. G. Ruck	15	0	287	75	19.13
M. R. Hatt	9	0	155	39	17.22
D. M. Burke	9	0	143	38	15.88
W. S. Fletcher	14	1	145	37	11.15

Bowling

	Overs	Maidens	Runs	Wickets	Average
C. G. Ruck	163.1	34	455	30	15.16
A. C. Howeson	189	39	542	35	15.48
B. A. Marsh	98.1	23	254	13	19.53
P. D. Hay	138	30	382	19	20.10

VICTORIA COLLEGE, JERSEY

Played 16, *Won* 4, *Lost* 9, *Tied* 1, *Drawn* 2, *Abandoned* 1

Batting

	Innings	Not outs	Runs	Highest inns.	Average
†R. J. de Ste. Croix	15	2	250	42	19.23
J. A. Moisan	14	0	202	42	14.42
W. N. Pennington	13	1	170	56	14.16
R. J. Brooks	15	1	188	30	13.42
M. R. Stokoe	13	0	144	24	11.07
R. F. Robins	13	2	108	25	9.81

Bowling

	Overs	Maidens	Runs	Wickets	Average
R. J. de Ste. Croix	205	44	503	43	11.69
A. G. Harper	143	28	452	24	18.83
W. M. Pennington	143	30	512	24	21.33
P. F. Moon	135	16	393	18	21.83

WALLASEY GRAMMAR SCHOOL

Played 12, *Won* 4, *Lost* 2, *Drawn* 6, *Abandoned* 2

Batting

	Innings	Not outs	Runs	Highest inns.	Average
A. Hughes	11	2	272	60*	30.22
P. H. Dunn	11	2	229	66	25.44
G. C. Stone	12	1	155	55	14.09
†G. Horner	12	0	162	32	13.50
J. A. Smith	12	2	134	39*	13.40
C. G. Bruce	12	1	129	33	11.72

Bowling

	Overs	Maidens	Runs	Wickets	Average
S. D. McGinity	109	21	319	31	10.29
J. A. Smith	147.4	44	360	23	15.65
C. A. Coulson	132	31	343	16	21.43
G. C. Stone	125.4	14	436	15	29.06

WARWICK SCHOOL

Played 13, *Won* 8, *Lost* 1, *Drawn* 4, *Abandoned* 2

Batting

	Innings	Not outs	Runs	Highest inns.	Average
V. G. Evans	11	3	228	61	28.50
M. E. Barnwell	11	5	154	31	25.66
D. S. Freeman	11	1	247	60	24.70
†D. I. Dollery	12	3	213	62*	23.66
R. P. Haddon	8	3	114	39	22.80
R. G. Steane	12	0	264	38	22.00
N. W. Harper	12	0	177	52	14.75

Bowling

	Overs	Maidens	Runs	Wickets	Average
D. I. Dollery	164	42	345	30	11.50
N. W. Harper	80	28	138	11	12.54
D. S. Freeman	52	11	141	11	12.81
R. G. Steane	256	48	418	30	13.93

WELLINGBOROUGH SCHOOL

Played 11, *Won* 1, *Lost* 6, *Drawn* 4

Batting

	Innings	Not outs	Runs	Highest inns.	Average
T. G. P. Wootton	11	1	119	26	11.90
D. J. H. Reddy	10	0	118	27	11.80
P. F. Bryant	11	1	109	22	10.90

Bowling

	Overs	Maidens	Runs	Wickets	Average
M. P. Hainsworth	65	8	195	10	19.50
†R. J. Dennison	93.1	13	290	14	20.71
B. J. Chisholm	113.4	4	495	19	26.05

WELLINGTON COLLEGE

Played 14, *Won* 0, *Lost* 6, *Drawn* 8

Batting

	Innings	Not outs	Runs	Highest inns.	Average
R. G. Carter	8	1	172	66*	24.57
D. J. McCaig	16	0	352	78	22.00
S. H. A. Potter	16	3	282	110*	21.69
C. G. T. Brown	15	1	294	94	21.00
C. N. A. Perkins	15	2	264	78*	20.30
†A. R. Oakley	11	0	128	29	11.63

Bowling

	Overs	Maidens	Runs	Wickets	Average
A. R. Oakley	113.2	29	309	20	15.45
T. M. Trembath	82	11	254	13	19.53
B. A. K. Wigram	147	40	463	23	20.13
C. G. T. Brown	92	12	308	12	25.66
D. E. L. Watt	111.5	33	260	10	26.00

WELLINGTON SCHOOL

Played 11, *Won* 4, *Lost* 5, *Drawn* 2

Batting

	Innings	Not outs	Runs	Highest inns.	Average
†D. Coley	10	2	245	86*	30.62
N. Cowan	10	1	154	51	17.11
B. Blaber	9	1	133	35	16.62

Bowling

	Overs	Maidens	Runs	Wickets	Average
R. Harman	100.5	22	235	23	10.21
N. Cowan	66	10	174	15	11.60
D. Jones	103.8	30	241	20	12.05

WHITGIFT SCHOOL

Played 18, *Won* 3, *Lost* 5, *Drawn* 10, *Abandoned* 1

Batting

	Innings	Not outs	Runs	Highest inns.	Average
N. J. G. Lack	18	0	389	91	21.61
M. C. Cook	19	1	382	45	21.22
J. L. Cooke	12	2	210	43*	21.00
R. T. Ibbotson	13	1	248	121*	20.66
P. J. Seear	19	1	306	68	17.00
S. J. Kennedy	7	0	104	30	14.85
P. J. J. Skeen	16	3	186	33	14.30

Bowling

	Overs	Maidens	Runs	Wickets	Average
A. W. Le Serve	249.3	63	373	40	9.32
D. M. Scott	75.4	27	151	10	15.10
P. J. J. Skeen	167.1	46	462	26	17.76
†R. A. Pennells	220.3	71	525	28	18.75
J. M. W. Hills	132	25	387	17	22.76

WINCHESTER COLLEGE

Played 12, *Won* 4, *Lost* 5, *Drawn* 3, *Abandoned* 1

Batting

	Innings	Not outs	Runs	Highest inns.	Average
†R. L. Burchnall	15	2	610	128*	46.92
S. G. B. Bartley	11	3	200	48	25.00
A. G. W. Jackson	15	3	280	39	23.33
R. M. W. Longmore	13	3	185	63	18.50
J. H. Marigold	8	0	124	46	15.50
J. M. Bebb	7	0	101	47	14.42
W. A. Bailey	10	0	141	53	14.10

Bowling

	Overs	Maidens	Runs	Wickets	Average
J. J. S. Hudson	181	46	462	40	11.55
O. J. C. Oakes	162.5	48	400	26	15.38
S. G. B. Bartley	103	32	280	16	17.50
A. M. D. Palmer	95	29	249	14	17.78
C. J. F. Sinclair	56.1	12	186	10	18.60

WOODHOUSE GROVE SCHOOL

Played 14, *Won* 9, *Lost* 1, *Drawn* 4, *Abandoned* 2

Batting

	Innings	Not outs	Runs	Highest inns.	Average
†J. G. Foster	14	2	354	87	29.50
P. B. Triffitt	11	4	181	56	25.85
M. A. Hillary	13	0	267	53	20.53
G. P. A. Clark	11	2	112	31	12.44

Bowling

	Overs	Maidens	Runs	Wickets	Average
T. D. Mason	183.3	59	298	50	5.96
R. D. Jones	49.0	16	75	12	6.25
P. D. Wilson	49.3	13	101	14	7.21
J. F. Marston	186.4	61	302	38	7.94

WORCESTER ROYAL GRAMMAR SCHOOL

Played 16, *Won* 12, *Lost* 3, *Drawn* 1

Batting

	Innings	Not outs	Runs	Highest inns.	Average
K. Griffith	16	5	454	70*	41.27
†N. W. Watkins	16	2	334	79*	23.85
G. K. Haslam	14	3	224	51*	20.36
K. Fidoe	11	4	128	39*	18.28
R. B. Hiles	16	1	195	49	13.00
P. J. Beckley	14	3	120	18	10.90

Bowling

	Overs	Maidens	Runs	Wickets	Average
J. C. H. Lee	137.1	39	278	37	7.51
K. Griffith	167	40	378	40	9.45
D. E. Perryman	203.4	60	435	42	10.35
R. P. Starkey	58.5	13	138	10	13.80
E. A. Baynham	121	43	222	15	14.80

WORKSOP COLLEGE

Played 13, *Won* 4, *Lost* 3, *Drawn* 6, *Abandoned* 1

Batting

	Innings	Not outs	Runs	Highest inns.	Average
T. C. Taylor	13	0	405	74	31.15
I. C. Dodson	14	0	327	71	23.35
†S. N. Birkett	13	0	285	54	21.92
R. S. Hill	14	3	236	46	21.45
P. D. Huddlestone	14	0	241	56	17.21
C. S. Ingham	14	1	157	39	12.07

Bowling

	Overs	Maidens	Runs	Wickets	Average
S. N. Birkett	120	20	321	27	11.88
M. R. Corker	167	42	342	27	12.66
S. C. Corlett	160	37	444	26	17.07

WREKIN COLLEGE

Played 18, *Won* 10, *Lost* 5, *Drawn* 3, *Abandoned* 2

Batting

	Innings	Not outs	Runs	Highest inns.	Average
R. C. Bush	20	6	493	101*	35.21
N. D. Little	20	1	558	99	29.36
E. M. Grace	20	3	371	62	21.82
[illegible]. H. G. Wright	10	1	184	75*	20.44
D. G. S. Wright	16	3	229	73*	17.61
C. A. Fergusson	12	1	167	46	15.18

Bowling

	Overs	Maidens	Runs	Wickets	Average
D. G. S. Wright	61.5	11	162	21	7.71
E. S. Dean	209.4	74	450	35	12.85
J. R. Thorburn	243.4	49	703	53	13.26
†J. R. Trevethick	211.1	31	651	42	15.50

WYCLIFFE COLLEGE

Played 12, *Won* 5, *Lost* 2, *Drawn* 5

Batting

	Innings	Not outs	Runs	Highest inns.	Average
S. M. Greaves	11	3	222	60*	27.75
B. T. Cockburn-Smith	12	1	259	56	23.54
K. M. Youde	9	1	104	18*	13.00
†I. K. Hamilton	12	1	122	34	11.09

Bowling

	Overs	Maidens	Runs	Wickets	Average
I. K. Hamilton	133.3	30	312	34	9.17
C. S. Raine	128.4	41	294	31	9.48
C. J. Gregg	116.4	19	320	22	14.54
B. T. Cockburn-Smith	84.5	20	273	17	16.05

WYGGESTON SCHOOL

Played 9, *Won* 1, *Lost* 5, *Drawn* 3

Batting

	Innings	Not outs	Runs	Highest inns.	Average
J. A. Corrall	9	2	125	35	17.85
†R. Ewen	8	0	106	31	13.25

Bowling

	Overs	Maidens	Runs	Wickets	Average
P. A. Gooch	87.2	14	254	18	14.11
M. J. Voss	57.4	16	174	10	17.40
J. A. Corrall	77	14	229	13	17.61

ETON v. WINCHESTER

At Agar's Plough, Eton, June 24, 25. Drawn. Rain interfered on both day and few batsmen did themselves justice, although on the first day the pitch offere no undue help to the bowlers. After Burchnall won the toss for Winchester th batsmen made slow progress against some splendid bowling by Lord Crowhur who took five wickets for 54. Bebb played soundly and Hudson, after retirin temporarily following a blow on the head, hit freely. A heavy downpour at fiv o'clock also damped the spirit of the Eton batsmen, who broke down again Hudson, six wickets falling for 34 before Lowndes and Fulton intervened and toc the score to 71. Next day, they raised their stand to 50 and Eton just managed t avoid the follow-on. Winchester led by 92 but apart from Burchnall, who h five 4's in making the top score of the match, they showed little confidence again the slower bowling of Wilson and Lawrie. At one stage only 10 runs came whi six wickets fell and in the end Eton were set to make 208 in just under three hour Unfortunately the rain returned at fifteen minutes to four and ruined any chan of an exciting finish.

Winchester

J. H. Marigold b Peebles	5 — c Wilson b Crowhurst	7
†R. Longmore c Fulton b Lawrie	6 — c Fawcett b Crowhurst	14
*R. L. Burchnall c Fulton b Wilson	25 — c Hodges b Wilson	54
A. G. W. Jackson b Crowhurst	24 — c Hodges b Wilson	17
J. M. Bebb c Fawcett b Crowhurst	47 — c and b Lawrie	4
S. G. B. Bartley b Fulton	6 — c Weekes b Lawrie	1
C. J. Sinclair c Peebles b Crowhurst	3 — c Smith b Wilson	2
B. E. T. Synge b Crowhurst	2 — c and b Wilson	3
A. Palmer c Lowndes b Crowhurst	0 — not out	0
J. J. S. Hudson not out	30 — not out	0
O. J. C. Oakes c Lowndes b Smith	22 — c Fawcett b Lawrie	10
B 7, l-b 10, w 3	20 L-b 3	3
1/6 2/37 3/41 4/75 5/96 6/103 7/114 8/114 9/153	190 1/12 2/35 3/95 4/96 5/99 6/102 7/103 8/105 9/115	(9 wkts., dec.) 115

Bowling: *First Innings*—Peebles 7—4—7—1; Crowhurst 27—12—54—5; Wilson 11—4—19—1; Lawrie 15—3—37—1; Smith 7.3—1—24—1; Fulton 7—0—29—1. *Second Innings*—Crowhurst 17—7—31—2; Peebles 8—2—14—0; Fulton 11—2—33—0; Lawrie 9—1—21—3; Wilson 7—2—13—4.

Eton

*D. M. Smith c Longmore b Bartley	0 — not out	6
P. M. Hodges c Bebb b Hudson	8 — not out	27
B. L. H. Powell c Synge b Hudson	3	
G. E. N. S. Wilson c Palmer b Bartley	1	
P. G. Lowndes c Longmore b Hudson	42	
C. A. Lawrie b Hudson	2	
H. R. B. Fawcett run out	4	
R. H. G. Fulton b Hudson	22	
Viscount Crowhurst c Burchnall b Hudson	0	
†R. C. Kinkead-Weekes c Burchnall b Oakes	9	
A. R. T. Peebles not out	2	
L-b 5	5 W 1	1
1/4 2/7 3/12 4/20 5/22 6/34 7/84 8/87 9/96	98	(No wkt.) 34

Bowling: *First Innings*—Hudson 22—8—42—6; Bartley 11—3—31—2; Palmer 4—2—7—0; Oakes 13.2—7—13—1. *Second Innings*—Hudson 5—1—25—0; Bartley 4—1—8—0.

Umpires: W. Southall and M. Pierce.

WESTERN PROVINCE WILLOWS

By Charles Burton

Western Province Willows, a young and enthusiastic South African side omprising 21 players, toured England for the first time in July. Whilst only three natches were won and seven were drawn of the ten matches played, another being ibandoned, in the space of 17 days, this was unquestionably a successful pioneer 'enture, considering that most of the matches were played on unfamiliar pitches ınd not always in the kindest of weather. Indeed, four games were ruined by rain.

The three victories were notable for their exciting finishes. Essex 2nd XI were ›eaten by one wicket with less than ten minutes to spare; Kent 2nd XI, who ncluded a number of players who had often assisted the 1st XI, were beaten by wo wickets with as many minutes to spare, and Buckinghamshire by four wickets ı the last over.

The strength of the side lay in its batting. Indeed, on occasions the batting rder was successfully reversed. The most consistent scorers were M. Lamb, V. Low, K. Ruthenberg and A. Duncan, Lamb's best effort being 131 against

Berkshire. Low made 53 on an unpleasant wicket against Kent 2nd XI. Duncan scored the first century of the tour, against Marlow. The captain, K. Heldsinger, the veteran of the side, made the third highest score of the tour, 78 (two 6's and eleven 4's) against Berkshire.

The Willows were fortunate in having two opening bowlers of the calibre of D. McCay and J. Freeman, both of whom have represented South African Universities. Both enjoyed their best performances in the same match—against Kent 2nd XI, Freeman taking six for 32 and McCay four for 20. The spin bowling honours were shared by the vice-captain, D. Whitefield and G. Chevalier.

The former bowled especially well against a strong Public Schools Wanderers side which included J. P. Fellows-Smith, the South Africa and Oxford University all-rounder, D. Varnals, another South African Test player, and F. S. Goldstein, the Oxford University opening batsman, while Chevalier was seen at his best against Essex 2nd XI and Middlesex 2nd XI. The tourists had three good wicket-keepers in G. Pfuhl, K. Anderson and H. Spiro, while the fielding was first class, especially the throwing from the deep.

Lastly, but by no means least, in Mr. David Harvey, the Willows had not only an able and genial manager, but a dedicated cricket enthusiast. The touring party comprised: K. Heldsinger (captain), D. Whitefield (vice-captain), J. Bell, G. Chevalier, D. Gowdy, K. Anderson, A. Duncan, C. Franz, J. Freeman, I. Goodman, J. Gurney, J. Herringer. M. Lamb, J. Langenegger, D. LeRoux, W. Low, D. McCay, J. Pepler, G. Pfuhl, K. Ruthenberg, H. Spiro.

RESULTS

At Hampstead, July 5. South Hampstead 101 for three (R. Ager 46; D. McCay three for 42). Drawn.

At Bishop's Stortford, July 6, 7. Hertfordshire 212 for eight dec. (P. Lord 51*; D. McCay three for 58) and 173 for eight dec. (T. Martins 59; J. Gurney four for 13); Western Province Willows 214 for eight dec. (J. Freeman 43, K. Ruthenberg 42; J. Appleyard three for 18) and 161 for nine (G. Pfuhl 44, A. Duncan 43). Drawn.

At Chelmsford, July 8. Essex 2nd XI 171 (J. Wallace 38; G. Chevalier three for 23); Willows 173 for nine (M. Lamb 37, D. Goudy 33; K. D. Boyce three for 23). Won by one wicket.

At Marlow, July 10. Willows 226 for six dec. (A. Duncan 100, J. Herringer 59; M. Horgan six for 47); Marlow 107 for seven (D. Whitefield three for 6). Drawn.

At Greenwich, July 11, 12. Kent 2nd XI 177 for eight dec. (J. M. Prodger 37) and 67 (J. Freeman six for 32, D. McCay four for 20); Willows 140 (W. Low 53; J. Shepherd four for 26) and 110 for eight (M. Lamb 36; J. Shepherd three for 30). Won by two wickets.

At Earley, July 13, 14. Willows 189 (K. Heldsinger 78; S. Baynes four for 52) and 274 for nine dec. (M. Lamb 131); Berkshire 241 for eight dec. (P. Watts 41*, S. Baynes 38) and 214 for seven (A. Davis 129; J. Pepler four for 51). Drawn.

At Shepherd's Bush, July 15. Public School Wanderers 154 for eight dec (F. S. Goldstein 42, R. Briance 36; D. Whitefield five for 41); Willows 79 for two (D. LeRoux 42*). Drawn.

At The Oval, July 16. Surrey 2nd XI 201 for six dec. (Mohammed Younis 125*; D. Whitefield three for 56); Willows 167 for nine (W. Low 39, M. Lamb 33 Mohammed Younis three for 28). Drawn.

At Slough, July 17, 18. Buckinghamshire 105 (P. Wood 33; D. Whitefield four for 28; W. Low three for 46) and 227 (N. Feasey 51*; D. Whitefield four for 54, W. Low three for 57, J. Freeman three for 81); Willows 267 (K. Ruthenberg 51 W. Low 46; W. Rawlings four for 84) and 66 for six. Won by four wickets.

At Ilford, July 19, 20. v. Club Cricket Conference. Abandoned, rain.

At Finchley, July 21. Middlesex 2nd XI 202 for five dec. (R. Harris 73 G. Chevalier three for 55); Willows 172 for eight (D. McCay 49; M. Manasseh three for 27, D. Ling three for 33). Drawn. Rain stopped play on first day.

WILFRED ISAACS' SOUTH AFRICANS' TOUR

By Charles Burton

Wilfred Isaacs, who has done so much for young cricketers in South Africa during the last fifteen years, brought an attractive side to England in July for a three weeks tour of seventeen matches. Just as five years earlier another South African touring side, Fezela, under the captaincy of Roy McLean, made their mark in English cricket by their attractive play, besides "blooding" such promising young players as Colin Bland and Dennis Lindsay, on English wickets, so Isaacs' side blazed the trail for more possible future South African players.

In addition to such well-tried Test players as D. J. McGlew, R. A. McLean, H. J. Tayfield, N. A. T. Adcock and K. J. Funston, the touring side included Test potentials in B. Richards, M. Proctor, P. Henwood, A. Bruyns and L. Irvine, all of whom were products of Nuffield Schools representative cricket.

The bare fact that the tourists were unbeaten in seventeen games, four of which were rained off, gives but a statistical indication of their success. Some of the victories were against the clock and moreover, against powerful opposition. Thus the side raised by Peter West was led by Richie Benaud and included the former England players, J. C. Laker and P. E. Richardson, yet was beaten by seven wickets. Then a full Glamorgan side was beaten at Cardiff, while a Parasites XI, including Laker, Richardson and Richard Hutton, was also accounted for.

There was no weak link in the team. As with Fezela, aggression was the keynote of the batting and the rate of scoring on many occasions would have made those inured to watching English County Cricket blink with amazement.

Seldom was the batting extended, for with McLean, McGlew, Richards, Procter, Bruyns, Irvine, Wesley and Mackay-Coghill all full of runs, the lower order was seldom called upon. The bowling matched the batting in strength, with the "veterans" Tayfield, Adcock, Cole and Hall reproducing their old skill plus the young brigade, Procter, Henwood and Watson, not forgetting McGlew's usefulness as a spinner. The tourists were also fortunate in having three wicket-keepers of the class of J. Ferrandi, Irvine and Bruyns. Nor must the parts played by Wilfred Isaacs (an enthusiastic captain and organiser), and Ronald Eriksen, an indefatigable manager, be overlooked when assessing the success of the tour on and off the field.

The touring party was: W. Isaacs (captain), R. A. McLean (vice-captain), N. A. T. Adcock, A. Bruyns, J. Cole, J. Ferrandi, K. J. Funston, P. Henwood, G. Hall, L. Irvine, D. Mackay-Coghill, D. J. McGlew, M. Procter, B. Richards, H. J. Tayfield, G. Watson, C. Wesley, R. Eriksen (manager).

RESULTS

At Sidmouth, July 7. Isaacs' XI 304 for six dec. (A. Bruyns 100, D. Mackay-Coghill 73; D. Frank three for 8); Sidmouth C.C. 66 (G. Watson four for 20, G. Hall three for 12). Won by 238 runs.

At Bournemouth, July 8, 9. Isaacs' XI 263 (D. J. McGlew 99, B. Richards 72; A. Wassell four for 82, G. L. Keith four for 36) and 133 for three dec. (M. Procter 56, B. Richards 46*); Hampshire 2nd XI 164 for seven dec. (G. L. Keith 51, D. A. Livingstone 36) and 159 (T. Jesty 44; J. Cole four for 26). Won by 73 runs.

At Bristol, July 10. v. D. A. Allen's XI. Abandoned, rain.

At Sherborne, July 11. Isaacs' XI 206 (M. Procter 55, B. Richards 46; C. Hunter three for 40, D. J. W. Bridge three for 60); R. A. W. Sharp's XI 162 (D. M. Daniels 58; H. J. Tayfield six for 77, G. Hall four for 31). Won by 44 runs.

At Marlborough, July 12. Isaacs' XI 170 for eight dec. (R. Benaud 35, D. C. S. Compton 32; P. Hough three for 44); D. R. W. Silk's XI 149 for eight (P. Hough 45; D. C. S. Compton three for 39). Drawn.

At Canterbury, July 13. Isaacs' XI 250 for six dec. (K. J. Funston 85, B. Richards 83; J. N. Graham three for 70); Kent 2nd XI 100 (H. J. Tayfield three for 42). Won by 150 runs.

At Cranbrook, July 14. Peter West's XI 172 (J. C. Laker 36, R. M. C. Gilliat 34; D. Mackay-Coghill five for 28). Isaacs' XI 173 for three (M. Procter 62, B. Irvine 47). Won by seven wickets.

At St. Albans, July 15. Club Cricket Conference 160 for eight dec. (L. G. Studds 66, P. M. Cordoray 38; J. Cole three for 37); Isaacs' XI 111 for four (A. Bruyns 30). Drawn, rain.

At Eton, July 16. Oxford Harlequins 189 (A. C. Walton 45, G. N. S. Ridley 41*; N. A. T. Adcock three for 22); Isaacs' XI 192 for three (B. Richards 89*, K. J. Funston 39, C. Wesley 37). Won by seven wickets.

At Cardiff, July 17. P. M. Walker's XI 173 (38 overs) (P. M. Walker 37; D. J. McGlew six for 50); Isaacs' XI 174 for nine (32 overs) (M. Procter 51; D. J. Shepherd four for 40). Won by one wicket.

At Eastbourne, July 18, 19. Isaacs' XI 293 (B. Richards 74, M. Procter 68, D. Mackay-Coghill 65, J. Cole 52; R. Benaud five for 73) and 199 for two dec. (R. A. McLean 118); Colonel L. C. Stevens's XI 201 for four dec. (R. A. Gale 84, A. H. Phebey 51) and 210 for nine (R. A. Gale 92). Drawn.

At Arundel, July 20 Isaacs' XI 167 for five dec. (A. Bruyns 81*; J. Thwaites three for 38); Sussex Martlets 42 for two. Drawn, rain.

At Hove, July 21. v. Sussex 2nd XI. No play, rain.

At Roehampton, July 22. Isaacs' XI 166 (L. Irvine 73, M. Procter 41; J. Denman five for 46, P. Watts three for 62); M. R. Ricketts' XI 100 for 8 (D. J. McGlew four for 15). Drawn.

At Stoke Green, July 23. Parasites 156 (J. C. Laker 39; H. J. Tayfield five for 50, G. Watson four for 32); Isaacs' XI 157 for three (R. A. McLean 62*, M. Procter 31). Won by seven wickets.

At Woolwich, July 24. Cambridge Quidnuncs 200 for eight dec. (J. M. Brearley 118; D. Carr four for 52); Isaacs' XI 28 for one. Drawn, rain.

At Leatherhead, July 25. Isaacs' XI 225 for five dec. (A. Bruyns 101, L. Irvine 62; J. F. Russell four for 59); Old Johnians 154 (S. Vallins 33; J. Cole three for 23, G. Hall three for 24, H. J. Tayfield three for 37). Won by 71 runs.

DE FLAMINGO'S TOUR, 1966

Although the tour was only moderately successful judged by results, it augured well for the future of Dutch cricket. The team acquitted themselves well and proved up to the standard of the best of English club sides. Their most attractive attribute was the batting, van Schouwenburg proved an accomplished opener and C. Bakker and Spits displayed a wide range of strokes; the former drove with great power and the latter was a splendid cutter of the ball. Spits was also the pick of a moderate set of bowlers and was unafraid to buy his wickets with wrist spin. Against the Privateers he performed the hat-trick and in his next over took two more wickets. The fielding was patchy and several important catches were missed but Mulder kept wicket most efficiently. Off the field the team made friends wherever they went and were worthy ambassadors of their country.

RESULTS

At Burton Court, August 8. De Flamingo's 214 (N. Spits 68, C. van Schouwenburg 55); Household Brigade 99 for nine (N. Spits seven for 35). Drawn.

At Winchester, August 9. De Flamingo's 83 for one (C. van Schouwenburg 72*) v. Old Wykehamists. Drawn (rain).

At Trinity College, Oxford, August 10. Oxford University XI 197 for seven dec. (A. A. K. Abbasi 51; N. Spits four for 74); De Flamingo's 126 for six. Drawn.

At Burton Court, August 12. De Flamingo's 159 (G. R. V. Robins five for 35, A. R. B. Neame four for 43); Arabs 160 for five (12-a-side). Arabs won by 5 wickets.

At Hurlingham, August 13, 14. De Flamingo's 229 for nine dec. (J. P. Leemhuis 50; P. A. Simpkins four for 77) and 166 (R. Heydeman 55*; D. S. Perrett four for 43); Free Foresters 235 for six dec. (A. L. Thackara 81; N. Spits four for 96) and 164 for five. Free Foresters won by five wickets.

At Buckhurst Park, Eton, August 15. De Flamingo's 276 for nine dec. (C. R. P. Bakker 70, N. B. Spits 71); Eton Ramblers 101 (H. A. Wijkhuizen six for 32). De Flamingo's won by 175 runs.

At Lord's, August 17. De Flamingo's 194 (A. Bakker 77); M.C.C. 198 for five (I. C. MacLaurin 53). M.C.C. won by five wickets.

At Amersham, August 18. De Flamingo's 185 for nine dec. (C. van Schouwenburg 88; L. J. Champniss seven for 54); Privateers 139 (N. B. Spits seven for 61, incl. hat trick). De Flamingo's won by 46 runs.

At Hampstead, August 19. De Flamingo's 179 for eight dec. Hampstead C.C. 180 for five (G. Goonesena 61). Hampstead won by five wickets.

R. P. C. Morgan.

M.C.C. TEAM IN AUSTRALIA AND NEW ZEALAND, 1965–66

By E. M. Wellings

M.C.C. had two objectives when they began their tour of Australia in October 1965. The winning of the Ashes is the ostensible purpose of all such tours. The other objective, which many considered more important, was, by playing with aggressive enterprise, to correct the impression left by the previous two M.C.C. teams that Englishmen now play their cricket only negatively on the defensive. Four months later, when their venture ended, they could claim a considerable measure of success. Had it ended three weeks earlier the impression left behind them would have been even more favourable. And, incidentally, the Test series would have been won. The final three matches, including two Tests, were not so satisfying. By then, however, the team led by M. J. K. Smith and managed by S. C. Griffith with the assistance of J. T. Ikin had done enough to persuade Australians that the spirit of adventure still flickers in the English.

Smith and his followers were indeed widely acclaimed as an enterprising side. Only one other post-war M.C.C. side, that of 1954–55, enjoyed such respectful kindness from the Australian Press. They established their reputation by their batting. Barber, the number one, played exclusively attacking cricket from start to finish and his 185 off only 255 balls in the Sydney Test was the superlative achievement of the whole tour. When he succeeded, the runs gushed like oil from a new strike. Even when he was out early, the policy was based on taking the initiative by going for scoring strokes. Even batsmen with reputations for treating big occasions with solemnity, notably Boycott and Barrington, played Test innings of splendid dash. Perhaps the players were fortunate to be able to form the desired impression almost entirely by their batting.

In the field Smith continued to be a cautious captain; his policy was based on defensive measures, which played on the patience of his opponents. Australian batsmen were occasionally blamed for slow play, when the root cause was the negative out-cricket of the Englishmen. Smith's great virtue lay in his ability as a tour leader to take the players along with him. He had no tricks of leadership—in the modern idiom no gimmicks. He was in fact somewhat self-effacing. Yet he had a flair for leading and binding a team together. This was not perhaps quite so apparent right to the end of the venture as it had been during the previous two winters, when he led M.C.C. in India and South Africa. Towards the end his leadership was flagging, and his cricketing form was expended.

Smith in Australia had more than a team to lead. Shortly

before Christmas he was joined by his wife and two small children. He had to think about them as well as his team and escort them round the country. Skippering on tour is a job on its own big enough for anyone. The addition of the cares of a family in a strange country, which Smith himself had not previously visited, is a crippling additional burden. Wide experience of touring during the past twenty years has firmly persuaded me that wives accompanying cricketers are a liability, however well they behave and aim to keep themselves in the background, as those in Australia did on this occasion. The husbands cannot leave them to fend for themselves. They must accordingly be a distraction to the cricketers. In the case of the skipper, whose responsibilities are greater, the distraction is more serious.

That the last three matches of the tour were something of an anti-climax was in part due to the fact that the captain was a spent force. His inspiration was obviously much less than during the period in which the reputation for playing enterprising cricket was being formed. Another, and more potent, reason was the unbalanced programme, which was cluttered with minor games between the third and fourth Tests. M.C.C. prepared for the fourth Test by playing a Country XI at Newcastle, Tasmania at Launceston and Tasmania plus three batsmen from the mainland in Hobart. For a fortnight the touring side was opposed by teams not good enough to keep them up to the mark. In the Test in Adelaide they were a side unwound, and the proud victors of the third Test lurched to an overwhelming defeat. Their blunted form on this occasion was not entirely unexpected. At the end of the year they suffered the unwinding process during a week spent toying with four Up-Country sides. They then spent the better part of their four-day game against South Australia re-conditioning themselves to first-class cricket before going into the second Test.

On this tour Griffith was more than manager. In effect M.C.C. appointed him Tour Overlord. He could have dictated to the captain. He was given wide powers because M.C.C. were determined that their representatives should play the right sort of cricket. In fact Griffith did not use his powers. He is not the sort of which dictators are made. He is, however, a very good persuader, backed by qualities of charm and tact. In that way he was able to have his way—the M.C.C. way—with this team. That he persuaded even stolid defensive batsmen that attack could be the best means of defence was, perhaps, the greatest of his successes on tour. And those successes were many and varied, for he was a sterling manager. He and Ikin closely studied the scoring rates of the batsmen, measured in runs per 100 balls, and also the over rates of the bowlers. When the side was in the field his influence was more remote. Hence this side fielding was not nearly so enterprising as it was while batting.

On one score—one that is vital to the health of the game—Smith must be roundly condemned. He did little, if anything, to stir dawdling bowlers and fielders to maintain a satisfactory over rate. In only one first-class match—the first against New South Wales—did this reach the bare minimum of satisfaction, 120 balls an hour. Its nearest approach subsequently was between 116 and 117 in the first Test. From that point it declined almost unchecked until in the final Test Smith and his accompanying dawdlers averaged only 96 balls an hour. In the fifteen first-class games the touring side's overall average was between 108 and 109 balls against just over 113 by their opponents. The men who wasted most time were Brown and Jones. On the third day of that final Test they managed only 71 and 77 balls an hour in two spells of bowling in partnership. Cricket cannot flow and maintain interest unless the tempo is brisk. Hence the slow tempo of this side must be regarded as a serious failure on the part of the captain.

Five of the fifteen first-class matches were won, two lost and eight left drawn. All but one of the definite results occurred during the first ten games. Two of the five Tests suffered the loss of a day or more, when rain fell. Draws on such occasions are almost inevitable, for the total covering of pitches eliminates sticky conditions which formerly allowed the bowlers to make up for lost time. Each side won once. In the other, the second of the series in Melbourne, England allowed a winning position to slip from their grasp. The Ashes, in fact, should have been regained, but such a result would have been an injustice to the Australians. Their one Test win was clear cut in Adelaide, where the playing conditions played no part in the result. England's success in Sydney was determined by the winning of the toss and first use of the pitch, which became more and more favourable to bowlers as the match progressed.

When the team was chosen, the batting was expected to be strong enough, and so it proved. The fears expressed concerned the bowling. A period of good fast bowling in English cricket had ended, and successors to Statham, Tyson and Trueman were far from obvious. England also suffered from a dearth of spin bowlers, quite simply because they had too long been discouraged in county cricket. Titmus and Allen, the off spinners, were the only two regular slow bowlers in the side. The advance hope was that Barber's fine natural ability as a leg spinner would be developed. If any Australian State captain had taken over the handling of this M.C.C. side in the field, the story of the tour would have been very different. All Australians recognised the potential of Barber's spin. They would have built up his confidence by using him regularly as a first line attacking bowler and, by keeping him hard at work in the middle, would have turned him into a considerable asset in the Tests. Smith merely pecked at the job, and Barber continued to be regarded as a luxury for occasional use at a probable high cost.

Bowling

	Overs	Maidens	Runs	Wickets	Average
D. R. Owen-Thomas	196.3	48	554	38	14.57
C. C. A. Zweigbergk	110.2	33	275	18	15.27
S. Reed	158.3	58	406	26	15.61
B. W. J. Kingston	47.4	12	161	10	16.10
S. C. Buchanan	76.7	17	210	12	17.50
W. G. Garbis	87	13	312	14	22.28

KING'S SCHOOL, BRUTON

Played 13, *Won* 4, *Lost* 4, *Drawn* 5

Batting

	Innings	Not outs	Runs	Highest inns.	Average
A. R. Nichols	14	2	376	55	31.33
G. O'Grady	14	2	314	59*	26.16
C. A. Beaman	8	0	189	60	23.62
C. A. Tilley	11	2	147	33	16.33
M. R. Carr	13	3	124	33	12.40
†F. N. Myatt	13	0	132	25	10.15

Bowling

	Overs	Maidens	Runs	Wickets	Average
C. A. Tilley	195	59	410	48	8.54
G. Pursey	93.5	28	162	18	9.00
A. W. Nichols	114.1	19	306	19	16.10

KING'S SCHOOL, CANTERBURY

Played 15, *Won* 3, *Lost* 7, *Drawn* 5

Batting

	Innings	Not outs	Runs	Highest inns.	Average
C. C. N. Bridge	11	1	299	64	29.90
†J. R. Kilbee	16	0	290	55	18.12
J. D. W. Wright	16	1	233	29	15.53
M. J. Gray	16	0	247	34	15.43
R. G. S. Draycott	11	0	161	49	14.63
J. R. Wilson	15	2	166	38	12.76
A. R. Amlot	9	1	101	28*	12.62
G. K. Jaggers	15	0	175	42	11.66

Bowling

	Overs	Maidens	Runs	Wickets	Average
J. D. W. Wright	185.1	42	510	36	14.16
J. Frankland	74.4	22	205	14	16.64
C. J. C. Rowe	161.3	24	478	25	19.12
J. R. Kilbee	120.3	28	311	16	19.43
M. J. Gray	121.4	26	357	16	22.31

KING'S SCHOOL, ELY

Played 13, *Won* 2, *Lost* 7, *Drawn* 4, *Abandoned* 1

Batting

	Innings	Not outs	Runs	Highest inns.	Average
D. N. Perrin	12	2	319	80*	31.90
†M. E. P. Yeend	13	1	305	84	25.41
P. L. Anderton	11	2	167	52*	18.55

Bowling

	Overs	Maidens	Runs	Wickets	Average
†M. E. P. Yeend	179.3	37	468	46	10.17
I. D. Pountain	170.3	30	501	21	23.85

Without him the side was short of penetrative bowling, except on those rare occasions when conditions suited Allen and Titmus.

Unfortunately Titmus was much less effective in the big matches than he had been three years earlier in Australia. As the tour progressed, and as he made more and more runs, for he had a splendid batting season, his bowling became more and more defensive, his trajectory flatter and flatter. Allen was the better attacking spinner, but as he was always regarded as number two to Titmus, against most of the evidence, he was not handled to the best advantage. This was most noticeable in the second Test in Melbourne. On the first day he bowled effectively from the Southern end and dismissed both Simpson and Lawry. After that successful spell he did not again bowl from that end in the match. Titmus was given the Southern end and finished the match with nought for 136.

Four pace bowlers were in the original side. One of them, Larter, was a passenger for most of the venture. When he suffered a bruise or a muscular strain, he spent an unconscionable time recovering. When he was in action, his bowling was short of resolution and purpose. Brown was also injury prone, and, when both these players were laid up just before the first Test, Knight was summoned from England to reinforce the team. It was a pity he was not an original choice, for he was a valuable all-rounder, who played some stirring innings and bowled so usefully that he played in two Tests. Brown and Jones, the left-hander, became the opening pair, and both improved during the season. Jones was the more successful in the Tests, but the eagerness and greater fire of Brown impressed me more. Indeed, at the end of the tour I was still not convinced that Jones was a Test class bowler. Nevertheless he improved and managed to correct his habit of following through close to the line of the stumps. During the first match against New South Wales he was frequently warned about this by the umpires and finally barred from bowling again in the innings by R. Burgess.

That was one of the few controversial events of the tour. Some condemned the umpire as being overzealous and officious. I considered his action was entirely justified, and believe he did Jones a good turn. The gash made by Jones in his follow through was some five feet in front of the batting crease and menacingly close to the line of the off-stump for bowlers at the other end. Justification for the action of Burgess could be found in those balls that subsequently landed in the offending footmarks. When Allen on one occasion provided a stumping chance, the ball pitched there, kicked and, entirely eluding Parks' gloves, went through to score byes.

The fourth pace bowler was Higgs, one of the two unlucky members of the party. He was an automatic choice for the Test side until he was laid low with the stomach complaint, which combined with muscular ailments to make the manager's lot unhappy during the first half of the season. That cost him his place in the second Test. That he never regained it was unfortunate. Higgs bowled admirably after recovering from a shaky start in Perth, and it was noticeable that the off spinners invariably seemed to bowl better when he was nagging away accurately at the other end. He would always have been in the side if I had chosen it. So would Russell, the other unlucky tourist. Russell played the most attractively polished cricket of anyone in Australia. Conditions there suited his smooth, straight-bat style perfectly. His leg glancing and off driving during his lengthy innings will surely be remembered when most other details of the season's play have been forgotten. He also lost his Test place unfortunately, when he twice suffered hand injuries in Brisbane, the second while playing in the first Test.

Russell's misfortune was good luck for Boycott and Edrich. The former had the unexpected opportunity of opening in that first Test, and he retained his position as Barber's partner throughout the series. Edrich slipped into the number three position, unchallenged when Russell was still out of the reckoning for the second Test. Boycott prospered in the first three Tests, helped early in both the second and third by badly missed catches off McKenzie. In the last two he fell away sadly. Boycott was not really the right partner for Barber, the brilliant go-getter who should have been given as much of the bowling as possible. Instead, Boycott liked to take more than a half share, whether he was batting well or badly. In the fifth Test, when his form was emphatically bad, he played 60 of the first 80 balls bowled. He scored only 15 out of 33 off them, thus giving the innings a pottering start. Then in the following over he called for a ridiculous run off the last ball, which would give him the bowling again, and ran out Barber.

Edrich was carried through by his splendid determination and temperament. When Barber and Boycott mastered the Australian bowling, he thumped home the advantage and thus scored two successive Test centuries. When they did not, he was in a tangle, but battled on and invariably sold his wicket dearly. Seldom can a batsman have played and missed so often, have so often threatened to get out and yet scored so well in Australia. Barrington, as usual, was a wonderfully reliable batsman on tour, no less so when he was persuaded to parade his scoring power, which he is usually at pains to conceal. His 115 in the fifth Test was an innings of fine dash and splendour, and again he finished at the top of the Test averages. Cowdrey was his usual contradictory self. He accomplished quite a lot, thriving conspicuously in Melbourne, where he has scored most of his centuries against Australia, but again not accomplishing all that his talents promise.

Another batsman ideally suited by Australian conditions was Parks. He batted so well and so aggressively that he was worth selection for the Tests as a specialist batsman, and it was mistaken policy to leave him as low as number seven throughout the series. He saved the side in the first Test and came off with the bat in each subsequent one except the third. The pity was that he was also required to keep wicket throughout, though Murray was so obviously his superior. His blunder in missing a simple off-side chance of stumping Burge off Barber in the second innings almost certainly cost England the second Test and with it the Ashes. It was unfortunate that one of the main tour successes should be thus so crucially at fault. The blame rather should rest with selectors who would not appreciate that bowlers deserve the best possible wicket-keeper irrespective of any other consideration.

Smith himself played fine cricket during the first half of the tour, and in a side that outfielded even the Australians, before the decline in the final two Tests, his catching at short leg was outstanding. Unfortunately his period of fine form virtually came to an end when the Test series began, and he did little in the big matches. In that his experience was similar to that of several famous English captains in Australia, including D. R. Jardine in 1932–33, W. R. Hammond in 1946–47 and L. Hutton in 1954–55. Nevertheless he set a fine example in the early matches, from which his team in general benefited. The final batsman was Parfitt, who for a second time failed to reproduce his true form in Australia. His fielding, however, was unimpaired, and he was the automatic twelfth man for all Tests. Subsequently, he recouped his batting losses during the subsidiary part of the venture in New Zealand.

Australia's side was not one of their strongest. They also suffered from a bowling shortage. Hawke was always a persistent attacker, and after falling out of favour McKenzie turned in a match-winning performance in Adelaide to re-establish himself. Both these key bowlers missed one Test, for Australia also were troubled by injuries. And they had no adequate substitutes for these two. Nor was their spin bowling even passable, for Philpott, the first choice leg spinner, lost his form, the left-handed Sincock was much too erratic, and Stackpole, who finally displaced them, was merely steady. Moreover, the off spin of Veivers was never menacing. The Australian batting, reinforced by Walters, one of the finest young prospects in world cricket, was very powerful. Lawry failed only once, and Simpson scored heavily after recovering from injury, which deprived him of most of the first half of the season. That Booth and Burge slipped back hardly mattered, for Cowper had come to the front, and Walters and Thomas, a superbly uninhibited stroke maker, were ripe for promotion. At nineteen Walters was a remarkably mature cricketer. He made a century in his first Test in Brisbane when four wickets had gone for 125, another in the second when he and Burge saved the match, and in the third he alone was able to fight long against Allen and Titmus on a turning pitch. His bowling also was useful enough for the selectors to dispense with a specialist third seamer.

The umpiring was of a high class, except briefly during the first State matches in Adelaide and Melbourne. In the Tests C. Egar and L. Rowan were a splendidly reliable pair. In all respects indeed the tour proceeded smoothly and pleasantly. There was talk of shortening it in future. That, I believe, would be a sad mistake. Tours involving England and Australia are the great events of cricket. If they are worth doing, they must be done thoroughly, without any skimping. That is not to say that the programme could not be improved, notably by starting the Tests earlier and spacing them out better, always ensuring that at least one genuinely first-class match is played between each of them. It could be improved also by reducing the up-country games to a maximum of three of one day's duration each. A team of first-class cricketers on tour deserves first-class opposition almost throughout. It is absurd to employ a pneumatic drill to pierce an almond. A tour of 16 first-class matches and three minor games would mean a tour of 18 weeks, and it should not be any shorter than that.

M.C.C. should also give some thought to travel. For the first time the team flew by fast jet aircraft all the way to Australia—and in the cramping discomfort of Economy class—and numerous players suffered stomach disorders and odd indispositions, which were grandly called virus diseases. Even the common cold was thus termed. The complaint was just the same but with a vital difference. Called a cold, it was too insignificant to keep a cricketer from playing. Described in high faluting fashion as a virus infection, it became grand enough to keep him out of action. Subsequently two other touring sides from Britain transported at high speed and great height to Australia, the Rugby Union and Rugby League teams, suffered in the same virulent way on arrival. It is a fair assumption that rapid transportation into different conditions is at least in part the cause of such maladies, which were not suffered when teams travelled more slowly by sea. In that event a further amendment to the tour travel arrangements seems necessary.

M.C.C. RESULTS IN AUSTRALIA

Test-Matches—Played 5; Won 1, Lost 1, Drawn 3.

First-class Matches—Played 15; Won 5, Lost 2, Drawn 8.

All Matches—Played 23; Won 13, Lost 2, Drawn 8, Abandoned 1.

Wins—Australia (one), Western Australia, South Australia, New South Wales, South Australia, Western Australia Country XI, Victoria Country XI, South Queensland Country XI, Prime Minister's XI, New South Wales Country XI, Southern N.S.W. Country XI, South Australia Country XI, Northern N.S.W. District XI.

Losses—Victoria, Australia (one).

Draws—Australia (three), Combined XI at Perth, Queensland, Tasmania, Combined XI at Hobart, New South Wales.

Abandoned—Victoria Country XI.

M.C.C. began with two one-day matches in Ceylon and after visiting Australia played four first-class matches in New Zealand including three Tests, finishing with two one-day games in Hong Kong.

ENGLAND BATTING AVERAGES IN THE TESTS AGAINST AUSTRALIA

	Matches	Inns.	Not Outs	Runs	Highest Inns.	Average
K. F. Barrington.......	5	8	1	464	115	66.28
F. J. Titmus...........	5	6	2	258	60	64.50
M. C. Cowdrey........	4	6	1	267	104	53.40
J. M. Parks............	5	6	0	290	89	48.38
J. H. Edrich...........	5	8	0	375	109	46.87
G. Boycott.............	5	9	2	300	84	42.85
R. W. Barber..........	5	9	1	328	185	41.00
D. A. Allen............	4	5	2	62	50*	20.66
M. J. K. Smith.........	5	7	1	107	41	17.83
I. J. Jones.............	4	5	2	29	16	9.66
B. R. Knight...........	2	2	0	14	13	7.00
D. J. Brown............	4	5	0	17	12	3.40

Played in one match: K. Higgs 4; W. E. Russell 0*.

* *Signifies not out.*

ENGLAND BOWLING AVERAGES IN THE TESTS AGAINST AUSTRALIA

	Overs	Maidens	Runs	Wickets	Average
K. F. Barrington.......	7.4	0	47	2	23.50
B. R. Knight...........	83.7	10	250	8	31.25
I. J. Jones.............	129	15	533	15	35.53
D. J. Brown............	108	14	409	11	37.18
G. Boycott.............	23	4	89	2	44.50
D. A. Allen............	137	33	403	9	44.77
K. Higgs...............	30	6	102	2	51.00
F. J. Titmus...........	210.3	52	517	9	57.44
R. W. Barber..........	55.1	2	261	3	87.00

Also bowled: M. J. K. Smith, 2—0—8—0.

AUSTRALIAN BATTING AVERAGES IN THE TESTS

	Matches	Inns.	Not Outs	Runs	Highest Inns.	Average
R. B. Simpson.........	3	4	0	355	225	88.75
W. M. Lawry..........	5	7	0	592	166	84.57
R. M. Cowper.........	4	6	0	493	307	82.16
K. D. Walters..........	5	7	1	410	155	68.33
G. Thomas.............	3	4	0	147	52	36.75
P. J. Burge............	4	6	0	159	120	26.50
K. R. Stackpole........	2	2	0	52	43	26.00
T. R. Veivers..........	4	5	1	83	56*	20.75
I. M. Chappell.........	2	2	0	36	19	18.00
B. C. Booth............	3	5	0	84	27	16.80
N. J. N. Hawke........	4	5	3	28	20*	14.00
G. D. McKenzie.......	4	5	1	51	24	12.75
P. I. Philpott...........	3	4	1	22	10	7.33
A. T. W. Grout........	5	5	0	34	16	6.80

Played in one match: A. N. Connolly 0 and 0*; I. R. Redpath 17; D. J. Sincock 29 and 27; P. J. Allan did not bat.

* *Signifies not out.*

AUSTRALIAN BOWLING AVERAGES IN THE TESTS

	Overs	Maidens	Runs	Wickets	Average
N. J. N. Hawke	142.7	29	419	16	26.18
G. D. McKenzie	133.4	20	467	16	29.18
K. D. Walters	79	8	283	9	31.44
R. M. Cowper	22	5	76	2	38.00
P. J. Allan	24	6	83	2	41.50
P. I. Philpott	100.1	9	371	8	46.37
K. R. Stackpole	32	5	116	2	58.00
T. R. Veivers	66.7	11	250	4	62.60
A. N. Connolly	38	5	128	1	128.00
I. M. Chappell	45	7	143	1	143.00

Also Bowled: R. B. Simpson 21—5—81—0; D. J. Sincock 20—1—98—0.

M.C.C. TEAM FIRST-CLASS BATTING AVERAGES IN AUSTRALIA

	Matches	Inns.	Not Outs	Runs	Highest Inns.	Average
K. F. Barrington	11	17	3	946	158	67.57
F. J. Titmus	10	12	4	528	80*	66.00
J. M. Parks	9	13	3	652	107*	65.20
W. E. Russell	8	14	4	580	110	58.00
B. R. Knight	6	9	2	370	94	52.85
M. C. Cowdrey	12	20	4	834	108	52.12
R. W. Barber	13	22	2	1,001	185	50.05
J. H. Edrich	12	21	1	977	133	48.85
G. Boycott	10	17	2	720	156	48.00
M. J. K. Smith	13	22	5	792	112*	46.58
J. T. Murray	7	10	1	255	110	28.33
D. A. Allen	11	12	5	181	54*	25.85
P. H. Parfitt	8	15	1	307	87	21.92
D. J. Brown	9	11	1	113	27	11.30
K. Higgs	10	7	4	30	12*	10.00
I. J. Jones	11	8	2	30	16	5.00
J. D. F. Larter	5	3	0	7	4	2.33

* *Signifies not out.*

M.C.C. TEAM FIRST-CLASS BOWLING AVERAGES IN AUSTRALIA

	Overs	Maidens	Runs	Wickets	Average
K. F. Barrington	32.4	1	149	6	24.83
F. J. Titmus	420.3	90	1,109	36	30.80
D. J. Brown	221	35	900	29	31.03
J. D. F. Larter	99.2	12	411	12	34.25
I. J. Jones	294.6	34	1,231	34	36.20
B. R. Knight	151.7	17	512	14	36.57
D. A. Allen	374.7	89	1,077	29	37.13
K. Higgs	279.3	28	980	24	40.83
G. Boycott	45	6	214	3	71.33
P. H. Parfitt	48.2	5	217	3	72.33
R. W. Barber	176.1	8	873	10	87.30

Also bowled: W. E. Russell 4—0—16—0; M. J. K. Smith 3—0—9—0; J. T. Murray 3—0—19—0; M. C. Cowdrey 1—0—7—0.

ENGLAND BATTING AVERAGES IN THE TESTS AGAINST NEW ZEALAND

	Matches	Inns.	Not Outs	Runs	Highest Inns.	Average
J. M. Parks	2	4	2	117	45*	58.50
D. A. Allen	3	3	1	104	88	52.00
M. C. Cowdrey	3	5	1	196	89*	49.00
M. J. K. Smith	3	5	0	209	87	41.80
P. H. Parfitt	3	5	1	137	54	34.25
B. R. Knight	2	3	1	50	25	25.00
W. E. Russell	3	5	0	123	56	24.60
D. J. Brown	2	2	0	44	44	22.00
J. H. Edrich	3	3	0	40	36	13.33
K. Higgs	3	3	2	8	8*	8.00
G. Boycott	2	2	0	13	5	4.33
I. J. Jones	3	2	0	0	0	0.00

Also batted: J. T. Murray 50.

* *Signifies not out.*

ENGLAND BOWLING AVERAGES IN THE TESTS AGAINST NEW ZEALAND

	Overs	Maidens	Runs	Wickets	Average
K. Higgs	128	50	157	17	9.34
I. J. Jones	122.3	40	242	14	17.29
P. H. Parfitt	28	9	58	3	19.33
D. J. Brown	61	14	126	6	21.00
D. A. Allen	190.5	72	359	13	27.62
B. R. Knight	69	32	105	3	33.00

Also bowled: G. Boycott 12—6—30—0; J. M. Parks 3—1—8—0; J. H. Edrich 1—0—6—0.

NEW ZEALAND BATTING AVERAGES IN THE TESTS

	Matches	Inns.	Not Outs	Runs	Highest Inns.	Average
B. W. Sinclair	3	6	0	218	114	36.33
B. E. Congdon	3	6	0	214	104	35.67
R. C. Motz	3	6	0	148	58	24.67
E. C. Petrie	3	6	1	115	55	23.00
R. S. Cunis	3	6	3	55	16*	18.33
N. Puna	3	5	3	31	18*	15.50
G. P. Bilby	2	4	0	55	28	13.75
M. J. F. Shrimpton	3	6	0	68	38	11.33
R. W. Morgan	2	4	0	33	25	8.25
G. A. Bartlett	2	4	0	10	6	2.50

Also batted: M. E. Chapple 15 and 0; T. W. Jarvis 39 and 0; B. R. Taylor 18 and 6.

* *Signifies not out.*

NEW ZEALAND BOWLING AVERAGES IN THE TESTS

	Overs	Maidens	Runs	Wickets	Average
B. R. Taylor	33	10	66	5	13.20
V. Pollard	25	6	61	4	15.25
M. E. Chapple	9	3	24	1	24.00
G. A. Bartlett	76.2	12	177	6	29.50
R. S. Cunis	121.5	32	248	7	35.43
R. C. Motz	114	27	271	7	38.71
N. Puna	80	20	240	4	60.00

M.C.C. TEAM BATTING AVERAGES—FIRST-CLASS MATCHES IN AUSTRALIA AND NEW ZEALAND

BATTING

	Matches	Innings	Not Outs	Runs	Highest Inns.	Average
K. F. Barrington	11	17	3	946	158	67.57
F. J. Titmus	10	12	4	528	80*	66.00
J. M. Parks	12	18	6	771	107*	64.25
M. C. Cowdrey	16	26	6	1,076	108	53.80
R. W. Barber	13	22	2	1,001	185	50.05
M. J. K. Smith	17	28	5	1,079	112*	46.91
W. E. Russell	12	20	4	709	110	44.31
J. H. Edrich	16	25	1	1,060	133	44.16
B. R. Knight	9	13	3	426	94	42.60
G. Boycott	13	21	2	784	156	41.26
D. A. Allen	15	15	6	285	88	31.66
J. T. Murray	9	11	1	305	110	30.50
P. H. Parfitt	12	21	2	565	121	29.73
D. J. Brown	11	13	1	157	44	13.08
K. Higgs	14	10	6	38	12*	9.50
I. J. Jones	14	10	2	30	16	3.75
J. D. F. Larter	5	3	0	7	4	2.33

* *Signifies not out.*

BOWLING

	Balls	Maidens	Runs	Wickets	Average
K. F. Barrington	260	1	149	6	24.83
K. Higgs	3,279	100	1,214	44	27.39
D. J. Brown	2,134	49	1,026	35	29.31
I. J. Jones	3,093	74	1,473	48	30.68
F. J. Titmus	3,363	90	1,109	36	30.81
D. A. Allen	4,546	186	1,594	47	33.91
J. D. F. Larter	794	12	411	12	34.25
B. R. Knight	1,728	55	658	19	34.63
P. H. Parfitt	662	20	325	7	46.43
R. W. Barber	1,409	8	873	10	87.30

Also bowled: G. Boycott 594—25—285—4; M. C. Cowdrey 8—0—7—0; J. H. Edrich 6—0—6—0; J. T. Murray 24—0—19—0; J. M. Parks 48—4—17—1: W. E. Russell 56—1—36—3; M. J. K. Smith 24—0—9—0.

Note: *Eight balls were bowled to the over in Australia and six to the over in New Zealand.*

M.C.C. FIELDING IN FIRST-CLASS MATCHES

J. M. Parks 38 (32 ct, 6 st); M. J. K. Smith 27; J. T. Murray 20 (17 ct, 3 st); M. C. Cowdrey, P. H. Parfitt 12; K. F. Barrington, R. W. Barber 10; D. A. Allen 9; W. E. Russell 8; F. J. Titmus 7; J. H. Edrich, B. R. Knight, G. Boycott 6; K. Higgs 5; I. J. Jones, J. D. F. Larter 4; D. J. Brown 1; sub. 2 (Titmus, Boycott).

HUNDREDS FOR ENGLAND AND M.C.C.

The following twenty-four three-figure innings were played for M.C.C.:

R. W. Barber (3):
185 v. Australia at Sydney (Third Test).
126 v. Western Australia at Perth.
113 v Combined XI at Perth.

K. F. Barrington (3):
158 v. Victoria at Melbourne.
115 v. Australia at Melbourne (Fifth Test).
102 v. Australia at Melbourne (Fourth Test).

J. H. Edrich (3):
133 v. Queensland at Brisbane.
109 v. Australia at Melbourne (Second Test).
103 v. Australia at Sydney (Third Test).

M. J. K. Smith (3):
164 v. Country Districts at Newcastle.†
112* v. Combined XI at Perth.
108 v. South Australia at Adelaide.

M. C. Cowdrey (2):
108 v. Tasmania at Launceston.
104 v. Australia at Melbourne (Second Test).

W. E. Russell (2):
110 v. Queensland at Brisbane.
101* v. New South Wales at Sydney.

G. Boycott (1):
156 v. Combined XI at Hobart.

J. T. Murray (1):
110 v. South Australia at Adelaide.

P. H. Parfitt (1):
121 v. President's XI at Wellington.

J. M. Parks (1):
107* v. Western Australia at Perth.

F. J. Titmus (1):
114 v. Country Districts at Newcastle.†

* *Signifies not out.* † *Not first-class.*

HUNDREDS AGAINST ENGLAND AND M.C.C.

The following twenty-five three-figure innings were played against M.C.C.:

W. M. Lawry (5):
166 for Australia at Brisbane (First Test).
153 for Victoria at Melbourne.
126* for Combined XI at Hobart.
119 for Australia at Adelaide (Fourth Test).
108 for Australia at Melbourne (Fifth Test).

R. M. Cowper (3):
307 for Australia at Melbourne (Fifth Test).
143* for Combined XI at Hobart.
122* for Combined XI at Perth.

K. D. Walters (3):
155 for Australia at Brisbane (First Test).
129 for New South Wales at Sydney.
115 for Australia at Melbourne (Second Test).

P. J. Burge (2):
120 for Australia at Melbourne (Second Test).
114* for Queensland at Brisbane.

P. C. Kelly (2):
119 }
108* } for Western Australia at Perth.

* *Signifies not out.*

R. B. Simpson (2):
225 for Australia at Adelaide (Fourth Test).
123 for New South Wales at Sydney.

C. Baker (1):
101 for Country Districts at Newcastle.†

I. M. Chappell (1):
113* for South Australia at Adelaide.

B. E. Congdon (1):
104 for New Zealand at Christchurch (First Test).

B. Richardson (1):
112 for Tasmania at Launceston.

A. B. Shiell (1):
202* for South Australia at Adelaide.

B. W. Sinclair (1):
114 for New Zealand at Auckland (Third Test).

G. Thomas (1):
129 for New South Wales at Sydney.

M. Vernon (1):
118 for Western Australia at Perth.

* *Signifies not out.* † *Not first-class.*

CEYLON C.A. PRESIDENT'S XI v. M.C.C.

At Colombo Oval, October 19. M.C.C. 198 for six dec. (R. W. Barber 64 not out, J. M. Parks 34, M. J. K. Smith 33; Abu Fuard four for 61); President's XI 156 for six (L. Fernando 40). Drawn.

CEYLON v. M.C.C.

At Colombo Oval, October 20. M.C.C. 127 (M. C. Cowdrey 47; N. Chanmugam five for 26, P. I. Peiris three for 40); Ceylon 77 for one (R. Reid 54 not out, Dr. B. Reid 16 not out). The brothers Reid put on 59 in their unbroken stand but rain ruined the finish. It was M.C.C.'s lowest score in Ceylon since 1891. Drawn.

WESTERN AUSTRALIA COUNTRY XI v. M.C.C.

At Moora, October 27. M.C.C. 232 for seven wickets declared (J. H. Edrich 66, J. M. Parks 48); Western Australia Country XI 150 (J. McCormack 64; R. W. Barber five for 64). M.C.C. won by 82 runs.

WESTERN AUSTRALIA v. M.C.C.

At Perth, October 29, 30, November 1, 2. M.C.C. won by nine runs. The touring team's most consistently aggressive batsmen hit the first two centuries. Barber, driving superbly, made his 126 out of 197 in 44 overs, with twelve 4's, and Parks, who hit one 6 and twelve 4's and drove handsomely over mid-off, needed only 35 overs for his 107. Though more restrained, Russell also played fluent cricket in a second-wicket stand of 106 with Barber, and after a quiet start Smith was confidently aggressive towards the end of an unfinished stand of 175 with Parks. Kelly, formerly of New South Wales, retorted with a century in each innings and altogether held up M.C.C. for nine and a half hours. Vernon, a left-hander with delightful attacking strokes, was another century maker in an attractive second innings of three and a quarter hours. Kelly retired hurt when 3, but he resumed at the fall of the third wicket and with Vernon put on 171. Western Australia then needed 77 in sixty-five minutes, but wickets fell as they pressed for runs, and M.C.C. rather fortunately gained a slender win on the point of time. The bowling on both sides was of moderate quality, but Jenner showed himself to be a leg-spinner of much promise.

M.C.C.

First innings		Second innings	
R. W. Barber c and b Jenner	126		
J. H. Edrich c Becker b Mayne	33	c Chadwick b Jenner	45
W. E. Russell c Becker b Mayne	81	b Mayne	1
P. H. Parfitt b Jenner	6	c Kelly b Jenner	48
M. C. Cowdrey c Lock b McKenzie	19	c Vernon b Jenner	1
*M. J. K. Smith not out	67	c Mayne b Jenner	1
†J. M. Parks not out	107	not out	37
D. A. Allen (did not bat)		not out	20
B 4, l-b 2, w 2	8	B 3	3
1/91 2/197 3/225 4/269 5/272 (5 wkts., dec.)	447	1/2 2/77 3/81 4/87 5/103 (5 wkts., dec.)	156

K. Higgs, I. J. Jones and J. D. F. Larter did not bat.

Bowling: *First Innings*—Mayne 24—1—105—2; McKenzie 21—2—88—1: Irvine 3—0—23—0; Lock 28—3—100—0; Jenner 26—4—107—2; Vernon 2—0—16—0. *Second Innings*—Mayne 7—1—33—1; McKenzie 13—1—34—0; Jenner 17—4—72—4; Lock 4—0—10—0; Kelly 1—0—4—0.

Western Australia

First innings		Second innings	
W. R. Playle b Allen	45	run out	14
P. C. Kelly c Parks b Jones	119	not out	108
M. Vernon c Parfitt b Barber	18	b Jones	118
*B. K. Shepherd run out	15	c and b Larter	11
G. D. McKenzie b Larter	25	c Smith b Higgs	11
D. Chadwick not out	52	c Parfitt b Larter	0
J. Irvine c Cowdrey b Jones	0	run out	0
†G. C. Becker c Higgs b Jones	18	c Higgs b Jones	6
T. Jenner c Parks b Jones	6	b Larter	0
G. A. R. Lock c sub b Jones	0	c Smith b Higgs	4
L. C. Mayne not out	0	c Parks b Larter	0
B 3, l-b 1, n-b 1	5	B 7, l-b 12	19
1/91 2/124 3/153 4/200 5/243 6/243 7/275 8/288 9/288 (9 wkts., dec.)	303	1/25 2/53 3/53 4/224 5/244 6/260 7/286 8/287 9/291	291

Bowling: *First Innings*—Larter 16—0—57—1; Higgs 17.2—2—61—0; Jones 19—3—59—5; Allen 37—7—80—1; Barber 12—2—32—1; Parfitt 2—0—9—0. *Second Innings*—Larter 11.3—2—49—4; Higgs 15—0—85—2; Allen 12—1—36—0; Jones 9—0—39—2; Barber 11—1—63—0.

Umpires: J. M. Meacham and N. Townsend.

COMBINED XI v. M.C.C.

At Perth, November 5, 6, 8, 9. Drawn. Rain cut nearly three hours from the playing time on the first two days, and not even three declarations could produce a definite result. The Combined team's gamble of sending in M.C.C. was an immediate failure, for in 20 overs Barber and Edrich, who batted more confidently in an innings lasting nearly three hours than in the first match, scored 74 for the first wicket. Subsequently, Smith, scoring more freely on the off side than usual, again batted finely for three hours, forty minutes. Titmus, his partner in a stand of 139, played the first of a series of robust innings. In one over Titmus drove Cowper to the off for three 4's. Combined XI, for whom Burge and Cowper batted soundly, declared as soon as they had avoided the follow-on, and Barber's second and still more aggressive century—113 off only 26 overs in one and three-quarter hours—

led to the third declaration. Again led by Cowper, who reached 100 inside two and a half hours, and Burge, the Combined XI scored so freely that, when Shepherd was fourth out at 248, they had eighty minutes in which to score 106. Two more lost wickets, however, put the brake on Cowper, and M.C.C. were not afterwards in danger. The batting on fast, true turf was again too good for the bowling. Higgs was not yet mastering his direction, and Jones was similarly erratic. Brown's energetic fast bowling was more encouraging.

M.C.C.

R. W. Barber run out	33	— c Shepherd b Lock	113
J. H. Edrich c Burge b Mayne	92	— c Shepherd b Jenner	10
P. H. Parfitt b McKenzie	0	— c Lock b McKenzie	24
K. F. Barrington c Vernon b Mayne	3		
M. C. Cowdrey c Lock b Mayne	31	— not out	24
*M. J. K. Smith not out	112	— b Mayne	24
†J. T. Murray lbw b Lock	5	— not out	8
F. J. Titmus st Becker b Lock	69		
D. J. Brown not out	25		
B 3, l-b 3, n-b 3	9	B 2	2
1/74 2/75 3/83 4/137 5/169 6/199 7/338 (7 wkts., dec.)	379	1/50 2/145 3/149 4/195 (4 wkts., dec.)	205

K. Higgs and I. J. Jones did not bat.

Bowling: *First Innings*—Mayne 19—0—98—3; McKenzie 26—0—99—1; Inverarity 2—0—10—0; Lock 25—5—79—2; Jenner 14—3—54—0; Cowper 7—1—30—0. *Second Innings*—Mayne 5—0—21—1; McKenzie 15—1—48—1; Jenner 7—0—65—1; Lock 6—0—32—1; Cowper 6—0—37—0.

Combined XI

M. Vernon c Parfitt b Jones	31	— c Murray b Titmus	44
P. C. Kelly lbw b Brown	15	— c Smith b Jones	33
R. M. Cowper c Smith b Higgs	89	— not out	122
R. J. Inverarity c Barber b Brown	5	— run out	13
P. J. Burge c Barber b Titmus	52	— c Murray b Barber	50
*B. K. Shepherd not out	29	— b Brown	39
†G. C. Becker not out	8		
G. A. R. Lock (did not bat)		— c Barber b Titmus	8
T. Jenner (did not bat)		— not out	12
W 1, n-b 1	2	L-b 1	1
1/47 2/47 3/67 4/165 5/216 (5 wkts., dec.)	231	1/71 2/79 3/166 4/248 5/265 6/296 (6 wkts.)	322

G. D. McKenzie and L. C. Mayne did not bat.

Bowling: *First Innings*—Jones 11—0—50—1; Higgs 16.2—4—41—1; Brown 13—4—44—2; Barber 10—0—43—0; Titmus 18—5—44—1; Parfitt 3—2—7—0. *Second Innings*—Jones 8—3—19—1; Higgs 9—0—59—0; Brown 10—0—56—1; Titmus 21—1—94—2; Barber 10—0—60—1; Parfitt 4—0—32—0; Smith 1—0—1—0.

Umpires: J. M. Meacham and N. Townsend.

SOUTH AUSTRALIA v. M.C.C.

At Adelaide, November 12, 13, 15, 16. M.C.C. won by six wickets. Cowdrey put South Australia in first on a rain-affected pitch and M.C.C. dismissed them in two and a half hours. Allen, who took three for 15 in his first four overs, and Brown secured the first six wickets before lunch for 86 and Larter skittled the tail. In improved conditions M.C.C. scored briskly, Boycott and Edrich making 116 together in 22 overs. Edrich hit his 61 in eighty-nine minutes. In his first match

Boycott, who fell ill with stomach trouble in Ceylon on the outward journey, batted with refreshing enterprise for two and three-quarter hours and hit ten 4's. Barrington more quietly also found his form. In the second innings Favell played magnificent attacking cricket. He made 96 with thirteen 4's from strokes all round the wicket during an opening stand of 150 with Marks, who stayed nearly three and a half hours. Shiell, a youngster in his second season of State cricket, played with exceptional promise for just on three and three-quarter hours. His fifth-wicket stand with Jarman added 94. Brown's bowling was again lively, and Higgs, who had tended to bowl down the leg side in Perth, regained his accuracy. In the final innings M.C.C. hit off the runs in 36 overs, Barrington making his sparkling 51 in less than an hour.

South Australia

*L. E. Favell c Parfitt b Allen	9	— b Higgs	96
L. Marks st Parks b Allen	30	— b Larter	67
I. M. Chappell b Brown	1	— lbw b Brown	0
D. Sharpe c Edrich b Allen	5	— b Brown	10
†B. N. Jarman c Parks b Brown	4	— b Higgs	61
A. B. Shiell b Larter	16	— b Brown	83
N. J. N. Hawke c Larter b Brown	14	— c Barrington b Brown	0
G. Griffiths not out	13	— lbw b Higgs	2
D. J. Sincock c Barrington b Allen	4	— c Barrington b Larter	9
B. Hurn c Parfitt b Larter	0	— not out	24
D. Robins b Larter	4	— c Parks b Higgs	6
B 3	3	L-b 5, n-b 1	6
1/25 2/26 3/39 4/38 5/52 6/66 7/88 8/99 9/99	103	1/150 2/159 3/171 4/194 5/288 6/291 7/298 8/315 9/350	364

Bowling: *First Innings*—Larter 8.7—2—29—3; Higgs 3—0—12—0; Allen 11—3—24—4; Brown 6—2—35—3. *Second Innings*—Larter 18—1—104—2; Brown 24—5—82—4; Higgs 29.7—3—99—4; Allen 18—5—51—0; Barrington 3—0—22—0.

M.C.C.

G. Boycott c Robins b Sincock	94		
J. H. Edrich c Hurn b Sincock	61	— c and b Sincock	29
W. E. Russell st Jarman b Sincock	3	— lbw b Hawke	11
P. H. Parfitt c Sharpe b Sincock	1	— b Hawke	27
K. F. Barrington c Jarman b Hawke	69	— c Robins b Sincock	51
*M. C. Cowdrey lbw b Hawke	11	— not out	30
†J. M. Parks c Marks b Sincock	2	— not out	4
D. A. Allen c Sharpe b Robins	31		
D. J. Brown run out	27		
J. D. F. Larter b Hawke	2		
K. Higgs not out	0		
B 4, l-b 5	9	L-b 6	6
1/116 2/125 3/131 4/174 5/199 6/202 7/257 8/305 9/309	310	1/19 2/61 3/93 4/143 (4 wkts.)	158

Bowling: *First Innings*—Hawke 22.5—3—71—3; Robins 13—2—45—1; Griffiths 6—0—40—0; Sincock 23—2—113—5; Chappell 5—0—23—0; Hurn 4—0—9—0. *Second Innings*—Hawke 14—3—49—2; Robins 6—0—21—0; Sincock 12—0—67—2; Hurn 2—0—7—0; Favell 1.6—0—8—0.

Umpires: C. Egar and F. Godson.

VICTORIA COUNTRY DISTRICTS v. M.C.C.

At Hamilton, November 17. Victoria Country XI 167 for six wickets declared (J. Kerr 50 not out; R. W. Barber four for 21); M.C.C. 264 (J. M. Parks 75, W. E. Russell 50; McKenzie four for 44). M.C.C. won by six wickets.

VICTORIA v. M.C.C.

At Melbourne, November 19, 20, 22, 23. Victoria won by 32 runs. Lawry, who batted for seven and a quarter hours in the two innings, was the architect of Victoria's first win against a M.C.C. touring side since the war. In the first innings—four hours and fifty minutes with nine 4's—he took part in stands of 104 with Redpath, 65 with Stackpole and 51 with Anderson. When he was 100 he trod on his wicket while playing Titmus, but neither umpire saw the incident and he stayed to make 53 more. When seven wickets had gone for 262, four having tumbled in seventeen minutes, mainly to Brown, who at that stage had taken four for 40, Watson and D. L. Cowper, older brother of the Test player who was playing his first State match as wicket-keeper, shared an unfinished stand of 122 in two hours. M.C.C., with the exception of Smith, batted without distinction and were caught on the run by the accurate leg spin of Stackpole. Thanks to the spin of Titmus and Barrington, M.C.C. hit back and on the last day seemed to be heading for a win when Barrington, who put on 75 with Russell and 160 with Cowdrey, hit sixteen 4's in a commanding innings of 158 lasting just over five hours. When he was fifth out at 279, however, M.C.C. collapsed against the medium pace of Watson and the fast-medium of Connolly.

Victoria

*W. M. Lawry st Murray b Titmus	153	— c Murray b Titmus	61
I. R. Redpath c Cowdrey b Barber	53	— b Higgs	17
R. M. Cowper b Brown	2	— b Higgs	8
K. R. Stackpole c Murray b Higgs	23	— c Smith b Titmus	9
D. J. Anderson c Russell b Brown	25	— b Titmus	5
G. Watson not out	59	— c Cowdrey b Barrington	17
P. Williams lbw b Brown	2	— b Barrington	29
J. W. Grant b Brown	2	— c Murray b Titmus	4
†D. L. Cowper not out	60	— not out	9
A. N. Connolly (did not bat)		— c Jones b Barrington	1
R. W. Rayson (did not bat)		— st Murray b Barrington	1
L-b 3, n-b 2	5	B 4	4
1/104 2/109 3/174 4/225 (7 wkts., dec.) 5/258 6/260 7/262	384	1/55 2/89 3/99 4/102 5/111 6/131 7/142 8/160 9/162	165

Bowling: *First Innings*—Brown 15—2—77—4; Jones 17—2—78—0; Higgs 17—0—72—1; Titmus 31—4—77—1; Barber 13—0—66—1; Barrington 4—0—9—0. *Second Innings*—Brown 5—0—24—0; Jones 7—0—23—0; Higgs 13—1—40—2; Titmus 21—3—50—4; Barrington 7—1—24—4.

M.C.C.

R. W. Barber c Williams b Watson	28	— c Stackpole b Connolly	0
J. H. Edrich lbw b Stackpole	46	— c Redpath b Connolly	1
W.E. Russell c R. M. Cowper b Stackpole	19	— lbw b Stackpole	42
K. F. Barrington c D. L. Cowper b Stackpole	12	— c D. L. Cowper b Connolly	158
M. C. Cowdrey c Williams b Grant	14	— c Anderson b Watson	52
*M. J. K. Smith not out	46	— c Grant b Watson	22
†J. T. Murray c and b Stackpole	7	— b Watson	0
F. J. Titmus c and b R. M. Cowper	24	— lbw b Connolly	9
D. J. Brown c R. M. Cowper b Connolly	8	— run out	0
K. Higgs c R. M. Cowper b Connolly	0	— not out	8
I. J. Jones b Rayson	0	— run out	1
W 1, n-b 6	7	B 4, l-b 5, w 2, n-b 2	13
1/39 2/72 3/105 4/108 5/125 6/138 7/170 8/200 9/202	211	1/0 2/7 3/82 4/242 5/279 6/280 7/289 8/289 9/303	306

Bowling: *First Innings*—Connolly 11—3—38—2; Grant 10—1—46—1; Watson 5—0—23—1; Stackpole 20—4—64—4; Rayson 3.6—0—19—1; R. M. Cowper 3—0—14—1. *Second Innings*—Connolly 26—5—84—4; Grant 9—1—30—0; Stackpole 26—5—74—1; Rayson 13—1—57—0; R. M. Cowper 5—1—18—0; Anderson 1—0—6—0; Watson 11.1—2—24—3.

Umpires: W. Smyth and K. Collicoat.

VICTORIA COUNTRY DISTRICTS XI v. M.C.C.

At Euroa, November 24. Abandoned owing to rain.

NEW SOUTH WALES v. M.C.C.

At Sydney, November 26, 27, 29, 30. M.C.C. won by nine wickets. An innings of 527 for six in six hours, fifty minutes guaranteed a win for M.C.C. on the Sydney pitch, which for some years has helped spin bowlers in the later stages. The foundation of the M.C.C. total was a superb opening stand of 151 in an hour and forty-two minutes by Barber and Russell. Barber hit his 90 in that time off only 85 balls, an innings of magnificently weighty stroke play. Russell, who batted two hours, forty minutes, played cultured cricket, the leg glance and off drive bringing most of his ten 4's, before he was stumped for 93. Cowdrey, Smith and particularly Parks, who made his 63 in seventy-five minutes, also played aggressively and finally Titmus and Allen hit 121 without being parted off only 17 overs. After a third-wicket stand of 142 between Booth and Walters in the first N.S.W. innings the off-spin of Titmus and Allen was conclusive. Nevertheless, the touring side had the first of several long looks at the nineteen-year-old Walters, who played finely in both innings. In the first he stayed four hours and hit fifteen 4's in 129. In the second when the ball was turning more awkwardly he batted resourcefully for two and a quarter hours.

M.C.C.

R. W. Barber run out	90	— c Renneberg b Rothwell	0
W. E. Russell st Taber b Philpott	93	— not out	0
P. H. Parfitt run out	16	— not out	2
M. C. Cowdrey c Taber b Philpott	63		
*M. J. K. Smith c Taber b Philpott	59		
†J. M. Parks c Taber b Renneberg	63		
F. J. Titmus not out	80		
D. A. Allen not out	54		
L-b 8, n-b 1	9		
1/151 2/195 3/207 4/237 5/328 6/406 (6 wkts., dec.)	527	1/0 (one wkt.)	2

D. J. Brown, J. D. F. Larter and I. J. Jones did not bat.

Bowling: *First Innings*—Renneberg 17—1—78—1; Leslie 16—1—93—0; Philpott 23—2—126—3; Walters 15—0—100—0; Martin 19—1—84—0; Goffet 5—0—33—0; Booth 1—0—4—0. *Second Innings*—Rothwell 0.2—0—2—1.

New South Wales

G. Thomas c Cowdrey b Larter	2	— lbw b Titmus	56
G. Goffet b Brown	0	— c Smith b Titmus	6
*B. C. Booth c Parfitt b Jones	80	— c Parks b Brown	11
K. D. Walters c Smith b Jones	129	— c Smith b Parfitt	39
B. A. Rothwell b Titmus	8	— c Russell b Allen	27
M. Hill c Jones b Allen	36	— c Smith b Titmus	40
P. I. Philpott c Jones b Allen	16	— run out	32
J. W. Martin c Barber b Titmus	1	— c Smith b Allen	0
†H. B. Taber not out	2	— c Smith b Titmus	7
P. Leslie c Russell b Titmus	0	— b Titmus	4
D. A. Renneberg b Jones	9	— not out	9
L-b 5	5	B 4, l-b 5	9
1/2 2/4 3/146 4/157 5/242 6/272 7/277 8/277 9/277	288	1/13 2/24 3/102 4/140 5/156 6/207 7/208 8/218 9/227	240

Bowling: *First Innings*—Larter 2—0—13—1; Brown 12—2—60—1; Jones 15.1—0—76—3; Allen 22—5—75—2; Titmus 20—6—54—3; Parfitt 1—0—5—0. *Second Innings*—Jones 4—3—4—0; Brown 16—4—75—1; Titmus 34.1—9—45—5; Russell 4—0—16—0; Allen 29—9—47—2; Parfitt 12—0—36—1; Barber 2—0—8—0.

Umpires: E. Wykes and R. Burgess.

QUEENSLAND v. M.C.C.

At Brisbane, December 3, 4, 6, 7. Drawn. The sickness which had dogged the touring side laid low Cowdrey and put him out of the Test that followed. It also affected Barber to a lesser extent. Moreover, Russell, who had clinched his Test place by more splendid batting, suffered a slight fracture of his right thumb. His batting during a stand of 201 with Edrich lasting 38 overs in two hours, thirty-seven minutes was as elegantly sure as in Sydney. Edrich attacked splendidly and hit three 6's and thirteen 4's in his 133 in three hours, twenty minutes. A three-hour innings by Barrington cemented their work, and Titmus again batted vigorously and well. He made 51 in seventy-two minutes as his contribution to an unfinished stand of 106.

Despite a resolute innings of nearly four hours by Burge, Queensland finished 230 behind, but Smith did not enforce a follow-on. Instead, Edrich and Russell shared another brisk stand, scoring 109 before Russell's injury compelled him to retire. Queensland were set to make 354 in just under five hours. But for bad light in the evening which finally ended the match they might have scored them, so aggressively did Burge and Veivers play with the sound support of Bull. Burge hit 60 in a second-wicket stand with Bull of 92 in just over an hour. Veivers hit three 6's and slammed 74 in eighty-two minutes. When he was fifth out at 285, wickets started to tumble in increasingly dull light, and the game was called off twenty minutes before the scheduled close.

M.C.C.

G. Boycott c Allan b Veivers	30	— c Grout b Allan	0
R. W. Barber retired ill	21		
W. E. Russell st Grout b Veivers	110	— retired hurt	45
J. H. Edrich c Duncan b Lillie	133	— not out	68
K. F. Barrington not out	80	— not out	9
*M. J. K. Smith b Allan	14	— c Mackay b Lillie	0
†J. T. Murray c Buckle b Mackay	10		
F. J. Titmus not out	51		
L-b 3	3	B 1	1
1/67 2/268 3/319 4/346 (5 wkts., dec.)	452	1/0 2/110 (2 wkts., dec.)	123

D. A. Allen, K. Higgs and I. J. Jones did not bat.

Bowling: *First Innings*—Allen 18—2—77—1; Duncan 21—2—99—0; Mackay 18—1—93—1; Veivers 21—2—83—2; Lillie 19—2—97—1. *Second Innings*—Allan 6—2—19—1; Duncan 12—0—42—0; Mackay 4—0—26—0; Veivers 5—0—16—0; Lillie 4—0—19—1.

Queensland

D. Bull c Smith b Allen	25	— c and b Allen	64
S. Trimble c Barrington b Titmus	34	— c Murray b Barber	31
W. Buckle c Smith b Titmus	0	— b Higgs	36
*P. J. Burge not out	114	— c Titmus b Allen	60
T. R. Veivers c Murray b Higgs	0	— c Allen b Jones	74
D. Hughson c Barrington b Barber	30	— b Titmus	3
†A. T. W. Grout c Allen b Barber	3	— c Barber b Titmus	19
J. Mackay lbw b Jones	6	— c Smith b Titmus	23
P. J. Allan c Allen b Higgs	5	— not out	1
D. Lillie lbw b Higgs	0	— not out	0
R. Duncan c Titmus b Jones	0		
B 2, l-b 2, n-b 1	5	B 2, l-b 2	4
1/59 2/59 3/61 4/62 5/160 6/164 7/210 8/221 9/221	222	1/65 2/157 3/157 4/178 5/285 6/300 7/314 8/315 (8 wkts.)	315

Bowling: *First Innings*—Jones 16.3—5—36—2; Higgs 17—3—35—3; Boycott 1—1—0—0; Allen 19—4—34—1; Titmus 21—3—79—2; Barber 8—2—33—2; *Second Innings*—Jones 11—0—59—1; Higgs 14—0—39—1; Allen 14—0—79—2: Boycott 1—1—0—0; Titmus 13—0—56—3; Barber 10—0—78—1.

Umpires: L. Rowan and J. Goodwin.

QUEENSLAND COUNTRY DISTRICTS XI v. M.C.C.

At Beaudesert, December 8. Country Districts XI 152 for seven declared (G. Jennings 77); M.C.C. 159 for three (R. W. Barber 56, G. Boycott 48 not out). M.C.C. won by seven wickets.

AUSTRALIA v. ENGLAND

First Test

At Brisbane, December 10, 11, 13, 14, 15. Drawn. Back trouble kept McKenzie out of Australia's side, and England were without Cowdrey. Russell was fit to play, but he split his right hand while fielding, and Boycott, who had been kept out of all but two of the first-class games by stomach trouble and sciatica, moved up from his intended position at number six to open with Barber. He seized the chance to re-establish himself in that position for the series by playing two sound innings. Rain cut the first day's play to two and three-quarter hours and washed out the second.

Except briefly midway through the England first innings a definite result was always out of the question, for Australia batted nearly nine and a half hours in the first innings, which ran into the fourth day. Fine, lively bowling by Brown, who took the first three wickets for 45 in 12.6 overs, reduced Australia to 125 for four. Lawry and Walters then added 187 in even time. Lawry, obdurate as ever, batted seven hours, his stubborn defence punctuated by outbreaks of leg-side hitting and drives through extra cover, which brought him twenty 4's in his 166. Walters, who became the ninth Australian to score a century in his first Test, and that in particularly testing circumstances, confirmed his class by his mature batting in an innings lasting five hours twenty-two minutes. With his quick footwork he played Barber's leg breaks particularly well. In one over he hit Barber for four 4's and later hooked him for 6. He also drove Titmus over mid-off for 6 and, in addition, hit eleven 4's.

England, unsettled by the leg spin of Philpott and the pace of Hawke and Allen, lost four wickets for 115, but Parks, who drove Veivers straight and to the off for three 6's, played such a fine attacking innings that his side afterwards was not in serious danger. Parks hit 52 in a stand of 76 with Barrington in sixty-eight minutes off 66 balls. Barrington batted over three hours for 53, and Titmus played so resolutely and well for two hours, forty minutes that England did not follow-on 163 behind until mid-afternoon on the last day. In the final innings Boycott, batting throughout the three and three-quarter hours, supplied the solidity while Barber, Edrich and Barrington, each of whom hit one 6, attacked successfully. Barber made his 34 off 37 balls in forty-five minutes, and Barrington, by contrast with his first innings, batted only fifty-four minutes for 38.

Australia

W. M. Lawry c Parks b Higgs	166	T. R. Veivers not out	56
I. R. Redpath b Brown	17	N. J. N. Hawke not out	6
R. M. Cowper c Barrington b Brown	22	L-b 2, n-b 3	5
P. J. Burge b Brown	0		
*B. C. Booth c and b Titmus	16	1/51 2/90 3/90 (6 wkts., dec.)	443
K. D. Walters c Parks b Higgs	155	4/125 5/312 6/431	

†A. T. W Grout, P. I. Philpott and P. J. Allan did not bat.

Bowling: Brown 21—4—71—3; Higgs 30—6—102—2; Titmus 38—9—99—1; Allen 39—12—108—0; Barber 5—0—42—0; Boycott 4—0—16—0.

England

R. W. Barber c Walters b Hawke	5	— c Veivers b Walters	34
G. Boycott b Philpott	45	— not out	63
J. H. Edrich c Lawry b Philpott	32	— c Veivers b Philpott	37
K. F. Barrington b Hawke	53	— c Booth b Cowper	38
*M. J. K. Smith b Allan	16	— not out	10
†J. M. Parks c Redpath b Philpott	52		
F. J. Titmus st Grout b Philpott	60		
D. A. Allen c Cowper b Walters	3		
D. J. Brown b Philpott	3		
K. Higgs lbw b Allan	4		
W. E. Russell not out	0		
B 4, n-b 3	7	B 2, l-b 2	4
1/5 2/75 3/86 4/115 5/191 6/221 7/232 8/253 9/272	280	1/46 2/114 3/168 (3 wkts.)	186

Bowling: *First Innings*—Allan 21—6—58—2; Hawke 16—7—44—2; Walters 10—1—25—1; Philpott 28.1—3—90—5; Cowper 7—4—7—0; Veivers 11—1—49—0. *Second Innings*—Allan 3—0—25—0; Hawke 10—2—16—0; Walters 5—1—22—1; Philpott 14—1—62—1; Veivers 12—1—37—0; Cowper 6—0—20—1.

Umpires: C. Egar and L. Rowan.

PRIME MINISTER'S XI v. M.C.C.

At Canberra, December 17. Prime Minister's XI 288 for seven declared (P. Sheahan 79, J. W. Burke 60, R. Benaud 45); M.C.C. 289 for eight (G. Boycott 95, M. C. Cowdrey 52, M. J. K. Smith 51 not out). M.C.C. won by two wickets.

N.S.W. COUNTRY DISTRICTS XI v. M.C.C.

At Bathurst, December 18. Country Districts XI 221 (K. F. Barrington six for 92); M.C.C. 256 for six (J. H. Edrich 67 not out, K. F. Barrington 61). M.C.C. won by five wickets and batted on.

N.S.W. COUNTRY DISTRICTS XI v. M.C.C.

At Albury, December 20. Country Districts XI 190 (G. Stacey 56 not out; K. F. Barrington four for 72); M.C.C. 253 for five (M. J. K. Smith 81, J. H. Edrich 76). M.C.C. won by six wickets and batted on.

SOUTH AUSTRALIA COUNTRY DISTRICTS XI v. M.C.C.

At Mount Gambier, December 22. South Australia Country Districts XI 176 for six declared (D. Fischer 40 not out); M.C.C. 223 for two (G. Boycott 99, P. H. Parfitt 52 not out). M.C.C. won by eight wickets and batted on.

SOUTH AUSTRALIA v. M.C.C.

At Adelaide, December 23, 24, 27, 28. M.C.C. won by six wickets. After a week up-country on a whistle-stop tour of four one-day games, M.C.C. needed time to re-acclimatise themselves to first-class cricket and owed their win to the generous declaration of Favell. In his first State match since joining the team as a reinforcement in Brisbane, Knight batted excellently and bowled usefully. South Australia lost their first five wickets for 133, but again young Shiell was in great form. In five hours he hit 202 not out with two 6's and nineteen 4's. Jarman, who hooked and square-cut strongly, was his partner in a stand of 146 in two and a half hours, and South Australia averaged 4.6 runs an over. M.C.C. also scored briskly after recovering from the loss of four wickets for 87. Smith made his 108 with fifteen 4's in under two and a quarter hours, and Knight hit 79 inside two hours. Murray struck his batting form for the first time in two tours of Australia in first-class company and batted almost three hours for 110, in which were eleven 4's. Before South Australia declared, leaving M.C.C. three hours and ten minutes in which to make 269, Chappell hit fourteen 4's in an innings of 113 in three hours, forty minutes. With Barber and Boycott hitting 138 in only 18 overs for the first wicket before falling in successive overs, M.C.C. sailed home with more than half an hour to spare. Knight hit 46 in forty-one minutes and Cowdrey 63 not out in seventy-seven minutes.

South Australia

*L. E. Favell c Allen b Knight	40	— b Knight	31
L. Marks c Parfitt b Jones	0	— c Murray b Higgs	11
I. M. Chappell st Murray b Allen	59	— not out	113
K. G. Cunningham c Barber b Higgs	0	— run out	46
H. N. Dansie run out	30	— c Boycott b Parfitt	43
A. B. Shiell not out	202		
†B. N. Jarman c Parfitt b Higgs	70		
G. Griffiths c and b Higgs	23		
D. J. Sincock not out	28		
B 3, l-b 2, n-b 2	7	B 4, l-b 3, w 1, n-b 1	9
1/3 2/58 3/48 4/122 5/133 6/279 7/330 (7 wkts., dec.)	459	1/34 2/79 3/181 4/253 (4 wkts., dec.)	253

D. Robins and A. Frost did not bat.

Bowling: *First Innings*—Jones 14.2—1—78—1; Higgs 21—2—82—3; Knight 15—1—89—1; Allen 18—4—75—1; Barber 20—0—87—0; Parfitt 5—1—15—0; Barrington 1—0—5—0; Boycott 5—0—21—0. *Second Innings*—Jones 8—0—62—0; Higgs 10—1—29—1; Knight 7—0—17—1; Allen 13—2—35—0; Barber 10—1—41—0; Parfitt 5.2—1—32—1; Boycott 4—0—28—0.

M.C.C.

G. Boycott c Chappell b Frost	0	— b Sincock	58
R. W. Barber c Griffiths b Robins	42	— c Cunningham b Chappell	77
P. H. Parfitt b Robins	6	— c Favell b Chappell	2
M. C. Cowdrey c Jarman b Sincock	18	— not out	63
*M. J. K. Smith c Cunningham b Sincock	108	— not out	15
K. F. Barrington st Jarman b Sincock	63		
†J. T. Murray c Sincock b Robins	110		
D. A. Allen b Chappell	1		
B. R. Knight b Robins	79	— c and b Griffiths	46
K. Higgs not out	4		
I. J. Jones b Chappell	0		
L-b 8, w 2, n-b 3	13	B 7, l-b 1, n-b 1	9
1/0 2/13 3/66 4/87 5/223 6/250 7/253 8/417 9/444	444	1/138 2/138 3/152 4/237 (4 wkts.)	270

Bowling: *First Innings*—Frost 21—2—89—1; Robins 18—1—69—4; Sincock 29—1—141—3; Chappell 17.1—3—77—2; Griffiths 7—0—44—0; Cunningham 1—0—6—0; Dansie 1—0—5—0. *Second Innings*—Frost 8—0—59—0; Robins 6—0—35—0; Sincock 8—0—59—1; Chappell 9—0—58—2; Griffiths 7—0—37—1; Dansie 1—0—5—0; Favell 0.3—0—8—0.

Umpires: C. Egar and F. Godson.

AUSTRALIA v. ENGLAND

Second Test

At Melbourne, December 30, 31, January 1, 3, 4. Drawn. Illness and injury kept Brown and Higgs out of the England side, and they were replaced by Jones and Knight. Hawke, whom minor injury had kept out of the South Australian side against M.C.C., was omitted from the Australian team, but Simpson had recovered from the broken wrist which kept him out of the first Test. He and Lawry made 93 stodgily for the first wicket, in two hours twenty-five minutes, but afterwards only a stubborn innings by Cowper which lasted three hours and twenty minutes, seriously held up England's substitute opening bowlers, who were well supported by Allen.

England scored very fast at the start of their innings. Barber and Boycott hit 98 before Boycott, who had the major share of the bowling and was badly missed in the slips in McKenzie's first over, was out in the sixteenth over after seventy-six minutes. Edrich, who batted more than five hours, cemented the fine start during stands of 118 with Barrington and 105 with Cowdrey. Yet, despite the large total of 558, the most was not made of the inspiring start. Only Cowdrey, who made his third Test century in Melbourne and his fourth against Australia, scored briskly, making his 104 in three and a quarter hours.

On the fourth day seventy minutes were spent adding 42 for the last three wickets. At the close of that day Australia were 131 for one. Simpson, playing much more fluently than in the first innings, made 67 of an opening partnership of 120 in two hours, twenty minutes. In the first eighty minutes of the final day three more wickets fell for 45, and, if Parks had not missed a simple off side chance of stumping Burge off Barber when he was 34, England would surely have won the match. Burge did not finally yield his wicket until he and Walters had assured their side of a draw. They put on 198 in just over three hours, and both played supremely well. Burge stayed four and a quarter hours and Walters a little longer. Burge in heavy-handed manner tamed the English attack, while Walters was content to play soundly in his support until the time came for him also to attack. After tea, when no definite result was possible, the last six wickets fell, and England had ten minutes batting before the close.

Australia

First Innings		Second Innings	
*R. B. Simpson c Edrich b Allen	59	c Barrington b Knight	67
W. M. Lawry c Cowdrey b Allen	88	c Smith b Barber	78
P. J. Burge b Jones	5	c Edrich b Boycott	120
R. M. Cowper c Titmus b Jones	99	lbw b Jones	5
B. C. Booth lbw b Jones	23	b Allen	10
K. D. Walters c Parks b Knight	22	c and b Barrington	115
T. R. Veivers run out	19	st Parks b Boycott	3
P. I. Philpott b Knight	10	b Knight	2
†A. T. W. Grout c Barber b Knight	11	c Allen b Barrington	16
G. D. McKenzie not out	12	run out	2
A. N. Connolly c Parks b Knight	0	not out	0
B 2, l-b 7, n-b 1	10	B 1, l-b 3, w 1, n-b 3	8
1/93 2/109 3/203 4/262 5/297 6/318 7/330 8/342 9/352	358	1/120 2/141 3/163 4/176 5/374 6/382 7/385 8/417 9/426	426

Bowling: *First Innings*—Jones 4—4—92—3; Knight 26.5—2—84—4; Titmus 31—7—93—0; Allen 20—4—55—2; Barber 6—1—24—0. *Second Innings*—Jones 20—1—92—1; Knight 21—4—61—2; Titmus 22—6—43—0; Allen 18—3—48—1; Barber 17—0—87—1; Barrington 7.4—0—47—2; Boycott 9—0—32—2; Smith 2—0—8—0.

England

G. Boycott c McKenzie b Walters	51	— not out	5
R. W. Barber c Grout b McKenzie	48	— not out	0
J. H. Edrich c and b Veivers	109		
K. F. Barrington c Burge b Veivers	63		
M. C. Cowdrey c Connolly b Cowper	104		
*M. J. K. Smith c Grout b McKenzie	41		
†J. M. Parks c Cowper b McKenzie	71		
B. R. Knight c Simpson b McKenzie	1		
F. J. Titmus not out	56		
D. A. Allen c Grout b Connolly	2		
I. J. Jones b McKenzie	1		
B 4, l-b 5, w 2	11		
1/98 2/110 3/228 4/333 5/409 6/443 7/447 8/540 9/551	558	(no wkt.)	5

Bowling: *First Innings*—McKenzie 35.5—3—134—5; Connolly 37—5—125—1; Philpott 30—2—133—0; Walters 10—2—32—1; Simpson 16—4—61—0; Veivers 12—3—46—2; Cowper 3—0—16—1. *Second Innings*—Connolly 1—0—3—0; McKenzie 1—0—2—0.

Umpires: C. Egar and W. Smyth.

AUSTRALIA v. ENGLAND

Third Test

At Sydney, January 7, 8, 10, 11, 12. England won by an innings and 93 runs. Illness put Simpson out of the Australian side again, and Booth, as in Brisbane, was the captain. On a pitch which turned more and more in favour of spin bowlers the toss was the decisive event. Barber's greatest innings of the tour and his opening stand of 234 with Boycott made certain that England would not lose the advantage of batting first. Again Australia paid a heavy price for dropping Boycott early. He was missed at backward short leg off the luckless McKenzie when he was 12. In two hours before lunch he and Barber made 93 off 36 overs. In the next two hours before Boycott at last fell to Philpott's leg spin they added 141.

When Barber was second out at 303 he had batted four minutes under five hours and hit nineteen 4's in an innings of magnificent aggression, a match-winning innings. His wicket started Hawke on a splendid new ball spell which swept aside England's middle batting. In eight overs he took three for 14, and with his first ball on the second morning he also dismissed Brown. Despite his fine bowling—seven for 105 in conditions which did not materially help pace—England made an unassailable total, for Edrich scored a second successive Test century in almost four and a quarter hours. Finally Allen, who made his not out 50 in eighty-eight minutes, and Jones put on 55 for the last wicket in 12 overs.

On a wearing pitch Australia were always struggling after a second-wicket stand of 81 by Thomas and Cowper. Thomas revealed his wide range of beautiful strokes while making 51 of those runs with seven 4's in just under one and three-quarter hours. Cowper by contrast batted four hours, ten minutes for 60 and meekly played his side into the hands of the English fast bowlers, Jones and Brown. On his return to the side, after recovering from muscular trouble, Brown took three wickets in his first over with the new ball at 174 and finished with five for 63.

In the follow-on the off spin of Allen and Titmus was decisive on a broken pitch. The longest stand was 46 for the first wicket by Thomas and Lawry, but Walters was again responsible for the best batting. For two hours he played the turning ball with rare skill, and so for the third time running he came off splendidly when his side were in difficulties. Sincock, the left-arm spinner who was brought in to increase Australia's attacking spin on the Sydney pitch, had an unfortunate match as a bowler, but in both innings he batted with admirable determination.

England

G. Boycott c and b Philpott	84
R. W. Barber b Hawke	185
J. H. Edrich c and b Philpott	103
K. F. Barrington c McKenzie b Hawke	1
M. C. Cowdrey c Grout b Hawke	0
*M. J. K. Smith c Grout b Hawke	6
D. J. Brown c Grout b Hawke	1
†J. M. Parks c Grout b Hawke	13
F. J. Titmus c Grout b Walters	14
D. A. Allen not out	50
I. J. Jones b Hawke	16
B 3, l-b 8, w 2, n-b 2	15
1/234 2/303 3/309 4/309 5/317 6/328 7/358 8/395 9/433	488

Bowling: McKenzie 25—2—113—0; Hawke 33.7—6—105—7; Walters 10—1—38—1; Philpott 28—3—86—2; Sincock 20—1—98—0; Cowper 6—1—33—0.

Australia

Batsman	First innings		Second innings	
W. M. Lawry	c Parks b Jones	0	c Cowdrey b Brown	33
G. Thomas	c Titmus b Brown	51	c Cowdrey b Titmus	25
R. M. Cowper	st Parks b Allen	60	c Boycott b Titmus	0
P. J. Burge	c Parks b Brown	6	run out	1
*B. C. Booth	c Cowdrey b Jones	8	b Allen	27
D. J. Sincock	c Parks b Brown	29	c Smith b Allen	27
K. D. Walters	st Parks b Allen	23	not out	35
N. J. N. Hawke	c Barber b Brown	0	c Smith b Titmus	2
†A. T. W. Grout	b Brown	0	c Smith b Allen	3
G. D. McKenzie	c Cowdrey b Barber	24	c Barber b Titmus	12
P. I. Philpott	not out	5	lbw b Allen	5
	B 7, l-b 8	15	B 3, l-b 1	4
	1/0 2/81 3/91 4/105 5/155 6/174 7/174 8/174 9/203	221	1/46 2/50 3/51 4/86 5/86 6/119 7/131 8/135 9/140	174

Bowling: *First Innings*—Jones 20—6—51—2; Brown 17—1—63—5; Boycott 3—1—8—0; Titmus 23—8—40—0; Barber 2.1—1—2—1; Allen 19—5—42—2. *Second Innings*—Jones 7—0—35—0; Brown 11—2—32—1; Titmus 17.3—4—40—4; Allen 20—8—47—4; Barber 5—0—16—0.

Umpires: C. Egar and L. Rowan.

NORTHERN N.S.W. COUNTRY DISTRICTS XI v. M.C.C.

At Newcastle, January 14, 15, 17. M.C.C. won by ten wickets. This match was not ranked as first-class.

Country Districts XI

Batsman	First innings		Second innings	
M. Fox	c Murray b Brown	11	absent ill	0
J. Scobie	c Parfitt b Larter	26	c Murray b Knight	36
I. Barton	c Murray b Knight	3	st Murray b Barber	20
C. Baker	c Edrich b Parfitt	101	c Barber b Titmus	19
M. Hill	lbw b Barber	98	c Smith b Titmus	8
B. Weissel	c Edrich b Barber	46	c Titmus b Brown	8
H. Crozier	c Murray b Barber	11	c sub b Titmus	0
C. Whitehead	not out	13	c Smith b Titmus	4
R. Holland	b Titmus	9	c Brown b Parfitt	13
L. Ellis	b Titmus	0	not out	14
G. Lammi	hit wkt b Barber	4	c Murray b Brown	0
	B 5, l-b 4, w 1, n-b 2	12	L-b 2, n-b 2	4
	1/43 2/46 3/48 4/242 5/279 6/299 7/310 8/323 9/323	334	1/57 2/67 3/81 4/88 5/88 6/95 7/99 8/99 9/126	126

Bowling: *First Innings*—Larter 10—1—44—1; Higgs 7—0—38—0; Knight 8—2—38—1; Brown 4—1—19—1; Parfitt 16—1—66—1; Barber 12.7—2—57—4; Titmus 12—1—60—2. *Second Innings*—Brown 6—0—25—2; Larter 9—1—36—0; Knight 4—1—14—1; Barber 7—2—11—1; Higgs 5—1—7—0; Titmus 7—3—29—4; Parfitt 2—2—0—1.

M.C.C.

R. W. Barber c Barton b Whitehead	48	— not out	11
W. E. Russell c Barton b Ellis	0		
D. J. Brown c Crozier b Ellis	0	— not out	2
J. H. Edrich c Hill b Whitehead	14		
P. H. Parfitt lbw b Weissel	26		
*M. J. K. Smith c Whitehead b Weissel	164		
F. J. Titmus lbw b Whitehead	114		
†J. T. Murray b Hill	16		
B. R. Knight not out	35		
K. Higgs c Crozier b Hill	5		
J. D. F. Larter c Whitehead b Lammi	19		
B 2, l-b 4, n-b 2	8		
1/9 2/15 3/43 4/76 5/106 6/366 7/378 8/394 9/404	449	(no wkt.)	13

Bowling: *First Innings*—Ellis 13—0—79—2; Whitehead 23—5—87—3; Lammi 8.5—0—61—1; Weissel 18—2—83—2; Holland 6—0—58—0; Hill 10—1—73—2. *Second Innings*—Ellis 1—0—9—0; Weissel 6—0—4—0.

TASMANIA v. M.C.C.

At Launceston, January 19, 20, 21. Drawn. Tasmania's batting was stronger than their bowling. M.C.C. bowled somewhat listlessly and never looked good enough to win the match. M.C.C. hit 371, Smith getting 96 in two hours, twenty minutes and Parks 91 in two and a quarter hours. An excellent aggressive innings by Richardson, who batted under two and a half hours for 112 and hit one 6 and fourteen 4's assured Tasmania of safety. When their innings ended only four and a quarter hours remained, and M.C.C. batted out time. Cowdrey played smoothly for 108 in three hours, and Knight spent only seventy-three minutes over his unfinished 51. While batsmen were generally in command Flint, a young leg spinner, bowled with much promise in both innings. He was not available for the next match in Hobart.

M.C.C.

R. W. Barber b Allen	19		
*M. J. K. Smith b Allen	96	— run out	17
P. H. Parfitt c Maddocks b Flint	25	— c Farrell b Allen	33
M. C. Cowdrey st Maddocks b Patterson	63	— c Brown b Flint	108
*J. M. Parks c Farrell b Patterson	91	— c and b Flint	58
. T. Murray b Flint	0	— c Maddocks b Patterson	7
B. R. Knight not out	45	— not out	51
D. A. Allen c Maddocks b Flint	2	— c Palfreyman b Flint	2
D. J. Brown b Allen	27	— lbw b Archer	9
. D. F. Larter b Hooper	1		
L-b 2	2	B 2, n-b 2	4
/23 2/109 3/157 4/230 (9 wkts., dec.) /231 6/329 7/332 8/370 9/371	371	1/46 2/54 3/160 (7 wkts.) 4/171 5/270 6/274 7/289	289

K. Higgs did not bat.

Bowling: *First Innings*—Hooper 12.3—0—52—1; Allen 13—0—63—3; Palfreyman 4—0—34—0; Flint 23—1—133—3; Patterson 16—1—87—2. *Second Innings*—Allen 10—0—37—1; Hooper 9—0—38—0; Patterson 14—2—54—1; Palfreyman 8—0—25—0; Flint 16—1—93—3; Farrell 2—0—13—0; Stokes —0—21—0; Archer 0.7—0—4—1.

Tasmania

K. Brown b Higgs 28
J. Archer lbw b Allen 17
R. Stokes st Parks b Parfitt 25
B. Richardson c Larter b Knight . . 112
G. Farrell b Brown 41
B. Palfreyman b Brown 6
B. Patterson not out 67
*†L. Maddocks lbw b Higgs 6
H. Allen c Parks b Higgs 0
K. Hooper b Allen 5
K. Flint st Parks b Allen 4
B 4, lb 5, w 1, n-b 1 11

1/49 2/52 3/140 4/227 5/232 322
6/237 7/251 8/251 9/274

Bowling: Brown 12—2—38—2; Higgs 17—2—57—3; Larter 20—4—64—0; Knight 10—3—26—1; Allen 22—9—41—3; Barber 2—0—20—0; Parfitt 9—1—46—1; Murray 3—0—19—0.

Umpires: H. B. West and Dr. J. Travira.

COMBINED XI v. M.C.C.

At Hobart, February 22, 24, 25. Drawn. Eight Tasmanians and three Test players from the mainland, Lawry, Cowper and Walters, formed the Combined XI, and the last three did nearly all their scoring. Titmus gained his best figures of the tour, and M.C.C. put out Combined XI in four and three-quarter hours. They themselves scored easily, starting with 107 from Russell and Boycott, who stayed over four hours and hit nineteen 4's in his 156. Cowdrey made 70 quickly, and Murray, in top form, scored 83 in as many minutes. On the last afternoon Lawry and Cowper batted together for almost four hours and put on 254 without being parted. On good batting pitches three days were insufficient to produce definite results to the matches in Tasmania.

Combined XI

*W. M. Lawry c Barrington b Titmus. 47 — not out 12
K. Brown c Barrington b Jones . . . . 2 — c Murray b Jones . . . .
R. M. Cowper c Cowdrey b Titmus . . . . . 53 — not out 14
R. Stokes c Murray b Jones 3
K. D. Walters run out 46
B. Richardson b Titmus 5
G. Farrell lbw b Higgs 11
B. Patterson lbw b Titmus 1
†L. Maddocks not out 8
H. Allen c Knight b Titmus 11
K. Hooper c Murray b Titmus 5
B 1, l-b 6 . . . . 7 B 4 . . . .

1/9 2/102 3/104 4/110 5/127 199 1/19 (one wkt.) 27
6/172 7/173 8/175 9/188

Bowling: *First Innings*—Jones 15—2—56—2; Higgs 17—1—45—1; Knigh 9—1—26—0; Titmus 23.7—6—65—6. *Second Innings*—Jones 11—0—59— Higgs 10—0—36—0; Titmus 7—1—28—0; Knight 8—2—23—0; Parfitt 7—0—35—0; Barrington 10—0—42—0; Boycott 7—0—39—0; Cowdrey 1—0—7—0.

M.C.C.

G. Boycott c Farrell b Walters 156
W. E. Russell b Hooper 48
J. H. Edrich lbw b Hooper 1
K. F. Barrington c Maddocks b Hooper 37
P. H. Parfitt c Patterson b Cowper. 20
*M. C. Cowdrey c and b Hooper . . 70
F. J. Titmus lbw b Hooper 37
B. R. Knight c Cowper b Allen . . . .
†J. T. Murray c Farrell b Patterson 8
K. Higgs not out 1
L-b 1 . . . .

1/107 2/109 3/199 (9 wkts., dec.) 4
4/254 5/267 6/370 7/371
8/379 9/471

I. J. Jones did not bat.

Bowling: Allen 22—0—111—1; Hooper 29—1—106—5; Walters 13—0—73—1; Patterson 23.4—2—123—1; Cowper 6—2—23—1; Stokes 3—0—20—0; Richardson 2—0—14—0.

Umpires: M. Thomas and K. Gorman.

AUSTRALIA v. ENGLAND

Fourth Test

At Adelaide, January 28, 29, 31, February 1. Australia won by an innings and nine runs in four days. The roles of the two sides were completely reversed in this match. England went into it soft after two weeks of holiday cricket. Australia were revitalised. They outfielded, outbatted and outbowled the victors of the previous Test. Simpson was fit to resume in charge of Australia and returned in buoyant mood and form. The side had four changes. Booth, Cowper, Philpott and Sincock were dropped for Simpson, Veivers and two young players, Chappell and Stackpole. A fifth change discarded also McKenzie, but a late injury to Allan caused his recall with happy consequences. The changes cleared away the cobwebs and stirred the survivors to keener effort.

The reprieved McKenzie turned in the match-winning performance on the first day. While there was some early life in the pitch he and Hawke took the first three English wickets for 33, and Australia never relaxed their grip on the game. Only during a third-wicket stand of 72 between Barrington and Cowdrey was there a suggestion of English recovery. They were playing well when Cowdrey mistook a call, as Barrington played the ball straight to mid-on, and rushed down the pitch to be run out. Though Barrington stayed three hours, twenty minutes, followed by ninety minutes of fluent cricket by Parks and the usual stout resistance of Titmus, McKenzie strode on strongly to his final triumph of six for 48, the finest bowling performance of the series.

England's 241 was exceeded by three before the first-wicket partnership of Simpson and Lawry was broken four and a quarter hours later. This great stand was Australia's highest for the first wicket in Test cricket. It was cemented by seventy-five minutes of fine stroke play by Thomas in a second-wicket partnership of 87, and Simpson went on until he had batted in commanding manner for nine hours and five minutes, scoring his 225 out of 480 with one 6 and eighteen 4's. Stackpole also batted admirably in his first Test and bowled effectively when England went in again 275 behind.

Again McKenzie and Hawke broke the early batting by taking the first three wickets for 32, and England were decisively defeated with more than a day to spare. On the fourth day England mistakenly used defensive tactics when only bold methods might have prised loose Australia's hold. Titmus alone appreciated that fact and hit his 53 in ninety-five minutes with eight 4's. Barrington stayed five and a half hours for a century that contained only four boundaries. Cowdrey, his partner while 82 were added, hit only two 4's in a pawky innings of over two and a half hours. This time Hawke was the outstanding bowler with five for 54. Together McKenzie and Hawke formed a match-winning combination.

England

G. Boycott c Chappell b Hawke	22	— lbw b McKenzie	12
R. W. Barber b McKenzie	0	— c Grout b Hawke	19
J. H. Edrich c Simpson b McKenzie	5	— c Simpson b Hawke	1
K. F. Barrington lbw b Walters	60	— c Chappell b Hawke	102
M. C. Cowdrey run out	38	— c Grout b Stackpole	35
*M. J. K. Smith b Veivers	29	— c McKenzie b Stackpole	5
†J. M. Parks c Stackpole b McKenzie	49	— run out	16
F. J. Titmus lbw b McKenzie	33	— c Grout b Hawke	53
D. A. Allen c Simpson b McKenzie	2	— not out	5
D. J. Brown c Thomas b McKenzie	1	— c and b Hawke	0
I. J. Jones not out	0	— c Lawry b Veivers	8
L-b 2	2	L-b 2, n-b 8	10
1/7 2/25 3/33 4/105 5/150 6/178 7/210 8/212 9/222	241	1/23 2/31 3/32 4/114 5/123 6/163 7/244 8/253 9/257	266

Bowling: *First Innings*—McKenzie 21.7—4—48—6; Hawke 23—2—69—1; Walters 14—0—50—1; Stackpole 5—0—30—0; Chappell 4—0—18—0; Veivers 13—3—24—1. *Second Innings*—McKenzie 18—4—53—1; Hawke 21—6—54—5; Walters 9—0—47—0; Chappell 22—4—53—0; Stackpole 14—3—33—2; Veivers 3.7—0—16—1.

Australia

*R. B. Simpson c Titmus b Jones	225
W. M. Lawry b Titmus	119
G. Thomas b Jones	52
T. R. Veivers c Parks b Jones	1
P. J. Burge c Parks b Jones	27
K. D. Walters c Parks b Brown	0
I. M. Chappell c Edrich b Jones	17
K. R. Stackpole c Parks b Jones	43
N. J. N. Hawke not out	20
†A. T. W. Grout b Titmus	4
G. D. McKenzie lbw b Titmus	1
B 3, l-b 4	7
1/244 2/331 3/333 4/379 5/383 6/415 7/480 8/501 9/506	516

Bowling: Jones 29—3—118—6; Brown 28—4—109—1; Boycott 7—3—33—0; Titmus 37—6—116—3; Allen 21—1—103—0; Barber 4—0—30—0.

Umpires: C. Egar and L. Rowan.

NEW SOUTH WALES v. M.C.C.

At Sydney, February 4, 5, 7, 8. Drawn. M.C.C. were still below par for most of this game, but a dashing display of batting on the last day after being forced to follow-on restored their spirit before the final Test. The Sydney pitch lasted well on this occasion, and batsmen had things much their own way. New South Wales averaged 4.4 runs an over, and only Allen and Knight made much impression on their batsmen, among whom Simpson, Thomas and Walters were again in fine form. Simpson batted three hours, twenty minutes for his 123, Thomas eight minutes under three hours for 129, in which were fourteen 4's, and together they put on 156 for the second wicket. M.C.C. batted moderately with the exception of Parfitt. For the first time on the tour he reproduced his English form and stayed three hours, twenty minutes for 87. In the second innings aggressive batting brought an average above five runs an over. Barber set the example with 75, including two 6's and eight 4's during an opening stand of 120, and at the end Knight hit 94 out of 120 in only seventy-one minutes. Another cultured exhibition of batting lasting three and three-quarter hours by Russell contributed to a lively final day's play in which 449 runs were scored. On the home side Davies, a young leg-break bowler and sound batsman, played with much promise in his first match against an international side.

New South Wales

*R. B. Simpson c Allen b Barber	123
N. C. O'Neill lbw b Knight	36
G. Thomas b Boycott	129
B. C. Booth c Smith b Knight	23
K. D. Walters c Allen b Knight	57
B. A. Rothwell c Murray b Larter	46
G. Davies c Larter b Allen	26
J. W. Martin c Boycott b Allen	25
†H. B. Taber not out	[illegible]
G. E. Corling c Parfitt b Allen	[illegible]
D. A. Renneberg b Allen	[illegible]
B 6, l-b 4, n-b 1	1[illegible]
1/77 2/233 3/315 4/318 5/418 6/428 7/473 8/482 9/482	48[illegible]

Bowling: Larter 23—3—95—1; Higgs 23—3—86—0; Knight 19—0—81—3; Allen 27.7—7—97—4; Barber 13—0—81—1; Boycott 4—0—37—1.

M.C.C.

G. Boycott c Booth b Renneberg	5	— c Thomas b Simpson	77
R. W. Barber c Taber b Renneberg	49	— c Renneberg b Simpson	75
J. H. Edrich c Walters b Martin	36	— st Taber b Simpson	47
W. E. Russell b Corling	26	— not out	101
*M. J. K. Smith c Thomas b O'Neill	40	— c Taber b Renneberg	64
P. H. Parfitt b Davies	87	— c Simpson b Corling	10
B. R. Knight c Taber b Simpson	35	— c and b Simpson	94
†J. T. Murray lbw b Davies	25		
D. A. Allen not out	9		
K. Higgs c Renneberg b Martin	2		
J. D. F. Larter c Simpson b Davies	4		
B 7, lb 4	11	L-b 3, n-b 1	4
1/33 2/66 3/106 4/122 5/176 6/231 7/309 8/316 9/323	329	1/120 2/181 3/204 4/309 5/322 6/472 (6 wkts.)	472

Bowling: *First Innings*—Renneberg 22—4—92—2; Corling 17—4—51—1; Martin 19—4—56—2; Simpson 14—4—45—1; O'Neill 9—2—32—1; Davies 12.7—0—42—3. *Second Innings*—Renneberg 13—0—70—1; Corling 13—2—49—1; Walters 9—0—61—0; Martin 17—3—123—0; Simpson 15.6—2—71—4; Davies 20—3—83—0; Booth 4—2—11—0.

Umpires: E. Wykes and K. Berridge.

AUSTRALIA v. ENGLAND

Fifth Test

At Melbourne, February 11, 12, 14, 15, 16. Drawn. The final Test, on which the series depended, was anti-climax and doomed to be indecisive before rain washed out all play on the fourth day. England increased their seam bowling by including Knight at the expense of Allen. Australia recalled Cowper in place of Burge. Up to a point England played with the necessary enterprise after a bad start. Boycott, though out of touch, took 60 of the first 80 balls bowled, then ridiculously ran out Barber and himself fell twenty minutes later. However, Barrington played his most aggressive Test innings; indeed he hit the fastest century of the series, for he needed only 122 balls for his first 102 inside two and a half hours. He hit two 6's and eight 4's. By contrast Edrich needed 160 balls for his first 50. Though Cowdrey and Parks batted well, putting on 138 together, the pace slackened, and finally Titmus needed over two hours for 42.

Thoughts of victory gave way to the urge to ensure against defeat, and in the field England averaged only 96 balls an hour. Such time wasting allowed Australia little chance of striking for a win, and they were content to play quietly. Lawry's 108, his fifth century against the English bowlers, lasted over six hours. During the season he batted over forty-one hours against the touring team and averaged under 24 runs an hour. He was an avid, but tedious, accumulator of runs, 979 in eleven innings. When he and Cowper had added 212 for the third wicket and batted together almost five and a half hours, the match was already half dead. Cowper matched Lawry's patience. His first 100 occupied five hours, ten minutes, his second three and three-quarter hours, and altogether he batted seven minutes over twelve hours for 307, a monumental innings in which were twenty 4's. Fear of losing frustrated the good intentions with which both sides doubtless entered this disappointing and quickly-to-be-forgotten match. It was a sour ending to a generally appetising tour in Australia.

England

G. Boycott c Stackpole b McKenzie	17	— lbw b McKenzie 1
R. W. Barber run out	17	— b McKenzie 20
J. H. Edrich c McKenzie b Walters	85	— b McKenzie 3
K. F. Barrington c Grout b Walters	115	— not out 32
M. C. Cowdrey c Grout b Walters	79	— not out 11
*M. J. K. Smith c Grout b Walters	0	
†J. M. Parks run out	89	
F. J. Titmus not out	42	
B. R. Knight c Grout b Hawke	13	
D. J. Brown c and b Chappell	12	
I. J. Jones not out	4	
B 9, l-b 2, n-b 1	12	L-b 2 2
1/36 2/41 3/219 4/254 (9 wkts., dec.) 5/254 6/392 7/419 8/449 9/474	485	1/6 2/21 3/34 (three wkts.) 69

Bowling: *First Innings*—McKenzie 26—5—100—1; Hawke 35—5—109—1; Walters 19—3—53—4; Simpson 5—1—20—0; Stackpole 10—2—43—0; Veivers 15—3—78—0; Chappell 17—3—70—1. *Second Innings*—McKenzie 6—2—17—3; Hawke 4—1—22—0; Walters 2—0—16—0; Stackpole 3—0—10—0; Chappell 2—0—2—0.

Australia

W. M. Lawry c Edrich b Jones	108
*R. B. Simpson b Brown	4
G. Thomas c Titmus b Jones	19
R. M. Cowper b Knight	307
K. D. Walters c and b Barber	60
I. M. Chappell c Parks b Jones	19
K. R. Stackpole b Knight	9
T. R. Veivers b Titmus	4
N. J. N. Hawke not out	0
B 6, l-b 5, n-b 2	13
1/15 2/36 3/248 4/420 5/481 6/532 7/543 8/543 (8 wkts., dec.)	543

†A. T. W. Grout and G. D. McKenzie did not bat.

Bowling: Brown 31—3—134—1; Jones 29—1—145—3; Knight 36.2—4—105—2; Titmus 42—12—86—1; Barber 16—0—60—1.

Umpires: C. Egar and L. Rowan.

PRESIDENT'S XI v. M.C.C.

At Wellington, February 19, 21, 22. Drawn. Determined defensive batting by the opposition held the M.C.C. bowlers in check, despite Allen taking five wickets for 96 on the first day when Shrimpton, Sinclair and Morgan performed creditably for the President's team. Heavy rain over the weekend delayed the resumption for an hour on the second day before Boycott and Edrich proceeded cautiously under difficult conditions. After tea Parfitt drove splendidly, hitting one 6 and eight 4's in his 121. He and Smith put on 189 in just over two and a half hours and on the third morning M.C.C. took their lead to 122, declaring forty minutes before lunch. Then on a dusty pitch, the openers, Bilby and Shrimpton, stayed together for seventy minutes and, with the other batsmen following their example, the New Zealanders became immune from defeat before bad light brought the game to an end forty minutes earlier than arranged.

President's XI

G. P. Bilby c Murray b Knight	5	— b Boycott	24
M. J. F. Shrimpton run out	58	— c Parks b Higgs	46
P. B. Truscott b Higgs	12	— c Knight b Higgs	22
*B. W. Sinclair c Russell b Allen	41	— c Boycott b Russell	46
R. W. Morgan not out	72	— c and b Parks	21
G. M. Turner lbw b Parfitt	5		
†A. E. Dick c Knight b Allen	13	— c Allen b Russell	10
P. R. Taylor b Allen	5	— b Russell	0
B. W. Yuile c Edrich b Allen	4	— not out	0
R. O. Collinge c Smith b Allen	0		
R. E. Sutton c Parfitt b Knight	12		
B 5, l-b 4, n-b 1	10	B 12, l-b 7	19
1/9 2/28 3/108 4/132 5/144 6/164 7/173 8/181 9/197	237	1/58 2/93 3/130 4/178 5/178 6/188 7/188 (7 wkts.)	188

Bowling: *First Innings*—Higgs 19—9—26—1; Knight 14.3—5—41—2; Allen 45—17—96—5; Parfitt 18—6—50—1; Boycott 11—7—14—0. *Second Innings*—Knight 2—2—0—0; Higgs 27—13—57—2; Allen 22—8—62—0; Boycott 16—6—27—1; Parks 5—3—9—1; Russell 4—1—20—3.

M.C.C.

G. Boycott c Sinclair b Yuile	51
W. E. Russell b Collinge	6
J. H. Edrich c Shrimpton b Yuile	43
P. H. Parfitt c Truscott b Taylor	121
*M. J. K. Smith c Shrimpton b Collinge	78
M. C. Cowdrey not out	46
B. R. Knight c Yuile b Taylor	6
J. M. Parks not out	2
B 2, l-b 4	6
1/16 2/97 3/105 4/294 5/313 6/333 (6 wkts., dec.)	359

†J. T. Murray, D. A. Allen and K. Higgs did not bat.

Bowling: Sutton 20—6—46—0; Taylor 35—3—131—2; Collinge 28—8—87—2; Yuile 21—4—78—2; Morgan 2—0—11—0.

Umpires: W. T. Martin and R. Allen.

NEW ZEALAND v. ENGLAND

First Test

At Christchurch, February 25, 26, 28, March 1. Drawn. Excitement ran high in this match. Twice New Zealand, by capturing the first four England wickets cheaply, seemed to have gained the upper hand, but in the end they collapsed and were in danger of being dismissed for less than 26, the record lowest total credited to them at Auckland in 1955 in Sir Leonard Hutton's last Test.

For the first time for many years New Zealand had a new captain in Chapple, Reid having retired after setting up a world record of fifty-eight consecutive Test appearances, previously jointly held by Frank Woolley and Peter May, each with fifty-two.

Although the pitch was soft after several days of rain and lowering cloud forecast trouble for batsmen, Smith, winning the toss, decided to bat. It was the captain, with Parfitt, who extricated the side from difficulties in a stand of 113 before Puna, an Indian, appearing in his first Test, made one of several brilliant catches. As the pitch eased the tail built up the score, Allen playing well for three and three-quarter hours for 88. Brown also shaped confidently for two and a quarter hours while the partnership realised 107.

Congdon kept the New Zealand innings on a firm basis and finished with the tenth Test hundred for his country against England which occupied nearly five and a half hours. Petrie signalled his return to Test cricket after five years, by playing soundly for 55 and finally Motz, two 6's and six 4's, hit magnificently so that New Zealand gained a first-innings lead of five.

Their cup of joy overflowed when by the end of the third day they had disposed of Boycott and Edrich for 32, but again they were thwarted by Smith and Parfitt and England set them to make 197 to win in two hours and twenty minutes.

Suddenly the England bowlers took charge and in nine overs Higgs claimed four wickets for five runs, but Pollard, hero of several innings in England in 1965 and Cunis, a well-built Rugby centre-threequarter, saved the day by defending successfully through the last thirty-five minutes.

Other highlights in the match were Parks' five catches behind the stumps in the first innings, equalling his own and Binks' England record and Cowdrey's easy catch at second slip from Chapple, which equalled W. R. Hammond's feat of one hundred Test catches. Moreover, Cowdrey held the ball on almost the same spot where Hammond claimed his hundredth victim.

England

G. Boycott c Petrie b Motz	4	— run out	4
W. E. Russell b Motz	30	— b Bartlett	25
J. H. Edrich c Bartlett b Motz	2	— lbw b Cunis	2
M. C. Cowdrey c Bilby b Cunis	0	— c Pollard b Motz	21
*M. J. K. Smith c Puna b Pollard	54	— c Bilby b Puna	87
P. H. Parfitt c Congdon b Bartlett	54	— not out	46
†J. M. Parks c Petrie b Chapple	30	— not out	4
D. A. Allen c Chapple b Bartlett	88		
D. J. Brown b Cunis	44		
K. Higgs not out	8		
I. J. Jones b Bartlett	0		
B 6, l-b 6, n-b 16	28	B 4, n-b 8	12
1/19 2/28 3/47 4/47 5/160 6/160 7/209 8/316 9/342	342	1/18 2/32 3/48 4/68 5/193 (5 wkts., dec.)	201

Bowling: *First Innings*—Motz 31—9—83—3; Bartlett 33.2—6—63—3; Cunis 31—9—63—2; Puna 18—6—54—0; Chapple 9—3—24—1; Pollard 5—1—27—1. *Second Innings*—Motz 20—6—38—1; Bartlett 14—2—44—1; Cunis 19—3—58—1; Puna 14—6—49—1.

New Zealand

G. P. Bilby c Parks b Higgs	28	— c Parks b Brown	3
M. J. F. Shrimpton c Parks b Brown	11	— c Smith b Allen	13
B. E. Congdon c Smith b Jones	104	— c Cowdrey b Higgs	4
B. W. Sinclair c and b Higgs	23	— c Parks b Higgs	0
V. Pollard lbw b Higgs	23	— not out	6
*M. E. Chapple c Cowdrey b Jones	15	— c Parks b Higgs	0
G. A. Bartlett c Parks b Brown	0	— c Brown b Parfitt	0
†E. C. Petrie c Parks b Brown	55	— lbw b Higgs	1
R. C. Motz c Parks b Jones	58	— c Russell b Parfitt	2
R. Cunis not out	8	— not out	16
N. Puna c Smith b Jones	1		
B 7, l-b 13, n-b 1	21	B 2, l-b 1	3
1/39 2/41 3/112 4/181 5/202 6/203 7/237 8/326 9/344	347	1/5 2/19 3/21 4/21 5/22 6/22 7/22 8/32 (8 wkts.)	48

Bowling: *First Innings*—Brown 30—3—80—3; Jones 28.3—9—71—4; Higgs 30—6—51—3; Allen 40—14—80—0; Boycott 12—6—30—0; Parfitt 3—0—14—0. *Second Innings*—Brown 4—2—6—1; Jones 7—3—13—0; Higgs 9—7—5—4; Allen 19—15—8—1; Parfitt 6—3—5—2; Parks 3—1—8—0.

Umpires: W. T. Martin and F. R. Goodall.

NEW ZEALAND v. ENGLAND

Second Test

At Dunedin, March 4, 5, 7, 8. Drawn. Cheerless conditions prevailed and so much time was lost through rain that a definite result never really appeared possible. With Chapple suffering from a damaged leg muscle, New Zealand had another new captain in Sinclair. The start was delayed for nearly two and a half hours and only three and a quarter hours' cricket took place on the first day when New Zealand lost five wickets while crawling to 83. The air was icy and the outfield sodden.

The second day was memorable for the excellent wicket-keeping of Murray—he took an amazing left-handed catch from Pollard far away to leg—and some more dazzling hitting by Motz. Allen tempted Motz, who hit him for 4 and three 6's in one over, and added four more 4's while making top score in under two hours. Altogether New Zealand occupied six and a quarter hours for their total of 192.

England, too, found batting a slow business; during a brief third day's cricket of less than two hours, Cowdrey reached fifty in three and a quarter hours while England's total was taken to 181 for five. Next day Smith declared when Cowdrey, having hit seven 4's and batted five and three-quarter hours, still wanted 11 for his century.

As Shrimpton had gone down with influenza, Pollard opened the New Zealand second innings with Bilby and though he failed they lost only three wickets in the next two hours for 75, but after tea Allen, three wickets in two overs, caused a breakdown before careful play by Petrie and Puna kept New Zealand out of danger. Puna, off-spin, was the pick of the New Zealand bowlers. Following criticism of Bartlett's action, B. R. Taylor was given his place in the final Test.

New Zealand

First innings		Second innings	
G. P. Bilby c Murray b Jones	3	— c Parfitt b Higgs	21
M. J. F. Shrimpton c Boycott b Higgs	38	— b Allen	0
B. E. Congdon c Murray b Jones	0	— b Parfitt	19
*B. W. Sinclair b Knight	33	— c Knight b Jones	39
V. Pollard c Murray b Higgs	8	— b Higgs	2
R. W. Morgan c Murray b Higgs	0	— c Smith b Allen	3
G. A. Bartlett c Parfitt b Allen	6	— c Knight b Allen	4
†E. C. Petrie c Smith b Jones	28	— not out	13
R. C. Motz c Higgs b Knight	57	— b Jones	1
R. S. Cunis c Boycott b Allen	8	— lbw b Allen	9
N. Puna not out	3	— not out	18
B 4, l-b 4	8	B 10, l-b 6, n-b 2	18
1/4 2/6 3/66 4/83 5/83 6/92 7/100 8/179 9/181	192	1/8 2/27 3/66 4/75 5/75 6/79 7/100 8/102 9/112 (9 wkts.)	147

Bowling: *First Innings*—Jones 26—11—46—3; Higgs 20—6—29—3; Knight 32—14—41—2; Allen 27.3—9—68—2. *Second Innings*—Jones 15—4—32—2; Higgs 13—7—12—2; Knight 3—1—3—0; Allen 33—17—46—4; Parfitt 17—6—30—1; Edrich 1—0—6—0.

England

G. Boycott b Bartlett	5
W. E. Russell b Motz	11
J. H. Edrich c Bilby b Cunis	36
M. C. Cowdrey not out	89
*M. J. K. Smith c Pollard b Bartlett	20
P. H. Parfitt c Pollard b Puna	4
†J. T. Murray c Sinclair b Puna	50
B. R. Knight c Bartlett b Motz	12
D. A. Allen b Cunis	9
K. Higgs not out	0
B 4, l-b 6, n-b 8	18
1/9 2/32 3/72 4/103 5/119 6/200 7/213 8/241 (8 wkts., dec.)	254

I. J. Jones did not bat.

Bowling: Motz 32—7—76—2; Bartlett 29—4—70—2; Cunis 28—7—49—2; Puna 14—2—40—2; Pollard 1—0—1—0.

Umpires: W. T. Martin and W. J. Gwynne.

NEW ZEALAND v. ENGLAND

Third Test

At Auckland, March 11, 12, 14, 15. Drawn. No one could blame the weather for yet another undecided contest. Both sides showed little enterprise and especially New Zealand. They were opposed to a side with only ten men, Edrich having been stricken down with appendicitis after the match began. Altogether the Test occupied twenty-four hours, but it produced only 806 runs—an average of 33 an hour—and these included 47 extras.

Sinclair, the New Zealand captain, had the satisfaction of hitting his third Test hundred, his first against England, but he needed three-quarters of an hour for his last 12 runs which gave him three figures. Higgs again bowled well for England and New Zealand's total at the end of the first day was 237 for six; Sinclair 103 not out.

England soon completed their immediate task, mainly through Allen, and then Taylor, with his first ball in Test cricket in New Zealand, removed Parfitt, the deputy opener. Russell and Cowdrey displayed style and confidence in a prolonged stand of 118, but the tail failed against Pollard and New Zealand gained a lead of 74.

This was soon discounted on Shrimpton and Jarvis departing without a run on the board and by the close of the third day New Zealand stood 179 runs ahead with four wickets left.

In the end England faced the task of getting 204 to win in four and a half hours and though at one period Sinclair set a defensive field for Motz, Taylor and Cunis, withdrawing the slips and leg trap, England never asserted any superiority against opponents who averaged only sixteen overs an hour. It was a poor show.

New Zealand

T. W. Jarvis c Parks b Jones	39	— c Parks b Jones	0
M. J. F. Shrimpton b Brown	6	— lbw b Brown	0
B. E. Congdon lbw b Higgs	64	— run out	23
*B. W. Sinclair c Russell b Jones	114	— b Higgs	9
R. W. Morgan c Russell b Allen	5	— lbw b Knight	25
V. Pollard c Knight b Allen	2	— c Parks b Jones	25
†E. C. Petrie c Smith b Higgs	12	— b Higgs	6
R. C. Motz c Jones b Allen	16	— c Smith b Jones	14
B. R. Taylor b Allen	18	— b Higgs	6
R. S. Cunis not out	6	— c sub b Allen	8
N. Puna c Russell b Allen	7	— not out	2
B 1, l-b 4, n-b 2	7	B 2, l-b 7, n-b 2	11
1/22 2/99 3/142 4/153 5/189 6/237 7/262 8/264 9/288	296	1/0 2/0 3/20 4/48 5/68 6/85 7/109 8/118 9/121	129

Bowling: *First Innings*—Brown 18—6—32—1; Jones 21—4—52—2; Higgs 28—13—33—2; Allen 47.5—12—123—5; Knight 16—8—40—0; Parfitt 2—0—9—0. *Second Innings*—Brown 9—3—8—1; Jones 25—9—28—3; Higgs 28—11—27—3; Allen 23.3—5—34—1; Knight 18—9—21—1.

England

P. H. Parfitt b Taylor	3	— b Taylor	30
W. E. Russell lbw b Motz	56	— c Petrie b Taylor	1
M. C. Cowdrey run out	59	— lbw b Puna	27
*M. J. K. Smith b Taylor	18	— lbw b Cunis	30
†J. M. Parks lbw b Taylor	38	— not out	45
B. R. Knight c Taylor b Pollard	25	— not out	13
D. A. Allen not out	7		
D. J. Brown b Pollard	0		
K. Higgs c Petrie b Pollard	0		
I. J. Jones b Cunis	0		
J. H. Edrich absent ill	—		
B 10, l-b 4, n-b 2	16	B 4, l-b 4, n-b 5	13
1/3 2/121 3/128 4/175 5/195 6/215 7/215 8/219 9/222	222	1/2 2/50 3/79 4/112 (4 wkts.)	159

Bowling: *First Innings*—Motz 15—4—42—1; Taylor 21—6—46—3; Cunis 25.5—8—45—1; Puna 22—2—70—0; Pollard 5—2—3—3. *Second Innings*—Motz 16—1—32—0; Taylor 12—4—20—2; Pollard 14—3—30—0; Cunis 18—5—33—1; Puna 12—4—27—1; Shrimpton 2—1—1—0; Jarvis 1—0—3—0.

Umpires: W. T. Martin and R. W. Shortt.

M.C.C. IN HONG KONG

Two matches in Hong Kong were arranged for M.C.C. on their way home The first was spoiled by rain:

At Hong Kong, March 18. M.C.C. 149 for seven (W. E. Russell 37, J. T. Murray 35; C. Metcalfe five for 41); President's XI did not bat. Drawn.

At Kowloon, March 19. M.C.C. 266 for six dec. (G. Boycott 108, W. E. Russell 59; M. C. Cowdrey 46); Hong Kong XI 193 (D. Coffey 88, P. Hall 41; I. J. Jones four for 5, D. A. Allen four for 28). M.C.C. won by 73 runs.

WORCESTERSHIRE IN JAMAICA, 1966

By Jack Anderson

Once again Carreras, of Jamaica, came forward to help the development of Jamaica sport by bringing Worcestershire, the English County Champions of 1964 and 1965, for a five match tour in March 1966 under the management of their secretary, Joe Lister. They were the second County Championship team to visit Jamaica, Yorkshire having toured in 1936. Worcestershire, led by Donald Kenyon, an England selector in 1966, proved to be fine ambassadors. The tour was confined to the rural areas, to help build the game in those parts, but one two-day match against a Jamaica Next XI was played in Kingston. All five matches played resulted in draws. The only first-class match was a four-day game against a Jamaica Invitation XI at Jarrett Park, Montego Bay.

The Jamaica team, besides having the West Indies captain Garfield Sobers in their midst, also included three other members of the West Indies 17 who later toured England.

Not until the final match did a local team manage to take first-innings lead over the tourists. Against the Invitation XI in the first innings Worcestershire managed to score the respectable total of 270, but after the local team had replied with 323, due mainly to a fine innings of 120 by Sobers, who hit two 6's and seventeen 4's, and an enterprising 73 by the young and promising Maurice Foster, the County Champions rallied with 259 for five. This included a fine knock pf 101 by the South African, Basil d'Oliveira, who hit one 6 and fifteen 4's. V. Fray batted promisingly both in the Next XI and Jamaica games.

Worcestershire were without Tom Graveney, their star player, who so successfully returned to the England side against the West Indies, but had to drop out of the tour at the last moment because of his wife's illness.

At Monymusk, Clarendon, March 18, 19. Jamaica Colts 166 (L. Dyer 59: D. N. F. Slade seven for 47); Worcestershire 229 for six (D. W. Richardson 56, J. A. Ormrod 53*, D. Kenyon 39; D. Lewis (aged 16) took three for 69 in 14 overs). Rain allowed less than two hours' play on the first day. Drawn.

At Kirkvine, Mandeville, March 21, 22. Worcestershire 201 for four dec. (R. G. A. Headley 63, B. d'Oliveira 47, M. J. Horton 37) and 80 for two dec. (M. J. Horton 39*); Southern Parishes 105 (B. d'Oliveira four for 17, N. Gifford three for 26) and 39 for three. Drawn.

At St. Ann's Bay, March 24, 25. Rain interfered with play, allowing only three hours and ten minutes play in the two days. Worcestershire 204 for five dec. (B. d'Oliveira 60*, D. Kenyon 45, J. A. Ormrod 41, M. J. Horton 36); Northern Parishes 79 for four. Drawn.

At Kingston, March 26, 28. Jamaica Next XI 247 (R. Grandison 68, V. Fray 58, H. Parris 36*; L. J. Coldwell three for 56); Worcestershire 287 for nine (R. Booth 74, B. d'Oliveira 54, M. J. Horton 52, J. A. Ormrod 50, L. Chambers five for 73). Drawn.

WORCESTERSHIRE v. JAMAICA INVITATION XI

At Jarrett Park, Montego Bay, March 30, 31, April 1, 2. Drawn.

Worcestershire

*D. Kenyon c Hendriks b Sobers	45	— b Hamilton	25
M. J. Horton st Hendriks b Foster	36	— c Fray b Hamilton	52
R. G. A. Headley c and b Levy	20	— c Hendriks b Hamilton	0
B. d'Oliveira c sub b Foster	9	— c Levy b Foster	101
D. W. Richardson b Hamilton	67	— c Fray b Sobers	28
J. A. Ormrod lbw b Hamilton	51	— run out	21
†R. Booth c McMorris b Cohen	1	— not out	29
D. N. F. Slade not out	16	— not out	0
B. M. Brain b Cohen	0		
L. J. Coldwell c Dyer b Cohen	1		
J. A. Flavell b Hamilton	8		
B 7, l-b 6, w 1, n-b 2	16	L-b 3	3
1/82 2/99 3/117 4/121 5/230 6/237 7/250 8/259 9/261	270	1/35 2/35 3/111 4/186 5/224 6/251 (6 wkts., dec.)	259

Bowling: *First Innings*: Cohen 23—1—73—3; Sobers 20—5—66—1; Hamilton 17.2—2—53—3; Levy 17—9—29—1; Foster 20—8—33—2. *Second Innings*—Cohen 11—0—42—0; Sobers 27—6—60—1; Hamilton 17—3—61—3; Levy 14—8—25—0; Foster 17—2—68—1.

Jamaica Invitation XI

V. Fray lbw b Coldwell	67	— not out	60
E. D. McMorris b Coldwell	4	— b Brain	0
T. Griffith c and b Horton	34	— c sub b Brain	36
M. Foster c Ormrod b Coldwell	73	— c Headley b Coldwell	9
G. S. Sobers b Flavell	120		
H. Bennett lbw b Coldwell	0	— not out	11
L. Dyer c Richardson b Flavell	4		
†J. L. Hendriks c Headley b Flavell	0		
L. Levy c Headley b Flavell	5		
R. A. Cohen c Richardson b Flavell	0		
J. Hamilton not out	8		
B 4, l-b 3, n-b 1	8	B 4, l-b 1	5
1/10 2/76 3/162 4/210 5/210 6/241 7/241 8/293 9/311	323	1/2 2/60 3/73 (3 wkts.)	121

Bowling: *First Innings*—Flavell 21.1—4—73—5; Coldwell 23—5—64—4; Brain 12—1—45—0; Slade 17—6—50—0; Horton 17—6—66—1; d'Oliveira 4—1—17—0. *Second Innings*—Flavell 1—0—1—0; Coldwell 9—0—34—1; Brain 7—0—35—2; Slade 6—2—19—0; Horton 5—0—18—0; Kenyon 1—0—9—0.

Umpires: D. Sang Hue and N. Sealey.

OVERSEAS CRICKET, 1965–66

AUSTRALIAN INTER-STATE MATCHES

By T. L. Goodman

SHEFFIELD SHIELD RESULTS

	Played	Won	Won on 1st Inns.	Drawn	Lost on 1st Inns.	Lost	Points
Points awarded.........	–	10*	4	2	–	–	–
New South Wales......	8	4*	0	0	1	3†	40
Western Australia......	8	2	4	0	2	0	36
South Australia........	8	2	1	0	3	2†	28
Victoria..............	8	2*	3	0	2	1	24
Queensland............	8	1*	1	0	1	5†	18

* Includes outright win (in the case of Victoria two outright wins) after being behind on 1st innings, for which 6 points only are awarded.

† Includes outright defeat (in the case of Queensland two outright defeats) after leading on 1st innings, for which 4 points are awarded.

New South Wales retained the Sheffield Shield and this performance was the more noteworthy because that State had suffered more than most others through absentees on duty in matches against the M.C.C. touring team.

This tour made it more difficult for the Inter-State series to be financially profitable.

Among many great individual performances was that of Queensland's pace bowler Peter Allan, who took all ten wickets in Victoria's first innings in Melbourne.

As in the previous summer, the Shield competition boiled up into a virtual "final" in the last match, New South Wales v. Western Australia, in Perth. Western Australia needed an outright victory (10 points) to win the competition for the first time since 1947–48. They managed to gain only first-innings points (four). This in itself was a splendid effort as New South Wales had totalled 458 runs after being 423 for six at the end of the first day. Western Australia declared at 459 for eight thanks to their right-handed opener, P. C. Kelly and left-hander M. Vernon, who bettered their State second-wicket Shield record by adding 203 runs. New South Wales, for whom K. D. Walters and N. C. O'Neill hit centuries in the first innings, had to stall for time in their second innings, having begun the last (fourth) day at 86 for five. H. B. Taber (the wicket-keeper) and P. T. Philpott resisted stubbornly and at one stage only 11 runs came from 15 overs. The fast bowler, G. D. McKenzie, finished with six wickets for 100 runs—a grand effort of perseverance in extreme heat. In the end, time beat Western Australia, who, 96 for one in the last innings, needed 126 more runs for outright victory.

New South Wales suffered three outright defeats in the competition, whereas Western Australia's only two reverses were on the first innings.

There was a vital game in Sydney, in which New South Wales beat South Australia by an innings after the first day and much of the second had been washed out by rain. Before this match, Western Australia led the competition with 32 points, having one match to play; New South Wales, 30 and South Australia, 28, each had two matches to play.

After South Australia's medium-paced swing bowler, D. Robins, had taken cheap wickets, the Test batsman Walters and a new young player, G. Davies made a stand of 199 for N.S.W. The fast bowler, D. A. Renneberg, quickly dismissed South Australia's openers in the second innings.

The competition opened with a remarkable match in Brisbane, where Queensland led New South Wales on the first innings by 199 runs, following a century by

P. J. Burge and the routing of New South Wales by the pace pair, Allan and R. Duncan, on a lifting pitch, for 108. New South Wales, following on, were virtually 0 for two when Simpson had his left fore-arm broken and O'Neill had been dismissed. The opening batsman, Grahame Thomas, played a magnificent innings for 182 runs at one a minute and Booth, Walters and Rothwell made valuable contributions. In the Queensland second innings Trimble and Burge quickly fell to Renneberg, who also threw down the wicket of Bull. Some exciting catching helped New South Wales to win by 27 runs.

Western Australia won all four away matches, after losing at home to Victoria. South Australia gained a fine win over New South Wales in an animated match in Adelaide, where the visitors were forced to follow-on. Victoria wiped off a first-innings deficit and won over New South Wales in Sydney, I. R. Redpath making the winning hit, to finish with 161 not out after an admirable innings. Queensland were disappointing, failing to back up splendid work by their pace bowlers, Allan, Duncan and Morgan.

Allan, against Victoria in Melbourne, became only the second bowler to capture all ten wickets in a Shield innings; another pace man, T. W. Wall (South Australia) took all ten New South Wales wickets in Sydney in 1932–3 (for 36 runs). Allan at the close of the first day had taken four wickets for 32 runs, with Victoria 76 for four; the next day he captured the remaining six wickets and the runs debited against him included five overthrows. His complete figures, for a superb effort of control of length, swing and pace, were: 15.6 overs, 3 maidens, 61 runs, 10 wickets.

Allan had put Victoria out for 130 runs—a first-innings deficit of 50 and Queensland then scored 336. An opening stand for 213 runs by Redpath and G. D. Watson proved the basis of Victoria's three-wicket win.

Allan and Duncan, who the previous season had shared 65 Shield wickets, were joined in Queensland's team midway through the 1965–6 season by another of their pace type, tall John Morgan, aged 20, who took five wickets in an innings in three of his five matches and with 25 wickets at 19.20 led the first-class averages.

The biggest wicket-takers in all first-class cricket during the season were the Test medium-pacer N. J. N. Hawke (S. A.), with 49; the English left-arm spinner G. A. R. Lock (W.A.) 44, J. W. Martin (N.S.W.) 41, G. D. McKenzie (W.A.) and D. J. Sincock (S.A.) each 40 and Allan 39; the last-named finished second to Morgan in the averages. Lock captured most wickets in the Shield series, 41.

Martin, another left-arm spinner, though in his case the stock ball turns from the off, took 39 Shield wickets. He reached a tally of 261 wickets in the inter-State games, of which 10 were secured in a season for South Australia. R. Benaud has taken most Shield wickets for New South Wales, 266. Martin had intended to retire from first-class cricket in the season under review; but he quickly found form, his sharp spin being assisted by his home pitch at Sydney. He went on to win a place in the Australian team to tour South Africa, ousting another left-hander, Sincock, who again had too many days of untidy bowling.

K. R. Stackpole (Vic.), whose stock ball was the top-spinner, supplemented strong batting with useful bowling performances and he also was selected for South Africa.

A feature was the success of the pace brigade. D. A. Renneberg (N.S.W.) and the left-hander J. Hubble (W.A.) produced some excellent bursts and were chosen to support McKenzie and Hawke in South Africa. A. N. Connolly did his customary solid work for Victoria. Along with Morgan in the medium to fast-medium department were I. Brayshaw (W.A.), G. D. Watson (Vic.) and D. Robins (S.A.). Watson, also a first-class batsman, hit a double-century opening partnership with Redpath—Brayshaw played some stalwart innings; Robins performed the " hat-trick " against New South Wales in Adelaide.

The heaviest run-getters in the first-class programme were Victoria's left-handed Test batsmen, W. M. Lawry (most runs, 1,445) and R. M. Cowper (1,418 runs, including his 307 in the fifth Test, and top average of 74.63). New South Wales' youthful K. D. Walters, who hit centuries in his first two Tests against England, totalled 1,332 runs; G. Thomas (N.S.W.) 1,171 and I. M. Chappell (S.A.) 1,019. Chappell's sound methods continued to make him a most interesting player.

Western Australia received full value from the former N.S.W. opener, P. J.

Kelly; he scored a century in each innings for a combined team against M.C.C. in Perth and later played many vigilant innings for the State. Kelly had a solid opening partner in the former New Zealand Test batsman, W. R. Playle. The presence of the left-handed M. Vernon in some home games was a great asset. Lawry and Redpath (Vic.) participated in further big stands; two experienced batsmen, S. C. Trimble (Qld.) and H. N. Dansie (S.A.) increased their notable list of centuries. Injuries and illness put the great New South Wales pair R. B. Simpson and N. C. O'Neill out of action for some time; Simpson missed the first Test through injury and the third through chicken-pox. B. C. Booth (N.S.W.), who led Australia in those two matches, had no luck during the season. Two young batsmen, A. B. Shiell (S.A.) and R. J. Inverarity (W.A.) confirmed their promise of the previous season; two 19-year-olds, P. Sheehan (Vic.) a tall right-hander from Melbourne University, and G. Davies (N.S.W.) showed excellent batting talent, and Davies did some useful leg-spin bowling.

Shiell was among four players who made double centuries (202 not out). Simpson's great 225 was scored in the fourth Test, in Adelaide. Thomas, following his exhilarating centuries in State games in Brisbane and Adelaide, played an explosive innings of 229 (run out) in four and a half hours against Victoria in Melbourne, on a day of enervating heat; in the same match J. Potter (Vic.) recovered top form with a fine innings of 221. Another notable effort was by the wicket-keeper B. N. Jarman (S.A.), who reached 196 against New South Wales in Adelaide and ran up 725 runs in first-class matches.

The Test batsman Walters, after completing the " big cricket " season was called up for two years of National Service in the Army and misses the South African tour, but he expects to be available for selection for the tour of England in 1968.

Western Australia's stalwart batsman and captain, B. K. Shepherd, has been transferred to Sydney in his employment and in future will be available for New South Wales; the South Australian spin bowler, D. J. Sincock, has also gone to Sydney.

Queensland and Western Australia continued to play on Sundays in matches against each other; in 1965–5 Victoria played their away matches with those States on Sundays.

Mr. Sydney Smith, C.B.E., retired from the presidency of the New South Wales Cricket Association, which he had held since 1935. Mr. Smith, now aged 86, was manager of the 1921 and 1926 Australian teams in England. He was succeeded as president of the N.S.W. Association by Mr. E. G. Macmillan, who at the time was chairman of the Australian Board of Control.

QUEENSLAND v. NEW SOUTH WALES

At Brisbane, October 29, 30, November 1, 2. New South Wales won by 27 runs. They fought back after being 199 runs behind on the first innings, and, following on, being virtually no runs for two wickets in the second innings, Simpson having retired with a broken left fore-arm and O'Neill having been dismissed. The recovery was inspired by Grahame Thomas, who in a magnificent innings scored 182 runs (one 6 and thirty-three 4's) in just over three hours. Thomas dominated a second-wicket stand of 236 runs. Booth contributing 54 not out to this partnership. Queensland, for whom Burge and Grout batted stout-heartedly in the first innings, were set 252 runs to win outright; but the fast bowler Renneberg quickly dismissed Trimble and Burge. Veivers hit ten 4's in making 54; but New South Wales prevailed over some dogged batting.

Queensland

First innings		Second innings	
S. C. Trimble c Taber b Renneberg	8	c Booth b Renneberg	6
D. F. Bull c Taber b Corling	0	run out	0
W. Buckle b Corling	20	b Renneberg	22
*P. J. Burge c Thomas b Renneberg	111	c Corling b Renneberg	0
T. R. Veivers c Philpott b Martin	46	st Taber b Martin	54
D. Hughson st Taber b Philpott	10	lbw b Martin	41
J. R. Mackay c Taber b Renneberg	0	c Martin b Philpott	42
†A. W. T. Grout c Booth b Philpott	91	lbw b Renneberg	8
D. Hale b Walters	17	c Booth b Philpott	9
P. J. Allan run out	0	c O'Neill b Philpott	20
R. Duncan not out	1	not out	10
B 1, l-b 2	3	B 9, l-b 3	12
1/8 2/8 3/48 4/179 5/188 6/193 7/217 8/300 9/301	307	1/1 2/18 3/18 4/39 5/96 6/111 7/154 8/185 9/195	224

Bowling: *First Innings* Renneberg 12—1—50—3; Corling 15—1—61—2; Walters 11—1—56—1; Philpott 14.7—2—92—2; Martin 8—0—39—1; O'Neill 1—0—6—0. *Second Innings*—Renneberg 17—5—37—4; Corling 6—1—29—0; Walters 4—0—18—0; Philpott 13.5—1—40—3; Martin 17—4—65—2; O'Neill 3—0—23—0.

New South Wales

First innings		Second innings	
*R. B. Simpson c Burge b Allan	0	retired hurt	0
G. Thomas c Grout b Duncan	17	c Grout b Veivers	182
N. C. O'Neill c Trimble b Duncan	1	c Burge b Allan	0
B. C. Booth c Allan b Veivers	29	st Grout b Veivers	56
K. D. Walters c Veivers b Duncan	2	c Buckle b Mackay	84
B. A. Rothwell c Bull b Allan	4	not out	75
P. I. Philpott c Grout b Duncan	2	lbw b Duncan	5
J. W. Martin b Allan	51	c Buckle b Mackay	23
†H. B. Taber not out	1	st Grout b Veivers	16
D. A. Renneberg b Allan	0	b Mackay	0
G. E. Corling c Burge b Veivers	1	lbw b Allan	7
		L-b 2	2
1/0 2/5 3/26 4/28 5/37 6/40 7/81 8/107 9/107	108	1/0 2/236 3/239 4/278 5/346 6/353 7/392 8/396 9/450	450

Bowling: *First Innings*—Allan 13—2—32—4; Duncan 12—2—42—4; Mackay 5—0—25—0; Veivers 5.3—1—9—2. *Second Innings*—Allan 23.5—1—128—2; Duncan 18—4—86—1; Mackay 21—2—118—3; Veivers 28—7—69—3; Hale 8—0—47—0.

Umpires: J. Goodwin and L. Rowan.

SOUTH AUSTRALIA v. VICTORIA

At Adelaide, November 5, 6, 8, 9. Victoria won on the first innings. Victoria overhauled South Australia's score of 401, thanks mainly to an exhilarating opening partnership of 204 runs in two and a half hours by Lawry and Redpath. The leg-spinner Rayson took ten South Australian wickets in the match, including three for three runs at one stage in the second innings, in which Jarman led a rearguard action. Chappell batted splendidly for 82 (ten 4's) in the first innings.

South Australia

First Innings		Second Innings	
*L. E. Favell c Connolly b Grant	48	st Jordon b Rayson	76
L. Marks lbw b Watson	35	lbw b Connolly	0
I. M. Chappell b Rayson	82	run out	25
K. G. Cunningham b Grant	8	c Grant b Rayson	16
D. A. Sharpe c Lawry b Rayson	72	c and b Rayson	15
A. B. Shiell c Connolly b Rayson	51	b Grant	0
N. J. N. Hawke c Lawry b Rayson	1	c Jordon b Rayson	3
G. Griffiths c Lawry b Rayson	13	c Jordon b Stackpole	34
†B. N. Jarman b Doble	52	not out	76
D. J. Sincock st Jordon b Rayson	23	c Doble b Connolly	29
D. Robins not out	2	c Grant b Anderson	16
L-b 5, w 3, n-b 6	14	B 2, l-b 1, n-b 2	5
1/69 2/103 3/142 4/236 5/263 6/266 7/285 8/376 9/390	401	1/3 2/62 3/117 4/120 5/121 6/124 7/167 8/171 9/240	295

Bowling: *First Innings*—Connolly 18—0—50—0; Doble 10.5—0—68—1; Grant 24—1—100—2; Watson 9—1—32—1; Rayson 23—3—97—6; Stackpole 11—2—38—0; Anderson 1—0—2—0. *Second Innings*—Connolly 11—2—40—2; Doble 6—0—48—0; Grant 15—1—68—1; Rayson 24.6—6—91—4; Stackpole 16—3—36—1; Anderson 4.1—2—7—1.

Victoria

First Innings		Second Innings	
*W. M. Lawry c Chappell b Robins	160		
I. R. Redpath b Sincock	107		
K. R. Stackpole c Marks b Sincock	54		
D. J. Anderson c Favell b Sincock	22	b Robins	0
G. D. Watson b Sincock	31	not out	18
P. Williams c Favell b Sincock	63	not out	8
†R. C. Jordon lbw b Chappell	23	b Hawke	2
J. W. Grant c and b Hawke	7		
A. N. Connolly c Sincock b Griffiths	5		
R. W. Rayson not out	0		
A. W. Doble c Chappell b Griffiths	0		
B 3, l-b 1, w 2	6	W 1	1
1/204 2/317 3/335 4/379 5/380 6/435 7/456 8/478 9/478	478	1/4 2/9 (2 wkts.)	29

Bowling: *First Innings*—Hawke 22—1—104—1; Robins 12—1—50—1; Chappell 17—1—71—1; Sincock 33—1—168—5; Griffiths 24.2—3—79—2. *Second Innings*—Hawke 3—0—8—1; Robins 3—0—11—1; Cunningham 2—0—5—0; Favell 1—0—4—0.

Umpires: C. J. Egar and J. C. Novak.

WESTERN AUSTRALIA v. VICTORIA

At Perth, November 12, 13, 14, 15. Victoria won on the first innings. Western Australia found the opposing fast bowlers, Connolly and Grant, hostile, though Grant was unlucky; the Victorian leg-spinner, Rayson, took good wickets. Cowper batted soundly to help Victoria to a lead, despite steady bowling by Lock. Cowper followed with a solid second innings of 113, in three and a quarter hours. Western Australia had recovered to reveal batting depth in their second effort after a three-figure opening stand by Kelly and Playle.

Western Australia

P. C. Kelly c Cowper b Connolly	0	run out 80
W. R. Playle c Connolly b Cowper	41	c Watson b Grant 48
M. Vernon c Stackpole b Connolly	7	st Williams b Stackpole 27
*B. K. Shepherd st Jordon b Rayson	58	run out 0
R. J. Inverarity run out	4	lbw b Grant 56
I. Brayshaw c Redpath b Rayson	31	b Grant 48
T. Jenner c Cowper b Connolly	25	b Rayson 36
†G. C. Becker c Jordon b Stackpole	11	b Watson 22
G. D. McKenzie not out	2	c sub b Watson 26
G. A. R. Lock b Stackpole	15	not out 28
L. C. Mayne b Rayson	5	not out 4
B 1, n-b 2	3	B 6, l-b 1, w 2, n-b 3 12
1/0 2/12 3/101 4/112 5/118 6/151 7/179 8/179 9/195	202	1/125 2/151 3/152 4/157 5/266 6/269 7/325 8/348 9/383 (9 wkts. dec.) 387

Bowling: *First Innings*—Connolly 14—2—48—3; Grant 14—3—29—0; Watson 3—1—13—0; Stackpole 9—2—22—2; Rayson 13.7—1—66—3; Cowper 10—4—21—1. *Second Innings*—Connolly 14—1—58—0; Grant 24—5—85—3; Watson 9—1—31—2; Stackpole 20—3—67—1; Rayson 15—1—89—1; Cowper 13—3—37—0; Anderson 3—0—7—0; Redpath 1—0—1—0.

Victoria

*W. M. Lawry run out	51	b McKenzie 11
I. R. Redpath hit wkt. b Mayne	20	c Becker b Brayshaw 25
R. M. Cowper c Berker b Mayne	63	c Jenner b Mayne 113
K. R. Stackpole c and b Lock	26	lbw b Lock 57
D. J. Anderson c Shepherd b Mayne	13	c Shepherd b Lock 45
G. D. Watson c Becker b Mayne	4	b McKenzie 0
P. Williams c Inverarity b Lock	14	not out 17
†R. C. Jordon not out	31	
J. W. Grant c Inverarity b Lock	35	not out 1
A. N. Connolly run out	1	
R. W. Rayson not out	1	
B 3 l-b 5	8	B 3, l-b 3, w 1 7
1/44 2/109 3/146 4/173 5/180 6/197 7/203 8/259 9/262 (9 wkts., dec.)	267	1/21 2/69 3/171 4/248 5/250 6/267 (6 wkts.) 276

Bowling: *First Innings*—McKenzie 25—3—74—0; Mayne 21.4—3—111—4; Lock 26—10—35—3; Jenner 6—0—26—0; Brayshaw 1—0—13—0. *Second Innings*—22—0—94—2; Mayne 13—0—74—1; Lock 18—3—57—2; Jenner 6—1—27—0; Brayshaw 4—0—17—1.

Umpires: N. Townsend and J. M. Meachem.

NEW SOUTH WALES v. WESTERN AUSTRALIA

At Sydney, November 19, 20, 22, 23. Western Australia won by four wickets. Western Australia, pursuing the home side's first innings of 270, to which the young left-hander Hill had contributed 61, owed much to the vigilance of their opening batsman Kelly, who had played a Shield game for New South Wales before transferring to Perth. In five and a half hours of unspectacular but valuable batting, including a century stand with Chadwick, Kelly scored 132. In the second innings, Shepherd steered his team through to their first-ever outright win in Sydney. The medium-paced Brayshaw had taken five wickets in New South Wales second innings. New South Wales were without their leg-spinner Philpott (broken left index finger) and pace-man Corling (bruised thumb) in Western Australia's first innings; but Phillpott took three wickets in the second innings.

New South Wales

G. Thomas c Inverarity b Brayshaw	44	— c Lock b Brayshaw	66
N. C. O'Neill lbw b McKenzie	28	— c Lock b Brayshaw	2
*B. C. Booth c and b Jenner	13	— lbw b McKenzie	54
K. D. Walters b McKenzie	0	— c Shepherd b Brayshaw	76
B. A. Rothwell st Becker b Jenner	46	— c Shepherd b Lock	22
M. Hill c Mayne b Lock	61	— c Shepherd b Brayshaw	0
P. I. Philpott c Inverarity b Brayshaw	23	— absent hurt	0
J. W. Martin b Jenner	0	— c Kelly b Brayshaw	39
†H. B. Taber c Shepherd b Jenner	0	— c Becker b McKenzie	13
G. E. Corling not out	42	— c Becker b Mayne	21
D. A. Renneberg not out	4	— not out	20
B 2, l-b 6, n-b 1	9	B 3, l-b 2	5
1/68 2/80 3/83 4/87 5/195 (9 wkts., dec.) 6/203 7/205 8/205 9/264	270	1/32 2/127 3/183 4/183 5/187 6/256 7/271 8/277 9/318	318

Bowling: *First Innings*—Mayne 12—0—74—0; McKenzie 19.6—0—64—2; Brayshaw 13—1—43—2; Lock 15—4—31—1; Jenner 17—6—49—4. *Second Innings*—Mayne 13—3—59—1; McKenzie 21—1—85—2; Brayshaw 15—2—66—5; Lock 14—1—38—1; Jenner 14—1—65—0.

Western Australia

W. R. Playle c Thomas b Martin	29	— c Walters b Renneberg	5
P. C. Kelly c Walters b Corling	132	— c Martin b Philpott	29
*B. K. Shepherd c Rothwell b Walters	32	— not out	88
B. Chadwick lbw b Martin	51	— lbw b Martin	3
R. J. Inverarity b Martin	0	— b Martin	13
I. Brayshaw c Taber b Walters	13	— c Booth b Philpott	30
†G. C. Becker lbw b Renneberg	56	— c Taber b Philpott	35
T. Jenner lbw b Corling	1	— not out	16
G. D. McKenzie c Taber b Renneberg	0		
G. A. R. Lock b Walters	44		
L. C. Mayne not out	1		
L-b 4, n-b 1	5	B 3, l-b 3	6
1/55 2/116 3/219 4/219 5/242 6/309 7/319 8/319 9/325	364	1/8 2/71 3/72 4/79 (6 wkts.) 5/137 6/202	225

Bowling: *First Innings*—Renneberg 20—4—53—2; Corling 6—0—33—2; Walters 21.3—2—76—3; Martin 27—4—77—3; Booth 9—1—28—0; O'Neill 9—0—72—0; Hill 5—1—20—0. *Second Innings*—Renneberg 7—0—27—1; Corling 3—0—11—0; Walters 3—1—14—0; Martin 11.6—0—80—2; Booth 2—0—6—0; Philpott 14—0—81—3.

Umpires: R. Burgess and E. Wykes.

QUEENSLAND v. WESTERN AUSTRALIA

At Brisbane, November 26, 27, 28, 29. Western Australia won on the first innings. Trimble, the opening bat, after some "lives", reached 140 (thirteen 4's) for Queensland, having a fourth-wicket stand of 129 with Veivers; Buckle scored a century in the second innings despite Lock's steady spin bowling. Patient, well-controlled batting had given Western Australia a lead of 16 runs, Inverarity fighting hard for a score of 109, with assistance from Irvine.

Queensland

Batsman	First Innings		Second Innings	
S. C. Trimble	c Lock b Mayne	140	c Irvine b Brayshaw	4
J. Brown	c and b Brayshaw	2	c Chadwick b Lock	24
W. Buckle	c Shepherd b Jenner	31	c Jenner b Lock	112
*P. J. Burge	c Becker b Mayne	8	c Becker b Lock	31
T. R. Veivers	b Brayshaw	70	c Playle b Lock	36
D. Hughson	lbw b Mayne	1	not out	27
†A. W. T. Grout	b Mayne	25	c Inverarity b Brayshaw	35
J. R. Mackay	c Becker b Brayshaw	7	b Inverarity	17
D. Hale	c Lock b Brayshaw	8	c Becker b Inverarity	2
P. J. Allan	not out	1		
R. Duncan	c Mayne b Brayshaw	7		
	B 2, l-b 8, n-b 1	11	L-b 4, n-b 2	6
	1/10 2/76 3/111 4/240 5/241 6/276 7/289 8/301 9/303	311	1/4 2/61 3/116 4/176 5/224 6/260 7/292 8/294 (8 wkts., dec.)	294

Bowling: *First Innings*—Mayne 28—3—94—4; Brayshaw 18.6—3—74—5; Irvine 3—0—17—0; Lock 18—4—43—0; Jenner 17—2—72—1; Kelly 1—1—0—0. *Second Innings*—Mayne 13—3—54—0; Brayshaw 16—1—88—2; Lock 31—4—91—4; Jenner 6—1—24—0; Inverarity 6.4—0—31—2.

Western Australia

Batsman	First Innings		Second Innings	
W. R. Playle	c Burge b Allan	5	b Duncan	1
P. C. Kelly	c Grout b Mackay	34	lbw b Mackay	46
†G. C. Becker	c Grout b Veivers	53	c Brown b Duncan	30
*B. K. Shepherd	c Trimble b Allan	6	b Allan	0
D. Chadwick	c and b Hale	62	b Allan	10
R. J. Inverarity	b Allan	109	not out	35
I. Brayshaw	lbw b Mackay	0	not out	25
J. Irvine	c Hughson b Hale	36		
T. Jenner	not out	19		
G. A. R. Lock	c. Veivers b Allan	0		
L. C. Mayne	c Brown b Hale	0		
	B 1, l-b 2	3	B 1, l-b 2	3
	1/32 2/61 3/69 4/117 5/194 6/195 7/308 8/312 9/312	327	1/1 2/51 3/52 4/74 5/91 (5 wkts.)	150

Bowling: *First Innings*—Allan 24—6—66—4; Duncan 23—4—69—0; Mackay 21—1—64—2; Veivers 19—6—40—1; Hale 16.5—0—85—3. *Second Innings*—Allan 14—2—51—2; Duncan 9—3—32—2; Mackay 3—0—12—1; Veivers 3—0—8—0; Hale 7—1—44—0.

Umpires: W. Priem and L. Rowan.

VICTORIA v. WESTERN AUSTRALIA

At Melbourne, December 4, 6, 7, 8. Western Australia won on the first innings. Three hours play was lost on the last day, the resumption being delayed by wet approaches. Victoria, sent in to bat, failed against the swing of Brayshaw and the spin of Lock. Brayshaw after lunch took three wickets in eight balls. Playle's 116 (eleven 4's), a dour innings of just over five hours, was his first century for Western Australia. Shepherd, batting number seven after being ill, played aggressively for 63, some of his nine 4's coming from hook strokes.

Victoria

*W. M. Lawry c Becker b Lock	32	— b Hubble	54
I. R. Redpath c Becker b Brayshaw	5	— c Chadwick b Brayshaw	17
R. M. Cowper c Becker b Brayshaw	32	— lbw b McKenzie	21
K. R. Stackpole c Becker b Brayshaw	9	— b Lock	24
J. Potter c Becker b Brayshaw	0	— c Becker b Hubble	0
G. D. Watson c Becker b Lock	47	— st Becker b Jenner	60
†P. Williams c and b Lock	1	— c Inverarity b Lock	1
J. W. Grant c Kelly b Lock	36	— c Becker b McKenzie	12
D. Cowper c and b Lock	3	— not out	22
A. N. Connolly not out	5	— lbw b Shepherd	24
R. W. Rayson run out	0	— not out	1
L-b 2, n-b 1	3	B 5, l-b 4, n-b 2	11
1/6 2/57 3/80 4/80 5/81 6/92 7/143 8/149 9/170	173	1/36 2/77 3/106 4/110 5/125 6/127 7/156 8/214 9/246 (9 wkts.)	247

Bowling: *First Innings*—McKenzie 12—3—40—0; Brayshaw 18—3—37—4; Lock 20.5—5—61—5; Hubble 3—0—18—0; Jenner 3—0—14—0. *Second Innings*—McKenzie 22—3—67—2; Brayshaw 8—1—25—1; Lock 31—12—38—2; Hubble 13—0—53—2; Jenner 12—2—37—1; Kelly 1—0—2—0; Chadwick 2—0—13—0; Shepherd 1—0—1—1.

Western Australia

W. R. Playle c Grant b Watson	116
P. C. Kelly c Watson b R. M. Cowper	57
†G. C. Becker b R. M. Cowper	20
D. Chadwick c Potter b Rayson	1
R. J. Inverarity lbw b Grant	11
I. Brayshaw b R. M. Cowper	27
*B. K. Shepherd c Williams b Rayson	63
T. Jenner lbw b Connolly	30
G. D. McKenzie c Watson b Rayson	10
G. A. R. Lock b Connolly	6
J. Hubble not out	1
L-b 3, n-b 2	5
1/112 2/152 3/155 4/193 5/225 6/257 7/319 8/333 9/340	347

Bowling: Connolly 15.2—2—62—2; Grant 17—2—50—1; Watson 13—3—31—1; Stackpole 14—2—47—0; R. M. Cowper 27—12—51—3; Rayson 21—4—85—3; Potter 6—1—16—0.

Umpires: K. Butler and J. Collins.

SOUTH AUSTRALIA v. WESTERN AUSTRALIA

At Adelaide, December 10, 11, 13, 14. Western Australia won on the first innings. They completed their fourth successive away victory; but had to produce some grim defence in the second innings to stave off defeat. Chappell was the leading batsman, with scores of 99 and 129. In South Australia's first innings he took part in a punishing second-wicket stand of 161 with the left-hander Marks, who reached 127. Kelly, Chadwick and Irvine made solid contributions towards Western Australia's narrow first innings lead; Chadwick, 110, held up the attack for three and a half hours.

South Australia

First Innings		Second Innings	
*L. E. Favell b Lock	35	lbw b McKenzie	20
L. Marks b McKenzie	127	b Lock	46
I. M. Chappell lbw b Jenner	99	run out	129
H. N. Dansie c Jenner b McKenzie	7	lbw b Lock	8
A. B. Shiell st Becker b Lock	53	st Becker b Lock	25
†B. N. Jarman c Inverarity b Brayshaw	27	c and b Lock	2
B. M. Hurn run out	5	c Shepherd b McKenzie	0
G. Griffiths b Brayshaw	16	not out	40
D. J. Sincock not out	1	b Lock	8
E. Freeman c Shepherd b Brayshaw	0		
D. Robins lbw b Lock	12	not out	11
B 1, l-b 2, w 3	6	L-b 6	6
1/80 2/241 3/251 4/275 5/318 6/332 7/373 8/375 9/375	388	1/36 2/84 3/122 4/170 5/174 6/188 7/191 8/278 (8 wkts., dec)	295

Bowling: *First Innings*—McKenzie 25—0—96—2; Brayshaw 24—2—88—3; Inverarity 2—0—10—0; Lock 29.6—5—100—3; Jenner 15—2—72—1; Irvine 2—0—16—0. *Second Innings*—McKenzie 18.5—0—70—2; Brayshaw 7—0—51—0; Lock 27—0—118—5; Jenner 10—1—50—0.

Western Australia

First Innings		Second Innings	
W. R. Playle lbw b Robins	22	lbw b Sincock	50
P. C. Kelly c Dansie b Freeman	85	st Jarman b Chappell	23
†G. C. Becker c Chappell b Sincock	12	b Freeman	10
*B. K. Shepherd c Chappell b Sincock	19	b Freeman	2
D. Chadwick c Freeman b Hurn	110	b Griffiths	18
R. J. Inverarity run out	66	run out	7
I. Brayshaw b Chappell	6	not out	32
J. Irvine c Chappell b Griffiths	31	c Jarman b Griffiths	22
T. Jenner c Jarman b Chappell	26	lbw b Chappell	46
G. D. McKenzie not out	4	not out	4
G. A. R. Lock not out	9		
B 2, l-b 7, w 2	11	B 5, l-b 4, n-b 1	10
1/50 2/87 3/121 4/161 5/320 6/320 7/335 8/386 9/386 (9 wkts., dec.)	401	1/37 2/52 3/56 4/88 5/102 6/127 7/157 8/210 (8 wkts.)	224

Bowling: *First Innings*—Freeman 17—4—76—1; Robins 23—1—80—1; Hurn 8—2—17—1; Sincock 23—0—121—2; Chappell 17—2—56—2; Griffiths 18—5—38—1; Dansie 1—0—2—0. *Second Innings*—Freeman 11—0—53—2; Robins 6—1—17—0; Sincock 17—4—50—1; Chappell 18—3—65—2; Griffiths 10—1—28—2; Dansie 2—1—1—0.

Umpires: A. T. Godson and J. C. Novak.

SOUTH AUSTRALIA v. NEW SOUTH WALES

At Adelaide, December 17, 18, 20, 21. South Australia won by four wickets. This animated match marked Simpson's return after six weeks absence through a broken fore-arm. South Australia won with half an hour to spare. In their first innings Jarman scored 196, his century (one 6 and twelve 4's) coming in two and a quarter hours. He had a big partnership with Griffiths, who in the second innings figured in a hard-hitting stand with Cunningham. Walters accomplished a splendid batting double for New South Wales, 113 not out and 84; in the second innings Thomas played a great innings of 131 (one 6, fourteen 4's). On the third day when 437 runs came in under five and a half hours, the medium-paced Robins performed the hat-trick for South Australia, Walters scored his third century in successive matches, and Martin hit a six on to the members' stand roof.

South Australia

	First Innings		Second Innings	
*L. E. Favell c Taber b Corling	19	—	lbw b Corling	14
L. Marks c Walters b Martin	39	—	lbw b Philpott	40
I. M. Chappell c Taber b Renneberg	54	—	b Martin	20
K. G. Cunningham c Taber b Martin	25	—	not out	78
H. N. Dansie run out	26	—	c Corling b Martin	3
A. B. Shiell c Taber b Renneberg	47	—	not out	20
†B. N. Jarman b Simpson	196	—	c Thomas b Martin	31
N. J. N. Hawke b Renneberg	4			
G. Griffiths run out	67	—	c Walters b Simpson	49
D. J. Sincock not out	27			
D. Robins c Taber b Renneberg	19			
L-b 4, n-b 1	5		L-b 2	2
1/28 2/91 3/138 4/142 5/179 6/283 7/305 8/466 9/485	528		1/23 2/56 3/72 4/84 5/147 6/233 (6 wkts.)	257

Bowling: *First Innings*—Renneberg 21.3—0—145—4; Corling 19—0—80—1; Philpott 24—4—83—0; Walters 8—1—29—0; Martin 24—1—97—2; Simpson 12—0—76—1; O'Neill 2—0—13—0. *Second Innings*—Renneberg 7—0—46—0; Corling 5—0—17—1; Philpott 9—0—59—1; Martin 12—0—91—3; Simpson 7.3—0—42—1.

New South Wales

	First Innings		Second Innings	
*R. B. Simpson c Jarman b Hawke	10	—	c Jarman b Robins	0
B. A. Rothwell lbw b Robins	2	—	c Chappell b Sincock	33
G. Thomas c Jarman b Robins	4	—	c Marks b Griffiths	131
N. C. O'Neill c Griffiths b Sincock	80	—	hit wicket b Griffiths	12
B. C. Booth c Jarman b Griffiths	49	—	run out	65
K. D. Walters not out	113	—	c Jarman b Hawke	84
J. W. Martin b Sincock	44	—	c Griffiths b Sincock	24
P. I. Philpott c Jarman b Robins	35	—	lbw b Hawke	34
†H. B. Taber b Robins	6	—	not out	16
G. E. Corling b Robins	0	—	not out	27
D. A. Renneberg c Jarman b Robins	0			
L-b 4	4		B 5, l-b 5	10
1/11 2/13 3/26 4/128 5/160 6/229 7/338 8/347 9/347	347		1/0 2/80 3/107 4/244 5/247 6/309 7/390 8/395 (8 wkts., dec.)	436

Bowling: *First Innings*—Robins 15.3—3—62—6; Hawke 19—3—72—1; Cunningham 2—0—9—0; Chappell 11—0—36—0; Sincock 20—0—120—2; Griffiths 11—0—44—1. *Second Innings*—Robins 11—1—59—1; Hawke 12—0—72—2; Cunningham 3—1—16—0; Chappell 14—0—74—0; Sincock 24—0—147—2; Griffiths 13—1—58—2.

Umpires: C. J. Egar and J. J. Ryan.

VICTORIA v. NEW SOUTH WALES

At Melbourne, December 23, 24, 27 and 28. New South Wales won by nine wickets. Two double centuries were scored in this match. Thomas, whose 229 for New South Wales was an enthralling innings, took part in double-century stands with Simpson (214 in two and a half hours) and O'Neill (215 in two hours) on the same day. New South Wales gave a display of power batting. Simpson reached 113 in a three-hour effort of concentration; he was joined by Thomas after Rothwell had retired, having been struck below the right eye when he tried to hook Grant. Thomas, fighting for Test recognition, made his first double hundred in first-class cricket; tremendous power was allied to brilliant stroke play. He was dropped at 130 and 187 and was run out after periods of exhaustion in 100 degrees heat.

He batted for nearly four and a half hours. In Victoria's first innings Stackpole reached 99 in an innings marked by emphatic driving and pulling; in the second innings Potter, showing his best form since his early return from the 1964 English tour, scored 221, many of the runs coming from well-placed drives.

New South Wales

*R. B. Simpson, st Jordon b Cowper	113	— not out	33
B. A. Rothwell retired hurt	3		
G. Thomas run out	229	— b Grant	8
N. C. O'Neill c Jordon b Kirby	108		
K. D. Walters b Connolly	9		
B. C. Booth c and b Kirby	26	— not out	46
J. W. Martin lbw b Connolly	8		
P. I. Philpott not out	60		
†H. B. Taber b Stackpole	20		
G. E. Corling c Redpath b Stackpole	1		
D. A. Renneberg lbw b Stackpole	1		
B 4, l-b 6, w 1, n-b 3	14	N-b 3	3
1/226 2/441 3/458 4/490 5/503 6/ 519 7/587 8/589 9/592	592	1/15 (1 wkt.)	90

Bowling: *First Innings*—Connolly 22—2—83—2; Grant 17—0—89—0; Watson 10—0—64—0; Kirby 23—0—149—2; Stackpole 11.1—0—53—3; Cowper 26—3—117—1; Potter 3—0—23—0. *Second Innings*—Connolly 5—0—24—0; Grant 3—0—15—1; Watson 1—0—2—0; Kirby 3—0—19—0; Stackpole 3.6—0—21—0; Cowper 2—0—6—0.

Victoria

*W. M. Lawry c Taber b Walters	43	— lbw b Corling	16
I. R. Redpath b Walters	10	— lbw b Renneberg	7
R. M. Cowper c Walters b Renneberg	0	— c Philpott b Simpson	87
K. R. Stackpole b Martin	99	— c Martin b Renneberg	17
J. Potter c Philpott b Walters	34	— b Walters	221
A. P. Sheahan st Taber b Philpott	62	— c Martin b Simpson	5
G. D. Watson c and b Martin	1	— st Taber b Martin	4
†R. C. Jordon lbw b Philpott	0	— b Renneberg	20
J. W. Grant lbw b Martin	4	— c Simpson b Renneberg	15
K. Kirby not out	3	— not out	17
A. N. Connolly c Simpson b Philpott	5	— lbw b Walters	0
L-b 5	5	B 2, l-b 4	6
1/48 2/49 3/57 4/111 5/222 6/238 7/239 8/248 9/260	266	1/23 2/25 3/50 4/228 5/244 6/249 7/311 8/354 9/415	415

Bowling: *First Innings*—Renneberg 15—1—62—1; Corling 9—0—37—0; Walters 8—0—52—3; Philpott 20.3—2—72—3; Martin 12—3—38—3; Simpson 3—3—0—0. *Second Innings*—Renneberg 23—3—74—4; Corling 5—0—19—1; Walters 14.4—1—78—2; Philpott 8—1—23—0; Martin 26—2—131—1; Simpson 24—4—76—2; Booth 5—2—8—0.

Umpires: W. Smyth and J. Collins.

NEW SOUTH WALES v. QUEENSLAND

At Sydney, January 1, 3, 4. New South Wales won by 192 runs, with a day to spare. Rothwell, who led New South Wales, played a rescuing century innings, after the young medium-paced Morgan, a late replacement in the Queensland team, had taken cheap wickets. Trimble, in his fiftieth Shield game, made 158 for Queensland, thus celebrating his first appointment as captain. Most of the visitors failed against the sharp spin on a responsive pitch of the jaunty left-hander Martin, who took nine wickets in the match besides playing aggressive innings for 46 and 76 not out. Yet the left-hander Crane, in his first big match, used his feet well to Martin, and was unlucky to miss a century by two runs.

New South Wales

G. Goffet c Cooper b Duncan	15	— b Duncan	4
†H. B. Taber c Bull b Morgan	1	— not out	45
G. Thomas c Bizzell b Morgan	4	— b Lillie	48
*B. A. Rothwell b Duncan	125	— c Cooper b Morgan	30
M. Hill c Crane b Morgan	8	— c Crane b Lillie	5
G. Davies c Buckle b Morgan	69	— b Lillie	14
K. Owen c Crane b Morgan	8	— c Mackay b Lillie	6
J. W. Martin b Duncan	46	— not out	76
R. Guy b Mackay	9		
D. A. Renneberg c Bizzell b Mackay	0		
P. Leslie not out	0		
B 4, l-b 5	9	B 1, l-b 7, n-b 1	9
1/1 2/9 3/51 4/87 5/227 6/227 7/257 8/286 9/286	294	1/8 2/71 3/79 (6 wkts.. dec.) 4/101 5/107 6/111	237

Bowling: *First Innings*—Morgan 20—4—99—5; Duncan 23.5—5—65—3; Mackay 17—3—48—2; Lillie 18—3—61—0; Crane 3—0—12—0. *Second Innings*—Morgan 9—1—37—1; Duncan 13—2—50—1; Mackay 9—1—30—0; Lillie 16—1—69—4; Crane 8—1—42—0.

Queensland

*S. C. Trimble c Thomas b Leslie	58	— b Renneberg	6
R. Crane st Taber b Martin	15	— c Thomas b Davies	98
W. Buckle b Martin	17	— c Owen b Martin	12
G. M. Bizzell b Martin	19	— b Martin	4
D. Hughson st Taber b Martin	5	— lbw b Davies	4
J. R. Mackay c Davies b Martin	4	— c Owen b Guy	0
J. Morgan c Taber b Guy	8	— c Hill b Davies	0
D. F. Bull b Guy	13	— c Taber b Martin	29
†L. Cooper not out	10	— run out	2
D. Lillie st Taber b Guy	6	— st Taber b Davies	0
R. Duncan c Guy b Martin	0	— not out	20
B 2, l-b 3, n-b 1	6	L-b 1, w 1, n-b 1	3
1/32 2/78 3/110 4/111 5/116 6/131 7/131 8/154 9/160	161	1/18 2/40 3/48 4/49 5/56 6/80 7/80 8/133 9/134	178

Bowling: *First Innings*—Renneberg 17—3—50—0; Leslie 8—1—31—1; Martin 23.5—10—44—6; Guy 7—4—16—3; Davies 3—0—14—0. *Second Innings*—Renneberg 5—1—10—1; Leslie 6—0—24—0; Martin 17—3—60—3; Guy 8—2—27—1; Davies 10.5—2—51—4; Hill 1—0—3—0.

Umpires: E. F. Wykes and R. Burgess.

WESTERN AUSTRALIA v. SOUTH AUSTRALIA

At Perth, January 1, 3, 4. South Australia won on the first innings. A second-wicket partnership by Favell and Chappell, 175 runs in two and three-quarter hours, with Chappell scoring his third century of the season, frustrated the spin of Lock and the pace of the left-hander Hubble. Then Hawke wrecked Western Australia's first innings, despite a sixth-wicket stand by Shepherd and Jenner. Later that tall batsman, Inverarity, with a tenacious innings of 177, averted outright defeat; Western Australia's remaining three wickets put on 160 runs on the last day, Inverarity being last out.

South Australia

*L. E. Favell c Hubble b Lock	95	— c Shepherd b Hubble	1
L. Marks c Becker b Hubble	4	— run out	23
I. M. Chappell c sub b Lock	134		
A. B. Shiell c and b Lock	9	— not out	10
H. N. Dansie st Becker b Lock	71		
K. G. Cunningham c Becker b Hubble	40	— not out	25
†B. N. Jarman c Hubble b Lock	15		
G. Griffiths run out	8	— c Kelly b Hubble	11
D. J. Sincock b Hubble	7		
D. Robins c Inverarity b Hubble	8		
N. J. N. Hawke not out	4		
B 5, l-b 9, n-b 3	17		
1/15 2/190 3/214 4/285 5/358 6/384 7/394 8/403 9/406	412	1/6 2/34 3/36 (3 wkts.)	70

Bowling: *First Innings*—Hubble 28—1—119—4; Massie 13—0—54—0; Hoare 18—2—72—0; Lock 31—4—93—5; Jenner 5—0—53—0; Shepherd 3—1—4—0. *Second Innings*—Hubble 5—1—20—2; Massie 3—0—17—0; Hoare 3—1—3—0; Lock 9—3—21—0; Jenner 8—4—9—0.

Western Australia

W. R. Playle c Shiell b Hawke	14	— lbw b Sincock	48
P. C. Kelly c Shiell b Hawke	0	— b Robins	19
†G. C. Becker c Sincock b Robins	14	— c Chappell b Sincock	27
*B. K. Shepherd c Chappell b Hawke	84	— c Hawke b Robins	1
D. Chadwick c Shiell b Hawke	4	— st Jarman b Chappell	38
R. J. Inverarity c Shiell b Cunningham	1	— c Robins b Favell	177
T. Jenner c Jarman b Hawke	69	— c Griffiths b Chappell	25
D. G. Hoare b Hawke	9	— c Dansie b Hawke	32
G. A. R. Lock c Jarman b Sincock	11	— c Chappell b Hawke	25
J. Hubble not out	0	— c Favell b Hawke	6
R. Massie st Jarman b Sincock	0	— not out	12
L-b 4, w 2, n-b 3	9	B 1, l-b 1, n-b 7	9
1/5 2/30 3/33 4/45 5/48 6/177 7/192 8/211 9/215	215	1/26 2/65 3/76 4/103 5/162 6/194 7/259 8/295 9/334	419

Bowling: *First Innings*—Hawke 19—3—62—6; Robins 10—3—25—1; Cunningham 7—1—27—1; Chappell 6—1—23—0; Griffiths 5—2—13—0; Sincock 8.6—0—56—2. *Second Innings*—Hawke 33—8—79—3; Robins 19—4—69—2; Cunningham 7—1—24—0; Chappell 23—2—81—2; Griffiths 10—4—24—0; Sincock 33—2—119—2; Dansie 8—3—14—0; Favell 0.7—0—0—1.

Umpires: N. Townsend and J. M. Meachem.

VICTORIA v. QUEENSLAND

At Melbourne, January 7, 8, 10, 11. Victoria won by three wickets. Victoria ended the first innings 50 runs in arrears, after the pace bowler Allan had taken all ten wickets (15.6—3—61—10). Allan's figures were four for 32 at the end of the first day, with Victoria 76 for four. Allan next day actually took six for 14, these runs including five overthrows. The Queensland left-handed opener Bull made fine scores of 78 and 167 not out; but Queensland in the first innings lost their last nine wickets for 57. Stackpole bowled his spin mixture impressively in each innings. An opening stand of 213 runs in three and a quarter hours by Redpath, 180, and Watson, 109 had helped Victoria to recover. Redpath survived three chances during a stay of six and a quarter hours.

Queensland

D. F. Bull lbw b Stackpole	78	not out	67
*S. C. Trimble c Sheahan b Grant	3	c and b Stackpole	97
W. Buckle c Swanson b Stackpole	44	c Swanson b Stackpole	0
G. M. Bizzell b Stackpole	9	b Stackpole	2
F. Crane c Watson b Connolly	1	b Stackpole	10
K. Ziebell c Connolly b Stackpole	9	c and b Grant	18
J. R. Mackay b Stackpole	3	run out	22
†L. Cooper lbw b Kirby	0	c Sheahan b Kirby	0
P. J. Allan not out	7	lbw b Swanson	8
J. Duncan b Kirby	4	lbw b Kirby	0
D. Lillie c Swanson b Kirby	13	c and b Swanson	4
B 6, n-b 3	9	B 4, l-b 2, w 1, n-b 1	8
1/12 2/123 3/140 4/141 5/141 6/144 7/154 8/156 9/166	180	1/169 2/169 3/177 4/187 5/249 6/301 7/315 8/325 9/334	336

Bowling: *First Innings*—Connolly 13—5—36—1; Grant 13—1—49—1; Watson 4—0—9—0; Kirby 13—5—39—3; Stackpole 19—8—38—5. *Second Innings*—Connolly 19—3—56—0; Grant 12—3—34—1; Watson 7—0—33—0; Kirby 25—5—73—2; Stackpole 33—8—80—4; Swanson 10—2—31—2; Potter 2—0—19—0; Anderson 1—0—2—0.

Victoria

I. R. Redpath lbw b Allan	20	c Buckle b Mackay	180
G. D. Watson c Trimble b Allan	8	c Mackay b Crane	109
D. Anderson c Bizzell b Allan	45	b Ziebell	45
*J. Potter c Cooper b Allan	5	c Cooper b Crane	24
K. R. Stackpole b Allan	1	c Crane b Mackay	15
†R. C. Jordon b Allan	27	c Mackay b Lillie	0
A. P. Sheahan c Cooper b Allan	0	run out	1
J. Swanson c Crane b Allan	0	not out	4
J. W. Grant c Crane b Allan	0	not out	8
K. Kirby c Trimble b Allan	18		
A. N. Connolly not out	0		
L-b 4, n-b 2	6	B 1	1
1/15 2/41 3/53 4/61 5/100 6/100 7/100 8/100 9/123	130	1/213 2/247 3/345 4/371 5/375 6/375 7/376 (7 wkts.)	387

Bowling: *First Innings*—Allan 15.6—3—61—10; Duncan 5—0—31—0; Mackay 1—0—12—0; Crane 9—5—20—0. *Second Innings*—Allan 11—0—63—0; Duncan 16—2—65—0; Mackay 24.6—3—78—2; Crane 10—0—47—2; Lillie 19—0—105—1; Bull 1—0—3—0; Ziebell 9—0—25—1.

Umpires: K. Butler and K. Collicoat.

SOUTH AUSTRALIA v. QUEENSLAND

At Adelaide, January 15, 17, 18, 19. South Australia won by six wickets. The medium-paced Test bowler, Hawke, dominated this match, taking ten Queensland wickets in the two innings. He followed his first innings six for 96 in 31 overs by making 48 not out in a whirlwind stand which helped South Australia to a first-innings lead. Cunningham and Jarman also scored well. The pace-bowler Allan twice dismissed Favell cheaply and the off-spinner Veivers took four wickets in the first innings. Chappell's 75 not out (nine 4's) in South Australia's second innings was a chanceless display.

Queensland

S. C. Trimble c Robins b Hawke	16	— lbw b Hawke	29
D. F. Bull b Robins	5	— b Hawke	7
W. Buckle c Favell b Hawke	4	— lbw b Sincock	45
*P. J. Burge c Sincock b Cunningham	21	— b Hawke	0
T. R. Veivers lbw b Hawke	61	— b Griffiths	6
R. Crane lbw b Hawke	56	— c Shiell b Sincock	31
†A. W. T. Grout c Cunningham b Hawke	24	— c Hawke b Sincock	11
J. Morgan st Jarman b Cunningham	55	— not out	16
P. J. Allan c Chappell b Robins	4	— lbw b Hawke	0
D. Lillie c Jarman b Hawke	20	— b Griffiths	17
R. Duncan not out	2	— c Jarman b Dansie	5
B 2, l-b 2, w 1	5	B 3	3
1/5 2/12 3/47 4/49 5/159 6/170 7/199 8/205 9/269	273	1/19 2/48 3/48 4/61 5/102 6/128 7/133 8/134 9/160	170

Bowling: *First Innings*—Hawke 31—3—96—6; Robins 19—3—62—2; Cunningham 3.6—2—12—2; Sincock 8—0—44—0; Chappell 12—2—44—0; Griffiths 2—0—10—0. *Second Innings*—Hawke 18—5—41—4; Robins 10—0—39—0; Sincock 13—1—46—3; Chappell 3—1—5—0; Griffiths 18—7—35—2; Dansie 0.5—0—1—1.

South Australia

*L. E. Favell c Grout b Allan	2	— b Allan	0
L. Marks c Crane b Veivers	45	— c Crane b Duncan	3
I. M. Chappell c Grout b Allan	24	— not out	75
A. B. Shiell c Burge b Morgan	17	— c and b Veivers	11
H. N. Dansie run out	6	— not out	6
K. G. Cunningham c Crane b Veivers	77		
†B. N. Jarman c Grout b Duncan	50		
G. Griffiths c Crane b Veivers	3		
D. J. Sincock b Veivers	2	— c Duncan b Veivers	50
N. J. N. Hawke not out	48		
D. Robins b Allan	17		
B 7	7	L-b 2	2
1/2 2/46 3/90 4/92 5/97 6/213 7/220 8/228 9/235	298	1/0 2/10 3/97 4/139 (4 wkts.)	147

Bowling: *First Innings*—Allan 17.2—1—81—3; Duncan 19—1—94—1; Morgan 9—1—31—1; Veivers 19—2—48—4; Lillie 6—0—37—0. *Second Innings*—Allan 7—2—23—1; Duncan 7—2—22—1; Morgan 5—1—11—0; Veivers 15.6—4—68—2; Crane 7—0—21—0.

Umpires: C. J. Egar and V. P. Bell.

WESTERN AUSTRALIA v. QUEENSLAND

At Perth, January 22, 23, 24, 25. Western Australia won by four wickets. Two dogged century innings marked this game. Trimble batted five hours for his 101 (nine 4's) for Queensland, and followed with 50 in the second innings. The Western Australia opener, Playle, by his solid display for 122 set his team on the way to a lead. Lock, with well-controlled spin, finished the Queensland second innings.

Queensland

First innings		Second innings	
D. F. Bull c Chadwick b McKenzie	2	c Becker b Hubble	30
S. C. Trimble c and b McKenzie	101	c Shepherd b Jenner	50
W. Buckle lbw b Hubble	13	b Lock	10
*P. J. Burge c Becker b Hubble	25	c Inverarity b Jenner	32
T. R. Veivers c Becker b Hubble	6	c and b Lock	16
R. Crane c Playle b Jenner	13	b Hubble	5
†A. W. T. Grout c Jenner b Lock	17	c Jenner b Lock	29
J. Morgan c Hubble b Jenner	18	b Hubble	37
D. Lillie st Becker b Lock	29	b Brayshaw	1
P. J. Allan c Becker b Brayshaw	10	c Inverarity b Lock	1
R. Duncan not out	8	not out	15
B 10, l-b 2, n-b 12	24	L-b 2, n-b 1	3
1/2 2/36 3/77 4/87 5/108 6/144 7/189 8/231 9/248	266	1/43 2/65 3/112 4/134 5/143 6/147 7/180 8/186 9/189	229

Bowling: *First Innings*—McKenzie 17—1—60—2; Hubble 21—2—72—3; Brayshaw 14—1—45—1; Jenner 15—3—32—2; Lock 13—3—33—2. *Second Innings*—McKenzie 14—3—40—0; Hubble 20.5—6—59—3; Brayshaw 6—0—11—1; Jenner 18—0—65—2; Lock 0—4—51—4.

Western Australia

First innings		Second innings	
W. R. Playle b Duncan	122	c Morgan b Duncan	28
M. Vernon c Grout b Morgan	38	b Morgan	22
†G. C. Becker c Grout b Allan	24	b Lillie	29
*B. K. Shepherd c Grout b Allan	64	not out	3
G. D. McKenzie c Veivers b Allan	3		
D. Chadwick c Lillie b Duncan	18	not out	18
R. J. Inverarity not out	35	c Grout b Veivers	17
T. Jenner c Buckle b Morgan	0	c Duncan b Crane	13
I. Brayshaw c Trimble b Morgan	16	b Veivers	1
G. A. R. Lock not out	39		
B 4, l-b 2, w 1	7		
1/65 2/127 3/245 4/253 5/261 6/278 7/279 8/315 (8 wkts., dec.)	366	1/37 2/75 3/79 4/102 5/116 6/123 (6 wkts.)	131

J. Hubble did not bat.

Bowling: *First Innings*—Allan 23—6—48—3; Duncan 21—4—88—2; Morgan 17—2—106—3; Veivers 16—1—59—0; Lillie 9—2—54—0; Crane 1—0—4—0. *Second Innings*—Allan 4—0—15—0; Duncan 5—1—31—1; Morgan 6—1—23—1; Veivers 6—3—9—2; Lillie 9—1—40—1; Crane 3—0—13—1.

Umpires: N. Townsend and J. M. Meachem.

NEW SOUTH WALES v. VICTORIA

At Sydney, January 28, 29, 31, February 1. Victoria won by five wickets. For New South Wales, Lee celebrated his return to big cricket with a punishing innings of 63 (two 6's, nine 4's) and had a partnership of 99 with the 19-year-old Davies. Anderson and Sheehan put on 101 in a fifth-wicket stand for Victoria. Potter having declared when 63 in arrears twenty minutes before "stumps", Booth successfully appealed against the light. However, New South Wales, despite tail-end rallies, were put out for 254; Hill was hit on the head when he ducked into a short ball from Grant. The opening bat, Redpath, in a chanceless 161 not out, made the winning hit for Victoria with twenty minutes to spare. He was comfortable against spin on a slow pitch. Connolly and Grant formed an impressive pace combination for Victoria, taking thirteen wickets all told.

New South Wales

Batsman	1st Inns		2nd Inns	
*B. C. Booth lbw b Grant	38	—	c Watson b Connolly	1
†H. B. Taber c Thomas b Grant	17	—	run out	12
B. A. Rothwell st Jordon b Rayson	65	—	c Swanson b Grant	23
N. C. O'Neill c Watson b Connolly	14	—	c Redpath b Grant	18
M. Hill c Rayson b Connolly	6	—	retired hurt	15
G. Davies c Jordon b Watson	60	—	c Jordon b Connolly	24
T. H. Lee c Potter b Grant	63	—	c Thomas b Connolly	11
J. W. Martin b Grant	13	—	c Jordon b Rayson	51
P. I. Philpott c Jordon b Connolly	13	—	c Watson b Rayson	55
G. E. Corling not out	0	—	c Redpath b Rayson	22
D. A. Renneberg b Grant	0	—	not out	17
B 1, l-b 1, w 1, n-b 4	7		B 1, l-b 2, n-b 2	5
1/54 2/57 3/92 4/116 5/163 6/262 7/275 8/294 9/296	296		1/1 2/38 3/38 4/62 5/107 6/108 7/198 8/227	254

Bowling: *First Innings*—Connolly 20—2—57—3; Grant 20.6—1—79—5; Watson 8—0—28—1; Swanson 16—2—55—0; Rayson 11—1—62—1; Anderson 1—0—1—0; Potter 2—1—7—0. *Second Innings*—Connolly 14—3—57—3; Grant 15—1—63—2; Watson 8—1—28—0; Swanson 15—5—39—0; Rayson 11.4—0—56—3; Anderson 1—0—5—0; Potter 1—0—1—0.

Victoria

Batsman	1st Inns		2nd Inns	
I. R. Redpath b Renneberg	12	—	not out	161
G. D. Watson c Philpott b Corling	20	—	b Martin	47
B. Thomas b Renneberg	14	—	c Philpott b Martin	8
*J. Potter c Lee b Philpott	0	—	c Booth b Philpott	26
A. P. Sheahan c Booth b Davies	44	—	lbw b Martin	5
D. Anderson b Davies	67	—	c Taber b Renneberg	48
J. Swanson c Booth b Davies	6	—	retired hurt	1
†R. C. Jordon c Lee b Renneberg	37	—	not out	17
J. W. Grant lbw b Martin	27			
A. N. Connolly not out	3			
R. W. Rayson not out	0			
B 3	3		B 4, l-b 1	5
1/14 2/43 3/43 4/51 5/152 6/164 7/173 8/224 9/233 (9 wkts., dec.)	233		1/78 2/92 3/154 4/167 5/271 (5 wkts.)	318

Bowling: *First Innings*—Renneberg 15.5—3—55—3; Corling 9—2—27—1; Philpott 14—4—38—1; Martin 17—4—52—1; Lee 6—2—17—0; Davies 7—1—41—3. *Second Innings*—Renneberg 19—2—71—1; Corling 8—0—42—0; Philpott 12—2—36—1; Martin 23—2—98—3; Lee 10—2—22—0; Davies 9—0—39—0; O'Neill 1—0—4—0; Rothwell 0.2—0—1—0.

Umpires: P. Berridge and E. F. Wykes.

QUEENSLAND v. VICTORIA

At Brisbane, February 4, 6, 7. Queensland won on the first innings. The second day was washed out by rain, and the match resolved into a first innings affair. Victoria, sent in to bat, compiled the respectable score of 271, Cowper contributing a stalwart 96 after the young pace-bowler Morgan had dismissed Lawry cheaply. Morgan went on to finish with five for 55. Trimble and Veivers pulled Queensland out of trouble, despite steady spin bowling by Stackpole.

Victoria

Batsman	1st inns		2nd inns	
*W. M. Lawry c Grout b Morgan	2	—	c Lillie b Duncan	12
I. R. Redpath lbw b Duncan	32	—	c Ziebell b Veivers	80
R. M. Cowper c Trimble b Lillie	96	—	c Grout b Duncan	17
K. R. Stackpole run out	37	—	c Morgan b Veivers	18
G. D. Watson st Grout b Lillie	21	—	not out	64
J. Potter b Morgan	31	—	c Grout b Morgan	14
D. Anderson c Grout b Morgan	13	—	not out	7
†R. C. Jordon b Morgan	7			
J. W. Grant c Grout b Duncan	19			
A. N. Connolly c Buckle b Morgan	4			
R. W. Rayson not out	0			
L-b 5, n-b 4	9		L-b 1, n-b 2	3
1/6 2/70 3/149 4/184 5/209 6/234 7/241 8/253 9/267	271		1/31 2/57 3/103 4/152 5/180 (5 wkts.)	215

Bowling: *First Innings*—Morgan 13—2—55—5; Duncan 20.4—2—92—2; Ziebell 9—1—41—0; Veivers 17—8—22—0; Lillie 10—2—52—2. *Second Innings*—Morgan 11—2—44—1; Duncan 7—1—21—2; Ziebell 4—0—17—0; Veivers 12—1—27—2; Lillie 15—0—77—0; Trimble 2—0—9—0; Crane 4—0—17—0.

Queensland

D. F. Bull lbw b Connolly	5
*S. C. Trimble c Rayson b Connolly	50
W. Buckle lbw b Stackpole	15
R. Crane lbw b Stackpole	9
T. R. Veivers c Potter b Cowper	76
D. King c and b Watson	28
K. Ziebell not out	37
†A. W. T. Grout c Grant b Cowper	9
J. Morgan c Stackpole b Cowper	25
D. Lillie not out	3
B 8, n-b 9	17
1/27 2/64 3/84 4/92 5/151 6/216 7/232 8/268 (8 wkts., dec.)	274

R. Duncan did not bat.

Bowling: Connolly 28—4—86—2; Grant 16—4—35—0; Watson 7—0—23—1; Stackpole 29—8—56—2; Cowper 18—8—31—3; Rayson 5—1—16—0; Potter 4—1—10—0.

Umpires: J. Newcombe and R. Wilkie.

QUEENSLAND v. SOUTH AUSTRALIA

At Brisbane, February 11, 12, 14, 15. Queensland won by 199 runs. Trimble and King enjoyed splendid batting doubles for Queensland and Trimble's determined 152 (fourteen 4's) in the second innings was his third century of the season and his fifteenth in Shield cricket. The South Australian veteran, Dansie, also made his fifteenth Shield century; but his team collapsed before a lively pace trio in the second innings; Allan took four of the first five wickets and Morgan finished with eight for 74 in the match.

Queensland

Batsman	1st inns		2nd inns	
*S. C. Trimble c Robins b Sincock	58	—	c Jarman b Frost	152
D. F. Bull c Sincock b Clark	34	—	b Frost	0
W. Buckle c Lill b Sincock	10	—	st Jarman b Sincock	56
R. Crane c Sincock b Frost	10	—	b Sincock	0
K. Ziebell lbw b Robins	53	—	b Griffiths	21
D. King lbw b Robins	56	—	not out	65
J. Morgan b Sincock	7	—	run out	41
D. Lillie c Lill b Frost	2	—	st Jarman b Sincock	1
P. J. Allan c Robins b Sincock	0	—	lbw b Robins	8
†L. Cooper not out	10	—	st Jarman b Sincock	11
R. Duncan c Jarman b Frost	5	—	c Clark b Sincock	7
B 2, l-b 1, n-b 4	7		B 6, l-b 5, w 4, n-b 7	22
1/71 2/98 3/105 4/119 5/220 6/231 7/237 8/237 9/241	252		1/0 2/37 3/133 4/133 5/223 6/285 7/361 8/362 9/371	384

Bowling: *First Innings*—Frost 13.1—2—42—3; Robins 13—1—43—2; Clark 11—1—46—1; Cunningham 5—1—24—0; Sincock 13—0—56—4; Dansie 3—0—22—0; Griffiths 4—2—12—0. *Second Innings*—Frost 24—4—74—2; Robins 16—3—47—1; Clark 13—3—31—0; Cunningham 6—1—21—0; Sincock 22.4—1—134—5; Dansie 2—0—8—0; Griffiths 16—1—47—1.

South Australia

*L. E. Favell c Buckle b Duncan	22	— c Crane b Allan	5
J. Lill b Morgan	11	— b Allan	1
D. J. Sincock c Bull b Morgan	17	— lbw b Duncan	0
K. G. Cunningham c Duncan b Crane	64	— b Allan	3
H. N. Dansie c King b Allan	106	— lbw b Allan	5
A. B. Shiell c Cooper b Morgan	10	— c Ziebell b Duncan	1
†B. N. Jarman b Allan	64	— not out	24
G. Griffiths c Cooper b Duncan	16	— c Ziebell b Morgan	10
G. Clark c Ziebell b Morgan	9	— c Ziebell b Morgan	14
D. Robins c and b Morgan	44	— b Duncan	2
A. Frost not out	5	— b Morgan	0
N-b 3	3	B 1	1
1/32 2/34 3/74 4/145 5/175 6/297 7/298 8/322 9/326	371	1/6 2/7 3/10 4/15 5/23 6/23 7/38 8/41 9/66	66

Bowling: *First Innings*—Allan 16—1—61—2; Duncan 20—1—96—2; Morgan 14.4—2—60—5; Ziebell 2—0—10—0; Crane 11—0—50—1; Lillie 15—0—91—0. *Second Innings*—Allan 7—2—25—4; Duncan 9—4—19—3; Morgan 3.4—0—14—3; Lillie 1—0—7—0.

Umpires J. Goodwin and L. Johnson.

NEW SOUTH WALES v. SOUTH AUSTRALIA

At Sydney, February 19, 21, 22. New South Wales won by an innings and 20 runs after rain had prevented play on the first day and had limited play on the second to two hours. New South Wales were 65 for four, the medium-paced Robins having dismissed Simpson, Thomas and Rothwell in 18 deliveries; but Walters, who survived four chances in hitting 168, made a stand of 199 runs with the young Davies. Then Martin, left-arm spin, routed South Australia; Renneberg soon dismissed the openers in the second innings and the leg-spinner Davies captured three wickets.

New South Wales

*R. B. Simpson b Robins	22
G. Thomas b Robins	31
B. A. Rothwell b Robins	2
B. C. Booth c Sincock b Hawke	5
K. D. Walters b Hawke	168
G. Davies c Jarman b Robins	79
T. H. Lee lbw b Robins	0
J. W. Martin lbw b Hawke	5
†H. B. Taber lbw b Robins	11
G. E. Corling not out	8
D. A. Renneberg b Hawke	1
B 4, l-b 3	7
1/51 2/56 3/57 4/65 5/264 6/268 7/301 8/318 9/338	339

Bowling: Frost 10—0—59—0; Hawke 22.2—3—86—4; Robins 19—5—58—6; Sincock 11—0—71—0; Chappell 12—1—58—0.

South Australia

*L. E. Favell c Lee b Corling	13	— c Taber b Renneberg	6
L. Marks c Martin b Renneberg	0	— c Walters b Renneberg	4
I. M. Chappell b Corling	6	— b Martin	39
K. G. Cunningham st Taber b Martin	47	— b Davies	40
H. N. Dansie c Booth b Renneberg	30	— run out	26
A. B. Shiell c Thomas b Corling	6	— c and b Martin	20
†B. N. Jarman c sub b Martin	8	— c Simpson b Davies	13
N. J. N. Hawke b Martin	24	— b Lee	10
D. J. Sincock c and b Martin	1	— st Taber b Davies	0
D. Robins c Renneberg b Martin	4	— run out	12
A. Frost not out	0	— not out	1
B 2, l-b 2, n-b 1	5	B 4	4
/1 2/14 3/25 4/67 5/74	144	1/4 2/11 3/84 4/90 5/135	175
5/107 7/124 8/130 9/144		6/141 7/160 8/162 9/166	

Bowling: *First Innings*—Renneberg 10—0—61—2; Corling 11—0—44—3; Martin 6—1—21—5; Davies 4—1—13—0. *Second Innings*—Renneberg 5—0—22—2; Corling 6—1—19—0; Martin 12—1—36—2; Davies 9.4—0—37—3; Simpson 5—0—27—0; Lee 10—2—28—1; Booth 2—1—2—0.

Umpires: R. Burgess and E. F. Wykes.

VICTORIA v. SOUTH AUSTRALIA

At Melbourne, February 25, 26, 28, March 1. Victoria won on the first innings. Victoria plundered the South Australian bowling, Sincock coming in for heavy punishment. Lawry and Redpath achieved their eighth century opening stand and the young batsman, Sheahan, hit splendidly for 106 not out. The medium-paced Watson dismissed six of the first seven South Australians, but Cunningham and Dansie enjoyed a productive fourth-wicket association. Chappell and Dansie in the follow-on added to their list of centuries after Favell in sparkling form, had scored 95 of the 142 runs in the opening stand.

ictoria

W. M. Lawry c Jarman b Robins	85	G. D. Watson st Jarman b Dansie	80
R. Redpath st Jarman b Sincock	85	†R. C. Jordon not out	17
. M. Cowper b Frost	79	B 11, l-b 6, w 1, n-b 5	23
. R. Stackpole b Chappell	19		
Potter lbw b Frost	54	1/173 2/185 3/236 (6 wkts., dec.)	548
. P. Sheahan not out	106	4/343 5/344 6/503	

W. Grant, R. W. Rayson and A. N. Connolly did not bat.

Bowling: Hawke 29—1—102—0; Frost 21—2—93—2; Robins 19—1—87—1; incock 27—3—140—1; Chappell 17—3—73—1; Cunningham 1—0—10—0; ansie 4—0—20—1.

outh Australia

. E. Favell lbw b Watson	29	— c Jordon b Connolly	95
. Marks c Potter b Stackpole	36	— c Stackpole b Watson	45
M. Chappell b Watson	10	— run out	113
. G. Cunningham c Lawry b Watson	95	— b Grant	2
. N. Dansie b Watson	81	— lbw b Watson	101
. B. Shiell c Jordon b Watson	4	— st Jordon b Cowper	12
. N. Jarman c Redpath b Watson	5	— c Watson b Cowper	27
. J. N. Hawke c Jordon b Stackpole	30	— not out	18
J. Sincock c Sheahan b Connolly	11	— not out	7
Robins b Connolly	0	— c Rayson b Potter	11
Frost not out	0		
L-b 2, n-b 3	5	B 6, l-b 2, n-b 2	10
33 2/44 3/94 4/256 5/256	306	1/142 2/159 3/168 (8 wkts.)	441
262 7/265 8/306 9/306		4/338 5/376 6/405	
		7/409 8/426	

Bowling: *First Innings*—Connolly 13.3—2—51—2; Grant 9—0—38—0; Watson 15—2—61—6; Stackpole 16—3—61—2; Cowper 14—3—35—0; Rayson 7—0—45—0; Potter 8—3—10—0. *Second Innings*—Connolly 14—0—68—1; Grant 10—0—53—1; Watson 19—4—39—2; Stackpole 18—2—60—0; Cowper 22—2—85—2; Rayson 10—0—91—0; Potter 6—0—32—1; Redpath 1—0—3—0.

Umpires: W. Smyth and J. R. Collins.

WESTERN AUSTRALIA v. NEW SOUTH WALES

At Perth, February 25, 26, 28, March 1. Western Australia won on the firs innings by one run after sending in New South Wales to bat. Wanting 222 run to win outright, in quick time, Western Australia found the task impossible Nevertheless the first innings lead was a fine achievement, as New South Wale had scored 423 for six on the first day. Simpson, Walters and O'Neill score heavily. McKenzie's six wickets for 100 runs in the second innings was an admi ably sustained effort in extreme heat. The tail-end batsmen Taber and Philpo stubbornly fought for time at one stage only 11 runs came from 15 overs. In th end the tactics paid. Earlier the left-handed Vernon, in one of his best innings, an Kelly created a second-wicket record of 203 runs for Western Australia agains New South Wales. It was Kelly's fourth hundred in first-class cricket in the seasor

New South Wales

G. Thomas c Vernon b McKenzie	41	— c Shepherd b McKenzie	3
*R. B. Simpson c and b Lock	91	— c Vernon b Hubble	
K. D. Walters c sub b Jenner	114	— b McKenzie	
N. C. O'Neill b Hubble	140	— run out	3
B. C. Booth c Vernon b Lock	16	— lbw b McKenzie	
B. A. Rothwell c Becker b Hubble	2	— run out	3
J. W. Martin c Lock b Brayshaw	7	— c Lock b McKenzie	
P. I. Philpott c Becker b Brayshaw	11	— b McKenzie	2
†H. B. Taber not out	11	— c Inverarity b Jenner	5
G. E. Corling c and b Lock	1	— not out	1
D. A. Renneberg b Lock	13	— b McKenzie	1
B 6, l-b 1, n-b 4	11	B 2, l-b 1, n-b 3	
1/74 2/186 3/303 4/358 5/386 6/420 7/426 8/436 9/438	458	1/13 2/16 3/44 4/50 5/80 6/98 7/112 8/150 9/201	22

Bowling: *First Innings*—Hubble 24—5—87—2; McKenzie 17—0—117— Brayshaw 16—0—71—2; Lock 20.3—3—89—4; Jenner 10—0—71—1; Shephe 1—0—12—0. *Second Innings*—Hubble 19—2—48—1; McKenzie 24.6—3— 100—6; Brayshaw 7—4—12—0; Lock 20—11—13—0; Jenner 16—5—43—1.

Western Australia

W. R. Playle c Booth b Corling	5	— not out	
P. C. Kelly c Taber b Corling	103	— c Thomas b Martin	
M. Vernon c Walters b Martin	173		
*B. K. Shepherd c Simpson b O'Neill	46		
†G. C. Becker lbw b Corling	34		
R. J. Inverarity c Walters b Corling	0		
T. Jenner run out	1	— not out	
I. Brayshaw not out	53		
G. A. R. Lock c Booth b Corling	26		
G. D. McKenzie not out	13		
L-b 3, w 1, n-b 1	5	B 4	
1/5 2/208 3/274 4/330 5/332 6/337 7/380 8/427 (8 wkts., dec.)	459	1/49 (1 wkt.)	

J. Hubble did not bat.

Bowling: *First Innings*—Renneberg 23—2—86—0; Corling 27—1—109—5; Walters 4—0—18—0; Philpott 23.4—3—95—0; Simpson 9—0—36—0; Martin 14—1—78—1; O'Neill 7—1—32—1. *Second Innings*—Renneberg 6—0—21—0; Corling 4—0—26—0; Martin 5—0—21—1; Rothwell 2—0—15—0; Thomas 1—0—9—0.

Umpires: N. Townsend and J. M. Meachem.

BATTING—ALL FIRST-CLASS MATCHES

(Qualification: Minimum of 300 runs)

	Inns.	Times Not Out	Runs	Highest Inns.	Average
R. M. Cowper (Vic.)	21	2	1,418	307	74.63
W. M. Lawry (Vic.)	21	1	1,445	166	72.25
K. D. Walters (N.S.W.)	21	2	1,332	168	70.11
R. B. Simpson (N.S.W.)	14	2	747	225	62.35
I. M. Chappell (S.A.)	19	2	1,019	134	59.94
G. Thomas (N.S.W.)	20	0	1,171	229	58.55
P. C. Kelly (W.A.)	17	1	904	132	56.50
M. Vernon (W.A.)	9	0	478	173	53.11
I. R. Redpath (Vic.)	17	1	848	180	53.00
S. C. Trimble (Qld.)	17	0	843	152	49.59
B. N. Jarman (S.A.)	17	2	725	196	48.33
K. G. Cunningham (S.A.)	15	2	566	95	43.54
G. D. Watson (Vic.)	17	3	590	109	42.14
W. R. Playle (W.A.)	17	1	642	122	40.13
N. C. O'Neill (N.S.W.)	12	0	473	140	39.42
R. J. Inverarity (W.A.)	16	2	549	177	39.21
H. N. Dansie (S.A.)	15	1	549	106	39.21
P. J. Burge (Qld.)	18	1	663	120	39.00
B. K. Shepherd (W.A.)	18	3	560	88*	37.33
A. B. Shiell (S.A.)	19	3	597	202*	37.31
J. Potter (Vic.)	11	0	409	221	37.18
B. A. Rothwell (N.S.W.)	17	2	545	125	36.33
T. R. Veivers (Qld.)	16	1	528	74	35.20
D. Chadwick (W.A.)	13	2	385	110	35.00
L. E. Favell (S.A.)	20	0	656	96	32.80
D. F. Bull (Qld.)	15	1	459	167*	32.79
L. Marks (S.A.)	18	0	555	127	30.83
D. Anderson (Vic.)	12	1	335	67	30.45
B. C. Booth (N.S.W.)	21	1	595	80	29.75
K. R. Stackpole (Vic.)	16	0	460	99	28.75

* Not out.

BOWLING—ALL FIRST-CLASS MATCHES

(Qualification: 15 wickets)

	Overs	Runs	Wickets	Average
. Morgan (Qld.)	108	480	25	19.20
. J. Allan (Qld.)	223.5	833	39	21.36
. Brayshaw (W.A.)	176.6	640	27	23.70
G. D. Watson (Vic.)	129.5	441	18	24.50
N. J. N. Hawke (S.A.)	378.6	1,261	49	25.73
G. A. R. Lock (W.A.)	406.5	1,134	44	25.77
. Hubble (W.A.)	140.5	476	17	28.00
D. Robins (S.A.)	238.3	879	30	29.30
K. R. Stackpole (Vic.)	283.7	833	27	30.85
. W. Martin (N.S.W.)	300.3	1,291	41	31.49

	Overs	Runs	Wickets	Average
T. R. Veivers (Qld.)	234	708	22	32.18
D .A. Renneberg (N.S.W.)	274	1,110	32	34.69
R. W. Rayson (Vic.)	159.7	774	22	35.18
G. E. Corling (N.S.W.)	163	654	18	36.33
A. N. Connolly (Vic.)	295.5	1,028	28	36.71
G. D. McKenzie (W.A.)	435.7	1,643	40	41.08
R. Duncan (Qld.)	261.1	1,044	25	41.76
L. C. Mayne (W.A.)	155.4	723	17	42.53
D. J. Sincock (S.A.)	346.6	1,750	40	43.75
P. I. Philpott (N.S.W.)	280.2	1,116	25	44.65
K. D. Walters (N.S.W.)	199.7	857	19	45.11
J. W. Grant (Vic.)	228.6	863	19	45.42
T. Jenner (W.A.)	241	1,007	20	50.35

SHEFFIELD SHIELD HONOURS

1892–93	**Victoria**	**1928–29**	**New South Wales**
1893–94	**South Australia**	**1929–30**	**Victoria**
1894–95	**Victoria**	**1930–31**	**Victoria**
1895–96	**New South Wales**	**1931–32**	**New South Wales**
1896–97	**New South Wales**	**1932–33**	**New South Wales**
1897–98	**Victoria**	**1933–34**	**Victoria**
1898–99	**Victoria**	**1934–35**	**Victoria**
1899–1900	**New South Wale**	**1935–36**	**South Australia**
1900–1	**Victoria**	**1936–37**	**Victoria**
1901–2	**New South Wales**	**1937–38**	**New South Wales**
1902–3	**New South Wales**	**1938–39**	**South Australia**
1903–4	**New South Wales**	**1939–40**	**New South Wales**
1904–5	**New South Wales**	**1940–46**	**No competition**
1905–6	**New South Wales**	**1946–47**	**Victoria**
1906–7	**New South Wales**	**1947–48**	**Western Australia**
1907–8	**Victoria**	**1948–49**	**New South Wales**
1908–9	**New South Wales**	**1949–50**	**New South Wales**
1909–10	**South Australia**	**1950–51**	**Victoria**
1910–11	**New South Wales**	**1951–52**	**New South Wales**
1911–12	**New South Wales**	**1952–53**	**South Australia**
1912–13	**South Australia**	**1953–54**	**New South Wales**
1913–14	**New South Wales**	**1954–55**	**New South Wales**
1914–15	**Victoria**	**1955–56**	**New South Wales**
1915–19	**No competition**	**1956–57**	**New South Wales**
1919–20	**New South Wales**	**1957–58**	**New South Wales**
1920–21	**New South Wales**	**1958–59**	**New South Wales**
1921–22	**Victoria**	**1959–60**	**New South Wales**
1922–23	**New South Wales**	**1960–61**	**New South Wales**
1923–24	**Victoria**	**1961–62**	**New South Wales**
1924–25	**Victoria**	**1962–63**	**Victoria**
1925–26	**New South Wales**	1963–64	South Australia
1926–27	**South Australia**	1964–65	New South Wales
1927–28	**Victoria**	1965–66	New South Wales

New South Wales have won the Shield 36 times, Victoria 19, South Australia 8, Western Australia 1, Queensland 0.

CRICKET IN SOUTH AFRICA, 1965–66

By Geoffrey A. Chettle

Transvaal, holding a commanding lead, appeared certain to win the Curri Cup for the first time since 1958–59, only for Natal to come from behind and shar the top position. At the other end of the table, Western Province in their Jubile Year struck their worst patch for many seasons and suffered the ignominy o relegation.

The South African Board of Control, in an effort to intensify the preparation for the 1966–67 Australian tour, decided to continue the Currie Cup Tournament as a two-section competition despite the presence of a touring team and planned the itinerary to ensure the completion of the majority of fixtures before the first Test. The country's leading cricketers will thus be given a far better opportunity of striking form than has been the case in the past.

In the "B" Section North-Eastern Transvaal, well ahead of their nearest rivals, may justly consider themselves unfortunate to miss promotion in view of the Board's policy to reduce "A" Section in the future to four teams.

Ably led by the experienced Jim Pressdee, the Glamorgan professional, and adequately supported by the Springboks Lindsay, Burke and Botten, the Pretoria team enjoyed one of their most successful seasons. With the addition of the former Springbok captain Trevor Goddard, and the promising Hylton Ackerman (Border) they faced the prospect of "A" section competition with confidence.

A disappointing feature of the season was the loss of form of Bland and Graeme Pollock, each of whom played only one characteristic innings. On the credit side, the 22-year-old University student, Berry Versfeld, emerged as a tremendous prospect. He scored 824 runs in eight matches, including two centuries and a brilliant 201 not out.

The two Natal youngsters, Richards and Proctor, fresh from a season with Gloucestershire, made an auspicious entry into the Currie Cup. Each had an aggregate of more than 400 runs in top company. Proctor enhanced his all-round value by capturing 17 wickets as a seamer.

H. R. Lance, one of the 1965 Springboks, enjoyed a tremendous season, the highlight being a new South African tenth-wicket record of 174 in partnership with his fellow Transvaaler, D. Mackay-Coghill, against Natal. This eclipsed the 71-year-old Transvaal record of 104 and the national record of 129 established in 1925–26 by F. Caulfield and L. R. Tuckett for Orange Free State v. Western Province.

Peter Pollock, with 32 wickets in seven matches, maintained the killer instinct he displayed on the short tour of England. Support at the opposite end is essential if opponents are to feel the might of Pollock at his best. The mantle may fall on the shoulders of the Springbok Lawrence (Rhodesia) or Trimborn, the Natal opening bowler, both of whom exceeded 30 wickets at a reasonable cost.

The three-year search for a successor to Hugh Tayfield continued, Seymour and D. B. Pithey were sent to Australasia to develop under the most rigorous conditions. They returned with 30 wickets apiece from twelve matches without in any way approaching the standard of subtlety of South Africa's former off-spinner.

CURRIE CUP

SECTION "A"

	Played	Won outright	Lost outright	1st Inns. Won	1st Inns. Lost	Points
Points awarded	–	6	–	3	1	–
Natal	6	2	–	2	2	20
Transvaal	6	2	–	2	2	20
Eastern Province	6	1	2	3	–	15
Rhodesia	5	1	1	1	2	11
Western Province	5	–	3	–	2	2

Note: The final match, Rhodesia v. Western Province at Salisbury, was abandoned without a ball being bowled, owing to the waterlogged state of the ground.

At Bulawayo, November 20, 21, 22. Rhodesia 195 (N. G. Frangos 53, E. F. Parker 39; A. H. McKinnon five for 59, A. F. Tillim three for 36) and 202 (E. F. Parker 45, N. G. Frangos 40, R. A. Gripper 31, R. B. Ullyett 31; H. R. Lance three for 28, R. Dumbrill three for 40); Transvaal 219 (R. C. White 58, H. R. Lance 44; E. F. Parker three for 65, J. T. Partridge three for 84) and 159 for nine wickets (H. R. Lance 41; G. B. Lawrence three for 28, D. B. Pithey three for 47). Transvaal won on first innings.

At Wanderers, Johannesburg, November 27, 29, 30. Eastern Province 221 (L. J. Nel 44, P. M. Pollock 35, M. Court 32, A. L. Wilmot 30) and 148 (A. L. Wilmot 34; R. Dumbrill four for 29); Transvaal 212 (B. J. Clark 76, J. H. B. Waite 31 not out; P. M. Pollock five for 63) and 161 for two wickets (A. Bacher 53 not out, G. G. Ritchie 38, R. Dumbrill 34 not out). Transvaal won by eight wickets.

At Police Ground, Salisbury. December 4, 5, 6. Rhodesia 450 (D. B. Pithey 143, R. B. Ullyett 135, J. H. du Preez 49, H. Gardiner 42 not out; A. Hector five for 121) and 38 for three wickets (M. Court three for 11); Eastern Province 487 (A. L. Wilmot 222 not out, E. J. Barlow 142, R. G. Pollock 53; E. F. Parker five for 76, J. T. Partridge three for 78). Eastern Province won on first innings.

At St. George's Park, Port Elizabeth, December 17, 18, 20. Eastern Province 224 (E. J. Barlow 87, A. L. Wilmot 30; R. S. Steyn four for 56, H. D. Bromfield three for 59) and 167 for three wickets (E. J. Barlow 64, N. W. Mallett 46, R. G. Pollock 39 not out); Western Province 163 (F. T. M. Drummer 44 not out, R. S. Steyn 44; E. J. Barlow three for 21, P. M. Pollock three for 30) and 145 for three wickets (A. Bruyns 50, L. J. Weinstein 30). Eastern Province won on the first innings.

At Jan Smuts Stadium, Pietermaritzburg, December 18, 20, 21. Rhodesia 359 (N. G. Frangos 85, A. J. Pithey 57, D. B. Pithey 57, K. C. Bland 51, R. A. Gripper 41; P. H. J. Trimborn four for 89) and 162 for five wickets (A. J. Pithey 59 not out, R. A. Gripper 35); Natal 299 (B. A. Richards 68, M. J. Proctor 56, B. Versfeld 48, T. L. Goddard 47, M. Parsons 30; D. B. Pithey five for 67) and 21 for no wickets. Rhodesia won on the first innings.

At Wanderers, Johannesburg, December 27, 28, 29. Natal 385 (B. Versfeld 128, M. J. Proctor 72, B. L. Irvine 49, D. J. McGlew 39, R. A. McLean 36; R. Dumbrill four for 78, G. L. Watson three for 65) and 184 for two wickets (B. L. Irvine 57, B. A. Richards 51, T. L. Goddard 33); Transvaal 378 (H. R. Lance 169, D. Mackay-Coghill 57 not out, A. Bacher 34, G. G. Ritchie 33; M. J. Proctor four for 90). Natal won on the first innings.

At Newlands, Cape Town, December 27, 28, 29. Western Province 194 (P. L. van der Merwe 61, L. J. Weinstein 32; J. T. Partridge five for 85; G. B. Lawrence three for 56) and 99 (L. J. Weinstein 36; G. B. Lawrence eight for 42); Rhodesia 172 (A. J. Pithey 38, J. H. du Preez 38, G. B. Lawrence 32 not out; J. McG. Cole five for 45) and 122 for four wickets (R. A. Gripper 51, A. J. Pithey 22). Rhodesia won by six wickets.

At St. George's Park, Port Elizabeth, January 1, 3, 4. Eastern Province 272 (E. J. Barlow 111, D. Gradwell 69, J. P. Harty 49; D. F. Parker four for 59, G. B. Lawrence four for 87) and 159 (R. G. Pollock 61; G. B. Lawrence five for 46); Rhodesia 236 (E. F. Parker 44, D. B. Pithey 40, K. C. Bland 30, R. A. Gripper 30; P. M. Pollock five for 45, E. J. Barlow three for 41) and 129 (D. B. Pithey 37; A. Hector four for 47). Eastern Province won by 66 runs.

At Newlands, Cape Town, January 1, 3, 4. Transvaal 349 (H. R. Lance 147, B. J. Clark 73, D. Mackay-Coghill 38; F. T. M. Drummer four for 51) and 229 (H. R. Lance 62, D. Mackay-Coghill 30; R. Steyn four for 64); Western Province 318 (E. Emary 66, L. Morby-Smith 65, A. Bruyns 56, A. W. Catt 44, P. L. van der Merwe 34; A. H. McKinnon six for 107, H. R. Lance three for 47) and 227 for nine wickets (P. L. van der Merwe 77, L. Morby-Smith 50, A. Bruyns 49; A. H. McKinnon five for 66, H. R. Lance three for 48). Transvaal won on the first innings.

At St. George's Park, Port Elizabeth, January 15, 16, 18. Eastern Province 233 (R. G. Pollock 88, E. J. Barlow 52, N. W. Mallett 36; T. L. Goddard three for 24, P. H. J. Trimborn three for 58) and 201 (E. J. Barlow 82; P. H. J. Trimborn four for 43); Natal 225 (T. L. Goddard 78, B. Versfeld 55; A. Hector four for 55, E. J. Barlow three for 34) and 177 for five wickets (B. A. Richards 77, B. Versfeld 36; A. Hector three for 62). Natal won on the first innings.

At Newlands, Cape Town, January 21, 22, 24. Natal 144 (M. Bowditch nine for 52 on Currie Cup debut) and 257 (M. J. Proctor 67, C. G. Burger 45, B. Versfeld 45, C. Wesley 41; H. D. Bromfeld three for 60, M. Bowditch three for 68); Western Province 83 (L. Morby-Smith 30; P. H. J. Trimborn five for 38, M. J. Proctor four for 19) and 85 (A. Bruyns 33; N. S. Crookes four for 14, P. H. J. Trimborn three for 39). Natal won by 233 runs.

At Kingsmead, Durban: February 11, 12, 14. Transvaal 290 (A. Bacher 94, H. R. Lance 74, L. Harris 37; P. H. J. Trimborn three for 51) and 190 for eight wickets declared (A. F. Tillim 41, R. Dumbrill 34; B. A. Richards three for 23); Natal 406 for six wickets declared (B. Versfeld 201 not out, M. J. Proctor 129, B. A. Richards 35; R. Dumbrill three for 90). Natal won on the first innings.

At Wanderers, Johannesburg, February 18, 19, 21. Western Province 285 (R. K. Muzzell 101 not out, P. L. van der Merwe 62, N. R. Budge 37; A. H. McKinnon five for 82) and 233 (P. L. van der Merwe 60, D. Louw 41, D. le Roux 33; R. Dumbrill four for 44); Transvaal 465 for nine wickets declared (R. C. White 117, H. R. Lance 96, B. J. Clark 52, R. Dumbrill 51, A. Bacher 32; N. R. Budge three for 67, M. Bowditch three for 83) and 56 for two wickets (H. R. Lance 34 not out). Transvaal won by eight wickets.

At Kingsmead, Durban, February 18, 19, 21. Natal 191 (B. A. Richards 67; J. E. Dumbrill five for 53) and 271 for five wickets (T. L. Goddard 83, M. J. Proctor 64 not out, B. A. Richards 61, B. Versfeld 34; A. Hector three for 83); Eastern Province 173 (A. L. Wilmot 67 not out) and 229 (E. J. Barlow 106, P. M. Pollock 39 not out; T. L. Goddard six for 68). Natal won by 60 runs.

At Police Ground, Salisbury, February 26, 27, 28. Rhodesia v. Western Province. Match abandoned. Ground waterlogged.

SECTION "B"

	Played	Won Outright	Lost Outright	1st Inns. Won	1st Inns. Lost	Points
Points awarded	–	6	–	3	1	–
North-Eastern T'vaal ..	5	4	–	–	1	25
Border..............	5	3	1	–	1	19
Natal "B"...........	5	1	–	4	–	18
Transvaal "B"........	5	1	2	1	1	10
Orange Free State.....	5	–	3	1	1	4
Griqualand West......	5	–	3	–	2	2

At Benoni, November 26, 27, 29. Transvaal "B" 322 (J. H. Baillie 76, L. R. Harris 67, G. Davies 56, G. Watson 47; J. S. Pressdee four for 70, J. Viviers three for 66) and 257 (L. R. Harris 116, A. W. Motley 49, A. Simon 31; J. T. Botten four for 77); North-Eastern Transvaal 368 (E. J. Brotherton 111, G. G. Hall 56, J. H. Corbett 55, C. I. Dey 46, D. Lindsay 43; G. Watson four for 82, K. A. Walter four for 89) and 212 for four wickets (D. Lindsay 91 not out, D. Hill 41, J. H. Corbett 32). North-Eastern Transvaal won by six wickets.

At Kimberley, November 27, 29, 30. Border 201 (E. C. Baker 94 not out, C. P. Wilkins 52; C. R. English five for 51, B. W. Burrow three for 72) and 180 (P. Heger 59; C. R. English four for 84, B. W. Burrow three for 36); Griqualand West 197 (R. A. Scurr 44, T. J. Heale 40; J. L. Fetting three for 17, N. Edwards three for 42) and 129 (N. Hunter four for 36). Border won by 55 runs.

At Bloemfontein, December 2, 3, 4. Border 259 (A. P. Haxton 72, W. S. Farrer 67, J. L. Fetting 31; O. van Niekerk three for 35, W. Strydom three for 54) and 361 (W. S. Farrer 207 (four and a half hours, thirty-two 4's), J. L. Fetting 36, C. P. Wilkins 35; J. Drew three for 56, P. Henwood three for 115); Orange Free State 361 (R. van der Poll 98, S. Strydom 66, N. Rosendorff 53; J. Sansom three for 80) and 223 (E. Hardiman 55, D. Heldsinger 42, R. van der Poll 38; N. H. Hunter five for 41). Border won by 36 runs.

At Loftus Versfeld, Pretoria, December 10, 11, 13. Griqualand West 194 (E. J. Draper 72 not out, C. W. Symcox 38; G. G. Hall five for 97, J. S. Pressdee three for 36) and 257 (E. J. Draper 75, C. W. Symcox 46, B. W. Burrow 35; J. S. Pressdee four for 68, G. G. Hall three for 67); North-Eastern Transvaal 415 for eight wickets declared (P. L. Corbett 146, J. A. Corbett 76, T. Rolfe 64, D. Lindsay 30; B. W. Burrow three for 121) and 38 for no wicket. North-Eastern Transvaal won by ten wickets.

At Kingsmead, Durban, December 27, 28, 29. Transvaal "B" 279 (T. Rex 70, K. Bond 61 not out, L. R. Harris 40, A. W. Motley 32, I. R. Fullerton 32; M. Smithyman three for 49, C. Sullivan three for 64) and 194 (L. R. Harris 56, I. R. Fullerton 44; D. Phillips three for 12); Natal "B" 323 (C. G. de V. Burger 86, U. Groom 77, M. Smithyman 47 not out, T. C. McDonald 36; M. J. Macaulay five for 80, K. A. Walter four for 88). Natal "B" won on the first innings.

At Jan Smuts Ground, East London, December 27, 28, 29. North-Eastern Transvaal 357 (J. A. Corbett 94, D. Lindsay 58, T. Rolfe 58, J. S. Pressdee 40, J. T. Botten 33, D. Hill 30; N. H. Hunter five for 100) and 221 for eight wickets declared (S. F. Burke 67 not out, C. I. Dey 33, J. T. Botten 30; P. D. Heger four for 64, J. Sansom three for 30); Border 223 (E. C. Baker 38, I. Harty 35, A. P. Haxton 34, C. P. Wilkins 33, H. M. Ackerman 30; G. G. Hall four for 81, J. S. Pressdee three for 32) and 96 (J. S. Pressdee three for 33). North-Eastern Transvaal won by 259 runs.

At Jan Smuts Ground, East London, January 1, 3, 4. Border 211 (C. P. Wilkins 55, A. P. Haxton 43; F. Palmer three for 26, C. Wesley three for 36) and 263 (A. P. Haxton 77, W. S. Farrer 60, V. C. Wild 43 not out, H. M. Ackerman 37; M. Smithyman three for 49, F. Palmer three for 124); Natal "B" 361 (P. R. Carlstein 102, D. Murdoch 90, T. McDonald 49, D. Phillips 38; P. Heger three for 67) and 67 for five wickets (C. P. Wilkins three for 29). Natal "B" won on the first innings.

At Vereeniging, Transvaal, January 1, 3, 4. Transvaal "B" 476 (J. H. Baillie 79, L. R. Harris 70, T. Rex 69, K. A. Walter 55, J. Horak 51, K. Bond 43, L. Rael 35, A. Simon 33; P. Henwood four for 99, N. Rosendorff four for 104) and 121 for one wicket (T. Rex 53, A. Simon 52 not out); Orange Free State 244 (S. Strydom 97; K. A. Walter four for 18) and 503 for nine wickets declared (S. Strydom 234, N. Rosendorff 88, L. Hardiman 57, O. van Niekerk 32 not out; L. Rael six for 105). Transvaal "B" won on first innings.

At Jan Smuts Stadium, Pietermaritsburg, January 15, 16, 18. Natal "B" 352 (C. Wesley 120, J. F. C. Palmer 74 not out, U. G. Groom 37, P. R. Carlstein 32; J. S. Pressdee four for 75, S. F. Burke three for 79) and 232 for six wickets declared (T. McDonald 60, D. D. Phillips 46 not out, U. G. Groom 38; J. S. Pressdee three for 71); North-Eastern Transvaal 227 (E. J. Brotherton 74, J. A. Corbett 39, P. L. Corbett 34; R. M. Nicholson four for 33, J. F. C. Palmer three for 54) and 256 (P. L. Corbett 51, C. I. Dey 42, D. Lindsay 39, J. A. Corbett 34, E. J. Brotherton 30, T. Rolfe 30; J. F. C. Palmer four for 81). Natal "B" won on the first innings.

At De Beers Stadium, Kimberley, January 21, 22, 24. Orange Free State 325 for seven wickets declared (N. Rosendorff 102, S. Strydom 66, E. W. Cronje 43, E. Hardiman 39; C. R. English five for 65) and 5 for no wickets. Griqualand West 246 (B. W. Burrow 94, G. Fleeton 32; W. Strydom three for 50). Orange Free State won on the first innings.

At Wanderers, Johannesburg, February 11, 12, 14. Transvaal "B" 119 (M. Henning 37; B. W. Burrow six for 48, G. Fleeton three for 33) and 374 for nine wickets declared (R. C. White 205, P. Flanagan 51, L. Rael 31; B. W. Burrow five for 119). Griqualand West 47 (K. A. Walter five for 19, F. Hankey four for 2) and 158 (C. W. Symcox 33, D. J. Schonegevel 28; K. A. Walter three for 49). Transvaal "B" won by 288 runs.

At Ramblers, Bloemfontein, February 12, 14, 15. Natal "B" 370 (G. C. Heath 122, D. Phillips 44, D. Murdoch 39; J. Drew five for 102) and 199 for four wickets declared (T. C. McDonald 80, G. C. Heath 67); Orange Free State 243 (E. W. Cronje 98, P. Strydom 62 not out, N. Rosendorff 45; N. McDonald five for 53, J. F. Palmer four for 76) and 176 (E. Crossman 38, N. Rosendorff 31; J. F. Palmer four for 78, R. Falkson three for 54). Natal "B" won by 150 runs.

At De Beers Stadium, Kimberley, February 17, 18, 19. Natal "B" 323 for nine wickets declared (N. McDonald 100 not out, K. Martin 54 not out, D. Murdoch 48, R. Nicholson 30; B. W. Burrow five for 85, H. Lubbe three for 93) and 220 for seven wickets declared (U. Groom 51, D. Phillips 35, J. F. Palmer 32 not out); Griqualand West 198 (D. J. Schonegevel 79 not out, E. J. Draper 33; J. F. Palmer five for 87, R. Nicholson three for 19) and 284 for nine wickets (D. J. Schonegevel 138 not out, B. W. Burrow 38; J. F. Palmer three for 105, N. McDonald three for 41, R. Falkson three for 57). Natal "B" won on first innings.

At Berea Park, Pretoria, February 18, 19, 21. North-Eastern Transvaal 399 (J. S. Pressdee 101, E. J. Brotherton 85, C. I. Dey 56, D. Hill 34, S. F. Burke 34, D. Lindsay 32; J. Drew three for 64, N. Rosendorff three for 68) and 229 for four wickets (D. Lindsay 83, F. A. Oosthuizen 81); Orange Free State 254 (N. Rosendorff 60, J. Drew 46; G. G. Hall seven for 137, J. S. Pressdee three for 68) and 145 (W. Strydom 40; J. S. Pressdee four for 36, G. G. Hall four for 95). North-Eastern Transvaal won by 229 runs.

At Jan Smuts Ground, East London, February 18, 19, 21. Border 362 (A. P. Haxton 89, B. Groves 76, C. P. Wilkins 42, N. H. Hunter 40, A. Greig 37, W. S. Farrer 30; K. A. Walter four for 92) and 155 for four wickets (C. P. Wilkins 79, B. Groves 35; K. A. Walter three for 72); Transvaal "B" 180 (A. Wilson 30, A. During 39; P. D. Heger six for 40, M. Scott three for 64) and 335 (D. J. Horak 111, P. J. D. Flanagan 78, G. Watson 51, M. Henning 37 not out; M. Scott four for 68, J. L. Fetting three for 50). Border required 154 runs in eighty minutes for victory and won by six wickets with eight minutes to spare. Border won by six wickets.

FIRST-CLASS MATCHES (OTHER THAN CURRIE CUP)

At Newlands, Cape Town, December 11, 13, 14. South African Universities XI. 383 for eight wickets declared (B. Versfeld 141, E. Emary 45, K. Tattersal 39, R. Steyn 32 not out, H. D. Bromfield three for 65, D. McMeeking three for 95) and 187 for six wickets declared (B. Versfeld 63 not out, E. Emary 34); Western Province 208 (L. Morby-Smith 64, N. R. Budge 34, A. W. Catt 31; R. K. Muzzell four for 60, P. de Waal three for 13) and 322 for nine wickets (P. L. van der Merwe 91, M. Giles 73; E. Emary five for 71). South African Universities XI won by 40 runs.

At Wanderers, March 4, 5, 7, 1966. North 204 (C. P. Wilkins 91, E. J. Brotherton 32; T. L. Goddard six for 30) and 166 (D. Mackay-Coghill 66, D. B. Pithey 37; P. M. Pollock five for 50, P. H. J. Trimborn four for 57); South 420 for nine wickets declared (T. L. Goddard 102, H. M. Ackerman 84, N. S. Crookes 61 not out, W. S. Farrer 56, R. G. Pollock 37; G. B. Lawrence three for 90). South won by an innings and 50 runs.

CURRIE CUP WINNERS

1890	Transvaal	1929–30	Transvaal
1891	Griqualand West	1931–32	Western Province
1892	Western Province	1933–34	Natal
1894	Western Province	1934–35	Transvaal
1895	Transvaal	1936–37	Natal
1897	Western Province	1937–38	Natal/Tvl (tied)
1898	Western Province	1946–47	Natal
1903	Transvaal	1947–48	Natal
1903–4	Transvaal	1950–51	Transvaal
1904–5	Transvaal	1951–52	Natal
1906–7	Transvaal	1952–53	Western Province
1908–9	Western Province	1954–55	Natal
1911	Natal	1955–56	Western Province
1912–13	Natal	1958–59	Transvaal
1920–21	Western Province	1959–60	Natal
1921–22	Tvl/Natal/W.P. (tied)	1960–61	Natal
1923–24	Transvaal	1962–63	Natal
1925–26	Transvaal	1963–64	Natal
1926–27	Transvaal	1965–66	Natal/Tvl (tied)

CRICKET IN NEW ZEALAND, 1965–66

By A. G. Wiren

PLUNKET SHIELD

(Won by Wellington)

	Played	Won outright	Won on 1st inns.	Lost outright	Lost on 1st inns.	Lead on 1st inns. but lost outright	Points
Points awarded	–	10	5	–	1	3	–
Wellington	5	3	2	0	0	0	40
Canterbury.......	5	2	2	0	1	0	31
Auckland	5	1	1	0	1	2	22
Otago..........	5	1	2	1	1	0	21
Central Districts ..	5	0	1	2	2	0	7
Northern Districts.	5	0	0	1	3	1	6

Plunket Shield Holders: Auckland 16 times, Canterbury 15, Wellington 14, Otago 6, Central Districts 1, Northern Districts 1.

An interesting Plunket Shield season was brought to a close with Wellington coming first, nine points above Canterbury, the runners-up.

To win the Shield it was necessary for Wellington to gain maximum points in their last two matches, otherwise Canterbury would have been the champions if they succeeded in gaining an outright win in their closing match against Otago. Wellington were successful in gaining outright wins in these two vital matches. In both games they had to score runs swiftly in the fourth innings of low-scoring contests. It was generally considered that the Wellington bowling would prove to be inadequate owing to the absence of J. R. Reid and R. W. Blair, both of whom had retired from first-class cricket after very successful careers.

The bowlers did their part well, supported by good fielding, and D. O. Neely (who succeeded J. R. Reid as captain) could scarcely have led the side better.

Canterbury and Auckland were evenly matched, filling second and third places. Otago tried hard but never appeared the likely winners. Northern Districts and Central Districts were unable to force any outright victories, and there was little between them in actual results. Bert Sutcliffe, who captained the Northern Districts team, announced his retirement from first-class cricket at the conclusion of the season. His first-class career commenced in 1942 and he is the record-holder for runs scored by a New Zealander in first-class cricket with an aggregate exceeding 16,000 runs.

The leading batsmen were: R. W. Sinclair 395 runs,average 56.4; G. M. Turner (a promising young batsman from Otago) 325 runs, average 54.1 and G. R. Bilby 333 runs, average 41.6.

In bowling, B. A. G. Murray 11 wickets, average 10.3, led the averages, followed by N. Puna 34 wickets, average 13.4 and R. C. Motz 24 wickets, average 14.6.

The wicket-keeping honours were shared between A. E. Dick (Wellington) and R. Schofield (Central Districts) each with 14 dismissals.

PLUNKET SHIELD DETAILS

At Basin Reserve, Wellington, December 25, 27, 28. Otago 187 (K. Ibadulla 65) and 180 (G. D. Alabaster 35; H. A. Morgan three for 44, L. C. Butler three for 51); Wellington 385 for four wickets, declared (G. P. Bilby 161, P. B. Truscott 77, B. W. Sinclair 67 not out, B. A. G. Murray 53). Wellington won by an innings and 18 runs.

At the Domain, Tauranga, December 25, 27, 28. Central Districts 232 (R. M. Schofield 47 not out, M. E. Chapple 37, B. E. Congdon 30; N. Puna five for 51) and 164 for eight wickets declared (B. E. Congdon 53, B. L. Hampton 34; N. Puna three for 48); Northern Districts 163 (G. V. Giles 64; B. W. Yuile five for 41) and 83 for five wickets (B. Sutcliffe 32 not out; V. Pollard four for 13). Central Districts won on the first innings.

At Lancaster Park, Christchurch, December 27, 28, 29. Auckland 321 (R. M. Harris 75, J. T. Sparling 67, R. S. Cunis 50 not out, R. W. Morgan 44; R. C. Motz three for 64, B. R. Taylor three for 69) and 129 (B. R. Taylor four for 28, G. A. Bartlett three for 32, R. C. Motz three for 38); Canterbury 287 (D. L. Gallop 124, K. Thomson 68, J. M. McIntyre 34; R. E. Sutton five for 42) and 164 for eight wickets (M. L. Ryan 43, I. R. Hartland 38; J. T. Sparling six for 56). Canterbury won by two wickets.

At McLean Park, Napier, December 30, 31, January 1. Wellington 352 (B. W. Sinclair 80, D. O. Neely 74, A. E. Dick 60, H. A. Morgan 33; R. O. Collinge six for 69) and 91 for five wickets declared (D. A. Kinsella three for 22); Central Districts 216 (M. J. F. Shrimpton 53, V. Pollard 43; A. R. Taylor four for 35, H. A. Morgan three for 27, L. C. Butler three for 67) and 89 for three wickets (M. J. F. Shrimpton 33 not out). Wellington won on the first innings.

At Carisbrook, Dunedin, December 30, 31, January 1. Otago 216 (K. Ibadulla 111; R. S. Cunis five for 48) and 22 for one wicket; Auckland 157 (N. S. Harford 50; F. J. Cameron four for 35, K. Ibadulla three for 22). Otago won on the first innings.

At Lancaster Park, Christchurch, December 30, 31, January 1. Northern Districts 244 (E. C. Petrie 48, B. Dunning 43, W. P. Bradburn 37, B. Sutcliffe 32; G. A. Bartlett four for 39, J. M. McIntyre four for 52) and 115 (R. C. Motz five for 31, G. A. Bartlett three for 36); Canterbury 172 (B. G. Hadlee 52 not out, R. C. Motz 38; A. J. Beuth five for 35) and 188 for seven wickets (B. R. Taylor 82 not out, M. L. Ryan 39; A. J. Beuth four for 41). Canterbury won by three wickets.

At Basin Reserve, Wellington, January 3, 4, 5. Canterbury 122 (K. Thomson 30; N. A. Huxford three for 24, L. C. Butler three for 28, H. A. Morgan three for 30) and 201 (B. F. Hastings 70, K. Thomson 39; A. R. Taylor three for 49, N. A. Huxford three for 55, H. A. Morgan three for 61); Wellington 163 (B. W. Sinclair 31, H. A. Morgan 30; R. C. Motz four for 56) and 74 for two wickets (G. P. Bilby 37 not out). Wellington won on the first innings.

At Eden Park, Auckland, January 3, 4, 5. Central Districts 168 (V. Pollard 60, M. E. Chapple 31; H. J. Howarth four for 34) and 246 for six wickets, declared (M. J. F. Shrimpton 96, B. L. Hampton 64; H. J. Howarth three for 63); Auckland 277 for seven wickets, declared (N. S. Harford 103 not out, R. S. Cunis 68, R. W. Morgan 45; B. W. Yuile three for 66) and 140 for six wickets (J. T. Sparling 33 not out; B. W. Yuile three for 72). Auckland won by four wickets.

At Carisbrook, Dunedin, January 3, 4, 5. Otago 171 (K. Ibadulla 47, S. N. McGregor 47; N. Puna six for 53, K. D. Kennedy four for 45) and 118 for five wickets (R. W. Hutchison 46, K. Ibadulla 33); Northern Districts 149 (A. J. Beuth 36, H. T. Schuster 30; G. D. Alabaster four for 42, F. W. Cameron three for 25). Otago won on the first innings.

At Eden Park, Auckland, January 7, 8, 10. Northern Districts 210 (W. P. Bradburn 107; R. W. Morgan three for 32, R. S. Cunis three for 39) and 189 for five wickets, declared (W. P. Bradburn 59, W. J. Mitchell 38, J. F. Bailey 30 not out; H. J. Howarth three for 59); Auckland 213 for six wickets, declared (T. W. Jarvis 73, A. R. Morrison 53, N. S. Harford 41 not out; N. Puna four for 68) and 165 for nine wickets (T. W. Jarvis 78; N. Puna four for 53). Auckland won on the first innings.

At Pukekura Park, New Plymouth, January 7, 8, 10. Canterbury 311 (G. A. Bartlett 72, J. W. Burtt 53, B. F. Hastings 47; B. W. Yuile nine for 101) and 177 for six wickets, declared (M. L. Ryan 88 not out, K. Thomson 44); Central Districts 178 (B. E. Congdon 43; J. M. McIntyre five for 49, G. A. Bartlett three for 38) and 238 for nine wickets (V. Pollard 62, D. H. Payton 40 not out; J. W. Burtt four for 49). Canterbury won on the first innings.

At Seddon Park, Hamilton. January 31, February 1, 2. Northern Districts 176 (G. V. Giles 81, E. C. Petrie 32; A. R. Taylor six for 47, L. C. Butler three for 56) and 174 for six wickets, declared (B. Sutcliffe 56, G. V. Giles 48, B. Dunning 43; B. A. G. Murray three for 51); Wellington 181 for seven wickets, declared (B. W. Sinclair 79, P. T. Barton 37 not out; A. J. Beuth three for 34, N. Puna three for 47) and 170 for eight wickets (D. O. Neely 35 not out; N. Puna three for 36). Wellington won by two wickets.

At Eden Park, Auckland, February 4, 5, 7. Auckland 225 (J. T. Sparling 44, R. W. Morgan 41, A. R. Morrison 37, R. M. Harris 32; B. A. G. Murray four for 43, L. C. Butler three for 57, A. R. Taylor three for 49) and 163 for eight wickets, declared (R. M. Harris 45; H. A. Morgan three for 19, A. R. Taylor three for 42); Wellington 160 (A. E. Dick 41, B. W. Sinclair 32; R. S. Cunis four for 35, R. E. Sutton three for 34) and 231 for seven wickets (G. P. Bilby 57, B. W. Sinclair 55, P. B. Truscott 39; R. S. Cunis three for 40). Wellington won by three wickets.

At Carisbrook, Dunedin, February 5, 7, 8. Otago 247 (G. H. Taylor 95, J. C. Alabaster 57; D. A. Kinsella three for 32) and 144 for seven wickets, declared (G. M. Turner 48 not out, J. C. Alabaster 32; V. Pollard three for 36); Central Districts 172 (M. E. Chapple 42, M. J. F. Shrimpton 32; J. C. Alabaster four for 67, F. J. Cameron three for 35) and 121 (G. D. Alabaster six for 45, J. C. Alabaster three for 48). Otago won by 98 runs.

At Lancaster Park, Christchurch, February 10, 11, 12. Canterbury 291 (G. A. Bartlett 58 not out, B. F. Hastings 46, K. Thomson 44, J. W. Burtt 35; F. J. Cameron four for 45) and 181 for seven wickets, declared (C. L. Bull 51; G. D. Alabaster five for 77); Otago 211 (S. N. McGregor 81, G. M. Turner 55, R. C. Motz four for 24) and 172 for three wickets (G. M. Turner 71 not out; S. N. McGregor 43, K. Ibadulla 31). Canterbury won on the first innings.

REPRESENTATIVE MATCH

N.Z. UNDER 23 XI v. PLUNKET SHIELD WINNERS

At Basin Reserve, Wellington, on March 25, 26, 28. Under Twenty-Three Team 173 (C. L. Bull 43, D. Moreland 36; L. C. Butler eight for 50) and 229 (S. R. Speed 73, B. D. Smith 65; G. T. McConnell five for 74). Wellington 251 (P. B. Truscott 51, B. A. G. Murray 39, H. A. Morgan 38, I. R. Mason 36, D. O. Neely 30; R. E. Redmond four for 54, J. Syme four for 64) and 153 for nine wickets (B. A. G. Murray 41, L. C. Butler 39; R. E. Redmond six for 56, S. R. Dunne three for 52). Wellington won by one wicket.

CRICKET IN INDIA, 1965–66

By P. N. Sundaresan

For the third time in post-war cricket in India there was no visit by an overseas side. The difficult foreign exchange position and the Pakistani hostilities resulted in the postponement of a tour from the West Indies team. This naturally was a keen disappointment for enthusiasts in India as they were eager to know how their players, who had come up considerably in the last five years, would acquit themselves against the strongest combination in the game at the present time. The only blot in fact on the otherwise creditable record for this period was the defeat at the hands of the Caribbeans in 1961–62 and there was keen anticipation about the outcome of another India–West Indies series.

The 1965–66 season was, however, no disappointment to the keen followers of the game in India. It proved indeed to be an extremely interesting one and afforded the opportunity to take stock of the talent available and assess the strength and weaknesses of our cricket. There is an abundance of batsmen, from the school stage to the topmost level, and an equal wealth in spin bowlers. The weakness is in pace bowling, with the prospect of discovering even one real fast bowler being quite bleak.

The general strength in batting could be gauged from the fact that batsmen of the calibre of A. L. Wadekar and Abbas Ali Baig would have to win a place in the Test side. There were also players at the University level like Ambar Roy who had been doing remarkably well in the national and zonal championships. We discovered a new off-spinner during the New Zealand team's visit in 1965 in S. Venkatraghavan but his position was soon seriously challenged by E. A. S. Prasanna, who made a splendid come-back during the season; this meant that there were two first-class off-spinners in the country. S. A. Durani and R. G. Nadkarni still led in left-arm spin but they were challenged by youngsters like P. K. Shivalkar, Rajinder Goel and Bishen Singh Bedi. I hope that India will not succumb to a modern policy and discard their leg-spinners, of the orthodox type, of whom C. G. Joshi had a very fine season. Of course, B. S. Chandrasekhar, the unorthodox in this line, did well again, despite a tendency to impart more speed than spin to his deliveries. R. B. Desai, though only half as good as in the past, still proved to be the best medium-paced bowler. C. K. Bhaskar and K. Gattani, the best among the younger set, failed to come up even to this standard.

Bombay retained the Ranji Trophy when R. G. Nadkarni led them to their eighth successive triumph in the final. South Zone, strengthened in batting by the switch-over of the Nawab of Pataudi from the North Zone, and backed up by the spinning combination of Chandrasekhar, Prasanna and Venkatraghavan, won the Duleep Trophy for the first time. The beautiful batting of V. L. Manjrekar in both these competitions deserved special mention. In the Duleep Trophy semi-final he played a grand knock of 91 not out for Central Zone whom he captained against East Zone and, in the company of Hanumant Singh, led his side to a great victory. In the Ranji Trophy semi-final Manjrekar again guided the destinies of Rajasthan against Mysore with a brilliant 175-run knock. Both were memorable performances from one who had announced his retirement from Test cricket during the series against New Zealand. The possibility of his return to the Test scene cannot be ruled out, as Manjrekar has said that he would not hesitate to respond to the call of the country, if the need arose.

The Irani Trophy match between the Ranji Trophy champions (Bombay) and the Rest of India, which heralded the season, proved disappointing with rain cutting short play. The trophy was shared as even the first innings were not completed.

The tour of a London Schoolboys team evoked considerable interest and provided the opportunity for a number of schoolboy players to gain invaluable experience. Another such team composed of boys from Sydney schools in Australia passed through the country on their way to East Africa and played a couple of matches. W. A. Oldfield, the great Australian wicket-keeper, accompanied the boys and gave pleasure to many by his genial presence.

Notable performances during the season:—

Ranji Trophy Championship

Century on debut: N. F. Saldana, 142, Maharashtra v. Saurashtra.

Over 500 runs in season in Ranji Trophy:—

	Innings	Not Outs	Runs	Highest Innings	Average
A. L. Wadekar (*Bombay*)	10	4	695	185	115.83
B. Awasthy (*Services*)..........	10	1	666	190	74.00

Highest score: A. Roy, 197, Bengal v. Orissa.

Century before lunch: B. Awasthy, 142, Services v. Jammu & Kashmir.

Hat-trick: Rajinder Pal, Delhi v. South Punjab.

Outstanding bowling: 13 for 128 (seven for 60, six for 68) A. Joshi, Maharashtra v. Gujerat.

E. A. S. Prasanna: 12 for 244 (five for 162, seven for 82) Mysore v. Rajasthan.

Duleep Trophy Championship

Outstanding bowling: 11 for 80 (six for 19, five for 61) E. A. S. Prasanna, South Zone v. Central Zone.

E. A. S. Prasanna and B. S. Chandrasekhar, the Mysore spinners, shared all the Central Zone wickets in this match.

RANJI TROPHY CHAMPIONSHIP

South Zone:

At Kothagudium, November 26, 27. Andhra 156 (M. Shyam 58, R. P. Gupta 37; Abid Ali four for 20, M. Jairam three for 33) and 127 (B. Ramprasad 55; Abid Ali three for 26, B. Mahendra Kumar five for 39); Hyderabad 357 for six dec. (Abid Ali 77, Abbas Ali Baig 121, B. Mahendra Kumar 47 not out, Wahid Yar Khan 41 not out). Hyderabad won by an innings and 74 runs.

At Bangalore, November 27, 28. Kerala 40 (B. S. Chandrasekhar four for 6, E. A. S. Prasanna four for 7) and 128 (P. V. Surendran 34 not out; B. S. Chandrasekhar four for 37, E. A. S. Prasanna four for 55); Mysore 316 for eight dec. (K. R. Rajagopal 62, S. Krishnamurthy 69, P. R. Ashok Anand 109, T. V. S. Mani three for 44). Mysore won by an innings and 148 runs.

At Madras, December 4, 5, 6. Kerala 51 (S. Venkatraghavan three for 7, K. S. Vaidyanathan four for 4) and 58 for seven (K. Madan Mohan 30 not out, S. Venkatraghavan four for 22, V. V. Kumar three for 27); Madras 81 for two dec. (P. K. Belliappa 41, R. Ramesh 35). Drawn. Rain.

At Eluru, December 10, 11, 12. Madras 207 (P. K. Belliappa 35, A. G. Milkha Singh 69; R. P. Gupta four for 43, T. V. Ramana four for 48) and 212 for five dec. (P. K. Belliappa 55, R. Ramesh 37, S. V. S. Mani 52; J. C. Patel 34); Andhra 108 (V. V. Kumar four for 37, S. Venkatraghavan five for 46) and 123 (K. Satyadev 36; S. Venkatraghavan six for 52, V. V. Kumar three for 45). Madras won by 188 runs.

At Secunderabad, December 11, 12, 13. Hyderabad 170 (Abid Ali 36, M. L. Jaisimha 46; B. S. Chandrasekhar five for 77, E. A. S. Prasanna three for 31) and 287 (Abid Ali 36, B. Mahendra Kumar 46, A. G. Kripal Singh 43 not out; E. A. S. Prasanna four for 85, B. S. Chandrasekhar five for 119); Mysore 330 (K. R. Rajagopal 43, S. Krishnamurthy 62, Najam Hussain 103; B. Mahendra Kumar four for 91) and 84 for six (Abid Ali four for 32). Drawn.

At Ananthapur, December 18, 19. Andhra 69 (Y. B. Patel three for 14, E. A. S. Prasanna three for 31, Najam Hussain four for 6) and 64 (B. S. Chandrasekhar four for 4); Mysore 273 (B. K. Kunderam 111 not out, V. Subramanyam 48). Mysore won by an innings and 140 runs.

At Ernakulam, January 1, 2, 3. Andhra 183 (Mastan Rao 30, M. Shyam 37, K. P. Ramamurthy 68; C. K. Bhaskar seven for 86) and 117 (M. Shyam 35; Manikantan four for 26); Kerala 179 (T. V. Ramana three for 42, Lakshmanan four for 45) and 122 for five (S. P. Mallick 54 not out, K. Madan Mohan 27). Kerala won by five wickets.

At Madras, January 1, 2, 3. Hyderabad 306 (M. Venkatesh 31, Abid Ali 40, Abbas Ali Baig 50, M. L. Jaisimha 86 not out, Habib Ahmed 41; V. Prabhakar Rao three for 90, V. V. Kumar three for 68) and 19 for three dec.; Madras 183 (P. K. Belliappa 39, V. Rajaram 30, S. Venkatraghavan 30; M. L. Jaisimha four for 54, B. Mahendra Kumar three for 2) and 74 for eight (B. Mahendra Kumar three for 19). Drawn.

At Bangalore, January 8, 9, 10. Mysore 256 (V. Subramanyam 74, A. V. Jagannath 85, Y. B. Patel 36; U. Prabhakar Rao six for 77) and 191 for six dec. (S. Krishnamurthy 30, P. R. Ashok Anand 49, Najam Hussain 51 not out); Madras 113 (A. G. Milkha Singh 50; B. S. Chandrasekhar four for 40, E. A. S. Prasanna three for 46) and 193 (A. G. Milkha Singh 115 not out; Y. B. Patel three for 32, B. S. Chandrasekhar four for 49, E. A. S. Prasanna three for 46). Mysore won by 141 runs.

At Ernakulam, January 8, 9. Kerala 114 (K. Madan Mohan 52; Govindaraj three for 43, B. Mahendra Kumar three for 34) and 181 (P. C. Moses 50; B. Mahendra Kumar six for 64); Hyderabad 388 for four dec. (Habib Ahmed 42, The Nawab of Pataudi 78, M. L. Jaisimha 72, B. Mahendra Kumar 104 not out, M. A. Baig 66 not out). Hyderabad won by an innings and 93 runs.

West Zone:

At Surat, November 6, 7, 8. Gujerat 268 (T. G. Surve 41, N. J. Contractor 32, R. F. Surti 81, H. Shah 46; R. G. Nadkarni three for 29, S. J. Diwadkar five for 80) and 101 (N. J. Contractor 45, R. F. Surti 33; M. S. Hardikar three for 49, R. G. Nadkarni four for 30); Bombay 324 (F. M. Engineer 27, D. N. Sardesai 73, A. L. Wadekar 157 not out; A. Joshi six for 103) and 48 for two. Bombay won by eight wickets.

At Rajkot, November 6, 7, 8. Baroda 360 (S. P. Gaekwad 74, J. W. Ghorpade 34, G. Kishenchand 96, J. M. Ghorpade 39, S. M. Fadnis 38; U. Joshi three for 63) and 165 (L. Fernandez 48; U. Joshi four for 50); Saurashtra 323 (K. S. Indrajitsinh 64, K. S. Chatrapal 35, K. S. Zahid 64, Prahladsinh 58, D. Parsana 38; J. M. Ghorpade three for 102) and 63 for four. Drawn.

At Bombay, November 13, 14, 15. Bombay 381 (S. G. Adhikari 110, R. G. Nadkarni 62, V. R. Bondre 32, S. V. More 38 not out; Kher three for 63) and 156 for four (A. L. Wadekar 101 not out; S. N. Mohol three for 16); Maharashtra 245 (H. S. Kanitkar 61, V. H. Bhosle 91, M. S. Gupte 34; R. B. Desai four for 61). Drawn.

At Junagadh, November 13, 14, 15. Gujerat 467 (R. Nagdev 57, T. G. Surve 32, N. J. Contractor 58, M. T. Chandrabhan 30, H. Shah 34, Naik 94, P. Sheth 96; U. Joshi five for 151); Saurashtra 137 (K. S. Indrajitsinh 38; A. Joshi three for 26) and 316 (K. S. Indrajitsinh 78, K. S. Chatrapal 31, K. S. Zahid 45, Prahladsinh 64; R. F. Surti three for 55). Gujerat won by an innings and 14 runs.

At Karad, November 20, 21, 22. Baroda 264 (J. W. Ghorpade 63, V. S. Indulkar 71; S. N. Mohol three for 97, A. Khan six for 57) and 179 (J. M. Patel 36; A. Shaikh five for 55); Maharashtra 308 for nine dec. (H. S. Kanitkar 116, C. G. Borde 57; C. R. Williams five for 106) and 45 for no wicket. Drawn.

At Bombay, November 21, 21. Saurashtra 100 (K. S. Indrajitsinh 32, R. B. Desai four for 27; Lele four for 37) and 104 (K. S. Indrajitsinh 40; S. J. Diwadkar six for 19); Bombay 314 for four dec. (F. M. Engineer 50, S. G. Adhikari 64, D. N. Sardesai 90, A. L. Wadekar 100). Bombay won by an innings and 110 runs.

At Baroda, November 27, 28, 29. Baroda 338 (R. R. Bhatt 60, J. M. Patel 106, G. Kishenchand 30, A. Fernandez 35) and 24 for three; Gujerat 218 (T. G. Surve 38, N. J. Contractor 69; C. R. Williams four for 59, J. M. Patel three for 55). Drawn.

At Nasik, November 27, 28, 29. Maharashtra 330 for nine dec. (H. S. Kanitkar 30, N. F. Saldana 142, V. H. Bhosle 32, M. S. Gupte 31) and 184 for nine dec. (N. F. Saldana 33, M. R. Salvi 43; U. Joshi four for 85, Antani three for 40); Saurashtra 185 (A. Chayya 58, U. Modi 34, J. Shah 50; A. Joshi four for 78, A. Shaikh five for 75) and 159 (J. Shah 67; A. Joshi four for 66, A. Shaikh three for 38). Maharastra won by 170 runs.

At Baroda, December 4, 5, 6. Bombay 299 (F. M. Engineer 88, A. L. Wadekar 45, S. V. More 30, V. R. Bondre 36; C. R. Williams four for 112) and 216 (A. L. Wadekar 47, R. G. Nadkarni 52, V. R. Bondre 35; C. R. Williams four for 90); Baroda 154 (J. Patel 57; R. G. Nadkarni four for 38) and 264 for seven (S. P. Gaekwad 47, J. W. Ghorpade 49, G. Kishenchand 36, A. Fernandez 51). Drawn.

At Vallabh Vidyanagar, December 11, 12, 13. Gujerat 206 (N. J. Contractor 58, R. F. Surti 60; A. Joshi seven for 60) and 180 (S. Trivedi 48, R. F. Surti 91; A. Joshi six for 68); Maharashtra 311 for eight dec. (H. S. Kanitkar 39, V. H. Bhosle 58, S. T. Kirtane 39; Zaveri five for 86) and 78 for three. Maharashtra won by seven wickets.

Central Zone:

At Nagpur, December 3, 4, 5. Vidharba 214 (V. Pimprikar 66; Bhave six for 55) and 301 for six dec. (V. Pimprikar 122 not out); Madhya Pradesh 361 (R. Bhatia 70, S. Saxena 80, A. K. Chaturvedi 64, A. Jagdale 82, M. Joshi 32 not out; Rahim four for 56, Ogiral three for 112) and 84 for four (A. K. Chaturvedi 53 not out). Drawn.

At Jaipur, December 5, 6, 7. Uttar Pradesh 210 (K. Chisti 30, K. V. R. Murthy 42; K. Ghattani four for 48) and 203 for seven dec. (K. Nautial 42, A. Mishra 37, K. Ghattani three for 40); Rajasthan 212 for nine dec. (A. K. Singh 30, Raj Singh 41 not out, G. R. Sunderram 39; Kasim four for 50) and 144 for one (P. C. Poddar 51 not out, K. M. Rungta 89). Drawn.

At Jaipur, December 11, 12, 13. Vidharba 247 (N. Murthy 60, V. Pimprikar 31, S. Sahu 30; Raj Singh three for 56, S. A. Durani three for 56, C. G. Joshi three for 24) and 196 (N. Murthy 41, P. N. Khot 59; K. Ghattani four for 44); Rajasthan 444 for seven dec. (P. C. Poddar 176, S. A. Durani 74, Hanumant Singh 34, K. M. Rungta 35, V. L. Manjrekar 54; M. S. Manian three for 120; R. N. Abhyankar three for 80). Rajasthan won by an innings and one run.

At Indore, December 11, 12, 13. Madhya Pradesh 332 for three (B. G. Kher 120, A. K. Chaturvedi 130 not out). Uttar Pradesh did not bat. Drawn. Rain on last two days.

At Nagpur, December 17, 18, 19. Uttar Pradesh 247 (M. Halim 48, K. V. R. Murthy 58, L. Hazaria 37; Ogiral three for 60) and 302 for nine (L. Hazaria 57, K. M. Tiwari 42, A. Kasim 70 not out, S. N. Puri 32 not out; Mani four for 38); Vidharba 342 (M. Rajan 92, S. Sahu 86, Imran Ali 77; M. Halim three for 67). Drawn.

At Jaipur, December 18, 19. Madhya Pradesh 104 (Raj Singh four for 23, S. A. Durani three for 16) and 214 (S. Saxena 49, Gulrez Ali 71, G. R. Sunderram five for 46); Rajasthan 211 (S. A. Durani 104, P. Sharma 41) and 108 for two (S. A. Durani 51 not out, Hanumant Singh 28 not out). Rajasthan won by eight wickets.

North Zone:

At Jullundur, December 1, 2, 3. North Punjab 377 for six dec. (S. Talwar 69, A. Khanna 46, Chaman Lal 77, Gurdip Singh 86, V. Sehgal 54); Jammu & Kashmir 160 (Bishen Singh Bedi three for 42, Chaman Lal three for 29) and 131 (Gurdip Singh five for 39; Bishen Singh Bedi three for 33). North Punjab won by an innings and 86 runs.

At Patiala, December 1, 2, 3. Services 313 (R. Dewan 61, B. Awasthy 41, M. Sharma 32, H. T. Dani 58; Daljit Singh six for 90) and 134 for three dec. (R. Dewan 41, B. Awasthy 63 not out); South Punjab 193 (M. P. Pondove 91; G. Inder Dev five for 78, M. R. Baig three for 39) and 104 (Megh Raj 38; G. Inder Dev five for 32). Services won by 150 runs.

At Ludiana, December 5, 6, 7. North Punjab 208 (A. Khanna 59, V. Sehgal 39; G. Inder Dev five for 63) and 269 (Chaman Lal 73, S. Luthra 101; M. R. Baig three for 46); Services 409 for six dec. (R. Devan 33, M. Sharma 170, H. T. Dani 84, V. Bhushan 70 not out; Bishen Singh Bedi four for 117) and 71 for one (R. Dewan 51 not out). Services won by nine wickets.

At Patiala, December 5, 6, 7. South Punjab 175 (A. Swaroop 36; A. Rauf five for 25, Mohiuddin five for 50) and 205 for seven dec. (M. P. Pondove 50 not out, Dharamvir 57); Jammu & Kashmir 137 (M. P. Pondove five for 41) and 92 (Daljit Singh six for 18). South Punjab won by 151 runs.

At Delhi, December 9, 10. Jammu & Kashmir 110 (A. Rauf 30; R. Goel six for 43) and 129 (R. Raina 45; A. Shukla six for 41; R. Goel three for 41); Delhi 290 (Akash Lal 84, R. Saxena 37, Gyneshwar 73; A. Rauf four for 88, Mohiuddin four for 125). Delhi won by an innings and 51 runs.

At New Delhi, December 13, 14. Services 440 for six dec. (B. Awasthy 142, H. T. Dani 64, G. Inder Dev 61 not out, Dharmalingam 79 not out); Jammu & Kashmir 135 (A. Rauf 45; H. T. Dani four for 22, G. Inder Dev three for 14) and 130 (A. Rauf 30; G. Inder Dev six for 47). Services won by an innings and 175 runs.

At New Delhi, December 17, 18. Jammu & Kashmir 126 (S. Jagdish four for 11) and 107 (V. B. Ranjane six for 24); Railways 406 for seven dec. (Y. M. Choudhry 100, S. Jagdish 91, Mushtaq Ali 44, Gurpal Singh 48, M. Mehra 49 not out, P. Bangara 55 not out). Railways won by an innings and 173 runs.

At New Delhi, December 21, 22, 23. Railways 248 (G. Murtaza 57, Y. M. Choudhry 36, S. Jagdish 28, Mushtaq Ali 34; R. Goel six for 78) and 201 for nine (S. Dharsey 42, Mushtaq Ali 33, W. Ghosh 52 not out; V. Mehra five for 23); Delhi 383 (V. Mehra 75, Sher Mohammad 109, R. Saxena 68, Daljit Singh 30; V. B. Ranjane three for 119, W. Ghosh three for 77). Drawn.

At Jullundur, December 21, 22, 23. South Punjab 304 (M. P. Pondove 65, Megh Raj 55, Rajinder Pal 45; Ramnath four for 55) and 164 for seven dec.; North Punjab 173 (Rajinder Pal six for 73) and 128. South Punjab won by 167 runs.

At New Delhi, December 26, 27. Services 346 (B. Awasthy 73, M. Sharma 44, G. Inder Dev 91, Dharmalingam 74; A. Shukla four for 78, Sher Mohammad three for 56) and 287 for seven (B. Awasthy 28, M. Sharma 28, H. T. Dani 83, V. Bhushan 86 not out; R. Goel four for 102); Delhi 286 (Sher Mohammad 101, A. Shukla 40, Gulshan Rai 36) and 188 for one (Akash Lal 64 not out, R. Saxena 122). Drawn.

At New Delhi, December 26, 27. Railways 399 for four dec. (N. Baxi 81, H. Ghosh 166 not out, Y. M. Choudhry 102; Bishen Singh Bedi three for 100); North Punjab 194 (S. Talwar 70, A. Khanna 30, Chaman Lal 42; W. Ghosh three for 27, S. Jagdish three for 26) and 191 (S. Talwar 69; W. Ghosh three for 48, V. Mehra three for 39). Railways won by an innings and 14 runs.

At New Delhi, December 29, 30. South Punjab 181 (Megh Raj 46; Gurpal Singh five for 42) and 23 for one. Railways 293 (N. Baxi 45, Y. P. Sidhaye 52, Mushtaq Ali 100; Rajinder Pal five for 71). Drawn.

At New Delhi, January 2, 3, 4. Services 403 (R. Dewan 46, M. Sharma 34, B. Awasthy 190; W. Ghosh six for 77) and 235 for eight (B. Awasthy 59, Harcharan Singh 33, Dharmalingam 62; S. Jagdish four for 100); Railways 323 (N. Baxi 68, Mushtaq Ali 49, Gurpal Singh 70). Drawn.

At Chandigarh, January 9, 10, 11. South Punjab 206 (Amrik Singh 34, R. Chauhan 37, M. P. Pondove 60; Ravinder Pal four for 34, Jain four for 59) and 193 (A. Swaroop 48, Daljit Singh 47; Ravinder Pal three for 41, Khatter three for 42); Delhi 203 (S. Hardas 71; Rajinder Pal five for 73) and 54 for six (Rajinder Pal three for 25). Drawn.

At Jullundur, January 14, 15, 16. Delhi 300 (Akash Lal 104, R. B. Mathur 32, R. Saxena 44, R. Saini 77; Bishen Singh Bedi four for 86) and 116 (Akash Lal 65); North Punjab 257 (S. Luthera 65, Chaman Lal 37, Bishen Singh Bedi 39; Sitaram three for 81, R. Goel four for 85, Gyneshwar three for 34) and 65 for one. Drawn.

East Zone:

At Cuttack, December 12, 13, 14. Assam 278 (M. P. Barua 46, T. Barua 58, A. Hussain 120; B. S. Alva three for 34) and 151 (A. Hussain 58, K. Barua 44; A. Patel seven for 48); Orissa 191 (N. N. Swamy 66, B. J. Godbole 48; K. Ahmed five for 68, A. Ghatak three for 63) and 201 for five (B. Jena 110; A. Ghatak three for 83). Drawn.

At Jamshedpur, December 18, 19, 20. Assam 190 (T. Baura 40, S. N. Quamar 36; S. Nagaswamy four for 26) and 259 (M. P. Barua 41, P. Bhattacharjee 52, Anwar Hussain 50, K. Ahmed 46 not out; S. Kapoor four for 43); Bihar 345 (R. Sanyal 121, M. Roy 59; A. Ghatak six for 98) and 108 for three (S. Bose 48 not out, R. Sanyal 34). Bihar won by seven wickets.

At Cuttack, December 18, 19, 20. Bengal 313 (A. Roy 197, S. S. Mitra 36; Satpathy six for 89); Orissa 129 (Shome three for 39, S. Guha four for 37) and 181 (K. N. Patro 31; T. J. Bannerjee five for 32). Bengal won by an innings and three runs.

At Cuttack, December 25, 26, 27. Orissa 169 (L. I. Parija 43, A. Jena 30; S. Nagaswamy five for 56) and 269 (B. K. Sikdar 105, A. Jena 48, K. Patel 32, Aloke Jena 48; S. Das six for 59); Bihar 193 (R. Sanyal 51, G. Ghosh 60; A. Patel five for 78) and 194 (S. Bose 37, S. Amin 49; A. Patel three for 49, D. S. Murthy five for 64). Orissa won by 51 runs.

At Calcutta, December 24, 25, 26. Bengal 426 (D. Mukerjee 42, P. Roy 43, A. Roy 52, S. S. Mitra 155, C. Goswami 42; Laskar three for 98, P. Chowdhury four for 95); Assam 105 (C. Goswami three for 12) and 153 (M. P. Barua 34, K. Ahmed 34; T. J. Bannerjee five for 39, C. Goswami four for 18). Bengal won by an innings and 168 runs.

At Jamshedpur, January 1, 2, 3. Bihar 308 (K. Chakravarthy 76, K. Mitra 42. Gopalakrishnan 47, S. Amin 46; S. Guha three for 60, J. Ghosh three for 53); Bengal 192 for two (D. Mukerjee 75, T. Roy 52, A. Roy 49 not out). Drawn.

Quarter-final:

At Jaipur, January 28, 29, 30. Services 156 (H. T. Dani 38, Harcharan Singh 52; Raj Singh three for 51; C. G. Joshi three for 32) and 268 (B. Awasthy 58, V. Bhushan 69 not out, R. Surendranath 33; G. R. Sunderram four for 83, Ramaswamy four for 51); Rajasthan 330 (Suryaveer Singh 31, Hanumant Singh 85, K. M. Rungta 128; G. Inder Dev three for 88) and 95 for three (Parathasarathy 32 not out, K. M. Rungta 44). Rajasthan won by seven wickets.

Semi-finals:

At Bombay, January 29, 30, 31, February 1. Bengal 109 (R. G. Nadkarni four for 10; Lele three for 53) and 252 (P. Roy 68, A. Roy 38, S. S. Mitra 80; V. R. Bondre three for 58); Bombay 254 (S. G. Adhikari 91, S. J. Diwadkar 88 not out; S. Guha seven for 59, C. Goswami three for 47) and 109 for one (D. N. Sardesai 50 not out, S. G. Adhikari 38). Bombay won by nine wickets.

At Bangalore, February 5, 6, 7, 8. Mysore 397 (K. R. Rajagopal 97, B. K. Kunderam 48, P. R. Ashok Anand 72, Najam Hussain 38, Y. B. Patel 50; C. G. Joshi four for 131) and 243 for seven dec. (P. R. Ashok Anand 46, K. H. Nagabushan 64 not out; C. G. Joshi four for 63); Rajasthan 458 (P. C. Poddar 51, Hanumant Singh 82, V. L. Manjrekar 175, P. Sharma 44, Raj Singh 44 not out; E. A. S. Prasanna five for 162) and 183 for nine (Hanumant Singh 32; E. A. S. Prasanna seven for 92). Rajasthan won by one wicket.

Final:

At Jaipur, February 17, 18, 19, 20. Rajasthan 165 (M. S. Hardikar six for 25) and 268 (R. N. Rungta 60, K. Ghattani 94, C. G. Joshi 30; R. B. Desai four for 72, M. S. Hardikar three for 69); Bombay 362 (A. L. Wadekar 185, D. N. Sardesai 99; C. G. Joshi six for 96) and 32 for two. Bombay won by eight wickets.

RANJI TROPHY HOLDERS

1934–35	Bombay	1950–51	Holkar
1935–36	Bombay	1951–52	Bombay
1936–37	Nawanagar	1952–53	Holkar
1937–38	Hyderabad	1953–54	Bombay
1938–39	Bengal	1954–55	Madras
1939–40	Maharashtra	1955–56	Bombay
1940–41	Maharashtra	1956–57	Bombay
1941–42	Bombay	1957–58	Baroda
1942–43	Baroda	1958–59	Bombay
1943–44	Western India	1959–60	Bombay
1944–45	Bombay	1960–61	Bombay
1945–46	Holkar	1961–62	Bombay
1946–47	Baroda	1962–63	Bombay
1947–48	Holkar	1963–64	Bombay
1948–49	Bombay	1964–65	Bombay
1949–50	Baroda	1965–66	Bombay

DULEEP TROPHY TOURNAMENT

At Bangalore, October 23, 24, 25. South Zone 480 for nine dec. (P. K. Belliappa 54, Abbas Ali Baig 159, The Nawab of Pataudi 44, M. L. Jaisimha 160; G. Inder Dev three for 155) and 185 for seven dec. (Abbas Ali Baig 65, The Nawab of Pataudi 34); North Zone 272 (V. Mehra 50, Akash Lal 53, H. T. Dani 52, Daljit Singh 50; B. S. Chandrasekhar five for 86, S. Venkatraghavan three for 63) and 103 for five. Drawn.

Semi-finals:

At Hyderabad, October 30, 31, November 1. West Zone 214 (V. H. Bhosle 41, R. F. Surti 51, R. G. Nadkarni 42; S. Venkatraghavan four for 64) and 238 for seven (A. L. Wadekar 76, M. L. Jaisimha five for 42); South Zone 487 (P. K. Belliappa 38, Abbas Ali Baig 73, The Nawab of Pataudi 132, M. L. Jaisimha 38, A. G. Milkha Singh 108, Wahid Yar Khan 61 not out; R. B. Desai three for 58, A. V. Mankad five for 126). Drawn.

At Calcutta, November 27, 28, 29. East Zone 392 (M. P. Barua 63, D. Mukerjee 63, A. Roy 93, S. S. Mitra 34, P. Roy 83; K. Ghattani four for 100); Central Zone 416 for four (P. C. Poddar 65, S. A. Durani 33, Raj Singh 36, Hanumant Singh 168 not out, V. L. Manjrekar 91 not out). Drawn.

Final:

At Madras, December 25, 26. Central Zone 123 (B. G. Kher 30; S. A. Durani 36; E. A. S. Prasanna six for 19) and 167 (S. A. Durani 40; E. A. S. Prasanna five for 61, B. S. Chandrasekhar five for 39); South Zone 310 (B. K. Kunderam 100, P. K. Belliappa 44, The Nawab of Pataudi 38, Abid Ali 56; S. A. Durani five for 120, C. G. Joshi three for 95). South Zone won by an innings and 20 runs.

MOIN UD DOWLA GOLD CUP TOURNAMENT

At Hyderabad, October 3, 4, 5. State Bank of India 446 (V. Mehra 87, B. K. Kunderam 81, Hanumant Singh 38, A. L. Wadekar 50, R. Saxena 34, V. Subramanyam 80, S. J. Diwadkar 50; M. S. Hardikar four for 144) and 172 for five (Hanumant Singh 67, A. L. Wadekar 30; A. Mankad three for 54); Maharana of Mewar's XI 363 (S. Dharsey 69, M. S. Hardikar 112, P. Sharma 41, Sridharan 38; B. P. Gupte three for 102, R. Goel three for 61). Drawn.

At Hyderabad, October 5, 6, 7. Hyderabad XI 403 (R. Venkatesh 44, Abid Ali 147, Abbas Ali Baig 47, Wahid Yar Khan 53; K. Ghattani four for 89, S. Venkatraghavan three for 126) and 182 for nine (M. L. Jaisimha 47, B. Mahendra Kumar 36; S. Venkatraghavan four for 39); Vazir Sultan Colts 337 (A. Roy 57, The Nawab of Pataudi 175, M. S. Gupte 31; B. Mahendra Kumar four for 62). Drawn.

Semi-finals:

At Hyderabad, October 8, 9, 10. State Bank of India 311 (V. Mehra 39, B. K. Kunderam 32, A. L. Wadekar 105, N. K. Tantra 31 not out; R. G. Nadkarni five for 88) and 187 for one (V. Mehra 46, B. K. Kunderam 101 not out); Associated Cement Company 306 (V. H. Bhosle 74, R. G. Nadkarni 34, P. R. Umrigar 66, W. A. DeSouza 50; R. Goel six for 77) and 91 for no wkt. (K. S. Indrajitsinh 44 not out, D. N. Sardesai 31 not out). Drawn.

At Hyderabad, October 11, 12, 13. Hyderabad XI 408 (M. L. Jaisimha 99, Abbas Ali Baig 97, B. Mahendra Kumar 42, Wahid Yar Khan 52, A. G. Kripal Singh 46; W. Ghosh three for 98) and 126 for four (Murtuza Ali Baig 38); Indian Starlets 202 (A. Shukla 56; G. Inder Dev five for 42). Drawn.

Finals:

At Hyderabad, October 15, 16, 17, 18. Hyderabad 433 (M. Sharma 81, M. L. Jaisimha 73, Habeeb Ahmed 43, Wahid Yar Khan 62, G. Inder Dev 103 not out; S. J. Diwadkar three for 138) and 304 (M. Sharma 48, M. L. Jaisimha 111, Habib Ahmed 63; R. Goel three for 65); State Bank of India 268 (A. L. Wadekar 108, V. Subramanyam 82; Abid Ali four for 75, M. Jairam three for 41) and 369 (B. K. Kunderam 30, R. Saxena 66, Hanumant Singh 106, S. J. Diwadkar 53; M. Jairam five for 139). Hyderabad won by 100 runs.

YESHWANT RAO MEMORIAL TOURNAMENT

At Indore, January 7, 8, 9. State Bank of India 142 (V. Mehra 38, R. G. Nadkarni four for 17) and 288 for five dec. (Abid Ali 140 not out, R. Saxena 97; V. R. Bondre three for 68); K. M. Rangnekar's XI 307 (V. J. Paranjpe 34, R. F. Surti 31, M. S. Hardikar 35, V. L. Manjrekar 53, M. S. Tamhane 49; Abid Ali three for 85) and 101 for three (S. Shetty 30, M. S. Hardikar 41 not out). Drawn.

At Indore, January 10, 11, 12. Prof. Deodhar's XI 447 (D. G. Kher 51, H. S. Kanitkar 42, V. H. Bhonsle 84, C. G. Borde 73, Y. P. Sidhaye 46, S. N. Mohol 38; Gupte three for 110); M.Y.C.C. XI 271 (K. S. Indrajitsinh 119, Subodh Saxena 82; D. G. Kher four for 48). Drawn.

Final:

At Indore, January 15, 16, 17, 18. K. M. Rangnekar's XI 459 (S. G. Adhikari 126, R. F. Surti 60, V. L. Manjrekar 119, R. G. Nadkarni 42; S. N. Mohol four for 112) and 78 for one (S. G. Adhikari 38 not out); Prof. Deodhar's XI 294 (H. S. Kanitkar 39, The Nawab of Pataudi 76, C. G. Borde 31, Y. P. Sidhaye 30 not out; R. G. Nadkarni three for 45) and 270 for seven (D. Kher 46, H. S. Kanitkar 71, Y. P. Sidhaye 83, C. G. Borde 33; V. R. Bondre three for 78). Drawn.

OTHER FIRST-CLASS MATCHES

At Panjim, March 25, 26, 27. Gujarat Governor's XI 317 for eight dec. (S. P. Gaekwad 72, N. J. Contractor 57, The Nawab of Pataudi 32, R. F. Surti 50. not out; S. N. Mohol three for 93) and 264 (M. L. Jaisimha 56, Jitendra Patel 47); Maharashtra Governor's XI 320 for eight dec. (S. J. Diwadkhar 103, D. N. Sardesai 62, B. K. Kunderam 57; M. L. Jaisimha three for 98) and 262 for seven (D. N. Sardesai 101, B. K. Kunderam 61). Maharashtra Governor's XI won by three wickets.

At Kolahpur, April 16, 17, 18. Maharashtra Small Savings Minister's XI 279 (S. P. Gupte 94, V. L. Manjrekar 47, R. F. Surti 32; E. A. S. Prasanna four for 81, R. B. Desai three for 65, R. G. Nadkarni three for 74) and 230 (R. F. Surti 57, V. B. Ranjane 42, S. P. Gaekwad 34; E. A. S. Prasanna four for 64, S. N. Mohol four for 72); L. I. C. Chairman's XI 280 for five dec. (A. L. Wadekar 127, M. S. Hardikar 46 not out, D. G. Kher 37; B. S. Chandrasekhar three for 64) and 170 (V. H. Bhosle 61, B. S. Chandrasekhar six for 58; S. Venkatraghavan four for 65). Minister's XI won by 59 runs.

At Poona, April 22, 23, 24. Maharashtra Small Savings Minister's XI 220 (V. H. Bhosle 85, A. L. Wadekar 52, M. S. Hardikar 30; S. N. Mohol six for 70, including a hat-trick) and 243 for nine dec. (F. M. Engineer 74, A. L. Wadekar 49; S. Venkatraghavan four for 73); Cricket Control Board President's XI 173 (V. L. Manjrekar 48; E. A. S. Prasanna five for 61, R. B. Desai three for 37) and 255 (Abbas Ali Baig 147, S. J. Diwadkar 34; M. L. Jaisimha three for 63). Minister's XI won by 35 runs.

CRICKET IN PAKISTAN, 1965–66

By Ghulam Mustafa Khan

QUAID-E-AZAM TROPHY

Karachi retained the Quaid-E-Azam Trophy for the sixth consecutive time by beating Lahore Greens by 105 runs. This was their seventh win in ten Championships held so far. Of the 27 teams which were to participate nine withdrew, Services before and D. I. Khan, Quetta, P.W.D., Hyderabad University and Board. Karachi University and Board, Rajshahi, Chittagong, Khulna, after the draws were announced, leaving only 18 teams to compete. These teams were divided into four Zones.

In the North, for Rawalpindi Greens (Senior String), the seam bowlers Fida (18 wkts. av. 13.09) and Zia Burney (17 wkts. av. 15.35) and the Test off-spinner Javed Akhtar (15 wkts. av. 19.06) shared 50 of the 59 wickets which fell to the bowlers. Siddiq Akbar (162 runs av. 81.00), Salim Asghar (253 runs av. 42.16) and Nayyar Husain (238 runs av. 47.60) were their leading run getters. Greens' best moments were when they beat the star-studded P.I.A. at Rawalpindi.

Lahore Greens dominated the Central Zone table. Railways, the other better team in the Zone, who had earlier defeated Punjab University and Lahore Board combined team and Sargodha, got a merciless treatment from Lahore Greens' batsmen, particularly Shakoor. He scored most runs in the tournament (501 av. 83.50) and was ably supported by Shafqat Rana. Iqbal Sheikh (19 wkts. av. 21.37) including the hat trick against Multan and Pervez Sajjad (16 wkts. av. 20.62) were the leading bowlers.

No team could measure its strength with Karachi Blues, the eventual winners of the Trophy in the South Zone. They scored 634 for four declared against Hyderabad (Wallis (228) and Salahuddin (169) hit their highest scores and Shahid made a century). Against Bahawalpur, the Blues ran up 632 for eight declared (including a century each by Masood Akhtar and Ijaz Mirza); 389 against Rawalpindi Greens (Semi-final) and against Lahore Greens in the Final 463 and 173. Wallis topped the tournament, batting with an average of 119.33 in three innings. Aftab Alam, Javed Burki, Salahuddin, Ijaz Mirza and Masood Akhtar all batted well for their team. Munawar took most wickets in the tournament. Wasim Bari's excellent wicket-keeping (11 ct. 5 st.) also contributed much to their success.

In the East Zone, the strong Karachi Whites (including four Test players) were beaten by Dacca who, however, lost to Lahore Greens at Karachi.

One unique record was a year's gap in Dacca's first match against Dacca University and Board combined team at Dacca (March 3, 4, 5, 1965) and their second match against Lahore Greens at Karachi (March 4, 5, 6, 1966). This was due to the New Zealand tour in Pakistan, the indifferent weather conditions and war with India.

As explained in *Wisden* 1966, page 894, three Quaid-E-Azam Trophy matches had not been played at the end of the 1964–65 season. The competition was completed as follows:—

Eastern Zone

At Dacca, March 4, 5, 6, 1966. Karachi Whites 211 (Masudul Hassan 76; Niaz three for 56, Mufasirul three for 50, Nasimul Ghani three for 41) and 152 for two (Naushad Ali 77*, Abdul Kadir 46); Dacca 310 (Muttaqi Hassan 74, Anwar 65, Nasimul Ghani 60, Rauf Ansari 32; Munir Malik four for 86, Saeed Ahmed three for 54). Dacca won on first innings.

Semi-final:

At Karachi, April 7, 8, 9, 10, 1966. Dacca 297 (Amirullah 62 not out, Nasimul Ghani 52, M. A. Latif 49; Pervez Sajjad four for 78) and 213 for six dec. (Muttaqi Hassan 39, Rehman Ali 35, Mahmoodul Hasan 34; Iqbal Shaikh four for 63); Lahore Greens 329 (Shafqat Rana 104, Asghar Quareshi 80, Zafar Altaf 51, Farooq Hamid 34; Nasimul Ghani six for 96) and 127 for two (Iftekhar Bokhari 71 not out). Lahore Greens won on first innings.

Final:

At Karachi, April 12, 13, 14, 16, 17, 1966. Karachi Blues 463 (Javed Burki 137, Aftab Alam 80, Shahid Mahmood 58, Ejaz Mirza 56; Pervez Sajjad three for 100) and 173 (Wasim 42, Ejaz Mirza 37; Iqbal Shaikh four for 60, Pervez Sajjad three for 35); Lahore Greens 268 (Shafqat Rana 110, Zafar Altaf 49; Shabbir Husain four for 34) and 263 (Shakoor Ahmad 150 not out, Pervez Sajjad 35; Shabbir Husain four for 95, Munawar Husain four for 93). Karachi Blues won by 105 runs.

AYUB TROPHY CRICKET TOURNAMENT—1966

At Rawalpindi, April 15, 16, 17. Rawalpindi received a walk-over from D. I. Khan.

At Peshawar, April 15, 16, 17. Peshawar 96 (Ahad Khan six for 33) and 31 for no wkt.; Railway Reds 297 (Arif Butt 75, Saeed Butt 57, Bashir Hyder 47; Ghulam Mohammad five for 67). Railway Reds won on first innings.

At Bahawalpur, April 15, 16, 17. Bahawalpur 375 (Iqbal Awan 118, Javed Bhatti 142; Khalid Khan six for 77); Multan 117 (Khalid Nisar 37; Azizur Rahman three for 17) and 176 for seven (G. Martin 39; Akbar three for 35). Bahawalpur won on first innings.

At Lahore, April 15, 16, 17. Sargodha 216 (Mohd. Iqbal 57, Hamid Nagra 50; Salim Altaf six for 89) and 24 for two; Punjab University 364 for 8 dec. (Aftab Gul 100, Waqar Husain 90, Salim Altaf 40 Mushtaq Nashmi 39; Sher Andaz four for 49). Punjab University won on first innings.

At Hyderabad, April 15, 16, 17. Hyderabad 351 (Khawar Nabi 131, Iqbal Shaikh 91, Bashir 57, Riaz Alam 36; Tahir Ali five for 109, Manzoor four for 98); Khaipur 161 (Ashraf 41, Anwar 38 not out; Razzaq five for 46). Hyderabad won on first innings.

At Karachi, April 15, 16, 17. Karachi University 135 (Afzal Shaikh four for 30) and 119 (Akhtar Sadiq 32; Sultan five for 21); Quetta 70 (Anwar Ali 30; Afzal Ahmad five for 21) and 164 (Riaz 30; Tariq Javed three for 15). Karachi University won by 20 runs.

At Rawalpindi, April 19, 20, 21. Railway Reds 295 (Ijaz Hussain 91, Saeed Butt 74, Anis Ahmad 41; Javed Akhtar five for 109) and 288 (Anis Ahmad 68, Ijaz Husain 57, Saeed Butt 57, Arif Butt 35; Anwar three for 44); Rawalpindi 147 (Daud Rabbani 38 not out, Munawar Ahmad 30; Mohammad Nazir six for 48) and 93 for four. Railway Reds won on first innings.

At Karachi, April 19, 20, 21. Hyderabad 138 (Khawar Nabi 29; Aslam Khan four for 42) and 175 (Talat Iqbal 40 not out, Bashir 39; Tahsin three for 40); Karachi Blues 283 (Ghulam Abbas 70, Wallis Mathias 51, Javed Burki 35, Wasim Bari 31, Asif Iqbal 30; Iqbal Ahmad three for 49) and 31 for one. Karachi won by nine wickets.

At Karachi, April 19, 20, 21. Karachi University 212 (Akhtar Sadiq 61, Tariq 38; Khalid five for 61) and 116 for five (Aftal Ahmad 51 not out; Mehtab three for 18); Railway Greens 262 (Bashir 74, Khizer Hayat 30). Railway Greens won on first innings.

At Lahore, April 21, 22, 23, 24. Lahore Greens 824 (Zafar Altaf 268, Majid Jahangir 241, Asghar Quareshi 100, Saddiq 58, Nasir Qizilbash 48; Javed Bhatti five for 193); Bahawalpur 360 (Iqbal Awan 111, Khalid Jamil 82, Afzal Bokhari 40; Khalid Quareshi three for 54). Lahore won on first innings. (Note: As the first innings was not decided on the third day, the match was extended to April 24.)

At Lahore, April 21, 22, 23. Karachi Whites 206 (Masudul Hasan 74, Abdul Dyer 73; Khalifa Rauf three for 41) and 179 for three (Fakir Aizazuddin 83, Masood Akhtar 51); Punjab University 344 (Aftab Gul 96, Mushtaq Hashmi 69, Khalifa Rauf 53; Munir Malik eight for 154). Punjab University won on first innings.

At Rawalpindi, April 23, 24, 25. Lahore Reds 93 (Gulraiz 38; Arif Butt six for 36) and 158 (Razi 39, Naved Cheema 34; Ahad Khan five for 59). Railway Reds 404 (Ijaz Husain 173, Saeed Butt 105, Arif Butt 55; Intikhab Ahmad five for 86). Railway Reds won by an innings and 153 runs.

At Karachi, April 23, 24, 25. Karachi Blues 512 (Wallis Mathias 278 not out, Asif Iqbal 85, Arshad Bashir 33; Khalid four for 154, Nazir four for 176); Railway Greens 147 (Aslam Khan five for 47; Tahsin four for 59) and 81 for four. Karachi Blues won on first innings.

At Lahore, April 29, 30, May 1. Lahore Greens 242 (Majid Jahangir 127 not out, Intikhab Ahmad 60; Salim Altaf seven for 69) and 201 (Shakoor Ahmad 60, Majid Jahangir 36; Salim Altaf four for 86); Punjab University 152 (Mushtaq Hashmi 50, Nasrullah 38; Iqbal Shaikh seven for 34) and 152 for two (Aftab Gul 76). Lahore Greens won on first innings.

At Dacca, May 21, 22, 23. Dacca 188 (Jewel 38, Salim 34; Sadiq four for 50) and 70 (Javed Hassan four for 6); P. W. D. 160 (Mehdi seven for 40) and 63 for four. (Match abandoned when ninety minutes play still remained and P.W.D. needed 36 to win with six wickets in hand. The local University players invaded the ground for their football match.)

At Dacca, May 24, 25, 26. P.I.A. received a walk-over from Chittagong.

At Karachi, September 19, 20, 21. P. W. D. received a walk-over from Dacca. (*Note: Following dispute in match between Dacca and P. W. D., played on May 21, 22, 23, 1966, a replay was arranged, but Dacca were late in reaching the venue.*)

At Karachi, September 24, 25, 26. P.I.A. 252 (Fiza Khan 51, M. Ilyas 43, Muttaqi Hassan 32; Mohammad Sadiq three for 38) and 115 for five (Mohammad Sadiq 44); P. W. D. 258 (Izhar Siddiqi 85, Khalid Rafiq 64; Mohsin Siddiqi three for 49). P. W. D. won on first innings.

Semi-finals:

At Lahore, September 23, 24, 25, 26. Railway Reds 307 (Ijaz Husain 158, Arif Butt 75; Nayyar Husain three for 36) and 109 (Iqbal Shaikh five for 25); Lahore Greens 225 (Khalid Aziz 55, Shakoor Ahmad 47, Javedur Rahman 30; Nazir six for 67) and 196 for six (Majid Jahangir 57, Intikhab Ahmad 46*). Lahore Greens won by four wickets.

At Karachi, September 30, October 1, 2, 3. P. W. D. 292 (Mohammad Sadiq 119, Khalid Rafiq 54, Anwar 30; Saeed Ahmad four for 89) and 134 (Rahman Ali 34, Aslam Khan five for 41); Karachi Blues 365 (Salahuddin 62*, Ghulam Abbas 62, Naushad Ali 58, Mushtaq Mohammad 44, Javed Burki 42; Nasimul Ghani six for 92) and 63 for three. Karachi Blues won by seven wickets.

Final:

It was decided to play the match after the visit of the M.C.C. Under Twenty-Five team in 1966–67.

OTHER MATCH

At Lahore, February 18, 19, 20, 1966. Governor's XI 290 for four dec. (Hanif Mohammad 73, Ijaz Butt 58, Shafqat Rana 51 not out, Majid Jahangir 38 not out) and 171 for eight dec. (Mohammad Ilyas 52, Arif Butt 42; Ashraf four for 53); Punjab University 231 for nine dec. (Aftab Gul 49, Khalifa Rauf 36; Sadiq Mohammad five for 70) and 191 for six (Waqar Ahmad 50, Irshad Ghafoor 41; Sadiq Mohammad four for 68). Drawn.

CRICKET IN CEYLON, 1965–66

By H. G. Vaidyasekera

The annual Saravanamuttu Trophy Tournament, the premier cricket tournament on the island, was suspended during the 1965–66 season, due to exceptional circumstances. This tournament had an unbroken record of fifteen years since its inception in 1950.

The Nondescripts Cricket Club, a premier cricket club, inaugurated the Cecil Horan Trophy instead, in memory of the great Ceylon left-arm blowler, Cecil Horan, related to the Horans of Australia. The Horan Trophy was won by the sponsors, Nondescripts, with the Burgher Recreation Club as runners-up.

P. Ian Peiris of the Sinhalese Sports Club, a former Cambridge Blue, headed the batting averages for the season; Fitzroy Crozier (Nondescripts) headed the bowling with 49 wickets taken at 7.76 runs apiece. Lariff Idrees (Ceylon University) scored two hundreds in the tournament. Eleven hundreds were hit, of which Nihal Kodituwakku's 159 v. Moors was the highest.

The Colombo Municipality won three trophies at the Government Services Cricket Association tournament—the "A" Division, the Veterans' Division and the Railway Centenary Cup for over 50's.

Anura Tennekoon, Schoolboy Cricketer for 1966 for the second year in succession and captain of St. Thomas's College and Ceylon Schools, won a Ceylon cap at the age of eighteen. Stanley Jayasinghe, the Leicestershire cricketer, returned home and gave added strength to Ceylon cricket.

The sparkling and interesting cricket played by the London Schoolboys in Ceylon in the early part of the year was witnessed by large crowds.

A strong Madras team captained by P. K. Belliappa won the M. J. Gopalan Trophy, gaining a lead on the first innings. This team included several well known players like S. Venketaraghavan, J. Patel, V. V. Kumar, S. V. S. Mani and the two brothers, A. G. Milkha Singh and A. G. Satwender Singh, sons of A. G. Ram Singh and brothers of A. G. Kripal Singh. They drew all the three matches played in Ceylon.

In the Quadrangular Tournament, the schoolboys, captained by Anura Tennekoon, created a startling upset by entering the Finals.

The admission of Ceylon to the International Cricket Conference as an Associate Member was warmly welcomed and regarded as an acknowledgment of the high standard of cricket in the island.

M.C.C., captained by M. J. K. Smith, on their way to Australia and New Zealand, played two one-day matches which naturally created great interest. Reference to these games will be found in the section dealing with the tour.

MADRAS TEAM IN CEYLON, APRIL 1966

Madras v. Dimbulla President's XI

At Radella, April 2, 3. Madras 273 for eight dec. (A. G. Milkha Singh 85, T. Doraiappan 45 not out, S. Jagdish 38) and 80 for two dec. (S. V. S. Mani 31 not out); Dimbulla 174 for six dec. (M. H. Tissera 75 not out, V. Tissera 44) and 101 for six (P. K. Dharmalingam three for 34). Drawn.

M. J. GOPALAN CRICKET TROPHY MATCH

Madras v. Ceylon President's XI

At the Colombo Oval, April 5, 6, 7. Madras 398 (A. G. Satwender Singh 89, S. Jagdish 80, P. K. Dharmalingam 73, S. V. S. Mani 35, P. K. Belliappa 33; N. Frederick three for 89) and 36 for three (S. Wimalaratna three for 16); President's XI 143 (A. Tennekoon 45, N. Chanmugam 30; S. Venketragahavan four for 48, Prabhakar Rao three for 31) and 345 (Dr. H. I. K. Fernando 102 not out, N. Kodituwakky 87, S. Wimalaratna 30; V. V. Kumar five for 67, S. Venketaraghavan three for 123). Drawn.

Madras v. Galle

At the Galle Esplanade, April 9, 10. Madras 255 for nine dec. (A. G. Satwender Singh 88, S. Venketaraghavan 37, V. Rajaram 33; F. B. Crozier four for 96) and 137 for three dec. (J. C. Patel 65); Galle 157 (L. Fernando 67, T. C. T. Edwards 31; V. V. Kumar five for 48, S. Venketaraghavan three for 58) and 126 for seven (Ranjit Fernando 47, A. Polonowita 33 not out; P. K. Dharmalingham five for 43). Drawn.

PENTANGULAR CRICKET TOURNAMENT 1966

ROBERT SENANAYAKA CHALLENGE TROPHY

Government Services v. Ceylon Schools

At the Sinhalese Spots Club Grounds, April 2, 3, 4. Government Services 242 (D. Weerasinghe 130, D. P. de Silva 56; A Withanachi six for 54, N. Samarasekera three for 63) and 228 (L. Fernando 129, B. Aliph 36; S. Rajapaksa six for 78); Ceylon Schools 344 (P. de Niese 85 not out, F. Dias 59, A. Tennekoon 46, S. Rajapaksa 38; A. Polonwita five for 82) and 127 for three (K. Ramanathan 40; M. Gunaratna three for 38) Ceylon Schools won by seven wickets.

Ceylon Schools v. The Rest

At the Sinhalese Sports Club Grounds, April 17, 18, 19. Ceylon Schools 157 (A. Tennekoon 55, S. Rajapaksa 32; N. Frederick six for 31) and 217 (A. Tennekoon 75; N. Frederick four for 37, R. de Silva three for 36); The Rest 142 (A. Tennekoon four for 28, S. Rajapaksa four for 38) and 212 (S. Seneviratna 67, S. Rajaratnam 53 not out, R. Hamer 30; N. Samarasekera four for 65, S. Rajapaksa three for 45). Ceylon Schools won by 20 runs.

Mercantile Services v. Combined Services

At the Nondescripts Cricket Club Grounds, April 17, 18, 19. Combined Services 192 (M. D. Fernando 97; N. Chanmugam five for 65, F. B. Crozier three for 72) and 121 (M. D. Fernando 55; N. Chanmugam four for 34, F. B. Crozier three for 32); Mercantile Services 363 (N. Chanmugam 71, S. S. Kumar 56, C. E. Reid 49, F. B. Crozier 37 not out, D. Heyn 35; H. D. Fernando three for 57, J. B. Francis three for 65). Mercantile Services won by an innings and 50 runs.

FINAL MATCH

Mercantile Services v. Ceylon Schools

At the Sinhalese S.C. Grounds, April 25, 26, 27. Ceylon Schools 190 (A. Tennekoon 81, S. Rajapaksa 49; F. B. Crozier three for 54) and 100 for five (P. de Niese 35); Mercantile Services 196 for eight dec. (S. S. Kumar 39; A. Withanachi three for 47). Mercantile Services won by two wickets on the first innings and carried off the Trophy.

ALL-INDIA STATE BANK TOUR OF CEYLON, 1966

Fifteen members of the State Bank of India cricket team visited Ceylon in August, 1966, on a three-week tour. The team included five Indian Test caps and were led by A. G. Milkha Singh, the turbaned Sikh. The other Test caps were Hanumant Singh, V. V. Kumar, B. K. Kunderam and Vijay Mehra. Mr. P. V. H. Bahu was the manager. The team played ten matches, winning six, drawing three and losing one. They lost the only three-day match to the Prime Minister's XI by nine wickets. Of the four two-day matches, they won one and drew three. They won all the five one-day matches, winning by seven runs in the fourth ball of the last over at Galle.

Waheedyar Khan was the most consistent batsman. Hanumant Singh began with two fifties but later fell off in form. The stylish Ramesh Saxena also made several useful scores with 98 as his highest. S. J. Diwadkar wound up the tour with two not-out fifties. Rajinder Goel, the left-hand spinner, was the mainstay of the bowlers and was ably assisted by Chandrasekharam, the other off-spinner.

At Colombo Oval, August 4, 5. President of Ceylon Cricket Association's XI 184 (N. Kodituwakku 44, S. B. Seneviratne 39, P. I. Pieris 36; R. Goel five for 53, V. V. Kumar four for 77) and 161 for eight wkts. dec. (P. I. Pieris 52*, S. Jayasingha 39, N. Kodituwakku 33); State Bank128 (Hanumant Singh 56; P. I. Pieris six for 27, N. Samarasekera three for 41) and 167 for eight wkts. (A. L. Wadekar 54, R. Saxena 31, V. Mehra 30; A. Polonowita three for 40, N. Samarasekera three for 43). Drawn.

At Colombo Oval, August 7, 8. Mercantile C.A. 217 (R. J. Reid 65, N. Chanmugam 36; R. Goel four for 78, S. J. Diwadkar three for 40, R. Chandrasekharam three for 50) and 237 for four wkts. dec. (Claude Reid 110*, Ranjit Fernando 73); State Bank 215 for five wkts. dec. (A. L. Wadekar 69*, V. Mehra 42) and 157 for three wkts. (R. Saxena 98, B. K. Kunderam 37). Drawn.

At Radella, August 10, 11. State Bank 110 for six wkts. dec. (R. Raghavan 44; U. de Silva three for 29) and 35 for three wkts.; Dimbulla President's XI 112 for three wkts. dec. (R. Morrel 59*, T. Witham 40). Drawn.

At the Colombo Oval, August 13, 14, 15. State Bank 96 (Waheedyar Khan 54; P. I. Pieris six for 30) and 255 (A. L. Wadekar 86, A. G. Milkha Singh 61; P. I. Pieris four for 58, N. Frederick four for 71); Prime Minister's XI 305 (S. Jayasinghe 55, A. Tennekoon 51, M. Tissera 32, N. Kodituwakku 30; R. Chandrasekeram four for 58, V. V. Kumar three for 115) and 49 for one wkt. Prime Minister's XI won by nine wickets.

At Colombo Oval, August 17, 18. Nationalised Services 222 (D. P. de Silva 50, S. Dias 47, C. Weerasinha 37, Tissa de Soysa 31, A. Gunasena 30; S. J. Diwadkar four for 68) and 152 for five wkts. dec. (C. Weerasinha 59*, D. P. de Silva 34); State Bank 234 for five wkts. dec. (A. L. Wadekar 118*, S. J. Diwadkar 50*) and 144 for six wkts. (R. Saxena 48). State Bank won by four wickets with five minutes to spare.

* *Signifies not out.*

CEYLON TOUR OF PAKISTAN, 1966

By GHULAM MUSTAFA KHAN and CHRISTIE SENEVIRATNE

With just a year and a half left before Ceylon's first tour of England in the summer of 1968, the Island's cricket received a severe blow by losing all three unofficial Tests overwhelmingly to Pakistan, two by an innings and the other by 10 wickets, and drawing the three representative games in the one month's tour of the sub-continent in November 1966.

Ceylon, whose cricket is normally confined to one and a half day games, showed their inability in four-day cricket, always forcing the pace trying to make the game bright and entertaining, and as a result they lacked the staying power and temperament which are so vital in big cricket.

Both Stanley Jayasinghe and Clive Inman, the Leicestershire county professionals, proved most unsuccessful, but Jayasinghe retrieved some of his form in the latter stages of the tour, with a sparkling Test hundred. The entire tour was a personal triumph for the left-arm spin bowler, Fitzroy Crozier, whose selection was criticised by the press and public. He alone snatched the major honours, both in bowling and batting, creating a new bowling record against Pakistan by capturing seven wickets for 135 runs.

For Pakistan the visit provided practice although the tourists were no match for Pakistan's full might. Intikhab Alam (17 wickets), Saeed Ahmad (13 wickets) and Salim Altaf (11 wickets) were the leading bowlers for Pakistan. In addition, Intikhab totalled 190 in three innings, including a hurricane 89 containing five 6's and seven 4's. Javed Burki, who scored 307 runs, average 102.33, was tried as an opening batsman in the last two matches. At Dacca, he and Ijaz made 94 for the first wicket and at Karachi, Burki and Ilyas began with a stand of 183.

At Bahawalpur, November 1, 2. Pakistan Board of Control XI 273 for six dec. (Ghulam Abbas 101, Javed Bhatti 52*, Masudal Hassan 36); Ceylon 209 for four (L. Fernando 74, A. Tennekoon 68). Drawn.

At Rawalpindi, November 4, 5, 6. Ceylon 331 (C. C. Inman 87, F. B. Crozier 60, D. Heyn 55*, S. Jayasinghe 51; Intikhab Alam four for 91) and 164 for five dec. (A. Tennekoon 51*, F. B. Crozier 43); Rawalpindi President's XI 172 (Iqbal Kashmiri 57; S. Wimalaratne four for 37) and 269 for eight (Abdul Latif 42, Wallis Mathias 34; B. W. R. Thomas four for 71). Drawn.

At Lyallpur, November 8, 9, 10. Ceylon 278 for nine dec. (C. C. Inman 102, M. Tissera 64; Asif Iqbal three for 51) and 206 for four (F. B. Crozier 46, N. Chanmugam 32; Zulficar three for 39, Pervez Sajjad three for 60); Governor's XI 204 for four dec. (Waqar Ahmad 53, Salah-ud-Din 41*, Aftab Gul 36, Hamid Nagra 35) and 170 for seven (N. Chanmugam four for 66). Drawn.

PAKISTAN v. CEYLON

First "Test": at Lahore, November 12, 13, 14, 15. Pakistan won by ten wickets. Pakistan 425 (Mushtaq Mohammad 101, Intikhab Alam 49, Mohammad Ilyas 48, Izaj Husain 44, Javed Burki 42; F. B. Crozier six for 133) and 40 for no wkt. Ceylon 189 (S. Wimalaratne 41*, H. I. K. Fernando 37; Intikhab Alam five for 69, Salim Altaf three for 26) and 275 (S. Jayasinghe 118, H. I. K. Fernando 46, N. Kodituwakku 31; Intikhab Alam four for 82, Saeed Ahmad three for 44).

Second "Test" at Dacca (East Pakistan), November 18, 20, 21. Pakistan won by an innings and 37 runs. Pakistan 517 for seven dec. (Mushtaq Mohammad 129, Hanif Mohammad 114, Intikhab Alam 89, Javed Burki 55, Saeed Ahmad 43, Izaj Hussain 39; B. W. R. Thomas three for 166). Ceylon 213 (C. C. Inman 48, A. Tennekoon 33, H. I. K. Fernando 33; Saeed Ahmad five for 48, Purvez Sajjad three for 61) and 267 (F. B. Crozier 57, C. C. Inman 48, A. Tennekoon 34; Saeed Ahmad five for 82).

Third "Test": At Karachi, November 26, 27, 28, 29. Pakistan won by an innings and 35 runs. Ceylon 178 (A. Tennekoon 31; Salim Altaf four for 56) and 270 (M. Tissera 120*; Intikhab Alam four for 55, Asif Iqbal three for 74); Pakistan 483 (Javed Burki 210, Asif Iqbal 61, Mohammad Ilyas 60, Intikhab Alam 52, Salah-ud-Din 49; F. B. Crozier seven for 135).

CRICKET IN WEST INDIES, 1965–66

Following the overthrow of Australia in the early part of 1965—the tour was fully reported in last year's *Wisden*—main interest in cricket in the West Indies centred on the Shell Regional Tournament which helped the selectors in choosing or completing the side to visit England under Garfield Sobers.

With Sobers present for a home tournament for the first time for ten years it was not surprising that he led his team, Barbados, to a sweeping success. They beat British Guiana, the reigning Champions, and Trinidad each by an innings.

As many as nine of the Barbados side gained places on the tour to England and most surprisingly M. R. Bynoe, their talented opening batsman, was left behind; both E. D. McMorris, who hit three hundreds for Jamaica, and M. C. Carew, the only representative from Trinidad, who had shone in an all-round capacity, being preferred.

Among the youngsters who did well but were left at home, were Clive Lloyd, who displayed much brilliance in hitting 107 against Barbados and 194 against Jamaica. He is a cousin of L. R. Gibbs and clearly a gifted player. Two off-spinners came to the fore, A. Howard (Barbados) and L. Levy (Jamaica) and the Combined Islands produced a most promising number three batsmen in Irving Shillingford. R. Collymore, the British Guiana left-arm slow bowler, was called five times for throwing by umpire Douglas Sang Hue in the match against Jamaica on February 26.

SHELL REGIONAL TOURNAMENT

WINDWARD AND LEEWARD ISLANDS v. JAMAICA

At St. John's, Antigua, January 27, 28, 29, 31. Jamaica 283 (E. H. C. Griffith 150, R. G. A. Headley 44, M. Foster 41; A. Freeland six for 49) and 285 for five dec. (E. D. McMorris 134, R. G. A. Headley 67, E. H. C. Griffith 44); Combined Islands 250 (I. Shillingford 55, L. Harris 41, C. John 40, E. Gresham 34; K. Barnett five for 51) and 264 for five (I. Shillingford 113 not out, L. Harris 52, C. John 47). Drawn.

TRINIDAD v. JAMAICA

At Port of Spain, February 2, 3, 4, 5. Trinidad 334 (B. Davis 81, A. Corneal 66, R. de Sousa 60, C. Davis 36; L. Levy three for 35, R. Cohen three for 80) and 213 for six dec. (M. C. Carew 66, C. Davis 58 not out, B. Davis 36, W. V. Rodriguez 33); Jamaica 236 (E. D. McMorris 127 not out; W. V. Rodriguez five for 71, J. Ali three for 52) and 35 for one wkt. Drawn.

BARBADOS v. WINDWARD AND LEEWARD ISLANDS

At Bridgetown, February 9, 10, 11, 12. Combined Islands 141 (I. Shillingford 48, H. Elwin 35; R. C. Brancker six for 39); Barbados 396 for five (S. M. Nurse 153, P. D. Lashley 92, M. R. Bynoe 62, D. W. Allan 42 not out, C. C. Hunte 39; K. Laurent four for 117). No play last two days, rain. Drawn.

TRINIDAD v. BRITISH GUIANA

At Port of Spain, February 12, 14, 15, 16. British Guiana 398 for nine dec. (J. S. Solomon 110, S. Comacho 106, V. Mayers 48, C. Collymore 35; W. V. Rodriguez four for 97, J. Ali three for 114); Trinidad 192 (C. Davis 61, W. V. Rodriguez 51; L. R. Gibbs three for 49, E. Mohamed three for 59) and 77 for two (B. Davis 36 not out). Drawn.

BARBADOS v. BRITISH GUIANA

At Bridgetown, February 18, 19, 21, 22. British Guiana 227 (B. F. Butcher 99, R. B. Kanhai 69; G. S. Sobers six for 56, C. C. Griffith three for 28) and 317 (C. Lloyd 107, J. S. Solomon 70, R. B. Kanhai 43; C. C. Griffith four for 49); Barbados 559 for nine dec. (G. S. Sobers 204, R. C. Brancker 132, P. D. Lashley 54, S. M. Nurse 52, C. C. Griffith 38; J. S. Solomon four for 46). Barbados won by an innings and 15 runs.

BARBADOS v. TRINIDAD

At Bridgetown, February 25, 26, 28. Trinidad 148 (K. Furlonge 41 not out; D. A. J. Holford four for 56, T. Howard three for 23) and 171 (E. Aleong 50, C. Davis 32; C. C. Griffith four for 41); Barbados 427 (P. D. Lashley 120, M. R. Bynoe 104, G. S. Sobers 76 not out, S. M. Nurse 33, R. Edwards 31; M. C. Carew five for 80). Barbados won by an innings and 108 runs.

JAMAICA v. BRITISH GUIANA

At Kingston, February 26, 28, March 1, 2. Jamaica 222 (F. Harvey 40, M. Foster 36; R. Collymore three for 38, R. Ramnarace three for 42) and 404 for nine dec. (E. D. McMorris 190, J. L. Hendriks 51, R. G. A. Headley 38, F. Harvey 32); British Guiana 421 for nine dec. (C. Lloyd 194, R. B. Kanhai 61, S. Camacho 32; R. Cohen three for 111, L. Levy three for 116) and 27 for no wkt. Drawn.

WINDWARD AND LEEWARD ISLANDS v. BRITISH GUIANA

At Basseterre, St. Kitts, March 4, 5, 7, 8. Combined Islands 176 (L. Harris 61, E. Gresham 43, H. Gilbert 34 not out; J. S. Solomon four for 28) and 251 (C. John 69, H. Benjamin 58; L. R. Gibbs six for 49, B. Saheed three for 44); British Guiana 307 (B. F. Butcher 98, C. Lloyd 40, R. Fredericks 37, R. B. Kanhai 36; A. Mellowe three for 49, M. Roach three for 78) and 122 for four (R. B. Kanhai 36, B. F. Butcher 36, R. Fredericks 31). British Guiana won by six wickets.

JAMAICA v. BARBADOS

At Kingston, March 5, 7, 8, 9. Jamaica 193 (R. G. A Headley 86; D. A. J. Holford four for 51) and 260 (M. Foster 71, F. Harvey 59, E. D. McMorris 40, J. L. Hendriks 30; D. A. J. Holford four for 80; G. S. Sobers three for 48); Barbados 421 for four dec. (S. M. Nurse 126, P. D. Lashley 121 not out, M. R. Bynoe 71, C. C. Hunte 61; L. Levy three for 112) and 36 for three (R. Cohen three for 15). Barbados won by seven wickets.

WINDWARD AND LEEWARD ISLANDS v. TRINIDAD

At Castries, St. Lucia, March 11, 12, 14. Combined Islands 266 (C. John 94, I. Shillingford 66, H. Elwin 38) and 145 (L. Harris 39, E. Gilbert 34; M. C. Carew five for 45, K. Roberts three for 33); Trinidad 295 (M. C. Carew 81, B. Davis 66, W. V. Rodriguez 55, R. de Sousa 54; K. Laurent four for 68, E. Gilbert three for 51) and 85 (A. Corneal 37; A. Mellowe four for 19, E. Gilbert three for 12). Combined Islands won by 31 runs.

CRICKET IN CANADA, 1966

By Donald King

One record Canadian cricket season continues to succeed another in this day and age and the 1966 season was unique in a number of different ways. Never, previously, had three teams from abroad toured Canada in the same year. In June, the popular Emu Club of New South Wales returned after five years and played 18 matches between Victoria, B.C. and Montreal, Quebec. A Bermuda representative team spent ten days in Ontario and Quebec in July, but, in view of the strength of this side, it was unfortunate that, on account of short notice given the Canadian Cricket Association, matches had to be contrived against club, as opposed to representative sides. In an effort to reciprocate much hospitality extended to Canadian Colts sides on tour in the United Kingdom biennially since 1957, an invitation was given to J. C. Marshall, the Oxford Blue of 1953, Cricket Master at Rugby School, England, to bring a team of schoolboys drawn from Rugby, Marlborough and Wellington, to Canada in August. A fifteen-man team was duly mustered and twelve games were staged against a variety of opposition during a three-week cross-country tour which covered 6,045 miles.

The fifth Junior Inter-Provincial Tournament since 1939, for boys under 21 years of age, took place at Vancouver, B.C. in July. For the first time five Provinces were represented and, in the case of Quebec, it marked the only occasion, to date, when a cricket team from that Province has visited British Columbia. Unseasonably cold and wet weather marred the proceedings, three days' play being rained out. British Columbia, who fielded a competent, well-balanced side, won the Junior Championship with Ontario, who gave them a tremendous battle for honours, runners-up.

The Toronto Cricket, Skating and Curling Club became the first Canadian side at club level to undertake a tour of England and France, this most ambitious and successful event taking place over a three-week period in July. Twenty-three club members participated and the side, which included three Canadian International players, more than held their own in 17 matches played against opposition ranging from County Club and Ground sides to village teams.

A Canadian representative team journeyed to Los Angeles, California, to oppose the United States in what was the first match in the 122-year-old International Series of games between the two countries to be held on the Pacific coast. A low-scoring encounter saw the United States victorious by 58 runs after the Canadian batting collapsed completely in the second innings when 98 runs were required to be made in two hours, thirteen minutes.

Organized cricket returned to eastern coastal regions this year after having been virtually moribund for almost half a century. In August, the Maritime Provinces Cricket Association, with headquarters in Halifax, Nova Scotia, came into being and was accepted, subsequently, as a corporate member of the Canadian Cricket Association with a representative on the Board of Control. Four teams are now in operation in Nova Scotia and New Brunswick. This number is likely to expand progressively.

Khan Mohammad, the Canadian Cricket Association's official professional coach, undertook a six-week tour of duty in Vancouver where he remained subsequently to be in attendance during the Inter-Provincial Tournament for junior players. Latterly, he held week-long courses for young players in Calgary, Edmonton and Winnipeg. V. Felix of Toronto, an Ontario-capped player, was engaged professionally in the Metropolitan Toronto area where four junior cricket centres are now established.

The Canadian Cricket Association is applying for Letters Patent to enable the Association to become an Incorporated Body without share capital. New by-laws, drawn up by the Association's legal adviser, will be considered by the Board of Control at the Canadian Cricket Association's Annual General Meeting due to be held in Montreal, Quebec, and a brief will be presented to the Secretary of State immediately thereafter.

After having served as Chairman of the Canadian Cricket Association Board of Control continuously since 1949, Lewis Gunn of Toronto, under whose able guidance the Association has increased both in stature and significance, withdrew from office at the end of 1965. As a tribute to his outstanding record of service to Canadian cricket, both as player and administrator, he was named President Emeritus of the Canadian Cricket Association, a new position created in his honour by his colleagues on the Board of Control.

CRICKET IN THE UNITED STATES, 1966

By John I. Marder

The two features of the season in the United States were the visit of the New South Wales "Emus" and the winning of the match with Canada for the first time since its revival. The Emus enjoyed their several matches, but none of the American clubs were able to extend them, and they won their games easily. A very exciting match with Canada was won by the United States by 58 runs, a result not even contemplated by any but the most enthusiastic American supporters.

In the eastern part of the country, Brooklyn C.C. won the New York and Metropolitan District League. In the first interzone game played at Fairmount Park, Philadelphia on August 13, 14 the South beat the East by eight wickets. East scored 158 (O. Larrier 37) and 138 (E. Fornaris 37); South 264 (R. S. Laurie 76, M. A. Stollmeyer 68) and 34 for two wickets. The East could not field their best side but the event opened a great new series which will be continued.

Staten Island beat the "Wagtails" XI of British schoolboys touring in North America, who made their only appearance in the United States in this match. The Staten Island club entertained the visitors at lunch prior to the match. The Wagtails scored 109 for nine dec. and Staten Island replied with 110 for five, beating their visitors by five wickets.

At Philadelphia on October 27 the members of the Forty Club resident in the United States held a dinner at Merion Cricket Club commemorating three of the living American cricketers who have participated in first-class cricket, Dr. J. A. Lester (94 years young) who captained the Philadelphians in 1903 and 1908 in their first-class tours of England; C. C. Morris (85) who scored the highest innings for an American in first-class cricket—164 for Philadelphia v. Nottinghamshire at Trent Bridge in 1903, and Charles H. Winter (75) who was reserve wicket-keeper in the 1908 team to England. The occasion was marked by an interchange of telegrams with the Forty Club who were holding their annual banquet at the London Hilton on the same evening.

In the Middle West, Melbourne C.C. of Chicago won their second Midwestern Cricket Conference title by a close margin over Louisville. In 1967 Northwestern University of Evanston, Illinois, will compete in the Conference for the first time. Winnetka undertook a tour of Eastern Canada under the captaincy of R. Jacques, winning one, drawing one and losing two games.

As late in the season as October 28, 29 a two-day match was played between Missouri and Illinois, at Saint Louis: Missouri 107 (P. L. Jeffrey 35) and 111 (P. L. Jeffrey 59); Illinois 77 and 89 for eight (G. Lytle 36*). In the first innings of Illinois, V. V. Masterton, an American-born player who appeared for the U.S.A. in 1963, took eight wickets for 17.

In the west, San Francisco cricketers celebrated Christmas by sending a team to Hawaii. The San Franciscans enjoyed their stay but lost all three one-day games by the same margin of four wickets.

Stanford University won the Northern California Cricket Association title after a close fight with University of California and Marin County. In the south, Pasadena were champions of the Southern California Association and the knock-out Williamson Trophy was won by Britamer who defeated Los Angeles in the Final. At Tilden Park, Oakland, California, on May 28, 29, Northern California drew with Southern California: Northern California 96 and 107 for nine; Southern California 69 and 80 for six. The scores were disappointing, having in mind the calibre of cricketers engaged, but the wicket was not in good shape.

The United States was represented for the first time at the meeting of the International Cricket Conference at Lord's. Despite criticism, the Conference was of great interest and served to bring the cricketing countries into closer co-operation.

Haverford College, Haverford, Pa., where cricket has been played for over a hundred years continuously is initiating an ambitious scheme to found a Cricket Library and Museum. Thirty thousand dollars is to be raised for the collection, which will have a special interest for cricketers all over the world. All cricket enthusiasts are asked to lend their support and to contribute items which have special American cricket interest to the new library. Donations of money and material should be sent to Dr. Howard Comfort at the College.

A one-day match was played at Westminster, California, between a United States Invitational XI and Southern California. The U.S. XI made 172 for three wickets declared, J. J. Reid scoring 112 not out; Southern California replied with 130 for eight before the game was drawn. A. Lashkari scored 37 and R. Severn 41 for Southern California.

All in all 1966 saw a great deal of enjoyable cricket played in the United States, and a further improvement everywhere in ground preparation could bring about a sharp increase in the standard of play in future years.

UNITED STATES v. CANADA

At Sir Aubrey Smith Field, Los Angeles, California, September 4, 5, 1966, in brilliant weather before a large crowd on both days, the United States beat Canada by 58 runs for their first win in international cricket since 1912. There were eight changes in the American side from the 1965 match. Canada included Van Twest and Winterlick of the 1965 Canadian Colts XI which toured England, and R. W. Wilson, the Oxford Blue of 1957.

Winning the toss the Americans batted, but after an attractive opening stand the batting became somewhat negative and a laboured innings of a little over four hours produced only 136 runs. Canada seemed to have the match well in hand when the score had reached 70 for three, but an hour on the second day sufficed to end their innings 27 behind, although Clarke played well.

No one was prepared for the exicting events of the second day when the fortunes of the match veered from side to side almost hourly and kept the large crowd in a frenzy of excitement. United States lost most of their best batsmen cheaply and five wickets were down for only 19. Bains and Hodgson redeemed the innings and Canada were left two and a half hours to score 99. At this point they looked certain winners but no one could cope with the fine bowling of Larrier of the Empire club of New York. With the score standing at 14 he clean bowled Hackett, Taylor and Campbell with successive balls for a brilliant hat-trick, the first in the long history of the match. With five wickets down for 14 the Canadians were hopelessly at sea but Dawson defended stubbornly. The innings was over in an hour and a half for only 40. Great enthusiasm was manifested. Larrier being "chaired" off the field.

United States

*J. J. Reid (*So. Calif.*) c Welcome v Van Twest	26	—	c Hackett b Lissett	0
C. Severn (*So. Calif.*) c Van Twest b Clarke	24	—	lbw b Campbell	8
M. A. Stollmeyer (*D.C.*) b Clarke	3	—	c Wilson b Tait	9
A. W. M. Cooper (*N. Calif.*) run out	22	—	b Lissett	1
R. Severn (*So. Calif.*) b Campbell	14	—	run out	3
O. Larrier (*New York*) run out	2	—	c Lissett b Tait	2
P. L. Jeffrey (*Missouri*) c Clarke b Wilson	16	—	lbw b Clarke	4
C. Hodgson (*N. Calif.*) c Van Twest b Wilson	1	—	c Lissett b Taylor	10
D. Kaufmann (*Kentucky*) c and b Wilson	6	—	not out	3
C. Bains (*So. Calif.*) not out	5	—	c Lissett b Taylor	19
W. A. Brook (*New York*) c Clarke b Wilson	4	—	c Van Twest b Taylor	0
B 6, l-b 5, n-b 2	13		B 2, l-b 4, w 1, n-b 5	12
1/48 2/51 3/59 4/92 5/93 6/97 7/108 8/123 9/128	136		1/0 2/8 3/10 4/17 5/19 6/28 7/31 8/60 9/71	71

Bowling: *First Innings:* Lissett 7—2—11—0; Campbell 12—2—34—1; Clarke 9—0—24—2; Tait 3—0—9—0; Van Twest 8—0—17—1; Wilson 17.7—10—17—4; Taylor 6—0—11—0. *Second Innings*—Lissett 7—1—19—2; Campbell 8—5—5—1; Clarke 5—2—5—1; Tait 4—0—12—2; Wilson 5—2—3—0; Taylor 8.7—2—15—3.

Canada

A. Welcome (*Sask.*) lbw b Larrier	0	— c Larrier b Brook	2
H. A. Clarke (*Ontario*) lbw b Cooper	50	— c Bains b Brook	1
J. W. S. Tait (*B.C.*) lbw b Brook	2	— b Cooper	19
H. Hackett (*Man.*) lbw b Cooper	9	— b Larrier	1
*V. K. Taylor (*Ontario*) c Hodgson b Cooper	9	— b Larrier	0
C. Campbell (*Sask.*) b Larrier	0	— b Larrier	0
R. L. Dawson (*Man.*) c Hodgson b Larrier	2	— not out	11
D. F. J. Winterlick (*B.C.*) c Stollmeyer b Larrier	4	— c Hodgson b Larrier	0
C. J. Van Twest (*B.C.*) c Stollmeyer b Cooper	10	— b Larrier	3
A. P. Lissett (*B.C.*) c C. Severn b Larrier	4	— b Larrier	0
R. W. Wilson (*Ontario*) not out	3	— b Reid	0
B 1, l-b 5, w 1, n-b 9	16	B 1, n-b 2	3
1/2 2/11 3/55 4/74 5/79 6/84 7/88 8/92 9/102	109	1/2 2/9 3/14 4/14 5/14 5/14 6/24 7/25 8/25 9/39	40

Bowling: *First Innings*—Larrier 14—1—41—5; Brook 4—0—9—1; Bains 2—0—16—0; Cooper 8.6—1—27—4. *Second Innings*—Larrier 10—2—15—6; Brook 4—0—16—2; Cooper 4—2—5—1; Reid 1.5—0—1—1.

Umpires: P. Cooney and L. Magnus (Southern California).

M.C.C. SCHOOLS IN SOUTH AFRICA

For the first time M.C.C. sponsored a Schools tour abroad and the visit to South Africa proved a tremendous success both on and off the field. There were fourteen players with Mr. M. R. Ricketts as manager. Four of the thirteen matches played were against strong men's teams, but nine were against Representative Schools XI's from the various Provinces. Of these M.C.C. won five, drew three and lost only one. This was a fine performance when one takes into account that the South Africans were in the middle of their season whereas the M.C.C. boys had to contend with a heat wave on arrival in Johannesburg, sickness, which hit one of the opening batsmen, D. W. Sharp, fatigue and strange conditions.

Walsh, the captain, proved a splendid leader and was a determined and dependable batsman. Cosh and Hooper played several fine innings, notable for stroke play, and Carter excelled as wicket-keeper with twenty-one victims in eleven matches. Although the pitches seldom offered encouragement to the bowlers, Jordan was fast and hostile, Denman steady and Palfreman tenacious, Acfield, off-spin, gave little away over long spells but Cattrall, leg-spin, gained his ten wickets mainly at the expense of tail-enders. The fielding was always reliable and often brilliant.

South African Schools cricket seemed far better organised than in England. Each Province holds its own week and the senior men's team play the selected eleven before the South African Schools hold their annual Nuffield week.

BATTING

	School	Innings	Not Outs	Runs	Highest Inns.	Average
N. J. Cosh	*Dulwich*	12	1	391	92	35.55
D. R. Walsh	*Marlborough*	13	2	371	91	33.73
J. M. M. Hooper	*Charterhouse*	13	0	397	93	30.54
A. M. Jorden	*Monmouth*	7	3	122	46	30.50
C. A. Richardson	*Stamford*	13	1	301	53*	25.08
D. R. Aers	*Tonbridge*	9	1	180	41*	22.50
J. R. A. Cragg	*Macclesfield*	10	2	140	28	17.50
C. E. P. Carter	*Radley*	6	1	77	28*	15.40
D. W. Sharp	*Moseley Hall*	6	0	71	27	11.83
P. W. Watts	*Bradfield*	6	1	36	14	7.20
A. B. Palfreman	*Nottingham H.S.*	5	0	36	24	7.20
J. Denman	*Ifield*	5	2	20	10	6.67

Also batted: P. J. Cattrall (*King's, Canterbury*) 0, 0*; D. L. Acfield (*Brentwood*) 0*, 1*, 0*.

* *Indicates not out.*

BOWLING

		Overs	Maidens	Runs	Wickets	Average
P. J. Cattrall ...	*King's, Canterb.*	62	18	154	10	15.40
J. Denman......	*Ifield*	123	37	281	15	18.74
A. M. Jorden	*Monmouth*	122.3	22	373	17	21.93
A. B. Palfreman.	*Nottingham H.S.*	104	29	287	13	22.08
D. L. Acfield....	*Brentwood...*	172	60	457	18	25.38
P. W. Watts.....	*Bradfield*	96	16	310	9	34.44
D. R. Aers......	*Tonbridge*	14	2	41	1	41.00

Also bowled: D. R. Walsh (*Marlborough*) 37—7—131—0; J. M. M. Hooper (*Charterhouse*) 4—0—10—0.

M.C.C. SCHOOLS' TEAM IN SOUTH AFRICA, 1965–66

Played 13, *Won* 6, *Lost* 4, *Drawn* 3, *Abandoned* 1.

At Pretoria, December 22. M.C.C. Schools 228 for eight dec. (N. J. Cosh 92); North Eastern Transvaal 168 for five (S. Bezuidenhout 71). Drawn.

At Johannesburg, December 23. Wilfred Isaacs' XI 223 for four dec. (A. Bacher 69, R. C. White 60); M.C.C. Schools 161. Isaacs' XI won by 62 runs.

At West Rand, December 28. M.C.C. Schools 155 (A. M. Jorden 46); Transvaal XI 159 for three (P. Kerr 58, A. During 42). Transvaal XI won by seven wickets.

At Johannesburg, December 30. M.C.C. Schools 197 for eight dec. (J. M. M. Hooper 52; P. Flanaghan four for 44); Transvaal Nuffield XI 111 (D. L. Acfield four for 20, A. B. Palfreman four for 46). M.C.C. Schools won by 86 runs.

At Durban, January 1. Natal Schools 193 for six dec. (D. G. Macleod 52*, R. D. Harvey 49); M.C.C. Schools 146 (I. Tayfield five for 49). Natal Schools won by 47 runs.

At Pietermaritzburg, January 3. M.C.C. Schools 207 for seven dec. (J. M. M. Hooper 66, D. R. Walsh 53; N. McDonald four for 60); Natal XI 139 (T. Falkson 40; D. L. Acfield five for 59). M.C.C. Schools won by 68 runs.

At Port Elizabeth, January 5. Eastern Province Nuffield XI 173 for eight dec. (A. Cawood 52, A. Short 45); M.C.C. Schools 176 for eight (C. A. Richardson 42). M.C.C. Schools won by two wickets.

At Cape Town, January 7. Western Province Colts 234 for one dec. (N. Budge 113*, D. Hugo 102); M.C.C. Schools 192 (J. M. M. Hooper 93; K. Meehan four for 30). Western Province Colts won by 42 runs.

At Cape Town, January 10. Rhodesia 223 for five dec. (R. Berry 70*, C. Fletcher 57); M.C.C. Schools 74 for four.

At Cape Town, January 11. M.C.C. Schools 189 for five dec. (D. R. Walsh 91); Griqualand West 86 (P. J. Cattrall five for 23). M.C.C. Schools won by 103 runs.

At Cape Town, January 12. M.C.C. Schools 211 for three dec. (D. R. Walsh 61*, C. A. Richardson 53*, J. M. M. Hooper 47); Orange Free State 86 (J. Denman five for 13, P. W. Watts four for 42). M.C.C. Schools won by 125 runs.

At Cape Town, January 13. Western Province 143 (J. Plimsoll 39*; A. M. Jorden six for 68); M.C.C. Schools 147 for four (N. J. Cosh 81*). M.C.C. Schools won by six wickets.

At Cape Town, January 14. M.C.C. Schools 188 for five dec. (N. J. Cosh 48, D. R. Aers 41*); Border 185 for five (H. Ackerman 118*). Drawn.

At Cape Town, January 17. Rain caused the match against the South African Nuffield Team to be abandoned without a ball bowled.

* *Signifies not out.*

LONDON SCHOOLS IN INDIA AND CEYLON, 1965–66

By A. R. Harris

The London Schools Cricket Association undertook a very successful two-month tour of India and Ceylon around Christmas and the New Year. The party comprised:

John Brooks (*East Ham Grammar School*), captain, Philip Carling (*Kingston G.S.*) vice-captain, Raymond Ambler (*Highbury G.S.*), Michael Boyers (*Sir Geo. Monoux G.S.*), Victor Brooks (*East Ham G.S.*), Christopher Brown (*East Ham G.S.*), David Laycock (*Crown Woods School*), Christopher Lewis (*Malory School*), Roy Lewis (*Tulse Hill School*), Roger Mayes (*Kingston G.S.*), Paul Moir (*St. Paul's School*), Paul Nash (*Salesian College, Battersea*), Christopher Payne (*Owen's G.S.*), Roy Payne (*Battersea G.S.*), Michael Selvey (*Battersea G.S.*), Alan Suffling (*William Ellis G.S.*).

Manager: A. R. Harris; secretary, C. J. Green; treasurer, F. J. Ingram.

Fourteen matches were played, including six representative or "Tests" and the side won three, drew ten and lost one. In the matches against the State and Zonal sides, the London boys enjoyed a definite supremacy. Three times they amassed 300 in under four hours, ten minutes, and on many other occasions they scored at a very considerable rate, notably 288 in two and a half hours at Madras.

Several batsmen distinguished themselves, in particular Victor Brooks, who scored 564 runs in 14 innings. His aggressive, fluent shots won him many admirers and the side much goodwill. Roy Lewis, who scored 482 in 15 innings, was an utterly dependable opening batsman, his great talent allied to iron concentration.

P. Carling did not find his best form, yet his skill was such that he collected 456 runs in 15 completed innings. C. Payne and D. Laycock, two very stylish batsmen, also scored over 400 each.

With Indian wickets slow and plumb, the bowlers for the most part were at the batsmen's mercy, as the figures often showed, P. Moir, the most successful bowler, took 36 wickets.

The best fast bowler was M. Boyers whose intelligence, hostility and stamina earned him 26 wickets.

The fielding was disappointing at the outset of the tour. The intense glare and rather irregular outfields posed problems, and it was nearly a month before the players found their touch in this department.

Socially, the tour did immense good in smoothing Anglo-Indian relations, and it certainly improved the cricket of both sides. The genuine friendship between the rival teams proved to many observers how much this first tour by schoolboys did to improve Commonwealth relations.

CHIEF BATTING AVERAGES

	Innings	Not Outs	Runs	Highest Inns.	Average
V. Brooks	16	2	556	128	39.71
R. Lewis	16	1	475	75*	31.66
P. Carling	16	1	459	91	30.60
C. Payne	18	3	452	100	30.13
D. Laycock	19	0	489	88	25.73
J. Brooks	16	2	345	63	24.64
C. Lewis	14	0	345	107	24.64
R. Payne	15	3	270	48	22.50
P. Nash	16	1	282	74	18.80

CHIEF BOWLING AVERAGES

	Overs	Maidens	Runs	Wickets	Average
R. Ambler	148.1	38	425	25	17.00
P. Moise	212	63	583	33	17.66
M. Boyers	174	33	537	25	21.48
V. Brooks	120	25	404	17	23.76
R. Lewis	83	15	251	10	25.10
R. Mayes	55	9	172	6	28.66
R. Payne	169	34	456	15	30.40
C. Brown	91	14	307	8	38.37
M. Selvey	45	9	160	4	40.00
A. Suffling	128	21	400	10	40.00

RESULTS

At Ahmedabad, Sardar Stadium, December 4, 5. West Zone 272 (A. Mankad 58; P. Moir five for 36) and 24 for 0; London 227. Drawn.

At Poona, Nehru Stadium, December 7, 8. London 363 for six dec. (D. Laycock 88, P. Nash 74, V. Brooks 67, J. Brooks 55*); Maharashtra 240 (V. Saldhana 76, V. Mudliar 74; M. Boyers three for 10) and 67 for three. Drawn.

At Bombay, Brabourne Stadium, December 10, 11, 12. All India 295 (S. Gavaskar 115, R. Nagdev 75) and 114 for four dec. (R. Nagdev 56); London 175 (V. Brooks 65) and 98 for eight. Drawn.

At Jaipur, Railway Ground, December 15, 16. Central Zone 250 for five dec. (Gulrej Ali 135) and 50 for three; London 368 (V. Brooks 97*, P. Carling 91; Gulrej Ali five for 122). Drawn.

At Delhi, Ferozeshah Kotla, December 18, 19, 20. All India 280 for seven dec. (M. Rege 113, S. Gavaskar 55; P. Moir three for 50) and 180 for six dec.; London 223 (P. Nash 50; A. Kumar five for 80) and 176 for seven. Drawn.

At Kanpur, Green Park. December 24, 25, 26. All India 236 (S. Amarnath 54; V. Brooks five for 36) and 202 for five dec. (R. Nagdev 67, S. Gavaskar 57); London 211 and 175 for five (P. Carling 62, R. Lewis 60). Drawn.

At Nowgong, December 29,30. London 97 (J. Biswas seven for 53) and 111 (K. Dutta seven for 41); East Zone 78 and 125 for nine (R. Ambler five for 45). Drawn.

At Calcutta, Eden Gardens, January 1, 2, 3. London 387 for nine dec. (V. Brooks 128, R. Lewis 75, D. Laycock 74); All India 135 for nine (M. Boyers four for 38). No play third day (rain). Drawn.

At Hyderabad, Fateh Maidan, January 5, 6. London 175 (C. Payne 51; Inder Kuma five for 55) and 141 for five (D. Laycock 60); Hyderabad 223 for seven. Drawn.

At Madras, January 8, 9. London 288 for seven dec. (C. Lewis 107, V. Brooks 74); Madras 110 (C. Brown four for 20) and 100. London Schools won by an innings and 78 runs.

At Ernakulam Fact, Eloor, January 11, 12. London 255 for seven dec. (C. Payne 100*); South Zone 214 for eight. Drawn.

At Bangalore Central College, January 14, 15, 16. All India 276 (E. Solkar 82, M. Rege 85, S. Amarnath 58; R. Ambler six for 54) and 157 for four dec. (R. Nagdev 100*); London 201 (A. Kumar four for 61) and 142 (C. Payne 51). All India Schools won by 90 runs.

At Colombo Oval, January 18, 19. Ceylon Schools 168 (T. Appurdurai 69) and 132 for nine dec. (T. Appurdurai 44); London 173 for four dec. (D. Laycock 61, C. Lewis 55) and 130 for seven (P. Wijesekera four for 50). London Schools won by three wickets.

At Colombo C.C., Maitland Place, January 20. Ceylon National Schools 119 (G. R. Senanayaka 47*, M. Seeriysbandara 44; M. Boyers four for 30); London 120 for three (C. Lewis 60). London Schools won by seven wickets.

SCOTTISH CRICKET IN 1966

After a poor start, Scotland ran into better form in their two home matches towards the end of the season. The old rivals, Ireland, were beaten at Raeburn Place, Edinburgh, by six wickets with less than ten minutes to spare in a match that had been reduced to two days because of the weather. A declaration by each side and the dismissal of Ireland for 114 in the second innings left Scotland to score 136 in two hours. They achieved it mainly through 73 not out by L. C. Dudman, who had scored 59 in the first innings.

The other home game should have been a two-day fixture against the West Indies at Hamilton Crescent, but rain washed out the first day and it was decided to play 60-overs-a-side on the second day. That, too, was affected by rain, but not before Scotland had dismissed the tourists for 193 in 48.1 overs. Only R. B. Kanhai, with 68, showed much assurance against the excellent fast-medium bowling of E. R. Thompson.

Scotland had lost their first game of the season by one wicket to Cambridge University at Fenner's. The visitors seemed assured of victory when with nine wickets down the University needed 42 to win, but an unbroken last-wicket stand by R. Roopnaraine and S. G. Russell carried Cambridge through.

In the other matches Scotland had the worse of draws, against Warwickshire at Edgbaston and against M.C.C. at Lord's. The Birmingham match will be remembered most by J. M. Allan, who earlier in the season had joined Warwickshire but was released to play for his country. In saving Scotland from having to follow on behind the county's 401 for four declared, Allan reached 1,000 runs for Scotland and thus became the only man who has so far done the double for the national team. Two other Scots, J. Brown and D. Barr, also reached 1,000 runs during the season, and R. H. E. Chisholm beat the Rev. James Aitchison's record of 69 appearances when he played against the West Indies.

Scotland brought in three new Internationals, H. K. More, G. Hutton, and K. M. Hardie, but only More played in all five matches, along with Brown, Chisholm, Dudman, J. G. Laing, Barr and Thompson. Altogether 18 players were called on, the others being T. B. Racionzer, G. F. Goddard, D. Livingstone, T. N. Gallacher, M. H. Denness, W. D. F. Dow, J. M. Allan, R. Ellis and J. M. C. Ford.

Perthshire, who contributed Brown, Dudman and Laing to the national team, became Scottish Counties' Champions for the eleventh time in fourteen years. They ran away with the championship, losing only to Forfarshire, who finished second.

Clydesdale won the Western Union title, and here, too, the Champions' only defeat was by the runners-up, Kilmarnock, who because of heavy rain were denied the chance on the last day of beating the leaders and thus winning the title. Heriot's F.P. won the East League for the first time, being run close by Melville College F.P. and Stenhousemuir.

Kelburne, who finished no higher than seventh out of ten in the Western Union, were unexpected first winners of the Rothman's Quaich knock-out competition, beating Ferguslie, Stenhousemuir, West Lothian and Perthshire. Because they did not finish in the first four of the league they did not qualify to defend the trophy next season.—W.M.McM.

Leading positions in the Leagues (first four places) were:—

WESTERN UNION

	P.	W.	L.	Drawn with pt.	Drawn w'out pt.	Pts.	Per cent
Clydesdale......	12	9	1	1	1	19	79
Kilmarnock.....	14	9	2	2	1	20	71
Uddington......	15	9	3	2	1	20	66
West of Scotland	13	8	4	0	1	16	61

SCOTTISH COUNTIES

	P.	W.	L.	D.	Pts.	Per cent
Perthshire	10	8	1	1	51	85
Forfarshire	11	6	3	2	42	63
West Lothian	9	5	3	1	33	61
Aberdeenshire	9	4	2	3	33	61

EAST LEAGUE

	P.	W.	L.	D.	Pts.	Per cent
Heriot's F.P.	7	6	1	0	18	87
Melville College F.P.	10	8	2	0	24	80
Stenhousemuir	10	7	0	3*	23	76
Royal H.S. F.P.	10	6	2	2	20	66

** Indicates draw point forfeited in one match.*

STRATHMORE UNION

	P.	W.	L.	D.	Pts.	Per cent
Strathmore	18	13	2	3	29	80
Forthill XI	13	8	3	2	18	69
Arbroath United	19	9	3	7	25	65
Meigle	18	7	6	5	19	52
Mannofield XI	20	6	5	9	21	52

GLASGOW AND DISTRICT LEAGUE

	P.	W.	L.	D.	Pts.	Per cent
Motherwell	10	7	0	3	50	63
Prestwick	10	5	1	4	41	63
Glasgow H.S. F.P.	11	5	2	4	42	63
Allan Glen's F.P.	9	3	2	4	27	50

BORDER LEAGUE

	P.	W.	L.	D.	Pts.	Per cent
Kelso	11	8	3	0	16	72
Selkirk	11	8	3	0	16	72
Hawick and Wilton	10	6	4	0	12	60
St. Boswells	10	6	4	0	12	60

IRISH CRICKET IN 1966

Ireland lost all three representative matches in 1966. Against Middlesex in Belfast in July this was naturally anticipated. Ten days later, against Scotland in Edinburgh, the match was reduced to two days by rain. It was obvious that the side which fielded first would almost certainly not be beaten—it was Scotland! The M.C.C. match in Dublin in September might have been won and should not have been so dispiritedly lost. Middlesex brought their five Test players for the two-day match, played in warm sunshine. They put Ireland in and bowled them out for 113 and 112. Middlesex scored 246, sufficient to win by an innings and 21 runs.

A new cap, the bearded I. Anderson of Queen's University, scored 36 and 37 by a combination of graft, watchfulness and sudden splendid stroke. It was a very good debut augmented by a wonderful fielding and throwing display. The off-spinner, Bick, was Ireland's undoing, taking three for 26 and six for 19, five of the six being caught by Titmus in succession. Parfitt (93) and Murray (50) put on 94 for Middlesex's fourth wicket. Ireland's best cricket in the match came in the field. Torrens, another new cap and a quickish bowler, took four for 77. D. R. Pigot, an opening batsman, also gained his first cap in this match at the age of 37. His father played twenty times for Ireland before the war.

And so to Edinburgh and a wet Saturday during which at least the World Cup Final could be enjoyed. On Monday, Ireland were put in for the second time in succession and declared at tea at 152 for seven. B. O'Brien and D. R. Pigot made artistic 30's while F. S. A. Hewitt contributed 36 more rustically. Scotland declared 21 runs behind after an hour's play on the last morning. Ireland took a long time to make 114 in their second innings, the runs only coming at two an over. The new young Scottish left-arm bowler, K. W. Hardie, took four for 23.

Scotland's ultimate task was 136 in just under two hours. They succeeded with six minutes and six wickets to spare. Dropped catches were the difference between defeat and a draw in this match.

J. F. Pretlove and J. A. Bailey won the match for M.C.C. in Dublin. Pretlove scored 81 in the first innings of 210 and this was by far the highest innings of the match. The wicket was affected by rain at the week-end and became progressively more difficult to bat on. Ireland made only 149 after being 107 for two. Anderson was again top scorer with 44 but Bailey and A. R. Duff were too much for the later batsmen. The wicket was now at its worst and M.C.C. were all out in 34 overs for 67 and it might well have been less. O'Riordan, the fast left-armer, was in great form. He took six for 35 and brought his tally of wickets for Ireland to 93 in 30 matches. Ireland needed 129 to win but were 39 for three after ninety minutes on the second day. Next morning Bailey and Duff continued to take wickets regularly and before lunch the match was over with Ireland 92 all out. Despite the helpful wicket it was a poor Irish batting display. Praise must go to J. A. Bailey who followed his five for 33 with no less than eight for 24 in 32.1 overs.

This match will be remembered with sadness for another reason. It was Ian Bedford's last first-class match; ten days later he collapsed and died playing in a club match. He was most popular in Irish cricketing circles, having played six times for M.C.C. against Ireland between 1955 and 1966.

Anderson was the only Irish batsman to end the season satisfied. In all he scored 159 runs, average 26.50. His 44 against M.C.C. was the highest Irish score of the season. O'Riordan had his best season since 1960 with the ball, taking 17 wickets at 15.58 runs. S. S. J. Huey, the 1960 captain, was reappointed captain and D. M. Pratt captained against Middlesex when Huey was not available. F. S. A. Hewitt reappeared in the team after a gap of eleven years.

The new Guinness Cup competition was a great success. Six selected teams competed, two from Dublin, two from Belfast, one from the North-West and one from Munster. The North-West unexpectedly and convincingly won the competition. Two of their bowlers, Huey and Torrens, were the top wicket takers with 15 each and their leading batsman B. Donaghey scored most runs, 173 (average 57.66). Donaghey was unfortunately unable to play for Ireland in any match.

Woodvale won the Northern Senior League in a close finish from Downpatrick. The latter compensated by beating Lisburn by 140 runs in the two-innings knock-out cup final, each innings being restricted to 60 overs. In this match R. Hutton scored 43 and 47 for Downpatrick and N. Ferguson had match figures of nine for 78.

A new trophy, the Rothman Cup, was competed for by the league and cup winners and was played under the same conditions as the cup final. Downpatrick won by 74 runs. N. Ferguson (Downpatrick) scored 99 in one hour fifty minutes in the first innings.

The season was a very wet one in Belfast as can be seen by the league table that follows. Each club should have played 14 matches—two managed nine!

In Dublin, after an exciting finish Dublin University won their fourth league title. They last won in 1948 and in 1949 the handicap system was introduced for them. They now play each other team once only. In their seven wins Dublin University, captained by C. D. Anderson, had two by one wicket, one by two runs and one by seven runs! A. Little, an all rounder, was their most valuable player.

For the third successive year Old Belvedere won the knock-out cup and each year their defeated opponents were Malahide. Old Belvedere have won the toss each year and in 1966 won by 210 (F. A. Daly 72) to 65 (A. J. O'Riordan seven for 23).

The Marchant Cup for batting was won by D. R. Pigot (Phoenix) who scored 630 runs (average 63). The O'Grady Cup for bowling went to A. J. O'Riordan for the seventh time in eight years. O'Riordan took 51 wickets (average 6.45) and beat J. C. Boucher's record of six wins in this cup. O'Riordan also won the Samuels Cup for all-rounders. Beyond all shadow of doubt he is the best cricketer in Ireland and is as yet only 26.—Derek Scott.

NORTHERN SENIOR LEAGUE (BELFAST) 1966

	Played	Won	Drawn	Lost	Points Possible	Points Obtained	Percentage
Woodvale (4)......	8	5	2	1	32	22	68.75
Downpatrick (7)....	9	6	–	3	36	24	66.66
Instonians (–)......	8	4	1	3	32	16	50.00
Lisburn (2)........	8	3	3	2	32	14	43.75
Lurgan (3).........	7	3	1	3	28	12	42.85
R.U.C. (5).........	9	3	–	6	36	12	33.33
N.I.C.C. (1)	5	1	1	3	20	6	30.00
Cregagh (6)........	8	–	4	4	32	6	18.75

(*a*) Figures in brackets denote final position in 1965.
(*b*) Waringstown relegated after 1965 will return for 1967 in place of Cregagh.

LEINSTER SENIOR LEAGUE (DUBLIN) 1966

	Played	Won	Drawn	Lost	Points Possible	Points Obtained	Percentage
Dublin University (6)	9	7	–	2	170	112	65.88
Leinster (3)........	15	7	6	2	150	88	58.66
Clontarf (9)........	15	7	4	4	150	82	54.66
Pembroke (5).......	16	6	7	3	160	81	50.62
Y.M.C.A. (1).......	16	6	6	4	160	78	48.75
Old Belvedere (7)...	14	4	8	2	140	64	45.71
Malahide (2).......	16	5	4	7	160	62	38.75
Railway Union (8)..	16	4	3	9	160	49	30.62
Phoenix (4)........	15	2	6	7	150	38	25.33
Merrion (10).......	14	–	6	8	140	18	12.85

(*a*) Figures in brackets denote final positions in 1965.
(*b*) Dublin University play only one round and their maximum percentage is 84.

WOMEN'S CRICKET IN 1966

By Netta Rheinberg

The 1966 season will be remembered mainly for the second visit of a New Zealand women's cricket team to England. Coming only three years after that of the Australians, it caused the Association much concern in regard to finance. In 1963 some £4,000 was raised for accommodation, travelling and entertainment. This time the task was more difficult, but £3,300 was duly collected. The immense efforts made by a small association in the span of four years to enable overseas visitors to be welcomed in a fitting way should certainly not go unrecognised and shows to a marked degree an enthusiasm and tenacity of purpose among the members of the Women's Cricket Association.

The tour itself was a mixed success. The New Zealand team was a capable one, though not as strong as the 1954 side. They were adept at defensive play, over-cautious, and seemed unwilling to take the necessary risks to open up and make the games entertaining. Similarly off the field the team were less gay than is normal, though the blame for this cannot be wholly theirs. The standard of cricket in the W.C.A. was not as good as in recent years, particularly as regards the bowling, there being no fast bowlers. The three Test matches were drawn, which was a great disappointment but this was mainly due, not so much to lack of cricketing ability, as to inexperienced captaincy on both sides.

For the first time in any women's international tour two managers accompanied the team, being in fact sisters-in-law, one dealing with the administrative side and the other being in charge of the cricket.

M.C.C. provided net practice at Lord's during the first week but owing to the weather, advantage of this could only be taken much later in the season. M.C.C. also entertained the team to dinner in August.

The Warwickshire Supporters' Club generously donated £250 to the hospitality fund, and another £250 at the end of the tour when it became evident that, owing to the bad summer, the match accounts showed a substantial loss. Various sports firms helped to entertain, and ground authorities everywhere strained themselves to provide the best pitches and facilities.

The tour was well publicised locally, but the coverage in the National Press was disappointing, owing to the World Cup and the Commonwealth Games. Broadcasting and television authorities showed some but no great interest.

As far as domestic affairs were concerned, a special committee was formed during the season to discuss the changes considered necessary to counteract a steady shrinkage of players and how best to take advantage of the statutory opportunities available. The outcome of their deliberations will not be apparent for some time but will be reported in due course and, it is hoped, will succeed in strengthening both the membership and the actual cricket.

NEW ZEALAND RESULTS

Played 20, *Won* 8, *Drawn* 12, *Abandoned* 2.

ENGLAND v. NEW ZEALAND

First Test

At Scarborough, June 18, 20, 21. Drawn. A gay century by R. Heyhoe, captaining England for the first time, was the highlight of this match. England looked superior, but failed to assess New Zealand's capacity for dour defensive cricket and, though nine bowlers were tried, they were unable to dislodge their opponents on the second day.

England finished in a satisfactory position at the close of the first day, having treated the crowd to an entertaining partnership of 121 between R. Heyhoe and E. Barker, following a slow but confident start. E. Barker distinguished herself by hitting a 6 off the first ball bowled by J. Burley with the new ball, but this was the only Test Match 6 of the series. The advantage of a declaration an hour before the end was pressed home by the capture of two wickets for 8 runs. New Zealand's fielding was poor, no fewer than seven catches being dropped.

New Zealand crawled to 165 for nine on the second day. J. Doull and C. Oyler resisted dourly in a partnership of 93, the former taking more than three hours for her 50 and four and a quarter hours for her 74. England broke through after tea when J. Moorhouse took four wickets, seven wickets in all falling to catches.

R. Heyhoe and E. Barker once again set the pace on the third day with a partnership of 74 in twenty-five minutes and set New Zealand 230 in two and three-quarter hours, but no attempt was made to go for the runs.

England

†S. Plant c Brentnall b Burley	46	— b Saulbrey	7
J. Whitney b Lord	29	— c Stonell b Maker	40
*R. Heyhoe c and b Burley	113	— not out	59
E. Barker b Saulbrey	54	— not out	28
O. Marshall not out	3		
A. Sanders not out	21		
J. Bragger b Blackler	5		
M. Pilling b Burley	0		
L-b 2	2		
1/54 2/96 3/217 4/249 5/249 6/264 (6 wkts., dec.)	273	1/25 2/60 (2 wkts., dec.)	134

J. Moorhouse, L. Clifford and E. Vigor did not bat.

Bowling: *First Innings*—Burley 36—9—68—3; Saulbrey 36—8—106—1; Maker 12—2—38—0; Lord 6—1—16—1; Blackler 10—0—43—1. *Second Innings*—Burley 21—7—62—0; Saulbrey 13—2—41—1; Maker 7—2—31—1.

New Zealand

J. Doull lbw b Pilling	74	— not out	33
J. Stonell b Pilling	3	— lbw b Vigor	8
B. Maker c Plant b Vigor	0		
C. Oyler c Bragger b Moorhouse	35	— not out	36
*P. McKelvey c Sanders b Moorhouse	10		
P. Blackler c Whitney b Moorhouse	14		
J. Stead c Plant b Moorhouse	0	— lbw b Vigor	0
†B. Brentnall c Heyhoe b Vigor	6		
J. Burley b Vigor	11		
J. Saulbrey c Marshall b Barker	9		
J. Lord not out	6		
B 6, n-b 4	10	B 2	2
1/4 2/8 3/21 4/114 5/130 6/135 7/140 8/146 9/163	178	1/11 2/19 (2 wkts.)	79

Bowling: *First Innings*—Pilling 38—27—26—2; Moorhouse 38—20—38—4; Clifford 9—6—6—0; Vigor 27—17—29—3; Bragger 20—9—21—0; Sanders 17—3—23—0; Barker 6.4—2—9—1; Marshall 3—0—8—0; Heyhoe 3—1—8—0. *Second Innings*—Pilling 2—1—1—0; Moorhouse 2—2—0—0; Clifford 5—1—10—0; Vigor 16—13—7—2; Bragger 1—0—3—0; Sanders 8—6—3—0; Barker 7—2—16—0; Marshall 5—3—4—0; Heyhoe 4—0—28—0; Whitney 4—1—5—0.

Umpires: Miss D. J. Ayres and Miss I. Nowell-Smith.

ENGLAND v. NEW ZEALAND

Second Test

At Edgbaston, July 10, 12, 13. Drawn. A match of fluctuations, promise and disappointment ended in a creditable draw for New Zealand, who collapsed on the first day, half the side being out before lunch after which England, on the attack and favoured by some luck, had them all out for 131 shortly after tea. Bowling honours were shared by J. Moorhouse and E. Vigor. England also made a bad batting start, but were rescued by their captain, R. Heyhoe, who ended the day at 54 not out, sharing a third-wicket stand of 71 in sixty-five minutes, with E. Barker. Starting the second day at 94 for four, and helped by R. Heyhoe's 85 and an energetic seventh-wicket stand between two Yorkshire members of the team, J. Moorhouse and L. Clifford, England were able to declare with a comfortable lead of 144. J. Lord, a spin bowler, one of the two New Zealand eighteen-year-old players, bowled 27 overs for her two for 56. The day ended with New Zealand 64 behind with nine wickets in hand and England were still in command, though the close of play score of 80 for one pointed to the pitch playing much more easily.

England's bowlers failed to penetrate on the third day and New Zealand were able to establish two records, B. Brentnall's not-out 84 being the highest individual New Zealand Test score to date, and their 300 in six and three-quarter hours being their highest Test total yet. Moreover it provided the opportunity for a first-ever Test declaration by New Zealand against England. Had this record score been made more quickly, New Zealand would have given themselves the time to force a win. As it was, their declaration left England sixty-five minutes in which to score 157 and all they could do was to take some batting practice.

New Zealand

First Innings		Second Innings	
J. Doull b Moorhouse	0	c Vigor b Marshall	12
J. Stonell b Vigor	12	c Plant b Barker	47
*P. McKelvey b Moorhouse	11	b Barker	37
B. Maker run out	3	lbw b Barker	2
C. Oyler c Heyhoe b Clifford	0	c Vigor b Bragger	36
P. Blackler b Thomas	32	run out	10
†B. Brentnall c Barker b Vigor	7	not out	84
J. Burley run out	22	b Barker	46
W. Coe lbw b Vigor	9	not out	6
J. Saulbrey not out	32		
J. Lord b Moorhouse	1		
L-b 1, n-b 1	2	B 17, l-b 1, n-b 2	20
1/0 2/16 3/26 4/26 5/30 6/66 7/68 8/86 9/124	131	1/20 2/96 3/98 4/117 5/134 6/187 7/277 (7 wkts., dec.)	300

Bowling: *First Innings*—Moorhouse 18—9—32—3; Pilling 11—4—19—0; Clifford 11—4—15—1; Vigor 19—10—24—3; Bragger 7—2—15—0; Thomas 13—9—9—1; Barker 6—1—15—0. *Second Innings*—Moorhouse 22—10—36—0; Pilling 19—11—39—0; Clifford 13—3—25—0; Vigor 30—15—37—0; Bragger 7—2—12—1; Thomas 21—12—27—0; Barker 44—16—94—4; Marshall 13—9—8—1; Whitney 3—1—2—0.

England

First Innings		Second Innings	
†S. Plant c Saulbrey b Burley	0	b Coe	8
J. Whitney b Coe	1		
*R. Heyhoe c Stonell b Saulbrey	85	c Oyler b Lord	26
E. Barker b Lord	31	b Lord	4
O. Marshall run out	0	not out	2
L. Thomas run out	58	not out	11
J. Bragger c Brentnall b Lord	7		
J. Moorhouse not out	50	b Coe	7
L. Clifford not out	31		
L-b 8, n-b 4	12		
1/3 2/5 3/76 4/78 5/168 6/185 7/199 (7 wkts., dec.)	275	1/8 2/21 3/28 4/47 (4 wkts.)	58

M. Pilling and E. Vigor did not bat.

Bowling: *First Innings*—Burley 26—11—53—1; Coe 18—5—59—1; Saulbrey 28—9—55—1; Lord 27—6—56—2; Maker 4—0—27—0; Blackler 3—0—13—0. *Second Innings*—Burley 5—2—11—0; Coe 12—3—30—2; Lord 7—2—17—2.

Umpires: Miss P. Culver and Miss M. Hughes.

ENGLAND v. NEW ZEALAND

Third Test

At The Oval, August 6, 8, 9. Drawn. This match looked, during the second day's play, like a certain first Test win for New Zealand but this was prevented by the tenacity on the third day of two Northerners, L. Clifford and J. Moorhouse, aided by number eleven, E. Vigor. The best performance of the match was by the New Zealand bowler, J. Burley, whose figures were 34.2 overs, 18 maidens, 41 runs, 7 wickets.

Had rain on the first day not largely spoilt the afternoon's play, which was finally abandoned at twenty minutes to four, the result might have been very different. England's score then stood at 138 for six, and their anxiety to put on runs under a grey sky and worsening weather lost them these wickets. They pursued the same policy with the same result the second day and only 16 runs had been added to the overnight score when they declared at 154 for nine. The afternoon's play was brightened by a record partnership of 93 for the fifth wicket in eighty-six minutes between P. Blacker and C. Oyler, made more easy by England's bowling and field placing, which were poor. After the declaration by New Zealand, England collapsed before close of play to the tune of 5 for three wickets and the third day consisted of more shocks followed by a dangerously fraught mixture of stoppages for rain and frustrations for New Zealand. England imperceptibly pulled the game round and at six o'clock their innings ended with a mere lead of 83, which was just sufficient to save the day.

England

First innings		Second innings	
†S. Plant b Burley	10	b Burley	0
J. Whitney lbw b Maker	4	c Moore b Burley	1
*R. Heyhoe c Brentnall b Lord	42	b Burley	31
E. Barker b Lord	7	lbw b Burley	18
A. Disbury c Lord b Saulbrey	44	c and b Saulbrey	25
O. Marshall b Saulbrey	0	b Burley	0
L. Thomas c Maker b Burley	42	c Brentnall b Maker	4
J. Moorhouse b Maker	1	c Moore b Saulbrey	18
L. Clifford c Blackler b Maker	4	c Moore b Burley	32
R. Goodchild not out	0	c Doull b Burley	1
E. Vigor (did not bat)	—	not out	16
		B 1, l-b 1, n-b 5	7
1/4 2/34 3/49 4/70 5/81 6/138 7/140 8/154 9/154 (9 wkts., dec.)	154	1/0 2/1 3/5 4/6 5/52 6/78 7/85 8/103 9/114	153

Bowling: *First Innings*—Burley 21—13—28—2; Maker 18—7—34—3; Lord 14—4—37—2; Saulbrey 16—8—24—2; Moore 9—2—31—0. *Second Innings*—Burley 34.2—18—41—7; Maker 23—13—26—1; Lord 26—11—28—0; Saulbrey 23—12—39—2; Blackler 8—3—12—0.

New Zealand

First innings		Second innings	
J. Doull run out	29	not out	20
J. Stead c Heyhoe b Goodchild	4	not out	14
*P. McKelvey lbw b Vigor	5		
P. Moore hit wkt b Vigor	11		
C. Oyler not out	67		
P. Blackler c Moorhouse b Barker	68		
†B. Brentnall b Goodchild	0		
J. Burley run out	0		
J. Saulbrey lbw b Barker	2		
B. Maker b Vigor	5		
J. Lord not out	25		
B 6, l-b 2	8	L-b 1	1
1/4 2/32 3/41 4/53 5/146 6/152 7/156 8/158 9/169 (9 wkts., dec.)	224	(no wkt.)	35

Bowling: *First Innings*—Moorhouse 18—9—37—0; Goodchild 24—10—40—2; Vigor 28—12—64—3; Barker 28—11—40—2; Thomas 9—2—27—0; Clifford 5—1—8—0. *Second Innings*—Moorhouse 4—0—13—0; Goodchild 3—0—8—0; Barker 1—0—5—0; Heyhoe 1—0—8—0.

Umpires: Mrs. D. M. Coysh and Miss S. Swinburne.

BIRTHS AND DEATHS OF CRICKETERS

To compress this list within reasonable bounds it has been necessary from time to time to take out the names of cricketers who died before certain dates. The following table indicates the issues in which details of cricketers may be found:

Deaths before 1851	*in the* 1933 *and earlier editions*	
Deaths between 1851 *and* 1855	„ „ 1936	„ „ „
„ „ 1856 „ 1899	„ „ 1940	„ „ „
„ „ 1900 „ 1919	„ „ 1947	„ „ „
„ „ 1920 „ 1925	„ „ 1952	„ „ „
„ „ 1926 „ 1935	„ „ 1956	„ „ „
„ „ 1936 „ 1945	„ „ 1959	„ „ „
„ „ 1946 „ 1955	„ „ 1965	„ „ „

Details of members of famous cricketing families and some personalities special interest have, in many cases, been retained. The qualification now is ten appearances in first-class cricket during one season in England, or the award of a County Cap or University Blue. Overseas cricketers are usually included only if they have represented their country in a tour of England. Although the distinction between the amateur and the professional in English first-class County cricket was abolished in 1963 the title "Mr." is retained here for those cricketers who were recognised as amateurs before that date.

Abberley, R. N. (Warwickshire), b. April 22, 1944

a Beckett, Mr E. L. (Victoria), b Aug 11, 1907

Abel, R. (Surrey), b Nov 30, 1857, d Dec 10, 1936

Abel, T. E. (Surrey and Glamorgan), b Sept 10, 1890, d Jan 23, 1937

Abel, W. J. (Surrey), b Aug 29, 1887, d March 23, 1934

Abell, Sir G. E. B. (Oxford Univ. and Worc.), b June 22, 1904

Aberdare, 3rd Lord (*see* Bruce, Hon. C. N.)

Acfield, D. R. (Essex), b July 24, 1947

Achong, Mr. E. (West Indies), b Feb 16, 1904

A'Court, D. G. (Glouc.), b July 27, 1937

Adam, Gen. Sir Ronald, 2nd Bart., President M.C.C., b Oct 30, 1885

Adams, Mr. G. C. A. (Hampshire), b May 24, 1909

Adcock, Mr. N. A. T. (South Africa), b March 8, 1931

Adhikari, Mr. H. R. (India), b Aug 12, 1919

Afaq, Hussain (Pakistan), b Dec 31, 1939

Ahl, F. D. (Worc.), b Nov 24, 1908

Ainsworth, Lt.-Cdr. M. L. Y. (Worc.), b May 13, 1922

Aird, Mr. R. (Camb. Univ. and Hampshire, Secretary M.C.C. 1953 to 1962), b May 4, 1902

Akers-Douglas, Mr. I. S. (Kent), b Nov 16, 1909, d Dec 16, 1952

Akhtar, J. (Pakistan), b Nov 21, 1940

Alabaster, Mr. J. C. (New Zealand), b July 11, 1930

Alcock, Mr. C. W. (Sec., Surrey C.C.C. 1872–1907), b Dec 2, 1842, d Feb 26, 1907

Alderman, A. E. (Derbyshire), b Oct 30, 1907

Aldridge, K. J. (Worc.), b March 13, 1935

Alexander, Mr. F. C. M. (Camb. Univ. and West Indies), b Nov 2, 1928

Alexander, Mr. H. (Victoria) b June 9, 1905

Alexander, Mr. W. C. (South Australia), b Sept 14, 1907

Alim-ud-Din (Pakistan), b Dec 15, 1930

Allcott, Mr. C. F. W. (New Zealand), b Oct 7, 1896

Allan, D. W. (West Indies), b Nov 5, 1937

Allan, Mr. J. M. (Oxford U., Kent, Scotland and War.), b April 2, 1932

Allen, Mr. A. W. (Camb. Univ. and Northants), b Dec 22, 1912

Allen, Mr. B. O. (Camb. Univ. and Glouc.), b Oct 13, 1911

Allen, D. A. (Glouc.), b Oct 29, 1935

Allen, Mr. G. O. (Camb. Univ. and Middlesex, President M.C.C. 1963–64), b at Sydney, Australia, July 31, 1902

Allen, M. H. J. (Northants and Derbyshire), b Jan 7, 1933

Alletson, E. B. (Notts.), b March 6, 1884, d July 5, 1963

Alley, W. E. (N.S.W. and Somerset), b Feb 3, 1919

Allom, Mr. M. J. C. (Camb. Univ. and Surrey), b March 23, 1906
Altham, Mr. H. S. (Oxford Univ., Surrey and Hampshire, President M.C.C., 1959–60), b Nov 30, 1888, d March 11, 1965
Amarnath, L. (India), b Sept 11, 1911
Amar Singh (India), b Dec 4, 1910, d May 20, 1940
Ames, L. E. G. (Kent), b Dec 3, 1905
Amir Elahi (India), b Sept 1, 1908
Amiss, D. L. (War.), b April 7, 1943
Andrew, F. J. (Glouc.), b May 29, 1937
Andrew, K. V. (Northants), b Dec 15, 1929
Andrews, Mr. T. J. E. (New South Wales), b Aug 26, 1890
Andrews, W. H. R. (Somerset), b April 14, 1908
Angell, F. L. (Somerset), b June 29, 1922
Anson, Mr. G. F. (Camb. Univ. and Kent), b Aug 10, 1922
Anson, Hon. Rupert (Middlesex), b Nov 7, 1889, d Dec 20, 1966
Appleyard, Mr. F. (Essex), b Sept 9, 1906
Appleyard, R. (Yorkshire), b June 27, 1924
Apte, A. L. (India), b Sept 24, 1934
Archer, Mr. R. G. (Queensland), b Oct 25, 1933
Arenhold, Mr. J. A. (Oxford Univ.), b May 9, 1931
Armstrong, Mr. E. K. (Queensland), b Feb 5, 1881
Armstrong, N. F. (Leic.), b Dec 22, 1894
Armstrong, T. R. (Derbyshire), b Oct 13, 1909
Armstrong, Mr. W. W. (Victoria), b May 22, 1879, d July 13, 1947
Arnold, E. G. (Worc.), b Nov 7, 1877, d Oct 25, 1942
Arnold, G. (Surrey), b Sept 3, 1944
Arnold, John (Oxfordshire and Hampshire), b Nov 30, 1907
Arnold, P. (Canterbury and Northants), b Oct 16, 1926
Arnott, Mr. T. (Glamorgan and Monmouthshire), b Feb 16, 1902
Asgarali, Mr. N. (West Indies), b Dec 28, 1922
Ashcroft, Dr. E. Maynard (Derbyshire), b Sept 27, 1875, d Feb 26, 1955
Ashdown, W. H. (Kent), b Dec 27, 1898
Ashman, J. R. (Yorkshire and Worc.), b May 20, 1926
Ashton, Sqdn.-Ldr. C. T. (Camb. Univ. and Essex), b Feb 19, 1901, d Oct 31, 1942
Ashton, Mr. G. (Camb. Univ. and Worc.), b Sept 27, 1896
Ashton, Sir H. (Camb. Univ. and Essex, President M.C.C., 1960–61), b Feb 13, 1898
Asif, Ahmed (Pakistan and Oxford Univ.), b April 1, 1942
Aspinall, R. (Yorkshire), b Nov 26, 1918
Astill, W. E. (Leic.), b Mar 1, 1888, d Feb 10, 1948
Astor of Hever, Col. Lord J. (Eton, Buckinghamshire, President M.C.C., 1937), b May 20, 1886
Atfield, A. J. (Glouc. and Wiltshire), b Mar 3, 1868, d Jan 1, 1949
Atkins, Mr. G. (Camb. Univ.), b May 14, 1938
Atkinson, Mr. B. G. W. (Northants, Middlesex and Scotland), b Sept, 1900, d Sept 4, 1966
Atkinson, Mr. C. R. M. (Somerset), b July 23, 1931
Atkinson, Mr. D. (West Indies), b Feb 26, 1925
Atkinson, G. (Somerset), b March 29, 1938
Atkinson, Mr. J. A. (Victoria and Tasmania), b April 4, 1896, d June 11, 1956
Atkinson, T. (Notts.), b Sept 27, 1930
Atkinson-Clark, Mr. J. C. (Middlesex), b July 9, 1912
Attewell, Thos. (Notts.), b Nov. 7, 1869, d July 6, 1937
Attewell, W. (Notts.), b June 12, 1861, d June 11, 1927
Austin, Mr. H. M. (Camb. Univ.), b March 8, 1903
Avery, A. V. (Essex), b Dec 19, 1914
Bacher, A. (South Africa), b May 24, 1942
Bacmeister, Mr. L. H. (Middlesex), b Nov 22, 1869
Badcock, Mr. C. L. (Tasmania and South Austrialia), b April 10, 1914
Badcock, Mr. F. T. (New Zealand), b Aug 9, 1898
Badcock, J. R. (Hampshire), b Oct 4, 1883
Baggallay, Mr. M. E. C. (Camb. Univ.), b Dec 7, 1887, d March 19, 1961
Baggallay, Lt.-Col. R. R. C. (Derbyshire), b May 4, 1884
Bagnall, Mr. H. F. (Camb. Univ. and Northants), b Feb 18, 1904
Baig, A. A. (Oxford Univ., India and Somerset), b March 19, 1939

Baig, M. A. (Oxford Univ.), b Nov 8 1941
Bailey, A. (Surrey, Somerset and Scotland), b March 14, 1872
Bailey, Mr. B. T. R. (South Australia), b Dec 5, 1874
Bailey, Sir D. (Bart.) (Glouc.), b Aug 15, 1918
Bailey, J. (Hampshire), b April 6, 1908
Bailey, Mr. J. A. (Essex and Oxford Univ.), b June 22, 1930
Bailey, R. R. (Northants), b May 16, 1944
Bailey, Mr. T. E. (Essex and Camb. Univ.), b Dec 3, 1923
Baily, Mr. R. E. H. (Camb. Univ. and Surrey), b June 6, 1885
Baiss, Mr. R. S. H. (Kent), b March 6, 1873, d May 2, 1955
Baker, A. (Surrey), b Nov 28, 1872, d April 29, 1948
Baker, C. S. (War. and Cornwall), b Jan 5, 1883
Baker, D. (Kent and Notts.), b July 26, 1935
Baker, Mr. E. C. (Camb. Univ., Sussex and Somerset), b Jan 7, 1892
Baker, Mr. E. S. (Worc.), b Nov 9, 1910
Baker, Mr. H. Z. (Kent), b Feb 7, 1880, d Aug 25, 1958
Bakewell, A. H. (Northants), b Nov 2, 1908
Balaskas, Mr. X. (South Africa), b Oct 15, 1910
Balderstone, J. C. (Yorkshire), b Nov 16, 1940
Baldry, D. O. (Middlesex and Hampshire), b Dec 26, 1931
Baldwin, C. (Surrey and Suffolk), b Dec 29, 1865, d May 2, 1947
Baldwin, H. (Hampshire), b Nov 27, 1860, d Jan 12, 1935
Baldwin, H. G. (Surrey), b March 15, 1893
Bale, E. (Surrey and Worc.), b Sept 18, 1878, d July 7, 1952
Bale, F. (Leic.), b Jan 9, 1893
Ballance, Major T. G. L., M.C. (Oxford Univ.), b April 21, 1916, d Dec 4, 1943
Baloo, P. (India), b March 19, 1876, d July 4, 1955
Banerjee, S. (India), b Oct 3, 1913
Bannerman, Mr. A. C. (New South Wales), b March 21, 1859, d Sept 19, 1924
Bannerman, Mr. Charles (New South Wales), b in Kent, July 3, 1851, d Aug 20, 1930
Bannister, A. F. (Worc.), b June 15, 1875
Bannister, Mr. H. M. (Leic.), b June 3, 1889, d June 18, 1959
Bannister, J. D. (War.), b Aug 23, 1930
Barber, Mr. A. T. (Oxford Univ. and Yorkshire), b June 17, 1905
Barber, Mr. R. W. (Lancashire, Camb. Univ. and War.), b Sept 26, 1935
Barber, W. (Yorkshire), b April 18, 1902
Bardsley, Mr. R. V. (Oxford Univ. and Lancashire), b June 28, 1890, d July 26, 1952
Bardsley, Mr. W. (New South Wales), b Dec 7, 1883, d Jan 20, 1954
Baring, Mr. A. E. G. (Hampshire), b Jan 21, 1910
Barker, A. H. (Oxford Univ.), b Aug 7, 1945
Barker, G. (Essex), b July 6, 1932
Barling, T. H. (Surrey), b Sept 1, 1906
Barlow, A. (Lancashire), b Aug 31, 1915
Barlow, Mr. E. A. (Oxford Univ., Lancashire and Denbighshire), b Feb 24, 1912
Barlow, E. J. (South Africa), b Aug 12, 1940
Barnard, Mr. F. H. (Oxford Univ.), b May 6, 1902
Barnard, H. M. (Hampshire), b July 18, 1933
Barnes, S. F. (Warwickshire, Lancashire and Staffordshire), b April 19, 1873
Barnes, Mr. S. G. (New South Wales), b June 5, 1916
Barnett, Mr. B. A. (Victoria and Buckinghamshire), b May 23, 1908
Barnett, C. J. (Glouc.), b July 3, 1910
Barnett, Mr. C. S. (Glouc.), b Feb 26, 1884, d Nov 20, 1962
Barnett, Mr. E. P. (Glouc.), b March 22, 1885, d Jan 1, 1922
Barnwell, Mr. C. J. P. (Somerset), b June 23, 1914
Baroda, Maharaja of (Manager, India in England, 1959), b Oct 10, 1928
Barratt, F. (Notts.), b April 12, 1894, d Jan 30, 1947
Barratt, R. J. (Leic.), b May 3, 1942
Barrett, Capt. E. I. M. (Hampshire) b June 22, 1879, d July 11, 1950
Barrick, D. (Northants), b April 28, 1926
Barrington, K. F. (Surrey), b Nov 24, 1930
Barron, W. (Durham, Lancashire and Northants), b Oct 26, 1917
Barrow, Mr. I. (West Indies), b Jan 6, 1911
Bartlett, Mr. E. L. (West Indies), b March 18, 1906
Bartlett, Mr. H. T. (Camb. Univ., Surrey and Sussex), b Oct 7, 1914

Bartlett, Mr. J. N. (Oxford Univ. and Sussex), b June 6, 1928
Barton, Mr. H. G. M. (Hampshire), b Oct 10, 1882
Barton, Mr. M. R. (Winchester, Oxford Univ., Norfolk and Surrey), b Oct 14, 1914
Barwell, T. E. (Somerset), b April 29, 1937
Bateman-Champain, Col. C. E. (Cheltenham and Glouc.), b March 30, 1875, d Oct 13, 1956
Bateman-Champain, Mr. F. H. (Glouc. and Oxford Univ.), b June 17, 1877, d Dec 29, 1942
Bateman-Champain, Brig.-Gen. H. F. (Cheltenham and Glouc.), b April 6, 1869, d Oct 7, 1933
Bates, D. L. (Sussex), b May 10, 1933
Bates, L. A. (War.), b March 20, 1895
Bates, W. E. (Yorkshire, Glamorgan and Cheshire), b March 5, 1884, d Jan 17, 1957
Baxter, Mr. A. D. (Devon, Lancashire, Middlesex and Scotland), b Jan 20, 1910
Baxter, Mr. A. G. (Notts.), b Sept 21, 1931
Bayes, G. (Yorkshire), b Feb 27, 1884, d Dec 6, 1960
Bear, M. J. (Essex), b Feb 23, 1934
Beattie, Mr. F. D. (Lancashire), b Aug 18, 1909
Beaumont, H. (Yorkshire), b Oct 14, 1916
Beaumont, Mr. R. (South Africa), b Feb 4, 1884
Beddow, A. M. (Lancashire), b Oct 12, 1941
Bedford, Mr. P. I. (Middlesex), b Feb 11, 1930, d Sept 18, 1966
Bedser, A. V. (Surrey), b July 4, 1918
Bedser, E. A. (Surrey), b July 4, 1918
Beet, G. (Derbyshire), b April 24, 1886, d Dec 13, 1946
Beet, G. H. (Derbyshire), b May 30, 1904, d Aug 22, 1949
Begbie, Mr. D. W. (South Africa), b Dec 12, 1914
Beldam, Mr. G. W. (Middlesex), b May 1, 1868, d Nov 23, 1937
Bell, Mr. A. J. (South Africa), b April 15, 1906
Bell, J. T. (Yorkshire and Glamorgan), b June 16, 1898
Bell, Mr. R. M. (London County and M.C.C.), b Jan 1, 1874, d June 11, 1953
Bell, R. V. (Middlesex and Sussex), b Jan 7, 1931
Bellamy, B. (Northants), b April 22, 1891
Belle, Mr. B. H. (Oxford Univ., Essex and Suffolk), b April 7, 1914
Benaud, Mr. R. (New South Wales), b Oct 6, 1930
Bencraft, Sir H. W. Russell (Hampshire), b March 4, 1858, d Dec 25, 1943
Benham, C. (Essex and Scotland), b June 24, 1881
Benke, Mr. A. F. (Camb. Univ.), b Sept 3, 1938
Benn, Mr. A. (Oxford Univ.), b Oct 7, 1912
Bennett, A. (Lancashire), b May 18, 1910
Bennett, Mr. C. T. (Camb. Univ., Surrey and Middlesex), b Aug. 10, 1902
Bennett, D. (Middlesex), b Dec 18, 1933
Bennett, Mr. G. M. (Somerset), b Dec 17, 1909
Bennett, Mr. N. H. (Surrey), b Sept 23, 1912
Bennett, R. (Lancashire), b June 16, 1940
Bennett, Mr. R. A. (Hampshire), b Dec 12, 1872, d July 16, 1951
Benskin, W. E. (Leic. and Scotland), b April 8, 1883
Benson, Mr. E. T. (Oxford Univ. and Glouc.), b Nov 20, 1907
Berkeley, Mr. G. F. H. (Oxford Univ.), b Jan 29, 1870, d Nov 14, 1955
Bernard, Mr. J. R. (Camb. Univ. and Glouc.), b Dec 7, 1938
Bernau, Mr. E. H. L. (New Zealand), b April 6, 1896, d Jan, 1966
Berridge, Mr. W. C. M. (Leic.), b Dec 2, 1894
Berry, F. (Surrey), b Feb 13, 1911
Berry, L. G. (Leic.), b April 28, 1906
Berry, R. (Lancashire, Worc. and Derbyshire), b Jan 29, 1926
Bessant, J. G. (Glouc.), b Nov 11, 1895
Bestwick, W. (Derbyshire and Glamorgan), b Feb 24, 1876, d May 3, 1938
Betham, Mr. J. D. (Author of "Oxford and Camb. Cricket Scores and Biographies"), b Feb 13, 1874, d Jan 1, 1956
Beton, S. (Middlesex), b Nov 22, 1895
Bettington, Mr. R. H. B. (Oxford Univ., Middlesex and New South Wales), b Feb 24, 1900
Beveridge R. (Middlesex), b Sept 16, 1909
Bick, D. A. (Middlesex), b Feb 22, 1936
Bickmore, Mr. A. F. (Oxford Univ. and Kent), b May 19, 1899
Biddulph, K. D. (Somerset and Durham), b May 29, 1932

Bignell, Lt.-Col. G. N. (Hampshire), b Dec 3, 1886, d June 10, 1965
Binks, J. G. (Yorkshire), b Oct 5, 1935
Bird, Rev. F. N. (Buckinghamshire, Glouc., Northants, Devon and Suffolk), b 1876, d March 3, 1965
Bird, H. D. (Yorkshire and Leic.), b April 19, 1933
Bird, Mr. M. C. (Lancashire and Surrey), b March 25, 1888, d Dec 9, 1933
Bird, Mr. R. E. (Worc.), b April 4, 1915
Birkenshaw, J. (Yorkshire and Leic.), b Nov 13, 1940
Birkett, Mr. L. S. (West Indies), b April 14, 1905
Birrell, Mr. H. B. (Oxford Univ.), b Dec 12, 1927
Birtles, T. J. (Yorkshire), b Oct 26, 1887
Birtwell, Mr. A. J. (Buckinghamshire and Lancashire), b Dec 17, 1910
Bisgood, Mr. B. L. (Somerset) b March 11, 1881
Bisset, Mr. J. J. (Natal), b Dec, 1882
Bisset, Sir M. (South Africa), b April 14, 1876, d Oct 24, 1931
Bissex, M. (Glouc.), b Sept 25, 1944
Blackham, Mr. J. McC. (Victoria), b May 11, 1853, d Dec 27, 1932
Blackie, Mr. D. J. (Victoria), b April 5, 1882, d April 21, 1955
Blackledge, Mr. J. F. (Lancashire), b April 15, 1928
Blaikie, Mr. K. G. (Oxford Univ. and Somerset), b May 8, 1897
Blair, Mr. R. W. (New Zealand), b June 23, 1932
Blake, Mr. D. E. (Hampshire), b April 27, 1925
Blake, Capt. J. P. (Camb. Univ. and Hampshire), b Nov 17, 1917, d June 3, 1944
Blake, Rev. P. D. S. (Oxford Univ. and Sussex), b May 23, 1927
Blaker, Mr. R. N. R. (Camb. Univ. and Kent), b Oct 24, 1879, d Sept 11, 1950
Blanckenberg, Mr. J. M. (South Africa), b Dec 31, 1893
Bland, K. C. (South Africa), b April 5, 1938
Bland, Mr. R. D. F. (Notts.), b May 16, 1911
Blaxland, Mr. L. B. (Derbyshire), b March 25, 1898
Bligh, Hon. and Rev. E. V. (Oxford Univ. and Kent), b Feb 28, 1829, d April 22, 1908
Bligh, Hon. and Rev. Henry (Kent), b June 10, 1834, d March 4, 1905
Bligh, Hon. Ivo, *see* Darnley, 8th Earl
Bligh, Mr. L. E. (Kent), b Nov 24, 1854, d May 16, 1924
Block, Mr. S. A. (Camb. Univ. and Surrey), b July 15, 1908
Blofeld, Mr. H. C. (Camb. Univ.), b Sept 23, 1939
Blomley, B. (Lancashire), b Nov. 1885
Bloodworth, B. S. (Glouc.), b Dec, 1893
Bloy, Mr. N. C. F. (Oxford Univ.), b Jan 2, 1923
Blundell, Mr. E. D. (Camb. Univ. and New Zealand), b May 29, 1907
Blunden, A. (Kent), b Sept 5, 1906
Blunt, Mr. R. C. (New Zealand), b Nov 3, 1900, d June 22, 1966
Blythe, C. (Kent), b May 30, 1879, d Nov, 1917
Boddington, Mr. R. A. (Lancashire), b June 30, 1892
Boden, Rev. C. A. (Leic.), b Dec 18, 1890
Bodkin, Mr. P. E. (Camb. Univ. and Hertfordshire), b Sept 15, 1924
Bolton, A. (Lancashire), b July 1, 1939
Bolton, Capt. R. H. D. (Dorset and Hants), b Jan 13, 1893, d Oct 3, 1964
Bolus, J. B. (Yorkshire and Notts.), b Jan 31, 1934
Bond, Mr. G. E. (South Africa), b April 5, 1910
Bond, J. D. (Lancashire), b May 6, 1932
Bonham-Carter, Sir M. (Oxford Univ. and Kent), b Oct 11, 1880, d June 7, 1960
Bonnor, Mr. G. J. (New South Wales and Victoria), b Feb 22, 1855, d June 27, 1912
Boobbyer, Mr. B. (Oxford Univ.), b Feb 25, 1928
Booth, A. (Yorkshire), b Nov 3, 1902
Booth, B. J. (Lancashire and Leic.), b Oct 3, 1935
Booth, Mr. B. C. (New South Wales), b Oct 19, 1933
Booth, F. S. (Lancashire), b Feb 12, 1907
Booth, R. (Yorkshire and Worc.), b Oct 1, 1926
Borde, C. G. (India), b July 21, 1934
Bosanquet, Mr. B. J. T. (Middlesex and Oxford Univ.), b Oct 13, 1877, d Oct 12, 1936
Boshier, B. (Leic.), b March 6, 1932
Boswell, C. S. R. (Essex and Norfolk), b Jan 19, 1911
Botten, J. T. (South Africa), b June 21, 1938
Boucher, Mr. J. C. (Ireland), b Dec 22, 1910

Bowden, J. (Derbyshire), b Oct 8, 1884, d March 1, 1958
Bowell, A. (Hampshire), b April 27, 1881, d Aug 28, 1957
Bower, W. (Notts.), b Jan 2, 1895
Bowes, W. E. (Yorkshire), b July 25, 1908
Bowles, J. J. (Worc.), b April 3, 1891
Bowley, E. H. (Sussex), b June 7, 1890
Bowley, F. J. (Leic.), b Feb 20, 1909
Bowley, F. L. (Worc.), b Nov 9, 1875, d May 31, 1943
Bowman, Mr. R. (Oxford Univ. and Lancashire), b Jan 26, 1934
Bowmer, Mr. H. E. (Derbyshire), b July 14, 1891
Boycott, G. (Yorkshire), b Oct 21, 1940
Boyes, G. S. (Hampshire), b March 31, 1899
Bracey, F. (Derbyshire), b July 20, 1887, d March 28, 1960
Bracher, Mr. F. C. (Glouc.), b Oct 25, 1868
Braddell, Mr. R. L. L. (Oxford Univ. and Suffolk), b Dec 14, 1888, d March 17, 1965
Bradley, J. (Notts.), b Oct 3, 1913
Bradley, Mr. W. M. (Kent), b Jan 2, 1875, d June 19, 1944
Bradman, Sir D. G. (New South Wales and South Australia), b Aug 27, 1908
Bradshaw, J. C. (Leic.), b Jan 25, 1902
Bradshaw, Mr. W. H. (Oxford Univ.), b Jan 22, 1909
Brain, B. M. (Worc.), b Sept 13, 1940
Brain, Mr. W. H. (Oxford Univ., Glouc. and Glamorgan), b July 21, 1870, d Nov 20, 1934
Brancker, R. C. (West Indies), b Nov 19, 1937
Brann, Mr. G. (Sussex), b April 23, 1865, d June 14, 1954
Branston, Mr. G. T. (Oxford Univ. and Notts.), b Sept 3, 1884
Braund, L. C. (Surrey and Somerset), b Oct 18, 1875, d Dec 22, 1955
Bray, Mr. C. (Essex), b April 6, 1898
Brazier, A. F. (Surrey and Kent), b Dec 7, 1924
Brearley, Mr. J. M. (Camb. Univ., Middlesex and Cambs.), b April 28, 1942
Brearley, Mr. W. (Lancashire and Cheshire), b March 11, 1876, d Jan 30, 1937
Brennan, Mr. D. V. (Yorkshire), b Feb 10, 1920
Brice, G. (Northants), b May 4, 1924
Brice, Mr. W. S. (New Zealand), b Nov 14, 1880, d May 6, 1959
Bridge, W. B. (War.), b May 29, 1938
Bridger, Rev. J. R. (Hampshire), b April 8, 1920
Bridges, Mr. J. J. (Somerset), b June 28, 1887, d Sept 26, 1966
Bridgman, Mr. H. (South Australia), b Feb 1, 1890, d Dec 3, 1953
Brierley, T. L. (Glamorgan and Lancashire), b June 15, 1910
Briggs, John (Lancashire), b Oct 3, 1862, d Jan 11, 1902
Briscoe, Mr. A. W. (South Africa), b Feb 6, 1911, d April 21, 1941
Broadbent, R. (Worc.), b June 21, 1924
Brocklebank, Sir J. M., Bart. (Camb. Univ. and Lancashire), b Sept 3, 1915
Brocklehurst, Mr. B. G. (Somerset), b Feb 18, 1922
Brockwell, W. (Surrey), b Jan 21, 1866, d July 1, 1935
Broderick, V. (Northants), b Aug 17, 1920
Brodhurst, Mr. A. H. (Camb. Univ. and Glouc.), b July 21, 1916
Brodie, Mr. J. B. (Camb. Univ.), b March 19, 1937
Brodrick, Mr. P. D. (Camb. Univ.), b May 11, 1937
Bromfield, H. D. (South Africa), b June 26, 1933
Bromley, Mr. E. H. (Victoria), b Sept 2, 1912
Bromley, P. H. (War.), b July 30, 1930
Bromley-Davenport, Mr. H. R. (Camb. Univ., Cheshire and Middlesex), b Aug 18, 1870, d May 23, 1954
Brook, G. W. (Worc.), b Aug 30, 1895, d July 24, 1966
Brooke, Lt.-Col. F. R. R. (Lancashire), b Oct 2, 1884, d June 20, 1960
Brooke, Rev. R. H. J. (Glouc., Oxford Univ. and Buckinghamshire), b June 6, 1909
Brookes, D. (Northants), b Oct 29, 1915
Brookes, Mr. W. H. (Editor of *Wisden* 1936 to 1939), b Dec 5, 1894, d May 28, 1955
Brooke-Taylor, Mr. D. C. (Derbyshire), b June 15, 1920
Brooke-Taylor, Mr. G. P. (Camb. Univ. and Derbyshire), b Oct 25, 1895
Brooks, E. W. J. (Surrey), b July 6, 1898, d Feb 10, 1960
Broughton, Mr. E. A. (Leic.), b April 22, 1905
Broughton, P. H. (Yorkshire and Leic.), b Oct 22, 1935
Brown, A. (Kent), b Oct 17, 1935

Brown, A. S. (Glouc.), b June 24, 1936
Brown, D. (Glouc.), b Feb 26, 1942
Brown, D. J. (War.), b Jan 30, 1942
Brown, E. (War.), b Nov 27, 1911
Brown, Mr. F. R. (Camb. Univ., Surrey and Northants), b Lima, Dec 16, 1910
Brown, G. (Hampshire), b Oct 6, 1887, d Dec 3, 1964
Brown, Mr. G. R. R. (Essex), b Dec 8, 1905
Brown, J. T. (Yorkshire), b Aug 20, 1869, d Nov 4, 1904
Brown, J. T. (Yorkshire), b Nov 24, 1874, d April 12, 1950
Brown, L. (Leic.), b March 12, 1874, d Oct 14, 1951
Brown, Mr. L. S. (South Africa), b Nov 24, 1910
Brown, S. M. (Middlesex), b Dec 8, 1917
Brown, W. (Leic.), b April 11, 1888
Brown, Mr. W. A. (New South Wales and Queensland), b July 31, 1912
Brown, Mr. W. C. (Northants), b Nov 13, 1900
Brown, Mr. W. S. A. (Glouc.), b May 23, 1877, d Sept 12, 1952
Browne, Mr. C. R. (West Indies), b Oct 8, 1890, d Jan 12, 1964
Browne, Rev. F. B. R. (Camb. Univ. and Sussex), b July 28, 1899
Brownlee, Mr. L. D. (Oxford Univ., Glouc. and Somerset), b Dec 17, 1882, d Sept 22, 1955
Bruce, Hon. C. N. (3rd Lord Aberdare), (Oxford Univ. and Middlesex), b Aug 2, 1885, d Oct 4, 1957
Brunton, Rev. J. du V. (Camb. Univ.), b July 23, 1869, d Nov 12, 1962
Brutton, Mr. C. P. (Hampshire and Denbighshire), b Jan 20, 1899, d May 11, 1964
Bryan, Brig. G. J. (Kent), b Dec 29, 1902
Bryan, Mr. J. L. (Camb. Univ. and Kent), b May 26, 1896
Bryan, Mr. R. T. (Rugby and Kent), b July 30, 1898
Bryant, E. (Somerset), b June 2, 1936
Buchanan, Mr. J. N. (Camb. Univ. and Buckinghamshire), b in South Africa, May 30, 1887
Buckenham, C. P. (Essex), b Jan 16, 1876, d Feb 23, 1937
Buckingham, J. (War.), b Jan 21, 1904
Buckston, Mr. R. H. R. (Derbyshire), b Oct 10, 1908
Budd, W. L. (Hampshire), b Oct 25, 1913
Bull, Mr. A. H. (Northants), b Jan 23, 1892
Buller, J. S. (Yorkshire and Worc.), b Aug 23, 1909
Bulsara, Mr. M. D. (India), b Sept 2, 1877
Bunce, Mr. N. (Somerset), b April 17, 1911
Burch, G. W. (Leic.), b April 12, 1937
Burden, M. D. (Hampshire), b Oct 4, 1930
Burge, Mr. P. J. (Queensland), b May 17, 1932
Burgess, G. (Somerset), b May 5, 1943
Burgess, Mr. J. (Leic.), b Nov 22, 1880, d 1953
Burke, Mr. C. (New Zealand), b March 27, 1914
Burke, Mr. J. W. (New South Wales), b June 12, 1930
Burki, Mr. J. (Oxford Univ. and Pakistan), b May 8, 1938
Burn, Mr. K. E. (Tasmania), b Sept 17, 1863, d July 20, 1956
Burn, Sir R. C. W. (Oxford Univ.), b Oct 29, 1882, d May 8, 1955
Burnet, Mr. J. R. (Yorkshire), b Oct 11, 1918
Burnett, Mr. A. C. (Camb. Univ. and Glamorgan), b Oct 26, 1923
Burns, James (Essex), b June 20, 1865, d Sept 11, 1957
Burnup, Mr. C. J. (Camb. Univ. and Kent), b Nov 21, 1875, d April 5, 1960
Burrough, Mr. H. D. (Somerset), b Feb 6, 1909
Burton, Mr. D. C. F. (Yorkshire), b Sept 13, 1887
Burton, Mr. R. C. (Yorkshire), b April 11, 1891
Burton, T. (West Indies), b Jan 31, 1878
Burtt, Mr. T. B. (New Zealand), b Jan 22, 1915
Buse, H. T. F. (Somerset), b Aug 5, 1910
Bush, Mr. J. E. (Oxford Univ.), b Aug 28, 1928
Bushby, Mr. M. H. (Camb. Univ.), b July 29, 1931
Buss, A. (Sussex), b Sept 1, 1939
Buss, M. A. (Sussex), b Jan 24, 1944
Buswell, J. (Northants), b July 3, 1911
Buswell, W. A. (Northants), b Jan 12, 1875, d April 24, 1950
Butcher, B. F. (West Indies), b Sept 3, 1934
Butler, H. J. (Notts.), b March 12, 1913
Butterworth, Mr. H. R. W. (Camb. Univ., Denbighshire and Lancashire), b Feb 4, 1909, d Oct 9, 1958

Buxton, I. R. (Derbyshire), b April 17, 1938
Buxton, J. H. (Notts), b Nov 20, 1914
Buxton, Mr. R. V. (Oxford Univ. and Middlesex), b April 29, 1883, d Oct 1, 1953
Byrne, Mr. J. F. (Warwickshire), b June 19, 1871, d May 10, 1954
Cadman, S. (Derbyshire), b Jan 29, 1880, d May 6, 1952
Cahn, Sir Julien, 1st Bart. (Notts. C.C.C.), b Oct 21, 1882, d Sept 26, 1944
Caine, Mr. C. Stewart (Editor of *Wisden* 1926 to 1933), b Oct 28, 1861, d April 15, 1933
Calthorpe, Hon. F. S. G. (Camb. Univ., Sussex and War.), b May 27, 1892, d Nov 19, 1935
Cameron, F. J. (New Zealand), b June 1, 1932
Cameron, Mr. H. B. (South Africa), b July 5, 1905, d Nov 2, 1935
Cameron, Mr. J. H. (Camb. Univ., Somerset and West Indies), b April 8, 1914
Cameron, Dr. J. J. (West Indies), b May, 1882
Campbell, Mr. I. P. (Oxford Univ. and Kent), b Feb 5, 1928
Campbell, Mr. I. P. F. (Oxford Univ. and Surrey), b Nov 25, 1890, d Dec 25, 1963
Campbell, Mr. P. (Essex), b Dec 26, 1887
Cangley, Mr. B. G. (Camb. Univ. and Cambridgeshire), b Sept 12, 1922
Cannings, V. H. D. (War. and Hampshire), b April 3, 1920
Caple, R. G. (Hampshire), b Dec 8, 1939
Cardus, Mr. Neville (Cricket Writer), b April 2, 1889
Carew, M. C. (West Indies), b Sept 15, 1937
Carey, P. A. D. (Sussex), b May 21, 1920
Carlin, J. (Notts.), b Nov 3, 1861, d Nov 28, 1944
Carlisle, Mr. K. M. (Oxford Univ.), b Aug 7, 1882
Carlstein, Mr. P. R. (South Africa), b Oct 28, 1938
Carpenter, D. (Glouc.), b Sept 12, 1935
Carr, Mr. A. W. (Notts), b May 18 1893, d Feb 7, 1963
Carr, Mr. D. B. (Oxford Univ. and Derbyshire), b Dec 28, 1926
Carr, Mr. D. W. (Kent), b March 17 1872, d March 23, 1950
Carrington, E. (Derbyshire), b March 25, 1914
Carris, Mr. B. D. (Camb. Univ. and Middlesex), b Oct 23, 1917
Carris, Mr. H. E. (Camb. Univ. and Middlesex), b July 7, 1909, d July 29, 1959
Carrol, Mr. E. V. (Victoria), b Jan 16, 1885
Carter, Mr. C. P. (South Africa and Cornwall), b April 23, 1881, d Nov 8, 1952
Carter, Mr. H. (New South Wales), b in Yorkshire, March 15, 1878, d June 8, 1948
Carter, R. (Derbyshire), b Nov 7, 1933
Carter R. G. (War.), b April 14, 1933
Carter, R. G. M. (Worc.), b July 11, 1937
Cartwright, Mr. Philip (Sussex), b at Gibraltar, Sept 26, 1880, d Nov 21, 1955
Cartwright, T. W. (War.), b July 22, 1935
Carty, R. A. (Hampshire), b July 28, 1922
Case, Mr. C. C. (Somerset), b Sept 7, 1895
Cass, G. R. (Essex), b April 23, 1940
Castell, A. T. (Hampshire), b Aug 6, 1943
Castle, Mr. F. (Somerset), b April 9, 1909
Castledine, S. W. T. (Notts.), b April 10, 1912
Catt, A. W. (Kent), b Oct 2, 1933
Catterall, Mr. R. H. (South Africa), b July 10, 1900, d Jan 2, 1961
Cave, Mr. H. B. (New Zealand), b Oct 10, 1922
Cawston, Mr. E. (Camb. Univ., Sussex and Berkshire), b Jan 16, 1911
Chalk, Mr. F. G. H. (Oxford Univ. and Kent), b Sept 7, 1910, d Feb 20, 1943
Challenor, Mr. G. (West Indies), b June 28, 1888, d July 30, 1947
Chamberlain, Mr. L. W. (South Australia), b Jan 15, 1889
Chambers, R. E. J. (Camb. Univ.), b Nov 19, 1943
Chaplin, Mr. H. P. (Sussex), b March 1, 1883
Chapman, Mr. A. P. F. (Camb. Univ., Berkshire and Kent), b Sept 3, 1900, d Sept 16, 1961
Chapman, Mr. J. (Derbyshire), b March 11, 1877, d Aug 12, 1956
Chapman, T. A. (Leic.), b May 14, 1919
Charlesworth, C. (War.), b Feb 12, 1877, d June 15, 1953
Charlton, Mr. P. C. (New South Wales), b April 9, 1867, d Sept 30, 1954

Cheetham, Mr. A. G. (N.S.W.), b Dec 7, 1915
Cheetham, Mr. J. E. (South Africa), b May 25, 1920
Chester, F. (Worc., Umpire), b Jan 20, 1896, d April 8, 1957
Chesterton, Mr. G. H. (Oxford Univ and Worc.), b July 15, 1922
Chignell, Mr. T. A. (Hampshire), b Oct 31, 1880, d Aug 25, 1965
Childs-Clarke, Mr. A. W. (Middlesex and Northants), b May 13, 1905
Chipperfield, Mr. A. G. (New South Wales), b Nov 17, 1905
Chowdhury, Mr. N. R. (India), b 1923
Christiani, Mr. C. M. (West Indies), b Oct 28, 1913, d April 4, 1938
Christiani, Mr. R. J. (West Indies), b July 19, 1920
Christopherson, Mr. J. C. (Camb. Univ. and Kent), b June 1, 1909
Christopherson, Mr. P. (Kent and Berkshire), b March 31, 1866, d May 4, 1921
Christopherson, Mr. Stanley (Kent, President, M.C.C., 1939–46), b Nov 11, 1861, d April 6, 1949
Christy, Mr. J. A. J. (South Africa and Queensland), b Dec. 12, 1904
Chubb, Mr. G. W. A. (South Africa), b April 12, 1911
Clark, Mr. D. G. (Kent), b Jan 27, 1919
Clark, E. A. (Middlesex), b April 15, 1937
Clark, E. W. (Northants), b Aug. 9, 1902
Clark, Mr. L. S. (Essex), b March 6, 1914
Clark, T. H. (Surrey), b Oct 5, 1924
Clarke, Dr. C. B. (West Indies, Northants and Essex), b April 7, 1918
Clarke, Mr. C. C. (Derbyshire, Staffordshire and Sussex), b Dec 22, 1910
Clarke, F. (Glamorgan), b Oct 8, 1936
Clarke, R. W. (Northants), b April 22, 1924
Clarke, W. (Notts.), b March 17, 1850, d May 29, 1935
Clay, Mr. J. C. (Glamorgan), b March 18, 1898
Clay, J. D. (Notts.), b Oct 15, 1924
Clayton, G. (Lancashire and Somerset), b Feb 3, 1938
Cliff, Mr. A. T. (Worc.), b Oct 27, 1878, d Jan 25, 1966
Clift, P. (Glamorgan), b Sept 3, 1919
Clifton, E. G. (Middlesex), b June 15, 1939
Clode, H. (Surrey and Durham), b Sept 7, 1878
Close, D. B. (Yorkshire), b Feb 24, 1931
Close, P. A. (Camb. Univ.), b June 1, 1943
Clube, Mr. S. V. M. (Oxford Univ.), b Oct 22, 1934
Clugston, D L. (War.), b Feb 5, 1908
Cobbold, Mr. P. W. (Camb Univ. and Suffolk), b Jan 5, 1875, d Dec 28, 1945
Cobbold, Mr. R. H. (Camb. Univ.), b May 22, 1906
Cobbold, Mr. W. N. (Kent), b Feb 4, 1863, d April 8, 1922
Cobden, Mr. F. C. (Camb. Univ.), b Oct 14, 1849, d Dec 7, 1932
Cobham, 8th Visct. (5th Baron Lyttelton) (Camb. Univ., President, M.C.C., 1886), b Oct 27, 1842, d June 9, 1922
Cobham, 9th Visct. (Hon. J. C. Lyttelton), (Worc., President, M.C.C., 1935), b Oct 23, 1881, d July 31, 1949
Cobham, 10th Visct. (Hon. C. J. Lyttelton), (Worc., President, M.C.C., 1954–55), b Aug 8, 1909
Cobley, A. (Leic.), b Oct 5, 1875
Cock, Mr. D. F. (Essex), b Oct 22, 1914
Cockett, Mr. J. A. (Camb. Univ.), b Dec 23, 1927
Coe, S. (Leic.), b June 3, 1873, d Nov 4, 1955
Coen, Mr. S. K. (South Africa), b Oct 14, 1902
Coghlan, Mr. T. B. L. (Camb. Univ.), b March 29, 1939
Cohen, R. A. (West Indies), b May 23, 1943
Colah, S. H. M. (India), b Sept 22, 1902, d Sept 11, 1950
Coldwell, L. J. (Worc.), b Jan 10, 1933
Cole, C. G. (Kent), b July 7, 1916
Coleman, C. A. (Leic.), b July 7, 1906
Collin, T. (War. and Durham), b April 17, 1911
Collinge, R. O. (New Zealand), b April 2, 1946
Collins, Mr. D. C. (Camb. Univ.), b Oct 1, 1887
Collins, G. (Kent), b Sept 21, 1889, d Jan 23, 1949
Collins, Mr. G. A. K. (Sussex), b May 16, 1909
Collins, Mr. H. L. (New South Wales), b Jan 21, 1889, d May 28, 1959
Collins, Brig.-Gen. L. P. (Oxford Univ. Berkshire and India), b Nov 27, 1878, d Sept 27, 1957

Collins, R. (Lancashire), b March 10, 1934
Comber, Mr. J. T. H. (Camb. Univ.), b Feb 26, 1911
Compton, D. C. S. (Middlesex), b May 23, 1918
Compton, L. H. (Middlesex), b Sept 12, 1912
Congdon, B. E. (New Zealand), b Feb 11, 1938
Connolly, A. N. (Victoria), b June 29, 1939
Conradi, Mr. E. R. (Camb. Univ.), b July 25, 1920
Considine, Mr. S. G. U. (Somerset), b Aug 11, 1901, d Aug 31, 1950
Constable, B. (Surrey), b Feb 19, 1921
Constant, D. J. (Kent and Leics.), b Nov 9, 1941
Constantine, Sir Learie (West Indies), b Sept 21, 1902
Constantine, Mr. L. S. (Trinidad), b May 25, 1874, d Jan 5, 1942
Contractor, N. J. (India), b March 7, 1934
Conway, A. J. (Worc.), b April 1, 1886, d Nov 1, 1954
Cook, C. (Glouc.), b Aug 8, 1921
Cook, Mr. G. W. (Camb. Univ. and Kent), b Feb 9, 1936
Cook, L. (Lancashire), b March 28, 1885, d Dec 2, 1933
Cook, T. E. (Sussex), b Feb 5, 1901, d Jan 15, 1950
Cook, W. (Lancashire), b Jan 16, 1882, d Dec 18, 1947
Cook, Mr. W. T. (Surrey), b Dec 6, 1891
Cooke, R. (War.), b May 25, 1900
Coope, M. (Somerset), b Nov 28, 1917
Cooper, E. (Worc.), b Nov 30, 1915
Cooper, F. (Lancashire and Worc.), b April 18, 1921
Cooper, G. C. (Sussex), b Sept 2, 1936
Cooper, H. (Derbyshire), b Dec 23, 1883
Copley, S. H. (Notts.), b Nov 1, 1906
Copson, W. H. (Derbyshire), b April 27, 1909
Corbett, Mr. L. J. (Glouc.), b May 12, 1897
Cording, Mr. G. E. (Glamorgan), b Jan 1, 1878, d Feb 2, 1946
Cordle, A. E. (Glamorgan), b Sept 9, 1943
Corling, G. E. (New South Wales), b July 13, 1941
Cornford, J. H. (Sussex), b Dec 9, 1911
Cornford, W. (Sussex), b Dec 25, 1900, d Feb 6, 1964
Cornock, W. B. (Leic.), b Jan 1, 1921
Cornwallis, Capt. Hon. W. S. (2nd Lord Cornwallis) (Kent), b March 14, 1892
Corrall, P. (Leic.), b July 16, 1906
Corran, Mr. A. J. (Oxford Univ. and Notts.), b Nov 25, 1936
Cosh, N. J. (Camb. Univ.), b Aug 6, 1946
Cottam, R. M. H. (Hampshire), b Oct 16, 1944
Cotter, Mr. A. (New South Wales), b Dec 3, 1883, d Oct 20, 1917
Cotton, J. (Notts. and Leic.), b Nov 7, 1940
Cottrell, G. A. (Camb. Univ.), b March 23, 1945
Coulson, S. S. (Leic.), b Oct 17, 1898
Court, R. C. (Hampshire), b Oct 23, 1916
Cousens, P. (Essex), b May 15, 1932
Coutts, Mr. I. D. F. (Oxford Univ.) b April 27, 1928
Coventry, Hon. J. B. (Worc.), b Jan 9, 1903
Coverdale, W. W. (Northants), b May 30, 1912
Cowan, Capt. C. F. R., R.N. (War.), b Sept 17, 1883, d March 22, 1958
Cowan, M. J. (Yorkshire), b June 10, 1933
Cowdrey, Mr. M. C. (Kent and Oxford Univ.), b Dec 24, 1932
Cowie, Mr. J. (New Zealand), b March 30, 1912
Cowper, R. M. (Victoria), b Oct 5, 1940
Cox, A. L. (Northants), b July 22, 1908
Cox, G., jun. (Sussex), b Aug 23, 1911
Cox, Mr. G. C. (Worc.), b July 5, 1908
Cox, G. R. (Sussex), b Nov 29, 1873, d March 24, 1949
Cox, Mr. H. R. (Notts.), b May 19 1911
Cox, Mr. J. L. (South Africa), b June 28, 1886
Cox, M. (Northants), b May 10, 1881
Coxon, A. (Yorkshire), b Jan 18, 1917
Coxon, Mr. A. J. (Oxford Univ.), b March 18, 1930
Crabtree, Mr. H. P. (Essex), b April 30, 1906
Craig, Mr. E. J. (Camb. Univ. and Lancashire), b March 26, 1942
Craig, Mr. I. D. (New South Wales), b June 12, 1935
Cranfield, L. M. (Glouc.), b Aug 29, 1910
Crankshaw, Major Sir E. N. S. (Glouc.), b July 1, 1885
Cranmer, Mr. P. (War.), b Sept 10, 1914
Cranston, Mr. K. (Lancashire), b Oct 20, 1917

Crapp, J. F. (Glouc.), b Oct 14, 1912
Crawford, Mr. J. N. (Surrey and South Australia), b Dec 1, 1886, d May 2 1963
Crawford, Mr. P. (New South Wales), b Aug 3, 1933
Crawford, Mr. R. T. (Leic.), b June 11, 1882, d Nov 15, 1945
Crawford, Mr. V. F. S. (Surrey and Leic.), b April 11, 1879, d Aug 21, 1922
Crawley, Mr. A. M. (Oxford Univ. and Kent), b April 10, 1908
Crawley, Mr. L. G. (Camb. Univ., Durham, Worc. and Essex), b July 26, 1903
Cray, S. J. (Essex), b May 29, 1921
Creber, H. (Glamorgan), b April 30, 1874, d March 27, 1939
Creese, W. L. (Hampshire), b Dec 28, 1907
Cresswell, Mr. G. F. (New Zealand), b March 22, 1915, d Jan 10, 1966
Crisp, Mr. R. J. (South Africa and Worc.), b May 28, 1911
Cristofani, D. R. (Aust. Services and N.S.W.), b Nov 14, 1920
Critchley-Salmonson, Mr. H. S. (Somerset), b Jan 19, 1894
Crockford, Mr. E. B. (War.), b Oct 13, 1888, d Jan 17, 1958
Croft, Mr. P. D. (Camb. Univ.), b July 7, 1933
Cromack, B. (Leic.), b June 5, 1937
Cromb, Mr. I. B. (New Zealand), b June 25, 1905
Cromer, 2nd Earl of (President, M.C.C., 1934), b Nov 29, 1877, d May 13, 1953
Crookes, Mr. D. V. (Camb. Univ.), b June 18, 1931
Crookes, N. S. (South Africa), b Nov 15, 1935
Croom, A. J. (War.), b May 23, 1897, d Aug 16, 1947
Cross, G. (Leic.), b Nov 15, 1943
Crosse, Mr. E. M. (Northants), b Dec 11, 1882, d June 28, 1963
Crossland, Mr. A. P. (Yorkshire), b Dec 10, 1862, d Feb, 1948
Crowe, Mr. G. L. (Worc.), b Jan 8, 1885
Crump, B. S. (Northants), b April 25, 1938
Crush, Mr. E. (Kent), b April 25, 1917
Crutchley, Mr. G. E. V. (Oxford Univ. and Middlesex), b Nov 19, 1890
Cuff, Mr. L. A. (New Zealand and Tasmania), b March 28, 1866, d Oct 9, 1954
Cullen, L. (Northants), b Nov 23, 1914
Cumberlege, Mr. B. S. (Camb. Univ., Northumberland and Kent), b June 5, 1891
Cumming, Mr. B. L. (Sussex), b July 11, 1916
Cunningham, Mr. W. (New Zealand), b Jan 23, 1900
Curgenven, Mr. H. G. (Derbyshire), b Dec 22, 1875
Curnow, Mr. S. H. (South Africa), b Dec 16, 1907
Curtis, J. S. (Leic.), b Dec 21, 1887
Cuthbertson, Mr. G. B. (Middlesex and Northants), b March 28, 1901
Cuthbertson, Mr. J. L. (Oxford Univ. and Surrey), b Feb 24, 1942
Cutmore, J. A. (Essex), b Dec 28, 1900
Da Costa, Mr. O. C. (West Indies), b Sept 11, 1907, d Oct 1, 1936
Dacre, C. C. (New Zealand and Glouc.), b May 21, 1900
Daer, Mr. A. G. (Essex), b Nov 20, 1906
Daer, H. (Essex), b Dec 10, 1918
Daft, H. B. (Notts.), b April 5, 1866, d Jan 12, 1945
Daily, C. (Surrey), b April 28, 1900
Dales, Mr. H. L. (Middlesex), b May 18, 1888, d May 4, 1964
Daley, J. V. (Norfolk, Surrey and Suffolk), b Feb 1, 1907
Dallas Brooks, Gen. Sir R. A. (Hants), b. Aug 2, 1896, d March 22, 1966
Dalmeny, Lord (6th Earl of Rosebery), (Buckinghamshire, Middlesex and Surrey), b Jan 8, 1882
Dalton, Mr. E. L. (South Africa), b Dec 2, 1906
Daniell, Mr. J. (Camb. Univ. and Somerset), b Dec 12, 1878, d Jan 24, 1963
Daniels, D. M. (Camb. Univ.), b March 29, 1942
D'Arcy, Mr. J. W. (New Zealand), b April 23, 1936
Dare, R. (Hampshire), b Nov 26, 1921
Darling, Mr. J. (South Australia), b Nov 21, 1870, d Jan 2, 1946
Darling, Mr. L. S. (Victoria), b Aug 14, 1909
Darnley, 8th Earl of (Hon. Ivo Bligh), (Camb. Univ., Kent and President, M.C.C., 1900), b March 13, 1859, d April 10, 1927
Dartmouth, 7th Earl of (President, M.C.C., 1932), b Feb 22, 1881, d Feb 28, 1958
Darwall-Smith, Mr. R. F. H. (Oxford Univ. and Sussex), b July 11, 1914
Datta, Mr. P. B. (Camb. Univ.), b 1925
David, Mr. R. F. A. (Glamorgan), b June 19, 1907

Davidson, Mr. A. K. (New South Wales), b June 14, 1929
Davidson, Mr. K. R. (Yorkshire and Scotland), b Dec 24, 1905, d Dec 25, 1954
Davidson, Rev. W. W. (Oxford Univ. and Sussex), b March 20, 1920
Davies, Dai (Glamorgan), b Aug 26, 1896
Davies, D. A. (Glamorgan), b July 11, 1915
Davies, Emrys (Glamorgan), b June 27, 1904
Davies, Mr. E. Q. (South Africa), b Aug 26, 1909
Davies, Mr. G. A. (Manager Australia in England 1953), b March 19, 1895, d Nov 27, 1957
Davies, H. D. (Glamorgan), b July 23, 1932
Davies, H. G. (Glamorgan), b April 23, 1913
Davies, Mr. J. G. W. (Camb. Univ. and Kent), b Sept 10, 1911
Davies, T. E. (Worc.), b March 14, 1938
Davies, W. G. (Glamorgan), b July 3, 1936
Davis, E. (Northants), b March 8, 1922
Davis, F. J. (Oxford Univ. and Glamorgan), b March 23, 1939
Davis, P. (Northants), b May 24, 1915
Davis, P. (Kent), b April 4, 1922
Davis, R. (Glamorgan), b Jan 1, 1946
Davis, Mr. R. A. (Tasmania), b Oct 22 1892
Davis, W. E. (Surrey), b Nov 26, 1880
Davison, I. (Notts.), b Oct 4, 1937
Dawkes, G. (Leic. and Derbyshire), b July 19, 1920
Dawson, Mr. E. W. (Camb. Univ. and Leic.), b Feb 13, 1904
Dawson, G. (Hampshire), b Dec 9, 1916
Dawson, Mr. O. C. (South Africa), b Sept 1, 1919
Day, Mr. A. P. (Kent), b April 10, 1885
Day, Mr. H. L. V. (Bedfordshire and Hampshire), b Aug 12, 1898
Day, J. W. (Notts. and Lincolnshire), b Sept 16, 1882
Day, Mr. S. H. (Camb. Univ. and Kent), b Dec 29 1878, d Feb 20, 1950
Dean, H. (Lancashire and Cheshire), b Aug 13, 1885, d March 12, 1957
Dean, T. A. (Hampshire), b Nov 21, 1920
de Caires, Mr. C. (Joint Manager with T. Pierce West Indies in England 1957), b Nov 25, 1917
De Caires, Mr. F. I. (West Indies), b May 12, 1909
de Courcy, Mr. J. H. (New South Wales), b April 18, 1927
Deed, Mr. J. A. (Kent), b Sept 12, 1901
Deighton, Major J. H. G. (Lancashire), b April 5, 1920
Delisle, Mr. G. P. S. (Middlesex and Oxford Univ.), b Dec 25, 1934
de Lisle, Mr. J. A. F. (Leic.), b Sept 27, 1891, d Nov 4, 1961
Dempster, Mr. C. S. (New Zealand, Scotland, Leic. and War.), b Nov 15, 1903
Dench, C. E. (Notts.), b Sept 6, 1873, d June 30, 1958
Denness, M. H. (Scotland and Kent), b Dec 1, 1940
Dennett, George (Glouc.), b April 27, 1880, d Sept 14, 1937
Dennis, F. (Yorkshire and Cheshire), b June 11, 1907
Dennis, Mr. J. N. (Essex), b Jan 4, 1913
Denton, David (Yorkshire), b July 4, 1874, d Feb 17, 1950
Denton, J. (Yorkshire), b Feb 3, 1865, d July 19, 1946
Denton, Mr. J. S. (Northants), b Nov 2, 1890
Denton, Mr. W. H. (Northants), b Nov 2, 1890
De Saram, Mr. F. C. (Oxford Univ. and Hertfordshire), b Sept, 1912
Desai, R. B. (India), b June 20, 1939
de Trafford, C. E. (Lancashire and Leic.), b May 21, 1864, d Nov 12, 1951
Devereux, L. N. (Middlesex, Worc. and Glamorgan), b Oct 20, 1931
Devereux, R. J. (Worc.), b Dec 24, 1938
Dewdney, Mr. T. (West Indies), b Oct 23, 1933
Dewes, Mr. J. G. (Camb. Univ. and Middlesex), b Oct 11, 1926
De Winton, Mr. S. (Glouc.), b Sept 5, 1869
Dews, G. (Worc.), b June 5, 1921
Dexter, Mr. E. R. (Camb. Univ. and Sussex), b May 15, 1935
Deyes, G. (Yorkshire and Staffordshire), b Feb 11, 1879
de Zoete, Mr. H. W. (Camb. Univ. and Essex), b Feb 14, 1877, d March 26, 1957
Dick, A. E. (New Zealand), b Oct 10, 1936
Dickinson, Mr. D. C. (Camb. Univ.), b Dec 11, 1929
Dickinson, Mr. P. J. (Camb. Univ. and Surrey), b Aug 18, 1919
Dilley, M. R. (Northants), b March 28, 1939

Dillon, Mr. E. W. (Oxford Univ. and Kent), b Feb 15, 1881, d April 25, 1941
Diment, Mr. R. A. (Glouc. and Leic.), b Feb 9, 1927
Dines, W. J. (Essex), b Sept 14, 1916
Dipper, A. E. (Glouc.), b Nov 9, 1887, d Nov 9, 1945
Divecha, R. V. (Oxford Univ., India and Northants), b Oct 18, 1927
Dixon, A. L. (Kent), b Nov 27, 1933
Dixon, Mr. E. J. H. (Oxford Univ. and Northants), b Sept 22, 1915, d April 20, 1941
Dixon, Mr. J. A. (Notts.), b May 27, 1861, d June 8, 1931
Dixon, Mr. J. G. (Essex), b Sept 3, 1895, d Nov 19, 1954
Docker, Mr. C. T. (Australian Imperial Forces Team), b March 3, 1884
Dodd, W. T. F. (Hampshire), b March 8, 1909
Dodds, T. C. (Essex), b May 29, 1919
Doggart, Mr. A. G. (Camb. Univ., Durham and Middlesex), b June 2, 1897, d June 7, 1963
Doggart, Mr. G. H. G. (Camb. Univ. and Sussex), b July 18, 1925
d'Oliveira, B. L. (Worc.), b Oct 4, 1934
Doll, Mr. M. H. C. (Hertfordshire and Middlesex), b April 5, 1888, d June 30, 1966
Dollery, H. E. (War.), b Oct 14, 1914
Dollery, K. R. (War.), b Dec 9, 1924
Dolling, Mr. C. E. (South Australia), b Sept 4, 1886, d June 11, 1936
Dolphin, A. (Yorkshire), b Dec 24, 1886, d Oct 24, 1942
Donnan, Mr. H. (New South Wales), b Nov 12, 1864, d Aug 13, 1956
Donnelly, Mr. M. P. (New Zealand, Oxford Univ., Middlesex and War.), b Oct 17, 1917
Dooland, B. (South Australia and Notts.), b Nov 1, 1923
Doughty, D. (Somerset), b Nov 9, 1938
Douglas, Col. A. P. (Surrey and Middlesex), b June 7, 1867, d Jan 24, 1953
Douglas, Mr. C. H. (Essex), b June 28, 1886, d Sept, 1954
Douglas, Mr. J. (Camb. Univ. and Middlesex), b Jan 8, 1870, d Feb 8, 1958
Douglas, Mr. J. W. H. T. (Essex), b Sept 3, 1882, d Dec 19, 1930
Douglas, Rev. R. N. (Camb. Univ., Surrey and Middlesex), b Nov 9, 1868, d Feb 27, 1957
Douglas, S. (Yorkshire), b April 4, 1903
Douglas-Pennant, Mr. S. (Camb. Univ.), b June 28, 1938
Dovey, R. R. (Kent and Dorset), b July 18, 1920
Dowding, Mr. A. L. (Oxford Univ.), b April 4, 1929
Dowling, G. T. (New Zealand), b March 4, 1937
Dowling, Mr. W. J. (Manager Australia in England, 1956), b Sept 23, 1904
Downes, Mr. K. D. (Camb. Univ.), b June 12, 1917
Drake, E. J. (Hampshire), b Aug 16, 1912
Druce, Mr. N. F. (Camb. Univ. and Surrey), b Jan 1, 1875, d Oct 27, 1954
Druce, Mr. W. G. (Camb. Univ.), b Sept 16, 1872, d Jan 8, 1963
Drybrough, Mr. C. D. (Oxford Univ. and Middlesex), b Aug 31, 1938
D'Souza, A. (Pakistan), b Jan 17, 1939
Ducat, A. (Surrey), b Feb 16, 1886, d July 23, 1942
Duckfield, R. (Glamorgan), b July 2, 1906
Duckworth, Mr. C. A. R. (South Africa), b March 22, 1933
Duckworth, G. (Lancashire), b May 9, 1901, d Jan 5, 1966
Duff, Mr. A R. (Oxford Univ. and Worc.), b Jan 12, 1938
Duleepsinhji, K. S. (Camb. Univ. and Sussex), b June 13, 1905, d Dec 5, 1959
Dumbrill, R. (South Africa), b Nov 19, 1938
Dunkley, M E. F. (Northants), b Feb 19, 1914
Dunning, Mr. J. A. (New Zealand), b Feb 6, 1903
Durnell, Mr. T. W. (War.), b June 17, 1901
Durose, A. J. (Cheshire and Northants), b Oct 10, 1944
Durston, F. J. (Middlesex), b July 11, 1894, d April 8, 1965
Dye, J. C. (Kent), b July 24, 1942
Dyer, A. W. (Oxford Univ.), b July 8, 1945
Dyer, Mr. D. V. (South Africa), b May 2, 1914
Dyson, A. H. (Glamorgan), b July 10, 1905
Dyson, Mr. E. M. (Oxford Univ.), b Oct 21, 1935
Dyson, J. (Lancashire), b July 8, 1934
Dyson, Mr. J. H. (Oxford Univ.), b Sept 26, 1913
Eagar, Mr. E. D. R. (Oxford Univ., Glouc. and Hants), b Dec 8, 1917

Eagar, Mr. M. A. (Oxford Univ., Glouc. and Ireland), b March 20, 1934
Eaglestone J. T. (Middlesex and Glamorgan), b July 24, 1923
Ealham, A. (Kent), b Aug 30, 1944
Earle, Mr. G. F. (Surrey and Somerset), b Aug 24, 1891
East, R. (Essex), b June 20, 1947
Eastman, G. (Essex), b April 7, 1903
Eastman, L. C. (Essex), b June 3, 1897, d April 17, 1941
Eaton, J. (Sussex), b June 19, 1904
Ebbisham, First Baron (George Rowland Blades) (Surrey Club, captain Lords and Commons), b April 15, 1868, d May 24, 1953
Ebeling, Mr. H. I. (Victoria), b Jan 1, 1905
Eckersley, Lt. P. T. (Lancashire), b July 2, 1904, d Aug 13, 1940
Ede, Mr. E. M. C. (Hampshire), b April 24, 1881
Edmeades, B. (Essex), b Sept 17, 1941
Edmonds, R. B. (War.), b March 2, 1941
Edrich, B. R. (Kent, Glam. and Oxfordshire), b Aug 18, 1922
Edrich, E. H. (Norfolk and Lancashire), b March 27, 1914
Edrich, G. A. (Norfolk and Lancashire), b July 13, 1918
Edrich, J. H. (Norfolk and Surrey), b June 21, 1937
Edrich, Mr. W. J. (Norfolk and Middlesex), b March 26, 1916
Edwards, F. (Surrey and Buckinghamshire), b May 23, 1885
Edwards, M. J. (Surrey), b March 1, 1940
Eele, P. J. (Somerset), b Jan 27, 1935
Eggar, Mr. J. D. (Oxford Univ., Derbyshire and Hampshire), b Dec 1, 1916
Eglington, Mr. R. (Surrey), b April 1, 1908
Elgood, Mr. B. C. (Camb. Univ. and Berkshire), b March 10, 1922
Elliott, C. S. (Derbyshire), b April 24, 1912
Elliott, H. (Derbyshire), b Nov 2, 1895
Ellis, H. (Northants), b March 13, 1885
Ellis, Mr. J. L. (Victoria), b May 9, 1891
Elviss, R. W. (Oxford Univ.), b July 19, 1945
Emery, Mr. S. H. (New South Wales), b Oct 16, 1886
Emmett, G. M. (Glouc.), b Dec 2, 1912
Endean, Mr. W. R. (South Africa), b May 31, 1924
English, Mr. E. A. (Hampshire), b Jan 1, 1864, d Sept 8, 1966
Enthoven, Mr. H. J. (Camb. Univ. and Middlesex), b June 4, 1903
Entwistle, R. (Lancashire), b Oct 20, 1941
Estcourt, Mr. N. S. D. (Camb. Univ.), b Jan 7, 1929
Etheridge, R. J. (Glouc.), b March 25, 1934
Evans, Mr. A. J. (Oxford Univ., Hampshire and Kent), b May 1, 1889, d Sept 18, 1960
Evans, D. L. (Glamorgan), b July 27, 1933
Evans, Col. D. MacN. (Hampshire), b Dec 12, 1886
Evans, Mr. E. N. (Oxford Univ.), b Dec 7, 1911, d Feb 12, 1964
Evans, Mr. G. (Oxford Univ., Leic. and Glamorgan), b Aug 13, 1915
Evans, Mr. J. (Hampshire), b July 14, 1891
Evans, J. B. (Glamorgan and Lincs.), b Nov 9, 1936
Evans, Mr R. G. (Camb. Univ.), b Aug 20, 1899
Evans, T. G. (Kent), b Aug 18, 1920
Evans, V. J. (Essex), b March 4, 1912
Evans, Mr. W. T. (Queensland), b April 9, 1876
Eve, Mr. S. C. (Essex), b Dec 8, 1925
Everett, Mr. S. C. (New South Wales), b June 17, 1901
Evers, Mr. H. A. (New South Wales. and West Australia), b Feb 28, 1876
Evers, Mr. R. D. M. (Worc.), b Aug 11, 1913
Every, T. (Glamorgan), b Dec 19, 1909
Eyre, J. R. (Derbyshire), b June 13, 1944
Eyre, T. J. P. (Derbyshire), b Oct 17, 1939
Fabian, Mr. A. H. (Camb. Univ.), b March 20, 1909
Fagg, A. E. (Kent), b June 18, 1915
Fairbairn, Mr. A. (Middlesex), b Jan 25, 1923
Fairbairn, Capt. G. A. (Camb. Univ. and Middlesex), b June 26, 1892
Fairfax, Mr. A. G. (New South Wales), b June 16, 1906, d May 17, 1955
Fairservice, C. (Kent and Middlesex), b Aug 21, 1909
Fairservice, W. J. (Kent and Northumberland), b May 16, 1881
Falcon, Mr. M. (Camb. Univ. and Norfolk), b July 21, 1888

Fallows, Mr. J. A. (Lancashire), b July 25, 1907
Fane, Mr. F. L. (Oxford Univ. and Essex), b April 27, 1875, d Nov 27, 1960
Fantham, W. E. (War.), b May 14, 1918
Farnes, P/O K. (Camb. Univ. and Essex), b July 8, 1911, d Oct 20, 1941
Farquhar, Mr. J. F. (Queensland), b Jan 1, 1887
Farrimond, W. (Lancashire), b May 23, 1903
Fasken, Mr. D. K. (Oxford Univ.), b March 23, 1932
Faulkner, Mr. G. A. (Transvaal), b Dec. 17, 1881, d Sept 10, 1930
Fazal Mahmood (Pakistan), b Feb 18, 1927
Fearnley, C. D. (Wor.), b April 12, 1940
Fellows-Smith, Mr. J. P. (Oxford Univ., Northants and South Africa), b Feb 3, 1932
Felton, Mr. R. (Middlesex), b Dec 27, 1909
Fender, Mr. P. G. H. (Sussex and Surrey), b Aug 22, 1892
Fenley, S. (Surrey and Hampshire), b Jan 4, 1896
Fereday, J. (Worc. and Staffordshire), b Nov 24, 1875
Ferguson, Mr. V. (Hampshire), b Jan 10, 1866, d Feb 23, 1956
Fernandes, Mr. M. P. (West Indies), b Aug 12, 1897
Fernie, Mr. A. E. (Camb. Univ. and Staffordshire), b April 9, 1877, d July 24, 1959
Fida Hussain (Manager Pakistan in England, 1954), b Dec 4, 1908
Fiddian-Green, Mr. C. A. (Camb. Univ., War. and Worc.), b Dec 22, 1898
Fiddling, K. (Yorkshire and Northants), b Oct 13, 1917
Field, F. E. (War.), b Sept 23, 1875, d Aug 25, 1934
Fielder, Arthur (Kent), b July 19, 1878, d Aug 30, 1949
Fillary, E. W. J. (Oxford Univ. and Kent), b April 14, 1944
Findlay, Mr. A. P. (Tasmania), b March 17, 1892
Findlay, Mr. W. (Oxford Univ. and Lancashire; Sec. Surrey C.C.C.; Sec. M.C.C., 1926 to 1936), b June 22, 1880, d June 19, 1953
Fingleton, Mr. J. H. (New South Wales), b April 28, 1908
Firth, J. (Yorkshire and Leic.), b June 27, 1918
Fisher, H. (Yorkshire), b Aug 3, 1903
Fishlock L. B. (Surrey), b Jan 2, 1907
Fitzroy-Newdegate, Cdr. Hon. J. M. (Northants), b March 20, 1897
Flamson, W. H. (Leic.), b Aug 12, 1905, d Jan 9, 1945
Flavell, J. A. (Worc.), b May 15, 1929
Fleetwood-Smith, Mr. L. O'B. (Victoria), b March 30, 1910
Fletcher, B. E. (War.), b March 7, 1935
Fletcher, D. G. W. (Surrey), b July 6, 1924
Fletcher, K. (Essex), b May 20, 1944
Flint, B. (Notts.), b Jan 12, 1893
Flint, W. A. (Notts.), b March 21, 1890, d Feb 5, 1955
Flood, R. (Hampshire), b Nov 20, 1935
Foenander, Mr. S. P. (Colombo), b April 11, 1883
Foord, C. W. (Yorkshire), b June 11, 1924
Forbes, C. (Notts.), b Aug 9, 1936
Ford, Mr. A. F. J. (Camb. Univ. and Middlesex), b Sept 12, 1858, d May 20, 1931
Ford, Mr. F. G. J. (Camb. Univ. and Middlesex), b Dec 14, 1866, d Feb 7, 1940
Ford, Mr. F. W. J. (Repton), b Oct 14, 1854, d Sept 11, 1920
Ford, Mr. H. J. (Repton), b Feb 5, 1860, d Nov 19, 1941
Ford, Very Rev. L. G. B. J. (Repton), b Sept 3, 1865, d March 27, 1932
Ford, Mr. N. M. (Oxford Univ., Derbyshire and Middlesex), b Nov 18, 1906
Ford, Mr. R. (Glouc.), b March 3, 1907
Ford, Mr. W. A. J. (Repton), b March 20, 1861, d Aug 21, 1938
Foreman, D. J. (Sussex), b Feb 1, 1933
Foster, Mr. B. S. (Middlesex and Worc.), b Feb 12, 1882, d Sept 28, 1959
Foster, Mr. D. G. (War.), b March 19, 1907
Foster, Mr. F. R. (War.), b Jan 31, 1889, d May 3, 1958
Foster, Mr. G. N. (Oxford Univ., Worc. and Kent), b Oct 16, 1884
Foster, Mr. H. K. (Oxford Univ. and Worc.), b Oct 30, 1873, d June 23, 1950
Foster, Mr. M. K. (Worc.), b Jan 1, 1889, d Dec 3, 1940
Foster, Mr. N. J. A. (Worc.), b Sept 28, 1890
Foster, Mr. N. K. (Queensland), b Jan 19, 1878
Foster, Mr. P. G. (Kent), b Oct 9, 1916

Foster, Mr. R. E. (Oxford Univ. and Worc.), b April 16, 1878, d May 13, 1914
Foster, Major W. L. (Worc.), b Dec 2, 1874, d March 22, 1958
Fowke, Major G. H. S. (Leic.), b Oct 14, 1880, d June 24, 1946
Fowler, A. J. B. (Middlesex), b April 1, 1891
Fox, J. (War. and Worc.), b Sept 7, 1904, d Nov 15, 1961
Fox, J. G. (War.), b July 22, 1929
Fox, W. V. (Worc.), b Jan 8, 1898, d Feb 18, 1949
Foy, F. G. (Kent), b April 11, 1915
Foy, Mr. P. A. (Somerset and Argentine), b Oct 16, 1891, d Feb 12, 1957
Frames, Mr. A. S. (Manager South Africa team in England, 1947), b Jan 7, 1891
Francis, G. N. (West Indies), b Dec 7, 1897, d Jan, 1942
Francis, H. H. (Glouc. and South Africa), d Jan 7, 1936, aged 65
Francis, Mr. T. E. S. (Camb. Univ. and Somerset), b Nov 21, 1902
Franklin, Mr. H. W. F. (Oxford Univ., Surrey and Essex), b June 30, 1901
Franklin, Mr. W. B. (Camb. Univ. and Buckinghamshire), b Aug 16, 1891
Fraser, Mr. J. N. (Oxford Univ.), b Aug 6, 1890
Fraser, Mr. T. W. (Camb. Univ.), b June 26, 1912
Freeman, A. P. (Kent), b May 17, 1888, d Jan 28, 1965
Freeman, E. C. (Essex), b Dec 7, 1860, d Oct 16, 1939
Freeman, E. J. (Essex and Dorset), b Oct 16, 1880, d Feb 22, 1964
Freeman, J. R. (Essex), b Sept 3, 1883, d Aug 8, 1958
Fry, Mr. C. A. (Oxford Univ., Hampshire and Northants), b Jan 14, 1940
Fry, Mr. C. B. (Oxford Univ., Surrey, Sussex and Hampshire), b in Surrey, April 25, 1872, d Sept 7, 1956
Fry, Mr. K. R. B. (Camb. Univ. and Sussex), b March 15, 1883, d June 21, 1949
Fry, Mr. Stephen (Hampshire), b May 23, 1900
Fuller, Mr. E. R. H. (South Africa), b Aug 2, 1931
Fullerton, Mr. G. M. (South Africa), b Dec 8, 1922
Fynn, Mr. C. G. (Hampshire), b April 24, 1898

Gaekwad, Mr. D. K. (India), b Oct 27, 1928
Gaekwad, Mr. H. G. (India), b Aug 29, 1928
Gale, R. A. (Middlesex), b Dec 10, 1933
Gallichan, Mr. N. (New Zealand), b June 3, 1906
Gamble, F. C. (Surrey and Devon), b May 29, 1906
Gamsy, D. (South Africa), b April 17, 1940
Ganteaume, Mr. A. G. (West Indies), b Jan 22, 1921
Gardner, F. C. (War.), b June 4, 1922
Gardner, L. R. (Leic.), b Feb 23, 1934
Garland-Wells, Mr. H. M. (Oxford Univ. and Surrey), b Nov 14, 1907
Garlick, R. G. (Lancashire and Northants), b April 11, 1917
Garnsey, Mr. G. L. (New South Wales), b Feb 10, 1881, d April 18, 1951
Garrett, Mr. T. W. (New South Wales), b July 26, 1858, d Aug 6, 1943
Garrett, Mr. W. T. (Essex), b Jan 9, 1877, d Feb 17, 1953
Garthwaite, Mr. P. F. (Oxford Univ.), b Oct 22, 1909
Gaskin, B. (Manager West Indies in England 1963), b March 21, 1908
Gauld, Dr. G. O. (Notts.), b June 21, 1873, d June 16, 1950
Gaunt, Mr. R. A. (Victoria), b Feb 26, 1934
Geary, A. C. T. (Surrey), b Sept 11, 1900
Geary, G. (Leic.), b July 9, 1893
Gehrs, Mr. D. R. A. (South Australia), b Nov 29, 1880, d June 1953
Gentry, Mr. J. S. B. (Hampshire, Surrey and Essex), b Oct 4, 1899
Gerrard, Major R. A. (Somerset), b Jan 18, 1912, d Jan 22, 1943
Ghazali, M. E. Z. (Pakistan), b June 15, 1924
Ghorpade, J. H. (India), b Oct 2, 1930
Ghulam Ahmed (India), b July 4, 1922
Ghulam Mahomed (India), b July 12, 1898, d July 21, 1966
Gibb, P. A. (Camb. U., Scotland, Yorks. and Essex), b July 11, 1913
Gibbons, H. H. I. H. (Worc.), b Oct 10, 1904
Gibbs, L. R. (West Indies), b Sept 29, 1934
Gibbs, P. J. K. (Oxford Univ. and Derby.), b Aug 17, 1944
Gibson, Mr. C. H. (Camb. Univ., Sussex and Argentine), b Aug 23, 1900
Gibson, D. (Surrey), b May 1, 1936

Gibson, Mr. I. (Oxford Univ. and Derbyshire), b Aug 15, 1936, d May 3, 1963
Gibson, Sir K. L. (Essex), b May 11, 1888
Giffen, Mr. George (South Australia), b March 27, 1859, d Nov 29, 1927
Giffen, Mr. Walter F. (South Australia), b Sept 10, 1863, d June 29, 1949
Gifford, N. (Worc.), b March 30, 1940
Gilbert, Mr. H. A. (Monmouthshire, Oxford Univ., Worc. and Radnorshire), b June 2, 1886, d July 19, 1960
Gilchrist, Mr. R. (West Indies), b June 28, 1934
Giles, R. J. (Notts), b Oct 17, 1919
Gill, A. (Notts.), b Aug 5, 1940
Gillespie, Mr. D. W. (Camb. Univ.), b April 26, 1917
Gillhouley, K. (Yorkshire and Notts.), b Aug 8, 1934
Gilliat, Mr. I. A. W. (Oxford Univ.), b Jan 8, 1903
Gilliat, R. M. C. (Oxford Univ. and Hants), b May 20, 1944
Gilligan, Mr. A. E. R. (Camb. Univ., Surrey and Sussex), b Dec 23, 1894
Gilligan, Mr. A. H. H. (Sussex), b June 29, 1896
Gilligan, Mr. F. W. (Oxford Univ. and Essex), b Sept 20, 1893, d May 4, 1960
Gillingham, Canon F. H. (Essex), b Sept 6, 1875, d April 1, 1953
Gilman, Mr. J (Camb. Univ., Middlesex and Northumberland), b March 17, 1879
Gimblett, H. (Somerset), b Oct 19, 1914
Gladwin, C. (Derbyshire), b April 3, 1917
Glover, Mr. E. R. K. (Glamorgan), b July 19, 1911
Goatly, E. G. (Surrey), b Dec 3, 1882, d Feb 12, 1958
Godambe, S. R. (India), b March 1, 1899
Goddard, Mr. J. D. (West Indies), b April 21, 1919
Goddard, Mr. T. L. (South Africa), b Aug. 1, 1931
Goddard, T. W. (Glouc.), b Oct 1, 1900, d May 22, 1966
Godsell, Mr. R T. (Camb. Univ. and Glouc.), b Jan 9, 1880, d April 11, 1954
Goldstein, F. S. (Oxford Univ), b Oct 14, 1944
Gomez, Mr. G. E. (West Indies), b Oct 10, 1919
Gooder, L. (Surrey), b Feb 11, 1876
Goodfellow, Mr. A. (Camb. Univ.), b Jan 8, 1940
Goodway, Mr. C. C. (Staffordshire and War.), b July 10, 1909
Goodwin, Mr. H. S. (Glouc.), b Sept 30, 1870, d Nov 13, 1955
Goodwin, J. (Leic.), b Jan 22, 1929
Goodwin, K. (Lancashire), b June 25, 1938
Goonesena, Mr. G. (Ceylon, Notts. and Camb. Univ.), b Feb 16, 1931
Gopalan, M. J. (India), b June 6, 1909
Gopinath, Mr. C. D. (India), b March 1, 1930
Gordon, Sir Home, 12th Bart. (Author of "Cricket Form at a Glance", etc.), b Sept 30, 1871, d Sept 9, 1956
Gordon, Mr. N. (South Africa), b Aug 6, 1911
Gorell-Barnes, Mr. R., 3rd Lord Gorell (Oxford Univ. and Suffolk), b April 16, 1884, d May 2, 1963
Gothard, Mr. E. J. (Derbyshire), b Oct. 1, 1904
Gouldsworthy, Mr. W. R. (Glouc.), b May 20, 1892
Gover, A. R. (Surrey), b Feb 29, 1908
Grace, Dr. Alfred, b May 17, 1840, d May 24, 1916
Grace, Dr. Alfred H. (Glouc.), b March 10, 1866, d Sept 16, 1929
Grace, Mr. C. B. (Clifton), b March 1882, d June 6, 1938
Grace, Dr. E. M. (Glouc.), b Nov 28, 1841, d May 20, 1911
Grace, Dr. Edgar M. (M.C.C.), son of E. M. Grace, b Oct 6, 1886
Grace, Mr. G. F. (Glouc.), b Dec 13, 1850, d Sept 22, 1880
Grace, Dr. Henry (Glouc.), b Jan 31, 1833, d Nov 15, 1895
Grace, Dr. H. M. (Father of W. G., E. M., G. F.), b Feb 21, 1808, d Dec 23, 1871
Grace, Mrs. H. M. (Mother of W. G., E. M., G. F.), b July 18, 1812, d July 25, 1884
Grace, Dr. W. G. (Glouc.), b July 18, 1848, d Oct 23, 1915
Grace, Mr. W. G., jun. (Camb. Univ. and Glouc.), b July 6, 1874, d March 2, 1905
Graham, H. C. (Leic.), b May 31, 1914
Grant, Mr. G. C. (West Indies and Camb. Univ.), b May 9, 1907
Grant, Mr. R. S. (West Indies and Camb. Univ.), b Dec 15, 1909

Graveney, J. K. (Glouc.), b Dec 16, 1924
Graveney, T. W. (Glouc. and Worc.), b June 16, 1927
Graves, P. J. (Sussex), b May 19, 1946
Gray, Mr. C. D. (Middlesex), b April 26, 1895
Gray, J. R. (Hampshire), b May 19, 1926
Gray, L. H. (Middlesex), b Dec 16, 1915
Greasley, D. G. (Northants), b Jan 20, 1926
Green, Mr. D. J. (Derbyshire and Camb. Univ.), b Dec 18, 1935
Green, Mr. D. M. (Oxford Univ. and Lancashire), b Nov 10, 1939
Green, Col. Leonard (Lancashire), b Feb 1, 1890, d March 2, 1963
Green, Brig. M. A. (Glouc. and Essex and Manager M.C.C. Team South Africa, 1948–49, Australia, 1950–51), b Oct 3, 1891
Greenhalgh, E. (Lancashire), b May 18, 1910
Greenhough, T. (Lancashire), b Nov 9, 1931
Greensmith, W. T. (Essex), b Aug 16, 1930
Greenstock, Mr. J. W. (Oxford Univ. and Worc.), b May 15, 1905
Greensword, S. (Leic.), b Sept 6, 1943
Greenwood, Mr. F. E. (Yorkshire), b Sept 28, 1905, d July 30, 1963
Greenwood, H. W. (Sussex and Northants), b Sept 4, 1909
Greenwood, P. (Lancashire), b Sept 11, 1924
Greetham, C. (Somerset), b Aug 28, 1936
Gregory, Mr. G. R. (Derbyshire), b Aug 22, 1878, d Nov 28, 1958
Gregory, Mr. J. M. (New South Wales), b Aug 14, 1895
Gregory, R. J. (Surrey), b Aug 26, 1902
Gregory, Mr. S. E. (New South Wales), b April 14, 1870, d Aug 1, 1929
Gregson, W. R. (Lancashire), b Aug 5, 1878, d 1963
Greig, Canon J. G., formerly Colonel (Hampshire), b Oct 24, 1871, d May 24, 1958
Greswell, Mr. E. A. (Somerset), b June 6, 1885, d Jan 15, 1962
Greswell, Mr. W. T. (Somerset), b Oct 15, 1889
Grierson, Mr. H. (Bedfordshire and Camb. Univ.), b Aug 26, 1891
Grieves, K. (New South Wales and Lancashire), b Aug 27, 1925
Grieveson, Mr. R. E. (South Africa), b Aug. 24, 1909
Griffin, Mr. G (South Africa), b June 12, 1939
Griffith, C. C. (West Indies), b Dec 14, 1938
Griffith, Mr. H. C. (West Indies), b Dec 1, 1893
Griffith, M. G. (Camb. Univ. and Sussex), b Nov 25, 1943
Griffith, Mr. S. C. (Camb. Univ., Surrey and Sussex, Sec. M.C.C., 1962), b June 16, 1914
Griffiths, Mr. C. (Essex), b Dec 9, 1930
Griffiths, J. V. C. (Glouc.), b Jan 19, 1931
Griffiths, S. S. (War.), b July 11, 1930
Griffiths, Mr. W. H. (Camb. Univ. and Glamorgan), b Sept 26, 1923
Grimmett, Mr. C. V. (Victoria and South Australia), b Dec 25, 1892
Grimshaw, N. (Northants), b May 5, 1912
Grimshaw, V. (Worc.), b April 15, 1916
Grimston, Lt-Col. G. S. (Sussex), b April 2, 1905
Grinter, Mr. T. G. (Essex), b Dec 12, 1888, d April 21, 1966
Gross, Mr. F. A (Hampshire), b Sept 17, 1902
Grout, Mr. A. T. W. (Queensland), b March 30, 1927
Grove, C. W. (War. and Worc.), b Dec 16, 1912
Grover, Mr. J. N. (Oxford Univ. and Northumberland), b Oct 15, 1915
Groves, M. G. M. (Oxford Univ. and Somerset), b Jan 14, 1943
Guest, M. R. J. (Oxford Univ.), b Nov 18, 1943
Guise, Mr. J. D. (India and M.C.C.), b Oct 31, 1872, d July 3, 1953
Guise, Mr. J. L. (Oxford Univ. and Middlesex), b Nov 25, 1903
Gunasekara, Dr. C. H. (Middlesex and Ceylon), b July 27, 1894
Gunn, G. (Notts.), b June 13, 1879, d June 28, 1958
Gunn, G. V. (Notts.), b June 21, 1905, d Oct 14, 1957
Gunn, J. (Notts.), b July 19, 1876, d Aug. 21, 1963
Gunn, T. (Sussex), b Sept 27, 1935
Gunn, W. (Notts.), b Dec 4, 1858, d Jan 29, 1921
Gupte, S. P. (India), b Dec 11, 1929
Hadingham, Mr. A. W. G. (Camb. Univ. and Surrey), b March 1, 1913
Hadlee, Mr. W. A. (New Zealand), b June 4, 1915
Hafeez, A. (India) (now A. H. Kardar), b Jan 17, 1925

Haig, Mr. N. E. (Middlesex), b Dec 12, 1887, d Oct 27, 1966
Haigh, Schofield (Yorkshire), b March 19, 1871, d Feb 27, 1921
Haigh Smith, Mr. H. A. (Hampshire), b Oct 21, 1884, d Oct 28, 1955
Haines, Mr. A. H. (Glouc.), b Aug 27, 1877, d May 30, 1935
Haines, Mr. C. V. G. (Glamorgan), b Jan 17, 1906, d Jan 28, 1965
Hake, Mr. H. D. (Hampshire), b Nov 8, 1894
Hale, I. E. (Sussex and Glouc.), b 1922
Hale, W. H. (Somerset and Glouc.), b March 6, 1870, d Aug 12, 1956
Halfyard, D. J. (Surrey and Kent), b April 3, 1931
Hall, A. E. (South Africa and Lancashire), b Jan 23, 1896, d Jan 1, 1964
Hall, C. H. (Yorkshire), b April 5, 1906
Hall, G. (Somerset), b June 1, 1941
Hall, I. W. (Derbyshire), b Dec 27, 1939
Hall, Mr. J. K. (Surrey), b July 29, 1934
Hall, Mr. P. J. (Camb. Univ.), b Dec 4, 1927
Hall, Mr. T. A. (Derbyshire and Somerset), b Aug 19, 1930
Hall, Mr. W. W. (West Indies), b Sept 12, 1937
Hallam A. W. (Lancashire, Notts. and Leic.), b Nov 12, 1872, d 1940
Hallam, M. R. (Leic.), b Sept 10, 1931
Hallam, T. H. (Derbyshire), b April 12, 1881, d Nov 24, 1958
Halliday, H. (Yorkshire) b Feb 9, 1920
Halliday, Mr. J. G. (Oxford Univ. and Oxfordshire), b July 4, 1915, d Dec 3, 1945
Hallows, C. (Lancashire), b April 4, 1895
Hambling, Mr. M. L. (Somerset), b Dec 6, 1893, d Aug, 1960
Hamence, Mr. R. A. (South Australia), b Nov 25, 1915
Hamer, A. (Yorkshire and Derbyshire), b Dec 8, 1916
Hamilton, Col. L. A. H. (Kent), b Dec 23, 1862, d March 14, 1957
Hammond, H. E. (Sussex), b Nov 7, 1907
Hammond, Mr. W. R. (Glouc.), b in Kent, June 19, 1903, d July 2, 1965
Hampden, 3rd Visct. (President, M.C.C., 1926), b Jan 29, 1869, d Sept 4, 1958
Hampshire, J. H. (Yorkshire), b Feb 10, 1941
Hampton, Mr. W. M. (War. and Worc.), b Jan 20, 1903, d April 7, 1964
Handford, J. (Derbyshire), b Feb 1, 1890
Handley, G. (Notts.), b Jan 10, 1876
Hands, Mr. P. A. M. (Oxford Authentics and South Africa), b March 18, 1890, d April 27, 1951
Hands, Mr. W. C. (War.), b Dec 20, 1886
Hanif, Mohammad (Pakistan), b Dec 21, 1934
Harbinson, Mr. W. K. (Camb. Univ.), b July 11, 1906
Harbord, Mr. W. E. (Yorkshire), b Dec 15, 1908
Harding, N. W. (Kent), b March 19, 1916, d Sept 25, 1947
Hardinge, H. T. W. (Kent), b Feb 25, 1886, d May 8, 1965
Hardisty, C. H. (Yorkshire and Northumberland), b Dec 10, 1885
Hardstaff, J. (Notts.), b Nov 9, 1882, d April 2, 1947
Hardstaff, J., jun. (Notts.), b July 3, 1911
Hardstaff, R. G. (Notts.), b Jan 12, 1863, d April 18, 1932
Harfield, L. (Hampshire), b Aug 16, 1905
Harford, Mr. N. S. (New Zealand), b Aug 30, 1930
Hargreaves, H. S. (Yorkshire), b March 22, 1913
Harkness, D. (Worc.), b Feb 13, 1931
Harman, R. (Surrey), b Dec 28, 1941
Harris, 4th Lord (Oxford Univ. and Kent, President, M.C.C., 1895), b West Indies, Feb 3, 1851, d March 24, 1932
Harris, A. (Glamorgan), b Jan 31, 1936
Harris, C. B. (Notts.), b Dec 6, 1908, d Aug 8, 1954
Harris, C. R. (Oxford Univ.), b Oct 16, 1942
Harris, Mr. G. W. (South Australia), b Dec 11, 1898
Harris, M. J. (Middlesex) b May 25, 1944
Harris, Mr. T. A. (South Africa), b Aug 27, 1916
Harrison, Mr. C. S. (Wor.), b Nov 11, 1915
Harrison, Mr. E. W. (Tasmania), b July 21, 1874
Harrison, H. S. (Surrey), b April 12, 1883
Harrison, L. (Hampshire), b June 8, 1922

Harrison, Mr. W. P. (Kent, Camb. Univ. and Middlesex), b Nov 13, 1885, d Sept 7, 1964
Harron, D. G. (Leic.), b Sept 12, 1921
Hart, G. E. (Middlesex), b Jan 13, 1902
Hart, Mr. T. M. (Oxford Univ. and Scotland), b March 1, 1909
Hartigan, Mr. G. P. D. (South Africa), b Dec 30, 1884, d Jan 7, 1955
Hartigan, Mr. R. J. (New South Wales and Queensland), b Dec 12, 1879, d June 7, 1958
Hartkopf, Dr. A. E. V. (Victoria), b Dec 28, 1889
Hartley, Col. J. C. (Oxford Univ. and Sussex), b Nov 15, 1874, d March 8, 1963
Harvey, J. F. (Derbyshire), b Sept 27, 1939
Harvey, J. R. W. (Camb. Univ.), b Feb 3, 1944
Harvey, P. F. (Notts.), b Jan 15, 1923
Harvey, Mr. R. L. (South Africa), b Sept 14, 1911
Harvey, Mr. R. N. (Victoria and New South Wales), b Oct 8, 1928
Haseeb Ahsan (Pakistan), b July 15, 1939
Hassett, Mr. A. L. (Victoria), b Aug 28, 1913
Hawke, 7th Lord (Camb. Univ. and Yorkshire, President, M.C.C., 1914–1918), b Aug 16, 1860, d Oct 10, 1938
Hawke, N. J. N. (Western Australia and South Australia), b Jan 27, 1939
Hawkins, D. G. (Glouc.), b May 18, 1935
Hawkwood, C. (Lancashire), b Nov 16, 1909, d May 10, 1960
Hawtin, Mr. A. P. R. (Northants), b Feb 1, 1883
Hay, Mr. Douglas (New Zealand), b Aug 31, 1876
Hayes, E. G. (Surrey and Leic.), b Nov 6, 1876, d Dec 2, 1953
Hayes, Mr. J. A (New Zealand), b Jan 11, 1927
Haynes, R. W. (Glouc.), b Aug 27, 1913
Hays, D. L. (Camb. U.), b Nov 5, 1944
Hayter, E. (Hampshire), b Sept 8, 1913
Hayward, T. W. (Surrey), b March 29, 1871, d July 19, 1939
Hayward, Mr. W. I. D. (Camb. Univ.), b April 15, 1930
Hazare, V. S. (India), b March 11, 1915
Hazell, H. L. (Somerset), b Sept 30, 1909
Hazlerigg, Lord, formerly Sir Arthur Grey, 13th Bart. (Leic.), b Nov 17, 1878, d May 25, 1949
Hazlerigg, Lord, 14th Bart., formerly the Hon. A. G. (Camb. Univ. and Leic.), b Feb 24, 1910
Headley, Mr. G. (West Indies), b May 30, 1909
Headley, R. G. A. (Worc.) b June 29, 1939
Heane, Mr. G. F. H. (Notts. and Lincolnshire), b Jan 2, 1904
Heap, J. S. (Lancashire), b Aug 12, 1883, d Jan 30, 1951
Hearn, P. (Kent), b Nov 18, 1925
Hearne, Alec (Kent), b July 22, 1863, d May 16, 1952
Hearne, Frank (Kent and South Africa), b Nov 23, 1858, d July 14, 1949
Hearne, G. (Bucks. and Middlesex), b May 15, 1829, d Dec 9, 1904
Hearne, Mr. G. A. L. (South Africa) b March 27, 1888
Hearne, George F. (Middlesex, Pavilion Clerk, Lord's), b Oct 18, 1851, d May 29, 1931
Hearne, George G. (Kent), b July 7 1856, d Feb 13, 1932
Hearne, Herbert (Kent), b March 15, 1862, d June 13, 1906
Hearne, J. T. (Middlesex), b May 3, 1867, d April 17, 1944
Hearne, J. W. (Middlesex), b Feb 11, 1891, d Sept 13, 1965
Hearne, Thomas (Buckinghamshire and Middlesex), b Sept 4, 1826, d May 13, 1900
Hearne, Thomas, jun. (Middlesex and Ground Superintendent at Lord's), b Dec 29, 1849, d Jan 29, 1910
Hearne, Walter (Kent), b Jan 15, 1864, d April 2, 1925
Hearne, Wm. (Buckinghamshire), b July 15, 1828, d July 17, 1908
Heath, Mr. A. B. (Hampshire), b Jan 19, 1865
Heath, D. M. W. (War.), b Dec 4, 1931
Heath, G. E. M. (Hampshire), b Feb 20, 1913
Heath, M. (Hampshire), b March 9, 1934
Hedges, B. (Glamorgan), b Nov 10, 1927
Hefferan, Mr. F. W. (Queensland), b May 25, 1901
Heine, Mr. P (South Africa), b June 28, 1929
Hemingway, Mr. W. M'G. (Camb. Univ. and Glouc.), b Nov 12, 1873
Henderson, Mr. D. (Oxford Univ.), b March 9, 1926
Henderson, Mr. M. (New Zealand), b Aug 2, 1895

Hendren, D. (Middlesex and Durham), b Sept 25, 1882, d May 30, 1962
Hendren, E. (Middlesex), b Feb 5, 1889, d Oct 4, 1962
Hendriks, J. L. (West Indies) b Dec 21, 1933
Hendry, Mr. H. L. (New South Wales and Victoria), b May 24, 1895
Henley, Mr. F. A. H. (Oxford Univ., Suffolk and Middlesex), b Feb 11, 1884, d June 26, 1963
Henley Welch, Mr. D. F. (Oxford Univ.), b July 21, 1923
Henson, W. (Notts.), b Dec 7, 1874
Herman, O. W. (Hampshire), b Sept 18, 1907
Herman, R. S. (Middlesex), b Nov 30, 1946
Hever, N. (Middlesex and Glamorgan), b Dec 17, 1924
Hewan, Mr. G. E. (Camb. Univ. and Berkshire), b Dec 23, 1916
Hewetson, Mr. E. P. (Oxford Univ. and War.), b May 27, 1902
Heygate, Mr. R. B. (Sussex), b May 13, 1883
Hibbert, W. J. (Lancashire), b July 11, 1874
Higgins, Mr. H. L. (Worc.), b Feb 24, 1894
Higgins, Mr. J. B. (Worc.), b Dec 31, 1885
Higgs, K. (Lancashire), b Jan 14, 1937
Higgs, Mr. K. A. (Sussex), b Oct 5, 1886, d Jan 21, 1959
Higson, Mr. T. A. (Derbyshire, Cheshire and Lancashire), b Nov 18, 1873, d Aug 3, 1949
Higson, Mr. T. A., jun. (Derbyshire and Lancashire), b March 25, 1911
Hilder, Mr. A. L. (Kent), b Oct 8, 1901
Hill, Mr. A. E. L. (Hampshire), b July 14, 1901
Hill, Mr. Clement (South Australia), b March 18, 1877, d Sept 5, 1945
Hill, Lt.-Col. D. V. (Worc.), b April 13, 1896
Hill, E. (Somerset), b July 9, 1923
Hill, G. (Hampshire), b April 15, 1913
Hill, G. H. (War.), b Sept 17, 1934
Hill, Mr. J. C. (Victoria), b June 25, 1923
Hill, Mr. J. E. (War.), b Sept 27, 1867, d Dec 2, 1963
Hill, M. (Notts. and Derby.), b Sept 14, 1935
Hill, Mr M. Ll. (Somerset and Glamorgan), b June 23, 1902, d Feb 28, 1948
Hill, N. (Notts.), b Aug 22, 1935
Hill, W. A. (War.), b April 27, 1910
Hiller, R. B (Oxford Univ.), b Oct 14, 1942
Hills, H. M. (Essex), b Sept 28, 1886
Hills, J. (Glamorgan), b Oct 14, 1897
Hill-Wood, Sir B. S. (Derbyshire), b Feb 5, 1900, d July 3, 1954
Hill-Wood, Mr. C. K. (Oxford Univ. and Derbyshire), b June 5, 1907
Hill-Wood, Mr. D. J. (Oxford Univ. and Derbyshire), b June 25, 1906
Hill-Wood, Sir S. H. (Derbyshire and Suffolk), b March 21, 1872, d Jan 4, 1949
Hill-Wood, Mr. W. W. (Camb. Univ. and Derbyshire), b Sept 8, 1901
Hilton, C. (Lancashire and Essex), b Sept 26, 1937
Hilton, J. (Lancashire and Somerset), b Dec 29, 1930
Hilton, M. J. (Lancashire), b Aug. 2, 1928
Hindlekar, D. D. (India), b Jan 1, 1909, d March 30, 1949
Hinds, Mr. S. A. (West Indies), b June 1, 1880
Hine-Haycock, Rev. T. R. (Oxford Univ. and Kent), b Dec 3, 1861, d Nov 2, 1953
Hipkin, A. B. (Essex and Scotland), b Aug 8, 1900, d Feb 11, 1957
Hirst, G. H. (Yorkshire), b Sept 7, 1871, d May 10, 1954
Hitch, J. W. (Surrey), b May 7, 1886, d July 7, 1965
Hitchcock, R. E. (Canterbury and War.), b Nov 28, 1929
Hoad, Mr. E. L. G. (West Indies), b Jan 29, 1896
Hobbs, Mr. J. A. D. (Oxford Univ.), b Nov 30, 1935
Hobbs, Sir J. B. (Cambridgeshire and Surrey), b Dec 16, 1882, d Dec 21, 1963
Hobbs, R. N. S. (Essex), b May 8, 1942
Hobson, Mr. B. S. (Camb. Univ.), b Nov 22, 1925
Hodgkinson, Mr. G. F. (Derbyshire), b Feb 19, 1914
Hodgkinson, Mr. G. W. (Somerset), b Feb 19, 1883, d Oct 6, 1960
Hodgson, G. (Lancashire), b April 16, 1904, d June 14, 1951
Hofmeyr, Mr. M. B. (Oxford Univ.), b Dec. 9, 1925
Holdsworth, Mr. R. L. (Oxford Univ., War. and Sussex), b Feb 25, 1899
Holdsworth, W. E. N. (Yorkshire), b Sept 17, 1928
Hole, Mr. G. B. (South Australia and New South Wales), b Jan 6, 1931

Holford, D. A. J. (West Indies), b April 16, 1940
Holland, F. C. (Surrey), b Feb 10, 1876, d Feb 5, 1957
Hollies, W. E. (War.), b June 5, 1912
Hollingdale, R. A. (Sussex and Scotland), b March 6, 1906
Hollins, Sir F. H., 3rd Bart. (Oxford Univ., Cumberland and Lancashire), b Oct 31, 1877, d Jan 31, 1963
Holloway, Mr. G. W. (Glouc.), b April 26, 1884
Holloway, Mr. N. J. (Camb. Univ. and Sussex), b Nov 11, 1889, d Aug 17, 1964
Holmes, Gr. Capt. A. J. (Sussex), b June 30, 1899, d May 21, 1950
Holmes, Mr. E. R. T. (Oxford Univ. and Surrey), b Aug 21, 1905, d Aug 16, 1960
Holmes, Percy (Yorkshire), b Nov 25, 1886
Holroyd, J. (Lancashire), b April 15, 1907
Holt, A. (Hampshire), b April 8, 1912
Home, Sir Alec Douglas (Middlesex), b July 2, 1903. President of M.C.C.
Hone, Mr. B. W. (South Australia, Oxford Univ. and Wiltshire), b July 1, 1907
Hooker, Mr. H. (New South Wales), b March 6, 1898
Hooker, R. W. (Middlesex), b Feb 22, 1935
Hooman, Mr. C. V. L. (Oxford Univ., Devon and Kent), b Oct 3, 1887
Hopkins, Mr. H. O. (Oxford Univ. and Worc.), b July 6, 1895
Hopkins, V. (Glouc.), b Jan 21, 1913
Hopley, Mr. F. J. V. (Camb. Univ. and Western Province), b Aug 27, 1883, d Aug 16, 1951
Hopwood, J. L. (Lancashire), b Oct 30, 1903
Hornby, Mr. A. H. (Lancashire), b July 29, 1877, d Sept 6, 1952
Hornby, Mr. A. N. (Harrow and Lancashire), b Feb 10, 1847, d Dec 17, 1925
Horner, N. F. (Yorkshire and War.), b May 10, 1926
Hornibrook, Mr. P. M. (Queensland), b July 27, 1899
Horrocks, W. J. (Lancashire), b June 18, 1905
Horsfall, R. (Essex and Glamorgan), b June 26, 1920
Horton, H. (Worc. and Hampshire), b April 18, 1924
Horton, J. (Worc.), b Aug 12, 1916
Horton, M. J. (Worc.), b April 21, 1934
Horwood, Mr. S. E. (Western Province), b July 22, 1877
Hosie, Mr. A. L. (Hampshire), b Aug 6, 1890, d June 11, 1957
Hossell, Mr. J. J., jun. (War.), b May 25, 1914
Hotchkin, Mr. N. S. (Camb. Univ., Lincolnshire and Middlesex), b Feb 4, 1914
Hough, Mr. G. de L (Kent), b May 14, 1894, d Sept 29, 1959
Houlton, G (Lancashire), b April 25, 1939
Hounsfield, Mr. T. D. (Derbyshire), b April 28, 1911
Howard, A. H. (Glamorgan), b Dec 11, 1910
Howard, Mr. B. J. (Lancashire), b May 21, 1926
Howard, J. (Leic.), b Nov 24, 1917
Howard, K. (Lancashire), b June 29, 1941
Howard, Mr. N. D. (Lancashire), b May 18, 1925
Howard, Major R. (Lancashire and Sec. Lancashire C.C.C.), b April 17, 1890
Howell, H. (War.), b Nov 29, 1890, d July 9, 1932
Howell, Mr. M. (Oxford Univ. and Surrey), b Sept 9, 1893
Howell, Mr. W. P. (New South Wales), b Dec 29, 1869, d July 14, 1940
Howitt, Mr. R. H. (Notts.), b July 21, 1864, d Jan 10, 1951
Howland, Mr. C. B. (Camb. Univ., Sussex and Kent), b Feb 6, 1936
Howorth, R. (Worc.), b April 26, 1909
Hubble, J. C. (Kent), b Feb 10, 1881, d Feb 26, 1965
Huddleston, W. (Lancashire), b Feb 27, 1875, d May 22, 1962
Hughes, Mr. D. W. (Glamorgan), b July 12, 1910
Hughes, G. (Glamorgan and Camb. Univ.), b March 26, 1941
Hughes, N. (Worc.), b Apr 6, 1929
Hughes, Mr. O. (Camb. Univ.), b July 7, 1889
Hughes, R. (Worc.), b Sept 30, 1926
Hughes-Hallett, Lt.-Col. N. M. (Derbyshire), b April 18, 1895
Huish, F. H. (Kent), b Nov 15, 1872, d March 16, 1957
Hulme, J. H. A. (Middlesex), b Aug 26, 1904
Human, Mr. J. H. (Camb. Univ., Berkshire and Middlesex), b Jan 13, 1912

Human, Capt. R. H. C. (Camb. Univ., Berkshire and Worc.), b May 11, 1909, d Nov 21, 1942
Hunt, F. (Kent and Worc.), b Sept 13, 1875
Hunt, G. (Somerset), b Sept 30, 1896, d Jan 22, 1959
Hunt, H (Somerset), b Nov 18, 1911
Hunt, Mr. R. G. (Camb. Univ. and Sussex), b April 13, 1915
Hunte, C. C. (West Indies), b May 9, 1932
Hunte, Mr. E. (West Indies), b Oct 3, 1905
Hunter, David (Yorkshire), b March 23, 1860, d Jan 11, 1927
Hunter, Mr. F. C. (Derbyshire and Cheshire), b Aug 23, 1886, d July 21, 1926
Hurd, Mr. A. (Camb. Univ. and Essex), b Sept 7, 1937
Hurst, Mr. C. S. (Oxford U. and Kent), b July 20, 1886, d Dec 18, 1963
Hurst, R. J. (Middlesex), b Dec 29, 1933
Hurwood, Mr. A. (Queensland), b June 17, 1902
Husain, Shafquat (India), b July 17, 1885
Hussain, Dilawar (India), b March 19, 1907
Hutcheon, Mr. J. S. (Queensland), b April 5, 1882, d June 18, 1957
Hutchings, Mr. K. L. (Kent), b Dec 7, 1882, d Sept 3, 1916
Hutchinson, J. M. (Derbyshire), b Nov 29, 1897
Hutton, Sir L. (Yorkshire), b June 23, 1916
Hutton, Mr. R. A. (Camb. Univ. and Yorkshire), b Sept 6, 1942
Hyder, Brig. R. G. (Manager Pakistan in England 1962), b April 30, 1920
Hylton, Mr. L. G. (West Indies), b March 29, 1905, d May 17, 1955
Hylton-Stewart, Mr B. D. (Somerset and Hertfordshire), b Nov 27, 1891
Hyman, Mr. W. (Somerset), b March 7, 1875, d Feb. 1959
Ibadulla, K. (War.), b Dec 20, 1935
Iddon, J. (Lancashire), b Jan 8, 1903, d April 17, 1946
Ijaz Butt (Pakistan), b March 10, 1938
Ikin, J. T. (Lancashire and Staffs.), b March 7, 1918
Ikram Elahi (Pakistan), b March 3, 1933
Illingworth, R. (Yorkshire), b June 8, 1932
Imlay, Mr. A. D. (Camb. Univ. and Glouc.), b Feb 14, 1885, d July 3, 1959
Imtiaz Ahmed (Pakistan), b Jan 5, 1928
Ingle, Mr. R. A. (Somerset), b Nov 5, 1903
Ingleby-Mackenzie, Mr. A. C. D. (Hampshire), b Sept 15, 1933
Ingram, Mr. E. A. (Middlesex and Ireland), b Aug 14, 1910
Inman, C. C. (Leic.), b Jan 29, 1936
Insole, Mr. D. J. (Camb. Univ. and Essex), b April 18, 1926
Intikhab Alam (Pakistan), b Dec 28, 1941
Ireland, Mr. J. F. (Camb. Univ. and Suffolk), b Aug 12, 1888
Iremonger, A. (Notts.), b June 15, 1884, d March 9, 1958
Iremonger, J. (Notts.), b March 5, 1876, d March 25, 1956
Irish, A. F. (Somerset), b Nov 23, 1918
Ironmonger, H. (Queensland and Victoria), b April 7, 1883
Irvine, Mr. L. G. (Camb. Univ. and Kent), b Jan 11, 1906
Isherwood, Capt. L. C. R. (Hampshire and Sussex), b April 13, 1891
Jackson, Mr. A. A. (New South Wales), b Sept 5, 1909, d Feb 16, 1933
Jackson, A. B. (Derbyshire), b Aug 28, 1933
Jackson, Mr. A. H. M. (Derbyshire), b Nov 9, 1899
Jackson, Rt. Hon. Sir F. S. (Camb. Univ. and Yorkshire; President, M.C.C., 1921), b Nov 21, 1870, d March 9, 1947
Jackson, Mr. G. R. (Derbyshire), b June 23, 1896, d Feb 21, 1966
Jackson, H. L. (Derbyshire), b April 5, 1921
Jackson, Mr. K. L. T. (Oxford Univ. and Berkshire), b Nov 17, 1913
Jackson, P. F. (Worc.), b May 11, 1911
Jackson, V. E. (Leic. and N.S.W.), b Oct 25, 1916, d Jan 28, 1965
Jacques, Mr. T. A. (Yorkshire), b Feb 19, 1905
Jagger, Mr. S. T. (Camb. Univ., Worc., Denbighshire and Sussex), b June 30, 1904, d May 30, 1964
Jahangir Khan, M. (India and Camb. Univ.), b Feb 1, 1910
Jai, L. P. (India), b April 1, 1902
Jaisimha, M. L. (India), b March 3, 1939
Jakeman, F. (Yorkshire and Northants), b Jan 10, 1921
Jakobson, Mr. T. R. (Oxford Univ.), b Dec 17, 1937
James, A. E. (Sussex), b Aug 7, 1924
James, K. C. (New Zealand and Northants), b March 12, 1905

James, Mr. R. M. (Camb. Univ.), b Oct 2, 1934
Jameson, J. A. (War.), b June 30, 1941
Jameson. Capt. T. O. (Hampshire), b April 4, 1892, d Feb 6, 1965
Jardine, Mr. D. R. (Oxford Univ. and Surrey), b Oct 23, 1900, d June 18, 1958
Jardine, Mr. M. R. (Oxford Univ. and Middlesex), b June 8, 1869, d Jan 16, 1947
Jarman, Mr. B. N. (South Australia), b Feb 17, 1936
Jarman, H. (Glouc.), b May 4, 1939
Jarrett, H. (War.), b Sept 23, 1907
Jarvis, T. W. (New Zealand), b July 29, 1944
Jaya Ram, Mr. B. (India and London County), b April 23, 1872
Jayasinghe, S. (Leic.), b Jan. 19, 1931
Jeacocke, Mr. A. (Surrey), b Dec 1, 1892, d Sept 25, 1961
Jeanes, Mr. W. H. (Secretary, Australian Board of Control), b May 19, 1883, d Sept 1, 1958
Jefferson, Mr. R. I. (Camb. Univ. and Surrey), b Aug 15, 1941
Jenkins, R. O. (Worc.), b Nov 24, 1918
Jenkins, Mr. V. G. J. (Oxford Univ. and Glamorgan), b Nov 2, 1911
Jenkins, Mr. W. L. T. (Glamorgan), b Aug 26, 1898
Jenner, F. D. (Sussex), b Nov 15, 1893, d March 31, 1953
Jennings, T. S. (Surrey), b Nov 3, 1896
Jephson, Rev. W. V. (Hampshire), b Oct 6, 1873, d Nov 12, 1956
Jepson, A. (Notts.), b July 12, 1915
Jessop, Mr. G. L. (Glouc. and Camb. Univ.), b May 19, 1874, d May 11, 1955
Jewell, Mr. M. F. S. (Sussex and Worc.), b Sept 15, 1885
Joginder Singh (India), b July 7, 1904
Johnson, A. (Notts.) b March 30, 1944
Johnson, Mr. G. H. (Northants), b Dec 16, 1894, d Jan 20, 1965
Johnson, Mr. H. H. (West Indies), b July 17, 1910
Johnson, H. L. (Derbyshire), b Nov 8, 1927
Johnson, Mr. I. W. (Victoria), b Dec 8, 1918
Johnson, L. A. (Surrey and Northants), b Aug 12, 1936
Johnson, Mr. P. R. (New Zealand, Camb. Univ., Devon and Somerset), b Aug 5, 1880, d July 1, 1959
Johnson, Mr. T. F. (West Indies), b Jan 10, 1917
Johnston, Col. A. C. Hampshire), b Jan 26, 1884, d Dec 27, 1952
Johnston, Mr. W. A. (Victoria), b Feb 26, 1922
Johnstone, Mr. C. P. (Camb. Univ. and Kent), b Aug 19, 1895
Jones, A. (Glamorgan), b Nov 4, 1938
Jones, Mr. A. O. (Notts. and Camb. Univ.), b Aug 16, 1872, d Dec 21, 1914
Jones, D. (Notts.), b April 9, 1914
Jones, Mr. E. (South Australia), b Sept 30, 1869, d Nov 23, 1943
Jones, E. (Glamorgan), b June 25, 1942
Jones, E. C. (Glamorgan), b Dec 14, 1912
Jones, Mr. G. L. (Hampshire), b Feb 11, 1909
Jones, I. J. (Glamorgan), b Dec 10, 1941
Jones, Mr. P. E. (West Indies), b June 6, 1917
Jones, P. H. (Kent), b June 19, 1935
Jones, Mr. S. P. (New South Wales), b Aug 1, 1861, d July 14, 1951
Jones, W. (Glam.), b Feb 2, 1912
Jones, W. E. (Glam.), b Oct 31, 1916
Jordan, J. (Lancashire), b Feb 7, 1932
Jorden, A. M. (Essex), b Jan 28, 1947
Jose, Mr. A. D. (Oxford Univ., Kent and South Australia), b Feb 17, 1929
Joshi, P. G. (India), b Oct 27, 1926
Jowett, Mr. D. C. P. R. (Oxford Univ.), b Jan 24, 1931
Jowett, Mr. R. L. (Oxford Univ.), b April 29, 1937
Joy, Mr. F. D. H. (Somerset), b Sept 26, 1880, d Feb 17, 1966
Joyce, Mr. F. M. (Leic.), b Dec 16, 1886
Joynt, Mr. H. W. (Oxford Univ.), b Jan 7, 1931
Judd, Mr. A. K. (Camb. Univ. and Hampshire), b Jan 1, 1904
Judge, P. F. (Middlesex and Glamorgan), b May 23, 1916
Julian, R. (Leic.), b Aug 23, 1936
Jupp, Mr. V. W. C. (Sussex and Northants), b March 27, 1891, d July 9, 1960
Kamm, Mr. A. (Oxford Univ. and Middlesex), b March 2, 1931
Kanhai, Mr. R. B. (West Indies), b Dec 26, 1935
Kapadia, B. E. (India), b April 9, 1900
Kardar, A. H. (formerly Abdul Hafeez) (India, Oxford Univ., War. and Pakistan), b Jan 17, 1925
Kaye, Lt.-Col. H. S. (Yorkshire), b Aug 9, 1882, d Nov 6, 1953

Kaye, Mr. M. A. C. P. (Camb. Univ.). b Jan 11, 1916
Keeton, W. W. (Notts.), b April 30, 1905
Keighley, Mr. W. G. (Oxford Univ. and Yorkshire), b Jan 10, 1925
Keigwin, Mr. R. P. (Camb. Univ. Essex and Glouc.), b April 8, 1883
Keith, G. L. (Somerset and Hampshire), b Nov 19, 1937
Keith, Mr. H. J. (South Africa), b Oct 25, 1927
Kelland, Mr. P. A. (Camb. Univ. and Sussex), b Sept 20, 1926
Kelleher, H. R. A. (Surrey and Northants), b March 3, 1929
Kelleway, Mr. C. (New South Wales), b April 25, 1889, d Nov 16, 1944
Kelly, Mr. G. W. F. (Oxford Univ. and Ireland), b April 2, 1877, d Aug 16, 1951
Kelly, J. (Lancashire and Derbyshire), b March 19, 1922
Kelly, J. (Notts.), b Sept 15, 1930
Kelly, Mr. J. J. (New South Wales), b May 10, 1867, d Aug 14, 1938
Kemp, Mr. M. C. (Oxford Univ. and Kent), b Sept 7, 1861, d June 30, 1951
Kemp-Welch, Capt. G. D. (Camb. Univ. and War.), b Aug 4, 1907, d June 18, 1944
Kennedy, A. S. (Hampshire), b Jan 24, 1891, d Nov 15, 1959
Kennedy, J. M. (War.), b Dec 15, 1931
Kenny, Mr. C. J. M. (Camb. Univ., Essex and Ireland), b May 19, 1929
Kent, Mr. K. G. (War.), b Dec 10, 1901
Kentish, Mr. E. S. M. (West Indies and Oxford Univ.), b Feb 21, 1916
Kenward, Mr. R. (Derbyshire and Sussex), b May 23, 1875, d Dec 24, 1957
Kenyon, D. (Worc.), b May 15, 1924
Kenyon, Mr. M. N. (Lancashire), b Dec 25, 1886, d Nov 21, 1960
Kerr, Mr. J. (Scotland), b April 8, 1885
Kerr, Mr. J. L. (New Zealand), b Dec 28, 1910
Kerr, Mr. J. R. (Scotland), b Dec 4, 1883
Kerslake, R. C. (Camb. Univ. and Somerset), b Dec 26, 1942
Kettle, M. K. (Northants), b March 18, 1944
Key, Sir K. J., 4th Bart. (Oxford Univ. and Surrey), b Oct 11, 1864, d Aug 9, 1932
Khalid Hassan (Pakistan), b July 14, 1937
Khalid Wazir (Pakistan), b April 27, 1936
Khan Mohammad (Pakistan), b Jan 1, 1928
Khanna, Mr. B. C. (Camb. Univ.), b June 22, 1914
Kidd, Mr. E. L. (Camb. Univ. and Middlesex), b Oct 18, 1889
Kidney, Mr. J. M. (Manager West Indies team in England, 1933, 1939, 1950), b Oct 29, 1888, dead
Killick, Ernest Harry (Sussex), b Jan 17, 1875, d Sept 29, 1948
Killick, Rev. E. T. (Camb. Univ. and Middlesex), b May 9, 1907, d May 18, 1953
Kilner, N. (Yorkshire and War.), b July 21, 1896
Kilner, R. (Yorkshire), b Oct 17, 1890, d April 5, 1928
Kimmins, Mr. S. E. A. (Kent), b May 26, 1930
Kimpton, Mr. R. C. M. (Oxford Univ. and Worc.), b Sept 21, 1916
King, B. P. (Worc. and Lancashire), b April 22, 1915
King, Mr. F. (Camb. Univ.), b April 6, 1911
King, I. M. (War. and Essex), b Nov 10, 1931
King, Mr. J. B. (Philadelphia), b Oct 19, 1873, d Oct 17, 1965
King, J. H. (Leic.), b April 16, 1871, d Nov 20, 1946
King, J. W. (Worc. and Leic.), b Jan 21, 1908
King, K. C. W. (Surrey), b Dec 4, 1915
King, L. A. (West Indies), b Feb 27, 1939
Kingsley, Sir P. G. T. (Oxford Univ. and Hertfordshire), b May 26, 1908
Kingston, Mr. C. A. (Northants), b Dec 5, 1865, d Oct 14, 1917
Kingston, Rev. F. W. (Camb. Univ. and Northants), b Dec 24, 1855, d Jan 30, 1933
Kingston, Rev. G. H. (Northants), b Feb 22, 1864, d Feb 17, 1959
Kingston, Mr. H. E. (Northants), b Aug 15, 1876, d June 9, 1955
Kingston, Mr. H. J. (Northants), b June 26, 1862, d April 14, 1944
Kingston, Mr. J. P. (Northants and War.), b July 8, 1857, d March, 1929
Kingston, Mr. W. H. (Northants), b Aug 12, 1874, d March 28, 1956
Kingston, Rev. W. P. (Northants), b 1867, d April 15, 1937
Kippax, Mr. A. F. (New South Wales), b May 25, 1897

Kirby, Mr. D. (Camb. Univ. and Leic.), b Jan 18, 1939
Kirk, Mr. L. (Notts.), b Nov 1, 1884, d Feb 27, 1953
Kirkman, M. (Camb. Univ.), b Feb 11, 1942
Kitchen, M. (Somerset), b Aug 1, 1940
Kitchener, F. (Hampshire), b July 2, 1871
Kitson, D. L. (Somerset), b Sept 13, 1925
Kline, Mr. L. F. (Victoria), b Sept 29, 1934
Knight, Albert E. (Leic.), b Oct 8, 1873, d April, 1946
Knight, B. R. (Essex), b Feb 18, 1938
Knight, Mr. D. J. (Oxford Univ. and Surrey), b May 12, 1894, d Jan 5, 1960
Knight, Mr. N. S. (Oxford Univ.), b March, 1914
Knight, Mr. R. F. (Northants), b Aug 10, 1879, d Jan 9, 1955
Knightley-Smith, Mr. W. (Middlesex, Camb. Univ. and Glouc.), b Aug 1, 1932, d July 31, 1962
Knott, A. (Kent), b April 9, 1946
Knott, Mr. C. (Hampshire), b Nov 26, 1914
Knott, Mr. C. H. (Oxford Univ. and Kent), b March 20, 1901
Knott, Mr. F. H. (Oxford Univ., Kent and Sussex), b Oct 30, 1891
Knowles, J. (Notts.), b March 25, 1910
Knowles, Mr. W. L. (Kent and Sussex, Sec. Sussex 1919 to 1943), b Nov 27, 1871, d Dec 1, 1943
Knox, Mr. F. P. (Oxford Univ. and Surrey), b Jan 23, 1880, d Feb 1, 1960
Knox, G. K. (Lancashire), b April 22, 1937
Knox, Major N. A. (Surrey), b Oct 10, 1884, d March 3, 1935
Kortright, Mr. C. J. (M.C.C. and Essex), b Jan 9, 1871, d Dec 12, 1952
Kotze, Mr. J. J. (South Africa), b Aug 7, 1879, d July 8, 1931
Kripal Singh, A. G. (India), b Aug 6, 1933
Lacey, Sir F. E. (Camb. Univ. and Hampshire; Secretary, M.C.C., 1898–1926), b Oct 19, 1859, d May 26, 1946
Lacy-Scott, Mr. D. G. (Camb. Univ. and Kent), b Aug 18, 1920
Lake, G. J. (Glouc.), b May 15, 1935
Laker, Mr. J. C. (Surrey and Essex), b Feb 9, 1922
Lall Singh (India), b Dec 16, 1909
Lamason, Mr. J. R. (New Zealand), b Oct 29, 1905, d June 25, 1961
Lamb, Mr. H. J. H. (Northants), b May 3, 1912
Lambert, G. E. (Glouc. and Somerset), b May 5, 1919
Lampard, Mr. A. W. (Australian Imperial Forces Team), b July 3, 1885
Lancashire, Mr W. (Hampshire and Dorset), b Oct 28, 1903
Lance, H. R. (South Africa), b June 6, 1940
Langdale, Mr. G. R. (Norfolk, Derbyshire, Somerset and Berkshire), b March 11, 1916
Langford, B. (Somerset), b Dec 17, 1935
Langford, W. (Hampshire), b Oct 5, 1875, d Feb 20, 1957
Langley, Mr. C. K. (War.), b July 11, 1888, d June 26, 1948
Langley, Mr. G. R. (South Australia), b Sept 19, 1919
Langley, Mr. J. D. A. (Middlesex and Camb. Univ.), b April 25, 1918
Langridge, Jas. (Sussex), b July 10, 1906, d Sept 10, 1966
Langridge, John (Sussex), b Feb 10, 1910
Langridge, R. J. (Sussex), b April 13, 1939
Langton, Mr. A. B. C. (South Africa), b March 2, 1912, d Nov 1942
Larter, J. D. F. (Northants), b April 24, 1940
Larwood, H. (Notts.), b Nov 14, 1904
Lashley, P. D. (West Indies), b Feb 11, 1937
Latchman, H. C. (Middlesex), b July 26, 1943
Latham, M. (Somerset), b Jan 14, 1939
Lavers, Mr. A. B. (Essex), b Sept 6, 1918
Lavis, G. (Glamorgan), b Aug 17, 1908, d July 29, 1956
Lawrence, A. A. K. (Sussex), b Nov 3, 1930
Lawrence, J. M. (Somerset), b Nov 7, 1940
Lawrence, J. W. (Somerset and Lincs.), b March 29, 1914
Lawrence, Mr. T. P. (Essex), b April 26, 1910
Lawrie, Mr. P. E. (Hampshire), b Dec 12, 1902
Lawry, Mr. W. M. (Victoria), b Feb 11, 1937
Lawson, H. M. (Hampshire), b May 22, 1914
Lawton, Mr. A. E. (Derbyshire, Lancashire and Cheshire), b March 31, 1879, d Dec 25, 1955

Leach, Cecil (Lancashire and Somerset), b Nov 28, 1897
Leach, C. W. (War.), b Dec 4, 1934
Leadbeater, E. (Yorkshire and War.), b Aug 15, 1927
Learmond, Mr. G. C. (Trinidad), b July 4, 1875
Leary, S. E. (Kent), b April 30, 1933
Leconfield, 3rd Lord (President, M.C.C., 1927), b Feb 17, 1872, d April 16, 1952
Le Couteur, Mr. P. R. (Oxford Univ.), b June 26, 1885, d June 30, 1958
Ledden, P. R. V. (Sussex), b July 12, 1943
Lee C. (Yorkshire and Derbyshire), b March 17, 1924
Lee, F. S. (Middlesex and Somerset), b July 24, 1907
Lee, G. M. (Notts. and Derbyshire), b June 7, 1887
Lee, H. W. (Middlesex), b Oct 26, 1890
Lee, J. W. (Middlesex and Somerset), b Feb 1, 1904, d July 1944
Lee, Mr. P. K. (South Australia), b Sept 14, 1904
Lees, Walter S. (Surrey), b Dec 25, 1876, d Sept 10, 1924
Legard, Mr. A. R. (Oxford Univ. and Worc.), b Jan 17, 1912
Legard, E. (War.), b Aug 23, 1935
Legge, Lt.-Cmdr. G. B. (Oxford Univ. and Kent), b Jan 26, 1903, d Nov 21, 1940
Lenham, L. J. (Sussex), b May 24, 1936
Lester, E. (Yorkshire), b Feb 18, 1923
Lester, G. (Leic.), b Dec 27, 1915
Lever, P. (Lancashire), b Sept 17, 1940
Leveson Gower, Sir H. D. G. (Oxford Univ. and Surrey), b May 8, 1873, d Feb 1, 1954
Levett, Mr. W. H. V. (Kent), b Jan 25, 1909
Lewis, A. E. (Somerset), b Jan 20, 1877, d March 1956
Lewis, Mr. A. R. (Camb. Univ. and Glamorgan), b July 6, 1938
Lewis, C. (Kent), b July 27, 1910
Lewis, Mr. D. J. (Oxford Univ.), b July 27, 1927
Lewis, E. (Glamorgan), b Jan 31, 1942
Lewis, Mr. E. B. (War.), b Jan 5, 1918
Lewis, K. H. (Glamorgan), b Nov 10, 1928
Lewis, Mr. L. K. (Camb. Univ.), b Sept 25, 1929
Lewis, Mr. P. T. (Oxford Authentics and South Africa), b Oct 2, 1884
Leyland, M. (Yorkshire), b July 20, 1900, d Jan 1, 1967
Liddell, A. G. (Northants), b May 2, 1907
Liddicut, Mr. A. E. (Victoria), b Oct 17, 1891
Light, E. (Hampshire), b Sept 1, 1874
Lightfoot, A. (Northants), b Jan 8, 1936
Lilley, A. A. (War.), b Nov 18, 1867, d Nov 17, 1929
Lilley, B. (Notts.), b Feb 11, 1895, d Aug 4, 1950
Lillywhite, James (Sussex), b Feb 23, 1842, d Oct 25, 1929
Lincoln, Earl of (Notts.), b April 8, 1907
Lindsay, Mr. J. D. (South Africa), b Sept 8, 1909
Lindsay, J. D. (South Africa), b Aug 4, 1939
Lindsay, Mr. N. V. (Transvaal), b July 30, 1887
Lindwall, Mr. R. R. (N.S.W. and Queensland), b Oct 3, 1921
Ling, Mr. W. V. (Griqualand West), b Oct 3, 1891
Linney, Mr. C. K. (Somerset), b Aug 26, 1912
Lipscomb, Mr. F. (Kent), b March 13, 1864, d 1952
Lister, Mr. J. (Yorkshire and Worc.), b May 14, 1930
Lister, Mr. W. H. L. (Lancashire), b Oct 7, 1911
Litteljohn, Mr. E. S. (Middlesex), b Sept 24, 1878
Livingston, L. (N.S.W. and Northants), b May 3, 1920
Livingstone, D. A. (Hampshire), b Sept 21, 1933
Livsey, W. H. (Hampshire), b Sept 23, 1894
Llewellyn, C. B. (Natal and Hampshire), b Sept 29, 1876, d June 7, 1964
Lloyd, D. (Lancashire), b March 18, 1947
Loader, P. J. (Surrey and Western Australia), b Oct 25, 1929
Lobb, B. (War. and Somerset), b Jan 11, 1931
Lock, G. A. R. (Surrey, Western Australia and Leic.), b July 5, 1929
Lock, H. (Surrey and Devon), b May 8, 1903
Locker, W. (Derbyshire), b Feb 16, 1867, d Aug 14, 1952
Lockhart, Mr. J. H. Bruce (Berkshire, Camb. Univ. and Scotland), b March 4, 1889, d June 4, 1956
Lockton, Mr. J. H. (Surrey), b May 22, 1892

Lockwood, W. H. (Notts. and Surrey), b March 25, 1868, d April 26, 1932
Lohmann, G. A. (Surrey), b June 2, 1865, d Dec 1, 1901
Lomax, J. G. (Lancashire and Somerset), b May 5, 1925
Long, A. (Surrey), b Dec 18, 1940
Longfield, Mr. T. C. (Camb. Univ. and Kent), b May 12, 1906
Longman, Lt.-Col. H. K. (Camb. Univ., Surrey and Middlesex), b March 8, 1881, d Oct 7, 1958
Longrigg, Mr. E. F. (Camb. Univ. and Somerset), b April 16, 1906
Lord, A. (Leicestershire), b Aug 28, 1888
Lord, W. A. (War.), b Aug 8, 1874
Louden, Mr. G. M. (Essex), b Sept 6, 1885
Love, Mr. H. S. B. (New South Wales and Victoria), b Aug 10, 1895
Loveday, F. (Essex), b Sept 14, 1894
Lowe, Wing-Cmdr. J. C. M. (Oxford Univ. and Warwickshire), b Feb 21, 1888
Lowe, Mr. R. G. H. (Camb. Univ. and Kent), b June 11, 1904
Lowndes, Mr. W. G. L. F. (Oxford Univ. and Hampshire), b Jan 24, 1898
Lowry, Mr. T. C. (Camb. Univ., Somerset and New Zealand), b Feb 17 1898
Lowson, F. A. (Yorkshire), b July 1, 1925
Loxton, Mr. S. J. (Victoria), b March 29, 1921
Lucas, Mr. A. P. (Camb. Univ., Surrey, Middlesex and Essex), b Feb 20, 1857, d Oct 12, 1923
Lucas, Mr. E. V. (Sussex and M.C.C.), b June 12, 1868, d June 26, 1938
Lucas, Mr. M. P. (Sussex and War.), b Nov 24, 1856, d July 9, 1921
Lucas, Mr. R. S. (Middlesex), b July 17, 1867, d Jan 5, 1942
Luce, Mr. F. M. (Glouc.), b April 26, 1878, d Sept 9, 1962
Luckes, W. T. (Somerset), b Jan 1, 1901
Luckhurst, B. W. (Kent), b Feb 5, 1939
Luckin, Mr. R. A. G. (Essex), b Nov 25, 1939
Lumsden, Mr. V. R. (Jamaica and Camb. Univ.), b July 19, 1930
Lupton, Major A. W. (Yorkshire), b Feb 23, 1879, d April 14, 1944
Luther, Major A. C. G. (Sussex and Berkshire), b Sept 17, 1880, d June 23, 1961
Lynes, J. (War.), b June 6, 1872
Lyon, Mr. B. H. (Oxford Univ., Wiltshire and Glouc.), b Jan 19, 1902
Lyon, Mr. M. D. (Camb. Univ., Wiltshire and Somerset), b April 22, 1898, d Feb 17, 1964
Lyttelton, 4th Lord (Camb. Univ.), b March 31, 1817, d April 18, 1876
Lyttelton, Rt. Hon. Alfred, M.P. (Camb. Univ., Middlesex and President, M.C.C., 1898), b Feb 7, 1857, d July 5, 1913
Lyttelton, Rt. Rev. the Hon. A. T. (Eton), b Jan 7, 1852, d Feb 19, 1903
Lyttelton, Hon. and Rev. A. V. (Worc.), b June 29, 1844, d April 4, 1928
Lyttelton, Hon. and Rev. C. F. (Camb. Univ. and Worc.), b Jan 26, 1887, d Oct 3, 1931
Lyttelton, Hon. C. G. (*see* 8th Visct. Cobham)
Lyttelton, Hon. C. J. (*see* 10th Visct. Cobham)
Lyttelton, Canon the Hon. Edward (Camb. Univ. and Middlesex), b July 23, 1855, d Jan 26, 1942
Lyttelton, Hon. G. W. (Eton), b Jan 6, 1883, d May 1, 1962
Lyttelton, Hon. G. W. Spencer (Camb. Univ.), b June 12, 1847, d Dec 5, 1913
Lyttelton, Hon. J. C. (*see* 9th Visct. Cobham)
Lyttelton, Gen. the Rt. Hon. Sir N. G. (Eton), b Oct 28, 1845, d July 6, 1931
Lyttelton, Hon. R. H. (Eton), b Jan 18, 1854, d Nov 7, 1939
Maartenoz, Mr. G A. (Hampshire), b April 14, 1882
McAdam, K. P. W. J. (Camb. Univ.), b Aug 13, 1945
Macartney, Mr. C. G. (N.S.W.), b June 27, 1886, d Sept. 9, 1958
Macaulay, G. G. (Yorkshire), b Dec 7, 1897, d Dec 14, 1940
Macaulay, M. J. (South Africa), b April 19, 1939
McBride, Mr. W. N. (Oxford Univ. and Hampshire), b Nov 27, 1904
MacBryan, Mr. J. C. W. (Camb. Univ. and Somerset), b July 22, 1892
McCabe, Mr. S. J. (New South Wales), b July 16, 1910
McCanlis, Mr. M. A. (Oxford Univ., Surrey and Gloucestershire), b June 17, 1906

McCarthy, Mr. C. N. (South Africa and Camb. Univ.), b March 24, 1929
McConnon, J. E. (Glamorgan), b June 21, 1923
McCool, C. L. (N.S.W., Queensland and Somerset), b Dec 9, 1915
McCorkell, N. (Hampshire), b March 23, 1912
McCormick, Mr. E. L. (Victoria), b May 16, 1906
McDonald, Mr. C. C. (Victoria), b Nov 17, 1928
McDonald, E. A. (Victoria and Lancashire), b in Tasmania, Jan 6, 1892, d July 22, 1937
McDonell, Mr. H. C. (Camb. Univ., Surrey and Hampshire), b Sept 19, 1882, d July 23, 1966
McGahey, Mr. C. P. (Essex), b Feb 12, 1871, d Jan 10, 1935
MacGibbon, Mr. A. R. (New Zealand), b Aug 28, 1924
McGirr, Mr. H. M. (New Zealand), b Nov 5, 1891, d April 14, 1964
McGlew, Mr. D. J. (South Africa), b March 11, 1929
Machin, Mr. R. S. (Camb. Univ. and Surrey), b April 16, 1904
McHugh, F. P. (Yorkshire and Glos.) b Nov 15, 1925
Macindoe, Mr. D. H. (Oxford Univ. and Bucks.), b Sept 1, 1917
McIntosh, Mr. R. I. F. (Oxford Univ.), b Aug 19, 1907
McIntyre, A. J. (Surrey), b May 14, 1918
McIver, Mr. C. D. (Oxford Univ. and Essex), b Jan 23, 1881, d May 13, 1954
Mackay, Mr. J. R. M. (New South Wales), b Sept 9, 1881, d June 13, 1953
Mackay, Mr. K. (Queensland), b Oct 24, 1925
Mackenzie, P. A. (Hampshire), b Oct 5, 1918
McKenzie, Mr. G. D. (W. Australia), b June 24, 1941
McKinna, Mr. G. H. (Oxford Univ.), b Aug 2, 1930
Mackinnon, Mr. F. A. (Camb. Univ. and Kent), b April 9, 1848, d Feb 27, 1947
McKinnon, Mr. A. H. (South Africa), b Aug 20, 1932
McLachlan, A. A. (Camb. Univ.), b Nov. 11, 1944
McLachlan, Mr. I. M. (Camb. Univ. and S. Australia), b Oct 2, 1936
MacLaren, Mr. A. C. (Lancashire), b Dec 1, 1871, d Nov 17, 1944
McLean, Mr. R. A. (South Africa), b July 9, 1930
MacLeod, Mr. K. G. (Camb. Univ and Lancashire), b Feb 2, 1888
McLeod, Mr. A. (Hampshire), b Nov 12, 1894
McMahon, J. W. (Surrey and Somerset), b Dec 28, 1919
McMorris, E. D. (West Indies), b April 4, 1935
McMurray, T. (Surrey), b July 24, 1911, d March 24, 1964
McRae, Mr. F. M. (Somerset), b Feb 12, 1916, d Feb 25, 1944
Maddocks, Mr. L. (Victoria), b May 24, 1926
Mahmood Hussain (Pakistan), b April 2, 1932
Mahomed, Gul (India), b Oct 15, 1921
Mailey, Mr. A. A. (New South Wales), b Jan 3, 1888
Majendie, Mr. N. L. (Oxford Univ. and Surrey), b June 9, 1942
Makepeace, H. (Lancashire), b Aug 22, 1881, d Dec 19, 1952
Malalasekera, V. P. (Camb. Univ.), b Aug 8, 1945
Makin, Mr. J. (Victoria), b Feb 11, 1904
Malik, Mr. H. S. (Sussex), b Nov 30, 1894
Mallett, Mr. A. W. H. (Kent and Oxford Univ.), b Aug 29, 1924
Manjrekar, V. L. (India), b Sept 26, 1931
Mankad, M. "Vinoo" (India), b April 12, 1917
Mann, Mr. E. W. (Camb. Univ. and Kent), b March 4, 1882, d Feb 15, 1954
Mann, Mr. F. G. (Camb. Univ. and Middlesex), b Sept 6, 1917
Mann, Mr. F. T. (Camb. Univ. and Middlesex), b March 3, 1888, d Oct 6, 1964
Mann, Mr. J. E. F. (Camb. Univ.), b Dec 2, 1903
Mann, Mr. J. P. (Middlesex), b June 13, 1919
Mann, Mr. N. B. F. (South Africa), b Dec 28, 1921, d July 31, 1952
Mannaseh, M. (Oxford Univ. and Middlesex), b Jan 12, 1943
Manning, J. S. (South Australia and Northants), b June 11, 1924
Manning, Mr. T. E. (Northants.), b Sept 2, 1884
Mansell, Mr. P. N. F. (South Africa), b March 16, 1920
Mantell, D. N. (Sussex), b July 22, 1934
Mantri, Mr. M. K. (India), b Sept 1, 1921

Maqsood Ahmed (Pakistan), b March 26, 1925
March, E. (Derbyshire), b July 7, 1920
Marks, Mr. A. (New South Wales), b Dec 10, 1910
Marlar, Mr. R. G. (Camb. Univ. and Sussex), b Jan 2, 1931
Marlow, F. W. (Staffordshire and Sussex), b Oct 8, 1867, d Aug 7, 1952
Marlow, W. H. (Leic.), b Feb 13, 1900
Marner, P. (Lancashire and Leic.), b March 31, 1936
Marriott, Mr. C. S. (Camb. Univ., Lancs. and Kent), b Sept 14, 1895 d Oct 13, 1966
Marshall, Mr. A. G. (Somerset), b April 17, 1895
Marshall, B. (Notts. and Scotland), b May 5, 1902
Marshall, Mr. J. C. (Oxford Univ.), b Jan 30, 1929
Marshall, J. M. A. (War.), b Oct 26, 1916
Marshall, N. D. (India), b Jan 3, 1905
Marshall, Mr. R. E. (West Indies and Hampshire), b April 25, 1930
Marsham, Mr. A. J. B. (Oxford Univ. and Kent), b Aug 14, 1919
Marsham, Rev. C. D. (Oxford Univ.), b Jan 30, 1835, d March 2, 1915
Marsham, Mr. C. H. B. (Oxford Univ. and Kent), b Feb 10, 1879, d July 18, 1928
Marsham, Mr. C. J. B. (Oxford Univ.), b Jan 18, 1829, d Aug 20, 1901
Marsham, Brig. F. W. B. (Kent), b July 13, 1883
Marsham, Mr. George (Kent), b April 10, 1849, d Dec 2, 1927
Marsham, the Hon. and Rev. John (Kent), b July 25, 1842, d Sept 16, 1926
Marsham, Mr. R. H. B. (Oxford Univ.), b Sept 3, 1833, d April 5, 1913
Marsland, Mr. G. P. (Oxford Univ.), b May 17, 1932
Martin, E. J. (Notts.), b Aug 17, 1925
Martin, Mr. F. R. (West Indies), b Oct 12, 1893
Martin, Mr. J. D. (Oxford Univ. and Somerset), b Dec 23, 1941
Martin, Mr. J. W. (Kent), b Feb 16, 1917
Martin, J. W. (New South Wales), b July 28, 1931
Martin, S. H. (Worc.), b Jan 11, 1909
Martindale, Mr. E. A. (West Indies), b Nov 25, 1909
Mason, A. (Yorkshire), b May 2, 1921
Mason, Mr. J. R. (Kent), b March 26, 1874, d Oct 15, 1958
Matheson, Mr. A. M. (New Zealand), b Feb 27, 1906
Mathews, Mr. J. K. (Sussex), b Feb 6, 1884, d April 6, 1962
Mathews, Mr. K. P. A. (Camb. Univ. and Sussex), b May 10, 1926
Mathias, W. (Pakistan), b Feb 4, 1935
Matthews, A. (Glouc.), b May 3, 1913
Matthews, Mr. A. D. G. (Northants and Glamorgan), b May 3, 1905
Matthews, C. S. (Notts.), b Oct 17, 1931
Matthews, F. C. (Notts.), b Aug 15, 1893, d Jan 11, 1961
Matthews, Mr. M. H. (Oxford Univ.), b April 26, 1914, d June 1, 1940
Matthews, Hon. R. C. (Sponsor, Canadian Cricket Tour in England, 1936), b June 14, 1871, d Sept 20, 1952
Matthews, Mr. T. J. (Victoria), b April 3, 1884, d Oct 14, 1943
Maudsley, Mr. R. H. (Oxford Univ. and War.), b April 8, 1918
Maxwell, Mr. C. R. (Notts., Middlesex and Worc.), b May 21, 1913
Maxwell, J. (Somerset and Glamorgan), b Jan 13, 1884
May, Mr. P. B. H. (Camb. Univ. and Surrey), b Dec 31, 1929
May, Mr. P. R. (Camb. Univ., London County and Surrey), b March 13, 1884, d Dec 6, 1965
Mayer, J. H. (War.), b March 2, 1902
Mayes, R. (Kent and Suffolk), b Oct 7, 1921
Mayne, Mr. E. R. (South Australia and Victoria), b July 4, 1883, d Oct 27, 1961
Mead, C. P. (Hampshire and Suffolk), b March 9, 1887, d March 26, 1958
Mead, Walter (Essex), b March 25, 1869, d March 18, 1954
Meads, E. A. (Notts.), b Aug 17, 1916
Meale, Mr. T. (New Zealand), b Nov 11, 1928
Medlicott, Mr. W. S. (Oxford Univ. and Wiltshire), b Aug 28, 1879
Meherhomji, R. P. (India), b March 4, 1877
Meherhomji, K. R. (India), b Aug 9, 1911
Mehta, A. H. (Parsees), b April 8, 1876
Melle, Mr. B. G. von B. (South Africa, Oxford Univ. and Hampshire), b March 31, 1891, d Jan 8, 1966
Melle. Mr. M. G. (South Africa), b June 3, 1930
Melluish. Mr. M. E. L. (Camb. Univ. and Middlesex), b June 13, 1932

Melsome, Brig. R. G. W. (Glouc.), b Jan 16, 1906
Melville, Mr. A. (Oxford Univ., Sussex and South Africa), b May 19, 1910
Melville, Mr. C. D. McL. (Oxford Univ.), b Oct 4, 1935
Mence, M. D. (War. and Gloucs.), b April 13, 1944
Mercer, J. (Sussex, Glamorgan and Northants), b April 22, 1895
Merchant, V. M. (India), b Oct 12, 1911
Merrick, Mr. H. (Glouc.), b Dec 21, 1887, d Aug 1961
Merritt, W. E. (New Zealand and Northants), b Aug 18, 1908
Merry, Mr. C. A. (West Indies), b Jan 20, 1911, d April 19, 1964
Meston, Mr. S. P. (Glouc. and Essex), b Nov 19, 1882, d Jan 9, 1960
Metcalfe, Mr. S. G. (Oxford Univ.), b June 20, 1932
Meyer, B. J. (Glouc.), b Aug 23, 1932
Meyer, Mr. R. J. O. (Camb. Univ. and Somerset), b March 15, 1905
Meyer, Mr. W. E. (Glouc.), b Jan 12, 1883, d Oct 1, 1953
Milburn, C. (Northants and Western Australia), b Oct 23, 1941
Miller, Mr. K. R. (Victoria, N.S.W. and Notts.), b Nov 28, 1919
Miller, Mr. L. S. M. (New Zealand), b March 31, 1923
Miller, M. E. (Camb. Univ.), b Dec 15, 1940
Miller, Mr. Neville (Surrey), b Aug 27, 1874
Miller, R. (War.), b Jan 6, 1941
Millman, G. (Notts. and Beds.), b Oct 2, 1934
Millner, D. (Derbyshire), b July 24, 1938
Mills, Mr. J. E. (New Zealand), b Sept 3, 1905
Mills, Mr. J. M. (Camb. Univ. and War.), b July 27, 1921
Mills, P. T. (Glouc.), b May 7, 1883, d Dec 8, 1950
Milner, J. (Essex), b Aug 22, 1937
Milton, C. A. (Glouc.), b March 10, 1928
Minnett, Mr. R. B. (New South Wales), b June 13, 1888, d Oct 21, 1955
Minnett, Mr. R. V. (New South Wales), b Sept 2, 1884
Minns, Mr R. E. F. (Oxford Univ. and Kent), b Nov 18, 1940
Mischler, Mr. N. M. (Camb. Univ.), b Oct 9, 1920
Misson, Mr. F. M. (N.S.W.), b Nov 9, 1938
Mistri, Col. K. M. (India), b Nov 7, 1874, d July 22, 1959
Mitchell, A. (Yorkshire), b Sept 13, 1902
Mitchell, Mr. B. (South Africa), b Jan 8, 1909
Mitchell, Mr. C. G. (Somerset), b Jan 27, 1929
Mitchell, Mr. Frank (Camb. Univ., Yorkshire and South Africa), b Aug 13, 1872, d Oct 11, 1935
Mitchell, F. R. (War.), b June 3, 1922
Mitchell, T. B. (Derbyshire), b Sept 4, 1902
Mitchell, Mr. T. F. (Kent), b Oct 22, 1907, d May 20, 1960
Mitchell, Mr. W. M. (Oxford Univ.), b Aug 15, 1929
Mitchell-Innes, Mr. N. S. (Oxford Univ., Somerset and Scotland), b Sept 7, 1914
Mobey, G. S. (Surrey), b March 5, 1904
Modi, R. S. (India), b Nov 11, 1924
Mohammad Aslam (Pakistan), b Jan 5 1920
Mohammad Farooq (Pakistan), b April 8, 1938
Moir, Mr. A. M. (New Zealand), b July 17, 1919
Moloney, Mr. D. A. R. (New Zealand), b Aug 11, 1910, d 1943
Monks, Mr. C. (Glouc.), b March 4, 1912
Montezuma, Mr. L. de (Sussex), b April 16, 1870
Montgomery, S. (Glamorgan), b July 7, 1920
Montgomery, W. (Surrey, Somerset, Wiltshire, Cheshire and Hertfordshire), b March 4, 1882, d Nov 14, 1952
Moon, Sir Cecil E., 2nd Bart. (London County and Wanderers, Chairman New Zealand Cricket Council, 1914–17), b Sept 2, 1867, d Feb 22, 1951
Mooney, Mr. F. L. H. (New Zealand), b May 26, 1921
Moore, Mr. D. N. (Oxford Univ. and Glouc.), b Sept 26, 1910
Moore, F. W. (Lancashire), b Jan 17, 1931
Moore, H. I. (Notts.), b Feb 28, 1941
Moore, J. (Hants), b April 29, 1891
Moore, Mr. R. H. (Hampshire), b Nov 14, 1913
Morcom, Mr. A. F. (Camb. Univ. and Bedfordshire), b Feb 16, 1885, d Feb 12, 1952
Mordaunt, Mr. D. J. (Sussex), b Aug 24, 1937

Mordaunt, Mr. G. J. (Oxford Univ. and Kent), b Jan 20, 1873, d March 5, 1959
Morgan, D. C. (Derbyshire), b Feb 26, 1929
Morgan, Mr. J. T. (Camb. Univ. and Glamorgan), b May 7, 1907
Morgan, M. (Notts.), b May 21, 1936
Morgan, Mr. M. N. (Camb. Univ.), b May 15, 1932
Morgan, R. W. (New Zealand), b Feb 12, 1941
Morgan, Mr. W. G. (Glamorgan), b Dec 26, 1907
Morkel, Mr. D. P. B. (South Africa), b Jan 25, 1906
Morris, Mr. A. R. (New South Wales) b Jan 19, 1922
Morris, Mr. H. M. (Essex), b April 16, 1898
Morris, Mr. R. J. (Camb. Univ. and Kent), b Nov 27, 1926
Morris, W. B. (Essex), b May 28, 1917
Morrison, Mr. J. S. F. (Camb. Univ., Northumberland and Somerset), b April 17, 1892, d Jan 28, 1961
Mortimer, Sir R. G. E. (Lancashire), b July 7, 1869, d May 3, 1955
Mortimore, J. B. (Glouc.), b May 14, 1933
Morton, A. (Derbyshire), b May 7, 1884, d Dec 19, 1935
Morton, Mr. F. L. (South Australia and Victoria), b Dec 21, 1901
Morton, Mr. H. G. S. (Queensland), b Oct 14, 1881
Moss, A. E. (Middlesex), b Nov 14, 1930
Moss, Rev. R. H. (Oxford Univ., Lancs., Beds and Worc.), b Feb 24, 1868, d March 19, 1956
Motz, R. C. (New Zealand), b Jan 12, 1940
Mountford, P. N. G. (Oxford Univ.), b June 21, 1940
Moyes, Mr. A. G. (South Australia and Victoria), b Jan 2, 1893, d Jan 18, 1963
Muddiah, V. M. (India), b June 8, 1929
Mulholland, Right Hon. Sir H. G. H., 1st Bart (Camb. Univ.), b Dec 20, 1888
Mulla, H. F. (India), b May 4, 1885
Muncer, B. L. (Middlesex and Glamorgan), b Oct 23, 1913
Munden, P. A. (Leic.), b Nov 5, 1938
Munden, V. (Leic.), b Jan 2, 1928
Munir Malik (Pakistan), b July 10, 1934
Murdin, J. V. (Northants), b Aug 16, 1891
Murdoch, Mr. W. L. (New South Wales and Sussex), b Oct 18, 1855, d Feb 18, 1911
Murray, Mr. A. L. (War.), b June 29, 1901
Murray, Mr. A. R. A. (South Africa), b April 30, 1922
Murray, D. L. (West Indies, Camb. Univ. and Notts.), b May 20, 1943
Murray, J. T. (Middlesex), b April 1, 1935
Murray Willis, Mr. P. E. (Worc. and Northants), b July 14, 1910
Murray Wood, Mr. W. (Oxford Univ. and Kent), b June 30, 1917
Murrell, H. R. (Kent and Middlesex), b Nov 19, 1880, d Aug 15, 1952
Mushtaq Ali (India), b Dec 17, 1914
Mushtaq Mohammad (Pakistan and Northants), b Nov 22, 1943
Musson, Mr. F. W. (Lancashire), b May 31, 1894, d Jan 2, 1962
Nadkarni, R. G. (India), b April 4, 1932
Nagel, Mr. L. E. (Victoria), b March 6, 1905
Naoomal Jeoomal (India), b April 17 1904
Nash, A. J. (Glamorgan), b Sept 18, 1873, d Dec 6, 1956
Nash, Mr. L. J. (Tasmania and Victoria), b May 2, 1910
Nasim-ul-Ghani (Pakistan), b May 14, 1941
Naumann, Mr. F. C. G (Oxford Univ. and Surrey), b April 9, 1892, d Oct 30, 1947
Naumann, Mr. J. H. (Camb. U. and Sussex), b Sept 9, 1893, d Dec 6, 1964
Navle, J. G. (India), b Dec 7, 1902
Nayudu, C. K. (India), b Oct 31, 1895
Nayudu, C. S. (India), b April 18, 1914
Nazir Ali, S. (India and Sussex), b June 8, 1906
Neale, W. L. (Glouc.), b March 3, 1904, d Oct 26, 1955
Neate, Mr. F. W. (Oxford Univ.), b May 13, 1940
Neblett, Mr. J. M. (West Indies), b Nov 13, 1901
Nelson, Mr. R P. (Camb. Univ., Middlesex and Northants), b Aug 7, 1912, d Oct 2, 1940
Neser, Mr. V. H. (Oxford Univ.), June 16, 1894, d Dec 22, 1956
Nevell, W. T. (Middlesex, Surrey and Northants), b June 13, 1916
Newham, Mr. W. (Sussex), b Dec 12, 1860, d June 26 1944
Newman, Mr. G. C. (Oxford Univ. and Middlesex), b April 26, 1904

Newman, J. (Hampshire), b Nov 12, 1887
Newson, Mr. E. S. (South Africa), b Dec 2, 1910
Newstead, J. T. (Yorkshire), b Sept 8, 1879, d March 25, 1952
Newton, Mr. A. E. (Oxford Univ. and Somerset), b Sept 12, 1862, d Sept 15, 1952
Newton-Thompson, Mr. J. O. (Oxford Univ.), b Dec 2, 1920
Nichol, M. (Worc.), b Sept 10, 1905, d May 21, 1934
Nicholas, Capt. F. W. H. (Essex and Bedfordshire), b July 25, 1893
Nicholls, Mr. C. O. (New South Wales), b Dec 5, 1901
Nicholls, D. (Kent), b Dec. 8, 1943
Nicholls, J. E. (Worc. and Staffordshire), b April 20, 1878
Nicholls, R. B. (Glouc.), b Dec 4, 1933
Nichols, M. S. (Essex), b Oct 6, 1900, d Jan 26, 1961
Nicholson, A. G. (Yorkshire), b June 25, 1938
Nicol, Mr. D. J. (South Africa), b Dec 11, 1887
Nimbalker, R. B. (India), b Dec 1, 1915
Nissar, Mahomed (India), b Aug 1, 1910, d March 11, 1963
Nitschke, Mr. H. C. (South Australia), b April 14, 1906
Noble, Mr. M. A. (New South Wales), b Jan 28, 1873, d June 21, 1940
Norbury, V. (Hampshire and Lancashire), b Aug 3, 1887
Norman, M E. (Northants and Leics.), b Jan 19, 1933
Norman, Mr. N. F. (Northants), b Feb 2, 1884
North, E. J. (Middlesex), b Sept 23, 1896
Northway, Mr. R. P. (Somerset and Northants), b Aug 14, 1906, d Aug 26, 1936
Nothling, Dr. O. E. (Queensland and N.S.W.), b Aug 1, 1900, d Sept 26, 1965
Nourse, Mr. A. D. (South Africa), b Jan 26, 1878, d July 8. 1948
Nourse, Mr. A. D., jun. (South Africa), b Nov 12, 1910
Nunes, Mr. R. K. (West Indies), b June 7, 1894, d July 22, 1958
Nunn, Mr. J. A. (Oxford Univ. and Middlesex), b March 19, 1906
Nupen, Mr. E. P. (South Africa), b Jan 1, 1902
Nurse, S. M. (West Indies), b Nov 11, 1933
Nutter, A. E. (Lancashire and Northants), b June 28 1913
Nye, J. K. (Sussex), b May 23, 1914
Oakes, C. (Sussex), b Aug 10, 1912
Oakes, J. (Sussex), b March 3, 1916
Oakley, L. (Worc.), b Jan 11, 1916
Oakman, A. S. M. (Sussex), b April 20, 1930
Oates, A. W. (Notts.), b Dec 9, 1908
Oates, T. W. (Notts.), b Aug 9, 1875, d June 18, 1949
Oates, W. F. (Yorkshire and Derbyshire), b June 11, 1929
O'Brien, Mr. L. P. J. (Victoria), b July 2, 1907
O'Brien, Mr. R. (Camb. Univ. and Ireland), b Nov 20, 1932, d Aug 26, 1959
O'Brien, Sir T. C., 3rd Bart. (Oxford Univ., Middlesex and Ireland), b Nov 5, 1861, d Dec 9, 1948
O'Byrne, Mr. W. F. T. (Sussex), b April 30, 1908, d Oct 23, 1951
Ochse, Mr. A. L. (South Africa), b Oct 11, 1899, d May 6, 1949
O'Connor, J. (Essex and Buckinghamshire), b Nov 6, 1899
O'Connor, Mr. L. P. D. (Queensland), b April 11, 1891
O'Halloran, J. (Victoria and Southland, N.Z.), b Jan 12, 1872
Oldfield, N. (Lancashire and Northants), b April 30, 1911
Oldfield, Mr. P. C. (Oxford Univ.), b Feb 27, 1911
Oldfield, Mr. W. A. (New South Wales), b Sept 9, 1897
Oldroyd, E. (Yorkshire), b Oct 1, 1888, d Dec 27, 1964
O'Linn, S. (Kent and South Africa), b May 5, 1927
Oliver, Mr. C. (New Zealand), b Nov 1, 1905
O'Neill, Mr. N. C. (N.S.W.), b Feb 19, 1937
Ord, J. S. (War.), b July 12, 1912
O'Reilly, Mr. W. J. (New South Wales), b Dec 20, 1905
Orlebar, Rev. A. ("Arthur," of "Tom Brown's Schooldays") (Bedfordshire), b June 14, 1824, d Sept 30, 1912
Ormrod, J. A. (Worc.), b Dec 22, 1942
Orr, Mr. J. H. (Scotland), b Oct 18, 1878
Outschoorn, L. (Worc.), b Sept 26, 1918
Ovenstone, Mr. D. M. (South Africa), b July 31, 1921
Owen, J. G. (Surrey and Bedfordshire), b Jan 23, 1909

Owen-Smith, Mr. H. G. O. (South Africa, Oxford Univ. and Middlesex), b Feb 18, 1909
Packe, Mr. M. St. J. (Leic.), b Aug 21, 1916
Padgett, D. E. V. (Yorkshire), b July 20, 1934
Page, Mr. D. A. C. (Glouc.), b April 11, 1911, d Sept 2, 1936
Page, J. C. T. (Kent), b May 20, 1930
Page, M. H. (Derbyshire), b June 17, 1941
Page, Mr. M. L. (New Zealand), b May 8, 1902
Pai, M. D. (India), b June 21, 1883
Paine, G. A. E. (Middlesex and War.), b June 11, 1908
Pairaudeau, Mr. B. H. (West Indies), b April 14, 1931
Palairet, Mr. L. C. H. (Oxford Univ. and Somerset), b May 27, 1870, d March 27, 1933
Palairet, Mr. R. C. N. (Oxford Univ. and Somerset), b June 25, 1871, d Feb 11, 1955
Palfreman, A. B. (Camb. Univ.) b Aug 27, 1946
Palia, P. E. (India), b Sept 5, 1910
Palm, Mr. A. W. (South Africa), b June 8, 1901
Palmer, Mr. C. (Camb. Univ. and Middlesex), b July 14, 1885
Palmer, Mr. C. H. (Worc. and Leic.), b May 15, 1919
Palmer, Mr. H. J. (Essex), b Aug 30, 1890
Palmer, K. E. (Somerset), b April 22, 1937
Pardon, Mr. Charles Frederick (five years Editor of *Wisden*), b March 28, 1850, d April 18, 1890
Pardon, Mr. Edgar S. (for twelve years associated with *Wisden*), b Sept 28, 1859, d July 16, 1898
Pardon, Mr. S. H. (Editor of *Wisden* from 1891 to 1925), b Sept 23, 1855, d Nov 20, 1925
Parfitt, P. H. (Middlesex), b Dec 8, 1936
Paris, Mr. C. G. A. (Hampshire), b Aug 20, 1911
Parker, C. W. L. (Glouc.), b Oct 14, 1884, d July 11, 1959
Parker, Mr. G. M. (South Africa), b May 27, 1899
Parker, Mr. G. W. (Camb. Univ. and Glouc.), b Feb 11, 1912
Parker, J. F. (Surrey), b April 23, 1913
Parker, Mr. J. P. (Hampshire), b Nov 29, 1902
Parkhouse, W. G. A. (Glamorgan), b Oct 12, 1925
Parkin, C. H. (Durham, Yorkshire and Lancashire), b Feb 18, 1886, d June 15, 1943
Parkin, J. (Notts.), b Oct 16, 1944
Parkin, R. (Lancashire), b March 17, 1908
Parkinson, L. W. (Lancashire), b Sept 15, 1908
Parks, H. W. (Sussex), b July 18, 1906
Parks, James H. (Sussex), b May 12, 1903
Parks, J. M. (Sussex), b Oct 21, 1931
Parr, F. D. (Lancashire), b June 1, 1928
Parry, Mr. D. M. (Camb. Univ.), b Feb 8, 1911
Parsons, A. B. D. (Camb. Univ. and Surrey), b Sept 20, 1933
Parsons, Canon J. H. (War.), b May 30, 1890
Partridge, Mr. N. E. (Camb. Univ. and War.), b Aug 10, 1900
Partridge, R. J. (Northants), b Feb 11, 1912
Pataudi, Nawab of (Oxford Univ., Worc. and India), b March 16, 1910, d Jan 5, 1952
Pataudi, Nawab of (Oxford Univ., Sussex and India), b Jan 5, 1941
Paterson, Mr. R. F. T. (Essex and Scotland), b Sept 8, 1916
Patiala, H. H. the Maharaja of (India), b Oct 12, 1891, d March 23, 1938
Patten, Mr. M. (Oxford Univ. and Scotland), b July 28, 1901
Pawle, Mr. J. H. (Camb. Univ. and Essex), b May 18, 1915
Pawson, Mr. A. C. (Oxford Univ.), b Jan 5, 1882
Pawson, Mr. A. G. (Oxford Univ. and Worc.), b May 30, 1888
Pawson, Mr. H. A. (Kent and Oxford Univ.), b Aug 22, 1921
Payn, Mr. L. W. (South Africa), b May, 6, 1915
Payne, Mr. A. U. (Camb. Univ. and Buckinghamshire), b Jan 28, 1903
Payne, Mr. C. A. L. (Oxford Univ. and Middlesex), b Aug 30, 1885
Payne, Mr. M. W. (Camb. Univ. and Middlesex), b May 10, 1885, d June 2, 1963
Paynter, E. (Lancashire), b Nov 5, 1901
Payton, Rev. W. E. G. (Camb. Univ., Notts. and Derbyshire), b Dec 27, 1913
Payton, W. R. D. (Notts.), b Feb 13, 1882, d May 21, 1943
Peach, C. W. (Kent), b Jan 3, 1900
Peach, H. A. (Surrey and Berkshire), b Oct 6, 1890, d Oct 8, 1961

Pearce, G. (Sussex), b Oct 27, 1908
Pearce, Mr. T. A. (Kent), b Dec 18, 1910
Pearce, Mr. T. N. (Essex), b Nov 3, 1905
Pearse, Mr. A. (Somerset), b April 22, 1915
Pearse, Mr. C. O. C. (South Africa), b Oct 10, 1884, d May 28, 1953
Pearse, Mr. G. V. (Natal and Oxford Univ.), b Sept 7, 1891, d Dec 19, 1956
Pearson, Mr. A. J. G. (Camb. Univ. and Somerset), b Dec 30, 1941
Pearson, D. B. (Worc.), b March 29, 1937
Pearson, F. (Worc.), b Sept 23, 1880, d Oct 11, 1963
Peat, Mr. C. U. (Oxford Univ. and Middlesex), b Feb 28, 1892
Peebles, Mr. I. A. R. (Oxford Univ., Middlesex and Scotland), b Jan 20, 1908
Peel, R. (Yorkshire), b Feb 12, 1857, d Aug 12, 1941
Pegler, Mr. S. J. (South Africa and Manager South African Team in England, 1951), b July 28, 1889
Peirce, Mr. T. (Joint Manager with C. de Caires, West Indies in England, 1957), b Dec 26, 1916
Pelham, Mr. A. G. (Camb. Univ., Sussex and Somerset), b Sept 4, 1911
Pellew, Mr. C. E. (South Australia), b Sept 21, 1893
Pennington, J. (Notts.), b June 24, 1881
Pepall, G. (Glouc.), b Feb 29, 1876, d Jan 8, 1953
Pepper, Mr. J. (Camb. Univ.), b Oct 21, 1922
Perkins, C. (Northants and Suffolk), b June 4, 1911
Perks, R. T. D. (Monmouthshire and Worc.), b Oct 4, 1911
Perrin, Mr. P. A. (Essex), b May 26, 1876, d Nov 20, 1945
Perry, Mr. E. H. (Worc.), b Jan 16, 1908
Pether, Mr. S. (Oxford Univ. and Oxfordshire), b Oct 15, 1916
Petrie, Mr. E. C. (New Zealand), b May 22, 1927
Pettiford, J. (New South Wales and Kent), b Nov 29, 1919, d Oct 11, 1964
Pewtress, Mr. A. W. (Lancashire), b Aug 27, 1891, d Sept 21, 1960
Phadkar, Mr. D. G. (India), b Dec 12, 1925
Phebey, A. H. (Kent), b Oct 1, 1924
Phelan, P. J. (Essex), b Feb 9, 1938
Phillipps, Mr. J. H. (Manager New Zealand teams in England, 1949 and 1958), b Jan 1, 1898
Phillips, E. F. (Leic.), b Jan 12, 1932
Phillips, Mr. F. A. (Essex, Somerset and Oxford Univ.), b April 11, 1873, d March 5, 1955
Phillips, Mr. J. B. (Oxford Univ. and Kent), b Nov 19, 1933
Phillipson, W. E. (Lancashire), b Dec 3, 1910
Piachaud, Mr. J. D. (Oxford Univ. and Hampshire), b March 1, 1937
Pickles, D. (Yorkshire), b Nov 16, 1935
Pickles, L. (Somerset), b Sept 17, 1932
Pieris, Mr. P. I. (Camb. Univ.), b March 14, 1933
Pierpoint, F. G. (Surrey and Norfolk), b April 24, 1915
Pierre, Mr. L. R. (West Indies), b June 5, 1921
Pilling, H. (Lancashire), b Feb 23, 1943
Pinch, Mr. F. B. (Glamorgan), b Feb 24, 1891, d Oct 9, 1961
Pitchford, L. (Glam.), b Dec 4, 1900
Pithey, Mr. A. J. (South Africa), b July 17, 1933
Pithey, Mr. D. B. (Oxford Univ. and Northants.), b Oct 10, 1936
Pitman, R. W. C. (Hampshire), b Feb, 21, 1933
Place, W. (Lancashire), b Dec 7, 1914
Platt, G. J. W. (Surrey), b June 9, 1882, d April 14, 1955
Platt, R. K. (Yorkshire and Northants), b Dec 21, 1932
Playle, Mr. W. R. (New Zealand and Western Australia), b Dec 1, 1938
Pleass, J. (Glamorgan), b May 21, 1923
Plimsoll, Mr. J. B. (South Africa), b Oct 27, 1917
Pocock, P. I. (Surrey), b Sept 24, 1946
Pollard, R. (Lancashire), b June 19, 1912
Pollard, V. (New Zealand), b Sept 7, 1945
Pollock, P. M. (South Africa), b June 30, 1941
Pollock, R. G. (South Africa), b Feb 27, 1944
Ponsford, Mr. W. H. (Victoria), b Oct 19, 1900
Pool, Mr. C. J. T. (Northants.), b Jan 21, 1876, d Oct 13, 1954
Poole, C. J. (Notts.), b March 13, 1921
Poole, K. J. (Notts.), b April 27, 1934
Poore, Brig.-Gen. Robert M. (Wiltshire, Hampshire and South Africa), b March 20, 1866, d July 14, 1938
Pope, A. V. (Derbyshire), b Aug 15, 1909

Pope, Mr. C. G. (Camb. Univ and Bedfordshire), b Jan 21, 1872, d Jan 31, 1959
Pope, D. F. (Glouc. and Essex), b Oct 28, 1908, d Sept 8. 1934
Pope, G. H. (Derbyshire), b Jan 27, 1911
Pope, Dr. R. J. (N.S.W. and M.C.C.), b Feb 18, 1864, d July 27, 1952
Popplewell, Mr. O. B. (Camb. Univ.), b Aug 15, 1927
Porch, Mr. R. B. (Somerset), b April 3, 1875, d Oct 29, 1962
Porter, Mr. A. (Glamorgan), b March 25, 1914
Pothecary, E. A. (Hampshire), b March 1, 1906
Pothecary, Mr. J. E. (South Africa), b Dec 6, 1933
Pothecary, S. (Hampshire), b May 6, 1890
Potter, Mr. G. (Lancashire and Cheshire), b Oct 3, 1878
Potter, G. (Sussex), b Oct 26, 1931
Potter, Mr. I. C. (Oxford Univ. and Kent), b Sept 2, 1938
Potter, J. (Victoria), b April 13, 1938
Potts, Mr. H. J. (Oxford Univ.), b Jan 23, 1925
Pountain, F. R. (Sussex), b April 23, 1941
Powell, Mr. A. G. (Camb. Univ., Essex and Suffolk), b Aug 17, 1912
Powell, Mr. W. A. (Kent), b May 19, 1885, d Jan 1, 1954
Poyntz, Col. H. S. (Somerset), b Sept 17, 1877, d June 22, 1955
Pratt, R. C. E. (Surrey), b May 5, 1928
Pratt, R. L. (Leic.), b Nov 15, 1938
Preece, C. A. (Worc.), b Dec 15, 1888, d Nov 11, 1966
Prentice, F. T. (Leic.), b April 22, 1912
Pressdee, J. S. (Glam.). b June 19, 1933
Prest, Mr. H. E. W. (Camb. Univ. and Kent), b Jan 9, 1890, d Jan 5, 1955
Preston, Mr. D. J. (Sussex), b Jan 12, 1936
Preston, Mr. Hubert (Editor of *Wisden* 1944 to 1951), b Dec 16, 1868, d Aug 6, 1960
Preston, H. J. (Kent and Scotland), b Oct 25, 1886, d April 23, 1964
Preston, K. C. (Essex), b Aug 22, 1925
Pretlove, Mr. J. F. (Camb. Univ. and Kent), b Nov 23 . 1932
Pretty, Dr. Harold C. (Surrey and Northants), b Oct 23, 1875, d May 31, 1952
Price, E. (Lancashire and Essex), b Oct 27, 1918
Price, J. S. E. (Middlesex), b July 22, 1937
Price, Mr. V. R. (Oxford Univ. and Surrey), b May 22, 1895
Price, W. F. (Middlesex), b April 25, 1902
Prideaux, Mr. R. M. (Camb. Univ., Kent and Northants), b July 31, 1939
Pritchard, G. C. (Camb. Univ. and Essex), b Jan 14, 1942
Pritchard, T. L. (New Zealand, War. and Kent), b March 10, 1917
Prodger, J. M. (Kent), b Sept 1, 1935
Proffitt, S. (Essex), b Oct 8, 1911
Proud, Mr. R. B. (Oxford Univ., Hampshire and Durham), b Sept 19, 1919, d Oct 27, 1961
Prouton, R. (Hampshire), b March 1, 1926
Pryer, Mr. B. J. K. (Camb. Univ. and Kent), b Feb 1, 1925
Pugh, Mr. C. T. M. (Glouc.), b March 13, 1937
Pullar, G. (Lancashire), b Aug 1, 1935
Pullinger, Mr. G. R. (Essex), b March 14, 1920
Purdy, H. (Derbyshire), b Jan 17, 1884, dead
Putner, F. W. (Middlesex), b Sept 26, 1912
Quaife, Mr. B. W. (War. and Worc.), b Nov 24, 1899
Quaife, Walter (Sussex, War. and Suffolk), b April 1, 1864, d Jan 18, 1943
Quaife, W. G. (Sussex and War.), b March 17, 1872, d Oct 13, 1951
Quick, Mr. A. B. (Essex), b Feb 10, 1915
Quick, Mr. I. W. (Victoria), b Nov 5, 1933
Quist, Mr. K. H. (New South Wales, Western Australia and South Australia), b Aug 18, 1875
Rabone, Mr. G. O. (New Zealand), b Nov 6, 1921
Radcliffe, Sir E. J. R H., 5th Bart. (Yorkshire), b Jan 27, 1884
Radcliffe, Lees (Lancashire and Durham), b Nov 23, 1871
Radley, C. T. (Middlesex), b May 13, 1944
Rae, Mr. A. F. (West Indies), b Sept 30, 1922
Rae, Mr. E. A. (West Indies), b Nov 8, 1897
Rahman, Major S. A. (Assistant Manager Pakistan in England 1962), b Dec 15, 1919
Raikes, Rev. G. B. (Oxford Univ., Hampshire and Norfolk), b March 14, 1873, d Dec 18, 1966

Raikes, Mr. T. B. (Oxford Univ. and Norfolk), b Dec 16, 1902
Rait Kerr, Col. R. S. (Rugby and R.M.A., Woolwich and Secretary, M.C.C. 1936–1952), b April 13, 1891, d April 2, 1961
Ralph, L. H. R. (Essex), b May 22, 1920
Ramadhin, Mr. S. (West Indies and Lancashire), b May 1, 1930
Ramaswami, C. (India), b June 18, 1896
Ramchand, Mr. G. S. (India), b July 26, 1927
Ramsamooj, D. (Northants), b July 5, 1932
Ramsay, Mr. R. C. (Camb. Univ. and Somerset), b Dec 20, 1861, d June 25, 1957
Ranjitsinhji, Kumar Shri, afterwards H.H. The Jam Saheb of Nawanagar (India, Camb. Univ., Cambridgeshire and Sussex), b Sept 10, 1872, d April 2, 1933
Ransford, Mr. V. S. (Victoria), b March 20, 1885, d March 19, 1958
Ransom, Mr. V. J. (Hampshire and Surrey), b March 17, 1918
Ratcliffe, Mr. A. (Camb. Univ., Denbighshire, Surrey and Buckinghamshire), b March 31, 1909
Ratcliffe, D. P. (Warwickshire), b May 11, 1939
Raybould, Mr. J. G. (Oxford Univ.), b July 26, 1934
Rayment, A. W. H. (Hampshire), b May 29, 1928
Read, Mr. A. H. (Essex), b Jan 24, 1880, d May 20, 1957
Read, Mr. H. D. (Surrey and Essex), b Jan 28, 1910
Read, J. Maurice (Surrey), b Feb 9, 1859, d Feb 17, 1929
Reay, Mr. G. M. (Surrey), b Jan 24, 1887
Reddick, Mr. T. B. (Middlesex and Notts.), b Feb 17, 1912
Reddish, J. (Notts.), b Dec 22, 1906
Reddy, Mr. N. S. K. (Camb. Univ.), b Oct 22, 1939
Redgrave, Mr. S. J. (New South Wales and Queensland), b Aug 5, 1878, d Aug 3, 1958
Redman, J. (Somerset), b March 1, 1926
Redpath, I. R. (Victoria), b May 11, 1941
Reed, B. L. (Hampshire), b Sept 9, 1937
Rees, A. (Glamorgan), b Feb 17, 1938
Rees-Davies, Mr. W. R. (Camb. Univ.), b Nov 19, 1916
Reeves, W. (Essex), b June 22, 1876, d March 22, 1944
Reid, Mr. J. R. (New Zealand), b June 3, 1928
Relf, A. E. (Norfolk and Sussex), b June 26, 1874, d March 26, 1957
Relf, R. R. (Berkshire and Sussex), b Sept 1, 1883, d April 28, 1965
Remnant, E. R. (Hampshire), b May 1, 1884
Revill, A. C. (Derbyshire and Leic.), b March 27, 1923
Reynolds, B. L. (Northants), b June 10, 1932
Rhodes, Mr. A. (Lancashire), b April 9, 1899
Rhodes, A. C. (Yorkshire), b Oct 14, 1906, d May 21, 1957
Rhodes, A. E. (Derbyshire), b Oct 10, 1916
Rhodes, H. J. (Derbyshire), b July 22, 1936
Rhodes, Mr. S. D. (Notts.), b March 24, 1910
Rhodes, Wilfred (Yorkshire), b Oct 29, 1877
Rhodes, W. E. (Notts.), b Aug 5, 1936
Richards, R. (Sussex), b Sept 10, 1908
Richardson, A. (Notts.), b Oct 28, 1926
Richardson, Arthur J. (South Australia and Western Australia), b July 24, 1888
Richardson, Mr. A. W. (Derbyshire), b March 4, 1907
Richardson, B. A. (War.), b Feb 24, 1944
Richardson, B. H. (Derbyshire), b March 12, 1932
Richardson, D. W. (Worc.), b Nov 3, 1934
Richardson, Mr. G. W. (Derbyshire), b April 26, 1938
Richardson, Mr. H. B. (Surrey and California), b March 10, 1873
Richardson, Mr. J. V. (Oxford Univ. and Essex), b Dec 16, 1903
Richardson, P. E. (Worc. and Kent), b July 4, 1931
Richardson, T. (Surrey and Somerset), b Aug 11, 1870, d July 2, 1912
Richardson, Mr. V. Y. (South Australia), b Sept 7, 1894
Richardson, Mr. W. E. (Worcestershire), b Dec 23, 1894
Riches, Mr. N. V. H. (Glamorgan), b June 9, 1883
Richmond, T. L. (Notts.), b June 23, 1892, d Dec 30, 1957
Riddell, Mr. V. H. (Camb. Univ.), b July 23, 1905
Riddington, A. (Leic.), b Dec 22, 1911
Ridgway, F. (Kent), b Aug 10, 1923

Ridley, G. N. S. (Oxford Univ. and Kent), b Nov 27, 1944
Rigg, Mr. K. E. (Victoria), b May 21, 1906
Riley, H. (Leic.), b Oct 3, 1903
Riley, T. M. N. (War. and Glouc.), b Dec 25, 1939
Riley, Mr. W. N. (Camb. Univ. and Leic.), b Nov 24, 1892, d Nov 20, 1955
Rimell, Mr. A. G. J. (Camb. Univ. and Hampshire), b Aug 29, 1928
Ring, Mr. D. (Victoria), b Oct 14, 1918
Rippon, Mr. A. D. E. (Somerset), b April 29, 1892, d April 16, 1963
Rippon, Mr. A. E. S. (Somerset), b April 29, 1892, d April 13, 1966
Rist, F. (Essex), b March 30, 1914
Roach, Mr. C. A. (West Indies), b March 13, 1904
Roberts, Mr. A. W. (New Zealand), b Aug 20, 1909
Roberts, Mr. A. W. (Glouc.), b Sept 23, 1874, d June 27, 1961
Roberts, Mr. D. (M.C.C. and Surrey), b Feb 5, 1894
Roberts, H. E. (Sussex), b Feb 8, 1890, d June 28, 1963
Roberts, H. J. (War.), b May 5, 1912
Roberts, W. B. (Lancashire), b Sept 27, 1914, d Aug 24, 1951
Robertson, J. D. (Middlesex), b Feb 22, 1917
Robertson-Glasgow, Mr. R. C. (Oxford Univ and Somerset), b July 15, 1901, d March 4, 1965
Robins, Mr R. V. C. (Middlesex), b March 13, 1935
Robins, Mr. R. W. V. (Camb. Univ. and Middlesex), b June 3, 1906
Robinson, A. G. (Northants), b March 22, 1917
Robinson, Lt.-Col. D. C. (Essex and Glouc.), b April 20, 1883, d July 31, 1963
Robinson, E. (Yorkshire), b Nov 16, 1883
Robinson, E. P. (Yorkshire and Somerset), b Aug 10, 1911
Robinson, Sir F. G. (Glouc.), b Sept 19, 1880
Robinson, G. W. (Notts.), b Feb 15, 1908
Robinson, Mr. H. B. O. (Oxford Univ.), b March 3, 1919
Robinson, Mr. J. J. (Camb. Univ.), b June 28, 1872, d Jan 3, 1959
Robinson, Mr. M. (Glamorgan and War.), b July 16, 1921
Robinson, P. J. (Worc. and Somerset), b Feb 9, 1943
Robinson, Mr. Theo (Somerset), b Feb 16, 1866, d Oct 4, 1959
Rochford, P. (Glouc.), b Aug 27, 1928
Rock, Mr. C. W. (War., Camb. Univ. and Tasmania), b June 9, 1863, d July 27, 1950
Rodriguez, W. V. (West Indies), b June 25, 1934
Roe, B. (Somerset), b Jan 27, 1939
Rogers, A. (Glouc.), b Feb 1, 1908
Rogers, Lt.-Col. F. G. (Glouc.), b April 7, 1897
Rogers, H. O. (Worc.), b Jan 21, 1891
Rogers, N. H. (Hampshire), b March 9, 1918
Rogers, Mr. S. S. (Somerset), b March 18, 1923
Roope, G. R. J. (Surrey), b July 12, 1946
Roopnaraine, R. (Camb. Univ.), b Jan 31, 1943
Root, C. F. (Derbyshire and Worc.), b April 16, 1890, d Jan 20, 1954
Rose, Mr. E. M. (Camb. Univ.), b Dec 4, 1936
Rose, M. H. (Camb. Univ. and Leic.), b April 8, 1942
Rosebery, 5th Earl of (Vice-President, Surrey C.C.C.), b May 7, 1847, d May 21, 1929
Rosebery, 6th Earl of (*see* Dalmeny, Lord)
Rotherham, Mr. G. A. (Camb. Univ. and Warwickshire), b May 28, 1899
Rought-Rought, Mr. D. C. (Camb. Univ. and Norfolk), b May 3, 1912
Rought-Rought, Mr. R. C. (Camb. Univ. and Norfolk), b Feb 17, 1908
Routledge, R. (Middlesex), b July 7, 1920
Rowan, Mr. A. M. B. (South Africa), b Feb 7, 1921
Rowan, Mr. E. A. B. (South Africa), b July 20, 1909
Rowe, E. J. (Notts.), b July 21, 1920
Rowe, Mr. W. (Queensland), b Jan 10, 1892
Rowley, Mr. Ernest (Lancashire), b Jan 15, 1870, d Oct 4, 1962
Roy, Mr. P. (India), b May 31, 1928
Rucker, Mr. C. E. S. (Oxford Univ.), b Sept 4, 1894, d Nov 24, 1965
Rudd, Mr. C. R. D. (Oxford Univ.), b March 25, 1929
Rudd, Mr. G. B. F. (Leic.), b July 3, 1894
Rudston, H. (Yorkshire), b Nov 22, 1879, d April, 1962
Rumbold, Mr. J. S. (Oxford Univ.), b March 5, 1920

Rumsey, F. E. (Worc. and Somerset), b Dec 4, 1935
Rundell, Mr. P. D. (South Australia), b Nov 20, 1890
Rushby, T. (Surrey), b Sept 6, 1881, d July 13, 1962
Rushton, F. (Lancashire), b April 21, 1906
Russell, A. C. (Essex), b Oct 7, 1887, d March 23, 1961
Russell, Mr. A. I. (Hampshire), b Feb 21, 1867, d Aug 20, 1961
Russell, S. E. (Middlesex and Glouc.), b Oct 4, 1937
Russell, S. G. (Camb. Univ.), b March 13, 1945
Russell, W. E. (Middlesex), b July 3, 1936
Rutherford, Mr. J. (Western Australia), b Sept 25, 1929
Ryan, F. (Hampshire and Glamorgan), b Nov 14, 1888, d Jan 6, 1954
Ryan, M. (Yorkshire), b June 23, 1933
Ryder, Mr. J. (Victoria), b Aug 8, 1889
Ryder, Mr. R. V. (Staffordshire and Sec. War. C.C.C.), b March 11, 1873, d Sept 1, 1949
Rymill, Mr. J. W. (South Australia), b March 20, 1901
Sabine, P. N. B. (Oxford Univ.), b Sept 21, 1941
Sadler, W. C. H. (Surrey and Durham), b Sept 24, 1896
Saeed Ahmed (Pakistan), b Oct 1, 1937
Saggers, Mr. R. A. (New South Wales), b May 15, 1917
Sainsbury, P. J. (Hampshire), b June 13, 1934
St. Hill, Mr. A. B. (West Indies), d Aug. 23, 1911
St. Hill, Mr. E. L. (West Indies), b March 9, 1904, d May 21, 1957
St. Hill, Mr. W. H. (West Indies), b July 6, 1893
Salam-ud-din, K. (India), b Oct 16, 1888
Sale, Mr. R. (Oxford Univ. and Derbyshire), b June 21, 1889
Sale, Mr. R., jun. (Oxford Univ., War. and Derbyshire), b Oct 4, 1919
Salmon, Mr. G. H. (Leic.), b Aug 1, 1894
Salter, Mr. M. G. (Oxford Univ. and Glouc.), b May 10, 1887
Samuel, Mr. G. N. T. W. (Glamorgan), b Oct 26, 1917
Sanders, W. (War.), b April 4, 1910, d May, 1965
Sandham, A. (Surrey), b July 6, 1890
Santall, F. R. (War.), b July 12, 1903, d Nov 3, 1950
Santall, J. F. E. (Worc.), b Dec 3, 1907
Santall, S. (Northants and War.), b June 10, 1873, d March 19, 1957
Sargent, M. A. J. (Leic.), b Aug 23, 1928
Sarwate, C. T. (India), b June 22, 1920
Saunders, Sir A. A. (Sussex), b Dec 15, 1892, d Feb 26, 1957
Saunders, C. J. (Oxford Univ.), b May 7, 1940
Savage, J. S. (Leic.), b March 15, 1929
Savill, L. A. (Essex), b June 30, 1935
Saville, G. J. (Essex), b Feb 5, 1944
Saville, Mr. S. H. (Camb. Univ. and Middlesex), b Nov 21, 1889, d Feb 22, 1966
Sayer, Mr. D. M. (Oxford Univ. and Kent), b Sept 19, 1936
Scaife, Mr. J. A. (Victoria), b Nov 14, 1909
Scorer, Col. R. I. (War.), b Jan 6, 1892
Scott, C. J. (Glouc.), b May 1, 1919
Scott, Mr. J. D. (New South Wales and South Australia), b Jan 24, 1890
Scott, Mr. M. D. (Oxford Univ.), b Nov 14, 1933
Scott, M. E. (Northants), b May 8, 1936
Scott, Mr. O. C. (West Indies), b Aug 25, 1893, d June 16, 1961
Scott, Mr. R. S. G. (Oxford Univ. and Sussex), b April 26, 1909, d Aug 26, 1957
Scott, Mr. V. J. (New Zealand), b July 31, 1916
Seabrook, Mr. F. J. (Camb. Univ. and Glouc.), b Jan 9, 1899
Sealey, Mr. B. J. (West Indies), b Aug 12, 1899
Sealy, Mr. J. E. D. (West Indies), b Sept 11, 1912
Seamer, Mr. J. W. (Somerset and Oxford Univ.), b June 23, 1913
Sedgley, J. G. (Worc.), b Feb 17, 1939
Seitz, Mr. J. A. (Oxford Univ. and Victoria), b Sept 19, 1883
Sellar, Lt.-Cmdr. K. A. (Royal Navy and Sussex) b Aug 11, 1906
Sellers, Mr. A. (Yorkshire), b May 31, 1870 d Sept 25, 1941
Sellers, Mr. A. B. (Yorkshire), b March 5, 1907
Sellers, R. H. D. (South Australia), b Aug 20, 1940
Semmence, D. J. (Sussex and Essex), b April 20, 1938
Sen, Mr. P. (India), b May 31, 1926
Sesha Chari, K. (India), b Jan 2, 1875
Sewell, Mr. C. O. H. (Natal and Glouc.), b Dec 19, 1874, d Aug 19, 1951

Sewell, Mr. E. H. D. (Bedfordshire, India, Essex and Buckinghamshire), b Sept 30, 1872, d Sept 20, 1947
Seymour, John (Sussex and Northants), b Aug 24, 1883
Shackleton, D. (Hampshire), b Aug 12, 1924
Shahid Mahmood (Pakistan), b March 17, 1939
Shakespeare, Mr. W. H. N. (Worc.), b Aug 24, 1893
Shakoor Ahmed (Pakistan), b Sept 15, 1928
Shardlow, W. (Derbyshire), b Sept 30, 1902, d June 21, 1956
Sharp, Mr. A. T. (Leic.), b March 23, 1889
Sharp, H. P. (Middlesex), b Oct 6, 1917
Sharp, Mr. J. (Lancashire), b Feb 15, 1878, d Jan 27, 1938
Sharp, Capt. R. H. (Essex), b June 11, 1893
Sharpe, P. J. (Yorkshire), b Dec 27, 1936
Shaw, Alfred (Notts. and Sussex), b Aug 29, 1842, d Jan 16, 1907
Sheffield, E. J. (Surrey and Kent), b June 20, 1908
Sheffield, J. R. (Essex), b Nov 19, 1906
Shelmerdine, Mr. G. O. (Camb. Univ. and Lancashire), b Sept 7, 1899
Shepherd, D. J. (Glamorgan), b Aug 8, 1927
Shepherd, T. F. (Surrey), b Dec 5, 1890, d Feb 13, 1957
Sheppard, Rev. D. S. (Sussex and Camb. Univ.), b March 6, 1929
Sherwell, Mr. N. B. (Camb. Univ. and Middlesex), b March 16, 1904, d Dec 29, 1960
Sherwell, Mr. P. W. (Cornwall and South Africa), b Aug 17, 1880, d April 17, 1948
Shields, Mr. J. (Leic.), b Feb 1, 1882, d May 11, 1960
Shipman, A. (Leic.), b March 7, 1901
Shipston, F. W. (Notts.), b July 29, 1906
Shirley, Mr. W. R. de la C. (Camb. Univ. and Hampshire), b Oct 13, 1900
Shirreff, Mr. A. C. (Camb. Univ., Hampshire, Kent and Somerset), b Feb 12, 1919
Shivram, P. (India), b March 6, 1878
Shortland, Mr. N. A. (War.), b July 16, 1916
Shrewsbury, A. (Notts.), b April 11, 1856, d May 19, 1903
Shuja-ud-Din (Pakistan), b April 10, 1930
Shuter, Mr. J. (Winchester, Kent and Surrey), b Feb 9, 1855, d July 5, 1920
Shuttleworth, Mr. G. M. (Camb. Univ.), b Nov 6, 1926
Shuttleworth, K. (Lancs.), b Nov 13, 1944
Sibbles, F. M. (Lancashire), b March 15, 1904
Sidwell, T. E. (Leic.), b Jan 30, 1888, d Dec 8, 1958
Siedle, Mr. I. J. (South Africa), b Jan 11, 1903
Sievers, Mr. M. W. S. (Victoria), b April 13, 1912
Silk, Mr. D. R. W. (Camb. Univ. and Somerset), b Oct 8, 1931
Sime, Mr. W. A. (Bedfordshire and Notts.), b Feb 8, 1909
Simpson, Mr. R. B. (New South Wales and Western Australia), b Feb 3, 1936
Simpson, Mr. R. T. (Notts.), b Feb 27, 1920
Sims, J. M. (Middlesex), b May 13, 1904
Sinclair, Mr. E. H. L. G. (Oxford Univ.), b Sept 10, 1904
Sinclair, B. W. (New Zealand), b Oct 23, 1936
Sinfield, R. A. (Glouc.), b Dec 24, 1901
Singh, S. (E. Punjab, Camb. Univ. and War.), b July 18, 1931
Singleton, Mr. A. P. (Oxford Univ. and Worc.), b Aug 5, 1914
Sinker, N. (Camb. Univ.), b April 19, 1946
Skeet, Mr. C. H. L. (Oxford Univ. and Middlesex), b Aug 17, 1895
Skelding, Alec (Leic.), b Sept 5, 1886, d April 17, 1960
Skene, Mr. R. W. (Oxford Univ.), b May 20, 1908
Skinner, Mr. A. F. (Derbyshire and Northants), b April 22, 1913
Skinner, Mr. D. A. (Derbyshire), b March 22, 1920
Skinner, I. J. (Essex), b April 1, 1928
Slack, Mr. J. K. E. (Camb. Univ.), b Dec 23, 1930
Slade, D. N. F. (Worc.), b Aug 24, 1940
Slade, W. (Glamorgan), b Sept 27, 1941
Smailes, T. F. (Yorkshire), b March 27, 1910
Smales, K. (Yorkshire and Notts.), b Sept 15, 1927
Small, Mr. J. A. (West Indies) b Nov 3, 1892, d April 26, 1958
Smart, C. C. (Glamorgan and War.), b July 23, 1898
Smart, Jack (War.), b April 12, 1894
Smedley, M. J. (Notts.), b Oct 28, 1941

Smith, Mr. A. C. (Oxford Univ. and War.), b Oct 25, 1936
Smith, Sir C. A. (Camb. Univ., Transvaal and Sussex), b July 21, 1863, d Dec 20, 1948
Smith, C. I. J. (Wiltshire and Middlesex), b Aug 25, 1906
Smith, Mr. C. S. (Lancashire and Camb. Univ.), b Oct 1, 1932
Smith, Denis (Derbyshire), b Jan 24, 1907
Smith, Mr. D. (Victoria), b Sept 14, 1884
Smith, Mr. D. J. (Camb. Univ.), b Oct 19, 1933
Smith, D. R. (Gloucestershire), b Oct 5, 1934
Smith, D. V. (Sussex), b June 14, 1923
Smith, E. (Derbyshire), b Jan 2, 1934
Smith, E. J. (War.), b Feb 6, 1887
Smith, Mr. F. B. (New Zealand), b March 13, 1922
Smith, Mr. G. (Kent), b Nov 30, 1925
Smith, G. J. (Essex), b April 2, 1935
Smith, Mr. G. O. (Oxford Univ. and Surrey), b Nov 25, 1872, d Dec 6, 1943
Smith, H. (Glouc.), b May 21, 1891, d Nov 12, 1937
Smith, H. A. (Leic.), b March 29, 1901, d Aug 7, 1948
Smith, Mr. H. E. (Transvaal), b April 21, 1884
Smith, Mr. H. T. O. (Essex), b March 5, 1906
Smith, I. W. (Worc.), b Oct 26, 1880
Smith, J. C. (Worc.), b Sept 26, 1894
Smith, K. D. (Leic.), b April 29, 1922
Smith, M. J. (Middlesex), b Jan 4, 1942
Smith, Mr. M. J. K. (Leic., Oxford Univ. and War.), b June 30, 1933
Smith, Mr. O. G. (West Indies), b May 5, 1933, d Sept 9, 1959
Smith, P. (Leic.), b Oct 5, 1934
Smith, R. (Essex), b Aug 10, 1914
Smith, R. (Somerset), b April 14, 1930
Smith, R. C. (Leic.), b Aug. 3, 1935
Smith, Mr. S. (Manager, Australian Teams, 1921 and 1926), b March 1, 1880
Smith, S. (Lancashire), b Jan 14, 1929
Smith, Mr. S. G. (West Indies, Northants and New Zealand), b Jan 15, 1881, d Oct 25, 1963
Smith, Mr. T. M. (Hampshire), b June 15, 1899
Smith, T. P. B. (Essex), b Oct 30, 1908
Smith, Mr. V. I. (South Africa), b Feb 23, 1925
Smith, Mr. W. A. (Leic.), b Feb 23, 1913
Smith, W. A. (Surrey), b Sept 15, 1937
Smithson, G. A. (Yorkshire and Leic.), b Nov 1, 1926
Smoker, H. G. (Hampshire and Cheshire), b March 1, 1881
Snary, H. C. (Leic.), b Sept 22, 1898
Snedden, Mr. N. C. (New Zealand), b April 3, 1892
Snellgrove, K. (Lancashire), b Nov 12, 1941
Snooke, Mr. S. D. (South Africa), b Nov 11, 1878, d April 4, 1959
Snooke, Mr. S. J. (South Africa), b Feb 1, 1881
Snow, J. A. (Sussex), b Oct 13, 1941
Snowden, Mr. A. W. (Northants), b Aug 15, 1913
Sobers, Mr. G. S. (West Indies), b July 28, 1936
Sohoni, S. W. (India), b March 5, 1918
Solbé, Mr. E. P. (Kent), b May 10, 1902, d Dec 28 1961
Solomon, J. S. (West Indies), b Aug 26, 1930
Somerset, Mr. A. P. F. C. (Sussex), b Sept 28, 1889
Southerton, Mr. S. J. (Editor of *Wisden* 1934–1935), b July 7, 1874, d March 12, 1935
Spanswick, J. (Kent), b Sept 30, 1933
Sparling, Mr. J. T. (New Zealand), b July 24, 1938
Spence, L. A. (Leic.), b Jan 14, .932
Spencer, A. H. (Worc.), b July 4, 1937
Spencer, C. T. (Leic.), b Aug 18, 1931
Spencer, T. W. (Kent), b Mar 22, 1914
Sperry, J. (Leic.), b March 19, 1910
Spicer, P. (Essex), b May 11, 1939
Spiller, Mr. W. (Glamorgan), b July 8 1886
Spofforth, Mr. F. R. (New South Wales, Victoria and Derbyshire), b Sept 9, 1853, d June 4, 1926
Spooner, Mr. A. F (Lancashire), b May 21, 1886, d Jan 11, 1965
Spooner, Mr. R. H. (Lancashire), b Oct 21, 1880, d Oct 2, 1961
Spooner, R. T. (War.), b Dec 30, 1919
Spring, A. W. (Surrey), b May 17, 1881
Springall, J. D. (Notts.), b Sept 19, 1932
Sprinks, Mr. H. S. (Hampshire), b Aug 19, 1905
Spry, E. (Glouc.), b July 31, 1881, d Nov 19 1958
Squires, H. S. (Surrey), b Feb 22, 1909, d Jan 24, 1950
Stacey, F. C. (Surrey), b April 27, 1878
Stainton, Mr. R. G. (Oxford Univ. and Sussex), b May 23, 1910
Standen, J. A. (Worc.), b May 30, 1935
Stannard, G. (Sussex), b July 9, 1894

Stanyforth, Major R. T. (Army, Capt. of M.C.C. in South Africa, 1927–1928, and Yorkshire), b May 30, 1892, d Feb 20, 1964
Staples, A. (Notts.), b Feb 4, 1899, d Sept 9, 1965
Staples, S. J. (Notts.), b Sept 18, 1892, d June 4, 1950
Starkie, S. (Northants), b April 4, 1926
Statham, J. B. (Lancashire), b June 17, 1930
Stead, B. (Yorkshire and Notts.), b June 21, 1939
Steel, Mr. A. G. (Camb. Univ. and Lancashire, President, M.C.C., 1902), b Sept 24, 1858, d June 15, 1914
Steel, Mr. D. Q. (Camb. Univ. and Lancashire), b June 19, 1856, d Dec 2, 1933
Steel, Mr. E. E. (Lancashire), b June 25, 1864, d July 14, 1941
Steel, Mr. H. B. (Lancashire), b April 9, 1862, d June 29, 1911
Steele, Dr. D. M. (South Australia), b Aug 17, 1893
Steele, D. S. (Northants), b Sept 29, 1941
Steele, Rev. J. W. J. (Hampshire), b July 30, 1905
Steele, Mr. R. (Manager, Australia in England 1964; Treas., 1961), b May 19, 1917
Stephens, E. J. (Glouc.), b March 23, 1910
Stephens, Mr. F. G. (War.), b April 26, 1889
Stephens, Mr. G. W. (War.), b April 26, 1889, d 1950
Stephenson, H. W. (Somerset and Devon), b July 18, 1920
Stephenson, Mr. J. S. (Oxford Univ. and Yorkshire), b Nov 10, 1903
Stephenson, Lt.-Col. J. W. A. (Essex and Worc.) b Aug 1, 1907
Stevens, Mr. G. T. S. (Oxford Univ. and Middlesex), b Jan 7 1901
Stevenson, Mr. M. H. (Camb. Univ. and Derbyshire), b June 13, 1927
Steward, E. A. W. (Essex), b June 27, 1941
Stewart, M. J. (Surrey), b Sept 16, 1932
Stewart, R. W. (Middx.), b Feb 28, 1945
Stewart, W. J. (War.), b Aug 31, 1934
Stewart-Brown, Mr. P. H. (Oxford Univ.), b April 30, 1904, d Dec 21, 1960
Steyn, Mr. S. S. L. (South Africa), b March 11, 1905
Stirling, Mr. W. S. (South Australia and Australian Imperial Forces Team), b March 20, 1891
Stocks, F. W. (Notts.), b Nov 6, 1918
Stoddart, Mr. A. E. (Middlesex), b March 11, 1863, d April 3, 1915
Stollmeyer, Mr. J. B. (West Indies), b March 11, 1921
Stollmeyer, Mr. V. H. (West Indies), b Jan 24, 1916
Storer, H. (Derbyshire), b Feb 2, 1898
Storey, S. J. (Surrey), b Jan 6, 1941
Stott, W. B. (Yorkshire), b July 18 1934
Straw, T. (Worc.), b Sept 2, 1872
Strudwick, H. (Surrey), b Jan 28, 1880
Studd, Mr. A. H. (Hampshire), b Nov 19, 1863, d Jan 26, 1919
Studd, Mr. C. T. (Camb. Univ. and Middlesex), b Dec 2, 1860, d July 16, 1931
Studd, Mr. E. J. C. (Cheltenham and M.C.C.), b Feb 13, 1849, d March 9, 1909
Studd, Mr. G. B. (Camb. Univ. and Middlesex), b Oct 20, 1859, d Feb 13, 1945
Studd, Brig-Gen. H. W. (Middlesex and Hampshire), b Dec 26, 1870, d Aug 8, 1947
Studd, Sir J. E. K., 1st Bart. (Camb. Univ. and Middlesex, President, M.C.C., 1930), b July 26, 1858, d Jan 14, 1944
Studd, Mr. P. M. (Camb. Univ.), b Sept 15, 1916
Studd, Mr. R. A. (Camb. Univ. and Hampshire), b Dec 18, 1873, d Feb 3, 1948
Sturman, W. (Leic.), b Aug 29, 1883
Sturt, Mr. M. A. S. (Somerset), b Nov 11, 1876
Styler, S. W. (Worc.), b Aug 26, 1908
Subba Row, Mr. R. (Camb. Univ., Surrey and Northants), b Jan 29, 1932
Sullivan, D. (Surrey and Glamorgan), b Jan 28, 1887
Sullivan, J. (Lancashire), b Feb 5, 1945
Sully, H. (Somerset and Northants), b Nov 1, 1939
Summers, D. W. L. (Worc.), b Oct 12, 1911
Summers, F. T. (Worc.), b Jan 25, 1887
Sunnucks, P. R. (Kent), b June 22, 1916
Surendranath, R. (India), b Jan 4, 1937
Surridge, Mr. W. S. (Surrey), b Sept 3, 1917

Susskind, Mr. M. J. (Middlesex and South Africa), b June 8, 1891, d July 9, 1957
Sutcliffe, Mr. B. (New Zealand), b Nov 17, 1923
Sutcliffe, H. (Yorkshire), b Nov 24, 1894
Sutcliffe, Mr. W. H. H. (Yorkshire), b Oct 10, 1926
Sutherland, T. (Hampshire), b Feb 17, 1880
Suttle, K. G. (Sussex), b Aug 25, 1928
Sutton, Mr. M. A. (Oxford Univ.), b March 29, 1921
Swallow, R. (Derbyshire), b June 15, 1935
Swanton, Mr. E. W. (Cricket Writer) (Middlesex), b Feb 11, 1907
Swetman, R. (Surrey and Notts.), b Oct 25, 1933
Swift, Mr. B. T. (Camb. Univ.), b Sept 9, 1937, d March 8, 1958
Sydenham, D. A. D. (Surrey), b April 6, 1934
Symington, Mr. S. J. (Leic.), b Sept 16, 1926
Tabart, Mr. T. A. (Tasmania), b Aug 10, 1879
Talbot, Mr. R. O. (New Zealand), b Nov 26, 1904
Tallon, Mr. D. (Queensland), b Feb 17, 1916
Tamhane, N. S. (India), b Aug 4, 1931
Tanner, Mr. A. R. (Middlesex), b Dec 25, 1889, d Aug 16, 1966
Tarbox, C. V. (Worc. and Hertfordshire), b July 2, 1893
Tarrant, F. A. (Victoria and Middlesex), b Dec 11, 1881, d Jan 29, 1951
Tasker, Mr. J. (Yorkshire), b Feb 4, 1887
Tate, C. F. (Derbyshire and War.), b May 1, 1908
Tate, E. (Hampshire), b Aug 30, 1877, d Jan 4, 1953
Tate, F. W. (Sussex), b July 24, 1867, d Feb 24, 1943
Tate M. W. (Sussex), b April 29, 1895, d May 18, 1956
Tattersall, R. (Lancashire), b Aug 17, 1922
Tayfield, Mr. H. J. (South Africa), b Jan 30, 1928
Taylor, B. (Essex), b June 19, 1932
Taylor, B. (Notts.), b June 16, 1875
Taylor, B. R. (New Zealand), b July 12, 1943
Taylor, Mr. C. H. (Oxford Univ., Leic. and Buckinghamshire), b Feb 6, 1904, d Jan 27, 1966
Taylor, D. (War.), b 1918
Taylor, Don. (War. and New Zealand), b March 2, 1923
Taylor, Mr. F. H. (Derbyshire), b June 14, 1890, d Dec 6, 1963
Taylor, Mr. G. R. (Hampshire), b Nov 25, 1909
Taylor, H. (Kent), b April 5, 1908
Taylor, Mr. H. W. (South Africa), b May 5, 1889
Taylor, Mr. J. M. (New South Wales), b Oct 10, 1895
Taylor, K. (Yorkshire), b Aug 21, 1935
Taylor, K. A. (War.), b Sept 29, 1916
Taylor, M. (Notts.), b Nov 12, 1942
Taylor, M. L. (Lancashire and Dorset), b July 16, 1904
Taylor, R. A. (Notts.), b March 25, 1909
Taylor, R. M. (Essex), b Nov 30, 1909
Taylor, R. W. (Derbyshire), b July 17, 1941
Taylor, Mr T L. (Camb. Univ. and Yorkshire), b May 25, 1878, d March 16, 1960
Taylor, Mr. W. H. (Worc.), b June 23, 1885, d July 25, 1959
Taylor, Mr. W. T. (Derbyshire, Secretary, Derbyshire C.C.), b April 14, 1885
Tebay, K. (Lancashire), b Feb 2, 1936
Teesdale, Mr. H. (Oxford Univ. and Surrey), b Feb 12, 1886
Tennyson, 3rd Lord (Hon. L. H.) (Hampshire), b Nov 7, 1889, d June 6, 1951
Thomas, A. E. (Northants), b June 7, 1893, d March 21, 1965
Thomas, R. (Lancashire), b July 15, 1871
Thomas, R. J. A. (Oxford Univ.), b March 13, 1942
Thompson, A. (Middlesex), b April 17, 1916
Thompson, E. C. (Essex), b Feb 27, 1907
Thompson, Mr. F. C. (Queensland), b Aug 1, 1890
Thompson, H. (Surrey), b Dec 6, 1870
Thompson, Mr. J. R. (Camb. Univ. and War.), b May 10, 1918
Thompson, R. G. (War.), b Sept 26, 1932
Thomson, N. I. (Sussex), b Jan 23, 1929
Thomson, Mr. R. H. (Camb. Univ. and Sussex), b Oct 19, 1938
Thornton, Mr. C. I. (Camb. Univ., Kent and Middlesex), b March 20, 1850, d Dec 10, 1929
Thorp, P. (Worc.) b May 6, 1911
Thursting, L. D. (Leic.), b Sept 9, 1916

Thwaites, I. G. (Camb. Univ.), b March 14, 1943
Tilly, H. W. (Middlesex), b May 25, 1932
Timms, B. S. V. (Hampshire), b Dec 17, 1940
Timms, J. E. (Northants), b Nov 3, 1907
Timms, Mr. W. W. (Northants), b Sept 28, 1902
Tindall, Mr. M. (Camb. Univ. and Middlesex), b March 31, 1914
Tindall, R. A. E. (Surrey), b Sept 23, 1935
Tindill, Mr. E. W. (New Zealand), b Dec 18, 1910
Tinsley, H. J. (Yorkshire and Lancashire), b Feb 20, 1865
Titmus, F. J. (Middlesex), b Nov 24, 1932
Todd, L. J. (Kent), b June 19, 1907
Toft, D. P. (Oxford Univ.), b March 1, 1945
Tolchard, R. W. (Leics.), b June 15, 1946
Tomlinson, Mr. D. S. (South Africa), b Sept 4, 1910
Tomlinson, Mr. W. J. V. (Camb. Univ. and Derbyshire), b Aug 10, 1901
Tompkin, M. (Leic.), b Feb 17, 1919, d Sept 27, 1956
Toone, Sir F. C. (Secretary, Yorkshire), b June 25, 1868, d June 10, 1930
Toppin, Mr. C. G. (Worc.), b April 17, 1906
Tordoff, Mr. G. G. (Camb. Univ. and Somerset), b Dec 6, 1929
Toshack, Mr. E. R. H. (New South Wales), b Dec 15, 1917
Towell, Mr. E. F. (Northants), b July 5, 1901
Towler, W. (Yorkshire), b Nov 12, 1866, dead
Townsend, A. (War.), b Aug 26, 1921
Townsend, A. F. (Derbyshire), b March 29, 1912
Townsend, Mr. C. L. (Glouc.), b Nov 7, 1876, d Oct 17, 1958
Townsend, Mr. D. C. H. (Oxford Univ. and Durham), b April 20, 1912
Townsend, L. F. (Derbyshire and Northumberland), b June 8, 1903
Trapnell, Mr. B. M. W. (Camb. Univ. and Middlesex), b May 18, 1924
Travers, Mr. B. H. (Oxford Univ. and Oxfordshire), b July 7, 1919
Treglown, Lt.-Col. C. J. H. (Essex), b Feb 13, 1893
Tremlett, M. F. (Somerset), b July 5, 1923
Tremlin, B. (Essex), b Sept 18, 1877, d April 12, 1936
Trestrail, Mr. K. B. (West Indies), b Nov 26, 1927
Tribe, G. E. (Victoria and Northants), b Oct 4, 1920
Tripp, G. M. (Somerset), b June 29 1932
Trueman, F. S. (Yorkshire), b Feb 6, 1931
Trumble, Mr. Hugh (Victoria), b May 12, 1867, d Aug 14, 1938
Trumble, Mr. J. W. (Victoria), b Sept 16, 1863, d Aug 17, 1944
Trumper, Mr. V. T. (New South Wales), b Nov 2, 1877, d June 28, 1915
Tuckett, Mr. L. (South Africa), b Feb 2, 1919
Tumility, Mr. L. R. (Tasmania), b June 12, 1884
Tunnicliffe John (Yorkshire), b Aug 26, 1866, d July 11, 1948
Tuppin, A. G. (Sussex), b Dec 17, 1911
Turnbull, Major M. J. (Camb. Univ. and Glamorgan), b March 16, 1906, d Aug 5, 1944
Turner, A. (Yorkshire and Scotland), b Sept 2, 1885, d Aug 29, 1951
Turner, C. (Yorkshire), b Jan 11, 1902
Turner, Mr. C. T. B. (New South Wales), b Nov 16, 1862, d Jan 1, 1944
Turner, R. E. (Worc.), b May 4, 1888
Twining, Mr. R. H. (Oxford Univ. and Middlesex, President M.C.C. 1964–65), b Nov 3, 1889
Tyldesley, E. (Lancashire), b Feb 5, 1889, d May 5, 1962
Tyldesley, Harry (Lancashire), b 1893, d Aug 30, 1935
Tyldesley, Jas. D. (Lancashire), Aug 10, 1889, d Jan 31, 1923
Tyldesley, J. T. (Lancashire), b Nov 22, 1873, d Nov 27, 1930
Tyldesley, Richard Knowles (Lancashire), b March 11, 1898, d Sept 17, 1943
Tyler, Mr. C. (Glouc.), b Jan 26, 1911
Tyler, Mr. C. H. (Northants), b Sept 13, 1887
Tyson, C. (Yorkshire and Glamorgan), b Jan 24, 1889, d April 4, 1940
Tyson, F. H. (Northants), b June 6, 1930
Udal, Mr. N. R. (Oxford Univ., Dorset and Devon), b Oct 16, 1883, d Feb 27, 1964
Ufton, D. G. (Kent), b May 31, 1928
Umrigar, Mr. P. R. (India), b March 28, 1926

Underwood, D. L. (Kent), b June 8, 1945
Unwin, Mr. F. St.G. (Essex), b April 23, 1911
Urquhart, Mr. J. R. (Camb. Univ. and Essex), b May 29, 1921
Utley, Father R. P. H. (Hampshire and R.A.F.), b Feb 11, 1906
Valentine, Mr. A. L. (West Indies), b April 29, 1930
Valentine, Mr. B. H. (Camb. Univ. and Kent), b Jan 17, 1908
Valentine, V. A. (West Indies), b April 4, 1908
Van der Byl, Mr P. G. (Oxford Univ. and South Africa), b Oct 21, 1907
Van der Gucht, Mr. P. I. (Glouc.), b Nov 2, 1911
Van der Merwe, Mr. E. A. (South Africa), b Nov 9, 1904
Van der Merwe, P. L. (South Africa), b March 14, 1937
Van Geloven, J. (Yorkshire, Leic. and Northumb'ld), b Jan 4, 1934
Van Ryneveld, Mr. C. B. (Oxford Univ. and South Africa), b March 19, 1928
Vann, Mr. D. W. A. (Northants), b Nov 21, 1916, d Jan 20, 1961
Vaulkhard, Mr. P. (Notts., Northumberland and Derbyshire), b Sept 15, 1911
Veivers, T. R. (Queensland), b April 6, 1937
Venn, W. H. (War.), b July 4, 1892, d Nov 23, 1953
Vere Hodge, Mr. N. (Essex), b Oct 31, 1912
Verity, Capt. Hedley (Yorkshire), b May 18, 1905, d July 31, 1943
Vials, Mr. G. A. T. (Northants), b March 18, 1887
Vidler, Mr. J. L. S. (Oxford Univ., Sussex and Oxfordshire), b March 30, 1890
Vigar, F. H. (Essex), b July 7, 1917
Vigar, H. E. (Surrey), b Nov 29, 1883
Viljoen, Mr. K. G. (South Africa), b May 14, 1910
Vincent, Mr. C. L. (South Africa), b Feb 16, 1902
Vincent, Mr H. G. (Camb. Univ.), b Nov 13, 1891
Vincett, J. H. (Sussex and Surrey), b May 24, 1883
Vine, J. (Sussex), b May 15, 1875, d April 25, 1946
Virgin, R. (Somerset), b Aug 26, 1939
Vivian, G. E. (N.Z.), b Feb 28, 1946
Vivian, Mr. H. G. (N.Z.), b Nov 4, 1912
Vizianagram, Maharaj Kumar, Sir Vijaya of (India), b Dec 28, 1905, d Dec 2, 1965
Voce, W. (Notts.), b Aug 8, 1909
Vogler, A. E. E. (South Africa), b Nov 28, 1876, d Aug 10, 1946
Waddington, A. (Yorkshire), b Feb 4, 1893, d Oct 28, 1959
Waddy, Rev. E. F. (N.S.W. and War.). b Oct 5, 1880, d Sept 23, 1958
Waddy, Mr. E. L. (N.S.W.), b Dec 3, 1878
Wade, Mr. H. F. (South Africa), b Sept 14, 1905
Wade, T. H. (Essex), b Nov 24, 1911
Wade, Mr. W. W. (South Africa), b June 18, 1914
Wainwright, W. (Yorkshire), b Jan 21, 1882, d Dec 31, 1961
Wait, Mr. O J. (Camb. Univ. and Surrey), b Aug 2, 1926
Waite, Mr. J. H. B. (South Africa), b Jan 19, 1930
Waite, Mr. M. G. (South Australia), b Jan 7, 1911
Walcott, Mr. C. L. (West Indies), b Jan 17, 1926
Walden, F. (Northants), b March 1, 1888, d May 3, 1949
Waldock, Mr. F. A. (Oxford Univ. and Somerset), b March 16, 1898, d July 4, 1959
Walford, Mr. M. M. (Oxford Univ., Durham and Somerset), b Nov 27, 1915
Walker, A. K. (New South Wales and Notts.), b Oct 4, 1925
Walker, C. (Yorkshire and Hampshire), b June 27, 1920
Walker, F/O C. W. (South Australia), b Feb 19, 1909, d Dec 21, 1942
Walker, G. A. (Notts.), b Jan 25, 1919
Walker, M. (Somerset), b Oct 14, 1933
Walker, P. (Glamorgan), b Feb 17, 1936
Walker, Willis (Notts.), b Nov 24, 1894
Wall, Mr. T. W. (South Australia), b May 13, 1904
Wallace, Mr. W. M. (New Zealand), b Dec 19, 1916
Walsh, J. E. (Leic.), b Dec 4, 1912
Walshe, Mr. A. P. (Oxford Univ.), b Jan 1, 1934
Walters, Mr. C. F. (Glamorgan and Worc.), b Aug 28, 1905
Walton, Mr. A. C. (Oxford Univ. and Middlesex), b Sept 26, 1933
Waqar Hassan (Pakistan), b Sept 12, 1932
Ward, D. J. (Glamorgan), b Aug 30, 1934

Ward, Mr. F. A. (South Australia), b Feb 23, 1909
Ward, Mr. J. T. (New Zealand), b March 11, 1937
Ward, W. (Warwickshire), b May 24, 1874, d Dec 13, 1961
Wardle, J. H. (Yorkshire and Cambs.), b Jan 8, 1923
Warne, F. (Victoria and Worc.), b Oct 3, 1908
Warner, Sir Pelham F. (Oxford Univ. and Middlesex), b in West Indies, Oct 2, 1873, d Jan 30, 1963
Waring, J. S. (Yorks.), b Oct 1, 1942
Warr, Mr. J. J. (Camb. Univ. and Middlesex), b July 16, 1927
Warren, A. R. (Derbyshire), b April 2, 1875, d Sept 3, 1951
Washbrook, C. (Lancashire), b Dec 6, 1914
Wass, T. (Notts.), b Dec 26, 1873, d Oct 27, 1953
Wassell, A. (Hampshire), b April 15. 1940
Waterman, Mr. A. G. (Essex), b May 13, 1911
Waters, Mr. A. E. (Glouc.), b May 8, 1902
Waters, Mr. R. H. C. (Oxford Univ. and Sussex), b Dec 6, 1937
Watkin, D. (Notts.), b June 28, 1914
Watkins, A. J. (Glamorgan), b April 21, 1922
Watkins, B. T. L. (Glouc.), b June 25, 1907
Watson, A. G. M. (Oxford Univ.), b Feb 27, 1945
Watson, F. (Lancashire), b Sept 17, 1899
Watson, G. S. (Leic. and Kent), b April 10, 1907
Watson, W. (Yorkshire and Leic.), b March 7, 1920
Watt, A. E. (Kent), b June 19, 1907
Watt, Mr. K. E (Tasmania), b Dec 12, 1891
Watts, E. A. (Surrey), b Aug 1, 1911
Watts, Mr. H. E. (Somerset and Camb. Univ.), b March 4, 1922
Watts, Mr. L. D. (Oxford Univ. and Glouc.), b May 2, 1935
Watts, P. D. (Northants), b March 31, 1938
Watts, P. J. (Northants), b June 16, 1940
Wazir Mohammad (Pakistan), b Dec 12, 1929
Webb, A. (Hampshire), b Aug 6, 1869
Webb, Mr H. E. (Oxford Univ. and Hampshire), b May 30, 1927
Webb, R. T. (Sussex), b July 11, 1922
Webb, Mr. S. G. (Manager, Australia in England 1961), b Jan 31, 1900
Webbe, Mr. A. J. (Oxford Univ. and Middlesex), b Jan 16, 1855, d Feb 19, 1941
Webster, Mr. J. (Camb. Univ. and Northants), b Oct 28, 1917
Webster, Dr. R. V. (Scotland and War.), b June 10, 1939
Webster, Mr. W. H. (Camb. Univ. and Middlesex), b Feb 22, 1910
Wedel, Mr. G. A. (Glouc.), b May 18, 1900
Weedon, Mr. M. J. H. (Camb. Univ.), b Oct 28, 1940
Weekes, Mr. E. D. (West Indies), b Feb 26, 1925
Weekes, Mr. K. H (West Indies), b Jan 24, 1912
Weeks, R. T. (War.), b April 30, 1930
Weir, Mr. G. L. (New Zealand), b June 2, 1908
Welch, T. B. G. (Northants), b July 31, 1906
Wellard, A. W. (Somerset), b April 8, 1903
Wellings, Mr. E. M. (Oxford Univ. and Surrey), b April 6, 1909
Wells, B. D. (Glouc. and Notts.), b July 27, 1930
Wells, Mr. C. M. (Camb. Univ., Surrey and Middlesex), b March 21, 1871, d Aug 22, 1963
Wells, Mr. T. U. (Camb. Univ. and Worc.), b Feb 6, 1927
Wensley, A. F. (Sussex and Scotland), b May 24, 1898
Wesley, Mr. C. (South Africa), b Sept 9, 1937
Westcott, A. H. (Somerset), b Nov 6, 1870
Wharton, A. (Lancashire and Leic.), b April 30, 1923
Whately, Mr. E. G. (Somerset and Hertfordshire), b July 27, 1882
Wheat, A. B. (Notts.), b May 13, 1898
Wheatley, Mr. G. A. (Oxford Univ. and Surrey), b May 28, 1923
Wheatley, K. J. (Hampshire), b Jan Jan 20, 1946
Wheatley, Mr. O. S. (Camb. Univ., War. and Glamorgan), b May 28, 1935
Wheelhouse, Mr. A. (Camb. Univ. and Notts.), b March 4, 1934
Whitcombe, Mr. P. A. (Oxford Univ. and Middlesex), b April 23, 1923
Whitcombe, Mr. P. J. (Oxford Univ. and Worc.), b Nov 11, 1928
White, Mr. A. F. T. (Camb. Univ., War. and Worc.), b Sept 5, 1915

White, Mr. A. H. (Camb. Univ.), b Oct 18, 1901
White, Mr. C. D. (Camb. Univ.), b April 4, 1937
White, D. W. (Hants). b Dec 14, 1935
White, Mr. E. S. (New South Wales), b April 17, 1913
White, Rev. H. (Northumberland and Oxford Univ.), b June 16, 1876, d Jan 11, 1965
White, Mr. J. C. (Somerset), b Feb 19, 1891, d May 2, 1961
White, M. E. (Worc.), b Jan 21, 1908
White, R. A. (Middlesex and Notts.), b Oct 6, 1936
White, Mr. R. C. (Camb. Univ. and Glouc.), b Jan 29, 1941
White, W. A. (West Indies), b Nov 20, 1938
Whitehead, A. (Somerset), b Oct 28, 1940
Whitehead, H. (Leic.), b Sept 19, 1875, d Sept 16, 1944
Whitehead, J. P. (Yorkshire and Worc.), b Sept 3, 1925
Whitehead, Ralph (Lancashire), b Oct 16, 1883
Whitfield, E. W. (Surrey and Northants), b May 31, 1911
Whiting, C. P. (Yorkshire), b April 19, 1890, d Jan 14, 1959
Whiting, N. H. (Worc.), b Oct 2, 1920
Whitington, Mr. R. S. (Adelaide Univ. and South Australia), b June 30, 1912
Whittaker, G. J. (Surrey), b May 29, 1916
Whittingham, B. (Notts.), b Oct 22, 1940
Whitty, Mr. W. J. (South Australia), b Aug 15, 1886
Whysall, W. W. (Notts.), b Oct 31, 1887, d Nov 11, 1930
Wigginton, S. H. (Leic.), b March 26, 1909
Wight, Mr. C. V. (West Indies), b July 28, 1902
Wight, Mr. O. S. (West Indies), b Aug 10, 1906
Wight, P. B. (British Guiana and Somerset), b June 25, 1930
Wilcox, Mr. A. G. S. (Glouc.), b July 7, 1920
Wilcox, Mr. D. R. (Camb. Univ. and Essex), b June 4, 1910, d Feb 6, 1953
Wilcox, J. (Essex), b Aug 16, 1940
Wild, J. (Northants), b Feb 24, 1935
Wild, Mr. J. V. (Camb. Univ.), b April 26, 1915
Wilenkin, Mr. B. C. G. (Camb. Univ.), b June 20, 1933
Wiles, Mr. C.A. (West Indies), b Aug 11, 1892
Wiley, Mr. W. G. A. (Oxford Univ.), b Nov 7, 1931
Wilkinson, Mr. C. T. A. (London County and Surrey), b Oct 4, 1884
Wilkinson, F. (Yorkshire), b May 23, 1914
Wilkinson, Mr. H. (Yorkshire), b Dec 11, 1877
Wilkinson, John (Glouc.), b July 16, 1876, d 1948
Wilkinson, L. L. (Lancashire), b Nov 5, 1916
Wilkinson, R. W. (Kent), b Dec 23, 1939
Wilkinson, Col. W. A. C. (Oxford Univ.), b Dec 6, 1892
Wilkinson, W. H. (Yorkshire), b March 12, 1881, d June 3, 1961
Willard, Mr. M. J. L. (Camb. Univ), b March 24, 1938
Willatt, Mr. G. L. (Camb. Univ., Notts., Derbyshire and Scotland), b May 7, 1918
Willett, M. D. (Surrey), b April 21, 1933
Williams, Mr. C. B. (West Indies), b March 8, 1926
Williams, Mr. C. C. P. (Oxford Univ. and Essex), b Feb 9, 1933
Williams, Mr. E. A. V. (West Indies), b April 10, 1914
Williams, Mr. Leo (Sussex), b May 15, 1900
Williams, Sir P. F. C., 2nd Bart. (Glouc.), b July 6, 1884, d May 6, 1958
Williams, Mr. P. V. (Sussex), b July 10, 1897
Williams, Mr. R. A. (Oxford Univ., Oxfordshire and Berkshire), b Feb 2, 1879, d Dec 1, 1958
Williams, Mr. R. H. (Worc.), b April 23, 1901
Williams, Mr. R. J. (South Africa), b April 12. 1912
Williamson, J. G. (Northants), b April 4, 1936
Willson, R. H. (Sussex), b July 14, 1933
Wilmot, K. (War.), b April 3, 1911
Wilmot, W. (Derbyshire), b Dec 25, 1872, d May 19, 1957
Wilson, A. (Lancs.), b April 24, 1921
Wilson, A. E. (Middlesex and Glouc.), b May 5, 1912
Wilson, Mr. A. K. (Sussex), b Aug 26, 1894
Wilson, B. B. (Yorkshire), b Dec 11, 1879, d Sept 14, 1957

Wilson, D. (Yorkshire), b Aug 7, 1937
Wilson, E. F. (Surrey), b June 24, 1907
Wilson, Mr. E. R. (Camb. Univ. and Yorkshire), b March 25, 1879, d July 21, 1957
Wilson, Mr. F. B. (Camb. Univ.), b Sept 21, 1881, d Jan 19, 1932
Wilson, Mr. G. (Camb. Univ. and Yorkshire), b Aug 21, 1895, d Nov 29, 1960
Wilson, Mr. G. (Worc.), b April 9, 1932
Wilson, Mr. G. A. (Yorkshire), b Feb 2, 1916
Wilson, G. A. (Worc.), b April 5, 1877, d March 3, 1962
Wilson, Mr. J. (South Australia), b Aug 20, 1922
Wilson, Mr. J. P. (Yorkshire), b April 3, 1889, d Oct 3, 1959
Wilson, J. V. (Yorkshire), b Jan 17, 1921
Wilson, R. C. (Kent), b Feb 18, 1928
Wilson, Mr. R. W. (Oxford Univ.), b July 15, 1934
Windows, Mr. A. R. (Camb. Univ. and Glouc.), b Sept 25, 1942
Winfield, H. M. (Notts.), b June 13, 1933
Winlaw, Sqdn.-Ldr. R. de W. K. (Camb. Univ., Bedfordshire and Surrey), b March 28, 1912, d Oct 31, 1942
Winn, Mr. C. E. (Oxford Univ. and Sussex), b Nov 13, 1926
Winning, Mr. C. S. (Australian Imperial Forces Team), b July 17, 1889
Winrow, H. (Notts.), b Jan 17, 1916
Winrow, R. (Notts. and Scotland), b Dec 30, 1910
Winslow, Mr. P. L. (South Africa, Rhodesia and Sussex), b May 21, 1929
Winter, Mr. C. E. (Camb. Univ.), b Sept 1, 1879, d July 20, 1964
Wisden, John (Sussex), Founder of John Wisden & Co. and *Wisden's Cricketers' Almanack*, b Sept 5, 1826, d April 5, 1884
Witherden, E. G. (Kent), b May 1, 1922
Wolton, A. V. (Berkshire and War.), b June 12, 1919
Wood, A. (Yorkshire), b Aug 25, 1898
Wood, B. (Yorks. and Lancs.), b Dec 26, 1942
Wood, Mr. C. J. B. (Leic.), b Nov 21, 1875, d June 5, 1960
Wood, D. J. (Sussex), b May 19, 1914
Wood, Mr. G. E. C. (Camb. Univ. and Kent), b Aug 22, 1893
Woodcock, Mr. R. G. (Oxford Univ.), b Nov 26, 1934
Woodfull, Mr. W. M. (Victoria), b Aug 22, 1897, d Aug 11, 1965
Woodhead, F. G. (Notts.), b Oct 30, 1912
Woodhouse, Mr. G. E. S. (Somerset), b Feb 15, 1924
Woods, Mr. S. M. J. (Somerset and Camb. Univ.), b April 14, 1868, d April 30, 1931
Wooler, C. (Leic.), b June 30, 1930
Wooller, Mr. W. (Camb. Univ. and Glamorgan), b Nov 20, 1912
Woollett, A. F. (Kent), b Sept 20, 1927
Woolley, C. N. (Glouc. and Northants), b May 5, 1886, d Nov 3, 1962
Woolley, F. E. (Kent), b May 27, 1887
Wormald, Major I. (Middlesex), b Feb 23, 1882, d Nov 14, 1957
Worrell, Sir F. M. (West Indies), b Aug 1, 1924
Worsley, Mr. D. R. (Oxford Univ. and Lancashire), b July 18, 1941
Worsley, Sir W. A., 4th Bart. (Yorkshire), President, M.C.C., 1961–1962), b April 5, 1890
Worthington, T. S. (Derbyshire), b Aug 21, 1905
Wreford-Brown, Mr. A. J. (Sussex), b Oct 26, 1912
Wreford-Brown, Mr. C. (Glouc.), b Oct 9, 1866, d Nov 26, 1951
Wright, A. (War.), b Aug 25, 1941
Wright, A. C. (Kent), b April 6, 1896, d May 26, 1959
Wright, Mr. C. C. G. (Camb. Univ.), b March 7, 1887, d Sept 9, 1960
Wright, D. V. P. (Kent), b Aug 21, 1914
Wright, L. (Worc.), b Jan 20, 1903, d Jan 6, 1956
Wright, Mr. P. A. (Camb. Univ. and Northants), b May 16, 1903
Wrightson, R. W. (Essex), b Oct 29, 1939
Wrigley, Mr. M. H. (Oxford Univ.), b July 30, 1924
Wyatt, Mr. R. E. S. (War. and Wor.), b May 2, 1901
Wykes, Mr. N. G. (Camb. Univ. and Essex), b March 19, 1906
Wyld, Mr. H. J. (Oxford Univ. and Middlesex), b April 16, 1880, d Dec 9, 1961
Yardley, Mr. N. W. D. (Camb. Univ. and Yorkshire), b March 19, 1915
Yarnold, H. (Worc.), b July 6, 1917
Yates, Major H. W. M. (Hampshire), March 25, 1883, d Aug 21, 1956

Yates, W. G. (Notts.), b June 18 1919
Yawar Saeed (Somerset), b Jan 22, 1935
Young, A. (Somerset), b 1890, d April 2, 1936
Young, Mr. D. E. (Oxford Univ. and Berks.), b May 7, 1917
Young, D. M. (Worc. and Glouc.), b April 15, 1924
Young, H. (Essex), b Feb 5, 1876
Young, J. A. (Middlesex), b Oct 14, 1912
Young, Mr. R. A. (Camb. Univ. and Sussex), b Sept 16, 1885
Yuile, B. W. (New Zealand), b Oct 29, 1941
Zulfiqar Ahmed (Pakistan), b Nov 22, 1926

THE NEW BALL

In the United Kingdom the new ball has been available as follows:

1902. Practice acknowledged of taking new ball if old damaged or if bowler had lifted seam to obtain better grip.
1907. Permitted after 200 runs "to clarify ambiguity".
1921. Permitted in Test Matches.
1923. After 200 runs in County Championship and Test Matches.
1939. After 200 runs in First-class or Minor county matches: optional in other grades.
1946. After 55 overs in first-class cricket.
1947. New Code said after 200 runs in first-class cricket and with prior consent in other games: Special Instructions continued 55-over experiment in first-class cricket.
1949. After 65 overs.
1952. New Code amended to permit new ball after 65 overs in first-class cricket in U.K. and with prior consent in other grades: elsewhere after 200 runs.
1954. Fresh special instruction amended new code to permit reversion to new ball after 200 runs in U.K. in first-class cricket.
1956. After 200 runs or 75 overs in first-class cricket.
1961. After 85 overs in first-class cricket: in Australian matches in this season; in 1964, after 200 runs or 85 overs.
1966. I.C.C. decision that, for two years, in all first-class cricket, new ball should be taken after a minimum of 75 overs, maximum 85 overs (six balls) at the discretion of the Home Authority.

OBITUARY, 1966

ANDREWS, WILLIAM, who died on December 22, aged 80, was a founder member and Past President of the Irish Cricket Union. Known as "The Grand Old Man" of Irish Cricket, "Willie" had been a member of the Northern Ireland Cricket Union for 59 years. In his playing days he appeared for Gentlemen of Ireland and for Ulster. He was at one time High Sheriff of County Down.

ANSON, THE HON. RUPERT, who died on December 20, aged 77, was in the Harrow XI of 1908. He was dismissed for 0, but by taking five wickets in the match for 81 runs, helped in the defeat of Eton by ten wickets. He occasionally played for Middlesex from 1910 to 1914, his best innings being 97 against Essex at Leyton in the last season. On that occasion, after Middlesex had been sent in to bat, he and F. A. Tarrant (250 not out) hit 235 for the opening stand and did much towards victory for their county in an innings with 156 runs to spare.

ATKINSON, BERNARD GERARD WENSLEY, who died in a London hospital on September 4, aged 65, played for Scotland, Northamptonshire and Middlesex. In the St. Paul's School XI from 1916 to 1919, he headed the batting averages in the last two years and while at Edinburgh Academy, where he taught for 37 years, hit many runs for Grange C.C. In 1934 for Middlesex against Surrey at Lord's, he hit a short-pitched ball from A. R. Gover for six with what was described as "an overhead lawn tennis smash". A first-rate Rugby footballer, he appeared at centre threequarter in a Cambridge Seniors' match but did not gain a Blue.

ATKINSON, NIGEL SAMUEL MITFORD, who died on October 24, was in the St. Paul's XI in 1916 and 1917, being second in the batting averages in the second year. His brother, B. G. W. Atkinson, who also died last year, was in the team at the same time. Sam took part in three matches for Middlesex in 1923, earning with medium-paced left-arm deliveries a match record of seven wickets for 106 runs against Cambridge University at Fenner's. He played club cricket for Hampstead for many years.

BAKER, WIRI AURUNUI, who died in Wellington, New Zealand, on July 1, aged 74, was the most prolific scorer in Wellington senior championship matches. A right-handed opening batsman, he hit 10,226 runs in 25 years of senior cricket. In addition, in first-class games for Wellington between 1911 and 1929, he obtained 1,835 runs, average 31.63.

BEASLEY, the REV. ROBERT NOBLE, who died on January 21, aged 83, played occasionally for Northamptonshire from 1907 to 1911. He was a first-class Rugby footballer.

BEDFORD, PHILIP IAN, who died on September 18, aged 36, after collapsing while batting for Finchley at Buckhurst Hill, captained Middlesex in 1961 and 1962. While at Woodhouse Grammar School, he made his debut for the county in 1947 at the age of 17 and in his first match, against Essex at Lord's, created a highly favourable impression when, with well-controlled leg-breaks and googlies, he took six wickets. That season Middlesex won the County Championship and Ian Bedford occupied second place in their bowling averages with 25 wickets at 19.36 runs apiece. He did not fare so well in the following season and after carrying out his National Service in the Royal Air Force, for whom he played, he returned to Finchley and met with marked success. When he was called upon to lead Middlesex upon the retirement of J. J. Warr, modesty prevented Bedford from bowling as much as he might, but he still achieved an occasional useful performance. Twice he toured South America and once visited Canada with M.C.C. teams.

BENNETT, MAJOR GEORGE GUY MARSLAND, who died on February 6, aged 82, was in the Harrow XI of 1902, helping in the defeat of Eton by eight wickets when scoring 52 not out—his highest innings of the season. While at Magdalen College, Oxford, he played an innings of 131 for the University against Worcestershire at Worcester in 1904, but did not gain a Blue. For over twenty years he did capital service for Berkshire. Besides being mentioned in despatches, he won the M.C. during the First World War.

BERNAU, ERNEST HENRY LOVELL, who died in January, aged 80, toured England with T. C. Lowry's New Zealand team in 1927. In first-class matches, he took 32 wickets with left-arm medium-pace bowling for 24.21 runs each, his best analysis being six for 35 in the first innings of Glamorgan at Cardiff. "Bill" Bernau achieved some excellent performances for Wanganui, Hawkes Bay and Wellington. In 1913 he took seven South Taranaki wickets for 57 runs in the first innings and five for 45 in the second and he did the "hat-trick" in the Town v. Country game of 1923. He was also a more than useful batsman, as he showed when hitting 117 for Wellington v. Auckland in his first Plunket Shield match in 1921–22.

BEVINGTON, TIMOTHY ARTHUR, who died in Vancouver in May, aged 85, was at Harrow without gaining a place in the XI. Brother of J. C. Bevington, who also played for the county, he appeared in four County Championship matches for Middlesex between 1900 and 1904. His highest innings was 27 in the last season, when he and J. H. Hunt stemmed a collapse against Gloucestershire at Lord's by adding 50 for the eighth wicket.

BLUNT, ROGER CHARLES, who died in London on June 22, aged 65, played in nine Test matches for New Zealand between 1929 and 1931, seven against England and two against South Africa. Beginning his career as a leg-break bowler, he developed into a very fine batsman. Against A. H. H. Gilligan's England team in New Zealand in 1929, he headed his country's Test bowling averages with nine wickets for 19 runs each. In the opening Test of that tour, which marked the entry of New Zealand into the top rank of cricket, he not only gained a match analysis of five wickets for 34 runs but, with 45 not out, was top scorer in a first innings of 112. In England in 1931, his 96 helped New Zealand to a highly creditable draw with England at Lord's after being 230 in arrears on the first innings. Until B. Sutcliffe surpassed his 7,769 runs in 1953, he was the highest-scoring New Zealand batsman in first-class cricket. In a dazzling display for Otago against Canterbury at Christchurch in 1931–32, he hit 338 not out, then the highest score ever achieved by a New Zealand cricketer, though Sutcliffe many years later made 355 and 385. Well-known in business circles in England and New Zealand, he was awarded the M.B.E. in 1965.

BRIDGES, JAMES J., who died in London on September 26, aged 79, bowled fast-medium for Somerset between 1911 and 1929. Before the 1914 war he played as a professional, but later he was one of the many popular amateurs who enjoyed cricket under the captaincy of John Daniell. He had a neat run-up and side-way action and took 685 wickets. When Jack Hobbs equalled W. G. Grace's record of 126 hundreds in 1925 at Taunton, Bridges had him caught at the wicket by M. L. Hill for 101. His bowling partner was usually R. C. Robertson-Glasgow, who tells in his *More Cricket Prints* how each considered himself the superior batsman; Daniell with rare judgement decided that they should toss for the last two places, a procedure which was regularly observed.

BROOK, GEORGE WILFRED, who died at Bournemouth on July 24, aged 70, did fine work as a leg-break bowler for Worcestershire from 1931 to 1935. Joining the county from the Kidderminster club at the age of 35, he enjoyed marked success in his first season. With such analyses as six wickets for 30 runs against Derbyshire at Kidderminster; six for 37 v. Leicestershire, six for 80 v. Nottinghamshire and six for 89 v. Lancashire, all at Worcester, he dismissed 128 batsmen in

Championship fixtures at an average cost of 21.41. Though he did not touch quite the same heights afterwards, he took 461 wickets, average 27.85, during a brief first-class career which terminated when he went to Keighley, the Yorkshire Council club.

BUTT, JOHN ALEC STEUART, who died on October 30, aged 74, did not get a place in the XI while at Marlborough, but played without much success in one match for Sussex in 1923.

CAHILL, KEYRAN WILLIAM JACK, who died in Launceston on March 7, aged 55, played in four first-class matches for Tasmania in 1931–32. His best performance was against H. B. Cameron's South African side when he hit 21 and 35 not out.

CHERRY-DOWNES, HUBERT MICHAEL ARTHUR, who died suddenly on March 28, aged 32, headed the Lincolnshire averages as a fast-medium bowler in 1957 when, with 65 wickets at 14.43 runs apiece, he dismissed more batsmen than any other player in the Minor Counties' Competition. In the Charterhouse XI in 1951 and 1952, he was top of the bowling averages in each year. He appeared for Nottinghamshire Second Eleven before joining Lincolnshire, whom he assisted from 1956 to 1964. Twice he represented the Minor Counties against touring teams from overseas.

CLARKE, JOHN, who died in a London hospital on June 17, aged 53, was leading cricket writer for the *Evening Standard* from 1958 till his death. The son of a doctor, he toured on behalf of his paper with England teams in Australia, South Africa, New Zealand and the West Indies.

CLIFF, ALFRED TALBOT, who died on January 25, aged 87, played as an amateur for Worcestershire from 1912 to 1920. His highest innings for the county was 59 not out against Leicestershire at Worcester in 1914, when he and M. K. Foster shared in a partnership of 166.

COOK, PERCY WILLIAM, who died in hospital on April 5, played for Kent Second Eleven in 1920 and 1921. He headed the bowling averages in 1920 with 21 wickets for 6.47 runs each, taking 15 of them for 53 runs at The Oval where Surrey Second Eleven, dismissed for 65 and 70, were beaten by an innings and 35 runs. Cook played most of his cricket for Gore Court C.C., Sittingbourne.

CREBER, ARTHUR B., who died in August, played in three matches for Scotland in 1937. Son of Harry Creber, the Glamorgan left-arm bowler, he took all ten wickets in an innings for Ferguslie in 1935 and for Heriot's F.P. in 1947. He was professional groundsman at George Heriot's School and later head groundsman at Rydal.

CRESSWELL, GEORGE FENWICK, who was found dead with a shot-gun at his side on January 10, aged 50, did not play in first-class cricket till he was 34. After only one trial match, he was chosen for the 1949 tour of England by New Zealand, and he did so well with slow-medium leg-theory bowling that he took 62 wickets in the first-class fixtures of the tour for 26.09 runs apiece. He played in one Test match that season, the fourth, disposing of six batsmen for 168 runs in an England total of 482. He also took part in the two Tests against F. R. Brown's England team of 1950–51. He played for Marlborough, Wellington and Central Districts.

CUNNINGHAM, ERNEST, who died on November 11, aged 86, played for North of Argentine and Brazil. He was father of the better-known O. T. ("Boy") Cunningham, who played in the same sides with him.

DALLAS BROOKS, GENERAL SIR REGINALD ALEXANDER, who died on March 22, aged 69, was in the Dover XI from 1912 to 1914 as a batsman and medium-paced bowler. In his last season he headed the School batting figures with 939 runs, of which he scored 187 in an innings against King's School, Canterbury, at an average of 62.62, and was also leading bowler with 36 wickets at 12.94 runs each. In 1919 and 1921 he appeared in a few matches for Hampshire, hitting 107 from the Gloucestershire bowling at Southampton in the first year. A fine all-round sportsman, he captained the Combined Services against touring teams from Australia, South Africa and New Zealand, led them at hockey, at which he played for England against Ireland and France and captained the Royal Navy at golf. Joining the Royal Marines on his eighteenth birthday, he earned the D.S.O. in the First World War for his part in the St. George's Day raid on Zeebrugge in 1918. He was Governor of Victoria from 1949 to 1963.

DICKENS, HENRY CHARLES, who died in November, aged 83, was the last surviving grandson of Charles Dickens. A keen cricketer, he was a member of M.C.C.

DOLL, MORDAUNT HENRY CASPERS, who died at Devizes on June 30, aged 78, was a hard-hitting batsman. In the Charterhouse XI from 1905 to 1907, he hit 195 against Westminster in the last season, when he and R. L. L. Braddell put on 214 together—180 of them in an hour. From 1912 to 1919 he played occasional matches for Middlesex and against Nottinghamshire at Lord's in 1913, scored 102 not out in an unfinished stand of 182 in two hours with H. R. Murrell. He toured the West Indies with the M.C.C. team captained by A. F. Somerset in 1912–13 and also appeared for Hertfordshire.

DUCKWORTH, GEORGE, who died on January 5, aged 64, was an outstanding character in first-class cricket in the period between the two World Wars, a time when the game possessed far more players of popular personality than at the present time. Small of stature, but big of heart and voice, Duckworth used an "Owzat" shout of such piercing quality and volume that his appeal alone would have made him a figure to be remembered.

But Duckworth possessed many other qualities. He was one of the finest wicket-keepers the game has produced; as a batsman he could be relied upon to fight in a crisis; he possessed wit and good humour which made him an endearing companion, and he was a sound judge of a player, an ability which served his native Lancashire well as a committee man in recent years.

Duckworth, born and resident in Warrington all his life, joined Lancashire in 1922. He made his debut a year later and ended his first-class career, perhaps prematurely, in 1938. He took up journalism, but hardly had time to establish himself before war broke out in 1939. Then he spent spells in hotel management and farming before his post-war career, which included journalism, broadcasting, and acting as baggage-master and scorer to M.C.C. teams abroad, and for touring countries here. He also took Commonwealth sides to India.

Duckworth received a trial with Warwickshire before arousing the interest of his native county with whom he quickly showed his talent by the confident manner in which he kept to such varied and demanding bowlers as the Australian fast bowler, E. A. McDonald, and the spin of C. H. Parkin and R. Tyldesley. By 1924 he had gained the first of 24 Test caps for England, a total which undoubtedly would have been much higher but for the competition of L. E. G. Ames of Kent, who in the 1930's usually gained preference because of his batting prowess. In his later days with Lancashire, Duckworth also faced strong competition from Farrimond, which he resisted successfully.

In Test cricket, Duckworth claimed 59 wicket-keeping victims, and he also hit 234 runs, with 39 not out as his highest. For Lancashire his number of victims was a record 921, and his highest score 75. In all first-class matches he helped in 1,090 dismissals, 751 catches and 339 stumpings. He dismissed 107 batsmen, 77 caught and 30 stumped, in his best season, 1928.

That season completed three Championship successes for Lancashire, captained by Leonard Green, who described Duckworth as "One of the smallest, but noisiest of all cricketing artists—a man born to squat behind the wicket and provide good humour and unbounded thrills day by day in many a glorious summer."

Lancashire won the Championship again in 1930, and 1934, so that Duckworth gained the honour of being a member of five championship teams. In 1949–50 Duckworth, a man of administrative ability, took his first Commonwealth team to India, Pakistan and Ceylon, and repeated the successful venture in 1950–51 and 1953–54. Then followed his duties as baggage-master and scorer, at home and abroad, where his jovial personality, wise counsel and experience were of benefit to many a team and individual cricketer. His radio and television commentaries, typically humorous and forthright, became well-known, both on cricket and on Rugby League, in which game he was a devoted follower of Warrington.

Among many tributes were:

H. Sutcliffe (Yorkshire and England): George was a delightful colleague, a great man on tours particularly. He had a vast knowledge of the game and he was always ready and willing to help any young player. As a wicket-keeper he was brilliant.

C. Washbrook (Lancashire and England): He was a magnificent wicket-keeper and a fighting little batsman. In his later years he became one of the shrewdest observers of the game and his advice was always available and eagerly sought by cricketers of every class and creed.

EARLE, GUY FIFE, who died at his home at Maperton, Wincanton, on December 30, aged 75, was a batsman who, while by no means a stylist, used his considerable physique to hit the ball tremendously hard. From 1908 to 1911 he was in the Harrow XI chiefly as a fast bowler, and he captained the School in the famous "Fowler's Match" of 1910 when Eton, only four runs ahead with nine wickets down, won by nine runs. He played two games for Surrey in 1911, but did not reappear in first-class cricket till turning out in 1922 for Somerset, with whom he stayed till 1931. In all first-class games he hit 6,303 runs, average 20.59, and took 109 wickets for 30.11 runs each. His highest innings for Somerset was 111 against Gloucestershire at Bristol in 1923; his biggest in first-class cricket was 130 for A. E. R. Gilligan's M.C.C. team against Hindus at Bombay in 1926, when he displayed his punishing powers to the full by hitting eight 6's and eleven 4's. He and M. W. Tate (50) put on 164 in sixty-five minutes. Earle was also a member of the first M.C.C. team which met New Zealand in official Tests in 1929–30 under the captaincy of A. H. H. Gilligan. His highest score on that tour was 98 in forty minutes, including three 6's and eleven 4's against Taranaki. On the way to New Zealand he punished Clarrie Grimmett for 22 in an over, including three 6's when M.C.C. met South Australia at Adelaide. Earle struck 59 in fifteen minutes against Gloucestershire at Taunton in 1929.

ENGLISH, EDWARD APSEY, who died on September 8, aged 102, was the oldest surviving county cricketer. He played as an amateur for Hampshire from 1898 to 1901. In the first season, "Ted" English hit his highest first-class innings, 98 against Surrey at The Oval, when he and A. Webb, by putting on 164 for the fifth wicket in the second Hampshire innings, rescued their side from a precarious position. He continued playing club cricket till 65 and remained an active sportsman till 1957. When 82 he holed in one on the Alton golf course and was 91 when he played his last game of golf. At 93 he reached the final of the Alton Conservative Club snooker championship. For 36 years he was Registrar at Alton.

EVANS BAILLIE, T. H., who died in hospital at Melrose, Roxburghshire, on April 19, aged 77, was a well-known sporting journalist. Educated at Haileybury and Oxford, "Bill" Baillie was a tea-planter before he took up journalism. Beginning with the *Morning Post*, he later wrote on cricket and Rugby football for the

Manchester Guardian and finally joined the *Daily Telegraph*, with whom he served for seventeen years till he retired and whose Northern Sports Editor he became. His tall figure and his monocle were familiar sights on many grounds and his genial manner and unfailing humour made him immensely popular. In his young days, he played Rugby for London Scottish and the Barbarians.

GALLOWAY, JACK OMAR, who died in a London hospital on July 30, aged 42, played cricket in Yorkshire and for the Royal Engineers, Mysore State, Sierra Leone and Singapore. For three years during the Second World War, he served as an officer in the Royal Indian Engineers; he was one of the original Council members and became President of the British Association of Corrosive Engineers.

GHULAM MOHAMED, who died in Karachi on July 21, aged 68, toured England with the Maharajah of Porbandar's All India team in 1932. He proved a big disappointment, taking only three wickets in first-class matches at a cost of 95.33 runs each, but on the matting pitches of his own country he achieved much success with left-arm deliveries of medium pace. He played for the Mohammadans in the Sind Pentangular and Bombay Quadrangular tournaments.

GODDARD, THOMAS WILLIAM JOHN, who died at his home in Gloucester on May 22, aged 65, was one of the greatest off-break bowlers the game has known. A big man, standing six feet three, with massive hands, he spun the ball to a remarkable degree and on a helpful pitch was almost unplayable. He bowled mostly from round the wicket and had such a command of length and flight that even on easy surfaces he kept batsmen apprehensive. His height enabled him to make the ball lift more than most spinners and the Gloucestershire combination of Goddard and the slow left-hander, Charlie Parker, was probably the most feared in Championship cricket.

The early days of Goddard's career gave no hint of the success he was later to achieve. Born on October 1, 1900, he first played for Gloucestershire in 1922 as a fast bowler. Despite his strong physique he made little progress and in six years took only 153 wickets at a cost of 34 runs each.

At the end of the 1927 season he left the county and joined the M.C.C. ground staff at Lord's. There he decided to experiment with off-breaks and his long, strong fingers were ideally suited to this type of bowling. Beverley Lyon, the Gloucestershire captain, saw him in the nets at Lord's and, immediately struck by Goddard's new-found ability, persuaded Gloucestershire to re-engage him. The effect was immediate and dramatic. In 1929 Goddard took 184 wickets at 16 runs apiece and he never looked back.

When he finally retired in 1952, at the age of 51, Goddard had taken 2,979 wickets, average 19.84 and in a period when off-break bowlers were not fashionable in Test cricket, he played eight times for England. He finished with six hat-tricks, the same number as his colleague, Parker, and only one less than the all-time record of seven, by D. V. P. Wright of Kent.

One of the hat-tricks came in a Test Match, against South Africa at Johannesburg on Boxing Day, 1938. His victims were A. D. Nourse (caught and bowled), N. Gordon (stumped) and W. W. Wade (bowled). This is still the only hat-trick achieved in Test cricket in Johannesburg. That match was drawn, but it also included two other remarkable performances by Englishmen, a century in each innings from E. Paynter, and 93 and 106 on his Test debut by P. A. Gibb.

Goddard appeared three times for England on that tour. His other Test appearances were once against Australia in 1930, twice against New Zealand in 1937 and twice against West Indies in 1939, all in England. His success was limited to 22 wickets, costing 26.72 runs each, but he enjoyed one fine performance, bowling England to victory by 130 runs against New Zealand at Old Trafford in 1937 with six for 29 in the last innings. He was among the thirteen England selected for Old Trafford against Australia in 1938 when rain prevented a ball being bowled.

On 16 occasions Goddard took 100 or more wickets in a season, four times reaching 200. His most successful year was 1937 when he claimed 248 victims.

Two years later he achieved the wonderful feat of taking 17 wickets in a day, against Kent at Bristol, nine for 38 and eight for 68. Only two other bowlers have equalled this, H. Verity of Yorkshire and C. Blythe of Kent.

In his big year, 1937, Goddard took all ten Worcestershire wickets in an innings for 113 at Cheltenham. He also obtained six for 68 in the first innings of that match. On seven occasions he finished with nine wickets in one innings.

One of the matches which gave Goddard most pleasure came at Bristol where Gloucestershire tied with the formidable Australian side of 1930. He played an important part in that thrilling match by taking three wickets in five balls at one stage and ended it by taking the final wicket, that of P. M. Hornibrook.

During the 1939 War, Goddard obtained a commission in the R.A.F. He was back at his best when first-class cricket resumed, but because of ill-health he announced his retirement in 1951. To help the county out of difficulties he returned in 1952 and despite his age he took 45 wickets in 13 Championship matches.

When he eventually gave up Goddard established a successful furniture shop in Gloucester in which he was active until about a year before his death.

His final tally of wickets places him fifth in the order of bowlers the game has known. Only W. Rhodes, A. P. Freeman, C. W. L. Parker and J. T. Hearne have taken more. Umpires over the years got to know Goddard's frequent and loud appeals. His first benefit, in 1936, brought him £2,097 and from his second, in 1948, he received £3,355.

GRINTER, TRAYTON GOLDING, who died on April 21, aged 80, played for Essex as an amateur in occasional matches between 1909 and 1921. While serving with the Artists' Rifles in the First World War, he was severely wounded in the left arm. Nevertheless he continued to play cricket for South Woodford and Frinton-on-Sea with marked success while virtually batting one-handed, and he put together more than 200 centuries in club matches. At the age of 50 he turned his attentions to golf and within a few weeks became a seven handicap player. Joining Cockburn and Co., the wine merchants, as office boy on Mafeking Day, 1900, he became chairman 33 years later.

GURUNATHAN, S. K., who died on May 6, aged 58, was Sports Editor of *The Hindu* and a well-known figure in sporting journalism in India. He wrote with authority on almost all games, but cricket was his speciality. He covered over 50 Test matches in which India took part, including the tour of England in 1952. He contributed to *Wisden* and to *The Times*, and was the author of many books, including *Story of The Tests* and *Indian Cricket*, an annual publication on the lines of *Wisden*.

HAIG, NIGEL ESME, who died in a Sussex hospital on October 27, aged 78, was a celebrated amateur all-rounder between the two World Wars. He did not gain a place in the XI while at Eton, but from 1912 until he retired from the game in 1934 he rendered splendid service to Middlesex, whom he captained for the last six years of his career. He was a member of the Championship-winning sides of 1920 and 1921. In addition, he played for England against Australia in the second of the disastrous Test series of 1921 and four times against the West Indies for the Hon. F. S. G. Calthorpe's M.C.C. team of 1929–30 without achieving much success. In all first-class cricket, Haig hit 15,208 runs, average 20.83, and with swing-bowling above medium pace he obtained 1,116 wickets for 27.47 runs each.

Six times he exceeded 1,000 runs, five times he took 100 or more wickets in a season and in 1921, 1927 and 1929 he did the "cricketers' double". An agile fieldsman, he held 218 catches. His batting style was scarcely classic, but a quick eye stood him in good stead and, despite his not very powerful physique, he could hit the ball hard. The highest of his twelve centuries was 131 against Sussex at Lord's in 1920, when he, P. F. Warner, H. W. Lee and J. W. Hearne, the first four Middlesex batsmen, each reached three figures—an unprecedented occurrence in first-class cricket which was repeated for the same county by H. L. Dales, H. W. Lee, J. W. Hearne and E. Hendren against Hampshire at Southampton three years later.

Seemingly built of whipcord, Haig, a nephew of Lord Harris, bowled for long spells without apparent signs of fatigue. Among his best performances with the ball was the taking of seven wickets for 33 runs in the Kent first innings at Canterbury in 1920. This was another eventful match for Haig, for he scored 57 in the Middlesex first innings and became the "second leg" of a "hat-trick" by A. P. Freeman in the second. In 1924 Haig took six wickets for 11 runs in Gloucestershire's first innings on Packer's Ground at Bristol, a game rendered specially memorable by the fact that C. W. L. Parker, the slow left-hander, twice accomplished the "hat-trick" at the expense of Middlesex. Haig was also a fine real tennis player, could hold his own with lawn tennis players of near-Wimbledon standard and was equally good at racquets, squash and golf. While serving with the Royal Field Artillery during the First World War, he won the M.C.

HARVEY, GEORGE, who died in June, aged 69, played on several occasions for Norfolk.

HEASLIP, JOHN GANLY, who died on May 23, aged 66, played as an all-rounder for many years for Hounslow C.C. He appeared for Gentlemen of Ireland, the Club Cricket Conference and for Civil Service.

HOLLOWAY, GEORGE JAMES WARNER, who died on September 24, aged 82, was in the Clifton XI of 1903. From 1908 to 1911 he played a few times for Gloucestershire.

HUNTING, GERARD LINDSAY, who died on September 4, aged 75, was a successful amateur batsman for Northumberland before and after the First World War. In the Loretto XI he headed the batting averages in 1910 and 1911.

JACKSON, CAPT. GUY R., who died in a Chesterfield hospital on February 21, aged 69, was a left-handed batsman who captained Derbyshire for eight years. While at Harrow, he appeared against Eton at Lord's, scoring 59—his highest innings of the season. After serving in the First World War, during which he was twice mentioned in despatches and awarded the M.C. and the Legion d'Honneur, he played for Derbyshire from 1919 to 1936, becoming captain in 1922. In four seasons he exceeded 1,000 runs. In all first-class cricket until his retirement from the game he scored 10,153 runs, including nine centuries, for an average of 23.07, and held 109 catches. He was joint managing director of the family iron and steel business, the Clay Cross Co., Ltd.

JEWELL, JACK EDMUND, who died at Knysna, Cape Province, on April 17, aged 75, was a brother of M. F. S. and A. N. Jewell, of Worcestershire. When in the XI at Felsted, he headed the School averages in 1907 and 1908. He later played for Surrey Second Eleven and Orange Free State.

JONES, CHARLES J. E., who died in hospital on September 1, aged 73, founded the London Counties war-time team of professional cricketers who played at Lord's and many other grounds around the Metropolis. Always a keen club cricketer, he was a Vice-President of Forest Hill after acting for many years as fixture secretary as well as being a most efficient umpire. Jones, who possessed an astute business brain—he was connected with the Inland Revenue—sponsored the first Sunday benefit match. It was for Harold Larwood, following the "body-line" tour of over thirty years ago. It took place at Forest Hill before a crowd of 5,000 and later that evening when Larwood was presented with a cheque for £100 he was so surprised that he showed his appreciation by giving back £25 to the club's funds. More recently, Jones sent to Lord's a scheme to bring all the Test match playing countries to England in the same season, embracing the Counties in a Championship as well as a full series of Test matches. He even drew up a list of fixtures with dates and grounds and stated that he felt sure that, if approached, big business firms would be willing to sponsor the whole affair. Now that firms like Gillette, Rothman's, Horlicks, Carreras and Charrington's are supporting cricket it seems that Jones was not, after all, far off the mark.

JOWETT, COLIN JOSEPH CADWALLADWR, who died on November 11, aged 75, was father of D. C. P. R. Jowett, the off-spin bowler who gained his Blue for Oxford from 1952 to 1955. Educated at Christ's Hospital, Colin played for Dorset for some years from 1923, being a fine bowler and useful batsman, and also served as secretary to the county for ten years after the Second World War. He was well known in Dorset, Somerset and Bristol club cricket.

JOY, FRANK DOUGLAS HOWARTH, who died in a Winchester nursing home on February 17, aged 85, was in the Winchester XI in 1895 and from 1897 to 1899. A fast-medium left-arm bowler, he took five Eton wickets for 21 runs in 1897. At Oxford, he played in the Freshmen's match of 1900, but did not gain a Blue. From 1909 to 1912 he occasionally turned out for Somerset, then predominantly amateur, his best match analysis being seven wickets for 72 runs against Yorkshire at Taunton in 1910, and he appeared for Bombay Presidency in 1908. As a captain in the Army, he was mentioned in despatches during the First World War. His daughter, Nancy, was author of *Maiden Over*, the standard history of women's cricket.

KNIGHT, BRUCE, who died on December 5, aged 93, played as a young man with W. G. Grace and G. L. Jessop for Witney Town C.C., Oxfordshire. He was formerly proprietor and Editor of the *Witney Gazette*.

LANGRIDGE, JAMES, of Sussex and England fame, died at his home at Brighton on September 10, aged 60. An all-rounder in the truest sense of the word, he could compare for both his left-hand batting and his slow left-arm bowling with the best in either field. He played for Sussex from 1924 until 1953, winning an England place on eight occasions. In his career he scored 31,716 runs, average 35.20, and took 1,530 wickets at 22.56 runs each, achieving the "double" feat of 1,000 runs and 100 wickets six times. He hit over 1,000 runs in twenty seasons, a total exceeded by only nine batsmen, and compiled forty-two centuries.

James Langridge—his Christian name was always employed to distinguish him from his brother, John, who opened the batting for Sussex for many years—was born at Newick on July 10, 1906. His early cricket was played first at the local school and then for the local club, where he displayed such potential that in 1923 he went to the Sussex Nursery on the county ground. The coach, A. Millward, rapidly realised that he had in his charge a batsman of considerable ability, though at the time his bowling skill had yet to manifest itself. Langridge appeared three times for the county in 1924, but could not gain a regular place until 1927. In that season he missed by eight scoring 1,000 runs and fell four short of a maiden hundred against Middlesex at Brighton. Next season he managed both targets comfortably.

Meanwhile his bowling made swift advances. His 35 wickets in 1928 proved expensive, but in the following year he took 81 wickets for less than 21 runs apiece. At the beginning of the 1930's his batting aggregate fell away, but his bowling proved immensely useful to Sussex, and in recognition of his promise as much as his achievements, *Wisden* chose him as one of the Five Cricketers of 1931. He amply justified the choice with a remarkable spell of bowling the following summer at Cheltenham, where he took seven Gloucestershire wickets for eight runs.

A year later came his first Test match, against the West Indies at Manchester. In the second innings of a drawn game he took seven wickets for 56 runs, including that of George Headley, whom he caught off his own bowling. This feat kept him in the side for the final Test and also earned him a place in the M.C.C. team in India that winter. He scored 70 in a draw at Calcutta when batting No. 4, and took five wickets for 63 runs in the last Test at Madras. His other three appearances on the Test field were in the home series of 1935, 1936, and 1946, and he went abroad again with E. R. T. Holmes' team to Australasia in 1935–36 and to India with Lord Tennyson in 1937–38.

Langridge would undoubtedly have been chosen more frequently for England but for the presence of Hedley Verity, of Yorkshire. After the Second World War, during which Langridge served with the National Fire Service, the England selectors, left without a left-arm spin bowler of Test class by the untimely death of Verity, turned to Langridge, then aged 40, for the tour of Australia.

He was one of several players to spend an unhappy time there in the cricketing sense. Chosen for the third Test at Melbourne, he injured a groin muscle at practice and thus missed his life's ambition. That virtually ended his tour and his representative career, though he continued to render splendid service to Sussex.

In 1950 he became only the second professional cricketer in recent years to be appointed the captain of a county side, the first being H. E. Dollery, of Warwickshire. He led Sussex for three seasons. His last match was against the 1953 Australians and he gained some slight consolation for the disappointment of Melbourne by materially assisting in preventing the tourists bringing off a win, when he batted for almost two hours in scoring 46.

Langridge could perhaps be cited as the typical professional of the pre-War era, skilled in all departments of the game to which he devoted his whole life. His batting style was as modest and unobtrusive as the man himself, most of his longer innings being patiently compiled. His bowling seldom troubled the best batsmen on good pitches, but, conversely, he was rarely heavily punished, so accurate was his length.

After his playing career ended, he continued to dedicate himself to the county he had served for thirty years, being coach from 1953 until 1959. In his later years he coached at Seaford College. His son, Richard, maintains the family's traditional link with Sussex cricket. Also a left-hand batsman, Richard has played for the county since 1957, gaining his "cap" in 1961.

McCormack, Vincent Charles, who died on April 8, aged 74, was a one-time Jamaican cricketer and former President of the Jamaican Cricket Board of Control. He was financial controller of the Jamaica Tourist Board.

McDonell, Harold Clark, who died on July 23, aged 82, was in the Winchester XI from 1899 to 1901. A leg-break bowler and a splendid fielder to his own bowling besides being a fair bat, he captained the school in the last two years. Against Eton in 1900, he gained match figures of eleven wickets for 111 runs. He got his Blue at Cambridge in 1903, 1904 and 1905, being top of the University bowling averages in the first and last years. In 1904 he took nine wickets for 125 runs in the University match. Next season at Lord's, though achieving little as a bowler, he played an innings which completely altered the course of the game. Facing first-innings arrears of 101, the Light Blues seemed destined to be beaten when they lost six wickets and were still 24 behind. Then McDonell (60) and L. G. Colbeck (107) added 143 in eighty-five minutes and, as A. F. Morcom (six wickets for 41 runs) followed with a remarkable spell of bowling, Cambridge snatched victory by 40 runs. McDonell's best bowling performance was in 1904 at Cambridge, where he took fifteen Surrey wickets for 138 runs—and was on the losing side. He turned out occasionally for Surrey in 1903 and 1904, heading their County Championship averages in the first season with 24 wickets in five matches at a cost of 17.87 runs each. From 1908 till 1921 he rendered good all-round service to Hampshire. He also represented Gentlemen v. Players in 1903 and 1904.

MacLaren, Geoffrey, who died on September 14, aged 83, played, like his elder brothers, A. C. and Dr. J. A. MacLaren, for Harrow and Lancashire. Against Eton in 1901, though taking four wickets for 84 runs, he was dismissed for 0; next year he helped in a win by eight wickets by hitting 41 and 9 and again dismissing four men for 84. He played in two matches for Lancashire in 1902 under the captaincy of A. C. MacLaren.

MARALANDA, ARMSTRONG PERCIVAL, who died on June 4, aged 62, was the greatest Ceylon schoolboy cricketer of the century. He was in the Trinity College, Kandy, XI from 1916, when 13, to 1922, in which time Trinity won the Inter-Collegiate Championship on four occasions. He was captain from 1920 to 1922. Besides being an astute leader, he was a stylish right-hand batsman and an accurate off-break bowler. He won prizes for batting, bowling and fielding and was awarded the coveted "Lion" both as a cricketer and as a Rugby wing threequarter. Unfortunately he was lost to Ceylon cricket after leaving school. He joined the Medical College in 1923 and at the time of his death was Deputy Director of Health Services.

MARRIOTT, CHARLES STOWELL, who died on October 13, aged 71, was one of the best leg-break and googly bowlers of his era. He learned his cricket in Ireland, where he was educated at St. Columba's, and gained a Blue at Cambridge in 1920 and 1921, meeting with remarkable success in the University matches. In 1920, when rain prevented play on the first two days, he took seven wickets for 69 runs and in the following season he played a leading part in a triumph for the Light Blues in an innings with 24 runs to spare by dismissing seven Oxford batsmen in the match for 111 runs.

In all first-class cricket he took 724 wickets at an average cost of 20.04 runs and his bowling skill so far exceeded his ability as a batsman that his victims exceeded his aggregate of runs by 169. Cunning flighting, allied to the ability to turn the ball sharply, made him a menace to batsmen even on good pitches and when the turf gave him help, he could be well-nigh unplayable. His action was high with a free, loose arm which he swung behind his back before delivery in a manner reminiscent of Colin Blythe. From 1919 to 1921 he appeared for Lancashire and when beginning a long association with Dulwich College as master-in-charge of cricket, he threw in his lot with Kent, whom he assisted during the school holidays from 1924 to 1937.

In his first season with the Southern county he distinguished himself by taking five wickets for 31 and six for 48 in the game with Lancashire at Dover and against Hampshire at Canterbury he returned figures of five for 66 and five for 44, and he achieved many other notable performances in later years.

He met with great success on the occasion of his one appearance in a Test match for England. That was at The Oval in 1933, when he so bewildered the batsmen that he took five wickets for 37 runs in the first innings and, with second innings figures of six for 59, hurried the West Indies to defeat by an innings and 17 runs—a feat described by *Wisden* of the time as one of the best accomplished by a bowler when playing for England for the first time.

"Father" Marriott, as he was popularly known, engaged in two tours abroad. In 1924–25 he was a member of Lord—then the Hon. Lionel—Tennyson's side in South Africa and in 1933–34 he went with D. R. Jardine's M.C.C. team to India, where, against Madras, he did the "hat-trick" for the only time in his first-class career. During the Second World War he served as an anti-aircraft gunner in the Home Guard.

MASSIE, ROBERT JOHN ALLWRIGHT, who died on February 14, was, as a 6 ft. 4 in. fastish left-hander for New South Wales, regarded as Australia's bowler of the future in 1914. Unhappily a wound received while on Army service during the First World War ended his cricket career. He represented New South Wales at cricket, Rugby football, athletics and rowing and was also amateur boxing champion of the State.

MELLE, DR. BASIL GEORGE VON BRANDIS, who died on January 8, aged 74, was among the earliest of leg-theory bowlers. He played in first-class cricket in South Africa, helping Western Province carry off the Currie Cup in 1908–09, before going up to Oxford, where he gained a Blue as a Freshman in 1913. High right-arm medium-pace in-swing to three short-leg fieldsmen so confounded Cambridge that he took six wickets for 70 runs in their first innings and two for 46 in the second.

"A genuine discovery" *Wisden* wrote of him, and indeed he was for, with little support, he headed the University averages that season with 55 victims for 15.90 runs each. Next year he broke a finger in an early game and the consequent loss of practice meant that he never became even a shadow of his previous self, though he again took part in the University match. From 1914 to 1921—the war intervened —he played for Hampshire, and though his bowling declined so much that he was seldom employed in the attack, his batting improved out of all knowledge. In 1919 he finished third in the county averages with 927 runs—110 of them in an innings against Gloucestershire at Bristol—for an average of 33.52. He was also a keen fieldsman.

NEATE, HORACE RICHARD, who died suddenly on November 12, aged 75, was chairman of Bedfordshire C.C.C. from 1938 to 1955, when he became President till ill-health compelled him to retire in 1964. For 40 years he served the Minor Counties' Cricket Association, acting as treasurer and chairman, and for a number of years was the Minor Counties representative on the Advisory County Cricket Committee.

NEWMAN, F. C. W., who died early in the year following a long illness, aged 72, played a few matches for Surrey in 1919 and 1921. A free-scoring batsman from his school days at Bedford Modern, he scored something like 30,000 runs in club cricket and hit over 60 hundreds. He made many runs for the Dulwich club and appeared in the Minor Counties Competition before the First World War for Bedfordshire. In 1926 he became private secretary to Sir Julien Cahn, for whose side he played regularly for many years. He also organised Cahn's tours to West Indies, South America, Denmark, Canada, U.S.A., Bermuda, Malaya and New Zealand.

O'NEILL, WILLIAM PAUL, who died on December 8 at Philadelphia, Pennsylvania, aged 86, had a notable career in cricket. He was a native Philadelphian and a graduate of Penn Charter School and the University of Pennsylvania. He came out in big cricket when he appeared for Philadelphia Colts v. Ranjitsinhji's touring team in 1899, taking six wickets for 70 with his slow off-spinners. He appeared on five occasions for the United States against Canada. O'Neill has a minor place in cricket history as the last American to get W. G. Grace's wicket! This occurred in 1911 when he toured England with the Germantown C.C. In a match against Blackheath, the famous W.G. appeared for the Kent club. O'Neill also toured England with the Philadelphia Pilgrims in 1921 but never found time to participate in any first-class tours with the Philadelphians. In 1913 he appeared for a Germantown XII v. Australia in which the American team snatched a famous victory by three wickets. In that match "Pete" O'Neill's fielding was legendary. He held ten catches during the game, one catch at second slip being held eighteen inches from the ground as he fell forward and reached out flat for the ball.

PREECE, CECIL ARTHUR, who died on November 11, aged 77, played as a professional for Worcestershire from 1920 to 1924. At a period when the county were far from strong, he headed the bowling averages in 1920 when taking with slow-medium deliveries 42 wickets at 30.11 runs each. He never again did as well, though against Warwickshire at Edgbaston in 1924 he performed the "hat-trick". He achieved occasional good work as a batsman, his best season being that of 1921, when he hit 505 runs, average 17.66. His highest innings was 69 for the Sussex bowling at Worcester in 1922.

PUCKLE, SIR FREDERICK HALE, who died suddenly on August 5, aged 77, was n the Uppingham XI of 1907 and 1908, being captain in the second year. He played much cricket in India and appeared for Lahore Europeans in 1924.

RAIKES, THE REV. GEORGE BARKLEY, who died on December 18, aged 93, was an Oxford Blue at both cricket and Association football. In the cricket XI at Shrewsbury from 1889 to 1892, he was captain and headed the batting averages in the last three years. He played in the University matches of 1894 and 1895 without achieving anything of note and from 1890 to 1897 he assisted Norfolk. From 1900 to 1902 he appeared for Hampshire, finishing second in the county averages in the first year, when he hit 77 from the Yorkshire bowling at Portsmouth. In 1904 he returned to Norfolk. "Ginger Beer", as, because of his initials, he was known to his intimates, was also a useful medium-paced bowler on occasion. He liked to tell the story of the time that he was invited to play for Nottinghamshire, but was compelled to decline because he was captain of Norfolk. As a footballer, he kept goal for Shrewsbury from 1890 to 1892; became a Corinthian in 1894; was in the Oxford side in 1894 and 1895 and in 1895 and 1896 gained four "full" International caps for England.

REES, ROBERT BLACKIE, who died at Bowmans Green, Herts., on September 20, aged 84, was a leg-break bowler of English birth who, between 1909 and 1913, took 57 wickets for South Australia in Sheffield Shield matches at an average cost of 27.92 runs each. He later returned to England and played for West Kent and Free Foresters.

REHMAN, RAY, who died as a result of a road accident on July 10, aged 26, was a Pakistani qualifying by residence for Leicestershire.

RIPPON, ARTHUR ERNEST SYDNEY, who died on April 13, aged 73, played as an amateur for Somerset between 1914 and 1937. At his best a brilliant batsman, on a number of occasions he opened the innings for the county with his twin brother, A. D. E. Rippon. In all, Arthur Rippon hit 3,833 runs, including six centuries, for an average of 21.17 and he held 46 catches. One of his best innings was that at Portsmouth in 1928, when he scored 112 and he and A. Young (92) made 197 in less than two and a half hours for the first wicket. J. C. White taking six wickets for 35 in the Hampshire second innings, Somerset triumphed in an innings with 28 runs to spare.

SAVILLE, STANLEY HERBERT, who died in an Eastbourne nursing home after a long illness on February 22, aged 76, gained his Blue as a batsman for Cambridge in four years from 1911 to 1914, being captain in the last season. He met with little success in the University matches, but he hit 101 against Free Foresters in 1913 and 141 not out from the Army bowling the following summer. He was in the Marlborough XI of 1907 and played a few times for Middlesex before and after the 1914 war. A fine hockey player at inside-right, "Sammy" Saville captained England and won 37 International caps at a time when matches were fewer than they are today. He had been President of the Hockey Association since 1951.

STANGER-LEATHES, CHRISTOPHER FRANCIS, who died on February 27, aged 84, was a hard-hitting batsman. In the Sherborne XI from 1896 to 1899, he headed the averages in the second and third seasons. For many years afterwards he played for Northumberland. A good Rugby footballer, he represented England at full-back against Ireland in 1905.

TAIT, JAMES, who died on February 1, aged 69, was masseur at Kennington Oval for 36 years. An injury during boyhood ended "Sandy" Tait's athletic aspirations and he turned his attention to ministering to the hurts of others. From 1916 to 1924 he served with Crystal Palace F.C. and later with Dulwich Hamlet and Kingstonian F.C.s. After joining Surrey he attended to England players and to those of some touring teams when they visited The Oval. A banjo-player and a humorist, he kept the Surrey players in good spirits in the dressing-room and when travelling. His father played at left-back in the Tottenham Hotspur F.A. Cup-winning team of 1901.

TANNER, ARTHUR RALPH, who died suddenly on August 16, aged 77, was an exceptionally good fieldsman close to the wicket. As an amateur for Middlesex between 1920 and 1929, he held 53 catches besides taking 71 wickets with slow bowling and scoring 764 runs.

TAYLOR, CLAUDE HILARY, who died on January 27, aged 61, achieved fame in 1923 when he became the first Freshman in history to hit a century in the University match. From 1918 to 1922 he was in the XI at Westminster, rendering splendid service as a solid, stylish batsman with an eminently straight bat and as a leg-break and googly bowler. In his last season at school, when *Wisden* said of him that he had "strong claims to be considered the best all-round school cricketer of the year", he headed the batting averages at 47.00 and was top of the bowling with 41 wickets for 12.73 runs each. Going up to Oxford, he got his Blue in 1923 and, with an innings of 109, bore a big part in the overthrow of Cambridge by an innings and 227 runs. He played in the University matches of the following three seasons without achieving anything like the same success. First playing for them in 1922 when at school, Taylor assisted Leicestershire till 1927, putting together four three-figure scores, the highest of which was 123 against Hampshire at Southampton in 1924—the only century obtained for the county that summer. After the Second World War, he appeared for Buckinghamshire. He was a master at Eton for many years and joint-author with D. H. Macindoe, another Oxonian and Eton master, of *Cricket Dialogue.*

OBITUARY, 1965

AWDRY, CHARLES EDWIN, who died on November 16, aged 59, was in the Winchester XI as a fast-medium bowler from 1923 to 1925, being captain in the last year. For some seasons from 1924 he assisted Wiltshire, taking nearly 300 wickets for them and scoring over 1,500 runs. He went to Egypt with H. M. Martineau's side in 1932 and 1933 and represented the Minor Counties against the 1937 New Zealanders. His father, C. S. Awdry, and his grandfather, Charles Awdry, were also in the Winchester XI of their time.

HINDE, BRIGADIER HAROLD MONTAGUE, who died suddenly in Italy on November 16, aged 69, was at Wellington before moving to Blundell's, where he gained a place in the 1912 XI. A fast bowler, he appeared for R.M.C. Sandhurst and between 1921 and 1932 he took 142 wickets for Berkshire. In 1927 he played for Egypt.

MANN, EDWARD JOHN, who died on December 17, was in the Marlborough XI from 1899 to 1901, being captain in the last year. He played for Cambridge University in 1905, but did not gain a Blue. He later appeared occasionally for Norfolk and Middlesex Second Eleven.

OBITUARY, 1964

HARRISON, WILLIAM PHILIP, who died on September 7, aged 78, ended a brief first-class career on a glorious note when, in his last innings, he hit 156 for Middlesex against Gloucestershire at Gloucester, where he and E. S. Litteljohn added 131 for the third wicket. In the XI at Rugby in 1902 and 1903, he hit 55 in the match with Marlborough at Lord's in the first year and 76 in the next, when he headed the school averages. He gained a Blue at Cambridge in 1907, but achieved little on the big occasion. He took part in seven matches for Kent in 1904 and 1905 and from 1906 to 1911 he played for Middlesex. In 1906–07 he toured New Zealand with the M.C.C. team.

Correction—In Obituaries in the 1965 edition, the Rev. Somerville Caldwell was incorrectly stated to have played for Somerset. In fact he played for Worcestershire, for whom his highest innings was 133.

CRICKETERS OF THE YEAR

Following is a complete alphabetical list of cricketers whose portraits and biographies have appeared in *Wisden* since, in the issue for 1889, the idea of publishing photographs of prominent players was first adopted. The number of cricketers selected for this feature has varied from time to time. Six bowlers of the year were chosen for the 1889 issue and in the following edition portraits of nine batsmen were given in the Almanack. A group of five representative wicket-keepers formed the subject of illustration for 1891 and photographs of five all-round cricketers were published in a subsequent issue.

Apart from a few exceptions, each successive *Wisden* has included portraits and biographical details of five players who, in the opinion of the Editor, most deserved the honour by reason of their accomplishments, especially during the previous season.

Abel, R. (Surrey), 1890
Adams, P. W. (Cheltenham), 1919
Adcock, N. A. T. (South Africa), 1961
Alley, W. E. (N.S.W. and Somerset), 1962
Ames, L. E. G. (Kent), 1929
Appleyard, R. (Yorks.), 1952
Armstrong, W. W. (Aust.), 1903
Ashton, H. (Winchester, Camb. U. and Essex), 1922
Astill, W. E. (Leics.), 1933
Attewell, W. (Notts), 1892

Bailey, T. E. (Dulwich, Camb. U. and Essex), 1950
Bakewell, A. H. (Northants), 1934
Barber, R. W. (Ruthin, Camb. U., Lancs. and War.), 1967
Bardsley, W. (Aust.), 1910
Barnes, S. F. (War., Lancs. and Staffs.), 1910
Barnes, William (Notts.), 1890
Barnett, C. J. (Glos.), 1937
Barrington, K. F. (Surrey), 1960
Bartlett, H. T. (Dulwich, Camb. U., Surrey and Sussex), 1939
Bedser, A. V. (Surrey), 1947
Benaud, R. (Aust.), 1962
Blackham, J. McC. (Aust.), 1891
Bland, K. C. (S.A.), 1966
Blunt, R. C. (N.Z.), 1928
Blythe, C. (Kent), 1904
Booth, M. W. (Yorks.), 1914
Bosanquet, B. J. T. (Middx.), 1905
Bowes, W. E. (Yorks.), 1932
Bowley, E. H. (Sussex), 1930
Boycott, G. (Yorks.), 1965
Bradman, Sir Donald G. (Aust.), 1931
Braund, L. C. (Surrey and Som.), 1902
Brearley, W. (Lancs.), 1909
Briggs, John (Lancs.), 1889
Brockwell, W. (Surrey, 1895
Brookes, D. (Northants), 1957
Brown, F. R. (Leys, Camb. U. and Surrey), 1933
Brown, J. T. (Yorks.), 1895
Brown, W. A. (Aust.), 1939
Bryan, J. L. (Rugby, Camb. U. and Kent), 1922
Bull, F. G. (Essex), 1898
Burge, P. J. (Aust.), 1965
Burke, J. W. (Aust.), 1957
Burnup, C. J. (Malvern, Camb. U. and Kent), 1903

Calder, H. L. (Cranleigh School), 1918
Cameron, H. B. (S.A.), 1936
Carr, A. W. (Notts.), 1923
Carr, D. B. (Repton, Oxf. U., Derby.), 1960
Carr, D. W. (Kent), 1910
Catterall, R. H. (S.A.), 1925
Chapman, A. P. F. (Uppingham), 1919
Close, D. B. (Yorks.), 1964
Compton, D. C. S. (Middx.), 1939
Constantine, L. N. (W.I.), 1940
Copson, W. H. (Derby.), 1937
Cowdrey, M. C. (Tonbridge, Oxf. U. and Kent), 1956
Crawford, J. N. (Repton and Surrey), 1907
Cuttell, W. R. (Yorks. and Lancs.), 1898

Darling, J. (Aust.), 1900
Davidson, A. K. (Aust.), 1962
Day, A. P. (Malvern and Kent), 1910
Dempster, C. S. (N.Z.), 1932
Denton, David (Yorks.), 1906
Dexter, E. R. (Radley, Camb. U. and Sussex), 1961
d'Oliveira, B. (Worcestershire), 1967
Dollery, H. E. (War), 1952
Donnelly, M. P. (N.Z. and Oxf. U.), 1948
Dooland, B. (Aust. and Notts.), 1955
Douglas, J. W. H. T. (Felsted School and Essex), 1915
Druce, N. F. (Marlborough, Camb. U. and Surrey), 1898
Ducat, A. (Surrey), 1920
Duckworth, G. (Lancs.), 1929
Duleepsinhji, K. S. (Camb. U. and Sussex), 1930

Edrich, J. H. (Surrey), 1966
Edrich, W. J. (Middx.), 1940
Evans, T. G. (Kent), 1951

Farnes, K. (Camb. U. and Essex), 1939
Fazal Mahmood (Pakistan), 1955

Fender, P. G. H. (St. Paul's School, Sussex and Surrey), 1915
Ferris, J. J. (Aust. and Glos.), 1889
Fielder, A. (Kent), 1907
Firth, J. E. D'E. (Winchester), 1918
Fishlock, L. B. (Surrey), 1947
Flavell, J. A. (Worcs.), 1965
Foster, F. R. (War.), 1912
Foster, H. K. (Malvern, Oxf. U. and Worcs.), 1911
Foster, R. E. (Malvern, Oxf. U. and Worcs.), 1901
Freeman, A. P. (Kent), 1923
Fry, C. B. (Repton, Oxf. U., Surrey and Sussex), 1895

Geary, G. (Leics.), 1927
Gibson, C. H. (Eton), 1918
Giffen, George (Aust.), 1894
Gilligan, A. E. R. (Dulwich, Camb. U. and Sussex), 1924
Gimblett, H. (Som.), 1953
Goddard, T. W. (Glos.), 1938
Gore, A. C. (Eton), 1919
Gover, A. R. (Surrey), 1937
Grace, W. G. (Glos.), 1896
Graveney, T. W. (Glos.), 1953
Gregory, J. M. (Aust.), 1922
Gregory, S. E. (Aust.), 1897
Griffith, C. C. (W.I.), 1964
Grimmett, C. V. (Aust.), 1931
Gunn, George (Notts.), 1914
Gunn, John (Notts.), 1904
Gunn, William (Notts.), 1890

Haigh, S. (Yorks.), 1901
Hall, L. (Yorks.), 1890
Hallam, A. (Lancs. and Notts.), 1908
Halliwell, E. A. (S.A.), 1905
Hallows, C. (Lancs.), 1928
Hallows, J. (Lancs.), 1905
Hammond, W. R. (Glos.), 1928
Hardinge, H. T. W. (Kent), 1915
Hardstaff, J. (junr.) (Notts.), 1938
Hartley, A. (Lancs.), 1911
Harvey, R. N. (Aust.), 1954
Hassett, A. L. (Aust.), 1949
Hawke, Lord (Eton, Camb. U. and Yorks.), 1909
Hayes, E. G. (Surrey), 1907
Hayward, T. (Surrey), 1895
Headley, G. (W.I.), 1934
Hearne, Alec (Kent), 1894
Hearne, J. T. (Middx.), 1892
Hearne, J. W. (Middx.), 1912
Hedges, L. P. (Tonbridge), 1919
Henderson, R. (Surrey), 1890
Hendren, E. (Middx.), 1920
Hewett, H. T. (Harrow, Oxf. U. and Som.), 1893
Hill, Clem (Aust.), 1900
Hilton, M. J. (Lancs.), 1957
Hirst, G. H. (Yorks.), 1901

Hitch, J. W. (Surrey), 1914
Hobbs, Sir J. B. (Surrey), 1909 and special portrait, 1926
Hollies, W. E. (War.), 1955
Holmes, E. R. T. (Oxf. U. and Surrey), 1936
Holmes, P. (Yorks.), 1920
Hunte, C. C. (W.I.), 1964
Hutchings, K. L. (Tonbridge an Kent), 1907
Hutton, Sir Leonard (Yorks.), 1938

Illingworth, R. (Yorks.), 1960
Insole, D. J. (Camb. U. and Essex), 1956
Iremonger, J. (Notts.), 1903

Jackson, Hon. Sir F. Stanley (Harrow, Camb. U. and Yorks.), 1894
Jackson, H. L. (Derby.), 1959
Jardine, D. R. (Winchester, Oxf. U. and Surrey), 1928
Jenkins, R. O. (Wors.), 1950
Jessop, G. L. (Camb. U. and Glos.), 1898
Johnstone, W. A. (Aust.), 1949
Jones, A. O. (Camb. U. and Notts.), 1900
Jupp, V. W. C. (Sussex and Northants), 1928

Kanhai, R. B. (W.I.), 1964
Keeton, W. W. (Notts.), 1940
Kelly, J. J. (Aust.), 1903
Kennedy, A. (Hants), 1933
Kenyon, D. (Worcs.), 1963
Kilner, Roy (Yorks.), 1924
Kinneir, S. P. (War.), 1912
Knight, A. E. (Leics.), 1904
Knight, D. J. (Malvern, Oxf. U. and Surrey), 1915
Knox, N. A. (Dulwich College and Surrey), 1907

Laker, J. C. (Surrey), 1952
Langley, G. R. A. (Aust.), 1957
Langridge, James (Sussex), 1932
Langridge, John (Sussex), 1950
Larwood, H. (Notts.), 1927
Lawry, W. M. (Aust.), 1962
Lees, Walter (Surrey), 1906
Leyland, M. (Yorks.), 1929
Lilley, A. A. (War.), 1897
Lindwall, R. R. (Aust.), 1949
Llewellyn, C. B. (S.A. and Hants), 1911
Loader, P. J. (Surrey), 1958
Lock, G. A. R. (Surrey), 1954
Lockwood, W. H. (Notts and Surrey), 1899
Lohmann, George (Surrey), 1889
Lyon, B. H. (Rugby, Oxf. U. and Glos.), 1931

Macartney, C. G. (Aust.), 1922
Macauley, G. G. (Yorks.), 1924
MacBryan, J. C. W. (Camb. U. and Som.), 1925
McCabe, S. J. (Aust.), 1935

McDonald, E. A. (Aust.), 1922
McGahey, C. P. (Essex), 1902
McGlew, D. J. (S.A.), 1956
MacGregor, G. (Uppingham, Camb. U. and Middx.), 1891
McKenzie, G. D. (Aust.), 1965
MacLaren, A. C. (Harrow and Lancs.), 1895
McLean, R. A. (S.A.), 1961
McIntyre, A. J. (Surrey), 1958
Mankad, M. (India), 1947
Marshal, Alan (Queensland and Surrey), 1909
Marshall, R. E. (W.I. and Hants), 1959
Martin, F. (Kent), 1892
Mason, J. R. (Winchester and Kent), 1898
May, P. B. H. (Charterhouse, Camb. U. and Surrey), 1952
Mead, C. P. (Hants), 1912
Mead, Walter (Essex), 1904
Melville, A. (Oxf. U., Sussex and S.A.), 1948
Mercer, J. (Glam.), 1927
Merchant, V. M. (India), 1937
Milburn, C. (Northants), 1967
Miller, K. R. (Aust.), 1954
Milton, C. A. (Glos.), 1959
Mitchell, B. (S.A.), 1936
Mitchell, Frank (Camb. U., Yorks. and S.A.), 1902
Mold, A. (Lancs.), 1892
Motz, R. C. (N.Z.), 1966
Morris, A. R. (Aust.), 1949
Murray, J. T. (Middlesex), 1967
Mushtaq Mohammad (Pakistan), 1963

Nayudu, C. K. (India), 1933
Newstead, J. T. (Yorks.), 1909
Nichols, M. S. (Essex), 1934
Noble, M. A. (Aust.), 1900
Nourse, A. D., junr (S.A.), 1948
Nurse, S. M. (West Indies), 1967

Oldfield, W. A. (Aust.), 1927
O'Neill, N. C. (Aust.), 1962
O'Reilly, W. J. (Aust.), 1935
Owen-Smith, H. G. (S.A.), 1930

Paine, G. A. E. (War.), 1935
Palairet, L. C. H. (Repton, Oxf. U. and Som.), 1893
Parfitt, P. H. (Middx.), 1963
Parker, C. (Glos.), 1923
Parkin, C. (Lancs.), 1924
Parks, J. H. (Sussex), 1938
Partridge, N. E. (Malvern), 1919
Pataudi, Nawab of (Chief's College, Lahore and Oxf. U.), 1932
Paynter, E. (Lancs.), 1938
Peebles, I. A. R. (Glasgow Academy and Middx.), 1931
Peel, R. (Yorks.), 1889
Perrin, P. A. (Essex), 1905
Pilling, R. (Lancs.), 1891
Pollock, P. M. (S.A.), 1966
Pollock, R. G. (S.A.), 1966
Ponsford, W. H. (Aust.), 1935
Poore, Major R. M. (Hants), 1900
Pullar, G. (Lancs.), 1960

Quaife, W. G. (Sussex and War.), 1902

Ramadhin, S. (W.I.), 1951
Ranjitsinhji, K. S. (Camb. U. and Sussex), 1897
Ransford, V. (Aust.), 1910
Read, M. (Surrey), 1890
Read, W. W. (Surrey), 1893
Reid, J. R. (N.Z.), 1959
Relf, A. E. (Sussex), 1914
Rhodes, W. (Yorks.), 1899
Richardson, P. E. (Worcs.), 1957
Richardson, T. (Surrey), 1897
Robertson, J. D. (Middx.), 1948
Robins, R. W. V. (Camb. U. and Middx.), 1930
Rotherham, G. A. (Rugby), 1918
Rowan, E. A. B. (S.A.), 1952
Russell, A. C. (Essex), 1923

Sandham, A. (Surrey), 1923
Schwarz, R. O. (Middx. and S.A.), 1908
Scott, S. W. (Middx.), 1893
Sellers, A. B. (Yorks.), 1940
Shackleton, D. (Hants), 1959
Sharpe, J. W. (Surrey and Notts.), 1892
Sharpe, P. J. (Yorks.), 1963
Sheppard, D. S. (Sherborne, Camb. U and Sussex), 1953
Sherwin, M. (Notts.), 1891
Shrewsbury, A. (Notts.), 1890
Simpson, R. B. (Aust.), 1965
Simpson, R. T. (Notts.), 1950
Smith, C. I. J. (Middx.), 1935
Smith, D. (Derby.), 1936
Smith, O. G. (W.I.), 1958
Smith, S. G. (W.I. and Northants), 1915
Smith, M. J. K. (Stamford Sch., Oxf. U., Leics. and War.), 1960
Smith, T. P. B. (Essex), 1947
Smith, W. C. (Surrey), 1911
Sobers, G. S. (W.I.), 1964
Spooner, R. H. (Marlborough and Lancs.), 1905
Staples, S. J. (Notts.), 1929
Statham, J. B. (Lancs.), 1955
Stevens, G. T. S. (University College School), 1918
Stewart, M. J. (Surrey), 1958
Stoddart, A. E. (Middx.),1893
Storer, William (Derby.), 1899
Strudwick, H. (Surrey), 1912
Subba Row, R. (Whitgift, Camb. U., Surrey and Northants), 1961
Sugg, F. H. (Yorks., Derby. and Lancs.), 1890

Surridge, W. S. (Emanuel and Surrey), 1953
Sutcliffe, B. (N.Z.), 1950
Sutcliffe, H. (Yorks.), 1920

Tallon, D. (Aust.), 1949
Tarrant, F. A (Victoria and Middx.), 1908
Tate, M. W. (Sussex), 1924
Tayfield, H. J. (S.A.), 1956
Taylor, H. W. (S.A.), 1925
Taylor, T. L. (Uppingham, Camb. U. and Yorks.), 1901
Tennyson, Lord (Eton and Hants), 1914
Thompson, G. J. (Northants), 1906
Titmus, F. J. Middx.), 1963
Townsend, C. L. (Clifton and Glos.), 1899
Townsend, L. (Derby.), 1934
Tribe, G. E. (Aust. and Northants), 1955
Trott, A. E. (Aust. and Middx.), 1899
Trott, G. H. S. (Aust.), 1894
Trueman, F. S. (Yorks.), 1953
Trumble, H. (Aust.), 1897
Trumper, V. (Aust.), 1903
Tunnicliffe, John (Yorks.), 1901
Turnbull, M J. (Downside, Camb. U. and Glam.), 1931
Turner, C. T. B. (Aust.), 1889
Tyldesley, E. (Lancs.), 1920
Tyldesley, J. T. (Lancs.), 1902
Tyldesley, R. (Lancs.), 1925
Tyson, F. H. (Durham U. and Northants), 1956

Valentine, A. L. (W.I.), 1951
Verity, H. (Yorks.), 1932
Vine, J. (Sussex), 1906
Voce, W. (Notts.), 1933
Vogler, A. E. (S.A.), 1908

Wainwright, E. (Yorks.), 1894
Walcott, C. L. (W.I.), 1958
Walters, C. F. (Glam. and Worcs.), 1934
Ward, A. (Yorks. and Lancs.), 1890
Wardle, J. H. (Yorks.), 1954
Warner, Sir Pelham (Rugby, Oxf U. and Middx.), 1904
and special portrait, 1921
Washbrook, C. (Lancs.), 1947
Watson, W. (Yorks.), 1954
Wass, T. (Notts.), 1908
Weekes, E. D. (W.I.), 1951
Wellard, A. W. (Som.), 1936
White, J. C. (Som.), 1929
Whysall, W. (Notts.), 1925
Wilson, J. V. (Yorks.), 1961
Wisden, John (Sussex). Special memoir and portrait, 1913
Wood, A. (Yorks.), 1939
Wood, H. (Surrey), 1891
Woodfull, W. M. (Aust.), 1927
Woods, S. M. J. (Camb. U., Som. and Aust.), 1889
Woolley, F. E. (Kent), 1911
Worrell, F. M. (W.I.), 1951
Worthington, T. S. (Derby.), 1937
Wright, D. V. P. (Kent), 1940
Wright, L. G. (Derby.), 1906
Wyatt, R. E. S. (War.), 1930

Yardley, N. W. D. (St. Peter's, Camb. U. and Yorks.), 1948

CENTURY AND FIVE WICKETS IN ONE TEST

J. H. Sinclair 106 and six for 26, 1898–9
South Africa v. England, at Cape Town.
G. A. Faulkner 123 and five for 120, 1909–10
South Africa v. England, at Johannesburg.
C. E. Kelleway 114 and five for 33, 1912
Australia v. South Africa, at Manchester.
J. M. Gregory 100 and seven for 69, 1920–21
Australia v. England, at Melbourne.
V. Mankad 184 and five for 96, 1952
India v. England, at Lord's.
K. R. Miller 128 and six for 107, 1954–5
Australia v. West Indies, at Kingston.
P. R. Umrigar 172 and five for 107, 1961–2
India v. West Indies, at Port of Spain.
B. R. Taylor 105 and five for 86, 1964–65
New Zealand v. India, at Calcutta.
G. S. Sobers 174 and five for 41, 1966
West Indies v. England, at Leeds.

THE LAWS OF CRICKET

(1947 Code—2nd Edition)

The term "Special Regulations" referred to in certain Laws are those authorised by M.C.C.. Overseas Governing Bodies or other Cricket Authorities in respect of matches played under their jurisdiction.

(A)—THE PLAYERS, UMPIRES AND SCORERS

SIDES

1.—A match is played between two sides of eleven players each, unless otherwise agreed. Each side shall play under a Captain who before the toss for innings shall nominate his players who may not thereafter be changed without the consent of the opposing Captain.

NOTES

1.—If a Captain is not available at any time, a Deputy must act for him to deal promptly with any points arising from this and other laws.

2.—No match in which more than eleven players a side take part can be regarded as First-class, and in any case no side should field with more than eleven players.

SUBSTITUTES

2.—A Substitute shall be allowed to field or run between the wickets for any player who may during the match be incapacitated from illness or injury, but not for any other reason without the consent of the opposing Captain; no Substitute shall be allowed to bat or to bowl. Consent as to the person to act as substitute in the field shall be obtained from the opposing Captain, who may indicate positions in which the Substitute shall not field.

NOTES

1.—A player may bat, bowl or field even though a substitute has acted for him previously.

2.—An injured batsman may be "Out" should his runner infringe Laws 36, 40 or 41. As *Striker* he remains himself subject to the Laws; should he be out of his ground for any purpose he may be "Out" under Laws 41 and 42 at the wicket-keeper's end, irrespective of the position of the other batsman or the substitute when the wicket is put down. When *not the Striker* the injured batsman is out of the game and stands where he does not interfere with the play.

THE APPOINTMENT OF UMPIRES

3.—Before the toss for innings two Umpires shall be appointed; one for each end to control the game as required by the Laws with absolute impartiality. No Umpire shall be changed during a match without the consent of both Captains.

NOTE

1.—The umpires should report themselves to the executive of the ground 30 minutes before the start of each day's play.

THE SCORERS

4.—All runs scored shall be recorded by Scorers appointed for the purpose; the Scorers shall accept and acknowledge all instructions and signals given to them by the Umpires.

NOTE

1.—The umpires should wait until a signal has been answered by a scorer before allowing the game to proceed. Mutual consultation between the scorers and the umpires to clear up doubtful points is at all times permissible.

(B)—The IMPLEMENTS OF THE GAME, AND THE GROUND

THE BALL

5.—The Ball shall weigh not less than 5½ ounces, nor more than 5¾ ounces. It shall measure not less than 8 13/16 inches, nor more than 9 inches in circumference. Subject to agreement to the contrary either Captain may demand a new ball at the start of each innings. In the event of a ball being lost or becoming unfit for play, the Umpires shall allow another ball to be taken into use. They shall inform the Batsmen whenever a ball is to be changed.

NOTES

1.—All cricket balls used in First-class matches should be approved before the start of a match by the umpires and captains.

2.—Except in the United Kingdom, or if local regulations provide otherwise, after 200 runs have been made off a ball in First-class matches, the captain of the fielding side may demand a new one. In First-class matches in the United Kingdom the fielding side may demand a new ball after 85 (6 ball) overs have been bowled with the old one. In other grades of cricket these regulations will not apply unless agreed before the toss for innings.

3.—Any ball substituted for one lost or becoming unfit for play should have had similar wear or use as that of the one discarded.

THE BAT

6.—The Bat shall not exceed 4¼ inches in the widest part. It shall not be more than 38 inches in length.

THE PITCH

7.—The Pitch is deemed to be the area of ground between the bowling creases, 5 feet in width on either side of the line joining the centre of the wickets. Before the toss for innings, the executive of the ground shall be responsible for the selection and preparation of the Pitch; thereafter the Umpires shall control its use and maintenance. The Pitch shall not be changed during a match unless it becomes unfit for play, and then only with the consent of both Captains.

THE WICKETS

8.—The Wickets shall be pitched opposite and parallel to each other at a distance of 22 yards from stump to stump. Each Wicket shall be 9 inches in width and consist of three stumps with two bails upon the top. The stumps shall be of equal and of sufficient size to prevent the ball from passing through, with their tops 28 inches above the ground. The bails shall be each 4 3/8 inches in length, and, when in position on the top of the stumps, shall not project more than ½ inch above them.

NOTES

1.—Except for the bail grooves the tops of the stumps shall be dome-shaped.

2.—In a high wind the captains may agree, with the approval of the umpires, to dispense with the use of bails (*see* Law 31, Note 3).

THE BOWLING AND POPPING CREASES

9.—The Bowling crease shall be in line with the stumps; 8 feet 8 inches in length; the stumps in the centre; with a Return crease at each end at right angles behind the wicket. The Popping crease shall be marked 4 feet in front of and parallel with the Bowling crease. Both the Return and Popping creases shall be deemed unlimited in length.

NOTE

1.—The distance of the Popping Crease from the wicket is measured from a line running through the centre of the stumps to the inside edge of the crease.

(C)—THE CARE AND MAINTENANCE OF THE PITCH

ROLLING, MOWING AND WATERING

10.—Unless permitted by special regulations, the Pitch shall not be rolled during a match except before the start of each innings and of each day's play, when, if the Captain of the batting side so elect, it may be swept and rolled for not more than 7 minutes. In a match of less than three days' duration, the pitch shall not be mown during the match unless "Special Regulations" so provide. In a match of three or more days' duration, the pitch shall be mown under the supervision of the Umpires before play begins on alternate days after the start of a match, but should the pitch not be so mown on any day on account of play not taking place, it shall be mown on the first day on which the match is resumed and thereafter on alternate days. (For the purpose of this Law a rest day counts as a day). Under no circumstances shall the Pitch be watered during a match.

NOTES

1.—The umpires are responsible that any rolling permitted by this Law and carried out at the request of the captain of the batting side, is in accordance with the regulations laid down and that it is completed so as to allow play to start at the stipulated time. The normal rolling before the start of each day's play shall take place not earlier than half an hour before the start of play, but the captain of the batting side may delay such rolling until 10 minutes before the start of play should he so desire.

2.—The time allowed for rolling shall be taken out of the normal playing time if a captain declare an innings closed either, (*a*) before play starts on any day so late that the other captain is prevented from exercising his option in regard to rolling under this Law, or (*b*) during the luncheon interval later than 15 minutes after the start of such interval.

3.—Except in the United Kingdom, if at any time a rain-affected pitch is damaged by play thereon, it shall be swept and rolled for a period of not more than ten consecutive minutes at any time between the close of play on the day on which it was damaged and the next resumption of play, provided that:—

(i) The umpires shall instruct the groundman to sweep and roll the pitch only after they have agreed that damage caused to it as a result of play after rain has fallen warrants such rolling additional to that provided for in Law 10.

(ii) Such rolling shall in all cases be done under the personal supervision of both umpires and shall take place at such time and with such roller as the groundman shall consider best calculated to repair the damage to the pitch.

(iii) Not more than one such additional rolling shall be permitted as a result of rain on any particular day.

(iv) The rolling provided for in Law 10 to take place before the start of play shall not be permitted on any day on which the rolling herein provided for takes place within two hours of the time appointed for commencement of play on that day.

COVERING THE PITCH

11.—The Pitch shall not be completely covered during a match unless special regulations so provide; covers used to protect the bowlers' run up shall not extend to a greater distance than 3½ feet in front of the Popping creases.

NOTE

1.—It is usual under this Law to protect the bowlers' run up, before and during a match both at night and, when necessary, during the day. The covers should be removed early each morning, if fine.

MAINTENANCE OF THE PITCH

12.—The Batsman may beat the Pitch with his bat, and Players may secure their footholds by the use of sawdust, provided Law 46 be not thereby contravened. In wet weather the Umpires shall see that the holes made by the Bowlers and Batsmen are cleaned out and dried whenever necessary to facilitate play.

(D)—THE CONDUCT OF THE GAME

INNINGS

13.—Each side has two innings, taken alternately, except in the case provided for in Law 14. The choice of innings shall be decided by tossing on the field of play.

NOTES

1.—The captains should toss for innings not later than 15 minutes before the time agreed upon for play to start. The winner of the toss may not alter his decision to bat or field once it has been notified to the opposing captain.

2.—This Law also governs a One-day match in which play continues after the completion of the first innings of both sides. (*See also* Law 22.)

FOLLOWING INNINGS

14.—The side which bats first and leads by 150 runs in a match of three days or more, by 100 runs in a two-day match, or by 75 runs in a one-day match, shall have the option of requiring the other side to follow their innings.

DECLARATIONS

15.—The captain of the batting side may declare an innings closed at any time during a match irrespective of its duration.

16.—When the start of play is delayed by weather, Law 14 shall apply in accordance with the number of days' play remaining from the actual start of the match.

START AND CLOSE OF PLAY AND INTERVALS

17.—The Umpires shall allow such intervals as have been agreed upon for meals, 10 minutes between each innings and not more than 2 minutes for each fresh batsman to come in. At the start of each innings and of each day's play and at the end of any interval the Umpire at the Bowler's end shall call "Play," when the side refusing to play shall lose the match. After "Play" has been called no trial ball shall be allowed to any player, and when one of the Batsmen is out the use of the bat shall not be allowed to any player until the next Batsman shall come in.

NOTES

1.—The umpires shall not award a match under this Law unless (i) "Play" has been called in such a manner that both sides can clearly understand that play is to start, (ii) an appeal has been made, and (iii) they are satisfied that a side will not, or cannot, continue play.

2.—It is an essential duty of the captains to ensure that the "in-going" batsman passes the "out-going" one before the latter leaves the field of play. This is all the more important in view of the responsibility resting on the umpires for deciding whether or not the delay of the individual amounts to a refusal of the batting side to continue play.

3.—The interval for luncheon should not exceed 45 minutes unless otherwise agreed (but *see* Law 10, Note 2). In the event of the last wicket falling within 2 minutes of the time arranged for luncheon or tea, the game shall be resumed at the usual hour, no allowance being made for the 10 minutes between the innings.

4.—Bowling practice *on the pitch* is forbidden at any time during the game.

18.—The Umpires shall call "Time," and at the same time remove the bails from both wickets, on the cessation of play before any arranged interval, at the end of each day's play, and at the conclusion of the match. An "Over" shall always be started if "Time" has not been reached, and shall be completed unless a batsman is "Out" or "Retires" within 2 minutes of the completion of any period of play, but the "Over" in progress at the close of play on the final day of a match shall be completed at the request of either Captain even if a wicket fall after "Time" has been reached.

NOTES

1.—If, during the completion of the last over of any period of play, the players have occasion to leave the field, the Umpires shall call "time." In the case of the last over of the match, there shall be no resumption of play and the match shall be at an end.

2.—The last over before an interval or the close of play shall be started, provided the umpire standing at square leg, after walking at his normal pace, has arrived at his position behind the stumps at the bowler's end before time has been reached.

SCORING

19.—The score shall be reckoned by runs. A run is scored:—

1st.—So often as the Batsmen after a hit, or at any time while the ball is in play, shall have crossed and made good their ground from end to end; but if either Batsman run a short run, the Umpire shall call and signal "One short" and that run shall not be scored. The Striker being caught, no run shall be scored; a Batsman being run out, that run which was being attempted shall not be scored.

2nd.—For penalties under Laws 21, 27, 29, 44, and boundary allowances under Law 20.

NOTES

1.—If while the ball is in play, the batsmen have crossed in running, neither returns to the wicket he had left except in the case of a boundary hit or a boundary from extras, or under Laws 30, Note 1, and 46, Note 4 (vii). This rule applies even should a short run have been called, or should no run be reckoned as in the case of a catch.

2.—A run is "short" if either, or both, batsmen fail to make good their ground in turning for a further run. Although such a "short" run shortens the succeeding one, the latter, if completed, counts. Similarly a batsman taking stance in front of his popping crease may run from that point without penalty.

3 (1).—One run only is deducted if both batsmen are short in one and the same run. (2).—Only if three or more runs are attempted can more than one run be "short" and then subject to (1) above, all runs so called shall be disallowed. (3).—If either or both batsmen deliberately run short, the umpire is justified in calling "dead ball" and disallowing any runs attempted or scored as soon as he sees that the fielding side have no chance of dismissing either batsman under the Laws.

4.—An umpire signals "short" runs when the ball becomes "Dead" by bending his arm upwards to touch the shoulder with the tips of his fingers. If there has been more than one "short" run, the umpires must instruct the scorers as to the number of runs disallowed. (*See* Note 1 to Law 4.)

BOUNDARIES

20.—Before the toss for innings the Umpires shall agree with both sides on the Boundaries for play, and on the allowances to be made for them. An Umpire shall call or signal "Boundary" whenever, in his opinion, a ball in play hits, crosses or is carried over the Boundary. The runs completed at the instant the ball reaches the Boundary shall count only should they exceed the allowance, but if the "Boundary" result from an overthrow or from the wilful act of a fieldsman, any runs already made and the allowance shall be added to the score.

NOTES

1.—If flags or posts are used to mark a boundary, the real or imaginary line joining such points shall be regarded as the boundary, which should be marked by a white line if possible.

2.—In deciding on the allowances to be made for boundaries the umpires will be guided by the prevailing custom of the ground.

3.—It is a "Boundary" if the ball touches any boundary line or if a fieldsman with the ball in hand grounds any part of his person on or over that line. A fieldsman, however, standing within the playing area may lean against or touch a boundary fence in fielding a ball (*see also* Law 35, Note 5).

4.—An obstacle, or person, within the playing area is not regarded as a boundary unless so arranged by the umpires. The umpire is not a boundary, but sightscreens within the playing area shall be so regarded.

5.—The customary allowance for a boundary is 4 runs, but it is usual to allow 6 runs for all hits pitching over and clear of the boundary line or fence (even though the ball has been previously touched by a fieldsman). It is not usual to allow 6 runs when a ball hits a sight screen full pitch, if the latter is on or inside the boundary.

6.—In the case of a boundary resulting from either an over-throw or the wilful act of a fieldsman, the run in progress counts provided that the batsmen have crossed at the instant of the throw or act.

7.—The umpire signals "Boundary" by waving an arm from side to side, or a boundary "6" by raising both arms above the head.

LOST BALL

21.—If a ball in play cannot be found or recovered any Fieldsman may call "Lost Ball," when 6 runs shall be added to the score; but if more than 6 have been run before "Lost Ball" be called, as many runs as have been run shall be scored.

THE RESULT

22.—A match is won by the side which shall have scored a total of runs in excess of that scored by the opposing side in its two completed innings, one-day matches, unless thus played out, shall be decided by the first innings. A match may also be determined by being given up as lost by one of the sides, or in the case governed by Law 17. A match not determined in any of these ways shall count as a "Draw."

NOTES

1.—It is the responsibility of the captains to satisfy themselves on the correctness of the scores on the conclusion of play.

2.—Neither side can be compelled to continue after a match is finished; a one-day match shall not be regarded as finished on the result of the first innings if the umpires consider there is a prospect of carrying the game to a further issue in the time remaining.

3.—The result of a finished match is stated as a win by runs, except in the case of a win by the side batting last, when it is by the number of wickets still then to fall. In a one-day match which is not played out on the second innings, this rule applies to the position at the time when a result on the first innings was reached.

4.—A "Draw" is regarded as a "Tie" when the scores are equal at the conclusion of play but only if the match has been played out. If the scores of the completed first innings of a one-day match are equal, it is a "Tie," but only if the match has not been played out to a further conclusion.

THE OVER

23.—The ball shall be bowled from each wicket alternately in Overs of either 8 or 6 balls according to the agreed conditions of play When the agreed number have been bowled and it has become clear to the Umpire at the Bowler's wicket that both sides have ceased to regard the ball as in play, the Umpire shall call "Over" in a distinct manner before leaving the wicket. Neither a "No Ball" nor a "Wide Ball" shall be reckoned as one of the "Over."

NOTE

1.—In the United Kingdom the "over" shall be 6 balls, unless an agreement to the contrary has been made.

24.—A Bowler shall finish an "Over" in progress unless he be incapacitated or be suspended for unfair play. He shall be allowed to change ends as often as desired, provided only that he shall not bowl two "Overs" consecutively in one innings. A Bowler may require the Batsman at the wicket from which he is bowling to stand on whichever side of it he may direct.

DEAD BALL

25.—The ball shall be held to be "dead"—on being in the opinion of the Umpire finally settled in the hands of the Wicket-keeper or of the Bowler; or on reaching or pitching over the boundary; or, whether played or not, on lodging in the dress of either a Batsman or Umpire; or on the call of "Over" or "Time" by the Umpire; or on a Batsman being out from any cause; or on any penalty being awarded under Laws 21 or 44. The Umpire shall call "Dead Ball" should he decide to intervene under Law 46 in a case of unfair play or in the event of a serious injury to a player; or should he require to suspend play prior to the Striker receiving a delivery. The ball shall cease to be "Dead" on the Bowler starting his run or bowling action.

NOTES

1.—Whether the ball is "finally settled" is a question of fact for the umpire alone to decide.

2.—An umpire is justified in suspending play prior to the striker receiving a delivery in any of the following circumstances:—

- (i) If satisfied that, for an *adequate* reason, the striker is not ready to receive the ball, and makes no attempt to play it.
- (ii) If the bowler drops the ball accidentally before delivery, or if the ball does not leave his hand for any reason.
- (iii) If one or both bails fall from the striker's wicket before he receives the delivery.

In such cases the ball is regarded as "Dead" from the time it last came into play.

3.—A ball does not become "Dead" when it strikes an umpire (unless it lodges in his dress), when the wicket is broken or struck down (unless a batsman is out thereby), or when an unsuccessful appeal is made.

4.—For the purpose of this and other Laws, the term "dress" includes the equipment and clothing of players and umpires as normally worn.

NO BALL

26.—For a delivery to be fair the ball must be bowled, not thrown or jerked: if either Umpire be not entirely satisfied of the absolute fairness of a delivery in this respect, he shall call and signal "No Ball" instantly upon delivery. The Umpire at the Bowler's wicket shall call and signal "No Ball" if he is not satisfied that at the instant of delivery the Bowler has at least some part of one foot behind the Bowling crease and within the Return crease, and not touching or grounded over either crease.

NOTES

1.—Subject to the provisions of the Law being complied with a bowler is not debarred from delivering the ball with both feet behind the bowling crease.

2.—The striker is entitled to know whether the bowler intends to bowl over or round the wicket, overarm or underarm, right or left handed. An umpire may regard any failure to notify a change in the mode of delivery as "unfair," if so, he should call "No ball."

3.—It is a "No Ball" if the bowler before delivering a ball throws it at the striker's wicket even in an attempt to run him out (*see* Law 46, Note 4 (vii)).

4.—If a bowler break the near wicket with any part of his person during the delivery, such act in itself does not constitute a "No Ball."

5.—The umpire signals "No Ball" by extending one arm horizontally.

6.—An umpire should revoke the call "No Ball" if the ball does not leave the bowler's hand for any reason.

27.—The ball does not become "Dead" on the call of "No Ball." The Striker may hit a "No Ball" and whatever runs result shall be added to his score, but runs made otherwise from a "No Ball" shall be scored "No Balls," and if no runs be made one run shall be so scored. The Striker shall be out from a "No Ball" if he break Law 37, and either Batsman may be run out, or given out if he break Laws 36 or 40.

NOTES

1.—The penalty for a "No Ball" is only scored if no runs result otherwise.

2.—Law 46, Note 4 (vii), covers attempts to run before the ball is delivered, but should the non-striker unfairly leave his ground too soon, the fielding side may run out the batsman at the bowler's end by any recognised method. If the bowler throws at the near wicket, the umpire does not call "No Ball," though any runs resulting are so scored. The throw does not count in the "Over."

WIDE BALL

28.—If the Bowler shall bowl the ball so high over or so wide of the wicket that in the opinion of the Umpire it passes out of reach of the Striker, and would not have been within his reach when taking guard in the normal position, the Umpire shall call and signal "Wide Ball" as soon as it shall have passed the Striker.

NOTES

1.—If a ball which the umpire considers to have been delivered comes to rest in front of the striker "Wide" should not be called, and no runs should be added to the score unless they result from the striker hitting the ball which he has a right to do without interference by the fielding side. Should the fielding side interfere, the umpire is justified in replacing the ball where it came to rest and ordering the fieldsmen to resume the places they occupied in the field before the ball was delivered.

2.—The umpire signals "Wide" by extending both arms horizontally.

3.—An umpire should revoke the call if the striker hits a ball which has been called "Wide."

29 —The ball does not become "Dead" on the call of "Wide Ball." All runs that are run from a "Wide Ball" shall be scored "Wide Balls," or if no runs be made one run shall be so scored. The Striker may be out from a "Wide Ball" if he break Laws 38 or 42, and either Batsman may be run out, or given out if he break Laws 36 or 40.

BYE AND LEG BYE

30.—If the ball, not having been called "Wide" or "No Ball," pass the Striker without touching his bat or person, and any runs be obtained, the Umpire shall call or signal "Bye"; but if the ball touch any part of the Striker's dress or person except his hand holding the bat, and any run be obtained, the Umpire shall call or signal "Leg Bye"; such runs to be scored "Byes" and "Leg Byes" respectively.

NOTES

1.—The umpire shall regard the deliberate deflection of the ball by any part of the striker's person, except the hand holding the bat, as unfair, and as soon as he is satisfied that the fielding side have no chance of dismissing either batsman as an immediate result of such action, he shall without delay call "Dead Ball". In deciding whether such deflection is deliberate the criterion shall be whether or not the batsman has attempted to play the ball with his bat.

2.—The umpire signals "Bye" by raising an open hand above the head, and "Leg Bye" by touching a raised knee with the hand.

THE WICKET IS DOWN

31.—The wicket shall be held to be "Down" if either the ball or the Striker's bat or person completely removes either bail from the top of the stumps, or, if both bails be off, strikes a stump out of the ground. Any player may use his hand or arm to put the wicket down or, even should the bails be previously off, may pull up a stump provided always that the ball is held in the hand or hands so used.

NOTES

1.—A wicket is not "down" merely on account of the disturbance of a bail but it is "down" if a bail in falling from the wicket lodges between two of the stumps.

2.—If one bail is off, it is sufficient for the purpose of this Law to dislodge the remaining one in any of the ways stated or to strike any of the three stumps out of the ground.

3.—If, owing to the strength of the wind, the captains have agreed to dispense with the use of bails (*see* Law 8, Note 2), the decision as to when a wicket is "down" is one for the umpires to decide on the facts before them. In such circumstances the wicket would be held to be "down" even though a stump has not been struck out of the ground.

4.—If the wicket is broken while the ball is in play, it is not the umpire's duty to remake the wicket until the ball has become "dead." A fieldsman, however, may remake the wicket in such circumstances.

5.—For the purpose of this and other Laws, the term "person" includes a player's dress as defined in Law 25, Note 4.

OUT OF HIS GROUND

32.—A Batsman shall be held to be "Out of his ground" unless some part of his bat in hand or of his person be grounded behind the line of the Popping Crease.

BATSMAN RETIRING

33.—A Batsman may retire at any time, but may not resume his innings without the consent of the opposing Captain, and then only on the fall of a wicket.

NOTE

1.—When a batsman has retired owing to illness, injury, or some other unavoidable cause, his innings is recorded as "Retired, Not Out," but otherwise as a completed innings to be recorded as "Retired, Out."

BOWLED

34.—The Striker is out "Bowled"—If the wicket be bowled down, even if the ball first touch his bat or person.

NOTES

1.—The striker, after playing the ball, is out "Bowled" if he then kicks or hits it on to his wicket before the completion of his stroke.

2.—The striker is out "Bowled" under this Law when the ball is deflected on to his wicket off his person, even though a decision against him might be justified under Law 39 L.B.W.

CAUGHT

35.—The Striker is out "Caught"—If the ball, from a stroke of the bat or of the hand holding the bat, but not the wrist, be held by a Fieldsman before it touch the ground, although it be hugged to the body of the catcher, or be accidentally lodged in his dress. The Fieldsman must have both his feet entirely within the playing area at the instant the catch is completed.

NOTES

1.—Provided the ball does not touch the ground, the hand holding it may do so in effecting a catch.

2.—The act of making the catch starts from the time when the fieldsman first handles the ball.

3.—The fact that a ball has touched the striker's person before or after touching his bat does not invalidate a catch.

4.—The striker may be "Caught" even if the fieldsman has not touched the ball with his hands, including the case of a ball lodging in the wicket-keeper's pads.

5.—A fieldsman standing within the playing area may lean against the boundary to catch a ball, and this may be done even if the ball has passed over the boundary.

6.—If the striker lawfully plays the ball a second time he may be out under this Law, but only if the ball has not touched the ground since being first struck.

7.—The striker may be caught off any obstruction within the playing area provided it has not previously been decided on as a boundary.

HANDLED THE BALL

36.—Either Batsman is out "Handled the ball"—If he touch it while in play with his hands, unless it be done at the request of the opposite side.

NOTES

1.—A hand holding the bat is regarded as part of it for the purposes of Laws 36, 37 and 39.

2.—The correct entry in the score book when a batsman is given out under this Law is "Handled the Ball," and the bowler does not get credit for the wicket.

HIT THE BALL TWICE

37.—The Striker is out "Hit the ball twice"—If the ball be struck or be stopped by any part of his person, and he wilfully strike it again, except for the sole purpose of guarding his wicket, which he may do with his bat or any part of his person, other than his hands. No runs except those which result from an overthrow shall be scored from a ball lawfully struck twice.

NOTES

1.—It is for the umpire to decide whether the ball has been so struck a second time legitimately or not. The umpire may regard the fact that a run is attempted as evidence of the batsmen's intention to take advantage of the second stroke but it is not conclusive.

2.—A batsman may not attempt to hit the ball twice, if in so doing he baulk the wicket-keeper or any fieldsman attempting to make a catch.

3.—This Law is infringed if the striker, after playing the ball and without any request from the opposite side, uses his bat to return the ball to a fieldsman.

4.—The correct entry in the score book when the striker is given out under this Law is "Hit the ball twice," and the bowler does not get credit for the wicket.

HIT WICKET

38.—The Striker is out "Hit wicket"—If in playing at the ball he hit down his wicket with his bat or any part of his person.

NOTES

1.—The striker is "Out" under this Law if:—

(i) In making a second stroke to keep the ball out of his wicket he hits it down.

(ii) While playing at the ball, but not otherwise, his wicket is broken by his cap or hat falling, or by part of his bat.

2.—A batsman is not out for breaking the wicket with his bat or person while n the act of running

L.B.W.

39.—The Striker is out "Leg before wicket"—If with any part of his person except his hand, which is in a straight line between wicket and wicket, even though the point of impact be above the level of the bails, he intercept a ball which has not first touched his bat or hand, and which, in the opinion of the Umpire, shall have, or would have, pitched on a straight line from the Bowler's wicket to the Striker's wicket, or shall have pitched on the off-side of the Striker's wicket, provided always that the ball would have hit the wicket.

NOTES

1.—The word "hand" used in this Law should be interpreted as the hand holding the bat.

2.—A batsman is only "Out" under this Law if *all* the four following questions are answered in the affirmative.

(i) Would the ball have hit the wicket?

(ii) Did the ball pitch on a straight line between wicket and wicket (and this case includes a ball intercepted full pitch by the striker), or did it pitch on the off-side of the striker's wicket?

(iii) Was it part of the striker's person other than the hand which first intercepted the ball?

(iv) Was that part of the striker's person in a straight line between wicket and wicket at the moment of impact, irrespective of the height of the point of impact?

OBSTRUCTING THE FIELD

40.—Either Batsman is out "Obstructing the field"—If he wilfully obstruct the opposite side; should such wilful obstruction by either Batsman prevent a ball from being caught it is the Striker who is out.

NOTES

1.—The umpire must decide whether the obstruction was "wilful" or not. The involuntary interception by a batsman while running of a throw in is not in itself an offence.

2.—The correct entry in the score book when a batsman is given out under this Law is "Obstructing the field," and the bowler does not get credit for the wicket.

RUN OUT

41.—Either Batsman is out "Run out"—If in running or at any time, while the ball is in play, he be out of his ground, and his wicket be put down by the opposite side. If the batsmen have crossed each other, he that runs for the wicket which is put down is out; if they have not crossed, he that has left the wicket which is put down is out. But unless he attempt to run, the Striker shall not be given "Run out" in the circumstances stated in Law 42, even should "No Ball" have been called.

NOTE

1.—If the ball is played on to the opposite wicket, neither batsman is liable to be "Run out" unless the ball has been touched by a fieldsman before the wicket is put down.

STUMPED

42.—The Striker is out "Stumped"—If in receiving a ball, not being a "No Ball," delivered by the Bowler, he be out of his ground otherwise than in attempting a run, and the wicket be put down by the Wicket-keeper without the intervention of another fieldsman. Only when the ball has touched the bat or person of the Striker may the Wicket-keeper take it in front of the wicket for this purpose.

NOTE

1.—The striker may be "Stumped" if the wicket is broken by a ball rebounding from the wicket-keeper's person.

THE WICKET-KEEPER

43.—The Wicket-keeper shall remain wholly behind the wicket until a ball delivered by the Bowler touches the bat or person of the Striker, or passes the wicket, or until the Striker attempts a run. Should the Wicket-keeper contravene this Law, the Striker shall not be out except under Laws 36, 37, 40 and 41 and then only subject to Law 46.

NOTE

1.—This Law is provided to secure to the striker his right to play the ball and to guard his wicket without interference from the wicket-keeper. The striker may not be penalised if in the legitimate defence of his wicket he interferes with the wicket-keeper except as provided for in Law 37, Note 2.

THE FIELDSMAN

44.—The Fieldsman may stop the ball with any part of his person, but if he wilfully stop it otherwise five runs shall be added to the run or runs already made; if no run has been made five shall be scored. The penalty shall be added to the score of the Striker if the ball has been struck, but otherwise to the score of Byes, Leg Byes, No Balls or Wides as the case may be.

NOTES

1.—A fieldsman must not use his cap, etc., for the purpose of fielding a ball.

2.—The five runs are a penalty and the batsmen do not change ends.

(E)—DUTIES OF THE UMPIRES

45.—Before the toss for innings, the Umpires shall acquaint themselves with any special regulations, and shall agree with both Captains on any other conditions affecting the conduct of the match; shall satisfy themselves that the wickets are properly pitched; and shall agree between themselves on the watch or clock to be followed during play.

NOTES

1.—Apart from "Special Regulations" (*see* Law 10), other conditions of play within the framework of the Laws are frequently necessary, *e.g.* Hours of play, Intervals, etc.

2.—The captains are entitled to know which clock or watch will be followed during play.

46.—Before and during a match the Umpires shall ensure that the conduct of the game and the implements used are strictly in accordance with the Laws; they are the sole judges of fair and unfair play, and the final judges of the fitness of the ground, the weather and the light for play in the event of the decision being left to them; all disputes shall be determined by them, and if they disagree the actual state of things shall continue. The Umpires shall change ends after each side has had one innings.

NOTES

1.—An umpire should stand where he can best see any act upon which his decision may be required. Subject to this over-riding consideration the umpire at the bowler's end should stand where he does not interfere with either the bowler's run up or the striker's view. If the other umpire wishes to stand on the off instead of the leg side of the pitch, he should obtain the permission of the captain of the fielding side and inform the batsman.

2.—The umpires must not allow the attitude of the players or spectators to influence their decisions under the Laws.

3.—A code of signals for umpires is laid down in the Notes to the relevant Laws; but an umpire must call as well as signal, if necessary, to inform the players and scorers.

4.—FAIR AND UNFAIR PLAY.

(i) The umpires are entitled to intervene without appeal in the case of unfair play, but should not otherwise interfere with the progress of the game, except as required to do so by the Laws.

(ii) In the event of a player failing to comply with the instructions of an umpire or criticising his decisions, the umpires should in the first place request the captains to take action, and if this proves ineffective, report the incident forthwith to the executives of the teams taking part in the match.

(iii) It is illegal for a player to lift the seam of the ball in order to obtain a better hold. In such a case the umpire will if necessary change the ball for one which has had similar wear, and will warn the captain that the practice is unfair. The use of resin, wax, etc., by bowlers is also unfair, but a bowler may dry the ball when wet on a towel or with sawdust.

iv) An umpire is justified in intervening under this Law should any player of the fielding side incommode the striker by any noise or motion while he is receiving a ball.

(v) It is the duty of the umpires to intervene and prevent players from causing damage to the pitch which may assist the bowlers.

(vi) The persistent bowling of fast short-pitched balls at the batsman is unfair if, in the opinion of the umpire at the bowler's end, it constitutes a systematic attempt at intimidation. In such event he must adopt the following procedure:—

(*a*) When he decides that such bowling is becoming persistent he forthwith "cautions" the bowler.

(*b*) If this "caution" is ineffective, he informs the captain of the fielding side and the other umpire of what has occurred.

(*c*) Should the above prove ineffective, the umpire at the bowler's end must:—

(i) At the first repetition call "Dead Ball," when the over is regarded as completed.

(ii) Direct the captain of the fielding side to take the bowler off forthwith. The captain shall take the bowler off as directed.

(iii) Report the occurrence to the captain of the batting side as soon as an interval of play takes place.

A bowler who has been "taken off" as above may not bowl again during the same innings.

(vii) Any attempt by the batsmen to *steal a run* during the bowler's run up is unfair. Unless the bowler throws the ball at either wicket (*see* Laws 26, Note 3, and 27, Note 2), the umpire should call "Dead Ball" as soon as the batsmen cross in any such attempt to run, after which they return to their original wickets.

(viii) No player shall leave the field for the purpose of having a rub down or shower while play is actually in progress.

5.—GROUND, WEATHER AND LIGHT.

(i) Unless agreement to the contrary is made before the start of a match, the captains (during actual play the batsmen at the wickets may deputise for their captain) may elect to decide in regard to the fitness of the ground, weather or light ' or play; otherwise, in the event of disagreement, the umpires are required to decide.

(ii) Play should only be suspended when the conditions are so bad that it is unreasonable or dangerous for it to continue. The ground is unfit for play when water stands on the surface or when it is so wet or slippery as to deprive the batsmen or bowlers of a reasonable foothold, or the fieldsmen of the power of free movement. Play should *not* be suspended merely because the grass is wet and the ball slippery.

(iii) After any suspension of play, the captains, or, if the decision has been left to them, the Umpires, unaccompanied by any of the players, will without further instructions carry out an inspection immediately the conditions improve, and will continue to inspect at intervals. Immediately the responsible parties decide that play is possible, they must call upon the players to resume the game.

APPEALS

47.—The Umpires shall not order a Batsman out unless appealed to by the other side which shall be done prior to the delivery of the next ball, and before "Time" is called under Law 18. The Umpire at the Bowler's wicket shall answer appeals before the other Umpire in all cases except those arising out of Laws 38 or 42 and out of Law 41 for run out at the Striker's wicket. In any case in which an Umpire is unable to give a decision, he shall appeal to the other Umpire whose decision shall be final.

NOTES

1.—An appeal, "How's that?" covers all ways of being out (within the jurisdiction of the umpire appealed to), unless a specific way of getting out is stated by the person asking. When either umpire has given a batsman "Not out" the other umpire may answer any appeal within his jurisdiction, provided it is made in time.

2.—The umpires signal "Out" by raising the index finger above the head. If the batsman is not out, the umpire calls "Not out."

3.—An umpire may alter his decision provided that such alteration is made promptly.

4.—Nothing in this Law prevents an umpire before giving a decision from consulting the other umpire on a point of fact which the latter may have been in a better position to observe. An umpire should not appeal to the other umpire in cases on which he could give a decision, merely because he is unwilling to give that decision. If after consultation he is still in any doubt, the principle laid down in Law 46 applies and the decision will be in favour of the batsman.

5.—The umpires should intervene if satisfied that a batsman, not having been given out, has left his wicket under a misapprehension.

6.—Under Law 25 the ball is "Dead" on "Over" being called; this does not invalidate an appeal made prior to the first ball of the following "Over," provided the bails have not been removed by both umpires after "Time" has been called.

NOTES FOR SCORERS AND UMPIRES

1. (*a*) Law 4 explains the status of the scorers in relation to the umpires.

(*b*) During the progress of the game, if two scorers have been appointed, they should frequently check the total to ensure that the score sheets agree.

(*c*) The following method of entering "No Balls" and "Wides" (Laws 27 and 29) in the score sheet is recommended:—

(i) If no run is scored from the bat off a "No Ball," the latter should be entered as an "Extra," and a dot placed in the bowling analysis with a circle round it to show that the ball does not count in the over.

(ii) If runs are scored from the bat off a "No Ball," they should be credited to the striker, and entered in the bowling analysis with a circle round the figure. Such runs count against the bowler in his analysis even though the ball does not count in the over.

(iii) All runs scored from "Wide Balls" are entered as "Extras," and inserted in the bowler's analysis with a cross to indicate that the ball does not count in the over.

2. The following code of signalling between the umpires and the scorers has been approved:—

Boundaries—by waving the hand from side to side.
A boundary six—by raising both arms above the head.
Byes—by raising the open hand above the head.
Leg Byes—by touching a raised knee with the hand.
Wides—by extending both arms horizontally.
No Balls—by extending one arm horizontally.
The decision "Out"—by raising the index finger above the head.
"One Short"—by bending the arm upwards and by touching the top of the nearest shoulder with the tips of the fingers of one hand.

3. If the above instructions are properly carried out, cases of disagreement as regards the scores and the results of matches should not occur.

It is, however, important that the captains should satisfy themselves of the correctness of the scores on the conclusion of play, as errors cannot subsequently be corrected.

It should be noted that, in general, by accepting the result notified by the scorers, the captain of the losing side has thereby acquiesced in the "playing out or giving up" of the match as stated in Law 22.

REGULATIONS

FIRST-CLASS MATCHES, 1966

HOURS OF PLAY

Test Matches

All of five days' duration, 11.30 a.m. to 6.30 p.m. on the first four days and 11 a.m. to 5.30 p.m. or 6 p.m. on the fifth day. Luncheon interval 1.30–2.10, subject to alteration by the captains or umpires. A tea interval shall be allowed as provided for inter-County matches below.

Inter-County Matches (Standard Hours)

1st and 2nd days	11.30 a.m. to 6.30 p.m. (see (d) below)
3rd day	11.30 a.m. to 6 p.m. with an extra 30 minutes on this day on the demand of either captain for the purpose of securing a result in the match or on the first innings.

Alterations in the above "Standard" hours shall only be permitted in the following circumstances and within the limits stated:—

(*a*) The total hours (including all intervals, stoppages and extra time) shall not exceed 21 hours, or be less than 20 hours in any match, and shall not exceed 7 hours (including extra time) on the third day, or 8 hours (excluding extra time) on any other day.

(*b*) On no day shall play commence earlier than 11 a.m. or end later than 7.30 p.m. (including extra time), on either of the first two days, or 6.30 p.m. (including extra time) on the third day.

(*c*) Subject to (*a*) and (*b*) above, the executive of the Home County may modify the "Standard" hours of play in order to facilitate travelling on the third day in those cases only in which a team will be unable to reach its next destination before midnight, in which case a match must not be scheduled to end earlier than 4.30 p.m. (including extra time) on the third day.

The "Standard" hours of play shall be adhered to as closely as possible, and any departure from them, mutually agreed between the two Counties will be notified to all concerned including the Press, before the commencement of the season and thereafter no alternative will be permitted, except to meet exceptional travelling difficulties of either team or the umpires. In the latter case the County requiring departure from the "Standard" hours, shall notify its opponents immediately, and the Home County will be responsible for giving notice of such alterations to the umpires and the Press.

(*d*) If, in the opinion of both captains 30 minutes extra time at the end of the first and/or second day's play would bring about a definite result on that day the umpires shall order the same. If, however, the captains disagree the decision shall be left to the umpires. Any time so claimed will not preclude either side demanding an extra 30 minutes on the third day for the purpose of securing a result in the match, provided the maximum of 21 hours allowed by sub-para. (*a*) is not exceeded. If the extra 30 minutes is ordered on the first and/or second days of a three-day match, the whole 30 minutes should be played out, even though the possibility of finishing the match may have disappeared before the 30 minutes has expired.

TEA INTERVAL

1. Subject to the provisions in sub-paras. (2) and (3)—

(*a*) A tea interval of 20 minutes shall be taken to START not earlier than 3.45 p.m. or later than 4.45 p.m.

(*b*) Tea shall be taken at 4.15 p.m. except in the following circumstances—

(i) If nine wickets are then down, play shall continue for a period not exceeding 30 minutes after which tea will be taken.

(ii) If at or after 3.45 p.m. an innings closes or play is suspended—this includes a suspension which may have begun before 3.45 p.m.—the tea interval of 20 minutes (to include the interval between innings) shall then be taken.

(iii) If before 3.45 p.m. an innings closes or the game is resumed after a stoppage, tea shall be taken at 4.15 p.m. or after 50 minutes' play, whichever is the later.

2. There shall be no tea interval on any day—

(i) If both captains agree to forgo it.

(ii) If the close of play on any day (excluding any extra time permitted) has been fixed at or before 5 p.m.

(iii) If there has been no play at all between 2.45 p.m. and 3.45 p.m.

3. The above timings shall apply in all cases, except when the close of play on any day has been fixed for 7 p.m. or later. In such cases all the timings in this Regulation shall be 15 minutes later.

Drinks shall not be taken on the field to the same team more than once in each period of play.

HOURS OF PLAY FOR SUNDAY COUNTY MATCHES

(i) Play shall not begin earlier than 1 p.m. nor end later than 7.30 p.m. (including extra time).

(ii) Lunch—Shall be taken before the start of play.

(iii) Tea—The Test Match tea interval regulation will apply, except that it will be of 30 minute duration. In the event of a match starting at 1.30 p.m. or before, all the timings in the regulation will be 15 minutes earlier.

UMPIRES

Test Matches

The chairman of the Selection Committee and the manager of the touring team shall be notified confidentially in advance of Test Matches of the names of the umpires appointed to stand. Any objection lodged against either umpire must be received within three days of the notice being issued, and will be dealt with by the Umpires' Committee whose decision will be final.

No member of either team will make any statement to the Press in connection with the appointment of umpires.

Both umpires shall report themselves to the Ground Authority at 10 a.m. on the first day, and at 9 a.m. on the remaining days of play. They must remain on the ground, unless released by the Ground Authority, until half an hour after the agreed time for drawing stumps; if adverse weather conditions bring about an abandonment of play for the day, they must remain to supervise any drying of the pitch which may be possible. If there is likely to be a long period of waiting before conditions become suitable for drying the pitch, they may be released by the Ground Authority, but must hold themselves subject to recall. Their address and telephone number for the duration of the match must be left with the Ground Authority so that they may be available on call at any time.

LAW 14—FOLLOW-ON

All Matches

The following experimental Law 14 will apply:—

The side which bats first and leads by 200 runs in a match of more than three days, by 150 runs in a match of three days, by 100 runs in a two-day match, or by 75 runs in a one-day match, shall have the option of requiring the other side to follow their innings

NEW BALL

All Matches

Law 5, Note 2, as applicable to first-class matches in the United Kingdom, will be in abeyance and the captain of the fielding side shall have the choice of taking the new ball after 85 overs have been bowled with the old one. The number of overs bowled will be put up singly from the beginning of an innings in Test matches. If this is not possible in County matches, after the 75th over, the scorers shall display a small white flag or signal, which shall be replaced by a yellow signal after the 80th over. At the commencement of the 85th over both signals shall be exposed, and left exposed until the new ball is taken. Alternatively some counties may prefer to display numbers indicating the overs bowled, commencing from the end of the 75th over up to and including the 85th over.

INTERFERENCE WITH THE BALL (Tests and All West Indies Matches)

The following experimental Note 4 (iii), to Law 46, will apply:—

(*a*) No one, other than the bowler, may polish the ball.

(*b*) No one (including the bowler) shall rub the ball on the pitch or ground or take any other action, save as permitted in section (*a*) of this clause, to alter the condition of the ball.

(*c*) Law 46, Note 4 (iii), is experimentally amended by the word "oils" being inserted after the words "resin, wax".

OTHER FIRST-CLASS MATCHES

The following experimental Note 4 (iii), to Law 46, will apply:—

No polishing or other interference with the natural condition of the ball shall be allowed. Wiping and cleaning the ball shall be allowed under the Umpires' supervision.

EXCHANGING TEAMS (All Matches)

The two captains before tossing shall give each other a list of the eleven selected to play together with the emergency fieldsman. Afterwards no alteration shall be made in either eleven or emergency player without the consent of the opposing captain.

PLAYERS LEAVING THE FIELD (ALL MATCHES)

No player on the fielding side shall leave the field for the purpose of having a rub down or shower whilst a match is actually in progress.

FITNESS OF PITCH, GROUND, WEATHER AND LIGHT (ALL MATCHES)

(i) *Pitch and Ground*
Except as provided for in the official Laws of Cricket, the two captains shall decide as to the fitness of the pitch and ground for play. In the event of their disagreement, the decision shall be left to the umpires.

(ii) *Weather*
During play the captains (the batsmen at the wicket may deputise for their captain) may elect to decide in regard to fitness of the weather for play; otherwise or in the event of disagreement, the umpires are required to decide. After a suspension of play on account of weather, the decision as to the resumption shall also be in the hands of the captains. In the event of disagreement, the umpires shall decide.

(iii) *Light*
The fitness of the light before the commencement of play in any session shall be entirely in the hands of the umpires. The umpires on appeal shall decide the fitness of the light for play. Only one appeal per batting side per session will be allowed; the fielding side shall have no right of appeal. If an interruption takes place in any session and play restarts before the next adjournment, the fitness of the light for play shall be in the umpires' hands until play commences after such adjournment.

(iv) After play has been suspended due to the light, should conditions improve, the umpires will, without waiting for instructions, call upon the players to resume the game.

DECLARATIONS (LAW 15 SHALL APPLY INCLUDING TESTS AND ALL MATCHES v. WEST INDIES)

(*a*) If under Law 16 a match becomes a one-day one, no side shall declare its first innings closed until it has batted for at least sixty minutes.

(*b*) Law 15 provides an option to the captain of a batting side only, and it is not the intention that any declaration should become the subject of an agreement between the captains. If the umpires have grounds for thinking that any such agreement has taken place, they shall report accordingly to the M.C.C., and if the M.C.C. Committee is satisfied that agreement is proved, any points scored shall not be counted in the Championship table.

(*c*) In County Championship matches a captain may forfeit his second innings. In this event, the interval between innings shall be ten minutes and his decision must be notified to the opposing captain and umpires in sufficient time to allow seven minutes rolling of the pitch.

BOUNDARIES (ALL MATCHES)

The length of the boundary shall be a matter for the Home Ground Authority to decide.

SCREENS

Sight screens shall be provided at both ends of all Test grounds and if practicable at all first-class match grounds.

LAW 35—CAUGHT (ALL MATCHES)

A fieldsman must have no part of his body grounded outside the playing area in the act of making a catch and afterwards.

DRYING THE PITCH

All Matches

If both captains agree, mats or blankets may be used off the pitch in wet weather in order to make possible an earlier resumption of play. These mats or blankets may remain on the ground while play is actually in progress. (See also Laws 10 and 11.)

RENOVATION OF BOWLERS' FOOTHOLDS (All Matches)

After consultation with the Ground Authority, the umpires shall see that wherever possible and whenever it is considered necessary, action is taken during all intervals in play to do whatever is practicable to improve the bowlers' footholds.

COVERING THE PITCH

Test Matches

(a) The whole pitch shall be covered:—

(i) The night before the match and, if necessary, until the first ball is bowled; and, whenever necessary and possible, at any time prior to that during the preparation of the pitch.

(ii) On each night of the match and, if necessary, throughout Sunday. In addition, in the event of rain during the specified hours of play, the pitch shall be completely covered from the time the umpires decide that no further play is possible on that day. When this decision is taken the captains shall forthwith abandon play for the day.

(b) The bowling ends will be covered to a distance of 4 feet in front of the popping creases, if, during the hours of play, the match is suspended temporarily, owing to weather or light conditions.

Matches Other Than v. West Indies

(a) As for Test Matches, or any less degree of covering at the discretion of the Home County subject to notification before the season starts to M.C.C. and the appropriate opponents in each case.

(b) The bowling ends will be covered to a distance of 4 feet in front of the popping creases:—

(i) If during the hours of play, the match is suspended temporarily, on account of weather or light conditions.

(ii) On each night of the match, if the pitch is not fully covered.

THE CONDUCT OF THE GAME (All Matches)

The attention of umpires is particularly drawn to the provisions of Law 46.

Time-Wasting

Umpires are reminded that any waste of time—a bowler wasting time, the fielders crossing over slowly between the overs and for left-handed batsmen; fielders throwing the ball to one another before returning it to the bowler, unless the bowler begins his walk back to his mark immediately after delivering the ball; captains being unduly deliberate in field placing and not starting such field placing until a new batsman has reached the wicket; incoming batsmen taking too long to reach the wicket—constitutes unfair play, and after consultation together and, where possible, after warning the captain concerned, they shall report such occurrences as above.

In the event of a bowler taking unnecessarily long to bowl an over, the umpire at the bowler's end, after consultation with the other umpire, shall take the following immediate action:—

(i) Caution the bowler and inform the captain of the fielding side that he has done so.

(ii) Should this caution prove ineffective:—

(*a*) Direct the captain of the fielding side to take the bowler off at the end of the over in progress. The captain shall take the bowler off as directed.

(*b*) Report the occurrence to the captain of the batting side as soon as an interval of play takes place.

(*c*) Send a written report of the occurrence to the secretary of M.C.C. and to the manager or secretary of the team to which the offending player belongs.

A bowler who has been "taken off" as above may not bowl again during the same innings.

Damage to Pitch

The attention of umpires is particularly drawn to Note 4 (v) to Law 46: and, purely as a guide, it is suggested that the "danger area" is an area contained by an imaginary line 4ft. from the popping crease and parallel to it, and within two imaginary and parallel lines drawn down the pitch from points 1ft. on either side of the middle stump and 4ft. from the popping crease.

In the event of a bowler contravening Law 46, Note 4 (v), the umpire will:—

(a) In the first instance caution the bowler.

(b) If this caution is ineffective, inform the captain of the fielding side and the other umpire of what has occurred.

(c) Should the above prove ineffective, the umpire at the bowler's end must:—

(i) At the first repetition call "Dead Ball" when the over is regarded as completed.

(ii) Direct the captain of the fielding side to take the bowler off forthwith. The captain shall take the bowler off as directed.

(iii) Report the occurrence to the captain of the batting side as soon as an interval of play takes place.

A bowler who has been "taken off" as above may not bowl again in the same innings.

LIMITATION OF THE NUMBER OF ON-SIDE FIELDERS—EXPERIMENTAL NOTE 3 TO LAW 44 (All Matches)

The number of on-side fieldsmen behind the popping crease at the instant of the bowler's delivery shall not exceed two.

In the event of an infringement of this Rule by the fielding side the square-leg umpire should call "No Ball."

Note.—The umpire may elect to stand on the off-side, provided he informs the captain of the fielding side and the striker of his intention to do so.

LAW 26. No Ball. (All Matches)

As an experiment in 1966 the following will apply:—

(a) For a delivery to be fair, the ball must be bowled not thrown: if, in the opinion of either umpire, a delivery is unfair in this respect, he shall call and signal "No Ball" instantly upon delivery. At the conclusion of every match, both umpires will submit reports to the secretary of M.C.C., on the fairness or otherwise of the actions of all bowlers in the match. In the event of an umpire expressing doubt as to the absolute fairness of a bowler's action, the secretary of M.C.C. shall inform the secretary of the County Club, or the manager of the Touring Team, concerned. The captains may also report, if they have any doubt about the fairness of the action of any bowler in the match.

The umpire at the bowler's wicket shall call and signal "No Ball" if, in the delivery stride, the bowler's front foot lands clear beyond the popping crease, or if he is not satisfied that the bowler's back foot has landed within and not touching the return crease or its forward extension.

(b) Add the following additional Note to the Law: A ball shall be deemed to have been thrown if, in the opinion of either umpire, the bowling arm, having been bent at the elbow, whether the wrist is backward of the elbow or not, is suddenly straightened immediately prior to the instant of delivery. The bowler shall nevertheless be at liberty to use the wrist freely in the delivery action.

(c) In conjunction with the above mentioned Experimental Law the following conditions shall apply:—

(i) The length of the return crease shall be 4 feet.

(ii) The popping crease shall extend 6 feet either side of the line of stumps.

(iii) The popping crease and return crease shall be re-drawn during each interval.

REGULATIONS FOR DRYING THE PITCH AND GROUND IN FIRST-CLASS MATCHES IN THE UNITED KINGDOM

N.B.—*These regulations are primarily designed for First-class Cricket, and their application in whole or in part in other grades of Cricket in the United Kingdom is at the discretion of the ground, etc., authorities.*

1. Except as provided below, the existing regulations in regard to the rolling of the pitch and the fitness of the ground for play shall apply. (*See* Laws 10, 12 and 46.)

2. (i) To enable play to proceed with the least possible delay after rain, the groundman shall adopt every practical means to protect or rid the surface of the ground, *other than the pitch*, of water or dampness at any time except while play is in progress.

(ii) Prior to tossing for choice of innings the artificial drying of the pitch and outfield shall be at the discretion of the groundman. Thereafter and throughout the match the drying of the outfield may be undertaken at any time by the groundman, but the drying of the pitch shall be carried out only on the instructions and under the supervision of the umpires. The umpires shall be empowered to have the pitch dried without a reference to the captains at any time they are of the opinion that it is unfit for play.

(iii) In wet weather, the umpires shall see that the foot-holes made by the bowlers and batsmen are cleaned, dried and filled up with sawdust at any time during the match, although the game is not actually in progress.

The groundman, without instructions from the umpires, may also clean out in this way foot-holes, provided they are not on any part of the pitch, more than 3 ft. 6 ins. in front of the popping creases.

The drying of the foot-holds on the pitch itself may be undertaken, as directed by the umpires, at any time. The umpires may also direct the groundman to protect against further rain marks made by the bowlers, even though they be more than 3 ft. 6 ins. in front of the popping creases, provided they are not between wicket and wicket, with loose sawdust, which, however, shall be removed prior to the resumption of play.

(iv) The umpires shall ascertain from the groundman before the commencement of a match what equipment is available for drying the pitch artificially.

Any roller may be used, if the umpires think desirable but only (except as laid down in paragraph (2) (v)) for the purpose of drying the pitch and making it fit for play, and not otherwise. This would allow umpires to roll the pitch after drying it, say with a light roller, for a minute or two, should they consider it desirable.

(v) When the artificial drying of the pitch, under the supervision of the umpires, coincides with any interval during the match, after the toss for choice of innings, the umpires, and not the captain of the batting side, shall select the roller to be used.

(vi) The fact that the umpires may have dried the pitch artificially does not take the decision as regards the fitness of the pitch and ground for play out of the hands of the captains, even though the umpires may have selected the roller to be used for the drying process. Law 46, Note 5 (i) is applicable in such cases.

INTERNATIONAL CRICKET CONFERENCE

In 1909, representatives of cricket in England, Australia and South Africa met at Lord's and founded the Imperial Cricket Conference. Membership was confined to the Governing bodies of cricket in countries within the British Commonwealth, where Test cricket was played. India, New Zealand and West Indies were elected additional members in 1926 and Pakistan in 1952. South Africa ceased membership on leaving the Commonwealth in May 1961

In 1965, the Conference was renamed The International Cricket Conference, and new rules were adopted to permit the election as full or associate members of countries outside the British Commonwealth. A full member is a country, or countries associated for cricket purposes, with a governing body for Cricket, recognised by the Conference, of which the representative teams are accepted as qualified to play official Test Matches. Associate members are countries with governing bodies for cricket recognised by the Conference, not qualifying as full members, but where cricket is fully recognised and organised.

The Conference normally meets once a year to approve official programmes for the interchange of visits between member countries, the qualification rules for players in Test Matches and other matters of common interest.

United States, Ceylon and Fiji were elected associate members in 1965 and Bermuda, Holland, Denmark and East Africa in 1966.

FIRST-CLASS MATCH DEFINED

A match of three or more days duration between two sides of eleven players officially adjudged first-class shall be regarded as a first-class fixture.

The following matches by this definition shall not be regarded as first-class: If either team has more than 11 players. If the duration of the match is shorter than three days.

The Governing body in each country shall decide the status of teams.

Any question arising under these rules shall be submitted to the International Cricket Conference, and their decision shall be final.

FUTURE TOURS

	Visits to U.K.		*Tours Abroad*
1967	India and Pakistan.	1967–68	M.C.C. to West Indies.
1968	Australia.	1967–68	India to Australia and New Zealand.
1969	West Indies and New Zealand.	1968–69	M.C.C. to South Africa.
1970	South Africa.	1968–69	West Indies to Australia.
1971	Pakistan and India.	1970–71	M.C.C. to Australia.
1972	Australia.	1971–72	M.C.C. to India and Pakistan

BOARD OF CONTROL OF "TEST" MATCHES AT HOME

DISTRIBUTION OF PROFITS

All monies taken at stands and enclosures at all Test matches together with gate money in respect thereof, less the opponents' 50 per cent share for each person paying admission at the outer gate, less expenses, shall be distributed as follows: 11 per cent between each Minor County; Oxford, Cambridge Univs. £2,250 each; Combined Services, Ireland, Scotland £250 each. To Lancashire, M.C.C., Nottinghamshire, Surrey, Warwickshire and Yorkshire, being the six clubs having recognised Test match grounds, £1,750; the balance of the distributable profit to be divided as to 50 per cent in equal shares between the six clubs having recognised Test match grounds and 50 per cent in equal shares between the remaining first-class counties. Television and Broadcasting fees from Test matches shall be distributed; £1,250 to each club having a recognised Test-match ground; the balance as to 95 per cent between the first-class counties and M.C.C. in equal shares and as to 5 per cent between each minor county.

TRAVELLING EXPENSES

A player or umpire will be paid the cost of a first-class railway fare from the ground on which he was last engaged or from his home, if he has not been engaged immediately prior to the Test Match. He will similarly be paid the cost of a first-class railway fare to the ground on which he is next engaged or to his home if he is not engaged. If a cricketer travels by private car he may claim 8d per mile instead of the railway fare.

HOTEL AND INCIDENTAL EXPENSES

The ground authority, when so requested, will arrange for hotel accommodation, and will pay the hotel account excluding expenses for guests, drinks, tobacco and other personal items.

Players who do not use the accommodation so provided will not be entitled to claim hotel or lodging charges.

All players and umpires will be allowed £3 for a five-day Test match for incidental expenses.

REMUNERATION OF PLAYERS, ETC.

	Test Match
Cricketers playing	£120 per match
12th man (on duty through Test)	£65 per match
12th man (1st and 2nd days)	£40
12th man (3rd, 4th and 5th days)	£25
Reserves	£25 per match
Umpires	£75 per match
Scorers	£25 per match
Emergency fieldsman	£5 per day

INSURANCE OF PLAYERS

The secretary M.C.C. will take out an insurance policy to cover the risk of accidents to cricketers (including 12th man and reserves) playing in Test or Trial matches.

REGISTRATION AND QUALIFICATION RULES IN COUNTY CRICKET

(As amended 9th December, 1963)

Definitions

(*a*) For the purposes of these Rules, a Colony, State, Province, or other overseas cricketing authority, shall be regarded as a County.

(*b*) The term "Residence" as used in these Rules shall mean a bona fide home, and not a mere acquirement or hiring of a tenement during a cricket season only.

(*c*) For the purpose of County Cricket, a player shall be qualified by birth for the County shown on his birth certificate. The residential qualification of a player shall be for that County in which he has resided during his qualifying period. The County of London shall not be regarded as a county. A player born or resident in the County of London shall be qualified for that County in which his place of birth or residence was situated prior to it being incorporated in the County of London.

Any doubtful cases shall be referred to the Registration Committee for decision.

Rule 1. Alteration to Rules

No alteration in, or addition to, the Advisory County Cricket Committee Rules governing the Registration and qualification of cricketers in County Cricket shall be made, except at a Meeting of the Advisory County Cricket Committee; and no such alteration or addition shall be made except by a vote of two-thirds of the representatives present at such Meeting.

Rule 2. Engagement and Registration of Cricketers

(a) Registration

No cricketer may play in a competitive cricket match under the control of the Advisory County Cricket Committee, unless he has been registered with M.C.C. by his County that season.

Before the beginning of each cricket season, each County Cricket Club shall send to the M.C.C. and to every other County Cricket Club, a list of the cricketers, with their respective qualifications, who are expected to play for the County during that season; and if, in the course of the season, a County wishes to play a cricketer not included in that list, his name and qualification shall be circulated in a similar manner forthwith.

Cricketers who have been specially registered for any County will continue, subject to the provisions of Rule 8(a) (i), to be shown as qualified under Rule 8, so long as they are on the playing strength of that County.

(b) County wishing to negotiate with a Cricketer qualified for another County

A County wishing to offer a trial to, to engage, to play or to register a cricketer, not qualified for that County, but who is qualified for another County (or Counties), must obtain written consent from the County (or Counties) for which the cricketer is qualified, before starting negotiations with him. Such consent shall not be unreasonably withheld. Unless a cricketer has been registered under Rule 5(c) or 5(f), qualification under these two rules may, for this purpose, be disregarded.

(c) Cricketer previously registered with one County wishing to qualify by residence for another County

Should a cricketer, who has been registered for one County wish to qualify by residence for another County, he must obtain written consent, which must not be ante-dated, from the former County. His residential qualification shall not begin to run until he has obtained this consent, which shall not be unreasonably withheld.

(d) Appeals referring to Rules 2(b) and 2(c)

If the cricketer or County referred to in Rules 2(b) or 2(c) above consider that consent has been unreasonably withheld, they may appeal to the Registration Committee.

(e) Cricketer wishing to play for the County of his birth

A cricketer who has been registered as in Rule 2(*a*) for another County or Counties and who wishes to play for the County of his birth, must give written notice to the last County for which he has been registered.

Rule 3. Cricketer not to Play for more than one County in a Calendar Year

A cricketer may not play for more than one English County within a Calendar Year in any competition organised by the Advisory County Cricket Committee; the penalty for the infringement of this Rule shall be disqualification for two years.

During the English off-season, this Rule shall not, however, debar a registered county cricketer from playing first-class cricket overseas, always provided that permission to do so has been obtained from the County for which he is registered. The County concerned, before granting such permission, shall ensure that the cricketer is not required for a major M.C.C. tour overseas. Should a registered county cricketer play for the country of his birth during a tour of the United Kingdom by that Country, he shall forfeit his County qualification.

Rule 4. Notice to Counties

Correspondence on all matters concerning the registration and qualification of cricketers will be addressed to the secretary and any notice sent to the secretary of a County Cricket Club shall be regarded as notice to that County.

Rule 5. Qualifications

Subject to the provisions of Rules 2, 3, 6 and 7, a cricketer shall be qualified for registration.—

(*a*) For the County of his birth.

(*b*) If born in the United Kingdom—for the County in which he has resided for the previous 12 consecutive months and in which he is still residing. The residence of a Master at a School shall count as residence for this purpose.

(*c*) For the County in which his boarding school is situated, whilst at school and thereafter.

(*d*) If born out of the United Kingdom, but having resided in the United Kingdom for the previous five consecutive years, for the County in which he has resided for the previous 12 consecutive months and in which he is still residing. In the event of such a cricketer not having resided in the United Kingdom for the required five consecutive years, the qualifying residential period shall be 24 consecutive months. During this residential qualification period, he shall not play cricket under any contract outside the County for which he is qualifying.

Note: (i) The County for which an overseas cricketer is qualifying by residence shall notify M.C.C. of the date on which this cricketer starts his residential qualification.

(ii) No County shall have more than two cricketers born overseas on their list of registered cricketers in any one season.

(*e*) For the County for which his father has played regularly for at least three years.

(*f*) For the County for which he is Specially Registered.

Rule 6. Re-Qualification

A cricketer already registered under Rule 2(*a*) for one County shall not be registered for another County unless qualified by:—

(*a*) Birth—Rule 5(*a*), or

(*b*) Continuous residence for the previous 24 months: provided that, if the County for which he is registered shall decide that it no longer requires him, such County shall forthwith remove his name from its list of Registered Players and the period of continuous residence shall then be reduced to 12 months. During this residential qualification period, he shall not play cricket under any contract outside the County for which he is qualifying. The provisions of Rules 2(*b*) and 2(*c*) shall apply, or

(*c*) Special Registration—Rule 8

Rule 7. Continuance and Cessation

(*a*) A cricketer who has been registered for a County shall be considered eligible to play for that County—subject to the terms of Rule 2(*a*)—until such time as he is registered by another County.

(*b*) A cricketer, in the course of qualifying by residence for a County, breaks his qualification for that County, if he is registered for another, including the County of his birth.

(*c*) A cricketer acquiring residential qualification for a County does not interrupt that qualifying period by undertaking Government Service or occasional winter work for business reasons outside the County in which his residence is situated.

(*d*) A cricketer born overseas who has resided in the United Kingdom for five consecutive years shall thereafter, for the purpose of these Rules, only as far as residential qualification is concerned, be regarded as if born in the United Kingdom.

RULE 8. SPECIAL REGISTRATION

The object of Special Registration is to safeguard the interests of a cricketer who is not required by the County or Counties for which he is qualified and, by enabling him to play for another County with the minimum delay, to retain him in the game. Before deciding to grant any Special Registration, the Registration Committee must be satisfied that their decision is in the best interests of County Cricket.

(*a*) The Registration Committee may specially register any cricketer always provided that:—

(i) The County applying for a Special Registration has not, during any cricket season, more than 10 cricketers shown as qualified under this Rule on their list of cricketers circulated in accordance with Rule 2(*a*). This number shall not include any cricketer who has been Specially Registered for a County, who has resided continuously in that County for a period of 5 years: but shall include any Cricketer granted Temporary Special Registration under paragraph (g) of this Rule.

(ii) Not more than two applications for Special Registration and for Temporary Special Registration for any County shall be approved in any Calendar Year, beginning on 1st January.

(iii) The County applying for a Special Registration shall undertake to make reasonable use of the cricketer's services, as far as these may be available, for at least three seasons. The Registration Committee shall, on appeal from the cricketer, be empowered to cancel a Special Registration in any case in which a County has failed to carry out its obligations to make reasonable use of a cricketer, or found itself unable to do so, but only if such a course is shown to be in the interest of the cricketer.

(iv) In the case of a cricketer being offered a written Contract, such Contract shall be for a minimum period of three years.

NOTE.—A cricketer born in the United Kingdom shall be eligible for Special Registration if he has no qualification for any County.

(*b*) The following shall not be eligible for Special Registration:—

(i) A cricketer born outside the United Kingdom, unless he has been resident in the United Kingdom for 10 consecutive years.

(ii) A cricketer who is required by the County for which he is qualified, unless the Registration Committee are satisfied that the circumstances are exceptional.

(*c*) Applications for Special Registration shall be made to the Registration Committee on the form provided for the purpose and shall be signed by the secretary of the County (or Counties) for which the cricketer is qualified, and by the cricketer himself.

The County applying for the Special Registration shall satisfy the Registration Committee that reasonable use is to be made of the services of the cricketer, and it shall be the duty of the Registration Committee to withhold approval to any application if of opinion that the engagement or move is not in the interests of the cricketer.

(*d*) In considering an application for Special Registration, it shall be open to the Registration Committee to withhold consent or to agree to the cricketer's immediate Special Registration for the County applying.

(*e*) Subject to Rule 3, a cricketer shall be eligible to play for a County as soon as the Special Registration has been approved. On receipt of the approval of a registration by the Registration Committee, the County concerned shall immediately carry out the provisions of Rule 2(*a*).

(*f*) Should the attention of the Registration Committee be called to any breach of the provisions of Rule 8, they shall be empowered to cancel the Special Registration granted under that Rule to any cricketer concerned.

(g) Temporary Special Registration

A cricketer born overseas, whilst in residence as an undergraduate of a University in the United Kingdom may be Specially Registered temporarily for a County. Such temporary Special Registration will continue until the end of the cricket season of his last year in residence at the University.

In the event of such a cricketer wishing to prolong his registration for the County for which he has been Temporarily Specially Registered, the County concerned shall make application to the Registration Committee who may grant such an extension for two seasons only. Should the cricketer wish to continue his registration for the County concerned when this period has elapsed, he must establish a residential qualification for that County. Should the cricketer wish to be registered for another County, he must qualify in accordance with Rule 6(*b*).

RULE 9. DOUBTFUL CASES OF QUALIFICATION

If required to do so, it is obligatory on the County for which a cricketer wishes to be registered to prove his qualifications to the satisfaction of the Registration Committee.

In the event of an infringement of Rules 2(*b*) or 2(*c*), the Registration Committee shall have authority to fix a date when the cricketer shall become qualified by residence.

RULE 10. APPEALS

Any appeal from a decision of the Registration Committee, shall be referred to M.C.C., whose decision shall be final.

MEETINGS IN 1966

The two reports issued by the D. G. Clark sub-committee which dealt with the problems and the future of County Cricket and also the full report of the Throwing Committee will be found among the feature articles in the early part of the Almanack.

THE 65 OVERS EXPERIMENT

The Advisory County Cricket Committee received the first report from the D. G. Clark sub-committee on March 1 and decided that in 1966 each county would play twelve matches with the first innings of each limited to 65 overs. The detailed arrangement and the list of matches involved are given under The County Championship on page 348. It was also decided that the team leading on the first innings and winning the match would retain the two points for first-innings lead, making it possible to take 12 points from the match.

By a 10–7 vote the Counties cast aside the 65-overs experiment as a failure after only one season's trial at their meeting on November 16.

SUNDAY CRICKET

Several counties having decided to play some matches on Sundays, it was agreed at the Advisory meeting at Lord's on March 16 that play would not begin before 1 p.m. and would end at 7.30 at the latest, with half an hour allowed for tea.

In certain conditions Sunday play would be permitted in the Gillette Cup.

TEST SELECTORS

The Board of Control reappointed the current Test selectors on March 16 for 1966: D. J. Insole (chairman), A. V. Bedser, D. Kenyon and P. B. H. May.

TOURING TEAM ARRANGEMENTS

The West Indies agreed that the existing system by which umpires were required to report doubtful actions of bowlers in County Cricket should apply to themselves in 1966.

The touring team also approved the new ball after 85 overs; local boundaries, the front foot rule for bowlers, and no limit to the number of on-side fielders, except two behind the batting crease.

COVERING OF PITCHES

As there was some support among the Counties for going back to uncovered pitches, it was decided that in 1966 Counties would be allowed to cover pitches each night and over the week-end, but there would be discretion for home counties to adopt less covering.

This regulation was slightly amended for 1967 when on November 16 the Advisory C.C.C. decided that Counties may either cover fully as for Test matches each night and at the week-ends, or not cover at all. Other regulations for 1967 regarding the new ball, polishing the ball, forfeiting of innings, boundaries, leg-side limitation, front foot and throwing remained unchanged.

QUESTIONNAIRE TO MEMBERS

The Advisory C.C.C. at their meeting on March 16 made no decision on the sub-committee's recommendation that the future structure of County Cricket should be either 16 three-day matches and 16 one-day matches in one Championship, or 20 three-day games and 16 one-day games in separate Championships. They desired to see, for one thing, how the 65-over experiment worked.

It was also considered desirable to question County members concerning the game's long-term future.

GOLD COIN FOR THE TOSS

Lord's Taverners presented to M.C.C. a golden sovereign having the date of the first England–Australia Test, 1877, to be used for the toss at home Tests between the two countries. A similar coin was presented to the Australian Board of Control for their home Tests.

THE H. J. RHODES CONTROVERSY

At the request of Derbyshire, the special committee set up on March 1 to deal with suspect throwers met at Lord's on March 25 to consider the bowling action of H. J. Rhodes. They watched several films before Rhodes, in his full cricketing kit, went to the practice ground and bowled for fifteen minutes with his full run of twenty yards at his fastest pace. He hit a single stump several times. Mr. W. E. Tucker, the surgeon, gave evidence, including demonstrations with the help of a human skeleton, which showed that Rhodes's right arm naturally bent back from the straight. Afterwards, the Committee issued this statement: The Committee unanimously considered his basic action to be fair, but were divided on the evidence before them as to whether or not his action was occasionally suspect. They intend therefore to have further films taken and to hold another meeting. This took place in June when the Committee accepted his basic action as fair though they were divided as to whether or not an occasional delivery contravened the law.

INTERNATIONAL CRICKET CONFERENCE

New Definition of a Throw

At the annual meeting of the International Cricket Conference at Lord's on July 14 the following definition of a throw, put forward by M.C.C., was adopted for all countries for one year, 1967:

> A ball shall be deemed to have been thrown if in the opinion of either umpire the process of straightening the bowling arm, whether it be partial or complete, takes place during that part of the delivery-swing which directly precedes the ball leaving the hand.

This definition will not debar a bowler from the use of the wrist in the delivery swing.

Among the experimental rules which the meeting agreed should be discussed by the various boards, with a view to being incorporated in the laws in the near future, was that concerning time-wasting. Offending bowlers should be warned by the umpire and, if necessary, the captain should be ordered to take off the bowler for the rest of the innings. There was no support for limiting the length of a bowler's run-up.

For two years all countries will experiment with the following new ball rule: a minimum of 75 overs, maximum 85 overs (six-ball) at the discretion of the Home Authority.

Four new associate members were elected—the Netherlands, Denmark, Bermuda and East Africa, making six full members and seven associates. South Africa did not apply to rejoin the conference. The leading Test match countries decided to set up a central fund so that coaches can be sent to associate member countries.

TEST PROFITS SHARE OUT

The five Tests in 1966 yielded a record profit of £188,400. The six Test centres, M.C.C., Nottinghamshire, Warwickshire, Yorkshire, Lancashire and Surrey each received £14,285. The twelve other first-class counties £7,019; Oxford and Cambridge Universities £2,250; nineteen Minor Counties £852 each; Combined Services, Ireland and Scotland £250 each.

No fewer than 8,300,000 people dialled UMP to find out the scores in the Tests between England and West Indies, yet paid County attendances dropped by 146,000 to the dismal figure of 513,578, compared with over two million paying at the turnstiles just after the war. Membership numbers also declined by nearly 5,000.

For 1967 the minimum Test admission fee was raised by the Board of Control at their meeting on November 16 from six shillings to seven and six. The Advisory C.C.C. put up the price for the Gillette Cup Final from ten to fifteen shillings; semi-finals to seven and six and the first three rounds to five shillings.

TEST DATES FOR 1968

Dates and venues for the England v. Australia Tests in 1968: June 6 at Old Trafford; June 20 at Lord's; July 11 at Edgbaston; July 25 at Headingley; August 22 at The Oval.

OVERSEAS QUALIFICATION STAYS RIGID

Lancashire and Nottinghamshire pleaded for the waiving of the qualification period in the case of one overseas player for each county, but it was feared that the richer counties would snap up the leading stars and the proposal met with a heavy defeat. It was argued that it would not be wise for counties to commit themselves to expensive long-term contracts if less cricket was eventually arranged. Some counties were also worried about an auction for the really big names and the possible introduction of a transfer system of stars if contracts were for a short period. Proposals to abolish the qualification period altogether or to reduce it from two years to one were also defeated.

UMPIRES FOR 1967

TESTS

With six Tests against India and Pakistan compared with five in 1966 it was decided to add A. E. Fagg and H. Yarnold to the panel of four, J. S. Buller, C. S. Elliott, W. F. Price and A. Jepson, who were retained.

FIRST-CLASS

One change was made, A. Gaskell (Yorkshire) replacing P. A. Gibb, who had been on the list since 1957. H. Mellows was appointed for the whole of 1966 when C. Cook withdrew. The 1967 list is: A. E. Alderman, J. Arnold, R. Aspinall, J. S. Buller, W. H. Copson, J. F. Crapp, C. S. Elliott, A. E. Fagg, A. Gaskell, L. H. Gray, O. W. Herman, F. Jakeman, A. Jepson, John Langridge, R. S. Lay, H. Mellows, C. G. Pepper, W. E. Phillipson, G. H. Pope, W. F. Price, A. E. Rhodes, W. F. Simpson, T. W. Spencer, P. B. Wight, H. Yarnold.

MINOR COUNTIES

The Minor Counties chose the following twenty-seven umpires: R. Alderson, F. Berry, W. L. Budd, T. C. Burrell, M. A. Cleaver, M. J. Downer, T. Drinkwater, C. E. Dunn, R. G. Evans, C. S. Hainsworth, J. H. Harding, W. H. Harvey, L. A. Hoff, P. Hough, D. R. Ingrey, A. A. J. Larby, S. H. Moore, J. O'Neill, H. W. Parks, W. J. Paulley, C. Petrie, R. O. Prouton, A. M. Pullinger, A. E. D. Smith, L. Tomlinson, W. H. Wignall, K. Wilson.

M.C.C. SECRETARY'S SPEECH

Welcoming the County Secretaries at their annual meeting at Lord's on December 6, Mr. S. C. Griffith, secretary of M.C.C., outlined the possible future structure of the Championship, which can be found in the D. G. Clark report, and also gave his views as to the way the players themselves can play their part in the improvement of the image of cricket.

"It is two years since I last had this opportunity to speak to you," he said, "and, in the meantime, I have had the good fortune to visit Australia and, as it were, to begin again to appreciate the views and feelings of present-day players. I am sure the experience has been of tremendous value in the work one tries to do at Lord's. It has, I think, given me a closer understanding of the problems involved in promoting first-class cricket in such a way as to maintain the intrinsic quality of the game, to satisfy the spectator, and to enable the player to retain his enthusiasm, enjoyment and skill.

"Incidentally, given the pitches to play on and an understanding of the requirements, no side could have made a greater effort than our team in Australia. Most of the cricket played was worth going a long way to see.That we did not achieve greater success threw up in the sharpest possible relief the old argument as to the best possible method of achieving success, and I am ignoring for the moment the question of whether or not the result is more important than the way it is achieved.

"I am a firm believer in the principle that good cricket, and by that I mean positive cricket, is more likely to bring success than the highly efficient but excessively dull policy of defence and containment. And, what is more, it is much more fun for players and spectators alike. Furthermore, cricket as a game was, I am sure, always meant to be played in a positive way. In other words, the approach of the players—constantly encouraged by the known and stated requirements of Committees—is all-important, and vital to the well-being of Test and County cricket whatever the structure of the latter.

"Lately, we have all been much engaged in considering the structure of County cricket—and shining like a beacon light through all the questionnaires, opinion polls and the like is the urgent need for players and Committees to ensure and insist upon good cricket. And it is particularly encouraging that, in the recent expression of opinion from the players, so conscientiously and carefully made, they, too, fully appreciate the part they must play; and how much a firmer line from their Captains and Committees would help.

"I recall one occasion last summer, on a seaside ground, on a good pitch, on a fine Saturday in July, with a good holiday crowd there, the side batting first managed some 140 runs for the loss of four or five wickets by tea time. Cricket utterly without point, and nothing as far as I know was said except by the Sunday newspapers. Again, a Captain on another occasion made it abundantly clear in front of a good crowd, that he disapproved of the 65-over limitation—and the cricket played as a result of this irresponsible fourth-form behaviour made a complete travesty of the game. I am not suggesting that the 65-over limitation was either a good or a bad thing. All I say is that such performances on a cricket field should never be allowed to happen.

"If we are going to consider a change of structure, and I, personally, very much hope we are, let us insist that the cricket played is good cricket and played on good pitches. And that the insistence comes to the players via the Committees and Captains."

CRICKET BOOKS, 1966

By John Arlott

Sixty-six titles of the usual wide range and variable quality argue another healthy year in the publishing of cricket books, and certainly they included the most ambitious book on the game published in modern times.

The World of Cricket (Joseph, 6 guineas) of which E. W. Swanton was the general, and Michael Melford the associate, editor, was originally planned as an even larger operation than its eventual single volume of 1,165 pages. No such encyclopaedic reference book on cricket has ever appeared before and, with over two thousand entries—some of them cross-references, but others of booklet length—it covers much ground. As with any reference book, it is possible for anyone who applies himself to the task to find errors and omissions. On the other hand, most readers—and writers—on the subject will be grateful for a collection which, in so rapidly changing a world as that of cricket, provides many and valuable statistics, but is sufficiently concerned with trends, ideas and history to survive beyond the records of the next Test series. England *v.* Australia was a natural entry. The Cheetham Case, Nigeria, Ravens. C.C., "Iffish" and Kelly-King were less obvious, and indicate the scope of the book. O. J. Wait's survey of the sources of University Blues, the late Arthur Wrigley's collection of career records, and the history of league cricket—in the Midlands and Wales as well as Lancashire, Cheshire and Yorkshire—are all valuable and original contributions to the chronicles of the game. Illustration—including a number of colour photographs by J. G. Dunbar—is generous, and the selection of the action photographs is extremely impressive. Most of the contributors are recognised authorities in their departments but among those less generally known, R. L. Arrowsmith, Geoffrey Bolton and a number who have contributed histories of their own particular clubs, have written with charm as well as knowledge. The editor describes his aim as covering history, biography, glossary of terms, bibliography, Directory, facts and figures (provided by the late Arthur Wrigley) and "miscellaneous". No doubt in due course we shall see a fresh edition of this book, meanwhile it affords the widest work of reference the game has yet had, and does so in attractive form.

More privately and not, so far as I can ascertain, for sale, Peter Wynne-Thomas has compiled and cyclostyled *A Complete Register of Cricketers to Represent Nottingham Old Club and Nottinghamshire County Cricket Club from 1821 to 1965.* The extent of his research indicates that this is the basis for a further and much larger record to add to the already extensive bibliography of Nottinghamshire cricket.

An important accession to South African cricket history is *Century at Newlands 1864–1964; A History of the Western Province Cricket Club* (Western Province C.C., Campground Road, Newlands, Cape Town, South Africa, Rands 2.50), compiled by S. E. L. West and edited by W. J. Luker. From the October day of 1864 when the *Cape Argus* announced "A cricket match will be played at Wynberg tomorrow between two teams of the newly formed Western Province Cricket Club", through the leasing of "Lot 27" of Mariendal farm—now, arguably, the loveliest cricket ground in the world—this book records the doings of a provincial side of memorable and friendly character, and both the representative cricket and the less publicised matches played on its pitch. The story is told concisely—at times one could wish for more expansive treatment—but also with sympathy, humour and a genuine feeling for tradition and people.

Another centenary is marked by *Basingstoke & North Hants Cricket Club, 1865–1965* (from the Secretary, B. & N.H.C.C., May's Bounty, Basingstoke, 10s. 6d.) by P. M. Bichard—holder of the club record for a season's aggregate—and B. R. S. Harrison, formerly of the Hampshire staff, who was responsible for the statistics. It is a sound and conscientious club history, firmly based on matches but with perceptive studies of the club's main figures, notably the remarkable Bert Butler, for fifty-two years groundsman at the Bounty, and who scored 21,451 runs and took 1,836 wickets for the first team, irrespective of his performances for the second team and the Thursday eleven—a mighty practitioner and enthusiast of cricket.

Although *Mayfield Cricket Club 1866–1966* (from the Secretary, Mayfield C.C., Sussex, 5s.) is described as a Centenary Souvenir, it produces evidence of Mayfield playing a match as long ago as 1751. It is a pleasant, friendly, well-produced booklet.

Armchair Cricket 1966 (B.B.C., 5s.), edited by Brian Johnston, is a revised and enlarged edition of *Armchair Cricket* (1955). Like its predecessor its main purpose is to increase the understanding and the pleasure of the radio listener or television viewer. It contains essays on the history of cricket commentary, radio and television production, the skills of commentary, the commentators, scoring, and a glossary of cricket terms. It also contains photographs and biographical notes on English county players and the touring West Indians, and main Test records.

One of the unusual items of the year is *Krieket vir die Tuisblyer* (South African Broadcasting Corporation, Johannesburg, 2s.) by Awie Labuschagne and Duggie Ettlinger. Written in Afrikaans, its declared purpose is "to explain cricket to persons whose sole knowledge of cricket is that it is a game"—a difficult task in any circumstances, the effort of bold men when attempted within 40 pages. As nearly as can be ascertained, however, a thoughtful

attempt has been made to achieve that aim. The need for such a book is explained in these terms: "The S.A.B.C. intend to provide continuous commentary in both of South Africa's official languages on every ball of all five Test matches (South Africa *v.* Australia) and it is anticipated that more South Africans will listen to the commentary in Afrikaans than to that in English."

H.C.C. "De Krekels" 1941–'66 (Haagsche Cricket Club, "De Krekels", Populierlaan 93, Rijswijk, Z.H., no price given) is an attractively presented 48-page quarto, in Dutch, about this Hague club's cricket, couched in happy vein.

Some of the most gentle, perceptive, humorous and nostalgic of all writing on the game is contained in *Crusoe on Cricket* (Ross, 36s.), a selection of the cricket writings of R. C. Robertson-Glasgow, sympathetically made and introduced by Alan Ross. "Crusoe" was at his best in the profiles of players which he published as *Cricket Prints* and some seventy of them form the most impressive part of the book, but a passage of autobiography, the light verse and sketches of *The Brighter Side of Cricket*, and a number of wise and witty essays, sustain an unusually high standard in a cricket book of 320 pages. Robertson-Glasgow was a sensitive man who suffered much. His cricket writing, however, was invariably warm, his touch cultured and light, and he had a true feeling for his fellow cricketers.

The Cricketer's Bedside Book (Batsford, 30s.) is described as edited by Ron Roberts, and it was originally planned by that widely travelled, kindly and enthusiastic cricket correspondent, the late R. A. Roberts. After his death the work was continued by his friends and dedicated to his memory, while the contributors ceded their fees to his memorial fund. Such contributors as Colin Cowdrey, Sir Neville Cardus, J. J. Warr, Ben Travers, Ray Robinson, John Woodcock, Alex Bannister, Richie Benaud, Alec Bedser, Alan Ross and A. A. Thomson among others are guarantee of a high standard of information and entertainment, while the make-up is in the high tradition of these publishers.

The Changing Face of Cricket (Eyre & Spottiswoode, 30s.)—which should not be confused with the book of the same title by the late A. G. Moyes—is a collaboration between Sir Learie Constantine and Denzil Batchelor. The authors are individualists with sharp minds, quick wits, inclination towards disputation and well developed senses of humour. The man does not live who is sufficiently mentally acrobatic to agree with both of them at every point, but in history, precept, criticism and recommendation for the future there is much to entertain and stimulate any cricketer.

I Was There (Collins, 15s.) is a symposium of twenty-one stories by *Daily Telegraph* and *Sunday Telegraph* reporters who were present at great sporting events. Two of the subjects are cricket matches, both Tests played at Lord's. England *v.* Australia

in 1930—the most impressive gathering of great players in a single match of modern times?—is described by E. W. Swanton, and the England–West Indies draw of 1963 by Alan Gibson; both are fine reports of stirring games.

The Michael Green Book of Coarse Sport (Hutchinson, 15s.) is, as one expects of Michael Green, funny—at times extremely funny. "My Grandfather Might Have Nearly Bowled W. G. Grace" reflects shrewd observation of the cricket bore and "The Rime of the Ancient Cricketer" contains some neat lines of parody.

Only three tour accounts have been sent for review but they prompted a look along the shelves of similar books of the past four decades, and the realization that, with few exceptions, the titles are vastly alike and lack a date, so that collectors and students of the future may well be baffled as to the precise series covered by a book called, say, *With the West Indies in Australia*, or *vice versa* or some such. If the date were added to the title—*on the spine as well as the title page*—as was done in the admirable *Fight for the Ashes* series, much confusion would be saved, particularly since Tests and the books about them continue to increase in number and frequency.

Few people, perhaps, would have expected Ken Mackay to become a reporter of cricket after his retirement from active play but, in *Quest for The Ashes* (Pelham Books, 25s.), "In collaboration with Frank O'Callaghan" he describes the M.C.C. tour in Australia, 1965–66, with characteristically shrewd observation and tactical and technical assessment. The collaboration, at times, leads to such contrasts within a few lines as "One cannot be dogmatic when running between wickets, even if empowered to make the call" and "Simmo looked ready to bite a piece out of his boot" but the story is illuminatingly told and the scores are given of all first-class matches.

The late John Clarke followed the same tour as cricket correspondent of the *Evening Standard* and called his book *With England in Australia* (Stanley Paul, 21s.). John Clarke never lost his enthusiasm for reporting cricket and that was always apparent in his writing; so, too, was his literary background. This book, like his others, is sympathetic, at times critical, but never seeking sensation, and it has the flavour of accomplished writing. All first-class scores and the tour averages are included.

John Clarke also undertook a book on the West Indies visit to England during 1966, but he saw only the first Test of the series and died shortly after the second began. Entitled *Everything That's Cricket* (Stanley Paul, 25s.) it was completed for him by Brian Scovell. Mr. Scovell is a highly professional cricket reporter and he carried out his task conscientiously. The "quotes", the facts and the background are all there and his summing-up chapter is both balanced and informed. Again there is an appendix of all first-class scores of the tour.

The Best of Cricket Fiction, Volume One (Macdonald, 35s.) is an anthology compiled by Leslie Frewin. Originally planned as a single book, it is now seen as the first of "more than one volume". It contains most of the familiar pieces, which are none the worse for being familiar; there probably is no other volume now in print which contains the majority of these stories or extracts, which is ample justification for making them freshly available to a generation which may not know them. A. G. MacDonell, Charles Dickens' Dingley Dell, Hugh de Sélincourt's Tillingfold, the game from Vachell's *The Hill*, Tom Brown's Last Match, and Siegfried Sassoon's *The Flower Show Match* are all there and no doubt many small boys will relish them as much as their fathers did.

Best Sports Stories (Faber, 18s.), edited by Paul Edwards, contains two cricket items—a small triumph of situation comedy by Samuel Sevlon, and an epilogue by C. L. R. James—both of them West Indians, which may indicate the direction of the current of present-day cricket.

Cricketers of Wombwell (The Wombwell Cricket Lovers' Society, 8s. 6d.) is a study of three Yorkshire cricketers from that town—Irving Washington, Roy Kilner and Norman Kilner—and their local background by A. Woodhouse, R. D. Wilkinson and J. Sokell. It is the most ambitious publication, thus far, of one of the most active and enthusiastic cricket societies in the world.

The year's biographies and appreciations—twelve of them—

are more wide-ranging than usual in both subject and treatment. *I Look Back* (The Hindu, 2–3 Salisbury Court, Fleet Street, E.C.4, 4s.) is the autobiography of Professor D. B. Deodhar, bound up from serial publication in the Indian magazine, *Sport and Pastime*. Professor Deodhar scored his first century—in an inter-school Shield Match—when he was fourteen; his last, for C. K. Nayudu's XI, in a Bengal Relief match in 1946, when he was 54, and he was still playing tennis at 74. He made hundreds, too, in unofficial Tests against Arthur Gilligan's and Lord Tennyson's M.C.C. teams of 1926 and 1937. His quality as a player of the older generation and manner of Indian cricket was unmistakably high and his integrity and wisdom are not to be doubted. He has been an unselfish but important figure in Indian cricket for fifty years and his book, clear and firm, is, in the best sense of the word, worthy.

Ted Dexter Declares: an Autobiography (Stanley Paul, 21s.) is something less than a full autobiography. Mr. Dexter has more than one good book left in him on his life to date. This became a widely—though not always fairly—talked-of book when, as a result of its publication, Mr. Dexter became the first player to be barred from playing cricket in England since, so far as I can ascertain, William Lambert more than a hundred years ago. When one contemplates the nonsense that has been "ghosted" and published under the names of famous cricketers in the past, any person of reasonable outlook must regard this punishment as inconsistent. There is no doubt that Mr. Dexter writes his own copy, and, if he can be trusted with the captaincy of England but not to state his opinions about the game, then it may be English cricket, and not Mr. Dexter, that is awry. Whatever may be the official verdict upon it, this is a book of both importance and interest.

The Trevor Goddard Story (Purfleet, Durban, Rands 2.10) is less convincing. No one would dispute that Trevor Goddard has been one of the most efficient, diligent and complete all-rounders in modern cricket. The facts of his career, too, are all gathered in orderly fashion and, if some might disagree with certain of the arguments, that is inevitable in modern international sport. It is, however, cloying to find a single sentence which runs—"Lill and Jarman had taken mighty swipes at the Springbok morale, and now Sobers and McLachlan rubbed salt into the wound: not only by being grassed early in their innings, but by pouncing on each bowler like fox terriers playing with a teddy bear, and shaking the stuffing out of them." No prize is offered for sub-editing.

W. G. Grace, 1848–1915 (from the Rev. A. N. B. Sugden, St. Peter's Vicarage, 13 Beech Grove, Harrogate, Yorkshire, 3s. post free) is a printing of extracts from the address, given by Mr. Sugden (then vicar of St. Mary's, Shortlands) on the fiftieth anniversary of the death of "W.G.", with a portrait of "The Champion" and a photograph of his grave in Elmers End Cemetery, Kent. Mr.

Sugden had earlier drawn attention to the neglected state of the grave and, as Englishmen may contemplate without pride, Mr. Ray Ingelse, a Dutch cricket enthusiast, organised a Memorial Fund to have it put in good condition.

Blasting for Runs (Souvenir Press, 18s.) is the autobiography of Rohan Kanhai, dedicated to John Gibson for working so closely on it. This is a lively, unaffected book with much pertinent criticism and straightforward argument. It is, too, a rare view of West Indian cricket through an inside eye, especially, and with genuine honesty, on their unsuccessful English tour of 1957.

Run-Digger—His Own Story, by Bill Lawry (Souvenir Press, 21s.) is "edited by Phil Tressider" but there is no doubt that Lawry has his say in it and makes the points he wants to make. The essence of a dry, honest book is to be found in its own words: "Me, Mrs. Lawry's little boy who never wanted anything more in life than to bat right through the lunch hour in the Thornbury public school playground while the other kids had to field."

Ron Roberts (from the Hon. Treasurer, Ron Roberts Fund, 135 Fleet Street, E.C.4, for a subscription to the Fund) is a dignified and well-made brochure which, in pictures and the recollections of those who knew him, captures glimpses of the life of one of the best of modern cricket journalists, a man at once capable, humorous, eager and without an enemy.

Captain's Story (Stanley Paul, 21s.), by Bobby Simpson, with acknowledgement to: "Ken Roberts for his help and assistance in the writing of this book", has already made headlines in most cricketing countries. It is difficult to escape the impression that, if a modern Test cricketer does not comment on unfair bowling, he is evading a major issue and that, if he does, he will be attacked. Mr. Simpson, as a working journalist in England during the summer of 1966, wrote some competent and responsible match reports and criticism. It is clear that much of the content of this book consists of his own opinions and observations. Anyone who doubts this should read the chapter headed "My Technique against Griffith". This is not a great book but much of it is unmistakably first-hand experience and it is hard for anyone who reads it *all* to regard it as exceptionable by comparison with a dozen other player-stories of recent years.

Garfield Sobers was a Test match player at sixteen, the greatest all-rounder in the world at twenty-nine—or perhaps earlier. In *Cricket Crusader* (Pelham Books, 25s.) he thanks R. A. Martin "for his collaboration in the writing of my story". It is such a story as anyone with a sense of plot or feeling for cricket would be delighted to write. The chapter on "Collie"—Collie Smith—is moving in its jerky semi-statement but, all through, there are absorbing situations, worthwhile ideas and illuminations of the great moments of recent Tests.

Vizzy Commemoration Souvenir (Vishal Press, New Delhi, Rupees 3), edited by K. Iswara Dutt and K. V. Gopala Ratnam, had been planned as a volume of tributes to mark, in the Hindu fashion, the sixtieth birthday of the Maharaj Kumar of Vizianagram, Shri Vijaya Anand. He died, however, while the volume was being compiled and it was changed to a series of obituary tributes, by cricketers and public figures from all over the world, to the enthusiastic, friendly man ("Call me Vizzy") who captained the 1936 Indian team to England and devoted a considerable proportion of his life to cricket as a player, administrator and broadcaster.

Peter Walker Benefit Souvenir Brochure (Glamorgan County Cricket Club, 2s. 6d.) is a much more elaborate publication than most beneficiaries' booklets. A foreword, nineteen feature articles about various aspects of cricket, generous illustration—and advertisements which should have increased the Fund handsomely—make up an attractive and readable book of 88 pages.

Close on Cricket (Stanley Paul, 18s.) falls, strictly speaking, under the heading of instructional books, and Brian Close divides it into the technical departments of the game, plus tactics and criticism, fitness, care of equipment and "Playing to win". In addition to much useful advice on the mechanics, strategy and mental processes of play, however, he uses for illustration and argument much astute, first-hand observation of first-class players and matches so that the ordinary reader will find it entertaining as well as educational.

The M.C.C. tour of Australia 1965–66 was marked, as usual, by the issue of *A.B.C. Cricket Book—M.C.C. Tour of Australia 1965–66* (The Australian Broadcasting Commission; available in the U.K. from E. K. Brown, Bevois Mount, Liskeard,Cornwall, 2s.) with essays by F. R. Brown and Alan McGilvray, biographical sketches of players on both sides, and plenty of records.

Rothmans Test Cricket Almanac, 1965–66 Series (Rothmans of Pall Mall, gratis) with a Foreword by Sir Donald Bradman and photos and brief notes on the players of both sides, included condensed scores of every match between England and Australia and the averages of every player for each country.

The usual *Playfair* souvenir, *Cricketers from the West Indies* (Dickens Press, 2s. 6d.) has a main essay by Gordon Ross and a neatly arranged statistical section, but its main emphasis is pictorial, with both portraits and action pictures of the West Indian players and photographs of historic significance in matches between the two countries.

Rothmans Test Cricket Almanack, England–West Indies 1966 (Rothmans of Pall Mall, gratis) carries a substantial biographical survey, an introduction by J. S. Barker, essays by Ian Wooldridge and Trevor Bailey, a statistical survey by Irving Rosenwater and plenty of illustrations, in a fresh-looking format.

Rothmans World Cup Cricket Tournament (Rothmans of Pall Mall, 1s. 6d.) deals with the three-day, England XI *v.* A Rest of the World XI match at Scarborough, and the triangular series of one-day matches between Rest of the World, West Indies and England for the World Cricket Cup, by means of notes on, and photographs of, the England and Rest players, and introductions by Sir Oliver Leese and Crawford White.

The current annuals may fairly be described as hardy; many of the frail growths of the immediate post-war years have disappeared but the surviving six English and four overseas titles are now firmly established and have been joined by two important new publications.

Cricket Fixtures 1966 From The Times (The Times, 1s. 6d.) had 48 pages (including three for notes) gave the fixtures for the County Championship, Minor Counties and Second XI Competitions, major dates in other sports for 1966 and, from 1965, the three league tables, leading first-class averages and Test results.

Wisden Cricketers' Almanack 1966 (Sporting Handbooks, 23s. 6d., limp edition; 27s. 6d. in cloth boards) is the 103rd edition and the fifteenth to be edited by Norman Preston. The increasing magnitude of his task is indicated by the fact that this issue contains details of eight major—i.e. Test-playing—and seven lesser, tours. Fifteen pages, too, are found for Gillette Cup scores and accounts. To condense all into 1042 pages is a substantial editorial achievement. The outstanding feature is an obituary appreciation of Walter Hammond by Sir Neville Cardus at his most majestic; "Welcome West Indies—World Cricket Champions" is by Sir Learie Constantine; "Cricket A Game—Not a Subject" is by Austin Matthews, and "The Great Years and Great Players of Kent" by R. L. Arrowsmith. The "Five Cricketers of the Year", chosen with sage objectivity, are the three South Africans who made such an impact on English cricket in 1965, R .G. Pollock, P. M. Pollock and K. C. Bland; R. C. Motz (New Zealand), and John Edrich. Debate about the "Births and Deaths" section may well rage as long as the game of cricket exists. The fact remains that it is possible to choose from players omitted an eleven which, by the standing of its members in their own day, might beat a team chosen from those included. It must, surely, be difficult to justify the inclusion of the 5th Earl of Rosebery—a Vice-President of Surrey—in preference to 'Silver Billy' Beldham, George Parr, John Small, Fuller Pilch, Albert Trott, 'Happy Jack' Ullyett, Billy Barnes or Billy Bates.

Cricket Spotlight 1966 (from Robert Baker, 2 Aynho Walk, Sunnyside, Northampton, 2s.) is Mr. Baker's tenth spirited effort—with county and Test scores, averages, reviews, biographies, fixtures and features by some of the best known writers—to produce profits for the English Schools Cricket Association. It is as lively and as satisfying as ever.

"Flagstaff" Cricket Annual 1966 (Flagstaff Press, 2s. 6d.) moves

into its fourteenth year, still under the editorship of Roy Lester. County reviews and biographies once more provide its main substance, but its double-spread, at-a-glance results-table for the county cricket of the preceding season remains unique and valuable, and it has much lively feature material, including an interview with Rohan Kanhai, by John Gibson.

Playfair Cricket Annual 1966 (Dickens Press, 3s.) edited by Gordon Ross, appeared for the fourth time in its "new" square format with its usual strong county section and major Test scores and records.

The Sports Argus Cricket Annual, Season 1966 (Sports Argus, Birmingham, 3s.) edited by R. Haynes, is, as usual, strong on the cricket of Warwickshire, Worcestershire and the Birmingham League, with features by W. G. Wanklyn and Tom Duckworth and orderly attention to the wider scene.

South African Cricket Annual 1965 (available in the U.K. from E. K. Brown, Bevois Mount, Liskeard, Cornwall, 11s. 9d. post free) under the editorship of Geoffrey A. Chettle, marked the 75th Anniversary of the South African Cricket Association which now, happily, associates itself with the publication, and thus gives it a reassuring air of continuity. Within 188 pages it includes due celebratory and historic recognition of the anniversary and, in addition to an adequate Currie Cup section and a "Who's Who" of South

African players and South African records, it includes full coverage of the South African tour of England in 1965.

South African Cricket Annual 1966 (available in the U.K. from E. K. Brown, Bevois Mount, Liskeard, Cornwall, 11s. 6d. post free), edited by Godfrey Chettle, is the thirteenth volume in this healthy series. It arrived in Britain earlier than usual, notwithstanding the fact that it had been printed late enough to salute Transvaal's first win over an Australian team, and Peter van der Merwe's appointment as captain of South Africa. There are sound biographical notes of the touring Australians, photographs of the Provincial teams of 1965–66, and the usual thorough "Who's Who". It continues to give that most valuable contribution to world cricket records, the complete coverage—full scores and accounts—of the Currie Cup series. Incidentally, the "Five Cricketers of the Year" include two players well known in English cricket in Jim Pressdee (formerly of Glamorgan who, in his first season after emigrating, captained the North Eastern Transvaal side which won the Currie Cup 'B' section), and R. C. White who played for Cambridge University and Gloucestershire before he went back to his native Transvaal. The other three chosen are S. Strydom, B. Versfeld and C. P. Wilkins.

Two other overseas annuals have brought publication up to date, that for New Zealand, reflecting its new sponsorship in the title—*The Shell Cricket Almanack of New Zealand 1965* and *The Shell Cricket Almanack of New Zealand 1966* (both available in the U.K. from E. K. Brown, Bevois Mount, Liskeard, Cornwall, 13s. 6d. each post free). These—in the eighteenth and nineteenth years of issue—are edited by the founder, Arthur H. Carman. The 1965 edition extends to 192 pages to cover the tours of New Zealand in India, Pakistan and England. The fixture between a New Zealand Under-23 team and the Plunket Shield winners—Canterbury—and "Glances" to fifty and a hundred years into the past are interesting, and the entire volume takes an honourable place as part of the chronicles of the world game. The 1966 issue is more domestic, dealing with the 1965–66 home season, a sad list of New Zealand obituaries, some absorbing play—not least in the under-23 Rothmans Tournament—and the awards of Batsman of the Year to B. E. Congdon and Bowler of the Year to N. Puna.

Indian Cricket 1965, edited by S. K. Gurunathan and *Indian Cricket 1966*, editor P. N. Sundaresan, both reached England in 1966 (both obtainable from Kasturi & Sons, 2–3 Salisbury Court, London, E.C.4, 7s. 6d. each). S. K. Gurunathan, a faithful historian and statistician, edited the first nineteen volumes of this full record of his country's cricket with fidelity and judgement: he died on 6th May, 1966, leaving this admirably sound annual and chronicle as his memorial. The volume for 1965 covered ten Tests played in India of which seven were official and three (with Ceylon) unofficial. As usual, the editor cast his net widely for contributors from England, Australia, New Zealand and the West Indies as well as dealing with the great volume of domestic play which includes three- and four-day matches, down to school level. One of the last words of Mr. Gurunathan's Preface recorded his thanks to Mr. Sundaresan who has now succeeded him in the editorship.

The 1966 issue begins with an obituary notice of Mr. Gurunathan and continues along the lines he had established. The Indian season of 1965–66 was concerned almost exclusively with domestic play but there is a special statistical feature on India–West Indies Tests and the usual articles on cricket in other countries. Again the basic duty of the annual—to provide full records of cricket in India—is faithfully discharged.

The new, and long awaited, addition to the list of yearly records is *Cricket Annual 1965* (Board of Control for Cricket in Pakistan; obtainable in U.K. from E. K. Brown, Bevois Mount, Liskeard, Cornwall, 11s.) edited by Bashir Ahmad, Secretary of the Board of Control, with statistics by Ghulam Mustafa Khan. This first effort consists of the full scores of all first-class matches played in Pakistan, or by Pakistan teams overseas, in the 1964–65 period. It is not inadequate but it has the air of being produced in a vacuum rather than with knowledge of the growing-pains and development of other national annuals. It should improve. The fact that it is an official publication gives good hope that it may continue regularly, unlike so many overseas annuals which have perished for lack of support. An issue dated 1966 is expected early in 1967. If continuity can be maintained, the next step is the publication of a volume—such as Luckin's *South African Cricket* or Reese's *New Zealand Cricket*—giving full first-class match scores from, in this case, Partition, to the start of the Annual. Thus Pakistan would have an enviably complete record.

Trinidad Cricket Council Year Book 1966 (available in U.K. from E. K. Brown, Bevois Mount, Liskeard, Cornwall, 9s. 6d. post free) is the third issue of a handbook which covers the cricket of its own island—at most levels—quite admirably, and gives full scores of the Australian tourists' matches there in 1965, the (undated) Tests of the same tour, and pays fair attention to West Indian Test records. Unfortunately it only summarises the scores of the West Indies Regional Competition. By a little concentration of text and expansion of space, this yearbook could become the effective annual of West Indian cricket—which now is the most serious lack in the chronicles of the modern game.

The Scottish Cricket Annual 1966 (Charlotte Publicity Service, Edinburgh, 9, 2s. 6d.) edited by A. M. C. Thorburn and George G. Lawrie, wisely and thoroughly concerns itself almost solely with domestic play, statistics and fixtures, clearly set out and well printed.

The Official Yearbook of Fixtures and Statistics 1965 (Manitoba Cricket Associations, no price stated) marks the centenary of cricket in Manitoba with letters from M.C.C. and Sir Donald Bradman, a historical survey of a hundred years of cricket there, and results and averages for 1964.

Cricket Year Book, 28th Edition (New South Wales Cricket Association; available in U.K. from E. K. Brown, Bevois Mount, Liskeard, Cornwall, 9s. 6d. post free) is more a national record of Australian cricket than a localised State publication. It provides full scores and averages of the Sheffield Shield competition 1964–65, Australia in England 1964 and in West Indies 1965, and Pakistan in Australia 1964–65, as well as inter-state Colts matches, N.S.W. Grade competitions and records.

M.C.C. Cricket Diary 1967 (Collins, 6s. 6d.), in its red leatherette binding is, once more, well set-out and provides much useful information not easily available elsewhere.

The annual year books of separate counties which follow are, in the usual fashion of these publications, wrappered, small octavo, with reports and scores of the previous season's matches of first and second teams, captain's and/or Committee's reports, statistics for the county and list of Officers. Only variations from this general shape are noted.

Glamorgan County Cricket Club Year Book (Glamorgan C.C.C., 2s.) has a forthright foreword, an appreciation of Peter Walker by Wilfred Wooller and a full list of members. Second XI scores, however, are not given, which is the more regrettable since that side won the Second XI Championship of 1965.

The Hampshire Handbook 1966 (Hampshire C.C.C., 2s. 6d.) continues under the editorship of Desmond Eagar to print a satisfying amount of feature writing. This edition has a sympathetic obituary by the editor, of Harry Altham, for so long the County Club's President and whose speech on John Nyren is also reprinted, the last of his many and accomplished contributions to this Handbook. Denys Treseder writes on E. A. English, the longest-lived first-class cricketer; Brian Hayward on Roy Marshall and the Hampshire season of 1965; E. A. James on Hampshire Schools Cricket, and H. N. P. Pepin on cricket at Dean Park. There are no scores of Second XI matches but Bernard Harrison contributes the extremely interesting averages for all Second XI matches of 1959–65.

Leicestershire 1966 Year Book (Leicestershire C.C., 2s.), edited by E. E. Snow and F. M. Turner, has 'potted' reports of Second XI matches, there is an essay by E. E. Snow on "The Grace Road Ground", to mark its acquisition by the county club—the first ground it has owned in its history—and a list of the birthplaces of all the county's Leicestershire-born players.

Sussex Cricket Handbook (Sussex C.C.C., 1s. 6d.) has appreciations of the Nawab of Pataudi, Ken Suttle and W. L. Creese, a study of cricket at Chalvington and Ripe by Esmund Esdaile, and histories of Brighton Electricity C.C., and the Eastbourne Cricket Tournament.

The Warwickshire C.C.C. Annual Report for 1965 (Warwickshire C.C.C., gratis to members) devotes its usual thorough and wise attention to the general cricketing scene before turning its attention to the county club's affairs—especially in relation to the Edgbaston Ground—and to appreciations of Mike Smith and Canon J. H. Parsons. Match scores are given in abbreviated form.

Dorset County Cricket Club Year Book 1966 (Dorset C.C.C., Sherborne, no price given) follows full match reports with essays on the origins of the county club, a history of Sherborne C.C., and a list of members.

Northumberland County Cricket Club Year Book 1966 (Dring, Newcastle upon Tyne, 2s.), edited by Robson Dring is, as usual, a well-produced book. It contains an obituary notice of the late C. F. Stranger-Leathes; "Northumberland Cricket Origins"; and "Bowling Problems in the 1940s", both by George Harbottle; "The Game of Games" by Basil Donne-Smith; a note on Jack van Geloven, formerly of Leicestershire who has now joined the Ashington club; a cheerful piece of light verse, and coverage of League and representative junior cricket in the county.

Midlands Club Cricket Conference 1966 Year Book (Midlands Club Cricket Conference, 3s. 6d.) edited by the unfailingly keen W. Leslie Jones, in addition to full scores of representative Conference matches and club details, includes some forty pages of varied and readable feature articles.

The South Wales Cricket Association Official Handbook 1966 (South Wales C.A., gratis to members) provides 128 pages of rules, records, reports and fixtures of play in this healthy competition.

Of the periodicals, *The Cricketer* (seventeen numbers in 1966; The Cricketer Ltd., 178–202 Great Portland Street, London, W.1, 2s. 6d. per copy) has undergone major changes. The former ownership has been merged with the Hutchinson Group of Companies with E. W. Swanton as editorial director, R. G. G. Anderson, business editor; John Reason and Irving Rosenwater, assistant editors, and Patrick Eagar as picture editor. That kindly, wise man, Arthur Langford, has retired from the editorial staff to which he belonged for half a lifetime but continues to write, out of deep and long knowledge, on club cricket. Of late, fresh minds have brought not only changes but greater variety of treatment to *The Cricketer*, and it has succeeded quite impressively in reflecting conflicting points of view about a number of controversial points in the contemporary game.

Playfair Cricket Monthly (The Dickens Press, 4 Upper Thomas Street, London, E.C.4; twelve monthly numbers a year, 2s. 6d. each), edited by Gordon Ross, maintained its generous pictorial bias, and has articles, both conversational and analytical, by a number of famous names.

The Cricket Quarterly (from The Editor, 95 Willingdon Road, Eastbourne, Sussex; annual subscription 30s. in 1966) completed its fourth year and volume under Rowland Bowen. In this year it provided 278 pages of research, statistics, reviews, history and comment of a devoted and absorbing quality. Sadly, the editor-publisher has had to announce that the magazine runs at a loss and that he will need an increase in the number of subscribers or in the subscription-rate—or both—if publication is to be maintained. *The Cricket Quarterly*—deliberately—is not "popular", but neither is it dull. If there is a place for scholarship in cricket, this is it. Neither does it shrink from plain speaking, controversy or, at times, genuinely rumbustious pamphleteering. It needs only a fair moneysworth of support from the cricket world to survive and serve that world well.

(As readers will gather from the advertisement for *The Cricket Quarterly* on page 1013, the magazine has obtained the required support from subscribers, and continues with unabated vigour.)

FIXTURES FOR 1967

** Indicates Sunday Play.*

GILLETTE CUP: First round to be completed by Friday, May 5.

Wednesday, April 26

Oxford Univ. v. Warwickshire

Saturday, April 29

*Derby Derbyshire v. Leics.
*Trent Bridge Notts. v. Kent
Edgbaston Warwick. v. Lancs.
Lord's M.C.C. v. Yorkshire
Cambridge Univ. v. Essex
Oxford Univ. v. Surrey

Wednesday, May 3

Worcester Worcs. v. India
Dartford Kent v. Gloucs.
Taunton Somerset v. Hampshire
Hove Sussex v. Lancashire
Edgbaston Warwicks. v. Leics.
Harrogate Yorkshire v. Glamorgan
Lord's M.C.C. v. Surrey
Cambridge Univ. v. Notts.
Oxford Univ. v. Northants.

Saturday, May 6

*Brentwood Essex v. Glamorgan
*Portsmouth Hampshire v. Leics.
*Old Trafford Lancashire v. Worcs.
Lord's Middlesex v. Derby.
*Taunton Somerset v. Notts.
The Oval Surrey v. Warwickshire
Bradford Yorkshire v. Kent
Cambridge Univ. v. Sussex
Oxford Univ. v. Gloucs.

Monday, May 8

Gravesend Club Conf. v. India (2 days)

Wednesday, May 10

Canterbury Kent v. India
Brentwood Essex v. Sussex
Bristol Gloucs. v. Warwick.
Leicester Leics. v. Glamorgan
Lord's Middlesex v. Lancs.
The Oval Surrey v. Hampshire
Hull Yorkshire v. Worcs.
Cambridge Univ. v. Northants.
Oxford Univ. v. Somerset

Saturday, May 13

Gillette Cup—Second Round

Oxford Univ. v. India
Cambridge Univ. v. Free Foresters

Wednesday, May 17

Edgbaston Warwick. v. India
Southampton Hampshire v. Derby.
Old Trafford Lancashire v. Essex
Northampton Northants. v. Surrey
Trent Bridge Notts. v. Gloucs.
Taunton Somerset v. Kent
Hove Sussex v. Glamorgan
Leeds Yorkshire v. Leics.
Cambridge Univ. v. Middlesex
Oxford Univ. v. Worcs.

Saturday, May 20

Lord's M.C.C. v. India
*Chesterfield Derbyshire v. Surrey
Pontypridd Glamorgan v. Gloucs.
Gravesend Kent v. Northants.
*Old Trafford Lancashire v. Warwick.
*Leicester Leicestershire v. Sussex
Worcester Worcs. v. Somerset
Bradford Yorkshire v. Notts.
Oxford Univ. v. Middlesex

Sunday, May 21

*Ilford Essex v. Hampshire

Wednesday, May 24

Cardiff Glamorgan v. India
Derby Derbyshire v. Sussex
Ilford Essex v. Worcs.
Bournemouth Hampshire v. Notts.
Gravesend Kent v. Somerset
Lord's Middlesex v. Gloucs.
Northampton Northants. v. Leics.
Nuneaton (Griff and Coton Ground) Warwick. v. Surrey

Saturday, May 27

Northampton Northants. v. India
Swansea Glamorgan v. Hants.
Bristol Gloucs. v. Somerset
Old Trafford Lancashire v Yorks.
Lord's Middlesex v. Sussex
Trent Bridge Notts. v. Derbyshire
*The Oval Surrey v. Essex
Edgbaston Warwick. v. Kent
Worcester Worcs. v. Leicestershire
Oxford Univ. v. M.C.C.

Wednesday, May 31

The Oval Surrey v. India
Chesterfield Derbyshire v. Glam.
Leicester Leicestershire v. Kent
Northampton Northants. v. Essex
Trent Bridge Notts. v. Hampshire
Edgbaston Warwick v. Sussex
Kidderm'ster Worcs. v. Yorkshire
Old Trafford Lancs. v. Lancs. League XI

Saturday, June 3

*Old Trafford Lancashire v. India
*Bristol Gloucs. v. Essex
Lord's Middlesex v. Yorkshire
*Kettering Northants. v. Notts.
*Bath Somerset v. Derbyshire
*Guildford Surrey v. Leicestershire
*Hove Sussex v. Hampshire
Worcester Worcs. v. Warwick.
Oxford Univ. v. Glamorgan

Wednesday, June 7

Derby Derbyshire v. Worcs.
Romford Essex v. Gloucs.
Cardiff Glamorgan v. Northants.
Basingstoke Hampshire v. Surrey
Lord's Middlesex v. Kent
Trent Bridge Notts. v. Lancashire
Bath Somerset v. Yorkshire
Hove Sussex v. Warwick.
Cambridge Univ. v. Leicestershire

Thursday, June 8

LEEDS ENGLAND v. INDIA (First Test—5 days)

Saturday, June 10

*Romford Essex v. Leicestershire
Swansea Glamorgan v. Yorks.
*Portsmouth Hampshire v. Gloucs.
Blackheath Kent v. Middlesex
*Old Trafford Lancashire v. Derby.
*Bath Somerset v. Northants.
*The Oval Surrey v. Sussex
Coventry (Courtaulds) Warwick. v. Notts.
Lord's M.C.C. v. Cambridge U.
Dublin Ireland v. Worcestershire (2 days)

Monday, June 12

Oxford Univ. v. Navy (2 days)

Wednesday, June 14

Gillette Cup—Third Round

Cambridge Univ. v. India
Glasgow Scotland v. M.C.C.

Saturday, June 17

*Southampton Hampshire v. India
*Buxton Derby. v. Lancashire
Cardiff Glamorgan v. Essex
Bristol Gloucs. v. Yorkshire
Tunbridge W. Kent v. Sussex
Leicester Leics. v. Somerset
*Northampton Northants. v. Warwick.
*Trent Bridge Notts. v. Middlesex
The Oval Surrey v. Worcs.
Lord's Downside v. Oratory (1 day)

Wednesday, June 21

Chesterfield Derby. v. Somerset
Swansea Glamorgan v. Sussex
Bristol Gloucs. v. Surrey
Tunbridge W. Kent v. Worcs.
Old Trafford Lancashire v. Notts.
Leicester Leics. v. Cambridge U.
Edgbaston Warwicks. v. Middx.
Sheffield Yorkshire v. Northants.
Aldershot Army v. Oxford Univ. (3 days, not first class)

Thursday, June 22

LORD'S ENGLAND v. INDIA (Second Test—5 days)

Saturday, June 24

*Colchester Essex v. Middlesex
*Lydney Glos. v. Glamorgan
*Bournemouth Hampshire v. Somerset
*Leicester Leics. v. Lancashire
*Peterb'ough Northants. v. Kent
*Trent Bridge Notts. v. Worcs.
Hove Sussex v. Oxford Univ.
Edgbaston Warwick. v. Derby.
Leeds Yorkshire v. Surrey

Wednesday, June 28

Derby Derbyshire v. India
Colchester Essex v. Pakistan
Bournemouth Hampshire v. Oxford U.
Old Trafford Lancashire v. Sussex
Northampton Northants. v. Gloucs.
Trent Bridge Notts. v. Warwicks.
Taunton Somerset v. Leics.
The Oval Surrey v. Kent
Worcester Worcs. v. Middlesex
Scarborough Yorks. v. Cambridge U.

Saturday, July 1

Sheffield Yorkshire v. India
Canterbury Kent v. Pakistan
Ilkeston Derby. v. Cambridge U.

Old Trafford	Lancashire v. Oxford U.
Leicester	Leics. v. Gloucs.
*Lord's	Middlesex v. Hampshire
*Glastonbury	Somerset v. Worcs.
*The Oval	Surrey v. Glamorgan
Hove	Sussex v. Notts.
Edgbaston	Warwicks. v. Essex

Thursday, June 29

Lord's	Eton v. Harrow (2 days)

Wednesday, July 5

Trent Bridge	Notts. v. India
Lord's	Middx. v. Pakistan
Neath	Glamorgan v. Somerset
Old Trafford	Lancashire v. Surrey
Leicester	Leics. v. Yorkshire
Northampton	Northants. v. Hants.
Hove	Sussex v. Derbyshire
Edgbaston	Warwicks. v. Camb'dge Univ.
Worcester	Worcs. v. Essex
Roehampton	Sth. African Univs. v. Oxford U. (3 days)

Saturday, July 8

*Leicester	Leics. v. India
*Taunton	Somerset v. Pakistan
Lord's	Oxford v. Cambridge
Chesterfield	Derbyshire v. Yorks.
*Gloucester	Gloucs. v. Notts.
*Southampton	Hants. v. Warwick.
*Folkestone	Kent v. Lancashire
*Northampton	Northants. v. Glam.
*The Oval	Surrey v. Middlesex
Worcester	Worcs. v. Sussex

Wednesday, July 12

Hove	Sussex v. Pakistan
Westcliff	Essex v. Somerset
Gloucester	Gloucs. v. Derbyshire
Portsmouth	Hants. v. Northants.
Southport	Lancashire v. Kent
Leicester	Leics. v. Surrey
Trent Bridge	Notts. v. Glamorgan
Sheffield	Yorks. v. Middlesex

Thursday, July 13

Edgbaston	ENGLAND v. INDIA (Third Test—5 days)

Saturday, July 15

The Oval	Surrey v. Pakistan
*Westcliff	Essex v. Warwick.
Cardiff	Glamorgan v. Lancs.
*Southampton	Hampshire v. Kent
*Lord's	Middlesex v. Northants.
*Newark	Notts. v. Leics.
*Hove	Sussex v. Gloucs.
Worcester	Worcs. v. Derbyshire

Wednesday, July 19

Gillette Cup—Semi-final

The Oval	Surrey v. Northants. (or Sept. 6)
Swindon (County Gd.)	Minor Counties v. Pakistan

Thursday, July 20

Lord's	Single Wicket Comp. 2 days (prov.)

Friday, July 21

Dublin or Cork	Ireland v. India (2 days)

Saturday, July 22

Edgbaston	Warwicks. v. Pakistan
*Ilkeston	Derbys. v. Notts.
Swansea	Glam. v. Middlesex
*Bristol	Glos. v. Sussex
*Maidstone	Kent v. Hampshire
*Liverpool	Lancashire v. Somerset
*Leicester	Leics. v. Essex
The Oval	Surrey v. Yorkshire
*Dudley	Worcs. v. Northants.
Lord's	Clifton v. Tonbridge (1 day)

Wednesday, July 26

Chesterfield	Derbyshire v. Essex
Maidstone	Kent v. Surrey
Old Trafford	Lancashire v. Middx.
Worksop	Notts. v. Northants.
Hastings	Sussex v. Leics.
Coventry (Courtaulds)	Warwicks. v. Gloucs.
Worcester	Worcs. v. Glam.
Bradford	Yorkshire v. Somerset

Thursday, July 27

Lord's	ENGLAND v. PAKISTAN (First Test—5 days)

Saturday, July 29

Cardiff	Glamorgan v. Derby.
Bournemouth	Hampshire v. Yorks.
*Leicester	Leics. v. Warwick.
*Northampton	Northants. v. Middlesex
*Trent Bridge	Notts. v. Surrey
*Yeovil	Somerset v. Essex
*Hastings	Sussex v. Kent
Worcester	Worcs. v. Gloucs.
*Old Trafford	Lancs. v. Scotland (3 days)

Wednesday, August 2

Leeds Yorks. v. Pakistan
Ebbw Vale Glamorgan v. Notts.
Bristol Gloucs. v. Middlesex
Bournemouth Hampshire v. Essex
Old Trafford Lancs. v. Northants.
Leicester Leics. v. Derby.
Hove Sussex v. Worcs.
Edgbaston Warwick. v. Scotland
Lord's Public Schools v. Eng. Schools C.A. (1 day)

Thursday, August 3

Lord's M.C.C. Schools v. Indian Schools (1 day)

Friday, August 4

Lord's M.C.C. Schools v. Combined Services (2 days)

Saturday, August 5

Swansea Glamorgan v. Pakistan
Derby Derby. v. Middlesex
*Leyton Essex v. Notts.
*Southampton Hampshire v. Sussex
*Canterbury Kent v. Leicestershire
*Northampton Northants. v. Somerset
*The Oval Surrey v. Gloucs.
Edgbaston Warwick. v. Worcs.
Sheffield Yorks. v. Lancashire

Monday, August 7

Lord's M.C.C. v. Holland (1 day)

Wednesday, August 9

Leyton Essex v. Northants.
Swansea Glam. v. Warwick.
Canterbury Kent v. Yorkshire
Blackpool Lancashire v. Hants.
Lord's Middx. v. Leics.
Weston-s-M. Somerset v. Sussex
The Oval Surrey v. Derbyshire
Worcester Worcs. v. Notts.

Thursday, August 10

Trent Bridge ENGLAND v. PAKISTAN (Second Test—5 days)

Saturday, August 12

*Leyton Essex v. Kent
Cheltenham Gloucs. v. Worcs.
Lord's Middlesex v. Notts.
*Wellingborough School Northants. v. Lancs.
*Weston-s-M. Somerset v. Glamorgan
*Hove Sussex v. Surrey
Edgbaston Warwick. v. Hants.
Bradford Yorks. v. Derbyshire
Belfast Ireland v. Scotland

Wednesday, August 16

Cheltenham Gloucs. v. Pakistan
Burton-on-T. Derbyshire v. Kent
Old Trafford Lancashire v. Glam.
Lord's Middlesex v. Essex
Northampton Northants. v. Sussex
Weston-s-M. Somerset v. Surrey
Edgbaston Warwick. v. Yorkshire
Worcester Worcs. v. Hampshire

Saturday, August 19

Worcester Worcs. v. Pakistan
*Chesterfield Derby. v. Warwick.
Cheltenham Gloucs. v. Lancs.
*Gillingham Kent v. Glamorgan
*Leicester Leics. v. Hampshire
*Lord's Middlesex v. Surrey
*Trent Bridge Notts. v. Somerset
*Eastbourne Sussex v. Northants.
Scarborough Yorkshire v. Essex

Wednesday, August 23

Chelmsford Essex v. Surrey
Cardiff Glamorgan v. Kent
Cheltenham Gloucs. v. Leicestershire
Portsmouth Hampshire v. Middx.
Northampton Northants. v. Derby.
Eastbourne Sussex v. Yorkshire
Edgbaston Warwick. v. Somerset
Worcester Worcs. v. Lancashire
Lord's Young Professionals v. Young Amateurs

Thursday, August 24

The Oval ENGLAND v. PAKISTAN (Third Test—5 days)
Lord's Services Festival (3 days)

Saturday, August 26

Derby Derby. v. Northants.
*Chelmsford Essex v. Lancashire
Portsmouth Hants. v. Glamorgan
Dover Kent v. Warwickshire
*Leicester Leics. v. Worcs.
Trent Bridge Notts. v. Yorkshire
*Taunton Somerset v. Gloucs.
Hove Sussex v. Middlesex

Monday, August 28

Lord's M.C.C. v. Ireland (2 days)

Wednesday, August 30

Old Trafford	Lancs. v. Pakistan
Colwyn Bay	Glamorgan v. Worcs.
Bristol	Gloucs. v. Hampshire
Dover	Kent v. Essex
Leicester	Leics. v. Northants.
Lord's	Middlesex v. Somerset
The Oval	Surrey v. Notts.
Middlesb'gh	Yorkshire v. Warwick.

Saturday, September 2

Lord's	Gillette Cup Final
Scarborough	T. N. Pearce's XI v. Pakistan

Wednesday, September 6

Lord's	Middlesex v. Worcs.
Taunton	Somerset v. Lancashire
The Oval	Surrey v. Northants. (if not played on July 19)
Harrogate	Yorkshire v. Gloucs.
Scarborough	England XI v. Rest of World

Saturday, September 9

Lord's	Rothman Cup: England XI v. Rest of World
Scarborough	Yorkshire v. M.C.C.

Monday, September 11

Lord's	Rothman Cup: Pakistan v. Rest of World

Tuesday, September 12

Lord's	Rothman Cup: England XI v. Pakistan

INDIA TOUR, 1967

MAY

3	Worcester	v. Worcestershire
8	Gravesend	v. Cricket Club Conf. (2 days)
10	Canterbury	v. Kent
13	Oxford	v. University
17	Edgbaston	v. Warwickshire
20	Lord's	v. M.C.C.
24	Cardiff	v. Glamorgan
27	Northampton	v. Northants.
31	The Oval	v. Surrey

JUNE

3	*Old Trafford	v. Lancashire
8	Leeds	v. ENGLAND (First Test—5 days)
14	Cambridge	v. University
17	*Southampton	v. Hampshire
22	Lord's	v. ENGLAND (Second Test—5 days)
28	Derby	v. Derbyshire

JULY

1	Sheffield	v. Yorkshire
5	Trent Bridge	v. Notts.
8	*Leicester	v. Leicestershire
13	Edgbaston	v. ENGLAND (Third Test—5 days)
21	Dublin or Cork	v. Ireland (2 days)

PAKISTAN TOUR, 1967

JUNE

28	Colchester	v. Essex

JULY

1	Canterbury	v. Kent
5	Lord's	v. Middlesex
8	*Taunton	v. Somerset
12	Hove	v. Sussex
15	The Oval	v. Surrey
19	Swindon (County Gnd.)	v. Minor Counties (3 days)
22	Edgbaston	v. Warwickshire
27	Lord's	v. ENGLAND (First Test—5 days)

AUGUST

2	Leeds	v. Yorkshire
5	Swansea	v. Glamorgan
10	Trent Bridge	v. ENGLAND (Second Test—5 days)
16	Cheltenham	v. Gloucestershire
19	Worcester	v. Worcestershire
24	The Oval	v. ENGLAND (Third Test—5 days)
30	Old Trafford	v. Lancashire

SEPTEMBER

2	Scarborough	v. T. N. Pearce's XI
9	—	v. Gillette Cup Winners
11	Lord's	v. Rest of World
12	Lord's	v. England XI

MINOR COUNTIES

Sunday, May 21

Penrith Cumberland v. Northumberland

Wednesday, May 24

Old Trafford Lancs. II v. Cheshire

Sunday, May 28

Jesmond Northumberland v. Durham

Monday, May 29

Grimsby (Town Ground) Lincolnshire v. Beds.
Scarborough Yorks. II v. Lancs. II

Wednesday, May 31

Bramhall Cheshire v. Staffs.

Monday, June 5

Harrogate Yorks. II v. Northumberland
Edgbaston Warwick. II v. Durham

Wednesday, June 7

Little Stoke Staffs. v. Durham
Bridgnorth Shrops. v. Cambs.

Wednesday, June 14

March Cambs. v. Beds.
Wallasey Cheshire v. Lancs. II
Driffield Yorkshire II v. Durham
Ellesmere College Shropshire v. Lincs.

Monday, June 19

Jesmond Northumbld. v. Staffs.
Knowle and Dorridge Warwickshire II. v. Shropshire

Wednesday, June 21

Jesmond Northumbld. v. Lancs. II
Appleby Cumberland v. Yorks. II
South Shields Durham v. Staffs.
Chatteris Cambs. v. Lincs.

Wednesday, June 28

Watford, West Herts. C.C. Herts. v. Bedfordshire
Hoylake (Ellerman's) Cheshire v. Warwick. II
Bourne Lincolnshire v. Shrops.

Sunday, July 2

Jesmond Northumbld. v. Cumbld.

Monday, July 3

Great Chell Staffs. v. Norfolk

Wednesday, July 5

Bradford Yorks. II v. Cumbld.
Fenner's Cambs. v. Norfolk

Sunday, July 9

Kendal Cumbld. v. Durham

Monday, July 10

Old Trafford Lancs. II v. Northumbld.

Wednesday, July 12

Luton (Wardown Pk.) Beds. v. Staffs.
Macclesfield Cheshire v. Yorks. II
Scunthorpe Lincolnshire v. Norfolk
Stevenage Herts. v. Cambs.
Penzance Cornwall v. Somerset II

Monday, July 17

Old Trafford Lancs. II v. Durham

Wednesday, July 19

Luton (Wardown Pk.) Beds. v. Cambs.
Jesmond Northumbld. v. Yorks. II
Hertford Hertfordshire v. Norfolk
Bury St. Edmunds (Victory Ground) Suffolk v. Lincolnshire
Wellington (St. George's) Shrops. v. Warwick. II
Swindon (County Gd.) Minor Counties v. Pakistan (3 days)

Monday, July 24

Mkt. Drayton Shrops. v. Somerset II
Bradford (Park Avenue) Yorks. II v. Lincs.
Millom Cumbld. v. Lancs. II

Wednesday, July 26

W. H'tlepool Durham v. Warwick. II
Norwich (Lakenham) Norfolk v. Cambs.

Friday, July 28

Camborne Cornwall v. Devon

Monday, July 31

Marlborough College — Wiltshire v. Berkshire
Norwich (Lakenham) — Norfolk v. Staffs.
Hitchin — Herts. v. Bucks.
Seaton — Devon v. Somerset II
Edgbaston — Warwick. II v. Cumbld.

Wednesday, August 2

Birmingham (M. & B. Ground) — Warwick. II v. Cheshire
Oxford (Sports Club) — Oxfordshire v. Wiltshire
Taunton — Somerset II v. Shrops.
Norwich (Lakenham) — Norfolk v. Bucks.
Weymouth — Dorset v. Berkshire
Blackhill — Durham v. Yorkshire II
Paignton — Devon v. Cornwall
Lincoln — Lincs. v. Cambs.

Friday, August 4

Taunton — Somerset II v. Wilts.
Ipswich Schl. — Suffolk v. Bucks.
Exeter (County Ground) — Devon v. Berkshire
Weymouth — Dorset v. Cornwall

Monday, August 7

Bedford Sch. — Bedfordshire v. Shrops.
Swindon (British Railways) — Wiltshire v. Oxfordshire
Norwich (Lakenham) — Norfolk v. Herts.
Maidenhead (Boyne Hill C.C.) — Berks. v. Bucks.
Old Trafford — Lancs. II v. Yorks. II
Taunton — Somerset II v. Cornwall
Whitehaven — Cambs. v. Warwick. II

Wednesday, August 9

Bedford Sch. — Bedfordshire v. Lincs.
Uttoxeter — Staffs. v. Cheshire
Salisbury — Wiltshire v. Cornwall
Sawston — Cambs. v. Herts.
Oxford (Sports Club) — Oxfordshire v. Bucks.

Friday, August 11

Bedford Sch. — Bedfordshire v. Herts.
Sherborne School — Dorset v. Wiltshire
Norwich (Lakenham) — Norfolk v. Suffolk
H. Wycombe — Bucks. v. Berks.

Sunday, August 13

Gateshead Fell — Durham v. Cumberland

Monday, August 14

Longton — Staffs. v. Lancs. II
Northwich — Cheshire v. Northumbld.
Chippenham — Wilts. v. Somerset II
Bishops Stortford or Tring — Herts. v. Suffolk
Reading (Earley C.C.) — Berkshire v. Dorset
Oxford (St. Edward's School) — Oxfordshire v. Devon

Wednesday, August 16

Wing, Ascott Park — Buckinghamshire v. Suffolk
Newcastle-under-Lyme — Staffs. v. Northumbld.
Reading (C.C. Ground) — Berkshire v. Devon
Grimsby (Ross Gp.) — Lincs. v. Yorks. II
Wisbech — Cambs. v. Shrops.
Henley (Brewery Ground) — Oxfordshire v. Dorset
Darlington — Durham v. Lancs. II

Friday, August 18

Reading Univ. — Berkshire v. Wiltshire
Dorchester — Dorset v. Devon
Slough — Bucks. v. Oxfordshire

Monday, August 21

Wellington — Shrops. v. Beds.
Jesmond — Northumbld. v. Cheshire
Norwich (Lakenham) — Norfolk v. Lincs.
Chesham — Bucks. v. Herts.
Old Trafford — Lancs. II v. Cumberland
Falmouth — Cornwall v. Dorset
Taunton — Somerset II v. Devon

Wednesday, August 23

Lichfield — Staffordshire v. Beds.
Bridlington — Yorks. II v. Cheshire
Lowestoft — Suffolk v. Norfolk
Windsor and Eton C.C. — Berkshire v. Oxfordshire
Torquay — Devon v. Dorset

Friday, August 25

Wadebridge — Cornwall v. Wiltshire
Felixstowe — Suffolk v. Hertfordshire
Witney (Smith's Industries Ground) — Oxfordshire v. Berkshire

Sunday, August 27

Chester-le-Street Durham v. Northumbld.

Monday, August 28

Devizes Wiltshire v. Dorset
Beaconsfield Bucks. v. Norfolk

Spalding (Grammar School) Lincolnshire v. Suffolk
Instow (North Devon C.C.) Devon v. Oxfordshire
Old Trafford Lancs. II. v. Staffs.

Wednesday, August 30

Blandford Forum Dorset v. Oxfordshire

SECOND XI CHAMPIONSHIP

Note: Gloucestershire and Somerset are playing as a combined side. The Bristol matches will be played on the Gloucestershire C.C.C. ground.

Monday, May 1

Old Trafford Lancs. v. Warwicks.

Wednesday, May 3

Guildford Surrey v. Hants. (3 days)
Nottingham (Police Ground) Notts. v. Warwicks.

Monday, May 8

Northampton Northants v. Lancs.
Winchmore Hill Middlesex v Warwicks.
Nottingham Notts. v. Worcs.

Wednesday, May 10

Beddington Surrey v. Glam. (3 days)
Hove Sussex v. Hants. (3 days)
Derby Derbyshire v. Warwicks.
Old Trafford Lancashire v. Notts.
Worcester Worcs. v. Somerset

Monday, May 15

Coventry and and N. Warwicks. Grd. Warwick. v. Northants.

Wednesday, May 17

Mitcham Surrey v. Northants. (3 days)
Leicester Leics. v. Derbyshire

Thursday, May 18

Sittingbourne (Gore Court) Kent v. Sussex

Monday, May 22

Bournville Warwickshire v. Lancs.

Wednesday, May 24

Hove Sussex v. Surrey (3 days)
Collingham Notts. v. Northants
Worcester Worcs. v. Warwickshire

Thursday, May 25

Bristol Somerset v. Hampshire

Monday, May 29

Derby Derbyshire v. Notts.
Cardiff Glamorgan v. Warwicks.
Hove Sussex v. Middlesex

Wednesday, May 31

Southgate Middlesex v. Surrey (3 days)
Bedworth Warwicks. v. Notts.

Thursday, June 1

Canterbury Kent v. Worcs.
Moreton-in-Marsh Somerset v. Northants.

Monday, June 5

Laverstoke Hampshire v. Kent
Worksop (College Grd.) Notts. v Lancashire

Wednesday, June 7

Portsmouth Hants. v Sussex (3 days)
Guildford Surrey v. Middlesex (3 days)
Formby Lancs. v. Northants.
Stratford Warwicks. v. Somerset
Leicester Leics. v. Notts.

Monday, June 12

Derby Derbyshire v. Worcs.
Southwell Notts. v. Glamorgan
Leamington (Lockheed) Warwickshire v. Hants.
Corby (Stewarts & Lloyds) Northants. v. Kent

Wednesday, June 14

Dartford Kent v. Gloucs.

Thursday, June 15

Birmingham (Mitchell & Butlers) Warwickshire v. Worcs.

Monday, June 19

Bristol Somerset v. Glamorgan
Wembley Middlesex v. Kent
Worthing Sussex v. Worcestershire

Wednesday, June 21

Chelmsford Essex v. Surrey (3 days)
Duston Northants. v. Derby.
Hove Sussex v. Warwicks.

Monday, June 26

Aylesford Kent v. Essex
Leamington (Town) Warwicks. v. Glamorgan
Worcester Worcs. v. Notts.

Wednesday, June 28

Pontypridd Glam. v. Surrey (3 days)
Hove Sussex v. Gloucs.
Leicester (Grace Rd.) Leics. v. Northants.

Monday, July 3

Retford Notts. v. Derbyshire
Bridgend Glamorgan v. Somerset
Worcester Worcestershire v. Kent
Northampton Northants. v. Middlesex

Wednesday, July 5

Folkestone Kent v. Surrey (3 days)
Braintree (Crittalls) Essex v. Northants. (3 days)

Monday, July 10

Derby Derbyshire v. Northants.
Ealing Middlesex v. Sussex
Nottingham (Player's Grd.) Notts. v. Surrey

Wednesday, July 12

Lord's Middlesex v. Hants.

Thursday, July 13

Worcester Worcs. v. Leicestershire
Northampton Northants. v. Notts.

Monday, July 17

Ashton Northants. v. Somerset

Thursday, July 20

Corringham Essex v. Sussex
Worcester Worcs. v. Derbyshire

Monday, July 24

Dagenham Cables Essex v. Kent
Newport Glamorgan v. Worcs.
Horton Northants. v. Warwicks.

Wednesday, July 26

Cranleigh Surrey v. Sussex (3 days)
Derby Derbyshire v. Lancs.
Walthamstow Essex v. Middlesex

Thursday, July 27

Abergavenny Glamorgan v. Notts.
Bristol Gloucs. v. Kent
Northampton Northants. v. Leics.

Monday, July 31

Sittingbourne (Bowaters) Kent v. Hampshire
The Oval Surrey v. Notts.

Wednesday, August 2

The Oval Surrey v. Kent (3 days)
Peterborough Northants. v. Essex

Monday, August 7

Hove Sussex v. Essex
Worcester Worcs. v. Glamorgan
Newark Notts. v. Leicestershire

Wednesday, August 9

Northampton Northants. v. Surrey (3 days)
Mill Hill Middlesex v. Essex
Nuneaton (Griff & Coton) Warwicks. v. Derbyshire

Thursday, August 10

Bournemouth Hampshire v. Somerset
Bexhill Sussex v. Kent

Saturday, August 12

The Oval Surrey v. Essex (3 days)

Monday, August 14

Greenwich (Metrogas) Kent v. Middlesex
Leicester Leics. v. Warwickshire
Worcester Worcs. v. Northants.

Wednesday, August 16

Bournemouth Hants v. Middx. (3 days)
The Oval Surrey v. Warwickshire (3 days)
Derby Derbyshire v. Leics.

Thursday, August 17

Broadstairs Kent v. Northants.

Monday, August 21

Southampton Hants. v. Warwickshire
Enfield Middlesex v. Northants.

Wednesday, August 23

Basingstoke Hants. v. Surrey (3 days)
Burnley Lancs. v. Derbyshire
Leamington (Lockheed) Warwickshire v. Leics.

Monday, August 28

Milford Hav. Glamorgan v. Gloucs.
Edgbaston Warwickshire v. Middx.

Wednesday, August 30

Edgbaston Warwicks. v. Surrey (3 days)
Taunton Somerset v. Worcs.

Monday, September 4

Bristol Somerset v. Warwicks.

GILLETTE CUP

First Round

Sunday, April 23: Chester-le-Street, Durham v. Nottinghamshire.

Wednesday, April 26: Taunton, Somerset v. Leicestershire; Luton, Bedfordshire v. Northamptonshire.

Saturday, April 29: Basingstoke, Hampshire v. Lincolnshire; Worcester, Worcestershire v. Sussex.

Wednesday, May 3: Wisbech, Cambridgeshire v. Oxfordshire.

Second Round

Saturday, May 13: Bedford or Northampton, Bedfordshire or Northamptonshire v. Durham or Nottinghamshire; Edgbaston, Warwickshire v. Somerset or Leicestershire; Brentwood, Essex v. Kent; Old Trafford, Lancashire v. Gloucestershire; The Oval, Surrey v. Derbyshire; Portsmouth or Lincoln, Hampshire or Lincolnshire v. Glamorgan; Bradford, Yorkshire v. Cambridgeshire or Oxfordshire; Worcester or Hove, Worcestershire or Sussex v. Middlesex.

---

limp 85020/0148. *cloth* 85020/0156

MADE AND PRINTED IN GREAT BRITAIN BY WILLIAM CLOWES AND SONS LTD., LONDON AND BECCLES